ENCYCLOPEDIA OF
BRITAIN

BAMBER GASCOIGNE
ENCYCLOPEDIA OF
BRITAIN

Macmillan Publishing Company
New York

Copyright © Bamber Gascoigne 1993

First published 1993 by Macmillan Press Ltd, London and Basingstoke
and in the USA by Macmillan Publishing Company
866 Third Avenue
New York, NY 10022

Library of Congress Cataloging-in-Publication Data
Gascoigne, Bamber.
The encyclopedia of Britain/Bamber Gascoiogne.
p. cm.
ISBN 0-02-897142-6 : $75.00
1. Great Britain — Encyclopedias. I. Title.
DA27.5.G37 1993
941'.003—dc20 93–1881
CIP

ISBN 0-02-897142-6

Designed by Robert Updegraff
Picture Research by Juliet Brightmore
Graph Design © Robert Updegraff
Typeset by Heronwood Press, Medstead, Hampshire
Printed and bound in Great Britain

For Christina

ACKNOWLEDGEMENTS

A great many people have played an essential part in shaping this book. One group includes all those who commented on my proposed list of headwords, making possible a limited consensus as to what constitutes general knowledge about Britain. Another group, some of whose members overlap with the first, is made up of those who generously gave expert advice on the first draft of my entries. The names of all who played either of these roles are listed at the end of these acknowledgements, and they have my profound thanks for their contribution.

Many others helped greatly by answering requests for brochures or for information about their cities, institutions, companies or buildings. For many months our postman, John Wheeler, uncomplainingly brought great bundles of such material to the door. My thanks to all of them, and to him.

Among those more directly responsible for the encyclopedia I am grateful first of all to Julian Ashby, who in 1989 asked me to consider doing a book of this kind for Macmillan; without him it would never have been. John Peacock and Jayne Jenkinson played a crucial role in ensuring that the project could be done from the start on computer. When it came to the stage of editing the completed text, I am immensely grateful to a hawk-eyed trio – my editor, Penny Warren, together with Caroline Ball and John English – who not only flushed out many inconsistencies and infelicities, but also made invaluable suggestions for improvements and additions. Robert Updegraff proved himself a designer of unfailing courtesy and flexibility when confronted with authorial niggles; Juliet Brightmore selected the illustrations with eye-catching flair; and Stephen Benaim shepherded us safely through a very tight production schedule.

Nearer home, I could not have got through the final stages without two local and ever-helpful sources of last-minute information: Diana Howard and her staff in the Richmond central reference library; and Helena Caletta and her assistants in our admirable local bookshop, the Open Book.

Peter Mullings, my producer and director on *University Challenge* for 25 years, kindly agreed to go through every entry in the book. He has sought out errors, misleading implications and areas of potential confusion with the thoroughness which he applied in the past to thousands of quiz questions. I am immensely grateful for his many excellent suggestions.

Finally, a more than usually heartfelt without-whom-this-would-never-have-been. My wife Christina not only put up for nearly four years with the obsessions of an encyclopedist, but in the last few months spent all her time checking details and chasing up elusive scraps of information. Many such scraps lurked in government departments or in the intricate minds of experts, and could only be extracted in long conversations. Since Christina is an Olympic-class telephonist, she was the ideal sleuth. My gratitude is unbounded.

The following are those who very kindly advised on headwords or on completed entries, or in some cases provided detailed information on specific subjects: Charles Aberconway, Caroline and Kit Ackroyd, Christopher Airy, Barrie Allcott, John Amis, Kingsley Amis, Alwyn Arkle, Robert Armstrong, Mary and Julian Ashby, Diana Baring, Francis Baring, Nicholas Baring, Anthony Beeson, Andrew Best, Kenneth Bradshaw, Steven Brindle, Melanie and Benedict Brogan, Jane and Colin Brown, Michael Brown, Andrew Brunt, Helena Caletta, Harry Carpenter, Edward Cazalet, Colette Clark, Gillian and Neil Clarke, Janet and Derek Cooper, Martha Crewe, Timothy d'Arch-Smith, Neil Deadman and family, Tim de Lisle, Bruce Donn, Helena Drysdale, Elizabeth Fenwick, Chris Fildes, Denis Forman, Michael Frayn, Sue Freathy, Philip French, Brian Gascoigne, Sue Gernaey, Dennis and Mark Griffiths, John Gross, John Hale, John Harrison, John Hemingway, Nicola and John Hilton, Godfrey Howard, Ralph Hyde, Elizabeth Ingles, Peter Jackson, Fred Kenett, Alvilda and James Lees-Milne, the Lion and Unicorn bookshop, Anthony Lloyd, Jessica and Robin Lough, Peter Lovering, Neil MacGregor, Raphael Maklouf, Anthony Marks, Timothy Motley, Toby Motley, Colin Nears, Chris Newbery, Elizabeth and Peter Offord, Simon O'Hagan, Derek Pearce, George Pinker, Ben Plowden, Veronica Plowden, William Plowden, Richard Pomeroy, John Prescott, William Reid, Kenneth Richardson, Richmond upon Thames College, Sarah Riddell, Anthony Russell-Roberts, Charlotte Ryton, Prunella Scales, Mark Sainsbury, John Sales, Basil Skinner, Jocelyn Starling, Jamie Stormonth-Darling, Roderick Suttaby, Norman Swallow, Jean Thow, Barry Turner, Michael Twyman, Marina Vaizey, Sebastian Walker, Marina Warner, Karen Watson, Timothy West, Eileen and Jonathan Wright Miller, Frank Wright, Brian Young.

My thanks to them all.

Bamber Gascoigne
April 1993

PREFACE

Twenty-five years spent checking the questions for a quiz game, *University Challenge*, have left me with two things – a good reference library and a fascination with the idea of general knowledge. This book is the fruit of both.

It is based on the belief that general knowledge is a real territory with boundaries that can be approximately defined. I developed a keen sense of these boundaries when asking the questions on the programme. The contestants were bright and highly competitive university students. It might happen that none of them knew the answer to a question. If it fell within the broad realm of general knowledge, there would be much banging of palms against foreheads, clicking of fingers, agonized grimaces and mutters of 'yes, yes, yes, what is that?'. But if the question rang no bell at all, the reaction would be very different – eight faces glaring at me as one, brimming with righteous indignation. It was clear then that the required fact lay outside the implicit boundaries, or at any rate the boundaries existing for their generation. The latter is an important proviso. A friend in his twenties, glancing at the list of headwords in this volume, said 'You can't include Aberfan, nobody's heard of that'.

The underlying principle can be demonstrated by compiling a hierarchy of names in any subject, listed in descending order of fame. The boundary of general knowledge falls where only a few people other than specialists respond to a name. Literature, Britain's chief export, can provide the easiest example. Everybody in Britain has heard of Shakespeare; almost everybody has heard of Dickens; most people have heard of Swift (if only because of *Gulliver's Travels*); many have heard of Sterne and *Tristram Shandy*, and quite a number of Sir Thomas Browne; but on the whole only students of literature will know the name of Robert Henryson.

Sterne, on this basis, is clearly part of general knowledge and Sir Thomas Browne is on the borderline. This encyclopedia was made possible by the realization that there is space within a single volume to reach Browne, and his equivalent in other subjects, while providing sufficient basic information to be of interest and use to the non-specialist. Browne is in, Henryson out.

In these borderline areas many readers will have strong subjective views on what should be in or out, just as there was inevitably a subjective element in my own choices. But there are objective guidelines too. Reference books, by which we are all much influenced, often give an unexpectedly clear indication of the boundaries, and in doing so perpetuate them. In the example used above, Browne and Henryson can be said to be of roughly equal interest to students of literature. But the *Oxford Dictionary of Quotations* includes 70 passages from Browne and not a

single one from Henryson. Such are the building blocks of fame.

Inevitably there are broader areas of difficulty as to what to include, and Ireland provides the outstanding example. As in real life, its division into two parts has been problematic. It is in the British Isles, but citizens of the Republic of Ireland might well take umbrage at finding themselves included under Britain; and yet it would be as eccentric to omit St Patrick as to include Mr Haughey. The politicians, authors, towns, houses or beauty spots of Northern Ireland clearly have to be in, and those of the republic just as clearly must not. But what of Trinity College, founded in Dublin by Elizabeth I in 1591 as an Anglican enclave in a Roman Catholic country? It was a borderline case; in the event it has been left out (except as one of the copyright libraries). By contrast the Anglo-Irish who made such a mark in British life in the 18th and 19th centuries had to be in – O'Connell and Parnell, and the great line of Irish authors, Swift, Goldsmith, Sheridan, Wilde, Shaw. Writers, as it happens, offer a natural demarcation line almost as clear as the political break of 1921. Shaw, born in 1857, made his career entirely in England; he seems more a British author than an Irish one and is naturally in. But Yeats (born 1865), Synge (1871) and O'Casey (1880) remained in Ireland and it was in Dublin that they made their names. They are excluded, as is Joyce (1882) who lived abroad – though never in Britain – but who wrote exclusively about Ireland.

In some categories it has been possible to establish rules for inclusion. Thus all British cities are in, all towns above a certain size, all Commonwealth countries, all prime ministers since the Reform Act, all plays by Shakespeare, all golf courses where the Open has been played since 1970, all places (however small) which are the administrative centres of counties. Similarly there is a place for anyone who has been in the cabinet in the past ten years and every chancellor of the exchequer, foreign secretary and home secretary of the past 20 years. Automatically included are the 50 largest British companies (a fluctuating category, but many of the next 50 are also in as household names), together with any pop group which has been in the charts more than a certain number of weeks, and so on.

But most candidates for inclusion do not fall into any such quantifiable area. In the majority of cases the final selection or rejection of rival entries has been based on what I might call a consensus of subjectivity. On each topic I circulated a list of my proposed entries to several people. I tried to include some who were expert in the subject, some who were broadly well informed and some who would not mind being described as average members of the public; the latter were clearly important in areas such as television and sport, but their views were immensely valuable in all fields since the criterion was the frontiers of general knowledge. Interestingly, as I transferred the ticks from individual lists to my master copy, a strong group preference frequently emerged between candidates who had seemed to me to have equal claims. And I hope that this pooling of subjective preferences will continue after the book is published. If an omission strikes anyone as particularly surprising, I shall be grateful to hear of it so that a readers' consensus may perhaps emerge before the next edition. It will carry more weight if accompanied by a suggestion as to which headword in the same category (an author for an author, an athlete for an athlete) should be dropped to make way for the newcomer.

Domicile and nationality presented particularly thorny problems of choice. What are the comparative claims of British people who made their careers abroad and of foreigners who lived in Britain and contributed greatly to the life of the country? With historical figures the consensus has long been established. Handel clearly has to be in a book of this kind – not because he became a British citizen, but for his contribution to specifically British music.

The choice becomes harder in our own time. How about Eamonn Andrews, an Irishman who lived in Britain, or Stan Laurel, born in England but with his entire adult career abroad? Or two foreigners of great distinction who have chosen to make England their home, Alfred Brendel and V.S. Naipaul? Of these four I originally included two, but at the last moment made space for a third. The reasons shed some light on the principles which I have followed.

Eamonn Andrews is included because anyone presenting two such long-running programmes as *What's My Line?* and *This Is Your Life* comes to seem part of the national fabric. Stan Laurel is included because his British origin is sufficiently widely known for it to be a source of pride, particularly in his home town of Ulverston where there is a museum in his memory.

By contrast Alfred Brendel, Austrian by nationality, is not in the book. My hunch, right or wrong, is that many devoted music lovers will be unaware that his home is in Hampstead; the life of an international concert pianist is by definition international, and where he settles between concerts is not a matter of great public concern. The principle is clarified by the fact that two other great musicians from abroad are in the book, Solti and Haitink. My reasoning here is that both have held lengthy appointments as musical directors of British opera houses and that this has given them a more unmistakably British presence. Solti does also happen to be British (since 1972), but this is not in itself a decisive reason for including him; the public is largely unaware of who has become naturalized, though a knighthood rather than an 'Hon. KBE' does demonstrate the fact in Solti's case.

For reasons similar to Brendel, Naipaul was originally not in the book. As with pianists, the lasting whereabouts of a writer is an elusive matter; he or she is more likely to be identified with the country in which the books are set. Thus Edna O'Brien, a resident of London, seems to me essentially an Irish writer and is excluded; and Naipaul (Indian in origin, Trinidadian by birth, writing for the most part about the Caribbean, India and Africa, but living in Wiltshire) was for the same reason omitted. But then, in March 1993, he became the first recipient of Britain's largest literary award, the David Cohen British Literature Prize. By the rules of the prize this identified him as a naturalized British citizen (a fact previously unknown to me and I suspect to most people), but again this was not the deciding factor. What brought him over the borderline and into the book was that the award gave wide publicity to his link with Britain. And it is just such a perceived link, resulting in the expectation of readers that someone will have an entry, that has been my yardstick.

Inevitably the realm of general knowledge includes many more examples of some species than of others. Current affairs and television are heavily represented; people today spend much of their time absorbing both. Literature plays a major part, and not only because it is the outstanding achievement of British culture; it looms large in general knowledge because it requires no specialist skills to enjoy a book or a play. Art and architecture also provide pleasure to the non-expert, but it takes time and money to sample them widely – part of the reason why relatively few great paintings or houses have won a secure place in general knowledge, compared with books of the same quality. And science is even less well represented.

The most frequent complaint about *University Challenge* was that we had too few science questions. We tried to include more, and were usually rewarded with those looks of blank indignation unless there happened to be an appropriate scientist on the team (appropriate because a physicist would be flummoxed by any but an easy biology question, and vice versa). The reason, unacceptable to many scientists but I believe inescapably true, is that science can never be part of general knowledge in the same way as arts subjects. Scientific books are not comprehensible to the non-specialist. Anyone can read and may well find enjoyment in an author as serious as George Eliot; it is impossible to understand a treatise on physics of comparable importance without years of study.

Using the test applied earlier to authors, far fewer scientists come above the line for inclusion. Everyone in Britain has heard of Newton; almost everybody has heard of Darwin; most of Rutherford; many of Priestley; quite a number of John Ray; but probably only specialists know the name of Charles Vernon Boys. In literature the guillotine fell between Browne and Henryson; here it divides Ray (in) from Boys (out). This principle has let into the book some 320 authors but only about 120 from the fields of science and technology.

The criteria for inclusion or exclusion have therefore been unashamedly populist. A headword is in the encyclopedia not because people ought to be looking it up, but because they are likely to do so – a question more of fame than of merit. This is not quite so startling as it sounds. In the vast majority of cases fame is based on merit.

To put the matter another way, I have tried to include most of the facts about Britain that most people are most likely to want to look up. Every specialist work of reference contains a small percentage of entries which are far more often looked up than the others. This book takes these most popular items from every subject and brings them together in a single volume. Nearly all the information included here can be quickly found by anyone in a good reference library. But most of us don't have that at home. And I believe that even those who do will find it useful to have the mainstream facts about Britain and the British gathered in one volume, as the natural first place to check a detail, settle an argument or clarify a sequence of events.

Some may argue that a national slice through general knowledge is jingoistic. I see the force of this but believe it to be wrong. Cultural identity within the developed world has been nation-based for some centuries, and the general knowledge of each nation differs greatly from that of others. The national slice is therefore the most valid of subdivisions. The full international spectrum of general knowledge requires a multi-volume encyclopedia, of which volume A–B is clearly useless on its own. An encyclopedia on literature or sport or the 18th century is useful, but it remains a specialist work of reference. By contrast an encyclopedia on a single nation can fit within one volume and is broad enough to be classed as general.

I cherish the thought that writers in other countries may produce similar volumes on their own national culture, preferably in the same format as this so that they can stand on the shelf as a set. Together they would add up to a general encyclopedia unlike any other in one crucial respect. Each volume would be worth owning separately.

Headwords These are given as far as possible in the form in which they are generally used and are most likely to be looked up. This is not as obvious as it sounds and is only gradually becoming normal practice. In the early 1970s the *Encyclopedia Britannica* still had its entry for the prime minister Herbert Asquith under 'Oxford and Asquith, earl of' (the title given him three years before his death) with a cross-reference from Asquith; every single reader in pursuit of Asquith must surely have had to look in both places. At the same period the *Oxford Companion to Sports and Games* had entries for two distinguished sportsmen under 'Moore, Robert' and 'Stewart, John'; it takes even a keen sports enthusiast a moment to realize that the footballer Bobby Moore and the racing driver Jackie Stewart are being described.

By the same token the writers George Gordon Byron, Gerard Manley Hopkins, Thomas Stearns Eliot and Anthony Dymoke Powell often appear in reference books in that entirely accurate form. But I believe it is of greater help to the reader to know that they are commonly referred to as Lord Byron, Gerard Manley Hopkins, T.S. Eliot and Anthony Powell; so these are the versions in the relevant headwords here.

I have used the method, which I hope will be found congenial, of putting the alphabetized headword in its correct place instead of first: 'Anthony Powell' rather than 'Powell, Anthony'. This derives from my own impatience with the strange inversions which we have all come to accept in reference books: *Midsummer Night's Dream, A,* for example. I believe it is just as easy to find one's way around with a clear running head at the top of the page and the individual headwords written normally.

Population figures These are given for towns and cities, counties and regions. It is stated in each case whether the figure is that of the 1981 or 1991 census. The 1991 census figures were only available, when this book went to press, for local authority areas. Where an urban district coincides with a town, it has been possible to give the 1991 figure for that town. But where the town is the centre of a large rural district, it has been necessary to give the 1981 figure for the town itself; the city of Durham, for example, had 26,000 inhabitants in the 1981 census, whereas the Durham local authority covers 86,000 people in the available 1991 figures.

Welsh, Scottish and Irish Since the English are by far the majority of the British population (more than 85%), it is only a matter of interest in national life if people come from one of the smaller constituent countries. In keeping with this, it is often mentioned in an entry that a person is Welsh, Scottish or Irish, but only rarely that he or she is English.

Honours and titles One of the oddities of British life is that distinguished people from time to time change the way in which they are addressed. Playgoers in recent decades have at various times been moved by Laurence Olivier, Sir Laurence Olivier and Lord Olivier. It is useful to know the timing of such a change, so the relevant details are given after the dates of birth and death. But in

the interests of economy I have limited this information to the first and last honours received in a lifetime. The duke of Wellington became a knight in 1804, viscount in 1809, earl and then marquess in 1812, duke in 1814; this cascade is compressed here to 'kt 1804, duke 1814'. Honours of this name-changing kind are the only ones to be included (and only for people given an entry of their own). The one exception is the nation's highest award for achievement, the Order of Merit.

Marriages As with honours and titles, details and date of a marriage are only automatically given where it explains the subject's name. The marriage of A.S. Byatt (born Antonia Drabble) is mentioned; that of her sister, Margaret Drabble, is not.

Cross references These are not automatically added before any word which has its own entry elsewhere in the book. Asterisks are placed only where the other entry contains closely related material, of a kind likely to follow on from the reader's original enquiry; or where a name or phrase may need explanation, which can be found in the related entry; or occasionally where it might not be clear under which word a phrase should be looked up (Stone of *Scone is an example).

Dates The dates given for books are those of publication; dates of plays and music are of the first performance. The date of writing or composition is mentioned only if it was several years earlier than publication or performance.

Dates of birth, and if appropriate death, are given at the start of an entry for a person; the only exception is living people who have chosen to conceal their date of birth in reference books such as *Who's Who*. Similar dates are added within an entry if there is a direct relationship between the person and the subject of the entry – for the architect when the entry is a building, for the author when the entry is a book, and so on. This applies only when there is not a separate entry, complete with dates, for the architect or author.

Location A distinction is made between places that readers might want to visit and institutions that they are more likely to wish to contact by letter or telephone. The former (castles, stately homes, villages) are located in terms of their distance and direction from a city or town which has its own entry in the book. The latter (charities, pressure groups, government departments) are given sufficient location – such as a postcode in London – to enable their address or telephone number to be easily found.

Abbreviations

ac	acres	d.	died
km	kilometres	min	minutes
b.	born	ft	feet
kph	kilometres per hour	mph	miles per hour
bn	billion	ha	hectares
kt	knight	oz	ounces
bt	baronet	hr	hours
lb	pounds	sq.km	square kilometres
c	century	in	inches
m	metres, miles,	sq.m	square miles
	million	kg	kilograms
cwt	hundredweight	yd	yards
m.	married		

Sources
Any general work of this kind relies on a multitude of other more specialized reference books. Those most frequently used are listed in the bibliography at the back, and on the whole my information is only as good as

theirs. If more specialist sources than mine agree that the Battle of Agincourt occurred in 1415, this book is not the place to query the received opinion (somewhere in Voltaire's voluminous output there can be found the compelling definition of history as the lie that historians have agreed upon). Nevertheless four sources have provided, between them, so much material not rapidly available in other books that they must be individually acknowledged.

Foremost is the *Oxford English Dictionary*, its profuse quotations from the past five centuries often provide invaluable insights into British social history. An annual treasure house of information is *Whitaker's Almanack*; it is less widely used than it should be, partly because its treasures are so varied and so dense that they tend to lie hidden until one knows the book well. The *Dictionary of National Biography* is often criticized for containing inaccuracies in its entries (not surprising in that the bulk of them were written a century ago); but it pioneered a short form of biography, perfectly suited to a work of rapid reference. Finally, I have made much use of the leading English-language encyclopedia, the *Encyclopaedia Britannica*, which was also my main source in checking *University Challenge* questions. For my present purposes the edition of 1972 proved most useful, for two reasons: it was the last edition before the very unhelpful division of the encyclopedia into two sections, *Micropaedia* and *Macropaedia*; and it was the last to retain a strong bias towards British material, which had somehow survived the 40 years since the American acquisition of the encyclopedia in 1929.

A

A1 see *Lloyd's Register of Shipping.*

A6 murder A crime which many believe led to a major miscarriage of justice. In August 1961 Michael Gregsten and his lover Valerie Storie were shot in their car in a lay-by off the A6 between Luton and Bedford. Gregsten was dead but Storie survived, paralysed from the waist down. The first suspect was Peter Alphon, a travelling salesman, but at an identity parade Storie picked out another man, known to be innocent. The next suspect was a 25-year-old petty criminal, James Hanratty. Storie picked him from an identity parade, and her identification was the main evidence which led to his being hanged in April 1962. In *Who Killed Hanratty?* (1971) the journalist Paul Foot concluded that Hanratty was innocent. Foot also revealed that Alphon had repeatedly told him he was the murderer. In 1992, on the 30th anniversary of Hanratty's death, Foot claimed that Alphon, living then in a run-down hotel in the King's Cross district of London, was still confessing to the crime.

AA (Automobile Association) Britain's largest motoring organization, founded in 1905, with a membership in the early 1990s of some 7 million. It is now used mainly for its breakdown service, but the chief duty of its first patrol-men, riding bicycles, was to warn members if policemen were lurking behind bushes with stopwatches, at a time when the nationwide speed limit was 20mph/32kph. The agreed signal was a failure to salute the member's car, identifiable by its AA badge.

AAA (Amateur Athletic Association, known as the three As) Body established in 1880 to organize amateur athletics in England and Wales, with all amateur clubs eligible for association; it finally merged in 1991 with the Women's Amateur Athletic Association, formed in 1922 when the AAA committee refused to allow women's clubs to affiliate. The late 19C was a time when many such athletic organizations were coming into being. The Northern Counties Athletic Association, formed in 1879 to represent clubs in the north of England, claims to be the oldest governing body for athletics in the world; Midland Counties followed in 1880, and Scotland in 1883. The first Amateur Athletic Championships were held in 1886, and the English Cross Country Championships in 1887. The AAA Championships have remained the main national annual athletics meeting. British involvement in international athletics is the responsibility of the *British Athletic Federation.

Abbey Dore (16km/10m SW of Hereford) Oddly shaped parish church, of unusual size and dignity. It is the surviving east end (chancel and transepts) of a 12–13C Cistercian monastery church, with a tower added in the 17C. It is one of very few Cistercian buildings still used for worship in Britain.

Abbey National Company deriving from what had been Britain's second largest *building society. It was formed in 1944 by the merger of the Abbey Road Building Society (originally a self-help group founded in 1874 in a Baptist church in London's Abbey Road) and the National (established in 1849). In 1989 more than 5 million members (the savers and the borrowers) voted to convert the society into a public limited company in which they would have shares, thus becoming the first building society to depart from the non-profit-making tradition. The head offices are on the site in *Baker Street associated with Sherlock Holmes.

Abbey Road (London NW6) Residential street which became famous when the *Beatles used the name in 1969 for an album recorded in the *EMI studios at 3 Abbey Road. A century earlier the local Baptist church established a friendly society which survives as part of the *Abbey National.

Abbots Bromley Horn Dance Ceremony performed every September in the Staffordshire village of Abbots Bromley. The dancers carry reindeer antlers (one pair has been carbon-dated to around AD 1000), and they mime the fighting of stags. It is believed to be the oldest surviving folk festival in Britain, but its origins and purpose are unknown. Equally mysterious is how the horns reached Staffordshire, where reindeer were extinct long before 1000.

The dancers at Abbots Bromley in about 1900.

Abbotsbury (16km/10m SW of Dorchester) Village near the Dorset coast with several claims to fame. The great tithe barn survives from a Benedictine monastery, as does the swannery, where hundreds of pairs nest every spring. The gardens contain many tender plants seldom grown elsewhere in Britain out of doors. And the traditional start of the mackerel season is still marked each May by an ancient ceremony in which garlands, blessed in the church, are thrown into the sea.

Abbotsford (52km/32m SE of Edinburgh) House built and largely designed by Walter *Scott in 1822–4 on the river Tweed. The Victorian-medieval style of the architecture, comfortably romantic and rich in detail, is in keeping with the great appeal at the time of his novels. With his possessions still in place, the house is today a most evocative memorial.

Abbot's Kitchen see *Glastonbury.

A, B, C1, C2, D, E Social classifications devised by the National Readership Survey to provide profiles of the readership of newspapers and magazines; they are also often used in discussion of voting patterns. Classification is based in most cases on the occupation of the 'head of the household', usually the main earner. The broad definition of each category is as follows: A, 3% of total, 'upper middle class', senior professional people and senior members of large firms and organizations; B, 14%, 'middle class', people at the top of smaller enterprises, or not quite at the top of professions or large organizations; C1, 22%, 'lower middle class', non-manual workers in the lower echelons of firms, the group traditionally described as 'white-collar workers'; C2, 28%, 'skilled working class', craftsmen and skilled manual workers; D, 18%, 'semi-skilled and unskilled working class', everyone else in regular employment, mainly in manual jobs; E, 15%, casual workers and those living on the basic old-age pension.

abdication crisis The events of the summer and autumn of 1936 leading up to the abdication of *Edward VIII. Rumours about the king's relationship with Wallis Simpson, a married American, came to a head in the summer when the couple went for a cruise together in the Adriatic. In October Mrs Simpson was granted a divorce and the king told the prime minister, Stanley Baldwin, that he intended to marry her. Baldwin, and probably the majority of public opinion, felt that marriage with a divorced woman was incompatible with the role of the monarch. On December 10 Edward signed an instrument of abdication (the only British monarch to have done so), and the following evening made his historic speech on the radio, frequently broadcast in extract ever since, explaining his decision to the nation: 'I have found it impossible to carry the heavy burden of responsibility and to discharge my duties as king as I would wish to do without the help and support of the woman I love.'

Frederick **Abel** see James *Dewar.

Aberdeen (190,000 in 1981) City and seaport on the northeast coast of Scotland; administrative centre of the Grampian region. Lying between the mouths of the Don and the Dee (its name means 'mouth of the Dee' in Gaelic), it is known as the 'granite city' from the stone of which it is largely built. It has long been Scotland's largest fishing port, and in recent decades has become the support centre for the oil-drilling operations in the North Sea.

The city developed from two separate settlements. One, known as Old Aberdeen, grew up around St Machar's Cathedral in the north; beyond it is the famous *Brig o' Balgownie. The other district, commercial Aberdeen,

developed in the south, round the harbour on the Dee. Castlegate, with its Mercat Cross (market cross) of 1686, was the original centre of this area; the nearby Town House (1868) incorporates part of the previous municipal building, the 17C Tolbooth. Two of the earliest houses, both once belonging to provosts of the city, are now museums. Provost Skene's House (c.1545) displays domestic items in rooms with period furniture; and Provost Ross's House (1593) is the home of the Maritime Museum. The main thoroughfare of modern Aberdeen, Union Street, running southwest from Castlegate, was begun in 1800 and was named after the Union with Ireland.

Aberdeen is a city of three cathedrals. St Machar's (14–15C, a ruin except for the nave which remains in use as a parish church) is named after a possibly legendary figure, the supposed founder of the Celtic Christian settlement around which Old Aberdeen grew up. St Andrew's Cathedral (opened 1814) is of particular interest as the mother cathedral of the Episcopal church of the USA. In newly independent America the notion that the English monarch was head of the Anglican church was offensive to many; so an American cleric, Samuel Seabury, was secretly consecrated by three bishops in Aberdeen and became the first Anglican bishop to owe no allegiance to the crown. St Mary's (1856–69) is the Roman Catholic cathedral.

The Art Gallery and Museum, founded in 1885, has been largely shaped by an unusual restriction. In 1900 a local granite merchant, Alexander Macdonald, bequeathed his collection and a large sum of money with the proviso that it must be spent on paintings not more than 25 years old. The result is an excellent collection of British sculpture and painting.

The university of Aberdeen was formed in 1860 by the merging of King's College (one of the oldest university colleges in Scotland, founded in 1494) and Marischal College (1593). Marischal's superb granite façade, with its Gothic pinnacles, was added in 1906.

Aberdeen, known as the Dons (Pittodrie Stadium, Aberdeen). Football club, formed in 1903, which made a great impact on the Scottish scene during the 1980s – challenging the long-standing supremacy of Rangers and Celtic. Aberdeen took the Scottish FA Cup four out of five years in 1982–6, and capped that success with a win over Real Madrid (2–1 in extra time) in the final of the European Cup Winners' Cup in 1983. Club victories: Scottish FA Cup 1947, 70, 82, 83, 84, 86, 90; League 1955, 80, 84, 85; League Cup 1956, 77, 86, 90; European Cup Winners' Cup 1983.

Lord **Aberdeen** (George Hamilton-Gordon, 1784–1860, 4th earl of Aberdeen 1801) Conservative politician, prime minister 1852–5. On the death of *Peel in 1850 he became leader of the 'Peelite' section of the Conservative party (those who approved of the repeal of the *Corn Laws), and in 1852 he formed a coalition government of Peelites and Liberals. His period in office was overshadowed by the *Crimean War, and was brought to an end by an adverse vote in the House of Commons on his conduct of the campaign.

Aberdeen Angus (also known simply as Angus) Scottish breed of black, hornless cattle, famous for its high quality beef. The strain was bred in the early 19C from aboriginal cattle in the adjacent areas of Aberdeen and Angus.

Aberdeenshire Until 1975 a *county in northeast Scotland, now part of the Grampian region.

Aberdeen terrier see *terriers.

Aberfan Coal-mining village in Mid Glamorgan. On 21 October 1966 a giant slag heap collapsed, burying the village school and other buildings; 116 children and 28 adults died.

Abernethy (14km/9m SE of Perth) Village which was an important Pictish centre. Of its 9C monastery there survives a well-preserved *round tower. The nearby Castle Law, an Iron-Age hill fort of about 500 BC, is one of the best examples of the Scottish 'timber-laced' technique, in which stone ramparts have an internal frame of wood.

Aberystwyth (9000 in 1981) Resort on the west coast of Wales, in Dyfed. The medieval town developed round a Norman castle, now a ruin. The first college of the University of Wales was established here in 1872, and the town was chosen in 1907 as the site for the *National Library of Wales. The Ceredigion Museum, housed in a restored Edwardian theatre, uses a collection of domestic and craft objects to recreate the history of the area. The mining of silver and lead played an important part in this, and the nearby Llywernog Silver-Lead Mine Museum includes a restored water-powered mine which was abandoned in the 1880s.

Abide with me One of the most popular of evening hymns, written in 1820 by a clergyman, Henry Francis Lyte (1793–1847), after being present at the deathbed of a friend. It has become a traditional part of the *Cup Final at Wembley, where the vast crowd sings it before the teams come on to the pitch.

abortion An area of the law not subject to quite such passionate controversy in Britain as in the USA or Ireland. It was legalized in the Abortion Act of 1967, introduced as a private member's bill by David Steel. Under its terms a pregnancy can only be terminated by a registered medical practitioner, and two medical practitioners must agree that it is necessary on one of two grounds – the physical or mental health of the mother, or the likelihood that the baby will be born with a serious physical or mental handicap. The last time at which abortion can be legally carried out is the 24th week of pregnancy (the only exception thereafter is if the continued pregnancy would cause 'grave permanent injury to the physical or mental health' of the woman). MPs voted in 1990 against proposals for various lower limits.

Abortions, in thousands

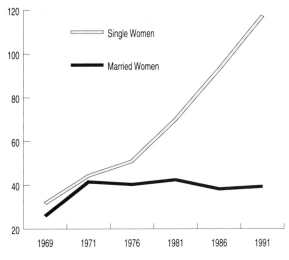

1969 was the first full year after the act of 1967 became effective in April 1968. *Source:* Social Trends (*see* *Central Statistical Office*).

Harold **Abrahams** (1899–1978) Sprinter who won the gold medal for the 100 metres in the Olympic Games of 1924, a feat celebrated in the film *Chariots of Fire*.

absentee landlords Term used in particular of English owners of estates in Ireland who rarely, if ever, visited them.

absolute monarchy see *divine right of kings.

Academy of Ancient Music Ensemble established by Christopher Hogwood in 1973 for the performance on authentic instruments of music of the 17–18C. The name was originally that of a musical society in 18C London.

Academy of St Martin-in-the-Fields Chamber orchestra founded in 1959 by a violinist, Neville *Marriner, as a string ensemble for baroque music. It played at that time without a conductor, and gave its first concerts in the London church of *St Martin-in-the-Fields. As the size of the orchestra grew, Marriner became the conductor (there has been no other in more than three busy decades, though Iona Brown and Kenneth Sillitoe lead some performances as first violins). The repertoire was long ago extended up to the 20C, and the Academy is now among the world's most recorded chamber orchestras. It played the sound track for the film of *Amadeus* (1984).

ACAS (Advisory, Conciliation and Arbitration Service) Government agency set up in 1975 to help avoid and resolve industrial disputes.

account day An account, in the *Stock Exchange, is the period (usually two weeks) during which transactions are made without payment being yet required. Account day, when payment must be made, is normally the second Monday after the end of the account.

acid bath murders Sensationally unpleasant series of murders which came to light in 1949, when John George Haigh was tried and convicted for the murder of an elderly widow whose body he had dissolved in a bath of sulphuric acid. He had committed other similar murders (about five, but the exact number is uncertain), and claimed to have drunk a cup of blood from each of his victims before dissolving them.

ack ack see *Royal Artillery.

acre see *area.

Act of Parliament The instrument by which laws are created. The government presents to the House of Commons a bill, in effect a first draft. The First Reading is a purely formal announcement of the bill. Debate and the possibility of amendment begin with the Second Reading, followed by the committee stage – a more intense scrutiny by a *committee of MPs. After the Report Stage, at which amendments by the committee are debated in the House, and the Third Reading (usually without debate), the bill is passed to the House of Lords, where it will go through similar stages. Any amendment by the Lords (not allowed on bills involving finance) will require further debate in the Commons. Once a bill has gone through this entire process, it requires only the *royal assent to become law as an act of parliament. (Bills can also start in the House of Lords, following a similar pattern before being transferred to the Commons.)

Since 1963 acts have been dated by the calendar year in which they received the royal assent. Previously the date was expressed as a regnal year – the year within the reign followed by the name of the monarch. Since the regnal year begins from the moment of accession, it invariably spans two calendar years. Thus 2 Victoria, the second year of her reign, lasted from 20 June 1838 to 19 June 1839.

Act of Settlement or **Supremacy** see Act of *Settlement or *Supremacy.

Lord **Acton** (John Acton, 1834–1902, baron 1869) English historian widely remembered for his statement in a letter of 1887 that 'power tends to corrupt and absolute power corrupts absolutely'.

Acton Burnell (13km/8m to the S of Shrewsbury) Village which takes its name from Robert Burnell, chancellor to Edward I. The red sandstone 'castle', which he started to build in 1284, was more of an elegant manor house. It was lived in for little more than a century and never altered; although now a ruin, it suggests well the domestic arrangements of a 13C grandee. Burnell also built the village church, in the Early English style, which is notable for one of the finest memorial *brasses in England, commemorating Sir William Burnell (d. 1382).

Acts and Monuments see *Foxe's Book of Martyrs.

Robert **Adam** (1728–92) By far the most influential architect of his period in Britain. His father, William (1689–1748), had himself been a leading architect in Scotland. Three of William's sons joined the profession; John (1721–92) maintained the Edinburgh end of the family practice, while Robert and James (1730–94) established themselves in London. A fourth son, William Jnr, looked after their business affairs.

Much of the famous *Adam style was the result of the two years (1755–7) which Robert spent in Rome, studying and drawing classical architecture. His success lay in adapting the classical tradition to provide the elegance and delicacy required by his patrons. He designed rooms down to the last details of furniture and fittings. Among the most famous of his many houses are *Kedleston, *Harewood, *Syon, *Osterley, and *Kenwood. In 1768 the brothers undertook together a vast project in London, the *Adelphi.

In his later years Robert Adam designed several important buildings back in Scotland, including the great sham castle *Culzean on the west coast and, in Edinburgh, *Charlotte Square, the University and the Register House for the *Scottish Record Office.

Adam Bede (1859) The first full-length novel by George *Eliot, which won her immediate fame for its strong realism. It is the story of the two women in the life of Adam Bede, a village carpenter – the flighty Hetty Sorrel and her cousin Dinah Morris, a Methodist preacher, whom Adam eventually marries.

'Adam delved and Eve span' see John *Ball.

Bodkin **Adams** (1899–1983) A doctor in Eastbourne whose trial for murder in 1956 caused great excitement. He was suspected of poisoning his elderly female patients, after a succession of them had included him as a substantial beneficiary in their wills. He was tried for the murder in 1950 of Edith Morrell, but was acquitted after the defence had been able to cast doubt on much of the prosecution's evidence.

Douglas **Adams** see *The *Hitch Hiker's Guide to the Galaxy.*

Gerry **Adams** see *Sinn Fein.

Richard **Adams** see *Watership Down.*

Cliff-top Culzean on the west coast of Scotland: one of Robert Adam's most spectacular creations.

Two soldiers of the Gordon Highlanders, photographed in Edinburgh Castle in 1845 by Adamson and Hill.

Robert **Adamson** (1821–48) Scottish photographer, responsible with David Octavius *Hill for many of the early masterpieces of portrait photography. Within not much more than a year of Fox *Talbot's patent of his calotype process (1841), the 22-year-old Adamson was in business taking portraits by this method in Edinburgh. His association with Hill, an artist, began in 1843. In the few years that remained of Adamson's life they together took some 1800 photographs, mainly portraits but also scenes in and around Edinburgh.

Adam style The style in interior decoration, furniture and ornament introduced by Robert *Adam and much copied. It retains the lightness of *rococo within a *neoclassical framework. Adam's characteristic colour scheme, particularly on ceilings, is often described as acid, akin to the range seen in assorted fruit drops.

Joseph **Addison** (1672–1719) Essayist whose easy conversational prose and instinct for subjects of serious but general interest contributed largely to the success of the *Tatler* and the *Spectator*. He was also author of a tragedy, *Cato* (1713), much admired in its time. His deistic ode to creation, *The spacious firmament on high* (based on Psalm 19 and published in the *Spectator*), has survived as a rousing hymn.

Addison's disease see *Guy's Hospital.

Addled Parliament Name given to a parliament which sat for two months in the spring of 1614 (5 Apr.–7 June) and hatched nothing. Not a single act was passed, because the Commons would not yield to the wish of James I to impose taxes, the king rejected any legislation favoured by the Commons and an aristocratic faction, at odds with parliament, had a vested interest in wrecking the session.

Adelphi (London WC2) Ambitious development by Robert *Adam and his brothers in 1768–73 of a large area stretching from the Strand down to the river. They named it after themselves (*adelphoi* is Greek for 'brothers'). The main terrace of riverside houses, raised on arches, was demolished in 1936–8. Only a few of the original buildings of the Adelphi now survive in the streets behind.

Aden Port at the southern tip of the Arabian peninsula, an important stopping place on the sea route through the Suez Canal to India. It was a British colony until 1967 and is now the independent state of South Yemen.

Kate **Adie** (b. 1945) Correspondent for BBC TV, specializing in trouble spots and war zones. She happened to be on an assignment in Libya in April 1986 when the USA made its unexpected air strike. Her reports from areas devastated by the bombs were criticized by Norman Tebbit (then chairman of the Conservative party) as being antigovernment and anti-American. She was vigorously defended by the BBC and was later given the Royal Television Society's award for the best international news coverage of that year. By 1992 she was less popular with the Libyans, and this time it was a Libyan government official who complained, begging the BBC (or so it was reported) to take her home; but then on that occasion she was investigating the case of the two *Lockerbie suspects.

*The **Admirable Crichton*** see J.M. *Barrie.

Admiral's Cup International yachting trophy presented in 1957 by the Royal Ocean Racing Club to encourage foreign yachts to race in British coastal waters. The event is held every other August and coincides with *Cowes week. Each nation is allowed to enter three boats, which compete in a series of inshore and offshore races off the south coast of England. The final event is the *Fastnet Race.

Admiral's Men An Elizabethan company of actors, so named because their patron was Lord Howard of Effingham, the Lord High Admiral who commanded the fleet against the Armada. Their leading actor was Edward *Alleyn.

Admiralty The governing body of the *Royal Navy from the reign of Charles II to 1964, when it was merged with the Ministry of *Defence. Its offices were at the northwest end of *Whitehall and its administrative structure was largely the creation of Samuel *Pepys.

Admiralty Arch (London SW1) Triumphal arch built in 1910 to complete the vista of Aston Webb's new design for the *Mall. It is so named because it is adjacent to the *Admiralty.

Lord **Adrian** (Edgar Douglas Adrian, 1889–1977, baron 1955) English physiologist, working mainly at Cambridge, who in 1932 shared a Nobel prize with *Sherrington for their work on nerve cells. Adrian's special field was nerve impulses, in relation to such topics as muscular control, the nature of sensation, and the electrical activity of the brain.

Adrian IV (Nicholas Breakspear, d. 1159) Pope from 1154, and the only Englishman to have achieved that position. Born near St Albans, and believed to have been the son of a monk, he made his way as a boy to France and was probably never again in England. He was long believed to have granted a bull to Henry II allowing him to conquer Ireland, but this is now thought to have been a forgery.

Adrian Mole The nation's best-known fictional school-boy of recent years, ever since his innermost thoughts were revealed in 1982 in *The Secret Diary of Adrian Mole Aged 13 3/4* – transcribed by Sue Townsend, then aged 36 1/2. *The Growing Pains of Adrian Mole* followed in 1984.

advocate The name in Scotland for a *barrister. The Faculty of Advocates in Edinburgh, established in the 16C, is the Scottish equivalent of the *Inns of Court. Its library became the *National Library of Scotland.

AEEU (Amalgamated Engineering and Electrical Union) Britain's second largest trade union when it was formed in 1992 by the merging of the AEU (Amalgamated Engineering Union) and the EETPU (Electrical Electronic Telecommunication and Plumbing Union). Both unions, with a combined membership of more than a million, were themselves the result of a long history of mergers. The oldest constituent part of the AEU was the Old Mechanics, formed as early as 1826; and the electricians created their union in 1889, in the early days of the *electricity industry (they attempted at that time to join the engineers' union but were rebuffed).

The merger caused considerable difficulties within the trade union movement, because the EETPU had been expelled from the *TUC in 1988 for signing single-union agreements and for allegedly poaching members from other unions. The EETPU had also been at odds with the rest of the movement in 1986 when its members printed the *Times* and other newspapers at the new plant in *Wapping, and thus broke the power of the traditional print unions.

Aerospace Museum (Albrighton, 13km/8m SE of Telford) Large collection of historic civil and military aircraft, with a display of the development of British Airways. Examples of enemy missiles which have won a lasting place in British demonology include the *V1 and V2, and a flying bomb of the type piloted by a Japanese *kamikaze* pilot.

Aesthetic Movement The conscious attempt by certain British writers and artists in the late 19C to live and dress in a manner which would set them apart from the practical and material concerns of Victorian England, and above all to create 'art for art's sake'. The phrase, which became the slogan of the movement, had been current since the beginning of the century in the more pithy French version *l'art pour l'art*. It meant that art should have no aim other than the creation of beauty, and above all no moral purpose.

While *Swinburne and Walter Pater contributed greatly to the movement as writers, and Dante Gabriel *Rossetti and *Burne-Jones as painters, the highest profiles were maintained by *Whistler and *Wilde; both were present in 1877 at the opening of the *Grosvenor Gallery. The aesthetes were satirized by W.S. Gilbert in *Patience*. Their ideas were closely related to the *Arts and Crafts movement and to *Art Nouveau.

AEU see *AEEU.

AFC see *DFC.

Afghan Wars Three wars in which Britain unwisely tried to impose an outsider's will on the people of Afghanistan. The first two (1838–42, 1878–81) were prompted by the fear of a Russian threat to India. Britain wanted a friendly buffer state in Afghanistan, but the two attempts to impose a sympathetic ruler, backed by British force, led in each case to the eventual massacre of a large number of British subjects. The third war (1919–21) was an equally ineffective effort to prevent the emergence of Afghanistan as an independent nation.

The **African Queen** see C.S. *Forester.

Age Concern (London SW16) Pressure group on behalf of the old, involved also in research and in direct care for the needs of the elderly through regional branches. It derives from the Old People's Welfare Committees, of which the first was set up in 1940 to cope with the problems of the elderly in the war. The name Age Concern has been used since 1971, though the more formal title is the National Council on Ageing. There are separate administrations for Scotland, Wales and Northern Ireland.

age of consent The age (16 years) at which a woman can first legally consent to sexual intercourse; a man having intercourse with a woman below the age of consent is therefore guilty of a crime, 'unlawful sexual intercourse' (there are certain exceptions and defences). Since the legitimization of *homosexuality between consenting adult males, the age of 21 has also become in that context an age of consent.

Agincourt (25 Oct.1415) Victory by Henry V and a small English army over the French in the middle period of the *Hundred Years' War. As at *Crécy, lightly armed men with *longbows wreaked havoc among the French in their unwieldy armour – killing some 1500 knights and 4500 other men-at-arms, at the cost of relatively few English casualties. The battle's fame in Britain (like that of St *Crispin) derives largely from its treatment by Shakespeare in *Henry V*. The modern French name of the village, about 50km/31m SE of Boulogne, is Azincourt.

Agricola see *Romans.

Ministry of **Agriculture, Fisheries and Food** (London SW1) Department established in its present form in 1954 to administer government policy in the given areas, with responsibility also for food safety. For ministers since 1983 see the *cabinet.

Andrew **Aguecheek** see *Twelfth Night*.

aid see *overseas aid.

Aesthetic art-lovers satirized in a Punch *cartoon of 1880 by George du Maurier.*

St Aidan (d. 651) Irish missionary who was instrumental in bringing Celtic Christianity to northeast England. He was a monk on *Iona until sent as bishop to the Anglo-Saxon kingdom of Northumbria, with its main stronghold at Bamburgh. Aidan established a church and monastery on the nearby island of *Lindisfarne, from which he made long journeys inland to set up missionary outposts. His feast day is August 31.

Ailsa Craig Granite island which rises steeply to 340m/ 1114ft off the west coast of Scotland at the southern end of the Firth of Clyde. Occasionally inhabited in the past, it is now a bird sanctuary. Its position on the sea route between Belfast and Glasgow gave it the nickname Paddy's Milestone, and it has been famous as the source of the best granite for *curling stones (sometimes known as Ailsas).

Aintree see the *Grand National.

Airbus Series of wide-bodied airliners made by a European consortium, Airbus Industrie, in production from the 1980s. *British Aerospace has a 20% stake in the project and is responsible for designing and manufacturing the wings.

Airedale Scenic valley in North Yorkshire, formed by the upper reaches of the river Aire. It is noted in particular for Gordale Scar, a deep ravine with waterfalls; and for Malham cove, a concave cliff from which the Aire emerges, already a river, from its subterranean sources.

Airedale terrier see *terriers.

Air Force Cross and **Medal** see *DFC.

Kriss Akabusi (b. 1958) British athlete of Nigerian descent whose career took off in 1987 after he changed from the 400 metres to 400 metres hurdles. In his new event he became the UK champion in 1987, and won gold medals at the Commonwealth Games in 1990 and then at the European Championships in the same year – the occasion on which he beat David *Hemery's 20-year-old UK record. He has subsequently broken his own record twice, when winning a bronze at the 1991 World Championships and another bronze in the 1992 Olympic Games.

Alabama claims see *Gladstone.

alabasters see *Nottingham.

Aladdin A favourite *pantomime subject, based on the story in The *Arabian Nights about a penniless small boy, Aladdin, who gets hold of a magic lamp. When he rubs it, genies appear (from *jinni*, the Arabic word for a demon); they help him to untold wealth, a vast palace, and the love of Badroulboudour, the sultan's daughter.

El Alamein Village on the north coast of Egypt which was the site of two important battles in *World War II. In June 1942 the German Afrika Corps, headed by Rommel, was storming east through north Africa and seemed likely to reach Cairo and the Suez Canal. They were held at El Alamein in July by the British 8th Army under *Auchinleck. By late October, when the 8th Army had been greatly reinforced and was under the command of *Montgomery, a counterattack was launched which was to be one of the turning points of the war. The battle lasted October 3–November 5, after which Rommel withdrew 1100km/700m to the west. The momentum had begun for the expulsion of the Germans from Africa, which was followed by the allied invasion of Italy.

Lord Alanbrooke (Alan Brooke, 1883–1963, KCB 1940, viscount 1946) Commander of the 2nd Army Corps at *Dunkirk. Subsequently, as chief of the Imperial General Staff (1941–6), he was Churchill's right-hand man in the conduct of most of World War II.

St Alban (died 3C) Venerated as Britain's earliest Christian martyr. The first known version of his story, dating from the 6C, relates that he was a Roman living in Britain who was executed for sheltering a fugitive Christian. *Bede improved on this by making him a Roman soldier who saved a priest's life by dressing in his clothes and dying in his place. There have been many learned guesses at the precise year in which this may have happened; all that is certain is that by 429 there was a church on the traditional site of his martyrdom (around it grew up the city of *St Albans). His feast day is June 22, but as the result of an ancient confusion was in the past commemorated in the Church of England on June 17.

Albany (London W1) The most select apartment block in London, on the north side of Piccadilly. The house facing the entrance yard was built by William Chambers in 1771–4; it was adapted in 1802–3 as apartments, and at the same time two long ranges of chambers were added behind the house by Henry Holland. Designed originally for bachelors, Albany retains something of the seclusion and severity of a university college – with the apartments giving off staircases to either side of a covered walkway. Its most distinguished residents, ranging from Byron and Gladstone to Edward Heath, have usually come from the arts and politics.

Prince Albert (1819–61) Husband of *Victoria, and from 1857 her prince consort. Born in Germany, he was the second son of the duke of Saxe-Coburg & Gotha. He married Victoria in 1840 and had a profound influence on her; indeed his stern moral approach to life affected the whole of Victorian society. He was much concerned with the fields of industry and applied art, and the *Great Exhibition was largely his achievement. His sudden death from typhoid devastated the queen, whose subsequent years of protracted mourning made her increasingly unpopular.

Albert and the Lion see Stanley *Holloway.

Albert Dock see *Liverpool.

Royal **Albert Hall** (London SW7) Domed hall, appearing round but in fact slightly oval, which was built in 1868–71 as a memorial to Prince *Albert. The design was by Francis Fowke (1823–65). The profits from the *Great Exhibition provided £50,000, but the greater part of the funds was raised by selling 999-year leases on more than 1300 seats. The owners of these still go free to all events apart from some 80 each year (by recent agreement). The hall has been used for a wide range of occasions and spectacles, including boxing matches. A notorious echo made it relatively unsuitable for music (it was said to be the only place where a British composer could be sure of hearing his work twice) until absorbent discs were suspended from the dome in 1968. The hall has been best known in the past half century as the home of the *Proms.

Albert Memorial (London SW7) The nation's memorial to Prince *Albert, built in 1863–72 on the south side of Kensington Gardens. The design was by George Gilbert *Scott in the style of a medieval reliquary. The ornamentation (the work of many sculptors) has the Victorian high seriousness of Albert himself. The splendid marble

The Albert Memorial from Kensington Gardens, with the Albert Hall in the background.

groups flanking the platform represent the continents of Europe, Asia, Africa and America. The 169 life-size figures round the base were selected as the most creative human beings known to history. On the next level are four groups depicting Agriculture, Commerce, Manufactures and Engineering. And under the canopy sits Albert, sculpted by John Foley (1818–74). He holds in his hand the catalogue of his own most creative contribution, the *Great Exhibition, which had taken place just nearby in Hyde Park.

Albert Memorial Chapel Lying to the east of the larger St George's Chapel in *Windsor Castle, it stands on the site of a chapel built by Henry III in 1340. Rebuilt by Henry VII in the 1490s, it soon fell again into disrepair. It was restored by Queen Victoria to house a memorial to her husband, Prince Albert, whose effigy in white marble is by Baron Triqueti. The most impressive tomb in the chapel is that of Edward VII's elder son (duke of Clarence, 1864–92), by Alfred *Gilbert.

Albion Poetic name for England or Britain, of either Celtic or Roman origin (sometimes explained as deriving from *albus*, the Latin for white, because of the cliffs of Dover). It is mainly remembered now in the phrase 'perfidious Albion', in common use in France since the *Napoleonic Wars and first recorded in a poem of 1793 by Augustin, Marquis of Ximenez, which recommends attacking *perfide Albion* at sea. But a link in French perception between perfidy and England is much older. In the 17c Bossuet even contrived to work the phrase *perfide Angleterre* into a sermon on the circumcision of Jesus.

*The **Alchemist*** (1610) Comedy by Ben *Jonson, in which Subtle, posing as an alchemist, fleeces various gullible visitors by promising them what they most long for. His victims include Sir Epicure Mammon, a wealthy knight addicted to conspicuous self-indulgence, and two Puritans, Ananias and Tribulation Wholesome. He is helped in the fraud by his whore, Dol Common, and by a servant, Face, who provides the premises for the fraud in his master's empty house.

Alcock and Brown (John Alcock, 1892–1919, KBE 1919; Arthur Whitten Brown, 1886–1948, KBE 1919)

British aviators who on 14–15 June 1919 achieved the first nonstop transatlantic flight. The journey taking 16hr 27min in a Vickers Vimy twin-engined biplane, from St John's in Newfoundland to Clifden on the west coast of Ireland, won them the £10,000 prize offered by the *Daily *Mail*. A few months later Alcock died from a fractured skull, sustained when landing near Rouen on a flight to Paris.

Alcoholics Anonymous (AA) International organization in which alcoholics are pledged to help each other stop drinking. Founded in Chicago in 1935 (in keeping with the principle of anonymity the two founders are referred to simply as Dr Bob and Bill W.), it arrived in 1947 in Britain, where there are now more than 2000 active groups.

Alcuin (*c*.735–804) English scholar, born at York where he was a teacher until his mid-40s. He then went to direct the palace school for Charlemagne at Aachen. He was largely responsible for the programme of studies which spread through Charlemagne's empire to become the basis of European medieval education. One phrase of his is frequently quoted, from a letter to Charlemagne in 800: *Vox populi, vox Dei* (the voice of the people is the voice of God). In isolation it sounds like an early call for democracy, but this was precisely the opposite of Alcuin's meaning. He urges the emperor that 'those people should not be listened to who keep saying *Vox populi, vox Dei*, since the riotousness of the crowd is always very close to madness'.

Aldeburgh (3000 in 1981) Resort on the east coast of England, in Suffolk. It is best known for its annual music festival, founded by Benjamin *Britten in 1948 and held each June. The major performances are now given 6.5km/4m away at Snape in an old industrial building, the Maltings, which was converted in 1967 into a superb concert hall (on the first night of the 1969 festival the Maltings burnt down, but it was rebuilt in time for the 1970 season). Aldeburgh itself is *The Borough* in the title of Crabbe's poem, from which Britten derived his story for *Peter Grimes*.

John **Alden** (*c*.1599–1687) One of the best known of the *Pilgrim Fathers because of various details, two of them legendary. The legends are that he was the first Pilgrim to set foot on Plymouth Rock, and that he wooed Priscilla Mullens as a proxy for his friend Myles Standish (a tradition made famous by Longfellow in his poem *The Courtship of Myles Standish*). It is a fact, however, that he married Priscilla (and had 11 children with her); and that when he died, he was the last survivor of those who had arrived in the *Mayflower*.

alderman Until 1974 the highest rank in local government after the mayor; aldermen, like mayors, were elected by their fellow councillors. The word is Anglo-Saxon, synonymous with 'elder'. The office was abolished in the Local Government Act of 1972 (effective from 1974), and it now survives only in the *City of London.

Aldermaston (16km/10m SW of Reading) Village in Berkshire where the Atomic Weapons Research Establishment was set up after World War II (it is known now as the Atomic Weapons Establishment). It was at Aldermaston, in the mid-50s, that research was carried out for Britain's H-bomb under William Penney (1909–91). The place became the subject of much public attention after the first bomb was tested in 1957, particularly in the annual Aldermaston marches organized by *CND from 1958.

Alderney see the *Channel Islands.

Aldershot (33,000 in 1991) Town in Hampshire associated more than any other in Britain with the army. It was established as a military camp in 1855.

A level see *exams.

Lord **Alexander** (Harold Alexander, 1891–1969, KCB 1942, earl 1952) Commander of the rearguard at *Dunkirk, of the army in Burma during the British retreat in 1942, and of the forces in the Middle East at the great turning point of World War II from the victory at El *Alamein to the German surrender at Tunis in May 1943. He remained in command of the Allied forces for the invasion of Sicily and the drive up through Italy in 1943–4. After the war he was governor general of Canada (1946–52) and minister of defence (1952–4).

Mrs **Alexander** (Cecil Frances Humphreys, 1818–95, m. William Alexander 1850) Irish author whose *Hymns for Little Children* (1848) contains three of the best-known hymns in the English language – *'All things bright and beautiful', 'There is a green hill far away' and 'Once in royal David's city' (popular also as a *carol).

Alexander I (*c.*1080–1124) King of Scotland from 1107, son of Malcolm III; he succeeded his brother Edgar. He seems to have acknowledged Henry I of England as his overlord, fighting with him against the Welsh and marrying his illegitimate daughter, Sibylla. He was succeeded by his brother David I (see the *royal house of Scotland).

Alexander II (1198–1249) King of Scotland from 1214, son of William I. His long reign coincided with the even longer one of the English king Henry III, whose sister Joan he married in 1221. The rival claims of the kings to parts of each other's territory were settled by the Peace of York in 1237, establishing the Scottish border along roughly its present line. He was succeeded by his son, Alexander III (see the *royal house of Scotland).

Alexander III (1241–86) King of Scotland from 1249, son of Alexander II. Betrothed at the age of one to the daughter of Henry III of England, and only seven when he inherited the Scottish throne, he was at first just a pawn in the frustrated efforts of Henry to take control of Scotland. Alexander's reign was later seen as the last in which Scotland had both independence and prosperity, before a prolonged period of warfare with England. He died after being thrown from his horse during a night journey. All his children had predeceased him, so he was succeeded by his 4-year-old granddaughter, Margaret the Maid of Norway (see the *royal house of Scotland).

Princess **Alexandra** (b. 1936) Granddaughter of George V (see the *royal family). In 1963 she married Angus Ogilvy (b. 1928). They have two children – James (b. 1964) and Marina (b. 1966, m. Paul Mowatt 1990). She lives in Thatched House Lodge in Richmond Park.

Queen **Alexandra** see *Edward VII.

Alexandra Palace (London N22) In 1862 London held a second international exhibition, hoping to repeat the success of the *Great Exhibition. The building was on the corner of Cromwell Road and Queen's Gate, where the Natural History Museum now stands. The materials were later reused, to a different design, to form the present Alexandra Palace in north London (much as the *Crystal Palace had been transferred to south London). It opened as an entertainment centre in 1873 (and reopened in 1875 after a disastrous fire), being named in honour of the princess of Wales, the future Queen Alexandra. Neither exhibition nor palace matched the earlier triumph. The fame of Alexandra Palace derives more from its use for television by the BBC, which from 2 November 1936 transmitted a regular service, making Alexandra Palace the world's first public TV station. In 1980 much of the building was again destroyed by fire. In 1984–8 it was expensively refurbished, but in the early 1990s it remained virtually unused while proposals for its future were the subject of local controversy.

Lithograph of a 'palace for the people': Alexandra Palace seen shortly after it was reconstructed in north London.

The **Alexandria Quartet** (1957–60) Four novels, set in Egypt and highly elaborate in texture and style, which established the reputation of Lawrence *Durrell. The separate books – *Justine* (1957), *Balthazar* and *Mountolive* (both 1958), *Clea* (1960) – describe from differing viewpoints the sexual and political schemes of a group of people in Alexandria in the late 1930s. The observer at the still centre of this turning world, as if in the position of Durrell himself (who was there a few years later), is a schoolteacher by the name of Darley.

Alf Garnett see *Till Death Us Do Part*.

Alfred Jewel (Ashmolean Museum) Small golden object of the 9C with the words *Aelfred mec heht gewyrcan* (Alfred had me made) running round the edge and an enamel image of a man in the centre. It ends in a socket which perhaps once held a pointer for following one's place in a manuscript, and the inscription makes it probable that it was made for *Alfred the Great. It was found in 1693 in Somerset.

Alfred the Great (849–99) King of *Wessex from 871, and the first man to be thought of also as king of all the English. Son of King Aethelwulf of Wessex, he was 16 at the time of the first great Danish invasion, in 865, and the main practical task of his life was preventing the *Danes from overrunning England. It was his success in this – by many victories on land, including the all-important recapture of London in 886, and by building up a navy – which caused him to be accepted as leader by all the *Anglo-Saxons not yet under Danish rule.

His fame today derives also from his patronage of learning. He had important Latin texts translated into English, and even translated some himself. He was thought of in English tradition as the ideal king; he is described in a 12C text as the 'darling of the English', and he remains the only English ruler to be known as 'the Great'.

The legend of the cakes is first recorded in the 11C. Alfred, after a brush with the Danes, is unrecognized by a cowherd's wife when he takes refuge in her hut. She sets him to watch the cakes, but the great king lets them burn and is roundly scolded.

Ali Baba and the Forty Thieves A story from *The *Arabian Nights* which has been much used as the basis for *pantomimes. Ali Baba sees thieves entering a cave after speaking the magic phrase 'Open Sesame'. He later uses it himself and acquires the wealth they have hidden there. The thieves' attempts to recover it are foiled by a female slave, Morgiana, who eventually kills them by pouring boiling oil into the jars in which they are hiding.

Alice in Wonderland (*Alice's Adventures in Wonderland* 1865) Children's book by Lewis *Carroll, illustrated by *Tenniel. It begins with Alice following the White Rabbit down his hole, then falling down a great well, at the bottom of which she drinks a liquid which makes her tiny and then eats a cake which makes her huge. Her comment, 'Curiouser and curiouser!', describes also the course her adventures will take. They include the hookah-smoking Caterpillar who makes her recite the poem *You are old, Father William* to prove she has not lost her memory; the Cheshire Cat, which can vanish, leaving its grin to the last; the Mad Tea-Party, with the Hatter, the March Hare and the Dormouse; the King and Queen of Hearts, on whose croquet-ground the mallets are flamingoes and in whose law court the trial is held to discover who stole the tarts; and the Mock Turtle and the Gryphon who sing and dance the Lobster Quadrille. The story ends when the Queen of Hearts shouts 'Off with her head!' and Alice wakens from her dream. Her later adventures in fantasy were told in *Through the Looking-Glass*.

Allan-a-Dale A minstrel and one of *Robin Hood's companions. Robin helps him rescue his future bride from an enforced marriage to a rich old knight.

'All animals are equal' see *Animal Farm*.

All Creatures Great and Small (BBC, intermittently from 1977) Television series about the experiences in the 1930s of a Yorkshire vet, played by Christopher Timothy. It is based on the experiences of James Wight (b. 1916), who in his fifties, under the pseudonym James Herriot, published a book of reminiscences (*If Only They Could Talk* 1970), which led to several others and a worldwide success.

'Gubby' Allen (George Oswald Browning Allen, 1902–89, kt 1986) All-rounder and a notable fast bowler, playing *cricket for Middlesex (1921–50) and for England (1930–48, captain 1936–7, 47–8). In subsequent years he was chairman of selectors (1955–61) and a leading administrator in English cricket. His nickname derived from the initials of his first three names.

Thomas **Allen** (b. 1944) English baritone who made his debut with Welsh National Opera in 1969. Britten's Billy Budd at Covent Garden in 1979 was one of his most

Alice squashed against the ceiling as she grows by magic: an illustration by Lewis Carroll in his original manuscript.

famous performances, and he now has an international reputation in a wide range of operatic parts. He is particularly well known in two Mozart roles, as the Count in *Figaro* and as Don Giovanni.

Lord **Allenby** (Edmund Allenby, 1861–1936, viscount 1919) The last great British leader of mounted cavalry. His victories against Turkish forces in World War I led to the capture of Jerusalem (1917) and Damascus (1918).

All England Badminton Championship Held annually since 1900 and played now at *Wembley. The tournament was long regarded as the unofficial world championship of *badminton until an actual World Championship contest, held every three years, was inaugurated in 1977.

All England Lawn Tennis and Croquet Club see *Wimbledon.

Edward **Alleyn** (1566–1626) One of the first two great English actors. Performing with the *Admiral's Men, he created the leading roles in the plays of Marlowe while his rival, Richard Burbage, was associated with Shakespeare. Alleyn owned several theatres, including the *Rose. He used his wealth to found *Dulwich College.

Allhallows Museum see *Honiton lace.

Alliance The name used by the *Liberal party and the *SDP from 1983–7 when campaigning together and voting together in parliament. In the 1983 election the Alliance polled nearly 8 million votes, only 700,000 less than the Labour party (but because of the British first-past-the-post *two-party system, these votes won the Alliance only 23 seats compared to 209 for Labour). The expectation of an effective centre force in British politics lasted until after the 1987 election, when disagreements about a merger led to a newly created *Liberal Democratic party coexisting during the next parliament with a much reduced SDP.

Allied-Lyons Group of companies manufacturing and distributing alcoholic and soft drinks and food. Most of the brewers and wine merchants in the group were founded in the 18–19c. J. Lyons and Co. is the company which in 1894 opened the first *Lyons teashop.

Allies Term for the group of nations of which Britain was a part in both world wars. The other principal Allies were the countries of the *Commonwealth, France, Russia and the United States. Italy and Japan were with the Allies in the first war, against them in the second.

alliterative verse The standard form of Old *English verse, which achieved powerful effects by the relentless repetition of consonants. It survived in some Middle English poems up to the 14c (e.g. *Gawain and the Green Knight, *Piers Plowman) and it lasted longest in Scotland. An example from William *Dunbar (late 15c) suggests well the effect. In his *Tua Mariit Wemen and the Wedo* it is hardly necessary to know the Scots words to appreciate what one of the married women thinks of her husband:

> I have ane wallidrag, ane worme, ane auld wobat carle,
> A waistit wolroun na worth bot wourdis to clatter.

allotments Patches of ground, each a quarter of an acre (0.1ha) in size, which can be rented from a local authority. The idea of providing land on which poor families could grow their own vegetables goes back several cen-

The Allies as seen in Punch *in the first days of World War I: a British and a French soldier at the front.*

turies, but in the late 19c it became a statutory obligation on local authorities to make such plots available – a process culminating in the Allotments Act of 1908. The number of allotments rose in World War I from 600,000 to 1.5 million, and there was a similar temporary increase in World War II. Allotments in urban districts have become increasingly important, being used in recent decades largely as a leisure activity.

Alloway Village on the river Doon, 5km/3m south of *Ayr and famous as the birthplace of Robert *Burns. The family cottage is kept today as a memorial to the poet, and the medieval Brig o' Doon still spans the river.

All people that on earth do dwell Metrical version of the 100th Psalm ('O be joyful in the Lord, all ye lands'), written by William Kethe and published in Geneva in 1561. Its tune is the *Old Hundredth.

All's Well that Ends Well (c.1603) Comedy by *Shakespeare, based on a story by Boccaccio, in which Helena uses devious means to win back her husband, Bertram, who has been misled by the braggart Parolles. Tragic in mood, it is only a comedy in that it does, as the title says, end well.

'All the world's a stage' see *seven ages of man.

All the Year Round see *Household Words.

All things bright and beautiful An immensely popular hymn of 1848 by Mrs *Alexander, which begins with the more acceptable side of Victorian complacency in the first verse:

> All things bright and beautiful,
>   All creatures great and small,
> All things wise and wonderful,
>   The Lord God made them all.

It drifts into a less attractive aspect of the theme in the third verse, nowadays usually omitted:

> The rich man in his castle,
>   The poor man at his gate,
> God made them, high or lowly,
>   And ordered their estate.

Almack's see *clubs.

A Victorian fantasy of sexual opportunities in ancient Greece: The Women of Amphissa *by Alma-Tadema.*

Lawrence **Alma-Tadema** (1836–1912, kt 1899) Dutch-born painter who worked in England from 1869. His favourite subject was beautiful Greek and Roman girls in marbled halls who invariably appear to be awaiting sexual adventure, a theme with immense appeal to Victorian patrons.

almshouse Originally the part of a monastery in which alms (charity for the poor) were distributed. After the *dissolution of the monasteries it became the custom for rich men to build almshouses (intended mainly as homes for the elderly poor) which would bear their names. Often in a grand architectural style, almshouses are a familiar feature of many English towns.

Alnwick (2500 in 1981) Town in Northumberland, on the river Aln, which has grown up round a Norman stronghold controlling the eastern coastal route to Scotland. Alnwick Castle has been the home since the 14c of the Percy family, one of whom was Harry Hotspur (see *Henry IV, Part 1*). Its interior, frequently altered, is notable now for some superb Victorian rooms and a fine collection of paintings.

Alph see *Kubla Khan*.

Althorp (11km/7m NW of Northampton) Belonging to the Spencer family since 1508, this is the ancestral home of the princess of *Wales. The 16c house now has a late-18c character, having been remodelled from 1786 in a neoclassical style by Henry *Holland.

Alton Towers (29km/18m to NW of Derby) Ruined Regency and Victorian mansion with 19c garden and conservatories, developed during the 1980s into a very successful leisure park. Aiming to be in the Disneyland league, with an Adventureland, Fantasy World and Kiddies Kingdom, it soon became Britain's second highest paying attraction (after Madame *Tussauds).

Amadeus (1979) Play by Peter *Shaffer in which the two main characters are Wolfgang Amadeus Mozart (presented as exaggeratedly childish and scurrilous, on the grounds of some infantile passages in his letters) and another historical figure, the craftsmanlike composer Antonio Salieri. The drama and the poignancy comes from the jealous Salieri being painfully aware that his rival is a genius. It was filmed in 1984 by Milos Forman.

Amadeus Quartet Britain's best-known string quartet in the decades after World War II. Three of its members – Norbert Brainin and Siegmund Nissel (violins) and Peter Schidlof (viola) – were teenage refugees from Vienna in 1938–9 and first met in an Isle of Man internment camp in the early years of the war. The quartet was formed in 1947 with Martin Lovett as the cellist, and it continued to perform until the death of Peter Schidlof in 1987. The remaining three created in 1988 the larger Amadeus Ensemble.

amateur Admiration for the amateur (doing a task for the love of it rather than for money, and preferably with an easy nonchalance) has been a long-standing and in many ways debilitating tradition in Britain. The word was used in this sense from the late 18c, mainly in the arts, and acquired its greatest force with the 19c cult of *games in the *public schools. The persistence of the amateur spirit is seen in the division between Gentlemen and Players in *cricket until 1962; and it was not till 1972 that the Football Association abolished the distinction. It still separates the two forms of *rugby (rugby union is amateur), and athletics remains officially an amateur sport – though in recent years complex arrangements have been made to enable rugby players and athletes to earn money from sponsorship without losing their 'amateur status'. In tennis, by contrast, Britain was in the forefront in abolishing the distinction; in 1968 *Wimbledon was the first of the Grand Slam tournaments to admit professionals.

Amateur Athletic Association see *AAA.

*The **Ambassadors*** (1533, National Gallery) Painting by
*Holbein of the French ambassador to London, Jean de
Dinteville, with his friend Georges de Selve. Famous not
only for its powerful realism as a double portrait, but also
for its wealth of detail, all of symbolic significance – and
in particular for the strange cautionary smudge across the
bottom which, if viewed from close to the canvas on
either side, tightens into the image of a skull.

Ambridge see *The *Archers*.

America From the 1570s there had been various English
attempts to colonize the coast of north America, promoted by men such as Walter *Raleigh. Most failed
immediately, the nearest to success being a colony on
Roanoke Island, off North Carolina, in 1587. There was
born there in that year the first New World child of
English parents, by name Virginia Dare. But three years
later no trace remained of the settlement. The first to survive permanently was Jamestown, settled in 1607 and
nursed through its early struggles by the leadership of
John *Smith. It developed into the colony of Virginia;
the general area had been named earlier after Elizabeth,
the Virgin Queen. Jamestown itself commemorates her
successor, James I.

Virginia was colonized with various motives, which
included expanding Britain's trade and checking the
advance in America of Spain and Portugal. In other
colonies there was a religious dimension, whether it was
Protestant radicals seeking a new life (the *Pilgrim
Fathers in Massachusetts, William *Penn in Pennsylvania)
or Roman Catholics in need of a haven – as was the case
with Maryland, established by the son of a Catholic convert, Lord Baltimore, and named after Henrietta Maria,
the wife of Charles I.

Meanwhile others were settling too. In the 1620s the
Dutch established a colony on what became the most
prosperous island of the eastern seaboard. They called it
New Amsterdam. But the English were now strong
enough to dominate this small group in their midst. New
Amsterdam was surrendered in 1664 and became New
York. By the end of the 17c 12 British colonies had been
established as separate entities; Georgia was added
in 1733.

A stronger European power than the Dutch posed a
greater threat to the British presence in America. The
French had been to the north, in *Canada, since the 16c;
now, in the early 18c, they settled to the south and west,
establishing New Orleans and the territory of Louisiana
(named after Louis XIV), for which they claimed all the
land drained by the Mississippi. In this way they threatened to confine the British to the eastern coast of the
continent.

In the 18c France and Britain were enemies in a series
of European wars (*Spanish Succession, *Austrian Succession, *Seven Years War). Each was also fought in
north America, and the result was that by the 1760s all
the French territories in America had been ceded to
Britain. This sudden expansion gave great confidence to
the British colonists, but also involved Britain in new
administrative and military expenses. In these changes lay
the beginning of the end of British rule.

The government in London devised various ways of
raising money from the colonies, causing particular
resentment in 1765 with a stamp duty (a tax on legal
documents and newspapers) and subsequently with other
duties on various everyday commodities. After furious
protest these were all repealed except the duty on tea,
which provoked in 1773 the *Boston Tea Party. Some in
Britain, such as Edmund *Burke, urged a conciliatory

approach, but two years of mounting tension ended with
the British government attempting to enforce its authority in America. The resulting War of *American Independence began in 1775 and led a year later to the
Declaration of Independence. Britain's first colonies thus
evolved into an independent country, the first of many to
share the English language and to inherit elements of
British culture.

***America**: A Personal History of the United States*
(BBC 1972) Thirteen-part TV documentary series, from
Columbus to Vietnam, written and presented by Alistair
*Cooke.

War of **American Independence** (also known as the
American Revolution, 1775–81) The war by which
Britain's colonies in *America became the independent
United States of America. Since their foundation the
colonies had not been taxed from Britain nor had they
sent representatives to parliament in London, but parliament imposed a tax on sugar (or molasses) in 1764 and
on legal documents and newspapers in 1765 – leading
to the slogan in the colonies 'no taxation without representation'. After much protest these taxes were
repealed, but a new tax on tea, introduced in 1773, led
directly to the *Boston Tea Party. Britain responded to
this insubordination in Massachusetts by closing the
port of Boston and sending in troops, thus sparking off
the revolution.

Armed hostilities began on 19 April 1775. British
troops on the way to seize a depot of colonial ammunition at Concord were confronted by a small party of
minutemen (militiamen, or part-time soldiers). It is not
known which side fired 'the shot heard round the world',
in Ralph Waldo Emerson's phrase, but eight Americans
died at Lexington and there was a larger battle at
Concord later in the day.

George Washington became commander-in-chief of
the colonial forces in June 1775. He suffered reverses
when the British under William Howe captured New
York in 1776 and for a few months in 1777–8 occupied
Philadelphia, the colonial capital, where the Declaration
of Independence had been issued on 4 July 1776. But the
tide was about to turn. On 17 October 1777 an entire
British army under John Burgoyne surrendered to
Horatio Gates at Saratoga in the state of New York – a
British defeat of profound political consequences, for it
persuaded France to recognize the independence of the
colonies and to send troops and ships. The final event of
the war was at Yorktown on the coast of Virginia, where
Washington with the support of a French army and a
French fleet besieged Lord Cornwallis. He surrendered
on 19 October 1781, but disengagement elsewhere took
some time. The British did not finally leave New York city
until 25 November 1783, though the treaty recognizing
the independence of the new country had been signed on
September 3 of that year.

American Museum see *Claverton Manor.

America's Cup The most coveted trophy in inter-
national yacht racing. Originally known as the Hundred
Guinea Cup, it was presented in 1851 by the Royal
Yacht Squadron of *Cowes for a race round the Isle of
Wight. The New York Yacht Club sent the schooner
America to compete, and she defeated all the British
contenders. The New York club renamed the trophy the
America's Cup and has subsequently accepted challenges
for it at varying intervals. Only once has a yacht of
another nation deprived New York of the cup.
Australia II did so in 1983, losing it again to *Stars &
Stripes* in 1987.

Hardy **Amies** (b. 1909, KCVO 1989) Fashion designer who set up in business in 1946. He was appointed dressmaker to the queen in 1955.

Kingsley **Amis** (b. 1922, kt 1990) Novelist and poet, whose disgruntled anti-establishment hero in *Lucky Jim* brought him immediate fame and an honorary place (rejected by Amis himself) in the media-created group of *angry young men. His later novels both celebrate and mock the appetites of the middle class and middle-aged. *The Old Devils* won the Booker prize in 1986, and *The Green Man* (1969) was adapted as a television series in 1990 with Albert Finney in the central role.

Martin **Amis** (b. 1949) English novelist and journalist, son of Kingsley *Amis. His novels, such as *Dead Babies* (1975) or *Money* (1984), satirize trendy urban life on both sides of the Atlantic with savage wit but also show considerable relish for its seedier aspects.

Amnesty International (London WC1) In 1961 a British lawyer, Peter Benenson, wrote an article in the *Observer* announcing the launch of Appeal for Amnesty, the aim being to campaign for the release of political prisoners – defined as those imprisoned for their beliefs who had not used or advocated violence. Thirty years later there are branches of Amnesty in nearly 50 countries, and it is the world's leading pressure group and source of information on torture and the violation of human rights, publishing annually the *Amnesty International Report*. It also campaigns against capital punishment.

Ampleforth College Roman Catholic *public school for boys. It is run by the Benedictine monks of Ampleforth Abbey, distant successors of those who in the Middle Ages taught in the school attached to Westminster Abbey. At the Reformation the abbey school was transformed into a Protestant establishment (the present *Westminster School), and the Benedictines escaped to the Continent. One of them started a new community, eventually with a school attached. It was this group which returned to England in the 1790s, under anti-clerical pressure from the French Revolution, and settled in 1802 in the Yorkshire village of Ampleforth (a parallel story is that of *Downside). The main buildings of today's school, together with the abbey church, were built from 1922 by Giles Gilbert Scott.

Amstrad Electronics firm founded in 1968 by Alan Sugar (b. 1947); his initials, AMS, and 'trading' provided the name. Its first success was with hi-fi equipment, but it became a household name in the mid-1980s when it brought the word processor and then the personal computer to a new range of customers by drastically undercutting the competition. Sugar floated the company on the Stock Exchange in 1980. In 1992, with the share price having collapsed to about one eighth of its 1988 value, he attempted to buy back the 65% of the company owned by others; but the shareholders rejected his offer of 30p per share.

ancient lights The right to receive unobstructed light through any window that has been in use for more than 20 years. It has been established in English law since the 17c.

The **Ancient Mariner** (*The Rime of the Ancient Mariner* 1798) Narrative poem by *Coleridge in ballad form, a landmark in the *Romantic movement. Its appeal is based on a seductive clarity of language and image, a fast-moving sense of drama, and a constant undercurrent of mystery and horror. These qualities are evident from the opening

The Ancient Mariner, bearing round his neck the dead body of the albatross: illustration from an edition of 1857.

couplet, which seizes the reader as brusquely as the Mariner himself grabs the wedding guest:

It is an ancient Mariner,
And he stoppeth one of three.
'By thy long grey beard and glittering eye,
Now wherefore stopp'st thou me?'

The mariner insists on telling how an albatross followed his ship in the Antarctic. For no particular reason he shot it with his crossbow, bringing a curse on the crew. Later, becalmed in the tropics, they ran out of water:

Water, water, everywhere,
And all the boards did shrink;
Water, water, everywhere
Nor any drop to drink.

All the crew die except the Mariner, round whose neck they have hung the dead albatross. Not till he has uttered a spontaneous blessing of the water-snakes in the moonlit sea, moved by the beauty of God's creatures, does he find that he can pray again; the dead bird falls from his neck and he sleeps. He is saved. But his penance is to wander the world seeking an ever-new audience for his ghastly tale.

ancient monuments see *English Heritage.

Elizabeth Garrett **Anderson** (Elizabeth Garrett, 1836–1917, m. James Anderson 1871) Pioneer female physician. She overcame numerous obstacles in her unorthodox determination to qualify as a doctor, and her crusading energies found a perfect cause in establishing the New Hospital for Women in London's Euston Road. Here, for the first time, women could receive medical attention from their own sex. The year after her death it was renamed the Elizabeth Garrett Anderson Hospital.

'And now for something completely different' see *Monty Python's Flying Circus.

Prince **Andrew** see Duke of *York.

St **Andrew** (1st century AD) Patron saint of Scotland, with a feast day on November 30. He was one of the

12 apostles and brother of St Peter. Bones said to be his were brought to *St Andrews in Scotland at some time before the 8C, and early medieval tradition asserted that he was crucified on an X-shaped cross at Patras, in Greece. Thus the X-shaped cross became his emblem and is one of the three constituent parts of the *Union Jack, representing Scotland.

Eamonn **Andrews** (1922–87) Genial Irish TV presenter. His early career was as a sports commentator on radio in Ireland (he had himself been a junior amateur All-Ireland boxing champion). He was on British television from as early as 1951, being particularly associated with *What's My Line? and *This is your Life.

Julie **Andrews** (stage name of Julia Wells, b. 1935) Actress whose career has been in musical comedy in the USA. After appearing in The Boy Friend on Broadway in 1954, she created the role of Eliza Doolittle in *My Fair Lady (1956). Her best-known film roles have been Mary Poppins (1964) and The Sound of Music (1965).

And when did you last see your father? (1878, Walker Art Gallery, Liverpool) One of the most famous of English narrative paintings, though few can remember the artist (William Frederick Yeames, 1835–1918). The poignancy of this *English Civil War scene derives from the tiny figure of the Cavalier boy – dead centre, and the picture's brightest patch of colour in his blue Van Dyck suit. He stands on a stool to face the almost kindly Roundhead officer asking the dangerous question in the painting's title, while his mother and sisters stand terrified in the background. The picture was for many years re-created as a life-size tableau in Madame Tussaud's.

Andy Capp Strip cartoon in the Daily Mirror since 1956, drawn by Reginald Smythe (b. 1917) and featuring the quintessential British working-class chauvinist. With a check cap pulled right down over his eyes and a permanent fag in his mouth, Andy is idle, self-indulgent, cunning and cheerfully outrageous in his manipulation of his long-suffering wife, Flo.

Angel Choir see *Lincoln.

Angel, Islington (London N1) The name, now attached to a crowded junction in south Islington, was from the 17C that of a coaching inn which stood there, on the main road north from London.

angels of Mons see *Mons.

Angles One of the three main Germanic tribes which together became known as the *Anglo-Saxons. They came from northwest Europe, possibly from the modern German region of Schleswig which still contains a district called Angeln. During the 5–6C they invaded and settled the entire eastern coast from East Anglia to Northumberland. Although they were only one part of the tribal mix in the country at that time, the words England and English derive from their name.

Anglesey (Ynys Môn in Welsh, 70,000 in 1991) Island off the northwest tip of the Welsh mainland, the largest in England and Wales (715sq.km/256sq.m). It was until 1974 a separate *county but is now part of Gwynedd. The island's prehistoric importance is seen in Wales's best burial chamber, *Bryn Celli Ddu. In later centuries it was a natural port of call both for Celtic monks from Ireland and for their Viking persecutors. The eventual Norman-English domination of this furthest outpost of Wales was powerfully demonstrated in the castle of *Beaumaris. In

modern times the island's main importance has come from Holyhead, on *Holy Island off the west coast, as an embarkation point for Dublin. It was the opening up of this route which made necessary the two magnificent 19C bridges over the *Menai Strait.

Anglia Medieval Latin word for the territory of the *Angles, used by extension for *England.

Anglican Communion Those churches in other countries which have a historic link with the *Church of England, sharing a heritage in which two important elements are the *Book of Common Prayer and the *Thirty-nine Articles. They are in communion with the see of Canterbury and every ten years their bishops attend the *Lambeth Conference.

angling Fishing has long been one of Britain's most popular pastimes, with a famous book in its praise from as far back as the 17C (The *Compleat Angler). Fishes are protected in most parts of the country during specific *close seasons. In 'coarse fishing' (the pursuit of anything other than salmon and trout, usually by means of a float and a submerged bait) it is now the custom to throw the fishes back alive into the river or lake – after keeping them in a net to be weighed at the end of the day if the angler is taking part, as is often the case, in a competition. Salmon and trout, fished for with a fly, are the expensive end of the sport (where it is conventionally called fishing rather than angling). The most desirable trout fishing is in the chalk streams of southern England, whereas the best salmon rivers are in Scotland.

Anglo-Catholicism A term first used in the 1830s to emphasize the continuity of the *Church of England from the pre-Reformation Roman Catholic Church, because of the apostolic succession – the unbroken chain of consecration, bishop to bishop, back to the apostles. The same tendency had earlier been called High Church (the new name was adopted at a time when restrictions on *Roman Catholics in England were at last being eased). The implication was not that there should be a reconciliation between the two churches, but that the Church of England could move closer to Roman Catholic ritual and theology without violating its own identity. This viewpoint (opposed by *Evangelicals) was strongly expressed in the *Oxford Movement and has remained an influential theme within the Church of England – though in 1993 many Anglo-Catholics were close to converting to Rome on the issue of the *ordination of women.

Anglo-Dutch Wars A series of three 17C conflicts between the two leading maritime and commercial nations of the time. Each was busy empire-building, with rival interests both in the Far East and in America, and each needed to protect its trade by asserting control over the English Channel.

The first war (1652–4) was essentially local, involving a series of skirmishes in the Channel between Robert Blake (1599–1657) and the Dutch admiral Maarten Tromp. The story of Tromp sailing up the Thames with a broom at his masthead (to demonstrate his power to sweep the seas) relates to a victory of his in 1652 but is probably apocryphal. The war ended, with advantages on the whole to Britain, in the treaty of Westminster (Apr. 1654).

The second war (1665–7) had more international aspects. It was partly provoked by the British capture in 1664 of the main Dutch possession in *America, the settlement of New Amsterdam on the island of Manhattan. The war spanned a period of double disaster in London (the Great Plague of 1665, the Great Fire of 1666) and it was a severe affront to national pride when a Dutch squadron sailed up the Medway in 1667 and destroyed several warships in Chatham dock. Both sides made concessions in the peace of Breda (July 1667); the most significant was the ceding to England of New Amsterdam, which was renamed New York.

The war of 1672–4 was part of a wider European conflict, in which England briefly sided with France in an attack on the United Provinces of the Netherlands; the Dutch remained at war with France until 1678, but England made separate terms in 1674 in the treaty of Westminster.

Anglo-Indians A term applied now to the community in India descended from mixed English and Indian parentage. In the past it was used also of British families living in India.

Anglo-Irish Irish people of English descent, in the centuries before the independence of the republic of *Ireland (1921). The term is sometimes applied to the descendants of the Norman barons, such as the Fitzgeralds, who were granted feudal lands in Ireland from the 12C onwards and who at the time of the Reformation remained Roman Catholic like the rest of Ireland. But these are more often called the Old English, leaving the name Anglo-Irish for the English families who settled in Ireland in the 16–17C and who were therefore Protestant. These people formed the Irish ruling class in the century before the Act of Union (1800), and it was they who provided so many talented writers, from Swift, Goldsmith and Sheridan to Wilde and Shaw.

Anglo-Irish Agreement Signed at *Hillsborough Castle on 15 November 1985 by the prime ministers of the United Kingdom and Ireland, Margaret Thatcher and Garrett FitzGerald. The agreement set up a regular inter-governmental conference of ministers and officials. It therefore gave the republic of Ireland a say, albeit oblique, in the affairs of *Northern Ireland. Widely welcomed by others, it was strenuously opposed in Ulster by many Unionists, particularly those of Ian *Paisley's faction.

Anglo-Irish War (1919–21, known in Ireland as the War of Independence) The formal name for the armed disturbances in Ireland popularly known as the *Troubles, which consisted of guerrilla and terrorist raids by the *IRA and often brutal reprisals by the British army and police, in particular the *Black and Tans. The unrest was the final violent stage of the long campaign for *Home Rule. The war ended when the Anglo-Irish Treaty of December 1921 recognized the independence of the Irish Free State (later the republic of *Ireland), with the six counties of Ulster remaining as *Northern Ireland within the United Kingdom – an uneasy compromise which 70 years later is no easier.

Anglo-Saxon see *English (the language) or *Anglo-Saxons (the people).

Anglo-Saxon Chronicle A narrative, surviving in seven different manuscripts, which is the main source of English history for the centuries leading up to the Norman Conquest. It was first compiled in the late 9C from earlier documents, including the work of *Bede. Unlike Bede's history it is in English rather than Latin, as a result of the campaign by *Alfred the Great to promote vernacular literature. The various manuscripts of the chronicle were continued sporadically after Alfred's reign, one having an entry as late as 1154.

Anglo-Saxon kingdoms The *Anglo-Saxons had by the 8C divided England into seven large and reasonably stable kingdoms known as the Heptarchy ('rule by seven' in Greek). The four smallest (Sussex, Kent, Essex and East Anglia) corresponded roughly to the areas still known by those names. The others were *Wessex, *Mercia and *Northumbria. The eastern kingdoms were conquered in the 9C by the *Danes.

Anglo-Saxons A group comprising all the Germanic tribes (mainly the *Angles, *Saxons and *Jutes) which moved into and controlled England between the departure of the Romans in the 5C and the arrival of the Normans in the 11C. The term was first used in pre-Norman times to distinguish the Saxons in England from those remaining on the Continent, but it has since been applied generally to the inhabitants of England in the centuries before the Norman Conquest.

angry young men Phrase coined by the press in 1956 after the great success of John Osborne's play *Look Back in Anger*. It was used to lump together several young writers who had little in common, except a shared impatience with the *Establishment. Apart from Osborne, the others most often described this way were Kingsley *Amis, Colin Wilson (because of his book *The Outsider*), and Kenneth *Tynan.

Anguilla Small island in the eastern Caribbean which is a British dependent territory. It was granted a measure of independence jointly with *St Kitts-Nevis, but it severed its links with them in 1967 (complaining of domination by St Kitts) and reverted to its dependent status.

Angus Until 1975 a *county on the east coast of Scotland, now part of the Tayside region. For Angus cattle see *Aberdeen Angus.

Animal Farm (1945) Satirical fable by George *Orwell on the process and pattern of revolution, particularly as seen in the Soviet Union. The farm animals revolt against the farmer, Mr Jones, and create their own Utopian community with slogans such as 'Four legs good, two legs bad' and 'All animals are equal'. But soon the pigs take control, with a power struggle developing between the ruthless Napoleon (Stalin) and the more idealistic Snowball (Trotsky). The good-natured carthorse, Boxer (the worker), believes everything he is told right up to the moment of his own dispatch to the knacker's yard. By the end Napoleon is living in Mr Jones's house and the slogans have been mysteriously transformed into 'Four legs good, two legs better' and 'All animals are equal, but some animals are more equal than others'.

Animal Liberation Front Organization which uses direct confrontation, sometimes involving criminal acts of terrorism, against any enterprise which it considers cruel to animals. It began in the early 1970s as the Band of Mercy, and was at that time committed to non-violence. The change of name came a few years later, coinciding with the adoption of a militant policy.

Anne (1665–1714) Queen of England, Scotland and Ireland from 1702; second daughter of James II and Anne Hyde; married 1683 Prince George of Denmark; succeeded her brother-in-law, *William III.

Anne's years as a princess were darkened by tragedies of childbirth. She suffered ten miscarriages, gave birth to four infants who died within weeks, and saw her only surviving child die at the age of 11 (William, duke of Gloucester, 1689–1700). Before she even ascended the throne, the Act of *Settlement had made provision for her to be succeeded by a distant cousin. Anne's comfort, in addition to that of a happy marriage, had been in her close friendship with Sarah Jennings; they were famous for dropping royal protocol to such an extent that Sarah addressed the princess as Mrs Morley and was called Mrs Freeman in return. After Sarah married the duke of *Marlborough the couple remained Anne's closest allies, until political differences intervened and Sarah was replaced as friend and favourite by Abigail Hill (Mrs Masham).

Internationally the dominant factor of her reign was the War of the *Spanish Succession. At home her policies were guided largely by her devotion to the Anglican church, a commitment which had caused her to welcome the Protestant William III when he replaced her Roman Catholic father on the throne. One of her most lasting acts as queen was to use the crown revenue from the church (originally taxes paid to the pope, appropriated by Henry VIII) to increase the livings of the poorer parish clergy. The fund, known as Queen Anne's Bounty, is now administered by the *Church Commissioners. Anne's death brought to an end the *Stuart dynasty. She was succeeded by George I and the house of *Hanover (see also the *royal house).

Princess **Anne** see the *Princess Royal.

Anne Boleyn (c.1507–36) Second wife of *Henry VIII and mother of Elizabeth I. She grew up at *Hever Castle. The king's infatuation with her (his love letters survive) coincided with his determination to divorce *Catherine of Aragon, who had failed to provide him with a male heir and was now in her forties. The couple married secretly in January 1533 and in May archbishop Cranmer pronounced the previous marriage with Catherine invalid (a decisive step in the English *Reformation). The birth of a girl in September was a disappointment to Henry, compounded when Anne had a late miscarriage, probably of a male child, in January 1536. In May of that year he sent her to the Tower, accused of adultery with several men, including her own brother (it is not known whether any of the charges were true). Her reputed lovers were executed on May 17 and she was beheaded on May 19. The next day Henry was betrothed to Jane Seymour, whom he married on May 30.

Anne Hathaway's Cottage (2km/1m W of Stratford-upon-Avon) Family home in which Anne *Hathaway grew up, in the village of Shottery, before marrying William *Shakespeare. An attractive half-timbered and thatched building, it is a substantial farmhouse rather than a cottage, for the Hathaways were a prosperous *yeoman family.

Anne of Cleves (1515–57) Fourth wife of *Henry VIII, who married her in January 1540. She was the daughter of a German duke, and Henry was hoping for a German alliance against the Catholic powers of Europe. His distaste at first sight of her (calling her the *'Flanders mare') led to his not consummating the marriage; he was therefore able to have it annulled six months later, by which time changes in Europe had also made the alliance less necessary. Anne, whose fault was probably being dull rather than ugly, was given a good pension and lived in apparent contentment in England through the rest of Henry's reign, and then through that of Edward VI and all but one year of Mary's.

Annie Laurie Scottish song whose origins are as misty as the love it expresses. Annie Laurie (1682–1764) was the daughter of Sir Robert Laurie of Maxwelton; it is said that she rejected the love of William Douglas of Fingland, who then wrote this lyric claiming that she gave him her promise true in Maxwelton braes. However the text first appears in a book of ballads in 1823 and its famous tune was not published until 1838. Lady John Scott later claimed to be author of the tune and adapter of William Douglas's words.

Pietro **Annigoni** (1910–88) Italian painter who became famous in Britain for his meticulously realistic portrait of *Elizabeth II, commissioned in 1954 by the Fishmongers, one of the *City Livery Companies.

Mary **Anning** see *Lyme Regis.

'annual income twenty pounds' The borderline in *David Copperfield* between happiness and misery, in the economic philosophy of Mr Micawber. 'Annual income twenty pounds, annual expenditure nineteen nineteen six, result happiness. Annual income twenty pounds, annual expenditure twenty pounds ought and six, result misery.'

another place Circumlocution used by speakers in either of the Houses of *Parliament when referring to the other, as a way round the convention that it is improper to comment on what has been said in the other chamber.

St **Anselm** (c.1033–1109) Monk and theologian who was archbishop of Canterbury from 1093. Born in northern Italy, he entered the monastery of Bec, in Normandy, where Lanfranc was teaching; Anselm succeeded the older man as prior at Bec and later at Canterbury. His years as archbishop were marked by a long battle with first William II and then Henry I over the relative powers of church and state, particularly in the matter of appointing bishops. Anselm was a prolific author and has remained highly regarded as a theologian. There is no record of his canonization, but pilgrimages to his shrine at Canterbury were common from the 12c. In 1720 he acquired the status of a saint through being declared a doctor of the church. His feast day is April 21.

Anthem for Doomed Youth Sonnet by Wilfred *Owen, written towards the end of World War I, which is a bleak indictment of the appalling slaughter. It begins with the question 'What passing-bells for these who die as cattle?', and concludes that they will be commemorated only in 'the tenderness of silent minds,/And each slow dusk a drawing-down of blinds'.

Antigua and Barbuda Member of the *Commonwealth since 1981, consisting of two small islands in the eastern Caribbean. Barbuda was colonized by English settlers in 1628 and Antigua in 1632. Barbuda was for two centuries the private property of the Codrington family, to whom it was granted by Charles II in 1680. The islands became internally self-governing in 1967 and independent in 1981.

antisepsis see Joseph *Lister.

Antonine Wall Roman protective earthwork, now largely destroyed, which ran 60km/37m across the entire width of Scotland from the Clyde (at Old Kilpatrick) to the Forth (at Bridgeness). Its construction was ordered in about AD 142 by the emperor in Rome, Antoninus Pius, thus pushing north the frontier of Roman Britain only 15 years after the building of *Hadrian's Wall. But the new line was one which the legions found hard to hold, and the Antonine Wall was abandoned before the end of the century. It was a turf rampart, on stone foundations, with a ditch in front and a military road running behind. There were forts every 3km/2m for the garrisons. The best preserved of these forts is Rough Castle, 8km/5m west of Falkirk.

Antony and Cleopatra (*c*.1607) Tragedy by *Shakespeare, based on the relationship in the 1st century BC between the Roman general, Mark Antony, and Cleopatra, queen of Egypt. The Roman is diverted from his duty not only by the charms of the queen but by the luxurious appeal of the east, expressed in the play's most famous speech when Enobarbus describes Antony's first glimpse of Cleopatra:

> The barge she sat in, like a burnish'd throne,
> Burnt on the water: the poop was beaten gold.

Defeated in battle, Antony falls on his sword and dies in Cleopatra's arms. She commits suicide by snake-bite, applying an asp to her breast.

Antrim County and town (21,000 in 1991) in Northern Ireland. With the reorganization of *local government in 1973, the town became a district within the *county. It contains, near the northeast corner of Lough Neagh, a superb example of a monastic *round tower, dating from the 10C.

Any old iron see Harry *Champion.

Any Questions? (BBC) Long-running radio discussion programme, on the air from 1948 and broadcast from a succession of different halls around the country. Four people form a panel to answer questions each Friday evening from a local audience. A high proportion of the panellists are politicians, and the questions (selected by the producer but coming as a surprise to the team) are on serious and usually topical subjects, with a few frivolous ones let through for variety. The series has been associated with two chairmen in particular – Freddie Grisewood (1948–67) and then David *Jacobs until 1984. They were followed by John Timpson (1984–7) and Jonathan Dimbleby. A selection of listeners' responses to what has been said makes up the following week's edition of *Any Answers?*. The television adaptation of the format is *Question Time.

Anzio Town on the west coast of Italy, 50km/31m south of Rome, where allied forces landed in *World War II (22 Jan. 1944) for a quick thrust up to the Italian capital. Instead they allowed themselves to be trapped at the coast and only just survived a German counter-attack in early February.

APEX see *GMB.

Apostles see the *Cambridge spies.

appeasement Term used in particular of the appeasing of Adolf Hitler's expansionist claims in the late 1930s, a policy closely identified with Neville *Chamberlain and most in evidence at *Munich. Popular with a majority of the British public at the time, and as widely vilified by a majority in the decades after World War II, the best defence of the policy has been that it delayed the war by a year and gave Britain time to rearm.

Appleby (2500 in 1981) Ancient town in Cumbria, with a Norman castle, best known now for the week-long horse fair which has been held there in early June since 1751. It is by far the largest annual gathering of Britain's *Gypsies.

apple charlotte A *charlotte* is a French dessert, in which fruit baked within a casing of bread remains firm enough to be turned out on a plate. It has been adapted to a rather different British pudding, baked until the apple is almost a purée and the buttered and sugared bread on top is crisp and golden.

apple-pie bed A children's bedtime joke in which a sheet is folded and tucked across the middle of the bed, preventing the occupant from getting more than half way in. The name may derive from the folded pastry of an apple turnover or from the French *nappe pliée*, meaning a folded cloth.

apple-pie order see *A was an apple pie.

Edward **Appleton** (1892–1965, KCB 1941) English physicist, awarded the 1947 Nobel prize for his research into the ionosphere. In 1924 he provided the first experimental evidence of the reflecting layer which had been postulated by *Heaviside and Kennelly. He later discovered a higher layer, known for a while as the Appleton layer but now more commonly called the F-layer.

Apprentice Boys' March see *Londonderry.

April Fool's Day The tradition of jokes at the expense of the gullible on the first day of April exists in many countries, but its origin is unknown. In Britain newspapers and television companies, in addition to children, make the most of the opportunity. The *Guardian* has published on that day detailed reports from the island of San Serife, and in 1957 BBC TV scored a notable success with Richard Dimbleby showing the long soft tendrils being picked from trees in the Italian spaghetti harvest.

APRS see *rural protection.

Apsley House (London SW1) Built by Robert *Adam in 1771–8, this house at Hyde Park Corner was the first imposing residence after entering London through the tollgates at Knightsbridge and so acquired the popular address 'No. 1 London'. It was bought in 1817 by the duke of *Wellington, who made major changes to the exterior. In 1947 his descendant gave it to the nation, and since 1952 it has been open to the public as the Wellington Museum.

Its main treasures are items presented to Wellington. These include the Sèvres Egyptian dessert service, and the huge marble statue by Canova of the duke's rival, Napoleon, as a heroic nude. The Waterloo Gallery contains many of the paintings which were honourable loot from the Peninsular War. Wellington captured them from the French, who had removed them from the Spanish royal collection, and he was told by the Spanish king to keep them for his pains. They include the superb early Velazquez of *The Waterseller of Seville*.

Aquae Sulis see *Bath.

aquatint see Paul *Sandby.

The Arabian Nights (short for *The Arabian Nights' Entertainments*) The name by which *The Thousand and One Nights*, an ancient collection of Arabic stories, is more commonly known in English. Both titles refer to the fictional device linking the stories. Shahrazad, or Scheherazade, is married to a king who kills each new bride the morning after consummating the marriage. Shahrazad saves herself by telling him a succession of cliff-hanging tales, so exciting that he cannot resist keeping her alive one more night to hear what comes next. Her repertoire includes *Aladdin, *Ali Baba and *Sindbad the Sailor. The best-known English translation is that of 1885–8 by Richard *Burton.

Arbroath (24,000 in 1991) Fishing port and resort in the Tayside region of Scotland. The abbey was founded in 1178 by William the Lion, king of Scotland, and was dedicated to Thomas *Becket, martyred eight years previously and already canonized. The Declaration of Arbroath was made here by a Scottish parliament in 1320 and was sent to the pope, informing him that Robert the Bruce was king of an independent Scotland. The main feature of the red sandstone ruins of the abbey church is a circular window, still intact, known as the 'round O of Abroath'.

arbroath smokie Haddock cured by smoking at Arbroath, a port on the coast of Scotland northeast of Dundee.

Jeffrey **Archer** (b. 1940, baron 1992) Conservative politician and author. He was MP for Louth (1969–74) but resigned his seat when the failure of a business venture threatened him with bankruptcy. He avoided that outcome by writing a novel about someone who fights his way out of a similar predicament (*Not a Penny More, Not a Penny Less* 1975), and the success of the book launched him on his new career. Subsequent bestselling titles, much helped by his own thorough promotional campaigns, have included *Kane and Abel* (1979), *First Among Equals* (1984) and a book of short stories, *A Twist in the Tale* (1988).

His political career seemed to take on a new lease of life in 1985 when Mrs Thatcher made him deputy chairman of the Conservative party, but it came to an abrupt end again with his resignation in 1986 after the *News of the World* broke the story of a bizarre incident, never fully explained. Reporting that Archer had sent £2000 in a bundle of £50 notes to a prostitute, Monica Coghlan, the paper maintained he was paying her to go abroad to avoid a scandal; Archer insisted that he had never met the woman, and that he was resigning 'for lack of judgement and that alone'. He subsequently won heavy libel damages (£500,000) against the *Daily Star* for stating that he had been seen visiting Coghlan's address. In addition to the salacious interest attached to Coghlan's unsuccessful attempts to prove that there had been an intimate friendship, the case became widely remembered for one phrase: the judge, Mr Justice Caulfield, emphasizing the strong support shown for her husband in court by Mary Archer, recommended her to the jury as someone notably 'fragrant' by comparison with other witnesses.

*The **Archers*** (BBC from 1950) The world's longest running broadcast serial, on BBC radio nationally with a 15-minute episode five days a week from 1 January 1951 (it had previously been heard for a few months in the Midland region). It was devised for a practical purpose – to convey useful information to the farming community – and 40 years on it still deliberately writes into the plot themes of topical concern to its audience. The original Archers were Dan and Doris, living at Brookfield Farm in Ambridge, and their descendants remain the central family; prominent among their neighbours are the trouble-prone Grundys. Ambridge is situated south of Borchester in the fictional county of Borsetshire, but in another sense it has a real location at Hanbury in Worcestershire; Brookfield Farm was based on the first producer's farm there, and various weddings in the series have been recorded in Hanbury church. The programme has a tradition of occasionally including real people: Princess Margaret visited Ambridge for a charity fashion show in 1984, as president of the NSPCC; and in 1992 Eddie Grundy got drunk on champagne in Britt Ekland's dressing room, when she was in the Borchester Christmas pantomime. The signature tune, 'Barwick Green', comes from *My Native Heath*, a suite written in 1922 by Arthur Wood.

Forest of **Arden** Forest in Warwickshire, long ago cleared and surviving at most in small isolated patches. The name has a wider resonance because the pastoral scenes in * As You Like It* are set in the Forest of Arden.

Mary **Arden** The mother of William *Shakespeare. She married John Shakespeare in about 1557 after growing up at Wilmcote, 8km/5m northwest of Stratford-upon-Avon. An antiquarian decided two centuries later, on no particular evidence, which house was hers. It has been shown as such to tourists ever since.

Edward **Ardizzone** (1900–79) Son of an Italian father and English mother, he illustrated more than 170 books by other authors and some 20 of his own – in particular a series about a small boy and his adventures at sea, which ran from *Tim and the Brave Sea Captain* (1936) to *Tim's Last Voyage* (1972).

Ardoch Roman Camp (19km/12m N of Stirling) The earthworks of a large military camp, active in the early 2nd century AD and probably in use as an outpost after the building of the *Antonine Wall to the south.

area Measurements of area are for the most part measurements of *length squared (see box for metric and *imperial equivalents). The exception is in defining medium-sized areas of land, where the traditional British unit is the acre – Old English for a field. The imperial acre (4840 square yards) shows at present little sign of yielding to the metric hectare (10,000 square metres).

Measurements of area		
Imperial		*Metric*
0.155 sq. inches	=	**1 sq. centimetre**
1 sq. inch	=	6.452 sq. centimetres
(144 sq. inches) **1 sq. foot**	=	929.03 sq. centimetres
(9 sq. feet) **1 sq. yard**	=	8361 sq. centimetres or 0.8361 sq. metre
1.196 sq. yards	=	**1 sq. metre** (10,000 sq. centimetres)
(4840 sq. yards) **1 acre**	=	4047 sq. metres or 0.4047 hectares
2.471 acres	=	**1 hectare** (10,000 sq. metres)
0.386 sq. miles or 247.1 acres	=	**1 sq. kilometre** (100 hectares)
(640 acres) **1 sq. mile**	=	2.59 sq. kilometres or 259 hectares

'Are you sitting comfortably?' see * *Listen with Mother*.

Argyll Until 1975 a *county on the west coast of Scotland, now mostly in Strathclyde with part in the Highland region.

Argyll Group Food retailer, formed as a company in 1977. Its most important supermarkets are the Safeway chain, acquired in 1987 and much expanded since. In 1986 Argyll was the loser in a £2.7bn takeover battle with Guinness for Distillers, the opponent's tactics later becoming exposed in the *Guinness affair.

Ariel see *The *Tempest*.

Arkle (foaled 1957) Irish-bred and trained bay colt which dominated English steeplechasing in 1962–6, winning three successive *Cheltenham Gold Cups (1964, 65, 66) and much else with Pat Taaffe (1930–92) in the saddle. His career was made doubly exciting by an intense rivalry (from which he emerged the clear winner) with a great English contemporary, *Mill House.

Ark Royal A name of great resonance in naval history, used mainly for aircraft carriers in the 20c but going back to Lord Howard of Effingham's flagship against the *Armada, which was also sometimes referred to just as the *Ark*.

Anonymous contemporary view of the Armada: Drake's Revenge *is bottom left and Howard of Effingham's* Ark Royal *bottom right.*

Richard **Arkwright** (1732–92, kt 1786) Outstanding example of the type of inventor-entrepreneur who drove forward the early stages of the *Industrial Revolution. Starting out as a travelling wig-maker, he became interested in the machinery for spinning cotton and made important technical advances. To put them into practice he built a factory at *Cromford, in Derbyshire, which was run by water power. It was the first of many, and in his later years he was employing some 5000 workers.

John **Arlott** (1914–91) Commentator on *cricket for BBC radio from 1947 to 1980, after being a detective sergeant with the Southampton police. His ability to evoke both the match and the surrounding scene, combined with the much imitated richness of his Hampshire accent, caused him to be described as the 'voice of English summer'.

Armada The word itself is merely the Spanish for 'armed'; the Armada of 1588 was called in full *La Flota Armada Invencible*, the armed invincible fleet. It was sent against England by Philip II of Spain for several reasons: to restore Roman Catholicism to the country previously ruled by his ardently Catholic wife, *Mary I; to end English assistance to the rebels in the Netherlands, who had been opposing Spanish rule there since 1567; and to keep English sailors away from his American possessions. In 1585–6 a fleet under *Drake had plundered the Spanish Caribbean. Drake then had the effrontery to attack the gathering Armada in Cadiz harbour in 1587 (an act which became known as 'singeing the king of

Spain's beard'). The Spanish ships at Cadiz were mainly galleys, the basic Spanish fighting ship, but this encounter convinced Philip that sails rather than oars were needed to match the agile English vessels. He rapidly assembled galleons, many of them converted merchant ships, and it was a somewhat unwieldy fleet of 130 vessels which sailed north in 1588 under the command of the duke of Medina Sidonia.

The plan was to pick up at Calais an army from the Spanish Netherlands (roughly Belgium) for an invasion of England. The English fleet was under the overall command of Lord Howard of Effingham (1536–1624); Drake was his vice admiral, *Hawkins the rear admiral. They harried the Armada in the English Channel, but the Spanish fleet reached Calais virtually intact – only to find that the promised army was not there. The English then sent fireships towards the anchored Spaniards, who cut their cables and moved in great disorder some 16km/10m northeast to Gravelines, where the only real battle took place. The more mobile English had destroyed at least three of the Armada and had severely battered the rest, without losing a single ship, when both sides ran out of ammunition. The wind then shifted from northwest to southwest and the Armada limped away into the North Sea; it continued round the tip of Scotland and into the Atlantic, losing almost half the fleet (51 ships went down or were wrecked) and thousands of men before reaching home. It was the first battle between fleets of sailing ships, inaugurating a form of warfare in which Britain excelled during the next two centuries, culminating in Trafalgar.

Armagh The name of one of the six *counties of Northern Ireland; also of one of the province's most ancient towns (14,000 in 1991) and Ireland's ecclesiastical centre. With the reorganization of *local government in 1973 the town of Armagh became a district within the county. Its history goes back to the 5C, when it was chosen by St *Patrick as his headquarters. It is the seat of two archbishops, Roman Catholic and Anglican, each head of his own community in both parts of Ireland and each bearing the title Archbishop of Armagh and Primate of all Ireland. The Anglican cathedral is of the 18–19C and the Catholic entirely 19C. Secular buildings of the 18C include one by Thomas Cooley housing the Royal School (founded by James I in 1608) and an Observatory which has been in use since 1791.

armed forces They consist of the *Royal Navy, the *Royal Marines, the *Army and the *Royal Air Force, with a total of about 265,000 men and 19,000 women serving in 1992. As the graph shows, numbers have declined steadily over the past 30 years, and the reduction will be more rapid during the 1990s (see *Options for *Change* for the proposed levels in the army). The officer in command of the armed forces is the chief of the defence staff, while political control lies with the secretary of state for *defence.

Armistice Term used in particular of the agreement which ended World War I. It was signed at 5 a.m. on 11 November 1918 in the railway carriage of the French field marshal Foch, at Rethondes in the forest of Compiègne. Hostilities were to cease at 11 o'clock that same morning (a moment of some resonance, being the 11th hour of the 11th day of the 11th month). On the first anniversary there began the custom of a two-minute silence at exactly that time, in remembrance of the dead. For many years people stopped at 11 a.m. on Armistice Day (known also as *Poppy Day) and stood quietly, wherever they might be; traffic and factories came to a halt, for an expression of national grief in which everybody had someone to mourn. After World War II Armistice Day was adapted to become a commemoration of the dead of both wars. The name became Remembrance Day, or Remembrance Sunday, and the date was moved to the second Sunday in

---

Relative ranks in the armed forces

Royal Navy	Army	RAF
Officers		
Admiral of the Fleet	Field Marshal	Marshal of the Royal Air Force
Admiral	General	Air Chief Marshal
Vice-Admiral	Lieutenant-General	Air Marshal
Rear-Admiral	Major-General	Air Vice-Marshal
Commodore	Brigadier	Air Commodore
Captain	Colonel	Group Captain
Commander	Lieutenant-Colonel	Wing Commander
Lieutenant-Commander	Major	Squadron Leader
Lieutenant	Captain	Flight Lieutenant
Sub-Lieutenant	Lieutenant/2nd Lieutenant	Flying Officer/Pilot Officer
Noncommissioned officers		
Fleet Chief Petty Officer	Warrant Officer Class 1	Warrant Officer
	Warrant Officer Class 2	
Chief Petty Officer	Staff Sergeant	Flight Sergeant/Chief Technician
Petty Officer	Sergeant	Sergeant
Leading Rate	Corporal	Corporal
	Lance-Corporal	

Armed Forces: total personnel, male and female

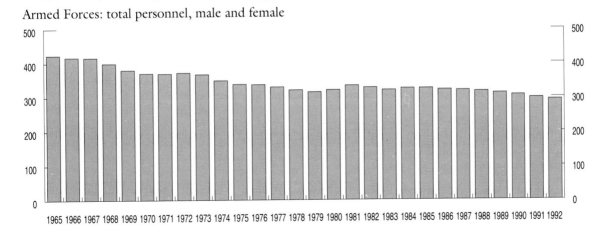

The proportions are approximately Royal Navy 20%, Royal Marines 2%, Army 50%, Royal Air Force 28%. Women, represented in all the services except the Marines, account for some 8% of the total. *Source: Annual Abstract of Statistics (see *Central Statistical Office).*

November. There are ceremonies at 11 a.m. on that day at war memorials all over the country, and in particular at London's *Cenotaph.

Armouries see *Royal Armouries.

Arms and the Man (1894) Play by George Bernard *Shaw which lightly mocks the conventional heroics of both love and war. A dishevelled Swiss mercenary officer, Captain Bluntschli, escapes from his pursuers by climbing into the bedroom of the young heroine, Raina. She feeds him chocolate creams, helps him to avoid discovery and later dreams of her 'Chocolate Cream Soldier'. He returns after the war, upsets the formal certainties of her life and replaces the pompous Sergius as her fiancé.

Armstrong Siddeley Company formed in 1919 by the amalgamation of two Coventry firms, Armstrong-Whitworth and Siddeley-Deasy. Cars were produced under this name, mostly at the top end of the market, until 1960. The company was also a major producer of aircraft engines, evolving in 1935 into *Hawker Siddeley.

Army Until the 17C there was no standing army in Britain. The larger of the two kingdoms, England, had always depended for defence on its navy – enlisting men for military campaigns only when required. Cromwell's *New Model Army of 1645 was the first step in a new direction. It was only a little later – at the Restoration – that the oldest regiments in today's regular army were established (the Grenadier, Coldstream and Scots Guards in the infantry, the Life Guards and Horse Guards in the cavalry, and the Royal Marines). Many regiments were founded in two subsequent periods of prolonged warfare, the early 18C and the early 19C. In recent years regiments have been increasingly merged as the size of the army shrinks (see *armed forces and *Options for Change); in 1992 the approximate numbers serving were 132,000 men and 8000 women.

The officer in command of the army is the chief of the general staff (CGS); and the government department controlling it, previously the War Office, is now the army department of the Ministry of *Defence.

Thomas **Arne** (1710–78) In his time the most successful composer of songs for London's theatres and pleasure gardens, best remembered now for *Rule, Britannia!

Arnhem Town in the Netherlands, on the north bank of the lower Rhine, which was the target of an ambitious operation in *World War II. The allied forces under Montgomery, pushing north, needed to capture the Rhine bridges. On 17 September 1944 paratroops and gliders of the British 1st Airborne Division were dropped beyond the Rhine to seize the north end of the bridge. But the main army, pressing up from the south, failed to reach them in time. On September 25 Montgomery ordered the advance troops to pull back across the river; only some 2400 of the original 10,000 had been able to do so before the remaining survivors were captured. The campaign was the subject of the film *A Bridge Too Far* (1977).

Dr **Arnold** (Thomas Arnold, 1795–1842) Headmaster of Rugby from 1827 till his death, and the single most formative influence on the development of the *public schools. He said on his appointment that his object would be to form Christian men ('Christian boys I can scarcely hope to make'), and the resulting emphasis was on the building of character. Arnold was quite plain about his priorities: 'first, religious and moral principles; secondly, gentlemanly conduct; thirdly, intellectual ability'. An idealized portrait of him is given by one of his boys, Thomas Hughes, in *Tom Brown's Schooldays*. Matthew *Arnold was his son.

Malcolm **Arnold** (b. 1921, kt 1993) Composer whose career began as a trumpeter (principal with the London Philharmonic till 1948). He has been prolific over a wide range, from symphonies to ballets and film music (winning an Oscar for his score for *Bridge on the River Kwai*).

Matthew **Arnold** (1822–88) Poet and critic, son of the Rugby headmaster, Thomas Arnold. His professional career was as an inspector of schools. Poetry was a main concern in the first half of his life (*The Scholar-Gipsy* 1853, *Dover Beach* 1867), but he turned later to wide-ranging works of prose criticism. The most influential of these has been *Culture and Anarchy* (1869), a collection of essays analysing the cultural and educational needs of a healthy society.

The Arnolfini Marriage (1434, National Gallery) Painting by Jan van Eyck which is believed to depict Giovanni di Arnolfini, an Italian merchant in the Belgian city of Bruges, with his bride Giovanna (who was long assumed to be pregnant, an impression caused only by the fashion of her dress).

The mirror on the wall shows two other figures, perhaps witnesses to the marriage ceremony, and the inscription above is taken to suggest that the artist was one of them, for it reads *Johannes de eyck fuit hic* (Jan van Eyck was here). The dog is probably a symbol of marital fidelity rather than their actual pet.

Arran Island and resort off the west coast of Scotland, in the Strathclyde region, with dramatic scenery of moor and glen rising to the peak of Goat Fell (874m/2866ft). The island's capital, Brodick, lies on the east, close to *Brodick Castle.

Arsenal, known as the Gunners (Highbury, London N5). Football club formed in 1884 among workers in the Royal Arsenal at *Woolwich (the name Arsenal was adopted in 1886). The club turned professional in 1891 and was elected that same year to Division 2 of the *Football League. Since 1904 they have played continuously in Division 1 apart from two years (1913–14), which were also the first two years after the move to Highbury in north London. Inspired by Herbert *Chapman, they were so successful in the 1930s that the local tube station, Gillespie Road, was renamed Arsenal in their honour. They have been League champions ten times (a record beaten only by Liverpool), and are one of only five clubs to have won the championship and the FA Cup in the same season (1970–1). In the early 1990s Arsenal acquired a very high-scoring striker in Ian Wright (b. 1963). Club victories: FA Cup 1930, 36, 50, 71, 79, 93; League Champions 1931, 33, 34, 35, 38, 48, 53, 71, 89, 91; League Cup 1987, 93; Fairs Cup (now UEFA Cup) 1970.

Art Deco The dominant international style between the wars, which had developed gradually from about 1905. The term became current only in the 1960s; it was derived from the first big international exhibition of design after World War I, held in Paris in 1925, *L'Exposition Internationale des Arts Décoratifs et Industriels Modernes* (The International Exhibition of Modern Decorative and Industrial Arts). The emphasis was on straight lines, firm curves and bright colours, suitable for mass production, in deliberate contrast to the more sinuous subtleties of *Art Nouveau. The best-known British designer in the style is Clarice *Cliff.

art for art's sake see *Aesthetic Movement.

Artful Dodger see *Oliver Twist.

King **Arthur** Britain's main contribution to legend. It is possible that Arthur had a historical origin, as a leader of the *Britons against the advancing *Anglo-Saxons in the early 6C, but he is first mentioned in this role by the chronicler Nennius in the 9C (the gap is equivalent to a first mention of Oliver Cromwell today). It was in Wales that stories about Arthur began to proliferate and they were brought together in the 12C by *Geoffrey of Monmouth. In his version Arthur was born at *Tintagel and is the son of Uther Pendragon, king of the Britons, and of his Cornish wife Igraine; he has mounted knights as his followers; he already has his sword, *Excalibur, and his faithful friend Gawain; mortally wounded fighting against his treacherous nephew Mordred, he is borne away to the island of *Avalon.

The success of Geoffrey's account carried Arthur's fame abroad, and it was writers in France in the following decades who completed his transformation into a hero of courtly romance; Wace, a Norman cleric, added the detail of the *Round Table, while Chrétien de Troyes introduced Lancelot and his love for Guinevere, together with the entire theme of the *Holy Grail. It was from these many sources that Malory compiled his *Morte d'Arthur*, the version in which the stories have been widely known ever since. There are several competing candidates for the site of Arthur's supposed capital, *Camelot.

Arthur's Seat see the Palace of *Holyroodhouse.

Art Nouveau (French for 'new art') The name for the style which was fashionable from 1890 to 1910, based on a sinuous line making much of the growth of vegetation and the flow of long female hair. The name was that of a shop in Paris, specializing in this fashion in the 1890s; the style was also associated with *Liberty's in London (it became known in Italy as *stile Liberty*). It was influenced by various earlier developments in Britain, including the William *Morris factory, the *Arts and Crafts movement, the art of *Burne-Jones and, more obliquely, the rediscovery of William *Blake with his emphasis on flowing line. Once the style was established, the leading British practitioners moved rapidly to a more severe version which prefigured much in 20C design. Examples are the illustrations of *Beardsley and the furniture of Charles Rennie *Mackintosh.

Arts and Crafts Movement A conscious return in the second half of the 19C to the romantic idea of medieval craftsmanship. Inspired by John *Ruskin's passionate rejection of the machine age and by the socialist ideals of William *Morris, the aim was, in Morris's words, to rediscover 'art made by the people, and for the people, as a happiness to the maker and the user'. The most effective example of the idea in practice was Morris's own firm, founded in 1861.

art schools The longest-established art school in Britain is that of the *Royal Academy, which today offers postgraduate courses in painting and sculpture. The free teaching of talented students was part of the academy's original purpose in 1768, and Blake, Lawrence, Turner and Constable were among the early pupils. The academy's emphasis was naturally on the fine arts, but the next wave of London art schools was a result of the mid-19C concern with industrial design.

The Royal College of Art descends from a Government School of Design set up in 1837 by the Board of Trade. It was greatly expanded in 1853, in the aftermath of the *Great Exhibition, when it became the National Art Training School (its premises, beside the Albert Hall, are in the district developed with the profits of the exhibition). It became the Royal College of Art in 1896, and in recent times has been purely a postgraduate college. It had a particularly lively period from the late 1950s, when Bridget Riley, Peter Blake and David Hockney were among the students.

Another school founded in the immediate aftermath of the Great Exhibition was Saint Martin's. It began, in 1854, as a local initiative by the vicar of St-Martin-in-the-Fields to teach design to local boys. It became an independent school in 1859 and remained so until merged, in 1989, with the Central School of Art and Design. The Central, established in 1896 by the London County Council as the Central School of Arts and Crafts, offered evening courses to apprentices and others, with an emphasis on the direct handling of tools and materials in the spirit of the *Arts and Crafts movement. The Central's buildings in Southampton Row are the premises for the merged Central Saint Martins College of Art and Design. In 1989 the combined college became one of five forming the London Institute, Europe's largest group for art and design education with some 20,000 students; the other four are the Camberwell College of Arts, the Chelsea College of Art and Design, the London College of Fashion and the London College of Printing and Distributive Trades.

The Slade School of Fine Art proclaims in its name a different approach, keeping to the high ground. Resulting from a bequest by Felix *Slade, it was established in 1871 as part of London's University College It was particularly influential around the turn of the century, when Augustus and Gwen John and Stanley Spencer were among the students.

The most distinguished of the many art schools elsewhere in the country is in Glasgow. Dating back to 1844, it is housed in famous premises designed by one of its own graduates, Charles Rennie *Mackintosh. He won the competition for the new building in 1896 and produced what is regarded as one of the masterpieces of Art Nouveau. Constructed over two periods (1897–9, 1907–9), the Glasgow School of Art still contains the furniture which Mackintosh designed for the library, director's room and board room.

Arts Council (of Great Britain) Independent public body, established in 1946, which receives each year a lump sum from the government and then distributes it to arts organizations (in particular music and the performing arts) throughout the country.

Arundel (2500 in 1981) Town in West Sussex on the river Arun. It developed on the slope of the hill rising from the river to the Norman castle, established in the late 11C as a stronghold to control much of the south coast. The castle has been inherited within just two related families since the 12C, but its interior is now largely of the 18–19C (including a superb neo-Gothic library). Since 1672 its owners, the dukes of Norfolk, have been hereditary *earl marshals of England.

Ascension Island of volcanic origin in the south Atlantic, administered from *St Helena (some 1125km/700m to the southeast). It was uninhabited until 1815, when Napoleon was sent to St Helena and Britain posted troops on Ascension. It later became an important link in communications systems (submarine cable and radio), and in the 1980s acquired a new prominence as a staging post to the *Falklands.

*The **Ascent of Man*** (BBC 1973) Thirteen-part television series telling the story of man's discoveries in agriculture, technology and science. Written by Jacob Bronowski (1908–74), and presented by him with an intensity which made the very processes of thought seem to live, it brought to a wide public the broad sweep of scientific history.

Roger **Ascham** (1516–68) Schoolmaster who was tutor for two years to the future Elizabeth I, from when she was 15. His book *The Schoolmaster*, published by his widow in 1570, lays out his liberal ideas on education. He believed that it can only succeed if the child finds it attractive. By the same token he was against corporal punishment.

Ascot (11km/7m S of Windsor) Racecourse famous in particular for its summer meeting, held for four days in June and known as Royal Ascot; the link with royalty goes back to 1711, when a race meeting here was founded by Queen Anne. Ascot remains a firm fixture in the royal family's calendar. Known for its display of fashion (with a minority tradition of outrageous hats), the meeting's most famous race is the Gold Cup (4-year-olds and upwards, run since 1807). But Ascot's biggest race, in terms of prize money and prestige, is run at the July meeting. It is the King George VI and Queen Elizabeth Diamond Stakes (for 3-year-olds and upwards), founded in 1951 to mark the Festival of Britain.

ASH (Action on Smoking and Health, London W1) Britain's first campaigning medical charity (and most successful acronym). ASH was founded by the Royal College of Physicians in 1971 to promote positive action against smoking after the publication of their report *Smoking and Health Now*. The charity acts as a pressure group by spreading information about the hazards of smoking and by public relations campaigns – such as the Butt of the Month Award introduced in 1973 for the most appalling tobacco advertisement. The ASH fact sheet justifiably claims *James I as one of the earliest known supporters of the cause.

Peggy **Ashcroft** (1907–91, DBE 1956) Actress with an exceptionally distinguished career of more than 60 years in a wide range of classic and modern roles. She first appeared at the Birmingham Repertory Theatre in 1926. In London she was Desdemona to Paul Robeson's Othello (1930) and Juliet in Gielgud's production of *Romeo and Juliet* (1935). She has been closely involved with all the important developments in postwar London theatre, starring in the first season of the *English Stage Company (*The Good Woman of Setzuan*), becoming a mainstay of the *Royal Shakespeare Company during the 1960s and 1970s, and then appearing frequently at the *National Theatre. Her career in television and films flourished in the 1980s, when she received awards for *The Jewel in the Crown* (1984) and for *A Passage to India* (1985).

Paddy **Ashdown** (Jeremy John Durham Ashdown, b. 1941) Politician, MP for Yeovil since 1983 (originally as a Liberal) and leader of the *Liberal Democrats from their formation in 1988. He served in the Royal Marines (1959–71) and in the diplomatic service (1971–6) and worked in industry before entering politics.

He was the victim in 1992 of a mysterious series of events apparently designed to harm the Liberal Democrats at the time of the general election. A thief broke into his solicitor's office and stole nothing except the petty cash and a confidential document about a love affair between Ashdown and his former secretary. The document was offered for money to the press and a scandal looked like developing, until Ashdown defused it by simply announcing that the affair had indeed taken place, several years in the past.

The nickname Paddy, traditional for anyone Irish, is the result of his spending much of his childhood in Northern Ireland; it became attached to him when he arrived with an Irish accent at an English public school.

In Affectionate Remembrance
OF
ENGLISH CRICKET,
WHICH DIED AT THE OVAL
ON
29th AUGUST, 1882,
Deeply lamented by a large circle of sorrowing friends and acquaintances.

R. I. P.

N.B.—The body will be cremated and the ashes taken to Australia.

The original notice which launched the notion of the Ashes, in the Sporting Times *of 1882.*

Ashes The mythical prize competed for in *Test matches between England and Australia. It derives from a mock obituary of English cricket which appeared in the *Sporting Times* after Australia had defeated England at the Oval in 1882. The memorial ended: 'The body will be cremated and the ashes taken to Australia.' A year later an English team won a Test series in Australia and a bail was cremated, the ashes of which are kept in a famous urn at *Lord's. But the Ashes which are won, lost or retained in each Test series between the two countries remain a disembodied concept.

The term is also now used in the same sense for *rugby football matches against Australia.

Daisy **Ashford** see *The *Young Visiters*.

*The **Ash Grove*** Traditional Welsh song in which the singer roves pensively 'down yonder green valley', remembering the sweet maiden whom he met there so recently and who is now there again – 'for she sleeps 'neath the green turf down by the Ash Grove'.

Laura **Ashley** see *Laura Ashley.

Ashmolean Museum (Oxford) Named after its founder, Elias Ashmole (1617–92), it is the oldest public museum in Britain, having opened its doors in 1683 in what is now the Museum of the History of Science. Its origins lie in the old tradition of the 'cabinet of curiosities', for Ashmole had been left an extensive cabinet by the *Tradescant family. A few specially curious curiosities are still on display – Guy Fawkes' lantern, for example.

The museum moved in 1845 into its present neoclassical building, designed by C.R. Cockerell (1788–1863). The broadly based collection, of outstanding quality, has among its antiquities the major surviving part of the famous Arundel marbles (classical sculptures collected by the earl of Arundel in the 17C) and exceptional material from Cyprus and Crete. The Heberden Coin Room contains more than 300,000 items. There is a broad spectrum of European painting from the Renaissance to the 19C, with a special emphasis on the Pre-Raphaelites. The decorative arts include such treasures as the *Alfred Jewel.

Frederick **Ashton** (1904–88, kt 1962) Britain's first great choreographer. His earliest works were for Ballet Rambert and the related Camargo Society (for whom he did *Façade* in 1931), but from 1933 he was with the company which evolved into the *Royal Ballet (as principal choreographer and then also as director, 1963–70). His career was closely linked with that of *Fonteyn, who created the leading roles in many of his ballets from *Le Baiser de la Fée* in 1935 through *Symphonic Variations* (1946) and *Ondine* (1958) to *Marguerite and Armand* (1963), which Ashton devised specifically for her new partnership with Nureyev. Having given up classical dancing early in his career, he continued in comic roles (notably as an ugly sister in his own *Cinderella*). He proved that his talents were undimmed when he created, in his seventies, the touching *A *Month in the Country*, which rapidly established itself as a modern classic. The choreography of his popular film *The Tales of Beatrix Potter* (1971) was transferred to the stage with equal success by the Royal Ballet in 1992.

Asians see *ethnic and religious minorities.

Arthur **Askey** (1900–82) Tiny bespectacled entertainer (1.6m/5ft3in), who after years of concert parties and after-dinner entertaining sprang to fame in 1938 in the BBC radio show *Band Waggon* with Richard Murdoch. Known as 'big-hearted Arthur', he later had a successful career in films and musicals.

AS level see *exams.

Michael **Aspel** (b. 1933) Radio and TV presenter since 1957, and since 1984 one of the most relaxed and intelligent of chatshow hosts in *Aspel and Company*. In 1988 he took over the long-running programme *This is Your Life*.

Herbert **Asquith** (1852–1928, earl of Oxford and Asquith 1925) Liberal politician, prime minister 1908–16. He entered parliament for East Fife in 1886 and was home secretary for three years (1892–5) in Gladstone's last administration. He was chancellor of the exchequer from 1906 under Campbell-Bannerman, whom he succeeded in 1908 as leader of the Liberal party and prime minister.

Asquith's administration laid the foundation of Britain's *welfare state, with radical legislation on pensions and unemployment benefit. But he was plunged into a major power struggle with the House of *Lords over the attempts of his chancellor, *Lloyd George, to raise taxes to pay for battleships in anticipation of the forthcoming war. The budget of 1909 was vetoed by the hereditary upper chamber. In 1910 Asquith called and won two elections on this constitutional issue, the upshot of which was that George V agreed to create enough new Liberal peers to carry through the upper chamber the Parliament Bill of 1911; the threat proved sufficient to persuade the existing House of Lords to pass the bill ending their own power of veto over any financial legislation.

The early stages of World War I brought criticism of Asquith as a war leader. He changed his cabinet to a coalition in May 1915, and eventually stood down in December 1916 in favour of Lloyd George. He nevertheless remained leader of the Liberal party for another ten years, a strange state of affairs by modern standards – even more so after he lost East Fife in 1918 and only returned to the House of Commons in a by-election in 1920.

Assay Office see *hallmarks.

assembly rooms Important part of 18C social life, being the place in any resort town to which 'polite persons of both sexes' would go in the daytime for 'conversation, gallantry, news, and play' (in the words of a contemporary account), and in the evening for dancing. Two well-known examples survive, at *Bath and in the rooms created by Lord *Burlington in York.

Associated British Foods One of Britain's largest food manufacturers and retailers, deriving from seven long-established grocery companies which merged in 1935 as Allied Bakeries; among the seven were Twining and

Johnny Town-Mouse and Mrs Tittlemouse in Ashton's Tales of Beatrix Potter, *danced by the Royal Ballet in 1992.*

Ryvita. The name was changed to Associated British Foods in 1960.

ASTMS see *MSF.

F. W. **Aston** (Francis William Aston, 1877–1945) English physicist and chemist, who by his development of the mass spectrograph at the *Cavendish Laboratory in 1919 was able to show that stable elements of low atomic weight contain mixed isotopes. Aston eventually identified 212 of the 287 naturally occurring isotopes. His apparatus is now in the Science Museum in London. In 1922 he was awarded the Nobel prize for chemistry.

Aston Martin Outstanding series of sports cars, particularly the DB range in the decades after World War II; DB are the initials of David Brown (b. 1904), who acquired the company in 1946. The DBR won at Le Mans in 1959. The first Aston Martin was built in 1914 by Lionel Martin and was named because of its success in a hill climb at Aston Clinton, on the edge of the Chilterns.

Aston Villa, known as the Villans (Villa Park, Birmingham). Football club formed in the spring of 1874 by members of a Wesleyan chapel in Aston, a suburb to the northeast of Birmingham. The club turned professional in 1885. A committee member, William McGregor, then put forward the idea that prominent sides in the Midlands should form a *Football League, and Villa became one of the original 12 League teams in 1888. They had an early period of extraordinary success (five wins between 1894 and 1900), since when there have been a few brief dips into Division 2. By 1992 their seven wins in the FA Cup were equalled by Manchester United but exceeded only by Tottenham Hotspur. Club victories: FA Cup 1887, 95, 97, 1905, 13, 20, 57; League Champions 1894, 96, 97, 99, 1900, 10, 81; League Cup 1961, 75, 77; European Cup 1982; European Super Cup 1982.

Nancy **Astor** (Nancy Langhorne, 1879–1964, m. Waldorf Astor 1906) American by birth, she became the first woman to sit in the House of Commons, as Unionist MP for Plymouth (1919–45). The seat had previously been held by her husband, and she won it in the by-election caused by his succeeding his father as the 2nd viscount Astor. She was a famous political hostess in the 1930s, entertaining at *Cliveden the prime minister, Neville *Chamberlain, and others who believed in the policy of *appeasement.

Astronomer Royal Office established in 1675, when Charles II appointed John *Flamsteed to set up the *Royal Observatory, responsibility for which remained with the astronomer royal until 1971. Edmund *Halley succeeded Flamsteed in 1720. The position is now largely honorary, but the astronomer royal for Scotland still has responsibility for the Royal Observatory in Edinburgh.

As You Like It (c.1599) Comedy by *Shakespeare in which various exiles from the corrupt court of a usurper live in the forest of Arden, at the informal court of the deposed ruler. The play satirizes the pastoral conventions of lovesick shepherds but celebrates at the same time the healing power of nature, for ill-will is dissipated in this forest; the finale provides four marriages and the restoration of the true court. The central character is Rosalind, who disguises herself as a boy, Ganymede, to follow her beloved Orlando de Boys into the forest. Comedy is provided at two very different levels – clownish with Touchstone and his wench Audrey, sophisticated in the company of the cynical Jaques (who describes the *seven ages of man).

Athenaeum (London SW1) The most academic of London's *clubs, with a bias towards science; the first chairman was *Davy and the first secretary *Faraday (there is a public misconception that most of the members are bishops). It was founded in 1824 and the building (1828–30) was commissioned from the young Decimus Burton (1800–81) on part of the site of the recently demolished *Carlton House. The cream and blue frieze below the roof line is in the style of the *Elgin marbles, at that time a new attraction in London. This lavish feature was created with money which many would rather have spent on an ice house for cool summer drinks, resulting in a rhyme at the expense of the member who had insisted upon it:

> I'm John Wilson Croker,
> I do as I please;
> Instead of an Ice House
> I give you – a frieze!

Athens of the north see *Edinburgh.

Tommy **Atkins** see *Tommy Atkins.

Rowan **Atkinson** (b. 1955) Comedian who made his name in *Not the Nine O'Clock News* and went on to create two very popular characters in TV series – *Blackadder, and subsequently Mr Bean.

Battle of the **Atlantic** (1940–43) The long struggle of British and later American warships against the German U-boats, which threatened the convoys bringing crucial supplies from Canada and the USA in *World War II. The fall of France in June 1940 gave the U-boats Atlantic harbours from which they could raid far into the ocean. Large numbers of merchant ships were sunk that summer. The situation improved with the introduction of disciplined convoys (the U-boats responded by hunting in packs) and with the development of sonar (known at the time as asdic, an acronym of Anti-Submarine Detection Investigation Committee) and later of radar. By the summer of 1943 the Allies had established control of the Atlantic. The conflict had included only one major surface encounter, when Germany's newest battleship, the *Bismarck*, ventured out in May 1941. She was sunk at the cost of the *Hood*, a British battle cruiser. Conditions in the Atlantic became familiar to a very wide post-war audience through the bestseller The *Cruel Sea*.

Atlantic Charter A joint statement on the rights of nations by Winston Churchill and the US president, F.D. Roosevelt, after a series of meetings in August 1941 on warships off the coast of Newfoundland. The unanswered purpose of the meeting was Britain's desperate need for American support (this was four months before the Japanese attack on Pearl Harbor brought the USA into *World War II), but the pious generalities of the Charter were at least a joint rebuttal of everything the Nazis stood for; and the following year its clauses were written into the Declaration of the *United Nations.

atomic energy see *nuclear power.

Astronomers Royal appointed in the 20th century	
1910	Frank Dyson
1933	Harold Jones
1956	Richard Woolley
1972	Martin Ryle
1982	Francis Graham-Smith
1991	Arnold Wolfendale

atomic theory see John *Dalton.

ATS see *WRAC.

David **Attenborough** (b. 1926, kt 1985) Broadcaster and naturalist, brother of Richard Attenborough. In the 1950s he made a famous series of *Zoo Quest* programmes but later became more involved with administration in the BBC. He returned to programme making in 1979 with a major series on evolution, * *Life on Earth*, which he followed with further bites at the same large cherry of animal behaviour (*The Living Planet* 1984, *The Trials of Life* 1990).

Richard **Attenborough** (b. 1923, kt 1976) Film actor, producer and director, brother of David Attenborough. He achieved early fame with his portrayal of the cowardly young sailor in * *In Which We Serve* (1942). He moved into production with *The Angry Silence* (1960) and into direction with * *Oh! What a Lovely War* (1969). The most successful of his many subsequent films as producer-director has been * *Gandhi* (1982), but *Chaplin* (1992) may prove a rival.

attendance centre Place to which offenders aged 17–21 may be ordered to report for a specified number of hours in the evenings or at weekends, if the court considers it more appropriate than a *young offender institution.

Clement **Attlee** (1883–1967, earl Attlee 1965) The first leader of the Labour party to come from the professional classes and the first Labour prime minister with an absolute majority in the House of Commons (1945–51). Trained as a lawyer, he entered parliament as MP for Limehouse in 1922. He was one of the few Labour members to hold his seat in the 1931 election, after which he became deputy to the new leader, George Lansbury (1859–1940), whom he succeeded in 1935. He served with Churchill in the wartime coalition cabinet and then defeated him heavily in the 1945 election.

Attlee's postwar government enacted a broad programme of socialist legislation in spite of conditions of austerity in which *rationing was extended even to bread and potatoes. By the end of 1946 acts had been passed nationalizing the Bank of England and laying the ground for extended national insurance and for the *National Health Service. The railways, the mines and the supply of gas and electricity soon followed into public ownership. Meanwhile Attlee had been closely involved in the process of dismantling the *British empire, with independence given to India, Pakistan, Ceylon and Burma. Yet he believed in Britain playing a strong role in world affairs; he accepted the need for British participation in the *Korean War and he set up the programme to develop an independent nuclear capability (ironic in view of his party's later conflicts on this issue). His majority was reduced to six in the 1950 election and he lost the election the following year, handing over the leadership of the party in 1955 to Hugh *Gaitskell.

Attorney General The senior law officer of the *crown in England, Wales and Northern Ireland (the *lord advocate is the equivalent for Scotland). His deputy is the solicitor general. Both are *MPs of the ruling party and *barristers by profession. The attorney general's responsibilities include advising the government on legal matters, answering on such topics in the House of Commons, supervising the office of the *Director of Public Prosecutions, and prosecuting personally in court on rare occasions when the case is held to be of national concern. Recent attorney generals have been Michael Havers (1979–87), Patrick Mayhew (1987–92), and since 1992 Nicholas Lyell.

Mabel Lucie **Attwell** (1879–1964) English illustrator, associated in particular with the cheerful, chubby babies which she provided to excess for books and greetings cards.

John **Aubrey** (1626–97) English biographer, known in his own time chiefly as an antiquary; he was the first to draw attention to *Avebury and the Aubrey holes at *Stonehenge were noted by him (he was also the first to put forward the influential but false theory that Stonehenge was connected with the *Druids). His fame today derives not so much from ancient stones as from the racy anecdotal style in which he recorded information and gossip about the eminent men of his own and recent times. His manuscript, deposited by him in the Ashmolean Museum, was not published until the 19C; his book was then given its present title, * *Brief Lives*.

Auchinleck (26km/16m E of Ayr) Village near the ancestral home of James *Boswell, whose father took the title Lord Auchinleck on becoming a judge. The parish church is now a museum in memory of Boswell, who is buried nearby in the family mausoleum.

General **Auchinleck** (Claude Auchinleck, 1884–1981, GCB 1945) World War II commander in the Middle East (from 1941), popularly known as the Auk. By the time of the first victory at El *Alamein he had also taken personal command of the 8th Army, but his approach was too cautious for Churchill. In the late summer of 1942 the 8th Army was given to *Montgomery and the broader Middle East command to *Alexander. Auchinleck spent the rest of the war as commander-in-chief in India (1943–7).

W.H. **Auden** (Wystan Hugh Auden, 1907–73) English-born poet who from his first published collection (*Poems* 1930) was seen as the leading figure of the generation after T.S. Eliot. His early work, much influenced by Anglo-Saxon *alliteration, gave way to a period of strongly political verse during the 1930s. He also wrote political drama in collaboration with Christopher *Isherwood, beginning with *The Dog Beneath the Skin* in 1935.

In 1939 both Isherwood and Auden emigrated to the USA (they became US citizens in 1946). Auden's poetry now became more religious (his family background had been devoutly Anglo-Catholic) and he reissued some of his political poetry in a revised form, arguing that the changes were to do with quality rather than content. His output had always been very varied, with a constantly teasing mix of solemnity and lightness. It was now extended to include opera libretti, such as the text for Stravinsky's *The Rake's Progress* (1951). This, like several other works of that time, was written in collaboration with the US poet Chester Kallmann, Auden's companion for the last 30 years of his life.

Audley End (24km/15m to the S of Cambridge) Huge Jacobean mansion, even though much reduced from its size when first built (1605–14). In the 18C the interior was altered by Vanbrugh and subsequently remodelled by Robert Adam, and the park was landscaped by Capability *Brown. It stands on the foundations of a Benedictine abbey, and its name derives from Sir Thomas Audley (1488–1544), lord chancellor to Henry VIII, who was granted the abbey in 1538.

Frank **Auerbach** (b. 1931) German-born painter, living in Britain since 1939. His work is characterized by extremely thick and roughly applied paint, almost sculptural in its depth, giving a disturbingly expressionistic feeling to his many portraits. He also paints townscapes, and has done versions in his own style of old master paintings, including a sequence after Titian.

Augustan Age Term applied now to English literature of the early 18C, the time of Pope and Swift, but used in their day less appropriately to describe the preceding *Restoration period. The implication is of a flowering of classically correct literature, for Virgil, Horace and Ovid were writing in the reign of the emperor Augustus (27BC to AD14).

St **Augustine** (of Canterbury, d. 604) Known as the apostle of England, he introduced Christianity to the southern part of Britain. He was sent from Rome by Pope Gregory I, with 30 or 40 monks, to convert the *Anglo-Saxons. Reaching England in 597, they were well received by the king of Kent, Ethelbert, whose wife Bertha came from a Frankish tribe on the Continent and was already a Christian. Ethelbert, soon converted, built Augustine a church in his capital city, *Canterbury, of which Augustine became the first archbishop. Augustine sent monks from Canterbury to establish other English sees. St Justus became the first bishop of Rochester in 604, and St Mellitus the first bishop of London in the same year. St Paulinus later went from Canterbury to become the first archbishop of *York. Augustine's feast day is May 26.

Auld Brig o' Don see *Brig o' Balgownie.

Auld Lang Syne (Lowland Scottish for 'old long since') Version by *Burns of a traditional song, now sung throughout Britain on *New Year's Eve and by Scots on many other occasions. Those singing it usually cross arms in front of the chest to hold hands on either side, raising and lowering the entire chain of arms to mark the rhythm.

Aunt Sally Popular feature of fairs from the mid-19C, consisting of a wooden head of a woman with a clay pipe in her mouth. Competitors threw objects at her to try and break the pipe. The phrase became used by extension for anyone on the receiving end of abuse.

Jane **Austen** (1775–1817) Novelist who established an influential new tradition in English fiction, through her use of understatement and irony in describing the everyday play of relationships within a small group of people in the leisured middle class. Daughter of a clergyman, she was born in the rectory at Steventon in Hampshire, which remained her home until her father's retirement, when she was 26. The last years of her short life were spent in the house of her brother Edward at Chawton, also in Hampshire (kept now as a museum).

It was in this family setting that she wrote continuously, from childhood on, using her relations as her enthusiastic public. Several of the finished novels were revisions of earlier books. *Sense and Sensibility* came out in 1811 at her own financial risk (she made a profit); it was followed by *Pride and Prejudice* (1813), *Mansfield Park* (1814), and *Emma* (1816). *Northanger Abbey* and *Persuasion* were published together in 1818, the year after her death from what has been retrospectively diagnosed as Addison's disease.

Austin Car company founded in 1905 by Herbert Austin (1866–1941) at Longbridge, south of Birmingham; he had previously designed cars for *Wolseley. In 1922 Austin produced the first British car for the popular market, the famous Austin Seven or 'Baby Austin'; it remained in production until 1939. In 1952 the company merged with Austin's great rival, *Morris, to become the *British Motor Corporation. In 1959 the *Mini was offered as a revival of the Austin Seven.

The Austin Seven as a member of the family: from the cover of a 1935 catalogue.

Australia Member of the *Commonwealth, with *dominion status from 1901. Various explorers in the 17C (most notably the Dutchman Abel Tasman) made brief contact with the west and south coasts of the Australian continent, but it was not until the first voyage of Captain *Cook in 1769–71 that the more hospitable eastern coast was visited by Europeans. Joseph *Banks, one of Cook's party, strongly recommended it for the settlement of convicts (they had previously been sent to America). As a result the 'First Fleet' of 11 vessels sailed from England in 1787 under the command of Arthur Phillip. It carried about 730 convicts, including some 160 women, accompanied by 250 or so passengers. The ships arrived in 1788 at the appointed destination of Botany Bay, named for the profusion of flowers that Banks had found there. Phillip considered the location unsuitable and moved 8km/5m north to Port Jackson, which became the nucleus of the city of Sydney.

The harsh nature of much of central Australia meant that settlements were developed round the coast, particularly to the south and east. Hobart, on the island of Tasmania, was established in 1804, to be followed by Brisbane (1824), Perth (1829), Melbourne (1835) and Adelaide (1836). Darwin, in the extreme north, was not settled until 1872. By the late 19C the continent consisted of six separate colonies (New South Wales, Tasmania, Queensland, Victoria, South Australia and Western Australia), which combined to form, from 1 January 1901, a single independent country, the Commonwealth of Australia.

War of the **Austrian Succession** (1740–8) Conflict provoked by the first great opportunistic move in the growth of Prussia. Frederick the Great became king of Prussia in 1740, when he was only 28. In that same year the

23-year-old Maria Theresa inherited the much larger neighbouring territories of Austria and Hungary. Gambling on the uncertainties attached to a female inheritance, Frederick marched into the nearest part of her empire, Silesia. Austria's ancient enemies sided with Prussia, prominent among them France and Spain. Britain, already at war with Spain (see *Jenkins' Ear), supported Austria – though with limited success. George II led his troops to a minor victory at *Dettingen in 1743, but his son (the duke of *Cumberland) was commander-in-chief of the allied British, Hanoverian, Dutch and Austrian army which was decisively defeated by the French in 1745 at Fontenoy. An offshoot of the main war was the *'45 Rebellion, an invasion of Britain launched with French support.

The peace agreed in 1748 at Aix-la-Chapelle restored to their original owners the various territories seized during the war with the notable exception of Silesia, which remained with Prussia (provoking strong Austrian grievance, which in turn contributed to the *Seven Years' War). Among the treaty's various clauses was French recognition of the *Hanoverian succession in Britain – an important detail in view of the recent reassertion of *Stuart claims in the '45 Rebellion. *Handel's *Music for the Royal Fireworks* was part of the peace celebrations.

Authorized Version see *Bible in English.

The ***Autobiography of a Super-Tramp*** (1908) The best-known book of the Welsh poet W.H. Davies (William Henry Davies, 1871–1940), recounting his life on the road and in dosshouses in England, America and Canada – where his leg was amputated after an accident when he was jumping a train.

Autolycus see The *Winter's Tale.

Automobile Association see *AA.

Autumn Leaves (1856, Manchester City Art Gallery) Painting by *Millais which evokes the Victorian obsession with transience and death. In the fading light of sunset a pile of red and brown leaves, beginning to burn, is tended by four young girls – their youth the only detail not yet claimed by autumn. Two of the four gaze at the leaves, but the others stare challengingly at the onlooker. The picture follows the *Pre-Raphaelite principles (painted from nature, serious in its theme), but it has at least as much to do with the sentimental mood of Victorian poetry.

autumn statement see *public spending round.

Avalon The island to which King *Arthur's body is carried after his death in battle and where his wounds are magically healed by Morgan le Fay. Geoffrey of Monmouth, who first mentions it, says that it means 'island of apples' (*afal* is the Welsh for an apple). It was a few decades after Geoffrey's book that *Glastonbury became linked with Avalon, to its considerable profit, when the monks identified some bones found there as Arthur's.

Avebury (10m/6km W of Marlborough) One of the largest and most important Stone Age monuments in Europe, probably created some time before 2000 BC. A great bank of chalk and an inner ditch, from which most of the material came, enclose 11.5ha/28.5ac including the village of Avebury. Just inside the ditch there was a ring of about 100 vast standing stones, many of them still upright today, and inside that ring are the remains of two smaller circles. The stones, known as sarsens and up to 50 tons in weight, are of sandstone from the local North Wessex *Downs. The scale of the operation caused the first serious student of Avebury, John Aubrey, to write that it as much surpasses *Stonehenge 'as a cathedral doth a parish church'. A processional route of paired stones, known as the West Kennet

Scottish soldiers (left) in the victorious French army at Fontenoy, in the year of the '45 Rebellion: painting by Horace Vernet.

Average weekly earnings in £s

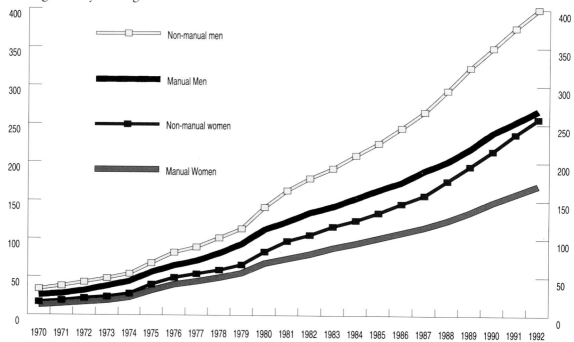

The figures given are for those in full-time employment, including overtime. One small element in the large discrepancy between male and female earnings is the greater number of hours worked by men on hourly rates: on average 42.2 hours per week as opposed to 37.5 by women in 1990.

Average earnings and retail prices

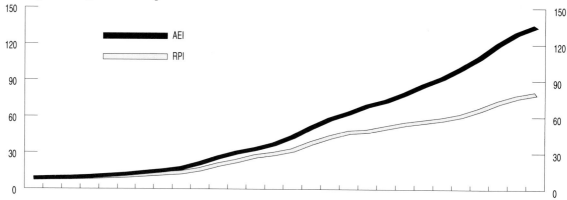

The upper line shows the increase since 1965 in average earnings (AEI, Average Earnings Index: 1988 = 100).
The lower line gives the equivalent rise in prices from 1965; it is the *RPI (Retail Prices Index) adjusted to the same 1965 figure as the earnings index. The gap between the two lines indicates the relative increase in prosperity.
Source: Annual Abstract of Statistics *(see *Central Statistical Office).*

Avenue and now partly restored, stretched about 2km/ 1m southwards, ending at a double circle of stones (the Sanctuary) which was destroyed in the 18c. The equally ancient *Silbury Hill is nearby.

The Avengers (ABC TV 1961–8) Comedy thriller series with a successful blend of chic, kinkiness, violence and a sense of not taking itself too seriously. Patrick MacNee played the male lead – the elegant secret agent Steed, with bowler hat and cane. His female colleague in 1961–3 was Honor Blackman (judo expert and devotee of black leather), followed by Diana Rigg (1965–7) and Linda Thorson (1968). In 1976 MacNee returned in *The New Avengers* with Joanna Lumley.

average earnings In recent decades British wages and salaries have risen faster than *productivity or prices (see *RPI), making for a rising standard of living not fully justified by the country's underlying economic performance. The figures usually quoted for average weekly earnings are those of full-time adult manual and skilled workers; they are assessed after the payment of overtime but before the deduction of income tax or national insurance contributions. By contrast the Average Earnings Index (AEI) is based on the pay of all employees, including those involved in clerical and administrative tasks.

Aviemore (53km/33m SE of Inverness) Resort on the river Spey which has greatly developed since the opening in the 1960s of a custom-built leisure centre. It offers year-round facility in many sports in addition to winter skiing in the Monadhliath range to the west and the Cairngorms to the east.

Avon (962,000 in 1991, administrative centre Bristol) *County in southwest England, formed in 1974 from parts of Gloucestershire and Somerset.

Avon Name of three English rivers (the word is Celtic for a river). The longest, sometimes called the Upper Avon (154km/96m), is the one connected with Shakespeare; it rises in Northamptonshire and flows through Warwick, Stratford-upon-Avon and Evesham to join the Severn near Tewkesbury. The next in length, further south and therefore the Lower Avon (120km/75m), rises in the Cotswolds and flows south to Bradford-on-Avon before turning northwest to Bath and Bristol; it joins the Severn after passing through the Clifton Gorge. The shortest of the three, sometimes known as the East Avon (about 96km/60m) rises in Wiltshire and flows south through Salisbury to enter the English Channel at Christchurch.

Earl of **Avon** see Anthony *Eden.

A was an apple-pie The most popular of the alphabet nursery rhymes, recorded as far back as the 17c. It continues with 'B baked it, C cut it, D dealt it', and so on down to Z. It is almost certainly the origin of the phrase 'apple-pie order', meaning perfect order.

Rev. W. **Awdry** see *Thomas, the Tank Engine.

Axminster (43km/27m E of Exeter) Town in Devon of which the name is much linked with carpets. A factory produced hand-made carpets here from 1755; in 1835 it went bankrupt and the equipment was moved to *Wilton. Soon after this the Wilton factory began mechanical weaving of carpets, in a technique patented in 1839 by James Templeton of Glasgow. The product was named Chenille Axminster, and the name Axminster later became standard for any carpet produced on a similar type of loom (the essential characteristic being that each tuft is inserted separately as in hand-weaving). One of the major advances in such looms was made at *Kidderminster in about 1900, and both Kidderminster and Wilton have continued to produce large quantities of Axminster carpets. A new factory was built at Axminster in 1937 and still manufactures carpets, but not of the Axminster type.

Alan **Ayckbourn** (b. 1939) Prolific and much performed English playwright. His comedies combine an often dark view of the oddities of middle-class manners with the magic of complex stagecraft, as in his trilogy *The Norman Conquests* (1974) in which the same action is repeated in successive plays but from a different viewpoint. Among his best-known plays are *Relatively Speaking* (1967), *Absurd Person Singular* (1973) and *A Chorus of Disapproval* (1985). Since 1971 he has been artistic director of the Theatre-in-the-Round company in Scarborough, where each of his plays is tested before coming to London.

A.J. Ayer (Alfred Jules Ayer, 1910–89, kt 1970) English philosopher whose reputation was established early with his *Language, Truth and Logic* (1936). His book brought into English-language philosophy the approach known as logical positivism, developed originally in Vienna. An extreme version of empiricism (the theory of which *Berkeley was the leading British advocate), logical positivism rejected not only metaphysical statements but moral judgements too. This ruled out many of the traditional concerns of philosophy. Of those that remained, Ayer made linguistic analysis his special concern.

Aylesbury (48,000 in 1981) Market town, administrative centre of Buckinghamshire. The original county hall survives (1723–40, by Thomas Harris), with its court room of that date unchanged. The Buckinghamshire County Museum, founded in 1862, is housed in a mainly 18c building which was the old grammar school. The town has been best known for its poultry, and in particular the Aylesbury duck.

Ayot St Lawrence Village in Hertfordshire in which George Bernard *Shaw lived for nearly 50 years. His house, called Shaw's Corner, belongs to the National Trust and is on show much as he lived in it.

Ayr (49,000 in 1981) Seaport and resort on the west coast of Scotland, in the Strathclyde region. Its history goes back to the Middle Ages, but it is best known now for its links with Robert *Burns, born in the nearby village of *Alloway and baptized in Ayr's Auld Kirk (old church). The old and new bridges which argue with each other in his poem *Twa Brigs* still span the river Ayr side by side, and an alehouse, believed to be the building in which *Tam o' Shanter begins his wild night of adventure, is now a museum in the poet's memory.

Ayrshire Until 1975 a *county on the west coast of Scotland, now part of the Strathclyde region. The brown and white Ayrshire cow, a major international dairy breed, was developed in the county in the 19c.

B

BA (Bachelor of Arts) The status of an undergraduate who has successfully completed a degree course (or graduated) in the arts or humanities. The equivalent for the sciences is BSc.

BA see *British Airways.

BA 149 British Airways flight from London to Kuala Lumpur which touched down at Kuwait airport in the early hours of 2 August 1990, when the Iraqi invasion (leading to the *Gulf War) had already begun. As a result the crew and 337 passengers were trapped in Kuwait; many of the British among them were later moved to Baghdad as part of Saddam Hussein's human shield. The mysterious failure to warn the pilot became the subject of unresolved controversy and much rumour (including the somewhat improbable theory that the British government was using the flight to get secret agents into Kuwait).

BAA Company *privatized in 1987 as the successor to the British Airports Authority. It owns and manages most of Britain's major airports, including London's trio of *Heathrow, *Gatwick and *Stansted and the airports of *Glasgow and *Edinburgh.

Baa, baa, black sheep Nursery rhyme first recorded in the 18C but probably much older. The black sheep admits to having three bags of wool, and the explanation of how they shall be divided is traditionally believed in the wool trade to date back to a new tax imposed in 1275 (the little boy presumably being the taxman):

> One for the master,
> And one for the dame,
> And one for the little boy
> Who lives down the lane.

Charles **Babbage** (1792–1871) Mathematician who spent much time and money in attempting to create an 'analytical engine', his concept for which is now accepted as the world's first digital computer. It relied on a system of punched cards, had a storage capacity or memory, was able to take account of its own previous calculations and had a print-out facility. Conceived in the 1830s, but never built, it was forgotten until his account of it was rediscovered in 1937.

Babbage did partially build in 1832 a sophisticated calculating machine which he called a 'difference engine'. A working version of this was created from his plans early in the 1990s by the Science Museum in London, and is on exhibition.

*The **Bab Ballads*** see W.S. *Gilbert.

Babington Plot (1586) An incompetent conspiracy to assassinate Elizabeth I, which led instead to the death of *Mary Queen of Scots. Anthony Babington (1561–86), a member of a Roman Catholic family, had been devoted to Mary since boyhood, when he had served as a page to her jailer, Lord Shrewsbury. He and other aristocratic Catholic friends together with a priest, John Ballard, conspired in 1586 to put Mary on the throne and so make England a Catholic country again. Babington's letter to Mary, outlining these plans, was intercepted by *Walsingham, as was Mary's reply. Babington and five others were executed before Mary herself went on trial.

Baccarat Scandal A libel case of 1891, caused by an accusation of cheating at baccarat made against a guest staying at Tranby Croft, the house of a Hull shipowner, Arthur Wilson. It was of interest only because the prince of Wales, the future Edward VII, was one of the party and gave evidence in the witness box. What chiefly shocked the nation was the amount of money for which the heir to the throne and his apparently dubious friends were in the habit of gambling.

J.C. Bach (Johann Christian Bach, 1735–82) Known as 'the English Bach', he was the 18th child and youngest son of Johann Sebastian Bach. He came to London in 1762 as opera composer at the King's Theatre and soon acquired various royal appointments. From 1764 he promoted (with Karl Friedrich Abel, 1723–87) the series of subscription concerts which for the next two decades were the centre of London's musical life. Bach's own orchestral works influenced both Haydn and Mozart.

backbencher Any *MP who does not hold office in the *government or have a shadow portfolio in the *Opposition, and therefore does not sit on either of the *front benches in the House of Commons.

Steve **Backley** (b. 1969) Javelin thrower who in 1992 held the world record with a throw of 91.46 metres (a length which happens to be almost exactly 100 yards), achieved in New Zealand in January of that year. There have been longer throws, including one over 100 metres (104.8m by Uwe Hohn in 1984), but the official specifications for a javelin have since been amended – in relation to centre of gravity and smoothness of surface. Backley's record throw was made with a javelin of the most recent (1991) specification.

Francis **Bacon** (1561–1626, kt 1603, viscount St Albans 1621) Politician, author and philosopher of science. Trained as a lawyer, he became a member of parliament in

1584, but it was not till the reign of James I that he progressed rapidly; he was made solicitor general in 1609, attorney general in 1613 and lord chancellor in 1618. But his public career came to an abrupt end in 1621; he was convicted of taking bribes when sitting as a judge.

As an author he is now best known for his *Essays* (successive collections in 1597, 1612 and 1625). His contribution to scientific thought is contained in *The Advancement of Learning* (1605) and *Novum Organum* (1620, Latin for 'The New Instrument'). In these he argues for a new science that will observe particular examples to establish general laws. Bacon is often quoted as having died in the service of this modern empirical method. Struck by the notion that it might be possible to preserve food by freezing it, he got down from his carriage near Highgate to stuff a chicken with snow and died of the resulting chill.

Francis **Bacon** (1909–92) English painter, born and brought up in Dublin, who achieved a major international reputation. Powerful, nightmarish imagery is his hallmark, and his first major work was *Three Studies for Figures at the Base of a Crucifixion* (1944, Tate Gallery). His most characteristic subject has been a single figure, often nude, seen in despairing isolation; the flesh distorts and distends in a macabre fashion but the body is held firmly in place by a piece of furniture, often a bed or chair, and is fixed in space by strong lines suggesting walls and floor. In 1989 one of his triptychs achieved easily the highest price for a living British artist ($6.27m) when sold at Sotheby's in New York.

Roger **Bacon** (*c.*1220–*c.*1292) Philosopher and scientist who combined a medieval measure of credulity on such topics as astrology and alchemy with a clear-eyed interest in astronomy and optics. He is seen as partly prefiguring

The origins of badminton: Girl with a Shuttlecock (1737) by Chardin, whose uncle manufactured tennis rackets.

the methods of modern science. Educated at Oxford and Paris, and from about 1257 a Franciscan friar, he spent his last years arguing for improved scientific education and attempting an encyclopedia of scientific knowledge. He was known later as the *doctor admirabilis*.

Baconian theory The argument that Shakespeare's plays were written by Francis *Bacon. First appearing in print in the mid-19C, the concept relies largely on the patronizing idea that a man educated at Stratford grammar school could not have written Shakespeare's masterpieces. Supporters have found statements of Bacon's authorship within the plays, concealed in elaborate cryptograms – invariably a minefield of self-delusion for those with theories to prove.

Lord **Baden-Powell** (Robert Baden-Powell, 1857–1941, kt 1909, baron 1929) Soldier and founder of the *Scouts. He became a national hero in 1900 for his 217-day defence of *Mafeking (1899–1900), thus acquiring an unexpectedly wide readership for his manual of military scouting techniques (*Aids to Scouting* 1899), which was published during the siege. The resulting public interest caused him to set up an experimental scouting camp for boys in 1907, on Brownsea Island in Poole harbour, Dorset. Its success led to the publication of *Scouting for Boys* (1908) and to the establishment in that year of the Scout movement.

Douglas **Bader** (1910–82, kt 1976) A hero of World War II, known as the 'legless ace'. Both his legs were amputated after an air crash in 1931. He rejoined the RAF in the war, flying at *Dunkirk and in the *Battle of Britain. By the time his Spitfire was shot down over France in 1941, he had destroyed 23 enemy aircraft and had won the DSO and the DFC, each with a bar (awarded twice). He spent the rest of the war in Colditz. In the film of his story (*Reach for the Sky* 1956) he was played by Kenneth More.

badminton Modern game for two or four players based upon the ancient pastime of using a taut leather racket (the battledore) to strike and keep in the air a light feathered object (the shuttlecock). It derives its name from the 1860s, when it was played at *Badminton House. By the mid-1870s it was popular with the British in India, and as early as 1878 there was a Badminton Club in New York (the membership consisting of men and 'good-looking' single girls). The game was developing in the same decade as lawn *tennis, for which it was in a sense an indoor alternative. The Badminton Association was formed in England in 1893 and from 1900 held annually what became known as the *All-England Championship. The international team championships, held every three years, are the Thomas Cup for men (held since 1949) and the Uber Cup for women (since 1957).

Badminton House (19km/12m N of Bath) Home of the dukes of Beaufort since 1682, originally 17C but much added to by William *Kent *c.*1740. Kent also laid out the grounds which were extended later by Capability *Brown. The kennels of the Beaufort hunt are at Badminton; this famous pack of foxhounds has always been a family concern, and since its beginnings in the 18C the duke of Beaufort has usually been the master. Since 1949 the most important of the British *three-day events has taken place in the grounds of Badminton House each May.

'bad money drives out good' see entry on Thomas *Gresham.

Baedeker raids German air raids on some of Britain's historic cities, such as York and Bath, in the summer of 1942 – so named because it was announced that Germany was planning to bomb any place which had three stars in the Baedeker guide to Britain.

Walter **Bagehot** (1826–77) Economist and critic whose best-known work, *The English Constitution* (1867), has become the classic analysis of political processes in Britain. His editing of the *Economist*, from 1860 until his death, gave it an international reputation and influence.

Bagheera see The *Jungle Book.

Bagpipe Music Satirical poem of the 1930s by Louis *MacNeice, a cheerful merry-go-round of garish images and jokes. It ends:

> The glass is falling hour by hour, the glass will fall for ever,
> But if you break the bloody glass, you won't hold up the weather.

bagpipes Although most famously associated with Scotland, bagpipes are an age-old instrument of folk music in many parts of Europe, Asia and Africa. The bag (originally an entire goat or sheep skin) is held under the arm; the piper blows into it, and then uses the pressure of his arm to squeeze air through the 'chanter' (on the finger-holes of which he plays the tune) and through the 'drones' (three in number in the Scottish version, tuned to provide an unchanging accompaniment). Originally used for festive occasions, and still an important element of *Burns Night, the pipes acquired another important role in Scottish military music, accompanied by drums to arouse the fervour of the infantry – along with *tartan they were for a while forbidden after *Culloden. The military use is now their most familiar role, a band of massed pipers in full *Highland dress providing a magnificent spectacle. The best-known example is the annual Military Tattoo at *Edinburgh Castle.

The Bahamas Member of the *Commonwealth since independence in 1973, consisting of some 700 islands (30 inhabited) to the southeast of Florida. They were first settled by English colonists from *Bermuda in the 1640s. The duke of Windsor was governor of the islands during World War II, after his abdication as *Edward VIII.

Bahrain Island in the Persian Gulf which has been ruled by the Khalifa family since 1783. By a treaty of 1861 Bahrain came under British protection; Britain agreed to defend the emirate against its neighbours in return for Bahrain not engaging in 'war, piracy or slavery'. This ended when Bahrain became an independent state in 1971.

David **Bailey** (b. 1938) Photographer who was responsible for the best-known images of the leading British model of the early 1960s, Jean *Shrimpton. He became the chief chronicler, in stark black and white images, of that very fashion-conscious decade – enshrining a broad mix of its famous faces in *David Bailey's Box of pin-ups* (1965, including the *Kray brothers as well as Beatles, Rolling Stones, Michael Caine and Rudolf Nureyev) and in *Goodbye Baby and Amen* (1969).

Bailey bridge Temporary bridge, capable of rapid construction, which was widely used by the Allied forces in *World War II. Designed by Donald Bailey (1901–85), it consisted of rectangular lattice-work steel sections, made from prefabricated standard parts, which could be joined together either as a fixed bridge or on floating pontoons.

Edward Hodges **Baily** (1788–1867) Sculptor, a pupil of *Flaxman, best known for the figure on top of *Nelson's Column.

John Logie **Baird** (1888–1946) Scottish amateur pioneer of television who was ahead of his rivals but whose system was inadequate to survive the competition. On 26 January 1926 he gave the world's first demonstration of television in his attic rooms in Soho; his makeshift apparatus, which scanned the image mechanically and transmitted a picture of 30 lines repeating 10 times per second, is now in London's Science Museum. In 1928 he succeeded in transmitting an image of himself (together with a certain Mrs Howe) across the Atlantic to the USA. He formed a company which the BBC employed from 1929 for private experimental broadcasting a few hours a day; the televising of the Derby in 1931 was one of the major successes. But from 1931 *EMI was developing a more sophisticated electronic system. When the BBC launched public TV in 1936, the EMI system (405 lines, 50 frames per second) and Baird's (by now up to 240 lines and 25 frames per second) were for a short while in competition, but Baird's was soon dropped.

Janet **Baker** (b. 1933, DBE 1976) Mezzo-soprano known both for her performances of baroque music, from Monteverdi to Handel, and for modern work (particularly Elgar and Britten). After performing with all the leading British companies, she retired from opera in 1982. But she continued with a busy career in concerts – the song cycles of Mahler are a speciality.

Kenneth **Baker** (b. 1934) Conservative politician, MP for Mole Valley since 1983 (previously for Acton 1968–70, St Marylebone 1970–83), who entered the *cabinet in 1985 as secretary of state for the environment. He moved in 1986 to education and science, and in 1989 became chancellor of the duchy of Lancaster and chairman of the Conservative party. In 1990, in the first administration of John Major, he was appointed home secretary.

Richard **Baker** (b. 1925) Broadcaster with a special interest in music, though best known to a wide public as a newsreader on BBC TV (1954–82). He was a regular panellist (1966–79) on the music quiz *Face the Music* (BBC2). On BBC radio he has introduced the Proms since 1960, and for many years (1970–87) chaired the regular Monday morning discussion programme *Start the Week*.

Samuel White **Baker** (1821–93, kt 1866) Explorer, big-game hunter and discoverer in 1864 of Lake Albert as one of the sources of the *Nile. His colourful adventures, described in his own books, were made even more dramatic by the fact that he was accompanied by his extremely courageous Hungarian wife, Florence.

baker's dozen A term now for 13 (in the past often 14), being the number of loaves or rolls given by a baker for the price of a dozen. The usual explanation, deriving from the 1864 edition of Hotten's *Slang Dictionary*, is that this was a precaution by bakers terrified of punitive laws against giving short measure. The earlier entry in Grose's *Dictionary of the Vulgar Tongue* ('Fourteen; that number of rolls allowed to the purchasers of a dozen') suggests a much more likely origin as a discount on quantity.

Baker Street (London W1) Road laid out from 1755 by William Baker, a speculative builder. It is best known for a connection with fiction. Sherlock *Holmes had rooms at 221B, an address at the north end of the street now absorbed within the head office of Abbey National. The 'Baker Street irregulars' are a bunch of street urchins who assist Holmes in *The Sign of Four* (1890).

Robert **Bakewell** (1725–95) Agriculturalist and pioneer of stock breeding. By new techniques, such as inbreeding, he greatly improved the local strain of both sheep and cattle in his native Leicestershire. His family inheritance of 178ha/440ac became much visited as a model farm, where his animals and his innovations in crop methods and irrigation could be inspected. He was also the first to establish a profitable stud, hiring out his rams and bulls for large sums.

Bakewell tart (originally known as Bakewell pudding) An open pastry tart lined with jam and then baked with a filling of eggs, butter and ground almonds. It was a speciality of the Rutland Arms at Bakewell, in Derbyshire, in the early 19C.

Balaclava helmet Tight woollen hood to cover the head and neck (like a terrorist's stocking but with a hole for the face). It is assumed to have been worn by soldiers in the *Crimean War, when Balaklava was the army's supply port on the Black Sea.

Balaklava see *Charge of the Light Brigade.

balance of payments The overall balance between the money that has moved into and moved out of a country during a given period, usually a month or a year. It is made up of the visible balance (the difference between the import and export of raw materials and goods) and of so-called invisible exports (transactions where only money is involved, as in payments for financial services such as banking and insurance). Invisible exports are an important part of the UK balance of payments (see above). An adverse visible balance is often referred to as a trade gap.

Michael **Balcon** (1896–1977, kt 1948) Film producer whose determination to promote a characteristically British film industry, rather than an imitation of Hollywood, bore fruit in the *Ealing comedies. He ran the Ealing Studios from 1938 to 1959.

Stanley **Baldwin** (1867–1947, earl Baldwin 1937) Conservative politician who was prime minister three times (1923–4, 1924–9, 1935–7) and whose terms of office included two major political crises, the *General Strike and the *abdication. His cultivated image of being a plain man, typical of the average citizen, was to some extent justified (in spite of considerable family wealth from coal

mines and steel mills) and it helped him in coping with each of these problems. He entered parliament in 1908. After various ministerial appointments in Lloyd George's coalition governments, he took a prominent stand against continuing the coalition when he supported Bonar *Law in the Carlton Club meeting of 1922; and when Law became prime minister after the resulting election, Baldwin was made chancellor of the exchequer. Illness then forced Law to resign (1923) and Baldwin succeeded him as prime minister. For the rest of his political career he alternated the premiership with Ramsay *MacDonald, serving under him in the *national government from 1931 to 1935 and then following him at its head. In 1937 he retired and was succeeded by Neville *Chamberlain.

A.J. **Balfour** (Arthur James Balfour, 1848–1930, earl of Balfour 1922) Conservative politician whose early career was closely linked with that of his uncle, Lord *Salisbury (his mother was Salisbury's sister). He became a member of Salisbury's cabinet in 1887, as chief secretary for Ireland, and in his uncle's later administrations (1891–2, 1895–1902) was leader of the House of Commons and first lord of the *Treasury – the only occasion in recent times when the latter office has not been held by the prime minister. With Salisbury leading the House of Lords, and acting as foreign secretary as well as prime minister, uncle and nephew together held the reins of government in an unprecedented fashion. In July 1902 Salisbury retired and Balfour succeeded him as prime minister (1902–5). After a string of by-election defeats he resigned in 1905, to be succeeded by the Liberal *Campbell-Bannerman, and in the election of 1906 a Liberal landslide cost Balfour his own seat. He was soon back in parliament, but Bonar *Law took over the party leadership in 1911. In the wartime coalition governments Balfour held various offices, including a spell as foreign secretary (1916–19) which was to have a resounding effect on world history through the *Balfour Declaration.

Balfour Declaration A milestone on the way to the creation of the state of Israel. In a letter of 2 November 1917 to Lord Rothschild, leader of the British Jewish community, *Balfour wrote that Britain favoured 'the establishment in Palestine of a national home for the Jewish people' provided that it did not prejudice 'the civil and religious rights of existing non-Jewish communities in Palestine'. The declaration was later included by the League of Nations in the terms of the British mandate for *Palestine. The British motives were a combination of imperial politics (the desirability of a friendly state near the Suez Canal on the route to India) and of religious idealism (support for a Biblical homecoming).

Balance of payments: in £ million (1990 prices)

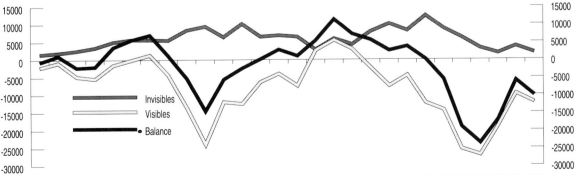

1965 1966 1967 1968 1969 1970 1971 1972 1973 1974 1975 1976 1977 1978 1979 1980 1981 1982 1983 1984 1985 1986 1987 1988 1989 1990 1991 1992

To make comparison valid between different years, the figures are adjusted for inflation to 1990 values.

Source: Economic Trends (*see* *Central Statistical Office).

John de **Baliol** (*c*.1250-1314) King of Scotland 1292–6. One of 13 claimants on the death of *Margaret, the Maid of Norway, he was first helped to the throne and then four years later removed from it by the English king, *Edward I, who imprisoned him in the Tower of London. His father, also John de Baliol, was the founder of Balliol College at Oxford. An independent Scottish kingdom was later re-established by *Robert the Bruce

John **Ball** (d. 1381) Radical English priest who was excommunicated and often imprisoned for advocating a classless society. He became one of the leaders of the *Peasants' Revolt and was reported to have preached to the rebels, taking as his text the popular verse:
> When Adam delved and Eve span,
> Who was then a gentleman?

After the collapse of the uprising he was captured and hanged.

ballad Any narrative poem which is handed down in an oral tradition, usually in short rhyming verses of a kind suitable for singing. An interest in preserving ballads developed in the 18C, the first major group being published in Thomas Percy's *Reliques of Ancient Poetry* (1765).

*The **Ballad of Reading Gaol*** (1898) Narrative poem by *Wilde, written after his release from prison. He deliberately borrows the rhythms and vivid imagery of *The *Ancient Mariner* to conjure up similar horrors, in this case those of prison life. The central event had happened while Wilde was himself in Reading jail – the hanging of a soldier who had slit his wife's throat. Part of Wilde's theme is that we are all guilty of cruelty, for 'each man kills the thing he loves', if not by violence then with a bitter look, a flattering word or a false kiss.

ballad opera see *The *Beggar's Opera*.

R.M. **Ballantyne** (Robert Michael Ballantyne, 1825–94) Scottish author of adventure stories for boys, the best known being *The *Coral Island*.

Ballet Rambert see *Rambert Dance Company.

ballot see *franchise.

Balmoral (80km/50m SW of Aberdeen) House in the *Scottish baronial style (and therefore called a castle), built 1853–6 for Queen Victoria and Prince Albert on the bank of the river Dee. The architect was William Smith of Aberdeen. The royal family has used Balmoral ever since as a holiday home, worshipping on Sundays in the local church of Crathie (where the second marriage of the *Princess Royal took place in 1992).

Baloo see *The *Jungle Book*.

Bamburgh (80km/50m N of Newcastle-upon-Tyne) Imposing castle on an isolated crag on the coast of Northumberland. An Anglo-Saxon fortress here was captured with great difficulty by William II in the late 11C. Of the Norman castle which then rose in its place, only the much restored walls and keep remain. The rest of the present building, dating from 1894–1903, is a rich example of Victorian medievalism. The village of Bamburgh achieved fame in 1838 as the birthplace of Grace *Darling.

Banbury (36,000 in 1981) Town in Oxfordshire, famous historically for the quality of its cakes and ale but best known now for its cross, the memory of which is kept alive by the nursery rhyme *'Ride a cockhorse to Banbury cross'. The stone cross stood in the market place, but was destroyed by Puritans in 1602. The present one is a replacement put up in 1858.

Band Aid see Bob *Geldof.

Banffshire Until 1975 a *county on the northeast coast of Scotland, now part of the Grampian region.

Bangladesh Member of the *Commonwealth since 1972. After the partition of *India it was part of *Pakistan, but in 1971 it declared independence as Bangladesh (the name means the 'Bengal nation'). Its freedom was achieved after India's intervention in the resulting civil war.

Bangladeshis see *ethnic and religious minorities.

Bangor (12,000 in 1991) Town on the northwest coast of Wales, opposite Anglesey, which can claim to be the oldest diocese in Britain. It seems likely that St Deiniol established a Celtic monastery here in 525 (more than 70 years before St Augustine arrived in Canterbury) and that he was appointed bishop in 546. The present cathedral dates back to the 14C but has been much altered and restored.

The town is also the home of the University College of North Wales. Founded here in 1883, it became in 1893 one of the five colleges of the University of Wales. The main buildings, forming a quadrangle on a hill above the town, were completed in 1910 to the designs of Henry Thomas Hare.

Bank Holidays	England & Wales	Scotland	Northern Ireland
January 1	*	*	*
January 2		*	
March 17			*
Good Friday	*	*	*
Easter Monday	*		*
First Monday, May	*	*	*
Last Monday, May	*	*	*
July 12			*
First Monday, August		*	
Last Monday, August	*		*
December 25	*	*	*
December 26	*	*	*

If a bank holiday falls on a Saturday or Sunday, the next working day becomes the holiday.

bank holiday The term in Britain for a public holiday. It derives from an act introduced in 1871 by Sir John Lubbock (1834–1913), which compelled the Bank of England and the clearing banks to close on specific days and thus established them as public holidays. Christmas Day and Good Friday were already common law holidays in England, Wales and Ireland; to them were added Easter Monday, Whit Monday, the first Monday in August (an entirely secular holiday known for a while as St Lubbock's Day) and *Boxing Day. The equivalent four bank holidays in Scotland were established as New Year's Day, the first Monday in May, the first Monday in August and Christmas Day. Subsequent legislation has amended the list, bringing the present annual total to eight. In Northern Ireland two extra holidays are recognized; March 17 (St Patrick's Day) and July 12, when the Battle of the

*Boyne is commemorated. In 1992 the government announced plans to abolish from 1995 the May Day bank holiday (introduced in 1978), replacing it with either an extra day in August or the last Monday in October.

Bank of England The central bank of the UK, nationalized in 1946. It was founded by a group of merchants in 1694, along lines proposed by William Paterson (1658–1719), with the immediate purpose of raising money to lend to William III. The link with government meant that it acquired during the 18c the status of a national bank even though remaining a private institution. Since 1734 it has been on *Threadneedle Street. Its main functions are: the managing of the *national debt; the implementation of government exchange-rate and interest-level policies; the issuing of the nation's paper currency; and acting as banker to the government itself, to the *clearing banks and to other commercial banks. It also has a responsibility as the regulating agency for banks and financial institutions in Britain. Recent governors have been Leslie O'Brien (1966–73), Gordon Richardson (1973–83) and Robin Leigh-Pemberton (1983–93) and Eddie George from 1993.

Bank of Scotland One of the *clearing banks. Founded in 1695, a year after the *Bank of England, it differs in having remained a commercial bank – largely because the Act of *Union followed soon after, leaving room for only one national or central bank.

bank rate see *MLR.

Gordon **Banks** (b. 1937) One of England's two outstanding goalkeepers in football; the other, Peter *Shilton, followed him in goal at Leicester City, where Banks played 1959–67. Banks then moved to Stoke City, where he stayed until a motor accident ended his career in 1972. His most distinguished appearances were in two successive World Cups – in 1966 when England won at Wembley, and in 1970 in Mexico where his interception of a header from Pele of Brazil has become part of the folklore of goalkeeping. He made 73 appearances in all for England.

Joseph **Banks** (1743–1820, bt 1781) Botanist and patron of science. He accompanied Captain *Cook on his journey to the Pacific in 1768, taking with him at his own expense the botanist Daniel Solander and two artists to record their finds. The superb series of copper plates depicting the plants, commissioned later by Banks, are now in the Natural History Museum in London; they were printed and published for the first time during the 1980s. Banks also played a major part in building up the collection of plants at *Kew Gardens.

Bankside (London SE1) The south bank of the Thames, near Southwark Bridge. Its importance historically is that the theatres were here in the time of Shakespeare (they were banned within the boundaries of the city of London, on the north bank, and this was the nearest congenial area). Here were the *Rose, Swan and *Globe, in addition to an arena for *bear-baiting.

Roger **Bannister** (b. 1929, kt 1975) Athlete who was the first to run a mile in four minutes. He was a medical student when he achieved a time of 3:59.4 at Oxford on 6 May 1954, with Christopher Chataway and Christopher Brasher pacing him. His time was bettered the following month by the Australian John Landy (with 3:58.0), but Bannister won the mile when the two met in the Commonwealth Games that August. He then retired to pursue his medical career, becoming a distinguished neurologist and (from 1985) master of Pembroke College in Oxford.

Spectators are overcome with emotion as Bannister breaks the tape for the first 4-minute mile.

bannock The word, Gaelic in origin, for a form of unleavened bread in Scotland and the north of England; it is baked on top of the stove on a griddle. Traditionally the bannock is home-made, in contrast to baker's bread, and uses barley meal (distinguishing it from the *oatcake). A Selkirk bannock, rich with lard and dried fruit, is an entirely different commodity, closer to the *lardy cake.

Bannockburn (24 June 1314) Notable victory of the Scots, led by *Robert the Bruce, over a much larger English army with Edward II at its head. The English were trying to relieve their garrison in *Stirling Castle, which was the only Scottish stronghold remaining in English hands (Bannockburn is a small town about 3km/2m to the south). *Scots, wha hae is an imaginary speech by Robert to his men on the eve of the battle.

Banqueting House (London SW1) The earliest building in the *Palladian style to be completed in Britain (1622), designed by Inigo *Jones for James I. It is also the only surviving part of *Whitehall Palace. The famous ceiling was commissioned by Charles I from Rubens in 1630 and depicts the apotheosis of the house of *Stuart in the person of Charles's father, James I. It was from the Banqueting House that Charles stepped out on to a scaffold in Whitehall for his execution in 1649.

Bantock House see *Wolverhampton.

BAOR (British Army of the Rhine) The British military force stationed in Germany from the end of World War II. In the early 1990s its strength was about 63,000, but numbers have been reduced with the easing of the Cold War.

bap Soft bread roll, a speciality of Scotland. The word, of unknown origin, first appeared in print in the 16c.

Baptists One of the world's major groups of Protestant Christians, which has evolved from congregations established in London in the early 17C. They differed from other radical Protestant sects in England at the time in their insistence that baptism must be a conscious choice made by believing adults rather than something imposed upon infants. In this they were following the much persecuted Anabaptist groups on the Continent, for whom adult baptism had been a central article of faith from the earliest years of the Reformation, in the 1520s.

The movement developed among separatists who escaped from Lincolnshire to the Netherlands in 1608. Some of them later became *Pilgrim Fathers. Others settled in Amsterdam, where under the leadership of John Smyth (d. 1612) they began practising adult baptism. At about the time of Smyth's death, members of his congregation returned from Amsterdam to establish the first Baptist church in London. Rival groups among them were soon preaching bitterly opposed versions of the faith, the main disagreement being between Calvinists and Arminians as to whether only the elect or all believers can be saved. But in one form or another Baptist churches spread. Roger Williams established the first in the USA in 1639; the first in Canada dated from 1763; the English Baptist Missionary Society, founded in 1792, evangelized Australia (1831) and New Zealand (1854). Each Baptist congregation retains a high degree of autonomy, but the majority in Britain combined in 1891 to form the Baptist Union. There are believed to be more than 38 million Baptists worldwide, with approaching a quarter of a million in the United Kingdom (for the numbers attending services in England see *Christians).

Bar Collective term for *barristers, who are described as having been called to the Bar. The bar in question is an imaginary line within a court of law, separating the area where the judge sits (the bench) from the body of the court. Only the officers of the court, *QCs (barristers who have been called within the Bar) and those personally involved in the litigation may enter this area. There is another similar bar in each of the Houses of *Parliament, though this is a physical rail; non-members may not go beyond it, and it is here that they stand if they have to address either House.

Barbados Member of the *Commonwealth since independence in 1966. The most easterly island of the West Indies, it was settled in 1627 by a British group led by Henry Powell. The early prosperity of the island was based on the production of sugar cane by slave labour, until the abolition of *slavery in 1834. Barbados became a separate independent state four years after the break-up of the *West Indies Federation.

Barbara Allen The cruel heroine of at least two *ballads, in each of which her admirer dies for unrequited love of her.

Barbarians (known as the Baa-Baas) *Rugby union football club which distinguished players are invited to join. Founded in Bradford in 1890, it has no clubhouse or ground of its own. There are six fixtures each year against English and Welsh clubs, and since 1948 international teams have usually finished a tour of Britain with a game against the Barbarians. The 1973 match against New Zealand at Cardiff provided one of the game's classic moments, with a run almost the length of the field involving six passes and ending with a try by Gareth *Edwards.

Anthony **Barber** (b. 1920, baron 1974) Conservative politician, MP for Doncaster 1951–64 and for Altrincham and Sale 1965–74. He was chancellor of the exchequer (1970–4) for all but the first month of Edward Heath's administration, being appointed after the sudden death of Iain *Macleod.

Barber Institute of Fine Arts (Birmingham) The institute was founded in 1932, in memory of Sir William Barber, to promote the study of art history in the university of Birmingham. A study collection of paintings has been built up, of wide range (from Simone Martini to Magritte) and of high quality, housed in a building by Robert Atkinson (1883–1953).

Barbican (London EC2) Large development in the *City, completed in 1982, on an area to the north of St Paul's which had been devastated in the *Blitz. Designed by Chamberlain, Powell and Bon, the concrete tower blocks provide apartments (rarities in this City of offices). The Barbican Centre includes an art gallery, a concert hall (home to the *London Symphony Orchestra), and a theatre which is the London base for the *Royal Shakespeare Company. The Centre, with its many-tiered public areas, rapidly became established as the hardest place in London to find one's way around.

bar billiards Form of *billiards played in pubs, with nine holes set in the surface of the table. They have different values from 10 to 200 – representing the score achieved when a ball is potted. To retain the element of skill on a small table, the game is complicated by skittles placed in front of the four most valuable holes; knocking over a skittle incurs penalties. The game first became popular between the wars.

John **Barbirolli** (Giovanni Battista Barbirolli, 1899–1970, kt 1949) English-born conductor of Italian descent. After beginning his career as a cellist, he conducted various orchestras before being appointed in 1943 to the Hallé, with whom he remained till his death. He married the oboist Evelyn Rothwell in 1939.

Barbour Makers of country clothing in South Shields (Tyne and Wear) since the 1890s. The company has specialized in waterproof garments of all kinds; and in recent years a Barbour jacket, characteristically in dark green, has become something of a fashion accessory.

Barchester Towers (1857) The second in *Trollope's Barsetshire series of novels, and the outstanding classic of clerical intrigue. A new bishop, Dr Proudie, has arrived in Barchester. He is under the influence of two ambitious but very different characters – his imperious wife and the unctuous Obadiah Slope, his chaplain. At first they are on the same side against the old guard in the Cathedral Close, led by Dr Grantly, but they fall out over who shall have the appointment at Hiram's Hospital left vacant at the end of The *Warden. Slope eventually falls victim to Mrs Proudie's schemes and is dismissed.

Barclays Bank One of the 'big four' *clearing banks, formed by the merging of more than 20 banks in 1896. The largest of them derived originally from the firm of John Freame, a goldsmith in London's *Lombard Street, whose son-in-law Robert Barclay joined the business in 1736.

Bardolph see *Henry IV.

bards It was a tradition among all *Celts to give an honoured status to bards, or poets, who were selected to celebrate the achievements of the leader and the tribe. This tradition flourished most strongly in Wales, where in the Middle Ages there was an elaborate hierarchy of bards. A later period of decline was brought to an end by the revival of the *eisteddfod.

Bardsey (Ynys Enlli in Welsh) Small rocky island in the Atlantic, 3km/2m off the end of the Lleyn peninsula in Gwynedd, which was the site of an early Celtic monastery and then of an Augustinian abbey. It became a place of pilgrimage, known as the island of 20,000 saints, and is now a bird sanctuary.

Barebones Parliament Abusive nickname for the parliament appointed by Cromwell in July 1653 after he had dismissed the rump of the *Long Parliament. Mainly strict Puritans (they had been chosen as 'God-fearing men'), they set about their business with more zeal than judgement. The nickname was based on that of a member, Praise-God Barbon (c.1596–1680), who in fact took little part. The parliament was dissolved in December 1653 and was replaced by the *Protectorate.

'the **barge she sat in**' see *Antony and Cleopatra.

Baring Brothers The oldest merchant bank in London, founded in 1763 by the grandson of a Lutheran pastor from Bremen, in Germany. From the early 19C Baring and *Rothschild were the two leading families in British banking, but Baring Brothers nearly came to an end in 1890 after heavy losses in Argentina. They eventually paid all debts and continue today as a leading institution in the *City.

Ronnie **Barker** (b. 1929) Comedian and character actor, known for the range of his comedy in the long-running series The *Two Ronnies, but also demonstrating his considerable acting abilities in *Porridge. He followed this with a portrayal of the owner of a small corner shop in Open All Hours (1976–82). Although still frequently on Britain's television screens in repeats, he announced his retirement in 1987.

'**Barkis is willin**' see *David Copperfield.

barley sugar Amber-coloured translucent and brittle sweet, often sold in the past in the form of a twisted stick. It was traditionally made by boiling sugar in water previously used for boiling barley.

barley wine Now just a term for an unusually strong type of beer, but in the 18C a concoction of white wine with lemon, sugar and boiled barley, bottled and left to mature.

Barlow Clowes Fraudulent investment company, the details of which came to light in 1988. It was founded in 1973 by Elizabeth Barlow (who later disappeared, owing £100,000) and Peter Clowes. The company's professed purpose was to invest in government stocks, but the interest paid to existing investors was met from new money coming in. The surplus was embezzled. Some £150m was missing when Clowes was arrested in 1988; he was sentenced in 1992 to ten years in prison. The government at first refused to consider compensation for the 18,000 investors, most of them elderly, who had lost their money; but in 1989 the full £150m was provided after the *Ombudsman identified maladministration by the Department of Trade and Industry.

Barnaby Rudge see *Gordon Riots.

Barnardo's (Ilford, Essex) Charity founded by Dr Thomas Barnardo (1845–1905), a Protestant missionary who established a home for destitute children in the East End of London in 1870. There were eventually more than 90 'Dr Barnardo's Homes', which astonishingly managed to maintain their stated principle – 'no destitute child ever refused admission'. Today the homes as such are not needed, but the charity does extensive work caring for disadvantaged children in the community, whether through foster parents or specialist day centres.

Julian **Barnes** (b. 1948) Novelist who found his own style of philosophical fancy in *Flaubert's Parrot* (1984) and developed it in *Staring at the Sun* (1986) and *A History of the World in 10 1/2 Chapters* (1989). He also writes thrillers under the pseudonym of Dan Kavanagh.

baron The fifth and lowest rank in the *peerage, but used also as a general term in medieval history for any member of the feudal nobility. A woman inheriting a barony which descends through the female line is a baroness. Since the Life Peerages Act of 1958 non-hereditary baronies have been granted to both sexes. Barons are invariably addressed as Lord (Lord Smith) and baronesses traditionally as Lady (Lady Smith); but some female life peers prefer to be called Baroness (Baroness Smith).

baronet The lowest rank of hereditary title. The honour was instituted in 1611 by James I, for unashamedly fundraising purposes. He decided to create 'a new dignity between barons and knights', to be awarded to any gentleman who would pay £1095 – the sum required to keep 30 soldiers for 3 years (the daily cost of the entire 30 being £1). Baronets and their wives are known as Sir and Lady in the same manner as *knights.

baroque Style which developed in Italy in the 17C and spread throughout Europe, though most powerfully in Roman Catholic countries. An abundance of form and feeling (the women in paintings by Rubens offer a good touchstone for the mood of baroque) is combined with a love of complexity. The extremes of baroque were too florid for Protestant England, but the architecture of *Wren and the carving of Grinling *Gibbons are restrained versions of the style. In the following century the buildings of *Vanbrugh and the furniture of William *Kent take English baroque to its limit.

The term is also applied to music of the same period, during which *Purcell and *Handel were the most important composers working in Britain.

Barra The most southerly of the main islands of the Outer *Hebrides. Its only town, Castlebay, takes its name from the castle of Kisimul (first recorded in the 15C but claimed to date in part from the 11C) which stands on a rock in the bay. Barra is unusual in having a predominantly Roman Catholic population, and it has acquired a late-20C fame as the location of the events narrated by Compton Mackenzie (himself buried on the island) in *Whisky Galore.

barrage balloon Elongated balloon with tail fins, filled with hydrogen and tethered to the ground by a steel wire – used in World War II as a defence against attack by low-flying aircraft. A barrage or obstruction of this kind had first been attempted late in World War I, when a shield of such balloons was known as a balloon apron.

Elizabeth **Barrett Browning** see Robert *Browning.

J.M. Barrie (James Matthew Barrie, 1860–1937, bt 1913) Scottish playwright, known above all for *Peter Pan* (1904). One of ten children of a handloom weaver, his first success came with a series of sentimental stories and novels about Scottish working-class life. Two of the best known among his plays for adults are The Admirable Crichton (1902), in which Crichton is a butler whose practical skills and ingenuity give him authority over his noble employer when the family is shipwrecked; and *What Every Woman Knows* (1908), where a self-made politician comes to discover the message of the title, which is that he could not have succeeded without the love of a good woman. Barrie's birthplace in Kirriemuir is kept as a museum.

Jonah **Barrington** (b. 1941) The outstanding British squash player of recent decades – indeed the only Briton since the 1930s to win the British Open Championship, which has otherwise been dominated by players from Egypt, Australia and Pakistan. He won six times, losing on only one occasion between 1967 and 1973 (in 1969 to the Australian player Geoff Hunt).

barrister A lawyer who has been called to the *Bar; he or she is also invariably a member of one of the *Inns of Court. The work of barristers is distinct from that of *solicitors, for they specialize in pleading the client's case in court (in addition to giving advice on all aspects and applications of the law). At present only barristers are allowed to plead in the higher courts, though this has recently been a subject of much debate as a restrictive practice. About one in ten barristers is a *QC. In Scotland the term for a barrister is an advocate.

Charles **Barry** (1795–1860, kt 1852) Architect of distinction in several styles, from the Gothic of St Peter's church (1823–6) in Brighton, through the Grecian classicism of the Royal Institution of Fine Arts (1824–35) in Manchester, to the Italian Renaissance manner of the *Travellers' and *Reform clubs in London. But by far his greatest achievement involved a return to the Gothic style, in the *Houses of Parliament.

Barsetshire Fictional county, with its cathedral town at Barchester, which is the setting for a sequence of six novels by *Trollope.

Bartholomew Fair (1614) Comedy by Ben *Jonson, following the fortunes of various visitors to London's very lively Bartholomew Fair. Held each year on and around St Bartholomew's Day (Aug. 24) at *Smithfield, the fair had originated in the 12C to provide funds for the adjacent priory of *St Bartholomew the Great. It became the country's greatest cloth fair and a famous centre of entertainment, with many theatrical booths and puppet shows (an important feature of Jonson's play). The fair lasted till 1855, when the site was cleared for the covered Smithfield market.

Barton Farm Tithe Barn see *Bradford-on-Avon.

Bart's (St Bartholomew's Hospital, London EC1) One of the two oldest hospitals in London (the other is *St Thomas's). It was founded in about 1123 by *Rahere, and the present building (1730–59) was designed by James *Gibbs. Bart's has been a teaching hospital since at least the 17C, but the 1992 Tomlinson inquiry into London's hospitals raised the possibility of its closure.

base rate The level of interest selected by individual banks (in most people's experience usually one of the *clearing banks) as the base for their loans to customers. The amount paid above base rate will vary according to the size and reliability of the customer; large and secure companies may be able to borrow at one percentage point above base rate, but small companies and private individuals will pay several points higher.
   The graph shows the rise and fall of base rates since 1965. The exact levels are only approximate at any point, but the cost of borrowing money (as for example for *mortgages) will have followed the same pattern of highs and lows – though usually a few points higher on the percentage scale.

basic English A proposed international language devised in the 1920s by two Cambridge dons, C.K. Ogden (1889–1957) and I.A. Richards (1893–1979). It consisted of 850 English words with a simplified grammar to make them serve 'for all the purposes of everyday language'. First explained in Ogden's *Basic English* (1930), the system was for a while widely followed. The title was an early but awkward acronym, standing for *British American Scientific International Commercial* English.

Basil Brush Glove puppet of a fox, a popular figure on children's television programmes from the early 1960s. He was one of several comic figures at the time to use 'Boom Boom' as a catch phrase to emphasize a joke.

Basildon see *Essex man.

John **Baskerville** (1706–75) Birmingham-based printer and publisher, responsible for many of the best-produced English books of the 18C. His name survives in the type which he designed – a clear-cut version of roman and italic, well suited to showing off the high quality of his printing and still in use today.

Bass The largest brewer in the UK, which became also the owner of the world's largest chain of hotels with the purchase of Holiday Inns in 1987–9. The original brewery was founded by William Bass in Burton-upon-Trent in 1777. In the 19C the company developed a thriving export trade with its India Pale Ale; there are even bottles on the bar of the Folies Bergère in Manet's famous painting. The Bass red triangle was the first trademark to be registered, in 1875.

Shirley **Bassey** (b. 1937) Welsh singer and cabaret star of vibrant voice and personality, born in Tiger Bay, Cardiff, daughter of a West Indian seaman. Of her many top 10 hits, only *As I Love You* (1958) reached no. 1. She recorded the theme songs of two James Bond films, *Goldfinger* (1964) and *Diamonds are Forever* (1971).

Bass Rock Precipitous circular rock of volcanic origin, 105m/350ft high, at the entrance to the Firth of Forth (about 2.5km/1.5m offshore from *Tantallon). It has been the site in the past of hermits' cells and of a castle, used in the 17C as a prison.

Basutoland see *Lesotho.

BAT (BAT Industries) British-American Tobacco was founded in 1902 and from the 1960s diversified widely outside the tobacco industry into such areas as paper

Base rates

Approximate % charged by selected high street banks.
Source: Economic Trends (*see* *Central Statistical Office*).

Bottles of Bass occupying a prominent position in A Bar at the Folies-Bergère *by Edouard Manet (1882, detail).*

manufacture (Wiggins Teape), insurance (Allied Dunbar and Eagle Star) and retail (Argos). This led in 1989 to Britain's largest takeover bid from Hoylake Investments (headed by James *Goldsmith, Jacob Rothschild and the Australian Kerry Packer), with the express intention of breaking up the group. The bid failed but some of the takeover group's proposals were put into effect, Wiggins Teape and Argos being floated off as independent companies.

Hester **Bateman** (1709–94) Silversmith who took over the workshop of her husband, John Bateman, after his death in 1760. Under her management and to her own designs the firm produced tableware of all kinds, including tea and coffee pots, characterized by an elegant simplicity, often with no decoration other than beaded edges.

H.M. **Bateman** (Henry Mayo Bateman, 1887–1970) Australian-born cartoonist who made his career in Britain. He is best remembered for his depiction of appalling social embarrassment, where one figure in the cartoon has transgressed in some way the convention of all the others.

Alan **Bates** (b. 1934) Actor who in his early career contributed to two of the most significant of London's theatrical first nights, playing Cliff, Jimmy Porter's friend, in *Look Back in Anger* (1956) and Mick in The *Caretaker (1960). His early film career was equally distinguished, including *A Kind of Loving* (1962), *Zorba the Greek* (1965) and *Women in Love* (1969). Subsequent highlights have included *Butley* (1972) on stage and screen, and on television *An Englishman Abroad* (1983).

H.E. **Bates** (Henry Ernest Bates, 1905–74) English novelist and writer of short stories, whose early work was rooted in the life of the English countryside. Many of these stories provided the basis for the plays in the TV series *Country Matters* (1972). Meanwhile his wartime experiences with the RAF had extended his range, as in *Fair Stood the Wind for France* (1944) about a bomber crew shot down in occupied France. In 1991 his fictional Larkin family scored a major popular success on TV in The *Darling Buds of May*.

Bath (85,000 in 1991) City and spa in Avon. It contains England's best Roman remains and is itself the country's most perfect example of an 18C town, almost unspoilt and built throughout in the lovely honey-coloured local limestone. It is the hot springs (49°C/120°F) which have brought visitors and prosperity to Bath. The Romans called the town *Aquae Sulis* (the waters of Sul, a local Celtic deity similar to the Roman Minerva), and they built extensive baths connected with a temple to Sul Minerva. These were rediscovered in 1755, by which time the waters of Bath had once again become fashionable under the expert supervision of Beau *Nash. The present Pump Room, where ladies and gentlemen both bathed in and drank the waters, was built in 1791–5 by Thomas Baldwin and John Palmer. The Assembly Rooms, to which visitors repaired for social amusements, are a little earlier – 1768–71 by John *Wood the younger (bombed in 1942, but restored).

The greatest glory of 18C Bath lies in the cumulative effect of its domestic Georgian streets, but it is also distinguished by many outstanding individual features. The Circus is a superb circular piazza (1754–70, by John Wood father and son); two crescents on the steep hillside (Royal Crescent, 1767–75 by the younger Wood; Lansdown Crescent, 1789–93 by John Palmer) are the finest in the country; and

Coloured aquatint by Rowlandson of visitors to Bath taking a medicinal plunge in his Comforts of Bath *(1798).*

Pulteney Bridge over the river Avon, surmounted by tiny Palladian houses (1769–74), is by Robert Adam.

Bath Abbey survives intact from a slightly earlier period, when the city's prosperity was based on the wool trade rather than the hot springs. There was a Benedictine monastery here from the 10C, but the present church was begun only in 1499; it is therefore an unusually consistent example of the Perpendicular style in Gothic architecture. The angels climbing ladders on either side of the west front had appeared in the dream which prompted the bishop, Oliver King, to build the church. Its interior is notable for the high-flown sentiments on the memorial stones of those who died here in the 18C.

In the old Sydney Hotel (1793–7) the Holburne of Menstrie Museum has an excellent display of paintings and the decorative arts, deriving from the collection of Sir William Holburne (1793–1874). The Victoria Art Gallery, founded in 1900, is Bath's municipal gallery; it has good holdings of the local artist known as Barker of Bath (Thomas Barker, 1769–1847). The Museum of Costume, established in 1963, is housed in the Assembly Rooms. Beckford's Tower survives as the last creation of the rich eccentric William *Beckford, who died in Bath, and *Claverton Manor is now the home of an American Museum.

Bath Rugby union football club, formed in 1865 and dominant on the English scene in recent years. It won the John Player/Pilkington Cup every year except two between 1984 and 1992; the exceptions were 1988 and 1991, both won by Harlequins.

Bath bun Sweet bun containing sultanas and candied peel, with blobs of crunchy melted sugar on top. It was first made in Bath during the 19C.

Bath Festival Founded in 1948 by the city council in conjunction with Glyndebourne. The original purpose was an annual celebration appropriate to *Bath, with performances of 18c chamber music in the city's 18c halls. Chamber music remains at the heart of each year's festival (held in May and June), but the entertainment has expanded over the years to include a wide range of orchestral music and opera (in the Theatre Royal) as well as jazz. The music directors – including Thomas Beecham in 1955, Yehudi Menuhin (1959–68) and Michael Tippett (1969–74) – have been of a stature to guarantee high standards.

bathing machine An invention of the 18C to enable the fashionable to enter the sea discreetly when bathing in resorts such as *Brighton. The bather, fully clothed, was enclosed in a hut on four wheels which was then drawn by horses into the sea. He or she changed inside before

The dippers of Brighton by Cruikshank, c.1830.

opening the door at the far end to descend some steps, where a 'dipper' would be standing in the water to ensure the bather's safety.

Bath Oliver A large, hard, pale unsweetened biscuit, invented by Dr William Oliver (1695–1764), a leading physician in Bath who believed that his patients were overeating and needed something nutritious but not rich. On his deathbed he gave his coachman the recipe, £100 and ten sacks of the finest flour. The coachman made a fortune and the biscuit (baked now by Huntley & Palmers at Aintree, near Liverpool) remains to this day the favourite of a few to accompany cheese.

Battersea Dogs Home (London SW8) In 1860 Mary Tealby founded a 'Temporary Home for Lost and Starving Dogs' in Holloway, and in 1871 it moved to its present premises in Battersea. The purpose of the home is to let owners recover their dogs and to find new homes for healthy unclaimed dogs. In an average week about 400 dogs are brought in. Of these approximately 60 are claimed, 240 are sold to new owners and 100 put down.

Battersea Power Station (London SW8) This landmark south of the Thames, with its four great corner chimneys, was designed by Giles Gilbert *Scott and was completed in 1937. Ceasing in the 1980s to have a practical function in the generating of electricity, it was acquired to house a theme park and was gutted before being abandoned when funds ran out. It stands, in the early 1990s, a vast and hollow shell.

Battle Abbey (8km/5m NW of Hastings) Benedictine abbey founded by William I to fulfil a vow made before the Battle of *Hastings. The altar of the abbey church was sited where his rival, Harold II, had fallen. There remain today the 14C gatehouse, standing in the market-square of the small town of Battle, and the abbot's hall (rebuilt in the 16C and now part of a girls' school).

Battle of Britain (June–Sept. 1940) The first turning point of World War II, in which the pilots of Britain's *Hurricanes and *Spitfires (known later as the *Few) denied the German *Luftwaffe* control of the air over the Channel and therefore made impossible Hitler's proposed invasion. In September the Germans changed to a new strategy of bombing British cities (the *Blitz).

Bayeux Tapestry Not in fact a tapestry but an embroidered strip of linen (68m/74yd long and on average about 50cm/20in high). It depicts in lively detail the events culminating in the Norman *Conquest in 1066. It is believed to have been made in southern England before 1082. Displayed for centuries in the nave of Bayeux Cathedral in Normandy, it is now on show nearby in a custom-built museum of its own.

Nicola **Bayley** (b. 1949) Illustrator of children's books, with an exceptionally delicate and detailed style, who made her name in 1975 with her *Book of Nursery Rhymes*. Since then she has specialized in stories about cats. The first was *Tyger Voyage* (1976, illustrating a story by Richard Adams, author of *Watership Down*); it has been followed by, among others, *The Patchwork Cat* (1981) and *The Mousehole Cat* (1990).

Lilian **Baylis** (1874–1937) Theatrical manager with a passionate commitment to making serious drama, opera and ballet widely available. Her energies gave the *Old Vic and *Sadler's Wells their greatest days, and led directly to the existence of English National Opera, the Royal Ballet and the Birmingham Royal Ballet.

Joseph **Bazalgette** (1819–91, kt 1874) Engineer whose great work was the sewers which discharge London's effluent into the Thames at a safe distance downstream. The project, which began in 1859, was given urgency by the *Great Stink of the previous year. Partly opened in 1865 and completed ten years later, Bazalgette's brick tunnels are still in good condition today. Part of the same undertaking was the *Embankment.

BBC (British Broadcasting Corporation) The nation's broadcasting service, publicly funded but independent of government control. It descends directly from the British Broadcasting Company, established in 1922 by a group of firms manufacturing wireless equipment. One of them, *Marconi, had opened a radio station in London earlier that year with the call sign '2LO', and it was from the 2LO studio in Savoy Hill (off the Strand) that the BBC began broadcasting. The company went on air on November 14 at 6 p.m., with the news read by Arthur Burrows. The first general manager (later called director general) was John *Reith, whose concept of public service broadcasting was given a seal of approval when the company received a royal charter in 1927 as the British Broadcasting Corporation. Its expenses have been met since then by licence fees, paid by anyone owning a radio or subsequently a television; the level of the fee is fixed annually by the government (it was ten shillings for radio in 1927, £80 for colour television in 1992). The royal charter has to be renewed from time to time. The next occasion is 1996, with the result that in the mid-1990s there is close scrutiny of the role of public service broadcasting in an era of proliferating channels of communication.

With headquarters at *Broadcasting House and *Bush House, the BBC acquired a high reputation for independence and integrity – giving it wide influence through its *World Service in occupied countries during World War II, and similarly since then in many places where truth remains hard to come by. Its motto, 'Nation shall speak peace unto nation', was adapted by Montague Rendall (1862–1950) from an Old Testament line, 'Nation shall not lift up a sword against nation' (*Micah* 4,3).

Within Britain the BBC had a monopoly of legitimate *radio until the first commercial station went on air in 1973. Meanwhile the BBC had launched in 1936 the first public *television service, but here its monopoly was shorter; the first commercial TV channels began transmitting in 1955. BBC television established extremely high standards over the whole range of programme-making (particularly drama and documentaries), setting a challenging benchmark for its commercial rivals.

Recent director generals have been Ian Trethowan (1977–82), Alasdair Milne (1982–7), Michael Checkland (1987–93) and John Birt from 1993.

BBC1 and **BBC2** see *television.

BBC Orchestras The BBC Symphony Orchestra was founded in 1930 and was rapidly brought to a high standard of adventure and excellence by its first chief conductor, Adrian Boult; in his long tenure (1931–50) he established the tradition of inviting distinguished contemporary composers to play or conduct their own work. He was followed by Malcolm Sargent (1950–57). Another particularly lively period was in the 1970s, when the French composer Pierre Boulez was chief conductor (1971–5). John Pritchard held the post from 1982 to 1989, and was followed by Andrew Davis. The orchestra's main annual showcase is the *Proms, during which its many performances invariably include the last night.

The original name in 1930 was simply the BBC Orchestra, and the 114 musicians were expected to provide smaller groups for theatre or palm court music. But

early success led to a need for specialization, and in 1931 the BBC Theatre Orchestra was created to concentrate on light music. It survives as the BBC Concert Orchestra – part of Radio 2, and playing in the Golders Green Hippodrome when at home in London.

A further development, also in the 1930s, was regional BBC orchestras. The BBC Northern Orchestra was formed in Manchester in 1934. Known since 1982 as the BBC Philharmonic (with a permanent home since 1980 in Manchester's Studio 7 Concert Hall), it has built a strong reputation for its performances of 20c British music. The BBC Scottish Symphony Orchestra was founded in 1935; it was launched in Edinburgh and has been a regular feature of the Edinburgh Festival, but it is based in the BBC's Glasgow headquarters. Plans were announced in 1992 for it to merge with the orchestra of Scottish Opera. The BBC Welsh Symphony Orchestra, based in Cardiff, was a general broadcasting orchestra until promoted to its present status during the 1980s; it is now recognized as Wales's national symphony orchestra.

All concerts given by the BBC Symphony Orchestra and the Philharmonic, and most of those by the Scottish and Welsh orchestras, are broadcast on Radio 3.

BCCI (Bank of Credit and Commerce International) Huge international private bank which collapsed in 1991 with liabilities estimated at around $5bn. It was founded in 1972 by a Pakistani, Agha Hassan Abedi, and its majority shareholder was the oil-billionaire Shaikh Sayed of Abu Dhabi. Depositors in Britain included some 40 councils (losing about £50 million between them) and many small businesses, the majority owned by Asian Muslims. It transpired that the bank had for years been systematically run as a criminal enterprise. Two reports in 1992, by Lord-Justice *Bingham and by a US senate subcommittee, strongly criticized the Bank of England and the British auditors Price Waterhouse for delay in taking action to prevent BCCI trading (for much of the time its headquarters were in London). In 1992 the liquidators, Touche Ross, arranged a deal with Abu Dhabi by which depositors would be compensated for about 33% of their losses.

BEA see *BOAC.

Beachcomber Humorous column in the *Daily Express*, written 1924–75 by J.B. Morton (John Bingham Morton, 1893–1979). Beachcomber's brilliantly eccentric humour centred on a cast of long-running characters, including Mr Justice Cocklecarrot, Captain Foulenough, the pedantic Prodnose and – best remembered of all – Dr Strabismus (Whom God Preserve) of Utrecht.

Beachy Head (34km/21m E of Brighton) Headland of sheer chalk cliffs, about 175m/575ft high, on the south coast of England. A short distance to the west of the headland are the cliffs known as the Seven Sisters.

Earl of **Beaconsfield** see *Disraeli.

HMS *Beagle* see Charles *Darwin.

beagling see *hunting.

Beaker folk Name given to people spread widely through continental Europe in about 3000 BC, characterized by the bell-shaped beakers or drinking vessels, with linear cord-like patterns on the surface, which are found in their tombs. They arrived in Britain some time before 2000 BC. They made much use of copper and may have been instrumental in the transition in Britain from the late *Stone Age to the *Bronze Age.

Beamish North of England Open-Air Museum
(13km/8m NW of Durham) Extensive recreation of
everyday working life in about 1900. Cottages, shops, a
farm, colliery buildings and a railway station have been
brought from neighbouring areas and rebuilt here in
81ha/200ac of countryside. People in period costume
work trams and steam engines and farm machinery, and
take visitors through the tunnels of a drift mine at the colliery. Beamish was voted European Museum of the Year
in 1987.

Beano Children's comic which has been published
weekly since 1938. Among its most memorable characters have been the irrepressibly awful child, Dennis the
Menace, who first appeared in 1951; and higher up the
social scale the top-hatted Lord Snooty, billed as 'the
Beano's longest serving star' until dropped in 1992.

bear A speculator who gambles that the stock market
will fall. The word was already in use in the early 18c but
was applied then to the stock sold by such a man, who
often did not own what he had sold but hoped to buy
it at a lower price before the delivery date. The analogy is
said to have been with a bearskin sold by a trader who has
not yet shot the bear. The companion word 'bull' (a
gamble on a rising market) entered the language a few
years later, possibly just as a natural companion from the
world of bear-baiting.

bear-baiting The baiting of both bears and bulls with
*mastiffs was a popular entertainment in England in the
17–18c. The baited animal was usually tethered to a post.
The London theatres of the time, of which the *Globe is
the best-known example, had the form of an enclosed
ring perfectly suited to animal baiting. A bear garden, later
to become a synonym for unruly violence, was merely the
term for any such place where the sport could be enjoyed.

*Beardsley's illustration of Salome with the head of John the
Baptist, for Wilde's* Salome *(1894).*

The baiting of animals was not banned by law in Britain
until 1835.

Aubrey **Beardsley** (1872–98) Artist and illustrator whose
brilliantly stylized black-and-white images, mostly designed for reproduction as line blocks, have become a predominant visual symbol of the *aesthetic 1890s. In a
prolific and tragically brief career his greatest achievements were two books which appeared in 1894, Wilde's
Salome and Malory's *Morte d'Arthur*; in that same year he
became art editor of the *Yellow Book*. His pornographic
illustrations to Aristophanes' *Lysistrata* (1896) were characteristically witty and elegant. He died of tuberculosis.

beating the bounds An annual procession round a
parish's boundaries, usually led by the vicar with much
ceremony. This was in earlier centuries a necessary territorial
act. In several places the custom still continues, more out of
sentiment than necessity now that maps are clear and
detailed. An equivalent in Scotland is the *common riding.

Beatles By far the most successful and influential of all
British pop groups, though only in existence for eight
years. All four were from Liverpool. John Lennon
(1940–80), Paul McCartney (b. 1942) and George
Harrison (b. 1943) were playing together in 1958 as the
Quarrymen (all three vocals and guitar). In 1960 they
formed a new group with Stuart Sutcliffe on guitar and
Pete Best on drums, calling themselves Long John & the
Silver Beatles, soon shortened to the Beatles. After work-
ing mainly in Hamburg and in the Cavern Club in
Liverpool, they had by 1962 found their lasting identity:
Stuart Sutcliffe had left to study art (he died in 1962);
Pete Best had been replaced by Ringo Starr (b. Richard
Starkey 1940, vocals and drums); Brian Epstein
(1934–67) had become their manager; and George
Martin (b. 1926) was their record producer at EMI.

Their first record, *Love Me Do*, reached no. 17 in October 1962; *Please Please Me* climbed to no. 2 in January
1963; and *From Me to You* was no. 1 in April 1963. In
the next 12 months they had three more no. 1 hits in succession – *She Loves You, I Want to hold your Hand* and
Can't buy me Love. A pattern was established of songs
with catchy tunes and often an almost surreal quirkiness
in the lyrics. This blend, combined with the personal
charm and irreverent humour of the quartet, proved to
have a wide appeal – Beatlemania was felt to some degree
by almost all age groups. The same fresh and unexpected
quality made a success of their first film, *A Hard Day's
Night* (1964), a gleeful indulgence in the oddness of their
own new helter-skelter lives, directed by Richard Lester.

1967 was their peak year. The first live TV global link-
up showed them recording *All you need is Love*, a deliberately simple lyric for an international audience; and the
most varied and brilliant of their LPs was issued, *Sergeant
Pepper's Lonely Hearts Club Band*, including such
psychedelic delights as 'Lucy in the Sky with Diamonds'.
But their manager died in that year; other interests were
assuming greater importance (including transcendental
meditation with an Indian guru, Maharishi); their personal lives were drifting apart; and both as composers and
performers they were feeling the need to launch out on
their own. By the end of 1970 all four had issued solo
LPs, and in that year the group officially broke up. Ringo
Starr made a few records of his own songs in the early
1970s. George Harrison continued more effectively with
a solo career, with an emphasis at first on eastern music
(and an early no. 1 hit, *My Sweet Lord*, in 1971); after a
period when his interest was more in film production
than pop music, he made an unexpected comeback in
1987 with *Got My Mind Set on You* (no. 2 in UK, no. 1 in
US). Meanwhile *McCartney created a new group,

One of the more exotic treasures of the National Motor Museum at Beaulieu: a brewer's delivery van of 1924.

Wings, and *Lennon had a varied and controversial career until his tragic death.

Nearly all the Beatles songs were written by Lennon and McCartney. It emerged later that their relationship had never been easy; but the number of their tunes to have found a place in the standard repertoire makes them probably the most successful song-writing partnership of all time.

Cecil **Beaton** (1904–80, kt 1972) Photographer remembered chiefly for half a century of royal photography, of which a selection was published in 1988 as *The Royal Portraits*. A different side of his skill was revealed in his wartime photography, the basis of several books in the 1940s. As a designer his greatest success was the costumes for *My Fair Lady, on both stage and screen.

Earl **Beatty** (David Beatty, 1871–1936, KCB 1914, earl 1919) Commander of the battle cruiser fleet which fought the first part of the Battle of *Jutland, successfully luring the Germans north towards the approaching Grand Fleet under Jellicoe. Later that year Beatty succeeded Jellicoe in command of the Grand Fleet.

Beaufort see *Badminton House.

Beaufort Scale A method for measuring wind force at sea. Still in use today, it was devised in 1805 by the captain of HMS *Woolwich*, Francis Beaufort (1774–1857), as a means of making his log entries more consistent. His yardstick was the amount of sail his ship could carry at each step on a wind scale from 0 to 12. Verbal descriptions of the sea later became the internationally accepted basis for the scale, from 0 (Calm – 'like a mirror') to 12 (Hurricane – 'air filled with foam and spray, sea completely white with driving spray').

Beaulieu (16km/10m S of Southampton) One of the major tourist attractions in Britain, largely because of the National Motor Museum. This superb collection of

vehicles includes an example of virtually every model of significance in the history of British motor and motorcycle manufacture, together with some splendid rarities and oddities. There is, for example: a car made by John Knight in 1895 in Farnham, Surrey, which is believed to be the first British petrol-driven car to have run on public roads; the oldest surviving Triumph motorcycle, dating from 1903; the *Golden Arrow* in which *Segrave broke the land speed record in 1929, and the *Bluebird* in which Donald *Campbell did the same in 1964; and, best of all the oddities, a 1924 Daimler delivery van in the shape of a bottle of Worthington's India Pale Ale.

Beaulieu was originally a Cistercian monastery of the 13c. Among the ruins stands Palace House, incorporating the original gatehouse of the abbey within a 19c mansion in the *Scottish baronial style.

Beaumaris (8km/5m NE of Menai Bridge) Town on *Anglesey which has grown up round the castle built for Edward I. Set in completely flat land, the castle relied for its defence on two great concentric walls and a moat filled by the tide from the Menai Strait. Work began in 1295 and within three years the fortifications were complete, thanks to 400 masons and 2000 labourers.

Bill **Beaumont** (b. 1952) Rugby union player who captained the England team in 1980 in its first Grand Slam victory for more than 50 years. He had 34 caps as a lock for England (1975–82) and seven for the *Lions (1977–80).

Beaumont and Fletcher The play-writing partnership of Francis Beaumont (1584–1616) and John Fletcher (1579–1625) was for a few years, from about 1609, so successful with the London public that the two have been spoken of in the same breath ever since. Their collaboration ended soon after 1613, when Beaumont married an heiress. The best-known of their plays is *The Maid's Tragedy* (c.1610). Fletcher is also believed to have collaborated with Shakespeare on two plays, **Henry VIII* and *The *Two Noble Kinsmen*.

'Beauty is truth, truth beauty' see *Ode on a Grecian Urn*.

*The **Beaux' Stratagem*** (1707) Comedy by George *Farquhar about two impoverished beaux, Aimwell and Archer, who pretend to be Lord Aimwell and his servant. Their prospects improve when Dorinda, daughter of the rich Lady Bountiful, falls in love with Aimwell. Her affection survives his admission of the fraud, but he then turns out to be Lord Aimwell after all; news comes of the death of his elder brother and his inheritance of the family title. The play ends with double happiness. Archer too has fallen in love – with Mrs Sullen, Lady Bountiful's daughter-in-law, whose drunken husband is persuaded to dissolve the marriage. More from the appropriateness of the name than from Farquhar's original character, the term Lady Bountiful was later applied, often satirically, to any woman dispensing charitable largesse in a country district.

Lord **Beaverbrook** ('Max' Aitken, 1879–1964, kt 1911, baron Beaverbrook 1917) Newspaper proprietor and politician. Born in Canada, son of a Scottish Presbyterian minister, he had made a fortune in business before he came to Britain in 1910. He was elected a Unionist MP that same year, for Ashton-under-Lyne. He bought the *Daily Express* in 1916, launched the *Sunday Express* in 1918 and acquired the *Evening Standard* in 1923. His papers were known for their popular crusading journalism (a masthead image of a crusader is a feature of the *Express*), and the most consistent campaign was support for the empire. Beaverbrook was brilliantly effective as minister in charge of aircraft production in 1940–1, a period which included the *Battle of Britain.

'Because it is there' see *Everest.

Becher's Brook see the *Grand National.

Bechuanaland see *Botswana.

Lord Beaverbrook by David Low in 1926; the following year Low became the cartoonist of the Standard.

Max, Lord Beaverbrook.

Thomas **Becket** (also known as Thomas à Becket and St Thomas Becket, *c*.1118–70) The king's chancellor 1154–62, and archbishop of Canterbury 1162–70. Born in London of Norman-French parents, he established a reputation in the household of the previous archbishop of Canterbury, Theobald, and was selected as chancellor by Henry II in 1154. A close friendship developed between the two men, but it did not long survive Henry's appointment of Thomas, against his will, to succeed Theobald at Canterbury in 1162. This was a period of constant friction between royal and ecclesiastical power, and Thomas's insistence on the rights of the church made it necessary for him to flee to France in 1164. He remained abroad for the next six years, upholding the papal cause by such measures as excommunicating those bishops in England who collaborated with the king.

In 1170 Thomas returned to Canterbury, to be greeted there with acclaim. According to verbal tradition, the king then asked the dangerous question 'Who will rid me of this turbulent priest?'. It was answered on 29 December 1170 by four knights (Hugh de Morville, William de Tracy, Reginald Fitzurse and Richard le Breton), who murdered Thomas in the north transept of his own cathedral. He was rapidly canonized (1173), and in 1174 the king did public penance at his tomb. His shrine turned Canterbury into one of medieval Europe's most popular places of pilgrimage, and in the 20c his martyrdom was made the subject of a major poetic drama, * *Murder in the Cathedral*. His feast day is the date of his death, December 29.

Margaret **Beckett** (Margaret Jackson, b. 1943, m. Lionel Beckett 1979) Labour politician, MP for Derby South since 1983 (previously for Lincoln 1974–9) and deputy leader of the party from 1992. She was the opposition front bench spokesman on health and social security (1984–9) and then on Treasury affairs (1989–92). In 1992 she became shadow leader of the House with an overall responsibility for Labour campaigns.

William **Beckford** (1759–1844) Eccentric of immense wealth who was a significant figure in early romanticism, both as the author of *Vathek* and as the builder of Fonthill Abbey. *Vathek*, written in French in a single trance-like spell of three days in 1781, indulges the contemporary fashion for orientalism; it is a Faust-like tale of a cruel eastern potentate who becomes a servant of the devil in his quest for the extremes of power and passion. An unproven homosexual scandal in 1794 caused Beckford to travel abroad for many years, during which he formed a great collection of pictures and books. On his return he commissioned James *Wyatt to rebuild his family home, Fonthill Abbey in Wiltshire, as a suitable setting for himself and his *objets d'art*. The new Fonthill, in which he lived as a recluse, became one of the famous follies of the age. Its 85m/278ft tower collapsed three months after completion, was rebuilt and collapsed again in 1825. Meanwhile Beckford had sold the house and had moved to Bath, where he built himself on Lansdown Hill a study with a tower of only 46m/150ft (Beckford's Tower, still standing). Of his vast fortune, from sugar plantations in the West Indies, only a fraction remained when he died.

Bedales Britain's oldest co-educational boarding school, in Hampshire. It was founded in 1893 as a boys' boarding school by John Badley (1865–1967), who had previously been a teacher at Abbotsholme in Staffordshire. Abbotsholme, founded in 1889, launched the movement in Britain for progressive education, with its ideal that a school should be a 'community' or 'miniature commonwealth'. Bedales introduced co-educational boarding at the surprisingly early date of 1898; Abbotsholme followed suit in 1969.

Beddgelert, meaning the 'grave of Gelert' (19km/12m SE of Caernarfon). Village on the river Glaslyn, in a green valley below wooded hills, which was the site of a Celtic monastery from the 6C and of an Augustinian priory founded by Llewellyn the Great in about 1300.

The village is best known now for a legend, according to which Gelert was Llewellyn's dog, slain by the king when he found his infant son missing and the dog covered in blood. Subsequently the child was found, alive and well, close to a dead and equally blood-stained wolf. Llewellyn gave the heroic dog a suitable burial, hence the village's name. An enterprising local publican in the 18C put together the stones which are now much visited as poor Gelert's grave.

Bede (also known as the Venerable Bede, c.673–735) Monk in the monastery of Jarrow, in Northumbria, whose lasting fame derives from his *Historia Ecclesiastica Gentis Anglorum* (History of the English Church and People). It briefly describes the Roman occupation of England, but concentrates on the centuries after their departure. These include the arrival of the *Anglo-Saxons and of two different waves of Christian missionaries, the Celtic and the Roman; the rival claims in ritual and dogma between these two groups had been resolved, shortly before his own birth, at the *Synod of Whitby. Many semi-legendary names from the early mists of English history, such as *Hengist and Horsa or *Caedmon, are known only from Bede, and he was used as a major source for later works such as the *Anglo-Saxon Chronicle*. Probably known as 'venerable' even in his own lifetime, he was canonized as a doctor of the church by Pope Leo XIII in 1899. His bones were moved in the 11C to *Durham, where there is a shrine to him in the Galilee Chapel.

Bedford (74,000 in 1981) Town on the river Ouse; administrative centre of the *county of Bedfordshire. It was already a town in Anglo-Saxon times, but the best-known incident in Bedford's long history is the imprisonment of John *Bunyan. The Bunyan Meeting is a chapel built in 1850 on the site of the barn in which he used to preach. The town is known also for its four schools, two for boys and two for girls, endowed in the 16C by Sir William Harpur and all still surviving. The Cecil Higgins Art Gallery and Museum is an exceptional private collection gathered by Cecil Higgins (1856–1941) and open to the public since 1949 in his own house; it is particularly strong in ceramics, glass and English paintings and watercolours.

Bedfordshire (534,000 in 1991, administrative centre Bedford) *County in south central England.

Bedgebury National Pinetum (19km/12m SE of Tunbridge Wells) Research plantation specializing in conifers native to Britain, established jointly in 1924 by *Kew Gardens and the *Forestry Commission, and now run by the Forestry Commission alone. The site was chosen because a wide range of ornamental conifers already existed there, planted in 1850–70 by a previous owner. The Pinetum suffered grave damage in the *Great Storm of 1987.

Bedlam The common name in past centuries for the Bethlehem Royal Hospital, which from the 14C was London's main lunatic asylum. The Priory of St Mary Bethlehem in Bishopsgate had been its first home (the site is now Liverpool Street Station); from 1676 it was in

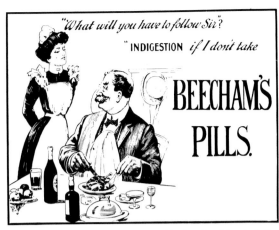
Someone with rather less than World War I on his mind, in a Beecham's advertisement of 1915.

a vast building in Moorfields, where it became a fashionable pastime for visitors to marvel at the lunatics; it moved in 1815 to what is now the *Imperial War Museum, and in 1930 to Beckenham. Today it is run jointly with the *Maudsley. For some considerable time (either causing the popular corruption or in response to it) its official name has been the Bethlem Royal Hospital.

Thomas **Beecham** (1879–1961, kt 1916, 2nd bt 1916) Conductor, famous for high musical standards combined with a caustic wit from the podium, and founder of two of Britain's leading orchestras, the *London Philharmonic and the *Royal Philharmonic. He spent his own fortune (deriving from *Beecham's pills) to promote music, his first major enterprise being an opera season at Covent Garden in 1910; in this he conducted the English premieres of Richard Strauss's *Salome* and *Elektra* and of *A Village Romeo and Juliet* by *Delius, of whom he was a passionate supporter and eventually, in 1958, the biographer.

Beecham's Pills Patent remedy to dispel that liverish feeling, which became Britain's best-known contribution to the family medicine cupboard. The formula was patented in 1847 by Thomas Beecham (1820–1907), who had a grocery and herbal remedy shop in Wigan, near Manchester; his ingredient was the recently discovered chemical compound aloin, a laxative extracted from aloes. The pills' subsequent international success brought Beecham much wealth and incidentally enabled his grandson, Thomas *Beecham, to spend a great deal of money promoting music. The family company went public in 1928 as Beecham Pills Ltd, and is now part of *SmithKline Beecham.

Beeching Report see *railways.

beefeaters Nickname used since the 17C for both the *Yeomen of the Guard and the yeoman warders of the *Tower of London.

Bee Gees Long-running pop group with no. 1 hits spanning 20 years (*Massachusetts* 1967, *You Win Again* 1987). The three brothers – Barry Gibb (b. 1946) and twins Robin and Maurice (b. 1949) – write their songs and sing them in piping voices. The group's name is variously explained as the initials of Barry Gibb or of the Brothers Gibb. Their greatest success was the soundtrack album for the film *Saturday Night Fever* (1978), which had worldwide sales of more than 30 million and provided three US no. 1 singles (*How Deep is your Love; Stayin' Alive; Night Fever*).

Self-portrait in 1906: Mr Max Beerbohm – somewhat overweighted by a Taplow Malmaison *(in his buttonhole).*

Max **Beerbohm** (1872–1956, kt 1939) Caricaturist and writer, half-brother of the actor Beerbohm Tree (1853–1917). His gently humorous caricatures, mainly of literary and artistic figures, are in a highly individual style with rounded lines and soft tones. Famous in his own time as a parodist, essayist and wit, his literary reputation now rests mainly on his satirical romance *Zuleika Dobson* (1911), in which the beautiful heroine turns her thoughts to Cambridge after every single undergraduate in Oxford has committed suicide for love of her.

Mrs **Beeton** (Isabella Mayson, 1836–65, m. Samuel Beeton 1856) Editor of *The Book of Household Management* (1861), an extremely influential collection of recipes and tips on all aspects of housekeeping. It appeared from 1859 (when Mrs Beeton was 23) in monthly issues of *The Englishwoman's Domestic Magazine*, a periodical published by her husband.

BEF see *British Expeditionary Force.

The Beggar's Opera (1728) Satirical work by John *Gay and the outstanding example of English ballad opera, in which the songs are set to existing popular tunes. The orchestration and overture were by Johann Pepusch (1667–1752). The story of Captain Macheath, a highwayman, was intended to satirize both the corruption of *Walpole's administration and the conventions of Italian opera; Macheath is betrayed by Peachum (his colleague in crime), is unscrupulous with the affections of two girls (Polly Peachum and Lucy Lockit), and is rescued from the gallows only by an obligatory happy ending. Staged

by the impresario John Rich (*c.*1682–1761), the show was immensely successful and gave rise to the tag that it had made Gay rich and Rich gay. A scene from it was painted by *Hogarth (Tate Gallery). Bertolt Brecht and Kurt Weill used it as the basis for *The Threepenny Opera* (1928).

Beilby family Two members of the family, William (1740–1819) and his sister Mary (1749–1797), working in Newcastle-upon-Tyne, achieved exquisite results in the decorative enamelling of glass. They painted mainly in white enamel on goblets and decanters, producing delicate rococo designs of birds, fruit or landscape, though sometimes they used a range of colours for armorial decoration. Their brother Ralph (1743–1817), a silversmith, had *Bewick as an apprentice.

Toby **Belch** see *Twelfth Night.*

Belfast (279,000 in 1991) Capital city of Northern Ireland on the northeast coast at the mouth of the river Lagan, where it enters the long inlet of the North Channel known as Belfast Lough. The town grew up around a Norman castle of the 12c (destroyed in 1315). By the 18c Belfast's two main industries were clearly identified: the manufacture of linen had been given a considerable boost by the arrival of refugee *Huguenot weavers in the late 17c; and the development of shipbuilding led eventually to the giant Harland and Wolff yard, where the *Titanic was launched.

By the Government of Ireland Act of 1920 Belfast became the seat of government for Northern Ireland, and a classical-style parliament building was provided at Stormont (1928–32, by Arnold Thornely). It has been out of use since 1972 when direct rule was imposed from Westminster because of the sectarian violence in the city. For the same reason two otherwise undistinguished Belfast streets have become familiar names throughout Britain, the Falls Road as a Catholic enclave and the Shankhill Road as the Protestant equivalent. Belfast's cathedral, St Anne's, is Protestant; begun in 1899 to the design of Thomas Drew, and continued by Charles Nicholson, it is still unfinished. Queen's University stands in what is still a largely Victorian suburb, with a central building in Tudor style by Charles Lanyon (1813–89); founded as Queen's College in 1845, it has had university status since 1908.

The Ulster Museum has a strong holding of the Belfast-born painter Sir John Lavery (1856–1941) and a splendid array of gold and silver, together with many more mundane objects, recovered in the 1960s from the *Girona*, a ship of the Spanish Armada which went down off the north Antrim coast.

HMS *Belfast* (London SE1) Cruiser in service with the Royal Navy through World War II, after being launched in 1938 (11,550 tons). Since 1971 she has been moored in the Thames, just upstream of Tower Bridge, and is open to the public as part of the *Imperial War Museum.

Belfast News Letter Britain's oldest surviving daily newspaper, launched as a single sheet in 1737. It had a major scoop in 1776, when it was the first in Britain with news of the American Declaration of Independence; a ship on its way to London, carrying copies of the declaration, had called in at Londonderry.

Belgravia (London SW1) Area to the west of Buckingham Palace which was developed from the 1820s by Thomas *Cubitt in conjunction with the Grosvenor family (later dukes of Westminster), who owned the land. The word derives from the most imposing of the squares, Belgrave Square, itself named from a village just north of Leicester, where the Grosvenors had an estate.

Belisha beacon Nickname given by the public to the flashing amber globe at each end of a pedestrian crossing (because it was introduced by Leslie Hore-Belisha when minister of transport in 1934–7).

Belize Member of the *Commonwealth since 1981. On the coast of central America, to the east of Guatemala, the region was one of constant dispute between the Spanish colonial powers and British settlers, who from 1638 plundered the hardwood forests and made the area a base for privateering raids into the West Indies. It was declared a colony in 1862 as British Honduras (the name was changed back to Belize in 1973), but territorial disagreements have continued ever since with Guatemala and are still unresolved. The country had internal self-government from 1964 on the way to full independence in 1981.

Alexander Graham **Bell** (1847–1922) Scottish-born inventor of the telephone. He lived in the USA from 1872 and became naturalized in 1874. His researches, begun in 1874, reached fruition on 10 March 1876 when he summoned his assistant with the first sentence ever transmitted by telephone, 'Mr Watson, come here; I want you'.

David **Bellamy** (b. 1933) Passionate and genial botanist, much involved with environmental causes and widely known to the TV audience through his programmes of popular science. His best-known series had a title aptly describing himself – *Botanic Man* (Thames TV 1978). *Bellamy's Backyard Safari* (BBC 1981) was a shorter series in every sense; he was ingeniously shrunk by trick photography to the height of a few millimetres, turning everyone's backyard into a huge jungle of living marvels.

Bellamy's veal pies see William *Pitt.

*La **Belle Dame sans Merci*** (1820) Short ballad by *Keats, using the title of a 15C French poem about a 'beautiful lady without mercy' but applying it to a quite different story. Keats's version is part of a medieval strain in the *Romantic movement which had a powerful appeal in Britain. His knight-at-arms, 'alone and palely loitering', was still a favourite type of subject for *Burne-Jones at the end of the century. The knight meets and lifts onto his 'pacing steed' a beautiful lady, a wild long-haired fairy's child, who tempts him into her elfin grotto. There he sees all her other victims in a dream before waking, incurably afflicted, from his vision.

Belleek ware Porcelain made since 1857 in the village of Belleek in County Fermanagh. It is known for its extremely thin almost eggshell quality, translucent and with a pearly lustre. Within a wide range of products, the most famous designs have been dishes in the form of shells and open-weave baskets decorated with flowers and leaves. Various factories in the USA later imitated the style and used the name.

Belle Vue Public gardens of great popularity in 19C Manchester; they opened in 1836, with a zoo as the chief attraction, but the area has now been built over. The nearby stadium has been used since 1987 for greyhound racing and speedway. Belle Vue was closely associated with the development of the *brass band movement, as the location of the British Open competition.

Bell Harry see *Canterbury.

Macheath in leg-irons in Hogarth's 1729 painting of The Beggar's Opera, *with aristocratic spectators seated on the stage.*

Hilaire **Belloc** (1870–1953) Prolific and versatile French-born author, educated in Britain and naturalized in 1902. He is best remembered now for his comic verse (*The Bad Child's Book of Beasts* 1896, *Cautionary Tales* 1907), for his discursive travel writing and for his ardent Roman Catholicism. The two latter themes were combined very successfully in *The Path to Rome* (1902), an account of a pilgrimage on foot from northern France.

Belshazzar's Feast (1931) Oratorio by William *Walton for baritone, chorus and orchestra, with text (arranged by Osbert Sitwell) taken mainly from the biblical account in the Book of Daniel.

Lord **Belstead** (John Ganzoni, b. 1932, 2nd baron 1958) Conservative politician, in the cabinet 1988–90 as leader of the House of Lords.

Beltane The spring festival of the ancient *Celts, celebrated on *May Day with bonfires and dancing. In parts of Scotland and Wales the Beltane festivities were held until the early 19C. The equivalent autumn festival was Samhain (see *Hallowe'en).

Belvoir Castle (pronounced *beever*, 29km/18m SE of Nottingham) Gothic Revival mansion of the early 19C, home of the dukes of Rutland, on the site of a Norman castle which dated back to the late 11C. The name, deriving from Norman French, means 'beautiful view'. James *Wyatt was the original architect of the present house, but his designs were much modified. There is an excellent collection of paintings, including five of a set of seven sacraments by Poussin. The kennels of the Belvoir, one of the oldest hunts in the *Shires, are at the castle.

BEM see *orders of chivalry.

Benefits Agency (Leeds) The largest of the executive agencies established under the *Next Steps programme, operating since 1991 within the Department of *Social Security and responsible for issuing social security payments from nearly 500 offices around the country. The bulk of the payments are *pensions, *income support and child benefit, but the agency is also responsible for all other state benefits except those issued by the *Employment Service.

Benenden School Independent girls' school in Kent, founded in 1923. Its name became widely known in the 1960s when Princess Anne was a pupil.

Bengalis see *ethnic and religious minorities.

Ben Gunn see *Treasure Island.*

Nigel **Benn** (b. 1964) Boxer who won the WBO middleweight title in 1990, defeating Doug de Witt in Atlantic City, but lost it six months later to Chris Eubank in Birmingham. He took the WBC super-middleweight title in 1992 from Mauro Galvano in Rome.

Tony **Benn** (b. 1925) Labour politician, MP for Chesterfield since 1984 (previously for Bristol SE 1950–60 and 1963–83). In 1960 he inherited the title of Viscount Stansgate, resulting in an automatic by-election for his seat in the House of Commons. From the mid-1950s he had waged a vigorous campaign for the right to renounce *peerages, and he now took the unprecedented step of standing in the by-election; he won by a large majority but was refused entry to the chamber of the Commons. His defeated opponent became MP in his place, resigning the seat (see *Chiltern Hundreds) when the 1963 law

enabled Benn to renounce his peerage and resume his career. He entered the cabinet in 1966 as minister of technology (1966–70) and continued in the next Labour government as secretary of state for industry (1974–5) and for energy (1975–9). There is an element of play acting in his image as a plain man of the people (including the foreshortening of Anthony Wedgwood Benn to Tony Benn), but his political views have been firmly within the historical traditions of the Labour party and there is no justification for the Tory tabloid depiction of him as an ogre from the loony left.

Alan **Bennett** (b. 1934) Author and actor, who first revealed in **Beyond the Fringe* his ear for the quirks of everyday English idiom. His most ambitious and best-known undertaking has been a series of six bleakly poignant monologues for television (*Talking Heads* BBC 1988). The *Cambridge spies provided the basis for two short plays – *An Englishman Abroad* (1983) about Guy Burgess in Moscow, and *A Question of Attribution* (1988) featuring Anthony Blunt among the queen's pictures (famous also for Prunella Scales' portrayal of Elizabeth II). His 1990 National Theatre adaptation of *The *Wind in the Willows* looks set to become a regular Christmas treat.

Arnold **Bennett** (1867–1931) Author whose best novels, notable for their detailed realism, are set in the *Five Towns of his own childhood and early youth (he was born in Hanley). His first success was *Anna of the Five Towns* (1902), followed by *The Old Wives' Tale* (1908) and by a series on the fortunes of the Clayhanger family which began with *Clayhanger* (1910).

Ben Nevis Mountain to the southeast of Fort William in the Highland region, which at 1343m/4406ft is the highest in the British Isles. It lacks a dramatic peak – indeed it has at its summit the ruins of an observatory which was in use from 1823 to 1904.

Jeremy **Bentham** (1748–1832) Philosopher who became the leading exponent of utilitarianism – the theory that any action should be judged only according to whether it promotes 'the greatest happiness of the greatest number'. It was a philosophy which became associated with a harshly practical view of life, popular with factory owners, because it seems to justify the 'lesser happiness' of the losers. Bentham is remembered also for his rational and influential design for a *prison, the 'panopticon', and for the eccentric clause in his will that his body was to be dissected in the presence of his friends. The skeleton was dressed in his own clothes and still sits today, in a glass-fronted case, in University College, London.

Bentley One of the greatest names among British sports cars. Designed in 1919 by William Owen Bentley (1888–1971), the 3-litre model had five victories at Le Mans (1924, 27, 28, 29, 30). The firm, with its factory at Cricklewood in northwest London, was bought in 1931 by *Rolls Royce, which has continued to manufacture Bentleys – now more associated with great luxury than with the rigours of Le Mans.

E.C. **Bentley** (Edmund Clerihew Bentley, 1875–1956) Journalist whose lasting fame is as an author of detective fiction (in particular *Trent's Last Case* 1913) and as the inventor of the clerihew. The first examples of this type of 4-line humorous verse, with the subject's name providing the rhyme for the opening couplet, appeared in his *Biography for Beginners* (1905, with illustrations by his close friend G.K. Chesterton). A typical biography runs:

Drawing of 1925 by G.K. Chesterton to illustrate the clerihew about Wren and St Paul's.

Sir Christopher Wren
Said, 'I am going to dine with some men.
If anybody calls
Say I am designing St Paul's.'

Such a verse became known as a clerihew because the volume was published under the pseudonym E. Clerihew, based on the author's first two names.

Bentley and Craig One of the most controversial of cases in the years preceding the abolition of *capital punishment. During the evening of 2 November 1952 two teenagers were apprehended by police on the roof of a building in Croydon. Derek Bentley, an illiterate 19-year-old with a mental age of 11, was already being held by one of the policemen when his 16-year-old companion, Christopher Craig, drew a gun. Bentley was then alleged to have shouted 'Let him have it, Chris'; Craig fired and killed PC Sidney Miles. The prosecution argued that Bentley's words were an incentive to Craig to shoot the policeman rather than to give him the gun. He was convicted of incitement to murder and was hanged. Craig, too young for the death penalty, went to jail and is alive today. The case has been kept in the public eye by a stream of books and films, and by the determination of Iris Bentley to win a pardon for her brother. She received a setback in 1992 when the home secretary, Kenneth Clarke, followed his predecessors in refusing either a retrospective pardon or a new enquiry.

Beowulf (probably 8C) By far the most important poem in Old *English, though its plot is set entirely in northern Germany and Denmark, areas from which the *Anglo-Saxons had come. The hero, Beowulf, confronts three dragons in the course of the very long poem (3182 lines). The first two exploits are in his youth, when he saves the court of the Danish king from the dragon Grendel and then from Grendel's mother. Rewarded with a kingdom and people of his own (the Geats), he dies late in life killing a dragon which is threatening them. The poem contains many historical references to an earlier period,

the 6C, but scholars date it in or near the 8C because Beowulf's pagan world of feasting heroes has been infiltrated by Christian images and morality. It is first known in a manuscript of the 10C.

Jack **Beresford** (1899–1977) Oarsman with the exceptional Olympic record of competing in five successive games and winning a medal in each – successively a silver in the single sculls (1920), a gold in the single sculls (1924), a silver in the eights (1928), a gold in the coxless fours (1932) and a gold in the double sculls (1936). In modern times Steve *Redgrave has a chance of equalling Beresford's total.

Svetlana **Beriosova** (b. 1932) Born in Lithuania, daughter of the ballet master Nicolas Beriozoff, she was trained in the USA and danced in Britain (now her home) from 1950. She began with the Sadler's Wells Theatre Ballet (now the *Birmingham Royal Ballet) and transferred in 1952 to the Royal Ballet. Known in particular for the elegance and nobility of her dancing in the classics, she also had many new roles created for her by Ashton, Cranko and MacMillan.

George **Berkeley** (also known as Bishop Berkeley, 1685–1753) Anglo-Irish philosopher, the leading exponent of empiricism (the theory that things exist only through being perceived), as expressed in his *Treatise concerning the Principles of Human Knowledge* (1710). He was the Anglican bishop of Cloyne in County Cork from 1734 to 1752.

Berkeley's lasting popular fame derives from a scene in Boswell's life of Johnson. The two men were outside a church in Harwich in 1763 and began discussing 'Bishop Berkeley's ingenious sophistry to prove the non-existence of matter'. Boswell observed that the theory was clearly wrong but impossible to refute, whereupon Dr Johnson kicked a large stone and said 'I refute it thus'. If anything, Johnson's stubbed toe would seem to demonstrate the bishop's theory about matter and perception, but he had also misunderstood the point. Berkeley, like Boswell, took it as obvious that matter continued to exist when unseen; but he considered this to be proof of the existence of God, whose entire creation was under His constant observation.

Lennox **Berkeley** (1903–89, kt 1974) Composer known for his elegant craftsmanship. One of his earliest works (after studying with Nadia Boulanger in Paris) was an orchestral suite of Catalan dances, *Mont Juic* (1937), written in collaboration with Benjamin Britten. He was a convert to Roman Catholicism and many of his pieces for voice or choir were religious in content.

Berkeley Castle (31km/19m SW of Gloucester) Medieval stronghold, unusually intimate in scale and setting, lived in by the Berkeley family since 1153. The interiors date mainly from an extensive rebuilding in 1340–50. By then the darkest deed in the castle's history, the murder of *Edward II, had already taken place.

Berkeley Square (London W1) Square laid out in the 1730s, which still has its 18C houses on the west side. Its fame derives from the song *A Nightingale sang in Berkeley Square*, written in 1940 by a British lyricist (Eric Maschwitz, 1901–69) and an American composer (Manning Sherwin, 1902–74).

Berkshire (753,000 in 1991, administrative centre Reading) *County in south central England.

Berkshire see *pigs.

Isaiah **Berlin** (b. 1909, kt 1957) Philosopher born in Russia, living in Britain from the age of ten. His best-known works are the essay *The Hedgehog and the Fox* (1953), which is a study of Tolstoy's view of history; *Four Essays on Liberty* (1969); and *Russian Thinkers* (1978), a collection of his essays on 19C Russian literature and thought (including a reissue of *The Hedgehog and the Fox*). He is a member of the Order of *Merit.

Bermuda Self-governing British colony in the west Atlantic, consisting of more than 100 small islands (about 20 inhabited). They were settled as the result of an accident. Sir George Somers, in command of a ship taking colonists to Virginia in America, was shipwrecked here in 1609 (the territory was long known as the Somers Islands); his account of his experiences partly inspired Shakespeare's *The *Tempest*, written two years later. Internal self-government was introduced in 1968, but the governor, appointed from Britain, remains responsible for security and external affairs.

Bertie Wooster see P.G. *Wodehouse.

Bertram Mills Britain's best-known circus until its final season in the winter of 1966. It was established by the owner of a coach-building firm, Bertram Mills (1873–1938), after he had bet a friend that he could put on a better show than what was then available at *Olympia. From 1920 his circus was the regular Christmas show at Olympia, and from 1929 it also toured each year in a big top; it was continued after his death by his two sons, Cyril and Bernard. One of the most popular attractions was its famous clown, Coco (Nicolai Poliakoff, 1900–74).

Berwickshire Until 1975 a *county in the extreme southeast of Scotland, now part of the Borders region.

Berwick-upon-Tweed (12,000 in 1981) Town in Northumberland, at the mouth of the river Tweed, which was a much disputed frontier post between Scotland and England, changing hands at least a dozen times before being finally recognized as English in 1482. Its character was inevitably that of a garrison. The ramparts, designed in 1555 in keeping with the latest Italian theories of fortification, are still complete. The barracks, built round a square in 1719 and possibly by Vanbrugh, are now used in part to house the Museum and Art Gallery. This includes excellent French 19C paintings given by Sir William Burrell before his better-known bequest of the *Burrell Collection to Glasgow. The 17C bridge from Tweedmouth, on the south bank, has had since 1928 a neighbour in concrete, the Royal Tweed bridge. The railway viaduct further upstream, the Royal Border bridge, 38m/126ft high with 28 arches (1847–50), is by Robert Stephenson.

BES see *Business Expansion Scheme.

Annie **Besant** (Annie Wood, 1847–1933, m. Frank Besant 1867) A whirlwind of energy in a wealth of causes. She campaigned with Charles *Bradlaugh for atheism and free speech; their publication of a deliberately provocative pamphlet on birth control led to prosecution and to her being deprived of her children. Later she was one of the founders of the *Fabian Society. These interests were dropped in 1889 when she discovered mysticism through the theosophy of Mme Blavatsky, and this in turn directed her attention towards India. By 1918 she was president of the Theosophical Society, president of the Indian National Congress and adoptive mother of a messiah-figure, Jiddu Krishnamurti (1895–1986), whom she proclaimed to be the reincarnate Buddha.

Henry **Bessemer** (1813–98, kt 1879) Versatile inventor with a pivotal role in the story of *iron and steel. His fame and fortune derived from the discovery that carbon can be removed from molten iron by blowing air through it – thus simplifying, in the technology of that time, the manufacture of steel. He perfected the Bessemer process during the years 1855–9, in time to benefit from the world-wide demand for steel caused by the spread of railways.

Besses o' th' Barn see *brass bands.

Bess of Hardwick (Elizabeth Hardwick, 1527–1608) Spirited Elizabethan who by four judicious marriages (Robert Barlow *c.*1543, Sir William Cavendish 1547, Sir William St Loe 1559, the earl of Shrewsbury 1567) rose from the minor Derbyshire gentry to become one of the richest people in England. She spent her last years and much of her wealth in creating a spectacular new house near her childhood home, *Hardwick Hall.

George **Best** (b. 1946) Northern Irish footballer who had a dazzling but relatively brief career, mainly with Manchester United (1963–73) where he was an important member of the team which won the European Cup in 1968. He is remembered for his brilliant dribbling skills as a winger and for an excitingly theatrical temperament (which later led to much publicized troubles in his private life). He had 37 caps for Northern Ireland, and his last playing years were in the embryonic Soccer League of the USA.

'best-laid schemes o' mice an' men' Phrase from *Burns' poem *To a Mouse; on turning her up in her nest, with the plough, November 1785*. Burns apologizes to the 'wee, sleekit, cowrin, tim'rous beastie' and expresses fellow feeling because the best-laid schemes of mice and men 'gang aft a-gley' (often go awry).

'best of times, worst of times' see A *Tale of Two Cities*.

Bethlem Royal Hospital see *bedlam.

Bethnal Green Museum of Childhood (London E2) Opened in 1872 as the Bethnal Green Museum, an outpost of the *Victoria and Albert Museum. The intention was to provide a general museum for the underprivileged *East End. Only gradually did the emphasis shift towards childhood. It was given its present name in 1974 and now has a major collection of toys, dolls, dolls' houses, games and children's books and costumes. One part of the museum is an airy metal structure originally put up in South Kensington, as part of the first temporary Victoria and Albert Museum, which was moved here in 1872.

John **Betjeman** (1906–84, kt 1969) Poet and architectural enthusiast whose endearing personality, both in his poetry and as a broadcaster, made him a household name. He was ahead of his time in seeing the beauties of Victorian architecture. His poetry casts a humorous eye on social habits: nostalgically in *A Subaltern's Love Song* to Miss Joan Hunter Dunn ('What strenuous singles we played after tea/ We in the tournament – you against me!'); satirically in *How to Get On in Society* ('It's ever so close in the lounge, dear,/ But the vestibule's comfy for tea'). *Slough* made him unpopular in the Berkshire town of that name ('Come, friendly bombs, and fall on Slough/ It isn't fit for humans now'). Even so, both his verse autobiography (*Summoned by Bells* 1960) and his *Collected Poems* (1958) were bestsellers. He was appointed *poet laureate in 1972.

The cartoon which launched a catch phrase: 'if you knows of a better 'ole, go to it.'

'better 'ole' In the *Bystander* for 24 November 1915 there appeared a cartoon of two British soldiers crouching in a small crater with shells falling all round them. The caption, 'Well if you knows of a better 'ole, go to it', became a World War I catch phrase. The cartoonist, Bruce Bairnsfather (1888–1959), was himself serving in the trenches. His two famous characters, featuring eventually in seven books of his *Bystander* cartoons, were Old Bill, a stoical cockney with a walrus moustache, and his feeble chain-smoking young companion, Bert.

''Tis **better to have loved and lost**/Than never to have loved at all' Couplet by Tennyson in *In Memoriam*, expressing grief for his friend Arthur Hallam.

Master William **Betty** see *infant prodigies.

Betws-y-Coed (23km/14m S of Conwy) Village which since the 19C has been a popular resort for the spectacular beauty of the surrounding countryside, now in the Snowdonia National Park. Three rivers, the Conwy, Llugwy and Lledr come tumbling down rocky courses to meet near here (the Swallow Falls on the Llugwy being perhaps the greatest local attraction). The name of the village means 'prayer house in the wood', relating to the mainly 14C Old Church which still survives. The stone Bridge of the Cauldron (*Pont-y-Pair*) over the Conwy dates from the 15C; the iron bridge crossing the Llugwy, by Thomas Telford, was named the Waterloo Bridge because it was built in 1815.

Aneurin **Bevan** (1897–1960) The most colourful and controversial Labour politician in the years after World War II, remembered in particular for his period as minister of health (1945–51), when he introduced the *National Health Service. The son of a miner, and himself down the mines from the age of 13, he became an active trade unionist and entered parliament in 1929 as MP for Ebbw Vale. During the 1950s he headed a large left-wing 'Bevanite' minority within the party, at odds with the leadership in particular on nuclear policy – though in 1957 he helped defeat a conference proposal for *unilateral disarmament, saying that it would send a British foreign secretary 'naked into the conference chamber'. He married Jennie *Lee in 1934.

Beveridge Report (1942) The report produced by the Committee on Social Insurance and Allied Services, chaired in 1941–2 by William Beveridge (1879–1963). Its wide-ranging proposals for a social security programme (providing insurance against the costs of illness, unemployment, old age and death) became the basis of the *welfare state established in Britain after 1945.

Beverley (16,000 in 1981) Ancient market town (the name of its main square is Saturday Market); administrative centre of Humberside. It is notable for two superb Gothic churches, St Mary's (14–15C) and Beverley Minster. On the site of a church first established in the 7C, the present *minster was begun *c.*1230 and took about a century to build. It is noted in particular for the twin towers of its west front, for its long nave with a double set of transepts, and for the Percy tomb with its elaborately carved canopy. Dating from the mid-14C, this is one of the greatest examples of English stone-carving.

Beverley Sisters Blonde sisters, Babs, Joy and Teddie, who established a big following in the 1950s as a harmonizing trio. Their most successful records were *I saw Mommy kissing Santa Claus* (1953) and *Little Drummer Boy* (1959).

Ernest **Bevin** (1881–1951) Trade unionist and Labour politician, of great stature in both fields. Working on farms from the age of 11, and then driving a horse and cart, he formed in 1910 a carters' branch of the dockers' union in Bristol. In 1921 he was instrumental in establishing the *TGWU, of which he became the first general secretary, and in 1926 he was the member of the council of the TUC charged with the organization of the *General Strike. As an opponent of *appeasement in the 1930s and a leading figure in the nation's industrial affairs, he was well qualified when Churchill brought him in 1940 into his wartime cabinet as minister of labour and national service – a post in which he deployed with great skill the nation's resources in men and women. In the postwar Labour government he became foreign secretary (1945–51), coping with the immediate crises of the Cold War (such as the Berlin airlift in 1948) and taking a leading part in the negotiations which led to the creation of *NATO.

Bevin boys Young men conscripted in World War II and then selected by ballot to work in the coal mines rather than join the armed forces. So named because the minister of labour and national service who introduced the scheme was Ernest *Bevin.

Bevis Marks Synagogue (London EC3) The oldest surviving synagogue in Britain, built in 1701 for Spanish and Portuguese Sephardic Jews. It retains its original interior, with much carved woodwork and with galleries supported on columns in a style very similar to Wren's contemporary London churches. It sounds to modern ears as though it commemorates a Jewish benefactor, but Bevis Marks has been since medieval times the name of an adjacent street.

'Beware the ides of March' see *Julius Caesar*.

Thomas **Bewick** (1753–1828) Engraver working in Newcastle-upon-Tyne who almost single-handedly established the craft of wood-engraving and at the same time revealed its artistic potential. His genius lay in the depiction of nature and of country scenes on a tiny scale, as seen in the illustrations of his two great works, *A General History of Quadrupeds* (1790) and *History of British Birds* (2 vols, 1797–1804). The family cottage in which he was born at Cherryburn, 18km/11m west of Newcastle, is kept as a museum.

Beyond the Fringe (1960) Entertainment which opened at the Royal Lyceum Theatre as part of the Edinburgh Festival of 1960, written and performed by Alan *Bennett, Peter *Cook, Jonathan *Miller and Dudley *Moore. Its great success, with long runs in the West End and on Broadway, coincided with the virtual end in the theatre of *revue.

beyond the pale see the *pale.

BhS (British Home Stores) Chain of nearly 140 stores (in the early 1990s). The first opened in the London district of Brixton in 1928. Financed by Americans, it was designed as a slightly less downmarket version of Woolworths; where Woolworths' top price for any item was sixpence, British Home Stores' was twice as high at a shilling (the level was raised in 1929 to five shillings to allow for drapery departments). The name was changed to BhS in 1986, with a new logo designed by Terence *Conran's group, after BhS had merged with Conran's Habitat and Mothercare to form Storehouse.

Bible in English One of the central themes of the *Reformation was that Christians should be able to read the Bible in their own languages. Manuscript translations had circulated among the *Lollards, but the first printed Bible in English was the translation by William Tyndale (*c*.1492–1536), published in parts in Germany (1525–31); the Old Testament in this version was never completed. Other famous 16C translations were similarly published by expatriates on the Continent. They include a Protestant version in Geneva in 1560 (commonly known as the Breeches Bible, because it used this word for the covering that Adam and Eve made for themselves from fig leaves); and the Roman Catholic Rheims-Douai version, made for the use of priests and published in 1582 (New Testament, at Rheims) and 1609–10 (Old Testament, at Douai).

From the point of view of the Church of England the most significant of these editions published abroad was that of Miles Coverdale (1488–1568), translator of the first complete printed Bible in English. His version of 1535, printed in Marburg, was made the basis of the Great Bible, a copy of which Henry VIII ordered to be placed in every church in 1539. But the royal initiative which provided the best-known and best-loved English Bible came from James I. In 1604 he presided over the Hampton Court Conference, which commissioned a new translation. Largely based on the earlier text by Tyndale, it was published in 1611 and became variously known as the King James Version (it was dedicated to him) and the Authorized Version (because its title page declared it to be 'Appointed to be read in Churches').

In the 19C the more archaic phrases in the Authorized Version were amended and the result was published (N.T. 1881, O.T. 1885) as the Revised Version. The New English Bible (N.T. 1961, O.T. 1970) is a translation by a committee of British Protestant scholars whose brief was to use the 'language of the present day'.

Biddulph Grange (11km/7m N of Stoke-on-Trent) Exotic Victorian garden, created over 20 years (from 1842) by James Bateman (1811–97). Trees and shrubs from distant parts of the world are planted among follies in appropriate architectural styles, as in the Chinese Garden or the Egyptian Court.

John **Biffen** (b. 1930) Conservative politician, MP for Shropshire North since 1983 (previously for Oswestry 1961–83). He entered the cabinet as chief secretary to the Treasury (1979–81) and continued as secretary of state for trade (1981–2) and leader of the House of Commons (1982–7).

Big Bang Name borrowed from cosmology and used of 27 October 1986, the day on which the deregulation of the *Stock Exchange came into effect. The major changes were the abolition of a minimum level of commission, the ending of the separate functions of brokers and jobbers, and the introduction of a computerized system of trading (Stock Exchange Automated Quotations, or SEAQ). Earlier in the year, in March, firms which were members of the Stock Exchange were allowed for the first time to be bought by other financial organizations such as banks and insurance companies, adding to a new atmosphere of free-for-all which brought major ups and downs for individual firms – particularly after the stock market crash of 19 October 1987 (a day known subsequently as Black Monday).

Big Ben The popular name used both for the clock above the *Houses of Parliament and for the tower which supports it (St Stephen's Tower). The name was given originally to the great bell (weighing about 13.5 tons) which strikes the hours and quarters. It was cast in 1858 and first chimed in the tower on 31 May 1859. There are two versions of the origin of the name, neither provable from any documentary source; one relates it to Sir Benjamin Hall, who was chief commissioner of works, and the other to a popular heavyweight boxer, Benjamin Caunt. The clock was exceptionally accurate for its period (within one second per hour was the specification) and the chimes of Big Ben have long been a symbol of the nation's time-keeping. They have been broadcast by the BBC since 1923.

'Big Brother is watching you' see *Nineteen eighty-four*.

Big Brum see *Birmingham.

'big four' see the *clearing banks.

Biggles Jingoistic hero of some 70 children's books by Captain W.E. Johns (1893–1968) which appeared from the 1930s. Like his author, Biggles was a pilot in the Royal Flying Corps in World War I. He went on to play a major part in the Battle of Britain, and after World War II travelled the world foiling the evil plots of an unreformed Hun, Erich von Stalhein. In this crusade he was invariably supported by two early flying companions, Algy and Ginger. His views on inferior races, and foreigners in general, made Biggles increasingly unpopular with adults, though his adventures have continued to excite children.

Bilbo Baggins see The *Hobbit.

Acker **Bilk** (Bernard Stanley Bilk, b. 1929) Clarinettist who in 1958 formed the Paramount Jazz Band, playing traditional Dixieland. His first hit was *Summer Set* (1960) but by far his greatest success has been his own composition *Stranger on the Shore* (1961). Acker is usually explained as rural slang for a 'mate'.

The first test, in 1856, of the first Big Ben; to improve the tone, the size of the clapper was gradually increased until the bell cracked in 1857. The present bell, in use from 1859, was recast from the same metal.

bill see *Act of Parliament.

The **Bill** (Thames TV from 1984) Police drama series (inspired by a 1983 television play, *Woodentop*), in which the detectives of Sun Hill police station tackle London crime; the 'bill' is London slang for the police. The programme was twice weekly until 1993, when a third episode was added.

billiards Game using a cue to strike a ball on a cushioned table. By the 16c it had emerged from obscure origins to become a fashionable court pastime in France and Britain (Mary Queen of Scots in captivity complained of being deprived of her billiard table). The game developed differently in the two countries, the French game (carom billiards) using a table without pockets. The English version, with six pockets, became the more widespread (particularly in the form known as pool, popular in the USA, involving 15 numbered balls and the cue ball). The traditional English game, using two white balls and one red, had a national champion from the early 19c (Jonathan Kentfield held the title 1825–49). In more recent times by far the best-known player has been Joe *Davis, who was instrumental in shifting attention towards the more complex game of *snooker.

Billingsgate Market (London EC3) Wharfs here, on the north bank of the Thames downstream from London Bridge, were in use from at least the 11c as markets for a wide range of commodities. From the 17c the Billingsgate wharf specialized in fish. It was famous also for bad language; to 'talk like a Billingsgate fishwife' became almost a national benchmark in these matters. The Renaissance-style building facing the river dates from 1874–7 (designed by Horace Jones), but the market itself was moved in 1982 to a new building on the Isle of Dogs.

Bill of Rights The name commonly used for the Act Declaring the Rights and Liberties of the Subject, passed by parliament in December 1689. Its concern was not with the rights of the individual subject. It dealt instead with the relationship between the monarch and parliament (the body representing his subjects). It incorporated the Declaration of Right, the document accepted by *William III and Mary II along with the crown. This declared illegal the arbitrary use of royal power which had characterized Stuart rule, and it thus became the accepted basis for *constitutional monarchy. The Bill of Rights also limited the succession to the throne, so as to exclude Roman Catholic claimants, but in this it was superseded by the Act of *Settlement.

Bill Sikes see *Oliver Twist*.

Billy Budd (1951) Opera with an all-male cast by *Britten, with libretto by E.M. *Forster and Eric Crozier (b. 1914) based on the novel by Herman Melville. Billy, enthusiastic and naive, is press-ganged into the navy in 1797 (during the *French Revolutionary Wars), and is hanged from the yardarm after unintentionally killing an officer who falsely accuses him of encouraging mutiny.

Billy Bunter Grossly fat bespectacled schoolboy in loud check trousers, created by Frank Richards (pen name of Charles Hamilton, 1876–1961). He made his first appearance in 1908 in the opening number of *Magnet*, a magazine which featured until 1940 a weekly story about Greyfriars School, where Bunter is the regular butt of a gang calling themselves the Famous Five. The driving force of the plot is usually Bunter's unscrupulous greed, leading almost inevitably to his own later cries of anguish – 'Yarooooh, you rotters! Oh crikey!'. Of his many illustrators, Charles Chapman became the best known.

Billy Liar (1959) Novel by Keith *Waterhouse about an undertaker's clerk in a northern town, a daydreamer who escapes from his drab life into a world of fantasy. A play based on it (by Waterhouse and Willis Hall) was staged in 1960 with Albert Finney; and in 1963 it was made into a film, directed by John Schlesinger, with Tom Courtenay as Billy.

Lord Justice **Bingham** (Thomas Bingham, b. 1933) Lawyer who became *Master of the Rolls in 1992. Earlier that year he produced the Bingham Report on *BCCI.

bingo The modern name for a simple game of chance, played in Britain from the 18C as 'lotto' and known in the early 20C as 'housey-housey'. Bingo halls swept Britain in the 1960s and 70s, but the game's popularity has declined. Each player stakes money and receives a card showing several numbers; the winners are those whose numbers come up first from a random sequence. The calling of the numbers used to be done with many ritual phrases (66, invariably announced as 'clickety-click', or 88, 'two fat ladies'), but electronic technology in modern halls has made these colourful details redundant.

David **Bintley** (b. 1957) Choreographer who since 1978 has created many ballets for the Sadler's Wells Royal Ballet (now the *Birmingham Royal Ballet) and for the Royal Ballet. His first was *The Outsider* (1978) and his first three-act piece was *The Swan of Tuonela* (1982). His two most popular works to date have been the humorous one-act *Still Life at the Penguin Café* (1988) and the full-length *Hobson's Choice* (1989).

Lord **Birkenhead** see F.E. *Smith.

Birmingham (995,000 in 1991) City in the West Midlands, the largest in Britain after London. From a small medieval town, specializing by the 16C in metal work, it grew at astonishing speed from the late 18C. It had always had natural advantages – an abundance of local coal and iron – but these could only be fully exploited once a transport system existed to make the most of Birmingham's geographical position at the very centre of England. This was achieved with the development of canals in the 18C and railways in the 19C. Three of the greatest figures of the early Industrial Revolution – Watt, Boulton and Priestley – all worked in the town. Together with other leading scientists and industrialists (including Herschel, Smeaton and Wedgwood) they were members of the famous Lunar Society, which met to discuss scientific and philosophical questions.

Birmingham's 19C prosperity was matched by new municipal standards, introduced in the 1870s by a pioneering mayor, Joseph *Chamberlain, whose reforms made it the best run city in the kingdom. From this period dates the great Council House (1874–9, by Yeoville Thomason), with its 49m/160ft clock tower known locally as Big Brum. Adjacent on the city's central Victoria Square is the slightly earlier Town Hall, in the style of a Greek temple (1831–3, by Joseph Hansom). Corporation Street, reflecting in its name the new civic pride, replaced in 1875–82 an area of slums; it is now largely redeveloped, but there are still at the north end the splendid Victoria Law Courts (1887–91, by Aston Webb). After World War II the city centre was not treated with the respect the Victorians gave it. Birmingham led the field in the 1950s in tearing down old streets to make way for traffic, though the modern Bull Ring and the related dual carriageways have recently made an unexpected contribution to the city's sporting life as the track for an occasional motor race.

The city became a diocese only in 1905. St Philip's,

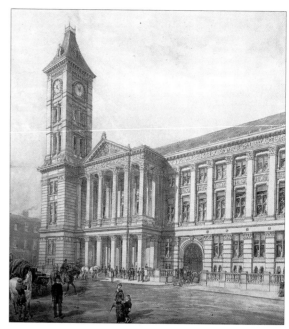

Big Brum beside the Museum and Art Gallery: watercolour of c.1885, when the gallery opened.

previously the parish church of the High Town, was made the cathedral. It is a baroque building of 1708–15 by Thomas Archer (c.1668–1743), with its interior now much enlivened by the stained glass windows of Burne-Jones, born nearby. When Birmingham's first Roman Catholic bishop was appointed in 1850, St Chad's (1839–41 by Pugin) was designated the cathedral.

The Museum and Art Gallery (1881–5, by Thomason) are next door to the Council House. Among the decorative arts there is special emphasis on silver (an important product of Birmingham in previous centuries) and ceramics, with excellent examples of William *De Morgan. The art gallery's greatest strength is the Pre-Raphaelite paintings, of which Ford Madox Brown's *The *Last of England* is one of the best known.

Birmingham played a leading part in the 20C repertory theatre movement, with the establishment by Barry Jackson (1879–1961) of a permanent company in 1913; the City of Birmingham Symphony Orchestra was founded in 1920; and in 1990 the city became the home of the Sadler's Wells Royal Ballet, known since then as the *Birmingham Royal Ballet. In the past two decades Birmingham has recovered its ancient civic pride and has constructed a series of major public buildings. The *National Exhibition Centre was opened in 1976 to the southeast; and at the heart of the city a new complex includes the International Conference Centre, the National Indoor Arena and the Symphony Hall.

*The **Birmingham Post*** The main daily newspaper of the Midlands, founded in Birmingham by John Feeney in 1857. Together with other Midlands papers (the *Evening Mail*, *Sunday Mercury* and *Coventry Evening Telegraph*) it was acquired by its own management in a buy-out organized in 1991.

Birmingham Royal Ballet Company which acquired this name when it moved in 1990 to the Hippodrome in Birmingham, under the artistic direction of Peter *Wright. It descends from the Sadler's Wells Theatre Ballet, founded in 1946 at *Sadler's Wells in London after the *Royal Ballet had moved to Covent Garden. Administered as a second company of the Royal Ballet, it was intended specifically for young dancers and had from the start a commitment to regular touring. A royal charter in 1956 transformed it into the Sadler's Wells Royal Ballet, the name under which it was known until the move to Birmingham. It still spends most of its season on tour (including visits to Sadler's Wells) and retains links with the Royal Ballet; both companies recruit their dancers from the Royal Ballet School in Richmond Park.

Birmingham Six Six Irishmen who were wrongly convicted of having planted the bombs which exploded on 21 November 1974 in two crowded Birmingham pubs, the Mulberry Bush and the Tavern in the Town, killing 21 and wounding more than 150. Patrick Hill, Gerry Hunter, Richard McIlkenny, William Power, John Walker and Hugh Callaghan were sentenced in August 1975 to life imprisonment. They began a long process of protesting their innocence, arguing that their confessions had been extracted by police violence. *World in Action* queried in 1985 the reliability of the *forensic evidence which had suggested the presence of nitroglycerine; shortly afterwards the forensic scientist in question, Dr Frank Skuse, was given early retirement. In 1986 a Labour MP, Chris Mullin, claimed in his book *Error of Judgement* that he knew the identity of the real bombers, who were living in Ireland. *ESDA tests subsequently revealed that the police notes on the case had been amended.

The six were released from prison in March 1991, and the home secretary immediately set up the Royal Commission on *Criminal Justice. In 1992 charges of conspiring to pervert the course of justice and of perjury were brought against three detectives from the West Midlands police force who had been closely involved in the case.

Birnam Wood see *Macbeth.

Birthday Honours see *orders of chivalry.

birth rate The birth rate in England, Wales and Scotland has halved since the beginning of the century, as a result of the availability of contraception (see Marie *Stopes) and the drop in *infant mortality. The relatively less steep decline in Northern Ireland's birth rate reflects the province's large Roman Catholic minority and the Vatican's ban on artificial methods of contraception.

Harrison **Birtwistle** (b. 1934, kt 1988) Composer with a special interest in theatre and opera. With Peter *Maxwell Davies he founded in 1967 the Pierrot Players, with the express purpose of performing music drama, and since 1975 he has been responsible for music at the National Theatre. His own work includes, in addition to

Birth rate

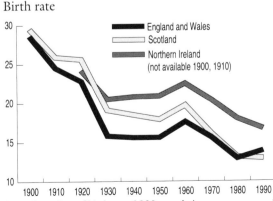

Annual number of births per 1000 population: compare graph of *infant mortality.
Source: Annual Abstract of Statistics (see *Central Statistical Office).

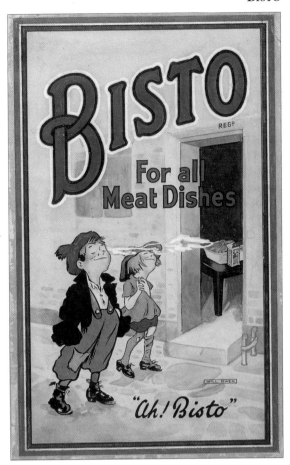

The original Bisto Kids, enjoying the aroma from someone else's pie in 1919.

many orchestral and chamber pieces, a dramatic cantata (*Down by the Greenwood Side* 1969) and four very successful operas (*Punch and Judy* 1968, *The Mask of Orpheus* 1985, *Yan Tan Tethera* 1986, *Gawain* 1991).

Bisham Abbey see *Sports Council.

Henry **Bishop** (1786–1855, kt 1842) Prolific composer of theatre music, with more than 80 operas to his credit. But he is remembered now chiefly for a single song, *Home, Sweet Home.

Bisley The main rifle shooting contest in Britain. It is held each July at Bisley Camp near Woking in Surrey, which has been since 1890 the headquarters of the National Rifle Association. The most prestigious event is the Queen's Prize (the King's Prize when the monarch is male).

Bisto A base for gravy, sold from 1910 in powder form and more recently as granules, which owes its fame to a brilliant poster of 1919 by the illustrator Will Owen (1869–1957). He showed two young street urchins, a boy and a girl, passing an open door and smelling the aroma which drifts from a pie on a table inside; their ecstatic expressions were accompanied by the caption 'Ah! Bisto'. The Bisto Kids became a part of British tradition, and since 1983 two children have been chosen in an annual competition to impersonate the original Bisto Kids in charity events for the NSPCC. Bisto had originally been devised as a substance which would brown, season and thicken the meat juices in a roasting pan; its name was derived from the slogan 'Browns, Seasons, Thickens in One'.

bitter The standard draught beer in a British pub, traditionally served (to the astonishment of foreigners) at room temperature. The name relates to a slight bitterness given by a high hop content. 'Bitter beer' was in contrast to 'mild beer'. Relatively little drunk now, mild is darker and is made with fewer hops. The two were often mixed in the glass as a 'mild and bitter'.

Cilla **Black** (stage name of Priscilla White, b. 1943) One of the few British stars to have made the transition from pop singer to mainstream entertainer. Born in Liverpool, she was on the fringe of the pop scene in the early days of the Beatles (literally on the fringe for a while, checking in coats at the Cavern Club), until she leapt to fame with two no. 1 hits in the spring of 1964 (*Anyone who Had a Heart*; *You're my World*). In the 1980s, after raising a family (she married her manager, Bobby Willis, in 1969), she emerged as a cheerful and engaging host of peak-time TV game shows (*Surprise Surprise*; *Blind Date*).

Joseph **Black** (1728–99) Scottish chemist and physicist, known in particular for his demonstrations of what he called 'fixed air' (carbon dioxide) and 'latent heat' (the heat absorbed, without a rise in temperature, while a solid is changing to a liquid or a liquid to a gas).

Blackadder Wise-cracking cynical character created by Rowan *Atkinson in successive series for BBC television, each of them set in a different historical period (from the Middle Ages to World War I). The first (*The Black Adder* 1983) was supposedly during the Wars of the Roses, but the character was more convincing in *Blackadder II* (1985), a nightmarish comic version of the court of Elizabeth I. Blackadder's long-suffering servant, Baldrick, is played by Tony Robinson.

Black and Tans Popular term of abuse for the armed auxiliary police force, sent to Ireland in June 1920 during the *Anglo-Irish War. The phrase (the name of a hunt in Munster) was appropriate because the men, rapidly recruited and clothed, had been issued with a mixture of police and army uniforms.

black-and-white see *timber-frame.

*The **Black and White Minstrel Show*** (BBC 1958–78) Television song-and-dance programme, reaching large audiences until it became politically unacceptable. The men were blacked up, leaving white around the eyes and mouth in the tradition of Al Jolson. The women were known as the Toppers. Versions of the show had long runs in the theatre, and there was an attempt in 1992 to revive it on tour.

Blackbeard see Edward *Teach.

Black Beauty: the autobiography of a horse (1877) Story which has delighted and moved successive generations of children, particularly girls, being the horse's own account of his experiences at the hands of different human owners. It was 'translated from the original equine' by Anna Sewell (1820–78), whose birthplace in Great Yarmouth is now a museum.

Blackburn (88,000 in 1981) Town in Lancashire which has long been an important weaving centre, for wool in the Middle Ages and for cotton since the 18C. The Lewis Textile Museum demonstrates the development of the spinning and weaving industries. St Mary's church (1818–31 in the Gothic Revival style, architect John Palmer) acquired the status of a cathedral when Blackburn became a diocese in 1927; it has since been

gradually enlarged. The Museum and Art Gallery, founded in 1862, has a collection of 19C British paintings and watercolours together with good holdings in unexpected fields, such as illuminated manuscripts and Japanese prints, which are the result of individual bequests.

Tony **Blackburn** (b. 1943) Disc jockey who began his *radio career on Radio Caroline in 1964, then moved to the rival Radio London (on a ship moored off the coast of Essex) and became a star when he was chosen to present the opening programme on Radio 1 in 1967. He is known for being exceptionally outspoken on air, on a wide range of topics, and for an unquenchable love of corny jokes.

Blackburn Rovers, known as Rovers or the Blue and Whites (Ewood Park, Blackburn). Unique among existing football clubs in having won the FA Cup in three successive years, albeit in the early days (1884–6); Wanderers, no longer surviving, had done so in 1876–8. Formed in 1874, Blackburn Rovers was a founder member of the Football League in 1888. The club won the FA Cup again in 1890, 1891 and 1928. In more recent times Rovers had languished in Division 2 or 3 (since 1966), until their fortunes took a sudden turn for the better in the early 1990s with the arrival of a multi-millionaire majority shareholder, Jack Walker, and the hiring in 1991 of Kenny *Dalglish as manager. With some massively expensive purchases – notably £3.6 million for Alan Shearer – the club achieved promotion to become a founder member of the *Premier League in 1992. In the early months of the new league's first season Blackburn reached the top position. Club victories: FA Cup 1884, 85, 86, 90, 91, 1928; League Champions 1912, 14.

black cap Ominous token which a judge placed on his head before passing sentence of death, in the days before the abolition of *capital punishment. Its black symbolism was accidental. The cap was part of the judge's full attire, necessary at such a solemn moment.

blackcock see *grouse.

Black Country The region stretching from Wolverhampton almost to Birmingham, straddling the south Staffordshire coalfields. The name was first used in the 18C, when the rich coal and iron resources led to rapid industrialization and to pollution of the entire district by the black coal smoke from the factory chimneys. The Black Country Museum (at Dudley, 10km/6m S of Wolverhampton) has reassembled ancient buildings from the district and has revived early machinery to give visitors a working glimpse of the region's many manufacturing trades and crafts.

Black Death (1348–51) The name later given to the most disastrous of the many outbreaks of bubonic plague, transmitted to humans by fleas that have fed on infected rats. This outbreak spread west from China, reaching Europe in 1347. It arrived in Britain when a ship from Calais brought it to Melcombe Regis in Dorset in August 1348. It was at its most violent in London in the spring of 1349, reaching Scotland in 1350. About a third of the population of Europe is believed to have died.

Black Dyke Mills see *brass bands.

Patrick **Blackett** (1897–1974, baron 1969) Physicist who did pioneering work in the use of Charles *Wilson's cloud chamber, winning the Nobel prize in 1948 for his contributions in this field – which included a major share in the discovery of the positron.

Blackheath (London SE3) Hilltop common near Greenwich which has historically been a gathering place for large groups approaching London from the southeast. It was here that Wat *Tyler concentrated his forces, and here that John *Ball is believed to have preached to them before they entered the city during the Peasants' Revolt; Jack *Cade's followers camped on Blackheath a century later. The flat terrain has also given the area significance in sporting history. *Golf was played on the heath in the early 17C; here, in the mid-19C, *hockey was first established as an organized game; and Blackheath was one of the first rugby football clubs, founded in 1858.

Black Hole of Calcutta An incident in June 1756 which has had wide currency in imperial history as an atrocity committed against the British. The young nawab of Bengal, Siraj-ud-Daulah, overwhelmed the British settlement at *Calcutta and locked those he had captured in the jail of their own fort. The first published account of the event appeared eight years later and stated that 145 men and one woman were locked into a tiny room with only two small windows in the heat of the Indian summer; by the morning only 22 men and the woman were alive. The story has been repeated with these details ever since. Lack of any contemporary evidence of British outrage suggests that this later version of the atrocity was exaggerated. But it seems likely that a less sensational accident did occur, with some British prisoners certainly dying in the jail.

Black Isle The name used (but never satisfactorily explained) for an area of Scotland which is neither an island nor in any evident sense black. It is a pleasant promontory, some 25km/16m long, stretching northeast between the Cromarty Firth and the Moray Firth, with the town of Cromarty at its northern tip.

Blackmail see Alfred *Hitchcock.

Black Monday see *Big Bang.

R.D. **Blackmore** see *Lorna Doone.*

Black Mountain and **Black Mountains** see *Brecon Beacons National Park.

Blackpool (150,000 in 1991) Seaside town and conference centre on the west coast, in Lancashire. Since the arrival of the railway in the mid-19C it has been the favourite holiday resort for the industrial towns of the northwest, famous for its illuminations, for its three *seaside piers, for its long sandy beach with 11km/7m of promenades (the single most visited attraction in the British Isles) and above all for the Blackpool Tower (built 1891–4, 158m/520ft high, in imitation of the Eiffel Tower in Paris). The town is calculated to accommodate some 8 million visitors each year in about 5000 hotels and boarding houses.

Black Prince (Edward, prince of Wales, 1330–76) Name by which the eldest son of *Edward III and Philippa of Hainaut is now commonly known. It was first used some two centuries after his death, and has been said to derive from the colour of his armour. He was famous in his own time as a knight of chivalry, living in great style but also distinguishing himself on the field of battle; under his father's command at Crécy (1346) he won the insignia associated ever since with the prince of *Wales, and at Poitiers (1356) he achieved a famous victory when in command of the English army. He died a year before his father, so it was his son who succeeded to the throne as Richard II. Edward's reclining effigy in gold armour, surmounting his tomb, is one of the treasures of Canterbury Cathedral.

Black Rod (short for Gentleman Usher of the Black Rod) Official of the Order of the Garter and of the House of Lords, whose symbol of authority is an ebony rod, surmounted by a golden lion, which he carries in his right hand, resting on his right shoulder. First appointed on the founding of the *Garter by Edward III, Black Rod still walks in front of the sovereign at the annual Garter ceremony at Windsor. His role in the House of Lords dates from the reign of Henry VIII, and is now seen most prominently at the *state opening of parliament. On this occasion he walks to summon the Commons into the monarch's presence in the Lords, has the door slammed in his face, and has to bang on it three times with the black rod to gain admittance. The ceremony reflects the long struggle of the Commons to assert their independence of the crown. MPs are now summoned in this way only on the opening and closing days of a parliamentary session, but until 1967 they were expected to attend every granting of the *royal assent in the House of Lords.

Blackstone's *Commentaries* see *common law.

black tie see *evening dress.

Black Wednesday see *exchange rate.

Blackwell's One of Britain's most distinguished bookshops, founded by Benjamin Henry Blackwell in Oxford in 1879 and still run by his descendants. It has two functions. The first, still operated on the site of the original small shop in Broad Street, is as the bookshop to the university. The larger unseen operation is that of supplying British books and learned journals to universities and libraries around the world, an operation which began with the market for British books in India.

Blaenavon (27km/17m N of Newport) Town in Gwent where coal has been mined since the 18C. The mine has now been adapted to become the Big Pit Mining Museum, where visitors may go deep underground to the coal face.

Tony **Blair** (b. 1953) Labour politician, MP for Sedgefield since 1983. In 1992 he came second (after Gordon *Brown) in the list of those elected to the shadow cabinet – usually taken as an indication of future political prospects, since a Labour shadow cabinet is elected by the party's MPs. His appointment in 1992 was as shadow home secretary.

Blair Castle (56km/35m NW of Perth) Stronghold of the dukes of Atholl, dating in part from the 13C but much altered. Turned in the 18C into as gracious a mansion as its great walls would allow, it later returned to a medieval appearance when the leading advocates of the *Scottish baronial style, David Bryce and his nephew John, were employed in 1869 to bring back the turrets. Blair was the last castle in Britain to withstand a siege; it was held in 1746 by royalist troops, whom the followers of Bonnie Prince Charlie failed to dislodge. A century later Queen Victoria, on a visit in 1844, gave her host a unique privilege which survives today; the duke of Atholl is the only citizen allowed to maintain a small private army, the Atholl Highlanders.

George **Blake** (b. 1922) Dutch-born British spy, unmasked in 1961. His family name was Behar, which he changed to Blake when he escaped to Britain in World War II after being a member of the Dutch resistance. He joined British naval intelligence, and was captured by the Communists during the Korean War. During his captivity he was persuaded to act as a double agent, an enterprise for which he had ample opportunity after being posted to Berlin in 1955. At his trial he was sentenced to an unprecedented 42 years in prison, but in 1966 he escaped from Wormwood Scrubs and managed to reach Moscow. It later transpired that he had been sprung from the jail by a petty Irish criminal inside (Sean Bourke) and by two peace protesters outside (Pat Pottle and Michael Randle). Pottle and Randle were friends of Bertrand *Russell and met Blake when they were in jail after accompanying Russell on a CND demonstration; they took part in his escape because they believed his sentence to be unjust. After years of police inactivity on the issue, they were prosecuted in 1991. They admitted their actions but pleaded justification, and the jury acquitted them.

Peter **Blake** (b. 1932) One of the leading figures in *pop art, who has produced bright images of singers and film stars, wrestlers and strippers, and even of people plastered with badges commemorating such heroes of popular culture. Where other pop artists worked their sources into collages, Blake went one better by grouping a large number of such inspirational objects and images behind an actual shop window with adjacent door (*The Toy Shop* 1962, Tate Gallery). His best-known single work is his *Sergeant Pepper* cover for the Beatles, and he has continued in this field of popular artwork with designs for the Live Aid poster and the Band Aid cover.

Quentin **Blake** (b. 1932) Illustrator with an expressive, scratchy line. He has illustrated his own books (such as *Mr Magnolia* 1980), and those of many other authors including Roald Dahl and Russell Hoban.

Robert **Blake** see *Anglo-Dutch Wars.

William **Blake** (1757–1827) England's most individual painter and poet. As a student at the Royal Academy he conceived a passionate hatred of authority and of the establishment, particularly as personified by *Reynolds. He studied engraving, which became his trade; but other forms of printmaking were also central to his art. In about 1788 he developed his famous method of relief etching, which enabled him to make a metal block for each page of a book, containing both his own hand-written verse and its illustration. It was in these 'illuminated books', such as *Songs of Innocence* (1789), that many of his best-known poems first appeared. When a copy was ordered, Blake and his wife, Catherine, would make up the book and colour it. Few were sold, so copies are now extremely rare and valuable. In these books he developed his very personal philosophy, contrasting the evils of materialism, conventional morality, organized religion and reason with the virtues of honest human experience, love, nature and imagination. His ideas were expressed in a blend of Christian imagery and an arcane mythology of his own invention.

His paintings, commissioned by a very few loyal patrons, were mainly of a kind which could have become engraved plates, being illustrations of scenes in the Bible or in the works of Milton, Bunyan and Dante. His flowing linear style is instantly recognizable, though owing something to the example of his friend *Fuseli. In different ways it anticipates the elegance of *Beardsley and even the zooming conventions of aerial travel in modern comics.

Blake's usual medium was watercolour. The main exceptions are the large colour prints of about 1795, known as the Lambeth prints because he was then living in that part of London. These superbly rich images, each existing in two or three slightly different forms because they are monotypes (taken from a surface on which the image is repainted in oils between each impression) are considered

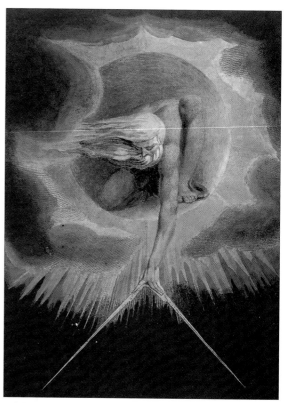

Blake's famous image of the Creator, called The Ancient of Days *from a phrase in the* Book of Daniel: *hand-coloured relief etching, the frontispiece to* Europe, a Prophecy *(1794).*

by many the peak of Blake's art. The most complete collection is in the Tate Gallery.

Late in life Blake was taken up by a group of younger artists (in particular Samuel *Palmer, Edward Calvert and John Linnell) who called themselves the 'Ancients' and regarded the older man as their master. Largely forgotten both as painter and poet in the later 19C (not a single poem of his appeared in The *Golden Treasury* in 1861), he is now seen as a major figure in both fields. It is a measure of the strength of his visionary imagination that *Jerusalem should have become probably the best-known and best-loved poem in the English language while being, at a literal level, almost incomprehensible.

PC **Blakelock** see *Broadwater Farm.

Danny **Blanchflower** (b. 1926) Northern Irish footballer (midfield), who was with Barnsley (1949–51) and Aston Villa (1951–4) but whose main career was with Tottenham Hotspur (1954–64); he captained the Spurs team which achieved the League and FA Cup double in 1961. He won 56 caps for Northern Ireland.

Blandings Castle see P.G. *Wodehouse.

blank verse Poetry without rhymes, characteristic of the greatest English literature of the 16–17C, particularly in the form of the iambic pentameter – a line of five feet or ten syllables, theoretically stressed on every other syllable but in practice much more fluid. First used in the 1540s, it became the standard line of *Marlowe, of *Shakespeare and of *Milton in his longer poems. Most 18C poets preferred rhymes, but blank verse was much used again in the 19C.

Blantyre see David *Livingstone.

Bleak House (1853) Novel by *Dickens, published in 1852–3 in monthly parts. At the centre of a complex plot is the case of Jarndyce versus Jarndyce, which has dragged on and on in the old court of Chancery (nowadays a division of the High Court) to the benefit of no-one but the lawyers. Litigation comes to a sudden end when it is discovered that the costs now equal the entire value of the estate under dispute. Among the many characters is Mrs Jellyby, whose obsessive philanthropy threatens to ruin her own family in much the same way as the lawyers have eaten up the Jarndyce inheritance.

Blenheim (13 Aug. 1704) A victory over the French, in the War of the *Spanish Succession, by the British under the duke of *Marlborough and the Austrians under Prince Eugene of Savoy; the village of Blenheim (German name Blindheim) is on the north bank of the Danube about 37km/23m northwest of Augsburg. The victory ended the French threat to Vienna, and was of great psychological importance as the first major defeat of a French army for half a century.

Blenheim World War II bomber. The Bristol Blenheim IV, with a crew of three, was the RAF's main daytime bomber in Europe in the early years of the war, the larger *Wellington being used for night sorties. It was a modified version of the Blenheim I, with the nose extended to accommodate the navigator, who also aimed the bombs. It entered service with the RAF in March 1939, and was claimed then to be the fastest bomber in the world at 475kph/295mph.

Blenheim orange Variety of apple, more gold than orange in colour, first grown during the 19C at *Blenheim Palace.

Blenheim Palace (16km/10m NW of Oxford) The most self-important building in Britain, adopting the tone of solemn grandeur pioneered by Louis XIV, whose defeat the palace celebrates. Designed by *Vanbrugh with the assistance of *Hawksmoor, and built 1705–22, it was the gift of a grateful parliament to the duke of *Marlborough after his victory at Blenheim. The vast courtyard and portico lead the visitor into a towering entrance hall beneath a ceiling (by Sir John Thornhill) in which the duke, in the guise of a Roman general, is presented with a laurel wreath by Britannia.

Another British hero is commemorated in a more modest fashion in the palace, for the bedroom is on show in which Winston *Churchill was born. The surroundings of the palace, originally formal in the style of the time, were given their present more romantic character by Capability *Brown.

Blickling Hall (24km/15m to the N of Norwich) Built around an earlier house in 1616–25, and added to in the 18C, Blickling nevertheless retains a powerfully Jacobean feeling with its warm red brick and large mullioned windows. The architect, Robert Lyminge (d. 1628), had recently completed *Hatfield House, of which this seems a more intimate cousin. His most striking feature is the Long Gallery, with its intricate plasterwork ceiling of heraldic and emblematic designs.

Blickling is also famous for its gardens, which have developed over three centuries. It is possible that Humphrey *Repton had a hand in the wider landscape garden. A sunken flower garden, the famous Parterre, nestles discreetly to the east side of the house; laid out in the 1870s, it was adapted to its present form by Norah Lindsay in the 1930s. Blickling was the first stately home to be given to the *National Trust.

The great banqueting hall at Blenheim, with trompe-l'oeil murals by Louis Laguerre of perpetual spectators at the feast.

Captain **Bligh** (William Bligh, 1754–1817) A man much mutinied against. On the first occasion he was in command of HMS *Bounty* in the Pacific in 1789, when a mutiny was led by the acting lieutenant, Fletcher *Christian. Bligh was set adrift in an open boat with 18 of his crew. After a journey of three months and some 5600km/3500m he brought them to safety on Timor, an island near Java. The next mutiny against him was in 1797, as part of the general unrest at the *Nore. And finally, as governor of New South Wales in Australia, he was arrested in 1808 by his deputy and sent back to England. On each occasion the courts vindicated Bligh. Although clearly an unpopular and overbearing commander, he may have been more unlucky than unusual for his time. Bligh was played by Charles Laughton and Christian by Clark Gable in the famous *Mutiny on the Bounty* of 1935.

Blighty Nostalgic slang term for Britain, used particularly by soldiers abroad in World War I. It derives from a word picked up by the British in the 19c in India, where *bilayit* (Hindustani for a distant province) was a name for Europe. A magazine called *Blighty*, specializing in pin-ups and cartoons, used to be a favourite with the troops, particularly in wartime; it was published 1916–20 and 1939–58.

Colonel **Blimp** A fat, pompous retired army officer, with a rooted objection to any new idea, who was created and used as a regular character (from 1934) by David *Low. The words 'blimp' and 'blimpish' have entered the language for anyone with similar attitudes. The colonel, bald and plump with long moustaches, was most often seen pontificating in a Turkish bath. His name was probably borrowed from a similarly soft, round and witless object, for 'blimp' was the common name for gas-filled aerial balloons of a kind first used in World War I.

*The **Blind Girl*** (1854–6, Birmingham City Art Gallery) Painting by *Millais, sentimental in mood but still in the hard, bright *Pre-Raphaelite style. A beautiful blind girl, probably a beggar, is basking in the warmth of the sun but is unable to enjoy the spectacular double rainbow seen in the sky behind her. To make the point, the child accompanying her peeps backwards for a glimpse of it. The landscape shows Winchelsea, in Sussex.

Arthur **Bliss** (1891–1975, kt 1950) Composer whose output covered a wide range of musical forms, including orchestral works, ballets (*Checkmate* 1937, *Miracle in the Gorbals* 1944) and film music (*Things to Come* 1936). He was appointed *Master of the Queen's Music in 1953.

'Bliss was it in that dawn' see William *Wordsworth.

Blitz The word used in English for the large-scale German bombing of London and other cities in World War II. The first such raid was on London during the night of 7 September 1940; it was described in the *Daily Express* of September 9 as 'blitz bombing'. The source was *blitzkrieg* (lightning war), the term coined by the Germans for their devastatingly successful military technique of a sudden attack with massive force.

bloater A herring, or occasionally a mackerel, which has been lightly smoked in the round (as opposed to the opened-up *kipper). The bloater is a speciality of Great Yarmouth, on the coast of Norfolk.

block vote see *Labour party.

Blondel de Nesle (late 12c) French troubadour whose fame derives from his legendary discovery of where *Richard I was held prisoner. Blondel sang beneath the walls of a castle the first verse of a song which he and Richard had written together. When he heard the second verse being sung inside, he had found his man.

Bloodless Revolution see *Revolution of 1688.

blood sports (also known as field sports) Any sport which involves killing, but in practice the term is used more often of those where the quarry is warm-blooded (*hunting and *shooting as opposed to fishing). In *angling the modern custom is to return the catch alive to the river or lake.

'blood, toil, tears and sweat' see Winston *Churchill.

Bloody Assizes see Judge *Jeffreys.

Bloody Mary A traditional term in Protestant England for *Mary I, which became applied in the mid-20c to a drink of vodka and tomato juice.

Bloody Sunday The term now used for two disastrous Sundays in British history when political demonstrations ended with the crowd being fired on by troops. On 13 November 1887 a socialist demonstration in Trafalgar Square ended with two dead. On 30 January 1972, in Londonderry in Northern Ireland, 13 died after paratroops of the British army opened fire on a banned civil rights march. There were provocative and stone-throwing groups among the marchers, but no proof has been found for the army's assertion that someone on the march opened fire or even that any were armed.

The subsequent report by Lord Widgery (April 1972) was widely regarded as a whitewash; it repeated the claim that IRA marchers had fired as many shots as the army and suggested only that the army's response had 'bordered on the reckless'. The disaster caused a sharp deterioration in community relations in *Northern Ireland, and led to a rise in terrorist violence and the imposition of direct rule from Westminster.

Bloody Tower One of many towers in the *Tower of London which have been used to hold distinguished prisoners. It acquired its name in the late 15c from the belief that the *princes in the Tower were murdered here.

Claire **Bloom** (b. 1931) Actress who in her early twenties was playing leading roles at the Old Vic and was already a film star opposite Charlie Chaplin in *Limelight* (1952). Subsequent films have included *Look Back in Anger* (1959) and *The Spy Who Came in from the Cold* (1966). One of her major television roles was in *Brideshead Revisited* (1981).

Bloomsbury (London WC1) The area lying east of Tottenham Court Road, which contains the *British Museum and the central buildings of London university.

Bloomsbury Group (nicknamed the Bloomsberries) A circle of talented young writers and artists who began meeting, in about 1905, in the house of Virginia *Woolf and her sister Vanessa Bell (at 46 Gordon Square, in the *Bloomsbury district of London). They had no specific programme, other than a rejection of Victorian notions of social and sexual propriety, and a belief in the paramount importance of human relationships and of art. The group, which continued to exercise influence in the years after World War I, had particularly strong links with Cambridge. Among the best-known members (not all involved from the start) were Lytton *Strachey, E.M. *Forster, Roger *Fry, Duncan Grant and Maynard *Keynes.

blue Term used both of an athlete representing Oxford or Cambridge and of the distinction achieved; a competitor can be described either as 'being a blue' (the more traditional usage) or as 'winning a blue'. It derives from the colour of the team caps, dark blue for Oxford and light blue for Cambridge. Games in which relatively few people play (polo is an extreme example) have the status only of a 'half-blue'.

Blue Arrow Recruitment agency of which the name became widely known after several employees of County NatWest were charged in 1991 with having conspired to mislead the market during an issue of Blue Arrow shares (part of an attempt to take over Manpower). County NatWest, a subsidiary of the National Westminster Bank, was advising Blue Arrow on the issue. The trial of five of them, with immensely complex financial details, lasted a year and was estimated to have cost some £40 million. It ended with acquittal for one and suspended jail sentences for four, who were then acquitted a few months later on appeal.

Bluebell Girls Troupe of high-kicking girls in the Folies-Bergère tradition, established in the 1930s by an Anglo-Irish dancer, Margaret Kelly, who was herself known as Miss Bluebell (apparently from the colour of her eyes). They began at the Folies-Bergère and still perform mainly in Paris, though many of the girls are British.

Bluebell Railway Stretch of previously disused railway line, 8km/5m long, between Sheffield Park and Horsted Keynes in East Sussex, on which vintage steam trains run through scenic countryside.

Bluebird see entries on Donald *Campbell and Malcolm *Campbell.

Blue Book see *Central Statistical Office and *white paper.

The *Blue Boy* see Thomas *Gainsborough.

blue chip see *gilt-edged.

Blue Circle The largest cement producer in the UK. In 1900 many small firms producing *Portland cement merged in a single company, Associated Portland Cement Manufacturers. They continued to market under their own brand labels until, in the 1920s, the Blue Circle was adopted as their standard trademark. The company name was changed to Blue Circle Industries in the 1970s.

Blue-Coat Schools Charity schools for poor children, whose traditional uniform from the 16c was a long blue gown. By far the best known is *Christ's Hospital, but an example of a much smaller establishment is the Blewcoat School in Caxton Street, Westminster – built in 1709 at the expense of a local brewer and now in use as a National Trust shop.

Blue Cross (London SW1) Animal welfare charity founded in 1897 as Our Dumb Friends' League. The change of name deliberately echoed the human Red Cross. An Animals' Hospital (still in existence today) was opened in 1906 in the Victoria district of London.

Blue Ensign see *ensign.

Blue Guides Series of detailed guide-books to Britain and foreign countries, launched in 1915 when Finlay and James Muirhead published *Blue Guide to London and its Environs*. This was later issued in French by Hachette as a *Guide Bleu*. Hachette in turn then produced a *Guide Bleu* to Paris, which was issued by Muirhead in English – the beginning of a two-way collaboration which lasted until 1933. The series has continued, published now by A&C Black. The 50th *Blue Guide*, to Tuscany, appeared in 1993.

blue john Multi-coloured variety of the mineral fluorspar, found only in the Peak District of Derbyshire. A spectacular cave system in these hills was mined in the past for this precious mineral, from which superb vases were carved – as far back as the Roman empire, but particularly in the 18–19c. Several of the caves, with extraordinary rock formations, are now open as tourist attractions. There is the Peak Cavern with its massive entrance hall, the Speedwell Cavern (entered by boat along a subterranean passage cut in the 18c), the Treak Cliff Cavern, and best of all the Blue John Cavern with a succession of chambers reaching some 3km/2m into the hillside.

Blue Peter (BBC from 1958) The most distinguished and long-lasting of the children's programmes on British television. Aiming at the 5–12 age group, and usually appearing twice weekly, it introduces a wide range of subjects and has made a speciality of charitable appeals. Among its best-known presenters has been Valerie Singleton (on the programme 1962–71). A 'blue peter' is a signal flag, blue with a white square at its centre, which a ship flies when it is about to leave port.

blue plaques Ceramic signs set into the façades of buildings in London where distinguished people have lived, giving the relevant dates and details. The first was placed by the LCC in 1901 on the house in which Macaulay died; there are by now nearly 400 blue plaques. From 1867 the Royal Society of Arts had been attaching memorial tablets to buildings on a similar basis, starting with the house where Byron was born.

Blue Riband The distinction (existing only in name) held by the ship which has made the fastest Atlantic crossing. It was hotly contested in the days of the great liners, such as the *Mauretania*. The last liner to hold it was the *United States* – achieving on her maiden voyage in 1952 a time of 3 days 10hr 40min. This speed was not bettered until Richard *Branson's crossing in 1986 in *Virgin Atlantic Challenger II*, with a time of 3 days 8 hr 31 min; this was improved in 1990 by the catamaran ferry *Hoverspeed Great Britain SeaCat*, with 3 days 7hr 54min; and that record was in turn shattered in 1992, by a margin of 21 hours, when the Italian-owned *Destriero* (a £17m speedboat with the Aga Khan among its sponsors) crossed in 2 days 10 hr 34 min. The concept of a blue ribbon is attached to the peak of achievement in several fields (the *Derby is called the Blue Riband of the Turf); it probably dervies from the blue ribbon of the *Garter, the highest order of chivalry in Britain.

Since 1935 there has been an actual trophy, the Hales Trophy, for the fastest crossing by a vessel designed for commercial passenger service. This is now held by *Hoverspeed Great Britain SeaCat*, which won it from the *United States*.

Blues and Royals see *Household Cavalry.

bluestocking Derogatory term for an intellectual woman, deriving by a circuitous route from evenings organized by Mrs Montague and other ladies in London in the mid-18c. Their intention was to promote conversation in place of card games. One of their guests, Benjamin Stillingfleet, liked to come in informal clothes, wearing blue worsted stockings instead of black silk ones. The evenings were mocked therefore as 'bluestocking' occasions, and the name stuck somewhat unjustly to the high-minded ladies.

Blue Vinney The traditional name for the blue cheese of Dorset ('vinney' derives from an old word for mould or mildew). Unusually hard for a blue cheese, with a low fat content, it was made on isolated farms by dairymen using a variety of odd methods to introduce the mould (such as storing the ripening cheese among damp and rotting boots). It is believed now to be extinct, according to experts who maintain that cheese sold today as Blue Vinney is probably substandard *Stilton. The search for a genuine Blue Vinney was a much publicized quest in the 1970s.

David **Blunkett** (b. 1947) Labour politician, on Sheffield City Council from 1970, a member of the *NEC from 1983 and MP for Sheffield Brightside since 1987. In 1988 he became Labour's front bench spokesman on the environment and local government, giving him a high profile on the issue of the poll tax. In 1992 he took over the shadow portfolio on health. His career and his command of detail is made even more impressive by the fact that he is blind. His guide dog is the only four-footed animal to have been officially admitted to the chamber of the House.

Anthony **Blunt** see *Cambridge spies.

Enid **Blyton** (1897–1968) Prolific bestselling children's author, commercially more successful than any other in Britain in the 20C. Her best-known series featured the *Famous Five, followed in 1949 by stories about the Secret Seven for younger children. Her most successful character was *Noddy – the main cause of a boycott of her work for many years by librarians, who argued that her books showed racial prejudice and were too undemanding. Nevertheless in the 1990s she is consistently among the two or three childrens' authors most often borrowed from public libraries.

BOAC (British Overseas Airways Corporation) State-owned airline created in 1939 by merging two private companies, Imperial Airways and British Airways. Each was itself a merger of smaller companies, formed in the days since a pioneer firm, Aircraft Transport and Travel, took off on its first scheduled flight from Hounslow to Le Bourget on 25 August 1919 with a full load consisting of a single passenger, a few newspapers, a consignment of Devonshire cream and some grouse. In 1945 the government created BEA (British European Airways) to cover domestic and European routes, leaving BOAC with intercontinental travel. In the following decades each company introduced two widely known British aircraft (the *Comet and the *VC10 flying with BOAC, the *Viscount and the *Trident with BEA). By the Civil Aviation Act of 1971 the two companies were merged as *British Airways, one of the last acts of BOAC being to place an order for five *Concordes.

Boadicea see *Boudicca.

Chris **Boardman** (b. 1969) Cyclist who won a gold medal in the 4000 metres individual pursuit at the 1992 Barcelona Olympics, riding a revolutionary design of bicycle pioneered by *Lotus. He moved so fast in the final that he achieved the rare feat of overtaking his opponent, who had started at the opposite side of the arena.

Board of Trade Established in 1696 as a committee of the *privy council, with responsibility for every aspect of Britain's trade. The Board developed over the centuries

EVERY IMPERIAL AIR LINER HAS

4 ENGINES FOR SECURITY

IMPERIAL AIRWAYS

in 1937 carried over 70,000 passengers and flew over 6,000,000 miles

The safer airline, with four engines: poster of 1938, just before Imperial Airways was merged into BOAC.

to become a large government ministry. It ceased to have independent existence in 1970, when it became part of the new Department of *Trade and Industry.

Boat Race Annual contest between the eights of the universities of Oxford and Cambridge, traditionally accepted as one of the nation's main sporting events. It was first rowed at *Henley in 1829 but has been held on the Thames in London since 1836. An annual contest from 1839 (apart from the war years), it is rowed over a distance of 6.779km (4 miles 374 yards) from Putney to Mortlake – upstream, but rowed on an incoming tide. By the mid-1970s Cambridge had a decisive lead on aggregate score, but since 1975 they have won only twice (1986, 93). After the 1993 result Cambridge had 70 wins and Oxford 68 (there was a dead heat in 1877). Susan Brown, coxing Oxford in 1981 and 1982, was the first woman to take part in the race. The record time was achieved by Oxford in 1984 (16 min 45 sec). Just before the race, the second eights compete over the same course – Oxford's boat being known as Isis and Cambridge's as Goldie.

Boat Show see *Earl's Court.

bobby Nickname for a policeman, particularly one in London. It is a familiar version of the first name of Robert *Peel, who as home secretary established London's *police force with his Metropolitan Police Act of 1828.

Bobby Shafto Nursery rhyme which is said to have been sung in support of Robert Shafto, an election candidate in

1761. But the verse was also sung with other names, and it seems more likely to be an older song which became well known after being adapted for that occasion. Apart from the catchy tune, its appeal lies in the romantic first verse which surely carries few electoral promises:

> Bobby Shafto's gone to sea,
> Silver buckles at his knee;
> He'll come back and marry me,
> Bonny Bobby Shafto!

BOC Founded in 1886 as Brin's Oxygen Company, the name was changed to British Oxygen Company in 1906. In the early years the only demand for oxygen was in the 'limelights' which provided theatrical lighting. Later it was sold for carbon dioxide in soda water syphons. But the mass market for oxygen came in the 20c with oxyacetylene welding and with developments in medicine and flying.

BOC now also manufactures the many other gases required by modern industry and science.

Boche World War I slang for a German, or for the Germans collectively, borrowed from a French word of uncertain origin.

Bodiam Castle (19km/12m N of Hastings) Castle of the late 14c, sitting square and proud in the middle of a stretch of artificial water that is more of a lake than a moat. Built rapidly as a protection against invasion from France, to the latest design and standards of comfort (no fewer than 28 lavatories were set in the walls, draining into the moat), the castle was in the event not needed and has remained unchanged and unspoilt.

Bodleian see *Oxford.

Bodmin Moor High heathland in Cornwall with granite outcrops or tors (highest point Brown Willy, 419m/1375ft). On the only road across the moor is the village of Bolventor, containing Jamaica Inn – made famous as a smugglers' resort in the fiction of Daphne du Maurier.

Bodnant (13km/8m S of Llandudno) One of the most magnificent gardens in Britain, created since 1875 by four generations of the family of Lord Aberconway. Its special beauties are made possible by two factors: the warm, damp climate of the Gulf Stream, and an extraordinary location.

There are distant views of Snowdonia from the formal terraces at the top of the garden. The visitor then gradually descends into the romantic ravine of the river Hiraethlyn, alive with waterfalls and a profusion of woodland plants and shrubs, with a special emphasis on camellias, azaleas and rhododendrons.

'body-line' see Harold *Larwood.

'body of a weak and feeble woman' A phrase used by *Elizabeth I on 9 August 1588 in a speech to her troops at Tilbury. The Spanish *Armada had been defeated two weeks earlier but invasion was still expected from another fleet allied with Spain, that of the duke of Parma. The queen said: 'I know I have the body of a weak and feeble woman. But I have the heart and stomach of a king, and of a king of England too; and think foul scorn that Parma or Spain, or any prince of Europe, should dare to invade the borders of my realm.'

Bodiam Castle, with its powerfully protected gateway (far end) and seven towers to complete the square.

Body Shop International chain of shops (about 750 in the early 1990s), with a product range focused on a very precise purpose – to 'cleanse, polish and protect the skin and hair' – and with a much publicized 'green' approach to ingredients and packaging. The first Body Shop was opened by Anita Roddick (b. 1942) in Brighton in 1976, selling a range of only 15 products. The rapid growth of the business was achieved through franchising.

Boer War (1899–1902) The name by which the South African War is known in Britain; *boer* is the Dutch for farmer, and the war was essentially the struggle of the Dutch farmers, the oldest European settlers in *South Africa, to avoid being dominated by the British settlers and the imperial parliament in London. It was to some extent personalized in a struggle between two men. Cecil *Rhodes was prime minister of the British Cape Colony in the southwest; he was also head of the British South Africa Company, busy developing what became Southern Rhodesia (now Zimbabwe) to the northeast. Between Cape Colony and Zimbabwe is the Transvaal, then an independent Boer republic with Paul Kruger as its president. To Rhodes the future lay in a unified British South Africa, easing the path of expansion northeast. To Kruger such plans represented a British encirclement and a threat to Boer (or Afrikaner) independence. Any hope of compromise between the two was ended by the fiasco of the *Jameson Raid.

A political point at issue between the British government and Kruger was the lack of rights of British settlers in the Transvaal; known as the *uitlanders*, many of them were recent arrivals searching for gold. Over this, and the question of British authority, both sides took intransigent positions. The attempted negotiations, conducted on Britain's side by Alfred *Milner, descended as if inexorably through threats and ultimatums to war. The only other Boer republic, the Orange Free State, sided with the Transvaal.

The outbreak of war in October 1899 was followed by immediate sieges of the British garrisons at *Mafeking

Ordinary Boers take up arms against the British: magazine illustration of 1900, engraved from a photograph.

and Kimberley, soon to be followed by Ladysmith. The broader military campaign also went badly, including three major defeats in the so-called Black Week of December 1899. But eventually sufficient forces were brought out from Britain. The Transvaal was invaded in May 1900 and was officially annexed in September. There followed a prolonged phase of guerrilla warfare. The country was finally subdued from corrugated-iron blockhouses built along the railway lines as temporary forts for British troops, with orders to destroy the produce and economy of the surrounding districts. A treaty was signed in May 1902 at Vereeniging, a place of which the name happened to mean 'union'. By its terms the two Boer provinces recognized Edward VII as their sovereign.

The campaign of the Boers gave the world the concept of *commandos. Meanwhile the British had invented concentration camps – *Kitchener's solution for the families displaced by his scorched earth policy. By the end of the war Britain had lost 22,000 men and the Boers 6000; but in addition to these casualties some 4000 women and 16,000 children had died of disease in the camps.

'boets and bainters' see *George I.

Dirk **Bogarde** (stage name of Derek van den Bogaerde, b. 1921, kt 1992) English actor and author, son of a Dutch journalist in London, best known in his early days for a series of comedy films about medical students (beginning with *Doctor in the House* 1954). His many serious film roles include *Victim* (1961, notable as an early treatment of a homosexual theme in the cinema), *The Servant* (1963) and *Death in Venice* (1971). He began a successful second career as an author with a volume of autobiography, *A Postillion Struck by Lightning* (1976, the first of four such books), which he followed with several novels.

bogey A British standard, introduced in the 1890s, for the number of strokes in which a good player should complete a given hole on a *golf course. The name is believed to derive from a song, *The Bogey Man*, which was popular at the time. It has been replaced now by the international system of 'par', more demanding on the longer holes. (Bogey is often now said to have been one stroke over par, but short holes are rated at three strokes under both systems.) See also *Colonel Bogey*.

Bognor Regis (40,000 in 1981) Seaside resort in West Sussex. Regis (Latin for 'of the king') was added to the name after George V had convalesced in 1929 at the nearby Craigweil House, which has since been demolished. An early and persistent rumour links Bognor with the king's dying words. The story goes that a doctor whispered to him on his deathbed 'Cheer up, Your Majesty, you will soon be at Bognor again' and got the curt reply 'Bugger Bognor'. The official version of his last words, reported in *The Times*, was 'How is the Empire?' – a question which he had certainly asked that morning, when receiving a group of Privy Councillors.

Bogside see *Londonderry.

The **Bohemian Girl** (1843) Opera by Michael Balfe (1808–70), with libretto by Alfred Bunn (*c*.1796–1860), remembered now chiefly for one number that has survived as a popular song – 'I dreamt that I dwelt in marble halls'.

Boiled beef and carrots see Harry *Champion.

Marc **Bolan** (stage name of Mark Feld, 1947–77) Pop singer and songwriter who formed Tyrannosaurus Rex in 1967 with Steve Peregrine-Took on drums. In 1970

Bolan expanded the group to a quartet, dropping Took and bringing in Mickey Finn, Steve Curry and Bill Legend; at the same time he changed from acoustic to electric guitar and shortened the name to T.Rex. He developed a knack for catchy tunes in a style that blended pop with rhythm and blues, and his glittering outfits put him in the vanguard of 'glam rock'. Four no. 1 hits followed in 1971–2 (*Hot Love; Get It On; Telegram Sam; Metal Guru*). In 1977 Bolan's car, driven by his girlfriend Gloria Jones, crashed into a tree on Barnes Common in London and he was killed. The tree has become a shrine in his memory.

Anne **Boleyn** see *Anne Boleyn.

Bolsover (11,000 in 1981) Town in Derbyshire, with striking hilltop ruins of Bolsover Castle – a 17c house on the site of an earlier fortress. The town is better known at present for its Labour MP, Dennis Skinner (b. 1932), whose bovver-boy tactics in the House of Commons have earned him a good deal of public affection and the title 'Beast of Bolsover'.

Robert **Bolt** (b.1924) Playwright who achieved wide fame with his play about Thomas More, A *Man for All Seasons* (1960). Its success launched him into films. His script for *Lawrence of Arabia* (1962) was followed by *Dr Zhivago* (1965) and then by *A Man for All Seasons* (1967) – each of the last two won him an Oscar. In 1967 he married the actress Sarah Miles; they divorced in 1976 and remarried in 1988.

Bolton (147,000 in 1981) Metropolitan district in Greater Manchester which was an important wool town in the Middle Ages and from the 18c a major centre in the cotton-spinning industry. Hall-i'-th'-Wood (a fanciful but officially used spelling of Hall in the Wood) is a half-timber 15c mansion in which Samuel *Crompton invented the spinning mule. The Tonge Moor Textile Museum displays early spinning machinery. The town's Museum and Art Gallery, founded in 1890 but now in a building of 1939, has a wide-ranging collection from ancient Egypt to 20c English painting, with an emphasis on local and industrial history.

Bolton Abbey (27km/17m W of Harrogate) Ruins of a 12c Augustinian priory (never in fact an abbey), famous for the beauty of the Wharfedale setting. The nave survived the *dissolution of the monasteries because it was in use, and still is, as the local parish church.

Bolton Wanderers, known as the Trotters (Burnden Park, Bolton). Football club formed in 1874 by boys of Christ Church Sunday School.The club took the name Bolton Wanderers in 1877, turned professional in 1880 and became a founder member of the *Football League in 1888. They had an exceptional run of success in the FA Cup in the 1920s, but in recent years have been often in Division 3 and once in Division 4. Club victories: FA Cup 1923, 26, 29, 58.

Bombay Island off the west coast of India, on which the old part of the city of Bombay stands. It was given to Charles II in 1661 by the king of Portugal as part of the dowry of his sister, Catherine of Braganza. In 1668 Charles leased it for £10 a year to the *East India Company, which built a fortified town there and made it the company's headquarters.

Bomber Command see 'Bomber' *Harris.

Andrew **Bonar Law** see Bonar *Law.

James **Bond** see Ian *Fleming.

Michael **Bond** see *Paddington Bear.

Margaret **Bondfield** (1873–1953) Labour politician, the first woman to be chairman of the *TUC (1923) and a member of the cabinet (minister of labour, 1929–31). She began her political career in the National Union of Shop Assistants, and first made an impression with a rousing speech when she was the only woman delegate to the TUC in 1899.

Bond Street (London W1) An architecturally undistinguished street, long famous as the capital city's most expensive shopping thoroughfare. It takes its name from Thomas Bond, a speculator involved in the 1680s in building the southern part, now Old Bond Street. New Bond Street, the extension to the north, was added in the early 18c.

bone china The English form of porcelain, introduced by *Spode in the 1790s. Most 18c English porcelain, including *Chelsea, *Bow and *Worcester, was of the kind known as artificial or soft-paste porcelain. This was white clay with the addition of ground glass – an attempt to imitate the translucency of true porcelain, which is a mixture of kaolin and petuntse (the secret of porcelain was discovered in China in about the 8c and at Meissen in the early 18c). This artificial porcelain was improved at Bow in about 1750 by the addition of white bone ash, a technique soon copied elsewhere. But true bone china depended on the secret of porcelain reaching England (it was first made here in Plymouth in 1768). It was to this genuine hard-paste porcelain that Spode added bone ash, thus achieving the version of bone china which later became the standard porcelain of the English factories.

St **Boniface** (*c.*673–754) Missionary who was instrumental in bringing Christianity to the pagan Germanic tribes and who is often known as the Apostle of Germany. Born in Devon and christened Wynfrith, he joined a monastery at the age of seven and remained a monk in England until he was over 40. He then began his great missionary journeys, which led to his being consecrated bishop in 722 and establishing his see at Mainz. He founded churches and monasteries throughout Germany, usually bringing monks and nuns from England. At the age of about 80 he was still carrying the faith to new territories; he was murdered by pagans at Dokkum, in the Netherlands. His feast day is June 5.

Chris **Bonington** (b. 1934) Mountaineer who led the successful 1970 attempt on the south face of Annupurna in the Himalayas, and also the British Everest expeditions of 1972 and 1975; the second of these achieved the first ascent of the southwest face. Bonington himself reached the summit of Everest in 1985. He has written several books on mountaineering.

Bonnie Prince Charlie see Charles Edward *Stuart.

Boodle's (London SW1) A *club founded in Pall Mall in 1762 and known by the name of Edward Boodle, its first manager. It moved in 1783 to its present building in St James's Street, designed in 1775 by John Crunden (1745–1835).

Booker One of Britain's largest companies, specializing in the production and distribution of food. It derives from a business which two brothers, George and Richard Booker, set up in 1834 in Demerara (see *Guyana) to trade in sugar; their ships sailed to Liverpool, where their elder brother Josias had established an office in 1829. John McConnell joined Booker Bros as a clerk in Demerara in 1846 and eventually became a partner; the company was known as Booker McConnell until 1986. In 1968 it launched a very successful promotional venture, the *Booker Prize.

Booker Prize The British literary prize which has most successfully achieved a high profile, as the first to offer a large sum of money (£5000 when first awarded in 1969, more than £20,000 in the 1990s) and the first to announce the winner on television (from 1981). It is awarded each autumn to a novel published in the previous 12 months and written in English by a member of the *Commonwealth. The six books on the short list, announced a few weeks before the award ceremony, are given considerable prominence in bookshops and have odds offered on them by bookmakers. The sales of the winning novel are greatly increased – the similar effect in France of prizes such as the Prix Goncourt was part of the inspiration for the scheme in the 1960s. The prize is financed by *Booker and administered by *Book Trust.

*The **Book of Common Prayer*** Order of service of the *Church of England, largely the work of Thomas *Cranmer. First published in 1549, and reissued in a more Protestant form in 1552, its final version dates from 1662. Cranmer's aim, in providing an English liturgy, was to strip away medieval accretions in the Roman Catholic rites and thus to return to the forms of early Christian worship. The beauty of his prose had a lasting effect on the English language and caused his Prayer Book to be much loved. There was considerable resistance when the church promoted in 1980 an *Alternative Service Book* in modern English, but this has now become the most widely used Anglican liturgy.

Book of Nonsense see Edward *Lear.

Book Trust Private organization founded in 1925 to promote the reading and buying of books. It was previously known as the National Book Council (1925–45) and the National Book League (1945–86). It administers several literary prizes, including the *Booker.

George **Boole** (1815–64) Mathematician who devised a method by which logical reasoning could be expressed in mathematical form, the resulting method being generally known as Boolean algebra. The simplest version of this algebra (two-valued, or binary) became a crucial element in the design of computers. His ideas were most fully expressed in *An Investigation of the Laws of Thought, on which are founded the mathematical theories of logic and probabilities* (1854).

William **Booth** see the *Salvation Army.

Betty **Boothroyd** (b. 1929) Labour politician, MP for West Bromwich West since 1973 and the first female *Speaker of the House of Commons (from 1992). Born in Yorkshire, and for two years from the age of 17 a *Tiller Girl, her combination of toughness, energy and wit make her well able to control several hundred MPs in often unruly mood.

Boots Britain's leading chemists. The company has developed from a small shop selling herbal remedies in Goose Gate, Nottingham, which was run by the mother of Jesse Boot (1850–1931, baron Trent 1929). Boot built up the business from 1877 by a combination of low prices and bold advertising. By the time he died he had nearly 1000 branches and had long been manufacturing most of the

products he sold. In 1968 Boots absorbed an older firm of chemists and hardware merchants, Timothy Whites (founded in 1848 in Portsmouth).

bo-peep An ancient baby-game, hiding behind hands or a garment and then peeping out, which probably developed into the 19C *nursery rhyme about Little Bo-peep (who has lost her sheep and doesn't know where to find them).

border collie see *collie.

Borders (104,000 in 1991, administrative centre Newtown St Boswells) Since 1975 a *region of southeast Scotland, comprising the former counties of Roxburgh, Peebles, Selkirk, Berwick and the southern tip of Midlothian.

borough Originally any fortified town, but the word was used later for an area entitled to send a representative to *parliament. Thus a 'pocket borough' was one where the electors were in the pocket of a local grandee, who could be sure of the seat for his nominee. A 'rotten borough' was an area which had dwindled in importance until it had so few electors that their votes could be bought. The most notorious of these was Old Sarum, which with just seven voters had two seats in parliament; this borough of rolling fields contained no building of sufficient dignity to house the returning officer, not even a barn. It was not until the *Reform Act of 1832 that such abuses were ended.

Today the word is applied only to certain authorities in *local government, in particular the 32 boroughs of *Greater London and any *district which has been granted a royal charter.

borstal A corrective institution introduced in 1902 as an alternative to prison for young offenders (aged 15–20). The name derives from the first of the kind, at Borstal in Kent. In 1983 borstals were replaced by detention centres, which have recently been renamed *young offender institutions.

Reginald **Bosanquet** (1932–84) The first star newsreader of ITN, on air from the beginning of the service in 1955 until 1979. He acquired a devoted following, the result of his own bluff charm but amplified by a reputation for a convivial private life – and the ever-present chance of its affecting his delivery of the news. His father (B.J.T. Bosanquet 1877–1936) was a celebrated Test cricketer and the inventor of the googly, a ball with a deceptive direction of spin which used to be known, after him, as a 'bosie'.

Boscobel (13km/8m NW of Wolverhampton) Site of the famous oak tree in the branches of which *Charles II hid for a night and a day when parliamentarians were searching for him after the battle of Worcester. He spent the following night in a priest-hole within Boscobel House, a building of the 17C which survives today (considerably altered). After the Restoration the king's birthday, May 29, was celebrated each year as Oak Apple Day; it remained a public holiday until the mid-19C. The oak shown now at Boscobel is believed to be a self-seeded sapling from an acorn of the original tree.

Boston (26,000 in 1981) Town in Lincolnshire, on the *Wash near the mouth of the river Witham, which was a major port in the Middle Ages. The huge tower of the 14–15C church of St Botolph, 88m/288ft high, is a landmark for miles around and is known as the Boston Stump. It was from here that the main group of *Pilgrim Fathers set off in 1608 on the travels which would take them eventually to the New World. In the Guildhall the cells are preserved in which they were imprisoned after their first abortive attempt to leave, in 1607. The city of Boston in the USA was named because many of the leading settlers had come from the district around this English coastal town.

Boston Tea Party (1773) Celebrated incident in the tense period leading up to the War of *American Independence. A tax on tea payable to Britain was deeply resented, and three ships of the East India Company were in Boston harbour, laden with the precious commodity. On December 16 a party of respectable Bostonians, lightly disguised as Indians, boarded the vessels and threw the tea overboard. It was both intended and taken as a deliberate affront to British authority. The result was an act of parliament closing Boston port, which served only to strengthen the opposition. An interesting by-product of this series of events is that tea was never again a popular drink in the USA.

James **Boswell** (1740–95) Scottish author, known first as the biographer of Dr *Johnson and more recently as an outstanding diarist. He met Johnson in London in 1763, and their friendship was maintained in Boswell's annual visits from Edinburgh, where he was employed as a lawyer. In 1773 the two of them visited the Hebrides. Boswell invariably noted in his journal the best of the great man's conversation, and after Johnson's death in 1784 he devoted himself to moulding this material into a biography. The first instalment was *The Journal of a Tour of the Hebrides* (1785), followed by *The Life of Samuel Johnson* (1791). It was only in the 1920s that Boswell's private papers came to light, in the possession of a descendant. His journal depicts with great immediacy the social life of the time, including his own often disastrous sexual adventures.

Bosworth Field (22 Aug. 1485) Battle in Leicestershire, some 5km/3m south of the town of Market Bosworth, in which *Richard III was defeated and killed by the man who then took the crown as *Henry VII. Few details are known about the battle itself, but a highly dramatic version of it provides the final scenes of Shakespeare's *Richard III*.

botanic gardens The concept of a scientific garden, in which living plants would be collected and studied (with a practical emphasis on their medicinal or physic properties), was given its impetus by the discovery of many unknown species in America in the 16C. Italy led the field, but three of Britain's surviving botanic gardens date from the 17C.

The earliest is at Oxford, founded in 1621 by Henry Danvers with a gift of £5000. Its scientific purpose was evident in its original shape, divided into four sections which were intended to accommodate separately the flora of the four known continents (Australia not yet being on the map). Half a century later came the garden at Edinburgh, established in 1670 by two physicians (originally where Waverley Station stands today, moved to its present site in 1823); with some 35,000 different plants, this Royal Botanic Garden is now one of the largest in the world. The *Chelsea Physic Garden was founded in 1673, acknowledging in its name the central purpose in this early study of plants. The botanic garden at Cambridge was not founded until 1762; it moved to its present site in the mid-19C.

Two of the later botanic gardens were much influenced by William *Hooker. As professor of botany at Glasgow he was closely involved with the botanic gardens started there in 1817 (the great glasshouse known as the Kibble Palace was brought to Glasgow in 1873 from the garden of John Kibble); and in 1840 Hooker became the first director of the newly established national institution at *Kew Gardens. Belfast's botanic gardens date from 1828, and contain a magnificent curving cast-iron and glass palm house (1839–52) by Charles Lanyon and Richard Turner; Turner was an innovative Dublin engineer and ironmaster who moved on from this project to the even more ambitious palm house at Kew.

Botany Bay see *Australia.

Ian **Botham** (b. 1955) Larger than life character who for the past two decades has been the most colourful figure in English *cricket – and its most successful allrounder of all time, as a big-hitting batsman, ceaselessly attacking bowler and nonchalant catcher. He has played for Somerset (1974–86), for Worcestershire (1987–91), for Durham (from 1992) and for England (from 1977, captain 1980-1). By 1992 he had played in 102 Test matches, and the records which he has broken are too numerous to list. But some of the most impressive demand a mention.

Only two cricketers in Test history have ever achieved more than 1000 runs, 100 wickets and 100 catches; they are Botham (5200 runs, 383 wickets, 120 catches) and Garry Sobers (8032 runs, 235 wickets, 109 catches). He is one of only three players of any nation to have scored a century and taken 10 wickets in a Test (against India in Bombay in the 1979–80 tour). No-one has ever hit a double century off fewer balls (220 balls against India at the Oval in 1982). On only six occasions has an England player scored a century and taken five or more wickets in an innings; on five of those occasions the player was Botham. In 1985 he passed Bob Willis's England record of 325 Test wickets; and in 1992 his career total of 383 Test wickets was second in the world (to the 431 of Richard Hadlee of New Zealand).

Botham is also a flamboyant figure off the pitch, known in particular for his marathon walks (on two separate occasions from John o'Groats to the south coast of England), which pass through the land with the razzmatazz of an itinerant circus and raise huge sums of money for leukaemia reseach. He is a fixture on the television quiz *A Question of Sport*.

Earl of **Bothwell** see *Mary Queen of Scots.

Botswana Member of the *Commonwealth since 1966, having previously been the British protectorate of Bechuanaland. A land-locked territory to the north of South Africa, it was threatened in the late 19C by pressure from the Boers of the Transvaal. British missionaries were well established in the area and in 1885 the Christian king, Khama III, arranged for his country to become a British protectorate. His grandson, Seretse Khama (1921–80), was much in the news in the 1950s after marrying a British woman, Ruth Williams. He was exiled from the protectorate by the British government to prevent his inheriting the tribal kingship, but he became the country's first president on its independence in 1966.

Bottom see A *Midsummer Night's Dream*.

Virginia **Bottomley** (Virginia Garnett, b. 1948, m. Peter Bottomley 1967) Conservative politician, MP for Surrey South-West since 1984. She entered the cabinet in 1992 as secretary of state for health. Her husband is also an MP.

Boudicca (d. *c.*AD 60) Queen of the Iceni tribe whose violent rebellion in AD 60 against the *Romans has given her the status of the first British heroine. Her husband,

Prasutagus, had cooperated with the Romans but on his death they seized his kingdom in what is now Norfolk. His widow led her tribesmen in a trail of destruction of Roman settlements, reaching as far south as London. After her eventual defeat she is believed to have taken poison. Until recent years she has been more commonly known by the Latin version of her name, Boadicea.

Adrian **Boult** (1889–1983, kt 1937) Conductor who first made his reputation performing the great English composers of his youth, Elgar, Vaughan Williams and Holst. Two great orchestras had the benefit of his skills in their formative years: the *City of Birmingham Symphony Orchestra (1924–30) and the *BBC Symphony Orchestra (1931–50). He was subsequently principal conductor of the *London Philharmonic (1951–7).

Boulting brothers (John and Roy, twins b. 1913, John d. 1985) Film producers known in particular for hard-hitting comedies satirizing British national characteristics, of which *I'm All Right Jack* was an outstanding example.

Matthew **Boulton** (1728–1809) Entrepreneur best known for his part in the development of the *steam engine, but also a leading manufacturer of decorative objects in metal. Son of a maker of buckles, he built in 1762 a new factory at Soho, just north of Birmingham, which was soon famous for its production of high-quality items in silver, Sheffield plate and ormolu. In 1775 he went into partnership with James *Watt, taking charge of the production and marketing of Watt's inventions. By the time Boulton retired in 1800, more than 500 Boulton and Watt steam engines had been installed round the country and abroad.

Boundary Commissions Four commissions (one each for England, Wales, Scotland and Northern Ireland) which are responsible for adjusting *constituency boundaries so that the number of electors in each does not vary excessively. The average size of a constituency for the House of *Commons is about 70,000 and for the *European Parliament about 565,000. The *Speaker of the House of Commons is chairman of each of the commissions.

The next constituency adjustments are expected in about 1994. Reflecting a population drift away from the inner cities, they are considered likely to bring an advantage of a dozen or more seats to the Conservative party.

Lady **Bountiful** see The *Beaux' Stratagem.

HMS *Bounty* see Captain *Bligh.

Bournemouth (145,000 in 1981) Resort and conference centre on the south coast, at the mouth of the Bourne in Dorset (until 1974 it was in Hampshire). It developed only in the 19C, with the increased popularity of bathing, and its air of gentility has made it a favourite place for retirement. The Russell-Cotes Art Gallery and Museum is housed in an extravagantly Italianate seaside villa (1894, by John Fogerty) which was built for the mayor of Bournemouth, Sir Merton Russell-Cotes. It was given by him to the town with his collection, mainly large academic paintings of the late 19C. The Bournemouth Symphony Orchestra, founded in 1893 and known for its encouragement of British composers, is now based in the Poole Arts Centre; it performs, when at home, in the 1600-seat Wessex Hall. The Bournemouth Sinfonietta, the related chamber orchestra, was founded in 1968.

Bournville (7km/4m S of Birmingham) Garden suburb founded when the *Cadbury brothers moved their chocolate factory in 1879 to a rural site on which stood

Bournbrook Cottage; *ville* was added to the name because the best chocolates then came from France. The Cadburys were Quakers with a conviction that social evils began with bad housing. The example of Bourneville, where the families had larger gardens than in the earlier experiment at *Saltaire, had great influence on the planning of suburban development.

Bovril Trade name of a concentrated extract of beef, the basis for a hot drink but also used as a flavouring or for gravy. It derived from a product pioneered in Canada in 1873 by a Scotsman, John Johnson, and sold as 'Johnson's Fluid Beef'. He launched it in Britain in the 1880s under a new name based on the Latin for a cow (*bos, bovis*) plus the word *vril* – a magic force (described as the 'unity in natural energic agencies') which had featured in a novel of 1871, *The Coming Race* by Edward Bulwer-Lytton. A very successful advertising campaign later recommended Bovril to avoid 'that sinking feeling'.

Bow Bells The bells of St Mary-le-Bow in London's Cheapside. The idea that a true *cockney must be born within the sound of them may derive from their having been used sometimes to ring a curfew in the Middle Ages. They have twice been replaced (burnt in the *Great Fire, bombed in 1941). 'Bow' was an old word for an arch and survives in the church's name because it was the first in London to be built above a crypt of stone arches.

Thomas **Bowdler** (1754–1825) His lasting place in the language, in the form of the verb to 'bowdlerize', derives from his 10-volume edition of Shakespeare (1818) in which he removed anything which could not 'with propriety be read aloud in a family'. This ranged from single words ('God' invariably became 'Heaven') to entire passages and characters, thus playing havoc with both sound and sense. But his edition was extremely popular. He then set about the equally daunting task of purging Gibbon's *Decline and Fall* of 'all passages of an irreligious or immoral tendency'.

Elizabeth **Bowen** (1899–1973) Irish writer who spent the middle years of her life in England and set many of her novels and short stories in London. She was adept at suggesting the subtle anxieties of everyday existence – she described her subject matter as 'the cracks in the surface of life' – and she found ideal material in the fashionable London world of the 1930s (seen through a child's eyes in *The Death of the Heart* 1938) and in wartime London (the setting of her most widely read book, *The Heat of the Day* 1949).

Bowes Museum Vast French château in the small town of Barnard Castle, in the county of Durham. It is one of England's strangest and most delightful museums, deriving from the collecting enthusiasm of John Bowes (1811–85) and of his wife Josephine, a French actress. Together they planned the building (1869–76) as a museum to house their treasures for the public. The design was by a French architect, Jules Pellechet.

In addition to paintings of the 15–19C (including works by El Greco, Tiepolo, Canaletto, Boucher, Goya, Courbet), there are excellent textiles, ceramics, glass, clocks and furniture. The museum's most famous exhibit, in the hall, is a silver mechanical swan of the 18C which bends its graceful neck (now only once a day) to swallow a fish from a rippling silver stream.

Bow Group Pressure group founded after World War II by young Conservatives, including Geoffrey Howe, with the aim of moving towards a more classless Conservative party, a free market economy and independence for the territories of the British empire. The name derived from the location of the first meeting, at 149 Bow Road in east London. In 1957 the group launched *Crossbow*, the magazine through which it has chiefly exerted an influence. The *Monday Club was a reaction within the party to the Bow Group's colonial policy.

Bowhill (65km/40m S of Edinburgh) House dating in its present form mainly from the early 19C. Its distinction is the superb collection of miniatures and paintings, of which the public's favourite – deservedly so – is *Winter*, Reynolds's enchanting portrait of Lady Caroline Scott, aged about three, in her outdoor clothes.

David **Bowie** (stage name of David Jones, b. 1947) Pop singer, songwriter and actor whose music has been innovative and influential but whose public persona has often been controversial (notably for sometimes wearing dresses and for supposed Fascist sympathies when he was researching a film on Goebbels). He acquired a weird extra-terrestrial image with his first success, *Space Oddity* (1969); partly inspired by the film *2001*, it benefited greatly from coinciding with the first landing on the moon; it introduced Major Tom, who later returned in a bigger hit single, *Ashes to Ashes* (1980). The style later known as glitter rock or glam rock was developed in the album *The Man Who Sold the World* (1970) and in the character of Ziggy Stardust, featured in records and on the stage. Bowie has also had an acting career, with one undoubted triumph – creating the part of John Merrick in *The Elephant Man* on Broadway in 1980.

bowler Stiff felt hat, usually black, with a domed crown and a narrow brim curving tightly upwards, said to be named after a London hatter, John Bowler. Introduced *c.*1850, it became in the 20C (and remained until the 1970s) the indispensable headgear for men working in the *City. Known in north America as a derby, it is familiar round the world as part of the costume of Charlie *Chaplin.

bowls The throwing or rolling of stones to hit a mark is among the earliest of recorded human pastimes but the aim has usually been to knock down the target, as in modern ten-pin bowling. In Britain during the Middle Ages the game developed of rolling the bowl on grass to end up near the mark (an annual tournament held in Southampton claims to date back to 1299). By the 16C the bias had been added to make the bowl travel in a curve. One of the most cherished legends of English history is that of Sir Francis *Drake being told of the approach of the Armada while playing bowls on Plymouth Hoe and replying: 'There is plenty of time to win this game and to thrash the Spaniards too.'

It was in Scotland that the game was taken most seriously (in effect as a summer version of *curling). Standardized rules were first established there in 1849 and it was mainly Scottish emigrants who took the game to other countries in the empire. It is included as a sport in the Commonwealth Games.

Bowls is usually played on a level lawn but some players in northern England use a 'crown green', which slopes gently away from a central mound and can be of less smooth turf. It is thought to derive from the time when many pubs had their own greens but were unable to make them perfectly smooth.

James **Bowman** (b. 1941) The leading British countertenor in the generation after Alfred Deller. In the early years of his career he mainly gave concert performances with the Early Music Consort. Subsequently he has been much seen in opera, both in Britain and abroad.

Bowood House (27km/17m NE of Bath) An 18C house with a beautiful south front, in the style of an orangery, by Robert *Adam. (An older and larger part of the house was demolished in 1955, except for one Adam room which was transferred to *Lloyd's of London.) Joseph *Priestley was employed as librarian here, and the laboratory where he discovered oxygen in 1774 is still shown. The park is considered one of the masterpieces of Capability *Brown.

Bow porcelain Wares made from the late 1740s at Stratford, on the other bank of the River Lea from Bow in what is now east London. A patent for porcelain had been taken out in 1744 by the founders of the factory, Edward Heylyn and Thomas Frye, but no surviving pieces of Bow have been dated earlier than 1750. The factory made a speciality of blue and white tableware in the Chinese style, and of figures of actors and actresses in favourite roles. But for the most part it followed continental models, though in a less sophisticated manner than *Chelsea. The factory closed in 1776; it is often said to have been bought and shut down by William Duesbury of the *Derby factory, but there is no documentary evidence of this.

Bow Street (London WC2) A street of importance in London's history because of the magistrates' court which stood on the west side in the 18C. When Henry *Fielding was magistrate here in the late 1740s, he established a system of volunteer thief-catchers. Known later as the Bow Street Runners, they were predecessors of the metropolitan *police. The well-known Bow Street police station and magistrates' court of modern times, on the east side of the road, was built in 1879–80 and continued in its original use until the early 1990s.

Box and Cox (1847) Farce by J.M. Morton (1811–91) about the results of a landlady letting the same room to John Box, a printer who works all night, and to James Cox, a hatter who works all day. The success of the play was such that 'box and cox' became a common phrase for any taking of turns.

Boxer see *Animal Farm*.

boxing Fighting with fists, which had been a part of athletics in ancient Greece and of gladiatorial entertainments in Rome, did not reappear as an organized sport until the early 18C in England, where prizefighters competed for a purse of money while others gambled on the result. These were prolonged and violent contests with bare fists and few rules. By 1719 the concept of a champion of England was already in existence, for in that year the title was claimed by James Figg (1695–1734). Jack Broughton (1704–89) was champion from 1734 to 1750

British Heavyweight Champions since 1959	
1959 Henry Cooper	1981 Gordon Ferris
1969 Jack Bodell	1981 Neville Meade
1970 Henry Cooper	1983 David Pearce
1971 Joe Bugner	1985 Hughroy Currie
1971 Jack Bodell	1986 Horace Notice
1872 Danny McAlinden	1989 Gary Mason
1975 Bunny Johnson	1991 Lennox Lewis
1975 Richard Dunn	(relinquished title)
1976 Joe Bugner	1992 Herbie Hide
1978 John L. Gardner	

Trade card by Hogarth for James Figg, c.1730, offering to teach gentlemen the noble science of defence.

and was the first to introduce an effective set of rules. Even so, it was not until the London Prize Rules of 1839 that kicking and biting and blows below the waist were declared to be fouls. Boxing was a fashionable sport in the early 19C, when enthusiasts were described as the Fancy and *Mendoza was the best-known practitioner. The *Queensberry Rules, which govern modern boxing, gradually came into use during the late 19C.

Boxing Day The day after Christmas, which has been a *bank holiday since 1871. In the church calendar December 26 is the feast of St Stephen, and it only became known as Boxing Day in the early 19C. The name derives from householders giving presents, or Christmas 'boxes', to servants and tradesmen on that day.

Charles **Boycott** (1832–97) English agent, on the Irish estate of the earl of Erne, whose name entered the language after an incident in 1880. Bad harvests in 1879 led to a demand by tenants for their rents to be reduced; Boycott responded by serving eviction notices; *Parnell then proposed, as a policy for similar cases throughout Ireland, that tenants should refuse to communicate in any way with those trying to evict them. The impasse on the Erne estate was the first to attract wide attention; and since the tenants' action was new, requiring a new word, Boycott's name was immediately and widely used to describe the isolation of someone by the removal of all contact.

Geoff **Boycott** (b. 1940) Outstanding batsman, playing *cricket for Yorkshire (1962–86) and England (1964–82, captain 1977–8). During 1981–3 he held the world record for the number of runs scored in *Test matches; his total of 22 Test centuries for England remains in 1992 the record (shared with Hammond and Cowdrey), and his 8114 runs were the England record until overtaken in

1992 by David *Gower. His reputation as an awkward character, much loved and much hated, was confirmed in Yorkshire's turmoil of the mid-80s; the club's committee dismissed him as a player in 1983, whereupon his supporters voted out the committee, appointed him to the new one and returned him for two more years to his place at the wicket.

The **Boy Friend** (1953) Musical by Sandy Wilson (b. 1924), affectionately mocking the mannerisms of the 1920s with clever lyrics, delightful tunes and a suitably silly plot (heiress Polly, at finishing school on the Riviera, meets aristocratic Tony disguised as messenger boy). From modest beginnings in London's Players' Theatre Club, the show went on to long runs in the West End and on Broadway (where it launched the career of Julie *Andrews). It was filmed in 1971 by Ken Russell with Twiggy and Christopher Gable.

Boy George (stage name of George O'Dowd, b. 1961) Pop singer whose appearance in frocks and make-up provoked outrage and amusement in just about the proportions intended. He formed the band Culture Club in 1981 with Mikey Craig, Roy Hay and Jon Moss. Each of their first two albums included no. 1 hit singles – 'Do you really want to hurt me?' on *Kissing to be Clever* (1982) and 'Karma Chameleon' on *Colour by Numbers* (1983). In 1987 he began recording on his own (beginning with a no. 1 hit, *Everything I Own*), but the novelty was beginning to wear off and his career was not improved by an admission of heroin addiction.

The **Boyhood of Raleigh** (1870, Tate Gallery) Painting by *Millais which chimed with the mood of Victorian imperialism by evoking the romantic beginnings of colonial expansion. The boy *Raleigh, who would later lead expeditions to both north and south America, sits on the beach with a young friend, listening intently to a sailor who points beyond the horizon.

Robert **Boyle** (1627–91) Chemist and physicist best known for his statement of the relationship between volume and pressure in gases, called in Britain and the USA Boyle's Law (at a constant temperature the pressure of a gas varies inversely with its volume). He researched in many fields, with a rigour in his experimental methods which was advanced for his time, and he put forward an atomic theory of the nature of matter in *The Sceptical Chymist* (1661). He was a founder member of the *Royal Society.

Battle of the **Boyne** (11 July 1690) Victory by William III and an army of some 35,000 men over the deposed *James II (with about 21,000); the site of the battle, in the republic of Ireland, was south of the river Boyne and about 40km/25m north of Dublin. James's flight from the battlefield and from Ireland ended his attempt to reclaim his crown. The victory is celebrated annually by Protestants in Northern Ireland on July 12, a public holiday sometimes referred to as the Glorious Twelfth. The error of one day in the date was the result of confusion about the change from Old Style to New Style (see *calendar). The OS date of the battle was July 1; the variance on dates in the 17C was ten days, so the NS date is July 11. But by the time Britain made the change to New Style (in 1752) the necessary adjustment for contemporary dates was 11 days. This number was added, incorrectly, to a date from the previous century.

Boys' Clubs The first clubs for boys and young men were founded in the mid-19C in the industrial cities, particularly London, Liverpool and Manchester, to provide for those who had few leisure facilities. A National Association was formed in 1925 and there are now more than 2000 clubs round the country, some with a mixed membership of boys and girls, for people aged between 11 and 19. Group activities are mainly in the countryside, from mountaineering and caving to all forms of water sports.

Boy Scouts see *Scouts.

Boy's Own Paper Magazine, at first weekly and then monthly, which was published for almost a century (1879–1967) by the Religious Tract Society. Though intended to be improving, with an emphasis on manly and Christian ideals, it sold extremely well because of the excitement of its adventure stories and public school serials (of which *The Fifth Form at St Dominic's* was the best known).

'The **boy stood on the burning deck**' see the Battle of the *Nile.

Boz see Charles *Dickens.

BP (British Petroleum) Founded in 1909, as the Anglo-Persian Oil Company, by *Burmah Oil in partnership with William Knox d'Arcy – a solicitor turned prospector who had discovered oil in southern Iran the previous year. His find was the beginning of the Middle East oil industry. In 1914 the British government took a majority shareholding to ensure a supply of fuel to the navy (the government share was progressively sold from 1979). In the 1930s the company extended its activities to Iraq and Kuwait, but in 1951 its wells and refineries in Iran were nationalized. It then reorganized as British Petroleum (from 1954), and developed more widely based oil interests – first in Alaska, where it discovered the USA's largest oil field in 1969 (an event which led to BP taking over Standard Oil in 1987), and then in the North Sea, where it is the largest oil producer.

BR see *railways.

Brabham Motor-racing and manufacturing team established in Britain in 1962 by the Australian driver Jack Brabham (b. 1926, kt 1979). He had previously won the world championship twice driving for *Cooper (1959, 60), and he achieved a unique feat when he won it again in 1966 in a car manufactured by himself (he also won the constructors' championship that year and again in 1967). In 1970 he sold his share in the company but it has continued to race under his name; Nelson Piquet won the world championship for Brabham in 1981 and again in 1983.

Lady **Bracknell** see The *Importance of Being Earnest.

Malcolm **Bradbury** (b. 1932) Professor of literature whose infrequent novels (one per decade) reflect both the comedy and the anxiety of changing intellectual trends. The first (*Eating People is Wrong* 1959) revelled in the dithering uncertainties of liberalism, while the latest (*Dr Criminale* 1992) is set in a fragmenting intellectual world shaken loose by fashions such as 'deconstruction' and by more tangible deconstructions such as the removal of the Berlin wall. His best-known novel is The *History Man* (1975, televised 1981) about an appalling lecherous left-wing lecturer in sociology, Howard Kirk.

Bradford (280,000 in 1981) City in West Yorkshire which from the Middle Ages was an important centre for the woollen and textile trades, though the rapid growth of the town dates only from the 19C (one of the first steam-powered mills was installed here in 1798). A famous extension of Bradford's industry was the experiment at *Saltaire, and from the same period there survives the large area of textile warehouses known as Little Germany (the reason for the name is not known). Two of the city's most grandiose buildings opened in 1873: Lister's Mill in Manningham, whose 76m/250ft chimney in the style of an Italian bell-tower is one of Bradford's best-known landmarks; and the Gothic City Hall, with a Venetian clock tower not much lower than the mill's chimney, by the local firm of Lockwood and Mawson. The same partnership had previously built the Wool Exchange (1867), an elaborately self-confident market-place in keeping with a time when much of the world's wool was traded here. Bradford Grammar School, one of the best known in the country, was founded in 1662; it is now an independent school.

The parish church (14–15C) became the cathedral when Bradford was made an Anglican diocese in 1919. Bolling Hall, a 15C manor house much altered and improved in the 18C, was opened in 1915 as a museum specializing in period furniture and decoration; and Cartwright Hall, completed in 1904, was built in Lister Park as a municipal art gallery to house a collection of mainly British paintings. The most recent addition to Bradford's museums is the *National Museum of Photography, Film and Television.

An offer of c.1880 to supply textiles direct from Bradford's looms, with 'all intermediate profits going to the consumer'.

Bradford-on-Avon (8000 in 1981) Town in Wiltshire known in particular for the tiny chapel on its bridge, which was used as the local prison cell from the 17C; and for the Saxon church, originally founded by St Aldhelm in about 700 and rediscovered in the 19C after being used as a school. Just south of the town is the superb Barton Farm Tithe Barn, a stone structure of the 14C with a roof supported by great arches of oak.

Charles **Bradlaugh** (1833–91) Atheist and freethinker, son of a solicitor's clerk, who was for many years a colleague of Annie *Besant in furthering unpopular causes. His most famous struggle came after his election in 1880 as an independent radical MP for Northampton, when he was unable to take his seat because he was neither allowed to affirm (legally a commitment as strong as an oath, but not involving the Bible) nor, as a known atheist, to take the oath (though he was willing to do so). He was re-elected four times before finally being permitted to take the oath and his seat in 1886.

Caroline **Bradley** (1946–83) Show jumper who was in the gold medal-winning British team, riding her famous Tigre, in the 1978 World Championships. She was again in the winning team at the 1979 European Championships.

Bradshaw The bible of the travelling classes in the great days of the railway. The first *Bradshaw's Monthly Railway Guide*, already in its characteristic yellow paper cover, appeared in 1839, published by George Bradshaw (1801–53), a Manchester engraver. Publication continued until May 1961, each issue giving complete railway timetables for the whole country. So much information in so little space prompted an aphorism from Sherlock Holmes: 'The vocabulary of Bradshaw is nervous and terse, but limited.'

Braemar Castle (14km/9m SW of Balmoral) Small, uncompromisingly military fortress which dates in this form only from 1748. It was rapidly constructed from an earlier ruin in the rush to suppress the Highlands after the *'45 Rebellion.

Braemar Gathering The best known of all the *Highland games, because members of the royal family usually come to it from nearby *Balmoral. It is held on the first Saturday of September in a park on the west side of the village of Braemar (known also for *Braemar Castle).

Melvyn **Bragg** (b. 1939) Author and TV presenter. As both editor and presenter since 1978 of The *South Bank Show, he has been influential in the popularizing of the arts through television. He has written biographies of Laurence Olivier and Richard Burton, but as a writer he is primarily a novelist, most of his fiction being set in his native Cumbria.

William and Lawrence **Bragg** Physicists, father (1862–1942, KBE 1920) and son (1890–1971, kt 1941), who shared the 1915 Nobel prize for their pioneer work in x-ray crystallography. They are the only father and son to have been awarded the prize together, and Bragg junior remains the youngest of Nobel laureates – at the age of only 25.

Dennis **Brain** (1921–57) Player of the French horn (and from 1951 of the German double horn) who revealed to an astonished postwar generation the potential of these instruments in the hands of a virtuoso. He was most widely known from his recordings of the Mozart horn concertos, but his brilliance also inspired several leading composers – including Britten and Hindemith – to create new works for him. He was killed in a car crash.

Brain of Britain (BBC from 1967) Radio quiz show, with difficult general knowledge questions, which leads to an annual winner, the 'brain of Britain'. It evolved from an earlier quiz, *What Do You Know?* (1953–67). Since 1973 Robert *Robinson has been the questionmaster.

The Brains Trust (BBC 1941–9) The most highbrow of discussion programmes, on which a regular panel of Julian *Huxley, Professor C.E.M. Joad and Commander A.B. Campbell were joined each Tuesday evening by two other conversationalists. The talk was prompted by questions, of an extraordinarily wide range, and for its first 18 months the name of the programme was *Any Questions*. In 1954–5 there was a version of *The Brains Trust* on BBC television; of the original trio only Julian Huxley took part.

Bramley (short for Bramley's seedling) Cooking apple believed to be named after Matthew Bramley, a butcher in *Southwell, who first grew it in his garden in the mid-19C.

Kenneth **Branagh** (b. 1960) Actor and director who formed his own company, Renaissance Theatre, in 1987; it was soon followed by Renaissance Films. His debut as a film director was particularly successful in 1989, with *Henry V*; he braved the comparison with Laurence Olivier's earlier achievement, directing himself with great flair as the central character of England's most nationalistic play. He is married to Emma *Thompson.

Brands Hatch (18km/11m SW of Rochester) Motor-racing circuit in Kent which began in the 1930s as a grass track for motorcycles. It opened for Formula Three racing in 1949 and in 1964 became the location for the *British Grand Prix, a position it retained in alternate years until 1986.

Bill **Brandt** (Hermann Wilhelm Brandt, 1904–83) German photographer who made his career in Britain from 1931. His work during the 1930s cast a coldly dispassionate eye over the social extremes (the upstairs and the downstairs) of English life. After the war he became known for photographs of nudes, or details of nudes, taken in close-up with a wide-angle lens to form distorted sculptural shapes often hard to recognize as flesh – a transformation heightened by his grainy and contrasty prints.

brandy butter Butter creamed with sugar and brandy, the traditional accompaniment to plum pudding.

Richard **Branson** (b. 1950) Entrepreneur and founder of the *Virgin group of companies (no-one since *Elizabeth I has done so much to give virginity a good name). His daring long-distance exploits have publicity value but are also considerable achievements. He captained *Virgin Atlantic Challenger II*, which for a while held the *Blue Riband for the fastest crossing of the Atlantic; and with Per Lindstrand he was the first to make hot-air balloon crossings of the Atlantic (1987, ditching in the sea off the coast of Northern Ireland) and of the Pacific (1991).

Brantwood see *Coniston Water.

brass bands Many countries have brass bands (which differ from military bands in having no woodwind instruments), but it was in Britain that a particularly strong tradition developed of amateur bands linked with places of work, particularly in Lancashire and Yorkshire. The Stalybridge Old Band, established by 1814, is usually quoted as the first brass band. The two oldest surviving bands, both frequent winners of competitions, existed for some decades as brass-and-reed bands before dropping the woodwinds in the 1850s; they are Besses o' th' Barn (the name of a village near Manchester) and Black Dyke Mills (in Queensbury, near Bradford). These date from 1853 and 1855 respectively. The next oldest, again from near Bradford and equally well known, is the Brighouse and Rastrick (1881). The main annual contests are the British Open, held at Belle Vue in Manchester since 1853; and the National Championship, held from 1900 at the Crystal Palace and since 1945 in the Albert Hall. Between the wars an exceptional dominance was established by the Foden Motor Works Band, founded in 1902 at Sandbach in Cheshire. In the early 1990s one of the most successful was the Grimethorpe Colliery Band, formed in 1917; they won the Open in 1991 and the National in 1992, but the colliery itself, at Grimethorpe in Yorkshire, was closed in 1992.

memorial **brasses** Sheets of brass set into church floors or walls, engraved with images (frequently a full-length representation of the deceased) and with texts. The sheets of brass and the technique came originally from the Netherlands, but it was in England that their use became widespread. The earliest to survive are those of Margaret and John de Valence (d. 1276, 1277) in Westminster Abbey. Brasses remained popular until the 17C (though many were destroyed in the 16–17C as graven images) and there was a revival in the 19C. Brass-rubbing is a method of acquiring a full-scale facsimile of a brass. Paper is spread over it and rubbed with heelball, graphite or chalk; the recessed lines of the engraved image remain unmarked by the substance and so appear in white on black.

John **Bratby** (1928–92) The leading artist of the *kitchen-sink school of the 1950s, using thickly applied paint and often garish colours to depict the objects of everyday life. The subject matter was a precursor of *pop art, though the rich application of paint was in a different tradition. Bratby also published several novels during the 1960s.

Brave New World (1932) Satirical novel by Aldous *Huxley set in a terrifying future (the year is 632 AF, or After Ford), where genetic engineering has led to a clinically stable society in which personal freedom is no more than a romantic idea from the past. The title is borrowed, with irony, from Shakespeare; when Miranda first sets eyes upon a group of courtiers in *The Tempest*, she cries 'O brave new world, that has such people in't!'.

Fanny **Brawne** see John *Keats.

Bray (8km/5m NW of Windsor) Village on the Thames known mainly for the legendary vicar of Bray, hero of a song dating from the 18C. He boasts that he has remained vicar through five reigns by changing his political complexion; he was a High Churchman under Charles II, a Papist under James II, a man of no principles at all under William III, a Tory under Anne, and now he is a Whig under George I. Such cheerful opportunism, combined with a very catchy tune, has made him a lasting favourite. He may have had an historical origin in Symon Symonds, who veered from Catholic to Protestant and back again twice between the reigns of Henry VIII and Elizabeth I, arguing that he was keeping true to his main principle, which was 'to live and die the vicar of Bray'.

'**Brazil, where the nuts come from**' see *Charley's Aunt*.

bread-and-butter pudding Recipe which appears in English cookery books from the early 18C. Slices of buttered bread are piled in a dish with sultanas between them and are then soaked in milk and eggs before being baked, the top slices turning brown and crisp in the oven.

bread sauce Crumbled white bread heated in milk and flavoured with onions and usually cloves, used as a sauce with turkey, chicken and roast game.

Nicholas **Breakspear** see *Adrian IV.

Julian **Bream** (b. 1933) Guitarist and lutenist, a leading influence in the revival of interest in Elizabethan lute music but also much involved in the creation of a modern repertoire for the guitar; Britten and Walton are among the composers who have written works for him. He formed in 1960 the Julian Bream Consort, and more recently has often performed with John *Williams.

Mike **Brearley** (b. 1942) Batsman who played *cricket for Middlesex (1961–83) and for England (1976–81, captain 1977–81). His greatest skill was his ability to get the best out of a team (he is a psychoanalyst by profession), and he led England to a record 11 victories against Australia – ending with three dramatic wins during the 1981 series. In that year Brearley was recalled for the game at Headingley after the first in the series had been lost and the second drawn. He won that match and the next two to retain the Ashes.

Scobie **Breasley** (b. 1914) Australian who was four times *champion jockey in Britain between 1957 and 1963. His successes included two Derbys in three years – 1964 on Santa Claus, 1966 on Charlottown.

Breathalyzer see *road safety.

Brechin (8000 in 1981) Town in the Tayside Region, with a cathedral founded by David I in 1150. Much altered over the centuries, it is now the parish church. It stands on the site of an earlier Celtic monastery, of which there survives the impressive *round tower adjoining the cathedral. This was built, probably by Irish masons, in the late 10C.

Brecon (Aberhonddu in Welsh, 7000 in 1981) Town in Powys which became in 1923 the cathedral town of the new diocese of Swansea and Brecon. The cathedral is 13–14C, with the Early English chancel its most impressive feature. This was unfinished, with a flat timber roof, until George Gilbert Scott completed it in 1862–5 with the appropriate stone vaulting. The Grecian-style Shire Hall (completed 1842, by Thomas Henry Wyatt and David Brandon) houses the Brecknock Museum, which has an extensive display of local history.

Brecon Beacons (Bannau Brycheiniog in Welsh) Area of mountains in south Wales, mainly of red sandstone, designated in 1957 a *national park (1,344sq.km/519sq.m). It includes, from west to east, the Black Mountain (highest peak Fan Brycheiniog 802m/2630ft); the Brecon Beacons (the main beacons are the twin peaks of Corn Ddu 873m/2863ft, and Pen-y-fan 886m/2906ft); and, most confusingly, another range which is called the Black Mountains (Waun Fach 811m/2660ft).

Breconshire (also known as Brecknockshire) Former *county in Wales, which has been part of Powys since 1974.

Breeches Bible see *Bible in English.

Rory **Bremner** (b. 1961) Satirical impressionist of great versatility and accuracy, with regular one-man shows on BBC TV since 1988.

St **Brendan** (*c*.485–*c*.578) Irish monk who founded the monastery at Clonfert in Galway and who certainly travelled as far as Scotland, but whose lasting fame derives from a 9C Latin narrative in which he is the hero of a great sea journey westwards to find the 'promised land of the saints'. This has led to excited speculation that the Irish might have reached America before any other Europeans. The Atlantic was crossed from Ireland in 1977 by Timothy Severin and others in a leather boat of a kind that existed in Brendan's time, proving that it was at least possible. His feast day is May 16.

Bren gun The light machine gun used by the British army in World War II. Based on the ZB, developed at Brno in Czechoslovakia, it was manufactured at *Enfield. Its British name combined the first two letters of the two towns.

Brent Walker see George *Walker.

Brewer's Dictionary of Phrase and Fable Treasure house of strange pieces of information, jotted down and collected over many years by Dr E. Cobham Brewer (1810–97) and first published in 1870. Revised and added to many times since then, it retains the original flavour of hours spent in a Victorian study – with lists, for example, of 'famous horses in myth and history' or of 'renowned misers'.

Brideshead Revisited (1945) Novel by Evelyn *Waugh in which a young Oxford undergraduate, Charles Ryder, becomes increasingly involved with a rich Roman Catholic family, the Flytes, whose ancestral seat is Brideshead. It was made by Granada TV into a very successful 13-part series, first shown in 1981, starring Jeremy Irons as Ryder and Anthony Andrews as Sebastian Flyte, with *Castle Howard standing in for Brideshead.

brides in the bath Famous murder case of 1915, in which George Joseph Smith, a Bristol antique dealer, was convicted of murdering three wives in succession by drowning them in the bath. A rich detail which has stuck in popular memory is his having gone into the sitting room, while the body of one bride was still in the bath, to play *Nearer, my God, to Thee* on the harmonium.

Frank **Bridge** (1879–1941) Composer and virtuoso viola player, known in particular for his chamber music – though one of his most popular pieces is a suite for orchestra, *The Sea* (1912). To his earlier romantic style he added in the 1920s elements of atonality, making him closer to the continental avant-garde than most British composers. *Britten was his pupil from the age of 12.

Bridge on the River Kwai (1957) Film directed by David *Lean, from a novel by Pierre Boulle, about British prisoners forced by the Japanese to build a crucial railway bridge in Burma during World War II. The drama centres on the British commander, played by Alec Guinness, whose perfectionism leads him to have such pride in the bridge itself that he opposes the British agents who are trying to blow it up. The music, by Malcolm Arnold, made stirring use of the traditional tune *Colonel Bogey,* and the film won Oscars for Arnold, Lean and Guinness, in addition to Carl Foreman (writer) and Jack Hildyard (photography).

Robert **Bridges** (1844–1930) Poet known in particular for his short lyric poems. He was appointed *poet laureate in 1913.

Carl **Bridgewater** Newspaper delivery boy, aged 13, who was killed by a shotgun blast after disturbing thieves in 1978 at Yew Tree Farm in Staffordshire. Four men were convicted of the murder (two cousins, Michael and Vincent Hickey, together with James Robinson and Patrick Molloy), largely on the basis of the confession of Molloy, who died in prison in 1981. The case was under review in 1992 as another possible miscarriage of *criminal justice; Molloy's confession was made to a detective who was later discredited, when he was a member of the *West Midlands Serious Crime Squad.

Bridgewater Canal see James *Brindley.

Brief Encounter (1945) Film written by Noel *Coward and directed by David *Lean, which has become a classic for the poignancy of its drab middle-class love affair. The encounter begins when a suburban housewife (played by Celia Johnson) and a doctor (Trevor Howard) meet in a station tea room; the station and its passing trains provide a continuing thread in their brief relationship, before they decide to part for ever. The music, from Rachmaninov's 2nd Piano Concerto, tugs at the heart strings in a manner which the protagonists themselves are too British to allow.

Brief Lives The title now commonly used for the collection of short and pithy biographies compiled in the 17C by John *Aubrey. They were made the basis of a successful one-man play, first performed by Roy Dotrice in 1969.

Richard **Briers** (b. 1934) Actor whose line in comedy involves much fluster and indecision. His best-known TV series have been The *Good Life and Ever Decreasing Circles (1984–8).

Brigadier Gerard (foaled 1968) Bay colt with an extraordinary record of 17 wins in 18 races, starting with the 2,000 Guineas in 1971. He was ridden by Joe Mercer (b. 1934) and named after a *Conan Doyle character. Excelling at the shorter distances, he was not entered for the Derby of 1971, which was won by *Mill Reef.

Brigg Fair see Frederick *Delius.

Raymond **Briggs** (b. 1934) Illustrator and author. His speciality has become the book in comic-strip form, beginning with *Father Christmas* (1973) about a Santa Claus who hates the cold conditions of his work. This was followed by *Fungus the Bogeyman* (1977), indulging children's love of everything unsavoury, and a post-nuclear parable for adults, *When the Wind Blows* (1982). The latter, like *The Snowman* (1978) and *Father Christmas,* was also successful as a cartoon film.

Brighouse and Rastrick see *brass bands.

John **Bright** (1811–89) English politician from a Quaker mill-owning family who was a founder in 1838 of the Manchester association against the *Corn Laws. He and Richard *Cobden emerged as leaders of the campaign. Elected MP for Durham in 1843 (and Manchester 1847–57, Birmingham 1858–89), he used his great powers of oratory not only against trade restrictions but also against military imperialism (telling the House of Commons during the Crimean War, 'The angel of death has been abroad throughout the land; you may almost hear the beating of her wings'). He was also a passionate advocate of parliamentary reform and the extension of the *franchise.

The main feature of the sea front at Brighton: the Palace Pier, built in the last years of the 19C.

Brighton (154,000 in 1991) Town in East Sussex, originally the fishing village of Brighthelmston, which began its transformation into England's leading seaside resort with the arrival in 1753 of Dr Richard Russell, author of *A Dissertation on the Use of Sea Water in Diseases of the Glands.* Under his guidance bathing became fashionable, and soon 'dippers', such as the celebrated Martha Gunn, made a profession of plunging the rich in the waves. Brighton's future was secured when the prince of Wales, the future George IV, moved there in 1783 and soon set about building the *Royal Pavilion.

From the prince's time there date the Theatre Royal (1807) and the nearby district of narrow streets known as the Lanes. Brighton has been famous for its piers; the Chain Pier, dating from 1823 and destroyed in a storm of 1896, was replaced by the present Palace Pier, while the West Pier was built in 1866. Also on the seafront is the Grand Hotel (1864), the scene of a terrorist attack when the prime minister and cabinet were staying for the Conservative party conference in 1984; during the night of October 11 an IRA bomb demolished part of the building, killing five people.

The Museum and Art Gallery, housed in a building in a Victorian Moorish style (1871–3, by Philip Lockwood) began with some good paintings, from 17C Dutch and Flemish to 19C English, and much commemorative pottery, given by Henry Willett. It has since extended into many other areas, in particular musical instruments, costume and 20C design.

Brighton Rock (1938) Novel by Graham *Greene about the last days of a 17-year-old hoodlum, Pinkie or 'The Boy', who commits an increasingly disastrous series of crimes and cynical follies (murder, marriage, fake suicide) in an attempt to establish himself as a gangland leader in Brighton. His dream is to rival an established racketeer,

Mr Colleoni (a name preceding by three decades the better-known Corleone, the gangster in *The Godfather*). Greene's Roman Catholicism adds another dimension to the book, for Pinkie's relentless will to evil is seen as pitted against divine grace. After Pinkie has come to a violent end, his pregnant girlfriend Rosie is told by a priest that no-one can imagine the 'strangeness of the mercy of God'.

Brighton Run Annual rally for veteran cars (strictly those built before the end of 1904) from Hyde Park in London to the promenade in Brighton, held usually on the first Sunday in November. It commemorates the Emancipation Run by motorists betweeen the two towns on 14 November 1896, the day on which the legal restrictions of the *Red Flag Act came to an end.

Bright's disease see *Guy's Hospital.

bright young things The gilded youth of the 1920s, with a reputation for outrageous behaviour. They were originally known as as the 'bright young people', but this version of the phrase soon became more common.

Brig o' Balgownie Scotland's oldest bridge, crossing the river Don to the north of Aberdeen – known also as the Auld Brig o' Don (old bridge of Don). Dating from about 1300, it is a single arched span of 19m/62ft. An extra excitement for those on the bridge in horse-riding times was the prediction that it would fall down if crossed by an only son riding a mare's only foal.

James **Brindley** (1716–72) The father of British canals. He built more than 300 miles of inland waterways, solving extraordinary engineering problems even though he was semi-literate and never committed any of his designs or calculations to paper. The son of a small farmer in Derbyshire, he made a name for himself repairing machinery for mills. In 1759 the duke of Bridgewater asked his advice on a proposed canal to take coal 16km/10m from the duke's mine at Worsley into Manchester. The duke had in mind a conventional system of locks down to the river Irwell. Brindley proposed instead an aqueduct to carry the barges over the Irwell at Barton; the ease of the resulting journey halved the cost of coal in Manchester and made the duke a fortune. This first part of the Bridgewater canal was completed in 1761; it was extended to Liverpool in 1776, joining the *Mersey at Runcorn. Brindley was immediately in demand for other canals, the most important of which was the Grand Trunk, joining the two coasts of England by linking the Mersey to the Trent.

Brink's-Mat Firm owning a security warehouse at Heathrow airport from which there was a violent theft in November 1983 of 3.4 tons of gold bullion (some 6800 ingots, worth £26m, belonging to Johnson Matthey, a firm of dealers in precious metals). It was at the time Britain's largest robbery – later outdone in this respect by the *Knightsbridge safe deposit case. The confession of a corrupt security guard gave police their first lead in an investigation which lasted nearly ten years and resulted in charges against some 30 people.

Bristol (393,000 in 1991) City and port on the confluence of the rivers Avon and Frome; administrative centre of the county of Avon. From early Norman times Bristol developed rapidly to become the major port on the west coast. It was from here that Sebastian Cabot sailed in 1497; the Society of Merchant Venturers was incorporated in 1552; and trade with the colonies in tobacco, sugar and slaves brought Bristol great prosperity until it began to lose its pre-eminence to Liverpool in the late 18c. Nevertheless in the 19c two of Brunel's massive ships, the *Great Western* and the **Great Britain*, were built and launched in the city.

The cathedral was originally the church of a 12c abbey, given this new role when Bristol became an Anglican diocese in 1542. The 12c chapter house, with elaborately carved linear decorations, is one of the best Norman interiors in Britain. The 14c choir and Lady Chapel survive from the abbey church; the present nave was discreetly added in the 19c by G.E. Street. More of a piece is the 14c St Mary Redcliffe, in the Perpendicular style and famous as probably the grandest parish church in all England; the three panels of the large altarpiece commissioned for this church from Hogarth in 1755 are displayed in St Nicholas, bombed in the war and now a museum of ecclesiastical art. The city also contains the world's first Methodist chapel, the New Room, built for John Wesley in 1739. The modernist Roman Catholic cathedral of SS Peter and Paul was consecrated in 1973. Bristol Grammar School, founded in 1532, is now an independent school.

The Corn Exchange (by John Wood the elder, 1741–3) is well known for the bronze 'nails', pillars set in the pavement outside, on which merchants are said to have completed their transactions – an explanation often given (without any evidence) for the phrase 'to pay on the nail', meaning to pay promptly. The Theatre Royal (1766) has been since 1943 the home of the Bristol Old Vic, and is the oldest theatre in the country in regular use.

The Museum and Art Gallery, founded in 1823, are housed together in a building of 1905. Suspended in the entrance hall is a full-scale replica of the city's contribution to early aviation, the Bristol Boxkite biplane of 1910. The museum is particularly strong in glass (Chinese and ancient Roman as well as English) and in ceramics, including the local Bristol delftware. The art gallery has a good general collection but is made exceptionally interesting by the work of local 19c painters, in particular Francis Danby (1793–1861).

An elegant residential district developed in the 18c and early 19c to the west of the city, in Clifton, with views over the Avon gorge which were later made even more spectacular by the addition of the *Clifton Suspension Bridge.

Bristol Channel Inlet of the Atlantic lying between Wales to the north and Cornwall, Devon and Somerset to the south. At its eastern end it merges with the *Severn estuary, where the channel narrows between Penarth and Weston-super-Mare.

Eric **Bristow** see *darts.

Britain The abbreviation of *Great Britain which is commonly used to mean the *United Kingdom.

Battle of **Britain** see *Battle of Britain.

Britannia The Roman name for the area of *Great Britain which Rome controlled, approximating to modern England and Wales. The female figure of Britannia, wearing a helmet and carrying a trident, has been on the reverse of many English coins since 1672 – in recent years on the old penny (see *currency) and then on the 50 pence piece. The original model was a mistress of Charles II (Frances Stuart, duchess of Richmond and Lennox, 1647–1702), who had appeared in this guise on medals struck for the king in 1667.

Britannia Britain's chief holiday airline and the largest in the world to specialize in charter flights. It began in 1962 as Euravia, operating three Lockheed Constellations from Luton airport (which remains its base). The airline adopted its present name in 1964, when it began to build up a fleet of Bristol Britannias. In 1965 it became part of the Thomson Organization, a major holiday tour group.

Britannia The royal yacht, built at the John Brown shipyards in *Glasgow and launched in 1953. With an overall length of 126m/412ft, and a reception room able to accommodate 250 guests, the ship was designed to function as a mobile royal palace (and to double as a hospital ship in wartime). Nowadays, for royal tours overseas, *Britannia* usually sails in advance and is in place when the royal party arrives by air.

Britannia Bridge see *Menai Strait.

Britannia metal Alloy of tin and antimony first produced in England in the 18c and later widely manufactured as a cheap alternative to pewter.

Britannia Royal Naval College see *Dartmouth.

The **British** Citizens of the *United Kingdom. See also *Britons.

British Academy (British Academy for the Promotion of Historical, Philosophical and Philological Studies) Body of distinguished academics, established in 1901 to do for the humanities what the *Royal Society does for science. Its main practical function in recent years has been allocating government funds to postgraduate research projects.

British Aerospace (written in abbreviation BAe) Group formed in 1977 to bring together various publicly owned aviation companies, including the British Aircraft Corporation (see *Vickers). BaE was privatized in 1985, and since then has acquired from the government the Royal Ordnance and the *Rover Group. The latter transaction, in 1988, became a subject of controversy when a hidden sweetener of £38m (contrary to EC regulations) was revealed in the purchase price and had to be paid back to the Treasury. Subsequently the National Audit Office reported its view that the Rover price tag of £150m had undervalued the company by at least £50m. By 1992 the company was in sufficient financial trouble to close its aircraft factory at Hatfield in Hertfordshire – a production plant associated with many of the most famous names in British aviation history, from the Tiger Moth to the Comet and Trident.

British Aircraft Corporation see *British Aerospace.

British Airways (BA) Britain's national airline, formed in 1971 to merge the publicly owned *BOAC and BEA (an operation completed by 1974). British Airways was *privatized in 1987; it took over *British Caledonian later that year and *Dan Air in 1992. It has acquired a reputation for unscrupulous business practices, after paying damages for dirty tricks campaigns against both *Laker and *Virgin.

British Antarctic Territory The name since 1962 of an area, previously known as the Falkland Islands Dependency, which has the shape of a slice of cake on the map of Antarctica. With its point at the south pole, it extends between longitudes 20°W and 80°W as far north as latitude 60°S. Within this area various research stations have a resident population of British scientists, numbering only about 60 in winter. Similar slices are claimed by Norway, Australia and several other countries. The situation was temporarily stabilized by the Antarctic Treaty of 1961, valid for 30 years, which was signed by the interested nations and by others including the USA and the USSR (each of whom made no claim but reserved the right to do so). Though now only of scientific interest, the continent risks future exploitation of its minerals. With this in mind a new Antarctic Treaty was signed in 1991; one of its clauses is a 55-year ban on mining.

British Association (British Association for the Advancement of Science) Body established in 1831 to promote interest in science and technology. Much of its work is done at school level, but it has been best known for the controversial topics discussed at its annual meetings – in particular the famous one at Oxford in 1860 on the theories of *Darwin.

British Athletic Federation Organization established in 1991 to be the governing body of athletics in the United Kingdom, with special responsibility for British teams in international events and for national training. It replaced the British Amateur Athletic Board, founded in 1932. Competitive events within Britain are under the control of the *AAA (Amateur Athletic Association).

British Caledonian Independent airline formed in 1970 when Caledonian (founded in 1961 as a long-range charter carrier) took over British United Airways (formed in 1960 from several smaller companies). In 1987 British Caledonian, flying by then to most parts of the world with about 100 flights a day, was itself taken over by the newly privatized *British Airways. The BCal aircraft livery and uniforms reappeared in 1988 when the holiday charter branch of British Airways was renamed Caledonian Airways.

British citizen Since the British Nationality Act of 1981 there have been three forms of British citizenship. The first, defined simply as a British citizen, is the status

of anyone born in Britain if one parent is either British or legally settled in the country; and of anyone born abroad with one British parent normally resident in Britain. It is also the form of citizenship acquired by anyone becoming naturalized.

British Dependent Territories citizen is a category applying mainly to residents of Gibraltar and Hong Kong, and it will be lost by those in Hong Kong when the territory is returned to China in 1997. British Overseas citizen is a status given in 1981 to all previous citizens of the UK and Colonies who did not come under either of the other two categories. British Dependent Territories citizens and British Overseas citizens are entitled to British citizenship if they establish residence in the UK, but there is no automatic right of immigration.

British Coal see *coal.

British Constitution A traditional phrase for testing someone's degree of intoxication (by asking them to say it clearly), but otherwise famous largely for not existing. Britain is one of very few countries without a written constitution, meaning that no single legal document or code of laws exists which is harder to change than any other. Instead, the constitutional procedures and the rights of citizens in the United Kingdom depend on an accumulation of separate statutes and unquestioned conventions.

British Council Independent public body established in 1934 and funded by the government for the purpose of representing British culture abroad. With offices in more than 80 countries, it arranges for visits by British artists, lecturers and performers, mounts exhibitions, teaches English and provides libraries of British books.

British Empire Two events in the 1490s began the process which led to the European empires of later centuries. In 1492 Columbus discovered America; and in 1497 Vasco da Gama sailed round the southern tip of Africa and opened the sea route to Asia. The double lure of new territories in the west and new trade with the east stimulated all the European countries bordering the Atlantic. Portugal and Spain moved first, followed by France, Holland and England. It was with its two nearest neighbours, France and Holland, that Britain found itself most directly competing, first in north America and then in India.

The growth of the empire was haphazard; indeed Britain lost her most significant colony before the main imperial expansion began. When *America became independent, the only other colonies were *Canada and various islands in the *West Indies which had been settled or seized in a piecemeal fashion, as part of the continuing naval process of exploration, privateering and warfare.

The next increase in territory, to the east, was the result of the trading activities of the *East India Company. These led to the gradual inclusion in the empire of the entire subcontinent of *India and to the establishment of secure ports of call on the way to China, in particular *Singapore and *Hong Kong. Other additions, strategic places on the sea route such as *South Africa and *Sri Lanka, were seized from Holland during the French Revolutionary Wars.

Meanwhile a new continent had been discovered. *Australia began to be settled in the late 18C, when British naval power was entering its greatest period. Here, as also in *New Zealand, Britain had no European rivals. This was not the case in Africa in the 19C, where there was intense competition with new imperial powers such as Germany and Belgium. The driving force in Africa came as much from *missionary endeavours as from trade.

The last additions to the empire, the most piecemeal of all, were themselves the by-product of British imperial

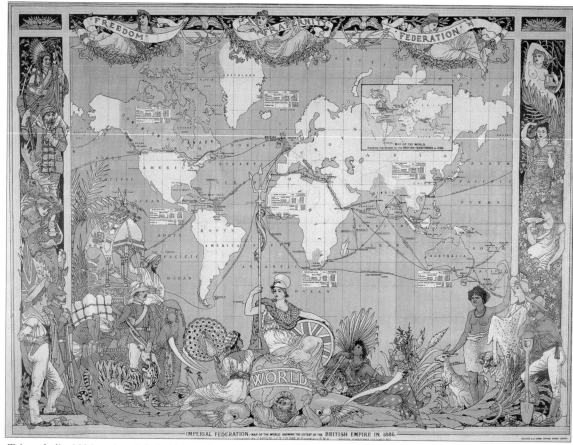

Triumphalist 1886 version of the British empire, with Britannia astride the world and 'British territories coloured red' in a firmly established convention.

strength. It sometimes suited other powers or rulers to allow Britain control over their territories in return for protection. It was this which created colonies as diverse and improbable as *Cyprus and *Fiji. The empire was traditionally marked red on British maps, and by the early 20C much of the world seemed that colour.

Meanwhile the unravelling of empire had begun with the independence of Canada in 1867. During the early years of the 20C Australia, New Zealand and South Africa also achieved *dominion status. The pattern was becoming clear by which the empire could be transformed into the *Commonwealth. In the decades after World War II the process was completed as more and more colonies were granted independence, though sometimes only after a period of agitation and terrorism. By the 1990s there were only a handful of dependent territories, of which the most important (the *Falkland Islands, *Gibraltar, *Hong Kong) were either about to undergo a change of sovereignty or were the subject of continuing controversy on that issue.

What was probably the most lasting achievement of the British empire only became evident in the second half of the 20C – the establishment of English as an international language.

British Empire Medal see *orders of chivalry.

British Expeditionary Force (BEF) The name used for the first British army sent to the Continent in each of the world wars. The BEF of 1914 (see *Old Comptibles) was the professional rapid-response force established by *Haldane. Under the command of Sir John French it landed at Boulogne on August 14; by August 23

it was involved at *Mons, followed by action at *Ypres in October. In December 1915 French was replaced as commander by *Haig. By then the original force of professional soldiers was being supplemented by hundreds of thousands of volunteers recruited into the army.

The BEF of 1939 was sent to France in September under the command of Lord Gort. The troops dug in during the winter along the French-Belgian border, but were outflanked by the rapid advance of the German army in May 1940. They were rescued at *Dunkirk, where the rearguard was under the command of General *Alexander.

British Film Institute see *National Film Theatre.

British Gas The Gas Light and Coke Company, founded in London in 1812, was the first to pipe *gas into people's homes. Rival concerns soon proliferated and there were more than 1000 suppliers by the time the industry was nationalized in 1948 under the Gas Council (from 1972 the British Gas Corporation). In recent decades the supply has changed from coal gas to natural gas from the North Sea, first piped ashore in 1967. The Corporation was *privatized as British Gas in 1986. In 1992 the regulatory body OFGAS (see *OFFER) argued that British Gas remained a monopoly and needed to be broken up into smaller competing elements.

British Grand Prix The sequence of Grand Prix motor races goes back to Le Mans in France in 1906 (hence the French name for the 'great prize' of the sport), but it only gradually developed into the present international contest; it differed from other top-level races in being from the start between manufacturers' rather than national teams. The first British Grand Prix was held at *Brooklands in 1926; there was then a series in the 1930s at Donington Park near Derby; but the first British Grand Prix in the present unbroken series took place at *Silverstone in 1950. The race was held at Aintree on a few occasions between 1955 and 1962, but the main other location has been *Brands Hatch.

In 1993 Britain acquired a second Grand Prix, with Donington Park selected as the location for the Grand Prix of Europe. The course has in recent years been the regular location for the British Motorcycle Grand Prix.

British Home Stores see *BhS.

British Honduras see *Belize.

British Indian Ocean Territory The islands of the Chagos Archipelago, established as a colony in 1965 in anticipation of the independence of *Mauritius and *Seychelles, with which they had previously been linked.

British Grand Prix

1950	Giuseppe Farina (Italy)	Alfa-Romeo
1951	José Gonzalez (Argentina)	Ferrari
1952	Alberto Ascari (Italy)	Ferrari
1953	Alberto Ascari (Italy)	Ferrari
1954	José Gonzalez (Argentina)	Ferrari
1955	Stirling Moss (UK)	Mercedes-Benz
1956	Juan Manuel Fangio (Argentina)	Lancia-Ferrari
1957	Stirling Moss & Tony Brooks (UK)	Vanwall
1958	Peter Collins (UK)	Ferrari
1959	Jack Brabham (Australia)	Cooper
1960	Jack Brabham (Australia)	Cooper
1961	Wolfgang von Trips (Germany)	Ferrari
1962	Jim Clark (UK)	Lotus
1963	Jim Clark (UK)	Lotus
1964	Jim Clark (UK)	Lotus
1965	Jim Clark (UK)	Lotus
1966	Jack Brabham (Australia)	Brabham
1967	Jim Clark (UK)	Lotus
1968	Jo Siffert (Switzerland)	Lotus
1969	Jackie Stewart (UK)	Matra
1970	Jochen Rindt (Austria)	Lotus
1971	Jackie Stewart (UK)	Tyrrell
1972	Emerson Fittipaldi (Brazil)	Lotus
1973	Peter Revson (USA)	McLaren
1974	Jody Scheckter (South Africa)	Tyrrell
1975	Emerson Fittipaldi (Brazil)	McLaren
1976	Niki Lauda (Austria)	Ferrari
1977	James Hunt (UK)	McLaren
1978	Carlos Reutemann (Argentina)	Ferrari
1979	Clay Regazzoni (Switzerland)	Williams
1980	Alan Jones (Australia)	Williams
1981	John Watson (UK)	McLaren
1982	Niki Lauda (Austria)	McLaren
1983	Alain Prost (France)	Renault
1984	Niki Lauda (Austria)	McLaren
1985	Alain Prost (France)	McLaren
1986	Nigel Mansell (UK)	Williams
1987	Nigel Mansell (UK)	Williams
1988	Ayrton Senna (Brazil)	McLaren
1989	Alain Prost (France)	McLaren
1990	Alain Prost (France)	Ferrari
1991	Ayrton Senna (Brazil)	McLaren
1992	Nigel Mansell (UK)	Williams

They are used as a naval support base by Britain and the USA.

British Isles Group of islands in the northeast Atlantic, including Ireland to the west, the Shetlands to the north and the Channel Islands to the south. By far the two largest islands are *Ireland and *Great Britain.

British Israelites Followers of a demented visionary, Richard Brothers (1767–1824), who believed that the British were descended from the biblical lost ten tribes of Israel and that he himself was the rightful prince of the Hebrews.

Royal **British Legion** Body established after World War I (in 1921) to represent the interests of ex-service men and women and their dependants; 'Royal' was added in 1971. Money is distributed to those in need through local branches, run by members, around the country; and the main fund-raising event is *Poppy Day.

British Leyland Motor manufacturing group formed in 1968 by Leyland Motors (makers of commercial vehicles since 1897), absorbing *Rover and the *British Motor Corporation to become the major part of the British car industry. The group was facing collapse when taken over by the government in 1975, and continued to lose money and to suffer appalling labour relations as a nationalized industry. It was *privatized during the 1980s, *Jaguar being sold separately in 1984 and the remainder, under the name of the Rover Group, going in 1988 to *British Aerospace.

British Library (London WC1 and NW1) The chief *copyright library and the nation's greatest collection of manuscripts and printed material. It was the library of the *British Museum until 1973; in that year it became an independent body, though still occupying the museum's famous round reading room. By then the collection was so large that parts of it were outhoused in more than a dozen other buildings around London. Plans were made for a purpose-built modern library; a site was acquired just west of St Pancras Station; and Colin St John Wilson (b. 1922) was chosen as architect. The project provoked considerable controversy as its costs spiralled above £400m. It is anticipated that it will open to readers during 1994 at the earliest.

British Lion see *Royal Arms and *Lions.

British Midland The second largest domestic airline in Britain, after British Airways. It derives from a flying school founded near Derby in 1938; after the war the school began to offer charter flights, and scheduled services were started in 1953 (first to the Channel Islands). The name was changed from Derby Airways to British Midland in 1964. International flights were added in 1967.

British Motor Corporation Company formed in 1952 by the merger of *Austin and *Morris, and itself absorbed in 1968 into *British Leyland.

British Museum (London WC1) The national collection of antiquities and one of the great museums of the world. Founded in 1753, initially to house the collection of Hans *Sloane, it was opened to the public in 1759 in Montague House. The present museum was built on the same site in 1823–47 to a design by *Smirke. The rapidly expanding collection covered all areas of knowledge, and was particularly strong in printed books and manuscripts. A magnificent round reading room was formed in 1852–7 by covering the central courtyard with a massive dome, thus creating the famous British Museum Library in which Karl Marx and scores of other famous writers have worked. But this section of the museum became independent in 1973 as the *British Library, which in the 1990s is moving to its own premises. The natural history collection had earlier moved out to become the *Natural History Museum. The *Museum of Mankind, by contrast, remains an attached department.

Among the best known of the British Museum's treasures are the *Elgin marbles, the *Portland vase, the *Rosetta stone, the *Mildenhall treasure, the *Sutton Hoo ship burial, the Lewis chessmen (see *Lewis with Harris) and, a very recent addition, *Lindow man.

British National Party see *neo-Nazis.

British Nuclear Fuels see entries on *nuclear power and *Sellafield.

British Rail see *railways.

British Steel In the economic difficulties of the 1930s Britain's steel companies (see *iron and steel) began to collaborate with each other and with the government, operating a cartel protected by tariff barriers. After World War II the major companies teetered in and out of state control before being finally nationalized in 1967 as the British Steel Corporation. This in turn was *privatized in 1988 as British Steel. The slimming of the industry to a few large plants had put the company into profit by 1989. After the closure of *Ravenscraig in 1992 the remaining steel works were *Port Talbot and Llanwern in Wales, Scunthorpe and Teesside in the northeast.

British subject By the British Nationality Act of 1948 this was a secondary status held by citizens of the UK and Colonies and by citizens of the independent countries of the Commonwealth. It is now replaced by *Commonwealth citizen for those categories, but it applies still to a few other groups included within the 1948 act.

British Summer Time see *Summer Time.

Britons The *Celtic people inhabiting England before and during the Roman occupation, who were driven west by the *Anglo-Saxons. They are often called ancient Britons, because the word by itself is also used of *British people today.

Leon **Brittan** (b. 1939, kt 1989) Conservative politician who has been in Brussels since 1988 as one of the commissioners of the EC – responsible for competition policy until the end of 1992, and then for external economic affairs. He was MP for Cleveland and Whitby (1974–83) and for Richmond in Yorkshire (1983–8). He entered the cabinet in 1981 as chief secretary to the Treasury, and continued as home secretary (1983–5) and as secretary of state for trade and industry from 1985. He resigned in 1986 as a result of the *Westland affair.

Benjamin **Britten** (1913–76, baron 1976) Leading British composer of the mid-20C, pre-eminent particularly in his writing for the voice. Precociously talented (and born on November 22, the feast day of St Cecilia, the patron saint of music), he studied composition from the age of 12 with Frank *Bridge, before becoming a pupil of John *Ireland at the Royal College of Music. He achieved international fame with the production of *Peter Grimes* in 1945; as in many of his subsequent operas and song cycles, the central role was created by his lifelong companion, the tenor Peter *Pears. Later operas which have continued to hold the stage were *Albert*

Herring (1947), **Billy Budd* (1951), *The Turn of the Screw* (1954), *A Midsummer Night's Dream* (1960) and *Death in Venice* (1973). Among the most powerful of his works is the choral **War Requiem* (1962).

Children's voices play an important part in many of Britten's compositions, such as the *St Nicholas* cantata (1948) or *Noye's Fludde* (1958). In 1946 he wrote the popular **Young Person's Guide to the Orchestra*.

In 1947 he settled in *Aldeburgh, where he created the annual music festival at which many of his own works were first heard.

BRM (British Racing Motors) Racing car launched at Silverstone in 1950 by Raymond Mays, who before the war had built the ERA (English Racing Automobiles). The BRMs were at first unsuccessful, but they hit a winning streak ten years later with Graham *Hill as their chief driver; they were top of the constructors' championship in 1962.

Broadcasting House (London W1) The headquarters of *BBC radio, custom-built in 1928–32 to provide soundproof studios in the heart of London. In his carving above the entrance Eric *Gill used a theme from *The *Tempest* to symbolize radio – Prospero sending the spirit Ariel out into the world.

Broadcasting Standards Council Body set up by the home secretary in 1988, after many years of pressure from Mary *Whitehouse and others, to investigate complaints relating to violence, sex and matters of taste or decency in broadcast programmes. Its powers of rebuke are limited to the publication of its findings. A separate Broadcasting Complaints Commission was established by the Broadcasting Act of 1990, to deal in a similar manner with issues of fairness and privacy.

Broadlands (13km/8m N of Southampton) Originally a 16C house, transformed into a Palladian one by Capability *Brown (in his less usual role of architect) with additions by his son-in-law, Henry *Holland. Brown also landscaped the park. This work was done for the father of Lord *Palmerston, and more recently Broadlands has been the home of Lord *Mountbatten. Both men are commemorated by displays in the house.

Broadmoor Prison near Crowthorne in Berkshire for the criminally insane (technically a special hospital). The building dates from 1863.

Broadwater Farm Housing estate in Tottenham, north London, which was the scene of a riot and of a violently gruesome murder on 6 October 1985. Hundreds of youths, most of them black, went on a rampage of destruction after the death of a West Indian woman, Mrs Cynthia Jarrett, who collapsed as police searched her house. Buildings were set on fire and the firemen were attacked as they tried to put them out. PC Keith Blakelock was attempting to protect the firemen when he was set on by the mob and hacked to death. Urgent police investigations led to sentences of between one and six years on 40 people, and to life sentences on three – the *Tottenham Three, whose convictions were later quashed.

Broadway (24km/15m NE of Cheltenham) Village with a long street of delightfully irregular old houses, in mellow Cotswold stone and with stone-tiled roofs and dormers – often quoted as perhaps the prettiest village in England, and correspondingly much visited. The Broadway Tower, a landmark on the hill above the village, is a folly put up in 1800 by the earl of Coventry, who wanted something extra in the view from his house 32km/20m away.

Broadwood Firm of piano makers, founded in 1728 and still in existence, which manufactured grand pianos from 1781. They came to be considered the best in Europe and Thomas Broadwood, meeting Beethoven in 1817 in Vienna, promised to send him one; it took six months on its journey from London, by sea to Trieste and then north by cart to Austria. Beethoven is believed to have hammered away at it throughout his remaining years. It is now in the National Museum in Budapest, presented by Liszt.

Brobdingnag see *Gulliver's Travels.*

brochs Iron-Age circular forts of a kind found only in Scotland. Of dry-stone construction, formed of an inner and outer wall often with a stairway rising between the two, they typically enclosed an area some 12m/40ft in diameter with walls also about 12m/40ft high. They were built during the centuries just before the Christian era, and several hundred are known. By far the best preserved is on *Mousa.

Ring of **Brodgar** see *Maes Howe.

Brodick Castle (3km/2m N of Brodick, on *Arran) Red sandstone castle, originally of the 13c but progressively altered up to the 19c. The interior has fine plaster ceilings, and the woodland garden is famous for its rhododendrons.

brogues Originally rough leather boots worn in Ireland and the Highlands of Scotland, but applied in the 20c to sturdy shoes with patterns of perforation in an upper layer of leather, worn in particular for such activities as shooting or golf.

Brompton Oratory (London SW1) Massive baroque Roman Catholic church, built 1878–84 to the design of Herbert Gribble (1847–94). It immediately played an important role in the re-establishment of Roman Catholicism, as London's largest and main place of worship until the opening of *Westminster Cathedral in 1903.

Brontë sisters Writers who exercise a special fascination not only through their work but from the unusual circumstances of their lives. Charlotte (1816–55), Emily (1818–48) and Anne (1820–49) were daughters of Patrick Brontë, the Irish-born rector of *Haworth in Yorkshire. Their mother died in 1821 and Charlotte and Emily were sent to join two older sisters at a dismal school for the daughters of clergy at Cowan Bridge in Lancashire (the school on which Charlotte based Lowood in *Jane Eyre*). Charlotte and Emily were removed after the two older girls sickened and died. Thereafter the children lived at home and developed their own imaginative world, set in the kingdoms of Angria and Gondal, which they chronicled in minute script in a series of tiny books. At this time the most artistic of the children seemed to be their brother Branwell (1817–48), but he later dissipated his talent in drink and opium.

As young adults, the girls took unsatisfactory jobs as teachers and governesses. In 1845 they decided to publish a joint volume of their poems at their own expense, choosing pseudonyms which reflected the initial letters of their names but gave no hint of their sex (Currer, Ellis and Acton Bell). They sold just two copies. They had also been writing novels, and each now found a publisher. Charlotte was the first in print with *Jane Eyre* (Oct. 1847); two months later came Emily's *Wuthering Heights* and Anne's *Agnes Grey*, to be followed in June 1848 by Anne's *Tenant of Wildfell Hall*. By the summer of 1848 public interest had forced the sisters to reveal their identities.

Their fame was rapidly followed by a series of tragedies. Branwell died in September of that same year, 1848. Emily fell ill immediately after his funeral and died in December, to be followed by Anne in May 1849. Charlotte published more novels (*Shirley* 1849, *Villette* 1853) while continuing to live with her father at Haworth. In 1854 she married his curate, Arthur Nicholls, and died the following year during her first pregnancy.

Charlotte and Anne were the most appreciated of the three in the 19c, but in modern times it is the wilder passion of Emily, both in her poetry and in *Wuthering Heights*, which has been increasingly admired.

Bronze Age The period following the *Stone Age, and the first in which metal was used (first copper by itself, and then the alloy of copper and tin which is bronze). The period lasted in Britain from about 2000 BC to 500 BC, when there was a gradual development into the *Iron Age.

Peter **Brook** (b. 1925) Director who had a brilliant early career in the commercial theatre, with a string of West End successes in his twenties. He followed these in the 1960s with some strikingly original productions – in particular the staging of Peter Weiss's *Marat/Sade* (1964) and a circus-like *Midsummer Night's Dream* (1970) with the lovers conversing on trapezes. In 1970 he moved to Paris to set up a research centre devoted to the study of ritualistic theatre. Its most ambitious project has been a version of the ancient Indian epic *The Mahabharata* (1985), amounting in performance to more than nine hours.

Peter **Brooke** (b. 1934) Conservative politician, MP for City of London and Westminster South since 1977. He became widely known as a conciliatory secretary of state for Northern Ireland (1989–92), though he accidentally gave offence in 1992 when he accepted an invitation to sing *Oh My Darling Clementine* on Irish television within hours of an IRA bomb killing several civilians in County Tyrone. He was omitted from the first cabinet after the 1992 general election, but a few months later he replaced David *Mellor at the Department of National Heritage.

Raja **Brooke** (James Brooke, 1803–68, KCB 1848) Soldier who founded a dynasty of English rajas in *Sarawak. After leaving the army and inheriting a fortune, he sailed east in 1838 with the intention of establishing a settlement in Borneo. He found the raja of Sarawak facing a rebellion, helped him put it down, and was himself then appointed raja with the right to name his successors.

Rupert **Brooke** (1887–1915) Poet whose charm and brilliance, together with his early death in World War I, made him a symbol of gilded Edwardian youth and its tragic fate. His fame as a poet was firmly established with the five 'war sonnets', published in 1915. They included *The Soldier*, which in its romantic patriotism was very different from the later mood of Wilfred *Owen but which tragically prefigured the poet's own death later that same year:

> If I should die, think only this of me:
> That there's some corner of a foreign field
> That is for ever England.

The foreign field turned out to be on the Greek island of Skyros, where Brooke was buried after dying of blood poisoning while serving in the navy. Among his other well-known poems are the nostalgic *The Old Vicarage, Grantchester* ('Stands the church clock at ten to three?/ And is there honey still for tea?') and the fanciful fish's-eye view of paradise in *Heaven*.

Cornering at relatively high speed on the banked curves of Brooklands in the early 1920s.

Brooklands The world's first custom-built motor-racing circuit, which opened near Weybridge in Surrey in 1907. It was designed as an oval course with heavily banked curves. It was also of great use to the British motor industry for the testing of cars, since a 32kph/20mph speed limit prevailed on the roads. In Brooklands' first year a record was established by Selwyn Edge for the distance travelled in 24 hours (2546km/1582m, at an average speed of 106kph/66mph, a figure unequalled for another 18 years). Racing continued at Brooklands until 1939, but the track was not restored after being used for aeroplane manufacture during World War II.

Anita **Brookner** (b. 1928) Art historian, specializing in 18C French painting, who began another career as a novelist in 1981 with *A Start in Life*. Since then she has published a novel every year, all of them quiet, witty, low-keyed studies of lonely people – for the most part middle-aged, middle-class and female. She acquired a wider and faithful readership after her fourth novel, *Hotel du Lac* (1984), won the Booker prize.

Brooks's (London SW1) A *club founded in Pall Mall in 1764, taking its name from its first manager, William Brooks. It moved in 1778 into premises in St James's Street, newly completed and designed by Henry *Holland. The late 18C was the club's most fashionable period. Its members were rich and dissolute (Charles James *Fox was their leader, giving the club a strong Whig association), and gambling was the favourite pastime; the stakes were high.

David **Broome** (b. 1940) The most successful of all British show jumpers, with gold medals in the World Championships (individual 1970, team 1978) and European Championships (individual 1961, 67, 69, team 1979), and with two individual bronze medals in the Olympic Games (1960, 68). He also has a record six wins in the King George V Gold Cup (1960, 66, 72, 77, 81, 91). The most famous of his many horses is probably Mister

Softee, which he rode from 1965, but his gold in the World Championship in 1970 was on Beethoven. Liz *Edgar is his sister.

brothel-creepers Term which became common in the 1950s to describe suede shoes with rubber soles, in the same vein as the earlier *co-respondents.

Jack **Broughton** see *boxing.

Arthur Whitten **Brown** see *Alcock and Brown.

Capability **Brown** (Lancelot Brown, 1716–83) Landscape gardener who acquired his familiar name because he assured so many prospective patrons that he could see capabilities in their estates. He became head gardener in 1841 at Stowe, where William *Kent was creating a landscape more gentle and romantic than the formal patterns which had previously been in favour. Brown was inspired to set up on his own, from 1751, as an 'improver of grounds'. In a career of unbroken success he improved more acres than any man before or since, transforming the parks of some 140 houses, of which Blenheim was merely the grandest (others include Badminton and Burghley). Where Kent had relied on architectural features such as temples or ruins, the main ingredients of Brown's palette were dark clumps of trees and bright patches of water to give emphasis to the green contours of a park's own natural landscape. He worked also as an architect, sometimes in partnership with his son-in-law, Henry *Holland.

Ford Madox **Brown** (1821–93) Painter who was closely linked with the younger men in the *Pre-Raphaelite Brotherhood, though never formally a member of their group. To some extent he anticipated their hard, bright style and their interest in medieval subjects. Two of his paintings are among the best known of Victorian images. *The Last of England* (1852–5, Birmingham Art Gallery) is a sombre comment on the wave of emigration at the time; depicting a young middle-class couple in the stern of a boat, with white cliffs in the background, it was inspired by the departure of the Pre-Raphaelite sculptor Thomas Woolner for Australia. The subject of *Work* (1852–65, Manchester City Art Gallery, with a smaller version in Birmingham) is more schematic. It shows many different kinds of work in progress in Heath Street, Hampstead, from the handsome navvies digging the road to the watching intellectuals (one of them is Thomas Carlyle). Brown's notes emphasize that though the brain-workers appear to be idle, they are 'the cause of well-ordained work and happiness in others'. In 1878–93 he painted a series of wall panels on the history of the city for the new town hall in Manchester.

George **Brown** (1914–85, baron George-Brown 1970) Labour politician and MP for the Belper division of Derby-shire (1945–70), who was defeated by Harold Wilson in the 1963 leadership election. In Wilson's government of 1964 Brown was the first secretary of state of a newly created Department of Economic Affairs (responsible for overall economic planning, abolished in 1969). He then became foreign secretary (1966–8), a post from which he resigned because of disagreements with the prime minis-ter. His reputation was of someone talented but highly erratic.

Gordon **Brown** (b. 1951) Labour politician, MP for Dunfermline East since 1983. In successive years during the early 1990s his fellow MPs gave him the highest num-ber of votes in elections to the shadow cabinet, causing him to seem the heir apparent to John *Smith – unless the party proves reluctant to elect two Scottish leaders in suc-cession. During the financial crises of 1992 he was shadow chancellor of the exchequer.

Joe **Brown** (b. 1930) Climber who made his reputation in 1954 when he achieved the west face of Petit Dru in France. He subsequently tackled a wide geographical spread of the world's highest peaks – Kanchenjunga in the Himalayas in 1955, Mount Communism in the Pamirs in 1962, Cotopaxi in Ecuador in 1979, Mount Kenya in Africa in 1984, Mount McKinley in Alaska in 1986, and the northeast ridge of Everest in 1986 and 1988.

Thomas **Browne** (1605–82, kt 1671) Physician and writer, whose enquiring mind and rotundity of phrase ('Half our days we pass in the shadow of the earth, and the brother of death exacteth a third part of our lives') have at all times won him faithful readers. His best-known works are *Religio Medici* (1642), an account of his religious convictions and personal philosophy; and *Urn Burial* (1658), in which the discovery of some funerary urns in Norfolk leads him into a wide-ranging discussion of burial practices and of death itself.

Brownies The junior section of the *Guides. Estab-lished in 1914, they were first called Rosebuds. The name Brownie was adopted in 1918, deriving from a book of 1870 by Juliana Ewing in which two children behave like brownies (elf-like creatures with the admirable habit of finishing the humans' housework at night). Mrs Ewing's book also provided the name Brown Owl, for the adult leader of the pack, and the elfin mythology led to each Brownie's obligation to attempt a good deed every day.

Robert **Browning** (1812–89) Poet whose work is for the most part dense in content and allusion though often conversational in tone. He is widely remembered for two of his slighter pieces, *The *Pied Piper of Hamelin* and *Home-Thoughts, from Abroad* ('Oh to be in England/ Now

Ford Madox Brown's carefully contrived cross-section of Victorian society: the Manchester version of Work.

that April's there'). In 1845 he met Elizabeth Barrett, a poet living the life of an invalid in the household of a tyrannical father; their love affair, which is chronicled day by day in secret letters, led to a clandestine marriage and elopement to Italy. Elizabeth then recovered her health, becoming better known to history as Elizabeth Barrett Browning (1806–61). They lived mainly in Florence until her death.

Christopher **Bruce** (b. 1945) Dancer and choreographer, with the Ballet Rambert from 1963 and its leading performer after it re-formed in 1966 to concentrate on modern dance. Some of his most successful roles were in *Pierrot Lunaire, L'Après-midi d'un faune* and **Cruel Garden*. His first ballet as choreographer was for Ballet Rambert (*George Frideric* 1969); he has subsequently created much new work for them and other companies, including *Ghost Dances* (1981), *Swansong* (1989) and *Rooster* (1991, to early Rolling Stones songs). In 1989 he became the resident choreographer of the Houston Ballet in Texas.

William **Bruce** (*c*.1630–1710, bt 1668) Leading Scottish architect of the late 17C; designer of the remodelled **Holyroodhouse and the original **Hopetoun.

Bruce's Cave The name of two caves, one near Kirkpatrick Fleming in Scotland and the other on the island of Rathlin off the north coast of Ireland, which are claimed to have sheltered **Robert the Bruce (and his spider) when he was a fugitive in 1306. It is certain that he did take refuge somewhere on Rathlin.

Bruges City in Belgium, the name of which has been associated in recent British politics with hostility to the **EC. In 1988 Mrs Thatcher gave a speech to students at the College of Europe there, expressing her reservations about further powers being given to the European Community. The Bruges Group was later formed by her supporters to exert political pressure on this issue.

Beau **Brummell** (George Brummell, 1778–1840) The epitome of the **Regency rake and dandy. A sharp wit, a good dress sense, a private fortune and the friendship of the prince of Wales (the future **George IV) made him in his twenties the arbiter of taste in London. But he was no royal sycophant. He quarrelled with his patron in 1812, and when meeting Lord Alvanley and the prince at a ball the following year is said to have asked Alvanley: 'Who's your fat friend?' By 1816 his gambling debts were such that he fled to France, where he lived a long and pathetic existence before dying in an asylum.

Brunei Member of the **Commonwealth since 1984, on the northwest coast of Borneo. A powerful Muslim sultanate from the 15C, it became a British protectorate in 1888. With great wealth from oil and natural gas, its population (less than 250,000) has an exceptionally high per capita income and the sultan is often said to be the world's richest man.

Isambard Kingdom **Brunel** (1806–59) The outstanding example of an entrepreneurial Victorian engineer, seen at his most memorable in front of the chains used to launch the *Great Eastern*. His father, the French-born engineer Marc Isambard Brunel (1769–1849), invented the tunnelling shield and with it constructed the world's first underwater tunnel, 366m/400yd long, under the Thames between Wapping and Rotherhithe; it is still in use as part of London's **underground. The younger Brunel was appointed resident engineer of the project at the age of 19. In 1833, when he was 27, he became chief engineer to the Great Western railway, building the line from Paddington to Bristol. His design for the new **Clifton suspension bridge had been accepted in 1831.

The boldest of his many endeavours were his three great ships, each the largest in the world when launched. The *Great Western*, a wooden paddle steamer, was the first steamship to be built specifically for the Atlantic; she made her inaugural crossing in 1838 in 15 days (the smaller *Sirius* had been by a whisker the first to steam across, reaching New York the previous day after a journey of 19 days). The iron-hulled **Great Britain* was launched in Bristol in 1843 and is now back there. The *Great Eastern* (1858) was a monster which almost literally killed Brunel. It was another half century before any ship exceeded her length of 211m/692ft or her displacement of 22,500 tons. She proved almost impossible to launch and then had an unsatisfactory career crossing the Atlantic (so much coal had to be carried that there was insufficient room for the intended 4000 passengers). She only came into her own when laying the Transatlantic telegraph cable in 1865.

Brunel was spared the pain of much of this saga; he suffered a stroke on board the ship just before her maiden voyage.

Frank **Bruno** (b. 1961) Britain's leading heavyweight boxer in the 1980s. He never challenged for the British title, but was European champion in 1985 (he relinquished the title the following year). In each of his two attempts on the world championship (against Tim Witherspoon in 1986 and Mike Tyson in 1989) he failed to go the full distance. Trouble with a retina led to retirement from the sport, but he returned in 1992 to defeat Pierre Coetzer in what was seen as an eliminator for another attempt on the world title.

Brut or **Brutus** The founder of Britain and the man from whom the word 'Britain' derives, according to medieval

A recreation by Frederick Barnard, in about 1880, of the vanished world of Brummell and the dandies.

The classic image of the Victorian engineer: Brunel in front of the chains used to launch the Great Eastern.

legends gathered by *Geoffrey of Monmouth. Brut was believed to be the great-grandson of the Trojan prince Aeneas and to have conquered England with a Trojan army, overcoming the giants then living here who were led by Gogmagog (an amalgamation of *Gog and Magog). He was also held to be the founder of London, which therefore became known as Troynovant or new Troy.

David **Bryce** (1803–76) The most influential architect in the *Scottish baronial style, whose works include *Blair Castle and *Fettes.

Bryn Celli Ddu (5km/3m to the SW of Menai Bridge, Anglesey) The best preserved prehistoric burial chamber in Wales, dating from about 2000 BC. It was a passage grave, with the entrance corridor and the polygonal chamber lined and roofed with large stones, all beneath a protective mound.

Brythonic see *Celtic languages.

BSA (Birmingham Small Arms) Munitions company which diversified in the first decade of the century into manufacturing motor cycles. Their first model, in 1908, was described in a magazine of the time as 'by no means a potterer'. By the 1920s BSA was a leading make, but in the 1960s it declined with the rest of the British *motor cycle industry and in 1971 production ceased. The name was subsequently revived for a new company, based in Gloucestershire, which makes relatively light models mainly for export.

BSc (Bachelor of Science) The status of an undergraduate who has successfully completed a degree course (or graduated) in any of the sciences. The equivalent for the arts and humanities is BA.

BSE (Bovine Spongiform Encephalopathy) An affliction affecting the nervous system of cattle, commonly known as mad cow disease because of its effect on their behaviour. An epidemic of BSE was indentified in Britain in 1986. It was discovered to be caused by cattle food containing the bone meal of sheep, which had themselves been infected with another disease, scrapie. In 1988 it was made illegal to recycle cattle or sheep in animal feed, and no animal eating meal produced after that date has been infected. But the incidence of BSE in cattle alive before 1988 has continued to rise, reaching a peak of 3000 cases a month in 1992. All such animals are destroyed and their owners compensated. There were scares that humans might suffer brain damage from handling or eating contaminated beef, but no evidence of this has been found.

BSI (British Standards Institution) Body established in 1901 in the engineering industry, and known under this name from 1931. It was created out of frustration at the range of incompatible components, from screw threads up to steel girders. As early as 1903 the kitemark (a symbol in the shape of a kite with an S in the middle) was introduced to identify goods produced to an established standard – it was first used on tramway lines. Over the decades the principle has been extended not only throughout manufacturing, but also to less tangible areas such as safety and management. In recent years standardization within the European Community has been the major issue.

BSkyB see *television.

B Special Part-time policeman in *Northern Ireland, member of a force composed mainly of Protestants which was disbanded late in 1969, because it was seen as provocative at a time of increasing sectarian unrest in the province. The name derives from the special police force created in 1920, during the *Anglo-Irish War, drawing many of its recruits from *Carson's Ulster Volunteers. The full-time members, the A Specials, were backed up by reserves who put in one night a week, the B Specials.

BST see *Summer Time.

BT (British Telecommunications) After the installation in 1879 of the first British telephone exchange (in London's Coleman Street), the *Post Office established itself as the largest of the rival suppliers of telephone lines and services. By 1912 the private companies had dropped out and the Post Office had a monopoly except in one or two places where the municipal authorities ran the service (most notably in Hull, where that remains the case). In 1981 the telephone system was made independent as British Telecom, and in 1984 it became the first public agency to be *privatized; *Mercury had meanwhile been licensed, to avoid a private telephone monopoly. By 1992 BT's profits were so large that OFTEL (see *OFFER) demanded a 7.5% reduction in prices in each of the following five years.

BTR One of Britain's largest manufacturing companies, established in 1924 as the British Goodrich Tyre Company. Rubber and more recently plastics have remained the core of the business, and *Dunlop was acquired in 1985. *Hawker Siddeley was taken over in 1991 with a successful bid of £1.5bn. The name was changed in 1934 to the British Tyre and Rubber Company. In 1957 it was stated that the same three initials now stood for British Thermoplastics and Rubber.

The use of Bubbles *which enraged John Everett Millais, artist and grandfather of the small boy.*

bubble and squeak Now usually a dish of potatoes and cabbage fried together, but in the 18–19C invariably beef and cabbage. The name is the sound they supposedly made while cooking, as in a verse of 1795,

> When midst the Frying-pan in accents savage,
> The Beef so surly quarrels with the Cabbage.

Bubbles (1886, Royal Academy on loan from A&F Pears) Painting by *Millais of his grandson Willie James (later Admiral Sir William James) blowing bubbles. It was bought by Messrs Pears, who published it as a chromolithograph on which they had added a bar of Pears soap at the child's feet. The indignation of the artist was sufficient for the soap to be removed from later issues of the print.

John **Buchan** (1875–1940, baron Tweedsmuir 1935) Scottish author and, in his later years, statesman (the climax of his public career was as governor general of Canada, 1935–40). He is best known for his adventure stories, jingoistic in tone but invariably exciting. The first was *Prester John* (1910). In *The *Thirty-Nine Steps* (1915) he introduced the secret agent, Richard Hannay, who with Sandy Arbuthnot and others reappeared in a succession of books starting with *Greenmantle* (1916).

Buckfast Abbey (19km/12m W of Torquay) Medieval abbey in Devon, a ruin since the 16C, known now exclusively for its modern history. Between 1907 and 1938 it was rebuilt on its old foundations by French Benedictine monks, who themselves were the masons and labourers.

Duke of **Buckingham** (George Villiers, 1592–1628, kt 1615, duke 1623) Handsome son of a Leicestershire knight who in 1614 came to the notice of the highly sus-

ceptible *James I, resulting in Villiers' rapid progress through the ranks of the peerage. In 1623 he accompanied the future *Charles I to Spain in search of a bride. At that time, and subsequently in the reign of Charles, he was allowed to busy himself with the highest matters of diplomacy and warfare, causing immense resentment. When parliament attempted to impeach him, Charles dissolved parliament. In 1628 he was assassinated in Portsmouth by John Felton, a disaffected officer with a grudge about his lack of preferment.

Buckingham Palace (London SW1) The chief residence of the monarch since the accession of Queen Victoria. Buckingham House was built in 1702–5 for the 1st duke of Buckingham, and was bought in 1762 by George III. The king lived there until his death, whereupon George IV employed John *Nash to rebuild the house. Neither the new king nor his brother, William IV, was able to live in the palace and it was barely ready for Victoria. Nash created a three-sided courtyard, open towards the Mall, with *Marble Arch forming its entrance. But he was dismissed on the accession of William IV and was replaced by Edward Blore (1787–1879), who constructed a fourth side to the courtyard and moved Marble Arch to its present site. It is Blore's wing that the public sees, though the actual façade was added in 1913 by Aston *Webb (as the final detail of his new design for the Mall). The *Changing of the Guard takes place on the parade ground in front of this eastern façade. Since 1962 a building with access from Buckingham Palace Road has been used for temporary exhibitions of items from the royal collection; it is known as the Queen's Gallery.

Buckinghamshire (640,000 in 1991, administrative centre Aylesbury) *County in south central England.

Buckland Abbey see Francis *Drake.

Buddhists A small proportion of Britain's *ethnic and religious minorities are Buddhists, mainly from Sri Lanka, Burma and China. There are also Indian Buddhists, immigrants to Britain from 'untouchable' communities which converted to Buddhism in India in 1948 to escape their status at the bottom of the Hindu caste system. In addition to these there is a flourishing group of European converts to Buddhism, part of a widespread interest since the 1960s in eastern religions. In the past two decades several monasteries have been established in Britain, following Tibetan, Thai or Japanese Zen Buddhist traditions. Estimates of the number of Buddhists in Britain range from 25,000 to 50,000.

Budget The annual statement on financial policy and taxation levels given to the House of Commons by the *chancellor of the exchequer (in recent years on a Tuesday in March, but from 1993 to be combined in December with the *public spending round). The word means a leather wallet of a kind to contain papers, and in the 18C the chancellor was said to be opening his budget when he presented his proposals. In token of this, when setting off to make his speech, each chancellor is still traditionally photographed holding up the battered budget box covered in red leather; it is believed to have been made for Gladstone during his 1859–66 spell as chancellor of the exchequer.

Buggins' turn Phrase for a benefit of some kind, particularly an appointment, going to the next in line rather than being awarded on merit. Its first recorded use is in 1901, and the origin is unknown. The oddity lies in such a rare name coming to stand for someone essentially ordinary; in the early 1990s there were only four people by the name of Buggins in the London telephone directory.

Joe **Bugner** (b. 1950) Boxer who achieved fame young, when he took Henry *Cooper's British, Commonwealth and European titles in 1971; but he lost them before the end of the year to Jack Bodell. He recovered the European title in 1972 and held it until 1975. He then retired, but in 1976 made a brief successful return – recovering all three titles in a defeat of Richard Dunn before almost immediately retiring again.

building societies Traditionally non-profit-making organizations, which in recent decades have made possible the great increase in *home ownership by means of *mortgages. The first building society was set up in Birmingham in 1775. Each member paid a regular subscription; lots were drawn as to whose house should be built first; once every member had a new home, subscriptions ended and the society was wound up. 'Terminating societies' of this sort were replaced in the mid-19C by 'permanent societies' in which investors (wanting interest on their money) were distinguished from borrowers (wanting a loan to build a house). There was no need for such a society to come to an end, and by the late 20C, with escalating house prices, they had grown to a massive size. In 1992 the largest in the UK, the *Halifax, had assets of almost £60bn. In 1989 the *Abbey National became the first building society to convert itself into a profit-making public company.

Bulgarian atrocities see *Gladstone.

The **Bulge** Term used in the 1920s for the unusually large number of children of school age resulting from the increase in birth rate after World War I. It was revived in the 1950s for the same phenomenon after World War II.

bull see *bear.

John **Bull** see *John Bull.

bulldog Stocky breed of short-coated dog, with broadly spread forelegs, a severely squashed nose and a huge head covered in folds of loose skin. It was bred centuries ago to bait bulls, which it did by clenching its jaws on the bull's muzzle and hanging on. It lost its original purpose when animal-baiting was made illegal in 1835, but enthusiasts bred out its more ferocious characteristics to preserve it as a domestic animal. As such it has retained considerable popularity, its phlegmatic appearance and tenacious qualities causing it to be thought of as peculiarly British.

The concept of the plucky 'British bulldog breed' features in the work of Charles *Kingsley in the mid-19C and was increasingly applied to British men rather than their dogs (as, eventually, with Sapper's *Bull-dog Drummond). The accidental echo of *John Bull no doubt contributed to this.

Bull-dog Drummond Dim but excessively patriotic ex-army officer in the books of Sapper (the pen name of H.C. McNeile, 1888–1937). From his first appearance (*Bull-dog Drummond* 1922) he was immensely popular – the James Bond of his age – featuring in a new thriller almost every year till his author's death. His chief adversary was Carl Peterson, an international criminal. Like Bond he featured in a great many films, more than 25 in all.

Bullers of Buchan (44km/27m N of Aberdeen) Spectacular natural feature on the east coast of Scotland. The path goes round the rim of a sheer 61m/200ft cavity (perhaps a great cave of which the roof has collapsed), with the sea surging at the bottom.

Bull Ring see *Birmingham.

Rowlandson and John Bull query Nash's bill for Buckingham Palace (seen with Marble Arch forming the entrance).

bull terrier Powerful breed of short-haired dog, of any colour but often pure white, with pointed ears and small eyes in a severely chiselled head. It was probably bred soon after 1835, when bull-baiting was banned, from the bulldog and a strain of terriers including the now extinct white English terrier. The purpose was to provide a dog more agile than the bulldog, better equipped for the sport of fighting other dogs in pits. The Staffordshire bull terrier, slightly smaller and with a less stark profile, was bred for the same reasons at much the same time, from the bulldog and from a line which probably included the black-and-tan terrier. A related American breed, the pit bull terrier, was singled out in 1991 as specially dangerous (see *dog registration).

bully beef see *corned beef.

bumping races Form of boat race pioneered at Oxford and Cambridge and in use elsewhere in Britain where rivers are too narrow to permit racing side by side. At the start of a race the eights are strung out in line, with the same distance between each. Traditionally if any eight catches the one in front before the end of the course (touching or 'bumping' it), both retire from the race and begin the next day with their positions reversed; nowadays overlapping rather an actual bump is expected. There are usually four days of racing, and the sequence at the end of the final day is carried over to the next year. The boat holding the front position is 'head of the river'.

Bunbury see The *Importance of Being Earnest.

bungalow Word used by the British in India in the 18–19c for their own one-storey homes, and applied in the early 20c to single-storey houses of a similar kind being built in Britain, mainly in the suburbs and in seaside resorts. The origin is uncertain but the word probably derives from *bangla* (Bengali), reflecting a British belief that such houses were characteristic of Bengal.

Bunter see *Billy Bunter.

John **Bunyan** (1628–88) Preacher and author, son of an itinerant mender of pots and pans. He followed his father's trade until being drafted during the English Civil War into the parliamentary army, a stimulating melting pot of Puritan ideas. He found his own spiritual home with the Baptists, becoming in the 1650s a preacher in his home town of Bedford. After the Restoration there were severe restrictions on *Nonconformists, and Bunyan spent 11 years in Bedford jail (1661–72) for preaching without a licence. In prison he wrote his spiritual autobiography, *Grace Abounding to the Chief of Sinners* (1666). The same concept of a guilt-ridden, self-denying quest, turned now into fable, lies behind his greatest work, The *Pilgrim's Progress.

BUPA (British United Provident Association) The leading provider of *private health insurance in Britain, giving cover in the early 1990s to about 3 million people. The British Provident Association was founded in 1923 and became BUPA after amalgamating with other regional societies in 1947. In addition to insurance, BUPA runs a network of more than 30 hospitals. It is non-profit-making, spending any surplus on developing its services.

Richard **Burbage** (c.1567–1619) The actor most associated with Shakespeare. He was the son of London's first professional theatre manager, James Burbage (c.1531–97), whose original theatre was rebuilt as the *Globe. In 1594 he became the leading actor of the newly formed *Chamberlain's Men, the company of which Shakespeare

was a member, and as such he created the roles of Richard III, Romeo, Henry V, Hamlet, Macbeth, Othello and Lear.

Burberry Trade name for the fabric of a waterproof outer garment manufactured since the early 20c by the London firm of Burberrys. Indispensable to early motorists in open cars, and used on polar expeditions, a Burberry was as fashionable for much of the 20c as the *Barbour has been in recent years.

William **Burges** (1827–81) A leading architect and designer of furniture in the *Gothic Revival style. His interiors, characterized by a wealth of sculpted and painted detail deriving from medieval models, are an important feature of *Cardiff Castle and *Castell Coch. In the same manner he built a domestic castle for himself in London, the Tower House, at no. 9 (now 29) Melbury Road.

Anthony **Burgess** (John Anthony Burgess Wilson, born 1917) Novelist of exceptional range and variety. His first three books, published 1956–9 and known later as *The Malayan Trilogy*, drew on his experiences as an education officer in Malaya and Brunei in 1954–9. The subsequent Enderby series (four novels 1963–84) follow in comic vein the adventures of Enderby, a poet, in England, Rome, Tangiers and New York. Burgess won a wide following with the short but bold *Clockwork Orange* (1962). *Earthly Powers* (1980) is an erudite and witty panorama spanning much of the 20c; it also has one of the most arresting opening sentences of modern fiction ('It was the afternoon of my eighty-first birthday, and I was in bed with my catamite when Ali announced that the archbishop had come to see me').

Burgess is a prolific reviewer for a wide range of newspapers, in particular the *Observer*. He is also much involved with music. He is a composer who has had symphonies performed, and he likes to use musical themes in fiction; one of his novels, *Napoleon Symphony* (1974), is based on the form of Beethoven's 3rd symphony, the *Eroica*.

Burgess and Maclean see *Cambridge spies.

burgh The Scottish spelling of *borough, retaining until 1975 a difference in meaning. It was used of towns which had a degree of self-government, usually conferred by royal charter – hence a 'royal burgh'. Since the reorganization of Scottish *local government in 1975, the word has been mainly of historical significance.

Burghclere (34km/21m SW of Reading) Village noted for Stanley *Spencer's Sandham Memorial Chapel. The murals (1927–32) depict camp and hospital scenes in World War I, culminating in Spencer's favourite theme, a Resurrection, on the east wall. The chapel commemorates Lieutenant Henry Sandham (d. 1919) who had served, like Spencer, in Macedonia.

Lord **Burghley** (William Cecil, 1520–98, kt 1551, baron 1571) Chief minister to Elizabeth I for 40 years, first as her principal secretary of state (1558–72) and then as lord treasurer. Trained as a lawyer, and serving as a member of parliament from 1543, he first made his mark in the administration of Somerset, the protector during the reign of Edward VI. From 1550 he was employed by Elizabeth to look after her personal property, and from the start of her reign he saw himself as her servant in fulfilling a shared commitment – to build up a strong and independent England, which would not be undermined by religious faction (whether Roman Catholic or Puritan) or by foreign interests. He was a great builder, though of his various creations only *Burghley House survives. He was followed as the queen's chief counsellor by his son, Robert *Cecil.

Burghley House (19km/12m NW of Peterborough) The most imposing of late Elizabethan mansions, built 1555–87 by Lord *Burghley, apparently to his own design, and still lived in by his descendants. Its traditional 16C exterior (central gatehouse, large heavily mullioned windows, flanking corner towers) conceals spectacular baroque interiors commissioned a century later, mainly from Antonio Verrio. Of his elaborately painted effects the most dramatic is the 'heaven room', in which figures tumble from the ceiling down the walls; in a very successful piece of trompe l'oeil they even seem to step from the walls on to the floor. The park as seen today was landscaped by Capability *Brown. Since 1961 Burghley has been the setting each September for the major autumn *three-day event, the Burghley Horse Trials.

*The **Burial of Sir John Moore*** (1817) The only poem of Charles Wolfe (1791–1823) to have caught and held the public's imagination. The account of the general being laid in the cold ground at *Corunna, under cover of darkness, without even coffin or shroud, in a place that tomorrow will be abandoned to the enemy, combines an undercurrent of patriotic celebration with some brutally down-to-earth details:

> We buried him darkly at dead of night,
> The sods with our bayonets turning.

Edmund **Burke** (1729–97) Irish politician and author, who made his career in London. He was a member of parliament from 1765 to 1794, but his main influence was as a political philosopher. His concern for a just relationship between rulers and the ruled caused him to argue for the rights of the American colonists and of the Irish and the Indians, who were all alike in being governed from a distant Britain. At Westminster he favoured an organized party system of government and opposition, in place of arbitrary *Tory and Whig factions depending for power on the royal whim (he was himself a Whig).

His most influential work was *Reflections of the Revolution in France* (1790), in which he rejected the revolutionaries' over-zealous destruction of much that was good in society in the name of inhuman abstractions. His treatise, a classic statement of pragmatic conservatism, provoked many replies – in particular *The Rights of Man* from Thomas *Paine.

Burke and Hare Two Irishmen whose enterprising response to the shortage of bodies for dissection by medical students in the early 19C led to the passing of the Anatomy Act of 1832, which regulated the supply of corpses. In 1827 Burke was living in a lodging house run by Hare in Edinburgh, a city noted for its surgery. The two men began digging up corpses in cemeteries to supply the needs of the medical schools. They soon found it easier to suffocate travellers in the lodging house, and they had killed about 15 before they were arrested. Hare escaped by turning king's evidence; Burke was hanged in 1829. To 'burke' rapidly became a word meaning to suffocate, and by extension to hush up.

Burke's Peerage and *Burke's Landed Gentry* Two of the best-known works of British genealogy. John Burke (1787–1848) published his first small pocket-sized edition of *Burke's Peerage* in 1826. With the 19C passion for anything medieval, this highly romanticized account of the origin of the country's oldest families was rapidly expanded into a fat quarto volume published annually

The secret work of 'resurrectionists' such as Burke and Hare: etching by Phiz, c.1850.

(with the regular addition of their lordships' latest offspring). Burke's son and grandsons ran the business until 1926. Of several other similar titles, the *Landed Gentry* was the most successful. Every glamorous anecdote about a family's origins was included in these works, enabling Oscar Wilde to describe *Burke's Peerage* as 'the best thing the English have done in fiction'. In the mid-20C both the *Peerage* and *Landed Gentry* were re-edited on a more scholarly basis, becoming reliable works of reference. But *Burke's Peerage, Baronetage and Knightage* (to give it its full title) has not been published since 1970.

Lord **Burlington** (Richard Boyle, 1694–1753, 3rd earl of Burlington 1703) Architect and chief promoter of the *Palladian style in 18C England. He was determined to base a native tradition on the isolated example of Inigo *Jones and on the ideas of Palladio. He commissioned Colen *Campbell to rebuild *Burlington House in Piccadilly; but his country villa, *Chiswick House, was his own design. Other ventures included the Assembly Rooms in York, a painstaking copy of an Egyptian Hall by Palladio. But Burlington's greatest influence was through the work of his friend and protégé, William *Kent.

Burlington Bertie One of the best-known songs in Vesta *Tilley's repertoire. A later male impersonator, Ella Shields (1880–1952), borrowed the name for a different song, *Burlington Bertie from Bow*.

Burlington House (London W1) Best known now as the home of the *Royal Academy, the house takes its name from the earl of *Burlington who in about 1717 employed Colen *Campbell to remodel it in the Palladian style. That part, considerably altered, is the building at the end of the courtyard. The other three sides were added in 1868–73 in a government scheme to house the various learned societies which now share the premises with the Academy.

Burma see *Myanmar.

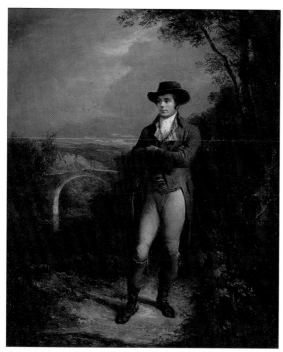

Imaginary portrait of Burns and the old bridge at Alloway: painting by Alexander Nasmyth, 1828.

Burmah Castrol Burmah Oil was founded in 1886 by a Scottish merchant, David Cargill, for the purpose of transporting lamp oil, easily available in Burma, to the markets of India. The company developed India's oil industry as well as Burma's, and with *BP was involved at the start of developments in the Gulf. It is now entirely international (it acquired Castrol in 1966) and has diversified into chemicals and other fields, including the transportation of millions of tons of liquefied natural gas each year from Indonesia to Japan.

Edward **Burne-Jones** (1833–98, bt 1894) Painter who developed the romantic side of the *Pre-Raphaelite movement, creating an exquisite but languid world of wistful maidens, distant descendants of those in Botticelli and chiming perfectly with the new spirit of the *Aesthetic movement. The first influence on him had been Dante Gabriel *Rossetti, and he was a close friend (from their time together as students at Oxford) of William *Morris. He did many designs for Morris's firm (stained glass in particular) and illustrated several books for the *Kelmscott press, the greatest of them being the famous Kelmscott Chaucer of 1896.

Frances Hodgson **Burnett** (Frances Hodgson, 1849–1924, m. Swan Burnett 1872) English author of children's books, remembered in particular for * *Little Lord Fauntleroy* and The * *Secret Garden*. Her husband was American, and she kept houses in both the USA and Britain.

Fanny **Burney** (1752–1840, m. Alexandre d'Arblay 1793) Novelist and author of extensive journals. She was the daughter of the music historian Charles Burney (1726–1814). Her first novel, a witty account of a young girl's entry into London society (*Evelina* 1778) was an immediate success, as was Fanny herself. She became part of the literary circle round Dr *Johnson and had a royal appointment at court. Both these worlds, and that of her French émigré husband, were described in detail in regular letters to her sister, Susan, which were later published as her journals.

John **Burningham** (b. 1936) Author and illustrator of children's books who achieved an immediate success with his first, *Borka, the Adventures of a Goose without Feathers* (1963). Subsequent stories have followed the adventures of Mr Gumpy, and in the mid-1970s he produced a series of 'little books' for children just beginning to read.

Robert **Burns** (1759–96) Scottish poet, the son of a poor farmer in *Alloway. His *Poems, chiefly in the Scottish dialect*, published at his own expense in 1786, were an immediate success and caused him to be lionized in Edinburgh. He there became much involved in collecting and writing Scottish songs for *The Scots Musical Museum* (6 vols, 1787–1803), in which many of his best-known lyrics appeared, including * *Auld Lang Syne* and * *Scots, wha hae*. After a busy love life, he married Jean Armour in 1788 in *Mauchline. The immediacy of his songs and longer poems (such as * *Tam o' Shanter*) and his use of the dialect which he called *Lallans (sufficient to deter many a *Sassenach) have ensured that Burns has remained Scotland's favourite poet. His birthday is celebrated each year as *Burns Night.

Burns Night (Jan. 25) Annual celebration held by Scots everywhere in the world to commemorate the birthday of Robert *Burns. The main dish is the *haggis ('Great Chieftain o' the Puddin-race' in Burns' phrase), which is whenever possible preceded into the room by someone playing the *bagpipes. The evening includes a succession of patriotic and elaborately humorous speeches, the recital of poems by Burns and the singing of * *Auld Lang Syne*.

Burrell Collection More than 8000 items bequeathed to Glasgow by the shipping magnate William Burrell (1861–1958). Covering a very wide range of fine and decorative arts, this extraordinary bequest is now housed in Pollok Park in a new museum designed by Barry Gasson (b. 1935). It opened in 1983.

Burton Clothing group which derives from a menswear shop opened in Chesterfield in 1900 by Montague Burton (1885–1952). Between the wars Montague Burton ('the tailor of taste', based in Leeds) had a large share of the nation's trade in men's bespoke tailoring. The name was changed to Burton in 1969, and the group had a period of rapid growth in the 1980s under the chairmanship of Ralph Halpern – the first of a new breed of highly paid executives, with a glamorous lifestyle much described in the tabloid press. Halpern was removed in 1990 in a boardroom coup, after a dramatic collapse in Burton's fortunes; even so he departed with a £2 million handshake and a pension of £456,000.

Richard **Burton** (1821–90, KCMG 1886) Author and explorer, whose brilliance at languages enabled him to mingle as a native in the bazaars of India and to make the pilgrimage to Mecca in 1853 disguised as a Muslim. He was a companion of *Speke during part of the search for the source of the Nile, though he later disputed Speke's claim to have found it. His chief literary monument is his unexpurgated translation of The * *Arabian Nights* (16 vols, 1885–8). His widow, Isabel, destroyed all his private papers and built him a marble tent as a memorial in Mortlake.

Richard **Burton** (stage name of Richard Jenkins, 1925–84) Welsh actor, son of a miner, who first appeared on stage at the Royal Court Theatre, Liverpool, in 1943. By the mid-1950s, when he was at the Old Vic, he was widely seen as Britain's leading young Shakespearean actor. His later career was largely in films (most notably *Look Back* *in Anger* 1959, *The Spy Who Came in from the Cold* 1965, *Who's Afraid of Virginia Woolf?* 1966). On radio his rich Welsh voice was perfectly suited to **Under Milk Wood*. After his marriage to Elizabeth *Taylor in 1964 (divorce 1974, remarriage 1975, redivorce 1976) his private life came to receive more attention than his acting.

Bury St Edmunds (29,000 in 1981) Town in Suffolk which was originally a Saxon settlement. It acquired its name after the bones of St Edmund the Martyr were transferred to a monastery here in about 910. He had been the last king of *East Anglia, killed by the Danes in 870 for refusing to deny Christianity. His shrine brought prosperity as a major place of pilgrimage in the Middle Ages.

The abbey is now a ruin except for two gateways, one of them set in a superb Norman tower. But two 15c parish churches survive on its periphery. St Mary's has a notable hammer-beam roof with carved angels; St James' has been since 1914 the cathedral of the diocese of St Edmundsbury and Ispwich, and is being gradually enlarged. Moyses Hall, a stone-vaulted domestic building of the 12c, was at successive periods a tavern, a workhouse and a prison before it became in 1899 a museum of Bury's extensive local history.

Much of 17–18c Bury survives, with striking buildings such as Cupola House and Angel Corner. The Unitarian chapel dates from 1711; the town hall (1774–80) is by Robert Adam; and the Theatre Royal (1819, by William Wilkins, with its interior unchanged) remains in use as a working theatre.

Matt **Busby** (b. 1909, kt 1968) The most consistently successful of British football managers. His own playing career was with Manchester City (1929–36, FA Cup win in 1934) and Liverpool (1936–9). In 1945 he became manager of *Manchester United, seeing them through a series of triumphs (5 League victories and 2 FA Cups) and one major disaster (the Munich air crash of 1958). The club won the European Cup in 1968, the year before his retirement.

Kate **Bush** (b. 1958) Pop singer and songwriter of glamorously pre-Raphaelite appearance whose first record, *Wuthering Heights* (1978), was her own reduction of the novel to three minutes; it reached the top of the UK chart before her 20th birthday. Later successes have included *Man with the Child in his Eyes* (1978), *Wow* (her catch phrase, 1979) and *Running up that Hill* (1985). Among her albums, *Never For Ever* (1980), *Hounds of Love* (1985) and *The Whole Story* (1986) all topped the charts, and *The Sensual World* (1989) reached no. 2.

Bush House (London WC2) Headquarters since 1940 of BBC radio's *World Service. The building is named after an American entrepreneur, Irving T. Bush, who opened it in 1935 as a luxurious trade centre but failed to make his vision pay.

Business Expansion Scheme (BES) Introduced in the Finance Act of 1983 to encourage investment in small companies, and discontinued from the end of 1993. The scheme allowed people to invest money tax-free (up to a given annual limit and on condition the investment was for at least five years) in British companies not quoted on the Stock Exchange.

Darcey **Bussell** (b. 1969) Dancer who achieved prominence with the *Royal Ballet at a young age; she was only 20 when she was appointed to the highest rank in the company (that of principal). She was selected in 1989 by Kenneth MacMillan to create the leading role in *The Prince of the Pagodas*, and she followed this two years

later with another major role for MacMillan – Masha in *Winter Dreams*. Unusually tall for a dancer, she found in 1992 a well-matched partner in the powerful Hungarian dancer Zoltán Solymosi.

but and ben In Scotland the traditional two-roomed cottage, consisting of an outer kitchen and living room (the but) and an inner room for sleeping (the ben).

Butcher Cumberland see duke of *Cumberland.

Bute Island off the west coast of Scotland, of importance from the Middle Ages because of the royal burgh of Rothesay and its castle, now a well-restored ruin. Until 1975 Bute was also a *county incorporating Arran and other islands in the Firth of Clyde; all are now part of the Strathclyde region.

Bute Park see *Cardiff.

Rab **Butler** (Richard Austen Butler, 1902–82, baron 1965) Tory politician and MP for Saffron Walden (1929–65), who held most of the great offices of state (chancellor of the exchequer 1951–5, home secretary 1957–62, foreign secretary 1963–4) and who was widely expected to succeed *Macmillan as prime minister in 1964. He failed to do so largely because of Macmillan's determined opposition.

Seen as an essentially reasonable man, a believer in consensus politics, his name formed part of *Butskellism. He was the wartime minister of *education (1941–5), and his most lasting piece of legislation – still often referred to as the Butler Act – was the Education Act of 1944. On retirement from politics he became master of Trinity College, Cambridge.

Samuel **Butler** (1835–1902) Author much influenced by a suffocating Anglican family background. He escaped from the threat of holy orders by taking up sheep farming in New Zealand, but an ambivalent fascination with religion and later with theories of evolution was to be a central theme of his books from **Erewhon* in 1872 to the autobiographical novel *The Way of all Flesh* (published in 1903, after his death), which recounts his escape as a young man from his family.

Butler Act see Rab *Butler.

Butlin's Britain's first and best-known chain of holiday camps. They were established by William Butlin (1899–1980), a successful showman in fairs and amusement parks. He opened his first Butlin's at Skegness in 1936. There was a great deal of jollity (a cry of 'Wakey, Wakey' over the tannoy to begin the day, and the famous redcoats to organize the entertainment). In the years after World War II a Butlin's holiday was an annual event for many families; holidays with pay had recently been introduced, and an early slogan was 'a week's holiday for a week's wage'.

Butskellism Consensus politics characteristic of the 1960s and 1970s, when there was a measure of agreement between the left wing of the Conservative party and the right wing of the Labour party. The word combines two representative middle-of-the-road figures, Rab *Butler and Hugh *Gaitskell.

Clara **Butt** (1873–1936, DBE 1920) Contralto who made her career in oratorio and on the concert platform rather than in the opera house, where her only appearance was as Orpheus (in Gluck's *Orfeo*) for Beecham at Covent Garden in 1920.

William **Butterfield** (1814–1900) Architect of almost 100 churches, in whose work the twin themes of *Anglo-Catholicism and the *Gothic Revival came powerfully together, harking back to an earlier more theatrical tradition of Christianity. Butterfield was drawn to the polychrome Gothic of Italy, and his churches – most notably All Saints, Margaret Street, in London – are known for their almost garish patterns of coloured bricks and tiles. His secular work, such as Keble College in Oxford or Rugby School, is in the same style.

butterscotch see *sweets.

butty (from buttered) An old word in northern England for a slice of bread and butter, used more recently to mean a *sandwich.

Buxton (21,000 in 1981) Spa town in Derbyshire, in the centre of the Peak District. As at Bath, its thermal springs brought the Romans here and made it fashionable again in the 18C; indeed its renewed appeal was much increased after John *Carr had built the Palladian Crescent (1779–84) in direct imitation of those in Bath. The town is particularly known for its music festival, held in late July and early August since 1979. It centres on two operas, linked by some theme and chosen for their relative rarity, which are given in the town's Edwardian opera house (1903, by Frank Matcham).

buzz-bomb see *V1.

A.S. **Byatt** (Antonia Susan Drabble, m. Ian Byatt 1959) Novelist whose early heroines suffer the tension of strong family and literary rivalries (Margaret *Drabble is her sister), but who later found her own idiom in a rich embroidery of fiction and literary allusion – her other profession is as a lecturer in English. This blend was seen first in two linked chronicle novels of the mid-20C (*The Virgin in the Garden* 1978, *Still Life* 1985). But it found its most effective expression in *Possession* (1990, Booker prize and Irish Times/Aer Lingus fiction prize), which bridges the 19 and 20C to combine the pleasures of academic detective work, literary pastiche and rediscovered romance.

by-election The election of an *MP at any time other than a *general election, caused by the death or resignation (see *Chiltern Hundreds) of the sitting MP.

Byerley Turk see *thoroughbred.

by-laws Regulations imposed by a local authority and applying only within its own area. Certain categories of legislation are delegated in this way, but a by-law comes into effect only when it has been approved by central government.

Admiral **Byng** (John Byng, 1704–57) A sailor famous only for his unfortunate end. He was shot on board HMS *Monarque* in Portsmouth harbour, after being convicted by a court martial of neglect of duty in failing to relieve the garrison on *Minorca from the hostile attentions of a French fleet. His execution prompted Voltaire's comment in *Candide* (1759) that in England it is thought wise to kill an admiral from time to time *pour encourager les autres* (to encourage the others).

William **Byrd** (1543–1623) The leading English composer of the generation after *Tallis, who was his teacher and his colleague in the Tudor musical establishment. Although a devout Roman Catholic, Byrd retained the favour of the court throughout his life and wrote for the Anglican church. He also wrote much secular music – songs and madrigals as well as pieces for strings (the viol consort) and for keyboard (the virginals). But the peak of his achievement was his settings of the Latin liturgy, published as *Cantiones Sacrae* (1575–91) and *Gradualia* (1605–7).

Lord **Byron** (George Gordon Byron, 1788–1824, 6th baron 1798) Poet and outstanding figure of the *Romantic movement, whose life and work reflect in heightened form the turmoil of excitement and despair in the early decades of the 19C. At the age of ten he inherited the family title and a romantic ruin of a house, Newstead Abbey near Nottingham. He was educated at Harrow and Cambridge, where he made a life-long friend, John Cam Hobhouse. Together they set off in 1809 on a tour through Spain and Greece to Turkey. Byron's experiences on these travels provided the material for the poem which in 1812 brought him instant fame, *Childe Harold's Pilgrimage*.

He became by far the most alluring young man in London: a moody bestselling poet, good-looking but with one pitiable physical defect (usually described as a club foot, but its nature is medically uncertain); a wildly unconventional peer with radical views (his maiden speech in the House of Lords in 1812 was a passionate plea on behalf of the Nottingham weavers); and a bisexual lover notorious for numerous adventures. He began an affair with Lady Caroline Lamb, who famously described him as 'mad, bad, and dangerous to know'. Soon there were rumours, probably correct, that he was having an incestuous relationship with his half-sister, Augusta Leigh.

Marriage in 1815 to the 22-year-old Anne Milbanke may have seemed something of an escape, but only a year later, after the birth of a daughter, she insisted on a separation, hinting that there were dark unspecified reasons. Byron's pleasant notoriety was curdling into scandal, and he went abroad in April 1816. He never returned to Britain. He lived mainly in Italy, starting to write *Don Juan* in Venice in 1818 and witnessing the cremation of *Shelley on the beach at Viareggio in 1822. In July 1823 he sailed for Greece to join the battle for independence from the Turks. At Missolonghi, in April 1824, he died of a fever. Newstead Abbey, 18km/11m north of Nottingham, is kept as a museum.

C

cabal Word deriving from the Hebrew *qabbalah* (the oral tradition within Judaism), which was much used in the mid-17c as a name for any secret clique. It then happened that a group of five ministers of Charles II had names which could be arranged in a sequence to spell 'cabal' (Clifford, Arlington, Buckingham, Ashley, Lauderdale). Relatively little was made of the coincidence at the time, and it has endured largely as a memorable nugget of information in school history books.

Cabinet The committee of ministers, headed by the *prime minister, which is the executive authority of the nation. The name derives from the 17c, when monarchs wished to rule through a smaller body than the *privy council. The chosen group of ministers met with the king in a more intimate room (a cabinet) and so became known as the cabinet council. Gradually this select body grew in power – particularly after the Hanoverian kings gave up attending its meetings, a change which in the long term increased cabinet independence. The size and membership of the cabinet is at the discretion of the prime minister. In recent years cabinets have numbered about 22 people and have normally met in 10 *Downing Street on Thursday mornings (for members since 1983 see next page).

Since 1916 there has been a cabinet secretary, also known as secretary of the cabinet – the most powerful *civil service appointment in Britain. The cabinet secretary is head of the *Cabinet Office and of the home civil service.

Cabinet Office (London SW1) Government department fulfilling several separate functions. It is the secretariat for members of the *cabinet in relation to cabinet business. It has been responsible for managing the *civil service since 1968, serving the prime minister in his or her role as minister for the civil service. And since 1992 it has incorporated the new Office of *Public Service and Science.

cabinet pudding A steamed suet pudding with currants. If there is a political origin for the name, it is unknown; a cookery book of 1822 calls it 'Cabinet Pudding or Chancellor's Pudding'.

Cabinet War Rooms (London SW1) Bomb-proof nerve centre for the conduct of World War II, built below the buildings of *Whitehall in 1938–9. There are about 70 rooms, of which the most important were opened to the public in 1984, furnished as when in use. They include the room where the war cabinet would meet during an air raid, the map room where information from every front was processed and coordinated, and the tiny bedroom in which Churchill was occasionally persuaded to sleep.

Cable and Wireless International communications company which has developed from Anglo-Mediterranean Telegraph, formed in 1868 to lay a cable under the sea from Malta to Alexandria. A global network of cable was in place by the time *Marconi's wireless telegraphy posed a major threat in the 1920s. The two enterprises merged in 1929 as Cable and Wireless. A large part of the company was nationalized in 1946; Marconi was bought at the time by English Electric and thus eventually became part of *GEC. Cable and Wireless was privatized in 1981, and *Mercury has been a subsidiary since 1984.

John **Cabot** (*c*.1450–*c*.1499) Italian explorer who in 1497 sailed west with a crew of 18 in the *Matthew* on behalf of the English king, Henry VII. Like Columbus (who had crossed the Atlantic five years earlier for Spain), he was hoping to establish a new trade route to the orient; and he believed the place where he landed (probably Newfoundland) to be the coast of north China. On his return to England he received a reward of £10 from Henry, and an annual pension of £20; his landfall later proved useful in Britain's claim to Canada. Cabot sailed again with a larger expedition in 1498, and contemporary accounts differ as to whether he died at sea or returned to England. His son Sebastian (*c*.1476–1557) followed a similar career, serving at different times both Spain and England.

Cadbury Schweppes Formed in 1969 by the merger of two very long-established British firms, of which Schweppes was the older. Jacob Schweppe was a German jeweller, living in Geneva, who in the 1780s established a business making aerated water, or soda water. In 1792 he moved to London, then sold most of his interest and returned to Geneva in 1799. The company launched its famous *tonic water in the 1870s and developed fizzy lemonade in the 1880s.

The firm of Cadbury developed from a grocery shop opened by a Quaker, John Cadbury (1801–89), in 1824 in Birmingham. His most popular items were cocoa and drinking *chocolate, ground by himself in a pestle and mortar; from this developed the huge chocolate enterprise which has continued to be managed by his descendants in an unbroken line. The industrial settlement of *Bournville was begun in 1879, and the company's two best-known products, Dairy Milk and Milk Tray, were launched in 1905 and 1915 respectively. In 1919 Cadbury absorbed Fry, an even older family firm of chocolate makers, also Quakers, which had been established by Joseph Fry in Bristol in the mid-18c.

Jack **Cade** (d. 1450) Leader of a Kentish rebellion in 1450 against high taxes and misgovernment under Henry VI. The rebels entered London and killed the king's treasurer

Members of the Cabinet since 1983

All cabinet posts are listed except two occasional offices: Paymaster General (Kenneth Clarke 1985-7) and Minister without Portf[...]

	1983	1984	1985	1986	1987	1988
Prime Minister	Thatcher	Thatcher	Thatcher	Thatcher	Thatcher	Thatcher
Chancellor of the Exchequer	Howe/Lawson	Lawson	Lawson	Lawson	Lawson	Lawson
Foreign Secretary	Pym/Howe	Howe	Howe	Howe	Howe	Howe
Home Secretary	Whitelaw/Brittan	Brittan	Brittan/Hurd	Hurd	Hurd	Hurd
Lord Chancellor	Hailsham	Hailsham	Hailsham	Hailsham	Hailsham/Havers/Mackay	Mackay
Agriculture	Walker/Jopling	Jopling	Jopling	Jopling	Jopling/MacGregor	MacGregor
Defence	Nott/Heseltine	Heseltine	Heseltine	Heseltine/Younger	Younger	Younger
Education	Joseph	Joseph	Joseph	Joseph/Baker	Baker	Baker
Employment	Tebbit/King	King	King/Young	Young	Young/Fowler	Fowler
Energy	Lawson/Walker	Walker	Walker	Walker	Walker/Parkinson	Parkinson
Environment	Heseltine/King/Jenkin	Jenkin	Jenkin/Ridley	Ridley	Ridley	Ridley
National Heritage						
Social Services	Fowler	Fowler	Fowler	Fowler	Fowler/Moore	
Health						Clarke
Social Security						Moore
Trade and Industry	Jenkin/Parkinson/Tebbit	Tebbit	Tebbit	Tebbit/Channon	Channon/Young	Young
Transport	King/Ridley	Ridley	Ridley	Ridley/Moore	Moore/Channon	Channon
Northern Ireland	Prior	Prior/Hurd	Hurd/King	King	King	King
Scotland	Younger	Younger	Younger	Younger/Rifkind	Rifkind	Rifkind
Wales	Edwards	Edwards	Edwards	Edwards	Edwards/Walker	Walker
Leader of the House of Commons	Biffen	Biffen	Biffen	Biffen	Biffen/Wakeham	Wakeham
Leader of the House of Lords	Whitelaw	Whitelaw	Whitelaw	Whitelaw	Whitelaw	Whitelaw/B[...]
Chief Secretary to the Treasury	Brittan/Rees	Rees	Rees/MacGregor	MacGregor	MacGregor/Major	Major
Chancellor of the Duchy of Lancaster	Parkinson/Cockfield	Cockfield/Gowrie	Gowrie/Tebbit	Tebbit	Tebbit/Clarke	Clarke/New[...]

before dispersing on promise of a pardon, but Cade continued his resistance and was himself killed. The rebels sympathized with the Yorkist branch of the royal family, and the civil disorder was part of the broader unrest in the country leading to the *Wars of the Roses.

Cader Idris (Welsh for 'chair of Idris') Mountain range near the west coast of Wales, in Gwynedd, rising gradually to the peak known as Pen-y-Gader (892m/2927ft). Idris is a legendary Welsh hero, whose stories feature a magic chair; anyone who sleeps in it wakes up as either a bard or a lunatic.

Cadiz see *Armada.

Cadwallader see *Geoffrey of Monmouth.

Caedmon (7c) Traditionally the first English poet, but nothing is known about him beyond what *Bede records in a chapter of his history. He says that Caedmon was an illiterate herdsman who one night saw a vision in which he was given the gift of poetry and was told to use it to praise God. He entered the monastery at Whitby and there he made 'melodious song' from the Bible stories, 'like one of the clean animals chewing the cud'.

Caerlaverock Castle (14km/9m S of Dumfries) Unusual triangular castle, with the entrance between twin towers at its apex. It is now an exceptionally beautiful red sandstone ruin in the waters of its moat. Within the 13c castle walls there was built, in about 1634, a stone mansion with large rooms and a Renaissance-style façade. Both it and the castle were abandoned after being largely destroyed by *Covenanters in 1640.

Caerleon (3km/2m N of Newport) Town in Gwent, on the river Usk. It was the site of the camp of the Roman 2nd Legion, established in the late 1st century AD. Their amphitheatre has been excavated, as have sections of the barracks. Finds from the area are on view in the Legionary Museum. The Romans called the place Isca (from the Usk), and its present name is a corruption of *castra legionis*, the camp of the legion. It also has a place in Arthurian legend, as one of the candidates for *Camelot.

Caernarfon (10,000 in 1981) Administrative centre of Gwynedd and a place of importance since Roman times, when the fort of *Segontium was established here. A wooden Norman keep followed in the 11c, and the motte (or mound) on which it stood is now within the castle built for Edward I in 1283–92. The castle walls, occupying a strategic site between the river Seiont and the Menai Strait, borrowed their theme of polygonal towers with horizontal stripes from distinguished predecessors – the city walls of Constantinople. Today the castle is little more than a magnificent shell. But it was here, in 1284, that the first *prince of Wales was born; and here, in 1969, that the present prince of Wales was invested.

(Lord Young 1984-5). Each minister has his or her own alphabetical entry.

1989	1990 (to 28 Nov.)	1990 (from 28 Nov.)	1991	1992	1993
Thatcher	Thatcher	Major	Major	Major	Major
Lawson/Major	Major	Lamont	Lamont	Lamont	Lamont
Howe/Major/Hurd	Hurd	Hurd	Hurd	Hurd	Hurd
Hurd/Waddington	Waddington	Baker	Baker	Baker/Clarke	Clarke
Mackay	Mackay	Mackay	Mackay	Mackay	Mackay
MacGregor/Gummer	Gummer	Gummer	Gummer	Gummer	Gummer
Younger/King	King	King	King	King/Rifkind	Rifkind
Baker/MacGregor	MacGregor/Clarke	Clarke	Clarke	Clarke/J.Patten	J.Patten
Fowler	Fowler/Howard	Howard	Howard	Howard/Shephard	Shephard
Parkinson/Wakeham	Wakeham	Wakeham	Wakeham	Wakeham	
Ridley/C.Patten	C.Patten	Heseltine	Heseltine	Heseltine/Howard	Howard
				Mellor/Brooke	Brooke
Clarke	Clarke/Waldegrave	Waldegrave	Waldegrave	Waldegrave/Bottomley	Bottomley
Moore/Newton	Newton	Newton	Newton	Newton/Lilley	Lilley
Young/Ridley	Ridley/Lilley	Lilley	Lilley	Lilley/Heseltine	Heseltine
Channon/Parkinson	Parkinson	Rifkind	Rifkind	Rifkind/MacGregor	MacGregor
King/Brooke	Brooke	Brooke	Brooke	Brooke/Mayhew	Mayhew
Rifkind	Rifkind	Lang	Lang	Lang	Lang
Walker	Walker/Hunt	Hunt	Hunt	Hunt	Hunt
Wakeham/Howe	Howe/MacGregor	MacGregor	MacGregor	MacGregor/Newton	Newton
Belstead	Belstead	Waddington	Waddington	Waddington/Wakeham	Wakeham
Major/Lamont	Lamont	Mellor	Mellor	Mellor/Portillo	Portillo
Newton/Baker	Baker	C.Patten	C.Patten	C.Patten/Waldegrave	Waldegrave

Caernarvonshire Former *county in Wales, since 1974 part of Gwynedd.

Caerphilly (43,000 in 1981) Town in Mid Glamorgan which dates back to a Roman fort of the 1st century AD. The ruined castle, begun in 1268 by Gilbert de Clare, is the largest in the country after Windsor. It is also one of the earliest examples in Britain of a concentric castle (copied from those seen by Crusaders in the Holy Land), in which a stronger ring of inner walls confronts any attacker who has breached the outer defences. Yet another distinction of this castle was the brilliance of its engineering works, the protective lake being formed by a great dam of some 365m/400yd which holds back the Nant-y-Gledyr stream. The southeast tower is famous for a tilt sufficient to rival Pisa, thought to be the result of a failed attempt by the Parliamentarians to blow it up in about 1648.

Caerphilly The best known of the Welsh cheeses, mild-flavoured and almost white. Though named from one town in Mid Glamorgan, it was widely made during the 19c throughout south Wales and is still produced on many farms today.

Julius Caesar (100–44 BC) Roman general and dictator (from 49 BC), and the first invader of Britain whose name is known to history. He spent the years 58–50 subduing Gaul (roughly present France and Belgium) and his two invasions of Britain, in 55 and 54 BC, were offshoots of that campaign. They were both raids, in which he came and saw but in no sense conquered. (There is an inaccurate but widely held belief that his slogan *veni, vidi, vici* applied to Britain.) His invasion brought English tribes within the sphere of influence of Roman Gaul, but it was almost another century before the *Romans returned to conquer Britain.

Café Royal (London W1) Restaurant established in 1865, which became a fashionable meeting place for writers and artists. Rebuilt with the rest of *Regent Street in the 1920s, the present Grill Room retains the style and atmosphere of the original Café Royal.

Michael **Caine** (stage name of Maurice Micklewhite, b. 1933) Film actor, whose offhand *cockney manner (he was born in London's Old Kent Road) first made him a star in such films as *The Ipcress File* (1965) and *Alfie* (1966). Subsequent successes have included *Sleuth* (1973) and *Educating Rita* (1982, and he won an Oscar in 1986 for *Hannah and her Sisters*. He has become associated with the catch phrase 'not many people know that' (also used as 'not a lot of people know that').

Cairngorms The chief mountain range in the British Isles, with several peaks over 1220m/4000ft (the highest is Ben Macdhui, 1309m/4296ft). It lies between Aviemore in the northwest (the chief ski resort for the area) and Braemar in the southeast, where the range merges with the less dramatic *Grampians. A variety of quartz found here (usually yellow, brown or grey and known simply as cairngorm) is used as a gemstone.

Cairnpapple Hill (32km/20m W of Edinburgh) Windswept open hill, with views for miles around, which is one of Scotland's most important archaeological sites. It was a place of ritual importance for some 2500 years. Here Stone Age man erected a ring of standing stones for religious purposes (contemporary with Stonehenge and Avebury, approximately 2500 to 1600 BC). In the early Bronze Age these stones were either removed or incorporated within a great burial cairn built on the hill, which remained in use until the early Iron Age or approximately the 1st century AD.

cairn terrier see *terriers.

Caithness Until 1975 a *county forming the extreme northeast tip of Scotland, now part of the Highland region.

Calais The nearest town to England on the mainland of Europe, and for several centuries the token of England's claim to the French crown. In 1347, during the *Hundred Years' War, Calais was captured by Edward III after a long siege (the occasion of the heroic offer by the six burghers of Calais to give up their own lives in return for the safety of the town). It remained for two centuries an English enclave in France, surrounded by its *pale. The final loss of it to the French in 1558 caused the English queen, Mary I, to declare: 'When I am dead and opened, you shall find "Calais" lying in my heart.'

Calcutta The largest city in India, established in the 1690s by merchants of the *East India Company on one of the mouths of the Ganges (a village in the area, Kalikata, gave the town its name). In 1696 they built Fort William, the scene in 1756 of the *Black Hole of Calcutta. The expedition by *Clive to recapture the town in 1757 turned out to be the first step in Britain's military and political domination of India. Calcutta itself grew rapidly in size and importance. In 1773 it became the capital of British India, retaining that position until 1912 when the seat of government was transferred to *Delhi.

Calcutta Cup Trophy played for annually between the *rugby union teams of Scotland and England. It has an unusual and romantic origin. Some old boys of Rugby school formed a club to play football in Calcutta in the 1870s. Closing it down for lack of support a few years later, they spent their remaining funds on an exotic Indian tankard with three snake handles and an elephant on the lid (made, it is said, from the actual silver rupees in the club's kitty). In 1878 they presented this cup for a contest between Scotland and England.

Calcutt Review see *privacy.

Caledonia The Roman name for the region of north Britain which remained outside their control, inhabited by a tribe called the Caledones. It corresponded roughly to modern *Scotland for which it has become a grander synonym, as in the many Caledonian societies around the world.

Caledonian Canal Waterway which joined the east and west coasts of Scotland by linking the lakes in the *Great Glen. Surveyed by James Watt from 1773, it was built by *Telford from 1803 with a total of 29 locks; it opened in 1822. Originally of great commercial benefit to Scotland, it is now used mainly by pleasure craft.

Caledonian Club (Edinburgh) A *club in Scotland's capital, formed by the merging of several earlier establishments – the first of which dates back to 1825.

calendar Two important historical changes have affected the calendar in Britain. The first concerned the time of the new year. In the early Middle Ages the year began on Christmas Day, but in the 12c the English Church began to calculate the new year from *Lady Day (March 25). This meant that January, February and most of March fell within the same calendar year as the preceding December; the day after 31 December 1220 was therefore 1 January 1220. The potential for confusion is lessened in modern works of history by writing such a year 1220/1 for its first three months (e.g. 1 Jan. 1220/1). It was not until 1600 in Scotland and 1752 in the rest of Britain that the official start of the new year was established as January 1.

The other great change was from the Julian calendar (introduced by Julius Caesar in 46 BC) to the Gregorian (brought in by Pope Gregory XIII in 1582). The Julian calendar was inaccurate by about 18 hours in a century; the Gregorian rectifies this by having a leap year only in those centennial years which are divisible by 400 (1900 was not a leap year, 2000 will be). All Roman Catholic countries made this change in the 16c. Great Britain, suspicious of anything papist, delayed till 1752. By then the error had accumulated to 11 days. To remedy this, September 3 in that year was renamed September 14 (causing much indignation among those who felt they had been robbed of 11 days of life).

Dates before 1752 are now described as New Style (NS) if they have been translated into the Gregorian calendar (to coincide with events abroad, or for anniversaries), or Old Style (OS) if they are left in the Julian calendar.

Caliban see The *Tempest.

Calke Abbey (14km/9m S of Derby) A house little known until the 1980s, when it was acquired by the National Trust and received wide publicity as a place where time had stood still. It had been owned since the 17c by the Harpur-Crewes, a reclusive family reluctant to throw anything away. Their jumble of accumulated objects, from carriages to natural history collections, included even a superb state bed, delivered to the house in 1734 and in pristine condition because it had not been unpacked. The house, half concealed in a romantic park, dates mainly from 1701–4.

James **Callaghan** (b. 1912, baron 1987) Labour politician, MP for Cardiff constituencies (1945–87) and prime minister 1976–9. His first career was as a tax officer in the Inland Revenue. He entered the cabinet as chancellor of the exchequer (1964–7) at the start of Harold Wilson's first administration, and in 1967 he had to advise the prime minister to devalue sterling (see the *pound in your pocket). Callaghan then became home secretary (1967–70). At the start of the next Labour administration he was foreign secretary (1974–6) and on Wilson's surprise resignation, in 1976, the party's MPs elected Callaghan as their leader; he therefore automatically succeeded Wilson as prime minister. His term in office was dominated by industrial unrest, culminating in the *winter of discontent.

On 28 March 1979 the government was narrowly defeated (311 votes to 310) on an opposition motion of no confidence. It was the first occasion since 1924 when a vote in the House of Commons had precipitated a general election, though one was due in any case within the next six months. Labour lost the election and in October 1980 Callaghan resigned as party leader, being followed by Michael *Foot.

called to the Bar see the *Bar.

Calton Hill A landmark in Edinburgh, 108m/355ft high, to the east of the New Town. It was used from the early 19C as a hill of monuments. The National Monument, which looks like the ruins of a Greek temple, is all that was built of a full-scale replica of the Parthenon in Athens (begun in 1822 as a memorial to the Scottish dead in the Napoleonic Wars). The Nelson Monument was erected in 1806–16, some 30 years before *Nelson's Column in Trafalgar Square.

Cambria Latin name for *Wales, coined in the Middle Ages and based on the Welsh name for the country, Cymru.

Cambrian see *geological periods.

Cambridge (90,000 in 1981) City on the river Cam; administrative centre of the county of Cambridgeshire. The town developed round an Anglo-Saxon bridge over the river (the tower of St Bene't's church survives from that period) and William I built a castle on the hill in 1068 (the round Church of the Holy Sepulchre is Cambridge's best Norman monument), but the city's identity and fame is as the home of the second oldest university in Britain.

The effective centre is King's Parade, a street with old houses down one side and the wide expanse of King's College on the other. At its north end are three of Cambridge's best-known buildings: the parish and university church of Great St Mary (15–16C); the Senate House (1722–30 by James Gibbs), in which formal university functions are carried out; and, the jewel of Cambridge's architecture, King's College Chapel. Begun in 1446 by the founder of the college, Henry VI, and complete by 1515, it is a perfect late example of the Perpendicular style, known in particular for its superb fan vaulting and for its stained glass, nearly all of the 16C.

Parallel to King's Parade, on the other side of King's College, are the Backs – a continuous stretch of riverside gardens and lawns linking half a dozen colleges, and the scene of many punting parties in summer. The bridge at the southern end linking two parts of St John's College is known as the Bridge of Sighs (1827–31) because of a similarity to the bridge in Venice which leads to the state prison. The wooden bridge at the north end, the Mathematical Bridge in Queens' College, is traditionally said to have been designed by Newton in such a manner that it stands without nails or pegs. As often, tradition is false. The bridge dates from 1749 (to a design by W. Etheridge), was rebuilt in 1867 and 1904, and has always had iron bolts at its main joints.

The precise beginnings of the university are obscure, but it is known that in 1209 a party of students arrived from *Oxford, where there had been disturbances. At this time students made their own arrangements with individual masters and lived in whatever lodgings they could find. It was not until 1284 that the first residential college, Peterhouse, was founded – following the example of Merton at Oxford. Individual self-governing colleges have remained the basis of the university structure. Fifteen others had been founded by the end of the 16C (most notably King's 1441, St John's 1511, Trinity 1544), but then there was a lull until the 19C, when four more were established – two of them the first colleges for women (Girton 1869, Newnham 1871). Since the 1950s there have been many new foundations, including Churchill in 1960. Nearly all the colleges now take students of both sexes.

The scientific achievements of the *Cavendish laboratory have brought the university great renown, and in the

*Fitzwilliam it has a superb museum and art gallery. It is also known for its *botanic gardens. The University Library, (1930–4, by Giles Gilbert Scott) is one of the six *copyright libraries. The Cambridge University Press has been active as a printer since 1534 and as a publisher since 1584 – enabling it to claim to be the oldest surviving printer and publisher in the world.

Cambridge mafia Term in use in the early 1990s to describe a group of senior Conservatives who were at Cambridge together in the early 1960s and were active in university politics. Five were in John Major's 1992 cabinet – Kenneth Clarke, John Gummer, Michael Howard, Norman Lamont, Peter Lilley – and Norman Fowler was then chairman of the party. Leon Brittan, another of the group, was in the cabinet at a slightly earlier period (1981–6).

Cambridgeshire (670,000 in 1991, administrative centre Cambridge) *County in southeast England, enlarged in 1974 by the inclusion of Huntingdonshire and Peterborough.

Cambridge spies The long-running saga of the Cambridge spies began when two British diplomats, Guy Burgess and Donald Maclean, defected to Moscow in 1951. It was discovered that they had been spies for the KGB. Rumours about the existence of a third and then a fourth man were confirmed when another diplomat defected (Kim Philby, 1963), and when it was revealed in 1979 that a senior establishment figure, Anthony Blunt, Surveyor of the Queen's Pictures, was one of the ring. The four were at Cambridge together in the 1930s (all of them in Trinity) and they shared a conviction, common among intellectuals at the time, that Communism was the only effective alternative to Fascism; two of the four, Burgess and Blunt, were homosexual. Speculation about the possibility of a fifth man has continued unabated.

This tale of treachery brought into temporary disrepute a Cambridge secret society of which Burgess and Blunt were members. Known as the Apostles, and established as long ago as 1820, it consists of a group of friends meeting regularly for discussion; it has included among its members Tennyson, Bertrand Russell and E.M. Forster.

Camden Town Group Group of artists, formed and named by *Sickert in 1911. Their purpose was to exhibit together. Camden Town is an area of north London, then largely working-class, in which Sickert had painted many of his pictures of nudes in drab boarding-house rooms. In the Group's first show he included two such paintings, calling them *Camden Town Murder Series No. 1 and No. 2*, though the link with some recent murders can only have been suggested for the sake of publicity. Other members included Robert Bevan, Harold Gilman, Charles Ginner, Spencer Gore, Augustus John and Wyndham Lewis. They had no strong identity in terms of style, though the majority shared Sickert's preference for everyday subjects. The exhibitions organized by Roger *Fry at this time introduced a strong influence from France. In 1913 they merged with others to form the larger and stylistically even more disparate London Group.

Camelot The legendary location of King *Arthur's court. There have been several candidates for its origin if the legends are based on fact. In the *Morte d'Arthur* it is at Winchester; when Malory was writing, the supposed *Round Table was already in the Great Hall there. Other leading claimants are *Caerleon and Cadbury Castle, an Iron Age hill fort in Somerset.

Julia Margaret **Cameron** (1815–79) The first great portrait photographer. Given a camera by her daughter in 1863, she set up a studio in the chicken house at her Isle of Wight home and converted a coal house into a dark-room. Choosing to concentrate on portraits, she made two crucial decisions; she would take close-ups and she would adjust the daylight for artistic effect rather than maximum intensity. This meant torture for her sitters (her average exposure lasted five minutes, and she scorned the conventional headrest), but the results – known later as her 'Rembrandt effect' – looked like real art and made possible a much greater sense of the sitter's character. She had distinguished friends, so her portraits have an added historical importance. Her sitters included Tennyson, Browning, Trollope, Carlyle, Darwin, Ellen Terry and, perhaps her single most powerful image, the astronomer Sir John Herschel.

Camillagate see *privacy.

Campaign for Nuclear Disarmament see *CND.

Colen **Campbell** (1676–1729) Architect who published *Vitruvius Britannicus* (3 vols, 1715–25), consisting of 100 engraved elevations of British buildings in the classical style. It was he who first interested Lord *Burlington in *Palladianism. The most imposing of his own buildings is *Houghton Hall.

Donald **Campbell** (1921–67) Specialist in speed who followed his father, Malcolm *Campbell, in attaining records on land (648kph/403mph in Australia in 1964) and on water (325kph/202mph on Ullswater in 1955; 418kph/260mph on Coniston Water in 1960; 444kph/276mph in Australia in 1964). He died in 1967 when his jet-powered *Bluebird* somersaulted at more than 480kph/300mph on Coniston Water. The *Bluebird* in which he broke the land speed record in 1964 is now at *Beaulieu.

Malcolm **Campbell** (1885–1948, kt 1931) Racing motor-ist who set many early speed records on land and water. He raised the land speed record from 235kph/146mph in 1924 to 484kph/301mph in 1935; his final water speed record was 228kph/142mph on Coniston Water in 1939. From 1927 all his vehicles, on either surface, were named *Bluebird* – a custom continued by his son, Donald *Campbell.

Naomi **Campbell** (b. 1970) London-born model, of Jamaican descent, who is the only British woman among the handful of so-called 'supermodels' of the early 1990s. She made her name modelling for the designer Azzedine Alaïa in Paris, and in 1988 became the first black cover girl for the French *Vogue*.

Mrs Patrick **Campbell** (Beatrice Tanner, 1865–1940, m. Patrick Campbell 1884) Actress who created the roles of Paula in *The Second Mrs Tanqueray* (1893) and of Eliza in *Pygmalion* (1914) – the play in which she caused a sensation with her delivery of the line 'Not bloody likely!'. Famous as a bewitching, witty and difficult woman (qualities evident in her long correspondence with Bernard Shaw), she is remembered for two characteristically spicy observations: that people's sexual practices are their own business, 'so long as they don't do it in the street and frighten the horses'; and that marriage is 'the deep, deep peace of the double bed after the hurly-burly of the chaise-longue'.

Henry **Campbell-Bannerman** (1836–1908, GCB 1895) Liberal politician, prime minister 1905–8. In 1868 he was elected MP for Stirling Burgh (a seat which he held till his death), and he first made his mark as secretary of state for war (1886, 1892–5) in two of Gladstone's administrations. He became leader of the party in 1899 and was invited by Edward VII to form a government when Balfour resigned in December 1905. In the subsequent general

One of the many Thames views by Canaletto: London Seen Through an Arch of Westminster Bridge *(1746–7, when the bridge was under construction).*

election the Liberals won a large majority, but many of their measures passed in the Commons were defeated by the Conservative majority in the House of *Lords – a continuing provocation which led to the Parliament Act of 1911, in which Campbell-Bannerman's successor, Herbert *Asquith, clipped the wings of the upper chamber.

Edmund **Campion** (1540–81, beatified 1886, canonized 1970) The best known of the Jesuit martyrs in the reign of Elizabeth I. Ordained in the Church of England, he converted to Roman Catholicism and became a Jesuit in Rome during the 1570s. In 1580 he was sent back to England to minister in secret to Roman Catholic congregations. But in 1581 he made a very unsecret gesture of defiance, attending a degree-giving ceremony at Oxford to distribute a pamphlet of his own attacking the Anglican church. Arrested two weeks later he was tortured, accused of conspiring against the queen and executed. His feast day is December 1.

CAMRA (Campaign for Real Ale, St Albans) Pressure group, founded by four friends on holiday in Ireland in 1971 who were alarmed that traditional ale, which continues to ferment in the cask, was being driven out of existence by the big brewers' pasteurized 'keg' beers. They originally called it a Campaign for the Revitalization of Ale, but the name was soon changed because nobody could say 'revitalization' after a few pints. The theme struck a chord, attracting the support of some 30,000 members in local CAMRA branches by the late 1970s. The result was that small traditional brewers were in many cases saved from takeover, and the larger firms found it prudent to revert to the old methods for some of their brands. The annual *Good Beer Guide* and Great British Beer Festival are part of an ongoing campaign.

Camulodunum see *Colchester.

Canada Member of the *Commonwealth and the first of Britain's colonies to have become independent as a *dominion. European settlement of Canada had begun with the arrival of the French explorer, Jacques Cartier, in 1534. From this there developed round the St Lawrence river a large area known as New France, of value primarily to the fur-traders (their main quarry being the Canadian beaver). From the late 17c the British were also active in the fur trade further north, after the foundation of the *Hudson Bay Company. But the main area of friction was on the southern border of Canada, between New France and the British colonies of *America. Tensions here led eventually to war, and the French territories were ceded to Britain after the capture of Quebec by *Wolfe in 1759 and of Montreal in the following year. The change was formalized by the treaty of Paris in 1763.

The forcible inclusion of some 60,000 French Canadians within a British colony led to problems which continue today, in the issue of Quebec and separatism. Meanwhile the British population in the area was being steadily increased, first by loyalists emigrating from the newly independent American colonies and later by waves of immigrants from Britain (in particular from Scotland). The inhabited areas of the country were extended west towards the Pacific, first by the fur-traders and then by the discovery of gold.

In 1864 the separate governments of the more advanced eastern colonies met to discuss a federal union. The result, after parliament in London had passed the British North America Act of 1867, was the establishing of a new country, the Dominion of Canada, consisting of Ontario, Quebec, Nova Scotia and New Brunswick. Other provinces soon joined (Manitoba and the Northwest Territories, 1870; British Columbia, 1871;

Prince Edward Island, 1873; Yukon Territory, 1898; Alberta and Saskatchewan, 1905; and eventually Newfoundland, in 1949). The new country remained a monarchy, recognizing the British king or queen as head of state and setting the pattern for all members of the Commonwealth until India became a republic in 1949.

Canaletto (Antonio Canal, 1697–1768) The leading Venetian painter of city views. His best patrons were English collectors, many of whom had visited Venice on the *Grand Tour. From 1746–55 he spent most of his time in England, supplying the same patrons with local views, particularly of river scenes in London and of their own stately homes. More than 200 of his paintings are in Britain.

canals A spate of canal-building was an important element in the early *Industrial Revolution. (There was nothing new about canals in themselves; the Chinese, who invented the lock, built their first Grand Canal in the 7th century AD.) The first English canal to be successfully completed was James *Brindley's for the duke of Bridgewater, in 1761. Its success sparked off great activity, until canal-building was brought to an end by the *railways in the 1830s. By then there were about 6840km/4250m of navigable waterways in Britain (including several marvels of engineering, such as *Pont Cysyllte). They long continued as a cheaper and slower system of transport, with carthorses ambling along the towpaths harnessed to the special 'narrow boats', thin barges designed so that two could pass. The canals are much used again in modern times for pleasure purposes, and the narrow boats have been adapted very successfully as holiday homes. With water shortages in parts of Britain in recent summers, it has been suggested that the canals might be used as a national water grid.

Canary Wharf (London E14) Prestige project in *Docklands, which underwent a major crisis in 1992 when the Canadian developers (Olympia & York, owned by the Reichmann brothers) filed for insolvency. The buildings were then complete but only half occupied. At the centre is the vast 244m/800ft Canary Wharf tower, visible from miles around (designed by Cesar Pelli). It stands on the site of the old West India Docks, straddling the Isle of Dogs – a long narrow peninsula on the north bank of the Thames, formed by a loop in the river.

'Can I do you now, sir?' see *ITMA.

George **Canning** (1770–1827) Prime minister for five months in 1827, but best known for his achievements as foreign secretary in the previous five years. His mother, widowed a year after his birth, became an actress to support the family – a fact often used against him by aristocratic political opponents. He entered parliament in 1793 as a protégé of William Pitt, but his career in the Tory party was blighted by the intense antipathy between himself and *Castlereagh. When Canning became foreign secretary, in 1807, Castlereagh was secretary of state for war. After a series of military disasters in 1809, beginning with *Corunna, Canning so undermined Castlereagh's position that the two men fought a duel (Canning was wounded in the thigh) and both resigned. For the next decade it was Castlereagh who was at the centre of affairs, but his suicide in 1822 led to Canning following him as foreign secretary.

His originality, in the charged atmosphere of liberation politics after the Napoleonic wars, was to support those demanding liberty – in Greece and above all in South America, where he protected Spain's rebellious colonies from European intervention. 'I called the New World into existence, to redress the balance of the Old', he said in a speech in 1826. After the resignation for reasons of health of the prime minister, Lord Liverpool, Canning was asked to form a government. He had barely done so (his caustic wit had made many enemies who would not serve under him, and his support for Catholic emancipation alienated others) before he himself died.

Cannock Chase Heathland plateau between Stafford and Lichfield. It was once a royal hunting preserve (since the time of the kings of Mercia), and there are still *deer – mainly fallow, but a few red. Originally an oak forest, most of the woodland was cleared in past centuries to provide fuel for the extensive local industries.

Canongate see *Edinburgh.

Canterbury (33,000 in 1981) City in Kent on the river Stour, the seat of the archbishop of Canterbury and centre of the *Anglican church. There was a heavily defended settlement here as early as 200 BC, and under the name of *Durovernum* it was important in the Roman period. It then became the capital of Ethelbert, king of Kent, whose conversion to Christianity by St *Augustine was the origin of Canterbury's ecclesiastical pre-eminence. Some of the foundations of Augustine's abbey, destroyed in the *dissolution of the monasteries, can still be seen. The medieval city walls survive round half the old town.

The cathedral stands on the site of the small church provided by Ethelbert for Augustine, and on the foundations of a Norman cathedral built in the decades after the Conquest. The crypt of this cathedral remains, with some magnificent carved animals on the capitals of the columns, but the present structure above ground was begun after a fire in 1174. It was a most propitious moment for rebuilding. In 1170 the archbishop, Thomas *Becket, had been murdered in the cathedral, and by 1173 he was already canonized; a large number of pilgrims, an important part of the medieval economy, could be expected. The new work was the introduction to England of the *Gothic style. The cathedral went on being altered and enlarged, past the time of Chaucer's pilgrims (see The *Canterbury Tales), until the great central tower, Bell Harry, was finally completed in 1503 (and so named because it contained just a single bell, known as Harry). Becket's shrine was appropriated by Henry VIII in 1538, when 26 cartloads of precious materials were transferred to his treasury. But the windows of the choir, including scenes of Becket's miracles, are the finest collection of 13C stained glass in the country.

Attached to the cathedral are the buildings of the *King's School, an independent boys' school which claims to be the oldest in the country, deriving from a monastic school founded by St Augustine in about 600.

Archbishop of **Canterbury** (Primate of All England) Senior prelate of the *Church of England and accepted by convention as the senior bishop of the international *Anglican Communion, in which role he presides at the *Lambeth Conference. He has a palace in Canterbury but his main residence is Lambeth Palace in London. The first

archbishop of Canterbury was St *Augustine, and when George *Carey was consecrated in 1991 he became the 103rd in direct and unbroken succession. The archbishop signs with his Christian name followed by *Cantuar.*

The **Canterbury Tales** (c.1387–1400) Collection of narrative poems by *Chaucer. Incomplete in the form he intended, it amounts nevertheless to some 17,000 lines of mainly rhyming verse. The prologue explains the scheme. Thirty pilgrims gather in London, at the Tabard in Southwark, to make a pilgrimage to *Canterbury with the host of the inn, Harry Bailly, as their guide. Each pilgrim is to tell two tales on the way out and two on the way back (with a free supper at the Tabard for whoever is judged to have told the best). Of the 120 proposed tales, Chaucer completed only 24 (two of them told by himself as one of the pilgrims).

The leading pilgrims are vividly described in the humorous vignettes of the prologue. They span a wide social range, from the knight and prioress down to unscrupulous pedlars of religion (friar and pardoner) and relatively humble figures (miller and cook). The best known of them all is the irrepressible five-times-married Wife of Bath. Each individual tale reflects the character of the pilgrim telling it, as in the courtly romance of the Knight's Tale or the scurrilous rival farces of the Miller's Tale and the Reeve's Tale, in which a reeve (or bailiff) and a miller respectively are cuckolded in comic and unabashed detail.

Canute (c.995–1035) A Dane who became king of England in 1016, winning the crown after a series of battles against Edmund Ironside, the son of *Ethelred the Unready. He was an extremely powerful figure in northern Europe, being also king of Denmark (from 1018) and of Norway (from 1028), and his firm reign was one of peace and prosperity. The legend of his attempting to turn back the waves of the sea first appeared in a chronicle of 1129, by Henry of Huntingdon. Remembered now as an example of idiotic pride, it was told then at the expense of the courtiers who assured Canute that everything in the world obeyed him; the moral of the tale was the drenching they received when he wickedly invited them to sit with him on the beach while he commanded the waves. Two of his sons briefly succeeded him on the throne, after which the English royal house returned in 1042 with *Edward the Confessor.

'Can you hear me, mother?' Radio's earliest catch phrase, popularized by the comedian Sandy Powell (1900–82). He came across it accidentally in about 1932, when he was doing a sketch supposedly broadcast from the North Pole. After reading one of the lines ('can you hear me, mother?'), he dropped his script; to cover the gap he repeated the same phrase until he had found his place, and from then on audiences wanted to hear it again and again.

capercaillie see *grouse.

Cape Wrath Craggy headland in Scotland, 159m/523ft high, which is the extreme northwest point of the British mainland. The lighthouse was built in 1828.

capital gains tax A tax on profits from an increase in the value of shares or property, introduced in 1965. Subject to exemption or reduction below a certain level, the rate was 30% up to 1988; it was then changed to each taxpayer's highest rate of *income tax, at that time either 25% or 40%. A person's house (or principal residence if more than one is owned) is exempt, and in recent decades this has been the main area of capital gain for many in the UK. Any capital gain from a *PEP is also exempt.

Archbishops of Canterbury since 1928

1928	Cosmo Gordon Lang
1942	William Temple
1945	Geoffrey Fisher
1961	Michael Ramsey
1974	Donald Coggan
1980	Robert Runcie
1991	George Carey

The execution reserved for aristocrats: the beheading on Tower Hill in 1554 of a rebel leader, Sir Thomas Wyatt.

capital punishment Like much else in Britain, execution has had class distinctions. Aristocrats were beheaded, usually with an axe but for women sometimes with a sword; the last to be so executed was Lord Lovat in 1747. The rest were hanged, which until the early 19C meant strangling to death on the end of a rope (a drop from the scaffold was later introduced, causing the neck to break). Traitors suffered the further horror of being hanged, drawn and quartered; they were taken down from the gallows while still alive, and were castrated and disembowelled (tradition maintains that at this point Thomas Harrison, one of the regicides of Charles I, rose and assaulted the executioner) before being beheaded and having the torso divided into four quarters, each attached to one limb. Scotland differed from the rest of the country in using, in the 16–17C, an early form of guillotine known as the Maiden.

The best-known place of execution in Britain from the late Middle Ages to the 18C was *Tyburn, where hangings provided Londoners with popular entertainment. From 1868 executions took place out of sight, within prison walls, until the abolition of capital punishment in Britain in 1965 (a temporary measure, not confirmed as permanent until 1969). The last woman to be hanged was Ruth *Ellis, and the last deaths by hanging were of two men on 13 August 1964. Capital punishment remains on the statute book for certain crimes (in particular treason and piracy with violence) and there have been regular attempts in the House of Commons to reintroduce it for acts of terrorism and murder of the police. On five separate occasions (in 1982, 83, 87, 88, 90) proposals to restore it have been voted down by MPs.

Capital punishment remained on the statute book in the *Isle of Man until a bill for its abolition was introduced to the Tynwald in 1992, but the only three recent death sentences (for murders in 1972, 1982 and 1991) were all commuted to life imprisonment by the use of the *royal prerogative.

Capital Radio see *radio.

capital transfer tax see *inheritance tax.

capping see *local taxes.

Caratacus or **Caractacus** (1st century AD) The Latin name for the Celtic chieftain Caradoc, who was son of the *Cymbeline of Shakespeare's play. When the *Romans invaded in AD 43, Caradoc led the resistance; but defeat in the southeast drove him back to Wales, where he was again defeated and finally captured. The emperor Claudius displayed him and his family in a triumphal procession in Rome, where they so impressed the onlookers by their dignity that they were allowed to live in honourable captivity in the capital.

Cardiff (Caerdydd in Welsh, 290,000 in 1991) City and administrative centre of both South and Mid Glamorgan, recognized in 1955 as the capital of Wales. The link by rail with the Welsh mining valleys caused Cardiff to grow at phenomenal speed in the 19C, from a small town with a population of about 1000 in 1800 to the world's largest coal-exporting port a century later. But Cardiff's history dates back to about 75 AD when the Romans built a fort here. The Normans later used the same site, and Cardiff castle has at its centre the 12C Norman keep astride its mound. The castle's most famous feature now is the extraordinary range of Gothic Revival interiors, created from 1867 for the 3rd marquess of Bute by William *Burges.

In 1899, in the area to the north of the castle known as Cathays Park, Cardiff began the creation of its Civic Centre, the most impressive municipal complex in Britain. The first two important buildings, completed in 1906, were the City Hall and the Law Courts, both designed by the firm of Lanchester, Stewart and Rickards. The *National Museum of Wales followed in 1927 (with later offshoots in the *Welsh Folk Museum and *Welsh Industrial and Maritime Museum). The Welsh National War Memorial (1928) stands in Alexandra Gardens, behind the City Hall, and is an open circular structure of Corinthian columns by Ninian Comper with bronze figures by Bertram Pegram. At the northwest end of Alexandra Gardens is the *Welsh Office (1938). The city's impressively large area of parkland (1093ha/2700ac) includes Bute Park and Sophia Gardens (on the east and west banks of the river Taff), and in the suburbs Roath Park and the wooded hillside of Cefn Onn Park. In a northwestern suburb is *Llandaff Cathedral.

Cardiff is the home of the *Welsh National Opera, based in the New Theatre (1906); St David's Hall, opened in 1985 and seating 2000, is Wales's chief concert hall. The city is also the centre of Welsh sport, with *Cardiff Arms Park, the National Sports Centre, and the Wales National Ice Rink (opened in 1987).

Cardiff Rugby union football club, formed in 1876, with its ground at *Cardiff Arms Park. The club has had five victories in the Schweppes Welsh Cup (1981, 82, 84, 86, 87).

Cardiff Arms Park Headquarters of *Cardiff and the centre of Welsh rugby football. The original ground, now the National Stadium, has been the location for all home internationals since 1954. Cardiff now play on an adjoining pitch.

Cardiff Three Three men cleared by the Court of Appeal in 1992, after being convicted in 1990 of the brutal murder of a Cardiff prostitute, Lynette White. The lord chief justice, Lord Taylor, stated that the confessions of the men (Stephen Miller, Yusef Abdullahi and Tony Paris) had been extracted from them in police interviews which were 'bullying and hectoring'.

cardigan Woollen garment, similar in shape to a waistcoat but with long sleeves, named after the earl of Cardigan who led the *Charge of the Light Brigade (the reason why it has his name is uncertain). It is believed to have been first devised to protect the soldiers against the bitter cold of a Crimean winter.

Lord **Cardigan** (James Brudenell, 1797–1868, 7th earl of Cardigan 1837) A martinet, deeply unpopular with his own officers, who led the *Charge of the Light Brigade down the wrong valley but was lionized as a hero on his return to Britain.

Cardiganshire Former *county in Wales, since 1974 part of Dyfed.

Neville **Cardus** (1889–1975, kt 1967) Manchester-born critic with the unusual distinction of writing equally well on cricket and music, mainly for the *Guardian*. In articles and books, in both fields, he expressed the warmth of his enjoyment in a richly allusive prose style.

The **Caretaker** (1960) The play which established the reputation of Harold *Pinter. It is about the shifting patterns of dominance in an ill-assorted male trio. Davies is an obsessive tramp who is surprised to find himself offered the post of caretaker in a flat which seems to belong to two brothers, Mick and Aston. He brilliantly plays them off against each other before finally being thrown out.

George **Carey** (b. 1935) Archbishop of *Canterbury since 1991, having previously been bishop of Bath and Wells (1987–91). He comes from a poor background in the East End of London and he left school at 15 – though his later return to full-time education resulted in a doctorate in early church history. He is considered to be on the evangelical wing of the Church of England, having introduced the 'charismatic' style of worship during his years as a vicar in Durham (1975–82). But his views are liberal on the church's dominant issue of the early 1990s – the *ordination of women – and he caused affront to the *Anglo-Catholic wing of the church when he declared in 1991, in an interview in *Reader's Digest*, that opposition to the concept of female priests was 'a most serious heresy'.

The staircase at Carlton House: watercolour by Charles Wild for Pyne's Royal Residences *(1819).*

Cargoes A much recited poem by *Masefield, published in *Ballads and Poems* (1910). Its three verses contrast the 'quinquireme of Nineveh', bearing a cargo of ivory and peacocks for Palestine; the 'stately Spanish galleon', bringing back jewels and gold from Latin America; and the 'dirty British coaster' in the Channel, with its load of coal, metal and cheap tin trays.

Carisbrooke Castle (2km/1m SW of Newport, Isle of Wight) Norman castle, on the site of a Roman fort, much altered in the 16C. Charles I was kept prisoner here for ten months (1647–8) after escaping from Hampton Court.

Carlisle (71,000 in 1981) City and administrative centre of Cumbria. Carlisle's position in the extreme northwest of England made it a frontier post from its time as the Roman garrison of Luguvallum (close to the western end of *Hadrian's Wall), through the building of the Norman castle (begun in 1092) and even into the 18C; the town's last experience of armed hostilities between the English and the Scots was in 1745, when it was taken by Prince Charles Edward Stuart and then soon recaptured.

The remains of the castle include the Norman keep. The 12–15C cathedral contains a superb east window in the Decorated style, the largest of its kind in the country, with medieval stained glass still in the sections of tracery. The 14C guildhall and the 18C town hall survive, and the city's Museum and Art Gallery (in Tullie House, 1689) has a collection as wide-ranging as Carlisle's history, from Roman artefacts to 20C British painting. The development of a cotton industry and a pivotal position in Britain's rail and motorway networks have been the basis of the city's more recent economy.

Carl Rosa Opera Company The leading company touring productions of opera in English round Britain in the first half of the 20C. It was founded in 1875 by a German violinist and conductor (originally Karl Rose,

1843–89) after the death of his wife, the Scottish soprano Euphrosyne Parepa (1836–74). It lasted until 1958, when its remnants merged with what later became the *English National Opera.

Carlton Club (London SW1) The *club of the *Conservative party, founded in 1832 to rally support after the Tories had fared badly in the long political struggle leading up to the *Reform Act of that year (their triumphant opponents were at the same time establishing the *Reform Club). The Carlton's first home was in *Carlton House Terrace, but from the late 1830s it occupied premises in Pall Mall between the present Reform and RAC clubs. This site was bombed in World War II, causing the move to St James's Street where the club was again damaged, with injuries to eight people, by an IRA bomb on 25 June 1990. One of the most dramatic political events in the Carlton's history was the formation of the *1922 Committee.

Carlton House The London palace in which the future *George IV lived in lavish style when prince regent. Originally an early 18C house, overlooking the northeast corner of St James's Park, it was reconstructed with a new magnificence from 1783 by Henry *Holland. Even so the prince considered it inadequate for a king. On inheriting the crown he commissioned John *Nash to improve *Buckingham Palace and to build the present Carlton House Terrace (1827–32), on the site of Carlton House.

Thomas **Carlyle** (1795–1881) Scottish essayist and historian who in his time had a major reputation as a sage, similar to that of Ruskin in the next generation. In 1826 he married Jane Welsh (1801–66) and in 1834 they moved to London, becoming part of the artistic world of *Chelsea; their house, 24 Cheyne Row, is kept as a museum with many of their possessions still in it. Carlyle's major work (*The French Revolution* 3 vols, 1837) suffered a famous disaster when the manuscript of the first volume was thrown on the fire by John Stuart

Whistler's Arrangement in Grey and Black, No. 2: Portrait of Thomas Carlyle *(1872–3)*.

Mill's maid; Carlyle cheerfully rewrote it. *On Heroes, Hero-Worship, & the Heroic in History* (1841) developed his favourite theme, that society needs strong charismatic leaders. One of his most fruitful legacies has been the *London Library.

Carmarthen (12,000 in 1981) Town on the river Towy in south Wales; administrative centre of Dyfed. It has always been a place of strategic importance (the Towy turns here sharply south to the sea, so this is the shortest route to southwest Wales without the need for a river crossing). The Roman presence is seen in part of an amphitheatre, and a 14C gatehouse survives from the Norman castle. An Augustinian priory was here from the 12–15C, best known now as the place where the earliest Welsh manuscript, the *Black Book of Carmarthen* (National Library of Wales) was written in the 12C; it is a collection of ancient poetry, some of it about King Arthur. With St Peter's church (12–14C) and an 18C Guildhall, Carmarthen has today the air of a pleasant market town.

Carmarthenshire Former *county in Wales, since 1974 part of Dyfed.

Carnaby Street (London W1) Street which rapidly became a fashion centre for the young, and consequently a tourist attraction, after John Stephen and others opened boutiques there in the late 1950s.

Andrew **Carnegie** (1835–1919) Scottish-born US philanthropist. His father, a weaver in *Dunfermline, emigrated with the family in the *'hungry forties' and settled in Pennsylvania. Starting as a 13-year-old bobbin boy in a cotton factory, Carnegie rose to become the immensely rich master of America's largest empire of steel works. In 1889 he published a famous essay, *The Gospel of Wealth*, in which he set out the principle that a man should spend the first part of his life accumulating wealth and the second distributing it ('the man who dies rich dies disgraced'). He fulfilled this ideal with astounding generosity. His benefactions in Britain were particularly important in the development of public *libraries, the first of his many gifts in this field being to Dunfermline in 1882.

Carnoustie Golf course on the east coast of Scotland, northeast of Dundee. *Golf has been played on this seaside area since the 16C, and the present course was laid out in the mid-19C. It has been the location of five *Opens during the 20C, but has not been used for the tournament since 1975.

Anthony **Caro** (b. 1924, kt 1987) Sculptor who from about 1960 developed a characteristic style, forming open abstract compositions from brightly painted girders and sheets of welded steel. He was a pioneer of the modern convention by which a sculpture lies directly on the floor, rather than being raised as an art object on a pedestal.

Caroline Word used for the reigns of Charles I or Charles II (*Carolus* in Latin), but for some reason much less common than *Jacobean for the preceding reign.

Caroline of Brunswick see *George IV.

carols The carols widely sung in the Christmas season today (most often in public places to collect money for charity) are of two distinct kinds.

Some are survivals of the original carols which flourished in Britain from about 1300 to 1550. These were popular songs on biblical themes, with catchy tunes. They tended to concentrate on the events connected with the twelve days of *Christmas, and to include much verbal repetition for ease of memory. A good example is *God rest you merry, gentlemen*, which tells the story of the shepherds and the Nativity in a mood of cheerful conviviality, with the chorus repeating its 'tidings of comfort and joy'. These traditional carols were suppressed in the *Reformation, surviving only in folk memory and on cheap broadsheets, printed to meet a continuing popular demand. But the 19C revival of interest in the Middle Ages and in folk music led to their being collected and published. A great many pastiche carols were also written in the same Victorian burst of enthusiasm, but they have mainly been discarded by now in favour of the traditional ones.

The other main element in the modern repertoire of carols is hymns borrowed from the Christmas section of the hymnal, such as *O come, all ye faithful* or *Hark! the herald angels sing.*

Harry **Carpenter** (b. 1925) Sports commentator, associated in particular with the BBC TV programmes *Grandstand* and *Sportsnight*. His own specialities as a commentator include tennis, golf and above all boxing, on which he has written several books.

John **Carr** (also known as Carr of York, 1723–1807) Architect in the *Palladian style who began his career as a mason but went on to design many stately homes, most of them in Yorkshire. The best known is *Harewood.

Robert **Carr** (b. 1916, baron 1975) Conservative politician (MP for Mitcham 1950–74) who entered the cabinet in 1970 as secretary of state for employment. He was subsequently leader of the House of Commons (1972) and home secretary (1972–4).

Carrickfergus (23,000 in 1991) Seaside town north of Belfast, on the inlet of the North Channel known as Belfast Lough. Its Norman castle is one of the best preserved in Ireland. Founded in about 1180 on a rock above the harbour, its square 5-storey keep now houses a museum.

Lord **Carrington** (Peter Carrington, b. 1919, 6th baron 1938) Conservative politician, unusual in modern times in having had a distinguished career while sitting in the House of Lords. He entered the cabinet in 1970 as secretary of state for defence, but was best known during his time as foreign secretary (1979–82). He resigned from this office at the start of the *Falklands War, when the Argentinians captured the islands in an attack which took the Foreign Office by surprise, saying that he accepted responsibility for 'a very great national humiliation'. He subsequently became secretary general of NATO (1984–8).

Lewis **Carroll** (pen name of Charles Dodgson, 1832–98) Author of two of the world's best-known children's books. He taught mathematics at Christ Church, Oxford, where he became friendly with the three young daughters of the dean, Henry Liddell, and in particular with Alice. He was a keen photographer and began telling stories to keep the children amused while he was taking their pictures. On a boating trip up the Thames, on 4 July 1862, when Alice was ten, he improvised for them a fantasy called *Alice's Adventures under Ground* and promised to write it out. He did so, with his own illustrations (the manuscript is now in the British Library), and it was published in 1865 as *Alice's Adventures in Wonderland.* Seven years later came *Through the Looking-Glass.* Carroll was to produce one more masterpiece of nonsense, *The *Hunting of the Snark* (1876). His photographs of young girls, occasionally nude, have given him a second reputation of lasting interest, both for the beauty of the photographs and for the psychological aspect of his long succession of child-friends (though none ever matched his feeling for Alice).

Jasper **Carrott** (stage name of Robert Davies, b. 1942) Comedian of the bar-stool monologue school, whose humour is based on deadpan amazement at the idiocies of the world. He has had regular solo TV series since the 1970s, and has issued a steady succession of albums; *Rabbits On and On* (1975) reached the top ten in the charts.

Carry On series Nearly 30 films, extremely popular with British audiences in the 1960s and 1970s, which offered vaguely farcical plots but relied rather more on camp performances and a stream of sexual double entendre. The first was *Carry on Sergeant* in 1958. Three of its cast became regulars – Kenneth Williams, Charles Hawtrey and Kenneth Connor. They were joined in most of the later films by Sid James, Hattie Jacques, Jim Dale and Joan Sims. The entire series was produced by Peter Rogers and directed by Gerald Thomas. The formula was revived for *Carry On Columbus*, made in 1992 with Julian Clary continuing the camp tradition.

cars see *road safety

Edward **Carson** (1854–1935, kt 1900, baron 1921) Irish lawyer and politician, notable both for his brilliance and his ruthlessness. His reputation in England was made by his devastating cross-examination of Oscar *Wilde in 1895, yet Wilde had been a fellow undergraduate at Trinity College, Dublin. And his orthodox political career (solicitor general 1900–6, attorney general 1915) did not prevent his raising in 1913 a large force of insurrectionary Ulster Volunteers and smuggling in illegal arms as part of his campaign against *Home Rule. It was almost entirely due to his efforts that the Home Rule bill of 1914 excluded Ulster and that the *six counties remained in 1921 part of the United Kingdom.

Willie **Carson** (b. 1942) Scottish jockey who in the 20C trails only Lester *Piggott in the number of *classics he has won. His total by the end of the 1992 season was 16, including the only occasion on which a jockey has won a classic on a horse which he himself had bred – a feat achieved with Minster Son in the 1988 St Leger. In 1977 he rode the Queen's filly Dunfermline to victory in both the Oaks and the St Leger; and Troy gave him an exceptional season in 1979, when they together won the Derby, the Irish Derby and the King George VI and Queen Elizabeth Diamond Stakes. He has been *champion jockey five times.

D'Oyly **Carte** see Richard *D'Oyly Carte.

Angela **Carter** (Angela Stalker, 1940–92, m. Paul Carter 1960) Writer whose talent for wild invention was blended with a love of the down-to-earth and the vulgar in a potently effective brew. Feminine sexuality was her abiding theme, dark and mysterious in the manner of Gothic fairy tales or exuberant in a tradition of circus and theatre. The screenplay for *The Company of Wolves* (1984) was her own, from one of her stories. Her two last books were among her best (*Nights at the Circus* 1984, *Wise Children* 1991).

Howard **Carter** (1873–1939) Archaeologist who in 1922 found the intact tomb of the 14th-century BC Egyptian pharaoh Tutankhamen, piled high with its treasures, in the Valley of the Kings at Thebes; the contents are now in the Cairo Museum. From 1907 Carter's

The working carthorse: a wood engraving from Thomas Bewick's General History of Quadrupeds *(1790).*

excavations had been paid for by the 5th earl of Carnarvon (1866–1923), who was bitten by a mosquito when in the Valley of the Kings in 1923; the bite turned septic and a month later he contracted pneumonia and died in Cairo, giving rise to much speculation about the revenge of the disturbed pharaoh's spirit.

carthorses Exceptionally strong horses were bred in the Middle Ages to carry heavily armoured knights into battle. The descendants of these horses were later adapted to the more mundane task of dragging ploughs or heavy carts. In Britain three local varieties, all established by the 18C, proved particularly successful. The Clydesdale was bred near Lanark, in the valley of the Clyde; its colour ranges from bay to black, invariably with white markings. The Suffolk, bred in that county and also known as the Suffolk Punch, is somewhat smaller and invariably chestnut in colour; all registered Suffolks descend from 'Crisp's Horse', foaled in 1768. The shire or shire horse (bred in the *Shires) is the largest of the three; with colour again ranging from bay to black, its white markings are limited to its lower legs. Both the Clydesdale and the shire are characterized by 'feathers' (long hair) falling over the hooves.

Barbara **Cartland** (b. 1901, DBE 1991) Romantic novelist credited in the *Guinness Book of Records* with the greatest number of books by any British author (some 570 by 1992) and the largest worldwide sales of any living author (more than 650 million copies). Her rate of production means that a new book is finished every two or three weeks; the purpose of each has been, in her own words, 'to give Morality, Beauty and Love to the world'. She is also known as an advocate of alternative medicine and health foods ('Due to my special Vitamins and Honey our marriage lasted for twenty-eight perfect years'). Certainly her own energy in her nineties is a powerful testimonial.

Roger **Casement** (1864–1916, kt 1911) British consular official and Irish nationalist, hanged for treason. His career in the consular service was distinguished by a series of reports on atrocities by European colonial powers in Africa and South America, which brought him fame and his knighthood. He retired to Ireland in 1912 (he was of Protestant Irish stock) and became a passionate opponent of Irish participation in World War I. He travelled to Germany to organize an invasion of Ireland which he believed would bring independence. Failing in this, he returned to Ireland in 1916 hoping to postpone the imminent *Easter Rising. But his movements were known, and he was arrested after a German submarine had landed him near Tralee. Controversy over his execution was heightened by the private circulation of his diary, containing accounts of homosexual activities. Its authenticity was widely doubted at the time, but modern scholars tend to agree that the handwriting is his.

Casket Letters A collection of eight letters and some sonnets, written by *Mary Queen of Scots to Bothwell and so called because they were found in a silver casket, where they had been placed supposedly by Bothwell. Their importance is that if genuine (and it has been argued that they are wholly or in part forgeries) they implicate Mary in the murder of her husband, Darnley, in 1567. In an attempt to prove her guilt, the letters were first revealed by her Protestant enemies later in that year. They are now known only from contemporary copies. The whereabouts of the supposed originals was a mystery from the 1580s, complicating the question of whether they were forged.

Cassandra Pen name under which William Connor (1909–67, kt 1966) wrote a column in the *Daily Mirror* from 1935 until his death. His hard-hitting prose, always opinionated but often unpredictable, won him a large and devoted readership.

Hugh **Casson** (b. 1910, kt 1952) Architect and watercolourist, who first achieved prominence as 'director of architecture' for the *Festival of Britain in 1951. Subsequent designs include the Arts Faculty building at Cambridge and the elephant and rhino pavilion (1962–5) at London Zoo. His delicate watercolours were very widely seen in a children's book which he illustrated in 1980, *The Old Man of Lochnagar*, written by the prince of *Wales; and he has published books of sketches of London (1983), Oxford (1988) and Cambridge (1992). He was president of the Royal Academy 1976–84.

Castell Coch (8km/5m NW of Cardiff) Gothic Revival castle built by William *Burges for the 3rd marquess of Bute on the foundations of a ruined 13C fortress (the name means the 'red castle' in Welsh). It was begun in 1875 and completed in 1891, after Burges's death. In spite of the drawbridge and arrow slits, the new castle was intended (but rarely used) for comfortable Victorian entertaining in Burges's highly decorated interiors.

Barbara **Castle** (b. 1910, baroness 1990) Labour politician, MP for Blackburn (1945–79) and MEP for Greater Manchester (1979–89). She entered the cabinet in Wilson's government of 1964 and is remembered in particular for her time as secretary of state for employment and productivity (1968–70), when she made courageous efforts to defuse the industrial confrontations of that period; her blueprint *In Place of Strife* was attacked by the unions and rejected by the party.

Castle Campbell (21km/13m E of Stirling) Romantic ruined castle (15–17C) at the head of a wooded glen. Its surroundings have a Bunyanesque quality, for it is in the parish of Dollar (or Dolour), while Gloom Hill and the streams of Sorrow and Care are nearby. The castle was largely destroyed by Cromwell's troops in 1654.

Castle Coole (2.5km/1.5m SE of Enniskillen) Severe neoclassical house built 1790–7 for the 1st earl of Belmore to the design of James *Wyatt. The Regency decoration and furnishings, still surviving, were provided by John Preston of Dublin.

The baroque splendour achieved by Vanbrugh and Hawksmoor in the great entrance hall at Castle Howard.

Castle Howard (24km/15m NE of York) Stately home in North Yorkshire, designed by *Vanbrugh and *Hawksmoor for the 3rd earl of Carlisle. The house was built in 1700–26 in an English version of *baroque, but the west wing (designed by the earl's son-in-law, Thomas Robinson) was added in 1753–9 in the subsequent *Palladian manner. The soaring entrance hall, as flamboyant as a church interior in Rome and with the dome painted ·by a Venetian artist, Pellegrini, was destroyed in a fire in 1940 but has been precisely restored. In the grounds are the Temple of the Four Winds, a belvedere designed by Vanbrugh in the last two years of his life; and, beyond it, a circular mausoleum by Hawksmoor.

Castle of Mey see *Queen Mother.

Castle of Otranto see Horace *Walpole.

Lord **Castlereagh** (Robert Stewart, 1769–1822, 2nd marquess of Londonderry 1821) Tory politician and long-serving foreign secretary (1812–22), known for most of his adult life as viscount Castlereagh, his *courtesy title. He made his political reputation as chief secretary in the Irish parliament (1798–1801), securing the passage of the Act of *Union against considerable opposition. In 1805 he became secretary of state for war in Pitt's government. There then developed a bitter rivalry with *Canning, the foreign secretary, whose secret schemes for the removal of Castlereagh after military reverses in 1809 led to a duel between the two men and their joint resignation.

In 1812 it was Castlereagh who returned to office as foreign secretary, and it was he who represented Britain in the peace settlement at the end of the *Napoleonic Wars.

In foreign policy he was against re-establishment of the old European order, but at home his name was increasingly linked with repression and he became profoundly unpopular with the public. He was leader of the House of Commons when the *Peterloo massacre occurred, provoking Shelley's couplet in *The Mask of Anarchy*:

I met Murder on the way –
He had a mask like Castlereagh.

In the last months of his life he was unstable and depressed to the extent that his doctor removed his razors. He committed suicide by cutting his throat with a pen knife.

Castle Ward (48km/30m SE of Belfast House built in the 1760s, famous for the clash of architectural styles which resulted from the differing tastes of Bernard Ward and his wife, Lady Anne. He preferred the classical style, while she was an early enthusiast for the *Gothic Revival. They split their house down the middle, the façades and interiors on either side being flamboyant examples of the rival orthodoxies. The marriage did not long survive this disagreement, Lady Anne retreating to spend the rest of her days, surprisingly, in the ultra-classical city of Bath.

Castlewellan (40km/25m S of Belfast) Town in County Down laid out with a broad main street and residential squares by the earls of Annesley in the 18C. The nearby park of their 19C baronial castle is notable for an arboretum established in 1740.

Casualty (BBC1 since 1986) Hospital soap opera in a tradition going back to *Emergency Ward Ten*. The main characters in the casualty department of Holby Hospital include the male nurse Charlie (played by Derek Thompson) and the very stern sister, Lisa Duffin or 'Duffy' (Cathy Shipton).

Cat and Mouse Act Popular name for the Prisoners (Temporary Discharge for Ill Health) Act of 1913. This was the government's very effective solution to the problem posed by *suffragettes on hunger strike in prison. To avoid their becoming martyrs, the act allowed them to be released from prison and then re-arrested when their health had recovered.

Cathays Park see *Cardiff.

Catherine of Aragon (1485–1536) Daughter of the Spanish rulers, Ferdinand and Isabella, and first wife of *Henry VIII. She married in 1501 his elder brother, Prince Arthur, who died a few months later. Henry married her in 1509. Their relationship, reasonably good for many years, foundered eventually because of her tragic failure to produce a male heir. (Of her six children only one, *Mary I, survived early infancy; of the five who were stillborn or died within weeks, three were boys.) Henry's conviction that the kingdom required a king was understandable – the only female heir in previous English history, *Matilda, had failed to make good her claim – and he became determined to end the marriage. His first efforts to do so, in 1527, were probably before the start of his passion for *Anne Boleyn. It was not until May 1533 that he finally had the marriage annulled by his archbishop, Thomas Cranmer (in defiance of the pope, thus provoking the English *Reformation). For the last few years of her life Catherine remained in England, defiantly insisting upon her status as the queen, though separated from her daughter and increasingly persecuted by her husband.

Catherine Howard (*c.*1521–42) Fifth of the wives of *Henry VIII. The king married her in July 1540, within three weeks of having his marriage to Anne of Cleves annulled. A year later he discovered that she had had previous affairs, and in February 1542 parliament passed a bill declaring it treason for an unchaste woman to marry the king. Two days later Catherine was beheaded in the Tower.

Catherine Parr (1512–48) Sixth and last wife of *Henry VIII. Twice widowed before she married the king in 1543, she was a civilized and congenial woman who for the first time brought together his three children from separate marriages to live within his household. After his death she was married for a fourth time (to Thomas Seymour, brother of the protector, the duke of Somerset), but she died shortly after giving birth to a daughter.

Catholic Herald Weekly newspaper founded as the *Glasgow Observer* in 1885, and adopting its present name when it moved to London in 1888. It takes an independent and often radical line on Roman Catholic issues – attacking, for example, the encyclical of 1968, *Humanae Vitae*, in which Pope Paul VI reasserted the Church's ban on contraception.

Cathy Come Home (BBC 1966) Documentary play about the plight of a homeless young mother, written by Jeremy Sandford and directed by Ken Loach. It has remained a famous example of the power of television, for it created public concern about a specific problem and gave an impetus to pressure groups such as *Shelter.

Cats (1981) Musical by Andrew *Lloyd Webber, directed by Trevor *Nunn, which succeeded in turning a book of poems, **Old Possum's Book of Practical Cats*, into a show which has run for years in several cities around the world.

Suffragette poster making powerful use of the popular name for the government legislation of 1913.

Catseye Trade name of the glass reflectors, in resilient rubber pads, which are set into the surface of a highway to provide safe markings at night. Designed in 1934 by Percy Shaw (1890–1976), they were inspired by his difficulties in driving along dark Yorkshire roads.

cattle The selective breeding of cattle began in England in about 1770, with pioneer work by Robert *Bakewell. His example was soon followed by the development of the *shorthorn in county Durham. Other British breeds now familiar in many parts of the world include the *Aberdeen Angus, the *Ayrshire and the *Hereford. The *Channel Islands have provided exceptional milk-producing cows in the Jersey and the Guernsey. Two aboriginal strains from the more rugged parts of Britain – *Highland cattle and Welsh black cattle – have survived as domesticated breeds. See also *Chillingham cattle.

Steve **Cauthen** (b. 1960) American jockey who had a very successful early career in the USA before moving in 1979 to Britain, where he was *champion jockey three times in the mid-1980s. His transatlantic successes enabled him to become the first man to win both the Kentucky Derby (1978 on Affirmed) and the Derby (1985 on Slip Anchor, 1987 on Reference Point).

Cavaliers Supporters of the royal cause in the *English Civil War. Like *Roundhead, the name was in use from the early 1640s as a term of abuse; deriving from a word for a horse-soldier or knight, it was first applied to swashbuckling followers of Charles I who seemed eager for war.

Edith **Cavell** (1865–1915) English nurse whose execution by the Germans in World War I made her a national heroine. She was matron of a Red Cross hospital in Brussels, where many Allied soldiers were trapped after the German occupation of Belgium. She had given refuge to some 200, and had helped them across the border into neutral Holland, before she was arrested in August 1915. She was court-martialled and on October 12 she was shot. Her words, spoken to the chaplain just before she faced the firing squad, later became famous: 'Standing, as I do, in the view of God and eternity, I realize that patriotism is not enough. I must have no hatred or bitterness towards anyone.'

Henry **Cavendish** (1731–1810) Chemist and physicist who identified hydrogen (or 'inflammable air') as a distinct substance, demonstrated that water was a compound rather than an element, and made a remarkably accurate assessment of the density of the earth. He also made important early experiments with electricity. Wealthy by inheritance, he lived the life of an eccentric recluse.

Cavendish Laboratory Centre for experimental physics founded at Cambridge in 1871 by the 7th duke of Devonshire in memory of a distinguished scientist in his own family, Henry *Cavendish. James Clerk *Maxwell was the first director, a post subsequently held by J.J. *Thomson (discoverer of the electron) and by *Rutherford (discoverer of the nucleus and the proton). *Chadwick was at the Cavendish when he discovered the neutron in 1932, and in the same year *Cockcroft achieved the first nuclear reaction induced by artificially accelerated particles. In the second half of the 20c the laboratory extended its range to include radio astronomy under Martin *Ryle (the Mullard Radio Astronomy Observatory was built in 1964) and for a while molecular biology – the field in which Cambridge scientists made one of the greatest breakthroughs of the 20c with the discovery in 1953 of the structure of *DNA.

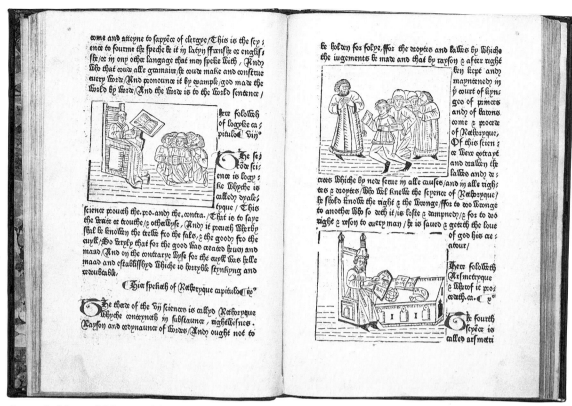

A spread of Caxton's Mirrour of the World *(c.1481), with lessons depicted in Logic, Rhetoric and Arithmetic.*

Cavern Club see the *Beatles.

Cawdor Castle (21km/13m E of Inverness A castle of great literary resonance because *Macbeth is promised by the witches in Shakespeare's tragedy that he will be thane of Cawdor. The present building dates from rather later (14–17c), but has remained the home of the earls of Cawdor.

William Caxton (c.1422–91) The first English printer. He spent most of his life trading as a merchant (1442–76) on the Continent, mainly in Bruges, where he set up a press in about 1474. He brought the press to England in 1476, and began printing in Westminster. Some of his most successful books were *The *Canterbury Tales* (c.1478); *The Mirrour of the World* (c.1481), an encyclopedia which is also the first printed book in English with illustrations; the *Fables of Esope* (1484); and the *Morte d'Arthur* (1485). After his death the business was carried on to increasingly high standards in *Fleet Street by Wynkyn de Worde (d. 1535), who had been his assistant since the first days in Bruges.

Cayman Islands Colony of three islands in the West Indies, lying northwest of Jamaica. The name derives from a statement in the log of the first English visitor, Francis *Drake, that there were *caymanas* (the local word for crocodiles). The islands were settled by the British spasmodically from about 1670 and permanently from 1734. After 1863 they were controlled from Jamaica. When that became independent, in 1962, the Caymans opted to remain a crown colony.

CB, CBE see *orders of chivalry.

CBI (Confederation of British Industry) Independent organization founded in 1965 to speak for the interests of British industry and commerce. It is funded by its members and its main task is to advise and where necessary to lobby the government.

CBSO see *City of Birmingham Symphony Orchestra.

Robert Cecil (1563–1612, kt 1591, earl of Salisbury 1605) Chief minister to Elizabeth I after the death of his father, Lord *Burghley, in whose footsteps he followed precisely (a legal training, a seat as an MP and then royal service). He was appointed secretary of state in 1596 and James I kept him in the same position when he came to the throne in 1603, making him lord treasurer in 1608. His elder brother inherited Burghley House and he built *Hatfield House, in which his descendants still live.

Cecil Higgins Art Gallery and Museum see *Bedford.

Cefn Onn Park see *Cardiff.

ceilidh (pronounced 'kayley') Gaelic word for a social visit, applied in Scotland to an evening of music, songs and stories.

Celsius see *temperature.

Celtic, known as The Bhoys (Celtic Park, Glasgow). Football club with a long history of rivalry with *Rangers. They share the honours as Scotland's two most successful teams, but Rangers has Protestant support whereas Celtic is Roman Catholic; it was founded in 1888 by Irish Catholics in the east end of Glasgow to raise money for needy children. In 1967 Celtic became the first British team to win the European Cup. By 1992 the club had won the Scottish FA Cup 29 times (Rangers 25), the Scottish League 35 times (Rangers 42) and the Scottish League Cup 9 times (Rangers 17).

Celtic cross Cross of the Latin type (the horizontal bar more than half way up the vertical) with a circle surrounding the point of intersection. The shape may have developed first in metal work but is known in particular from the stone crosses of the 8–10c in Ireland, richly carved with patterns of interlacing lines or small biblical scenes.

Celtic languages The *Celts were driven west across Britain some 1400 years ago by the *Anglo-Saxons, and variants of their ancient language survive now only on the west coasts of Wales, Scotland and Ireland. The dialects are divided into two groups: Goidelic, the northern variety, which covers the *Gaelic spoken in Ireland and Scotland and until recently in the Isle of Man; and Brythonic, in the south, which includes *Welsh, Cornish and Breton, the language of Brittany in northwest France.

Celts The Greek name for a barbarian people occupying central Europe in the 6th century BC. The following centuries saw their energetic expansion; they sacked Rome in about 390 BC, and spread west through France and Britain to Ireland. They were the dominant group in both France and England (where they were the original *Britons with *druids as their priests) before the extension of the *Roman empire northwest during and after the 1st century BC. After the Romans came the *Anglo-Saxons, and the result of these pressures was that the Celts retreated to the western extremities of France (Brittany) and of Britain (Cornwall, Wales, the west of Scotland and Ireland). These have remained the only strong areas of Celtic influence, a fact reflected in the survival there of the *Celtic languages. The vigorous art of the Celts, characterized by intricate patterns of interlacing lines, is evident in *Celtic crosses and in the manuscripts illustrated in Irish monasteries. It was Celtic missionaries, following the lead of St *Patrick, who brought Christianity to northern Britain and much of continental Europe.

Cenotaph (London SW1) The national monument to the men and women who died in the services in both world wars (the word means 'empty tomb' in Greek). Standing in the middle of *Whitehall, it is a slightly curving vertical block of Portland stone, adorned with the flags of the three services and the merchant navy, and with the simple inscription 'To the Glorious Dead'. It was designed by *Lutyens and was completed in 1920 in time for the second *Armistice Day, which was also the occasion when the coffin bearing the *Unknown Warrior passed on its way to burial in Westminster Abbey. The dates of World War II were added to the monument in 1946. On each Remembrance Sunday, the successor to Armistice Day, the two-minute silence is followed by the *Last Post; then wreaths are laid at the foot of the Cenotaph by the royal family, the leaders of the main political parties and many other representatives of national institutions.

censorship Those in power have always attempted to suppress information or opinions harmful to their own interests, and their task became both more urgent and more difficult after the invention of printing in the 15c. In Britain the Tudor monarchs introduced controls over both the printed and the declaimed word. From the 1530s every book had to be licensed, a function carried out from 1557 by the Stationers' Company; licensing was extended in the 17c to the first newspapers; it ended in 1695, but a charge of seditious libel then became the favoured method for silencing adversaries (for example *Wilkes, *Paine and *Cobbett). It can be argued that the modern system of *D-notices carries the risk of being used in this way. The need for a *Freedom of Information Act (as introduced in the USA in 1966) is a topical issue in Britain in the 1990s. The classic work in the long argument against censorship of the press is Milton's *Areopagitica* (1644). Censorship of literature on the grounds of obscenity was successfully challenged in the case of *Lady Chatterley's Lover*.

The licensing of plays was carried out in the Tudor period by the Master of the Revels. It later passed to another royal official, the *lord chamberlain, and it remained one of his duties – an astonishing anachronism – until 1968.

census The first country to establish a systematic and regular count of the *population was the USA in 1790, followed by France and Britain in 1801. The UK census has taken place every ten years since then, with the single exception of 1941 (during World War II). Each householder has a legal obligation to fill in certain details about anyone resident in the house on a particular night, together with anyone normally resident but temporarily away; 21 April 1991 was the most recent census date. From being originally a simple head count, the modern census collects information on a wide variety of topics: the size, condition and amenities of the house itself; and the age, sex, marital status, health, country of birth, ethnic origin (for the first time in the 1991 census) and economic status of each person, together with the occupation, hours and mode of travel of those in work.

CENTO (Central Treaty Organization) Middle-Eastern alliance for military, economic and technological cooperation which began with the Baghdad Pact of 1955 between Iraq and Turkey. Later that year Britain, Iran and Pakistan joined, but in 1958 Iraq withdrew (after a revolution); the headquarters then moved to Ankara and the name was changed to CENTO. The USA was never a full member but was closely involved. In 1979 Iran and Pakistan withdrew and the alliance was brought to an end.

Central (267,000 in 1991, administrative centre Stirling) Since 1975 a *region of central Scotland, comprising the former county of Clackmannan, most of Stirling and parts of Perth, Fife and Kinross.

Central Criminal Court see *Old Bailey.

Central Office of Information (COI, London SE1) Executive agency (see *Next Steps) which handles all government publicity and advertising, and distributes press notices for nearly all government departments. The exception is the prime minister's office, for which the press secretaries in Downing Street are responsible.

Central Saint Martins College of Art see *art schools.

Central School of Speech and Drama see *drama schools.

Central Statistical Office (CSO, London SW1) Executive agency (see *Next Steps) which derives from the government department set up in 1941 by Winston Churchill to provide better statistics for managing the war economy. The office has since then researched on an increasingly wide range of economic and social subjects, though it is only since 1989 that it has had responsibility for the index which attracts the most attention, the *RPI. The CSO publishes the monthly *Economic Trends* and its leading annual titles are: *Annual Abstract of Statistics, Social Trends, Regional Trends,* and *United Kingdom Annual Accounts,* known as the Blue Book. The department was greatly enlarged in 1989, when it absorbed the

A large and lively ancient image in the Dorset landscape: the Cerne Giant, dating from c.500.

Business Statistics Office (BSO) and other research groups previously in the Department of Trade and Industry, and also the section working on retail prices in the Department of Employment. The CSO reports to the chancellor of the exchequer.

For anyone needing British statistics, an invaluable introduction to what is available is provided in *Guide to Official Statistics*, published by *HMSO for the Central Statistical Office.

Ceredigion Museum see *Aberystwyth.

Cerne Giant (10km/6m N of Dorchester) Britain's best-known phallic image, on a hillside above the village of Cerne Abbas in Dorset. This uncompromising figure of male virility is 55m/180ft tall and is composed of lines cut in the green turf, exposing the white chalk beneath. It is believed to have been created some 1500 years ago, after the Roman occupation, with the club in the giant's right hand perhaps deriving from Hercules.

Ceylon see *Sri Lanka.

CGS see *Army.

CGT see *capital gains tax.

CH see the Order of the *Companions of Honour.

Mr **Chad** Stylized figure, quick and easy to draw, of a bald head, a pair of eyes and a long nose appearing over a wall with the question 'wot no . . . ?' (whatever you cared to fill in). Chad was the most popular of graffiti in Britain

in World War II, as a humorous outlet for complaints about shortages. No-one knows his origin or by what long process he was perfected. The *Times* declared in 1946 that he could claim no one man as his creator and might well complain 'Wot no father?'.

James **Chadwick** (1891–1974, kt 1945) Physicist who worked at the Cavendish Laboratory with *Rutherford and in 1932 discovered the neutron – the uncharged particle which is a pair, in subatomic physics, to the proton previously identified by Rutherford. The discovery of the neutron, which can penetrate the nucleus of atoms because it lacks any electrical charge of its own, opened the way to nuclear fission; Chadwick worked in the USA in 1943–5 on the development of the atomic bomb. He was awarded the Nobel prize for physics in 1935.

Chained Library see *Hereford.

HMS *Challenger* Wooden corvette which covered some 127,600km/79,300m in 1872–6, carrying out an exploration of the oceans undertaken jointly by the Admiralty and the Royal Society. The director was Charles Wyville Thomson (1830–82). The *Report on the Scientific Results* (50 vols, 1880–95) provided a wealth of material on oceanography and marine biology which is still of use today.

Austen **Chamberlain** (1863–1937, KG 1925) Son of Joseph *Chamberlain (by his first wife) who followed his father into politics, becoming a Unionist MP in 1892 and remaining closely associated with him on most issues. They served together in Balfour's cabinet of 1902, in which Austen became chancellor of the exchequer in 1903. He was briefly leader of the Conservative party (1921–2, after Bonar *Law's resignation for health reasons) until ousted by the *1922 Committee. His greatest achievement was as foreign secretary (1924–29), when his efforts to settle and guarantee Germany's disputed western frontiers led to his sharing (with his US colleague Charles Gates Dawes) the Nobel peace prize in 1925.

Joseph **Chamberlain** (1836–1914) Politician who first came to prominence as a reforming mayor of Birmingham (1873–6), where he introduced improvements in sanitation, housing and the supply of water and gas. His efforts not only transformed Birmingham but gave an example to the rest of the country. He made such a success of the family business that he was able to retire with a fortune in 1874 and devote himself to politics. He became Liberal MP for Birmingham in 1876, and was in Gladstone's cabinet from 1880 as president of the Board of Trade. He split from the Liberals in 1886 on the *Unionist issue. His vision of a united and strong empire was influential when he was secretary of state for the colonies in 1895–1903, a period which included the *Boer War. His belief in mutual self-interest within the empire lay behind the major campaign of his later years, to introduce tariff advantages for the colonies. Both his sons, Austen and Neville, were prominent in politics.

Neville **Chamberlain** (1869–1940) Conservative politician, prime minister 1937–40. Son of Joseph *Chamberlain by his second wife, he followed his father in a business career and in city politics in Birmingham. He became MP for the Ladywood division of Birmingham in 1918 (he was already in his 50th year), changing in 1929 to the Edgbaston division which he held until his death. By 1923 he was chancellor of the exchequer in Stanley Baldwin's brief first government, a post he held again (1931–7) in the *national governments of Ramsay MacDonald and Baldwin. When Baldwin retired in 1937, Chamberlain was his natural successor as prime minister.

By then there was a single dominant issue in world affairs – the aggressive intentions of Nazi Germany under Adolf Hitler. The majority in Britain hoped that a peaceful solution could be found for Germany's claims on areas of other countries with German populations, and Chamberlain was a willing spokesman for this policy of *appeasement. With the agreement at *Munich in 1938 he effectively abandoned Czechoslovakia (whose trouble with its German citizens he described as 'a quarrel in a far-away country between people of whom we know nothing'). But he immediately accelerated Britain's rearmament programme and the following year declared that Britain would defend Poland against German attack. This commitment led, in September 1939, to the start of *World War II.

Chamberlain brought into his war cabinet the leading opponent of appeasement, Winston *Churchill. The failure of the campaign in Norway in April 1940 caused criticism of Chamberlain's leadership and he resigned on May 10, being succeeded by Churchill. Chamberlain was already an ill man, and he died later the same year.

Chamberlain's Men The leading company of actors in the late Elizabethan and early Jacobean period. Both Shakespeare and Burbage were prominent members from 1594, the year in which the *lord chamberlain provided his patronage, and Shakespeare wrote nearly all his plays for the company. They were based at the *Globe from 1599; from about 1608 they also had a covered theatre at Blackfriars for winter performances. On his accession in 1603 James I took them under his personal protection, and from then on they were known as the King's Men.

Chamber of Horrors see *Madame Tussaud's.

Chambers By pure coincidence a name which has twice been of importance in the history of British encyclopedias. The first of its kind was the *Cyclopaedia; or, an Universal dictionary of arts and sciences* (2 vols), published in London in 1728 by Ephraim Chambers; it was the inspiration for the famous French *Encyclopédie* of 1751–80. The better known *Chambers's Encyclopaedia* had no connection with the earlier work. It was first issued in 1860–68 by the Edinburgh firm of W. and R. Chambers (in weekly numbers costing three halfpence each, which were later printed as ten volumes) and it continued to be published until the 1970s.

William **Chambers** (1723–96, kt 1770) Architect of Scottish descent who was the chief rival in his day of another Scotsman, Robert *Adam. Chambers' success began in 1755 when he was appointed architectural tutor to the future George III, whose mother then commissioned him to provide classical temples and follies (including the famous pagoda) in *Kew Gardens. His real buildings, mostly in the prevailing *Palladian style, tended to be more conventional than Adam's. The most ambitious was *Somerset House in London.

Bob **Champion** see the *Grand National.

The elegant entrance from the Strand, leading into the courtyard of William Chambers' Somerset House.

Champion jockeys since 1946

	Flat	National Hunt		Flat	National Hunt
1946	Gordon Richards	Fred Rimmell	1970	Lester Piggott	Bob Davies
1947	Gordon Richards	Jack Dowdeswell	1971	Lester Piggott	Graham Thorner
1948	Gordon Richards	Bryan Marshall	1972	Willie Carson	Bob Davies
1949	Gordon Richards	Tim Molony	1973	Willie Carson	Ron Barry
1950	Gordon Richards	Tim Molony	1974	Pat Eddery	Ron Barry
1951	Gordon Richards	Tim Molony	1975	Pat Eddery	Tommy Stack
1952	Gordon Richards	Tim Molony	1976	Pat Eddery	John Francome
1953	Gordon Richards	Fred Winter	1977	Pat Eddery	Tommy Stack
1954	Doug Smith	Dick Francis	1978	Willie Carson	Jonjo O'Neill
1955	Doug Smith	Tim Molony	1979	Joe Mercer	John Francome
1956	Doug Smith	Fred Winter	1980	Willie Carson	Jonjo O'Neill
1957	Scobie Breasley	Fred Winter	1981	Lester Piggott	John Francome
1958	Doug Smith	Fred Winter	1982	Lester Piggott	John Francome & Peter Scudamore
1959	Doug Smith	Tim Brookshaw	1983	Willie Carson	John Francome
1960	Lester Piggott	Stan Mellor	1984	Steve Cauthen	John Francome
1961	Scobie Breasley	Stan Mellor	1985	Steve Cauthen	John Francome
1962	Scobie Breasley	Stan Mellor	1986	Pat Eddery	Peter Scudamore
1963	Scobie Breasley	Josh Gifford	1987	Steve Cauthen	Peter Scudamore
1964	Lester Piggott	Josh Gifford	1988	Pat Eddery	Peter Scudamore
1965	Lester Piggott	Terry Biddlecome	1989	Pat Eddery	Peter Scudamore
1966	Lester Piggott	Terry Biddlecome	1990	Pat Eddery	Peter Scudamore
1967	Lester Piggott	Josh Gifford	1991	Pat Eddery	Peter Scudamore
1968	Lester Piggott	Josh Gifford	1992	Michael Roberts	Peter Scudamore
1969	Lester Piggott	Bob Davies & Terry Biddlecome			

Harry **Champion** (stage name of William Crump, 1866–1942) Cockney star of the *music hall, whose paunchy and battered appearance was belied by an act of whirlwind energy in which he reeled off a repertoire of favourite songs, accompanying them with a frantic jigging dance. They included *Boiled beef and carrots*, *Any old iron* and *I'm Henery the Eighth I am*.

champion jockey There are two champion jockeys in Britain each year, the title going in each case to the rider who has won the greatest number of races in his category. The season's champion National Hunt jockey is known by the end of May, after the winter's *steeplechases; the champion jockey for flat races is known in November, after a summer of racing on the turf.

Chancellor of the Duchy of Lancaster An obsolete medieval office (since 1399 every monarch has been duke of Lancaster, thanks to *John of Gaunt). It is now used as a wild card in the cabinet. By this device the prime minister can appoint someone to concentrate on a specific task, free (if so required) of departmental duties. A holder of the office in the 1930s recorded that his work as chancellor took him about half an hour a week. The existence of the duchy is reflected in the form of the *loyal toast in Lancashire.

Chancellor of the Exchequer The minister with responsibility for the nation's finances, though technically only no. 2 in the *Treasury. The name dates back to the 12C, when the king's treasurer and his advisers met round a table with a chequered cloth; the squares were a form of abacus, enabling relatively rapid financial calculations to be made on the spot.

In recent decades the chancellor has made an autumn statement, announcing the results of the *public spending round, and has followed this with his *budget in the spring. But it was announced in 1992 that in future the two would be merged each December, beginning in 1993.

Chancery Division see *High Court.

Changing the Guard Two separate ceremonies in London which take place daily in the summer and on alternate days in winter. At 11.00 a.m. (10.00 on Sundays) a troop of mounted guards from the *Household Cavalry takes over in the courtyard on the Whitehall side of *Horse Guards; and at 11.30 a company of infantry, usually from one of the regiments of *Foot Guards, replaces the old guard with a ceremony in the forecourt of *Buckingham Palace.

Channel see *Strait of Dover.

Channel 3 and **4** see *television.

Channel Islands (133,000 in 1991) Group of islands off the northwest coast of France, which became attached to the British crown at the time of the *Conquest as part of the dukedom of Normandy. They have remained

Chancellors of the Exchequer since 1945

1945	Hugh Dalton
1947	Stafford Cripps
1950	Hugh Gaitskell
1951	R.A. Butler
1956	Harold Macmillan
1957	Peter Thorneycroft
1958	Derick Heathcoat Amory
1960	Selwyn Lloyd
1963	Reginald Maudling
1964	James Callaghan
1967	Roy Jenkins
1970	Iain Macleod
1970	Anthony Barber
1974	Denis Healey
1979	Geoffrey Howe
1983	Nigel Lawson
1989	John Major
1990	Norman Lamont

linked with Britain ever since (the only part of Normandy of which this is true) and are now crown dependencies. They have internal self-government, which includes making their own tax laws, and for purposes of administration they are divided into two bailiwicks. One is Jersey (capital St Helier); and the other Guernsey (capital St Peter Port) with Alderney, Great and Little Sark, Brechou, Herm, Lihou and Jethou as dependencies. In addition each island has its own parliament, known as the States (except on Sark, where it is called the Chief Pleas). Sark is also unique in retaining a feudal system with a hereditary overlord of considerable power, known as the Seigneur when male and the Dame when female.

The population is mainly of Norman descent, though Alderney has a majority of English settlers, and both French and English are spoken throughout the islands. Farming and fishing have provided the traditional economy. The famous local varieties of dairy cow, the Jersey and the Guernsey, notable for the high butterfat content of their milk, were recognized as breeds from the 18c, when laws were passed preventing the import of any cattle to the islands except for slaughter. Small and usually fawn-coloured, they are believed to have descended from the indigenous cattle of the nearest parts of the mainland, Normandy and Brittany. Jersey's skill in knitwear is reflected in the widespread use of the word *'jersey', and the island is famous also for its Jersey Royal potatoes. In recent times greenhouse tomatoes have become a major crop, particularly on Guernsey. Tourism and tax benefits are of importance in the economy of the islands.

The islands were the only part of the British Isles to be occupied by the Germans in World War II, from July 1940 to 9 May 1945.

Channel Tunnel The first agreement between France and Britain to cooperate in the construction of a tunnel beneath the *Channel was signed in 1875, after some 20 years of preparatory work by engineers – including at the start Brunel and Robert Stephenson. The scheme soon foundered and was not revived until 1957. Discussions and reports led to an announcement in 1966 that work would begin in 1968 and that the tunnel would be open by 1975. In the event no serious progress was achieved until the mid-1980s, when a firm commitment was made to a privately funded twin-track rail tunnel (with drive-on facilities for cars). At Lille in January 1986 and at Canterbury the following month Mrs Thatcher and President Mitterand met to complete the formalities. The company undertaking the project was Eurotunnel, and the contractors carrying out the work were a consortium of ten British and French firms operating together as Transmanche Link (subsequent disputes over cost between these two groups amounted to sums in excess of £1bn).

Drilling through the chalk sea bed began at points northeast of Folkestone and southwest of Calais. In October 1990 the two tunnels met and the first narrow borehole was broken through to link them. Meanwhile there had been much confusion and controversy about the route of the rail link for high-speed trains from the tunnel to London, with the result that a fully effective British service will be delayed long after the French equivalent. In 1992 the tunnel was scheduled to open for shuttle trains between Calais and Folkestone during the winter of 1993–4 and for services between London and Paris in the summer of 1994.

Paul Channon (b. 1935) Conservative politician, MP for Southend West since 1959. After being minister for the arts in 1981–3, he entered the cabinet in 1986 as secretary of state for trade and industry (1986–7) and was then secretary of state for transport (1987–9).

A compressed-air boring machine, expected in 1882 to speed up work on the Channel Tunnel.

chapel see *Nonconformists.

Charlie **Chaplin** (1889–1977, KBE 1975) The greatest comic actor of the silent cinema. Born in London to parents who were in the *music hall, Chaplin's first public performance was at the age of eight in a *clog dancing act. He was on stage with the Fred *Karno company from 1906. When performing on tour in New York in 1913, he was offered a part in one of the Keystone company's short slapstick films; he never returned to the stage and the rest of his career, until the 1950s, was in the USA.

For his second film with Keystone, *Kid Auto Races at Venice* (1914), Chaplin improvised the costume of baggy trousers, walking cane, bowler hat and moustache which soon provided both his trademark and his character in films. His special appeal lay in his timing in slapstick farce together with the pathos which he found in the character of the tramp. The combination turned him into one of the cinema's first great stars, with sufficient wealth and power to form a production company, United Artists, in partnership with two other actors, Mary Pickford and Douglas Fairbanks.

The best of his shorter films was *The Kid* (1921), while his great silent features were *The Gold Rush* (1925), *City Lights* (1931) and *Modern Times* (1936). In *The Great Dictator* (1940), a satire on Hitler, Chaplin spoke coherent dialogue for the first time. He later added narrative sound-tracks to the silent films but his patronizing attitude to the 'little fellow' does them considerable disservice.

Chaplin was among those persecuted for supposed Communist sympathies in the Hollywood witch-hunts of the 1950s. In 1952 he moved to Switzerland, not setting foot again in the USA until 1972 when he returned to receive an honorary Oscar. His life was made the subject of a major film in 1992, directed by Richard *Attenborough.

Herbert **Chapman** (1875–1934) One of football's legendary managers, for his ability to deploy a team to the best tactical advantage on the field and for his achievements with two clubs in particular. He took over Huddersfield Town in 1921; the club won the FA Cup in 1922 and became League champions in each of the following three years. He moved in 1925 to Arsenal and guided them to victories in the League (1931, 33) and in the FA Cup (1930); after his death Arsenal carried on to win the League in 1934 and 1935 and the FA Cup in 1936.

Chapman's *Homer* see John *Keats.

Charge of the Light Brigade (25 Oct. 1854) The best-known incident in the Battle of Balaklava, and indeed in the entire *Crimean War. The Russians had captured artillery posts on heights to either side of a valley north of Balaklava. The British army commander, Lord Raglan, sent an order for the Light Brigade (cavalry on nimble horses, lightly armed with sabres or lances) to attack the Russians on one of the isolated heights. The order became garbled in the delivery and the commander of the brigade, Lord *Cardigan, led his men down the valley between the heights. In the resulting slaughter, a third (247 of 637) were killed or wounded. The fame of the event is partly due to the speed of communication in the age of the electric telegraph. It was only six weeks later that *Tennyson's poem *The Charge of the Light Brigade* appeared in London, in the *Examiner* of 9 December 1854.

> Cannon to right of them,
> Cannon to left of them,
> Cannon in front of them,
> Volley'd and thunder'd.

His lines include the tell-tale phrase 'someone had blundered' (as had indeed been reported by *Russell of the *Times*) together with his famously bleak image of a soldier's duty:

> Their's not to reason why,
> Their's but to do and die:
> Into the valley of Death
> Rode the six hundred.

Yet the overall theme of the poem was drama and heroism, with a last verse beginning: 'When can their glory fade?'

Charing Cross The last of the *Eleanor crosses, where the queen's body rested on the final night before her burial in Westminster Abbey. It stood where Whitehall now joins Trafalgar Square, and was pulled down by order of parliament in 1647. A replica was created in 1863 and was placed in the forecourt of Charing Cross station.

Charing Cross Road (London WC2) A thoroughfare created in the 1880s by the widening of narrow slum streets leading north from Trafalgar Square. It became associated in particular with second-hand bookshops, a reputation widely publicized by the book and play *84 Charing Cross Road*, based on Helene Hanff's correspondence from New York with the firm of Marks and Co. (which ceased trading in 1970 when the site was redeveloped).

Charing Cross Station (London WC2) The mainline terminal closest to the centre of London, designed by John Hawkshaw (1811–91) for the South Eastern Railway. It opened in 1864. In the early 1990s the station was encased within a new building by Terry *Farrell.

Chariots of Fire (1981) Film directed by Hugh Hudson about the 1924 Olympics, at which Harold *Abrahams won the 100 metres. It won an Oscar as best picture.

Charity Commission (London SW1) Public body established in 1853, and in its present form deriving from the Charities Act of 1960. It keeps a register of Britain's charities (there are some 170,000) and decides on new applications for charitable status, as well as providing advice and checking on abuses. There are five charity commissioners, of whom three are full-time; at least two of the five must be lawyers.

Charlecote Park (8km/5m E of Stratford-on-Avon) Only the gatehouse remains unaltered of the mansion built in the 1550s by Thomas Lucy; the rest was reconstructed during the 19c in the Victorian idea of an Elizabethan style. Much of the furniture was brought from *Beckford's Fonthill, itself an even more ambitious exercise in historical fantasy.

Glamour has long been added to Charlecote by the tradition (early in origin though unsupported by hard evidence) that the young Shakespeare was caught poaching deer in the park, that he was brought before Sir Thomas Lucy as the local magistrate, and that the shameful incident caused the lad to remove to London, where he found fame and fortune. He is also believed to have satirized Sir Thomas in the character of Justice Shallow, who in *The *Merry Wives of Windsor* accuses Falstaff of having killed his deer.

Prince **Charles** see the Prince of *Wales.

Charles I (1600–49) King of England, Scotland and Ireland from 1625; second surviving son of James I and Anne of Denmark; married in 1625 Henrietta Maria, sister of the French king Louis XIII.

Charles became heir to the throne when his elder brother Henry died in 1612. In 1623 he travelled incognito to Spain with his father's favourite, the duke of *Buckingham, in the hope of marrying the Spanish princess Maria, sister of Philip IV. But the projected alliance failed, causing the French marriage to be adopted as an alternative two years later.

The history of Charles's reign was one of increasing hostility between himself and parliament. He retained the intensely unpopular Buckingham as his chief minister and twice dissolved parliament (in 1626 and 1628) to forestall attempts to impeach him. The next parliament, which passed motions criticizing the king's own conduct,

Linen shirt, with drawn threadwork borders, which Charles I is believed to have worn on the scaffold.

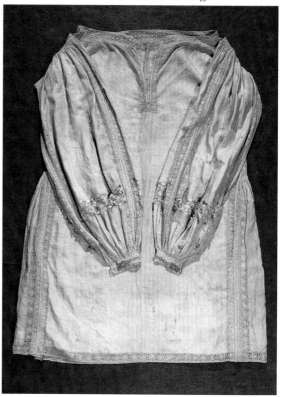

was dismissed in 1629. Charles then ruled for 11 years without parliament. But he summoned two parliaments in 1640 when urgently in need of funds after the opposition to *ship money and his defeat in Scotland by the *Covenanters. It was his relationship with the second of these parliaments, the *Long Parliament, which led to the *English Civil War and to his own eventual capture in 1647.

In January 1649 he was put on trial in Westminster Hall, charged with high treason as the personal cause of England's troubles. He refused to plead, denying that a king could legally be tried by such a court. On January 30 he was beheaded on a scaffold erected in Whitehall, in front of Inigo Jones's Banqueting House. He was succeeded by his son Charles II, though it was another 11 years before he was able to ascend the throne.

Charles was among the most civilized of British monarchs. He built up one of the best collections of paintings in Europe (dispersed in the Commonwealth), and was a patron of Rubens and in particular of Van Dyck – in whose portraits the king, the queen and their courtiers retain a living presence unmatched in any reign before or since.

Charles II (1630–85) King of England, Scotland and Ireland from 1660; eldest surviving son of *Charles I and Henrietta Maria; married Catherine of Braganza in 1662.

Living abroad from 1646 (in France, the Netherlands, Spain), Charles made only one military attempt to recover his throne after the execution of his father in 1649. With the promise of support from the *Covenanters, he landed in Scotland in June 1650 and was crowned at Scone in January. A march south ended in defeat by Cromwell at Worcester (3 Sept. 1651), from which Charles escaped after hiding in an oak tree at *Boscobel. The Commonwealth was now secure under Cromwell. But after Cromwell's death there was a gradual drift towards anarchy, and in 1660 parliament opened negotiations with Charles for his return.

Politically his reign was dominated by religion. He was by nature tolerant, partly because he wished to heal national wounds and partly because the influence of his years in exile predisposed him to freedom for Roman Catholics. But the Cavalier Parliament (1661–79) was in a vindictive mood against Roundheads and passed the acts known collectively as the *Clarendon Code, restricting Nonconformists and Catholics alike. Anti-Catholic feeling was whipped up in 1678 by the *Popish Plot, and this was immediately followed by a campaign to exclude the king's heir (his brother, the future James II), from the succession because he was a Roman Catholic – a bitter dispute which introduced *Tories and Whigs into British politics.

The *Restoration period, one of licentiousness and cynicism, was a reaction against the drab years of the Commonwealth but also reflected the king's own pleasure-loving character. No other monarch has spawned so many new ducal families from the offspring of his acknowledged mistresses, of whom the best known were Barbara Villiers (Countess of Castlemaine and Duchess of Cleveland, 1641–1709), Louise de Kéroualle (Duchess of Portsmouth, 1649–1734) and Nell *Gwyn.

Charles became a Roman Catholic, typically late and rather casually, on his deathbed. He is credited with two last sayings, both very human: 'Let not poor Nelly starve', and the hope that the bystanders would excuse him for being 'an unconscionable time dying'.

Charley's Aunt (1892) Farce by Brandon Thomas (1856–1914), in which a male friend of two Oxford undergraduates dresses up as his rich aunt from Brazil, to provide a compliant chaperone when they entertain a pair of young ladies to tea. The opportunities for disaster are compounded when the real rich aunt arrives. 'Brazil, where the nuts come from' is the play's most famous and most often repeated line.

Charlie and the Chocolate Factory (1964) Children's book by Roald *Dahl in which young Charlie Buckett, poor and hungry, finds himself on a tour of a strange chocolate factory owned by Willy Wonka, where the workers are pygmies (the Oompa-Loompas) and greedy children can come to a very sticky end.

Charlotte Dundas see *steam.

Charlotte Square The outstanding architectural feature of *Edinburgh's New Town, designed in 1791 by Robert Adam and built (with certain modifications) in 1792–1807. The north side of the square is entirely his. The central house, no. 6, is the official residence of the secretary of state for Scotland. No. 7, the 'Georgian House', is furnished and on display as an example of a rich Edinburgh residence in the late 18C.

Bobby **Charlton** (b. 1937) Footballer (midfield) for Manchester United (1954–73), known in particular for often spectacular shots at goal. He was a survivor of the Munich air disaster, and was in the teams which won the League in 1957, 1965 and 1967 and the FA Cup in 1963. But his greatest fame came with his performance in the England team which won the 1966 World Cup. He made in all 106 international appearances; his record of 49 goals for England was threatened but not equalled in 1992 by Gary *Lineker.

Jack **Charlton** (b. 1935) Elder brother of Bobby *Charlton and a footballer (centre back) for Leeds United (1952–73), where his great height and long neck brought him a nickname, the Giraffe. His international career began late, in 1964 (when he was 29), but he was in the team which won the World Cup in 1966 and he eventually made a total of 35 appearances for England. He has had a successful second career as manager, most notably of Ireland's national team since 1986.

Charter 88 Pressure group which was launched with a document, *Charter 88*, issued in 1988. This argued that a number of specific reforms were urgently needed in Britain. Prominent among these were a written *British constitution; a bill of rights (or, as a first step, the European Convention on Human Rights written into British law); *devolution to a Scottish assembly; *proportional representation; and *freedom of information (which turned out to be the issue on which the public felt most strongly). The movement canvases support by persuading an increasing number of people to sign the charter and by vigils to publicize the cause. The name reflected the rather more courageous Czech example of Charter 77, but it also acknowledged an important British constitutional centenary in 1988 – that of the *Revolution of 1688.

Charterhouse Boys' *public school, which since 1872 has been in the country near Goldalming in Surrey. It moved there from London, where it was founded in 1611 on the site of a Carthusian monastery destroyed in the Reformation – hence the name Charterhouse and the reason why boys from the school are known as Carthusians. The founder of the school was a rich merchant, Thomas Sutton (1532–1611), who at the same time established an adjacent almshouse (the Charterhouse pensioners still live on the original site). Since 1972 girls have been admitted to Charterhouse for the final two years, in the sixth form.

Wood engraving based on a depiction of Chaucer himself in an early manuscript of The Canterbury Tales.

Leslie **Charteris** see the *Saint.

Chartists Supporters of the People's Charter, which was drawn up in London in 1838 and which made six specific demands for political reform. The hard economic conditions of the following ten years caused Chartism to develop into the first nationwide working-class political movement. But agitation, occasional violence and a petition with 3 million signatures failed to move parliament to action, and after the repeal of the *Corn Laws in 1846 the immediate pressure for reform dwindled. Nevertheless only one of the six demands in the Charter (for a *general election every year) has not since been met. The others all now seem an indispensable part of democracy: a vote for all adults (males only in the Charter), constituencies of roughly equal size, a secret ballot, payment for MPs and no property qualification to become an MP.

Chartwell (26km/16m NW of Tunbridge Wells) Home of Winston *Churchill from 1922 till his death. A redbrick Victorian house was remodelled for him by the architect Philip Tilden (1887–1956). Some of the rooms are kept now as he lived in them, including the study where he wrote his books; others are a museum of memorabilia, with cigar boxes, wide-brimmed hats, his wartime *siren suits (several of them in in velvet) and many of his paintings. The gardens contain long stretches of wall that he built himself (one of his more unusual hobbies) and the studio in which he painted. On the lake are descendants of his black swans, originally a gift from Australia.

Chatham (62,000 in 1981) Town in Kent, near the mouth of the river Medway, which has been important in British naval history since Henry VIII established a royal dockyard there. Over the centuries many of the navy's most famous ships were built at Chatham, including HMS *Victory. The dockyard was finally closed in 1984,

and is now a museum. The town also has close associations with Charles *Dickens.

Earl of **Chatham** (William Pitt, known as Pitt the Elder, 1708–78, earl 1766) Politician in charge of British policy in the *Seven Years' War (1756–63). After entering parliament in 1735 for Old Sarum, Pitt established a reputation as a brilliant young rebel. At the same time he carefully nurtured a following in the country, becoming known as the Great Commoner. By the 1750s his reputation was such that he seemed the natural leader in time of war, though two dukes (Devonshire and Newcastle) were in turn the nominal head of government. In 1766 Pitt briefly headed a ministry of his own, but his part in public life was soon reduced by the onset of mental illness. Nevertheless in 1777 he made impassioned speeches in the House of Lords against the American war, insisting that the colonists' grievances be redressed because 'You cannot conquer America'. The Great Commoner has become best known to history as Chatham only because his son was an even more distinguished William *Pitt.

Chatsworth (14km/9m W of Chesterfield) One of the greatest of Britain's stately homes, seat of the dukes of Devonshire. It was built for the 1st duke in 1686–1707 on the site of an earlier house, the main design being by William Talman (1650–1719). Changes in the surroundings were made for the 4th duke by James Paine (1717–89), who built the very stately stable block and the bridge, an important feature in Capability *Brown's design of the park. Finally the house itself was greatly extended for the 6th duke in the 1820s by *Wyatville.

In the grounds the famous Cascade, with water tumbling down a long succession of steps, survives from the formal garden laid out for the 1st duke, as does the Sea Horse Fountain. The other great water feature, the *Emperor Fountain, was devised in the 19c by the most famous of Chatsworth's gardeners, Joseph *Paxton. He also built here in 1836–40 (well before the *Crystal Palace) the Great Conservatory (91m/300ft long) which was demolished in 1920.

Thomas **Chatterton** (1752–70) Boy poet, born in Bristol, whose pseudo-medieval poetry was an important part of the early *Romantic movement. At a time when *Ossian was still believed to be genuine, Chatterton invented a 15c priest, Thomas Rowley, whose poems he claimed to have discovered. Coming to London and finding himself alone and unrecognized, he committed suicide in an attic room when still only 17 – a tragic scene later immortalized in one of the best-known Pre-Raphaelite paintings, by Henry Wallis (1856, Tate Gallery).

Geoffrey **Chaucer** (c.1343–1400) The greatest poet in England before Shakespeare, and the first to make English, rather than French or Latin, the main language of his poetry. The son of a rich London wine merchant, his career was closely involved with the royal court; he was variously employed on diplomatic missions, as controller of customs, and as clerk of the works. The palace and the households of great nobles also provided his audience; it was in such gatherings that he read his poems, which then circulated in manuscript. It was not till nearly a century after his death that *Caxton brought him a wider readership.

A learned and bookish man, his genius ranged from the courtly elegance of *Troilus and Criseyde to the rumbustious vigour of the most popular scenes in The *Canterbury Tales. Much admired in his own time, he was granted the honour of burial in Westminster Abbey, where his tomb later became the nucleus of *Poet's Corner.

Cheddar Britain's best-known cheese, due to the name becoming a general term for any that is smooth, medium-hard and pale or yellow. The general run of packaged cheddar has given the original version a bad name – indeed it used to be widely known as 'mousetrap'. But a traditional farmhouse Cheddar, increasingly in demand again in the 1990s, can be deliciously tangy and moist. Cheddar was only one of many Somerset villages making cheese of this kind from at least the 16C; but sales were mainly to visitors to the famous *Cheddar Gorge, so the rest of the world came to know Somerset cheese by that name.

Cheddar Gorge (11km/7m NW of Wells) Ravine winding for about 3km/2m through the Mendips between limestone cliffs (in places 130m/425ft high) before emerging at Cheddar. The cliffs are riddled with hundreds of caves, inhabited in prehistoric times. The two most dramatic, with their stalactites and stalagmites, are Gough's Cave and Cox's Cave. Jacob's Ladder is a steep flight of 322 steps up one face of the gorge. A smaller nearby gorge, Burrington Combe, is believed in local tradition to have inspired the famous hymn *Rock of Ages.

Cheddleton Flint Mill (16km/10m NE of Stoke-on-Trent) The water wheels of two mills face each other across a mill race on the river Churnet. The north mill was built about 1756–65, probably by James *Brindley, to grind flint for the Staffordshire potteries (the addition of powdered flint whitened the wares); it remains much as when in use. The south mill, an older corn mill adapted to grinding flint, houses a museum of the raw materials used in the ceramics industry.

Chedworth Roman Villa (11km/7m to the NE of Cirencester) The best preserved *Roman villa in Britain (*Fishbourne being more of a palace), with good mosaic floors in the dining room and in the range of rooms for bathing. Household objects are on show in the museum.

Chelmsford (58,000 in 1981) Market town and administrative centre of Essex. From the 13C this was where Essex's law courts were held and where the county's taxes were collected. But it was not until 1914 that Chelmsford became a diocese and the parish church of St Mary (15C, much rebuilt) acquired the status of a cathedral. The neoclassical Shire Hall, completed in 1792, is by John Johnson (1754–1814), who designed several buildings in the town. *Marconi established his business here in the early years of the century and electronics has become the main local industry.

Chelsea (London SW3 and SW10). Area in west central London on the north bank of the Thames. It was a village when Thomas More built himself a country house here in the 16C and when the *Chelsea Hospital was built in the 17C. Its reputation as London's artistic quarter derives from the late 19C, when Whistler and Rossetti lived by the river. In the 1980s the *King's Road was where tourists went in search of *punks.

Chelsea, known as the Blues (Stamford Bridge, London SW6). Football club founded in 1905 and in Division 1 for much of the time since 1907. Club victories: FA Cup 1970; League Champions 1955; League Cup 1965; European Cup-Winners' Cup 1971.

Chelsea Arts Club (London SW3) A *club founded in 1891 by a group of artists – including *Whistler, who had been instrumental in *Chelsea becoming a district associated with painters. The club moved in 1902 to its present premises in Old Church Street, adapted from two 18C cottages with a large garden. It was best known to the outside world through the famous Chelsea Arts Ball. With magnificent costumes and elaborate decorations by London art students, the ball was held from 1910 at the Albert Hall – until 1921 on Shrove Tuesday and then on New Year's Eve. But the annual event became so rowdy that after 1958 it was discontinued (there was an October revival of it at the Albert Hall in 1992). In the 1960s members other than practising artists were for the first time admitted to the club.

Chelsea bun Square currant bun made in *Chelsea as early as the 17C, recognizable by two very distinct characteristics. It is made from a coil of sweet dough with the currants between the coils, and its edges are white and fluffy where it has been separated from its neighbour on the baking tray.

Chelsea Flower Show The annual show of the *Royal Horticultural Society, held for four days in May in the gardens of *Chelsea Hospital.

Chelsea Hospital (London SW3) The name by which the Royal Hospital in *Chelsea is more commonly known. Commissioned by Charles II (traditionally prompted by Nell *Gwyn, but there is no evidence for this) and built in 1682–92 by *Wren, the imposing building with its wings reaching down towards the Thames was designed to house 440 old soldiers. It is still home for about that number. They are known as the Chelsea Pensioners and are a familiar sight in the district in their uniforms of scarlet in summer, dark blue in winter.

Chelsea Pensioners see *Chelsea Hospital.

Chelsea Physic Garden (London SW3) The third oldest *botanic garden in the country, founded in 1673 by one of the *City Livery Companies, the Apothecaries' Society, for purposes of teaching and research. In 1681 the Society installed Britain's first heated greenhouse (visited and much admired by John Evelyn in 1684). Hans *Sloane acquired the garden in 1712, linking it with the Royal Society and greatly enhancing its use both to botany and medicine.

Chelsea porcelain The earliest English porcelain, made in *Chelsea from at least 1745 (the year of the first clearly dated pieces). The success of the factory was due to Nicholas Sprimont (1716–71), by trade a silversmith. He produced both tableware and ornamental figures, relying heavily on existing continental models (at first Meissen, later Sèvres). The factory was also known for the so-called 'Chelsea toys', miniature pieces such as scent bottles. Chelsea porcelain is dated in a succession of periods, identifiable by marks on the base: a triangle (up to 1750), raised anchor (1750–2), red anchor (1752–6) and gold anchor (after 1756). In 1770 the firm was bought by the *Derby factory. The wares of the two factories were marketed together until the Chelsea site was closed down in 1784, the years 1770–84 being known as the Chelsea-Derby period.

Cheltenham (73,000 in 1981) Town in Gloucestershire which has preserved the spacious and elegant feeling of its period of greatest prosperity, the 18C and early 19C. It was a market town until the discovery of mineral springs in 1718 set it on course to become a fashionable spa. The Pump Room in Pittville Park (1825, by John Forbes) became in 1983 a museum of costume and jewellery. The Art Gallery and Museum, a general collection but with an emphasis on the Cotswold school of early 20C furniture, is in a building of 1899 by W.H. Knight.

An 1823 caricature of Cheltenham spa: Effects of the Cheltenham Waters, or 'tis Necessary to Quicken your Motions.

The house in which Holst was born is now a museum in his honour. The town is known for its many schools, which include one of the leading public schools for girls, Cheltenham Ladies' College, founded in 1853. The redoubtable Miss Beale (1831–1906) was headmistress from 1858 until her death.

Famous since the early 19c for its superbly situated racecourse, Cheltenham now holds its National Hunt Festival each March. The most important steeplechase is the Gold Cup (for 5-year-olds and upwards), established in 1924 and run over 5.2km/3.25m.

Cheltenham Festival There are two annual cultural events under this name at *Cheltenham. The music festival, held in June or July, was established immediately after World War II; the composers taking part in 1945 included William Walton, Benjamin Britten and Arthur Bliss. The emphasis has tended to be on contemporary British music, and for a while there was a particularly strong link with the Hallé orchestra and Barbirolli; they appeared at 15 successive festivals from 1947. The other Cheltenham Festival, founded only slightly later (1949), is concerned with literature; held each autumn, it has developed into Britain's major annual gathering of writers and their readers.

Walter **Chepman** see Androw *Myllar.

Chepstow (21km/13m E of Newport) Town in Gwent on the river Wye, with a very early Norman castle straddling a rocky bluff above a curve in the river. The central 2-storey tower was built in about 1070 by William FitzOsbern, one of William the Conqueror's closest circle of friends. Unusually for the time, he built in stone rather than wood. Much enlarged in the 13c, the castle is now a ruin.

Chequers (in full Chequers Court) Official country residence of the prime minister. An old house in the Chilterns, to the west of London, it was largely rebuilt in the 16c and was given neo-Gothic trimmings in the 19c. It was bought in 1909 by Arthur Hamilton Lee (1868–1947, Conservative MP for Fareham 1900–18, viscount Lee of Fareham 1922). He restored it, furnished it, and in 1917 gave it to the nation with a large endowment for its present purpose. The first prime minister to use it was Lloyd George in 1921.

Cherry ripe Setting by Charles Horn (1786–1849) of a poem by *Herrick in which the rough cry of a street trader is adapted to the most delicate and desirable of cherries, in a girl's complexion.

Lord **Cherwell** (Frederick Lindemann, 1886–1957, baron Cherwell 1941, viscount 1957) Physicist who had great influence during World War II as Churchill's personal assistant and scientific adviser, holding the post of paymaster general in 1942–5 (he was more widely known as 'the Prof'). In World War I he worked out on scientific principles how to bring a plane out of a previously fatal spin, and then courageously demonstrated the technique in the air.

Cheshire (967,000 in 1991, administrative centre Chester) *County in the northwest of England.

Leonard **Cheshire** (1917–92, baron 1991) World War II hero and provider of refuge for the incurably handicapped; by the early 1990s there were some 270 Cheshire Homes in 49 countries. As a pilot in Bomber Command he received the *Victoria Cross in 1944 – not, as in other cases, for a single act of bravery but for his role in a long succession of dangerous missions (many of them with the *Dam Busters squadron, of which he became leader shortly after their famous raid).

The Cheshire Homes started almost accidentally. After 18 months in hospital with TB, and a conversion to Roman Catholicism, he attempted to establish a community home for ex-servicemen. Instead, finding himself in possession of a large empty house (Le Court, in Hampshire), he gave shelter to an incurable patient from a local hospital – the first of many. In 1959 Cheshire married another tireless crusader in a similar cause, Sue *Ryder.

Cheshire Cat see *Alice in Wonderland*.

Cheshire cheese A pale cheese, mild in flavour and crumbly in texture. Cheshire is the oldest named district for cheese-making in Britain (it is mentioned in this context in the Domesday Book), and traditional farmhouse Cheshire is still made in the county. The loose texture of the cheese, and the local custom of using skewers to drain the whey, made it easily infiltrated by mould. In previous centuries cheese going green or blue with mould was thrown away (or used in small quantities for medicinal purposes on wounds and sores), but from the 1920s it began to be sold as the now very popular blue Cheshire.

Cheshire Cheese (London EC4) A pub of great antiquity, just off Fleet Street, with many writers and artists among its past patrons. Even Samuel Johnson is claimed to have been of their number, though hard evidence is lacking. A more certain regular was a parrot at the time of World War I. On Armistice night it repeated some 400 times its trick of imitating the pop of a champagne cork, before collapsing from temporary exhaustion.

Chesil Bank Shingle strip 29km/18m long on the coast of Dorset, separating an elongated lake (the Fleet) from the sea and reaching to the Isle of *Portland. Nature has mysteriously sorted the pebbles by size; at the northern end they are smaller than ping pong balls and at the southern too large for tennis.

Chester (58,000 in 1981) One of England's oldest and best preserved cities; administrative centre of Cheshire. It was founded by the Romans in the 1st century AD, on a curve of the river Dee, as the chief base for their legions in the northwest. The Roman name for the town itself was *Deva*, but 'Chester' derives from the first word of the Latin *Castra Devana* (camp on the Dee).
Chester is the only city in England where the entire circuit of the medieval city wall survives. In the Middle Ages it was a prosperous port, until the Dee silted up. That was the period, too, of Chester's cycle of *mystery plays, revived in modern times outside the cathedral. This was originally the church of a Benedictine abbey (11–16c, much restored in the 19c). It acquired the status of a cathedral in 1541, when Chester became an Anglican diocese.
The east gate of the city wall is surmounted by the Eastgate Clock, an elaborate wrought-iron timepiece presented to the city in 1897 to commemorate the diamond jubilee of Queen Victoria. But the most striking of all Chester's attractions are the Rows, a unique architectural feature in which the houses – many of them black and white *timber-frame buildings of the 16c – include at first-floor level a continuous covered shopping arcade. The Grosvenor Museum opened in 1886 in a Renaissance-style building designed for the purpose by a local architect, Thomas Lockwood (1830–1900). It specializes in local items, including decorative arts and paintings, and has a particularly strong collection from Chester's Roman period.
The Roodee, a meadow by the river, has been used for horseracing since the 16c, making Chester races England's oldest meeting.

Earl of **Chester** see Prince of *Wales.

Cheltenham Gold Cup: winners since 1960

	Winner	Jockey
1960	Pas Seul	Bill Rees
1961	Saffron Tartan	Fred Winter
1962	Mandarin	Fred Winter
1963	Mill House	Willie Robinson
1964	Arkle	Pat Taaffe
1965	Arkle	Pat Taaffe
1966	Arkle	Pat Taaffe
1967	Woodland Venture	Terry Biddlecome
1968	Fort Leney	Pat Taaffe
1969	What a Myth	Paul Kelleway
1970	L'Escargot	Tommy Carberry
1971	L'Escargot	Tommy Carberry
1972	Glencaraig Lady	Frank Berry
1973	The Dikler	Ron Barry
1974	Captain Christy	Bobby Beasley
1975	Ten Up	Tommy Carberry
1976	Royal Frolic	John Burke
1977	Davy Lad	Dessie Hughes
1978	Midnight Court	John Francome
1979	Alverton	Jonjo O'Neill
1980	Master Smudge	Richard Hoare
1981	Little Owl	Jim Wilson
1982	Silver Buck	Robert Earnshaw
1983	Bregawn	Graham Bradley
1984	Burrough Hill Lad	Phil Tuck
1985	Forgive'n'Forget	Mark Dwyer
1986	Dawn Run	Jonjo O'Neill
1987	The Thinker	Ridley Lamb
1988	Charter Party	Richard Dunwoody
1989	Desert Orchid	Simon Sherwood
1990	Norton's Coin	Graham McCourt
1991	Garrison Savannah	Mark Pitman
1992	Cool Ground	Adrian Maguire
1993	Jodami	Mark Dwyer

Chesterfield (71,000 in 1981) Ancient industrial town in Derbyshire, where lead was mined in Roman times, widely known now for the crooked spire of the 14c parish church of St Mary and All Saints. Beneath a lead covering it is constructed of timber, which has warped and twisted to bring the top 2.4m/8ft out of the vertical.

Lord **Chesterfield** (Philip Stanhope, 4th earl of Chesterfield, 1694–1773) Politician and author, now remembered largely through Dr Johnson's abuse of him. His unfulfilled promises provoked Johnson's famous attack on *patrons; and his *Letters to his Son* (private letters to the boy, with advice on all aspects of behaviour in polite society, published in 1774 after both father and son were dead) were dismissed with the Johnsonian comment that they taught 'the morals of a whore and the manners of a dancing master'.

Chesters see *Hadrian's Wall.

G.K. Chesterton (Gilbert Keith Chesterton, 1874–1936) Author best known now for his short stories featuring an unassuming but brilliantly intuitive amateur detective, Father Brown (a Roman Catholic parish priest who first appeared in *The Innocence of Father Brown* 1911). He is also remembered for some of his poems. These include *The Rolling English Road* ('The rolling English drunkard made the rolling English road') and *The Donkey*, in which 'the devil's walking parody on all four-footed things' reminds the reader that he too had his hour, in Jerusalem, with palms before his feet. Chesterton, a close friend of Hilaire Belloc, converted to Roman Catholicism in 1922; he was received into the church by Father John O'Connor, who had been the inspiration for Father Brown.

Chetham's see *Manchester and *music schools.

Albert **Chevalier** (1861–1923) Actor who became a star of the *music hall, singing sentimental *cockney songs. *My old Dutch* is addressed to the 'dear good old gal' he has been married to for forty years; 'duchess', abbreviated to Dutch, was *rhyming slang for 'wife' (from the duchess of Fife, daughter of Edward VII), but Chevalier always maintained that he called his wife this because her face reminded him of an old Dutch clock. This song, like many of his best (including *Knocked 'em in the Old Kent Road*), was written by himself with music by his brother-in-law, Charles Ingle.

Cheviots Range of rounded hills, mainly in Northumberland, which for about 56km/35m form the border between England and Scotland. The Cheviots were for centuries the scene of border warfare, reflected in the ballad *Chevy Chase. The central road north passes through Carter Bar, and the highest peak is the Cheviot itself (816m/2676ft). The *sheep bred in the hills have soft pliable wool, excellent for spinning, and the name cheviot has become a general term for any similar wool or fabric.

Chevy Chase A *ballad of border warfare between the English family of Percy and the Scottish family of Douglas. The title refers to a hunt in the *Cheviots, in which Percy deliberately provokes Douglas by hunting deer on the Scottish side of the hills. In the ensuing battle both leaders die, together with most of their men.

Chichester (24,000 in 1981) County town and administrative centre of West Sussex. The Roman origins of the town (with *Fishbourne Roman Palace nearby) are reflected in the four straight streets which quarter the city and meet at the central Market Cross, an elaborately carved structure of 1501. Established as a diocese in 1075, Chichester's cathedral was built in the 11–15c. The free-standing bell tower was added in the 15c to relieve the central tower of the weight of bells, but in spite of this the tower and spire collapsed dramatically through the roof in 1861 and have been reconstructed. The tapestry behind the high altar is by John Piper.

St Mary's Hospital, founded in the 12c and used since the 16c as an almshouse, has a superb medieval great hall. But the predominant atmosphere of the city is of the 18c, particularly in the southeast quarter known as the Pallants; an outstanding building here is Pallant House, completed in 1713 for a prosperous wine merchant and now open to the public, with a permanent collection in the house and temporary exhibitions in an adjoining gallery. Outside the walls to the north is the Festival Theatre (1962, by Powell and Moya), which had Laurence Olivier as its first director and which continues to mount distinguished summer seasons of new productions.

Francis **Chichester** (1901–72, KBE 1967) English aviator and yachtsman. In 1929–30 he made a solo flight from Britain to Australia in a Gipsy Moth biplane. He used the same name for his yachts when he took up ocean sailing, at the age of 51. In *Gipsy Moth III* he won the first solo transatlantic race in 1960. He was 65 when he set off from Plymouth on a solo round-the-world voyage (27 Aug. 1966 – 28 May 1967) in the 16.5m/54ft *Gipsy Moth IV*. He was knighted on his return by Elizabeth II with the sword of Francis *Drake. *Gipsy Moth IV* now lies at *Greenwich beside the *Cutty Sark*.

Chi-Chi see *London Zoo.

chief and **chieftain** Head of a Scottish *clan, a position hereditary within a family. The words are often used indiscriminately, but sometimes 'chief' is kept for the head of an entire clan and 'chieftain' for the leader of a subsidiary group. The chief is referred to by a repetition of the clan name; thus the chief of the Macleod clan is the Macleod of Macleod.

Chief of Air Staff see *Royal Air Force.

Chief of Defence Staff see *armed forces.

Chief of General Staff see *Army.

Chief of Naval Staff see *Royal Navy.

Chief Rabbi (Chief Rabbi of the United Hebrew Congregations of the British Commonwealth of Nations) Though widely accepted as the religious spokesman for all *Jews in Britain, the Chief Rabbi's direct pastoral authority is only over the Orthodox section of the community. Immanuel *Jakobovits was succeeded as chief rabbi in 1991 by Jonathan *Sacks.

Chief Secretary to the Treasury An office of cabinet rank, technically third in seniority within the *Treasury, created in 1961 to ease the burden on the chancellor of the exchequer. The specific responsibility of the chief secretary is the control of public expenditure, and it is he who conducts each autumn's *public spending round. For holders of the office since 1983 see the *cabinet.

child abuse A highly controversial subject in Britain since the late 1980s. The NSPCC reported during the 1980s a steady increase in cases of sexual abuse of children, but the matter first received national attention when two paediatricians in Cleveland (Marietta Higgs and Geoffrey Wyatt) declared that a surprisingly large number of children in their region were being sexually abused at home – their conclusion was based on the results of one particular test (children's anal dilation). Others argued that they had misinterpreted the evidence. In 1987 an enquiry was set up under Lord Justice Butler-Sloss to investigate what had by then become known as the Cleveland scandal. In 1988 the Northern Regional Health Authority banned Marietta Higgs from working in the field of child abuse and severely reprimanded Geoffrey Wyatt.

In her Cleveland report Dame Elizabeth Butler-Sloss made specific recommendations as to how social workers should conduct such cases, but she later complained that these were widely disregarded. There was soon a new element to complicate the issue. Ritual or satanic abuse of children was suddenly discovered in a variety of places, shortly after American 'experts' had publicized the problem and its symptoms. In 1990 14 children in Rochdale were taken into care by social workers in dawn raids on their homes, on the suspicion of having suffered ritual sexual abuse. In February 1991 the same thing happened to nine children in the Orkneys. In both cases courts later ordered the immediate return of the children to their families – though only 10 of the 14 in Rochdale. (A court of appeal in Scotland subsequently judged that the sheriff had reacted too hastily in sending the Orkney children home, but a 1992 report by Lord Clyde roundly condemned the procedures which had led to the children being removed in the first place).

There had as yet been no firm proof anywhere of satanic abuse. Those who believed in its existence were confident that it would be put beyond doubt in a trial of three men and two women in November 1991, charged

Thomas Bewick's celebrated 1789 wood engraving of The Chillingham Bull.

with ritual abuse of two sisters, aged 10 and 14, in Epping Forest. But in the middle of the case the judge instructed the jury to bring in verdicts of not guilty, on the grounds that the crucial evidence of the younger girl was unreliable (she had described being forced to eat the flesh of sacrificed babies).

Childe Harold's Pilgrimage (1812–18) The poem which made *Byron's reputation and launched on the world the Byronic hero – a moody and rebellious character, Byron himself in real life and Childe Harold in this autobiographical poem. Written in the verse form of Spenser's *Faerie Queene*, and with its title and opening sections mock-medieval in spirit ('Whilome in Albion's isle there dwelt a youth . . . Childe Harold was he hight'), it soon settles down into a richly detailed account of a young man's responses to some of the most romantic places in Europe, all recently visited by Byron. The first two cantos were an instant success in 1812 ('I awoke one morning and found myself famous'). Cantos 3 and 4 followed in 1816 and 1818.

Children's Hour (BBC 1922–64) The main children's radio programme for two generations in Britain, beginning in the first year of the *BBC's existence and broadcast early every evening. For many years it had regional editions, and presenters round the country became much loved as Uncle or Aunt; the best known was London's Uncle Mac (Derek McCulloch, 1897–1967). It was he who played the part of Larry the Lamb in the programme's famous *Toytown* series, which began in 1929. There were widespread protests when *Children's Hour* was brought to an end in 1964; audiences were falling because of the rise of television and the success of programmes such as *Blue Peter*.

Chillingham cattle Famous herd of wild white cattle, survivors of a native British breed, which have lived in the grounds of Chillingham Castle in Northumberland for some 700 years. *The Chillingham Bull* is the largest and most famous of Thomas *Bewick's woodcuts.

Chiltern Hundreds A parliamentary oddity. No member of the House of Commons is allowed to resign his or her seat during the course of a parliament. But equally no member is allowed to occupy any 'office of profit' belonging to the crown. Since the 18C these two restrictions have been neatly combined. A member wishing to resign a seat applies to become steward either of the Chiltern Hundreds (the three 'hundreds' or small areas of Stoke, Desborough and Burnham in the Chilterns) or of the Manor of Northstead; both offices once carried a salary from the crown, both are now defunct. The member who applies for either does nothing and is paid nothing but must relinquish the seat in parliament; he or she then resigns the stewardship to make it available for another applicant.

Chilterns Range of chalk hills (highest point Coombe Hill, 251m/825ft) running about 64km/40m northeast from the Thames near Reading. Famous for their fine beech woods, they have long been considered a very desirable residential area as the closest range of hills to the west of London.

Chindits (also known as Wingate's Raiders) Guerrilla force, combining British, Gurkha and Burmese troops, which operated behind the Japanese lines in Burma from 1943. They were organized by Orde *Wingate, who also suggested their name – from *chinthé*, a mythical Burmese lion which they used as a badge.

The modestly sized Chiswick House with its vastly impressive entrance: Burlington's elegant model of Palladianism.

Chinese The longest-established ethnic minority in Britain apart from the *Jews. There was a Chinese community in the port of Liverpool from the early 19C as a result of the trade in tea and silk with Canton, and the Chinese laundry soon came to feature in music-hall songs as an established part of working-class culture. Nevertheless more than half Britain's relatively small Chinese population (about 140,000 in the early 1990s) are immigrants, mainly from Hong Kong. A related import from Hong Kong is the Triad, a form of organized crime similar to the Mafia and with equally strong historical roots. Four Triad gangs are known to operate in Britain, extorting protection money from Chinese businesses.

Chinese Chippendale see Thomas *Chippendale.

chinoiserie Decorative style which swept Europe in the 17–18C, when Chinese figures, pagodas, dragons and birds became the fashion in ceramics, fabrics, furniture, silver and wall coverings. Among the best-known English applications of the style are Chinese *Chippendale and the *willow pattern, while the most prominent surviving example, late in the day, is the interior of the *Royal Pavilion in Brighton. The pagoda in *Kew Gardens is a large-scale expression of the same theme.

chintz Printed cotton fabric, often in floral patterns. The word derives from the Hindi *chint* meaning 'many-coloured', and the original 'chints' were hand-painted cloths imported from India in the 17C. With a new spelling, the word became applied to printed cotton made in Britain, usually glazed.

Thomas Chippendale (1718–79) The best-known English cabinet-maker of the mid-18C, largely because he published in 1754 an unusually detailed and wide-

ranging collection of furniture designs, known as the *Director* (in full *The Gentleman and Cabinet-Maker's Director*). The designs are mainly *rococo in style, one particularly influential section indulging the taste for *chinoiserie in what became known as Chinese Chippendale. There is no clear evidence as to how many of the designs were Chippendale's own (as opposed to being commissioned from other designers or lifted from foreign sources), and pieces were immediately produced to these patterns by other cabinet-makers. Therefore most mid-18C Chippendale is merely furniture based on one of the plates in the *Director* or done in a similar style. But in some great houses (*Nostell Priory, for example) documents survive to authenticate pieces as having come from Chippendale's own workshop in St Martin's Lane, London.

From about 1770 he adopted the *neoclassical style under the influence of Robert *Adam, providing superb furniture for Adam's decorative schemes in such houses as *Harewood. The firm continued into the 19C under its founder's son, also Thomas Chippendale (1749–1822).

chips see *fish and chips.

Chirk aqueduct see *Pont Cysyllte.

Chirk Castle (34km/21m SW of Chester) Solid and rather squat castle, built 1290–1310 for Roger Mortimer. It has been lived in continuously since then and so has acquired Tudor and 18–19C internal features without ever denying its medieval character. The superb wrought-iron entrance gates of 1719–21 are the work of the Davies brothers of Bersham, near Wrexham.

Chiswick House (London W4) Villa built 1725–9 by Lord *Burlington in the grounds of his Jacobean mansion (no longer surviving) in the countryside just west of London. A notable example of his commitment to *Palladianism, it is based mainly on Palladio's Villa Capra, near Vicenza. Of great formal elegance but surprisingly small, its purpose was to house his paintings and books and to provide a meeting place for his friends. In the interior decoration and in the design of the garden Burlington was assisted by William *Kent.

chloroform see James *Simpson.

chocolate The Aztecs and others in central America used crushed cocoa beans as the basis for a drink, and Columbus took some beans back to Spain in 1502. The Spaniards kept this expensive delicacy to themselves, and it was not until the 17C that it began to spread. The first shop in London selling chocolate opened in 1657. The first *coffee house was then also new, and the two drinks were in the following decades an essential part of social life for the richer classes (both drinks were expensive). The addition of milk, much improving chocolate as a drink, was a London innovation in about 1700. It was not until the 19C that bars of sweetened chocolate were first sold for eating, a market in which the *Cadbury family established an early lead. The Cadburys (like other famous chocolate families, such as Fry and Rowntree) were Quakers, and the sale of cocoa and chocolate as drinks was seen as part of the fight against alcohol.

Christian see *The *Pilgrim's Progress*.

Fletcher Christian (dates unknown) Acting lieutenant or second-in-command on HMS *Bounty*, and leader of the mutiny in 1789 against Captain *Bligh. He subsequently sailed the ship to Tahiti, and later moved on again with some of the mutineers, accompanied by Tahitian men and women. No more was heard of them until one survivor and the English-speaking descendants of the group were discovered on *Pitcairn Island in 1808. The survivor said that Christian had died on Pitcairn, but there were persistent rumours in the early 19C that he returned to Britain. He has been portrayed on film by Clark Gable in 1935 and by Marlon Brando in 1962.

Christian Aid (London SE1) The relief and development agency of the British Council of Churches, working in more than 70 countries. It derives from an initiative by British churches in 1944 to raise money for relief in a Europe shattered by war. The first Christian Aid week, with door-to-door collections throughout the country, was held in 1957 and has become a familiar annual fixture. The charity itself adopted the name Christian Aid in 1964.

Christians The first Christians in Britain arrived with the *Romans, and the religion found many followers among the well-to-do. The *chi-rho* monogram (formed of the first two letters of the Greek word for Christ) is featured in the Roman villas at Chedworth and *Lullingstone and on spoons in the *Mildenhall and *Hoxne treasures; it also appears on the earliest known representation in Britain of Christ himself, in a 4C mosaic pavement found at Hinton St Mary in Dorset (now in the British Museum). But this first veneer of Christianity did not long survive the departure of the Romans.

The lasting conversion of Britain depended on two separate missionary endeavours. One derived from the efforts of St *Patrick in Ireland, influencing Scotland and northern England from *Iona and *Lindisfarne. The other came from Rome, with the arrival of St *Augustine in Kent. The rival claims of these two strands of Christianity were resolved at the *Synod of Whitby in 664, with the victory going to Rome.

Roman Catholicism remained the Christianity of Britain until the 16C, when the *Reformation resulted in two different forms of the faith in the *Church of England and the *Church of Scotland. During the 17–18C several of the most important breakaway Christian groups had their origins in England, in particular the *Baptists, *Quakers and *Methodists.

Classed as *Nonconformists, these sects lived under severe restrictions until the 19C, as did the surviving small minority of *Roman Catholics. By contrast Ireland had been relatively little affected by the Reformation, in spite

Linford Christie in red, white and blue after his triumph at the 1992 Barcelona Olympics.

of strenuous efforts from England, and it remained largely Roman Catholic. The exception was the northern province of *Ulster, which was settled during the 17C with Protestants, mainly from Scotland, as a deliberate colonial policy – a measure which still has disastrous results in *Northern Ireland today.

The 19C saw a great revival of Christian fervour in the educated classes in England, with the rise of *Anglo-Catholicism, but the inhabitants of the new industrial cities were drifting increasingly outside the reach of the churches. And the 20C has seen a steady decline in churchgoing, particularly in the Church of England; by the 1970s there were more Roman Catholics than Anglicans in church on an average English Sunday. The most recent figures for church attendance derive from a census carried out on Sunday 15 October 1989 in all places of Christian worship in England (it did not extend to other parts of Britain). Adult churchgoers on that day numbered 1,304,600 Roman Catholics, 1,143,900 Anglicans, 396,100 Methodists, 199,400 Baptists, 114,000 in the United Reformed Church, 95,200 Pentecostal, 68,500 Afro-Caribbean, 57,300 Salvation Army, 12,300 Seventh-Day Adventists, 9400 Orthodox, 4700 Lutheran, 1800 Moravian, 1500 Society of Friends (Quakers); and 292,800 grouped together as Independent churches. All the major groups had declined in number from ten years previously apart from the Afro-Caribbeans, the Pentecostalists and (by far the largest increase) the Independents; these are many small groups, characterized above all by the House Church Movement, worshipping in people's own homes.

Christian Scientists Followers of the teaching of the American Mary Baker Eddy (1821–1910), as expressed in her *Science and Health with Key to the Scriptures* (1906). The sect lays great emphasis on the Bible and on spiritual healing (the resulting rejection of conventional medicine being its most controversial aspect). Mrs Eddy founded the First Church of Christ, Scientist, in Boston. There are now some 2500 branch churches and societies internationally, of which about 215 are in Great Britain.

Christian Socialism see *muscular Christianity.

Agatha **Christie** (Agatha Miller, 1890–1976, m. Archibald Christie 1914, DBE 1971) The most successful English writer of detective fiction since Conan Doyle, and the creator of two very different detectives – the Belgian Hercule Poirot, who featured in her first book (*The Mysterious Affair at Styles* 1920) and the elderly Miss Marple, who made her bow in *The Murder at the Vicarage* (1930). Both have become widely known to film and television audiences. Their author's reputation was firmly established in 1926 with *The Murder of Roger Ackroyd*. According to the *Guinness Book of Records* she is the all-time bestselling writer of fiction; her 78 crime novels are estimated to have sold two billion copies in 44 languages.

Agatha Christie was also a phenomenally successful playwright, most notably with *Witness for the Prosecution* (1953) and *The *Mousetrap*. After her first marriage ended in divorce, she married Max Mallowan, an archaeologist. A famous mystery in her own life was a much publicized and still unexplained disappearance for a few days in 1926.

Julie **Christie** (b. 1940) Film actress, whose international career was established early with **Billy Liar* (1963), *Darling* (1964, bringing her an Oscar) and *Dr Zhivago* (1965).

Linford **Christie** (b. 1960) Britain's finest sprinter, winner of the gold medal for the 100 metres at the 1992 Olympic Games with a time of 9.96 seconds. He is only the third Briton ever to have won this event, after Harold

*Abrahams in 1924 and Alan *Wells in 1980. His Olympic gold was added to the European and Commonwealth titles, both of which he won in 1990. His fastest time has been 9.92 seconds, but this brought him only fourth place in the 1991 World Championships in Tokyo.

Christie's (Christie, Manson and Woods, London SW1) Auctioneers established in London by James Christie in 1776. Starting with general furniture and household effects, he soon began to specialize in fine art, a field in which the firm held an undisputed lead until challenged by *Sotheby's in the mid-20C. His son James moved to the present address in 1823. William Manson became a partner in 1831, and Thomas Woods in 1859.

Christ in Majesty see *Llandaff.

Christmas Christmas derives originally from two pagan sources, both celebrating the return to health of the sun after its shortest day (the winter solstice, December 21 or 22). The Roman emperors had chosen December 25 as the birthday of *Sol Invictus*, the unconquered sun, with which they identified themselves; and in Rome this was the season too of the Saturnalia, a period of revelling and present-giving. Meanwhile the pagan tribes of northern Europe enjoyed a 12-day winter festival called Yule, with its own traditions of trees and mistletoe. Christianity adopted and adapted both (easier than launching a new festivity).

The medieval Christmas was a prolonged event, the period of Yule having turned into the *twelve days of Christmas (a concept which survives now mainly in the secular carol of that name). Twelfth Night, the night of January 6, was the climax of the revels, after which life had to return to normal. The *Puritans, recognizing the pagan origins of the Christmas revels, did their best to suppress them. They were successful in Scotland, where the most important winter festivity became the *New Year.

The modern English Christmas retains the elements of feasting and present-giving, much overlaid with additions from the 19C (these include the *Christmas card, the *Christmas tree, and *Father Christmas). The Christmas meal is essentially now a family affair, and is usually held at midday. The ingredients have become surprisingly standardized. Where a joint of beef or a goose once provided the main course, it is now almost invariably a turkey, well stuffed (often with sage and onion at one end, chestnut at the other) and accompanied by *bread sauce and cranberry sauce. It is followed by *plum pudding and *mince pies.

The table is decorated with crackers, which first made their appearance in early Victorian times. Their contents were originally sweets with a motto or a poem, but now are trinkets with punning jokes, the awfulness of which is a large part of their appeal.

The traditional decoration for the living room at Christmas has been holly (which must be taken down on Twelfth Night but not before); it probably dates back to pagan times as a symbol of the revival of life, being evergreen and bearing berries in midwinter. In the same spirit a branch of mistletoe has provided a time-honoured place for kissing under. It was the old custom that any man who claimed a kiss beneath it removed one berry, and when there were no more berries the kissing had to stop.

Since 1932, when George V first spoke to the nation on radio, an integral part of Christmas Day has been the king's or queen's Christmas message at 3 p.m. It has been broadcast on television since 1956.

Christmas is a *bank holiday, as are *Boxing Day (Dec. 26) and New Year's Day. Since a weekend is bound to fall between December 25 and January 1, the entire period is increasingly taken as a midwinter holiday by many in Britain, returning almost to the medieval tradition of the twelve days of Christmas.

Christmas cake Rich fruit cake, traditionally with marzipan and white sugar icing. It is more likely to be eaten during the Christmas season than on Christmas day itself, where pride of place goes to the Christmas pudding, made of similar ingredients.

Christmas cards The first Christmas card was designed by John Callcott Horsley in 1843 for Henry Cole (an important figure in the early days of the *Victoria and Albert Museum). A thousand copies were printed. It depicted a happy family gathering which caused some offence to the temperance lobby, for the young children were shown with wine glasses.

A Christmas Carol (1843) A cautionary tale for Christmas, by Charles *Dickens. On Christmas Eve the miserly Scrooge sees visions of Christmasses past, present and future, including a glimpse of his own likely end if he dies despised and hated. He wakes up on Christmas morning a reformed character, and promptly sends a turkey to his underpaid clerk, Bob Cratchit. The great success of the story caused Dickens to publish a Christmas book in several of the following years.

Christmas Day in the Workhouse see *Poor Laws.

Christmas pudding A rich, dark pudding made of flour, suet, eggs, currants and other dried fruit, spices, ale and brandy. It usually has the upturned shape of the bowl in which it has been steamed, but sometimes is a complete sphere. It is served as the pudding course on Christmas day, accompanied by *brandy butter; traditionally a sprig of holly crowns it, lucky silver charms and coins are concealed within it, and flaming brandy is poured over it just before it is served. The old custom was for all the family to take a turn at stirring the Christmas pudding with a wooden spoon on Stir-Up Sunday – a day in late November on which the Anglican collect requests the Lord to 'stir up the wills' of His faithful people, that they may bring forth 'the fruit of good works'.

The Christmas pudding is also known as a plum pudding. In the late 17C, when a pudding of this kind is first mentioned (already in connection with Christmas), the word 'plum' was used for dried currants and raisins.

Christmas stocking see *Father Christmas.

Christmas tree A decorated fir tree in the house at Christmas was an established custom in Germany long before it began to spread in the 19C. It was also in occasional use in England before the marriage of Prince *Albert to Victoria in 1840. But it was his addition of it to the royal Christmas which gave it sudden and wide popularity. The best-known Christmas tree in Britain is the one which goes up in Trafalgar Square. It has been an annual gift since 1947 from the city of Oslo, in commemoration of friendship in World War II – when the king of Norway was in London with a government in exile.

Christopher Robin The central character in the children's books of A.A. *Milne, based on his own son. Christopher Robin Milne has described (in *The Enchanted Places* 1974) the difficulties associated with this unusual type of fame.

Christ's Hospital Independent school for boys and girls, founded by Edward VI in 1552 for the education of poor London children. It was established in buildings in Newgate Street which had belonged to the Franciscans, or Greyfriars. During the 18C the girls were moved to Hertford, and in 1902 the boys' school transferred to its present site at Horsham in West Sussex; here the girls rejoined them in 1985, reuniting the school in its original form after more than two centuries.

The boys still wear the traditional *blue-coat uniform of charity children, with yellow stockings under their long blue robes, but the girls now have a newly designed blue dress (old pupils of both sexes are known as Old Blues). Christ's Hospital had a distinguished literary period in the late 18C, when its pupils included Coleridge and Lamb.

Church Army Evangelical organization, much involved with social work, founded in the slums of London in 1882 by an Anglican clergyman (Wilson Carlile, 1847–1942). It is in effect the Church of England's answer to the *Salvation Army.

Church Commissioners The administrators of the property and investments of the Church of England, the income from which is used mainly for the salaries and pensions of the clergy. The commission was established in 1948 by merging the administration of Queen *Anne's Bounty (established in 1704) with the Ecclesiastical Commissioners (1836).

Winston **Churchill** (1874–1965, KG 1953) Prime minister 1940–45 and 1951–5, and perhaps the most determined and inspirational war leader in Britain's history.

Born in Blenheim Palace, grandson of the duke of Marlborough, his background was one of privilege. It was also political. His father, Lord Randolph Churchill (1849–95), was a brilliant orator and a controversial leader of a splinter group within the Conservative party. His mother, Jennie Jerome, was the daughter of a flamboyant American speculator.

After an unhappy time at Harrow, Churchill became an officer in the 4th hussars. Posted to Cuba, India, the Sudan and South Africa, he supplemented his income with newspaper articles; and it was as a journalist that he achieved sudden fame in 1899–1900, when his dramatic reports from the Boer War for the *Morning Post* included an account of his own escape from a Boer prison camp. Throughout his life he derived his main income from writing, in particular his massive personal histories of the World Wars, *The World Crisis* (6 vols, 1923–31) and *The Second World War* (6 vols, 1948–54). He was awarded the Nobel prize for literature in 1953.

Churchill had unsuccessfully contested the seat of Oldham as a Conservative in a by-election in 1899, but he returned from South Africa to win it in the *'khaki' election of 1900. He held it until 1906, and later was MP for Manchester (1906–8), Dundee (1908–22), Epping (1924–45) and Woodford (1945–64). He is rare among modern politicians in having crossed the floor of the House twice, defecting to the Liberals in 1904 and back to the Conservatives in 1924.

He rapidly achieved high office, becoming president of the Board of Trade in 1908. As home secretary (1910–11) he became an ogre for the left through sending troops to deal with strikes in the Welsh mines and through his personal involvement in the *Sidney Street siege (this reputation was later reinforced by his militant response to the *General Strike in 1926). His energies as first lord of the Admiralty (1911–15) did much to prepare the navy for World War I, though his bold plan for *Gallipoli ended in disaster. At the same period he gave influential support to a new invention, the *tank.

His time as chancellor of the exchequer (1924–9) is remembered chiefly for his disastrous decision to put Britain back on the *gold standard (a policy abandoned in 1931 after insupportable pressure on the currency).

All behind you, Winston: cartoon by Low in 1940, when Churchill took over as prime minister. Attlee and Bevin are beside him, followed by other members of his cabinet.

During the 1930s he was in the political wilderness, his pugnacious attitude to Nazi Germany being at odds with the fashionable policy of *appeasement. If Churchill had died in 1939, history would have remembered him as a brilliant maverick.

On the outbreak of *World War II Chamberlain appointed him to the very post he had held during the previous war, first lord of the Admiralty. But on 10 May 1940, after the failure of the Norwegian campaign, Chamberlain resigned. Churchill was the natural man to succeed him. And it was during that darkest summer of 1940 that his astonishing oratory seemed to rally the nation, from his opening statement to the House of Commons on May 13 that he had 'nothing to offer but blood, toil, tears and sweat'. Each successive crisis produced phrases that have resounded ever since, from the danger of invasion after *Dunkirk ('their *finest hour') to the *Battle of Britain (his tribute to the *Few). With his oratory went his personal trademarks – the large cigar, rarely seen in a much reduced state, and his famous *V-sign.

Churchill lost the general election in June 1945 (in his own words, 'all our enemies having surrendered unconditionally or being about to do so, I was immediately dismissed by the British electorate from all further conduct of their affairs'), but he returned to Downing Street in 1951, finally retiring in 1955. One certainty in a frequently uncertain career had been his very happy marriage, in 1908, to Clementine Hozier (1885–1977); and somehow he had found time to remain an enthusiastic amateur painter.

His death, on 24 January 1965, was followed by the rare honour of lying in state in Westminster Hall and a state funeral in St Paul's Cathedral. He was buried in the small churchyard of Bladon, near Blenheim.

Church in Wales see the *Church of England.

Church of England
The established church in England, which came into being with the Act of *Supremacy in 1534. Henry VIII's quarrel with Rome was more political than theological, and among the Protestant churches this is the most closely related to Roman Catholicism, retaining bishops and much of the Roman basis of the litany in the *Book of Common Prayer. More radically Protestant measures under Edward VI were followed by a brief return to Roman Catholicism under Mary I.

The lasting form of the Anglican church was established in the reign of Elizabeth as a middle way, expressed in the *Thirty-nine Articles; these declared Elizabeth to be Supreme Governor of the Church of England, a position held by English monarchs ever since. From the late 17c the Church of England encompassed two extremes: the High Church party laid emphasis on the authority of bishops and on the importance of ritual; those in the Low Church were closer to the Protestantism of the *Nonconformists. The same distinction has existed in more recent times between *Anglo-Catholics and *Evangelicals.

Since 1970 the governing body has been the General Synod (previously the Church Assembly), consisting of three houses (bishops, clergy, laity) and presided over by the archbishops of Canterbury and York; it meets three times a year.

Offshoots of the Church of England in other parts of the British Isles are the Episcopal Church in Scotland, the Church in Wales and the Church of Ireland. The archbishop of Canterbury is also accepted as the leader of the wider *Anglican Communion. The majority of people in Britain are nominally Anglican, but on an average Sunday the number attending church is not much above a million (see *Christians).

Church of Ireland see *Church of England.

Church of Scotland The national church in Scotland, *presbyterian in structure unlike the episcopal *Church of England. Scotland was strongly influenced in the 16c by John *Knox, but the Stuart kings later favoured that part of the Scottish church which had retained its bishops. With the deposition of *James II the episcopal cause was lost, and in 1690 the Presbyterians were made the established church, their opponents surviving as the independent *Episcopal Church in Scotland. The established link with the state was removed in 1921. A major rift within the church which took place in 1843 (see the *Free Church of Scotland) was mended in 1929. The governing body of the church is the General Assembly presided over by the Moderator, who is elected to serve for one year.

chutney Originally a strong spicy relish of pickled fruit or vegetable, but now usually sweet (mango chutney is a typical example). Discovered by the British in India (*chatni* is a Hindi word), it has been widely used in Britain since the 19c.

CID see *police.

Cider with Rosie (1959) Poetic reminiscence by Laurie Lee (b. 1914) of his childhood in a Cotswolds village during and after World War I, evoking the way of life of rural England at the last moment before its transformation by the motor car.

Cinderella One of the most popular of *pantomimes. The story (a traditional fairy tale published by *Mother Goose in 1697) has all the desirable ingredients: the rags-to-riches story of the heroine who begins in kitchen drudgery and ends by marrying the prince; the opportunity for spectacular transformations (such as the pumpkin turning into a coach); the glamour of a court ball and rich dresses; the excitement of the search for the tiny foot (Cinderella's) which will fit into the glass slipper, all that remained of her after she vanished from the ball on the stroke of midnight; and the low comedy of her jealous ugly sisters, played by men and therefore providing a double ration of the usual pantomime *dame.

Cinderella (1948) Ballet by *Ashton, the first full-length work by an English choreographer. Sergey Prokoviev had written the music during the war (1941–4), and the first of several ballets created to it was presented in Moscow in 1945, with choreography by Zakharov. In Ashton's version, which has won a secure place in the repertoire of the Royal Ballet, the part of Cinderella was intended for Fonteyn, but an accident kept her out of the role for the first performances; instead it was created by Moira *Shearer, with *Somes as the prince and *Helpmann and Ashton as the ugly sisters.

Cinque Ports (pronounced 'sink ports') Group of five (*cinque* in old French) ports on the south coast of England which in the 11–14c had a joint responsibility to provide a royal fleet for the defence of the realm. The original five were Hastings, New Romney, Hythe, Dover and Sandwich; after the Norman Conquest two further towns, Winchelsea and Rye, were added. The group retained a ceremonial identity long after their practical function had ended. Their chief officer, the Lord Warden of the Cinque Ports, is also the constable of Dover Castle and has an official residence in Walmer Castle. Recent Lord Wardens have been Sir Winston Churchill (1941–65), the Australian statesman Sir Robert Menzies (1965–78) and, since 1978, the Queen Mother.

circuits The six areas into which England and Wales have long been divided for the purpose of administering justice. A group of judges is appointed to travel within each circuit, sitting in both *county courts and the *Crown Court. The circuits are the Midland and Oxford (in which the first-tier centres are Birmingham, Lincoln, Nottingham, Oxford, Stafford and Warwick); the North Eastern (Leeds, Newcastle-upon-Tyne, Sheffield, Teesside); the Northern (Carlisle, Liverpool, Manchester, Preston); the South Eastern (Greater London, Lewes, Norwich); Wales and Chester (Caernarfon, Cardiff, Chester, Mold, Swansea); and the Western (Bristol, Exeter, Truro, Winchester).

Circumlocution Office see *Little Dorritt.*

Cirencester (16,000 in 1981) Gloucestershire market town which was one of the most important Roman towns in Britain, under the name *Corinium.* The foundations of the forum and of a basilica and amphitheatre have been excavated, and the Corinium Museum displays many of the finds, including mosaics. The wealth of Cirencester in the Middle Ages, deriving from the wool trade, is seen in the superb Perpendicular church of St John the Baptist (15–16c), one of the largest parish churches in the country and known in particular for its great 3-storey porch on the market square, built in about 1500 to provide ecclesiastical office space.

Citizens Advice Bureau (CAB) Network of more than 1300 offices around Britain, where members of the public can seek free and confidential advice on any subject. About 90% of those staffing the offices are trained volunteers, and in an average year they answer some 7 million questions; family breakdown, debt, legal rights and the complexity of the benefits system are among the most common problems. The service, funded mainly by local authorities and the Department of Trade and Industry, was set up in 1939 to cope with family problems in wartime when children and husbands were likely to be far from home as evacuees and servicemen.

citizen's arrest Each of us has the right to arrest someone committing or suspected of committing an arrestable offence (one carrying a prison sentence of five years or more), but it is a right more easily exercised in the imagination than in practice.

Citizen's Charter *White paper published in July 1991, setting out a programme designed to improve the accountability and the service to the public of government departments and executive agencies (see *Next Steps). The proposals had the direct personal backing of the prime minister, John Major. They included further *privatization and contracting out of services, with an emphasis on more performance-related pay for the providers of services and more choice for the consumers, the public. Each department and agency was instructed to produce its own specialist charter and a set of targets; there have subsequently been charters for patients and parents and passengers, among many others. Members of the public soon found themselves referred to as clients or customers in a wide range of contexts, from people drawing unemployment benefit to passengers delayed on a British Rail train. After the election victory of 1992 John Major set up a new department, the Office of *Public Service and Science, to push forward the implementation of his charter.

Citizens Theatre (Glasgow) Built originally as a music hall in 1878, in the Gorbals district, it is now a distinguished repertory theatre. The first Citizens Theatre was established here in 1945, by the Scottish playwright James Bridie and others. The present company, dating from 1970, has been one of remarkable stability; in the early 1990s it is still run by the three directors who founded it, Giles Havergal, Philip Prowse and Robert David MacDonald.

city The term applies officially in Britain only to those towns which have been incorporated as cities by royal charter. In the past all such cities had cathedrals, and by extension it became the informal custom to describe any town with a cathedral as a city. The first large town without a cathedral to be granted the status of a city was Birmingham, in 1889.

City (City of London, 4000 in 1991) The area of the original walled city of *London, not much more than 2.5sq.km/1sq.m in size and known colloquially as 'the square mile'. It is administered from the *Guildhall by the Corporation of London, headed by the *Lord Mayor (whose residence is the *Mansion House). As the centre of the nation's business and financial activities, the City has for a century or more consisted of little other than office buildings – which explains why the resident population is so small.

City and Guilds (City and Guilds of London Institute, London W1) Body established in 1878 by the Corporation of the *City of London and by the *City Livery Companies to further technical and scientific education. From its very first year it conducted exams in technical subjects, and it established a college of engineering – the City and Guilds College – which is now part of the *Imperial College of Science and Technology.

City Challenge Method of channelling central government funds to *inner city areas, introduced in 1991 by Michael Heseltine as secretary of state for the environment. Local authorities are invited to put forward schemes for regenerating urban areas. These are then judged in competition with all the other submitted schemes, resulting in outright winners who receive the necessary finance and losers who get nothing (in the second contest, in 1992, there were 20 winners and 34 losers). The proposed schemes must involve private money and have the active support of voluntary organizations in the region, in addition to that of the local authority. The competition is intended to be an annual event.

City Livery Companies The descendants of London's medieval craft guilds. Originally sharing the aim of modern trade unions, to promote the well-being of their members, they exercise now mainly a charitable and social function. In recent times it has become the custom to establish new companies for new professions (the Air Pilots' and Air Navigators' Guild, for example) and there are now 94 companies in all. The Great Twelve are, in order of precedence: the Mercers, Grocers, Drapers, Fishmongers (who still exercise their original function, with control over London's fish markets), Goldsmiths (they too retain craft responsibilities, for *hallmarks and for the *Trial of the Pyx), Merchant Taylors and Skinners (alternating in sixth and seventh places after a dispute over precedence in the 15c, or being 'at *sixes and sevens'), Haberdashers (great founders of schools, with eight thriving around the country), Salters, Ironmongers, Vintners and Clothworkers.

City of Birmingham Symphony Orchestra (CBSO) Founded in 1920, with its first symphony concert conducted by Elgar. It benefited from an early spell with Adrian Boult as conductor (1924–30). In recent years it has achieved international status under Simon *Rattle, and in 1991 it acquired the added boost of Birmingham's new custom-built *Symphony Hall.

City Technology Colleges A government initiative, announced in 1986 by Kenneth Baker when secretary of state for education, to create new state secondary schools in inner city areas, specializing in science and technology. Funded directly by central government and by sponsorship from commerce and industry, they were to be outside *LEA control and were in this sense forerunners of the later government policy of *opting out. The first CTC opened in Solihull in the West Midlands in 1988, and by the autumn of 1991 there were 13 in existence. It seemed by that time that rather less private sponsorship had been provided than was originally promised or expected.

Civic Trust (London SW1) Charity set up by Lord Duncan-Sandys in 1957 as a pressure group to improve standards in townplanning and the environment. Supported by membership fees and sponsorship, it advises on environment legislation, publishes pamphlets and reports, and acts as the national voice for almost 1000 local amenity societies.

Civilisation (BBC 1969) Thirteen-part TV documentary series on western art from the early Middle Ages to the 19C, written and presented by Kenneth *Clark. Rich visual pleasures of this kind in the living room had only recently become possible with the arrival of colour television. The series was the first to show the potential of such material if well filmed and presented in an easy but nevertheless serious manner.

Civil List The annual payment by parliament to meet the expenses of the royal household. In 1760 George III surrendered the hereditary income from royal property (now known as the Crown Estate) in return for the civil list, and this arrangement is renewed at the start of each reign. In the early 1990s the annual net income from the Crown Estate was in excess of £60m; the queen's civil list was fixed for each year of the 1990s at £7.9m. Ten other members of the *royal family have also until recently received public funds (usually referred to as part of the civil list, though technically separate parliamentary annuities). The total cost of these was fixed for the 1990s at an annual figure of £1.89m, but in 1992 the queen declared that she would in future pay the expenses of nearly all of them.

Two royal possessions, the duchies of Lancaster and Cornwall, were excluded from the Crown Estate. The income of the duchy of Lancaster provides the privy purse, used by the monarch for semi-official purposes; and that of the duchy of Cornwall meets the expenses of the prince of Wales (also duke of Cornwall), who receives no funds from the civil list. The queen's personal wealth (a matter of constant speculation in the press, though the figure is inflated to unreal levels by the inclusion of the value of palaces and paintings) is applied to her private expenses. It became a matter of some controversy in the 1990s that she was the only person in the realm to be exempted from tax (a concession granted to her father and continued in the present reign). The matter was resolved in 1992, when the prime minister announced her agreement that her income and capital gains should be taxed.

Civil Service Collective name for the civilian officials working in the departments of central government. The term originated in the 18C in the *East India Company, to describe those British employees of the company engaged in administration in India (as opposed to those in the military service). In 1968 the post of minister for the civil service was created; it is held by the prime minister.

Civil War see *English Civil War.

Clackmannanshire Until 1975 a small inland *county in the centre of Scotland, now part of the Central region.

clan Important social group in Scotland, particularly in the Highlands. The members of a clan come originally from the same region and share the same surname but are not directly related. The system may have developed when the *Scots were establishing control in the 9C. It was the clans who supported the Young Pretender in 1745, and the power of their chieftains was deliberately broken after *Culloden. The existence of a clan *tartan plays an important part in the modern sense of group identity.

Clapham Junction Railway station in south London, opened in 1863, the busiest in the country (and for a time in the world) with about 2200 trains passing through each day. On 12 December 1988 it was the scene of a major accident when an express ran into a stationary commuter train carrying more than 900 passengers, of whom 35 died. The cause was signal failure due to faulty rewiring.

Clapham omnibus The man on the Clapham omnibus has been a phrase for the ordinary man since the 1890s (when the word 'omnibus' was already archaic, replaced by the abbreviation 'bus' for the horse-drawn vehicle of those days). The choice of the omnibus from Clapham into London, rather than from any other terminus, seems accidental. It may perhaps derive from an article of 1857 in the *Journal of the Society of Arts* about London's traffic, where the author says congestion has become so normal that the passenger on the roof of a Clapham omnibus can be stuck on London Bridge for half an hour without complaining.

Clapham Sect The name given to a group of influential Anglicans, most of them living in the London district of Clapham, who devoted much money and effort to missionary causes. They were formed in the 1790s and met in the Clapham house of the banker Henry Thornton (1760–1815), with whom *Wilberforce was lodging at the time. Prominent among their activities was the campaign for the abolition of the *slave trade.

Eric **Clapton** (b. 1945) Rock guitarist, known for trying to keep a lower profile than his skill will allow. After playing with several groups, notably the Yardbirds and Cream, he issued his first solo album, *Eric Clapton*, in 1970. *Layla*, his best-loved song, appeared in the same year, ostensibly by Derek and the Dominos (Eric attempting concealment as Derek). After absence with a drug problem he returned in 1974 with a hit under his own name, *I shot the Sheriff* (no. 1 in the USA, 9 in the UK). He still has a wide and enthusiastic following, with annual appearances in recent years at the Albert Hall. His albums *August* (1986) and *Journeyman* (1989) reached nos. 3 and 2 respectively in the charts.

Anthony **Clare** (b. 1942) Irish psychiatrist who elicits intimate self-revelation from those who face him on his radio programme *In the Psychiatrist's Chair* (Radio 4 from 1982).

Claremont (8km/5m SW of Kingston-upon-Thames) The earliest surviving example of *landscape gardening in Britain. Claremont broke with the previous rigid formalities of garden design in successive stages. From about 1715 *Vanbrugh and Charles Bridgeman created a garden here which was rural but still geometrical, with a turf amphitheatre and circular lake. In the 1730s *Kent gave these features a more natural outline, and later in the century Capability *Brown made further modifications as well as contributing to the design of the house (now a school) which was built in the park for a new owner, Clive of India.

Clarence House (London SW1) A house adjacent to St James's Palace, designed by John *Nash for the duke of Clarence (later William IV) and completed in 1828. It has always been used as the private residence of a member of the royal family, and since 1953 has been the home of the *Queen Mother.

Earl of **Clarendon** (Edward Hyde, 1609–74, kt 1643, earl 1661) Politician and historian, lord chancellor 1660-7. Appointed guardian to the 15-year-old prince of Wales in 1645, he accompanied him during the years of exile and was the main influence on him when he returned, as Charles II, at the *Restoration. The king and his chancellor were tolerant in religious matters and the misnamed *Clarendon Code reflects not so much his views as those of the vindictively Anglican parliament, known as the Cavalier Parliament. Clarendon gradually lost the favour of the king, who did nothing in 1667 to prevent his impeachment by political rivals. He fled abroad, where he wrote his own *Life* and completed his *History of the Rebellion and Civil Wars in England*, begun during his previous long spell of exile. He left his manuscripts to the university of Oxford, and the profits from his *History* were used to build a new printing house, the Clarendon Press. In 1660 his daughter Anne married the future James II; he thus became grandfather of two queens, Mary II and Anne.

Clarendon Code Term popularized by historians in the past to cover four acts passed by parliament while the earl of *Clarendon was lord chancellor. The purpose of the acts was to restrict *Nonconformists, but the term is inaccurate in that Clarendon himself was not in favour of the measures. The Corporation Act (1661) ruled that all holding office in town corporations must have previously taken the sacrament in an Anglican church. The Act of Uniformity (1662) forced all clergy to accept the *Thirty-nine Articles, thus successfully removing from their livings some 2000 sectarians who had been appointed during the *Commonwealth. The Conventicle Act (1664) made worship illegal outside an Anglican church if more than a very small number were present. And the Five-Mile Act (1665) prevented Nonconformist ministers from coming within five miles of any town or place where they had previously ministered. These precise restrictions were later replaced by the more general discrimination of the *Test Acts.

claret A word of long and varied history. Deriving from Norman French for any 'clear' wine, it was for some centuries used of intermediate wines between the unmistakable extremes of white and red. From about 1600 it inclined to the red side. Only in the past century or so has it had its exclusive modern meaning, restricted to red wine from the vineyards of Bordeaux.

Claridge's (London W1) One of London's most famous hotels. Originally established in 1812, it was known until the mid-19C by the name of James Mivart, its manager. He incorporated a succession of adjacent houses on the present Brook Street site, and when he retired in the 1850s the enterprise was taken over by William and Marianne Claridge – who had previously been running another small adjacent hotel. The present building dates from 1894–8.

Clarissa see Samuel *Richardson.

Dave **Clark** (b.1942) Drummer and film stuntman who in 1958 formed a pop group, the Dave Clark Five, after advertising in *Melody Maker* for fellow musicians. The other four eventually stabilized as Mike Smith (b. 1943, vocals and keyboards), Lenny Davidson (b. 1944, guitar), Denis Payton (b. 1943, saxophone) and Rick Huxley (b. 1942, guitar). Their first and only no. 1 hit in the UK was *Glad All Over* (1963), but *Over and Over* (1965) reached the top in the US. Their many other singles in the top ten included *Bits and Pieces* (1964) and *Everybody Knows* (1967). They split up in 1970.

Jim **Clark** (1936–68) Scottish racing driver who established a phenomenally successful partnership with *Lotus in the 1960s (he won the *British Grand Prix in a Lotus every year but one between 1962 and 1967). He was world champion in 1963 and 1965. He was killed in a Formula Two race at Hockenheim in Germany, when his car suddenly swerved off the track into trees; the reason was never discovered but is thought to have been a puncture.

Kenneth **Clark** (1903–83, KCB 1938, baron 1969) Art historian whose combination of authority and wit made an international success of his TV series *Civilisation* (1969). In addition to his many books on art, he was author of a lively two-volume autobiography (*Another Part of the Wood* 1974, *The Other Half* 1977).

Michael **Clark** (b. 1962) Dancer and choreographer with a considerable cult following. His entertainments combine well-honed classical technique (he was a star pupil of the Royal Ballet School) with a deliberately outrageous punk element of four-letter words, bare bottoms, dildoes and phalluses, deafening music (sometimes that of the Sex Pistols themselves) and, in one famous case, a goldfish taken from its bowl and apparently swallowed alive. Much of this was in his *New Puritans* (1984); a more recent show has been *Mmm...* (1992, to Stravinsky's *Rite of Spring*). Whatever the views on the trappings, critics agree that underlying them is a brilliant and original dancer.

Petula **Clark** (b. 1932) Singer and actress who was a wartime child star on the radio show *It's All Yours* at the age of nine. To a successful career on stage and screen she added pop stardom from the mid-50s. Her first success was *The Little Shoemaker* (1954), to be followed by *Sailor* (1961) and above all *Downtown* (1964).

Arthur C. **Clarke** (b. 1917) Science-fiction author, born in Somerset, who has lived since the late 1950s in Sri Lanka. He is known for the firm grasp of scientific reality underlying his fantasies – demonstrated most famously in an article of 1945, in which he described the technology of communications satellites many years before they became a commonplace of modern life. Space travel has been his theme from one of his first published books, *The Sands of Mars* (1951), to later works such as *Rendezvous with Rama* (1973). A short story, 'The Sentinel', was the basis for the work by which he is most widely known – the Stanley Kubrick film *2001: A Space Odyssey* (1968).

Kenneth **Clarke** (b. 1940) Conservative politician, MP for the Rushcliffe division of Nottinghamshire since 1970. Son of a Derbyshire coal miner (who later kept a small shop in Nottingham), Clarke became a prominent member of the *Cambridge mafia. He entered the *cabinet in 1985 as paymaster general and minister for employment (1985–7), and was then chancellor of the duchy of Lancaster (1987–8). His performance as secretary of state in two of the most high-spending and politically sensitive departments (Health 1988–90, Education and Science 1990–2) established him as a no-nonsense minister who would not be deflected from his purposes. He became home secretary after the general election of 1992.

The **Clash** *Punk rock group formed in 1976 by Mick Jones with Joe Strummer and Paul Simonon (all b. 1955); in 1977 Nicky 'Topper' Headon replaced their original drummer, Terry Chimes. An appropriately anarchic career of live performances was accompanied by a succession of singles in the charts (none in the top 10) and by albums including *London Calling* (1979), *Sandinista* (1980) and *Combat Rock* (1982). Headon was jailed for 15 months for heroin offences in 1987, but the band had broken up in the previous year.

Classic FM see *radio.

Classics Britain's five leading flat races, all long established: the *1,000 Guineas, *2,000 Guineas, *Derby, *Oaks and *St Leger.

Claude or **Claude Lorrain** see *landscape gardening, *picturesque, Richard *Wilson and J.M.W. *Turner.

Clause 4 see *Labour Party.

Clause 28 A clause in the Local Government Act of 1988, making it illegal for local authorities to 'promote homosexuality'. It provoked much controversy, partly for its implicit attack on gay rights but also because it threatened the subsidy of a wide range of cultural activities which might be said to have some homosexual content or link.

Clava Cairns (10km/6m to the E of Inverness) Important group of three large cairns or burial mounds, spanning the transition between the Stone and Bronze Ages (approx. 2000–1500 BC). They are unusual in that all three are ringed by standing stones.

Claverton Manor (5km/3m E of Bath) Neoclassical villa of *c.*1820 by Wyatville which since 1961 has housed the American Museum; 18 rooms are decorated and furnished in the styles of different periods and regions of the USA.

Clean Air Act (1956) The turning point in the improvement of London's atmosphere. Since the 19C London in winter had been notorious for its dense smoky fog, a phenomenon now known worldwide as *smog but locally at that time as a 'peasouper'. The act, making anything but smokeless fuel illegal in central zones, improved conditions rapidly and set a pattern for other cities. London's last peasouper, in the autumn of 1952, reduced visibility in places to a few feet and was calculated to have caused some 4000 deaths.

clearing banks The high-street banks, providing facilities for members of the public to write cheques (in addition to other services). The name refers to membership of the London Bankers' Clearing House, an institution in which all the cheques drawn on any day are balanced against each other so that only the net result is credited or debited to each bank's account with the *Bank of England. In 1992 the clearing banks were the English 'big four' (Barclays, Lloyds, Midland and National Westminster) together with Abbey National, the Bank of Scotland, Clydesdale, Co-operative, Coutts, Girobank, Royal Bank of Scotland, TSB and Yorkshire.

Art deco in the ballroom: a dancing couple in Clarice Cliff's Bizarre series, late 1920s.

John **Cleese** (b. 1939) Author and performer of manic comedy. He was a mainstay of two classic TV series, *Monty Python's Flying Circus* and *Fawlty Towers*. Films in similar vein have included *The Life of Brian* (1978) and *A Fish Called Wanda* (1988). He has also written, with Robin Skynner, a work of popular psychology (*Families and How to Survive Them* 1983).

John **Cleland** see *Fanny Hill.

Cleopatra's Needle (London WC2) Egyptian obelisk on the north bank of the Thames, one of a pair originally put up in about 1500 BC at Heliopolis, close to modern Cairo (the link with the much later Cleopatra is spurious). A single piece of granite, about 18m/60ft high and weighing some 189,000kg/186tons, it was presented to Britain by the Turkish viceroy of Egypt in 1819. It was not till 1877 that a method was devised for transporting it to London, where it was erected in 1878. Its companion is in Central Park in New York.

clerihew see E.C. *Bentley.

Cleveland (557,000 in 1991, administrative centre Middlesbrough) *County in northeast England, formed in 1974 from parts of Durham and North Yorkshire.

Cleveland child abuse case see *child abuse.

Clickhimin Broch (2km/1m S of Lerwick) One of the best preserved brochs (stone towers of the Bronze and Iron Ages) in Scotland. It stands on an island at the end of a causeway in Loch Clickhimin, with space around it for a small settlement. Built in about the 5th century BC, and in use for perhaps 1000 years, its walls (5.5m/18ft thick) still stand 4.5m/15ft high from an original height of probably three times as much.

Clarice **Cliff** (1899–1972) Designer of ceramics, whose brightly coloured hand-painted wares, often in geometric designs, have become one of the best-known features of *Art Deco in Britain. Born in the *Potteries, she emerged as a successful designer in 1928 when her 'Bizarre' range of products was launched by the Newport Pottery.

Clifford's Tower see *York.

Clifton Suspension Bridge (western outskirts of Bristol) Marvel of Victorian engineering which at the time was the longest and highest span attempted (214m/702ft wide and 75m/245ft above high tide), even though the original design by Isambard Kingdom *Brunel had been reduced by the cautious judges of the competition. The work began in 1836 when a continuous wrought-iron bar, 305m/1000ft long and 3.8cm/1.5in thick, was slung across so that a trolley carrying men and materials could be suspended from it. Brunel died before the bridge was completed in 1864, and his Egyptian designs for the supporting piers were never built. But this single span over the craggy Avon gorge continues to amaze and delight.

Clink A prison in use in the 16–17C in London, in Clink Street near the south end of London Bridge, remembered only because its name became a slang term for any jail.

Robert **Clive** (1725–74, baron 1762) Soldier and administrator who laid the foundations of the British empire in *India. At the age of 18 he went out to Madras as a 'writer' (a superior form of clerk) in the *East India Company, but he was soon revealing a military talent in the Company's constant skirmishes with the French. The turning point of his career came in 1757 when he was sent to recover *Calcutta from the nawab of Bengal. He did so, and in the subsequent Battle of Plassey (1757) defeated the nawab. He replaced him with a puppet ruler, introducing the system of British government from behind the scenes which later spread through most of India.

Clive also set a pattern of personal corruption which stained the early years of the British raj. During 1757–60 he accepted a total of some £234,000 in cash together with land worth about £30,000 a year – a record which hardly helped him when, in a second term in Bengal (1765–7), he urged higher standards upon his subordinates. An attempt to convict him of corruption failed after he had defended himself before his peers in an all-night sitting in the House of Lords in 1772. But depression, exacerbated perhaps by an addiction to opium, led to his suicide two years later. His Indian collection is exhibited at *Powis Castle.

Cliveden (13km/8m NW of Windsor) House built in the 1850s by Charles *Barry in the style of an Italian Renaissance palace, with formal gardens and spectacular views down to the Thames. It has twice had a high profile in British political life, first when Nancy *Astor played hostess here in the 1930s to the 'Cliveden set' (supporters of *appeasement) and then, in the 1960s, as the location of the party scenes in the *Profumo affair.

*A **Clockwork Orange*** (1962) Short novel by Anthony *Burgess in which Alex, a 15-year-old Beethoven-loving hooligan in some future totalitarian state, describes how he is brainwashed into passive respectability after an orgy of vandalism. He speaks in 'nadsat', a cocktail of English, cockney slang and bits of Russian – cunningly devised so that the reader soon gets the hang of it. After abjectly demonstrating his new docility, he is left alone to enjoy the Ninth of his beloved 'Ludvig van'. The scherzo soon has him dreaming of 'carving the whole litso of the creeching world with my cut-throat britva' – suggesting the double-edged hope that brainwashing can never be absolute. The book was filmed in 1971 by Stanley Kubrick with Malcolm McDowell as Alex.

Watercolour by Samuel Jackson of the proposed Clifton Suspension Bridge (c.1836), showing Brunel's Egyptian arches at each end.

clog dance Traditional dance in which the wooden soles of the clogs are used to beat out complex rhythms. It was particularly popular in Ireland and northern England. Danced competitively on table tops or as an entertainment in theatres (the infant Charlie Chaplin first appeared before the public with a clog dance), it later had considerable influence on the more sophisticated tap dancing of the USA.

Charles **Clore** (1904–79, kt 1971) Financier, son of immigrants from Russia, who built up a large commercial empire including real estate, manufacturing companies (his British Shoe Corporation was the country's largest maker of footwear) and many retail businesses (among them Selfridges), which he grouped together under the name of Sears. He established the Clore Foundation, which has made many large charitable donations – most notably the Clore Gallery at the *Tate.

closed shop A familiar feature of British industry and of certain professions until the 1980s. *Trade unions had closed-shop agreements either preventing non-members from getting employment (a pre-entry agreement) or forcing everyone in employment to join the union (post-entry agreement). A succession of employment acts during the 1980s established the freedom of the individual not to join a union and removed legal immunity from any union involved in a *strike in defence of a closed shop.

close seasons The times during which it is illegal in Britain to kill game birds or fishes. People are naturally more aware of the other period, the season during which they may legally shoot or fish, and those are the dates given here:

> Grouse: August 12–December 10
> Partridge: September 1–February 1
> Pheasant: October 1–February 1

The law also forbids the shooting of these birds in England and Wales on any Sunday and on Christmas Day. The two so-called game fishes may be caught (with some local variations) during the following periods:

> Salmon: February 1–October 30
> Trout: March 1–September 30

Other freshwater fishes, known collectively as 'coarse', have no close season in southwest England but are protected during March and April in Yorkshire and from March 15 to June 15 in the rest of the country.

'Close your eyes and think of England' A catch phrase used by the British from the late 19C when they found themselves in unpleasant conditions in faraway corners of the empire. The idea that it was once sexual advice to Victorian young ladies seems only a modern joke. A letter written to Eric *Partridge from Australia in 1975, reproduced without comment in his *Dictionary of Catch Phrases*, quotes from a supposed 1912 journal by an unspecified Lady Hillingdon: 'When I hear my husband's steps outside my door I lie down on my bed, close my eyes, open my legs and think of England.' The phrase 'open my legs' is in itself enough to make a date of 1912 highly improbable.

clotted cream (also known as Devonshire or Cornish cream) A speciality of the southwest of England, and in particular Devon and Cornwall. Formed on the surface of milk kept just below boiling point, it is an essential ingredient of a *cream tea.

cloud chamber see Charles *Wilson.

Brian **Clough** (b. 1935) Known now as a football manager, he was also a very effective player; in his Division 2

career (for Middlesbrough and Sunderland) he averaged nearly a goal per appearance, scoring 251 in 274 games. Injury ended his playing career. With Peter Taylor, his assistant, he became manager of Hartlepool United (1965-7), Derby County (1967-73) and Nottingham Forest (1975-93). He took Derby County to victory in the League in 1972, and under his control Nottingham Forest have won the League once, the League Cup four times and the European Cup twice. His son, Nigel Clough, has been with Nottingham Forest since 1984 and has played for England.

clubs The characteristic English club (sometimes called a gentlemen's club to distinguish it from a *working men's club), which developed in its present form in the 18C. Male London society had previously met in the more informal *coffee houses. The new clubs differed in being open only to members, whereas a payment of a penny or twopence gained access to a coffee house. The transition was gradual and the oldest surviving London club, *White's, developed from one to the other.
    The leading entrepreneur of 18C club life was William Almack (d. 1781). In 1762 he opened Almack's club at 50 Pall Mall, where he provided his members with dinner, newspapers and opportunities to gamble; his manager there was Edward Boodle. Two years later he began a club next door, at no. 49, for 27 young aristocrats calling themselves the Macaronis; this one was managed by William Brooks. Each manager soon took his own members elsewhere, to form the independent *Boodle's and *Brooks's. But Almack was meanwhile busy with the even more successful Assembly Rooms which he opened in 1765 in King Street. Known simply as Almack's, these rooms were the site of fashionable balls and gatherings until the mid-19C.
    If the 18C clubs were unashamedly for aristocrats interested in drinking and gambling, those founded in the 19C tended to have a membership sharing more serious interests: science, medicine and literature at the *Athenaeum, politics at the *Reform and the *Carlton, drama and the arts at the *Garrick, travel at the *Travellers. They all occupy magnificent buildings, where members can read, write, play cards, drink and talk, have lunch or dinner and entertain friends. They remain for the most part resolutely masculine, opening certain rooms to women as guests but not allowing them membership. The Reform has been the exception, with female members since 1981; the Athenaeum debated the question and decided against, while the Garrick said a resounding 'no' in 1992.

clumber spaniel see *spaniels.

Clwyd (414,000 in 1991, administrative centre Mold) Since 1974 a *county in Wales, formed from Flintshire, most of Denbighshire and part of Merionethshire.

Clyde The river which has been the heart of Scotland's industry. It rises in the Lowther Hills, in the extreme south of the Strathclyde region, and flows north past New Lanark. There, in the Falls of Clyde, it drops 75m/250ft in 6km/4m – providing crucial energy for cotton mills in the 18–19C and hydroelectric power today. Continuing northwest through Glasgow the river reaches the area known as Clydeside, with many miles of shipbuilding yards, a source of great prosperity in the past but increasingly uneconomic in the late 20C. The length of the Clyde is calculated as 170km/106m from the source of its main headwater, the Daer, to Dumbarton; it there becomes the Firth of Clyde, which stretches about 105km/65m (first west and then south) to the rocky island of Ailsa Craig which is considered its outer limit.

Clydesdale see *carthorses.

CMG see *orders of chivalry.

CND (Campaign for Nuclear Disarmament) Pressure group founded in London in 1958, after Britain had tested its first H-bomb in the Pacific the previous year. In April 1958 the first Aldermaston march took place; 9000 people walked all or part of the 80km/50m from London to the government's Atomic Weapons Research Establishment at *Aldermaston in Berkshire, in a protest repeated as an annual event for several subsequent years. The chief aims of CND have been to achieve *unilateral disarmament by Britain and the removal of American nuclear bases. The ending of the Cold War deprived CND of some of its support. But it has from the start had the subsidiary aim of progressive non-nuclear disarmament, and it has campaigned against *nuclear power. In the early 1990s the organization had about 60,000 members. Its famous symbol (a circle, containing a shape like an aircraft with swept back wings) has become widely used internationally; it was designed by Gerald Holton for the first Aldermaston march.

Coade stone Artificial stone made from the 1760s at a factory in Lambeth, London, belonging to Mrs Eleanor Coade. A form of terracotta with the addition of finely ground glass or quartz, it was cast rather than carved and was used for statues and reliefs as well as for decorative work around windows and doors. The factory closed in 1840.

coal The commodity which more than any other made possible Britain's lead in the *Industrial Revolution. There is believed to have been surface mining of coal in Roman Britain, and by the 13c it was a source of fuel in many regions. It became of economic importance only in the 15–16c, when its increasing use for firing bricks led in turn to brick hearths in which it could be more efficiently burnt as fuel. By the 17c there was a major trade in coal down to London and the south of England from the first area of large-scale mining, *Tyneside. Improvements in the smelting of iron by Abraham Darby and others in the mid–18c led to a surge of industrialization in Staffordshire and the *Black Country. By then Britain was the world's leading producer of coal, with new mines being developed throughout the country – in particular in Scotand, Yorkshire and the valleys of south Wales.

The appalling working conditions and the economic importance of their industry caused miners to take a leading role in the *trade union movement, a position maintained in the *General Strike of 1926. In 1947 the mines were nationalized under the National Coal Board (now British Coal), since when the industry has been much reduced. *Miners' strikes involved major political confrontations in 1974 and 1984. By the mid-1980s the number of collieries had shrunk from nearly 1000 after World War II to about 170; and the number of miners from about 700,000 to 200,000. Fears of future savage reductions in the industry were a major theme of the 1984 miners' strike; if they seemed exaggerated at the time, they were to be fully justified by subsequent events.

By 1992 there were 50 collieries and about 50,000 men working in the industry. In October of that year British Coal made a sudden announcement of a drastic plan; 30 of the remaining 50 pits were to close within six months. There were immediate political repercussions. The reaction at Westminster and among the public forced the government to agree to an enquiry, with the possibility of a reprieve for all but ten of the pits (those earmarked for immediate closure). In December a judge ruled that British Coal and the president of the Board of Trade,

Michael Heseltine, had acted with illegal haste in relation to the closure of the ten. Opponents suspected that the British Coal programme was part of a government scheme to slim the industry down for *privatization. But the underlying fact remained that the domestic market for coal had shrunk far below what the 50 pits could produce – though the chief underlying reason for that had been the decision of the privatized electricity industry to buy gas rather than coal for the nation's power stations.

Coalbrookdale see entries on *Ironbridge and *Coalport porcelain.

Coalport porcelain Wares were produced in the Staffordshire village of Coalport from the mid-1790s by John Rose (c.1772–1841), and some of them were stamped with the name of neighbouring Coalbrookdale (about 5km/3m upstream on the Severn). The term Coalbrookdale has also been generally applied to any Coalport piece which is heavily encrusted with flowers. Coalport porcelain flourished, with a wide range of wares including lavish pieces in imitation of Sèvres, and it is still produced at a factory in *Stoke-on-Trent. The original factory in Coalport is preserved as part of the *Ironbridge Gorge Museum.

coals to Newcastle see *Newcastle.

Eric **Coates** (1886–1957) Composer known in particular for some very famous pieces of incidental music. *By the Sleepy Lagoon* (1930) became the signature tune for *Desert Island Discs. His march *Knightsbridge* (1932) was used to introduce the radio programme *In Town Tonight* (1933–60). *Calling All Workers* began each day's version of *Music While You Work. And the *Dam Busters march featured in the score for the 1954 film.

Cobb see *Lyme Regis.

John **Cobb** (1899–1952) Rival of the two Campbells, father and son, in the pursuit of speed records on land and water. He was the first to drive at more than 400 mph, reaching 649kph/403mph on the Bonneville Salt Flats in Utah in 1947. His average over the required two measured miles was below 400 mph (634kph/394mph), and it was this which was registered as the official record; it lasted until improved on in 1964 by Donald *Campbell. Cobb died when his jet-propelled speedboat disintegrated at more than 320kph/200mph on Loch Ness.

William **Cobbett** (1763–1835) English journalist and politician, with a down-to-earth commonsensical character and a marvellously direct prose style (Carlyle called him the very pattern of *John Bull). He was also a prime example of the radical journalist, instinctively writing in opposition to whoever was in power. His savage attacks on authority got him into frequent trouble – two years in jail for example, in 1809, for 'sedition' in denouncing the flogging of some soldiers who had complained about unjust deductions from their pay. His vast output was mainly published in his own journal, the weekly *Political Register*, which he started in 1802. Here he introduced in 1803 an account of parliamentary debates, which developed into *Hansard; and here there appeared during the 1820s the pieces which formed his most lasting work, published in 1830 as *Rural Rides*. As Cobbett travels through the southern counties, deploring the changes in the country way of life brought about by corrupt politicians and officials and by the baleful influence of metropolitan London (which he calls 'the great Wen'), his observations provide a vivid picture of England in the years just before the *Reform Act of 1832. In the first reformed parliament he was briefly MP for Oldham.

Richard **Cobden** (1804–65) The chief 19c advocate, with John *Bright, of the principle of free trade. Having established his own textile business, he was drawn into politics in opposition to the *Corn Laws, leading the argument in the House of Commons after being elected MP for Stockport in 1841. He remained an MP, for various constituencies, until his death, continuing to campaign for a broader international abolition of tariffs.

Charles **Coborn** (1852–1945) Performer who had in his repertoire two of the best-known of all *music-hall songs, *Two Lovely Black Eyes* (1886, words and music by himself) and *The Man who Broke the Bank at Monte Carlo* (1890, his own music but words by Fred Gilbert).

Charles **Cochran** (1872–1951, kt 1948) Impresario whose promotions ranged from boxing, wrestling and roller-skating, through rodeo at Wembley and *The Miracle* at Olympia, to ballet and serious drama. But he is remembered above all for his brilliant succession of *revues between the wars.

cock-a-leekie A Scottish soup deriving its name from its two main ingredients, chicken and leeks.

John **Cockcroft** (1897–1967, kt 1948) Scientist who in 1932 at the *Cavendish Laboratory, together with the Irish physicist Ernest Walton, achieved the first artificial disintegration of an atom by means of accelerated protons. The protons were directed at lithium nuclei with the resulting release of alpha particles (helium nuclei). It was the start of nuclear fission, and Cockcroft was later closely involved with Britain's *nuclear power programme; he became in 1946 the first director of the atomic energy research establishment at Harwell. He and Walton shared the 1951 Nobel prize for physics.

Christopher **Cockerell** see *hovercraft.

cocker spaniel see *spaniels.

Arthur **Cockfield** (b. 1916, kt 1973, baron 1978) Statistician, businessman and Conservative life peer who was in the *cabinet as secretary of state for trade (1982–3) and as chancellor of the duchy of Lancaster (1983–4).

cockfighting From the 16c to the 19c one of the most popular gambling sports in Britain. Two birds, made more deadly by the addition of sharpened steel spurs, were set to fight to the death in a small enclosed area (the cockpit), often with large bets placed on their chances. Cockfighting was banned in 1849, but still continues in some places illegally.

cockles see *whelk stall.

cockney As with many words, this was a term of ridicule which came later to be used with pride. A cockney was originally any spoilt child brought up in the soft ways of the town rather than the country. By the 17c it was being applied specifically to Londoners and the theory already existed that a true cockney must have been born within the sound of *Bow Bells. The traditional image of the cockney is of someone streetwise and cheeky; in keeping with this, the cockney accent rattles along paying scant attention to consonants.

Coco see *Bertram Mills.

cod wars Disputes in the 1970s between Britain and Iceland, and between the fishing fleets of the two nations, over cod in the north Atlantic. It was eventually agreed, in 1976, that an average of 24 British trawlers a day would be allowed to fish within the 200-mile zone of coastal water claimed by Iceland.

Sebastian **Coe** (often known as Seb Coe, b. 1956) Britain's greatest middle-distance runner in terms of medals won and records broken; he also had exceptional crowd appeal as a deceptively slight figure with the power to destroy all comers. He was spurred on by a very creative rivalry with Steve *Ovett, but Coe had the better of it (12 world records, for example, to Ovett's five). It was in 1979 that Coe first showed his class in dramatic fashion. In the space of six weeks that summer he established new world records for the 800 metres, the 1500 metres and the mile. The following year he added the 1000 metres, as well as bettering his own earlier times at the other lengths; his eventual tally of 12 world records consisted of 9 outdoors and 3 indoors. His career in the Olympic Games was equally impressive – gold for the 1500 metres and silver for the 800 metres in 1980, and the same two medals again in 1984. Coe failed to be selected for the 1988 Olympic games, and soon after the 1990 Commonwealth Games he retired to take up a career in politics.

In 1992 he was elected as the Conservative MP for the Cornish constituency of Falmouth and Camborne. At that time two of his 1981 world records still held after 11 years: 1:41.73 for the 800 metres and 2:12.18 for the 1000 metres.

Coeur de Lion see *Richard I.

C of E Abbreviation for *Church of England.

coffee The drinking of coffee in Arab countries goes back to at least the 15c and it began to spread through Europe in the 16c. The first coffee house in London opened in 1652, and soon the social life and much of the business of the capital city was being conducted in such establishments (where other new drinks, *tea and *chocolate, were also available). They became much like *clubs, linked with particular interests or professions. Edward *Lloyd's coffee house, where ship owners and sea captains congregated, developed into London's market for marine insurance; Jonathan's became the *Stock Exchange; and Francis *White's chocolate house, a favourite haunt of aristocratic gamblers in St James's Street, evolved into the club of that name. By the mid-18c the coffee houses were declining, partly because genuine clubs with members were taking their place, and it was not until the arrival of espresso bars in the 1950s that they again played an important part in British life.

C of S Abbreviation for *Church of Scotland.

Donald **Coggan** (b. 1909, baron 1980) Archbishop of Canterbury 1974–80, after being bishop of Bradford (1956–61) and archbishop of York (1961–74). His training was as an academic (Semitic languages and New Testament studies) and he is the author of many books on the Christian faith.

Coggeshall Grange Barn (16km/10m W of Colchester) The oldest surviving timber-framed barn in Europe, built in the 12c as part of a Cistercian monastery.

Robert **Cohan** (b. 1925) American-born choreographer who was co-founder of the influential *London Contemporary Dance Theatre. His career as a dancer was in the USA with the Martha Graham company, but his many ballets as a choreographer have been created for LCDT. They include *Cell* (1969), *Stages* (1971) and *Class* (1975).

COHSE see *Unison.

COI see *Central Office of Information.

coins see *currency.

Edward **Coke** (1552–1634, kt 1603) Parliamentarian and lawyer. As attorney-general (from 1594) he was a ferocious prosecutor on the royal behalf (in the cases of *Essex, *Raleigh and the *Gunpowder Plot conspirators) and yet at the same time he remained an implacable opponent of any attempt by the monarch to encroach on the *common law (his robust defence of which is seen as his greatest achievement). From 1613 to 1616 he was lord chief justice, the first to be so called. In his later years his determination to oppose the Stuart assertion of the *divine right of kings made him one of the leaders of the parliamentary cause, the *Petition of Right being largely his work.

Coke of Norfolk (Thomas·Coke, 1754–1842, earl of Leicester 1837) Agriculturalist who greatly advanced the cause of scientific farming by introducing improved new methods on his estate at *Holkham, and by demonstrating that they brought financial benefits.

Colchester (82,000 in 1981) Town in Essex on a ridge above the river Colne. Before the Roman invasion it was the capital city of the ruler of much of southern England, Cunobelin; he is better known as Shakespeare's Cymbeline and as the father of *Caratacus. Captured by the emperor Claudius in AD 44, Colchester (*Camulodunum*) became the earliest Roman town in Britain. Sections of the Roman walls survive and the temple of Claudius later provided the foundations for the vast Norman keep, the largest in Europe, begun in about 1080. Appropriately the castle now houses a museum of Roman antiquities. Colchester later thrived as a centre of the cloth trade, with many Flemish weavers settling there in the 16–17c, and it has long been famous for its oysters from the Colne estuary. There is no historical basis for the theory that Old King Cole, of the nursery rhyme, is reflected in the name of the town.

Cold Comfort Farm (1932) Novel by Stella Gibbons (1902–89) which set out to parody the earthy rural fiction then in vogue (Mary Webb's *Precious Bane* of 1924 being the prime example), but which achieved its own lasting fame as a comic masterpiece. The horrors of country life are discovered by a town girl, Flora Poste, when she goes to stay with her appalling rustic relations, the Starkadder family, in deepest Sussex; typical is Aunt Ada Doom who once, as she endlessly repeats, saw 'something nasty in the woodshed'.

Coldstream see *Foot Guards.

George **Cole** (b.1925) Comedy actor whose early films included several based on Ronald *Searle's St Trinian's. He starred on radio and television in the series *Life of Bliss*, but he is best known as Arthur Daley in *Minder* (and as a similarly colourful Cockney in TV commercials for the Leeds Building Society).

John **Cole** (b. 1927) Political editor of the BBC from 1981 until his retirement in 1992. His rich Belfast accent and vibrant tweed overcoat, combined with reliable political insights, made his reports from Westminster a favourite feature of BBC television news for many viewers.

David **Coleman** (b. 1926) Sports commentator of unbridled enthusiasm, whose high profile is reflected in the *Private Eye* column named after him ('Colemanballs', an anthology of unintended humour from sports commentators speaking at speed without a script) and in his explosively overheated persona on *Spitting Image*. He has been involved in particular with the BBC TV programmes *Grandstand* and *Sportsnight*; his own specialities as a commentator are football and athletics. Since 1970 he has chaired a quiz, *A Question of Sport* (BBC TV), in which sporting celebrities are the very knowledgeable contestants.

Samuel Taylor **Coleridge** (1772–1834) One of the leading poets of the *Romantic movement, whose *Ancient Mariner* and *Kubla Khan* are among the best-known poems in the language. Born in Devon, the son of a clergyman, he was educated at *Christ's Hospital and at Jesus College, Cambridge. From his early adult life he was closely involved with other leading poets of his generation. With Southey he developed in 1794 a political creed, pantisocracy, the purpose of which was to establish a utopian community in America; and he and Southey married two sisters, Sara and Edith Fricker (Coleridge's relationship with Sara was somewhat reluctant from the start and the marriage was not a success). With Wordsworth he published in 1798 a joint selection of their poems, *Lyrical Ballads*, in which Coleridge's contribution included The Ancient Mariner. The great love of Coleridge's life, Sara Hutchinson, had a sister, Mary, who married Wordsworth. In 1800 he moved to Keswick, to be near Wordsworth in the Lake District, but he stayed there only till 1804.

In his twenties he became addicted to opium, the only good result of which was *Kubla Khan*. His struggle against addiction, the distress of his waning poetic powers and the pain of his love for the other Sara are movingly recounted in journals and private papers, published in the 20c as his *Notebooks*. Throughout his life he was also a prolific and profound literary critic.

Coliseum (London WC2) The largest theatre in the West End, seating more than 2500, with an extravagant interior of 1904 by Frank Matcham (1854–1920). Since 1968 it has been the home of *English National Opera.

College of Arms (also known as Heralds' College, London EC4) The college, headed by the *Earl Marshal, is responsible for matters of heraldry and genealogy, in particular the granting of new arms (except in Scotland, which has its own establishment in the Court of the *Lord Lyon). The heralds retain medieval titles; there are, for example, three Kings of Arms (called respectively Garter, Clarenceux, and Norroy and Ulster) and four Pursuivants (Portcullis, Bluemantle, Rouge Croix and Rouge Dragon). The college itself is an attractive red-brick building dating from just after the *Great Fire.

collies Lean and intelligent dogs, bred originally in Scotland for herding sheep and closely related to other *sheepdogs. There are distinct long-haired and short-haired breeds; it is believed that the long-haired were used to herd the sheep in the wilder conditions of the hills, while the short-haired had the easier task of accompanying them to market. All have some white in their coat, combined usually with reddish brown, grey or black. The word 'collie' has been in use for centuries, but its origin is not known. The American film star Lassie, first seen in *Lassie Come Home* (1943), rapidly became the world's most famous collie.

The border collie is a slightly smaller and distinct breed, usually black with white markings, originating from the border regions between England and Scotland. Its extraordinary skills in herding and separating sheep on whistled commands have become familiar in Britain through the

TV programme *One Man and his Dog* (BBC). The bearded collie is an old breed (though only recognized as distinct in 1944), related in origin both to the collie and to the Old English sheepdog – but more nearly resembling the latter, with shaggy hair covering even the paws.

Admiral **Collingwood** (Cuthbert Collingwood, 1750–1810, baron 1805) Nelson's second-in-command at *Trafalgar. In the *Royal Sovereign* he was the first to engage the enemy and he took command after Nelson's death.

Joan **Collins** (b. 1933) Actress best known for her appearances during the 1980s in the role of Alexis, the ruthless beauty in the US television serial *Dynasty*.

Phil **Collins** Drummer and singer who came to fame with *Genesis, as drummer from 1970 and as lead singer from 1975. His first solo album, *Face Value* (1981), went straight to no. 1 in the UK and stayed in the charts for more than five years. Of his four subsequent albums two reached no. 1 (*No Jacket Required* 1985, . . . *But Seriously* 1989) and the others halted at no. 2 (*Hello I Must Be Going* 1982, *Serious Hits . . . Live!* 1990). In 1988 he played the lead role in *Buster*, a film about Buster Edwards – one of those convicted for the Great Train Robbery of 1963.

Wilkie **Collins** (1824–89) Writer who achieved wide popular success with the The *Woman in White*, and whose The *Moonstone* is the first full-length English detective novel.

Colman's Mustard see *Reckitt & Colman.

Colonel Bogey March tune written in 1914 by Kenneth Alford (pseudonym of a military bandmaster, Frederick Ricketts, 1881–1945), to which some morale-boosting scurrilous words became attached in World War II:
> Hitler has only got one ball,
> Goering has two but very small,
> Himmler is somewhat similar,
> But poor old Goebbels has no balls at all.

The tune was used for *Bridge on the River Kwai*.

St **Columba** (*c*.521–97) The most influential of the early Irish missionary saints through his founding of the monastery on *Iona. He went there with 12 disciples in 563 and used it as a base from which to convert the *Picts in mainland Scotland. His feast day is June 9.

St **Columban** (*c*.543–615) Irish monk who was already in his mid-40s when he set off with 12 companions to take Celtic Christianity to the continent of Europe. He founded several monasteries, most notably at Luxeuil in France and Bobbio in northern Italy. His feast day is November 23.

Colwyn Bay (8km/5m SE of Llandudno) Resort on the north coast of Wales, in Clwyd. Its long sandy beach has made it a favourite place for holiday-makers from the Midlands.

The **Comedy of Errors** (*c*.1593) The earliest comedy by *Shakespeare, based on the Roman farces of Plautus. The comic errors are those of mistaken identity. Maximum opportunities for confusion are provided by a pair of identical twins, each called Antipholus, who employ another pair of identical twins, each called Dromio. To give the plot the necessary element of danger, Syracuse and Ephesus are in a state of hostility and one identical master-and-servant pair comes from each place.

Come into the garden, Maud (1856) One of the most popular of Victorian drawing-room songs, a setting by Michael Balfe (1808–70) of a section of Tennyson's recently published *Maud*.

Comet The world's first commercial jet aircraft, manufactured by the de Havilland Aircraft Company and put into service by *BOAC in 1952. With flight times suddenly halved, it promised a golden age for both the manufacturer and the airline. Two unexplained crashes early in 1954 put an end to this hope. After months of investigation it was discovered that the cause was metal fatigue (a problem foreseen in Nevil *Shute's *No Highway* six years earlier). A redesigned Comet was back in the air in 1958, in time to operate the first transatlantic jet service just a few days ahead of its ultimately more successful rival, the Boeing 707.

Comic Relief Charitable enterprise in the tradition pioneered by Bob *Geldof and Band Aid. The first Comic Relief was broadcast live from a refugee camp in the Sudan on Christmas Day 1985. Subsequent ventures included the 1986 hit single *Living Doll* with Cliff Richard and the Young Ones, and a succession of Red Nose Days in which people bought a small red nose for themselves or a large red nose for their cars. By 1993 Comic Relief had raised more than £77 million.

coming of age The acquiring in law of adult status, or majority. Anyone below the given age is unable to sign legal documents or to marry without parental consent. The age was 21 until reduced to 18 by the Family Law Reform Act of 1969. The same reduction was made, also in 1969, in the minimum voting age. (The *age of consent, concerned only with the law on sexual intercourse, has no connection with coming of age.)

'coming through the rye' The refrain of an old song, *The Bob-tailed Lass*, which was used as the first line of a poem by *Burns. His are the words which are now well known in the song of this title.

commando Word used by the Boers in South Africa to mean a military company formed of drafted civilians. The name was adopted in Britain in 1940 to describe units, made up of volunteers from army regiments, which were trained to land from the sea in enemy-occupied territory. From 1942 commandos were increasingly formed from the *Royal Marines, and after the war the role became exclusively theirs. The name was soon used for a soldier within such a unit (wearing the distinctive green beret) rather than for the unit itself.

Commercial Union Major insurance company, founded in 1861 as the result of a fire which destroyed a group of warehouses near London Bridge. The resulting claims caused the existing companies to raise their premiums dramatically, prompting a group of merchants to form their own commercial union to undertake insurance.

The **Committee** (Channel 4, 1991) Television documentary about Northern Ireland which in 1992 brought the makers, Box Productions, and the transmitter, Channel 4, before the High Court under the terms of the *Prevention of Terrorism Act. An unnamed loyalist terrorist was the programme's source for allegations that there was collusion between the security services and Loyalist paramilitaries in planning the murder of members of the IRA. The television companies were prosecuted for contempt of court in refusing to name their source. The judge ruled that they could not cite public interest or the threat of retaliation as a reason for breaking the law; he fined them £75,000 for flouting the order, but refrained from insisting that they comply with it.

parliamentary committees There are three distinct forms of committee in the House of *Commons. In the process leading to an *act of parliament the bill is discussed in detail at its 'committee stage' by some 40 or 50 MPs, referred to as a standing committee. The phrase is misleading in that the membership changes with each new bill under discussion, according to its subject and the expertise required; but the balance of members from the political parties in a standing committee invariably reflects their relative strength in the House. All financial bills, and any others considered of great national importance, are debated at their committee stage in the chamber of the House, with every MP eligible to take part; this is known as a committee of the whole House. Finally there are select committees, usually comprising between 10 and 15 MPs, responsible for looking into specific subjects. This specialization, on such topics as health, education or foreign affairs, means that the average select committee is concerned with the performance of a particular government department. Select committees have the right to question ministers, senior civil servants and any other relevant witnesses.

The House of Lords may also become a committee of the whole House, but the Lords equivalent of a standing committee (known as a Public Bill Committee) is rarely used. The two most important select committees in the Lords are on the European Communities and on Science and Technology. Most of the House's judicial work is transacted in the Appeal and Appellate Committees.

Common Agricultural Policy see *EC.

Common Entrance see *public school.

common land There are many places in Britain where a motorist still drives over a cattle grid to enter a 'common' on which cows or sheep are grazing. These open spaces are what survive from centuries of struggle between landlord and tenant. Under the early medieval *open-field system, the local people held in common the right to graze cattle, catch fish or collect wood and peat on any land not under cultivation. Powerful lords of the manor in Norman times began to claim that the lord actually owned the common land, while the peasants had only specific rights to use it. An inevitable next step was for the lord to attempt to frustrate these rights by physically enclosing his land. Beginning in the 13c, enclosure reached a peak in the 18–19c (the fences adding excitement to the new British passion for *hunting), until steps were taken to prevent it in the Enclosure Act of 1852 and the Commons Act of 1876.

Even today commons remain frequently under threat, from development and other demands, in spite of the supposedly final Commons Registration Act of 1965. The Commons Preservation Society, Britain's oldest conservation group (founded 1865), has been in the forefront of the ongoing campaign; it now calls itself the Open Spaces Society. In the early 1990s the government announced plans for a new Commons Act, based on proposals put forward in 1983 by the Common Land Forum.

common law The body of English law which has been built up in the centuries since the Norman Conquest by the custom and practice of judges dealing with specific cases (it is also known as case law), as opposed to statute law established by act of parliament. Inevitably the body

of material became impossibly unwieldy, and an important part has been played by jurists selecting and annotating the most significant judgements. A formative span of British history, from the Tudors to the Hanoverians, produced three outstanding commentators of this kind: Edward *Coke, whose *Institutes of the Laws of England* appeared in 1628; Matthew Hale (1609–76), whose *History of the Pleas of the Crown* (1685) and *History of the Common Law of England* (1713) were published after his death; and William Blackstone (1723–80), author of the famous *Commentaries* based on his lectures at Oxford (*Commentaries on the Laws of England* 1765–9).

Common Market see *EC.

*Book of **Common Prayer** see *Book of Common Prayer.

common riding An annual custom in parts of Scotland, particularly just north of the border, in which the boundaries of common land are marked out by riders headed by a young man with a banner. As with the English *beating the bounds, what was once a practical necessity is now a festive event.

House of Commons The lower but more powerful chamber in *parliament, made up of the *MPs who won a seat at the most recent *general election or *by-election. The number of seats in the House has varied: in 1983 the total was increased from 635 to 650 (523 for England, 38 for Wales, 72 for Scotland and 17 for Northern Ireland); an extra seat was added in England in 1992 (Milton Keynes became two constituencies), bringing the total to 651.

The early Norman rulers gathered their funds from nobles and bishops (the members of the House of *Lords who owed the monarch direct feudal allegiance), but from the 13c the financial needs of the kings compelled them to involve knights from the shires and citizens from the increasingly rich towns. From the 14c the Commons sat in a separate chamber. Their ability to provide money

Overall majorities in the House of Commons after each general election since 1945

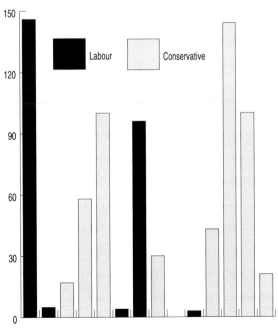

gave them power first over the monarch and then over the upper house; by the end of the 17c it was accepted that the Lords could reject but not amend money bills, and since 1911 they have had no powers at all over financial legislation. In the early 20c the convention was also established that the *prime minister should invariably be in the Commons; the last to hold that office in the Lords was the marquess of Salisbury (up to 1902).

The independence of the House of Commons was dramatically expressed when Charles I came to arrest the *Five Members, an incident which also emphasized the importance of the *Speaker. The sacrosanct nature of the chamber itself is symbolized by the Bar of the House, two rods which can be drawn across between the end benches (the furthest from the Speaker); anyone summoned to appear before the House stands at the Bar. The benches run the length of the House, facing the central aisle. Since the 18c the party in power has sat on the left (if one is facing the Speaker) with the Opposition on the right; the leading members of each party sit on the *front benches. These arrangements have become widely familiar with the televising of debates, which began in 1989 after years of delay and controversy (they had been broadcast on radio occasionally from 1976 and on a regular basis from 1978). Sittings normally begin at 2.30 p.m. from Monday to Thursday and at 9.30 a.m. on Fridays.

The chamber was destroyed by bombs on the night of 10 May 1941, but was rebuilt to the same dimensions – with seats for only 437 of the members, thus creating an exciting sense of crush with many having to stand during an important debate.

Commonwealth (1649–1660 The period between the execution of *Charles I and the *Restoration. England was declared a commonwealth on the day of Charles's death, 30 January 1649. For four years the House of Commons ran the country, but in 1653 the army gave power to Oliver *Cromwell as Lord Protector, a role in which his son Richard succeeded him for eight months after Cromwell's death. The years 1653–9 are therefore also known separately as the Protectorate.

Commonwealth (of Nations) The loose association of independent countries which has emerged from the *British empire. The earliest recorded use of the phrase made the link long before it was a reality: in a speech in 1884 the earl of Rosebery declared that 'the British empire is a commonwealth of nations'. All the members were at one time colonies or dependencies of Britain.

The idea of the modern Commonwealth, that of consultation and cooperation between equals, was formalized in the Statute of Westminster (1931). The main political forum is the Commonwealth Conference, a meeting of the prime ministers of all the member states which is held every two years. Trade advantages which had previously been given to fellow members had to end when Britain joined the *EC in 1973.

It was taken for granted that all members would retain the British monarch as head of state, until India in 1949 decided to become a republic but wished to remain in the Commonwealth. The solution adopted was that members should acknowledge the monarch as head of the Commonwealth. Ireland (1949) and South Africa (1961) have withdrawn; Pakistan withdrew in 1972 and rejoined in 1989. In 1992 there were 50 member states. Shridath Ramphal (b. 1928, CMG 1966) of Guyana was secretary general from 1975 to 1990, when he was succeeded by Chief Emeka Anyaoku (b. 1933) of Nigeria.

Commonwealth citizen By the British Nationality Act of 1981 this became the secondary status held by *British citizens (together with British Overseas and

The traditional shape of the chamber in the Commons: painting by K.A. Hickel of Pitt addressing the House in 1793.

British Dependent Territories citizens) and by citizens of the independent countries of the Commonwealth, replacing the former status of *British subject.

Commonwealth Conference see *Commonwealth (of Nations).

Commonwealth Day In 1902, at the end of the Boer War, an annual celebration of the achievements of the *British Empire was informally established, mainly for schoolchildren. May 24 was chosen, being the birthday of the late Queen Victoria. It was called Empire Day, and was given official recognition in 1916. Reflecting the evolution of Empire into *Commonwealth, the name was changed in 1958. It is now celebrated on the second Monday in March.

Commonwealth Games Athletics contest held every four years and open to all citizens of the *Commonwealth. The first games were at Hamilton in Canada in 1930. They were then called the British Empire Games, the name being changed to the British Commonwealth Games in 1970. In team events the four parts of the United Kingdom compete separately as England, Wales, Scotland and Northern Ireland.

Commonwealth Institute (London W8) The educational and cultural centre of the *Commonwealth. Each member country has a permanent display in the building, where events of many kinds are organized to foster an understanding of this unique alliance of nations. The institute is the successor of the Imperial Institute, established in 1887 to celebrate Victoria's golden jubilee. It occupied a magnificent building in Exhibition Road, opened in 1893 but demolished in the late 1950s (all but its 85m/280ft bell tower) to make way for new buildings for the Imperial College of Science and Technology. The Commonwealth Institute, formally renamed by an act of parliament in 1958, moved at that time to a site between Kensington High Street and Holland Park. Its distinctive tent-like building (by Matthews & Johnson-Marshall) was opened in 1962.

Commonwealth War Graves Commission see Commonwealth *War Graves Commission.

Communist Party of Great Britain The United Kingdom, home at various times to *Marx and *Engels, had early links with communism; but it was not until 1920 that a British Communist Party was formed. It had an early success, with two members in parliament by 1922, but the momentum was not maintained. In the 1945–50 parliament there were again two Communists, but they were to be the last in the House; one of them, William Gallacher (1881–1965), had held a seat in Fife since 1935. The Communists continued to fight general elections but usually every candidate lost the deposit. In 1991 the majority of the party (which by then had a membership of only about 5000) voted to change the name to the Democratic Left. At the same time there was an official admission that in the 1960s and 1970s large annual payments had been received from Moscow to foster industrial unrest.

A minority decided in 1991 to continue as the Communist Party of Great Britain and in 1992 they revived the *Daily Worker*. This had been launched in 1930 as the party's newspaper, but its name was changed in 1966 to the *Morning Star*.

community charge see *poll tax.

community council see *local government.

Commonwealth

The 50 member states in 1993 (each has its own entry)

Monarchies with Elizabeth II as head of state	Republics
	Bangladesh
	Botswana
Antigua and Barbuda	Cyprus
Australia	Dominica
The Bahamas	The Gambia
Barbados	Ghana
Belize	Guyana
Canada	India
Grenada	Kenya
Jamaica	Kiribati
New Zealand	Malawi
Papua New Guinea	The Maldives
St Christopher and Nevis	Malta
St Lucia	Mauritius
St Vincent and the	Namibia
Grenadines	Nauru
Solomon Islands	Nigeria
Tuvalu	Pakistan
United Kingdom	Seychelles
	Sierra Leone
Monarchies (or similar systems) with other heads of state	Singapore
	Sri Lanka
	Tanzania
Brunei	Trinidad and Tobago
Lesotho	Uganda
Malaysia	Vanuatu
Tonga	Zambia
Swaziland	Zimbabwe
Western Samoa	

community-service order A sentence of up to 240 hours of unpaid work, of a socially useful kind and carried out under the supervision of a probation officer, which can be imposed on an offender instead of a prison sentence. Typical tasks are decorating the homes of the elderly or building adventure playgrounds for children.

Order of the **Companions of Honour** The most recent of the *orders of chivalry, established in 1917 and awarded to people of distinction in any field (most often politics and the arts). Apart from an occasional honorary foreign member, the number is limited to 65. The order confers no title, but members place the letters CH after their names.

'Comparisons are odorous' see *Much Ado About Nothing*.

151

*The **Compleat Angler**, or the Contemplative Man's Recreation* (1653, 2nd enlarged edn 1655) The chief work of Izaak *Walton and the outstanding classic of British angling. It takes the form of a dialogue, in which a fisherman (Piscator) persuades a hunter and a fowler of the superior pleasures of his sport. The book offers practical tips on angling within an idealized vision of English rural life.

comprehensive school Type of *state secondary school introduced from the 1950s. Comprehensives are committed to taking all children, of whatever ability, from a given area; they were devised to avoid the guillotine of the eleven-plus in the selection of children for *grammar schools and secondary moderns. Nearly all provide facilities for pupils to stay beyond the age of 16 to take A levels. In the early 1990s about 90% of secondary places in the state system were in comprehensive schools. It remains to be seen what effect the introduction of *opting out will have.

Denis **Compton** (b. 1918) Precociously talented batsman, scoring more than 1000 runs at the age of 18 in his first season in first-class *cricket and scoring a century at the age of 20 in a *Test match. He is still (in 1992) the youngest English player to have achieved either feat. In addition he holds the record for the greatest number of runs scored in an English season (3816 in 1947). He played for Middlesex (1936–58) and for England (1937–57). He was also a talented footballer, appearing in wartime teams for both Arsenal and England.

Ivy **Compton-Burnett** (1884–1969, DBE 1967) Novelist who with *Pastors and Masters* (1925) and *Brothers and Sisters* (1929) staked out the narrow but intense territory which she made characteristically her own – that of characters in a confined context, usually an Edwardian country house, playing out ruthless struggles of dominance and cruelty which are revealed almost entirely through dialogue.

Compton Verney Location near Stratford-upon-Avon where an annual opera festival is planned in the grounds of an early-18C house (in the style of Vanbrugh). Aiming to provide the Midlands with an equivalent of *Glyndebourne, the project had in 1992 a proposed opening date of 1995.

Compton Wynyates (14km/9m W of Banbury) The most romantic of England's large Tudor mansions, an uneven jumble of redbrick towers and chimneys round a courtyard, nestling in a wooded valley. It has been in the hands of the Compton family since the 12C. Half way through their eight centuries on the site they rebuilt the house in its present delightful form (1480–1520).

Arthur **Conan Doyle** (1859–1930, kt 1902) Author remembered mainly for the creation of Sherlock *Holmes. But his prolific output included also historical novels, science fiction and a series of books about another highly memorable character, Brigadier Gerard, an endearingly boastful French officer in the Napoleonic wars.

concentration camps see *Boer War.

Concorde The only supersonic airliner flying in the early 1990s. The first test flight was on 2 March 1969 and the first scheduled service on 21 January 1976. With a capacity of 128 passengers, Concorde cruises at up to Mach 2 (2333kph/1450mph). It was designed and manufactured jointly by the British Aircraft Corporation in Britain and by Aerospatiale in France, as the result of an agreement between the two governments signed in 1962. Its noise level caused early opposition (particularly in New York) and it has remained a noisy beast, but a very beautiful one.

Supersonic passenger flights began in the Soviet Union in 1975 with the Tupolev Tu-144 (so similar in appearance to the Concorde that it became known as the Concordski), but the plane was withdrawn from service in 1983.

*The **Condition of the Working Class in England*** see *Engels.

Congregationalists The main group of English *Puritans other than the *Presbyterians. In the 16C they rejected the presbyterian hierarchy of elders, who together had authority over more than their own immediate church, insisting that every Christian congregation must be entirely independent (they were known also as the Independents). It was from a group of English Congregationalists that the *Pilgrim Fathers came; and it was with the support of the largely Congregationalist army that Oliver *Cromwell took sole power in 1653. In the Restoration they suffered with Presbyterians and others the restrictions placed upon *Nonconformists. English Congregationalists and Presbyterians came together in 1972 in the *United Reformed Church.

Congress House see the *TUC.

William **Congreve** (1670–1729) Aristocratic playwright, one of the leading figures in *Restoration comedy. He made his name with *The Old Bachelor* (1693), which he followed with *The Double Dealer* in the same year, and then *Love for Love* (1695) and The *Way of the World (1700).

Coniston Water Long narrow lake (8km/5m by about 0.5km/0.3m) in the *Lake District. Its length and relatively sheltered position among the hills caused it to be chosen by both Malcolm and Donald *Campbell for attempts on the water speed record. On the eastern shore is the home of John *Ruskin in his last years. At the northern end is the village of Coniston beneath the local peak, the Old Man of Coniston (802m/2630ft). During the summer a steam yacht (*Gondola*, first launched in 1859) carries passengers the length of the lake.

Connaught (London W1) Hotel known in particular for its excellent restaurant. Dating back to the early 19C, though with a succession of changes of name, it supposedly became fashionable with the hypochondriac aristocracy in the 20C because it lay almost on a straight line between *Harley Street and Buckingham Palace.

Sean **Connery** (b.1930) Scottish actor who leapt to fame as the creator on screen of James Bond. Beginning with *Dr No* in 1962, he made four more Bond films up to *You Only Live Twice* in 1967, and then subsequently returned for two others (*Diamonds are Forever* 1971, *Never Say Never Again* 1983). Although Bond has dominated his public image, he has frequently proved himself an excellent actor in other roles – such as *The Man Who Would Be King* (1975) with Michael Caine.

Billy **Connolly** (b. 1942) Large and loud Scottish stand-up comedian, whose early reputation was much enhanced among his fans by material and language guaranteed to outrage the prim. He is widely known (though more, it seems, in England than in Scotland) as 'the Big Yin'.

The **Conquest** (1066) The usual term in Britain for the Norman Conquest, the last successful invasion of the island and the event which has made 1066 the most famous date in English history (as in * *1066 and all that*). William, duke of Normandy, had some expectations of inheriting the crown of England on the death of *Edward the Confessor. Instead it went to *Harold II. William landed with his fleet at Pevensey in East Sussex on 28 September 1066, and some two weeks later he defeated the English at the Battle of *Hastings. The new king (see *William the Conqueror) consolidated his hold over England with remarkable speed; successive rebellions were rapidly put down (particularly in Northumbria in 1069) and by 1070 the Normans held firm control, which they consolidated through the military structure of *feudalism.

Joseph **Conrad** (the name adopted in England by Teodor Józef Konrad Korzeniowski, 1857–1924) Novelist who became a master of English prose, though he first learnt the language in his twenties. Born an aristocrat in a part of Poland under Russian rule, he left home at 17 to go to sea. His adventures brought him eventually into the British merchant navy, and he was naturalized in 1886. His experiences around the world, particularly in the Far East and Africa, provided the settings for many of his novels and short stories, such as * *Lord Jim* and * *Heart of Darkness*; but the subject matter is not so much the exotic location as the self-awareness, often of a most depressing kind, which his central characters experience in these remote conditions. * *Nostromo*, often considered his masterpiece, is untypical in depicting a broader canvas of a society in upheaval.

Terence **Conran** (b. 1931, kt 1983) Designer and entrepreneur, whose style was influential from the 1960s through Habitat – a chain of furniture shops which extended through the UK, and then to the USA and France, after he opened the first in London's Fulham Road in 1964. He is also known in London as a restaurateur, owning Bibendum in the famous Michelin building on Fulham Road and Le Pont de la Tour at Butler's Wharf. Habitat was merged in 1982 with *Mothercare, and in 1986 the two joined *BhS to form the Storehouse group – from which Conran retired as chairman in 1990. Storehouse subsequently sold Habitat.

conscientious objectors Historically many groups have espoused pacifism, but only *conscription brings them into direct conflict with the state. The first occurrence of this in Britain was in World War I. It resulted in much injustice from inadequate methods for identifying genuine cases of conscience; and the public war hysteria found in the 'conchies' a perfect target. The most effective solution was that of the Friends Ambulance Unit, established by pacifist *Quakers, through which many conscientious objectors provided first aid on the battlefield. By World War II the position of conscientious objectors was better understood and methods were in place for them to be properly identified.

conscription The first occasion on which men were drafted by act of parliament into the British armed forces was in March 1916, during World War I; the call-up involved men between 18 and 40 (later raised to 45 and then 50). Conscription was reintroduced on 3 September 1939, the day on which World War II was declared, this time for men between 18 and 41 (later raised to 51). Women between 21 and 31 were drafted from 1941. After the war the call-up continued for all young men, who were enlisted for a 2-year period known as national service. The final batch finished their service in 1962.

Conservative Party In electoral terms by far the most successful British party over the past century and a half (see *parliament). The name Conservative was adopted by the *Tories under the leadership of Peel in the 1830s, to suggest a party which would conserve the traditional British values in contrast to the more radical *Liberals. The present full name of the party (Conservative and Unionist party) is the result of an alliance in 1886 with the *Unionists; these were Liberals defecting because of Gladstone's support of *Home Rule for Ireland. A firm support for Anglicanism as the established religion was also a consistent strand in party policy, leading to the jibe that the *Church of England is the Conservative party at prayer – though this has ceased to be valid in recent years, when Anglican bishops and archbishops have often spoken forcefully against the divisive social effects of Conservative policies.

During the 19c support for Conservatives or Liberals was not class-based. Broadly speaking the Conservatives had more support in country districts and the Liberals were stronger in the industrial towns, but they leapfrogged each other in their attempts to appeal to the lower classes of society. In the late 19c the Conservatives seemed the party of the working man, for it was they who extended the *franchise in 1867. By the early 20c the position was reversed, when the Liberals were laying the foundations of the *welfare state.

By then the Conservative party had become associated with capitalist interests, in addition to its traditional rural support. This helped to ensure the party's survival, for there now emerged the first class-based party in British politics, the *Labour party. The newcomers increasingly seemed the natural opposition to the Conservatives, and the pressures of a *two-party system caused Liberal support to crumble.

For most of the 20c the electorate's only realistic choice was between the Conservative and Labour parties, and voting was for the most part in terms of traditional class interest. But this simple pattern of allegiances has recently changed. Not one of the three leaders chosen by the Conservative party since the mid-1960s (Edward Heath, Margaret Thatcher, John Major) has come from the upper or upper-middle classes; and many of the radical policies of Mrs Thatcher, such as the sale of council houses to their tenants, appealed strongly to the very section of society, the skilled working class, that was first drawn into the fold when the Conservatives extended the franchise a century earlier.

The party headquarters are in *Smith Square.

Consolidated Fund The nation's account with the *Bank of England, into which tax revenues are paid and from which government expenditure is drawn. Until 1786 these functions had been divided between several funds, which were then 'consolidated' into one.

John **Constable** (1776–1837) Painter whose largely uneventful life was devoted to capturing on canvas the natural landscape, with its flicker of light on leaf and water and grass. To this end he made hundreds of oil sketches, studying changes in the weather or in clouds, which he used when working up his large exhibition canvases. Though relatively unappreciated in his own time (he caused more of a stir in France than in England), his pictures now seem to offer the essential image of the English landscape, direct and rich in tone, free from the fashions of the *picturesque. His home was on the border between Suffolk and Essex (his father was a rich miller in East Bergholt), and his paintings of the river Stour have immortalized not only the district but even particular buildings on the bank; of these Flatford Mill and Willy Lot's cottage were presented to the nation in 1928. Two

Stratford Mill *(1820), one of a series of large paintings by Constable of scenes on the river Stour. The foreground group of children has given the painting an alternative title –* The Young Waltonians, *from Izaac Walton and his* Compleat Angler. *The mill, which made paper, was pulled down in 1840; it stood about two miles from Flatford Mill.*

other areas feature in many of his paintings – Salisbury, with many views of its great cathedral from the surrounding countryside, and Hampstead, where he lived from 1821.

constituency An area electing one *MP. The number of constituencies, and therefore of seats in the House of *Commons, has been rising in recent decades; it was increased to 630 in 1955, 635 in 1970, 650 in 1983 and 651 in 1992. Since the 1970s England, Wales and Scotland have also been divided into 78 larger constituencies each of which sends one *MEP to the European Parliament. It is the responsibility of the *Boundary Commissions to keep the number of electors in each constituency roughly balanced.

constitutional monarchy The rule by a king or queen based on statutes which limit the monarch's power. The basis of all modern European monarchies, the concept was pioneered in Britain in the late 17C when the absolute monarchy associated with the *divine right of kings was made impossible by a series of measures beginning with the *Bill of Rights in 1689. It was the *Reform Act of 1832 which finally gave *parliament a sufficiently strong democratic mandate for the monarch's role to be gradually reduced to its present largely symbolic status.

Consumers' Association see * *Which?*

John **Conteh** (b. 1951) Boxer who won the European light heavyweight title from Rudige Schmidtke in March 1973, and two months later added the British and Commonwealth titles when he beat Chris Finnegan; both fights were at the Empire Pool, Wembley. In 1974, again

at Wembley, he defeated the Argentinian Jorge Ahumada to become WBC world light heavyweight champion. He fought successfully three times in defence of the title, but he forfeited it in 1977 after a succession of hand injuries had kept him out of the ring for long periods.

Continental System see *Napoleonic Wars.

Conwy (13,000 in 1981) The Welsh spelling, now standard, for a town on the north coast of Gwynedd previously spelt Conway in English. There was a Norman fortification here and a Cistercian abbey of the 12C, but the present town and castle are the creation of Edward I. Together they form one of the most complete surviving fortified settlements of that time in Europe. The castle, now internally a ruin but still impressive in its great walls, was built in only about five years, from 1283. At the same time Edward was enclosing the adjacent land within town walls (some 1280m/1400yd long, with 21 towers), which are still intact.

Increased travel on the scenic route along the north coast of Wales prompted the construction of two magnificent early metal bridges over the estuary of the river Conwy. The suspension bridge carrying the road was built in 1824–6 by *Telford, and the tubular railway bridge in 1846–8 by Robert *Stephenson. A road tunnel under the estuary was opened in 1991.

A.J. **Cook** see the *General Strike.

Captain **Cook** (James Cook, 1728–79) Explorer who made many important discoveries in the Pacific. Born the son of a labourer in Yorkshire, he learnt his seamanship in vessels trading from Whitby and then joined the navy. In

1768 he was put in command of HMS *Endeavour*, which had been built in Whitby as a collier. His instructions were to take readings of the transit of Venus, as seen from Tahiti in June 1769, and then to search for a continent believed to exist in the south central Pacific. In his party was Joseph *Banks, whose botanical observations were one major achievement of the voyage. Another was Cook's charting of New Zealand and of the east coast of Australia, not previously visited by any European. Returning to England in July 1771, he set off again a year later with the *Resolution* and the *Adventure*. This voyage (1772–5) proved conclusively that there was no undiscovered continent north of the ice fields of the Antarctic, and added many new groups of islands to the map of the Pacific. On his third voyage (1776, again in the *Resolution*) Cook explored the Pacific coast of north America in the hope of finding a northwest passage from the Atlantic. He then wintered in Hawaii, where he was killed in a skirmish with natives.

He had been the first explorer to take a consistently scientific approach, whether in charting treacherous coasts, in the use of the newly improved chronometer for better navigation, or in the care of his crew. Cook's insistence on a supply of fresh vegetables and fruit meant that these were the first voyages of comparable length to be free of scurvy. His birthplace at Marton, near *Middlesbrough, is kept as a museum.

Peter **Cook** (b. 1937) Comic author and performer who was a central figure in the satire boom of the early 1960s, as a member of *Beyond the Fringe*, as one of the founders of *Private Eye*, and as the joint owner of the Establishment,

Detail from a 1776 portrait by Nathaniel Dance of Captain Cook, with a modest hint of his extensive journeys.

a cabaret nightclub. He became known to a wider public as half of Dud and Pete, the pair of philosophical layabouts in his TV series with Dudley *Moore (*Not Only But Also* BBC 1965–71).

Robin **Cook** (b. 1946) Labour politician, MP for Livingston since 1983 (previously for Edinburgh Central, 1974–83). As the opposition front bench spokesman on health from 1987, he had a prominent part in the long-running dispute over funding and reforms of the National Health Service. In 1992 he took over the shadow portfolio on trade and industry.

Thomas **Cook** (1808–92) Inventor of the package tour, which evolved from his zeal for the temperance movement. Wanting to get teetotallers from Leicester to a rally in Loughborough, he hired and advertised a special train on the Midland railway; 570 people responded and made the return journey for a shilling on 5 July 1841. Within a few years Cook was organizing attractive holiday tours; 350 tourists, for example, paid a guinea to travel by train and steamer to Glasgow, where they had vouchers for their hotels and were greeted with brass bands and the firing of cannons. The natural next step was tours abroad. Under his son (John Mason Cook, 1834–99) and grandsons, the firm developed into the international travel agency of today. In 1992 it was bought by LTU, a German travel and air charter group.

Alistair **Cooke** (b. 1908) British-born journalist and broadcaster, who became an American citizen in 1941. He has interpreted the USA for the British for more than half a century, in his articles for the *Guardian*, in his long-running radio programme *Letter from America*, and in his documentary series *America*. Since 1971 he has also done the same in reverse, with his introductions on American TV to British plays shown in *Masterpiece Theater*.

Cookham (16km/10m NW of Windsor) Village on the Thames best known for its link with Stanley *Spencer, who depicted it in many of his visionary paintings such as *Christ Preaching at Cookham Regatta* or *The Resurrection, Cookham*. He was born in Cookham, spent much of his working life there, and is commemorated now in the village's Stanley Spencer Gallery.

Catherine **Cookson** (Catherine Fawcett, b. 1906, DBE 1993, m. Thomas Cookson 1940) Author, one of the most popular in Britain, who did not publish a book until she was 44. Her novels are naturalistic stories, romantic rather than sentimental, of everyday life during her youth in her own part of England, the northeast. They have tended to be written in series, following a particular character or family for a while and then turning to another. The main characters, in sequence, have been Mary Ann, the Mallen family, Tilly Trotter and Bill Bailey.

'The **cook was a good cook**' see *Saki.

Co-op The popular name for any retail outlet of the *Cooperative movement. In spite of strong competition in recent decades from supermarket chains, there are still some 4700 Co-ops round the country in the 1990s.

Cooper Company with notable successes in motor racing in the 1950s and 1960s. Charles Cooper and his son John began designing and constructing racing cars in Surbiton, in Surrey, after World War II. Stirling *Moss won many Formula Three races in Coopers (particularly the Cooper 500), and he came first in the Argentine Grand Prix of 1958 in a Cooper Climax – the combination with which the company subsequently won the constructors' championship, in 1959 and 1960, when *Brabham was their winning driver. The next development was one for which the firm became even better known – the transformation of the *Mini into a sports car, the Mini-Cooper, which won the Monte Carlo rally in 1964, 1965 and 1967.

Henry **Cooper** (b. 1934) The most successful British boxer of the postwar years, popularly known as 'our 'Enery'. He held the British heavyweight title for a record unbroken spell of ten years and five months, winning it in 1959 from Brian London and losing it in 1969 to Jack Bodell; he won it back from Bodell the following year, but lost it to Joe *Bugner in 1971. Meanwhile his ten successful fights had given him an unprecedented three *Lonsdale belts. During this whole period the Commonwealth title was also his, and he was European champion in 1964, 1968–9 and 1970–1. On the world stage he failed in his two fights with Muhammad Ali, but in one of them he floored the great man just before the bell.

Tommy **Cooper** (1921–84) Much loved comedian and conjuror, a shambling figure in a red fez who liked to accompany the final collapse of a trick with the catch phrase 'just like that'. He was a regular at the London Palladium, and for many years had his own television series, *It's Magic*. Only an extremely accomplished conjuror could have achieved his chaotic effects; he was a senior member of the exclusive Magic Circle.

Cooperative Movement Inspired by the ideas of Robert *Owen, many cooperative ventures were founded in early 19c Britain, with the profit from joint endeavours shared between the members. The most lasting in its influence was the Rochdale Society of Equitable Pioneers, formed in 1844 in Rochdale (then in Lancashire, now part of Greater Manchester). From it has descended the worldwide Cooperative Movement, following what are known as the Rochdale Principles; these include open membership, democratic control and a dividend on purchases. The dividend, in effect a discount to members on goods bought at the *Co-op, has been the main reason for the great success of the enterprise; but the early ideals of mutual help within a community also provided a powerful impulse. The movement has remained a coalition of local societies, each with its own members and responsible for its own finances. But the pressures of competition have caused many to merge in recent decades. In 1960 there were some 900 retail societies in the country; in the early 1990s the number is closer to 60.

The Rochdale Pioneers and other retail cooperatives found it difficult to buy the goods they needed; so in 1863 they formed the Cooperative Wholesale Society (CWS), which in 1873 also began manufacturing. The CWS now has extensive factory and farming enterprises, producing 60% of the goods sold in the Co-op outlets. The Cooperative movement is also involved in insurance, banking, publishing and education.

Cooperative Party Political party resulting from a decision of the Cooperative Congress, in Swansea in 1917, to ensure that the interests of the *Cooperative movement were represented in parliament. One of the first group of Cooperative candidates was elected in 1918, and he allied himself in the House of Commons with the Labour party. It was the beginning of a long and close link between two parties with many shared interests, though the Cooperative party had a particular concern for the consumer. They soon made a formal alliance, agreeing to sponsor some joint candidates both at Westminster and in local government. As a result the Cooperative party has had a low profile with the public, but in every parliament there are a few MPs taking the Labour whip whose affiliation is officially described as Cooperative-Labour or Labour-Cooperative.

Jonathan **Cope** (b. 1962) Dancer with the *Royal Ballet, known for a noble presence in the classical roles. He retired in 1990, in spite of developing a strong partnership with Sylvie Guillem, but he returned to the company in 1992.

Copenhagen (2 Apr. 1801) Naval engagement in the *Napoleonic Wars, a pre-emptive strike by Britain after a league with France had been formed by various Baltic states including Denmark. *Nelson was second in command of a fleet sent to the Baltic. He boldly took a group of relatively small ships into shallow and heavily defended waters close to Copenhagen, and proceeded to bombard the shore defences and the ships in the harbour. After heavy fighting his commander in chief, Sir Hyde Parker, flew a signal ordering retreat; this was the famous occasion on which Nelson put the telescope to his blind eye and thus pretended he had not seen the signal. His action, successfully completed, was followed by an armistice with the Danes.

Copley Medal The earliest and most distinguished of the awards made by the *Royal Society. Sir Godfrey Copley, an MP and member of the society, bequeathed £100 in 1709 to go towards experiments or any other purpose. The medal was established in 1731 and is awarded annually to honour distinguished scientific research.

Lord **Copper** see *Scoop.

copperplate Flowing style of handwriting, with elongated loops, based on the lettering of copperplate engravings. Popularized by George Bickham's *Universal Penman* (1733–41), in which the examples of writing were engraved, it was taught to children in Britain until the mid-20c.

copyright An exclusive right to reproduce or allow others to reproduce certain categories of intellectual material. This legal property (now belonging automatically to anyone who writes or draws anything, no matter how slight) has been gradually established over the centuries. From Tudor times printers were granted by the crown an exclusive licence to print and sell particular works. The position of authors was improved by an act of 1709 which allowed them sole rights over a new book for 14 years from its first publication; an act of 1842 extended this period to 42 years from the book's publication or seven years from the author's death, whichever was longer; and an act of 1911 introduced the law prevailing today, by which an author's copyright (which may be sold or inherited in any work, in part or in whole) lasts until 50 years after his or her death. Copyright in engravings was secured in 1735, largely by the efforts of *Hogarth.

Nowadays copyright extends not only to the traditional areas of art, literature, drama and music, but also to radio, film and television (inventions, however, are covered by the laws of *patent). An extension of copyright in Britain in 1979 was the concept of *Public Lending Right.

copyright libraries Six libraries to which publishers must send free of charge, if so requested, a copy of every book. By an act of 1666 printers were required to deliver three copies, one each for the King's Library and the universities of Oxford and Cambridge. Further acts added copies for the Advocates' Library in Edinburgh (1709),

Trinity College in Dublin (1800, following the Act of Union) and the National Library of Wales (1911). The six copyright libraries today, descended directly from those first granted this privilege, are the *British Library (the only one to which a copy must be sent without being requested), the Bodleian at *Oxford, the University Library at *Cambridge, the *National Library of Scotland, the *National Library of Wales and Trinity College, Dublin.

coracle (from the Welsh *corwgl*) The one-man fishing boat of ancient Britain, still in use in parts of Wales. It is light enough to be carried on the back, where it looks much like a tortoise's shell. The structure is open wickerwork, covered originally with hides but now with canvas.

The Coral Island (1858) Story by R.M. *Ballantyne. Three boys (Ralph Rover, Jack Martin and Peterkin Gay) are shipwrecked on a South Sea island. Their adventures involve a shark, cannibals, a pirate and much sailing about before they are rescued by missionaries. The book directly inspired *Lord of the Flies.

cor anglais (French for 'English horn') Only the name wins this orchestral instrument a place in this book, for it is not in fact English; nor is it a horn. It is a woodwind instrument, a member of the oboe family, deriving from Italy in the 18C. The early versions were somewhat horn-like in shape, but no convincing explanation has been found for the supposed link with England; the most common suggestion is that the angle between the reed and the instrument caused it to become known as *angl*é (for 'angled'), but the word does not exist in French.

Ronnie **Corbett** (b. 1930) Scottish comedian, diminutive in size but boundless in energy and optimism, best known in the long-running TV series *The *Two Ronnies. During the 1980s he also starred as an over-age mother's boy in a BBC TV situation comedy, *Sorry!*

Cordelia see *King Lear.

co-respondents (short for co-respondent's shoes) Term in the 1930s for men's shoes in two tones of leather, one of them white or cream. A co-respondent was the third party cited in a divorce case; the wife being divorced was the respondent to the charge, and her lover the co-respondent. A similar implication was later attached to *brothel-creepers, footwear apparently being a prime indication of moral turpitude.

Corfe Castle (34km/21m SE of Dorchester) Ruins of one of the strongest of England's Norman castles (12–13C), in a commanding hilltop position near the south coast. The castle became famous during the English Civil War for its spirited defence by Lady Bankes, in the absence of her husband, against a parliamentary army. Parliament ordered its demolition in 1646, after capturing it by trickery.

corgi (also known as Welsh corgi) Either of two similar but distinct breeds of cattle-driving dogs, with short legs, long bodies and fox-like features, in use on Welsh farms for many centuries before becoming more widely known as pets. Their name derives from the Welsh *cor* (dwarf) and *ci* (dog). The Cardigan Welsh corgi has a long tail, whereas that of the Pembroke Welsh corgi is docked. The latter is by far the better known as a result of being the favourite dog of Elizabeth II; she was given a pair by her father, George VI, and now there are usually seven or eight in the royal entourage.

Corinium see *Cirencester.

Coriolanus (*c*.1608) One of the last and most stark of *Shakespeare's tragedies. The brilliant but arrogant general Caius Martius, known as Coriolanus from his capture of the Volscian town of Corioli, is Rome's natural leader but is too proud to disguise his scorn for the common people. He is banished and in revenge offers his services to the Volscians, whom he leads to the very walls of Rome. The Romans plead for mercy in vain, until they send out to him his aged mother. At her request he turns back, and is himself killed by the Volscians.

corn circles (also known as crop circles) Flattened areas of corn, in circular and other patterns, which appeared first in Wiltshire in 1980 and by the end of the decade were a regular summer phenomenon in the surrounding region, in increasing numbers and ever more varied shapes. Those who were already interested in UFOs and ley lines responded eagerly to new evidence of unseen forces; others maintained that the crops were flattened by localized whirlwinds, resulting from freak weather conditions. By the early 1990s it was clear that many of the circles, if not all, had been made by hoaxers.

corned beef Now an alternative name for bully beef, though in origin they were different. Bully (deriving from the French for boiled, *bouilli*) was a boiled and pressed concoction; Smollett, offered some in 1753, described it as looking like the flesh of Pharaoh's lean cattle 'stewed into rags and tatters'. Corned beef was taken a stage further; the corns were grains of salt, forming the brine in which it was pickled.

Cornish beam engine The largest and simplest form of steam engine, developed in the 18C for pumping water out of mines in Cornwall. A great metal beam, pivoted at the centre, lies horizontally across the top of the engine, attached at one end to the steam cylinder and at the other to the pumping cylinder; it links the actions of the two as it tilts up and down. The largest beam engine still in operation (a diameter of 229cm/90in in the steam cylinder) can be seen at the Kew Bridge Steam Museum, where it was installed in 1846 to circulate water through the pipes of west London.

Cornish pasty Meat and vegetables (particularly potatoes, turnips, onions) in a case of shortcrust pastry, formed by folding a full circle in half and pinching it together round the edges. Traditionally a single large pasty was made in Cornwall when the whole family ate at home. There were smaller versions on weekdays for the men to take to the mines or fields; individual variations in seasoning and contents were thus possible, and the initial letter of the man's name would be baked on the corner of his pasty to avoid confusion. The women would even put a savoury filling at one end of the pasty and a sweet one, such as apple, at the other – to make a complete meal.

Corn Laws Laws regulating the import and export of grain, to ensure a sufficient home-grown supply, were a feature of British policy from the Middle Ages. But the disadvantage of restrictions on import was that prices were kept artificially high in times of shortage. The issue became politically sensitive in the 19C for two reasons: the Napoleonic Wars and bad harvests caused successive periods of shortage; and the landowners in parliament, benefiting from high prices for the grain from their own estates, were perceived to be following naked self-interest in their support for the restrictive laws. The Anti-Corn Law League, set in motion by a small group in Manchester in 1838, was developed by *Cobden and *Bright into a nationwide pressure group of the industrial and urban classes against the land-owning aristocracy. The failure of the Irish potato crop of 1845 and the resulting *Great Famine finally caused the prime minister, Robert *Peel, to act. With great difficulty, and splitting the Conservative party, he forced through the repeal of the Corn Laws on 25 June 1846.

Cornwall (475,000 in 1991, administrative centre Truro) *County at the extreme southwest tip of England, including the *Scilly Isles.

Duke of **Cornwall** see Prince of *Wales.

Coronation Since 1066, a year in which two monarchs were crowned (Harold II and William I), every coronation has taken place in *Westminster Abbey. The ceremony begins with the archbishop of Canterbury presenting the monarch to the assembled company, who respond with shouts of acclamation. The monarch then takes an oath, which since the 16c has included a commitment to maintain the *Church of England. There follows the anointing, for which the monarch sits in a plain white robe on the *Coronation Chair, while the choir sings *Handel's anthem *Zadok the Priest* (it was Zadok who anointed Solomon). Various symbols of dignity and power are then heaped upon the monarch (coronation robes, golden spurs, a jewelled sword, bracelets, a cloth of gold, an orb, a ring, a glove, two sceptres), to be followed by the crown itself. After a shout of 'God save the Queen (or King)' the monarch receives homage from the *Lords Spiritual and Temporal and then takes Holy Communion, bringing the ceremony itself to an end.

Until the reign of William IV the coronation was followed by a banquet in Westminster Hall, into which the King's Champion rode in full armour to challenge any who would dispute his right to this title (the failure to reinstate this colourful medieval ceremony for Victoria provoked the *Eglinton tournament). Two kings, Edward V and Edward VIII, reigned for so little time that they were not crowned.

Coronation Chair Oak chair in Westminster Abbey, made for Edward I and incorporating the Stone of *Scone beneath the seat. It has been used for every *coronation since that of Edward II in 1308.

Coronation chicken Cold chicken with a curry sauce, accompanied by a salad of rice and peas – so named because it was recommended as a dish which would avoid the need for cooking on the day of the coronation of Elizabeth II in 1953.

Coronation Street (Granada from 1960) Britain's favourite soap opera and most successful television programme, following the lives of the people in an ordinary street supposedly on the outskirts of Manchester. Devised by Tony Warren (only 23 at the time), it went on air on 9 December 1960 as a twice-weekly half-hour show. It was described that month by the *Daily Mirror* as 'doomed from the outset, with its grim scene of a row of terraced houses'. Instead it has usually been first and second in the week's ratings (even first, second and third since it added an extra weekly episode in 1989), and it has on occasion drawn audiences of more than 20 million. Famous characters have included Ena Sharples (played by Violet Carson), Elsie Tanner (Pat Phoenix), Annie Walker (Doris Speed), Albert Tatlock (Jack Howarth) and Ken Barlow (William Roache, who in 1992 was the only survivor from the original cast). Life on 'the street' centres on the pub, the Rovers Return, and both pub and street, constructed behind Granada's studios in Manchester, have themselves become tourist attractions. Unlike other soaps, *Coronation*

Street has appealed to a wide range of fans; one of the most passionate in his support was the poet laureate, John Betjeman, who compared it to *Pickwick Papers*.

coroner The name derives from the Middle Ages, when a coroner looked after the private property of the crown. The function of a coroner today is to hold inquests in two areas – the cause of any violent or unexplained death, and cases of *treasure-trove. Appointments to the office are limited to lawyers or doctors, and in practice coroners usually have qualifications in both fields.

corporal punishment Flogging was in past centuries a common punishment within the law, particularly in the navy, and birching and caning were a characteristic part of discipline in the *public schools – with the oddity of *le *vice anglais* as a possible by-product. When Lord Goddard went to Buckingham Palace in 1932 on appointment as a judge of the King's Bench, George V said he hoped he would not hesitate to sentence violent criminals to flogging – a sentiment with which Goddard agreed, for as lord chief justice he opposed the abolition in 1948 of corporal punishment in the British criminal system. In the Isle of Man it remained on the statute books in the early 1990s, but local magistrates were advised not to sentence anyone to birching after the European Court of Human Rights pronounced it to be 'cruel and unusual'.

During the 1980s there was strong pressure from teachers to ban the caning of children, and in 1986 a bill to outlaw corporal punishment in state schools was narrowly passed in both Houses of Parliament (by two votes in the Lords and by one in the Commons).

corporation tax The tax charged on the annual profits of a company, payable nine months after the end of the accounting period. The rate of tax was 52% during the period 1973–82 and was then reduced in stages to 35% in 1986. In 1990 it came down to 34% and in 1991 to 33%; it remained at that level in 1992, with a reduced rate of 25% for companies showing profits of less than £250,000, and then a sliding scale up to profits of £1.25m.

Corrective Party A campaign for licensed brothels in Britain, with the stated aims of avoiding kerb crawling and preventing the spread of Aids. It was launched in 1988 by Lindi St Clair (b. c.1950), a London prostitute and brothel keeper known also as Miss Whiplash. She first stood as a candidate at a by-election in Richmond in Yorkshire in 1989. She has subsequently argued her case in more than half a dozen other by-elections and in the 1992 general election – achieving considerable publicity but not many votes. In January 1993 she vanished in mysterious circumstances, after announcing that she was about to reveal the names of her clients in public life; her car was abandoned in such a way as to suggest either suicide or murder, but she was discovered a week later at Fort Lauderdale in Florida.

corridors of power A phrase for the places in which high-level decisions are taken, probably already current when used by C.P. Snow in a novel of 1956 (*Homecomings*) and widely familiar after he made it the title of a later novel (*Corridors of Power* 1964).

Corunna (16 Jan. 1809) A minor incident in the *Peninsular War. Sir John Moore (1761–1809) was in command of a British army retreating from an unsuccessful campaign and expecting to be picked up by a fleet at Corunna (La Coruña in Spanish), a port at the northwest tip of Spain. The pursuing French army reached Corunna a little earlier than the British fleet. The relatively light casualties in the battle included the death of Moore himself. The fleet had meanwhile arrived, and the army embarked safely the next day. The lasting fame of the event derives from a poem, *The *Burial of Sir John Moore.*

Cotswolds Range of gently rolling limestone hills much intersected by small deep valleys, stretching about 80km/50m northeast from Bath. The area has been rich since medieval times, originally thanks to the wool of the Cotswold sheep. Stone quarried here weathers to a lovely pale grey, resulting in many exceptionally attractive small towns and villages, comfortably settled in the landscape, which have given the region its high reputation for charm and beauty.

cottage pie see *shepherd's pie.

Cottesmore see the *Shires.

cotton The commodity which best combined the advantages of Britain's worldwide trading network with the opportunities of the *Industrial Revolution, bringing great wealth in the 19c to northwest England. Lancashire was the natural place for the development of a cotton industry. It was close to Liverpool, where the raw material arrived from America; it had reliable rivers to provide the early mills with water power; it was close to plentiful supplies of coal, from the Midlands, in the subsequent era of the steam engine.

The inventive skill of men such as *Kay, *Hargreaves and *Crompton, combined with the productivity of regimented workers in mechanized factories, meant that the finished products exported from Lancashire could undercut hand-made goods even in the cotton-producing countries. This ceased to be the case from the late 19c, when others borrowed the technology and benefited from a cheaper supply of labour. The result was prolonged recession in Lancashire during much of the 20c.

Britain's last steam-powered cotton mill, with engine and looms built in 1894, remained in operation in Burnley, Lancashire, until the early 1990s. It is to be preserved as a museum.

Billy **Cotton** (1899–1969) Popular bandleader who began each show with a piercing cry of 'Wakey, Wakey!'. Alan Breeze (b. 1909) sang for many years with the band, and *The Billy Cotton Band Show* ran on BBC radio from 1949 and on television from 1956 until Cotton's death.

Henry **Cotton** (1907–87, kt 1987) The dominant British golfer between the wars, winning the Open in 1934 and 1937 (and again after the war in 1948). He was also a golfing journalist and author of several books. In his later years he designed golf courses, of which the best known is at Penina in Portugal.

council The elected body at each level of *local government.

council houses and flats Dwellings built by the council, or local authority, and let to tenants at a subsidized rent. From the mid-19c there was an awareness of the need to clear the insanitary slums of the industrial cities and to build better working-class housing. Several acts were passed enabling local authorities to do so, but little progress was made until after World War I. Between the wars some 1.5 million council houses were built; about 4.5 million houses and flats (many in tower blocks) had been added by the early 1980s. In the Housing Act of 1980 the Conservative government introduced the right of council tenants to buy their houses. By 1992 approximately 1,350,000 had done so; only about 350,000 new council dwellings had been built in the same period,

representing a large overall reduction in local authority housing. The government prevented local authorities from spending more than 25% of the capital receipt from the sales, the rest of the money being set aside as a reduction of public debt.

Council of Europe A body with its headquarters in Strasbourg, founded in 1949. Its 23 members are European states (the smallest being San Marino). It has been best known for the work of the European Court of Human Rights, which it established in 1950. It is distinct from the *European Council.

Council of Ministers (Council of Ministers of the European Communities) The main decision-making body of the *EC, based in Brussels. It consists of one government minister from each of the member states. On broad international issues this will be the foreign minister, on more specialized matters the minister concerned. The presidency of the Council is held by member states in rotation, for a period of six months.

council tax The form of *local tax which in 1993 replaced the *poll tax. It is similar to the rates (themselves replaced by the poll tax) except that the level of tax paid by a household depends not on the house's notional rental value but on its capital value, assessed according to where it falls in a range of eight price bands (with a built-in protection for the richer households, the highest tax level being limited to three times the lowest). The other main difference, aiming to remedy the undue burden of the rates on those living alone, is a 25% reduction where there is only one adult in the household.

countess see *earl.

Country Gardens see Percy *Grainger.

Country Life Weekly magazine founded in 1897 as a revival of *Racing Illustrated*. It aimed to follow its predecessor in making the most of new technology for printing black-and-white photographs, but with more varied country interests. Within a few years it had found its most distinctive theme – serious and well illustrated architectural studies of buildings, particularly country houses. Its other famous feature over many decades has been the frontispiece black-and-white portrait of a society bride-to-be, smiling at the camera and almost invariably wearing pearls; the last picture of this kind appeared in 1991, being subsequently replaced by colour photographs of a wider range of aristocrats.

The Country Wife see *Wycherley.

county The most ancient territorial division in the British Isles. The word itself is Norman in origin but the system is older (the earlier word being 'shire'). Three of the present counties – Essex, Kent and Sussex – are survivals from the *Anglo-Saxon kingdoms.

In England the ancient counties remain the basis for *local government. The Local Government Act of 1972 brought into being (from 1974) six *metropolitan counties around the large cities; and it made minor modifications to the existing English counties, establishing the present number at 39. In Wales the same act created eight new counties in place of the previous 13. In Scotland the Local Government Act of 1973 introduced (from 16 May 1975) nine new *regions and three islands areas where there had previously been 33 counties. Northern Ireland, also known as 'the six counties', retains these original counties but since 1973 has had a different basis for its local government. (See maps on next spread.)

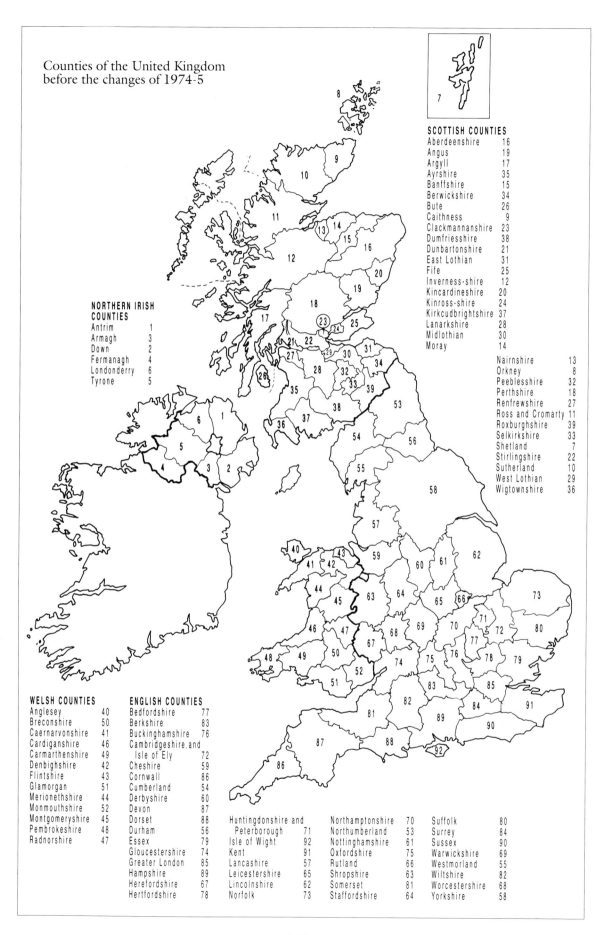

Counties of the United Kingdom
before the changes of 1974-5

SCOTTISH COUNTIES

Aberdeenshire	16
Angus	19
Argyll	17
Ayrshire	35
Banffshire	15
Berwickshire	34
Bute	26
Caithness	9
Clackmannanshire	23
Dumfriesshire	38
Dunbartonshire	21
East Lothian	31
Fife	25
Inverness-shire	12
Kincardineshire	20
Kinross-shire	24
Kirkcudbrightshire	37
Lanarkshire	28
Midlothian	30
Moray	14

Nairnshire	13
Orkney	8
Peeblesshire	32
Perthshire	18
Renfrewshire	27
Ross and Cromarty	11
Roxburghshire	39
Selkirkshire	33
Shetland	7
Stirlingshire	22
Sutherland	10
West Lothian	29
Wigtownshire	36

NORTHERN IRISH COUNTIES

Antrim	1
Armagh	3
Down	2
Fermanagh	4
Londonderry	6
Tyrone	5

WELSH COUNTIES

Anglesey	40
Breconshire	50
Caernarvonshire	41
Cardiganshire	46
Carmarthenshire	49
Denbighshire	42
Flintshire	43
Glamorgan	51
Merionethshire	44
Monmouthshire	52
Montgomeryshire	45
Pembrokeshire	48
Radnorshire	47

ENGLISH COUNTIES

Bedfordshire	77
Berkshire	83
Buckinghamshire	76
Cambridgeshire and Isle of Ely	72
Cheshire	59
Cornwall	86
Cumberland	54
Derbyshire	60
Devon	87
Dorset	88
Durham	56
Essex	79
Gloucestershire	74
Greater London	85
Hampshire	89
Herefordshire	67
Hertfordshire	78
Huntingdonshire and Peterborough	71
Isle of Wight	92
Kent	91
Lancashire	57
Leicestershire	65
Lincolnshire	62
Norfolk	73
Northamptonshire	70
Northumberland	53
Nottinghamshire	61
Oxfordshire	75
Rutland	66
Shropshire	63
Somerset	81
Staffordshire	64
Suffolk	80
Surrey	84
Sussex	90
Warwickshire	69
Westmorland	55
Wiltshire	82
Worcestershire	68
Yorkshire	58

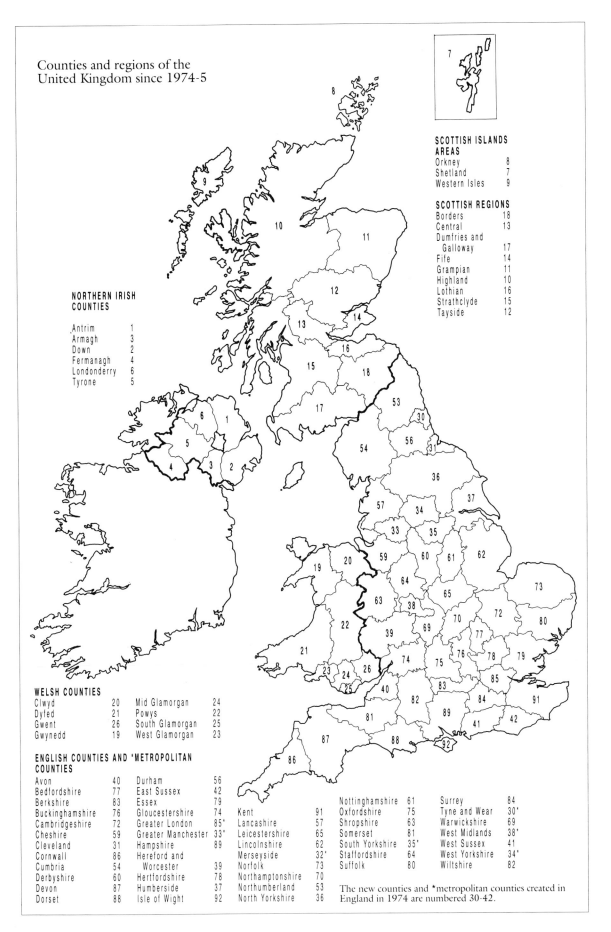

Counties and regions of the
United Kingdom since 1974-5

7

SCOTTISH ISLANDS AREAS

Orkney	8
Shetland	7
Western Isles	9

SCOTTISH REGIONS

Borders	18
Central	13
Dumfries and Galloway	17
Fife	14
Grampian	11
Highland	10
Lothian	16
Strathclyde	15
Tayside	12

NORTHERN IRISH COUNTIES

Antrim	1
Armagh	3
Down	2
Fermanagh	4
Londonderry	6
Tyrone	5

WELSH COUNTIES

Clwyd	20	Mid Glamorgan	24
Dyfed	21	Powys	22
Gwent	26	South Glamorgan	25
Gwynedd	19	West Glamorgan	23

ENGLISH COUNTIES AND *METROPOLITAN COUNTIES

Avon	40	Durham	56
Bedfordshire	77	East Sussex	42
Berkshire	83	Essex	79
Buckinghamshire	76	Gloucestershire	74
Cambridgeshire	72	Greater London	85*
Cheshire	59	Greater Manchester	33*
Cleveland	31	Hampshire	89
Cornwall	86	Hereford and	
Cumbria	54	Worcester	39
Derbyshire	60	Hertfordshire	78
Devon	87	Humberside	37
Dorset	88	Isle of Wight	92

		Nottinghamshire	61	Surrey	84
Kent	91	Oxfordshire	75	Tyne and Wear	30*
Lancashire	57	Shropshire	63	Warwickshire	69
Leicestershire	65	Somerset	81	West Midlands	38*
Lincolnshire	62	South Yorkshire	35*	West Sussex	41
Merseyside	32*	Staffordshire	64	West Yorkshire	34*
Norfolk	73	Suffolk	80	Wiltshire	82
Northamptonshire	70				
Northumberland	53				
North Yorkshire	36				

The new counties and *metropolitan counties created in
England in 1974 are numbered 30-42.

County championship: winners since 1946

1946	Yorkshire	1962	Yorkshire	1978	Kent
1947	Middlesex	1963	Yorkshire	1979	Essex
1948	Glamorgan	1964	Worcestershire	1980	Middlesex
1949	Middlesex & Yorkshire (shared)	1965	Worcestershire	1981	Nottinghamshire
1950	Lancashire & Surrey (shared)	1966	Yorkshire	1982	Middlesex
1951	Warwickshire	1967	Yorkshire	1983	Essex
1952	Surrey	1968	Yorkshire	1984	Essex
1953	Surrey	1969	Glamorgan	1985	Middlesex
1954	Surrey	1970	Kent	1986	Essex
1955	Surrey	1971	Surrey	1987	Nottinghamshire
1956	Surrey	1972	Warwickshire	1988	Worcestershire
1957	Surrey	1973	Hampshire	1989	Worcestershire
1958	Surrey	1974	Worcestershire	1990	Middlesex
1959	Yorkshire	1975	Leicestershire	1991	Essex
1960	Yorkshire	1976	Middlesex	1992	Essex
1961	Hampshire	1977	Kent & Middlesex (shared)		

county championship The main annual competition in *cricket. County teams were playing each other from as early as the 18C and a championship was held from 1873, but it was only in 1890 that the contest was formally organized on a points system. Eight counties were then competing – *Gloucestershire, *Kent, *Lancashire, *Middlesex, *Nottinghamshire, *Surrey, *Sussex and *Yorkshire. Between 1891 and 1905 another eight teams were admitted – *Derbyshire, *Essex, *Hampshire, *Leicestershire, *Northamptonshire, *Somerset, *Warwickshire and *Worcestershire. *Glamorgan, the only club from Wales, played first in 1921; and after a very long gap *Durham joined in 1992, bringing the total to 18. Games in the championship last three or four days (for a trial period from 1993 all are to be four days), and teams also now play *one-day cricket. Matches between teams in the county championship (sponsored by Britannic Assurance since 1984 and by Schweppes 1977–83) are defined as *'first-class' cricket. Since 1895 other counties have competed in what was originally known as the Second Class County Championship and is now called the Minor Counties Cricket Championship.

county court A court exclusively for civil (i.e. non-criminal) cases. Since 1846 a network of county courts has been established throughout England and Wales (the nearest equivalent in Scotland is the *sheriff court). A county court deals with all forms of litigation from land and tenancy through financial disputes to divorce and adoption. Cases where less than £1000 is involved are usually dealt with by arbitration as *small claims, while any of exceptional legal complexity, together with all involving more than a certain level of money, will begin in the *High Court (see *courts of law).

County Hall (London SE1) Imposing building on the south bank of the Thames, almost opposite the Houses of Parliament, which was the headquarters of the *London County Council and of the *Greater London Council until 1985. Designed by Ralph Knott (1878–1929), it was built 1909–33. In 1992 it was sold to a Japanese company planning to turn it into a hotel; a rival contender for the premises had been the London School of Economics.

county town A phrase which has become ambiguous. When first used, it was applied to the chief historic town in a county which was also, in those days, the seat of county government. With changing population patterns in the 19–20C county government has in many cases been moved to other towns, referred to officially as 'administrative centres'. 'County town' is therefore generally now reserved for the historic centre of a county. In many cases the two are still the same. Shrewsbury is both the county

town and the administrative centre of Shropshire. But while Lancaster is the county town of Lancashire, Preston is the administrative centre.

coupon election see *Lloyd George.

Courier Dundee's daily newspaper, originally established in 1816 as the *Dundee Courier and Argus*. It was bought in the 1870s by William Thomson (1817–96), a local shipowner, whose descendants built up the publishing empire which has given *Dundee its reputation for journalism. The *Courier* was the last major newspaper in the country to follow the old tradition (first broken by the *Express* in 1900) of devoting the front page to advertisements; it was not until 1992 that its readers were confronted with news in that prominent position.

coursing see *greyhound racing.

Courtauld Institute (London WC2) Britain's first institute for the study of the history of art and architecture. Part of the university of London, it was established by the gift in 1930 of £100,000 from the industrialist Samuel Courtauld (1876–1947). He followed this with the remainder of the lease of his house at 20 Portman Square, built by Robert Adam in 1773–5. The new Institute was installed here in time to take its first students in 1932. The end of the lease in 1982 made necessary a new home. This was found in *Somerset House, to which the Institute moved in 1990.

Courtauld was also a great collector, particularly of French Impressionists, and some 60 of his masterpieces (including Manet's *Bar at the Folies-Bergère*) form an important part of the Institute's superb collection. This is now on show in Somerset House.

Courtaulds Textile firm which developed from a small mill for spinning silk established in Essex in 1816 by Samuel Courtauld (1793–1881), descendant of a Huguenot family which had arrived in the late 17C. Its rapid growth resulted from the Victorian preoccupation with death, for Courtaulds became the leading manufacturer of black silk crape, an essential part of every lady's wardrobe in periods of mourning. When this fashion passed, the company pioneered man-made textiles in the early 20C – in particular the artifical silk known as rayon. Diversification was followed by the separation in 1990 of textile and non-textile products into two companies, Courtaulds Textiles and Courtaulds. See also the *Courtauld Institute.

courtesy title Any title used by a member of the *peerage which has no legal significance (such as 'The Hon' used by children of peers), but in particular a title used by the eldest son of a duke, marquess or earl. This is invariably a second and lower-ranking title held by the father. Thus the first duke of Wellington was also created marquess of Douro, which has since been used as the courtesy title of the eldest son.

Court of Appeal The division of the *Supreme Court which hears appeals in both civil and criminal cases (see *courts of law). The civil court is presided over by the *Master of the Rolls and the criminal court by the *lord chief justice.

Court of St James's The official name of the royal court of Britain, because *St James's Palace was the main royal residence in London during the 18c, when the phrase was established. Diplomats from foreign countries are described as being accredited to the Court of St James's, though new ambassadors present their credentials to the queen in a ceremony at Buckingham Palace.

Court of Session The highest civil court in Scotland, instituted by James V in 1532 and equivalent to the civil side of the *Supreme Court in England and Wales. Exact parallels cannot be made, but broadly speaking the Court of Session's Outer House corresponds to the English High Court; and the Inner House to the Civil Division of the Court of Appeal. Judges of the Court of Session also sit as the *High Court of Justiciary. The lower court, with greater powers than a county court in England, is the *sheriff's court (see *courts of law).

courts of law In England and Wales the courts of law for criminal and civil cases are separate. On the criminal side the lowest level is the *magistrates' court; from this the more serious cases are referred to the *Crown Court (as are most appeals unless on a specific point of law, in which case the appeal may go to the Queen's Bench Division of the High Court); an appeal from the Crown Court continues up to the Criminal Division of the *Court of Appeal.

On the civil side *small claims may be dealt with by arbitration. Full litigation begins in a *county court, with larger cases being heard in one of the three divisions of the *High Court. Appeals from both the county courts and the High Court go to the Civil Division of the Court of Appeal. Beyond the Court of Appeal, on either criminal or civil matters, the last resort is to the House of *Lords – which only considers cases involving a point of law of general public importance.

Scotland, with its own *law, has different courts. The lowest criminal court, the equivalent of the magistrates' court, is the district court; it can impose no sentence more severe than 60 days in prison. The *sheriff courts hear both criminal and civil cases. The highest civil court peculiar to Scotland is the *Court of Session; its judges also sit on the highest criminal court, the *High Court of Justiciary (beyond which there is no further appeal). The House of Lords, as the court of last appeal in civil cases, is the only one in common between Scotland and the rest of the country. There are differences also in the *jury system in Scotland.

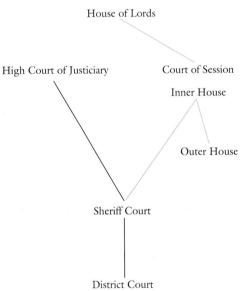

Courts of Law (England and Wales)

House of Lords

Court of Appeal

Criminal Division   Civil Division

Crown Court   High Court   High Court   High Court
Queen's Bench   Chancery   Family
Division   Division   Division
(criminal)   (civil)

Magistrates' Court   County Court

Courts of Law (Scotland)

House of Lords

High Court of Justiciary   Court of Session

Inner House

Outer House

Sheriff Court

District Court

The diagram shows the pyramid of courts in England and Wales leading up to the final court of appeal, the House of Lords.
The dotted line is followed when an appeal in a criminal case is on a specific point of law. Such an appeal is presented in written form, and the case is described as being "stated". It goes from either a magistrates' court or a crown court to the Queen's Bench Division of the High Court.
Beyond that it can go only to the House of Lords.

The High Court of Justiciary differs from the High Court in England, in that it is a court of first trial for serious crimes in addition to being a court of appeal.

The black lines show the channel of appeal in a criminal case, and the blue lines in a civil case.

Robin Cousins (b. 1957) Athlete who won a gold in the figure skating at the 1980 Olympics, retaining for Britain the medal which John *Curry had won at the previous games.

Coutts One of the oldest of the *clearing banks and by far the smallest, with only 19 branches in 1992. Its headquarters have been at various addresses in the Strand, in London, ever since John Campbell set up as a goldsmith and banker there in 1692. In 1755 James Coutts married Campbell's niece. He later secured George III as a customer, since when Coutts have remained bankers to the royal family. Though a subsidiary of the *National Westminster since 1969, the bank retains some time-hallowed customs; managers wear frock coats (a formal garment of the 19C) and a few traditionally-minded customers still begin letters to the bank with the single word 'Gentlemen'.

Covenanters Presbyterians who pledged themselves to maintain their form of worship and church government in Scotland. The first important bond between them was the National Covenant of 1638, formed in opposition to a new liturgy which Charles I was attempting to foist upon Scotland. In the resulting conflict (known as the Bishops' Wars, 1639–40) Charles was defeated. Three years later, when the king was at war with his English parliament, the Scots made a new extended pact, the Solemn League and Covenant (1643), by which they gave their support to

A Scottish Covenanter on a 17C playing card, having a difference of opinion with an English Congregationalist.

parliament in return for a guarantee of a presbyterian church in Scotland and (so they hoped) in England too. When this pledge was not honoured by Cromwell, the Covenanters changed their support to the Stuarts. This left no-one with any great obligation to them, and their cause seemed lost when Charles II re-imposed bishops upon Scotland. But their original purpose was finally achieved, after the revolution of 1688, when William III established a presbyterian *Church of Scotland.

Covent Garden (London WC2) The name derives from the area having been a 'convent garden' belonging to Westminster Abbey. It was developed as a Palladian piazza in the early 17C, with Inigo *Jones as architect, though all that survives from his original scheme is the church on the southwest side (St Paul's, known as the actors' church from its long association with the profession). The centre of the piazza was used for the sale of flowers and vegetables from the 17C until 1974, when the market moved to Nine Elms in southwest London. The market building was designed by Charles Fowler in the 1830s; saved from demolition in the 1970s, it is now the centrepiece of London's liveliest district of small shops and cafés. To the northeast is the *Royal Opera House, which is itself often referred to as Covent Garden.

Coventry (306,000 in 1991) City and district of the West Midlands. It grew up around a Benedictine monastery founded in 1043 by Leofric, the earl of Mercia, and his wife Godgifu, better known in legend as Lady *Godiva. Its medieval prosperity was based on cloth-making. The 14C St Mary's Hall, built for the Merchant Guild, has in its great hall the Coventry Tapestry which is believed to commemorate the visit of Henry VII and his queen in 1500.

In modern times transport has provided the basis of the city's industry. James Starley (1830–81), known as the 'father of the cycle industry', invented here the tensioned wire spoke which made possible the *penny-farthing. In 1896 Coventry pioneered the British manufacture of cars, with the 3-wheeled Coventry Motette appearing in that year and the first English Daimler in 1897.

Coventry has been known as the city of three tall spires. One still has its church attached, the 14–16C Holy Trinity. The second is all that remains of the church of the Grey Friars, destroyed in 1539. And the third is the only part of the medieval cathedral to have survived Coventry's night of destruction, 14 November 1940, the first instance of the carpet-bombing of a city. The shell of the old building has been kept as a memorial beside the new cathedral, designed by Basil *Spence, which was consecrated in 1962. A wealth of art was commissioned for it, most notably the bronze sculpture of St Michael and the Devil on the exterior by Epstein; the glass entrance screen engraved by John Hutton (1906–78); the stained glass in the baptistry window by John Piper; and above the altar the great tapestry of Christ in Glory by Graham Sutherland.

The phrase 'sent to Coventry' (meaning shunned or not spoken to) is of unknown origin. In *Clarendon's *History of the Great Rebellion* some prisoners are taken in Birmingham and are 'sent to Coventry'. This verbal coincidence is often quoted, not very convincingly, as the origin of the phrase. But perhaps the incident stuck in the public mind and later became adapted to its present meaning.

Coventry plays see *mystery plays.

Miles **Coverdale** see *Bible in English.

Coverley see Sir *Roger de Coverley.

Noel **Coward** (1899–1973, kt 1970) Playwright and actor who personified an elegant, witty and faintly outrageous way of life betwen the wars. He first achieved fame starring in his own play *The Vortex* in 1924, which he followed with.* *Hay Fever* (1925) and * *Private Lives* (1930). A patriotic vein evident in his stage extravaganza *Cavalcade* (1931) came into its own with the wartime film * *In Which We Serve* (1942); from the same period is his classic * *Brief Encounter* (1945). He was also an accomplished cabaret performer, singing at the piano his own lyrics such as *Mad Dogs and Englishmen* (the only two forms of life to go out in the midday sun).

Colin **Cowdrey** (b. 1932, kt 1992) Outstanding batsman and slip catcher, playing *cricket for Kent (1950–76) and for England (1954–75, captain 1959–61, 66–9). His score of 154 in a 1957 *Test against the West Indies at Edgbaston was part of a 4th wicket stand with Peter *May of 411 runs, which remains England's record stand. Another England record, shared with Hammond and Boycott, is his 22 Test centuries. He has been since 1989 the chairman of the International Cricket Council. He was destined from birth for the game, a cricket-mad father having given him the initials *MCC (Michael Colin Cowdrey).

Cowes (20,000 in 1981) Port and yachting centre on both banks of the Medina estuary at the northern tip of the Isle of Wight. The yachting activities in the Solent culminate in the fashionable Cowes week in early August. Of the many clubs in the region the earliest and most exclusive is the Royal Yacht Squadron, established in 1815. Its members have the unique privilege of being allowed to fly the white *ensign. Since 1856 the Squadron has had its headquarters in Cowes castle – one of Henry VII's coastal defences, dating from 1540 but rebuilt.

William **Cowper** (pronounced *cooper*, 1731–1800) Poet whose recurring bouts of depression and occasional insanity were mitigated by an evangelical faith, powerfully expressed in one of the most popular of English hymns, *God moves in a mysterious way*. His best poetry is a subtle evocation of nature and the countryside, but he is most widely remembered for *John Gilpin*, a comic tale about a Cheapside linen draper's unintended ride to Ware and back; it was told to Cowper by a friend to cheer him up.

Cox's orange pippin Widely held to be the best English apple, first grown in about 1825 by Mr Cox, a retired brewer, in his garden near Slough, in Berkshire. Pippin was a common word for apple; as to orange, a Cox's skin is in fact more dark red and greeny brown in colour.

CPRE and **CPRW** see *rural protection.

CPRS and **CPS** see *think-tank.

CPS see *Crown Prosecution Service.

George **Crabbe** (1754–1832) Poet and clergyman born at Aldeburgh, in Suffolk. His long poems about country life, such as *The Village* (1783), use traditional rhyming couplets and yet give a harshly realistic picture. *The Borough* (1810) brings together several stories set in Aldeburgh and was the inspiration for Britten's * *Peter Grimes.*

Lord **Craigavon** see *Northern Ireland.

Craigievar Castle (43km/27m W of Aberdeen) The most perfect of the Scottish tower houses, six storeys high with a profusion of turrets at its upper levels. It remains miraculously unchanged from when it was built in 1610–26 for William Forbes, a merchant trading with the Baltic. The magnificent plasterwork of the interiors is in marked contrast to the defensive exterior.

Craigmillar Castle (SE outskirts of Edinburgh) Imposing ruins of a castle (15–17C) which was one of the favourite residences of Mary Queen of Scots.

Steve **Cram** (b. 1960) Athlete who followed hard on the heels of *Coe and *Ovett in dominating the world scene in middle-distance running. He won gold medals for the 1500 metres in the European Championships and Commonwealth Games in 1982, and won at the same distance in the 1983 inaugural World Championships. The Olympic Games of 1984 brought him a silver at the same distance, but 1985 was his miracle year; during it he set new world records for the 1500 metres, the mile and the 2000 metres (his mile record of 3:46.32 was still unbeaten in 1992). In 1986 he successfully defended his 1500 metres titles in both the European Championships and Commonwealth Games, and added a gold for the 800 metres in the European event.

Cramond (8km/5m NW of Edinburgh) Attractive seaside village on the Firth of Forth with medieval remains and 18C houses. A Roman fort, of which the foundations have been revealed, was built in about AD 142 to guard a harbour here, at a time when the *Antonine Wall was being constructed from a point further west along the firth.

Walter **Crane** (1845–1915) Illustrator whose bold designs in flat blocks of colour (somewhat in the style of Japanese prints) were influential in the development of colour-printed children's books – particularly in his famous series of sixpenny and shilling 'toybooks'. He was much involved with the Arts and Crafts movement and in the development of art schools.

Cranford (1853) Vignettes by Mrs *Gaskell, serialized in * *Household Words* 1851–3. They add up to a delightful novel, low-keyed but sharp-eyed, about a group of middle-aged and middle-class people, almost all female, in a fictionalized version of the small town of Knutsford, in Cheshire, where the author herself grew up. The central character is Matilda Jenkyns, known as Miss Matty.

John **Cranko** (1927–73) Choreographer, born in South Africa, who in the 1950s created many works for the Sadler's Wells Theatre Ballet (* *Pineapple Poll* 1951, *The Lady and the Fool* 1954) and for the Royal Ballet. In 1961 he moved to Stuttgart, where he achieved what became known as the 'Stuttgart Ballet Miracle', building up a company of world class and creating for it a scintillating repertoire. *Cranks*, which he wrote and directed in London in 1956, was a highly original *revue.

Thomas **Cranmer** (1489–1556) Archbishop of Canterbury from 1533 (the first in the reformed *Church of England), and a major influence on the English *Reformation. He was one of a group of young priests at Cambridge in about 1520 who were inspired by the ideas of Martin Luther. From 1529 he was employed by *Henry VIII to further his divorce from Catherine of Aragon. Appointed archbishop in 1533, he immediately annulled the royal marriage and validated the new one to Anne Boleyn (which he would in turn annul three years later). He continued to act with considerable compliance to his master's whims in all fields except theology, where he bravely opposed the royal tendency to revert to Roman Catholic doctrine. Meanwhile Cranmer was gradually laying the foundation of the Anglican church; the *Book of Common Prayer was largely his work, and he provided the basis of the *Thirty-nine Articles.

He moved to a more radical Protestant position in the reign of Edward VI, with the result that he inevitably suffered in the swing back to Roman Catholicism under *Mary I. He had also, at the dying king's insistence, supported the claim of Lady Jane *Grey. This enabled his enemies to charge him with treason as well as heresy, and they believed that they had finally discredited Protestantism when they persuaded the archbishop to sign a document denying his previous beliefs. Just before being burnt he was to make his recantation public in Oxford's university church. Instead he used the occasion to deny the authority of the pope, disclaiming his recantation; and at the stake in Broad Street he thrust into the flames his right hand ('this was the hand that wrote it, therefore it shall suffer first punishment'). His act of defiance was a lasting inspiration to Anglicans, as has been the superb language of his litany.

Cranwell Village in Lincolnshire, location of the Royal Air Force College which since 1920 has trained officers for the RAF.

Crathes Castle (24km/15m SW of Aberdeen) Tower house of 1553–1602, with additions in the early 18C, built by the Burnett family. They had been granted land here by Robert the Bruce in 1323 for their support at Bannockburn; the ancient Horn of Leys, still to be seen in the castle, is believed to have accompanied this grant. The interiors are distinguished by painted wooden ceilings, in a strong primitive style, completed in 1602. The eight separate but adjacent gardens, planted for a range of effects at every season, were created in the early 20C by Sir James and Lady Burnett.

Crathie see *Balmoral.

Michael **Crawford** (b. 1942) Actor who first became known for playing comically pathetic roles, notably in the long-running TV series *Some Mothers Do 'Ave 'Em* (BBC 1974–9) about an exceptionally incompetent young man confronted with the prospect and experience of marriage. In the 1980s he achieved a major international career in musicals, first with *Barnum* (1981) and then *The Phantom of the Opera* (1986).

Crazy Gang Group of comedians who first appeared together in a *music-hall show of 1932, called *Crazy Week*, and who continued as a team until 1962. The Gang was made up of three double acts: Bud Flanagan (1896–1968) and Chesney Allen (1894–1982); Jimmy Nervo (1890–1975) and Teddy Knox (1896–1974); Charlie Naughton (1887–1976) and Jimmy Gold (1886–1967). Chesney retired in 1946, and from 1956 'Monsewer' Eddie Gray (1897–1969) was a member.

CRE see Commission for *Racial Equality.

cream tea Afternoon tea with scones, jam and *clotted cream, originally a speciality of Devon and Cornwall.

Crécy (26 Aug. 1346) Victory by Edward III over the French during the first phase of the *Hundred Years' War, at Crécy-en-Ponthieu (50km/31m S of Boulogne). It was the first demonstration of the power of the *longbow, with which the English archers devastated a larger and more heavily armed French force.

Creggan see *Londonderry.

Crewe (48,000 in 1981) Town in Cheshire which developed in the 19C as a major railway junction.

Crimes recorded by the police, per thousand population

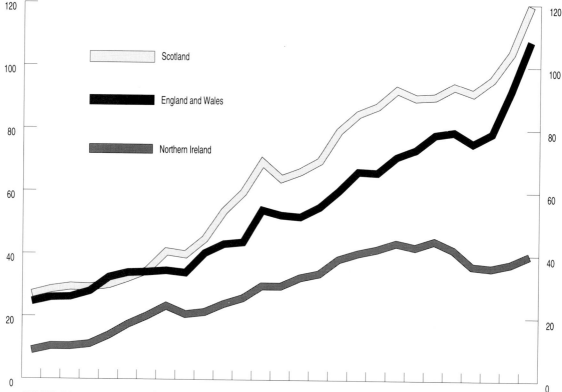

Scotland

England and Wales

Northern Ireland

1965 1966 1967 1968 1969 1970 1971 1972 1973 1974 1975 1976 1977 1978 1979 1980 1981 1982 1983 1984 1985 1986 1987 1988 1989 1990 1991

Source: Annual Abstract of Statistics (*see* *Central Statistical Office*).

Crichton Castle (24km/15m SE of Edinburgh) Ruined castle (14–16C) set in rolling open country and notable for an Italianate interior courtyard with an arcade. This feature was the result of a visit to Italy in the 1570s by the 5th earl of Bothwell, whose uncle had been the husband of Mary Queen of Scots.

Francis **Crick** see *DNA.

cricket England's national summer game, relatively little played in Scotland, Ireland or Wales. It involves two teams of eleven, but the encounter is essentially between a batsman, who with his wooden bat must defend a wicket (consisting of three stumps or upright pieces of wood on which two smaller pieces, the bails, loosely rest), and a bowler, who projects the ball (with a straight arm and nowadays overarm, though this was illegal until 1864) towards the wicket. The bowler's purpose is either to knock the bails off the wicket or to tempt the batsman into hitting the ball in such a way that it can be caught before it reaches the ground. The game must originally have been a simple country pastime (there is a theory that it was played by shepherd boys, the wicket being a low gate into the sheep pen). It is first mentioned in the 16C and was developed into a formalized and skilful game in southeast England during the 18C. The most important elements in this development were the *Hambledon Club, the *MCC and *Lord's.

Competition became regional, from village cricket up to the *county championship. Most county players were paid for their services, but meanwhile the game had been introduced with great success into the *public schools, resulting in many talented amateurs. Thus began a strange division in English cricket between Gentlemen (the amateurs) and Players (the professionals). They played together in county and national teams, but every summer competed against other in the Gentlemen v. Players match at Lords (last played in 1962, after which the distinction was ended).

Cricket was exported to the colonies, and the international *Test matches date back as far as 1877.

Cries of London More than 150 of the calls of street-sellers hawking their wares in the capital were collected before they ceased to be heard, and they have sometimes been incorporated by English composers in their works. The phrase was used as the title for several series of prints of itinerant traders. The best known are the stipple engravings of 1793–7 based on sentimental paintings by Francis Wheatley (1747–1801).

crime The number of criminal offences recorded by the police has risen inexorably in recent decades. Part of the explanation may be that a greater percentage of crimes is now notified to the police; another relevant factor has been high levels of unemployment. In certain regions the police have declared that teenage crime (and even theft by children) has reached unprecedented levels. But overall the youth element in crime is nothing new. In 1965 51% of males convicted of indictable offences in England and Wales were aged under 21; in 1990 the equivalent figure was 36%.

It is probably a common perception in all societies at all times that everyday life is becoming more violent and more crime-ridden. There may be some truth in the impression that Britain in the mid-20C was relatively law-abiding (with violence enough in two world wars), but the Victorian era was far from gentle. In about 1870 an author, Blanchard Jerrold, wanted to visit the Whitechapel district for a book on London, to be illustrated by Gustave Doré. Before doing so, he took what he considered the necessary precautions; he put on his shabbiest clothes and arranged for a police escort.

Crimean War (1854–6) War fought by Great Britain, France and Turkey against Russia in the Crimea, a large peninsula on the north coast of the Black Sea. The underlying struggle was for control of the Black Sea and the eastern Mediterranean. Britain and France sent a force to destroy the Russian naval base at Sebastopol, and the main action of the war was the prolonged Russian attempt to relieve the besieged city. The two major engagements were the battles of Balaklava (25 Oct. 1854, remembered in particular for the *Charge of the Light Brigade) and of Inkerman (5 Nov. 1854). The Russians evacuated Sebastopol in September 1855, and the war ended with various Russian concessions in the treaty of Paris (1856).

From the public's point of view this was the first modern war. Telegraph brought back almost instant news. Recording the events brought fame to the first great war reporter, *Russell of the *Times*, and the first war photographer, Roger *Fenton. But by far the best-known figure to emerge was Florence *Nightingale.

criminal justice The procedure by which the *police and the *courts of law bring those guilty of crime to conviction and sentence. A spate of miscarriages of justice and of quashed convictions in the early 1990s (among them the *Guildford Four, the *Birmingham Six and the *Maguire Seven) caused the home secretary to appoint in 1991 a Royal Commission on Criminal Justice. Chaired by Lord Runciman, its report was scheduled for June 1993. Areas of special concern are police intimidation of suspects and fabricating of evidence (the *West Midlands Serious Crime Squad was the extreme case); the reliance on uncorroborated confessions (such as that of Judith *Ward); the misuse of *forensic evidence; the non-disclosure to the defence of relevant information known to the police; and unnecessary obstacles in the appeal procedure.

Dr **Crippen** (Hawley Harvey Crippen, 1862–1910) American doctor whose poisoning of his wife, a would-be music hall artiste calling herself Belle Elmore, was one of the most sensational cases of the early 20C. It had a double

The dramatic arrest of Crippen and of Ethel le Neve, disguised as his son: from a French magazine of 1910.

appeal. It was a very middle-class crime of passion in a respectable area of north London; Crippen's mistress Ethel le Neve moved into his home at 39 Hilldrop Crescent, where Belle's body was hidden in the coal cellar. And the manner of the couple's arrest was extremely dramatic. When remains of the body were found, in 1910, they fled to Canada disguised as Mr Robinson and his son. But the captain of the SS *Montrose* was suspicious; he sent a message to Scotland Yard by wireless telegraphy (it is the first known use of radio in making an arrest). Chief Inspector Dew set off in pursuit in a faster ship and boarded the *Montrose* in the St Lawrence River. Meanwhile the use of telegraphy meant that newspapers on shore were able to report every stage of the chase before the culprit even knew he had been discovered. Crippen was hanged but Ethel was acquitted; she lived until 1967.

Stafford **Cripps** (1889–1952, kt 1930) Labour politician and MP for Bristol East (1931–50), remembered in particular as the chancellor of the exchequer (1947–50) who kept tight control during Britain's years of austerity after World War II. A barrister by profession (appointed attorney general in 1930), he was sent by Churchill as ambassador to Russia (1940–2) and had a place in the war cabinet in charge of aircraft production (1942–5).

'Crisis? What crisis?' see *winter of discontent.

St **Crispin** Saint whose legend states that he and his brother, Crispinian, were shoemakers, martyred in the 3rd century AD. He is remembered in Britain only because his feast day (Oct. 25, shared with his brother) happened to be the date of the Battle of *Agincourt, giving Shakespeare the opportunity to put into the king's mouth in *Henry V* the rousing speech about 'we few, we happy few, we band of brothers' who fought together 'upon Saint Crispin's day'.

Crockford (*Crockford's Clerical Directory*) The *Who's Who* of Anglican clergy in Britain, with an entry for every clergyman in the Church of England, the Church in Wales, the Scottish Episcopal Church and the Church of Ireland. First published in 1858, it now appears every other year. It is named after John Crockford, about whom little is known; even his role in launching the directory is uncertain.
In 1987 a controversy and a tragedy brought *Crockford* to the attention of many who had never previously heard of it. An unsigned preface in that year's edition took the unprecedented step of criticizing the archbishop of Canterbury. A week after publication, and after much furore, it was announced that the author was a clergyman, Gareth Bennett, and that he had committed suicide the previous day.

Cromford Mill (27km/17m N of Derby) The first cotton mill in which water power was successfully applied to spinning, built in 1771 by *Arkwright and restored in the 1980s. The town of Cromford was also the first in Britain specifically created to house factory workers.

Richmal **Crompton** (pen name of Richmal Crompton Lamburn, 1890–1969) The author of some 40 books about *William. She was classics mistress at Bromley High School when she became severely disabled by polio in 1923. But *Just – William* had been published in the previous year, and she had found her new career.

Samuel **Crompton** (1753–1827) Inventor of the spinning mule, which he perfected in about 1779. A great improvement on *Hargreaves' spinning jenny (which

tended to break the yarn), it enabled almost all types of yarn to be spun at high speed. It acquired its popular name as a pun. A jenny is also the word for a female ass; Crompton had combined elements of the spinning jenny and of another machine being used by *Arkwright, making the new hybrid naturally a mule.

Oliver **Cromwell** (1599–1658) Ruler of the whole of Great Britain as Lord Protector during the central years of the *Commonwealth, from 1653 to 1658. Born in *Huntingdon into a family prominent in local affairs, his first public career was in politics – as an MP for Huntingdon in 1628 and then for Cambridge in the *Long Parliament of 1640. With the start of the *English Civil War, Cromwell raised a troop of cavalry in Cambridgeshire on behalf of parliament. He rapidly proved himself a brilliant soldier and was largely responsible for the successes of the *New Model Army. Prominent among those demanding the execution of Charles I, and one of the political leaders of the new *Commonwealth, he was also appointed commander-in-chief of the parliamentary army sent to put down unrest in *Ireland in 1649. He did this with considerable severity, intended as an example (in particular in the massacre of the royalist garrison at Drogheda in September). A similar campaign in Scotland (1650–1) was equally effective, and he capped these successes with the defeat of Charles II at the battle of Worcester in 1651.
By now there were deep religious differences between parliament (presbyterian and inclined to the suppression of all dissent) and the army, in which there were many mutually tolerant sects, linked by the Congregationalist doctrine that each group had the right to be self-governing. Cromwell, by now the most powerful man in the land, sided with the army and in 1653 personally ejected the rump of the *Long Parliament from the House of Commons. He replaced it with the *Barebones Parliament, the failure of which led rapidly to his own supreme power under the *Protectorate.
In religious matters he ruled with a considerable degree of tolerance (allowing the *Jews to return, for example, after nearly 400 years) and a new efficiency brought Britain successes abroad, particularly in the *Anglo-Dutch Wars. Cromwell died in 1659 of malaria, first contracted during his campaigns in Ireland. Many of his domestic reforms were repealed in the *Restoration, when the high feeling against him led to his body being exhumed from Westminster Abbey. It was hung in chains at Tyburn and his head was stuck on a pole on top of Westminster Hall, where it remained for some 25 years.

Richard **Cromwell** see the *Protectorate.

Thomas **Cromwell** (*c*.1485–1540, earl of Essex 1540) Chief minister of Henry VIII during the 1530s. His life, like that of *Wolsey, demonstrates the high level both of opportunity and risk in any Tudor career. Cromwell, whose father is variously described as a London blacksmith, brewer or clothmaker, rose in Wolsey's service. He then followed his master as the king's counsellor, completing the break with Rome through the Act of *Supremacy and enriching the royal coffers by the *dissolution of the monasteries. He had meanwhile vastly improved the central administration, laying the basis for what was in effect a civil service. His mistake was to press upon Henry a German alliance, personified in *Anne of Cleves who proved personally displeasing to the king. This error of judgement, combined with hostility to him from a conservative faction at court, was sufficient to lead to Cromwell's downfall. He was executed as a heretic and traitor less than four months after being created earl of Essex.

THE ROYALL OAKE OF BRITTAYNE

Oliver Cromwell supervising the destruction of the royal oak of England: a royalist engraving published after the king's death.

A.J. Cronin (1896–1981) Scottish novelist, who trained as a doctor in Glasgow and practised medicine in a mining community in Wales. The success of his first novel, *Hatter's Castle* (1931), enabled him to become a full-time writer. Like nearly all his work it contained much autobiography. *The Citadel* (1937) was a fierce attack on the greed of the fashionable doctors of Harley Street. But it was his account of a rural medical practice which reached the widest audience, for he was the creator of the television series *Dr Finlay's Casebook*.

William **Crookes** (1832–1919, kt 1897) Chemist and physicist who in 1861 discovered the element thallium by observing a green line in the spectrum of selenium (the element was first isolated in France the following year, by Claude-Auguste Lamy). He invented the radiometer known by his name, in which lightweight vanes blackened on one side revolve in a near-vacuum when light or other radiant energy falls upon them. In his later years he did pioneering work on cathode rays.

croquet Game using a mallet to knock a ball through hoops, and thus an extension of the French medieval game of *paille-maille* (reflected in the name of *Pall Mall in London). In its modern form, played on grass, it seems to have developed in Ireland shortly before spreading to England in about 1850. It rapidly became a popular game with the middle classes and in 1869 the All England Croquet Club was founded at *Wimbledon. Today the Hurlingham Club in London is the headquarters of the sport in Britain.

Anthony **Crosland** (1918-77) Labour politician and author who established himself with *The Future of Socialism* (1956) as the leading theorist of the middle ground in

left-wing politics. He held various cabinet posts during the Labour government of 1964–70 and had been Callaghan's foreign secretary for just ten months when he died of a brain haemorrhage in 1977.

cross-benches Seats in the House of Lords which are arranged along the short end of the rectangular debating chamber. Since the two main parties confront each other from opposite sides of the chamber, these seats imply a position of independence. Only in the Lords do members frequently have no expressed allegiance to a political party, and the idea of the 'cross-bencher' developed in the 19c to describe peers of this kind.

Cross Fell see the *Pennines.

Crossing the Bar (1889) Poem by *Tennyson, written while crossing the Solent. Crossing the harbour bar and putting out to sea is presented as a journey through death and into the afterlife:

> I hope to see my Pilot face to face
> When I have crost the bar.

crossing the floor Term for a member of parliament changing from one party to another. It derives from the rectangular shape of the chambers in the Houses of Parliament. With the two main parties confronting each other across a central divide, a change of allegiance does literally involve crossing the floor of the House.

Crossroads (ATV/Central 1964–88) Soap opera set in a motel in the Midlands. It began five nights a week, was gradually reduced to four and then to three. There was an outcry from fans when Noele Gordon, playing the manager of the motel, was written out of the series in 1981.

Croydon airport in 1929, with two French passenger planes on the tarmac: painting by Kenneth McDonough.

The Crown The legal entity which is the supreme power in the *United Kingdom. It is embodied in the reigning king or queen; but with royal powers delegated to parliament under *constitutional monarchy, the term now effectively means the government.

Crown Court The court above a *magistrate's court in the hearing of a criminal case in England and Wales (see *courts of law). Crown Courts were established in 1970, replacing the previous assizes and quarter sessions. Guilt or innocence is decided by a *jury but the sentence is at the discretion of the judge, within the limits set by law. The Crown Court is one of three divisions of the *Supreme Court.

Crown Derby see *Derby porcelain.

Crown Estate see *Civil List.

crown green see *bowls.

Crown Jewels The phrase is normally used of the British crown jewels, kept in the *Tower of London. Apart from one or two of the lesser items these go back no further than the 17C, the previous royal insignia having been destroyed during the *Commonwealth. Two crowns are used during a *coronation, the heavy St Edward's crown made for Charles II, followed by the lighter imperial state crown, made for Queen Victoria, which is also used for the *state opening of parliament. The most famous stones in the crown jewels are the *Kohinoor and the Star of Africa (cut from the *Cullinan diamond).

There is another far older set of crown jewels in Britain, the so-called Honours of Scotland – now in Edinburgh Castle. Among these Scottish regalia, the oldest in Europe, is the crown refashioned for James V in 1540; it is believed to contain within it a circlet with which Robert the Bruce was crowned at Scone in 1306.

Crown Prosecution Service (CPS) Organization which in 1986 took over from the police the responsibility for deciding on and conducting the majority of prosecutions in England and Wales. It is headed by the *director of public prosecutions (DPP).

Croydon airport London's airport from 1920 to 1946, when it was replaced by *Heathrow. Situated in the south London borough of Croydon, it was the starting point for Amy *Johnson's great flight of 1930.

Crucible Theatre see *Sheffield.

Cruel Garden (1977) Full-length surrealist ballet based on the life and works of the Spanish poet Lorca. Conceived by Lindsay Kemp and choreographed by Christopher *Bruce for the Ballet Rambert, it was first presented on a thrust stage in London's Round House, a converted railway engine shed. The music, by Carlos Miranda, is based on traditional Spanish songs. A televised version (BBC 1982) won the Prix Italia Music Award.

The Cruel Sea (1951) Bestselling novel of World War II by Nicholas Monsarrat (1910–79). It reflected his own experiences on corvettes and frigates, accompanying convoys in the long drawn-out battle of the *Atlantic.

Crufts (Crufts Dog Show) Annual event dating back to a show organized at the Royal Agricultural Hall in Islington in 1891 by Charles Cruft (1852–1938), an ex-salesman of Spratt's 'dog cakes'. By the time of his death Crufts was a fixture in the national calendar. It was then taken on by the *Kennel Club. From 1948 it was held at Olympia; in 1979 it moved to Earl's Court; and in 1991 it went for the first time out of London, to the National Exhibition Centre at Birmingham. Each year's show, now lasting four days and attended by much publicity, results in a winner for each breed and one supreme champion.

George **Cruikshank** (1792–1878) The leading English caricaturist of the generation after Gillray and Rowlandson. Beginning his career during the social and political excesses of the *Regency, he had easy targets for ridicule. The skill of his etched line, with an abundant ability to suggest humour and character in tiny crowded scenes, made him much in demand for book illustration, the plates for *Oliver Twist* being perhaps his best known. He was later a keen supporter of the Temperance movement and published narrative series of cautionary prints, such as *The Drunkard's Children* (1848). It was discovered in 1992 that in his later years he lived a fascinating double life. At the age of 61 he seduced a young housemaid, Adelaide, who was working for himself and his wife; when she became pregnant, he secretly set her up in a house two minutes walk away; by the time he died, 15 years later, Adelaide had given birth to 11 children. Mrs Cruikshank, who first heard of their existence at his deathbed, did much to support them over the following years.

Crumlin Road Prison in Belfast where republican and loyalist suspects are held when on remand, facing terrorist charges. There has been much friction between the two groups; a loyalist remand prisoner was killed and eight others injured in 1991 by a bomb in the jail. Crumlin Road also holds top security prisoners, and an underground tunnel connects it with one of Belfast's main courts.

crumpet see *muffin.

Crusades The series of military expeditions which set out from Europe in the 11–14c to recover the holy places of Christianity from the Muslims. Many British knights took part as individuals from the first crusade (1095–9) onwards, but it was only in the third (1188–91) that they played a prominent role. One of the three official leaders was *Richard I, whose adventures later became much embroidered in legend. In reality little was achieved, except a further deterioration in the relationship between Christians and Muslims in Palestine. Richard's own contribution to this process included his allowing the massacre, after the capture of Acre, of some 2600 Muslim prisoners.

Crusaid (London SW1) Charity founded in 1986 to raise money for the victims of Aids, with special emphasis on helping sufferers to continue to live at home through the provision of day centres, medical care and financial support.

Crystal Palace Vast glass and metal building (564m/ 1850ft long and 124m/408ft wide, covering four times the ground area of St Peter's in Rome), which was designed by *Paxton for the *Great Exhibition of 1851. It was in several ways a revolutionary concept – the first building in which the entire load-bearing structure was an iron frame, the first made from prefabricated units, the first with glass curtain walls. It was designed in nine days and put up on the south side of Hyde Park in six months (Paxton was knighted on its completion). It enclosed three large elms together with their resident sparrows, a messy threat to the exhibits but safe from shot guns in a glasshouse; it was the duke of Wellington who provided the solution when he advised the queen 'Try sparrowhawks, ma'am'. The building was taken down in 1852 and reconstructed as the centrepiece of a new park in south London, at Sydenham. In 1936 its fittings and contents caught fire and it was destroyed.

But the park survives, still enlivened by its original set of life-size prehistoric monsters (iron and brick covered with painted stucco); the half-completed iguanadon was large enough for 21 people to dine inside it in 1854. Part of the park was used in 1956–64 to build one of the national sports centres run by the *Sports Council.

CSE see *exams.

CSO see *Central Statistical Office.

CTC see *city technology colleges.

CTT see *inheritance tax.

Thomas **Cubitt** (1788–1855) Carpenter turned speculative builder who made a fortune constructing large parts of 19c London, most notably *Belgravia. He was unusual in hiring his craftsmen on a permanent basis. The need to keep them employed caused him to buy up tracts of land for development in the rapidly expanding city. The designs were usually by himself or by members of his firm, which for a while included his brother Lewis (1799–1883).

Cubs Short for Cub Scouts, the junior branch of the *Scouts, established for 8–10-year-olds in 1914 and known as Wolf Cubs until 1966. The adult leader of a Cub Pack is known as Akela (after the head of the wolf pack which adopts Mowgli in The *Jungle Book).

Cullinan diamond The world's largest diamond, weighing 3106 carats when found in 1905 in South Africa in a mine started three years previously by Thomas Cullinan. The Transvaal government presented it to Edward VII. It was cut into nine large stones and about 100 smaller ones, all now in the *crown jewels. The largest of them is in the sceptre – the pear-shaped Star of Africa (at 530 carats the world's largest cut diamond).

Culloden (16 Apr. 1746) Battle between some 5000 Scots under Charles Edward *Stuart and a government army of about 9000 under the duke of *Cumberland. Taking place on an exposed moor 5km/3m east of Inverness (kept now as a memorial), it put a decisive end

The crown jewels in a coronation photograph of Elizabeth II by Cecil Beaton (1953); the Cullinan diamond is in the sceptre.

to the *'45 Rebellion and was the last battle fought on British soil. In addition to being outnumbered, the Scots were exhausted after marching throughout the previous night in a futile attempt to surprise the enemy. The battle lasted less than an hour and ended in the complete rout of the Pretender's army. The disaster was re-enacted in an influential drama-documentary (*Culloden* BBC 1964) directed by Peter Watkins.

Nicholas **Culpeper** (1616–54) Physician noted for his early study of the medicinal properties of herbs. His *Complete Herbal* was first published in 1652 under the title *The English Physitian, or an Astrologo-physical discourse of the vulgar herbs of this nation. Being a complete method of physick, whereby a man may preserve his body in health; or cure himself, being sick.*

Culross (35km/22m NW of Edinburgh) Town in Fife, on the north shore of the Firth of Forth, which dates back to a 6c monastic settlement but which is known now as a superbly preserved small Scottish burgh of the 16–17c thanks to restoration by the National Trust for Scotland. The most notable buldings are the 17c Town House and the late-16c 'Palace' (in fact a merchant's house). The choir of the Cistercian abbey, dating originally from the 13c but rebuilt in 1633, is used as the parish church.

Culzean Castle (23km/14m SW of Ayr) One of the masterpieces of Robert *Adam and a precursor of the many 19c stately homes disguised as castles. It was built in 1777–87 for the Kennedy family, on the site of an earlier tower house at the top of a craggy cliff facing the Atlantic. The round drawing room in the great castellated tower and the oval staircase in the centre of the house are two of Adam's most impressive creations. His home farm of 1777 is now the visitors' centre for a large country park. An apartment in the house, given in 1946 to General Eisenhower in recognition of his achievements in World War II, is kept as a memorial to him.

Cumberland Former *county in northwest England, merged in 1974 with Westmorland and part of Lancashire to form Cumbria.

Duke of **Cumberland** (William Augustus, 1721–65) Second surviving son of George II, active as an army commander (1742–57). In 1745 he was in command of the allied forces at Fontenoy, a major setback in the War of *Austrian Succession. But he defeated Bonnie Prince Charlie decisively at *Culloden in 1746, acquiring his nickname, Butcher Cumberland, from the severity with which over the next three months he pursued and punished the rebels. Handel's oratorio *Judas Maccabaeus* was written to greet him on his return to London; its best-known chorus, 'See, the conquering hero comes', was added when Handel later extended the work.

Cumbernauld see *new towns.

Cumbria (490,000 in 1991, administrative centre Carlisle) *County in the extreme northwest of England, formed in 1974 from Cumberland, Westmorland and part of Lancashire.

Samuel **Cunard** (1787–1865, bt 1859) Founder of the greatest of the shipping lines of the steam age. Born in Canada, he came to Britain in 1838 and set up the British and North American Mail Steam Packet Company. He introduced the first regular transatlantic postal service when the *Britannia* left Liverpool on 4 July 1840, arriving in Boston 14 days later (one day better than the previous record set by *Brunel's *Great Western*). Renamed the

Cunard Line, the company built and operated many of the most famous British liners – including the *Mauretania*, the *Lusitania* and the three Queens (*Queen Mary, Queen Elizabeth, *QE2).

Jack **Cunningham** (b. 1939) Labour politician, MP for Copeland since 1983 (previously for Whitehaven, Cumbria, from 1970). He was first elected to the shadow cabinet in 1983, becoming opposition spokesman on the environment (1983–9) and shadow leader of the House of Commons (1989–92). In John Smith's first shadow cabinet, from 1992, he held the foreign affairs portfolio.

Cunobelin see *Cymbeline.

Cup Final The main event of the English football year, when the two teams surviving from the knock-out competition of the *FA Cup meet at *Wembley, usually on a Saturday in early May. The game is preceded by the performance of massed bands and by much communal singing among the spectators. The final of the *Scottish FA Cup is held at *Hampden Park, often on the same day.

curate's egg A phrase for anything that is a mixture of good and bad. It derives from a cartoon by *du Maurier in *Punch* on 9 November 1895, in which the bishop says to a nervous curate at breakfast 'I'm afraid you've got a bad egg, Mr Jones' and gets the reply 'Oh no, my Lord, I assure you! Parts of it are excellent!'

'Curiouser and curiouser' see *Alice in Wonderland.

'the **curious incident** of the dog in the night time' One of Sherlock *Holmes's best-known insights, the curious element being that the dog in the stable did not bark during the night of the crime (in the story 'Silver Blaze'). Holmes reasons that the dog must have known whoever removed the racehorse Silver Blaze, which leads him to suspect the dead trainer.

curling Traditional winter game in Scotland and in several other countries with a cold climate. It is in effect bowls on ice, with the players sliding smooth heavy stones (known as 'granites') towards a fixed mark, the tee; to increase the distance travelled by the stone, the surface of the ice in its path may be swept with a brush or broom. It is a matter of dispute whether the game began in Scotland or the Netherlands. Many early curling stones have been found in Scotland (the earliest, with the engraved date 1511, is in the Smith Institute in Stirling); but the game is first depicted in scenes by Pieter Brueghel (*c*.1525–69) in Flanders, where no such stones have been found. The explanation may be that the Dutch and Flemish played with lumps of frozen earth or even ice, with a stick stuck in for the handle. The earliest book on curling (*An Account of the Game of Curling* 1811) was written by a Scottish minister, John Ramsay, a member of the Duddingston Curling Society. The central international body for curling is the Royal Caledonian Curling Club in Edinburgh, founded in 1838 (as the Grand Caledonian Curling Club) 'to unite curlers throughout the world'. By that time there were clubs in Canada (Montreal 1807) and the USA (Orchard Lake in Michigan 1831).

currency The present system of decimal coinage, introduced in 1971, consists of a pound made up of 100 pence. Money is written in the form £12.79 (12 pounds and 79 pence). The pound was the unit of currency taken over from the previous system, in which it consisted of 20 shillings, each of 12 old pence (see *£.s.d.). Although shillings and pence had long been the basic subdivisions of the pound, there were until 1971 two other coins in circulation with distinctive names. These were the half-crown (2 shillings and 6 pence, the crown being an old coin worth 5 shillings) and the florin (2 shillings). The *guinea was also still in use as a notional sum of money.

At the time of decimalization, in 1971, those coins remained in circulation which translated exactly into new pence. These were the two-shilling piece or florin (the equivalent of 10 new pence), the shilling (5p) and the six-pence (2½p). They were joined by four new decimal coins, one 'silver' (in fact cupro-nickel) and three bronze: 50p, 2p, 1p and ½p. Inflation soon made a half penny irrelevant; the 2½p coin, the old sixpence, ceased to be legal tender in 1980 and it was followed by the decimal halfpenny itself in 1984.

Four new coins introduced since 1982 have completed the decimal coinage. First came the silver 20p (seven-sided like the 50p); then Britain's first £1 coin of recent years (an alloy of copper, nickel and zinc to look like gold in memory of the *sovereign); and finally two small silver coins for 5p and 10p. The previous versions of 5p and 10p, which ceased to be legal tender in December 1990 and June 1993 respectively, still included the surviving shillings and florins; so their removal from circulation severed the last links with the old coinage. The coins in everyday circulation are now £1, 50p, 20p, 10p, 5p, 2p and 1p.

curriculum see *national curriculum.

Edwina **Currie** (b. 1946) Flamboyant Conservative politician, MP for Derbyshire South since 1983, whose career came to a halt, at least temporarily, when she resigned as under-secretary of state for health in December 1988. She had stated in a TV interview that most of Britain's egg production was infected with salmonella. A leading egg producer began legal proceedings for losses caused by her remarks, and her resignation was followed by a government announcement of a £19 million package to help the egg industry recover from the salmonella scare.

curry Any dish prepared with hot spices, of a kind which has become popular in Britain through the country's involvement with India; the word derives from *kari* ('sauce' in Tamil), a spicy concoction of vegetables, fish or meat adding flavour to a meal of rice. By the early 19c curry powder was available, providing ground turmeric and other mixed spices in a convenient form.

John **Curry** (b. 1949) Athlete whose grace and flair brought the quality of ballet to figure skating. He won the European Championship in 1976, following it in that same year with a gold medal at the Olympics and then in the World Championship. He subsequently turned professional, setting up his own ice dance spectacular.

Curtis Cup see *golf.

Lord **Curzon** (George Nathaniel Curzon, 1859–1925, baron 1898, marquess 1921) Viceroy of India (1899–1905) and foreign secretary (1919–24). His most lasting contribution is to be seen in India, where the restoration of many of the subcontinent's ancient monuments was undertaken during his period as viceroy.

HM **Customs and Excise** (London SE1) Government department responsible for collecting duty on imports (customs) and tax imposed on goods produced internally such as alcohol or tobacco (excise). Since 1973 the department has also collected *VAT.

St **Cuthbert** (*c*.635–87) Born in northeast England, he was a monk at *Melrose and in his last years bishop at *Lindisfarne. His reputation for saintliness caused his bones to be regarded as very sacred relics. They were removed from Lindisfarne because of *Viking raids, and after two centuries of uncertain travel found a final resting place in *Durham. His feast day is March 20.

Cutty Sark The last survivor of the great three-masted tea-clippers, designed to sail at maximum speed to the London market with a precious cargo of fresh tea from China. Launched in Scotland (Dumbarton 1869), and named after the provocative young witch in *Tam o' Shanter*, she has been in dry dock at *Greenwich and open to visitors since 1957.

CVO see *orders of chivalry.

Cwmbran (45,000 in 1981) Town in south Wales; administrative centre of Gwent. This area in the Llwyd valley, consisting at the time of small industrial villages, was designated in 1949 the site for a *new town, with an intended eventual population of 55,000.

Cwm Idwal (11km/7m SE of Bangor) Glacial valley, overhung by the precipice of Glyder Fawr with the great fissure known as the Devil's Kitchen. Welsh legend says that the Kitchen is haunted by a murderous foster-father who drowned Prince Idwal in the nearby lake. The area was designated a nature reserve in 1954.

Cymbeline (*c*.1609) Play by *Shakespeare about love tested to melodramatic limits and surviving. A faithful wife, Imogen (daughter of an early British king, Cymbeline) undergoes a series of horrifying experiences. She is the victim of a pretended seduction by Iachimo (who hides in a trunk in her bedroom to discover details such as a mole on her breast which will back up his lies); she then escapes an attempted murder arranged by her jealous husband, Posthumus, and has a spell hiding in Wales, disguised as a male page (Fidele), during which she wakes to find beside her a headless corpse which she takes to be that of her husband. With something of a strain to credulity, all ends happily.

Cymbeline, known to historians as Cunobelin, was king of the region round Colchester early in the 1st century AD. He was father of *Caratacus and of Adminius, whose tomb was possibly the one discovered at *Verulamium in the early 1990s. Another royal tomb, assumed to be of a member of Cunobelin's family, was excavated near Colchester in 1992.

Cymru The name in Welsh of *Wales.

Cyprus Member of the *Commonwealth since 1960. The island was part of the Turkish empire from 1573 to 1878, when the Turks ceded control (though not sovereignty) to Britain in return for British defence against a threat by sea from Russia. Britain annexed the island in 1914, when Turkey was an enemy in World War I. Cyprus then became a crown colony, but it was troubled by constant unrest between the Greek majority and Turkish minority; this culminated in a period of prolonged terrorism, sparked off after World War II by an aggressive Greek campaign for *enosis* (union with Greece). The leader of the Greek cause was Archbishop Makarios (1913–77), who became president of an independent Cyprus in 1960. The constitution, supposedly strengthened by guarantees from Britain, Greece and Turkey, was intended to share power between the two communities and thus to avoid partition. It soon proved unworkable. In 1975 the Cypriot Turks, led by Rauf Denktash, declared their own state in the northern part of the island. A United Nations peace-keeping force, sent to Cyprus in 1964, has remained to preside over an uneasy impasse.

D

Dad's Army (BBC 1968–77) One of the most endearing of TV comedy series, following the exploits of a platoon in the *Home Guard. The pompous platoon commander, Captain Mainwaring, constantly struggling to assert his authority over his shambling band of incompetents, was played by Arthur Lowe; and his long-suffering deputy, Sergeant Wilson, by John Le Mesurier.

daffodil see national *emblems.

Roald **Dahl** (1916–90) Author born in Wales of Norwegian parents. His exotic and often cruel imagination was well suited both to mystery stories for adults and to books which would fascinate children. *James and the Giant Peach* (1962) was rapidly followed by his greatest success *Charlie and the Chocolate Factory.* In the 1990s he is consistently among the two or three authors whose books are most borrowed from children's libraries.

Daily Express, Mail etc see under Daily *Express, Daily *Mail.

Daily Worker see *Communist Party of Great Britain.

Daimler Coventry firm which began making cars in 1897 under licence from the German pioneer Gottlieb Daimler (1834–1900). In 1900 a 6hp model was bought by the future Edward VII, thus beginning the long link between the royal family and the British firm of Daimler. The company was bought in 1960 by *Jaguar.

Daleks see *Dr Who.

Dales Valleys in the *Pennines (*dael* was an Old English word for a low place), famous for their beauty. Applied mainly to the Yorkshire dales, the term is used also of the valleys further south in Derbyshire.

Kenny **Dalglish** (b. 1951) Scottish footballer and manager, with a sparkling career in both contexts. He played first for his home team, Celtic (1970–7), and then moved to Liverpool (1977–90) where he followed Kevin Keegan as the club's star player during an almost unbroken run of successes. In 1985 he became the team's player manager (taking over on the day after the *Heysel tragedy), and he led Liverpool to its League and FA Cup double in 1986. The League was won again in 1988 and 1990 and the FA Cup in 1989, but Dalglish then astonished everyone by retiring in February 1991, for reasons of stress, with just three months of the season to go. He rapidly re-emerged from retirement, in October of that same year, to sign on as manager of *Blackburn Rovers, then in Division 2; by the end of the season he had won them

promotion to the top division (renamed the *Premier League), where they immediately prospered. In his international career Dalglish won a record 102 caps; and he holds (jointly with Denis Law) the record of 30 goals scored for Scotland.

Dalmeny House (11km/7m W of Edinburgh) One of the first *Gothic Revival buildings in Scotland, completed in 1817 to a design by *Wilkins. Its treasures have recently been supplemented by the best items from *Mentmore Towers.

Dalriada Kingdom of the *Scots which in the 5C united northeast Ireland and western Scotland under a single rule. Viking invasions weakened the Irish side and by the 9C, under *Kenneth I, the kingdom existed only in Scotland.

Hugh **Dalton** (1887–1962, baron 1960) Labour politician who was in Churchill's wartime government (responsible for 'economic warfare' and then for trade) and who became the first chancellor of the exchequer (1945–7) in the postwar Labour government. His time in this office came to an abrupt and sad end in November 1947. On his way into the chamber of the Commons, where he was to deliver his budget, he answered some questions (off the record, as he thought) from the lobby correspondent of the *Star.* The details were on sale on the street a few minutes before they were announced in the House and Dalton resigned. He returned to the cabinet in June 1948 as chancellor of the duchy of Lancaster.

John **Dalton** (1766–1844) Self-taught chemist who was the first to provide an account of the atomic theory which is central to modern chemistry. The notion that matter is made up of independent atoms goes back to ancient Greece as a philosophical concept, and it began to enter the realm of material science with the recognition of elements as irreducibly pure substances (a process in which Robert *Boyle's *Sceptical Chymist* of 1661 was an important step). But it was Dalton who suggested a coherent scheme in which different elements have atoms of differing size and weight – atoms which are themselves indestructible but which combine in new arrangements to form compounds. He made out a first brief table of relative atomic weights in 1803, and described the system more fully in *A New System of Chemical Philosophy* (1808), thus putting in place the structure which was developed by others into the full periodic table.

The red-green colour blindness known as daltonism was a disability from which Dalton himself suffered. He described it in a paper of 1794 to the Manchester Literary and Philosophical Society.

Cardinal **Daly** (Cahal Daly, b. 1917) Roman Catholic archbishop of *Armagh since 1990, having previously been bishop of Ardagh and Clonmacnois (1967–82) and of Down and Connor (1982–90). He was made a cardinal in 1991. He is known for the vehemence of his condemnation of the activities of the IRA; like his Anglican counterpart, Robert *Eames, he was educated in Belfast.

Dam Busters The air crews of 617 Squadron, who flew the mission on the night of 16 May 1943 to destroy the Möhne and Eder dams, providing electricity for Germany's industrial Ruhr valley. The 19 Lancasters were under the command of Guy *Gibson and the bouncing bombs were designed by Barnes *Wallis. Only 11 of the planes returned, but the dams were put out of action for a year. A film, *The Dam Busters*, was made in 1954, directed by Michael Anderson, with Richard Todd as Gibson and Michael Redgrave as Wallis, and with music by Eric *Coates.

dame Traditionally an elderly female role played by a man in *pantomime. Since 1917, when the Order of the British Empire was founded for both men and women, the title 'Dame' has been familiar in British life as the female equivalent of 'Sir' for men (see *orders of chivalry).

Dan-Air Britain's second largest airline until financial troubles in the early 1990s threatened bankruptcy. In October 1992 it was saved from closure by the announcement that BA (British Airways) would absorb its fleet and some of its crews (for a notional £1 and the acceptance of debts amounting to £35 million). The name Dan-Air was based on the initials of Davies and Newman, a ship-broking firm which launched the airline in 1953. It prospered at first with package tours to the Mediterranean, and expanded in the 1970s into scheduled flights.

*A **Dance to the Music of Time*** see Anthony *Powell.

Dance Umbrella Festival of contemporary dance, presenting British and foreign companies at several locations in London and on tour. First held in 1978, it is now an annual event lasting several weeks each autumn.

Dan Dare (Pilot of the Future) The spaceman hero of *Eagle, whose eternal enemy was the tiny green-headed extraterrestrial Mekon.

Dandie Dinmont see *terriers.

Dandy Children's comic published weekly since 1937. Its undoubted star has been Desperate Dan, a cowboy of rugged jaw and limited intelligence, whose great strength depends on a regular supply of cow pies.

Danegeld Tax levied in the *Anglo-Saxon kingdoms to buy off the invading Danes, in particular between 991 and 1013. It provided Kipling (in his poem *Dane-Geld*) with a telling couplet on appeasement. He concludes:

> That if once you have paid him the Dane-geld
> You never get rid of the Dane.

Danelaw see *Danes.

Danes The name used in English history for those *Vikings who conquered the eastern and northern parts of England in the 9C, and who came mainly from Denmark and Norway.

Spasmodic coastal raids throughout the early 9C were followed by full-scale conquest (from 865) of the *Anglo-Saxon kingdoms of Northumbria and East Anglia, with inroads into Mercia. Danish control of the whole of England looked probable until their advance was halted by *Alfred the Great. The result was that they were contained to the north of a line running roughly from London to Chester, and by the early 10C they had accepted the overlordship of the newly established kings of England (see *Wessex). The area in which the Danes had settled became known as Danelaw. The chief town within Danelaw was Nottingham, others of importance being Leicester, Stamford, Derby and Lincoln.

The first half of the 10C saw relatively peaceful co-existence between Danelaw and southern England, but from 980 there were renewed Danish invasions on English coasts. This time the invaders were temporarily bought off with the payment known as *Danegeld. Then, in 1013, the Danish king Sweyn I invaded and conquered the entire country. Under his son and grandson, *Canute and Harthacanute, England and Denmark were joined as one kingdom. Danish rule ended with the succession to the throne in 1042 of *Edward the Confessor, though there now began the intrusion of a different group of Viking descendants, the *Normans. The last Danish invasion was in the same year as the Norman Conquest; in September 1066 Harold Hardraade landed on the east coast and was defeated at Stamford Bridge by *Harold II, who died the following month at the Battle of Hastings. But Danish influence survived in many ways (the 'ridings' of Yorkshire, for example, date back to their rule), and in Norman times Danelaw was still the term for the entire eastern section of England where Danish laws and customs prevailed.

Thomas **Daniell** (1749–1840) Topographical artist who went out to India in 1794 with his nephew William Daniell (1769–1837). Their series of large aquatints, published in six parts as *Oriental Scenery* (1795–1808), were largely responsible for the vogue for Indian architecture which began with *Sezincote. William later published an equally famous series of small aquatints of British coastal scenes (*A Voyage round Great Britain* 1814–25).

Dan Dare confronting the sinister Mekon ('Silence him!') in an August 1954 issue of Eagle.

Paul Daniels (b. 1938) Conjuror whose first television appearance was on *Opportunity Knocks* in 1970, and who went on to become one of the most popular entertainers of the 1980s with his *Paul Daniels Magic Show*.

John Dankworth (b. 1927) Saxophonist, bandleader and composer. He formed the Johnny Dankworth Seven in 1950; in 1953 he expanded the group into a large jazz orchestra (Cleo *Laine, whom he married in 1958, was the vocalist). His jazz career has overlapped with mainstream orchestral music (in 1985 he became the Pops Music Director of the London Symphony Orchestra), and he has had a successful career composing film scores – including *Saturday Night and Sunday Morning* and *The Servant* (1963).

Dan-yr-Ogof (40km/25m NE of Swansea) Cave system discovered in 1912, with impressive rock formations. It is believed to be the longest accessible sequence of caves in Britain (about 2.5km/1.5m are open to the public).

Abraham **Darby** see *Ironbridge.

Darby and Joan Any idealized old couple, living in marital harmony. The names (used particularly in Darby and Joan clubs for the elderly) derive from a ballad by Henry Woodfall, first published in 1735.

Dardanelles see *Gallipoli.

dark lady of the sonnets see The *Sonnets.

Darkness at Noon (1940) Novel by *Koestler, published in an English translation from his German original. Inspired by the Moscow trials of 1936–8, it was influential as the first work of imaginative power to draw attention to the realities of Stalin's regime. It recounts the experiences of an old party member, N.S. Rubashov. His arrest in the middle of the night by No. 1's secret police leads inexorably, after lengthy interrogations, to his secret execution in the prison cellar. Koestler himself had spent some months in a Spanish jail in 1937, daily expecting death at the hands of the Fascists.

'dark Satanic mills' see *Jerusalem.

Darley Arabian see *thoroughbred.

Grace **Darling** (1815–42) Having grown up in the lighthouse kept by her father on Longstone, one of the most remote of the treacherous Farne Islands off the coast of Northumberland, she became a national heroine after a dramatic exploit in 1838. Grace rowed with her father through tumultuous seas to rescue survivors from the steamboat *Forfarshire*, who were stranded on a rock. Her instant fame led to more requests for locks of her hair than nature could reasonably provide. She made several expeditions to the mainland; but she always came back, in the words of the *Dictionary of National Biography*, 'with such reports of the outer world as deterred her from marriage'. The boat she used is preserved in the *RNLI memorial museum in *Bamburgh.

The **Darling Buds of May** (Yorkshire TV from 1991) Series which achieved great popularity from its first episode, partly in a mood of escapism to a supposedly carefree world of the 1950s. Pop Larkin (father of the family, played by David *Jason) indulges himself to excess in the pleasures of food, alcohol and sex – and further demonstrates his freedom of spirit by refusing to pay income tax. His favourite word of approval, 'perfick', also caught on. The series is based on novels by H.E. *Bates.

Darlington see *Stockton and Darlington railway.

Earl of **Darnley** see *Mary Queen of Scots.

Peter **Darrell** see *Scottish Ballet.

Dartington (26km/16m NW of Dartmouth) Village in Devon where Leonard and Dorothy Elmhirst established in the 1920s a trust specializing in agriculture, rural crafts and education. Its centre is the 14c Dartington Hall (a manor house with a surviving great hall), and its best-known element has been the progressive Dartington School. This closed in 1987 but many of the craft activities continue, in particular the blowing of glass (in north Devon, at Great Torrington).

Dartmoor Area of high moorland in Devon, designated in 1951 a *national park (945sq.km/365sq.m). The district is known for its semi-wild ponies and for its crags (or tors) of granite which rise from the heather. The highest peaks, side by side in the north, are Yes Tor (618m/2028ft) and High Willhays (621m/2039ft).

The small town of Princeton has grown up round Dartmoor prison, built in the *Napoleonic wars to house French prisoners. Since 1850 it has been in use as a conventional prison, considered one of the most secure because of the exposed surrounding countryside. In 1992 the chief inspector of prisons, Judge Stephen Tumim, was strongly critical of conditions in Dartmoor and recommended that the prison should be closed unless improvements were made.

Dartmouth (6000 in 1981) Ancient port and now a yachting resort on the west bank of the estuary of the river Dart in Devon. The castle guarding the entrance to the estuary was begun in 1481 and was designed so that a chain could be stretched across to the companion fort on the opposite bank at Kingswear. The town's museum, housed in the 17c Butterwalk, is particularly strong in models of ships. The Britannia Royal Naval College, an imposing building by Aston Webb on the hillside above the town, has been since 1905 a preliminary training college for officers in the Royal Navy; previously they had studied on board HMS *Britannia*, moored in the Dart.

darts There are records of darts being thrown by hand at a target in England in the 16c (in effect a form of indoor archery), and the Pilgrim Fathers amused themselves with such a game on the *Mayflower*. But it was only in the first half of the 20c that the game became formalized as a favourite pastime in British pubs, after Brian Gamlin (of Bury in Lancashire) had devised in 1896 the present scoring system. The round darts board is divided into 20 equal segments, like slices of a cake, numbered in random sequence from 1 to 20. Each segment contains two small sections, one scoring double and the other treble; thus the top score for a single dart is 60 (in the treble section of the 20 segment), making a maximum of 180 for the three darts which each of the two players throws in turn. The space at the centre scores 50 for the inner circle (the bullseye) and 25 for the surrounding ring.

In 1928 the *News of the World* inaugurated an annual contest which became accepted as the world championship. It continued until 1990, when the newspaper withdrew its support, but by then its status had been usurped by the Embassy World Professional Championship, launched in 1978. The televising of this competition (held since 1986 at the Lakeside Country Club, Frimley Green, Surrey) gave darts a new standing and created its first celebrities. Pre-eminent among these has been Eric Bristow (b. 1957), who won the title five times during the 1980s. Others with impressive records have been John Lowe (b. 1945) and Jocky Wilson (b. 1950).

Charles **Darwin** (1809–82) Naturalist known in particular for his theory of evolution by natural selection. This was inspired by observations made during the voyage of HMS *Beagle*, surveying the islands and coasts of the southern hemisphere in 1831–6. The commander of the ship, Captain Robert Fitzroy (1805–65), took Darwin along as unpaid naturalist to the expedition. The varieties within a single species from one island to another in the Galapagos group convinced Darwin that evolution of some kind must be involved; and his later reading of the theories of *Malthus, on population growth and food supply, prompted the idea that accidental variations might make some variants better equipped in the struggle for life. The well-known phrase to sum up this process, the 'survival of the fittest', was coined in 1864 by another writer on evolution, Herbert Spencer.

Darwin published his *Journal* of the voyage in 1839 and over the next 20 years gradually collected evidence to support his theory. Then, on 18 June 1858, he received what is probably the most famous unpleasant shock in the history of science. The postman delivered an article which had been sent to Darwin for his opinion by someone personally unknown to him, Alfred Russell *Wallace (who had recently begun collecting specimens for Darwin in Malaya). The article expounded precisely the theory of evolution arrived at, but as yet unpublished, by Darwin himself. Darwin was anxious not to take advantage of Wallace's action, and a solution was found when Wallace's paper was read to the Linnaean Society on 1 July 1858 together with earlier private letters by Darwin on the subject. Darwin then set about preparing for publication his own extended account of the theory, known now as *The Origin of Species* (in full *On the Origin of Species by means of Natural Selection, or the Preservation of favoured races in the struggle for life* 1859).

The entire edition of 1250 copies was sold on the first day amid a turmoil of indignation at the threat to the biblical account of creation and at the suggested link between human beings and apes. In a notorious debate at a meeting of the British Association in Oxford in 1860, Bishop Wilberforce – son of William Wilberforce, and known as Soapy Sam – asked Darwin's most energetic disciple, T.H. *Huxley, whether he was descended from an ape on his grandfather's or his grandmother's side.

Darwin published many other books in his later years, the majority on evolution in plants. *The Descent of Man, and selection in relation to sex* (1871) was a sequel to *The Origin of Species*.

Erasmus **Darwin** (1731–1802) Physician and poet, remembered in particular as an early theorist on the subject which his grandson, Charles *Darwin, made his own – evolution. His conclusions, stated in *Zoonomia* (1794–6), were those which his grandson discredited, for he argued that species can adapt to new surroundings and then pass on their acquired characteristics to their offspring (a theory more often associated with the later work of Lamarck). Another grandson was Francis *Galton.

Elizabeth **David** (Elizabeth Gwynne, 1913–92, m. Ivor David 1944) Cookery writer, combining a scholarly approach with very personal enthusiasms. She had a major and beneficial influence on British culinary standards from the 1950s, particularly with *French Country Cooking* (1951), *Italian Food* (1954) and *French Provincial Cooking* (1960).

St **David** (6C) The patron saint of Wales, about whom very little is known except that he established several Welsh monasteries. His headquarters, where he was both abbot and bishop, was at Mynyw, now *St David's. His feast day, March 1, is celebrated as Wales's national day, when it is traditional to wear the national *emblem of a leek, or in some cases recently a daffodil.

Darwin and a distant cousin consider the family likeness: satirical cartoon of 1874.

David I (*c*.1084–1153) King of Scotland from 1124. The youngest son of Malcolm III and Margaret, he succeeded his brother Alexander I. He grew up at the English court of Henry I, who had married his sister, and he introduced Norman-French culture to Scotland, giving lands in the Lowlands to many Norman barons. He went to war unsuccessfully against Stephen on behalf of his niece *Matilda. At home his foundation of numerous abbeys and priories caused him to be venerated later in Scotland as a saint. He married Matilda, daughter of the earl of Northumbria; he was succeeded by a grandson, Malcolm IV (see the *royal house of Scotland).

David II (1324–71) King of Scotland from 1329; son of Robert the Bruce and Elizabeth de Burgh; married first in 1328 (when he was four) Joanna, the infant sister of Edward III, and second in 1363 Margaret Drummond. His long reign was one of almost unbroken disaster. Edward III, in spite of being his brother-in-law, supported a rival for the Scottish throne. David spent seven years in exile in France and 11 years as a captive of the English, after which he was financially crippled by the agreed ransom. He was succeeded by his nephew Robert II (see the *royal house of Scotland).

David Copperfield (1850) Semi-autobiographical novel by Charles *Dickens, published in monthly parts from May 1849. The main characters in the young David's life are: his old nurse Clara Peggotty, who marries the phlegmatic carrier Barkis (his proposal to her is the cryptic message, 'Barkis is willin''); David's childhood sweetheart, little Em'ly, who is related to Peggotty; his schoolfriend, the handsome and brilliant Steerforth; the impecunious but eternally optimistic Mr Micawber, whose economic philosophy in relation to his *'annual income' has become famous and in whose house David lodges after being sent by his brutal stepfather to a life of drudgery in London, where he pastes labels onto bottles for a living; his wealthy but eccentric aunt, Betsey Trotwood, who previously rejected her nephew for not being a niece but who now helps him; and the lawyer, Mr Wickfield, whose daughter Agnes falls in love with David.

Not at first appreciating Agnes, David marries the pretty but childish Dora Spenlow. Meanwhile David himself is becoming a successful author; Steerforth has persuaded little Em'ly to run off with him to foreign parts and has there abandoned her; and Agnes's father has fallen into the clutches of his clerk, Uriah Heep, the hand-wringing master of false humility (' I am well aware that I am the umblest person going').

In the end Steerforth is drowned in a shipwreck, Em'ly is safely recovered by her family, Mr Micawber is instrumental in frustrating the schemes of Uriah Heep (who ends up in prison with a life sentence) and David, whose wife has died young, marries Agnes.

Lynn Davies (b. 1942) Welsh athlete who broke a string of long-jump records in the 1960s. In 1962 he established a new British record of 7.72m (25ft 4in), and in 1964 he set his first Commonwealth record of 8.01m (26ft 3³/₄in); over the years he consistently pushed up the Commonwealth record to an eventual 8.23m (27ft) in 1968. Meanwhile he had won the gold medal at the 1964 Olympic Games; in 1966 he added to his Olympic gold both the Commonwealth and European titles, becoming the first athlete ever to hold all three at the same time.

Sharron Davies (b. 1962) Swimmer who was in the 1976 Olympics as a 14-year-old and who won a gold medal in the 440 yards individual medley at the Commonwealth Games two years later, following this with silver in the 400 metres individual medley at the 1980 Olympics.

She then retired, disenchanted with the routine of a top-level swimmer, but returned ten years later to the rigours of training to qualify for the 1992 Olympics.

W.H. **Davies** see *The *Autobiography of a Super-Tramp*.

Andrew **Davis** (b. 1944) Conductor who has been musical director of Glyndebourne since 1988, known in particular for his interpretations of operas by Richard Strauss. He is also chief conductor of the BBC Symphony Orchestra (from 1989) and previously held the same position with the Toronto Symphony Orchestra (1975–88).

Colin **Davis** (b. 1927, kt 1980) Conductor who has been particularly connected with opera, at Sadler's Wells (1959–65, see the *English National Opera) and at the Royal Opera House (1971–86). The orchestras with which he has been most connected, as principal guest conductor, are the Boston Symphony Orchestra (1972–84) and the London Symphony Orchestra (since 1974).

Fred **Davis** (b. 1913) The younger brother of Joe *Davis, and the leading British snooker player for some years after Joe's retirement; he won the World Professional Championships three times (1948, 49, 51) and its breakaway replacement, the Professional Match-Play Championship, five times (1952–6). He was still playing on the circuit in his late seventies, and he won the World Professional Billiards Championship as recently as 1980.

Joe **Davis** (1901–78) The greatest of British snooker players, dominating the game throughout his career. He had won the World Professional Billiards Championship four times (1928, 29, 30, 32), when he realized that the future lay with the more challenging game of snooker – in which he was instrumental in setting up a separate World Professional Championship. He won this its first year (1927) and was never subsequently defeated, holding his title until 1946 and then retiring from championship play. Inevitably most of his exhibition games had to be on a handicap basis. He only lost four level snooker matches in his entire career – all of them to his younger brother, Fred *Davis. In 1955 Joe became the first player to achieve in public the perfect score of 147 (see *snooker).

Steve **Davis** (b. 1957) The dominant figure in world snooker during the 1980s, as the winner in more than half the years of the decade of both the UK Open (1980, 81, 84, 85, 86, 87) and the World Professional Championship (1981, 83, 84, 87, 88, 89). In the 1982 Lada Classic he became the first man to achieve the perfect score of 147 (see *snooker) while being televised – a sequence frequently shown. He is not related to Joe *Davis.

Davis Cup see *tennis.

Humphry **Davy** (1778–1829, kt 1812) Chemist whose experimental methods led to the discovery of sodium and potassium. He first made a reputation in 1801 with a series of public lectures at the Royal Institution in London. His special interest was in the link between electricity and chemical reaction, arguing that electrolysis was the most likely method of breaking down substances to their elements. It was by this means that he was able to isolate sodium and potassium in 1807, following these with magnesium, calcium, strontium and barium in 1808. His widest fame has been for a practical invention, the Davy lamp. Explosions were caused in mines by methane gas coming into contact with the naked flames of the miners' lamps. Davy protected the flame with a double cylinder of metal gauze. His solution was in use everywhere until the arrival of the electric lamp in the 20c.

Davy (holding the bellows) conducts a public demonstration of chemistry at the Royal Institution: caricature by Gillray (1802).

Davy lamp see Humphry *Davy.

Robin **Day** (b. 1923, kt 1981) Political commentator and interviewer on radio and TV, associated particularly with *Panorama, *Question Time and election broadcasts. He was one of the pioneers in Britain of the aggressive political interview, in his case usually tempered with wit.

C. **Day-Lewis** (Cecil Day-Lewis, 1904–72) Poet and author of detective fiction. Between the wars he was a member of the group of left-wing poets led by W.H. Auden, but he later became more of an establishment figure and was appointed *poet laureate in 1968. He used the pseudonym Nicholas Blake for his novels, in which the detective (Nigel Strangeways) was loosely based on Auden.

daylight saving see *Summer Time.

DBE, DCB, DCMG, DCVO see *orders of chivalry.

D-day A phrase, already in use at the time for the first day of any operation, which has become linked in particular with 6 June 1944 – the start of 'Overlord', the code name in *World War II for the Allied invasion of Normandy. Originally planned for May, the day finally chosen was June 5 but the operation was delayed for 24 hours by bad weather. Troops from the entire southern coast of England converged on the northern beaches of Normandy, with massive air cover. The Germans, uncertain whether the invasion would be here or by the shortest sea route to Calais, were relatively unprepared. By that evening 156,000 men had landed and established beachheads. At Portsmouth, the naval base due north of the beaches, there is a D-day museum containing the *Overlord embroidery. The invasion was re-enacted in the film *The Longest Day* (1962).

'Dead! and he never called me mother' see *East Lynne.*

Dead March in Saul The popular name for the funeral march from Handel's oratorio *Saul* (1739), used on certain solemn occasions such as state funerals.

dead parrot sketch Probably the most widely remembered highlight of *Monty Python, in which an irate John Cleese brings a dead parrot (a Norwegian Blue) back to the 'boutique' from which he bought it less than half an hour before. The shopkeeper (Michael Palin) insists that it is resting, or perhaps pining for the fiords. Cleese responds with a frenzied list of euphemisms for death, ending with 'It's rung down the curtain and joined the choir invisible. This is an ex-parrot.'

Forest of **Dean** Ancient forest of oak and beech between the Severn and Wye, stretching some 32km/20m north from the junction of the two rivers. A royal hunting reserve in medieval times, and more recently the scene of small-scale coal mining, it was in 1938 declared Britain's first National Forest Park.

death duties see *inheritance tax.

Death on the Rock (Thames TV 1988) Controversial documentary about a controversial event in 1988, the killing of three suspected IRA terrorists – Daniel McCann, Sean Savage and Mairead Farrell – by the SAS in Gibraltar. The deaths sparked off a terrifying escalation of violence in Northern Ireland; a loyalist gunman fired on the funeral of the three and killed three of the mourners; a few days later, at the funeral of one of those three victims, two British off-duty corporals, David Howes and Derek Wood, were dragged from their car (they had driven into the path of the funeral) and were gruesomely murdered.

The documentary accused the SAS of having shot the three in Gibraltar when they could have arrested them; this enraged the government, which tried and failed to prevent the programme from being transmitted. The inquest on the incident exonerated the SAS, but an independent enquiry later supported Thames TV over the film (the enquiry's findings were vigorously rejected by Mrs Thatcher and the government).

'Death, thou shalt die' see John *Donne.

Debrett's The familiar name for the *Peerage and Baronetage*, which is the only current work of reference on Britain's titled families. It dates back to *The New Peerage*, published by John Almon in 1769. John Debrett (1753–1822) took on Almon's business in 1784; he first put his own name on the *Peerage* in 1802 and on the *Baronetage* (then a separate publication) in 1808. From 1866 to 1971 the *Peerage and Baronetage* was published annually. Since 1980 it has appeared every five years, with an edition scheduled for 1995.

decimalization The change of the *currency from the old system of *£.s.d. to one based on a pound of 100 new pence. It came into effect on 15 February 1971.

Declaration of Right see *Bill of Rights.

Decline and Fall (1928) The greatly successful first novel of Evelyn *Waugh, charting the comic decline and fall of an Oxford theology student, Paul Pennyfeather. His job at an appalling boarding school (with a particularly horrifying sports day) is followed by high life in the circle of Margot Beste-Chetwynde, mother of one of the pupils, and by a spell in prison ('Anyone who has been to an English public school will always feel comparatively at home in prison') before returning to his theology.

Decline and Fall of the Roman Empire (*The History of the Decline and Fall of the Roman Empire*, 6 vols, 1776–88) Account by Edward *Gibbon of a great swathe of European history from Rome in the 1st century AD to the fall of Constantinople to the Turks in 1453. The most ambititous and distinguished historical work in English literature, it is also famous for the precisely pinpointed moment of its conception: 'It was at Rome, on the 15th of October, 1764, as I sat musing amidst the ruins of the Capitol, while the barefoot friars were singing vespers in the Temple of Jupiter, that the idea of writing the decline and fall of the city first started to my mind.' Much of his theme was a lament for rational and classical thought, falling victim in the medieval Christian centuries to the superstitious predecessors of those barefoot friars, in a process which he described as 'the triumph of barbarism and religion'.

Decorated style see *Gothic.

Dedham Vale Valley of the river Stour near Dedham, on the border of Essex and Suffolk. Beautiful in its own right (it was designated in 1970 an Area of Outstanding Natural Beauty), it is also famous as the landscape in many of the paintings of *Constable.

Dee The name of three rivers in Britain. The longest (about 140km/87m) rises in the Cairngorm mountains and flows east past Braemar and Balmoral to enter the North Sea at Aberdeen. Another, in Dumfries and Galloway, flows south for some 80km/50m to enter the Solway Firth at Kircudbright. The third (113km/70m) rises in Wales, flows north for some way as the border between Wales and England, passes round Chester and then is confined to an artificial channel for its final passage to its estuary and the Irish Sea.

John **Dee** (1527–1608) Mathematician of eccentric brilliance, who made important contributions in astronomy and navigation while also acquiring a sinister reputation for his alchemical experiments and supposed sorcery.

deed of covenant The most effective way of giving money to a charity, making the gift tax free. £100 donated by covenant to a charity costs the donor £75 if he or she pays tax at a standard rate of 25%, and only £60 if tax is paid at a higher rate of 40%. The payment has to be made on an annual basis over a period of at least four years, but it is legal to pay the entire sum in advance as an interest-free loan. Since 1990 single gifts to charities have also been free of tax, under a scheme known as Gift Aid, if above a certain level; the minimum net payment has been gradually reduced from £600 to £250.

Deep Purple Influential rock-metal group, formed in 1968, disbanded in 1976 and reformed in 1984. The chief members have been Ian Gillan (b. 1945, vocals), Ritchie Blackmore (b. 1945, guitar), Jon Lord (b. 1941, keyboards), Roger Glover (b. 1945, bass) and Ian Paice (b. 1948, drums). Their album *Deep Purple in Rock* (1970) was in the British charts for more than a year but only reached no. 4; it was followed by three no. 1 albums (*Fireball* 1971, *Machine Head* 1972, *Deepest Purple* 1980).

deer Only three species of deer are native or long-established in Britain. The largest, the red deer (the proud stag of the *Monarch of the Glen*), has its habitat in high moorland regions; it is stalked in the Highlands of Scotland and is hunted on Exmoor. The small and delicate roe deer, also native, lives in woodlands and is considered vermin because of the damage it does to young trees. Fallow deer, probably introduced by the Romans, are intermediate in size between the other two and live mainly in what survives of the ancient forests, such as Epping. Herds of red and fallow deer can be seen in many of the parks surrounding grand houses in Britain, while some other species have escaped from stately homes in the past century and are now living in the wild – notably two very small deer, the Asian muntjac and the Chinese water deer, both of which were brought in about 1900 to *Woburn (the home also of Père David's deer).

deerstalker Close-fitting cloth hat, usually of tweed, with identical peaks in front and behind, and with ear flaps turned up and tied over the crown. It has been associated above all with Sherlock *Holmes.

Ministry of **Defence** (London SW1) The government department responsible for the *armed forces, formed in 1964 by merging the Admiralty, War Office and Air Ministry. For secretaries of state since 1983 see the *cabinet.

Defender of the Faith see *FD.

Daniel **Defoe** (1660–1731) Prolific author and pamphleteer, born in London, who became one of the first writers of realistic fiction with *<i>Robinson Crusoe</i> and *<i>Moll Flanders</i>. He had an extraordinary career: he was engaged in a wide variety of commercial enterprises, mainly unsuccessful; he founded and almost single-handedly wrote a thrice-weekly periodical, *The Review* (1712–13); he was the chief pamphleteer for successive governments (not necessarily of the same political persuasion) and he travelled widely as a semi-secret agent collecting political information. This experience resulted in his valuable description of the country, *A Tour thro' the Whole Island of Great Britain* (3 vols, 1724–7). His investigative and imaginative skills came together in *Journal of the Plague Year* (1722), a fictional account of London during the *Great Plague of 1665 based on surviving contemporary documents.

Geoffrey **de Havilland** (1882–1965, kt 1944) Aircraft designer and manufacturer, who set up his own company in 1920 after designing fighter planes in World War I. The de Havilland works at Hatfield, in Hertfordshire, produced many of Britain's best-known aircraft including the *Tiger Moth, the *Mosquito, the *Comet and the *Trident. The company was taken over by Hawker Siddeley in 1959 and eventually became part of *British Aerospace; the Hatfield works were closed in 1992.

Len **Deighton** (b. 1929) Author who introduced a new down-to-earth element in spy stories, with *The Ipcress File* (1962) and *Funeral in Berlin* (1964). They featured the agent Harry Palmer, performed by Michael Caine in the films of the two books. Deighton used a documentary technique, rich in everyday and often mundane detail, to give the stories a humdrum authenticity; he later applied the same method to very different subjects, such as *Bomber* (1970) about a crew going out on a raid in World War II.

Walter **de la Mare** (1873–1956) Author of poems, novels and short stories, many of them for children, with an inclination towards mystery and melancholy. One of his best-known books, *Memoirs of a Midget* (1921), is a poetic fantasy about the world as viewed by the tiny Miss M.

New **Delhi** Capital of the republic of India since 1947 and previously of British India from 1912, when it replaced Calcutta. A succession of cities on the site of

Delhi date back to 1500 BC. The present one was laid out on a geometrical plan devised by *Lutyens, with broad avenues and plenty of space for villas with large gardens. The design of the government buildings, deliberately combining European and Indian architectural traditions, was shared between Lutyens and Herbert Baker (1862–1946). The most impressive is the Viceroy's House by Lutyens (now Rashtrapati Bhavan, the presidential palace).

Frederick **Delius** (1862–1934) Composer, born in Yorkshire, whose parents were German immigrants and who spent most of his adult life on the Continent, but whose music is often considered to capture the spirit of the English countryside. Of his operas *A Village Romeo and Juliet* (1907) has held the stage best; its famous intermezzo, 'Walk to the Paradise Garden', was added in 1910 to cover a scene change at the request of *Beecham, Delius's chief champion in Britain. His short orchestral works remain much performed, in particular *Brigg Fair* (1907, based on Lincolnshire folk tunes), *In a Summer Garden* (1908, a response to his own garden at Grez-sur-Loing, near Fontainebleau) and *On Hearing the First Cuckoo in Spring* (1912). In the 1920s Delius became blind and paralysed but was able to continue composing when a young English musician, Eric Fenby (b. 1906), offered to write down the works from dictation.

Alfred **Deller** (1912–79) Countertenor whose strength and purity of voice led to a revival of interest in the castrato roles of the 17–18c being sung by men. He formed in 1948 the Deller Consort for the authentic performance of baroque music. In 1960 he created the role of Oberon in Benjamin Britten's *Midsummer Night's Dream*.

De Lorean Fraud in which an American, John De Lorean, persuaded the British government in 1978 to subsidize his setting up a sports car factory in Belfast. He involved Colin Chapman of *Lotus in developing the first model. The government had put £77 million into the project by the time it went bankrupt in 1982. De Lorean was arrested later that year and was charged with plotting to distribute cocaine worth £18 million (in an attempt, it was argued, to save his factory). He was acquitted on this charge, but in 1992 a warrant was issued in Belfast for his arrest after a former senior executive with Lotus was jailed for three years and fined £2.25 million; he had admitted conspiring with De Lorean and Chapman (who died in 1982) to defraud the Belfast company of more than £9 million.

Democratic Left see *Communist Party of Great Britain.

William **De Morgan** (1839–1917) Designer of ceramics, and in particular of tiles. His bold designs of plants and animals make his work extremely distinctive. He was a friend of William *Morris, whose ideas he largely shared. Giving up pottery for reasons of ill health, he turned in old age to writing fiction and produced a series of successful novels, beginning with *Joseph Vance* (1906).

Denbighshire Former *county in Wales, since 1974 divided between Clwyd and Gwynedd.

Judi **Dench** (b. 1934, DBE 1988) Actress who made her name during a series of Old Vic seasons (1957–61), perhaps above all with her performance of Juliet. Among her best-known roles in a very full career, mainly in the theatre, are Lady Macbeth and Juno (in O'Casey's *Juno and the Paycock*), in both cases with the Royal Shakespeare Company. A successful series on television during the

1980s, *A Fine Romance* (LWT), was about a couple of gauche middle-aged people falling awkwardly in love; the man was played by her husband in real life, Michael Williams.

Lord **Denning** (Alfred Denning, b. 1899, kt 1944, baron 1957) Lawyer who was *Master of the Rolls (1962–82). In 1963 he produced the Denning Report on the *Profumo affair.

Dennis the Menace see the *Beano*.

Depression The slump throughout the capitalist world in the early 1930s, the worst in the series of recurring recessions which have been a feature of capitalist history. The international trigger was the US stock market crash; Black Thursday, the worst single day, was 24 October 1929. Britain was already weak after the *General Strike of 1926. The number of unemployed rose to more than two million, bringing an unprecedented level of *national insurance payments. In 1931 the mounting government debt provoked an international loss of confidence in sterling, and the crisis caused the coalition *national government to be in power until World War II. There was little economic improvement during the 1930s, as witnessed by the series of hunger marches of which *Jarrow was only one example.

De Profundis (1897) A long letter of self-discovery and of recrimination, written by Oscar *Wilde from Reading jail to his lover, Lord Alfred Douglas, whose silence after the prison sentence seemed a painful betrayal. The Latin title that Wilde had in mind for it was *In Carcere et Vinculis* (In Prison and in Chains), but when it was published in 1905 his literary executor used the two Latin words which begin Psalm 130, meaning 'Out of the depths'.

Deptford (London SE8 & SE14) Area on the south bank of the Thames, west of Greenwich, which was a fishing village until Henry VIII chose it as the site for a royal dock, in which his navy was built and maintained. It retained its importance as a shipyard until the 19c. It was here that the Russian emperor, Peter the Great, worked incognito as a carpenter for three months in 1698 to gather ideas on design for his own navy.

Thomas **De Quincey** (1785–1859) Author of the autobiographical *Confessions of an English Opium-Eater* (1821 in the *London Magazine*, 1822 much revised as a book). He was for some years a close friend of Wordsworth, whom he followed as the occupant of *Dove Cottage.

André **Derain** (1880–1954) The Thames and Westminster feature at their most cheerful in frequently reproduced paintings by this French artist, who lived in London during the period (1906–7) when he was working in the startlingly bright colours of Fauvism.

Derby (223,000 in 1991) City in central England, on the river Derwent. It was the furthest point south in the advance into England in 1745–6 of Charles Edward *Stuart. In the same decade it began making the product for which it is most famous, *Derby porcelain. From 1907 to 1939 all *Rolls-Royce cars were produced here.

All Saints Church, which has been Derby's cathedral since 1927, has a 16c tower and a nave added by James Gibbs in 1722–7. The Museum and Art Gallery (1876–9) has an outstanding collection of paintings by the local artist, Joseph *Wright, while the Royal Crown Derby Museum (attached to the working porcelain factory) displays examples of the city's wares through two and a half centuries.

Lord **Derby** (1799–1869, 14th earl 1851) Prime minister for three relatively brief periods – 1852, 1858–9 and 1866–8. His early political achievements related to Ireland, where his family had extensive estates. An MP from 1820, he entered the cabinet in 1831 as chief secretary for Ireland, and passed a bill much in advance of its time introducing a system of state education in the province. In 1846 he became the leader of the Conservative majority which parted company with Peel on the issue of the *Corn Laws. His administration of 1858 took in hand the government of *India and removed the political restrictions on Jews, enabling Lionel Nathan *Rothschild to take his seat in the House of Commons. Something of a brilliant amateur, Derby was less dynamic than his deputy in the House of Commons, *Disraeli, who succeeded him when ill health forced Derby to resign in 1868. Together they had pushed through the Reform Act of 1867, the first extension of the *franchise since 1832.

Sage **Derby** (or Derby sage) A pale cheese, deriving from Derbyshire and similar in kind to *Cheshire cheese; it is mottled with green by being coated with sage leaves in an early stage of production. The traditional sage Derby was composed of alternating layers of sage-tinted and plain cheese.

The **Derby** Britain's foremost flat race, for 3-year-old colts and fillies, run over 2.4km/1.5m at *Epsom on the first Wednesday in June. The race was first run in 1780, taking its name from the 12th earl of Derby (1752–1834) who was prominent among those promoting it. In recent decades an extraordinary Derby record was achieved by Lester *Piggott, winner nine times and second on four occasions. The *suffragette Derby took place in 1913. The day has a more festive atmosphere than any other in Britain's racing calendar, with vast crowds and the mood of a fun fair. The tradition derives from Victorian times when it was seen as an unofficial holiday for Londoners of all classes – an occasion captured in minute detail in William *Frith's *Derby Day*.

Derby County, known as the Rams (Baseball Ground, Derby). Football club formed in 1884 by members of the *Derbyshire County Cricket Club – partly to raise funds in the winter to support their cricket. The club was professional from the start and was a founder member of the *Football League in 1888. Club victories: FA Cup 1946; League Champions 1972, 75.

Derby Day see William *Frith.

Derby porcelain High quality porcelain figures were produced between 1750 and 1756 at a Derby factory run by Andrew Planché. They tend to have an unglazed rim round the base and are known as 'dry-edge Derby'. In 1756 Planché was joined in a new venture by William Duesbury (1725–86), who soon became the dominant partner and built up a successful business, mainly imitating the *Chelsea figures of the time (themselves based on Meissen). In 1770 he bought the Chelsea factory. The original firm at Derby lasted until 1848. It was followed by two separate ventures, which finally merged in 1935. One was set up in King Street in 1848 by a group of craftsmen from the earlier firm. The other was founded in Osmaston Road in 1877 as the Derby Crown Porcelain Company (from 1890 the Royal Crown Derby Porcelain Company, as it remains today). A crown was the main element of the Derby mark from the 1770s, but the phrase 'Crown Derby' – now in general use by non-specialists for any Derby product – was not part of the name of any of the companies until the late 1870s.

Derbyshire (940,000 in 1991, administrative centre Matlock) *County in central England.

Derbyshire County Cricket Club Founded in 1870 and in the *county championship on a regular basis from 1895; it has won only once, in 1936. In *one-day cricket Derbyshire won the NatWest Bank Trophy in 1981 and the Sunday League in 1990. The county ground is in Derby, and the county plays also at Chesterfield and Heanor.

Derry see *Londonderry.

Derwentwater One of the most beautiful of the lakes in the *Lake District, running north between crags and wooded slopes from Borrowdale to Keswick, and dotted with several small islands.

DES see Department for *Education.

*The **Deserted Village*** see Oliver *Goldsmith.

Desert Island Discs (BBC) Britain's longest running record programme, first broadcast on 29 January 1942. Until his death the programme was presented by the man who devised it, Roy Plomley (1914–85). His first guest was the comedian Vic Oliver, and the extremely successful formula has never varied. The week's castaway chooses eight favourite pieces of recorded music or sound to provide solace on the desert island; in between the musical extracts the life of the subject, and the reason for the choice of music, is brought out in an interview. Two details were added some years later; the castaway is asked to choose a book other than the Bible and Shakespeare (both already on the island) and one luxury item (the

A shepherd in Derby biscuit porcelain (fired but unglazed), modelled by J.J. Spangler in the 1790s.

Derby: winners since 1945

	Winner	Jockey		Winner	Jockey		Winner	Jockey
1945	Dante	Billy Nevett	1962	Larkspur	Neville Sellwood	1979	Troy	Willie Carson
1946	Airborne	Tommy Lowrey	1963	Relko	Yves Saint-Martin	1980	Henbit	Willie Carson
1947	Pearl Diver	George Bridgland	1964	Santa Claus	Scobie Breasley	1981	Shergar	Walter Swinburn
1948	My Love	Rae Johnstone	1965	Sea Bird II	Pat Glennon	1982	Golden Fleece	Pat Eddery
1949	Nimbus	Charlie Elliott	1966	Charlottown	Scobie Breasley	1983	Teenoso	Lester Piggott
1949	Galcador	Rae Johnstone	1967	Royal Palace	George Moore	1984	Secreto	Christy Roche
1951	Arctic Prince	Charlie Spares	1968	Sir Ivor	Lester Piggott	1985	Slip Anchor	Steve Cauthen
1952	Tulyar	Charlie Smirke	1969	Blakeney	Ernie Johnson	1986	Shahrastani	Walter Swinburn
1953	Pinza	Gordon Richards	1970	Nijinsky	Lester Piggott	1987	Reference Point	Steve Cauthen
1954	Never Say Die	Lester Piggott	1971	Mill Reef	Geoff Lewis	1988	Kayhasi	Ray Cochrane
1955	Phil Drake	Freddie Palmer	1972	Roberto	Lester Piggott	1989	Nashwan	Willie Carson
1956	Lavandin	Rae Johnstone	1973	Morston	Eddie Hide	1990	Quest for Fame	Pat Eddery
1957	Crepello	Lester Piggott	1974	Snow Knight	Brian Taylor	1991	Generous	Alan Munro
1958	Hard Ridden	Charlie Smirke	1975	Grundy	Pat Eddery	1992	Dr Devious	John Reid
1959	Parthia	Harry Carr	1976	Empery	Lester Piggott	1993	Commander in	
1960	St Paddy	Lester Piggott	1977	The Minstrel	Lester Piggott		Chief	Michael Kinane
1961	Psidium	Roger Poincelet	1978	Shirley Heights	Greville Starkey			

latter providing wild opportunities for self-revealing fantasies). Michael Parkinson presented the programme for a while (1986–8) and was followed in 1988 by Sue Lawley. The theme music has been the same from the start – Eric *Coates's *By the Sleepy Lagoon*, with accompanying seagulls.

Desert Orchid (foaled 1979) Grey gelding with more than 30 victories as a steeplechaser, including the Cheltenham Gold Cup (1989) and the King George VI Chase three times (1986, 88, 89).

desert rats Nickname originally used for soldiers who served with the British 7th Armoured Division in the North Africa campaign of 1941–2; it derived from the badge which the division had adopted, that of a rat which lives in hot sandy places (the jerboa). The desert rats were prominent among the British troops sent to *Kuwait in 1990, though reduced by then to the 7th Armoured Brigade.

Design Centre (London SW1) The headquarters in the Haymarket of the Design Council, known to the public chiefly as a location for exhibitions. The council was established in 1944 to improve design in British industry – precisely the motive which in the previous century prompted the *Great Exhibition and the *Victoria and Albert Museum. In keeping with this tradition the council had responsibility for all the official exhibitions in the *Festival of Britain (1951).

Desperate Dan see the *Dandy.

detention centre see *young offender institution.

Dettingen (1743) Inconclusive victory by George II over the French in Bavaria during the War of the *Austrian Succession, remembered chiefly as the last occasion on which a British monarch led his troops into battle.

Deva see *Chester.

Ninette de Valois (stage name of Edris Stannus, b. 1898, DBE 1951) A founding figure of modern British ballet, known to all in the ballet world as 'Madam'. Born in Ireland, she danced first in pantomimes at the Lyceum Theatre in London (1914–18) before appearing as a prima ballerina at Covent Garden in 1919. She later

joined Diaghilev's Ballets Russes (1923–6), and in 1926 she began her profoundly influential partnership with Lilian *Baylis. She began by teaching movement to the actors at the Old Vic, and then enlarged her activities to encompass a ballet school and, from 1931, the Vic-Wells Ballet – which performed at Sadler's Wells. From these initiatives there have developed the Royal Ballet School, the *Royal Ballet and the *Birmingham Royal Ballet. During the 1930s de Valois was a prolific choreographer, her many ballets including *The *Rake's Progress* (1935) and *Checkmate* (1937, with music by Arthur Bliss). She remained the director of the Royal Ballet until 1963, and was appointed in 1992 to the Order of *Merit.

devaluation see *exchange rate.

Devil's Bridge (16km/10m SE of Aberystwyth) Village where the river Mynach tumbles over spectacular waterfalls to join the Rheidol, with a gorge spanned by three bridges one above the other. The highest is an iron bridge of 1901; below this is a stone bridge of 1753; and closest to the water is another stone bridge, the Devil's Bridge itself, possibly dating from the 12C. The legend tells of an old woman gambling with the devil for her soul in return for his making a bridge to bring across her cow.

George **Devine** see the *English Stage Company.

Arthur **Devis** see *Preston.

Bernadette **Devlin** (b. 1947, m. Micheal McAliskey 1973) Politician who came to prominence through the civil rights movement in *Northern Ireland in the late 1960s. She became the youngest MP at Westminster when she won a by-election in Mid Ulster in 1969, standing as an Independent Unity candidate; she held the seat until 1974. In 1969, when already an MP, she was sentenced in Londonderry to six months in prison for incitement to riot. In 1981 she and her husband were shot and wounded in a terrorist attack.

devolution Greater regional powers for Scotland and Wales have been on and off the political agenda since the recommendation by a *royal commission, in 1973, that both countries should have separate assemblies and that there should be advisory regional councils in England. Scotland sends a high proportion of *Labour MPs to Westminster, and the Labour party embraced devolution as a self-protective measure because of the growing strength of the *SNP (a party committed to full Scottish independence). In a referendum in March 1979 approximately 33% of Scots on the electoral register said yes to devolution and 31% said no; the number in favour had to be at least 40% of the electorate and so the issue was dropped (in Wales there was a 4:1 majority against).

Devolution was subsequently little discussed until it became a major issue in the election of 1992, when the SNP was able to argue that smaller countries were the pattern of the future (with the re-emergence of the Baltic states, for example, from the disintegrating USSR) and that Scotland's natural identity was as an independent state within the EC. The election manifestoes of both the Labour party and the Liberal Democrats included a pledge to introduce a Scottish parliament, but the Conservatives remained emphatically opposed, pointing out that Scotland already had a considerably devolved administration in the form of the *Scottish Office. The electoral results, in which the SNP did worse than expected and the Conservatives better, suggested that the issue would again be dormant for a while.

For half a century (1921–72) *Northern Ireland provided an example of a devolved parliament functioning within the framework of the United Kingdom.

Devon (also called Devonshire, 1,040,000 in 1991, administrative centre Exeter) *County in southwest England between the English Channel and the Bristol Channel.

Devonian see *geological periods.

Devonshire cream see *clotted cream.

Devonshire Hunting Tapestries (Victoria and Albert Museum) Four large tapestries (on average about 4.3m/14ft high and 10m/33ft wide) depicting courtly figures in spectacularly lavish costumes, engaged in the pursuit of boars, bears, deer and other animals. They were made in the 15c in northern France or Belgium, probably either at Arras or Tournai. Before coming to the V&A they used to hang in the long gallery at Hardwick Hall, one of the houses of the dukes of Devonshire.

James **Dewar** (1842–1923, kt 1904) Scottish physicist and chemist, known in particular for his research at very low temperatures. To keep liquid gases cool, he used a surrounding vacuum as insulation. The Dewar flask became more widely familiar in its household application as the Thermos flask. In 1889 he and Frederick Abel (1827–1902) together developed cordite as an explosive.

Ted **Dexter** (b. 1935) Batsman who played *cricket for Sussex (1957–68) and for England (1958–68, captain 1961–4), known in particular for his courage and aggression against fast bowling. Widely referred to as Lord Ted, he has been since 1989 the chairman of the English selectors for Test teams.

DFC and **DFM** (Distinguished Flying Cross and Medal) Decorations for gallantry when flying in an engagement against an enemy; the DFC is given to officers and warrant officers, and the DFM to lower ranks. The AFC and AFM (Air Force Cross and Medal) were instituted in the same year (1918) for acts of courage when flying in any other context.

DFE see Department for *Education.

DG REG (or REX) The letters appearing with the monarch's head on coins of the realm. They stand for *Dei Gratia Regina (Rex)*, Latin for 'By the grace of God, Queen (King)'. They are followed by *FD.

DHSS see Department of *Health and Department of *Social Security.

Diamond Sculls see *Henley.

Princess **Diana** see Princess of *Wales.

Dianagate see *privacy.

*The **Diary of a Country Parson*** The title given to the published version (5 vols, 1924–31) of the diary of James Woodforde (1740–1803). He lived in his parish of Weston Longeville in Norfolk for his last 27 years, and the great appeal of the diary lies in the matter-of-fact enthusiasm with which he records the details of everyday country life (with special and prolonged emphasis on his own meals).

*The **Diary of a Nobody*** (1892) Fictional diary of a suburban anti-hero, Charles Pooter, serialized in *Punch* from April 1891. It begins when he and his wife Carrie move into their new London house (The Laurels, Brickfield Terrace, Holloway), where they are soon joined by their appalling son Lupin – markedly lacking in respect for his father. Mr Pooter's constant fear of social embarrassment, a fear usually justified, is suggested with such delightful comic detail that the book somehow avoids being condescending. It was written by the brothers George and Weedon Grossmith (1847–1912; 1854–1919), with illustrations by Weedon.

Dick Barton (Special Agent) Hero of a BBC radio serial which ran from 1946 to 1951. With the regular help of Jock and Snowy he foiled a wide range of criminal enterprises, in a tradition which has since become the staple fare of television.

Charles **Dickens** (1812–70) Novelist who combined to an exceptional degree literary genius and popular appeal. His father was an improvident government clerk who was eventually imprisoned in the Marshalsea for debt. His mother and the younger children lived in the prison with him, while the 12-year-old Dickens was boarded out and put to work labelling bottles in a London shoe-blacking factory. These were experiences which scarred his childhood but gave him much material for his fiction. At 16, after learning shorthand, he began four years of reporting law cases and debates in parliament. His first literary efforts were a series of comic sketches, mainly about London life, which he contributed to newspapers under the pseudonym 'Boz'. They were published as *Sketches by Boz* (1836) with illustrations by Cruikshank. In that same year there appeared the first monthly issues of the work which brought the 24-year-old author fame and fortune, *Pickwick Papers*.

Over the next few years he worked with extraordinary intensity, producing *Oliver Twist* (1837–8), *Nicholas Nickleby* (1838–9), *The Old Curiosity Shop* (1840–1), *Barnaby Rudge* (1841), A *Christmas Carol* (1843) and *Martin Chuzzlewit* (1843–4). All but A *Christmas Carol* were published as serials in monthly or weekly parts. From 1850 to the end of his life Dickens was himself the editor of magazines publishing fiction in this way, first *Household Words* and then *All the Year Round*.

With *Dombey and Son* (1846–8) Dickens began to plan each book more as a whole, instead of the earlier improvisational approach with cliff-hangers at the end of episodes. He now entered the period of his greatest achievement, writing *David Copperfield* (1849–50), *Bleak House* (1852–3), *Little Dorrit* (1855–7), *Great Expectations* (1860–1) and *Our Mutual Friend* (1864–5). Two powerful melodramas, one social and political (*Hard Times*

1900. It has been kept up to date with a supplement each decade, recently reduced to a span of only five years with the publication of a volume covering 1981–5.

Dido and Aeneas (1689) Opera by *Purcell, to a libretto by Nahum Tate (1652–1715), based on the sequence in Virgil's *Aeneid* where Aeneas dallies with Dido, queen of Carthage, but then leaves her and sails for Italy. Dido commits suicide after her famous lament, 'When I am laid in earth'. The opera's powerful combination of simplicity and intensity is surprising for two reasons: it is virtually the first English opera, and it was written to be performed at a girls' boarding school in Chelsea.

'**Die, my dear doctor**, that's the last thing I shall do!' see Lord *Palmerston.

Dieu et mon droit see the *Royal Arms.

digestive Traditional form of sweet wheatmeal biscuit, sold under that name from the mid-19C.

Dignity and Impudence see Edwin *Landseer.

Charles **Dilke** (1843–1911, 2nd bt 1869) Politician on the radical wing of the Liberal party, who served in Gladstone's cabinet (1882–5) and was considered likely to succeed him as leader. In 1886 the Liberal MP for Lanark, Donald Crawford, cited Dilke as co-respondent in a divorce case against his wife. Dilke protested his innocence to the end of his life, and in two trials no evidence was produced other than a highly coloured account of their affair by the 22-year-old Virginia Crawford (much of it proved to be fabrication). But Dilke's reputation was tarnished and he never again held office.

Dimbleby family Britain's first broadcasting dynasty. Richard Dimbleby (1913–65), after a pioneering career as a correspondent for BBC radio, gave television its first widely remembered broadcast with his commentary on the coronation in 1953. His resonant phrases, reinforcing each viewer's unprecedented experience of seeming to be present at such an occasion, provided for many in Britain their introduction to an exciting new medium. Dimbleby was also the anchor man on British television's first major political programme, *Panorama. Twenty-five years after his early death, from cancer, he was given an honour unprecedented for someone known for the spoken rather than the written word, that of a memorial in *Poets' Corner. His eldest son David (b. 1938) has followed very precisely in his footsteps, both in a long connection with *Panorama* and in becoming a commentator on great royal and state occasions. Jonathan (b. 1944) also specializes in political broadcasting and current affairs, and has chaired *Any Questions?* since 1987.

Dinky Toys see *Meccano.

dinner A word which is rivalled only by *tea in its potential for social confusion, describing two quite different meals depending on class and to a certain extent on region. Throughout most of the 20C it has meant a midday meal in working-class families, and that remains to a large extent the case in northern England. During the same period it has been an evening meal for the professional classes. It is the manual workers who have been consistent, for it was always the custom to dine in the middle of the day (a lighter evening meal being supper). But during the 18–19C the well-to-do steadily postponed their main meal. Pepys, in the late 17C, dined at noon; a century later Parson Woodforde sat down at 3.00; and by

Dickens, the international author, seen bringing his wares to Paris in a French caricature of the 1860s.

1854) and the other historical (A *Tale of Two Cities 1859), date from the same period.

In 1836 Dickens had married Catherine Hogarth, with whom he had ten children, but their relationship was virtually over by 1857 when he bought Gad's Hill in Kent. This was a great house which he had admired from the outside as a boy (he had lived from the age of four to eleven, the only happy part of his childhood, in Chatham, where his father worked in the naval dockyard). Dickens and Catherine separated in 1858, and during his last years he had a young mistress, Nelly (Ellen) Ternan. He had always been much involved in public affairs as a campaigning author and journalist, but he now developed a different sort of public life, giving extremely successful readings from his works on both sides of the Atlantic. His sudden death at Gad's Hill made a literal and lasting mystery of his final novel, *The Mystery of Edwin Drood* (1870). Only six of the twelve monthly episodes were written, so the reasons for Edwin Drood's disappearance will never be known.

Dickens' birthplace in Portsmouth (393 Old Commercial Rd) is kept as a museum, as is the house in London (48 Doughty St) where he and Catherine lived in the early years of their marriage. Stage, film and television adaptations have extended Dickens's already vast following. Probably not even Shakespeare has created so many characters with a secure place in the nation's collective memory.

*The **Dictionary of National Biography*** (DNB) An ongoing project by Oxford University Press, founded in 1882 to provide brief but factually detailed biographies of all 'noteworthy inhabitants of the British Isles and the Colonies (exclusive of living persons) from the earliest historical period to the present time'. The first editor was Leslie Stephen (1832–1904), the father of Virginia Woolf. Starting with the letter A in January 1885, and published in sections four times a year, Z had been reached by the late 19C the time for dinner was 7.00. It has shifted less rapidly since then, being now at about 8.00.

As the gap between breakfast and dinner extended, the fashionable began to feel the need for something in the interim. The result was luncheon, derived from a word for a lump of bread or meat. In its first known appearance, in 1652, luncheon is clearly just a snack for it is described, splendidly, as 'intermealiary'. By the early 19C it had become established as lunch, a full-scale meal. Such it has remained, fixed for the moment at about 1.00 p.m. In the coming years it will probably drive out entirely the original midday meaning of dinner.

Supper is now used as an alternative term for the evening meal, though still with the implication that it is lighter and less formal than dinner.

dinner jacket see *evening dress.

Paul **Dirac** (1902–84) Theoretical physicist who made a major contribution to the development of quantum mechanics. In 1928 he produced a mathematical theory of elementary particles which reconciled quantum mechanics and relativity, and in 1930 he predicted the existence of the positron (later verified experimentally by others). His *Principles of Quantum Mechanics* (1930) is a classic in the field. He shared the Nobel prize for 1933 with the Austrian Erwin Schrödinger.

Director of Public Prosecutions (DPP) The head of the *Crown Prosecution Service. The decision whether to bring a prosecution rests in England and Wales with the DPP, resulting in a great deal of public attention when it is uncertain whether charges will be pressed in a controversial case. He or she is appointed by and answerable to the *attorney general. In Scotland it is the crown agent who advises the *lord advocate on questions of prosecution.

The office was much in the news in 1991 when the DPP, Sir Allan Green, resigned after being cautioned by police for approaching prostitutes in the King's Cross district of London. He was succeeded by the first woman in the post, Barbara Mills.

direct rule see *Northern Ireland.

Dire Straits Pop group formed in 1977 by guitarist and singer Mark Knopfler (b. 1949) and named in recognition of its early financial situation; the only other lasting member is John Illsley (b. 1949, bass). With a more intimate, craftsmanlike sound than most pop at the time, the group had several hit singles (*Sultans of Swing* 1979, *Private Investigation* 1982, *Walk of Life* 1986), and two exceptional albums, *Dire Straits* (1978) and *Brothers in Arms* (1985). By 1987 the latter was the most successful LP of all time in Britain, with sales of more than 3 million.

Dirleton (33km/21m NW of Edinburgh) Ruined castle (13–17C) on an outcrop of rock with houses clustered around. The effect has caused Dirleton to be often described as Scotland's prettiest village.

'dirty British coaster' see *Cargoes.*

Disappearing World (Granada TV) Series of separate documentaries, made at irregular intervals from the 1970s, in which a camera crew lives for several weeks with a remote tribe whose way of life is endangered.

Discovery see Captain *Scott and Henry *Hudson.

Disgusted, Tunbridge Wells Hypothetical signature for any indignant anonymous letter to a newspaper,

suggesting blimpish outrage. It is not known when or where the joke began, but it is not popular in Tunbridge Wells.

dispatch box In the past an everyday container in which to carry papers, surviving now as two separate features of British political life. One is the locked red-leather boxes in which papers are delivered to cabinet ministers and others. The other, deriving probably from such boxes used by speakers needing documents in the Houses of Parliament, is a permanent part of the furniture in both chambers. On the central table of each there are two wooden boxes, one on each side, from which ministers and leading opposition members speak. Their contents (oath cards, affirmation cards and various versions of the Old and New Testaments) relate solely to the swearing-in of members.

Benjamin **Disraeli** (1804–81, earl of Beaconsfield 1876) Author and Conservative politician, prime minister in 1868 and 1874–80. His Italian-Jewish grandfather (the name was then spelt D'Israeli) emigrated to England. His father, Isaac D'Israeli, quarrelled with the *Bevis Marks synagogue and decided to have his children baptized as Christians. Disraeli would otherwise not have had a political career, for Jews could not sit in the House of Commons until legislation was introduced in 1858 by Disraeli himself and Lord *Derby.

His early career was a flashy mixture of financial speculation (disastrous, leaving him with heavy debts) and over-ambitious literary undertakings. But in 1837 he won a seat in parliament and in 1839 he secured himself a reliable income and a large house in London by marrying a wealthy widow, 12 years older than himself. It was a calculated match which developed into a happy marriage. His wife put it well when she said 'Dizzy married me for my money, but if he had the chance again he would marry me for love'.

His literary success preceded and prefigured his political achievements. His two best novels (*Coningsby; or, The*

The Queen at Hughenden: *lithograph of 1887, after Disraeli's death, commemorating the queen's affection for her prime minister.*

New Generation 1844, *Sybil; or, The Two Nations* 1845), expressed the ideas of a group of politicians who became known as 'Young England'. In these books Disraeli put forward a romantic view of Conservatism in which there was a natural alliance between the aristocracy and the people; the failure of modern society was that it had split into the 'two nations' (basically the rich and the poor) of the subtitle of *Sybil*.

His maiden speech in the House of Commons was howled down (both his manner and appearance were over-elaborate), but he shouted a final prophetic sentence – 'I will sit down now but the time will come when you will hear me'. Over the years he gradually asserted his authority; and when Peel split from the Conservative party over the *Corn Laws, taking with him its senior members, Disraeli emerged as the leader in the House of Commons with Lord Derby as head of the party. Disraeli was chancellor of the exchequer in each of Derby's three brief administrations, and succeeded him as prime minister for a few months in 1868. He lost the election that autumn to the Liberals, and his great rival *Gladstone came in for his first term. The two men disliked each other and for the first time the parties had clearly different identities – particularly on foreign policy where Disraeli was motivated by imperialist concerns and Gladstone more by moral issues.

Disraeli won the general election of 1874 and began, at the age of 70, the term of office on which his reputation rests. In foreign policy he effected a brilliant coup by buying a cheap half share in the *Suez Canal with money borrowed from the Rothschilds, against Foreign Office advice and before he could get parliamentary approval. His firm but controversial stand on the *Eastern Question (the occasion of the original *jingoism) led to the curtailment of Russia's ambitions against Turkey. Disraeli himself attended the congress of Berlin in 1878 where the final terms were agreed, returning in triumph with the claim that he had achieved 'peace with honour'. In home affairs he put through legislation improving housing and sanitation for the urban poor, in keeping with the concept of one-nation Conservatism.

His period as prime minister was marked by his close relationship with Queen Victoria (a friendship between the country's leading widow and widower, for his wife had died in 1872). The queen fell willing victim to the charm which is so evident in all photographs of Disraeli and which he used without scruple; 'everyone likes flattery,' he told Matthew Arnold, 'and when it comes to royalty you should lay it on with a trowel'. Victoria made him an earl in 1876 so that he could lead the government with less strain from the House of Lords, and when he died she travelled to Hughenden Manor to lay a wreath on his coffin. His wife and he had bought this house near High Wycombe in 1848, and it is kept today much as they lived in it.

Dissenters Historically an alternative name to *Nonconformists for those who dissent from the orthodoxy of the *Church of England. The word was first used during the mid-17C struggle between Anglicans and Presbyterians.

Dissolution of the Monasteries The destruction of the monasteries, abbeys and priories of England in 1536–41 and the seizing of their lands for the crown. To the other practical advantages derived by Henry VIII from the *Reformation, this policy added a major economic windfall. It was ruthlessly executed on the king's behalf by Thomas *Cromwell. A survey in 1535 of all ecclesiastical property was rapidly followed by inspectors looking into allegations of monastic corruption and licentiousness; the evidence in the second survey was used to justify seizing what had been listed in the first. The

smaller establishments were closed down in 1536 (provoking the *Pilgrimage of Grace) and the remainder suffered in a second wave up to 1541. The abbey churches were destroyed and the secular buildings were usually sold to private citizens, which is why many romantic abbey ruins in England have a grand country house of the late 16C in the near vicinity.

Distinguished Flying Cross and **Medal** see *DFC.

Distinguished Service Cross and **Medal** see *DSC.

Distinguished Service Order see *DSO.

district Established by an act of 1894 as the middle tier of *local government. An urban district council is responsible for an entire town or small city of up to about 250,000 inhabitants. Rural district councils usually cover enough ground to bring the inhabitants up to between 50,000 and 100,000, though in some sparsely inhabited districts to only about 30,000. Since 1985 the metropolitan district councils (those in the *metropolitan counties) have been single-tier authorities with in one case (Leeds) more than 700,000 inhabitants. Districts granted a royal charter are called *boroughs.

divine right of kings The theory that a king or queen governs by divine authority, without human restraints, as God's anointed ruler. Reaching a later peak in the absolute monarchy of Louis XIV in France, divine right was taken for granted early in the 17C in England by James I and Charles I (and above all by *Laud on the royal behalf). The tendency of Charles I to rule in a correspondingly absolute manner was an underlying cause of the *English Civil War. During the following half century the concept was replaced in Britain by *constitutional monarchy.

divorce Although Henry VIII is usually described as having divorced Catherine of Aragon, he in fact arranged for Cranmer to annul his marriage – to declare not that it had ended, but that it had never begun. Subsequently parliament became the only body in Britain which could end a marriage by divorce, but this process was so lengthy and expensive that it was only open to the very rich; in more than 250 years, from 1602 to 1859, there were only 317 parliamentary divorces. The breakdown of a marriage more often resulted in a *common law action brought by the husband against another man for the offence of crim. con. Short for criminal conversation, and meaning adultery, this crime had the legal status of trespass – on the husband's property, his wife. This was the charge brought unsuccessfully by George Norton against Lord *Melbourne.

Crim. con. was rendered obsolete by the Matrimonial Causes Act of 1857, which for the first time made it possible to obtain a divorce in the courts on the grounds of adultery. But this was available only to the husband, for whom it was enough to prove a single act of infidelity on his wife's part; the wife, by contrast, had to prove that an adulterous husband was also cruel, or had committed sodomy, rape, incest or bigamy, or that he had deserted her for two years or more. This inequality survived until 1923, when a single act of adultery by the husband became sufficient for the wife to obtain a divorce. Subsequent campaigns, boosted by A.P. Herbert's satirical novel *Holy Deadlock* (1934), added cruelty and desertion as grounds for divorce even if adultery was not proved. But any couple wishing to divorce simply because their marriage had failed still had to go through an embarrassing charade, in which the husband would arrange to meet a woman and a private detective in a seedy hotel so that the court could be provided with apparent evidence of adultery.

The Divorce Reform Act of 1969 introduced the concept which is central to modern divorce law in Britain – the right to a divorce, if both partners wish it, without legal guilt on either side. All that the court required under the new law was proof of the irretrievable breakdown of the marriage. In addition to the previous ways of proving this, such as adultery or cruelty, it became sufficient for the couple to have lived apart for two years (if both parties wanted the divorce) or for five years (if only one wanted it). The act ruled out divorce within the first three years of marriage, but this period has subsequently been reduced to one year. Divorces are granted in two stages: the decree nisi is a provisional divorce (*nisi* is Latin for 'unless'), which may be cancelled if good cause is shown; the decree absolute, completing the process, usually follows six weeks later.

The number of divorces in Britain soon doubled after the 1969 act, as people trapped in unhappy marriages took the first easy opportunity to break free. The annual rate continued to drift up during the 1970s, but it has remained fairly level since about 1980. A loose but widely quoted statistic states that one marriage in three in Britain now ends in divorce.

Divorced beheaded died, divorced beheaded survived Old schoolroom mnemonic for the fate, in sequence, of the six wives of *Henry VIII.

Dixon of Dock Green (BBC 1955–76) The first and the longest-lasting British police series on television. George Dixon, an avuncular old copper in London's East End, first appeared in a 1949 film, *The Blue Lamp*; in the story he trained a young recruit and was then killed in a shoot-out. The character was revived for the television series (written by Ted Willis, 1918–92) and was played by the same actor, Jack Warner (1895–1981), who was in his eighties when the series ended. His catch phrase, 'Evening all', began each programme.

Dixons By far the largest retailer on Britain's high streets of electronic, photographic and electrical consumer goods; in addition to about 350 Dixons shops, the group has another 1000 or more under the names Currys, Supasnaps and Silo. The enterprise began in 1937 when Charles Kalms (1897–1978) opened the first Dixons photographic studio in Southend. His business prospered greatly during the war, when the families of people away from home in the services were steady customers. Later Kalms specialized in the sale of cameras and accessories, building up a large mail-order business. The company grew with the electrical and electronic markets. It went public in 1962 and since 1967 the chairman has been Stanley Kalms (b. 1931), the son of the founder.

DNA (deoxyribonucleic acid) The main constituent of chromosomes in living creatures, carrying the genetic code which passes on hereditary characteristics. The race to unravel the structure of this stuff of life was one of the great dramas of 20c science, hotly contested between two teams. One, at the *Cavendish Laboratory in Cambridge, included Francis Crick (b. 1916) and an American scientist, James Watson (b. 1928); the other, at King's College in London, was headed by Maurice Wilkins (b. 1916). In the event, with the borrowed help of x-ray pictures taken by Wilkins' colleague Rosalind Franklin (d. 1958), the Cambridge team were the first to discover, in 1953, that DNA has a double-helix structure. In 1962 Crick, Watson and Wilkins shared a Nobel prize. Their discovery made possible the numerous subsequent developments in genetic medicine.

DNB see The *Dictionary of National Biography*.

D-notice A notice sent to the media by the government's Defence, Press and Broadcasting Committee (established for the press in 1912), putting a block on the publication of certain information in the interests of security; the prohibition does not have legal force but has been traditionally accepted. In recent years the D-notice procedure has been controversial because of suspicions that the security in question may sometimes be that of the government rather than the nation. It was officially under review at the end of 1992.

Docklands The name by which Londoners now know the area of the old London docks, stretching miles along the north bank of the Thames; the *urban development corporation formed to revive the region was given the name London Docklands. The docks, once the heart of London's commercial activity, had become unviable by the mid-1960s – larger modern ships needed deep-water berths and there was no remaining advantage in unloading so far up the Thames. Much attention has been focused on the area during its development. *Wapping became the scene of violent events in 1986–7, when the new offices of the *Times* were besieged; the financial problems of *Canary Wharf were headline news in 1992; and the corporation itself was the subject of controversy in 1992, when it was revealed that in the period 1987–92 it had received almost as much in government grants as the other nine urban development corporations put together. The area's troubles have been increased by transport problems. The Dockland's Light Railway proved inadequate, running small tram-like automatic trains without drivers; and the proposed extensions of the Light Railway and of the Jubilee line were delayed when the original developers of Canary Wharf failed to provide an agreed £400m for the project.

Marriages and divorces in the UK, in thousands

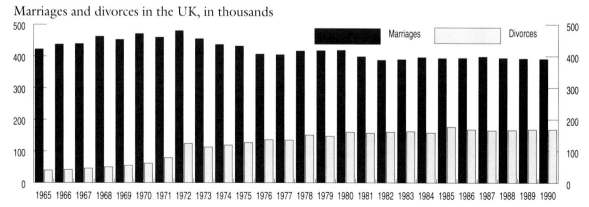

In March 1993 comparative figures for 1991 and 1992 were not yet available from the Office of Population Censuses and Surveys.
Source: Annual Abstract of Statistics *(see *Central Statistical Office).*

Doctor Faustus (*The Tragical History of Dr. Faustus, c.*1590) Tragedy by *Marlowe, not published until 1604 but written and produced in about 1590. It is based on a bestselling book of 1587, the *Faustbuch*, which brought together many tales about a German magician and charlatan who had died in 1540. Faustus sells his soul to the devil, in the form of Mephistopheles, in return for 24 years of indulging every whim. His most famous fancy is to have Helen of Troy as his paramour, greeting her apparition with 'Was this the face that launched a thousand ships?', a line soon followed by 'Sweet Helen, make me immortal with a kiss'. The part of Faustus was first performed by Edward *Alleyn.

Dr Finlay's Casebook (BBC, 1959–66) Television series which ran to more than 150 episodes, following the adventures of two doctors – Dr Finlay (Bill Simpson) and Dr Cameron (Andrew Cruickshank) – who live with their housekeeper Janet (Barbara Mullen) in the small fictional town of Tannochbrae. Set in the 1920s, it derived from the personal experiences of its creator, A.J. *Cronin. In 1993 Scottish TV broadcast an update of the series, as *Dr Finlay*, setting it in the years after World War II and using Auchtermuchty in Fife as the location.

Doctor Foster went to Gloucester Nursery rhyme which first appeared in the mid-19C. There is no known historical origin for the doctor, who stepped in a puddle right up to his middle and never went there again.

'Dr Livingstone, I presume' see Henry Morton *Stanley.

Dr Who (BBC 1963–89) Science-fiction television serial, aimed at older children but with a cult status among many adults. It followed the adventures of a Time Lord, Dr Who, who has the power to travel through both time and space in his Tardis (a vehicle disguised as a police box and an acronym for Time And Relative Dimension In Space). His main opponents are the Daleks, a race of robots with staccato mechanical voices. The first Dr Who was William Hartnell, followed by Jon Pertwee, Patrick Troughton, Tom Baker and others.

Ken **Dodd** (b. 1931) Comedian and singer who is the leading example, in the postwar generation, of the traditions of the *music hall. Like many of his great predecessors, he successfully combines outrageous comedy with buckets of sentiment. His comic props include (in addition to nature's gift of a toothy profile) wild hair, outlandish clothes, a tickling stick and a miniature chorus of Diddymen; even his home address, Knotty Ash in Liverpool, is made part of the joke. Meanwhile his plaintive tenor voice has given him many hit singles, such as *Love is like a Violin* (1960), *Happiness* (1964) and above all *Tears* (1965). His acquittal in the Liverpool Crown Court in 1989 no doubt added to his popularity, after he had been charged with tax fraud involving more than £8 million.

Charles **Dodgson** see Lewis *Carroll.

DOE see Department of the *Environment.

Dogberry see *Much Ado About Nothing.

'dog comes, cat goes' Specifically English-language mnemonic for the phases of the moon. A waxing or coming half moon has the shape of a D, a waning or going one the shape of a C.

Dogger Bank Sandbank in the North Sea, about 100km/60m off the northeast coast of England, rising some 20m/65ft above the surrounding sea bed and forming a relatively shallow area which has been known for centuries as a good fishing ground. It is 250km/155m long and up to 100km/60m wide.

Doggett's Coat and Badge The oldest annual sporting contest in Britain, instituted in 1715 by the comedian Thomas Doggett (*c.*1670–1721) to celebrate the accession of the house of *Hanover in the previous year. It is rowed by young Thames watermen over a 7.25km/4.5m course upstream from London Bridge to Chelsea. The winner gets (and wears thereafter on ceremonial occasions) a distinctive red coat in 18C style and a large silver badge.

dog registration A controversial topic in the early 1990s. Dog licences were introduced in 1796 to raise money for the French Revolutionary War and were abolished in 1988 on the grounds that they achieved nothing and cost a great deal to administer (the annual licence, which had not risen with inflation, cost by then the derisory sum of 37 pence). The *RSPCA has campaigned strongly for a more thorough system of dog registration by which the owners of stray dogs could be traced, pointing out that there are half a million strays on the streets of Britain (in spite of 1000 being put down every day). A series of horrifying attacks by dogs on children caused the government to rush through the very limited Dangerous Dogs Act of 1991, by which four breeds (only one of which, the pit bull terrier, is widely owned in Britain) had to be registered, neutered and tagged by the insertion of a microchip; the legislation was followed by a great deal of confusion and argument as to whether particular dogs were or were not pit bulls.

Dolaucothi (40km/25m NE of Carmarthen) Site mined intermittently for gold from Roman times to the 20C. The remains of the Roman mine and aqueduct can be seen.

Anton **Dolin** (stage name of Patrick Kay, 1904–83, kt 1981) English dancer, choreographer and pioneer of British ballet. He danced first with Diaghilev's Ballets Russes; by 1924 he was a soloist, creating a leading role in that year in Nijinska's *Le Train Bleu*. In 1930 he was a founder member of the Camargo Society, and in 1935 he began a fruitful partnership with *Markova. They formed several companies together, most notably the one which became the *English National Ballet.

Dr **Dolittle** An unconventional doctor, expert in animal languages who takes the part of animals against human beings. He is the hero of a series of children's books by Hugh Lofting (1886–1947), beginning with *The Story of Doctor Dolittle* (1920). Lofting, who was born in Britain and who conceived Dolittle when serving in the trenches with the Irish Guards, spent most of his life after World War I in the USA. He illustrated the books himself in a very precise linear style.

Domesday Book The written record of the survey of land holdings in England, carried out for *William the Conqueror during 1086 and summarized in this form in 1087. The entire country was covered except for the extreme north (the area that is now Northumberland, Durham and Cumbria). An unexplained omission is the two main cities of the realm, London and Winchester (the capital).

The main purpose of the survey was to ascertain the extent and taxable value of the king's lands and of land held as fiefs by his vassals (see *feudalism), but it has also been of great historical importance as the first detailed account of England and the earliest record of many place names. It consists of two volumes: the Great Domesday, which is the summary of all but three of the counties; and the more detailed Little Domesday, consisting of the un-abbreviated returns for Essex, Norfolk and Suffolk. Both are on show in the *Public Record Office. Referred to by contemporaries simply as the 'description of England', it was already known in the 12C as the Domesday Book. The analogy was with the Day of Judgement, there being no appeal against the findings of either.

Dominica Member of the *Commonwealth since 1978. A volcanic island in the eastern group of the West Indies, Dominica was named from the Latin for Sunday, the day of the week on which Columbus discovered it in 1493. Claimed by the French from 1632, it changed hands between France and Britain several times before coming finally under British control in 1805. After membership of the *West Indies Federation, the island exercised internal self-government from 1967 as a step towards full independence in 1978. (The Dominican Republic, also in the West Indies but not in the Commonwealth, is a separate independent state, sharing the island of Hispaniola with Haiti.)

dominion status A concept devised in 1867 to express the new identity of *Canada, independent but retaining certain links with Britain. Other countries also called dominions for a certain period were New Zealand, Australia, South Africa, Ireland (as the Irish Free State, from 1921) and Newfoundland (prior to its becoming part of Canada in 1949). Dominion status was never precisely defined, but in 1921 Lloyd George identified three characteristics of a dominion: it shared with Britain an allegiance to the monarch; it was equal with Britain, not being subordinate in any aspect of internal or external affairs; and it was freely associated, like Britain, with the *Commonwealth of Nations. These ideas were more formally enshrined in the Statute of Westminster (1931). The concept later became irrelevant, as the Commonwealth adjusted to include republics with their own national head of state.

Doncaster (82,000 in 1981) Town on the river Don in South Yorkshire, dating back to the Roman settlement of *Danum* but deriving its character from its modern industrial role as a coal-mining and railway centre. It is known above all for racing, for it is here that the oldest classic, the *St Leger, has been run since 1776; the earliest grandstand at the course, designed by John Carr, dates from that same year. The Mansion House (1745–48, one of the earliest in the country) is by James Paine.

Lonnie Donegan (Anthony Donegan, b 1931) Singer and guitarist in the skiffle style. He played in jazz bands with Ken Colyer and Chris Barber before his first solo success in 1956 with *Rock Island Line*. Later hits in the same style included *Cumberland Gap* and *Puttin' on the Style* (both 1957) and *My Old Man's a Dustman* (1960), each of which topped the UK chart.

The **Dong with a Luminous Nose** (1877) Nonsense song by Edward *Lear about a lovesick Dong who has strapped a lantern on his nose so that he can roam the great Gromboolian plain by night, searching for his beloved Jumbly Girl, 'with her sky-blue hands, and her sea-green hair'. She had mysteriously arrived and then departed again with the other Jumblies, 'who went to sea in a sieve'. An earlier nonsense song by Lear, *The Jumblies* (1871), describes their 20-year journey.

Donington Park see *British Grand Prix.

Don Juan (1819–24) *Byron's longest poem, published in parts from 1819 but incomplete at his death (though

by then amounting to 16 cantos or some 500 pages). The hero is amorous but not predatory, unlike his famous namesake. His drifting adventures – on a Greek pirate island, in the courts of Turkey and Russia, and eventually in London – provide the poet with a broad canvas on which to record his comments on life. The mood is satirical, with mockery constantly undermining pretension (including that of poetry itself – 'Hail, Muse! *et cetera*' are the opening words of Canto 3). A few subjects remain too serious for deflation. One such is Greek independence, the theme of verses in Canto 3 which have become widely known under the title of their opening words, *The Isles of Greece*.

The **Donkey** see G.K. *Chesterton.

John Donne (pronounced *dunn*, 1572–1631) Poet and preacher whose reputation has soared in the 20C, as leader of the *Metaphysical poets and as a master of rhetorical prose. His early life, as a law student in London, was fashionable and frivolous (he was described as 'a great visitor of Ladies, a great writer of conceited Verses'). The verses were conceited in the sense of being full of literary conceits, sometimes ironic, often erotic. He was ordained in 1615 (born a Roman Catholic, he became an Anglican in his twenties) and the same intelligent and passionate ingenuity was then adapted to sacred verse (the proud challenge of 'Death, thou shalt die', for example). In 1621 he became dean of St Paul's and during the next ten years preached many sermons in or outside the cathedral and at court. His most famous passage of prose, frequently read now in church, comes from a book (*Devotions* 1624) which he wrote during a serious illness. It involves each of us in the death of all: 'No man is an island, entire of itself; . . . and therefore never send to know for whom the bell tolls; it tolls for thee.'

Steve Donoghue (1884–1945) Jockey who won the Derby six times (a record second only to that of Lester *Piggott) and who had the unique distinction of riding two *triple crown winners – Pommern in 1915 and Gay Crusader in 1917.

Do not go gentle into that good night (1951) Poem by Dylan *Thomas, addressed to his dying father and published in his *Collected Poems* (1952). It is a villanelle in form, meaning that two lines (the opening line, which is also the title, and 'Rage, rage against the dying of the light') are repeated as alternating refrains.

Don't dilly-dally on the way see Marie *Lloyd.

'don't frighten the horses' see Mrs Patrick *Campbell.

doodle-bug see *V1 and V2.

Eliza **Doolittle** see **Pygmalion*.

Doomsday Book see *Domesday Book.

Dorchester (14,000 in 1981) Market town of great antiquity; administrative centre of Dorset. *Maiden Castle is nearby and on the southern outskirts of the town are Maumbury Rings, a Stone Age circle adapted by the Romans to an amphitheatre. Excavation has revealed much of the Roman town of *Durnovaria*, remains of which are on show in the Dorset County Museum. The town has a hallowed place in trade union history, because it was in the Shire Hall that the *Tolpuddle Martyrs were sentenced in 1834. And its literary fame is secure thanks to its local author, Thomas *Hardy, who in his novels called it Casterbridge.

therefore a higher proportion of skimmed milk) and the richer double cheese (made with the cream from the evening and morning milking). It is orange-coloured and mild in flavour.

Doubting Castle see *Pilgrim's Progress.*

Douglas (20,000 in 1981) Seaport and resort, capital of the *Isle of Man since 1869, when it replaced Castletown. A town rich in Victorian domestic architecture, from the period of its first prosperity, it acquired also a busy financial sector in the late 20C because local levels of taxation, the responsibility of the *Tynwald, were more lenient than in the UK. The Manx Museum has an excellent collection of stone carvings from the early Christian and the Viking periods, in particular an extraordinary Crucifixion of the 8C on a slab of local slate which was found on the Calf of Man, a small island off the coast. The *TT Races start and finish at Douglas.

Lord Alfred **Douglas** (1870–1945) Spoilt young aristocrat, with the nickname of 'Bosie', who indirectly caused the downfall of his lover, Oscar *Wilde. Wilde's *De Profundis was addressed to him from prison. Douglas was himself a minor poet, responsible for one widely remembered phrase – 'the *love that dare not speak its name'.

Alec **Douglas-Home** see Lord *Home.

Doulton pottery and porcelain Products of a firm in the Lambeth district of London, which John Doulton joined in 1815; by 1820 he and John Watts were its joint owners. The factory soon made a commercial success with glazed stoneware; it specialized, from 1846, in the ceramic drainpipes, basins and lavatories required for the mid-19C revolution in drainage and sanitation. It achieved a more respectable prominence in the 1870s

Crucifixion scene of the 8C, in low relief on Manx slate: one of the treasures of the Manx Museum in Douglas.

Dorchester (London W1) One of London's best-known hotels, overlooking Hyde Park from Park Lane. It was built 1929–31, replacing a Victorian Italianate private palace called Dorchester House.

Dormouse see *Alice in Wonderland.

Dorset (663,000 in 1991, administrative centre Dorchester) *County on the southern coast of England.

Dorset Horn see *sheep.

Dotheboys Hall see *Nicholas Nickleby.

Do they know it's Christmas? see Bob *Geldof.

Douai Bible see *Bible in English.

double cube room see *Wilton House.

double-decker The characteristic London bus, deriving ultimately from the two tiers of the horse-drawn omnibus (the two-sided bench known as the knife-board was first placed on the roof of a London omnibus in 1847). The best-known version is the Routemaster, introduced in the 1950s and designed by Douglas Scott (1913–90), with the great merit of an open platform at the back for ease of access. This excellent model unfortunately requires a conductor as well as a driver and so has been gradually phased out since the 1980s, replaced by fully enclosed double-deckers operated by the driver alone (cheaper but much slower, since he has to deal with tickets before driving on from a bus stop).

'Double, double toil and trouble' see *Macbeth.

Double Gloucester The only well-known English variety to preserve, at least in name, the distinction between a single cheese (made with the cream of only one milking and

A combined bath and shower by Doulton, hi-tech and elaborately decorated: from a catalogue of about 1890.

with its 'artistic' wares, involving students from the Lambeth School of Art in the decoration and design of the products. The best known of the artists were the Barlow sisters, the Martin brothers and George Tinworth. At the same period the company began producing porcelain at Burslem in Staffordshire, which has been the source of all Doulton china since the closure of the Lambeth pottery in 1956; there is a Doulton museum near the factory. The company was authorized by Edward VII to trade as Royal Doulton (the mark on its wares since 1901).

Doune Castle (14km/9m NW of Stirling) An important stronghold of the Stewarts (later *Stuarts), who built it in the 14c and in whose hands it remains. Roofless from neglect by the 18c but sensitively restored in the late 19c, it is today a very well preserved ruin with its interior sufficiently intact to suggest vividly how its occupants lived. Also at Doune is a motor museum, with a collection of rare and early cars.

Dounreay Village on the extreme north coast of Scotland, in the Highland region, which has been the site of Britain's experimental 'fast reactor' nuclear programme, operated by the Atomic Energy Authority. The first reactor became operational in 1959 and closed in 1977; a larger version, the Prototype Fast Reactor, came into operation in 1974 and is scheduled to close in 1994 (bringing the Dounreay experiment to an end).

Dove Cottage The home from 1799 to 1808 of William *Wordsworth and his sister Dorothy, in the village of *Grasmere. It was subsequently occupied by Thomas de Quincey.

Dovedale The valley of the river Dove is a limestone gorge in the Peak District, forming the boundary between Staffordshire and Derbyshire. Rocks and peaks have weathered into shapes which have acquired romantic names – Lover's Leap, the Twelve Apostles, Jacob's Ladder. The presiding spirit of the valley is Izaak Walton, for whom this was a favourite place to fish.

Dover (33,000 in 1981) Seaport on the south coast of England, in Kent, which is the nearest English town to the mainland of Europe. As such its history has been much tied up with the crossing of the *Strait of Dover. In modern times this has included its role as the main embarkation point for Channel ferries, as a starting point for attempts at *swimming the Channel, and as a terminal of the *Channel tunnel. But in the past it meant being a first line of defence against invasion.

A Bronze Age ship, dating from about 1000 BC, was discovered in 1992 some 7m/23m below the present ground level in the centre of Dover; about 15m/50ft long, and one of the oldest surviving boats in the world, it probably sank in an estuary which long ago silted up.

Julius Caesar landed here in 55 BC, and in later centuries Dover developed as the Roman town of *Dubrae* or *Dubris*; a Roman lighthouse is still incorporated in the castle (mainly Norman in origin but much altered). The profusely ornamented large cannon aiming out to sea from the castle (more than 7m/23ft long and known as Queen Elizabeth's Pocket Pistol) was given to Henry VIII by Charles V, the Holy Roman Emperor. The town's strategic position caused it to become the chief of the *Cinque Ports. The famous white cliffs of Dover, a gleaming wall of chalk in places 114m/374ft high, have acquired great symbolic status as the last and first glimpse of England; they were the subject of one of Vera *Lynn's most popular songs during World War II.

Lord **Dowding** (Hugh Dowding, 1882–1970, KCB 1933, baron 1943) Airman in charge from 1936 of the newly created Fighter Command of the RAF. He was responsible for providing radar stations round the south coast and an effective fighting force of *Hurricanes and *Spitfires in time for World War II. As overall commander during the *Battle of Britain, much of the strategic credit was his. In 1988 a statue of him was placed in front of *St Clement Danes.

Anthony **Dowell** (b. 1943) Dancer who joined the *Royal Ballet in 1961. Three years later he danced the first role created for him and also began his most famous partnership; in Ashton's *The Dream* (1964) Dowell was Oberon and Antoinette *Sibley was Titania. He went on to create many other roles with Ashton (in particular Beliaev in A *Month in the Country) and with MacMillan (des Grieux in *Manon to Sibley's Manon). In the late 1970s he was frequently a guest artist with the American Ballet Theatre in New York, and in 1986 he was appointed director of the Royal Ballet – which under his leadership has gone from strength to strength.

John **Dowland** (c1562–1626) Composer, lute-player and singer who spent much of his life in courts on the Continent before entering the service of James I in 1612. His fame now derives from his solo compositions for lute, from his songs (of which *Fine Knacks for Ladies* is one of the best known), and from his instrumental pieces for viols and lute in the collection published as *Lachrimae* (1604).

Down One of the six *counties of Northern Ireland, but since 1973 no longer an administrative unit in *local government.

Down and Out in Paris and London (1933) Narrative by George *Orwell of his life in the late 1920s, struggling to make a living in Paris by giving English lessons and working as a *plongeur* (washer-up), and then taking to the road as a tramp back in England. An inside account of a submerged section of society, rich in detail and dialogue, his book was as much an education for the reader as the experiences had been for Orwell. He concludes: 'I shall never again think that all tramps are drunken scoundrels, nor expect a beggar to be grateful when I give him a penny . . . That is a beginning.'

Down at the Old Bull and Bush A favourite *music-hall song which sounds quintessentially English but was in fact American in origin. Written by Harry Von Tilzer (1872–1946) as *Down Where the Wurzburger Flows*, it was first sung in Britain by Florrie *Forde in 1903. Criticized for singing about a German river, she commissioned new words and scored a lasting hit.

Edward **Downes** (b. 1924, kt 1991) Conductor who was artistic director and principal conductor of the BBC Philharmonic Orchestra (1980–91) and who has an unbroken 40-year association with Covent Garden, where he first conducted in 1953. In 1993 his performance there of *Stiffelio* triumphantly restored to the repertoire a long-neglected Verdi opera.

Downing Street (London SW1) Cul-de-sac off the west side of *Whitehall. Its fame derives from no. 10 being the official residence of the *prime minister. Indeed 'Downing Street' and 'No. 10' are used as synonyms for the prime minister's office.

The street was built in about 1680 by a member of parliament, George Downing (c.1623–84). In 1732 George II bought no. 10 and offered it as a gift to Walpole, who was effectively the first prime minister. He accepted it not as his own but as linked with his office, and it has gone with it ever since. In the early 19C the crown also acquired nos. 11 and 12, now respectively the residence of the *chancellor of the exchequer and the office of the chief *whip. (These are the only three houses which remain of the original street.) Until the recent dangers of IRA violence, the public had free access to Downing Street and children could even be photographed on the steps of No. 10. In 1989 the public was excluded even more firmly than before by the placing of heavy iron gates across the entrance from Whitehall.

Downs A term misleading in its implication of something low rather than high. It comes from the Old English *dun* meaning 'hill', and is applied to the rolling chalk uplands, grassy and treeless, which are characteristic of much of southern England. The North Downs stretch from southwest of London to the coast near Dover, where the chalk ridge is broken off to form the famous white cliffs. The South Downs, running close to the coast through most of Sussex, reach the sea round Beachy Head. The Berkshire Downs lie south of the Chilterns, separated from them by the Thames valley. The North Wessex Downs are round Marlborough, and the West Wiltshire Downs stretch west from Salisbury.

At sea the anchorage protected by the *Goodwin Sands is also known as the Downs.

Downside School Boys' *public school which is run by Benedictine monks of Downside Abbey. The community derives from one established at Douai in France in 1606 by a group of English and Welsh monks from Continental monasteries. They developed there a school to teach English Catholic boys. As with the *Ampleforth community, the French Revolution caused them to flee to England. They arrived in 1794 and eventually settled at Downside, near Bath, in 1814. The abbey church, built from the 1870s and completed by Giles Gilbert Scott in 1925, is the largest of the many neo-Gothic Roman Catholic churches built in England since the mid-19C.

Down Your Way (BBC 1946–87) Radio programme which during five decades was a Sunday teatime favourite for many, with the presenter visiting a different place in Britain each week and talking to the locals about their community and its history. There were only four presenters during the entire period – Stewart MacPherson (1946–50), Richard Dimbleby (1950–5), Franklin Engelmann (1955–72) and Brian Johnston (1972–87).

Conan **Doyle** see Arthur *Conan Doyle.

Richard **D'Oyly Carte** (1844–1901) Impresario who made a fortune presenting the *Savoy operas, and who built the *Savoy theatre and hotel. Theatrical companies bearing his name, and managed by his heirs, continued until quite recently to tour traditional productions of Gilbert and Sullivan.

DPP see *Director of Public Prosecutions.

Margaret **Drabble** (b. 1939) Novelist who has chronicled the emotional and intellectual development of a succession of middle-class heroines, in background and experience usually similar to herself. In her first book (*A Summer Bird-Cage* 1962) the narrator is Sarah, whose elder sister Louise is getting married; the central character of the next (*The Garrick Year* 1964) is Emma, married to an actor and with a young baby; and so on to the books of recent years in which the characters are middle-aged, like the three women who in *The Radiant Way* (1987) look back on their younger selves. She edited the 5th edition of *The Oxford Companion to English Literature* (1985).

Dracula (1897) Horror story by the Irish author, Bram Stoker (1847–1912), whose main employment was as Henry Irving's manager. The tale, launching the Transylvanian count and vampire on his astonishing career, contains as much spine-chilling hokum as any of its countless successors.

Francis **Drake** (*c*.1541–96, kt 1581) The first sea captain to sail round the world. Son of a Protestant naval chaplain (from a farming family in Devon) and related to *Hawkins, he first proved himself in the English sport of raiding the Spanish main (the coast bordering the southern part of the Caribbean Sea). In 1577 he was put in command of an expedition to plunder Spanish trade in the Pacific and then to complete a circumnavigation of the globe – a feat achieved only once before, in 1519–22, by one of Magellan's ships (Magellan himself died on the voyage in 1521). Drake set off with five ships. Of these only his own, the *Golden Hind* (renamed from the *Pelican*), completed the journey in 1580. He was knighted by the queen on board his ship at Deptford, where the *Golden Hind* remained for another century or so as a tourist attraction, in a special dock. With his share of the profits from the voyage Drake bought Buckland Abbey, in Devon, which now contains a museum in his honour. He was prominent in the campaign against the *Armada, commanding the *Revenge* and taking the leading role in the attack at Gravelines. (His legendary remark when playing *bowls on Plymouth Hoe does not appear in print until 1736.) He died in the Caribbean, still busy plundering the Spanish.

drama schools The earliest of London's drama schools is LAMDA (London Academy of Music and Dramatic Art), established in 1861. In spite of the 'music' in its name, it trains only actors, stage managers and theatre technicians; it moved in 1963 into custom-built premises on the Cromwell Road, with its own fully adaptable small theatre.

The Guildhall School of Music and Drama dates from 1880 and is now housed in the Barbican (see *music schools). RADA, or the Royal Academy of Dramatic Art, was founded in 1904 by the actor-manager Beerbohm Tree. It has perhaps the highest prestige of all the schools and has benefited greatly from Bernard Shaw's bequest of one third of his royalties; its Vanbrugh Theatre, on Malet Street, was opened in 1954. The Central School of Speech and Drama, dating from 1906, differs from the others in including courses for speech therapists and teachers; it has the use of a late-Victorian theatre, the Embassy, in Swiss Cottage.

The Bristol Old Vic School was opened in 1946, in conjunction with the recently established Old Vic company in *Bristol; it has had its own premises in Clifton since 1956. In Glasgow the Royal Scottish Academy of Music added drama to its curriculum in 1968 (see *music schools).

Drambuie Scotland's whisky liqueur, which claims romantic origins in the *'45 Rebellion. It is said to have been the personal drink of Bonnie Prince Charlie, and the story goes that when in hiding in Skye (see Flora *Macdonald) he rewarded a faithful follower, Captain John MacKinnon, by giving him the secret recipe. The MacKinnon family kept the drink to themselves until they decided, in 1906, to manufacture it commercially. The precise method of making the liqueur remains a family secret, but the ingredients are a blend of Scotch whiskies together with honey and a herbal extract. The name derives from the Gaelic *an dram buidheach*, meaning 'the drink which pleases'.

HMS **Dreadnought** British battleship, launched in 1906. Displacing 17,900 tons and capable of 21 knots, it was the first of the massive vessels, armed exclusively with big guns, which dominated naval warfare until the end of World War II. 'Dreadnought' became a general term for ships of this class, but the name has had a longer and ongoing place in British naval history; ships called *Dreadnought* fought against the Armada and at Trafalgar, and a submarine was launched with that name in 1960.

The **Dream of Gerontius** (1865) Poem by John Henry *Newman, a dramatic monologue by a just soul confronting death, with choruses of angels and devils. The poem was set for solo voices, chorus and orchestra by *Elgar in 1900.

'Drink to me only with thine eyes' see Ben *Jonson.

dripping The fat that has dripped from roasting meat. It was popular spread on bread, like butter, in the days before cholesterol was much heard of.

driving licences see *Swansea.

Droeshout portrait see William *Shakespeare.

Drones Club see P.G. *Wodehouse.

'Dropping the Pilot' Cartoon by *Tenniel which appeared in *Punch* on 29 March 1890 after the young kaiser, William II, had demanded the resignation of his 74-year-old chancellor, Bismarck. A subcaption explained: 'The Prussian Bully has no further use for Prince Bismarck.'

drop scone see *scone.

druids The priests of the ancient *Celts. Little is known about their ceremonies, except that they took place in sacred groves (oak and mistletoe being particularly significant) and that they involved human sacrifice; it is possible that *Lindow Man was a victim. Their supposed link with the much earlier *Stonehenge derives from a mistaken assumption by the antiquary John *Aubrey. Various

self-appointed groups perform modern druidical rituals at the summer solstice. The earliest was the United Ancient Order of Druids, founded in London in 1781 as something akin to a masonic order (with groves instead of lodges), but operating since 1833 mainly as a *friendly society.

Drum Castle (16km/10m SW of Aberdeen) Massive tower keep of the late 13C (one of the earliest in Scotland), with a mansion attached to it in the 17C.

Drumlanrig Castle (32km/20m NW of Dumfries) Four-square and somewhat severe stately home built 1679–90 for the 1st duke of Queensberry. The house contains excellent furniture and paintings.

Drury Lane (Theatre Royal Drury Lane, London WC2) London's oldest theatrical site, with an unbroken record of production since 1663 (Nell *Gwyn first appeared on the stage here in 1665). The present theatre is the fourth. It opened in 1812, to a design by Benjamin Wyatt (son of James *Wyatt), but the interior was rebuilt in 1922. Since World War II the theatre has been the home of a succession of long-running musicals, most of them American.

Dryburgh Abbey (64km/40m to the SE of Edinburgh) Founded in the 12C, in a lovely setting by the river Tweed, for Premonstratensian canons (from Prémontré in northern France). In the ruins of the abbey church lie the graves of Walter *Scott and Earl *Haig. The other monastic buildings are relatively well preserved, giving an unusually clear idea of how the monks lived.

John **Dryden** (1631–1700) Dramatist and poet whose literary life was closely linked with the Restoration court; he was made *poet laureate in 1668. But his first career was in the public theatre. Of his many plays, the one that has lasted best is *All for Love* (1677), a reworking of Shakespeare's *Antony and Cleopatra* along the lines of the classical drama fashionable in France at the time. He later discovered a talent for mock-heroic poetry. *Absalom and Achitophel* (1681) uses a biblical story to parallel the contemporary struggle between *Tories and Whigs as to whether the future James II should be excluded from the throne as a Roman Catholic. Faithful to his court position, Dryden brilliantly satirized the Whigs. When James did succeed to the throne, in 1685, Dryden himself converted to Roman Catholicism and wrote a long poem (*The Hind and the Panther* 1687) about the religious issues of the day.

DSC and **DSM** (Distinguished Service Cross and Medal) Decorations for gallantry in the Royal Navy, instituted in 1914 and extended in 1942 to the merchant navy. The DSC is awarded to officers below the rank of captain and to warrant officers, the DSM to chief petty officers and below. The DSC was a continuation under a new name of the Conspicuous Service Cross, established for the same purpose by Edward VII in 1901.

DSO (Distinguished Service Order) Bestowed since 1886 on commissioned officers of the Navy, Army and Air Force (and of the merchant navy since 1942) for special distinction in action.

DSS see Department of *Social Security.

DTI see Department of *Trade and Industry.

Dubrae see *Dover.

The **Duchess of Malfi** (c.1613) Tragedy with elements of black comedy by John *Webster. The duchess, a young widow, sets the plot spinning by secretly marrying

Interior of the Drury Lane theatre which burnt down in 1804: aquatint published in Microcosm of London *(1808).*

her honest steward, Antonio, in direct opposition to the wishes of her powerful and evil brothers, a duke and a cardinal. They place a spy, Bosola, in her household. By the end of the play, after much cruelty and torment, the machinations of Bosola and the brothers have led to the death of all five main characters.

ducking stool An unpleasant method of punishment, devised in the late 16C, in which the culprit was strapped in a chair on the end of a pivoted arm and was ducked in a lake or river. The number of immersions was specified by the magistrate, but the length of each – of greater concern to the victim – was no doubt unpredictable. It was most commonly the punishment for women who had offended in some way, but it was also often the fate of dishonest traders. Ducking stools were familiar devices in the 17C and were last used in the early 19C.

Dudley (188,000 in 1981) Ancient mining and smelting town in the West Midlands, sometimes known as the capital of the *Black Country. Dudley Zoo has been in the grounds of the ruined Norman castle since 1935. An excellent small museum, specializing in the history of glass, was opened in 1980 in Broadfield House; and the Black Country Museum is 2km/1m to the north of the town.

William **Duesbury** see *Derby porcelain.

duffle coat Traditional style of short coat, of thick woollen material, fastened with toggles and usually with an attached hood, which was widely worn in the 1950s and 1960s. 'Duffle' was the name of the material, originally a product of Duffel in Belgium; there are references to 'duffle coats' and 'duffle cloaks' as far back as the 17C.

duke The highest rank in the *peerage. A dukedom is traditionally given to younger sons of the monarch (including in previous centuries illegitimate sons) and to men of great distinction, such as the duke of Wellington.

Geoff **Duke** (b. 1923) Racing motorcyclist who became world champion in 1951–2 riding for Norton (350cc 1951, and 1952, 500cc 1951). He was subsequently 500cc champion three years running (1953–5), when he rode for the Italian Gilera team. He also won the Isle of Man Senior TT for Norton in 1950 and 1951, and for Gilera in 1955.

Duke of Edinburgh's Award Scheme Programme in existence since 1956, deriving from the ideas of Kurt Hahn at *Gordonstoun and promoted by the duke of *Edinburgh. Its purpose is to encourage young people (originally 14–18, but now up to 25) to tackle a wide range of challenges and adventures, usually involving physical skills, endurance or service to the community.

Dulwich College Boys' *public school in south London, founded in 1619 by the actor Edward *Alleyn. His endowment also provided another school surviving today, Alleyn's, which was separated from the main college in 1882. Among the wittiest of Dulwich's old boys was P.G. Wodehouse.

Dulwich Picture Gallery (London SE21) Britain's oldest public art gallery, which opened in 1814 in a building designed by *Soane to accommodate a bequest of 371 paintings to Dulwich College. It has remained a relatively small collection of exceptionally high quality, particularly strong in the 17C (Poussin, Claude, Rubens, Van Dyck, Rembrandt, Murillo) and in English portraits of the 18C.

Daphne **du Maurier** (1907–89, DBE 1969) Novelist who lived most of her life in Cornwall and reached a very wide audience with her thriller-romances set in the West Country. The best known is *Rebecca, but its narrative skills are equalled by *Jamaica Inn* (1936), *Frenchman's Creek* (1941) and *My Cousin Rachel* (1951). Her chilling short story 'The Birds' was filmed in 1963 by Alfred Hitchcock. She was the daughter of the actor-manager Gerald du Maurier (1873–1934) and the granddaughter of George *du Maurier.

George **du Maurier** (1834–96) Cartoonist and novelist, son of an English mother and French-born father. He became best known for his society pictures in *Punch*, detailed drawings of the social life of the rich, accompanied by often over-elaborate humorous captions (his best known is the *curate's egg). He had an immensely successful second career as a popular novelist, in particular with *Trilby*.

dumb-waiter A piece of furniture introduced in England in the mid-18C so that food and drink could be at hand in the dining room without the need for a servant. It consisted of two or three circular revolving trays, set above each other on a central column with tripod legs. The first recorded use of the word is in *Fanny Hill*, where the piece of furniture serves a very precise purpose. Fanny explains that 'a bottle of Burgundy, with the other necessaries, were set on a dumb-waiter', enabling the landlady to remain outside the room while Fanny is seduced by H . . ., brother to the earl of L . . .. The word was later applied (first in the USA) to a concealed system of ropes and pulleys bringing food up from the kitchen to other floors in the house.

dum-dum A soft-nosed bullet, designed to spread on impact and cause maximum injury; it was named after the town of Dum-Dum, just north of Calcutta, where it was first manufactured by the British in the 19C. Dum-dums were outlawed by the Hague Conference of 1899.

Dumfries (32,000 in 1981) Town in southwest Scotland, sometimes known as 'Queen of the South'; administrative centre of the Dumfries and Galloway region. Frequently damaged in border warfare with the English, its most distinguished building is Midsteeple (1707), which originally was the town hall. The Footbridge, the oldest of the five bridges over the river Nith, dates from the 15C but has been considerably rebuilt. The town's traditional industries are hosiery and knitwear.

Robert Burns lived here for the last five years of his life, and his house is kept as a memorial. The Dumfries Museum (on local subjects) is housed in an 18C windmill with a camera obscura on its roof. The Gracefield Arts Centre has a collection of 20C British paintings, and Shambellie House is a museum of costume.

Dumfries and Galloway (148,000 in 1991, administrative centre Dumfries) Since 1975 a *region of southwest Scotland, comprising the former counties of Dumfries, Kirkcudbright and Wigtown.

Dumfriesshire Until 1975 a *county on the southwest coast of Scotland, bordering England, now part of the Dumfries and Galloway region.

Dunadd (66km/41m S of Oban) Bleak hilltop near the village of Cairnbaan which has evocative associations in Scottish history. It was the main stronghold of the kingdom of *Dalriada, and according to tradition the Stone of *Scone was the coronation throne here before it began its complicated journeys. In the area just to the north of

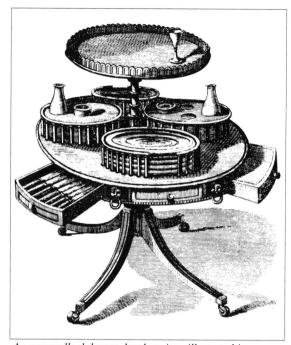

An unusually elaborate dumb-waiter, illustrated in Thomas Sheraton's Cabinet Dictionary (1803).

Dunadd there is an extraordinary concentration of prehistoric sites, with numerous standing stones and cairns from the Stone and Bronze Ages.

William **Dunbar** (c.1460–c.1520) Scottish poet, at the court of James IV. Little is known of his life but he was master of a wide range of poetic styles, including *alliterative verse. His lament for dead poets (*Lament for the Makaris*) is deliberately chilling, as the list of distinguished names creeps closer to his own generation; each verse ends with the refrain *Timor mortis conturbat me* (Latin for 'the fear of death disturbs me'). He has been remembered with affection south of the border for a poem in praise of the English capital, including the line 'London, thou art the flower of cities all', but it is now thought not to be by him.

Dunbartonshire Until 1975 a *county in the west of Scotland, to the north of the Clyde estuary, now part of the Strathclyde region.

Dunblane (11km/7m N of Stirling) Town on the Allan Water, crossed here by a single-span 16C bridge, in the Central region of Scotland. It is known in particular for its cathedral, which has been used since the Reformation as the parish church. Founded by David I in about 1150, the building dates mainly from the 13C with considerable restoration in the early 20C. The west front is a very fine example of the Early English style, and was singled out for special praise by John Ruskin. As a result the oval window beneath the gable is now known by his name.

Duncan I (d. 1040) King of Scotland from 1034, whose lasting fame derives from Shakespeare's *Macbeth*. Although the innocent victim in the play, his claim to the throne was no greater than *Macbeth's and possibly less.

The **Dunciad** (bks 1–3 1728, bk 4 1742) Mock-heroic poem by *Pope celebrating the triumph of Dullness, a device enabling the author to ridicule all the pedants and scribblers who had criticized his works.

Dundee (175,000 in 1981) City on the north shore of the Firth of Tay, close to the two *Tay bridges; administrative centre of the Tayside region. A town of importance since the 13C, its chief growth was in the 19C when it became Britain's centre for the manufacture of goods from imported jute. It has often been said that 'jute, jam and journalism' are Dundee's specialities. The jam for which the city is best known is *marmalade. The national consumption of Dundee's journalism has been mainly by children, for it is here that D.C. Thomson & Co. have published Britain's most successful comics, ranging from *Rover*, *Wizard* and *Hotspur* to *Beano* and *Dandy*. Shipbuilding has also been important, and the special dock made for the construction of Captain Scott's *Discovery* can still be seen; the *Discovery* herself is moored in Craig Harbour. In the Victoria Dock is the *Unicorn*, a wooden frigate launched in 1824 and by now the oldest British warship still afloat.

St Paul's, the episcopal cathedral, is by George Gilbert *Scott on the site of Dundee's castle, destroyed in the 14C; St Andrew's (19–20C) is the Roman Catholic cathedral. The Museum and Art Gallery, with emphasis on Scottish painters of the 19–20C, is in a building of 1871–3 by George Gilbert Scott. Dundee High School, an extremely ancient institution (founded in 1239), is now an independent fee-paying school.

Dundee cake Fruit cake decorated on top with split almonds. The name first appears in print in the late 19C, by which time it had no exclusive link with Dundee.

Dundee United, known as the Terrors (Tannadice Park, Dundee). Football club founded in 1909 as Dundee Hibernian (renamed Dundee United in 1923) which has had a run of successes during the 1980s. These included reaching the finals of the UEFA Cup in 1987. Club victories: Scottish League Champions 1983; Scottish League Cup 1980, 81.

Dundrennan Abbey (42km/26m SW of Dumfries) Ruins of a 12C Cistercian abbey with a particular poignancy in Scottish history, because it was here that *Mary Queen of Scots spent her last night on Scottish soil (15 May 1568) before crossing the Solway Firth in a small fishing boat to England and captivity.

Dunfermline (52,000 in 1991) Town in Fife which had a long and close connection with the Scottish royal family. Malcolm III and his wife St Margaret built a palace here and founded a Benedictine priory (later raised to the status of an abbey). They were both buried in the abbey grounds, as were many later kings of Scotland including *Robert the Bruce. The 12C Romanesque nave of the abbey had a new choir added to it in 1817–22 (by William Burn), and this is now the parish church.

Dunfermline was the birthplace of Andrew *Carnegie, and the small cottage where he was born is preserved as a museum. His father worked in Dunfermline's main trade, the weaving of damask linen.

Dunkeld (1000 in 1981) Town in the Tayside region. Beneath wooded hills on the river Tay, this was the site of a Celtic monastery from at least the 9C and probably earlier. It became the seat of a bishopric in the 12C and the cathedral dates from the 14–15C; apart from the choir, which remained in use as a parish church, it has been a romantic ruin since the Reformation. The 'Little Houses' lining the approach to the cathedral are of the early 18C, and the nearby bridge over the Tay was built by Telford in 1809.

Dunkirk Town on the north coast of France, 40km/25m east of Calais, at which the British snatched victory of a sort from the jaws of defeat in *World War II. The rapid German advance in May 1940 had forced the *British Expeditionary Force and other Allied troops back to the coast. Evacuation began from Dunkirk on May 26. The next day the harbour was bombed, so the main operation was moved to a long stretch of beach east of the town, where only small craft could come in close enough to pick up the soldiers. A fleet of peacetime vessels (fishing boats, private cruisers, river ferries) was rapidly assembled. It had been expected originally that only some 10,000 could be saved from falling into German hands. In the event the motley fleet of 860 vessels had by June 4 ferried over to England 200,000 British and 140,000 French troops.

John **Dunlop** (1840–1921) Scottish inventor of the pneumatic tyre. He moved in 1867 to Belfast, where he established a successful practice as a vet. In 1887 his 9-year-old son complained about riding his solid-wheeled tricycle over cobbles, and Dunlop began experimenting with a rubber tube filled with air. In 1888 he patented the idea and in 1889 production begun with a Dublin company (the Pneumatic Tyre and Booth's Cycle Agency), which evolved into the Dunlop Rubber Company and is now part of *BTR. Dunlop himself played only a small part in the development of his invention and profited little from it. There were legal difficulties after it was discovered that the idea of a pneumatic tyre had been patented earlier (in 1846) but not exploited.

Dunmow Flitch One of Britain's oldest popular ceremonies, dating from at least the 14C. In the Essex town of Dunmow a flitch (a cured and salted side of pork) is given to a couple who can prove that not once in a year and a day have they regretted marrying. One of the earliest references is in The *Canterbury Tales*, where the Wife of Bath boasts that none of her five husbands would have dreamt of claiming the flitch. At various times the custom died out, but it has been continuous (held now in each leap year) since it was revived in 1885 with the addition of a mock court involving judge, jury and witnesses.

Dunnet Head The most northerly point on the British mainland, though *John o'Groats (some 19km/12m to the east) is popularly thought of as having this distinction. The most northerly part of the British Isles is *Unst.

Dunnottar Castle (27km/17m S of Aberdeen) Scotland's most dramatically sited castle, on a high rocky promontory thrusting out into the sea. The main buildings, now ruined, are a 14C keep and a 16C gatehouse.

John **Duns** (known as Duns Scotus, c.1265–1308) Theologian and Franciscan friar, born in the village of Duns in the Borders region of Scotland. His writings, full of so many nice distinctions that he became known as the 'subtle doctor', are Britain's main contribution to medieval scholastic philosophy. By the 16C his followers, still splitting hairs, had become objects of ridicule – inspiring the excellent word 'dunces'. He was beatified in 1993.

Dunsinane see *Macbeth*.

St **Dunstan** (c.909–88) Abbot of Glastonbury from about 943 and archbishop of Canterbury from 959. A man of considerable learning, he is credited with effecting a revival in monastic standards. Contrary to popular assumption, he was not blind (see *St Dunstan's). His feast day is May 19.

Dunster Castle (5km/3m SE of Minehead) Standing out boldly on a wooded hillside in Somerset, Dunster was lived in by the Luttrell family for nearly six centuries

The three great towers of Durham Cathedral, with the western pair rising almost sheer above the river Wear.

(1405–1979). Some 17c interiors survive, with richly plastered ceilings, but so do the less fortunate alterations to the exterior, done in the 19c. The castle is traditionally visited on the afternoon of May Day by the hobby horse from neighbouring *Minehead.

On the river Avill, beneath the castle, the 18c Dunster watermill was restored in 1979 and is now on show as a working mill, producing wholewheat flour.

Dunvegan Castle (NW coast of Skye) Stronghold on a rocky inlet, the home of the chieftains of the Macleod clan since the 13c. Much added to and rebuilt over the centuries, particularly in the past 150 years, the fabric of the castle is now less interesting than the contents accumulated by the family over eight centuries. The best known of these is the Fairy Flag, a stretch of tattered silk which legend claims to have been given as a farewell gift to the Macleod chieftain in about 1400 by a fairy who had lived with him as his wife; history suggests, with hardly less romance, that it is a holy relic brought back from the Crusades, when it was probably believed to be part of a saint's garment.

Jacqueline **Du Pré** (1945–87) Brilliant cellist whose career struck a profound chord with the public, first through her early success and later because of her tragically early retirement, at the age of 28, as a victim of multiple sclerosis. She had her debut recital in 1961 at the Wigmore Hall and first appeared at the Festival Hall in the following year, performing Elgar's cello concerto – a work with which she became particularly associated. In 1967 she married Daniel Barenboim.

Duran Duran Pop group formed in Birmingham in 1978, consisting eventually of Simon le Bon (b. 1958, vocals), Andy Taylor (b. 1961, guitar), Nick Rhodes (b. 1962, keyboards), John Taylor (b. 1960, bass) and Roger Taylor (b. 1960, drums); surprisingly, the three Taylors are unrelated. Playing a more romantic rock than the punk fashion of the time, the group rapidly became a teenage cult. Each of their first two albums (*Duran Duran* 1981, *Rio* 1982) was in the British charts for nearly two years; no. 1 hit singles soon followed (*Is there something I should know?* 1983, *The Reflex* 1984).

Viviana **Durante** (b. 1967) Italian-born dancer, living in Britain from the age of ten, who emerged in the late 1980s as a leading talent with the *Royal Ballet. Since 1990 she has developed a brilliant partnership with the Russian dancer Irek Mukhamedov, particularly in works by Kenneth MacMillan (*Romeo and Juliet, Manon, Mayerling*). Together they created the leading roles in MacMillan's last ballet, *The Judas Tree* (1992).

Durham The name both of a *county in northeast England (604,000 in 1991) and of the ancient city (26,000 in 1991) which is its administrative centre.

The castle and cathedral of Durham stand side by side on a superb natural site, a high rocky peninsula formed by a long U-bend in the river Wear. William the Conqueror chose this place in 1072 for a fortress against the Scots. He entrusted it to the Bishop of Durham, thus creating a peculiar hybrid, the famous prince bishops of Durham. Through the Middle Ages bishops would ride out from here at the head of armies to protect the English realm, and it well suited the monarch that this immensely powerful position was not hereditary. The castle became the bishop's palace. Much altered through the ages, it has been since 1837 the home of Durham university, founded five years earlier on the initiative of the last prince bishop.

In Norman times Durham was already a place of great ecclesiastical importance, for it was here that the sacred remains of St *Cuthbert were at last brought to a place of safety, three centuries after his death. The Anglo-Saxon cathedral built to house them was pulled down by the Normans, to be replaced by the present building (begun in 1093, largely completed in the next half century). It is the greatest example of *Romanesque architecture in England and one of the best in Europe, notable for the introduction of *rib-vaulting. The Galilee Chapel at the west end (late 12C) contains the remains of the Venerable *Bede.

Bishop of Durham One of the five *Lords Spiritual who sit, regardless of seniority, in the House of Lords. He signs with his Christian name followed by *Dunelm*. The bishop consecrated in 1984 (David Jenkins, b. 1925) became a controversial figure because of his liberal views. While many Anglicans might agree that the Virgin Birth is a myth, there were fewer who shared his view that it is possible to be a Christian without believing in the physical reality of the Resurrection.

Durham County Cricket Club Founded in 1882, on the initiative of the South Shields club, and an original member in 1895 of the minor counties championship. By 1990, when its application to become the 18th team in the *county championship was successful, it had won the lesser contest nine times – a record shared with Buckinghamshire. The club's first season in the championship was 1992, and it was disappointed to finish in bottom place. Its new ground at Chester-le-Street is due to open by 1996.

Durham Miner's Gala Britain's best-known annual demonstration of trade-union pride and solidarity, established in 1871 and held on the second Saturday in July. Each lodge of the local union, led by its colliery band, marches through the city of Durham bearing a painted banner. The destination is the old Durham racecourse, where there have traditionally been speeches by leading politicians of the *Labour party, followed by general festivities. In recent years two factors have reduced the size and importance of the gala – the fall in the number of pits (see *coal), and the reluctance of Labour politicians to maintain their close links with the union movement.

during Her Majesty's pleasure see *McNaughten Rules.

Durovernum see *Canterbury.

Gerald **Durrell** (b. 1925) Zoologist and author, younger brother of Lawrence *Durrell. He has travelled widely on expeditions to collect animals for zoos, and his books and television series combine the pleasures of autobiography, faraway places and natural history. Among the best known are *The Bafut Beagles* (1954) and *My Family and Other Animals* (1956).

Lawrence **Durrell** (1912–90) Poet, novelist and travel-writer who spent the middle years of his life in the eastern Mediterranean. Corfu was his home in the 1930s and was the subject of the first of his island books, *Prospero's Cell* (1945); in the 1950s it was Cyprus which gave him his material for *Bitter Lemons* (1957). With the German occupation of Greece in World War II he moved to Egypt and from 1944 was head of the British Information Office in Alexandria; the ancient city with its polyglot population gave him his material for the *Alexandria Quartet*. His younger brother is Gerald *Durrell.

Dutch elm disease (*Ceratocystis ulmi*) Suffocating fungus which grows beneath the bark of elm trees and is spread by beetles. It was first identified in Holland in 1919, and since then has destroyed many of the world's elms. It was particularly virulent in Britain in the 1970s. Of some 30 million elms in the country, two thirds were calculated to have died by the early 1980s.

Joseph **Duveen** (1869–1939, kt 1919, baron 1933) Art dealer and patron, the first to demonstrate quite how much money great art could fetch in the hands of a great dealer. Several of the leading American collections were formed around European and British masterpieces shipped west by Duveen (*Gainsborough's *Blue Boy* is perhaps the best-known example). But if he reduced the country's store of art, he greatly improved its art institutions – with major benefactions to the National Gallery, the Tate Gallery and the British Museum, where the Duveen Gallery houses the Elgin marbles.

Duxford (14km/9m S of Cambridge) Duxford airfield was an important base for Spitfires during the Battle of Britain. Since 1976 it has been a branch of the *Imperial War Museum, with more than 100 aircraft on display together with military vehicles and other items such as midget submarines.

DVLC see *Swansea.

Anthony van **Dyck** (1599–1641, kt 1632) Painter of the Flemish school, whose stay in England for the last nine years of his life influenced the style of English portraiture for the next two centuries. Born in Antwerp, he was in his teens an assistant in the studio of *Rubens before firmly establishing his brilliance as a portraitist during five years in Genoa (1622–7). Settling in London in 1632, he was immediately made principal painter to Charles I and to the queen, Henrietta Maria. It is his images that now bring to mind the ill-fated royal pair and their Cavalier court, capturing a languorous elegance and barely concealed conviction of natural superiority. That easy arrogance was dented by the English Civil War, but Van Dyck's relatively informal full-length portraits, in sumptuous clothes and often in landscape settings, inspired later painters such as *Gainsborough. He was buried in St Paul's Cathedral, but his monument there was destroyed in the Great Fire.

D'ye ken John Peel? The most popular of hunting songs, celebrating the most enthusiastic of huntsmen. John Peel (1776–1854) was a Cumberland farmer who maintained his own pack of hounds for more than 50 years. The lyric, by Peel's friend John Graves (1795–1886), is said to have been written impromptu when the two men were in a pub and someone enquired as to the correct words of this old Cumberland folk tune. If so the final verse, lamenting Peel's death, is clearly a later addition.

Dyfed (351,000 in 1991, administrative centre Carmarthen) Since 1974 a *county in Wales, formed from Carmarthenshire, Pembrokeshire and Cardiganshire.

'dying beyond my means' see Oscar *Wilde.

J.B. **Dykes** (John Bacchus Dykes, 1823–76) Anglican clergyman with an improbable middle name who wrote several of the most familiar hymn tunes, including those for *Lead, kindly Light*, *Praise to the Holiest in the height* and *The King of love my Shepherd is*.

Dyson Perrins Museum see *Worcester porcelain.

E

'each man kills the thing he loves' see The *Ballad of Reading Gaol.

Eagle Boy's comic founded in 1950 by Marcus Morris, a clergyman. Its ulterior motive was revealed by the presence of St Paul, whose journeys at first occupied the back page, but it sold on the appeal of *Dan Dare and to a lesser extent on the humorous adventures of the incompetent Harris Tweed, Extra Special Agent (a reference to the contemporary character *Dick Barton). In the early years *PC 49 was also a regular. Eagle lasted until 1969 and was revived in a different format in 1982.

Ealing comedies Numerous films were made by Ealing Studios (run by Michael *Balcon at Ealing in west London), but the term 'Ealing comedies' is used in particular of a very successful group in the late 1940s. They brilliantly combined anarchy and British eccentricity, as seen in The *Lavender Hill Mob, *Whisky Galore, *Kind Hearts and Coronets or *Passport to Pimlico. The last three all came out in May–June 1949.

Robert **Eames** (b. 1937) Anglican archbishop of *Armagh since 1986, having previously been bishop of Derry and Raphoe (1975–80) and of Down and Dromore (1980–6). Like his Roman Catholic counterpart, Cardinal *Daly, he was educated in Belfast.

earl The third rank in the *peerage. Until the 18C earldoms were always attached to a place (Earl of Devon) but then an alternative custom developed of using the family name (Earl Russell). An earl's wife is a countess, as also is a woman inheriting an earldom which descends through the female line.

Earl Grey see Earl *Grey.

Earl Marshal An officer of state who is head of the *College of Arms and is responsible for all major ceremonial events, such as coronations and royal marriages and funerals. From 1316 the post was held mainly by the earls and dukes of Norfolk, and since 1672 it has been hereditary in their family. By a paradox of history their religion, as Britain's leading Roman Catholic family, made it impossible for them to fulfil their high office until the *Emancipation Act of 1829.

Earl's Barton (10km/6m E of Northampton) Village with a magnificent Saxon church (All Saints, 10C). The west tower is famous for its 'long and short work' (alternating vertical and horizontal slabs at the outer edges of the tower) and for the decorative stone strips on the flat surfaces, in patterns similar to wood on the exterior of a timber-frame building.

Earl's Court (London SW5) District taking its name from the court held here in the middle ages by the earls of Warwick and Holland, who were lords of the manor. It is best known now for the great exhibition hall, opened in 1937, where events such as the *Boat Show, the *Ideal Home Exhibition and the *Royal Tournament are held. The midwinter event is the Boat Show, held in early January every year since 1960 (with many of the craft afloat). It had previously been at Olympia, from 1955; before that, from 1921, boats had been included in the Motor Show.

early English style see *Gothic.

earnings see *average earnings.

'Earth has not anything to show more fair' see *Westminster Bridge.

Eas a'Chùal Aluinn Highest waterfall in the British Isles with a fall of 200m/658ft, at the head of Loch Glencoul in the Highland region of Scotland.

East Anglia Low-lying area of eastern England between the Wash in the north and the Thames estuary in the south, loosely defined but including the counties of Norfolk and Suffolk and parts of Cambridgeshire and Essex. The flat watery landscape of the *Fens and the *Norfolk Broads, with vast expanses of sky, has inspired many English painters and in particular Constable. East Anglia was one of the seven *Anglo-Saxon kingdoms, but was overrun by the Danes in the 9C.

East End The area to the east of the old walled city of London, stretching from the Tower of London along the north bank of the Thames. Much of it lies within the modern borough of Tower Hamlets. As the home of the *cockneys, the East End (named in contrast to the *West End) has historically had an image of poverty tempered by great vitality. The London docks, now defunct, were an essential part of the area's economy and the modern *Docklands development will inevitably much alter the district.

EastEnders (BBC from 1985) Twice-weekly soap opera with which the BBC has challenged the long-established pre-eminence in the ratings of *Coronation Street. The BBC soap is set in a similar working-class urban area – a fictional London square (Albert Square in the supposed borough of Walford) rather than a fictional Manchester street – but from the start it made a point of dealing with more controversial issues and allowing more provocative language than Coronation Street. Dirty Den, played by Leslie Grantham, has been among the most popular characters, as are Michelle and Pauline Fowler (Susan Tully, Wendy Richard).

Eastern Question The source of continuous friction throughout the 19c, as the European powers jockeyed to benefit from the crumbling of the Ottoman Turkish empire. At the start of the century this stretched from Greece all the way round the Mediterranean to Egypt. Britain's most active involvement in the resulting conflicts was in the *Crimean War, but it continued with the *jingoism of the 1870s.

Easter Rising (24–29 Apr. 1916) The most dramatic of the events in the struggle for *Home Rule in Ireland. The uprising had been planned by several of the radical nationalist groups and it began with the seizing of the General Post Office in Dublin's great thoroughfare, O'Connell Street. From its pillared portico Patrick Pearse read out a proclamation announcing the birth of the Irish Republic. Sniping and shelling in the streets lasted until the end of the week, when the rebels surrendered. Pearse, James Connolly and a dozen others were executed, their martyrdom (unlike their uprising) serving to create much sympathy for their cause.

East India Company Granted a charter by Elizabeth I in 1600 to trade with the East Indies, the company soon concentrated on India where competition with the Dutch was less intense. By 1700 it was trading from fortified townships at *Bombay, Madras and *Calcutta, which subsequently became the capital cities of the company's three presidencies.

In the 18c the power of the company was for the first time extended by military means, particularly under Robert *Clive. With almost unlimited opportunities for corruption, company officials were soon returning with vast fortunes to Britain, where they became known as 'nabobs' (a version of the Indian word *nawab*, a princely ruler). Resentment of the nabobs played a large part in the impeachment of Warren *Hastings.

The company extended its power through India by war and by a series of protective alliances with individual kingdoms, until by the 19c (when it was known colloquially as John Company) it had become a vast administrative and military organization. The cost of running this was increasingly supported by an unsavoury trade, the export of opium from India to sell in China – a prolonged abuse which led to the *Opium Wars.

The company lasted until 1858, by which time the *Indian Mutiny had persuaded the government in London to take direct charge of Indian affairs.

'Oh, East is East, and West is West, and never the twain shall meet' The opening of *The Ballad of East and West* (1889) by Rudyard *Kipling. The poem is an action-packed tale, with a galloping rhythm, about the Colonel's son riding out after the bandit Kamal, who has stolen the Colonel's favourite mare in the northwest territory of India, near the Khyber Pass. Each man learns to respect the other, allowing the conclusion that there is neither East nor West 'when two strong men stand face to face, though they come from the ends of the earth'.

East Lothian Until 1975 a *county on the east coast of Scotland, to the south of the Firth of Forth, now part of the Lothian region.

East Lynne (1861) First novel by Mrs Henry Wood (1814–87), which became the basis of the most popular of all *melodramas on the Victorian stage. The plot concerns a disgraced mother, later disfigured beyond all recognition in a railway accident, who returns secretly home and is employed as governess to her own dying child – making possible the play's most famous line, 'dead, dead, dead! and he never knew me, never called me mother!'.

The imperial Russian bear embraces Turkey: Punch*'s view, in 1853, of the underlying danger in the Eastern Question.*

'East of Suez' see *Mandalay*.

East Pakistan see *Bangladesh.

East Sussex (717,000 in 1991, administrative centre Lewes) Since 1974 a *county on the south coast of England, previously part of Sussex.

'Eating *pâtés de foie gras* to the sound of trumpets' see Sydney *Smith.

Eboracum see *York.

EC (European Community) The origins of the EC date back as far as 1950, just five years after the end of World War II, when the French foreign minister, Robert Schuman, put forward a far-sighted plan to merge the coal and steel industries of France and Germany – a measure calculated to have both economic and peace-keeping benefits. By 1952 this idea had developed into the European Coal and Steel Community (ECSC), in which six countries (France, Germany, Italy, Belgium, the Netherlands, Luxembourg) formed a common market, without tariff barriers, in coal and steel. In 1957, with the Treaty of Rome, the same six countries established the European Economic Community (EEC). Often referred to in Britain as the Common Market, this extended the level of international cooperation to cover free trade in all commodities, free movement of labour, and a commitment to steadily greater economic integration between the member states.

The European Community was created in 1967 to bring together the EEC, the ECSC and the European Atomic Energy Community (EURATOM), enabling them to share the same political and administrative institutions. These include the *European Commission, which is the executive branch; the *Council of Ministers, the main decision-making body; the elected *European Parliament; and the *European Court of Justice.

Negotiations were begun in 1961 for four of the *EFTA countries (United Kingdom, Ireland, Denmark and Norway) to join the Community, but this development was vetoed by the French president, General de Gaulle – in 1963 and again in 1967. In 1973 the United Kingdom, Ireland and Denmark did finally join (the people of Norway had decided not to do so in a referendum in 1972). In Britain a Labour government came to power in 1974 and held in 1975 the country's first referendum, posing the question whether to stay in the EC; the vote went 2 to 1 in favour of doing so. Greece (1981) and Spain and Portugal (1986) have brought the number of members to 12. By early 1993 formal applications for membership had also been received from Sweden, Finland, Austria, Malta, Turkey, Cyprus and Norway; the Norwegian application, presented in November 1992, was the fourth time the country had embarked on the process of joining.

In 1962 the Community introduced a Common Agricultural Policy (CAP) to protect farmers against the import of cheaper foodstuffs. The inefficiencies of this system, which led to vast subsidies and overproduction (the notorious 'butter mountain' being followed by similar surpluses of wheat and wine), dominated Community politics until the mid-80s, when reforms began to be introduced. Since then the main topic of disagreement has been the speed of advance towards full economic integration. The *EMS (European Monetary System) was introduced in 1979. The longer-term plan is for EMU (Economic and Monetary Union), with a European bank and a single currency. A broad consensus on the way forward was agreed between member states, with considerable difficulty, at *Maastricht in December 1991. A single market was introduced on 1 January 1993, in principle establishing the completely free passage of goods between nation states and the ending of border formalities within the community for EC nationals.

Eccles cake A filling of moist currants enclosed within flaky pastry. It is a speciality of Eccles in Greater Manchester.

Eclipse (foaled 1764) Chestnut colt which was the most successful racehorse of the 18C, named because he was foaled during a total eclipse of the sun. He ran 18 recorded races, winning them all (a win/loss record still unbeaten). Three of the first five *Derby winners were sired by him and he is the ancestor of the majority of *thoroughbreds. His skeleton is preserved in the National Horseracing Museum at Newmarket. The Eclipse Stakes, named in his honour in 1886, is run at *Sandown Park.

'economic miracle' A concept believed in by many in Britain in the late 1980s, during the artificial boom presided over by Mrs Thatcher as prime minister and Nigel Lawson as chancellor of the exchequer (he used the phrase during the budget debate in 1988). By the early 1990s, with recession in danger of turning into slump, the two words had retreated within ironic quotation marks.

economical with the truth A phrase which entered everyday language after being used in Australia by Robert Armstrong, then secretary of the cabinet, in his evidence in the *Spycatcher case. He used it of a letter to the publisher of an earlier but related book, in which he had not mentioned that he already knew its contents (from a proof copy acquired before publication, legitimately but in confidence). The phrase was widely taken to be his own invention and a euphemism for lying. In fact he was quoting Edmund *Burke who, in one of his *Letters on a* *Regicide Peace*, argues that there is sometimes genuine need for an 'economy of the truth'.

The phrase acquired a new version in 1992 when the former trade minister Alan Clark admitted, during the trial of Matrix Churchill executives for supplying arms to Iraq, that he had advised the company to be 'economical with the *actualité*' when applying for an export licence.

The Economist Weekly journal on economic and political matters, founded in 1843 to promote the cause of *free trade in the campaign for the repeal of the *Corn Laws. It became very influential under the editorship, from 1860, of Walter *Bagehot. With a large international readership and a circulation of about 500,000 (nearly half of it in the USA), the *Economist* is now printed each Thursday night in six regions of the world (UK, Holland, Switzerland, USA, Singapore, Hong Kong).

ECSC see *EC.

ECU (European Currency Unit) Currency established by the *EMS (European Monetary System), used for payments between member states. Its value fluctuates according to a weighted value of currencies in the system.

Pat **Eddery** (b. 1952) Irish jockey who has for many years been prominent in British racing. In his twenties he was *champion jockey in four successive years (1974–7) and he had another run of successive championships from the late 1980s. In 1990 he became the first jockey since Gordon *Richards (in 1947) to ride more than 200 winners in a British flat-racing season.

Paul **Eddington** (b. 1927) Comedy actor known in particular for two successful TV series, The *Good Life and * Yes, Minister.

Eddystone lighthouses The Eddystone Rocks, at the western end of the English Channel (23km/14m from Plymouth), were sufficient hazard to prompt the construction of the world's first offshore lighthouse. This was a wooden tower (1696–9); it was swept away in a storm in 1703 together with its designer, Henry Winstanley (1644–1703), and his crew. A replacement of wood and iron was completed in 1708 but destroyed by fire in 1755. The third attempt, designed by John *Smeaton in a technique of dovetailed stones which was to become standard, lasted from 1759 for more than a century, until the rocks below it began to crumble. In 1882 it was replaced by the present lighthouse, designed by James Douglass (1826–98).

Anthony **Eden** (1897–1977, KG 1954, earl of Avon 1961) Conservative politician, prime minister 1955–7. His career, which ended in misfortune, had begun early and brilliantly. He entered the House of Commons in 1923 as MP for Warwick and Leamington and in 1935, at the age of 38, became foreign secretary in Baldwin's coalition government. He resigned from this office in 1938 in protest at the attempts by the new prime minister, Neville Chamberlain, to appease Hitler. Under Churchill he returned for two later spells as foreign secretary (1940–5 and 1951–5). He succeeded Churchill as prime minister but had not made his mark before being overwhelmed by the *Suez Crisis. The dramatic failure of this military adventure led to a collapse in his already frail health and to his resignation.

Edgar (c.1075–1107) King of Scotland from 1097, the first of three sons of Malcolm III and Margaret to inherit the throne. He accepted William II of England as his overlord. Dying unmarried, he was succeeded by Alexander I.

Edinburgh Castle on its rock above the National Gallery of Scotland, with the Scott monument and Princes Street on the right.

Liz Edgar (Liz Broome, b. 1943, m. Ted Edgar 1964) Show jumper with a record number of five wins in the most prestigious of women's contests, the Queen Elizabeth II Cup at the *Royal International Horse Show (1977, 79, 81, 82, 86). David *Broome is her brother.

Edgbaston (Birmingham) Suburb best known for its cricket ground, the home of *Warwickshire County Cricket Club which acquired the land in 1886. A Test match was first played at Edgbaston in 1902, and it has remained a regular Test venue.

Edgehill (23 Oct. 1642) Inconclusive battle in Warwickshire which was the first engagement in the *English Civil War, with Charles I at the head of the royalist army against the parliamentarians under the earl of Essex.

Edinburgh (419,000 in 1981) Capital of Scotland. The old part of the city is dominated by *Edinburgh Castle, high on its rock. From the 11c a town developed around this, particularly on the route down the hill along Lawn Market, High Street (with *St Giles and the John *Knox house) and Canongate. Together these are known as the Royal Mile. At the bottom or east end of this was the abbey of Holyrood, founded in the 12c; in its grounds stands the Palace of *Holyroodhouse. With its courtyards of tall tenement houses on the steep slope, the Old Town retains a medieval atmosphere. But by the 18c, when Edinburgh's sophistication earned it the nickname 'Athens of the north', the need was felt for a more dignified modern city.

South of the Royal Mile is Edinburgh's ancient educational district. The university, established in 1582, now has as its central building the Old College designed in 1789 by Robert Adam. The Heriot-Watt university derives from the School of Arts and Mechanics Institute established in 1821. And George Heriot's School was founded in 1628 from the bequest of a rich jeweller and banker to James I and VI; it occupies a very striking 17c building in a Scottish Renaissance style.

The New Town, built on open space to the north of the old city, was launched by an act of parliament in 1767. The competition for its design was won by a young Scottish architect, James Craig (c.1740–95), who put forward the simple grid design which survives today. It is based on three parallel streets, *Princes Street, George Street and Queen Street. The most distinguished single feature of the New Town is usually considered to be *Charlotte Square, at the west end of George Street. The Mound, a causeway across the valley between new and old Edinburgh, was created by dumping some 2 million cartloads of earth excavated in 1781–1830 during construction of the New Town.

In the early 1990s another new area is being added to the west of the city, with the intention of replacing the New Town as Edinburgh's business and financial district. To be known as Edinburgh Park, it is being laid out within a broad design by the American modernist architect Richard Meier.

Edinburgh contains many of Scotland's most important institutions, such as the *National Gallery of Scotland, the *National Library of Scotland and the *Royal Museum of Scotland; it also has the second oldest *botanic gardens in Britain. Every August the city becomes an international arts centre with the *Edinburgh Festival.

Duke of **Edinburgh** (also known as Prince Philip, b.1921) The husband of *Elizabeth II. His father was Prince Andrew of Greece and his mother Princess Alice of Battenberg (sister of Lord *Mountbatten). Educated at *Gordonstoun and as a naval cadet at Dartmouth, he served in the Royal Navy in World War II. In February 1947 he took British nationality and adopted his mother's family name of Mountbatten; in November of that year he married Princess Elizabeth in Westminster Abbey. He remained on active service as a naval officer until her accession to the throne in 1952. He was created duke of Edinburgh and styled *HRH from just before his marriage, but was not accorded the status of a British prince until 1957. Prominent among his many spheres of interest have been projects for the young (the *Duke of Edinburgh's Award Scheme) and nature conservation (in particular the World Wide Fund for Nature). He has represented Britain on several occasions in the sport of four-in-hand carriage driving.

Edinburgh airport In origin one of Britain's earliest surviving airports, dating back to a grass strip at Turnhouse used for training by the Royal Flying Corps during World War I. It remained a military airport until 1947, when BEA began the first commercial service between London and Edinburgh; but it was not until 1976 that an appropriate terminal building was opened. Edinburgh is now second only to Glasgow among Scotland's airports.

Edinburgh Castle There were fortifications on the great rock at Edinburgh from the 7c, but the present castle was begun in the 11c by Malcolm III. Its oldest surviving building, St Margaret's Chapel, is named after his wife and was built either by her or by her son.

The castle is approached across the broad Esplanade, the site of the famous Military Tattoo during the Edinburgh Festival but noted also for its macabre Witches' Well, where more than 300 women were burned as witches between 1479 and 1722. Crown Square is the summit of the castle and is flanked by the main parts of the palace (15–17c), including the great banqueting hall (known as the Old Parliament Hall, because the Scottish parliament sat here until 1639) and the Crown Room, with a permanent display of the *crown jewels of Scotland. In the dungeons beneath is *Mons Meg. The west side of Crown Square is occupied by the Scottish United Services Museum, established in the 1920s and linked in origin with its neighbour on the north side – the Scottish National War Memorial (1927, by Robert Lorimer), with the marble Stone of Remembrance set on an outcrop of bare rock.

Edinburgh Festival Running for three weeks in August every year since 1947, the Edinburgh International Festival of Music and Drama claims now to be the largest arts festival in the world. This is due to the growth of the so-called Fringe, formed of literally hundreds of small companies which crowd in to add their performances to those more officially on offer. The most famous show to have emerged from the festival, * *Beyond the Fringe*, was in spite of its title an official production.

Edinburgh Gazette The government's bulletin for Scotland, in which official announcements are made. It was founded in 1699 and appears twice a week. The equivalent for the rest of Britain is the * *London Gazette*.

Edinburgh Zoo Established by Thomas Gillespie and opened to the public in 1913 – four years after the founding of the Zoological Society of Scotland. It became famous in 1919 for its successful hatching of a king penguin chick. The penguins, the first seen outside the Antarctic, had been received in 1914 from a whaling expedition; and the resulting colony is still a special pride of the zoo.

Edmund Ironside see *Canute.

Aunt **Edna** Name coined by Terence *Rattigan (in a 1953 preface to his collected plays) for the typical middle-aged and middle-class woman in a matinée audience. A similarly average Edna was developed at the same moment, in the mid-1950s, by the Australian performer Barry Humphries (b. 1934), when he created an antipodean housewife, Edna Everage (the name was coincidental, being based on an Edna who was once his nanny). In

Humphries' outrageously flamboyant and witty impersonation, this other Edna grew rapidly in stature; she eventually acquired the title of Dame and became a Housewife Superstar, practising the art of the put-down on assorted celebrities in peak-time television programmes.

education The earliest schools in Britain were the *grammar schools, from which there gradually emerged the *public schools. From the 17c onwards many educational establishments were founded by rival Christian sects, while at a village level simple instruction was on offer in the so-called dame schools, where a local woman taught children for a small fee. In the 19c the state gradually began to accept responsibility for the nation's education. The most important of the early education acts was that of 1870, also called Forster's Act from the MP who introduced it; it set up a network of free secular primary schools alongside the existing sectarian schools, to provide education up to the age of 11. A subsequent act (1880) made attendance compulsory, and another in 1891 established that state schools must be entirely free of even subsidiary charges.

In modern times the Education Act of 1944 extended the principle of free compulsory schooling to secondary education, raising the school-leaving age to 15; it gave local authorities the obligation to provide secondary modern schools for all who failed to gain admittance to *grammar schools. The school-leaving age was raised to 16 in 1963. Education is now compulsory from 5 to 16 in England, Wales and Scotland, and from 4 to 16 in Northern Ireland. There is no legal requirement for education below those ages, but most local authorities cater for this age group; in the early 1990s about 50% of children at the ages of 3 and 4 go to a public sector school of some kind.

In the 1960s there were two major reports on education. The Newsom Report of 1963 (chaired by John

Schooling at village level, at the hands of a strict disciplinarian, in the days before the education acts (c.1820).

Education: government expenditure, in £bn

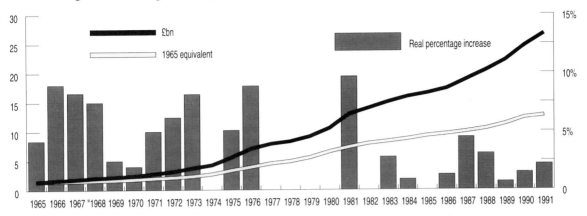

The lower line is the 1965 figure adjusted each year for inflation; the gap between the lines is therefore the cumulative real increase in expenditure.   *Source:* Annual Abstract of Statistics *(see *Central Statistical Office).*

Newsom) dealt with secondary education, placing special emphasis on the needs of children of average and below average ability; the Plowden Report of 1967 (chaired by Bridget Plowden) did the same for primary education. By the late 1970s grammar schools and secondary moderns had been largely replaced by *comprehensive schools under local authority control. A recent swing of the political pendulum away from this system has been the Conservative policy of *opting out. See also *examinations; and for further education see *universities and *TECs.

Department for **Education** (DFE, London SE1) Government department responsible for the broad system of schooling in England and Wales, from primary level to universities. (The same responsibilities for Scotland are covered by the *Scottish Office.) The department was established in 1964, as a result of the Robbins Report and the Newsom Report. Until 1992, when scientific research was moved to the new Office of *Public Service and Science, the department was known as the DES (Department of Education and Science). It has since been called the DFE (Department for Education). For secretaries of state since 1983 see the *cabinet.

Prince **Edward** (born 1964) The youngest child of Elizabeth II (see the *royal family). After being educated at Gordonstoun and at Jesus College, Cambridge, he joined the Royal Marines in 1986 but in 1987 resigned his commission. Since then he has been professionally involved in theatrical production and has taken an active part in the *Duke of Edinburgh's Award Scheme.

Edward I (1239–1307) King of England from 1272; eldest son of *Henry III and Eleanor of Provence; married in 1254 Eleanor of Castile, who died in 1290 and for whom he put up the *Eleanor Crosses.

Edward's reign was marked by an aggressively expansionist policy against both Wales and Scotland. In Wales he succeeded in overwhelming *Llewelyn ap Gruffydd and in holding down his territories with a ring of rapidly constructed but massively strong castles (Caernarfon, Harlech, Conwy, Beaumaris). In Scotland he was given an opportunity to intervene when the death of Margaret, the Maid of Norway, left the country without an obvious heir. Edward invaded in 1296, removing to Westminster the famous Stone of *Scone, but with opponents of the quality of William *Wallace and *Robert the Bruce he found himself engaged in years of ineffectual campaigning.

At home he showed great skill in his control of the barons. He used parliament to mobilize support for his policies and summoned in 1295 what later became known as the *Model Parliament. One group to suffer from his ruthless methods was the Jews, who were first stripped of their wealth and then in 1290 expelled from the country. Edward died in 1307 on his way north to attempt to reconquer Scotland. He was succeeded by his son Edward II (see the *royal house).

Edward II (1284–1327) King of England from 1307; fourth but oldest surviving son of Edward I and Eleanor of Castile; married in 1308 Isabella, daughter of Philip IV of France.

It is not surprising that Edward's life, a dramatic blend of sexual and political intrigue, was made the subject of one of England's earliest history plays, *Edward II* by Christopher Marlowe. The resentment of the barons at the king's long-standing favourite Piers Gaveston, with whom he is assumed to have had a homosexual relationship, ended with the murder of Gaveston. Later the power of a new favourite, Hugh le Despenser, provoked Queen Isabella and her lover Roger Mortimer to a rebellion which ended in the imprisonment of Edward. He was deposed in January 1327 in favour of his son, Edward III (see the *royal house), and was moved to Berkeley Castle. He died there in September, almost certainly murdered. Within a few years the gory tradition was already in circulation, fuelled by rumours of the king's homosexuality, that the instrument of death had been a red-hot skewer up the anus.

The chief military problem of Edward's reign had been the presence of a strong ruler in Scotland, *Robert the Bruce, who inflicted a major defeat on Edward at *Bannockburn in 1314 and so was able to drive the English south of the border.

Edward III (1312–77) King of England from 1327; eldest son of Edward II and Isabella of France; married in 1328 Philippa of Hainaut.

Once he was free of the influence of his mother (see *Edward II) and of her lover (Roger Mortimer, whom he seized and executed in 1330), the young Edward set about reasserting the expansionist policies of his grandfather, *Edward I. He had some success in Scotland, but his main thrust was towards France, to the throne of which he laid claim through his mother. The resulting sporadic conflict, prolonged far beyond his reign, was known later as the *Hundred Years' War.

There was no conclusion or profit in that struggle with France, in spite of individual English victories such as Crécy (1346) and Poitiers (1356), but Edward's reign later came to seem something of a golden age with the romance of medieval chivalry – whether in the exploits of his son, the *Black Prince, or in the founding of the Order of the *Garter.

It was also the last period of stability in England for more than a century. The Black Prince died before his father, causing Edward to be succeeded by a 10-year-old grandson, Richard II (see the *royal house). It was the descendants of two of Edward's other sons, the dukes of Lancaster and of York, who later fought for the throne in the *Wars of the Roses.

Edward IV (1442–83) King of England from 1461, except for six months in 1470–1; eldest surviving son of Richard, duke of York, and Cicely Neville; married in 1464 Elizabeth Woodville.

He was the first Yorkist king (the dukedom of York being his hereditary title) and his accession to the throne was achieved in the turmoil of the *Wars of the Roses. He was descended from two of the sons of Edward III (see the *royal house), but his claim became strong only through the weakness of his cousin *Henry VI. Edward's greatest advantage was that he was related, through his mother, to the most powerful baron in England, *Warwick the Kingmaker. In 1461 Henry VI fled to Scotland and Edward was crowned in London.

There were several reverses ahead. Edward lost the support of Warwick through marrying a commoner, Elizabeth *Woodville, and giving to her family the royal favour which had previously been Warwick's. With Warwick's help Henry VI was now returned to the throne (Oct. 1470), but Edward defeated Warwick at Barnet in April 1471, after which he had Henry murdered.

Edward had proved himself a brilliant general, using tactics such as unexpected forced marches (on one occasion of more than 64km/40m). In 1475, in the final gasp of the *Hundred Years' War, he landed a vast army in France; but he brought his soldiers home, without a blow being struck, in return for a fat French pension for life. With the benefits of peace he was soon making improvements in both finance and administration, but he died of a sudden illness when he was only 40. He was succeeded briefly by his 12-year-old son, Edward V (see the *royal house).

Edward V (1470–83?) King of England from April to June 1483; son of *Edward IV and Elizabeth Woodville. The beginning and end of his short life reflected alike the violence of the times. He was born in the sanctuary of Westminster Abbey where his mother had taken refuge when his father was briefly deposed. Two months after his own accession to the throne, in 1483, a preacher at St Paul's argued that his father's marriage had been invalid, that Edward was therefore a bastard and that the rightful heir was his father's younger brother Richard, duke of Gloucester. Three days later (June 25) an assembly at Westminster invited the duke to take the crown, which he did as *Richard III (see the *royal house). The 12-year-old Edward and his younger brother were last seen in the Tower of London, and the fate of the two *princes in the Tower has been a matter of conjecture ever since.

Edward VI (1537–1553) King of England and Ireland from 1547; the only son of Henry VIII; his mother, Jane Seymour, died 12 days after he was born.

The policy of the reign was at first dictated by the young king's uncle, Edward Seymour (c.1500–52), who became protector and duke of Somerset in 1547. Somerset was moderate in his religious policy; Cranmer's first *Book of Common Prayer, for example, imposed on the country in 1549, was not extreme in its Protestantism.

Edward VI, at the age of about nine, holding a Tudor rose: studio of William Scrots, c.1546.

But Somerset was ousted in that year by John Dudley, duke of Northumberland (1502–53), who had him imprisoned and later executed.

Northumberland was unscrupulous and his policies were more aggressively anti-Catholic. Enriching himself with Roman Catholic properties, he married his son to Lady Jane *Grey (a great-granddaughter of Henry VII) and then persuaded the dying 16-year-old king to write a will bequeathing her crown. The plot failed, and Edward was succeeded by his sister, Mary I, who executed Northumberland for treason.

Edward VII (1841–1910) King of Great Britain and Ireland from 1901; eldest son of Victoria and of Albert of Saxe-Coburg-Gotha; married in 1863 Alexandra, daughter of the heir to the throne of Denmark.

When he was only a month old his mother created him prince of *Wales, so he was known as this for all but the last decade of his life. His enjoyment of slightly *risqué* society, of gambling (the *baccarat scandal) and of racing (on two occasions a horse of his won the Derby and the St Leger in the same season) was not well calculated to please Victoria, who much preferred the earnest ways of his father. So Edward was excluded from any serious public role until his accession, by which time he was nearly 60. A caricature by Max Beerbohm suggests perfectly the awkwardness of his relationship with his mother.

His reign of nine years introduced a mood of sumptuousness and enjoyment which was in marked contrast to the late Victorian era, contributing to his considerable popularity as king. He travelled a great deal, making use of the fact that nearly all the royal families of Europe were his cousins. He particularly encouraged closer ties with France and Russia. He was succeeded in 1910 by his second son, George V.

Edward VIII (1894–1972) King of Great Britain and Northern Ireland 20 January–11 December 1936; eldest son of George V and Mary of Teck; married Wallis Warfield Simpson in 1937.

He was invested as prince of *Wales at Caernarfon in 1911. He had been educated at the Royal Naval College (first at Osborne, then at Dartmouth), but nevertheless served in World War I in the army (Grenadier Guards), as ADC to Sir John French and then to Lord Cavan. After the war he made a very successful series of tours to all parts of the empire. His brief reign was dominated by the *abdication crisis, as a result of which he was succeeded by his brother (as George VI) and was himself created duke of Windsor. On the night of his abdication speech to the nation on radio, he left Portsmouth on a naval destroyer and went to France. There, some six months later, he married Mrs Simpson; but on cabinet advice George VI denied the duchess royal status. Apart from the war years, when the duke was appointed governor of the Bahamas, the couple lived in France. The duchess died in 1986.

Edward, the Black Prince see the *Black Prince.

Edward the Confessor (St Edward, *c.*1003-1066) King of England from 1042; son of Ethelred the Unready and of Emma, daughter of the duke of Normandy; married in 1045 Edith, daughter of Godwin, earl of Wessex.

He spent his formative years (1016–41) in Normandy, and during his reign offended the English by favouring Normans at court. He was opposed by his powerful father-in-law, Godwin. Edward, who had no children, seems to

Caricature by Max Beerbohm: The rare, the rather awful visits of Edward, Prince of Wales, to Windsor Castle.

have promised his crown to William, duke of Normandy. But on his deathbed he named as his heir Godwin's son, whose accession as *Harold II was followed by the Norman *Conquest.

Edward had a reputation for holiness and for working miracles (he is the first king known to have touched for the *king's evil), and he was canonized in 1161 with a feast day on October 13. He was later called the Confessor, meaning one who bears witness to the Christian faith in his life but is not martyred. The name distinguished him from an earlier English king, Edward the Martyr (962–78), who was murdered in his teens and whose remains were held to have miraculous powers.

Edwardian Used specifically of the reign of *Edward VII (1901–10), most often in relation to fashion and social customs. The period, with its sweeping dresses, broad-brimmed hats and parasols, but with the horrors of World War I looming ahead, has acquired the nostalgic flavour of a sunlit interlude before the abrupt end of an era.

Gareth **Edwards** (b. 1947) Rugby union player, at scrum half, for Cardiff – with 53 caps for Wales (1967–78) and ten for the *Lions (1968–74). He first played for Wales before his 20th birthday, and became the youngest captain of the national team less than a year later. His try for the *Barbarians against the New Zealand All Blacks at Cardiff in 1973 is considered one of rugby's hallowed moments. His 53 Welsh caps were in consecutive matches, an unbroken series which is a record in the international game (whether it is equalled by 53 successive Irish caps in the career of Willie John *McBride depends on differing interpretations of what constitutes a fully international event).

Nicholas **Edwards** (b. 1934, baron Crickhowell 1987) Conservative politician, MP for Pembroke 1970–87. He entered the cabinet in 1979 as secretary of state for Wales (1979–87).

Edzell Castle (56km/35m SW of Aberdeen) Ruined castle, famous for the survival of its 'pleasance' or secret garden. This was laid out in 1604, with a series of allegorical sculptures set into the surrounding walls.

EEA (European Economic Area) Trading area merging the *EC and *EFTA nations into a single market. Preliminary agreement as a first stage towards establishing it was reached in 1992.

EEC see *EC.

Eeny meeny miney mo The most popular of children's counting rhymes, particularly when a child has to be chosen for some role in a game, the choice falling with the last syllable. (The traditional but unconvincing theory has been that it derives from the *Druids choosing a victim for human sacrifice.) The opening line, found in similar form in other languages, is believed to relate back to an otherwise forgotten set of early numerals. The British version of the second line used to be 'catch a tinker by his toe', but this was ousted by the American 'catch a nigger'. Since this is now unacceptable, a rhyming character from A.A. Milne's *The House at Pooh Corner* has been pressed into service in at least some parts of Britain, the result becoming:

> Eeny meeny miney mo,
> Catch a tigger by his toe;
> If he squeals, let him go,
> Eeny meeny miney mo.

EETPU see *AEEU.

Eeyore see A.A. *Milne.

EFA (European Fighter Aircraft) Joint project by Germany, Italy, Spain and the UK, designed to be ready to go into service with the national air forces by the year 2000. Germany proposed in 1992 to withdraw, on the grounds that the plane was too expensive, but was persuaded to continue with a revised version, about 15% cheaper, which was named the NEFA (New European Fighter Aircraft).

EFTA (European Free Trade Association) Organization established in 1960 by seven European countries (Austria, Denmark, Norway, Portugal, Sweden, Switzerland, United Kingdom) to achieve benefits similar to those of the European Economic Community. Iceland and Finland later joined, but in 1973 the UK, Denmark and Portugal left to join the *EC. The headquarters are in Geneva.

Eglinton Tournament (28 Aug. 1839) An elaborately reconstructed medieval tournament, held at Eglinton in the Strathclyde region of Scotland. On what turned out to be a day of torrential rain, young Victorian aristocrats jousted in the lists before a Queen of Beauty in a mood of nostalgia for a more glamorous past inspired by the novels of Walter *Scott.

Egypt Britain's close involvement with Egypt began in 1875, when the bankrupt Egyptian khedive sold most of his *Suez Canal shares to the British government. British intervention to control a series of uprisings led to effective occupation of the country from 1883 to 1914. In spite of the British presence, Egypt was still nominally a part of the Ottoman empire. But in 1914, with Turkey on the opposing side in World War I, Britain declared Egypt a British protectorate. In 1922 the country became an independent monarchy, which lasted until the second king, Farouk, was deposed by the army in 1952. The disastrous culmination of this long involvement was the *Suez crisis.

Eikon Basilike (Greek for 'image of a king', 1649) Collection of meditations and prayers, supposedly written by *Charles I in captivity, published on the day of the executed king's burial. The book had an immense effect, which parliament attempted to counter with a less successful reply later in the same year – *Milton's *Eikonoklastes* ('Image Breaker').

Eilean Donan (coast of mainland opposite Skye) One of the most romantically sited castles in Scotland, on a rocky island just offshore at the mouth of Loch Duich, an inlet on the west coast. There was a castle here at least from the 13C, but the present building is a careful reconstruction (1912–32).

eisteddfod (Welsh for a 'sitting' or 'session') Any gathering of poets and musicians in Wales is an eisteddfod, in a tradition going back to the medieval *bards. The best-known is the National Eisteddfod of Wales (now in full the Royal National Eisteddfod). Since its revival in the 19C this has been held annually, with its location varying in rotation between north, central and south Wales. It now involves several different arts but the climax is still the chairing of the bard, the poet whose work in the traditional Welsh bardic form has been awarded the top prize. The Eisteddfod is run by the Gorsedd (or Court) which announces the competition, at least a year and a day in advance, in a druidic ceremony accompanied by harp music in a specially laid circle of stones.

An International Music Eisteddfod is also held each year at *Llangollen. Since 1992 it has been staged in an imaginative tent-like structure, the Royal International Pavilion, designed by D. Y. Davies Associates.

Elan Valley Mountain valley in Powys which for 100 years has supplied Birmingham with water along an aqueduct some 117km/73m long. The great dams for the first reservoirs here, trapping some of the headwaters of the Wye, were built in 1892–1904. The nearby Claerwen reservoir was added in 1952.

Mark **Elder** (b. 1947) Conductor known in particular as music director of the English National Opera (1979–93).

Eleanor crosses A series of carved stone crosses put up in memory of Eleanor of Castile (1246–90), the wife of *Edward I. She had accompanied him on crusade and was believed to have saved his life when he was wounded at Acre in 1274. When she died in Nottinghamshire, her body was brought down to London. Wherever it had rested, on each evening of that sad journey, he later had one of these crosses built. There were twelve, of which only three survive – at Geddington and Hardingstone in Northamptonshire, and at Waltham in Essex. The most famous of them, *Charing Cross in London, exists today as a replica.

Eleanor of Aquitaine (*c*.1122–1204) One of the most powerful figures of the 12C, wife of two kings and mother of two more, famous in her time for her great possessions, her beauty and her patronage of the arts. She was heiress to the vast lands of Aquitaine in southwest France. Her first marriage, to Louis VII of France, was annulled in 1152. Within two months she had married Henry of Anjou, who in 1154 became *Henry II of England. It was through this marriage that most of southwest France became attached to the English crown, later one of the causes of the *Hundred Years' War. Her family life was turbulent, for she supported her sons against their father in 1173, as a result of which she spent the next ten years in virtual imprisonment. But she remained a force to be reckoned during the reigns of her sons, Richard I and John.

Electoral Reform Society Pressure group formed in 1884 to campaign for change in the British electoral system – from first-past-the-post to a specific form of *proportional representation (the single transferable vote in multi-member constituencies). It was not until the 1980s that the society found a wide measure of public support for PR, but it had meanwhile made itself an indispensable advisory body for any group or organization in Britain needing to count and record votes in an orderly fashion.

Elector of Hanover see house of *Hanover.

electricity Single buildings were lit by electricity (through the installation on the premises of a steam-driven generator) before there was any public supply of current. Joseph *Swan had been the first scientist to give a display of electric light sufficiently reliable for domestic use, at Newcastle-upon-Tyne in 1878; the *Savoy Theatre then made history in 1881 as the first public building to be lit by this method; the first systems delivering power to subscribers' homes were installed in London in January 1882 and in New York in September of that year.

The spread of electric power in Britain was the piecemeal achievement of private companies and municipal councils. Each separate enterprise built its own power station and connected it to the houses of the surrounding district. By the time the industry was *nationalized, in 1948, there were 195 private and 367 municipal concerns, working alongside a Central Electricity Board which operated a national grid and some 300 national power stations. All towns and nearly all villages had by then a supply of electricity, but most farms and prosperous isolated houses relied on their own diesel generators, while country cottages were still lit by paraffin lamps. It was not until the 1960s that electricity in the house was normal throughout Britain. By then *nuclear power stations were providing a small part of the nation's supply, as a supplement to those fired by *coal.

The nationalized electricity industry in England and Wales consisted of a Central Electricity Generating Board and 12 area electricity boards. It was this structure which was *privatized in 1991. The country's power stations were divided between two competing companies, National Power and PowerGen, and the area boards became 12 regional electricity companies; the near-monopoly powers of the 12 are subject to regulation by *OFFER (the monopoly is not quite absolute, in that large consumers have a right to buy direct from the generating company or even from another regional supplier, a right which is supposedly to be extended to domestic customers from 1998). Scotland's electricity was similarly reorganized as two private companies. The future costs of dismantling obsolete nuclear power stations made it impossible to sell that part of the industry, which has remained state-owned as Nuclear Electric and Scottish Nuclear.

Electric Light Orchestra (ELO) Pop group formed in 1971 by Ron Wood (b. 1946) and other musicians from a Birmingham group, The Move, together with Jeff Lynne (b. 1947), playing in the style then known as progressive rock. They evolved into a mainstream pop band with 'classical' touches. Two albums were in the charts for two years (*A New World Record* 1976, *Out of the Blue* 1977); these were followed by two no. 1 albums (*Discovery* 1979, *Time* 1981) and by *Secret Messages* (1983) and *Balance of Power* (1986).

electroplate In 1842 George Elkington, a Birmingham manufacturer, patented a method for coating a cheaper metal with silver by electrolysis. He almost immediately ruined trade in the more expensive *Sheffield plate. Electroplating has remained the method for all silver plate since the 1850s, the cheaper underlying metal usually being the alloy known as nickel silver (copper, zinc and nickel).

Elegy written in a Country Church Yard see *Gray's *Elegy*.

'Elementary, my dear Watson' A phrase popularly held to have been used by Sherlock *Holmes when explaining a brilliant piece of detection to his slower-witted assistant. It seems to have evolved from a single use of the word in 'The Crooked Man', one of the stories in *The Memoirs of Sherlock Holmes* (1894). Watson, as usual, is the narrator: ' "Excellent!" I cried. "Elementary", said he.'

Elephant and Castle (London SE1) Name of a major road junction, south of the Thames, deriving from an 18c tavern which stood there. Its origin has caused much speculation. An elephant with a castle on its back has long been a feature of both chess and heraldry, and is the sign of the Cutlers' Company (one of the *City Livery Companies). More fanciful is the theory that the name comes from the Infanta of Castile, who was in the 1620s a prospective bride for Charles I.

eleven lost days see *calendar.

The London highway, past the Mansion House and towards the Royal Exchange, lit by electricity in 1881.

eleven-plus see *grammar school.

Edward **Elgar** (1857–1934, kt 1904) Widely thought of as the most English of composers. He was born in Lower Broadheath near Worcester (where the house of his birth is kept as a museum) and his first success was local, with works for choral societies and for the *Three Choirs Festival. Wider recognition came with *Enigma Variations* (1899) and The *Dream of Gerontius* (1900). A tune from the first of his *Pomp and Circumstance* marches (1901) reappeared in 1902 as *Land of Hope and Glory*. He was appointed *Master of the King's Music in 1924; his orchestral *Nursery Suite* (1931) was dedicated to the princesses Elizabeth and Margaret Rose, daughters of the future George VI. One reason for the great appeal of his music is his ability to treat large themes in an exhilarating and popular style.

Elgin (19,000 in 1991) Scottish town, previously the county town of Morayshire but now in the Grampian region. Its cathedral (13–15c), of which the great western towers and entrance still provide an imposing ruin, was one of the finest in Scotland. The High Street contains two much restored 17c crosses, the Muckle Cross and the Little Cross.

Elgin marbles (British Museum) Marble sculptures of the 5th century BC from the frieze of the Parthenon in Athens. They were brought to England in 1801–11 by the earl of Elgin (1766–1841), with permission from the Turks (then ruling Greece) to whom he was ambassador. He sold the sculptures to the British government in 1816 for £35,000. They are housed now in specially constructed galleries given by Joseph *Duveen. In recent years there has been pressure from the Greek government, and

The Elgin marbles in the British Museum, three years after their purchase by the nation: painting of 1819 by Archibald Archer.

in particular from the actress Melina Mercouri (when minister of culture), for them to be returned to Greece.

Elia see Charles *Lamb.

George **Eliot** (pen name of Mary Ann Evans, 1819–1880) Writer whose first novel, *Adam Bede* (1858), revealed the blend of detailed realism and moral passion which became her hallmark and caused her to be recognized immediately as a major literary figure. Her later books include *Mill on the Floss* (1860), the short *Silas Marner* (1861), *Felix Holt* (1866), and her masterpiece, *Middlemarch* (1871–2). Her personal life was bravely unconventional, for she made public her atheism and lived openly with a married man, George Henry Lewes (1817–78), who was unable by the laws of those days to divorce his wife. It was he who first encouraged her to write fiction. After his death, and in the last year of her own life, she married a young banker, John Walter Cross, who had looked after her investments.

T.S. **Eliot** (Thomas Stearns Eliot, 1888–1965) American-born British poet, who lived in England from 1914 and was naturalized in 1927. His first book of poems (*Prufrock, and other observations*) was published in 1917, but it was the brilliantly fragmented expression of contemporary disillusion in The *Waste Land* (1922) which brought him fame. The *Four Quartets* (1944) was the culmination of his development as a poet. Like much of his later work it was specifically Christian in theme, after his confirmation in 1927 in the *Anglo-Catholic wing of the Church of England.

Eliot had also been the leading figure in the mid-century revival of poetic drama, with *Murder in the

Cathedral (1935) followed by *The Family Reunion* (1939) and *The Cocktail Party* (1949). In addition he had great influence on the British literary scene both as critic and publisher; he founded a quarterly review, the *Criterion*, in 1922, and subsequently built up a very strong poetry list for Faber and Faber. After his death his *Old Possum's Book of Practical Cats* (1939) became the basis of the immensely successful musical comedy *Cats. He was awarded the Nobel prize for literature in 1948.

Elizabeth I (1533–1603) Queen of England and Ireland from 1558; second daughter of Henry VIII, her mother being Anne Boleyn.

Arguably England's greatest monarch, she only came to the throne because of the deaths of her younger brother Edward VI and her elder sister Mary I. She inherited a country torn between the Puritans who had prospered under Edward and the Roman Catholics who had benefited under Mary. It was typical of Elizabeth's attitude and qualities that she contrived to establish a moderate *Church of England, reasserting authority without the previous extremes of persecution.

Religion dominated foreign as well as home affairs, with other rulers and their factions constantly trying to restore a Roman Catholic to the English throne. This was the thorn in Elizabeth's long and difficult relationship with her cousin *Mary Queen of Scots, and it was the underlying cause of the greatest external threat, the *Armada. The queen had a genius for keeping the affection and loyalty of the talented administrators, soldiers and sailors who were also her courtiers. Some, such as the earl of *Leicester, were her wooers as well, and she astonished her contemporaries by remaining resolutely the

Virgin Queen. But a royal husband from abroad (she turned down Philip II of Spain) or a loyal English subject would each, in different ways, have cramped her freedom to rule. Instead, even in her very last years (with the earl of *Essex), there was an element of flirtation with her favourites.

Elizabeth presided over a period during which England was stabilized after a long period of upheaval. There were the beginnings of expansion abroad, in the journeys of Raleigh and others. And her last decade saw the birth of England's great theatrical tradition, with Marlowe and Shakespeare. Her greatest talent was her ability to inspire and unite her people, often playing upon their affections. Few monarchs have spoken in such direct and emotional terms, whether in her speech to rally the troops at Tilbury in 1588 (where she described herself as having the *'body of a weak and feeble woman' but the 'heart and stomach of a king') or in the mood of farewell which formed part of her so-called 'golden speech' to members of the House of Commons in 1601: 'This I account the glory of my crown, that I have reigned with your loves . . . And though you have had, and may have, many mightier and wiser princes sitting in this seat, yet you never had, nor shall have any that will love you better.' It hardly seems to matter that the occasion was a royal demand for more taxes.

She was succeeded by her Scottish cousin, James I and VI (see the *royal house).

Elizabeth I as a devout and studious girl of about 13: detail of painting attributed to William Scrots, c.1546.

Elizabeth II (b. 1926) Queen of Great Britain and Northern Ireland from 1952; elder child of George VI and of Queen Elizabeth, now the *Queen Mother. On 20 November 1947 she married in Westminster Abbey her distant cousin, Philip Mountbatten, who was created Duke of *Edinburgh on the eve of the wedding. They were together in Kenya in the Sagana Hunting Lodge when news reached them, on 6 February 1952, that her father had died of a heart attack.

Queen Elizabeth has been the very model of a constitutional monarch, much in evidence and always non-controversial. Her reign has seen the completion of the process by which the *British empire has transformed itself into the *Commonwealth, a family of nations in which she has taken great interest and pride. Her four children are Charles, Prince of *Wales; Anne, *Princess Royal; Andrew, Duke of *York; and Prince *Edward. Her residences are Buckingham Palace, Windsor Castle, Sandringham, Holyroodhouse and Balmoral.

Queen **Elizabeth**, the Queen Mother see *Queen Mother.

Elizabethan Term used almost invariably of the reign of Elizabeth I rather than Elizabeth II. Architectural historians apply it to the English version of the continental Renaissance style, seen in such houses as *Longleat or *Hardwick. It is more popularly used of *timber-frame houses, particularly of the black-and-white variety, which in fact were built for many years before and after the Elizabethan period.

Peter **Elliott** (b. 1962) Athlete who won silver medals in the 800 metres at the 1987 World Championships and in the 1500 metres at the 1988 Olympic Games, following these with a gold medal in the 1500 metres at the 1990 Commonwealth Games.

Havelock **Ellis** (1859–1939) Pioneer in the study of human sexual behaviour. He wrote many books for general readers, such as *Man and Woman* (1894) and *The Erotic Rights of Women* (1918), but his major scientific work – *Studies in the Psychology of Sex* (7 vols, 1897–1928) – was for many years published only in the USA, after a bookseller had been prosecuted in Britain in 1898 for stocking the first volume.

Ruth **Ellis** (1926–55) The last woman to be hanged in Britain. She was sentenced to death for the basic *crime passionel*, the murder of a lover who was unfaithful to her. Her story has been the subject of two feature films – *Yield to the Night* (1956), filmed immediately after her execution with Diana Dors in the central role, and *Dance with a Stranger* (1985).

Elsie Tanner see *Coronation Street*.

Elsinore see *Hamlet*.

Ben **Elton** (b. 1959) Stand-up comedian with a reputation for 'comic correctness', after his 1986 attack on Benny *Hill's more traditional routines for being sexist and dealing in stereotypes.

Ely (10,000 in 1981) Cathedral town in Cambridgeshire, on the river Ouse. Until the draining of the Fens the site was an island, the Isle of Ely, and as such was used as a defensive position against the Normans by Hereward the Wake. The cathedral, visible for miles across the flat landscape, was built in the 11–14C. Its most famous feature is the great central octagon, spanning the entire width of the nave in an exceptionally bold piece of 14C design; the wooden lantern surmounting it required oak corner-posts

19.2m/63ft long. A museum of stained glass was opened in part of the cathedral in 1979.

Close by is the King's School, founded as a monastic school in 970 and re-established by Henry VIII after the *dissolution of the monasteries.

Emancipation Act (1829) The act which removed most of the barriers preventing *Roman Catholics from holding public office, from which they had been excluded since 1678 in the hysteria following the fictitious *Popish Plot. Earlier attempts at emancipation had led to the *Gordon Riots of 1780 and the resignation of *Pitt in 1801. The act of 1829 was prompted by the election to the House of Commons of the Irish leader Daniel *O'Connell and was promoted by *Peel; its crucial clause dropped the requirement of an oath denying the spiritual authority of the pope. The act also enabled Roman Catholic peers to take their seats in the House of Lords, one of the first to do so being the *Earl Marshal.

Embankment Road along the north bank of the Thames from Westminster to Blackfriars, built out into the river by *Bazalgette in 1864–70. It was designed to accommodate the District line, an addition to London's new *underground, in the layer immediately below the road; and below the underground lay Bazalgette's new sewer. Its full name is the Victoria Embankment, distinguishing it from two others built further upstream, also by Bazalgette – the Albert Embankment (1866–70, on the Lambeth bank) and the Chelsea Embankment (1871–4).

Embassy World Professional Championships see *darts and *snooker.

emblems The shamrock, for Ireland, is said to derive from St *Patrick having used it (three leaflets on one stem) to explain the mystery of the Trinity when converting the Irish. The leek, for Wales, supposedly relates back to a Welsh habit (introduced by St *David, it is said) of wearing a leek in the cap as identification in a battle. (Since the early 20C some in Wales, with the active encouragement of Lloyd George, have adopted a daffodil in place of the leek – the precise reason is unclear, unless it is a verbal link between daffy and *Taffy.) The thistle, for Scotland, is supposed to have helped the Scots rather more physically in battle, when an enemy soldier in a surprise attack trod on such a plant and gave the game away with his yell. The rose, for England, has been provided with no such fanciful explanation but has long been an important symbol in English history, as in the *Wars of the Roses.

Other symbols with a national connection are the *Welsh dragon, the Irish *harp and the British *bulldog.

Emergency Ward Ten (ATV 1957–67) One of the earliest soap operas on British television, set in a hospital ward and transmitted twice weekly.

EMI (Electric and Musical Industries) Company formed in 1931 by the merger of two rivals in the gramophone industry – the London-based Gramophone Company and the Columbia Graphophone Company, whose roots went back to the early talking machines patented in the USA by Thomas Edison. The merger brought together many of the best-known labels, including Columbia, Parlophone and the Gramophone Company's *HMV. In the same year, 1931, Elgar opened EMI's famous studios in *Abbey Road, at that time the largest building in the world devoted entirely to recording. From the start the new company took a leading role in the development of television; its 405-line system was adopted by the BBC in place of the earlier but less sophisticated technology of John Logie *Baird.

EMI (European Monetary Institute) Interim organization charged with preparing for the establishment of the European Central Bank – the main financial institution of the *EC once a single currency is introduced (by the *Maastricht timetable at some point between 1996 and the end of the century). The city in which the EMI is to be sited was under negotiation between the EC countries at the end of 1992.

Eminent Victorians (1918) Short biographical essays by Lytton *Strachey on four much revered Victorians. In probing behind the façades, often with caustic wit, Strachey pioneered an influential approach to biography. His subjects were Cardinal Manning (1808–92), Florence *Nightingale, Dr *Arnold and General *Gordon.

Emma (1816) Novel by Jane *Austen. The heroine, Emma Woodhouse, is a self-satisfied manipulator of other people's affections and aspirations, in particular those of the pretty but socially inferior Harriet Smith. After many painful complications caused by Emma's meddling, the naturally suited couples do at last come together – Harriet and the young farmer Robert Martin, Emma herself and the eligible Mr Knightley.

'emotion recollected in tranquillity' see *Lyrical Ballads*.

Emperor Fountain Britain's tallest fountain, installed by *Paxton in 1844 at *Chatsworth, reaching originally a height of 79m/260ft. A lake was created on the hill behind the house to provide the water pressure. It still plays, though nowadays not quite so high.

Empire Day see *Commonwealth Day.

Empire Loyalists (short for United Empire Loyalists) American colonists who left the United States after the War of American Independence, retaining their allegiance to Britain. The majority went to Canada, where they became known by this name.

Empire Pool Swimming pool at *Wembley, opened in 1934 for the Empire Games (now called *Commonwealth Games) and last used for the Olympic Games in 1948. It was then adapted to become the Wembley Arena, used for events such as ice spectaculars and show jumping.

empiricism The philosophical theory which more than any other has been characteristic of the British tradition in philosophy, as seen in *Locke, *Berkeley and *Hume. The empiricist argues that experience rather than intellectual reasoning is the basis of human knowledge.

Department of **Employment** (London SW1) Government department which in 1968 replaced the former Ministry of Labour. Its main tasks are to improve skills and training and to promote an efficient and competitive labour market. Its responsibilities in industrial disputes are delegated to an independent agency, *ACAS. For secretaries of state since 1983 see the *cabinet.

Employment Service (Sheffield) Executive agency under the *Next Steps programme, established in 1991 within the Department of Employment. It has two main functions: to distribute *unemployment benefits; and to help the unemployed find work through a network of *Jobcentres.

Empress of Blandings see P.G. *Wodehouse.

EMS (European Monetary System) Voluntary system, introduced in 1979, for members of the *EC to achieve greater economic stability. Its most important element is the ERM (Exchange Rate Mechanism), which prevents member currencies from floating more than 2.25% either side of a given exchange rate. This was originally expressed in terms of the *ECU (European Currency Unit, introduced at the same time), but the ECU was later replaced by the strongest currency within the system, the German mark; a currency's permitted band of fluctuation is therefore defined either side of an agreed central exchange rate with the mark. The United Kingdom accepted the broad aims of the EMS but did not enter the ERM until 8 October 1990; it was subsequently forced out again by the weakness of the pound on 16 September 1992 (for the sequence of events see *exchange rate).

Lord **Emsworth** see P.G. *Wodehouse.

EMU see *EC.

enclosure see *common land.

Encounter Literary and political journal, founded in 1953, with ten issues a year until it ceased publication in 1990. It proved something of an embarassment when the magazine, a leading critic of repressive Communist regimes, was discovered to have been indirectly funded by the CIA (via the Congress for Cultural Freedom).

Encyclopaedia Britannica The leading English-language encyclopedia, first published in Edinburgh in 1768–71 by a 'Society of Gentlemen in Scotland'. Since 1929 it has been published in the USA.

Endeavour see Captain *Cook.

'**end of the beginning**' Winston *Churchill's description of the situation after El *Alamein in a speech at the Mansion House on 10 November 1942. 'This is not the end. It is not even the beginning of the end. But it is, perhaps, the end of the beginning.'

Department of **Energy** (London SW1) Government department created in 1974, in the wake of the *oil crisis, a *miners' strike and the three-day week, to oversee the nationalized coal, gas and electricity industries (previously dealt with by the *Department of Trade and Industry). The programme of *privatization in the 1980s left it with much diminished responsibilities, and in 1992 it was merged back into the DTI. For secretaries of state from 1983 to 1992 see the *cabinet.

Enfield District to the north of London where the Royal Small Arms Factory was established in 1815. It *oil crisis, a *miners' strike and the three-day week manufactured several well-known weapons – in particular the Lee-Enfield rifle, used in both world wars, and the *Bren.

Friedrich **Engels** (1820–95) German author and the leading theorist, after *Marx himself, of 19c Communism. His father owned a textile factory in Germany and had a share of one in Manchester, where the young Engels was sent to work (1842–4). His experience of the human misery behind Britain's industrial wealth caused him to write, when only 24, a classic of political sociology, *The Condition of the Working Class in England* (1845 in German, but no British edition until 1892).

England (land area 129,720sq.km/50,085sq.m, population 47.1 million in 1991) The largest of the three territories which together form the island of *Great Britain.

The entire area of England was for the first time under single control during the *Roman occupation. In the next few centuries the *Angles (from whose name the word England derives) were one of the invading tribes from northern Europe. The process of reunification into one England, recognizing a single king, began under *Alfred the Great.

Over the centuries England became the dominant force within the *British Isles. *Wales was merged with the English crown in 1536. *Ireland, occupied by the English for many centuries, was finally incorporated in a Union lasting 1801–1921. *Scotland was never dominated militarily in the same way; but the crowns of England and Scotland were joined in 1603 when the Scottish king, James VI, inherited the English throne as *James I; and the two countries were merged politically by the Act of Union in 1707. There is a tendency (much resented by the other regions) for the English to use England as a synonym for the wider *United Kingdom, as for example in referring to Elizabeth II as the queen of England.

'**England expects that every man will do his duty**' The signal flown from the masts of HMS *Victory* before the Battle of *Trafalgar. The signals lieutenant, John Pasco, wrote later that Nelson asked him to send the message starting with 'England confides' but that he persuaded the admiral to substitute 'expects' – because it had its own flag in the signals book, whereas 'confides' would have to be spelt out.

'**England is a nation of shopkeepers**' A remark reported to have been made by Napoleon when living on St Helena. The phrase itself had been in currency for half

Nelson's famous signal printed by the Daily Mail *as a rallying cry during World War I.*

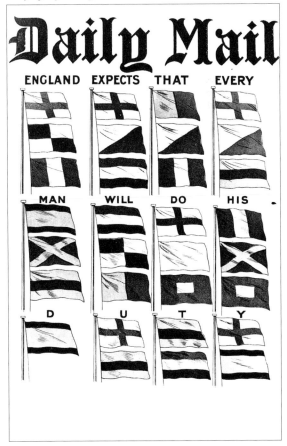

a century. Adam Smith wrote in *The Wealth of Nations* (1776): 'To found a great empire for the sole purpose of raising up a people of customers, may at first sight appear a project fit only for a nation of shopkeepers.'

English The first language of the United Kingdom and of Ireland, and of several other countries throughout the world as a result of British colonial activities. Also by now the second language of a great many other nations, with the result that it has become the leading international language.

English is a member of the Indo-European family of languages, and more specifically of the Germanic sub-group. It takes its name from the *Angles who in the 5–6c arrived from what is now northwest Germany. Dialects of their language were spoken by the other invading tribes, the Jutes and the Saxons, and their common culture is now called Anglo-Saxon. So was their language until recently, but it is now generally referred to as Old English (the language of *Beowulf*). This lasted until about 1100, when the influence of Norman French caused it to develop into Middle English (culminating in *Chaucer). This in turn evolved around 1500 into Modern English.

The English Those *British citizens who were born in or now live in *England. The term has very little ethnic meaning since centuries of invasion (forcing the early *Britons in the region ever further to the west) were followed by centuries of immigration. The nearest to an indigenous English people are probably the descendants of the *Anglo-Saxons.

English bond Method of laying bricks in which one row or course is made up entirely of bricks with their sides showing (stretchers) and the next of bricks with their ends showing (headers). This was the usual English method up to the 18c, when it was replaced by the Flemish bond (sometimes called Dutch bond), where headers and stretchers alternate within each course. Modern brick houses, with cavity walls, usually have courses entirely of stretchers (known as running bond).

English breakfast A concept now surviving in the breakfast rooms of hotels rather than in British homes. An English breakfast is distinguished by a cooked course, consisting traditionally of fried eggs, bacon and sausage – with sometimes fried mushrooms, potatoes and in the north of England black pudding. This is in addition to a choice of fruit juice, cereal, and toast or rolls with butter and marmalade, which on their own are described as 'continental'. Both forms of breakfast are accompanied by tea or coffee.

English Channel The stretch of water along the entire south coast of England, separating it from France. Some 560km/350m long, it narrows at its eastern end to become the *Strait of Dover.

English Civil War (1642–51) The conflict between the king, *Charles I (whose supporters became known as the *Cavaliers) and parliament (the *Roundheads). The underlying reasons were partly political, resulting from the mutual antipathy between Charles and a powerful group of politicians, led by *Pym, who feared that the king was moving towards a form of absolute rule (a logical extension of his *divine right). And they were partly religious, in the clash between the Anglican and Puritan concepts of a Christian society. But the immediate cause was the refusal of the *Long Parliament to meet the demands put upon it by Charles.

The king's attempt to arrest the *Five Members brought matters to a head in 1642. Charles moved north

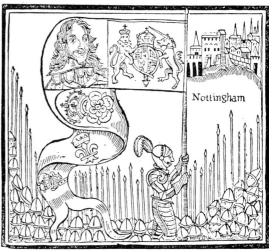

The raising of the royal standard of Charles I at Nottingham in 1642, depicted in a contemporary pamphlet.

and raised his standard at Nottingham, to rally support to the royal cause. With two now incompatible sources of authority, the country both drifted and bustled into war. Different counties, cities, manor houses, families and even individual members of families made their own decisions as to whom to support. London was strongly parliamentarian. If anything the south and east of the country inclined to parliament, with more support for the king in the west and north. But there were fragmented patterns of allegiance within every region.

The early months of the war involved many local skirmishes, while both sides concentrated on building up their forces. Each had some professional soldiers, but the main task was that of mobilizing, arming and training civilians (the notable success being parliament's *New Model Army). Prince *Rupert emerged as a gifted commander on the royalist side, as did Thomas *Fairfax and Oliver *Cromwell for parliament. These were the three who clashed in the first full-scale battle, two years after the start of the war, at *Marston Moor in 1644. Like *Naseby in the following year, this was a victory for parliament. The first stage of the conflict ended with the capture of the king in 1647.

Negotiations were begun. But unsuccessful uprisings on behalf of Charles strengthened the hostility of parliament, resulting in the execution of the king in 1649 and the establishment of the *Commonwealth. The final stage of the war was the attempt of the king's son, *Charles II, to recover the throne, culminating in his defeat at Worcester in 1651. The Commonwealth lasted until the *Restoration in 1660.

English disease Term used in continental Europe in the 1960s and 1970s to explain the sluggish state of the British economy. The symptoms were seen as strikes, restrictive practices, absenteeism and prolonged tea breaks. In the 1980s the same term was applied to *soccer hooliganism.

English Heritage (Historic Buildings and Monuments Commission for England) Established by the National Heritage Act of 1983, English Heritage took over from the Department of the *Environment the responsibility for maintaining some 400 ancient monuments and historic properties in England, and for ruling on all planning applications which involve listed buildings. Its brief includes promoting the public enjoyment of the sites in its care, and to this end it has adopted a higher profile than its predecessor. It produced in 1992 a controversial plan to devolve responsibility for half its properties to local authorities or other regional groups.

English horn see *cor anglais.

English law see *law.

'an **Englishman's home is his castle**' Popular phrase deriving from the *Third Institute* of Edward Coke (see *common law), where he states that 'a man's house is his castle'. It remains a cornerstone of the law that not even the police have the right to enter anyone's house without a warrant.

English National Ballet Touring company which was known until 1989 as the London Festival Ballet and before 1969 as Festival Ballet. It began as a company formed by *Markova and *Dolin, which gave its first performances in London in the autumn of 1950 – a few months before the *Festival of Britain. A regular place of performance in London is the Festival Hall, and its repertoire is a mix of the classics and modern works. Its artistic directors have included John *Gilpin, Beryl *Grey and Peter Schaufuss (1984–90).

English National Opera (ENO) London-based company which has performed opera in English since 1931, first at *Sadler's Wells and since 1968 at the *Coliseum. Founded by Lilian *Baylis as the Vic-Wells Opera, the name was soon changed to Sadler's Wells Opera and then, in 1974, to English National Opera. In 1978 the company established an offshoot in Leeds, known as *Opera North.

English setter see *setter.

English-Speaking Union (London W1) Independent organization, with branches and members all over the world, devoted to fostering international understanding and friendship through a shared use of the English language. Founded in 1918, its original purpose was as a bond between Britain and the USA; this was soon extended to the Commonwealth and in recent years to many other countries, with the increasing acceptance of English as the international language. The ESU's main activities are social and cultural events, and the providing of scholarships for young people to travel.

English Stage Company Established specifically to present contemporary drama, in particular by writers new to the theatre, the company opened in 1956 under the direction of George Devine (1910–66) at the *Royal Court Theatre in London, which has remained its home. Its first season was a spectacular success because it included *Look Back in Anger. John Osborne's play sparked off a revival in the British theatre in which the English Stage Company has continued to play a leading role.

English vice see le *vice anglais.

Enigma Variations (1899) The name commonly used for *Elgar's orchestral *Variations on an Original Theme*, because the word 'enigma', printed at the head of the first of 14 variations, poses two riddles. One is a well-known tune which, according to Elgar, goes with the music but is not played. It has been much guessed at, with *Auld Lang Syne emerging as the favourite. The other is the identity of 'my friends pictured within', to whom the work is dedicated and each of whom is depicted in one of the subsequent 13 variations. Hinted at in the score by initials or nicknames, they have all been identified. The friends were together pictured on the stage in 1968 in *Enigma Variations*, a ballet to Elgar's music by *Ashton.

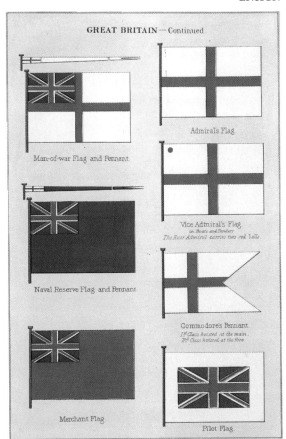

Page of British naval flags, published in 1882, with the white, blue and red ensigns on the left.

Enniskillen (formerly Inniskilling, 11,000 in 1991) County town of Fermanagh in Northern Ireland. Established as a garrison town on an island in the river Erne, it held out in 1689 against *James II and retains a strongly Protestant character. It was the home of two famous regiments, the Royal Inniskilling Fusiliers and the Inniskilling Dragoons. The Portora Royal School includes Oscar Wilde and Samuel Beckett among its past pupils. Enniskillen was subjected to a terrorist attack in 1987 when an IRA bomb exploded among a crowd gathered for a Remembrance Day service, killing 11 and injuring 63.

ENO see *English National Opera.

ENSA (Entertainments National Service Organization) Production enterprise, with its headquarters in London's Drury Lane Theatre, which throughout World War II provided entertainment, from solo acts up to full-length dramas, for the troops abroad and for camps and factories at home. ENSA was known affectionately at the time as Every Night Something Awful.

ensign Word for a flag, deriving from the same root as 'insignia' and therefore used in particular for flags of identification flown by the armed forces. In the army the regimental standard is known as the ensign, and the word is also used by extension for the officer who carries it. In the navy the complex use of personal standards by the commanders of individual ships gave way in the 18c to red, white and blue flags for the three squadrons of a fleet drawn up for battle. In the 19c this in turn was replaced by the present system: the White Ensign is flown only by ships of the Royal Navy and by members of the Royal

PUNCH, OR THE LONDON CHARIVARI.—April 22, 1914.

AFTER TEN YEARS.

Ten years of friendship between a rather masculine Britannia and her winsome French equivalent, Marianne.

Yacht Squadron (a privilege granted in 1829 to several yacht clubs, but withdrawn from all the others); the Blue Ensign is flown by auxiliary vessels of the Royal Navy, by other ships employed in the public service and by certain yacht clubs; and the Red Ensign is flown by the merchant navy. The Royal Air Force ensign, flown at air force bases, is a variant in RAF blue of the naval ensign, with the addition of the RAF triple circle (or roundel) in red, white and blue.

Entente Cordiale ('friendly understanding' in French) The name commonly given to an agreement between France and Britain in 1904. It resolved colonial antagonism between the two countries in various parts of the world, in particular giving a free hand to France in Morocco and to Britain in Egypt. It also brought them into a tacit alliance against German interests, a pact which held through the next decade and into World War I.

Enterprise Neptune see *National Trust.

Enterprise Oil Independent company which expanded dramatically during the 1980s from its exploration and production of *North Sea oil. It was floated on the London stock market in 1984.

enterprise zones Government-designated areas, particularly in decayed inner cities, into which new industrial and commercial enterprises are enticed by financial and tax incentives and by reduced planning controls. The scheme was introduced in 1981. Its most high-profile off-shoot has been the ten *Urban Development Corporations.

*The **Entertainer*** (1957) Play by John *Osborne about a down-at-heel music-hall comedian, Archie Rice, who communicates with his family in a string of gags and only comes alive when engaging the audience with his old routines ('Why should I care?' is his favourite number). In the end even the routines fail him, after his son has been killed at Suez and his father, a more dignified entertainer of the old school, has died. Archie provided a magnificent part for Laurence Olivier, both on stage and film (1960).

E number One of a series of numbers, each preceded by E (for Europe) and each defining under *EC regulations a specific food additive. Any which have been added to a processed food must be listed on the packaging.

Department of the **Environment** (DOE, London SW1) Government department created in 1970 by merging three previous ministries (Housing and Local Government, Public Building and Works, and Transport). Of these the Department of *Transport became independent again in 1976. The DOE is responsible for all matters of planning, land use, housing and conservation, and has authority over *local government. For secretaries of state since 1983 see the *cabinet.

Episcopal Church in Scotland Autonomous branch of the *Anglican Communion, called 'episcopal' because it has bishops (*episcopi* in Latin) in contrast to the *Church of Scotland.

Epping Forest Some 2400ha/6000ac of forest just to the north of London, in Essex, surviving from the large primeval forest which once covered most of East Anglia. Preserved as a royal hunting ground for many centuries, Epping Forest was famous for its herds of fallow *deer, which have now almost died out.

Epsom (69,000 in 1981) Town in Surrey, famous for the racecourse (with its sharp left-hand turn at Tattenham Corner) which is home to the *Oaks and the *Derby. Epsom became a resort after the discovery in about 1618 of mineral springs (from which Epsom salts, used originally as a laxative, were extracted by evaporation). Racing had become a permanent feature by 1730.

Jacob **Epstein** (1880–1959, kt 1954) Born in New York of Russian-Polish parents, he settled in London in 1905. *The Rock Drill* (1914) was the outstanding work of *Vorticism (only the torso of the figure survives, cast in bronze – there is an example in the Tate). His early public commissions often caused outrage, in particular his 1912 space-age angel on the tomb of Oscar Wilde in Paris. But two of the best-known Christian monuments in Britain today are his – the bronze *St Michael and the Devil* on the wall of *Coventry Cathedral, and the aluminium *Christ in Majesty* in *Llandaff Cathedral. He was also a skilful and prolific portraitist in bronze.

Equal Opportunities Commission Set up in 1975 under the Sex Discrimination Act, the Commission's role is to monitor the working of that act and of the Equal Pay Act of 1970, striving to promote equal opportunities regardless of sex or marital status.

equal pay see *Equal Opportunities Commission.

equity see *law.

Equity (British Actors' Equity Association Trade union established in 1930 for the acting profession, later extended to include performers in most fields of entertainment; the Variety Artistes' Federation was absorbed in 1967. The name and many of the principles were adopted from the already existing American Equity. In the decades after World War II the union established a closed shop in the West End theatre, but this ended as a result of employment acts during the 1980s.

E^{II}R The royal cypher, used on royal and state documents and seen in public on vans of the Royal Mail, on certain pillar boxes and on fittings, such as cast-iron bollards, where the land belongs to the Crown Estate. The royal cypher in the previous reign was G^{VI}R. The initials stand for Elizabeth II Regina and George VI Rex (*regina* and *rex* being Latin for queen and king).

ERA see *BRM.

Erddig (21km/13m SW of Chester) House in Clwyd, built in the 17–18C, remarkable for the preservation of its outhouses and of the servants' quarters, complete with furniture and contents. The formal garden, symmetrically arranged round a canal, has recently been restored as it appears in an engraving of 1740.

Erewhon (1872) Novel by Samuel *Butler in which the narrator's experiences in a remote land are used to satirize arrangements nearer home. The title, an anagram of 'nowhere', links it with the 'no place' of *Utopia*. The narrator eventually escapes in a balloon with his host's beautiful daughter. In the sequel (*Erewhon revisited* 1901), it is revealed that the narrator's name is Higgs. He returns to Erewhon 20 years later to find that the manner of his previous departure has given him the status of a god.

'er indoors' see *Minder*.

ERM see *EMS.

Ermine Street The *Roman road which ran north from London to the east Midlands, ending at York. The name is an Anglo-Saxon one, which was also used for a lesser road running east-west from Silchester (near Reading) to Gloucester.

Ernie The name chosen in 1956 to humanize the computer which chooses the winning numbers of *premium bonds. The friendly acronym was achieved somewhat awkwardly from Electronic Random Number Indicator Equipment.

Eros Britain's most famous statue, surmounting the Shaftesbury Memorial Fountain in *Piccadilly Circus. Designed by Alfred *Gilbert, and cast in aluminium, it was unveiled in 1893. It commemorates the great philanthropist, Lord *Shaftesbury, and was intended to represent the angel of Christian Charity. It rapidly acquired its present name from its similarity to Cupid (his Greek name is Eros), who seemed to be aiming his arrow of love into a public place which was then much frequented by prostitutes.

ESDA (Electrostatic Detection Apparatus) A technique which has discredited police evidence in a wide range of cases, from the *Guildford Four and the *Birmingham Six in 1974 to the *Tottenham Three in 1985; it also led to the quashing of many convictions secured by the *West Midlands Serious Crime Squad. Invented in the late 1970s by two research scientists (who have developed it as a successful commercial enterprise), ESDA uses an electrostatic process similar to xerox. Black dust, concentrating in the lines indented in a sheet of paper by the pressure of the ballpoint pen writing on the sheet above, reveals whether the sheets came in the correct sequence from a police pad and whether any subsequent alterations have been made. The law states that the police must note down at the time what a suspect says; any later amend-

ments count as fabrication of evidence and may imply a conspiracy to pervert the course of justice.

Esq Abbreviation for 'Esquire', often placed after a man's name on an envelope (John Smith, Esq). Originally a social distinction applied to someone below the *peerage in rank (compare *gentleman), it has become a meaningless convention and is gradually giving way to other forms (Mr John Smith, or simply John Smith).

Essex (1,549,000 in 1991, administrative centre Chelmsford *County on the east coast of England, north of the Thames estuary. Its name derives from the East Saxons, a slightly enlarged version of the present area having been one of the *Anglo-Saxon kingdoms.

Earl of **Essex** (Robert Devereux, *c.*1567–1601, 2nd earl 1576) The youngest favourite of Elizabeth I and the only one to be executed in her lifetime. His glittering career at court was interspersed with a series of dashing military and naval expeditions. His most important command was as lord lieutenant of Ireland from 1599, during which he lost the queen's favour by making an unauthorized treaty and by returning to England without her permission. Isolated and petulant, he launched a half-hearted rebellion for which he was tried and beheaded (see also *Richard II*).

Essex County Cricket Club Founded in 1876 and in the *county championship since 1895. It had never finished higher than third until victory in 1979 began an extraordinary winning streak (champions again in 1983, 84, 86, 91, 92). In *one-day cricket the club won the NatWest Bank Trophy in 1985; the Benson and Hedges Cup in 1979; and the John Player League in 1981, 84, 85. The county ground is at Chelmsford, and the county also plays at Colchester, Ilford and Southend.

Essex man Phrase coined in a 1990 *Sunday Telegraph* profile of a fictional right-wing working-class Tory – the voter who more than any other had kept the Conservatives in power during the *Thatcher years. Headed 'Mrs Thatcher's bruiser', the article defined Essex man as ruthlessly self-interested, philistine, lager-swilling, racist, and a likely Rottweiler-owner if only he had time to walk the animal. The link with Essex was two-fold: it is the nearest country area for the upwardly mobile to move into from the East End of London; and in recent elections the county had sent many Tory hard-liners to Westminster, Norman *Tebbit being defined as 'ur-Essex man'. Subsequently Essex girl became the butt of a string of sexist and snobbish jokes.

Basildon, a town in Essex, reinforced the stereotype at the 1992 general election. It was the first constituency to declare a result, and it accurately implied a stronger level of Conservative support in the country than the polls had predicted.

The **Establishment** A term long applied to those holding power in any community, which became increasingly used in the late 1950s to describe the tightly-knit circles perceived to be in control of Britain. The word was applied to the 'governing classes' by A.J.P. Taylor in the *New Statesman* in 1953 and was much enlarged upon by Henry Fairlie in 1955 in the *Spectator* (the article which gave the term its wider currency). In the early 1960s it was used as the name of a satirical nightclub in London.

estate duty see *inheritance tax.

estates of the realm A phrase surviving from the Middle Ages, when the clergy, the nobility and the common people were the three estates. The concept has no real meaning in modern life, though it is roughly reflected in the composition of *parliament (formed of the Lords Spiritual, the Lords Temporal and the Commons). Since the early 19C the press has been described as the fourth estate. The first clear use of the phrase in this context was by Macaulay, who applied it in 1828 to the gallery of the House of Commons in which the reporters sat.

Eternal Father strong to save (1860) Hymn with words by William Whiting (1825–78) which, in a seafaring nation, has become a favourite. It is known as the navy's hymn, with its refrain rising and falling like a wave:

> O hear us when we cry to Thee
> For those in peril on the sea.

Ethelred the Unready (c.968–1016) King of England from 978. The popular fame of Ethelred II, compared with the many other Ethelberts, Ethelfriths and Ethelreds of Anglo-Saxon England, is the accidental result of his being called 'unready'. The word derives from the Old English *unraed*, meaning that he received 'bad advice'. Certainly his reign was a disaster, with constant attacks from the Danes leading to the notorious *Danegeld. Soon after his death his throne was seized by a Dane, *Canute, who married Ethelred's widow, Emma. But a son of Ethelred and Emma, *Edward the Confessor, later recovered the throne.

ethnic and religious minorities The *Jews are by far the longest established ethnic group in Britain to have remained identifiable (a strong Celtic element survives on the west coast of Britain, but nobody thinks of himself primarily as a Celt). However the term 'ethnic minority' is commonly used only of groups which have arrived by *immigration since World War II. Since the majority of these came from the New Commonwealth – particularly the West Indies and the subcontinent of India – the phrase implies also a distinction of colour and in many cases of religion.

The 1991 *census revealed that the number in Britain of Caribbean (or West Indian) descent was about 500,000, and that there were some 380,000 other black people from Africa and elsewhere; the Asian groups included 825,000 Indians, 500,000 Pakistanis, 165,000 Bangladeshis, 165,000 Chinese. The total of all the ethnic minorites in the country, including some 500,000 not in any of the above categories, was in the region of 3 million or about 5.5% of the population. About half of these were born in Britain. The problem of prejudice and discrimination against the ethnic minorities is monitored by the Commission for *Racial Equality.

People of Caribbean origin are nearly all Christian (with a very small minority of *Rastafarians), but the Asian community is divided between *Muslims, *Sikhs and *Hindus (with, again, a very small minority of *Buddhists).

Eton College Probably the best-known of Britain's *public schools, on the opposite bank of the Thames from Windsor. It was founded in 1440 by Henry VI. He built a superb chapel in the Perpendicular style (as at King's, *Cambridge), but at Eton only the choir was completed; murals of the 15C have survived on its walls. Eton has provided some 20 prime ministers from Walpole to Macmillan and Home. The duke of Wellington was at the school and supposedly said that 'the Battle of Waterloo was won on the playing fields of Eton' (a remark first attributed to him shortly after his death). The boys have worn tail coats as a school uniform since about 1850, accompanied until the 1940s by top hats.

Eton took the lead in the 19C in developing rowing as a school sport. The famous *Eton Boating Song* (by William

Johnson, 1823–92) celebrates 'Jolly boating weather/ And a hay harvest breeze', urges the boys to 'Swing, swing together', and proclaims:

> Harrow may be more clever,
> Rugby may make more row,
> But we'll row, row for ever,
> Steady from stroke to bow.

Etruria see *Wedgwood.

E-type One of the most successful of all British sports cars, outstanding for its streamlined design, its performance (0–160kph/100mph in under 16 secs) and its price when launched by *Jaguar in 1961 (£2200). It remained in production until 1975.

Chris **Eubank** (b. 1966) Boxer who by the end of 1992 was undefeated in 34 professional fights. Ten of those were world championship contests, after he won the WBC middleweight title in March 1990 against Hugo Corti and the equivalent WBO title in November of that year against Nigel Benn. His fight against Michael *Watson in September 1991 ended in tragedy, when Watson nearly died and went into a prolonged coma.

EURATOM see *EC.

The **European** Weekly newspaper launched in 1990 by Robert *Maxwell, and bought after his death by Frederick and David Barclay. Specializing in subjects of European interest, it is on sale each Thursday throughout the European Community.

European Atomic Energy Community see *EC.

European Coal and Steel Community see *EC.

European Commission (Commission of the European Communities) The executive wing of the *EC, based in Brussels and equivalent to the *civil service at a national level. There are 17 commissioners (the larger member states appointing two each and the others one), serving for a renewable 4-year period, each of whom takes responsibility for a specific area of EC activity.

European Community see *EC.

European Council The official name for the periodic meetings of the heads of government of the member states of the *EC; these events are more commonly referred to as European summits. The European Council is distinct from both the *Council of Ministers and the *Council of Europe.

European Court of Human Rights see *Council of Europe.

European Court of Justice The court which rules on all matters connected with *EC legislation. It sits in Luxembourg and consists of 13 judges and six advocates-general, appointed by the governments of the member states for renewable 6-year terms.

European Cup (in full European Champion Clubs' Cup) Annual knock-out competition, first played in 1956, between the winners of the equivalent of the *Football League in the UEFA countries (see also *UEFA Cup).

European Cup-Winners' Cup Annual knock-out football competition, played since 1961 between the winners of the equivalent of the *FA Cup in the UEFA countries (see also *UEFA Cup).

European Currency Unit see *ECU.

European Economic Community see *EC.

European Fairs Cup see *UEFA Cup.

European Free Trade Association see *EFTA.

European Monetary System see *EMS.

European Parliament The elected authority of the *EC. There are (in 1993) 518 seats apportioned roughly in accordance with the size of individual countries. The United Kingdom has 81 (66 for England, 8 for Scotland, 4 for Wales and 3 for Northern Ireland); the Northern Ireland seats are allotted by *proportional representation, but the others have a first-past-the-post system with large *constituencies. Members are elected for five years, and the first election was held in 1979; there had previously been an unelected assembly fulfilling similar functions. The opinion of the parliament is sought by the *Council of Ministers, but its vote on most issues is not binding (the chief exception is that it can reject a proposed Community budget). The sessions of the parliament itself are held in Strasbourg, but its committees sit in Brussels and the secretariat is in Luxembourg.

Eurovision Song Contest Annual competition on TV, launched by BBC Television in 1956, in which a country enters a singer or group with a new song. In a somewhat interminable finale, a jury in each of the competing nations awards points to the entries. Sandie Shaw won for Britain in 1967 with *Puppet on a String*. Subsequent British winners have been Lulu in 1969 (*Boom bang-a-bang*, joint with three other countries), Brotherhood of Man in 1976 (*Save your Kisses for Me*) and Bucks Fizz in 1981 (*Making your Mind Up*). Terry *Wogan does the commentary for British TV in what is by now a well-established tone of subdued ridicule.

Eurythmics Pop duo formed late in 1980 by Annie Lennox (b. 1954) and Dave Stewart (b. 1952); they had previously worked together as the Tourists, with Pete Coombes. They established themselves with their quirky, largely electronic second LP, *Sweet Dreams (Are Made of This)* (1983), off which the title track and 'Love is a Stranger' became hits. Later successes included *Sex Crime (Nineteen Eighty Four)* (1984) and *There must be an Angel (Playing with my Heart)* (1985) – titles with parentheses were something of a trademark.

Euston Road School Group of artists, led by William Coldstream (1908–87), Victor Pasmore (b. 1908) and Claude Rogers (1907–79), and named from the art school which they founded in London's Euston Road in 1937. They rejected the two extremes of academicism and modernism, favouring naturalistic studies of life and landscape.

Euston Station (London NW1) London's earliest and until recently grandest terminus, which opened in 1837 and was designed by Philip Hardwick (1792–1870) for Robert *Stephenson's London and Birmingham railway. To suggest the importance of this new iron road to the industrial heart of the kingdom, the station was approached through a vast Doric arch, completed in 1838. In 1846–9 there was added the Great Hall, the concourse at which passengers arrived, designed by Hardwick's son, P.C. Hardwick. This splendour was all swept away in 1963, in spite of much protest, to make way for the present drearily functional station.

euthanasia see *Exit and *Hillsborough.

Evangelicals Term used for those in the *Church of England who place maximum emphasis on an essentially Protestant theme – that each believer's salvation depends solely on his or her personal faith and on the authority of scripture, without benefit of ritual, sacrament or good works. This wing of the church derives from the spiritual revival led by John *Wesley in the 18c (Methodist and Evangelical were used interchangeably in the early 19c). The emergence of *Anglo-Catholicism in the mid-19c brought the difference of opinion sharply into focus, and Evangelicals and Anglo-Catholics have remained two contrasting strands within the Anglican Church.

Arthur **Evans** (1851–1941, kt 1911) Archaeologist who discovered and excavated Knossos, the palace of the rulers of Crete from about 3000 to 1200 BC. He also coined the term Minoan (from Minos, the legendary king of Crete) to describe this early Greek civilization. The site yielded a large number of clay tablets in the script known as *Linear B.

Edith **Evans** (1888–1976, DBE 1946) Actress who was employed as a milliner before making her first amateur appearance on stage, as Viola in *Twelfth Night*, at the age of 22. Her professional career began two years later. She excelled in portraying strong and slightly eccentric characters; Millamant in *The Way of the World* in 1924 was her first major success with the public, and Lady Bracknell in *The Importance of Being Earnest* became by far her best-known role.

Geraint **Evans** (1922–92, kt 1969) Welsh baritone whose career was centred on Covent Garden, where he made his debut in 1948 and eventually gave more than a thousand performances; abroad, it was probably in San Francisco and Chicago that he was a most regular visitor. He was known in particular for his comic roles, among them Mozart's Figaro and Papageno, Verdi's Falstaff, Wagner's

British clubs which have won the European Cup	
1967	Celtic
1968	Manchester United
1977	Liverpool
1978	Liverpool
1979	Nottingham Forest
1980	Nottingham Forest
1981	Liverpool
1982	Aston Villa
1984	Liverpool

British clubs which have won the European Cup-Winners' Cup	
1963	Tottenham Hotspur
1965	West Ham United
1970	Manchester City
1971	Chelsea
1972	Rangers
1983	Aberdeen
1985	Everton
1991	Manchester United

Beckmesser and Bottom in Britten's *Midsummer Night's Dream*. He gave his farewell performance at Covent Garden in 1984 in a part which he had made his own in his later years, Donizetti's Dulcamara in *L'Elisir d'Amore*.

Godfrey **Evans** (b. 1920) Outstanding wicket-keeper, playing *cricket for Kent (1939–67) and England (1946–59). Until 1976 he held the world record for *Test dismissals by a wicket-keeper (219). His batting was notable for its extreme variations in speed. He holds (in 1992) two violently contrasting Test records: the longest period at the wicket before scoring his first run (95 minutes in Adelaide in 1947); and the fastest score before lunch (98 at Lord's in 1952).

Mary Ann **Evans** see George *Eliot.

Timothy **Evans** see *Rillington Place.

John **Evelyn** (1620–1706) Author of one of the two great English diaries of the 17C, very different in kind from the other – that of *Pepys, who was a friend of Evelyn's. Where Pepys has left an intensely personal document, Evelyn's is a record of the public life of his time from someone singularly well placed to observe it. He was part of the court circle, was a founding member of the Royal Society and had a breadth of interest which enabled him to write books on subjects as varied as engraving (*Sculptura* 1662) and forestry (*Sylva* 1664). The diary was published first in 1818 and in an authoritative 6-volume edition in 1955.

evening dress For a woman this conventionally means a long dress. To specify male dress for an evening occasion, British invitation cards use one of two phrases. 'Black tie' means a dinner jacket (tuxedo in American) with a black bow tie. 'White tie' means white bow tie, wing collar, starched shirt and tails. This was normal evening dress in Victorian and Edwardian times, but is now worn only on very grand occasions. In Scotland *Highland dress is worn as formal dress in the evening.

Evening Standard see Evening *Standard.

The Eve of St Agnes (1820) Medievalist poem by *Keats based on the legend that on St Agnes' Eve a virgin may see and entertain her lover in a vision. In this case Madeline, hoping for such delights, wakes to find her beloved Porphyro in person beside her bed; together they elope. The subject greatly appealed to the *Pre-Raphaelites, being painted by Holman Hunt and by Arthur Hughes.

Everest The highest mountain in the world has held a fascination for the British, perhaps because so tantalizingly close to India. It was named, in 1863, after George Everest (1790–1866); as surveyor general of India he had completed an exceptionally detailed and accurate survey of the subcontinent.

The obsession with reaching the peak (8848m/29,028ft above sea level) began in earnest during the 1920s. Between the wars there were five attempts on the summit, all by British groups. The first was in 1922. But it was the second, in 1924, which captured the public imagination: on June 8 two members of the party, George Mallory and A.C. Irvine, set off on the final stage to the summit; they were last seen, progressing strongly, just before the mist closed over them. Many at the time believed they must have reached the top before they died but this is now thought improbable, with greater knowledge of the mountain. Mallory had also been a member of the 1922 expedition, and on a lecture tour in the USA in 1923 he had coined a famous phrase; to the frequent question 'Why do you want to climb Mount Everest?', he answered simply 'Because it is there'.

The first two attempts after the war, both in 1952, were by a Swiss group. Then, in 1953, the Royal Geographical Society sent out an expedition led by John Hunt (b. 1910). The final ascent was left to the New Zealand climber Edmund Hillary (b. 1919) and the Sherpa guide Tenzing Norgay (c.1914–86); Tenzing had also accompanied the Swiss expedition of the previous year. On May 29 Hillary and Tenzing reached the south summit at about 9 a.m.; they were standing on the peak shortly before noon. By June 2 the entire expedition was back at the base camp, and on that same morning the news was on the front page of Britain's newspapers; it happened, by a glorious coincidence, to be the day of the coronation of Elizabeth II.

Between 1953 and the early 1990s more than 200 other expeditions have reached the top of Everest, leading to one of the world's most unlikely environmental problems. The Nepal Mountaineering Association has calculated that some 50 tons of rubbish now litter the summit.

Everton, known as the Toffeemen or Toffees (Goodison Park, Liverpool). Football club formed by the St Domingo Sunday School in 1878; it changed its name to Everton the following year and turned professional in 1885, becoming a founder member of the *Football League in 1888. From 1884 they played at Anfield Road, and it was their departure to Goodison Park in 1892 which led to the formation of a new club in the district, *Liverpool. Club victories: FA Cup 1906, 33, 66, 84; League Champions 1891, 1915, 28, 32, 39, 63, 70, 85, 87; European Cup-Winners' Cup 1985.

Everyman (c.1500) The best-known English morality play, meaning one in which the characters are allegorical abstractions rather than the biblical figures of *mystery plays. An earlier Dutch text provided most of the plot, in which Everyman learns to distinguish between true and false values. Facing Death, he is abandoned by former friends such as Fellowship and Goods. Only Good Deeds can actually accompany him into the grave. But Knowledge speaks a reassuring couplet which became widely familiar through being printed on the first page of each volume in Everyman's Library, published from 1906:

Everyman, I will go with thee, and be thy guide,
In thy most need to go by thy side.

Winifred **Ewing** (Winifred Woodburn, b. 1929, m. Stewart Ewing 1956) One of the leading Scottish nationalist politicians, whose by-election victory at Hamilton in 1967 was a triumph for the *SNP. She lost the seat in 1970 but then represented Moray and Nairn (1974–9); she has been MEP for the Highlands and Islands since 1979.

exams Until a generation ago all children in Britain took, by the age of 13, a single exam of decisive importance. Those in the state system sat the eleven-plus (deciding once and for all their chance of getting into a *grammar school), which was in most areas phased out with the introduction of *comprehensive schools. Others sat the common entrance, and this remains still the competitive form of entry to any *public school. An innovation in the early 1990s has been SATs (standard assessment tasks). These are tests which children in the state system take at the ages of 7, 11 and 14 to give teachers and parents an indication of their progress on a national scale of achievement (see the *national curriculum). The opposition of many teachers to the tests, both on principle and in detail, led to confrontation between unions and government during 1993.

In the last few years of schooling in England, Wales and Northern Ireland there are two groups of formal examinations which are taken by children in both the state and private system.

The first is the GCSE (General Certificate of Secondary Education), which pupils sit at the age of about 16 in sometimes as many as ten subjects. The results were originally classified in seven grades, from A to G, but from 1994 these are to be replaced by grades from 10 down to 4, representing the top levels of the national curriculum. Introduced as an exam in 1988, the GCSE differs from its predecessors in that it is taken by children of all levels of ability. It replaced the O level and the CSE; the O level (Ordinary level of the General Certificate of Education) had previously been reserved for the more academic pupils, while the less demanding CSE (Certificate of School Education) was taken by the rest.

The merged GCSE was welcomed by teachers, since it avoided the damage done to any child stuck in the wrong stream. It subsequently became the subject of dispute between the profession and the government on two counts. In the first year there was a high proportion of marks for course work (awarded by the pupils' own teachers for work done over a long period at school), which the government has insisted on reducing to achieve a more formal written exam; and from 1994 special papers can be taken by the brightest pupils, which critics say represents a reintroduction by the back door of the old two-level system. The exam also proved controversial on the subject of standards. After pupils achieved exceptionally good GCSE results in 1992, there were accusations that the examining boards were being more lenient than in previous years. This fear was compounded by concern that comparison with past standards would become impossible from 1994, because the new levels were not designed to tally exactly with the previous grades. The closest available link was that levels 10 and 9 would be equivalent to grade A; 8 to B; 7 and 6 to C, D, E; 5 to F; and 4 to G.

The other exam is the A level (Advanced level of the General Certificate of Education), taken by the majority of those who stay on at school after 16 and seen primarily as a credential for a place at a university. Most pupils only have time to prepare for A levels in three subjects, so a new exam was introduced in 1989 to broaden the range; the AS level (Advanced Supplementary) is of the same standard as the A level but its courses are narrower, enabling sixth-formers to tackle more subjects. The five grades in A levels and AS levels (from A to E in both cases) are translated into an overall score of points by *UCAS in the competition for university places. An innovation in 1992, attempting to counteract the academic bias of A levels and AS levels, is the GNVQ (General National Vocational Qualification). From September 1992 students can take courses in subjects such as business, manufacturing, or leisure and tourism; their GNVQs (first awarded after exams in 1994) are intended to be the equivalent of A levels as an entry requirement for university education. A new non-academic scale of examinations for those already in work is the *NVQ.

In November 1992 the government published the first comparative tables of schools' examination results in GCSE, A-levels and AS-levels. All state schools were included and some independent schools (in future years all are to be covered). The intention is to help parents in choosing a school for a child, but opponents argued that the information was misleading without equivalent data on the standards of children entering each school ('value added' being the relevant yardstick). However this will be available after a few years of the scheme, when SAT results have been recorded.

As in so many areas of British life, Scotland is different and has its own system of exams. Broadly speaking the SCE (Scottish Certificate of Education) is equivalent to the GCSE, while the SCE Higher grade approximates to the A level. The CSYS (Certificate of Sixth Year Studies) is a supplementary and more specialized qualification.

Exbury Gardens (24km/15m SW of Southampton) Woodland garden of 81ha/200ac created since 1919, famous for its rhododendrons. More than 1200 of the well-known Exbury hybrids grow in the woods.

Excalibur The sword of King *Arthur, first mentioned by *Geoffrey of Monmouth (by whom it is called Caliburn). The legends include two versions of how Arthur came by it. In one he alone, as a boy, is able to draw it from the stone in which it is fixed; in the other he receives it from the Lady of the Lake. Its end fits the second version. When wounded in his final battle, Arthur tells Sir Bedivere to throw Excalibur into the lake. An arm rises from the water to catch it, brandishes it three times, and vanishes.

exchange controls One of the first acts of the new Conservative administration in 1979 was to remove all exchange controls (except in relation to Rhodesia, which was subject to UN sanctions). Since that time the British have been able to take money out of the country without restriction. By contrast in the late 1960s (from July 1966 to January 1970) there was a limit of £50 for anyone going abroad other than on business.

exchange rate The prevailing rate at which one currency is exchanged for another, and therefore in British terms the level at which *sterling is traded. From 1821 to 1914 the pound was a cornerstone of the international currency system because it was on the *gold standard, meaning that it had a consistent value in relation to gold; as other countries joined the gold standard, a stable exchange rate between their currencies was automatically established. After World War II, in keeping with agreements made in 1944 in the USA (at Bretton Woods), a similar system was established with the dollar as the central currency. The USA guaranteed to exchange dollars for gold at a fixed rate, while other countries wishing to maintain a stable exchange rate pegged their currency to the dollar. Sterling was at a fixed rate of $2.80 to the pound until the devaluation of 1967 brought the level down to $2.40 (a fall of 14%). In 1971 the USA, bearing the costs of the Vietnam War and running a major balance of payments deficit from its currency obligations, temporarily suspended the convertibility of the dollar into gold while it negotiated a new agreed level. This introduced an era of fluctuation in currency markets, followed by successive efforts to restore semi-fixed parities.

In 1972 the countries of the European Community established the European currency snake, or the 'snake in the tunnel'. The currencies were to be allowed to fluctuate against each other within a margin of 2.25% (the snake) and the entire group was to remain within 4.45% either side of the dollar (the tunnel). But the system soon collapsed. By June 1972 speculative selling of sterling had forced the pound below the snake's limits; Britain left the system and became the first major currency in the postwar period to 'float', with its value decided directly by market forces. The snake was disintegrating and the tunnel itself was soon to vanish; in 1973 the dollar was allowed to float. The EC responded in 1979 with the *EMS, in which the exchange rate mechanism (ERM) tied the member currencies to the ECU and subsequently to the German mark.

Britain did not join the ERM in 1979, but in an attempt to reduce Britain's rate of inflation (by the external discipline of the system) Mrs Thatcher and John

Major, as prime minister and chancellor, took the country into the ERM in October 1990. The central value of the pound was fixed against the mark at DM2.95 (which many later argued was too high), with an allowed fluctuation of 6% as opposed to the 2.25% to which most member states were limited. This placed the pound's lowest permitted level at just below DM2.78.

In September 1992 another ERM currency, the Italian lira, was devalued. Shortly afterwards, on Tuesday September 15, speculators began selling sterling in large quantities. On that afternoon the pound hit its floor and the Bank of England spent £10bn purchasing sterling to maintain that level. On the Wednesday (soon to be known as Black Wednesday) the chancellor, by then Norman Lamont, raised interest rates by 2% and later in the day by a further 3% – but without improving sterling's value. The pound was then taken out of the ERM and allowed to float. By the end of the week it had fallen to DM2.62, and three weeks later it reached DM2.44 – a devaluation of 12% from its lowest ERM level and a loss (at that point) of more than £1bn of the money spent by the Bank of England in propping it up.

Exchange Rate Mechanism see *EMS.

Exchequer see *Chancellor of the Exchequer.

Exclusive Brethren see *Plymouth Brethren.

Exeter (105,000 in 1991) City on the river Exe; administrative centre of the county of Devon. From pre-Roman times it was of importance as the lowest point at which the river could be crossed and therefore as the gateway to the southwest tip of England. By the 13C sea-going vessels from the English Channel could no longer come this far up the river, but an exceptionally early canal, still surviving, was constructed from 1563 to link the city with the estuary.

Exeter was the centre of a diocese in late Anglo-Saxon times and a Norman cathedral was begun soon after the Conquest. Two Norman towers survive, surmounting in an unusual fashion the two ends of the transept. Between them there was built in the 13–14C the nave and choir of the present cathedral, an exceptionally consistent example of the Decorated style with a splendid west façade. The

Exeter Book, in the cathedral library, is an important collection of Old English poems, compiled in about 940 and given by Leofric, who in 1050 became Exeter's first bishop.

The Guildhall (dating from 1330, considerably rebuilt in the 15C and with a pillared exterior of the 16C) remains in use after nearly seven centuries. The Royal Albert Memorial Museum, by John Hayward (1808–91), was built 1865–6 as a civic museum, art gallery and library. Its collection is strong in lace, English ceramics and silver.

Exit (London W8) The name commonly used for the Voluntary Euthanasia Society, formed in 1935 by a group of doctors. Their purpose was to campaign for a change in the law so that doctors could legally help terminally ill patients who wanted to die. In 1961 suicide ceased to be illegal in Britain, but giving assistance to anyone committing suicide remains a criminal offence. The society distributes a 'living will', increasingly accepted by the medical profession, by which people can record in advance that in certain circumstances they do not wish to be artificially kept alive. Exit was the first of its kind, but there are now some 30 right-to-die societies around the world.

The issue of euthanasia acquired a new topicality in Britain in 1992 when a jury convicted a doctor, Nigel Cox, of attempted murder. He had given a lethal injection to a terminally ill patient, in extreme pain, who had begged him to do so. Dr Cox was given a suspended sentence and was allowed by the General Medical Council to continue in medical practice. See also *Hillsborough.

'Exit, pursued by a bear' see The *Winter's Tale.

Exmoor Area of high moorland bounded by steep wooded valleys, on the border of Somerset and Devon. It was designated in 1954 a *national park (686sq.km/ 265sq.m). Its rock formations are mainly of slate or sandstone, the highest peak being Dunkery Beacon (520m/ 1705ft). The moor is famous for its wildlife, supporting red deer (still hunted in the 1990s and the subject of much controversy), the Exmoor horned sheep and the famous Exmoor ponies – one of the oldest native British breeds.

Exchange rate of sterling against the US dollar and German mark: annual averages

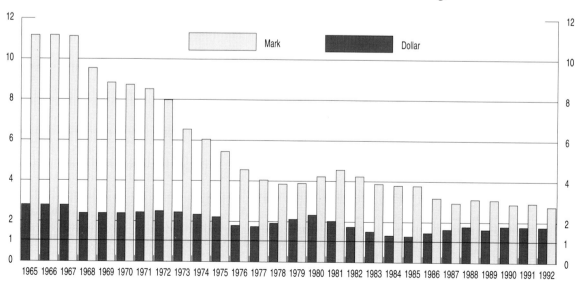

Source: Economic Trends (*see* *Central Statistical Office).

The entrance hall of the old Daily Express *building, with bold fan vaulting for the central light.*

Express The name of two of Britain's leading national newspapers. The *Daily Express* first appeared in April 1900 and made an immediate splash as the first daily paper to carry news instead of advertisements on its front page. Founded by Arthur Pearson (1866–1921), it was bought in 1916 by Lord *Beaverbrook, who two years later launched its sister paper, the *Sunday Express*. It was Beaverbrook who introduced in 1930 the logo of a crusader which still appears on each of the papers today. In 1936 the *Daily Express* had the largest circulation in the world (2.25 million copies). By then Beaverbrook had commissioned the magnificent Daily Express building in Fleet Street, with its sheer black glass façade (1931–2 by Ellis and Clarke) and extravagant Art Deco interiors (1936–9 by Owen Williams). This remained the office and printing plant of Express Newspapers until they moved in 1989 to Blackfriars Road.

Richard **Eyre** (b. 1943) Theatre and film director, since 1988 the artistic director of the *National Theatre. Among his own best-known productions have been *Guys and Dolls* (1982) and *Richard III* (1990) in the theatre, *Tumbledown* (BBC 1987) on television, and *The Ploughman's Lunch* (1983) in the cinema.

F

Fabian Society Founded in 1884 with the aim of working towards a democratic socialist state. The name was taken from the Roman general Fabius Cunctator (Fabius the Delayer), who in the 3rd century BC used a process of attrition to undermine Rome's enemy, Hannibal. The idea was to take the same long-term approach to changing Britain. Early members included George Bernard *Shaw (whose *Manifesto* of 1884 was one of their first pamphlets), Sidney *Webb and Annie *Besant. These and others contributed to the influential *Fabian Essays in Socialism* (1889), edited by Shaw. The society was one of the groups which helped to create the *Labour party, with which it retains close links, and its members were instrumental in establishing the *London School of Economics.

Façade (1921–3) Entertainment with music by William *Walton to a series of staccato poems by Edith *Sitwell, declaimed originally by the poet herself to specific and syncopated rhythms. Composed in 1921, it was performed privately in 1922 and in public in 1923. The music was used in 1931 for a ballet of the same name by *Ashton, which has been a popular item in the repertoire ever since.

'face that launched a thousand ships' see *Doctor Faustus*.

Face to Face (BBC 1958–60) Series of television interviews conducted by John Freeman, famous for the unprecedented directness of his questioning – on one occasion he caused Gilbert *Harding to break down and cry. Many of the guests who submitted themselves to this interrogation were immensely distinguished; they included Bertrand Russell, Edith Sitwell, Carl Jung and the notoriously prickly Evelyn Waugh. The title was revived in the early 1990s for a more relaxed series of interviews conducted by Jeremy Isaacs.

Factory Acts The unregulated mills and factories of the early *Industrial Revolution exploited cheap labour, particularly that of women and children, and reformers in the 19c fought a long campaign to outlaw the worst excesses. The first Factory Act (1802) limited to twelve the hours an apprentice child could work each day. Significant improvements were made, after a long struggle, in the act of 1833: children under 9 were not to work; children aged 9–13 were limited to eight hours a day and the 13–18 group to twelve hours; those between 9 and 13 were to be educated for two hours each day (the first compulsory education in Britain); and inspectors, albeit at the start only four for the whole country, were to be allowed into the factories. The next milestone, again long

fought for (particularly by Lord *Shaftesbury), was the act of 1847 which limited the working day for women and children to ten hours. By then the principle of legislative control was well established, and subsequent Factory Acts were often more concerned with making the control effective.

'Facts alone are wanted in life' see *Hard Times*.

Faculty of Advocates see *advocate.

FA Cup Knock-out competition established by the *Football Association in 1871, with 15 teams in the 1871–2 contest (won by Wanderers). Originally for amateur teams only, the professionals were allowed to compete after they had established their own separate *Football League. Since 1923 the *Cup Final has been held at Wembley. By the end of 1992 Tottenham Hotspur had the highest number of victories (8, of which 6 had been achieved in the years since 1960), followed by Aston Villa and Manchester United with 7 each.

The Faerie Queene (1590–6) Epic poem by Edmund *Spenser combining moral allegory with praise of England and of Elizabeth I. The six books that appeared (three in 1590, three in 1596) were part of a longer projected work, to be built around a courtly framework of 12 adventures on behalf of the queen by 12 of her knights. The verse is in what became known as the Spenserian stanza (8 lines of 10 syllables followed by one of 12 syllables, rhyming *ababbcbcc*). This verse form was often later revived, as for example by Byron for *Childe Harold's Pilgrimage*.

Fagin see *Oliver Twist*.

Fahrenheit see *temperature.

'Fain would I climb' see Walter *Raleigh.

Thomas **Fairfax** (1612–71, kt 1640, 3rd baron 1648) The leading general, with Oliver Cromwell, on the parliamentary side during the *English Civil War. The two scored their first notable success at *Marston Moor (1644). In 1645 Fairfax was given the task of forming the *New Model Army, and he and Cromwell (his second-in-command) were victorious together at *Naseby (1645). Politically Fairfax was moderate. He was appointed one of the judges of Charles I, but refused to sit; he was later an active supporter of the Restoration, but objected to the body of Cromwell being exhumed and hung in chains. He spent most of his time after 1650 in retirement in Yorkshire.

Fairford (13km/8m E of Cirencester) Town in Gloucestershire with a church in the Perpendicular style (St Mary's, 15c), containing a superb series of 28 stained-glass windows. Dating from the 16c, they tell the Bible story from the Creation to the terrifying Last Judgement at the west end of the nave.

Fair Isle The most southerly of the Shetlands, in an isolated position halfway towards the Orkneys. Best known in the past for the intricate multi-coloured patterns in which the islanders have knitted their wool, it now has increasing importance as a centre for the study of migrating birds.

fair shares for all A resonant phrase associated now with the ideals of the *Labour government of 1945. It was in fact devised by the Board of Trade, in 1941, as a slogan to prepare the public for clothes rationing.

Adam **Faith** (stage name of Terry Nelhams, b. 1940) Pop singer and actor who was one of Britain's leading pop stars in the early 1960s, having topped the charts with both his first two singles (*What do you Want?* 1959, *Poor Me* 1960). He became something of a spokesman for youth, discussing eternal verities with the archbishop of York on television and being interviewed on *Face to Face*. In the late 1960s he turned to acting, and achieved his greatest success as a sharp cockney character in the central role of the TV series *Budgie* (1971–3).

Nick **Faldo** (b. 1957) In the early 1990s the best golfer in Britain and many would say in the world; in 1992 he easily headed the world rankings and his tally of five major tournaments since 1987 is unrivalled. He has won the Open three times (1987, 90, 92), and the US Masters twice (1989, 90). He failed on his last putt to clinch the US Open in 1988, and went on to lose the play-off.

Finalists in the FA Cup since 1950

1950	Arsenal	2	Liverpool	0	
1951	Newcastle United	2	Blackpool	0	
1952	Newcastle United	1	Arsenal	0	
1953	Blackpool	4	Bolton Wanderers	3	
1954	West Bromwich Albion	3	Preston North End	2	
1955	Newcastle United	3	Manchester City	1	
1956	Manchester City	3	Birmingham City	1	
1957	Aston Villa	2	Manchester United	1	
1958	Bolton Wanderers	2	Manchester United	0	
1959	Nottingham Forest	2	Luton Town	1	
1960	Wolverhampton Wanderers	3	Blackburn Rovers	0	
1961	Tottenham Hotspur	2	Leicester City	0	
1962	Tottenham Hotspur	3	Burnley	1	
1963	Manchester United	3	Leicester City	1	
1964	West Ham United	3	Preston North End	2	
1965	Liverpool	2	Leeds United	1	
1966	Everton	3	Sheffield Wednesday	2	
1967	Tottenham Hotspur	2	Chelsea	1	
1968	West Bromwich Albion	1	Everton	0	
1969	Manchester City	1	Leicester City	0	
1970	Chelsea	2	Leeds United	1	(on replay)
1971	Arsenal	2	Liverpool	1	
1972	Leeds United	1	Arsenal	0	
1973	Sunderland	1	Leeds United	0	
1974	Liverpool	3	Newcastle United	0	
1975	West Ham United	2	Fulham	0	
1976	Southampton	1	Manchester United	0	
1977	Manchester United	2	Liverpool	1	
1978	Ipswich Town	1	Arsenal	0	
1979	Arsenal	3	Manchester United	2	
1980	West Ham United	1	Arsenal	0	
1981	Tottenham Hotspur	3	Manchester City	2	(on replay)
1982	Tottenham Hotspur	1	Queen's Park Rangers	0	(on replay)
1983	Manchester United	4	Brighton & Hove Albion	0	(on replay)
1984	Everton	2	Watford	0	
1985	Manchester United	1	Everton	0	
1986	Liverpool	3	Everton	1	
1987	Coventry City	3	Tottenham Hotspur	2	
1988	Wimbledon	1	Liverpool	0	
1989	Liverpool	3	Everton	2	
1990	Manchester United	1	Crystal Palace	0	(on replay)
1991	Tottenham Hotspur	2	Nottingham Forest	1	
1992	Liverpool	2	Sunderland	0	
1993	Arsenal	2	Sheffield Wednesday	1	(on replay)

Falkirk (37,000 in 1991) Industrial town in the Central region of Scotland. Its position at the northern end of the shortest line between the firths of Clyde and Forth gave it strategic importance from Roman times (the *Antonine Wall passes through it), and it has been the site of two major battles between the English and the Scots. On 22 July 1298 Edward I defeated the army of Sir William Wallace in an encounter which first proved the devastating effect of the English longbow. And on 17 January 1746 Prince Charles Edward Stuart achieved a welcome victory over the English forces in pursuit of him as he withdrew northwards towards the decisive encounter at Culloden.

The town became Scotland's chief cattle market in the 18C, and later developed into a centre for metal industries and the casting of iron.

Falkland (27km/17m SW of Perth) Small town which grew up round a favourite palace and hunting lodge of the early Stuart kings. James II began to build the palace in the mid-15C; a century later James V gave it French Renaissance trappings at the time of his marriage to the daughter of the French king, Francis I. From the early 18C the palace became derelict. What is seen today is largely the restoration carried out in the late 19C by the 3rd marquess of Bute.

Falkland Islands Group of islands in the south Atlantic, forming a British colony some 400km/250m east of the southern tip of Argentina. The history of settlement and of territorial claims is of immense complexity. The English were the first to land, but the French were the first to establish a colony (1764). The French sold the islands in 1766 to the Spanish (by whom they were known as the Islas Malvinas), and the Spanish lost them in 1820 to their newly independent colonists in Argentina. Meanwhile the British had maintained a fort on one of the smaller islands (from 1765) while laying claim to the whole. In 1833 they expelled the Argentinians, established a new capital at Stanley on East Falkland and brought in British settlers as cattle and sheep farmers. The Argentinian claim led eventually to a United Nations demand in 1966 for negotiations. These had made little progress when the Argentinian occupation of the islands in 1982 provoked the *Falklands War. The British victory was followed by a massively expensive build-up of a resident garrison to establish what became known as Fortress Falklands.

The previous Falkland Islands Dependencies are now administered separately as *South Georgia and the *British Antarctic Territory.

Falklands War (1982) Conflict resulting from the unresolved Argentinian claim to the *Falkland Islands. In March 1982, 60 Argentinians landed on South Georgia to collect scrap metal; they then hoisted the Argentinian flag and left some of their number on the island. There soon followed the news that an Argentine naval force was heading towards the Falklands, and on April 2 it was confirmed that the islands had been invaded and captured by some 5000 Argentinian troops; the governor, Rex Hunt, and the garrison of 81 Royal Marines were their prisoners (they were flown back to Britain a few days later). On April 3 the prime minister, Mrs Thatcher, announced that a large task force was being assembled to recapture the islands. The foreign secretary, Lord *Carrington, resigned in acknowledgement that the foreign office had been taken by surprise.

Air engagement over the Falklands began on April 30 with attacks by British Vulcan bombers. Britain had declared a 200-mile exclusion zone round the islands, within which any ship or aircraft would be assumed to be hostile, and the most controversial event of the war came with the torpedoing on May 3 of the Argentinian cruiser *General Belgrano* with considerable loss of life; the ship was subsequently said to have been outside the exclusion zone and moving away from it. The following day a British destroyer, HMS *Sheffield*, was hit by an Exocet missile with the loss of 20 men.

By May 21 Royal Marine Commandos and the Parachute Regiment had established a bridgehead on East Falkland; by May 28 the town of Port Darwin and the nearby Goose Green airstrip had been recaptured; and on June 14 it was announced that British troops were in Port Stanley, the capital, and that the Argentinians had surrendered. A total of 255 men of the task force had been killed during the war (and 655 Argentinians). Some of the heaviest casualties were on the landing ships *Sir Galahad* and *Sir Tristram*, which were bombed as they were unloading supplies near Fitzroy settlement. A few days after the ceasefire *Sir Galahad* was towed out to sea and sunk as a war grave.

The defeat of Argentina led to the immediate overthrow of the military junta which had conducted the war; four years later, in May 1986, General Galtieri and two of his closest colleagues were stripped of their rank and given jail sentences. It was not until October 1989 that Britain and Argentina formally ended hostilities.

Falstaff Shakespeare's fat knight, created in *Henry IV* and brought back by public demand in The *Merry Wives of Windsor*. His death in his bed, babbling of green fields, is described by Mistress Quickly in *Henry V*.

The most impressive early example of fan vaulting: the cloisters of Gloucester Cathedral, late 14C.

Rocky shore in the Farne Islands, with one of the pups of the colony of grey seals.

Family Division see *High Court.

Famous Five Heroes of 21 books by Enid *Blyton, from *Five on a Treasure Island* (1942) to *Five Are Together Again* (1963). The gang, tireless in the frustration of assorted villains and their evil schemes, consists of two boys (Julian and Dick), two girls (Anne and George, short for Georgina) and the dog Timmy. An earlier Famous Five were at school with *Billy Bunter.

Fanny Hill (1749) The title now generally used for *Memoirs of a Woman of Pleasure* by John Cleland (1709–89). A modern unexpurgated edition was banned on its publication by Mayflower Books in 1963, after trials in London and Manchester. Reissued in 1970, this time without being prosecuted, it sold widely as the first piece of pornography openly available in British bookshops as a work of literature. Fanny is a poor country girl from Lancashire who describes her sexual adventures in London in a tone of almost pastoral innocence but with an unblushing wealth of sexual detail.

Fantasia on a Theme by Thomas Tallis (1910) Composition by *Vaughan Williams for string quartet and double string orchestra. The theme is a psalm tune, one of nine composed by *Tallis for a metrical psalter published in 1567.

Fantasia on British Sea Songs (1905) Arrangement of songs by Henry *Wood, compiled for a concert to celebrate the centenary of *Trafalgar. Its nine sections include *Tom Bowling, Home, Sweet Home, See, the conquering hero comes* and finally *Rule, Britannia!* The piece is now always played at the last night of the *Proms, where the audience join in singing *Rule, Britannia!*

fan vaulting Intricate roof pattern introduced in England in the late 14C, the earliest major example being the cloisters of *Gloucester Cathedral. The ribs spray out from the base of the vault in a fan-like pattern which is decorative rather than structural; it is in effect an extension of the stone tracery in the windows, characteristic of the later stages of *Gothic architecture.

Michael **Faraday** (1791–1867) Experimental physicist responsible for important disoveries in electromagnetism. The son of a blacksmith, he was largely self-educated and only acquired training in science after applying for a job as *Davy's assistant at the *Royal Institution in 1812. Until the age of 30 he was primarily a chemist (his discoveries included benzene), but from 1831 he was fascinated by the relationship between magnetism and electricity. His experiments led him to electromagnetic induction (simultaneously discovered in the USA by Joseph Henry), which was an essential step on the way to the dynamo and transformer; his study of the laws of electrolysis provided such familiar modern concepts and words as electrode, anode and cathode; and his idea of lines of force led *Maxwell towards modern field theory. Faraday had a genius for communicating the excitement of science, particularly in the famous Friday Evening Discourses which he began to give in 1826 at the Royal Institution. His laboratory at the institution is kept as a museum.

'far, far better thing' see A *Tale of Two Cities.

Far from the Madding Crowd (1874) Novel by Thomas *Hardy in which the patient love of Gabriel Oak for Bathsheba Everdene, the wayward owner of the farm on which he works, triumphs at last over the posturings of her other admirers. Gabriel proposes at the start of the book and is only accepted at the end. Meanwhile Bathsheba has married the bombastic Sergeant Troy; he is shot by her next frenetic suitor, Farmer Boldwood, who in turn is imprisoned as criminally insane. The title is from *Gray's *Elegy*, where the poet praises those country people who keep the tenor of their own way amid the ignoble strife of the crowd.

Farmer George see James *Gillray.

Farnborough Air Show Event held every other year in the first week of September at Farnborough in Hampshire – the home of the Royal Aircraft Establishment. It is a trade show for the sale of aircraft, with a flying display each afternoon as a public entertainment. The first show was held at Olympia in 1918; in 1932 the exhibition moved to Hendon, north of London, where it was for the first time linked with flying displays; and since 1948 it has been at Farnborough. It was held each year until 1962, when it became biennial (alternating with the Paris Show).

Farne Islands Group of uninhabited rocky islands off the coast of Northumberland, a notable bird sanctuary and home to a colony of grey seals. St *Cuthbert died on the largest island in 687, but the group is best known for the connection with Grace *Darling.

George **Farquhar** (1678–1707) Irish playwright who added a much-needed dash of realism to the artificial conventions of *Restoration comedy. He was born in Londonderry and moved to London in 1697, achieved lasting success only with the plays written in the final two years of his life, The *Recruiting Officer* (1706) and The *Beaux' Stratagem* (1707).

Tommy **Farr** (1913–86) Welsh boxer who became British and Commonwealth champion when he beat Ben Foord in the Harringay Arena in March 1937. In June of that year Joe Louis knocked out James Braddock to become world champion, and in August Farr was his first challenger for the title. He astonished everyone by losing narrowly on points; the next seven fighters rash enough to challenge the Brown Bomber were all knocked out. Farr relinquished his titles and stayed in the United States to capitalize on his sudden fame.

Terry **Farrell** (b. 1938) Architect associated with a colourful post-Modernism, first noticed in his studios for *TV-am, where the early-morning theme was suggested by egg cups on the roofline and a sunrise-coloured entrance. Other buildings include a temple-like pavilion for the *Henley Royal Regatta, and most recently a structure enclosing Charing Cross Station (completed 1991) and a new headquarters for MI6 near the south end of Vauxhall Bridge (1992).

farthing see *£.s.d.

Fastnet Race Yachting race over a 975km/605m offshore course from Cowes on the Isle of Wight, round Fastnet Rock (off the southwest coast of Ireland), and back to Plymouth. Established in 1925, it is held every other August, during Cowes week, with a wide range of boats competing. The race of 1979 was a reminder that the dangers are real; appalling weather capsized many yachts and caused 15 deaths. Since 1957 the race has included a top class of custom-built racing yachts, for it doubles now as the final event of the *Admiral's Cup.

Father Brown see G.K. *Chesterton.

Father Christmas A bearded figure of this name has been attached to Christmas festivities in England since at least the 17C, but in his present form he was imported from the USA in the early 19C. The Dutch in New York had the tradition of Sinterklaas, a corruption of St Nicholas (a saint of the 4C, whose legends include his throwing a golden dowry into the bedroom of three impoverished sisters). Sinterklaas filled the shoes of Dutch-American children with presents on his saint's day, December 6. English-speaking families in New York seem to have adapted this custom to Christmas. A poem by Clement Clarke Moore, *A Visit from St Nicholas*, was published in the USA in 1823 and has all the ingredients of the modern British custom: a stocking put out on Christmas Eve, a sleigh drawn by reindeer arriving on the roof, and St Nicholas, clad in fur, coming down the chimney with a sack of toys. When the poem reached England, its details became attached to the existing figure of Father Christmas (Santa Claus, the usual name now for Sinterklaas in the USA, remains a less common alternative in Britain). The multiple appearance of Father Christmas, in parties, streets or shops, dates from the Edwardian period.

Father of the House Title given to the MP who has sat in the House of Commons for the longest uninterrupted period (even if for different constituencies). It carries no duties or responsibilities. The Father of the House after the 1992 election was Edward *Heath.

Father William see *Alice in Wonderland*.

fathom see *length.

Guy **Fawkes** see *Gunpowder Plot.

Fawlty Towers (BBC 1975–9) Television comedy series which has lodged in the nation's collective memory so securely that it is hard to believe there were only 13 half-hour programmes (six in 1975, seven in 1979). The programmes were written by John *Cleese and Connie Booth, who were married at the time. Cleese played Basil Fawlty, the frantic owner of the hotel in which the sketches were set; Prunella *Scales was his stern wife, Sybil; Connie Booth was the receptionist; and the spectacularly incompetent Spanish waiter, Manuel, was performed by Andrew Sachs.

FD or **FID DEF** One or other of these abbreviations of *Fidei Defensor* (Latin for Defender of the Faith) has appeared on every British coin since the reign of George I, in a somewhat cheeky perpetuation of a title granted to Henry VIII in 1521 by Pope Leo X. Henry was being hailed as a defender of the Roman Catholic faith, because of a pamphlet he had written attacking Luther. When Henry himself later broke with Rome, the papacy stripped him of his title; but in 1543 Henry was able to persuade the English parliament to vote it back to him and to his successors in perpetuity, as defenders now of the *Church of England.

The female of the species (1911) Poem by Rudyard *Kipling with the refrain 'The female of the species is more deadly than the male'.

Fenians (known also as the Irish Republican Brotherhood) Irish insurrectionary group, established in both Ireland and the USA in the late 1850s and taking its name from the *Fianna*, the band of warriors of the legendary Irish hero Finn McCool. The Fenians introduced into Irish politics a strand of violence which survives in the north. Their numbers dwindled in the late 19C, after the failure of an abortive uprising in Ireland in 1867, but they renewed their efforts in World War I when Britain's difficulties seemed to offer opportunities for insurrection. They were prominent among those planning the *Easter Rising of 1916, and among the survivors of that event who formed the *IRA early in 1919.

Fens Low-lying coastal area in eastern England, about 120km/75m north to south from Lincoln to Cambridge, and in places extending some 50km/30m inland from the *Wash (of which the region is a silted up extension). The Fens were peaty marshland with occasional firm islands (most notably *Ely) until drainage was undertaken in the 17–19C. They are now rich agricultural land.

Roger **Fenton** (1816–69) The first war photographer whose work has survived. He was sent out to the *Crimean War early in 1855 by a Manchester publisher, Thomas Agnew, who issued his photographs in five portfolios later that year. Fenton took with him a converted winemerchant's delivery vehicle, which was both his caravan and his darkroom. Marked 'Photographic Van', it became an object of great curiosity to the troops. Working with large glass plates, and exposure times from 3 to 20 seconds, his images were posed groups rather than action shots. But it was the first time the public at home had any such direct glimpse of a theatre of war.

Photograph by Fenton of his caravan and dark room in the Crimea, with his assistant Marcus Sparling (1855).

Fermanagh One of the six *counties of Northern Ireland, and the only one to have remained an administrative unit in *local government as the district of Fermanagh.

Fern Hill One of the best known of the poems of Dylan *Thomas, published in *Deaths and Entrances* (1946). He evokes the happiness and sense of freedom of a child in the countryside, 'as I was young and easy under the apple boughs'. Fern Hill was an isolated farm near Llangain where Dylan often stayed with a much loved aunt, his mother's sister Annie Jones.

Kathleen **Ferrier** (1912–53) Contralto who established herself as one of Britain's best-loved singers in a tragically brief career before her death from cancer. Her talent was recognized in her first London appearance, in Handel's *Messiah* in Westminster Abbey in 1943. Best known for her concert performances of song cycles and of works such as Mahler's *Das Lied von der Erde*, she also performed the title roles in Britten's *The Rape of Lucretia* and Gluck's *Orfeo* at Glyndebourne in 1946–7. She made memorable recordings of English folk songs, such as *Blow the wind southerly*.

Royal **Festival Hall** (London SE1) The capital city's main concert hall, on the south bank of the Thames, designed 1949–51 by Robert Matthew (1906–75) and Leslie Martin (b. 1908) for the *Festival of Britain. The *South Bank complex grew around it. Since 1992 the *London Philharmonic has been the resident orchestra.

Festival of Britain (1951) Exhibition and season of festivities held on the south bank of the Thames in central London, marking the centenary of the *Great Exhibition and celebrating postwar Britain. The *Festival Hall is the only feature of it to survive, though the event launched the *South Bank as an area for the arts. Other central features were the Dome of Discovery and the Skylon, a futuristic version of an obelisk.

Fettes College One of Scotland's leading *public schools, situated in Edinburgh. It was founded in 1870 according to the terms of a bequest by William Fettes (1750–1836), a wine and tea merchant who was twice Lord Provost of Edinburgh. The school buildings are a bizarre combination of French chateau and *Scottish baronial, by David Bryce.

feudalism System of administration, standard in England after the Norman *Conquest, by which the upper levels of a military society assign land to those below them in return for military service when required. The process begins when a king, at the peak of the feudal pyramid, entrusts large areas of newly conquered or confiscated land to individual barons, as *William the Conqueror did after 1066; these territories are then subdivided as each lord assigns fiefs (parcels of land from which income can be derived) to his own vassals. This is a rapid and effective way of controlling an area, trouble arising only in later generations when those who have inherited fiefs may have less personal loyalty to their lord or king.

Feudalism developed among the Franks under Charlemagne in the 8c and spread eventually through most of Europe. When the Vikings conquered northwest France in the 10c they adopted the system, and it was their Norman descendants who accelerated its development in England (there is evidence of earlier beginnings of a native feudalism among the Anglo-Saxons).

At the bottom of feudal society were the peasants, who worked the land on the *open-field system. They fell into two classes. Free peasants paid for their right to farm the land by performing military service when required, or agricultural service at other times; the villeins (or serfs) were tied to the land, for their payment was a given number of days of work on the fields of the lord of the manor. From the 12c the obligations of both groups began to be commuted for payment of a cash 'quitrent', enabling the lord to hire full-time labourers of his own. A free peasant taking this option held his land as a freehold of the manor, and a villein as a 'copyhold' (a less secure tenure). By the second half of the 14c the free peasants had been transformed into the distinctly non-feudal *yeomanry, and many of the villeins were wage labourers capable of such equally non-feudal gestures as the *Peasants' Revolt.

The Few The young pilots of the *Battle of Britain. After they had won the first respite in the battle, *Churchill told the House of Commons, on 20 August 1940, that 'never in the field of human conflict was so much owed by so many to so few'.

Ffestiniog Railway Narrow-gauge railway running 23km/14m from Porthmadog, on the west coast of Wales, up the vale of Ffestiniog to Blaenau Ffestiniog. It opened in 1836 for horse-drawn wagons bringing slate down to the harbour. The line was adapted to a passenger service with steam engines in the 1860s. In recent decades enthusiasts have gradually brought the old engines and rolling stock back into use.

FID DEF see *FD.

The Field With its subtitle 'Magazine for the Country', it has been providing comment on country life and sports since its first issue in 1853. In addition to shooting, fishing and farming, the *Field* has traditionally paid particular attention to all horse-related activities (Surtees, the creator of *Jorrocks, was involved in its launch). It also has the distinction of having provided the original prize at *Wimbledon. The magazine was weekly until 1986, when it became a monthly.

Henry **Fielding** (1707–54) Playwright, journalist, lawyer and above all novelist. His first career was in the theatre (and his greatest success the mock-heroic farce *Tom Thumb* 1730), but his satirical attacks on Walpole provoked a more rigorous censorship of the stage from 1737, bringing his theatrical career to an end. His polemics were then confined to journalism, but meanwhile he resumed his legal studies. In 1748 he was appointed magistrate in London's Bow Street court, a post which he took with unprecedented seriousness, making detailed studies of London's underworld (others in the post had been more concerned with the perks). In about 1750 he was joined on the bench by his blind half-brother, John Fielding (d. 1780). Together they established the *Bow Street runners.

But Fielding's fame rests primarily on his fiction. The success of *Pamela*, Samuel *Richardson's novel of virtue, provoked Fielding to write *Shamela* – a lampoon, anonymous but almost certainly his, which retells Richardson's story with less virtuous implications. It also inspired his own first novel, *Joseph Andrews* (1742). Joseph is the brother of Richardson's Pamela, who also appears in the book. In its rough but colourful world, of a kind well known to Fielding, virtue is found not among the respectable, as in *Pamela*, but in a handful of everyday characters who happen to be honest, generous and warm – most notably the absent-minded Parson Adams. The broad canvas of *Joseph Andrews*, as Joseph and Adams travel the country together, established a new pattern for the English novel which was triumphantly extended in Fielding's best-known work, *Tom Jones* (1749).

The old and the new in 1838: Turner's contrasting image of a paddle-steaming tug and the Fighting Téméraire.

Field of Cloth of Gold (7–24 June 1520) Series of meetings near Calais between Henry VIII and Francis I of France, famous for the splendour of the setting. Each king stayed in a temporary palace of timber and canvas; and there was much jousting and tilting and banqueting. Henry was expressing general goodwill rather than attempting an alliance, because he immediately afterwards engaged in similar but less lavish festivities in Kent with Francis's great rival, the Holy Roman Emperor Charles V.

Gracie **Fields** (stage name of Grace Stansfield, 1898–1979, DBE 1979) *Music-hall performer from Lancashire who became a national star ('Our Gracie') after being seen in London in *Mr Tower of London* (1924). Her film career began in 1931 with *Sally in our Alley* (featuring the famous 18C song of that name) and included *Sing As We Go* (1934), which she chose as the title of her autobiography.

field sports see *blood sports.

Ranulph **Fiennes** (Ranulph Twisleton-Wykeham-Fiennes, pronounced *fines*, b. 1944, 3rd bt 1944) Indefatigable polar adventurer whose expeditions to the earth's extremities have resulted in danger, frostbite, much media attention and funds for the Multiple Sclerosis Society. In 1993 he and Michael Stroud (b. 1955) became the first to cross Antarctica without external support.

Fife (341,000 in 1991, administrative centre Glenrothes) A *region on the east coast of central Scotland, lying between the firths of Tay and Forth. Until 1975 roughly the same area was a *county of the same name (a small part of it is now in the Central region).

'15 Rebellion (also known simply as the Fifteen) The first of two military attempts to recover the throne for the *Stuarts from the house of *Hanover. An uprising began in Scotland in September 1715, and the rebels had suffered two defeats (at Preston and Sherrifmuir) before James *Stuart himself landed at Peterhead on December 22. He went to *Scone where his coronation was being prepared, but the approach of the English and the weakness of his own position caused him to beat a hasty retreat. He was back in France by February 10. Thirty years later his son's equivalent effort in the *'45 Rebellion was less of a fiasco.

James **Figg** see *boxing.

Fighter Command see Lord *Dowding.

The **'Fighting Téméraire'** *Tugged to her last Berth to be broken up* (1838, National Gallery) Painting by *Turner of a great gilded man-of-war towed by a small black steamer, belching smoke, against the background of a brilliant sunset. The *Téméraire*, launched at Chatham in 1798, became known as *The Fighting Téméraire* after distinguishing herself at Trafalgar. Sold for scrap in 1838, Turner shows her being towed up the Thames to London docks.

Fiji Member of the *Commonwealth from 1970 to 1987. It is an archipelago in the southwest Pacific, consisting of more than 800 islands of various sizes. It was in a state of anarchy in 1874 when the paramount chief, Cakobau, invited Britain to assume sovereignty. Fiji was a crown colony until independence in 1970. After two military coups in 1987, the country allowed its membership of the Commonwealth to lapse.

*La **Fille Mal Gardée*** Ballet of 1789 by Jean Dauberval, known now in Britain in the version of 1960 choreographed by *Ashton (to music of Hérold, adapted by John Lanchbery). A mix of rustic romance and comedy, it tells the story of Lise, whose love for Colas is until the last minute frustrated by the efforts of her mother, Widow Simone (a *travesti* role, danced by a man), to marry her off to the half-witted but wealthy Alain.

film certificates The British Board of Film Classification grades films within categories. U (for Universal) means that the film is suitable for everyone; PG (Parental Guidance) warns that certain scenes may be considered unsuitable for young children; the numbers 12, 15 and 18 limit the audience to people above those ages. R18 indicates a sex film, restricted to specialist cinemas where no-one under the age of 18 may be admitted. There are similar classifications for videos, with the addition of Uc (particularly suitable for children).

Financial Times Britain's leading financial daily newspaper. It was founded in 1888, and in 1893 adopted the pink paper which subsequently became a distinguishing mark (at the time another newspaper was already famous for this colour, the *Sporting Times*, popularly known as the 'Pink 'Un'). In 1945 the paper merged with its only serious rival in the City, the *Financial News*, founded in 1884; it was actually the *News* which bought the *Times*, but the latter had a larger circulation (not to mention its famous pink paper), so its name was kept. The present owners, *Pearson, bought the *Financial Times* in 1957. By then it was broadening its range and had introduced an arts page which won a high reputation for the quality of its critics. Today the *Financial Times* reaches an international daily readership, being printed – in all cases on pink paper – in Germany, France, the USA and Japan in addition to Britain.

Financial Times Indices The longest-running index of *Stock Exchange prices in the **Financial Times* is the Ordinary Share Index, known also as the 30-Share Index. It began in the *Financial News* in 1935 (1 July 1935 = 100) and continued in the *Financial Times* when the papers merged in 1945; it tracks a selection of 30 leading British industrial shares. This remained the standard daily yardstick of share price movement until the mid-1980s, when it began to be upstaged by the FT-SE 100-Share Index, commonly known as Footsie. Based on minute-by-minute market details supplied by the Stock Exchange, Footsie reflects every movement in the share values of the 100 largest British companies, with their influence on it

weighted according to each company's size; it was launched in January 1984 (30 Dec. 1983 = 1000). The other main index still in use in the early 1990s was the FT-Actuaries All-Share Index, based on a much broader range of quoted securities (though not actually all shares, as the name suggests). When launched in 1962 (10 Apr. 1962 = 100), it took 594 equities into account – about 60% of the total.

In 1992 two new FT-SE indices were launched. The FT-SE 250 index (base 2000 in 1985) reflects the share prices of the 250 next largest companies after those in the FT-SE 100 index; and the FT-SE 350 index (base 1000 in 1985) combines the market movements in the FT-SE 100 and 250 indices.

financial year For a company the financial year is a 12-month accounting period which can begin at any point in the calendar. For the assessment of *income tax the financial year ends on April 5. This strange date derives indirectly from the late medieval *calendar, when the new year began on March 25 (Lady Day). In 1752, with the introduction of the Gregorian calendar, 11 days were removed from September; and so that there should be no accusation of annual taxes being levied on a short year, the government extended the end of the 1752–3 financial year by those 11 days to April 5. The government's own financial year was tidied up in 1854 to begin, with the start of a new month, on April 1.

'finest hour' The climax of a peroration to the House of Commons on 18 June 1940 (coincidentally the anniversary of the Battle of Waterloo), in which *Churchill warned that the *Battle of Britain was about to begin and that failure would mean a new Dark Age for Europe. 'Let us therefore', he concluded, 'brace ourselves to our duties and so bear ourselves that if the British Empire and its Commonwealth last for a thousand years men will still say, "This was their finest hour" '.

Fingal's Cave The best-known cave on *Staffa, some 69m/76yd long and with its roof formed of straight-sided basalt columns. The floor of the cave is well below sea level even at low tide. Mendelssohn visited Staffa in 1829 and his *Hebrides Overture* (first performed in London in 1832) soon became known as *Fingal's Cave*. Fingal was a pseudo-legendary Scottish hero, invented in the 18c in one of the greatest of British literary frauds (see *Ossian).

fingerprints The use of fingerprint classification for criminals was introduced by the British in India in 1897, and subsequently at *Scotland Yard in 1901. It was first

Share prices: the two main Financial Times Indices

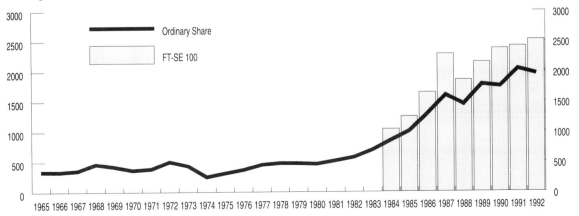

The figures for the Ordinary Share index are an average for the year; those for the FT-SE 100 are the level at mid-year.

proposed theoretically in 1880 that every person had a unique fingerprint. Francis *Galton verified this through systematic studies, for which he used a classification system based on arches, loops and whorls (*Finger Prints* 1892). Galton's method was improved by the inspector general of police in Bengal, Edward Henry (1850–1931), and it was the Henry system which became standard throughout most of the world (Spanish-speaking countries are the exception, using the Vucetich system).

Ian Hamilton Finlay (b. 1925) Scottish artist who first became known for his concrete poetry (in which the appearance of the poem is a large part of its point) and then moved on to carved inscriptions, conceptual sculpture and landscape gardening. The sculpture garden which he has created at Stonypath (or Little Sparta), his home in Strathclyde, became the subject of a distinctly conceptual dispute between the local council and himself. The council classified it as a commercial art gallery, liable to rates; Finlay declared it to be a temple, immune from payment.

finnan haddie Smoked haddock, deriving its name from Findon, a seaside village south of Aberdeen where the particular method of curing was originally practised.

Albert Finney (b. 1936) Actor whose reputation on stage and screen was firmly established in 1960. In that year he appeared in London in the title role of *Billy Liar* and starred in *Saturday Night and Sunday Morning*. He followed these successes with the title role in John Osborne's *Luther* (1961, and 1963 in New York). Subsequent films have included *Tom Jones* (1963) and *Murder on the Orient Express* (1974, as Hercule Poirot).

Tom Finney (b. 1922) Footballer (right winger) for Preston North End (1937–59), known as the Preston Plumber because that had been his trade. Only a few years younger than Stanley *Matthews, who played in the same position on the field, Finney had a similar ability to follow a long run down the wing with a very precise pass. When the two men played together for England, Finney switched to the left wing with a versatility which caused many to consider him the greater of two great players. He was capped 76 times for England.

Ronald Firbank (1886–1926) Novelist who became a cult figure through his stylishly fantastic plots, his oblique methods of narrative and his sly dialogue. He was as exotic as his books; a wit, a dandy, a homosexual, a convert to Roman Catholicism and a rich invalid, he spent much of his short life travelling for his health. His best-known book is *Valmouth* (1919), set in a British spa town where people have unusually long and active sex lives; the central character is a sensual black masseuse, Mrs Yajñavalkya.

Fireworks Music see George Frideric *Handel.

First Blast of the Trumpet see The *Monstrous Regiment of Women.

first catch your hare see Hannah *Glasse.

first-class cricket In general use this term has referred to *cricket played by national teams and by teams featuring in the *county championship, but it was formally defined in 1947 as applying to matches lasting three days or more. For those compiling statistical records, first-class cricket is deemed to have started in 1815.

First Cuckoo in Spring see Frederick *Delius.

First Fleet see *Australia.

First Folio The name given to the collected edition of 36 plays by *Shakespeare, published in 1623 by two of his fellow actors (John Heminge 1556–1630, Henry Condell d. 1627). The volume was printed by William Jaggard (d. 1623) and includes commemorative verses by, among others, Ben *Jonson. Another edition, the Second Folio, was published in 1632, to be followed by a third and fourth in 1663 and 1685. About half the plays had previously been printed as separate *quartos.

first-footing see *New Year.

First Lord of the Admiralty see *Royal Navy.

First Lord of the Treasury see *Prime Minister.

first past the post see *two-party system.

First Reading see *Act of Parliament.

First Sea Lord see *Royal Navy.

fish and chips Britain's traditional fast food, consisting of deep-fried fillets of fish in batter and potato chips. In the old days, as an early form of takeaway, the fish and chips were carried from the shop in a twist of newspaper. The first recorded use of the phrase is surprisingly early (1876). Perhaps less surprisingly, it is a complaint: 'Fish and chip shops were a considerable source of nuisance'.

Fishbourne Roman Palace (2km/1m W of Chichester) The largest Roman building to have been discovered in Britain. The find was made in 1960 when a water main was being dug. Excavations revealed the remains of a palace and its gardens covering 4ha/10ac, dating from the 1st century AD and believed to have belonged to Cogidubnus, the ruler of a local British tribe who collaborated with the invading Romans and was suitably rewarded. The palace, which was destroyed by fire in the late 3C, had superb mosaic floors – in particular the so-called 'dolphin mosaic', with its centrepiece of Cupid riding a dolphin.

Geoffrey Fisher (1887–1972, baron 1961) Archbishop of Canterbury 1945–61, having previously been bishop of Chester (1932–9) and of London (1939–45); before his bishopric at Chester he was headmaster of Repton school for 18 years. He was the first archbishop of Canterbury to become widely known to the public through television, beginning with the coronation of Elizabeth II in 1953. His tenure of office also included a historic moment in the relationship between the Roman Catholic and Anglican churches; when he visited Pope John XXIII in the Vatican in 1960, it was the first time since the Reformation that a pope and an archbishop of Canterbury had met.

John Fisher (1469–1535) Bishop and saint, who was beheaded two weeks before Thomas *More and on the same charge of treason, for refusing to accept the Act of *Supremacy. Fisher, who had been bishop of Rochester since 1504, was a scholar of European stature, a friend of Erasmus and a leading polemicist against Luther. His support was therefore essential to Henry VIII, but he had been considerably more outspoken than More in rejecting the proposed divorce of Catherine of Aragon. He was canonized in 1935; his feast day is the date of his martyrdom, June 22.

fishing see *angling.

Fisons Pharmaceutical company which grew spectacularly during the 1980s but was faring less well in the early 1990s, largely because of difficulties in getting two of its most profitable drugs licensed in the USA. James Fison, a village baker in 18c Suffolk, was the founder of a family enterprise in agricultural produce which in the mid-19c became a leading producer of artificial fertilizers. The company's rapid growth during the 1980s stemmed from a decision to close down this traditional side of the firm's activities and to concentrate on pharmaceuticals, scientific equipment and gardening products.

'fit for heroes' The promise of a land fit for heroes, offered to the nation after the appalling sacrifices of World War I, was far from fulfilled in the decades of the *General Strike and the *Depression. It was made by *Lloyd George in a speech of November 1918: 'What is our task? To make Britain a fit country for heroes to live in.'

Gerry **Fitt** see *SDLP.

Edward **FitzGerald** see *Omar Khayyám.

Mrs **Fitzherbert** see *George IV.

Fitzwilliam Museum (Cambridge) Founded in 1816 by the bequest of the collection and library of Lord Fitzwilliam (1745–1816). He also left money for the building, designed by George Basevi (1794–1845), which opened in 1848. The breadth of Fitzwilliam's interests made his own collection museum-like in its scope, and extensive additions along the same lines have formed what has been called the 'finest small museum in Europe'. Among the antiquities, ceramics, musical manuscripts and ivories, it is the paintings which are perhaps the most impressive of all, including superb Venetian works of the 16c.

Five Members Members of parliament, leaders of the opposition to Charles I, whom the king tried to arrest for treason on 3 January 1642. Arriving with 400 men, Charles forcibly entered the House of Commons (a grave breach of parliamentary privilege). The five had been forewarned and had made their escape, but when the king asked the Speaker, William Lenthall, whether he saw any of them in the chamber, he received a reply which has won a secure place in parliamentary history: 'I have neither eye to see, nor tongue to speak here, but as the House is pleased to direct me'. The five members were John Pym, John Hampden, Arthur Haselrig, Denzil Holles and William Strode. The king's high-handed action was widely seen as a turning point in the events leading to the *English Civil War.

Five-Mile Act see *Clarendon Code.

'Five Nations' tournament Annual round of international matches in *rugby union football between England, Wales, Scotland, Ireland and France. The four British nations competed against each other from 1883 and France joined in 1910. Each nation plays each of the others once in the season, and the tournament is won on points. But two forms of outright win are hotly contested: the internal triple crown when one of the British teams beats the other three; and the grand slam, when one nation beats all the rest. By 1992 England had pulled ahead of Wales in grand slams and had an equal number of triple crowns, after achieving the rare feat of two grand slams in succession (1991, 92). But Wales was still ahead in the total number of tournament wins, and in 1993 England failed to complete an unprecedented trio of successive grand slams.

Triple Crowns and Grand Slams in the Five Nations tournament

	Triple Crown	Grand Slam
1883	England	
1884	England	
1891	Scotland	
1892	England	
1893	Wales	
1894	Ireland	
1895	Scotland	
1899	Ireland	
1900	Wales	
1901	Scotland	
1902	Wales	
1903	Scotland	
1905	Wales	
1907	Scotland	
1908	Wales	Wales
1909	Wales	Wales
1911	Wales	Wales
1913	England	England
1914	England	England
1921	England	England
1923	England	England
1924	England	England
1925	Scotland	Scotland
1928	England	England
1933	Scotland	
1934	England	
1937	England	
1938	Scotland	
1948	Ireland	Ireland
1949	Ireland	
1950	Wales	Wales
1952	Wales	Wales
1954	England	
1957	England	England
1960	England	
1965	Wales	
1968	France	
1969	Wales	
1971	Wales	Wales
1976	Wales	Wales
1977	Wales	France
1978	Wales	Wales
1979	Wales	
1980	England	England
1981	France	
1982	Ireland	
1984	Scotland	Scotland
1985	Ireland	
1987	France	
1988	Wales	
1990	Scotland	Scotland
1991	England	England
1992	England	England

Total wins for each nation

Tournament	Triple Crown	Grand Slam
Wales 32	Wales 17	England 10
England 29	England 17	Wales 8
Scotland 21	Scotland 10	France 4
Ireland 18	Ireland 6	Scotland 3
France 17	Ireland 1	

Slipware plate of Charles II and Catherine of Braganza: an early product of the Five Towns region of Staffordshire, c.1675.

fives There were several ancient games known as fives (possibly from the five fingers), in which the ball was struck with the open hand. The two main varieties surviving today, played with a small hard ball and padded gloves, were formalized at *public schools during the 19C. The more eccentric of the two, Eton fives, developed from a game which the boys played while waiting to go into chapel. The courts, of which the first was built in 1840, duplicated the chapel's buttresses and projections and even the drain at the foot of the entrance steps, resulting in a game in which the ball bounces at strange angles from a multiplicity of surfaces. Rugby fives, by contrast, is played in a rectangular court similar to a squash court.

Five Towns A term for the Potteries in Staffordshire, where the ceramic industry was concentrated in five closely linked towns (Tunstall, Burslem, Hanley, Stoke-upon-Trent and Longton), which were merged in 1910 as *Stoke-on-Trent. The phrase is associated in particular with Arnold *Bennett, who set many of his novels in the five towns, renaming them respectively Turnhill, Bursley, Hanbridge, Knype and Longshaw.

flags see *Union Jack and *Welsh dragon.

Flamborough Head (32km/20m SE of Scarborough) Chalk promontory of broken cliffs (about 122m/400ft high) jutting out into the North Sea.

John **Flamsteed** (1646–1719) English astronomer and, at the age of 29, the first *Astronomer Royal. In the newly established *Royal Observatory he made the systematic observations which led to his 3-volume *Historia Coelestis Britannica* (British Celestial History), published posthumously in 1725. This included his *British Catalogue* of 2935 stars observed at Greenwich, which forms the basis of all subsequent star catalogues.

Barry **Flanagan** (b. 1941) Sculptor characterized by a playful manner with materials and form, whether in shapes contrived by the weight of sand in tubes of cloth, or in roughly shaped fragments of stone, or in his best-known work – a fanciful series of leaping hares.

Flanagan and Allen see *Crazy Gang.

Flanders and Swann Cabaret duo who had a great success with their revue *At the Drop of a Hat* (London 1957–9, New York 1959–60). It consisted entirely of their own songs, with the composer (Donald Swann b. 1923) at the piano and the lyricist (Michael Flanders 1922–75) in the wheelchair to which he had been confined by polio.

Flanders fields Phrase for the battlefields of World War I, and the origin of the Flanders poppy to commemorate the dead (see *Armistice). It derives from a poem, *In Flanders Fields*, written by John McCrae in May 1915 at the Ypres salient:

> In Flanders fields the poppies blow
> Between the crosses, row on row,
> That mark our place.

'Flanders mare' The phrase used, according to Thomas Cromwell, by Henry VIII when he set eyes on his fourth bride, *Anne of Cleves; he had gone in disguise to get a first glimpse of her as she journeyed from the coast to London. The tradition that he believed himself to have been misled by *Holbein's portrait is not mentioned until the 18C.

Harry **Flashman** The bully in *Tom Brown's Schooldays*, who roasts Tom in front of the fire and is eventually expelled for drinking. He has become widely known in recent years through the series of picaresque novels by George MacDonald Fraser (b. 1925), which recount Flashman's wild adventures in later life.

Flatford Mill see John *Constable.

flattery with a trowel see *Disraeli.

Holbein's portrait, in 1539, of the unfortunate Anne of Cleves – somewhat unjustly known to history as the Flanders mare.

Fleet Air Arm The flying force of the Royal Navy, taking off from aircraft carriers. It descends from the RNAS (Royal Naval Air Service) of World War I. From 1915 seaplanes were carried on warships and were lowered into the water for take-off. The first vessel to be adapted as an aircraft carrier in the modern sense, with an extended deck for take-off and landing, was the cruiser HMS *Furious*. She was ready by July 1918 to launch six Sopwith Camels against some German Zeppelin sheds – the first carrier air strike in history.

In 1918 the RNAS was absorbed into the RAF, and it acquired the name of Fleet Air Arm in 1924; in 1939 it was transferred back to the navy. A Fleet Air Arm Museum was opened in 1964 at Yeovilton, in Somerset, with a full range of aircraft from the early Sopwith biplanes to today's Sea Harriers.

Fleet prison Jail which stood from the 12C beside the Fleet river in London's Farringdon Street. It was used for those convicted in the *Star Chamber and later as one of the main prisons for debtors; the ending of clandestine marriages by impoverished clergy in the Fleet brought prosperity to *Gretna Green. The appalling conditions were described in *Pickwick Papers* just before the prison was closed; but the Fleet also had the unusual distinction, as Mr Pickwick discovered, of being an important centre for the game of *rackets. It was demolished in the 1840s.

'the fleet's lit up' Phrase lodged in the public mind from the most famous of broadcasting blunders. Commander Tommy Woodrooffe was commentating live for the BBC from the Coronation Naval Review at Spithead in 1937. 'Lit up' was a standard euphemism for being drunk, and listeners were variously outraged or delighted when Woodrooffe rambled on with such comments as 'the whole fleet's lit up . . . when I say lit up, I mean lit up by fairy lamps . . . the whole thing is lit up by fairy lamps . . . it's just . . . fairy land'. After a few minutes he was taken off the air in mid-sentence, and he was suspended by the BBC for six months; but he resolutely denied that a day of hospitality on his old ship HMS *Nelson* had taken its toll, insisting that he had been working too hard and that his mind had gone blank.

Fleet Street (London EC4) Street associated with printing from about 1500, when Wynkyn de Worde moved *Caxton's press here from Westminster. Until recently it was the centre of Britain's national press, containing the often very grand headquarters of the great newspapers; the Daily *Express building, in particular, has a superb Art Deco interior. But papers began to move to new premises elsewhere in the 1980s, to meet the demands of modern technology and to sidetrack the powerful printing unions associated with Fleet Street. It seems likely that the traditional link with printing and writing, seen also in *St Bride's and in pubs such as the *Cheshire Cheese, will soon be a matter of history.

Fleetwood Mac Pop group formed in London in 1967 by Peter Green (guitar and vocals), Mick Fleetwood (drums), John McVie (bass) and Jeremy Spencer (guitar and vocals). It had several early successes (particularly *Albatross* which reached no. 1 in 1968), but the record-breaking days of the group came after it moved to the USA in the mid-1970s and incorporated Lindsey Buckingham and Stevie Nicks. Their album *Fleetwood Mac* reached the top of the US charts in 1976; its successor, *Rumours* (1977), sold 15 million copies worldwide and was in the UK charts for more than eight years.

Alexander **Fleming** (1881–1955, kt 1944 Bacteriologist who discovered the first mass-produced antibiotic,

penicillin (which he named from *penicillium*, New Latin for a tufted mould). In 1928 he noticed that a mould had accidentally formed on a culture of staphylococcus and that it had killed the surrounding bacteria. He isolated the mould and was able to prove its antibiotic qualities, but it was H.W. Florey (1898–1968) and E.B. Chain (1906–79) who solved the problems of bringing penicillin into clinical use. The three men shared a Nobel prize in 1945.

Ambrose **Fleming** (1849–1945, kt 1929) Inventor in 1900 of the thermionic valve, or diode, which remained an essential part of radio and other electronic equipment until supplanted by the transistor. He is also remembered for the Fleming rules, which use the thumb and first two fingers of each hand to indicate the relative directions of motion, field and current in a dynamo and a motor. The thumb (the only word with an M) is the Motion; the First Finger is the Field; and the second finger (the only one with a C) is the Current. If the three are held at right angles each to the next (thumb up, first finger pointing, second finger jutting out from the palm), the right hand gives the relationship in a dynamo; and the left does the same for a motor.

Ian **Fleming** (1908–64) Creator of fiction's best-known secret agent, James Bond, whose number (007) indicates that he is licensed to kill. Fleming was a journalist by profession but he worked in naval intelligence during World War II. Bond made his first appearance in *Casino Royale* (1953), and thereafter a new Bond thriller appeared every year; Fleming wrote one each winter at his holiday home in Jamaica. The books were immediately popular with their seductive blend of ingredients – exotic locations, ruthless enemies, elaborate gadgetry, much emphasis on the trappings of luxury, and above all the suave character of Bond himself with his retinue of beautiful and willing women, many of them villains under the skin. But it was the films, starting with *Dr. No* in 1962, which made Bond an international superstar – in the mould of John *Buchan's Richard Hannay and *Sapper's Bull-dog Drummond, but much more successful than either. He was performed first by Sean *Connery, subsequently by Roger *Moore and others. Fleming's love of gadgets was also evident in his stories for children, collected as *Chitty-Chitty-Bang-Bang* (1964, filmed 1968); the title is the name of a magic flying car, in which two children outwit Joe the Monster.

'fleshly school of poetry' see *Rossetti.

Flight of the Earls see *Ireland.

'flinging a pot of paint' see *Grosvenor Gallery.

flint Much used in the past as an exterior surface for cottages in East Anglia. The flints are set either with the pale outer curve of the complete cobble showing or with a flat black surface where one has been split (knapped flint). Framed by bricks (needed to provide firm edges at corners or around windows), the material makes very attractive patterns.

Russell **Flint** (1880–1969, kt 1947) Scottish painter, mainly in watercolours, whose best work was in landscape but who is more widely known from the many reproductions of his scenes with scantily clad women.

Flintshire Former *county in Wales, since 1974 part of Clwyd.

Flodden (9 Sept. 1513) Battle between the Scots and English which ended as a disastrous defeat for Scotland. In keeping with the terms of a Scottish alliance with the

French, *James IV marched into England in August 1513 after Henry VIII had invaded France. An English army under the earl of Surrey moved north in response, and the forces met on Flodden Field, near Branxton, about 20km/12m southwest of Berwick-upon-Tweed. James led about 30,000 men and Surrey some 20,000. Both armies had primitive artillery, but it was the English pikes and arrows which got the better of the Scottish spears. As many as 10,000 Scots were left on the field, including the king himself – a tragedy commemorated in the lament *The *Flowers o' the Forest*.

Flook Strip cartoon drawn by *Trog which appeared in the *Daily Mail* from 1949 to 1984 and was then transferred for a while to the *Daily Mirror*. It was written by several authors including Humphrey *Lyttelton and George *Melly. Flook is a furry animal with a white face and a snout, loosely resembling a baby elephant on its hind legs but with magical powers. His companion is a boy, Rufus. Intended originally for children, Flook and Rufus developed into a couple of innocents whose experiences in swinging London provided good opportunities for adult satire and comedy.

Florence Court (13km/8m SW of Enniskillen) House built 1756–64 by John Cole, probably to his own design; he named it Florence after his mother. The stone central block is flanked by colonnades leading to pavilions. The interior, famous for its delicate rococo plasterwork, was much damaged by fire in 1955 but has been restored. The park was landscaped in about 1778–80 by William King, in the informal manner of Capability Brown. Nearby is the original Florence Court yew, still living, which in the 18C was discovered to have an upright rather than a spreading habit. This characteristic survives if propagated by cuttings (but reverts to normal if planted as a seed), and the tree now grows throughout Ireland.

'Flores in the Azores' see Richard *Grenville.

florin see *currency.

*The **Flower of Scotland*** Song written and performed in the late 1960s by the Corries, a Scottish pop duo (Ronnie Brown and Roy Williamson). By the 1980s it was the favourite song at football and rugby matches north of the border, replacing *Scotland the Brave* as the unofficial Scottish anthem.

*The **Flowers o' the Forest*** Traditional lament for the Scots who fell at *Flodden, played by pipers as part of the Remembrance Sunday ceremony. The best-known words to the tune, including the line 'The flowers of the forest are a' wede away', were written by Jane Elliot (1727–1805).

Fluellen see *Henry V.

flying shuttle see John *Kay.

Flying Squad see *police.

Foden Motor Works see *brass bands.

folios see *quartos and folios.

follies Buildings of no practical purpose, constructed purely to amuse or delight the viewer. Large numbers were created in Britain in the 18C. They were a feature of the new informal fashion in *landscape gardening, in which part of the pleasure of a walk round the grounds was chancing upon a hermit's cell, a grotto, a ruined Gothic tower, a classical temple or a pagoda.

Fontenoy see War of the *Austrian Succession.

Margot **Fonteyn** (stage name of Margaret Hookham, 1919–91, DBE 1956) Britain's most distinguished ballet dancer, who at the age of 16 created her first major role as the Bride in *Ashton's *Le Baiser de la Fée* (1935) with the Vic-Wells company. Many other Ashton roles were created for her at Sadler's Wells in the remaining years before the war; and afterwards, when the company evolved into the *Royal Ballet, she continued to give some of her greatest performances in new Ashton ballets (among them *Symphonic Variations* in 1946 and *Ondine* in 1958). By the early 1960s she seemed to be coming to the end of an immensely distinguished career, outstanding not so much for her technique as for an exceptional ability to convey emotion through the flow of her line and phrasing, together with a natural ease in almost any role.

She then, astonishingly, began a new chapter in which those talents seemed even more remarkable – in her partnership with Rudolf Nureyev, who defected from Russia in 1961. She first danced with him in *Giselle* in 1962 and they went on to create a succession of famous pairs of lovers, including *Marguerite and Armand* (1963) for Ashton and *Romeo and Juliet* (1965) for Kenneth MacMillan. A favourite guest artist throughout the world, Fonteyn received on her 60th birthday in 1979 a very rare tribute; the Russian ballet establishment named her *prima ballerina assoluta*, a title given officially to only three other ballerinas in the entire history of the Russian ballet. She suffered one major tragedy in her personal life. Her husband, the Panamanian diplomat and politician Roberto Arias, was the victim in 1964 of an assassination attempt which left him totally paralysed. He died two years before her, in 1989.

Fonthill Abbey see William *Beckford.

*The **Food Programme*** (Radio 4 from 1979) Weekly programme, devised and presented by Derek Cooper (b. 1925), which began with an emphasis on cookery and recipes but has developed into a topical examination of a wide range of often controversial issues relating to agriculture, marketing and the environment.

Fool see *King Lear.

fool Purée of stewed fruit mixed with cream or custard. In the 16C a fool was a dish of clotted cream; a *trifle at that time was similar, and the two names may share an implication of having little substance. It was not until the 18C that the fool acquired its link with fruit.

'Fools rush in where angels fear to tread' see entry on Alexander *Pope.

foot see *length.

Michael **Foot** (b. 1913) Author and Labour politician, MP for Ebbw Vale (1960–83) and Blaenau Gwent (1983–92). He entered the cabinet in 1974 as secretary of state for employment (1974–6) and was then leader of the House of Commons (1976–9). In 1980 he became leader of the Labour party, in succession to James *Callaghan, and led the opposition for the rest of that parliament. He resigned after the general election defeat of 1983 and was followed by Neil *Kinnock. A brilliant orator, he nevertheless seemed an eccentric choice as leader of a national party; and he left it in a sorry state, wedded to unpopular policies (such as *unilateral disarmament) and threatened by internal disruption from the *Militant Tendency. Of his many books the most ambitious is the two-volume life (1962, 1973) of Aneurin Bevan, whom he succeeded as MP for Ebbw Vale.

football The inclination to kick a round object about is no doubt as old as the human race, but the game now played internationally resulted from developments in 19C England. Boys at the *public schools had been encouraged to join in competitive games, and different varieties of school football had developed – the main distinction being whether or not a player was allowed to handle the ball. In 1863 a group of London clubs, many of them formed by old boys of schools who wished to continue their sport, met to try and agree a set of rules. They called themselves the *Football Association. Their first draft rules allowed holding the ball and 'hacking' (deliberately kicking an opponent's shin) but these were both banned in the final version, provoking those who wanted to carry the ball into forming their own *Rugby Football Union in 1871.

Football Association (FA) Organization founded in 1863 to clarify the rules of *football, the resulting version of the game becoming known as soccer (Oxford undergraduate slang from the second syllable of Association). In 1871 it inaugurated the *FA Cup. It has remained responsible for all football in Britain apart from games in the *Football League. In 1992 it poached the top clubs from the league with the creation of its own *Premier League – supporting its right to do so with the argument that the top clubs provide the players of the England team, for which the FA is responsible.

football hooliganism see *soccer hooliganism.

Football League Competition on a points system (nowadays 3 for a win, 1 for a draw) launched in 1888 for professional clubs, the *Football Association having made a principle of amateurism. There were 12 clubs in the 1888–9 season (won by Preston North End). A 2nd division was added in 1892, a 3rd in 1920 and a 4th in 1958. Liverpool has been by far the most successful League club, with 18 wins by 1992 (nearest rivals Arsenal with 10 and Everton with 9). From the 1992–3 season the clubs of the 1st division formed a separate *Premier League.

Football League Cup Knock-out competition for the teams in the *Football League, first played in the 1960–1 season. Since 1967 the final has been at *Wembley. Known since 1992 as the Coca-Cola Cup, it was previously the Rumbelows Cup (1991–2), the Littlewoods Cup (1987–90) and the Milk Cup (1982–6). By 1992 Liverpool and Nottingham Forest had the greatest number of wins, with 4 each, followed by Aston Villa with 3.

Foot Guards The sovereign's personal bodyguard and the elite of the British infantry, dating back to the *Restoration. The First Regiment of Foot Guards, the Grenadiers, derives from a bodyguard formed at Bruges in 1656 during the exile of Charles II. The second, the Coldstream, is older in its foundation but not in the service of the sovereign; it was raised by Cromwell in 1650 as a regiment for General *Monck, and derives its name from the march south with him in 1660 from Coldstream, a small town on the Scottish border. The Scots Guards, raised in 1662, have been linked with the other two regiments since the Act of *Union (1707). The name of the 1st Guards was changed to Grenadiers in 1815 as a token of their defeat of Napoleon's Grenadiers at Waterloo. They adopted at the same time the French bearskin as a headdress, subsequently taken up by the other regiments. The Irish Guards were formed in 1900 and the Welsh Guards in 1915, to complete the present Guards Division. Between them they carry out the daily event of *changing the guard at Buckingham Palace; and a battalion of one of the regiments performs the annual ceremony of *trooping the colour.

Football League: champions since 1950	
1950	Portsmouth
1951	Tottenham Hotspur
1952	Manchester United
1953	Arsenal
1954	Wolverhampton Wanderers
1955	Chelsea
1956	Manchester United
1957	Manchester United
1958	Wolverhampton Wanderers
1959	Wolverhampton Wanderers
1960	Burnley
1961	Tottenham Hotspur
1962	Ipswich Town
1963	Everton
1964	Liverpool
1965	Manchester United
1966	Liverpool
1967	Manchester United
1968	Manchester City
1969	Leeds United
1970	Everton
1971	Arsenal
1972	Derby County
1973	Liverpool
1974	Leeds United
1975	Derby County
1976	Liverpool
1977	Liverpool
1978	Nottingham Forest
1979	Liverpool
1980	Liverpool
1981	Aston Villa
1982	Liverpool
1983	Liverpool
1984	Liverpool
1985	Everton
1986	Liverpool
1987	Everton
1988	Liverpool
1989	Arsenal
1990	Liverpool
1991	Arsenal
1992	Leeds United
1993	Manchester United

The year given is the one in which each season ended.

Footsie see *Financial Times Indices.

Anna **Ford** (b. 1943) TV presenter and in 1978 the first woman to read the news on *ITN (Angela *Rippon had preceded her in 1976 on the BBC). She was one of the group of distinguished presenters who won the franchise for *TV-am in 1980.

Florrie **Forde** (stage name of Florence Flanagan, 1876–1940) Australian singer who was a great success in British *music hall, with a knack for choosing memorable songs. Her repertoire included *Down at the old Bull and Bush, Has anybody here seen Kelly?, Hold your hand out, naughty boy* and two favourites of World War I, *It's a long way to Tipperary* and *Pack up your troubles in your old kit bag.*

Foreign Office (London SW1) Government department responsible for British embassies abroad and for relations with all foreign and Commonwealth countries; in 1968 the Foreign Office and the Commonwealth Office were

Foreign Secretaries since 1945	
1945	Ernest Bevin
1951	Herbert Morrison
1951	Anthony Eden
1955	Harold Macmillan
1955	Selwyn Lloyd
1960	Lord Home
1963	R.A. Butler
1964	Patrick Gordon Walker
1965	Michael Stewart
1966	George Brown
1968	Michael Stewart
1970	Lord Home (as Sir Alec Douglas-Home)
1974	James Callaghan
1976	Anthony Crosland
1977	David Owen
1979	Lord Carrington
1982	Francis Pym
1983	Geoffrey Howe
1989	John Major
1989	Douglas Hurd

merged, and the official name now is Foreign and Commonwealth Office. It is housed in the Government Offices, designed by George Gilbert *Scott. There has been a foreign secretary since 1782, when the work of the two *secretaries of state was reorganized so that one was responsible for home and the other for foreign affairs.

forensic evidence The results of scientific tests, presented as evidence to a jury in a court of law. Incompetence and distortion in the use of forensic evidence contributed greatly to the concern in the early 1990s about the administration of *criminal justice. In the cases of the *Birmingham Six and Judith *Ward a government scientist, Dr Frank Skuse, wrongly maintained that a Greiss test proved there were traces of nitroglycerine on their hands; it was known at the time that shoe polish could give the same results, and it was shown later that even ordinary soap could do so. Tests conducted by the Royal Armaments Defence Research Establishment (RARDE) in the *Maguire Seven case were similarly revealed to be less than conclusive and were criticized for being presented in such a way as to help the prosecution. Dr Skuse was retired early, in 1986, as being of 'limited efficiency'. After the freeing of Judith Ward in 1992 the Crown Prosecution Service began investigating charges that two members of the forensic section of RARDE had in 1973 concealed forensic evidence which would have made her conviction unlikely.

C.S. Forester (Cecil Scott Forester, 1899–1966) Novelist who was already well established before the first appearance of his most successful character, Hornblower. (*The African Queen*, published in 1935, became a very successful film in 1951 starring Humphrey Bogart and Katharine Hepburn.) Hornblower makes his entrance in *The Happy Return* (1937) as a midshipman in the British navy in 1793. A further 11 novels, meticulous in their detail of ships and naval conditions, follow the self-doubting hero through the Napoleonic Wars until he reaches the rank of admiral. There is much in him of Horatio Nelson, a biography of whom Forester had published in 1929.

Forestry Commission (Edinburgh) Government agency established by the Forestry Act of 1919 in response to the timber shortage suffered during World War I. Its original task was to create forests for strategic purposes, and the eventual target of 2 million hectares (nearly 5m acres) by the year 2000 was achieved ahead of time in 1983. The Commission's aims had meanwhile broadened to include the recreational use of forests, a national advisory role on forestry and timber, and commercial forestry on its own account.

'for ever England' see Rupert *Brooke.

George Formby (stage name of George Booth, 1904–61) *Music-hall entertainer from Lancashire who became a national favourite and a successful film star, by projecting a cheerfully gormless character with a wide toothy grin. He strummed on a ukulele-banjo to accompany his faintly saucy patter songs, such as *When I'm cleanin' windows*. His father had been in music hall before him, using the same name.

E.M. Forster (Edward Morgan Forster, 1879–1970) Novelist who observed with a cool eye the attitudes of the cultivated middle classes, often as revealed in a foreign setting. Italy is the background for *Where Angels Fear to Tread* (1905) and *A Room with a View* (1908), while misunderstandings between east and west gave him his greatest success in *A *Passage to India* (1924). Disconnections within English society are the theme of *Howard's End* (1910). During his lifetime he circulated privately a partly autobiographical novel about a homosexual relationship, *Maurice*, which was published in 1971 just after his death. Highly successful films have been made in recent years from his books, which offer attractive locations and a wealth of cameo characters.

The Forsyte Saga The title under which various novels and fragments by *Galsworthy chronicling the Forsyte family were published together in 1922 (the main separate ingredients were *The Man of Property* 1906, *In Chancery* 1920, *To Let* 1921). Soames Forsyte, a successful solicitor, marries Irene in the 1880s and builds a house for her, Robin Hill. Love affairs, infidelities and remarriages frustrate the expected increase in wealth and happiness. Forty years on, after two generations of upset and disappointment, Robin Hill is empty and to let. The saga, rich in incident and detail, was the first to prove the great potential of such novels on television; it was dramatized by the BBC in 26 episodes in 1967 with Eric Porter as Soames and Nyree Dawn Porter (no relation) as Irene.

Frederick Forsyth (b. 1938) War correspondent who became a writer of brilliantly researched thrillers in up-to-date political contexts. His first, *The Day of the Jackal* (1971), achieved the extraordinary feat of maintaining a high level of excitement in a plot, about an assassination attempt on De Gaulle, which the reader knew could only end in failure. He achieved an equally convincing level of documentary realism in his next book, *The Odessa File* (1972), in which a journalist uncovers a network of former Nazis smuggling arms to Arab terrorists in Israel.

Forte Hotel and catering group formed in 1970 by the merger of a hotel chain, Trust Houses, with the varied enterprises of Charles Forte (b. 1908, kt 1970, baron 1982). Born in Italy, Forte moved with his family to Scotland at the age of five (his father was a successful caterer); he launched his own business in London in 1934, building it up by the purchase of restaurants and hotels and, from the 1950s, through early involvement in the growth areas of airport, in-flight and motorway catering. Trust Houses derived from an initiative in the early 20c to improve the standard of country inns in Britain; the Public House Trust Company was formed in 1904 to buy and rehabilitate local hostelries on a county by county basis.

Forth River which flows 105km/65m east from the Central region of Scotland into the Firth of Forth; the firth stretches a further 77km/48m to the North Sea. The river is tidal to Stirling, but the firth is taken as starting further downstream at Kincardine. At its narrowest point (Queensferry, where it is 1.6km/1m wide) it was crossed in 1890 by the great cantilever railway bridge, with two central spans each of 521m/1710ft. This was designed by John *Fowler with a very wide margin of safety because of the recent collapse of the *Tay bridge. It is part of British folklore that the task of painting the bridge is unending; the steel struts have a combined surface area of 55ha/135ac. A little way upstream is the suspension bridge carrying the road, with a central span of 1005m/3300ft, which was opened in 1964 (designed by Gilbert *Roberts).

Forth-Clyde Canal Long-disused canal of great importance when first built (1768–90 by *Smeaton), because it enabled boats and barges to cross Scotland from one coast to the other. It linked the Forth at Grangemouth to the Clyde at Bowling, a distance of 61km/ 38m between almost exactly the two points joined, for a different reason, by the *Antonine Wall. From 1802 the canal had the benefit of Britain's first tug powered by *steam.

Fortnum and Mason (London W1) Shop with a reputation for lavish and exotic food. William Fortnum was a footman in the service of Queen Anne, and Hugh Mason was a small shopkeeper. With Fortnum's palace connections they built up a business which later thrived by supplying food to British officers abroad. The famous Fortnum hampers, containing a suitable selection of food and drink, are a tradition which began in 1851 – to supply the needs of visitors to the Great Exhibition. The shop in Piccadilly was entirely rebuilt in 1923–5, and the animated clock on the façade (with Messrs Fortnum and Mason turning on the hour to bow to each other) was installed in 1964.

Fort William The name of two famous forts built in the 1690s, both named after William III, one in *Calcutta and the other at the foot of Ben Nevis in Scotland. The site of the original Indian fort is now Calcutta's main post office; the present Fort William was built further south in 1757–81. The Scottish Fort William was pulled down in the 19C to make way for the railway. The town of the same name, which grew up around it, is now an important centre for tourism in the southern Highlands.

'45 Rebellion (also known simply as the Forty-Five) The second and last of the military attempts, by supporters of the Jacobite cause, to recover the throne for the Stuart dynasty. Launched with French encouragement during the War of the *Austrian Succession, it came much nearer to success than the *'15 Rebellion.

Bonnie Prince Charlie (Charles Edward *Stuart) landed in Inverness-shire in August 1745 and the Highland clans were called out in his support. They marched south through Perth and entered Edinburgh, where on September 17 he proclaimed his father king, as James VIII of Scotland (he was in Rome – see James *Stuart). The prince installed himself in Holyroodhouse, and on September 21 won a decisive victory over a royal army at Prestonpans, a few miles east of Edinburgh. He then headed south. The city of Carlisle was captured in November and by December 4 the army had reached Derby. Here, with increasing defections and difficulties of supply, the prince was persuaded by his officers to turn north again.

A long retreat back to Inverness culminated in the disaster of *Culloden on 16 April 1746. The Stuart claimant had received little support in the Lowlands or in England, and the English now set about reducing any spirit of resistance in the Highlands. Military roads and forts were established and attempts were made to break the clan system, reducing the power of the chiefs and even banning the wearing of *tartan.

Forty Years On see *Harrow School.

The end of the '45 Rebellion: the duke of Cumberland at Culloden, with his lines of redcoats to the right.

'**for whom the bell tolls**' see John *Donne.

Fosse Way The Roman road which crossed the whole of England from the coast in south Devon to a point near Lincoln, where it joined *Ermine Street. Its name is said to derive from its having a fosse, or ditch, on either side.

Brendan **Foster** (b. 1948) Britain's leading middle-distance runner of the 1970s. He won a gold medal for the 5000 metres in the 1974 European Championships, a bronze for the 10,000 metres in the 1976 Olympics, and a gold for the 10,000 metres in the 1978 Commonwealth Games.

Norman **Foster** (b. 1935, kt 1990) Architect who won wide public attention in the 1970s with two striking designs in East Anglia, the Sainsbury Centre near *Norwich and the Willis Faber building (the head office of Willis, Faber & Dumas) in Ipswich; this hillside creation of curving glass has the rare distinction of being made a Grade 1 *listed building within less than 30 years of its completion (1975). In 1979 he won an international competition for the new headquarters in Hong Kong of the Hongkong and Shanghai Bank. His more recent work includes the airport terminal at *Stansted, new galleries at the *Royal Academy and major plans for the areas of *King's Cross and *Spitalfields.

Fountains Abbey (6km/4m W of Ripon) The largest and one of the best preserved of the abbeys destroyed in the *dissolution of the monasteries. Its beautiful position on the wooded banks of the river Skell, in North Yorkshire, is further enhanced by the proximity of *Studley Royal. The long 12c nave is in the severe style characteristic of the Cistercian order. The monastery was founded in 1132 by a group of monks dissatisfied with the lax ways of a Benedictine abbey in York, and three years later they aligned themselves with the more rigorous Cistercians. The nearby Fountains Hall (1598–1611) was built partly with stone from the abbey.

'**four legs good**' see *Animal Farm.

Four Quartets (1944) Four poems by T.S. *Eliot, which he saw as a single work though each had already been published separately. 'Burnt Norton' (1935), 'East Coker' (1940), 'The Dry Salvages' (1941) and 'Little Gidding' (1942) combine to form a complex meditation on human experience and memory; the theme of 'time present and time past' is announced in the opening words of 'Burnt Norton'. The tone is specifically Christian, very different from the nihilism of The *Waste Land. Each of the four poems relates to a specific place: Burnt Norton is a garden in the Cotswolds; East Coker a Somerset village which had been the home of Eliot's ancestors; the Dry Salvages a group of rocks off the coast of Massachusetts; and Little Gidding a village in East Anglia, where Nicholas Ferrar established a utopian Christian community in the 17c.

fourth estate see *estates of the realm.

John **Fowler** (1817–98, KCMG 1885, bt 1890) Civil engineer who did much of the early work on London's *underground and was responsible for the *Forth railway bridge. His Central Station in *Manchester has recently become a major exhibition centre.

Norman **Fowler** (b. 1938, kt 1990) Conservative politician, MP for Sutton Coldfield since 1974 (previously for Nottingham South from 1970). He entered the *cabinet in 1981 as secretary of state for transport (1981) but rapidly moved to social services (1981–7) and then to employment (1987–90). After the general election of 1992 he became chairman of the Conservative party. He is the oldest member of the so-called *Cambridge mafia.

Fowler's *Modern English Usage* (1926) A dictionary of guidelines by a former schoolmaster, H.W. Fowler (Henry Watson Fowler, 1858–1933), as to what he considered correct in written English. It has been a work of considerable influence in the use of the language. A second edition, revised by Ernest Gowers, was published in 1965.

John **Fowles** (b. 1926) Novelist who began with a highly compressed psychological thriller (*The Collector* 1963) about a butterfly-collector who in similar fashion 'collects' a young art student, kidnapping and eventually murdering her. His next novel was the sprawling *The Magus* (1966, revised in 1977), a conjuror's blend of sex and mystery on a Greek island which was sufficiently arcane to acquire a cult following. But it was with The *French Lieutenant's Woman* (1969) that he reached his widest readership.

Charles James **Fox** (1749–1806) Politician and leader of the Whig party whose reputation, both in his own time and now, derives not so much from any practical achievements as from his powers as an orator and his personal charm. To these was added a dissolute image very much in keeping with his period (he was an obsessive gambler and a close friend of the future *George IV), together with a tendency to espouse causes which were unpopular at the time but later came to be seen as liberal. He opposed, for example, the war to suppress American independence from Britain, and he campaigned against the slave trade; more controversially he was almost alone among British politicians in welcoming the French Revolution.

The thread which linked these themes was an emotional commitment to liberty. It was this which caused him to be the leading critic of the powers of the monarch; and the resulting enmity of George III kept him out of office apart from a few brief spells as foreign secretary. (He was the first to hold that post, in 1782, when the *Foreign Office became the province of a separate *secretary of state, and he held it briefly again in 1783 and 1806). Added to these disadvantages was the extraordinary dominance of *Pitt. For the last 20 years of his life Fox was confined to leading the Whig opposition in the House of Commons.

George **Fox** (1624–91) Founder of the Society of Friends, widely known as the *Quakers. Born in Leicestershire, he wandered the countryside from the age of 19, seeking God and interrupting preachers whom he considered to be in error. He was frequently imprisoned for troublemaking or for blasphemy, but his own preaching – together with his courage, honesty and simplicity – soon made converts to his view of religion, that each man should listen to God within himself. One of his earliest followers was Margaret Fell, whom he later married, and it was around her house (Swarthmore Hall in Lancashire) that in the 1650s an organization began to develop which became the Society of Friends. Fox continued to travel and preach for the rest of his life, not only in Britain but in Europe and even North America.

Foxe's Book of Martyrs The name commonly used for *Acts and Monuments of these Latter and Perilous Days*, a compilation by John Foxe (1516–87) of the frequently gory deaths suffered by Protestant martyrs during the reign of *Mary I. The book, steadily growing in size, was

¶ The burnyng of sixe godly Martyrs in one fire.

Protestants pray as they burn during the reign of Mary: typical of the inflammatory images in Foxe's Book of Martyrs.

reissued many times after its first Latin edition (Strasbourg, 1554). It was first published in English in 1563. Widely read in the 16–17c, and more dramatic than accurate in its approach, it contributed greatly to a long-lasting anti-Catholic hysteria in Britain.

Foxhunter One of the most fondly remembered horses in British equestrian history, largely because of the faultless final round which clinched the gold medal for Britain's show-jumping team at the 1952 Olympic Games. His rider was Harry Llewellyn, and the pair held numerous other distinctions – such as the horse-and-rider record of three wins in the King George V Gold Cup at the *Royal International Horse Show (1948, 50, 53).

fox-hunting see *hunting.

fox terrier see *terriers.

Foyle's (London WC2) Bookshop which had a high reputation in the mid-20c for the size of its stock, and which still has miles of shelving on five floors among which customers can browse. It was established in Charing Cross Road in 1906 by two brothers, William and Gilbert Foyle (1885–1963, 1886–1971). The Foyle's literary luncheon is a social event open to the public, with a sprinkling of distinguished guests of honour, in celebration of a newly published book; the first lunch was organized in 1930 by Christina Foyle, whose close involvement has continued into the 1990s.

franchise The first important step in the long campaign to extend the franchise (the right to vote) was the *Reform Act of 1832; previously the electoral system had been both chaotic and corrupt, as seen in the extreme case of the rotten *boroughs. The act of 1832 gave the vote to any male householder occupying a property above a stated freehold, leasehold or rental value. The levels chosen had the effect of enfranchising the middle classes. Legislation in 1867 reduced the qualifying levels and thus gave the vote to the urban working man, while further amendments in 1884 did the same for rural workers. Meanwhile the Ballot Act of 1872 had introduced the essential democratic element of a secret ballot. The Representation of the People Act of 1918 removed all financial constraints, substituting residence as the sole qualification; it also, for the first time, gave the vote to women, but only to those over 30 (as opposed to 21 for men). Universal suffrage was finally achieved in the UK in 1928, when the age limit for women was reduced to 21. The voting age was further reduced to 18 in 1969; and since 1989 Britons living abroad have been entitled to vote in British elections for up to 20 years from their last time of UK residence. The few important categories of people without a vote are peers, certified lunatics and those in prison.

In the Isle of Man the *Tynwald was in the forefront of electoral reform when it gave the vote to certain women as early as 1881.

Clare **Francis** (b. 1946) Yachtswoman who crossed the Atlantic single-handed in 1973 in 37 days; by 1976, when she was the fastest woman in the Observer Transatlantic Race, her time was down to 29 days. She is also a novelist.

Dick **Francis** (b. 1920) Bestselling thriller writer, whose first career was as a National Hunt jockey. He was *champion jockey in 1954, and his narrow failure to win the 1956 *Grand National provided one of the most famous moments in the history of the race. He retired in 1957 and in the same year published his first book, an autobiography (*Sport of Queens*). Since then there have been almost annual thrillers of crime and corruption in the racing fraternity; among the best known are *Whip Hand* (1979) and *Hot Money* (1987).

John **Francome** (b. 1952) The leading National Hunt jockey of the early 1980s. He was *champion jockey seven times, with an unbroken run from 1981 to 1985. In 1984 he exceeded the previous record number of wins (Stan Mellor's 1035) and when he retired in 1985 his total was 1138 – which remained the record until overtaken in 1989 by Peter *Scudamore.

franglais A word combining *français* (French) and *anglais* (English), coined in 1964 to describe the creeping and much resented intrusion of English words into the French language. Official French efforts to discourage it have had little success. An extreme example is a sign supposedly seen on a garment in the window of a Paris menswear shop: *Très snob, presque cad*.

Frankenstein, or the modern Prometheus (1818) The story which has inspired so many horror films was written by the 19-year-old Mary *Shelley as part of a ghost-story competition, organized by Byron when he and the Shelleys were staying together in Switzerland. Frankenstein is a Swiss scientist who creates an artificial man of great strength. The original story is more subtle than its imitators because it is largely about the monster's need for affection. It is his rage, when denied a mate of his own kind, which causes him to chase Frankenstein to the

Arctic and to murder him there before walking off into the frozen wastes.

The story was filmed several times in the early days of the cinema, but first became a cult after the 1931 version with Boris *Karloff.

Frankie Goes to Hollywood Pop group of five men, all but one born in Liverpool, which was formed in 1980 with Holly Johnson and Paul Rutherford (vocals), Brian Nash (guitar), Mark O'Toole (bass) and Peter Gill (drums). They acquired a valuable reputation for being outrageous when their first success, the single *Relax* (1983), was excluded from BBC radio and TV on the grounds of obscenity. It climbed to no. 1, where it was followed by *Two Tribes* and *The Power of Love* and by an album, *Welcome to the Pleasure Dome* (all three in 1984).

John **Franklin** (1786–1847, kt 1829) Arctic explorer, credited with the discovery of the *northwest passage. He had led two land-based expeditions to map the extremely complex north coast of Canada (1819–22, 1825–7) before being given command of an expedition in 1845 to search for the elusive passage itself. He sailed on May 18 with 129 men in two ships, the *Erebus* and *Terror*, which had previously been used by James Clark *Ross. They were last seen entering Lancaster Sound on July 26. From 1847 some 40 expeditions were sent out to look for traces of them (adding vastly to the knowledge of the region) but it was not till 1859 that some remains were found. With them was a document revealing that Franklin had died, in 1847, in the knowledge that only a few miles of ice now separated him from waters already charted from the west.

Michael **Frayn** (b. 1933) Journalist, novelist and playwright. He first became known as a satirical columnist in the *Guardian* and *Observer* in the early 1960s. He subsequently devoted himself mainly to novels (*The Russian Interpreter* in 1966 and *Towards the End of the Morning* in 1967 being particularly successful), but in the 1970s he abandoned fiction for the theatre. Easily his most popular play has been the farce * *Noises Off* (1982). He has recently returned to novels with *The Trick of It* (1989) and *A Landing on the Sun* (1991).

James **Frazer** (1854–1941, kt 1914) Scottish anthropologist, whose *Golden Bough* (2 vols 1890, enlarged to 12 vols by the 3rd edn of 1907–15) is a massive compilation of other people's researches into ritual and religious customs. It remains a rich and fascinating treasure house, though Frazer's central thesis (that human thought processes have progressed from magic through religion to science) is no longer accepted.

Free Church of Scotland The largest group to have seceded from the *Church of Scotland, and the most dramatic in its departure. On 18 May 1843 a group of 203 ministers (out of some 1200) marched out of the General Assembly in Edinburgh in protest against ministers being appointed by the patrons of livings rather than chosen by their congregation. The number of dissidents grew over the next days and weeks to 474. They disclaimed any rights to church income, property or buildings (an act of courage which had an unexpected effect on the history of photography, through David Octavius *Hill). Instead they set about building a new church organization from scratch. They succeeded so well that later in the century other groups, which had seceded earlier from the Church of Scotland, wished to join them. The creation of the resulting United Free Church of Scotland in 1900 caused in its turn some of their own members to walk out, continuing to call themselves the Free Church and becoming

Freemason emphasizing that his lips are sealed, with masonic symbols in his right hand: Meissen porcelain figure, late 18C.

known as the Wee Frees ('wee' in the sense of little). The larger secession came to an end when the United Free Church reunited in 1929 with the Church of Scotland.

freedom of information An area in which many people feel that Britain (with its *D-notices and *thirty-year rule) lags too far behind other countries, such as the USA, where legislation tends to protect rather than restrict the public's right of access to information. This is one of the themes on which *Charter 88 campaigns vigorously, and in 1993 a private member's Freedom of Information Bill was before parliament; it also proposed a 'public interest' defence for *whistle-blowers prosecuted under the *Official Secrets Act.

Alan **Freeman** (b. 1927) Australian disc jockey, on the BBC's Light Programme from 1960 – presenting *Housewives' Choice* and from 1962 *Pick of the Pops* (on which he developed his catch phrase 'Greetings, pop pickers'). He joined Radio 1 in 1972, and during much of the 1980s was at Capital. He broadcast his final *Pick of the Pops* in 1992.

John **Freeman** (b. 1915) Politician, journalist and diplomat (high commissioner in India 1965–8, ambassador in Washington 1969–71), but best remembered by the public for his superb series of TV interviews, *Face to Face*.

Freemasons Members of a secret society which derives in its present form from England and Scotland in the 18C but which has much older roots. Medieval masons were itinerant, often working in remote parts of the country (building monasteries, for example); it suited them to have a secret guild, with a sign or word known only to initiates which would act like a membership card in a modern trade union. There is evidence that until the 17C all freemasons were still craftsmen involved in cutting stone. Then, initially in Scotland, aristocratic names began to feature. By the early 18C the masonic lodges were becoming highly fashionable associations of gentlemen with shared philosophical interests, often of a free-thinking nature (which caused strong opposition from the Roman Catholic church).

The Grand Lodge, founded in London in 1717, gradually acquired a position of authority over all the other English lodges, which it still retains; and the Grand Lodge of Scotland (1736) has the same authority north of the border. An early link with the royal family (two of the sons of George II became freemasons) continues to this day; there have been eight royal Grand Masters of the Grand Lodge, including the present duke of Kent (since 1967). During the 18C British enthusiasts carried freemasonry to India, to the West Indies and to America, as well as throughout Europe. It remains a thriving worldwide organization, though often now suspected by outsiders of existing largely for the mutual commercial benefit of its members.

free trade International trade without restrictive tariffs was a major plank of British foreign policy from the repeal of the *Corn Laws in 1846 until World War I – a period during which Britain was the world's leading trading nation. The inter-war years and the *Depression saw the reintroduction of tariffs to protect local industry, but the tendency since World War II has again been towards free trade, promoted by organizations such as *GATT, *EFTA and the *EC.

French and Saunders Title used for successive television series by a duo of comedy writers and performers, Dawn French and Jennifer Saunders. They first made their names in *The Comic Strip* (Channel 4, 1982–6).

The British lion enjoying the effects of free trade: a rosy and prosperous future predicted in a Punch *cartoon of 1846.*

French cricket A simple game in which a ball is tossed at the legs of a child, who defends them with a cricket bat held vertically in front of them; the child's turn lasts until his or her legs are struck by the ball. The game shares with *cricket only the concept of defending a wicket, and its name was presumably a joke at France's expense. It is first mentioned in the early 20C.

French leave This 18C phrase is now used to mean absence without permission and is therefore assumed to be critical of the French. But it originally described a French social custom which was widely admired – that of slipping away discreetly from a large gathering, without disturbing it by taking leave of the host and hostess. The French, whether ironically or not, return the compliment; the equivalent phrase for an unauthorized departure is *filer à l'anglaise* (making off in the English way).

*The **French Lieutenant's Woman*** (1969) Novel by John *Fowles, set in the 1860s and indulging in the narrative richness of 19C story-telling while also titillating the modern reader with documentary scraps and teasing diversions about the nature of fiction – there is even a choice of endings. The subject is the obsessive love of a rich man, Charles Smithson, for Sarah Woodruff, a governess treated as an outcast after being jilted by a French lieutenant. It was filmed in 1981 by Karel Reisz, with a screenplay by Harold Pinter and with Meryl Streep and Jeremy Irons in the central roles.

French Revolutionary Wars (1792–1802) Conflict between France and, at different times, virtually every other European power. The French revolutionary creed, adopted from 1789 and held with a crusading zeal, was combined with more traditional expansionist tendencies – giving France's royalist enemies double cause for alarm. Austria and Prussia attacked in 1792; by mid-1793 all Europe except Switzerland and the Scandinavian countries had joined in. Britain contributed no more than a few thousand men (under the ineffective duke of *York) to the campaigns on land, which were marked by many successes for the large French armies – the first in history raised by national conscription. Separate countries were in succession either occupied by the French or were forced to make peace. By the end of 1797 Britain and France were the only two powers still at war.

France was a long-standing rival of Britain for control of the sea, and Britain had concentrated her war effort on naval strategy. But at the start of 1797 the country faced an unusual threat; Spain and the Netherlands were now allied with France, so that the navies of three maritime powers were ranged in a hostile alliance. The situation was eased by British victories over the Spanish fleet off Cape St Vincent in February, and over the Dutch at Camperdown in October.

By now there was a dominant new figure in France – Napoleon Bonaparte, a young general who had conducted a brilliant campaign in Italy against the Austrians, leading to a treaty in October 1797 which brought peace to the Continent for the first time since 1792. Late in 1797 he took command of an army poised to invade Britain, but he concluded that this was impractical until the French had control of the sea. He decided instead to invade Egypt, in an attempt to spoil Britain's trade in the Middle East and even perhaps pose a threat to India. The resulting campaign brought Britain her greatest victory of the war, that of Nelson in 1798 at the *Nile.

Internal upheavals in France resulted in Napoleon becoming first consul in 1799. He was in effect dictator, and historians have often taken this as the end of the French Revolutionary Wars. But there is a more natural break with the short-lived peace of Amiens in 1802. In

1799 Austria, Russia and Turkey had re-entered the war against France, but they were soon forced by French successes to come to terms. By early 1801 the struggle was once more between Britain and France. Again the danger of a concerted naval invasion was frustrated, this time by Nelson's action at *Copenhagen.

Both sides were now weary of war (the expense of which had led to the introduction of *income tax in Britain) and a treaty was signed at Amiens in March 1802. But the underlying tensions had not been resolved. The peace was much enjoyed by British tourists, able to cross the Channel for the first time in almost ten years, but Napoleon continued to give unmistakable signs of his wider imperial ambitions. In May 1803 the British declared war again, starting another 12 years of conflict – the *Napoleonic Wars.

French's see *Samuel French.

Lucian **Freud** (b. 1922) German-born painter, a grandson of Sigmund Freud, living in Britain since 1933. His portraits and nudes have a brutal realism, emphasized in the early years by a coolness of palette and hard precision of line; more recently a violent application of the paint and the often ungainly poses of his subjects achieve a similarly distancing effect. He first came to fame with a large painting of a man in a raincoat, clenching his fist, alone in the corner of a room with a gloomy yucca (*Interior in Paddington* 1951, Walker Art Gallery). One of his most famous images, a small 1952 portrait of Francis Bacon belonging to the Tate, was stolen in 1988 when on exhibition in Germany.

Friar Tuck The fat, jovial father-confessor to *Robin Hood.

friendly societies Groups organized for mutual benefit, locally based and often secret, which were common in Britain from the 18C. They were formed partly for social reasons but primarily to provide members and their families with financial support in case of sickness or on death. One of the oldest and most widespread is the Oddfellows, founded at some time before 1745. The number and importance of the societies decreased after the introduction of the *welfare state.

Society of **Friends** see *Quakers.

Friends of the Earth (London N1) Environmental pressure group, originating in the USA and existing in Britain since 1970. It first achieved prominence with a campaign of 1971 in which thousands of non-returnable bottles were dumped on the doorstep of Schweppes. Recycling is now just one of a dozen ongoing campaigns, from the rain forests and global warming to local issues such as water pollution.

'Friends, Romans, countrymen, lend me your ears' see *Julius Caesar.

Fringe see *Edinburgh Festival.

Elizabeth **Frink** (1930–93, DBE 1982) Sculptor who made her reputation with menacing bronzes of predatory birds, but whose main subsequent themes have been horses (often with nude male riders) and masked or helmeted men. She is also an accomplished printmaker.

William **Frith** (1819–1909) Painter whose fame rests on his lively crowd scenes, in settings well chosen for their significance in English life of the time, such as *The Railway Station* (1862, Royal Holloway and Bedford New College), *Ramsgate Sands* (1854, Royal Collection) and above all *Derby Day* (1858, Tate Gallery).

Martin **Frobisher** (c.1539–94, kt 1588) English sailor and explorer. He sailed in 1576 to find the *northwest passage, and returned to Canada in 1577 and 1578 to search for gold and to attempt to found a colony in Canada, in what is now Frobisher Bay. He commanded the *Triumph* against the Armada in 1588, and was knighted at sea during the campaign.

Frogmore House in *Windsor Home Park, built in the 1680s and enlarged in the 1790s. In its gardens is the mausoleum (1862–71) which *Victoria built for Prince Albert and in which she is buried beside him; it is open to the public each year on three days in May.

Frog Service see *Wedgwood.

front bench The front row of seats on either side of the House of *Commons, occupied by senior members of the two main parties. Government ministers sit on the left-hand side looking towards the Speaker (their bench is sometimes referred to as the Treasury bench), while the shadow cabinet of the *Opposition sit facing them. Occupants of the front benches stand at the *dispatch box to speak. On the floor in front of each bench there is a line which members must not cross when debating. There is traditionally said to be a distance of two sword-lengths between the two lines; this conjures up an exciting image of more volatile days, but is a variable measurement for which there seems no known authentic origin.

David **Frost** (b. 1939, kt 1993) Television personality and tycoon, who shot to fame in 1962 as the cheeky front man of *That Was The Week That Was. He revealed another side to his talent in 1966 when he invited a group of the most powerful people in public life, including the prime minister, Harold Wilson, to have breakfast with him at the Connaught Hotel; and they turned up. Access to the famous, for interviews of which his own company is often the producer (notably his *Nixon Interviews* of 1976, the president's first lengthy appearance after his disgrace) has underpinned a lasting career on both sides of the Atlantic. He is capable of savagery in an interview – as in his controversial 'trial by television' in 1967 of Emil Savundra, who was later imprisoned for fraud.

frost fairs The narrow arches of old *London Bridge slowed down the ebb and flow of the Thames sufficiently for the river to freeze in very cold spells; and the impromptu fairs which then took place on the ice were a popular London tradition. The greatest frost fair of all lasted for ten weeks from the beginning of December 1683. There was a whole street of booths selling food and fancy wares; an ox was roasted; and as a souvenir you could have your name printed on a press set up on the ice (a sheet done in this way for Charles II and his party survives in the London Museum). The last great frost fair was in the winter of 1813–14, before old London Bridge was replaced in 1831.

Christopher **Fry** (b. 1907) The leading playwright, with T.S. Eliot, in the postwar revival of poetic drama. His comedies, with their exuberant word play, offered joyful escapism in a society still drab and rationed. The most successful were The *Lady's Not For Burning* (1948) and *Venus Observed* (1950).

Elizabeth **Fry** (Elizabeth Gurney, 1780–1845, m. Joseph Fry 1800) Quaker philanthropist who was the leading figure in early 19C prison reform. The plight of women

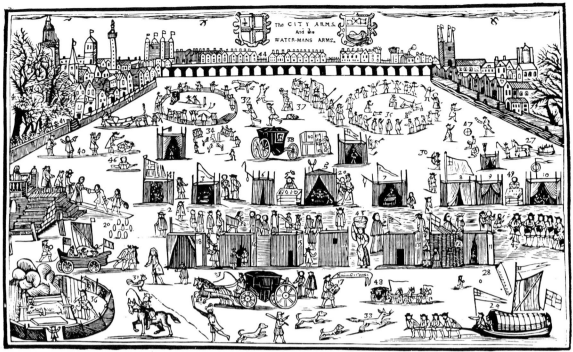

The frost fair of 1683, with London Bridge in the background and a street of tradesmen's stalls on the ice.

prisoners in *Newgate prompted her to a campaign demanding segregation of the sexes, female supervision and improved conditions. She made the case so powerfully that she was soon invited to visit prisons and to make recommendations for improvement throughout Britain and much of Europe.

Roger **Fry** (1866–1934) Member of the *Bloomsbury Group and the most influential art critic of his time, known in particular for his advocacy of Cézanne and the Post-Impressionists in two influential exhibitions (1910 and 1912) at the Grafton Galleries in London. In 1913 he founded the *Omega Workshops.

FT-SE 100-Share Index see *Financial Times Indices.

Vivian **Fuchs** (b. 1908, kt 1958) Geologist who led the first land crossing of the Antarctic in 1957–8 on an expedition connected with the International Geophysical Year. His 12-man team travelled with snow tractors and teams of dogs from the Filchner Ice Shelf to the McMurdo Sound in 99 days.

fudge see *sweets.

Sergeant **Fulton** (A.G. Fulton, 1887–1972) Outstanding marksman, a sniper in World War I and the only man to have won the King's Prize at *Bisley three times (1912, 26, 31). Accuracy was in his blood. His father won the Queen's Prize, as it then was, in 1888; and his son did so in 1958.

fund-holders see *National Health Service.

Fungus the Bogeyman see Raymond *Briggs.

furlong see *length.

Furry Dance see *Helston.

Billy **Fury** (stage name of Ronald Wycherley, 1941–83) Liverpool rock star in the Elvis Presley mould, who progressed from working as a deckhand on Mersey tug boats in 1958 to a long run of hit singles (though never a no. 1) beginning with *Maybe Tomorrow* in 1959. *Halfway to Paradise* (1961) was longest in the charts. He died of a heart attack, the result of rheumatic fever in childhood.

Henry **Fuseli** (Johann Heinrich Füssli, 1741–1825) Swiss painter who settled in London in 1779. His feverish imagination and sinuous line make him an important figure in the early *Romantic movement. Women in exotic clothing and scenes from Shakespeare and Milton were among his favourite subjects. His style has much in common with that of William Blake, 16 years his junior. In spite of Blake's hatred of the Royal Academy, where Fuseli was for many years a professor, Fuseli won the friendship and approval of the younger man, who wrote of him:

> The only man that e'er I knew
> Who did not make me want to spew.

Fylingdales Isolated spot in the North York Moors national park which became in the early 1960s the site of the government's Ballistic Missile Early Warning Station. Three eerily beautiful geodesic domes, visible for miles around, were designed to give a four-minute warning of nuclear attack from the USSR. Both the technology and the threat were obsolete by the early 1990s. In 1992 English Heritage mounted an unsuccessful campaign to prevent the demolition of the 'radomes'.

Fyvie Castle (56km/35m NW of Aberdeen) Castle continuously added to from the 13c to 19c and known in particular for its five tall towers, each named after one of the families who have owned Fyvie. They are, in sequence, the Preston, Meldrum, Seton, Gordon and Leith towers (only the last two were actually built by the family in question). The house contains a famous 17c 'wheel' staircase, rising five floors with stone steps 3m/10ft wide.

G

G7 (Group of Seven) The seven largest capitalist economies (Canada, France, Germany, Italy, Japan, UK, USA), the leaders of which have held since 1976 a regular series of meetings, approximately annual, known also as economic summits.

Christopher **Gable** see *Northern Ballet Theatre.

Dennis **Gabor** (1900–79) Hungarian-born physicist, working in Britain from 1933, who in 1947 invented holography. The first holograms were crude, having to rely on conventional light waves, but they rapidly improved after the invention of the laser (1960) – to become the most popular example of scientific magic. Gabor was awarded the Nobel prize in 1971.

Peter **Gabriel** (b. 1950) Singer who was with *Genesis until 1975. From 1977 he produced four solo albums, all called *Peter Gabriel* (the third included his anti-apartheid song 'Biko'), but it was in 1986 that he had his greatest success – with *So*, which was in the UK album charts for 76 weeks and reached no. 1. His music includes ethnic influences from many parts of the world, and in 1982 he launched WOMAD (World of Music Arts and Dance), a festival at Shepton Mallet, in Somerset, which became an annual event.

Gaelic The variants of the *Celtic language which are still spoken as a native tongue by some people on the west coasts of Ireland and Scotland. Records of Gaelic date back as far as the 5th century AD in the *Ogham inscriptions. At about that time Gaelic crossed from Ireland to Scotland, where it later developed into virtually a distinct language. It was also the language of the Isle of Man, where the last native speaker died in 1974; but Manx Gaelic was kept alive by enthusiasts, and from 1992 began to be taught again in schools on the island. In the republic of Ireland Gaelic is the first of two official languages (the other being English) and it is taught in Irish schools.

Gaiety Girls The chorus girls, noted for their good looks, who sang and danced in a string of successful musical comedies presented at the Gaiety Theatre in the Strand in London during the 1890s. Each show had 'girl' in the title (*The Shop Girl* 1894, *The Circus Girl* 1896, and so on). The Gaiety was demolished in 1903 for the development of the Aldwych.

Thomas **Gainsborough** (1727–88) English painter rivalled only by *Reynolds as a portraitist in the 18C and sharing with Richard *Wilson a dominant position at the start of British landscape painting. He was born in Suffolk (at Sudbury, where the family house is now a museum),

and landscape was his first love as a painter. But it was portraiture which paid the bills. He had a studio in Ipswich from 1752 and moved in 1759 to fashionable Bath. Here he increasingly modelled himself on Van *Dyck, one of his most famous paintings being his 1779 portrait of the young Jonathan Buttall in a costume of Van Dyck's period (usually known as *The Blue Boy*, and now in the Huntington Art Gallery in Los Angeles). In 1774 he established himself in London. His style had now evolved to a shimmering delicacy which could suggest fabric or foliage with an insubstantial lightness of touch. Portraits of elegant women, full-length in spectacular dresses against a hint of woodland background, gave him many of his greatest successes.

Hugh **Gaitskell** (1906–63) Labour politician and MP for Leeds South (1945–70). In 1950 he became chancellor of the exchequer in Attlee's government, and in 1955 he succeeded Attlee as leader of the Labour party. In this role he strenuously opposed those advocating unilateral nuclear disarmament, calling on fellow members to 'fight and fight and fight again to save the party we love'; and he strove to replace the commitment to public ownership (Clause 4) with a more flexible ideal, that of the pursuit by any available means of greater equality and prosperity throughout society. He died suddenly, the year before the general election victory which made Harold Wilson prime minister in his place.

Galahad The purest of the knights of the *Round Table, son of Lancelot and of Elaine the Fair, daughter of King Pelles. It is Galahad who completes the quest of the *Holy Grail.

Gallipoli (also known as the Dardanelles, 1915–16) Disastrous campaign of *World War I, boldly conceived by Winston *Churchill but bungled in execution. Gallipoli is the peninsula forming the western side of the Dardanelles, a narrow strait leading up from the Mediterranean towards the Turkish capital of Istanbul, beyond which lies the Black Sea. Turkey, which had entered the war on Germany's side, was blocking the best Allied supply route to southern Russia. The plan was for the British fleet to bombard its way through the heavily defended strait, while an Allied army captured the Gallipoli peninsula. Neither happened, owing to miscalculation and incompetence. The fleet withdrew after three battleships were sunk in an undetected minefield, and the troop landings on 25 April 1915 were gallant but ineffectual (the bridgehead held by the Australian and New Zealand Army Corps, known as ANZAC, is commemorated each year on that day). The allies withdrew in January 1916, having lost more than 200,000 men.

gallon see fluid *volume.

gallows or pox see John *Wilkes.

John **Galsworthy** (1867–1933) Novelist and playwright, a member of a large and ambitious legal family in many ways resembling the one depicted in *The *Forsyte Saga*. His plays were realistic dramas on contemporary social problems, the best known being *Strife* (1909), about the effects of a strike. He was awarded the Nobel prize for literature in 1932.

Francis **Galton** (1822–1911, kt 1909) Scientist who was a pioneer in statistical analysis. His first interest was in meteorology (he was involved in the establishment of the *Meteorological Office), and his gathering of worldwide data led to his discovery of anticyclones. The publication of *The Origin of Species* by *Darwin (a cousin) prompted him to use statistical analysis to discover the relative importance of inherited and environmental factors; he inclined to heredity (*Hereditary Genius* 1869) and advocated the dangerous theory of 'eugenics' (a term coined by him for selective human breeding). Lasting results of his techniques of measurement were *fingerprints and the correlation coefficient, his statistical device for comparing two sets of variables.

James **Galway** (b. 1939) Northern Irish flute player whose performances and recordings have given his instrument a star quality not normally associated with it. His recorded repertoire covers the range of 18–20C classics, but it is his collections of virtuoso showpieces which have reached the wider audience with titles such as *The Man with the Golden Flute* (he plays an A.K. Cooper 14-carat gold flute).

The hit show at the Prince of Wales in 1894 – the model for many subsequent successes at the Gaiety.

Gambia (officially The Gambia) Member of the *Commonwealth since 1965 and a republic since 1970. From the 16 to 19C the French and the British fought over trading settlements along the Gambia river on the west coast of Africa. In 1889 it was finally agreed that Britain should control the land 10km/6m either side of the river, as an enclave within the surrounding French colony of Senegal. This arrangement defined the unusual shape of the narrow territory, stretching some 320km/200m inland, which became independent in 1965 as The Gambia.

Michael **Gambon** (b. 1940) Actor known to a wide audience through his central role in the 1986 TV series *The *Singing Detective*. He has been closely linked in the West End with many successes by Alan Ayckbourn (beginning with *The Norman Conquests* 1974), and he won a large number of awards for his performance in the London revival of Arthur Miller's *A View from the Bridge* (1987).

games Sports and games of various kinds feature largely among Britain's most successful 19C exports. Some were already well-established by that time in Britain, notably *golf and *cricket. Others emerged from the *public schools, in which large numbers of young men needed exercise and discipline. Team games were found to provide both, and the result was organized versions of ancient activities such as *football, *rugby football and *hockey. In other contexts new games emerged at the same period from older ones (*squash from *rackets, *snooker from *billiards, and modern *darts from its informal predecessors), while some were invented afresh, meeting the needs of the newly leisured middle classes; examples are *croquet and the trio of lawn *tennis, *badminton and *table tennis. Even *rounders can legitimately claim to have been exported as baseball.

Gandhi (1982) Spectacular film biography of the man whose life task was the peaceful removal of the British from India. Distinguished above all by an extraordinary performance from Ben Kingsley in the title role, the film collected eight Oscars (including one for Kingsley and two for Richard *Attenborough, as producer and director).

Gangway A corridor crossing the chamber of the House of Commons about half way along its length. Minority parties and dissenting groups within the main parties tend to sit beyond this corridor (as seen from the Speaker's chair), in a position known as 'below the gangway'.

garden city A phrase already applied to certain towns in the USA before being put forward by Ebenezer Howard (1850–1928) in a book of 1898 as the urban ideal of the future. His campaign for *new towns of about 30,000 people (with a well-balanced mix of civic and industrial buildings, protected by an outer belt of agricultural land) led directly to the founding of Letchworth in 1903 and Welwyn in 1919, both of them in Hertfordshire.

Gardeners' Question Time (Radio 4 from 1947) Hardy weekly programme which began as *How Does Your Garden Grow?* (the name was changed in 1951). Using the same format as another programme of the same vintage, *Any Questions?*, it is recorded in a succession of village halls around the country, with a panel responding to questions from the audience. The gardening programme differs in having a permanent panel of experts, and for 30 years (from 1951) the trio never changed – Fred Loads, Bill Sowerbutts and Professor Alan Gemmell.

Gardeners' World (BBC2 since 1968) Television programme which shares with viewers the practical secrets of gardening. Its stars for many years were Percy Thrower (1913–88), usually seen in his own garden (the Magnolias) at Shrewsbury; and Arthur Billitt (1902–92) at Clack's Farm. More recently the most regular of the presenters has been Geoff Hamilton, in charge of the programme's own garden at Barnsdale in the Midlands.

John Eliot **Gardiner** (b. 1943) Conductor who has specialized in the performance of early music on period instruments, for which he founded the English Baroque Soloists in 1978. He first became known as an interpreter of Monteverdi, founding the Monteverdi Choir in 1964 (while still a student) and the Monteverdi Orchestra in 1968.

Leon **Garfield** (b. 1921) Author of novels, mainly for older children. Most of them are set in the 18–19c and they are in the richly detailed tradition of *Fielding and *Dickens, full of mystery and surprise. His first, *Jack Holborn* (1964), was soon followed by two which have remained among his most popular – *Smith* (1967) and *Black Jack* (1968). Twelve short linked novels about London apprentices were published in 1976–8, beginning with *The Lamplighter's Funeral*; they were issued in a single volume in 1982 as *The Apprentices*. Many of his books have been illustrated by Antony Maitland (b. 1935).

Garibaldi biscuit see *squashed flies.

Alan **Garner** (b. 1934) Children's author in whose work the past and its legends entangle with present-day life in a complex and challenging way. In *The Owl Service* (1967) there are three threads – the story of some modern adolescents, a related sequence in their parents' generation, and a layer of myth from the *Mabinogion*. The short novels known as *The Stone Book Quartet* (1976–8) focus on four periods in the history of his own family of craftsmen in a Cheshire village over the past century and a half.

David **Garrick** (1717–79) The leading British actor and theatre manager of the 18c. He grew up in Lichfield and became one of the few students at Samuel *Johnson's academy, before the two men went to London together in 1737. He set up in the wine trade and dabbled in amateur acting until, on a legendary night in British theatre history, his performance as Richard III in a small London theatre took the town by storm (1741). The reason was a new naturalness which he brought to acting, in place of the prevailing pomposity. He quickly established himself and remained for the rest of his career at the head of his profession, both in tragedy and comedy. His long period as manager of the Drury Lane theatre (1747–76) brought many reforms, including the removal of privileged spectators from the stage and major improvements to the stage lighting.

Shakespeare was Garrick's passion, though he was not above drastic amendments to the text. He organized the first Shakespeare festival at *Stratford-upon-Avon in 1769; he put up a temple to the bard on his Thames-side lawn at Hampton (still there, and open to the public); and he commissioned the statue of Shakespeare by Roubiliac which is now in the British Museum. He also wrote plays and songs; *Heart of Oak* is still sung. With a grand town house (he was one of the first residents of the *Adelphi) and a country mansion at Hampton, with a wide circle of friends in fashionable and literary circles, and with artists of the calibre of Reynolds, Gainsborough and Zoffany to paint him and his wife, Garrick was the first to prove the point, often repeated since, that an actor can live the life of a gentleman. He was buried in Westminster Abbey, in *Poets' Corner.

Garrick Club (London WC2) A *club named in honour of David *Garrick, founded in 1831 as a place where 'actors and men of refinement' might meet on equal terms and where 'easy intercourse' could be promoted between artists and patrons. It moved in 1864 to the present building, designed by Frederick Marrable (1818–72); its walls are lined with the club's famous collection of theatrical portraits. The membership is drawn largely from theatre and television, literature and journalism, publishing and the law – a catchment area suggesting enlightenment. Nevertheless, on an issue which generated wide outside interest, the club voted heavily in 1992 against admitting women as members.

Order of the **Garter** (in full The Most Noble Order of the Garter) The senior *order of chivalry, founded by *Edward III in 1348, with its motto *Honi soit qui mal y pense* (French for 'Shame on whoever thinks evil of this'). Legend has both the order and the motto deriving from the garter of a countess, dropped at a ball in Calais and chivalrously picked up by Edward who then wore it on his own calf (knights today in full attire still wear the blue garter of the order below the left knee). Historians think it more probable that the garter is a version of a sword-belt; and that the motto perhaps relates to Edward's claim to the throne of France, which provoked the *Hundred Years' War.

St *George is the patron saint of the order and *St George's in Windsor Castle is its chapel, where the annual Garter ceremony takes place – normally on the Monday of Royal *Ascot week. Apart from members of the royal family and distinguished foreigners, the number of knights (officially Companions) is limited to 24, who put KG after their names; the non-royal members of the order were invariably men until 1990, when Lavinia, Duchess of Norfolk, became the first Lady Companion (LG).

gas During the late 18c there were several successful attempts in Europe to derive gas from coal for lighting. Employees of *Boulton and Watt were the first to achieve a sustained practical application. William Murdock (1754–1839) lit his cottage by gas in 1792, and illuminated the firm's Soho factory in Birmingham to celebrate the Peace of Amiens in 1802; his assistant Samuel Clegg (1781–1861) set up as an independent gas engineer in 1805. The first gas company was established in London in 1812. In 1814 Westminster Bridge was lit by gas; by 1817 it was used both for the stage and front-of-house areas of Drury Lane theatre; and as early as 1826 there was installed in Leeds the first 'gasometer' (the popular term for a gas-holder), expanding and contracting like a telescope. With mains laid throughout the larger cities, gas soon became the standard method of lighting for all who could afford it; and in 1841 Alexis Soyer introduced cooking by gas in London's Reform Club. Its other 20c application, for heating, was only developed after the more convenient *electricity had replaced it for domestic lighting.

In 1948 *nationalization merged more than 1000 municipal and private gas companies into what eventually this was *privatized as *British Gas. The industry received a boost in the early 1990s (and *coal a corresponding blow) when the electricity-generating companies favoured a rapid conversion to gas-fuelled power stations – in what became known as the 'dash for gas'.

Paul **Gascoigne** (commonly known as Gazza, b. 1967) English footballer, always boisterous and often clownish (or 'daft as a brush'), who played for his local team, Newcastle United (1985–8), before transferring for £2 million to Tottenham Hotspur. He acquired huge fame in the World Cup in Italy in 1990. He performed in the midfield with great flair, but it was an unexpected event in the semi-final against West Germany which clinched his legend. After a foul against Berthold, Gascoigne was shown a yellow card. It was his second of the tournament, and would have prevented his playing in the final if England had won this game. In front of the television millions Gazza wept. A new-style hero was born, and suddenly everyone in Britain could spell the name Gascoigne. In 1991 the Italian club Lazio offered a record £7.9m for him, but this was reduced to £5.5m when he injured his knee playing for Spurs in the 1991 Cup Final. After a year of convalescence he joined Lazio in the summer of 1992.

Mrs **Gaskell** (Elizabeth Stevenson, 1810–65, m. William Gaskell 1832) Novelist of everyday life, especially in the northwest. Her mother died when she was one month old and she was brought up by a maternal aunt at Knutsford, in Cheshire, the setting for her best-known novel, *Cranford*. Her husband was a Unitarian minister in Manchester, where she saw at close quarters the poverty and misery of the *hungry forties, the decade in which *Engels was noting the condition of the working classes in this same great industrial city. This was the raw material of her first novel, *Mary Barton: a Tale of Manchester Life* (1848), in which the heroine is the daughter of a trade unionist. Coming out in Europe's year of revolutions, the book was greeted with fury by Manchester mill-owners but won her the immediate respect of other writers. Another new novelist of great distinction, first published in the previous year, was Charlotte *Brontë. Mrs Gaskell became her firm friend and, in 1857, her first biographer.

Gateshead (81,000 in 1981) Industrial town on the south bank of the river Tyne, historically overshadowed by its larger rival to the immediate north, *Newcastle-upon-Tyne. Gateshead has excellent paintings in the Shipley Art Gallery, based on the collection of a Newcastle solicitor, Joseph Shipley (1822–1909). It also has the Gateshead International Stadium, opened in 1955 and gradually developed since then to become a major national location for athletics events and for large open-air pop concerts. The Metro Centre was Britain's largest shopping centre when it opened in 1985.

'Gather ye rose-buds while ye may' The opening line of *Herrick's irresistibly titled poem, *To the Virgins, to make much of Time*. Set to music by William Lawes (1602–45), it rapidly became one of the most popular of 17c songs.

GATT (General Agreement on Tariffs and Trade) International organization, set up by a treaty of 1948 and with headquarters at Geneva, which provides a permanent forum for discussions aimed at removing tariff barriers. In the early 1990s 105 countries were participants, responsible between them for some 90% of world trade.

GATT negotiations are conducted in 'rounds', which last several years and are known by the place where the talks began. The latest has been the Uruguay Round. Started in 1986, it very nearly foundered in 1992 through disagreement between the USA and the EC over European farm subsidies under the Common Agricultural Policy. The broader issue became focused on a dispute between the USA and France over oilseeds. In November 1992 the USA threatened to launch a trade war, with tariffs against European imports; but the two sides pulled back from the brink and seemed likely to achieve a compromise.

Mike **Gatting** (b. 1957) Batsman with a boisterously aggressive style who has played *cricket for Middlesex

from 1975 and for England from 1977. He captained England in 1986–8 and was embroiled in a major row over umpiring at Faisalabad during a tour of Pakistan; his captaincy ended later, ostensibly because of an improbable fuss about his relationship with a barmaid during the 1988 series in England against the West Indies. He then led a rebel tour to South Africa (1989), which resulted in a five-year ban from Test cricket; it was lifted in time for him to take part in the 1993 tour of India.

Gatwick (43km/27m S of London) The capital city's second major airport, serving about 21 million passengers a year in the early 1990s. A field here was first licensed for recreational use by light aircraft in 1930. It was developed as a commercial airport in 1934–5, and was the first in the world to have its own rail link (still a notable feature of Gatwick); the Southern Railway opened a station in 1935, joined to the terminal building by a subway. In the 1950s it was designated London's second airport, and a new terminal was opened in 1958. Gatwick subsequently became the world's busiest single-runway airport, but in the mid-1990s there are plans for a second runway.

Gaumont see J. Arthur *Rank.

*Sir **Gawain and the Green Knight*** (late 14c) Narrative poem consisting of 2530 lines of *alliterative verse. It is in four 'fitts' or sections. In the first Gawain responds to a green knight, who arrives at King *Arthur's court one Christmas and invites anyone to strike him with an axe and to receive the blow back a year later; Gawain cuts off the head of the knight, who rides away with it. In the second fitt, Gawain travels north through a wintry landscape and arrives at a castle. In the third, he and the green knight agree to exchange whatever the knight kills on the hunting field for whatever Gawain gets in the castle; Gawain duly trades the kisses which he wins from the knight's wife, but he withholds a magic girdle which she says will save him from violent death. In the fourth, the green knight only pretends to cut off Gawain's head but he does nick his neck in gentle rebuke over the girdle. Gawain returns to Arthur's court wearing the girdle as a sign of shame, but the courtiers are delighted and adopt it as their badge (it has been suggested that the anonymous poem may have been written to celebrate the new Order of the *Garter). In 1991, as *Gawain*, it was turned into an opera by Harrison *Birtwistle.

John **Gay** (1685–1732) Poet and playwright, remembered in particular for one outstanding success, *The *Beggar's Opera*. His reputation was high enough for him to be buried in Westminster Abbey, where the epitaph which he wrote for himself suggests his easy and cynical wit:

Life is a jest; and all things show it.
I thought so once; but now I know it.

Gay News The largest-circulation homosexual newspaper in Britain, launched in 1972. It was prosecuted for blasphemy in 1977 in a widely publicized private case brought by Mary *Whitehouse, after the publication of a poem by James Kirkup about Christ on the cross; the judgement was that the editor, Denis Lemon, was guilty of publishing a 'blasphemous libel' (he was fined and given a suspended sentence). *Gay News* ceased publication for a while in 1983, but since 1984 has been incorporated in *Gay Times*.

'making Gay rich and Rich gay' see *The *Beggar's Opera*.

gazumping A more splendid word of the 1920s, 'gazoomphing', was of unknown origin but meant the perpetrating of a swindle. In its modern duller form it became widely used in the 1970s. By then it was limited to real estate, and meant offering a property at a higher price to a new purchaser after verbal agreement had been reached with another – an abuse little seen in the more recent property market (see *house prices).

GBE, GCB, GCMG and **GCV0** see *orders of chivalry.

GC see *George Cross.

GCE and **GCSE** see *exams.

GCHQ (Government Communications Headquarters, Cheltenham) The centre of Britain's global intelligence-gathering network, designed to eavesdrop on the conversations carried on the world's airwaves. The system, employing some 10,000 people in the early 1990s, was set up after World War II in partnership with the US National Security Agency. Any information considered of importance is sent to the Joint Intelligence Committee, a group reporting to the *cabinet office and including the heads of *MI5 and MI6. GCHQ is under the control of the Foreign Office and became the subject of controversy after the foreign secretary announced in 1984 that workers there could no longer belong to a trade union. A compensation of £1000 was offered to each employee, and within a month 90% had accepted. A minority (eventually just 18 people) refused to give up membership, and their case was fought by the civil service unions until it was finally rejected by the European Court of Human Rights in 1987.

GDP (gross domestic product) The total value of goods and services produced by the nation within a given period (usually a year), calculated as an aggregate of the market values paid by the consumer or final purchaser. The only other potential wealth accruing is the net balance between money received from British assets abroad and money paid out on assets owned by foreigners in Britain.

To date this has always been a positive sum. It is added to the GDP to provide the GNP (gross national product).

The level of annual percentage growth in the GDP is a standard yardstick of the state of the economy, with a declining GDP indicating *recession.

GEC (General Electric Company) Britain's largest manufacturer of electrical goods, deriving from an enterprise set up in London in 1886 by two young men, Hugo Hirst and Gustav Byng, in the first years of the commercial exploitation of *electricity. At first they marketed other people's products, but soon they were making light fittings, bells and bulbs. In 1920 the company constructed an 'All-Electric House' at the *Ideal Home Exhibition, including machines for washing clothes and dishes, a vacuum cleaner, a toaster, a hair dryer and a 'medical vibrator'. Later in the same decade hydro-electric equipment was installed in the Dalai Lama's palace in Tibet. Television sets were manufactured when the BBC launched its service in 1936. GEC expanded greatly in the 1960s, with a series of company acquisitions which included English Electric and *Marconi.

Jenny **Geddes** see *St Giles' Cathedral.

Geffrye Museum (London E2) Museum of furniture and interior design, opened in 1914 in a row of early 18C almshouses. The collection is shown mainly in a series of rooms decorated and furnished in contemporary styles from 1600 to 1939.

Archibald **Geikie** (1835–1924, kt 1891) Scottish geologist whose literary skills brought the subject to a wider audience, in such works as *The Scenery of Scotland* (1865), *The Ancient Volcanoes of Great Britain* (1897) and *The Founders of Geology* (1897).

Bob **Geldof** (b. 1954, Hon KBE 1986) Irish pop singer who in 1984 formed Band Aid in London. He had founded a *punk rock group, the Boomtown Rats, in Dublin in 1975. The next year they moved to England and had

Gross Domestic Product, in £bn

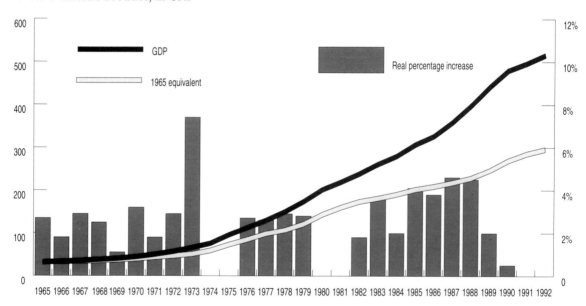

The GDP figures in the upper line are at factor cost, which means market prices less 'factor cost adjustment' (the removal of the distortion in the market price caused by taxes on expenditure and by subsidies). The lower line represents the 1965 GDP adjusted each year for inflation; the gap between the two lines is therefore the cumulative real growth in the economy.
Source: Economic Trends *(see *Central Statistical Office).*

General elections since 1945

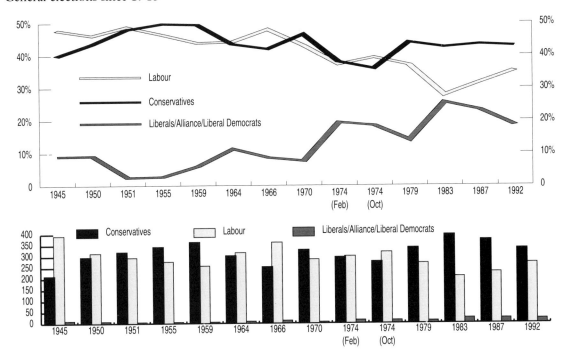

Percentage of the vote gained by each of the main parties and the resulting number of seats in the House of Commons.

no. 1 hits with *Rat Trap* (1978) and *I don't like Mondays* (1979). In 1984 he was inspired by a TV film about famine in Ethiopia to bring together a galaxy of pop stars (collectively described as Band Aid) to record *Do They Know It's Christmas?*, written by Midge Ure and himself. Launched with an Ethiopia Benefit concert at the Albert Hall, it became the biggest-selling single of all time in Britain (more than 3 million copies in the first few weeks). Geldof followed it up in 1985 with Live Aid, a vast pop concert broadcast live on international TV, and then with Sport Aid in 1986. These activities and their spin-offs raised more than £100m for Africa, as well as providing the inspiration for *Comic Relief.

Adeline **Genée** (stage name of Anina Jensen, 1878–1970, DBE 1950) Danish-born dancer who acquired great popularity at London's Empire Theatre in 1897–1907, particularly as Swanilda in *Coppélia*. She lived the rest of her life in England and contributed greatly to the development of ballet training in Britain.

General Accident One of Britain's major insurance companies and the largest Scottish company of any kind. Its headquarters are in Perth, where the business was established in 1885.

General Assembly see *Church of Scotland.

general election The election during a single day of an *MP for each *constituency in the UK. Polling booths are open from 7 a.m. to 10 p.m. The candidate elected is the one with the greatest number of votes, on a simple first-past-the-post principle. Almost every British, Irish or Commonwealth citizen aged 18 or more is entitled to vote in a constituency if he or she is listed on the register of electors (compiled annually) as residing there. From 1985 the *franchise was extended, with certain restrictions, to British citizens living overseas. The timing of a general election is at the discretion of the prime minister, but it must be called within five years of the previous one. Tactical considerations usually bring an election after about four years.

The money spent by each candidate during the election campaign is limited to a fairly small sum, to which a few pence are added for each registered elector; the candidate must also put down a deposit which is forfeited if he or she polls less than 5% of the votes cast. The figures in 1992 were: election expenses (excluding the candidate's personal expenses) of not more than £4144, plus 3.5 pence for each elector in an urban constituency or 4.7 pence in a county constituency; and a deposit of £500.

General Electric see *GEC.

General Strike (1926) The single largest conflict in British industrial history. In 1925 the owners of the coal mines, whose markets were shrinking after an earlier boom, demanded longer hours and a cut in wages. The miners were led by a brilliant orator, A.J. Cook (Arthur James Cook, 1883–1931). They were ready to strike, going into battle with Cook's telling slogan 'Not a penny off the pay; not a minute on the day'. The government defused the issue with a temporary subsidy, but when this came to an end in 1926 the situation was as before. At the end of April the mine owners initiated a lock-out. In response the newly organized General Council of the *TUC called a general strike. About three million people came out on strike from May 4, in transport and in all the main industries. The mine owners then offered a compromise which the TUC considered reasonable. They called off the strike after nine days, on May 12, but failed to get the new terms accepted by the miners themselves, who remained on strike for another five months before giving in. There were no comparable confrontations until the *miners' strikes of 1972 and 1984.

General Stud Book see *thoroughbred.

General Synod see *Church of England.

Genesis Progressive rock group formed originally in 1966 by boys at Charterhouse School, of whom three – Tony Banks (keyboards), Mike Rutherford (guitar, bass and vocals) and Peter *Gabriel (vocals) – were the central figures when the group began to succeed professionally. Phil *Collins joined on drums in 1970 and became the lead singer when Gabriel left to go solo in 1975. Famous for their outrageous clothes as well as their individual sound, Genesis have never been higher than no. 4 with a single (*Mama* 1983), but they have had five albums at the top of the charts (*Duke* 1980, *Abacab* 1981, *Genesis* 1983, *Invisible Touch* 1986, *We Can't Dance* 1991).

Geneva Bible see *Bible in English.

Geneva Convention The name commonly used for the combined provisions of a series of agreements signed in Geneva and accepted by the majority of states. The first, in 1864, was linked with the establishment of the Red Cross and was mainly concerned with the protection of sick and wounded soldiers. Additions in 1925 and 1929 coped with problems which had emerged in World War I – banning gas and bacteriological warfare and laying down codes for the treatment of prisoners of war. The 1949 Convention brought in the new issues of World War II, attempting in particular to protect civilians with regulations about the bombing of cities.

Genevieve (1954) Comedy film about two veteran cars (one of them is Genevieve) in a friendly race on the way home from the *Brighton Run. The two couples, coaxing their unreliable vehicles towards the Westminster finishing line, were played by Kenneth More and Kay Kendall in one car, John Gregson and Dinah Sheridan in the other. Written by William Rose and directed by Henry Cornelius, the film also has a famous harmonica score by Larry Adler.

gentleman Historically the term for a man in a specific social class, below the nobleman but above the *yeoman. It is sometimes still used of a man showing qualities of courtesy supposedly associated with such a class, but for the most part it is now just a formal word for men in general – as in 'Ladies and Gentlemen' (the conventional opening words of a speech) or 'Gentlemen' (the usual label on the door of a lavatory for men).

The **Gentleman's Relish** A stylish trade name registered in the late 19C for a product which also bears on its label a spoof Latin phrase, *Patum Peperium*. It is in fact not a pepper paste but an anchovy paste – salty, highly spiced and usually spread thinly on toast.

Gentlemen and Players see *cricket.

Geoffrey of Monmouth (d. 1155) Author of *Historia Regum Britanniae* (History of the Kings of Britain), a collection of medieval legends about the origins of the nation. He begins with the founding of Britain by *Brut, continues with stories of individual rulers (including Shakespeare's Lear) and ends with the death of a last legendary British king, Cadwallader, and the dominance of the Anglo-Saxons. His book became the most influential source for stories of King *Arthur.

geological periods In the 1830s there was a concentrated effort in Britain to identify the correct sequence of early fossil-bearing rock strata (the work of James *Hutton in the previous century had opened the door to this kind of scientific approach). Two great geologists were in the vanguard, sometimes complimenting each other's work and sometimes clashing. Adam Sedgwick

Geological periods identified by fossil-bearing rocks in Wales and Devon		
	Types of fossil	*Approximate period*
CAMBRIAN	Marine invertebrates	570–480 million years ago
ORDOVICIAN	Primitive fishes	480–435 million years ago
SILURIAN	First land plants and animals	435–405 million years ago
DEVONIAN	First amphibians, numerous fishes	405–340 million years ago

(1785–1873) began investigating the rocks of north Wales in 1831 and gave the name Cambrian (from *Cambria*, new Latin for Wales) to what he considered the oldest fossil-bearing stratum. In the same year Roderick Murchison (1792–1871) began work in the border districts of south Wales; he identified a more recent group of strata which he called Silurian (from the Silures, a Celtic tribe so named by the Romans).

The friendship between Sedgwick and Murchison at this period was evident when they together identified and named, in 1839, the Devonian period – more recent again, and seen in the rocks of south Devon. Their famous dispute came later, over where the dividing line lay between their respective Cambrian and Silurian periods. It was not resolved until 1879, after both their deaths, when Charles Lapworth (1842–1920) proposed an intermediate period which he called Ordovician (from the Ordovices, another Welsh tribe).

It is the fossil record which identifies a period. The accompanying table shows the periods established by Sedgwick and Murchison, each with its characteristic fossils and approximate time scale; the sequence shown is

The start of scientific geology: James Hutton face to face with some tempting strata (caricature of 1787 by John Kay).

the first third of the Paleozoic Era, the later periods of which (Carboniferous and Permian) were characterized by the first reptiles and by coal deposits from forests. The subsequent two eras are the Mesozoic (the time of the dinosaurs) and the still continuing Cenozoic (the arrival of mammals).

Geordie Nickname for anyone from *Tyneside. The word is locally a diminutive of George, and was first applied to miners in the district (and to the safety lamp designed for them by George *Stephenson); it was also used of coal ships and their crews plying from Newcastle. Geordies are known for a strong local sense of identity and, in extreme cases, for an almost impenetrable accent.

St George Patron saint of England, with a feast day on April 23. Although there is no historical record of his existence, he was venerated from at least the 6C as a soldier who had been one of the early martyrs. His killing of the dragon to rescue a maiden is a medieval invention. Edward III made him patron saint of the Order of the Garter, which is probably why he began to be thought of as England's saint and to feature prominently in the *mummers' plays. His emblem of a red cross on a white ground became one of the three constituent parts of the *Union Jack. In 1969 the Vatican, with a greater regard for historical truth than for English sensibilities, removed him from the official calendar of saints.

George I (1660–1727) Elector of Hanover from 1692 and king of Great Britain and Ireland from 1714, as the first monarch of the house of *Hanover; eldest son of Ernest Augustus of Hanover and of Sophia, daughter of the *Winter Queen; married Sophia Dorothea of Celle (1682).

His claim to the British throne came through his mother, a granddaughter of James I (see the *royal house), and it was confirmed by the Act of *Settlement. George was a long-established and successful German monarch, with a particular skill in military matters, when he inherited the British crown at the age of 54. He took a more positive role in British affairs than has often been suggested, but he was always seen in Britain as a foreigner – a condition emphasized by his failure to learn fluent English.

The new king's private life also made him unpopular. He had divorced his wife in 1694 and was known to be keeping her a prisoner in the castle of Ahlden; he suspected her of infidelity with the Graf von Königsmark, whose unexplained assassination added a sinister twist to the tale. To add to this, George arrived in Britain with his two favourite German mistresses. They were hated alike for their ugliness and for the greed with which they profited from power; the thin one, created duchess of Kendal, was known as the Maypole, while the plumper countess of Darlington became the Elephant. Another strand in this unfortunate family scene was the hatred between George and his son, the future *George II. Their mutual hostility shaped British politics, with an opposition to the king's chosen ministers forming around the prince of Wales (a pattern repeated in the next two reigns). It was largely to avoid meeting the prince, after a major quarrel between them in 1717, that George I gave up attending *cabinet meetings.

Dislike of the new regime was not sufficient for the *'15 Rebellion to find much support, but the scandal of the *South Sea Bubble added further opprobrium in 1720 (the king was closely involved, and the German mistresses made large sums before the crash). However, by the end of the reign the prime minister, *Walpole, had achieved sufficient stability for George II to inherit the throne without disturbance. Traditional charges against

George I have included philistinism (with the reported remark 'I hate all boets and bainters'), but he was a lover of music.

George II (1683–1760) King of Great Britain and Ireland and elector of Hanover from 1727; only son of George I and Sophia Dorothea; married Caroline of Ansbach (1705).

The years preceding his inheritance of the crown were marked by prolonged hostility between himself and his father. A quarrel in 1717 over a trivial matter (the godparents of a newly born son) led to the prince's children being removed while he was confined to his house. But on his accession to the throne George retained his father's chief minister, *Walpole, whose skills over the next 15 years put the reign on a stable basis. The other great influence was that of his wife, Caroline, an intelligent woman who strongly supported Walpole; she died in 1737. George's own interests, like those of his father, were connected largely with the army. He was himself a keen soldier, fighting with courage and distinction in battles from Oudenarde in 1708 to *Dettingen in 1743.

George was like his father in two other respects. He was a lover of music, being in particular an enthusiastic patron of *Handel. And he detested his eldest son, Frederick Louis (1707–51), whose early death prevented his inheriting the crown. George was succeeded by his grandson, as George III (see the *royal house).

George III (1738–1820) King of Great Britain and Ireland and elector of Hanover from 1760; eldest son of Frederick Louis, Prince of Wales, and Augusta of Saxe-Gotha; married Charlotte of Mecklenburg-Strelitz (1761).

His father died when George was 12, making him heir to his grandfather, *George II. His first decade on the throne, from the age of 22, was unsettled; there was a lack of public confidence in the mentor chosen for him, his first prime minister, the earl of Bute (1713–92); and there were devastating attacks on all in authority by *Wilkes. Matters improved after George found in 1770 a prime minister with whom he could work, Lord North (1732–92), whose term in office lasted until 1782. This period included the entire War of *American Independence, an expensive national disaster for which North and the king shared the public opprobrium, though it was in fact the king who was more resolute than his minister in continuing the conflict to the bitter end.

North fell from power because of the war, and political squabbles and uncertainties immediately returned; but a year later the king appointed another prime minister with whom he achieved an even longer working relationship, William *Pitt. Pitt's first spell in office lasted from 1783 to 1801 and ended because of one particular issue, the emancipation of the Roman Catholics, which was strongly opposed by the king because of his oath on accession to protect the Church of England.

In 1788 George suffered the first serious attack of the mental illness which eventually made him unfit to govern. His contemporaries saw the king when in this condition as quite simply mad; modern medical opinion, not unanimous, diagnoses the cause as porphyria, a rare imbalance of the corpuscles of the blood which can have this effect. His son, the future George IV (see the *royal house), was about to be appointed regent in 1789 when the king suddenly recovered – postponing the beginning of the regency for another 22 years, until 1811. A lasting legacy of George III is his superb collection of books, now part of the *British Library.

George IV (1762–1830) Prince regent from 1811 and king from 1820 of Great Britain, Ireland and Hanover (a kingdom from 1814); eldest son of George III and

Caricature by Gillray of the grossly self-indulgent prince of Wales, at the age of 30 in 1792.

Charlotte of Mecklenburg-Strelitz; married Maria Anne Fitzherbert (1785) and Caroline of Brunswick (1795).

His reputation as the most dissolute of Britain's monarchs was well earned. Reacting against the virtuous family life of his father and the public rectitude of *Pitt, George established at *Carlton House a court of pleasure which included Pitt's rival, Charles James *Fox, and later Beau *Brummell. In 1785 he married Mrs Fitzherbert (1756–1837), a Roman Catholic widow and perhaps the only woman for whom he felt lasting affection. The marriage was illegal since no member of the royal family could marry under the age of 25 without the king's consent; had it been legal and therefore valid, a Roman Catholic wife would have cost George his right to the succession under the terms of the Act of *Settlement. But in any case the marriage remained a secret.

In 1795, as part of a strategy to persuade parliament to pay his debts, he married a German cousin, Caroline of Brunswick (1768–1821), daughter of his father's sister Augusta. His first remark on setting eyes on her ('Harris, I am not well, pray get me a glass of brandy') suggests that the marriage was a disaster from the start. A daughter, Charlotte, was born in 1796 but in that same year the parents separated. Caroline spent much of her time travelling abroad, but when George inherited the throne in 1820 she returned to become queen. He attempted to get a bill through parliament divorcing her on the grounds of adultery with an Italian member of her retinue, Bartolomeo Pergami (often written Bergami). The bill met such opposition that it was withdrawn, but the door of Westminster Abbey was closed against Caroline when she tried to gain admission to the coronation in 1821. An embarrassing situation was resolved by her death three weeks later. These scandalous events, together with the king's known inclination to drink, gambling and wild extravagance, did little to endear him to his subjects.

In practice he had been ruling as prince regent since 1811, when his father's mental condition came to seem irreversible. It was a period of reactionary policies. George continued his father's opposition to the emancipation of the Catholics. The example of the French Revolution, combined with economic hardship after the Napoleonic Wars, gave the authorities a terror of radical agitation (an attitude resulting in the *Peterloo massacre). And there were still attempts to preserve Britain's corrupt political system, soon to be swept away by the *Reform Act.

It is as a patron of architecture that George is best remembered. His decision to live on the south coast brought prosperity and elegance to *Brighton, a town which still glories in the *Royal Pavilion, the king's greatest single creation. And his employment of John *Nash in London resulted in Regent Street (now altered out of recognition) and *Regent's Park.

His only child, Princess Charlotte, married Leopold of Saxe-Coburg in 1816 and died giving birth to a stillborn son the following year (her memorial is in *St George's Chapel). George was therefore succeeded by his brother as William IV (see the *royal house).

George V (1865–1936) King of Great Britain and Ireland from 1910; second son of Edward VII and Alexandra; married Mary of Teck (1893).

At the age of 12 he joined the training ship *Britannia* at *Dartmouth, beginning the modern link of the royal family with the navy. He was a naval commander in 1892 when his life was changed by the sudden death of his elder brother, Albert Victor, from pneumonia. Created duke of York that summer, George became engaged to his dead brother's fiancée Mary of Teck, known then as May but more familiar now as Queen Mary (1867–1953). After his father died, in 1910, the new king and his queen began their reign with a spectacular visit to India for the coronation durbar of 1911 – the only occasion on which a British king-emperor visited the subcontinent. At home his reign was unsettled by a series of crises – *Asquith's clash with the House of Lords, then *Home Rule, *World War I, the *General Strike and the *Depression. In his final years he was shocked by the relationship between the prince of Wales and Mrs Simpson which led after his death to the *abdication crisis.

The important development of the empire into the *Commonwealth of Nations occurred in his reign, with the Statute of Westminster (1931); and he was consciously addressing the entire Commonwealth in 1932 when he made the first of the traditional broadcasts by the monarch on *Christmas Day. From his twenties he was a keen philatelist and he built up an unparalleled collection of stamps of Britain and the Commonwealth. He had six children (see the *royal family) and was succeeded briefly by his eldest son as Edward VIII.

George VI (1895–1952) King of Great Britain and of Northern Ireland from 1936; second son of George V and Mary of Teck; married in 1923 Elizabeth Bowes-Lyon (now the *Queen Mother).

He followed the example of his father and elder brother (the future Edward VIII) in training as a naval cadet, first at Osborne and then Dartmouth; he then served at sea for much of World War I, seeing action at Jutland. Known as a child by his first name, Prince Albert, he was created duke of York in 1920. Between the wars his main concern was welfare and industrial relations (the Duke of York's Camps brought together boys from industrial areas and from *public schools), until he was suddenly elevated to the throne by the *abdication crisis. A shy man, for whom public speaking was torture because of his stammer, he seemed unsuited to the role in very difficult times. Events proved otherwise.

World War II gave the country its lasting impression of the new king and queen, who stayed in London through the bombing and became inspirational figures in the civilian war effort; in 1940 the king instituted the *George Cross in token of the courage being shown by civilians. By the time peace returned the royal family had acquired a historically unprecedented popularity.

The independence of *India brought changes to the monarchy in the late 1940s. The king ceased to be an emperor and 'Ind. Imp.' was dropped from the coins. More important, India's wish to become a republic but to remain within the *Commonwealth of Nations gave the British sovereign a new and more significant position as head of the Commonwealth and symbol of a free association of nations – a role taken very seriously by the king's daughter, Elizabeth II, who succeeded him in 1952 after illness had led to his death at the young age of 56. His only other child (see the *royal family) was Princess Margaret.

George Cross (GC) The highest award for heroism that can be awarded to civilians, ranking second only to the *Victoria Cross among all orders and decorations. It was instituted by George VI in 1940, the first year of the German bombing of British cities. In 1942 it was awarded to the entire island of *Malta. Suspended from a dark blue ribbon, it consists of a plain silver cross with, at its centre, a medallion showing St George and the Dragon and bearing the words 'For Gallantry'.

George Inn see *Southwark.

George Square see *Glasgow.

George Street see *Edinburgh.

Georgian A term which differs in meaning according to its context. In architecture and the decorative arts, such as furniture or silver, it applies to the reigns of George I to George IV (1714–1830); in practice it is often limited to the 18C, after which *Regency intervenes. It is much used to describe the elegantly simple terrace houses with sash windows which emerged then as the distinctive feature of British towns; but many grander styles also evolved in the Georgian period, including *Palladian, *rococo, *neoclassical and *Gothic Revival.

In poetry the word relates to the reign of George V (1910–36), particularly the early years. It derives in this sense from an influential anthology entitled *Georgian Poetry*, which was published in several volumes between 1911 and 1922 and included Rupert *Brooke, John *Masefield and Walter *de la Mare.

John Paul Getty Jnr (b. 1932) American philanthropist, resident in Britain, who in the past two decades has made a series of major donations to British institutions. He is the son of the oil billionaire J. Paul Getty (1892–1976). Among the chief beneficiaries of his generosity have been the Imperial War Museum, the MCC, the Museum of the Moving Image and the National Gallery.

Ghana Member of the *Commonwealth since 1957 and a republic since 1960. From as early as the 15C trading fortresses were built by the Portuguese in this part of west Africa, known to Europeans as the Gold Coast. By the 17C slaves were an even more valuable export than gold, and the Netherlands, Denmark and Britain were all involved in the area. The territories making up modern Ghana gradually came under British control from about 1850. Kwame Nkrumah (1909–72) was elected in 1952 as the first prime minister of the colony of the Gold Coast. He continued to lead Ghana from independence in 1957 until he was ousted in a coup in 1966.

Giant Despair see *Pilgrim's Progress*.

Giant's Causeway Promontory in northern Ireland, in County Antrim, formed of vertical stone columns, most of which are irregular hexagons. They are the result of the rapid cooling of molten basalt, forced some 60 million years ago through a volcanic rift which stretches due north under the sea to *Staffa, where the same shapes occur. The name derives from the ancient legend that these are stepping stones laid by a giant so that he could cross the sea. Dr Johnson, a reluctant traveller to Scotland, said of the fascinating natural phenomenon at Staffa that it was 'Worth seeing, yes, but not worth going to see' (a very precise anticipation of the later distinction in Michelin guides between *vaut la visite* and *vaut le détour*).

Edward **Gibbon** (1737–94) English historian, author of *The *Decline and Fall of the Roman Empire*. Apart from a spell as a notably inactive MP (1774–82), his life's work was his great history. He was the recipient of a remark often quoted as an extreme example of English philistinism. He gave the second volume of *Decline and Fall* to the duke of Gloucester, younger brother of George III, only to receive the response, 'Another damned, thick, square book! Always scribble, scribble, scribble! Eh! Mr Gibbon?'.

Grinling **Gibbons** (1648–1721) Woodcarver of consummate skill, particularly in his limewood wall panels of fruits, leaves and vegetables (a peapod was long considered to be a signature, but it was not invariably his). He worked also in stone and bronze. There is much of his carving in St Paul's Cathedral, including wooden choir stalls inside and stone decorative swags on the exterior. He contributed to many stately homes of the period, but the single most impressive display of his work is in the Carved Room at *Petworth.

Orlando **Gibbons** (1583–1625) The most brilliant keyboard player of his time, both on the virginals and the organ (he was organist of the Chapel Royal from the age of 21). His fame as a composer derives in particular from his anthems and madrigals, of which *The Silver Swan* is one of the best known.

An outstanding example of Grinling Gibbons' skill in suggesting different textures in carved limewood, c.1685.

James **Gibbs** (1682–1754) Scottish architect who studied in Rome before starting a practice in London in 1709. His experience of Roman *baroque and his admiration for the work of Wren prevented his adopting the new *Palladian orthodoxy as fully as his younger contemporaries, and he remained an extremely individual architect. His best-known buildings are *St Martin-in-the-Fields in London; the Radcliffe Camera in *Oxford; and, in *Cambridge, the Senate House and the Fellows' Building in King's College (known locally as the Gibbs Building). He published in 1728 *A Book of Architecture*, through which his designs, and in particular that of St Martin-in-the-Fields, had a wide influence.

Gibraltar Rocky promontory at the southern tip of Spain which is an internally self-governing British dependent territory. Captured from Spain in 1704, during the War of the *Spanish Succession, it was ceded to Britain in 1713 by the treaty of Utrecht. The most active Spanish attempt to recover it was the Great Siege of 1779–83. Its already great military importance, guarding the entrance to the Mediterranean, was much increased for Britain when the opening of the Suez canal in 1869 made this the sea route to India. Spanish claims on it intensified in the 1960s; but in a referendum of 1967 the people of Gibraltar voted overwhelmingly to preserve the link with Britain. In 1969 Spain closed the border, reopening it partly in 1982 and fully in 1985. In March 1988 Gibraltar was the scene of a controversial event when two men and a woman, members of the IRA, were shot by the SAS – a sequence of events investigated in *Death on the Rock*. Tourism is an important part of the economy of the Rock, famous in particular for its Barbary apes.

Alexander **Gibson** (b. 1926, kt 1977) Principal conductor and musical director of the Scottish National Orchestra (1959–84), and founder of *Scottish Opera. From 1954 to 1959 he was with Sadler's Wells Opera (which became the *English National Opera), and it was this experience – combined with the inspiring example of what *Welsh National Opera had achieved – which prompted him to establish Scotland's own opera company, of which he was artistic director from the first season in 1962 until 1985.

Guy **Gibson** (1918–44) One of the outstanding pilots of World War II. At the age of 24 he led the *Dam Busters on their famous raid and was awarded the VC for his part in the action. He died when his Mosquito crashed, for reasons unknown, in Holland.

Mike **Gibson** (b. 1942) Northern Irish rugby union player, usually at centre or flyhalf, with 69 caps for Ireland (1964–79) and 12 for the *Lions (1966–71); the total of 81 is the highest of any international player in the game, beating by one the previous record of his fellow countryman Willie John *McBride.

John **Gielgud** (b. 1904, kt 1953) The great survivor from a generation of great British actors; he made his name sooner than his contemporaries Ralph Richardson and Laurence Olivier, and was working long after them. Theatre was in his family (Ellen Terry was his great aunt), and by 1929 he had established himself as a magnificent Shakespearean actor. In that year he played for the first time, at the *Old Vic, his most famous role of all, Hamlet; he is known for his mellifluous voice and classical style of verse-speaking. He also has a drily effective way with comedy; Jack Worthing in *The Importance of Being Earnest* became one of his best-known parts in the theatre, and he delighted the much larger TV audience with his performance in *Brideshead Revisited*. In his later years he

One of W.S. Gilbert's Bab Ballads *sketches: an elderly father ('a prophet by trade'), cursed with a precocious baby.*

played many leading roles in new British plays, such as David Storey's *Home* (1970) and Harold Pinter's *No Man's Land* (1975) – in both cases with Ralph Richardson. His numerous films include an Oscar-winning performance in *Arthur* (1981) and a leading role as recently as 1991 in *Prospero's Books*.

Gift Aid see *deed of covenant.

Alfred **Gilbert** (1854–1934, kt 1932) The leading British sculptor of the late 19c, best known for *Eros. His greatest work, mainly completed in the 1890s, is the tomb to the duke of Clarence in the *Albert Memorial Chapel, an extraordinarily elaborate monument in polychromed bronze and aluminium.

Humphrey **Gilbert** (c.1539–83, kt 1570) English soldier and colonizer who claimed St John's, Newfoundland, for Elizabeth I in 1583. But the colonists he had taken with him decided almost immediately against staying. On the return voyage Gilbert went down in a storm with the tiny 10-ton *Squirrel* in which he had, eccentrically, insisted on travelling.

William **Gilbert** (1544–1603) The author of the first English book of fully experimental science. He was a doctor by profession, physician to both Elizabeth I and James I. He made magnetism his special study, publishing in 1600 *De Magnete, magneticisque corporibus, et de magno magnete tellure* (Latin for 'Of the magnet, of magnetic bodies, and of the earth as a great magnet'). He describes his experiments with magnetized metal bars, concluding that the earth has magnetic poles near the geographical poles and that it exercises an influence on other bodies in the solar system. The gilbert, the modern unit of magnetomotive force, is named after him.

W.S. **Gilbert** (William Schwenck Gilbert, 1836–1911, kt 1907) Librettist of the *Savoy operas. By profession a barrister, he contributed comic verse illustrated with his own drawings to the magazine *Fun* from 1861, using the pseudonym 'Bab'. Skilful both in rhythm and rhyme, these verses were published in book form as *The Bab Ballads* (1869). A moderate career as a playwright was transformed by the string of comic opera successes with *Sullivan. He died of a heart attack after saving a young woman from drowning in the 'swimming lake' which he had built in the grounds of his house.

Gilbert and Ellice Islands see *Kiribati and *Tuvalu.

Gilbert and George (Gilbert Proesch, b. 1943; George Passmore, b. 1942) Artists who began with performance art, presenting themselves in various guises as the art object, and then progressed to large wall pieces – again usually containing their own images.

Giles (Carl Ronald Giles, b. 1916) Cartoonist from 1943 for the *Daily* and *Sunday Express*, whose work has been reissued as an annual every year since 1945. His wartime cartoons, often featuring Hitler and Mussolini with their cronies, were already in the crowded format, full of Dickensian character and incident, which is his trademark. Subsequently the large and chaotic Giles family became his theme, centring on the squat little figure of Grandma; only a fraction of her pugnacious bespectacled face is visible between her black coat and hat, but the glint in her eyes is enough to suggest that she may erupt at any moment.

Eric **Gill** (1882–1940) English sculptor and wood-engraver who had a major influence on typography and book design. From carving letters on tombstones he moved into low-relief sculpture, as in the *Stations of the Cross* (1914–18) for Westminster Cathedral. His work as typographer and illustrator ranged from small editions of books for the Golden Cockerel Press (his famous *Four Gospels* came out in 1941, just after his death) to mass-circulation typefaces such as his Perpetua range (from 1925) or the Gill Sans-Serif (1927), commissioned by Monotype. In his illustrations a brilliant clarity of line is used in attenuated and often fanciful figures reminiscent of early medieval manuscripts. His personal reputation was dented by the publication in 1989 of extracts from a diary in which he recorded his indulgence in incest and paedophilia.

Gillow Family of cabinet-makers, based in Lancaster, who provided elegant well-made furniture in the Georgian and Regency periods and who were the first English firm to stamp their name on some of their pieces (from the 1760s). Robert Gillow (1703–73) established the business, which was extended into London under his sons, Richard and Robert.

James **Gillray** (1756–1815) English political caricaturist, with a savagery of attack and a freedom of etched line that have rarely been equalled. His most famous targets were George III (whom he ridiculed as the boorish Farmer George) and the prime minister, William Pitt. For much of his life Gillray lived and worked above the shop in St James's Street where his publisher, Mrs Humphrey, sold his prints. Crowds would gather on the pavement to buy straight from the press his up-to-the-minute satires on the political scene.

John **Gilpin** (1930–83) Dancer who had a successful career as a child actor before joining Ballet Rambert in 1945. In 1950 he moved to the London Festival Ballet (now the English National Ballet), of which he later became the artistic director (1962–5). A virtuoso dancer, he appeared as a guest with companies all over the world.

gilt-edged Term used now for government stocks, implying that money in them is safe because the stated interest will be paid and the stock redeemed at par on the given date. It was applied originally to any stock grand enough to have a certificate with gilded edges. The equivalent 'blue chip' for an almost equally safe share in a commercial company derives from the colour of a high chip used in poker. Both terms were current in the USA before being adopted in Britain.

Gimcrack (foaled 1760) Grey colt which first raced at Newmarket in 1765 and went on from that first victory to another 26 wins. He appears in at least four paintings by Stubbs. Two of his rare defeats were at York, where the Gimcrack Stakes is run in his honour at the August meeting.

gin A liquor distilled from grain and flavoured with juniper berries. It was developed in the Netherlands in the 17C, and a taste for it was probably brought to England by soldiers returning from Marlborough's campaigns in the early 18C. By 1720 London was addicted. Gin was cheap, bearing no tax, and there was no restriction on the sale of it. It was said that anybody could be 'drunk for a penny and dead drunk for twopence'. The resulting horrors were depicted by Hogarth in his engraving *Gin Lane*, published in February 1751. The Gin Act was passed that same summer, and the combination of a heavy duty and a licence fee eventually solved the problem. Gin became popular in the 20C in a new combination, the gin and *tonic.

Gipsy Moth see Francis *Chichester.

Girl Guides see *Guides.

The **Girl I left behind me** Tune traditionally played by a military band when a battalion or regiment is departing. The words of the song and the tune (known also as 'Brighton Camp') date from the 18C.

Gin Lane: Hogarth's polemical engraving of the poverty, debauchery and violence caused by cheap gin (1751).

Gladstone, man of the people, in a public omnibus – by contrast with the private hansom cab (Alfred Morgan, 1885).

Girl's Own Paper Magazine published 1880–1965 by the Religious Tract Society as a companion to the **Boy's Own Paper*. With much emphasis on home economics, it was aimed at young women as well as girls.

Girobank A *clearing bank established in 1968 to operate as part of the *Post Office. It offers the services associated with any other bank but uses the local post offices (outnumbering all the high-street banks put together) as its retail outlets. The same concept was behind the establishment a century earlier of *National Savings.

'Give us the tools, and we will finish the job.' Winston *Churchill's message to President Roosevelt in a radio broadcast on 9 February 1941. The policy of *lend-lease was passed by Congress the following month.

William **Gladstone** (1809–98) Politician who was four times prime minister (1868–74, 1880–5, 1886, 1892–4) and who shaped the *Liberal party. He entered parliament as a Tory in 1832 and during the next 30 years served in cabinets of Peel, Aberdeen, Palmerston and Russell, becoming chancellor of the exchequer in 1852–5 and 1859–66. In the extremely fluid political situation of the mid-19C these leaders opposed each other on specific issues or refused to serve in each other's administrations, but together they represented a gradual move towards Liberalism. Some had come from a Whig tradition. Others, like Gladstone himself, moved out of the Tory party with Peel over the *Corn Laws. But it was only under Gladstone that the Liberal position became clarified. He believed in self-government for the colonies (an attitude which extended to Home Rule for Ireland), a minimum of sabre-rattling abroad (both of these in marked contrast

to *Disraeli's imperial vision), a reduction in government expenditure and intervention, and an emphasis on individual freedom and political rights. A Liberal slogan of his time summed it up as 'Peace, Retrenchment, Reform'.

A good example of Gladstone's unaggressive stance cropped up during his first administration in the case of the *Alabama*. This was a warship, privately built and equipped in Britain, which was used on behalf of the Confederate side in the American Civil War, doing much damage to Federal shipping. The US government claimed heavy damages against Britain for not having prevented this unfriendly act. The matter was allowed to go to arbitration and Gladstone agreed in 1872 to pay $15,500,000 in gold. He was criticized at the time, but it is now seen as an early triumph of international law.

He virtually retired from politics after Disraeli won the election of 1874, but again it was a moral matter which brought him back. He was appalled by the atrocities committed against the Bulgarians by their Turkish overlords, and was distressed that Disraeli overlooked this aspect in his pro-Turkish and anti-Russian policy on the *Eastern Question. Gladstone's pamphlets and oratory on the issue gradually built up moral indignation in a previously indifferent electorate and contributed largely to the defeat of Disraeli in 1880.

In his last years *Home Rule became his dominant theme. All his attempts to push it through parliament failed, but it was the support of Irish MPs which gave him his last electoral victory, in 1892, when he was in Queen Victoria's words 'an old, wild, and incomprehensible man of eighty two and a half'. The queen had never liked him, preferring the warmth of Disraeli and complaining that Gladstone 'speaks to me as if I was a public meeting'. His moral conviction made him seem aloof or fanatical to many, but he had a happy marriage and eight children. His famous method of relaxation, felling trees, seems less eccentric nowadays, even if his other quirk of behaviour, wandering the streets at night to offer advice and protection to prostitutes, would still be considered unusual in a prime minister.

Glamis Castle (19km/12m N of Dundee) Imposing baronial castle, originally 14c but much added to up to the 19c. The central part is of the 17c, including the great spiral staircase set in an angle of the building, the long drawing room with its barrel-vaulted ceiling of decorative plaster, and the wood-panelled chapel with a ceiling by Jacob de Wet. Glamis has always been the home of the Lyon family, which includes the present *Queen Mother. Since her marriage in 1923, the rooms now called the Royal Apartments have been kept for her use.

Glamorgan Former *county in Wales, split since 1974 into Mid Glamorgan, South Glamorgan and West Glamorgan.

Glamorgan County Cricket Club Founded in 1888 and in the *county championship from 1921. They won the championship in 1948 and 1969, but by 1992 had no trophies for *one-day cricket. The county ground is in Cardiff, and the county also plays at Swansea, Neath and Abergavenny.

Glasgow (762,000 in 1981) Scotland's largest city, a port on the river Clyde; administrative centre of Strathclyde. It is believed to have grown up round a Christian settlement established in the late 6c by St *Mungo, whose church was probably on the site of the present cathedral; his tomb is in the crypt or Lower Church of the 13–14c Gothic building. Opposite the cathedral is Glasgow's oldest surviving house, the 15c Provand's Lordship, now a museum of mainly medieval material. The city's real prosperity began when the Clyde was developed as a port in the late 18c, enabling it to share with Liverpool and Bristol the profits from transatlantic trade. Shipbuilding followed, and the area became in the 19c a major industrial region; the world's last surviving sea-going paddle steamer, the *Waverley*, still takes passengers on the Clyde; and it was at the John Brown shipyards that the *Cunard liners, the *Queen Mary*, *Queen Elizabeth* and *QE2*, were built, in addition to the royal yacht *Britannia*.

This traditional side of Glasgow's economy suffered a major decline in the late 20c, but riches in other fields were sufficient to make it European City of Culture in 1990. The city was at the forefront of design in the early years of the 20c, as seen still in the buildings and furniture of Charles Rennie *Mackintosh, who took Art Nouveau forward into the beginnings of modernism. The Art Gallery and Museum, a very strong collection founded in 1854, is housed in a magnificently self-confident Victorian building by John W. Simpson (1858–1933) and E.J. Milner Allen (1859–1912); the surrounding Kelvingrove Park, laid out in the 1850s, was the scene in 1888 of an International Exhibition, the profits from which paid for the building. A much larger park to the southwest, Pollok Park, includes Pollok House (excellent Spanish paintings) and, since 1983, the *Burrell Collection.

The *Hunterian Museum and Art Gallery belongs to the university of Glasgow, founded in 1451 and the second oldest university in Scotland (St Andrews is earlier); the Gothic main university building, opened in 1870 and dominating one side of Kelvingrove Park, was designed by George Gilbert *Scott. The city's other university, Strathclyde, is one of the world's earliest colleges of technology; though only having university status since 1964,

it derives from the late 18c Anderson's Institution. Glasgow also has Scotland's two oldest schools. The High School of Glasgow is believed to have been founded in 1124, as the town's grammar school; it was given its present name when the town council took on its administration in 1834. Closed by the Glasgow Corporation in 1976, in a programme of merging schools into comprehensives, it was immediately revived as an independent school. Hutchesons' Grammar School is also now independent; founded for 12 poor orphans in 1641 by two brothers prominent in Glasgow, George and Thomas Hutcheson, it now has some 1700 pupils.

Glasgow Green (a municipal park from 1662, and as such the oldest in Britain) offers another kind of educational establishment – the splendid People's Palace, a late-Victorian cultural centre for the poor of Glasgow's East End (used now as a museum of social history), with a great conservatory attached as its winter gardens. Another impressive conservatory is the Kibble Palace in the *botanic gardens, while a recent and original piece of social history can be seen in the Tenement House in Buccleuch Street. Agnes Toward, a typist, lived in this building from 1911 to 1965, making few concessions to modern fashion; kept as when she died, her flat provides a vivid window on to the past. A notorious area of slums, the Gorbals, has been cleared and rebuilt in recent decades; the district includes the *Citizens Theatre.

Sauchiehall Street is Glasgow's main shopping street, but the city's centre is George Square; its east end is occupied by the huge and opulent civic building, the City Chambers, constructed in 1883–8 in an Italian Renaissance style to the design of William Young. An outstanding public reference library, the Mitchell, is named after Stephen Mitchell, a tobacco merchant who founded it in the 1870s. The Theatre Royal has been since 1975 the home of *Scottish Opera, and the *Glasgow Royal Concert Hall opened in 1990.

In sport Glasgow has Scotland's national stadium, *Hampden Park, and two football teams whose deepseated rivalry has traditionally included a sectarian element – *Rangers being Protestant and *Celtic Roman Catholic. Since 1988 Kelvin Hall, opposite the Kelvingrove Art Gallery, has housed a sports complex and the National Museum of Transport; it was previously Glasgow's main exhibition hall, until superseded in 1985 by the new Scottish Exhibition and Conference Centre on the north bank of the Clyde. Glasgow was the first city after London to instal an *underground railway.

Archbishop of **Glasgow** The senior Roman Catholic prelate in Scotland, president of the Bishop's Conference of Scotland, the church's governing body. Since 1974 the archbishop has been Thomas Winning (b. 1925).

Glasgow airport Scotland's largest airport and the fourth busiest in the UK (after Heathrow, Gatwick and Manchester). Opened in 1966, on a site previously used for a naval air station, it has gradually replaced in importance Scotland's other west coast airport, *Prestwick; this was established in 1935 and for many years had a monopoly on transatlantic flights from Scotland.

Glasgow Royal Concert Hall Designed by Leslie Martin (b. 1908), with a capacity of nearly 2500, the concert hall is on Sauchiehall Street. Opened in 1990, it is where the *Royal Scottish Orchestra now plays when at home in Glasgow.

Glasgow School Group of architects and designers who trained at the Glasgow School of Art in the late 1880s. They evolved an elegantly attenuated version of *Art Nouveau which had great influence abroad. One of the group, the metal-worker Margaret Macdonald, married in 1900 the most talented among them, Charles Rennie *Mackintosh.

The term is also applied to a slightly earlier group of painters working in the city, though they preferred to call themselves the Glasgow Boys (or simply the Boys). They were the first to break away from the academic tradition in Scottish painting, often working in the open air; some used a bright palette, though Whistler was also an important influence. Among many others the rather loose group included James Guthrie (1859–1930), John Lavery (1856–1941), Arthur Melville (1855–1904) and George Henry (1858–1943), whose *Galloway Landscape* (1889, Glasgow Art Gallery) is considered the masterpiece of the movement. The Boys were an important influence on the *Scottish Colourists.

Glasgow School of Art see *art schools.

Hannah **Glasse** (18C) The most influential cookery writer in English before the arrival of Mrs Beeton, though nothing is known of her beyond what can be deduced from her books. *The Art of Cookery Made Plain and Easy* (1747) went through many editions, amply justifying the bold claim on its original title page that it 'far exceeds any Thing of the kind ever yet Published'. Mrs Glasse is widely believed to have begun a recipe with the words 'First catch your hare'. In fact this is an old proverb; the nearest she comes to it is the instruction 'Take your hare when it is cased'.

Glastonbury (7000 in 1981) Town in Somerset which was of importance in early English Christianity and which has a leading role in both Christian and Arthurian legend. The Benedictine abbey appears to have been founded before the Anglo-Saxon period. It prospered greatly and is recorded in the Domesday Book as having the lordship of manors in five counties. The main feature of the ruins now is the very striking 14C Abbot's Kitchen, with its pointed octagonal stone roof.

In the 13C there first appears the legend that Joseph of Arimathea (the rich Jew in the Gospels who arranges for the burial of Jesus) had come to Glastonbury with the *Holy Grail. An even later story says that the Glastonbury thorn, which supposedly flowers each Christmas, sprang from Joseph's staff. The town also has its Arthurian legends. In 1191 bones were discovered which were believed to be those of Arthur and Guinevere. They were reburied before the altar of the abbey church in the presence of Edward I, and from then on Glastonbury was widely held to have been *Avalon.

The town's air of satisfying mystery is completed by the Glastonbury Tor, a weirdly conical hill which rises steeply nearby. And an informal pop concert held in 1970 has developed into a three-day Glastonbury Festival of rock music each summer, with the visitors creating a temporary township of tents.

Glaxo Britain's leading pharmaceutical company, and one of the largest companies of any kind in the country. It derives from an export-import business set up in New Zealand in 1873 by Joseph Nathan (1835–1912), son of a London tailor. A London office was opened in 1876 and a UK company was formed in 1899. Dairy products made up a high proportion of the goods imported by the company to Britain, and the company's breakthrough was its purchase of a patent for producing powdered milk. Drying machines were installed in New Zealand, and in 1906 a new trade name, Glaxo, was registered in London; it copied the recent example of *Oxo, but with milk (*galacticos* is 'milky' in Greek) as its declared ingredient instead of beef.

It was in the 1920s that Glaxo moved into chemicals, securing a licence to extract vitamin D from fish-liver oil. In its subsequent growth (in the 1990s it is the world's second largest pharmaceutical company) it absorbed several of Britain's oldest firms in this field; in 1958 it bought what is believed to be the oldest of all, Allen and Hanbury's (founded in London in 1715), and in 1963 it acquired J.F. Macfarlan, established in Edinburgh in 1780.

GLC see *Greater London.

Glencoe Village where Glen Coe, a long rugged valley in the Highland region, reaches an inlet of the sea on the west coast of Scotland. It was the scene of one of the most shameful episodes in British history. Clan leaders had been ordered to make their formal submission to William and Mary by the last day of 1691, but the local MacDonald chieftain had done so a few days late. The government seized the opportunity of making an example in the Highlands, where dissatisfaction with the change of regime after the *Revolution of 1688 had been strongest. A company of soldiers, mainly Campbells, had been living among the MacDonalds for nearly two weeks when they received orders to massacre their hosts. They began to do so at 5 a.m. on 13 February 1692, killing 38 men, women and children before the rest escaped.

Owen **Glendower** (Owain ap Gruffydd in Welsh, *c*.1354–*c*.1416) Rebel against English rule in *Wales, siding from 1400 with the English opposition to Henry IV. By 1404 he was in control of sufficient territory to declare himself prince of *Wales. But he was gradually driven from his strongholds by the young man who held that title more legitimately, the future Henry V. Glendower was eventually reduced to leading little more than a band of guerrillas. The last mention of him, still refusing to make terms, dates from 1416. His name remains widely known because of his dramatic appearance in Shakespeare's *Henry IV*, where he is a mad Welsh wizard in love with rhetoric.

Gleneagles Hotel golf course in the hills southwest of Perth, famous for offering very pleasant golf in a landscape of great beauty. The two courses, the King's and the Queen's, were laid out just before World War I.

Glenfinnan Monument (27km/17m W of Fort William) Round tower, 20m/65ft high, built by Alexander Macdonald in 1815 to mark the spot where Charles Edward *Stuart raised his standard 70 years earlier, on 19 August 1745, to gather the clans and begin the *'45 Rebellion. The figure of a Highlander, sculpted by John Greenshields, was placed on top in 1834.

glengarry (short for Glengarry bonnet) Brimless headgear, with a crease down the centre and often with ribbons hanging from the back, best known in the tartan version worn by certain Scottish regiments. The name derives from Glen Garry, a valley in the Grampians west of Blair Atholl.

Glen More see the *Great Glen.

Glenrothes (33,000 in 1981) One of Scotland's first *new towns, founded in 1948; since 1976 the administrative centre of Fife. Created as the town for new collieries in the district, it succeeded in bringing in other industries when the mines proved uneconomical. It is known for the generous provision of modern sculpture in its public places.

Gary **Glitter** (stage name of Paul Gadd, b. 1944) Singer known in the 'glam rock' era of the early 1970s for his outrageous costumes; he has been described as the Liberace of British pop. He had three no. 1 hit singles in the UK in rapid succession – *I'm the Leader of the Gang (I Am)* (1973), *I Love You Love Me Love* (1973), *Oh Yes! You're Beautiful* (1974).

Globe The theatre in which most of Shakespeare's greatest plays had their first performances. It was built in 1598–9 south of the river Thames on Bankside, the main entertainment area at that time, by Cuthbert and Richard *Burbage. They re-used the timbers of London's earliest theatre (called simply the Theatre and built north of the city by their father, James Burbage, in 1576). The Globe was round – *Henry V*, which has in its prologue the phrase 'this wooden O', may have been one of the first plays performed in it. It had three tiers of galleries for seated spectators around the open area on which the 'groundlings' stood to watch the play. There was a thatched roof above the galleries and over the stage, which was a rectangular platform projecting into the yard. In 1613 a spark from a cannon, fired during a performance of *Henry VIII*, set the thatch alight and the Globe burnt to the ground.

By the next year it had been rebuilt (with tiles on the roof), and as such it appears in the 1647 'Long View' of London by Hollar. But the lettering was wrongly added to the print. The Globe is the building on the left, marked 'Beere bayting' (the double roof over the stage is clearly visible). The building marked 'The Globe' was in fact the Hope, which had been built for *bear baiting but which put on plays as well while the Globe was out of action. Along with the other London theatres the Globe was closed by the *Puritans in 1642. It was pulled down in 1644; in 1989 traces of its foundations were discovered. A full-scale reconstruction of it near the original site has been planned since the 1970s by the American actor Sam Wanamaker; by 1992 building was under way, with talk of performances from about 1995.

Part of Bankside in Hollar's 1647 view: the Globe, wrongly identified, is the theatre marked 'Beere bayting'.

Glorious First of June (1 June 1794) The British name for a battle fought in the Atlantic during the *French Revolutionary Wars. The British commander, Lord Howe (1726–99), was attempting to prevent a convoy of 130 merchant ships, loaded with American grain, from reaching France. About 640km/400m from the coast of Europe he engaged the French escort, which like himself had 26 *ships of the line. Howe captured six and damaged many more, but the convoy got through – leaving little but glory for the British to commemorate.

Glorious Revolution see *Revolution of 1688.

Gloucester (104,000 in 1991) City on the river Severn; administrative centre of Gloucestershire. The Roman settlement of *Glevum* was established here in the late 1st century AD to protect the river crossing west into Wales. The town's later importance derived from the abbey founded in 681. At the *dissolution of the monasteries the abbey church (11–15c) became the cathedral of a new diocese. The predominantly Romanesque nave with massive pillars leads into a delicate Perpendicular choir; its east window, the largest of its period, has stained glass given in 1352 to commemorate the victory at *Crécy. Even more spectacular Perpendicular stonework is in the cloisters (late 14c to early 15c), with the earliest large-scale *fan vaulting in the country. This is one of the locations of the *Three Choirs Festival, and the first *Sunday school was also in Gloucester.

The City Museum and Art Gallery, in an Elizabethan-style building of 1893, has mainly local material apart from the Marling Bequest of 18c British painting and decorative art. Part of the city's docks have been adapted to form the National Waterways Museum, with a floating collection of historic boats and an accompanying exhibition in the 19c Llanthony warehouse. The Robert Opie Collection is an evocative museum of advertising and packaging materials from the mid-19c to the present.

Gloucester Rugby union football club, formed in 1873. It has won the John Player/Pilkington Cup outright twice (1972, 78) and has shared it once (1982 with Moseley).

Duke of **Gloucester** (Prince Richard, b. 1944) Grandson of George V (see the *royal family). His elder brother, Prince William (1941–72), was killed when his plane crashed in Staffordshire during an air race. In 1972 he married Birgitte van Deurs (b. Denmark 1946), and they have three children – Alexander, Earl of Ulster (b. 1974), Davina (b. 1977) and Rose (b. 1980).

Gloucester Old Spot see *pigs.

Gloucestershire (539,000 in 1991, administrative centre Gloucester) *County in west central England bordering on Wales.

Gloucestershire County Cricket Club Founded in 1871 and one of the original teams in the *county championship. Thanks to W.G. *Grace the club was very successful in the early years (champions 1873, 76, 77), but has not finished first since the points system was introduced in 1890. Their other most distinguished player has been Wally *Hammond. In *one-day cricket they have won the Gillette Cup (1973) and the Benson and Hedges Cup (1977). The county ground is the Phoenix in Bristol, and the county also plays in Gloucester and Cheltenham.

Jane **Glover** (b. 1949) Conductor and TV presenter of music programmes. Since 1983 she has been music director of the London Choral Society, and in 1984–91 was artistic director of the London Mozart Players.

Elinor **Glyn** (Elinor Sutherland, 1864–1943, m. Clayton Glyn 1892) Romantic novelist, remembered chiefly because of an anonymous rhyme inspired by a tiger skin which features in numerous scenes of passion in her book *Three Weeks* (1907): 'Would you like to sin/ With Elinor Glyn/ On a tiger skin?/ Or would you prefer/ To err/ With her/ On some other fur?'.

Glyndebourne House in Sussex which has provided, since 1934, one of the most brilliant oddities of the English summer. In that year the owner, John Christie (1882–1952), presented two Mozart operas in a theatre which he had built in the garden, with his wife, the soprano Audrey Mildmay (1900–53), playing Susanna in *The Marriage of Figaro*. From the start the standard was extremely high, and as run by the next generation (George Christie, b. 1934) Glyndebourne has continued to be at the forefront of British opera. The repertoire extends from Monteverdi to newly commissioned works, but keeps Mozart as its central concern. Evening dress is worn by the audience (causing strange early-afternoon scenes at Victoria Station), and many bring elaborate picnics to eat in the gardens during the interval – the resulting chaos in stormy weather is also traditional. Tickets, though pricey, are almost impossible to buy, so during 1993 the old theatre is being replaced by a larger building, scheduled to open in 1994. Each autumn, after the season at Glyndebourne, the company's productions go on tour with a different cast.

GMB The most characteristic example of a *super-union, with members in virtually every field of employment, whether industrial, white-collar or service. Its constituent unions, stretching far back into the 19C, have represented boilermakers, blacksmiths, Jewish tailors, Belfast collar workers, felt hat trimmers, women clerks and almost everyone else. The most recent merger, in 1989, was between GMBATU (General, Municipal, Boilermakers and Allied Trade Union) and APEX (Association of Professional, Executive, Clerical and Computer Staff). The name chosen, GMB, does not so much stand for three words as echo past history, and the union describes itself as 'Britain's General Union'. In the early 1990s it had about 850,000 members.

GMT see *Greenwich Mean Time.

gnomes of Zurich A phrase for the international banking community, coined by Harold Wilson in a speech to the House of Commons in 1956 ('all the little gnomes of Zurich and the other financial centres'). It was revived when his Labour government faced a balance of payments crisis on coming to power in 1964.

GNP see *GDP.

The **Go-Between** (1953) Novel by L.P. Hartley (1895–1972) about a 12-year-old boy, Leo, on holiday in a country house during an idyllic Edwardian summer. He carries secret messages to and fro between two lovers, the daughter of the house and a tenant farmer, becoming increasingly disturbed by the passion of which he is the bewildered channel. The film of 1970 was an immaculate and nostalgic recreation of that lost world; directed by Joseph Losey, it had a script by Harold Pinter and starred Alan Bates and Julie Christie.

gobstopper see *sweets.

God be in my head Beautifully simple short hymn which first appears in a book printed in London in 1544 (by Richard Pynson), where it is said to derive from Salisbury.

Lord **Goddard** (Rayner Goddard, 1877–1971, kt 1932, baron 1944) Lord chief justice from 1946 to 1958, a strong believer in the deterrent value of both *corporal and *capital punishment. He presided over one of the most controversial murder trials of the period, that of *Bentley and Craig; the law compelled him to pronounce the death sentence on Bentley, but he was said to have been surprised that the home secretary granted no reprieve (the jury had recommended mercy).

Lady **Godiva** Historical figure connected with *Coventry in the 11C, whose fame derives from a legend first appearing in a 13C chronicle. This states that in 1057 her husband, irritated by her complaints that his taxes on the people of Coventry were too harsh, replied provokingly that he would reduce them if she would ride naked through the crowded marketplace. She did so, preserving her modesty with her long hair. The attractive story was much repeated; one 14C version added that the tax on horses was the only one not reduced, presumably as a punishment on Godiva's accomplice. The extra detail of Peeping Tom (who disobeyed an order not to look at her nakedness and was struck blind) first appeared in 1678, the year in which a Godiva procession became part of Coventry's annual fair. Both respectable and titillating, Godiva was a favourite with Victorian painters. The statue of her by Reid Dick (1879–1961) in the centre of Coventry, at Broadgate, was put up in 1949.

God moves in a mysterious way see William *Cowper.

Godolphin Arabian see *thoroughbred.

God rest you merry, gentlemen see *carols.

God Save the Queen see the *national anthem.

Gog and Magog Names in the biblical *Revelation*, representing nations which will fight each other at the time of the apocalypse. In the medieval legends about the founding of Britain by *Brut, the two names were rolled into that of a single giant, Gogmagog. By the 15C they were separate again in the form of two large painted wooden statues, Gog and Magog, which took part in London processions and were kept in the *Guildhall. The pair of them are still there, though they have twice been replaced – after being destroyed in the Great Fire of 1666 and by bombing in 1940.

Goidelic see *Celtic languages.

Gold Coast see *Ghana.

Gold Cup see *Ascot and *Cheltenham.

The **Golden Bough** see James *Frazer.

Golden Hind see Francis *Drake.

Golden Miller (foaled 1927) Bay gelding with the exceptional record of five successive wins in the Gold Cup at *Cheltenham (1932–6), in addition to finishing first in the *Grand National in 1934.

golden retriever see *retriever.

The **Golden Treasury** The most influential anthology of English poetry until eclipsed by The *Oxford Book of English Verse. The selection was by Francis Turner Palgrave (1824–97), with assistance from Tennyson. The first edition appeared in 1861, and there have been frequent revisions and enlargements since.

Lady Godiva, almost overwhelmed by modesty on her public-spirited outing: painting of c.1898 by John Collier.

Goldie see *Boat Race.

***Goldilocks** and the Three Bears* Goldilocks herself was the final addition to this much retold story, first printed in the early 19C as a tale of an old woman visiting the house of the three bears and trying their porridge and their beds. By 1850 the intruder was a more sympathetic little girl, called Silver-Hair. Later she became Golden Hair, and in the early 20C finally emerged as Goldilocks. Her story is sometimes made the basis for *pantomime.

William **Golding** (b. 1911, kt 1988) Novelist, much concerned with the nature of evil, who with his first book planted in the nation's mind (and on every school syllabus) a powerful fable on human savagery – * *Lord of the Flies* (1954). In his subsequent books he has taken many bold leaps of the imagination. His second, *The Inheritors* (1955), is a story of primitive men and women threatened by a more aggressive Neanderthal species; *Pincher Martin* (1956) takes place in the dying moments of a drowning man; and *The Spire* (1964) follows in intricate detail the stages by which an obsessive medieval architect drives ever higher an over-ambitious cathedral spire. Golding won the Booker prize with *Rites of Passage* (1980), in which a young man loses his innocent optimism in the confined environment of a shipload of passengers sailing out to Australia in the early 19C. He was awarded the Nobel prize for literature in 1983.

James **Goldsmith** (b. 1933, kt 1976) Larger-than-life character whose amorous, litigious and financial adventures have continued to fascinate gossip columnists and public alike. He was front-page news at the age of 20 when he eloped with a Bolivian tin-heiress. His successful action against * *Private Eye* in 1983 for criminal libel, one of the most publicized civil cases of recent times, was followed by the establishment of the satirical magazine's

Goldenballs Fund to pay Goldsmith his £85,000 damages and costs. His reputation for financial acumen, with a reputed personal fortune of between $1bn and $2bn by the early 1990s, was much boosted by the news that he had sold all his shares just weeks before the 1987 stock market crash; but a massive corporate raid led by him against *BAT failed in 1989, and in 1990 he announced that he was retiring from active business. In the 1990s he is building himself a retreat, complete with its own airstrip, in the Mexican jungle.

Oliver **Goldsmith** (c.1730–74) Irish author, in London from about 1756, who became a close member of Dr *Johnson's circle. He has the unusual distinction of having contributed to English literature a classic in each of three different forms: a novel (*The *Vicar of Wakefield*), a play (* *She Stoops to Conquer*) and a poem, *The Deserted Village* (1770). The poem is an evocation of an idealized rural life before the enclosure of *common lands and the beginning of the *Industrial Revolution had caused the fictional village of Auburn to become deserted (the inevitable untruth in such nostalgia provoked *Crabbe into the harsher realities of *The Village*). Goldsmith was known among his friends for the difference between his ease in print and his awkward conversation, a contrast summed up in Garrick's impromptu epitaph:

> Here lies Nolly Goldsmith, for shortness called Noll,
> Who wrote like an angel, but talked like poor Poll.

gold standard Economic system in which a country's paper currency is supported by gold, anyone having the right to demand from the national bank the same amount of gold as the face value of a bank note. Britain was on the gold standard from 1821 to 1914, and on a modified version of it for a period between the wars. Now the promise on a bank note means only that it will be treated as legal tender for the stated sum.

golf Game associated in particular with Scotland, where its first mention dates from the 15C. A decree of 1457, in the reign of James II, banned 'fute-ball and golfe' so that greater attention should be paid to the necessary sport of archery. Similar decrees were issued in the reigns of James III and James IV, suggesting that both football and golf were immensely popular. A game using a stick or club to strike a ball had been played in many parts of Europe since Roman times, and the earliest representations are outside Scotland – the figure of a single player in the great 14C east window of Gloucester Cathedral, and a group of three golfers on a putting green in an early 16C Flemish manuscript (now in the British Library). But it was the Scottish game which spread round the world. Among its greatest enthusiasts were the 16C Stuart kings (in spite of the prohibitions of their immediate ancestors), and James VI made it fashionable in London after he became James I of England. He is recorded as having played on Blackheath common, and a society of golfers was established there in 1608. It is on this rather inconclusive evidence, and with that year as its foundation date, that the Royal Blackheath is often described as the world's oldest surviving golf club.

More solid milestones are the founding of the Gentlemen Golfers of Leith in 1744 (see *Muirfield) and of the Society of St Andrews Golfers in 1754 (known from 1834 as the *Royal and Ancient). The courses of these clubs on the east coast of Scotland established 'links' (undulating sandy ground) as the classic golf terrain. During the 19C the Royal and Ancient became accepted as the international authority on the rules of the game. Since 1920 the club has managed the annual *Open and amateur championships. Three important biennial team competitions with the USA were launched between the wars: in 1922 the Walker Cup (amateur men, British and Irish against the Americans), with a trophy donated by George Herbert Walker, president of the US Golf Association; in 1927 the *Ryder Cup; and in 1932 the Curtis Cup (amateur women, British and Irish against the Americans) with a trophy given by two sisters, Margaret and Harriet Curtis, who had both won the amateur championship in the USA.

golliwog Black doll created as a character for children by Florence Upton (1873–1922), an illustrator born in the USA of English parents. She was living in England by the time *The Adventures of two Dutch dolls and a Golliwogg* appeared in 1895, with verses by her mother, Bertha Upton (1849–1912). It was the first of a long series, and Golliwog himself rapidly became a craze. He was based on a favourite doll of Florence's childhood. In World War I she put the two Dutch dolls and Golliwog up for auction to buy an ambulance. The purchasers presented them to *Chequers, where they remained for many years – until Golliwog's political incorrectness made them unsuitable. They are now in the Bethnal Green Museum of Childhood.

E.H. Gombrich (Ernst Hans Gombrich, b. 1909, kt 1972) Austrian-born art historian, in Britain since the 1930s, who has had a major influence on public perception both through his books on how we see (in particular *Art and Illusion* 1960) and through his bestselling general history *The Story of Art* (1950). He is a member of the Order of *Merit.

The Gondoliers or, The King of Barataria (1889) A *Savoy opera by Gilbert and Sullivan, set in Venice where one of two gondoliers, Marco and Giuseppe, is supposedly the prince of Barataria. The duke of Plaza Toro, an impoverished and very unmilitary aristocrat ('He led his regiment from behind,/ He found it less exciting') arrives to marry his daughter Casilda to whichever is the prince. But Casilda loves her father's attendant Luiz; and happily it turns out that he, a changeling, is the one with the royal blood.

Graham **Gooch** (b. 1953) Batsman who has played *cricket for Essex (from 1973) and for England (1975–82 and from 1985, captain from 1988). The three-year gap in his Test career was the result of being banned after leading a rebel tour to South Africa in 1982. He holds one record which is unlikely to be equalled. In a Test match against India at Lord's in 1990 he scored 333 in the first innings and 123 in the second, becoming the first player in the history of both Test and first-class cricket to score a triple century and a century in the same match.

Reginald **Goodall** (1901–90, kt 1985) Conductor, mainly of opera. One of his great moments was the first performance of *Peter Grimes at Sadler's Wells in 1945. He subsequently became known for his interpretations of Wagner, in particular a very successful *Ring* cycle from 1973 for English National Opera.

Goodbye Mr Chips (1934) Novel by James Hilton (1900–54), following the career of a teacher in an English *public school from persecution by the boys in his early years to eventual high status as an elderly eccentric. It was filmed in 1939 with Robert Donat (1905–58) in the title role, and in 1969 with Peter O'Toole.

Goodbye to All That (1929) Vivid and provocatively down-to-earth account by Robert *Graves of his first 30 years. Though it includes life at a *public school (Charterhouse) and at Oxford in the 1920s, it is mainly set in the trenches and is best known for its account of the horrors of war. The disillusioned author explains his title in the last sentence: 'So I went abroad, resolved never to make England my home again.'

Goodbye to Berlin see Christopher *Isherwood.

The Good Companions (1929) Novel by J.B. *Priestley which gives a warmly affectionate panorama of contemporary England as seen in the experiences of three strangers, from very different backgrounds, who come together to form a small theatrical company. Jess Oakroyd is a carpenter who has walked out of his job in a Yorkshire mill; when her aged father dies, Miss Trant leaves her Cotswold village for an open-ended holiday; and Inigo Jollifant, piano player and would-be writer, gives up his job in an East Anglian school to try a new life. Together, three enthusiastic amateurs, they set up a professional 'concert party', calling themselves the Good Companions. The scene is expertly set to enable the reader to share in the excitement of small-scale theatrical life.

Good Food Guide Restaurant guide of an unusual kind in that it is written by the customers. It was launched in 1949 by Raymond Postgate (1896–1971), using a team of volunteers. Once the guide was published, every purchaser became automatically a member of a notional Good Food Club. Members can send in reports of meals eaten or restaurants discovered, and their comments may be quoted verbatim in the next annual edition after being checked by a team of specialist inspectors. Since 1963 the guide has been published by the Consumers' Association (see *Which?).

Duncan **Goodhew** (b. 1957) Winner of the gold medal in the 100 metres breaststroke at the 1980 Olympics. His subsequent career as a personality has been much helped by the instant recognizability conferred by his entirely bald head.

*The **Good Life*** (BBC 1975–7) TV series which extracted comedy from the beginnings of the green movement, in the friction between a young couple who are attempting to lead a life of ecological self-sufficiency (played by Felicity *Kendal and Richard *Briers) and their more conventional neighbours (Penelope *Keith, Paul *Eddington).

*The **Good Old Days*** see *music hall.

Goodwin Sands Dangerous strip of shifting sandbanks, exposed at low tide and lying about 10km/6m off the eastern tip of Kent. The deeper water between them and the coast, known as the Downs, has been an important anchorage. Legend describes the sands as the remains of an island, Lomea, which supposedly belonged to Godwin, the father of Harold II.

Goodwood House (6km/4m NE of Chichester) House which has developed from a hunting lodge bought in 1697 by the 1st duke of Richmond, the illegitimate son of *Charles II and Louise de Kéroualle. The present building is largely the creation of the 3rd duke, who in 1760 commissioned *Chambers to rebuild the house and later employed James *Wyatt to enlarge it. He also brought back many of its most precious contents from his time as ambassador to Louis XV – French furniture, Sèvres china and Gobelin tapestries on the theme of Don Quixote.

In the last years of his life the same duke inaugurated the races on top of the downs, to the north of the house, which have been an annual event since 1801. The main meeting, traditionally known as Glorious Goodwood, is held over five days in July. The oldest race, the Goodwood Cup, has been held since 1812; but the Stewards' Cup (first run in 1840) and the Sussex Stakes (1841) now have a higher profile. From 1948 to 1966 Goodwood was also the scene of top-class motor racing, on the perimeter of a wartime airfield, until the greater speed of modern cars made the track too dangerous.

Goonhilly Downs see the *Lizard.

*The **Goon Show*** (BBC 1952–60) Probably the most celebrated of all comedy shows on British radio (*ITMA would be its only rival). It was written largely by Spike *Milligan, whose fellow performers were Peter *Sellers, Harry *Secombe and, at the start, Michael Bentine. The same team had begun a similar programme in 1951 under the title *Crazy People*, and the beginning of *The Goon Show* was in fact little more than a change of name. The series encapsulated, more than any other, the unpredictable lunacy which has been a hallmark of British comedy on radio and television.

Goossens family Distinguished group of British musicians in the late 19c and 20c. Eugene Goossens (1845–1906) was a Belgian conductor who lived in England from 1873, conducting the Carl Rosa Opera (1882–92). His son and grandson were both Eugene (1867–1958, 1893–1962) and both conductors; the son became in his turn principal conductor of the Carl Rosa (1899–1915); the grandson was also a violinist and composer. Another grandson, Leon (1897–1988) was a virtuoso oboist, for whom Elgar and Vaughan Williams wrote pieces; and two granddaughters (Marie 1894–1991, Sidonie b. 1899) became distinguished harpists.

Gorbals see *Glasgow.

General **Gordon** (Charles Gordon, 1833–85) A heroic figure in Victorian Britain even before his death at Khartoum completed the legend. He first came to public attention through the events which gave him his popular name, 'Chinese Gordon'. The Europeans in Shanghai (of whom there were an increased number after the second *Opium War) were threatened in 1863 by a violent uprising, the Taiping rebellion. Gordon was put in command of some 4000 untrained Chinese and proved himself, in an 18-month campaign, to be an inspired and fearless leader of irregular troops. The subsequent highlights of his career all shared this element of derring-do on the frontiers of empire.

From the 1870s Britain had close links with the khedive of *Egypt. Gordon became governor (1877–80) of the vast and unruly Egyptian province of the Sudan, where he succeeded in pacifying the area. But after his return to England a charismatic popular leader emerged in the region, calling himself the Mahdi (in very broad terms the Muslim equivalent of a Messiah). His followers threatened the Egyptian garrisons in the Sudan, and Gordon accepted a call to relieve them. Instead, he found himself besieged in Khartoum. In a final extraordinary demonstration of his leadership he inspired a feeble garrison to withstand a 10-month siege, while the prime minister, Gladstone, dithered in London over whether to send a relief force. On 26 January 1885 the city wall was breached and the entire garrison slaughtered. The relieving army arrived two days too late. The Mahdi's followers then made their capital city at Omdurman, on the opposite bank of the Nile, from which they were dislodged by *Kitchener 13 years later.

Gordon Riots (2–8 June 1780) A week of violence in London which involved much destruction of property and ended with some 300 deaths. The disorder began with a huge march to the House of Commons, led by Lord George Gordon (1751–93), to protest against the measures of Catholic *emancipation which had been enacted in a bill of 1778 (they were minimal, being mainly concerned with rights of ownership). Parliament deferred its response and the crowd began burning Catholic premises. Their attention later turned to other establishments, including the Bank of England and various prisons (they released the inmates of *Newgate, after which looting became the main concern of the mob). The effective terrorizing of London ended only when troops were brought in, causing deaths and injury among the rioters.

Gordon himself was an eccentric and unstable character, but there was no proof that he approved of the violence and he was acquitted of a charge of high treason. Ironically he himself spent the last five years of his life in Newgate, on other charges, living in extravagant ease, entertaining his friends to daily dinners and fortnightly dances. The riots feature prominently in Dickens' novel *Barnaby Rudge* (1841).

Gordonstoun Scottish *public school near Elgin, until 1972 for boys only, founded in 1934 by Kurt Hahn (1886–1974) with a special commitment to building character (through a strict regime in Spartan conditions) as well as training the intellect. Its best known pupils have been the duke of Edinburgh and the prince of Wales.

Gorsedd see *eisteddfodd.

'Gotcha!' Notorious headline in the *Sun* on 4 May 1982, above the story of the sinking of the *General Belgrano* in the *Falklands War.

Gothic Derogatory term, coined in Italy during the *Renaissance, for the entire period of architecture which had intervened since the fall of Rome (sacked by the Goths in 410) and the end of classicism. The earlier centuries were later redefined as *Romanesque after the pointed

A Gothic Revival drawing room, at Eastnor Castle near Hereford, with design and furniture of c.1850 by Pugin.

arch, making possible a new elegance and lightness, had become recognized as the essential Gothic characteristic.

Such arches, originating in France, first appeared in England with the rebuilding of the east end of Canterbury Cathedral in 1175. During the next 250 years the English version of Gothic went through three distinct phases. It is in church windows that the difference is most clearly seen.

The first phase, known as Early English (up to *c.*1300) has very tall, narrow windows, simple and severe, with sharply pointed tops. In the next, Decorated (*c.*1300–1370), the tops of the windows are fragmented into curving lace-like stonework (known as tracery); at the same time the stone surfaces are much decorated with patterned carving. Finally in Perpendicular (*c.*1350–1550) the windows become vast, filling almost the entire wall, and they revert to more severely vertical partitions (the 'perpendicular' element), providing rectilinear spaces which can accommodate glorious expanses of stained glass. The decorative stonework now moves up into the roof with the development of *fan vaulting.

Gothic Revival (also called neo-Gothic) The reintroduction of the *Gothic style in architecture of the 18–19C. There had in fact been no break in a continuing Gothic tradition, only a slowing down, and historians distinguish between survival and revival. The two overlap in the 18C. The revival was characterized by a new fascination with the Middle Ages and a certain playfulness – elements which appeared at the same time in literature, though here playfulness took the form of the macabre. Horace *Walpole was a pioneer in both fields, *The Castle of Otranto* (1765) being the first Gothic novel and *Strawberry Hill (begun in 1750) one of the earliest Gothic Revival houses.

In the mid-19C the movement became more historical and less playful, though there were elements of play in the fantastic creations of William *Burges. More central was

the solemnity of *Pugin and *Ruskin. By the end of the century there were new Gothic churches all over Britain, promoted first by the discovery of the church commissioners in the 1820s that the Gothic style was cheaper to build than the classical (with its expensive stone lintels) and then boosted by *Anglo-Catholicism. Meanwhile in town halls, hotels and railway stations Gothic seemed the perfect medium for civic or commercial pride.

Bryan **Gould** (b. 1939) New Zealand-born Labour politician, in Britain from 1962. He entered parliament in 1974 as MP for Southampton Test, and since 1983 has represented Dagenham. A member of the shadow cabinet from 1986, he has been the front bench spokesman for trade and industry (1987–9) and for the environment (from 1989). He challenged John Smith for the leadership of the party in 1992, and resigned from the shadow cabinet later that year over the party's policy on Europe and its lack of opposition to the *Maastricht treaty.

Government The executive wing of the ruling political party or parties (whoever can command a majority of the votes in the House of *Commons). The government consists of those MPs or members of the House of *Lords who have been appointed *ministers. In common usage the word is often extended to include the departments of the civil service under their control.

government expenditure The total amount spent by the government in any *financial year. Until 1993 the amounts available for each government department were decided each autumn in the *public spending round and the taxation levels to raise the necessary money were set in the spring in the *budget; from 1993 the two processes are merged in the final months of each year. By far the largest single element of government expenditure is social security (mainly pensions and unemployment benefit), which in 1992 amounted to 29% of the total; this is followed by the National Health Service and related social services (15% in the same year), education (12%) and defence (9%). Government expenditure also includes interest (7% of the total in 1992) payable on the accumulated *national debt. If expenditure exceeds the total raised by taxation (see *tax burden), the deficit is the *PSBR.

Ian **Gow** (1937–90) Conservative politician, MP for Eastbourne from 1974. He was parliamentary private secretary to the prime minister, Mrs Thatcher, from 1979 to 1983. In 1985, when he was a minister of state at the Treasury, he resigned from the government over the *Anglo-Irish agreement. In 1990 he was murdered outside his home by an IRA car bomb.

David **Gower** (b. 1957) Left-handed batsman of classic elegance who has played *cricket for Leicestershire (1975–89), for Hampshire (from 1990) and for England (from 1978, captain 1983–6). In 1992 he broke two major England records, passing Colin Cowdrey's total of 114 Test appearances and Geoff Boycott's aggregate of 8114 runs in Test matches. By the end of that year Gower had played in 117 Test matches and had hit 8231 runs. Often accused of taking an over-relaxed attitude to the game, he enraged his critics in 1991 when he hired a Tiger Moth biplane and flew low over the ground in Queensland on which his colleagues were playing during a tour of Australia. His non-selection for the 1993 tour of India provoked an equal measure of indignation among his supporters.

Gower Peninsula Designated in 1956 an area of outstanding natural beauty, the peninsula stretches some 24km/15m west into the Bristol Channel from Swansea. It consists of a high plateau edged by a dramatically rocky coastline. The Mumbles, two small islands off the south coast, have given their name to the adjacent promontory (Mumbles is said, not entirely convincingly, to derive from *mamelles*, the French for breasts). The peninsula has many traces of occupation by prehistoric man (part of a skeleton found in 1823 has a carbon-dated age of about 18,000 years) and the caves have yielded animal remains including mammoth, rhinoceros and hippopotamus.

Lord **Gowrie** (Grey Hore-Ruthven, b. 1939, 2nd earl of Gowrie 1955) Conservative politician, in the *cabinet 1984–5 as chancellor of the duchy of Lancaster and as minister for the arts.

Gowrie conspiracy (1600) An event mysterious in its own time and still unexplained. After a day's hunting James VI (later *James I and VI) visited the house in Perth of the earl of Gowrie (*c.*1577–1600). He was unexpected but was accompanied by Gowrie's younger brother. In a scuffle later that night Gowrie and his brother were killed. The official version was that they were conspiring to seize the king; others have maintained that it was part of a complex royal plot to murder Gowrie.

GP (General Practitioner) The standard term in Britain for the local or family doctor, who has a 'general practice' rather than being a specialist. Changes to the *National Health Service in 1990 gave GPs the choice of becoming independent 'fund-holders'.

GPMU (Graphical, Paper and Media Union) Trade union formed in 1991 by the amalgamation of the two major printing unions, NGA (National Graphical Association) and SOGAT '82 (Society of Graphical and Allied Trades 1982). Each of these was itself the result of many successive mergers of smaller unions in the fields of printing, packaging, papermaking, bookbinding and design. The new union had on its formation some 300,000 members.

GPO see *Post Office.

W.G. **Grace** (William Gilbert Grace, 1848–1915) The best-known player in the history of *cricket, immediately recognizable in photographs with his thick moustache and chunky beard. He was a qualified doctor but cricket was his life, and he did more than anyone to make it popular. His team was Gloucestershire, which he captained 1870–98; he played for England 1880–99 and was captain 1888–99. In a career in first-class cricket spanning 1865–1908, he scored 54,896 runs (including 126 centuries) and took 2876 wickets.

Grâce Dieu Warship built for Henry V at Southampton in 1418, one of the largest of the new 'men-of-war' which were designed to carry cannon. She was struck by lightning and burnt out before she had put to sea. She

Government Expenditure, in £bn

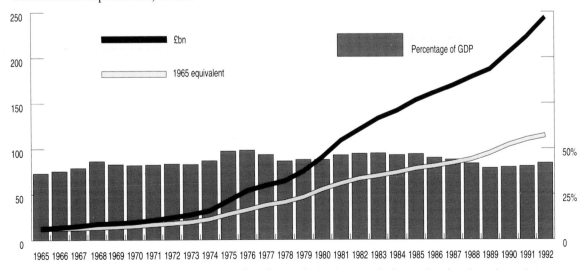

The lower line is the 1965 figure adjusted each year for inflation; the gap between the lines is therefore the real cumulative increase in government expenditure.

Source: Autumn Statement (*HM Treasury, November 1992*).

probably had three masts, and the remains of her hull (discovered in the river at Hamble in 1933) revealed that she was more than 38m/125ft in length. The *Henry Grâce à Dieu*, better known as the *Great Harry*, is a different ship built in the following century.

The Graces see *Woburn Abbey.

Gradgrind see *Hard Times.

Thomas **Graham** (1805–69) Pioneer in the chemical study of colloids (mixtures in which one substance is suspended in another) and in the processes which he called osmosis and dialysis. Graham's Law, named after him, states that the rate of diffusion of a gas is inversely proportional to the square root of its density.

Kenneth **Grahame** (1859–1932) Scottish author of one of Britain's most lasting classics for children, *The *Wind in the Willows*. He had previously published two very successful books of stories about childhood (*The Golden Age* 1895, *Dream Days* 1898). His professional career was in the Bank of England, where he rose from being a clerk in 1879 to Secretary of the Bank in 1898.

Grail see the *Holy Grail.

Percy **Grainger** (1882–1961) Australian-born composer who lived most of his life in the USA, but whose years in Britain before World War I resulted in several pieces with a strongly local flavour – in particular *Country Gardens* (1919, based on the folk tune to which *The Vicar of *Bray* is sung) and *Handel in the Strand* (1930, variations on Handel's tune *The Harmonious Blacksmith*). He collected English folk music, and it was he who brought 'Brigg Fair' to the notice of *Delius.

grammar school Originally the term for any school in medieval Europe. The schools taught Latin grammar and were religious institutions, many of them attached to cathedrals and monasteries, others founded as an act of charity. It has been calculated that by the 14C there were some 400 grammar schools in England and Wales for a population of about 2.5 million. Such schools were also often called high schools, particularly in Scotland; the term was first used for one established in 1519 in Edinburgh.

These schools were free, and by the 16C they were widely referred to as public schools – by contrast with the smaller and more elementary private schools, for which a fee was charged. Later many of the greatest grammar schools evolved into the modern *public schools (essentially fee-paying establishments), leaving the original name of grammar school for those in which tuition had remained free. In the modern world the major part of any free school's funding has come not from charitable sources but from government grants, and so they have become known as grant-aided or direct grant schools.

The high standard of grammar school education meant great pressure on the available places, and in the mid-20C selection was made by an examination which children in all *state schools sat at the age of 11 or 12 – the so-called eleven-plus. Those who passed won a place at a grammar school, with education to the age of 18 and a good chance of going on to university; the rest were offered a lesser standard of education to the age of 15 at secondary modern schools ('modern' in their curriculum, compared with the classical tradition of the grammar schools). The finality of this judgement at such an early age, potentially unjust and socially divisive, led to the gradual introduction from the 1950s of *comprehensive schools. Many of the best-known grammar schools (such as Manchester and the original King Edward's in Birmingham) chose to become public schools rather than abandon the principle of selection. By the late 1980s about 90% of state secondary schools in Britain were comprehensive, leaving only 10% of children divided between the surviving grammar and secondary modern schools. See also *education and *opting out.

The Grand National at Aintree in 1845, when the race was known as the Liverpool Grand Steeplechase.

Grand National: winners since World War II

	Horse	Jockey		Horse	Jockey
1946	Lovely Cottage	Bobby Petre	1970	Gay Trip	Pat Taaffe
1947	Caughoo	Eddie Dempsey	1971	Specify	John Cook
1948	Sheila's Cottage	Arthur Thompson	1972	Well To Do	Graham Thorner
1949	Russian Hero	Leo McMorrow	1973	Red Rum	Brian Fletcher
1950	Freebooter	Jimmy Power	1974	Red Rum	Brian Fletcher
1951	Nickel Coin	Johnny Bullock	1975	L'Escargot	Tommy Carberry
1952	Teal	Arthur Thompson	1976	Rag Trade	John Burke
1953	Early Mist	Bryan Marshall	1977	Red Rum	Tommy Stack
1954	Royal Tan	Bryan Marshall	1978	Lucius	Bob Davies
1955	Quare Times	Pat Taaffe	1979	Rubstic	Maurice Barnes
1956	E.S.B.	Dave Dick	1980	Ben Nevis	Charlie Fenwick
1957	Sundew	Fred Winter	1981	Aldaniti	Bob Champion
1958	Mr What	Arthur Freeman	1982	Grittar	Dick Saunders
1959	Oxo	Michael Scudamore	1983	Corbière	Ben De Haan
1960	Merryman II	Gerry Scott	1984	Hallo Dandy	Neale Doughty
1961	Nicolaus Silver	Bobby Beasley	1985	Last Suspect	Hywel Davies
1962	Kilmore	Fred Winter	1986	West Tip	Richard Dunwoody
1963	Ayala	Pat Buckley	1987	Maori Venture	Steve Knight
1964	Team Spirit	Willie Robinson	1988	Rhyme'N'Reason	Brendan Powell
1965	Jay Trump	Tommy Smith	1989	Little Polveir	Jimmy Frost
1966	Anglo	Tim Norman	1990	Mr Frisk	Marcus Armytage
1967	Foinavon	John Buckingham	1991	Seagram	Nigel Hawke
1968	Red Alligator	Brian Fletcher	1992	Party Politics	Carl Llewellyn
1969	Highland Wedding	Eddie Harty	1993	*no result*	

Grampian (504,000 in 1991, administrative centre Aberdeen) Since 1975 a *region of northeast Scotland, comprising the former counties of Kincardine, Aberdeen, Banff and most of Moray.

Grampians A term used rather loosely for the range of hills and mountains running northeast across Scotland from Oban. The *Cairngorms are an extension to the north in central Scotland. It was probably just short of the eastern part of the range that the Romans won the victory of Mons *Graupius, of which the name Grampian is a corruption.

Granada Commercial *television company, based in Manchester, which is the earliest survivor and the most distinguished of the ITV franchise-holders. It went on air in May 1956 and over the years has won a high reputation for quality programmes, both in the documentary field (*Disappearing World*, *World in Action*) and in drama (*Brideshead Revisited*, *Jewel in the Crown*).

War of the **Grand Alliance** see *William III.

Grand Challenge Cup see *Henley.

Grand Hotel see *Brighton.

Grand Metropolitan (Grand Met) Major food and drinks company which has developed from a chain of small hotels established after World War II by an estate agent, Maxwell Joseph (1910–82). The group was given the name Grand Metropolitan Hotels in 1962, and for some years during the 1980s its hotel interests included the Inter-Continental chain. More recently it has concentrated on the manufacture and retailing of food and drink, a side of its business which grew rapidly with the purchase of Express Dairy in 1969, of Watney Mann (including International Distillers and Vintners) in 1972 and of the US Pillsbury group in 1989.

Grand National (short for the Grand National Steeplechase) One of the greatest sporting events in the British calendar, and for many people the only occasion when they risk a bet. A steeplechase of 7.25km/4.5m over 30 fences (for 6-year-olds and upwards), its appeal lies in the challenge it makes to the courage and stamina of horses and jockeys alike; what starts each year much like a cavalry charge ends with only a few finishing (and sometimes dead horses among the fallen, a controversial issue). It takes place on a Saturday in April at Aintree, a course north of Liverpool which was opened for flat-racing in 1829. Steeplechasing was soon introduced (on the urging of Captain Becher, an enthusiast who fell from his horse into a brook in 1839, and whose name is now immortalized in the most dangerous of the jumps, Becher's Brook). The Grand National has been run at Aintree since about 1838, and has been known by that name since 1847. The race was cancelled in 1993 after two chaotic false starts.

By far the most famous horse in the history of the race has been *Red Rum; a winner of outstanding courage was Bob Champion (b. 1949), who overcame cancer to win on Aldaniti in 1981; and one of the most dramatic moments was the sudden and still unexplained collapse of the Queen Mother's Devon Loch in 1956, when in the lead and only 50 yards from the winning post, with Dick *Francis in the saddle.

Grand Panjandrum A character first appearing in nonsense lines said to have been composed by Samuel Foote (1720–77) to test the actor Charles Macklin, who claimed to be able to memorize any text on a single hearing. It is what we would now call a shaggy-dog story (featuring as it happens a 'great she-bear') and it introduces many weird characters, ending with 'the Grand Panjandrum himself, with the little round button at top, and they all fell to playing the game of catch as catch can, till the gun powder ran out at the heels of their boots'.

Grand Prix see *British Grand Prix.

grand slam Term used in various sports (deriving from bridge, where it means the bidding and winning of every trick). In rugby union it is applied to any country beating all four others in the *'Five Nations' tournament. It is used in tennis when any player wins the four most prestigious contests in the same season: *Wimbledon and the US, Australian and French championships. In golf it applies to a player winning all four *majors.

A memento of the Grand Tour: William Gordon of Fyvie, painted by Batoni in 1766 among Roman ruins and in his tartan (forbidden at the time in Scotland).

Grand Tour The obligatory finishing school for any fashionable young British gentleman in the 18C. The destination was Rome, where the young man was expected to become acquainted with the classical beginnings of civilization. Likely highlights on the journey were Paris and Versailles, Nîmes (the Pont du Gard and Maison Carrée) and the scenery of the Alps. After a visit to Venice, the journey continued through Florence and on to Rome. An excursion further south to Naples might be followed by an easterly route home through Switzerland, Germany and the Low Countries. The young men were away for about three years and usually set off in their late teens or early twenties, travelling with a tutor and several servants. Many had a riotous time, socialized almost exclusively with other young British noblemen, and returned home little improved. But a minority acquired the taste which resulted in Britain's *stately homes being furnished with a wealth of continental treasures – the profusion of works by *Canaletto being just one example.

Grand Union Canal The main inland waterway in the south of England, known under this name only since 1929 – when a company acquired control of various existing canals linking the Thames (west of London) to Birmingham. The southern section had previously been known as the Grand Junction Canal.

Stewart Granger (stage name of James Stewart, b. 1913) Actor who was an established romantic lead on stage and screen in Britain before his Hollywood career began. His first American success was in a remake of Rider Haggard's *King Solomon's Mines* in 1951.

granite city see *Aberdeen.

Cary **Grant** (stage name of Archibald Leach, 1904–86) Hollywood leading man, famous for his debonair good looks and clipped vocal mannerism. He was born in Bristol and began his career in the Bristol Hippodrome as a callboy, fetching actors from dressing room to stage in time for their cues. He first went to the USA in 1920, singing, dancing and juggling in a troupe of acrobats. His Hollywood career began in the 1930s.

Granta Cambridge undergraduate magazine which was transformed in the late 1970s into a major literary periodical, now published quarterly. The original *Granta* had expired in 1977; it was revived with wider ambitions in 1979 by two Cambridge students, Bill Buford and Peter de Bolla. Their first issue, entitled 'New American Writing', staked a claim to literary significance which has been successfully maintained. Penguin began distributing *Granta* in 1983, and in 1989 Granta Books was launched as a publishing house.

Grantchester (4km/2.5m SW of Cambridge) Village on the river Cam, also known as the Granta, made famous by Rupert *Brooke's poem about the Old Vicarage, his family home from 1910.

grant-maintained school see *opting out.

Grasmere (8km/5m NW of Lake Windermere) Village in Cumbria particularly associated with *Wordsworth. He is buried in the churchyard, and lived in various houses nearby – in particular *Dove Cottage and Rydal Mount (4km/2.5m to the south, his home from 1813 until his death). Both are kept as museums.

Grassmarket Ancient market place in Edinburgh, immediately below the castle. The city's gallows stood at its east end, and in a nearby alleyway was the lodging house where *Burke and Hare selected their victims.

Mons **Graupius** (Latin for Mount Graupius) Battle in AD 83, in which the *Romans under Agricola defeated the Scottish tribes; they thus established, albeit briefly, the furthest point north of Roman power. The battle is described by the historian Tacitus (who had married Agricola's daughter), but his *Mons Graupius* has never been identified. It is known to have been north of the Firth of Tay, and the hills inland from Stonehaven (south of Aberdeen) are a possibility. The name of the *Grampians is the result of a misreading of Graupius, the site of the battle being shown on a map of 1527 as Mons Grampius.

Robert **Graves** (1895–1985) Poet and author of a wide variety of prose works. He expounded his view of the poet in *The White Goddess* (1948), in which he argues that poetry derives from a feminine principle which has been suppressed in civilization by male values of reason and logic. The directness of his prose was strikingly seen in his early autobiography, *Goodbye to All That* (1929). Of his many historical novels the first, *I, Claudius* (1934), remains the best known. For much of his life he lived in Majorca.

'The **Grave's a fine and private place**' see Andrew *Marvell.

Thomas **Gray** (1716–1771) Poet of exceptionally small output, whose *Elegy Written in a Country Church Yard* (1751, commonly known as *Gray's *Elegy*) is a precursor of the *Romantic movement. He was a schoolboy at Eton, where his two close friends were Horace *Walpole and Richard West. The death of the latter, in 1742, prompted *Ode on a Distant Prospect of Eton College* (published 1747), an early example of Gray's wistful melancholy. Walpole was indirectly responsible for another often quoted poem, *Ode on the Death of a Favourite Cat, Drowned in a Tub of Gold Fishes* (1747); the unfortunate Selima, immortalized in this ode, was a cat which had toppled into a Chinese vase at Strawberry Hill. Gray lived an extremely secluded life at Cambridge, lodging in Peterhouse until 1756. In that year he was the butt of a practical joke by undergraduates, who knew of his terror of fire and placed a barrel of water under his window before raising a false alarm; he moved as a result to Pembroke. His mother lived from 1742 at Stoke Poges, in Buckinghamshire. Gray is buried beside her in the churchyard.

Gray's Anatomy The common name for *Anatomy, descriptive and surgical* by Henry Gray (1825–61), a surgeon at St George's Hospital in London. First published in 1858, it rapidly established itself as a basic medical textbook and has gone through more than 30 editions with a succession of editors.

Gray's Elegy (written 1742–50, published 1751) The name commonly used for the *Elegy written in a Country Church Yard* by Thomas *Gray, one of the most often quoted of English poems. The gentle pastoral melancholy of the verses, imagining the innocent unknown country people in their graves, made the poem an instant and lasting success. It is generally assumed that the churchyard was that of Stoke Poges in Buckinghamshire, where Gray himself was later buried.

Gray's Inn see *Inns of Court.

Great Bed of Ware (Victoria and Albert Museum) Massive oak four-poster bed of *c.*1580, about 3.4m/11ft square, made originally for an inn at Ware, in Hertfordshire. It was a famous monster even in its own time, having the status of a tourist attraction for those travelling on one of the main roads north from London. In Shakespeare's *Twelfth Night* Sir Andrew Aguecheek is urged to write down enough lies to fill a sheet 'big enough for the bed of Ware'.

Great Britain (land area 227,453sq.km/87,820sq.m, population 54.9 million in 1991) The largest island of the *British Isles, comprising England, Scotland and Wales. The name was not much used until *James I and VI inherited the crowns of both England (already incorporating Wales) and Scotland, so becoming the first ruler of the entire island and being described as king of Great Britain. The inclusion of Ireland, effective from 1801, caused the country to be known as the *United Kingdom. But in some contexts, such as certain international sports, Great Britain is still used to describe the nation, including Northern Ireland.

Great Britain Iron steamship designed by *Brunel which inaugurated the age of transatlantic liners, being the first to be driven by a screw propeller (admittedly augmented by sails on six masts). She was built in a special dry dock at Bristol, was floated in 1843 and made her first voyage to New York in 1845 (14 days 21 hours, average speed 9.4 knots). After service in many parts of the world, she was eventually abandoned in the Falkland Islands. In 1970 she was brought home on a vast pontoon to Bristol docks, where she is now being restored and is on view.

Great Commoner see earl of *Chatham.

Great Coxwell Barn (32km/20m SW of Oxford) One of the earliest and most impressive stone tithe barns in England, built for Cistercian monks in the 13C.

Great Eastern see *Brunel.

Greater London (6,680,000 in 1991) Area consisting of 32 London *boroughs, established in 1963 by the London Government Act (effective from 1965). Those parts of neighbouring counties to which London's conurbation had spread were now added to the central districts previously controlled by the *London County Council. The new area of some 1660sq.km/610 sq.m was about 56km/35m east to west and 45km/28m north to south. The

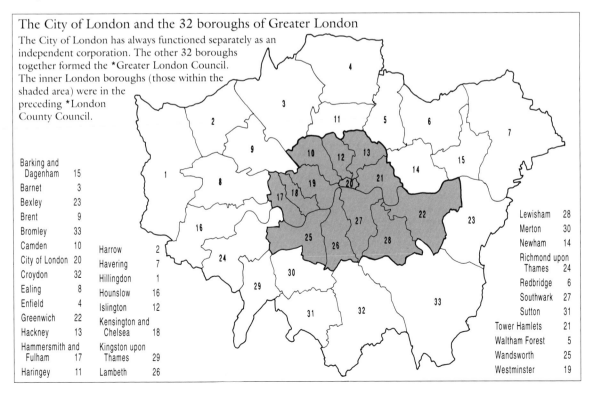

The City of London and the 32 boroughs of Greater London

The City of London has always functioned separately as an independent corporation. The other 32 boroughs together formed the *Greater London Council. The inner London boroughs (those within the shaded area) were in the preceding *London County Council.

Barking and Dagenham	15
Barnet	3
Bexley	23
Brent	9
Bromley	33
Camden	10
City of London	20
Croydon	32
Ealing	8
Enfield	4
Greenwich	22
Hackney	13
Hammersmith and Fulham	17
Haringey	11

Harrow	2
Havering	7
Hillingdon	1
Hounslow	16
Islington	12
Kensington and Chelsea	18
Kingston upon Thames	29
Lambeth	26

Lewisham	28
Merton	30
Newham	14
Richmond upon Thames	24
Redbridge	6
Southwark	27
Sutton	31
Tower Hamlets	21
Waltham Forest	5
Wandsworth	25
Westminster	19

Greater London Council (GLC) was the highest local authority for this region from 1 April 1965 to 30 March 1985, when its function was brought to an end under the provisions of the London Government Act of 1983 (after a high-profile clash of wills between the Labour leader of the council, Ken Livingstone, and the Conservative prime minister, Margaret Thatcher). Since then Greater London has been controlled by the individual boroughs operating as a single-tier system of *local government.

Greater Manchester (2,499,000 in 1991) *Metropolitan county in northwest England, consisting of ten *districts – Bolton, Bury, Manchester, Oldham, Rochdale, Salford, Stockport, Tameside, Trafford and Wigan.

'greatest happiness of the greatest number' see Jeremy *Bentham.

Great Exhibition of the Works of Industry of all Nations (London 1851) The full title explains what was in the mind of Prince *Albert when he chaired, in January 1850, the committee which in effect set about planning the first world fair (fixing in advance an opening date just 16 months away). A competition for the design of the building produced 245 designs, from which the committee then produced a composite one of their own, a brick building with a dome. News of this unsuitable edifice caused Joseph *Paxton to submit, uninvited, a brilliant solution – the *Crystal Palace. The exhibition was an outstanding success, with its marvellous array of products from all over the world and with some 6 million visitors between May 1 and October 15, including on frequent occasions the queen. It ended with a large financial profit, much of which was used for the *Victoria and Albert Museum.

Great Expectations (1861) Novel by *Dickens, serialized 1860–1 in *All the Year Round*. In an intensely dramatic opening scene a young boy, Pip (Philip Pirrip), is accosted in a churchyard by Abel Magwitch, an escaped convict with irons on his legs. Pip agrees to bring him a file and some food. The great expectations are those of Pip himself, who later begins to receive money from a mysterious source, enough to take him to London and to give him the life of a gentleman. He assumes the money comes from a wealthy recluse, Miss Havisham, whose ward, Estella, does not fully return Pip's love for her. But it is sent by Magwitch, who has made a fortune in Australia. Both Pip and Estella (Magwitch's daughter, it turns out) reveal their worst selves in rich London life; Pip now scorns Joe Gargery, the good-hearted blacksmith who has brought him up, and Estella marries an upper-class oaf, Bentley Drummle, who mistreats her but dies in an accident. Adversity improves them both. Pip is penniless after the supply of money from Magwitch ends, but he then makes a career abroad. The two meet again in the last scene with an implicit promise, to the reader, that they will marry. Dickens' more bleak original ending, which he changed on a friend's advice, left Pip facing the rest of his life alone.

A very successful film of the novel (1946) was directed by David Lean with John Mills as the adult Pip.

Great Famine (1845–7) In 1845 the potato crop failed disastrously in Ireland, where potatoes were the staple diet, because of a previously unknown blight (*phytophthora infestans*). The next year's crop was as badly infected. The immediate effects of the suffering were the repeal of the *Corn Laws and a huge increase in emigration from Ireland, particularly to the USA. The population fell from 8.5 million in 1845 to nearer 6.5 million in 1851, the loss being about half and half through death and emigration.

Great Fire (3–4 September 1666) Fire which devastated London, starting early in the morning in Pudding Lane, in the shop of a baker by the name of Farriner. By the end of the next day some 13,000 houses had been destroyed and 87 churches, including old St Paul's Cathedral, but amazingly only nine people had died.

Great Glen (also known as Glen More) Geological fault across the entire width of the Highlands of Scotland, running southwest from Inverness to Fort William. Its three lakes (Loch *Ness, Loch Oich and Loch Lochy) were joined in the early 19C to form the *Caledonian Canal.

'Great God! this is an awful place' see Captain *Scott.

Great Harry The familiar name for the *Henry Grâce à Dieu*, one of the largest warships of its day (about 1000 tons). She was launched for Henry VIII at his Woolwich dockyard in 1514. The ship was accidentally burnt, also at Woolwich, in 1553.

Great North Road The historic main road north from London, up through the centre of England, keeping to the east of the Pennines. Its route was very approximately that of the present A1.

Great Ormond Street (London WC1) Street which contains the Hospital for Sick Children, commonly referred to as the Great Ormond Street Hospital. When founded in 1852 by Dr Charles West (1816–98), it was the first children's hospital in Britain. It received a major

Part of the Crystal Palace being hoisted into place, just five months before the opening of the Great Exhibition.

source of income in 1929 when J.M. Barrie gave the copyright in *Peter Pan* (normally the term of copyright would have ended in 1988, but it was extended by act of parliament). The main building dates from 1938, with a major extension due to open in 1994.

Great Plague (1665) Plague which killed some 70,000 Londoners (representing about 1 in 7 of the city's population). Although plagues were common occurrences, spread by the fleas from rats in crowded urban conditions, this was by far the worst outbreak since the *Black Death. Daniel *Defoe's *Journal of the Plague Year* is a semi-fictional account. In the following year London suffered another disaster, the *Great Fire.

Great Stink The name popularly given to the appalling stench rising from the Thames during the summer of 1858, caused by hot weather and the quantity of sewage discharged by a new but ill-advised system of sewers. Conditions became so unpleasant in the riverside *Houses of Parliament that swift political action ensued, resulting in *Bazalgette's improvements to London's sanitation.

Great Storm Term now used for the hurricane which swept through southern England in the early hours of 16 October 1987, resulting in the loss of several lives and a vast number of trees. The damage was compounded in some areas by an equally severe storm on 25 January 1990.

Great Tom see *Lincoln and *Oxford.

Great Train Robbery The name (borrowed from a famous silent film of 1903) which became attached to a crime in England in 1963. Early in the morning of August 8 a gang stopped a Post Office train from Glasgow when it was passing through Buckinghamshire. The thieves hit the driver on the head with an iron bar (he later died) and took mailbags containing £2,631,684 in old bank notes, on their way to London for pulping. After hiding up for a few days at Leatherslade Farm, near Oakley, they escaped with the money – of which very little was ever recovered. Several of the gang became well-known figures in the following years – in particular Ronald Biggs (who escaped from Wandsworth prison in 1965 and who has managed to foil a succession of attempts to extradite him from Barbados and Brazil) and Buster Edwards (the subject of the 1988 feature film *Buster*).

Great Universal Stores (GUS) Major retailing company which has developed from a mail order firm, Universal Stores, established in Manchester in 1900 by George Rose. The upturn in its fortunes began when an employee, Isaac Wolfson (1897–1991), bought out Rose in 1932; GUS has been since then in the control of the Wolfson family. Mail order remains its central business, with many illustrated catalogues (of which Kays is the most important) published each year. But it has also had a large presence on the high street through the purchase of retail chains. In the late 1970s, with 2200 shops, GUS was the UK's largest high-street retailer. Many have been sold since, but in the early 1990s the company retains Burberrys and Scotch House.

Great Unknown see *Waverley novels.

Great West Road The historic road leading west from London to Bath and Bristol, roughly following the course of the modern A4.

Great Yarmouth (48,000 in 1981) Port and resort on the east coast of Norfolk. It was badly bombed in the war but many of its oldest parts have been restored, including

A message in 1855 for Father Thames, whose condition was already giving concern – three years before the Great Stink.

the characteristic Rows (narrow streets of fishermen's houses running down at right angles to the sea) and the 12–13C St Nicholas, said to be the largest parish church in the country. The birthplace of Anna Sewell, author of *Black Beauty*, is now a museum; and south of the town is a superb monument to Nelson which long predates London's *Nelson's Column.

Jimmy **Greaves** (b. 1940) Footballer for Chelsea (1957–61), Tottenham Hotspur (62–70) and West Ham (70–71). He was known as a prodigious goal-scorer. He had put more than 100 into the net for Chelsea before he was 21; he scored 44 in his 57 matches for England; and six times he headed the charts for the highest number of goals scored in a season in Division 1. After retirement he made a second career as a presenter on television, being best known from 1985 on *Saint and Greavsie*.

Greek Revival A second stage in *neoclassicism, which had initially been influenced – at any rate in architecture – more by Roman than by Greek examples. A pioneer, as reflected in his nickname, was 'Athenian' Stuart (James Stuart, 1713–88), who returned in 1755 after spending several years in Greece. His Temple of Theseus in the grounds of Hagley Hall (West Midlands) dates from as early as 1758 and was soon followed by his work at *Shugborough. But the spread of the style resulted more from his four-volume *Antiquities of Athens* (1762–1816). The heyday was the early 19C, with *Smirke's British Museum the most impressive single building and with Thomas *Hope designing furniture based on Greek examples.

An architect who carried the style on into a period dominated by Gothic Revival was 'Greek' Thomson (Alexander Thomson, 1817–75), whose churches in Glasgow in this manner were built in the 1850s and 1860s.

Lucinda **Green** (Lucinda Prior-Palmer, b. 1953, m. David Green 1981) Three-day event rider who has won gold medals in the World Championships (individual and team

1982) and in the European Championships (individual 1975, 77). She was a member of the team which won silver in the 1984 Olympics. She has also been particularly successful at Badminton, with a record six victories (1973, 76, 77, 79, 83, 84).

Kate **Greenaway** (1846–1901) Illustrator whose charming and slightly stilted scenes of children, dressed anachronistically in clothes of the early 19C, made her work immensely successful in late Victorian Britain (a great period for colour-printed children's books). They even caused a 20C fashion for what became known as Kate Greenaway dresses.

green belt A strip of countryside, around a town or city, in which development is restricted. The concept of towns being closely surrounded by agricultural land was part of the *garden city movement, but the phrase derives from the 1930s when specific areas round London and other cities were designated as green belt. Encroachment on these areas has been a controversial issue ever since.

Graham **Greene** (1904–91) Novelist whose mastery of the traditional skills – such as narrative, suspense, comedy and character – brought to a very wide public his obsessive concerns with failure and moral ambiguity. Two important factors in his own life were his dramatically depressive tendencies (bizarre suicide attempts at school, Russian roulette on several occasions when he was about 20) and his conversion in 1926 to Roman Catholicism. The result was a lifelong compulsion to travel, observe, sympathize, share guilt. He once used a quotation from Robert Browning to describe what interested him – 'the dangerous edge of things, the honest thief, the tender murderer, the superstitious atheist'.

He only needed to travel as far as Brighton to find the seedy underworld of gang warfare for *Brighton Rock* (1938), but it was Mexico that gave him The *Power and the Glory* (1940); West Africa (Greene worked as an agent for MI6 in Sierra Leone in 1941–3) provided an unspecific background for *The Heart of the Matter* (1948), while Vietnam is the setting for *The Quiet American* (1955), Cuba for *Our Man in Havana* (1958), the Congo for *A Burnt-Out Case* (1961), Haiti for *The Comedians* (1966) and Paraguay for *The Honorary Consul* (1973). Greene divided his novels into 'entertainments' and the rest; some of his most delightful books do fall firmly into the entertainment category (*Our Man in Havana*, or *Travels with my Aunt* 1969), but with many the distinction seems blurred because entertainment and deeper relevance is so well mixed.

One of the most successful of those classed as entertainment was The *Third Man*, written as a treatment for the film of 1949. In the following decade Greene made a successful diversion into the theatre with three plays (*The Living Room* 1953, *The Potting Shed* 1957, *The Complaisant Lover* 1959). He has often been described as the most distinguished writer not to have been awarded the Nobel prize for literature.

'Green grow the rushes O' The refrain of the *Dilly Song*, an ancient and still very popular folk song, which repeats (usually *accelerando*) a sequence of numerical items from 'one is one and all alone' up to 'twelve for the twelve apostles'. One God, four gospel makers, ten Commandments and twelve apostles are recognizable from Christian sources. Others, such as the 'two lily-white boys, clothed all in green O', may suggest more mysterious pagan origins. But ingenious Christian explanations have been found for all of them: the lily-white boys are said to be Jesus and John the Baptist, the three rivals the persons of the Trinity, and so on.

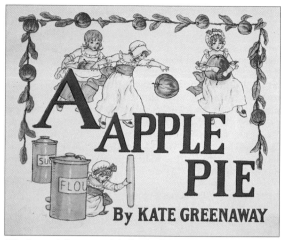

The letter A from an alphabet book by Kate Greenaway, with the children in 'Kate Greenaway' dresses.

Greenham Common RAF base in Berkshire which became the site of a prolonged political protest by the 'Greenham women'. It was announced in 1980 that American Cruise nuclear missiles were to be sited there. In September of the following year there was a peace march from Cardiff to Greenham, after which a large number of women camped outside the wire perimeter of the base. They were still there to block the arrival of the first missiles in November 1983, and a small number – including some veterans from the original march – were there in 1991 when the last of the missiles was removed (in compliance with a disarmament treaty between the USA and the USSR). Some even stayed on to celebrate the tenth anniversary of the camp in September 1991, protesting now in general terms against war. Over the years the struggle had become ritualized in a repeated sequence of cutting the wire to enter the camp, being arrested for trespass and malicious damage, serving a prison sentence and then returning to the cause.

green paper see *white paper.

Green Party Britain was late on the scene with its Green party. There was a Green member in the Swiss parliament in 1979, nine were elected in Belgium in 1981 and 28 won seats in the German Bundestag in 1983. In 1989 the British Green party, nurtured by Sara Parkin (b. 1946) and Jonathon Porritt (b. 1950), surprised the nation by coming from almost nowhere to take 2.3 million votes (15% of the poll) in the election for the European parliament. Another prominent figure among the Greens has been David Icke (b. 1952), an ex-footballer and sports broadcaster who in 1991 declared himself 'an aspect of the Godhead'. Amid much wrangling between those for and against Icke, the party began to show signs of disintegration and it won only 1.3% of the vote in the 1992 general election (the German Greens suffered a similar reversal of fortune in 1990).

Greensleeves A tune continuously popular in England since the 16C. Several mentions of it survive from the 1580s when it first acquired a name (from a ballad set to it, in which the singer loves the faithless Lady Greensleeves), but the tune itself is almost certainly older – though there is no foundation for the popular belief that it was written by Henry VIII.

Greenwich (London SE10) Historic area on the south bank of the Thames downstream from London. There was a royal palace here from the 15C, when Greenwich

Park was enclosed. Henry VIII, Mary I and Elizabeth I were born in the palace, which survived till the 17C; it was used as a biscuit factory during the Commonwealth. Greenwich contains Britain's earliest classical building, the *Queen's House; the *Royal Observatory and the *Royal Naval College (on the site of the old palace) date from the late 17C. The district has retained strong links with the sea in the *National Maritime Museum. Also on display are the *Cutty Sark and Francis *Chichester's Gipsy Moth.

Greenwich Mean Time The time as calculated by the movement of the sun in relation to the *Greenwich meridian. It is the local time in the British Isles, except when *Summer Time applies, and it is used internationally to define relative time zones; thus Tokyo is said to be nine hours ahead of GMT and New York five hours behind. Until 31 December 1924 a time given as 0001 GMT was one minute after noon, but GMT then changed to the now familiar 24-hour system starting at midnight.

Greenwich meridian The line of longitude passing through the *Royal Observatory at Greenwich, where its position is marked by a brass rail set in concrete. It was accepted internationally in 1884 as the prime meridian, or 0° longitude, from which other lines of longitude are calculated in degrees east or west.

Germaine **Greer** (b. 1939) Australian author and gardening enthusiast, living in Britain since the 1960s. She made her name with one of the classics of feminism, *The Female Eunuch* (1970); later books on related issues have been *Sex and Destiny* (1984, on the politics of contraception) and *The Change* (1991, on the menopause). She first went public as a gardener in the Rose Blight column in *Private Eye*.

Grenada Island in the Caribbean which, with several nearby smaller islands, has been a member of the *Commonwealth since 1974. Visited by Columbus in 1498, it was fought over by the French and British in the 17-18C before being ceded to Britain in 1783. From 1958 Grenada was a member of the *West Indies Federation; it became independent in 1974. Although part of the Commonwealth, the island was invaded by the USA after the murder in 1983 of the Marxist prime minister, Maurice Bishop, by a rival Marxist faction. An interim government was then set up under the British governor general until new elections were held in 1984.

Grenadiers see *Foot Guards.

Joyce **Grenfell** (Joyce Phipps, 1910–79, m. Reginald Grenfell 1929) Comedienne who from 1939 established a reputation in revue with quirky monologues on the oddities of human behaviour. By 1954 she was touring the world with her own one-woman two-hour show. She also became a well-known character actress in films (particularly in the series based on Ronald *Searle's St Trinian's), and in her later years she was a regular panellist on a TV music quiz, *Face the Music*.

Richard **Grenville** (1542–91, kt c.1573) Naval commander, cousin of Raleigh, who is remembered for a gallant death, commemorated by Tennyson in *The Revenge* (1880). The poem's first line is sufficiently arresting to have stuck in the nation's mind: 'At Flores in the Azores Sir Richard Grenville lay.' He was in command of the *Revenge* (*Drake's flagship three years earlier at the Armada), on an expedition to capture Spanish treasure. When the English were forced to withdraw in the face of a larger Spanish fleet, the *Revenge* was becalmed in the lea of a galleon. His crew fought for 15 hours, often hand-to-hand, until most of them, including Grenville, were dead or dying.

Greenwich in 1842, with the Observatory (on the left), Queen's House, Royal Naval College and view upstream to London.

Thomas **Gresham** (1519–79, kt 1559) Merchant banker who built, largely at his own expense, London's first *Royal Exchange. He is wrongly credited with the so-called Gresham's Law ('bad money drives out good'), a principle well understood before his time. The law describes the situation (true of Tudor England) in which coins bearing the same face value contain differing quantities of precious metal. It states the obvious – that people will use the intrinsically less valuable coins (the bad money) for their purchases, while either hoarding or melting down the good money, thus driving it out of circulation and debasing the currency.

Gretna Green (16km/10m NW of Carlisle) Village just over the border into Scotland which benefited greatly from the Marriage Act of 1753, prohibiting in England 'clandestine' marriages – meaning those solemnized outside authorized Christian places of worship. Also known as Fleet marriages, such ceremonies had traditionally been conducted by clergy who were in the *Fleet prison for debt. It was this abuse which was now stopped. Scottish law required only a declaration in front of witnesses, and the blacksmith's anvil at Gretna Green became the fashionable location for runaway couples. From 1856 a new law required one of the pair to live in Scotland for three weeks, and in 1940 these marriages were declared illegal. But the anvil is still there and is still a powerful centre of attraction.

Beryl **Grey** (b. 1927, DBE 1988) Dancer who joined the Sadler's Wells Ballet (now the Royal Ballet) in 1941 and was a prima ballerina from 1942 until she left the company in 1957 to go freelance. She was the first western ballerina to dance with the Bolshoi company (1957–8) and with the Chinese Ballet in Peking and Shanghai (1964). She was artistic director of the London Festival Ballet in 1968–79.

Earl **Grey** (Charles Grey, 1764–1845, 2nd earl 1807) Politician who succeeded Charles James Fox in 1806 as

A clandestine marriage of the type banished in 1753 to Gretna Green: illustration of a fictional scene (c.1840).

Greyhound racing since 1965

	Derby	Grand National
1965	Chittering Clapton	I'm Crazy
1966	Faithful Hope	Halfpenny King
1967	Tric-Trac	The Grange Santa
1968	Camera Flash	Ballintore Tiger
1969	Sand Star	Tony's Friend
1970	John Silver	Sherry's Price
1971	Dolores Rocket	Sherry's Price
1972	Patricia's Hope	Sherry's Price
1973	Patricia's Hope	Killone Flash
1974	Jimsum	Shanney's Darkie
1975	Tartan Khan	Pier Hero
1976	Mutts Silver	Weston Pete
1977	Balliniska Band	Salerno
1978	Lacca Champion	Top O' The Tide
1979	Sarah's Bunny	Top O' The Tide
1980	Indian Joe	Gilt Edge Flyer
1981	Parkdown Jet	Bobcol
1982	Laurie's Panther	Face The Nutt
1983	I'm Slippy	Sir Winston
1984	Whisper Wishes	Kilcoe Foxy
1985	Pagan Swallow	Seaman's Star
1986	Tico	Castelyons Cash
1987	Signal Spark	Cavan Town
1988	Hit the Lid	Breck's Rocket
1989	Lartigue Note	Lemon Chip
1990	Slippy Blue	Gisme Pasha
1991	Ballinderry Ash	Ideal Man / Ballycarney Dell } *dead heat*
1992	Farloe Melody	Kildare Slippy

leader of the Whig party. He was prime minister from 1830 to 1834, at the head of a coalition cabinet committed to parliamentary reform. His place in history is assured by his having steered the *Reform Act of 1832 through parliament against strong opposition.

The very popular blend of China tea known as Earl Grey is said to derive from a special mixture which he received from China – a present, the story goes, from a grateful mandarin whose life had been saved by a member of an embassy sent out by Lord Grey.

Edward **Grey** (1862–1933, 3rd bt 1882, viscount 1916) Liberal politician who was foreign secretary (1905–16) during the period leading up to and into World War I, in the governments of Campbell-Bannerman and Asquith. It was he who said (on 3 Aug. 1914, the day before Britain declared war), 'The lamps are going out all over Europe; we shall not see them lit again in our lifetime'.

Lady Jane **Grey** (1537–54) Queen of England for nine days (10-19 July 1553) and one of the most tragic figures in English history. Famous in her own time for her childhood proficiency in Greek and Latin, she was thrust unwillingly into public affairs in the last months of the reign of *Edward VI because of a distant claim to the throne through her grandmother, a daughter of Henry VII (see the *royal house). The duke of Northumberland married her to his son, Lord Guildford Dudley, and persuaded the young and dying king to make Jane his heir. Her new father-in-law proclaimed her queen a few weeks later, on 10 July 1553, after Edward's death. She was still only 15. It was a coup with little chance of success. Northumberland's support evaporated and the rightful heir to the throne, Edward's sister, was proclaimed on July 19 as *Mary I. Jane pleaded guilty to high treason and was executed in the Tower of London in February 1554, on the same day as her husband and some six months after her father-in-law.

greyhound racing The pursuit of game with dogs is among the most ancient of sports, and the greyhound was a breed already known in ancient Egypt and Greece. The organized racing of greyhounds developed in Britain in the 18C, in the form known as coursing – the competitive chase of a live hare by a pair of dogs, the winner being the one which catches it. The first rules for a race meeting of this sort were drawn up in 1776, and the sport is still practised in Britain (nowadays in such a way that most of the hares escape through prepared routes where the dogs cannot follow, the winner being judged purely on speed and agility). The chief event of the coursing year is the Waterloo Cup, which has been held since 1836 on farm land at Great Altcar, near Southport in Merseyside; it took its name from the nearby Waterloo Hotel, where the owners dined on the first day of the meeting. Since 1857 the contest has been between 64 dogs, competing in a knock-out tournament over three days.

Mechanical racing dates from an event near Hendon, north of London, in 1876, which was described as 'coursing by proxy'. The proxy hare was pulled along a straight rail over a course of 366m/400yd. It proved a dull event, and little more was heard of this form of greyhound racing until a circular track (offering much more challenge to the skill of the dogs) was opened in California in 1919. During the 1920s dog racing developed rapidly into a popular sport. The first meeting in Britain with a mechanical hare (which the dogs pursue by scent) was at Belle Vue in Manchester in 1926. The two most prestigious British races, the Greyhound Derby and the Grand National (over hurdles), were first run at White City in London in 1927, and remained there until 1984; since then the Derby has been held at Wimbledon and the Grand National at Hall Green, Birmingham. The only dogs to have won the Derby more than once are Mick the Miller (1929, 30) and Patricia's Hope (1972, 73). One dog has had three victories in the Grand National (Sherry's Prince, 1970, 71, 72), while several have won twice (Juvenile Classic 1938, 40; Blossom of Annagura 1949, 50; Top O' The Tide 1978, 79).

John **Grierson** (1898–1972) Scottish pioneer of documentary films in Britain. He directed his first, *Drifters*, in 1929. Thereafter he became leader of a production team for a succession of films including *Industrial Britain* (1933), *The Song of Ceylon* (1934), *Coal Face* (1935) and *Night Mail* (1936). Among the directors he employed was the American Robert Flaherty, who with his *Nanook of the North* (1922, on the life of the Eskimos) had effectively invented the documentary genre.

Jane **Grigson** (Jane McIntire, 1928–90, m. Geoffrey Grigson) Cookery writer for the *Observer*, whose *English Food* (1974) succeeded in being both informal and scholarly.

Joseph **Grimaldi** (1778–1837) Regarded as the classic English clown, he is credited with introducing the traditional white-faced make-up. For most of his career he was the resident clown at the *Sadler's Wells theatre. It was in memory of him that a 'joey' became a general name for a clown.

Grimethorpe Colliery Band see *brass bands.

Jo **Grimond** (b. 1913, baron 1983) Author and Liberal politician, MP for Orkney and Shetland 1950–83. He was leader of the Liberal party from 1956 to 1967 and saw the party's votes rise from about 700,000 in 1955 to more than 3 million in 1964. But this increase added only three parliamentary seats, bringing the figure up from six to nine (see the *two-party system). His first two books outlined his vision for the party – *The Liberal Future* (1959) and *The Liberal Challenge* (1963). He was succeeded as leader in 1967 by Jeremy *Thorpe.

Grimsby (92,000 in 1991) England's main fishing port, in Humberside, on the south shore of the Humber estuary. There was an important settlement of Danes here in the 9C, and the name is believed to derive from Grim, a fisherman in Danish legend. In recent years the town has suffered from the *cod wars and from restrictions on fishing. The waterfront is dominated by the great Dock Tower, an 1852 replica of the tower in Siena.

Atkinson **Grimshaw** (1836–93) Painter whose talent as a portraitist in the manner of *Tissot is relatively little known, because of the great success of his formula for urban landscapes, with strong verticals diffused in a shimmer of lamplight and fog and cobblestones.

grog Rum diluted with water, issued until recently on ships of the royal navy. It derives its name from an improbable but authentic series of events. Edward Vernon (1684–1757) commanded a squadron in the West Indies in 1740 and was given the nickname Grog because he wore a cloak of grogram (a coarse fabric stiffened and made waterproof with gum). Sailors in Europe were allowed an astonishing daily ration of alcohol, a gallon of beer or a quart of wine. In the West Indies this became a pint of the local rum (a half pint for boys), with predictable consequences when distributed neat at midday. There was initial resentment at Vernon's order that the same ration be diluted and issued morning and evening, and 'grog' must originally have been a derisive term for the new drink. But the reform had excellent effect, and grog itself became a hallowed part of naval heritage after being officially adopted by the Admiralty.

Joey Grimaldi in his garish thigh-length pantaloons: in one form or another these were his standard costume.

The ration was reduced during the 19C and from 1918 was limited to ratings, to whom the issue of grog continued until 1970.

gross domestic product see *GDP.

George and Weedon **Grossmith** see *Diary of a Nobody.*

Grosvenor Gallery Establishment which opened in 1877 in New Bond Street and immediately became associated with the *Aesthetic movement. The opening show included a night scene by Whistler entitled *Nocturne in Black and Gold: The Falling Rocket*, of which Ruskin wrote: 'I have seen, and heard, much of Cockney impudence before now; but never expected to hear a coxcomb ask two hundred guineas for flinging a pot of paint in the public's face.' Whistler sued him and was awarded a farthing's damages. Oscar Wilde, present at the opening, was later parodied as the aesthetic Bunthorne in *Patience* with the lines:

A pallid and thin young man,
A haggard and lank young man,
A greenery-yallery, Grosvenor Gallery,
Foot-in-the-grave young man.

The gallery survived until 1903, when its premises were coverted to a concert room, the Aeolian Hall.

The aesthetic Whistler, shortly after the Grosvenor Gallery incident: caricature by Spy in Vanity Fair *(1878).*

groundnut scheme An attempt promoted by the Labour government in 1946 to grow groundnuts (another name for peanuts) on unused land in Africa (at Kongwa in Kenya). By 1949 it had proved an expensive failure. The sheer improbability of the scheme as a government venture, together with its cost to the taxpayer, ensured its place in the public's memory as a famous fiasco.

grouse A large family of game birds, the Tetraonidae, which are distributed throughout the northern hemisphere. The species most associated with British moors, particularly in Scotland and Yorkshire, is the red grouse (*Lagopus scoticus*). Its *close season ends before that of any other game bird, on August 12; the 'glorious Twelfth' has therefore had a special significance in shooting circles. Other species of grouse living in Britain are the black grouse (the male is a blackcock and the female a greyhen); the ptarmigan, which lives on the highest ground and changes to its white winter plumage in the snow; and the largest of all, the capercaillie, the male of which can reach the size of a turkey (a fact reflected in its name, from the Gaelic *capull coille*, 'horse of the woods'). The capercaillie was shot to extinction in Britain during the 18C; it was reintroduced into Scotland from Sweden in 1837.

Grove The shortened name commonly used for the *Dictionary of Music and Musicians*, compiled originally by George Grove (1820–1900) and published by Macmillan in four volumes (1879–89). An engineer by trade, Grove was led by his love of music to write the programme notes for concerts at the *Crystal Palace for 40 years, and he became in 1883 the first director of the Royal College of Music. His dictionary has been regularly expanded and updated. The 6th edition, an entirely new work (*The New Grove Dictionary of Music and Musicians*), came out in 1980 in 20 volumes, edited by Stanley Sadie – who is also the editor of the similarly comprehensive *New Grove Dictionary of Opera*, first published in 1992.

Charles **Groves** (1915–92, kt 1973) Conductor who was a familiar part of British musical life for several decades as the musical director or conductor of a succession of regional orchestras – the BBC Northern Orchestra (1944–51), the Bournemouth Symphony Orchestra (1951–61), the Welsh National Opera (1961–3) and the Royal Liverpool Philharmonic (1963–77).

Grub Street Street in London which in the mid-17C was the centre of a new phenomenon, a lively pamphleteering press. It became known as a place where you could get a hack author to write anything, and so came to stand for the worst in cheap journalism. It survives as Milton Street (the name was changed in 1830), close to the modern Barbican.

Grundys see The *Archers.*

The **Guardian** Newspaper founded in 1821 as the weekly *Manchester Guardian*. It became a daily in 1855 but did not acquire a significant national status until the very long editorship (1872–1929) of C.P. Scott; in 1936 the Scott Trust was formed to ensure that the paper could not be influenced by proprietors (a fate to which most of its rivals are prone). In 1959 the name was changed to the *Guardian* and in 1964 the headquarters were transferred to London. With most of Britain's press strongly supportive of the Conservative party, the *Guardian* has traditionally taken a left-of-centre stance.

Guards see *Foot Guards and *Household Cavalry.

Guernsey and **Guernsey cattle** see *Channel Islands.

Guide Dogs for the Blind Association (Windsor) The use of guide dogs for the blind was pioneered in Germany after World War I. Associations were established in Switzerland and the USA in 1928, and the British branch trained its first dogs in 1931. There are now about 4000 trained dogs working with blind people in Britain.

Guides The girls' branch of the scouting movement, founded in 1910 by Agnes, the sister of *Baden-Powell (who had been somewhat surprised when a large contingent of girls insisted on joining his first rally of scouts at Crystal Palace). The name was originally Girl Guides, changed to Guides in 1992. There are now some 8.5 million Guides in more than 100 countries. From 1914 girls aged 8–11 were admitted as *Brownies; and a new category of Rainbow Guides was established in 1988 for the 5–7 age group.

Guildford (57,000 in 1981) Cathedral town on the river Wey, historically the county town of Surrey but not in recent times the administrative centre. It has been a diocese since 1927. The redbrick cathedral, on a hilltop site to the northwest of the town, was designed by Edward Maufe (1883–1974) and was consecrated in 1961. The 12c keep survives of the Norman castle, and the town's steep High Street (famous for the clock projecting from the 17c Guildhall) contains several distinguished buildings – in particular the early 17c almshouse, Abbot's Hospital. The Royal Grammar School, founded in 1552 and now an independent school, still has its 16c library of 89 chained books.

Guildford Four A group given life sentences in 1975 for the 1974 IRA bombing of pubs in Guildford and Woolwich. They were released in 1989 after their convictions were quashed. The four were Carole Richardson, Patrick Armstrong, Paul Hill and Gerard Conlon. It emerged from *ESDA tests that police notes of their interrogation, in particular that of Patrick Armstrong, had been altered by the Surrey police. In February 1991 charges of conspiracy to pervert the course of justice were brought against three officers, leading to much controversy when the charges were dropped in June of that year; it was said that the lapse of time and adverse publicity would prejudice the chance of a fair trial. The case against the officers was revived by the attorney general in January 1992, and after a further succession of delays was scheduled to be heard during 1993.

Guildhall (London EC2) The civic building of the *City of London. Dating from the 15c, it was considerably damaged in the *Great Fire of 1666 and again in an air raid in 1940, but it retains its medieval shape and much of its fabric. The statues of *Gog and Magog in the west gallery are limewood carvings, by David Evans, replacing those destroyed in 1940.

Guildhall School of Music and Drama see *music schools.

guillotine A procedural device, in occasional use since the early 20c, by which the government can speed up the passage of legislation through the House of *Commons. A guillotine motion is passed, in advance of a bill being debated, which allots a maximum number of days to each stage on the bill's way to becoming an *act of parliament. When the time limit on any stage is reached, debate is abruptly cut off.

guinea Gold coin first struck in the 1660s and named because gold from the Guinea Coast in Africa was used to mint the early examples. Its value fluctuated until fixed in

The curious incident of the ostrich which did not put its head in the sand: a famous poster from the classsic period of Guinness advertising, in the 1930s.

1717 at one pound and one shilling (see *currency). It has not been in circulation since 1816, but until 1971 it remained the unit in which the accounts of certain long-established professions (such as lawyers, doctors, tailors) were presented – an easy way of adding 5% to the bill. In the 1990s thoroughbred horses are still auctioned by *Tattersalls in guineas.

Guinevere King *Arthur's queen, whose liaison with *Lancelot is presented in the early accounts as an example of the medieval ideal of courtly love, but in later tradition becomes an adulterous impurity which prevents his completing the quest for the *Holy Grail.

Guinness A leading international company in the manufacture of alcoholic drinks. It derives from a brewery established by Arthur Guinness in Dublin in 1759. The firm's brand of rich, dark, somewhat bitter stout acquired a wide following – Dickens in *Sketches by Boz* (1836) writes of a 'large hamper of Guinness's stout' – and by the 1930s Dublin could not meet the international demand. The first Guinness brewery outside Ireland was opened in 1936 at Park Royal in northwest London. In more recent years Guinness has purchased a wide range of distilling companies and has become the international leader in sales of whisky (including Johnnie Walker) and gin (with Gordon's). It was a takeover battle in this market which led to the *Guinness Affair.

The building of the brewery in Britain followed Guinness's launch of its first advertising campaign in 1928. The admirably simple slogan 'Guinness is good for you' was used in various forms until the 1970s, with variants such as 'My Goodness, My Guinness' enabling distinguished cartoonists to depict the glass of dark liquid in a wide range of perilous contexts (including, perhaps most famous of all, half way down the neck of an ostrich). Another brilliant marketing idea, the *Guinness Book of Records, has led to Guinness's publishing branch – a profitable sideline which keeps the brand name on popular reference books in fields such as sport and pop music, where records of achievement require annual updating.

Alec **Guinness** (b. 1914, kt 1959) Actor famous for the way in which he can submerge himself in an astonishing variety of roles – a talent taken to its bravura extreme when he played all eight murder victims in *Kind Hearts and Coronets. He was already a leading stage actor, known for his Shakespearean roles (including a modern-dress Hamlet in 1938), when his performance as Fagin in David Lean's Oliver Twist (1948) launched him on his cinema career. Among his best-known subsequent films have been The *Lavender Hill Mob (1951), The *Bridge on the River Kwai (1957, an Oscar-winning performance), Tunes of Glory (1960) and Star Wars (1977). For TV audiences his greatest role has been as John Le Carré's world-weary spy master, Smiley, in Tinker, Tailor, Soldier, Spy (1979) and its successor Smiley's People (1982).

Guinness Affair Series of events during the £2.7bn take-over of Distillers by *Guinness, which resulted in criminal trials. The offences concerned measures taken to inflate Guinness's share price so as to enhance the company's chance of success against the rival bidders, *Argyll. The four main defendants, convicted and sentenced in August 1990, were Ernest Saunders, the chairman and chief executive of Guinness (five years); Gerald Ronson, chairman and chief executive of Heron Corporation (one year and a fine of £5m); Anthony Parnes, a stockbroker (two years six months); and Sir Jack Lyons, chairman of London Properties (a fine of £3m); the sentences of Saunders and Parnes were later reduced.

Other defendants, in three subsequent trials connected with the affair, either had the charges against them dropped or were found not guilty. The subsequent claim of Argyll against Guinness, for costs and lost profits, was eventually settled out of court by a payment of £100m, to which the company's advisers, Morgan Grenfell and Cazenove, were each believed to have contributed about £5m.

*The **Guinness Book of Records*** Compilation of the smallest, largest, lowest, highest, least or most in every conceivable field. The first edition was commissioned by the managing director of *Guinness and appeared in 1955, edited by the twins Norris and Ross McWhirter (b. 1925; Ross was shot by IRA terrorists in 1975). Since 1960 it has been published annually and in 1974 it earned its own place in the records, becoming the top-selling copyright book in the world. By the early 1990s the aggregate global sales were approximately 70 million in nearly 40 languages.

Gulf Stream Current of water flowing east across the Atlantic from the Caribbean. Recent discoveries suggest that it is greatly boosted by another body of warm water, the Agulhas Current, which flows from the Indian Ocean, round the Cape of Good Hope and then up through the Atlantic.

As the Gulf Stream moves east towards Europe and Africa it splits into several strands, one of which turns north past the British Isles. The current retains enough of its original warmth to affect the climate of adjacent areas, with the result that coastal gardens in southwest England, Wales and western Scotland are able to grow many plants which would not survive elsewhere in Britain.

Gulf War (1990–1) On 2 August 1990 Iraq invaded its southern neighbour, Kuwait, and rapidly occupied the country; its reasons included long-standing claims to all or part of *Kuwait, and a more recent dispute over oil prices and the extraction of oil near the border. The UN Security Council immediately condemned this aggression and applied trade sanctions against Iraq. As Iraqi troops massed on the Saudi Arabian border, the USA and the UK decided to send troops to protect the Saudis and to enforce UN resolutions concerning Iraq's withdrawal. Twelve Arab nations also agreed to join the allied UN force, as did France and Italy.

President Saddam Hussein of Iraq rounded up all the westerners he could find in Kuwait and took them to Baghdad (among them were the British passengers from flight *BA 149), saying that he would deploy them as a human shield against air attack. During the autumn of 1990 a succession of foreign dignitaries visited Baghdad to plead on behalf of the hostages (including Edward *Heath from Britain and Willy Brandt from Germany), each returning with some they had rescued; Saddam Hussein then surprised everyone, on December 6, by releasing all the remaining western hostages.

The United Nations gave 16 January 1991 as the final deadline by which Iraq must withdraw from Kuwait; Saddam Hussein merely promised in return the 'mother of battles'. Air strikes on Iraqi positions in Kuwait and on selected military targets in Iraq began during the night of January 16–17 – it was the start of Operation Desert Storm. Soon, on television screens around the world, US guided missiles were seen seeking out their targets with uncanny precision. Iraq in return launched Russian-supplied Scud rockets against Israel and Saudi Arabia, most of which were intercepted and destroyed during flight by US Patriot missiles.

By late January the Iraqis were pumping vast quantities of Kuwaiti oil into the gulf to form a huge slick, and in February they began setting fire to Kuwaiti oil fields. An allied ground offensive began on February 24, and met very little resistance. Kuwait City was liberated on February 26. And on February 27 the allies engaged the best trained and equipped of Saddam Hussein's forces, the Republican Guard, in a final tank battle west of the city of Basra in southern Iraq; it was during this engagement, on the last day of the war, that nine British soldiers were killed in their armoured vehicles when they were fired on in error by US planes. The allied offensive was suspended in the early hours of the following morning. The total number of British casualties was 24.

There then began years of frustrating effort in the attempt, still incomplete in 1993, to force Saddam Hussein to comply with the UN requirement that his war machine be destroyed; this included research establishments working on nuclear and chemical weapons. At the same time it proved necessary to take steps to protect Iraq's large minorities – the Kurds in the north and the Shias in the south – from their president's savage attentions.

Gulliver's Travels (1726) Jonathan *Swift's most famous satire takes the form of a narrative by a ship's surgeon, Lemuel Gulliver, under whose name it first appeared with the title Travels into Several Remote Nations of the World. Each of his four voyages is calculated to provide a differing satirical perspective on ourselves.

In Lilliput, where the people are six inches high, it is Gulliver who peers down and marvels at their petty ways. In Brobdingnag, where the people are giants, the position is reversed; Gulliver tells the king about the manners and institutions of Europe, and is surprised at his reaction that we sound like 'little odious Vermin'. The flying island of Laputa is inhabited by philosophers and scientists, who make a predictable mess of things. By contrast in the land

Robert Winter | Christopher Wright | John Wright | Thomas Percy | Guido Fawkes | Robert Catesby | Thomas Winter

Bates

A cheerful Guy Fawkes (third from right) with his fellow Gunpowder Plot conspirators: anonymous engraving of 1606.

of the Houyhnhnms (a very passable attempt by Swift to spell the neighing of a horse) all the inhabitants are animals; but the ruling Houyhnhnms are rational and admirable horses, whereas the Yahoos (beasts in human shape) are brutal and oafish.

The vividness of Swift's imagination has caused his savage satire to be enjoyed also as a fantasy for children, keeping Gulliver's adventures fresh for each new generation.

John **Gummer** (b. 1939) Conservative politician, MP for Suffolk Coastal since 1983 (previously for Eye 1979–83 and for Lewisham West 1970–74). One of the *Cambridge mafia, he entered the cabinet in 1989 as minister for agriculture and still held the same job in 1992. He was a member of the General Synod of the Church of England from 1979 until his resignation, in 1992, over the issue of the *ordination of women.

gunboat diplomacy A phrase now commonly applied to aggressive acts of Victorian imperialism, such as the Don *Pacifico incident. But it seems to have been coined only in the 20C, probably in the USA and with particular reference to foreign intervention in China.

Sally **Gunnell** (b. 1965) Athlete who first made an international mark when she won the gold medal for the 100 metres hurdles at the 1986 Commonwealth Games; she followed this with another gold, this time for the 400 metres hurdles, at the next Commonwealth Games in 1990 (taking the silver in her defence of the 100m title). In the 1991 World Championships she came second in the 400 metres hurdles, with her best time of 53.16 seconds. In 1992 she took the gold medal for the same event in the Olympic Games, with a time of 53.23 seconds.

Gunpowder Plot The name from the late 18C (previously it had been called the Gunpowder Treason) for a conspiracy in 1605 by Robert Catesby and other Roman Catholics. Their plan, the prelude to a proposed Roman Catholic coup d'état, was to blow up the House of Lords on the opening day of the new session of parliament, when the king and queen would be present with peers

and MPs. A soldier, Guy Fawkes (1570–1606), was entrusted with placing the explosives in the vault after an underground passage had been dug from a nearby cellar; he brought in 36 barrels of gunpowder. The plot failed because a conspirator, Francis Tresham, sent an anonymous message to his brother-in-law, Lord Monteagle, warning him not to attend the opening. The relevant day was November 5, and the barrels were discovered during the night of November 4 with Guy Fawkes alone among them (causing the annual festivities on November 5 to become known later as *Guy Fawkes Night.) Catesby and three others were killed resisting arrest, Tresham died in prison, and eight including Fawkes were tried and hanged. Some historians have suggested that ministers knew about the plot from the start and let it run its course to discredit the Catholics.

Gurkha The ruling house of Nepal, and the name in common use for any citizen of Nepal serving in the British army. The Nepalese are famous for their martial spirit, and there were Gurkhas in the army in India from 1815. Gurkha regiments distinguished themselves in both world wars, and after the independence of India several battalions remained as regular soldiers within the British army. In recent years they have mainly been stationed in Hong Kong and Brunei. In the early 1990s the Brigade of Gurkhas numbered some 4000 men.

Guyana Member of the *Commonwealth since 1966, having previously been known as British Guiana. This part of the north coast of South America was settled by the Dutch from the 17C, with occasional interventions by the French and British. Britain seized it in 1796, during the French Revolutionary Wars, and in 1814 bought the three territories of Demerara, Essequibo and Berbice from Holland. They were grouped together as the crown colony of British Guiana in 1831, and became independent in 1966.

Guy Fawkes Night Annual celebration on November 5, decreed by parliament as an occasion of national thanksgiving after the discovery of the *Gunpowder Plot. The central feature is the bonfire on which an effigy of Guy Fawkes is burnt, though in modern times fireworks play a larger part. 'Penny for the guy' is the traditional plea of children collecting money in the preceding days. There are tales that in centuries past live cats were put inside the guy to make his end more exciting, but nowadays the original anti-papist theme is forgotten except in one rare and unpleasant survival, at *Lewes, where an effigy of the pope is burnt to cries of 'No Popery'.

Guy's Hospital (London SE1) The founder, Thomas Guy (c.1645–1724), was a successful publisher and printer; the building of the hospital began shortly before his death. In the early 19C the physicians at Guy's included an exceptional trio, each remembered by diseases named after them. Richard Bright (1789–1858) pioneered diagnostic methods for disorders of the kidney; Thomas Addison (1793–1860) identified the malfunction of the adrenal glands; and Thomas Hodgkin (1798–1866) used the methods of pathology to discover a disorder of the lymph nodes and the spleen. In 1990 Guy's was the most prominent hospital in the first group to be granted *trust status, and rapidly became the most controversial when it immediately made large reductions in its budget estimates and staff levels. A report published in 1992 recommended that Guy's should be merged with St Thomas's, with the loss of one of their sites.

Guy the gorilla see *London Zoo.

Gwent (population of 447,000 in 1991, administrative centre Cwmbran) Since 1974 a *county in Wales, formed from much of Monmouthshire, part of Breconshire and the former county borough of Newport.

GWR see *railways.

Nell **Gwyn** (1650–87) Illiterate daughter of a brothel keeper near Covent Garden, seller of oranges in the theatre, actress, and finally a rarity among royal mistresses in endearing herself to the crowd – in her own time but also to posterity. Her success, both on the stage and in the affections of Charles II, derived from a delightfully direct quality combined with vivacity and wit (in Pepys's phrase she was 'pretty witty Nell'). A good example is the remark with which she disarmed a hostile crowd, mobbing her carriage in the belief that she was another royal mistress, the Roman Catholic Louise de Kéroualle: 'Pray, good people, be civil,' she shouted, 'I am the Protestant whore.'

She was on the stage from the age of 14 and became the king's mistress at 19, giving up the theatre the following year. He set her up in a fine house in Pall Mall, where she entertained lavishly. Of the two sons she bore the king, one died in childhood and the other was created duke of St Albans (her direct descendant today is the 14th duke). James II honoured his brother's dying wish ('Let not poor Nellie starve') and provided her with a pension.

Gwynedd (240,000 in 1991, administrative centre Caernarfon) Since 1974 a *county in Wales, formed from Anglesey, Caernarvonshire, much of Merionethshire and part of Denbighshire.

gymkhana A word invented by the British in India in the mid-19C, probably to give 'gymnasium' a more Indian

Gypsy family with their caravan in the south of England in about 1890: photograph by John Thompson.

flavour. It was applied to a place where games of any kind could be played. Back in Britain it later came to mean more specifically an event with competitions on horseback. As such the gymkhana has become a central feature of *pony club life.

Gypsies Their name in English and in several other languages reflects a mistaken belief that they were Egyptian in origin. They are now believed to have come from India. The first reference to them in Europe is in the 14C, and a group of some 200 is known to have arrived in Germany in 1417. Gypsies were soon being expelled from a succesion of countries (England 1531, Scotland 1541). Spain was more tolerant than most, flamenco being a notable result of the Gypsy presence there.

Any country which allowed the Gypsies to stay has tended to try and force them to settle. Their refusal to abandon their nomadic ways, relying on crafts and skills which enabled them to keep moving, has amounted over the centuries to an astonishing story of successful resistance – though the modern state, determined to bring higher standards of health and education to all children, is a formidable opponent. It is thought that there are about 50,000 Gypsies in Britain, many of whom now call themselves Travellers. The traditional Gypsy language, Romany (related to Indian languages), is largely extinct in Britain.

H

habeas corpus The first two words of an ancient Latin writ in English common law, telling the person in receipt of the writ that 'you should have the body' brought before a court of law. The writ is issued to the custodian in charge of the 'body' (a living person), and the best known of its many applications is when a court wishes to decide whether the imprisonment of the person is lawful. Since *Magna Carta decreed that no free man should be seized without due process of law, it has been widely assumed to have introduced habeas corpus. In fact it was not till the reign of Henry VII that the writ acquired this main purpose, of freeing people unjustly imprisoned by the *Privy Council. The assertion of habeas corpus as a right of the citizen against royal power was an important part of parliament's struggle against the supposed *divine right of kings claimed by the Stuarts. The *Petition of Right (1628) was followed by the Habeas Corpus Act of 1679, which laid down strict rules to make the writ fully effective.

John **Habgood** (b. 1927) Archbishop of York since 1983, after being bishop of Durham (1973–83). The title of one of his books suggests the very Anglican middle way which he represents – *Confessions of a Conservative Liberal* (1988).

Habitat see Terence *Conran.

hackney The hackney carriage and a hackneyed phrase share a common derivation in the medieval French word *haquenée* for an ambling female horse (having nothing to do with the London district of Hackney). Such an inferior horse was the kind generally offered for hire, and so 'hackney' became a term for anything worn out by general use, including in the past prostitutes as well as cabs and clichés.

Haddo House (40km/25m N of Aberdeen) Palladian mansion designed for the 2nd earl of Aberdeen in the 1730s by William *Adam but much altered and added to in the 19C. The Haddo House Choral Society, which organizes annual concerts with distinguished guest artists, has made Haddo in recent years a local centre for the arts.

Haddon Hall (26km/16m SW of Sheffield) Stone medieval house which grew up from the 12C round an upper and lower courtyard and which gives a powerfully coherent impression of baronial life, with a 14C banqueting hall and a chapel with 15C murals. The Long Gallery was given its present form in the early 17C. By 1700 the Manners family had abandoned the house – just before the two 'improving' centuries. Haddon was therefore unspoilt when the 9th duke of Rutland began restoring it in the early 20C.

Hadrian's Wall Defensive barrier, stretching 117km/73m coast-to-coast across northern England (from Bowness on the Solway Firth to Wallsend on the Tyne), which was built as the northern frontier of Roman Britain. The construction of the huge wall (originally about 4.6m/15ft high, 2.7m/9ft wide, and of solid masonry for most of its length) was ordered by the emperor Hadrian when he visited Britain in AD 122; the work was largely complete by 130. There were small forts every Roman mile (1000 paces), and 17 larger garrisons in which the troops lived. Of these Chesters (the Roman *Cilurnum*, housing 500 cavalry) and Housesteads (probably *Vercovicium*, for 1000 infantry) are the best preserved; each has its own museum.

However it is the Roman fort of *Vindolanda*, a few miles to the southwest of Housesteads, which has recently

The surviving base of Hadrian's Wall, broad and sturdy, snaking its way west through the northern English countryside.

emerged as the most important site of all. A large oak palace of some 50 rooms, many with elaborate murals, was discovered there in the early 1990s. As yet only partly excavated, it has been dated to about AD 120; it is therefore believed likely to be the headquarters from which Hadrian supervised the construction of the wall.

The next emperor, Antoninus Pius, moved the frontier further north to the *Antonine Wall, making Hadrian's Wall temporarily obsolete. On three later ocasions, when the garrison was partly withdrawn south of Hadrian's Wall (in 197, 296 and 367), it was much damaged by tribes from the north; and it has often been plundered for stone. Even so it remains for much of its length a most impressive feature.

Rider **Haggard** (1856–1925, kt 1912) Author of a great many adventure novels, remembered now in particular for *King Solomon's Mines* and *She.

haggis Highly esteemed in Scotland as the national dish. It consists of minced offal of sheep or calf, mixed with oatmeal, suet and seasoning, cooked and served in the skin of the animal's stomach. It is the invariable dish of honour at any *Burns Night celebration. Traditionally an object of horror to *Sassenachs, those who dare sample it usually find it more palatable than expected.

Earl **Haig** (Douglas Haig, 1861–1928, KCVO 1909, earl 1919) Commander-in-chief from December 1915 of the British army fighting on the western front in *World War I. It was he who directed the campaign of slow attrition, from the battles of the *Somme onwards, which cost hundreds of thousands of lives but eventually wore down the German opposition. After the war he campaigned strongly for a fair deal for the returning troops and was instrumental in the creation of the *British Legion, of which he became the first president.

Lord **Hailsham** (Quintin Hogg, b. 1907, baron 1970) Conservative politician, MP for Oxford City (1938–50) and for St Marylebone (1963–70). The gap in his House of Commons career was the result of his succeeding his father, as Viscount Hailsham, in 1950; he disclaimed his *peerage as soon as it was possible, in 1963. A barrister by profession, he held high office as lord chancellor for the best part of two recent decades (1970–4, 1979–87).

'Hail to thee, blithe spirit!' see *To a Skylark.

Mike **Hailwood** (b. 1940) Racing motorcyclist who dominated the sport in the mid-1960s, with nine world championships – three for Honda in the 250cc class (1961, 66, 67), two for Honda at 350cc (1966, 67) and four for MV Agusta at 500cc (1962, 63, 64, 65). He also had an exceptional run of victories in the Isle of Man Senior TT, winning in 1961 for *Norton, in 1963–5 for MV Agusta, in 1966–7 for Honda and in 1979 for Suzuki.

Bernard **Haitink** (b. 1929) Dutch conductor who has been much involved with music in Britain, as principal conductor and musical director of Glyndebourne (1977–88), of the London Philharmonic (1967–79) and of the Royal Opera House since 1987. From 1964 to 1988 he was also artistic director and permanent conductor of the Concertgebouw Orchestra of Amsterdam.

Richard **Hakluyt** (c.1552–1616) The first historian of British exploration overseas. An interest from boyhood in travellers' tales led to the compilation of his main work – *The principall navigations, voiages and discoveries of the English nation*, published first in 1589 and then in a much expanded 3-volume edition (1598–1600).

Haldane Scottish family prominent for two generations in public life and in science. Richard Burdon Haldane (1856–1928, viscount 1911) was a barrister and Liberal MP for East Lothian (from 1885). His greatest contribution was as secretary of state for war in 1905–12, when he set up an easily mobilized expeditionary force and founded the *territorial army – developments of great importance in the coming war. His sister Elizabeth Sanderson Haldane (1862–1937) was also much involved in public life, mainly on welfare issues, and was the first woman JP in Scotland. Their brother John Scott Haldane (1860–1936) was a physiologist whose researches into the chemical aspects of breathing were of great importance in the mining industry. The latter's son J.B.S. Haldane (John Burdon Sanderson, 1892–1964) was a geneticist of distinction, specializing in heredity and the evolution of entire populations. He was a prominent Marxist in the 1930s and was chairman (1940–50) of the editorial board of the *Daily Worker*.

Kathleen **Hale** see *Orlando the Marmalade Cat.

Matthew **Hale** see *common law.

half-crown see *currency.

half-timber see *timber-frame.

Halifax (87,000 in 1981) Town in West Yorkshire, on the river Hebble, which was a major centre of English cloth production in the late Middle Ages; it was also known at the time for its own form of capital punishment, the Halifax gibbet (last used in 1650), which was an early

A cliff-hanging scene in a Rider Haggard novel: Leo saves his companion in the nick of time in She.

version of the guillotine. With its long industrial history, Halifax is now rich in related museums. The Calderdale Industrial Museum occupies a 19C mill; on an adjacent site the pre-industrial history of the wool trade is displayed in the Piece Hall, a large colonnaded building (completed in 1779), which was the cloth market to which the cottage weavers brought their finished 'pieces' of cloth for sale. The rural side of pre-industrial economy can be seen in the West Yorkshire Folk Museum at Shibden Hall, a partly timber-framed manor house with a magnificent 17C barn. A stimulating addition to Halifax's museums opened in 1992 in the form of Eureka!, Britain's first interactive museum for children; funded by the Duffield and Clore Foundations, it involves 5–12-year-olds in a 'hands-on experience' of many aspects of everyday life.

The **Halifax** Britain's biggest *building society, a position it has held since 1913. It was founded in 1853 in Halifax, West Yorkshire, as the Halifax Permanent Benefit Building and Investment Society.

Henry **Hall** (1898–1989) Bandleader who formed the BBC Dance Orchestra in 1932 and became a national figure from 1934 with his weekly *Guest Night*. His signing-off tune at the end of each programme was a song written by himself, either *Here's to the Next Time* (1932) or *It's Time to say Goodnight* (1934).

Peter **Hall** (b. 1930, kt 1977) Theatre director who has run the country's two leading companies – the *Royal Shakespeare Company (1960–8) and the *National Theatre (1973–88). In addition to numerous productions from the classic repertoire (including a chronological sequence of seven Shakespeare history plays for the 400th anniversary celebrations at Stratford in 1964), he has directed the premieres of several important contemporary works – among them Harold Pinter's *The Homecoming* (1965) and *No Man's Land* (1975) and Peter Shaffer's *Amadeus* (1979). He has also been much involved with opera, particularly at Glyndebourne. The publication of his *Diaries* (1983) ruffled a few theatrical feathers.

Arthur **Hallam** see *In Memoriam*.

Hallé Orchestra Manchester's principal orchestra, founded in 1858 by Charles Hallé (1819–95), a German pianist and conductor who had moved to England in 1848. Until his death he continued to conduct the orchestra's annual series of concerts (of which Manchester's Free Trade Hall became the home) and to perform as the piano soloist. The longest-serving conductors since then have been Hamilton Harty (1920–33), John Barbirolli (1943–70) and James Loughran (1971–83).

Hallelujah Chorus see *Messiah*.

Edmond **Halley** (first name often spelt Edmund, 1656–1742) Astronomer who at the age of 20 travelled to St Helena to spend two years cataloguing the stars of the southern hemisphere, to complement the work that *Flamsteed was doing for the northern hemisphere. The publication of his catalogue in 1679 established him among the leading scientists in the early years of the *Royal Society. He became a close friend of *Newton and personally provided the funds which enabled the Society to print his *Principia*. He succeeded Flamsteed as *astronomer royal in 1720.

Like all scientists of his time his interests were wide (the pattern of the earth's winds, the salinity of the sea, the age of the earth and much else in addition to the normal concerns of astronomy), but he is remembered in

The most commonly found hallmarks: the standard marks of England and Scotland, and the assay marks of London, Birmingham, Sheffield and Edinburgh.

particular for the comet which now bears his name. Observing the orbit of a comet in 1682, he saw a resemblance to others reported in 1531 and 1607. He argued that this was a single comet with a period of about 76 years, and correctly predicted that it would return in 1758. The most recent reappearance of Halley's comet, more intensely studied than ever before, was in 1986.

hallmarks The marks impressed in objects of silver and gold (and since 1975 platinum). The most important is the standard mark, which signifies that the metal has been assayed (tested) and found to be of *sterling quality. In silver this is a purity of 92.5%. The standard mark on English silver has been, since 1544, a lion passant (walking with the right foreleg raised). On silver assayed in Edinburgh it was from 1759 to 1974 a thistle, and since then has been a lion rampant (standing on hind legs).

The assay office mark gives the city in which the silver was assayed; the four now in operation are London (a leopard's head), Birmingham (an anchor), Sheffield (until 1974 a crown, now a rose) and Edinburgh (a castle). The other marks are the initials of the silversmith, a single letter for the year, and at certain periods the monarch's head for the reign.

The assay office marks are the same on gold, with minor exceptions, but the standard marks have differed since 1798 (on most gold items, such as wedding rings, the hallmarks are too small to be identified with the naked eye). Gold differs from silver in being assayed at various levels of purity, defined in carats. Pure gold is 24 carats, and the standard of gold is marked either as carats or as a percentage of 24. Thus an 18-carat gold ring will have on its inner surface either the number 18 or 75.0 (for 75%).

Hallowe'en (Oct. 31) The name means 'Allhallows even' or the eve of All Saints' Day, but the reason for the spooky traditions associated with this night is that the next day, November 1, was the Celtic festival of Samhain. This was the autumn equivalent of *Beltane in the spring. On the eve of this important day, the beginning of winter, the spirits of the pagan dead were much in evidence. They were the reason for the church enlisting all the saints to try and pre-empt the occasion for Christianity. For children this was 'mischief night', when pranks could be blamed on the spirits. This custom, surviving in northern England, travelled in the past to the USA and has recently returned to these shores with the American refinement of 'trick or treat'. The importance of Hallowe'en has over the years been much reduced in Britain, partly because of the proximity of *Guy Fawkes Night.

An early cricket match: anonymous 18C painting, long associated with Hambledon (the distant church suggests wrongly so).

Hambledon Cricket Club The most famous club from the early days of *cricket. Hambledon is a village in Hampshire, north of Portsmouth. For a period from the 1760s the village club was a match for all-comers. On their celebrated field, Broadhalfpenny Down (the turf from which was moved in about 1782 to Windmill Down), they even beat teams representing the rest of England. The club's achievements were recorded by John Nyren, son of one of the players, in *The Cricketers of My Time* (published in *The Young Cricketer's Tutor* 1833).

Ham House (19km/12m SW of central London) Red-brick house on the south bank of the Thames which is the most perfect surviving example of *Restoration taste. Built originally in 1610, it was enlarged and completely redecorated by the duke and duchess of Lauderdale in the 1670s. Their lavish wood inlays and carvings and their leather wall hangings survive (and even some satin and silk), together with much of the furniture mentioned in three contemporary inventories.

Lady **Hamilton** (Amy Lyon, c.1765–1815, m. William Hamilton 1791) Daughter of a blacksmith, William Lyon, who was using the name Emma Hart by the time she was the 15-year-old mistress of the owner of *Uppark. There she met and became attached to a young aristocrat, Charles Greville, who introduced her to his friend George *Romney – which is why we have so many paintings of the young temptress. Greville had heavy debts and he passed Emma on to his rich uncle Sir William Hamilton (1730–1803) in return for his debts being settled. Hamilton, a noted collector of classical antiquities, was British envoy to the court of Naples, where Emma became a celebrity, famous for her 'attitudes' (poses in classical scenes). *Nelson met her there in the 1790s and by 1799 was her lover. The relationship ended Nelson's own marriage but Sir William tolerated it, and in 1802–3 the Hamiltons and Nelson lived together in a house at

Merton, now in southwest London. Emma had a daughter by Nelson, christened Horatia (1801–81).

Richard **Hamilton** see *pop art.

Hamlet (c.1601) Tragedy by *Shakespeare which has provided literature's leading example of a moody young man, brilliant but indecisive, with dark obsessions in his response to women. Hamlet's central problem is that his mother, Gertrude, has married his father's brother, Claudius, within weeks of Claudius killing Hamlet's father, the king of Denmark, and usurping the throne. The young prince parades his grief by wearing black at his uncle's court at Elsinore, but he is prompted to take more violent action by the appearance of his father's ghost, demanding vengeance. The prince seizes every opportunity of avoiding action and of rebuking himself for inaction. Even after Claudius has demonstrated his guilt (in his response to a play called *The Mousetrap*, depicting the murder, which Hamlet persuades some travelling players to present at court), the prince cannot bring himself to kill his uncle when he next finds him alone – because he is praying and Hamlet will not send his soul to heaven.

Hamlet vents his frustrations on *Ophelia, who loves him and is driven insane by his obsessive cruelties. In a passionate scene in the bedroom of his mother he upbraids her violently for her betrayal of his father. He is now clearly dangerous and Claudius arranges for two courtiers, Rosencrantz and Guildenstern, to take Hamlet to England and there to kill him. He escapes and returns, chancing on the way upon a gravedigger who finds for him the skull of a favourite jester, Yorick, which sets the prince musing once more ('Alas, poor Yorick'). There then arrives in the graveyard the funeral procession of Ophelia, who has fallen into a stream in her madness and has been drowned. Hamlet brawls in the grave with her brother, Laertes, and the drama moves at last to a conclusion. Claudius tries to kill Hamlet by organizing a fencing match with Laertes, who has a poisoned rapier (which Hamlet turns on Laertes); and then by offering him a poisoned drink (which Hamlet forces on Claudius himself, after Gertrude has unwittingly drunk from it). Hamlet has himself been nicked by the rapier and he too dies. 'The rest is silence' are his final words.

Shakespeare makes great use in this play of soliloquies, a device entirely appropriate to the introspective nature of his central character, traditionally known in theatrical circles as 'the moody Dane'. In two of them, beginning respectively 'O, that this too too solid flesh would melt' and 'To be, or not to be: that is the question', Hamlet contemplates suicide. In an extremely complex plot other important characters include Horatio, Hamlet's faithful confidant; and Polonius, the pompous court chamberlain, father of Ophelia and Laertes, who is the butt of much humour but has one of the play's best-known speeches, including the line *'Neither a borrower nor a lender be'.

Hamley's (London W1) Britain's best-known toy shop. William Hamley began selling toys in London in 1760, calling his premises Noah's Ark, and the firm moved to its present Regent Street premises in 1906. A model of Noah's Ark over the door recalls its origins.

hammer-beam roof A form of construction for timber roofs, in use in the 14–16C and peculiar to England. The hammer beams are short thick timbers projecting inwards from the side walls at the base of a sloping roof. They support vertical hammer posts up to the next tier of the structure, as well as braces which arch inwards to the centre. Though weaker than a tie beam reaching across the full width, the system makes possible a much more open roof structure with maximum opportunities for carved decoration. The best-known hammer-beam roof, and the earliest surviving large-scale example, is the one in *Westminster Hall by the master carpenter Hugh Herland.

Wally **Hammond** (1903–65) The greatest English batsman and all-rounder in the years between the wars, playing *cricket for Gloucestershire (1920–51) and for England (1927–47, captain 1938–47). His 905 runs in a *Test series (Australia, 1928–9) are still (early in 1993) a record for England, as are his 22 Test centuries (a record shared with Cowdrey and Boycott).

John **Hampden** (1594–1643) Parliamentarian who led the opposition to Charles I over *ship money, refusing the payment due from him in 1636 on his estates in Buckinghamshire. One specific levy (20 shillings on Stoke Mandeville) was heard as a test case before 12 judges, who decided narrowly for the king. The effect was to cause many others to withhold payment. Hampden was prominent in the Long Parliament, and was one of the *Five Members. He died of musket wounds after a skirmish with Prince Rupert's cavalry near Oxford during the English Civil War.

Hampden Park (Glasgow) Scotland's national football stadium which is also, surprisingly, the ground of an amateur club, *Queen's Park. It is the club's third ground on the site. Completed in 1903, to grander dimensions than any other stadium in Scotland, it became the venue for international matches and for the Scottish Cup Final.

Hampshire (1,579,000 in 1991, administrative centre Winchester) *County on the south coast of England.

Hampshire County Cricket Club Representing the county which had produced the most famous early cricket club (the *Hambledon), Hampshire CCC was founded in 1863 and joined the *county championship in 1895. It

has won the championship twice (1961, 73). Victories in *one-day cricket have been the NatWest Trophy (1991), the Benson and Hedges Cup (1988) and three wins in the Sunday League (1975, 78, 86). The county ground is in Southampton, and the county also plays at Bournemouth, Basingstoke and Portsmouth.

Hampstead (London NW3) As the nearest hilly region to the city, lying just a few miles to the northwest, Hampstead and its famous heath (today 273ha/676ac of open countryside) provided rich Londoners with a place of refuge from the plague long before becoming fashionable in the 18C for medicinal waters. In modern times the district has been a favourite residential area for writers and musicians.

Hampton Court Palace (24km/15m SW of central London) Built by Cardinal *Wolsey in 1514–21 to be the most impressive house in England (some 280 beds were kept available for strangers), it was given by him to Henry VIII a few years later in an attempt to retain the royal favour. Of Wolsey's creation the first two courts survive (the Base Court and Clock Court). Henry built the present Great Hall, much embellished the Chapel and placed the *King's Beasts at the entrance to the first court.

In 1689 William and Mary wanted something more modern. They commissioned *Wren, who added very rapidly (before 1694) the south and east fronts round the Fountain Court, linking them to the Tudor palace by the continuing use of red brick. The interiors were not complete until well into the next century. The outstanding feature is the King's Staircase, for which the Italian artist Antonio Verrio began painting the illusionistic murals in 1700. After the death of George II, in 1760, the palace was never again used as a royal residence. Queen Victoria opened it to the public in 1838. A fire considerably damaged the 17C King's Apartments in 1986, but they were restored and open again by 1992.

Fountain Court, added to Hampton Court Palace by Christopher Wren in the early 1690s.

The gardens contain a *real-tennis court; a famous Maze, created in the 1690s for William III; the Great Vine, planted in 1768 and still flourishing; and, round the Privy Garden, the most splendid display of wrought iron in Britain, the 12-panel screen made in about 1693 by the French Huguenot blacksmith Jean Tijou.

Tony **Hancock** (1924–68) Comedian whose *Hancock's Half Hour* (BBC radio from 1954, TV from 1956) focused on the semi-autobiographical hang-ups of a fictional Anthony Aloysius St John Hancock, resident at 23 Railway Cuttings, East Cheam. The character's blend of paranoia and aggression proved irresistible in brief classics such as *The Blood Donor*. But there were similar problems in Hancock's own life, leading to his eventual suicide.

George Frideric **Handel** (1685–1759) German-born composer who was by far the most distinguished musician in 18C Britain; he lived here from soon after 1710 and was naturalized in 1727. His early years in London were spent composing and directing Italian opera (he had a considerable success in 1711 with *Rinaldo*), but in general English audiences were suspicious of this elaborate foreign fare. Handel met their needs with a new form, the English oratorio, using biblical subjects, dramatic in content but designed for concert performance and sung in English. The best known of them all is *Messiah. Some were written to catch the national mood on specific occasions, such as the triumphalist *Judas Maccabaeus* (1747) which greeted Butcher *Cumberland on his return to London.

Handel had long been closely connected with royal occasions. His *Water Music* may have been written to accompany a boating party given on the Thames by George I in 1717; for the coronation of George II in 1727 he composed four anthems, of which *Zadok the Priest* has been performed at every *coronation since; and the *Music for the Royal Fireworks* was played in 1749 in London's Green Park during the festivities for the end of the War of the *Austrian Succession (it had previously had a public rehearsal in *Vauxhall Gardens). Handel was buried in Westminster Abbey, with a monument by *Roubiliac in Poets' Corner.

Handel in the Strand see Percy *Grainger.

Handel's Largo General name given to any instrumental arrangement of the aria 'Ombra mai fu' from Handel's opera *Xerxes* (1738). It relates to the musical notation *largo*, meaning slow and stately, though the passage is in fact marked with the less sombre *larghetto*.

A Handful of Dust (1934) Novel by Evelyn *Waugh in which Tony Last escapes from marital and financial troubles in England by making a journey up the Amazon. Deep in the interior of Brazil he falls into the hands of Mr Todd, illiterate but the proud owner of a set of Dickens which he inherited from his English father. He loves being read to and starts Tony off on *Bleak House* – the beginning of a life sentence as it turns out, for by a trick Mr Todd convinces the eventual rescue party that Tony is dead. The title comes from The *Waste Land – 'I will show you fear in a handful of dust'.

Tommy **Handley** see *ITMA.

hanged, drawn and quartered see *capital punishment.

hangmen The names of three hangmen have lodged in the public mind. The first two can better be described as

executioners, since the most prominent part of their duty was beheading aristocratic offenders. Richard Brandon, the executioner of Charles I, died in 1649 – the same year as his famous victim. John Ketch (d. 1686) had such a vile reputation that 'Jack Ketch' was for the next two centuries a common term for any hangman; however, his notoriety seems to have been caused not so much by any unusual barbarity as by his becoming a character in the *Punch and Judy shows, new in England at the time. Finally Albert Pierrepoint is remembered, partly because he was hangman for a quarter of a century (1931–56) within living memory but also because he later became an opponent of *capital punishment. In his autobiography (1974) he argued that the deterrent effect of the gallows was disproved by the courage of the condemned: 'All the men and women whom I have faced at that final moment convince me that in what I have done I have not prevented a single murder.'

Richard **Hannay** see John *Buchan.

House of **Hanover** (1714–1901) The descendants on the throne of Britain of Ernest August, the elector of Hanover, and his wife Sophia, who was a granddaughter of James I (see the *royal house). The Act of *Settlement had limited the inheritance to Sophia and her heirs. The first five of the dynasty (George I, George II, George III, George IV, William IV) also inherited the throne of Hanover. Thereafter the *Salic law separated the two thrones, for the next in line in Britain was a woman, Victoria. Her son, Edward VII, following the dynastic line of his father Prince Albert, was of the house of *Saxe-Coburg-Gotha.

The 18C rulers of Hanover were 'electors' in a fanciful survival of a medieval custom by which certain German princes elected the Holy Roman Emperor. It was by then meaningless, for ' Holy Roman Emperor' had become a hereditary title in the ruling house of Austria. Even as a fiction the empire was formally brought to an end in 1806, when Austria was threatened by the imperial ambitions of Napoleon, and Hanover was reclassified as a kingdom at the congress of Vienna in 1814.

James **Hanratty** see *A6 murder.

Hansard The colloquial name for the *Official Report* of debates in parliament. Verbatim accounts of speeches are published in daily and weekly editions. The name derives from Luke Hansard (printer to the House of Commons 1774–1828), whose son Thomas acquired in 1810 the *Parliamentary Debates* which had been started by *Cobbett. The reports did not become verbatim until 1909.

Joseph **Hansom** (1803–82) Architect and designer, who in 1834 patented his idea for a 'safety cab'. The eventual result was the light and fast hansom cab (familiar in mid-19C images of the streets of London), though his concept had been much altered by others before the vehicle came into general use. A more lasting achievement was his 1831 design for the new town hall in *Birmingham.

Hanson Enterprise which has grown, through a series of takeovers, into one of Britain's largest companies. The process began in 1964 when a public company, Wiles Group, bought a lorry firm and put its two owners, James Hanson (b. 1922) and Gordon White (b. 1923), on the board. The following year Hanson and White acquired control of Wiles, which then became their takeover vehicle; its name was changed to Hanson Trust in 1969. In 1973 White set up the US side of the business, and in 1987 Hanson Trust became a public company as Hanson.

A subsequent clear out of assets left the company with £1 billion of available cash in 1988, and by 1991 Hanson was in a position to contemplate (though not in the event to carry through) a raid on mighty ICI. An attempt in the following year to win control of Ranks Hovis McDougall was similarly frustrated.

Happy Families Card game in which the pack is made up of families of four cards (father and mother, son and daughter), each based on a trade and appropriately named – Mr Bun the Baker, Mrs Bun the Baker's Wife and so on. The purpose is to collect them as complete families. The game was marketed from the mid-19C and had a predecessor called Spade the Gardener.

Keir **Hardie** (James Keir Hardie, 1856–1915) The first Labour MP and the founding father of the *Labour party. He was born in Lanarkshire and began working in the mines at the age of ten. His trade union activities led to his standing for parliament in 1888, unsuccessfully, as an independent Labour candidate. But he became an MP in 1892 for West Ham South, and immediately established a strong public image, much loved and much hated. His arrival at the House of Commons in a tweed suit and cloth cap caused a sensation and he soon became known as the 'member for the unemployed'. (The deerstalker, with which he had earlier been associated in his open-air campaigning, was replaced by the cloth cap with its stronger working-class associations.) He lost his seat in 1895, but was returned in 1900 for Merthyr Tydfil, which he held till his death. By 1906 there were enough Labour MPs to form a parliamentary party, of which he was elected leader. He resigned in 1911 (owing to a combination of ill health and a lack of aptitude for this new role), and was succeeded by Ramsay *Macdonald.

Gilbert **Harding** (1907–60) The first man in Britain to acquire the status of a television 'personality'. He became well known on radio, chairing *Round Britain Quiz* and *Twenty Questions*, but it was as a panellist on the TV game *What's My Line?* that he really appealed to the public – largely because of his grumpy character, which the audience hoped (often with good reason) might lead him into downright rudeness. One of the most widely remembered moments from the early years of British TV was Harding's breaking down on *Face to Face*, when a question about his mother unexpectedly touched a raw nerve.

'Hard pounding this, gentlemen' see entry on Battle of *Waterloo.

Hard Times (1854) Novel by *Dickens, serialized in *Household Words* from April 1854. It contrasts the worlds of Fact and Fancy. Materialism is heavily satirized in the person of Thomas Gradgrind, a merchant of Coketown who brings up his children on supposedly utilitarian principles: the book opens with his peremptory words 'Now what I want is Facts', and he enlarges the theme later with the statement 'Facts alone are wanted in life'. A diet of hard Facts brings misery and stunted emotions to Gradgrind's children, by contrast with the warm Fancy to be found with Sissy Jupe and among the members of Sleary's circus troupe.

Hardwick Hall (16km/10m S of Chesterfield) The Elizabethan house which carries further than any other the passion of the time for large areas of window. Glass was expensive and therefore a status symbol ('Hardwick Hall, more glass than wall' runs the jingle). It was built in the 1590s by *Bess of Hardwick, whose initials ES (Elizabeth, countess of Shrewsbury) surmount each of six corner towers, and it was almost certainly designed by Robert *Smythson. Many of the original furnishings, listed in an inventory of 1601, are still in place – most notably a superb range of embroidered fabrics, and the set of tapestries around which the great chamber was designed.

Thomas **Hardy** (1840–1928) Novelist and poet, associated more than any other with the English countryside and in particular with Dorset, the county in which he was born and lived. Trained as an architect, he first achieved popular success as an author in 1874 with *Far from the Madding Crowd*. It was also the book which introduced Wessex, the fictional county in the West Country which provides the setting for many of his novels and poems, with Casterbridge (Dorchester) as its county town. The best known among the novels which followed are *The Return of the Native* (1878), The *Mayor of Casterbridge* (1886), *Tess of the D'Urbervilles* (1891) and *Jude the Obscure* (1896). The subject matter and treatment of the last two were highly controversial, in particular *Jude* – a study of the clash between the flesh and the spirit, offering a morbid view of both sex and Christianity. The public response caused Hardy to devote himself exclusively to poetry for the last third of his life.

In 1904–8 he published the three parts of *The Dynasts*, a poetic drama set in the Napoleonic Wars. He followed this with several volumes of lyric poems drawing on the same material as his novels – the forces of nature in his beloved Wessex. In 1885 he and his first wife Emma (d. 1912) moved into Max Gate, a house which he built near Dorchester and lived in for the rest of his life (he married again in 1914). The thatched cottage in which he was born in Higher Brockhampton is kept in his memory.

hare and hounds A cross-country sport popular in *public schools from the early 19C, in which a couple of runners (the hares) are given a head start on their pursuers (the hounds). It is also called a paper-chase, since the hares usually scatter fragments of paper as the equivalent of the scent, enabling the hounds to track them. Many British athletic clubs, with their origins in this sport, still call themselves Harriers – the word for dogs trained to hunt hares.

Harefield Hospital Britain's leading hospital for heart and heart-and-lung transplants, situated in the countryside about 32km/20m west of central London. A specialist surgical team was established there in 1980, led by Magdi Yacoub (b. 1935). By the late 1980s, with an average of 150 transplants performed every year, the Harefield programme was the largest in the world. Harefield Park, in which the hospital stands, was the home of the founder of the *Lancet.

Lord **Harewood** (George Lascelles, b. 1923, 7th earl of Harewood 1947) Grandson of George V (see the *royal family) and son of Princess Mary, who in 1932 was created *Princess Royal. He has had a distinguished career in opera, being at various times closely involved with several of the national opera companies and editing the recent editions of *Kobbé's Complete Opera Book*. His divorce from his first wife in 1967 was the first in the British royal family since Henry VIII (*George I divorced his wife while still only elector of Hanover).

Harewood House (11km/7m N of Leeds) Palladian mansion built 1759–71 for Edwin Lascelles by John *Carr, with interiors by Robert *Adam. Furniture commissioned for the house from *Chippendale and a park landscaped by Capability *Brown complete Harewood's immaculate pedigree for its period. Today Adam's columned entrance hall has a centrepiece with a rather different pedigree, a massive alabaster sculpture of the original Adam by *Epstein. In 1922 the Lascelles became linked with the royal family when the 6th earl of Harewood (1882–1947) married the *Princess Royal, daughter of George V.

James **Hargreaves** (*c*.1720–78) Lancashire spinner who in about 1764 invented the spinning jenny. An overturned spinning wheel, continuing to spin with the spindle vertical, gave him the idea that several spindles could be worked simultaneously from a wheel in this position. He developed a version with eight spindles for use by his own family, multiplying output eight times (news of which caused local spinners in Blackburn to invade his house and smash his machines). By the time of his death there were 20,000 hand jennies in England, each by then with 80 spindles; but they were about to be superseded by *Crompton's mule. The traditional explanation for the name of his machine is that the daughter who inspired him, by knocking over her spinning wheel, was called Jenny.

Hark! the herald angels sing see Charles *Wesley.

Harlech (88km/55m N of Aberystwyth) Town in Gwynedd which grew up below the most spectacularly sited of Edward I's concentric Welsh castles, perched on its rock above what was then the shore line (now receded by some 800m/900yd). Built in 1283–9, its outer walls are still largely intact. A Lancastrian garrison was besieged here for seven years by the Yorkists in the *Wars of the Roses – a brave resistance usually said to have inspired the March of the Men of Harlech. However the words to which the song is now sung (by Thomas Oliphant, 1799–1873) describe a victory by the ancient Britons of Wales at a much earlier period, the 7–8c, when they were being threatened by the Anglo-Saxons.

Harlequin The foppish young lover of Columbine in 18c *pantomime, who went about his courtship dressed in a tightly fitting suit made of bright silk diamond patches. Although he borrowed his name from Arlecchino, a quick-witted servant in the Italian *commedia dell'arte*, he was exclusively a part of English stage tradition. During the 19c he was gradually crowded out of pantomime by the principal boy and the dame.

Harlequins Rugby union football club, formed in 1866 and based in Twickenham. It won the Pilkington Cup in 1988 and 1991, and has been the most successful club in its local Middlesex Sevens.

Harley Street (London W1) Street built in the mid-18c, and associated in the 20c almost exclusively with medical consulting rooms.

harling see *pebble dash.

Harmsworth brothers see Lord *Northcliffe.

Harold II (*c*.1022–1066) The last *Anglo-Saxon king of England, reigning for ten months. He had succeeded his father, Godwin, as earl of Wessex in 1053. The death of *Edward the Confessor in January 1066, after naming Harold at the last moment as his successor, caused two rivals to invade the country. The first was Harold Hardraade, king of Norway. Harold II defeated him in the northeast at Stamford Bridge, on September 25, but then had to march hurriedly down to the south coast where *William the Conqueror landed on September 28. Harold died in the resulting Battle of *Hastings, on October 14.

harp The Welsh harp and the Irish harp are specific variants of this extremely ancient musical instrument, and in both these Celtic regions the harp has been of almost mystical significance. It is the heraldic symbol of Ireland, on Irish coins from the 16c and representing Ireland in the *royal arms. It was also the symbol of office of Welsh *bards.

Harpers & Queen Monthly women's magazine, specializing in fashion and society. It is the result of a 1970 merger

Harlech Castle on its high bluff: when it was built, the sea reached the foot of the rock.

between *The Queen* (founded in 1861 by the husband of Mrs *Beeton) and *Harpers Bazaar* (launched in 1929). Its most famous feature is 'Jennifer's Diary', a description and photographic record of parties attended, written for 47 years (1944–91) by Betty Kenward.

*The **Harp that once through Tara's halls*** see Thomas *Moore.

Harrier The Harrier jump jet, introduced in the RAF in 1969, was the first plane capable of vertical take-off and landing (VTOL); it therefore won a place in many of the world's air forces. The first model, the GR1, was manufactured by Hawker Siddeley; subsequent versions have been made by British Aerospace. The RAF in recent years has been equipped with the GR3, and the Fleet Air Arm uses the Sea Harrier on aircraft carriers.

harriers see *hare and hounds.

Harris see *Lewis with Harris.

'Bomber' **Harris** (Arthur Harris, 1892–1984, KCB 1942, bt 1953) Airman in charge from 1942 of the RAF's Bomber Command. Originally formed in 1936, this was built up by Harris into the formidable fighting machine which blasted German military and civilian targets from 1943. He has been criticized in recent decades for the enthusiasm with which he continued 'area bombing' (particularly of Dresden in 1945), after more precise night-time targeting had become possible. The placing of a statue of him in front of *St Clement Danes caused controversy in 1992.

Rex **Harrison** (1908–90, kt 1989) Actor noted for his crisp comic portrayal of often rather smooth characters. A gloriously crusty exception was his Professor Higgins in both the stage and screen versions of *My Fair Lady*.

Tony **Harrison** (b. 1937) Poet born in Leeds and much inspired by the clash between his working-class origins and the middle-class world into which his talent and his degrees (in classics and linguistics) have propelled him. As even the title proclaims, this is the theme of *Them & [uz]* – a poem which he often performs in public. Theatre has also been an important strand. He was resident dramatist at the National Theatre in 1977–9, and his 1981 version of *The Oresteia* by Aeschylus was a celebrated production there.

Harris tweed The best-known of all varieties of *tweed, taking its name from the southern part of *Lewis with Harris. Originally made only for local use, it became widely popular in the late 19C. In the 20C, under threat from cheaper imitations, genuine Harris tweed has been defined as cloth made from pure Scottish wool, spun and dyed in the outer Hebrides, and woven by the islanders in their own homes. In recent years there has been pressure to allow the introduction of power looms in small factories on the island.

Harrods (London SW1) Britain's most famous department store, seen in its heyday as the ultimate in luxury. It derives from a small grocery shop on the same site which was taken over in 1849 by Charles Henry Harrod (1800–85). It was his son Charles Digby Harrod (1841–1905) who expanded the business. The present store, occupying the entire block, was built in 1894–1912. Two of its most famous features – the terracotta façade on the Brompton Road (lit by 11,500 bulbs) and the decorative tiles in the food halls – were produced by the *Doulton pottery at Lambeth. In 1985 Harrod's was the subject of

Hygeia, a Greek goddess of health, gives her endorsement to Harrogate in an early 20C poster.

a bitterly contested takeover battle between Al-Fayed and *Lonrho. The Egyptian Al-Fayed brothers won the day, but Lonrho's persistent accusations of financial irregularity (reinforced by a critical 1990 report on the takeover by the Department of Trade and Industry) have kept the dispute in the public eye for nearly a decade.

Harrogate (66,000 in 1981) Spa town in North Yorkshire. From the 17C visitors came to take the waters from some 88 separate mineral springs. The Royal Pump Room (1842) is now a museum.

Harrow School One of the best-known of boys' *public schools, which took in its first pupils in 1615 in Harrow-on-the-Hill – at that time a small town a few miles to the northwest of London. The school was founded and endowed under the will of John Lyon, who had died in 1592. Harrow has had many distinguished pupils, including Byron and Robert Peel, but the best known of all was an unsuccessful schoolboy, Winston Churchill. There is a strong tradition of games; the annual cricket match against Eton at Lord's dates back to 1805, and it was at Harrow that *squash was invented. It also has the most famous of school songs, written in 1872 by two masters (words Edward Bowen, tune John Farmer):

Forty years on, when afar and asunder
Parted are those who are singing today,
When you look back, and forgetfully wonder
    What you were like in your work and your play,
Then, it may be, there will often come o'er you,
Glimpses of notes like the catch of a song –
Visions of boyhood shall float them before you,
    Echoes of dreamland shall bear them along.

Prince **Harry** see the Prince of *Wales.

Norman **Hartnell** (1901–79, KCVO 1977) Fashion designer who was dressmaker to two successive queens – the present Queen Mother and her daughter, Elizabeth II. He made Princess Elizabeth's wedding dress in 1947 and also the dress for her coronation in 1953. The firm of Hartnell continued after his death; in 1990 Marc Bohan, previously in charge of Christian Dior in Paris, was appointed the design director.

Hart's Rules The standard set of conventions used by printers and publishers of books in English. Horace Hart (1841–1916) was a printer who began compiling his own set of rules in 1864. From 1883 he was in charge of the *Oxford University Press, where his book was privately printed in 1893 as *Rules for Compositors and Readers*. It was first published in 1904.

Hamilton **Harty** (1879–1941, kt 1925) Northern Irish conductor and composer, known in particular for his time with the *Hallé Orchestra and for his orchestrations of *Handel's *Water Music* and *Fireworks Music*.

Harvest Festival The old ceremony of 'harvest home', celebrating the gathering of the final stook of corn, was a convivial and often disorderly banquet for the harvesters. But in the respectable mid-19C the event was gradually taken over by the church; 'Come, ye thankful people, come,/Raise the song of Harvest-home', in the words of a hymn of the time. Nowadays, when the gathering of the harvest is largely mechanical, the produce itself has become the centre of attention – with a profusion of vegetables and loaves of bread arranged round the altars of country churches.

William **Harvey** (1578–1657) Physician who discovered the circulation of the blood. He announced his discovery in the learned manner of the day in a Latin text – *Exercitatio anatomica de motu cordis et sanguinis in animalibus* 1628 (Anatomical treatise on the movement of the heart and blood in animals). Harvey's researches were ahead of their time in being supported by detailed evidence from experiments on a wide range of animals, including dogs, pigs, snakes, frogs, fishes, lobsters, shrimps, oysters and even the humble slug.

Harwell see *nuclear power.

Hastings (14 Oct. 1066) Battle which launched the Norman *Conquest on its successful course. The two protagonists, *Harold II and *William the Conqueror, each had about 7000 men; but whereas the English had only foot soldiers with hand weapons (swords, axes, spears, slings), the Normans had archers and cavalry. The Normans spent all day trying to dislodge the English from the ridge, some 16km/10m northwest of Hastings, on which now stand the abbey and town of *Battle. Harold was killed in the late afternoon (according to tradition by an arrow through the eye) and at dusk the English fled. The battle is the main event depicted in the *Bayeux tapestry, where the image of Harold just before his death seems to show the fatal arrow – the only near-contemporary evidence of that famous detail.

Warren **Hastings** (1732–1818) The first governor general of India (1772–85), largely responsible for transforming the *East India Company from an organization of armed traders to a full-scale civil administration. Members of his council in Calcutta waged a personal feud against him for many years, and on his return to England they contrived to have him impeached. Though guilty of high-handedness (most famously in his recovery of money and land from the 'begums of Oudh', the mother and grandmother of the ruling nawab), he was rare among the British in India at that time in not being corrupt. His impeachment was heard before the House of Lords on 145 days spread over seven years (1788–95). He was acquitted on all charges.

Hatchard's (London W1) Bookshop which has been a feature of Piccadilly ever since John Hatchard (1769–1849) founded it in 1797. In its early years it was more like a club, a place where gentlemen would read the newspapers and browse among the latest publications. After Hatchard's death it was run by his son Thomas, but it has long ceased to be a family firm.

Hatfield House (10km/6m E of St Albans) The most imposing of Jacobean houses, built from 1608 for Robert *Cecil. There had previously been a Tudor palace here belonging to Elizabeth I (one wing survives, long used as stables but now with its great hall restored). In the first decade of the 17C the new king, James I, forced Hatfield on Cecil in exchange for the more impressive Theobalds, which Cecil had inherited from his father. At Hatfield he immediately began to build a new house, designed mainly by his head carpenter, Robert Lyminge (d. 1628); it survives unchanged today and is still lived in by his descendants. Its most famous features are the magnificent hall (paved in black and white marble), the elaborately carved oak staircase and the long gallery. In the gallery are many mementoes of the family's links with Elizabeth, and two portraits of the queen hang in the marble hall. The Cecils recovered a leading role in the country's political life when Lord *Salisbury became prime minister in the late 19C.

The gardens of Hatfield were planted in the early 17C by John *Tradescant, and in recent decades they have been restored to the style and the range of plants of that period. The sunken knot garden was created in the early 1980s.

Anne **Hathaway** (1556–1623) Wife of William *Shakespeare, whose name is widely remembered for two reasons: her family home survives (*Anne Hathaway's Cottage) and is much visited; and Shakespeare left her in his will his 'second best bed'. This bequest (his only mention of his wife in the document, written as an after-thought between the lines) has caused much amusement and scholarly speculation. But common law automatically secured for Anne the family house and a third of the estate. And it has been argued in Shakespeare's defence that the best bed may have been the one kept for guests, making this the marital bed.

Engravings from Harvey's treatise of 1628, revealing the flow of blood through the veins of the lower arm.

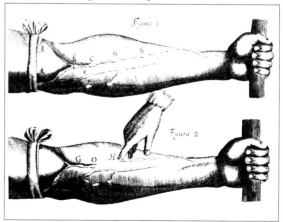

The harvest festival, usurped by the respectable in honour of God and Queen (VR for Victoria Regina): wood engraving, 1863.

Roy **Hattersley** (b. 1932) Labour politician, MP for the Sparkbrook division of Birmingham (since 1964) and deputy leader of the party (1983–92). He entered the cabinet in 1976 as secretary of state for prices and consumer protection (1976–9), and during the 1980s was shadow home secretary and shadow chancellor. He is also an author and journalist (selected by *What the Papers Say* in 1982 as columnist of the year).

hat trick Now used of any triple achievement, the phrase was first used in *cricket when a bowler took three wickets on three successive balls. This rare feat traditionally entitled him to a new hat at the expense of his club.

Have A Go see Wilfred *Pickles.

Michael **Havers** (1923–92, kt 1972, baron 1987) Conservative politician, MP for Wimbledon 1970–87. A barrister by profession, he was attorney general (1979–87) and was briefly lord chancellor in 1987.

Lord **Haw-Haw** Nickname of William Joyce (1906–46) given to him because of the plummy *Oxford accent in which he broadcast Nazi propaganda from Germany to the UK during World War II (he began each programme with 'Jairminny calling, Jairminny calling'). The name was coined in the first month of the war by Jonah Barrington, in the *Daily Express*, to describe another German propagandist (Joyce was not as yet on the air). But it was to Joyce that it soon stuck.

He was hanged by the British for treason, although he was an American citizen of Irish descent. He was judged to owe allegiance to Britain, an essential condition of treason, because he had lived in the country for much of his adult life (he formed the National Socialist League in London in the 1930s) and because he had an unexpired British passport, which he had obtained by illegally declaring himself a British subject.

Hawick Rugby union football club, formed in 1873 and recently by far the most successful in Scotland. By 1992 it had achieved ten victories in the Scottish club championship (the McEwans League, introduced in 1974), while its nearest rivals, Gala and Melrose, had only two each.

Hawker Siddeley The company which developed from Tommy *Sopwith's aviation enterprise and which in its time produced such classic military aircraft as the *Hurricane and the *Harrier. In 1991 it was taken over by *BTR.

Stephen **Hawking** (b. 1942) Theoretical physicist who has made major contributions to the study of the origin of the universe and of black holes; his calculations have supported the big-bang theory of how time and space began. In addition to his scientific achievements and his post as Lucasian professor of mathematics at Cambridge, his life has been remarkable in two other respects. He wrote a popular but by no means easy account of his subject (*A Brief History of Time* 1988), which became a runaway bestseller; and he has suffered, since his student days, from motor neuron disease, which for many years made it progressively harder for him to communicate. He relied on barely comprehensible sounds, and later on only the slightest of movements, until a computerized voice synthesizer restored to him the power of speech.

John **Hawkins** (1532–95, kt 1588) The first English slave trader, making three expeditions from Africa to the Caribbean in the 1560s. The last, in 1567–8, provoked the first of England's major naval confrontations with Spain. Of six ships in the expedition, the Spanish destroyed four; only those commanded by Hawkins and his younger kinsman, Francis *Drake, returned. From 1577 Hawkins was treasurer of the navy, and in that capacity greatly improved the fleet in time for the *Armada (in which campaign he commanded the *Victory*). He died two months before Drake, on an expedition which they had undertaken together to raid the Spanish West Indies.

Nicholas **Hawksmoor** (1661–1736) Baroque architect who had a hand in virtually every important English building in the decades around 1700 – first as *Wren's assistant (on Chelsea Hospital, Greenwich Hospital, St Paul's Cathedral) and then as *Vanbrugh's (Castle Howard, Blenheim Palace). Since Vanbrugh had no architectural training, Hawksmoor's contribution to his buildings must have been large. His own work includes half a dozen highly original churches in London (each of them an idiosyncratic blend of competing architectural influences), a superb mansion in Northamptonshire (Easton Neston, begun c.1702), the mausoleum at Castle Howard and the west towers of Westminster Abbey.

John **Hawkwood** (c.1320–94) English soldier of fortune who served Edward III in the early campaigns of the *Hundred Years' War and then was the leading mercenary (or condottiere) of his day in Italy. From 1378 to 1392 he commanded Florence's army, becoming a Florentine citizen in 1391. His image on horseback, painted in 1436 by Paolo Uccello, is one of the most striking features of the interior of the cathedral in Florence. Contemporary documents refer to him as a knight, but it is not known when or where he was knighted.

Haworth (14km/9m NW of Bradford) Village in West Yorkshire, on the edge of the moors, which was the home of the *Brontë family. Their parsonage, at the top of the steep cobbled Main Street, is kept as a museum and the surrounding landscape is that of Wuthering Heights. At the bottom of the hill, Haworth station is on the Keighley and Worth Valley railway, closed in 1961 and reopened by enthusiasts in 1968. Veteran steam locomotives are run on the 5-mile stretch from Keighley to Oxenhope, which was used for the film The Railway Children (1970).

Mike **Hawthorn** (1929–58) Racing driver who sprang to fame, driving a Ferrari, when he beat Fangio by a few feet to win the 1953 French Grand Prix. He remained one of the great man's chief rivals in subsequent years (Fangio won the world championship every year from 1954 to 1957) and succeeded him as champion in 1958 after Fangio's retirement. At the end of that year Hawthorn was killed in a road accident.

Nigel **Hawthorne** (b. 1929) Actor best known for his suavely manipulative role as Sir Humphrey in the *Yes, Minister TV series. In 1989–91 he played the lovesick C.S. Lewis in Shadowlands (West End and Broadway) and he had a great success at the National Theatre in 1991 as George III in Alan Bennett's The Madness of George III.

Haxey Hood A flexible leather cylinder, about two feet long, which is the centrepiece of a violent athletic contest each January 6 (the old twelfth night of *Christmas) between the neighbouring villages of Haxey and Westwoodside, on the border between Humberside and Lincolnshire. After due ceremonies by the Lord, his Fool and the 12 attendant Boggans (in effect the referees of the game), the Hood is carried to a hillside equidistant from the two villages and is thrown into the middle of the Sway, a scrummage of scores of violent young men. For several hours the Sway surges back and forth in the winter mud until the Hood has been delivered to a pub in one or other village. The victorious pub will serve free drink that evening and keep the Hood for the following year. Local tradition dates the game back to an incident in the 13c, when the Mowbray family were lords of the manor.

Joseph **Haydn** see *London Symphonies and *Nelson Mass.

Tubby **Hayes** (1935–73) The best-known jazz musician of his generation in Britain, on tenor sax and vibes. One of his early groups, in the mid-1950s, was the Jazz Couriers (with Ronnie *Scott). He died when undergoing heart surgery.

Hay Fever (1925) Comedy by Noel *Coward, making the most of the eccentricities of an artistic family. Judith Bliss is an actress and her husband David a novelist; they and their two eccentric children, Sorel and Simon, each invite a guest for the weekend. The comedy derives from the indignities suffered by four ordinary people in this inconsiderate bohemian setting; the Bliss family are so absorbed in their mutual bickering that they fail to notice the departure of their guests.

The Hay Wain (1821, National Gallery) The best-known of *Constable's paintings, typical of his subject matter and method. It shows the river Stour in Suffolk, seen from Flatford Mill with Willy Lot's cottage on the left. The unforced composition, with the hay cart and its draft horses blending unobtrusively into the colours of the river and woodland, is in keeping with the impression that this is an actual English summer day which has been observed and captured.

Hayward Gallery (London SE1) Designed by Greater London Council architects in the *South Bank arts complex, and opened in 1968 as London's main gallery for loan exhibitions of 19–20c art. Its concrete New Brutalist exterior is not universally loved by Londoners.

William **Hazlitt** (1778–1830) Literary critic and essayist, capable of treating a serious critical argument with the same informality of tone as he applied, for example, to 'The Fight', his famous account of a boxing match at Hungerford. Table Talk (1821), The Spirit of the Age (1825) and The Plain Speaker (1826) contain most of his best-known essays.

H-blocks see the *Maze.

Headingley (Leeds) The home of Leeds Rugby League Club and the county ground of *Yorkshire County Cricket Club. A sports ground was established here by the Leeds Cricket, Football and Athletic Company in 1890, and both rugby league and county cricket were played on it from the start. Headingley has been one of the locations most regularly used for Test matches (the first occasion was in 1899).

Denis **Healey** (b. 1917, baron 1992) Labour politician, MP for South East Leeds (1952–5) and Leeds East (1955–92) and deputy leader of the party 1980–3. He entered the cabinet in 1964 as secretary of state for defence (1964–70) and in the next Labour administration was chancellor of the exchequer (1974–9). Known as a tough political fighter (see *'savaged by a dead sheep'), he is also an author and keen photographer (Healey's Eye 1980).

Department of **Health** (London SW1) Formed in 1988 when the Department of Health and Social Security was split in two (they had been merged in 1968). The department's prime responsibility is the *National Health Service. For secretaries of state since 1983 see the *cabinet.

Seamus **Heaney** (b. 1939) Northern Irish poet, in whose work the rich continuity of rural Ireland (he grew up on a farm in County Derry) underlies the acute unease of present-day troubles (he is a Catholic). *Death of a Naturalist* (1966) first brought him wide attention; and *The Haw Lantern* (1987) is one of his most important recent collections. In *Sweeney Astray* (1984) he specifically bridged Ireland's centuries; it is his version of a medieval poem, *Buile Suibhne*, about a legendary mad king.

Heartbreak House (1920) Chekhovian comedy by George Bernard *Shaw. Written either before or during World War I, and first performed in New York in 1920, it uses the muddle-headed and for the most part appalling guests of an elderly eccentric, Captain Shotover, as an image of a community, by implication Britain, which has lost its sense of identity and purpose.

Heart of Darkness Story by *Conrad, written in 1899 and published with two others in *Youth* (1902). A disturbing and very personal insight into Africa and colonial exploitation, it is closely based on Conrad's own experiences during a journey up the Congo in 1890. The narrator, Marlow, describes how he penetrated deeper and deeper into the continent in search of a mysterious Mr Kurtz, the most successful agent of a company trading in ivory. He finds him, at the very heart of darkness, surrounded by human heads on stakes but enjoying an almost god-like status among the local tribe. Kurtz dies with a despairing cry ('The horror! The horror!'), but back in Europe Marlow feels constrained to tell Kurtz's girlfriend that her name was the last word he spoke.

Heart of Midlothian, known as Hearts or the Jam Tarts (Tynecastle Park, Edinburgh). Edinburgh's oldest surviving football club (1874). Club victories: Scottish FA Cup 1891, 96, 1901, 06, 56; Scottish League Champions 1895, 97, 1958, 60; Scottish League Cup 1955, 59, 60, 63.

The **Heart of Midlothian** (1818) Novel by Sir Walter *Scott, set in Edinburgh. The title is the popular name of the prison (the Old Tolbooth in *Parliament Square) in which the innocent Effie Deans awaits trial for murdering her child. She is pardoned after her half-sister, Jeanie, walks to London and pleads in person with Queen Caroline. The story centres on a historical event, the Porteous riot, which led to the storming of the prison in 1736.

Heart of Oak Patriotic song written by *Garrick for a pantomime (*Harlequin's Invasion* 1759). It celebrates 'this wonderful year', in which there had been several victories in the *Seven Years' War. The heart of oak is the wood the British ships are made of, and so by extension the quality of the British sailors ('Heart of oak are our ships,/Heart of oak are our men'). The tune is by William Boyce (1710–79).

Edward **Heath** (b. 1916, KG 1992) Conservative politician, MP for Bexley and Sidcup since 1950 and prime minister 1970–4. He entered the cabinet in 1960 as lord privy seal (with Foreign Office responsibility, since the foreign secretary, Lord Home, was in the Lords), and he was then briefly president of the Board of Trade (1963–4). In 1965 he followed Home as leader of the Conservative party (the first to be elected rather than mysteriously selected). A passionate European, he succeeded during his premiership in effecting Britain's entry to the *EC. In 1973 he coined a useful phrase which has become standard – 'the *unacceptable face of capitalism'.

The domestic economy was thrown into chaos in his last months of office by the *oil crisis and by a *miners' strike, which provoked him into calling the election of February 1974. The party lost the election, and a year later Heath was challenged and defeated for the leadership by

Margaret *Thatcher. As a pro-European and a consensus politician (the first of the *'wets'), he was an isolated figure during her years of power; but in the different atmosphere of the early 1990s it was he who seemed more in tune with the times. Having chosen to remain in the Commons, he had – after the 1992 election – the added satisfaction of being *Father of the House.

Ted **Heath** (1900–69) Trombonist and bandleader who established the Ted Heath Band in 1944, imitating the US big-band style of Glenn Miller. He wrote his own theme song *Listen to My Music* (1944), which was also the title of his 1957 autobiography. In London the band was a regular feature of the Hammersmith Palais de Danse. Their hit singles included *Hot Toddy* (1953) and *Swingin' Shepherd Blues* (1958).

Heathcliff see *Wuthering Heights.*

Heath Robinson (William Heath Robinson, 1872–1944) Cartoonist and illustrator who worked with great skill in several styles, but who particularly caught the public's fancy with his drawings of ludicrously elaborate machinery designed to achieve the most elementary of tasks. As a result any primitive and spindly device, relying on the equivalent of pieces of string, is described now as 'heath robinson'. His two brothers were also talented illustrators.

Heathrow (24km/15m W of London) The capital city's main airport and the world's busiest for international flights – with some 43 million passengers a year in the early 1990s, about 80% of them on non-domestic routes.

Working overtime for Christmas in the half-crown department of the Mint: a typically Heath Robinson industrial process (1925).

It is situated on Hounslow Heath, first used as an aerodrome by the Royal Flying Corps in World War I. Their primitive strip became London's civilian international airport in 1919, but it lost that role to Croydon in the early 1920s. It was not until 1944 that Heathrow was selected, from several other candidates around the city, as the site for London's postwar airport.

Its first flight took off on New Year's Day 1946, carrying ten passengers and a crew of six to Portugal. Its subsequent growth, intimately connected with the stories of *BOAC and BEA, required three terminals by 1961 and a fourth in 1986. In the mid-1990s there are controversial plans for a fifth. Terminal 5, if built, will increase Heathrow's annual capacity to 70 million passengers and 400,000 aircraft movements.

Oliver **Heaviside** (1850–1925) Self-taught English physicist whose only gainful employment was 14 years as a telegrapher. His speculations on electricity were of importance in several fields, but he is best remembered for having postulated the existence of the ionosphere to explain the working of long-distance radio telegraphy. It was known at first as the Heaviside layer (or the Kennelly-Heaviside layer, having been independently proposed by A.E. Kennelly in the USA). Its existence was first demonstrated in 1924 by *Appleton.

Hebrides Islands off the west coast of Scotland. *Skye is the most northerly and the largest island of the Inner Hebrides, the group closer to the coast; *Lewis with Harris is similarly the largest and most northerly island in the Outer Hebrides. The missionaries of St *Columba reached the islands in the 6C; from the 8C *Viking raiders dominated the area, eventually establishing an independent kingdom which ended in the 13C (after the Battle of *Largs). The title Lord of the Isles was then created for the feudal lord of the area; it was forfeited to the Scottish crown in 1493 and is now held by the eldest son of the sovereign.

Johnson and *Boswell were famous tourists to the Hebrides, and the islands inspired the overture by Mendelssohn now linked more specifically with *Fingal's Cave.

William **Hedley** see *Puffing Billy.

Cardinal **Heenan** (John Heenan, 1905–75) Archbishop of Westminster from 1963 until his death, after being bishop of Leeds (1951–7) and archbishop of Liverpool (1957–63). It was during his years in Liverpool that work began on the new cathedral of Christ the King. He was made a cardinal in 1965, by which time he was spending much of his time in Rome as a prominent member of the second Vatican Council. His main task during the rest of his life was putting into practice in Britain the council's many reforming decrees.

Heights of Abraham see General *Wolfe.

Hellfire Club Deliberately outrageous fraternity of the mid-18C which met from time to time among the ruins of Medmenham Abbey, a 13C Cistercian monastery near Marlow in Buckinghamshire. The 'Medmenham monks' were believed to indulge in Rabelaisian orgies; certainly they parodied Roman Catholic ritual. John *Wilkes, a guest, alarmed the company during one such mock service by releasing a baboon, which was briefly mistaken by some of the participants for the devil in person.

Hello! British version of the Spanish magazine ¡Hola!, which was launched in the UK in 1988 and rapidly acquired a large circulation by providing undiluted good news about famous people.

Robert **Helpmann** (1909–86, kt 1968) Australian-born dancer, choreographer and actor who joined the Vic-Wells Ballet at Sadler's Wells in 1933 and remained with the company until 1950. During that time he was a frequent partner of Margot Fonteyn, as well as choreographing several ballets in which he danced the leading male role, including *Hamlet* (1942) and *Miracle in the Gorbals* (1944); he also choreographed the ballet extracts in the film *The Red Shoes* (1948). During the 1950s he concentrated on acting, playing many of the leading Shakespearean roles at Stratford and at the Old Vic in London. In 1965 he returned to Australia to become director of the Australian Ballet.

Help the Aged (London EC1) Charity providing aid and support internationally to the old, particularly in relation to problems of poverty and isolation. As the Help the Aged Refugees Appeal, it was set up in 1961 by Cecil Jackson-Cole (1901–79), a businessman who had also been a leading member of the group launching *Oxfam in 1942.

Helston (21km/13m E of Penzance) Town in Cornwall, known in particular for its Furry Dance (a name often said to be a version of 'floral' but more probably linked to an annual 'fair'). The event is held on May 8, or the previous day if that is a Sunday, and the festivities include four separate processional dances in which couples move through the streets and in and out of houses. For the main dance, at noon, the gentlemen wear *morning dress and the ladies long formal dresses and hats. The Furry Dance is recorded from the early 17C and is probably much older.

Helvellyn see *Lake District.

Mrs **Hemans** (Felicia Dorothea Browne, 1793–1835, m. Alfred Hemans 1812) Poet remembered in particular for her lines on the *stately homes of England, and for the boy who stood on the burning deck at the Battle of the *Nile.

David **Hemery** (b. 1944) Athlete who set a world record when he won gold in the 400 metres hurdles at the 1968 Olympic Games; his time of 48.1 seconds was unbeaten for another four years and lasted as the British record until 1990. In the 1972 Olympics he won bronze in the same event and silver in the 4x400 metres relay. He also won the individual event at the Commonwealth Games in 1966 and 1970.

Stephen **Hendry** (b. 1969) Scottish snooker player who in the early 1990s edged Steve *Davis out of the top place in world rankings. After winning the Scottish amateur championship at the age of 15, he continued with a succession of 'youngest' records – including the youngest winner of a ranking professional tournament (Rothmans Grand Prix) in 1987. He won the Embassy World Professional Championship in 1990 and again in 1992; on the latter occasion he was trailing Jimmy White 8–14 but went on to take the next ten frames for the match.

Hengist and Horsa (5th century AD) Two semi-legendary brothers, supposedly leaders of the first *Anglo-Saxons in Britain. They make a tentative first appearance in the work of *Bede ('the first chieftains are said to have been the brothers Hengist and Horsa'), but the later *Anglo-Saxon Chronicle* states that they landed in 455 in Kent, that Horsa was killed in that year, that Hengist died in 488 and that his descendants became the kings of Kent. Hengist was the word for a stallion; so even if he existed, it seems unlikely that the short-lived 'horsa' was anything more than his verbal double.

Henley (Henley-on-Thames, 11,000 in 1981) Town in Oxfordshire, famous as the location for rowing races – for which it is particularly well suited, having a straight stretch of the Thames 2.1km/1.3m long. For this reason it was chosen for the first university *Boat Race in 1829. The Henley Royal Regatta, held in early July, was founded in 1839; the most prestigious among the dozen or so trophies are the Grand Challenge Cup for eights (also the oldest, raced for since the first year) and the Diamond Sculls (first competed for in 1844). The oldest rowing club, *Leander, has its headquarters here. The bridge over the Thames, the natural grandstand for the early regattas, is an elegant 5-arch structure dating from 1786.

'He nothing common did or mean' see Andrew *Marvell.

Lenny **Henry** (b. 1958) Britain's leading black comedian, whose characters include Delbert Wilkins (a Brixton wideboy), Theophilis P. Wildebeest (described as a one-man sex machine) and Grandpa Deakus (with a taste for Guinness). He first made his name in the late 1970s on children's television (in *Tiswas*), and became popular with adults through *Three of a Kind* (1981–3) and subsequently in his own *Lenny Henry Show*.

William **Henry** (1774–1836) Chemist remembered in particular for the law named after him, stating that the amount of gas absorbed by a liquid is proportional to the pressure of the gas on the liquid.

Henry I (1068–1135) King of England from 1100, duke of Normandy from 1106; third surviving son of William the Conqueror and Matilda of Flanders; married Matilda, daughter of Malcolm III of Scotland (1100).

After the death on the hunting field of his brother *William II (in which he was probably implicated), Henry immediately rode to Winchester, seized the royal treasure, and within three days had been crowned in Westminster Abbey, thus pre-empting the better claim of his eldest brother Robert Curthose, duke of Normandy (c.1054–1134). The following year Robert unsuccessfully invaded England. In 1106 Henry in turn invaded and conquered Normandy. Robert spent the rest of his long life the prisoner of his younger brother; and the English crown acquired the first of those territories in France which caused friction until after the *Hundred Years War.

Henry continued the severe rule of his father and brother, but with better administration and greater justice. A charter of liberties issued at the time of his coronation can be seen as a precursor of Magna Carta; and his judges, sent out to try cases in the provinces, were the basis of the slightly later system of judges on circuit. Henry's determination to appoint his own men as bishops led to a clash with *Anselm and with Rome; but a compromise agreed in 1107 left the king with considerable power in the matter. His nickname of Beauclerk, meaning 'good scholar', was not given to him until the 14C, but it reflected the fact that he was more literate than his predecessors.

The disaster of the *White Ship left the king without a male heir. Though he persuaded the barons in 1127 to accept his daughter *Matilda as his successor, she did not inherit his crown. But his grandson later did, as Henry II (see the *royal house).

Henry II (1133–89) King of England from 1154, duke of Normandy from 1150; founder of the house of *Plantagenet, son of Geoffrey Plantagenet and Matilda; married *Eleanor of Aquitaine (1152).

His grandfather, Henry I, had intended Henry's mother, *Matilda, to inherit the throne of England but it was

seized in 1135 by *Stephen. Henry invaded in 1153 to assert his rights. By then he had huge possessions in France: not only the dukedom of Normandy, but Anjou (inherited from his father) and Aquitaine (the territory of his wife). His strength caused Stephen to make a treaty, at Westminster in 1153, acknowledging Henry as his heir in place of his own son. Stephen died the following year.

The new king, still only 21, rapidly reasserted royal authority over the barons after a period of anarchy. His attempts to do the same over the church were for a while frustrated, to Henry's surprise and fury, by his friend Thomas *Becket. The main territorial expansion of royal power in his reign was into *Ireland, where English dominance was for the first time clearly established. But it was in the administration of justice that he left his most lasting mark; his reinforcement of his grandfather's system of itinerant judges (on circuit), his establishment of a permanent court at Westminster to deal with a wide range of cases (the Court of Common Pleas), and important developments in the *jury system have all contributed to his reign being seen as the effective beginning of *common law.

Henry's determination to safeguard the rightful succession (denied to him) prompted the unorthodox device of having his son, also Henry, crowned in his own lifetime (in 1170) as the Young King. But this son died before him, in 1183. After the murder of Becket, Henry survived a rebellion by his younger sons in league with their mother and the kings of both Scotland and France. He was succeeded by his eldest surviving son as Richard I (see the *royal house).

Henry III (1207–72) King of England from 1216; son of King *John and Isabella of Angoulême; married Eleanor of Provence (1236).

At the age of nine he inherited from his father a kingdom in chaos, which was only gradually recovered for him by a council of regency with papal support; and in his later years his extravagance and lack of judgement alienated his barons to such an extent that they for a while took power. It was therefore only in the middle section of his long reign that he effectively ruled. The barons forced his acceptance in 1258 of the Provisions of Oxford, by which he and a council of 15 barons were to share power. It was his subsequent denial of this agreement which provoked the uprising led by Simon de *Montfort, who captured Henry at Lewes in 1264. De Montfort was defeated in the following year by Henry's son, Edward. It was to him that the king left the control of the country in his final years, and it was he who succeeded as Edward I (see the *royal house).

Henry IV (1366–1413) King of England from 1399, taking the crown from Richard II; son of John of Gaunt and Blanche of Lancaster; known as Bolingbroke from the Lincolnshire castle in which he was born; married Mary de Bohun (c.1380) and Joan of Navarre (1403).

During Henry's early years his father, *John of Gaunt, was the most powerful man in the country, protecting his inadequate nephew *Richard II from his many opponents. Foremost among these opponents was Henry, a year older than the young king (his cousin) and far more a man of action. In 1398 Richard banished him. The following year, on John of Gaunt's death, Richard also confiscated Henry's Lancastrian possessions, an unwise act which provoked Henry to invade England. The king had few remaining supporters, and in August 1399 he surrendered at Conway. In September parliament declared Richard deposed and Henry king, signalling the start of the house of *Lancaster.

Henry's rule was threatened by a succession of rebellions, continuing the unrest of Richard's reign but with the added ingredient that the new king was a usurper. The two most significant uprisings were those of the Percy family in Northumberland (one of whom was the Hotspur of *Henry IV) and of Owen *Glendower in Wales. Meanwhile *parliament exacted a price for having handed the king his crown. Henry accepted the concept of governing through parliament, and the important principle was established in 1407 that revenue was the responsibility of the House of Commons. Henry suffered during the last years of his life from a serious disease, described by his contemporaries as leprosy. He died in the Jerusalem chamber of Westminster Abbey and was succeeded by his son Henry V (see the *royal house).

Henry IV, *Parts 1 and 2* (c.1597-8) Two self-contained history plays by *Shakespeare which together add up to a rich panorama of English life. The historical thread is provided by the plots and uprisings against the usurping *Henry IV. These include an uneasy alliance between Owen *Glendower and Henry Percy, son of the earl of Northumberland. Known as Hotspur, and by nature hotheaded, Percy is a man of action. He is contrasted with the king's son, Prince Hal (the future *Henry V), who drinks and jests in the company of one of Shakespeare's greatest creations, the self-indulgent but witty Sir John Falstaff. Their favourite London tavern is the Boar's Head, where Mistress Quickly is the hostess. Falstaff's disreputable companions include the ignorant Bardolph, famous for his flaming red nose, and the bombastic exsoldier Pistol.

In Part 1 the rebellion of Hotspur is brought to an end when Hal, redeeming himself, kills him in single combat on the field of battle. (Falstaff, coming across the dead body, immediately claims the deed as his own.) Hal reverts to his earlier ways in Part 2, where Falstaff's recruiting campaign in the Cotswolds brings in a new rural dimension and introduces the doddery Justice Shallow, one of Falstaff's cronies from college days. When news comes of Henry IV's death, Falstaff hurries to London and waits with Shallow outside the coronation to receive honours and wealth from his boon companion, the new king. Henry V's opening words to him are some of the most chilling in drama: 'I know thee not, old man; fall to thy prayers'. But Falstaff had other friends. Public demand (and, it was said, a private request from Elizabeth I) gave him a new lease of life in The *Merry Wives of Windsor.

Henry V (1387-1422) King of England from 1413; eldest son of Henry IV and Mary de Bohun; married Catherine of France (1420). More than any other English monarch he has come to symbolize the patriot and warrior, thanks to Shakespeare's play *Henry V. His reign was largely devoted to capturing territory in northern France, during the *Hundred Years' War. His first autumn of campaigning in 1415 brought the victory of *Agincourt, and by 1420 he was able to force the French to accept him, in the treaty of Troyes, as bridegroom to the king's daughter, Catherine, and as heir to the French throne. Henry's death just two years later, from fever in his camp, left his ambitious plans in ruins and an 8-month-old baby, *Henry VI, on the throne of England (see the *royal house).

Henry V (1599) Historical drama by *Shakespeare, a patriotic celebration of the campaigns of Henry V in 1415-20. The early part of the play sets out to establish good reasons for invading France; French provocation is established dramatically when a gift of tennis balls arrives from the dauphin for the young English king. At the heart of the drama are the two great victories of 1415, the siege of Harfleur (the occasion for 'Once more unto the breach, dear friends, once more') and the Battle of

*Agincourt. The later scenes prepare for Henry's marriage to the French princess. Comic relief is provided by national rivalries within Henry's army, as when the Welsh captain Fluellen makes the English braggart Pistol eat the leek that he has mocked. The play was superbly filmed at a time of national crisis (1944) with Laurence Olivier in the title role, and again in 1989 with Kenneth Branagh.

Henry VI (1421-71) King of England 1422-61 and 1470-1, the last ruler of the house of *Lancaster; son of Henry V and Catherine of France; married Margaret of Anjou (1445).

The successes in France of his father, *Henry V, meant that he inherited the thrones of France and England, both of them before his first birthday. He was crowned at Westminster in 1429 and in Paris in 1431. The latter was a hollow gesture because the tide had turned against England in the *Hundred Years' War. In a similar way the *Wars of the Roses, largely provoked by Henry's inadequacies as a ruler, ended his power at home. The wars began with a defeat of the royal army by the Yorkists at the battle of St Albans in 1455. At the second battle of St Albans, in 1461, Henry himself was captured. His Yorkist rival was proclaimed king as *Edward IV (see the *royal house). Henry fled to Scotland, but in 1465 was captured and imprisoned in the Tower of London. He was restored to the throne by *Warwick the Kingmaker for a brief period from October 1470, until Edward IV defeated Warwick at Barnet, entered London and returned Henry to the Tower, where he was murdered on 21 May 1471. Meanwhile his legitimate heir, Prince Edward (1453-71), had been killed on May 4 in the Battle of Tewkesbury. Henry's most lasting achievements were his foundations at *Eton and King's College, *Cambridge.

Henry VI, *Parts 1, 2 and 3* (c.1590-92) Three history plays by *Shakespeare covering the period of the *Wars of the Roses. With *Titus Andronicus they represent his earliest work, and there has been much debate as to whether they are wholly or only partly by Shakespeare.

Henry VII (1457-1509) King of England from 1485; son of Edmund Tudor, earl of Richmond, and of Margaret Beaufort; married Elizabeth of York (1486).

Born Henry Tudor, three months after his father's death, he had no more than a tenuous claim on the English throne (see the house of *Tudor and the *royal house). But the deaths in 1471 of *Henry VI and his son meant that Henry was the only male claimant on the Lancastrian side. His uncle, the earl of Pembroke, took him in that year to Brittany for safety. Henry's opportunity came when the Yorkist camp was split by the illegal accession of *Richard III. He invaded in 1485, defeating and killing Richard III at the Battle of Bosworth Field. He was immediately crowned, and his marriage the following year to the daughter of the first Yorkist king, Edward IV, was intended to demonstrate that the rift between the rival houses was now healed and the *Wars of the Roses over. The choice of Arthur as the name for their first son (1486-1502) harked back to the legendary beginnings of the English royal line.

But after so much turmoil, ambitious rivals were not to be deterred by symbolism. Henry's rule was disturbed by uprisings and invasions, including those fronted by the pretenders Lambert *Simnel and Perkin *Warbeck. Henry defeated these and other threats, while building up a stable kingdom. His strong control over finance amassed considerable wealth for the realm, and his skill in foreign alliances gave international protection. Among his children, Mary was betrothed to the future emperor Charles V; Margaret became the wife of the Scottish king, James IV;

and Arthur married the Spanish princess Catherine of Aragon in 1501 (but died the following year). Henry's surviving son succeeded to the throne in 1509 as Henry VIII without opposition (see the *royal house).

Henry VIII (1491–1547) King of England from 1509; son of Henry VII and Elizabeth of York; married Catherine of Aragon (1509), Anne Boleyn (1533), Jane Seymour (1536), Anne of Cleves (1540), Catherine Howard (1540) and Catherine Parr (1543).

Henry became the heir apparent at the age of 11, in 1502, when his elder brother Arthur died. Arthur's 17-year-old widow, *Catherine of Aragon, was too valuable a potential queen to lose in the chess game of international diplomacy (she was daughter of the king of Spain), so she was soon betrothed to her dead husband's brother. He married her on his accession to the throne, when he was 18. Her failure to provide him with a male heir (in spite of the birth of three infant sons) was to have a profound influence on events.

For most of Henry's reign the balance of power in Europe was between Francis I (the king of France) and Charles V (the Holy Roman Emperor, ruling Austria, Spain and much of the Netherlands and Italy). Henry's political power was as the third force, alliance with whom could tip the balance. He played this card most notably in 1520, feasting with Francis at the *Field of Cloth of Gold and then deliberating with Charles more discreetly in Kent.

The rival spheres of influence also affected Henry's divorce from Catherine, which he had determined upon in the hope of a male heir. That she had been the widow of his brother gave possible theological grounds for annulling the marriage. Unfortunately annulment depended on the pope; and the pope was reluctant to offend Charles V, who was Catherine's nephew and would not welcome his aunt being divorced in order to keep his cousin (Catherine's daughter, the future Mary I) off the English throne. But if the pope was unhelpful, could Henry not become head of the church of England and through the archbishop of Canterbury grant his own divorce? In the turmoil of the *Reformation anything seemed possible (it was now some 15 years since Luther had made public at Wittenberg his 95 Theses).

The drift of events was political rather than religious (Henry had in 1521 written a pamphlet against Luther, earning from the pope the title of Defender of the Faith), and the developing scenario brought profound political consequences. One was a change in the chief ministers to the crown, who had always been clerics and now became laymen (*Wolsey being followed by Thomas *More and Thomas *Cromwell). Another was the *dissolution of the monasteries, bringing huge wealth into the royal coffers and contributing to the strong centralization of power which was an essential feature of Tudor rule.

The political impetus in turn shaped much of England's religious development. The Act of *Supremacy of 1534 gave the country the anomaly, still surviving today, of a monarch who is head of a church (it also gave the Catholics two notable martyrs in Thomas More and John *Fisher, who refused to swear acceptance of this act). The early example of *Cranmer, Henry's wise but compromising archbishop, set the future tone for the *Church of England.

Henry married *Anne Boleyn in 1533. Her first child was a girl (the future Elizabeth I) and this disappointment was followed by a miscarriage. His next wife, *Jane Seymour, died after giving birth to the longed-for male heir, the future Edward VI. Marriage to the 'Flanders mare', *Anne of Cleves, was a diplomatic alliance which foundered on aesthetics, followed by an unconsidered reflex in the immediate embrace of *Catherine Howard.

One of the best of Holbein's characteristically chunky and brutal images of Henry VIII, c.1536.

Only *Catherine Parr seems to have been chosen for the comforts of matrimony, which lasted until Henry's death (making her the survivor in the mnemonic which begins *'divorced beheaded died').

With a constant stream of high officials, petty felons, bystanders, wives and relations going to the block or gallows (see Cardinal *Pole for an example), Henry's reign was undeniably one of terror. But he left England strong and united after the previous century, that of the *Wars of the Roses. And his passionate interest in the navy, as witnessed by the *Great Harry or the *Mary Rose, later stood the country in good stead against the Armada. It was religious differences, often inflamed by foreign interests, which remained the underlying problem – to be fought over and resolved in the successive reigns of his three children (see the *royal house).

The resolutely four-square image by which the king is known to posterity is the work of *Holbein.

Henry VIII (1613) One of Shakespeare's last works, if not the last. It was included in the *First Folio, but its uneven quality has caused some to see it as a collaboration, perhaps with John Fletcher (see *Beaumont and Fletcher). A performance of the play was the indirect cause of the destruction of the *Globe. The plot deals with the fall of Wolsey, the king's divorce and the advancement of Anne Boleyn.

Henry Smith's Kensington Estate Charity (London SW7) One of Britain's largest charitable foundations thanks to a far-sighted investment in the 1620s. The charity was established by a philanthropic London salter (who listed among his purposes the freeing of 'poor captives, being slaves under the Turkish pirates'). His trustees bought a farm in Kensington, now one of the most fashionable districts of London. The charity specializes in health and social welfare.

Hen Wlad fy Nhadau see *Land of my Fathers*.

Audrey **Hepburn** (1929–93) Actress born in Belgium of a British father and Dutch mother. A tentative beginning in *revue and musical comedy on the West End stage was transformed into a major international career by the title role in *Gigi* on Broadway (1951) and by the film *Roman Holiday* (1953). She devoted the last years of her life to working for the United Nations children's relief organization, UNICEF.

George **Hepplewhite** (d. 1786) Although now one of the best-known names among English cabinet-makers, not a single piece of furniture by Hepplewhite has been identified. He became famous two years after his death, when his widow published nearly 300 of the firm's working drawings under the title *The Cabinet-Maker and Upholsterer's Guide*. The designs adapt to more simple everyday purposes the *neoclassical style introduced by Robert Adam. The Hepplewhite patterns (it is not known if they were actually by him) were intended to 'unite elegance with utility, and blend the useful with the agreeable'. As such they were widely copied by cabinet-makers all over the country.

Heptarchy see *Anglo-Saxon kingdoms.

Barbara **Hepworth** (1903–75, DBE 1965) Sculptor of abstract forms, usually curving and sensual, who with Henry *Moore and the painter Ben *Nicholson (her husband at the time) formed in the 1930s the leading group of young British artists with an interest in abstraction. She went fully in this direction while Moore retained a strong figurative element. From 1939 she lived at *St Ives; her studio (where she died in a fire) and her garden are now a museum.

The Herald Glasgow's daily newspaper, one of the oldest in Britain (only the *Belfast News Letter* and the *Press and Journal* have earlier origins). It was founded in 1783 as the *Glasgow Advertiser*; in 1802 the name was changed to *The Glasgow Herald*, which it remained until 1992. Glasgow was then dropped from the title because of an ambiguity in the previous masthead statement, 'The Glasgow Herald – Scotland's Newspaper'. The *Herald's* great rival in this broader claim is the Edinburgh-based *Scotsman*.

Herald of Free Enterprise Townsend Thoresen car ferry which capsized on 6 March 1987 just outside the Belgian port of Zeebrugge as it sailed for Dover. It settled on its side on the sea bed, half out of the water; the death toll was 189, with four more reported missing. The ferry was of the roll-on roll-off type and had sailed without its car doors being closed. In 1990 seven employees of the company were put on trial for manslaughter, but during the case the charges were dropped and the jury was instructed to find them not guilty.

heralds see *College of Arms.

herbaceous border Long flower bed, usually with a background of a wall or hedge, planted with flowers which die down in the winter and which are carefully grouped for displays of colour. Such borders have been favourites in England since the 19C, particularly in country houses

and university colleges. As early as 1822 John *Loudon devoted a chapter of one of his books to 'herbaceous border-flowers'.

A.P. **Herbert** (Alan Patrick Herbert, 1890–1971, kt 1945) Author, wit and crusader. He first reached a wide public as a regular contributor to *Punch*, where his 'Misleading Cases' (published as a book in 1927) ridiculed certain aspects of court procedure. His crusading zeal was seen in his years as an MP for Oxford university (1935–50), particularly in his successful campaign for reform of the *divorce laws. He lived on the bank of the Thames at Hammersmith, and river life was another of his abiding interests – as seen in his most successful novel, *The Water Gipsies* (1930).

George **Herbert** (1593–1633) One of the leading *metaphysical poets. An aristocrat by birth, with many opportunities for worldly advancement, and a conscientious parish priest by choice, he wrote only devotional poems. A mood of simple piety transcends the subtle torments of spiritual conflict, a combination which brought Herbert many admirers in his own century and again in ours. His poems circulated only in manuscript during his life and were published after his death in a single volume, *The Temple* (1633).

Hereford (51,000 in 1991) City on the river Wye in Hereford and Worcester, until 1974 the administrative centre of Herefordshire. It was founded by Anglo-Saxons in the 7C as an outpost on the border with Celtic Wales, and it became at that time a diocese. The cathedral, of which the earliest parts are 12C, contains some striking Romanesque details. The *Mappa Mundi* has traditionally hung in the north aisle of the choir (it is now exhibited in the crypt). The cathedral's other famous treasure is up a flight of stairs from the north transept – the Chained Library, the largest of its kind in the country with some 1500 chained books (the earliest from about 800). The cathedral school, still in existence, was founded in 1384. The city's main street, High Town, contains the Old House, a distinguished building of the early 17C. Hereford boasts a *Nelson Column which was put up decades before the one in London. The Art Gallery, in a Gothic building of the early 20C, has a good collection of English watercolours.

Hereford Breed developed by local farmers in the 18C from the indigenous cattle of the Herefordshire region, with an emphasis on good beef production. Herefords were imported to the USA in the early 19C and are now widespread throughout the world. The breed had its own herdbook from 1846. Of various colours listed at that time, only the characteristic red with a white face survives today.

Hereford and Worcester (686,000 in 1991, administrative centre Worcester) *County in west central England bordering on Wales, formed in 1974 from the merging of Herefordshire and Worcestershire.

Herefordshire Former *county in west central England on the border with Wales, merged in 1974 with Worcestershire to form Hereford and Worcester.

Hereward the Wake (11C) Anglo-Saxon rebel hero who attempted an uprising in 1070 against *William the Conqueror. He made his headquarters on the Isle of *Ely, which became a famous place of refuge until recaptured by William. Hereward was believed to have escaped, and to have lived on with a royal pardon. Legend later provided him with a wide range of daring exploits against the Normans. The name 'the Wake', which is believed to have meant 'the watchful one', was a later addition.

Her Majesty's Stationery Office see *HMSO.

Herman's Hermits Pop group formed in Manchester in 1963 with Peter Noone (b. 1947, vocals), Derek Leckenby and Keith Hopwood (both b. 1946, guitars), Karl Green (b. 1947, bass) and Barry Whitwam (b. 1946, drums). Their main successes were cheerful old-fashioned songs. *I'm into Something Good* (1964) was a no. 1 single in the UK, but the Hermits' two best-known numbers, both reaching the top of the charts in 1965 in the USA, were not released as singles in Britain (*Mrs Brown, You've Got a Lovely Daughter* and Harry *Champion's music-hall song *I'm Henery the Eighth I am*). The group moved to the USA in the early 1970s.

Hermitage Castle (48km/30m NE of Carlisle) Ruggedly four-square tower house in the Borders region of Scotland. Begun in the 14C, it became the stronghold of Bothwell (lover and later husband of *Mary Queen of Scots), but was a ruin by the 18C. With its exterior walls now well restored, it is a powerful sight in its rolling Cheviot countryside. Brother William, a monk from Kelso Abbey, established the nearby hermitage in the 12C and so gave the area its name.

Herne the Hunter see *The *Merry Wives of Windsor*.

Herod see *thoroughbred.

Robert **Herrick** (1591–1674) Master of the lyric poem in miniature, as in his widely known *Cherry ripe* and *Gather ye rose-buds*. As a young man he was pleasure-loving and worldly-wise, but he spent his life from the age of 38 as the bachelor vicar of a quiet Devon parish (except for the Commonwealth years, when he was deprived of his office because of his royalist sympathies). Some 1200 of his poems, in an exceptionally wide range of forms but nearly all short, were published in 1648 under the title *Hesperides*.

James **Herriot** see **All Creatures Great and Small*.

Herschel Distinguished family of astronomers. William Herschel (1738–1822, kt 1816) was born in Hanover and came to England in 1757 as a professional musician. His private interest lay in constructing ever larger telescopes with which to view the heavens. With one of these he observed in 1781 the first new planet to be added to the five known since classical times; he called it *Georgium sidus* (the Georgian star) in honour of the king, but it became known as Uranus. His subsequent discoveries included the existence of double stars revolving round each other, the broad dimensions of the Milky Way, and the movement of the solar system through space.

His son, John Herschel (1792–1871, kt 1831), spent 1834–8 at the Cape of Good Hope cataloguing the nebulae, star clusters and double stars of the southern hemisphere as his father had done for the north. He was also a brilliant chemist and an important pioneer of photography. The earliest surviving glass negative is his; it was he who introduced hypo (hyposulphite) to fix the image; and he coined the terms 'negative' and 'positive'.

Herstmonceux see *Royal Observatory.

Hertford (21,000 in 1981) County town and administrative centre of Hertfordshire, on the river Lea. A settlement from before Roman times, with the remains of a Norman castle, Hertford is now a pleasant country town

Engraving of the largest of Herschel's great instruments, the 40-foot reflecting telescope erected at Slough in 1789.

with buildings of the 17–18C which include the Shire Hall of 1767–9 by James Adam.

Hertfordshire (990,000 in 1991, administrative centre Hertford) *County in southern England lying immediately to the north of Greater London.

Michael **Heseltine** (b. 1933) Conservative politician, MP for Henley since 1974 (previously for Tavistock 1966–74). He entered the *cabinet in 1979 as secretary of state for the environment (1979–83) and was defence secretary from 1983; as such he resigned in 1986 (literally walking out of a cabinet meeting) over *Westland. As a back-bencher during the following years he was Mrs Thatcher's most prominent opponent within the party, and in November 1990 he challenged her for the leadership – the day after Geoffrey *Howe had made a powerful speech criticizing her in the House of Commons. Two weeks later, in the second ballot of the resulting leadership election, Heseltine came second to John *Major.

Heseltine accepted the post of secretary of state for the environment in Major's cabinet, and in 1992 moved to trade and industry (a post in which he revived the title of president of the Board of Trade and rapidly became entangled in a government crisis over *coal). He combines a certain impetuosity (the Westland affair, and the *mace) with an appetite for painstaking political graft – a powerful combination, though many at the grass roots of the Tory party are reluctant to forgive his central role in Margaret Thatcher's downfall. His popular nicknames have fallen within a limited heroic range – Tarzan and Hezza (an echo of Gazza for Paul Gascoigne).

Myra **Hess** (1890–1965, DBE 1941) Pianist who made her London debut at the age of 17 playing Beethoven's fourth concerto, with Beecham as conductor. She organized the famous lunchtime concerts at the National Gallery during World War II, and was herself one of the regular performers. Her piano transcription of a Bach chorale, *Jesu, joy of man's desiring*, became immensely popular.

Heveningham Hall (37km/23m NE of Ipswich) House built 1778–84 with a *Palladian exterior by Robert Taylor (1714–88) and with interiors by James *Wyatt in his own version of the *Adam style. The most famous room is the

The romance of the Highlands: a scene near the west coast of Scotland, in Glencoe.

hall, with its barrel ceiling interrupted by fan-faulted alcoves; the pattern is echoed below in the marble floor. The park was laid out in 1780 by Capability *Brown.

Hever Castle (16km/10m NW of Tunbridge Wells) Rectangular stone castle in a moat, its exterior walls dating from the 13C. It was at Hever that Henry VIII courted *Anne Boleyn. The interiors which saw the beginnings of that ill-fated romance were dilapidated when the castle was bought in 1903 by the American millionaire William Waldorf Astor. He restored it, added the 'Tudor village' to house his guests and created the lake and gardens.

'He would, wouldn't he?' see *Profumo affair.

Hexham (35km/22m W of Newcastle-upon-Tyne) Town in Northumberland noted in particular for its priory church. The crypt survives from the 7C Saxon church of St Wilfrid, but the outstanding features are the Early English choir and extensive transepts from the priory of Augustinian canons founded in 1113. In the south transept is the famous Night Stair, a broad flight of steps leading to the dormitory above, used by monks attending night-time services.

Georgette **Heyer** (1902–74) Historical novelist, whose books are set in many different periods but who made the *Regency her particular territory. The language is a pastiche of Jane Austen and the plots, with love finally surmounting every obstacle, may have elements of *Mills and Boon, but the period details have considerable authenticity.

Heysel Stadium disaster The most appalling single incident of British *soccer hooliganism. The Heysel Stadium in Brussels was the location on 29 May 1985 for the European Cup Final between Liverpool and the Italian club Juventus, from Turin. A drunken charge by

Liverpool fans caused a crush of fleeing spectators and the collapse of a wall and fence; 38 people died and 454 were injured; 14 British fans were subsequently found guilty in the Belgian courts of manslaughter. The incident caused English clubs to be banned from playing in Europe, a ban not lifted until the 1990–1 season.

Hibernian, known as Hibs or the Hibees (Easter Road, Edinburgh). Football club formed in 1875 by Irishmen in Edinburgh, which in 1991 was rescued from bankruptcy and in the following season won its first major trophy for nearly two decades – the Scottish League Cup. Club victories: Scottish FA Cup 1887, 1902; Scottish League Champions 1903, 48, 51, 52; Scottish League Cup 1973, 92.

Hickstead (All England Jumping Course) Location of many of Britain's main showjumping events, including the annual Hickstead Derby and the Nations Cup (for national teams). Douglas Bunn (b. 1928) was a member of the British showjumping team when he bought Hickstead Place in Sussex and set about turning an open field into an arena suitable for international competition. He organized the first Hickstead meeting in 1960, and the first Derby was held in 1961.

Hidcote Manor Garden (16km/10m S of Stratford-upon-Avon) Garden created by Lawrence Johnston between 1907 and 1948, round a stone Cotswold manor house. His originality (much copied since) was to divide the area into about 20 'rooms' of different sizes and shapes, separated by a wide variety of hedges, each of which could be planted with its own colour or character, ranging from the formal to the pleasing turmoil of a cottage garden.

Henry **Higgins** The name of the leading male character in *Pygmalion and also of Britain's first professional matador. The real-life Henry Higgins made a name for himself fighting bulls in Spain in the late 1960s.

'Hurricane' **Higgins** (Alex Higgins, b. 1949) Northern Irish snooker player who became in 1972 the youngest to win the World Professional Championship (a title he regained in 1982), and whose colourful temperament helped to make him the first of the modern stars in the game.

Jack **Higgins** One of several pseudonyms of Harry Patterson (b. 1929). As Jack Higgins he has written his best-known thrillers, including *The Eagle Has Landed* (1975, about a wartime plot to assassinate Churchill). He also writes under his own name (variously Harry Patterson and Henry Patterson), and as Martin Fallon and Hugh Marlowe.

High Church see *Church of England.

High Commissioner The term used for an ambassador from one *Commonwealth country to another. It was first used of the Canadian representative in London, after Canada acquired *dominion status in 1867.

High Court (in full High Court of Justice) The section of the *Supreme Court which deals with civil cases (see *courts of law). It is itself split into three divisions. The Chancery Division is concerned with such matters as trusts, probate, company law, patents and bankruptcy. The Queen's Bench Division concentrates on commercial litigation and on damages, whether caused by breach of contract or any other wrong. The Family Division specializes, as its name states, in such matters as divorce and the custody of children. There are some areas in which the High Court also becomes involved in criminal cases; the Queen's Bench Division, for example, hears certain appeals from *magistrates' courts.

High Court (in full High Court of Justiciary) The highest criminal court in Scotland, differing from the English *Court of Appeal in that it is also a trial court, hearing all cases likely to incur a heavy penalty. It is the court of last appeal, with no further appeal to the House of Lords. The judges are those of the *Court of Session. Less serious cases go before a *sheriff's court (see *courts of law).

Highland (204,000 in 1991, administrative centre Inverness) Since 1975 a *region of northern Scotland, comprising the former counties of Caithness, Sutherland, Ross and Cromarty (except Lewis), Inverness and Nairn, with small parts of Moray and Argyll.

Highland cattle The most hardy breed of British cattle, believed to be direct descendants of the aboriginal cattle of the *Highlands. With long horns and shaggy coat, usually reddish-brown in colour, the domesticated animal still looks an entirely natural inhabitant of its rugged terrain.

Highland Clearances The removal of people during the 19C from their crofts (small tenanted farms) in the *Highlands of Scotland, often by force, in one of the most shameful sagas of Scottish history. The crofters paid only a small rent to their landlords – who were in many cases their own *clan chieftains – and a higher return was available if the land was turned over to large-scale sheep farming or even used for the stalking of red deer. Evictions continued sporadically from the early 19C. Faced with ever-higher rent demands, the remaining crofters turned to violence in the 1880s (the so-called Crofters' War). An act of parliament in 1886 finally gave them security of tenure.

Highland dancing see *reels.

Highland dress The full costume worn in the past by clansmen in the *Highlands of Scotland, surviving now in the uniform of certain regiments and as the Scottish equivalent of male *evening dress. The distinctive elements are the kilt (a knee-length pleated *tartan skirt, wrapped around and fixed at the waist), the sporran (a pouch, usually covered in fur, which is suspended from the waist to hang in front of the kilt) and the *sgian-dhu* or *skean-dhu* (literally 'black knife' but in practice a more ornamental dagger) tucked into the top of a knee-length stocking. The full outfit, worn as a uniform, includes the plaid (a long piece of tartan cloth worn over the shoulder) and a bonnet.

Highland fling An energetic solo male dance in Scotland, possibly originating as a victory dance and now much performed in competition at *Highland games. It consists of a series of complex steps danced on one spot, usually with one hand above the head and the other on the hip. In the most characteristic step the dancer hops on one foot while moving the pointed toe of the other rapidly to and fro round the calf.

Highland games Term commonly used for what the Scots themselves more often call gatherings or meetings. They derive originally from informal competitions at clan assemblies, but in their modern form they date from a revival in the mid-19C, part of the romantic discovery of Scotland prompted by Sir Walter Scott and fostered by Queen Victoria. The main ingredients of such an occasion, of which the *Braemar gathering is the best known, are *bagpipes, Highland dancing, and a wide range of athletic contests including *tossing the caber. The most demanding event is unique to the Fort William gathering – a 13-mile race, in effect a half-marathon, up and down *Ben Nevis.

Highlands Mountainous region of northern Scotland which has no exact boundaries on the map. It is usually

Highland dress, by Kenneth MacLeay: one of a series of drawings done by him for Queen Victoria (c.1865).

said to be that part of the mainland lying north of a line between Dumbarton on the Firth of Clyde and Stonehaven on the east coast; but it excludes the relatively flat coastal areas round Aberdeen (the Grampian region) and includes the Inner Hebrides. So the Highlands approximate to the present *Highland region and the northern part of *Strathclyde. The dramatic landscape for which the area is famous has made it relatively hard for hostile outsiders to penetrate (unlike the *Lowlands) and has contributed to the sense of self-contained independence underlying many of the local characteristics – *clan loyalty, the survival of a certain amount of *Gaelic, and a strongly Scottish identity expressed in *Highland dress and *Highland games. Together with all this has gone a profound distrust of England, seen in the traditional *Jacobite sympathies of the region.

high school see *grammar school.

High Sheriff An official in each *county of England, Wales and Northern Ireland, appointed for one year by royal patent, whose main task now is ensuring the safety and comfort of High Court judges when the court is sitting within the county. The office of sheriff dates back to before the Norman Conquest, as the local representative of royal authority and the chief executive of the law (celebrations were held in 1992 to mark the supposed 1000th anniversary of the office). The sheriff remains the principal legal officer of the *crown in a county, and still has certain legal responsibilities; but these are in practice carried out by a professional civil servant, the undersheriff. The sovereign's personal representative in a county is the *lord lieutenant. The *sheriff in Scotland has an entirely different function from the English sheriff.

high tea see *tea.

Highway Code Booklet published by *HMSO since 1931, giving guidance and rules on all aspects of road use. It mainly concerns motorists, and knowledge of it is an essential part of a driving test, but it deals with related subjects as varied as getting safely off a bus and how best to herd animals after sunset.

*The **Highwayman*** Poem by Alfred Noyes (1880–1958) which is a favourite with many (particularly perhaps the young and female) for its old-fashioned virtues of rhythm and romance. It tells of the stormy night on which the highwayman comes 'riding – riding – riding' up to the old inn door, beyond which there waits 'the landlord's black-eyed daughter'.

*A **High Wind in Jamaica*** (1929) The very successful first novel of Richard Hughes (1900–76), often quoted as a breakthrough from an idealized Victorian view of childhood and the beginning of a tradition leading to *Lord of the Flies*. Five children are seized by pirates in the West Indies; during their adventures on the pirate ship a 10-year-old girl, Emily, murders a fellow captive. Rich descriptions of tropical scenery, together with the children's heightened but distorted perception of events, give the book a quality which is both poetic and down-to-earth.

Benny **Hill** (1924–92) Comedian and impersonator who brought to television the lively tradition of the *seaside postcard. His long-running *Benny Hill Show* (BBC from 1955, Thames TV 1967–89) was written by himself; it was known not only for its blue jokes and scantily clad Hill's Angels, but also for considerable technical wizardry. As early as 1961 he played all four panel members on a *Juke Box Jury* skit, and for good measure impersonated the chairman, David Jacobs, as well. In that same year

one of his best-known characters gave him a no. 1 hit in the pop charts (*Ernie, the Fastest Milkman in the West*). In 1989 Thames TV abruptly ended his show, after criticism of its content by Ben *Elton and other young comedians.

David Octavius **Hill** (1802–70) Scottish landscape painter who became a pioneer portrait photographer. The reason was connected with the foundation of the *Free Church. Hill felt moved to attempt a vast group portrait of the ministers who had broken away from the Church of Scotland, and he enlisted the young Edinburgh photographer, Robert *Adamson, to help with the detail of so many faces. The resulting images, powerful in their own right, inspired him to continue with Adamson. Hill's expertise in composition and the use of light, backed up by Adamson's technical skills, made their portraits much in demand. When Adamson died, less than five years after their first collaboration, Hill returned to painting.

Graham **Hill** (1929–75) Racing driver associated in particular with the *BRM team. He won the world championship with them in 1962, and was runner up in each of the three following years. He was champion again in 1968, driving for *Lotus. He is the only Formula One champion to have achieved the grand slam of motor racing by also winning the other two major events – Indianapolis in 1966 and Le Mans in 1972. He died in a air crash when piloting his own plane. His son Damon (b. 1960) followed the same career and had his big break when invited to be Alain Prost's co-driver for the Williams team in the 1993 Grand Prix season (the year after *Mansell became world champion with Williams).

Octavia **Hill** (1838–1912) Pioneer in housing reform, whose innovation was to buy and manage, in 1864, some slum property in the Marylebone district of London. Instead of her tenants being visited weekly for the rent by the agent of a slum landlord, they now saw the representative of a benevolent organization. The experiment paid its way, and her concept of a housing association became widely imitated. Her knowledge of urban slums made her a campaigner for the preservation of open spaces, and as such she was one of the founders of the *National Trust.

Rowland **Hill** see *Post Office.

Hill House (Helensburgh, 37km/23m NW of Glasgow) The largest and most complete surviving house by Charles Rennie *Mackintosh. Commissioned in 1902 by the publisher Walter Blackie, the exterior is in the

Official hand signals for use when driving a horse-drawn vehicle: illustration from the first Highway Code *(1931).*

No. 5. " I am going to TURN."

Rotate the whip above the head ; then incline the whip to the right or left to show the direction in which the turn is to be made.

No. 5

Scottish tradition of turrets and harled surfaces (with just a hint of modernism in the placing of the windows). But the interiors, down to the tiniest details of decoration and furniture, are a clear and unified statement of the Mackintosh style.

Nicholas **Hilliard** (1547–1619) The first great English painter of portrait *miniatures, a form which had been introduced by artists from the Continent and brought to a high state of perfection by *Holbein. The son of an Exeter goldsmith, Hilliard was appointed court miniaturist by Elizabeth I in about 1570. More than 200 of his miniatures of leading Elizabethan figures survive, the best collection being in the *Victoria and Albert Museum. He wrote a treatise on his craft, *The Art of Limning* (not published until 1912), in which he named Holbein as his inspiration.

Hillsborough The ground in Sheffield of one of the two local football clubs, Sheffield Wednesday. On 15 April 1989 it was the scene of a major disaster before the FA Cup semi-final between Liverpool and Nottingham Forest. At the Leppings Lane end of the ground 95 people were crushed to death and some 200 injured, nearly all of them Liverpool fans, when police opened a gate to ease pressure outside the ground. The disaster was attributed in the *Taylor Report to a 'failure of police control', making it a matter of some controversy when disciplinary charges were later dropped against the two senior policemen responsible on the day.

The tragic case of one fan, Tony Bland, later raised important issues of medical ethics. The disaster left him in a coma with irreversible brain damage, a condition technically described as a persistent vegetative state (PVS). In February 1993 five law lords in the House of Lords ruled that he should be allowed to die (bringing the Hillsborough total of deaths to 96). Since euthanasia remains illegal in Britain, this could not be achieved by an injection but only by the stopping of artificial feeding – resulting in a slow (but painless) death. The law lords emphasized that parliament should debate as a matter of urgency these areas of moral ambiguity.

Hillsborough Castle (21km/13m SW of Belfast) House of the late 18c which from 1925 to 1972 was the residence of the governor of *Northern Ireland. It was here that the *Anglo-Irish Agreement was signed.

James **Hilton** see *Goodbye Mr Chips and *Shangri-La.

Hindus There are believed to be in Britain about 350,000 Hindus – followers of the ancient religion of the Indian subcontinent, which was established at some time before 1200 BC and of which the most important gods (among many) are Brahma, Vishnu and Shiva. Some of Britain's Hindu families arrived by *immigration in the years after World War II, from India and Sri Lanka; others came later from East Africa, where Indians had played an important part in economic life until they were expelled from Kenya and Uganda in the early 1970s. The main Hindu communities in Britain are in London, Birmingham, Bradford and Leicester.

Hinton St Mary see *Christians.

His Master's Voice see *HMV.

*The **History of Mr Polly*** (1910) Novel by H.G. *Wells about Alfred Polly, a fat draper's assistant turned unsuccessful shopkeeper, who escapes from his drab existence after a failed suicide attempt has resulted in his burning down his own shop. He has always been a dreamer and he

now finds a new life in an idealized rural England, helping the landlady (as plump as himself) in a country pub, the Potwell Inn.

Alfred **Hitchcock** (1899–1980, KBE 1980) Film director known for thrillers laced with wit. *Blackmail* (1929) was the first successful British talkie. Films such as *The *Thirty-Nine Steps* and *The *Lady Vanishes* secured him a high reputation in the British film industry, but he moved in 1940 to the USA, attracted by the greater facilities. (Technical challenges were always a stimulus; *Rope* was constructed in 1948 from unedited 10-minute takes.) *Strangers on a Train* (1951) and *North by Northwest* (1959) were successes in his established style, but horror drove out the comedy in *Psycho* (1960) and *The Birds* (1963). Never one for maintaining a low profile, Hitchcock kept audiences on the look-out (from as early as *The Lodger*, 1926) for his trademark, the single brief appearance of his own short and portly figure in every film. His flat London accent and deadpan wit became widely known through his introductions to his TV thriller series (*Alfred Hitchcock Presents* 1955–61, *The Alfred Hitchcock Hour* 1961–5). The trend to regard him as a master of modern cinema was pioneered by French critics in the 1950s.

*The **Hitch Hiker's Guide to the Galaxy*** (1979) The first book of Douglas Adams (b. 1952). A highly eccentric form of space fiction, it was based on his radio series of the same name. He has developed the theme in several more books, as well as on radio and television.

HMI see *OFSTED.

HMS The initials, standing for Her (or His) Majesty's Ship, which precede the name of any vessel in the Royal Navy.

HMSO (Her Majesty's Stationery Office, Norwich) Agency established in 1786 to provide printing, stationery and office supplies to government departments. It is best known to the public in its role as the government's publisher and bookseller, with its own retail shops in London and various other cities.

HMV (His Master's Voice) The best-known name to have survived from the early days of the British recording industry. The Gramophone Company was founded in 1898, initially to import the newly invented gramophones and gramophone records from Germany. By the end of that year it was making its own recordings in London, and it soon found an appropriate image in a painting entitled 'His Master's Voice' by Francis Barraud. The company bought the picture, asked Barraud to repaint the gramophone so that the terrier was listening to one of its own models, and used the image thereafter as a label. In 1931 the Gramophone Company merged with others to form *EMI.

Thomas **Hobbes** (1588–1679) Philosopher who for most of his life was tutor to the Cavendish family. From 1647 to 1651 he taught *Charles II in exile in Paris. His great work, *Leviathan*, appearing just after the *English Civil War and during the *Commonwealth, was an analysis of the most burning topic of the day, the relationship between subjects and government.

*The **Hobbit*** (1937) Fantasy for children by *Tolkien about a race of small rather domestic people called hobbits, and in particular about one of them, Bilbo Baggins, who leads a campaign against a dangerous dragon – sometimes with the help of Gandalf, a wizard. The story brings the ingredients of folk tales and Norse mythology into a minutely detailed rural setting, which Tolkien later developed on the broader canvas of *The *Lord of the Rings*.

Jack **Hobbs** (1882–1963, kt 1953) England's greatest pre-war batsman. Born the son of the groundsman at Jesus College, Cambridge, and known from his effortless style as 'the Master', he played *cricket for Surrey (1905–34) and for England (1907–30). His aggregate of 61,237 runs in *first-class cricket, and his 197 centuries (98 of them after he was 40) still stand as records by a wide margin.

Hobson's choice A phrase meaning no choice at all, deriving from the business methods of Thomas Hobson, a carrier in 17C Cambridge, who insisted that each customer hire whichever horse was next in line.

Hobson's Choice (1915) Play by Harold Brighouse (1882–1958), one of the so-called 'Manchester school' of realistic dramas of the early 20C. The traditional *Hobson's choice means no choice, which is the predicament of the drunken and domineering Henry Hobson, owner of a boot shop in Salford, when his daughter Maggie marries his best craftsman Will Mossop and sets up in business against him. By the end of the play the firm of Mossop and Hobson is running his shop as well as theirs. The play was filmed by David Lean in 1953 with Charles Laughton as Hobson and John Mills as Mossop; and in 1989 it was made the basis of a three-act ballet by David Bintley.

hockey Hitting a ball about with sticks has been as ancient a pastime, all over the world, as primitive football. But as with football, it was in English *public schools during the early 19C that hockey first became formalized as a game. The first adult club to be formed was the *Blackheath Football and Hockey Club, some time before 1861. Their version of hockey was rough and ready, played on the open heath with a black cube of rubber as the ball. The game was much refined in the 1870s when the Teddington Cricket Club, to the west of London, took it up as a winter sport, using a cricket ball on smooth grass. A national governing body, the Hockey Association, was formed in 1886; and by 1895 international matches were being played between England, Ireland and Wales. It has remained a purely amateur game. It was included in the Olympic Games at the White City in 1908 and rapidly became popular throughout the British Empire – to such an extent that the only non-Commonwealth country ever to win the men's Olympic gold medal has been Germany (1972, 92). Even more remarkably, no less than eight of those gold medals have gone to India and three to Pakistan.

David **Hockney** (b. 1937) The best-known British painter of his generation, not only for his talent in a wide range of fields but also because of his colourful lifestyle and blunt Yorkshire wit (he was born in Bradford). He achieved instant fame as a *pop artist when still at the Royal College of Art. An early series of etchings, *The Rake's Progress* (1961–3), demonstrated his skill as a printmaker; and the same subject was his introduction to another career, when he designed the sets for Stravinski's *Rake's Progress* at Glyndebourne in 1975. In the 1980s he pioneered a collage technique with colour photographs, giving a fragmented and cubist effect to everyday images of people and places.

His move to California in the mid-60s resulted in the famous series of paintings of swimming pools, with their characteristic ripples of light and naked young men; one of them, *A Bigger Splash* (1967), provided the title for a film made about him in 1975. **Mr and Mrs Clark and*

My Parents *by David Hockney (1977)*.

Percy is an outstanding example of Hockney's severely classical portraits of his friends.

Howard **Hodgkin** (b. 1932) Painter who is known for his vibrant colours, often extending to include the frame. Although the compositions are almost abstract, he identifies specific places or encounters between people as his source of inspiration. He won the *Turner prize in 1985.

Hodgkin's disease see *Guy's Hospital.

Gerard **Hoffnung** (1925–1959) German-born tuba player and illustrator, in Britain from childhood. He established a double reputation, as a cartoonist (often with musical subjects as the basis for his humour) and as an organizer of humorous concerts, specializing in musical parody; in these he extended the range of instruments to include such items as watering cans and a length of garden hose (played by no less a musician than Dennis *Brain).

William **Hogarth** (1697–1764) The first great British-born painter on a grand scale. He was trained as an engraver and it was with detailed realistic scenes, of a kind suitable for engraving, that he made his name. The earliest was his 1729 view of a scene from London's recent theatrical success, *The *Beggar's Opera*. In 1731 he painted *A Harlot's Progress* (destroyed in a fire in 1755), the first of his characteristic narrative series; it was followed by *The *Rake's Progress*, *Marriage à la Mode* (1743–5, National Gallery) and the *Election* series (1754–5, Sir John *Soane's Museum). All these were intended as subjects for engraving, but the piracy of the first series caused him to delay publication of *The Rake's Progress* until he had promoted, in 1735, an act of parliament protecting copyright; it is still known as Hogarth's Act. There was always a strong moral theme in Hogarth's work, and his engraving of the effects of cheap *gin led to immediate legislation. His house in west London, at Chiswick, is kept as a museum.

Hogmanay see *New Year.

Hog's Back Chalk ridge in Surrey between Guildford and Farnham, a westward extension of the North *Downs.

Hans **Holbein** the Younger (*c*.1497–1543) Painter born in the German town of Augsburg, whose years in London gave portraiture in England a late but distinguished start. His father, also Hans, and his uncle and elder brother were all painters. The younger Hans established himself first in Switzerland, at Basel. In 1526 he visited England with a letter of introduction from Erasmus to Sir Thomas More, who took him into his household. His painting of More's family, now surviving only in early copies, was the earliest European image of a family seen at home in a full natural setting.

Holbein came back to England again in 1532, after the Swiss Calvinist version of the Reformation had made life in Basel difficult for a painter. This time he settled, soon finding employment with Henry VIII. The massively four-square image by which posterity remembers the king was Holbein's, though again surviving only in versions which are probably copies. In 1538-9 he was sent abroad to paint *Anne of Cleves, due to become the king's fourth bride.

Holbein produced a great number of portraits of the courtiers of Henry VIII, and many of his preparatory drawings are in the Royal Collection at Windsor (widely known through being reproduced in 1792 as colour stipple engravings, themselves now much treasured). In his last years he also tried his hand at portrait *miniatures, and brought this relatively new form to a high standard. He died in London during one of the many epidemics of the plague.

Holburne of Menstrie Museum see *Bath.

Raphael **Holinshed** (d. *c*.1580) English historian who is remembered chiefly because his *Chronicles of England, Scotland and Ireland* (1577) were much used by Shakespeare as a source for material in his history plays.

Holker Hall (19km/12m NW of Lancaster across Morecambe Bay) Stately home dating in part back to the 17c but of interest mainly for the ornately detailed Elizabethan-style west wing, built in the 1870s to the design of two Lancaster architects, Paley and Austin. The gardens and pleasure grounds now contain many attractions, including the Lakeland Motor Museum.

Holkham Hall (58km/36m to the NW of Norwich) The greatest and least changed Palladian mansion in Britain. It was commissioned in 1734 by Thomas Coke (1697–1759, earl of Leicester 1744), who had met his architect, William *Kent, when on the Grand Tour in Italy. Kent's patron *Burlington undoubtedly had an influence on the architecture, but the interiors and furnishings are unique for the time in being designed by Kent himself as part of a unified concept. Many of the rooms contain pictures brought back by Coke from Italy, such as the Claudes in the Landscape Room. The most spectacular of the interiors is the great entrance, the Marble Hall, intended to suggest a Roman temple of justice. A Norwich architect, Matthew Brettingham (1699–1769), was Kent's assistant and completed the house after his death.

In the grounds is a very endearing triumphal column, of the same date as Nelson's in Trafalgar Square and almost as tall. It commemorate's Coke's great-nephew, the agriculturalist *Coke of Norfolk. On top stands not the hero himself but a sheaf of wheat, and in place of lions at the base are a Devon ox and some Southdown sheep.

Henry **Holland** (1745–1806) Architect who worked in a neoclassical style more restrained than that of Robert *Adam, who was one generation older. In 1771 he became the partner of Capability *Brown, and in 1773

The Devon ox and Southdown sheep at Holkham, commemorating the great agriculturalist Coke of Norfolk.

married his daughter. He did much work, no longer visible, for the Prince Regent; his Marine Pavilion at Brighton (1787) was absorbed within Nash's *Royal Pavilion, and *Carlton House was demolished in 1827. But *Brooks's Club and *Albany survive in central London, and he contributed greatly to *Althorp, *Broadlands and *Woburn.

Holland House (London W8) Jacobean house which was a famous salon in the early 19C, when Lord Holland (a nephew of Charles James Fox) and his formidable wife entertained a galaxy of writers and politicians. The house was bombed in World War II. Its remains and the surrounding Holland Park were bought in 1952 by the London County Council for the use of the public.

The **Hollies** Rock group formed in Manchester in 1961 by two schoolfriends, Allan Clarke (b. 1942, vocals) and Graham Nash (b. 1942, guitar), together with Eric Haydock (b. 1943, bass). When they turned professional, in 1963, they were joined by Tony Hicks (b. 1943, guitar) and Bobby Elliott (b. 1942, drums). They had a string of hit singles through the 1960s, though they only reached no. 1 with *I'm Alive* (1965). *He ain't Heavy, He's my Brother* was no. 3 in 1969 but topped the charts when it was reissued in 1988.

Holloway (London N7) The country's main prison for women, completed in 1852 in the style of a Gothic castle. Mrs Pankhurst and other *suffragettes were imprisoned here. In the 1970s it was entirely rebuilt, with the blocks surrounding an open space on the principle of a village green. Holloway was the first women's prison in Britain to have accommodation for mothers and babies, but the conditions in which they lived were severely criticized in 1992 by the Chief Inspector of Prisons.

Stanley **Holloway** (1890–1982) Actor, singer and entertainer who first became famous with his comic monologues, delivered in a deadpan Lancashire accent (though he was himself a Londoner). The earliest, in 1927, was *Sam, pick oop tha musket*, but by far the best known was *The Lion and Albert*, the story of how Albert Ramsbottom was swallowed by the lion in Blackpool Zoo ('Well, I am vexed' is his mother's response when she hears the news). His stage career included *music hall, *revue and straight theatre (even Shakespeare and Shaw), and he appeared in numerous films. But his crowning achievement was the creation of the cockney dustman Alfred Doolittle in *My Fair Lady*.

Holme Pierrepont see *Sports Council.

Sherlock **Holmes** The world's best-known private detective, created by *Conan Doyle. He featured in Conan Doyle's first novel, A Study in Scarlet (published in *Beeton's Christmas Annual* for 1887), but he only reached a wide public with the short stories which began in 1891 in the new *Strand Magazine*. These were collected in two volumes (*The Adventures of Sherlock Holmes* 1892, *The Memoirs of Sherlock Holmes* 1894). In the last story of the second volume, 'The Final Problem', Holmes and the arch-villain, Professor Moriarty, together plunge to their deaths at the Reichenbach Falls. But public demand eventually persuaded Conan Doyle to return to his most popular creation. In *The Hound of the Baskervilles* (1901–2 in the *Strand Magazine*) he recounted an early case of the dead detective. And in 1903 he revealed, in 'The Empty House', that Holmes had used his knowledge of Japanese wrestling to throw Moriarty over the precipice before faking his own death to put other vengeful criminals off the track. The flow of short stories could continue.

The ambiguous death struggle of Holmes and Moriarty at the Reichenbach Falls: illustration in the Strand Magazine *(1893).*

All the cases are narrated by the good-hearted and unsophisticated Dr Watson (*'Elementary, my dear Watson'), who eventually moves in with Holmes at 221B Baker Street; he is the perfect foil to the deviously brilliant detective with the razor-sharp powers of deduction. Holmes has certain unvarying props (pipe, dressing gown, violin, deerstalker), of which the strangest in modern terms is the syringe for calming his nerves with a shot of cocaine.

Gustav **Holst** (1874–1934) English composer of Swedish descent. For most of his career he combined composing with the teaching of music (at St Paul's Girls' School and Morley College). Like others of his generation he was at first much influenced by English folk music, but he was more attuned than most to new developments on the Continent – as seen in his best-known work, *The *Planets* (1914–16). The house where he was born in Cheltenham is kept as a museum.

Victoria **Holt** The best-known of the many pseudonyms under which Eleanor Hibbert (c.1910–93) wrote historical novels of romance, mystery or suspense. Others are Jean Plaidy (whose books are only marginally less popular than Victoria Holt's, according to the numbers borrowed from public libraries), Eleanor Burford, Ellalice Tate, Elbur Ford, Kathleen Kellow and Philippa Carr.

Holy Grail In medieval legend the cup used by Jesus at the Last Supper. Joseph of Arimathea was believed to have caught drops of Christ's blood in it at the Crucifixion and to have brought it to *Glastonbury. Only the purest of King *Arthur's knights may succeed in their quest for the Grail. So Lancelot (impure because of his affair with Guinevere) is unable to come fully into its presence; his perfect son Galahad does so and dies in ecstasy.

Holy Island Of various islands called Holy off the coast of Britain, the two most important are *Lindisfarne and the island linked by a causeway to the west coast of *Anglesey. Both derive their name from the presence of Celtic Christian monks in the 6–8c.

Holy Loch Inlet leading northwest off the Firth of Clyde, near Dunoon, which became the subject of controversy in 1961 when US nuclear submarines began to use it as a base. They continued to do so until 1992.

Palace of **Holyroodhouse** Palace in Edinburgh which stands beside the ruins of Holyrood Abbey (founded by David I in 1128 in gratitude for his escape from a stag indignant at being hunted). It is the official residence of the monarch when in Edinburgh, but at other times is open to the public. A palace was first established here by James IV in 1498, but the present structure was mainly built for Charles II in the 1670s to a design by William *Bruce. The superb park surrounding the palace includes Edinburgh's most prominent feature, Arthur's Seat, a hill 251m/822ft high, with a magnificent view over Edinburgh.

Lord **Home** (Alec Douglas-Home, b. 1903, 14th earl of Home 1951, KT 1962, baron 1974) Conservative politician and prime minister (1963–4) with a complex career between the two Houses of Parliament. He was an MP in Lanarkshire from 1931 until he inherited an earldom in 1951; he then sat in the House of Lords, with a spell as foreign secretary (1960–3). In 1963, at the end of *Macmillan's premiership, Lord Home emerged from secret consultations as leader of the party (Rab Butler had been the expected successor). He disclaimed his *peerage, an option first available in that year, and became prime minister as Sir Alec Douglas-Home; he returned to the House of Commons after winning a by-election in Kinross and West Perthshire. The anachronistic impression of smoke-filled rooms caused the party to adopt in 1965 a new procedure by which MPs would elect the leader, as in the Labour party. The Conservatives lost the election of 1964, and in 1965 Douglas-Home resigned as leader of the party. He was succeeded by Edward *Heath, in whose administration he served again as foreign secretary (1970–4). In 1974 a life peerage brought him back to the House of Lords – once again as Lord Home, but now a baron rather than an earl.

Home Counties Phrase used since the late 19c for the *counties surrounding London – Kent, Surrey, Berkshire, Buckinghamshire, Hertfordshire, Middlesex and Essex. It is sometimes extended to include East Sussex.

Home Guard The name given in 1940, on Churchill's suggestion, to the Local Defence Volunteers who had been formed earlier that year as a citizens' army of last defence. They underwent part-time training and eventually acquired reasonable equipment, but in their first summer they were described by Churchill as 'bands of determined men armed with shot-guns, sporting rifles, clubs and spears'. A less flattering portrait became popular, decades later, in the form of *Dad's Army.

homeless During the 1980s considerable numbers of people began sleeping rough on the streets of British cities, particularly London – an image of late-20c Britain which many found hard to believe and harder to accept. A large proportion of them were young; 'homeless and hungry' was the standard text on the accompanying placard, as they begged during the day. A contributory factor was the 1986 Social Security Act, which from April 1988 made those under 25 entitled to only a reduced rate of income support; a modification (from Sept. 1988) denied entitlement at any level to those under 18 who were not enrolled on a *YT scheme.

Home Office (London SW1) Government department with a somewhat miscellaneous group of responsibilities in England and Wales, including police and prisons, immigration, fire and civil emergency services, and the relationship between church and monarch and state. There has been a home secretary since 1782, when the work of the two *secretaries of state was reorganized to make one responsible for home affairs (which at the time included Ireland and the colonies) and the other for foreign affairs. All the new departments in the subsequent growth of government have taken over tasks previously done (if done at all) by the home secretary, whose present responsibilities are largely whatever happens to be left.

home ownership There has been a steady trend in Britain since World War II towards the purchase rather than the rent of housing. This was prompted by the tax advantages attaching to a *mortgage and by the dramatic rise in *house prices during the 1970s and early 1980s; a further boost was added by the specific commitment of the Thatcher government to the creation of a home-owning democracy, with encouragement to tenants to purchase their *council houses. In the early 1990s more than two thirds of dwellings in Britain were owner-occupied, but recent buyers were by then suffering from a collapse in house prices leading to an unprecedented level of repossessions by banks and building societies.

Home Rule The question of whether the Act of Union of 1800 should be repealed, giving *Ireland back a parliament in Dublin, was on the agenda at Westminster from the day when *O'Connell took his seat in 1829; and it became the single most burning issue of the late 19c. A Home Rule party was established in 1870, and was led from 1880 by *Parnell. In 1886 Gladstone introduced the first Home Rule bill. The issue split his Liberal party, leading to the emergence of the *Unionists. His second attempt, in 1893, was passed in the Commons but rejected in the Lords. The third Home Rule bill, brought in by Asquith in 1912, seemed certain to pass, since the Lords' power of veto had been curtailed the previous year. But it provoked a serious threat of insurrection and civil war from *Carson and the Unionists. As a result Ulster, with its Protestant majority, was excluded from

Home Secretaries since 1945	
1945	Chuter Ede
1951	David Maxwell Fyfe
1954	Gwilym Lloyd-George
1957	R.A. Butler
1962	Henry Brooke
1964	Frank Soskice
1966	Roy Jenkins
1967	James Callaghan
1970	Reginald Maudling
1972	Robert Carr
1974	Roy Jenkins
1976	Merlyn Rees
1979	William Whitelaw
1983	Leon Brittan
1985	Douglas Hurd
1989	David Waddington
1990	Kenneth Baker
1992	Kenneth Clarke

the bill which was finally passed in 1914. Its implementation was delayed until after World War I, by which time the *IRA were violently emphasizing that limited autonomy within the United Kingdom, as provided by Asquith's bill, was no longer enough for southern Ireland. The Anglo-Irish Treaty of 1921 established the Irish Free State (now the republic of Ireland) but excluded the six counties of *Northern Ireland.

Home Service see *radio.

Home, Sweet Home Song with the refrain 'There's no place like home'. The music is by Henry *Bishop and the words by the American playwright J.H. Payne (1791–1852). It first appeared in their opera *Clari, or, the Maid of Milan* (1823), but two years earlier Bishop had published the tune without words as a 'Sicilian air'.

homosexuality Male homosexual practices were on the statute book in Britain as criminal offences from the mid-19C (Oscar *Wilde being the most famous victim of the law in this respect), but homosexuality between females, or lesbianism, has never been illegal. The *Wolfenden Report (1957) recommended that homosexual acts in private between consenting adults should cease to be a criminal offence, and a law was finally passed to this effect in 1967 (21 being selected as the age of consent). More recent legislation on homosexuality, representing something of a backlash against the advances of the permissive society, has included *Clause 28. In 1992 the *Isle of Man remained in this respect, as in several others, an exception; it was by then the only place in western Europe where homosexual acts between consenting adults in private were still illegal.

The **Hon.** (abbreviation of The Honourable) A *courtesy title for sons and daughters in the peerage – used in writing but only rarely in any other context.

Hong Kong British crown colony (until 1997) on the south coast of China, consisting of the island of Hong Kong (with some smaller islands) and a large area on the adjacent mainland. The island was mainly a haunt of pirates until British vessels, engaged in the opium trade, began harbouring there in the 1820s. It was occupied by Britain in the first *Opium War, and was ceded by China in 1842 in the treaty of Nanking; in 1860 the second Opium War similarly yielded the small mainland peninsula of Kowloon. In 1898 the much larger New Territories were leased for 99 years. Preparing for the end of this lease, the British and Chinese governments negotiated in 1984 an agreement that Hong Kong would become a special administrative zone in China with its currency and legal system preserved for 50 years. If this is honoured, and China remains Communist, Hong Kong will indeed be a very special zone – for it has become, in the period since World War II, one of the world's most intensively active centres of capitalism.

Honi soit qui mal y pense see Order of the *Garter.

Honiton lace The best early English lace was made at Honiton in Devon in the 17C (the skill had been brought by Protestant refugees from Flanders). But the Honiton lace most familiar now, with its strong floral motifs against a net background, is machine-made and derives from the 19C revival of the local craft. It is still made in neighbouring villages and the technique is demonstrated in the Allhallows Museum in Honiton.

The royal christening robe, made for Victoria's first child in 1841 and used for most royal christenings in recent generations, is of Honiton lace.

The Poonah Grape: *watercolour by William Hooker, dated 1820 (when he became professor of botany at Glasgow).*

Honourable Artillery Company (HAC) Britain's oldest regiment, now part of the *Territorial Army, which derives from a body of citizen *archers trained to defend London and granted a charter in 1537 by Henry VIII. Their name then was the Artillery of Longbows, Crossbows and Handguns; 'Honourable' was applied to them informally from 1685, though not officially until the 19C. Volunteers from the company have fought in foreign wars from the Armada to World War II; they also fulfil ceremonial duties in London pageants such as the Lord Mayor's Show.

Honourable Member Phrase used between MPs in the House of *Commons, who address each other not by name but as the Honourable Member – sometimes adding the detail of the relevant constituency.

honours see *orders of chivalry.

Honours of Scotland see *crown jewels.

Captain **Hook** see *Peter Pan.

Robert Hooke (1635–1703) Scientist who made important contributions in a wide range of subjects (physics, optics, gravity, astronomy, microscopy, palaeontology), and who excelled as a deviser of instruments and experimental methods, but whose ideas tended to be carried to their conclusions by others. A founder member of the *Royal Society, he was largely responsible for its early professional standards; but his employment there as curator must have contributed to the disruption of his own researches, for he was required to demonstrate 'three or four considerable experiments' at each weekly meeting. The discovery named after him, Hooke's Law, concerns elasticity.

Hooker Family of botanists much involved with the *botanic gardens of the 19C. William Hooker (1785–

1865, kt 1836) was professor of botany at Glasgow from 1820 and in 1841 became the first director of *Kew Gardens. He was succeeded in that post in 1865 by his son Joseph Hooker (1817–1911, kt 1877), who in his early years had been a highly adventurous traveller in search of plants. He went with *Ross to the Antarctic in 1839–43 and spent 1847–51 in north India and the Himalayas. These expeditions resulted in several major works of botanical taxonomy.

hooligan Word which suddenly appeared in press reports in the summer of 1898, referring to disorderly young men who described themselves as part of the 'Hooligan' gang or gangs. No certain explanation has been found, but the most likely link is with a music-hall song of the 1890s about the activities of a rowdy Irish family called Hooligan.

Hope see G.F. *Watts.

Anthony **Hope** (pen name of Anthony Hope Hawkins, 1863–1933, kt 1918) Prolific novelist, known now only for his first two books, the romantic thriller *The Prisoner of Zenda* (1894) and its sequel *Rupert of Hentzau* (1898). They recount the adventures of an intrepid Englishman, Rudolph Rassendyll, in the fictional country whose name is Hope's greatest contribution to the language – Ruritania.

Thomas **Hope** (1769–1831) Collector whose fame now derives from the uncompromisingly 'antique' furniture which he himself designed for the houses in which he kept his collection of antiquities, and which he published in his *Household Furniture and Interior Decoration* (1807). His designs include chairs copied from Greek vases as well as painted Egyptian pieces, part of the revival of interest in ancient Egypt which had begun with Napoleon's campaign there in 1798–9.

Hopetoun House (19km/12m NW of Edinburgh) Mansion begun for the 1st earl of Hopetoun in 1699 by William *Bruce. His west front survives, but the rest was encased and vastly increased in size from 1721 by William Adam (1689–1748), who provided the imposing east front with its projecting pavilions in a version of the current *Palladian fashion. The interior decoration was completed after his death by his sons, John and Robert *Adam.

Anthony **Hopkins** (b. 1921) Composer and broadcaster, widely known through his series *Talking about Music* (on radio from 1954). He has written several chamber operas and much incidental music for radio, television and theatre.

Anthony **Hopkins** (b. 1937, kt 1993) Welsh actor of great emotional power (Laurence Olivier was something of a mentor), who returned to Britain in 1984 after ten years in California and immediately began a string of major stage successes. His role as the brutal newspaper tycoon in *Pravda* (1985) brought him many awards and was followed by highly acclaimed performances as King Lear (1986) and Mark Antony (1987) at the National Theatre. He won an Oscar for his portrayal of the serial killer Hannibal Lecter in *The Silence of the Lambs* (1991).

Gerard Manley **Hopkins** (1844–89) Poet of great originality, virtually unpublished in his lifetime. At Oxford he converted to Roman Catholicism and in 1868 became a Jesuit. He then burnt his early poems, but the death of five nuns in the *Deutschland*, a German ship heading for the USA which ran aground off Kent in 1875, prompted him to write *The Wreck of the Deutschland*. It was in what he called 'sprung rhythm', a form of his own relying on stress rather than strict metre and having much in common with medieval *alliterative verse. He continued

to write in this way, often in short poems expressing an intense experience of nature. *The Windhover* opens with a glimpse of a kestrel which suggests the style: 'I caught this morning morning's minion, kingdom of daylight's dauphin, dapple-dawn-drawn Falcon'. His collected poems were published in 1918.

hopscotch Children's game, known in England from at least the 18c but international and much earlier in origin. It is played in various forms, all involving hopping over the lines (or scotches) in a pattern of boxes marked on the ground, while getting a small object of some kind into a particular box.

Horatius see *Lays of Ancient Rome.

Michael **Hordern** (b. 1911, kt 1983) Actor often seen in quirky character parts but also with a solid career in many of the major Shakespearean roles, particularly Lear and Prospero.

Hornblower see C.S. *Forester.

Hornby see *Meccano.

Kenneth **Horne** (1907–69) Businessman who established a secondary career with the success of *Much-Binding-in-the-Marsh*. He continued in business until he had a stroke in 1958, after which he devoted himself to radio – *Beyond Our Ken* (1958–64) and *Round the Horne* (1965–9). His immense air of respectability enabled him to make increasingly risqué jokes with seeming innocence.

Horniman Museum (London SE23) Ethnographic collection started by a tea merchant, Frederick Horniman (1835–1906), as he travelled the world during the 1870s. He gave it to London in 1901 as a free museum, in an Art Nouveau building designed for the purpose by

One of a set of four armchairs designed in 1800–4 by Thomas Hope, for an Egyptian Room in his own house.

311

House prices: average price of a new house, in £s

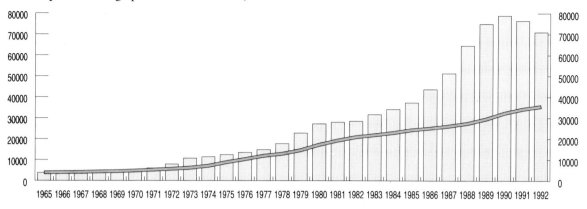

The line is the 1965 price adjusted for inflation: the gap is therefore the cumulative amount by which the rise in house prices has exceeded inflation.   *Source: Economic Trends (see *Central Statistical Office).*

C. Harrison Townsend (1851–1928). Horniman was interested (rather ahead of his time) in 'primitive' art, and in musical instruments – two areas in which the museum has continued to improve its holdings.

hornpipe A jigging solo male dance, once popular in most parts of Britain but particularly associated with sailors. It takes its name from the primitive wind instrument which traditionally provided the accompaniment.

'A horse! a horse! my kingdom for a horse!' see *Richard III.*

Horse Guards (London SW1) Building on Whitehall constructed for the royal cavalry in 1750–8 to a design by William Kent. The *changing of the guard takes place each morning in the small courtyard on the Whitehall side of the archway. The large parade ground on the other side is the site of the annual ceremony of *trooping the colour.

Horse of the Year Show Competitive equestrian event lasting several days in October, presented by the British Show Jumping Association and widely followed on television. It was first presented at the Harringay arena in 1949; it moved in 1959 to the *Empire Pool at Wembley, where it has remained each year since then.

Bob **Hoskins** (b. 1942) Chunky character actor who made his name with the leading role in the six-part TV serial *Pennies from Heaven* (1978). His subsequent films include *Mona Lisa* (1986) and *Who Framed Roger Rabbit?* (1988).

hospice movement The provision of hospices for the terminally ill, particularly those dying of cancer. In this modern sense St Christopher's, at Sydenham in southeast London, is often quoted as the first hospice; it was founded in 1967 by Cicely Saunders (b. 1918, DBE 1980) and has been widely imitated. In 1969 St Christopher's extended its activities to home care. Whether in the hospice or the patient's home, an important innovation has been the use of drugs to prevent rather than relieve pain. Since 1977 St Christopher's has run an information service, which by the early 1990s was listing more than 100 independent in-patient hospices in Britain. There are also now hospices for those with Aids.

Hospital for Sick Children see *Great Ormond Street.

hostages In 1990 there were two different groups of western hostages in the Middle East. One consisted of those working in Iraq in the period before the *Gulf War; held by Saddam Hussein after his invasion of Kuwait, they and their families were released gradually between September and December 1990. The longer-term victims were those held by terrorist groups in Beirut. The release of some of them had been secured by Terry Waite, the special envoy of the archbishop of Canterbury, before he himself was seized in January 1987. Over the following years British hopes and fears were focused on four hostages in particular. Brian Keenan, a Belfast-born teacher, had been kidnapped in April 1986 and was released in August 1990. Jackie Mann, a retired pilot in his late seventies, was seized in May 1989 and freed in September 1991. John McCarthy, a journalist, was taken in April 1986; it was his friend Jill Morell who did most to keep the issue of the hostages in the public eye, lobbying politicians and organizing vigils at the Fleet Street church, St Bride's; McCarthy was finally released in August 1991, after more than five years in captivity. Finally, after almost as long a period, Waite himself was freed in November of that year.

'host of golden daffodils' see *Wordsworth.

Hot Chocolate Pop group formed in 1969 in the Brixton district of London, centred on a pair of song-writing performers born in the West Indies, Errol Brown (b. 1948, vocals) and Tony Wilson (b. 1947, bass and vocals). They had a string of top ten hits in the 70s and early 80s, with one at no. 1 (*So You Win Again* 1977). By 1987 the group had broken up and Brown was recording on his own.

hot cross bun Round bun containing raisins, mixed spices and candied peel, marked on the top with a cross made of two strips of almond paste or of shortcrust pastry. The reason for the cross is that the bun is traditionally eaten on Good Friday. The nursery rhyme 'One a penny, two a penny, hot cross buns' derives from the street cry of vendors selling them on Good Friday morning.

Hotspur see *Henry IV.*

Hotspur Adventure comic for boys, launched in 1933 and continuing until the early 1980s. Its best-known character was Wilson the Wonder Athlete, whose outdoor vegetarian life made him so healthy that even at the age of 128 he still looked young. He could break the world record in any sport, but his modesty kept him out of the limelight.

Houghton Hall (23km/14m NE of King's Lynn) Palladian mansion built 1722–35 for Robert *Walpole, to designs by Colen *Campbell modified by Thomas Ripley (d. 1758). It survives virtually unchanged, with magnificent interiors by William *Kent who also painted the murals flanking the mahogany staircase and provided much of the furniture. The centrepiece of the state rooms is the Stone Hall, a precise cube (12m/40ft in each dimension) adorned with cherubs and portrait busts.

Houghton Mill (5km/3m SE of Huntingdon) Mill on the river Ouse which was recorded in the 10c, milled corn until 1930, and still has its internal machinery intact. The building itself dates from the 17–19c.

*The **Hound of the Baskervilles** see Sherlock *Holmes.

House at Pooh Corner see A.A. *Milne.

Household Cavalry The sovereign's mounted bodyguard, dating from the *Restoration and formed originally from troops of cavalry which had accompanied Charles II and the duke of York (the future James II) in their exile during the Commonwealth. These were the Life Guards, known familiarly as the 'Tins'. They were soon joined by another group, the Royal Horse Guards (descending partly from a unit of the *New Model Army which disbanded in 1660 and immediately re-enlisted for the king); they became known as the 'Blues'. Together these two regiments (the senior units of the British army) made up the Household Cavalry until the addition in 1969 of the 1st Royal Dragoons; they were amalgamated with the Horse Guards, forming the Blues and Royals. All these are now mechanized armoured units, but together they maintain one mounted regiment (at Knightsbridge Barracks) which is responsible for ceremonial duties in London, in particular at *Horse Guards.

Household Words (1850–9) Weekly magazine founded, owned and edited by *Dickens, combining journalism with fiction. In it he serialized some of his own work (*Hard Times* for example) and novels by other writers such as Mrs Gaskell. He followed it with *All the Year Round*, which he edited 1859–70 and in which he published the best of Wilkie Collins.

house prices Until the early 1990s it was an accepted fact of British life that house prices rose faster than inflation and that *home ownership was therefore the best possible investment. Between 1965 and 1990 the price of the average new house (measured at the stage when a *mortgage was approved) rose from £3820 to £78,917, an increase of 1966%; in the same period inflation was only 752% (see the *pound in your pocket). As a result it was a major shock to recent purchasers when house prices fell during 1992 by about 7%.

Houses of Parliament (London SW1) The magnificent Victorian Gothic building, standing on the bank of the Thames by Westminster Bridge with *Big Ben at its northern end, was made possible by the fire of 1834 which destroyed most of the *Palace of Westminster. Charles Barry's design was selected from 97 submitted for a new building 'in the Gothic or Elizabethan' style, to contain both the House of *Commons and the House of *Lords'. The imposing structure with its delicately ribbed façades is his, but he brought in *Pugin to provide the Gothic interiors. Immensely elaborate and now once again fashionable, these survive except in the chamber of the Commons and in the adjoining lobby, which were destroyed by bombs in 1941. They were rebuilt by Giles Gilbert *Scott in the same dimensions but with simpler ornamentation.

The tall square tower at the southern end of the building, at the other extreme from Big Ben, is the Victoria Tower. The Union Jack is flown above it from sunrise to sunset when parliament is sitting.

Housesteads see *Hadrian's Wall.

*The **House that Jack built** Nursery rhyme in which each verse adds one more of the events leading up to the cat killing the rat that ate the malt that lay in the house that Jack built. First printed in the mid-18c, it is certainly much older – if only because the Roman Catholic priest, 'all shaven and shorn', must predate the Reformation. An ancient Aramaic rhyme, *Had Gadyo*, has been suggested as the origin; but it is as likely to be a parallel case, for stories on this pattern exist in several languages.

housing In the decades up to the 1970s the number of houses completed in any year was taken as an indication of the state of the economy and the competence of the government. In the 1980s government priorities changed, with a twin policy of *council house sales and restrictions on local government expenditure. Between 1980 and 1990 the annual number of dwellings completed by local authorities was reduced by 80%, reaching about the same level as that achieved by the housing associations.

Housing associations – run by voluntary committees, often with tenant representation – are concerned with maintaining and administering dwellings in addition to building new ones. In the early 1990s there were some 2300 housing associations responsible for about 600,000 homes. They are controlled and provided with central funding by the Housing Corporation, established by parliament in 1964.

A.E. Housman (Alfred Edward Housman, 1859–1936) Distinguished classical scholar at Trinity College, Cambridge, who regarded the fame resulting from A *Shropshire Lad* as almost an unwelcome distraction.

Housing: permanent dwellings completed, in thousands

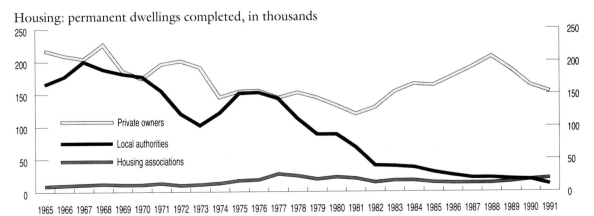

Houyhnhnms see *Gulliver's Travels.*

hovercraft (also called air-cushion vehicle or ACV) Machine using jets of air, within a protective skirt, to provide a cushion on which it travels over any relatively flat surface, such as water, marsh or desert. It was developed from 1953 by Christopher Cockerell (b. 1910); his original working model used a hair dryer and two coffee tins. The first full-scale hovercraft was successfully tested at Cowes in 1959, and since then they have been used in many contexts all over the world. The largest is the SR.N4, which carries 60 cars and 400 passengers across the English Channel at a speed of up to 77 knots – making it the fastest sea-going vessel of its size in the world.

Hovis Trade name registered in 1890 for a flour with extra wheat germ – developed by Richard Smith, a miller at Macclesfield in Cheshire. He launched a competition for the name and chose Hovis, based on the Latin *hominis vis*, meaning 'strength of man'; trade names of this learned sort were then much in fashion (compare *Bovril). The brown rectangular loaves baked from his flour have had their present shape from the start, with a slightly spreading top and the letters HOVIS embossed along the side in the baking.

Catherine **Howard** see *Catherine Howard.

John **Howard** (1726–90) The first English prison reformer. As *high sheriff of Bedfordshire in 1773, he was horrified by the condition of the prisoners in Bedford jail; and he was shocked to discover that some, already acquitted in the courts, were detained because they could not pay the charges imposed on them (the staff had no salaries and depended on whatever fees could be extracted from the prisoners). The following year Howard persuaded parliament to pass two acts attempting to redress

Spelling games in the service of marketing: an advertisement for Hovis in the magazine Bubbles *(1893).*

these particular abuses. For the rest of his life he made it his personal mission to visit and inspect prisons, and his work is carried on by the *Howard League for Penal Reform.

Leslie **Howard** (stage name of Leslie Stainer, 1890–1943) Actor who was seen, particularly in the USA in the 1930s, as the quintessential Englishman. On the screen he played Blakeney in *The Scarlet Pimpernel* (1934) and Higgins in *Pygmalion* (1938). He died when his plane was shot down returning in 1943 from neutral Portugal, where he had gone to lecture for the British Council and to make diplomatic contacts.

Michael **Howard** (b. 1941) Conservative politician, MP for Folkestone and Hythe since 1983. He was the last of the *Cambridge mafia to enter the *cabinet – as secretary of state for employment in 1990, and then for the environment from 1992.

Howard League for Penal Reform Pressure group formed in 1866 and named after the great 18C prison reformer, John *Howard. The league, relying entirely on private donations, has campaigned vigorously on moral issues such as the abolition of capital punishment. But its central theme remains as urgent as ever, with conditions in Britain's overcrowded and antiquated *prisons widely agreed to be in need of reform.

Lord **Howard of Effingham** see *Armada.

Howard's End (1910) Novel by E.M. *Forster about the split in Edwardian middle-class life between the cultured (represented by two sisters, Margaret and Helen Schlegel) and the practical (the Wilcox family, whose house is Howard's End). Friendships and love affairs between the two groups are the basis of the plot, and personal relationships are revealed as all-important (a *Bloomsbury theme). The book's most famous sentence, 'Only connect', relates to the broader issue of the two contrasted types of people. It is the message of Margaret to her husband, Henry Wilcox, just after she has married him: 'Only connect! . . . Only connect the prose and the passion, and both will be exalted, and human love will be seen at its highest.'

The book was made into a very successful film in 1992, directed by James Ivory, with Emma Thompson and Anthony Hopkins as Margaret and Henry.

'How different, how very different from the home life of our own dear queen!' Apocryphal comment supposedly made by a lady in a Victorian audience, while watching Sara Bernhardt writhing on the floor in a tantrum of amorous rage during a performance of *Antony and Cleopatra.*

Geoffrey **Howe** (b. 1926, kt 1970, baron 1992) Conservative politician, MP for Reigate (1970–4) and for Surrey East (1974–92). A barrister by profession (solicitor general 1970–2), he was shadow chancellor of the exchequer from 1975 and entered the *cabinet as chancellor (1979–83); he was subsequently foreign secretary (1983–9) and leader of the House of Commons (1989–90). In November 1990 he resigned from the cabinet in protest against Mrs Thatcher's attitude to the European Community. He followed this with a resignation speech to the House of Commons expressing strong criticism of her style of leadership. On the next day Michael *Heseltine made his challenge, and before the end of the month John *Major was prime minister.

Lord **Howe** see *Glorious First of June.

Frankie **Howerd** (1922–92) Camp comedian with an unrivalled ability to dwell, with lingering amazement and disapproval, upon an audience's response to an innuendo; 'titter ye not', he would rebuke them. He acquired a cult status in the 1960s from his appearances at the Establishment (a satirical nightclub founded by Peter Cook) and on *That Was The Week That Was*. But he was more at home in the *Carry On* films, in the mock-Roman frolics of the stage musical *A Funny Thing Happened on the Way to the Forum* (1963), or on television in *Up Pompeii* (BBC 1971).

How Green was my Valley (1939) Bestselling novel by Richard Llewellyn (1907–83), set in a Welsh mining community in the second half of the 19c as the slag heaps began to smother the valleys. The humour, warmth and resilience of the characters in their bleak surroundings touched a powerful chord during World War II.

'How is the empire?' see *Bognor Regis.

'Howl, howl, howl, howl!' see *King Lear*.

Hoxne Treasure The largest hoard of Roman gold and silver as yet unearthed in Britain. It was found in November 1992, at Hoxne in Suffolk, by someone using a metal detector to search for tools which had fallen off a tractor. Dating from a little after 400 AD, the treasure included about 1000 gold and 5000 silver coins, approximately 100 silver spoons (many with the *chi-rho* emblem of the early *Christians) and several gold bracelets and chains.

Hoy see the *Orkneys.

Hoylake Golf course of the Royal Liverpool Golf Club, on the sea at the northwestern tip of the promontory between the estuaries of the Mersey and the Dee. Built in 1879 and famous for its severity, Hoylake was the venue for the first Amateur Championship in 1885. Ten Opens have been played there, but the most recent was in 1967.

Fred **Hoyle** (b. 1915, kt 1972) English astronomer, working mainly at Cambridge, well known to the public both for his role in important controversies and for his successful popularization of astronomy. From 1948 he was the leading advocate of the steady-state theory (that there is continuous creation at the centre of the expanding universe), but subsequent discoveries have tended to discredit this in favour of the big-bang explanation associated with Martin *Ryle. Hoyle has also been a prolific author of science fiction.

HP Sauce Britain's most famous sauce has a precise origin. In 1899 Edwin Samson Moore, owner of the Midland Vinegar Company in Aston, a suburb of Birmingham, was visiting a creditor in the hope of getting a bill paid. Moore liked the smell of a sauce that was brewing in the room behind the grocer's shop, and he liked even more its name: HP Sauce. The grocer said he called it that because someone had seen a bottle of his sauce in the Houses of Parliament. Moore cancelled the debt, and for £150 bought the name and the recipe (a blend of spices and malt vinegar).

The product was relaunched in 1903 and was marketed with great flair. Eye-catching square-shaped green bottles, with the Houses of Parliament on the label, were delivered to grocery shops by a fleet of tiny wagons drawn by donkeys. In 1917 Moore added an exotic touch to the label – a description of the sauce in French, the language of smart menus. The paragraph about 'cette sauce de premier choix' and the assurance that 'elle est absolument pure' provided for decades the only French phrases known

George Hudson, a king with a smoke stack for a crown, goes off the rail in a Punch *view of the 1847 collapse.*

to many people in Britain; and there was a public outcry in 1984 when a later generation of marketing men dropped this detail. Meanwhile the product had received its most famous piece of free publicity; in 1964 Mary Wilson, wife of the newly elected prime minister Harold Wilson, let slip in an interview her irritation at the way he smothered everything she cooked in HP Sauce.

HRH (His or Her Royal Highness) Title reserved for the sovereign's children and the children of any son of a sovereign. It is not given to the children of the daughters of a sovereign, whose surname is their father's rather than that of the royal house of *Windsor. The wives of any royal highness and the husband of a sovereign are also accorded the title HRH. Those who are royal highnesses by birth use the title Prince or Princess; but whereas the wife of a prince is known as a princess, the husband of a princess does not become a prince.

Trevor **Huddleston** (b. 1913) Anglican priest and member of a celibate order, the Community of the Resurrection, known from their Yorkshire base as the Mirfield Fathers. The community is much involved in South Africa, where Father Huddleston became prominent in the early 1950s in the fight against apartheid. He has been bishop of Masai (1960–8), suffragan bishop of Stepney in London (1968–78), and simultaneously bishop of Mauritius and archbishop of the Indian Ocean (1978–83).

George **Hudson** (1800–71) Known as the 'railway king', he was the prime example of the fortunes that could be won and lost in the *railway mania of the mid-19c. A Conservative politician in York, he became chairman in 1837 of a company building a local railway. Its success brought him other companies and by 1844 he controlled more than 1600km/1000m of track. Shares soared in any enterprise with which he was involved, bringing him vast personal wealth. But in 1847 the market collapsed, revealing financial irregularities in his companies which led to his ruin.

Henry **Hudson** (d. 1611) Explorer commemorated in the names of the Hudson River, Bay and Strait. His first three expeditions (1607–9) were to the north of Russia, to find a northeast passage to China. He diverted on the third to look for a northwest passage, and on this occasion sailed 240km/150m up the Hudson River (as far as present-day Albany) before deciding that it did not lead through to the Pacific. He sailed west on the *Discovery* for his final voyage in April 1610, and spent the following winter in James Bay, the southernmost pocket of Hudson Bay. In June 1611, when they had broken out of the ice, the crew mutinied and set Hudson, his son and seven others adrift in a small boat.

Hudson's Bay Company The oldest chartered company still trading. It was established in 1670 with a charter from Charles II to 'the Governor and Company of Adventurers of England trading into Hudson's Bay'. The company's fur traders provided the first regular British presence in *Canada. Their rivals in this lucrative business were the French, until the ceding of French Canada to Britain in 1763. Later another English group, the North West Company of Montreal, became a serious threat; in the early 19C a virtual war broke out between employees of the two enterprises, ending only when the older company absorbed its opponent in a merger. On the Pacific coast the joint company established the colony of British Columbia, which in 1871 became part of the new Dominion of Canada. Since then the Hudson's Bay Company has continued to prosper as a trading concern, much enriched in the 20C by oil rights on its extensive properties. It remained British until 1970, when the headquarters were transferred to Canada.

hue and cry see *police.

Hughenden Manor see *Disraeli.

Richard **Hughes** see A *High Wind in Jamaica.

Shirley **Hughes** (b. 1927) Prolific author and illustrator of children's books (she has illustrated as many as 200). Her books find humour in the everyday situations of children's lives in an urban and multi-racial setting; among the most popular are those with a small boy, Alfie, as the central character.

Ted **Hughes** (b. 1930) Yorkshire-born poet whose imagery is vividly cruel and violent – in keeping with the everyday life of the wild animals which have been, in the tradition of fable, his main characters. He received immediate admiration for his first collection, *The Hawk in the Rain* (1957), and for its successor, *Lupercal* (1960). His best-known subsequent volume has been *Crow* (1970). He has also written much for children, and his story *The Iron Man* (1968, entitled *The Iron Giant* in the USA) has achieved the status of a classic. Appointed *poet laureate in 1984, he has taken the job in its traditional spirit – providing poems such as *Rain-Charm for the Duchy: a Blessed, Devout Drench for the Christening of His Royal Highness Prince Harry* (1984). His first wife was Sylvia *Plath.

Thomas **Hughes** see * *Tom Brown's Schooldays.*

Huguenots French Protestants, many of whom came to Britain in the last two decades of the 17C after prolonged persecution under Louis XIV. This had culminated in 1685 in the revocation of the Edict of Nantes, a law passed in 1598 to guarantee religious freedom for the Protestants. Some of those who came were expert craftsmen in silver, an area in which the Huguenots set new

standards in Britain; in the following generation Paul de Lamerie (1688–1751) became the best-known of English silversmiths. Other craftsmen ensured the success of *Spitalfields silk. There has been much elaborate speculation (but no firm conclusion) as to the origin of the word Huguenot, which was in use from the 16C.

Hull (Kingston-upon-Hull, 263,000 in 1991) City and port in Humberside, where the river Hull flows into the Humber estuary. It was selected by Edward I as the location for a harbour in the 13C. The parish church of Holy Trinity, begun at that period and one of the largest in England, is notable for its early use of brick. William *Wilberforce was born in Hull and his 17C family home has been turned, together with neighbouring houses, into a historical museum with special emphasis on the slave trade. The Ferens Art Gallery, donated by Thomas Ferens (1847–1930) with contributions from Joseph *Duveen (another native of Hull), has a European collection but specializes in British painting.

An oddity for which Hull has become famous is the retention of its own municipal telephone system, which survived the many years during which the rest of the country's network was nationalized. Hull's extensive modern docks stretch for miles along the Humber, but the older Town Docks form an inlet to the heart of the city at Queen Victoria Square, where their history is commemorated in the Town Docks Museum.

The **Human League** An early synthesizing pop group formed in Sheffield in 1977 by two computer operators, Martin Ware and Ian Craig Marsh, who left in 1980 to form Heaven 17. By the time the group was having major successes (top album *Dare* and top single *Don't You Want Me*, both 1981), the line-up was Philip Oakey (lead singer), Suzanne Sulley and Joanne Catherall (vocals), Adrian Wright and Jo Callis (synthesizers) and Ian Burden (bass).

Humber Deepwater estuary in northeast England, with Hull on the north bank as its major port. It begins at the confluence of the rivers Ouse and Trent and stretches about 68km/42m to the North Sea. The Humber Estuary Bridge, crossing just to the west of Hull, was opened in 1981; in 1992 it still retained its record as the world's longest span (1410m/4626ft).

Humberside (874,000 in 1991, administrative centre Beverley) *County on the east coast of England, formed in 1974 from the southeast part of Yorkshire and a section of northern Lincolnshire.

Humble Petition and Advice see the *Protectorate.

humbug see *sweets.

Cardinal **Hume** (Basil Hume, b. 1923) Benedictine monk who has been archbishop of *Westminster since 1976. Almost his entire previous life was spent in the monastery school of *Ampleforth, as pupil, teacher, housemaster and abbot (1963–76).

David **Hume** (1711–76) Scottish philosopher whose work forms an important part of the British tradition of *empiricism. His ideas were fully expressed in his ambitious first book, *A Treatise of Human Nature* (3 vols, 1739–40). His political and economic theories (which had some influence on his younger contemporary and friend, Adam *Smith) were developed in *Essays, Moral and Political* (2 vols, 1741–2).

In his own time and for many decades after his death he was most widely admired for his *History of England*

(6 vols, 1754–62), spanning the entire period from Julius Caesar to the Revolution of 1688.

John **Hume** (b. 1937) Northern Irish politician, leader of the *SDLP since 1979. He was MP for Foyle (1969–72) in the Stormont parliament, and when the SDLP was formed in 1970 he became deputy leader to Gerry Fitt. In 1979 he was elected to the *European Parliament as one of Northern Ireland's three MEPs, a seat which he held in the elections of 1984 and 1989. Since 1983 he has also represented Foyle at Westminster.

Engelbert **Humperdinck** (stage name of Arnold George Dorsey, b. 1936) Pop singer working in pubs and clubs before he was spotted in 1967 and was given a grander name, plucked from a musical dictionary (the original E.H. was a 19c German composer). His first single, *Release Me* (1967), was an immediate hit, going to no. 1 and staying in the charts for more than a year. It was followed by many other top-ten records during the 1960s; since then he has had a busy cabaret career.

Humpty Dumpty Egg-shaped nursery-rhyme character who falls off a wall and cannot be put together again (because no-one can mend a broken egg). The rhyme first appeared in print in the early 19c, but many European countries have egg-characters with similar double names, and rhymes and games about them are probably very ancient. Humpty's fame in Britain derives largely from his long conversation with Alice in *Through the Looking-Glass*.

100-Share Index see *Financial Times Indices.

hundredweight see *weight.

Hundred Years' War (1337–1453) The name given by historians to a prolonged but intermittent struggle between England and France. Rivalries between such powerful neighbours were inevitable, but they were also fuelled by the complex territorial claims arising from marriages between princely families in England and France (marriages which had in the 12c brought Anjou and Aquitaine under English control).

The immediate cause was the death in 1328 of Charles IV, the king of France, without a male heir. The throne passed to his first cousin, Philip VI. In 1337 Philip confiscated large areas of southwestern France, round Gascony, which belonged by inheritance to the English crown (see *Eleanor of Aquitaine). The king of England, Edward III, responded by pressing his own claim to the throne of France, being a closer relation of the late king (a nephew rather than a cousin), albeit through the female line. The *Salic law was not then formally established in France, and did not apply in England.

Long periods of inactivity separated the English campaigns in France. A famous victory by Edward III at *Crécy in 1346 led to no great advantage; the king merely returned to England after besieging and capturing Calais. A campaign by his son, Edward the Black Prince, brought another victory at *Poitiers in 1356; the French king, John II, was captured and held hostage for four years until a large ransom and major territorial concessions were agreed (the agreement was soon revoked).

The most energetic English campaign was undertaken by Henry V and included the victory of *Agincourt in 1415. It ended with his marriage to Catherine, the daughter of the king of France, and his being accepted as heir to the French throne. But he died two months before his father-in-law, and the English successes were soon reversed by the most striking figure of the entire saga. A French peasant girl in her late teens, Joan of Arc,

inspired the French to a series of victories beginning with the recapture of Orléans in 1429. She was herself eventually captured, was tried for heresy and in 1431 was burnt at the stake by the English. But the tide had turned.

The war petered out after some final engagements in 1453. An invasion of France in 1475 by a large English army was bought off by the French. No treaty was ever signed. As things were left, the English retained only Calais out of all their French possessions. Even so, English kings continued until 1801 to describe themselves also as kings of France.

Hungerford massacre Disaster in August 1987 when Michael Ryan went berserk over a few hours in and around the town of Hungerford, in Berkshire. He shot and killed 13 people and wounded several others (two of whom later died) before shooting himself.

hunger strikes see *suffragettes and the *Maze.

hungry forties A phrase for the 1840s, characterized by the poor harvests and widespread economic distress which made the country a fertile ground for the message of the *Chartists. The years 1845–7 saw the *Great Famine in Ireland, after the potato crop was blighted in two successive years.

David **Hunt** (b. 1942) Conservative politician, MP for Wirral West since 1983 (previously for Wirral 1976–83). He joined the *cabinet in 1990 as secretary of state for Wales.

An image of the hungry forties: starving Irish peasants glean for potatoes in a field which has been harvested.

From a 16C manuscript in the Hunterian in Glasgow: John Banister uses skeleton and corpse to demonstrate a point.

Holman **Hunt** (William Holman Hunt, 1827–1910) One of the founding members of the *Pre-Raphaelite Brotherhood, who painted some of the best-known images of Victorian England including The *Light of the World* and The *Scapegoat*. He is characterized by intense realism, bright and sometimes garish colours, with often a lightly concealed moral or symbolic meaning – as in the sheep tempted by forbidden delights in *The Hireling Shepherd* (1851, Manchester City Art Gallery) or in the human moment of guilty self-realization in *The Awakening Conscience* (1854, Tate Gallery).

James **Hunt** (b. 1947) Racing driver who won the world championship for *McLaren in a cliff-hanging finale in 1976; he clinched his victory by a single point when he came third in the last race of the season, the Japanese Grand Prix. He retired soon after, and since 1980 has been a commentator on motor racing for the BBC.

Hunterian Museum (London WC2) Collection of anatomical specimens gathered by John Hunter (1728–93), a Scottish surgeon. The items, numbering more than 13,000 at his death, were selected to demonstrate the structure and function of organs in a wide range of animals. Owned by the Royal College of Surgeons, the collection suffered considerable damage from bombing in 1941. The *Hunterian Museum and Art Gallery in Glasgow commemorates Hunter's elder brother.

Hunterian Museum and Art Gallery (Glasgow) Named after a distinguished Scottish anatomist, William Hunter (1718–83), whose rich and varied treasures, bequeathed to the university of Glasgow, form its nucleus. The museum, notable for Hunter's collection of coins, is

housed in the main university building. The art gallery is in a modern building (1980). Hunter had some exceptional paintings (including two by Stubbs and three by Chardin); to these have been added the estates of *Whistler (some 80 of his oil paintings and many prints and drawings) and of Charles Rennie *Mackintosh, four of whose interiors from his own house have been built into the new gallery. The *Hunterian Museum in London is the anatomical collection of William's younger brother.

hunting The term is used in Britain only of the pursuit of a quarry with dogs, the killing of animals with a gun being described as *shooting (or stalking, when deer are shot with a rifle). And in practice it applies only to hounds which follow the trail by scent; hunting by sight with greyhounds, or *coursing, has developed into something closer to a sporting contest. Fox-hunting, particularly associated with Britain, is historically the most recent variety.

The hunting of deer was a royal pursuit from Anglo-Saxon times, with areas such as *Cannock Chase reserved for the purpose; in later centuries artificial hunting grounds such as *Richmond Park were enclosed for royal pleasure. Stag-hunting with horses and hounds is still practised in a few parts of Britain, most notably on Exmoor. The hunting of hares became popular in the 16C. For this the larger hounds, known as harriers, have usually been accompanied by hunters on horseback; beagles, considerably smaller, are followed on foot. Of the two, beagling is by now the more common.

Fox-hunting was first taken seriously as a sport in the second half of the 17C, particularly in the *Shires, and was made more exciting by the need to jump the fences which increasingly enclosed *common land. It rapidly became a favourite country pursuit, providing a fine spectacle with the red or scarlet coats of the huntsmen – which it has been the fashion to describe as 'pink' in hunting circles since at least the early 19C (by contrast the traditional colour for beagling is green). The sport has also given rise to a wide range of paintings, prints, books and characters (*Jorrocks), songs (*D'ye ken John Peel), a boisterous social life (hunt balls), much hallowed jargon (the fox's tail has to be called a brush but the hound's is a stern) and a certain amount of ceremony – a rider at his first kill is likely to be given the fox's brush and others may be honoured with the animal's mask (its head) or pad (one of its feet). The most widely known custom, in which a newcomer to the kill was 'blooded' by having the fox's blood smeared on his face, is now rarely practised out of deference to modern sensibilities.

The hunting season starts on November 1 and continues until March. In recent decades a vigorous campaign against hunting in all its forms has been mounted by the *League Against Cruel Sports. The hunting of otters was banned by law in 1981. In 1992 a bill to ban the hunting of any mammal failed by only 12 votes to pass its second reading in the House of Commons.

Huntingdon (17,000 in 1981) Town in Cambridgeshire on the north bank of the Great Ouse, linked by a 14C bridge with Godmanchester on the south bank. *Ermine Street crossed the river here on its way north to York. Huntingdon's more recent fame is its connection with Oliver *Cromwell. The parish register recording his birth bears the marks of a pithy addition, later erased: 'England's plague for 5 years' (referring to 1653–8 when he was lord protector). The school where he was educated is now a museum in his memory.

Huntingdonshire and Peterborough Former *county in central England, since 1974 part of Cambridgeshire.

*The **Hunting of the Snark*** (1876) Nonsense poem by Lewis *Carroll in eight 'fitts' (see *Gawain and the Green Knight*). A shipload of characters, led by the energetic Bellman, set off to find a Snark. Unfortunately the Baker chances upon the only dangerous kind and therefore vanishes – 'For the Snark was a Boojum you see' (the last line of the poem, and the one which Carroll said inspired him to write all that went before). The illustrations are by Henry Holiday (1839–1927).

Benjamin **Huntsman** (1704–76) Inventor in *Sheffield in the late 1740s of a method for making steel of much improved quality, by means of a crucible. The Sheffield cutlers rejected his metal as too hard to work. They then tried to prevent his exporting it to France, finding that French knives and scissors, reimported into Britain, were outselling their own. By about 1750 his secret was discovered and others in Sheffield began using his method.

Douglas **Hurd** (b. 1930) Conservative politician, MP for Witney since 1983 (previously for Mid-Oxon 1974–83). A diplomat by profession, his involvement with national politics began as private secretary to Edward Heath when he was leader of the opposition (1968–70), followed by a post as his political secretary when he was prime minister (1970–4). He joined the *cabinet in 1984 as secretary of state for Northern Ireland (1984–5), subsequently becoming home secretary (1985–9) and foreign secretary (since 1989). He entered the leadership contest in 1990 after Mrs Thatcher had decided not to stand in the second ballot, but he came third – behind Michael Heseltine and John *Major.

hurling The national game of the republic of Ireland, played also in Northern Ireland. It is of extremely ancient origin, skill in the game being mentioned in ancient legends as an attribute of heroes. It became an organized sport with the foundation of the Irish Hurling Union in 1879 and the Gaelic Athletic Association in 1884.

The game shares elements of both hockey and lacrosse, in that the stick (hurley in English, *caman* in Gaelic) can strike the ball along the ground but also has a broad enough head for the ball to be balanced in the air and

The distribution of parts of the fox as trophies at the end of a hunt: handcoloured aquatint, c.1820.

passed from player to player. There are 15 players in a team. The goals have uprights continuing above the crossbar as in rugby; hitting the ball above the crossbar scores one point, and a goal (below the crossbar) scores three. A version of the game crossed long ago to Scotland to become the basis of *shinty.

'hurly-burly of the chaise-longue' see Mrs Patrick *Campbell.

hurricane see *Great Storm.

Hurricane The chief plane used in the *Battle of Britain, with far more of them in service than the later and faster *Spitfire. When the prototype of the Hawker Hurricane flew in 1935 (only a year before the Spitfire) it was the first plane to exceed 300 mph (483 kph) in level flight and fully loaded.

Geoff **Hurst** (b. 1941) Footballer (playing forward) who leapt to fame in his first year in international football. He was a reserve for the England team in the first three matches of the 1966 World Cup. Given a place in the quarter-final against Argentina, he scored the only goal; and he went on to score three goals in England's victory against West Germany at Wembley, a record for a World Cup final still unequalled in 1992. His club was West Ham until he moved to Stoke City (1972–5), after which he was a year with West Bromwich Albion. He also played first-class cricket for Essex.

Hush-a-bye, baby, *on the tree top* The most popular lullaby in Britain, first printed in *Mother Goose's Melody* of about 1780 and sung to a version of *Lilliburlero*. There have been frequent attempts to find a historical origin for the baby and its fall from the tree top. The rhyme probably reflects an old country habit of suspending a cradle from a branch to have it rocked by the wind.

William **Huskisson** see *Liverpool and Manchester railway.

James **Hutton** (1726–97) Regarded as the founder of modern geology, his originality lay in observing that the mingled strata of rocks round his native Edinburgh could not have derived from isolated catastrophic events (as the biblical account required) but showed signs of long processes of sedimentation, erosion and volcanic eruption of a kind still continuing. He could see, in his much quoted phrase, 'no vestige of a beginning, no prospect of an end'.

Len **Hutton** (1916–90, kt 1956) One of the greatest English batsmen, playing *cricket for Yorkshire (1934–55) and for England (1937–55, captain 1952–5). His 364 runs against Australia at the Oval in 1938 remain (early in 1993) the highest England innings in a *Test match and only one run short of the world record (365 by Sobers in 1958). In 1952 Hutton became the first professional to captain England since Arthur Shrewsbury in 1886–7.

Huxley English family of great distinction in science and literature. T.H. Huxley (Thomas Henry Huxley, 1825–95) first established himself with his studies of surface life in tropical seas, carried out as a sideline when he was in southeast Asia as naval surgeon on HMS *Rattlesnake*. He became the chief champion of the evolutionary theories of Charles *Darwin, fighting for the cause with such persistence that he became known as Darwin's bulldog. In his later years he campaigned against what he considered the untenable claims of religion, coining the excellent word 'agnostic' (from the Greek for 'unknowing') for the

viewpoint that neither the existence nor the non-existence of God can be known on any rational basis.

His son Leonard (1860–1933) was a biographer and was himself father of three distinguished sons. Julian (1887–1975, kt 1958) was a zoologist who did pioneer work in the scientific study of animal behaviour and, like his grandfather, made evolution a speciality; he was an excellent popularizer of science, and was known to a wide public during World War II as a member of the *Brains Trust; in 1946 he became the first director-general of UNESCO.

Aldous (1894–1963), an author, mocked his contemporaries in a series of brilliant and cynical novels from *Crome Yellow* (1921) to *Point Counter Point* (1928). But his best-known work, *Brave New World* (1928), was more savagely pessimistic. In later life he became a controversial early advocate of the liberating power of drugs – describing his experiments with mescalin and LSD in *The Doors of Perception* (1954) and *Heaven and Hell* (1956).

Andrew (b. 1917, kt 1974) is a physiologist specializing in the study of nerve impulses and muscle contraction; he shared a Nobel prize with others in this field in 1963, and is a member of the Order of *Merit.

Hyde Park Large open space adjoining the *West End of London, forming with the adjacent *Kensington Gardens an unbroken 249ha/616ac of countryside. Hyde was the name of a piece of land here belonging to Westminster Abbey. At the *dissolution of the monasteries it was appropriated by Henry VIII, who turned it into a royal deer park. Open to the public from 1635, it became the haunt of highwaymen and duellists. Its present character derives from landscape gardening done for Queen Caroline, wife of George II; in 1730 she had the Westbourne stream dammed to form the lake known as the Serpentine (location of a 100-yd swimming race, the Peter Pan Cup, held each Christmas morning). *Rotten Row runs along the south side of the park. The southwest corner was the site of the *Crystal Palace; in the southeast corner is *Achilles*, a nude heroic figure by *Westmacott erected in 1822 in honour of Wellington and his companions by 'their countrywomen' (it is placed so as to be visible from the duke's nearby residence, *Apsley House); and to the northeast there is *Marble Arch and *Speakers' Corner.

Jack **Hylton** (1892–1965) Bandleader who was popular in both Britain and the USA during the 1930s. His signature tune was *She shall have music*, and 'Jack's back' became his catch phrase.

Hymns Ancient and Modern (1861) Collection of hymns compiled by Henry Baker (1821–77), with William Henry Monk (1823–89) as the musical editor (each hymn was printed with its tune). It rapidly became the hymnal most used in Anglican churches, even though Baker himself had controversially *Anglo-Catholic views; he caused some offence by including a hymn of his own to the Virgin Mary which begins 'Shall not we love thee, Mother dear'. The volume has been considerably added to (and subtracted from) in subsequent editions.

Nicholas **Hytner** (b. 1956) Stage director who has had some of his greatest successes in opera and musicals. His 1985 version of Handel's *Xerxes* is among the most celebrated of English National Opera productions, and *Miss Saigon* began a long run at Drury Lane in 1989. He staged *Carousel* in 1992 for the National Theatre, where his 1990 *Wind in the Willows* has secured a firm place in the repertory.

I

Iago see *Othello.

IBA see *ITC.

ICA (Institute of Contemporary Arts, London SW1) Founded in 1947 to promote the cause of modern art through exhibitions and lectures, the Institute was in Dover Street until moving to its present premises in the Mall in 1968.

Ice Age Term commonly used to mean the most recent of several glacial periods in which the cooling of the earth resulted in the polar ice cap extending far southward. A related and equally significant effect was the sinking of the sea level, as more of the earth's water was piled high as ice. In the last ice age, which ended about 10,000 years ago, the ice cap reached almost to the south of Britain (to a line roughly between the Bristol Channel and East Anglia) and dry land joined England to France between Dover and Calais. Humans crossed from the Continent and lived in caves, hunting the large hairy mammals such as the mammoth and the woolly rhinoceros which thrived in those conditions but became extinct with the thaw. The cycles of ice ages are not fully understood, but the current estimate is that the next one will begin in about 23,000 years.

Iceni see *Boudicca.

Ich dien see Prince of *Wales.

ICI (Imperial Chemical Industries) Company formed in 1926 by the merger of Britain's four largest chemical concerns at that time, with the express purpose of creating a group of major international status – a role which ICI has successfully maintained, though sometimes with the reputation of a slumbering giant (an image which in 1991 attracted the attention of *Hanson). The founding partners in 1926 were Brunner Mond, manufacturers of alkali; United Alkali, in the same field; Nobel Industries, an explosives company set up in 1870 by Alfred Nobel, the inventor of dynamite; and British Dyestuffs. In 1992 ICI announced a plan to split into two: commodity chemicals, paints and explosives were to remain with the existing company; and a new company, Zeneca, was to take over the speciality chemicals, drugs, agrochemicals and seeds businesses.

Icknield Way Prehistoric track which followed the high ground southwest from the *Wash, through the hills of East Anglia and the Chilterns to the Berkshire Downs. It then joined another route, to continue to the Stonehenge area and probably on to the south coast. The section through East Anglia and the Chilterns is still much used by walkers.

Ickworth (5km/3m SE of Bury St Edmunds) One of the strangest of English houses, built from 1795 for an improbable character – the 4th earl of Bristol (1730–1803), an avid collector and traveller (any Hotel Bristol on the Continent is named after him), who was simultaneously the free-spending and free-thinking bishop of Derry in Ireland. The great oval rotunda which is the central feature of Ickworth was to a design by an Italian architect (Mario Asprucci), modified by Francis and Joseph Sandys. The earl, who died before the completion of the house in 1829, had intended to live in the state rooms of the rotunda and to keep his art collection in the wings which are linked to it by long curving passages.

I, Claudius (1934) Historical novel by Robert *Graves, in which Claudius narrates an endearing version of his own eccentric path to the imperial throne through the horrors of Rome in the 1st century AD. Together with its sequel, *Claudius the God* (also 1934), it provided the material for a 13-part BBC drama series (*I, Claudius* 1976) with Derek Jacobi as the central character.

Ideal Home Exhibition Britain's largest annual exhibition of products connected with the home, sponsored by the *Daily Mail*. The first was held at *Olympia in 1908. The exhibitions have been annual since 1923, apart from the war years, and have been at *Earl's Court since 1979. In addition to the several hundred firms exhibiting their wares, each Ideal Home Exhibition includes some complete show houses built for the occasion.

'I dreamt that I dwelt in marble halls' see entry on The *Bohemian Girl.

Idylls of the King (1859–85) Series of 12 linked poems by *Tennyson, the first four of which were published under this title in 1859. The king is *Arthur, and the material is taken mainly from the *Morte d'Arthur* and the *Mabinogion*. Misty legends, medieval costume and Victorian sentiment combined to make them immensely successful with Tennyson's public.

IEA see *think-tank.

If Poem by *Kipling, published in *Rewards and Fairies* (1910) and rivalled only by Polonius's *'Neither a borrower nor a lender be' as a popular poetic collection of commonsense advice. But whereas Polonius is an old fool, Kipling is entirely serious. His 'ifs' are those tests which a boy must pass if he is to be a man (the poem begins, 'If you can keep your head when all about you/Are losing theirs . . .'). The ideals are those of the English *public school and the stiff upper lip: not even your closest friend should be able to

321

hurt you, don't look too good or talk too wise, dream but not too much, feel but not too much, think *but not too much*. Lindsay Anderson's film *If . . .* (1968) is set in a public school of which every flaw is writ exceptionally large.

'If music be the food of love, play on' see *Twelfth Night*.

Ightham Mote (18km/11m N of Tunbridge Wells) Moated manor house built round a courtyard, mainly in the 14–16C. The Great Hall, surviving from the earliest range of buildings, dates from the 1340s.

'ignorance is bliss' A quotation which has long appealed to schoolchildren, unaware of its original meaning or that it was first applied directly to them. It comes from Thomas *Gray's *Ode on a Distant Prospect of Eton College* (1742, publ. 1747). The poet envies the schoolboys their childish ignorance of the sorrows which will come with adult life:

> Where ignorance is bliss,
> 'Tis folly to be wise.

'Ignorance, madam, pure ignorance' The disarming reply of Dr *Johnson on being asked by a woman why, in his *Dictionary*, he had defined 'pastern' as the knee of a horse.

Ilkley (24,000 in 1981) Town in *Wharfedale in West Yorkshire, best known for the moor stretching to the south which features in the popular song *On Ilkla Moor baht'at* (meaning 'On Ilkley Moor without a hat').

*The **Illustrated London News** (ILN) Magazine of great significance in that its first issue – on 14 May 1842 – introduced the era of illustrated journalism. It was the brainchild of a printer, Herbert Ingram (1811–60), who had made money as a sideline from the sale of a laxative, Parr's Life Pills. His concept – news stories made more immediate by specially commissioned wood engravings – was an instant success. The paper was also made eye-catching by having news and pictures on the front page where others had only advertisements. Its content was challenging too; the second issue placed pictures of the domestic life of the young queen beside others of children working in the mines. When there was revolution in the streets of Paris in 1848, the editor sent an artist over with instructions to rush drawings back for the wood engravers – the first example of frontline image-gathering, now familiar in journalism. The ILN published illustrated stories of interest on any subject, as it still does today, but from the early years one specialization began to emerge – archaeology. This has traditionally been the journal where archaeologists first publish illustrations of their discoveries, including Howard *Carter's treasures of Tutankhamen in the 1920s.

The magazine remained for well over a century under the direct control of the Ingram family; the founder's grandson, Bruce Ingram, was editor for an extraordinary span of 63 years (1900–63). By the end of that period the ILN was in decline, partly because its old appeal of immediacy with pictorial news had been replaced by both television coverage and illustrated daily papers. It was a weekly from its launch in 1842; in 1971 it became a monthly and since 1989 has appeared only every other month.

I'm All Right Jack (1959) Satirical film by the *Boulting brothers which aimed at many targets, from corrupt management to idle workers, but which was seen above all as an attack on the trade unions. The reason was the brilliant performance of Peter *Sellers as Fred Kite, a ludicrously self-important shop steward.

The Illustrated London News *at its most exuberant: a colour plate of 1897 on the triumph of steam and electricity.*

'I may be some time' see Captain *Oates.

IMF (International Monetary Fund) Organization for promoting monetary stability, based in Washington, D.C., and conceived in 1944 at the conference at Bretton Woods (in New Hampshire). More than 150 countries are now members. One of its functions is to help member states with *balance of payments difficulties, while insisting on the measures necessary to resolve the underlying causes. In 1976 the UK agreed to large cuts in public expenditure in return for stand-by credit from the IMF.

I'm Henery the Eighth I am see Harry *Champion and *Herman's Hermits.

immigration A politically charged subject in Britain since the 1960s. In the years immediately after World War II, when the country had need of cheap labour, immigration from within the Commonwealth was made easy. The new arrivals came first from the West Indies and then from the Indian subcontinent. But alarm in some quarters at their numbers led to a Commonwealth Immigration Act in 1962. In 1968 the Commonwealth Immigrants Act further restricted the number of Asians arriving from Kenya. By then it was possible for politicians to play on prejudices against ethnic minorities. It was the year of Enoch *Powell's 'rivers of blood' speech, and *neo-Nazis were making their appearance in Britain.

The present law derives from the Immigration Acts of 1971 and 1988 and from the British Nationality Act of 1981. The combined effect of these has been to limit permanent entry to *British citizens, citizens of the republic of Ireland and certain Commonwealth citizens (those born before 1983 with at least one British parent); meanwhile EC regulations allow residence to citizens of other EC countries. Any outside these categories who are allowed to settle either have skills in short supply in Britain or have been granted political asylum.

A recent area of friction has resulted from the established custom by which many Asians return to their country of origin to marry. Marriage to a British citizen automatically conferred the right of abode until the act of 1981 introduced the 'primary purpose' rule – an obligation on foreigners marrying British citizens to prove that the primary purpose was not residence in Britain. This is stricter than the equivalent law in other EC countries, and a ruling by the *European Court of Justice in 1992 made it possible that its legality will be challenged.

'immortal with a kiss' see *Doctor Faustus.

Imperial College of Science and Technology Britain's leading college of science, part of *London University (though in the early 1990s there was talk of its becoming independent). Established on Exhibition Road in 1907, on land bought with the profits of the *Great Exhibition, it was an amalgamation of the Royal College of Science (founded in 1845), the Royal School of Mines (1851) and the *City and Guilds College.

Imperial War Museum (London SE1) Established by the government in 1917 to display the history of World War I and to receive the work produced by the official war artists, the museum opened in 1920 in the Crystal Palace. It transferred to its present building (previously *Bedlam) in 1936. Its theme has remained the history of war since 1914. A huge holding of modern British art (the largest outside the Tate Gallery) is supplemented by documents, weapons and vehicles. Outposts of the museum are HMS *Belfast, *Duxford airfield and the *Cabinet War Rooms.

imperial weights and measures The standards in use in Britain until the 1980s, when they began to be replaced by the metric system for *weight and fluid *volume (some imperial measures of *length, such as the mile, are proving more tenacious). Until the 18C, weights and measures were a chaotic collection of local standards, many of them extremely ancient. By the early 19C the imperial measurements had become general, but they were not precisely defined in their eventual form until later in the century. The word 'imperial' was first applied to a new gallon of 277.4 cubic inches, introduced in 1824; it replaced two existing gallons, the wine gallon of 231 cubic inches (which is still the gallon of the USA) and the ale gallon of 282 cubic inches. The measurements of length and weight were scientifically established in the Weights and Measures Act of 1878. This put an end to the old system of *troy weight, except for jewels and precious metals.

*The **Importance of Being Earnest** (1895) The last and most brilliant of Oscar *Wilde's comedies. The play concerns Algernon Moncrieff's courtship of Cecily Cardew and his friend Jack Worthing's of Gwendolen Fairfax (a pursuit made hazardous by the sharp tongue of her mother, Lady Bracknell). The frivolous young men ease their social life with the help of invented characters; Jack is known as Ernest when he is in town, while Algy has created Bunbury, a sickly relation in the country, whom he pretends to visit to avoid dreary London engagements. The play succeeds through its flow of epigram, but the plot is neatly tied together when it is revealed that Jack as a baby was accidentally left by Miss Prism, the governess, in a handbag at Victoria station; that he is Algy's brother; and that his real name is indeed Ernest, which happens to be Gwendolen's favourite. The 'importance of being earnest' (the final phrase of the play) thus applies both to his real identity and to the ending of frivolity as the couples at last come together.

inch see *length.

Inchcape Group formed in 1958 to bring together various enterprises, the majority of which had been established by Scottish merchants in the 18–19C to trade with the east. Several of them had been shaped or merged by James Mackay, created earl of Inchcape in 1911. It was his grandson who formed Inchcape in 1958. Now one of Britain's largest companies, the group is involved in worldwide marketing of goods (vehicles, business machines, drinks) and services.

Immigration: annual balance of immigrants and emigrants in the UK, in thousands

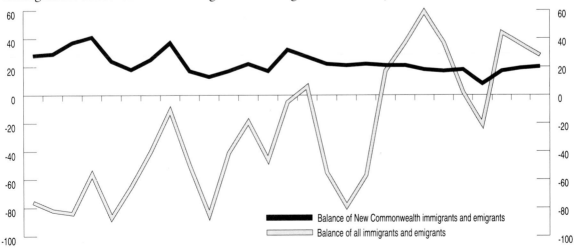

The New Commonwealth includes the entire present-day Commonwealth except Canada, Australia and New Zealand. Immigrants from Pakistan are included during the years when the country was not in the Commonwealth.
Source: Annual Abstract of Statistics (see *Central Statistical Office).

income support The main form of social security for those not eligible for *unemployment benefit. Issued by the *Benefits Agency, it goes to anyone whose income is below a certain level. In such cases housing benefit is also likely to be available, to help with the rent. Income support was known before 1988 as supplementary benefit (which in 1965 replaced the earlier national assistance, introduced in 1948).

income tax Great Britain was the first country to introduce income tax. In 1799 William Pitt, needing funds for the war against France, levied 10% per annum on incomes over £200, with a reduced rate for lower incomes and exemption below £60. The tax was lifted at the end of the Napoleonic Wars in 1815. It was next imposed in 1842, again as a temporary measure and now at only about 3%. But this time it stuck. In World War I it reached the unprecedented level of 30% with a surcharge on high incomes. The pattern was thus set for a standard tax up to a certain level and then a succession of higher rates. These have at times become excessive. In 1976 the standard rate was 35% and the highest rate on earned income was 83%; but there was a surcharge of 15% on income from investments, bringing the top rate of tax to 98%. This surcharge was abolished in 1984; the highest rate was reduced in 1979 to 60%; and the standard rate came down to 30% in 1979, 29% in 1986 and 27% in 1987. In 1988 the number of bands was reduced to two, a basic rate of 25% and a higher rate of 40%. A lower rate of 20% on the first small slice of taxable income was introduced in 1992.

In 1990 a long-standing anomaly was removed. Until then a husband was responsible for ensuring that tax was paid on his wife's income, and their earnings were normally assessed together. Now they are treated as two individual taxpayers. See also *PAYE.

*The **Independent*** The first serious national daily newspaper to be established in Britain in the 20C. Conceived in some secrecy by three journalists on the *Daily Telegraph* (one of whom, Andreas Whittam Smith, became the paper's first editor), it was launched in 1986 in direct competition with the *Times*, *Telegraph* and *Guardian*. The new paper was committed to independence in two forms – financial (the money was raised from some 30 City institutions so that there should be no press baron in control) and political (readership research had revealed a widespread desire for a newspaper of no particular allegiance). A sister paper, *The Independent on Sunday*, was first published in 1990.

independent school see *public school.

India Member of the *Commonwealth since 1947. Britain's involvement with the Indian subcontinent began in the 17C, and for the next 150 years was largely the history of the *East India Company. After the *Indian Mutiny (1857) the British government took control, appointing a viceroy to rule in the name of Queen Victoria; she herself was proclaimed Empress of India in 1876, adding the title 'Ind. Imp.' (from the Latin *Indiae Imperatrix*) to her coins from 1893.

At this same period a movement for independence was beginning. The first Indian National Congress met in Bombay in 1885; from it developed the Congress party, which has been the main force in Indian politics in the 20C. In 1906 the Muslim League was formed, to safeguard the interests of the subcontinent's large minority of Muslims.

The leading figure in the later independence movement was Mahatma Gandhi (1869–1948). Living in South Africa from 1893 to 1915, he developed there a political technique of passive resistance to win rights for the oppressed. Back in India his similar campaigns of civil disobedience proved an effective weapon against British rule. They undoubtedly speeded up the eventual withdrawal of the British (in 1947), but that was achieved at a cost which to Gandhi was a tragedy – the cost of partition. He believed that the Hindu and Muslim communities could together share a single democracy, but the Muslim League was committed to the creation of an independent Muslim country, *Pakistan, and the British government came to the conclusion that this was the only solution. Violence erupted in the period immediately before the British withdrawal and the process of partition was accompanied by widespread communal massacres, with a million or more deaths. Gandhi devoted all his energies to reconciling the communities. It was not a Muslim but a Hindu fanatic who assassinated him in 1948.

The excellence of Anglo-Indian relationships at this final stage is suggested by the fact that the last viceroy, Lord Mountbatten, was invited to stay on as the first governor general. The family of the first prime minister of independent India, Jawaharlal Nehru (1889–1964), remained in power for most of the following half century, with his daughter Indira Gandhi (no relation to the Mahatma) and his grandson Rajiv Gandhi in turn holding the premiership. Both, tragically, were assassinated, in 1984 and 1991.

Indian Mutiny (also known as the First War of Indian Independence, 1857–8) The most serious uprising in the history of British *India. There had been a long build-up of resentment against the western and Christian values being introduced by the British, but the immediate flashpoint was the cartridge for a new Enfield rifle. This came in greased paper which had to be bitten before use by the soldier (or sepoy). Animal rather than vegetable fat had foolishly been used, and the conviction soon spread among the Hindu soldiers that it was the fat of cows (a sacred animal) and among the Muslims that it was pig fat (unclean). Sepoys shot their European officers in a succession of incidents. They first captured Delhi, then Lucknow and other garrison cities. After much brutality on both sides, order was restored by the summer of 1858. The administration was to be much improved by this unpleasant shock. All the British in India, including even the soldiers, were at this time still employees of the *East India Company. The Indian army and the Indian civil service were now placed under government control.

Indians see *ethnic and religious minorities.

Ind. Imp. see *India.

Industrial Revolution A term first used in the mid-19C to describe the process by which Britain, during the previous 100 years, had been transformed from a society in which most people lived in the country, and most goods were produced by hand, to one in which urban living and machine production were the norm. Many different factors contributed to Britain being the first nation to go through this process, but they can be broadly divided into natural and political causes.

Nature had provided England with an abundance of two essential ingredients, *iron and *coal. A third natural commodity, water, played its part in several ways. There were reliable streams to drive the machinery of the early textile mills; the island's coastal waters simplified the distribution of fuel, raw materials and finished goods; the development of the *canal system greatly improved inland transport; and the moist climate and soft water of Lancashire were peculiarly well suited to the manufacture of *cotton goods, which were at the forefront of the revolution.

The political advantages stemmed from the *Revolution of 1688, which made possible the beginnings of a middle class with capital to invest, eager for more wealth and willing to take risks. Inventors and entrepreneurs were able to rise from quite humble beginnings to reap the rewards of their energies (*Arkwright was an outstanding early example), and the process was fostered by a strong Nonconformist tradition of hard work and thrift. There was also a ready-made economic advantage in Britain's available market, larger than any other nation's at the time; the Act of *Union had made England, Wales and Scotland an unusually large tariff-free internal zone, and the developing *British empire provided wide opportunities abroad.

A further boost came in the early 19C with the extension of *steam power, increasing output from the mills and improving methods of transport (see *railways). Britain's emerging industrial society was long blemished by the exploitation of cheap labour – an abuse gradually redressed in the series of *Factory Acts.

infant mortality The death of young babies was a familiar tragedy in past centuries at all levels of society (see Queen *Anne for an example), and it is only in the 20C that the figures have been drastically reduced by improved medical care. As the chart shows, the number of deaths in the first 12 months of life have fallen from 142 out of every 1000 babies in 1900 to just 8 per 1000 in 1990. The average *life expectancy at birth in 1990 was 72 years for boys and 78 for girls.

Infant Phenomenon see * *Nicholas Nickleby*.

infant prodigies In recent years childhood precocity in mathematics has been to the fore: first Ruth Lawrence (b. 1971, A level at 10, undergraduate at Oxford at 12) and then Ganesh Sittampalam (b. 1979, A level at 9, undergraduate at the university of Surrey at 11, Britain's youngest-ever graduate at 13, with first-class honours). But the most famous infant prodigy in English history was an actor, Master William Betty (1791–1874). Known as the young Roscius (from the most admired actor of ancient Rome), he caused hysteria among London audiences when he was only 13. Pitt even adjourned the House of Commons so that members could see Master Betty as Hamlet.

infant school see *state school.

Infant mortality

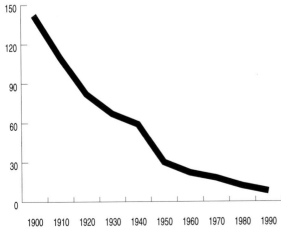

Deaths of infants under one year per thousand live births: compare graph of *birth rate.
Source: Annual Abstract of Statistics (*see* *Central Statistical Office*).

inflation Britain had its highest postwar rates of inflation during the 1970s – see *RPI and the *pound in your pocket. During the 1980s it became the overriding priority of the Conservative government to bring inflation down. It was argued that high *unemployment and high interest rates (see *base rate) were necessary evils in pursuit of an essential economic stability.

Ingleborough Cave (64km/40m NW of Bradford) Spectacular series of limestone stalactite-and-stalagmite caves. Further up the hillside is Gaping Gill, a cavern into which a stream plunges 104m/340ft.

*The **Ingoldsby Legends**; or, Mirth and marvels, by Thomas Ingoldsby, Esquire* Humorous poems on medieval subjects, with rattling rhythms and rhymes, written by a clergyman, R.H. Barham (Richard Harris Barham, 1788– 1845), and published from 1837. The only poem from the collection to remain at all widely known is *The Jackdaw of Rheims*, about a cheeky bird who steals the cardinal's ring but then repents of his crime and dies years later 'in the odour of sanctity'.

inheritance tax The name since 1986 of the tax on wealth transferred on a person's death. Up to 1975 it was known as estate duty (colloquially as death duties) and then as Capital Transfer Tax. The main differences are that estate duty was levied when a husband or wife died and their estate passed to the surviving partner, which has not been the case since 1975; and that both estate duty and CTT were paid on a steeply sliding scale, whereas inheritance tax has a large exempt slice, index-linked to the *RPI, with a flat rate payable above it (in 1992 £150,000 exempt and then 40% tax).

Inheritance tax, like CTT before it, is also payable on wealth transferred during a person's lifetime. There are many exemptions, including all payments to charities. Lifetime gifts between individuals are exempt below certain levels. Any number of separate gifts may be made to different people as long as each gift is worth not more than £250. Gifts of greater value are accumulated for tax purposes, and each person may give an accumulated total of £3000 in any one year without incurring tax (the figure has been at that level since 1981). Husbands and wives may each give the full amount, and any part of an unused allowance can be carried forward for one year – bringing the possible maximum of exempt gifts for a couple up to £12,000 in a given tax year.

Inkerman see the *Crimean War.

INLA see *terrorism.

Board of **Inland Revenue** (London WC2) Executive agency (see *Next Steps) deriving from a government department established in 1849 for the collection of taxes and excise.

Excise was transferred to the Board of *Customs in 1909, leaving the Inland Revenue to collect direct taxes – in particular *income tax, *capital gains tax, *inheritance tax, *corporation tax and *stamp duty. It is answerable to the chancellor of the exchequer.

*In **Memoriam** A.H.H.* (1850) The poem by *Tennyson which appealed more than any other to Victorian sensibilities. An elegy for his friend Arthur Hallam (1811–33), it is a compilation of many short passages written in the intervening 17 years, reflecting the poet's varying response to the young man's death and to his own grief. The dominant tone is of doubt and despair, but it moves towards a more optimistic ending and Tennyson's readers were able to see it as an affirmation of faith.

inner cities Since the early 1980s a succession of riots has drawn much public attention to underprivileged areas in many of Britain's cities, characterized by concrete tower blocks and a very high level of unemployment, particularly among the young. There has also often been a racial element, with black communities claiming discrimination against them by the police and others. The areas most involved have been Brixton in London (riots in 1981, leading to a public enquiry by Lord *Scarman, others in 1982 and 1985, and violent protests against the *poll tax in 1990); Toxteth in Liverpool, where the goverment's urgent response to riots in 1981 did not prevent a lesser repetition in 1985; Handsworth in Birmingham in 1985; and the St Paul's district of Bristol in 1980 and 1986, followed by trouble on the Hartcliffe estate in 1992. The single most horrifying event was on the *Broadwater Farm estate in London in 1985.

Responses by the government have included *enterprise zones in 1981, *City Challenge in 1991 and (active from 1993) an Urban Regeneration Agency – run by Lord Walker, with the primary purpose of bringing back into use 60,000ha/150,000ac of derelict land in Britain's towns and cities.

Innerpeffray (26km/16m SW of Perth) Scotland's first lending library. David Drummond (d. 1692) began the collection of books in the 1670s and left a bequest in his will for the library to be maintained 'for the improvement and education of the population'. The present building, in the grounds of Innerpeffray Castle, dates from 1762. The ledger of loans to local people survives from 1747 onwards, but the policy of lending was ended in 1968.

Inner Temple see *Inns of Court.

Inns of Court Collegiate institutions in London, surviving from the Middle Ages, to which all *barristers belong. The inns are believed to derive from hostels for those studying the common law, a subject not taught in the universities. The early rule that a student must reside for a number of terms was gradually replaced by a requirement that a given number of dinners must be eaten; three dinners were judged to equal one term. It is usual today for 24 meals to be consumed – normally over a two-year period, but by 'double dining' the task can be completed in one.

There are four inns, all occupying grounds to the west of the old walled *City of London. They are first mentioned in documents of the 15C, but certainly existed in the previous century. Lincoln's Inn is believed to derive its name from premises rented in the 14C from Thomas de Lincoln. Gray's Inn was associated from the same period with an eminent legal family, the de Greys. The Inner Temple and the Middle Temple together occupy a site which belonged to the Knights Templar until the suppression of the order in 1312. They share responsibility for an architectural treasure inherited from their predecessors – the Temple Church, one of the few round Norman churches in England, built in the late 12C in a transitional style between the Romanesque and the Gothic.

The equivalent of the inns of court in Scotland is the Faculty of *Advocates.

insider dealing The buying or selling of shares when in possession of privileged information, not as yet known to the public, which will predictably affect the price. This clearly unfair advantage, resulting in an eventual real loss to the other party in the transaction, was first made illegal by the Company Securities (Insider Dealing) Act of 1985. The first person to be prosecuted, in July 1987, was Geoffrey Collier, the former joint managing director of Morgan Grenfell Securities; he was fined £25,000.

An Inspector Calls see J.B. *Priestley.

Inspector Morse (Central TV 1987–93) Self-contained 2-hour murder mysteries, set in and around Oxford, starring John Thaw as the gloomy inspector (devoted to real ale and Mozart) and Kevin Whateley as his long-suffering assistant, Sergeant Lewis. Based originally on the novels of Colin Dexter, with complex stories noted more for Morse's musings over a pint than for action and violence, the programmes became a surprise international hit. The 1993 series, declared as the final one, brought the total number of episodes to 28.

Institute of Contemporary Arts see *ICA.

Instrument of Government see the *Protectorate.

Inter-cities Fairs Cup see *UEFA Cup.

interest rates see *base rate and *MLR.

International Monetary Fund see *IMF.

internment The detention without trial of people suspected of *terrorism in Northern Ireland was introduced by the Stormont parliament in August 1971. The move strengthened Roman Catholic hostility to Stormont and led to a marked increase in republican acts of terrorism, which in turn sparked off an upsurge of loyalist retaliation. Some of the internees engaged in violent protests in Long Kesh (later renamed the *Maze). The policy was ended in 1975 by Merlyn Rees, the secretary of state for Northern Ireland, who released in December of that year the last 73 internees (1,981 men and women had at various times been held).

The nationalist and loyalist terrorists in the Maze since that time have all been charged with or convicted of criminal acts, mainly murder. A renewed upsurge of terrorism in the early 1990s led some to argue for the reintroduction of internment.

'In the name of God, go!' A phrase used on two dramatic occasions in the House of Commons. It was first spoken by Oliver Cromwell in 1653 when forcibly ejecting the remaining members of the *Long Parliament: 'You have sat too long here for any good you have been doing. Depart, I say, and let us have done with you. In the name of God, go!' In a deliberate echo of the past, the passage was used by Leo Amery on 7 May 1940 in his attack on Neville *Chamberlain.

Intimations of Mortality from Recollections of Early Childhood (1807) Ode by *Wordsworth interpreting the intensity of childhood experience as a hint of another existence, preceding and succeeding our own.

Inveraray (500 in 1981) Town and castle in Strathclyde, planned as an entity in the 18C. The delightful small town has the rational elegance of its origins, with buildings by various members of the *Adam family. The plan was drawn up by Roger Morris (1695–1749), who was also responsible for the exterior of the castle with its early Gothic Revival details. The interiors are by Robert Mylne (1733–1811), in a more delicate neoclassical style. Inveraray is the ancestral seat of the dukes of Argyll, chieftains of the clan Campbell.

Inverewe (134km/83m NW of Inverness) Garden on a headland on the northwest coast of Scotland, created between 1862 and 1952 by Osgood Mackenzie and his daughter. It is said that when he bought the property the only thing growing on it was a dwarf willow (treasured for many years but now dead). Thanks to a century of imaginative planting, the kindly influence of the *Gulf Stream and protective windbreaks of Corsican pine and Scots fir, there is now a profusion of improbably exotic plants.

Inverness (40,000 in 1991) Town on the river Ness at the head of the Moray Firth; administrative centre of the Highland region of Scotland. Its commanding position made it one of the chief strongholds of the *Picts. Apart from the 16C Abertarff House and the 18C High Church, the main buildings today are all of the 19C – in particular the castle, the Town House and the episcopal St Andrew's Cathedral.

Inverness-shire Until 1975 a *county crossing northern Scotland from coast to coast, now part of the Highland region.

invisible exports see *balance of payments.

In Which We Serve (1942) War film which was the first collaboration between Noel *Coward (writer and director) and David *Lean (co-director). From the recollections of the survivors of a torpedoed destroyer it weaves a rich fabric of wartime life on shore and on the ship. The captain was played by Noel Coward, the petty officer by Bernard Miles, and two of the crew members by John *Mills and Richard *Attenborough.

Iona Small island in the Inner *Hebrides, off the southwest tip of Mull, which acquired great religious importance with the establishment of a monastery by St *Columba in 563. It was from here that St *Aidan took Christianity to the opposite coast of Britain, at *Lindisfarne. Recent excavation suggests that in the following centuries Iona may have developed into a sizable community, more like a small university town than a monastery.

The island experienced a modern revival in 1938 when George Macleod, a minister of the Church of Scotland, founded the Iona Community, a missionary group dedicated to emulating the practical Christianity of the early Celtic fathers. The first task was restoring the abbey, reconsecrated in 1959, but the mission was also extended to other places, in particular industrial parishes in Scotland. Large numbers of Christian groups now work and worship on the island each summer.

IPPR see *think-tank.

Ipswich (119,000 in 1991) County town and administrative centre of Suffolk, at the head of the estuary of the river Orwell. Its position as a safe harbour on an inlet of the North Sea has caused it to be much involved with the continent of Europe, from the early days of Danish settlements and Viking raids to the extensive shipping activities of its modern docks. It was the birthplace of Cardinal *Wolsey (Wolsey's Gateway is all that survives of the college he established here in 1536) and it was where *Gainsborough had his first studio in the 1750s. The town's best-known link with the 19C is in fiction; the Great White Horse Hotel, still in business, features prominently in *Pickwick Papers (Mr Pickwick has an adventure there with a lady in yellow curlpapers).

The Ancient House in Buttermarket, also known as Sparrowe's House, was built in the 1560s and has on its exterior an excellent 17C example of East Anglia's decorative speciality, *pargeting. Christchurch Mansion, a Tudor mansion of 1548–50 in a parkland setting, has interiors of the 17–18C; it contains a display of decorative art and paintings with a local emphasis, including work by the area's two great painters, Gainsborough and Constable.

A Celtic cross (St John's Cross, 10C but much restored) near the abbey church on Iona.

Ipswich Town, known as the Blues or Town (Portman Road, Ipswich). Football club formed in 1878 which did not turn professional until 1936. Elected to Division 3 of the *Football League in 1938, they had a meteoric rise during the years when Alf *Ramsey was manager, winning Division 2 in 1961 and, astonishingly, Division 1 the very next year. They had another successful period under the future England manager, Bobby *Robson. Club victories: FA Cup 1978; League Champions 1962; UEFA Cup 1981.

IRA (Irish Republican Army) Paramilitary organization formed early in 1919 to use guerrilla tactics against the British in *Ireland. It was the direct successor of a similar group formed in 1913 as the Irish Volunteers, but others such as the *Fenians (or Irish Republican Brotherhood) were also involved, particularly in the *Easter Rising. The IRA campaign (the *Anglo-Irish War of 1919–21) resulted in the creation of the Irish Free State. Those in the IRA who accepted this solution became the nucleus of the new state's army; those who rejected it, following the policy of *Sinn Fein, were known as the Irregulars and became the opposing side in the Irish civil war of 1921–3, in which they were defeated. This rump of the IRA continued to support Sinn Fein (itself much reduced by parting company with its leader, de Valera, in 1926), and it has been an illegal organization in Ireland since 1931.

In 1969 the Provisional IRA and Provisional Sinn Fein split from the parent bodies on various issues – including the use of *terrorism, which the Provisional IRA (Provisionals or Provos) have carried out since then in Northern Ireland and occasionally in mainland Britain and on the Continent. Close links between the two organizations are explained as Sinn Fein being the 'political wing' of the IRA – a distinction which many find hard to accept.

Iranian embassy siege see *SAS.

Iraq Administered by Britain as a *mandated territory from 1920 until its independence in 1932. The region of Mesopotamia had previously been ruled as three provinces within the Turkish empire, so it was only during the mandate that Iraq took shape as a nation. The British appointed Faisal I (1885–1933) as king in 1921, and the country remained a monarchy until the assassination of his grandson Faisal II (1936–58). See also *Gulf War and *Matrix Churchill.

Iraqi supergun In April 1990 customs officers on Teesside, in Cleveland, seized some very large steel cylinders which they believed might be part of a supergun; manufactured by two British firms, Sheffield Forgemasters and Walter Somers of Halesowen, the cylinders were on their way to Iraq. Subsequent investigations revealed that a vast gun with the codename Project Babylon had been designed for Saddam Hussein by a Canadian ballistics expert, Gerald Bull (in 1990 he was murdered in his Brussels flat, some said by Mossad, the Israeli secret service). After the Gulf War one version of the gun was found assembled up the edge of a hillside in Iraq; with a barrel 52m/170ft long, it could have fired chemical, biological or nuclear warheads to a distance of 1600km/1000m. The attempted export of the sections from Britain, contravening an embargo on supplying arms to Iraq, caused political embarrassment because the Department of Trade and Industry, the Ministry of Defence and MI6 had been previously warned that the steel sections might be for a gun and not, as the Iraqis claimed, for an oil pipe. In 1992 Customs and Excise presented the seized sections to the Imperial War Museum.

Ireland The second largest island of the British Isles, much influenced by the *Celts for whom this was the last point in their long migration westwards through Europe. After the conversion of the Irish by St *Patrick, it was Ireland which exerted pressure and influence on Britain – first in the missionary journeys of St *Columba and others, then in the expansion of the kingdom of the *Scots. But the pattern changed a century after the Norman Conquest. From then until 1921 it was more a case of constant pressure from Britain provoking constant Irish grievance.

In 1171 Henry II landed in Ireland and spent the winter in Dublin, receiving the homage of most of the Irish kings and granting large tracts of Irish land to his English followers. Dublin became the centre of English rule, though its authority often extended no further than the surrounding *pale. The first king to establish firm administrative control over Ireland was Henry VIII, in 1541. In the Elizabethan period a succession of rebellions by Irish hereditary chieftains resulted in vast areas of their land being confiscated and handed over to English adventurers. Meanwhile the Reformation, which had made no headway in a strongly Roman Catholic Ireland, caused any friction between the Irish and the English to be seen also as a clash between Catholics and Protestants.

Four years after Elizabeth's death the incident known as the flight of the earls took place. The earls of Tyrone and Tyrconnell, vassal lords of large crown territories in *Ulster, had engaged in rebellion against the queen. Reinstated in their lands, but under conditions which they found intolerable, they fled from Ireland to Roman Catholic Europe in September 1607 with about 100 other northern chieftains and their families. They thus provided the perfect opportunity for Britain to alter the balance in Ireland to its own advantage. English and Scottish Protestants were settled on the lands of the departed chieftains, giving northern Ireland a strong and favoured Protestant minority.

A rising of the Catholics in Ulster in 1641 led to a broader Irish war which only aggravated the situation. The English parliament raised an army by promising confiscated land in Ireland to those who would provide troops or money; Oliver *Cromwell himself conducted the later stages of the campaign. The Irish Catholics had one last chance to redress their grievances in war, when they marched in 1689 in support of James II. His defeat at the *Boyne condemned them to decades of severe

Tudor view of the Irish: a chieftain dines out of doors to the accompaniment of a harp (woodcut, c.1580).

restrictions under a parliament in Dublin which was limited to Protestants and which was in any case little more than a mouthpiece for London.

For the next two centuries Ireland was culturally a part of the United Kingdom. The elegance of 18c Dublin, much of which survives, is in the style of other British cities of the time; and a succession of brilliant Anglo-Irish Protestant writers (Swift, Goldsmith, Sheridan, Wilde, Shaw) lived in England and adorned English literature, a pattern broken only when Yeats and Synge made a special theme of their Irishness. But in the political context Irish aspirations remained fresh, stimulated by the examples of the American War of Independence and of the French Revolution. The latter led to the formation of societies of United Irishmen, urging Catholic emancipation, and to armed insurrection by Wolfe Tone (1763–98) with assistance from France. It was this unrest which persuaded Pitt that Ireland should be part of the United Kingdom, and the Act of Union was passed in 1800 with effect from 1 January 1801.

The political arena moved now from Dublin to London, with Irish members of parliament at Westminster. The election of Daniel *O'Connell in 1828 led directly to the Emancipation Act of 1829, admitting Roman Catholics to public offices. And although the *Great Famine of the 1840s had the temporary effect of reducing nationalist pressure, *Home Rule was the most consistently urgent topic in London from the 1870s. In Ireland the *Fenian movement was founded in 1858 and *Sinn Fein in 1902. The final stages of the long slow process towards Home Rule, violently opposed by *Carson, were only postponed by World War I.

The war offered the more radical nationalists an opportunity for action, with possible support from Germany (as sought by Roger *Casement). The result was the *Easter Rising of 1916, followed by the emergence of what became the *IRA and the period known as the Troubles (more formally the *Anglo-Irish War).

The Government of Ireland Act of 1920 provided for separate parliaments in Dublin and Belfast, each with limited local autonomy. Such a parliament came into effect in *Northern Ireland. But Sinn Fein rejected the proposal for the south, and violence continued until the Anglo-Irish Treaty of 6 December 1921; this finally recognized the whole island (except the *six counties of Ulster) as the independent Irish Free State, with *dominion status in the British empire.

The name of independent southern Ireland was changed to Eire in 1937, and to the Republic of Ireland in 1948. By the same act of 1948 Ireland withdrew from the *Commonwealth.

John **Ireland** (1879–1962) Composer known in particular for his songs and song cycles. *Sea Fever* (1913) set Masefield's words; *The Land of Lost Content* (1920–1) and *We'll to the Woods No More* (1926–7) are based on poems by Housman.

The **Irish** The inhabitants of *Ireland, both north and south. The majority are Roman Catholics, descendants of people who were in Ireland before the *Reformation; but there is a minority of Protestants, concentrated in *Northern Ireland (where they are a majority), descending from English and Scottish settlers in more recent centuries. The Northern Irish are British citizens, and people from the republic of Ireland have for historical reasons been allowed the right to live and vote in the UK (see *immigration). The Catholic Irish form one of Britain's main immigrant communities, particularly in the west coast cities of Liverpool and Glasgow.

Irish National Liberation Army see *terrorism.

Irish potato famine see the *Great Famine.

Irish Republican Army see *IRA.

Irish Sea The water between Ireland and Britain, linked with the Atlantic by the North Channel to the north and St George's Channel to the south.

Iron Age The period following the *Bronze Age, when the use of iron for tools and weapons replaced bronze (which could only be cast, whereas iron could be heated and shaped, or wrought). In Britain the Iron Age began around 500 BC.

iron and steel New developments in metal technology from the 18c played an important part in Britain's lead in the *Industrial Revolution. Early ironworks were invariably sited in forests because the smelting process required large quantities of charcoal. This dependence ended with the discovery by the Darby family (commemorated at *Ironbridge) that cast iron, also called pig iron, could be smelted with coke. Wrought iron made a similar advance with the puddling technique (a heating and stirring process which isolated a hard core of almost pure iron), patented in 1784 by Henry Cort (1740–1800). Cort also introduced the system of passing the hot metal through rollers, eliminating the need for much of the hammering. These two developments left the rapidly developing industries of the early 19c with a choice between cast iron (hard but brittle) and wrought iron (strong, in the sense of resisting shocks, but relatively soft). New applications, such as railway tracks, required a material both hard and strong. The answer was steel – iron strengthened with a small proportion of carbon.

Steel was already being produced in small quantities (for items such as cutlery and in particular at *Sheffield) by cottage-industry methods involving somewhat haphazard regulation of the carbon content of the iron. Mass production of a reliable product was made possible from the 1850s by the *Bessemer process, in which the entire carbon content of the molten iron was removed and the required proportion then reintroduced. Further improvement followed in the 1860s with the open-hearth method of *Siemens, in which a higher and better-controlled temperature in the furnace enabled the process to be stopped as soon as the carbon content was correct. The third stage in the growth of the 19c steel industry was the development in the 1870s by Sidney Thomas (1850–85) and his cousin Percy Gilchrist (1851–1935) of a furnace lining which made possible the use of more widely available iron ores with a high phosphorus content.

These techniques gave Britain a strong lead in world steel production in the late 19c. By the 1920s this had been eroded by foreign competition. Economic difficulties between the wars led to the developments which have resulted in today's *British Steel.

Ironbridge The world's first cast-iron bridge. It was constructed over the river Severn in 1777–9, a short distance downstream from Coalbrookdale in Shropshire, by the Darby family of ironmasters. They had already established a leading position in the industry when Abraham Darby (1677–1717) pioneered in 1709 the technique of smelting iron ore with coke. It was his grandson, also Abraham Darby (1750–91), who put up the iron bridge. It gave its name to the village which grew up round the toll house, a name now internationally known through the Ironbridge Gorge Museum. Founded in 1967, this is Britain's leading museum of industrial archaeology, preserving many separate features in this cradle area of the *Industrial Revolution. Apart from the bridge itself, the sites include the original coke-smelting furnace at

Ironbridge and its furnaces: De Loutherbourg's apocalyptic vision in Coalbrookdale by Night *(1801)*.

Coalbrookdale, the slightly later Bedlam Furnaces which appear in action in De Loutherbourg's *Coalbrookdale by Night*, and several locations connected with mining, tile-making and ceramics.

iron curtain Although the phrase had been in earlier use, it was Winston Churchill who gave it wide currency in his speech at Fulton, Missouri, on 5 March 1946. He pointed out that the demarcation line between the Soviet and western spheres of influence had created a new Europe very different from the one the Allies had fought to save; 'From Stettin in the Baltic to Trieste in the Adriatic an iron curtain has descended across the Continent.' In the divided world which had resulted from *Yalta, he now argued that 'a special relationship between the British Commonwealth and the United States' was the only safe remedy. The wall dividing Berlin later came to symbolize the iron curtain, which was effectively lifted when the wall was demolished in 1989.

Iron Duke see Duke of *Wellington.

Jeremy **Irons** (b. 1948) Actor who has played several leading roles with the Royal Shakespeare Company and who established himself on Broadway in Tom Stoppard's *The Real Thing* (1984). His best-known TV role is Charles Ryder in *Brideshead Revisited* (1981). Highlights of his film career have been *The French Lieutenant's Woman* (1981) and *Reversal of Fortune* (1990), in which he won an Oscar for his portrayal of Claus von Bulow.

Ironsides see *Marston Moor.

Henry **Irving** (stage name of John Henry Brodribb, 1838–1905, kt 1895) The outstanding actor of the late-Victorian theatre, and the first in his profession to be awarded a knighthood. Several years of touring in the provinces were followed by appearances in London from 1866, but his first major success was with a play and in

a theatre central to his career; at the Lyceum in 1871, performing in his own production of a *melodrama (*The Bells* by Leopold Lewis), he achieved a run of 150 nights. He made the Lyceum famous, managing it from 1879 to 1901 with Ellen *Terry as his leading lady. Shakespeare was the mainstay of their joint fame, but many modern plays were produced and *The Bells* remained in the repertory to the end; Irving's acting was mannered and melodramatic in style, and such a play evidently suited him. He was buried in Westminster Abbey.

Christopher **Isherwood** (1904–86) English-born novelist, best known for his autobiographical fiction set in Berlin during the period when Hitler was rising to power. *Mr Norris Changes Trains* (1935) was followed by *Goodbye to Berlin* (1939), a collection of sketches of which one, about the delightfully eccentric cabaret artist Sally Bowles, later became the basis for the musical comedy *Cabaret* (1968).

Isherwood collaborated with *Auden during the 1930s on three political dramas and on a book about their visit to China (*Journey to a War* 1938). They emigrated together to the USA in 1939 and were both naturalized in 1946. *A Single Man* (1964) and *Christopher and His Kind* (1976) were accounts of his own homosexuality. His companion, the artist Don Bachardy, published in 1990 his drawings of Isherwood during his last illness.

Isis The name by which the Thames is known at Oxford, perpetuating an ancient academic fallacy. The Roman name for the river was *Tamesis*. In about the 14c scholars decided that this was a combination of Thames and Isis; they therefore assigned the name Thames to the river below Dorchester and Isis to the upper reaches. Isis is also Oxford's second crew, competing before the main event on the day of the *Boat Race.

islands area Area of *local government since 1975 in the islands of Scotland, equivalent to a *region on the mainland. The three islands areas are Orkney, Shetland and Western Isles.

Isle of Dogs see *Canary Wharf.

Isle of Man (Ellan Vannin in Manx Gaelic, 65,000 in 1981) Large island (588sq.km/227sq.m) in the Irish Sea, roughly equidistant from Ireland, England and Scotland, with Douglas as its capital. It has mountainous scenery (highest peak Snaefell, 612m/2034ft). The island was much visited from the 6C by Celtic missionaries from Ireland; it was part of the territory of the Viking rulers of Dublin (10–13C); then for nearly a century it was governed from Scotland; and from 1333 it has been linked with England, first as the feudal territory of various great nobles (in particular the Stanley family, the earls of Derby) and since 1765 as the property of the crown. But it has never been entirely absorbed within the United Kingdom. It is a self-governing crown dependency and as such retains its own parliament, the *Tynwald. The heraldic device of three running legs, joined at the centre, has been in use since at least the 14C. The island is most widely known for the *TT races and the *Manx cat.

The Tynwald led the world as the first parliament to give votes to women (in 1881, see *suffragettes), but a century later the Isle of Man was notoriously backward in its legislation; bills to end *capital punishment and to legalize *homosexuality were at last introduced in 1992, but *corporal punishment was also at that time still on the statute book.

Isle of Wight The largest island off the south coast of England (380sq.km/147sq.m). It is also an English *county (127,000 in 1991, administrative centre Newport.

The **Isles of Greece** see *Don Juan.

Alec **Issigonis** (1906–88, kt 1969) British designer, of Greek descent, responsible for two of the most successful British cars – the Morris Minor (1948) and the *Mini (1959). He joined *Morris as a suspension engineer in 1936.

ITC (Independent Television Commission) Body established by the Broadcasting Act of 1990 to licence and regulate the commercial television companies. Its first task was the allocating of the licences which came into force at the start of 1993. The ITC replaced the Independent Broadcasting Authority (IBA), which had previously fulfilled the same function for both commercial television and radio. The IBA's responsibilities for radio were taken on by a new Radio Authority.

ITMA (1939–49) The first of the BBC's zany weekly radio shows to win a secure place in public memory. Its quirky characters and their catch phrases kept Britain amused throughout and after the war until the death of the star, Tommy Handley (1892–1949). The title, standing for 'It's That Man Again!', referred to Hitler – unspeakable but unavoidable in 1939. Much of the action took place in a ghastly wartime bureaucracy, the Office of Twerps. Notable among many popular characters were the lugubrious Mona Lott ('It's being so cheerful as keeps me going'), Mrs Mopp ('Can I do you now, sir?') and Colonel Chinstrap, eager for liquid refreshment ('I don't mind if I do').

ITN (Independent Television News) The organization which provides the news programmes broadcast by the regional independent *television companies (Channel 3) and by Channel 4. It was set up in 1955 as a non-profit making enterprise, to be jointly owned and funded by the regional companies. The Broadcasting Act of 1990 changed its status to that of an independent enterprise, and it now contracts with the broadcasting companies for its services.

It's a long way to Tipperary *Music-hall song which has never lost the great popularity it acquired in World War I. Written and first sung in 1912 by Jack Judge (1878–1938), it was made popular by Florrie *Forde. Its theme of longing for a girl back home (remembered in the song by an Irishman visiting London) exactly fitted the national mood at a time of millions of forced separations.

ITV see *television.

Ivanhoe (1819) Novel by Walter *Scott, set in the time of the crusades. Amid a turmoil of tournaments and sieges, Ivanhoe is loved by rival heroines – Rowena, descended from King Alfred, and the beautiful Rebecca, daughter of Isaac the Jew. The princess wins the knight, but it is Rebecca who wins the reader's heart.

Iveagh Bequest see *Kenwood House.

'I will be good' see *Victoria.

Advertisement in 1959 for the revolutionary Mini of Alec Issigonis, with an improbably spaced three in the back.

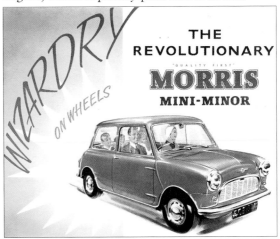

J

Jabberwocky see **Through the Looking-Glass.*

Jack and Jill One of the most popular of nursery rhymes. The first verse, in which the two children go up the hill to fetch a pail of water and then come tumbling down, was published on its own in the 18C. Frequent attempts, all unconvincing, have been made to find political or other explanations.

Jack and the Beanstalk Folk tale found in different versions round the world, but first published in English in 1734 as a parody of popular nonsense. It survived to become a favourite story for *pantomimes. Jack is a spoilt boy in King Alfred's time who is tricked by a butcher into selling his mother's cow for some beans. From them grows a huge beanstalk. Jack climbs it, and finds living at the top a giant who killed Jack's father; he steals from the giant his hen that lays golden eggs, his money bags and his harp which cries out to warn its master. Pursued down the beanstalk, Jack cuts it down just in time and the giant falls to his death.

The ***Jackdaw of Rheims*** see The **Ingoldsby Legends.*

Jack Ketch see *hangmen.

Tony **Jacklin** (b. 1944) Golfer who won the Open in 1969 and followed it with the US Open in 1970, becoming the first British player to win the US title for 70 years and the first to hold both titles simultaneously since Harry *Vardon in 1900. He came tantalizingly close to winning the Open again at Muirfield in 1972, but was robbed in a famously dramatic moment at the 17th when Lee Trevino holed his chip shot from a position beyond the green. Jacklin later had considerable success as the captain (1983–9) of the European *Ryder Cup team.

Jack Russell see *terriers.

jacks (short for jackstones) Modern version of a game going back to prehistory, of which the essential detail is throwing up and catching in a single hand a number of small objects, traditionally five. In Britain it is now primarily a girls' game.

Glenda **Jackson** (b. 1936) Actress who had a successful career on stage (frequently with the Royal Shakespeare Company) and on screen. Two of her film performances won her Oscars – *Women in Love* (1969) and *A Touch of Class* (1973). In the early 1990s she set aside acting to enter politics, and in 1992 she was elected Labour MP for Hampstead and Highgate.

Jack the Giant Killer Hugely successful story compiled in about 1700 from various folk tales. Jack is a cheeky Cornish lad in the time of King Arthur who by various clever tricks rids Britain of all its giants. One of these, unable to see Jack because he is wearing a coat of invisibility, roars the memorable lines (partly used also by Shakespeare in *King Lear*):

> Fe, fi, fo, fum,
> I smell the blood of an Englishman,
> Be he living or be he dead
> I'll grind his bones to be my bread.

Jack the Ripper The popular name, coined in 1888, for the unknown murderer who in that year and the next cut the throats of seven women, all prostitutes, in the Whitechapel district of London. He mutilated most of them in a way which implied to the authorities that he had some specialist knowledge of human anatomy, and a series of taunting notes were sent to the police from someone

Up-to-the-minute pictorial journalism: the Penny Illustrated Paper *in 1888 on two of Jack the Ripper's victims.*

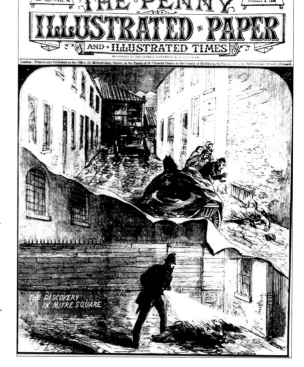

claiming to be the murderer. The gruesome killings ended as suddenly as they had begun. Remaining unresolved, they have exercised a great fascination ever since; fingers have been pointed at numerous suspects (including even the queen's grandson, the duke of Clarence), but there is no conclusive evidence. A horror novel on the subject – *The Lodger* (1913) by Marie Belloc Lowndes – has been several times filmed.

Jacobean The term can be used of any James (*Jacobus* in Latin) but is by convention limited to the reign of James I (1603–25). The architecture of this period follows on from the *Elizabethan Renaissance style but tends towards a more dislocated (or 'mannerist') application of individually striking elements. In furniture the characteristic material is a dark heavily carved oak. Late in the reign Inigo Jones introduced the isolated beginnings of *Palladianism.

Derek **Jacobi** (b. 1938) Actor whose early career was with the National Theatre; his skill was brilliantly demonstrated on TV in the title role of *I, Claudius* (1976).

Jacobite (from *Jacobus*, Latin for James) A supporter of *James II after his deposition in 1688 (or of his descendants after his death in 1701) as the rightful king of both Scotland and England. Support was always strongest in Scotland, the *Stuart homeland, where both the *'15 and *'45 Rebellions began. To a Jacobite James II was James VII and II (i.e. James VII of Scotland and II of England). By the same token his son James *Stuart was James VIII and III.

David **Jacobs** (b. 1926) Broadcaster on radio and TV, whose career has ranged from disc jockey (*Pick of the Pops* on radio, *Juke Box Jury* and *Top of the Pops* on TV) to the discussion programme *Any Questions?*, of which he was chairman 1967–84.

Jaguar Car company founded in 1945 by William Lyons (1901–85). It evolved from his Swallow Sidecar Company, established in 1922, and became famous both for its sports cars and its saloons. The XK roadsters, introduced in 1948, were followed by C- and D-type racing sports cars (five wins at Le Mans) and in 1961 by the *E-type. In 1966 the company merged with the *British Motor Corporation. It became independent again in 1984, and was bought by Ford in 1989.

The sports car tradition of the Jaguar name was thriving in 1992 at Bloxham in Oxfordshire, where JaguarSport was completing the first XJ220s – said to be the fastest production car ever built, with a top speed of over 355kph/220mph and a price tag of £340,000.

Immanuel **Jakobovits** (b. 1921, kt 1981, baron 1988) The *Chief Rabbi from 1967 to 1991, after being Chief Rabbi of Ireland (1949–58) and rabbi of the 5th Avenue Synagogue in New York (1958–67).

Jamaica One of the largest of the Caribbean islands, a member of the *Commonwealth since 1962. Visited by Columbus in 1494 and conquered by Spain in 1509, Jamaica was captured by the English in 1655 and was ceded to England in 1670. The island was a member of the *West Indies Federation from 1958 but seceded with Trinidad in 1962 to become separately independent, thus setting the future pattern for many neighbouring Commonwealth nations much smaller than itself.

Clive **James** (b. 1939) Australian with a high profile on British television from the early 1980s, known in particular for humorously jaundiced anthologies of other nations' television programmes, for personal travel documentaries and for chat shows more intelligent than most. He has chronicled his own life in a series of *Unreliable Memoirs*.

Henry **James** (1843–1916) American novelist who from 1876 lived most of his life in England, becoming naturalized in 1915 as a gesture of solidarity in World War I. Well travelled himself, his recurring theme was the interaction between Europe and Americans (in the earlier novels young American women in particular). He treated his material in fine analytical detail, causing him now to be seen as a precursor of modern introspective fiction but provoking Mrs Henry Adams (wife of the American historian) to complain that his problem was not so much biting off more than he could chew as chewing more than he had bitten off. Lamb House, where he lived 1898–1916 in Rye, Sussex, is kept partly as a museum.

Naomi **James** (b. 1949, DBE 1979) The first woman to sail single-handed round the world, which she did in nine months from September 1977 to June 1978 (one particular part of the journey was also a first, for no woman had sailed alone round Cape Horn). She was subsequently the fastest woman, in a new record time, in the 1980 Observer Transatlantic Race.

P.D. **James** (Phyllis Dorothy James, b. 1920, baroness 1991) The leading British writer of detective fiction in the generation after Agatha Christie. She was a civil servant in the administration of the National Health Service when she published her first book (*Cover Her Face* 1962), and from 1968 to 1979 she was in the Home Office specializing in forensic science and police work. The murders in her books tend to be more sinister than Agatha Christie's, and her fastidious detective, Adam Dalgleish, often finds elements of his work distasteful. In the past ten years many of her books have been televised, including *Cover Her Face*, *Shroud for a Nightingale* (published 1971), *The Black Tower* (1975), *Death of an Expert Witness* (1977) and *Devices and Desires* (1989).

James I (1394–1437) King of Scotland from 1406; son of Robert III and Annabella Drummond; married Joan Beaufort (1424).

Sent by his father to France in 1406, his ship was intercepted by an English vessel and he spent 18 years as a well-treated captive at the English court. In 1424 he married Joan Beaufort, a granddaughter of John of Gaunt, and returned to Scotland. He suppressed the anarchy prevailing among the nobles, and established a group of permanent judges which developed into the *Court of Session. He is generally held to be the author of *The Kingis Quair* (the king's book), a long poem much influenced by Chaucer but in a northern dialect. It was discovered in 1783. The main link is its supposedly autobiographical content, being an account of a royal prisoner who falls in love with a beautiful woman whom he sees walking in the garden below. James was assassinated in 1437 and was succeeded by his son James II (see the *royal house of Scotland).

James I and VI (1566–1625) King of Scotland from 1567 as James VI and of England and Ireland from 1603 as James I; son of *Mary Queen of Scots and of Henry Stewart, Lord Darnley; married Anne of Denmark (1589).

He was only one when his mother was deposed and he was proclaimed king of Scotland. The regency and the early years of his own rule were dominated by the struggle between Catholics and Protestants. James himself inclined towards the Catholics but never so far as to alienate *Elizabeth I, whose throne he could expect to inherit; though only her first cousin twice removed (see the *royal house), he was nevertheless her nearest relation.

The future James II soon after the royal return to Britain at the Restoration: miniature by Samuel Cooper (1661).

He had established effective royal control over the rival factions in Scotland before the English throne became his in 1603, in the so-called *union of the crowns. In England both religious groups had hopes of him but both were disappointed. The Puritans failed to win the reforms they wanted at the Hampton Court Conference of 1604 (an occasion of importance for the *Bible in English) and they suspected Catholic sympathies when James made peace with Spain in that same year. Yet it was Catholic hostility which lay behind the *Gunpowder Plot.

The greater tension of his reign in England was the battle with parliament, which was to dominate the first half of the 17C. James, rare among monarchs in being a writer, had published two books (*The True Lawe of Free Monarchies* 1598, *Basilikon Doron* 1599) in which he expounded the theory of the *divine right of kings. The response of serious-minded parliamentarians to such claims was not improved by a succession of handsome but otherwise unqualified young royal favourites – in particular Robert Carr (*c.*1590–1645) and the duke of *Buckingham. The antagonisms which brought to an end the reign and life of James's son, *Charles I, were already in place.

Modern attitudes to smoking have given a topicality to the king's best known work, *A Counterblast to Tobacco* (1604), in which he describes the habit as 'loathsome to the eye, hateful to the nose, harmful to the brain, dangerous to the lungs, and in the black, stinking fume thereof, nearest resembling the horrible Stygian smoke of the pit that is bottomless'.

James II (1430–60) King of Scotland from 1437; son of James I and Joan Beaufort; married Mary of Gueldres (1449).

His reign was dominated by struggles with the powerful Douglas family. James proved more than a match for them, stabbing one earl of Douglas to death himself in spite of a safe conduct and relieving them of much of their land and wealth. He died from the explosion of a cannon when he was besieging the English in Roxburgh Castle, and was succeeded by his son James III (see the *royal house of Scotland).

James II (1633–1701) King of England, Scotland (as James VII) and Ireland 1685–8; second surviving son of Charles I and Henrietta Maria; married Anne Hyde (1660) and Mary of Modena (1673).

James was known for most of his life as the duke of York, the title given him soon after birth. During the Commonwealth he lived abroad, like his elder brother Charles II, and fought with distinction in the French army. After the Restoration he had a successful public life, concerning himself in particular with naval and colonial matters (New York was named after him in 1664). His brother's lack of legitimate children meant that attention increasingly focused on James as the likely heir to the throne. In the tense religious atmosphere of the period there was alarm when he became a Roman Catholic (in about 1669, though he continued to attend Anglican services until 1676). But his two daughters by Anne Hyde (both future queens, Mary II and Anne) were being brought up as Protestants, and the crisis did not become urgent until James married the Roman Catholic Mary of Modena in 1673 (Anne Hyde had died in 1671).

In the hysteria following the *Popish plot (1678) there were demands that James be excluded from the succession to the throne. (It was the clash between his supporters and their opponents which formed Britain's two first political parties, the *Tories and the Whigs.) Nevertheless he succeeded his brother peacefully in 1685, though the rebellion of the duke of *Monmouth followed later in that year. In 1687, with the Declaration of Indulgence, he suspended the laws which prevented Roman Catholics and Nonconformists from holding office – a gesture of religious toleration with partisan motives. Two events in June 1688 provoked the final crisis. Mary of Modena gave birth to a boy (widely suspected at the time of being a *warming-pan baby), which meant that the heir to the throne was now Roman Catholic; and seven bishops, including the archbishop of Canterbury, were acquitted of the charge of libel brought against them by the king because of a petition which they had published against his policies. In the resulting *Revolution of 1688 so many of James's Protestant officers deserted to *William III that battle was never joined. James, with Mary and the baby prince (James *Stuart), escaped in December to France.

In 1689 James landed in Ireland, where a parliament summoned in Dublin acknowledged him as king, but his defeat the following year at the Battle of the *Boyne ended any chance of recovering the throne. He died in France. For two more generations his *Jacobite followers remained passionate in their support of his descendants (see the *royal house).

James III (1452–88) King of Scotland from 1460; son of James II and Mary of Gueldres; married Margaret, daughter of Christian I, king of Denmark, Norway and Sweden (1469).

He was the third successive king to inherit the throne as a child. Like his predecessors he was plagued by unruly nobles, and in his case by ambitious brothers – one of whom, Alexander Duke of Albany, was for a while recognized as the Scottish king by Edward IV. But the dowry of James's Scandinavian bride brought useful gains, in particular the ceding to Scotland of Norway's rights in the Orkneys and Shetlands. Defeated by rebels near Stirling in 1488, James was murdered in the immediate aftermath of the battle. He was succeeded by his son James IV (see the *royal house of Scotland).

James IV (1473–1513) King of Scotland from 1488; son of James III and Margaret of Denmark; married Margaret Tudor (1503).

At the age of 15 James was with the rebels who defeated and then murdered his father in 1488 (a deed for which he was said to have worn an iron belt all his life as a penance), yet he became the first Scottish monarch for several generations to exert full control over his own nobles. He also greatly improved material conditions in Scotland and was a patron of learning and the arts. His antipathy to England misled him into supporting Perkin *Warbeck, but a few years later he married Margaret, the eldest daughter of Henry VII – an alliance which later united the crowns of England and Scotland (see the *royal house). Relations deteriorated with the accession of Henry VIII. In 1513 James invaded northern England and died in the disaster at *Flodden. He was succeeded by his son James V.

James V (1512–42) King of Scotland from 1513; son of James IV and Margaret Tudor; married Madeleine of France (1537, she died later that year) and Mary of Guise (1538).

With a one-year-old James V on the throne after the disaster of *Flodden, Scotland was faced with a long minority during which there was constant friction between factions favouring alliance with England or with France. James himself, in control from 1528, took the side of France and the papacy against his uncle, Henry VIII (Margaret Tudor was Henry's elder sister). In 1542 Henry sent an army against Scotland and won an easy victory at Solway Moss. James died three weeks later in Falkland palace. For the second time running the Scottish crown passed to an infant; James's daughter, *Mary Queen of Scots, was six days old (see the *royal house of Scotland).

James VI see *James I and VI.

James VII see *James II.

James VIII & III The title used by the *Jacobites for James *Stuart, meaning that he was the rightful James VIII of Scotland and James III of England.

James Bond see Ian *Fleming.

Jameson Raid Invasion of the Transvaal from Mafeking on 29 December 1895 by Dr Jameson and some 600 men; it ended ignominiously, four days later and 23km/14m short of Johannesburg, with 16 dead and Jameson arrested. The raid was a major factor in the build-up to the *Boer War, particularly when it became known that *Rhodes, the prime minister of a neighbouring state, was ultimately responsible. The plan had been for the raid to coincide with an uprising of disaffected British (the *uitlanders*) in the Transvaal, but this never materialized. Leander Starr Jameson (1853–1917) was a doctor in the Kimberley diamond-mining camp before becoming a close colleague of Rhodes. He spent several months in London's Holloway jail for the raid, but returned to South Africa and by 1903 was occupying Rhodes's previous position as prime minister of the Cape Colony.

jam tomorrow A useful phrase which has entered the language from *Through the Looking-Glass*, where the White Queen's terms of employment for a lady's maid include 'jam tomorrow and jam yesterday – but never jam today'.

Jane Strip cartoon character in the *Daily Mirror* who acquired a devoted following among the troops during World War II – largely thanks to her perennial difficulty in keeping her clothes on, and to the curvaceous shapes revealed whenever she failed. She first appeared in the paper in 1932, drawn by Norman Pett. He continued until 1949 and other artists kept Jane alive for a further ten years; she was revived from 1985 to 1990.

Jane Eyre (1847) The first published novel by Charlotte *Bronte. Jane's early life reflects that of her author, with years at a dreadful girl's school (Cowan Bridge in reality, Lowood in the novel) followed by employment as a governess, looking after Adèle, the ward of the broodingly romantic Mr Rochester. Edward Rochester and Jane fall in love, but their marriage ceremony is interrupted by that moment of drama which every wedding guest must often have imagined – the voice from the body of the church saying yes, there is an impediment. It turns out that Rochester already has a wife, a mad Creole living in the attic. Jane escapes to a new life with the family of a clergyman, St John Rivers; he is discovered to be her cousin, together they inherit a fortune, and she is about to marry him and go to India as a missionary when she hears the voice of Rochester mysteriously calling her. She returns to find his house, Thornfield, burnt down and Rochester blinded from his attempt to save his wife. All impediment removed, and with an added spur to her compassion, Jane begins the final chapter with one of fiction's best-known romantic statements: 'Reader, I married him'.

Jane Grey see Lady Jane *Grey.

Jane Seymour (*c*.1509–37) Queen of England from 1536, as the third wife of *Henry VIII. She was the daughter of a Wiltshire knight, and became lady-in-waiting to Catherine of Aragon and then to *Anne Boleyn. Her rejection of the king's advances, unless made honourable by an offer of marriage, no doubt hastened her mistress's end; Jane became betrothed to the king the day after Anne's execution. She gave birth to the future Edward VI in October 1537 and died 12 days later.

Jane's Fighting Ships Annual publication giving an illustration and technical details of every ship of significance in every navy of the world. Its originator was Fred T. Jane (1870–1916), whose interest in the subject dated from the drawings he made, as a 17-year-old schoolboy, of eight battleships involved in a bombardment of Alexandria. A career as a naval journalist enabled him to continue sketching warships and in 1898 he published *All the World's Fighting Ships*, with a silhouette index to help in identification. It was such a success that an updated edition was published each year. The title was soon shortened to *Fighting Ships* and from 1901 sketches were replaced by photographs. Since 1909 there has been a companion volume, *All the World's Aircraft*.

japanning The term applies mainly to the 17–18c technique of imitating oriental lacquer by giving several layers of varnish to wooden furniture. But it is used also for a quite different craft developed in Britain in the late 17c, particularly at Bilston in Staffordshire and at *Pontypool. This process used tin-plated sheet iron for its base, and fused to it several layers of a varnish based on coal tar. The surface became hard and heat-resistant, and with added floral decoration proved a most attractive material for snuffboxes, teapots, urns and above all trays.

Jaques see *As You Like It*.

Jardine Matheson Major international company, with its interests primarily in the Far East, which has developed from the trade with China established by two Scottish merchants, William Jardine (1784–1843) and Nicolas Matheson (1796–1878), who set up business in Canton in 1832. Their early success was based on smuggling opium into China, in collaboration with the *East India Company – a highly profitable undertaking defended by Britain in the *Opium Wars.

Jarlshof (southern tip of Mainland, *Shetlands) Site showing continuous occupation from the Bronze Age (probably earlier than 1000 BC) through the Iron Age, followed by Norse settlements, a medieval farmstead and finally a 16c manor house. The misleading name, limiting the importance of the place to one period (it is Norse for 'earl's court'), was the invention of Walter Scott, who set part of his novel *The Pirate* here.

Jarrow (27,000 in 1981) Town in Tyne and Wear, on the south bank of the Tyne, which was the site of the 7c monastery where the Venerable *Bede spent most of his life; part of the original monastery church is incorporated in St Paul's, most notably the lower part of the tower. The name of Jarrow acquired a different resonance in the 1930s, when the local shipyards were hit by the Depression and unemployment reached more than 60%. Marches had been undertaken in other places to highlight economic need, but the Jarrow hunger march of 1936 became the best known of them all. Some 200 unemployed men marched 441km/274m south to petition the House of Commons in London.

David Jason (b. 1940) Comedy actor who acquired a large TV following as Del in *Only Fools and Horses*. He further increased it with *The *Darling Buds of May* and, from 1992, as Jack Frost in Yorkshire TV's police drama series *A Touch of Frost*.

Jedburgh (4000 in 1981) Town in the Borders region of Scotland, known in particular for the red sandstone ruins of its abbey. It was founded for Augustinian canons in the 12c by David I, and after being frequently damaged in border warfare was finally destroyed by the English in the 1540s.

Jeeves see P.G. *Wodehouse.

Judge Jeffreys (George Jeffreys, c.1645–89, kt 1677, baron 1685) Lawyer whose evil reputation derives from the

The unemployed of Jarrow marching south in 1936, in suitably gloomy weather, to the music of mouth organs.

Bloody Assizes of 1685. A career of rapid success (lord chief justice at 38, lord chancellor at 41) was largely the result of vigorous legal activity in the royal interest. It was in this role that he went in 1685 to the west of England, where *Monmouth's support had been strongest in the recent rebellion against James II. In a succession of assizes in different towns Jeffreys condemned about 200 people to death and many more to transportation. Justice tended then to be brutal, and his notoriety can be partly explained by Hanoverian historians making the most of this final fling of Stuart despotism. After James II's flight to France, Jeffreys disguised himself as a sailor to make his own escape, but was recognized and arrested in Wapping. He died in the Tower before being brought to trial.

Gertrude Jekyll (1843–1932) The most distinguished garden designer of her generation. She pioneered the use of flowers and shrubs to create a pleasing profusion and disorder which nevertheless remains firmly within an underlying structure. The charm of cottage gardens was an acknowledged influence. Coming late to gardening (she was primarily a painter until her fifties), she had a long and successful partnership with *Lutyens, who provided the architectural framework in which her plants could run wild but not too wild. One of their first collaborations involved her own home at Munstead Wood in Surrey, where she designed the garden around the house which he built for her in 1895–7.

Jekyll and Hyde Widely used names for the contrasting sides of a single personality, deriving from Robert Louis *Stevenson's psychological horror story *The Strange Case of Dr Jekyll and Mr Hyde* (1886). Jekyll is fascinated by the good and evil aspects of his own nature, and develops a drug which will isolate the evil part of himself as the repulsive Mr Hyde. But Hyde acquires an almost independent demonic career and eventually commits a murder, while Jekyll finds it harder and harder to escape back to his own full identity. On the verge of his secret being discovered, he commits suicide.

Earl Jellicoe (John Jellicoe, 1859–1935, KCVO 1907, earl 1925) Commander of the Grand Fleet at *Jutland.

jellied eels see *whelk stall.

Patrick Jenkin (b. 1926, baron 1987) Conservative politician who was MP for Wanstead and Woodford (1964–87). Entering the *cabinet in 1979, he was secretary of state for social services (1979–81), for industry (1981–3) and for the environment (1983–5).

Roy Jenkins (b. 1920, baron 1987) Labour politician who was subsequently one of the founders of the *SDP. He entered parliament as MP for Central Southwark (1948–50) and then represented Stechford in Birmingham (1950–76). In Harold Wilson's governments he was home secretary (1965–7, 1974–6) and chancellor of the exchequer (1967–70). He went to Brussels in 1977 as president of the European Commission (1977–81). He was the first leader of the SDP, returning to parliament as MP for Glasgow Hillhead (1982–7). He is also an author, specializing in political biography (*Mr Attlee* 1948, *Asquith* 1964, *Baldwin* 1987). In 1987 he was elected chancellor of the university of Oxford.

War of Jenkins' Ear (1739) Name given to hostilities between Britain and Spain in the Caribbean in 1739. It derives from an English sea captain, Robert Jenkins, who in 1738 produced for a House of Commons committee what he claimed to be his ear, cut off by Spaniards who had boarded his ship in the West Indies in 1731; it was on record that he had reported the incident at the time. His story inflamed already existing public hostility to the Spanish (clashes between the colonial powers in the Caribbean were constant), and it contributed to the government's decision to declare war on Spain in 1739. The conflict was almost immediately merged in the larger War of the *Austrian Succession, in which the two countries were again on opposing sides.

Edward **Jenner** (1749–1823) English country doctor who discovered vaccination against smallpox. Aware of a local tradition that cowpox gave protection against smallpox, he took the alarming risk in 1796 of inoculating an 8-year-old boy with cowpox and then a year later with smallpox. The more serious disease failed to develop. Jenner published his theory in 1798 (*An Inquiry into the Causes and Effects of the Variolae Vaccinae*). After some initial opposition the technique spread rapidly. It is believed that by 1800 some 100,000 people had been vaccinated (the new word was based on *vacca*, Latin for cow). In 1806 President Jefferson wrote to Jenner: 'Future generations will know by history only that the loathsome smallpox existed and by you has been extirpated.' In 1980 the World Health Organization declared that it had indeed been finally extirpated throughout the world.

Pat **Jennings** (b. 1945) British footballer with the record number of international appearances (119 for Northern Ireland) until overtaken by fellow goalkeeper Peter *Shilton in 1990. He kept goal for Watford (1963–4), Tottenham Hotspur (1964–78), and Arsenal (1978–86).

Jerome K. **Jerome** see *Three Men in a Boat.*

jersey A general term now for a wide-range of machine-knitted fabrics, deriving from the strong knitting tradition of Jersey in the *Channel Islands (the word was applied to knitwear, particularly stockings, from at least the 16C). Since the 19C it has been also used in Britain for a woollen garment, usually with sleeves, which is pulled on over the head – based originally on the versions worn by Jersey fishermen.

Jersey and **Jersey cattle** see *Channel Islands.

Jerusalem Poem by William *Blake, from the preface to his book *Milton* (1804–8). It follows a passage in which he attacks the classicism of his age, with its emphasis on Greece and Rome and the cult of reason, contrasting it with 'our own Imaginations, those Worlds of Eternity in which we shall live for ever in Jesus our Lord'. It was in this sense that Jerusalem must be built in 'England's green and pleasant land'. But the poem's more general vision of an England corrupted by 'dark Satanic mills', which could nevertheless be improved by brave and resolute effort, has given it an almost magic potency. It is best known in the musical setting of 1916 by *Parry, which has become an indispensable part of the last night of the *Proms.

Jesu, lover of my soul see Charles *Wesley.

jet engine see Frank *Whittle.

Jethro Tull Eccentric rock band, in a style known as 'art rock', deriving from a group formed in Blackpool in 1963 by Ian Anderson (b. 1947, vocals and flute). They had moved to London by the time the name Jethro Tull was adopted, late in 1967 (from the agricultural pioneer *Tull); Anderson was by then accompanied by Mick Abrahams (b. 1943, guitar), Glenn Cornick (b. 1947, bass) and Clive Bunker (b. 1946, drums). In the next five years they had six top-ten albums, including the no. 1 *Stand Up*

A New Way of Applying Dr Jenner: *one aspect of vaccination, in a* Punch *cartoon of 1870.*

(1969) and an ambitious rock opera, *Aqualung* (1971).

Jewel in the Crown (Granada TV, 1983) Adaptation for television, in 13 parts, of Paul *Scott's *Raj Quartet*. The story focuses on the British community in *India in the five years leading up to independence in 1947. Leading characters are Daphne Manners (played by Susan Wooldridge), whose rape in the Bibighar Gardens in Mayapore is the spark which sets off the drama; Hari Kumar (Art Malik), who is wrongly imprisoned for the crime; Ronald Merrick (Tim Pigott-Smith), an inhibited and severe police officer; and Barbie Batchelor (Peggy Ashcroft), a retired missionary teacher who owns the old chromolithograph, entitled *The Jewel in Her Crown*, which once hung in a missionary schoolroom. It shows Queen Victoria surrounded by people of all classes from her Indian empire, for India herself was the jewel. The series had an exceptional critical and popular success.

Jewel Tower see *Palace of Westminster.

The **Jewish Chronicle** The oldest surviving Jewish newspaper in the world, established in London in 1841 by Isaac Vallentine (1793–1868). Published every Friday, it is known for its foreign news – with a natural emphasis on the affairs of the Middle East – and for its coverage of the arts.

Jews England was the last of the major European countries to be reached by the Jews in the gradual spread of the Diaspora from Palestine; it was also the first to expel them. They arrived in the wake of the Norman *Conquest and soon became a prosperous community through money-lending (an activity which Christians despised as usury, but also one of the few activities open to the Jews, who were excluded from the Christian craft guilds). Persecution of the Jews began later in England than in central Europe, but took a particularly unpleasant and hysterical form. It was here that the dangerous legend began of Jews killing children in ritual sacrifices. The first case was William, a boy found murdered in Norwich in 1144, whose death was blamed on the Jews. More famous was the 9-year-old Hugh of Lincoln, found in a well in 1255. These children became the cause both of pilgrimage and pogrom. Meanwhile Italians were becoming money-lenders, and the state had less need of the Jews. In 1290 Edward I made it illegal for them to live in England, a law which remained in force until it was repealed in the

1650s, during the Commonwealth. It is a strange fact, therefore, that there were no Jews in London when Shakespeare created Shylock in The *Merchant of Venice.

Within 50 years of their return the two Jewish communities of Europe were well established again in London. The Ashkenazim (Jews from central Europe) founded in 1690 their Great Synagogue in Aldgate; it was bombed in World War II. Not far from Aldgate is the *Bevis Marks Synagogue, built in 1701 for the Sephardim (Jews from Spain, Portugal and north Africa). The 19C saw the beginnings of a much closer involvement of Jews in British public life. In 1804 Nathan Meyer *Rothschild opened in London one of the most important branches of the family bank; in 1858 his son Lionel Nathan took a seat in the House of Commons and ended the restriction on Jews holding public office.

Poverty and persecution in Russia and central Europe brought Ashkenazim in large numbers to Britain in the late-19C and 20C, the East End of London and Manchester being where the majority settled. Religiously they divide into two communities (Orthodox and Reform) in a split dating back to the early 19C in Germany. The first Reform group in England was established in 1840 at the West London Synagogue. The *Chief Rabbi is the leader of the Orthodox community.

Numbering now some 300,000, the Jewish community has made a contribution to the artistic and business life of Britain out of all proportion to its size.

Jew's House see *Lincoln.

jig Energetic folk dance, usually solo and related to the *hornpipe, which was popular from the 16C in many parts of the British Isles. The steps were improvised, with elaborate footwork but with the upper half of the body relatively static (it is from the dance that the verb to 'jig' comes). When several people were performing it at the same time, the effect must have been not unlike a modern disco.

Jimmy Porter see *Look Back in Anger.

Jimmy's (St James's Hospital, Leeds) The largest hospital in the country, widely known by its popular local name because of the Yorkshire TV documentary series, Jimmy's, which is filmed in its wards and follows case histories of the patients. The oldest building on the 50-acre site dates from 1846 and was the school of the Leeds Union Workhouse. The workhouse later concentrated on medical treatment and became the Poor Law Infirmary, which in 1925 was renamed St James's Hospital.

jingoism Term for aggressive imperialism which has a precise historical origin. 'By jingo' had been in use since the 17C as a phrase of emphasis (deriving from the conjuror's 'hey jingo', akin to 'hey presto'). It happened to feature in the chorus of a music hall song of 1878, supporting *Disraeli's controversial decision to send a British fleet into Turkish waters to deter Russian expansionism:

We don't want to fight, but by jingo if we do,
We've got the ships, we've got the men, we've got
    the money too.
We've fought the Bear before, and while Britons
    shall be true,
The Russians shall not have Constantinople.

Supporters of Disraeli immediately became known as jingoes, and their policy as jingoism.

Joan Hunter Dunn see John *Betjeman.

Jobcentres Offices in the shopping districts of British towns, responsible for helping the unemployed to find work. Run by the *Employment Service, they aim to be a

King John hunting deer in the midst of a rabbit warren: manuscript illustration of the 14C.

less forbidding version of the old-fashioned labour exchange. In addition to the basic task of matching applicants and vacancies, Jobcentres operate short courses to train the longer-term unemployed in the skills of applying for a job. Those wishing to train for specific employment are referred to *TECs.

Jock Colloquial term for anyone from Scotland, Jock being the familiar version there of the most common Christian name, John (Jack is the equivalent in England). It was first used specifically of Scottish sailors.

Jockey Club Until recently the all-powerful governing body of British flat racing. It began in about 1750 as a typical London *club, a social gathering of rich men with an interest in the turf. Needing a place to meet at *Newmarket, the centre of British racing, the club leased a plot of land there in 1752 and a building (the 'Coffee Room') was constructed. Over the years the Jockey Club expanded, until it owned all the land at Newmarket used for racing and training; by the same token it became accepted as the regulating and disciplinary committee for all flat racing in the country. In recent years it has come to seem an anachronism that a self-elected aristocratic club should be in charge of the multi-million-pound racing industry, and in the early 1990s the Jockey Club yielded control of most aspects of the sport to a newly formed British Horseracing Board.

jodhpurs Riding breeches, fitting tightly below the knee and flaring above it, which became popular in Britain from the 1890s. The name derives from the princely state of Jodhpur in India, where a similar-shaped garment in white cotton was normal male attire.

Jodrell Bank (Nuffield Radio Astronomy Laboratories) Site in Cheshire, 32km/20m south of Manchester, where

Bernard *Lovell supervised the construction (1953–7) of what was then the world's largest fully steerable radio telescope, with a dish reflector 76m/250ft in diameter. Jodrell Bank, a department of the university of Manchester, has been in the forefront of the study of distant radio sources, discovering several new pulsars and quasars. It also tracks artificial satellites and it received the first photographs of the surface of the moon, transmitted from the Soviet Luna 9 probe in 1966.

John (1167–1216) King of England from 1199, succeeding his elder brother Richard I; youngest son of Henry II and Eleanor of Aquitaine; married Isabella of Gloucester (1189) and Isabella of Angoulême (1200).

As a child he was given the nickname Lackland by his father, whose favourite he was and who did his best to provide him with appropriate territories (they included Ireland). John's early adult years were marked by an alternating pattern of support and treachery towards his brother, Richard. His own reign was dominated by two major struggles. One was with the papacy over whether Stephen *Langton should be archbishop of Canterbury; it ended with a compromise, and John became soon afterwards a vassal of the pope. The other, with his own barons, had a famous outcome in 1215 in *Magna Carta*. Later that same year, at John's request, the pope annulled the new charter and excommunicated the baronial leaders. The result was civil war, and the country was in a state of armed upheaval when John's 9-year-old son succeeded as Henry III (see the *royal house).

Augustus **John** (1878–1961) Welsh painter, younger brother of Gwen *John, who in the early years of the century was seen as Britain's leading bohemian. He lived a wandering life – he was fascinated by gypsies – and he often painted his favourite model (Dorelia McNeill, his second wife) as a lone traveller in a landscape. By the 1920s he also had a thriving career as a fashionable portraitist.

Barry **John** (b. 1945) Rugby union player, at fly half for Llanelli and then for Cardiff – with 25 caps for Wales (1966–72) and five for the *Lions (1968–71). At both club and international level he formed a famous partnership with Gareth Edwards, earning himself the title 'King' John for his brilliant running and kicking. He was at his very best in the 1971 Lions tour of New Zealand.

Elton **John** (stage name of Reginald Kenneth Dwight, b. 1947) Rock singer, pianist and composer whose flamboyant persona as he sings at the piano (usually in outrageous clothes and spectacles) has contributed to his becoming a superstar on both sides of the Atlantic, in spite of a distinctly uncharismatic appearance. His appeal in the record shops was demonstrated by four successive UK no. 1 albums in 1973–4. His classic songs, written with lyricist Bernie Taupin, include *Your Song* (1971), *Rocket Man* (1972), *Candle in the Wind* (1974) and *Sacrifice* (1989). He made a famous film appearance as the Pinball Wizard in *Tommy* (1975); his outsize boots for the role fetched a winning bid of £11,000 in a 1988 Sotheby's sale of his personal memorabilia. He was the first western pop star to do a solo tour of the USSR (recorded in the film *To Russia with Elton* 1980) and the first since the Beatles to be enshrined at Madame Tussaud's. A famous sideline in his career has been his ownership of Watford Football Club.

Gwen **John** (1876–1939) Welsh painter, elder sister of Augustus *John, whose style is as reserved as his was flamboyant. She spent most of her life in or near Paris, where she studied with Whistler – whose muted tones influenced her palette – and had a long affair, from 1904,

with Rodin. Her subtle introspective studies, most often of a woman alone, have brought her a steadily increasing reputation. In their lifetime the esteem was all her brother's; now the situation is largely reversed.

John Bull The personification of the English nation. He first appeared in print in 1712 in a pamphlet by John Arbuthnot (1667–1735), where he is contrasted with Lewis Baboon (representing the French) and other foreign characters. Arbuthnot describes him as an 'honest plain-dealing fellow, choleric, bold and of a very inconstant temper'. The same century produced someone who has often seemed the essential flesh-and-blood version – Dr Johnson, described by Boswell as 'at bottom much of a John Bull, much of a blunt true-born Englishman'.

John Lewis Partnership The most successful example in Britain of a utopian experiment in profit sharing among a company's employees (the *Co-op, by contrast, returns profits to the customers). John Lewis (1836–1928) opened a small draper's shop in London's Oxford Street in 1864 and built it up into a department store; and in 1905 he bought *Peter Jones in Sloane Square. It was his son, Spedan Lewis, who in the 1930s turned the business into a partnership of its employees. After a reasonable dividend has been paid on invested capital, profits are distributed among the partners as a percentage of their annual pay. In the early 1990s there were some 33,000 employee partners; the distributed profits had ranged over the previous two decades from 11% to 24% of salary.

In 1937 the partnership acquired a small group of grocery shops founded in 1908 by Messrs Waite and Rose.

John Bull with his bulldog: a patriotic pair sold as a colour print for scrapbooks or screens, c.1880.

By the early 1990s these had been developed into nearly 100 Waitrose supermarkets round the country. In addition the John Lewis chain included by then more than 20 department stores.

John Moores Exhibition An exhibition of paintings, linked to a competition, held every two years since 1957 at the Walker Art Gallery in Liverpool. The event was established by the founder of Littlewoods football *pools. The prize money (£1000 in 1957, £20,000 in the early 1990s) purchases the winning painting for the Walker Art Gallery. The result is an excellent and growing collection of contemporary British art.

John Murray Publisher with a longer and more distinguished literary record than any other in Britain. The firm was founded in 1768 in Fleet Street by John Murray (1745–93); it has been run ever since by direct descendants, each called John Murray (the present chairman is John Murray VII). Byron was the turning point. The success of *Childe Harold's Pilgrimage* enabled John Murray II to buy the 18C house in Albemarle Street (London W1) from which successive John Murrays have contrived to keep abreast of the times – as in the remarkable feat of publishing Darwin's *Origin of Species* and Samuel Smiles' *Self-Help* on the same day in 1859, or a century later in launching the first of the television book-of-the-series successes, Kenneth Clark's *Civilisation* (1969).

John of Gaunt (1340–99) Son of Edward III, father of Henry IV (see the *royal house) and the ancestor of the Lancastrians in the *Wars of the Roses. In 1359 Gaunt married Blanche, the heiress of a powerful northern baron, the duke of Lancaster. He inherited her lands and after his father-in-law's death was himself created duke of Lancaster. With his son's accession to the throne in 1399 the duchy of Lancaster became attached to the crown and has remained so ever since. Gaunt's public image is almost entirely the creation of Shakespeare in *Richard II*, where he is given the great patriotic speech about this *'precious stone set in the silver sea'. Even the name by which Gaunt is now known (deriving from the fact that he was born in Ghent) is due to Shakespeare; it was used in his lifetime only until he was three.

John o'Groats The site of a legendary house in Scotland. It is famous as the northern end of the longest possible land journey in Britain, *Land's End to John o'Groats (about 1408km/875m by road). The journey can in fact be continued another 3km/2m northeast to Duncansby Head, a craggy promontory which is the most northeasterly point of mainland Britain; but this lacks the romantic associations of John o'Groats. The strange name is traditionally explained by a story which first appeared in 1793. This states that three centuries earlier a Dutchman, Jan de Groot, settled in this remote spot with two of his brothers. When an argument over precedence broke out between eight members of the family, Jan built an 8-sided house (or perhaps room) with eight doors leading to seats at an 8-sided table, making it impossible for anybody to upstage anyone else. The suppposed location of this miracle of tact is now marked by a mound bearing a flagpole. (For the most northerly point on the mainland see *Dunnet Head.)

Amy **Johnson** (1903–41) Pioneer aviator who captured the nation's imagination with an extraordinary solo flight to Australia. Her previous longest flight had been from London to her home in Hull. She set off from *Croydon aerodrome on 5 May 1930 in a tiny Gipsy Moth, reaching India in six days (a record) and Australia in 19. She continued to make record long-distance solo flights during

Amy, *a song composed in 1930 to celebrate 'the homecoming of the heroine': Miss Johnson with her Gipsy Moth.*

the 1930s as well as double flights with James Mollison, whom she married in 1932. She was reported missing over the Thames estuary when flying for the Air Ministry in 1941.

Dr **Johnson** (Samuel Johnson, 1709–84) The most omnipresent of English authors, apart from Shakespeare, because so many of his pithy sayings have been implanted in the national consciousness by *Boswell's *Life*.

Johnson was born in Lichfield, son of a bookseller. At the age of three he was taken to London to be touched for the *king's evil, a condition which left him pockmarked for life. In 1735 he started a school near Lichfield, where his very few pupils included David *Garrick; and in 1737 he and Garrick rode together to London to seek their fortune. Johnson's never materialized, though a lifetime of extraordinarily varied literary activity brought him an increasing reputation. His first success was *London*, a long poem in the manner of Pope, published anonymously in 1738. By 1746 he was sufficiently well known for a group of booksellers to commission the greatest single task of his life, his *Dictionary of the English Language*; published in 1755, it was a marked improvement on earlier dictionaries both in the clarity of the definitions and in the copious quotations, from Johnson's wide reading, which were included as examples.

Meanwhile he had been earning his keep through the essays which were his form of journalism. The *Rambler* appeared twice weekly for two years (1750–2) as a publication written, with very few exceptions, by Johnson alone; he followed it with two years of the 'Idler', a piece contributed weekly to the *Universal Chronicle* (1758–60). His poem *The Vanity of Human Wishes* (1749) followed the success of *London*; a poetic tragedy, *Irene*, was acted in the same year; *Rasselas* (1759) had considerable impact as a philosophical fable; and his edition of Shakespeare (1765) was a prelude to his most lasting work of literary biography and criticism, *The Lives of the Poets* (1779–81). But more than any of this, it was

Johnson's conversation and personality which fascinated a few people in his time and a great many since.

He met Boswell in 1763. The following year Johnson and Joshua Reynolds together founded The Club – a group which gathered regularly to dine. The original members included Goldsmith and Burke, while Garrick, Boswell, Gibbon and Charles James Fox were among those later elected. In that same year, 1764, Johnson met Henry Thrale, a rich Southwark brewer, and his wife Hester, who provided him for a while with an alternative home. An essentially convivial man (though moody and depressive on his own), he had now found the circle of friends through whose reports we seem to know him so well – aggressive but warm-hearted, frequently perverse and provocative in his views yet with a bedrock of wisdom, deeply serious about his Christian faith but blessed with a wit capable of undermining all pretension. He is the nation's literary *John Bull.

Of several houses occupied by Johnson in London, one is kept as a museum to him – his home from 1746 to 1759, at 17 Gough Square, just north of Fleet Street. The traditional description of him as Dr Johnson derives from honorary doctorates conferred by Trinity College, Dublin (1765), and by Oxford (1775).

Jolly Roger The name, from at least the 18C, for the traditional flag hoisted by pirates, showing a white skull and crossbones on black. The reason for the name is unknown.

Ann Jones (Ann Haydon, b. 1938, m. Pip Jones 1962) Tennis player who won the French championship twice (1961, 66) and the Italian title (1966) before winning at Wimbledon in 1969. She subsequently became a commentator for BBC television.

Gwyneth **Jones** (b. 1936, DBE 1986) Welsh soprano, known in the powerfully dramatic roles. She made her British debut with Welsh National Opera in 1963 as Verdi's Lady Macbeth, and first became widely noticed as Leonora in *Il Trovatore* at Covent Garden in 1964. Her most regular appearances abroad have been in Vienna and Munich. In recent years she has been much seen as Wagner's Brünnhilde and Puccini's Turandot.

Inigo **Jones** (1573–1652) Architect and stage designer who introduced new and influential Italian styles to England. After his first visit to Italy, some time before 1603, he began designing for court *masques. In them he used the perspective scenery which he had seen in Florence; this gradually became the dominant scenic convention in the English theatre and remained so until the 19C. He returned a committed *Palladian from his second Italian journey (1613–14); his subsquent buildings pioneered the classical themes which have remained such a major part of British architecture. These were first seen in the *Queen's House at Greenwich and then in Whitehall's *Banqueting House. In the 1630s he laid out London's first formal square in *Covent Garden. He trained as his assistant a nephew by marriage, John Webb (1611–72), best known for his work at *Wilton.

Tom **Jones** (stage name of Thomas Jones Woodward, b. 1940) Welsh pop and cabaret singer with a big voice and presence, whose second single (*It's Not Unusual*

Dr Johnson supposedly strolling out in Scotland (in 1773, touring with Boswell): engraving of 1786, just after his death.

Two entries from Johnson's Dictionary, more convincing on the camel than the camelopard (the 18C name for a giraffe).

CA'MEL. *n. f.* [*camelus*, Lat.] An animal very common in Arabia, Judea, and the neighbouring countries. One fort is large, and full of flefh, and fit to carry burdens of a thoufand pounds weight, having one bunch upon its back. Another have two bunches upon their backs, like a natural faddle, and are fit either for burdens, or men to ride on. A third kind is leaner, and of a fmaller fize, called dromedaries, becaufe of their fwiftnefs ; which are generally ufed for riding by men of quality. See DROMEDARY.

   Camels have large folid feeet, but not hard ; in the fpring, their hair falls entirely off, in lefs than three days time, when the flies are extremely uneafy to them. *Camels*, it is faid, will continue ten or twelve days without eating or drinking, and keep water a long time in their ftomach, for their refrefhment. It is reported, that nature has furnifhed them, for this purpofe, with a very large ventricle, with many bags clofed within the coats of it, round about it, for referving the water. But the Jefuits in China, where they diffected feveral *camels*, found no fuch bags. When a *camel* is upon a journey, his mafter follows him, finging and whiftling ; and the louder he fings, the better the *camel* goes. The flefh of camels is ferved up at the beft tables, among the Arabians, Perfians, and other eaftern nations ; but the ufe of it was forbid the Hebrews, they being ranked by Mofes among the unclean creatures, *Deut.* xiv. 7. *Calmet.*

       Patient of thirft and toil,
  Son of the defart ! even the *camel* feels,
  Shot through his wither'd heart, the fiery blaft. *Thomfon.*

CAME'LOPARD. *n. f.* [from *camelus* and *pardus*, Lat.] An Abyffinian animal, taller than an elephant, but not fo thick. He is fo named, becaufe he has a neck and head like a camel ; he is fpotted like a pard, but his fpots are white upon a red ground. The Italians call him *giaraffa*. *Trevoux.*

CA'MELOT. } *n. f.* [from *camel*.] A kind of ftuff originally made
CA'MLET. } by a mixture of filk and camels hair ; it is now made with wool and filk.

   This habit was not of camels fkin, nor any courfe texture of its hair, but rather fome finer weave of *camelot*, grogain, or the like ; in as much as thefe ftuffs are fuppofed to be made of the hair of that animal. *Brown's Vulgar Errours.*
          Mean-

Vegetable market in Inigo Jones's Covent Garden, with his St Paul's church: painting by Balthasar Nebot, c. 1750.

1965) was a huge success. He had another no. 1 single with *Green Green Grass of Home* (1966), and his album *Delilah* was top of the charts in 1968. The album *Tom Jones Live in Las Vegas* (1969) reached no. 3 on both sides of the Atlantic and pointed the way ahead; Jones settled in the USA in the early 1970s and became a regular attraction in Nevada's gambling paradise. In 1987 he made a comeback in Britain with a top-ten hit *A Boy from Nowhere*, followed by *Kiss* (1988).

Ben **Jonson** (1572–1637) Poet and playwright, as varied as Shakespeare in the range that he attempted but holding the stage now only with his comedies – in particular **Volpone*, The **Alchemist* and **Bartholomew Fair*. During the reign of James I he was the chief writer of **masques for the court. He claimed a new literary status for the drama when he published, in 1616, a folio edition of his works (seven years before the **First Folio of Shakespeare); and in that same year the king gave him an official pension, causing Jonson to be regarded as the first **poet laureate. One of his poems – *To Celia*, beginning 'Drink to me only with thine eyes' – has remained a widely known song (the tune is anonymous). Though inclined to be quarrelsome, Jonson was a leading figure in the group of writers frequenting the **Mermaid tavern. He was buried in Westminster Abbey, where he is commemorated in an epitaph of the utmost directness and brevity: 'O rare Ben Jonson'.

Michael **Jopling** (b. 1930) Conservative politician, MP for Westmorland since 1964 (the constituency has been called Westmorland and Lonsdale since 1983). A farmer by profession, he was in the **cabinet as minister of agriculture, fisheries and food (1983–7).

Jordan see **Transjordan.

Jorrocks A sporting cockney grocer and the outstanding character in the literature of fox hunting. He was created by R.S. Surtees (Robert Smith Surtees, 1805–64) in a series of sketches for the *New Sporting Magazine*, published in book form as *Jorrocks's Jaunts and Jollities* (1838) with illustrations by **Phiz. In *Handley Cross* (1843) Surtees wrote his first and most successful novel featuring Jorrocks, by then a master of foxhounds with a grand house in the country.

Jorvik Viking Centre see **York.

Keith **Joseph** (b. 1918, 2nd bt 1943, baron 1987) Conservative politician (MP for Leeds North East 1956–87), whose theories were an important influence on Margaret Thatcher. In 1974 they together founded the Centre for Policy Studies, a right-wing **think-tank; and his book *Reversing the Trend* (1975), which coincided with her becoming leader of the party, was a critique of past Conservative economic and social policies. Joseph had served in Heath's **cabinet as secretary of state for social services (1970–4); in Mrs Thatcher's he was secretary of state for industry (1979–81) and for education and science (1981–6).

Joseph Andrews see Henry **Fielding.

Joseph of Arimathea see **Glastonbury.

Brian **Josephson** (b. 1940) Physicist who in 1962 predicted theoretically, while he was still a research student at Cambridge, the behaviour of an electric current between two superconducting materials across a very thin insulating barrier. Now known by his name, the Josephson effect has many applications in precision measurement of electromagnetic effects and in high-speed switches for computers. He shared a Nobel prize in 1973.

James **Joule** (1818–89) Physicist, born the son of a Lancashire brewer, who was taught science by John *Dalton and then experimented in a laboratory set up for him in his parents' house. In 1840 he announced his first major discovery, known now as Joule's Law (the heat produced by an electric current is proportional to the resistance of the conductor times the square of the current). In 1843, after long and painstaking experiment, he published a figure for the mechanical equivalent of heat; in doing so he incidentally demonstrated the first law of thermodynamics, that a constant amount of energy is required to produce a given quantity of heat and can equally be derived from it. By 1849 Joule had refined his figure to 772 ft-lb required to raise 1 lb of water by 1° Fahrenheit (the equivalent British thermal unit in use today is 778 ft-lb). In the 1850s he experimented with William *Thomson on gases; the Joule-Thomson effect describes the drop in temperature caused by an expanding gas and is the principle of household refrigerators. In modern science a joule is the derived SI unit of work or energy.

The **Journal** The daily newspaper of Newcastle-upon-Tyne, dating back to the *Newcastle Weekly Journal*, launched in 1832. It became a daily in 1860, and after several mergers with other local papers adopted its present brief title in 1958.

Journey of the Magi Probably the most widely known short poem by T.S. *Eliot, published in his *Collected Poems* of 1936. One of the three kings remembers, years later, the difficult journey to Bethlehem at dead of winter, with the camels sore-footed and refractory. They found the place just in time: 'it was (you may say) satisfactory'. But then he wonders whether he went all that way for a birth or a death. He witnessed a birth; but with it an old world died in him, painfully, and now all he longs for is another death.

Journey's End (1928) The most successful British play about World War I, written by R.C. Sherriff (1896–1975) who himself served in the trenches from 1917. Set in a claustrophobic dugout before a big offensive, it struck home to audiences because of the simple reality of its characters – in particular Raleigh, who has come straight from school into this hellish environment, and Stanhope, the brave captain whom he hero-worships but who has lost his nerve.

William **Joyce** see *Lord Haw-Haw.

JP (Justice of the Peace) A person of distinction in the local community, but of no formal legal training, who is appointed to sit with one or more other *magistrates on an unpaid and part-time basis. In the larger cities (and in Northern Ireland) professional lawyers are also employed as full-time magistrates, and they are empowered to pass judgement on their own.

jubilees The original jubilee, among the ancient Hebrews, was a celebration every 50th year. The Roman Catholic Church introduced jubilee years, for special pilgrimage to Rome; the interval between was soon reduced, for sound commercial reasons, to 25 years. The same reduction has occurred with royal jubilees in Britain. The first, in 1809, marked the beginning of the 50th year of George III's reign. Victoria celebrated a golden jubilee in 1887 for 50

completed years, and a diamond jubilee in 1897. In this century there have been two, each after only 25 years – in 1935 for George V and in 1977 for Elizabeth II. Jubilees tend now to be celebrated round the country in local street parties.

Jules Rimet Trophy see *World Cup.

Julius Caesar see Julius *Caesar.

Julius Caesar (1599) Tragedy by *Shakespeare, depicting the events before and after the assassination in 44 BC of Julius Caesar. He goes to the Capitol in Rome in spite of the warning of a soothsayer to 'beware the ides of March' (March 15, the day on which he was killed). The central character is Brutus, a republican who feels that by killing Caesar he is saving Rome from dictatorship. He dies in the ensuing civil war after the skilful oratory of Mark Antony ('Friends, Romans, countrymen, lend me your ears') has turned public opinion against the conspirators.

Jumblies see *The *Dong with a Luminous Nose*.

The **Jungle Book** (1894) Collection of short stories by *Kipling about Mowgli, a boy who is brought up by a pack of wolves after Shere Khan, a tiger, has frightened away his human parents. He is taught the Law of the Jungle by Baloo, a brown bear, and its skills by Bagheera, a panther. The life of the animals is given a simple dignity when compared with the chaotic human world to which Mowgli returns at the end. *The Second Jungle Book* (1895) added more stories about Mowgli's time among the animals.

junior school see *state school.

Junius The pen name of the unknown author of a series of letters savagely attacking the ministers of George III (and even the king himself in Letter XXXV). The letters appeared between 1769 and 1772 in the *Public Advertiser*; the publisher, Henry Woodfall, was prosecuted for seditious libel on account of the letter against the king, but he was acquitted. It was a political necessity for the author to keep his identity secret, which he did so successfully that some 50 candidates have been put forward by historians over the years. The most likely is now thought to be Philip Francis (1740–1818), a waspish character who went to

Cotton handkerchief to commemorate one of Queen Victoria's jubilees, probably that of 1887.

Kipling's own Just So *drawing of how the camel got his hump (a penalty for having too little to do).*

India in 1773 and later took a prominent part in the attempt to impeach Warren Hastings.

junket Specifically English manner of eating curds and whey. Normally the curd is broken up and drained of whey. Junket is the same substance in its undisturbed state, white, smooth and fragile like a delicate blancmange. Made by curdling warm milk with rennet (extracted from the stomachs of calves), it has been served since at least the 17c with a layer of clotted cream and cinammon on top. A supposed connection with Devon is relatively recent, a false deduction perhaps from the clotted cream.

jury system Trial by jury is now almost exclusively a characteristic of societies influenced historically by Britain, in particular the USA. The involvement of lay people in the process of law goes back to Charlemagne and was brought to England by the Norman kings. In the 12c Henry II required 12 men to be present in court to name persons suspected of serious crime and by the 14c this accusatory role had evolved into one of weighing the evidence. Majority verdicts were then occasionally accepted by judges, but unanimity soon became a requirement (in England, though not in Scotland). This lasted until 1967, since when the judge may allow a verdict if 10 out of 12 jurors agree after a minimum of two hours' deliberation. It is a crucial part of the system that the jury must assume the defendant to be innocent unless guilt seems proved 'beyond reasonable doubt'. All serious cases in Britain were at one time tried before juries, but this is now only invariably true of criminal law together with a few extra categories such as *libel.

Juries in Scotland (15 jurors for a criminal case) may return a verdict of Not Proven where guilt seems probable but is not established beyond reasonable doubt. The practical result is the same as Not Guilty; the charge is dropped and the accused cannot be tried again for the same offence.

Justice of the Peace see *JP.

Just So Stories *for Little Children* (1902) Tales and poems by *Kipling, illustrated with his own black-and-white drawings, offering fantastic accounts of the origin of animals, such as 'How the Camel got his Hump' and 'How the Leopard got his Spots'.

Jutes One of the three main Germanic tribes which together became known as the *Anglo-Saxons. They came from northwest Europe (traditionally from modern Denmark, but recent opinion suggests further south, around the Rhine), and they settled during the 5–6c in Kent and southeast England.

Battle of **Jutland** (31 May 1916) The only full-scale battle of World War I between the heavily armoured British and German fleets. It took place in the North Sea, west of Jutland (north Denmark). The German High Seas Fleet was smaller than the British Grand Fleet, and the German strategy was to redress the balance by engaging half the British fleet under *Beatty before *Jellicoe could bring the rest from *Scapa Flow. In the event the entire Grand Fleet reached the scene of battle and the Germans escaped with some difficulty in the early hours of the following morning. But they had inflicted more damage than they had suffered, causing the day to be claimed as a German victory. It was also seen as a victory in Britain, because the balance of power was unchanged and the German fleet remained in harbour for the rest of the war.

juvenile court see *youth court.

K

Kaleidoscope (BBC from 1973) Daily programme on Radio 4, combining reviews and interviews in all the various art forms including literature. Until 1990 the late-night programme was live, making possible instant comment on that evening's first nights, and there was a repeat the following afternoon. Since 1990 the afternoon programme has had priority, with a repeat in the evening, acknowledging the greater size of the daytime audience and giving time for more considered responses to plays or concerts.

Boris **Karloff** (stage name of William Pratt, 1887–1969) British character actor who spent most of his career in Hollywood and became known for one part in particular – that of the monster in *Frankenstein*, which he first played in 1931. He continued to have a varied career in other films, on Broadway and at the end of his life on British TV, but it is as the monster that he is remembered.

Fred **Karno** (1866–1941) Impresario who in the early years of the 20c toured companies performing slapstick comedy. Both Charlie *Chaplin and Stan *Laurel first visited the USA in his shows. 'We are Fred Karno's army' was a self-deprecating song popular with the British infantry in the shambles of World War I. Even so, the lyric predicted that when they got to Berlin the kaiser would say 'Hoch, hoch, mein Gott, Vot a bloody fine lot'.

Loch **Katrine** Lake in the Central region of Scotland which became a major tourist attraction after the success of Scott's The *Lady of the Lake. Ellen's Isle is named after the heroine of the poem, Ellen Douglas. A steamer built in 1900 and called *Sir Walter Scott* now cruises the lake.

The Trossachs, often applied to the entire scenic area around the lake, is more precisely the name of the narrow wooded valley at its southeast end, leading to Loch Achray.

Gerald **Kaufman** (b. 1930) Labour politician, MP for Manchester Gorton since 1983 (previously for Manchester Ardwick 1970–83). He was shadow home secretary (1983–7) and shadow foreign secretary (1987–92).

John **Kay** (1704–64) Lancashire-born inventor of the flying shuttle, patented in 1733, which could pass mechanically back and forth across the loom, representing a major step forward in the mechanization of weaving and thus in the development of the *cotton industry. It was much faster than a hand-operated shuttle, and a single weaver could now work a broad-cloth loom which had previously required one on each side.

KBE, **KCB**, **KCMG** and **KCVO** see entry on *orders of chivalry.

KC The equivalent of *QC when the monarch is a king.

Edmund **Kean** (*c*.1789–1833) Actor whose ability to project a sense of danger and dark passion made him as much a typical figure of the *Romantic movement as his exact contemporary, Lord Byron. An illegitimate child, he started young in the theatre and struggled for years in the provinces before succeeding in London, as Shylock at Drury Lane in 1814. Audiences were thrilled by his intensity, particularly in villainous parts, though his sudden outbursts of passion caused Coleridge to compare the experience to 'reading Shakespeare by flashes of lightning'. His private life was as violent and unstable as his performances, and alcohol was increasingly a refuge. He died a few weeks after collapsing on stage at Covent Garden, when playing Othello to the Iago of his son Charles (1811–68). Charles went on to become a distinguished actor-manager, known in particular for the careful historical accuracy of his Shakespearean productions.

John **Keats** (1795–1821) A major poet of the *Romantic movement, whose creative profusion was cut short by his death at the age of 26. Living an uneventful existence in London, his imagination was released by accidents of art and nature. A good example is his earliest well-known poem, written when he was 20. A friend and he had spent an excited evening reading the translation of Homer by George Chapman (*c*.1560–1634). Early the next morning the friend received the sonnet *On first looking into Chapman's Homer*, beginning 'Much have I travelled in the realms of gold' and ending with a sense of kinship with early explorers, staring in wonder at the Pacific, 'silent upon a peak in Darien'.

Keats' extraordinary year of creativity was 1819, when the circumstances of his life gave an intensity tinged with melancholy to his work. His brother Tom had died the previous year of tuberculosis; Keats himself was passionately in love with Fanny Brawne, his next-door neighbour, to whom he became engaged; and his own recurrent bouts of illness were coming to seem increasingly like tuberculosis. It was in such a mood that he contrasted the eternal qualities of nature (*Ode to a Nightingale*) and of art (*Ode on a Grecian Urn*) with the transience of human happiness. He found an escape too in fantasies of medievalism (The *Eve of St Agnes, La *Belle Dame sans Merci*) which were to have great influence on poets and painters later in the century. All these poems were published together in 1820, just seven months before his death.

He was sent to Italy for his health. Early in 1821 he died in Rome, in lodgings at the foot of the Spanish Steps (a floor of the building is now owned by the *Landmark Trust). The pair of semi-detached houses in Hampstead, the homes in 1819 of the poet and of Fanny Brawne, are kept as a museum.

John **Keble** (1792–1866) Clergyman and poet who was one of the leaders of the *Oxford Movement. He published in 1827 *The Christian Year*, probably the century's bestselling volume of sacred verse. A great many of its poems were later adapted as hymns, among them *New every morning is the love*. Keble College at Oxford was founded in his memory four years after his death.

kedgeree Anglicized version of an Indian word and dish. In India *khichri* was rice mixed with lentils and spices; in Britain kedgeree became rice with shredded fish and chopped hard-boiled eggs. It has been traditionally a breakfast dish.

Kedleston Hall (6km/4m NW of Derby) Stately home of the Curzon family, built from 1759 in a style developing from the *Palladian to the *neoclassical. Matthew Brettingham (1699–1769) produced the balanced Palladian design seen in the formal north front with its projecting wings, and he was briefly followed as architect by James Paine (1717–89). But from 1760 the young Robert *Adam was in charge. Recently returned from Italy, he was able to put into effect here many of his new ideas. The central axis through the house follows Roman themes, from the pillared Marble Hall to the circular Saloon (based on the Pantheon) and then out to the north front, which has as its centrepiece a version of the arch of Constantine. In the decoration of the rooms to either side the young architect introduced what became known as the *Adam style.

Robert **Kee** (b. 1919) Broadcaster and author. Starting on *Panorama* in 1958, he has been involved with a wide range of political programmes and documentaries. He has made Irish history a speciality, both on TV (*Ireland; a television history*, 1981) and in books. He was one of the five presenters who together won the franchise for *TV-am in 1980.

Kevin **Keegan** (b. 1951) Footballer who made a major contribution as a striker to *Liverpool during six years (1971–7) which included 3 League victories, an FA Cup, a European Cup and a UEFA Cup. He captained both Liverpool and England (a total of 63 caps). He was also one of the first British players to make his mark playing elsewhere in Europe; he was named European Footballer of the Year in two successive years (1978–9) while with Hamburg. He returned to English football to play for Southampton (1980–82) and *Newcastle United (1982–4). He subsequently transformed Newcastle after being appointed manager in 1992.

Keep right on to the end of the road see Harry *Lauder.

Keep the Home Fires Burning see Ivor *Novello.

Kegworth see *M1 air crash.

Keighley and Worth Valley Railway see *Haworth.

Penelope **Keith** Actress best known for the comedy which she can extract from haughtiness and disdain, as seen to excellent effect in the TV series *The *Good Life* and *To the Manor Born* (1979–81).

Kelmscott Press The last great enterprise of William *Morris. In 1890 he installed presses at Hammersmith near Kelmscott House (named from his Elizabethan country manor) and began designing books which were

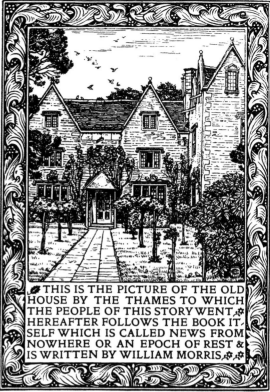

Frontispiece of Morris's News from Nowhere, *printed in 1892 at his Kelmscott Press and showing his 16c Kelmscott Manor.*

intended to rival the high standards of medieval manuscripts and early printing. Fifty-three titles were published, all in limited editions on handmade paper and with expensive bindings. The most successful was the last, the Kelmscott Chaucer (1896), with woodcuts by *Burne-Jones.

kelpie A creature of Scottish legend, first mentioned in print in the 18c, which was believed to haunt lakes and rivers, usually in the form of a horse, and to specialize in the drowning of travellers.

Kelso (4000 in 1981) Town in the Borders region of Scotland, at the junction of the Teviot with the Tweed, famous for the spectacular ruins of its once great Benedictine abbey. Founded by David I in 1128, it was destroyed by an English army in 1545.

Lord **Kelvin** see William *Thomson.

Fanny **Kemble** (Frances Anne Kemble, 1809–93) Actress and author, who delighted London from 1829 in performances both of tragedy and comedy, and subsequently gave pleasure to generations of readers with her fresh and lively journals and volumes of autobiography; these covered not only her early years of success in London but also her experiences in America as the wife of a plantation owner in Georgia (she left him because of her passionate opposition to slavery). She was a member of England's leading theatrical family of the time; her father (Charles Kemble, 1775–1854), her uncle (John Philip Kemble, 1757–1823) and her aunt (Mrs *Siddons) were merely the best known of her many relations on the stage.

Felicity **Kendal** (b. 1946) Actress who grew up touring India in her parents' Shakespeare company (the group seen in the 1965 film *Shakespeare Wallah*, in which she appeared). In Britain her career has been mainly in the theatre, including much Shakespeare, but she became widely known to the TV audience through The *Good Life.

Kenilworth Castle (6km/4m S of Coventry) Imposing ruin of one of the most powerful English castles of the Middle Ages. It was held by *John of Gaunt and later by the earl of *Leicester, who in 1575 entertained Elizabeth I here for the most lavish festivities of her reign; he is thought to have spent £100,000 making the accommodation suitable for the queen and then another £1000 for each of the 19 days of merrymaking.

Ludovic **Kennedy** (b. 1919) Broadcaster and author. On television he has presented many of the major political and current-affairs programmes, for both BBC and ITV. As an author and journalist he has specialized in the investigation of prominent criminal cases where injustice seems to have been done, beginning with the unfortunate Timothy Evans in Ten *Rillington Place (1961). He is married to Moira *Shearer.

Nigel **Kennedy** (b. 1956) Violinist whose job-lot wardrobe and pop-star platform manner outrage the purists, but whose performances of mainstream classics have reached unprecedentedly large audiences. His Elgar violin concerto with the London Philharmonic did well in 1985, but it was the 1989 recording of Vivaldi's Four Seasons (with the English Chamber Orchestra) which was in a different league of popular success; it reached no. 3 in the pop charts for albums and eventually sold more than 2 million copies. He followed it with Brahms's violin concerto in 1991 and with Beethoven's in 1992. In 1992 he announced that he was retiring from orchestral concert performances.

Kennel Club (London W1) Organization established in London in 1873 as the result of a newly popular type of event, the dog show; the first of its kind, held at Newcastle-upon-Tyne in 1859, was a competition for pointers and setters. As the number of shows increased, it became evident that some national system for registering the breeds and names of competing dogs was required. The founders of the Kennel Club aimed to fill this gap and saw their first task as the compiling of a register of pure-bred dogs and their pedigrees; the Kennel Club Stud Book has been an annual publication from 1874. Since 1948 the club has organized the main event of the canine year, *Crufts Dog Show.

Kenneth I (d. 858) Son of Alpin (known also therefore as Kenneth MacAlpin), he inherited from him Dalriada, the kingdom of the *Scots. By battle and alliance he also gained control over the *Picts. He thus for the first time brought under one rule the whole of mainland Britain north of a line from the Clyde to the Forth. This domination by the Scots led eventually to the entire area being known as Scotland.

Kensington Gardens (London W8) Now forming an uninterrupted western extension of *Hyde Park, they were originally the private grounds of Kensington Palace. George II allowed access on Saturdays to any who were 'respectably dressed' and the gardens have been fully open to the public since the reign of William IV. The Round Pond in front of the palace dates from 1728. There are two well-known statues: Physical Energy, a naked rider on a horse by G.F. *Watts; and *Peter Pan by George Frampton (1860–1928). At the southeast corner of the gardens is the *Albert Memorial.

Anonymous painting of the late 16C, traditionally said to show Leicester and Elizabeth dancing at Kenilworth.

Kenwood and its lake (beside which open-air concerts are now given), in an engraving of 1793.

Kensington Palace (London W8) An early 17c house on this site was bought by William III in 1689. *Wren was instructed to adapt it for royal use, with *Hawksmoor as clerk of the works. Improvements continued over several decades; *Kent painted the gallery of watching courtiers on the King's Staircase in the 1720s. In the 19c the palace was particularly associated with Victoria. In it she was born, christened, brought up and told of her accession; on her 70th birthday, in 1889, she opened the state apartments to the public (*Kensington Gardens had been open since the 1830s). Members of the royal family have continued to live in other parts of the palace, including in recent years Princess Margaret and the prince and princess of Wales.

Kent (1,539,000 in 1991, administrative centre Maidstone) *County on the south coast of England, to the southeast of London. It was one of the seven *Anglo-Saxon kingdoms in the 8c but was later absorbed by *Wessex.

Duke of Kent (Prince Edward, b. 1935) Grandson of George V (see the *royal family). His father served in the RAF in World War II and was killed when his plane crashed in Scotland. In 1961 the duke married Katharine Worsley (b. 1933) in York Minster, and they have three children: George, Earl of St Andrews (b. 1962), Helen (b. 1964) and Nicholas (b. 1970). He has been since 1967 Britain's leading *freemason, as Grand Master of the Grand Lodge.

Prince Michael of Kent (b. 1942) Grandson of George V (see the *royal family). In 1978 he married Marie-Christine von Reibnitz (b. 1945), who was divorced and a Roman Catholic (the latter causing him to lose his right of succession, by the Act of *Settlement). She is now known as Princess Michael of Kent. They have two children, Frederick (b. 1979) and Gabriella (b. 1981).

William **Kent** (*c.*1685–1748) Painter, architect, furniture designer and landscape gardener. Painting was his first profession (the murals at *Kensington Palace are his main work in this field). While studying in Italy (1709–19) he met Lord *Burlington, who became his life-long patron and turned his interests towards architecture in the Palladian style. One of his earliest projects with Burlington was *Chiswick House, where he was responsible for the interior decoration and the garden. His skill in these two fields is best seen in the interiors of *Houghton Hall and *Holkham Hall and in the revolutionary landscape garden at *Stowe. He was cheerfully eclectic in style and his furniture is much more heavily baroque than true Palladian principles should allow. In the National Maritime Museum at Greenwich there is a state barge designed by him, lavishly ornamented and gilded.

Kent County Cricket Club Founded in 1870 and one of the original members of the *county championship, Kent had a remarkable winning streak in the early years of the 20c and then again in the 1970s (champions 1906, 09, 10, 13, 70, 77, 78). The club's best-known players have been Colin *Cowdrey and two great wicket-keepers who were also fine batsmen – Leslie Ames and Alan Knott. There have been frequent triumphs in *one-day cricket (Gillette Cup 1967, 74; Benson and Hedges Cup 1973, 76, 78; John Player League 1972, 73, 76). The county ground is the St Lawrence in Canterbury, and the county team also plays at Folkestone, Tunbridge Wells and Maidstone.

St **Kentigern** see St *Mungo.

Kent's Cavern (2km/1m E of Torquay) Limestone cave on the south Devon coast used by Stone Age hunters. In addition to human remains and implements, fragments have been found of several extinct animals, including the mammoth, woolly rhinoceros and sabre-toothed tiger.

'Kent, sir – everybody knows Kent – apples, cherries, hops and women.' An observation by Mr Jingle in *Pickwick Papers*.

Kenwood House (London NW3) House on Hampstead Heath, which was built in about 1700 but owes its present appearance to the remodelling by Robert *Adam in 1767–8 for the 1st earl of Mansfield. Adam added the entrance portico on the north side and the library on the east, to balance the already existing orangery. In 1925, when Kenwood was threated with demolition, it was bought by the 1st earl of Iveagh (Edward Cecil Guinness, 1847–1927), who filled it with his own outstanding collection of pictures and bequeathed to the nation both house and contents – known together as the Iveagh Bequest. The landscape garden, dating from the 18C, is London's main location for outdoor concerts.

Kenya Member of the *Commonwealth since 1963, and a republic since 1964. European involvement in this part of east Africa began in the mid-19C, and was originally limited to missionaries and explorers. By the 1880s Germany and Britain were beginning to develop the interior; an agreed line of demarcation made a southern region (now *Tanzania) a German sphere of influence, leaving the northern area, Kenya, to the British. The excellent upland farming regions were extensively settled, becoming known as the White Highlands. In the 1950s a guerrilla movement, Mau Mau, was launched against British rule by the largest African tribe, the Kikuyu. The uprising reached alarming proportions. Only about 100 Europeans died, but the Mau Mau killed some 2000 Kikuyu who were considered to be collaborators and lost more than 11,000 of their own members. The supposed leader of the Mau Mau, Jomo Kenyatta (c.1891–1978), was imprisoned from 1952 to 1961, before becoming in 1963 the prime minister (and from 1964 president) of the newly independent country.

Kew Bridge Steam Museum see *Cornish beam engine.

Kew Gardens The name by which the Royal Botanic Gardens are commonly known. A royal garden was created in the mid-18C at Kew (16km/10m west of central London) by Frederick Prince of Wales and his wife Augusta, and it was later extended by their son, George III. It was Augusta who employed William *Chambers to beautify the garden with buildings and follies, of which the Orangery and the 10-storey Chinese Pagoda are the best known.

Under the guidance of Joseph *Banks plants were brought here from all over the world, and it was as a *botanic garden of scientific importance that Kew was given to the nation in 1840. Its reputation was further enhanced by the work of its first director, William *Hooker (the most dramatic story of propagation in his time being of *Victoria Amazonica).

Though primarily a centre for botanical research, Kew is also a very popular public garden of 121ha/300ac, attracting more than a million visitors each year. In addition to the beauties of botany and landscape there are architectural delights: a small redbrick mansion of 1631, sometimes known as the Dutch House but also as Kew Palace; the Queen's Cottage, a summerhouse built for Queen Charlotte in about 1771; and a magnificent early conservatory (the Palm House, 1844–8, by Decimus Burton and Richard Turner). Since 1965 *Wakehurst Place has been planted and administered as a companion garden to Kew.

John Maynard **Keynes** (1883–1946, baron 1942) Economist whose views were so influential that from World War II to the late 1970s 'Keynesian economics' were the widely accepted orthodoxy. He first came to prominence with *The Economic Consequences of the Peace* (1919), in which he accurately predicted that the terms of the Versailles Treaty would cripple Germany. His most influential work, *The General Theory of Employment, Interest and Money* (1936), was a response to the long *Depression of the 1930s which seemed to deny the classical theory of economic cycles.

Keynes argued that governments could spend their way out of recession by doing what the free market was supposed to do when labour was cheap – invest (by commissioning work on public projects) and encourage consumers to spend (by increasing the available *money supply). A reaction against this approach, on the grounds that it leads to *inflation, became influential in Britain during the 1980s when *monetarism was for a while an equally strong orthodoxy. Keynes was a prominent member of the *Bloomsbury group.

House of **Keys** see *Tynwald.

KG see Order of the *Garter.

khaki The cloth which became standard uniform in many armies. It was first worn by certain British regiments during the *Indian mutiny, replacing the bright plumage of the *redcoats. The word means dust-coloured in Hindi.

Londoners enjoying their local jungle in 1852, only four years after the great Palm House opened in Kew Gardens.

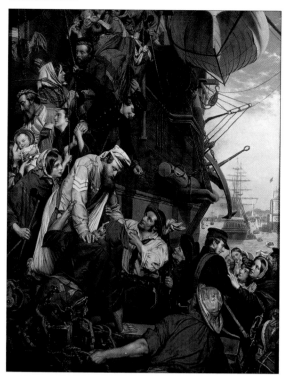

The new khaki worn by soldiers returning from the Indian Mutiny: painting by Henry Nelson O'Neil (1859).

The original 'khaki election' was that of 1900, when the Conservatives benefited from recent successes in the Boer War; and the phrase was later used of the 1945 election, much influenced by the vote of the troops at the end of World War II.

Khartoum see General *Gordon.

Captain **Kidd** (William Kidd, c.1645–1701) Sea captain who turned pirate after being a privateer (master of a private armed vessel employed by a government). As a privateer he had a commission from Britain to put down piracy in the Indian ocean. As a pirate himself he seized several ships, the most valuable of which, the *Quedagh Merchant*, was never seen again after he abandoned her in 1699 in the Caribbean – giving rise to subsequent legends that her treasure still lies somewhere buried. He was hanged at Wapping.

Kidderminster (51,000 in 1981) Town in Hereford and Worcester which from 1735 produced the type of carpet known by its name; it was a double cloth carpet (meaning flat-ribbed, without pile, and with the pattern in reversed colours on the back, of a kind also known in later forms as ingrain or Scotch). It was the first carpet to be produced partly by machine. Since the late 19C the town has been a major producer of machine-made *Axminster. A particular type of Axminster loom (the gripper) was developed in Kidderminster in about 1900.

Kidnapped (1886) Adventure story by Robert Louis *Stevenson. David Balfour, a Scottish boy in his late teens, is kidnapped and sent off to slavery in America by his uncle Ebenezer, who has usurped David's inheritance. The year is 1751, just after the failure of the *'45 Rebellion. Shipwreck saves David from the slavers and brings him into contact with Alan Breck, a spy for the *Jacobite cause. Together the pair have a series of dangerous brushes with the law in Scotland before David exposes his uncle and

recovers his estate, while Alan is promised safe passage to France. *Catriona* (1893) was a sequel, again involving David and Alan.

Pass of **Killiecrankie** Narrow wooded valley in the Tayside region of Scotland where, on 27 July 1689, *Jacobites massacred the remnants of an army supporting William III after defeating them in a battle just outside the pass. The Jacobites failed to exploit the victory because their leader John Graham, Viscount Dundee ('Bonnie Dundee', 1648–89), died in the battle.

Kilpeck (11km/7m SW of Hereford) Village with a 12C church, St Mary and St David, known for the vigour and profusion of its Romanesque carved-stone decoration – particularly on the south door, and on the corbels which project from the exterior walls just below the line of the roof.

kilt see *Highland dress.

Francis **Kilvert** (1840–79) Clergyman whose diary, discovered in the 1930s, gives a detailed account of life in Wales in the 1870s. He was curate in Clyro and then St Harmon (both in Powys) before becoming vicar of Bredwardine (Hereford and Worcester). He died of peritonitis within a few weeks of marrying. His wife and a niece destroyed between them more of the diary than survives, though what remains (covering most of 1870–9) is in itself extensive.

Kim (1901) Novel by *Kipling about a small boy, Kimball O'Hara, son of a sergeant in the British army, who is brought up by a half-caste woman after the death of his parents. Soon more at ease in the bazaar than among the British, he is perfectly placed to play a central role in a story of spying between the two communities. As well as being an exciting story, the book is rich in the details familiar to Kipling from his years in India as child and journalist.

Kincardineshire Until 1975 a *county in east Scotland, now part of the Grampian region.

Kind Hearts and Coronets (1949) One of the *Ealing comedies, a brilliantly debonair account of a young man (played by Dennis Price) murdering in turn the eight eccentric members of the Ascoyne d'Ascoyne family who stand between him and a dukedom. The film's stroke of genius is that all the victims, male and female alike, are played by Alec *Guinness.

Tom **King** (b. 1933) Conservative politician, MP for Bridgwater since 1970. He entered the *cabinet in 1983 and was in rapid succession secretary of state for the environment (Jan.–June), for transport (June–Oct.) and for employment. He remained at employment until 1985, and was then secretary of state for Northern Ireland (1985–9) and for defence (1989–92).

King Charles spaniel see *spaniels.

King Edward's Schools Many schools were founded by Edward VI during the last year (1552–3) of his short life, when he was himself only 15. They include King Edward's Schools at Bath and at Witley, the King Edward VI School in Southampton and *Christ's Hospital. The most fruitful of his foundations was King Edward's in Birmingham, long famous as one of the country's greatest grammar schools. It is now an independent fee-paying school, as is its companion the King Edward VI High School for Girls, founded in 1883. Prudent investment of the original endowment had made possible not only the girls' school but also, in the 1870s, no fewer than five King Edward VI grammar schools in different parts of Birmingham; all survive, offering free education within the state system.

Kingfisher Company formed in 1982 to buy the ailing *Woolworths for £310 million (the name was changed from Woolworth Holdings to Kingfisher in 1989). Its success in reviving the store chain was demonstrated by its ability to resist, in 1986, a £1bn bid by Dixons. By the early 1990s Kingfisher was among Britain's largest companies.

King George V Gold Cup see *Royal International Horse Show.

King George VI and Queen Elizabeth Diamond Stakes see *Ascot.

*The **Kingis Quair*** see *James I of Scotland.

King James version see *Bible in English.

King John (*c*.1595) One of *Shakespeare's least performed plays. It concerns the attempts of John to remain on the English throne from 1199 in spite of the better claim of a young nephew, Arthur.

King Lear (*c*.1605) The most elemental of *Shakespeare's tragedies, much of the later action taking place on an open heath with the protagonist drifting into madness as he discusses wild and weighty topics with the Fool, his licensed jester.

The tragedy is set in motion when Lear, a legendary king of Britain, proposes to divide his kingdom between his three daughters; the unscrupulous Regan and Goneril get half each because Cordelia refuses to engage in a public display of exaggerated love for her father. Dependent now on the evil sisters' charity, the king is treated steadily

The south door of the church at Kilpeck, with its vigorous and well-preserved 12c carving.

worse until he escapes to join Cordelia, who has married the king of France. A parallel story concerns the earl of Gloucester, who takes pity on Lear but is equally unwise about his own children. He has trusted his bastard son, Edmund, and has rejected the legitimate Edgar. But it is Edgar, himself living on the heath in the guise of madness as poor Tom, who protects his father after Regan's husband has gouged his eyes from their sockets (one of them with the line 'Out, vile jelly!').

Lear is reunited with Cordelia (she has landed near Dover with a French army) but soon they are both captured. Edmund, now the lover of both Regan and Goneril, orders that Cordelia shall be hanged. Edgar challenges and defeats him in single combat (while jealous Goneril poisons Regan and then kills herself), but the restoration of order comes too late to save Cordelia. Lear carries her body on to the stage crying 'Howl, howl, howl, howl!' and himself dies.

*The **King of love my Shepherd is*** see *The *Lord's my Shepherd*.

King's Beasts A set of ten heraldic sculptures on either side of the bridge leading into *Hampton Court. Each of the beasts holds a coat of arms, five of them relating to the ancestry of Henry VIII and five to Jane Seymour, mother of his only son, Edward VI. They are modern versions of ten of the twelve commissioned for the bridge by Henry in 1536. The original set was destroyed in the late 17c. Ten installed in 1909 became so eroded that they were replaced by the present carvings in 1950. A similar group, that of the *Queen's Beasts, was created in 1953.

King's Champion see *Coronation.

King's College, London Founded in 1828 by the two archbishops and by 30 bishops of the Church of England in response to the 'godless' affront of *University College, which has traditionally remained King's great rival; both are now part of *London University. The godly college did not insist on the undergraduates being Anglicans, but the professors had to be. Its building on the Strand (1829–31) was designed by *Smirke, and from 1839 there was a linked King's College Hospital. The hospital moved in 1913 to its present location on Denmark Hill in southeast London.

King's Cross (London N1) Area named after a monument to *George IV, which stood briefly at the main crossroads of the district. Put up in 1836 (the king was on top of an 18m/60ft monument), the object caused so much hostility that it was down again by 1845. King's Cross Station was built in 1851–2 to a design by Lewis Cubitt (1799–1883). In the early 1990s the station area was scheduled for redevelopment as a terminus for the *Channel Tunnel. British Rail's plan, designed by Norman *Foster, includes a futuristic station concourse and a large new park leading north towards a pair of skyscrapers.

In November 1987 the King's Cross underground station was the scene of a disaster when a fire, starting beneath an escalator, resulted in 31 deaths.

King's (or Queen's) English Grammatically correct English. An early use of the phrase is in Shakespeare's *Merry Wives of Windsor*, where a French physician, described as abusing the king's English, asks angrily, 'Do intend vat I speak?'. The outdated 20c phrase Oxford English referred only to an *'Oxford accent', but Queen's English is sometimes now used abroad to mean an accent that is English rather than American.

King's evidence see *Queen's evidence.

King's evil A name for scrofula (tuberculosis of the lymphatic glands at the side of the neck, with ulceration of the skin), because it was believed that the touch of a king could cure the condition. Touching for the king's evil is thought to have been practised as early as the 11C, by Edward the Confessor, and it continued until the reign of Queen Anne. In 1712 she touched the 3-year-old Samuel Johnson for the disease.

Charles **Kingsley** (1819–75) Clergyman, novelist and children's writer, remembered now chiefly for *Westward Ho!* and *The *Water-Babies*, and as the chief proponent of *muscular Christianity (a term which he himself hated).

King's Lynn (33,000 in 1981) Town in Norfolk, on the Great Ouse about 5km/3m from its entry to the Wash, of importance from medieval times both as port and market town. The market places are still the two main squares. Saturday Market is flanked by the 12–14C church of St Margaret (containing two spectacular 14C *brasses) and by the early 15C Guildhall of the Holy Trinity, with a chequerboard façade of flint and stone. Facing Tuesday Market is St George's Guildhall, also early 15C, the largest surviving medieval guildhall in the country. The town's continuing prosperity is revealed in a great many excellent houses of the 17–18C, chief among them the Customs House of 1683, designed by a local architect who was also mayor, Henry Bell (1647–1711). The town is more often referred to locally as Lynn, the royal addition being granted only in a charter of 1537 from Henry VIII.

King's Men see *Chamberlain's Men.

King Solomon's Mines (1885) Adventure story by Rider *Haggard, deliberately trying to rival the recent success of *Treasure Island* and even following the same narrative pattern. Allan Quatermain and two friends set off with a map to find the reputed treasure of the biblical Solomon. African tribal life, rather than the allure of pirates, provides in this case the necessary ingredients of exoticism and danger.

King's pattern The design used more than any other on silver spoons and forks in the Victorian period. The handles, heavily ornamented on both sides, have a scallop shell motif at the end which is repeated on the underside where the handle broadens into the bowl of the spoon or the prongs of the fork.

The queen's pattern has minor differences of decoration but is closely related.

King's Road (London SW) The main thoroughfare through *Chelsea. From the late 17C to 1830 it was for much of its length the king's private road towards royal properties upstream at Hampton Court and Kew. Its modern fame as a shopping street derives from *Peter Jones at its eastern end and, since the 1960s, from its many boutiques. In the 1980s *punks became the local exotica, attracting tourists with their weird and colourful display and then charging for a photograph.

King's Schools The various *public schools with this name were founded or refounded by Tudor kings. The two oldest (*Canterbury and *Rochester, dating from the first decade of the 7C) were monastic schools which were given a new charter by Henry VIII after the *dissolution of the monasteries.

King's (or **Queen's**) **shilling** The coin given, until 1879, to each new recruit in the British army. Taking the king's shilling (see *£.s.d.) was therefore a term for enlisting.

Kingston (Kingston upon Thames, 137,000 in 1991) Borough of Greater London; administrative centre of the county of Surrey. Much rebuilt in recent decades, it has been a town of importance from Anglo-Saxon times as a place where the Thames could be forded. There has been a bridge since the 13C. The local museum contains a surprising bequest – the photographic archives of a native of Kingston who emigrated to the USA, Eadweard *Muybridge.

Kingston Brooch (County Museum, Liverpool) Circular Anglo-Saxon jewel of gold, set with garnets, blue glass and shell, which was found in a 7C burial site at Kingston in Kent.

Kingston Lacy (18km/11m NW of Bournemouth) House built in red brick in 1663–5 for Sir Ralph Bankes whose previous family home (*Corfe Castle, a few miles to the south) had been destroyed after a famously brave defence by his mother against a parliamentary army. The original architect was Roger Pratt (1620–85, kt 1668), but the present stone-clad exterior and much of the interior, including the marble staircase, is the work of Charles *Barry in major alterations of 1835–41 for William John Bankes (whose superb collection of pictures is one of the great glories of the house).

Kingston-upon-Hull see *Hull.

King's Troop The mounted troop of the *Royal Artillery, seen displaying their ancient skills when giving *royal salutes or in the Royal Tournament. By the 1930s the whole of the Royal Horse Artillery was mechanized, but after World War II a Riding Troop was re-established for ceremonial duties. It was named the King's Troop in 1947, and on her accession in 1952 Elizabeth II ordered that it keep that name in memory of her father.

The **Kinks** Rock group formed in London in 1963 (originally as the Ravens) by Ray Davies and his brother Dave (b. 1944 and 1947, both vocals and guitar) with Peter Quaife (b. 1943, bass) and Mick Avory (b. 1944, drums). Their third single, *You Really Got Me*, reached no. 1 in 1964, to be followed in that spot by *Tired of Waiting for You* (1965) and *Sunny Afternoon* (1966); *Lola*, no. 2 in 1970, became perhaps their best-known number. Most of the group's songs, noisy in style but very English and rather nostalgic in mood, were written by Ray Davies. Still recording and performing together in the 1990s, the Kinks are among the great survivors from the early days of British rock.

Neil **Kinnock** (b. 1942) Welsh politician, MP for Islwyn since 1983 (previously for Bedwellty 1970–83), who was leader of the *Labour party and leader of the Opposition in parliament from 1983 to 1992. He was elected leader after the party had been through a chaotic period under Michael Foot (with defections to the *SDP), and he applied himself very successfully to tackling two themes unpopular with the voters – infiltration from the extreme left, as represented by the *Militant Tendency, and a commitment to *unilateral disarmament. The Labour party was therefore in much better shape by the 1992 general election, which the opinion polls predicted would carry Kinnock and his wife, Glenys, to Downing Street. He resigned as leader almost immediately after being disappointed in the election result, and was succeeded by John Smith.

Kinross-shire Until 1975 an inland *county in east central Scotland, now mostly in the Tayside region with part in Central.

Rudyard **Kipling** (1865–1936) Author whose somewhat jingoistic views on empire prejudiced his reputation in the mid-20C but who is now increasingly appreciated as a distinctly original poet and brilliant prose writer, particularly for children. Born in India, he was sent to a boarding school in England (described in *Stalky & Co) and worked from 1882 as a journalist in Lahore (the setting of *Kim). He published many short stories before returning to England in 1889. His growing reputation was enhanced by Barrack-Room Ballads (1892), a collection of lively poems in a soldier's vernacular (it included *Mandalay. His best books for children came out in the next ten years – The *Jungle Books and The *Just So Stories. *If, one of the most popular poems in the language, was published in 1910. By now he seemed the nation's unofficial laureate, serving for example as literary adviser to the Imperial *War Graves Commission. From 1902 he lived at Bateman's in East Sussex (24km/15m NW of Hastings), which is kept as a museum. He was awarded the Nobel prize for literature in 1907.

kipper A herring which has been sliced through from its underside, stopping just short of the skin on its back; it is then opened up flat like a book and cured by smoking. A technique used originally for salmon, it was adapted to the smaller fish by John Woodger at Seahouses, in Northumberland.

Kipps: the story of a simple soul (1905) Novel by H.G. *Wells about Arthur Kipps, an inarticulate draper's assistant whose life becomes a series of comic and embarrassing mishaps when he inherits a fortune. He marries his equally underprivileged first love, Ann Pornick.

Kiribati Republic and member of the *Commonwealth since independence in 1979. These 36 coral islands in the Pacific, of which 17 are the Gilbert Islands, were visited by British merchant ships from the late 18C. In 1892 they were made part of the protectorate of the Gilbert and Ellice Islands (the Ellice Islands became independent as *Tuvalu).

Kirkcudbrightshire Until 1975 a *county on the southwest coast of Scotland, now part of the Dumfries and Galloway region.

Kirkwall (6000 in 1981) Town on the island of Mainland; administrative centre of Orkney. The massively proportioned Romanesque cathedral (12–15C) was founded in 1137 by Rognvald, a Viking ruler, in honour of his uncle Magnus – a man known for his piety who was murdered in 1116 and was then adopted as patron saint of the *Orkneys. Two skeletons found in the cathedral in 1926, one with a fractured skull, are assumed to be those of Magnus and Rognvald. The Bishop's Palace and the ruined Earl's Palace date from the 16C. The museum, in the 16C Tankerness House, covers some 5000 years of Orkney archaeology and history.

kissing hands A ceremony for newly appointed privy councillors and government ministers. The hand is the monarch's, held out to be lightly kissed on the back of the fingers by the kneeling official. A new prime minister (as also a British ambassador or governor general appointed to a new post abroad) is described in the court circular as having 'kissed hands', but in this case the ceremony as such does not take place; the phrase is merely used for a particular type of royal audience.

'Kiss me, Hardy' see Battle of *Trafalgar.

Kit-Cat Club Early 18C club of leading Whig politicians and writers, which derived its name from a London

pastrycook, Christopher Cat – either because they first met in his house, or because they relished his mutton pies (known as kit-cats), or perhaps both. The club's fame has been assured by *Kneller, who painted portraits of 42 of his fellow members. The pictures, now in the National Portrait Gallery, are of identical size (91x71cm/36x28in), usually with just one hand showing. This short half-length was apparently made necessary by the low ceiling of the dining room in which the club met. 'Kit-cat size' later became a standard term in portraiture.

Lord **Kitchener** (Herbert Kitchener, 1850–1916, KCMG 1894, earl 1914) Soldier who was secretary of state for war at the start of World War I. He had first become well known from events in the Sudan. He was a member of the 1885 expedition which failed to relieve *Gordon at Khartoum, and he became determined to avenge Gordon's death – an ambition achieved in 1898 when he defeated the Mahdi's followers at the Battle of Omdurman (Sept. 2) and established British-Egyptian rule over the Sudan. From November 1900 he was the British commander-in-chief in the *Boer War, conducting the campaign with a ruthlessness which included the introduction of concentration camps. He commanded the British army in India (1902–9) and administered British Egypt (1911–14) before being appointed to the cabinet as secretary for war; his is the face on the best known of all recruiting posters, pointing imperiously at the viewer with the statement 'Your country needs you'. He died when the cruiser HMS *Hampshire*, taking him on a mission to Russia, struck a mine near the Orkneys.

kitchen-sink school Term coined by David Sylvester in *Encounter* in 1954 to describe John *Bratby, Derrick Greaves, Edward Middleditch and Jack Smith, whose paintings depicted everyday household objects ('Everything but the kitchen sink? The kitchen sink too'). By extension a certain kind of play became known as kitchen-sink drama – the work of playwrights such as Arnold *Wesker, author of The Kitchen (1959).

Godfrey **Kneller** (Gottfried Kniller, c.1646–1723, kt 1692) German-born painter who settled in England c.1675 and rapidly succeeded *Lely as the leading portrait painter. His best-known work is his series of portraits of the *Kit-Cat Club. The great house survives which he built for himself at Whitton, to the west of London; it was largely rebuilt in the 19C and is now, as Kneller Hall, the home of the Royal Military School of Music.

Kneller Hall see *military bands.

knight A non-hereditary rank awarded as an honour. Recipients use Sir in front of their names, and their wives Lady (Sir John and Lady Smith). Some knighthoods are awarded within the *orders of chivalry but the majority, known as knights bachelor, are separate and individual creations. The equivalent rank for women is that of *Dame.

Laura **Knight** (1877–1970, DBE 1929) Painter best-known for her circus and theatre pictures from between the wars, but more impressive in the brightly coloured Cornish scenes from her earlier years at *Newlyn (1907–18). As an official war artist she provided some powerful images of the accused in the dock at the Nuremberg trials.

Knightsbridge (London SW1) Street running west from Hyde Park Corner, famous (somewhat inaccurately) for its high-class department stores. Harvey Nichols is indeed in the street, but *Harrods (describing itself as 'of Knightsbridge') is in the Brompton Road.

Knightsbridge safe deposit boxes Britain's largest robbery. Items variously estimated between £30m and £40m in value were stolen in July 1987 from the deposit boxes in the Knightsbridge Safety Deposit Centre in London. The managing director of the centre, Parvez Latif, was one of four men convicted of the crime; he was sentenced to 18 years in prison.

Knightshayes Court (26km/16m N of Exeter) Victorian Gothic mansion built 1869–83 for the Heathcoat-Amory family, whose wealth derived from their lace factory at nearby Tiverton. The architect was William *Burges, but the extravagance of his proposed designs proved too daunting and most of the interiors were handed over to J.D. Crace (1838–1917). Knightshayes is best known now for its garden, originally laid out by Edward Kemp (1817–91) but greatly extended into the neighbouring woodlands after World War II by Sir John and Lady Amory.

Knocked 'em in the Old Kent Road see entry on Albert *Chevalier.

'Knock, knock, knock!' see *Macbeth*.

Knole (18km/11m N of Tunbridge Wells) Vast house round a succession of courtyards (traditionally held to contain a room for each of the 365 days in the year), built in the late 15C as a palace for Thomas Bourchier, archbishop of Canterbury. It was later appropriated by Henry VIII and was given by Elizabeth I to the Sackville family, with whom it remained. After remodelling the house in 1603–8 and filling it later in the century with magnificent objects, the Sackvilles made very few changes. As a result Knole contains an unrivalled collection of 17C furniture (complete with many of the fabrics) in a contemporary setting. The best-known pieces are the original 'Knole settee' (high-backed with arms which hinge down, much copied in the 20C); and, in the King's Room, the set of silver furniture and the state bed, with its matching chairs and stools in gold and silver brocade.

knot The unit of speed for a ship at sea. One knot is a speed of one nautical mile per hour (1.85kph/1.15mph). The name relates to a system introduced on British ships some time before 1633, the earliest recorded use of the term. It had long been the custom to assess a boat's speed by the amount of line pulled overboard by a floating object in a given time. The innovation first mentioned in 1633 was the tying of knots in the line at specific intervals to give a quicker and more accurate measurement. In the 20C the knot, already the international unit of speed at sea, was adopted also for aircraft.

John **Knox** (c.1514–72) Leader who secured the early successes of the presbyterian *Church of Scotland at the time of the *Reformation. Ordained a Catholic priest, he was converted to Protestantism by Scotland's first great reformer, George Wishart (c.1513–46), who was burnt at the stake in St Andrews in 1546. It was at St Andrews, the following year, that Knox emerged as a religious leader. He was among the Protestants besieged there after the prolonged turmoil following Wishart's death, and his preaching to the beleaguered town revealed his powerful qualities. When the town fell to the Catholics and their French allies, he was sentenced to serve as a galley slave on French ships. It was 19 months before he was released.

After being closely involved in England in the Protestant policies of Edward VI's reign, Knox avoided the Roman Catholic backlash under Mary I by escaping to the Continent. He spent the happiest years of his life (1556–9) as pastor to the community of English exiles in Calvin's

The silver furniture in the King's Room at Knole, believed to have been supplied c.1676 by the cabinet-maker Gerrit Jensen.

Geneva, which he called a 'perfect school of Christ'. It was there that he wrote his unfortunate tract on *The *Monstrous Regiment of Women*, which accidentally prevented his ever returning to England. But he was back in Scotland in 1559 to take part in the closing stages of the uprising by Protestants against Scottish and French Catholic forces. With English support the Protestants won, and Knox spent his remaining years establishing the structure of Scotland's reformed church and writing his *History of the Reformation in Scotland*. But those final years included one famous personal clash which held great potential danger. In 1561 the 19-year-old Roman Catholic *Mary Queen of Scots returned from France to Edinburgh. There was a famous series of encounters in Holyroodhouse between the wilful young queen and the outspoken reformer, ending in deep personal animosity between the two. In the event the other troubles which engulfed Mary left Knox free to continue with the work of reform.

The John Knox House on the Royal Mile in Edinburgh is kept as a museum. It is one of the earliest surviving domestic buildings in the Old Town (15C with additions up to the 17C). Knox is believed to have lived here during the last decade of his life, when he was minister at St Giles'.

Robin **Knox-Johnston** (b. 1939) The first man to sail non-stop and single-handed round the world, which he did in *Suhaili* in ten months from June 1968 to April 1969 – thus winning the Golden Globe, a trophy offered by the *Sunday Times* to whoever first achieved this feat. In 1993 he and six others set off from the Solent in *Enza New Zealand*, in an attempt to sail round the world in 80 days.

Arthur **Koestler** (1905–83) Hungarian-born author, living in England from 1940 and a British citizen from 1948. His experiences as a member of the Communist party (1931–8) led to the novel for which he is best known, *Darkness at Noon*. He wrote a wide range of non-fiction, including several books on science, such as *The Case of the Midwife Toad* (1971). His interest in parapsychology (*The Roots of Coincidence* 1972) led him to leave £500,000 for a chair in the subject; this was eventually established at the university of Edinburgh. He also funded annual arts prizes for people in prison. A keen supporter of *Exit, he committed suicide when suffering from Parkinson's disease and leukaemia; more controversial was the fact that his third wife, Cynthia, 22 years younger, killed herself with him.

Kohinoor (*koh-i-noor*, 'mountain of light' in Persian) A large diamond in the *crown jewels. It was presented in 1849 by the Sikh ruler of the Punjab to Sir John Lawrence, the British commissioner. Lawrence forgot it and left it for six weeks in his waistcoat pocket, but it eventually reached London in time to become a prize exhibit in the Great Exhibition of 1851.

Oskar **Kokoschka** (1886–1980) Austrian-born artist who fled to London in 1938 and became a British citizen in 1947. His paintings done in Britain include portraits and the high-angle townscape views in which he specialized, all done in a heavily expressionistic style. He lived in Switzerland from the 1950s.

Kop see *Liverpool football club.

Alexander **Korda** (adopted name of Alexander Kellner, 1893–1956, kt 1942) Hungarian-born film producer who settled in England in 1931. In 1932 he formed London Film Productions, with Big Ben as its trademark, which established its reputation with Charles *Laughton in *The Private Life of Henry VIII* and *Rembrandt*, and scored many other successes such as *The *Scarlet Pimpernel*, **Things to Come* and *The Four Feathers* (1939). After the war, from new studios at Shepperton, there came *The *Third Man* and Laurence Olivier in **Richard III*.

Korean War (1950–3) Conflict which was a direct aftermath of World War II. Korea, an ancient country at the northeast tip of China, was forcibly annexed by Japan in 1910. In 1945 the USSR received the surrender of Japanese troops in Korea north of the 38th parallel, while the USA did so south of that line – a state of affairs which soon led to ideologically opposed governments in the north and south. In 1950 a North Korean army invaded the south. In response to this aggression the Security Council of the United Nations sent out a multinational force to push back the invaders; about half the army was from the USA, the rest coming mainly from Australia, Britain, Canada and Turkey. By November 1950 the UN force had pressed forward to Korea's northern border with China, provoking a massive response from a Chinese Communist army. Early in 1951 the UN forces were pushed south again to below the 38th parallel, and by that summer a military stalemate was established close to that line. Fighting continued for two more years between virtually fixed positions in the hills. The armistice of July 1953 left two bitterly opposed countries, North and South Korea, with a heavily defended border along the 38th parallel.

Kray twins Gangsters, Reginald and Ronald (b. 1934), who in the 1960s ran protection rackets in an Al Capone style in London's East End. In 1969 they were sentenced to life imprisonment (with a recommended minimum of 30 years) for the murder of Jack 'The Hat' McVitie. *The Krays*, a feature film about their exploits, appeared in 1990.

Hans **Krebs** (1900–81, kt 1958) German-born biochemist who came to Britain in 1933. At Freiburg he had identified the 'urea cycle', by which the liver forms urea; at Sheffield he discovered the central process of metabolism (later known as the Krebs cycle), by which cells break down the carbohydrate in food in a succession of changes to release carbon dioxide, water and energy. In 1953 he shared the Nobel prize for medicine with Fritz Lipmann, an American scientist who had worked out important details of the cycle.

Krogers see *Portland spies.

KT see Order of the *Thistle.

Kubla Khan or, *A Vision in a Dream* (1797) Fragment of a poem by *Coleridge which he published, on the urging of Byron, in the same volume as *Christabel* in 1816. Coleridge introduces the poem with his famous account of its inspiration and interruption. He was in a lonely farmhouse in Somerset in 1797, under the influence of opium, and he fell asleep when reading in Purchas's *Pilgrimage* how Kubla Khan had built a great palace in the 13c at Xanadu in northern China. In his sleep he composed between 200 and 300 lines. On waking he began immediately to write them down, with their magnificent opening image:

> In Xanadu did Kubla Khan
> A stately pleasure-dome decree:
> Where Alph, the sacred river, ran
> Through caverns measureless to man
> Down to a sunless sea.

When he had completed only 54 lines, he was 'called out by a person on business from Porlock'; and by the time he got back to his desk, the rest of the poem 'had passed away like the images on the surface of a stream into which a stone has been cast'.

The surviving lines are a potent romantic brew, intermingling deep chasms and mighty fountains, sunny pleasure domes and caves of ice, a damsel with a dulcimer and a woman wailing for her demon lover.

Kuwait The ruling Al-Sabah dynasty, established in 1756, made a treaty with Britain in 1899 for protection against the Turkish empire. In 1914 Kuwait was recognized as an independent state under British protection, and in 1961 the country became fully independent. Iraq immediately claimed sovereignty over its smaller neighbour and threatened invasion. British military aid was sent (at the time Kuwait provided more than 20% of Britain's oil) and in 1963 Iraq recognized Kuwait's independence, though the line of the border was never formally agreed. It was against this background that Iraq invaded and annexed Kuwait in 1990, an action leading to the *Gulf War.

Kynance Cove Rocky inlet on the west coast of the *Lizard, with dramatic caves hollowed out by the Atlantic rollers. A crack in the cliff, known as the Devil's Bellows, causes roaring sounds and clouds of spray as the tide flows in and out.

L

Ministry of **Labour** see Department of *Employment.

Labour Party The political party which since the 1920s has provided the alternative to the *Conservatives under Britain's *two-party system. Its working-class inspiration derived distantly from the *Chartists and more immediately from the activities of independent radical politicians, among them Keir *Hardie (one of the founders of the Scottish Labour party in 1888 and of the Independent Labour party in 1893). An important intellectual input came from the *Fabian Society.

The party was established in 1900 at a conference of *trade unions and was called the Labour Representation Committee. It won only two seats in the election of that year, but 29 members were returned in 1906 when the name was changed to the Labour party. The pacifism of its first two leaders, Keir Hardie and Ramsay *MacDonald, reduced support in the years around World War I, but 142 seats in 1922 made Labour the official Opposition. The election of 1923 gave MacDonald 191 seats, enough to form a brief coalition government with the Liberals, and in 1929 he led for the first time the largest party in the House. But it was not until the landslide victory of 1945 that Labour had an overall majority.

In this postwar government, under *Attlee, Labour was able to achieve many of its stated policies, putting into place much of the *welfare state and nationalizing the country's major industrial resources. In the following decades two issues in particular seemed to distinguish Labour from the Conservatives, and neither was popular with the voters. The party was committed by Clause Four of its constitution to a continuing programme of nationalization; and there was a strong grass-roots inclination towards unilateral nuclear disarmament, in a tradition going back to the pacifism of the early leaders. Hugh *Gaitskell fought against both but lost on Clause Four, though the commitment to public ownership has been quietly dropped in recent years.

The party had periods of government in the 1960s and 1970s under Wilson and Callaghan, but in 1979 began a long spell in opposition (with Michael Foot, Neil Kinnock and John Smith as successive leaders). During the 1980s two main threats to Labour's electoral chances were identified. One was the *Militant Tendency, whose intrusions were eventually dealt with – though not before the left-wing and unilateralist trends within the party had provoked defectors into forming the *SDP. The other was the trade unions. Since the unions were instrumental in forming the party in 1900 and have funded it ever since, it is not surprising that they have retained a powerful influence. This is expressed at the annual conference, which elects the *NEC and votes on resolutions which have in the past been allowed to constitute party policy.

The delegates from the unions cast block votes (relating to the number of their members), giving an impression of baronial power which has seemed increasingly out of keeping with modern democracy. The party headquarters are in *Walworth Road.

Labrador see *retriever.

Lacock Abbey (23km/14m NE of Bath) From the 13c to the *dissolution of the monasteries this was a convent for Augustinian nuns. A considerable amount of the old building survives among alterations of the Tudor period; the early Gothic Revival additions are by Sanderson Miller (1717–80). The house is best known as the home of Fox *Talbot.

Ladbroke Betting firm which has grown to become one of Britain's largest companies, with interests extending from racing to hotels (in 1987 it acquired Hilton International, representing all Hiltons outside the USA). The company goes back to the village of Ladbroke in Warwickshire, where a horse trainer and his friend set up in the 19c as bookmakers. In London from the turn of the century, 'Ladbroke's' took bets placed on the telephone by rich account-holders – betting with cash was then illegal except at racecourses. The Betting and Gaming Act of 1960 made cash betting legal at licensed betting shops in the high street, and this was the opening which enabled Ladbroke to begin its rapid expansion; it became a public company in 1967.

Lady Title used by the wives of knights, baronets and barons, and in informal contexts by higher-ranking female members of the *peerage (with the exception of duchesses).

*The **Lady*** Britain's oldest women's magazine, founded in 1885 by Thomas Gibson Bowles and still owned by his descendants. The first issue declared the *Lady*'s intention 'to cover the whole field of womanly action' and to be 'at once a valuable friend and a delightful companion'. It has evidently achieved both while remaining plain, practical and resolutely unglossy, though it still aims – as its title implies – at the more privileged and old-fashioned section of the market.

Ladybird Children's publisher, known in particular for its small or 'pocket-sized' books, first produced in 1940. With an emphasis on learning to read, most of the firm's numerous titles are aimed at the 3–8 age group. The enterprise was developed by small commercial printers in Leicestershire, Wills & Hepworth, who in World War I began to produce picture books for children under the name Ladybird.

Lady Chatterley's Lover (1928) Novel by D.H. *Lawrence, printed privately in Florence in 1928. The book is noted for its detailed but highly poeticized descriptions of the act of love and for its use of four-letter words. It was first published in Britain in an unexpurgated version in 1960 (it had survived prosecution in the USA the previous year), and the acquittal of its British publishers, *Penguin, on a charge of *obscenity became an important turning point in the freedom of the press; it also brought Penguin a sale of 2 million copies in the six weeks after the verdict. One question from the trial has long outlived the event; the counsel for the prosecution, Mervyn Griffith-Jones, astonished the jury by asking if this was the sort of book they would wish their wives or their servants to read.

The central character is Constance Chatterley, whose war-wounded husband Sir Clifford is impotent. She has a passionate affair (rather later in the book than some of the eager first purchasers expected) with Sir Clifford's gamekeeper, the forthright Oliver Mellors – a typically Lawrentian figure, in touch with nature and therefore innocent of the falsities of modern society.

Lady Day (March 25) One of the *quarter days, important also for its role in the medieval *calendar. It is an abbreviation of Our Lady's Day, for it is the Feast of the Annunciation (nine months before Christmas).

Lady Lever Art Gallery see *Port Sunlight.

The Lady of the Lake (1810) Narrative poem by Walter *Scott about frustrated love and mistaken identities among warring chieftains in 16C Scotland, in the same vein as his earlier *Lay of the Last Minstrel. It was even more successful, causing such a rush of tourists to the lake in question (Loch Katrine) that a new hotel had to be built.

The Lady of the Lake in *Morte d'Arthur is a shadowy figure who gives *Excalibur to Arthur.

Lady of the Lamp see Florence *Nightingale.

The Lady of Shalott (1833, revised and reissued in 1842) One of *Tennyson's earliest Arthurian successes, about a mysterious lady in an island castle who never raises her eyes from her loom until Lancelot passes by on his way to Camelot; she looks out of the window at him and dies. The jingling rhythm and repetitive rhymes (particularly of Camelot, Shalott and Lancelot) make the poem attractive for reading aloud but also give it more than a little in common with the humorous verses of Edward Lear.

The Lady's Not for Burning (1948) Verse comedy by Christopher *Fry in which affection blossoms, amid verbal pyrotechnics, between a woman accused of witchcraft and murder (Jennet Jourdemayne) and a man (Thomas Mendip) so world-weary that he wants to die in her place until he discovers that he loves her. At the Conservative party conference in 1980 the title provided Mrs Thatcher with a widely remembered phrase. She ruled out any prospect of a U-turn on her policies with the words: 'You turn if you want; the lady's not for turning.'

The Lady Vanishes (1938) Comedy thriller by *Hitchcock, in which a young couple (played by Margaret Lockwood and Michael Redgrave) try and discover the link between a murdered Tyrolean street singer and the old lady who vanishes on a train journey back to England.

Cleo **Laine** (b. 1927) Singer and actress, whose jazz career has been much linked with that of her husband, Johnny *Dankworth, but who has also had a successful recording career with a wide range of other musicians; her bestselling album was *Best of Friends* (1978) with the guitarist John *Williams. She has also starred in several musicals, beginning with Sandy Wilson's *Valmouth* in 1958.

Lake District Area of exceptional beauty in Cumbria, designated in 1951 a *national park (2292sq.km/885sq.m). The lakes include *Windermere, *Ullswater, *Derwentwater and *Coniston Water. Among the peaks are Helvellyn (950m/3118ft) and *Scafell Pike, the highest point in England. The region acquired a specific link with the Romantic movement through the *Lake Poets.

Lakeland terrier see *terriers.

Lake Poets A name given at least as early as 1816 to *Wordsworth, *Coleridge and *Southey, leading members of the Romantic school who had all lived (Coleridge much less than the others) in the *Lake District. The term has sometimes been extended to include *De Quincey.

Freddie **Laker** (b. 1922, kt 1978) Founder in 1966 of Laker Airways and a hero with the travelling public for pioneering cheap air travel, particularly with his Skytrain service to the USA – which began in 1977 with a walk-on single ticket for £59. The collapse of his company in 1982 was followed by litigation against the major airlines on the grounds that they had conspired to force him out of business. British Airways and the other defendants settled out of court, giving him personally in excess of £5 million as well as paying all his creditors. Early in 1992 he set up a new Laker airways, flying from the Bahamas to various US cities; and he announced plans to fly again between Britain and the USA from the end of 1993.

Jim **Laker** (1922–86) Exceptionally successful off-spin bowler who played *cricket for Surrey (1946–59), Essex (1962–4) and England (1947–59). His most extraordinary achievement was in the 4th *Test against Australia at Old Trafford in 1956, where he set two records still standing in 1992 – the only occasion on which all 10 wickets have been taken by the same bowler in a Test match innings (10 for 53), and the highest number of wickets taken in any *first-class match (19 for 90).

Lallans (Scottish for Lowlands) Term used by *Burns for Scots, the Lowland Scottish dialect of English in which he wrote and which has a tradition going back to writers such as *Dunbar in the 15–16C. In the mid-20C there was an attempt by *MacDiarmid and others to revive it as a literary language.

Caroline **Lamb** see Lord *Melbourne.

Charles **Lamb** (1775–1834) Author remembered chiefly as an essayist. Educated at *Christ's Hospital, where he became a close friend of Coleridge, he made his career with the East India Company. In 1796 he was at home when his sister Mary, in a sudden fit of insanity, stabbed and killed their mother. She was allowed out of the asylum on condition that Charles took care of her; they spent the rest of their lives together, publishing in 1807 their immensely popular *Tales from Shakespeare*, the stories of the plays told for children. In 1820 Lamb was invited to contribute to the new *London Magazine*. He wrote an account of his early days at work and signed it with the name of an Italian clerk in the office, Elia. It was the first of the essays, about everyday things but often fanciful in tone, which were published in book form as *Essays of Elia* (1823).

Constant **Lambert** (1905–51) Conductor and composer who was closely involved with the early years of British ballet. He was still a student when he was commissioned

Daniel Lambert in acres of textile and an outsize chair: detail of a painting by Benjamin Marshall, c.1807.

by Diaghilev to write his first ballet (*Romeo and Juliet* 1926), and he was musical director of the Vic-Wells ballet from its beginnings in 1931 (see *Royal Ballet). His *Rio Grande* (1928) is a setting for chorus, piano and orchestra of a poem by Sacheverell Sitwell.

Daniel **Lambert** (1770–1809) Keeper of the jail in Leicester, whose name became a byword in Britain for obesity. In 1806 he resigned his post and moved to London to exhibit himself. At his death he weighed nearly 53 stone (337kg). His waistcoat is in the Leicester museum.

Lambeth Conference Assembly of bishops of the worldwide *Anglican Communion under the chairmanship of the archbishop of *Canterbury. The first conference was held in 1876 at Lambeth Palace, which remained the venue until 1968 when the number of bishops attending became so great (462) that the assembly was moved to Church House, Westminster. In modern times the conference has settled into a pattern of convening every ten years. In 1978 and again in 1988 it was held at the university of Kent in Canterbury, making possible a residential or collegiate dimension to the gathering.

Lambeth Palace (London SE1) Residence of the archbishop of *Canterbury, on the south bank of the Thames almost opposite the Houses of Parliament. Archbishop Hubert Walter was the first to feel that England's chief prelate should have a base close to the centre of royal power in London; he began building at Lambeth in about 1200. The earliest surviving parts, including the Tudor gatehouse, are of the 15c. The palace was largely rebuilt in 1828–34 and was badly damaged by bombs in 1941.

Lambeth Walk (London SE11) Street near Lambeth Palace, made famous by a song and a dance in *Me and My Gal*, a musical of 1937. With a catchy tune and simple steps (supposedly imitating a cockney walk), both song and dance were a craze during the war:

> Any time you're Lambeth way,
> Any evening, any day,
> You'll find us all
> Doing the Lambeth Walk – Oi!

LAMDA see *drama schools.

Paul de **Lamerie** see *Huguenots.

Norman **Lamont** (b. 1942) Conservative politician, in origin from the Shetlands but representing a southern English constituency (Kingston-upon-Thames since 1972). A member of the *Cambridge mafia, he entered the *cabinet in 1989 as chief secretary to the Treasury. In 1990 he succeeded John Major as chancellor of the exchequer – a position which he still held at the time of the *exchange rate crisis of September 1992.

A tabloid press saga of some embarrassment began in April 1991 when the *News of the World* ran a story under the headline 'Chancellor's flat is a vice den'. It transpired that, unknown to him, the tenant to whom he had let part of his house (on moving into 11 Downing Street), was a sex therapist. Controversy over the matter rumbled on into 1993, after it was revealed that the Treasury had paid £4,700 towards his costs in evicting her.

Suzy **Lamplugh** Estate agent who disappeared in 1986 after showing a property to a male client, who had given his name as Mr Kipper. She is assumed to have been abducted and murdered. Her mother, Diana Lamplugh, subsequently set up the Suzy Lamplugh Trust to promote the personal safety of women at work.

'The **lamps are going out all over Europe**' see Edward *Grey.

Lanarkshire Until 1975 an inland *county in south central Scotland, now part of the Strathclyde region.

Lancashire (1,408,000 in 1991, administrative centre Preston) *County on the northwest coast of England, much reduced in size in 1974 by its most populous areas becoming the *metropolitan counties of Merseyside and Greater Manchester.

Lancashire County Cricket Club Founded in 1864 (in reaction to the establishment of Yorkshire's club in 1863), and one of the original teams in the *county championship. The club won or tied the championship several times before 1890, and since then has had seven victories (1897, 1904, 26, 27, 28, 30, 34) in addition to tying with Surrey in 1950. In *one-day cricket it has won a record five times in the Gillette Cup and NatWest Bank Trophy (1970, 71, 72, 75, 90), twice in the Benson and Hedges Cup (1984, 90) and three times in the Sunday League (1969, 70, 89). Among the club's best-known players have been Cyril Washbrook and Brian *Statham. The county ground is *Old Trafford in Manchester, and the county also plays at Liverpool, Lytham, Blackpool and Southport.

Lancashire hotpot A mutton stew with potatoes and onions, now usually made with more tender but less tasty lamb.

Lancaster (46,000 in 1981) City and county town of Lancashire, at the head of the estuary of the river Lune. The castle, on the site of a Roman camp, was strengthened in the 14c by *John of Gaunt, through whom the duchy of Lancaster became a royal possession (its importance at that time still being reflected in the office of the *chancellor of the duchy of Lancaster); much altered inside, the castle contains the Shire Hall of 1796 in which assizes are held. The church of St Mary (mainly 15c) belonged to a Benedictine priory founded in the 11c. The Roman Catholic cathedral, St Peter's, was consecrated in 1859. Lancaster was the home of the *Gillow family of furniture makers, whose wares are displayed in two museums occupying historic houses – the Judges' Lodgings (17C) and the Old Town Hall (1781–3).

Lancaster Britain's main heavy bomber in World War II, with a crew of seven or eight; it was manufactured by Avro and was used in operations from 1942. Only the Lancaster could carry the enormous Grand Slam, a bomb of 10,000kg/22,000lb introduced in 1945. It was the plane of the *Dam Busters.

House of **Lancaster** (1399–1461) The descendants on the throne of England of John of Gaunt, duke of Lancaster, who was the third surviving son of Edward III. They were Henry IV, Henry V and Henry VI. See the *royal house and the *Wars of the Roses.

Osbert **Lancaster** (1908–1986, kt 1975) Cartoonist, set designer and author. His 'pocket cartoons' in the *Daily Express* (from 1939) found humour in the affairs of the moment as seen through the eyes of his affectionately satirized upper-class characters, in particular Maudie Little-hampton. He wrote and illustrated several books (serious in intent, comic in approach) about English architecture and the community, the first of which was *Progress at Pelvis Bay* (1936). From 1951 he designed the sets for many theatrical productions, mainly of opera and ballet.

Lancaster House (London SW1) Palatial mansion in the stable yard of St James's Palace, bordering Green Park. It was begun in 1825 for the duke of *York (to a design by Benjamin, son of James *Wyatt) but was sold before it was completed. The name was changed to Lancaster House by Lord *Leverhulme, in honour of the county of his birth; he bought the building in 1912 and in 1913 gave it to the nation, originally as a home for the London Museum (which remained there until World War II). It is now used for government entertainment and for conferences, being best known in recent years for the talks in 1979 which gave independence to Zimbabwe.

Lancelot (of the Lake) Brought up to be a perfect knight by a fairy in a lake, he was a leading member of the knights of the *Round Table until his affair with *Guinevere. This precipitated the warfare that destroyed King *Arthur's court. The king besieged Guinevere and her lover in Lancelot's castle of Joyous Gard and then pursued Lancelot to France; returning in haste (to prevent Mordred usurping the kingdom) Arthur was killed in the ensuing battle. Guinevere became a nun and Lancelot a priest. His carnal love handicapped him in the quest for the *Holy Grail, which was successfully achieved by his son *Galahad.

The **Lancet** (London WC1) Britain's oldest surviving medical journal, published weekly. It was founded by a young surgeon, Thomas Wakley (1795–1862), who issued the first number in October 1823. He made it a crusading and controversial journal, as in his famous publication in 1851 of chemical analyses of a wide range of food and drink on general sale; the horrifying details led eventually to the Adulteration of Food and Drink Act of 1860. In the early 1990s the journal has a large overseas circulation, the UK only accounting for about 20% of its readers.

land girls Women drafted for agricultural work in each of the two World Wars. The first land girls were the members of the Women's Land Army, established in 1917.

Landmark Trust (Maidenhead, Berkshire) Organization which provides an invaluable service by saving unusual buildings threatened with demolition, restoring them and letting them out as holiday homes. Founded in 1965 by John Smith (b. 1923), it now has some 200 properties including cottages, castles, lighthouses, follies, a railway station and the entire island of *Lundy.

Land of Hope and Glory see *Pomp and Circumstance*.

Land of my Fathers (*Hen Wlad fy Nhadau* in Welsh) Song, with words by Evan James (1809–78) and tune believed to be by his son James James (1833–1902), which was published in 1860 and has become the national anthem of Wales. The last line of the refrain states a theme of great importance to many in Wales today: *O bydded i'r heniaith barhau* (O may the old language endure).

Land Rover see *Rover.

landscape gardening The creation of a pleasing domestic landscape, around a palace or house, dates back thousands of years to the earliest potentates in the middle

The perfect blend of classical and romantic in English landscape gardening: the Pantheon beside the lake at Stourhead.

and far east. It was not until the 18c that the British made a distinctive contribution. At the start of that century English noblemen were following the portentously formal style which derived from Versailles, with straight walks and rectangular beds. Various influences caused the break. A greater informality in English life led to a wish that gardens should themselves be informal, places of surprise and delight. Meanwhile those returning from the *Grand Tour had acquired a taste for the paintings of Claude Lorrain (1600–82), who although French had spent his life working in Rome. They brought home his pictures (there are more in Britain than in any other country) and they set about recreating in real life his ideal landscapes of woods and water and classical temples. The designer who best achieved this was William *Kent, who was much involved with the garden at *Stowe. Another superb example in this style is *Stourhead.

Later in the century another fashion followed – that of the *picturesque, in which nature could fend for herself without the help of architecture. The leading designer now was Capability *Brown, whose innovations were developed and modified by Humphry *Repton. During the 19c the emphasis turned away from the broader landscape, concentrating more on the garden and on the creative mingling of flowers and trees. Early advocates of this change were John and Jane *Loudon. A certain wildness and a natural feel to a garden has remained the chief theme of leading designers, such as Gertrude *Jekyll, up to the present day.

Edwin **Landseer** (1802–73, kt 1850) The leading animal painter of the 19c, with a tendency to make his animals perform. He is at his best when the drama is one of natural savagery, as in *Man Proposes, God Disposes* (1864, Royal Holloway College), inspired by the disaster of *Franklin's expedition to the Arctic and showing two

polar bears tearing at the wreck of a sailing ship. Less satisfactory are the coy scenarios such as *Dignity and Impudence* (1839, Tate Gallery), with a bloodhound and a tiny terrier sharing a kennel. His best-known image is *Monarch of the Glen* (1851), in which a magnificent stag poses like a tragic actor. Painted for the refreshment room of the House of Lords, it is now owned by John Dewar and Sons, makers of whisky. In the last years of his life he sculpted the great lions at the base of *Nelson's Column in Trafalgar Square.

Land's End Low granite promontory in Cornwall which is the most westerly point of mainland Britain (the most southerly is the *Lizard). The dangerous reefs which continue out from it into the Atlantic are marked by the Longships lighthouse. Land's End to *John o'Groats is used as a phrase to mean the length and breadth of the land.

Lord **Lane** (Geoffrey Lane, b. 1918, kt 1966, baron 1979) Lord chief justice whose period in office (1980–92) coincided with mounting public unease about the reliability of *criminal justice in Britain. His own reputation was one of opposition to change, and his words when dismissing the 1987 appeal of the *Birmingham Six were subsequently much quoted: 'The longer the case has gone on, the more this court has been convinced that the jury was correct.'

Lanfranc (*c*.1005–1089) Archbishop of Canterbury from 1070. Born in north Italy, he founded a monastic school at Bec in Normandy. There he became a trusted ally of William, the future Conqueror. He remained on excellent terms with him in England, where Lanfranc reformed and strengthened the church – though his measures did involve replacing most of the Anglo-Saxon clergy with

Landseer working on his full-scale model for the bronze lions in Trafalgar Square: Illustrated London News, *1868.*

Normans. After Lanfranc's death William II left the see of Canterbury vacant for four years and plundered its revenues until the appointment of *Anselm in 1093.

Cosmo Gordon **Lang** (1864–1945, baron 1942) Archbishop of Canterbury 1928–42, after being archbishop of York from 1909. His time at Canterbury included the *abdication crisis.

Ian **Lang** (b. 1940) Conservative politician, MP since 1979 for Galloway (known as Galloway and Upper Nithsdale since 1983). One of only a handful of Conservative MPs with seats north of the border, he entered the *cabinet in 1990 as secretary of state for Scotland.

William **Langland** see *Piers Plowman.

Stephen **Langton** (d. 1228) Archbishop of Canterbury from 1207, though the opposition of John, the English king, kept him out of his see until 1213. He encouraged the barons to demand *Magna Carta and was instrumental in persuading Henry III to reissue it when he came of age, in the definitive version of 1225. He had been a powerful support and influence throughout the young king's minority.

Lillie **Langtry** (Emilie Le Breton, 1853–1929, m. Edward Langtry 1874) Known as the Jersey Lily (she was born there, daughter of the dean of Jersey), she caused a sensation in 1881 when she became the first society woman to go on the stage, in She Stoops to Conquer at the Haymarket Theatre in London. An extra touch of excitement was added by her being a mistress of the prince of Wales, the future Edward VII. From 1901 she had her own company, playing in London and on tour.

Language, Truth and Logic see A.J. *Ayer.

Lanhydrock House (48km/30m W of Plymouth) A house partly of the 17C (including a detached gatehouse and a 35m/116ft gallery with a barrel-vaulted plaster ceiling depicting Old Testament scenes) and partly the result of grandiose rebuilding in the 19C. The 38 clipped yews standing sentinel in front of the house were planted in 1857 and came from *Florence Court. The house is known for its extensive shrub and woodland gardens.

Laputa see *Gulliver's Travels.

lardy cake Bread enriched with lard, sugar and dried fruit, which traditionally was a celebration loaf at harvest time.

Large White see *pigs.

Largs (9000 in 1991) Seaside resort in Strathclyde, near the southern end of the Firth of Clyde. The elaborately carved and painted Skelmorlie Aisle (1636) is the mausoleum of Robert Montgomerie of Skelmorlie. Just south of the town at Bowen Craig is the 'Pencil', a monument commemorating the Battle of Largs (1263), in which Alexander III defeated the Norwegian king Haakon IV, who was attempting to assert Norway's traditional rights over the Hebrides and the Isle of Man; as an indirect result both were ceded to the Scottish crown.

The Lark Ascending Composition for violin and orchestra by *Vaughan Williams, called by the composer a 'romance'. Inspired by *Meredith's poem, it was written in 1914 but not performed until 1921.

Philip **Larkin** (1922–85) Poet who has become probably the most widely enjoyed of his generation, largely because a very easy surface to the verse entices the reader in before revealing its resonances. Single lines to demonstrate the point can be chosen almost at random: 'Home is so sad. It stays as it was left'. From 1950 he was librarian of the Brynmor Jones Library of the university of Hull. His best-known lines, opening the 1967 poem Annus Mirabilis, have a topical rather than a typical wit:

> Sexual intercourse began
> In nineteen sixty-three
> (Which was rather late for me) –
> Between the end of the Chatterley ban
> And the Beatles' first LP.

Harold **Larwood** (b. 1904) Extremely fast and accurate bowler, playing cricket for Nottinghamshire (1924–38) and England (1926–33). He became a controversial figure on the 1932–3 tour of Australia, when his captain (Douglas Jardine, 1900–58) devised the 'body-line' strategy which won the series against a side including Don Bradman. Larwood, who took Bradman's wicket in four of the five matches, was instructed to bowl with maximum speed at the leg stump (in effect therefore at the batsman's body). The controversy unjustly ended Larwood's Test career, and he emigrated to Australia in 1950.

Denys **Lasdun** (b. 1914, kt 1976) Architect of the *National Theatre, the last major building in central London in an uncompromisingly modernist tradition; its profile is composed entirely of rectangular blocks and it uses exposed concrete for both the exterior and interior surfaces. His other designs include the Royal College of Physicians in Regent's Park (completed 1964) and the university of East Anglia (1968).

Lass of Richmond Hill Song to a tune by James Hook (1746–1827), with words probably by Leonard McNally (1752–1820). Richmond in Surrey and Richmond in Yorkshire have both been keen to claim the 'sweet lass of Richmond Hill' as their own, but opinion inclines to Yorkshire.

The Last of England see Ford Madox *Brown.

Last of the Summer Wine (BBC from 1974) Television comedy series about three old schoolfriends in a Yorkshire village who consciously set about making the most of their twilight years. The actors in the early series were Bill Owen (Compo), Peter Sallis (Clegg) and Michael Bates (Blamire); more recently the third member of the trio has been Brian Wilde (Foggy). Nora Batty, in her wrinkled stockings, is played by Kathy Staff.

Last Post Bugle call at the end of the day (10 p.m.) in British army establishments. It has become charged with profound emotion through being sounded also at military funerals and at the end of the two-minute silence commemorating the dead on Remembrance Sunday.

The Last Rose of Summer see Thomas *Moore.

Hugh **Latimer** see *Oxford.

William **Laud** (1573–1645) Archbishop of Canterbury from 1633. By his vigorous efforts to suppress *Puritan forms of worship, and to impose on the country a royalist Anglican church, he did much to provoke the antagonisms which erupted in the English Civil War. His declaration that the king had a divine right to rule, and that to oppose him entailed damnation, was made in 1640, the year in which the *Long Parliament assembled. Before the year was out, parliament had impeached Laud for treason. His trial did not begin until 1644, and by that stage of the

Caricature by H.M. Bateman suggesting the somewhat grotesque Scottishness of Harry Lauder's stage persona, 1915.

war the proceeedings were a travesty of justice. Without apparent legal justification he was condemned and beheaded on Tower Hill.

Harry **Lauder** (1870–1950, kt 1919) Scottish *music-hall entertainer, born near Edinburgh and working as a miner before becoming known locally as a performer. When first seen in London, in 1900, he was an immediate success in his kilt, outrageous bonnet and profuse Highland trimmings, with a twisted knobbly stick. His songs, such as *Roamin' in the Gloamin'* and *Keep right on to the end of the road*, were written by himself. He was knighted for his work entertaining the troops in World War I.

The **Laughing Cavalier** (1624, Wallace Collection) Portrait by Frans Hals, probably the best-known painting in Britain. It was bought by the 4th marquess of Hertford in Paris in 1865. Nothing is known of the sitter (who is smiling rather than laughing) except his age, inscribed on the canvas; he looks older than his 26 years.

Charles **Laughton** (1899–1962) Plump character actor with an exceptionally mobile and expressive face. A career on the West End stage was followed by international success in films in the 1930s – particularly in the title roles of *The Private Life of Henry VIII* (1933, for which he received an Oscar), *Rembrandt* (1936) and *The Hunchback of Notre Dame* (1939), and as Captain Bligh in *Mutiny on the Bounty* (1935). He was married to the British actress Elsa Lanchester; they moved together to Hollywood in 1940.

Laura Ashley Company based in Wales, designing and manufacturing clothes, fabrics and furnishings which conform to a traditional country style. It derived from small beginnings in 1953; on a kitchen table in a London flat Bernard Ashley (b. 1926) started printing scarves and other small items designed by his wife Laura (1925–85). The family moved to Wales in 1961 and the first Laura Ashley shop was opened in London in 1968. By 1990 there were nearly 500 worldwide, though the company was by then showing signs of being over-extended. Meanwhile the Laura Ashley look, reassuringly old-fashioned, had much influenced the interior decoration of many British homes.

Stan **Laurel** (stage name of Arthur Jefferson, 1890–1965) Slapstick comedian who started in the *music hall

before joining Fred *Karno's company, with which he visited the USA in 1910. His career there in vaudeville and silent films took off after he teamed up in 1927 with Oliver Hardy (1892–1957). In their anarchic films the errors of the long-suffering Laurel, aggravated by the impatience of Hardy, lead to ever-escalating chaos. There is a Laurel and Hardy museum in Ulverston, the town in Cumbria where Laurel was born.

The **Lavender Hill Mob** (1951) One of the *Ealing comedies, in which a mouse of a bank clerk (played by Alec Guinness) masterminds a bullion robbery with the help of a down-at-heel businessman (Stanley Holloway) and some Cockney spivs. They disguise the gold as Eiffel Tower paperweights.

lavender list The dissolution honours awarded by Harold *Wilson after he had resigned as prime minister in 1976. It acquired that name after Wilson's press secretary, Joe Haines, claimed that it had been written on lavender-coloured paper in the hand of the prime minister's private and political secretary, Marcia Williams (herself recently ennobled as Baroness Falkender), with only a few corrections added by Wilson himself. The supposed implication was that the choice of people had been her's, though she could just as well have been writing down a list dictated by Wilson. Those honoured included James *Goldsmith and Joseph Kagan, maker of the prime minister's favourite Gannex raincoat.

Lavenham (37km/23m W of Ipswich) The best preserved of the Suffolk towns which grew rich in the 15c from the wool trade, with unspoilt streets of half-timber houses (the early 16c Guildhall is the outstanding example). The parish church of St Peter and St Paul, with its huge tower and excellent interior carving, was built between 1480 and 1530.

laver bread Seaweed which is sold already boiled to a spinach-like purée. Once popular all round Britain's coasts, it has now become a speciality of Wales; it is usually cooked with oatmeal in hot flat cakes, or is spread on toast. Laver is the common name for *Porphyra*, a seaweed much eaten in many parts of the world, particularly in the Far East.

law Roman law and English law, both widely influential, are characterized by very different approaches. In broad terms Roman law follows a coherent written code and a set of principles, while English law relies more on case law (an accumulation of previous decisions by judges, known as precedents). The division is seen within the United Kingdom itself, where Scotland is strongly influenced by Roman law.

There is no evidence that any trace of their legal system survived the departure of the *Romans from Britain, and in the succeeding centuries of settlement by *Anglo-Saxons and *Danes the law was largely a matter of local tribal customs. It was the strong centralized rule of the *Normans which introduced the basis of English law. Itinerant judges, sent round the country to standardize legal practice, gradually formed the *common law (in the sense of common to the whole kingdom). Common law was linked with the *inns of court; university lawyers at the time concentrated on canon law, the legal structure of the Roman Catholic church.

The developing common law was mainly concerned with penalties and damages after an offence was committed. It therefore often conflicted with people's sense of natural justice (where there was a need, for example, for a contract to be enforced or for legal authority to prevent something happening). This led to another strand of law known as equity (fairness); such cases, where the common law offered no remedy, began to be referred to the lord chancellor (the Court of Chancery). The third element, developing with the growth of *parliament, has been statute law – the accumulated body of laws established by successive *acts of parliament.

The Roman element in Scottish law is the result of major legal reforms in the 17C, when Scotland looked to France and Holland for its models. The Scots and the English therefore had different legal systems at the time of the Act of Union in 1707, a situation resulting in their differing *courts of law today.

Bonar Law (Andrew Bonar Law, 1858–1923) Conservative politician from an Ulster family, born in Canada, who made a fortune as an iron merchant in Glasgow – a blend of influences which made him a follower of Joseph *Chamberlain's imperialism and a firm ally of *Carson in opposition to *Home Rule for Ireland. He entered parliament in 1900 and in 1911 succeeded *Balfour as leader of the party. From 1915 he was in the coalition governments of Asquith and Lloyd George (he was chancellor of the exchequer 1916–19). In 1921 ill health forced his resignation (he was followed as leader of the party by Austen *Chamberlain), but in 1922 he was the moving spirit in the stormy meeting of Conservative MPs which ended the coalition, created the *1922 Committee and reinstated him as leader. The Conservatives easily won the resulting election. Law became prime minister in October 1922 but resigned again from ill health the following May.

Denis Law (b. 1940) Scottish footballer who was an important goal-scoring member of the *Manchester United team during their run of successes in the 1960s. He began with Huddersfield Town (1957–60) and moved briefly to Manchester City and then Torino before his spell with United (1962–73). For the final year of his career (1973–4) he returned to Manchester City. He was playing for City against United, in April 1974, when he scored a famous goal which left him with mixed feelings; for it had the effect of relegating his old club for a year to the 2nd division. He had 55 caps playing for Scotland and shares the record of 30 goals with Kenny Dalglish (who played nearly twice as many international games).

Law Courts (London WC2) The name commonly used for the Royal Courts of Justice. The imposing building in the Strand (by G.E. Street, 1824–81) opened in 1882. It was designed to bring under one roof all the civil actions being heard by the *High Court in London. Nowadays pressure on the *Old Bailey means that some criminal cases are heard in the Law Courts; and the Law Courts themselves have extended to premises other than the Strand.

'the law is a ass' Observation by Mr Bumble, the beadle in *Oliver Twist, on hearing that he is even more guilty than Mrs Bumble in the matter of Oliver's mother's missing locket and gold ring because 'the law supposes that your wife acts under your direction'. 'If the law supposes that', rejoins Bumble, 'the law is a ass – a idiot.'

Sue Lawley (b. 1946) TV and radio presenter, who first made her name on *Nationwide* (1972–83). She subsequently read the news for some years on BBC TV but recently has been best known on radio, becoming in 1988 the interviewer on *Desert Island Discs*.

Law Lords The common term for the Lords of Appeal in Ordinary, *life peers who since 1876 have been appointed to provide the judicial functions of the House of *Lords as the nation's final court of appeal. Originally only four, their numbers have steadily increased over the years (to nine in the early 1990s).

Lawnmarket see *Edinburgh.

D.H. Lawrence (David Herbert Lawrence, 1885–1930) Novelist and poet whose high critical reputation was ensured by F.R. *Leavis. The son of a Nottinghamshire miner, he portrayed his youth in one of his most successful novels, *Sons and Lovers* (1913). *The Rainbow* (1915) and *Women in Love* (1920) chronicle a Nottinghamshire family, the Brangwens, concentrating with a poetic intensity typical of Lawrence on their sexual relationships and feelings. *The Rainbow* was seized by the police in Britain and banned; *Women in Love* had to wait four years after its completion before being published in New York. *Lady Chatterley's Lover* (1928), famous for other reasons, is less of a unified whole than the earlier books. All share a moral earnestness which can slip into preaching.

In 1912 Lawrence met his future wife Frieda (an aristocratic German, born von Richthofen), who was married at the time to a Nottingham professor. They spent most of the rest of his life travelling abroad until his death of tuberculosis.

Gertrude Lawrence (stage name of Gertrude Klasen, 1898–1952) Actress and singer who made her name in the 1920s in *revue. In straight theatre she was particularly associated with Noel Coward, most notably in *Private Lives.

Ruth Lawrence see *infant prodigies.

T.E. Lawrence (Thomas Edward Lawrence, known also as Lawrence of Arabia, 1888–1935) Author and leader of irregular troops. He was posted to Saudi Arabia in 1916 to support an uprising against Turkish rule. Dressing in Arab costume, he joined Faisal (the future king of *Iraq) in mounting a guerrilla campaign which helped *Allenby to capture Jerusalem and Damascus. Lawrence described these events in *The Seven Pillars of Wisdom*

Drawing by Augustus John of T.E. Lawrence in 1919, when he was newly famous for his achievements in Arabia.

(begun 1919, published privately 1926). Famous after the war from reports of his exploits, he attempted in 1922 to plunge back into anonymity, joining the RAF as aircraftman Ross and the following year (after Ross had been unmasked) enlisting in the Royal Tank Corps as T.E. Shaw. Noel Coward gently mocked this camouflage, beginning a letter to him: 'Dear 338171 (may I call you 338?)'. Lawrence died as a result of a motorcycle accident near Clouds Hill, his cottage in Dorset which is kept as a museum. His desert adventures were made the subject of a spectacular film (*Lawrence of Arabia* 1962), directed by David Lean with Peter O'Toole in the title role.

Thomas **Lawrence** (1769–1830, kt 1815) The leading portrait painter of the generation after Reynolds and Gainsborough, noted for the ease and rapidity of his style. He was astonishingly precocious and was only 21 when commissioned to do the portrait of Queen Charlotte, now in the National Gallery. The image in the public mind of the prince regent, the future George IV, derives almost entirely from Lawrence's fluent brush.

Lawrence of Arabia see T.E. *Lawrence.

Nigel **Lawson** (b. 1932, baron 1992) Journalist and Conservative politician, MP for Blaby in Leicestershire 1974–92. He entered the cabinet in 1981 as secretary of state for energy, and became chancellor of the exchequer in 1983. He had two main areas of disagreement with his prime minister, Mrs Thatcher: he wanted to enter the ERM (see *EMS) in the mid-1980s (which many have subsequently judged to have been the right time), but she vetoed this; and he resented the influence of her rival economic adviser, the *monetarist Alan Walters. His response on the first issue was to peg the pound to the German mark from 1987, as if it were in the ERM – a policy strongly criticized by Walters. The tension led to the resignation of both men in October 1989. The boom created in Lawson's final years at the exchequer (by major reductions in *income tax in 1987 and 1988, and by the

easy credit which followed *Big Bang) has been widely blamed for the depth of the subsequent *recession.

Austen Henry **Layard** (1817–94, GCB 1878) Archaeologist who excavated two important sites in Iraq. The first was at Nimrud, which he wrongly believed to be Nineveh. It yielded many treasures from the palace of the Assyrian king, Ashurnasirpal II, including the great human-headed winged lions which are now in the British Museum. The second site was indeed Nineveh, where Layard's assistant, Henry Rawlinson, later discovered the palace of Ashurbanipal. Here were found the great bas reliefs of a royal lion hunt, also now in the British Museum.

The **Lay of the Last Minstrel** (1805) Narrative poem by Walter *Scott. The story, told by an ancient minstrel who is the last of his race, concerns the obstacles in the path of true lovers from rival Scottish houses in the 16c. After much complication, all ends happily.

Lays of Ancient Rome (1842) Poems by *Macaulay turning episodes from Roman history into stirring ballads. The best known, *Horatius*, begins with the resonant verse:

> Lars Porsena of Clusium
> By the nine gods he swore
> That the royal house of Tarquin
> Should suffer wrongs no more.

It goes on to tell how Horatius, gallant captain of the gate, held the bridge over the Tiber to protect Rome against the followers of the deposed house of Tarquin.

LBC see *radio.

LCC see *London County Council.

LEA (Local Education Authority) The department of *local government responsible for the *state schools in a district. Schools have received the major part of local authority expenditure since the Education Act of 1944 (see *education), and reducing the power of the LEAs has

Layard at ground level (top right) supervising the removal of one of the great winged lions from Nimrud.

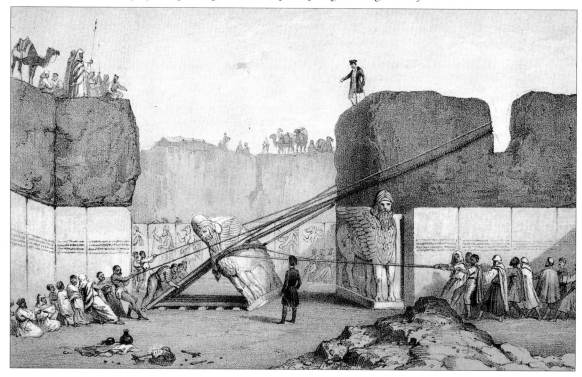

been a central theme of government policy in recent Conservative administrations. The introduction of *city technology colleges was a first step in this direction, but the major change came with the encouragement of *opting out.

Bernard **Leach** (1887–1979) Potter who profoundly influenced British ceramics by introducing Japanese skills and styles. He went to Japan in 1909 to teach etching and discovered pottery in 1911 at a tea party, where each of the guests was invited to throw a pot. Returning to Britain in 1920, he established his studio at *St Ives. His work, characterized by sturdy forms, often rough in texture but with subtle glazes, inspired many later potters such as Lucy *Rie. He described his methods in *A Potter's Book* (1940).

Leader of the House of Commons Member of the cabinet responsible for the conduct of business in the House of *Commons. The office emerged in the 19c during those periods when the prime minister was a member of the House of *Lords. At other times the function was carried out by the prime minister himself, until in World War II Churchill delegated the task to a cabinet minister. On Thursdays the leader announces the business of the House for the following week. The leader of the House of Lords, also in the cabinet, fulfils a similar function in the upper chamber. Each office has usually been combined with that of lord president of the Council or lord privy seal. For holders since 1983 see the *cabinet.

Leader of the House of Lords see *Leader of the House of Commons.

Leader of the Opposition see *Opposition.

Lead, kindly Light see Cardinal *Newman and J.B. *Dykes.

League Against Cruel Sports (London SE1) Pressure group formed in 1924 to campaign against all forms of *hunting. Its activities also include opposition to coursing (see *greyhound racing) and efforts to stamp out the illegal activity of badger baiting. Private bills to ban hunting have as yet failed to win a majority in parliament, but public opinion seems to be moving against the sport – a trend no doubt accentuated by the League's 1992 video of the *Quorn.

League of Nations Organization, with headquarters at Geneva, established after World War I as an international attempt to preserve peace. Foremost among its creators was the US president Woodrow Wilson, and an early blow to the League's effectiveness came from the rejection of his plans by a hostile Senate; the USA never became a member. Nevertheless the League had considerable influence during the 1920s, until the rise of Fascism made talk of peace increasingly irrelevant. Germany and Japan withdrew in 1933, Italy in 1937. But the League had provided an example to be built upon and improved by the *United Nations, which replaced it after World War II.

Leakey family Anthropologists who have made many significant discoveries relating to early man in east Africa. Louis Leakey (1903–72) and his wife Mary (Mary Nichol, b. 1913, m. 1936) worked mainly at Olduvai Gorge in northern Tanzania. In 1959 they found a skull of *Australopithecus*, believed to be about 1.75 million years old; in 1964 they discovered skull fragments of another extinct species of early man, which they named *Homo habilis* (handy man). After her husband's death Mary Leakey began excavating at Laetolil, 40km/25m south of Olduvai,

UP-HILL WORK.
JOHN BULL. "EVEN THOUGH IT'S ONLY HALF A LEAGUE, IT MUST GO ONWARD."

The League of Nations, as seen in Punch *in 1935, with Japan and Germany already out and Italy looking insecure.*

and found remains of a species of man dated to about 3.75 million years ago. Meanwhile their son Richard (b. 1944) had begun working at Lake Turkana in northern Kenya; his best-known find there, in 1972, was an almost complete skull of *Homo habilis*.

Royal **Leamington Spa** (43,000 in 1981) Town in Warwickshire, on the river Leam, with chalybeate and saline springs which made it, from the late 18c, a fashionable place to take the waters. The Parade dates from 1810–30 and the Royal Pump Room was opened in 1814 (restored 1953). Queen Victoria, visiting in 1838, designated it a royal spa.

David **Lean** (1908–91, kt 1984) Director whose earlier experience as cameraman and editor give his films a particular polish. He began, from 1942, with four collaborations with Noel Coward, including *In Which We Serve* and *Brief Encounter*. These were followed by two Dickens adaptations, *Great Expectations* and *Oliver Twist*. His later projects were increasingly large-scale and infrequent, but some were very successful – *Bridge on the River Kwai* and *Lawrence of Arabia* both won Oscars. They were followed by *Dr Zhivago* (1965), *Ryan's Daughter* (1970) and *A Passage to India* (1984).

Leander (Henley-on-Thames) Britain's oldest and most prestigious rowing club. Both the club and the name are said to derive from a day in 1818 when a group of young men hired a boat called *Leander* from Searle's boathouse, near Westminster Bridge, to go rowing on the Thames; they liked the boat so much that they formed a club for its continued use. By mid-century *Henley, rather than the London reach of the Thames, had become the main location for competitive regattas; Leander moved its headquarters there, to a newly built clubhouse, in 1897. The club's eight won gold for Britain in the Olympics of 1908 and 1912.

One of 42 superb hand-coloured lithographs in the 20-year-old Lear's Family of the Psittacidae *(1832).*

Lear see **King Lear.*

Edward **Lear** (1812–88) Painter and nonsense author. His first career was as an ornithological artist. His large coloured images of parrots were published in 1832, when he was only 20, and in that same year he was first employed by the 13th earl of Derby to draw his menagerie at Knowsley. It was to amuse the earl's grandchildren that Lear began to write nonsense verse. *A Book of Nonsense* appeared in 1846, consisting entirely of limericks illustrated with Lear's own distinctive drawings. *Nonsense Songs* (1871) introduced the longer type of poem for which he is best known – 'The **Owl and the Pussy-Cat'* in this volume, and 'The **Dong with a Luminous Nose'* and 'The **Pobble who has no Toes'* in *Laughable Lyrics* (1877). In about 1835 his interest as a painter turned to landscape, usually in watercolour, and for the rest of his life he travelled widely round the Mediterranean and in the Middle East, painting topographical views in a bold and often bright range of colours.

F.R. **Leavis** (Frank Raymond Leavis, 1895–1978) Critic who had great influence on the teaching of English literature in the mid-20C, insisting on moral seriousness as an essential yardstick of an author's importance, and demanding from the student close attention to the text rather than a biographical interest in the author. The poets who received his highest acclaim in *New Bearings in English Poetry* (1932) were Gerard Manley Hopkins, Ezra Pound, T.S. Eliot and to a lesser extent W.B. Yeats; the novelists to emerge in the same way from *The Great Tradition* (1948) were Jane Austen, George Eliot, Henry James and Joseph Conrad. D.H. Lawrence was championed in a book of 1955, and Dickens was re-evaluated (having earlier been dismissed) in a work of 1970.

The latter was written in collaboration with his wife Queenie (1906–81), herself a distinguished critic and always his close collaborator, particularly in the editing of *Scrutiny* (1932–53). Much of Leavis's own writing was first published in this quarterly review; it was through it and through the 'Leavisites' (his students at Downing College, Cambridge) that his influence spread. He saw a rigorous study of English literature as a bulwark against modern materialism. An unattractive aspect of his approach was a tendency to separate authors into two groups, the saved and the damned, in a manner more characteristic of small puritanical sects.

LECs see **TECs.

John **Le Carré** (pen name of David Cornwell, b. 1931) Writer of spy novels who pioneered a cool unromantic version of the genre with *The **Spy Who Came in from the Cold* (1963). He spent four years in the Foreign Office (1960–4) and there is a humdrum civil-service authenticity about the world of spies featured in his books. His best-known character is George Smiley, a retired master of espionage whose help is enlisted in difficult situations. Played by Alec Guinness, Smiley became a favourite with the television audience in the 1979 series made of *Tinker, Tailor, Soldier, Spy* (published 1974), which was followed in 1982 by *Smiley's People* (1980).

Led Zeppelin Rock group formed in 1968 by Robert Plant (b. 1948, vocals), Jimmy Page (b. 1944, guitar), John Paul Jones (b. 1946, keyboard) and John Bonham (b. 1948, drums); the name derived from the idea of a bad gig 'going down like a lead Zeppelin'. They had rapid success, with a heavy-metal sound and exceptionally noisy climaxes. Their second album, *Led Zeppelin II* (1969), was in the British charts for 138 weeks; and each of their next seven albums (up to *In Through the Out Door* 1979) followed it to the no. 1 spot. *Led Zeppelin 4* contained what became their best-known song, *Stairway to Heaven*. Bonham's death in 1980 brought the group to an end, but its influence has continued.

Jennie **Lee** (1904–88, baroness 1970) Labour politician, married to Aneurin **Bevan, remembered for her success as Britain's first minister for the arts (1967–70).

Leeds (706,000 in 1991) City in West Yorkshire on the river Aire, which by the 16C was an important centre of the woollen industry. In the 19C it won a dominant position, which it still holds, in the manufacture of clothing. The wealth of Leeds at that time is revealed in its Town Hall (1853–8), a massively confident Victorian building in the classical style by a then unknown Yorkshire architect in his thirties, Cuthbert Brodrick (1822–1905); he also designed the Corn Exchange (1861–3). The city's industrial history is displayed in Armley Mills, a fulling mill dating from 1806; and the ruins of Kirkstall Abbey, a 12C Cistercian house, now include in their gatehouse a museum of local domestic history. The City Art Gallery, founded in 1888, is particularly strong in British art of the 20C. In 1993 a major new institute and gallery devoted to sculpture was opened (the Henry Moore Sculpture Institute) and from 1996 the city will be the home of the **Royal Armouries.

A wide range of painting and the decorative arts is displayed in two nearby country houses, Temple Newsam (a Tudor exterior with interiors of several later periods) and the mainly Edwardian Lotherton Hall. The grammar school, now independent, was founded in 1552. The Leeds International Piano Competition was founded in 1963 and is held every three years.

Leeds One of the original clubs in rugby league football in 1895. Ten victories in the Challenge Cup (1910, 23, 32, 36, 41, 42, 57, 68, 77, 78) have put Leeds overall in second place behind **Wigan. The club ground is **Headingley.

The **Leeds** (Leeds Permanent) One of Britain's largest *building societies, founded in Leeds in 1848.

Leeds Castle (30km/19m W of Canterbury) Superbly situated on two islands in a lake formed from the river Len. A stone castle was begun here in 1119, on a site previously occupied by a wooden Saxon castle. It was given to Edward I in 1278 and remained in royal hands until the reign of Henry VIII, who gave it to Anthony St Leger, his long-serving lord deputy in Ireland. Henry built most of the rooms in the so-called Gloriette. This occupies the smaller island and is the oldest surviving part of the castle; the rest was much altered in 1822.

Leeds International Piano Competition Established in 1963 by Fanny Waterman and Marion Harewood (now Thorpe), and held every three years. It is open to professional pianists under the age of 30. The semi-finals (solo piano) and the finals (piano concertos) are in the Leeds Town Hall, and the finals are seen on television; in recent years the orchestra has been the CBSO under Simon Rattle. Past winners have included Radu Lupu in 1969 and Murray Perahia in 1972.

Leeds pottery A factory was established in Hunslet, near Leeds, in the mid-18c. It produced ware of many kinds but became particularly known for its cream-coloured earthenware, or creamware, often characterized by pierced work (patterns with holes right through the thickness of the china). The original Leeds Pottery went bankrupt in 1820. Until 1878 the old moulds continued to be used with less skill by others; from 1888 more skilful reproductions of the early models were produced.

Leeds United, known as United (Elland Road, Leeds). Football club formed in 1919 when an earlier team, Leeds City, was expelled from the *Football League after allegations of illegal payments to players. United had their greatest successes during the years when Don *Revie was manager (1961–74). After a long spell in Division 2 from 1982, they returned to Division 1 in 1990 and won the championship in 1992. Club victories: FA Cup 1972; League Champions 1969, 74, 92; League Cup 1968; European Fairs Cup 1968, 71.

leek see national *emblems.

legal aid System introduced by the Legal Aid and Advice Act of 1949, by which legal assistance is paid for out of public funds for those involved in civil legislation or facing criminal charges who cannot themselves meet the cost. In 1992, when the public outlay on the scheme had been rising faster than inflation and had reached an annual figure approaching £1bn, the lord chancellor proposed reforms which were strongly opposed by the legal profession; they included a flat rate for cases instead of hourly pay, and reduction of the income level at which people become eligible for aid.

Leicester (280,000 in 1991) City and administrative centre of Leicestershire, on the river Soar. The importance of the Roman settlement here, where the *Fosse Way crossed the river, is revealed in the size of the Jewry Wall (the reason for the name is not known), with its masonry and brickwork of the 2nd century AD; the site is now an archaeological museum. From the late medieval period there survive the timber-frame Guildhall (15–16c) and the Newarke, an area added to the castle precincts in the 14c and including two 16c buildings which have been combined into the Newarke Houses Museum of local domestic history. The 12–13c church of St Mary de Castro is less altered than the old parish church of St Martin, now mainly 19c, which in 1927 became the cathedral of the new diocese of Leicester. The Museum and Art Gallery, founded in 1847, has a broadly based collection of paintings and decorative arts but is particularly strong in German Expressionism. The traditional industry of the city has been stockings, with boots and shoes as an added speciality since the 19c. In recent decades Leicester has become the home of a large minority

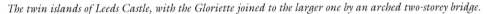

The twin islands of Leeds Castle, with the Gloriette joined to the larger one by an arched two-storey bridge.

from the subcontinent of India, mostly Hindus and Jains (it contains the only Jain temple in Britain).

Leicester Rugby union football club, formed in 1880. Its four wins in the John Player/Pilkington Cup (1979, 80, 81, 93) have been bettered only by Bath.

Earl of **Leicester** (Robert Dudley, c.1532–88, earl 1564) The first favourite of *Elizabeth I and the one she came nearest to marrying, even sounding out diplomatic opinion on the matter in 1561. This was soon after the mysterious death of Dudley's wife, Amy Robsart, who broke her neck falling downstairs – an event which made a royal marriage possible and yet probably out of the question, with the inevitable rumours of murder. A speculative account of the incident provides the plot of Walter Scott's novel *Kenilworth*. It was at *Kenilworth, his impressive castle in the Midlands, that Leicester lavished upon the queen in 1575 the most spectacular entertainment of her reign. With a few ups and downs he remained in favour to the end of his life.

Leicestershire (891,000 in 1991, administrative centre Leicester) *County in central England.

Leicestershire County Cricket Club Founded in 1879 and in the *county championship from 1895, a contest which the club has won only once (1975). It has been more successful in *one-day cricket (Benson and Hedges Cup 1972, 75, 85; John Player League 74, 77). Its best-known player has been David *Gower. Grace Road in Leicester was the county ground until 1900 and has been so again since 1946; the county plays also at Hinckley.

Vivien **Leigh** (stage name of Vivian Hartley, 1913–67) Actress whose distinguished career in the theatre is overshadowed by the fame of her Oscar-winning performance

as Scarlett O'Hara in *Gone with the Wind* (1939). At the Old Vic and at Stratford-upon-Avon she often acted opposite Laurence Olivier, whom she married in 1940. In 1949 she played Blanche Dubois in the London production of *A Streetcar Named Desire*, later winning another Oscar for the same role in the film.

Lord **Leighton** (Frederic Leighton, 1830–96, kt 1878, baron 1896) The undisputed leader of late Victorian art and the only painter to have received a peerage. The first painting he exhibited at the Royal Academy, the huge *Cimabue's Madonna carried in Procession through the streets of Florence* (1855, Royal Collection, on loan to the National Gallery), was bought by Queen Victoria. His most characteristic works are large paintings of Greek classical subjects, done in his own version of a high Renaissance style. In 1866 he moved into a house designed largely by himself in Holland Park Road (London W14), to which he added in 1877–9 an Arab Hall decorated with tiles collected in Egypt and Syria. Now known as Leighton House, it is kept as a museum.

Peter **Lely** (1618–80, kt 1680) Dutch painter who came to England in the early 1640s and was naturalized in 1662. His name was Peter van der Faes; 'Lely' seems to have been the family house in Holland. He achieved the unusual feat of prospering equally during the English Civil War, the Commonwealth (during which his best known commission was to paint Oliver Cromwell *'warts and all') and the Restoration, becoming principal painter to Charles II in 1661. He adapted the style of Van *Dyck to suit the new fashions, pleasing equally with his portraits of court beauties (such as the ten 'Windsor Beauties' at Hampton Court) and with his masculine subjects (the 12 Admirals or 'Flagmen' who had fought in an engagement of 1665 against the Dutch, now in the National Maritime Museum).

The house which Lord Leighton designed for himself in London, with the famous Arab Hall on the right.

Measurements of length

Imperial		Metric
0.3937 inches	=	1 centimetre
1 inch	=	2.54 centimetres
(12 inches) 1 foot	=	30.48 centimetres (0.3048 metre)
(3 feet) 1 yard	=	0.9144 metres
(39.37 inches) 3.2808 feet	=	1 metre
100 yards	=	91.44 metres
109.36 yards	=	100 metres
(220 yards) 1 furlong	=	201.17 metres
(440 yards) quarter mile	=	402.37 metres
(0.621 mile) 1093.6 yards	=	1 kilometre (1000 metres)
(1760 yards, 8 furlongs) 1 mile	=	1.6093 kilometres

lend-lease System devised by the USA, before its entry into World War II, for supplying equipment to the Allies for use against Germany. Congress passed the Lend-Lease Act in March 1941 and by the end of the war some $50bn of aid had been shipped. Not until 1972 did payments in settlement come to an end.

Ginny **Leng** (Virginia Holgate, b. 1955, m. Hamish Leng 1985) Three-day event rider who had an unprecedented run of individual golds in the biennial European Championships (1985, 87, 89). She won an individual Olympic bronze in 1984 and again in 1988, and on both occasions was a member of the team which won silver. She has won three times at Badminton (1985, 89, 93).

length The *imperial system prevails still in Britain for measurements on the ground (miles for distance, cubic feet for office space) and in describing people's height. But *metric is now usual for the dimensions of anything retailed commercially. The young have learnt in school to think metric, but the majority of people in Britain still use imperial measurements, from force of habit, in everyday life.

The smallest imperial unit of length is the inch: there are 12 inches in a foot, 3 feet in a yard, 1760 yards in a mile. In some contexts other measurements are commonly used. The length of a horse race is given in furlongs (one eighth of a mile) and the depth of water is expressed sometimes in terms of the fathom (6 feet). The speed of a boat in the water is calculated in *knots.

John **Lennon** (1940–80) His career after the break up of the *Beatles was much influenced by his marriage in 1969 to Yoko Ono. The couple became familiar figures in the international protest movement; *Give Peace a Chance* was recorded during a 'bed-in' which they staged in a Montreal hotel in 1969. Of Lennon's solo work during the 1970s, the most successful album was the 1971 *Imagine* (particularly its title song); it contained a veiled attack on Paul McCartney in *How Do You Sleep?* On 8 December 1980 Lennon was shot by a mentally disturbed fan, Mark Chapman, as he and Yoko Ono were entering their New York apartment block. Two books published in his twenties (*John Lennon in his Own Write* 1964, *A Spaniard in the Works* 1965) reveal his surrealist talent as a writer – evident also in the lyrics of the Beatles songs.

Dan **Leno** (stage name of George Galvin, 1860–1904) *Music-hall entertainer, born into the business, trained as an acrobat and contortionist by his parents, and for a while a champion *clog dancer before he eventually settled into his vastly successful routine of rambling personal anecdotes, told very fast and interspersed with songs. His

broad straight mouth and bright mischievous eyes were essential ingredients of the fun. He was also famous for his yearly appearances as a dame in *pantomime.

Leonardo Cartoon (*c.*1498, National Gallery) The name commonly given in Britain to a full-scale preparatory drawing (or cartoon) by Leonardo da Vinci, which shows the Virgin with the Child on her knee, her mother St Anne behind her, and the infant John the Baptist to one side. It is believed to be an early preparation for a similar painting in the Louvre. The cartoon was bought in 1962, with the help of a public appeal, and was damaged in the area of the Virgin's breast when a man fired a shotgun at it in 1987. It has since been most expertly restored.

Lerwick (7000 in 1981) Britain's most northerly town and the administrative centre of Shetland, on the island of Mainland. The antiquity of the area is demonstrated by the nearby *Clickhimin Broch. A more recent fortress at the other end of the town, Fort Charlotte, was built in 1653 by troops from a Cromwellian fleet. The Shetland Museum, in a modern building, depicts the long history of the islands. The strong Viking connection is enacted every winter in the festival of *Up-Helly-Aa.

Lesotho Member of the *Commonwealth since 1966, previously known as Basutoland. A mountainous landlocked country, entirely surrounded by South Africa, it was the region which the Basuto tribes had managed to defend first against the Zulus and then against the Boers. Their leader, Moshoeshoe (*c.*1790–1870), won British protection against the Boers in 1868, and in 1884 Basutoland was made a crown colony. It became independent in 1966 as Lesotho, a constitutional monarchy with Moshoeshoe II as head of state.

Doris **Lessing** (Doris Tayler, b. 1919, m. Gottfried Lessing 1945) Novelist who grew up in Southern Rhodesia, now Zimbabwe. She left the country in 1949 and moved to London, where she published in 1950 her first book, *The Grass is Singing* – about the tense and ultimately tragic relationship between a white woman and her black servant. Martha Quest is Lessing's heroine in a sequence of five semi-autobiographical novels (1952–69, entitled collectively *The Children of Violence*). *The Golden Notebook* (1962), probably her most ambitious undertaking, analyses in a complex structure the pain of Anna Wulf, writer of a series of interconnecting notebooks; Anna lives in a male-dominated world and the book was hailed by many, rather too simply, as a feminist tract. With *Canopus in Argos* (1979) Lessing began a series of science-fiction novels.

'Lest we forget' A phrase which now has great resonance as applied to the dead of both World Wars, though in fact written long before World War I. It is the refrain of the poem *Recessional* (1897) by Rudyard *Kipling, in which it is God who must not be forgotten.

Letchworth see *garden city.

'Let not poor Nelly starve' see *Charles II.

Letter from America Weekly talk by Alistair *Cooke on topical matters in the USA, which has been on BBC radio since 24 March 1946. It is the longest-running solo performance in the history of broadcasting.

Leuchars (10km/6m NW of St Andrews) Village noted for the rich stone decoration of the 12c apse and choir of its church, probably the best surviving *Romanesque work in Scotland.

Levellers Political agitators in the 1640s whose ideas were far ahead of their time – and indeed were still too advanced when many of the same demands were put forward by the *Chartists two centuries later. The Levellers wanted regular parliaments elected by all adult males, with power exercised by the House of Commons to the exclusion of the Lords; decentralized government on many issues; and free trade. Under the leadership of John Lilburne (1614–57) they gained so much support in the *New Model Army that they were forcibly suppressed.

Loch **Leven** Lake in the Tayside region of Scotland, an important nature reserve for wildfowl. It contains Loch Leven Castle, used as an island prison for Mary Queen of Scots in 1567. After 11 months she escaped in a boat with the help of a devoted 16-year-old, Willy Douglas. Another Loch Leven is an inlet of the sea on the west coast, north of Oban.

Levens Hall (24km/15m N of Lancaster) House which has grown up round a *peel tower of the 13C. The main rooms, added in the late 16C, have superb Elizabethan panelling and patterned plaster ceilings. But the greatest treasure of Levens Hall is its topiary garden, laid out in the 1690s and miraculously preserved in a developed version of its original form.

Lord **Leverhulme** (William Lever, 1851–1925, bt 1911, viscount 1922) Industrialist who from modest beginnings, manufacturing bars of Sunlight soap in 1885 in a Warrington factory, built up the firm which developed into *Unilever. In 1888 he moved his factory to *Port Sunlight. The Leverhulme Trust, established by him, is one of Britain's largest charitable foundations, specializing in research and education.

Leviathan (1651) Treatise by Thomas *Hobbes on the nature of human society, which he presents as a vast living organism, comparing it to the world's largest creature – the biblical leviathan, or whale. Hobbes's thesis, in his widely remembered phrase, is that in a state of nature the life of man is 'solitary, poor, nasty, brutish and short', a chaos of rival self-interests. The only solution, for both the individual and the common good, is a contract of subordination to a supreme authority, whether it be 'one Man or . . . one Assembly of men'. The alternatives were diplomatic in a book published during the *Commonwealth and just two years after the execution of Charles I.

Bernard **Levin** (b. 1928) Journalist known in particular for his parliamentary commentaries as 'Taper' on the *Spectator* (1957–62) and for his columns in the *Times* (since 1971). His elaborate prose is as well suited to ridicule of politicians or trade unionists as to hymns in praise of Wagner or good food. He is also well known on television, from the iconoclast of *That Was The Week That Was* to the quirky traveller crossing the Alps in Hannibal's footsteps (1985) or following the course of the Rhine (1987) and of Fifth Avenue (1989).

Lewes (14,000 in 1981) County town and administrative centre of East Sussex. Its importance derived from the Norman castle, begun in the late 11C but largely destroyed in the 17C (apart from an impressive 14C barbican). It was at Lewes that Simon de *Montfort won his crucial victory over Henry III in 1264. The town, on its hill site, consists now of a very pleasant mixture of architecture spanning several centuries. It is noted for its great procession and bonfire on *Guy Fawkes Night, an event which is undeniably spectacular but tainted by displays of anti-papist bigotry in the burning of specifically Catholic effigies.

C.S. **Lewis** (Clive Staples Lewis, 1898–1963) Author who reached a wide readership in three different fields. His study of courtly love (*The Allegory of Love* 1936) remains the best known of his academic books. As a committed Christian, he was able in his science fiction and in *The *Screwtape Letters* to confront the ordinary reader in a very lively manner with the challenge of his faith. And his attempt to stimulate the imagination of children in a similar direction was triumphantly successful in the *Narnia books.

Lennox **Lewis** (b. 1965) Boxer who is Britain's first in this century to hold any version of the world heavyweight championship. He went with his mother to Canada when he was 12, and it was as a Canadian that he beat the American Riddick Bowe for the Olympic gold medal in 1988. He then returned to England and began an unbroken succession of victories, taking the European title in 1990 and the British in 1991. In 1992 a second-round knock-out of Donovan 'Razor' Ruddock left Lewis as the number one contender for the undisputed world title, newly won at the end of that year by Riddick Bowe. When Bowe failed to make arrangements to fight Lewis in his first title defence, the World Boxing Council declared that it would transfer the WBC title by default to Lewis; Bowe pre-empted this by ceremonially dropping the WBC championship belt into a waste bin at a London press conference.

Wyndham **Lewis** see *Vorticism.

Lewis with Harris The largest and most northerly island of the Outer *Hebrides. Lewis is the larger northern part

The sentimental benefits of cleanliness: an early Port Sunlight poster for Lord Leverhulme's famous soap.

Knight, queen and bishop: three pieces in the British Museum from the set of 12C Lewis chessmen.

of the island, containing Stornoway, the only town. The Lewis chessmen (67 in the British Museum, 11 in the Royal Museum of Scotland) are ivory pieces of the 12C which were discovered in sand dunes on the island in 1831. They were carved from walrus tusks, almost certainly in Scandinavia (the Hebrides were ruled by Norway until the 13C), and are assumed to have been lost in a shipwreck.

Harris is separated from Lewis by a range of hills running between inlets of the sea (Loch Resort to the west, Loch Seaforth to the east). Its most famous product has been *Harris tweed.

ley lines Straight lines forming a network across the landscape and connecting prehistoric sites, according to a theory put forward by Alan Watkins in *Early British Trackways* (1922). Modern believers tend to describe them as lines of geopathic energy, resulting from the earth's magnetic field. The argument is that our primitive ancestors, more sensitive than us to unseen influences, sited their holy places on the ley lines – and that traces of their ancient tracks can reveal where the lines run. Some water diviners claim they can locate them by traditional methods of dowsing.

LG see Order of the *Garter.

libel and slander Acts of defamation, respectively in written form (though libel is now extended to include film and broadcasting) and by the more transitory spoken word. It was established by the Libel Act of 1792 that anyone sued for libel or slander has the right for the case to be heard before a *jury (unusual among civil cases). Moreover the jury decides the level of damages. There have been some extraordinary decisions in recent years, such as the £600,000 originally awarded to the wife of the *Yorkshire Ripper, and these have made the system increasingly controversial.

Slander is treated in English law (though not in Scottish) as an offence different from libel, requiring more stringent conditions to be actionable. In broad terms material or financial loss has to be shown, rather than just damage to the plaintiff's reputation – though there are major exceptions to this rule, as when the damaged reputation is connected with a person's profession or a woman's chastity. Actions for slander are extremely rare (recently only three or four in any decade), partly because it is difficult to prove that the words were actually spoken. But as with

libel, juries have awarded very high damages: £44,000 against the bookmakers William Hill in 1983, £150,000 against Dr Alanah Houston in 1991.

In the early 1990s reform was under discussion. The lord chancellor issued in 1991 a consultation document which included the suggestion that many defamation cases could be settled by arbitration, and that those which came to court should have the level of damages set by the judge rather than the jury.

Liberal Party Political party which developed in the mid-19C among the Whigs (see *Tories and Whigs). The name was first applied to radical Whigs as a term of abuse, suggesting a link with the liberation movements familiar in many countries after the Napoleonic Wars. But by the late 1830s Lord John Russell was using it of the Whigs as a whole. The Liberal principles which gradually developed, finding their fullest expression in the Gladstone administrations, were against government controls (the agitation against the *Corn Laws being in effect a Liberal campaign), were strong in defence of the individual and his rights (the Don *Pacifico adventure was an exaggerated instance), and were in favour of what we would now call devolution (the issue of *Home Rule).

After being the natural opposition to the *Conservatives for nearly a century, the Liberals found themselves replaced in that role after World War I by the *Labour party. Since then Liberal influence has been greater than their small number of seats in the House of Commons would suggest, for their traditional principles, with the emphasis on the individual and on 'grass-roots' politics, acquired a radical appeal in the corporate decades of the mid-20C, when the Conservatives seemed to be dominated by business interests and the Labour party by the trade unions.

Under the leadership of Grimond, Thorpe and Steel a succession of sweeping by-election successes continued to raise hopes for an increased share of the poll in general elections. This did not materialize until the Liberal partnership with the SDP, which led to a large vote for the *Alliance in 1983. On 17 September 1987 the Liberals voted at their annual conference to dissolve the party and to merge with the SDP, ending a century and a half of Liberal history. But the new party will almost certainly come to seem a continuation of the old, for the name of the Social Liberal Democratic party was soon officially shortened to *Liberal Democrats.

Liberal Democratic Party New political party formed in March 1988 through merging the *Liberal party and the *SDP. Called originally the SLD (Social and Liberal Democrats), the name was shortened in October 1989 to the Liberal Democrats. Paddy *Ashdown was elected leader in July 1988. The party has been consistently more pro-European than its rivals, and for reasons including self-interest has campaigned strongly for proportional representation. It had not by 1992 recovered the early support enjoyed by the *Alliance (there were some 8 million votes for the Alliance in 1983 and 6 million for the Liberal Democrats in 1992). The party's headquarters are in Cowley Street (London SW1).

Liberty (National Council for Civil Liberties) Pressure group formed in 1934 by Ronald Kidd (1889–1942), as a result of witnessing the police treatment of hunger marchers in London. It has remained an independent non-political organization, campaigning against any restrictions on civil liberty and often taking test cases to court. Topical issues in recent years have included sexual and racial discrimination, prisoners' rights, privacy and freedom of information. Known as the NCCL until 1989, the council has campaigned since 1989 under the name of Liberty.

Liberty's (London W1) Shop founded in 1875 by Arthur Liberty (1843–1917, kt 1913), which had great influence on fashion in the late 19c, particularly in popularizing *Art Nouveau. Liberty first specialized in oriental wares (reflected in the roofline frieze on the present building of 1924–5, which shows goods travelling by camel and elephant towards an image of Britannia), before becoming personally involved with the *Arts and Crafts movement. A famous outcome of this interest was the Liberty tradition of hand-printed fabrics; the emphasis in the early years was on silks, but the range was soon extended to cotton fabrics for furnishing and clothes.

libraries The widespread provision of public libraries, from which anyone living in the district can borrow books free of charge, dates back to the Public Libraries Act of 1850. This enabled towns to spend money from the rates for this purpose, but progress was slow until private charity – most notably that of Andrew *Carnegie – forced the pace. The trust set up by Carnegie provided library buildings (eventually more than 2800 in the English-speaking world), but with the essential proviso that the local authority would be responsible for the running costs. Borrowing has remained free, but from 1984 payments have been made under *Public Lending Right to the authors of the books borrowed. See also *copyright libraries.

Libyan embassy siege On 17 April 1984 a machine gun was fired from a window of the Libyan embassy in London at a crowd outside, demonstrating peacefully against the Libyan leader, Colonel Gaddafi. Twelve Libyan demonstrators were wounded and a British woman police constable, Yvonne Fletcher, was killed; there is now a memorial to her on the pavement in St James's Square where she fell. Police besieged the embassy building until April 27, when its occupants – including the unidentified killer of WPC Fletcher – were allowed to fly home after the government had broken off diplomatic relations with Libya. British diplomats and their families had during the

An early alternative to the public libraries: the Warrington Mechanics' Institution Perambulating Library, c.1830.

same period been besieged by hostile crowds of demonstrators in Tripoli, the capital city of Libya.

'licence to print money' see Roy *Thomson.

licensing laws see *pub.

Lichfield (26,000 in 1981) Cathedral town in Staffordshire, centre of a diocese ever since St Chad (d. 672) became the first bishop. The present cathedral with its three spires (known as the Ladies of the Vale) was built in the 13–14c and considerably restored in the 19c. The Lady Chapel is the most distinguished part of the interior, with nine great windows in the Decorated style; seven of them contain 16c stained glass from the Cistercian abbey of Herkenrode in Belgium, brought here in the early 19c. The city's most famous association is with Samuel *Johnson, whose birthplace is now kept as a museum. It was from Lichfield that he and *Garrick set off together to walk to London in 1737.

Patrick **Lichfield** (Patrick Anson, b. 1939, 5th earl of Lichfield 1960) Society photographer producing very stylish images in portraits (including many of the royal family) and in fashion work.

Alvar **Lidell** (1908–81) The voice of BBC radio in the early years. As newsreader and announcer (1932–69), it was he who introduced any momentous event – including the abdication message of Edward VIII in 1936 and Chamberlain's words in September 1939, telling the nation it was at war.

'Lie heavy on him, Earth!' see *Vanbrugh.

'lies, damned lies' By far the best-known remark on statistics is the one supposedly made by Disraeli (attributed to him in Mark Twain's *Autobiography*): 'There are three kinds of lies: lies, damned lies and statistics.' It is an opinion reinforced among the electorate by the ability of politicians to use statistics to prove diametrically opposite points.

There were protests from some statisticians during the 1980s at the government's tendency to alter the statistical basis on sensitive issues such as *unemployment, causing comparisons between different periods to become blurred. Such discrepancies are among the hazards of statistics as a science. But it is statistics as an art which cause the greatest confusion to the public. In this context the trick is to use the figures selectively. An elementary example can be seen in statistics of growth. If there is a substantial fall during a year (in industrial output or share prices or any other such indicator), one politician can point to a subsequent low rate of growth by taking a starting point before the fall; another can prove a much higher rate of growth over almost the same period by beginning the comparison after the fall.

life expectancy One of the most basic changes in western societies has been the vastly increased life expectancy of the population, leading to an unprecedented imbalance towards the elderly. *Engels, writing about Manchester in the 1840s, said that the average age of death (including *infant mortality) was 35 in professional families, 22 in the families of higher craftsmen, and just 15 in the families of labourers. Today a male is given an average life expectancy of about 72 at birth, and a female of about 78. In reality the figures will be higher, since these project forward the present-day statistics of death; as health and medicine improve, so does everyone's life expectancy. The graph, projected forward on a similar basis, shows the average expected age of death of men and women in each age group.

Life expectancy

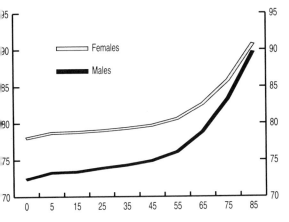

At each stage in a person's life, there is an average probability as to how many years remain (based on present-day statistics). To discover the average expectation of life at any age for a man or woman, select the age along the bottom and read the appropriate line of the graph against the vertical scale.

Source: Annual Abstract of Statistics *(see* *Central Statistical Office).*

Until her death in March 1993 the oldest person in Britain was Charlotte Hughes (b. 1877), with the greatest age of anyone in British history since reliable records began; she had passed on 25 February 1992 the previous figure of 114 years and 6 months. The oldest recorded man in British history was John Evans (1877–1990), who was fitted with a pacemaker when he was 108 and died two months short of his 113th birthday (an age far exceeded by the semi-legendary *Old Parr).

'Life is a jest' see John *Gay.

Life on Earth (BBC 1979) Thirteen-part TV series on evolution, written and presented by David *Attenborough – a vast undertaking, superbly filmed. The accompanying book achieved the unique distinction of being at the same time, in different editions, nos. 1 and 2 in the UK nonfiction bestseller list.

life peers Men and women granted non-hereditary *peerages, as barons and baronesses. The first were created in 1876, as *Law Lords. The principle was extended in 1958 to people of distinction in public life, with some degree of expectation that they will take an active part in the House of *Lords. There is a disparity in the resulting forms of address for spouses. If John Smith becomes a life peer, he is Lord Smith and his wife Lady Smith. If Mary Smith is similarly honoured, she is known as either Lady Smith or Baroness Smith but her husband remains plain Mr Smith.

The Light of the World (1851–3, Keble College, Oxford) Painting by Holman *Hunt which became, through engravings and photographs, one of the best-known images in 19c Britain. The figure of Jesus, bearing a lantern on a moonlit night, knocks on the door of a house. His eyes look directly – half inviting, half accusing – at the viewer. There are other versions, painted by Hunt himself, in Manchester City Art Gallery and in St Paul's Cathedral.

Light Programme see *radio.

Lili Marlene The outstanding song of World War II. Based on a poem by a German soldier in World War I (Lili Marlene was the girl waiting for him outside the barrack gate), it was set to music in 1938. It became a favourite with the German troops – particularly in north Africa, where it was adopted (from German radio broadcasts) by the British 8th army. The best-known version in both languages was the recording by a German-born American, Marlene Dietrich – the name Marlene, shared with Lili, was merely a happy coincidence.

Lilleshall see *Sports Council.

Peter **Lilley** (b. 1943) Conservative politician, MP for St Albans since 1983. The youngest member of the *Cambridge mafia, he entered the *cabinet in 1990 as secretary of state for trade and industry and in 1992 became secretary of state for social security.

Lilliburlero (also spelt Lillibullero) Tune which became a craze at the time of the *Revolution of 1688. It was first printed, without words, in 1686; the following year verses were written to it, satirizing James II's papist lord lieutenant in Ireland (Richard Talbot, earl of Tyrconnel), with the mocking refrain 'lilliburlero'. The tune retains a strong link with the *Orange movement in Northern Ireland, in the form of a song called *Protestant Boys* (see p. 384). It is also, in a simplified version, the tune of *Hush-a-bye, baby.* It is widely familiar among listeners to the BBC World Service, where it is used as a signature tune just before the news.

Lilliput see *Gulliver's Travels.*

limerick The most popular verse form in Britain for improvised humorous poetry and also the main vehicle for risqué rhymes. It was a medium for comic verse from the early 19c, though the name has not been found in print before the 1890s – by which time people were already perplexed as to its origin (no convincing explanation has been found). The rhythm (*tittytum tittytum tittytum*) and the rhyme scheme (*aabba*) make the limerick instantly recognizable. Its wide popularity must derive to some extent from Edward *Lear; he used it for every poem in his first published work, *A Book of Nonsense* (1846), supplying each one with its own illustration.

Lime Street The central station in Liverpool, where the 61m/200ft span of the roof was briefly the largest in the world when built in 1867 (it was soon outdone by St Pancras in London). The very grand station hotel (1868–71, now used as offices) is by *Waterhouse.

Typical limerick from A Book of Nonsense, *with Edward Lear's own very characteristic drawing.*

There was an Old Man in a tree, who was horribly bored by a bee;
When they said, "Does it buzz?" he replied, "Yes, it does!
It's a regular brute of a bee!"

The Angel Choir at the east end of Lincoln Cathedral, added in the second half of the 13C with carved angels above the arches on either side.

limey Slang term in other English-speaking countries for an immigrant from Britain, and hence for anyone British. It was originally applied to British sailors, who were forced to drink a daily measure of lime juice. Captain *Cook's remedy for scurvy had led to compulsory lemon juice on ships from 1795; this was replaced from 1865 by the cheaper and slightly less effective lime juice.

limited liability A concept of great importance in the raising of capital for business, introduced in the Joint-Stock Companies Act of 1856. The act also imposed an obligation on companies to register details about themselves so as to avoid fraudulent promotions (the memory of the *South Sea Bubble long haunted British legislators). The essence of limited liability is that an investor can lose no more than the money spent in purchasing the shares. A company thus becomes an independent entity, solely responsible for its own debts. (The most extreme modern example of the dangers of unlimited liability has been the crippling losses suffered in the early 1990s by many members of *Lloyd's of London).

To warn creditors of the new restriction of liability, the act of 1856 specified that the word Limited (usually abbreviated to Ltd) had to follow the name of the company. Since 1980 this term has been reserved for private companies and for subsidiary elements of larger groups, not separately quoted on the Stock Exchange. For public companies, whose shares are traded on the open market, Ltd has been replaced by PLC (often printed plc), standing for Public Limited Company.

Lincoln (84,000 in 1991) City and administrative centre of Lincolnshire, on a hill above the river Witham. It was founded as the Roman fortress of *Lindum*, established in AD 47. *Ermine Street passed through here; the north gate of the settlement survives intact as the Newport arch, one of the most complete Roman remains in Britain and the oldest arch still to have traffic passing beneath it.

The medieval importance of Lincoln began with the Norman castle, started as early as 1068 by William the Conqueror. The superb cathedral, lying immediately beside the castle, was begun just four years later. Its exterior is famous for its three towers, each once surmounted by a spire; the central spire, at 160m/525ft, was much higher than that of *Salisbury, but it fell in 1548. The huge central tower contains a 5.5-ton bell, Great Tom of Lincoln. Of the Norman church only the west front survives. The main body of the cathedral, in Early English style, was built from 1192 by St Hugh, bishop of Lincoln. Its greatest glory, the Angel Choir, was added at the east end in 1255–80 to contain his shrine. Its name derives from the 28 angels looking down from above the arches on either side. Squatting above one of the pillars between the arches is the small cheeky figure of the Lincoln Imp, a stonemason's joke which still gives much pleasure.

Lincoln had an influential community of Jews in the Middle Ages, remembered in the 12C Jew's House (one of the oldest domestic buildings in Britain) and in the career of the powerful financier Aaron of Lincoln. They were brutally persecuted in 1255 when they were blamed for the murder of a 9-year-old boy, another Hugh of Lincoln, later venerated by pilgrims as Little St Hugh. The city's medieval prosperity was based on wool (Lincoln green long being a famous cloth), but in more recent times it has specialized in engineering. The Usher Gallery, established in 1927 by James Ward Usher, has a strong collection of Peter de Wint, who lived in the city. The National Cycle Museum opened in Lincoln in 1984.

Lincolnshire (592,000 in 1991, administrative centre Lincoln) *County on the east coast of England.

Lincoln's Inn see *Inns of Court.

Lindisfarne (also known as *Holy Island) Part-time island in northeast England, linked to the coast of Northumberland at low tide by a 5km/3m causeway. Its holiness dates from the 7C when St *Aidan established a monastery here and was soon followed by St *Cuthbert. Their settlement fell victim to *Viking raiders, and the monks abandoned the island in 875. The present ruins are of a Benedictine priory founded in early Norman times and destroyed in the *dissolution of the monasteries.

The castle was built in the mid-16C as a military fortress against invasion from Scotland. Never used in battle, it was turned by Lutyens into the country house, notably lacking in comforts, which survives today.

Lindisfarne Gospels (British Library) Illuminated Latin manuscript of the four Gospels. A note added on the last page, and believed to be accurate, says that the book was written in honour of St *Cuthbert by Eadfrith, who was bishop on *Lindisfarne from 698 to 721. Cuthbert's body, exhumed in 698, was found to be uncorrupted, greatly adding to his reputation for sanctity, and this event may have prompted the creation of the manuscript. It is notable for combining Celtic decoration with a Byzantine convention of figure painting, seen in the images of the evangelists; and for the complex interlace patterns of its so-called carpet pages.

Lindow man (British Museum) The body of a man discovered in 1984 in a bog, Lindow Moss in Cheshire, in a remarkably well preserved state because of the surrounding peat (he was immediately named Pete Marsh or Lindow Pete in the popular press). The man had been stripped naked except for a fox-fur band on his left arm; he was then struck on the head from behind and was garrotted with a cord around his neck, after which his throat was cut. Radiocarbon dating revealed that he lived at some point between about 300 BC and the same number of centuries AD. It is thought probable that he was a sacrificial victim in the rites of the Celtic *druids. The severed head of a woman, similarly preserved, had been found nearby in 1983.

Lindum see *Lincoln.

Linear B The script of an early form of Greek used on Crete and in southern Greece in about 1300 BC, which remained a mystery until deciphered by a British architect, Michael Ventris (1922–56). He had been intrigued by the challenge since the age of 14, when he heard Sir Arthur *Evans lecture on the clay tablets from Knossos. He announced his solution on a BBC radio programme only three months before he was killed in a car crash. An earlier Cretan script, known as Linear A, is still undeciphered.

Gary **Lineker** (b. 1960) The most brilliant striker of his generation and England's most popular footballer in recent years. He began his career with Leicester City (1978–85), was briefly with Everton (1985–6) and then Barcelona (1986–9) before joining Tottenham Hotspur (1989–92). His six goals in the 1986 Mexico World Cup (including three against Poland) made him the top scorer of any nation; and by 1992 his total of goals for England, in 80 internationals, was just one short of Bobby Charlton's record of 49. In 1993 he began a new career playing in Japan.

Linlithgow (10,000 in 1981) Town in Lothian, site of the ruined but impressive Linlithgow Palace, which in appearance is more of a castle. The present structure was begun in 1425 by James I, after a fire had destroyed previous buildings on the site, and it was completed in the following century by James V; his daughter, Mary Queen of Scots, was born here in 1542. The palace was accidentally burnt in 1746 when troops of the duke of Cumberland were camping in it. The adjacent church of St Michael (15–16c, in the Decorated style) was also begun by James I on an earlier foundation.

Lion and unicorn Traditional antagonists found in the stories of many cultures. The English nursery rhyme in which they feature must partly reflect their coming together in the *royal arms:

> The lion and the unicorn
>   Were fighting for the crown;
> The lion beat the unicorn
>   All round about the town.

Lions (British Lions) The name given to *rugby teams representing the British Isles, including Ireland; they turn out in red shirts, white shorts and blue socks with green tops (a colour for each of the four home countries). The name has been in use since at least 1950, but is traditionally said (without contemporary evidence) to date back to the team which toured South Africa in 1924 and to derive from the lion symbol on their ties.

*The **Lion, the Witch and the Wardrobe*** see *Narnia.

liquorice allsorts Mixture of white and brightly coloured soft sweets, in a variety of shapes but all with bars or bands of black liquorice. They have been marketed under this very effective name since the early 20c.

listed buildings The national list of buildings of architectural importance, approved until 1992 by the secretary of state for the Environment (subsequently by the secretary of state for National Heritage). It includes all which survive relatively unaltered from before 1700; most such buildings up to 1840; and buildings of character and quality, or by significant architects, up to modern times. About 1% of these are given a special status as Grade 1; the rest are Grade 2, though an asterisk is added to the most important within this group (known as 'Grade two star'). Other grades are now obsolete. Special consent is required from the local authority for any alteration to a listed building.

*The **Listener*** Weekly magazine launched by the BBC in 1929 to preserve in print the best of its radio talks. This remained the basis, but arts reviews and general features were soon added. As a leading cultural and literary magazine, the *Listener* had a circulation in the 1950s of about 150,000. By the 1990s this had fallen to less than 20,000, and the last issue was published in January 1991.

Listen with Mother (BBC 1950–82) Radio programme for children under five, consisting of stories, songs and nursery rhymes. It achieved a very large audience in its early years, when it occupied the 15-minute slot just before *Woman's Hour*. The opening words of each programme were always the same and have entered the nation's collective memory: 'Are you sitting comfortably? Then I'll begin.'

Joseph **Lister** (1827–1912, bt 1883, baron 1897) Surgeon who introduced the principles of antiseptic surgery.

A jubilant Lineker, after one of his many goals for Spurs.

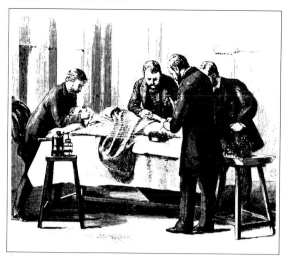

Surgery in about 1870 on Lister's new principles: before an operation his students would intone 'Let us spray'.

There was a great increase in the number of operations after the use of chloroform had been pioneered by *Simpson in 1847, but many patients then died of 'hospital gangrene'. Lister, professor of surgery at the university of Glasgow, demonstrated in 1865 that infection could be prevented if carbolic acid were applied to the wound. The precise antiseptic substance was later much improved, but his discovery was a milestone on the path towards safer surgery.

Little Black Sambo (*The Story of Little Black Sambo* 1899) Book for young children, written in India by the Scottish wife of an army doctor, Helen Bannerman (1862–1946), and illustrated by her in simple bright colours. The character and the story were immediately popular. Sambo goes into the jungle with a red coat, blue trousers, purple shoes and green umbrella. Four tigers deprive him of these and he only escapes when they chase each other so fast round a tree that they turn into melted butter, which he takes home for tea. In recent decades the book has been much criticized on racial grounds, and in the early 1990s it was not in print in Britain.

Little Bo-Peep see *bo-peep.

Little Dorrit (1857) Novel by *Dickens, published in monthly parts from December 1855. William Dorrit is 'father of the *Marshalsea', where he has lived for many years as a debtor; his youngest daughter, little Amy Dorrit, was even born in the prison. The hero is the middle-aged Arthur Clennam, who tries to help the family and with whom Little Dorrit falls in love. Like Amy's father, Clennam becomes hopelessly entangled in the obstructive bureaucracy of the Circumlocution Office – Dickens's bitter satire on a government department, from the period when the term *red tape entered the language. Dorrit is found to be heir to a fortune and leaves the Marshalsea; meanwhile Clennam, victim of a fraud, loses all his money and enters the prison, where he is visited and comforted by Little Dorrit (now rich, but the only one of her family not to be spoilt by wealth). Finally the Dorrit fortune is lost again, making it possible for the impoverished Clennam to ask Amy to marry him. Among the many minor characters is the very precise governess, Mrs General, who recommends the words 'papa, potatoes, poultry, prunes and prism' for giving a pretty shape to the lips, but 'especially prunes and prism'.

little Em'ly see *David Copperfield.

Little Englanders Pejorative phrase of the 1890s for those who disliked the policies of imperial expansion which were then being robustly advocated by men such as Cecil *Rhodes. The phrase was given prominence (and may even have been coined) by Joseph Chamberlain in a speech of July 1895.

Little Jack Horner Rhyme about a boy who puts his thumb in a Christmas pie and pulls out a plum. It is often said to refer to Thomas Horner who in the 16C (after the *dissolution of the monasteries) acquired the manor of Mells in Somerset, which had previously belonged to Glastonbury Abbey. The theory is highly improbable – there is no link other than the surname. The connection was first made in the 19C and is typical of attempts to find historical origins for *nursery rhymes.

Little John The most stalwart follower of *Robin Hood, named ironically for his size and strength.

'A little learning is a dangerous thing' see Alexander *Pope.

Little Lord Fauntleroy (1886) Children's novel by Frances Hodgson *Burnett about a young American boy, with long golden curls and in a velvet knickerbocker suit, who becomes Lord Fauntleroy when he is discovered to be the heir to an English earl. He travels to his English castle, has much trouble with the cantankerous old nobleman and is almost displaced by a young impostor. The huge success of the book caused unfortunate boys on both sides of the Atlantic to be forced into suits of velvet and lace.

Little Moreton Hall (14km/9m N of Stoke-on-Trent) The most spectacular of Britain's *timber-frame houses. Begun in about 1450 for Richard de Moreton, it was added to piecemeal until the early 17C but has not been altered since. The irregularity of its constituent parts is

A New York studio photograph of a small boy in the 1890s, trapped in the velvets of Little Lord Fauntleroy.

enhanced by a wonderful range of decorative patterns, both in the exterior timbers and in the leading of the windows.

Joan **Littlewood** (b. 1914) Founder in 1945 of Theatre Workshop, a touring company for working-class audiences which in 1953 settled in the Theatre Royal, Stratford (in the east end of London). There she developed an improvisational style of theatre which bore fruit in highly successful productions such as *Oh What A Lovely War.

Live Aid see Bob *Geldof.

Penelope **Lively** (b. 1933) Author who has written fiction with equal success for children and adults, in each case usually making her theme the interaction between past and present. For children this was brilliantly achieved, in comic vein, in the *The Ghost of Marjorie Kempe* (1973). She began her adult fiction with *The Road to Lichfield*; this was shortlisted in 1977 for the Booker prize, which she won ten years later with *Moon Tiger*.

Liverpool (475,000 in 1991) City and port in Merseyside, on the north bank of the estuary of the Mersey. First used as a harbour in the 13C for sending supplies to Ireland, it only became of major importance in the 18C with the development of manufacturing industry in Lancashire. This enabled Liverpool's merchants to benefit from the import of raw materials and the export of finished goods as well as enjoying extra profit from slaves on the middle section of the *triangular trade. The superb docks, and in particular the redbrick warehouses of Albert Dock (1841-5), fell into decay with the decline of the port but have recently been restored as museums – among them a northern extension of London's Tate Gallery, the Merseyside Maritime Museum and a museum describing a local success story, the *Beatles. On the waterside stands a building of 1910 which is the city's best-known landmark – the Royal Liver Building, with its two towers surmounted by the legendary Liver Birds (pronounced for some reason *lie-ver*) which supposedly gave Liverpool its name.

Liverpool's public collections of the 19C are of outstanding quality. The County Museum, founded in 1860 by William Brown (1784–1864, bt 1863) and standing in the street named after him, has among its treasures the *Kingston Brooch. Next door the Walker Art Gallery, the gift in 1877 of Andrew Barclay Walker (1824–93, kt 1877, bt 1886), has a broadly based collection of European painting of the 14–20C of a quality unrivalled in England outside London; the remarkable early works came from the collection of the Liverpool historian and connoisseur William Roscoe (1753–1831). The Gallery is the setting for the biennial *John Moores Exhibition. On the other side of the street, and completing the great array of Victorian classical buildings in the heart of the city, is St George's Hall, originally providing a concert room and assize courts (begun in 1839 to a design of Harvey Lonsdale Elmes, 1813–47). It acquired in 1870 a confident new Victorian neighbour of a different kind, *Lime Street Station.

In 1900 Liverpool had no cathedral (it had been a diocese only since 1880). It now has two. The Anglican cathedral, designed by Giles Gilbert *Scott, is the largest church in the country, in a severe Gothic style; it was completed in 1978. The Roman Catholic Metropolitan Cathedral of Christ the King is very different; a round tent-like structure in the shape of a crown (by Frederick Gibberd, 1908–84), it was built in 1962-7 above the crypt of an abandoned project by *Lutyens.

In recent years economic and political troubles have given Liverpool unwelcome publicity. Riots in 1981 in the black community of Toxteth focused attention on inner-city problems and racial discrimination. And the city was seen as the prime example of the threat posed to the Labour party by the *Militant Tendency, particularly while Derek Hatton (b. 1948) was deputy leader of the council.

Liverpool, known as the Reds (Anfield Road, Liverpool). Far and away England's most successful football club, with a total by 1992 of 27 wins in major UK tournaments (their nearest rivals, Aston Villa, scoring only 17). Yet Liverpool was formed in 1892 only as a replacement team, to occupy Anfield Road after *Everton had quarrelled with the landlord and departed. Elected to Division 2 of the *Football League in 1893, and winning in their first year, Liverpool have since then been almost continuously in Division 1. Their greatest successes began when Bill *Shankly was manager (1959–74), and continued apace under his successor, Bob *Paisley (1974–83). This was the period which saw the signing of Kevin *Keegan, followed by that of Kenny *Dalglish. From 1976 the Reds won an astonishing 10 League victories in 15 years (1976–90). The standing area for Liverpool supporters at one end of the Anfield Road ground has itself become a well-known feature of British football; it is known as the Kop, short for Spion Kop. Club victories: FA Cup 1965, 74, 86, 89, 92; League Champions 1901, 06, 22, 23, 47, 64, 66, 73, 76, 77, 79, 80, 82, 83, 84, 86, 88, 90; League Cup 1981, 82, 83, 84; European Cup 1977, 78, 81, 84; UEFA Cup 1973, 76.

Lord **Liverpool** (Robert Jenkinson, 1770–1828, 2nd earl of Liverpool 1808) Tory politician who was prime minister (1812–1827) during a fraught period in British history. His time in office included the end of the *Napoleonic Wars and the subsequent years of internal unrest which saw the *Peterloo massacre and an increasing need for the *Reform Act. A modest and cautious man with a wealth of experience (foreign secretary 1801–4, home secretary 1807–9, secretary for war and the colonies 1809–12), he came to office after the assassination of Spencer *Perceval. His skill lay in holding together a party which included others more talented and more temperamental than himself (among them *Canning, *Castlereagh and *Peel). Disraeli described him in *Coningsby* as 'the Arch-Mediocrity' – unjust, but the label stuck.

Liverpool and Manchester railway The first public railway to use exclusively steam locomotion (the *Stockton and Darlington had retained horse-drawn carriages for passengers). From 1826 the line was laid by George *Stephenson. Its route of 50km/31m included two major difficulties – the crossing of a bog, Chat Moss, and the creation of a cutting through Olive Mount. The choice of locomotive was decided in open competition at the *Rainhill trials. The railway opened with great ceremony on 15 September 1830 when a procession of eight of the Stephenson engines (all based on *Rocket*) travelled the length of the line, each drawing carriages packed with dignitaries (including the duke of Wellington, who was then prime minister). It was the occasion also of the first famous railway accident. One of the MPs for Liverpool, William Huskisson, was run over and mortally wounded by a locomotive, the *Dart*.

Liverpool Philharmonic see the *Royal Liverpool Philharmonic.

Liverpool Street Railway station in London, serving East Anglia. Designed by Edward Wilson, it was opened in 1874 as the terminus of the Great Eastern Railway and was very successfully modernized in 1991.

David **Livingstone** (1813–73) Scottish missionary and explorer who opened up the centre of Africa to European interests. Born in a one-room tenement in Blantyre in Lanarkshire (kept now with adjoining houses as a museum) and working in a cotton mill from the age of ten, he began to educate himself and took a medical degree in 1840. He then joined the London Missionary Society and was sent to South Africa. Expeditions into unknown parts of Africa filled the rest of his life, first to establish more mission centres, then to find trade routes which would bring prosperity to central Africa and so undercut the economic basis of the slave trade, and finally for purposes of pure exploration – in particular to find the sources of the three great African rivers, the Zambezi, Congo and Nile. In 1855 he discovered the Victoria Falls on the Zambezi (described in his *Missionary Travels* 1857), and in 1859 he found Lake Nyasa.

The world thought him lost on an expedition begun in 1866, until his famous discovery by H.M. *Stanley. His final journey across Africa was as dramatic as any. He died in swamps near Lake Bangweulu, whereupon two of his servants carried his embalmed body some 480km/300m before they made contact with a British expedition. Their action made it possible for him to be buried in Westminster Abbey.

Ken **Livingstone** (b. 1945) Labour politician, MP for Brent East since 1987. On the left wing of the party, he first came to wide public attention as leader of the *Greater London Council (1981–6) in the final years before its abolition – with the Tory tabloid press promoting an exaggerated image of 'red Ken', a dangerous revolutionary.

Lizard Peninsula in Cornwall with spectacular coastal scenery, the tip of which (Lizard Point) is the most southerly part of the British mainland. It has been particularly associated with communications. From Poldhu, on the west coast, *Marconi's equipment transmitted in 1901 the first transatlantic radio signal. And on Goonhilly Downs, in the centre of the promontory, stands the Earth Station, the Post Office's main installation for receiving and transmitting signals bounced off satellites. In 1962 the station received and broadcast the first live translantic TV progamme, via the Telstar satellite.

Llanberis Wild and dramatic valley in Wales, a rocky defile through the mountain range to the northeast of Snowdon.

Llandaff Ancient town and the oldest bishopric in Wales, now effectively a northern suburb of Cardiff. The first bishop was St Teilo, in the 6c, and the cathedral was built on the site of his church. The present structure dates from the 13c but has been frequently restored, most recently after extensive damage from an air raid in 1941. It was then that the famous central feature was added, an organ loft bearing a sculpture by *Epstein of Christ in Majesty.

Llandrindod Wells (3500 in 1981) Fashionable spa in the 19c, now the administrative centre of Powys. It was known for its medicinal springs from the 17c, but only developed with the arrival of the railway. The Roman fort known as Castell Collen was nearby to the northwest, and there are finds from there in the local museum.

Llandudno (19,000 in 1981) The largest resort in Wales, on the north coast of Gwynedd. It developed with the arrival of the railway in the mid-19c, providing holidays for the new industrial towns of the Midlands and the north of England. The long curving beach of the bay is flanked by two limestone headlands. The larger, Great Orme, is at the western end; it can be ascended by tram, funicular railway or cable car, and it has at its foot the traditional Victorian *seaside pier.

Llanelli Rugby union football club, formed in 1872. It has been the leading club in the Schweppes Welsh Cup, with nine victories (1973, 74, 75, 76, 85, 88, 91, 92, 93).

Llanfairpwllgwyngyllgogerychwyrndrobwllllan-tysiliogogogoch Village in Anglesey with an undisputed claim to the longest name in British topography. The name was probably introduced in the 19c as a tourist

Livingstone rescued from a lion: contemporary book illustration of the dangers faced by the great missionary in Africa.

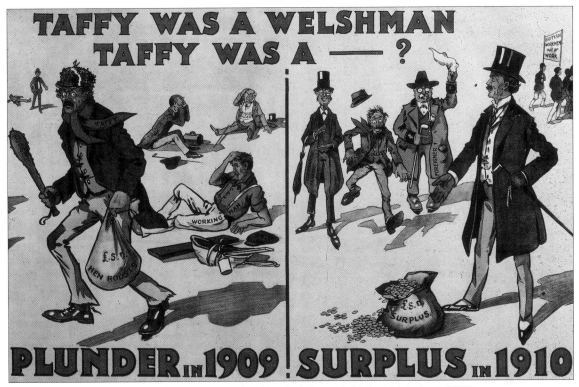

Poster in 1910 protesting at the tax increases introduced by Lloyd George in his 'people's budget' of 1909.

attraction, being Welsh for a phrase which seems more of an address than a place name: 'St Mary's church in the hollow of the white hazel near the rapid whirlpool of Llantysilio of the red cave'. Llanfairpwllgwyngyll or even just Llanfair P.G. are the commonly accepted abbreviations. The village had the distinction of forming the first *Women's Institute in Britain.

Llangollen (43km/27m NW of Shrewsbury) Town in Clwyd on the river Dee, where the International Music *Eisteddfod has been held in July since 1947. The Llangollen Steam Railway is a short section of line, closed in 1968 and restored by enthusiasts from the late 1970s – the 3km/2m to Berwyn was opened first, with plans to extend it the 16km/10m to Corwen. The 'Ladies of Llangollen' were two eccentric Irishwomen, Eleanor Butler and Sarah Ponsonby, who lived for half a century from 1779 in Plas Newydd, a house just southeast of the town, where they received many distinguished literary visitors. It was they who gave the house its neo-Gothic character; the black-and-white timbering was added later.

Llantrisant see the Royal *Mint.

Harry **Llewellyn** see *Foxhunter.

Llewelyn ap Gruffydd (d. 1282) Grandson of *Llewelyn ap Iorwerth who reasserted his family's authority in *Wales after an intervening period of disorder. By 1258 he was in a position to receive the homage of the other Welsh leaders and to proclaim himself Prince of *Wales, a dignity in which he was the first to be recognized by England (in 1267). Welsh independence did not long survive the accession of *Edward I. Resisting demands to submit to the English crown, Llewelyn died in battle in 1282. He was briefly succeeded by his brother David ap Gruffydd (d. 1283), but it was Llewelyn's death which brought Wales finally under English domination.

Llewelyn ap Iorwerth (known as Llewelyn the Great, d. 1240) Ruler of Gwynedd who established control over the greater part of *Wales, receiving feudal homage from the other Welsh princes. He was succeeded by his son David ap Llewelyn (*c.*1208–46), who was the first to assume the title of Prince of *Wales.

Marie **Lloyd** (stage name of Matilda Wood, 1879–1922) Perhaps the greatest of all *music-hall stars. Her speciality was warm-hearted songs about everyday life, made saucy with the help of her famous wink (or sometimes even without it – *She'd never had her ticket punched before* was one of her early numbers). The favourites in her repertoire were *A little of what you fancy does you good*, *Oh, Mr Porter*, in her last years *One of the ruins that Cromwell knocked about a bit* – and, above all, *Don't dilly-dally on the way*.

David **Lloyd George** (1863–1945, earl Lloyd-George 1945) Liberal politician and the dominant British figure during the years either side of World War I. He made his name as a young lawyer representing Welsh Nonconformists (his own background) and in 1890 was elected MP for Caernarfon, a seat he held till he was created a peer three months before his death. Apart from the brief interlude of Rosebery's government (1894–5), it was to be 15 years before there was a Liberal administration. When it finally arrived, in 1905, Lloyd George went straight into the cabinet as president of the Board of Trade. In 1908 Asquith made him chancellor of the exchequer. His 'people's budget' of 1909 caused a furore, introducing new taxes on the rich to strengthen the navy (the likelihood of war was now evident). The Conservative majority in the House of Lords had vetoed much Liberal legislation over the past few years but their rejection of this budget was the last straw, leading to a constitutional crisis solved only by *Asquith's Parliament Act of 1911. In that same year Lloyd George introduced compulsory *national insurance in certain industries, an important step towards the *welfare state.

The 'loss book' at Lloyd's of London, when the sums were rather smaller than today: wood engraving of the 1870s.

During the early part of World War I he was minister of munitions, a post in which he cut through much red tape to ensure an adequate supply of arms to the front. By the end of 1916 there was discontent with Asquith's management of the war, and Lloyd George schemed secretly with the Conservatives in the coalition government to take his place as prime minister – a coup for which the Liberal party did not forgive him for many years. For the remainder of the war he succeeded in streamlining the political command, working with an inner cabinet of just five people, but he was unable to effect much improvement among the generals with whom (particularly Haig) he remained frequently at odds.

After the war Lloyd George decided to continue the coalition. He and Bonar *Law went to the country together in 1918 in what became known as the 'coupon' election (because Asquith derided as a coupon the letter, signed by both leaders, which every coalition candidate carried as a certificate of authenticity). But it proved a coupon to success. The independent Liberals were reduced to just twenty-eight MPs, and even Asquith – still the leader of the party – lost his seat.

The main postwar issue was Ireland, where Lloyd George brought to a partial end the long-running problem of *Home Rule by giving independence in 1921 to the Irish Free State. The period also saw the honours scandal, in which he was accused of selling peerages, baronetcies and knighthoods; his doing so was partly an attempt to form his own political fund, for the Liberal party machine remained in Asquith's control. Conservative discontent with the coalition came to a head at a famous meeting at the Carlton Club in 1922, and there was an easy Conservative victory in that year's election. Lloyd George never again held office, though in spite of past animosities he did succeed Asquith as leader of the much reduced Liberal party (1926–31). His wife died in 1941 and in 1943 he married Frances Stevenson, who had been his private secretary since 1913. There is a

memorial museum to him at Llanystumdwy, in Gwynedd, where he had spent much of his boyhood and to which he returned in his last years.

Lloyds One of the 'big four' *clearing banks, founded in Birmingham in 1765 by a Unitarian button maker, John Taylor (1711–75), and a Quaker ironmaster, Sampson Lloyd (1699–1779). In 1771 the sons of the founders established a separate enterprise in London which was not absorbed into the older bank until 1884. The London company was then at a Lombard Street address which had been associated with banking since 1677 and was identified by the sign of a black horse – the beginning of the Lloyds link with this now widely featured animal.

Lloyds Abbey Life Group formed in 1988 when Abbey Life merged with several of the subsidiary businesses of *Lloyds Bank, including Black Horse Financial Services and Black Horse Agencies. Abbey Life was founded in 1961 to sell life insurance; it grew rapidly from 1963, when it pioneered unit-linked endowment policies. The combined operation was by the early 1990s among Britain's largest companies.

Lloyd's List One of the oldest newspapers in Britain, published by Lloyd's of London weekly from 1734, twice weekly from 1737 and daily since 1837. Originally a list of ships and their movements, it now covers all matters of interest to the insurance industry.

Lloyd's of London (London EC3) Unique insurance enterprise which has evolved from the transactions carried on in the 1680s between shipowners, merchants and insurers in the coffee house of Edward Lloyd (1648–1713). The risk is taken and the profit shared between a large number of members (known as 'names'), whose entire personal wealth is theoretically available to back up the risk accepted by the professional underwriters. In the early 1990s a series of bad years resulted in some heavy losses and much acrimony, but at other times members have been accustomed to receive a sizable annual bonus while their capital continues to earn interest elsewhere.

A famous feature of Lloyd's is the Lutine bell. The *Lutine* sank off Holland in 1799 carrying £200,000 of bullion insured with Lloyd's; in the 1850s the ship's bell and £25,000 were recovered from the sea bed. The bell used to be rung when any important news was received (one stroke for bad news, two for good). Since 1986 Lloyd's has occupied a spectacular new building by Richard *Rogers, in his hi-tech style with the tubes and conduits exposed (causing some to grumble that it was a bit much to start out in a coffee house and end up in a percolator). On the 11th floor Rogers incorporated a room by Robert Adam from *Bowood, which had already been in use as the Lloyd's council room in the previous building on the site.

Lloyd's Register of Shipping A published classification of ships according to their method of construction. The first *Register* was compiled by underwriters at Edward Lloyd's coffee house in 1760. The third edition (1775) introduced the rating of ships by a letter for the condition of the hull and a number for the standard of equipment; A1, which has entered the language as a general phrase for excellence, was therefore the highest grade. Although *Lloyd's Register* has always been closely linked with *Lloyd's of London, it is published by a separate organization.

Andrew **Lloyd Webber** (b. 1948, kt 1992) Britain's most successful composer of musicals, usually with several long-running shows on at the same time in the West End of London. His first success was *Joseph and the Amazing Technicolour Dreamcoat* (1968), followed by *Jesus Christ Superstar* (1970) and *Evita* (1976); all these had lyrics by Tim Rice. Subsequent and even greater hits have included *Cats* (1981) and *Phantom of the Opera* (1986). His production enterprise, the Really Useful Theatre Company, was named after James the Really Useful Engine, a bad-tempered colleague of *Thomas the Tank Engine; it included Prince Edward among its employees for two years from 1988. In 1992 Lloyd Webber saved from export an important Canaletto of a British scene (*The Old Horse Guards, London, from St James's Park*), buying it at auction for more than £10 million; he subsequently lent it to the Tate Gallery.

Llywernog Silver-Lead Mine see *Aberystwyth.

LMS see *railways.

LNER see *railways.

'loadsamoney!' The catch phrase of a character created in the mid-1980s by the comedian Harry Enfield (b. 1961), often seen on television in *Friday Night Live* (Channel 4). Enfield intended his noisy lout, waving wads of banknotes (he was a plasterer, much paid in cash), to be a satire of the big-money culture of the Thatcher years; but many viewed him more in a mood of celebration.

Local Education Authority see *LEA.

local government The four parts of the United Kingdom have slightly differing structures for their local authorities, in a framework established by the Local Government Acts of 1972 and 1973.

In England, outside the main cities, there is a three-tier system based on the ancient *counties, which are subdivided into *districts and then again into *parishes, separate councillors being elected for councils at each of the three levels. The seven main conurbations (six *metropolitan counties and *Greater London) have by contrast only a single tier of local government. This is the district council in the metropolitan counties and the *borough council in Greater London.

In Wales the three tiers are similar to England except that since 1974 the third level, below county and district, has been not the parish but the community.

The counties in Scotland were replaced in 1975 by nine *regions and three *islands areas. The regions have a two-tier system (regional councils and district councils), whereas the islands have only a single level, the islands council.

Northern Ireland retains its six ancient counties in name, but for local government purposes there is a single tier of smaller local authorities, variously called district and borough councils.

In almost all cases councillors are elected for a fixed term of four years. The terms run between different dates in different areas, and in some authorities only a proportion of the seats come up for election at one time. So there is no single day when the whole country is voting for local authorities, unlike the *general election for national government.

A Local Government Commission was appointed in 1992 to consider further reforms of the system. It is probable that the number of tiers of local government will be reduced, and possible that some of the more unpopular changes of the 1970s will be annulled – in particular the imposition at that time of new counties such as Avon. But one recent development seems unlikely to be reversed for a while. During the 1980s Conservative legislation progressively reduced the power and freedom of local authorities, first by introducing the capping of *local taxes and then by encouraging schools to *opt out (*education takes the largest part of local government expenditure). One result of this process is that in the early 1990s power is centralized in *Whitehall as perhaps never before.

local taxes For centuries, until 1989, local taxes were raised in Britain as rates. These were originally levied for specific purposes (the poor-rate, the church-rate), but in modern times householders were accustomed to paying a single annual sum known as 'the rates'. They paid relatively more or less according to a notional rental value of their property, based on the district and on the quality of the accommodation.

By the late 1970s the rates had become a main target for reform by the Conservative party, on two counts: that a few left-wing councils had been setting the tax at a very high level; and that the system took no account of the number of people paying the tax (the most often quoted example of an unfairly penalized rate-payer was a little old lady, widowed in a large house). The Conservative party conference of 1980 called for two measures: the imposing of limits by central government on local authority expenditure; and abolition of the rates as the method of funding *local government.

The result of the first was 'rate-capping', introduced in 1985, which gave the secretary of state for the environment the power to set an upper limit for the highest-spending councils. The second produced a succession of new taxes to replace the rates. The *poll tax, officially known as the community charge, was introduced in 1989 in Scotland and in 1990 elsewhere. It took no account of property or income, but charged each person equally (with a reduction for a few categories). Its profound unpopularity led to the introduction, from 1993, of the *council tax. Meanwhile capping, known as charge-capping during the years of the poll tax, remains in the mid-1990s one of the powers of central government.

Lochinvar The hero of a song which is part of *Marmion* (1808), a long narrative poem by Walter *Scott. Lord Lochinvar rides 'out of the west' to snatch from the bridal feast his beloved Ellen, who is about to be married to 'a laggard in love, and a dastard in war'.

Loch Ness Monster see Loch *Ness.

John **Locke** (1632–1704) Philosopher whose theories were a prelude to the 18C mood of enlightened optimism. His ideas on the nature of mind and knowledge were expressed in *An Essay concerning Human Understanding* (1690), an important text of English *empiricism. There appeared in the same year his main contribution to political theory, *Two Treatises of Government*. This was topical, in the aftermath of the *Revolution of 1688, in that it refuted the concept of the *divine right of kings; it also argued that the natural state of human existence is harmonious and that the purpose of government is only to safeguard the liberty and rights of the subject, thus making possible the proper functioning of society. This was in direct contrast to the theory put forward by Hobbes in *Leviathan* (1651) during the previous period of national upheaval. Hobbes's pessimism made strong rule essential; Locke's optimism argued for democracy and contained the seeds of liberalism.

Similar attitudes on religious matters are revealed in *The Reasonableness of Christianity* (1695) and in his three *Letters* (1689–92) on religious toleration – though he was sufficiently a man of his time to feel that tolerance should stop short of atheists and Roman Catholics.

Lockerbie Small town in Dumfries and Galloway, in southwest Scotland, of which the name is now associated with a major act of international terrorism. On 21 December 1988 a bomb exploded on Pan Am 103, a Boeing 747 which had recently taken off from Heathrow en route from Frankfurt to New York. The blast shattered the plane in mid-air, killing all 259 people on board and strewing wreckage over a distance of 130km/80m. The major sections of the plane and most of the dead fell on Lockerbie, killing a further 11 people on the ground. Two years of detective work ended by implicating Libya – with the motive assumed to be revenge for the US bombing of Tripoli in 1986. In February 1992 the USA and Britain named two Libyan security agents as the men who had planted the bomb – Al-Amin Khalifa Fhimah and Abdel Baset Ali Mohammed al-Megrahi. Britain demanded their extradition for trial in the UK, the country in whose airspace the murders occurred. Libya offered to let them stand trial in Libya or in a neutral third country. By the end of 1992 the issue was not yet resolved.

Lucy **Lockit** see The *Beggar's Opera.

David **Lodge** (b. 1935) Academic literary critic and novelist, best known for books deriving comedy both from fashionable intellectual trends and from the everyday social life of universities. *Changing Places* (1975) portrays the mutual culture shock when Philip Swallow, lecturer at Britain's Rummidge University, has a year's exchange with the brash Morris Zapp of Euphoria State University in the USA; the pair reappear on the circuit of academic conferences in *Small World* (1984). Several of Lodge's other novels – including *The British Museum is Falling Down* (1965) and *How Far Can You Go?* (1980) – chart the moral dilemmas of Roman Catholics in Britain, caught between the permissive society and the unpermissive Vatican.

Hugh **Lofting** see Dr *Dolittle.

logarithms see John *Napier.

Christopher **Logue** (b. 1926) Poet and author of wide-ranging output, including at one extreme the fortnightly 'True Stories' column in *Private Eye* (continuously for more than three decades, from the magazine's launch in 1961). Adept at short witty poems and songs, he is also known for an ambitious undertaking – a version of Homer's *Iliad* which is being published in parts (Books 16–19, *War Music* 1981; Books 1–2, *Kings* 1991).

Lollards The followers of the heretical ideas of John *Wycliffe (*c.*1330–84). In the early years there were many prominent Lollards, most notably Sir John Oldcastle, but after his execution in 1417 the movement went underground. It survived, particularly among skilled craftsmen, and surfaced again to contribute to the *Reformation. The name derived from a Dutch word for 'mumblers', used of heretics and relating probably to the mumbling of prayers.

lollipop lady or **man** A person who helps groups of schoolchildren across pedestrian crossings, bringing the traffic to a halt by raising a round sign on a pole, similar in shape to the sweet on a stick which is a lollipop.

Lombard Street (London EC3) The centre of banking in the *City of London since the 12c, when moneylenders from Lombardy in north Italy began to supplant the *Jews in this role.

Loch **Lomond** Lake in the Strathclyde region of Scotland, the largest in mainland Britain. The dramatic scenery, with Ben Lomond (973m/3192ft) to the east and Ben Vorlich (942m/3092ft) to the west, has provided only part of the lake's romantic image. The rest derives from

The City of London's main pageant, the Lord Mayor's Show, passing the Royal Exchange (William Logsdail, 1888).

the traditional Scottish song about Loch Lomond, in which the singer remembers the times he spent there ('by yon bonnie banks and by yon bonnie braes') with the true love he will never meet again. The lyric provides no explanation, but it is said to be the lament of a Scotsman who has died in some faraway place; when he says that by taking the low road he will get to Scotland first, this supposedly relates to a popular belief that the souls of the dead travel home underground.

Londinium see *London.

London (6,803,000 in 1991) Capital of the *United Kingdom. The historic heart of the city has been *London Bridge, for London was the furthest point downstream at which a bridge could be built over the *Thames. The Romans made a strategic settlement here in the 1st century AD, calling the place *Londinium*.

The medieval city grew up around the first *St Paul's Cathedral, founded as early as the 7c. In the 11c London's importance was recognized when William the Conqueror built his powerful White Tower, the nucleus of the *Tower of London, just outside the city wall (London became at this time the joint capital with *Winchester). Over the following centuries the wealth of the city guilds, known today as the *City Livery Companies, gave them increasing power. Their elected leader became the *Lord Mayor of London. The area of the original walled city is still known as the *City of London, as distinct from the rest of modern London.

London suffered a double disaster in the 1660s, the *Great Plague followed in the next year by the *Great Fire. As a result of the fire, little of medieval London survives. The rebuilt churches and the present St Paul's bear instead the mark of the great architect who supervised the reconstruction, Sir Christopher *Wren.

By the 18c the fashionable district was to the west, in the area now known as the *West End. The city had now spread so far as to include *Westminster and the old area of royal authority at *Whitehall. London's growth was further accelerated in the next century by the world's first *underground railway. The creation of the *London County Council in 1888 officially incorporated many ancient outlying villages which had been engulfed by the metropolis, and from 1965, under the *Greater London Council, the city was extended to an area about 48km/30m across. The Greater London Council was abolished in 1986, paradoxically leaving one of the largest cities in the world without any overall civic authority.

London has held the dominant position in British life, both politically and commercially, to a greater extent and over a longer period than is true of almost any other capital city. As a result it contains a high proportion of Britain's best-known landmarks, whether they be buildings (*Westminster Abbey, *Buckingham Palace, *Houses of Parliament, *Big Ben), shops (*Harrods, *Liberty's, *Fortnum and Mason, *Foyle's), hotels (*Ritz, *Savoy), streets and intersections (*Oxford Street, *Piccadilly Circus, *Shaftesbury Avenue, *Trafalgar Square), open spaces (*Hyde Park, *Regent's Park), districts (*Mayfair, *Soho, *Covent Garden) or institutions (*British Museum, *National Gallery, *Tate, *Madame Tussaud's). As so often it is Dr Johnson, a devoted inhabitant of the city, who provides the appropriate comment: 'When a man is tired of London, he is tired of life; for there is in London all that life can afford.'

Bishop of London One of the five *Lords Spiritual with a seat *ex officio* in the House of Lords. His cathedral is *St Paul's, dedicated when St Mellitus became the first bishop in 604. The bishop from 1981 to 1991 was Graham Leonard (b. 1921), a leading figure of the conservative wing of the Church of England. He was followed by David Hope (b. 1940). The Bishop of London signs with his Christian name followed by *Londin*.

London Bridge Crossing point over the Thames a few hundred yards upstream from the Tower of London. A wooden bridge was built here by the *Romans soon after AD 43. The first stone bridge was begun in 1176. Lasting for some 650 years, with tall, narrow houses built upon it, it became one of the most famous sights of London. It was replaced in 1831 by a bridge designed by John *Rennie, which in the 1960s was dismantled and reconstructed in Arizona as a tourist attraction. The present bridge was completed in 1972.

London Bridge is falling down Nursery rhyme relating not to any specific incident in the history of London but to the ancient and widespread game of a falling bridge – the upraised arms beneath which the children must pass, always with the fear that it is on them that the arms will descend.

London Contemporary Dance Theatre (LCDT) Britain's leading modern dance company, founded in 1967 by Robin Howard (1924–89) and Robert *Cohan. Howard was a passionate enthusiast for the work of the American pioneer of modern dance, Martha Graham, and Cohan had been one of her pupils. The two men also established a school (now the London Contemporary Dance School), from which most of the company's dancers are recruited. The LCDT tours widely, but both company and school have their base at the Place Theatre in London. Many of Britain's leading choreographers of contemporary dance developed their talents with the company – including Richard Alston (b. 1948), Siobhan Davies (b. 1950) and Robert North (b. 1945).

London County Council (LCC) The local authority which controlled London from 1889 to 1965, when it was replaced by the *Greater London Council. It made its headquarters at *County Hall, and built the *Festival Hall as its contribution to the Festival of Britain. It introduced in the 1930 the policy of London's *Green Belt.

Londonderry The name of one of the *six counties and also of the second largest city (72,000 in 1991) of Northern Ireland. The city is a port and garrison town on the river Foyle just before it flows into Lough Foyle (a north coast inlet of the sea); it is believed to be where St Columba founded a monastery in 564. The town was known as Derry (and is still usually called this, particularly by Roman Catholics) until granted in 1611 to the City of London, with the intention that it should be settled with English Protestants. This was carried out so successfully that in 1689 the inhabitants withstood a siege of 105 days, from April to August, by the army of the Roman Catholic *James II. The raising of the siege is commemorated each year on August 12, with much *Unionist triumphalism, in the Apprentice Boys' March; and the apprentices are celebrated because on 7 December 1688, four months before the start of the siege, they had forcefully indicated Londonderry's Protestant loyalty by closing the town gates in the face of James II's deputy in Ireland, the earl of Tyrconnel.

The city walls are virtually intact, as built in the 17c by the newly arrived Londoners; Roaring Meg, a brass cannon of 1642 which played its part in the great siege, stands on them still at the Double Bastion. The Diamond is the central square of the old city within the walls, and near the 18c arch known as Bishop's Gate is the Protestant cathedral, St Columb's (17–19c). The Roman Catholic cathedral, St Eugene's (19c), is outside the walls to the north of Bogside.

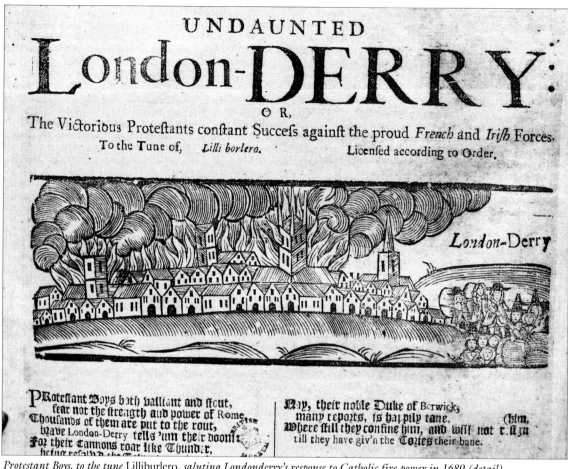

UNDAUNTED London-DERRY:

OR,

The Victorious Proteftants conftant Succefs againft the proud *French* and *Irish* Forces.

To the Tune of, *Lilli borlera.* Licenfed according to Order.

London-Derry

PRoteftant Boys both valliant and ftout,
fear not the ftrength and power of Rome,
Thoufands of them are put to the rout,
brave London-Derry tells 'um their doom:
For their Cannons roar like Thunder,
being refolv'd...

Nay, their noble Duke of Berwick,
many reports, is happily tane,
Where ftill they confine him, and will not r.ign (him,
till they have giv'n the Tories their bane.

Protestant Boys, to the tune Lilliburlero, *saluting Londonderry's response to Catholic fire power in 1689 (detail).*

Londonderry Air Folk tune from northern Ireland, published in a collection of 1855. An arrangement based on it by Percy *Grainger is entitled *Irish Tune from County Derry* (1927).

London Festival Ballet see *English National Ballet.

London Gazette The government's bulletin, in which official announcements are made. It was founded in 1665 (being known as the *Oxford Gazette* for the first 23 numbers) and it appears now four times a week. Scotland has its own equivalent in the *Edinburgh Gazette*.

London Library (London SW1) Britain's largest and most distinguished private library, open to anyone on payment of a subscription. It was launched in 1840, with Thomas Carlyle as the most energetic of its founders. Since then the library has bought all books of any significance published in English (other than specialist works in science and law), together with many in foreign languages, to form a working collection of well over a million volumes.

London Palladium (London W1) Theatre which was opened in 1910, with a lavish interior by Frank Matcham (1854–1920) and the novelty of box-to-box telephones. It was intended for *music hall and variety and has remained London's main theatre for such entertainment – topping the bill at the Palladium being a yardstick of success. *Sunday Night at the London Palladium* (ATV 1955–65) was an extremely popular television show, consisting of an hour of variety transmitted live each week. Tommy Trinder and Bruce Forsyth were the best known

of the comperes. The show was revived for a while in the 1970s but with rather less success.

London Philharmonic Orchestra founded with his own funds by *Beecham in 1932 (it is said in a fit of pique that the direction of the new BBC Symphony Orchestra had been given to Adrian Boult). Beecham's ownership of the orchestra ended with a financial crisis in 1939, after which it became a players' cooperative. In 1950 the musicians invited Boult to become principal conductor (1951–7), and others of great distinction in that role have been John Pritchard (1961–6), Bernard Haitink (1967–79) and Georg Solti (1979–83). In the early 1990s the London Philharmonic was selected as the first resident orchestra at the Festival Hall, taking effect from the 1992–3 season. The principal conductor since 1990 has been Franz Welser-Möst.

London Review of Books Fortnightly literary periodical, launched in 1979 when the year-long strike at the *Times* had also put out of circulation the *Times Literary Supplement*. Based on the concept of the *New York Review of Books* (and for the first issues distributed with the New York paper), the London version soon became independent and was strong enough to survive the return of the TLS.

London School of Economics and Political Science (LSE) Britain's first college in the political sciences, part of *London University. It was established in 1895 after a member of the *Fabian Society, Henry Hunt Hutchinson, left money in his will with the instruction that Sidney *Webb and others should use it for socially progressive purposes. The LSE, which occupies several cramped buildings close to the Aldwych, put in a strong but unsuccessful claim in 1992 for grander premises in *County Hall.

London Symphonies The last 12 symphonies of Joseph Haydn, commissioned by Johann Peter Salomon (1745–1815) and first performed in London. Salomon, a German-born violinist, settled in London in 1781 and soon became the capital's leading musical impresario. He travelled to Vienna in 1790 to persuade Haydn to make the journey to London. The composer made two visits, in 1791–2 and 1794–5, and was fêted in Britain as never before. The symphonies are also known as the Salomon Symphonies, the term London Symphony sometimes being reserved, for no very good reason, for the last of the 12 (no. 104).

London Symphony Orchestra (LSO) Founded in 1904 by four brass players from Henry *Wood's orchestra, indignant at the threat to their pockets from his stopping the practice of musicians sending a deputy when more profitable work was offered elsewhere. The orchestra was therefore self-governing from the start (it had a lucky escape on its pioneering 1912 tour of the USA – the original travel plans had included a crossing on the maiden voyage of the *Titanic*). The LSO was the first British orchestra to record the music for a film (Bliss's score for *Things to Come* in 1936), and more recent sound tracks have included *Star Wars*, *Superman* and *Close Encounters of the Third Kind*; the orchestra has also made more of an impact on the popular market than most, with a series of successful albums under the title *Classic Rock*. In 1982 the LSO became the resident orchestra at London's Barbican Hall. Recent principal conductors have been André Previn (1968–79), Claudio Abbado (1979–87) and, since 1988, Michael Tilson Thomas.

'London, thou are the flower of cities all' see William *Dunbar.

London Transport (LT) Body set up in 1969 to run London's *underground and bus services on behalf of the *Greater London Council. In 1984, a year before the abolition of the GLC, the services were transferred to London Regional Transport, answerable to the secretary of state for transport, though the name in everyday use remains London Transport. The monopoly of public transport in central London dates back to 1933 when the London Passenger Transport Board was established with power to take over all bus, tram, trolleybus and underground railway services. The monopoly is due to end in the mid-1990s, with the deregulation of central London bus routes.

The original underground companies, of which the Metropolitan Railway was the first in 1863, formed themselves in 1902 into a single operation, the Underground Group. It was this group which in 1927 commissioned the famous building above St James's Park station which is now LT's headquarters. Designed by Charles Holden (1875–1960) and his partners, it was the tallest office building in London at the time; sculptures were carved on location on its exterior walls by leading artists, including Jacob Epstein, Eric Gill and Henry Moore.

London buses have a history dating back to a horse-drawn service between Paddington and the Bank in 1829. In 1855 a French concern, trading in Britain as the London General Omnibus Company, began buying up the small individual bus firms; it adopted, in 1905, the wheel-and-bar symbol which is now widely known as London Transport's logo. The last horse-drawn bus retired in 1914. Its motorized *double-decker successor

later became one of the characteristic sights of London's streets.

In 1980 LT's extensive collection of road and rail vehicles, posters and other memorabilia was opened as the London Transport Museum, housed in a Victorian flower market in Covent Garden. Veterans of London Transport play a time-honoured role on Remembrance Sunday (see *Armistice), when they are the final group parading past the Cenotaph; their presence on the parade reflects not only their courage in keeping London's transport system moving throughout the *Blitz, but also the extraordinary fact that in World War I employees of London Transport drove troops to the front in double-decker buses.

London University Central organization of a large number of semi-independent colleges in and around London. It was established in 1836 for the purposes of conducting examinations; by then *University College and *King's College were already in existence. Of the many others which now make up the university the best-known are the *Imperial College of Science and Technology and the *London School of Economics. The university's first offices were in Somerset House; from 1869 it was in the building which is now the Museum of Mankind; and in 1936 it moved to its present Senate House in Bloomsbury.

In 1992 the Imperial College of Science and Technology announced plans to secede from the university and become a fully independent institution, a course which it seemed other major colleges might also follow.

London Zoo The establishment in 1826 of the Zoological Society of London was largely the achievement of Stamford *Raffles, but he died before its gardens were established in 1828. The original small collection of animals in Regent's Park was soon supplemented by the

The rivalry of the many small omnibus companies in mid-19C London: cartoon in Town Talk, *1858.*

THE RIVAL OMNIBUS COMPANIES.

"None but the Brave deserve the *Fare.*"

arrival of the royal menagerie, previously housed at Windsor and the Tower of London. The many animals to have caught the public's fancy in the zoo's history have included the first Jumbo, a very large African elephant whose numerous admirers tried to prevent his being sold to the American showman Phineas T. Barnum in 1882; Chi-Chi, the giant panda whose intimate problems with An-An, her Soviet fiancé, fascinated the world's media in the 1960s; and Guy the gorilla, so popular with Londoners in the 1970s that a statue of him was put up in the zoo after his death.

Meanwhile the zoo had pioneered the world's first reptile house (1849), aquarium (1853) and insect house (1881). It was stylish in its commissioning of architects; Decimus Burton (1800–81) laid out the gardens and designed the original buildings; the hillside and rocks for the bears and goats (Mappin Terraces, 1913) were devised by the distinguished firm of Belcher and Joass; the modernist penguin pool of 1934 was by Tecton (in particular Berthold Lubetkin); and two striking buildings completed in 1965 were by Lord Snowdon (the aviary) and Hugh Casson (the elephant and rhino pavilion).

In the early 1990s the zoo was in serious financial difficulties with rising costs and falling attendance. In 1992, after facing the possibility of closure at the end of that season, it decided to concentrate its resources on the breeding of endangered species. Its country branch, more in keeping with modern notions of animal conservation, is at *Whipsnade.

The *Loneliness of the Long Distance Runner* (1959)
Volume of stories by Alan *Sillitoe. The title story is a monologue by a Borstal boy, Colin Smith, as he trains for a cross-country race against a public school team. His resentment against authority, and his unyielding determination not to comply with its wishes, lead to his gesture of defiance – the deliberate losing of the race. The story was filmed in 1962 by Tony Richardson with Tom Courtenay in the central role.

Richard **Long** (b. 1945) Sculptor, or 'land artist', whose large formal arrangements on gallery floors (grouping great shards of slate or boulders of chalk) make very striking compositions. His accounts of his own long-distance walks, in the form of annotated ordnance survey maps and printed lists, are also exhibited on art gallery walls; they seem to imply self-importance at least as much as reverence for the landscape.

longbow A form of bow, probably developed in Wales in the 12C, which gave a distinct advantage to English armies from the early 14C, as first seen at *Crécy. Its length, which was about the height of the archer, gave it greater strength and range than shorter bows (it also made possible a longer and more lethal arrow), while the simplicity of its action gave the skilled archer more speed and mobility than an enemy cranking the more penetrating crossbow. The best longbows were made of yew. A good archer could shoot six accurate arrows per minute (some might achieve double that rate) with a range of about 180m/200yd. The study of the longbow has been much advanced by the survival of 138 bows and more than 3500 arrows in the *Mary Rose*.

longevity see *life expectancy.

Henry **Longhurst** (1909–79) Golf journalist and broadcaster (and in his youth a successful amateur player), who became known to a wide audience as the pioneer of TV coverage of golf for the BBC.

Long John Silver see *Treasure Island*.

Long Kesh see the *Maze.

Longleat House (30km/19m S of Bath) The earliest and, in its exterior, one of the most satisfying of the great Elizabethan houses. It was built for John Thynne, with Robert *Smythson as master mason, and was completed

The camel house, well established within ten years of the opening of London Zoo: lithograph by George Scharf, 1835.

Longleat, with its Elizabethan mullioned windows, tall chimneys and roof pavilions (Jan Siberechts, c.1675).

in 1580. Only the Great Hall retains its Elizabethan appearance. The interiors of the state rooms were created for the 4th marquess of Bath, who in the 1870s attempted to turn his English Renaissance house into an Italian Renaissance palace. The park was landscaped by Capability *Brown, the lakes being formed from the stream which gave the house its name (the Long Leat). Britain's first *safari park was established here in 1966, when the lions of Longleat rapidly became a major tourist attraction.

Long Meg and her daughters (29km/18m SE of Carlisle) Stone circle near the village of Little Salkeld. Of about 60 original *standing stones, 27 are still upright. Long Meg, about 3.6m/12ft high, dominates the group from the southwest side. Little Meg is a nearby circle of 11 stones.

Long Melford (45km/28m W of Ipswich) A Suffolk town which grew rich from wool. Its name reflects its famous main street, some 3km/2m long. The 15c church of the Holy Trinity has excellent contemporary stained glass in the aisles and fine monuments in the Clopton Chantry. In the chancel there is an alabaster effigy to William Cordell (d. 1581), speaker of the House of Commons, who built the nearby turreted redbrick mansion, Melford Hall.

Long Parliament The parliament called by Charles I in November 1640, which can be said to have lasted either till 1653 or 1660. The king needed the MPs' support in raising funds (to pay for his recent unsuccessful campaign in Scotland) and in providing troops (to put down a rebellion in Ireland). But from the start the parliament proved uncooperative, impeaching the king's most prominent supporters, the earl of *Strafford and Archbishop *Laud. Charles took an aggressive line in return, with his attempt to arrest the *Five Members in

1642. Soon the two sides were in arms against each other in the *English Civil War.

The Long Parliament was much reduced in Pride's Purge of 1648, when Colonel Thomas Pride (on behalf of the army) expelled about 140 of the less radical members, leaving only some 60. These, sometimes known as the Rump Parliament, later voted for the trial and execution of the king and the declaration of the *Commonwealth. They were themselves ejected from the House of Commons in 1653 (see *'In the name of God, go!'). The Rump was recalled in 1659, followed by the expelled members of the Long Parliament in 1660. Their one remaining task was to legislate for their own disssolution. A new parliament was then assembled to prepare for the *Restoration.

Longstone lighthouse see Grace *Darling.

Lonrho Company founded in 1909 as the London and Rhodesian Mining and Land Company; the name was changed to Lonrho in 1963. From the 1970s Lonrho expanded under a colourful chief executive, Tiny Rowland, to become one of Britain's largest companies, with worldwide interests in manufacturing, agricultural and service industries (including even newspapers – the *Observer* was bought in 1981). But a collapse in the company's share price in 1992 meant that it dropped out of the FT-SE 100 index. From 1985 Rowland waged a bitter public vendetta against the Al-Fayed brothers over the manner in which they purchased *Harrods (defeating a bid from Lonrho, which had been delayed by the involvement of the Department of Trade and Industry).

Anita **Lonsbrough** (b. 1941) Swimmer with a spectacular breaststroke career in the years either side of 1960. Her many successes included three Commonwealth gold medals (110 yards 1962, 220 yards 1958 and 1962) and an Olympic gold medal for the 200 metres in 1960.

Gordon **Lonsdale** see *Portland spies.

Lonsdale Belt Trophy awarded to a boxer winning any British title bout, at any weight. The first was presented by the 5th earl of Lonsdale in 1909. Any boxer winning three title bouts within the same division retains the belt. Several have kept two belts, but only Henry Cooper has taken home three.

Look Back in Anger (1956) The play which more than any other became identified with the mood of the *angry young men and inaugurated a new wave in the British theatre. The first work by John *Osborne to be seen in London, it was the outstanding feature of the first season of the *English Stage Company. The play is fuelled by the high-octane rhetoric of Jimmy Porter (working-class university graduate, now manning a sweet stall) as he rails at his wife Alison (a colonel's daughter) and ridicules the posh Sunday papers and a string of other targets identified as middle-class.

Look Back in Anger was filmed in 1959 with Richard Burton playing the lead, and Osborne portrayed Jimmy Porter nearly 40 years on in his play *Déjà Vu* (1992).

Lord Title used by barons and in informal contexts by higher-ranking male members of the *peerage (with the exception of dukes).

Lord Advocate The equivalent in Scotland of the *attorney general in the rest of Britain, with the exception that he does not play as full a political role and is not necessarily an *MP.

Lord Chamberlain The official in charge of the royal household. Historically he has had another notorious role in British life, as the official censor of the theatre – a task which evolved from his responsibility to provide entertainments for the monarch. Until the Theatres Act of 1968 all play scripts had to be presented to the palace before being performed in public, and playwrights found themselves forced into compromises over phrases or incidents deemed unacceptable.

Lord Chancellor (in full Lord High Chancellor) The most historic of the surviving great offices of state. From the 12C he was the right-hand man of the monarch, charged with keeping the Great Seal (a metal matrix of an image of the sovereign, used for making an impression in wax for attachment to royal documents). Usually held in earlier times by clerics, the post has become exclusively the preserve of lawyers; Thomas Becket, Cardinal Wolsey and Thomas More are among past holders of the office. Today the lord chancellor is a member of the *cabinet, head of the judiciary and Speaker of the House of Lords – where, unlike his counterpart in the Commons, his chairmanship is largely formal. He sits on the *Woolsack, but can step aside from it to address the House; and he does not have the task of maintaining order during a debate, considered unnecessary in the upper chamber. Traditionally no Roman Catholic could be lord chancellor (seen as keeper of the conscience of the monarch, head of the Church of England), but this restriction was abolished in 1974.

Lord Chief Justice Second only to the *lord chancellor in the legal hierarchy. He is the chief judge of the Queen's Bench Division of the *High Court and presides over criminal cases in the *Court of Appeal. In 1992 Lord *Lane ended his term of office as lord chief justice and was succeeded by Lord *Taylor.

Lord Jim (1900) Novel by *Conrad about an idealistic young mate of a steamship, the *Patna*, who on an uncharacteristic impulse jumps into a lifeboat ahead of the passengers. Disgraced at the court of enquiry (though in the event no-one died), he withdraws to ever more remote places, ending up as agent at a trading post, Patusan, in an inaccessible part of Malaya. Here he wins the respect of the elderly chief, Doramin, and becomes known as Lord Jim. But he fails in an honourable attempt to avoid bloodshed, when the community is threatened by a marauding gang led by Gentleman Brown. Jim has pledged his life on the outcome and willingly allows himself to be shot by Doramin, who has lost his own son in the violence. Death for a failed ideal wipes out the earlier failure to live up to an ideal. Like *Heart of Darkness*, the story is related by Marlow – though he is here only a friend and observer.

Lord Lieutenant The representative of the sovereign in a *county, appointed until retirement at the age of 75. The office was introduced in the 16C, originally to take over the military duties of the *high sheriff; the lord lieutenant became chief executive and magistrate of the district and remained responsible for the *militia until 1871. The office is now largely ceremonial, mainly in connection with royal visits, but it does still involve the recommendation of local justices of the peace.

Court of the **Lord Lyon** (Edinburgh) The equivalent in Scotland of the *College of Arms for the rest of Britain. It is presided over by Lord Lyon King of Arms.

Lord Mayor Title granted to the mayors of the major cities (the equivalent in Scotland is Lord Provost). Historically the most important among them has been the Lord Mayor of London, where the list goes back to 1192 and includes Dick *Whittington. Although now largely a ceremonial office, the Lord Mayor of London is still head of the corporation which governs the *City of London.

Lord Mayor's Banquet Annual event in the *City of London, dating back to the Middle Ages. Taking place in the Guildhall on a Monday in November, two days after the new Lord Mayor has taken office, it is officially given in honour of his retiring predecessor. But the event has acquired national importance as an occasion on which the prime minister gives a major speech on the theme of Britain's international role and policy.

Lord Mayor's Show Annual procession on the second Saturday of November, with floats and entertainments, accompanying the new *Lord Mayor of London to St Paul's Cathedral and then to the Law Courts, where he is presented to the lord chief justice.

Lord of the Flies (1954) The first published novel by William *Golding, inspired by *Coral Island* but taking a more jaundiced modern view of what would actually happen in an isolated community of small boys. In this version the well-meaning efforts of Ralph and Peterkin (the

Lord Chancellors since 1945	
1945	Lord Jowitt
1951	Lord Simonds
1954	Lord Kilmuir
1962	Lord Dilhorne
1964	Lord Gardiner
1970	Lord Hailsham
1974	Lord Elwyn-Jones
1979	Lord Hailsham
1987	Lord Havers
1987	Lord Mackay

latter transformed into the fat boy and victim, Piggy) are powerless against the ferocious dictatorship of Jack when they are all stranded on an island after an air crash. The lord of the flies (a literal translation of the Hebrew name for the devil, Beelzebub) is here a fly-blown pig's head, turned by the boys into an object of worship.

Lord of the Isles see the *Hebrides.

*The **Lord of the Rings*** (1954–5) Sequel by *Tolkien to his children's book, The *Hobbit. It developed into an epic for adults occupying three volumes, *The Fellowship of the Ring, The Two Towers* and *The Return of the King*. The characters of the earlier book reappear, but the hobbit hero this time in the long fight against evil is Frodo. Set in Middle-Earth, a fantasy world imagined in astonishing detail (lengthy appendices explain its chronology, genealogy and etymology), the book rapidly became a cult, selling millions of copies in many languages.

Lord President of the Council The cabinet minister responsible for the *privy council, presiding at its rare formal meetings. The modern history of the office has been similar to that of the *lord privy seal; it was used in the mid-20C to bring into the cabinet a minister charged with a new and specific task, but in recent years it has gone to either the *leader of the House of Commons or the leader of the House of Lords. For holders of the office since 1983 see the *cabinet.

Lord Privy Seal A high office of state to which appointments are still made even though it no longer bears any specific responsibilities. It dates back to the 13C when the holder was in charge of the king's private seal (used in transacting royal business) and therefore had great power. In the mid-20C it was used as a cabinet appointment for a minister carrying out a specific and perhaps temporary task. More recently it has gone with the job of either *leader of the House of Lords or leader of the House of Commons. For holders of the office since 1983 see the *cabinet.

Lord Protector see *protector.

Lord Provost see *Lord Mayor.

Lord's (London NW8) The world's best-known *cricket ground, home of the *MCC and of *Middlesex County Cricket Club. It derives its name from Thomas Lord (1755–1832), on whose London pitch (now Dorset Square) the newly formed MCC played from 1787. Lord twice moved his precious turf before laying it in 1814 at the present ground in St John's Wood. Since 1884 a match in every English *Test series has been played at Lord's. The scoreboard in the middle of the Grand Stand is surmounted by a famous weathervane of Father Time.

House of Lords The upper chamber in *parliament, consisting of the *Lords Spiritual and Temporal. All hereditary members of the *peerage may, if they wish, take their seats (an anachronism which has provoked many proposals for reform), but the majority of those taking part in debates are *life peers. A gradual loss of power to the House of *Commons culminated in the Parliament Acts of 1911 and 1949. The first deprived the Lords of any powers over financial legislation; the second made it impossible for them to reject any legislation passed by the Commons, leaving only the power to delay (by not more than a few months) and to propose amendments. In spite of this the debates in the Lords and the amendments passed on controversial issues can have a considerable impact, as was several times demonstrated during the Thatcher years of the 1980s. The House of Lords is also Britain's highest court of appeal, with the *lord chancellor and the *law lords constituting the court.

Lord's Day Observance Society (Bromley, Kent) The leading pressure group against secular activities on Sundays. Founded in 1831 by Anglican clergy and laymen, it has fought an energetic rearguard action to protect people from being diverted on Sundays by visits to the zoo or trips on the Thames (two of its earliest campaigns), or in more recent times by the cinema (in the 1930s), by advertisements on television (the 1950s) or by Sunday cricket matches (the 1960s). A notable reverse, about which the society protested strongly, was the tendency (first observed in the 1950s) of the duke of Edinburgh to play polo on the Lord's Day. In the 1990s the society's long-running battle against *Sunday trading looks as though it will finally be lost.

*The **Lord's my Shepherd*** Now a favourite hymn in England, it was not in any Anglican hymn-book until 1965. Its popularity can be dated precisely to 1947, when it was included in the marriage service of Princess Elizabeth, the future Elizabeth II. Written for the Scottish Psalter of 1650, as a metrical version of Psalm 23, it had long been popular north of the border. It is sung now to the 19C tune known as *Crimond*.

Lords of Appeal see *Law Lords.

Lords Spiritual The 26 leading clergy of the *Church of England, who sit in the House of *Lords. They consist of the archbishops of Canterbury and of York; the bishops of London, Winchester and Durham; and the 21 senior bishops by order of election to a diocese. The other members of the *peerage are defined by contrast as the Lords Temporal.

Loretto One of Scotland's leading *public schools for boys, near Musselburgh on the Firth of Forth. It was founded in 1827 by a clergyman, the Rev. Thomas Langhorne (d. 1848). It is unusual in having its own junior school, on the other side of the river Esk. Since 1981 girls have been admitted to the senior school for the last two years, in the sixth form.

Lorna Doone (1869) Romantic novel by R.D. Blackmore (Richard Doddridge Blackmore, 1825–1900), set on Exmoor in the 17C and including historical events such as the rebellion of *Monmouth and the assizes of Judge *Jeffreys. The evil Doone clan have murdered the father of young John Ridd. He eventually destroys them, rescuing his beloved Lorna who turns out to be the kidnapped daughter of a noble family. In this violent world she is shot at the altar even as he marries her, but she recovers to live happily ever after.

Joe Loss (1909–90) Violinist and bandleader who established his first band in 1932 at London's Astoria Ballroom. His first big hit was *Begin the Beguine* (1939) with Chick Henderson as singer; *In the Mood* (1940) became his signature tune. His band was a favourite choice for private parties given by the royal family at Buckingham Palace and Windsor Castle.

*The **Lost Chord*** One of the most popular of Victorian drawing-room songs, telling of a chord 'like the sound of a great Amen' which is accidentally played by an organist who can never again rediscover it. The poem, by Adelaide Ann Procter (1825–64), was set to music by Arthur *Sullivan in 1877, when he was mourning the death of his brother.

Ten varieties of convolvulus *and* ipomoea, *described by Mrs Loudon in her* Ladies' Flower Garden.

gay Lothario Term for a ladies' man, or seducer, which entered the language from the 'haughty, gallant, gay Lothario' in *The Fair Penitent*, a play of 1703 by Nicholas Rowe (1674–1718).

Lothian (population 726,000 in 1991, administrative centre Edinburgh) Since 1975 a *region of Scotland, formed from West Lothian, East Lothian and the greater part of Midlothian.

lottery In December 1992 the government published a National Lottery Bill, with the intention of having a lottery in operation by the autumn of 1994. The proposal is that a private operator should run the various games (from scratch cards for small prizes to weekly computerized draws for jackpots of up to £1 million), while overall responsibility rests with the director general of a new Office of the National Lottery. Britain had been the only country in the EC not to have a lottery, and the timing reflected the fact that tickets from other national lotteries could be sold in the UK from 1993 under the terms of the single market.

The proceeds of the lottery, forecast as up to £1bn after prizes and expenses have been paid, are to be distributed by an independent National Lottery Charities Board – with the funds divided equally between charities, the arts, sport, the national heritage and the Millennium Commission (the Commission's brief is to select major projects suitable for Britain's celebration of the year 2000).

Lotus Manufacturer of racing and sports cars, with an outstanding record in Formula One. It won the constructors' championship seven times (1963, 65, 68, 70, 72, 73, 78). By 1992 this score had been bettered only by Ferrari (with eight wins) and equalled by *McLaren.

The company was founded by Colin Chapman (1928–82), who from 1947 built and raced his own trial cars; the badge which appears on all Lotus cars is formed from his initials, ACBC (Anthony Colin Bruce Chapman). The first production sports cars were sold in 1957. They were the Lotus Elite and the Lotus Seven (produced in kit form, for assembly by the owner); the Lotus Elan followed in 1962 (driven in its first year by Emma Peel in *The *Avengers*). Meanwhile Lotus had begun its run of Formula One successes. The Monaco Grand Prix of 1960 was the first victory, with Stirling Moss at the wheel, but it was Jim *Clark who drove the cars to their first championship wins (both drivers' and constructors') in 1963 and 1965. The company's reputation under Chapman was later tarnished by its involvement in the De *Lorean scandal; details emerged only after Chapman's death, but a senior Lotus executive from that period was jailed in 1992 for his part in the fraud.

Lotus scored a notable triumph in a new field in 1992 with its LotusSport pursuit bicycle, a revolutionary monocoque design by Mike Burrows on which Chris *Boardman won a gold medal at the Barcelona Olympics.

Mr and Mrs Loudon (John Claudius, 1783–1843, m. 1830 Jane Webb, 1807–58) Horticultural authors who did much to promote Victorian interest in gardening. His most important work, which he published himself and which bankrupted him, was *Arboretum et Fruticetum Britannicum* (8 vols, 1838); and she was best known for *The Ladies' companion to the flower garden* (1841).

Love divine, all loves excelling see Charles *Wesley.

Richard **Lovelace** (1618–58) Cavalier soldier and poet, twice imprisoned for his support of the royalist cause. He is remembered in particular for two lyrics: *To Althea, From Prison* ('Stone walls do not a prison make/Nor iron bars a cage') and *To Lucasta, Going to the Wars* ('I could not love thee, Dear, so much,/Loved I not honour more').

Bernard **Lovell** (b. 1913, kt 1961) English astronomer, pioneer of radio astronomy and founder of *Jodrell Bank. Having done research on *radar during World War II, he acquired surplus radar equipment in 1945 and set it up on open ground at Jodrell Bank to study meteor showers. The immediate success of this new device, the radio telescope, led to increasing support for his researches. Anticipating the age of spacecraft, Lovell was ready with greatly improved equipment to track the first Russian sputnik in 1957 – an achievement which made both Jodrell Bank and Lovell himself household names.

Love on the Dole (1933) The first novel of Walter Greenwood (1903–74), using his own experience of unemployment in the Lancashire cotton industry as the basis for the fictional troubles of the Hardcastle family and their daughter Sally. It rapidly became established as the classic fictional account of working-class life in the Depression. It was dramatized in 1934 and filmed in 1941, with Deborah Kerr as Sally.

Love's Labours's Lost (*c*.1595) The most fantastical of *Shakespeare's comedies. The courtly lovers (the king of Navarre and the princess of France) engage in high-flown literary conceits; minor but more memorable characters include Armado (a ludicrous Spaniard) and Holofernes (a pedantic schoolmaster).

'love that dare not speak its name' Homosexual love, in a phrase coined by Lord Alfred Douglas (the lover of Oscar *Wilde) in the early 1890s in his poem *The Two Loves*.

David **Low** (1891–1963, kt 1962) New Zealand political cartoonist who worked from 1919 in England. His cartoons have a powerful clarity both of line and concept. The majority appeared in the *Evening Standard* (1927–50), where his most enduring characterizations were Colonel *Blimp and the carthorse symbolizing the *TUC.

Low Church see the *Church of England.

John **Lowe** see *darts.

Lowlands In common usage that part of Scotland which is not the *Highlands, applying to the entire southern region – drained by the rivers Clyde, Forth and Tay – in which by far the greater part of the population lives. The English dialect of this region, known as *Lallans, has provided the idiom of much Scottish poetry.

L.S. **Lowry** (Laurence Stephen Lowry, 1887–1976) Painter who depicted the industrial northwest as a bleak urban landscape in which tiny stick-like figures go in a lonely and detached manner about their business. Born in Manchester, he often painted in the adjacent city of Salford, which now owns the main collection of his work (City Art Gallery). Until retirement he painted only in the evenings, having a full-time job in a property company and progressing in his career from rent collector to chief cashier.

Loyalists Those Protestants in *Northern Ireland whose politics are shaped by loyalty to the British crown. They have been known by this name since the beginning of the *Unionist cause in the late 19C. In recent decades the term has been tainted by an association with *terrorism, since Protestant groups perpetrating sectarian violence are now usually described as 'loyalist paramilitary' organizations.

loyal toast At formal banquets or dinners the loyal toast is given towards the end of the meal. People rise to their feet (except in the Royal Navy, where the tradition is to remain seated), and the toast is simply 'The Queen' or 'The King'. In Lancashire the toast is 'The Queen, Duke of Lancaster' (see *chancellor of the duchy of Lancaster), and there are similar variants in the Isle of Man and the Channel Islands. It is a convention that no-one shall smoke until after the loyal toast.

£.s.d. The British *currency until decimalization in 1971, being the initial letters of Latin words taken to be the equivalents of the pound, the shilling and the penny. £ is a fanciful L for *libra* (*librae* in the plural); s is for *solidus* (*solidi*); and d for *denarius* (*denarii*). Sums of money were until 1971 written in this triple form, £10 15s. 6d. representing 10 pounds, 15 shillings and 6 pence. A sum less than one pound was written 15/6 (15 shillings and 6 pence). There were 20 shillings to the pound and 12 pence to the shilling. A farthing (legal tender until the end of 1960) was a quarter of a penny.

LSE see *London School of Economics.

LSO see *London Symphony Orchestra.

LT see Order of the *Thistle.

Ltd see *limited liability.

Lord **Lucan** Peer who vanished in 1974 after Sandra Rivett, his children's nanny, had been murdered. At the inquest into her death it was concluded that she had been killed by Lucan, who mistook her for his wife. His own disappearance has never been solved, nor has his body been found, but it has been suggested that he drowned himself at sea.

Luck of Edenhall (Victoria and Albert Museum) A glass drinking vessel, in shape like a tumbler with a flared top, decorated with Islamic patterns in coloured enamel. Made in Syria in the 13C, it is believed to have been brought back by a crusader. It was owned by the Musgrave family of Edenhall in Cumbria, and its name derives from a legend that it·was entrusted to them by a fairy king who warned that the luck of Edenhall would end if the glass ever broke. It has been in the V&A since 1958.

Lucky Jim (1954) First novel by Kingsley *Amis, chronicling the mishaps of Jim Dixon, a young English lecturer in a provincial university (Amis was then teaching English at Swansea). Its brilliant scenes of farce ensured the novel's success, while Jim's irreverence and deflation of pomposity caused both him and his creator to be classed as *angry young men.

Luddites Rioters who in the early 19C smashed the textile machines which they saw as a threat to their livelihood; they struck at night and were usually masked. The attacks began in Nottingham in 1811 and soon spread. The leader or leaders preserved anonymity by using the name King Ludd. The origin of the name is unknown, but an unsubstantiated account in 1847 traced it back to a simpleton, Ned Lud, who was supposed to have smashed two machines in Leicestershire in about 1779. Hangings and transportation seemed to have brought the movement to an end in 1813, but there was another outbreak in 1816.

The Luck of Edenhall: an outstanding example of medieval enamelled glass, probably made c.1250 at Aleppo in Syria.

Ludlow (7000 in 1981) Hillside town in Shropshire notable for its profusion of excellent houses of the 16–18C, many of them in Broad Street. The Feathers Hotel, in the Bull Ring, is outstanding among the half-timber buildings. The castle, one of the great fortresses of the *Marches but a ruin since the 18C, was begun in the late 11C to hold down the recently conquered Welsh. In 1634 Milton's *Comus*, a pastoral entertainment with music, was performed in the castle to welcome a new president of Wales and the Marches.

Lullingstone Roman Villa (23km/14m W of Rochester) Excavations at the villa (3–4C) have revealed a fine mosaic floor and a room with Christian symbols, in effect a chapel, one of the earliest pieces of evidence of the presence of *Christians in Britain.

Lunar Society see *Birmingham.

lunch see *dinner.

Lundy Rocky island, 5km/3m long, lying 19km/12m off the north coast of Devon. It was originally a pirate island, but the 13C castle was built for Henry III; there are 19C houses, cottages, lighthouses and a church. Owned by the National Trust since 1969, it is administered by the *Landmark Trust. *Lunde* is the Old Norse word for a puffin, and puffins still breed on the island.

Lusitania Launched by *Cunard in 1906 as a sister ship to the **Mauretania*. Her fame derives from her tragic end. On 7 May 1915 she was on a regular passenger run from New York to Liverpool (but was also carrying munitions). She was only a few miles off the southern coast of Ireland when hit by a torpedo from a German U-boat; 1198 people were drowned, including 128 US citizens. The disaster was one of the factors influencing the gradual American move away from neutrality in *World War I.

Lutine bell see *Lloyd's of London.

Luton Hoo (16km/10m N of St Albans) House designed by Robert *Adam 1767–74, much altered by *Smirke from about 1815 (adding the *Greek Revival portico), and devastated by fire in 1843. Its present appearance is largely the result of rebuilding in 1903–7 for Julius Wernher (1850–1912), a South African diamond and gold magnate whose magnificent collection of paintings and decorative art can be seen in the house today. The park is by Capability *Brown.

Edwin **Lutyens** (1869–1944, kt 1918) The leading British architect of the early 20C. An important early influence was his friendship with Gertrude *Jekyll, for whom he built Munstead Wood near Godalming in 1896. At that time he was working in a version of English medieval domestic architecture, deriving from the Red House by Philip Webb for William *Morris. He later used a variety of styles for a wide range of commissions. These included New *Delhi and the *Cenotaph in Whitehall. A minor masterpiece is *Queen Mary's Dolls' House.

Elizabeth **Lutyens** (1906–83) One of the most 'modern' British composers of her generation, and one of the first to use the 12-note system. She was also a prolific composer of scores for radio and film. She was a daughter of Edwin *Lutyens.

LVO see *orders of chivalry.

Lycidas (1638) Poem by *Milton, prompted by the death of a fellow student at Cambridge, Edward King, in a shipwreck of 1637 in the Irish Sea. It was printed in a volume of poems in the young man's memory. Written in a formal pastoral convention, it is nevertheless a very personal meditation on mortality – perhaps Milton's own more forcefully than Edward King's, who had been an acquaintance rather than a close friend.

Lydford Gorge (48km/30m N of Plymouth) Deep wooded ravine of the river Lyd, stretching 2km/1.5m to the White Lady waterfall and including a turmoil of water in the Devil's Cauldron.

Lydia Languish see The *Rivals.

Charles **Lyell** (1797–1875, kt 1848) Geologist whose *Principles of Geology* (1830–3) became the classic 19C textbook on the subject, establishing as orthodox the 'uniformitarian' theory first put forward by James *Hutton. He was prominent among the scientists who identified the epochs of the Tertiary period (70–10 million years ago) in terms of the surviving species which were then alive; and it was he who coined the names in use today (Eocene, Miocene, Pliocene).

Sandy **Lyle** (b. 1958) Scottish golfer who won the Open in 1985 and went on to become, in 1988, the first British player ever to win the US Masters.

Lyme Regis (5000 in 1981) Fishing town and resort in Dorset, fashionable from the 18C and known in particular for the Cobb, an ancient stone breakwater curving far out into the sea (it features in *Persuasion*). The cliffs between here and neighbouring Charmouth became a favourite hunting ground for palaeontologists after a 12-year-old local child, Mary Anning (1799–1847), discovered a 6.4m/21ft fossil of an ichthyosaur (now in London's Natural History Museum). The addition of Regis (Latin for 'of the king') was granted in 1285 by Edward I.

Lymeswold An invented blue creamy cheese, with a mock-rustic English name, which was launched in 1982 with a fanfare of publicity by Dairy Crest, a subsidiary of the Milk Marketing Board. Produced at Aston in Cheshire, and intended to compete with similar continental cheeses, it had a few years of success before demand collapsed. Production ceased in 1992.

Vera **Lynn** (b. 1917, DBE 1975) By far the most popular British singer of World War II, known as 'the Forces'

The geologist's hunting ground: rocks by the sea (vignette in Lyell's Principles of Geology, *1830).*

The popular 19c craze for fossils and geology, at Lyme Regis and elsewhere, satirized in an etching of 1855.

sweetheart', with hits such as *We'll Meet Again* and *White Cliffs of Dover*. After the war *Auf Wiederseh'n* reached the top of the American charts and eventually sold more than 12 million copies worldwide.

Lyonesse Mythical submerged land between Cornwall and the Scilly Isles. As legends go, this one is recent. To an old and not improbable tradition that Cornwall and the Scillies were once joined, there was added in the 16c the concept of Lyonesse as a lost kingdom. The name, that of the supposed birthplace of *Tristan, had featured in Malory's *Morte d'Arthur*.

Lyon King of Arms see Court of the *Lord Lyon.

Lyons' teashops Familiar feature in English towns in the early 20c. The first teashop was opened in 1894 in London, at 213 Piccadilly, by the Salmon and Gluckstein families, who had previously been retail tobacconists. A friend, Joseph Lyons (1855–1917), became the first chairman of their new company and gave it his name as J. Lyons and Co. (now part of *Allied-Lyons). The formula of light refreshments in pleasant surroundings with fast and friendly service (by waitresses known as 'Nippies') led to a chain of more than 200 teashops round the country by the 1930s. Meanwhile, in 1907, Lyons had moved into the restaurant business with their first Corner House in London's Coventry Street. Each Corner House offered

catering on a vast scale, with several restaurants in the same building. Coventry Street in its heyday could seat 4500 customers.

Lyrical Ballads (1798) Joint volume of poems by *Coleridge and *Wordsworth which was a milestone in the *Romantic movement. It was a reaction against the artificiality of 18c verse and an attempt to use the language of everyday conversation for poetry. Coleridge applied this principle to 'supernatural or at least romantic' subjects, while Wordsworth's aim was to find poetic appeal in familiar things. The two best-known works published in the collection, The *Ancient Mariner and *Tintern Abbey, reflect this difference. A second edition in 1801 included many new poems by Wordsworth, together with a preface in which he expounded his theories of natural diction and of poetry as 'emotion recollected in tranquillity'.

Humphrey **Lyttelton** (b. 1921) Jazz player and author who grew up at Eton, where his father was a housemaster. He composes many of the pieces performed by his own band, which he formed in 1948 and in which he plays the trumpet. *I play as I please* (1954, illustrated by himself) was the first of several volumes of autobiography. Since 1950 he has presented numerous programmes of jazz records on radio, and in recent years has been the chairman of the Radio 4 comedy series *I'm Sorry I Haven't a Clue*.

M

M0–M5 see *money supply.

M1 air crash On 8 January 1989 a Boeing 737, on a British Midland flight from London to Belfast, crashed on the M1 motorway near Kegworth in Leicestershire, killing 47 of those on board. It transpired that one of the two engines had been malfunctioning and that the pilots had in error shut down the other. There was subsequent criticism not only of their action but of the layout of the instruments on the cockpit panel.

M50 murder Marie Wilks, 22 years old and seven months pregnant, was abducted and murdered in 1988 as she telephoned for assistance after her car broke down on the M50 in Hereford and Worcester. The man convicted of the crime, Edward Browning, went on hunger strike in 1991 to protest his innocence. Late in 1992 his case was referred to the Court of Appeal and was scheduled for a hearing in 1993.

M62 coach bomb IRA terrorist atrocity in February 1974, when a bomb exploded on a coach carrying British soldiers and their families from Manchester to Catterick on the M62 motorway. Nine soldiers, a woman and two children died, and many were injured. Judith *Ward was jailed for the crime in November 1974 and had her sentence quashed in 1992.

Maastricht City in the Netherlands where the leaders of the 12 *EC countries signed in February 1992 a treaty intended to speed up the process of European integration. It included specific plans to move towards a single currency (by 1999 at the latest), to establish a common citizenship and to implement a common foreign and security policy. Britain secured the right to differ from the other 11 in not assenting to the 1989 Social Charter – a policy on employment conditions to which the Conservative party is opposed – and also insisted on the freedom to opt out when the time comes for a single currency.

The treaty had to be ratified by each nation, and its future looked uncertain after the Danish people rejected it (by a tiny margin of about 1%) in a referendum in June 1992; a French referendum approved it, equally narrowly, in September; and in Britain the first stage of legislation on the treaty was carried by only three votes in the House of Commons in November. At a European summit in Edinburgh in December compromises were reached which, it was hoped, would enable the ratification of the treaty to proceed more smoothly during 1993. Labour party opposition to the British government's position centred on the Social Charter (an issue also described as the Social Chapter, in reference to the relevant chapter of the Maastricht treaty).

*The **Mabinogion*** A collection of 11 tales on legendary and heroic subjects, written in Welsh in the 11–13c but based on earlier oral traditions. They all appear in the manuscript known as the Red Book of Hergest (*c*.1400, in Jesus College, Oxford) and several are in the earlier White Book of Rhydderch (*c*.1320, National Library of Wales). They were first published in an English translation (1838–49) by Lady Charlotte Guest (1812–95).

John **McAdam** (1756–1836) Engineer who invented a road surface, first put into general use in 1815 in the Bristol region, which proved much more durable than the alternatives. The principle of the 'macadamized' road was that the surface should be well drained and raised slightly above ground level. McAdam achieved this by laying graded stones, with the largest at the bottom. There were usually three layers, each compacted by the road being opened to carriage traffic for several weeks before the next was laid. The addition of tar later in the century provided the tar macadam road, and that in turn led to *'tarmac', a trade name for a related process.

Thomas **Macaulay** (1800–59, baron 1857) Historian who was from the start a precocious child (answering at four a kind enquiry after he had hurt himself with 'Thank you, madam, the agony is abated' and writing at eight a *Compendium of Universal History*). He won literary fame in his twenties with essays contributed to the quarterly *Edinburgh Review*. His *Lays of Ancient Rome* (1842) were immediately popular and *The History of England* (4 vols, 1849–55) sold as no book of history ever had before. Its narrative excitements compensated for its very narrow range compared to the broad claims of the title; intended originally to run from 1688 to 1830 (as an account of pre-Reform constitutional monarchy), it progressed no further than the end of the 17c.

Dave **McAuley** (b. 1961) Northern Irish boxer who won the IBF world flyweight title by defeating Duke McKenzie in 1989. He made seven successful defences of his title before losing it in June 1992 to Rudolfo Blanco.

Macbeth (d. 1057) King of Scotland from 1040, after killing *Duncan in battle near Elgin (rather than murdering him in bed, as in Shakespeare's play). He and Duncan were cousins, each with a roughly equal claim to the throne through their mothers. After a relatively peaceful reign of 17 years, Macbeth was in turn killed in battle by Duncan's son, *Malcolm III.

Macbeth (*c*.1606) Tragedy by *Shakespeare about *Macbeth, a historical figure of the 11c. Three witches, whom he encounters on a heath, prophesy that he will be king of Scotland. With this encouragement, and egged on by his ruthless wife, Lady Macbeth, he murders in his bed the present king, *Duncan, who is a guest in his castle. The moment of discovery of the deed is postponed by a comic scene in which the drunken Porter delays opening the castle gate with his repeated complaint of 'Knock, knock, knock'. The drama then becomes a crescendo of fear, as Macbeth kills anyone who might endanger his throne (Banquo, and the family of Macduff); and of guilt, which drives Lady Macbeth mad. In the sleepwalking scene she reveals her obsession with blood on her hands: 'Out, damned spot!'.

On a return visit to the witches (who stir their pot with the refrain 'Double, double toil and trouble/Fire burn; and, cauldron, bubble'), Macbeth is reassured by the promise that he will never be vanquished 'till Birnam Wood remove to Dunsinane'. The two places are 19km/11m apart near Perth, but Duncan's son Malcolm, advancing to attack Macbeth at Dunsinane, tells his men to pick branches from Birnam Wood and to march with them as camouflage. Before the battle, in which he dies, Macbeth is told of Lady Macbeth's death. His response, on the transience of human life, must be a record even for Shakespeare in its density of memorable and often quoted phrases:

> Tomorrow, and tomorrow, and tomorrow,
> Creeps in this petty pace from day to day,
> To the last syllable of recorded time;
> And all our yesterdays have lighted fools
> The way to dusty death. Out, out, brief candle!
> Life's but a walking shadow; a poor player,
> That struts and frets his life upon the stage,
> And then is heard no more: it is a tale
> Told by an idiot, full of sound and fury,
> Signifying nothing.

There is a long-standing theatrical superstition that *Macbeth* brings bad luck, even in the mention of the name, with the result that it has traditionally been referred to in the profession as 'the Scottish play'.

Willie John McBride (b. 1940) Northern Irish rugby union player, a powerful lock, with a record number of 17 caps for the *Lions (1962–74); combined with his 63 for Ireland (1962–75), this gave him the world's highest number of international rugby appearances until narrowly overtaken by Mike *Gibson in 1979. If a consecutive run of 53 of his matches are all accepted as full internationals, he equals in that respect the record of Gareth *Edwards for Wales.

Paul McCartney (b. 1942) After the break up of the *Beatles, McCartney formed Wings in 1971 – with his wife (Linda Eastman, whom he married in 1969), Denny Laine, Henry McCullough and Denny Seiwell. By far their most successful number commercially was *Mull of Kintyre* (1977), which was the biggest-selling single in the UK (2.5 million copies) until outdone by *Do They Know It's Christmas?* (Bob *Geldof and Band Aid, 1984). In 1991 his *Liverpool Oratorio*, co-written with Carl Davis, was performed by the Royal Liverpool Philharmonic; the piece was commissioned for the orchestra's 150th anniversary.

Liz McColgan (Liz Lynch, b. 1964, m. Peter McColgan 1987) Scottish long-distance runner who won the gold medal for the 10,000 metres at the 1986 Commonwealth Games and retained her title in 1990. Over the same distance she was the Olympic silver medallist in 1988 and won the gold medal in the 1991 World Championships. In 1991 she began to run marathons, winning the first that she entered (New York). In 1992 she set the world indoor 5000 metres record, with a time of 15:03.17.

Alec McCowen (b. 1925) Actor best known for his stage performances, and in particular for a solo *tour de force* in which he narrates the entire Gospel according to St Mark.

Donald McCullin (b. 1935) Photographer who has specialized in scenes of violence and destruction, particularly in war. London street gangs provided his first material, and Cyprus in 1964 was his first war. Whether in Vietnam or the Congo, Biafra or Cambodia, his lens sought out compelling images of horror; and his early career coincided with the heyday in Britain of the first Sunday colour supplements, eager to print such stark essays in photojournalism. McCullin was with the *Sunday Times* from 1965 to 1983.

Hugh MacDiarmid (pen name of Christopher Murray Grieve, 1892–1978) Scottish poet, much involved with Scottish nationalism and left-wing politics, who defined his duty as a poet as being not 'to lay a tit's egg, but to erupt like a volcano, emitting not only flame but a lot of rubbish'. In the 1920s he began to write in an artificially revived version of a Scots dialect (see *Lallans), looking for his model not to *Burns but much further back, to *Dunbar; he was particularly successful with this idiom in the long poem *A Drunk Man Looks at the Thistle* (1926). In 1928 he was a founder member of the *SNP, and in 1934 he joined the *Communist Party of Great Britain (his output at this period included two 'hymns to Lenin'). Expelled from the party in 1938 for 'national deviation', he demonstrated his cussedness by rejoining in 1957, a year after Russia's invasion of Hungary.

Flora Macdonald (1722–90) Scottish heroine famous for her part in the escape of Bonnie Prince Charlie (Charles Edward *Stuart) in 1746. She met him when he was in Benbecula, in the outer Hebrides, and she arranged for him to cross to greater safety in Skye as a member of her party; he was in female disguise and was described as Betty Burke, an Irish spinning maid. After the prince had

Macbeth with Banquo on the heath, where the three witches tell him he will be king: painting by Fuseli, 1793–4.

slipped through the English net, suspicion fell on Flora; she was brought to London and was briefly imprisoned in the Tower. She emigrated to North Carolina in 1774, but returned to Scotland in 1779.

Ramsay **MacDonald** (James Ramsay MacDonald, 1866–1937) The *Labour party's first prime minister, in 1924 and 1929–35. Born the illegitimate son of a farm servant in a Scottish *but and ben, he made an early name for himself in radical politics and was in 1900 the first secretary of the newly formed Labour Representation Committee (the original name of the party). He became MP for Leicester in 1906 and succeeded Keir *Hardie as leader in 1911. He was without a seat from 1918 (his pacifism had lost him much public sympathy in the war) but was elected for Aberavon in 1922. The election of 1923 returned 258 Conservatives, 191 Labour members and 159 Liberals, enabling MacDonald to become prime minister with Liberal support in January 1924.

The Conservatives recovered an overall majority later in 1924 (in an election influenced by the *Zinoviev letter), but in 1929 Labour was for the first time the largest party. MacDonald's new government had to grapple with the problems of the *Depression, and a financial crisis in 1931 caused him to offer his resignation to the king. Instead he was persuaded to stay on as head of a 'national' government, a coalition with the Conservatives and the Liberals. His own Labour party became the Opposition, headed now by Arthur Henderson (1863–1935). They lost nearly all their seats in the election later in 1931, a sequel for which many in the party never forgave MacDonald. In 1935 he resigned the premiership to another member of the national government, Stanley *Baldwin.

mace Of three maces used in *parliament, the best known is that of the *Speaker of the House of Commons. It dates from 1660, the mace used in earlier reigns having been destroyed during the *Commonwealth. At the head of the silver-gilt shaft is a crown with an orb and sceptre, for the mace symbolizes the royal authority delegated to the Speaker. The symbolic aura surrounding the mace was evident in the outrage provoked by Michael *Heseltine when, in 1976, he picked it up and brandished it in the chamber.

There are two maces in the House of *Lords because the lord chancellor fulfils two separate functions, one as Speaker and the other when presiding over the House in its judicial capacity (see *courts of law). Maces were originally offensive weapons – clubs with heavy spiked heads – and these ceremonial versions may have developed in the Middle Ages from weapons carried in procession by guards.

Ian **McEwan** (b. 1948) Author of short stories and novels, whose early work dealt with macabre subject matter in prose of a chilling elegance. In more recent books, from *The Child in Time* (1987) to *Black Dogs* (1992), the themes are still intensely dark but less overtly shocking – though a dismemberment scene in *The Innocent* (1990) provoked a degree of outrage.

Donald **McGill** (1875–1962) English cartoonist and the unrivalled master of the *seaside postcard. His brash colours and grossly curving human anatomies (a late descendant of similarly vulgar pleasures in *Rowlandson) combine perfectly with a suitably jolly level of sexual innuendo.

William **MacGonagall** (1830–1902) Dundee weaver who recited his own doggerel in public houses and who acquired wide posthumous fame after his verses (published by himself as *Poetic Gems* in 1890) were reissued in

the 1950s and ran through many impressions. They proved him a strong contender for the title of the world's worst published poet. The lines most often quoted in support of this claim are his response to the *Tay Bridge disaster of 1879:

Beautiful Railway Bridge of the Silv'ry Tay!
Alas, I am very sorry to say
That ninety lives have been taken away
On the last Sabbath day of 1879,
Which will be remember'd for a very long time.

John **MacGregor** (b. 1937) Conservative politician, MP for South Norfolk since 1974. He has had a wide range of posts since entering the *cabinet in 1985 – chief secretary to the Treasury (1985–7), minister of agriculture, fisheries and food (1987–9), secretary of state for education and science (1989–90), leader of the House of Commons (1990–2) and secretary of state for transport from 1992.

Barry **McGuigan** (b. 1961) Irish boxer who grew up in the border town of Clones, in Monaghan (becoming known as the Clones Cyclone). In 1982 he became a British citizen, and the following year defeated Vernon Penprase in Belfast for the British featherweight championship. Later the same year, again in Belfast, he took the European title from Valerio Nati. And in London in 1985 he won against Eusebio Pedroza to become WBA world champion – a title he held in two defences until losing it in 1986 to Steve Cruz in Las Vegas. He had been famous for his admiration of his Northern Irish manager, Barney Eastwood – 'Thank you Mr Eastwood' had been ridiculed as something of a catch phrase after each fight – but the two fell out over the finances of the Las Vegas fight, and engaged in prolonged and expensive litigation.

Macheath see *The *Beggar's Opera*.

Archie **McIndoe** (1900–60, kt 1947) Plastic surgeon, born in New Zealand, known for his magnificent work on airmen who were severely burned in World War II. His base was the tiny Queen Victoria Hospital at East Grinstead in Sussex, which he built up into a major centre for plastic surgery. His grateful patients formed a club, McIndoe's Guinea Pigs, which continued to meet annually after the war.

Lord **Mackay** (b. 1927, baron 1979) Scottish barrister who was appointed lord chancellor in 1987 (he had previously been lord advocate of Scotland, 1979–84). He has been sympathetic to the argument of *solicitors that they should be free to plead in the higher courts, but he clashed with the profession in 1992 over his proposed reform of *legal aid. An insight into Scottish puritanism was provided in a widely reported event of 1989 when Lord Mackay, a member of the Free Presbyterian Church of Scotland, was expelled for having attended a Roman Catholic requiem mass.

Ian **McKellen** (b. 1939, kt 1991) Actor with a wide repertoire in the theatre but known in particular as the leading Shakespearean performer of his generation; among his early successes were a pair of related performances, in 1968–9, as Shakespeare's Richard II and Marlowe's Edward II. He has worked relatively little in film or television. He is also a prominent campaigner for gay rights and in support of those suffering from Aids.

Compton **Mackenzie** (1883–1972, kt 1952) Prolific author in many fields, but known above all as a novelist. The semi-autobiographical *Sinister Street* (2 vols, 1913–14) was long popular as a racy account of the life of the affluent young at Oxford and in London. He is probably best known now for *Whisky Galore* (1947), inspired by a wartime incident when he was living on the Hebridean island of Barra.

Leo **McKern** see *Rumpole.

Charles **Mackerras** (b. 1925, kt 1979) Australian conductor, resident in Britain from the late 1940s. He has been much involved with the various opera companies (Sadler's Wells 1949-53, English National Opera 1970-7, Welsh National Opera 1987-92) and he introduced Janàcek to Britain – with *Katya Kabanova* at Sadler's Wells in 1951. He arranged Sullivan's music for the ballet *Pineapple Poll.*

mackintosh Now used for any raincoat, the word relates back to the waterproof fabric patented in 1823 by Charles Macintosh (1766-1843). This consisted of two layers of cloth cemented together with rubber dissolved in naphtha. It won immediate favour with passengers travelling on the outside of stage coaches. A raincoat similarly popular with passengers in early motorcars was the *Burberry.

Cameron **Mackintosh** (b. 1946) Impresario specializing in stage musicals, responsible for many of the best-known recent hits – including *Cats* (1981), *Les Misérables* (1985), *Phantom of the Opera* (1986) and *Miss Saigon* (1989).

Charles Rennie **Mackintosh** (1868-1928) Scottish architect and designer. After studying at the Glasgow School of Art he won in 1894 the competition for their new building, the first part of which opened in 1899 and brought him immediate fame. It is considered the earliest *Art Nouveau building in Britain. Meanwhile he had begun designing interiors and furniture for a series of Glasgow tea rooms (eventually four) owned by Miss Cranston. The angular and elongated chairs (the comfort of her patrons was not his first consideration) were in keeping with the furniture he designed for his own house, several rooms of which are now in the *Hunterian Museum; equally characteristic interiors survive in the *Hill House. In the quirkily refined and geometrical nature of his work, and in his muted colour schemes, he prefigured much in 20c design. He was invited to exhibit at the Secession show in Vienna in 1900.

McLaren The most successful British motor-racing team, sharing with *Lotus the British record of seven victories in the constructors' championship (1974, 84, 85, 88, 89, 90, 91) but outdoing Lotus by far in the number of Grand Prix races won; McLaren's tally was 99 by the end of the 1992 season. The company was founded by the New Zealand racing driver Bruce McLaren (1937-70), who died after a crash during testing at the Goodwood circuit. With nine victories in the drivers' championship, the team's greatest successes have been with Alain Prost (1985, 86, 89) and Ayrton Senna (1988, 90, 91); but one of its earliest wins was with James *Hunt in 1976. McLaren used Honda engines from 1988, and the two companies achieved an unprecedented run of four consecutive constructors' championships until defeated decisively by *Williams in 1992.

Alistair **MacLean** (1922-87) Scottish author of a string of bestselling thrillers, including *The Guns of Navarone* (1957) and *Where Eagles Dare* (1967). His publishers were fined in 1991 under the trading laws after MacLean's ideas for plots, unused by him at the time of his death, were turned into books by others but marketed under his name. The results became known in the book trade as MacLones.

Iain **Macleod** (1913-70) Conservative politician, MP for Enfield West from 1950, who was the first chancellor of the exchequer in Edward Heath's government of 1970, holding office for only a month before he died of a heart attack. An articulate member of the liberal wing of the party, Macleod speeded up the independence of the African colonies when he was colonial secretary (1959-61) under Macmillan, but in doing so he offended the right wing of his party and damaged his own leadership chances.

Harold **Macmillan** (1894-1986, earl of Stockton 1984) Conservative politician, MP for Stockton-on-Tees (1924-9, 1931-45) and for Bromley (1945-64), foreign secretary 1955, chancellor of the exchequer 1955-7, prime minister 1957-63. An outspoken opponent of *appeasement in the 1930s, he was given his first government post by Churchill in 1940, in the Ministry of Supply. In 1942 he was sent as minister to the Allied Mediterranean Command, and so for three years he was involved in the political side of the campaigns in Africa, Italy and Greece. It was a job in which he found himself dealing with two men who were to share the world stage with him in the late 1950s, Eisenhower and de Gaulle.

He was in the cabinet from 1951, when the Conservatives returned to power, and as chancellor he introduced *premium bonds in 1956. When Eden resigned after the *Suez crisis, Macmillan had overwhelming support in the party as his successor. His focus as premier was very much on foreign affairs. With two US presidents (Eisenhower an old friend and Kennedy a new one) he repaired the rift created by Suez and secured for Britain cooperation on issues of nuclear defence and a supply of Polaris missiles. Paradoxically his success with the USA jeopardized his efforts to get Britain into the European Economic Community (see *EC) – for it was one of the reasons why de Gaulle, who wanted a Europe free of transatlantic links, vetoed in 1963 Britain's application to join. In two major tours of the Commonwealth (1958 and 1960) Macmillan emphasized the need to abandon

The useful nickname acquired by Macmillan in his early years as prime minister: cartoon by Vicky, 1958.

colonial concepts, coining his best-known phrase when he told the South African Houses of Parliament in 1960 that 'the wind of change is blowing through this continent'.

After early successes at home as well as abroad (he acquired the nickname Supermac), his party was returned with an increased majority in 1959. The later years of his administration were clouded by economic troubles, the EC veto and the *Profumo scandal. But it was illness which caused him to resign in 1963. He took an active part in ensuring that he was followed by Lord *Home rather than Rab *Butler.

His manner, that of a bumbling Edwardian amateur, masked a ruthlessness which was evident in the *night of the long knives. It was also the vehicle for a sleepy-seeming but sharp wit which made him an excellent orator – a skill still evident in his extreme old age when, in a long and impromptu-seeming speech on the first day that the House of Lords was televised (Jan. 1985), he attacked Mrs Thatcher, the great privatizer, for not knowing the difference between capital and income. Many of his acquaintances, he said, had made the same mistake; the nicest of fellows, but they had mostly ended up in dreary lodging houses. (The 'family silver' speech was a different occasion – see *privatization.) However, the credit he is often given for his mock-populist phrase of 1957 ('most of our people have never had it so good') is undeserved; 'You never had it so good' was the election slogan of the Democrats in the USA five years earlier.

Another important strand in his life was publishing, for he was closely involved in the firm of Macmillan, established by his grandfather Daniel Macmillan (1813–57).

Kenneth **MacMillan** (1929–92, kt 1983) Britain's leading choreographer of the generation after Frederick Ashton, with an extraordinary range from the romanticism of *Romeo and Juliet (1965 or *Manon (1974) to the inner landscape of *Winter Dreams* (1991) and the sexual violence of *Mayerling (1978) or *The Judas Tree* (1992). He discovered in all of them new extensions of classical movement to express intense emotion or psychological unease. He formed a strong creative partnership with Lynn *Seymour, whom he first cast in *The Burrow* in 1958; she went with him to the Deutsche Oper in Berlin, where he was director of ballet from 1966 to 1969. In 1965 he created one of his most powerful works, (*Song of the Earth* to Mahler's music) at Stuttgart, where John *Cranko was director of the company. From 1970 to 1977 MacMillan was director of the Royal Ballet. He died of a heart attack, backstage at Covent Garden, during the first night of a triumphantly successful revival of *Mayerling*.

McNaughten Rules (sometimes spelt McNaghten or M'Naghten) The rules for the treatment of defendants who plead insanity. They derive from the case of Daniel McNaughten, tried in 1843 for murdering the prime minister's secretary whom he mistook for the prime minister. Suffering from delusions of persecution, he was acquitted as 'not guilty by reason of insanity'. The original statute defining the rules said that such persons must be detained in a hospital 'during Her Majesty's pleasure'. It was in effect a life sentence for murder, and the importance of this form of verdict was much reduced with the abolition of *capital punishment.

Louis **MacNeice** (1907–63) Northern Irish poet, linked with *Auden and *Spender in the 1930s though less political than them; his *Autumn Journal* (1939) is a personal poetic diary of the events up to and surrounding *Munich. He was an accomplished writer of radio documentaries and plays, notably *The Dark Tower* (published with other radio scripts under that title in 1947). His best-known single poem is probably *Bagpipe Music*.

William **Macready** (1793–1873) Actor who in his early years was the only rival to Edmund Kean. As manager at different times of both Covent Garden and Drury Lane he greatly improved standards, insisting on increased rehearsal time with the entire cast and not just the leading players, so that a production came together as a whole – something taken for granted now but unusual then.

Madame Tussaud's (London NW1) Waxworks museum which in recent years has regularly topped the charts among Britain's fee-paying tourist attractions. It derives from a museum established in Baker Street in 1835 by Madame Tussaud (Marie Grosholtz, 1761–1850, m. François Tussaud 1795). Her mother had been housekeeper to a modeller in wax; Marie studied with him as a child and helped him with his wax museum, which she inherited in 1794. She moved in aristocratic circles, as an art tutor at Versailles, and during the French Revolution she made a speciality of providing death masks from guillotined heads. She came to England in 1802 and toured her collection round the country until settling it in London in 1835. It moved to its present site in the Marylebone Road in 1884, where a second attraction – Britain's first planetarium – was opened in an adjoining building in 1958.

Newly famous figures in British life – politicians, pop stars, footballers – rapidly appear in wax at Madame Tussaud's, and the visit of the living person to view the meticulously detailed life-size replica is a well-established photo opportunity. There are also famous tableaux and permanent exhibitions, enlivened nowadays by elaborate lighting and sound effects. They include a scene on a gun deck of HMS *Victory* during the Battle of Trafalgar, and the perennial Chamber of Horrors – offering bloody glimpses of torture through the ages, with representations of a *bride in the bath or a victim of *Jack the Ripper.

'**Mad, bad, and dangerous to know**' see Lord *Byron.

mad cow disease see *BSE.

Maddermarket Theatre see *Norwich.

Mad Dogs and Englishmen see Noel *Coward.

Madeira White wine from Portugal's Atlantic island of Madeira, fortified with brandy for its travels. In 18–19c Britain it was as popular as the closely related *port. The madeira cake, of plain or lemon-flavoured sponge and served now with tea, was originally a favourite accompaniment to a glass of Madeira.

Mad Hatter see *Alice in Wonderland*.

Maes Howe (Mainland, *Orkneys) Huge prehistoric burial mound, the largest and best preserved of its kind in Europe. It has an 11m/36ft passage leading into a great central chamber which is surrounded by open tomb cells. Built some time before 1000 BC, it was looted in about AD 1150 by Norsemen who left runic inscriptions describing how they had removed the tomb's treasures over three nights. Nearby are remains of two great circles of prehistoric standing stones, the stones of Stenness (only four upright, plus the nearby isolated Watch Stone) and the Ring of Brodgar, with 27 of about 60 stones still standing.

Mafeking Garrison town founded in 1885 in the extreme north of Cape Colony in South Africa, as a base for administering a new protectorate (which became *Botswana). It was from here that the *Jameson Raid crossed into the Transvaal. The garrison, under the command of *Baden-Powell, was immediately besieged at the start of the

*Boer War. News of the relief of Mafeking (17 May 1900, after 217 days) was greeted in Britain with scenes of hysteria, and the event became the predominant popular memory of the war.

magistrates' court The lowest level of criminal court at which all minor (summary) offences are heard, and at which serious (indictable) offences are given their first hearing, before magistrates sitting without a jury (see *courts of law). In most cases the bench consists of two or more *JPs, but in the major cities these are sometimes replaced by a single professional (or stipendiary) magistrate. Magistrates can pass sentence on summary offences, but must commit the defendant to the *Crown Court on most indictable offences if they decide that there is sufficient evidence. The longest sentence of imprisonment which can be imposed by magistrates is 12 months. The equivalent in Scotland is the district court, where the JPs can impose no more than 60 days in prison.

Magna Carta (Latin for the Great Charter) The imminent danger of finding himself at war with his own rebellious barons persuaded King *John to fix his royal seal (on 15 June 1215 'in the meadow called *Runnymede between Windsor and Staines') to this charter, which limited his own power and which has been considered in English-speaking countries as the first touchstone of individual liberty.

The document attempted to lay down regulations for a feudal society, and much of it soon became outdated. By the same token the concessions of lasting importance were probably of minor interest to the king and his barons. Chief among these were clauses 39 and 40 (38 and 39 in later versions), which said that no free man would be imprisoned or punished without prior judgement by the law of the land; and that justice would not be denied, delayed or sold. This uncompromising statement of the supremacy of the law has given *Magna Carta* its lasting and almost magic status (also causing it to be thought of, incorrectly, as the origin of *habeas corpus).

Four copies of the 1215 *Magna Carta* survive (two in the cathedrals where they were first deposited, Lincoln and Salisbury, and two in the British Library), but the document was subsequently revised and reissued on several occasions. The version which became established in English law, being frequently reprinted in part or whole, is that issued by Henry III when he became of age in 1225.

St **Magnus** see *Kirkwall.

Magnus **Magnusson** see *Mastermind*.

Maguire Seven One of the cases which caused serious concern about the state of *criminal justice in Britain. It arose directly from another such case, that of the *Guildford Four. The arrest of Gerry Conlon in 1974, as a suspect in the IRA bombing of pubs at Guildford and Woolwich, caused police to search the home of his aunt, Anne Maguire. No explosives were discovered, but traces of nitroglycerine were said to have been found on the hands of her family and on plastic gloves. As a result the Maguires were charged with running an IRA bomb factory, and in 1976 the seven were jailed for between 4 and 14 years; they were Anne Maguire, her husband Patrick, her sons Vincent and Patrick (aged 15 and 13 at the time), her brother Sean Smyth, her brother-in-law Giuseppe Conlon (father of Gerry), and a family friend, Patrick O'Neill. Giuseppe Conlon died while still in prison. In 1991 his name was cleared posthumously, when his sentence was quashed along with those of the other six.

The case cast doubt on the use of *forensic evidence. Chemists at the Royal Armament Research and Development Establishment were shown to have been incompetent and possibly deceitful in their testimony to the court that the traces found on the Maguires' hands could only have been nitroglycerine.

The **Maiden** see *capital punishment.

Maiden Castle (4km/2.5m SW of Dorchester) Vast Iron Age fort, the most impressive in Britain. The hilltop site is believed to have been occupied first in about 2000 BC, but the fortification dates from *c*.300 BC. A series of terraced earth ramparts, rising to a height of about 25m/80ft and with a circumference of some 3.2km/2m, once enclosed a sizable town. Its store of ammunition, excavated in the 1930s, included 22,000 pebbles from Dorset beaches, suitable for shooting from slings. They were of little use against the armour of the Romans, who captured Maiden Castle in AD 43.

maiden speech The first speech of an *MP in the House of *Commons. By convention it is on a non-controversial topic (no longer always the case) and is listened to without interruption. The phrase is used by extension of first speeches in the House of *Lords and elsewhere.

Maid Marian Female character in the *May Day games and in *morris dances. *Robin Hood was later introduced into these, so Maid Marian became thought of as his sweetheart and was included in the Robin Hood stories.

maid of honour Small tart with an almond-flavoured curd filling, originally made only in Richmond, in Surrey, where there is an early 18C terrace called Maids of Honour

Maiden Castle, occupying a chalk ridge in Dorset: the ramparts were shaped in this form in about 300 BC.

Row. The terrace is named after its first inhabitants, the ladies-in-waiting to the princess of Wales, wife of the future George II.

Maid of Norway see *Margaret, the Maid of Norway.

Maidstone (72,000 in 1981) County town and administrative centre of Kent, on the river Medway. On the bank of the river is the 14–15c church of All Saints, in the Perpendicular style. Nearby stood the medieval palace of the archbishops of Canterbury, much adapted when it became a private house in the Elizabethan period; the surviving 14c stable block now houses a collection of horse-drawn carriages. The Museum and Art Gallery, founded in 1858 and occupying the mainly 16c Chillington Manor, has a broadly based collection of archaeology, decorative arts and painting.

*Daily **Mail*** Britain's first popular newspaper, launched by Alfred Harmsworth (later Lord *Northcliffe) in 1896. Selling for a halfpenny, it was the first paper to be described as *'tabloid'; and with immediate sales of nearly 400,000, the circulation was above a million by 1902. The *Mail* also engaged in promotional activities of a kind which have since become familiar, offering £1000 for the first cross-Channel flight (won by Blériot in 1909) and £10,000 for the same feat across the Atlantic (won by *Alcock and Brown). The *Mail*'s great rival in the middle of the market has been the *Express; in the early 1990s the *Mail* was ahead in circulation.

*The **Mail on Sunday*** Launched in 1982 as a sister paper to the *Daily Mail* and a rival to the *Sunday Express*. It recovered from a shaky start and ten years later had a circulation of more than 2 million.

Mainland see the *Orkneys and *Shetlands.

maintained school see *state schools.

John **Major** (b. 1943) Conservative politician who progressed with unprecedented speed through the high offices of state during the late 1980s, becoming prime minister in 1990 only three years after entering the *cabinet. His early life was both colourful and underprivileged. His father worked in vaudeville and circus, performing as clown, conjurer, singer and even trapeze artist, but by the time of Major's early childhood his attempts at business (including the manufacture of garden gnomes) had gone so badly that the family was living in poverty in Brixton, in south London. Major left school at 16 with just two O-levels, and began a career in banking; his main talent at the time seemed to be cricket, but any thought of a professional career was ended when a car crash in 1967 badly damaged a knee. In 1968 he won a seat on the Lambeth borough council, and in 1979 was elected MP for Huntingdonshire – the seat which he still holds (since 1983 it has been called Huntingdon).

He entered Mrs Thatcher's cabinet in 1987 as chief secretary to the Treasury; in 1989 he was briefly foreign secretary; and later in that year he became chancellor of the exchequer. A rapid succession of events in November 1990 brought him to 10 Downing Street. On November 1 Geoffrey *Howe resigned from the cabinet, following this on the 13th with a speech to the Commons which was a thinly veiled attack on Mrs Thatcher; on the 14th Michael *Heseltine challenged for the leadership; on the 20th Mrs Thatcher failed narrowly to win enough votes to avoid a second ballot; on the 22nd she said she would not be standing in the second round, whereupon Major and Douglas *Hurd entered the contest; on the 27th Major received 185 votes (to 131 for Heseltine and 56 for Hurd) and the other two withdrew, offering him their support.

Major enjoyed great popularity in his early months as prime minister (above all for seeming to care rather more than Mrs Thatcher about ordinary people), and he won the general election of April 1992 against the predictions of the opinion polls. But by the end of that year his premiership was in a trough where nothing seemed to go right: his determination to stay in the ERM (entered when he was chancellor, see *EMS) had been thwarted when pressure on sterling forced Britain out of the system and brought about an effective devaluation; his achievement at *Maastricht had led to profound divisions within the Conservative party; attempts to force immediate closure on a large number of mines (see *coal) were followed by a hasty climb-down and an impression of muddle; there was a rumbling crisis over arms sold to Iraq (see *Matrix Churchill); and the longest *recession since the war, falling entirely within his spell as chancellor and prime minister, showed little sign of ending. In January 1993 he served a libel writ on the *New Statesman and others for publishing unfounded rumours about his private life.

*Major **Barbara*** (1905) Play by George Bernard *Shaw which turns upside down easy preconceptions about where virtue lies. It contrasts the arms manufacturer Andrew Undershaft with his daughter Barbara, who has become a major in the Salvation Army in protest against the evil source of their family wealth. She receives a double shock, first in hearing that the shelter she runs for the poor has been funded by profits from whisky and then in discovering that her father is a model employer.

majority see *coming of age.

majority verdict see *jury system.

Majors The term in golf for the four most important tournaments, of which the *Open is the oldest and perhaps still the most prestigious. The others are the US Open (first held 1895), the US PGA (Professional Golfers' Association 1916) and the US Masters (1934).

Mrs **Malaprop** see *The *Rivals.

Malawi Member of the *Commonwealth since 1964, and a republic since 1966. This part of east central Africa was explored by David Livingstone, who urged missionaries and traders to settle there to undermine the slave trade. The region was proclaimed a British protectorate in 1891 and was named Nyasaland in 1907. It was a part of the Federation of *Rhodesia and Nyasaland before becoming independent in 1964 as Malawi. Hastings Banda (b. 1905) was the first prime minister and was declared president for life in 1971.

Malaya The British link with the Malay peninsula began in 1786, when the East India Company established a port of call on the island of Penang, off the west coast, for vessels plying between India and China. The next major step was the founding of *Singapore off the southern tip of the peninsula in 1819. During the 19c large-scale production of both tin and rubber was developed, while political control was achieved through treaties with the rulers of the separate states of the peninsula. These states together joined the *Commonwealth in 1957 as the independent federation of Malaya, being enlarged in 1963 to become *Malaysia.

Malaysia Member of the *Commonwealth since 1963. It was formed by the merging of Malaya with the newly independent territories of Singapore, Sarawak and Sabah (previously British North Borneo). In 1965 *Singapore seceded to become an independent state. The federation now consists of 11 states in the Malay peninsula and two states lying some 800km/500m across the sea in north Borneo. These two states, Sarawak and Sabah, themselves surround another member of the Commonwealth, *Brunei. The rulers of the 13 constituent states of the federation elect one of their own number to be head of state for a five-year term.

Malcolm III (also called Malcolm Canmore, c.1031–93) King of Scotland from 1057, founder of a dynasty which ruled for more than 200 years (see the *royal house of Scotland). He was the son of *Duncan I, and he secured the throne after killing *Macbeth in battle at Lumphanan, near Aberdeen (not at Dunsinane as in *Macbeth). In a life of almost constant warfare, with frequent expeditions into northern England, he established Scotland as a strong kingdom, though he did homage to William I in 1072 and to William II in 1091. He was killed in an ambush near Alnwick on one of his raids south. In about 1070 he married Margaret, later St *Margaret of Scotland. Three of their sons succeeded to the throne, the first being Edgar.

Malcolm IV (known as the Maiden, 1141–65) King of Scotland from 1153. He was only 11 when he succeeded his grandfather, David I; his father, David's only surviving son, had died the previous year. Henry II of England took advantage of the king's minority to demand back the northern fiefs of Northumberland and Cumberland, ceded to David I for his support of Henry's mother, *Matilda. Malcolm later served with Henry, campaigning in France. He was succeeded by his brother, William the Lion (see the *royal house of Scotland).

The **Maldives** Group of more than 1000 coral islands, about 200 inhabited, lying some 640km/400m southwest of Sri Lanka. Ruled by a sultan since the 12C, the islands were made a British protectorate in 1887. They became independent in 1965, abolished the sultanate in 1968 and became a full member of the *Commonwealth in 1985.

The **Mall** (London SW1) The capital city's main processional route, providing the first stage of the sovereign's journey either to the Houses of Parliament or to the parade ground at Horse Guards. Stretching from the *Victoria Memorial in front of Buckingham Palace to *Admiralty Arch at the other end, it was designed in its present form in 1903–4 by Aston *Webb and was seen as the national memorial to Queen Victoria. But the Mall had first been laid out as a broad avenue in the 1660s, when it immediately became London's most fashionable promenade.

Mallard see *National Railway Museum.

Mallory and Irvine see *Everest.

Thomas **Malory** see *Morte d'Arthur*.

Malta Small island in the Mediterranean, south of Sicily, which with neighbouring Gozo has been a member of the *Commonwealth since 1964 and a republic since 1974. It was ruled by the Knights of St John from 1530 until 1798, when it was captured by Napoleon. The island was relieved two years later by the British after a long siege. In 1802 the Maltese refused to allow the return of the Knights and declared the king of Great Britain to be their sovereign; in 1813 Britain acknowledged the Maltese as British subjects, a state of affairs ratified in 1814 by the treaty of Paris. In both world wars the island was a vitally important naval base for the Allies, and the heroic resistance of the Maltese to prolonged siege and bombardment was acknowledged in 1943 when George VI awarded the *George Cross to the 'Island Fortress of Malta'. There had been self-government of a kind since the 19C, but internal disagreement on constitutional matters delayed full independence until 1964.

The Mall as the place to see and be seen, with Westminster Abbey in the distance on the right (engraving of 1750).

The hills above Great Malvern (out of sight to the right), looking north from the Worcester Beacon.

Thomas **Malthus** (1766–1834) Author of *An Essay on the Principle of Population as it Affects the Future Improvement of Society* (1798), in which he argued that poverty is inescapable because the population (increasing geometrically) grows faster than production (increasing arithmetically); population growth is therefore only kept in check by famine, war and disease. This economic pessimism was for many a welcome argument against the promptings of charity, but it did inspire the evolutionary theories of both *Wallace and *Darwin.

Maltings see *Aldeburgh.

The **Malverns** Several villages and one town (Great Malvern) on the slopes of the Malvern Hills, a granite ridge stretching 14km/9m north and south in Hereford and Worcester (highest point Worcester Beacon, 425m/ 1395ft). Springs provide very pure water, bottled and widely sold as Malvern water. Great Malvern grew up round a Benedictine priory of the 11C. The priory church still has its Norman nave, within a Perpendicular exterior of the 15C; it is known in particular for its stained glass of the 15–16C and for the local 15C tiles set into the choir screen. The healthy reputation of this spa town made it a favourite place for schools, notably two *public schools, Malvern College (1865) and Malvern Girls' College (1893). Between the wars Malvern held an annual theatre festival (from 1929), with a special emphasis on the plays of Bernard Shaw.

Malvolio see *Twelfth Night.

Isle of **Man** see *Isle of Man.

Man and Superman (published 1903, first performed 1905) Play by George Bernard *Shaw which reverses the Don Juan theme by having the hero, John Tanner, relentlessly pursued by the heroine, Ann Whitefield. The evolutionary 'life force' is on her side, and the play ends with their decision to marry, but not without a great deal

of Shavian discussion of alternative programmes for mankind (such as the emergence of the Nietzschean Superman). Much of this is in the Act 3 dream sequence, 'Don Juan in Hell', which is sometimes omitted in performance.

Manchester (433,000 in 1991) City in Greater Manchester on the east bank of the river Irwell; on the west bank, though the river is too small to provide a noticeable line of demarcation, stands the separate city of Salford. From AD 79 Manchester was the Roman fort of *Mancunium*, and its inhabitants are still known as Mancunians. The link with the textile industry began in the 14C when Flemish weavers settled here, but the transformation of a market town into the great metropolis of *cotton began only in the 18C. James *Brindley's Bridgewater canal brought cheap coal into the city in 1761; steam power was first used in Manchester in 1789 for the spinning of cotton; and the opening of the *Liverpool and Manchester railway in 1830 and of the *Manchester Ship Canal in 1894 made possible the export of vast quantities of finished goods.

The wealth of the city, combined with the pioneering efforts of its mill owners in the exploitation of factory workers, gave Manchester a radical edge. It was here that the *Peterloo massacre took place in 1819; it was in Manchester's mills that the political ideas of the young *Engels were formed. But the employers were radical too in their impatience with Britain's protectionism; the campaign of *Bright and Cobden against the Corn Laws was centred in Manchester (commemorated in the Free Trade Hall of 1856, the home of the *Hallé orchestra). The *Manchester *Guardian*, the leading English newspaper of liberal views, was founded in 1821.

Manchester is famous for its libraries. Chetham's, founded by Humphrey Chetham (1580–1653), is the oldest free public library in England; it is attached to the school of the same name (see *music schools). The John Rylands library, a superb collection of rare books, is housed in an appropriately splendid Gothic building by Basil Champneys (1842–1935). The circular Central

Library (1934) is England's largest municipal library, with a round reading room which can almost rival the one in the British Museum.

Nearby, in Albert Square, is one of the greatest of Victorian town halls, Gothic in style with a huge clock tower, built 1867–76 to the design of Alfred *Waterhouse; the Great Hall has 12 murals by Ford Madox *Brown depicting the city's history. In keeping with its new dignity Manchester was made a diocese in 1847, whereupon the 15C parish church became the cathedral; it is known in particular for its finely carved choir stalls and misericords. The City Art Gallery, in a building of 1824–34 by Charles *Barry, has a European collection spanning the 14–20C but is strongest in British painting of the 19C – both pre-Raphaelite and high Victorian. Platt Hall, a Palladian house of the mid-18C, has one of the largest displays in the country illustrating the history of costume. The Whitworth Art Gallery, a broadly based collection founded in memory of the engineer and inventor Joseph *Whitworth, has been since 1958 a part of the university of Manchester – which emerged from the earlier Owens College (1851) and was granted independent university status in 1904. Manchester Grammar School is now a *public school; founded in 1515, its high academic standards had long given it the reputation of being the country's leading grammar school.

Two of Manchester's historic railway stations have recently been put to new uses. The site of the original passenger station for the *Liverpool and Manchester railway is now part of a Museum of Science and Industry. On a larger scale, the Central Station – opened in 1876 to the design of John *Fowler, with a single-span roof of 64m/210ft – has been turned into G-Mex, the Greater Manchester Exhibition and Events Centre. In 1992 the new Metrolink transport system was launched, reintroducing trams to link the road and rail networks. At the same period the city was planning a major sports stadium as part of its bid to stage the Olympic Games in the year 2000. One of England's foremost cricket grounds is Manchester's *Old Trafford.

Manchester airport The main international airport for the Midlands and north of England, and the busiest in the country after Heathrow and Gatwick. Manchester became in 1929 the first British municipality to have its own licensed aerodrome, which was moved in 1939 to the present site at Ringway. A major new terminal was opened in 1962, capable of dealing with 2.5 million passengers a year; it was the first in Europe where the passengers could walk all the way to the aircraft under cover.

On 22 August 1985 a British Airtours Boeing 737 burst into flames at Manchester when taking off for Corfu, resulting in 55 deaths.

Manchester City, known as the Blues (Maine Road, Manchester). Football club formed in 1894 but with roots going back to a church team in West Gorton in 1880. In Division 1 for most of the time since 1899 (but with two dips in the 1980s), City had their greatest run of successes after Joe Mercer became manager in 1965. Club victories: FA Cup 1904, 34, 56, 69; League Champions 1937, 68; League Cup 1970, 76; European Cup-Winners' Cup 1970.

Manchester Evening News Manchester's evening paper was launched in 1868 and steadily built up a strong regional following while the city's morning paper, the *Guardian*, was developing national stature. The two have been in the same ownership since 1924.

Manchester Guardian see *Guardian*.

Manchester Ship Canal Constructed in 1887–94, it enabled ocean-going vessels of up to 15,000 tons to leave the Mersey estuary (through a lock at Eastham on the south bank) and to go inland a distance of 57km/36m via Runcorn and Warrington to *Manchester.

Romanticized view of women at work in a Manchester cotton mill: hand-coloured steel engraving after Thomas Allom (1834).

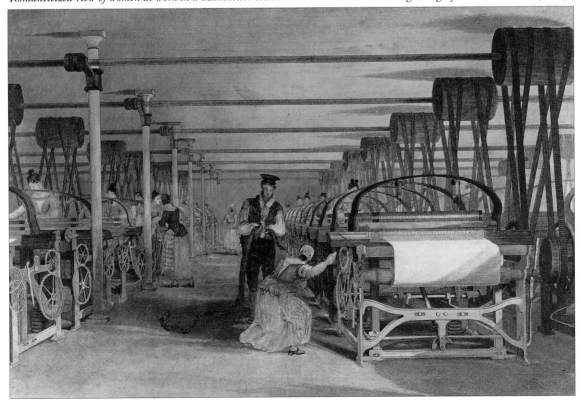

Manchester United, known as the Red Devils (Old Trafford, Manchester). Football club founded in 1902, but with origins in a club formed in 1878 by employees of the Lancashire and Yorkshire Railway. Its first period of brilliance began with the appointment of Matt *Busby as manager in 1945, but his young team was shattered in the air disaster of 1958. On February 6 their plane crashed on take-off from Munich during the return journey from a match in Belgrade; eight of the players died. Busby built the club up again for a new series of triumphs culminating in the first English win in the European Cup, in 1968, with Bobby *Charlton and George *Best in the team (and with Denis *Law playing until the final, which he missed through injury). By 1992 the club's seven wins in the FA Cup were equalled by Aston Villa but exceeded only by Tottenham Hotspur. United also achieved a successful return for England to European competition (after the ban following the *Heysel Stadium disaster) with their 1991 win in the Cup-Winners' Cup. Club victories: FA Cup 1909, 48, 63, 77, 83, 85, 90; League Champions 1908, 11, 52, 56, 57, 65, 67, 93; League Cup 1992; European Cup 1968; European Cup-Winners' Cup 1991.

Mancunium see *Manchester.

Mandalay One of *Kipling's *Barrack-Room Ballads* (1892), encapsulating much of the popular romance of empire. An ex-soldier, working now in the City of London, dreams of the road to Mandalay, 'where the flying fishes play' and where he imagines his Burmese girl still sitting 'by the old Moulmein Pagoda'. Sick of the English drizzle, all he wants is to be shipped somewhere 'east of Suez'.

mandated territories Those parts of the empires of Germany and Turkey which after World War I were administered, under mandate from the League of Nations, by individual members of the Allied group of nations. Each mandate was seen as a period of trusteeship leading towards independence. The most important were the Turkish provinces of the Middle East, which had at the time no national boundaries. The area was apportioned as three mandated territories; *Iraq and *Palestine (including *Transjordan) were administered by Britain, and Syria (including Lebanon) by France. The mandates ended with the independence of Iraq in 1932, of Syria and Lebanon in 1941, of Jordan in 1946 and Israel in 1948.

*A **Man for all Seasons*** (1960) Play by Robert *Bolt about the efforts of Thomas *More to save his neck without compromising his conscience on the issue of whether Henry VIII or the pope was head of the church. The play was filmed in 1967, winning a clutch of Oscars. Paul *Scofield played More on both stage and screen.

Man Friday see **Robinson Crusoe*.

Manon (1974) Ballet by Kenneth *MacMillan, setting the story of the Abbé Prévost's *Manon Lescaut* (1731) to music pieced together from more than 20 different works by Massenet. The parts of Manon and des Grieux were created for Antoinette *Sibley and Anthony *Dowell.

Manpower Services Commission (MSC) Body set up by an act of 1973 to run all public services connected with employment and training. It was progressively dismantled from 1987. In the early 1990s much of the MSC's previous role in employment is carried out by the *Employment Service, and its training functions have been devolved to *TECs.

Nigel **Mansell** (b. 1953) The most successful of British racing drivers, though his record would have looked very different if he had kept to his 1990 decision to retire. By then he had been runner-up twice in the world championship (1986–7). His first near-miss had been particularly distressing; he only needed to come third in the Australian Grand Prix at Adelaide to secure the title (driving for Williams), and he was safely in that position in the closing stage of the race when a rear tyre exploded and put an end to his hopes.

Frank Williams persuaded him to change his retirement decision in time for 1991. That year, from a late start, he came up fast behind Ayrton Senna in the championship but once again finished as runner-up. The break-through was in 1992, when the Williams car was technically far ahead of the opposition. Mansell set about demolishing a string of records. At the San Marino Grand Prix he became the first driver to win the first five races in a season; at the French Grand Prix he equalled Jackie *Stewart's British record of 27 Grand Prix victories; and the following week he bettered it with a win in the British Grand Prix. By the end of the year he was world champion, with a career total of 30 wins and a record nine in a single season. He had been eager to defend his title in 1993, but much publicized difficulties in reaching an agreement with Williams prompted a second decision to withdraw from Grand Prix racing – subsequently confirmed when he signed to compete in the Indycar series of races in the USA.

Mansfield Park (1814) Novel by Jane *Austen, about the level-headed Fanny Price who refuses to engage in the flirtatious behaviour of the Bertram family, her cousins, with whom she has grown up at Mansfield Park. She even turns down a proposal of marriage from the eligible Henry Craw-ford – to the fury of the head of the household, Sir Thomas Bertram, until Henry's running off with a married woman proves the soundness of Fanny's judgement. She loves Sir Thomas's son Edmund, a clergyman, who finally tires of the frivolities of social life, falls for Fanny and marries her.

Mansion House (London EC2) The residence of the *Lord Mayor of London. It was built in a Palladian style by George Dance (1695–1768) and was completed in 1753. Its best-known interior is the banqueting room, called the Egyptian Hall.

Mantovani (Annunzio Paulo Mantovani, 1905–80) Italian-born conductor, in Britain from the age of 16. His international fame came after World War II, with the formation of an orchestra of 45 players, including 32 strings, to produce his famous sound – the shimmering cascade of 'singing strings'. *Charmaine* (1951) sold a million copies, the first of a succession of hit singles and albums.

*The **Man who broke the bank at Monte Carlo*** see Charles *Coborn.

Manx cat Tailless cat, usually with a coat in two colours, which has been bred for perhaps as much as three centuries in the *Isle of Man. The legend is that their two ancestors only just got on to the Ark, losing their tails when Noah slammed the door. In practice most litters have some tailless kittens (known as 'rumpies') and others with very short tails ('stumpies'). Kittens are often stillborn if rumpies are too consistently interbred.

Mappa Mundi (Hereford Cathedral) Circular map of the world, painted on a large piece of vellum (prepared calf skin). It is believed to have been completed in about 1290, and has been in Hereford since at least the 17c. In the medieval tradition of map making, it shows Jerusalem at the centre of the world with the three known continents around it; Asia occupies the top of the map and Europe and Africa share the lower half. Europe and Africa were named the wrong way round by the artist, who signs himself Richard and fills his map and its margins with lively drawings of the marvels to be found in this world and the next. The *Mappa Mundi* (Latin for 'map of the world') was the subject of wide publicity in 1989 when the cathedral authorities planned to raise much-needed funds by selling it. Means were found to return it to its traditional home.

marathons As in other western countries, the British sporting calendar is now full of marathons and half-marathons. The length of a marathon, 26 miles and 385 yards (42.195km), is that of the race run at the *White City Olympics of 1908; it was adopted as the international standard in 1924. The London marathon, Britain's largest, was established in 1981 by Christopher Brasher who was an Olympic gold medallist in 1956 in the 3000 metres steeplechase; by contrast the Boston marathon in the USA has been an annual fixture since 1897, only a year after the race was invented in the first modern Olympics.

Marathon is a plain about 42km/ 26m northeast of Athens. The race commemorates the legendary feat of a soldier, Pheidippides, who was said to have run from Marathon to Athens in 490 BC and to have died immediately after declaring the good news that the Greeks had defeated the Persians.

Marble Arch (London W1) Designed by John *Nash, and supposedly inspired by the arch of Constantine in Rome, it was put up in 1828 as the entrance to the new *Buckingham Palace. It was moved in 1851 to its present position, at the northeast corner of Hyde Park, serving until 1908 as an entrance for traffic. The reliefs on the north side are by *Westmacott, and on the south by *Baily.

Marble Hill House (19km/12m to the W of London) Palladian villa built on the north bank of the Thames in 1723–9 for Henrietta Howard, later the countess of Suffolk, who was the mistress of the future George II. The original design was probably by Colen *Campbell, adapted by Lord Herbert (1693–1751) and Roger Morris (1695–1749).

The **Marches** England's border districts with Wales (also with Scotland, though less often used in this sense), which in the Middle Ages were in a constant state of petty warfare. The Lords Marcher, those barons with castles in the Marches, were given special privileges to compensate for their front-line position.

March Hare see *Alice in Wonderland.*

Marchioness Thames pleasure boat which sank after being hit from behind by the dredger *Bowbelle* in the early hours of the morning of 20 August 1989. There was a birthday party in progress on the *Marchioness* and 51 of those on board were drowned. The disaster prompted stricter safety procedures and brighter markings for public craft on the Thames. The captain of the *Bowbelle* was charged in 1991 with failing to keep a proper lookout but the jury was unable to agree on a verdict.

Guglielmo **Marconi** (1874–1937) Italian pioneer of radio telegraphy who based his career and his company in Britain. Finding little support for his ideas in Italy, he came to London in 1896 and filed his first patent in June of that year. He soon sent a radio signal 14km/9m across the Bristol channel, and in 1899 he achieved several striking successes: he signalled 50km/31m from England to France; British battleships communicated with his equipment at a distance of 121km/75m; and, most sensational from the public's point of view, reports were sent from sea to New York on the progress of the America's Cup. His greatest single triumph came in 1901 when he received in Newfoundland the first transatlantic radio message, transmitted from his equipment on the coast of the *Lizard in Cornwall. He continued to be in the forefront of experiment, particularly in short-wave radio, and the company he founded in Britain (trading as Marconi's Wireless Telegraph Company from 1900) grew into an international concern. It launched in 1922 the radio station 2LO, which later in that year became the first studio of the *BBC. The Marconi company was much in the news in 1990 when four of its executives were charged with making excessive profits on defence contracts, but the prosecution case collapsed after the trial had run for six weeks.

Princess **Margaret** (Countess of Snowdon, b. 1930) Daughter of George VI and Queen Elizabeth, and the younger sister of Elizabeth II (see the *royal family). As a child she was often known by both her names as Princess Margaret Rose. A constitutional crisis was caused by her wish in 1953, when she was third in line of succession to the throne, to marry Group Captain Peter Townsend; he had a senior royal appointment (equerry to the queen) but he had been divorced the previous year. Princess Margaret withdrew when it was decided that she could only marry him as a private citizen, requiring parliament to pass special legislation. In 1960, in Westminster Abbey, she married the photographer Tony Armstrong-Jones, who the following year was created Earl of *Snowdon. She has two children: David, Viscount Linley (b. 1961) and Sarah (b. 1964). She and Lord Snowdon were divorced in 1978; it was the first divorce so close to the throne, but the first in the royal family had been that of Lord *Harewood. Princess Margaret has taken an active interest in the performing arts, particularly music and dance. She lives at Kensington Palace and has a house on Mustique, one of the islands of St Vincent and the Grenadines.

St **Margaret** of Scotland (c.1045–93) A princess of the Anglo-Saxon royal house (great granddaughter of Ethelred the Unready). She and her family fled from the Normans in 1067 to the Scottish court, where in about 1070 she married the king, *Malcolm III. She was known both for her culture and for her piety; St Margaret's Chapel in *Edinburgh Castle is named after her. She was canonized in 1250. Her feast day in Scotland is November 16, the anniversary of her death, but it is held elsewhere on June 10.

Margaret, the Maid of Norway (c.1282–90) Queen of Scotland from 1286, inheriting the throne because her deceased mother had been the daughter of the Scottish king *Alexander III. Her father was king of Norway, and she sailed from Norway at the age of eight after a marriage had been arranged with the son of Edward I of England. She died during the journey, in the Orkneys, thus ending a stable dynasty which had stretched back to Malcolm III two centuries earlier (see the *royal house of Scotland).

Maria Marten see The *Red Barn.*

Four **Maries** (also known as the Queen's Maries) Four Scottish girls, all about the same age as the 6-year-old queen, who were the chief companions of *Mary Queen of Scots when she went to France in 1548. Of the four (Mary Fleming, Mary Seton, Mary Beaton and Mary

Livingston), it was Mary Seton who remained longest in the service of the queen. She was still with her, in captivity in England, 35 years later.

Mari Lwyd A hobby horse which is still carried through the streets in certain parts of south Wales at the midwinter season. The men accompanying Mari gain admittance to closed houses after a dialogue with those inside, conducted in partly improvised Welsh verse. Once inside, Mari misbehaves until her attendants are given food and drink. Many explanations have been suggested for the name Mari Lwyd, but *llwyd* is Welsh for grey and it may simply imply a 'grey mare'.

King **Mark** see *Tristan and Iseult.

Alicia **Markova** (stage name of Lilian Alice Marks, b. 1910, DBE 1963) The first British ballerina to dance the great classical roles (noted above all for her Giselle). She danced with Diaghilev's Ballets Russes from her midteens (1925–9), creating the title role in Balanchine's *Le Rossignol* in 1926. With Ballet Rambert and the Vic-Wells Ballet (which became the Royal Ballet) she created many of the early *Ashton roles. In 1935 she formed the first of several companies with Anton *Dolin. She was later a guest ballerina with many companies abroad until her retirement in 1962.

Marks & Spencer Britain's most widely known high street retailer, with a reputation for reliable quality – originally in clothing, but in recent decades increasingly in food. The huge enterprise (nearly 700 stores worldwide in the early 1990s) derives from very small beginnings. In 1882 a Jewish immigrant from Poland, calling himself Michael Marks, began selling haberdashery from a tray around his neck in the villages of northeast England. Two years later he was confident enough to borrow £5 from a wholesaler, Isaac Dewhirst (the firm of Dewhirst is still a major supplier to Marks & Spencer) and to take a stall in Leeds market; his eye-catching notice said 'Don't ask the price – it's a penny'. The success of this approach led to a small chain of stalls called Marks' Penny Bazaar. The penny limit lasted until World War I, but by then the name had changed; in 1894, to enable further expansion, Marks took in a partner, Thomas Spencer, who had been a cashier with Dewhirst. In 1926 Marks & Spencer became a public company, with a price limit by then of five shillings.

In 1924 the company began a policy of buying clothes direct from manufacturers, rather than through wholesalers, making possible much greater control of quality; and in 1928 the St Michael trademark was introduced on all goods produced to Marks & Spencer specifications (an astonishingly large number of people in Britain now carry the two words St Michael on their underwear). The company overtook *Woolworths in 1968 as Britain's largest retailer, a role in which it was itself replaced by *Sainsbury's in 1992.

Duke of **Marlborough** (John Churchill, 1650–1722, baron 1682, duke 1702) Soldier and politician who dominated the early years of the War of the *Spanish Succession. His first advancement was typical of the *Restoration court; his sister was the mistress of the king's brother (the future James II), and Churchill himself became the lover of one of Charles II's most influential mistresses, Lady Castlemaine. An even more important thread of intrigue began with his marriage early in 1678 to Sarah Jennings (1660–1744), well established as the favourite of the future Queen *Anne.

It was in Anne's reign that Churchill's period of greatest influence began. A successful military campaign in Germany in 1702 brought him his dukedom, and after his great victory at *Blenheim the queen granted him an estate at Woodstock and secured £100,000 of public money for him to build on it *Blenheim Palace. His subsequent victories (Ramillies 1706, Oudenarde 1708, Malplaquet 1709) were all in the region to the north of France. The high cost in lives at Malplaquet proved that a military advance on Paris, long favoured by Marlborough, was not an acceptable option; this undermined his position in London, as did the queen's rejection of Sarah as her favourite. In 1710 there was a change of ministry to the Tories, who were in favour of peace negotiations. In 1711 Marlborough was dismissed from all his offices. He was reappointed after the Hanoverian succession in 1714, but ill health made him ineffective in his final years.

Marlborough House (London SW1) Built by Wren in 1709–11 on the north side of St James's Park for Sarah, wife of the duke of *Marlborough. The French painter Louis Laguerre was employed to paint the murals of the duke's victories – Ramillies and Malplaquet on the stairs, Blenheim in the huge two-storey saloon. The land was leased to the duchess by Queen Anne, and in 1817 the house reverted to the royal family. From 1863 it was the London home of the prince of Wales; and in the 20c two widowed queens, Alexandra and Mary, have lived there. In 1959 it was given to the government as a centre for various Commonwealth purposes.

Christopher **Marlowe** (1564–93) The first great English dramatist. Unlike Shakespeare he was university-educated (at Cambridge) and his life is relatively well documented because of his troubles with the law – in prison in 1589 after an incident in which someone was killed, bound over to keep the peace in 1592, in constant danger for suspected atheism, and arrested in 1593 just 12 days before being killed in a tavern dispute (when still short of his 30th birthday).

With *Tamburlaine and *Doctor Faustus (produced 1587 and c.1590, shortly before Shakespeare's first plays), Marlowe inaugurated the greatest period of English theatre and of *blank verse. The Jew of Malta (c.1590) is a characteristic revenge tragedy of the time, in which the wrongs done to the Jew provoke him to an orgy of slaughter. And Edward II (c.1592) is England's first sophisticated history play – roughly contemporary with Shakespeare's more primitive Henry VI, but soon to be outshone by his Richard III.

marmalade Orange jam, best made with bitter Seville oranges, which since the early 20c has been a staple ingredient of the British breakfast. The name derives from a form of quince, the main ingredient of the original marmalade. It was later made from many different fruits, and was boiled sufficiently dry to be cut into pieces.

Dundee and Oxford are recognized as the main staging posts on the route to modern marmalade. In the early 18c James Keiller of Dundee bought a cheap cargo of Seville oranges. He was unable to sell them because of their bitter taste, so his wife made a sweet jam including strips of the peel. Marmalade of this kind became a mainly Scottish speciality until Mrs Cooper, wife of an Oxford grocer, began making it in the 1870s. The popularity of her product at undergraduate breakfast tables led to its wider use.

Marmite A tangy yeast spread, eaten usually on buttered bread or toast. Made from brewers' yeast, a byproduct of brewing, it was produced from 1902 by the Marmite Food Extract Company at Burton-upon-Trent. Its name is that of the trademark on the label, a *marmite* or French earthenware cooking pot.

Miss **Marple** see Agatha *Christie.

marquess see *peerage.

Marriage Guidance Council see *Relate.

marriages Two social changes in recent decades affect the number of marriages, and they pull in opposite directions. The marriage figures are reduced by an increasing tendency for couples to live together and have children without marrying; but this is to some extent offset by the greater ease of divorce and the resulting number of second marriages. The annual marriage and divorce figures in the UK are compared in the entry on *divorce.

Neville **Marriner** (b. 1924, kt 1985) Conductor and founder of the *Academy of St Martin-in-the-Fields, which has remained his chief concern. In the USA he has been music director of the Los Angeles Chamber Orchestra (1968–77) and of the Minnesota Orchestra (1979–86).

Marsden (Royal Marsden Hospital, London SW3) Founded in 1851 by William Marsden (1796–1867), and occupying from 1862 its present building in the Fulham Road, the original purpose of the Marsden was to offer free admission to those with cancer. It was the world's first hospital specifically for cancer patients, and was from the start in the forefront of cancer research. William Marsden had previously founded the *Royal Free.

Terry **Marsh** (b. 1958) Boxer who won the world light-welterweight title in 1987 and then became involved in a complex tangle of litigation. Marsh brought his own career to an end, later in 1987, with an announcement that he was suffering from epileptic fits. He was subsequently sued for libel by his manager, Frank Warren, on the grounds that he had implied on television that Warren knew of his epilepsy when fixing up a fight for him; Marsh won the case when it eventually came to court in 1992. Meanwhile, in November 1989, Warren had been shot and wounded by a mysterious masked gunman; Marsh was charged with the crime and was acquitted in November 1990.

Marshall Plan The name by which the European Recovery Programme became known. In 1947 the US secretary of state, George C. Marshall (1880–1959), proposed in a lecture at Harvard that a unified plan for European recovery after World War II should be financed by economic aid from the USA, part of the intention being to deter the spread of Communism. The OEEC (Organization for European Economic Cooperation) was set up to channel the funds to 16 European countries; a total of about $13.5bn in Marshall Aid was distributed in the period 1948–52, including about £1.5bn to Britain. The OEEC was later expanded to become the *OECD.

Marshalsea Prison in Southwark, south of the river in London, in use from at least the 14c. In later centuries it was mainly used for debtors. Dickens' father was imprisoned here for debt in 1824, and the prison features largely in *Little Dorritt. It was closed in 1842.

marshmallow see *sweets.

Marston Moor (2 July 1644) The first major parliamentary victory in the *English Civil War. Thomas Fairfax and Oliver Cromwell inflicted a heavy defeat on the army of Prince Rupert some 11km/7m west of York, thus effectively ending royalist control of the north of England. It was after this battle that Rupert gave Cromwell the nickname Ironside or Ironsides, which was later extended to his troops.

Martello Towers Circular stone towers, with room for a garrison inside and two guns on top, built along the south coast from Beachy Head to Folkestone as defence against invasion in the *Napoleonic Wars. Of the original 74 towers constructed in the early 19c, as many as 27 are still intact. The design and the name derived from a similar tower at Mortella in Corsica, where the French had put up an effective resistance to British bombardment in 1794.

John **Martin** (1789–1854) Painter noted for his apocalyptic images, whether on vast canvases or in the small-scale but intense theatricality of his mezzotint illustrations

Martello Towers at Hythe, in Kent, guarding the English beach at one of its closest points to France.

Satan on the Burning Lake: *one of John Martin's visionary mezzotints illustrating* Paradise Lost *(1825).*

to Milton's *Paradise Lost* (1827). His best-known works, the three *Judgement* paintings of scenes from Revelation (Tate Gallery), demonstrate the switchback course of his now high reputation. They were valued after his death at £8400 and were sold for £7 in 1935.

Andrew **Marvell** (1621–78) Now seen as an outstanding *metaphysical poet, he was known in his lifetime only as a minor public figure. His early employment was as tutor in leading parliamentary families (those of both Fairfax and Cromwell). A growing admiration for Cromwell led to his entering government service; in 1657 he became a fellow secretary with *Milton in the department concerned with foreign affairs. From 1659 to his death he was an MP for Hull and was known as a firm parliamentarian, watchful for any abuses of royal power.

The manuscripts of his lyric poems were found in his lodgings after his death and were published in 1681, though they only acquired their present high reputation during the 20C. Among the best known are *The Garden*, a green hymn to the pleasures of solitude in nature; and *To his Coy Mistress*, in which he presses a sense of urgency upon his loved one if together they are to enjoy life's delights ('The Grave's a fine and private place,/But none I think do there embrace'). His manuscripts included several poems in honour of Cromwell, considered too dangerous for publication until the 18C. The best of them, *An Horation Ode upon Cromwell's Return from Ireland*, reveals the level-headedness of Marvell's response to the great events of his time. It includes the most famous of all descriptions of Charles I on the scaffold:

> He nothing common did or mean
> Upon that memorable Scene.

Karl **Marx** (1818–83) Political and economic theorist who was expelled from Germany in 1849 as a dangerous revolutionary. He spent the rest of his life in London, where he and his family lived in considerable poverty (his friend *Engels, with his English connection, was a support). Their two rooms in Soho had the merit of being close to the *British Museum. In its domed reading room Marx found the texts and the statistics which he needed to write *Das Kapital* (of which only the first volume came out in his lifetime, in 1867). He was buried in Highgate cemetery, where his tomb remained a place of pilgrimage for many on the political left until the discrediting of Communism in the 1990s.

Queen **Mary** see *George V.

Mary I (1516–58) Queen of England and Ireland from 1553, succeeding her brother Edward VI; daughter of Henry VIII and Catherine of Aragon; married Philip of Spain (1554).

Mary was treated harshly by her father, *Henry VIII, for resisting the annulment of his marriage to her mother; she then suffered in the intolerant atmosphere of the reign of her brother, *Edward VI, for remaining true to Roman Catholicism; and her accession to the throne was briefly frustrated by the incident of Lady Jane *Grey. Mary began her reign with leniency towards her enemies, but her determination to restore Roman Catholicism soon provoked resistance. An early affront was her marriage in 1554 to the heir to the throne of Spain, the future Philip II. His arrival was closely followed by that of Cardinal *Pole, sent by the pope to absolve England and to receive her back into the Catholic fold.

The next few years were marked by severe persecution of Protestant heretics, causing the queen to become known as Bloody Mary. Some 300 were burnt at the stake, including Nicholas Ridley (1503–55) and Thomas *Cranmer. Their suffering, dramatically recorded in *Foxe's Book of Martyrs*, became a powerful inspiration to later Protestants. The main external event of the reign was a brief war in 1557 against France, which was urged upon Mary by her husband and which ended with the loss of *Calais. She had no children and was succeeded by her sister Elizabeth I (see the *royal house).

Mary II (1662–94) Queen of England, Scotland and Ireland, ruling jointly with her husband, from 1689; elder daughter of *James II and Anne Hyde; married William of Orange (1677).

Although her father became a Roman Catholic during her childhood, she continued to be brought up as a Protestant and was married to her Protestant Dutch cousin, William of Orange (see the *royal house). After his unopposed invasion of England in the *Revolution of 1688, they were proclaimed joint king and queen in April 1689. Pious and much loved by those who knew her, she deferred on public matters to her husband, *William III. She died of smallpox at the age of 32, without children, so her sister *Anne became her husband's heir.

Mary Barton see Mrs *Gaskell.

Mary had a little lamb One of the best-known nursery rhymes in Britain, but in origin a poem written for children in 1830 by an American author, Sara Josepha Hale (1788–1879). Based on a real incident, the narrative has a simple consistency quite unlike the surrealist folk ingredients of traditional nursery rhymes.

Marylebone Cricket Club see *MCC.

Mary Queen of Scots (also known as Mary Stuart, 1542–87) Queen of Scotland 1542–67; only child of *James V and Mary of Guise (also called Mary of Lorraine); married the French dauphin Francis (1558), the earl of Darnley (1565), the earl of Bothwell (1567).

From the melodrama of her youth to her tragic last years, Mary's life has always had huge popular appeal. Her very first week brought drama; the death of her father made her queen of Scotland when she was six days old. Her mother arranged for her to be brought up at the French court (accompanied by her 'four *Maries'), and in France sophistication was added to the natural appeal of a tall red-headed beauty. She was married to the dauphin in 1558. In 1559 his father died and so, at the age of 16 (her birthday was in December), Mary was queen of France – in addition to being queen of Scotland and next in line to *Elizabeth I on the throne of England (see the *royal house).

This giddy wheel of fortune turned again at the end of that year when her husband died, in December. A widow at 17, she returned two years later to a Scotland now racked with the struggles of the Reformation. But if the young queen's French Catholic ways did not please reformers such as *Knox, there were many who welcomed a glamorous court in Edinburgh. The future disasters were not inevitable. They were brought on primarily by her own impetuous actions.

At the political level these included open and frequent statements of her ambition to win the crown of England, if necessary by invasion (the Catholic view that the marriage of Henry VIII to Anne Boleyn was invalid made Elizabeth illegitimate and gave Mary a prior claim); naturally, in view of this, Elizabeth took the threat from Scotland very seriously. Meanwhile the chaos of Mary's personal life included the brutal murder of her secretary David Rizzio (often spelt Riccio) by her new husband, Lord Darnley, in 1566; the murder in the following year of her husband, probably organized by the earl of Bothwell with her connivance (if the *Casket Letters are correct); and then her marriage three months later to Bothwell.

These events provoked the Scottish Protestant nobility into deposing Mary in 1567 in favour of her one-year-old son by Darnley (see *James I and VI). With continuing lack of judgement, but perhaps not with many other options, Mary turned to Elizabeth for help, arriving in England in 1568. Her cousin contrived to keep her captive for the next 19 years, while nevertheless allowing her the dignity of a queen. She lived in a succession of castles with a retinue of at least 30 of her own people, and for most of the time her jailer was the relatively sympathetic earl of Shrewsbury. But she now engaged in a series of conspiracies, each involving the planned assassination of Elizabeth. These caused the English queen's advisers to call for her death many years before Elizabeth finally signed the warrant.

The end came as a result of the *Babington plot. Mary was tried in the great hall of Fotheringay Castle in Northamptonshire on 14–15 October 1586, and was executed there on 8 February 1587. Her courage and dignity on both occasions rounded off a life so full of drama that it has remained a favourite subject of fiction and theatre – most notably in Schiller's *Maria Stuart* (1800).

Mary Rose (Royal Dockyard, Portsmouth) Oak warship built for Henry VIII at Portsmouth in 1509–10, and rebuilt there to an enlarged size of 700 tons in 1536. She was swamped and sank in 1545, just 2km/1.25m off Portsmouth harbour, when sailing to engage a French fleet.

Her wreck was first discovered by pioneer divers in 1836; and in 1982 the surviving timbers of her hull were lifted, in a most delicate operation, from the sea bed. An entire side has been preserved, with projecting fragments of its deck timbers, offering a fascinating cross section of the interior of an early warship. Relics of the ship's contents are also on display – among them eating utensils, musical instruments, gaming boards, fragments of clothing, longbows and cannon.

John **Masefield** (1878–1967) Poet whose apprenticeship was in the merchant navy and whose first book of poems in 1902 included *Sea Fever*; it was followed by *Cargoes* in a volume of 1910. His long narrative poem *The Everlasting Mercy* (1911) shocked many because of its use of everyday and sometimes profane language. He was made *poet laureate in 1930.

Dan **Maskell** (1908–92) The voice of tennis in Britain for nearly half a century, as the BBC's chief commentator on international tournaments until his retirement in 1992. He was on radio from 1949, on television from 1951. In his previous career he was a tennis professional and the country's leading coach.

James **Mason** (1909–84) Actor who became a major star of British films in the 1940s, in particular with *The Man in Grey* (1943), *The Seventh Veil* (1945) and *Odd Man Out* (1947). Subsequent roles included two ageing men lusting after younger women, in *Georgy Girl* (1966) and – a more extreme case – *Lolita* (1962).

masque Form of theatre deriving from entertainments at court or in noblemen's houses, when disguised players entered a banqueting hall to perform. The masque reached a peak of sophistication in the early 17c court performances for James I and Charles I. These were elaborate confections of words (most often by Ben *Jonson) and music, with scenery by Inigo *Jones. The brilliance of Jones's scenery, machinery and costumes caused the element of spectacle to develop at the expense of the words, and Jonson eventually withdrew complaining that painting and carpentry had become 'the soul of masque'.

Pleasures of the masque: costume design by Inigo Jones for a fiery spirit in a performance of 1613 for James I.

Such a privileged form of entertainment did not survive the English Civil War, but the staging techniques of the masque later became standard in the public theatres; and the lavishness survived in opera and ballet.

Masquerade (1979) Book written and illustrated by Kit Williams (b. 1946), which for three years involved millions of readers around the world in the pursuit of a golden hare. The illustrations contained hidden clues as to where Williams had buried it (at Ampthill in Bedfordshire). In 1982 it was found, almost by accident, just before two other treasure hunters located the exact spot – the only two to have cracked the book's very precise puzzle.

Mass-Observation A sociological enterprise launched in 1937. Described as 'an anthropology of ourselves', its aim was to gather a wealth of everyday detail about the British. It was based primarily on interviews and questionnaires, but people were also encouraged to keep diaries. The original survey lasted until the late 1940s. The undertaking was revived in 1981 under the auspices of the university of Sussex, and in the early 1990s there were about 600 regular contributors supplying written material about their daily lives.

Mastermind (BBC from 1972) Television quiz with a spotlit empty black chair as its opening image. The contestants suffering the inquisition must answer for two high-pressure minutes on a subject of their choice (often extremely esoteric) and then for another two minutes on general knowledge. The interruption of a question by the final bell has given the show its catch phrase, 'I've started so I'll finish'. The question master is Magnus Magnusson (b. 1929), Icelandic by birth but resident in Scotland.

Master of the Queen's (or King's) Music Royal appointment for life, carrying a token salary and a vague obligation to provide a piece of music from time to time for a state occasion. Originally the appointment was as director of the monarch's private orchestra. The first incumbent was Nicholas Lanier, who held the post for Charles I from 1626 and for Charles II from 1660. The recent holders have been *Elgar (1924–34), Walford Davies (1934–41), Arnold Bax (1942–53), Arthur *Bliss (1953–75) and since 1975 Malcolm *Williamson. Nicholas Lanier's annual salary in the 1660s was £200; Malcolm Williamson's today is £100.

Master of the Rolls The judge who presides over civil cases in the *Court of Appeal. His title goes back to the 16C, reflecting a responsibility for the legal records (the rolls). This link was revived in 1838 when he was given control of the newly created *Public Record Office (transferred in 1958 to the lord chancellor). The Master of the Rolls now chairs the Advisory Council on Public Records. Since 1992 the office has been held by Lord Justice *Bingham.

mastiff A large and powerful breed of dog, with short coat and massive head, which probably existed in Britain before the arrival of the Romans. It is believed that they took mastiffs back to Rome to pit them in arenas against wild animals and even gladiators. When *bear baiting became a popular sport in England, it was again mastiffs which did the baiting. The slightly smaller bull mastiff, bred in the 19C to discourage poachers, was a cross between the mastiff and the *bulldog.

Matchem see *thoroughbred.

Matilda (known also as the empress Maud, 1102–67) Daughter of *Henry I, and his only legitimate child after the death of her brother in the *White Ship. Henry persuaded the barons to accept her as his heir, though no woman had then reigned in either England or Normandy. But on his death in 1135 a rapid coup brought her cousin *Stephen to the throne (see the *royal house). She spent the next 13 years in desultory warfare against Stephen before retiring to Normandy, but she survived to see her son succeed to the throne in 1154 as Henry II (see house of *Plantagenet). She is known as the empress Maud (a variant of Matilda) because her first marriage was to the Holy Roman emperor, Henry V, who died in 1125.

Matlock (21,000 in 1991) Administrative centre of Derbyshire, on the river Derwent. The town itself is at the entrance to the dramatic limestone ravine through which the river flows south past Matlock Bath (famous as a spa in the 19C) to *Cromford; on either side of the ravine are High Tor (on the left bank) and the wooded Heights of Abraham, said to have been named by a soldier who was with General *Wolfe at Quebec.

Matrix Churchill Company of which three directors were prosecuted in 1992 for having exported material of military value to Iraq in 1988, in contravention of the British government's official embargo. The case against them collapsed when Alan Clark, who had been minister for trade at the time, admitted in court that he had advised the company to emphasize the potential peaceful use of the items and to be 'economical with the *actualité*' in their application for export licences. The question of who in the government had known that the guidelines were being breached (illegally but to the benefit of Britain's balance of payments) subsequently became the subject of much political controversy.

Stanley **Matthews** (b. 1915, kt 1965) The first footballer to be knighted and the first superstar of the game, famous for his long and dazzling dribbles down the right wing followed by a well-placed pass into the centre. He played his first League game for Stoke City in 1931, when he was 16; he then went to Blackpool (1947–61); and finally returned to Stoke, playing his last match for them at the age of 50 in 1965. His skill has been widely seen in the film of the 1953 Cup Final, when Blackpool beat Bolton. He appeared 54 times for England, many of them with Tom *Finney on the other wing.

Mauchline (18km/11m NE of Ayr) Village where *Burns married Jean Armour in 1788. The house in which they lived is kept as a museum.

Maud (1855) Poem by *Tennyson, telling in a wide variety of verse-forms the ups and downs of the narrator's life; down into family destitution after his father's death; up again through love of Maud; down into madness after killing Maud's brother in a duel; and finally up in a somewhat misplaced outburst of patriotism over the *Crimean War, seen as an antidote to Britain's materialism. The stanzas beginning *'Come into the garden, Maud' became famous as a song.

Empress **Maud** see *Matilda.

Maudie Littlehampton see Osbert *Lancaster.

Maudsley Hospital (London SE5) Psychiatric hospital, founded with money from Dr Henry Maudsley and opened in 1916. The Maudsley has been a medical school of London University since 1924 and is now (as the Institute of Psychiatry) the main centre for postgraduate education in the field.

Somerset **Maugham** (1874–1965) Novelist and playwright whose first book, *Liza of Lambeth* (1897), was a fictional account of the working-class London life which he had seen as a medical student at St Thomas's Hospital. His first real successes came in the theatre, beginning with *Lady Frederick* in 1907. His light witty comedies were so appealing that by the next year he had four plays running in the West End.

He returned to fiction with his most important book, *Of Human Bondage* (1915), an autobiographical novel in which Maugham's own handicap, a severe stammer, is reflected in the club foot of the hero, Philip Carey. He published several volumes of short stories, starting with *Orientations* (1899), and this was perhaps where his greatest skill lay. One story in particular, 'Rain' (in *The Trembling of a Leaf* 1921), has become a classic; set in steamy tropical Samoa, it recounts the relationship between a Scottish missionary and a lively American prostitute, Sadie Thompson. From 1928 he lived in the south of France, and in 1947 he established the Somerset Maugham Awards, providing funds to enable young writers to travel. The painting of him by Graham *Sutherland is one of the most striking of modern portraits.

Mau Mau see *Kenya.

Maundy money Specially minted silver coins given by the sovereign to a selected number of poor people on Maundy Thursday (the Thursday before Easter). It is a survival of a medieval church ritual commemorating the Last Supper and the washing by Jesus of the disciples' feet; the name derives from the Latin *mandatum*, which was the first word of the foot-washing ceremony. The coins are minted in the values of 1, 2, 3 and 4 pence and nowadays the ceremony exactly reflects the sovereign's age. In 1992, when Elizabeth II was in her 66th year, 66 men and 66 women each received coins amounting in face value to 66 pence.

Mauretania The outstanding ship of the *Cunard Line, launched in 1906 as a sister ship to the *Lusitania*. They were the first liners to be driven by *steam turbines, and the *Mauretania* held the *blue riband for an unprecedented 22 years (1907–29). She was broken up in 1935.

Mauritius Island in the Indian ocean, about 880km/550m east of Madagascar, which has been a member of the *Commonwealth since 1968. Though visited by Portuguese and Dutch ships, it was not permanently inhabited until the French settled it in the early 18C with African slaves to work sugar plantations. It was captured by Britain in 1810 during the Napoleonic wars, was ceded in 1814 by the treaty of Paris, and became independent in 1968.

Hiram **Maxim** (1840–1916, kt 1901) American-born inventor, naturalized in 1900 and known for the machine

Sail greets steam in a 1920s Cunard poster advertising the Mauretania's services from the USA to Europe.

gun which he developed in London in the 1880s; it was adopted by the British army in 1889. The first fully automatic gun (in the sense that the recoil was used to eject the spent cartridge and then insert and fire the new one), it achieved the extraordinary rate for the time of ten rounds per second. Manufactured by *Vickers, it became known as the Vickers Maxim.

James Clerk **Maxwell** (1831–79) Physicist whose mathematical development of *Faraday's proposals laid the basis for modern field theory. In a series of papers beginning with *On Faraday's Lines of Force* (1856) he provided a mathematical model for electromagnetism; this was followed by his *Treatise on Electricity and Magnetism* (1873), and the 'Maxwell equations' remain the cornerstone of the subject. His researches provided him with a further momentous conclusion. Confirming experimentally that the speed of an electric current through a wire is much the same as the speed of light, he was the first to assert that light is itself a form of electromagnetic radiation. In a different area, he also made an important contribution to the kinetic theory of gases. In 1871 he became the first Cavendish Professor of Physics at Cambridge, and it was he who set up the famous *Cavendish Laboratory.

Robert **Maxwell** (1923–91) Corrupt entrepreneur, whose death in 1991 (by drowning, after going overboard from his luxury yacht *Lady Ghislaine*) was followed by the discovery of the extent of his thefts; he had removed more than £400 million from the pension funds of the Mirror Group of newspapers to prop up his bankrupt companies. Born Jan Hoch, in Czechoslovakia, he was in Britain from 1940. He won an MC in the war, after which his first fortune came from his Pergamon Press; it published scientific research journals, for which a small number of institutions were willing to pay large sums.

In 1969 a Board of Trade investigation into the finances of Pergamon concluded that Maxwell was not a suitable person to head a publicly quoted company (he was at the time Labour MP for Buckingham, 1964–70). In spite of this he managed to build an ever-expanding empire, and his most glamorous purchase was of the *Daily Mirror* and its sister newspapers in 1984. By nature a bully, quick to stifle criticism with the threat of litigation, he also had a blustering panache which endeared him to many as 'Captain Bob'. In June 1992 his sons Kevin and Ian, who worked with him, were charged with criminal offences. In September of that year Kevin was declared bankrupt to the sum of £406.5 million, a British record by a wide margin.

Peter **Maxwell Davies** (b. 1934, kt 1987) Prolific composer, many of whose works have had their first performances with his chamber music ensemble, the Fires of London; this evolved from the earlier Pierrot Players which he founded in 1967 with Harrison *Birtwistle. Since 1970 he has lived on the island of Hoy, in the Orkneys, where the annual St Magnus Festival (established by him in 1977) also premieres his work, much of it written for local children. His operas include *Taverner* (1970) and *The Lighthouse* (1979).

Peter **May** (b. 1929) The most successful batsman of his generation in English *cricket, playing for *Surrey (1950–63) throughout the period in which they had their unparalleled run of seven consecutive championship victories. His *Test career (1951–61, captain 1955–61) was equally exceptional: he still holds (in 1992) the record for the most Tests and the most victories as captain (a total of

The beginnings of the modern May Day, with children dancing round a maypole in the New Forest (wood engraving, 1852).

41, with 35 in an unbroken sequence and 21 wins); and his stand of 411 with *Cowdrey at Edgbaston in 1957 (his own score was 285) remains the highest 4th wicket stand in Test cricket and England's highest stand for any wicket.

May Day All primitive societies at any distance from the equator are likely to have held a spring festival to celebrate the triumph of light over darkness, and this event became stabilized on May 1 (some ten days after the equinox) in the regions of northwest Europe. The earliest known British tradition of this kind was the *Beltane of the Celts. The present-day central feature, the maypole, is believed to have arrived with the Anglo-Saxons. By the Middle Ages the festivities included *morris dancing and a bawdy May King, often linked with *Robin Hood. These robust revelries came to an end in the 16–17c under Puritan influence, and their revival in a more genteel form was part of 19c medievalism. In modern village celebrations (usually on the first Saturday in May) the shy May Queen is a schoolgirl, and the lacing of the maypole with ribbons attached to its top is a well-rehearsed routine. Traces of wilder origins survive in the hobby horses of *Minehead and *Padstow. By contrast an entirely calm start to the day is provided in the May Singing on Magdalen College tower in Oxford; in a tradition of disputed origin but dating back to least the 17c, the college choir greets the dawn of May with madrigals and a Latin hymn.

The link betweeen May Day and Socialism derives from its adoption as a workers' holiday by the Second International in Paris in 1889. In Britain May Day was introduced as an extra *bank holiday in 1978, but is to be dropped again from 1995.

Mayerling (1978) Three-act ballet by Kenneth *MacMillan, to music by Liszt, about the sexual and psychological torment leading up to the suicide at Mayerling in 1889 of the Austrian crown prince Rudolf and his mistress, Mary Vetsera. The ballet, with its violently expressive love scenes, was created for David Wall and Lynn Seymour.

Mayfair (London W1) Consistently the most expensive area of residential London since it was first developed in the late 17c. It derives its name from an annual fair held for two weeks in May; this took place, around what is now Curzon Street, from the 1680s until it was closed down in the mid-18c. The area forms a neat rectangle, bounded by four famous thoroughfares – *Piccadilly, *Regent Street, *Oxford Street and *Park Lane.

Mayflower see the *Pilgrim Fathers.

Patrick **Mayhew** (b. 1929, kt 1983) Conservative politician, MP for Tunbridge Wells since 1974. He was attorney general (1987–92) before entering the *cabinet in 1992 as secretary of state for Northern Ireland.

The *Mayor of Casterbridge: the life and death of a man of character* (1886) Novel by Thomas *Hardy, recounting the bleak story of Michael Henchard who begins the book drunk (selling his wife and daughter for five guineas at a fair) and ends it destitute (dying in a hut on Egdon Heath). In the intervening years this man of character, turned sober and respectable, has risen to become the prosperous mayor of Casterbridge. Through his own obstinacy he gradually loses everything once again, this time to his energetic Scottish manager, Donald Farfrae – who marries in turn Henchard's intended new wife (Lucetta Le Sueur) and his supposed daughter Elizabeth-Jane (discovered not to be his), as well as becoming mayor and taking over Henchard's business and his house.

Maypole and Elephant see *George I.

maypole and **May Queen** see *May Day.

Maze Prison in Northern Ireland, to the west of Belfast, which was opened in 1971 as the Long Kesh *internment camp (the name was soon changed to the Maze). The internees lived there like prisoners of war, wearing their own clothes and doing no prison work. After the end of internment in 1975, the convicted terrorists in the prison began a long campaign to be allowed the same political or 'special category' status. Their methods included the 'dirty protest' (smearing excrement on the walls of the H-blocks, named from the shape of each block as seen from the air) and a long series of hunger strikes. Eventually ten republican convicts starved themselves to death. The first was Bobby Sands, who died on 5 May 1981, less than a month after winning (from prison) a parliamentary by-election for Fermanagh and South Tyrone on an 'anti-H-block' ticket. In 1983 there was a mass break-out by 38 IRA prisoners, during which one prison officer died and six others were shot or stabbed. It was announced in 1991 that the Maze would close as soon as a replacement could be built.

MBE see *orders of chivalry.

MC and **MM** (Military Cross and Medal) Decorations for gallantry in the army, instituted in 1914 and 1916. The MC is awarded to junior officers (captain and below) and to senior noncomissioned officers, and the MM to lower ranks.

MCC (Marylebone Cricket Club) Club founded in 1787, with its headquarters at *Lord's, which rapidly became the accepted authority in *cricket (a role in which it succeeded the *Hambledon club). With the development of county cricket its importance as a playing club reduced, and in 1877 it persuaded the *Middlesex County Cricket Club to share its ground. In the late 19c the MCC administered the *county championship and *Test matches in England, and from the early 20c the club selected and managed teams playing for England abroad (Test teams travelled as the MCC until 1977). In 1968 these administrative roles were taken on by the Cricket Council and the Test and County Cricket Board (which meet at Lord's), but the MCC remains responsible for the laws of cricket.

mead Alcoholic drink made from fermented honey and water, a speciality of both Celts and Anglo-Saxons. It was the most common liquor in England until replaced in the late Middle Ages by home-grown ales for the majority and by imported wines for the rich.

Richard **Meade** (b. 1938) The most successful of Britain's three-day-event riders at the Olympic Games, with an individual gold medal in 1972 and team golds in 1968 and 1972. He was also in gold-medal teams at the World Championships (1967, 71, 81), and he has won at both Badminton (1970, 82) and Burghley (1964).

Meadowbank Sports Stadium (Edinburgh) Opened in 1970 in time for the Commonwealth Games of that year, the stadium was again the location when the games returned to Britain in 1986. With one large outdoor arena and several smaller ones under cover, Meadowbank is used for more than 30 different sports in addition to being the home ground of Meadowbank Thistle football club. At the New Year it is the location of the *Powderhall sprint.

Measure for Measure (c.1604) Play by *Shakespeare which is a comedy in that it has a happy ending, but is so dark in tone that it is often described (like *All's Well of the same period) as a 'problem' play. Vincentio, duke of Vienna, hands over control to his deputy, Angelo, and disguises himself as a friar to watch the results. Angelo begins by introducing extreme puritan measures but in no time is suggesting that he will spare the life of Claudio if he can sleep with his sister, Isabella, a novice nun. After further villainies the disguised duke declares himself and then wraps matters up by insisting upon four marriages, at least two of them totally unsuitable.

measurements see *area, *length, fluid *volume and *weight.

Meccano Children's engineering construction kit of girders, bolts and pulleys, patented in Liverpool in 1893 by Frank Hornby (1863–1936). He marketed Meccano from 1901, and Meccano Ltd later became the parent company producing his famous Hornby trains (from 1920) and Dinky Toy model cars (from the 1930s). The Hornby range became part of Triang Railways in 1964. Meccano continued to be manufactured in Liverpool until the factory closed in the early 1990s.

Peter **Medawar** (1915–87, kt 1965) Immunologist whose researches made possible the development of transplant surgery. During World War II he worked on skin grafts for burn victims, and he subsequently pioneered methods of avoiding the body's natural rejection of transplanted tissue – building on the discovery of the Australian scientist Macfarlane Burnet that the ability to produce antibodies (the agents of rejection) is not innate but is acquired during the foetal stage of development. Burnet and Medawar shared the Nobel prize for medicine in 1960.

Medway River in Kent, about 110km/70m long, flowing north to enter the Thames at Sheerness. Its estuary begins at Rochester and a little further downstream is Chatham.

Lord **Melbourne** (William Lamb, 1779–1848, 2nd viscount Melbourne 1828) Whig politician whose time as prime minister (1834, 1835–41) is largely remembered for his avuncular relationship with the young queen, Victoria, who said that he made her feel 'safe and comfortable'. His private life had been less satisfactory. His virtually deranged wife (Lady Caroline Lamb, 1785–1828) had an affair with *Byron in 1812–13 which became a very public scandal; and when prime minister he had to appear in court to face a charge (unsuccessful and probably unjust) that he had committed adultery with his friend Caroline Norton. He was home secretary (1830–4) during the period which saw the passing of the *Reform Act, but he took a repressive line with the *Tolpuddle martyrs.

Mellerstain (64km/40m SE of Edinburgh) House begun for the Baillie family by William *Adam in 1725. He provided only the two wings, which remained disconnected until his son Robert was commissioned in about 1770 to complete the house. He gave it the castellated roofline which was then coming into fashion. The interiors, in particular the library, are outstanding examples of the *Adam style.

David **Mellor** (b. 1949) Conservative politician, MP for Putney since 1979. He entered the cabinet in 1990 as chief secretary to the Treasury. In 1992 he became the first secretary of state in the new Department of *National Heritage, involving (among much else) responsibility for the media. In July of that year the tabloid press made much of his affair with an actress, Antonia de Sancha. With the firm support of the prime minister, Mellor survived calls for

him to be moved to another job; his opponents had argued that there was now a conflict of interest in his deciding on issues of *privacy and the press. But there was a second wave of public interest in his fitness for high office when it was revealed that he had accepted holiday airline tickets for himself and his family from someone connected, albeit obliquely, with the PLO (Palestine Liberation Organization). This time Tory backbench pressure led to his resignation, in September 1992.

Mellors see *Lady Chatterley's Lover.

George **Melly** (b. 1926) Jazz singer, author and something of a living art object in a wide repertoire of large and violently coloured suits. He sang first with Mick Mulligan's jazz band (1949–61) and has been since 1974 with John Chilton's Feetwarmers. His other career, as a wit and raconteur, has included writing the strip cartoon *Flook and some racy books of autobiography (Owning Up 1965, Rum, Bum and Concertina 1977).

melodrama Term used from the early 19C for plays, usually of a sensational kind, interspersed with the occasional song (melos in Greek). As the century progressed, the songs were dropped. Heroines in melodrama were always pure, while villains (the real stars of the entertainment) were of the deepest hue. Real crimes often provided a popular plot (such as The *Red Barn), and even the greatest actors were not above making the most of melodrama's possibilities (*Irving, for example, in The Bells). The most performed of them all was *East Lynne.

Melody Maker Weekly paper founded in 1926, originally covering both music and dance and for a while including jazz. In recent decades it has been entirely concerned with pop music.

The most famous moment in all melodrama: 'dead! and never called me mother!' (see East Lynne).

A section of box girder for Robert Stephenson's railway bridge over the Menai Strait: lithograph after G. Hawkins, 1849.

Melrose (60km/37m SE of Edinburgh) Small town, on the river Tweed, which was a monastic site from the first Celtic settlement in the 7C to the final days of the Cistercian abbey destroyed by the English in 1545. The present extensive ruins date from the 14–15C. Part of the abbey's attraction is the romantic tradition that the heart of *Robert the Bruce lies buried here, where the high altar once stood beneath the east window.

Menai Strait Channel separating *Anglesey from Wales. Its narrowest point (about 185m/200yd wide, at the northeast end near Bangor) has been crossed by two historically important bridges. The road bridge, built 1819–26 by Thomas *Telford, was the first suspension bridge to be attempted on this scale. Nearby is the Britannia railway bridge (1846–50), in which Robert *Stephenson pioneered his box-girder or tubular design (severely damaged by fire in 1970, it has been rebuilt with a road above the railway). A pair of similar but shorter bridges, by the same two engineers, carry road and rail across the river at Conwy.

Mencap (Royal Society for Mentally Handicapped Children and Adults, London EC1) Charity which began as a pressure group to improve services for mentally handicapped children after a correspondence between frustrated and anxious mothers in *Nursery World* in 1946. Its activities were soon extended to include similarly handicapped adults. In 1982 Mencap opened its first residential home, of which there are now more than 300. It has an energetic leader in Brian *Rix, who became secretary general in 1980 and has been chairman since 1988.

Mendips Limestone range of hills in Somerset (highest point 326m/1068ft), running some 40km/25m north-west from just north of Wells. There are many dramatic caves, in particular *Wookey Hole and those of the *Cheddar Gorge.

Daniel **Mendoza** (1764–1836) Jewish pugilist, from the days of bare-knuckle fights, who became the first British boxer to be widely remembered. He had a more scientific approach than his predecessors, writing a short book on the subject (*The Art of Boxing* 1789) and following this with his memoirs (1816). He was British champion 1791–5.

menhirs see *standing stones.

Menin Gate see *Ypres.

Men of Harlech see *Harlech.

Mensa Social organization founded in Oxford in 1946 by two barristers, restricting its membership to those with an IQ equal to the top 2% of the population. The society grew rapidly from the 1960s in the USA, and in the early 1990s has about 100,000 members worldwide. The name (Latin for table) was chosen to reflect Mensa's *'round table' nature, composed of equal members without a hierarchy.

Mentmore Towers (13km/8m NE of Aylesbury) House of spectacular Victorian opulence, imitating the prodigy houses of the Elizabethan age and modelled in particular on *Wollaton. It was built 1852–4 by *Paxton for Baron Meyer de Rothschild (1818–74), a great collector who filled it with treasures. In 1878 his only daughter married Lord *Rosebery. Their descendants sold the contents in a famous auction in 1977, after removing the best items to

*Dalmeny House. Mentmore itself was bought by the Maharishi Mahesh Yogi for use as a college of transcendental meditation.

Yehudi **Menuhin** (b. 1916, KBE 1965) American-born British violinist, the outstanding child prodigy of the 20c. He gave his first public recital in San Francisco at the age of seven, playing Mendelssohn's violin concerto. He made his European debut in Paris at the age of ten, and at 11 caused a sensation in New York playing the Beethoven concerto under Fritz Busch. At 12 he appeared in Berlin and London playing concertos by Bach, Beethoven and Brahms in a single programme. As an adult virtuoso he had works composed for him by Bartók, Walton and others. After World War II he settled in England and in 1963 founded a boarding school for musically gifted children at Stoke d'Abernon in Surrey (its most successful pupil has been Nigel *Kennedy). He is a member of the Order of *Merit.

MEP (Member of the European Parliament) Member elected to represent one of the 78 *constituencies of England, Wales and Scotland at the *European Parliament, or elected by proportional representation as one of the three members for Northern Ireland. The first direct elections to the parliament were in 1979, and they have been held at 5-year intervals since. The letters MEP are placed after a member's name.

Joe **Mercer** see *Brigadier Gerard.

Merchant Adventurers' Hall see *York.

*The **Merchant of Venice*** (c.1596) Play by *Shakespeare in which a Venetian merchant, Antonio, borrows money from Shylock the Jew to enable Bassanio to marry Portia. It is Shylock who dominates the play; presented on one level as a figure deserving ridicule and hatred, he acquires in Shakespeare's hands a tragic stature. His bond, if the money is not repaid, is a pound of the merchant's flesh. Antonio's ships are delayed and Shylock claims his due. Portia disguises herself as a lawyer to plead for Antonio, with her famous speech beginning 'The quality of mercy is not strained'. But Shylock insists. His evil intent is defeated only by Portia's legalistic argument that his bond is described as flesh and that if he spills a drop of blood in taking it he must die. Subplots include the courting of Portia and of Jessica, Shylock's daughter. Portia, an heiress, can only be won by a suitor who decides correctly whether her portrait is in a casket of gold, silver or lead (Bassanio wins with lead). Jessica elopes with a Christian, to the horror of Shylock who is forced to leave her his wealth and to turn Christian himself.

Mercia One of the most powerful of the *Anglo-Saxon kingdoms, occupying the centre of England. By the 8c, when it was ruled by Offa (the builder of *Offa's Dyke), it extended from the Humber in the north to the Thames in the south and from the frontiers of Wales to those of East Anglia. With neighbouring rulers to some extent accepting his supremacy, Offa came closer than anyone since the departure of the Romans to re-establishing England as a political entity. Mercia subsequently declined, under pressure from Danish invasions in the east and the rise of *Wessex in the south.

Mercury Telecommunications company set up in 1981, when the government ended the Post Office's monopoly of the national telephone system and invited applications for a licence to compete with *BT. Mercury, the only applicant, became in 1984 a wholly owned subsidiary of *Cable and Wireless. In that year it began to lay a network of fibre optic cables alongside railway lines. Mercury's public telephone boxes, introduced on Waterloo Station in 1988, have become familiar sights around the country; and in the early 1990s the company began to extend its customer range from commercial to domestic subscribers.

George **Meredith** (1828–1909) Novelist and poet, whose first successful works were written after his wife left him in 1857. Both the novel *The Ordeal of Richard Feverel* (1859) and the sequence of poems *Modern Love* (1862) start with the pain of failed love; the novel, following its young hero through successive relationships, caused initial offence by its frankness. *The Egoist* (1879) has as its central character a conceited aristocrat, Sir Willoughby Patterne, who cannot understand why he is jilted by a succession of young women who were at first drawn to him. Meredith's most popular novel, *Diana of the Crossways* (1885), recounts the adventures of the attractive and impulsive Diana Warwick in the world of politics. One of his poems, The *Lark Ascending, has become better known in a wordless form, for it inspired the 'romance' by Vaughan Williams.

Merionethshire Former *county in Wales, since 1974 part of Gwynedd.

Order of **Merit** An unusual *order of chivalry in that it ranks very high (after the Garter, the Thistle and the Bath) but does not confer knighthood; members, limited to 24 British men and women plus an occasional honorary foreigner, merely place OM after their names. Instituted in 1902 by Edward VII, and in the personal gift of the sovereign, it is intended for those who have made an 'exceptionally meritorious' contribution in any field, with

---

Members of the Order of Merit in 1993

The Sovereign
The Duke of Edinburgh 1968

Dorothy Hodgkin 1965
Dame Veronica Wedgwood 1969
Sir Isaiah Berlin 1971
Sir George Edwards 1971
Sir Alan Hodgkin 1973
Lord Todd 1977
Lord Franks 1977
Revd Owen Chadwick 1983
Sir Andrew Huxley 1983
Sir Michael Tippett 1983
Frederick Sanger 1986
Sir Frank Whittle 1986
Sir Yehudi Menuhin 1987
Sir Ernst Gombrich 1988
Max Perutz 1988
Dame Cicely Saunders 1989
Lord Porter of Luddenham 1990
Baroness Thatcher 1990
Dame Joan Sutherland 1991
Francis Crick 1991
Sir Michael Atiyah 1992
Dame Ninette de Valois 1992

Honorary Member, Mother Teresa 1983

a stated emphasis on 'the Arts, Learning, Literature and Science'. The scientists in the first dozen appointments were of undeniable distinction (they included Joseph Lister and William Thomson), but the first artist has lasted less well – G.F. Watts. Florence Nightingale was the first woman to be appointed, in 1907.

Merlin Magician who appears with varying characteristics in the Arthurian legends (the variety is due more to inconsistent local traditions than to his own magical skills). His chief role is as adviser to *Arthur and to Arthur's father, Uther Pendragon. It was Merlin's idea that Uther's successor should be revealed by whoever could draw *Excalibur from the stone. In one story the building of Stonehenge is credited to his magic.

Mermaid A tavern in London (it stood in Bread Street), which was frequented by Shakespeare, Ben Jonson, John Donne and other poets. It was destroyed in the *Great Fire. The name was revived for the Mermaid Theatre, which opened in 1959 as the first new theatre in the *City since the time of those celebrated writers.

*The **Merry Wives of Windsor*** (c.1600) Comedy by *Shakespeare, written in response to the great success of the character of Falstaff in *Henry IV*. The plot centres on Falstaff's plan to secure funds by seducing two rich wives of Windsor, Mistress Ford and Mistress Page. Rumbling his scheme (they have received identical love letters), they subject him to a series of humiliations. In the last he is persuaded to dress as Herne the Hunter, a horned spectre haunting Windsor Park, in the hope of an assignation beneath an oak tree. There he is cruelly pinched by young fairies dressed up by Mistress Page for the occasion.

Mersey River, about 115km/70m long, which rises on the western slopes of the Pennines and flows north and west, passing just south of Manchester, to enter its broad estuary at Runcorn. The chief port and city on the estuary is Liverpool, on the north bank. There are three tunnels under the Mersey, one for the underground railway (1886) and two for roads (1934, 1971).

Mersey beat Term coined for the British style of rock music which emerged in Liverpool (on the river Mersey) in the mid-60s, the leading exponents being the *Beatles.

Merseyside (1,404,000 in 1991) *Metropolitan county in northwest England, on both sides of the estuary of the Mersey, consisting of five *districts – Knowsley, Liverpool, St Helens, Sefton and Wirral.

Mesopotamia see *Iraq.

Messiah (1742) Oratorio composed by *Handel to verses from various parts of the Bible. Performed in Dublin in April 1742, it was first heard in London at Covent Garden theatre in March 1743. The Hallelujah Chorus, at the end of Part 2, acquired on that occasion a lasting tradition: George II rose to his feet as it began, in a gesture followed by British audiences ever since. The work only gradually acquired its status as one of the most popular pieces of English music, largely through the annual performances for charity which Handel gave at London's Foundling Hospital.

The *Messiah* has been the occasion of a notable piece of academic snobbery. By those in the know it is considered deeply ignorant to use 'the' in front of *Messiah*, as at the start of this paragraph – in spite of its being the more natural usage in English. The uninitiated can take heart from the advertisement for the first performance in Dublin,

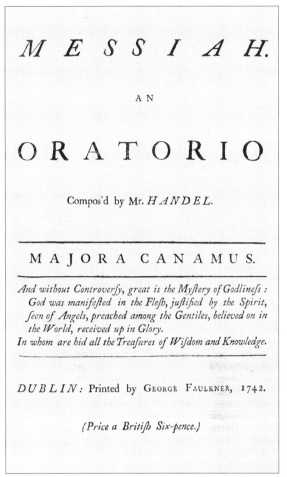

Title page of the first edition of Messiah, *published in 1742 in Dublin and sold for 'a British sixpence'.*

which announced a performance of 'Mr. Handel's new Grand Oratorio, called the *Messiah*'; and later that year Handel himself wrote to a friend promising to send him 'the printed Book of the Messiah'.

'messing about in boats' see The *Wind in the Willows.

metaphysical poets An imprecise term applied to *Donne, *Herbert, *Marvell and others of the 17c who shared a love of intellectual ingenuity, literary allusion and paradox, and who used language, images and rhythms of a kind not conventionally 'poetic' to startle the reader into thought; they were criticized in their own time for taking 'metaphysics' as their subject. They acquired a high reputation in the 20c after winning T.S. Eliot as both champion and disciple.

Meteor The only jet aircraft in service with the Allied forces in World War II. The first Gloster Meteor, with a top speed of 670kph/415mph, was delivered to the RAF in July 1944. Meteors spent the rest of that year pursuing *V1s over Britain (but only shooting down 13 in all). The first German jet, the Messerschmidt Me 262, also entered service in 1944 (before the Meteor).

Meteorological Office (also known as the Met. Office) Organization with its headquarters at Bracknell in Berkshire. It was founded in 1854 as a department within the Board of Trade, with Captain Fitzroy (previously of HMS *Beagle*) as its first director. Its brief was to provide

Miniature anticipating elements of the metaphysical poets (see previous page): portrait of Henry Percy by Hilliard, c.1595.

information on weather conditions and currents (the *shipping forecast remains a central responsibility). The information behind the weather forecasts is collected from nearly 300 stations around Britain, from balloons and satellites, and from a voluntary international fleet of some 7000 ships and rigs; it is combined with data from previous records before being processed by computer. The weather forecasts on television, presented by employees of the Met. Office, are the aspect of its work best known to the public. Under the *Next Steps programme it became, in 1990, an executive agency within the Ministry of Defence.

Methodists Members of the Christian church which derives from the 18c evangelical movement led by John and Charles *Wesley. Wesleyan preachers were most influential in deprived industrial areas; the great centres of Methodism became the Welsh mining valleys (where singing in the chapel has been a strong tradition) and the factory towns of the Midlands (Methodism features prominently in the novels of Arnold *Bennett). During the 19c the Methodists split into several mutually disaffected groups, but the most important of these (including the Primitive Methodists and the Wesleyan Methodists) united again in 1932 to form the present Methodist Church in Great Britain. Its governing body is the Conference, meeting annually and dating back to the occasion in 1744 when John Wesley first summoned his itinerant preachers to come together and confer. The founders of the movement took Methodism to the USA in the 18c; and the Wesleyan Methodist Missionary Society, founded in Britain in 1813, spread the message further afield. There are now believed to be about 54 million Methodists worldwide, with slightly fewer than half a million in

Britain (for the numbers attending church in England see *Christians).

metric system The system which in the late 20c is gradually replacing *imperial weights and measures in Britain. It is based on a supremely logical concept first put forward in France in 1670 (by the vicar of a church in Lyons) and eventually introduced by the National Assembly during the Revolution (in 1791). The essence of the system is not only a decimal relationship between each grade of units; it is that a single unit was made the basis for measurements of length, weight and volume. The unit chosen was the metre, defined as one ten-millionth of the distance from the equator to the north pole. The unit of weight, the gram, was then defined as the weight of a cube of water measuring one hundredth of a metre in each dimension; and the unit of liquid volume, the litre, was defined as the amount which would fit in a cube one tenth of a metre all round (or, stated differently, the space occupied by one kilogram of water, which amounts in this elegant edifice to the same thing). With improved techniques of measurement the definition of the metre has changed – it is now 1,650,763.73 wavelengths of the orange-red line of krypton-86 – but by 1791 the system itself was in place.

metropolitan county Administrative area created by the Local Government Act of 1972 (effective from 1974). Six major English conurbations (Greater Manchester, Merseyside, South Yorkshire, Tyne and Wear, West Midlands, West Yorkshire) were removed from their previous *counties to become separate metropolitan counties, each subdivided into up to ten *districts. They had a two-tier system of *local government (metropolitan county council and district council) until the Local Government Act of 1985 (effective from 1986). This abolished the metropolitan county councils along with the *Greater London Council, leaving the six metropolitan counties and London with a single tier of local authority.

Castle of **Mey** see *Queen Mother.

mezzotint see Prince *Rupert.

MG Britain's best-known series of relatively cheap sports cars. They were developed by Cecil Kimber, the manager of Morris Garages (the origin of the initials MG). He commissioned six in 1923 using the Morris-Cowley chassis, and two years later began producing custom-built cars for sporting competition from a factory at Abingdon in Berkshire. The enterprise remained part of the *Morris group, and as such became absorbed in 1952 in the *British Motor Corporation.

MI5 and **MI6** The government agencies responsible for security at home and abroad. Their names, standing for Military Intelligence sections 5 and 6, were once official. They survive in popular use, but MI5 is now called the Security Service and MI6 the Secret Intelligence Service. The traditional division of roles has been that MI5 operates within the United Kingdom as counter-intelligence, responsible for domestic security against hostile agents and spies; MI6 works abroad and is itself an intelligence-gathering or espionage agency. The end of the Cold War led to much discussion in the early 1990s of how their roles should be altered and whether they should be merged. In 1992 MI5 took over from the Special Branch (see *police) the leading role in intelligence gathering against IRA terrorist activity.

Until very recently public information about either agency was severely restricted, as seen in the government's attempts in 1987 to suppress *Spycatcher*. But the

Security Service Act of 1989 put MI5 for the first time on a statutory basis, with a commissioner overseeing its activities and reporting, through the prime minister, to parliament. In 1992 a similar level of exposure to public scrutiny was promised for MI6, which has traditionally been even more invisible; officially its very existence was until then denied, even though a large and very eye-catching building by Terry *Farrell was constructed near Vauxhall Bridge in the early 1990s as its new headquarters.

The head of MI6 has been referred to as C – short for CSS, or Chief of the Secret Service – ever since the first Secret Service Bureau was set up in 1909. He is said to be the origin of a similar and more widely known figure, M, who heads the agency employing Ian *Fleming's James Bond. A tradition of official secrecy about the identity of those in charge of the two services was recently ended, first with the public appointment in 1991 of Stella Rimington (b. 1935) as head of MI5 (the first female director of any major Western intelligence agency) and then with the announcement in 1992 that Sir Colin McColl (b. 1932) was to stay on for two more years in charge of MI6.

Mr **Micawber** see *David Copperfield.

George **Michael** (stage name of Georgios Panayiotou, b. 1963) Pop singer and songwriter, born in London the son of a Greek Cypriot father and an English mother. He is the only superstar to have emerged in British pop since the 1970s. In 1981 he formed Wham! with his schoolfriend Andrew Ridgeley, and they had four no. 1 hits before splitting up in 1986. Michael's biggest success by then had been a single on his own, *Careless Whisper* (1984); this was followed by *A Different Corner* (1986). His first solo album, *Faith* (1987), written, arranged and produced by himself (and performed by him on a variety of instruments), was no. 1 in both the UK and the US, where three of its tracks also topped the singles charts. *Faith* was followed by the less commercial *Listen Without Prejudice* (1990).

*The **Microcosm of London** see Thomas *Rowlandson.

Middle English see *English.

Middleham Jewel (Yorkshire Museum, York) Important piece of English jewellery of the 15C, consisting of a diamond-shaped gold pendant engraved with an image of the Trinity and embellished with a large sapphire. It was discovered in 1985 near Middleham Castle, on the edge of the Yorkshire Dales. In 1991 the Yorkshire Museum launched an appeal for £2.5m to save it from leaving the country.

***Middlemarch**, a study of provincial life* (1871–2) Novel by George *Eliot which, as its subtitle states, provides a detailed panorama of life in Middlemarch, a provincial town in Loamshire. The central character is the idealistic Dorothea Brooke. She makes a disastrous marriage to the pedantic Edward Casaubon (working on an interminable *Key to All Mythologies*) and gradually discovers her affection for his cheerful young cousin, Will Ladislaw; Casaubon attempts to ruin her future by a codicil denying her his fortune if she marries Will, but after his death they acknowledge their love and renounce the money. Prominent also in the town are Tertius Lydgate, a talented doctor whose life is ruined by the social pretensions of his wife, Rosamund; her brother Fred and his childhood sweetheart, Mary Garth; and Mr Bulstrode, a hypocritical banker with a shady past. But the novel's densely woven fabric, offering many other characters with almost equal demands on the reader's interest, results in Middlemarch itself becoming the theme of the book.

Middlesbrough (144,000 in 1991) Port and industrial town on the south bank of the Tees estuary; administrative centre of Cleveland. It developed rapidly from a tiny fishing village when the *Stockton and Darlington railway was extended to the coast in 1830. Export of coal from the Durham mines brought the first growth, boosted by

MI6 keeping the opposite of a low profile in the 1990s: the new Thames-side headquarters by Terry Farrell.

the discovery in the 1850s of iron ore in the Cleveland Hills. The Dorman Museum tells the history of the area's development; the city's Art Gallery has specialized in British painting of the 20C; and a little to the south, at Marton, Captain Cook's birthplace is kept as a museum.

Middlesex Former *county to the northwest of London which ceased to exist, except in postal addresses and in various county activities such as cricket matches, when it was wholly absorbed in 1965 within *Greater London. Its name goes back to *Anglo-Saxon times, when it lay in the 'middle' between the East Saxons of Essex and the West Saxons of Wessex.

Middlesex County Cricket Club Founded in 1864, and one of the original teams in the *county championship; it won once (1866) before the points system was introduced in 1890, and subsequently has had eight victories (1903, 20, 21, 47, 76, 80, 82, 85) in addition to tying in 1949 with Yorkshire and in 1977 with Kent. In *one-day cricket the club has won the Gillette Cup and NatWest Bank Trophy four times (1977, 80, 84, 88) and the Benson and Hedges Cup twice (1983, 86). Among Middlesex's best-known players have been 'Plum' *Warner, 'Gubby' *Allen and Denis *Compton. The county ground is *Lord's, shared with the *MCC since 1877, and the county plays also at Uxbridge.

Middlesex Sevens see *rugby football.

Middle Temple see *Inns of Court.

Mid Glamorgan (542,000 in 1991, administrative centre Cardiff) Since 1974 a *county in Wales, formed from parts of Glamorgan, Breconshire and Monmouthshire.

Midland Bank One of the *clearing banks, established in Birmingham in 1836 by a young Cornishman, Charles Geach. The Midland acquired two London banks during the 1890s, the Central and the City, and moved its headquarters to Threadneedle Street in 1898. In 1930 a spectacular new headquarters was opened in Poultry, designed by Lutyens. Midland pioneered low-cost telephone banking in Britain in 1989 with its First Direct service, but by the early 1990s it was the weakest of the 'big four' clearing banks. In 1992 Lloyds attempted to take it over so as to merge and reduce in number their joint high-street outlets, but Midland was acquired in that year by the Hongkong and Shanghai Banking Corporation.

Midlands The central area of England, which became heavily industrialized during the 19C. It is approximately enclosed within a ring (starting in the west and moving clockwise) formed by Wolverhampton, Stoke-on-Trent, Derby, Nottingham, Leicester, Northampton, Stratford-upon-Avon and Worcester.

Midlothian Until 1975 a *county in southeast Scotland, on the southern shore of the Firth of Forth, now part of the Lothian region (except for its southern tip, which is in the Borders region).

*A **Midsummer Night's Dream*** (c.1596) Play by *Shakespeare in which three very different sets of characters intermingle in a wood near Athens. The king of the fairies, Oberon, is angry with his queen, Titania, because she will not give up to him a changeling Indian boy. He employs his spirit servant *Puck to play a trick on her. As she sleeps, Puck squeezes into her eyes the juice of a wild pansy (love-in-idleness); she will now fall in love with whoever she first sees on waking.

Another group has come into the wood to rehearse a play. They are Athenian craftsmen – Quince the carpenter, Snug the joiner, Flute the bellows-mender, Snout the tinker, Starveling the tailor and the irrepressible Bottom the weaver. Puck puts an ass's head on Bottom ('Bless thee, Bottom . . . thou art translated', says Quince), and it is he whom Titania sees and dallies with when she wakes.

The third group is from the Athenian court. The duke, Theseus, is about to marry Hippolyta, the queen of the Amazons. Two young couples (Hermia and Lysander, Helena and Demetrius) enter the wood. Puck with his magic flower spins them through a labyrinth of misplaced affections before all comes right. As part of the wedding celebrations Bottom and his fellows perform their spectacularly incompetent play of Pyramus and Thisbe.

In 1960 the play was used as the basis for an opera of the same name by Benjamin Britten.

*The **Mikado** or, The Town of Titipu* (1885) One of the *Savoy operas by Gilbert and Sullivan, set in the Japanese town of Titipu. The chief characters are: Ko-Ko, the Lord High Executioner ('I've got a little list'); the girl he plans to marry, Yum Yum, who is one of his three wards ('Three little girls from school are we'); Yum Yum's beloved, the musician Nanki-Poo ('A wandering minstrel I'), who is in fact the Mikado's son in disguise; and the Mikado himself, emperor of Japan, who has a whimsical interest in finding ways to 'let the punishment fit the crime'.

mild see *bitter.

Mildenhall Treasure (British Museum) Hoard of Roman silver of the 4th century AD, discovered during ploughing near Mildenhall in Suffolk in the early 1940s. Its chief glory is the vast and purely pagan 'great dish', but some of the smaller items (for example several spoons) are of interest for being marked with symbols revealing that they were owned by *Christians.

mile see *length.

Milford Haven (14,000 in 1981) Town in Dyfed, established in the 1790s beside the natural harbour from which it takes its name. This had been for many centuries the normal place of departure for armies crossing to Ireland, and it was here that Henry VII landed in 1485 to make his bid for the crown. The town has had a new lease of life in the second half of the 20C as an oil terminal, since the deep waters of the harbour can accommodate vast modern tankers.

Militant Tendency The most active far-left group in Britain in recent decades, Trotskyite in its policies but aiming to work from within the *Labour party. Formed in the early 1960s as the Revolutionary Socialist League, it used the public name of Militant Tendency (from its newspaper, *Militant*). Evidence emerged in 1980 of the group's efforts to gain control of Labour constituency and regional organizations, as well as trade union branches and trades councils. Considerable damage was done to the public image of the Labour party, particularly after the NEC recommended in December 1980 that various right-wingers (who later founded the *SDP) should be expelled from the party but that no action should be taken against the left-wingers of Militant. Subsequently the Militant Tendency was judged by Labour to be a separate party, making its adherents ineligible for Labour party membership; Neil Kinnock then undertook the task of rooting out Militant, beginning with the expulsion of five leading members in 1983. The peak of Militant's power was its control during the 1980s of *Liverpool City Council.

military bands Term used of any band, almost invariably from a branch of the armed forces, which uses brass, woodwind and drums. (It was by dropping the woodwind that *brass bands emerged in the 19C.) Standards were much improved after the establishment in 1857 of the Royal Military College of Music at Kneller Hall, a large 18C house in Twickenham built for himself by *Kneller. The navy formed its own school of music in 1903, and the air force in 1949. Instead of a military band, Scottish regiments use a massed band of bagpipes and drums, as seen in the Military Tattoo at *Edinburgh Castle. Such groups are for public display. On less formal occasions the army still marches to the intimate sound of fife and drum (a small flute and a side drum), first used for this purpose by Swiss mercenaries in the 16C.

Military Cross and **Medal** see *MC and MM.

military ranks see *armed forces.

Military Tattoo see *Edinburgh Castle.

militia Part-time civilian soldiers, trained for active service and available to be enlisted when required. The experience of the *English Civil War and the example of the *New Model Army left many in England with a distrust of any strong standing army. It seemed safer to rely on a citizen army, and in the 18C each county was required to give a month's training each year to a local militia of a specified size. From 1803 young men could be forced to join (after selection by ballot), but there were always enough volunteers for this not to apply. The modern equivalent is the *Territorial Army.

Milk Race The name by which the Tour of Britain, the country's leading long-distance cycle race, has been known since the Milk Marketing Board began sponsoring the event in 1958. It had been launched in 1951, with the support of the *Daily Express*, on the pattern of the Tour de France. The race is over 12 days and has varied in length between 1475km/922m and 2424km/1515m. As in the French race, the yellow jersey is awarded each day to the race leader, the competitor who has completed the course to date in the shortest total time. The red jersey (King of the Mountains) goes to whoever has been quickest up to the hill peaks.

John Stuart Mill (1806–73) Philosopher who wrote classic statements of 19C liberalism in such works as *On Liberty* (1859). His *Autobiography* (1873) describes the extraordinary education given him by his father. At three he started Greek, and by eight was reading Aesop, Xenophon, Herodotus and Plato in the original. At the age of 20 he experienced a spiritual crisis which convinced him that this rational approach disregarded the poetry in human beings – a change of emphasis prefiguring much in the Victorian age.

John Everett Millais (1829–96, bt 1885) The most talented of the founding members of the *Pre-Raphaelite Brotherhood, but in later life the most conventional. The jewelled clarity of his early style is seen in such works as *Ophelia* and The *Blind Girl*. The latter uses brilliantly dramatic lighting to give an edge to an intrinsically sentimental scene, and the same can still be said of *Autumn Leaves*, but in the most famous of his later paintings, *Bubbles*, sentiment has carried the day. In 1855 he married Effie Gray, previously the wife of *Ruskin. He was the first painter to be made a baronet.

Jonathan Miller (b. 1934) Theatre director who first made his name as a comedian, notably in *Beyond the Fringe*.

He is a trained doctor and has used that background to popularize medical knowledge, as author and presenter of the BBC television series *The Body in Question* (1978). But his main career has been as a director, with a special emphasis in recent years on opera. His gangster *Rigoletto* (1982), set in New York's district of Little Italy in the 1950s, has become one of English National Opera's most celebrated productions.

Max Miller (stage name of Harold Sargent, 1895–1963) One of the last great *music-hall comedians, earning the title 'The Cheeky Chappie' by the verve with which he told a string of risqué jokes.

Mill House (foaled 1957) Irish-bred and English-trained bay gelding which had the misfortune to be an exact contemporary of *Arkle. He beat his rival in their first encounter (Hennessy Gold Cup at Newbury, 1963) but thereafter was overshadowed in a duel which nevertheless continued to thrill the public.

Spike Milligan (b. 1918) Frenetically eccentric comedian, whose input as author and performer was the most significant element in the zany farrago of the *Goon Show*. He has also been a prolific author of comic books, many of them with a World War II theme (*Adolf Hitler, My Part in his Downfall* 1971, *Monty, His Part in my Victory* 1976, *Mussolini, His Part in my Downfall* 1978).

The Mill on the Floss (1860) Novel by George *Eliot about Maggie and Tom Tulliver, who grow up together in a mill on the river Floss. Maggie, too intelligent for her environment, makes friends with Philip Wakem, the deformed son of a local lawyer. But her rough father hates the lawyer and with Tom's help brings the friendship to an end. After Tulliver's death, Maggie stays for a while in the nearby town of St Ogg's. There she is made to seem compromised by the behaviour on a boating party of Stephen Guest, due to marry her cousin Lucy, and her brother Tom turns her out of the mill. She finds refuge with friends, but when the river suddenly floods she returns to the mill to rescue Tom. Together they are swept to their death in a boat, after reconciliation has brought them into a final embrace – an end too abrupt for many readers, in a novel which begins with such a long and tender account of their childhood.

Mill Reef (foaled 1968) Bay colt which won 12 of his 14 races, including the 1971 Derby. One of his two defeats was by his even greater contemporary *Brigadier Gerard, in the 1971 2,000 Guineas.

John Mills (b. 1908, kt 1976) Film actor who was second only to James Mason in popularity with British audiences during the 1940s, in war movies such as *Waterloo Road* (1944) and *The Way to the Stars* (1945) and then as the adult Pip in David Lean's *Great Expectations* (1946). He won an Oscar as best supporting actor in *Ryan's Daughter* (1970).

Mills & Boon The leading British publishers of romantic fiction. The firm was founded as a general publisher in 1908 by Gerald Mills and Alan Boon, and it was not until the Depression years of the 1930s that it began to specialize in escapist romances. Its rapid growth in the past two decades has been based on creating and marketing the books as a reliable brand-name product. Mills & Boon paperbacks are written to a formula – with specified length, tone, nature of plot and resolution, all described in a manual for the authors entitled *Behind the Hearts and Flowers*. The books are much sold in newsagents and supermarkets, and by mail order, as well as in bookshops.

A.A. **Milne** (Alan Alexander Milne, 1882–1956) Scottish author and playwright whose lasting fame has come from his children's books. The main characters in *Winnie-the-Pooh* (1926) and *The House at Pooh Corner* (1928) are Milne's son, Christopher Robin, and three animal dolls in his nursery – a bear, small pig and donkey. Milne's brilliance lay in giving these animals vividly distinct characters, revealed mainly in dialogue. Pooh is genial and absent-minded, Piglet chirpy and timid, Eeyore infinitely lugubrious. Later animals (Kanga and Roo, Tigger) were added to the real-life nursery partly for the sake of the stories. Almost equally successful were two collections of children's verse, *When We Were Very Young* (1924) and *Now We Are Six* (1927). All four books were illustrated by E.H. *Shepard. Milne was also a playwright and in 1929 adapted The *Wind in the Willows* for the stage.

Alfred **Milner** (1854–1925, KCB 1895, viscount 1902) British high commissioner in South Africa at the time of the *Boer War, contributing to the inevitability of that war by his determination that the Boers should submit to British colonial policy. The so-called 'Milner kindergarten' was the group of young administrators whom he recruited in Oxford to take over the administration of the Transvaal after the defeat of the Boers.

Milton see *Whitaker family.

John **Milton** (1608–1674) The greatest epic poet in the English language, whose life and work fall into three distinct sections. In the first, up to 1640, he was the brilliant Cambridge scholar, known as 'the Lady of Christ's' (his college) because he was so fastidious. While still at the university, he wrote three medium-length poems revealing his precocious skills – *On the Morning of Christ's Nativity* (1629) and the contrasted pair in praise of the merry and the contemplative, *L'Allegro* and *Il Penseroso* (1631). *Comus*, a masque, was written for performance at Ludlow Castle in Shropshire in 1634, and *Lycidas* was published in 1638.

After leaving Cambridge, Milton spent his time reading and travelling. But this changed abruptly in the second period of his life (1640–60), when the great issues of the day diverted his energies into a stream of polemical prose pamphlets in the cause of parliament, puritanism and liberty. The best known are *Eikonoklastes* (1649), defending the regicides against the powerful impact of *Eikon Basilike*; and *Areopagitica* (1644), his great argument for freedom of the press, provoked by parliament imposing a censorship no less strenuous than the king's. From 1649 Milton had an active role in government, as Latin secretary to Cromwell's council; he was responsible for foreign corrrespondence, Latin being the international language.

A succession of personal tragedies had meanwhile darkened his life. In 1642 an unsuitable marriage, to a woman half his age, was rapidly followed by her abandoning him and returning home; in response he published four controversial pamphlets (1643–5) advocating divorce. His wife later returned and they had three daughters before she died in 1652. By then his long-failing eyesight had entirely gone, prompting the stoical sonnet *On His Blindness* which begins 'When I consider how my light is spent' and ends 'They also serve who only stand and wait'. A second marriage, in 1656, lasted only two years before his wife died.

The final phase began in 1660 with the Restoration. Milton's political record meant that his life was now in danger, but he was allowed to retire unmolested; and in retirement he produced his greatest works. His daughters, now young adults, read to him and took their turns with others in writing down the soaring blank verse which he carried in his head, usually composed during the previous night. He had begun dictating *Paradise Lost* in 1658; it was complete by 1663. In that year Milton married for the third time, and in 1665 he and his family fled from London's Great Plague to settle in a cottage at Chalfont St Giles in Buckinghamshire, today a museum. Their cottage economy survived not without family friction but almost without money (the publication of *Paradise Lost* brought only £10). But the work continued. *Paradise Regained* and *Samson Agonistes* were published together in 1671, just three years before his death.

Milton Keynes see *new towns.

mincemeat Confusingly, there is now no meat in mincemeat. It is a mixture of currants, raisins, sultanas, chopped apples and almonds, candied peel and brandy, and is used for the stuffing of *mince pies. By contrast meat that is minced is called minced meat or just mince (particularly when cooked). But in the old days meat was sometimes included in the sweet filling for mince pies. Mrs *Beeton gives a recipe which includes raw minced rump steak, together with the currants and other sweet ingredients.

mince pie Small round tart of shortcrust pastry, filled with *mincemeat and covered with a pastry lid. Eaten in winter and in particular on Christmas day.

MIND (London W1) Charity which campaigns to improve the quality of care available to mentally ill people. Founded in 1946 as the National Association for Mental Health, it changed its name in 1971 to MIND, launching under the new banner its first national campaign to raise both funds and public awareness of the issues.

Minder (Thames TV from 1979) Comedy series starring George *Cole as Arthur Daley, a Cockney rogue with a wide range of speculative ventures any of which might turn into a 'nice little earner'. An unseen character is the wife he refers to merely as ''er indoors'. The original writer was Leon Griffiths (1928–92) and for many years Dennis Waterman co-starred as Arfur's minder (his henchman), a role which Gary Webster took over in 1991.

'mind your p's and q's' Phrase in use from at least the early 19C, meaning to pay attention and behave properly. It derives from advice given to apprentice printers, for the piece of type for 'p' looks to the eye like a 'q' (it becomes reversed in the printing). The phrase is often said to derive from handwriting, but only in a 20C hand can the two letters be confused; in *copperplate the vertical of the 'p' extended above and below the line.

Minehead (8000 in 1981) Ancient harbour, now a resort, on the coast of Somerset. On *May Day and the two following evenings an unusual hobby horse (a long boat-shaped framework, with painted hangings reaching almost to the ground, carried on the shoulders of an unseen man) dances through the town and surrounding district, threatening passers-by until they pay a contribution.

miners' strikes (1972, 1974, 1984–5) The miners were at the heart of the *General Strike of 1926, when the TUC called other unions out in their support. The three major industrial confrontations of the postwar years have also centred on the miners, but on these occasions they fought the battle alone – though some other unions did take steps to prevent the movement of coal.

Early in January 1972 the executive of the *NUM called a strike in support of a 47% wage claim, after holding a secret ballot of members; in February a state of emergency was declared and four-hour power cuts were imposed around the country on a rota basis (resulting in nearly two million workers being laid off); later that month a court of enquiry recommended large wage increases which were accepted in a national ballot of miners; work resumed at the pits on the last day of February.

The miners again went on strike in 1974. Their challenge to the government this time followed the *oil crisis and the imposition of a three-day week. On February 4 the miners voted for a national strike; on February 7 the Conservative prime minister, Edward Heath, called a general election on the issue of who runs Britain; on February 28 he lost the election; and on March 6 the strike ended when the new Labour government awarded the miners a 35% pay increase. In 1977 Mrs Thatcher, by then leader of the Conservative party, declared that if she were in office and faced with a similar situation, she would consider holding a single-issue referendum to 'let the people speak'.

The expected confrontation came in 1984, five years after she entered office, and it was widely seen as a personal clash between two 'conviction' politicians – Mrs *Thatcher and Arthur *Scargill, president of the NUM. In 1982 Scargill had declared that the National Coal Board had secret plans to close a large number of pits, and in 1984 it was officially announced by the NCB that 20,000 jobs would go in the next year. Scargill's original claim had led to spasmodic strikes in individual pits and to an NUM ban on overtime from November 1983; the official announcement provoked an increase in local industrial action, and in April 1984 the NUM called all miners out (there had been no national ballot of the members). The strike soon involved violent confrontation between police and miners – outside power stations, and at pits where men wanted to cross the picket line and work. The nation, watching on television, was appalled by the violence but also increasingly distressed by the suffering of the families of miners as the strike dragged on for a year.

In October the NUM had all its assets sequestered by the High Court after it had refused to pay a £200,000 fine for contempt of court, arising from a case brought against it by two Yorkshire miners. By that time miners in various pits were beginning to drift back to work, in a process that accelerated during the winter. In March 1985, by a narrow majority, delegates of the NUM voted to end the strike and to return to work without having achieved any negotiated settlement with the NCB. Unlike the previous strikes, this was clearly a victory for the government; it was seen as a turning point in Mrs Thatcher's long campaign against union power. But events proved Scargill's warning more than justified, with pit closures by the early 1990s exceeding his predictions (see *coal). Meanwhile a sizable part of Scargill's union had branched off on its own as the *UDM.

Mini Britain's bestselling car of all time (5.3 million by 1992) and one of the two outstanding designs by Alec *Issigonis. When launched by the *British Motor Corporation in 1959, the Mini was a sensation on two counts: its price, just under £500; and its size for a four-seater car (3.05m/10ft long, achieved by placing the 848 cc engine sideways under the bonnet). It also held the road superbly, with its front-wheel drive and independent suspension. The car was at first marketed under both the Morris and Austin labels (there were straight lines on the radiator grille of the Morris Mini and wavy lines on an Austin). From 1961 a faster version, designed by John *Cooper, was available as the Mini-Cooper.

miniatures The word was originally used only of paintings in illuminated manuscripts (deriving from the Latin *minium* for the red paint which gave emphasis to certain capital letters), but it is more generally applied now to portrait miniatures. In the 16–18C these tiny likenesses were an important and highly skilled tradition in British art. At first they were often worn about the person, as tokens or jewels. Later they were kept in folding cases, often oval, which could be slipped into the pocket, or else in frames for display around a drawing room. In either form they fulfilled the role of a modern photograph.

The earliest English master was Nicholas *Hilliard, and the other leading names are Isaac Oliver (c.1565–1617), Samuel Cooper (1609–72) and Richard Cosway (1742–1821). Nearly all miniatures were painted on vellum until the early 18C, when ivory became the standard material.

Minimum Lending Rate see *MLR.

miniskirt (often abbreviated to mini) Skirt or dress with a very high hemline, introduced in about 1960 and deriving its name from the *Mini. At one point a miniskirt was defined as being at least 10cm/4in above the knee.

minister Any politician holding a *government office. Specific terms are used for ministers at diferent levels of the hierarchy. Those in charge of major departments are in most cases secretaries of state; below them are ministers of state; and then parliamentary under-secretaries of state.

There is one further distinction. Ministers of the crown are senior members of the government, chosen by the prime minister but appointed by the monarch; junior ministers are directly appointed by the prime minister. In practice the ministers of the crown and the members of the *cabinet are usually the same people.

Minorca The most easterly of the Balearic Islands, in the western Mediterranean, about 200km/125m off the coast of Spain. The deep-water harbour of its capital, Mahón, has been of great strategic importance. It was captured by Britain in 1708 and was retained at the end of the War of the *Spanish Succession. It was returned to Spain under the Treaty of Amiens in 1802. An unsuccessful naval action here in 1756 led to the execution of Admiral *Byng.

Self-portrait by the earliest master of the English miniature: Nicholas Hilliard at the age of 30, in 1577.

minster Originally a name for a monastery church, it survives as the term for a few English cathedrals or exceptionally large churches – in particular *York and others in its original diocese, such as *Beverley or *Southwell.

*The **Minstrel Boy*** see Thomas *Moore.

Royal **Mint** The government agency which manufactures the coins of the realm (see *currency). From 1300 to 1810 it operated within the Tower of London, and then in a building nearby on Tower Hill. It has now moved to Llantrisant in Mid Glamorgan, where coins were first minted in 1968. Under the *Next Steps programme it became in 1990 an executive agency, answerable to the chancellor of the exchequer – who has been since 1870 the *ex officio* master of the mint.

Minton pottery and porcelain Wares made at the *Stoke-on-Trent factory founded in 1793 by Thomas Minton (1765–1836), the probable designer of the conventional *willow pattern. The firm is still in business and over two centuries has produced a massive output in a very wide range of styles (visible today in a chronological display in the factory's museum). French Sèvres was among the most important influences, and Minton was the only English factory to use the Sèvres technique of *pâte-sur-pâte*, in which a design in white relief is built up by painting on layers of slip, or liquid clay.

mint sauce An infusion of chopped mint leaves, with sugar and vinegar, often served in Britain with roast lamb. A sweeter alternative is mint jelly.

miracle plays see *mystery plays.

*Daily **Mirror*** Founded in 1903 by Alfred Harmsworth (later Lord *Northcliffe) as a newspaper for women. It almost foundered in this form, but revived when it was rapidly transformed into an illustrated paper. As such it was soon rivalling the circulation of Harmsworth's other popular daily, the *Mail*. By the time of World War II the *Mirror* was the troops' favourite paper (*Jane being no small part of the attraction), and from the landslide 1945 election victory onwards it became the only *tabloid to give consistent support to the Labour party; it was by then the largest circulation daily (an astonishing 7 million copies were sold on the morning of the coronation in 1953). *Cassandra was its star columnist and *Vicky its political cartoonist. During the 1980s its rival in the tabloid market was the *Sun*, and in 1992 both papers were roughly level (just below 3.7 million) in spite of the grievous damage done to the *Mirror* by Robert *Maxwell. A sister paper, the *Sunday Pictorial*, was renamed the *Sunday Mirror* in 1963.

miscarriages of justice see *criminal justice.

Miss and **Mrs** Both words are abbreviations of 'mistress', from the time when that word was the feminine of 'master'. Since the late 17C unmarried women have been called 'Miss' and married women 'Mrs' (pronounced 'missis', though the written form is an abbreviation of the full 'mistress'). Both titles were at that time limited to women of the upper and middle class, likely to become mistress of a household employing servants. In most European countries unmarried women above a certain age are addressed as married women (*madame* rather than *mademoiselle*). The British have rigidly kept to 'Miss' regardless of age, making the elderly spinster a characteristic figure of national life and literature. In the 1970s and 1980s the American 'Ms' was often used to avoid this intrusive distinction, but a more recent trend has been to dispense with prefixes altogether, addressing people by their given and family names (Mary Smith rather than Ms Smith).

missionaries The Jesuit order of the Roman Catholic church sent vigorous missions around the world from the mid-16C, but Protestants were slower to proselytize. Britain's oldest missionary societies date from the late 17C – the Society for Promoting Christian Knowledge (SPCK) was formed in 1698, and the Society for the Propagation of the Gospel in Foreign Parts in 1701 – but they were mainly concerned with the spiritual welfare of British people living in remote parts of the infant empire. It was the evangelical fervour of the *Methodists which gave a new impetus in the late 18C, crystallized in William Carey's *Enquiry into the Obligations of Christians to Use Means for the Conversion of the Heathens* (1792). Carey formed in 1792 the Baptist Missionary Society, which was soon followed by the London Missionary Society (interdenominational 1795), the Church Missionary Society (Anglican 1799) and the Wesleyan Methodist Missionary Society (1813).

With these organizations in place Britain was poised to send out a steady stream of men and women, setting off around the world with considerable courage and unassailable certainty (doubts about imposing one's beliefs and customs on others are a modern phenomenon). Intrepid British missionaries were soon arriving in the Far East, the South Sea Islands and Africa, with some medicine and a plentiful supply of Bibles, to set up hospitals and schools; David *Livingstone was only the most famous among thousands. The same energy and enthusiasm was later applied to the heathen recently discovered in Britain's own backyard slums, most notably in the efforts of the *Salvation Army.

mistletoe see *Christmas.

Warren **Mitchell** (b. 1926) Actor almost inextricably identified with his mesmerizing portrayal of Alf Garnett in *Till Death Us Do Part*, but capable also of powerful straight performances – as he proved with his Willie Loman in the National Theatre's *Death of a Salesman* (1979).

Mitford family Of the six daughters of David Freeman-Mitford (later Lord Redesdale), four led careers which kept the family in the public eye – in the case of two of them, because of their Fascist sympathies. Hitler was present at the wedding of Diana (b. 1910) to Oswald *Mosley in 1936. Unity (1914–48) was a close friend of the Führer and almost fatally injured herself in an attempt to commit suicide in Munich. By contrast the youngest daughter, Jessica (b. 1917), was on the far left of the political spectrum in the late 1930s. Her first book (*Hons and Rebels* 1960) offered a vivid image of the life of the Mitford children. She lives in the USA and her subsequent career has been, in her own words, that of a 'muckraker', writing polemical investigations of such topics as the funeral industry (*The American Way of Death* 1963).

The most distinguished of the sisters was Nancy (1904–73), who had great success with her witty and lightly satirical novels. The books feature the girls of the Radlett family (closely resembling the Mitfords and featuring in Uncle Matthew a famous portrait of their father), following them and their circle through a shifting pattern of marriages and affairs; Nancy's first great success was aptly named *The Pursuit of Love* (1945). This was followed by *Love in a Cold Climate* (1949) and *The Blessing* (1951). Thereafter she concentrated mainly on biography, writing books on Mme de Pompadour, Voltaire and Louis XIV; she lived in Paris from 1947. In 1956 she edited and contributed to *Noblesse Oblige: an enquiry into* *the identifiable characteristics of the English aristocracy.* The intention was satirical but many read it for tips on etiquette, with the result that *U and non-U were launched on their dreary course.

Mithraism Iranian cult involving a sun god and a sacred bull, which had many followers in the *Roman army. A large temple to Mithras, in use during the 1–4c, was discovered below Queen Victoria Street in London in 1954.

Mitre Tavern which stood in London's *Fleet Street, famous because it was Dr Johnson's favourite. It was here that he and Boswell had supper together for the first time, on 25 June 1763, sitting till past 1 a.m. over two bottles of port. It ceased to be a tavern in 1788 and was pulled down in 1829.

MLR (Minimum Lending Rate) The term, current until 1981, for the minimum rate of interest charged by the *Bank of England (acting as lender of last resort) on a variety of transactions which affect the entire money market. Unlike the earlier bank rate, which it replaced in 1971, MLR did not compel commercial banks to follow suit. But in practice any movement in MLR was soon followed by interest rates in general, including *mortgages and *base rates. The regular use of MLR was discontinued in 1981, but adjusting the Bank of England's rate of lending on commercial bills remains the government's method of influencing interest rates throughout the economy.

MM see *MC and MM.

Model Parliament The name given by historians to the *parliament summoned by Edward I in 1295, because it established the pattern for the future by including elected members of the Commons, together with the clergy and the nobility. The Commons had been involved in earlier parliaments (Simon de *Montfort's, for example, in 1265), but on this occasion they were more representative of the nation, with two knights elected from each shire, two citizens from each city and two burgesses from each borough.

Moderator see *Church of Scotland.

mods and rockers Rival teenage styles during the 1960s. The mods were characterized by the neatness of their conventional dress and hair; their name (short for 'modern') reflected a contrast with the *teds, who had imitated the fashion of an earlier Edwardian generation. But the real rivals to the mods were the rockers, proclaiming in their name a love of rock and roll music and in their appearance (long hair, leather jackets) a mood of anarchy in direct contrast to the very precise mods. The mods used scooters and the rockers motor bikes; on bank holidays both liked to ride in large numbers to resorts such as Brighton in the hope of confrontation.

Mold (Wyddgrug in Welsh, 9000 in 1981) Town in northeast Wales; administrative centre of Clwyd. The church, mainly 15c, is known for its carved capitals and its mural paintings of animals. Daniel *Owen was a native of the town and there is a museum in his honour.

Mole see The *Wind in the Willows.

moles The popular term for civil servants who leak politically embarrassing documents, in contravention of the *Official Secrets Act. The number of such leaks increased considerably during the 1980s, perhaps because of an unusually doctrinaire stance by the government

itself. The two most prominent moles of the decade were Sarah Tisdall and Clive Ponting. In 1983 Tisdall, working in the Foreign Office, passed to the *Guardian* secret papers relating to the arrival in Britain of Cruise missiles; the *Guardian* eventually complied with a court order to reveal its source, and Tisdall was jailed for six months. Clive Ponting, a civil servant in the Ministry of Defence, leaked documents about the sinking of the *Belgrano* in the *Falklands War and admitted his action; in 1985 he was acquitted by a jury, after being charged with breaching the Official Secrets Act. In the early 1990s moles in less sensitive areas have been given some official encouragement as *whistle-blowers.

Moll Flanders (in full *The Fortunes and Misfortunes of the Famous Moll Flanders* 1722) Novel by *Defoe in the form of a rambling autobiography. Moll, the supposed author, was born in Newgate jail and has fluctuating fortune through her marriages and affairs, with prolonged spells in London's underworld and in the plantations of Virginia, to which both she and her mother are in turn transported. She looks back from a prosperous and supposedly repentant old age on a life story which holds the reader through richness of character and detail rather than from any compelling plot.

Molly Maguires Terrorists using female disguise in Ireland in the 1840s. Their targets were officers of the law and their purpose to prevent evictions for non-payment of rent. The name was used 20 years later by Irish terrorists in the USA, sabotaging coal mines in Pennsylvania.

James **Molyneaux** (b. 1920) Ulster Unionist politician, MP at Westminster for Lagan Valley since 1983 (previously for Antrim South, 1970–83). He has been leader of the Ulster *Unionist party in the House of Commons since 1974.

MOMI see *Museum of the Moving Image.

'I am **monarch of all I survey**' Opening line of William Cowper's *Verses Supposed to be Written by Alexander Selkirk* (1782). The famous historical castaway (the original of *Robinson Crusoe) comes down heavily against the delights of solitude:

> Better dwell in the midst of alarms,
> Than reign in this horrible place.

Monarch of the Glen see Edwin *Landseer.

monarchy see entries on *constitutional monarchy and *royal house.

General **Monck** (George Monck, 1608–70, duke of Albemarle 1660) Professional soldier whose level-headed integrity somehow made it possible for him to fight as a royalist in the *English Civil War, then to give his services in support of Cromwell during the *Commonwealth and *Protectorate, and finally to be the chief architect of the *Restoration. He successfully kept control in Scotland during the 1650s (interrupted by a brief spell as a naval commander during the first *Anglo-Dutch war), and it was from Coldstream, on the Scottish border, that he led an army south in January 1660. His immediate purpose was to prevent other generals imposing military rule after the collapse of the Protectorate. He reassembled the *Long Parliament and then persuaded it to make way for a newly elected assembly. The wish of the majority for the return of *Charles II could now be met and Monck acted as the chief intermediary. He received a dukedom, and part of his army became the Coldstream regiment of *Foot Guards in the royal service.

Monday Club Political pressure group formed in 1961 to assert 'traditional conservative values'. In addition to the uncontroversial themes of family, monarchy and Christianity, there was an assertion of empire, opposition to immigration and rejection of a multi-racial society (the club was to some extent a reaction to the success of the *Bow Group in spreading more liberal attitudes on these issues). Meetings were originally held on Mondays.

Claude **Monet** (1840–1926) The great French impressionist painted almost 100 canvases of the Thames in London, a few in 1870–1 (when he had left France to escape the Franco-Prussian war) but by far the majority as a result of three visits in the winters of 1899–1901. Many were painted from his room in the Savoy Hotel, with a view both up and down the river. These superb images are perhaps the only good result of London's notorious *smog. 'What I like most of all in London is the fog', said Monet. 'Without the fog, London would not be a beautiful city.'

monetarism The theory that control of the *money supply is the only means by which government should attempt to manage the economy. It assumes that market forces are the best natural regulators of economic activity, and it therefore goes back to the classical economics of David *Hume and Adam *Smith. A central purpose of controlling the money supply is the avoidance of *inflation, and Mrs Thatcher – coming to power at the end of Britain's most inflationary decade – was a passionate devotee of monetarism (the high priest of which has been the US economist Milton Friedman). For a while in the mid-1980s her personal guru on the subject was the American-based British economist Alan Walters (to the evident displeasure of her chancellor, Nigel *Lawson). The chief opposing theory derives from *Keynes, who favoured government intervention to boost a flagging economy.

money supply The amount of money circulating in the economy, the control of which is the main theme of *monetarism. It can be defined in several ways, depending on how much of people's savings or of money earning interest is considered to be in circulation. Theorists have varied as to which version they choose to emphasize. The definitions are in very broad terms as follows: M0, notes and coins in circulation plus the banks' own holdings to service this circulation; M1, these plus current accounts and deposit accounts from which money can be immediately withdrawn; M2 and M3, these plus differing categories of money on longer term deposit; M4 and M5 (previously known as private-sector liquidity), M0 plus virtually all sterling deposits with UK institutions. In recent years M0 and M4 have been most often used, as representing the 'narrow' and 'broad' versions of the money supply.

Monitor (BBC 1958–64) The formative arts magazine programme on British television, setting a pattern and standard which has influenced later versions such as *The *South Bank Show*. It was very much the creation of its editor and main presenter, Huw *Wheldon.

Monmouth (8000 in 1991) Town in Gwent on the river Wye. Of the Norman castle only the 12c keep remains, traditionally said to be where Henry V was born. The most impressive medieval survival is the 13c Monmow Bridge, surmounted by its own fortified gatehouse.

Duke of **Monmouth** (James Scott, 1649–85, duke 1663) Illegitimate son of *Charles II, born to his mistress Lucy Walter during his exile in the Netherlands. The boy was married in 1663, when he was 14, to a Scottish heiress, Anne Scott; he took her surname and was created a duke. Opponents of the Roman Catholic duke of York (the future *James II) favoured Monmouth, a Protestant, as heir to the throne. But the king stood by his brother, repeatedly denying the rumour that he had married Lucy Walter. A few months after the accession of James II, Monmouth landed at Lyme Regis in Dorset with just 82 followers. Protestants failed to rally to his cause in the numbers hoped for, and he was defeated by the royal army at Sedgemoor, in Somerset, on 6 July 1685. Monmouth was beheaded on Tower Hill, while those few who had supported him were treated in the Bloody Assizes with the severity which gave Judge *Jeffreys his lasting reputation.

Monmouthshire Former *county in Wales, forming since 1974 the major part of Gwent.

Monopolies and Mergers Commission (London WC2) Originally set up by the Monopolies and Restrictive Practices Act of 1948, the commission is charged with investigating possible restrictions on fair trade. The relevant legislation includes the Fair Trading Act of 1973, the Restrictive Practices Act of 1976 and the Competition Act of 1980.

Monopoly Board game in which each player's purpose is to bankrupt the others by buying up property and charging them rent. To the British the game is indelibly associated with places in London, but in origin it is American (invented by Charles Darrow in 1933) and the original board features the streets of Atlantic City in New Jersey.

Mons Town in southwest Belgium which was the scene of the first battle between the British and the Germans in *World War I. (Coincidentally it was only 40km/25m from where British troops had last fought on the Continent, 99 years earlier, at Waterloo.) On 23 August 1914 the *Old Contemptibles held off an attack by much heavier forces before beginning the retreat from Mons to the Marne. Their almost miraculous escape prompted a journalist to imagine St George and angels in the clouds with flaming swords, encouraging the British to hold back the Germans. The 'angels of Mons' caught the public imagination and soon many believed that there had indeed been a heavenly pro-British apparition.

Mons Meg Historic 15c cannon in Edinburgh Castle, made of long metal bars hooped together. The origin of its name is not known (there is no evidence that it was made at Mons in Belgium), but its first recorded use was in 1497 – by James IV against Norham Castle in Northumberland. Its barrel burst in 1682 when firing a salute in honour of the duke of York, later James II and VII.

Monster Raving Loony Party A comic sideshow in British politics, founded by Screaming Lord Sutch (David Sutch, b. 1942), a pop singer who found a quicker route to national fame through the media attention at by-elections. Whenever he stands as a candidate, it is virtually certain that he will lose his deposit but also certain that he will make a splash on television, in his cheerfully outlandish clothes, while the candidates are seen awaiting the result. In local elections, for district and town councils, the party has actually won some seats.

*The **Monstrous Regiment of Women*** (*First Blast of the Trumpet against the Monstrous Regiment of Women* 1558) Pamphlet written by John *Knox in Geneva, arguing that the regiment (meaning rule) of women is unnatural and improper. It was aimed at three Roman Catholics – the English queen Mary I, Mary of Guise (regent in Scotland) and her young daughter, Mary Queen of Scots. Unfortunately for Knox the pamphlet came out in 1558 just as another woman, the Protestant Elizabeth I, succeeded to the throne of England. She took it personally and never allowed him back into her realm.

Montacute House (37km/23m SE of Taunton) Imposing Elizabethan mansion, built in the 1590s for Sir Edward Phelips (later speaker of the House of Commons) in honey-coloured stone and to a strictly symmetrical design. The architect is believed to have been a Somerset mason, William Arnold. The house has survived virtually unaltered except for the addition in 1786 of a beautiful west front, very much in keeping because decorated with Tudor stonework and carvings from a nearby house, Clifton Maybank, which was then being demolished. The Long Gallery contains a display of Tudor portraits on loan from the National Portrait Gallery.

Monte Cassino Benedictine monastery on a hill about 140km/85m southeast of Rome, of great significance both in Christian history and in *World War II. The monastery is considered the cradle of western monasticism, for it was the headquarters of St Benedict himself in the 6c. The monastery buildings (of the 16–17c) were a key feature in the Gustav Line of defence, at which the Germans delayed by several months the Allied advance up Italy in 1944. In the course of the fighting the monastery was entirely demolished, together with many of its treasures. It has been rebuilt to the same design.

Simon de **Montfort** (*c*.1208–65) Leader of the more radical barons against his brother-in-law *Henry III (de Montfort had married the king's sister, Eleanor, in 1238). He defeated and captured Henry at Lewes in 1264, but lost baronial support by behaving like a military dictator. To provide another base for his authority he summoned

in 1265 his famous *parliament, calling to Westminster knights from the shires and citizens from the towns. Later that year he was defeated and killed at Evesham by an army led by the king's son, the future Edward I.

General **Montgomery** (Bernard Montgomery, 1887–1976, KCB 1942, viscount 1946) Considered by many the most inspirational British soldier of World War II. In August 1942 he was given command of the 8th army in north Africa. He rapidly invigorated troops demoralized by Rommel's successes, and prudently delayed his offensive until he had the advantage in numbers. A series of victories beginning with El *Alamein turned him into a national hero, popularly known as 'Monty' and famous for quirks such as his beret with twin badges. He achieved similar results in command of the ground forces on *D-day and through the early stages of the Normandy invasion. He was less successful as the campaign developed, finding it hard to play a subordinate role to the supreme commander, General Eisenhower.

Montgomeryshire Former *county in Wales, since 1974 part of Powys.

*A **Month in the Country*** (1976) Ballet by *Ashton, based on Turgenev's play and choreographed to a selection of piano music by Chopin, arranged by John Lanchbery. The part of the lady of the house, Natalia Petrovna, was created by Lynn *Seymour; and that of Beliaev, the tutor whose romantic effect on both Natalia and her ward Vera disrupts the household, by Anthony *Dowell.

Lord **Montrose** (James Graham, 1612–50, 5th earl of Montrose 1626, 1st marquess 1644) The most brilliant of the royalist commanders in Scotland during the *English

Montgomery, with twin badges in his beret, indicates an area of the Normandy campaign: portrait by Frank Salisbury, 1945.

Civil War. In 1644 he rallied the clans in the Highlands and won a rapid series of victories in the north until support drained away after the defeat of Charles I at *Naseby. From exile in France he returned to Scotland in 1650 to raise support for Charles II, but he was captured and subsequently hanged in Edinburgh.

Montserrat Island in the Caribbean which is a British crown colony. Visited by Columbus in 1493, it was first settled in 1632 by a British party consisting mainly of Irish Roman Catholics. It has been the only member of the *West Indies Federation to revert on a long-term basis to the status of crown colony.

Monty Python's Flying Circus (BBC 1969–74) The outstanding example of zany humour in television revue, with a status similar to *The *Goon Show* on radio. Outstanding among the author-performers were John *Cleese and Michael *Palin, and their *dead parrot sketch has become the single most widely remembered item. The material was deliberately fragmented, making much use of its famous catch phrase to move rapidly from nowhere in particular to somewhere else – 'And now for something completely different'. The graphics, characterized by a boot descending to obliterate the previous image, were the work of Terry Gilliam – another of the author-performers on the series.

Monument (London EC2) Designed by Wren, the Monument was erected by order of parliament in 1671–7 'to preserve the memory of this dreadful Visitation' (the *Great Fire). The inscription states that the fire began 202 ft (62m) to the east, and that 202 ft is the height of the column. It is surmounted by a flaming urn of gilt bronze, and 311 steps bring visitors up to a balcony beneath the urn.

Monymusk Reliquary see *Royal Museum of Scotland.

*The **Moonstone*** (1868) Novel by Wilkie *Collins, first published as a serial in *All the Year Round*, which is an important early example of detective fiction. The moonstone is a huge diamond. Stolen originally from an Indian temple, it disappears after being given to an English girl, Rachel Verinder, on her 18th birthday. The crime is unravelled with the help of a London detective, Sergeant Cuff.

Bobby **Moore** (1941–93) One of the greatest of English defenders on the football field, at centre back, and captain of the team which won the World Cup in 1966. His club career was almost entirely with West Ham United (1958–74); it included victories in the FA Cup in 1964 and in the European Cup Winners' Cup the following year. He captained England from 1963 (the youngest captain ever, at the age of 22) and his total of 108 caps when he retired in 1973 was at the time a record. He spent the last years of his League career with Fulham (1974–7).

Dudley **Moore** (b. 1935) Multi-talented comedian, actor and musician. His first success was in *Beyond the Fringe*. He then acquired a television following in Britain with Peter Cook as the rambling pair of down-and-out conversationalists, Dud and Pete, in *Not Only But Also* (BBC 1965–71). Next he established himself as a bantamweight heart-throb in a succession of Hollywood films (among the most popular '10' 1979, *Arthur* 1981). Meanwhile he has yet other careers as a composer of film scores and as a jazz and concert pianist, as seen in a 1992 Albert Hall performance with the BBC Concert Orchestra.

Gerald **Moore** (1899–1987) The leading accompanist in Britain to singers of two generations, from Kathleen

The Monument with alternative tops, Charles II or the flaming urn (the one selected): engraving after a drawing by Hawksmoor.

Ferrier to Janet Baker. One of his books has as its title the accompanist's perennial worry, *Am I Too Loud?* (1962).

Henry **Moore** (1898–1986) Sculptor with a major international reputation, whose most characteristic works – reclining semi-abstract figures, often made up of separate parts – evoke simultaneously the human body and eroded landscape forms. These compositions, often themselves large enough to assume a dominant position in a landscape, were the main theme of his later years. Much of his best-known work from the middle period of his life was more directly figurative, including the famous *Madonna and Child* (1943–4, commissioned for a church in *Northampton) and the *King and Queen* (1952–3) who sit facing out over the landscape near Dumfries in Scotland. Moore was also an excellent draughtsman; his crayon drawings of people sheltering in the London underground during World War II are among the most evocative images of that period. In the early 1990s there was litigation between his daughter, Mary Moore, and the Henry Moore Foundation over the foundation's plans to develop the sculptor's studio and garden at Perry Green in Hertfordshire as a study centre.

John **Moore** see *Corunna.

John **Moore** (b. 1937, baron 1992) Conservative politician, MP for Croydon Central (1974–92). He held *cabinet posts during the 1980s as secretary of state for transport (1986–7), for social services (1987–8) and for social security (1988–9).

Patrick **Moore** (b. 1923) Author of many books of popular astronomy and known to a wide audience as the genially eccentric presenter of *The Sky at Night*; he has done every monthly issue since its start on BBC TV in 1957, a period unrivalled in Britain by any other programme with a single presenter.

Roger **Moore** (b. 1927) Actor best known for having taken over the role of James Bond, starting with *Live and Let Die* (1973); he continued in another five, until *Octopussy* (1983). His credentials for the role had included some 114 TV episodes as the *Saint.

Thomas **Moore** (1779–1852) Poet who in his *Irish Melodies* (1808–34) set his own words to existing tunes. The book launched many of the best known 'traditional' songs, including *The Minstrel Boy, The Harp that once through Tara's halls* and *The Last Rose of Summer.*

Moorfields (Moorfields Eye Hospital, London EC1) Institution deriving from a dispensary for the poor, the first in London to specialize in diseases of the eye, which opened in 1805. It was prompted by the large number of soldiers returning from Egypt with trachoma in the Napoleonic Wars. In the 1820s, known then as the Royal Ophthalmic Eye Hospital, it moved into a new building by Robert Smirke in Lower Moorfields. It moved again in 1899, to its present site in the City Road; but the Moorfields location had by then provided its popular name, which was made official in 1956.

Moorgate disaster see *underground.

Adrian **Moorhouse** (b. 1964) Swimmer with numerous successes in breaststroke events during the 1980s, including three Commonwealth gold medals (100 metres 1982 and 1990, 200 metres 1986) and the gold for 100 metres in the 1988 Olympics. In the 1989 European championships he narrowly improved on the world 100 metres breaststroke record, with a time of 1:01.49; twice subsequently he exactly equalled his own record.

Moors murders Britain's most horrifying murders of recent times, in which children were tortured, in some cases tape-recorded and photographed in their last moments, and then were buried on the moors near Oldham, northeast of Manchester. In 1966 Ian Brady and Myra Hindley were convicted of the crimes and sentenced to life imprisonment. In 1987 they were taken back to the moors to help police search for two of their victims whose bodies had not been discovered.

morality plays see *Everyman*.

Moral Rearmament Evangelical Christian movement launched by an American Lutheran pastor, Frank Buchman (1878–1961). He won some support at Oxford University in the late 1920s, causing his followers to be known as the Oxford Group – a name officially changed to Moral Rearmament in 1938. The campaign was notably active in the 1950s and 1960s at the height of the Cold War, for the chief villain in its demonology was Communism. This was followed a close second by homosexuality, the two frequently being linked in the group's pamphlets and plays.

'**morals of a whore**' and the manners of a dancing master' see Lord *Chesterfield.

Moray Until 1975 a *county on the northeast coast of Scotland, now mostly in Grampian with part in the Highland region.

Moray Firth Inlet of the North Sea in northeast Scotland, reaching in as far as Inverness and the start of the *Caledonian Canal.

Kenneth **More** (1914–82) Actor who became a major star in Britain in 1954, with *Genevieve* and as one of the medical students in *Doctor in the House*; he followed these with the role of Douglas *Bader in *Reach for the Sky* (1956). His many subsequent performances, nearly all of them very 'British', never quite recaptured these early successes; but he won a large TV following as Young Jolyon in *The Forsyte Saga* (1967).

Thomas **More** (1478–1535, kt 1521) Statesman, author and saint. Born the son of a judge, and educated for the law, More was one of the first scholars in England to play an important part in the international humanism of the *Renaissance. Erasmus was a close friend; *Holbein stayed in More's house in Chelsea and painted his family; and More's Latin fable about a rational society, *Utopia*, was an immediate success throughout Europe.

His public career began in 1504 when he was elected a member of parliament; he was in the king's privy council by 1517, was at the *Field of Cloth of Gold in 1520 and became Speaker of the House of Commons in 1523. He helped *Henry VIII write his Latin attack on Luther in 1521 and became a personal friend of the king, even entertaining him at Chelsea. When Wolsey fell from favour in 1529, More succeeded him as lord chancellor; he was the first in that office to be neither cleric nor nobleman. He resigned in 1532, claiming ill health. He did so perhaps to sidestep the controversial issue of the day, the king's authority over the church. But even as a private citizen More was too prominent to avoid the question.

He was content to accept the validity of the king's marriage to Anne Boleyn, but he would not deny the supremacy of the pope. The distinction became urgent with the Act of *Supremacy of 1534. More's refusal to swear the oath led to his conviction and execution for treason in 1535; at his trial in Westminster Hall he had used the legalistic argument that his silence implied assent. He was canonized in 1935. His feast day used to be July 9, but he now shares June 22 with John *Fisher. More is the central character of A *Man for all Seasons.

The **Morecambe and Wise Show** Something of a national institution on television (ATV 1961–8, BBC till 1978, subsequently Thames TV). Eric Morecambe was the stage name of Eric Bartholomew (1926–84, born in Morecambe), as was Ernie Wise of Ernest Wiseman (b. 1925). The pair first met and formed a double act as teenagers, in 1941, but they were separated when Morecambe went down the mines as a Bevin boy and Wise was drafted into the merchant navy. They joined up again in 1947 and gradually shaped the act in which Wise was the anchor ('my buddy Ern with the short fat hairy legs') round whom Morecambe cavorted, both verbally and physically. One of many popular catch phrases was Morecambe's question and answer about the show: 'What do you think of it so far?' 'Rubbish!' Morecambe suffered a serious heart attack as early as 1968 and had open-heart surgery in 1979.

Morgan The most eccentric sports car available in Britain, with the company's basic model holding the world record for the longest production period; the Morgan 4/4 was first marketed in 1935 and there is still a waiting list of several years for a new one. It was the first four-wheel car produced by the company, previously well known for its racing three-wheelers. The original Morgan was developed in 1908–9 in the school workshops of Malvern College, where the engineering master and H.F.S. Morgan together produced a three-wheeler design which remained in production, little changed, until 1950. All Morgan cars (the 4/4 has more powerful stablemates, the Plus 4 and Plus 8) are made with a wooden frame, of ash.

Cliff **Morgan** (b. 1930) Rugby union player, at fly half, with 29 caps for Wales (1951–8) and four for the *Lions (1955). After his retirement he became a successful television commentator.

Henry **Morgan** (c.1635–88, kt 1674) Welsh buccaneer whose devastating raids on Spanish territories in the Caribbean were consistent, by the standards of the time, with positions of trust in the service of the crown – as witness his knighthood from Charles II and his position for the last years of his life as lieutenant-governor of Jamaica.

Professor **Moriarty** see Sherlock *Holmes.

Mrs **Morley** and Mrs Freeman see *Anne.

Robert **Morley** (1908–92) Portly actor, much of whose comedy was based on erupting with indignation or mock surprise. He had two qualities well calculated to make him a household name (he was instantly recognizable and reliably outrageous) and he explained with characteristic wit why he appeared in so many bad films: 'I am not an actor who has ever got into the habit of refusing film roles, holding that if one doesn't read the script in advance, or see the finished product, there is nothing to prevent one accepting the money.'

morning dress Male outfit consisting of a black or grey tail coat and top hat, now worn only at weddings or on certain royal occasions (such as *Ascot). It derives from late Victorian and Edwardian times when this was a gentleman's daytime dress in city life, as opposed to the differently cut black tail coat and white bow tie of *evening dress.

Morning Star see *Communist Party of Great Britain.

Morpeth (14,000 in 1981) Market town on the river Wansbeck; administrative centre since 1981 of Northumberland. It grew up round a Norman castle, of which only the 15c gatehouse survives. The church of St Mary is mainly 14c, with a contemporary 'tree of Jesse' window.

Norman **Morrice** (b.1931) Dancer and choreographer, with Ballet *Rambert for most of his career. He moved successfully into choreography with *Two Brothers* (1958), and was responsible for the company's change of emphasis to modern dance from 1966. He was director of the Royal Ballet 1977–86.

Morris Car company founded by William Morris (later Lord *Nuffield) in Oxford in 1912. His first machine, the two-seater Morris Oxford, became a bestselling model, known affectionately as the Bullnose Morris from the shape of its radiator. The factory was just south of Oxford at Cowley, which was the name of the next model, also bull-nosed and launched in 1915. Both the Oxford and Cowley remained in production until 1926, while the *MG was an offshoot of the same period. The years after World War II saw two immensely successful designs by *Issigonis, the Morris Minor (launched in 1948, re-using a name from 1929) and in 1959 the *Mini. By then the company had merged with *Austin to form the *British Motor Corporation.

William **Morris** (1834–96) Designer, poet, entrepreneur and socialist whose high seriousness about the importance of art and whose vision of a pre-industrial utopia owe

William Morris's painting of Jane Burden, whom he married the following year, as Queen Guinevere in her bedroom (1858).

much to the influence of *Ruskin. At Oxford he made a life-long friend of *Burne-Jones, who later designed for Morris's various enterprises. The first of these, founded in 1861 and developing into Morris & Co. (which lasted until 1940), produced embroideries, wallpapers, stained glass, textiles of all kinds and furniture. All were made to a high standard of craftsmanship and cost too much for the ordinary people whom Morris liked to think of as his market; but the strong and simple designs (notably Morris's own floral wallpapers and textiles) survived to become in the late 20c a familiar feature in many British homes. Morris's publishing venture, the *Kelmscott Press, was equally far removed from everyday pockets. The natural successor of his enterprises in these various fields was the *Arts and Crafts movement.

In 1859 he married Jane Burden, whose shock of hair, palely severe features and Cupid's bow of a mouth feature in dozens of paintings by Dante Gabriel *Rossetti; Morris's only known oil painting is also a portrait of her (*Queen Guinevere* Tate Gallery). The couple lived first in the Red House, at Bexleyheath in Kent, built for them in a simple medieval style by Philip Webb (1831–1915). In 1871 they settled at Kelmscott Manor, a 16c stone manor house on the Thames upstream from Oxford; Morris later borrowed the name for an 18c redbrick house on the Thames at Hammersmith, his London home from 1878, calling it Kelmscott House.

His best-known work of poetry, *The Earthly Paradise* (4 parts, 1868–70), links 12 medieval and 12 classical stories in a dream-like escape from the horrors of Victorian industrial society. In the 1880s Morris tried to alleviate those horrors by campaigning in the streets on behalf of socialism, even forming his own Socialist League in 1884, but *Bloody Sunday in 1887 brought disillusion with active politics. His childhood home in Walthamstow, to the northeast of London, is kept as a museum.

morris dance In the 15C, and probably earlier, the term 'morris' was applied to a wide variety of popular entertainments, including *mummers and even sword dancers. It is believed to derive from 'moorish' (similar dances on the Continent were known as *moresque* or *moresca*), and the reason may be that many of the performers disguised themselves with black faces. Like many popular art forms, morris dancing had almost died out by the late 19C. The present enthusiastic revival derives from the recording by Cecil Sharp (1859–1924) of a few surviving dances that he came across in the Cotswolds region. The familiar morris dance of today (performed by male dancers in white, with bells on their calves, clashing sticks and waving handkerchiefs) is therefore in origin just one regional variant.

Herbert **Morrison** (1888–1965, baron 1959) Labour politician and MP (with intervals) for South Hackney from 1923 and East Lewisham from 1945. He was prominent in the postwar Labour government – as leader of the House of Commons (1945–51) and briefly foreign secretary in 1951. As minister of transport in 1931 he was responsible for the bill which established *London Transport. His background was in London politics, leading the Labour group in the *London County Council between the wars.

Van **Morrison** (b. 1945) Northern Irish singer and songwriter who is one of the most individual talents in pop music, creating his own Celtic and nostalgic blend of blues, folk music and rock. One of his best-known early songs was 'Brown-Eyed Girl', issued as a single in 1967 and featuring later that year on his first album, *Blowin' Your Mind*. His next album, the mystical *Astral Weeks* (recorded in 48 hours in New York in 1968), has come to be considered a classic. He has continued to produce a steady succession of albums, and two of the most recent – *Enlightenment* (1990), *Hymns to the Silence* (1991) – have reached the top ten in the UK.

Morrissey (Steven Morrissey, b. 1959) Singer and lyricist who acquired a cult following in the 1980s, particularly among students, after forming the Smiths with Johnny Marr on guitar. His songs had a seductive mood of adolescent gloom (*Heaven Knows I'm Miserable Now* 1984). In 1987 he went solo and his first album *Viva Hate* (1988) went to the top of the UK charts.

Morte d'Arthur (c.1470) Prose narrative in English, printed by *Caxton in 1485, which brought together many separate strands of the legend of King *Arthur, taking them from French sources. Nothing is known of the author beyond what he himself reveals in the closing words of his text – that he is Thomas Malory, a knight, writing in 1469–70 while in jail. The most likely candidate is a knight of that name in Warwickshire, much in and out of prison in the 1450s for violence, theft and rape.

mortgage The loan of money to purchase a house against the security of the house itself; the loan is usually from a *building society. The interest on mortgages in the UK is tax deductible up to a given limit per borrower (in 1992 the limit was £30,000). The tax concession has been controversial on several counts – that it inflates house prices, that it is an unjust subsidy for the property-owning classes, and that the higher-rate taxpayer receives a greater subsidy on the same amount of interest (an inequity adjusted in April 1991, since when relief has been limited to the basic rate of tax). But in an increasingly *home-owning democracy, politicians have preferred not to meddle. For a rough indication of the rise and fall in the cost of a mortgage since 1965, see *base rate.

Mortgages were much in the news for a different reason in the early 1990s. Political encouragement of home ownership, and the exposure of the building societies to wider competition after the deregulation surrounding *Big Bang, resulted in exceptionally large mortgages being easily available (sometimes for almost 100% of the value of the house). A collapse of house prices and a rise in unemployment subsequently led to many people having their houses repossessed, and to others being unable to move because their home was suddenly worth less than the money which they owed on it.

Angela **Mortimer** (b. 1932) Tennis player who won the French championship in 1955 and the Australian in 1958 before becoming the Wimbledon champion in 1961.

John **Mortimer** (b. 1923) Barrister and author who has often drawn on the law for his material. His first play was the one-act *Dock Brief* (1957) about the relationship between a murderer and the barrister whose sheer incompetence causes the case to be dismissed; and his best-known character, *Rumpole, is a barrister. Mortimer himself had a high profile in the courts when he specialized in defending publishers and editors (including those of *Oz* and *Gay News*) against charges such as obscenity. A play about his relationship with his father (*A Voyage Round My Father* 1970) was later televised in the family home and garden, with Laurence Olivier as the father. Two recent novels (*Paradise Postponed* 1985, *Summer's Lease* 1988) have been turned into television series.

Mortlake tapestries The best English tapestries were made at Mortlake (now in southwest London) from 1619 by Flemish weavers. The *Raphael cartoons were acquired for this enterprise in 1623, and many copies of them were woven. The factory closed in 1703. By then several of the weavers had gone to factories in the Soho region, and 18C pieces woven in London are broadly known as Soho tapestries.

Morton's Fork A device of Tudor taxation which has lodged in the public mind for its memorable name and its fiscal elegance. The phrase was in use from at least the early 17C to describe a two-pronged argument supposedly offered to potential taxpayers by Henry VII's lord chancellor and archbishop of Canterbury, John Morton (c.1420–1500): an extravagant lifestyle proves that you have enough to pay, and a parsimonious one that you have set aside enough to pay.

Oswald **Mosley** (1896–1980, 6th bt 1928) Fascist leader in Britain during the 1930s. His previous political career had been chameleon-like; he sat as a Conservative MP (1918–22), as an independent (1922–4), and then for Labour (1926–31). He founded the British Union of Fascists in 1932 after a visit to Mussolini's Italy. By 1934 he was more influenced by the Nazis and his followers were increasingly anti-Semitic and hooligan (see *neo-Nazis). In 1936 he married Diana, a member of the *Mitford family. Both he and his wife were interned from 1940 to 1943 as Nazi sympathizers.

Mosquito One of the most versatile aircraft of World War II, twin-engined and acting as fighter, reconnaissance plane and fast lightweight bomber. Variously known as the Mozzie or the Wooden Wonder, it was made of wood, by de Havilland, with a total production of nearly 8000. It was in service with the RAF from 1941 to 1955.

Stirling **Moss** (b. 1929) Racing driver who was runner-up in the world championship in four successive seasons (1955–8), the first three times to Fangio and then to

Mike Hawthorn; he had previously had many successes in Formula Three with *Cooper. In 1955 he used the most painstaking professionalism to win the famous Italian Mille Miglia, which was raced – as the name states – over a distance of approximately 1000 miles on ordinary roads. Moss had logged every corner of the route, noting speeds and gears; his partner in the Mercedes (Denis Jenkinson, acting as navigator) read the charts and conveyed the information by hand signals. They won by the huge margin of 32 minutes over Fangio in the other Mercedes, with an average speed of 158kph/98mph – breaking the previous record by nearly 16kph/10mph.

Moss Bros (London WC2) Britain's best-known firm for the hiring of formal clothes, and in particular *morning dress for weddings. It derives from a new and second-hand clothes business established in 1860 by Moses Moses, and his descendants are still closely involved. New ready-made suits have always been the main trade, and it was not until the 1920s that the hiring out of clothes became significant; Monty Moss, great grandson of the founder, includes in his lecture on the firm's history a catalogue of items found in the returned morning suits (including wedding rings and on one occasion a glass eye). In the early 1990s the famous Moss Bros building in Covent Garden was being rebuilt.

Moss Side Area of south Manchester developed from the late 19C as a district of working-class terrace houses. Many were replaced by modern blocks in the 1970s. There were riots in July 1981, and by the early 1990s – with an extremely high level of unemployment – Moss Side had become notorious for drugs-related violence. In calmer days the district produced the first *Tiller girls.

Mothercare Chain of stores specializing in everything needed by the mother-to-be and by her child up to the age of eight. Mothercare was founded by Selim Zilkha (b. 1927), who had noticed this gap in the market. He opened his first shop in Kingston upon Thames in 1961; in the early 1990s there were some 250 stores in the UK, together with a large international mail order and franchise operation. In 1986 the chain merged with *BhS and Habitat to form the Storehouse group.

Mother Goose Old woman of magical powers, usually in a pointed witch's hat, who is a favourite character in *pantomime. She emerged in France in 1697 as the supposed author of a collection of traditional fairy stories, *Contes de ma mère l'Oye* (Tales of Mother Goose), which had been gathered together by Charles Perrault (1628–1703). These included several tales which became staples of British pantomime, including *Puss in Boots and *Cinderella. They first appeared in English, under Mother Goose's name, in an edition of 1729. She was later enlisted to present the most influential early collection of *nursery rhymes.

Mothering Sunday The middle or fourth Sunday in Lent, on which it was the tradition to 'go a-mothering'. This involved visiting one's parents and either giving or receiving a cake, in particular a *simnel cake. In recent years the term Mother's Day has become more common, borrowed from the USA (where it applies to the second Sunday in May).

'mother of Parliaments' see *Parliament.

Mother's Day see *Mothering Sunday.

Mothers' Union International organization of Anglican women, with membership open also to women of other Christian denominations. With a central aim of promoting the virtues of Christian family life, it derives from meetings held in 1876 by Mary Sumner (1828–1921), wife of the rector of Old Alresford, a village near Winchester.

Moto-cross (also known as scrambling) The motorcyle equivalent of a cross-country race, with the riders and their bikes plunging, leaping and slithering round a rugged circuit of natural hazards. First attempted in 1924 at Camberley, in Surrey, it became an international sport after World War II and there has been a world championship since 1957.

motorcycles A product in which British manufacturers suffered a catastrophic collapse from the 1960s, having previously been world leaders with makes such as *BSA, *Norton and *Triumph. The industry decided to concentrate in the 1960s on the most powerful bikes, just when the public was becoming interested in cheaper and lighter machines. The Japanese filled the gap, starting with the Honda Super Cub of 1959. After becoming established at the bottom end of the market the Japanese then challenged the home manufacturers with the more powerful 750cc-and-above 'superbikes', notably the Honda CB750 in 1968. By 1980 Japan had 75% of the British market and domestic producers had just 1%. Ten years later there were tentative signs of a comeback, and in 1992 the Isle of Man *TT was won for the first time in many years by the make which once dominated the event, a Norton.

motor racing From early in the 20C the British showed a keen interest in the sport, with the first custom-built track opening at *Brooklands in 1907. But it was 1958 which saw the beginning of a sequence of major successes. In that year Mike Hawthorn was the first of more than half a dozen British drivers to become world champion; and 1958 was the start of the constructors' championship, in which Cooper, Lotus, Brabham, Tyrrell, McLaren and Williams have all had distinguished records.

Motor Show Britain's most important display of the latest models of cars and commercial vehicles. The exhibition is presented by the Society of Motor Manufacturers and Traders, a trade organization founded in 1902. It put on its first Motor Show in 1903 at *Crystal Palace, and moved the event in 1905 to *Olympia; as more space was needed the location subsequently changed to *Earl's Court in 1937 and to the *National Exhibition Centre in Birmingham in 1978. From that year it became biennial instead of annual. It is held in October (apart from a 1990 experiment with September).

MOT test (Ministry of Transport test) An examination carried out on all features of a car which might affect its performance on the road (brakes, steering, tyres etc.). It is compulsory on any car more than three years old, and the car's vehicle licence cannot be renewed without a valid MOT certificate.

Mottisfont Abbey (19km/12m W of Winchester) Originally an Augustinian priory of about 1200, now mainly 18C in character, the house is known above all for the trees in its grounds (including a giant plane) and for a notable recent addition – a collection of old-fashioned roses in a walled garden, begun in 1972 and now unrivalled in its range of varieties.

Marion **Mould** (Marion Coakes, b. 1947, m. David Mould 1969) Show jumper who became famous in partnership with one of the most popular horses on the circuit, the

Motor racing

	World Champions	Constructors' Championship
1950	Giuseppe Farina (Ita)	
1951	Juan Manuel Fangio (Arg)	
1952	Alberto Ascari (Ita)	
1953	Alberto Ascari (Ita)	
1954	Juan Manuel Fangio (Arg)	
1955	Juan Manuel Fangio (Arg)	
1956	Juan Manuel Fangio (Arg)	
1957	Juan Manuel Fangio (Arg)	
1958	Mike Hawthorn (UK)	Vanwall
1959	Jack Brabham (Aus)	Cooper-Climax
1960	Jack Brabham (Aus)	Cooper-Climax
1961	Phil Hill (USA)	Ferrari
1962	Graham Hill (UK)	BRM
1963	Jim Clark (UK)	Lotus-Climax
1964	John Surtees (UK)	Ferrari
1965	Jim Clark (UK)	Lotus-Climax
1966	Jack Brabham (Aus)	Brabham-Repco
1967	Denny Hulme (NZ)	Brabham-Repco
1968	Graham Hill (UK)	Lotus-Ford
1969	Jackie Stewart (UK)	Matra-Ford
1970	Jochen Rindt (Aut)	Lotus-Ford
1971	Jackie Stewart (UK)	Tyrrell-Ford
1972	Emerson Fittipaldi (Bra)	Lotus-Ford
1973	Jackie Stewart (UK)	Lotus-Ford
1974	Emerson Fittipaldi (Bra)	McLaren-Ford
1975	Niki Lauda (Aut)	Ferrari
1976	James Hunt (UK)	Ferrari
1977	Niki Lauda (Aut)	Ferrari
1978	Mario Andretti (USA)	Lotus-Ford
1979	Jody Scheckter (SAf)	Ferrari
1980	Alan Jones (Aus)	Williams-Ford
1981	Nelson Piquet (Bra)	Williams-Ford
1982	Keke Rosberg (Fin)	Ferrari
1983	Nelson Piquet (Bra)	Ferrari
1984	Niki Lauda (Aut)	McLaren-Porsche
1985	Alain Prost (Fra)	McLaren-TAG
1986	Alain Prost (Fra)	Williams-Honda
1987	Nelson Piquet (Bra)	Williams-Honda
1988	Ayrton Senna (Bra)	McLaren-Honda
1989	Alain Prost (Fra)	McLaren-Honda
1990	Ayrton Senna (Bra)	McLaren-Honda
1991	Ayrton Senna (Bra)	McLaren-Honda
1992	Nigel Mansell (UK)	Williams-Renault

small but irrepressible Stroller. Together they won the Queen Elizabeth II Cup in 1965 (and again in 1971), the Hickstead Derby in 1967 and the silver medal at the 1968 Olympic Games. Marion Mould was the first woman to win an individual Olympic show jumping medal (a sport in which men and women compete on equal terms).

Lord **Mountbatten** (Louis Mountbatten, 1900–79, KCVO 1922, Earl Mountbatten 1947) Uncle of the duke of *Edinburgh and cousin of Elizabeth II (through his maternal grandmother, a daughter of Queen Victoria). In 1943 he became Supreme Allied Commander of South East Asia and established his base in Ceylon for the recapture of Burma and Malaya. In 1947 he was viceroy of *India at the time of partition, and he stayed on into 1948 as governor general. He was murdered in 1979 by an IRA bomb concealed in his fishing boat off the west coast of Ireland. His family name was Battenberg, changed in 1917 to a literal English translation because of anti-German sentiments during World War I. He was known to his family and friends as 'Dickie', though not one of his five Christian names was Richard.

Mount Stewart (16km/10m E of Belfast) The earlier part of the house was designed by Frederick Dance the Younger (1741–1825) for the 1st marquess of Londonderry, whose son Lord *Castlereagh grew up here. The central part, with its heavy classical portico, was added from about 1825 by the appropriately named William Vitruvius Morrison (1794–1838). Mount Stewart is particularly known for its gardens, created by Edith Londonderry from the 1920s to the 1950s. Nearby, overlooking Strangford Lough, is the Temple of the Winds, a tiny two-storey neoclasssical banqueting house of 1782–5 by James 'Athenian' Stuart (1713–88).

Mousa Uninhabited island in the *Shetlands, known for the best preserved of all *brochs. The walls of the broch still stand 14m/45ft high.

*The **Mousetrap*** (1952) Thriller by Agatha *Christie which holds by a wide margin the record for the world's longest-running play. It opened in London on 25 November 1952 at the Ambassador's Theatre and in 1974 moved next door to the St Martin's. The evening of its 40th anniversary, in 1992, was the 16,648th performance. The title is that of the play-within-a-play in *Hamlet.

Mowgli see *The *Jungle Book.

MP (Member of Parliament) A slightly misleading term in that it applies only to the members who form one of the two Houses of Parliament, the House of *Commons. Each has been elected, either in a *general election or a *by-election, to represent a single *constituency. The letters MP are placed after a member's name.

Mr The written version of Mister (derived originally from Master), which is placed before a man's name.

Mr and Mrs Clark and Percy (1971, Tate Gallery) Painting by *Hockney which is one of the most reproduced images of contemporary British art. It shows Ossie Clark and Celia Birtwell, fashion designers at whose wedding Hockney was best man. The white cat on Ossie's lap, the detail which probably makes the painting so popular, is in bitter truth a fraud; she is Blanche, not Percy (Hockney changed her name to Percy, that of another cat owned by the Clarks, because he felt it sounded better in the title).

Mrs see *Miss.

Mrs Dale's Diary (BBC 1948–69) Radio soap opera about the family life of Mary Dale and of her husband Jim, a doctor, in the fictional south London suburb of Parkwood Hill. The name was changed to *The Dales* when the family moved, in 1962, to a new town called Exton in the Home Counties.

Mrs Mopp see *ITMA.

MSF (Manufacturing, Science and Finance Union) Britain's largest trade union for professional and skilled workers, with members in a wide range of enterprises. It was formed in 1988 by the merger of ASTMS (Association of Scientific, Technical and Managerial Staff) and TASS (Technical, Administrative and Supervisory Staff). In the early 1990s the union had some 650,000 members.

Much Ado About Nothing (c.1599) Comedy by *Shakespeare in which the main plot concerns Claudio and his beloved Hero (female, in spite of her name). They are separated by the deceptions of the evil Don John, until the villain is unmasked by a comic bumbling constable, Dogberry – a predecessor of Mrs Malaprop, with his observations such as 'comparisons are odorous'. The better-known subplot follows the bantering relationship between Benedick and Beatrice, whose barbed hostilities become a smoke screen for love.

Much-Binding-in-the-Marsh (BBC 1947–53) Radio comedy series, written by and starring Kenneth *Horne and Richard Murdoch (1907–90), which was supposedly set in an RAF station doubling as a country club. Each programme ended with the whole cast singing a humorous jingle about Much Binding, to a tune by Sidney Torch.

Muckle Flugga see *Unst.

muffins and crumpets Often confused, but alike only in that both are circular, flat, cooked on a griddle rather than baked, and toasted before serving. The muffin ('toasted English' in the USA) is made from a dough similar to bread and is split through the middle before being buttered on the inside surfaces; it is eaten at either breakfast or tea. The crumpet uses a batter which becomes riddled with holes when cooked, enabling it to be saturated with melted butter; it is only eaten at tea time.

Muffin the Mule Popular puppet on BBC children's television in the years after World War II (from as early as 1946), performing beside Annette Mills (d. 1955) who wrote and narrated the stories.

Malcolm **Muggeridge** (1903–90) Journalist and broadcaster, notable for the trenchant wit with which he was able to undermine the certainties of those with whom he disagreed. The targets of this wit changed dramatically during his life. The young Muggeridge was left-wing, self-indulgent and sceptical; the older man, known to some as St Mugg, was reactionary, ascetic and a committed Christian; but at neither extreme was he pompous.

Frank **Muir** see *Take It From Here.*

Jean **Muir** Fashion designer with her own business since 1966. Her clothes tend to be restrained, and sombre in colour, but are made soft and flowing by skilful cutting (on the cross, in technical terms) and by the use of fabrics such as silk jersey.

Muirfield Golf course on the coast east of Edinburgh. It belongs to the world's oldest *golf club, the Honourable Company of Edinburgh Golfers, founded in 1744 as the Gentlemen Golfers of Leith. It was they who established the first rules of the game. They played until 1836 on the links at Leith, then moved east for a while to Musselburgh and in 1891 east again to Muirfield. The course at Muirfield was laid out by Tom Morris Snr, winner of four *Opens in the first eight years of the contest. It was on his new course at Muirfield that the first 72-hole Open was played in 1892, and it has remained one of the regular locations for the championship.

Mulberry harbours Two massive artificial harbours, capable of berthing large ships, which were constructed in Britain (comprising more than a million tons of steel and concrete) and were floated across in sections to be assembled on the Normandy beaches just after *D-day. Gales severely damaged them in late June, and the remains of one were used to repair the other (they were ten miles apart).

mulligatawny A spicy soup, curry-flavoured and made usually now with chicken stock, which was adopted and brought home by the British in India. The name is Tamil for 'pepper water'.

Mulready envelope see *Post Office.

Mumbles see *Gower Peninsula.

mummers Performers of a midwinter folk play, once common in most parts of Britain and still surviving in a few places. The actors are local amateurs, traditionally all men. They usually wear costumes which conceal their faces and they speak their doggerel verses in a deadpan manner, stepping into the circle formed by the onlookers to perform a play which has a very consistent central theme. A hero, most often St George or King George, engages in single combat with an adversary (Bold Slasher and the Turkish Knight are leading candidates). One of them is killed, whereupon a comic doctor steps forward; he professes to have all sorts of cures and is much concerned with being paid, but he does manage to revive the dead man. The play is probably a survival of a midwinter festival, celebrating or encouraging the renewal of life in the coming season, with many of the specific details added during the 18c.

St **Mungo** (d. c.612) The traditional founder of *Glasgow, though little is known of him except from very late sources. These state that his real name was Kentigern (Mungo being said to be a nickname meaning 'dear friend'); that he established a Christian settlement in Glasgow; and that he spent a period also in Wales when the local ruler in Scotland reverted to paganism. The ring and the fish in Glasgow's coat of arms are details from one of the miracles described in his legend. His feast day is January 14.

Munich The usual abbreviation in Britain for the Munich conference or pact of 29 September 1938, in which Neville *Chamberlain and the French premier Edouard Daladier agreed to Hitler's annexation of the Sudetenland (an area of Czechoslovakia with a German-speaking majority) in return for his making no further territorial demands. Chamberlain was regarded as a national hero by most people in Britain, though not by the opponents of *appeasement, when he landed in London and waved a piece of paper which he said represented 'peace for our time . . . peace with honour' (he was echoing words used by Disraeli in 1878, after he had negotiated peace between Russia and Turkey). Hitler's betrayal of the Munich agreement, by marching into the rest of Czechoslovakia in March 1939, finally resolved Chamberlain to replace appeasement with a firm commitment to defend Poland, the next likely victim, against aggression.

In 1992 John Major and the Czech president, Vaclav Havel, signed a declaration annulling the 1938 Munich agreement – by which Britain had in effect, until then, been acknowledging a German right to part of Czechoslovakia.

Alfred **Munnings** (1878–1959, kt 1944) Painter of horses and of racecourse scenes, who shared with the *Newlyn school a commitment to painting out of doors. He is remembered as a controversial figure because as president of the Royal Academy he used his speech at the annual dinner, in 1949, to attack all forms of modern art. His house at Dedham in Essex is kept as a museum.

Munros The 277 mountain peaks in Scotland which are above 3000 feet (914m). They are named after a Victorian eccentric, Hugh Thomas Munro (1856–1919), who published a list of them in 1891. It has become a familiar chal-

A beguiling challenge: two of the Munros in the Five Sisters range, above Glen Shiel near the west coast of Scotland.

lenge among enthusiasts to climb all 277. Munro himself died with one still to go, but it is said that some 800 people have completed the entire list. The best-known contender at present is John *Smith, whose score was 96 when he became leader of the Labour party in 1992.

*The **Muppet Show*** (ATV 1976–80) Television comedy series featuring puppets of all shapes and sizes (the smallest being a green glove with large eyes and a pink mouth, the show's compere, Kermit the Frog). The Muppets, created by Jim Henson (1936–90), began on the American children's programme *Sesame Street*, and were adapted in Britain to adult entertainment. Each show was ostensibly put on by the puppets in a theatre, with the elderly and dissatisfied Statler and Waldorf watching from a box. Comfortable Fozzie Bear and the impossibly vain Miss Piggy were popular favourites, and a human celebrity was usually introduced as a victim.

Roderick **Murchison** see *geological periods.

Murder in the Cathedral (1935) Poetic drama by T.S. *Eliot, commissioned for performance in the chapter house of Canterbury Cathedral. The play focuses on the inner conflict of Thomas *Becket as he contemplates martyrdom (the fear of pride in such a fate holds him back). The women of Canterbury, forming a chorus, discover a new self-awareness through his example. At the end the four assassins address the audience, using modern political arguments in self-justification.

Iris **Murdoch** (b. 1919, DBE 1987) Philosopher and author of some 25 novels by the early 1990s. The relationships and sexual tensions of her characters – usually professional people – are revealed in complex patterns of myth and symbolism beneath a surface realism. One of her best-known novels, *The Bell* (1958), is set among an eccentric lay community in a country house. *The Sea, the Sea* won the Booker prize in 1978.

Richard **Murdoch** see *Much Binding in the Marsh.

Rupert **Murdoch** (b. 1931) Australian-born international media tycoon, now a US citizen, who has a high profile in British life because of the extensive newspaper and television holdings of his UK company, News International. He made his first purchases of British newspapers in the lower range of the present *tabloids, buying the *News of the World* and the *Sun* in 1969. These were balanced from 1981 by the *Times* and its supplements, together with the *Sunday Times*. In 1987 *Today* was added to the collection. By then Murdoch was planning his entry into satellite *television; Sky went on air with four channels in 1989 and subsequently merged with its only satellite rival to become BSkyB, of which News International owns half. In 1992 Murdoch's personal attention was focused on Hollywood, where he had recently bought Twentieth Century Fox and taken over as executive chairman of the studio.

John **Murray** see *John Murray.

Murrayfield (Edinburgh) Scotland's national *rugby stadium, where all home international matches are now played (the first was a *Calcutta Cup engagement in 1925). In 1959 Murrayfield became the first ground to install electric heating cables beneath the turf, to make it playable even in severe frost. In the early 1990s the stadium is being considerably enlarged. The district of Murrayfield also contains *Edinburgh Zoo.

muscular Christianity Term applied derisively from the 1850s to vigorously Christian efforts to tackle social problems, as pioneered in the Christian Socialism of F.D. Maurice (1805–72) and Charles *Kingsley.

Museum of London (London EC2) Museum collecting and exhibiting many aspects of the capital city's history. It opened in 1976 in a new building by the firm of

Powell and Moya, adjacent to a section of London's city wall (dating back to Roman fortifications of the 3rd century AD). The museum was formed by the merging of two earlier collections. The Guildhall Museum was established in 1826 by the corporation of the City of London; and the London Museum had opened in Kensington Palace in 1912, returning there in 1951 after spending the period from 1914 in Lancaster House. The two were bitter rivals in the pursuit of London's past treasures until they were merged in their new home.

Museum of Mankind (London W1) Museum created to house the ethnographic collection of the *British Museum, which was moved there in 1970. The building, by James Pennethorne (1801–71), was designed in the 1860s as the administrative centre for London University.

Museum of the Moving Image (MOMI, London SE1) Collection tracing the history of cinema and television. It opened on the *South Bank in 1988 in premises under the arches of Waterloo Bridge, next door to the *National Film Theatre. The items on display, with a wealth of equipment and costumes and film clips, move chronologically from shadow puppets and peepshows to the latest developments in satellite broadcasting.

Thea **Musgrave** (b. 1928) Scottish composer, whose works offer virtuoso opportunities for the solo instrumentalist, as seen in her clarinet concerto of 1969, her horn concerto of 1971 and her violin concerto of 1973. She is also a successful composer of operas, notably *Mary, Queen of Scots* (1977) and *Harriet, the Woman called Moses* (1984).

music hall (also called variety) The main popular entertainment in Britain in the second half of the 19C, surviving in places into the mid-20C. With its origins among tavern performers, music hall gradually expanded until large new theatres were required to cater for a vast audience. Performers such as Dan *Leno, Vesta *Tilley, George *Robey, Harry *Lauder and Marie *Lloyd toured the country as stars, with a national following. Safe from the mass exposure of radio and television, they needed only a small repertoire of endlessly repeated but much loved numbers.

The old-time pleasures were brought to the television audience in successive series (from the 1950s) of *The Good Old Days*, a nostalgic programme of music hall broadcast from the City Varieties Theatre in Leeds, with even the audience in Victorian clothes. And on a small scale the traditions have been kept alive by places such as the Players Theatre in London.

Musicians' Union Trade union formed in 1921 by the merger of two similar groups, both established in 1893. Virtually all professional musicians in Britain are members, whether in pop groups, dance bands or concert orchestras.

music schools Britain has only one full-scale music school for children (aged 7 to 18); it happens also to be by far the oldest of the institutions now specializing in music. Chetham's, in Manchester, was founded in 1656 (by a bequest from Humphrey Chetham, 1580–1653) for the free education of 40 poor boys. Occupying a superb 15C building near the cathedral, it had grown by the mid-20C to a school of some 250 boys. Known for the standard of its music, and confronted by the need to go either *comprehensive or independent, Chetham's took the bold step of becoming the country's first specialist school for young musicians. It is co-educational, and combines publicly funded and fee-paying pupils; all admissions are dependent on a musical audition. Offering a general education,

though with music as each pupil's main subject, the school has acquired a high reputation.

The other leading music establishments are all colleges for undergraduates or graduates. The oldest is the Royal Academy of Music, formed in London in 1822 (at that time for just ten boys and ten girls). It moved in 1911 to its present premises in Marylebone Road. The Royal College of Music, situated behind the Albert Hall, was founded in 1883 by the prince of Wales; its grandiose Victorian building (1889–94 by Arthur Blomfield) is on land bought with the profits of the Great Exhibition. Slightly earlier is the Guildhall School of Music and Drama, set up by the Corporation of the City of London in 1880; it moved in 1977 into purpose-built premises in the Barbican, with its own theatre and concert hall.

Outside London the oldest college is the Royal Scottish Academy of Music and Drama. Its origins, shared with the Glasgow School of Art, go back to the Glasgow Athenaeum of 1847; it was formally established in 1891 as the Athenaeum School of Music and has been the Royal Scottish Academy of Music since 1944 (drama was added to the name in 1968). The youngest of the four royal schools is the Royal Northern College of Music, formed in 1973 by the amalgamation of the Northern School of Music and the Royal Manchester School of Music; like the Guildhall School in London, it has its own modern premises near the city centre complete with theatre and concert hall.

Music While You Work (BBC 1940–67) Radio programme, consisting of a non-stop medley of popular tunes, devised at the lowest ebb of Britain's fortunes in World War II (June 1940) to enthuse the workers in the factories. The music was played by a different band each day and was introduced by an Eric *Coates signature tune, *Calling All Workers*.

Muslims There are thought to be in Britain about 1.2 million Muslims – believers in Islam, the religion revealed in the Koran (or more accurately *Qur'an*), which Muslims believe to have been dictated by God (*Allah*) to the prophet Muhammad in the early 7C. The majority of British Muslims are members of families who *immigrated in the decades after World War II from *Pakistan and Bangladesh.

The largest communities of Muslims in Britain are in London, Birmingham, Bradford, Liverpool, Manchester, Cardiff, Edinburgh and Glasgow. Unlike other *ethnic and religious minorities, they have adopted a high political profile on the basis of their religion. Certain British Muslims took a controversial and widely criticized line in supporting the Iranian death sentence on Salman *Rushdie, and an unelected Muslim 'parliament' was formed in January 1992. There has also been a strong demand for separate Muslim *state schools (on the same basis as existing Christian and Jewish schools), and legislation proposed in 1992 makes this a likely development.

mustard Two distinct types of mustard seed, the white and the black, are among the oldest recorded spices, cultivated for at least 5000 years. The white seed gives a hot sensation on the tongue, while the black sets the nose ablaze. English mustard is a blend of both seeds, producing both effects; it is traditionally kept in powder form and is made by adding water just before use. French mustard, the other variety widely available in British restaurants, is made from the black seed and is blended with vinegar, wine and herbs.

Eadweard **Muybridge** (1830–1904) Photographer who first revealed the exact patterns of movement of horses and other creatures, using a series of cameras with their shutters linked to trip wires. Born plain Edward Muggeridge in Kingston upon Thames (which now has his archives), he emigrated in his twenties to the USA and it was there that he built his career.

MVO see *orders of chivalry.

Myanmar (the name since 1989 of Burma) Country which became independent from Britain in 1948 and decided not to join the Commonwealth. Three wars between British India and the neighbouring kingdom of Burma (in 1824–6, 1852, 1885) led to the annexation of the country as a province of India in 1886. Largely through Kipling's poem *Mandalay*, Burma came to seem one of the most romantic parts of the empire. The Japanese occupation in World War II was a major reverse for the Allies, cutting off the Burma Road (from Lashio in Burma to Chongqing in China), which was the main supply route to the Chinese.

My Fair Lady Possibly the most successful American musical of all time (lyrics by Alan Jay Lerner, music by Frederick Loewe), earning a place in this book through a strong British element. It was based on *Pygmalion* and opened on Broadway in 1956 with Rex *Harrison, Julie *Andrews and Stanley *Holloway in the leading roles. They repeated them in London in 1958. The two men also starred in the film (1964), where the part of Eliza was taken by Audrey *Hepburn.

Androw **Myllar** (fl. *c*.1508) Scotland's equivalent of *Caxton, as the country's pioneer of printing. He learned the craft in Rouen and brought French printers with him back to Edinburgh, where he and Walter Chepman (*c*.1473–*c*.1538) were granted in 1507 a joint licence and monopoly for the printing and selling of books in Scotland. The first title they issued, in 1508, was John Lydgate's *Complaint of the Black Knight*.

My old Dutch see Albert *Chevalier.

mystery plays The outstanding theatrical achievement of the Middle Ages, consisting of short scenes, each enacting an incident from the Old or New Testament, which together tell the Bible story. Throughout Europe plays of this kind developed in the 13C. The form they took in England, particularly in northern regions, was unusual in two respects: the scenes were played on carts which could be moved to different locations in a town, so that the entire sequence unfolded before a succession of audiences during the course of a day; and each scene was acted by a different trade guild, sometimes with an appropriate link (the shipwrights, for example, presenting Noah and the Ark).

The performances were part of the great festival of Corpus Christi, held on the Thursday after Trinity Sunday and established in the 13C to celebrate the doctrine of transubstantiation (the real presence of the body of Christ in the consecrated Communion wafer). This doctrine was anathema in the Reformation. The Corpus Christi procession was therefore suppressed in 16C England, and together with it the mystery plays.

Of many local cycles of plays, only four have survived – those of Chester (probably the earliest), York, Wakefield (also known as the Towneley plays, from the family which owned the manuscript), and Coventry (probably not in fact from there, but of unknown origin). At York and Chester the plays are now regularly performed again.

They have been variously known in the past as miracle plays and as mystery plays (originally from a Latin word for the church service and not, as often said, because they were performed by the 'mysteries' or guilds). The modern convention is to use mystery play for purely biblical sequences and miracle play for dramas which also include the lives and miracles of the saints.

'My words are my own' see Lord *Rochester.

N

NAAFI (Navy, Army and Air Force Institutes) The new name given in 1921 to what had previously been the Navy and Army Canteen Board. The NAAFI provides shops and recreation facilities for British service personnel wherever they are posted.

nabobs see *East India Company.

V.S. **Naipaul** (Vidiadhar Surajprasad Naipaul, b. 1932, kt 1990) Novelist and essayist of Indian descent, born in Trinidad and living in Britain since the 1950s. He first became known for his novels of life in the Caribbean (in particular *A House for Mr Biswas*, 1961). Later work has included fiction about the culturally uprooted (*In a Free State*, which won the Booker prize in 1971) and the politically exploited (*A Bend in the River* 1979); *The Enigma of Arrival* (1987) reflects his own adjustment over four decades to life in Britain. In 1993 he won the David Cohen British Literature prize, awarded for a lifetime's contribution to literature.

Nairnshire Until 1975 a *county on the northeast coast of Scotland, now part of the Grampian region.

NALGO see *Unison.

Namibia Member of the *Commonwealth since 1990. This coastal region in southwest Africa was a German protectorate from 1880 to 1915. After World War I it was administered by South Africa, a situation which provoked international opposition and local unrest in the 1970s. In 1988 an agreement was reached for South African troops to be withdrawn in return for the simultaneous ending of the Cuban presence in Angola, to the north. Namibia decided to join the Commonwealth on becoming independent.

Nantgarw porcelain A factory was founded in 1813 by William Billingsley (1758–1828) at Nantgarw, just southwest of Caerphilly, and for a few years made a translucent porcelain now much prized by collectors. In 1819 the enterprise was sold to the *Coalport factory.

John **Napier** (1550–1617) Scottish mathematician, laird of Merchiston Castle near Edinburgh, renowned for the invention of logarithms – which he published in 1614 in *Mirifici logarithmorum canonis descriptio* (Description of the wonderful rule of logarithms). His tables substituted addition and subtraction for multiplication and division, by providing the appropriate power for each number in relation to a given base. Logarithms remained the quickest way of making complex calculations until the arrival of the computer and pocket calculator.

Napoleon see *Animal Farm*.

Napoleonic Wars (1802–15) European conflict, a continuation of the *French Revolutionary Wars, provoked by Napoleon's imperial ambitions and ending only with his defeat at Waterloo. The invasion of Britain was at first a central part of Napoleon's strategy (causing the building of the defensive *Martello towers along the south coast of England) and he mustered an army of 100,000 for the purpose. But a force of this size could not cross the Channel while Britain's navy retained its power at sea. French efforts to distract or destroy the fleet were unsuccessful, and in 1805 Napoleon moved his army east to attack Austria. The combined French and Spanish fleet was attempting to enter the Mediterranean to lend support when it was annihilated by Nelson at *Trafalgar – a victory which put an end to any thought of invasion. Napoleon switched his strategy to squeezing Britain economically through a blockade – the so-called Continental System, by which he attempted to close all continental ports to British ships.

Napoleon's land war was, by contrast, entirely successful in the early years. He defeated Russia and Austria at Austerlitz (1805) and Prussia at Jena (1806). Austerlitz prompted William Pitt's accurate prediction that Napoleon would now dominate the entire continent: 'Roll up that map of Europe; it will not be wanted these ten years.' By early 1808 all the major countries of continental Europe were either controlled by Napoleon through puppet rulers or had been forced into alliances with him, committing them to the blockade of Britain. The last to close its harbours was Portugal, in 1807. This completion of the blockade provoked Britain's first involvement on land and the beginning of the *Peninsular War. Napoleon continued to have successes in central Europe during 1809–12, but the Peninsular War was a continuous drain on his resources. He sealed his fate with the disastrous invasion of Russia in 1812; of about 600,000 men who entered Russia that summer only 100,000 returned, in the depths of winter. Even so, Napoleon raised new armies and fought on until March 1814, when the allies entered Paris and he abdicated. He was exiled to Elba, while the leaders of the European powers gathered in Austria to agree among themselves, at the congress of Vienna, the details of a post-Napoleonic Europe.

They were still at their deliberations when Napoleon escaped from Elba and arrived back in Paris (20 Mar. 1815), to begin the extraordinary reign of a 'hundred days' which ended with his defeat at *Waterloo. A month after the battle he went on board a British ship, HMS *Bellerophon*, handing the captain a letter to the Prince Regent (later George IV), in which he announced his retirement and asked if he might seat himself 'at the hearth of the British people'. He was sent instead to the island of *St Helena.

Narnia An imaginary country, reached through a wardrobe, in which C.S. *Lewis set seven children's books from *The Lion, the Witch and the Wardrobe* (1950) to *The Last Battle* (1956). Events in Narnia have their own internal consistency, but Lewis was also consciously providing a parallel to the Christian story.

narrow boats see *canals.

Naseby (14 June 1645) Decisive battle in the *English Civil War, fought in the northern tip of Northamptonshire between a royalist army of 10,000 under Prince Rupert and a parliamentary one of 14,000 under Thomas Fairfax and Oliver Cromwell. In addition to the advantage in numbers, it was the greater discipline of the *New Model Army (and in particular Cromwell's control of the cavalry) which won the day. This was the end of effective resistance to the parliamentary forces.

Beau **Nash** (Richard Nash, 1674–1762) Dandy and arbiter of fashion in the two leading 18c resorts. He was living by his wits as a gambler when he arrived in 1705 in *Bath, where he was soon elected master of ceremonies. He immediately set about improving the tone of the place, even posting a Code of Manners in the Pump Room. He was widely referred to as the King of Bath, and from 1735 he exercised the same beneficial control over *Tunbridge Wells.

John **Nash** (1752–1835) The favourite architect of George IV, responsible for the *Royal Pavilion at Brighton and for the rebuilding from 1825 of *Buckingham Palace. His greatest single project was the creation of *Regent's Park and its surrounding terraces together with the processional route through the west end of London, linking the park via Portland Place (already existing) and *Regent Street to *Carlton House.

Paul **Nash** (1889–1946) Painter who absorbed surrealist and cubist influences within an overriding concern for landscape. He was a war artist in both world wars. One of his most powerful images is *Totes Meer* ('Dead Sea' 1941, Tate Gallery), based on a dump of wrecked German aircraft near Oxford.

'nasty, brutish and short' see *Leviathan*.

national anthem (*God save the Queen* or *King*) The origin of both words and tune is obscure. The words, evidently already traditional, are first recorded as being sung at Drury Lane theatre on 28 Sept. 1745 as part of the patriotic fervour provoked by the *'45 Rebellion. The music on that occasion was by Thomas *Arne, but the now familiar melody is probably a folk tune; variants of it feature in several early 17c works, most notably a keyboard piece by the aptly named John Bull (*c*.1562–1628). By 1861 words and tune featured as a three-verse hymn in *Hymns Ancient and Modern*. When sung as the national anthem, the first verse alone is used. In the present reign the words are:

> God save our gracious Queen,
> Long live our noble Queen,
>   God save the Queen.
> Send her victorious,
> Happy and glorious,
> Long to reign over us;
>   God save the Queen.

Modern hymn books, in keeping with modern sensibilities, either omit the second verse or add an asterisk meaning 'May be omitted'. Its words are more appropriate to the partisan certainties of the 18c:

> O Lord our God, arise,
> Scatter our enemies,
>   And make them fall;
> Confound their politics,
> Frustrate their knavish tricks;
> On Thee our hopes we fix;
>   God save us all.

Sussex Place, one of the grandest of John Nash's terraces, overlooking the southwest side of Regent's Park.

National Army Museum (London SW3) Collection devoted to displaying the history of the British army. It was first brought together and opened in 1960, in a former riding school at Sandhurst. It moved in 1971 to a new custom-built museum next door to the Chelsea Hospital.

National Art Collections Fund Britain's largest art charity, funded by donations and by the subscriptions of some 30,000 members. It was founded in 1903 in response to the amount of art leaving the country. The first triumph was the purchase in 1905 of the *Rokeby Venus*, which was then given to the National Gallery. Since then the Fund has contributed to the cost of more than 10,000 items in the fine and decorative arts, all of which are now in public museums, galleries or historic houses.

National Book League see *Book Trust.

National Curriculum Group of ten 'foundation' subjects established by the Educational Reform Act of 1988 as compulsory for all children aged 5–16 in *state schools in England and Wales. The subjects are English, mathematics, science, technology, history, geography, music, art, physical education, and a modern foreign language (for children aged 11–16). Special emphasis is placed on the first three, which are defined as the 'core' subjects. Children are assessed on their progress at the ages of 7, 11, 14 and 16, partly by their own teachers' assessments and partly by a national test (see also *exams). The selection of material to be studied provoked considerable controversy, particularly in the fields of English and music.

National Debt The total amount of money borrowed at any time by the government. The debt goes back to the founding of the *Bank of England in the late 17C and was close to £200bn in the early 1990s. Vast though this seems, it was only about 40% of *GDP. Nearly all the debt is money borrowed from UK citizens (through the sale of government bonds and securities, and to a lesser extent of savings certificates) so the interest paid is an internal circulation of money. Each year's addition to the national debt is known as the *PSBR (public sector borrowing requirement).

National Economic Development Council Body set up in 1962 to bring together government, management and trade unions in discussion of matters relating to economic growth. It was discontinued in 1992. The council was informally known as Neddy (from the initials NEDC), and from 1964 until the 1980s there were several 'little Neddies' (Economic Development Committees) dealing with specific industries.

National Executive Committee see *NEC.

National Exhibition Centre Custom-built exhibition and conference centre, 10km/6m southeast of Birmingham. It opened in 1976 and stages more than 100 exhibitions each year; since 1978 it has been the location of the biennial *Motor Show. Its indoor arena can seat up to 12,000 people for conventions or sporting events.

National Film Theatre (NFT, London SE1) Cinema on the *South Bank, deriving from the temporary Telekinema set up nearby in 1951 as part of the *Festival of Britain. This had been organized by the British Film Institute, a body formed in 1933 to encourage the development of cinema. The Institute, which is also responsible for the National Film Archive, allowed the very popular Telekinema to continue after the Festival was over and moved it in 1956, with a new name, to a permanent

home under the arches of Waterloo Bridge. The National Film Theatre has continued to show programmes of the best British and foreign films of all periods, and it is the setting each winter for the London Film Festival. A related enterprise, established next door in 1988, is the *Museum of the Moving Image.

National Front see *neo-Nazis.

National Gallery (London WC2) One of very few collections in the world where the entire development of western painting, from the 14C to the early 20C, is represented with a balanced selection of masterpieces from every important school. The collection was started relatively late, in 1834, when the government purchased 38 paintings from the estate of John Julius Angerstein (1735–1823). He was particularly fond of the 17C (Claude, Van Dyck, Rubens, Rembrandt), as were several other collectors who bequeathed or sold their paintings to the gallery in the early years; it was the directors in the mid-19C who added superb Renaissance paintings of both the Italian and the northern schools. Among the best-known works in the collection are the *Wilton diptych, the *Arnolfini Marriage*, the *Leonardo cartoon, The *Ambassadors*, the *Rokeby Venus*, The *Hay Wain*, The *'Fighting Téméraire'* and *Rain, steam and speed*.

The main building fronting Trafalgar Square is by *Wilkins and was completed in 1838. Adjoining it on the west is the Sainsbury Wing, an extraordinarily generous gift to the nation by three brothers, John, Simon and Timothy Sainsbury. It was designed by the American architect Robert Venturi (b. 1925) specifically to house the Gallery's exceptional Renaissance collection. The wing opened in 1991.

In World War II, when the paintings had been removed to a cave in a Welsh slate quarry, the National Gallery was the location for a famous series of lunchtime concerts (a total of 1698 between 1939 and 1946) organized by Myra *Hess.

National Gallery of Scotland (Edinburgh) Collection of European art, from the 14C to the late 19C, housed on the Mound in a classical building of the 1850s by William Henry Playfair (1790–1857); it was opened to the public in 1859. Among the best known of the gallery's masterpieces are Gerard David's triptych *Three Legends of St Nicholas*, Velasquez's *An Old Woman Cooking Eggs*, Van Dyck's *The Lomellini Family*, Rembrandt's *A Woman in Bed*, Gainsborough's *The Hon. Mrs Graham*, Degas' *Portrait of Diego Martelli* and Gauguin's *The Vision after the Sermon*. Two of the most popular images are in the Scottish collection, *Raeburn's informal glimpse of a skating clergyman and *Ramsay's portrait of his wife. Since 1946 a magnificent group of paintings has been on long-term loan from successive dukes of Sutherland; they include five Titians, three Raphaels and a set of seven sacraments by Poussin. On loan since 1912 from the royal collection is the *Trinity Altarpiece* by Hugo van der Goes.

National Garden Festivals Five large horticultural festivals, each creating new public gardens for a single summer, with displays, competitions and other entertainments. The idea, put forward by Michael Heseltine when secretary of state for the environment in the early 1980s, derived from similar enterprises in Germany, reclaiming sites devastated by bombing. The intention was that the British festivals should also be on derelict ground, and this was true of all but one. The first (Liverpool 1984) was on a municipal rubbish dump on the north bank of the Mersey; the second (Stoke-on-Trent 1986) covered a waste area of iron and steel slag and of refuse from coal mines and potteries; the third (Glasgow 1988) did not fulfil the dereliction test, being on a clear site on the south bank of the Clyde; but the fourth and fifth (industrial wasteland on the south bank of the Tyne at Gateshead in 1990, and the disused Welsh mining valley of Ebbw Vale in 1992) brought visitors and at least a temporary injection of new life to run down areas. The Ebbw Vale festival was planned as the last in the series.

National government Coalition of three parties (Labour, Conservative, Liberal) formed in response to the financial crisis of 1931, with Ramsay *MacDonald at its head. It lasted until 1940. The prime ministers after MacDonald were *Baldwin (1935–7) and Neville *Chamberlain. MacDonald and Baldwin fought the elections of 1931 and 1935 on a national government ticket, but the Conservative element within the coalition was predominant in 1935–40. The national government was much criticized for underestimating the threat from Hitler and for delaying rearmament. It was replaced in May 1940 by the new government of Winston Churchill. This was also a coalition, for wartime purposes, but it dropped the discredited 'national' tag.

National Health Service (NHS) The most cherished part of Britain's *welfare state. Inspired by the *Beveridge Report, and introduced by Aneurin *Bevan in the National Health Service Act of 1946, it came into effect in 1948 – providing free medical, dental and hospital services for everyone. Originally even pharmaceutical products were entirely free if prescribed by a doctor, but a standard charge per prescription was introduced in the 1960s – with exemptions for children, the old and certain other categories. Subsequently a rising scale of charges was made for dental treatment (in the richer areas of the southeast it has become increasingly hard to find NHS dentistry, as more and more dentists have decided to take only private patients), and in the late 1980s charges were introduced for the testing of eyesight. But the central core of the NHS – the services of the *GP and treatment in hospital – remains free to the patient and politically sacred. It was electorally important for the Conservatives in 1992 to refute claims that they had a hidden agenda to privatize the health service.

The suspicion that this might be so had resulted from changes introduced in the National Health Service and Community Care Act of 1990. The new 'internal market', introduced in April 1991, is an attempt to apply market disciplines to ever-spiralling health costs; it offers greater financial freedom to both GPs and hospitals. GPs with more than 9000 patients in their practice can now apply for 'fund-holding status'; this means that they have

their own budget from NHS funds, with which to shop around for the best medicine and treatment for their patients.

In a similar development any NHS hospital may apply for *trust status, becoming a 'self-governing trust' run as a business by a board of directors. Opponents of the scheme argue that trust hospitals have an incentive to encourage private treatment at the expense of NHS patients, particularly in the sensitive matter of patients paying to get an operation at an earlier date (long waiting lists in certain areas and for certain treatments have been a major NHS problem). There were much publicized teething troubles with some of the first trust hospitals – notably *Guy's – but the changes are as yet too recent for any conclusive judgement to be made. A total of 156 hospitals, about a third of the health service capacity, were trusts by the autumn of 1992; and some 400 practices, about 10% of the total, had by then become fund-holding GPs.

Department of **National Heritage** (London SW1) New government department set up in 1992 to combine a wide range of responsibilities: for the Arts Council, the national museums and galleries and the British Library (all previously dealt with by the Office of Arts and Libraries); for the media, both press and broadcasting (previously Home Office); for sport (previously Department of Education and Science); for tourism (previously Department of Employment); and for more conventional heritage matters such as listed buildings (previously Department of the Environment); in addition it was charged with launching the national *lottery. The department was immediately nicknamed the Ministry of Fun. The first secretary of state was David *Mellor, shortly followed by Peter Brooke.

National Heritage Memorial Fund Established by parliament in 1980 as a memorial to all who have died for Britain, with the broad purpose of preserving anything judged to be of importance in the national heritage. The range is wide, from securing historic houses, great paintings or important documents such as *Mappa Mundi, to the raising of the *Mary Rose and the saving of historic vehicles, including one of the last surviving World War I *tanks and the *Bluebird* in which Donald *Campbell broke the land speed record in 1964. Independent trustees dispense the proceeds of investment funds and grants provided by the government.

National Horseracing Museum see *Newmarket.

National Indoor Arena see *Birmingham.

National Health Service: government expenditure, in £bn

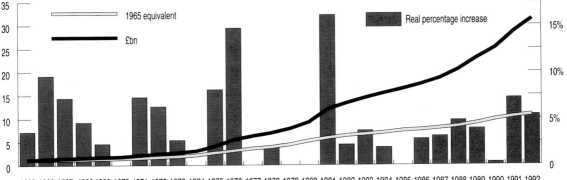

The lower line is the 1965 figure adjusted each year for inflation; the gap between the lines is therefore the cumulative real increase in public expenditure on education.
Source: Annual Abstract of Statistics *(see *Central Statistical Office).*

National Hunt General term for professional horse racing over hurdles or jumps, also known as *steeplechasing. It is short for National Hunt Committee, the body which regulates the sport. The committee was set up in 1866 to fulfil a function equivalent to that of the *Jockey Club in flat racing.

national insurance State scheme providing old-age pensions, benefits for the unemployed and for those out of work through sickness, support for families whose income is below a given level, and a wide range of other allowances for cases of special need. Together with the *National Health Service it is the main feature of Britain's *welfare state. The beginnings of the scheme came in the National Insurance Act of 1911, introduced by the Liberals, but this covered only a few selected industries. Among many later improvements the most extensive was the postwar Labour government's National Insurance Act of 1946. Contributions, part of which go also towards the cost of the National Health Service, are paid by all in employment (with an additional sum paid by the employer) and by the self-employed.

nationalization The gathering of public utilities into public ownership in Britain was a long and piecemeal process. Public utilities can be broadly defined as the basic services essential to the functioning of an entire community, such as communications, transport and the provision of power and fuel. A central element in communication, the *Post Office, was publicly owned from its creation in the 17C; and the same was true in broadcasting, with the creation of the *BBC in 1927. But the majority of utilities – such as the telegraph and telephone, the canals and the railways, the distribution of water, gas and electricity – were pioneered in the 18–19C by small independent companies. In the interests of efficiency these tended to

Promotional material for the new National Health Insurance stamp, at the time of the 1911 National Insurance Act.

merge; and for the same reason many were later taken over by local authorities, well placed to supply water, gas or electricity to their own communities. Similarly Britain's pioneering private airlines had all been merged by 1939 into *BOAC.

Many services were therefore in public ownership by the time Britain had its first government with the commitment and power to legislate on an ideological basis. This was the Labour administration of 1945, which put into effect a vigorous programme of nationalization; it brought into public ownership the *Bank of England (1946), *railways and *coal (1947), *gas and *electricity and many docks and canals (all 1948). The national ownership of hospitals, which came into effect in 1948 with the creation of the *National Health Service, was a different case since hospitals are in origin charitable institutions rather than commercial enterprises. The most controversial industry in terms of nationalization was steel; Labour's efforts to nationalize it and a Conservative commitment to denationalize it remained high on the political agenda until it was brought into public ownership in 1967 (see *British Steel).

Many of these industries had been ailing in private ownership, as were those in a second wave of nationalization in the 1970s; the government, for example, rescued *Rolls Royce when it was bankrupt in 1971 and took a majority stake in *British Leyland in 1975. But from 1979 Mrs *Thatcher introduced a new political ideology – the first in effect since 1945. It brought with it a new orthodoxy, *privatization.

National Library of Scotland (Edinburgh) One of the six *copyright libraries, founded in 1689 as the Advocates' Library. It was already more than a library for lawyers when it acquired, by an act of 1709, the right to a free copy of every book printed in Britain. In 1922 the Faculty of Advocates offered the library to the nation, and in 1925 an act of parliament gave it its present name. Its main building is by Reginald Fairlie (1883–1952).

National Library of Wales (Aberystwyth) One of the *copyright libraries, established by royal charter in 1907 to collect material in Welsh or Celtic languages, or relating to the Welsh or Celts, but also with the obligation to provide a general library suitable for the recently founded University of *Wales. The imposing classical building on Penglais Hill was begun in 1911, to a design by Sydney Greenslade (1866–1955).

National Maritime Museum (Greenwich, London SE10) Established by act of parliament in 1934, and opened in 1937 in the *Queen's House, the museum has an unrivalled collection of paintings and objects (including quite large sea-going vessels) connected with the history of seafaring. In recent decades it has incorporated the buildings of the *Royal Observatory.

National Monument see *Calton Hill.

National Motor Museum see *Beaulieu.

National Museum of Antiquities of Scotland see *Royal Museum of Scotland.

National Museum of Photography, Film and Television (Bradford) Large collection of equipment and photographs, incorporating the Kodak Museum, which opened in 1983 in a building designed as a theatre in the 1960s by Richard Seifert. Its most famous feature is the giant IMAX screen, as high as a five-storey house, in front of which viewers are almost literally engulfed in the moving image.

Scenery in one of Britain's most dramatic national parks: view from Snowdonia, looking northwest towards Llanberis.

National Museum of Wales (Cardiff) Wide-ranging collection covering archaeology, natural history, industry, social history and art, with special emphasis on the development of Wales. In the field of ceramics there is a fine collection of Nantgawr and Swansea wares, and leading Welsh painters (in particular Richard Wilson, Thomas Jones, Augustus and Gwen John) are well represented. The Davies Bequest of 1951 brought some excellent 19C French paintings, of which Renoir's full-length *Parisian Girl* is the best known. The classical-style building, by Smith and Brewer, has been opened in stages since 1922, and the museum has developed several branches in other locations, in particular the *Welsh Folk Museum and the *Welsh Industrial and Maritime Museum.

national parks Areas of outstanding natural beauty protected by the National Parks and Access to the Countryside Act (1949). During the 1950s ten such areas in England and Wales were selected, amounting to 13,651sq.km/ 5269sq.m of moorland, lake, mountain and coastal scenery; they are *Brecon Beacons, *Dartmoor, *Exmoor, the *Lake District, *Northumberland, the *North York Moors, the *Peak District, the *Pembrokeshire Coast, *Snowdonia and the *Yorkshire Dales. In 1992 the *New Forest was given the status of a national park, to protect it from increasing pressures for development. The act did not apply to Scotland or Northern Ireland, but in recent years there have been proposals to extend the scheme to Scotland.

National Portrait Gallery (London WC2) Collection begun in 1856 with the intention of assembling portraits of people distinguished in British history. From miniatures by Hilliard to contemporary paintings by Lucian Freud and others, they are often also of artistic importance. In recent years portrait photographs by distinguished photographers have been included. The building, adjacent to the National Gallery, was designed for the purpose by Ewan Christian (1814–95) and opened in 1896.

A number of portraits from the collection are on long-term loan for display at Beningbrough Hall near York, at Gawthorpe Hall in Lancashire, at Bodelwyddan Castle in Clwyd and at *Montacute House.

National Power see *electricity.

National Railway Museum (York) Museum which opened in 1975, combining the holdings of the previous LNER museum at York and of the British Transport Commission's museum at Clapham, in London. The collection of railway carriages includes those used by Queen Victoria and subsequent monarchs; and among the locomotives is *Mallard*, holder of the record for a steam engine with a speed of 203kph/126mph over a short distance in 1938.

National Savings The name since 1969 of what was previously called Post Office Savings. The use of the post offices as outlets for a national savings scheme dates back to the Post Office Savings Bank Act of 1861. Over the next century the Savings Bank introduced a succession of schemes to persuade people to put aside part of their wages, including savings stamps for sticking into books (or, for the patriotic in World War II, for sticking on the side of tanks or bomb casings as a contribution to the war effort), savings certificates and *premium bonds. In 1969, when the Post Office became a separate nationalized industry, savings remained within the civil service as the Department for National Savings. By the early 1990s the high-street banks had been added to the post offices as retail outlets and the total invested in National Savings was approaching £40bn.

national service see *conscription.

Royal **National Theatre** (London SE1) Building on the South Bank, designed by Denys *Lasdun, which opened in 1976. There had been plans for a national theatre from as long ago as 1848, but it was not until 1963 that a company was established – with Laurence *Olivier as its first artistic director. The Old Vic was used as a temporary home, with Peter O'Toole as Hamlet for the inaugural performance. In 1976 the Lyttelton was the first of the National Theatre's three auditoria to open (this time with Albert Finney as Hamlet); the Olivier and the Cottesloe followed over the next 12 months. Peter Hall had become director in 1973, to be followed by Richard Eyre in 1988. In that year, to mark the 25th anniversary of the first performance, the company was granted the title 'Royal'; but it is rarely referred to as anything other than the National Theatre.

National Trust (National Trust for Places of Historic Interest or Natural Beauty, London SW1) Britain's foremost conservation body, owning in England, Wales and Northern Ireland about 200 houses which are open to the public (including some of the greatest *stately homes), more than 100 gardens, 50 villages and 230,000ha/570,000ac of countryside. It began as a private venture, founded by Octavia *Hill and others in 1895. The first two properties came through the gift of a small scenic coastal area in north Wales, and the purchase, for £10, of a 14c timber-frame clergy house in Alfriston, East Sussex. Open spaces and small houses remained the theme until the 1930s, when a threat to the nation's stately homes became evident. *Blickling Hall in Norfolk was the first to be given, with its contents, garden and lands. The pattern became established that only houses of the first quality would be accepted, that they must usually be given with sufficient endowment to cover all their costs, and that whenever possible the family should continue to live in the house with due access given to the public. In 1965 the Enterprise Neptune appeal was launched and the Trust now preserves more than 800km/500m of Britain's most beautiful stretches of coastal scenery.

The Trust was incorporated by act of parliament in 1907 but remains an independent body, raising its own finances from endowments, admission charges and the annual subscriptions of a membership which has now risen to over two million.

National Trust for Scotland Body established in 1931 for the same purposes and along the same lines as the older *National Trust. It has grown with equal success, and it pioneered an influential technique in its Little Houses Improvement Scheme, launched in the late 1950s. Small town houses in places such as *Culross, derelict or in danger of demolition, are bought, restored, modernized in an acceptable manner and then put back on the market with restrictive safeguards, thus enabling the capital in a revolving fund to be used again for similar projects.

National Velvet (1930) A children's story by Enid Bagnold (1889–1981) which fulfils the daydream of every pony-club teenage girl. Velvet Brown wins The Piebald in a raffle, and together they go on to win the *Grand National. The film (1944) starred the 12-year-old Elizabeth *Taylor as Velvet.

National Waterways Museum see *Gloucester.

National Westminster Bank (NatWest) Formed in 1970 by the merger of the National Provincial and the Westminster, an event which reduced the 'big five' *clearing banks to the present 'big four'. Both the merged companies brought with them a large slice of British banking history. The National Provincial was formed in 1833 with the specific purpose of creating a network of offices throughout England and Wales (Gloucester was the first to open, in 1834); in 1920 the National Provincial acquired *Coutts; and in 1962 it absorbed the District Bank, established in Manchester in 1829. The London and Westminster Bank was set up in 1833; it merged in 1918 with Parr's Bank, dating back to a private banking partnership in the 18c in Cheshire. The National Westminster branch in London's Bishopsgate is a distinguished Victorian building (1864–5) by John Gibson; behind it there now soars one of the City's landmarks, the 183m/600ft National Westminster Tower by Seifert and Partners.

National Youth Orchestra Organization founded in 1947 by Ruth Railton (b. 1915) for teenagers (every player must be under 20) who are not in full-time music education. It is formed anew each year from auditions held in September. The new orchestra, 150 strong, begins to rehearse after Christmas and reconvenes for rehearsals and performances in each of the school holidays. As evidence of the orchestra's extremely high standard, it has long had an annual engagement at the Proms and since 1990 has played on BBC TV accompanying the finalists in the *Young Musician of the Year* competition.

National Youth Theatre Organization founded in the East End of London in 1956 by Michael Croft (1922–88), with the purpose of involving young people, between the ages of 14 and 21, in theatrical productions of a high standard. Members of the company are selected by an audition process which begins in 13 cities around the country. Performances are given in London each summer and the NYT has toured as far afield as New York and Moscow.

'nation of shopkeepers' see *'England is a nation of shopkeepers'.

'Nation shall speak peace unto nation' see *BBC.

Nationwide Britain's second largest *building society, formed in 1987 by the merger of Nationwide and Anglia. Those two names were themselves recent. The Cooperative Permanent Building Society, founded in 1883 as part of the *cooperative movement, called itself Nationwide from 1970; and Anglia was the name chosen in 1967 when the Northampton Building Society (formed in 1848) merged with the Leicestershire Building Society.

NATO (North Atlantic Treaty Organization) Defensive alliance set up by 12 nations in 1949, in response to the descent of the *iron curtain and the domination of eastern Europe by the USSR. The 12 were Belgium, Canada, Denmark, France, Iceland, Italy, Luxembourg, the Netherlands, Norway, Portugal, the UK and the USA; they agreed to treat an attack on any as an attack on all. Greece and Turkey joined in 1952 and the Federal Republic of Germany in 1955. The rearming of West Germany in 1955 caused the USSR to form the Warsaw Pact with East Germany and its other allies in that same year. NATO reached its present level of 16 nations when the newly democratic Spain joined in 1982.

France has played a lesser role in NATO than other members since 1966 when President de Gaulle, irritated at US dominance within the alliance, insisted that all NATO personnel leave French soil. The NATO headquarters was moved from France to Brussels. France took no further part in the routine business of NATO, but has remained within the alliance.

In 1990 the NATO countries redefined their purpose in response to the ending of the Cold War (see *iron curtain). It was agreed to reduce NATO forces by up to 30% and to create a new streamlined corps capable of rapid reaction to a crisis.

Natural History Museum (London SW7) The natural history holdings of the British Museum, built up around the collections of *Sloane and *Banks, were moved here in 1881 and the Natural History Museum became an independent institution in 1963. Vast numbers of zoological and botanical specimens, together with fossils and minerals, occupy a spectacular building (1873–80) by *Waterhouse, with terracotta reliefs of animals set into the walls inside and out. The nearby Geological Museum, in Exhibition Road, is a department of the Natural History Museum.

Nature Magazine launched by Macmillan in 1869 as 'a weekly illustrated journal of science' – a description which still applies, though the illustrations are now more colourful and the science infinitely more complex.

'Nature, red in tooth and claw' Tennyson's powerful phrase in *In Memoriam* for the natural condition of the animal world. He contrasts this with Man, Nature's 'last work' and supposedly more interested in love and God; but he does also cast some doubt on that consoling notion.

Nauru Republic and one of the smallest members of the *Commonwealth, consisting of some 9000 people on a coral island (21sq.km/8sq.m) in the Pacific, northeast of Australia. First visited by British ships in 1798, the island was annexed by Germany in 1888. From 1928 it was a British *mandated territory, administered by Australia. It became independent and joined the Commonwealth in 1968.

Navy see *Royal Navy.

Lough Neagh Lake in northern Ireland, the largest in the British Isles (382sq.km/147sq.m), with five of the *six counties sharing its shoreline (all but Fermanagh).

Anna Neagle (stage name of Marjorie Robertson, 1904–86, DBE 1969) Actress known for musical comedy and for historical roles on film (*Victoria the Great* 1937, *Nurse Edith Cavell* 1939, *The Lady with the Lamp* 1951). In 1943 she married the film producer Herbert Wilcox.

Airey Neave (1916–79) Conservative politician, MP for Abingdon from 1953, who was murdered by an IRA bomb which exploded in his car as he drove from the underground car park at the House of Commons. He was head of Mrs Thatcher's private office and the shadow secretary of state for Northern Ireland.

NEC (National Executive Committee) The administrative authority in the *Labour party. It has 26 members, of which two are ex officio (the leader and deputy leader); one is a youth member elected at the national youth conference; and the other 23 are elected at the party's annual conference (12 by the trade union delegates and the rest by various other groups).

NEDC or **Neddy** see *National Economic Development Council.

The Needles Three rocky peaks of chalk jutting like sharp white teeth from the sea off the western extremity of the Isle of Wight. There has been a lighthouse at the outer end of the third one since 1859.

Arthur Negus (1903–85) Fine-art auctioneer, with the Gloucester firm of Bruton Knowles, who first demonstrated the popular appeal of antiques on television through his appearances on the BBC quiz *Going for a Song* (1968–77).

'Neither a borrower nor a lender be' The most widely remembered line from the speech of Polonius to his son Laertes in *Hamlet*. Foolish though the old man is, his advice is excellent (though financially cautious), ending with 'to thine own self be true'.

Brian Nelson (b. 1947) Undercover agent in Northern Ireland, whose case emerged as a result of the Stevens enquiry (see *RUC) into allegations that members of the security forces were collaborating with UDA *terrorists to target IRA victims. Nelson was a member of the UDA in the mid-1970s, when he was first recruited by military intelligence; but his main period of activity was in the late 1980s, as a senior figure in the UDA's Belfast intelligence unit. In this role he was perfectly placed to provide his handlers with advance warning of UDA murder plots, and he did so; but in several cases, for whatever reason, the killings were not prevented.

Nelson was arrested by English detectives working for Stevens and was charged with conspiracy to murder; he was sentenced to ten years in jail. The case raised major questions about the role of undercover agents and also about communications in Northern Ireland between the army and the RUC, the body ultimately responsible for security in the province.

Lord Nelson (Horatio Nelson, 1758–1805, KB 1797, viscount 1801) Admiral whose victory and death at Trafalgar is remembered as the high point of British naval history. At sea from the age of 12, he was a captain before he was 21 and was a senior naval officer by the time the *French Revolutionary Wars began in 1793. He lost the sight of his right eye in 1794 when attacking Calvi, in Corsica, and his right arm was shattered in an assault on Tenerife in 1797. By 1798 he was in command of a fleet in the Mediterranean and scored his great victory at the *Nile. Throughout this period he was frequently at Naples, a port open to the British, and it was there that he met Lady *Hamilton. A respite from the *Napoleonic Wars in 1802–3 (the result of the peace of Amiens) meant that he was briefly able to enjoy with her the pleasures of London. His final two years brought him success at *Copenhagen as well as the tragic triumph of *Trafalgar, the scene of his death. His body was brought back to England, preserved in a cask of spirits, and lay in state in the Painted Hall of the *Royal Naval College at Greenwich before being buried in St Paul's Cathedral.

Nelson Mass Nickname which became attached to Haydn's Mass in D minor. News of Nelson's great victory over Napoleon at the Battle of the *Nile reached Austria on 15 September 1798, the day of the mass's first performance. Austrians, to whom Napoleon was the enemy, immediately attached Nelson's name to the piece – which Haydn himself called *Missa in angustiis* ('mass in troubled times').

Nelson's Column (London WC2) Monument to *Nelson, designed by William Railton (c.1801–77) and more formally known as the Nelson Column. The 51m/168ft Corinthian column of Devonshire granite, with a bronze capital, was put up in Trafalgar Square in 1839–42; the 5m/17ft statue of the admiral, by E.H. *Baily, was placed on top of it in 1843; but the four famous bronze lions at its base, sculpted by *Landseer, were not added until 1867.

This is the best known of the many monuments to Nelson, but others in the country were much earlier. Glasgow's was up by 1806, within a year of his death; Hereford put up in 1806–9 a column designed by Thomas Hardwick; in Edinburgh the Nelson Monument, a tower in the shape of a telescope on Calton Hill, was

The view from Nelson's Column to Big Ben: watercolour of Trafalgar Day in 1896, by William Alister MacDonald.

completed in 1816; and the great Doric column which can be climbed at Great Yarmouth (44m/144ft high) was in place by 1819.

Nemo me impune lacessit see Order of the *Thistle.

neoclassicism Style which developed in the mid-18C from the earlier *Palladianism. It was inspired by increasing knowledge of classical antiquities in the era of the *Grand Tour and was also a reaction against the frivolity of *rococo. The move was towards geometric forms, sharp edges and historical accuracy. Robert Adam returned from Rome in 1758 with the ideas which led to the very influential *Adam style. Developing at the same time, but later in its widespread architectural influence, was the *Greek Revival. In the decorative arts Greek vases were an inspiration to Josiah *Wedgwood, though he believed them to be Etruscan; and one of Wedgwood's designers, John *Flaxman, became the leading English sculptor in the neoclassical style. Among the many designers of furniture who aimed at exact re-creation of Greek or Egyptian examples, none aimed for more perfect accuracy than Thomas *Hope.

neo-Gothic see *Gothic Revival.

Neo-Nazis Like other European countries, Britain still has groups peddling the hate-filled certainties of Fascism; but they have only a small (if sometimes noisy) following. Among their predecessors in the 1930s the most active was Oswald *Mosley's British Union of Fascists, which provoked considerable violence by staging marches in Jewish areas of east London; there were also the National Socialist League, founded by William Joyce (see *Lord Haw-Haw) and Arnold Leese's Imperial Fascist League.

In the postwar decades the most prominent group has been the National Front. Formed in the 1960s, and later much associated with *skinheads, it achieved a high profile in the 1970s through the violence resulting from its demonstrations in areas with large black and Asian populations. The National Front still exists; in 1992 it put up 14 candidates for the general election, of whom the most successful received 665 votes. The National Front leader in 1980, John Tyndall, left the party at that time to set up a rival – the New National Front, known now as the British National Party. The best-known member of the far right in modern Britain is David Irving, a historian who argues that reports of the holocaust are greatly exaggerated; there was a furore in 1992 when the *Sunday Times* employed him to translate and edit previously unknown sections of Goebbels' diary, discovered in Moscow.

E. Nesbit (Edith Nesbit, 1858–1924) Author of novels for children which have acquired the status of classics. She was a general writer, and an enthusiastic early Socialist, until she discovered in middle age the talent for which she is famous. In 1899 she published *The Story of the Treasure Seekers*; it introduced the Bastable family, whose children reappear in several later books. *The Railway Children* (1906) features Roberta, Peter and Phyllis, who by their initiative rescue their father from unjust imprisonment. In *Five Children and It* (1902), the first of her fantasy books, 'it' is a rather dank, small, magic creature, the Psammead, which grants the children their wishes with often embarrassing consequences.

Loch Ness Lake at the northeast end of the *Great Glen, some 36km/22m long and in part 230m/754ft deep. It is known in particular for the Loch Ness Monster, the world's most elusive tourist attraction, affectionately known as Nessie. Numerous sightings have been reported since a road was built along the lake edge in the 1930s, and there have even been serious scientific investigations (though very deep lakes elsewhere do also tend to have rumoured monsters). Enthusiasts trace the first sighting back to St *Columba in the 6C; his early biographer, St Adamnan, tells how he used the sign of the Cross to repel a savage monster in the river Ness.

netball Game much played in girls' schools in Britain, similar to the American basketball from which it developed. Basketball was invented in 1891 to exercise a group of male students at a YMCA college in Springfield, Massachusetts. In 1895 an American, visiting a physical training college for girls in Hampstead, taught them a version which they played with wastepaper baskets hung at each end of the hall. The rules of basketball were still imprecise, and netball is merely the game established in a set of rules drawn up on this side of the Atlantic in 1901. It was the accident of its first English home which made it above all a game for girls.

'never had it so good' see Harold *Macmillan.

'Never in the field of human conflict . . .' see the *Few.

Never Never Land see *Peter Pan*.

'never said a foolish thing' see Lord *Rochester.

New Age travellers Nomads who in recent years have frequently clashed with police in their attempts to gather for festivals of music and to assemble at *Stonehenge for the midsummer solstice. The New Age philosophy, relating back in origin to the hippies of the sixties, rejects the materialism and fragmented nature of modern society – yearning instead for earlier ways of existence which seem closer to nature. A resulting interest in religions older than Christianity leads to the fascination with Stonehenge.

Newcastle United, known as the Magpies (St James' Park, Newcastle-upon-Tyne). Football club formed in 1881 and in the *Football League from 1893. The team had a run of successes in the first decade of the 20C and then again in the 1950s, when Jackie Milburn was the chief goal scorer. In 1985 they found (and rapidly sold) one of modern English football's greatest stars, the local boy Paul *Gascoigne. The Magpies had a remarkable recent revival after appointing Kevin *Keegan as manager, in February 1992. At that time they were floundering in Division 2; but they began the 1992–3 season with 11 successive wins (in what had been renamed Division 1) on the way to victory in the division and promotion for 1993–4 to the Premier League. Club victories: FA Cup 1910, 24, 32, 51, 52, 55; League Champions 1905, 07, 09, 27; European Fairs Cup 1969.

Newcastle-upon-Tyne (192,000 in 1981) City and port in Tyne and Wear, on the north bank of a shallow gorge of the river Tyne, about 13km/8m from its mouth (the town on the opposite bank is *Gateshead). This area has been the gateway to the northeast since Roman times, when the first bridge was built here and Hadrian's Wall ran nearby. Bridges over the Tyne have remained a famous feature of Newcastle (there are now eight). The Swing Bridge, constructed in 1876, is on the site of the Roman bridge and of its medieval successors; lying low, it swings open for ships to move up or down river. The High Level Bridge, designed by Robert Stephenson and opened in 1849, carries road and railway well above the masts of any vessel. The Tyne Bridge (1928) has become the city's best-known feature because of the dramatic single arch of girders from which the road is suspended.

The Norman castle, which gave the city its name, was evidence of its continuing military importance. A wooden fortress was built here in 1080 by Robert Curthose, eldest son of William the Conqueror, and was later replaced in stone; the impressive square keep dates from the 1170s. In the 16C Newcastle's importance became industrial, as the port for *Tyneside's coal; its near monopoly in this trade is remembered still in the common phrase for a useless activity, 'carrying coals to Newcastle'. The boats came back with sand as ballast, which led in turn to glass-making, Newcastle's other great industry in the early period of the industrial revolution. Shipbuilding and engineering followed later (George Stephenson set up here in 1823). The city's 19C wealth is reflected in the streets laid out by a speculative builder, Richard Grainger (1798–1861), with architecture mainly by John Dobson (1787–1865). Grey Street stands today as the most striking example of their work. At its end is Grey's Monument, the city's focal point, with Lord *Grey on a high column to commemorate the Reform Act (1832). The architects of the monument, John Green (1787–1852) and his son Benjamin, also built the nearby Theatre Royal.

Newcastle became a diocese in 1882 and the very large 14–15C parish church of St Nicholas was then promoted to the status of cathedral. Its outstanding feature is the tower with its 'crown spire' – an openwork structure of buttresses and small steeples to form a crown (dating from the mid-15C, and so about 25 years earlier than the more famous equivalent on St Giles' in Edinburgh). St Mary's, the Roman Catholic cathedral, was completed in 1844 to a design of *Pugin. The Laing Art Gallery has a collection of British paintings and specializes in the local decorative arts, particularly glass by the *Beilby family. The Museum of Science and Engineering uses early working models to commemorate the region's contribution to technology, which in addition to the Stephensons has included Parsons, whose *steam turbines were produced locally, and *Swan, who first demonstrated his electric light filament in Newcastle. The city's *underground railway, the Tyne and Wear Metro, opened in 1980.

New Club (Edinburgh) A *club in Scotland's capital, founded in 1787 by a group of committed claret drinkers.

Newcastle's vista of bridges: the first three are the Tyne Bridge, the Swing Bridge and Robert Stephenson's High Level Bridge.

It has occupied its present site in Prince's Street since 1837, though now in a building of 1969.

Thomas **Newcomen** see *steam.

New English Bible see *Bible in English.

New every morning is the love Hymn consisting of verses selected from a much longer poem in John *Keble's *The Christian Year*. It is usually sung to an earlier tune by Samuel Webbe (1740–1816), a London cabinet-maker and organist.

New Forest Area of woodland, heath and bog in south-west Hampshire (38,000ha/93,000ac) which was declared a royal hunting ground by William the Conqueror in 1079. All three varieties of British *deer still live wild there, as do the famous New Forest ponies. The Rufus Stone stands near the spot where *William II is believed to have been killed when hunting. In 1992 the forest was given the unofficial status of a *national park, the only lowland area in the country to have that protection.

Newgate London's most notorious prison, which from the 12c occupied a succession of buildings on the same site (to the northwest of St Paul's). It was from here that Jack *Sheppard made his extraordinary escapes. Later in the same century Newgate was attacked and burnt by the *Gordon rioters, in 1780. Shortly after that event the gallows were moved here from *Tyburn; executions were held outside the prison in front of large crowds until 1868, when they were transferred inside. It was the appalling conditions of female prisoners in Newgate which inspired Elizabeth *Fry's work of reform. The jail was pulled down in 1902 to be replaced by the *Old Bailey.

The *Newgate Calendars*, published at various times between 1773 and 1826, were accounts of the most notorious crimes. They made popular reading and provided plots for many Victorian novels and *melodramas.

New Lanark (48km/30m SE of Glasgow) Industrial village by the *Clyde, founded in 1784, which in the early 19c was the scene of Robert *Owen's experiments in improved housing and education. It survives virtually unspoilt.

Newlyn Fishing village on the south coast of Cornwall, near Penzance, where a colony of artists settled in the 1880s. Their leader was Stanhope Forbes (1857–1947), who was strongly committed to painting everyday scenes in the open air. The school founded there by Forbes and his wife Elizabeth (also a painter, 1857–1912) continued to attract artists of the next generation, such as *Knight and *Munnings.

Cardinal **Newman** (John Henry Newman, 1801–90) Influential figure in 19c *Anglo-Catholicism and the leading Anglican convert to the Church of Rome. Ordained as an Anglican in 1825, he caused a furore with his tracts for the *Oxford Movement, arguing that there was no essential incompatibility between Rome and the *Church of England. He converted in 1845 and was ordained a priest in Rome the following year, returning to Britain to found the Oratory in Birmingham. It was in response to attacks on his sincerity, most notably by the original *'muscular Christian', Charles Kingsley, that Newman wrote his influential spiritual autobiography, *Apologia pro Vita Sua* (1864). He was made a cardinal in 1879. Several well-known hymns were extracted from his poetry, including *Lead, kindly Light* (1834) and *Praise to the Holiest in the Height* (verses from The *Dream of Gerontius); the tunes for both were written by J.B. *Dykes.

Newmarket (16,000 in 1981) Town in Suffolk which is the historic centre of English racing and the home of the *Jockey Club. Horses have been raced here since the time of James I, but it was the personal involvement of Charles II which gave Newmarket its pre-eminence. Rowley Mile, the older of the two courses on Newmarket Heath, is named after the king, whose nickname was Old Rowley (itself deriving, appropriately, from the name of a favourite horse). On it are run the two first Classics of the season, the *1,000 Guineas and the *2,000 Guineas, at the spring meeting in late April. The autumn meeting, also on the Rowley Mile, has two famous handicap races, the Cambridgeshire and the Cesarewitch. The summer meeting is on the July Course. The National Stud was established at Newmarket in 1967; and in 1983 the National Horseracing Museum was opened in the Regency Subscription Rooms on the High Street.

New Model Army England's first trained professional army, established by parliament in 1645 on the urging of Oliver *Cromwell. Its skill and discipline proved a decisive factor in the *English Civil War. The concept of a disciplined force was emphasised by every infantryman wearing a scarlet tunic, which remained the uniform of the British army until replaced by *khaki. Thomas Fairfax was the commander and he drafted Cromwell as his second-in-command just before the crucial engagement at *Naseby. But a highly organized professional force is not easily disbanded, and the army played an increasingly political role during the *Commonwealth – an experience often quoted as lying behind later British reluctance to give much power to the military.

New Musical Express see *NME.

Newport (105,000 in 1981) Cathedral town on the river Usk in Gwent, close to the Roman settlement at *Caerleon and itself of importance from Norman times. The castle, though little remains of it, was first built in the 12c. The cathedral of St Woolos, on top of Stow Hill, is believed to stand on the site of a church of the 6c; the name is a corruption of Gwynllyw, who was supposedly the father of a Welsh Christian leader of that period, St Cadoc. The romantically narrow entrance to the nave, known as St Mary's Chapel, combines Saxon and early Norman elements; the church became the cathedral of the new diocese of Monmouth in 1921. The town itself developed largely in the 19c as a port for the coal being mined in the Welsh valleys. Tredegar House, set in a park 4km/2.5m southwest of the city centre, is a very fine red-brick mansion of 1664–72; it has recently been restored by the local council. The Newport Museum and Art Gallery, founded in 1888 but now housed in a modern building, has a good collection of Roman material excavated locally.

Newport (24,000 in 1981) Administrative centre of the Isle of Wight, situated in the middle of the island at the head of the long estuary of the river Medina. Many of its buildings are of the 18–19c, notably the Guildhall by John Nash. Parkhurst, a prison since 1838, is in Parkhurst Forest to the northwest of the town.

New Scientist Weekly magazine, founded in 1956 (on the initiative of Maxwell Raison), to provide a popular account of developments in science and technology. Sometimes described as half way between a newspaper and a learned journal, it not only covers new areas of research but focuses also on the political aspects of science and the environment.

New Scotland Yard see New *Scotland Yard.

Newsnight (BBC2 from 1980) Current-affairs television programme covering the day's topics in late-night interviews. Peter Snow has been one of the presenters from the start. In 1989 Jeremy Paxman brought to the programme a notably aggressive style of interviewing.

News of the World Britain's largest selling newspaper, with sales in the early 1990s approaching 5 million each Sunday. Launched in 1843 by John Browne Bell, it soon came to specialize in the themes which have kept it popular – crime, sport and scandal (the latter nowadays connected as often as possible, and however remotely, with the royal family). The paper was bought in 1969 by Rupert *Murdoch.

Newsom Report see *education.

New Statesman Political weekly founded in 1913 by Beatrice and Sidney *Webb, with active support from Bernard Shaw and other leading members of the Fabian Society. Its main rival has consistently been the *Spectator*, each has offered a lively mix of political opinion and arts coverage, the *New Statesman* from the left and the *Spectator* from the right of centre. Their fortunes have somewhat depended on the prevailing political mood (the eighties favoured the *Spectator*). Over the years the *New Statesman* has absorbed several other distinguished periodicals – notably the *Nation and Athenaeum* in 1931 (the first year of the reign of its most famous editor, Kingsley Martin, who remained in the post until 1960), and more recently *New Society* (1988) and *Marxism Today* (1991). In January 1993 the magazine was sued for libel by the prime minister, John Major, for giving prominent publicity (including a cover spread) to persistent unfounded rumours of a relationship between himself and the owner of a successful catering business, Clare Latimer.

Newstead Abbey see Lord *Byron.

New Street Birmingham's main railway station, entirely rebuilt in the 1960s. The original terminus for the London and Birmingham railway, which opened in 1838, was further from the centre of the town, at Curzon Street. The railway reached New Street in 1850.

New Style see *calendar.

Isaac **Newton** (1642–1727, kt 1705) Britain's greatest scientist, who made major contributions in several fields. He was born at Woolsthorpe Manor in Lincolnshire (kept now as a museum) and was a student at Trinity College, Cambridge. The Great Plague of 1665 led indirectly to his most creative period, for it caused the university to close for 18 months. During that period, in the isolation of his Lincolnshire home, Newton laid the basis for all his great discoveries.

In the field of pure mathematics he developed the binomial theorem and differential calculus (the latter was also being worked on independently by the German mathematician, Leibniz). There followed the experiments in which he showed that white light is made up of all the colours, and that these can be separated into the spectrum by refraction through a prism; from this derives the whole modern field of spectral analysis. But it is gravity which is most associated with that garden at Woolsthorpe, largely because of the story (first told in the next century by Voltaire, who claimed to have had it from Newton's step-niece) that Newton got the idea from seeing an apple fall. For years the supposed tree was shown to visitors in the Lincolnshire garden.

It was in fact the moon which had prompted his enquiries. What prevents the moon from flying out of its orbit round the earth, as a ball will if the string breaks on which it is being whirled around? Attempting to calculate the force required to hold the orbiting moon in place, Newton found that it approximated to the force causing an object to fall. He thus introduced the concept of gravity – the great unifying principle of classical physics, capable of explaining in one mathematical law the motion of the planets, the movement of the tides and the fall of an apple.

The university reopened in 1667; and in 1669, when still short of his 27th birthday, Newton became the Lucasian professor of mathematics. Working now on optics, he invented the reflecting telescope – the principle used in all the most powerful telescopes until the introduction of radio astronomy. Newton presented an example of his telescope to the Royal Society, of which he became a fellow in 1672. His discoveries were known only through his lectures at Cambridge and in papers submitted to the Royal Society until the publication in 1687 of his great work on gravity, the *Principia* (in full *Philosophiae Naturalis Principia Mathematica*, 'the mathematical principles of natural philosophy'). Edmond *Halley was instrumental in persuading him to write it and even paid for its publication.

Newton's researches on light and colour were published in *Opticks* (1704). From 1696 he took an active part in reforming the chaotic and corrupt system of the nation's coinage, and from 1699 till his death he held the lucrative post of Master of the *Mint.

Tony **Newton** (b. 1937) Conservative politician, MP for Braintree since 1974, who entered the *cabinet in 1988 as chancellor of the duchy of Lancaster (and minister of trade and industry). He was then secretary of state for social security (1989–92), and in 1992 became leader of the House of Commons.

new towns Concept pioneered by the Labour government after World War II (with influence from the *garden city movement), as a way of coping with population overspill from large cities. The New Towns Acts of 1946, 1947 and 1950 designated 12 areas in England and Wales and two in Scotland to become self-contained new towns with a balanced mix of industrial, residential and leisure areas; by the 1990s there were about 30 new towns in the United Kingdom. Each has been built up by a development corporation, which eventually disbands and hands over local administration to the people of the town. Prominent have been Glenrothes and Cwmbran, which thrived sufficiently to become the administrative centres of Fife and Gwent; Cumbernauld near Glasgow, which has won awards for its architecture; Telford in Shropshire, covering an area of early industrial importance and notable for its Ironbridge Gorge Museum; and the largest of them, Milton Keynes in Buckinghamshire (179,000 in 1991), which like Telford has become a household name through its high-profile efforts to persuade people and businesses to move there. It is also widely known as the administrative headquarters of the *Open University.

Newtown St Boswells (1000 in 1981) Administrative centre since 1975 of the Borders region of Scotland, and previously of Roxburghshire. In spite of these modern dignities it remains essentially the old St Boswells, a village lying just to the south of the ancient Melrose Abbey.

New Year By contrast with the private celebration within the family at *Christmas, New Year festivities in Britain tend to be more public, out in the streets or at parties with friends. The best known gathering places on the night of December 31 are Trafalgar Square in London, George

Square in Glasgow and the area round Tron Church in Edinburgh. The most widespread custom on the stroke of midnight is the singing of *Auld Lang Syne.

In Scotland the New Year and its celebrations are collectively known as Hogmanay, a word of uncertain origin which first appeared in the 17C. There and in northern England the tradition of first-footing survives, with the old belief that the good or bad luck of the coming year will be affected by whoever first steps through the door after midnight (a dark tall handsome man is the luckiest). On a more practical level those going first-footing are traditionally expected to bring something for the fire, something for the table and, most important of all, something in a bottle, usually whisky.

New Year's Day (Jan. 1) is a *bank holiday. For the changes in the date of the new year see *calendar.

New Year Honours see *orders of chivalry.

New Zealand Member of the *Commonwealth, having previously had *dominion status from 1907. The islands were first discovered by the great Dutch explorer Abel Tasman in 1642, but they received no further attention from Europe until Captain *Cook charted the coast in 1769–70 and published (in 1777) an enthusiastic account of the territory and its Maori inhabitants. In the following decades New Zealand was increasingly visited by whalers, traders, escaped convicts from Australia and then missionaries – who provided alarming reports of the interaction between these unscrupulous settlers and the Maoris. In 1837 a private British venture, the New Zealand Association, began rapidly acquiring land, and the government decided to intervene in a potentially unruly situation. A naval officer, William Hobson, was sent out. He made a treaty with the Maoris for North Island and claimed South Island by right of discovery. In 1841 New

Portrait of a Maori: watercolour by Sidney Parkinson, who visited New Zealand in 1769–70 with Captain Cook.

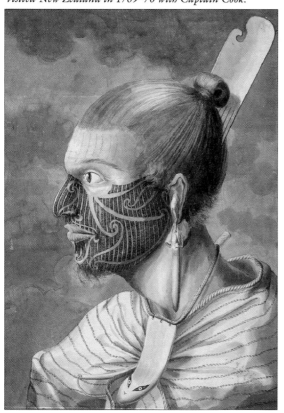

Zealand was declared a British colony, with Hobson as governor. It became independent in 1907.

Next Chain of retail stores which grew at phenomenal speed in the mid-1980s and as rapidly collapsed at the end of the decade. Based on the concept of providing designer-style clothes at relatively cheap prices to a generation flush with money, its early success was the achievement of George Davies (b. 1941). In a boardroom coup at the end of 1988 Davies was ousted as chairman and chief executive, after which the company attempted to retrench under new management.

Next Steps Government programme to reform the administration of the *civil service, introduced in 1988. Chosen sections were turned into semi-autonomous units (described as 'executive agencies'), with increased freedom of decision over how best to deliver a service to the public within an agreed budget and with built-in financial incentives. By the summer of 1992 there were 76 agencies, including HMSO, the Meteorological Office, the Ordnance Survey and even the Inland Revenue. Next Step agencies differ from *privatized bodies in that they remain part of the civil service, responsible to the relevant departmental minister.

NGA see *GPMU.

NHS see *National Health Service.

Nicholas Nickleby (*The Life and Adventures of Nicholas Nickleby* 1839) Novel by *Dickens with illustrations by *Phiz, published in monthly parts from April 1838. It describes the attempts of Nicholas and his sister Kate to make their way in life after their father has died and left them penniless. Nicholas teaches at an appalling school (Dotheboys Hall, where Wackford Squeers is headmaster) from which he escapes, taking with him a devoted halfwit, Smike. Together they find work with a tenth-rate but endearing theatrical company, headed by Vincent Crummles and starring his 15-year-old daughter as the Infant Phenomenon. Meanwhile Kate has been apprenticed to a dressmaker, Madame Mantalini, but improper approaches are made to her by colleagues of her uncle, Ralph Nickleby, a crooked financier and the real villain of the story. Nicholas, after finding work with the honest Cheeryble brothers, frustrates his uncle's various schemes. Smike, who dies of tuberculosis, turns out to have been Ralph Nickleby's son – a revelation which causes Ralph to commit suicide.

Loosely structured, and prone to melodrama and sentiment, the novel lives by its gallery of rich characters – among them the endlessly talkative Mrs Nickleby, mother of Nicholas and Kate. A dramatization of the novel in 1980 was one of the great successes of the *Royal Shakespeare Company.

Ben **Nicholson** (1894–1982) The only British painter to win an international reputation in a fully abstract style during the 1930s (he married in 1932 the abstract sculptor Barbara *Hepworth). He began with reliefs of circles and rectangles – in particular his series of *White Reliefs* – and moved on to painted abstracts, mostly serene in mood with rectangular patterns of solid colour. His father was the painter William Nicholson (1872–1949), who is widely known still for his bold poster-like prints of the late 1890s (including a famous portrait of Queen Victoria).

Harold **Nicolson** see Vita *Sackville-West.

Nigeria Member of the *Commonwealth since 1960 and a republic since 1963. This region on the west coast of Africa was a highly developed part of the continent,

A frail figure unmistakably in charge: Florence Nightingale receiving the wounded at Scutari in 1856, *by Jerry Barrett.*

with early civilizations such as the Benin and the Hausa, but it was also the area from which Europeans exported slaves. During the 19C Britain attempted to end the *slave trade and to develop a local economy based mainly on palm oil. Increasing British involvement and a succession of local treaties led to the establishment of Nigeria in 1914 as a single unified colony. It became independent in 1960 but tribal frictions caused the Ibo, in the southeast, to attempt secession as the separate state of Biafra. They were defeated in the ensuing civil war (1967–70).

Florence **Nightingale** (1820–1910) The founder of modern nursing. At the time when she decided to train as a nurse, against strong opposition from her respectable family, it was seen as a disreputable profession, linked in the public mind with prostitution. She first proved her organizing abilities in a Harley Street hospital. Then came the reports of *Russell of the *Times*, calling for 'devoted women' to come and tend the wounded in the *Crimea. At the same time a friend in the cabinet (Sidney Herbert, the secretary of state for war) urged her to go out and take charge.

The main British military hospital was at Scutari (known today as Uskudar), on the Bosphorus opposite Istanbul. She found the place an insanitary shambles, but by relentless and inspirational hard work she rapidly improved conditions. Her nightly inspection of the wards brought her the name by which she became widely known, the Lady of the Lamp. She was soon a heroine not only to the troops but to people at home, and after the war a public subscription was raised. She used it to found the first professional school of nursing, attached to *St Thomas's Hospital. For the rest of her long life she considered herself an invalid, but the energy which she put into her chosen causes – the well-being of troops in the army and public sanitation, in addition to nursing – suggests that her main complaint was hypochondria. In 1907 she became the first woman to be appointed to the Order of *Merit.

A *Nightingale sang in Berkeley Square* see entry on *Berkeley Square.

night of the long knives Used in British politics of 13 July 1962, when Harold *Macmillan sacked a third of his cabinet (7 people) after a disastrous by-election. The original night of the phrase was rather more drastic. It was that of 30 June 1934, when Hitler had many of his colleagues murdered.

Nijinsky (foaled 1967) Irish-trained bay colt which in 1970 achieved the rare feat of winning the *triple crown of English classics, ridden in all three races by Lester *Piggott.

Nile The quest for the source of the White Nile became an obsessive real-life adventure story for the British from the 1850s. Tales of a great inland sea, from which the river flowed, led to expeditions by *Burton and *Speke (1856–9), by Speke and James Grant (1860–3) and by *Baker and his wife (1862–5). The answer was found, though not immediately accepted, in the discovery and naming of Lake Victoria by Speke and of Lake Albert by Baker.

Battle of the **Nile** (1 Aug. 1798) Naval engagement during the *French Revolutionary Wars, in which Nelson surprised and destroyed the French fleet in Aboukir Bay, near the western mouth of the Nile. He thus effectively stranded in Egypt a French army under the command of Napoleon. One heroic detail of the battle was later celebrated in an English poem. The French flagship *L'Orient* caught fire but Jacques de Casabianca, the 10-year-old son of the wounded captain, refused to leave his father's side and died with him on board. Mrs *Hemans' poem *Casabianca* appeared in 1829, beginning:

> The boy stood on the burning deck
> Whence all but he had fled.

999 The number dialled in Britain by anyone requiring police, ambulance, fire or rescue services in an emergency. It was introduced in 1937 and the number was chosen as being the easiest to find in the dark (on the old circular dialling system nine was the bottom circle, closest to the finger stop). There were plans in the early 1990s to introduce an additional number, 112 (the emergency number in Germany), as a standard service throughout Europe.

Nineteen Eighty-Four (1948) George *Orwell's nightmare fable of a ruthless totalitarian regime, set in a near future – 1984 was chosen for its numerical link with the year of publication, 1948. The society depicted is only a little more horrifying (because more sophisticated in its techniques) than the gruesome Fascist and Communist dictatorships of the mid-20C. In the book Orwell coined many terms which have become current: 'doublethink' for the ability to hold contradictory beliefs, required of all party members; 'Newspeak' for the language created by the party to help it conceal truth; and Big Brother, the possibly non-existent party leader whose image is everywhere, with the slogan 'Big Brother is watching you'.

The story takes place in a Britain forming part of a superstate, Oceania, which is always fighting Eurasia or Eastasia in ever-shifting combinations of two against one. The central character is Winston Smith, a minor party member, who transgresses by having a warmly human love affair with Julia. The resulting thought-crimes have to be eradicated, but Winston's interrogator, O'Brien, only succeeds in breaking his spirit after he has submitted him to Room 101. This is where each person is confronted by his or her ultimate dread. In Winston's case it is rats. When a cage of these creatures is about to be strapped to his face he finally betrays Julia, saying let it happen to her, not me. She, he later discovers, has similarly betrayed him. When they meet again they are in no danger, for they no longer love each other. They love Big Brother.

1922 Committee The entire body of *backbenchers in the Conservative party. It takes its name from a meeting of Conservative MPs in the *Carlton Club in October 1922. Though chaired by Austen *Chamberlain, the meeting voted against his policy of remaining in *Lloyd George's coalition government – a decision which caused his downfall as leader of the party. This sudden taste of power suggested the need for an organization through which backbenchers might continue to exert influence. The executive of the Committee meets weekly when the House is sitting and the chairman, a senior member of the party, has direct access to the leader.

St **Ninian** (c.360–c.432) A somewhat shadowy figure with a claim to have long preceded St *Columba as a missionary in western Scotland. According to *Bede he was a Briton who was instructed in Rome and returned to build a church which became known as *Candida Casa* (the white house), because it was built of stone. It has traditionally been identified as *Whithorn. His feast day is September 16.

Peter **Nissen** (1871–1930) Engineer who invented the simple form of hut known by his name, made of curving strips of corrugated iron and widely used since World War I.

David **Niven** (1910–83) Actor who spent much of his career portraying a quintessentially elegant, tall, sardonic Englishman. Such a stereotype was seen at its best in such films as *A Matter of Life and Death* (1945), but his ability to act more complex roles was recognized by his Oscar as the self-deluding army officer in *Separate Tables* (1958).

His way with an anecdote made a great success of his two volumes of memoirs (*The Moon's a Balloon* 1971, *Bring on the Empty Horses* 1975). He was born in London – a fact not worth mentioning except that the Hollywood publicity machine has slipped into the reference books a more romantic Scottish place of birth, Kirriemuir.

NME (*New Musical Express*) The main newspaper of British pop music, published every Saturday. A previous *Musical Express* folded in February 1952. Two weeks later it was relaunched by a London agent, Maurice Kinn, as the *New Musical Express*. An early innovation was Britain's first chart based on the sale of records rather than sheet music. The paper was well established in time to champion the distinctively British pop of the early 1960s, with the arrival of the Mersey sound and the Beatles.

No. 10 see *Downing Street.

'the **noblest prospect which a Scotchman ever sees**' On 6 July 1763, at the Mitre Tavern, the Rev. John Ogilvie was unwise enough to praise, in Dr *Johnson's presence, the noble and wild scenic prospects of his native Scotland. He received the withering rejoinder that 'the noblest prospect which a Scotchman ever sees, is the high road that leads him to England'.

Noddy The best known of the characters created by Enid *Blyton. A wooden figure of a small boy, whose head nods when he speaks, Noddy first appeared in 1949 in *Little Noddy goes to Toyland*. In Toyland he made friends with Big-Ears the Brownie and the two reappeared together in countless books, drawn at first by a Dutch artist, Harmsen van der Beek, and after his death in 1953 by others copying his creations. Noddy was immediately much criticized by adults, for general inanity and because *golliwogs sometimes appeared in the stories as villains, but the response of children remained enthusiastic. In all new editions from 1987 the golliwogs were replaced by gnomes.

Noises Off (1982) Play by Michael Frayn deriving convulsive humour from the chaos and vanities of theatre itself. After watching an incompetent company rehearse a totally appalling farce, the real audience is treated to a glimpse of the backstage frenzy while a performance is being given to imagined spectators beyond.

'**No man is an island**' see John *Donne.

Non Angli sed Angeli (not Angles but angels) A remark supposedly made by Pope Gregory the Great, on being told that some fair-haired boys on sale as slaves in Rome were *Angles. The flattering anecdote, which has naturally had a prominent place in English tradition, first appears in *Bede's *Ecclesiastical History* (though the neatness of Gregory's eventual epigram is a later improvement on Bede's account). The incident was traditionally believed to have prompted Gregory to send *Augustine to convert the English.

Nonconformists Protestants who did not accept the orthodoxy of the *Church of England. The term was first used in the 1660s for those not conforming to the *Clarendon Code. The Act of Uniformity of 1662, by insisting upon the *Thirty-nine Articles, removed some 2000 clergy from their livings. The Toleration Act of 1689 established the right of Nonconformists to worship freely; but they continued to suffer severe restrictions, which they shared with Roman Catholics, in such areas as education (excluded from universities) and politics (ineligible for elected office), until the acts of the 17C were gradually repealed during the 19C. The Noncomformist ranks were greatly enlarged in the 18C by a new dissenting sect, the *Methodists. The word 'chapel' – originally applied to any place of worship which was not the 'church' of an Anglican parish – was by the 19C associated strongly with the Nonconformists.

Nonconformist attitudes, characterized by moral conviction, hard work and a respect for material success, have provided an important strand in British history.

Nonjurors Anglican clergy in England, and Episcopalians in Scotland, who refused after the *Revolution of 1688 to deny their oath of allegiance to James II and to swear a new one to William III and Mary II. They numbered about 400 in England, including the archbishop of Canterbury, William Sancroft. For some decades they maintained a separate church of their own, continuing the process of ordination and consecration in a line of succession which lasted until the last nonjuring bishop died in 1805.

Nonsuch Palace Extravagantly ornamented hunting palace built near Epsom in Surrey by Henry VIII in 1538. Its name suited its bombastic style, proclaiming that there was 'none such'. It was demolished in the 1680s, but the site survives as Nonsuch Park.

'There's **no place like home**' see *Home, Sweet Home.*

Denis **Norden** see *Take It From Here.*

The **Nore** Sandbank in the Thames estuary, opposite the mouth of the river Medway, which was the first in Britain to be marked with a lightship (1732). The name is also applied to the anchorage between the sandbank and the north coast of Kent, much used by naval fleets in the 17–18C. It was here that sailors mutinied over their conditions in May 1797, during the French Revolutionary Wars, two weeks after their colleagues at *Spithead.

Norfolk (759,000 in 1991, administrative centre Norwich) *County on the east coast of England. Its chief physical characteristic has been firmly fixed in the public mind by a brief line in Noel Coward's *Private Lives*: 'Very flat, Norfolk'.

Norfolk Broads Area to the east of Norwich, containing sluggish rivers (the Yare, Waveney and Bure) which meander between the broads (large lagoons of shallow water, the flooded sites of old peat workings) to converge on Breydon Water before reaching the east coast at Great Yarmouth. The region is an important nature reserve and Britain's favourite place for boating holidays, two functions which are to some extent incompatible. Wroxham Broad is considered one of the most beautiful. Hickling Broad, the largest, is a bird sanctuary – as also is Ranworth Broad, with its floating conservation centre.

Norman architecture see *Romanesque.

Norman Conquest see the *Conquest.

House of **Normandy** (1066–1154) The first four monarchs after the Norman conquest – William the Conqueror, his sons William II and Henry I, and his grandson Stephen (see the *royal house). They were followed by the house of *Plantagenet.

Normans (from Norsemen, or Northmen) The descendants of those *Vikings who had established themselves by the early 10C in northwest France, in the region which became known as Normandy. The close involvement of the dukes of Normandy in the affairs of England began with the reign of *Edward the Confessor. Confusion over his rightful successor provided the pretext for the Norman *Conquest and the establishment of the house of *Normandy.

A century of settled existence in France had not robbed the Normans of their Viking vigour, but they had also adopted much that they found there, including the French language, *Romanesque architecture and the well-organized system of *feudalism – all elements which later had a profound effect on English culture and development.

Roger **Norrington** (b. 1934) Conductor who specialized originally in music of the 17–18C, as director of the Schütz Choir of London from 1962 and of the London Classical Players from 1978. He was also principal conductor of Kent Opera (1966–84).

Norsemen see *Vikings and *Normans.

Lord **North** see *George III.

The **North** or **North Country** Terms used for the entire north of England, above a line stretching roughly from Chester in the west to Hull in the east. The area therefore includes the counties of Cheshire, Lancashire, Cumbria, Yorkshire, Durham and Northumberland, together with the heavily populated metropolitan areas of the region. The Northwest means usually Lancashire and Cumbria, the Northeast Durham and Northumberland.

Northallerton (10,000 in 1981) Historically the county town of the north *riding of Yorkshire and since 1974 the administrative centre of North Yorkshire. The town has held a weekly agricultural fair since 1205. The 12–13C church of All Saints, with a fine Perpendicular tower, survives little changed from that period apart from its Victorian chancel.

Northampton (157,000 in 1981) Administrative centre of Northamptonshire, on the river Nene. The Norman castle was demolished in the 17C, but medieval churches survive. The early 12C St Sepulchre's, based on crusaders' reports of the Holy Sepulchre in Jerusalem, is one of only four round Norman churches in England; and St Peter's, dating from later in the same century, is a fine example of its period. During the 1940s the vicar of the 19C St Matthews commissioned some outstanding modern art for his church, notably *Moore's *Madonna and Child* and a *Crucifixion* by *Sutherland. The Roman Catholic cathedral, opened in 1864, is by one of the sons of *Pugin.

Northampton's main industry, the manufacture of shoes, began in the 17C. The town's museum, housed in the former county jail (1846), contains the world's largest collection of boots and shoes from Roman times to the present. The Museum of Leathercraft, opened in 1978, surveys in a similar fashion the story of leather.

Northamptonshire (587,000 in 1991, administrative centre Northampton) *County in central England.

Northamptonshire County Cricket Club Founded in 1878 and in the *county championship from 1905 (as yet without taking the prize). In *one-day cricket the club won the Gillette Cup in 1976 and the Benson and Hedges Cup in 1980. The county ground is in Northampton, and the county plays also at Luton and Wellingborough (on the ground of Wellingborough School).

Northanger Abbey (1818) Novel by Jane *Austen, not published until the year after her death though it was begun in 1798 and had been completed by 1803. It satirizes the fashion for the Gothic novel (see *Gothic Revival) and was probably inspired by the success of *The Mysteries of Udolpho* (1794) by Mrs Ann Radcliffe (1764–1823). Catherine Morland is invited to stay in the romantic Northanger Abbey, ancestral home of Henry Tilney, with whom she has fallen in love; but the atmosphere of the house, combined with her taste for romantic fiction, makes her imagine that General Tilney, Henry's father, is involved in a macabre and criminal plot. The embarrassment is compounded by the general's mistaken belief first that Catherine is very rich and then that she is extremely poor. All ends well, with marriage and paternal approval.

North Channel see *Irish Sea.

Lord **Northcliffe** (Alfred Harmsworth, 1865–1922, bt 1903, viscount Northcliffe 1917) The first of the newspaper barons. He introduced the era of popular journalism when he founded the Daily *Mail in 1896, following it in 1903 with the Daily *Mirror. His younger brother Harold (1868–1940, bt 1910, viscount Rothermere 1919) was his partner in their ventures, which they named the Amalgamated Press.

Northeast see the *North.

Northern Ballet Theatre Dance company founded in 1969 to tour classical ballet. Based originally in Manchester, its headquarters are now in Halifax. Since 1987 the company's artistic director has been Christopher Gable (b. 1940); he was a leading dancer with the Royal Ballet (the part of Romeo in MacMillan's *Romeo and Juliet* was created for him) and he then had a career as an actor (including the title role in the film of The *Boy Friend*).

The **Northern Echo** The morning paper of much of northeast England, based in Darlington. It was founded in 1870 with the intention of putting forward 'advanced liberal opinions', and it maintains to this day a robust tradition of crusading journalism.

Northern Ireland (13,483sq.km/5206sq.m, population 1.6 million in 1991) The *six counties forming the northeast part of *Ireland, which were given a measure of local autonomy within the United Kingdom by the Government of Ireland Act of 1920. The first parliament met in 1921 in *Belfast. The prime minister was James Craig (1871–1940, Viscount Craigavon 1927) and he held this position until his death. The Protestant settlement of the six counties in the 17c had resulted in political and economic power being heavily concentrated in *Unionist hands. In the late 1960s the growth of the international civil rights movement coincided with the period in office of a more liberal-minded prime minister (Captain Terence O'Neill, 1914–90). The result was large-scale Catholic demonstrations, distorted by the involvement of the *IRA (in a continuation of the earlier *Troubles), which in turn provoked retaliation from Protestant paramilitary organizations. The province has by now suffered more than two decades of continuing *terrorism, and since 1969 British troops have been on active duty. In 1972 (the year of *Bloody Sunday) the parliament at Stormont was suspended and Northern Ireland was placed under direct rule from Westminster. Recent attempts to resolve the situation have centred on the *Anglo-Irish Agreement.

Northern Ireland Office (London SW1) The government department which has been responsible for *Northern Ireland since the introduction of direct rule in 1972, with particular concern for constitutional developments, security, and law and order. For secretaries of state since 1983 see the *cabinet.

Northern Sinfonia Chamber orchestra established in Newcastle-upon-Tyne in 1958; it is the only full-time professional orchestra touring regularly in northeast England. The Austrian cellist and conductor Heinrich Schiff became the Sinfonia's artistic director in 1990.

North Sea The entire stretch of water lying between the east coasts of England and Scotland and the land mass of the continent of Europe, from the Strait of Dover in the south to the Shetlands in the north. Beyond the Shetlands the North Sea merges into the Norwegian Sea.

North Sea oil and gas The first indication of major oil and gas reserves beneath the North Sea came in 1959, when natural gas was discovered in shallow water off the Netherlands. In 1966 reserves were found in deeper water off southeast England. Offshore drilling subsequently became a major industry. The search for oil and gas was licensed by the government to commercial firms in return for a tax on revenue (set in 1975 at 45%). The gas was mainly piped to the domestic market by *British Gas. The flow of oil began when the first North Sea crude came ashore in April 1976 from the Forties field. The sea between Scotland and Norway proved to be the area richest in oil, bringing temporary prosperity to east coast ports from Aberdeen up to Sullom Voe in the *Shetlands. Estimates of how long the supply will last have constantly been revised as new fields are found, but production peaked in the mid-1980s. The oil funds went with other tax revenue into the government's current account, and some have wondered whether this unrepeatable national windfall has been well used. A major disaster in the oil fields was the explosion in 1988 of *Piper Alpha.

Manor of **Northstead** see *Chiltern Hundreds.

Northumberland (also called Northumbria, 307,000 in 1991, administrative centre Morpeth) *County in the extreme northeast of England. The Northumberland *National Park, designated in 1956, comprises 1031sq.km/398sq.m of hill country, running in a narrow strip through the centre of the county from Hadrian's Wall in the south to the Cheviots and the Scottish border in the north.

Duke of **Northumberland** see *Edward VI.

Northumbria The most powerful of the *Anglo-Saxon kingdoms in the 7c, when its rulers controlled an area

North Sea Oil, in thousand tonnes

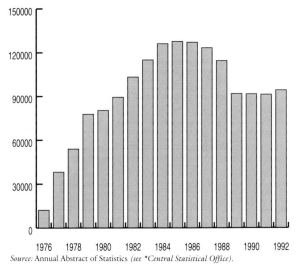

Source: Annual Abstract of Statistics (see *Central Statistical Office).

from coast to coast across the country, stretching from the Clyde and the Forth in the north to the Mersey and Humber in the south. Northumbria was noted for the learning and culture of its monasteries, particularly those on the east coast; *Bede wrote his history at Jarrow; the *Lindisfarne Gospels derive from Holy Island; and the Northumbrian decision on Christian ritual at the *Synod of Whitby set the pattern for the rest of England. The kingdom was much reduced from the late 9C by Danish invasions in the east and by pressure from the Scots in the north. In the mid-10C Northumbria ceased to exist as an independent kingdom and became an earldom within an England dominated by *Wessex.

Northwest see the *North.

Northwest Passage The quest for a sea route north of Canada to the Pacific tantalized explorers, many of them British, for five centuries. Among the best known have been *Frobisher in the 16C, *Hudson in the 17C, *Cook, who explored from the Pacific side in the 18C, and *Franklin (credited now as its discoverer) in the 19C. The first to complete the passage, in a 3-year voyage (1903–6), was the Norwegian Roald Amundsen.

North York Moors Area of moorland and woodland designated in 1952 a *national park (1433sq.km/ 553sq.m). It lies almost entirely within North Yorkshire, with just its northern tip extending into Cleveland. The North York Moors Railway is a private venture which since 1973 has run steam trains on the 29km/18m scenic journey between Pickering and Grosmont, a line built in the 1830s.

North Yorkshire (721,000 in 1991, administrative centre Northallerton) *County on the east coast of England, the largest in the country, formed in 1974 from most of the north *riding of *Yorkshire and parts of the other two ridings.

Norton One of the great names of the British *motorcyle industry, producing machines which for decades dominated racing; the original company was formed by James Norton in Wolverhampton in 1898. The Isle of Man Senior *TT, the most prestigious of events, was won by Nortons ten times between the wars and then every year from 1947 to 1954. The company declined in the 1960s and went into liquidation in 1974, but the name was relaunched on an ambitious scale in Lichfield in 1988. The new models have succeeded on the race track – winning the Senior TT in 1992 – but they have moved rather more slowly in the commercial market.

Norwich (125,000 in 1991) City on the river Wensum; administrative centre of Norfolk. It has been a regional centre of importance since Anglo-Saxon times and the city centre retains a medieval feeling, particularly around Elm Hill. The cathedral, begun in 1096, is notable from a distance for its soaring 15C spire (at 96m/315ft second in England only to *Salisbury); its interior is distinguished by the way the sturdy Norman arches of the lower levels merge into the delicate Gothic fan vaulting above, added in the 15C to replace the earlier timber roof. The 14C cloisters are unusual in consisting of two storeys.

The castle, begun like the cathedral shortly after the Norman Conquest, has housed since 1894 the city's museum and art gallery. This is particularly strong in its holdings of the so-called Norwich School of landscape painters, prominent among them John Crome (1768–1821) and John Sell Cotman (1782–1842). Another distinguished art gallery just outside the city is the Sainsbury Centre for the Visual Arts, the gift of Robert and Lisa

Interior of the early 18C doll's house at Nostell Priory, possibly made by the young Chippendale.

Sainsbury, in which a collection ranging from tribal art to modern painting and sculpture is displayed in a hangarlike structure by Norman *Foster (completed in 1978 with an extension in 1991); it is part of the university of East Anglia, founded in 1961 in Earlham Park with buildings designed by Denys *Lasdun. The Norwich Players are a long-established amateur theatre company, performing in the Elizabethan-style Maddermarket Theatre designed for them in 1921 within an older building.

Norwich City, known as the Canaries (Carrow Road, Norwich). Football club formed in 1902, largely on the initiative of two local schoolmasters. The club turned professional in 1905 and became a founder member of Division 3 of the *Football League in 1920. It has been in and out of Division 1 since 1972 and was one of the teams forming the Premier League in 1992–3. Club victories: Football League Cup 1962, 85.

Nostell Priory (10km/6m SE of Wakefield) House begun for Sir Rowland Winn in about 1736 and completed for his son, of the same name, in 1766–77. The father employed as his architect a precocious 19-year-old, James Paine (1717–89), who was responsible for the *Palladian design of the main block. The son, on inheriting in 1765, switched to the newly fashionable *neoclassicism of Robert *Adam, who completed most of the interior decoration and added the northeast wing with its pillared portico. The house's most interesting connection is with *Chippendale, for it contains an unparalleled collection of furniture provided by him together with much of the original documentation. Tradition in the Winn family adds, quite plausibly, that Chippendale began his career as an apprentice on the estate and that he made the exquisite furnished doll's house of about 1735 which is one of Nostell's treasures. The name derives from a 12C Augustinian priory which stood nearby.

Nostromo (1904) Novel by *Conrad about a fatal obsession with a horde of silver. In an imaginary South American country in the throes of revolution, Martin Decoud (a journalist) and Nostromo (an Italian adventurer) are asked to remove bullion from a silver mine for safe keeping. With great difficulty they manage to get it to an island, where they bury it. Decoud goes mad and drowns himself, weighted down with silver. Over the years Nostromo returns to the island to retrieve it bit by bit, stealing it for himself; Charles Gould, manager of the mine, has accepted the story that it was lost at sea. When Nostromo is shot on the island, mistaken for a casual intruder, the secret of the silver dies with him.

'no such thing as society' see Margaret *Thatcher.

'not a penny off the pay, not a minute on the day' see the *General Strike.

'nothing to declare except my genius' see Oscar *Wilde.

not proven see *jury system.

John **Nott** (b. 1932, KCB 1983) Conservative politician, MP for Cornwall St Ives 1966–83, who entered the cabinet in 1979 as secretary of state for trade (1979–81). He became widely known to the public on television in his next appointment, as secretary of state for defence (1981–3), because the Falklands War occurred during his period in office.

Not the Nine O'Clock News (BBC 1979–82) Satirical television revue series which launched the careers of Rowan *Atkinson, Pamela Stephenson, Mel Smith and Griff Rhys Jones (the latter subsequently known as a pair through *Smith and Jones*).

Nottingham (276,000 in 1991) City on the river Trent; administrative centre of Nottinghamshire. The name derives from the Anglo-Saxon settlement of Snotingaham (the village, or ham, of Snot's people). Occupied by the *Danes in the 9C, it became their most important centre; and its regional status was confirmed by the Normans, who built a castle here on a high outcrop of rock soon after the Conquest. The medieval town is traditionally linked with *Robin Hood, whose legendary band of merry men roam and rob in nearby *Sherwood Forest and whose chief enemy is the wicked sheriff of Nottingham. In more recent centuries the town's importance has been as a centre of the textile industry, specializing in lace and hosiery. Its early industrialization provoked the actions of the *Luddites, who had an articulate local champion in Lord *Byron (his ancestral home, Newstead Abbey, is nearby). Nottingham is also the birthplace of *Boots.

The Old Market Square (surprisingly large at 2.3ha/5.5ac) has been the town centre since Norman times and until 1928 was the site of Nottingham's annual Goose Fair in early October; originally a trade fair for the sale of livestock, this has long been a purely festive occasion and is now held on a site about a mile to the north. The medieval castle was almost entirely dismantled during the Commonwealth; the mansion which then replaced it was burnt during riots in 1831, part of the agitation leading to the Reform Act; and it was the ruins of this which were restored in the 1870s to become the Museum and Art Gallery. Among many treasures the art gallery has a particularly good collection of Richard Bonington (1802–28), who was born locally; and the museum displays many examples of the alabaster carvings (usually relief panels for altar-pieces) for which Nottingham was famous in the 14–15C. The rock on which the castle stands is riddled with passages and caves, many of them inhabited at times in the past. At the foot of the rock are Ye Olde Trip to Jerusalem (claiming to be oldest inn in England, established

in 1189) and Brewhouse Yard – a group of 17C cottages adapted to a museum of daily life. A natural history museum is housed in nearby *Wollaton Hall.

Nottingham is not an Anglican diocese, but has a Roman Catholic cathedral by *Pugin. *Trent Bridge is one of Britain's foremost cricket grounds.

Nottingham Forest, known as the Reds (City Ground, Nottingham). One of the oldest football clubs in Britain, formed in 1865 as the Forest Football Club when the members of an existing 'shinney' club (a type of hockey) decided to change their sport; they gave themselves a club identity by wearing red caps on the field. The only club in the League with a longer history is also local, *Notts County. Nottingham Forest joined Division 1 of the *Football League in 1892, and after an uneven career was consistently in the top division from 1977 until relegation in 1993. Club victories: FA Cup 1898, 1959; League Champions 1978; Football League Cup 1978, 79, 89, 90; European Cup 1979, 80.

Nottinghamshire (1,016,000 in 1991, administrative centre Nottingham) *County in central England.

Nottinghamshire County Cricket Club Founded in 1841 and one of the original teams in the *county championship. The club had ten victories in the championship before the points system was introduced in 1890, and has won four times since then (1907, 29, 81, 87). Among its best-known players has been the fast bowler Harold *Larwood. In *one-day cricket it has won the Gillette Cup in 1976, the Benson and Hedges Cup in 1980 and the Sunday League in 1991. The county ground is *Trent Bridge in Nottingham, and the county plays also at Worksop.

Notting Hill (London W11) Area developed during the 19C and famous in the late 20C for its annual carnival during the August *bank holiday weekend. Launched as a small local event in 1966, this has become Britain's largest black festival, based upon the carnivals of the Caribbean and like them drawing vast crowds of visitors.

Notts County, known as the Magpies (County Ground, Meadow Lane, Nottingham). The oldest professional football club in Britain. It existed on an informal basis from 1862 and was established in 1864, as the Notts Football Club. It was a founder member of the *Football League in 1888, but was in Division 2 by 1893 and has spent most of its history out of the top division. Club victories: FA Cup 1894.

Not Waving But Drowning see Stevie *Smith.

Ivor **Novello** (name taken by deed poll in 1927 by David Ivor Davies, 1893–1951) Composer, actor and playwright who was immensely popular between the wars in light musical and theatrical entertainment. In 1914, when only 21, he found fame and fortune with his song *Keep the Home Fires Burning*. He starred in many of his own comedies, but had the greatest success in his musicals – in particular *The Dancing Years* (1939), which ran through much of the war and survived his own absence for a month in 1944, when he was in prison for evading petrol restrictions.

NS see *calendar.

NSPCC (National Society for the Prevention of Cruelty to Children, London EC1) The Society was founded in 1884, when the law had no power to intervene between parents and children. Its activities led to the Prevention of

Cruelty to Children Act of 1889, and in 1904 parliament gave its officers the power to take children into care on the authority of a magistrate. The Society's local inspector, known popularly as the 'cruelty man', became a familiar figure in each district.

nuclear power Britain's research programme in atomic energy began with the establishment in January 1946 of the Harwell laboratory on a disused wartime airfield some 23km/14m south of Oxford. Scientists there devised a gas-cooled reactor using uranium rods housed in a casing of magnesium alloy (magnox), which produced electrical power and also the plutonium needed for the atomic weapon establishment at *Aldermaston. A magnox reactor, designed to achieve both these purposes, was built at Calder Hall on the *Sellafield site; it opened in 1956 as the world's first large-scale nuclear power plant. Subsequently many other magnox reactors were built in Britain, differing from Calder Hall in that they were designed only to generate power. An experimental 'fast reactor' was started at *Dounreay in 1959. And in 1979 the government announced a major expansion of Britain's nuclear power programme, switching to a US water-cooled design known as a pressurized water reactor. The declared intention was to build one such reactor a year for ten years, but by 1992 only one was under construction, at *Sizewell.

The magnox reactors have never produced electricity at a price to compete with coal-fired power stations, and the huge cost of dismantling them at the end of their working lives prevented the nuclear part of the *electricity industry from being privatized in 1991 along with the rest. The Dounreay reactor is closing down in 1994. But the state-owned Nuclear Electric believes that pressurized water reactors can be competitive and has plans for expansion at Sizewell. One part of the nuclear power industry, involved with the reprocessing of nuclear waste at Sellafield and other sites, was hived off as a separate state-owned enterprise in 1971 under the name British Nuclear Fuels (BNFL).

nuclear submarines Britain's independent nuclear deterrent has consisted of nuclear-powered submarines armed with US rockets (Polaris and Trident) carrying British nuclear warheads. Four Polaris submarines were equipped and launched in the 1960s, and were updated in a £1 billion programme during the 1970s. In 1980 the government announced a plan to build a replacement fleet of four submarines, carrying the latest US Trident missiles, to serve as Britain's deterrent during the 1990s; the cost was to be £5 billion over 15 years. HMS *Vanguard*, the first of the Trident submarines, was launched for its sea trials in October 1992 from the VSEL shipyard at Barrow-in-Furness, in Cumbria.

Lord **Nuffield** (William Morris, 1877–1963, bt 1929, viscount 1938) Britain's most successful car manufacturer, who set up in business at the age of 16 with a bicycle repair shop behind his home at Cowley, in Oxford. He was soon constructing and racing his own bicycles, which he followed with a motor bicycle in 1902. At the *Motor Show of 1912 he announced a car of his own make, the Morris-Oxford, and took 400 orders; the first was delivered in 1913, and the rest is the history of *Morris cars.

In his last three decades Nuffield concerned himself chiefly with philanthropy. He gave away some £30 million during his life, mainly to projects connected with medicine and the relief of suffering. His two greatest memorials have been the Nuffield Foundation (over the years one of Britain's largest charitable trusts) and Nuffield, the college which he founded in 1937 at Oxford.

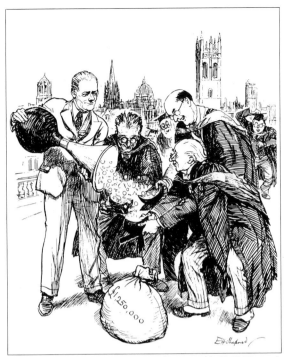

The motor horn as cornucopia: Punch *cartoon by E.H. Shepard in 1936, reflecting Lord Nuffield's generosity to Oxford.*

NUJ (National Union of Journalists) Trade union established in 1907, at a meeting at the Acorn Hotel in Birmingham, as a breakaway group from the Institute of Journalists. It became the largest union in the newspaper and magazine field, with photographers as well as writers among its members.

NUM (National Union of Mineworkers) Until 1985 the trade union for all coal miners in Britain. It was formed in 1944 as a national organization to replace the federated group of local unions, the MFGB (Miners' Federation of Great Britain), which had been established in 1889 and had represented the miners in the *General Strike of 1926. With coal at the heart of the nation's economy, the NUM became a symbol both of union power and of the unions' ability to disrupt. In the ten years following the nationalization of *coal (1947) the miners accounted for 33% of all days lost through industrial action even though they represented only 4% of the nation's workforce; the NUM (with Joe Gormley as president) subsequently took on the government in two *miners' strikes in the 1970s; and in Arthur *Scargill it had by 1981 a new president bent on further confrontation. The strike of 1984 resulted in Nottinghamshire miners leaving the NUM to found the *UDM. This defection, combined with the relentless closure of pits, resulted in the membership of the NUM dropping from 250,000 in the early 1980s to about 50,000 a decade later.

No. 1 London see *Apsley House.

Number Ten see *Downing Street.

Trevor **Nunn** (b. 1940) Theatre director who has spent most of his career with the *Royal Shakespeare Company. He joined it in 1964, became its artistic director in 1968 and remained in charge until 1987. His many productions included the company's greatest international success – the musical *Les Misérables* (1985), which has been restaged all over the world. Musicals are also a field in which he has excelled in the commercial theatre, directing

The Italian fountain and elaborate yew topiary at the heart of the Wall Garden at Nymans.

three of Andrew Lloyd Webber's (*Cats* 1981, *Starlight Express* 1984, *Aspects of Love* 1989). In opera he has directed notable productions of *Porgy and Bess* (1986) and *Cosi Fan Tutte* (1991) for Glyndebourne.

NUPE see *Unison.

NUR see *RMT.

nursery rhymes Verses for singing or reciting with young children. The first collection of English rhymes was *Tommy Thumb's Song Book* (1744), but the most influential was *Mother Goose's Melody* (1780 or earlier); *Mother Goose was already famous for her fairy stories. Some of the best-known traditional rhymes, such as *Jack and Jill*, appeared in these early collections; others (for example *Mary had a little lamb*) have been written since. It is often held that nursery rhymes (e.g. *Ring a ring o' roses* or *Little Jack Horner*) relate to specific events in the past, but there is rarely any evidence for this.

nursery school see *education.

NUS see *RMT.

NUT (National Union of Teachers) The earliest of the trade unions in the field of education, formed in 1870 as the Elementary Teachers' Union and renamed the National Union of Teachers in 1889. It represents teachers in England and Wales, and is strongly committed to the principle of *comprehensive schools.

NVQ (National Vocational Qualification) A new form of grading in craft and technical skills, introduced in the late 1980s. It attempts to establish a more standardized national scale than the previous range of traditional trade qualifications; at the start there were four grades, with plans to add a fifth. The scheme is supervised by the National Council for Vocational Qualifications, set up in 1986, but training is at places of work and examinations are conducted by such bodies as *City and Guilds, the *Royal Society of Arts or the more recently established BTEC (Business and Technician Education Council). A similar scheme of SVQs (Scottish Vocational Qualifications) is supervised by the Scottish Vocational Education Council.

Nyasaland see *Malawi.

Nymans (27km/17m N of Brighton) Garden and pinetum begun by Ludwig Messel in 1890, famous for its superb collection of trees and shrubs. It was much damaged in the *great storm of October 1987, but it is being painstakingly replanted.

O

Oak Apple Day see *Boscobel.

Oaks Flat race for 3-year-old fillies over 2.4km/1.5m, held at *Epsom on a Saturday in early June, three days after the *Derby. First run in 1779, in imitation of the recently established *St Leger, it was named after the house at Epsom leased by the 12th earl of Derby.

oast house Characteristically English design of kiln for the drying of hops (an essential ingredient in the flavour of beer), and a picturesque feature in the landscape of *Kent and neighbouring counties. An oast house is a brick building, either round or square, with a tapering roof leading up to an inclined wooden cowl which can be swivelled to improve the flow of air. The hops are laid on a slatted floor and are dried by a heated draught passing through them.

oatcake Coarsely textured, unleavened and unsweetened biscuit of oatmeal, usually associated with Scotland but also traditional in Ireland, the north of England and Wales.

Captain **Oates** (Lawrence Oates, 1880–1912) Member of Captain *Scott's expedition to the Antarctic, who won a lasting place in the nation's memory by the understatement of his last words. Knowing that his frost-bitten feet were delaying the party in their desperate struggle back to safety, he walked out of the tent into a blizzard with the remark 'I am just going outside and may be some time'.

Titus **Oates** see the *Popish Plot.

oats see *porridge.

Oban (8000 in 1991) Port and resort on the west coast of Scotland, in the Strathclyde region. It developed during the 19c as the base for excursions to the *Hebrides, a role which it still fulfils. The Roman Catholic cathedral of St Columba is by Giles Gilbert *Scott.

OBE see *orders of chivalry.

Oberon see A *Midsummer Night's Dream.

Prince **Obolensky** (Alexander Obolensky, 1916–40) Rugby union player and Russian aristocrat, brought to Britain at the age of one in the year of the Russian revolution. He had only four caps for England, all in 1936, but he is remembered for one particular moment, 'Obolensky's try', which he scored at Twickenham after a long diagonal run through the entire New Zealand defence. He died as a Hurricane pilot in 1940.

obscenity An obscene publication is defined in British law as anything that tends to deprave or corrupt, and the law covers magazines, books and videos. The issue becomes of topical importance only when there is disagreement on a question of merit. The Obscene Publications Act of 1959 introduced the concept of the 'public good' as a legitimate defence; experts could be called to argue that a publication had scientific, literary or artistic importance. Penguin was the first publisher to test the new law, publishing *Lady Chatterley's Lover in 1960 and being acquitted in the resulting prosecution on grounds of literary merit. *Fanny Hill, delightful but undeniably pornographic, failed at its first attempt in 1963 but was cleared in 1970. These two cases have made it unlikely that a work of any pretension to literary merit will be prosecuted for obscenity.

The **Observer** Britain's oldest Sunday newspaper, founded in London in 1791 by a young Irishman, W.S. Bourne. It entered its most distinguished period when a polemical

Captain Oates on board the Terra Nova *in the Antarctic, with two of the expedition's Siberian ponies.*

journalist, James Garvin (1868–1947), became editor in 1908 – a post he retained until 1942, becoming famous for his lengthy political editorials. The paper was owned for much of the 20c by the Astor family, and was bought in 1981 by *Lonrho.

O come, all ye faithful Hymn which is much sung now as a *carol. It is a direct translation by Frederick Oakeley (1802–80) of a Latin hymn having the same rhythm (*Adeste fideles, Laeti triumphantes; Venite, venite in Bethlehem*). The Latin seems to have been written by an unknown author in either France or Germany in the 18c, as a hymn for Christmas.

Daniel **O'Connell** (1775–1847) Irish lawyer and politician whose election to parliament in 1828 prompted the *Emancipation Act – passed because civil war seemed likely in Ireland if he was prevented from taking his seat. He was also the first to agitate for *Home Rule, in a series of massive popular gatherings throughout Ireland in the early 1840s. In the tradition of radical politics of the time he became known (like Bolívar in South America) as the Liberator.

Oddfellows see *friendly societies.

Odd Man Out (1947) Film directed by Carol *Reed, based on a novel by F.L. Green, about the last hours of a wounded IRA gunman on the run in Belfast. The black-and-white photography (evocative shadows in dark wet streets) and the tightening of the net on the fugitive (played by James Mason) prefigure another Reed film of two years later, *The Third Man*.

Odeon see J. Arthur *Rank.

Ode on a Grecian Urn (1820) Poem by *Keats, envying the unchanging bliss of the scene on a Greek vase, in which a youth plays the pipes to his loved one ('For ever wilt thou love, and she be fair'). It is the vase which speaks the much quoted and much debated final couplet, addressed to living human beings as they waste into old age:
> Beauty is truth, truth beauty – that is all
> Ye know on earth, and all ye need to know.

Ode to a Nightingale (1820) Poem by *Keats, inspired by the song of a nightingale in his Hampstead garden. The bird's free rapture is contrasted with the realities of everyday life ('Where youth grows pale, and spectre-thin, and dies'). The thought that the same song has been heard through the centuries (even perhaps lifting the heart of the biblical Ruth, 'when sick for home,/She stood in tears amid the alien corn') encourages him to dream of the same liberation through his poetry.

Ode to the West Wind (1820) Poem by *Shelley, inspired in Florence during a walk on a windy day in October 1819 and written that same afternoon. Shelley identifies with the violence of the 'wild West Wind' which both destroys and preserves, blowing to destruction the old leaves and settling into their winter lair the seeds of new life for the spring. As the last line asks, 'If Winter comes, can Spring be far behind?'.

OECD (Organization for Economic Cooperation and Development) Institution, based in Paris, which was established in 1961 to further economic and social cooperation between its member states, replacing the earlier OEEC which had been set up to administer the *Marshall Plan. The membership has since grown, but at first it consisted of the USA, Canada, Spain and West Germany together with the original 16 nations of the OEEC (Austria, Belgium, Denmark, France, Greece, Iceland, Ireland, Italy, Luxembourg, the Netherlands, Norway, Portugal, Sweden, Switzerland, Turkey and the UK).

OED see *Oxford English Dictionary.

Offa's Dyke Earthwork in eastern Wales running south from the Irish sea, near Prestatyn, to the Bristol Channel at Chepstow. It was built in the 8c by Offa (d. 796), the ruler of Mercia, one of the most powerful of the *Anglo-Saxon kingdoms. Built as a protection against the Britons to the west, it effectively defined the area of Wales.

OFFER, OFGAS, OFTEL, OFWAT Regulatory agencies with space-age names, which became part of the national scene in the wake of *privatization. Their brief includes safeguarding the interests of the consumer (at the mercy otherwise of what are in effect private monopolies). The electricity industry is regulated by OFFER (Office of Electricity Regulation), and British Gas, BT (British Telecom) and the water industry are kept in line by the other bodies with more recognizable acronyms. The regulators soon proved that that they were prepared to take a tough line. OFTEL, in response to BT's large profits, imposed on the company an annual reduction in its call charges of 7.5% in real terms (i.e. 7.5% less the rate of inflation) in each year from 1993 to 1997.

Martin **Offiah** (b. 1965) The outstanding rugby league player in the modern game, as an exceptionally fast winger. He transferred from Widnes to *Wigan early in 1992 (the £440,000 price was a record). In May of that year he was the main factor in Wigan's unprecedented fifth successive victory in the Challenge Cup final at Wembley (he narrowly failed to become the first man to score three tries in a final, when his third was disqualified because of a knock-on). A week later he achieved the astonishing feat of 10 tries in a match, against Leeds. The record is 11 by George West in 1905, but that was against an amateur side. Offiah's nickname, Chariots, derives from the film *Chariots of Fire*.

Official Secrets Act The first Official Secrets Act was passed in 1911 and there have been frequently amended versions, the most recent of which was in 1989. Apart from its general prohibition on spying, the main burden of the act is in section 2 – which makes it a criminal offence for government employees to divulge certain categories of information. It was under this act that the civil service *moles Sarah Tisdall and Clive Ponting were prosecuted. The author of *Spycatcher would be liable under its terms if he returned to Britain.

OFGAS see *OFFER etc.

Cardinal **Ó Fiaich** (Tomás Ó Fiaich, 1923–90) Roman Catholic archbishop of *Armagh from 1977 until his death. Born in the Northern Irish border town of Crossmaglen, he spent most of his career teaching at the Roman Catholic seminary of Maynooth in the republic of Ireland. He was much involved in attempts to restore the Irish language; indeed the Gaelic spelling of his own name was part of this campaign, for his parents were simply Patrick and Annie Fee. He died while on pilgrimage to Lourdes.

O for the Wings of a Dove Aria from Mendelssohn's *Hear My Prayer* (1844), which became particularly well known in Britain through the bestselling HMV record on which it is sung by the 15-year-old boy soprano Master Ernest Lough. It was recorded in 1927 in London's Temple Church, where Lough was a member of the choir until his retirement in 1972.

OFSTED (Office for Standards in Education) A new government department, established in 1992, which is charged with keeping a register of qualified independent inspectors of schools and contracting out to them (on the basis of competitive tenders) the regular work of inspection. It therefore takes on and semi-privatizes the responsibilities of HMI (His or Her Majesty's Inspectorate), the body which since Victorian times has reported on the state of the nation's schools and which had Matthew Arnold as its most distinguished employee. OFSTED is answerable directly to the secretary of state for education.

OFTEL, OFWAT see *OFFER etc.

Ogham The alphabet used in *Gaelic inscriptions on stones of about the 5th century AD. It consists of groups of short notches cut on either side of a straight line.

O God, our help in ages past Hymn written by Isaac *Watts in 1714, at a time when Queen Anne was mortally ill and there was national anxiety about the succession. The words are a loose paraphrase of Psalm 90. Watts began his first line with the words 'Our God' but John Wesley changed this to 'O God' in a collection published in 1737; Wesley's version was followed in *Hymns Ancient and Modern* (1861), where the now familiar tune of the early 18c (known as St Anne) was first attached to the hymn. It has become particularly associated with Remembrance Sunday, being sung in churches throughout the land and at the Cenotaph.

OHMS The initials, standing for On Her (or His) Majesty's Service, which are used in many contexts by the civil service, the armed forces and other state-funded bodies.

'Oh, to be in England' see Robert *Browning.

Oh What a Lovely War (1963) Entertainment devised by Joan *Littlewood and her Theatre Workshop company which achieved a powerful effect (satirical and yet sentimental) by enacting the story of World War I in the form of an end-of-pier entertainment, interspersed with the highly evocative songs and music-hall routines of the period. It was directed by Richard *Attenborough as a film in 1969.

Oil Crisis The unsettling effect on western economies caused by the steep increase in oil prices imposed in the mid-1970s by OPEC (Organization of Oil Exporting Countries). In 1973–4 oil prices rose by 300%. Government response in Britain included two major fuel-saving measures: the introduction of a three-day week in factories and offices, which lasted from January to March 1974 (this period also included a *miners' strike); and a 50 mph speed limit on all roads, imposed in December 1973 and lifted in May 1974.

Old Bailey (London EC4) The name commonly used for the Central Criminal Court, being that of the street on which it stands. In 1902 *Newgate prison was demolished to make way for this building (by E.W. Mountford, opened 1907). Central London's *Crown Court sits at the Old Bailey, hearing criminal cases, whereas the High Court sits at the *Law Courts in the Strand.

Old Bill see 'a *better 'ole'.

old boy network Phrase which became widely current in the mid-20c, at much the same time as the *Establishment, to describe an aspect of the same phenomenon. It reflected the fact that many of those appointing each other to positions of power in Britain's institutions were, and still are, 'old boys' of the same few *public schools and universities.

Judicial proceedings in the previous Old Bailey, replaced by the present building in 1907. Trials took place on a site adjacent to Newgate prison from the 16c, and in 1834 this was designated the Central Criminal Court.

Old Codgers Fictional pair of old men who for 54 years (1936–90) answered readers' letters and queries in the *Daily Mirror*, making 'Live Letters, Conducted by the Old Codgers' one of the longest-running features in British journalism.

Old Contemptibles Popular name adopted by the *British Expeditionary Force in World War I. It derived from reports that the Kaiser had called them a 'contemptible little army'.

Old English see *English.

Old English sheepdog see *sheepdogs.

Bruce **Oldfield** (b. 1950) Fashion designer who grew up in a *Barnardo's home in Yorkshire. From the mid-70s he was designing for film stars, and in 1975 he launched the first of his ready-to-wear collections. Oldfield fashion shows were the basis of two royal charity galas, in 1985 and 1988, to raise money for Barnardo's.

Mike **Oldfield** (b. 1953) Rock musician and composer whose life has been dominated by the phenomenal success of the album *Tubular Bells* (1973) – the basis of *Virgin's fortunes as well as his own. An instrumental sequence of more than 45 minutes (on which Oldfield played a wide range of stringed instruments and keyboards), the album with its bell motif was in the UK charts for five years and is calculated to have sold more than 10 million copies worldwide; a sequence from it was used as the theme of the film *The Exorcist* (1973). As if in a movie tradition of follow-ons, Oldfield eventually produced *Tubular Bells II* (1992), which also went to no. 1. Other successful LPs of the 1970s were *Hergest Ridge* (1974, no. 1) and *Ommadawn* (1975).

Old Firm Joint term for Glasgow's two perennial football rivals, Celtic and Rangers, an engagement between them being described, for example, as an 'Old Firm match'.

Old Hundredth The tune used for *All people that on earth do dwell*, described as the 'old' tune for the 100th Psalm when retained in a new psalter of 1696.

Old King Cole Nursery rhyme about a king who is a merry old soul, calling for his pipe and his bowl and his fiddlers three. His identity has been much debated since the early 18C. There have been two main contenders, neither with much except surmise to support his case. One is a legendary British king supposedly commemorated in the name of Colchester. The other is a rich cloth merchant of Reading by the name of Thomas Colebrook, who was stated in the 16C to have been a historical character.

Old Moore's Almanack An annual published since 1700 when Francis Moore (1657–1715), a doctor and astrologer in Lambeth, printed his astrological predictions for the next year under the title *Vox Stellarum* (Latin for *Voice of the Stars*). Like astrology itself, and equally mysteriously, Old Moore has gone from strength to strength, selling in the millions while still hedging its bets in the time-honoured way; 'Banana skins are waiting for he who thinks he can dominate the international stage' is the type of recurrent prediction which has a near-certainty of coming true.

Old Mother Riley Irish washerwoman with a strong line in comic abuse, the creation in the *music hall of Arthur Lucan; his wife Kitty McShane played Old Mother

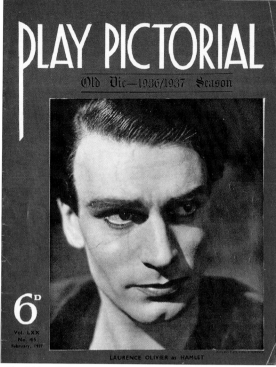

The Old Vic's heart throb in 1937, when Olivier's Hamlet was the highlight of the season.

Riley's daughter, Kitty. They became known to a much wider audience through the cinema. Between 1937 and 1952 there were 14 Mother Riley films.

Old Mother Hubbard Nursery rhyme about Mother Hubbard's shopping expeditions to buy food and clothes for her very eccentric dog. The nonsense verses were first published in 1805 and were credited to Sarah Catherine Martin (1768–1826), but it is not known whether she was adapting existing verses or writing entirely new ones. Mother Hubbard herself was already a popular character in the 16C.

Old Parliament Hall see *Edinburgh Castle.

Old Parr (Thomas Parr, d. 1635) Famous for having supposedly lived 152 years. He was brought from Shropshire to London in 1635 to be shown to Charles I and was then exhibited publicly at a tavern in the Strand. The strain killed the old man. He was buried in Westminster Abbey, where an inscription declares that he was born in 1483 and lived in ten reigns. Clearly that enticingly round number of reigns had influenced the supposed date of his birth. Edward IV died in 1483, and a child born in that year had lived in four reigns by the age of two (Edward IV, Edward V, Richard III, Henry VII). For established records of longevity in Britain see *life expectancy.

Old Possum's Book of Practical Cats (1939) Poems by T.S. *Eliot, introducing a gallery of feline characters now famous to a very wide audience through the musical *Cats. They include Growltiger, the barge cat who is the Terror of the Thames; Old Deuteronomy, an ancient cat; Skimbleshanks, the railway cat; and above all Macavity, mystery cat and Napoleon of Crime. The book was reissued in 1940 with illustrations by Nicolas Bentley (1907–78).

Old Pretender see James *Stuart.

Old Style see *calendar.

Old Trafford (Manchester) The name of an almost adjacent cricket ground and football ground. The cricket ground was opened in 1857 as the home of the Manchester Club and a few years later was taken on by the newly formed *Lancashire County Cricket Club. It is a regular location for *Test matches. The football ground is that of *Manchester United, who have played there since 1910.

Old Vic (London SE1) Theatre which has twice played a leading role in the nation's theatrical history. Lilian *Baylis became the manager in 1912 and turned it into a Shakespeare theatre (by 1923 an entire cycle of his plays had been performed). In 1931 she extended her activities to a similar programme for north London at *Sadler's Wells, but from 1934 Sadler's Wells concentrated entirely on ballet and opera while drama continued at the Old Vic. The other great period was 1963–76, when this was the first home of the *National Theatre under its founder director, Laurence Olivier.

The Old Vic originally opened in 1818 as the Royal Coburg. It was renamed the Royal Victoria in 1833 in honour of the young princess, and later in the 19C it acquired its lasting nickname.

O level see *exams.

Oliver Twist; or, the Parish boy's progress (1838) Novel by *Dickens with illustrations by *Cruikshank, published as a monthly serial in *Bentley's Miscellany* from February 1837. Oliver's mother dies giving birth to him in the workhouse, where as a child he dares to ask for more gruel, outraging the parish beadle, Mr Bumble (who later observes, at the time of his own downfall, that the *'law is a ass'). Oliver is sucked into London's underworld through a chance meeting with another child, the skilled pickpocket Jack Dawkins, better known as the Artful Dodger. The Dodger enrols him in the gang of child thieves run by an old Jew, Fagin; others involved in their operations are Bill Sikes and his girlfriend, Nancy, a prostitute. These are the characters the reader remembers, but there is a separate respectable world (that of Mr Brownlow and Mrs Maylie) to which Oliver turns out to be somewhat improbably connected. To help Oliver, Nancy liaises with this other world and is murdered by Bill Sikes. In the resulting chase Sikes accidentally hangs himself. Fagin ends on the gallows, and Oliver is adopted by Mr Brownlow.

Dickens aimed for a brutally realistic account of London's slums and criminals, but the appeal of his young thieves has given a more romantic edge to the many adaptations of the book. Outstanding have been the film of 1948, directed by David Lean with Alec Guinness as Fagin and Robert Newton as Bill Sikes; and *Oliver!* (1960), the stage musical by Lionel Bart (b. 1930).

Laurence **Olivier** (1907–89, kt 1947, baron 1970) Perhaps the last great actor in the old tradition of heroic self-indulgence. He played every part with a frank enjoyment of theatricality which made the experience even more memorable for his audience. In the 1930s he established himself as a wide-ranging Shakespearean actor – alternating Romeo and Mercutio with John Gielgud at the New Theatre in 1935, and playing Hamlet, Henry V, Sir Toby Belch, Iago and Coriolanus at the Old Vic from 1937. By the end of that decade he had also demonstrated a powerful screen personality in *Wuthering Heights* (1939). His marriage in 1940 to Vivien Leigh (his second wife) seemed to complete the image of the romantic star.

From the mid-40s he excelled in directing himself in Shakespeare on film. The dramatically shot *Henry V*

(1944), with its timely excesses of patriotism, was followed by *Hamlet* (1948) and finally by the melodramatically sinister *Richard III* (1956). When the new wave of British drama began in the late 1950s, Olivier was immediately part of it – giving one of his most brilliant performances as the world-weary music-hall comedian, Archie Rice, in John Osborne's The *Entertainer* (1957).

As an actor of such wide range, and a successful producer and director, Olivier was a natural choice to bring the *National Theatre into existence in 1963. Together with his new wife Joan Plowright (they had married in 1961), he built up a brilliant company and repertoire at the Old Vic, scene of many of his past successes. He wisely involved Kenneth *Tynan in the choice of plays. Olivier played cameo roles in the company with as much zest as the blockbusters (which included his celebrated portrayal of the father in Eugene O'Neill's *Long Day's Journey into Night*). He handed over to Peter Hall in 1973, three years before the National's move to its custom-built home on the South Bank (where the main auditorium is called the Olivier in his honour).

Olivier subsequently busied himself mainly with television and films (including *Sleuth* 1972, *Marathon Man* 1976, *The Boys from Brazil* 1978). In 1970 he became the first actor to be given a peerage, just as Irving had been the first to be knighted – a link reflecting the outstanding position of both in their profession.

Olympia (London W6) The earliest of London's great exhibition halls, built in Hammersmith in 1884. It was the home of spectacular live entertainment (in particular *Bertram Mills Circus), and it housed the *Motor Show from 1905, the first *Royal International Horse Show in 1907 and the first *Ideal Home Exhibition in 1908, though recently it has lost these events to more modern halls.

The biggest annual attraction at Olympia between the wars: poster for the Bertram Mills Circus in 1922.

British gold medallists at the Olympic Games since World War II

1948 London
Rowing *Coxless pairs:* 'Ran' Laurie and John Wilson
Double sculls: Richard Burnell and Bertie Bushnell
Yachting *Swallow class:* Stewart Morris and David Bond

1952 Helsinki
Equestrian *Prix des Nations, team:* Wilfred White on Nizefella, Douglas Stewart on Aherlow, Harry Llewellyn on Foxhunter

Oslo
Winter Games *Figure skating:* Jeannette Altwegg

1956 Melbourne
Boxing *Flyweight:* Terry Spinks
Lightweight: Dick McTaggart
Fencing *Individual foil:* Gillian Sheen
Swimming *100 metres backstroke:* Judith Grinham
Track & field *3000 metres steeplechase:* Christopher Brasher

Stockholm
Equestrian *Three-day event, team:* Frank Weldon on Kilbarry, Laurence Rook on Wild Venture, Albert Hill on Countryman III

1960 Rome
Swimming *200 metres breaststroke:* Anita Lonsbrough
Track & field *50 kilometres walk:* Don Thompson

1964 Tokyo
Track & field *800 metres:* Ann Packer
20 kilometres walk: Ken Matthews
Long jump: Lynn Davies
Long jump: Mary Rand

Innsbruck
Winter Games *Two-man bobsleigh:* Tony Nash and
Robin Dixon

1968 Mexico City
Boxing *Middleweight:* Chris Finnegan
Equestrian *Three-day event, team:* Derek Allhusen on Lochinvar, Richard Meade on Cornishman V, Reuben Jones on The Poacher
Shooting *Clay pigeon:* Bob Braithwaite
Track & field *400 metres hurdles:* David Hemery

Acapulco
Yachting *Flying Dutchman:* Rodney Pattisson and Iain MacDonald-Smith

1972 Munich
Equestrian *Three-day event, individual:* Richard Meade on Laurieston
Three-day event, team: Richard Meade on Laurieston, Mary Gordon-Watson on Cornishman V, Bridget Parker on Cornish Gold
Track & field *Pentathlon:* Mary Peters

Kiel
Yachting *Flying Dutchman:* Rodney Pattisson and Christopher Davies

1976 Montreal
Modern Pentathlon *Team:* Jim Fox, Danny Nightingale, Adrian Parker
Swimming *200 metres breaststroke:* David Wilkie

Kingston
Yachting *Tornado:* Reg White and John Osborn

Innsbruck
Winter Games *Figure skating:* John Curry

1980 Moscow
Swimming *100 metres breaststroke:* Duncan Goodhew
Track & field *100 metres:* Allan Wells
800 metres: Steve Ovett
1500 metres: Sebastian Coe
Decathlon: Daley Thompson

Lake Placid
Winter Games *Figure skating:* Robin Cousins

1984 Los Angeles
Rowing *Coxed fours:* Martin Cross, Richard Budgett, Andrew Holmes, Steve Redgrave, Adrian Ellison
Shooting *Small-bore rifle, three positions:* Malcolm Cooper
Track & field *1500 metres:* Sebastian Coe
Decathlon: Daley Thompson
Javelin: Tessa Sanderson

Sarajevo
Winter Games *Ice dance:* Jayne Torvill and Christopher Dean

1988 Seoul
Rowing *Coxless pairs:* Andrew Holmes and Steve Redgrave
Shooting *Small-bore rifle, three positions:* Malcolm Cooper
Swimming *100 metres breaststroke:* Adrian Moorhouse
Team games *Hockey:* Ian Taylor, Veryan Pappin, David Faulkner, Paul Barber, Stephen Martin, Jon Potter, Richard Dodds, Martyn Grimley, Stephen Batchelor, Richard Leman, James Kirkwood, Kulbir Bhaura, Sean Kerly, Robert Clift, Imran Sherwani, Russell Garcia.
Yachting *Star:* Mike McIntyre and Bryn Vaile

1992 Barcelona
Cycling *4000 metres individual pursuit:* Chris Boardman
Rowing *Coxless pairs:* Matthew Pinsent and Steve Redgrave
Coxed pairs: Jonny Searle, Greg Searle and Garry Herbert
Track & field *100 metres:* Linford Christie
400 metres hurdles: Sally Gunnell

Olympic Games The modern Olympic Games, taking place every four years, were inaugurated in Greece in 1896. This was achieved largely on the initiative of a French baron, Pierre de Coubertin, who hoped to revive in Europe the manly ideals which he felt were represented in the ancient Greek games, held at Olympia from at least 776 BC (they lasted 1000 years, until banned by a Roman emperor in about AD 393). Women athletes took part in the modern games from 1928. The range of competitive events was small at first but has steadily extended – including now, to the amazement of many, synchronized swimming with clips on the competitors' noses. The games have been held in Britain only twice, on each occasion in London (1908 in the newly completed *White City, 1948 at Wembley). Manchester has mounted a strong campaign to secure the millennium games in 2000.

Although the credit for establishing the modern games goes rightly to Coubertin, the idea itself was not his. The Greeks had made several attempts during the 19C to revive the Olympics, and the baron had a British predecessor of whom he was well aware. At Much Wenlock, in Shropshire, a local doctor and MP – William Brookes – established in 1850 the Wenlock Olympian Society, with the stated aim of improving the moral, physical and intellectual well-being of the local people by awarding prizes at an annual athletics contest. There were laurel crowns, and medallions depicting the Greek goddess of victory; and in 1890 the Wenlock games made a considerable fuss of a distinguished visitor, Baron Pierre de Coubertin. In an article later that year, entitled *Les Jeux Olympiques à Much Wenlock*, Coubertin wrote that the real impetus for the Olympic revival had come, 40 years earlier, from Dr Brookes. But after the heady success of the Greek games in 1896, Much Wenlock had no further mention in the baron's reminiscences. Meanwhile the Shropshire town continues to hold each year what it calls the Wenlock Olympian Games.

A parallel Olympic movement, the Paralympic Games, has been closely linked with the main event since Rome in 1960. This has a more direct origin in Britain, at *Stoke Mandeville in 1948.

OM see Order of *Merit.

Omar Khayyám Persian poet of the 12C who became a household name in Victorian times through the very free translation by Edward FitzGerald (1809–83) of his four-line verses, or *rubáiyát* in Persian. First published in 1859, they were reissued with considerable revisions by Fitz-Gerald in 1868, 1872 and 1879 (the reason why quoted versions of the same passage so frequently differ). The languid verses, sensual, fatalistic, laced with homely truths and exotic names, appealed to the 19C fascination with the orient and offered an antidote to an increasingly materialistic and hard-working age. The most popular quatrain of all has been the one offering a romantic escape into the life of a bohemian:

> Here with a Loaf of Bread beneath the bough,
> A Flask of Wine, a Book of Verse – and Thou
> Beside me singing in the Wilderness –
> And Wilderness is Paradise enow.

Ombudsman An official appointed from the early 19C in Sweden to protect the legal interests of a group. In the 20C an official of this kind, charged with protecting the public, was established in other Scandinavian countries. The idea was adopted in New Zealand in 1962 and in Britain in 1966, when Sir Edmund Compton was appointed the first Parliamentary Commissioner for Administration. Popularly known from the start as the Ombudsman, his brief was to investigate complaints against government departments, passed to him by MPs

on behalf of their constituents. Recent Ombudsmen have also held the post of Health Service Commissioner, looking into complaints against the National Health Service. In the late 1980s, in the deregulation surrounding *Big Bang, non-statutory financial ombudsmen were set up in the City of London in the fields of banking, insurance and the building societies.

Omdurman see Lord *Kitchener.

Omega Workshops Enterprise established in 1913 in Fitzroy Square, London, by Roger *Fry with the intention of producing furniture, fabrics and ceramics designed by artists, particularly those connected with the *Bloomsbury Group. A latter-day version of the more successful undertaking by William *Morris, it lasted only until 1920.

Omnibus (BBC since 1967) Arts programme which succeeded *Monitor; it has been in recent years the rival of The *South Bank Show on independent television. The name was previously used for a similar programme in the USA (ABC 1952–61), introduced by Alistair Cooke.

Once in royal David's city see Mrs *Alexander.

'**Once more unto the breach**' see *Henry V*.

Ondine (1958) Ballet by Frederick *Ashton, setting the story of *Undine* (1811, by Friedrich de la Motte Fouqué) to music commissioned from Hans Werner Henze. The part of Ondine, a sprit of the waters who has no soul until she marries a mortal and bears his child, was created by Margot *Fonteyn with sinuously liquid movements; her lover, Palemon, was danced by Michael *Somes.

one-day cricket Matches introduced in 1963 to enliven professional cricket. Most of the teams playing are those in the *county championship. There are three competitions: the NatWest Bank Trophy (known as the Gillette until 1980); the Benson and Hedges Cup; and a league played on Sundays, known as the Refuge Assurance League (1987–91) and previously as the John Player League (1969–86).

One Foot in the Grave (BBC from 1990) Television situation comedy which reached record audience levels with its third series, in 1993. Its appeal is based on the ever-mounting indignation of elderly Victor Meldrew at the imperfections of modern life. Victor is played by Richard Wilson, and his wife Margaret by Annette Crosbie.

Captain **O'Neill** see *Northern Ireland.

'**one of us**' see *wets.

One Thousand Guineas see under Thousand.

'**Only connect!**' see *Howard's End*.

Only Fools and Horses (BBC from 1981) Comedy series about a pair of low-life brothers, Del and Rodney Trotter (played by David *Jason and Nicholas Lyndhurst), which grew steadily in popularity during the 1980s. Its special editions had become Christmas favourites by the early 1990s.

Arthur **Onslow** see *Speaker.

Onward, Christian Soldiers One of the most self-confident of Victorian hymns, though its tone is largely explained by its origin. It was written in 1864 by Sabine Baring-Gould (1834–1924), to be sung by children

Winners of the Open since World War II

1946	Sam Snead (USA)	St Andrews		1970	Jack Nicklaus (USA)	St Andrews
1947	Fred Daly (UK)	Hoylake		1971	Lee Trevino (USA)	Royal Birkdale
1948	Henry Cotton (UK)	Muirfield		1972	Lee Trevino (USA)	Muirfield
1949	Bobby Locke (SAf)	Sandwich		1973	Tom Weiskopf (USA)	Troon
1950	Bobby Locke (SAf)	Troon		1974	Gary Player (SAf)	Royal Lytham
1951	Max Faulkner (UK)	Portrush		1975	Tom Watson (USA)	Carnoustie
1952	Bobby Locke (SAf)	Royal Lytham		1976	Johnny Miller (USA)	Royal Birkdale
1953	Ben Hogan (USA)	Carnoustie		1977	Tom Watson (USA)	Turnberry
1954	Peter Thomson (Aus)	Royal Birkdale		1978	Jack Nicklaus (USA)	St Andrews
1955	Peter Thomson (Aus)	St Andrews		1979	Seve Ballesteros (Spa)	Royal Lytham
1956	Peter Thomson (Aus)	Hoylake		1980	Tom Watson (USA)	Muirfield
1957	Bobby Locke (SAf)	St Andrews		1981	Bill Rogers (USA)	Sandwich
1958	Peter Thomson (Aus)	Royal Lytham		1982	Tom Watson (USA)	Royal Troon
1959	Gary Player (SAf)	Muirfield		1983	Tom Watson (USA)	Royal Birkdale
1960	Kel Nagle (Aus)	St Andrews		1984	Seve Ballesteros (Spa)	St Andrews
1961	Arnold Palmer (USA)	Royal Birkdale		1985	Sandy Lyle (UK)	Sandwich
1962	Arnold Palmer (USA)	Troon		1986	Greg Norman (Aus)	Turnberry
1963	Bob Charles (NZ)	Royal Lytham		1987	Nick Faldo (UK)	Muirfield
1964	Tony Lema (USA)	St Andrews		1988	Seve Ballesteros (Spa)	Royal Lytham
1965	Peter Thomson (Aus)	Royal Birkdale		1989	Mark Calcavecchia (USA)	Royal Troon
1966	Jack Nicklaus (USA)	Muirfield		1990	Nick Faldo (UK)	St Andrews
1967	Roberto de Vicenzo (Arg)	Hoylake		1991	Ian Baker-Finch (Aus)	Royal Birkdale
1968	Gary Player (SAf)	Carnoustie		1992	Nick Faldo (UK)	Muirfield
1969	Tony Jacklin (UK)	Royal Lytham				

carrying banners in a traditional Whit Monday procession in the parish where he was curate. He used a tune from Haydn. The one to which the hymn is now sung was composed for it by Arthur *Sullivan in 1871.

007 see Ian *Fleming.

The **Open** The world's oldest international golf championship, played annually since 1860, when the first event was held at *Prestwick. The only missing years have been during the two world wars and in 1871. The reason for the lack of contest in 1871 was that the original trophy, a championship belt, had been won outright in 1870 after three successive wins by Tom Morris (he and his father, also called Tom Morris, had between them won 7 of the first 11 championships). The Open resumed in 1872 with the present trophy, the famous silver claret jug, donated jointly by Scotland's three leading clubs, Prestwick, the Honourable Company of Edinburgh Golfers and the Royal and Ancient. The contest was originally played over 36 holes, but since 1892 has been over 72 holes.

Open Brethren see *Plymouth Brethren.

open-field system (also known as strip-farming) Method of agriculture, widespread in medieval Europe and from Anglo-Saxon times in arable areas of Britain, particularly in the Midlands. Each peasant had several long strips of land, in separate parts of large open fields, on which to grow his family's food. This arrangement shared out with some degree of fairness the areas of better and worse soil. His planting was part of a communal plan, because crop rotation was organized field by field. The development of a market economy and of wages (instead of days worked on the lord's own land) meant that the open fields became divided among tenant farmers, and gradually much of the *common land was also enclosed.

Open Spaces Society see *common land.

Open University A pioneering educational venture, introduced in 1969 by the Labour government under Harold Wilson; it has proved a great success. The university offers part-time degree courses which are open to

anyone, without need for formal academic qualifications. Tuition is by correspondence and through television and radio broadcasts, supplemented by video cassettes; and there is a network of study centres where tutors and fellow students can be contacted. There is no time limit by which exams must be taken, but the degrees awarded are of the same standard as at conventional universities. In the early 1990s about 75,000 people of all ages were enrolled as undergraduates. The administration is at Milton Keynes in Buckinghamshire.

Opera North The youngest of the five major opera companies in Britain. It was founded in 1978 as a northern branch of *English National Opera, and became fully independent in 1981. Its home is the Grand Theatre in Leeds, but it tours throughout the Midlands.

Ophelia Character in *Hamlet and the subject of a painting in the Tate Gallery by *Millais, who depicted her floating to her death in a stream, garlanded with flowers, as described by Gertrude in the play. Millais painted the flowers and stream from nature, according to strict *Pre-Raphaelite principles. The figure was Elizabeth Siddal (later the wife of *Rossetti) lying in a bath of water, kept warm by lamps beneath it.

Peter and Iona **Opie** Husband and wife team (Peter 1918–82, m. 1943 Iona Balfour, b. 1923) who made a major contribution to the study of children's folklore and literature. They published in 1951 the definitive study of nursery rhymes (*The Oxford Dictionary of Nursery Rhymes*). Travels round the country to record the present-day activities of children, many of which are firmly rooted in the past, resulted in *The Lore and Language of Schoolchildren* (1959) and *Children's Games in Street and Playground* (1969).

Opium Wars (1839–42, 1856–60) Two of the more shameful episodes in British imperial history. On each occasion China was invaded to protect the illegal but immensely profitable opium trade, a major part of the commercial enterprise of the *East India Company. Victory in the first war brought *Hong Kong into British hands; the second war, fought by Britain and France together, ended with the capture of Peking and the sacking of the emperor's summer palace. The effect and underlying purpose of each war was the opening up of China to western interests, thus beginning decades of exploitation.

Opposition The largest political party in the House of *Commons other than the one in power, with a duty to criticize the actions of government and to be ready when the time comes to form a government. The term was in use from the early days of the *two-party system, but the formal parliamentary concept of His (or Her) Majesty's Opposition first emerged during a debate in 1826. In 1937 the office of the leader of the Opposition was officially recognized and the holder was granted a state salary in addition to that earned as an MP. He or she presides over the shadow cabinet, a group of ministers-in-waiting who are allotted portfolios corresponding to those in the real *cabinet and who lead from the *front bench in debates on their own subject. A Conservative shadow cabinet is chosen by the leader of the Opposition, but a Labour shadow cabinet is elected by the party's members of parliament.

opting out A central theme of Conservative policy in the early 1990s in two areas, health and education. The intention is to introduce in hospitals and schools a measure of market discipline and increased customer choice. Hospitals choosing to opt out are more often described as having taken *trust status.

Secondary *state schools, and primary schools with more than 300 pupils, were encouraged under the Education Reform Act of 1988 to apply to become independent of *LEA (local education authority) control, with considerable cash incentives to cover the cost of the change. A school can only apply to opt out after a majority of the parents has voted in favour; permission then depends on the secretary of state for education. Any

school allowed to do so is run by a board of governors, among whom parents are strongly represented, and it becomes responsible for its own budget and its own admissions policy. Such schools are still paid for out of public funds and are known as grant-maintained – to distinguish them from maintained schools, those under LEA control. The first two to be given permission to opt out, in February 1989, were the Skegness Grammar School in Lincolnshire and the Audenshaw High School in Greater Manchester.

The free-market theory is that the better schools will expand, as more parents choose them, while the worse will correspondingly shrink and fade away. Critics argue that the better schools will cream off the brighter children (bringing back the injustices associated with the eleven-plus), with the result that children already socially disadvantaged will be restricted to the schools withering for lack of funds. However it transpired that many of the first schools to opt out were planning to retain the *comprehensive principle of automatic admission for children within a catchment area.

Teething troubles of a more organizational nature were revealed in 1992 at Stratford School in east London, where there were prolonged hostilities between the headteacher, Anne Snelling, and her board of governors; solving the problem was complicated by the fact that, with no LEA involvement, a very local problem became the direct responsibility of the secretary of state for education. Legislation before parliament late in 1992 proposed a solution in the form of a Funding Agency for Schools, with responsibility for the grant-maintained sector. By that stage approximately 340 state secondary schools had become grant-maintained, and parents in about the same number had voted to follow suit (out of some 4200 schools in all). But the government remained confident that the majority would eventually opt out, announcing a target of 1500 by April 1994.

Ophelia *by Millais, ultra-realistic both in the plants and in the semi-submerged young woman (Elizabeth Siddal).*

Options for Change The name given to government proposals, announced by the secretary of state for defence in 1991, for reducing and restructuring the army in response to the end of the Cold War. The planned reduction was from 144,000 regular trained personnel in 1991 to 104,000 in the mid-1990s, cutting back from 55 infantry battalions to 39 and from 19 armoured regiments to 11. The first new grouping, in 1992, involved the *Ulster Defence Regiment. In February 1993 the secretary of state for defence, Malcolm Rifkind, announced that because of extra commitments in Bosnia and elsewhere the proposed reduction in numbers would be less than originally planned.

opus anglicanum (Latin for 'English work') The medieval term for English embroidery, used now in particular of the superb work done in the 13–14C. With its bright and lively figures, and rich use of silver gilt thread, this embroidery was recognized at the time as the best in Europe and was widely exported for church vestments.

Orange Town in the south of France, north of Avignon, which was the centre of a small independent principality in the Middle Ages. The title of prince of Orange was inherited in the 16C by a man whose life and career had no direct connections with the area – William the Silent, the leader of the Dutch in their struggle for independence from Spain. Orange was equally remote from the life of his great-grandson, the prince of Orange who became king of England in 1689 as *William III. But the name has survived in British history through the significance attached by Protestants in Northern Ireland to William's victory at the *Boyne. A secret order of Orangemen was founded in 1795 to uphold Protestant supremacy against Irish nationalism; and Orange lodges have remained a feature of life in Ulster, organizing marches and processions on July 12, the supposed date of the Battle of the Boyne.

Oranges and Lemons Nursery rhyme which imitates the chimes of bells in various London churches. It accompanies a game in which children pass under an arch of raised arms. As with *London Bridge is falling down*, the excitement is that at a certain moment the arms will descend to trap a child – in this case after the recitation of 'Chop, chop, chop, chop, *chop!*'. The title comes from the best-known of the many verses ('Oranges and Lemons, say the bells of St Clement's'). Two London churches claim to be the one in question. *St Clement Danes has won the argument in the public's mind, but St Clement's Eastcheap is the stronger contender; it stands near the wharves where citrus fruit used to be unloaded.

Baroness **Orczy** (Emma Orczy, 1865-1947) Author, born in Hungary the daughter of Baron Felix Orczy. She lived in England from 1880. She made her name with *The *Scarlet Pimpernel*, but wrote many other historical romances, thrillers and detective stories.

orders of chivalry Apart from the *peerage, the system of honours in Britain is based on the medieval concept of orders of knighthood – though only one order, the Garter, dates from that period. The majority of honours are awarded on two occasions each year, in the New Year Honours and the Birthday Honours (announced on the *Queen's Birthday). At the end of each *parliament the prime minister also recommends a list of Dissolution Honours.

In 1993 John Major announced proposals to reduce the number of honours awarded automatically to senior members of the armed forces and of the foreign and civil service, and to reward instead any exceptional contribution to the community, particularly if done on a voluntary basis. But knighthoods for those who contribute to party political funds seemed likely to continue. Political honours became the subject of particular scandal in 1922 when Lloyd George, through his agent Maundy Gregory, established a tariff – £10,000 for a knighthood, £30,000 for a baronetcy and up to £100,000 for a peerage.

The orders of chivalry in regular use today, in sequence of precedence, are: the Most Noble Order of the *Garter; the Most Ancient and Most Noble Order of the *Thistle; the Most Honourable Order of the Bath (founded in 1725); the Order of *Merit; the Most Distinguished Order of St Michael and St George (1818); the Royal Victorian Order (1896); the Most Excellent Order of the British Empire (1917); and the Order of the *Companions of Honour. Appointments to the Garter, the Order of Merit, the Thistle and the Royal Victorian Order are in the personal gift of the monarch. The others are on the recommendation of the prime minister.

The four orders in which the majority of honours are awarded all have a similar hierarchy, reflected in the letters which members of the order may place after their names. The final letters in each case are B for Bath, MG for St Michael and St George, VO for the Royal Victorian Order and BE for the British Empire. The hierarchy, in descending order, is:

GCB (GCMG, GCVO, GBE)	Knight or Dame Grand Cross
DCB (DCMG, DCVO, DBE) and	Dame Commander and
KCB (KCMG, KCVO, KBE)	Knight Commander
CB (CMG)	Companion
CVO (CBE)	Commander
LVO	Lieutenant
OBE	Officer
MVO (MBE)	Member

The greatest number of appointments are to the Order of the British Empire, in which there has also been a lower and widely conferred honour, the British Empire Medal (BEM). Described as for those who did not qualify by rank for the higher grades of the Order, the BEM was abolished in John Major's 1993 reforms – to be in effect merged, for future recipients, with the MBE.

Those appointed Dame use it in front of their names (Dame Mary Smith), whereas knights use Sir (Sir John Smith).

ordination of women The issue which has proved most divisive within the *Church of England in recent years. George *Carey, archbishop of Canterbury, at one point declared it a 'serious heresy' to oppose this development; on the other side a cabinet minister, John *Gummer, resigned in 1992 from the General Synod when the vote finally went in favour of ordination.

The English parent body of the worldwide *Anglican Communion had lagged behind its offspring on this matter. In the USA a woman became an Anglican priest in 1981, and there has been a female bishop there since 1989; there is also now a female bishop in New Zealand. In Britain the General Synod agreed in 1985 to allow women to take holy orders as deacons (the lowest level of the priesthood) and the first female deacons were ordained in 1986. As such they were able to conduct all services except for certain solemn moments which are reserved for priests; these include the Prayer of Consecration in the communion service and the Blessing.

There were two main strands of opposition. The *Anglo-Catholic wing of the church follows the lead of the Vatican in rejecting women priests. At the other extreme certain fundamentalist *Evangelicals argue that the Bible rules out the concept. Opponents united under the name of the Cost of Conscience movement, which claimed some 3000 clergy among its supporters.

Ordnance Survey (Southampton) Government department responsible for providing maps of Britain (in scales ranging up to 1:1250, or 50 inches to the mile, for densely populated areas). It was founded in 1791 to chart the country for the ordnance (the artillery) and it rapidly acquired a sense of urgency because of the threatened invasion by Napoleon; for this reason the first county map to be published, in 1801, was of Kent. That was one inch to the mile, but by 1848 London was being mapped at 60 inches to the mile. Since World War II the entire country has been surveyed on a metric National Grid, giving every place a precise reference point; this involved the setting up of nearly 20,000 triangulation stations (commonly known as trig points, many of them marked by a concrete trig pillar). In 1971 the information began to be stored in digital form on computer, and this is increasingly how it is supplied to other mapmakers. Under the *Next Steps programme, the Ordnance Survey became in 1990 an executive agency reporting to the secretary of state for the environment.

Origin of Species see Charles *Darwin.

Orkney (20,000 in 1991, administrative centre Kirkwall) Since 1975 the *islands area covering the Orkneys.

Orkneys Group of islands in the north of Scotland, separated from *John o' Groats by the Pentland Firth. The largest island is Mainland; on it is the capital, Kirkwall, and a quite exceptional group of prehistoric monuments (*Skara Brae, *Maes Howe, the Stones of Stenness and the Ring of Brodgar). The second largest of the group, Hoy, is the only one to have dramatic scenery – most notably the Old Man of Hoy (a detached sandstone pillar rising 137m/450ft from the sea) and St John's Cliff (a sheer cliff of 347m/1140ft). The Dwarfie Stone, also on Hoy, has chambers hollowed out in prehistoric times and is believed to be a rock tomb. The sheltered anchorage between Hoy and Mainland is *Scapa Flow.

The Orkneys were raided from the 8C by *Vikings, who settled in the 9C. The jarls (or earls) who ruled the islands were vassals of the kings of Norway or Denmark until the 15C, when the Orkneys came to the Scottish crown (with the *Shetlands) as part of the dowry of a Danish princess, betrothed to James III.

Orlando the Marmalade Cat The central character of a series of children's books written and illustrated by Kathleen Hale (b. 1898), which began with *Orlando the Marmalade Cat: A Camping Holiday* (1938) and continued until *Orlando the Marmalade Cat, and the Water Cats* (1972). The early volumes were notable for their large and bright pages of colour lithography, making much of Orlando's marmalade fur.

Joe **Orton** (1933–67) The great anarchist of modern British theatre, both in his life and his plays. From his time at RADA in the 1950s he lived with Kenneth Halliwell, seven years his senior. Together they aspired to become writers; together they went to jail in 1962 for defacing public library books with mocking images and comments. Prison seems to have focused Orton's anarchic talent. He emerged to write a series of brilliantly outrageous farces, brimming with epigrams and using the shock of laughter to seduce audiences into accepting the unacceptable. His first full-length play, *Entertaining Mr Sloane* (1964) was followed by *Loot* (1965) and *What the Butler Saw* (produced posthumously in 1969). Unlike their earlier work together, these plays did not have Halliwell as co-author. Jealous of Orton's success (and of his promiscuity), Halliwell killed him in 1967 by battering his head with a hammer; he then took an overdose of sleeping pills.

George **Orwell** (pseudonym of Eric Blair, 1903–50) Novelist, essayist and author of two of the most successful political fables of the 20C. Born in India and educated at Eton, he returned to the east for his first employment – with the British police in Burma (1922–7). It was a formative but most unsuitable setting for a man of his political sympathies, and he reacted by spending the following years in the vagrancy which he described in *Down and Out in Paris and London*. His observations of everyday working-class conditions during the Depression were expressed in *The *Road to Wigan Pier*, and he described in *Homage to Catalonia* (1938) his experiences fighting on the Republican side in the Spanish Civil War. Although a committed Socialist, he was never a man to toe a party line; and hatred of repressive orthodoxy of any kind lay behind his two last books, the fables which brought him a far wider readership than before, *Animal Farm* and *Nineteen Eighty-Four*.

OS see *calendar and *Ordnance Survey.

John **Osborne** (b. 1929) Playwright whose *Look Back in Anger* (1956) brought a breath of much needed fresh air into the English theatre and saddled him with the reputation of being the leading *angry young man. He followed it immediately with an equally brilliant play, *The *Entertainer*, subsequent successes included *Luther* (1961) and *Inadmissible Evidence* (1964). He has published two volumes of characteristically candid autobiography – *A Better Class of Person* (1981), *Almost a Gentleman* (1991).

Osborne House (1km/0.5m SE of East Cowes) In the early 1840s Queen Victoria and Prince Albert, with a young family, were looking for a property on the Isle of Wight which would be, in her words, 'a place of one's own, quiet and retired'. In 1845 they bought Osborne, pleasantly situated with a private beach, and employed Thomas *Cubitt to build for them the present house, replacing an earlier one. It was completed by 1851, with its two towers imitating medieval Italian bell towers. The wooden Swiss Cottage was built in the grounds in 1853–4 for the royal children, as a place for educational experiments in housekeeping and cookery, and the extraordinary Durbar Room with its Indian interior was added to the house by Cubitt's firm in 1890–3. Osborne with all its contents, surviving just as when Victoria and her family lived there, was given to the nation by Edward VII in 1902.

Kitty **O'Shea** see Charles Stewart *Parnell.

Ossian The Scottish name for the semi-legendary Irish poet, Oisin, son of the warrior hero Finn McCool. The name became widely known after the success of *Fingal, an Ancient Epic Poem composed by Ossian*, published in 1762 by James Macpherson, who presented it as a translation of an ancient Gaelic manuscript. It was proved later to be entirely his own work, apart from a few scraps of old ballads. It was he who had turned Ireland's warrior, Finn, into a Scottish ruler, Fingal. But the Celtic twilight imagined by Macpherson chimed perfectly with the beginnings of the *Romantic movement, and his invention led to such lasting Scottish features as *Fingal's Cave. Within a few years there followed the similar fabrications of *Chatterton.

Osterley Park (20km/12m W of central London) House built originally for Thomas *Gresham in the 1570s, and extensively remodelled by Robert *Adam in 1761–80. The façade acknowledges the span of two centuries, with the redbrick Tudor corner towers linked by a

Overseas aid, in £bn

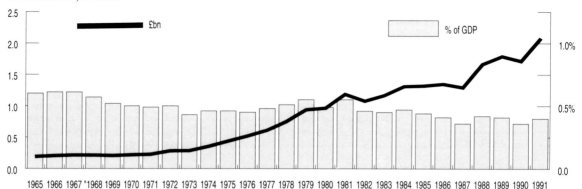

Source: Annual Abstract of Statistics (see *Central Office of Statistics).

pillared portico, but the superb interiors are entirely of the 18c. The sequence of state rooms survives as a virtually unaltered display of the *Adam style.

***Othello*, the *Moor of Venice* (*c*.1603) Tragedy by *Shakespeare on the theme of the 'green-eyed monster', jealousy. Othello, a Moor (meaning that he comes from north Africa), has risen to high rank in the service of Venice and has married Desdemona, the daughter of a senator. He is sent to command the Venetian forces in Cyprus, where Iago, an officer in the army, sets about destroying him. Iago's resentment derives from Othello having promoted Cassio rather than himself, and his scheme is aimed at both of them. He insinuates into Othello's mind the dark suspicion that Cassio is having an affair with Desdemona, so that innocent requests by Desdemona on Cassio's behalf come to seem sinister. Iago tricks his own wife, Emilia (Desdemona's lady's maid), into procuring for him a handkerchief given by Othello to Desdemona, a token of his love; and he arranges for it to come into Cassio's possession. The sight of it seems final proof to the increasingly demented Othello. After a poignant bedtime scene in which Desdemona sings the willow song (obliquely about her own predicament), Emilia leaves her to sleep. Othello enters and strangles her ('put out the light, and then put out the light'). Emilia reveals all, Iago is killed, and Othello – fully aware now of Desdemona's innocence – stabs himself.

The play became the basis for another great work of art, Verdi's opera *Otello* (1887).

Peter **O'Toole** (b. 1932) Actor who is best known on film, but who also has a virtuoso presence in the theatre – in recent years, for example, in Keith Waterhouse's *Jeffrey Bernard is Unwell*. It was his portrayal of T.E. *Lawrence in *Lawrence of Arabia* which brought him stardom in 1962, followed by such films as *The Lion in Winter* (1968) and *Goodbye Mr Chips* (1969).

ounce see *weight.

Ouse The name of several rivers in England, of which the most important, the Great Ouse (about 257km/160m), rises in Northamptonshire and flows sluggishly northeast, draining the *Fens and entering the Wash at King's Lynn. For much of its last 60km/37m it is contained in a straight artificial channel, the main section of which is known as the New Bedford River.

The Yorkshire Ouse (92km/57m) joins the Trent to form the Humber estuary. The Sussex Ouse (48km/30m) flows into the English Channel at Newhaven.

'Out, damned spot!' see *Macbeth.

'Out, vile jelly!' see *King Lear.

Outward Bound (Rugby) Organization set up in 1941 by Kurt Hahn (founder also of *Gordonstoun) and Lawrence Holt (the owner of a shipping line) with the purpose of providing physical and mental challenges for young people. Each year about 12,000 men and women attend courses at five outdoor centres in Britain, and there are now more than 35 such training centres in other countries.

The **Oval** (London SE11) The county ground of *Surrey County Cricket Club, and – with Lord's – one of the two most regular locations for *Test matches. The area was already called the Kennington Oval, from the shape of the surrounding streets, before it was turned into a cricket ground in 1845. That same year the Surrey club was founded, and it played its first county match at the Oval (against Kent) in 1846; the first Test match here was in 1880 (against Australia). The most historic moment on the Surrey pitch has been *Hutton's record Test score for England in 1938.

Three great middle-distance runners in the 1984 Olympics: Steve Ovett, Steve Cram, Sebastian Coe.

Education and refinement thanks to Robert Owen: quadrille dancing by the girls of New Lanark (aquatint of 1825).

Ovaltine The name under which the Swiss malt extract Ovomaltine (with its main ingredients eggs and malt) was registered in 1906 in Britain. It is said that the change was a slip of the pen by a ministry clerk, but Ovaltine has subsequently become the drink's name in many other parts of the world. Its fame was greatly increased by the Ovaltiney half hour, broadcast from 1935 on Radio Luxembourg. The show led to the formation of a children's club, the League of Ovaltineys.

'over here' The third and most serious objection by British males to US soldiers and airmen posted in Britain during World War II. They were described as 'over-paid, over-sexed and over here'.

Overlord see *D-day.

Overlord embroidery Vast embroidery depicting the events of *D-day. Designed by Sandra Lawrence and created in 34 panels by women of the Royal School of Needlework, it is 15m/49ft longer than the *Bayeux tapestry and consciously rivals its great predecessor, celebrating a successful return encounter – an invasion of Normandy to match the Norman Conquest. It hangs now in the D-day Museum at Portsmouth.

overseas aid During the 1970s the United Nations proposed that the developed countries should give 0.7% of their gross national product in aid to the Third World. At the end of that decade the UK was giving about 0.5%; the national figure in the early 1990s is closer to 0.3%.

Steve **Ovett** (b. 1955) Athlete who for a while played leapfrog with Sebastian *Coe in breaking world records over 1500 metres and a mile. Between 1980 and 1983 Ovett set new world figures for 1500 metres on three occasions and for the mile twice. Meanwhile at the 1980 Olympic Games he had won gold for the 800 metres and silver for the 1500, with Coe taking the silver and gold respectively. As a measure of Ovett's versatility, he won gold at the 1986 Commonwealth Games in the 5000 metres.

Owain ap Gruffydd see Owen *Glendower.

Daniel **Owen** (1836–95) The leading novelist in the Welsh language. Born in *Mold, the son of a miner, he was by trade a tailor and had become a preacher before he began to write. The strong narrative, humour and lively characterization in his scenes of contemporary life have caused him to be compared to Dickens. His novels include *Hunangofiant Rhys Lewis, Gweinidog Bethel* (Autobiography of Rhys Lewis, minister of Bethel, 1885) and *Profedigaethau Enoc Huws* (The trials of Enoc Huws, 1891).

David **Owen** (b. 1938, baron 1992) Politician who retained his seat in the House of Commons (Plymouth Devonport 1974–92, previously Plymouth Sutton 1966–74) in spite of leaving the Labour party in 1981 to become one of the founders of the *SDP. In his career with the Labour party he had entered the cabinet in 1977 as an exceptionally young foreign secretary. He led the SDP from 1983 until it was disbanded in 1990. In 1987 he advised his followers not to accept the proposed merger with the Liberals; the majority voted the other way, and he was left at the head of a much diminished rump of the SDP. This was disbanded in 1990, and Owen did not contest his Plymouth seat in the 1992 general election. Later that year he was appointed joint chairman (with Cyrus Vance) of the international conference charged with attempting to end the war in what was formerly Yugoslavia.

Robert **Owen** (1771–1858) Industrialist, reformer and utopian socialist. Son of a Welsh postmaster, he made an early reputation managing a cotton mill in Manchester. He then bought the mills at *New Lanark on the Clyde and turned them into a model industrial community: his workers were well housed, goods were provided in the village store at little more than cost price, and the children were educated (he opened the country's first infant school there in 1816). New Lanark was profitable and became the object of widespread interest. Owen's thoughts moved on to common ownership, and several utopian communities were fostered by him (most notably at New Harmony in the USA), but none survived for long. He was regarded with increasing suspicion by the ruling classes (particularly after he had declared his rejection of conventional religion), but his ideas were influential in the development of the *cooperative movement and the *trade unions.

Wilfred **Owen** (1893–1918) The outstanding British poet of World War I. He was invalided home from the Somme in 1917 and in hospital met Siegfried *Sassoon, who later arranged the publication of his poems (1920). Owen returned to the trenches in 1918 and died attempting to cross a canal under machine-gun fire on November 4, a week before the armistice. No-one else expressed with such passionate intensity the utter waste of the war (so fully proved in his own short life and death), in such poems as *Anthem for Doomed Youth* and *Strange Meeting*. Benjamin Britten set nine of Owen's poems in his *War Requiem*.

*The **Owl and the Pussy-Cat*** (1871) The first and probably the best known of the nonsense songs by Edward *Lear. The two characters go to sea in a beautiful pea-green boat (with honey and plenty of money, wrapped up in a five-pound note). After some musical courtship they buy the ring in a pig's nose and get married by a turkey, before eating mince and slices of quince with a runcible spoon.

Oxbridge Term coined in the mid-19C for the combined traditions and products of Britain's two oldest universities, Oxford and Cambridge. 'Camford', an alternative name from the same period, failed to catch on.

Helen **Oxenbury** (b. 1938) Illustrator who in a famous series of 'board books' (from 1981) achieved wordless images which somehow hold the attention of children not much more than a year old.

Oxfam (Oxford) Britain's largest aid agency, founded in 1942 as the Oxford Committee for Famine Relief. This was a response by a group of people in Oxford to the distress caused in German-occupied countries by the British trade embargo. Aid was sent first to the starving in Greece in 1943. The name Oxfam, informally used for many years, was officially adopted in 1965. An influential initiative was the opening of an Oxfam shop in 1948 in Oxford's Broad Street (it is still there, the first of more than 500). Immediate aid to disaster areas remained the most widely publicized part of the work, but over the years a different priority gained in importance – long-term development projects to tackle the roots of poverty. Oxfam is now actively involved in a large number of Third World countries.

Oxford (99,000 in 1981) City and site of Britain's oldest university; administrative centre of Oxfordshire. The medieval town, first mentioned in the 10C, grew up in the angle formed by the junction of two rivers – the Thames (called locally the *Isis) and the Cherwell. The central crossroads of the old town is still known as the Carfax, a word deriving from the Latin for 'four forks'. The university, which began in the 12C, provides Oxford's main identity; but there has been considerable industrial development in the 20C, the result of *Morris setting up his car factory in the suburb of Cowley.

The first students found what accommodation they

could, and the earliest surviving college – University College – was originally a student hostel. Merton, founded in 1264, set the collegiate pattern which became standard in both Oxford and Cambridge, that of a self-governing institution in which teachers and students live together as a community. Each college was a private haven entered through a gatehouse and built around courtyards, known in Oxford as quadrangles or quads. A steady succession of such colleges was founded until the early 17C. There was then a gap (apart from Worcester in 1714) until the late 19C, when several new foundations included Oxford's first two colleges for women, Lady Margaret Hall (1878) and Somerville (1879). In the early 1990s nearly all the colleges are open to both sexes. This is true even of the most exclusive and brilliant of Oxford's colleges – All Souls, founded in 1438 and limited to a small number of graduates who win a place by competitive examination.

The college with the greatest number of individual claims to fame is Christ Church, known as 'the House'. Its original founder, Cardinal Wolsey, wanted it to have Oxford's largest quadrangle (Tom Quad) and largest dining hall, two distinctions which it retains. Its chapel serves, surprisingly, as the seat of the bishop of Oxford. A building of the 12–13C with a fan-vaulted roof of the late 15C, it had been the church of a priory which Wolsey closed down to build his college; when Henry VIII made Oxford a diocese in 1542, the college chapel became England's smallest cathedral. The entry to the quadrangle is through Tom Tower, an elaborate structure by Wren (1681) surmounting Wolsey's gateway and containing Great Tom, a huge bell recast from an earlier one in 1680. Christ Church also has an exceptional collection of old master paintings and drawings on display in its own picture gallery.

The main public building of the university, the Sheldonian Theatre (1663), was the first important architectural undertaking by *Wren; he based it on the Theatre of Marcellus in Rome. The striking domed Italian baroque building of the next century, the Radcliffe Camera (1737–49), was paid for from the bequest of a fashionable doctor, John Radcliffe (1650–1714) and was designed as a library by James *Gibbs; it is now part of the university library, the Bodleian, named after the man who revived Oxford's library in the early 17C, Thomas Bodley (1545–1613, kt 1604). The oldest section of the Bodleian, one of the six *copyright libraries, is Duke Humfrey's library, completed in 1488 to house the books (later dispersed) of Humfrey, duke of Gloucester (1391–1447).

The university church is the 15C St Mary's, whose tall spire is one of the many for which Oxford is famous ('that sweet city with her dreaming spires', in Matthew Arnold's phrase). It was in St Mary's that *Cranmer, Nicholas Ridley (1503–55) and Hugh Latimer (1485–1555) were tried for heresy. All three were burnt in Oxford and in 1841 the Martyrs' Memorial, designed by George Gilbert *Scott, was put up near the spot.

The original 17C building of the *Ashmolean Museum now houses the Museum of History and Science, which has an exceptional collection of scientific instruments. The university also has outstanding ethnographic holdings in the Pitt Rivers Museum. The *botanic gardens are the oldest in the country.

Oxford accent An old-fashioned phrase sometimes used, inaccurately, to mean *Received Pronunciation. In use from the early 20C, it was often derogatory in intent – the tones of Oxford undergraduates being considered affected and divisive. Winston Churchill was praised in 1940 for 'lacking the Oxford accent' and speaking 'as a Briton to Britons'.

Oxford bags Unusually broad trousers, fashionable in the university of Oxford between the wars.

The ***Oxford Book of English Verse*** Anthology edited by Arthur Quiller-Couch (1863–1944), which first appeared in 1900 and has been several times revised and enlarged. As the most widely read anthology during most of the 20C, it has had great influence in establishing the canon of the best-known English poetry.

Oxford English Dictionary (11 volumes, 1884–1933) Massive undertaking by the *Oxford University Press, conceived in 1858. The entries for A were published in 1884 but Z was not reached until 1921 (the final volume of 1933 contained the sources). The original title was *A New English Dictionary on Historical Principles*, and the vast labour consisted in gathering the quotations (nearly 2 million) which underpinned the definitions and were printed with them. The editor for the greater part of the work was James Murray (1837–1915). A supplement, adding new words and new examples of old ones (4 vols, 1972–86), was edited by R.W. Burchfield (b. 1923). The original edition and supplement were integrated and published as the second edition in 1989. Shortened and concise versions of the Oxford dictionary have also been much used as standard works of reference.

Oxford Group see *Moral Rearmament.

Oxford Movement The earliest and most vigorous expression of *Anglo-Catholicism, so named because its leading figures – John Henry *Newman, John *Keble and Edward Pusey (1800–82) – were fellows of Oriel College, Oxford. Adherents were also known as Puseyites or Tractarians, the latter because they published their views in a series of *Tracts for the Times* (1833–41). The series ended when no. 90, by Newman, caused an outcry with its argument that the *Thirty-nine Articles were compatible with Roman Catholic doctrine. The movement's influence was seen in increased ritual, ornately decorated Victorian churches and the establishment of Anglican monastic communities.

Oxfordshire (578,000 in 1991, administrative centre Oxford) *County in central England.

Oxford Street (London W1) Street which in the late 19C acquired London's highest concentration of department stores (*John Lewis and *Selfridges are the two main survivors). Today it is the capital city's centre for mass-market retail and is correspondingly crowded. Originally a main route west from the old city of London, and known sometimes as the 'road to Oxford', its name nevertheless became established for a different reason – in 1713 the earl of Oxford bought the land on the north side of the road.

Oxford University Press Publishing house with a continuous history from 1690 (there had been Oxford printers from the 1580s, but not under the direct control of the university). An early and profitable venture was *Clarendon's *History* (3 vols, 1704). In the second half of the 19C the press undertook two major projects of lasting importance, the *Oxford English Dictionary and the *Dictionary of National Biography. The *Oxford Book of English Verse* (1900) became the most influential anthology of modern times, while such works as the *Oxford Companion to English Literature* (1932) and the *Oxford Dictionary of Quotations* (1941) established a tradition of popular works of reference on a wide range of subjects. Over the centuries the Bible has been OUP's bestseller, but it is followed in second place by the *Oxford Advanced Learner's Dictionary* (1948, with four editions and sales of 16 million copies by the 1990s). *Hart's Rules were originally the internal guidelines for Oxford's printers.

Oxo The name given in Britain in 1899 to Liebig's Extract of Beef, a concentrated essence of beef for use in making the drink known as 'beef tea'. A method of extracting some of the nutritional value from beef had been devised in the 1840s by the German chemist Justus von Liebig. His extract was manufactured from the 1860s in Argentina, where beef was cheap, and it was on sale in Britain from 1865. It is not known precisely how the inspired name of Oxo came into being, but the word was soon familiar all over Britain – particularly on the characteristic enamelled advertisements at railway stations. Oxo cubes soon followed; 'chocolate would be very welcome, also Oxo tablets' writes a soldier from the front in 1915.

Oyez! Oyez! see *town crier.

Oz Underground hippy-style magazine (founded in London in the 1960s by an Australian, Richard Neville), the name of which became widely known through the 1971 prosecution of Neville and two co-editors for 'conspiracy to corrupt morals' – a common law offence which has since been discarded. The offending issue of the magazine had not been edited by the three; they had handed it over to a group of schoolchildren. A cartoon in this so-called 'schoolkids' issue' caused particular outrage by dealing with the subject of Rupert Bear's sex life. The case came to seem one of a series in which the establishment tried to shore up its defences against irreverent anarchy (others involved *Lady Chatterley's Lover* and *Gay News*), and the defence counsel was something of a specialist on these issues, John *Mortimer. The editors were convicted and given prison sentences, but these were quashed on appeal.

Ozymandias (1818) Sonnet by *Shelley, one of the best-known short poems in the language. A massive statue of the Egyptian pharaoh Rameses II, recently acquired by the British Museum, inspired Shelley with his image of mile upon mile of desert surrounding a fragment of just such a monument, bearing on its base the inscription:

'My name is Ozymandias, king of kings:
Look on my works, ye Mighty, and despair!'

PA see *Press Association.

Don Pacifico Incident (1847–50) An event which polarized mid-19C attitudes to British foreign policy. David Pacifico, known as Don Pacifico, was a Portuguese Jew trading in Athens, but was a British subject by virtue of being born in Gibraltar. In 1847 an anti-Semitic crowd burnt his house. He sued the Greek government for damages, and in 1850 the prime minister, *Palmerston, sent a British naval squadron to seize Greek ships to the value of the claim. Censured in the House of Lords, Palmerston won a majority in the Commons where he argued that 'a British subject, in whatever land he may be, shall feel confident that the watchful eye and the strong arm of England will protect him against injustice and wrong'.

Pack up your troubles in your old kit bag (1915) One of the most popular of World War I *music-hall songs, with its consoling message of 'What's the use of worrying?' and 'Smile, smile, smile'. With music by Felix Powell (1878–1942) and words by his brother George (pen name George Asaff, 1880–1951), it was part of the repertoire of Florrie *Forde.

Paddington London's main railway station for trains to the west, built for the Great Western Railway in 1850–4. The station itself, with a roof of glass and wrought iron supported on wrought iron pillars, was by Brunel and was partly inspired by the contemporary example of the *Crystal Palace. The Great Western Hotel was designed at the same time by Philip Hardwick, the architect of *Euston. Paddington replaced the original terminus of the GWR, a wooden structure a few hundred yards to the west which had opened in 1838.

Paddington Bear The hero of numerous books and TV series by Michael Bond (b. 1926). He is so named because in the first book (*A Bear Called Paddington* 1958) he is found by the Brown family on Paddington Station in London with a label saying 'Please look after this bear'. They take him home and all else follows, including eventually the sale of huge numbers of teddy bears wearing Paddington's characteristic hat, duffel coat and wellington boots.

Padstow (40km/25m N of Truro) Town in north Cornwall, on the estuary of the river Camel. It is known for the Padstow hobby horse, a *May Day festivity recorded here since the early 19C but no doubt of earlier origin. The 'horse', consisting of a man concealed within a circular tent of black tarpaulin topped by a mask, dances through the streets. He is teased by the crowd, and from time to time will make a dash to try and corner a young girl. If he succeeds, he will envelop her in his long black cloak and pinch her – a certain sign of good luck, guaranteeing a husband or a baby in the near future.

Frederick Handley Page (1885–1962, kt 1942) Aircraft designer and manufacturer, whose London-based Handley Page company – established at Barking in 1909 and moved in 1912 to Cricklewood – produced the first twin-engined bomber, the 0/100, which went into service in November 1916. He followed this in 1918 with a four-engined version, designed to carry a three-ton bomb from England to Berlin; the war ended before it was used. The Handley Page Halifax was the RAF's main bomber at the start of World War II, and only the *Lancaster flew more missions.

James Paget (1814–99, bt 1871) Surgeon at *Bart's who is considered one of the founders of pathology. His name remains in everyday medical use through two conditions, each known as Paget's disease, which he was the first to identify: one, a chronic eczema around the nipple, is an early indication of cancer; the other (*osteitis deformans*) is a bone disease which results in deformity.

The image of Paddington Bear (without the wellingtons), as created by his first illustrator, Peggy Fortnum.

page-three girl The semi-nude featured on page three of the *Sun*, in a stylized pose with much emphasis on highly developed breasts. The first topless page-three girl appeared on 17 November 1970, the first anniversary of the paper's relaunch by Rupert Murdoch, with a simple justification in the caption – 'Birthday Suit!'. The idea was copied for a while by the *Mirror* and was adopted in a more blatant form by the *Star*. By far the best known of the page-three girls has been Samantha Fox, who made her debut in the *Sun* in 1983 at the age of 16. In the early 1990s the page-three girl was becoming a less prominent feature in the *Sun*, sometimes being relegated to other pages and on occasion not appearing at all.

Thomas **Paine** (1737–1809) Radical author and politician, most of whose dangerous ideas are now commonplace. He emigrated to America in 1774, where he published a pamphlet (*Common Sense* 1776) advocating immediate independence from Britain; it sold in large numbers. In 1787 Paine returned to England, where he wrote *The Rights of Man* (1791–2). This began as an answer to Burke's hostile *Reflections on the Revolution in France* (it used the telling line that Burke 'pities the plumage, but forgets the dying bird'); the book went on to advocate a social contract guaranteeing freedom for the individual, full democracy, a graded income tax, old age pensions, family allowances, free education and a reduction in levels of armament.

The result was a charge of treason and Paine's hasty escape to France, where he was elected to the revolutionary convention. But his opposition to the execution of the French king (he argued for exile) soon placed his own life in danger. In prison he wrote *The Age of Reason* (1794–5), an attack on conventional Christianity, mocking 'debaucheries' in the Old Testament and inconsistencies in the New. In 1802 Paine returned to America, where he died. In 1819 another English radical, William Cobbett, made the pious gesture of exhuming his body and bringing the bones back to England.

Painshill Park (15km/9m NE of Guildford) *Landscape garden of the mid-18C, created by Charles Hamilton with a range of natural vistas and artificial follies around its lake and islands. Once a worthy rival to Stowe and Stourhead, it had fallen into neglect until recovered in recent years by an ambitious programme of restoration. The Gothic Temple, the Chinese Bridge, the Grotto, the Water Wheel and the Ruined Abbey are now once again much as Hamilton intended.

Paisley (85,000 in 1981) Town just to the west of Glasgow which grew up round an abbey founded in the 12C. Its wider reputation derives from the 19C when it produced soft woollen plaids and printed cottons in the famous paisley pattern. Although usually described as a 'pine cone' motif, the essential characteristic of the pattern is a repeated oval with a curving end, made up of floral and leaf-like details. It was copied from Kashmiri shawls brought back from India by British soldiers. Paisley remains one of the world's leading producers of cotton thread. The Museum and Art Gallery was founded by the Coats family, leading Paisley threadmakers, and was opened in a succession of buildings from 1867 to 1904; in addition to a good collection of paintings by Scottish artists, there is an extensive historical display of Paisley shawls.

Bob **Paisley** (b. 1919) The most successful of all British football managers in terms of trophies. He became Bill Shankly's assistant at *Liverpool in 1959 (he had himself played for the club until 1954), and succeeded him as manager in 1974. Between then and his retirement in

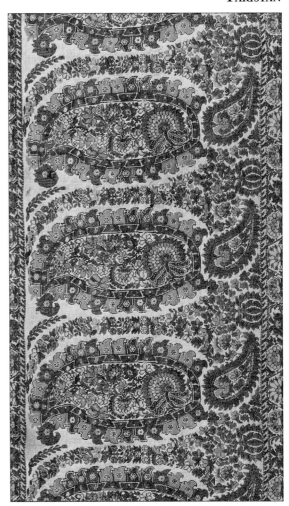

Border of an early 19C shawl, made up of the repeated 'pine cone' motif which is characteristic of Paisley fabrics.

1983 Liverpool won the League Championship six times, the League Cup three times, the European Cup three times and the UEFA Cup once.

Ian **Paisley** Presbyterian minister and *Unionist politician who first achieved wide publicity for his anti-papist cause when he travelled to Rome in 1962 to protest against observers from the Protestant World Council of Churches attending the Roman Catholic Council, Vatican II. He hit the headlines with his description of John XXIII as 'old redsocks'. A similar pungency has ensured wide coverage for his provocatively partisan responses to Ulster's political problems, but he has also had mainstream platforms on which to expound his theme; since 1970 he has represented Antrim in the House of Commons, and since 1979 has simultaneously been one of the three MEPs for Northern Ireland in the European Parliament. He is the leader of the Democratic Unionist Party, of which he was a co-founder in 1971. His party takes a more intransigent stance than the Ulster Unionists on sectarian issues and on relationships with the Republic of Ireland; it was particularly hostile to the *Anglo-Irish agreement of 1985. Ordained a minister in 1946, he established in 1951 his own sect – the Free Presbyterian Church of Ulster.

Pakistan Member of the *Commonwealth 1947–72 and since 1989. The creation of Pakistan ('land of the pure') was part of the political process by which the subcontinent of *India gained independence. The Muslim leader,

Muhammad Ali Jinnah (1876–1948), had come to believe that the interests of India's Muslim minority could only be safeguarded in a separate state. He convinced the British government of the necessity of this, and the two areas which were predominantly Muslim (the provinces bordering Iran and Afghanistan in the west, and East Bengal in the east) became independent in 1947 as a new country, Pakistan; its two territories, West and East Pakistan, were some 1500km/930m apart. East Pakistan declared its own independence in 1971, as *Bangladesh, during a civil war which West Pakistan lost after the intervention of India. West Pakistan, by then the entire country of Pakistan, withdrew from the Commonwealth on Bangladesh becoming a member, but recognized Bangladesh in 1974 and rejoined the Commonwealth in 1989.

Pakistanis see *ethnic and religious minorities.

Palace of Westminster (London SW1) The area between Westminster Abbey and the Thames has been the seat of executive power in England since the 11C, when Edward the Confessor built a palace there. William I and his successors lived in it; and as their chief residence it became the normal place for the king's council and later for *parliament to meet. In the 16C Henry VIII moved his palace a short distance north to *Whitehall, but the two houses of parliament remained in their improvised Westminster quarters. The Lords met in the White Chamber; the Commons eventually settled in St Stephen's Chapel, debating from the choir stalls.

This arrangement came to an accidental end in 1834, when it was decided to burn a quantity of old wooden tally sticks in a basement. The fire got out of hand and demolished the entire palace except for *Westminster Hall and the 14C Jewel Tower on the other side of the road. This fortunate mishap made possible the building of the present *Houses of Parliament, still officially described as the Palace of Westminster.

Palace Pier see *Brighton.

Pale The word, which means a fence or fenced area, became used for two beleaguered patches of English territory in the 14–16C, round Calais and Dublin. 'Beyond the pale' thus came to mean beyond the bounds of civilized behaviour, as in the earliest recorded reference (16C) to the Irish pale: 'Ireland is divided in two parts – one is the English pale, and the other the wild Irish.'

Palestine Area controlled by Britain after World War I as a *mandated territory, covering the entire region now occupied by Israel and Jordan. The land lying to the east of the river Jordan, known then as *Transjordan, was administered as a separate part of Palestine. The *Balfour Declaration, which it was Britain's responsibility to implement to the west of the Jordan, proposed a homeland for the Jews which would not prejudice the interests of the Palestinians. These two ideals proved irreconcilable. After much unrest and terrorism Britain in 1947 handed the problem over to the United Nations, which produced an unworkable proposal turning the area into a patchwork of territories shared out between Jews and Palestinians; the only admirable part of the plan was that Jerusalem should be administered separately as an international city.

The Jews accepted the UN solution; the Palestinian Arabs, a majority then within Palestine, rejected it; but the British insisted on the mandate ending on 15 May 1948. In the months leading up to the British withdrawal there was sporadic civil war between the communities, in which the Jews gained control over parts of the territories earmarked for the Arabs. On May 14 Israel declared itself an independent state, and on May 15 a joint Arab army of forces from Jordan (still known then as Transjordan), Syria, Iraq and Egypt crossed the river Jordan into the west bank area, the major part of the territory allotted by the UN to the Palestinians. Their intention was both to support the Palestinians and to prevent the emergence of the state of Israel. By the end of the resulting war roughly half the west bank was in Israeli hands and half in Jordanian. The Jordanian part was captured by Israel in the war of 1967. The west bank remains the major element in any initiative in the 1990s of bargaining 'land for peace'.

Francis **Palgrave** see *The *Golden Treasury.

Michael **Palin** (b. 1943) Author, actor and television presenter. He was a central member of the *Monty Python team and of their subsequent films. More recently he has made a successful new career as a television traveller, undertaking two vast journeys for the BBC in search of local colour and light relief. In *Around the World in 80 Days* (1989) he followed the route of Jules Verne's Phileas Fogg east from London, and in *Pole to Pole* (1992) he travelled from north pole to south through Europe and Africa.

Palladianism Style in architecture, based on the example of the 16C Italian architect Andrea Palladio, who himself was consciously reviving the classical forms described in the works of Vitruvius, a Roman architect of the 1st century BC. It was briefly introduced to England by Inigo *Jones, and then was more thoroughly promoted in the early 18C by Lord *Burlington. The style evolved later in the century into the more varied forms of *neoclassicism.

Pall Mall (London SW1) Street of clubs housed in grandiose buildings – among them the *Athenaeum, the *Travellers', the *Reform and the *Royal Automobile Club. It was laid out as a road in 1661 on the site of a pall mall alley. The game of pall mall, fashionable in Restoration London, combined elements of croquet and skittles; a ball was struck with a mallet to run down an alley and through a metal hoop.

Samuel **Palmer** (1805–81) Painter known in particular for a series of small rural scenes with figures, painted in his twenties with an intensity of detail and a richly vibrant light which invariably cause them to be described as visionary. They were painted at Shoreham, in Kent, where Palmer lived from 1827 to 1834. He was the leading member of the Ancients, a group inspired by medieval themes and by the example of William *Blake.

Lord **Palmerston** (Henry John Temple, 1784–1865, 3rd viscount Palmerston 1802) Politician who as foreign secretary (1830–4, 1835–41, 1846–51) and as prime minister (1855–8, 1859–65) came to represent the blunt sabre-rattling assertion of British interests abroad, to the great benefit of his popularity at home. He entered parliament as a Tory in 1807 (his viscountcy was in the Irish peerage and did not prevent his sitting in the House of Commons). He remained from 1809 to 1828 in the relatively obscure position of secretary-at-war, responsible for the financial administration of the army. In 1830 he became foreign secretary in the coalition cabinet headed by Lord Grey, a Whig. He subsequently held the same position under two later Whig prime ministers, Lord Melbourne and Lord John Russell, and thus gradually transferred his own allegiance to the group emerging as the *Liberal party.

If there was no conflict with British interests, Palmerston was a firm supporter of Liberal causes in the original meaning of the word (the liberation of people and nations from control by others); he assisted the independence of Belgium in 1831, was on the side of constitutional movements in Spain and Portugal in 1834, and supported insurgents in several countries in the unrest after 1848. But it was his *gunboat diplomacy that appealed rather more to the electorate. The most extreme example was the Don *Pacifico incident, but he was also involved in both the *Opium Wars. As prime minister he successfully coped with two conflicts not of his own making, the *Crimean War and the *Indian Mutiny. The final words attributed to him have often been quoted for the aptness of their wit: 'Die, my dear doctor, that's the last thing I shall do!'

Pamela see Samuel *Richardson.

Pancake Day see *Shrove Tuesday.

Pandarus see *Troilus and Cressida*.

Pandemonium see *Paradise Lost*.

P&O (Peninsular and Oriental Steam Navigation Company) The main link from the mid-19C between Britain and the East. The company was formed in 1837 by Arthur Anderson (1792–1868) and Brodie McGhie Willcox (1786–1862). Their first regular destination was Portugal and Spain, the 'peninsular' part of the name; 'oriental' was soon added, as the steam ships began services to the eastern Mediterranean. Soon the company also had ships in the Indian Ocean so that passengers and mail, after making the land journey across the Egyptian desert from Alexandria, could continue by sea to India and Hong Kong. By the time the Suez Canal opened, in 1869, P&O was well placed to become the main carrier on the full oriental route.

Meanwhile ocean cruising had been pioneered by the company from 1844, and its luxury white liners remain a familiar feature in that market. In modern times P&O has diversified into many other fields, including exhibitions (it owns both Earl's Court and Olympia in London) and the construction industry.

Panjandrum see *Grand Panjandrum.

Mrs Pankhurst (Emmeline Goulden, 1858–1928, m. Richard Pankhurst 1879) Leading *suffragette and founder in 1903 of the WSPU (Women's Social and Political Union). She was responsible for an increasing militancy in the women's campaign, prompted by an occasion in 1905 when her daughter Christabel (1880–1958) was thrown out of a Liberal meeting in Manchester for asking a question about votes for women, and was then arrested and imprisoned for assaulting the police. Both mother and daughter were frequently in prison in subsequent years.

Panorama (BBC since 1957) The flagship current-affairs programme of BBC television. For nearly four decades *Panorama* has presented each week a documentary on a subject of topical concern. It has had many presenters, but there has been a particularly strong link with the *Dimbleby family.

Pantiles see *Tunbridge Wells.

pantomime Traditional theatrical entertainment for the Christmas season, an important element in every provincial theatre's finances. Pantomimes became popular in Britain in the 18C. They derived from the Italian *commedia dell'arte*, but added a new central character in *Harlequin and made much use of stage machinery for elaborate transformation scenes. The modern pantomime emerged during the 19C, when the most important characters became the dame (a comic elderly female performed by a man) and the principal boy (the 'male' romantic lead, played by an actress wearing a close-fitting tunic and tights). A limited number of fairy stories and oriental tales have become the favourite vehicles to accommodate a succession of largely irrelevant routines and topical jokes (now for the most part deriving from television). Among the most popular are *Aladdin, *Cinderella, *Jack and the Beanstalk, *Puss in Boots and Dick *Whittington.

Andrzej **Panufnik** (1914–92, kt 1991) Polish-born British composer who had been conductor of both the Cracow and Warsaw Philharmonic Orchestras before he left Poland in 1954 and settled in Britain. The wide range of his compositions included, unusually for a contemporary composer, no fewer than ten symphonies. His tenth was commissioned by Georg Solti to commemorate the 1991 centenary of the Chicago Symphony Orchestra.

Eduardo **Paolozzi** (b. 1924, kt 1989) Scottish-born sculptor and printmaker, of Italian descent, who first became known for his surrealist collages juxtaposing improbable images from popular culture; they prefigured the later *pop art. His sculpture has similarly used incongruous fragments of machinery (or casts of them) to compose robot-like standing figures. The most 'popular' application of his art has been his glass mosaics for London's Tottenham Court Road underground station.

Papplewick Pumping Station (11km/7m to the N of Nottingham) The most perfect surviving example of the lavish care with which the Victorians embellished their machinery. The pumping station was opened in 1884 to improve Nottingham's water supply, using two great beam engines (designed by the firm founded originally by James *Watt). These survive unaltered and in working condition, housed in a shrine-like setting of cast-iron ornament and stained glass. The exterior of the building is no less romantic, reflected in the waters of its functional cooling pond.

Papua New Guinea Member of the *Commonwealth since 1975. This eastern part of New Guinea (the western half was in the Dutch empire and is now part of Indonesia) was annexed by Britain in 1888, together with the adjacent islands. The area was mandated to Australia in 1921 and a gradual move towards full independence took place between 1970 and 1975.

Papworth Hospital about 19km/12m west of Cambridge which was the first in the country to specialize in heart surgery. It led the way by inserting the country's first heart valve in a patient in 1962, following this with the first permanent pacemaker in 1967.

Parachute Regiment Section of the army, consisting of three regular battalions in the early 1990s, which was founded in 1940 during the Battle of Britain as the direct result of a memo from Churchill ('We ought to have a Corps of at least 5000 parachute troops . . . Pray let me have a note from the War Office on this subject'). At the same time a glider force was established for landing infantry from the air, and the two together formed the Army Air Corps. The Paras' reputation for toughness, well earned in enterprises such as *Arnhem (1944), has been seen in another light by the Catholic population of Northern Ireland since *Bloody Sunday (1972). Known for their red berets, the Paras have also been famous to the public in recent years through the performances of the *Red Devils.

An outstanding example of pargeting: 17C plaster decoration on the Ancient House at Clare in Suffolk.

Paradise Lost (1667) Epic poem by John *Milton, conceived in the 1640s, dictated 1658–63, but not published until 1667. The opening lines proclaim that its subject is 'man's first disobedience' and its purpose to 'justify the ways of God to man'. Using the first three chapters of *Genesis* as his springboard, Milton builds mighty edifices from the fall of Satan and his rebel angels (he coined the name Pandemonium for their kingdom), the struggle between them and the archangels, the promise of redemption through Christ, the innocence and temptation of Adam and Eve, and their expulsion from paradise.

Paradise Regained (1671) is a much shorter work, concentrating on the temptation of Christ in the wilderness. Paradise is regained through Christ's resisting Satan, just as it had originally been lost when Adam and Eve succumbed to him.

pargeting The covering of the exterior surface of a timber-frame building with a tough plaster, often decorated with elaborate patterns. The technique is seen particularly in East Anglia.

Parian ware see *Spode pottery and porcelain.

parish Historically the smallest administrative unit of the Church, being the area served by a single church building and by one priest. It was also the local political unit, with matters such as relief for the poor being dealt with at parish level (hence the phrase 'on the parish'). In those days there was no village hall and the local dignitaries met in the vestry, the room in the church where the priest's robes and the vessels for the service were kept. So the vestry became the name for the local authority in villages and small towns.

In rural areas of England the parish remains the third tier of *local government. An act of 1894 established that any parish of more than a certain size (now 200 adults) must elect a council. However a parish council may, if it considers the name more appropriate, resolve to call itself a town council and its leader a mayor.

Merle **Park** (stage name of Merle Bloch, b. 1937, DBE 1986) Dancer, born in Southern Rhodesia (now Zimbabwe), who joined the Royal Ballet in 1954. She was a leading member of the company until 1982, creating many roles in Ashton and MacMillan ballets and being chosen in 1968 by Nureyev to partner him in his new production of *The Nutcracker*. Since 1983 she has been the director of the Royal Ballet School.

Mungo **Park** (1771–1806) Scottish explorer who made two expeditions to west Africa to investigate the Niger river, of which the outlet to the sea was a mystery. His first journey, in 1795–7, resulted in *Travels in the Interior of Africa* (1799), a classic of its kind. He returned in 1805 and, as before, reached the interior by travelling up the Gambia river. He and his companions were last seen in November of that year on the Niger near Ségou. It was later discovered that they had travelled a further 1600km/1000m down the Niger before an attack by natives in which Park was drowned.

Parkhurst see *Newport, Isle of Wight.

Cecil **Parkinson** (b. 1931, baron 1992) Conservative politician (MP for Enfield West 1970–4, Hertfordshire South 1974–83, Hertsmere 1983–92), who entered the cabinet in 1981 as paymaster general. He was subsequently chancellor of the duchy of Lancaster (1982–3) and secretary of state for trade and industry (1983), for energy (1987–9) and for transport (1989–90). The gap in his career after 1983 was the result of his former secretary, Sara Keays, announcing that she had had an 11-year affair with him, that she had been given the impression that he was going to marry her and that she was expecting his baby. His resignation followed, but a succession of events brought renewed press attention – including the publication in 1985 of a book on the issue by Miss Keays (*A Question of Judgement*) and her winning libel damages in 1992 of £105,000 against *New Woman* for implying that the book was a 'kiss-and-tell' story.

James **Parkinson** (1755–1824) Surgeon who was the first to describe the disease named after him, in his *Essay on the Shaking Palsy* (1817).

Norman **Parkinson** (adopted name of Ronald Parkinson, 1913–90) Photographer who in 1934 set up a portrait studio in London with a partner, Norman Micklewhite, calling it Norman Parkinson. He became an extremely stylish fashion photographer, associated in particular with *Vogue*, and in 1947 he met – and later married – the model who inspired much of his work, Wenda Rogerson. He became one of a small group of royal portrait photographers and in 1973 took the official photographs for the wedding of Princess Anne and Mark Phillips.

Parkinson's Law The proposition that 'work expands so as to fill the time available for its completion'. These were the opening words of *Parkinson's Law* (1958), a bestselling satirical analysis of political and social economy by C. Northcote Parkinson (1909–93).

Park Lane (London W1) The western extremity of Mayfair, facing Hyde Park. Its name became associated with great wealth because it was the most fashionable address in London during Britain's richest period, the 19C. The great houses of that time have largely been replaced by hotels, of which the *Dorchester was one of the first.

Parliament The legislative assembly of the United Kingdom, consisting of the House of *Lords and the House of *Commons, both of which have their chambers at Westminster in the *Houses of Parliament. The word (deriving from the French *parler*, to speak) is also applied to the life-span of such an assembly from the time of its being summoned until it is officially dismissed. Nowadays this means the period between one *general election and the next. The life of a parliament is divided into separate sessions, each beginning with a *state opening of parliament.

All rulers, however autocratic, have a council of some kind. The history of the English parliament is essentially the prolonged struggle of such a council to become first independent and then more powerful than the monarch. England was the first country to undertake and achieve this aim, causing John *Bright, in a speech in 1865, to declare her the 'mother of parliaments'.

The word parliament (from the French *parler*, to speak) was first used in England in the 13C of an assembly convened by the monarch. It was in this same century that Simon de *Montfort introduced the beginnings of popular representation, and that the pattern of the future was established in the *Model Parliament of 1295.

Over the next two centuries parliament, and in particular the Commons, steadily acquired more power. From 1341 the Commons sat in their own chamber; from 1377 they had their own elected *Speaker; from 1407 they were granted priority over the Lords in the matter of voting funds for the monarch (since the greater part of the burden fell on them); and from 1414 it was accepted that when the Commons had drafted a bill and sent it for royal approval, the monarch could accept or reject it but not amend it. By the end of the 15C the strength of the Commons was considerable, and in an oblique manner it increased during the 16C. The Tudor monarchs were autocratic, but it suited them to rule through parliament; and so, though members were unduly compliant to the royal will, the practice of parliamentary government steadily developed. Under the next dynasty, the Stuarts, the House of Commons finally flexed its muscles. The

The Houses of Parliament, fronting the Thames from the Victoria Tower on the left to Big Ben on the right.

struggle against *Charles I ended with the execution of the king and the establishment of the *Commonwealth.

The introduction of *constitutional monarchy after the revolution of 1688 led to a century or more in which parliament was at last undeniably the power in the land. But it was increasingly corrupt, representative only of upper-class interests; and the active support of the king was essential if a *prime minister was to remain in power. The final stage in the creation of the modern parliament was the *Reform Act of 1832, inaugurating a gradual extension of the *franchise in a process not finally completed until 1928.

Since 1832 power in parliament has continued to alternate on a *two-party system. The *Conservative party has at all times been one of the contenders; its rival was the *Liberal party until World War I and subsequently the *Labour party.

Parliament Act (1911) see Herbert *Asquith.

Parliamentary Private Secretary (usually abbreviated to PPS) A *backbencher appointed to assist a secretary of state or a minister of state, particularly in relation to the business of the House of Commons.

parliamentary privilege Freedom of speech and freedom from arrest were the privileges fought for by *parliament in its long struggle with the crown. Today the only privilege of importance is that a member is not liable to the law of slander on any statement made in parliament, nor can the reporting of it in print be prosecuted as libel. The privilege ceases to apply if the same statement is repeated outside the Houses of Parliament.

Parliamentary Under-Secretary of State see entry on *minister.

Parliament House (Edinburgh) Building of 1632–40 in *Parliament Square, to which the Scottish parliament moved in 1639 from its previous meeting place in *Edinburgh Castle. When the parliament ceased to exist in 1707 (with the Act of *Union), Parliament House became home to the two highest courts of law in Scotland, the Court of Session and the High Court of Justiciary. The adjacent Parliament Hall, a Gothic building with a hammer-beam roof, is used as a public concourse by those involved in the business of the courts.

Parliament Square The name of squares in Edinburgh and London, both of which are flanked by ancient cathedrals and parliament buildings.

*St Giles' Cathedral in Edinburgh has High Street (part of the Royal Mile) to the north and is surrounded by Parliament Square on the other three sides. To the west stood the Old Tolbooth, known as the *Heart of Midlothian, demolished in 1817. To the south is *Parliament House. And to the east is the Mercat Cross, the centre of the city's public life in the Middle Ages and still the site for royal proclamations.

Parliament Square in London is more recent, laid out in the mid-19C as a suitable approach to Barry's new *Houses of Parliament, with *Westminster Abbey on the south side. The grass in the centre has statues of distinguished statesmen, that of Winston Churchill by Ivor Roberts-Jones (b. 1913) being the most recent addition, in 1973.

Charles Stewart Parnell (1846–91) Irish politician who came from a Protestant landed background but passionately espoused the cause of Irish nationalism; it was he who put *Home Rule firmly on the political agenda. He entered parliament in 1875 as the member for Meath and

by 1880 was the leader of the Home Rule party in the House of Commons. His alliance with Gladstone brought the first Home Rule bill before parliament in 1886, but in 1890 Parnell's career was shattered when he was cited as corespondent in a divorce case brought by a fellow MP, Captain William O'Shea, against his wife Kitty (Parnell and Kitty had been lovers for ten years). Gladstone refused to continue the alliance with Parnell as leader, and the majority of the Home Rule party abandoned him.

Catherine **Parr** see *Catherine Parr.

Thomas **Parr** see *Old Parr.

John **Parrott** (b. 1964) Snooker player who won the European Open Championship in 1989 and again in 1990, and followed this with the Embassy World Professional Championship in 1991.

Hubert **Parry** (1848–1918, kt 1898) Composer known in particular for his choral works, such as *Blest Pair of Sirens* (1887), a cantata for chorus and orchestra to words by Milton. He has achieved a lasting place in British popular culture with his setting of Blake's *Jerusalem. First performed in the middle of World War I (in 1916), with a choir singing in unison about 'England's green and pleasant land', this was tailor-made for its present status as almost an alternative national anthem. It is a feature of the last night of the *Proms and is much sung by large crowds cheering English teams at sporting events.

'parshial to ladies' see The *Young Visiters.

Charles **Parsons** see *steam.

Parson's Pleasure One section of the river Cherwell in Oxford, reserved for men only and for naked bathing.

Eric **Partridge** (1894–1979) New Zealand-born lexicographer who specialized in the underbelly of language, past and present. His main work was his *Dictionary of Slang*, first published in 1937 and frequently revised and extended. It was followed by, among many other books, *Shakespeare's Bawdy* (1947) and *A Dictionary of Catch Phrases* (1977). He had a faithful group of informants writing to him from around the world, whose contributions sometimes seem more colourful than reliable (see *'close your eyes and think of England').

*A **Passage to India*** (1924) Novel by E.M. *Forster about cultural misunderstandings between Indians and British under the *Raj. Adela Quested, a prim but liberal-minded young woman visiting India, tries to get beyond the prejudices of the British community. Her companion, Mrs Moore, makes friends with Aziz, a westernized Muslim doctor who arranges an expedition to the Marabar Caves. Disaster strikes when Adela accuses Aziz of having made a sexual advance to her in the caves. He is arrested and stands trial, but Adela now admits she was mistaken. Aziz, jolted into radicalism, concludes that there can be no personal friendship between Indians and British until the end of British rule. Prominent among the many other characters is the unworldly Brahmin, Professor Godbole. A film of the book was directed by David *Lean in 1984.

Passchendaele see *Ypres.

*Passport to Pimlico** (1949) One of the *Ealing comedies, beginning with the discovery of a document which proves the London area of Pimlico to be legally all that remains of ancient Burgundy. The resulting struggle between Whitehall bureaucracy and the new state (with

Stanley Holloway as its prime minister) turns into a joyful rejection of the bleak austerities of postwar Britain. Margaret Rutherford plays a small part as an eccentric expert on Burgundian history.

Paston Letters The largest and most detailed body of correspondence surviving from the 15C. The letters were written by three generations of the Paston family, whose rise in Norfolk society was hastened by their unexpected inheritance of Caister Castle. But their good fortune also brought years of turmoil, as local aristocrats backed up their lawsuits against the Pastons with attempts by bands of armed men to evict the upstarts. The letters provide a stark insight into the anarchy of England in the century of the *Wars of the Roses, together with fascinating details of family life and household economy. Most of the original letters are now in the British Library.

patent The exclusive right to manufacture or market a new invention for a given period of time. The concept of a patent arose in Britain as an exception to the Statute of Monopolies (1624), which declared all existing monopolies to be invalid except for grants giving 14 years' exclusivity to inventors of 'any manner of new manufactures within this Realm'. Today patents are granted by the *Patent Office. If the inventor can show that the idea is new, is not obvious, and is capable of practical use, he or she will be granted a patent which lasts for 20 years from the date of application.

Patent Office (Newport, Gwent) Government department set up in 1852, responsible for the registration of *patents and subsequently of trademarks and industrial designs. In 1989 the office moved from London to Newport, and under the *Next Steps programme it became in 1990 an executive agency reporting to the secretary of state for trade and industry. It is best known to the public through the scientific and technical library built up from 1855 and housed in Southampton Buildings (London WC2). Since 1966 this has been the Science Reference Library, a department of the British Library.

Paternoster Row (London EC4) Street running along the north side of the churchyard of St Paul's Cathedral, associated with bookselling from the early days of printing. The precise reason for the name is not known, but it derives from the first two words of the Lord's Prayer in Latin (*Pater Noster* Our Father). The street was destroyed by bombing in World War II, and the north end was re-built as a pedestrian precinct under the name Paternoster Square. Rival schemes for redevelopment (in modernist or in 'classical' post-modernist style) were the subject of much controversy in the early 1990s.

Patience or, Bunthorne's Bride (1881) One of the *Savoy operas by Gilbert and Sullivan. It satirizes the *Aesthetic movement, with the character of Grosvenor said to be based on Swinburne and that of Bunthorne on Oscar Wilde – though at the first performance Bunthorne was acted with the appearance and mannerisms of Whistler.

St Patrick (5th century AD) Patron saint of Ireland with a feast day on March 17. Born somewhere on the west coast of Britain, he was captured at the age of 16 by Irish raiders and taken as a slave to Ireland. Six years later he escaped, but returned to preach the gospel, establishing his headquarters at *Armagh and making Ireland the firm base from which Christianity later spread back through England and into northern Europe. He wrote two short works which are unusual for the period in being accepted now as wholly authentic. *Confessio* (Confession) is his spiritual autobiography, and *Epistola* (Letter) a protest against the ill-treatment of Irish Christians by the soldiers of an invading British chieftain. There are many legends about him. One explains the absence of snakes in Ireland (he drove them out); another relates why the shamrock is Ireland's *emblem, widely worn on St Patrick's Day (he used its three parts to explain the mystery of the Trinity). The cross of St Patrick is one of the three elements of the *Union Jack.

'patriotism is not enough' see Edith *Cavell.

patrons They have acquired a bad name in English literary tradition because of Dr *Johnson's famous attack on Lord *Chesterfield. When Johnson published his *Plan* for a dictionary in 1747, he dedicated it to Chesterfield and received £10 from him. Chesterfield then took little further interest until 1754, when he wrote two essays in the *World* eagerly anticipating the publication of the finished work. It was these which prompted Johnson's memorable but somewhat unjust response; his letter was private, and was first published by Boswell in his life of Johnson. The celebrated passage runs: 'Is not a Patron, my Lord, one who looks with unconcern on a man struggling for life in the water, and, when he has reached ground, encumbers him with help? The notice which you have been pleased to take of my labours, had it been early, had been kind; but it has been delayed till I am indifferent, and cannot enjoy it; till I am solitary, and cannot impart it; till I am known, and do not want it.'

Christopher **Patten** (b. 1944) Conservative politician, MP for Bath 1979–92, who entered the *cabinet in 1989 as secretary of state for the environment. From 1990 he was chancellor of the duchy of Lancaster and chairman of the Conservative party. In the latter role he directed the successful Conservative campaign in the 1992 general election, but he lost his own seat at Bath. A few months later he was appointed governor of *Hong Kong, with responsiblity for the last few years before the 1997 hand-over to China. His early attempts to introduce more democracy in the crown colony provoked instant hostility from Beijing.

John **Patten** (b. 1945) Conservative politician, MP for Oxford West and Abingdon since 1983 (previously for City of Oxford, 1979–83), who entered the *cabinet in 1992 as secretary of state for education.

St **Paulinus** see archbishop of *York.

pax Britannica (Latin for the 'British peace') Term in use from the 19C for the peace imposed within the *British empire by the strength of imperial power. It was a version of *pax Romana*, used in classical times for the similar order imposed on Europe by Rome.

Joseph **Paxton** (1801–65, kt 1851) Son of a small farmer, he was appointed in 1826 superintendent of the gardens at *Chatsworth. It was there that he designed the Great Conservatory, making possible his sudden leap to fame with the *Crystal Palace. The commission for *Mentmore Towers soon followed. In 1854 he became MP for Coventry, as a Liberal, and held the seat until his death.

PAYE (Pay As You Earn) System by which the *income tax of anyone in employment is collected. It is the responsibility of the employer to deduct the appropriate amount of tax from the wages or salary of each employee and to pay it to the Inland Revenue, the employee's 'take-home' pay therefore being net of tax.

Paymaster General Office created in 1835, to simplify the payment of the armed forces. In modern times the department still distributes public money, particularly public service pensions, but the duties of the paymaster general are light. The office has been used as a way of bringing someone into the *cabinet on a temporary basis. This was done most recently in 1986, when Kenneth Clarke was in the cabinet as minister of employment because his secretary of state, Lord Young, sat in the House of Lords.

Cynthia **Payne** A London brothel-keeper whose quaint arrangements delighted the nation when it was revealed in court that those visiting her house in Streatham in the 1970s (many of whom were said to be distinguished old gentlemen) were sold £25 luncheon vouchers, entitling them to food, drink, a striptease and a trip upstairs with a girl of their choice. She subsequently styled herself Madam Cyn or Madam Cynthia Payne LV.

'pay on the nail' see *Bristol.

PC Abbreviation both for police constable and *privy councillor.

PC 49 Hero of the first long-running British police series, on radio from 1947 to 1953. Played by Brian Reece, the London bobby was somewhat improbably called Archibald Berkeley-Willoughby (he had been to a public school). The villains had more characteristic names, such as Knocker Dawson and Slim Jiggs. PC 49 also featured for most of the 1950s in cartoon form in *Eagle*.

'peace with honour' see *Disraeli and *Munich.

Polly **Peachum** see The *Beggar's Opera.

Peak District An area of high moors, dales and peaks, forming the southern section of the *Pennines. The district was designated in 1951 a *national park (1404sq.km/542sq.m). Lying mainly in Derbyshire, it reaches north to the high ground between the industrial areas of Manchester and Sheffield.

Pearly Kings and Queens London's cockney royalty. The costermongers of the past, selling food (originally apples) from barrows, were known for the profusion of pearl buttons on their clothes. When they chose leaders to represent their interests, in the equivalent of a guild, the buttons were seen as a badge of office. Modern-day pearly kings and queens, shimmering all over, make appearances mainly for charity.

Peter **Pears** (1910–86, kt 1978) Singer known in particular for his creation of all the leading tenor roles in the operas of Benjamin *Britten; they were written specifically for his voice. In 1948 he was the co-founder with Britten of the *Aldeburgh festival, which he continued to direct after Britten's death.

Pears Cyclopaedia Annual which was first published in 1897 as an advertisement for Pears soap; its long survival demonstrates, like *Bubbles, the firm's genius at that time for publicity. The original *Pears Shilling Cyclopaedia* promised 'a mass of curious and useful information about things that everyone ought to know in commerce, history, science, religion, literature'. Modern editions continue to be packed with information on these and many other topics, though the long-established convention of separating the material into different sections makes much of it elusive to a newcomer. The link with Pears ended in 1960.

Pearson Major company which has developed from a Yorkshire firm described in the mid-19C as 'sanitary tube

and brick makers and contractors for local public works in and around Bradford'. Under the leadership of Weetman Pearson, the first Viscount Cowdray (1856–1927), the family firm extended its construction activities abroad – in particular to Mexico, where it acquired valuable oil interests. Subsequent diversification has led to major newspaper holdings (in particular the *Financial Times* and a half share in the *Economist*), and to participation in banking (Lazard Brothers), manufacturing (Doulton china) and entertainment (Madame Tussaud's, Alton Towers). The firm has been quoted on the Stock Exchange since 1969, when the family first sold a share of the equity to the public.

Peasants' Revolt (1381) The first great popular protest in English history. There were two immediate causes of resentment: an attempt to hold down wages in the scarce labour market resulting from the *Black Death; and the recent imposition of a poll tax of one shilling a head. Rebel forces marched on London from Essex and from Kent. The young king, Richard II, met the Essex men outside the city and made some major concessions. Meanwhile the Kentish men, led by Wat *Tyler, had entered London; they destroyed property and murdered two high officials held to be responsible for the poll tax. On the following day, at a meeting with Richard II, Tyler was wounded in a scuffle; he was later beheaded. The uprising gradually petered out and the king's concessions were immediately forgotten. But until the 1980s politicians in Britain tended to steer clear of any form of *poll tax.

peasouper see *Clean Air Act.

pebble dash (also called rough cast, and in Scotland harling) Surface for exterior walls, achieved by throwing gravel or small pebbles against the cement while it is still wet.

The pearly king of Hornsey, in north London, with colleagues at a charity event.

Wat Tyler, leader of the Peasants' Revolt, being struck down in the presence of Richard II (15C manuscript).

Pebble Mill Radio and television studio in Birmingham, which opened in Pebble Mill Road in 1971. BBC programmes originating there include *Pebble Mill* (broadcast live from the foyer studio), the lunch-time magazine programme *Pebble Mill at One*, drama series such as *All Creatures Great and Small* and – most venerable of all – *The Archers*.

'Peccavi' The most brief and brilliant example of a favourite British form of humour, the pun. In 1843 Sir Charles Napier conquered the Indian province of Sind (now southeast Pakistan), and was criticized in parliament in 1844 for his ruthless campaign. A girl in her teens, Catherine Winkworth (1827–78), remarked to her teacher that Napier's despatch to the governor general of India, after capturing Sind, should have been *Peccavi* (Latin for 'I have sinned'). She sent her joke to the new humorous magazine **Punch*, which printed it as a factual report under Foreign Affairs. As a result the pun has usually been credited to Napier.

Peeblesshire Until 1975 an inland **county in south central Scotland, now part of the Borders region.

John **Peel** see **D'ye ken John Peel?*

John **Peel** (radio name of John Ravenscroft, b. 1939) Disc jockey who is seen as Radio 1's intellectual of pop. He has been with the station since its start in 1967 (the only survivor of the original line-up) and in his *Top Gear* programme has specialized in featuring lesser-known groups of quality – often helping them on their way by his attention.

Robert **Peel** (1788–1850, 2nd bt 1830) Prime minister 1834–5 and 1841–6. Born the son of a Lancashire cotton manufacturer and Tory politician, Peel was himself a Tory MP from the time when he came of age, in 1809. For six years from 1812 he was secretary of state for Ireland, where the strong line which he took to suppress Catholic agitation earned him the inevitable nickname of Orange Peel (see **Orange*). Members of the **police force which he set up in Ireland were called 'peelers' from his surname, just as their London equivalents were later known as 'bobbies' from his first name. His establishment of the metropolitan police in 1829 was part of a major series of reforms in the criminal justice system which he carried out as home secretary (1822–7 in Liverpool's administration, 1828–30 in Wellington's). His other great achievement of that decade was pushing through parliament the **Emancipation Act, also passed in 1829. Peel's years in Ireland had made him an opponent of Catholic emancipation, but the deteriorating political situation there altered his views – a statesmanlike flexibility which lost him many supporters on this issue, as later also on the Corn Laws.

The passing of the **Reform Act in 1832 left the Tories weak and in disarray. Peel emerged as the new leader, and it was under him that the Tory party transformed itself into the modern **Conservative party; his manifesto to the electors of his Tamworth constituency in Staffordshire, before the election of 1834, has often been seen as the classic statement of reforming Conservative principles. He won that election but only held office for a few months before being defeated by a coalition of Whigs, radicals and Irish nationalists. When he returned as prime minister, after the general election of 1841, the problems he faced were associated still with those three groups: the Whigs were agitating for free trade and the repeal of the *Corn Laws, to which Conservative landowners were strongly opposed; the demands of the *Chartists were receiving passionate and often violent support in depressed industrial areas; and *O'Connell was holding massive rallies in Ireland against British rule.

In Ireland Peel took a strong line with civil disturbances but again balanced this with measures to promote Catholic opportunities and education. On free trade he was already making concessions, against the interests of his party, before the *Great Famine persuaded him to go further and to repeal the Corn Laws in their entirety in 1846. This action improved conditions in Britain and thereby reduced Chartist agitation, but it split the Conservative party. The act was passed by a minority of Conservatives with support from Whigs and radicals, after which Peel's government fell. The Conservatives who had supported him, known from then on as the 'Peelites', remained a separate faction, led after his death by Lord *Aberdeen; many of them eventually joined the *Liberal party. Peel died of injuries sustained when he was thrown from his horse on Constitution Hill, the road running along the edge of Buckingham Palace. In the last three decades of his life he formed a fine collection of paintings, mainly Dutch and Flemish of the 17c, more than 70 of which are now in the National Gallery.

peel tower (also called just a peel, and often spelt pele) Fortified house consisting of a square thick-walled tower, usually with a vaulted chamber on the ground floor for cattle and living accommodation above. Built in the 13–16c, peel towers are characteristic of both sides of the Scottish border.

Peeping Tom see Lady *Godiva.

peerage The peerage in Britain consists of five ranks – duke, marquess, earl, viscount, baron. These together are the Lords Temporal, sitting in the House of *Lords with the *Lords Spiritual. (Archbishops take precedence above dukes, bishops above barons.)

All ranks of the peerage were hereditary until 1856, when the first *life peers were created. The majority of hereditary titles pass only through the male line, but a few can be inherited by women. These include the oldest surviving British title, the earldom of Mar, created in about 1115. Although referred to formally with their full titles, peers and peeresses below the rank of duke and duchess are addressed in everyday life as Lord or Lady (followed by the place or name of their title).

The existence of a title is reflected also in the names of the children. The eldest son of a duke, marquess or earl is likely to have a *courtesy title of his own. Daughters of those three senior ranks are styled Lady, using the family surname; thus the surname of the duke of Wellington is Wellesley, and a daughter would be Lady Mary Wellesley. Younger sons of dukes and marquesses are styled Lord in the same way. Younger sons of earls and all the children of viscounts and barons are styled 'the Honourable' (the Hon. John Smith, the Hon. Mary Smith). In Scotland the eldest son of a baron is known as 'the Master' of whatever place is the family's baronial title.

Until 1963 it was not possible for a peer or peeress to disclaim a title. This issue came to a head when a Labour MP, Tony *Benn, inherited a viscountcy and had to relinquish his seat in the House of Commons. By the terms of the Peerage Act (1963) anyone inheriting a peerage now has a period of one year during which he or she may decide to surrender it for life, reverting to the status of a commoner; in such a case the peerage remains dormant, to be inherited by the heir on the person's death.

Clara **Peggotty** see *David Copperfield.

pele see *peel tower.

Pembroke (16,000 in 1981) Town in Dyfed, notable for the castle which bestrides a promontory in the tidal reach of the Pembroke river. Its great walls enclose a tall and sturdy cylindrical keep, built in about 1200. The castle was the birthplace and childhood home of Henry Tudor, who seized the crown as *Henry VII.

Pembrokeshire Former *county in Wales, since 1974 part of Dyfed.

Pembrokeshire Coast Area of Dyfed designated in 1952 a *national park (583sq.km/225sq.m). It includes the entire coastline of the southwest extremity of Wales together with several offshore islands.

Penguin The most influential imprint in British publishing history. It was founded in 1935 by Allen Lane (1902–70), with an initial list of ten paperbacks selling at sixpence each. The innovation was not that they were paperbacks or cheap, but that cheap paperbacks were of literary quality – the ten included work by André Maurois, Ernest Hemingway, Eric Linklater, Dorothy Sayers, Agatha Christie and Compton Mackenzie. Finding initial resistance from bookshops, Lane made many of his early sales through Woolworths. Puffin, an equally successful children's imprint, was introduced in 1941 with Worzel Gummidge as the first title. All quality paperbacks in Britain were from the Penguin stable until the emergence of rival firms in the 1960s. Penguin itself had started that decade with a bold decision and a massive commercial success, in the publication of *Lady Chatterley's Lover.

penicillin see Alexander *Fleming.

Peninsular War (1808–14) Campaign of the *Napoleonic Wars in Portugal and Spain, and the only part of the war on land in which Britain took a significant part until 1815. It was provoked by Napoleon's Continental System, an attempt to deny Britain the use of every port in continental Europe. Portugal, friendly to Britain, was a loophole which he closed by invading the country in 1807. Spain was already in the French alliance, but Napoleon pressed matters further in 1808 when he forced the Spanish royal family to abdicate and placed on the throne his own brother, Joseph Bonaparte.

British troops landed in Portugal in August 1808, captured Lisbon, and marched into Spain to support a widespread Spanish insurrection; but this first campaign ended in disaster when Sir John Moore's army had to retreat rapidly to *Corunna before escaping to England. In 1809 the remaining British forces in Portugal were placed under the command of *Wellington, whose strategy was to build heavily fortified defences stretching some 40km/25m from the Atlantic on the west, past Torres Vedras, to the broad river Tagus on the east. Lisbon, 40km/25m to the south, was secure behind these lines, giving Wellington an unusually large stronghold for his base. In the subsequent campaigns his two crucial victories were on 22 July 1812 at Salamanca (180km/112m NW of Madrid) and on 21 June 1813 at Vitoria (100km/62m from Spain's Atlantic border with France). At Vitoria the entire baggage train of Joseph Bonaparte was captured, accounting for many of the treasures now at *Apsley House.

Penlee lifeboat In December 1981 the crew of eight on the lifeboat operating from Penlee (just north of Mousehole in south Cornwall) were lost when trying to reach survivors on the wrecked coaster Union Star.

William **Penn** (1644–1718) English *Quaker and the founder of Pennsylvania. He was one of the first members of the upper class to throw in his lot with the Society of Friends; he was imprisoned in 1667 for attending a meeting in Ireland. In 1681 Charles II granted Penn extensive lands in North America, in compensation for a debt to his late father which had remained unpaid. There Penn established the 'holy experiment' of Pennsylvania, a name meaning Penn's woodland. The colony was committed by its first code of law to religious toleration, and for many years it was a haven for religious dissidents persecuted elsewhere.

Pennies from Heaven (BBC 1978) Six-part television drama serial by Dennis *Potter about a sheet-music salesman of the 1930s, played by Bob Hoskins. Its unusual feature is that the cast keep breaking into song and dance, miming to contemporary recordings of the songs which were the central character's stock in trade.

Pennines Range of limestone hills, frequently interrupted by valleys or dales, which stretch some 400km/250m north from Derbyshire, stopping just short of the *Cheviots. They thus form a central spine to northern England. The highest peak is Cross Fell (893m/2930ft) in Cumbria. Almost the entire length of the range is accessible to pedestrians on a footpath known as the Pennine Way, which starts at Edale in Derbyshire and reaches right up to the Cheviots, ending at Kirk Yetholm in the Borders region of Scotland.

penny see *currency.

Penny Black see *Post Office.

penny dreadfuls Sensational stories of gruesome events (the equivalent in print of *melodrama), serialized from the 1830s in weekly parts costing a penny. They made heroes of historical characters such as Jack *Sheppard and

Dick *Turpin, and added memorable inventions of their own, notably *Sweeney Todd. They fed the same Victorian appetite for fiction which at a higher level enabled *Dickens and others to be published in a similar weekly fashion.

penny-farthing The usual name now for the bicycle known in its own time as the Ordinary, the large front wheel and small back one bringing to mind a large and small everyday coin of recent times (see *£.s.d.). The Ordinary evolved from the Ariel, designed by James Starley (1831–81) and produced in Coventry from 1871. It remained the standard bicycle throughout the 1880s, until replaced in the 1890s by early versions of the modern machine (the Safety bicycle), which used a chain to achieve the gearing of the Ordinary's large wheel. The term 'penny-farthing' seems not to have been coined until the 1920s.

penny plain, twopence coloured see *toy theatre.

penny post see *Post Office.

Penrhyn Castle (3km/2m E of Bangor) Neo-Norman castle built and furnished in 1820–35 by Thomas Hopper (1776–1856) for George Dawkins-Pennant, whose fortune derived from the Penrhyn slate mines and from sugar plantations in Jamaica. The exterior makes a tolerably restrained use of Romanesque themes, but the interiors (in particular the grand staircase) are a riot of medieval decorative motifs, culled from the books of ornament then becoming fashionable and thrown together with a dizzy and exhilarating sense of abandon.

Penshurst Place (9km/6m NW of Tunbridge Wells) Rambling house of many periods, famous for its great hall, known as the Baron Hall, which was built for Sir John de Pulteney in the 1340s. Its superbly carpentered roof timbers are unusual in being of chestnut rather than

Waiting for the Pistol: *the start of a penny-farthing race, with assistants keeping the riders upright (caricature, c.1880).*

oak. The house contains excellent early portraits of the Sidney family, into whose possession it came in 1552 – just two years before Sir Philip *Sidney was born there.

pensions The old-age pension in Britain is paid from traditional retirement ages, 60 for women and 65 for men. But the amended Sex Discrimination Act of 1986, following a judgement of the European Court, made it illegal for firms to retire the sexes at different ages; this was followed by a European Court ruling in 1991 that the pensionable age must not discriminate between women and men. The government's Social Security Advisory Committee recommended in 1992 that the best solution would be to raise the pension age for women to 65, phasing it in over 15 years from 2000 and using the considerable savings to provide extra social security for the most needy.

The state pension is paid to anyone who has made *national insurance contributions (or whose partner has), but many in Britain also have earnings-related occupational pensions – organized by their companies with contributions from both employee and employer. A similar state scheme, SERPS (State Earnings-Related Pension Scheme), came into force in 1978; graded contributions provide different levels of supplement to the basic state pension. Both employers and individual employees are free to join SERPS or to opt out.

Pentland Firth see *Orkneys.

Penzance (20,000 in 1981) Port and resort in Cornwall; the most westerly town in England, it is only 15km/9m from *Land's End. The influence of the *Gulf Stream gives it subtropical vegetation. The early 19C Egyptian House, with its exotic façade in Chapel Street, is a rare example in architecture of the decorative fashion deriving from the Egyptian campaigns in the *French Revolutionary Wars.

*The **People*** Sunday newspaper founded in 1881 to support the Conservative cause. It had a succession of owners during the 20C and reached the very high circulation of more than 5 million around 1950. It later became part of the Mirror group of newspapers, and as such its future was uncertain after the death in 1991 of Robert *Maxwell.

People's Palace see *Glasgow.

PEP (Personal Equity Plan) Scheme introduced in January 1987 to encourage people to invest in UK shares (or equities). Subject to certain limits (from January 1992 a maximum of £9000 of new investment in any one tax year), dividends and capital gains from a PEP are free of tax.

Samuel **Pepys** (pronounced *peeps*, 1633–1703) The greatest diarist in the English language. His talents made him a man of considerable influence, through his work at the *Admiralty and as a fellow of the *Royal Society. But he would be forgotten today, except by specialist historians, if he had not responded to a new decade and the likelihood of a new era (the *Restoration) by buying a notebook, bound in calf, in which he made his first daily entry on Sunday, 1 January 1660. From then until 31 May 1669 (when he closed the diary because of trouble with his eyes) Pepys recorded the most intimate details of his private life, intermingled with public events in one of London's most eventful decades. Typical of this mixture is the drama of the *Great Fire, during which he takes the precaution of burying his parmesan cheese in the garden. The diary is in the Shelton system of shorthand, widely used at the time. In sections where Pepys feels a greater need for secrecy he lapses into garbled French or Spanish:

'To supper with my wife, very pleasant, and to bed – my mind, God forgive me, too much running upon what I can *faire avec la femme de Bagwell demain*' (19 Dec. 1664). The next day we learn, again in French, that he did what he wanted with Bagwell's wife.

Pepys left his magnificent library, including the diary, to his old college at Cambridge, Magdalene. Extracts from the diary were first printed in 1825, prompted by the recent publication of *Evelyn's. By the 1890s it was all in print, apart from some expurgated passages, and a full modern edition was completed in 11 volumes in 1983.

Spencer **Perceval** (1762–1812) Tory politician, whose name is remembered mainly for being the only British prime minister (1809–12) to have been assassinated. He was shot in the lobby of the House of Commons by John Bellingham, a demented bankrupt with a grievance against the government.

perfidious Albion see *Albion.

Pericles, Prince of Tyre (c.1608) Play by *Shakespeare in which an immensely complex plot, involving a succession of sea voyages and shipwrecks, results in Pericles temporarily losing both his wife, Thaisa, and his infant daughter, Marina. Their reunion after an interval of several years prefigures Shakespeare's more successful treatment of the same theme in *The Winter's Tale*. The *First Folio did not include *Pericles*, but it had been published earlier in a quarto edition with Shakespeare's name on the title page. It is possible that the first two acts are largely by another author.

William Henry **Perkin** (1838–1907, kt 1906) Discoverer and manufacturer of aniline or synthetic dyes. He found the first in 1856, as an accidental by-product of an attempt to synthesize quinine; he called it aniline purple, but the name given to it in France, *mauve* (French for mallow, the flower), soon became international. His son, also William Henry (1860–1929), followed his father's profession and made important discoveries in organic chemistry.

Perpendicular style see *Gothic.

Fred **Perry** (b. 1909) Tennis player who was Wimbledon champion for three successive years (1934–6) and who is still, 60 years on, the most recent British player to win the men's singles. He also won the championship in the USA (1933, 34, 36), Australia (1934) and France (1935), becoming the first player to win all four major titles – three of them in 1934, leaving him just one short of the first grand slam. He was world champion at table tennis in 1929 before beginning his tennis career.

'person from Porlock' see *Kubla Khan*.

Persuasion (1818) The last novel of Jane *Austen, written 1815–16 and published after her death. The heroine is the quiet, honest and faithful Anne Elliot, who differs greatly from her self-important family (in particular from her father, Sir Walter Elliot of Kellynch Hall, whose favourite reading is his own entry in the *Baronetage*). The story concerns the gradual coming together of Anne and Captain Frederick Wentworth, who meets her again some eight years after she refused his offer of marriage – a refusal much regretted since by her. She believes that he is now attached to Louisa Musgrove. An accident to Louisa on an expedition to the Cobb at *Lyme Regis – where Louisa is concussed after flirtatiously insisting on Captain Wentworth 'jumping her down' from the top – serves to delay the moment when Wentworth discovers, from a

Manchester Heroes: *the carnage of Peterloo in an etching of September 1819, three weeks after the atrocity.*

conversation in Bath, that his feelings for Anne are reciprocated. She accepts his renewed proposal.

Perth (42,000 in 1981) City on the west bank of the river Tay, flanked by two large riverside parks, North Inch and South Inch. The nine-arched bridge crossing the river just downstream of North Inch was built in 1766–71 by *Smeaton.

Deriving its early importance from the proximity of *Scone, Perth was considered the capital of Scotland in the 13–15C. The sermons preached here against idolatry in 1559 by John *Knox (in the 15–16C church of St John) unleashed the wave of iconoclasm which destroyed Scotland's religious art and sculpture. It was in Perth, in 1600, that the *Gowrie Conspiracy occurred. The town's best-known building derives its fame from fiction. Walter Scott, in *The Fair Maid of Perth* (1828), described a real house in North Port as the home of his 14C heroine, Catherine Glover. It is now officially called the Fair Maid's House. The Museum and Art Gallery, opened in 1935, specializes in 19–20C British painting and in 19C Scottish silver. Perth's oldest traditional industry has been the manufacture of dyes.

Perthshire Until 1975 an inland *county in central Scotland, now mostly in Tayside with part in the Central region.

Peterborough (115,000 in 1981) City in Cambridgeshire, on the river Nene. It derives from a Benedictine abbey founded here in about 650 by an Anglo-Saxon king of Mercia. The surviving abbey church was built mainly in the 12–13C; after the *dissolution of the monasteries it became, in 1542, the cathedral of a new Anglican diocese. The Norman nave is its greatest glory, surmounted by an early 13C painted roof; contemporary with the roof is the extraordinary west front, with three massively tall Gothic arches, like gaping mouths; the so-

called New Building, added as an extension behind the altar in the early 16C, is famous for its fan vaulting.

Apart from the cathedral and its immediate surroundings, little remains of Peterborough's past. It became an industrial town in the 19C and has been much rebuilt in the late 20C. Until 1965 it retained one medieval privilege, being administered as a separate county, the Soke of Peterborough.

Peter Grimes (1945) Opera by Benjamin *Britten which set post-war British music off to a flying start with its first performance at Sadler's Wells in June 1945. The story derives from *The Borough* (1820), a long poem by George Crabbe about life in his home town of Aldeburgh. Britten links two of Crabbe's characters: Peter Grimes, a solitary fisherman whose obsession with his work causes him to mistreat the boys he takes on as apprentices; and Ellen Orford, the schoolmistress who tries to befriend him. After two of his apprentices have died in accidents, local hostility to Grimes is so great that he is persuaded (by now himself in an unbalanced frame of mind) to sail his fishing boat far out to sea and to end his life by scuttling her. The richly atmospheric orchestral passages which punctuate the drama have become popular independently as *Four Sea Interludes*.

Peter Jones (London SW1) Department store housed since 1936 in one of the earliest and best examples of the modernist movement in Britain (designed by William Crabtree, 1905–91). Peter Jones (1843–1905) opened a drapery shop on part of the Sloane Square site in 1877, and his business was bought in 1905 by *John Lewis.

Peterloo (16 Aug. 1819) Popular name for a disaster symptomatic of the unrest and repression in Britain after the Napoleonic Wars. At a time of recession and high food prices a demonstration was held in Manchester on St Peter's Fields (where the Free Trade Hall now stands) to demand the reform of parliament. The crowd was peaceful and unarmed, but its unexpected size (some 60,000) alarmed the magistrates, who ordered troops to clear the area. They did so by charging and laying about them with their sabres. The exact figures are uncertain, but some 500 were injured and 11 killed. The name combined St Peter's Fields with the recent carnage of Waterloo.

***Peter Pan**, or The Boy Who Wouldn't Grow Up* (1904) Play for children by J.M. *Barrie which has become an enduring part of theatrical tradition, with a Christmas production in London every year except 1940 and a long succession of famous actresses playing the part of Peter.

Peter arrives mysteriously in the night nursery of the three Darling children, teaches them to fly and takes them back with him to the Never Never Land. Here the characters include the pirate Captain Hook (pursued and eventually eaten by the crocodile which bit off his hand and so got a taste for the rest of him) and the fairy Tinker Bell, who will fade away unless the children in the audience clap and shout that they believe in fairies. Peter eventually brings the children back to their parents and their nursemaid (a huge dog, Nana). The name of the eldest Darling child, Wendy, has since become a popular name for girls. It was coined by Barrie because a small child always called him her 'wendy' when trying to say her 'friend'.

In 1929 Barrie gave the royalties of the play to the *Great Ormond Street Hospital. There is a very popular statue of Peter Pan in *Kensington Gardens.

'Peter Piper picked a peck of pickled pepper' The first line of a tongue-twister which has been popular ever since published in *Peter Piper's Practical Principles of Plain and Perfect Pronunciation* (1813). The other three lines ring the changes on the same six prickly words.

Peter Rabbit see Beatrix *Potter.

Mary **Peters** (b. 1939) Northern Irish athlete who at her third Olympic Games, in 1972, won the gold medal for the pentathlon with a world record number of points (4801); she had finished fourth in 1964 and ninth in 1968. She also won the gold medal in the 1970 Commonwealth Games and successfully defended her title in 1974.

Petition of Right (1628) Declaration by both Houses of Parliament, asserting among other things that only parliament could authorize taxation and that only the due process of law could imprison anyone, two limits on the royal power which Charles I reluctantly accepted. It has been described as the greatest single constitutional advance in the four centuries following *Magna Carta.

Flinders **Petrie** (1853–1942, kt 1923) Archaeologist who excavated many sites in Egypt, most notably at Al Fayyum, Abydos and Memphis, and who was an important pioneer in the use of scientific method in field work.

Pet Shop Boys Pop duo consisting of Neil Tennant (b. 1954, vocals) and Chris Lowe (b. 1959, keyboards) who had a major international hit single with *West End Girls* (1985), topping the charts in the UK, USA and six other countries. Subsequent no. 1 hits in Britain have been *It's a Sin* (1987), *Always on my Mind* (1987) and *Heart* (1988).

Petticoat Lane (London E1) Thriving and long-established Sunday street market in and around Middlesex Street in the *East End, selling goods of all kinds. The market dates back at least to the 18C and retains the original name of the road (changed from Petticoat Lane to Middlesex Street in about 1830). After many attempts to close it down for illegal *Sunday trading, a special exception was made for it by an act of parliament in 1936.

Petworth House (23km/14m to the NE of Chichester) Medieval house largely rebuilt in 1688–93 for the 6th duke of Somerset, to the design of an unknown architect. Only the Marble Hall survives from the late 17C. The staircase, with murals by Laguerre, was rebuilt after a major fire in 1714. The famous Carved Room, looking very much of the 17C because of its panelling and the magnificent picture surrounds by Grinling *Gibbons, was in fact created in this form in 1794–5. J.M.W. *Turner frequently stayed at Petworth and there is an entire room of his paintings; the 3rd earl of Egremont was his major patron and provided the artist with a studio in the house. The park, laid out in 1752–6, is one of the masterpieces of Capability *Brown.

Nikolaus **Pevsner** (1902–83, kt 1969) German-born architectural historian who came to Britain in 1933. Among numerous other activities as author and lecturer, he was responsible for two major projects. One, launched in 1953 and still continuing, was *The Pelican History of Art*, aiming to cover the entire history of art and architecture in about 50 volumes; of this he was the editor. The other, even more daunting in that he undertook the entire work himself, was *The Buildings of England*, a minutely detailed description, county by county and place by place, of English architecture. The first volume was published in 1941 and the 46th, completing the series, in 1974. Widely referred to just as *Pevsner*, it stands as his monument.

Phantom of the Opera (1986) Musical by Andrew *Lloyd Webber, with lyrics by Richard Stilgoe and Charles Hart. It is based on a much filmed book by the French detective writer Gaston Leroux (1868–1927), about a hideously disfigured man, concealing his face behind a mask, who abducts an opera singer with whom he has become obsessed. The original production starred Sarah Brightman, Lloyd Webber's wife at the time, and Michael *Crawford.

Kim **Philby** see *Cambridge spies.

Philharmonia London-based orchestra founded in 1945 by Walter Legge (1906–79). Beecham conducted the first performance and Herbert von Karajan was much involved in the early years, but the orchestra developed its strongest link with Otto Klemperer (principal conductor from 1959). Subsequent principal conductors have included Riccardo Muti (1973–82) and, since 1984, Giuseppe Sinopoli. The orchestra, self-governing since 1964, tours a great deal abroad and is the resident orchestra both at the Taormina Festival in Sicily and at the Théâtre du Châtelet in Paris.

Philharmonic Hall see entry on the *Royal Liverpool Philharmonic.

Prince **Philip** see Duke of *Edinburgh.

Mark **Phillips** (b. 1948) Three-day event rider who was a member of Britain's gold-winning teams for the World Championships (1970), European Championships (1971) and Olympic Games (1972) – though the latter success was more technical than real, since he fell twice and his was the discounted score. He was in the team which won silver at the 1988 Olympics, and has had an exceptional record at Badminton with four wins (1971, 72, 74, 81). He married the *Princess Royal in 1973; they divorced in 1992.

One of Phiz's etchings of the portly bespectacled Samuel Pickwick (who a moment later falls through the ice).

Phiz Pseudonym used by Hablot Knight Browne (1815–82) as an illustrator of books. It was devised to go well with 'Boz', the pen name of Dickens, who chose Browne in 1836 to illustrate *Pickwick Papers*. The works of Dickens have given Phiz his lasting reputation, for he went on to illustrate *Nicholas Nickleby* (1839), *Martin Chuzzlewit* (1844), *Dombey and Son* (1848), *David Copperfield* (1850), *Bleak House* (1853), *Little Dorrit* (1857) and *A Tale of Two Cities* (1859).

phony war see *World War II.

Piccadilly (London W1) The main thoroughfare of the *West End, stretching from Piccadilly Circus to Hyde Park Corner. The name Piccadilly, the subject of endless conjecture since the 17C, probably derives from Piccadilly Hall, a house built nearby in about 1615 by a tailor, Robert Baker; and his house seems to have acquired that nickname because he had made a fortune selling piccadils (stiffened projecting borders worn at the neck, shoulders and wrists). In the 1640s the first houses were built along this road west from London; for a while it was called Portugal Street, but Piccadilly was the name which stuck.

When Nash drove *Regent Street through Piccadilly, he gave the intersection rounded edges to form a genuine 'circus'; the present broken shape of Piccadilly Circus (famous above all for *Eros) is the result of *Shaftesbury Avenue being added to the northeast in the 1880s, and of the other sides being redeveloped without regard for the circular groundplan.

picketing Reform of the laws on picketing was a feature of successive employment acts during the 1980s. The main changes were that pickets lost their immunity from civil legal action if the *strike was undertaken without a prior ballot of the members of the union concerned, or if the picketing was part of an attempt to enforce a *closed shop. In most cases secondary picketing (the picketing of an employer who is not an immediate party to the dispute) became illegal.

Wilfred **Pickles** (1904–78) Yorkshire broadcaster who was the first BBC newsreader with a strong regional accent. He became a national favourite as the host (assisted by his wife Mabel) of the most popular of Britain's radio quiz shows – *Have A Go* (1946–67). The answers and the prizes ('Give 'er the money, Barney!' was Pickles' catch phrase to his producer, Barney Colehan) were less important than the reminiscences and anecdotes which Pickles coaxed from his contestants.

'pick oop tha musket' see Stanley *Holloway.

Pickwick Papers (*The Posthumous Papers of the Pickwick Club* 1837, after being published in 20 monthly parts from April 1836) The work which made *Dickens's reputation, when he was 25. The fragmented nature of the book was deliberate, for it is merely an account of the comic adventures of the club founded by Samuel Pickwick (his fellow members are Tracy Tupman, Augustus Snodgrass and Nathaniel Winkle). Pickwick's own cheerful incompetence, the cause of many of the disasters, is offset by the sharp wit of the most successful character, his cockney servant Sam Weller. The text was commissioned to accompany sporting illustrations by Robert Seymour (*c.*1800–36), whose suicide after the second number caused Dickens to bring in *Phiz.

Picts People first mentioned in a Roman text of the 3rd century AD as the *Picti*, which may be a version of their

The cover photograph chosen for the first issue of Picture Post *in October 1938 (and used again for the last in 1957).*

name or may describe a habit of painting or tattooing their bodies (the word in Latin means 'painted people'). At that time they were the dominant group in northern Scotland and very effective raiders of Roman Britain. Their ethnic identity is uncertain but their language contained pre-Celtic elements, so they may have been earlier inhabitants of Britain driven north by the *Celts. Celtic Christianity reached them from Ireland by the late 6C, and in the 9C they were absorbed within a unified kingdom by the *Scots. Their art survives in their carved memorial stones and crosses.

The **Picture of Dorian Gray** (1891) Novel by Oscar *Wilde, first published in a somewhat different version in 1890 as a serial in *Lippincott's Monthly Magazine*. It is a notable expression of the sentiments of the *Aesthetic movement, depicting both the delights and consequences of self-indulgence. Dorian Gray is a beautiful young man whose evil genius is Lord Henry Wotton; the only influence for good in his life is Basil Hallward, the painter of the picture in the title. Dorian sells his soul to remain eternally youthful, allowing the corrupting effects of age and debauchery to disfigure instead the portrait, which he keeps in a locked upstairs room. He eventually murders Hallward; and in disgust at his appalling appearance in the portrait, stabs that too. He falls to the ground, dead, old and disgusting, while the image in the picture returns to its original perfection.

Picture Post The most celebrated weekly magazine in the history of British photo-journalism, though it survived for only a relatively short time. It was launched in 1938 by Edward Hulton (1906–8), and in the years immediately after the war had a circulation of more than 1.3 million. It closed in 1957, by which time the circulation had halved, but its legacy is a remarkable pictorial record of two decades.

picturesque The quality which people looked for in nature in late 18C Britain, greatly influencing the British *watercolour tradition. It derived from an interest in 17C artists such as Claude and Salvator Rosa, and developed with the romantic trend in *landscape gardening. But it was the Rev. William Gilpin (1724–1804) who popularized it through his accounts of his own sketching tours, beginning with *Observations on the river Wye . . . relative chiefly to Picturesque Beauty* (1782). Gilpin was the original of Dr *Syntax.

pidgin English Any form of English using a greatly reduced vocabulary and with grammatical rules of its own, developed originally for commercial transactions. The word 'pidgin' is believed to derive from the attempt of the Chinese in Canton to say 'business', the subject of their discussions with the British in the early 19C. Today people are more inclined to learn correct English, but pidgin has survived as a separate language in several parts of the world – most notably New Guinea, where the term for the British queen is said to have evolved as Big Fella Number One Missus.

The **Pied Piper of Hamelin** (1842) Poem by Robert *Browning, published in *Dramatic Lyrics*. The piper saves the town of Hamelin from a plague of rats by getting them to follow him as he pipes, but his fee is not paid. In revenge he works the same magic on the children of Hamelin, who dance behind him until all but one vanish into a cave. The legend, widely known from the Middle Ages, may be a folk memory of the hysteria of 1212, when thousands set off on the so-called Children's Crusade to the Holy Land and few returned.

Piers Plowman (late 14C) Allegorical poem in *alliterative verse by William Langland, about whom nothing is

A rare smile after Lester Piggott's 30th Classic victory, winning the 2,000 Guineas in 1992.

The Gloucester Old Spot pig, painted in Staffordshire by an unknown artist of the English naive school, early 19C.

known beyond what can be deduced from this one work; he was possibly a friar or other minor cleric, from the Midlands but living in London. He revised his poem in several versions, some of them amounting to more than 7000 lines. Piers the ploughman is one of a group of characters searching for Christian truth in the complex setting of a dream. The work includes sharply observed details of what Langland sees as the corrupt materialism of his time.

Lester **Piggott** (b. 1935) One of the most successful British jockeys of all time. In the years 1948–85 he won the Derby nine times (the first when he was only 18) and the St Leger eight times, including the rare feat of a *triple crown on Nijinsky in 1970. He was *champion jockey for an unbroken run of eight seasons from 1964, and the number of his victories in races worldwide exceeds 5200. In 1987 he was convicted of tax evasion involving £3.25 million and was sentenced to three years in prison, of which he served one. Against all expectations he started a second career as a jockey in 1990, and immediately proved that neither age nor adversity had diminished his brilliance. In 1992 he won the 2,000 Guineas to give him a record 30 *Classic victories; no other jockey since the 1880s has won even as many as 20.

Piggy see *Lord of the Flies*.

Piglet see A.A. *Milne.

pigs The wild boar was indigenous to the entire Eurasian landmass from western Europe to China, and the domestic pig was independently derived from it at various places (probably first in China). Out of some 300 breeds existing today, the best-known of those developed in Britain are the Berkshire (black with small patches of white on face, legs and tip of tail); the Gloucester Old Spot (white with black spots, now relatively rare); the Tamworth (golden red all over, deriving from Tamworth in Staffordshire and descended directly from the Old English forest pig); the Yorkshire or Large White (the nearest of all these to the conventional 'pink' pig of popular imagination,

bred in the 18C by crossing an English strain with a Chinese); and the Wessex Saddleback (black with white forelegs and a white band over the back).

Pilgrimage of Grace (1536) Uprising in Yorkshire, led by Robert Aske (*c*.1501–37), which was provoked by various aspects of the *Reformation but in particular by the start of the *dissolution of the monasteries. The rebels gathered a large army and captured York, but disbanded after being misled into believing that attention would be paid to their grievances and that there would be a general pardon. More than 200 were executed, including Aske himself, who was hanged, drawn and quartered in York.

Pilgrim Fathers The name given in the 19C to the first shipload of English settlers in Massachusetts, known until then as the Old Comers or Forefathers. Of the 102 in the party, 35 were Puritans who had sailed from *Boston in Lincolnshire in 1608 to establish their own church at Leiden, in the more tolerant Protestant Netherlands. In 1620 they decided to move to the New World and hired an English vessel, the *Mayflower*. They and the other settlers sailed from Plymouth on September 16 and landed on December 26 at a place to which they gave the same name, Plymouth.

*The **Pilgrim's Progress** from this world, to that which is to come* (1678–84) Allegory by John *Bunyan – one of the most read and best-loved of English books, because while unmistakably an improving religious work it also has the excitement of a folk tale and the rich characters of a novel. Part I (1678) tells how the pilgrim, Christian, sets off with his burden of sins upon his back to make his way to the Celestial City. His path takes him through the Slough of Despond, past the tempting delights of Vanity Fair, and into temporary imprisonment by Giant Despair in Doubting Castle. In Part 2 (1684) he is followed on the journey by his wife, Christiana, with their children. Three verses from Part 1, spoken by Mr Valiant-for-truth and beginning 'Who would true valour see', have been used as a hymn since the early 20C.

A communal version of the stocks, for four pairs of legs, in a woodcut of the 16C.

Pilgrims' Way Prehistoric track travelling along high ground from the coast in Kent towards Wiltshire, following the *Downs and the *Hog's Back. Though pre-Christian in origin, its present name reflects its use by medieval pilgrims, for two important religious centres, Canterbury and Winchester, are on the route.

Pilkington Firm which has manufactured glass at St Helens, in Lancashire, since 1826. In that year two brothers, Richard and William Pilkington, were among the original investors in the St Helens Crown Glass Company; by 1849 the company was known as Pilkington Brothers. It remained a family firm until 1970, when public shares were issued. By then it had long been a major international glass firm, but its greatest success had come in 1959 with the launch of its revolutionary float glass technology. Invented by Alastair Pilkington (b. 1920), the process involves floating glass on the surface of molten metal. Licensed in numerous countries, this soon became the standard method of manufacturing flat glass.

Pilkington Cup see *rugby football.

pillar box see *Trollope.

pillory and **stocks** Instruments of punishment in use in Britain from at least the 13C, in which offenders were exposed to public abuse and sometimes missiles. The culprit stood in the pillory, with head and hands held fast through holes in a cross-bar; the head was shaved in the case of a man, and the hair usually cut short for a woman. The stocks were slightly less unpleasant in that the miscreant could sit out the sentence with only the ankles trapped. Peter Bossy was the last to stand in the pillory (one hour for perjury at the Old Bailey in 1830), and the punishment was abolished by law in 1837.

Piltdown man One of the most successful of scientific forgeries. In 1912 an amateur geologist, Charles Dawson (1864–1916), revealed that he had found parts of the skull of an early man in a gravel formation at Piltdown, near Lewes in Sussex, together with fossil remains of extinct animals. The reconstructed skull appeared to share characteristics of both man and ape, and so was eagerly accepted by many scholars (but far from all) as the missing link in the evolution between our ape ancestors and ourselves. In honour of its finder, this early species of man was given the scientific name *Eoanthropus dawsoni* (Greek for 'Dawson's dawn man'). It was not until 1953 that improved methods of testing made the fraud unmistakable. Piltdown man exhibited the two sets of characteristics because the fragments combined a human skull and the lower jaw of an orang-utan, both of them scientifically treated to suggest fossilization.

Pimm's Summer drink in which lemonade, sliced fresh fruit and ice cubes are added to a base of Pimm's. The name derives from a restaurant belonging to James Pimm in the late 19C in Poultry, a street in the City of London. Pimm offered his customers a choice of six fruit cups, each using a different spirit for its alcohol content, and the drink became so popular that his recipe was marketed commercially. Nowadays a Pimm's almost invariably uses the gin-based No. 1 Cup, though No. 3 (vodka) is also available.

Pineapple Poll (1951) Ballet by *Cranko to music by Arthur Sullivan, arranged by Charles Mackerras, which was first performed at Sadler's Wells. The story was devised by Cranko from a poem by Sullivan's partner, W.S. Gilbert. It is based on the bumboat woman's story from *The Bab Ballads*, in which the girls of Portsmouth disguise themselves as sailors to go on board the gunboat *Hot Cross Bun*.

Arthur Wing **Pinero** (1855–1934, kt 1909) Playwright whose first successes were all farces (particularly *The Magistrate*, 1885), but who established himself as a serious dramatist in 1893 with *The *Second Mrs Tanqueray*. Of his later plays the best known is a comedy, **Trelawny of the 'Wells'*.

Pinewood Studios see J. Arthur *Rank.

ping pong see *table tennis.

Pink Floyd Psychedelic rock band formed in 1965 by Roger Waters (b. 1944, vocals and bass), Rick Wright (b. 1945, keyboards), Nick Mason (b. 1945, drums) and Syd Barrett (b. 1946, vocals, guitar). They were the first band to perform with light shows and projected slides, issuing their first single (*Arnold Layne*) in 1967. In 1968 Barrett left the group (he had a drug problem with LSD) and his place was taken by Dave Gilmour (b. 1944). Subsequent albums reaching the top of the UK chart were *Atom Heart Mother* (1970), *Wish You Were Here* (1975) and *The Final Cut* (1983). But *Dark Side of the Moon* was their greatest success; though it only reached no. 2, it was in the charts for nearly six years.

pink gin A drink fashionable in Britain in the mid-20C, consisting of gin, a little water and a dash of 'pink' (Angostura bitters, a dark red extract of gentian and spices, known from the 1820s at Angostura in Venezuela but now made in Trinidad).

pint see fluid *volume.

Harold **Pinter** (b. 1930) Playwright whose works have a characteristic blend of menace and humour, expressed in richly detailed but seemingly inconsequential dialogue. This was first seen in *The Birthday Party* (1958), but it was *The *Caretaker* which brought him success, followed by *The Homecoming* (1964), *Old Times* (1971) and *No Man's Land* (1975). He has also written many screenplays, including *The Servant* (1963) and *The *French Lieutenant's Woman* (1981). In recent years he has concentrated largely on directing plays.

Pip see **Great Expectations.*

John **Piper** (1903–92) Artist and author, with a particular interest in English architecture. He was a leading abstract painter in the 1930s, but found his characteristic style during the war in brooding images of bombed and burnt out buildings. These placed him in the rich landscape tradition which he explored in his book *British Romantic Painters* (1942); he later painted many churches and country houses in the same style. The same interests led him towards stained glass; probably the best known of his many windows is the one in *Coventry Cathedral. In the years after the war he was also busy in the theatre, particularly in collaboration with Benjamin Britten. From *The Rape of Lucretia* (1946) to *Death in Venice* (1973) Piper designed the sets for seven Britten operas, three of which had libretti by his wife Myfanwy.

Piper Alpha North Sea oil rig belonging to Occidental Petroleum which exploded on 6 July 1988 killing 167 men, including three rescuers. This worst of all North Sea accidents was investigated by Lord Cullen; his report made 106 recommendations, all accepted by the government, for improving safety in the offshore oil industry.

pips The term commonly used for the time signal on BBC radio, heard whenever a precise time is being given on the hour. The pips have been broadcast since 1924. Until 1990 they were known officially as the Greenwich Time Signal, because supplied by the *Royal Observatory, but the BBC now generates them itself. The signal consists of five short pips followed by a longer peeep, the exact stated time being at the start of the long final sound.

Camille **Pissarro** (1830–1903) French impressionist painter who, like *Monet, moved to London in 1870–1 to escape the Franco-Prussian War (the Prussians had overrun Pissarro's village and destroyed nearly all his paintings). He lived in south London (Lower Norwood) and has left many evocative images of the semi-rural suburbs of that time. His son Lucien, also a painter, settled in London in 1890.

Pistol A bombastic soldier who is one of Falstaff's disreputable companions in the second part of **Henry IV* and in *The *Merry Wives of Windsor.* By the time of **Henry V* he is married to Mistress Quickly.

Pitcairn Islands Group of small islands in the Pacific, halfway between New Zealand and Panama, which are a British dependent territory. The only inhabited island, Pitcairn, is a fertile volcanic rock about 5sq.km/1.9sq.m in size. It was settled in 1790 by Fletcher *Christian and other mutineers from the *Bounty.* The community in the early 1990s consists of about 50 people.

Pitlochry (42km/26m NW of Perth) Resort town in the Tayside region of Scotland, known for its summer festival (May to October) of plays and concerts. First held in 1951 in a marquee, productions are now in the riverside Festival Theatre (opened 1981). At the southern end of the nearby Loch Faskally is a ladder of 34 successive pools where salmon can be watched making their way upstream (it was created when the loch was dammed in 1950 for hydro-electric purposes).

Pitman's For many years the most widely used form of shorthand in English. It was devised by Isaac Pitman (1813–97), who published his method in *Stenographic Sound-Hand* (1837). His originality lay in basing it, to a much greater extent than any of his predecessors, on the sound rather than the spelling of words.

Pitmedden (26km/16m N of Aberdeen) Formal garden in the French 17c style, created from 1675 by Alexander Seton and restored in the 1950s within the surviving walled areas. The main features are four geometrical parterres with the frames (including lettering) provided by low box hedges. The intricate coloured patterns are created each summer by bedding out some 40,000 annual flowers in May.

William **Pitt** (also known as Pitt the Younger, 1759–1806) Statesman of exceptional precocity; he became prime minister at 24, and when he left office, 18 years later, he was still younger than any other prime minister in history beginning his or her first term. He was born into a political family, as the second son of the earl of *Chatham, and a seat in the House of Commons was found for him in 1781. He immediately made a mark with forceful speeches urging parliamentary reform, and by 1783 he was chancellor of the exchequer. In 1784, as the result of a political impasse largely caused by George III's hatred of Charles James *Fox, the king asked Pitt to form a government. Pitt did so initially with some difficulty, but early success in a general election kept him in power, combined with the essential element of the king's support.

His policies were pragmatic. He followed what he considered to be Britain's best interests without any overriding principle – an approach which has caused him to be seen as prefiguring the eventual transition from the *Tories into the *Conservative party. His first task was to restore the nation's finances after the expense of the War of American Independence. He succeeded in this by a variety of financial reforms and by reintroducing a sinking fund (a device nowadays called amortization, first used in 1716, by which a fund is built up so that its interest can be used to reduce a debt, in this case the national debt). These housekeeping improvements were later offset by the expense of the *French Revolutionary Wars, in response to which Pitt brought in *income tax.

The example of revolution in France led to radical agitation throughout the British Isles. In general Pitt's response was repressive, *habeas corpus even being suspended in 1794 (till 1801), but unrest in Ireland prompted more positive solutions. He was ahead of his time in trying to pass an *emancipation act for Catholics (the issue on which he resigned in 1801 because of widespread opposition, including that of the king), but he was able to force through the Act of *Union in 1800.

He was replaced as prime minister by the ineffectual Henry Addington (1757–1844), until the threat of French invasion caused George III to invite Pitt to form a new government in 1804. Pitt wanted a coalition with the Whigs, but he bowed to the king's outright rejection of Fox, thus making it impossible for other leading Whigs to accept office. This second ministry included the triumph of *Trafalgar, but Napoleon was still growing in strength when Pitt died in office after several years of illness.

He was a lonely man, known for his personal integrity (in an age when most were clubbable and corrupt), and the rival versions of his dying words suggest the extent to which his personal life was restricted to politics. One has him saying 'Oh my country! how I leave my country!', another substitutes 'how I love my country!', while in a third he murmurs that he could eat 'one of Bellamy's veal pies'. Even this has a political flavour, for John Bellamy was the first man to run a refreshment room in the House of Commons, which he opened in 1773.

Pitt the Elder see earl of *Chatham.

Pitt the Younger see William *Pitt.

plaid see *Highland dress.

Plaid Cymru (Welsh for 'the party of Wales') Political party committed to achieving self-government for Wales. It was founded in 1925 by six men in Pwllheli, in Gwynedd; they met in an upstairs room of a temperance hotel during the National *Eisteddfod. Plaid Cymru first contested a parliamentary seat in the general election of 1929 but did not achieve its first victory until its president, Gwynfor Evans (b. 1912), won a by-election at Carmarthen in 1966. The election of 1992 gave the party its highest representation yet in the House of Commons, with four seats. By an agreement of 1986 Plaid Cymru forms a bloc at Westminster with Britain's other nationalist party, the *SNP. The surge of nationalism in Scotland and Wales was rewarded with the referendum of 1979 on *devolution, but the concept was heavily rejected in Wales. A greater success for Plaid Cymru was its campaign for a Welsh-language television channel, *S4C. While independence for Wales remains the party's main theme, its broader political stance is socialist. Since 1991 Dafydd Wigley (b. 1943, MP for Caernarfon from 1974) has been president of the party and parliamentary leader.

Jean **Plaidy** see Victoria *Holt.

*The **Planets*** Orchestral suite by *Holst, written 1914–16 and first performed in its entirety in 1920. Each of the seven movements is named after one of the nine major planets (Earth was the only deliberate omission, for Pluto was not discovered until 1930). It is unusual among English music of the period in reflecting the influence of avant-garde composers such as Stravinsky.

planning permission The permit required before a new building can be constructed in Britain and before the use of an existing building can be much altered. The concept of a single planning permission was introduced in an act of 1947, replacing many separate *by-laws on subjects such as light and sanitation; the present regulations derive from the Town and Country Planning Act of 1990. Application for planning permission is made to the local authority (see *local government). The restrictions have sometimes been eased in specific development areas.

House of **Plantagenet** (1154–1399) Name which later became used for the descendants on the English throne of Geoffrey Plantagenet, Count of Anjou, who married *Matilda, daughter of Henry I. They were Henry II, Richard I, John, Henry III, Edward I, Edward II, Edward III and Richard II (see the *royal house).

Plas Newydd (SE coast of Anglesey) House facing the Menai Strait, built in its main features in 1793–9 by James *Wyatt. Most of the rooms are in a neoclassical style, but the two most spectacular are Gothic Revival – the Music Room and the Gothick Hall. The dining room, remodelled in the 1930s, has a huge landscape mural by Rex *Whistler with trompe l'oeil foreground details. Another house called Plas Newydd (Welsh for 'new place') is at *Llangollen.

Plassey see Robert *Clive.

Plas y Brenin see *Sports Council.

Sylvia **Plath** (1932–63) American author who became part of the British scene after marrying Ted *Hughes in 1957. She had published only one volume of poems (*The Colossus* 1960) and an autobiographical novel (*The Bell Jar* 1963) by the time she committed suicide in London in 1963. But several posthumous volumes – in particular *Ariel* (1965) – consolidated her reputation as a poet blending wit and tightly controlled distress.

David **Platt** (b. 1966) Footballer, at various times striker and midfield, who became one of Britain's most expensive transfers when bought by the Italian club Bari from Aston Villa in 1991 for £5.5 million; in May 1992 Bari sold him to Juventus of Turin for £7 million. He began his career with Manchester United in 1984, and in the following year was given to a Division 4 club, Crewe Alexandra, in a free transfer. He moved to Aston Villa in 1987 and was in the England team by the time of the 1990 World Cup.

'Play up! play up! and play the game!' The line which epitomizes the amateur spirit in British sport. It comes from a poem by Henry Newbolt (1862–1938), vividly suggesting a cricket match at the turn of the century:

> There's a breathless hush in the Close to-night –
> Ten to make and the match to win –
> A bumping pitch and a blinding light,
> An hour to play and the last man in.
> And it's not for the sake of a ribboned coat,
> Or the selfish hope of a season's fame,
> But his Captain's hand on his shoulder smote –
> 'Play up! play up! and play the game!'

The exceptionally obscure title of the poem, *Vitai Lampada* (Latin for 'the torch of life'), is – somewhat typically – borrowed from a poet of the 1st century BC, Lucretius.

PLC or **plc** see *limited liability.

Plimsoll line Painted on the hull of ships to mark the water line when the ship is carrying its maximum permitted load. Its name commemorates a Liberal politician and social reformer, Samuel Plimsoll (1824–98), who made safety at sea his special crusade. His book *Our Seamen* (1873), a hard-hitting attack on unscrupulous shipowners, led to the Merchant Shipping Act of 1876; this established the load line and gave the Board of Trade new powers of inspection on board ship.

Roy **Plomley** see *Desert Island Discs*.

ploughman's lunch Modern term for a plate of bread, cheese and pickles, served at midday in a *pub.

Plowden Report see *education.

Joan **Plowright** (b. 1929) Actress whose talent for rich and warm characterizations was first seen with the English Stage Company, in productions such as *The Country Wife* (1956) and *Roots* (1959). She married Laurence Olivier in 1961 and was a leading member of his original National Theatre company.

plum pudding see *Christmas pudding.

plus fours Loose breeches with an overhang at the knee, fashionable from Edwardian times for golf and shooting (nowadays only the latter). The name refers to the extra four inches of material needed by the tailor to achieve the overhang. More recently a version not so loose about the knees has been known as plus twos.

PLUTO (acronym for Pipe Line Under The Ocean) Project which was essential to the Normandy invasion in *World War II. In its early version pipelines from out at sea ran to the beachheads, enabling ships to deliver fuel without having to dock. Later, undersea pipelines were laid to carry petrol the full distance from Dungeness to Boulogne and from the Isle of Wight to Cherbourg.

Plymouth (254,000 in 1991) City, port and naval dockyard on the south coast of Devon, between the mouths of the rivers Tamar and Plym. The original town grew up in Anglo-Saxon times round Sutton Harbour, where the fishing boats still land their catches on the Barbican. Plymouth's importance began with the development in the 15–16C of larger ships for exploration and war; Plymouth Sound, an inlet of the English Channel with Plymouth at its head, was the perfect place to shelter a fleet of sailing ships, relatively safe but ready for action. It was here that the English fleet awaited the arrival of the Armada, and it is on the Hoe – Plymouth's level hilltop overlooking the Sound – that Drake is supposed to have played his famous game of *bowls. The *Pilgrim Fathers set sail across the Atlantic from the Barbican in 1620.

A royal dockyard was established at Devonport to the west, on the Tamar, in 1690. It remains in operation and the adjacent area of the Tamar estuary, known as the Hamoaze, is used as a harbour for British naval vessels. For this reason Plymouth was heavily bombed in World War II. The present city centre is entirely modern, designed around two main thoroughfares, Armada Way and Royal Parade.

Plymouth Brethren Christian sect deriving from a congregation established in Plymouth in 1831. Particular emphasis is laid on the text of the Bible and on the imminence of the Second Coming of Christ. The most influential leader was John Nelson Derby (1800–82), whose followers split from the main body (known subsequently as the Open Brethren) to become the Exclusive Brethren. The latter are so strict in their righteousness that they reject contact with anyone outside the sect, including even members of their own families.

Plymouth Sound see *Plymouth.

PM see *Prime Minister.

The Pobble who has no Toes (1877) Nonsense song by Edward *Lear about a Pobble who loses his toes when swimming the Bristol Channel, in spite of all the precautionary measures suggested by his Aunt Jobiska (who later maintains that Pobbles are happier without their toes).

Pocahontas (*c*.1595–1617) American Indian princess, daughter of the chief Powhatan, who was seized in 1613 and taken to Jamestown, the first successful English colony in *America. She was baptized a Christian and in 1614 she married one of the colonists, John Rolfe. In 1616 the couple and their infant son were brought to London. They were entertained in the royal palace at Whitehall and Pocahontas delighted London society. It was at this point that John *Smith first told the story of how he had been captured in 1608 by Powhatan's tribe and was about to be put to death, with his head already on the sacrificial stone, when Pocahontas intervened and saved his life. His timing has always cast some doubt on the incident, for he had four years earlier published an account of the colony in Virginia without mentioning this dramatic event. Pocahontas died just before returning to America.

pocket borough see *borough.

Poet Laureate The official poet of the royal household, originally with an obligation to write for public occasions (it is no longer a requirement, but most modern incumbents have produced some ceremonial verse). Ben *Jonson is considered the original English poet laureate (from 1616), though the first to be appointed as such was *Dryden in 1668; his annual salary was £200 and a butt of wine (an imprecise measure, but not less than 50 gallons). *Southey, *Wordsworth and *Tennyson were laureates in succession in the 19C. The most recent holders of the office have been *Masefield (1930–67), *Day-Lewis (1967–72), *Betjeman (1972–84) and since 1984 Ted *Hughes. Inflation has reduced the salary to a token amount, but Betjeman suggested and received the reinstatement of an annual allowance of wine.

Poets' Corner Part of the south transept of *Westminster Abbey, which became the most desirable burial place for poets after Chaucer was interred there in 1400. In 1740 a memorial was added to Shakespeare (buried in Stratford-upon-Avon), and since then it has been the custom to commemorate in this way the nation's great poets. The honour is conferred by the dean of Westminster, and so the lifestyle of certain poets (such as Burns, Byron or Shelley) has often caused a delay of many years before their admittance to the shrine. The most recent to have been honoured are *Auden and Dylan *Thomas. An unusual departure was the inclusion in 1990 of the great broadcaster Richard *Dimbleby, though it seems likely that the relatively ephemeral nature of the spoken word will make his name something of a mystery to future generations visiting the Abbey.

point-to-point Horse race over birch fences on a temporary race course, organized by a local hunt. The riders

A section of Poets' Corner, with monuments including those of Ben Jonson, Milton and Pope.

are amateurs and the horses must have been regularly used in the hunting field. The name reflects an origin similar to that of the related *steeplechase, from the days when such races were run between two given points in the countryside.

Hercule **Poirot** see Agatha *Christie.

Polaris see *nuclear submarines.

Cardinal **Pole** (Reginald Pole, 1500–58) Papal diplomat who became, in 1556, the last Roman Catholic archbishop of Canterbury. He was abroad when required to comment on *Henry VIII's divorce from Catherine of Aragon, but he sent a long treatise dismissing the supposed grounds and insisting on submission to papal authority. The result was that Henry executed Pole's elder brother and his mother. Pole remained in Italy, prominent among those trying to reform the church in response to the Protestant challenge, until he was sent as a papal legate to *Mary I. When Cranmer was dismissed from office and burnt, Pole succeeded him as archbishop of Canterbury. He was himself declared a heretic in 1557 by a reactionary new pope, Paul IV. He died in England, stripped of his papal authority, on the same day as Mary (17 Nov. 1558).

Polesden Lacey (14km/9m NE of Guildford) House built in the 1820s to a design of Thomas *Cubitt. It is of interest now as a lavish Edwardian country house and garden, created from 1906 by Mrs Ronald Greville. She used her fortune (her father founded the McEwan brewery in Scotland) to equip Polesden Lacey with excellent paintings and furniture as a setting in which to entertain Edward VII.

police The preserving of public order in medieval times was the responsibility of the *high sheriff of each county, while at a local level the parish constable brought offenders before a justice of the peace; Shakespeare provides the best-known early examples of each, in both cases comic, with Dogberry (the constable in *Much Ado About Nothing*) and Shallow (justice of the peace in *Henry IV Part 2*). The pursuit of a fugitive felon was a case of 'hue and cry', an established procedure in which those already in the chase called out to others to do their duty by joining in.

Such an amateurish system was inadequate to cope with the criminals of 18c London, and the first step towards a regular police force was the establishment in the 1740s of the *Bow Street Runners. But the foundation of a modern police force was the achievement of Robert *Peel – first in Ireland in 1814 with the predecessors of the *RUC (the 'peelers'), but above all in 1829 with London's Metropolitan Police Force (the 'bobbies').

The new Metropolitan Police needed premises close to the Home Office, and a building was chosen at 4 Whitehall Place in *Scotland Yard. In 1842 Scotland Yard established a specialist force of six detectives, calling them the Criminal Investigation Department. The CID now employs some 3500 detectives and itself contains several specialist departments well known by name to the public.

The Special Branch was formed in 1883 to combat *terrorism – at that time the enemy were the *Fenians, predecessors of the *IRA. Other duties have come to include protecting government ministers and foreign dignitaries visiting Britain, guarding against the activities of spies, and investigating offences against the *Official Secrets Acts. In 1992 the Special Branch relinquished to *MI5 much of its intelligence work against the IRA.

Probably the best-known department of the CID, through its fictional exploits on television, is the Flying Squad – reorganized in 1978 as the Central Robbery Squad, but still popularly known as the Sweeney (its name in Cockney *rhyming slang, from Sweeney Todd). It was set up in 1918 to patrol dangerous areas of London and it acquired in 1920 two motor vans to help in the task; it was they which won it the nickname of the Flying Squad.

The Fraud Squad was formed in 1946, staffed by officers from the Metropolitan Police together with the *City of London Police. Its remit was to tackle complex fraud cases, many of which have been dealt with since 1987 by the *Serious Fraud Office.

Although the Metropolitan Police are London's force, the CID takes a leading role in many national police activities – particularly against terrorists, drugs traffickers or forgers of currency – and Scotland Yard's National Identification Bureau is the central file of criminal records and fingerprints. But from around 1840 each county in Britain established its own police force, and they retain considerable autonomy. The regional police are accountable to local watch committees, composed of elected councillors and of magistrates, but the home secretary has been responsible for the Metropolitan Police. However, Home Office proposals were put forward in 1993 to restructure police authorities in England and Wales and to place the Metropolitan Police under a new authority of a similar kind.

In recent years the public image of the police has fared badly. Unrest in the inner cities from the early 1980s led to charges of racial prejudice within the force, and to the impression that police patrolling in cars had become too remote – a perception which led to a new emphasis on community relations and the 'bobby on the beat' (in official terms the Home Beat Officer). More recently confidence in the good faith of the police has been shaken by a series of cases – in particular several involving officers of

Bull's Eye on Bobby: cartoon in Punch *in 1877, with John Bull suspecting corruption in Scotland Yard.*

the *West Midlands Serious Crime Squad – in which police fabrication of evidence was revealed by *ESDA. Widespread concern led to the setting up in 1991 of a Royal Commission on *Criminal Justice.

Police Pop trio which was formed in 1977 by Sting (Gordon Sumner, b. 1951, vocals and bass), Stewart Copeland (b. 1952, drums, percussion and vocals) and Andy Summers (b. 1942, guitar and vocals). Performing in what became known as a white reggae style, they had two no. 1 hit singles in 1979 (*Message in a Bottle*; *Walking on the Moon*), and began in that year an unbroken succession of no. 1 albums – *Regatta de Blanc* (1979), *Zenyatta Mondatta* (1980), *Ghost in the Machine* (1981), *Synchronicity* (1983). In 1985 Sting issued a solo album, *The Dream of the Blue Turtles*, and his new career led to the break-up of the group. Of his subsequent albums ... *Nothing like the Sun* (1987) and *The Soul Cages* (1991) reached the top of the UK charts.

political parties The *two-party system which has prevailed in British politics goes back to the early *Tories and Whigs, who evolved in the 19C into the *Conservatives and the *Liberals. In the early 20C the *Labour party displaced the Liberals as the main rival to the Conservatives. The *Alliance of two centre parties, the Liberals and the SDP, demonstrated the size of the centre vote in the elections of 1983 and 1987 but did not win a corresponding number of seats; these parties later merged to become the *Liberal Democrats.

The *Unionist issue in Northern Ireland provides the main political plank of the Ulster Unionists and the Ulster Democratic Unionists; the opposite stance, aiming for a united Ireland, is that of the *SDLP and of the more radical *Sinn Fein. The nationalist parties campaigning for independence in Scotland and Wales are the *SNP and *Plaid Cymru.

Pollock's Toy Museum see *toy theatre.

Pollok Park see *Glasgow.

poll tax A tax levied by 'poll' or head of population, a method notorious in English history for having partly provoked the *Peasants' Revolt. It was similarly unpopular and only marginally less dramatic in its effects when imposed by the Conservative government in the 1980s under the euphemism of 'community charge'. Its supporters, among whom Mrs Thatcher was prominent, argued that it was fair (in the limited sense that everybody paid the same) and that it had the advantage of making all adult citizens aware of the level of *local taxes (these had impinged only on householders under the previous system of rates). Its more manifest unfairness was that it took no account of ability to pay, apart from a few categories of people eligible for an 80% reduction.

The poll tax was introduced with relatively little trouble in Scotland in 1989; but the approach of the first collection of the tax in England and Wales in the spring of 1990 led to a riot in the West End of London, followed by an orchestrated campaign of nonpayment. After the replacement of Mrs Thatcher as prime minister, later in 1990, the Conservative administration spent large sums of money in softening the impact of the tax and replaced it as soon as possible (in 1993) with a new *council tax. Meanwhile councils had been left with the massively expensive task of attempting to collect the poll tax from defaulters (liability orders were served on 2.8 million people for the 1991–2 tax year), and there was some evidence that the tax had affected the 1992 general election by deterring a significant number of potential voters from declaring themselves on the electoral register.

Polly Peck Small East End clothing firm bought in the early 1960s by a Turkish Cypriot, Asil Nadir (b. 1941). He built it up into one of Britain's largest companies, with activities ranging from fresh fruit to electronics. Valued early in 1990 at nearly £2bn, Polly Peck crashed spectacularly later that year. Nadir was declared bankrupt and was subsequently charged with theft and false accounting offences involving some £160 million.

Polonius see *Hamlet.

polytechnics see *universities.

pommy Mildly abusive slang term in Australia and New Zealand for an immigrant from Britain, and hence for anyone British. Its origin is unknown and all the main theories lack conviction. One is that it is short for 'pomegranate', which could be yelled as a rough rhyme for 'immigrant'; another is that it is a version of tommy (from *Tommy Atkins), introduced by Australian soldiers returning from the Boer War; and a third that it comes from the initial letters of Prisoner of Mother England, referring to the convict settlers of Australia.

Pomp and Circumstance A phrase borrowed from Shakespeare (in *Othello*) and used by *Elgar as the title for a set of five marches (1901–30). It is said that Edward VII, hearing the first of these, suggested that the tune of the trio section would be very fine if set to words. These were soon provided (by A.C. Benson, 1862–1925), and the tune and words formed the finale of Elgar's *Coronation Ode* (1902) under the title *Land of Hope and Glory*. The version of this published on its own (with words differing from those in the *Coronation Ode*) rivals *Jerusalem* as England's favourite patriotic song – and features with it on the last night of the *Proms.

ponies Several breeds of small horse have developed in different parts of Britain, where they live semi-wild. The three main areas are the New Forest, Dartmoor and Exmoor. Other separate strains are the Highland pony from Scotland (used by stalkers for carrying deer) and the Dales and Fell ponies from northern England. By far the best-known British breeds internationally are the Shetland and the Welsh mountain ponies. The Shetland or 'sheltie' is the smallest of the traditional pony breeds (only the modern miniature varieties, such as the Falabella of Argentina, are smaller). The Welsh mountain pony was brought down from the hills in the 19C to the indignity of working underground in the coal mines, but is now widely used for riding.

Pont Cysyllte (5km/3m E of Llangollen) Cast-iron aqueduct by *Telford, carrying the Shropshire Union Canal over the valley of the Dee. Barges move along in a great metal gutter, 307m/1007ft long and resting 37m/121ft up in the air on 19 stone arches. This extraordinary feat of engineering was begun in 1795 and completed in 1805. Telford was simultaneously (1796–1801) building a shorter and lower aqueduct, to a similar design, to carry the canal over the Ceiriog valley at Chirk.

Clive **Ponting** see *moles.

Pontin's The main rival to *Butlin's in the holiday camp business, with the staff known as bluecoats instead of redcoats. The chain was established in 1946 by Fred Pontin (b. 1906), who opened his first site in that year at Brean Sands near Weston-super-Mare.

Pontypool (37,000 in 1981) Town in Gwent, historically the centre of the Welsh iron industry, with smelting done there from 1577. In the 18C Thomas Allgood and his son Edward established the product for which the town has been best known, the famous *japanned Pontypool ware.

Pontypridd (33,000 in 1981) Town in Mid Glamorgan, at the southern end of the Rhondda valley, both known and named for a famous bridge (*pontypridd* is Welsh for 'bridge near the earthen hut'). The bridge spans the river Taff in a single stone arch of 43m/140ft. It was built in the 1750s by a local stonemason, William Edwards.

Pony Club A backbone of British country life for middle-class children. Organized in 1929 as a junior branch of the Institute of the Horse, the purpose of the club was to encourage children to ride. The nation was divided into districts, based wherever possible on local hunts, and the present-day pattern of branch activities was soon established, with its tests and badges, summer camps, *gymkhanas and rosettes.

Pooh see A.A. *Milne.

pools (short for football pools) Britain's nearest equivalent to a national *lottery, prior to the introduction of an actual lottery during the 1990s. Coupons for betting on the results of football matches were on sale before World War I, but the present nationwide postal system dates back to the 1920s when both the leading pools were founded. Littlewoods began in 1923 when three young Manchester telegraph operators printed 4000 copies of a coupon and succeeded in selling just 35 of them outside Manchester United's football ground. At the end of a gloomy first season only one of the three persevered, John Moores (b. 1896); his own name is now more widely known through the *John Moores Exhibition. Vernons, the other leading firm, also began in Lancashire – it was founded in Liverpool in 1925 by A.E. Sangster.

People betting on the pools vary the amount of their stake by the number of lines which they fill on the coupon, and they gather points by correct predictions of the match result. In the most popular method of playing, the Treble Chance, high points are scored by predicting draws. On a new scale introduced in 1993 there are 3 points for a draw with one goal on each side; $2^{1}/_{2}$ points for a draw of 2–2 or above; 2 points for a no-score draw (0–0); and $1^{1}/_{2}$ for a win, whether at home or away. The available kitty or 'pool' is shared between the highest-scoring coupons in various categories, with the result that a small stake can sometimes bring a very large prize. The first Littlewoods win of more than £1 million, in 1984, came from an outlay of £1.32.

Poor Laws The Poor Law of 1601 codified the method for coping with the needy which had evolved in local areas during the 16C. It had been widely realized that the problem could only be solved by a compulsory levy on householders within a district, and the act established the relevant district as the *parish. It took a long time before the law was effective nationally, but over the next two centuries it gradually became accepted that parishioners were responsible for the well-being of the poor in their midst. The poor naturally tended to gravitate towards richer or more generous parishes, and a familiar aspect of the poor laws in the 18C was a widespread obsession with keeping out or throwing out the needy from neighbouring districts.

Economic conditions during and after the Napoleonic Wars led to alarming increases in the poor rates, causing the entire system to be brought into question. As a result the new Poor Law of 1834 changed the emphasis; it introduced, on rigorously *Benthamite principles, a much

The first known use of Pop in pop art: Paolozzi's collage of c.1947, I was a Rich Man's Plaything.

more stern and disapproving view of those applying for help. A relatively little used element of the previous system had been the workhouses, in which the able-bodied poor were supposed to be provided with work of a kind useful to the parish. After 1834 these became a central part of the scheme. They were redefined as institutions which had to be more uncomfortable than the lowest level of subsistence in the outside community, with discipline and hard work to reinforce the message.

By mid-century the workhouse was established in the public mind as a terrifying place of last refuge, as the legislators of 1834 had intended. Later in the century humanity reasserted itself in most such institutions, and many workhouses became pioneers of health care and education for the poor. But the public hatred of the system was powerfully expressed in a poem of 1903, *Christmas Day in the Workhouse* by George Sims. It depicts a dramatic moment when an inmate thrusts away the Christmas meal so charitably brought by the guardians and their ladies, and then roundly abuses them for their patronizing cruelty; exactly a year ago, he tells them, his starving wife died after he had been denied a crust of bread for her at the door of this same workhouse – on the grounds that they never gave 'out relief', but would instead admit her to the institution.

A Royal Commission investigated the poor laws in 1909, and a minority of four members recommended scrapping the system entirely (one of them, Beatrice *Webb, wrote the minority report). The Poor Law of 1930 finally altered the emphasis to that of social security, under the national control of the minister of health, and in 1948 the postwar Labour government established the right of the poor to national assistance (now known as *income support).

Mr **Pooter** see *The *Diary of a Nobody*.

pop art Movement in painting and sculpture which began independently in Britain and the USA during the 1950s, as a reaction against the solemnity of 'high' art and the remoteness of abstraction. The images were bright, jazzy and vulgar, using the everyday clichés of advertising and packaging.

The first recorded use of the word 'pop' in art is in a collage of about 1947 by Eduardo *Paolozzi (b. 1924 in Scotland); the work is entitled *I Was a Rich Man's Plaything* and 'POP!' appears from the barrel of a gun aimed at the luscious plaything herself. In 1956 Paolozzi, Richard Hamilton (b. 1922) and others exhibited together as the Independent Group, and a small collage in the exhibition by Hamilton (*Just what is it that makes today's homes so different, so appealing?*) is often quoted as the first icon of the movement. By then the phrase 'pop art' had been coined by the British critic Lawrence Alloway (in about 1955), but he applied it to the visual ingredients of popular culture itself – not, as it was later used, to the art created from them.

The pioneers were followed by a second wave of slightly younger artists who were students at the Royal College of Art, among them Peter *Blake and David *Hockney. It was their work, seen in a series of 'Young Contemporaries' exhibitions, which brought pop art to the attention of a wide public in the early 1960s. Over much the same time span a similar progression had happened in the USA, from the work of Jasper Johns and Robert Rauschenberg in the second half of the 1950s to the emergence in the early 1960s of the best-known pop artists of all, Andy Warhol and Roy Lichtenstein.

Alexander **Pope** (1688-1744) The most brilliant poet of the *Augustan age. He began life, the son of a linen merchant, with a double disadvantage: as a *Roman Catholic he was excluded from the major schools and from university, so that much of his education was at home; and a curvature of the spine meant that he had a height of only 4ft 6in (1.37m). But his wit and his charm (to those he

was not savaging in print) soon made him a prominent figure in society.

An Essay on Criticism (1711) revealed his brilliant way with a memorable phrase, introducing to the language such often quoted lines as 'A little learning is a dangerous thing' or 'Fools rush in where angels fear to tread'. The **Rape of the Lock* appeared in the following year and in 1713 he published *Windsor Forest*, praising the reign of Queen Anne just as Virgil had celebrated that of the emperor Augustus. With his translations of the *Iliad* (1715–20) and the *Odyssey* (1725–6), both published by subscription, he earned enough to live the rest of his life in considerable style.

Pope moved to *Twickenham in 1717. Pioneering a fashion for riverside villas, he enlarged an existing house for himself and his mother and added a famous grotto (a tunnel under a nearby road, leading to his garden). He was now considered something of an authority on *landscape gardening, and was a welcome guest in many stately homes, such as Stowe, where the grounds were being developed. But his success and his sharp pen brought him as many enemies as friends; the former were vigorously attacked in the **Dunciad* (1728, final version 1743).

Nearly all Pope's poetry is in heroic couplets (pairs of rhyming lines, each of ten syllables), and his mastery of this form allowed him a wide range of surprises, contrasts, touches of bathos and other comic or satirical effects. The *Moral Essays* (1731–5) and the *Epistle to Dr Arbuthnot* (1735) were the most brilliant of his later works, the *Essay on Man* (1733-4) being as polished but less original.

Pop goes the weasel! Popular song of the 1850s, with words (attributed to W.R. Mandale) which have caused endless speculation. The first verse states that the money goes 'Up and down the City Road,/ In and out the Eagle'. This certainly relates to the Eagle Tavern, an early *music hall in London's City Road. The usual explanation is that the money spent at the music hall has come from 'popping' (pawning) the 'weasel' (said to be an obscure tool used by tailors or hatters). It seems more likely that 'pop goes the weasel' was already current as a

Pope's villa at Twickenham, turned into an even grander mansion by its next owner: detail of painting by Samuel Scott, c.1755.

United Kingdom population since 1801; census figures, in millions			
	UK	England and Wales	Scotland	Northern Ireland
1801	n/a	8.893	1.608	n/a
1811	13.368	10.165	1.806	1.397
1821	15.472	12.000	2.092	1.380
1831	17.835	13.897	2.364	1.574
1841	20.183	15.914	2.620	1.649
1851	22.259	17.928	2.889	1.443
1861	24.525	20.066	3.062	1.396
1871	27.431	22.712	3.360	1.359
1881	31.015	25.974	3.736	1.305
1891	34.264	29.003	4.026	1.236
1901	38.237	32.528	4.472	1.237
1911	42.082	36.070	4.761	1.251
1921	44.027	37.887	4.882	1.258
1931	46.038	39.952	4.843	1.243
1941	n/a	n/a	n/a	n/a
1951	50.225	43.758	5.096	1.371
1961	52.709	46.105	5.179	1.425
1971	55.515	48.750	5.229	1.536
1981	55.848	49.155	5.131	1.533
1991	56.467	49.890	4.999	1.578

There was no census in Northern Ireland in 1801, and none anywhere in the UK in 1941.

Source: Annual Abstract of Statistics (see *Central Statistical Office).

nonsense phrase (it is the name of a country dance) and that appropriately nonsensical rhymes became attached to it. Certainly the later verses, about a pudding of rice and treacle and a monkey knocked off a table, have little to do with pawnshops or tools of the trade.

Popish Plot (1678) Fictitious Jesuit plot to murder *Charles II and place *James II on the throne. Its existence was dreamt up by Titus Oates (1648–1705), a failed Anglican clergyman who had also partly trained as a Catholic priest in Spain and France. His experience gave his story just enough authentic detail for it to be believed in an age when religion was the tinderbox of politics. He was treated with high honour as the saviour of the nation and given a pension. His false accusations sent some 35 people to their deaths before the deception was realized. Convicted of perjury in 1685, his own punishment was only flogging and imprisonment.

Karl **Popper** (b. 1902, kt 1965) Austrian-born philosopher who went to New Zealand in 1937 and in 1945 took a post at the London School of Economics, which sub-

sequently remained his base. His approach, much of it against prevailing fashion, has been to apply philosophical enquiry to areas such as science and society rather than linguistics. His works have included *The Logic of Scientific Discovery* (German 1934, English 1959), *The Open Society and its Enemies* (1945) and *The Poverty of Historicism* (1957).

Poppy Day The name by which *Armistice Day became known because of the custom of wearing a red cloth poppy, in token of the famous poppies of the fields of Flanders where so many had died. The poppies proved a brilliant fund-raising as well as commemorative device. They are made and sold by the *British Legion, and the proceeds go to their charities for ex-service men and women.

population Population figures for any period before the 19C are academic guesses, achieved for the early centuries by calculating a total from surviving scraps of isolated evidence and later through the registration of baptisms and burials. It is usually said that the population of England in the late 11C, at the time of the *Domesday Book, was a little over one million; that it grew to about 4m by 1300, before being greatly reduced in the 1340s by the *Black Death; that it did not recover to the 4m level until the mid-16C; and that it reached nearly 5m by 1600, and 6m by 1700.

The first *census to count the population was taken in 1801. It gave a figure of nearly 9m for England and Wales, with another 1.6m in Scotland. By 1851 the population had doubled: there were 18m people in England and Wales and nearly 3m in Scotland; Northern Ireland (not counted in 1801) added almost 1.5m making a total of over 22m in the area of the present UK. This had almost doubled again by 1901, with a UK figure of more than 38m. Growth during the 20C has been much slower, increasing less than 50% in 90 years to reach 56.5m in the census of 1991.

porcelain see *bone china.

pork pie Cold pie of minced pork in pastry, often in a small enough form to be an individual helping. Together with the *Scotch egg it used to be a staple in *pubs, but improved standards of pub food in recent years have made both less common.

Porlock (10km/6m W of Minehead) Village on the coast of Somerset, remembered in particular as the home of the person who interrupted *Kubla Khan.

porridge Oatmeal boiled to a soft consistency and eaten nowadays as a breakfast dish, with milk or cream. Historically it was a staple diet in Scotland (hence the definition in *Johnson's dictionary of oats as 'a grain which in England is generally given to horses, but in Scotland supports the people'). Customs sometimes attached to porridge in Scotland have included the tradition that salt may be added when eating it but not sugar, and that it should be consumed standing up.

Porridge (BBC TV 1974–7) Situation comedy set in a British prison, written by Ian La Frenais and Dick Clement and starring Ronnie *Barker as Fletcher, the old lag with the ability to manipulate the system to his comfort and advantage. His cell mate was played by Richard Beckinsale; his enemy, the ramrod-backed chief warder, by Fulton McKay; and the well-meaning, gullible warder by Brian Wilde. A single series of *Going Straight* (1978) followed Fletcher in his efforts to adapt to life outside. 'Doing porridge' is slang for serving a prison sentence.

port Red wine from the valley of the Douro in Portugal, fortified with brandy, which like the white *Madeira fulfilled an 18c British passion for sweet wines. The majority of the firms shipping port from the Portuguese harbour of Oporto (from which it gets its name) were established by British families and have British names. Roughly once every three years the wine is good enough for the shippers to declare a 'vintage'; the port of these years is bottled early, matures slowly in the bottle, and is referred to by the name of the shipper and the year of the vintage. The wine of other years, known as wood port, matures more rapidly in wooden casks. The best of the wood port, left to a considerable age, becomes pale and is called 'tawny'. The rest is ordinary port, sometimes known as ruby port, which in the early 20c was a favourite winter drink in British pubs.

Vintage port has traditionally been much drunk in aristocratic and academic circles after dinner, with a certain degree of ceremony – in particular the taboo that the decanter must circulate in a clockwise direction. White port, relatively rare and in colour much like sherry, is made from white grapes and is drunk as an aperitif.

porter see *Whitbread.

Portia see The *Merchant of Venice.

Michael **Portillo** (b. 1953) Conservative politician, MP for Enfield Southgate since 1984, who entered the *cabinet in 1992 as chief secretary to the Treasury.

Isle of **Portland** Rocky peninsula, 6km/4m long, off the Dorset coast, with Portland Bill as its craggy southern tip.

Portland cement The standard modern cement, differing from earlier varieties in that the mixture of limestone and clay (or shale) is heated in manufacture; the resulting cement will harden even underwater. It is so named because Joseph Aspdin, taking out a patent for it in 1824, maintained that its colour when set resembled the very desirable Portland stone.

Portland spies Espionage network uncovered in 1961. Two clerks at the Underwater Weapons Establishment at Portland, in Dorset, had been regularly bringing secret documents up to London; they were Harry Houghton and his mistress Ethel Gee, widely known as Bunty. They regularly handed them over near the Old Vic to Gordon Lonsdale, who took them to a house in Ruislip where Peter and Helen Kroger kept what passed at the time for an extremely hi-tech espionage establishment – including a transmitter hidden beneath the floor, and photographic equipment by which the documents could be reduced to microdots. Peter Kroger dealt in second-hand books and the documents travelled to Russia as microdots pasted over full stops. The Krogers were actually two Canadians, Morris and Lona Cohen, and Lonsdale was a Russian (Konon Trofimovich Molody). Lonsdale received a 25-year sentence, the Krogers 20 years and Houghton and Gee (who married when they came out of prison) 15 years. Lonsdale had served only part of his sentence when he was exchanged in 1964 for Greville Wynne, a British businessman imprisoned as a spy in Russia because he had brought out material from a Soviet double agent, Oleg Penkovsky.

Portland stone A limestone quarried on the Isle of *Portland and much used as a prestige building material, as for example for St Paul's Cathedral.

Portland Vase (British Museum) Roman vase of cameo glass, deep blue with the raised figures in white, dating

Engraved ticket to see Wedgwood's ceramic version of the Portland Vase, exhibited in his London showroom in 1790.

from the late 1st century BC. It was bought by the duke of Portland in the 18c and from 1810 was on loan to the British Museum. In 1845 it was smashed by an Irish visitor, known only by the false name of William Lloyd. Reconstructed from about 200 pieces, it was finally bought by the museum in 1945. In 1987 it was taken to pieces and was reassembled using modern adhesives – a process which took a year and was recorded in a *Chronicle* television documentary. The vase has been often reproduced, most notably by *Wedgwood.

Portmeirion (8km/5m N of Harlech across the bay) Fantasy village on the coast of Wales, privately owned, to which day visitors are charged an admission fee. It was created from 1925 by the architect Clough Williams-Ellis (1883–1978), who set out to build on this craggy and lushly wooded peninsula a place as delightful as the seaside village of Portofino in Italy. He designed his own pastel-washed Italianate structures, and added to them older buildings saved from demolition elsewhere. Most are let out now as holiday homes. The visual delights of Portmeirion became widely known through its use as the setting for the TV serial The *Prisoner.

Portobello Road (London W11) Street which was once a track leading to Porto Bello farm, named to celebrate the British capture of Porto Bello on the coast of Panama from the Spaniards in 1739. It has been known for its market since the 1870s. Originally gypsies and costermongers sold here, but in recent decades it has been taken over by antique dealers. The northern end is relatively cheap and goods are heavily marked up as they progress southwards. The chief market day is Saturday, when the road is one of London's major tourist attractions.

Porton Down The name commonly used for the government's Chemical and Biological Defence Establishment at Porton in Wiltshire. It was first established in World War I in response to the poison gas used by the Germans against British and French troops at *Ypres in 1915.

Portsmouth (185,000 in 1991) City, port and naval dockyard on the south coast of England, in Hampshire. The city occupies a promontory to the east of a large natural harbour; the town on the western side of the narrow entrance channel is Gosport. Portsmouth's importance derives from Henry VII establishing a dockyard here in 1496, and it remains Britain's chief naval station (known to sailors as Pompey). The Royal Dockyard occupies a large section of the city and is closed to the public except for access to the Royal Naval Museum and Portsmouth's three great ships from the past, the *Mary Rose, *Victory and *Warrior. The cathedral is the old church of St Thomas (its main parts variously 13C, 17C and 20C), which was promoted to this status when Portsmouth became a diocese in 1927.

Port Sunlight (8km/5m S of Liverpool through Mersey tunnel) Model village built from 1888 by William Lever, later Lord *Leverhulme, for the workers at his Sunlight Soap factory. He founded the Lady Lever Art Galley in memory of his wife, who died in 1913. The custom-built museum (by William and Segar Owen) contains his very personal choice of furniture and decorative arts, mostly of an exceptional standard, with some excellent pre-Raphaelite and Victorian paintings.

Port Talbot (51,000 in 1991) Port and town on the north shore of the Bristol Channel, in West Glamorgan. It is the site of Britain's largest steel-producing complex in the early 1990s, with blast furnaces, coke ovens and rolling and strip mills extending some 7km/4m along the coast. A deep-water harbour was completed in 1970.

posh Word meaning rich and classy which first appeared in *Punch* in 1918 and for which many explanations have been put forward, all lacking in proof. Undoubtedly the most beguiling is that the initials stood for Port Out Starboard Home, those being the north-facing sides of a ship making the journey to India and back (offering therefore the coolest and most desirable cabins). Etymological sleuths have checked on cabin prices and interviewed passengers who made the journey at the time but have found no evidence of the word's use in this sense. But it is far simpler and more elegant than most guesses at derivation and deserves perpetuating for that reason alone.

postage stamps see *Post Office.

postcode Britain's version of the US zip code, introduced by the Post Office in 1968. The first two letters indicate one of the main regional sorting offices, and subsequent figures and letters narrow the area covered by the postcode to only about 15 houses.

Postman Pat (BBC from 1981) A television cartoon character for small children, created by John Cunliffe (b. 1933) and Ivor Wood (b. 1932). Postman Pat also features in a series of picture books.

Post Office (until 1969 the General Post Office or GPO) Organization responsible for postal services in Britain. Established in 1635 by Charles I as a public service under royal monopoly, and already known in the 17C as the General Post Office, it ceased to be a government department in 1969. Its monopoly powers have since been considerably reduced.

By the late 18C the postal service was highly organized, and improved roads were making for impressive delivery speeds. In 1784 the first regular mail coach was established, from London to Bath and Bristol. Soon coaches were leaving London each evening at 8 p.m. for a variety of destinations, accompanied by armed guards. Letters

Mail coaches leaving the General Post Office in 1830: the impressive building (designed by Smirke, completed 1829, demolished 1912) stood to the north of St Paul's. (Aquatint after James Pollard.)

reached Edinburgh in less than 48 hours, but postage was expensive and the method of payment inefficient. The cost depended on the distance travelled and the number of sheets (resulting in some very cramped writing); moreover the charge was made on delivery, so the letter had to make an expensive return journey if not accepted.

In 1840 Rowland Hill (1795–1879) swept away these restrictions in a single bold scheme, much ridiculed when he first proposed it, which laid the basis for all modern postal services. His new 'penny post' levied a uniform charge by weight (a penny per half ounce) for any letter or package travelling any distance within Britain. Even more crucial, it introduced prepayment. For this Hill proposed special envelopes, designed for him by the artist William Mulready (1786–1863). But the Mulready envelopes were not popular. What the public preferred was a subsidiary idea of Hill's – small pieces of paper, stating the sum paid and with a 'glutinous paste' on the back for sticking on to one's own envelope. With the Penny Black and the Two Pence Blue the world's first postage stamps had arrived. The monarch's head was considered sufficient national identification, and Britain remains the only country in the world not to be named on its stamps.

The penny post lasted until 1918, but price stability for the first 58 years of the service has been followed by inflation of some 5000% in the subsequent 75 years. In 1968 a distinction was introduced between first- and second-class postage; letters paying the first-class rate are supposed to be delivered to most of the country the following day.

The large network of post offices (some 20,000 in the early 1990s) has been used for *National Savings and for the *Girobank. Potential methods of privatizing the Post Office were under discussion early in 1993.

potato Native to South America, and cultivated by the Incas, the potato was brought to Spain in the second half of the 16C. It was some while before it changed from an expensive curiosity (with the supposed power of curing impotence) to a basic food, and the change seems to have come first in Ireland, where by the end of the 17C it was a major crop. (It had possibly been first planted there on the estates of Walter *Raleigh.) The potato soon became the basic food of the Irish peasant. The spread of the crop was encouraged by hardship and warfare; the potato yields far more food from the same area of ground than a grain crop, can be harvested when convenient, and is less likely to be destroyed by enemy or storm. But the dangers of total reliance on it were also first seen in Ireland, in the *Great Famine.

Pot Black (BBC 1969–86) The programme which first showed *snooker on television and thus transformed the game from a minority pursuit to one of the nation's most popular sports. In the 15-minute *Pot Black* programmes the competitors won or lost on a single frame – considered an unacceptable lottery in the modern era of multi-frame duels lasting several hours. The first *Pot Black* champion, in 1969, was Ray Reardon.

Potsdam Town southwest of Berlin where the Allied leaders held their final conference of *World War II (17 July–2 Aug. 1945). Roosevelt had died in April, so Truman took part as the US president. Churchill began the conference but was replaced before the end by Attlee, who had won the general election in Britain. Stalin again represented the USSR. Now that the final postwar positions of the western and Soviet armies were established, there was greater disquiet than at *Yalta about Russia's exclusion of her allies from the affairs of eastern Europe. From Potsdam an ultimatum went to Japan demanding immediate surrender, sent in the names of Truman, Churchill and Chiang Kai-shek, who had given his agree-

Peter Rabbit disobeys his mother and visits Mr MacGregor's garden: illustration by Beatrix Potter (1902).

ment by radio. The ultimatum was soon followed by the first atom bomb.

Percivall **Pott** (1714–88) Surgeon at Bart's whose treatises on the practice of surgery were influential in their time, but who is remembered for a fracture of bones in the ankle – of a kind known now by his name – which he himself suffered when he was thrown from his horse in Southwark in 1756.

Beatrix **Potter** (1866–1943) Author of a series of enduring classics for young children. The stories are deceptively simple, told with a certain irony and allowing the animals strongly differentiated characters; Beatrix Potter's delicate watercolour illustrations are based on close observation of nature and of the habits of her many pets. The early books emerged from stories in illustrated letters to the children of her former governess, sent in the 1890s when she was living with her parents in London. Her pets at the time included a rabbit and a hedgehog called respectively Peter and Mrs Tiggy. *The Tale of Peter Rabbit* (1902) was her first published success. Its very first scene demonstrates what made her books amusing and pleasantly alarming to young children. Mrs Rabbit tells her offspring not to go into Mr MacGregor's garden and explains why: 'Your father had an accident there; he was put in a pie by Mrs MacGregor.'

Characters whose tales were told in similar style in the following years included Benjamin Bunny, Mrs Tiggy-Winkle, Jeremy Fisher, Tom Kitten, Jemima Puddle-Duck and Samuel Whiskers. After 1913 she was less productive. In that year she married William Heelis, a local solicitor who had helped in her purchase of a farm near Sawrey in the Lake District. She now settled down to 30 years as an active farmer, specializing in the breeding of Herdwick sheep, a local variety. Her house, Hill Top, is kept as a museum; and a selection of her drawings and watercolours is exhibited in the building where her husband had his office, in nearby Hawkshead.

Dennis **Potter** (b. 1935) Television dramatist with a wide-ranging output. Two early plays (*Vote Vote Vote for Nigel*

503

Barton and *Stand Up Nigel Barton*, both 1965) were autobiographical – about a working-class Oxford graduate attempting to make a career in left-wing politics. *Blue Remembered Hills* (1979) achieved a disturbing dislocation by casting adult actors as a group of children playing together during World War II. **Pennies from Heaven, The *Singing Detective* and *Lipstick on Your Collar* (1993) are ambitious and lengthy exercises in a technique which he has made very much his own, with cheerful popular music erupting within fairly bleak drama.

Stephen **Potter** (1900–69) Author and broadcaster, remembered in particular for his humorous studies of competitive behaviour. Each of his two best-known books added a word to the language: *The Theory and Practice of Gamesmanship; or the Art of Winning Games without actually Cheating* (1947) and *One-Upmanship* (1952).

The **Potteries** Region, known also as the *Five Towns, in which *Staffordshire pottery has been made since the 17C.

John **Poulson** (1910–93) Architect who was at the centre of a major scandal about corruption in local government. He and a senior civil servant, George Pottinger, were sentenced in 1974 to five years in jail for bribery in connection with the winter sports centre at Aviemore. A month later Poulson was convicted on further charges which also brought a six-month jail sentence for T. Dan Smith, a former leader of Newcastle-upon-Tyne city council. The proceedings caused the resignation of the home secretary, Reginald Maudling (1917–79), because his ministerial responsibility for the police was incompatible with a slight personal involvement; he had at one time been chairman of two of Poulson's companies.

pound An imperial measurement of *weight and also the basic unit of British *currency. The two were originally linked, at a time when 240 silver pennies, known as *sterlings, weighed one pound.

pound in your pocket A useful phrase which became current after a much criticized broadcast by Harold Wilson in 1967, on the devaluation of sterling, in which he assured the public that 'the pound here in Britain, in your pocket or purse or in your bank' had not been devalued – true only until the owner tried to spend it on imported goods.

The relative value of the pound in your pocket at different periods is a subject of great interest but of even greater inexactitude, because the cost of goods in relation to each other is always changing. Basic commodities tend to go up in price, while manufactured products come down; an early black-and-white TV set cost a great many more pints of beer or loaves of bread than its colour equivalent today, and in the 1950s a ball-point pen was a suitable coming-of-age present.

The *RPI (Retail Prices Index) attempts to counteract this by regularly adjusting its balance of commodities. The ready-reckoner (below) for the pound in your pocket since 1950 is based on this index (see the RPI entry for the annual percentage changes).

'pound of flesh' see The *Merchant of Venice.

'pour encourager les autres' see Admiral *Byng.

Powderhall Stadium in Edinburgh of which the name is widely known from the Powderhall Sprint, a race over 130 yards (119m) first run there in 1870. A famous Edinburgh New Year event since those days, the sprint transferred in 1970 to the city's new *Meadowbank Stadium; the distance was then altered to 110m/120yd. Officially known now as the New Year Festival Sprint, the race is for professionals (with a top prize of £2000 in the early 1990s) and it attracts heavy betting; but a system of handicapping means that the fastest sprinter is not necessarily the winner. The Powderhall Stadium is still used for speedway and greyhound racing.

Anthony **Powell** (b. 1905) Novelist best known for his sequence of 12 books entitled *A Dance to the Music of Time* (1951–75). Together they offer a panorama of the experiences of Powell's own generation – members of the upper and middle classes who were young after World War I. The most striking character in a large cast is the

The Pound in your Pocket									
	1950	*1955*	*1960*	*1965*	*1970*	*1975*	*1980*	*1985*	*1990*
1950	**£1.00**	1.32	1.50	1.78	2.23	4.10	8.03	11.36	15.15
1955	0.76	**£1.00**	1.14	1.35	1.69	3.11	6.09	8.62	11.49
1960	0.66	0.88	**£1.00**	1.19	1.48	2.73	5.36	7.58	10.10
1965	0.56	0.74	0.84	**£1.00**	1.25	2.30	4.50	6.37	8.49
1970	0.45	0.59	0.67	0.80	**£1.00**	1.84	3.61	5.10	6.80
1975	0.24	0.32	0.37	0.43	0.54	**£1.00**	1.96	2.77	3.69
1980	0.12	0.16	0.19	0.22	0.28	0.51	**£1.00**	1.41	1.89
1985	0.09	0.11	0.13	0.16	0.20	0.36	0.71	**£1.00**	1.33
1990	0.07	0.09	0.10	0.12	0.15	0.27	0.53	0.75	**£1.00**
	1950	*1955*	*1960*	*1965*	*1970*	*1975*	*1980*	*1985*	*1990*

Choose on the left of the chart the nearest year to when the pound was in your pocket; then move horizontally along the line to discover its value in other years.

NB. The figures have no significance if read in vertical columns.

appalling Kenneth Widmerpool, whose naked ambition to better himself is first seen as comic but then turns sinister as he becomes steadily more powerful. The title is that of a painting by Poussin in the *Wallace Collection, which the narrator of the books, Nicholas Jenkins, acknowledges as an influence.

Enoch **Powell** (b. 1912) Conservative politician (MP for Wolverhampton SW 1950–74, and for South Down 1974–87 as an Ulster Unionist), who has been one of the most eccentric figures on the recent political scene. A professor of Greek and author of several scholarly works and books of poems, he was also the leading demagogue on the issue of *immigration. He was dismissed from Edward Heath's shadow cabinet in 1968 after what became known as his 'rivers of blood' speech in Birmingham; within days there were strikes by workers in sympathy with him and hundreds of dockers marched to Westminster in his support. It was typical that his actual words had been drily pedantic and seemingly far removed from the passions he inflamed: 'As I look ahead, I am filled with foreboding. Like the Roman, I seem to see "the river Tiber foaming with much blood".'

*The **Power and the Glory*** (1940) Novel by Graham *Greene which is the most powerful statement of his central concerns. It was inspired by his visit in 1937 to Mexico, where the Catholic Church was banned by a left-wing regime. The story balances two representative figures, both unnamed: a whisky-sodden priest, lustful father of a child, whose vocation somehow enables him to transcend his failings; and a lieutenant, a well-intentioned humanist, coolly dedicated to serving the best interests of the state. The priest reaches safety across the border, but is enticed back to give the last rites to a dying man and is cornered and executed by the lieutenant. The most unlikely of saints has suffered martyrdom.

'power corrupts' see Lord *Acton.

PowerGen see *electricity.

Powis Castle (30km/19m W of Shrewsbury) House in the county of Powys, in a commanding position looking out over the Severn towards England; it has developed over the centuries from the 13C fortress of a dynasty of Welsh princes. The interiors are of many periods, with some fine Elizabethan rooms and a baroque grand staircase. The marriage in 1784 of a Powis heiress to the son of Lord *Clive brought an excellent Indian collection as well as the wealth of a nabob, with which many of the house's impressive contents were purchased. The gardens are famous for four Italianate terraces, blasted from the rock of the hillside in the 1690s and surviving unaltered today, though the yews now bulge delightfully over the edges in a way of which the formal 17C would not have approved.

Powys (119,000 in 1991, administrative centre Llandidrod Wells) Since 1974 a *county in Wales, formed from Montgomeryshire, Radnorshire and the greater part of Breconshire.

John Henry **Poynting** (1852–1914) Physicist who was professor at Birmingham from 1880 until his death, remembered in particular for his work in electromagnetism. The Poynting theorem, published in 1884, states that the flow of electromagnetic energy at a point can be expressed as a product (the Poynting vector) of the separate electric and magnetic field intensities.

PPP (Private Patients Plan, Tunbridge Wells) Non-profit-making medical insurance company, launched in London in 1943 as the Hospital Service Plan; the name was changed in 1962 to Private Patients Plan. Unlike BUPA, its larger rival, PPP does not build and run hospitals.

PPS see *Parliamentary Private Secretary.

PR see *proportional representation.

Praise to the Holiest in the height see Cardinal *Newman.

'precious stone set in the silver sea' Britain, as described in the best known of all passages celebrating the nation. Spoken by *John of Gaunt in Shakespeare's *Richard II, it is part of a single-sentence speech of 21 lines made up of nothing but phrases describing England: 'this sceptred isle . . . this other Eden, demi-Paradise . . . this blessed plot, this earth, this realm, this England . . . this dear dear land'. The eulogy rolls irresistibly on, to reveal only at the end its bitter purpose – a lament for the present contrary state of things.

Premier League The name, from the 1992–3 season, of what had previously been Division 1 of the *Football League. It is a break with tradition in various ways. It is run by the *Football Association rather than the League (its creation had been opposed by the League but favoured by many of the break-away top clubs); and an exclusive Premier League *television deal was signed with BSkyB, which has meant that for the first time League matches by the best clubs are not available live and free to British viewers (extracts are shown later on the BBC). Other innovations include Sunday afternoon and Monday night matches, and the half-time interval extended from 10 to 15 minutes. In the first season the number of clubs was 22, with plans to restrict the League in the future to 20.

premium bonds A *savings scheme introduced in 1956 and the only government-sponsored *lottery in Britain until the introduction of a national lottery in the mid-1990s. The amount of prize money distributed is equivalent to a given rate of interest on the whole fund, and the winning numbers are selected by *Ernie. In the early 1990s there was more than £2bn invested in premium bonds.

Prentice Pillar see *Roslin Chapel.

prep school see *public school.

Pre-Raphaelites In 1848 three students at the Royal Academy schools, Holman *Hunt, *Rossetti and *Millais, formed the Pre-Raphaelite Brotherhood, aiming to create art which expressed important ideas and which derived from a direct study of nature. Their inspiration, in reacting against the murky academic art of their own time, was the brightly lit and minutely detailed narrative painting of the 15C, which had ended with Raphael. To express the solidarity of the brotherhood they added the letters PRB as a monogram on their pictures. It was partly this hint of a secret group which caused a storm to break about their heads, together with the outrage caused by Millais' realistic treatment of the Holy Family in *Christ in the House of His Parents* (1850, Tate Gallery). But they found an immediate champion in *Ruskin, and a year later Millais' *Return of the Dove to the Ark* (1851, Ashmolean Museum) was a great success.

The sharply observed clarity of these images was influential, and soon other artists were exhibiting works now described as Pre-Raphaelite. Ford Madox *Brown, older than the three in the brotherhood, can be seen as a precursor, for he was already painting in a closely related

The mystical strain in the Pre-Raphaelite movement: Rossetti's early and influential Ecce Ancilla Domini *(1850).*

style; Charles Allston Collins (*Convent Thoughts* 1851, Ashmolean) was linked almost from the start; among the best known of the others are Arthur Hughes (*April Love* 1855, Tate; *Home from Sea* 1862, Ashmolean) and Henry Wallis (*The Death of Chatterton* 1856, Tate; *The Stonebreaker* 1857, Birmingham City Art Gallery).

From the start there was a more mystical feeling in the work of Rossetti (for example his Annunciation scene, *Ecce Ancilla Domini* 1850, Tate), and this element of Pre-Raphaelitism also had prolonged influence – above all on *Burne-Jones.

Presbyterians Originally those in the English and Scottish *Reformation who wished to follow the example of Calvin in Geneva. In a presbyterian system authority resides in elected pastors and lay elders, rather than in the bishops of the episcopal *Church of England (*presbyter* and *episcopus* are Latin for an elder and a bishop). The Presbyterians were thus the original *Puritans, until they themselves were opposed by more radical reformers, the *Congregationalists. Parliament was Presbyterian in the *English Civil War. Presbyterians were persecuted in the Restoration as *Nonconformists, but it was they who in 1690 became the established *Church of Scotland. In England they have been part of the *United Reformed Church since 1972.

John **Prescott** (b. 1938) Labour politician, MP for Hull East since 1970, who has at various times been opposition front bench spokesman on employment, on energy and – since 1988 – on transport. He has been a member of the shadow cabinet since 1983.

Preseli Hills Range of hills close to the west coast of Wales, in Dyfed, known in particular as the site from which the blue stones were somehow brought to *Stonehenge.

Press and Journal Aberdeen's daily newspaper and the oldest in Britain after the *Belfast News Letter. James Chalmers published the first issue of *Aberdeen's Journal* in 1748, and the present name derives from a merger in 1892 with the *Aberdeen Free Press.*

Press Association (PA) Britain's national news agency, launched in 1868 by the regional newspapers as a joint news-gathering operation. The shares are still largely owned by the non-London press (the association was founded when the whole of Ireland was within the UK, so it includes newspapers in the Irish republic). In the early 1990s about 250 full-time journalists and 1000 stringers were employed. Until recently all news and photographs went by wire to the newsdesks, but since 1990 the information has increasingly been distributed by direct broadcast or via satellite. In 1941 the PA became owners of about 40% of *Reuters, bringing a windfall to its shareholders in 1984.

Press Complaints Commission see *privacy.

Preston (144,000 in 1981) Port at the head of the estuary of the river Ribble, and the administrative centre of Lancashire. Of strategic importance from Roman times as a river crossing, and rich from the weaving of wool in the Middle Ages, its modern importance has been as one of the first cotton-spinning towns of the *Industrial Revolution. The Harris Museum and Art Gallery, opened in 1893, occupies a spectacularly grand classical building by a local architect, James Hibbert (1853–1903). It has an outstanding collection of another local man, the painter Arthur Devis (*c.*1711–87), who is known for the period charm of his stilted conversation pieces; they reflect the custom of the time by which painters used flexible wooden figures or dolls to compose the picture. Every 20 years (most recently in 1992) the Preston Guild Merchants hold a great festivity on the first Monday after August 29, celebrating the founding of their guild in 1179.

Preston North End, known as the Lilywhites or North End (Deepdale, Preston). Football club formed in 1881 when the North End Cricket and Rugby Club (established in 1863) decided to give up the other games. The club was a founder member of the *Football League in 1888 and immediately won its place in football history by winning both the League and the FA Cup in the same season – a feat achieved on only four other occasions (Aston Villa 1897, Tottenham Hotspur 1961, Arsenal 1971, Liverpool 1986). The club's more recent history has not been so illustrious; it has not played in the top division since 1961. Club victories: FA Cup 1889, 1938; League Champions 1889.

Prestonpans see the *'45 Rebellion.

Prestwick Golf course on the west coast of Scotland, a little to the north of Ayr, which is the original home of the *Open. The tournament was played here in each of its first 12 years, from 1860, and on several subsequent occasions (the last in 1924). The nearby Prestwick airport, once well known to transatlantic passengers, has now been replaced in that role by *Glasgow and is used mainly for freight.

Prevention of Terrorism Act Temporary measures introduced in 1984 to curtail *terrorism originating in Northern Ireland; the full title was the Prevention of Terrorism (Temporary Provisions) Act. It was replaced in 1989 by another act of the same name, which during the early 1990s has been extended for a further 12 months each March. The act gives the *police extra powers of arrest and interrogation where a terrorist link is suspected, and the right to deny suspects entry to Britain; it classifies certain groups as 'proscribed organizations'; and it enables the courts to demand any information which may help in the prevention of terrorism. This can greatly inhibit the work of journalists in Northern Ireland; a test of the issue occurred in 1992, with the prosecution of Channel 4 over the programme *The *Committee.

Margaret Price (b. 1941, DBE 1993) Welsh soprano who made her debut as Mozart's Cherubino with Welsh National Opera in 1962 and at Covent Garden in 1963. She soon became known as a leading performer of Mozart in most of the opera houses of the world. Her repertoire also includes many of the soprano roles of Verdi and Richard Strauss.

Pride and Prejudice (1813) Novel by Jane *Austen with the best-known opening sentence in English fiction: 'It is a truth universally acknowledged that a single man in possession of a good fortune must be in want of a wife.' An early version of the book was written in 1796-7 under the title *First Impressions*. Of various

A typical detail from Preston's local painter, Arthur Devis: Francis Vincent, charming but wooden, shows signs of being based on a mechanical figure (1763).

wrong first impressions, the most important is that which the lively and intelligent Elizabeth Bennet forms of FitzWilliam Darcy; like his friend Charles Bingley (to whom the opening sentence applies), Darcy is a single man in possession of a very good fortune. But his haughtiness and Elizabeth's dignity (his is the pride, hers the prejudice) keep them apart until the end of the book, when at last they come happily together – as do a more easy-going couple, Bingley and Elizabeth's sister Jane. Meanwhile a third sister, Lydia, has eloped with an endearing adventurer, George Wickham. Mr and Mrs Bennet, the parents, are an ill-matched couple; he is a detached and wise friend to Elizabeth, while her mother remains relentlessly shallow and ambitious. Subsidiary characters include the self-important clergyman, William Collins, who pays court to Elizabeth; and the imperious Lady Catherine de Bourgh, Darcy's aunt and the patron of Mr Collins.

Pride's Purge see the *Long Parliament.

J.B. Priestley (John Boynton Priestley, 1894–1984) Novelist and playwright, born in Bradford and fond of projecting the image of a plain blunt Yorkshireman. He achieved very large sales with his first novel, *The *Good Companions* (1929), and in adapting it for the stage (1931) he began another successful career. Several of his early plays use narrative dislocations and tricks with time to good theatrical effect (*Dangerous Corner* 1932, *I have been here before* 1937, *Time and the Conways* 1937), but it is his moral mystery tale *An Inspector Calls* (1947) which has held the stage most effectively. In the darkest year of the war, 1940, Priestley began his famous radio broadcasts, 'Postscripts' after the news bulletin on Sunday evenings. His bluff commonsense, his strong voice, his humour, his very Englishness all contributed to bringing him a large and responsive audience.

Joseph Priestley (1733–1804) Experimental chemist and dissenting minister, as radical in his approach to science as to religion. His first studies were in electricity, but an interest in gases was prompted by observing fermentation in a brewery next door to his chapel in Leeds. In 1773 he was employed as librarian at *Bowood, where he was able to continue his researches. In 1774 he isolated oxygen and went on to discover several other gases including nitrogen (he cannot claim priority for either, because Scheele had independently prepared oxygen and nitrogen about two years earlier in Sweden). Priestley also did pioneering work on photosynthesis.

In 1780 he became minister of a nonconformist congregation in *Birmingham, where he was a prominent member of the Lunar Society. But his radical views (attacking conventional Christianity, supporting the American and French revolutions) made him an object of popular hostility. On 14 July 1791, the second anniversary of the fall of the Bastille, a mob burnt his chapel, house and laboratory. He moved first to London and then in 1794 to the USA, where he remained for the rest of his life.

priest's hole see *Roman Catholics.

primary schools *State schools for children from 5 up to the age of 11, which was the upper limit for free *education under the act of 1870. Schools for children above this age (not compulsory until 1944) became known by contrast as secondary schools.

Primate of All England see Archbishop of *Canterbury.

Primate of All Ireland see *Armagh.

Prime Ministers

(All have their own entries except those whose dates are given here.)

1721	Walpole	1828	Wellington	1902	Balfour
1742	Lord Wilmington (1673–1743)	1830	Grey	1905	Campbell-Bannerman
1743	Henry Pelham (1675–1754)	1834	Melbourne	1908	Asquith
1754	Duke of Newcastle (1693–1758)	1834	Peel	1916	Lloyd George
1756	Duke of Devonshire (1720–64)	1835	Melbourne	1922	Law
1757	Duke of Newcastle	1841	Peel	1923	Baldwin
1762	Earl of Bute (1713–92)	1846	Russell	1924	MacDonald
1763	George Grenville (1712–70)	1852	Derby	1929	Baldwin
1765	Marquess of Rockingham (1730–82)	1852	Aberdeen	1929	MacDonald
1766	Chatham	1855	Palmerston	1935	Baldwin
1767	Duke of Grafton (1735–1811)	1858	Derby	1937	Chamberlain
1770	North	1859	Palmerston	1940	Churchill
1782	Marquess of Rockingham	1865	Russell	1945	Attlee
1782	Earl of Shelburne (1737–1805)	1866	Derby	1951	Churchill
1783	Duke of Portland (1738–1809)	1868	Disraeli	1955	Eden
1783	Pitt	1868	Gladstone	1957	Macmillan
1801	Henry Addington (1757–1844)	1874	Disraeli	1963	Douglas-Home (Lord Home)
1804	Pitt	1880	Gladstone	1964	Wilson
1806	Lord Grenville (1759–1834)	1885	Salisbury	1970	Heath
1807	Duke of Portland	1886	Gladstone	1974	Wilson
1809	Perceval	1886	Salisbury	1976	Callaghan
1812	Liverpool	1892	Gladstone	1979	Thatcher
1827	Canning	1894	Rosebery	1990	Major
1827	Viscount Goderich (1782–1859)	1895	Salisbury		

Primate of England see Archbishop of *York.

Prime Minister The leader of the party or coalition in power and the nation's chief executive, presiding over the *cabinet. The office developed almost accidentally in the 18C. The monarch had taken cabinet meetings until the accession of George I, who spoke no English. In his absence someone had to take the chair, and this politician became known as the prime minister. Sir Robert *Walpole is considered the first to have held the office. He did so for 21 years (1721–42), longer than any of his successors.

The positions held jointly by Walpole were first lord of the Treasury and chancellor of the exchequer. The former has remained the office held by all prime ministers, for it was not until 1905 that the rank of prime minister itself was formally acknowledged. (Since 1968 each prime minister has also been the minister for the *civil service.) In the 18–19C prime ministers were as often in the House of *Lords as the House of *Commons, but the last to sit in the Lords was the marquess of Salisbury. The official residence since Walpole's time has been 10 *Downing Street, with *Chequers as a country house since 1921.

In recent years a cabinet minister has sometimes been designated deputy prime minister, usually as a political sop. The office has no constitutional authority and does not imply (unlike the vice-presidency of the USA) any right of succession should the prime minister die.

Prime Minister's Questions see *Question Time.

*The **Prime of Miss Jean Brodie*** (1961) Novel by Muriel *Spark about the effect of an unusual schoolmistress on a group of teenage girls in the 1930s. Miss Brodie, well-meaning but deeply pretentious, is determined that the Brodie set shall follow her own example (she is now in her prime) and become 'the crème de la crème'. Unfortunately she is devoted to Italy and the splendid example of 'Mussolini and his *fascisti*' – an obsession which leads to her downfall. The story was filmed in 1969 with Maggie Smith as a perfect Jean Brodie.

Prince and **Princess** see *HRH.

Prince Consort Title conferred on Prince *Albert by Victoria in 1857. It was of importance in terms of precedence, making him first in rank after herself and of a corresponding position in relation to foreign royalty. The title has not been conferred on the only other husband of a queen in recent history, the duke of *Edinburgh.

Prince of Wales see Prince of *Wales.

Prince Regent see *George IV.

Princes in the Tower Edward V, the 12-year-old king of England, and his younger brother, Richard. They were together lodged in the *Tower of London when their uncle was proclaimed king as Richard III, on 25 June 1483. They were seen from time to time playing in the garden, and then glimpsed occasionally through windows, but it was not long before the boys effectively disappeared. It is generally assumed that they were murdered, probably in August, on the orders of Richard. In 1674 a wooden chest was discovered beneath a staircase in the Tower, containing the bones of two children. These were placed in an urn in Westminster Abbey, and a scientific analysis in 1933 revealed that they were the remains of children of the correct ages.

Princess Royal The title of the eldest daughter of the monarch, but one which is not invariably conferred. It was held from 1932 until her death in 1965 by Princess Mary, only daughter of George V (see Lord *Harewood), and has been since 1987 the title of Princess Anne.

*The **Princess Royal*** (Princess Anne, b. 1950) The second child and only daughter of *Elizabeth II (see the *royal family). She was educated at *Benenden. An excellent three-day event rider, she won the individual gold at the European Championships in 1971 and represented Britain at the 1976 Olympics in Montreal. Her most prominent public role has been as the President of the Save the Children Fund. In 1973 she married Mark *Phillips; they have two children, Peter (b. 1977) and Zara (b. 1981). They divorced in 1992, and later that year she married Commander Tim Laurence (b. 1955) in a quiet family ceremony at Crathie church near Balmoral. The title of *Princess Royal was conferred on her in 1987.

Princes Street The main street of Edinburgh, named after the prince of Wales (the future George IV), possibly in conjunction with one or more of his brothers. It was one of the three original streets of the 18C New Town, but the buildings of that time along the north side have long since been replaced. What gives the street its great distinction is that there are no houses on the south side, allowing a superb view over an open valley (the Princes Street Gardens) to the Old Town and the castle on its rock. The most striking of the monuments on the south side is that of Walter Scott, erected in 1840–4 with a 61m/200ft Gothic spire above a statue of the writer (with his dog Maida) by John Steell (1804–91). Beyond the east end of the street rises another of Edinburgh's landmarks, *Calton Hill.

principal boy see *pantomime.

Principia Mathematica see entries on Isaac *Newton and Bertrand *Russell.

Prinny Familiar version of 'prince', widely used as a nickname for the future *George IV when prince of Wales.

James **Prior** (b. 1927, baron 1987) Conservative politician, MP for Lowestoft 1959–83 and Waveney 1983–7, who entered the *cabinet as minister of agriculture in 1970 and was then lord president of the council and leader of the House of Commons (1972–4). He was subsequently secretary of state for employment (1979–81) and for Northern Ireland (1981–4).

Lucinda **Prior-Palmer** see Lucinda *Green.

Miss **Prism** see The *Importance of Being Earnest.

prison conditions Until the late 18C prisons were chaotic and insanitary places, with both sexes thrown together and the comforts of the inmates depending entirely on how much they could pay the warders. Notorious examples in London were the *Fleet, the *Marshalsea and *Newgate. Conditions began to improve through the work of reformers such as John *Howard and Elizabeth *Fry. Most 19C prisons were custom-built, based on contemporary theories both of security and correction. Jeremy *Bentham published a prison design which he called the 'panopticon', in which prisoners in separate cells on different landings could all be watched from a central point. Modified versions of this idea were put into practice in many Victorian prisons, starting with London's Pentonville in 1842.

A large number of Britain's prisons survive from the 19C, when most of them were designed for fewer inmates than they now contain. Antiquated conditions (including the notorious slopping out of chamber pots) and overcrowding (prisoners often locked up two or three to a cell for all but a few hours a day) have been contributory factors in the large number of prison riots in recent years – of which *Strangeways in 1990 was the worst. The violence at Strangeways led to a report by Lord Justice Woolf; his recommendations, accepted by the Home Office, emphasized the need for better physical standards

(and eventually for smaller jails, containing not more than 400 people), and for easier contacts between prisoners and their families through increased visiting rights, proper access to telephones and an end to the routine censorship of letters. In 1992 the first *privatized prison opened. At the same period *tagging was among the proposals to reduce overcrowding in prisons.

*The **Prisoner*** (ATV 1967) Seventeen-part television series, hallucinatory in tone, following the experiences of a British secret agent who is subjected to brainwashing in a mysteriously self-contained civilization. The central character, Number Six, is played by Patrick McGoohan (b. 1928), who also wrote and directed the first and last episodes. The series has acquired a cult status, greatly increasing the number of visitors to the location where it was filmed, *Portmeirion.

*The **Prisoner of Zenda*** see Anthony *Hope.

prison sentences In British courts the sentence is decided by the judge after the jury has declared on the question of innocence or guilt (for lesser offences *magistrates can give both verdict and sentence, to a maximum of one year in prison). A prisoner may serve less than the full amount of his sentence by two methods. Parole, or release on licence, is available to most long-term prisoners after serving a third of their sentence; local review committees consider each case and advise the home secretary; if parole is granted, the prisoner is released on certain conditions but may be recalled at any time up to the point at which he or she would have been eligible for remission. Remission is possible in most cases for up to a third of the given sentence; equivalent to the cancelling of the remainder of the sentence, it is given for good behaviour while in prison.

No remission is allowed for prisoners serving a life sentence. 'Life' became the mandatory sentence for murder after the abolition of *capital punishment, but it can also be given for other crimes including arson, manslaughter and rape. In practice the length of a life sentence is usually regarded as being 15 years, but judges will often recommend a minimum time for the offender to serve (sometimes as much 35 years); the home secretary usually follows this recommendation when considering release. A prisoner serving life is released only through the granting of parole, and there is an informal tariff on the moment at which parole is first considered; normally after 15 years for the average murder, but this is likely to be extended to 20 years for categories such as acts of terrorism or sadism.

John **Pritchard** (1921–89, kt 1983) Conductor who was much involved from early in his career with Glyndebourne, of which he eventually became musical director (1969–77). He was also musical director of the Royal Liverpool Philharmonic (1957–63) and of the London Philharmonic (1962–6). The two posts which he held until his last year were as chief conductor of the BBC Symphony Orchestra (from 1982) and of the Cologne Opera (from 1978).

V.S. **Pritchett** (Victor Sawdon Pritchett, b. 1900, kt 1975) Author best known for his criticism and short stories. The raw material of his fiction is the quirks of everyday life, which he views with a dispassionate and ironic eye. A collected edition of his stories was published in 1990.

privacy There has been no legal right to privacy in English law, but the possible need for it has been under discussion since the late 1980s because of intrusive behaviour by the press. In 1989 Sir David Calcutt was asked to enquire into the matter. The Calcutt Report (1990) recommended

Privatization proceeds, in £bn

The figures relate to the 12 months ending on March 31 in the given year. Those after 1993 are Treasury predictions.
Source: Autumn Statement *(HM Treasury, November 1992)*

the setting up of a body, composed of members of the press and others. For a trial period of 18 months this body would deal with complaints and establish a code of press behaviour; its performance would reveal whether 'non-statutory self-regulation can be made to work effectively'. The result was the creation of the Press Complaints Commission early in 1991, replacing the earlier Press Council.

The summer of 1992, at the end of the 18-month period, saw an unprecedented series of of what seemed to many to be unacceptable invasions of privacy. Serialization by the *Sunday Times* of a book about the marital difficulties of the Princess of Wales was followed by the *Sun*'s invitation to readers to telephone a number and hear the so-called Dianagate tape of a private telephone conversation said to be between the princess and a male friend, who called her Squidgy. Meanwhile a paparazzo with a long lens had taken photographs of the Duchess of York sunbathing topless on holiday with her financial adviser. Early in July the secretary of state responsible for the press, David *Mellor, warned newspapers that they were 'drinking in the last-chance saloon' and announced that he was asking Calcutt to renew his enquiry; within weeks the *People* published a photograph of Mellor leaving the flat of an actress early in the morning.

Calcutt's *Review of Press Self-Regulation*, published early in 1993, proposed laws to protect privacy and recommended that the Press Complaints Commission should be replaced by a statutory body with power to fine newspapers up to 1% of their annual revenue for transgressing a code of practice. His suggestions were fiercely opposed by editors and journalists. Some argued that any restriction on the press was dangerous; others emphasized the lack of any corresponding proposal for a law to guarantee *freedom of information. The debate happened to coincide with an extreme example of intrusion on privacy – the publication of the so-called Camillagate tape, an intimate late-night telephone conversation allegedly between the Prince of Wales and Camilla Parker Bowles.

Private Eye Satirical magazine, founded in 1961, which has benefited from a network of journalists eager to release facts or rumours too dangerous for their own mainstream papers. Its merit has been in breaking stories which politicians and financiers would rather suppress; it has been less admirable in its cavalier way with people's private lives. City Slicker has been the vehicle for financial scandal; Lord Gnome is the magazine's very own press baron (loosely linked with Peter Cook, who was a major investor in the project), and its most sustained flight of brilliance has been *Dear Bill* – indiscreet letters of everyday life at No. 10, supposedly written by Denis Thatcher, husband of Margaret, to a fellow drinker. Of the magazine's many libel cases, those brought by James

*Goldsmith and by the wife of the *Yorkshire Ripper have been the most sensational.

private health insurance Around 7 million people in Britain have private medical cover, many of them through group schemes organized by their employers. Some schemes pay for all hospital treatment – either in a private hospital or in a 'pay bed', an equivalent private room in a *National Health Service hospital. Others only cover treatment which the NHS cannot provide within a given period, amounting therefore to little more than a way of avoiding waiting lists. In practice everyone involved in a medical emergency in Britain – such as a car accident or a serious heart attack or stroke – is likely to be treated in an NHS hospital. The two leading medical insurers are *BUPA and *PPP.

Private Lives (1930) Noel *Coward's most successful comedy. Two glamorous and brilliant characters, Elyot and Amanda, are divorced from each other; but honeymooning in their new marriages, they find that they have adjacent balconies. The old attraction reasserts itself, and they depart together for Paris. Here they rapidly sink into violent quarrels, in which they are discovered by their new partners. After further complications Elyot and Amanda convince themselves that such aggression must be a sign of love, so they sneak off together once again. They were played in the first production by Coward himself and Gertrude *Lawrence.

Private Member's Bill A bill introduced in the House of Commons by a *backbencher. The first 20 MPs drawn in a ballot (held at the start of each parliamentary session) may present a bill. The procedure is the same as for any other bill attempting to become an *act of parliament, but relatively few private members' bills reach that final stage, since they usually lack government support and the time allotted to them is short.

private school see *public school.

privatization The return to private control of enterprises previously run by the public sector. In the 1980s the USA and Britain were in the forefront in this policy; it was associated personally with President Reagan and Mrs *Thatcher. By the early 1990s it had been taken further in Britain than anywhere else. But the signs are that it will prevail widely, in view of the increasing dislike of state intervention both in capitalist countries and in regions emerging from Communism.

Privatization in Britain began with the government selling its stake in quoted companies; 80 million of the nation's *BP shares were on the market within six months of Mrs Thatcher's first victory in 1979. The next stage was the sale of fully *nationalized enterprises. Some, such as British Aerospace or Cable and Wireless, were floated in the normal way on the Stock Exchange. With others, of which British Telecom was the first in 1984, a major effort was made to attract members of the public who would not normally buy shares; an elaborate advertising campaign resulted in the £3.9bn issue of BT shares being four times oversubscribed. There was a similar response to the issues of TSB and British Gas in 1986, but the sale of the nation's ten water companies in 1989 and of the electricity industry in 1991 was less easy. Nevertheless there was a major financial incentive underpinning the ideology of privatization; by the end of the 1992–3 financial year the Treasury had received about £50bn from this source.

Meanwhile some critics argued that the nation's assets were being sold off too cheaply; the transfer of the Rover Group to *British Aerospace was a much quoted example. Others had a more rooted objection to this disposal of capital wealth, which Harold Macmillan likened in November 1985 to selling the family silver: 'First of all the Georgian silver goes, and then all that nice furniture that used to be in the saloon. Then the Canalettos go.'

A lesser form of privatization is contracting out. Services such as the collection of household refuse have increasingly been undertaken on behalf of local authorities by private contractors. An application of a similar principle in central government has been the *Next Steps programme, and a continuing move in this direction is a central theme of the *Citizen's Charter. In the early 1990s the contracting out of prisons to private companies was a controversial new departure; the first two were the Wolds in Humberside (1992) and Blakenhurst in Hereford and Worcester (1993), but the government's intention is that others should follow (the rebuilt *Strangeways was the next to be selected). The Queen's Speech in 1992 announced that private rail companies would soon be given access to British Rail's network, and in 1993 the sale of separate parts of the Post Office is also under discussion.

Privy Council Nowadays a body of largely formal status, though officially still the private council of the sovereign. There are usually between 300 and 400 privy councillors, appointed for life. They include all cabinet ministers (sworn in when first taking office) and others of distinction in such fields as politics, the law and the church. Some members are always from the *Commonwealth.

In its origin the council was a body of great power, being from the 14c the executive through which the sovereign ruled. But it was already losing power in the early 17c to a smaller group, the *cabinet; and with the arrival of *constitutional monarchy it was the cabinet which became pre-eminent. The words 'The Right Honourable' (usually abbreviated to Rt Hon.) are placed before a privy councillor's name, and the letters PC after it. 'Privy councillor' is now the usual spelling, but the older and official form is 'privy counsellor' – meaning someone giving private advice, rather than someone on the private council.

Privy Purse see *Civil List.

procurator fiscal Legal officer in Scotland, employed as a civil servant within the Crown Office. A procurator fiscal has two quite separate areas of responsibility: to decide on prosecutions and act as prosecuting counsel in the *sheriff courts; and to fulfil the duties carried out by a *coroner in England in relation to any violent or suspicious death.

productivity The output per head of those in employment. It has improved considerably in Britain since the 1970s.

Profumo Affair (1963) The most extensive political scandal in Britain in the postwar years. John Profumo (b. 1915) had been secretary of state for war (a non-cabinet post) since 1960 in the Macmillan government. Rumours began circulating that he was involved with a prostitute, Christine Keeler, who was also sleeping with Yevgeny Ivanov, a naval attaché at Russia's London embassy. In March 1963 Profumo assured the House of Commons that there was no truth in this. In June he confessed that he had lied and resigned his seat.

The doubts cast upon the efficiency of the security service almost caused the fall of the government, and details began to emerge of a political lifestyle unsuspected by the public. Profumo, it seemed, had first met Keeler when she was bathing naked at Lord Astor's mansion, *Cliveden. They had been introduced by an artist and osteopath, Stephen Ward, who had a cottage there. Another girl in Ward's entourage, Mandy Rice-Davies, had shared a flat with Keeler and had been the mistress of *Rachman (it was through the resulting publicity that Rachman's unsavoury activities came to the surface).

Stephen Ward was charged with living off immoral earnings, and his trial in July exposed further titillating

Productivity: output per person employed (1985 = 100)

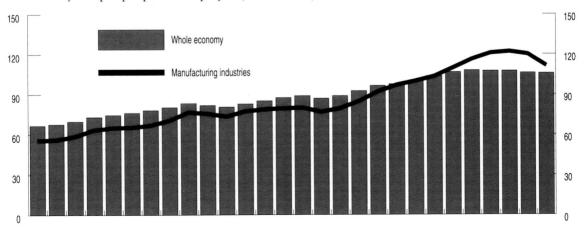

Source: Economic Trends (see *Central Statistical Office).

details. It also launched on its career one very useful phrase: when Mandy Rice-Davies was informed that Lord Astor had denied her allegations, she replied 'He would, wouldn't he?' Before the trial had ended, Ward committed suicide.

In September Lord Denning published his report on the affair, concluding that security had not been affected but that the government had been lax in responding to the issue. Denning also assured the public that an anonymous man, much discussed because of his peculiar fancy (waiting on dinner parties naked except for a mask), was not a government minister. Keeler was jailed for nine months later that year for perjury in another case. Profumo, over the following years, established a new reputation in social work and adult education (for which he was awarded the CBE in 1975).

Proms Promenade concerts, originally with the audience walking about, have been held at various times in London since 1838. The term is now used of an unbroken series, still continuing, which was launched by Henry *Wood in 1895. These are too crowded for perambulation, but a large part of the audience stands. Since 1927 the Proms have been sponsored and broadcast by the BBC. They were held in the Queen's Hall until it was bombed in World War II; since 1941 they have been in the *Albert Hall, where the eight-week season (July–Sept.) offers an astonishing wealth of musical performance. Wood died in 1944 and was succeeded by Malcolm *Sargent (until his own death in 1967). Since then there has been no principal conductor.

On the last night of the Proms the orchestra is invariably the BBC Symphony Orchestra. The occasion is a traditional one of jingoistic jollity, with much flag-waving from the promenaders who join in the choruses of three final works, now an inseparable part of the occasion: *Land of Hope and Glory*, deriving from the first of Elgar's *Pomp and Circumstance* marches; Henry Wood's *Fantasia on British Sea Songs*, which includes *Rule, Britannia!*; and Parry's *Jerusalem*.

Marjorie **Proops** (Marjorie Rayle, m. Sidney Proops 1935) Britain's senior agony aunt, writing the advice column on the *Daily Mirror* since the early 1960s and extending to the *Sunday Mirror* in 1993. In a 1993 autobiography, *Marje: The Guilt and the Gingerbread*, she revealed that from 1958 until her husband's death in 1988 she led a secret double life with a *Mirror* lawyer as her lover – making her, surely, even better equipped to advise those agonizing in her column.

proportional representation (PR) Any of various systems by which the balance of elected representatives reflects accurately the balance of opinion among the electorate. Britain, with its *two-party system, has always used the very different first-past-the-post electoral method, by which a candidate wins a constituency outright even if he polls only one vote more than his nearest rival. This makes no attempt to mirror at all precisely the voters' combined wishes, but it does at least tend to give the winning party a clear working majority. An accompanying disadvantage is seen in the many 'safe seats' around Britain, where one party or the other has an unassailable majority – meaning that a vote against their candidate might as well not have been cast. This is not only frustrating for the minority voter; it causes general elections to be decided in a small number of marginal seats.

From its foundation more than a century ago, the *Electoral Reform Society has campaigned for proportional representation as a matter both of logic and justice. Broader support had to await the arrival of genuine three-party contests in the 1980s. In the 1983 general election

the *Alliance received 26% of the vote in England, Wales and Scotland but won less than 4% of the seats in the House of Commons. For obvious reasons both the major parties have resisted proportional representation, but a fourth successive Conservative victory in 1992 prompted a change of heart among some in the Labour party – boosted by the knowledge that adjustments by the *Boundary Commission, due in the mid-1990s, are likely to benefit the Conservatives. One of the aims for which *Charter 88 was founded is electoral reform.

The variety of PR systems makes the subject seem alarmingly complex, but they can be reduced to two broad categories. In one of these the parties draw up lists of their candidates in order of party preference; members are then elected from the lists according to the number of votes cast for each party. An election by this method can be achieved from the lists alone (as in Israel), abandoning any link between MPs and constituencies; or the list can be used merely to adjust the more random balance of members elected on a first-past-the-post system in individual constituencies (the so-called Additional Member System or AMS, used in Germany).

The other main method, favoured by the Electoral Reform Society, is the Single Transferable Vote (STV). This avoids party lists; it does so by enlarging constituencies until it is possible for the correct balance to be approximately achieved within each constituency. In practice this means that each constituency in Britain would have to be about five times its present size, allowing five candidates to be elected from one set of ballot papers. Voters number their preferred candidates in order of preference. When the votes are counted, a candidate is elected as soon as he or she has the minimum number of first-choice votes needed to be sure of winning one of the seats; the second choices on this candidate's unneeded ballot papers, and on those of the candidate dropping out at the bottom with the least number of first-choice votes, are then distributed; the process continues, with successive candidates either being elected or dropping out until every ballot paper is part of the minimum bundle of votes needed to elect one candidate. Each voter has therefore cast only a single vote, progressively transferred until it has become effective. This system has been in use in Northern Ireland, since 1979, for elections to the European Parliament.

Prospect of Whitby (London E1) Ancient riverside tavern, at Wapping. Built in 1520, and a favourite resort of Pepys in the 17C, it was given its present name in 1777 after a ship moored off it, registered in Whitby and called the *Prospect*, had become a local landmark.

Prospero see *The *Tempest*.

protector A word for anyone taking charge of a kingdom during the minority or absence of a monarch (as with the duke of Somerset in the reign of *Edward VI), but used particularly in British history in relation to the *Protectorate.

Protectorate (1653–9) The period during the *Commonwealth in which Great Britain was ruled by Oliver *Cromwell as Lord Protector and then briefly by his son Richard (1626–1712). The Protectorate was established, immediately after the dissolution of the *Barebones Parliament, by a document known as the Instrument of Government (1653). This gave control for his lifetime to Cromwell, who was to govern with a nominated council and occasional parliaments. The second of these parliaments extended his rule with another document, the Humble Petition and Advice (1657), giving him the right to appoint his successor. He nominated his son, who gov-

PSBR (Public Sector Borrowing Requirement), in £bn

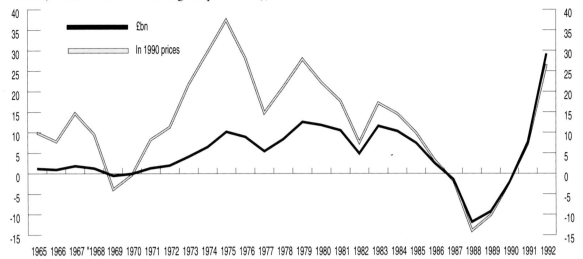

Where the lines are below zero, in 1969–70 and 1987–90, the government's balance sheet was in surplus by those amounts – causing a temporary reduction in the *National Debt.　　　　　*Source:* Economic Trends *(see *Central Statistical Office).*

erned from his father's death in September 1658 to May 1659, when he was eased out of power among increasing hostilities between parliament and the army. Military rule seemed probable until prevented by the decisive action of General *Monck.

'I am the **Protestant whore**' see Nell *Gwyn.

Mrs **Proudie** see *Barchester Towers*.

Provisionals see *IRA.

Prudential Insurance company, founded in 1848, which from 1854 pioneered the sale of life insurance to the industrial working classes through the door-to-door collection of regular premiums, usually every four weeks. By the end of the century one out of three families in Britain was insured with the company and 'the man from the Pru' was an established feature of national life. In the early 1990s Prudential remains Britain's largest insurance group, though by now offering a more conventional spread of insurance and financial services.

Prufrock The character through whom the talent of T.S. *Eliot was introduced to the world. *The Love Song of J. Alfred Prufrock* was the first of his mature poems to be published (in the American magazine *Poetry* in 1915), and it became the title poem of his first book, *Prufrock, and other observations* (1917). The nervous indecision of the middle-aged narrator is expressed in Eliot's characteristic blend of lyricism and mundane detail. Prufrock recognizes that he is not Prince Hamlet but at best an attendant lord, and goes on to lament:

　　I grow old . . . I grow old . . .
　　I shall wear the bottoms of my trousers rolled.

'**prunes and prism**' see *Little Dorritt*.

p's and q's see *'mind your p's and q's'.

PSBR (Public Sector Borrowing Requirement) Amount by which *government expenditure exceeds revenue in any year – in effect the excess of the expenditure agreed in the *public spending round over the amount of taxes raised in the *budget. If the necessary sum is raised by borrowing (the issuing of government bonds), the sum becomes an addition to the *national debt; it can also be raised by printing money, causing a growth in M4 (see *money supply). A negative PSBR (as in the years 1987–90) represents a reduction in the national debt.

ptarmigan see *grouse.

pub (short for public house) The main social gathering place in Britain, the equivalent of a bar or café in other countries. Pubs acquired their distinctive character in the 19c and many in the larger cities have gloriously ornate Victorian façades. Until fairly recently they sold little other than alcohol and in some areas were used exclusively by men, but now food and a family atmosphere have become more normal. Many pubs still have one area called the 'public bar' and others with names such as 'saloon bar' or 'lounge bar', a survival from times when there were class distinctions between drinkers. Of the games traditionally played, *darts and *bar billiards are now the most popular. Foreigners used to be amazed to find that the licensing laws forced pubs to close for two or three hours in the middle of the day; new regulations (1988) allow each pub in England and Wales to stay open for any hours it chooses between 11 a.m. and 11 p.m. on weekdays (12–3 and 7–10.30 on Sundays); there are minor variations on these times in Scotland and Northern Ireland. Alcohol cannot be sold to anyone under the age of 18, and those under 16 are only allowed to eat and drink in the garden or forecourt of a pub. But in 1993 government proposals were announced to allow children into pubs and to license cafés for the sale of alcohol.

Pubs in the old days were known by the signs hanging outside them and so their names reflect the images used (pub signs are a lively tradition in popular art). Typical is the King's Head, but national figures such as Lord Nelson were also pressed into service. One of the most common pub names used to be the Marquess of Granby, that of a famously bald 18c general who was an easy subject for the sign-painters. Other names tend to be country pursuits (the Hare and Hounds) or symbols from legend and heraldry (the Golden Fleece, the White Cross, the Red Lion).

public holidays see *bank holidays.

Public Lending Right (PLR) Principle established in 1979 by which authors are paid for each loan of their books from public *libraries. The money, from central government, has been distributed annually since 1984 according to the titles borrowed in some 30 representative libraries throughout the UK (the sampling libraries change each year). The estimated number of loans in a year is about 600 million.

Public Record Office The national archive of England and Wales, gathered together under this name in 1838 and placed then under the care of the *Master of the Rolls. The earlier documents (going back to the *Domesday Book of 1086) are kept in the 19C Tudor-style building which was created for them in Chancery Lane; more recent records are in a modern custom-built repository at Kew, where government documents are subject to the *thirty-year rule. The equivalent archive for Scotland is the *Scottish Record Office.

public school The first pitfall for anyone trying to understand the British system of *education is that 'public school' and 'private school' mean the same thing, both referring to fee-paying establishments. By contrast a school providing a free education is called a *state school or a maintained school. The exception, as so often in British life, is in Scotland where the term public school means what it says – a free state school, open to all.

The confusion results from a gradual development among the ancient *grammar schools, which offered free education and were known for that reason as public schools. Over the centuries several of the best-known began taking fee-paying pupils in addition to the central core of scholarship boys for whom they had been founded. An act of 1867 'for the better government of certain public schools' specifically concerned itself with Eton, Winchester, Westminster, Harrow, Rugby, Charterhouse and Shrewsbury. The name stuck, and for many years the act gave these seven a special status among public schools.

By then these ancient establishments had already pioneered the system which came to be considered characteristic of a public school – that of the older boys being responsible for much of the administration and discipline (as seen in *Tom Brown's Schooldays), including ritualized canings administered by prefects. This boys' own culture resulted in an emphasis on manliness and skill at games, together with a certain distrust of the intellect – all qualities which came to be associated with a public-school education. The success of these schools led to a harmful division within British education, and consequently within the community. The richer classes increasingly sent their children to public schools, where they acquired recognizable characteristics of accent and behaviour, while everyone else was educated in state schools.

In spite of very high fees, the pressure on the limited places at the best public schools is still such that children are often put down for a place at birth. This does not exempt them from a competitive examination at 12 or 13 (the Common Entrance), and most are sent from the age of about eight to fee-paying schools which specialize in preparing children for this test (preparatory or prep schools). From the late 19C increasing numbers of public schools for girls were founded, and many boys' public schools are now coeducational in the sixth form (16–18). The number of public schools was much increased in the decades after World War II, when many of the leading grammar schools chose to go private rather than become *comprehensives.

Schools in the private sector, from the nursery level upwards, now call themselves independent rather than 'public' or 'private', though the term has not yet become widely used. In the early 1990s independent schools were educating about 7% of Britain's children between the ages of 5 and 18. This amounted to some 600,000 boys and

Majolica plate designed by Pugin for Minton, c.1850, in a characteristically Victorian version of a medieval style.

girls (the majority boys), of whom about 36,000 had their fees wholly or party paid under the government's Assisted Places Scheme.

public sector borrowing requirement see *PSBR.

Office of **Public Service and Science** (OPSS, London SW1) Government department set up in 1992 within the *Cabinet Office to supervise the implementation of the *Citizen's Charter. It has also taken on the existing Cabinet Office responsibility of managing the civil service (supporting the prime minister as minister for the civil service), and it has the responsibilities for science previously held by the old Department of Education and Science. The first minister was William *Waldegrave.

public spending round The annual negotiation by ministers in charge of government departments to fix the level of their funding for the coming financial year. The process is conducted by the *chief secretary to the Treasury, and is held in September. In recent times the *chancellor of the exchequer's autumn statement has announced the figures agreed in the public spending round, while his *budget in the following spring has revealed how the necessary funds will be raised in taxation. But it was declared in 1992 that expenditure and revenue decisions would in future be announced together each December, starting in 1993.

In an attempt to hold down public or *government expenditure, the Treasury introduced a new device in 1992. In the past, public expenditure was the sum total of the amounts the chief secretary had been able to agree with departmental ministers. Under the new system an overall figure will be agreed in advance by the cabinet, so that ministers will compete for slices of a cake of known size.

'Publish and be damned' see Harriette *Wilson.

Puck A spirit full of tricks, originally identified with the devil but from the 16C seen more as a mischievous goblin. In this form he acquired the alternative name of Robin Goodfellow and is best known from Shakespeare's treatment of him in A *Midsummer Night's Dream.

Pudding Lane see *Great Fire.

Puffing Billy (Science Museum) The world's first steam locomotive running on smooth rails, instead of the previous rack rails. Designed by William Hedley (1779–1843), *Puffing Billy* began work in 1813, hauling coal on the 8km/5m journey from Wylam colliery in Northumberland to wharves on the river Tyne. Another version, made at much the same time and known as *Wylam Dilly*, is in the Royal Museum of Scotland.

Augustus Welby **Pugin** (1812–52) Architect, designer and a leading figure in the second stage of the *Gothic Revival. His father (Augustus Charles Pugin, 1762–1832) was an architectural illustrator and teacher, with a special interest in the Gothic. The younger Pugin's passionate belief in the spiritual aspects of medieval architecture coincided with the *Roman Catholic revival in Britain, and he himself became a convert in 1835. Thereafter his brief but extremely productive career was shaped by the demand for new Catholic churches. He built what are now the cathedrals in Newcastle, Nottingham, Birmingham and Southwark, and his two architect sons provided Roman Catholic cathedrals in Northampton, Shrewsbury, Wrexham, Cardiff and Motherwell. Pugin's most famous church (St Giles in Cheadle, Staffordshire) has a richly decorated interior of a kind which most of his patrons could not afford; but it is for just such decorative design, in the *Houses of Parliament, that he is now best known.

Pulteney Bridge see *Bath.

punch A drink mixing alcohol (most often wine) with fruit juice and spices, usually now served hot. It was much drunk by British sailors in the 17C and was associated in particular with India (the origin of the name is unknown but an early theory was that a punch should have five ingredients, *panj* being an Indian word for five). A French definition of 1653 is irresistible: '*Bolleponge est un mot Anglois, qui signifie une boisson dont les Anglois usent aux Indes faite de sucre, suc de limon, eau de vie, fleur de muscade, & biscuit rosty*' (Bowl-punch is an English word, signifying a drink which the English use in India made of sugar, lemon juice, brandy, muscatel, and roast biscuit).

Punch, or the London Charivari The leading vehicle in Britain for cartoonists, whether political or purely humorous, for the greater part of 150 years. Founded in 1841, the magazine soon included artists such as *Tenniel and *du Maurier among its regular contributors. It took its name from the puppet character Punch, who until 1954 appeared with his dog Toby on the cover (drawn by Richard Doyle, 1824–83).

In the mid-20C *Punch* was an indispensable item in every dentist's waiting room, but falling circulation led to its demise in 1992.

Punch and Judy The archetypal British puppet play, still frequently performed at the seaside or at children's parties. A hump-backed and hook-nosed string-puppet called Punchinello (deriving rather distantly from Pulcinella in the Italian *commedia dell'arte*) arrived in England in about 1662 and soon became simply Punch. He acquired a wife, known at first by various names but eventually settling down as Judy. Violent aggression, wife-beating tendencies and regular clashes with authority (policeman, doctor, priest, hangman) had become the central elements of his character by the late 18C. He then went out of fashion, but resurfaced later in country fairs in his present form as a glove-puppet. His only friend is his dog, Toby, traditionally a live terrier with a white ruff sitting on the edge of the stage throughout the performance. Mr Punch's appearance and name were prominent for 150 years in the magazine named after him, *Punch.

punk Movement of the young and outrageous which began in pop music, as punk rock, and moved into fashion. The first punk groups were deliberately amateurish bands in the USA in the 1960s. Punk resurfaced more energetically in Britain in the late 1970s, with groups such as the *Sex Pistols. The accompanying style in clothes was described in 1977 as 'short ragged hair with short, ragged leather jackets', but it evolved in the 1980s into much more elaborate plumage, with clothes suggesting bondage and grotesquely spiked and coloured hairdos. The name derives not from the old English word for a prostitute but from an American term for anything rotten and worthless (originally rotten wood from a tree).

Henry **Purcell** (1659–95) Composer who in his brief career was intensely involved in many aspects of the musical life of his time. He started as a chorister in the Chapel Royal; at the age of 15 he was tuning the organ in Westminster Abbey; at 18 he was appointed composer to Charles II's string orchestra; at 20 he became organist of Westminster Abbey. He was a prolific composer of songs and of 'fancies' for viols, together with trio sonatas and harpsichord suites; his church music includes the famous anthem *My heart is inditing*, written for the coronation of James II. Some of his music for the public theatres is still occasionally performed (for example *The Fairy Queen*, a masque of 1692 based on *A Midsummer Night's Dream*), but his most lasting contribution to the stage is Britain's earliest opera, **Dido and Aeneas*.

purchase tax An indirect tax introduced in 1940, levied on wholesale prices and with higher rates for luxury goods. It was replaced in 1973 by *VAT.

The pleasures of punk, complete with a token padlock.

Puritans First used in the 1560s as a term of abuse for those Protestant reformers who wished to 'purify' the *Church of England of all taints of Roman Catholicism. In the way of radical movements they soon split into many opposing sects, the chief of which were the *Presbyterians and the *Congregationalists.

Edward **Pusey** see *Oxford Movement.

Puss in Boots One of the tales of *Mother Goose, which became a favourite subject for *pantomime. A miller's son grumbles that all he has inherited from his father is a cat, but by a series of brilliant tricks Puss makes his master appear to be a great nobleman and wins for him the hand of the king's daughter.

Pussy cat, pussy cat, where have you been? Popular nursery rhyme in which the cat answers that it has been to London to look at the queen, and that it frightened a mouse under her chair. First published in 1805, it was popularly believed to refer to an actual incident in the reign of Elizabeth I.

David **Puttnam** (b. 1941) Film producer and campaigner on behalf of the British film industry who made his name with *Bugsy Malone* (1976) and *Midnight Express* (1978), but had his greatest success with *Chariots of Fire* (1981, Oscar for best picture). In a spell as chairman and chief executive of Columbia Pictures (1986–8) he found himself at cross-purposes with the demands of Hollywood.

Pygmalion (1913) Comedy by George Bernard *Shaw about an expert in linguistics, Professor Henry Higgins, who launches into society a Covent Garden flower girl, Liza Doolittle, after giving her an immaculate upper-class accent. But he has overlooked the content of polite conversation, and Eliza (as she now is) causes consternation at her first tea party by intoning with perfect precision 'Not bloody likely', when asked if she is planning to walk home. Her father, the dustman Alfred Doolittle, describes himself frankly as 'one of the undeserving poor'. The play has been one of Shaw's most popular – particularly in the form of the extremely successful musical

Woodcut from an anti-Puritan tract of 1641: Nick Froth the Tapster and Rulerost the Cook lament the effect on trade of the Puritan Sunday.

comedy based on it, **My Fair Lady* (1956). It also was an outstanding film of 1938, directed by Anthony Asquith with Leslie Howard as Higgins, Wendy Hiller as Eliza and Wilfrid Lawson as Doolittle.

Francis **Pym** (b. 1922, baron 1987) Conservative politician, MP for Cambridgeshire 1961–83 and Cambridgeshire South East 1983–7, who entered the cabinet as secretary of state for Northern Ireland (1973–4). He was subsequently secretary of state for defence (1979–81), leader of the House of Commons (1981–2) and foreign secretary (1982–3).

John **Pym** (*c*.1583–1643) Parliamentary leader from the start of the Long Parliament. He instigated the impeachment of both *Strafford and *Laud, and was one of the *Five Members whom Charles I tried to arrest. He was responsible until his death for the broad strategy of parliament's campaign in the English Civil War.

Pytchley see the *Shires.

Pyx see *Trial of the Pyx.

Q

QC (Queen's Counsel) A senior *barrister, appointed on the recommendation of the *lord chancellor. He or she sits within the *Bar when in court and wears a silk gown; hence the term 'silk' for any QC (or KC when the monarch is a king). The letters QC are placed after the name.

QE2 (*Queen Elizabeth II*) The third of the great *Cunard liners built on Clydeside and launched by a British queen – in this case Elizabeth II in 1967 – in the tradition of the *Queen Mary* and *Queen Elizabeth*. The QE2 (294m/963ft long and displacing 66,450 tons) was in 1975 retired from the transatlantic route to become a cruise ship. She took part in the *Falklands War, carrying 3000 troops to the south Atlantic. In August 1992 her hull was considerably damaged when she ran aground off Cape Cod, on a day trip from New York to Martha's Vineyard.

Q-ships (named apparently from Q for 'query') Vessels with the outline of merchant ships but carrying concealed guns, used in both World Wars as decoys to lure German submarines to their destruction.

Quakers Christian sect founded in the 1650s by George *Fox, called by him (and by Quakers themselves) the Society of Friends. The term 'Quaker' was applied to several of the religious visionaries and eccentrics characteristic of the mid-17c, deriving from their fits of ecstasy; it was possibly reinforced by Fox's bidding everyone to tremble at the word of the Lord. It has remained the term used by outsiders for the Friends, though it is no longer derogatory in intent.

The movement spread rapidly; by 1662 as many as 60 Quaker missionaries had crossed to North America. Like Fox and his followers in England, they were frequently imprisoned and persecuted for their uncompromising rejection of established religion and for their often eccentric and violent behaviour. Meanwhile a few members of the higher classes in society began to join the cause, most notably William *Penn.

It was in the calmer 18c that Quakers acquired the reputation which has remained with them, that of quiet strength. They have played a prominent part in British philanthropy and have led the cause of pacifism (as well as being noted makers of *chocolate). Today there are about a quarter of a million practising Quakers in the world, faithful still to George Fox's original vision – that true religious experience is not the pomp and ceremony of liturgy, but a quiet meeting of friends who will allow the voice of God to be heard in and through each of them. Their term for this is the Inward Light. (For the number of Quakers in England, see *Christians.)

'quality of mercy' see The *Merchant of Venice*.

quango Acronym from 'quasi-autonomous non-government organization', applied to any semi-public administrative body functioning outside the civil service but funded by the government. The concept and the word began in the USA in the 1960s. Quangos proliferated in the 1970s in Britain, where the name was sometimes said to derive from 'quasi-autonomous national government organization'; their number was reduced in the early 1980s, but had greatly risen again by the 1990s with the removal of an increasing number of responsibilities from elected local government.

Mary **Quant** (b. 1934) The most influential British fashion designer of the 1960s, associated in particular with the short-haired and mini-skirted look. She began in the 1950s with Bazaar, a boutique in the King's Road, Chelsea. By the late 1960s she and her husband, Alexander Plunket Greene (1933–90), had built up a Mary Quant empire – extending to fashion accessories, and above all cosmetics – which thrives internationally in the 1990s.

'quarrel in a far-away country' see entry on Neville *Chamberlain.

Quarry Bank Mill see *Styal.

quart see fluid *volume.

quarter days Days in the year, deriving from the medieval church calendar, when certain payments such as rents fall due. In England, Wales and Northern Ireland they are *Lady Day (March 25), Midsummer (June 24), Michaelmas (September 29) and Christmas (December 25). In Scotland, where they are known as term days, they are Candlemas, Whitsunday, Lammas and Martinmas; until 1991 these were February 2, May 15, August 1 and November 11 (the correct fixed days in the Christian calendar except for Whitsunday, which moves with Easter). In 1991 the term days were tidied up. While keeping their traditional names, they became February 28, May 28, August 28 and November 28.

quartos and folios Two technical terms for book sizes from the early days of printing; in the smaller quarto the printed sheet was folded twice, in the folio only once. They are widely known from their connection with *Shakespeare. During his lifetime 18 of his plays were published individually as quartos. Some were accurate versions but several are what are known as 'bad' quartos, pirated versions probably reconstructed from memory by an actor or prompter. It was not till after his death that his colleagues brought out a collected edition in the larger format, the *First Folio.

Queen in concert, with Freddie Mercury in the spotlight.

Quatre Bras see *Waterloo.

Quebec see General *Wolfe.

Queen Rock group formed in 1970 by Freddie Mercury (1946–91, vocals), Brian May (b. 1947, guitar), John Deacon (b. 1951, bass) and Roger Taylor (b. 1949, drums). Queen's first major success came with the LP *A Night at the Opera*, which reached the top of the charts; one number from it, 'Bohemian Rhapsody', became a major hit single and one of the first successful pop videos. *A Day at the Races* followed in 1976, and other albums to reach the top spot included *The Game* (1980), *A Kind of Magic* (1986), *The Miracle* (1989) and *Innuendo* (1991). Freddie Mercury died a few hours after issuing a public statement that he had Aids.

Queen Anne Stylistic term applied to architecture and to a small number of the leading crafts in the reign of Anne (1702–14), among them furniture characterized by cabriole legs and *Huguenot silver. The phrase is now used also of an architectural revival, beginning in the late 1860s, of which Norman *Shaw was a leading practitioner. This took many of the details of the Dutch-influenced English architecture of the late 17C (earlier than Anne) and exaggerated them in a fanciful manner. The characteristic ingredients are red brick, Dutch gables, tall dormer windows and high chimneys.

Queen Anne's Bounty see *Anne.

Queen Elizabeth see *Queen Mary.

Queen Elizabeth II Cup see the *Royal International Horse Show.

Queen Elizabeth's Pocket Pistol see *Dover.

Queen Mary and *Queen Elizabeth* The two great luxury liners built by *Cunard in the 1930s, each launched on Clydeside by a queen and named after her – the *Queen Mary* in 1934 by the wife of George V and the *Queen Elizabeth* in 1938 by the present *Queen Mother. Each was at the time the largest liner ever built, a record still held by the *Queen Elizabeth* (*Queen Mary* 311m/1020ft in length displacing 81,237 tons, *Queen Elizabeth* 314m/1031ft in length displacing 82,998 tons). The *Queen Mary* first sailed with passengers in 1936 and won the *blue riband in 1938 with a time of 3 days 21hr 48min. The newly fitted out *Queen Elizabeth* was immediately involved in World War II, in which both ships were used as troop carriers. They were retired from transatlantic service in 1967 and 1968, and were sold as hotels and tourist attractions. The *Queen Mary* has been moored since then at Long Beach in Los Angeles, but the *Queen Elizabeth* was destroyed by fire in 1972 while anchored in Hong Kong.

Queen Mary's Dolls' House (Windsor Castle) A miniature miracle which was presented in 1924 to Queen Mary, the wife of George V. The house itself was designed by Lutyens and the garden by Gertrude Jekyll. All the exquisitely detailed contents were made by craftsmen or firms specializing in the full-scale equivalents. Everything is on a scale of an inch to a foot, so the taps in the bathrooms, the tennis rackets and golf clubs in the games cupboard, the wine bottles in the cellar or the cars in the garage are all one-twelfth of life size. Famous artists provided tiny drawings and prints for the cabinet in the library, and famous authors wrote miniature books to be minutely bound in leather. Conceived as a present from the nation to the queen (an avid collector) after the trauma of World War I, the dolls' house was ready in time to be a centre of attention at the British Empire Exhibition at *Wembley in 1924.

Queen Mother A title sometimes used by the widow of a monarch who is also the mother of the reigning monarch. It has been held since 1952 by Queen Elizabeth, the widow of *George VI. Born in 1900 as Elizabeth Bowes-Lyon, the youngest daughter of the earl of Strathmore, her family home was *Glamis Castle. She married the duke of York, the second son of George V, in Westminster Abbey in 1923. Her husband became king as a result of the *abdication crisis. It was a change which she was said not to welcome, but as queen during the war and during her long widowhood she has inspired great public affection, particularly in her very lively old age. Her two children are *Elizabeth II and Princess *Margaret. In 1952 she bought the 16C castle of Mey, on the north coast of Scotland about 10km/6m west of *John o' Groats. Her London residence is *Clarence House.

*The **Queen of Hearts*** Nursery rhyme, first published in 1782 but probably older, about the king of hearts calling for the tarts made by the queen, only to find that they have been stolen by the knave. It was given added fame by *Alice in Wonderland*, where the trial of the knave of hearts is the setting for the final nonsensical scene and is shown in Tenniel's frontispiece.

Queen's Awards for Export and Technology Annual awards, under a scheme established in 1965, to organizations that have contributed significantly to Britain's industrial or commercial performance. The original single category (Queen's Awards to Industry) was split in 1976 to become separate awards for Export Achievement and for Technological Achievement. In an average year between 100 and 200 awards are made. Each allows a Queen's Award emblem to be used by the company for five years.

Queen's Beasts A set of ten heraldic figures, reflecting the ancestry of *Elizabeth II. Inspired by the example of the *King's Beasts, they were modelled in plaster by James Woodford in 1953. The original set was placed that summer outside Westminster Abbey for the Coronation. Copies in Portland stone now stand in Kew Gardens.

Queen's Bench see *High Court.

Queensberry Rules The rules governing modern *boxing, being a modification by John Chambers of the previous rules of the London Prize Ring. To give them added authority they were published in 1867 under the name of an aristocratic patron of boxing, the marquess of Queensberry (1844–1900, known also in relation to Oscar *Wilde). They were only gradually adopted by professionals, being considered soft by many (particularly in respect of fighting with gloves instead of bare fists), but they have been standard since their use in the world heavyweight bout between John Sullivan and Gentleman Jim Corbett in New Orleans in 1892.

Queen's Birthday (or King's) In the 18C the monarch's birthday was celebrated on the actual day, but the custom later developed of designating a more convenient official birthday for public celebrations. This is now invariably a Saturday in June. It is the occasion of the Birthday Honours (see *orders of chivalry) and is marked by *trooping the colour.

Queen's Club Sporting club in Hammersmith, west London, founded in 1886 for a wide range of activities but with an emphasis on real tennis, rackets and the relatively new game of lawn tennis. Since 1890 the London Grass Court Championships have been held at the club. The tournament now brings the world's top tennis internationals to Queen's each June – acclimatizing themselves to grass a fortnight before Wimbledon.

Queen's Counsel see *QC.

Queen's English see *King's English.

turning **Queen's evidence** or **King's evidence** Used of someone, accused of a crime, who gives evidence against his accomplices in return for leniency. The phrase relates to the fact that any criminal case is brought by the crown and is described in terms of *Regina* (or *Rex*) *versus Smith* (Latin for the Queen, or King, against Smith).

Queen's Gallery see *Buckingham Palace.

Queen's House (London SE10) Centrepiece of the 17C buildings at *Greenwich, with a view to the river in one direction and across Greenwich Park in the other. The earliest use in Britain of the *Palladian style, it was designed in 1616 by Inigo *Jones for one queen (Anne of Denmark, wife of James I) and was completed in 1629–40 for another (Henrietta Maria, wife of Charles I). Extensive wings, connected by colonnades, were added in 1807–9 to commemorate *Trafalgar. In 1934 the building became the home of the *National Maritime Museum.

Queen's pattern see *King's pattern.

Queen's Park, known as the Spiders (Hampden Park, Glasgow). Scotland's oldest football club, founded in

The last of the Queens: the QE2 *at Portsmouth in 1990, with the royal yacht* Britannia *in the foreground.*

1867. It played in the first years of the *FA Cup and was the moving spirit in founding the *Scottish FA Cup, which it won for the first three years (and ten times in all by 1893). The club won no more major trophies for it kept resolutely to its amateur status, but it was champion of the Scottish 2nd division in 1923, 1956 and 1981. The club's ground, *Hampden Park, is Scotland's national stadium.

Queen's (or **King's**) **Regulations** Code of conduct for members of the armed forces, issued in book form.

Queen's Speech see *State Opening of Parliament.

*A **Question of Sport** see David *Coleman.

Question Time An hour (2.30–3.30 p.m.) at the start of the day's sitting every Monday to Thursday in the House of *Commons, during which members can ask questions of government ministers. The questions are submitted in advance, to allow the minister's department to prepare the answer. The majority are answered in writing, the text being printed in *Hansard, but as many are dealt with orally as time allows. After the answer has been given, the member may ask a supplementary question, giving the opportunity to score an advantage over an unprepared adversary. Since 1961 the prime minister has answered questions on Tuesdays and Thursdays between 3.15 and 3.30. Members who start with a standard question about the prime minister's engagements for the day are using a device which allows almost any topic to follow as the supplementary question. A limited number of questions is also put at the start of each day's session in the House of Lords.

Question Time (BBC from 1979) The television version of **Any Questions?*, which rapidly became an important forum for leading politicians (a chance to show a human face in discussion of important issues before a large national audience). It was chaired from the start by Robin *Day with a fine balance of geniality, wit and aggression. He was followed in this role in 1989 by Peter *Sissons.

Questors Amateur theatre company in Ealing, west London, which has acquired a high reputation for the standard of its productions. It was founded in 1929 by a group of friends, among them Alfred Emmet (1908–91) who led the company through its years of growth – including the building of a permanent 350-seat theatre, the Playhouse, which opened in 1964.

Quiberon Bay see *Seven Years' War.

Mistress **Quickly** see **Henry IV*, *Falstaff and *Pistol.

Quorn Already one of the country's best-known hunts (see the *Shires) before an event in 1991 gave it unwelcome extra publicity. The Quorn was infiltrated by a member of the *League Against Cruel Sports, who made videos of its activities. One showed a fox being thrown live to the hounds after it had been dug from its earth; this was contrary to the hunt's own regulations and several of the joint masters resigned because of the incident. The footage, widely seen on television, almost certainly had the League's intended effect of increasing opposition to hunting.

Quorn A food launched on the market in Britain in 1984. It was the result of a joint research programme by Ranks Hovis McDougall and ICI to develop a protein food grown from cereal. The basic ingredient is a tiny plant occurring naturally in soil and the scientific name of the product is mycoprotein (fungus protein). Quorn is slightly chewy, similar in that respect to breast of chicken; its own taste is mildly savoury, but it readily takes on the flavour of whatever it is cooked with. Production by 1993 was 5000 tonnes a year.

R

R-38 The first of two British airship disasters (the other being the *R-101). The R-38 was built at Cardington in Bedfordshire, commissioned by the US navy. On its fourth flight, on 24 August 1921, its frame crumpled and ruptured the skin, causing the hydrogen to escape and ignite. The airship fell into the Humber, killing 44 of the 49 British and US service personnel on board.

R-101 The disaster which put an end to the use of airships in Britain. In spite of the *R-38 tragedy, the government commissioned two huge rigid airships in 1924. The R-100, designed by Barnes *Wallis, entered service safely in 1929, carrying 100 passengers. The larger R-101, carrying only 50 passengers but intended for the long-distance route to India, set out on its maiden voyage on 1 October 1930 with an official party on board which included the secretary of state for air. At 2 a.m. the following morning it touched the ground on its approach to Beauvais, caught fire and exploded. Only four of those on board survived. The R-100 was scrapped the following year.

RAC see *Royal Automobile Club.

Racal Electronics group deriving from a two-man consultancy founded in London in 1950 by Raymond Brown (1920–91) and Calder Cunningham (d. 1958). From the launch in 1957 of its first product, a high-frequency radio receiver, Racal has grown to become one of Britain's largest companies. The purchase of Chubb in 1984 took it into security, and in 1985 it launched Britain's first commercial cellular telephone service, Vodaphone. The cellular radio side of the business was floated in 1988 as a separate company – Racal Telecom, known from 1991 as the Vodaphone Group.

Peter **Rachman** Landlord in Notting Hill in London, whose name entered the language in 1963 in the form of Rachmanism – meaning the purchase of cheap houses with sitting tenants, followed by the use of threats or violence to drive the tenants out, thus greatly increasing the value of the property. Rachman had in fact died, in 1962, before he became notorious for activities of this kind. It was a past connection with the women in the *Profumo affair which brought his name to public attention.

Commission for **Racial Equality** (London SW1) Public body established by the Race Relations Act of 1976, responsible for promoting harmony and equal opportunity in the UK's multiracial society. It was the successor to the Race Relations Board, set up under an earlier Race Relations Act (1965) to improve the lot in Britain of the large ethnic minorities resulting from recent high levels of *immigration. A report published by the RRB in 1967 revealed much discrimination – against blacks and Asians in particular – in employment, housing and the provision of public services. Two decades later, unemployment among Britain's young black population and a sense of racial discrimination are still high among the problems of the *inner cities. Comparative figures give a stark picture. Unemployment levels in 1991, across the country, were 8% among whites, 12% among Indians, 15% among West Indians, and 25% among Pakistanis and Bangladeshis. A survey in 1987–9 revealed that 6% of white households had more than one person to a room, compared to 12% of West Indian, 22% of Indian and 43% of Pakistani or Bangladeshi.

Racing Post National daily newspaper launched in 1986 as a rival to the long-established *Sporting Life*. It concentrates on racing, but also gives form and odds on other major sports. Since 1988 its editor has been one of Britain's best-known racing commentators, Brough Scott.

rackets One of the fastest of British ball games, played with a racket and a hard ball in a large rectangular court enclosed on all four sides. It is now played by only a few because of the expense of such a court and of the number of rackets that get broken in modern play, but its origins go back a long way to more humble circumstances. It was a favourite game from the 18C wherever an open courtyard was available with suitably high walls. These were often found in the yards of taverns and there was one in use at Harrow School; but the best known of all was in the *Fleet prison, which provided many of the best early players (restricted inevitably to home matches). The sport is second only to boxing in having an acknowledged list of champions from a very early date, in this case 1820. The first custom-built court was completed in 1853 in Hans Place in west London, and its dimensions (18.3m/60ft by 9.15m/30ft) became the standard size. *Squash emerged at Harrow as an offshoot of rackets.

Arthur **Rackham** (1867–1939) Prolific illustrator of books in an angular and convoluted style (a Gothic version of Art Nouveau) which was particularly well suited to such subjects as fairies and hobgoblins. His first great success was *The Fairy Tales of the Brothers Grimm* (1900). His last illustrations, which he was working on when he died, were for a new edition of *The Wind in the Willows* – a book which he had long regretted turning down for its first publication, in 1908, on the grounds that he was too busy.

RADA see *drama schools.

The Church of Scotland at its most effortlessly elegant: Raeburn's portrait of the Reverend Robert Walker.

radio In the early 1920s small broadcasting stations were established in many cities of the world. In 1922 *Marconi set up one near the Strand in London, which began all its transmissions with the signal '2LO calling'. Later that year this became the first studio of the *BBC, which by 1927 was established as a public corporation with a national monopoly of the medium. 2LO remained the BBC channel until 1930 when it expanded to two services, calling them the National Programme and the Regional Programme; London had the first regional programme in that year, and other areas round the country developed their own during the 1930s. All this output was merged into a single new Home Service in 1939 – a time when transmission to foreign countries from *Bush House was about to be of major importance. The Home Service was again given a new name in 1967, becoming the present Radio 4.

In 1940 the BBC introduced a special light entertainment programme for British servicemen and women, calling it the Forces Programme; this became the Light Programme in 1945, and was renamed again in 1967 to become the present Radio 2. An innovation in 1946 was the Third Programme, with a brief to present serious talks and the best in drama and music. It acquired a high reputation and gradually transformed itself into the present Radio 3 – a name acquired in the same major reshuffle of 1967, which also added Britain's first legitimate pop station, Radio 1.

The launch of Radio 1 was prompted by the success in the mid-1960s of pirate radio stations, broadcasting pop music and advertisements to Britain from ships moored off the east coast. The first and best known was Radio Caroline, which won a huge following after its launch in 1964. In spite of a succession of disasters, including on one occasion being boarded by creditors and on another hitting a sandbank and sinking, Radio Caroline continued to transmit intermittently until 1990.

Meanwhile listeners in Britain had long been able to enjoy the world's most famous commercial radio station, which used British disc jockeys and was transmitted from Luxembourg. Launched in 1933, Radio Luxembourg pioneered many aspects of commercial broadcasting including the sponsored show, of which *Ovaltine's was the most successful example. The programmes were recorded in Britain on wax discs and transported to Luxembourg for transmission. The company broadcast on its famous 208 metres medium wave from 1951 to the end of 1991; it continued for a while via satellite, but ceased operation at the end of 1992.

The Sound Broadcasting Act of 1972 at last made commercial radio legal within Britain. The two London stations were the first on the air in 1974 – LBC (London Broadcasting Company) and, just a few days later, Capital Radio. Many others followed around the country, and by the early 1990s there were almost 100 local broadcasting companies.

Two new national stations were launched in the early 1990s. The BBC started Radio 5 in 1990. Ranging widely from sport and children's programmes to adult education and material originating on the *World Service, it came into being partly because of a reallocation of wave lengths. 1992 saw the arrival of the first national commercial radio station, when Classic FM began broadcasting selections of popular classical music.

Radio Authority see *ITC.

Radio Caroline and **Luxembourg** see *radio.

Radio Times The *BBC's weekly listing magazine for its programmes, launched in 1923 when newspapers refused to print full details of what could be heard on the radio; in the event *Radio Times* became a bestselling magazine, and readers came to demand the same information on a daily basis in their newspapers. Television listings were included in the *Radio Times* from the beginning of the new medium, but without the name being changed to acknowledge the intruder. From the start of commercial television (and subsequently radio) viewers needed to buy also the rival *TV Times*, until copyright restrictions on listings were outlawed in the late 1980s. Since 1991 both magazines have listed all the available radio and television programmes, including those of the satellite stations.

Radnorshire Former *county in Wales, since 1974 part of Powys.

Henry **Raeburn** (1756–1823, kt 1822) Scottish portrait painter who was the first to establish himself as a major artist without making his career in London. He was famous for working without a preliminary drawing on the canvas, developing instead a rugged style of broad brush strokes with his sitters usually seen against dark backgrounds. An early and untypical picture, *The Reverend Robert Walker Skating on Duddington Loch* (c.1784, National Gallery of Scotland), is rightly a popular favourite and has become one of Scotland's best-known images.

RAF see *Royal Air Force.

Raffles Gentleman thief who was the hero of many books by E.W. Hornung (Ernest William Hornung, 1866–1921). He first appeared in *The Amateur Cracksman* (1899), 'cracksman' being 19C slang for anyone skilled in breaking into houses.

Stamford **Raffles** (1781–1826, kt 1817) The founder of *Singapore. Employed by the East India Company, he was a model colonial administrator in the seriousness of his approach to local culture and traditions. His spell as governor of Java (1811–15) led to his authoritative *History of Java* (1817), and he was only later prevented from doing the same for Borneo and Sumatra through the loss by fire of his vast collection of notes and specimens during the journey home in 1824. His final efforts were on behalf of the *London Zoo, of which he was the first president.

*The **Ragged Trousered Philanthropists*** Classic fictional account of labour conditions and labour relations in the early 20C, written by Robert Tressall. This was the pen name of Robert Noonan (*c.*1870–1911), a house painter. His book, based on his time working for a builder in Hastings, was left in the care of his daughter and was published in an abridged form in 1918; the rediscovery of the manuscript in 1946 led to a full edition in 1955. The author is strongly critical not only of the grasping and corrupt employers in the fictional town of Mugsborough, but also of the uncomplaining workers – for they are the 'philanthropists' who so generously toil away to make money for others.

raglan sleeve One where the sleeve meets the neck of the garment, instead of joining a shoulder seam. The term 'raglan' was in use from the 1860s for an overcoat with sleeves of this kind, deriving from Lord Raglan (1788–1855), the commander of the British army in the Crimea. If he was indeed the first to wear a coat of this cut, the reason may have been his loss of an arm at Waterloo.

Ragley Hall (16km/10m W of Stratford-upon-Avon) House built in the early 1680s to a design by Robert Hooke (1635–1703). The main addition to the exterior is the portico added in 1780 by James *Wyatt, but both Wyatt and before him *Gibbs made major changes to the interior – Gibbs's Great Hall is outstanding, with its richly decorative plasterwork against a plain background. The south staircase is notable for a very large mural, painted in 1969–83 in a traditional style by Graham Rust.

Rahere (d. 1144) Often described as court jester to Henry I, he seems rather to have been a worldly cleric who moved in royal circles. His lasting fame derives from his building of *St Bartholomew the Great and his founding of *Bart's. Each was the result of his contracting malaria on pilgrimage to the Holy Land and vowing to build a hospital if he returned safely; St Bartholomew was said to have appeared to him in a vision, requesting a church as well.

Robert **Raikes** see *Sunday schools.

rail gauge see *standard gauge.

'railway king' see George *Hudson.

railways The use of wooden rails to smooth the passage of coal wagons in the collieries of northeast England goes back to the 16C, and cast iron rails and wheels offered increased efficiency by the 18C. The first *steam engines were too heavy to be used for traction, but in the early 19C several public railways opened using horses; the first was the Surrey Iron Railway Company in 1803, running between Wandsworth and Croydon (now both within London). The introduction of *Puffing Billy in 1813 signalled the direction in which railways would develop. Landmarks thereafter were the *Stockton and Darlington (1825) and the *Liverpool and Manchester railway (1830). By 1838 there were 89 companies in Britain operating some 800km/500m of line. There were uneasy cycles of boom and slump (see George *Hudson), but the era of cheap public travel had arrived.

By 1921 there were 120 companies and about 39,000km/24,000m of track. The Railway Act of that year combined these companies into four groups: the GWR (Great Western), the LMS (London, Midland and Scottish), the LNER (London and North Eastern) and the SR (Southern Railway). These four were in their turn nationalized in the Transport Act of 1947, eventually becoming known jointly as British Rail.

The reduction of the rail network began with the rise of the car but was much hastened by the Beeching Report of 1963 (officially *The Reshaping of British Railways*), in which the chairman of the British Railways Board, Richard Beeching, recommended the reduction of the surviving 29,000km/17,800m of route open for traffic by more than 50% and the closure of 2300 stations (out of more than 6000). His proposals were not implemented in full, but in the early 1990s there remained only about 16,500km/10,250m of route open for passenger traffic and some 2500 stations. In 1992 the government announced a complex plan to *privatize parts of the system, and the draft of a related Railways Bill was published in January 1993.

*The **Rainbow*** see D.H. *Lawrence.

rainfall Rain and lush pastures have long seemed part of Britain's image, whether in the clown's final song in *Twelfth Night* ('With hey, ho, the wind and the rain, . . . For the rain it raineth every day') or Blake's vision in *Jerusalem* of 'England's green and pleasant land'. But in several dry summers since the mid-1980s there has been talk of drought, with restrictions on the use of water in parts of England. There are two reasons. Modern society, with its washing machines, uses more water than ever before; and the most populated area of Britain, the southeast, is relatively dry, while the northwest has more rain

The early romance of the railways: frontispiece to John Bourne's 1846 account of the Great Western Railway, built by Brunel.

Annual rainfall, in millimetres

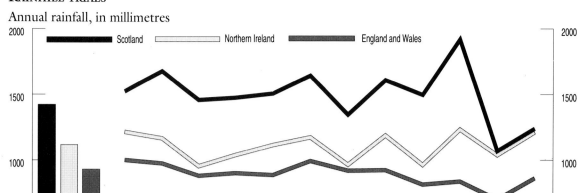

Source: Annual Abstract of Statistics (see *Central Statistical Office).

than it can use. The charts reveal an unusual aspect of Britain's rainfall. In all parts of the country the drier period is not high summer (July and August) but February to June.

Rainhill trials The competition held on 6–14 October 1829 at Rainhill, near Liverpool, to choose the design of locomotive for the *Liverpool and Manchester railway. The contenders (Robert *Stephenson's *Rocket*, Timothy Hackworth's *Sans Pareil* and John Braithwaite and John Ericsson's *Novelty*) had to run at least 113km/ 70m in a day at an average speed of not less than 16kph/ 10mph, back and forth over a 3km/2m level course. On the first day *Rocket* achieved 19km/12m in 53 minutes, and was eventually awarded the £500 prize. Eight versions of it (the original is now in the Science Museum in London) were ready for the opening of the railway a year later.

Rain, Steam and Speed – *The Great Western Railway* (1844, National Gallery) An extraordinary vision of the steam age by *Turner. It shows a train, a black intrusion in the hazy gold of a river scene, crossing the Thames at Maidenhead. Ahead of it a hare runs down the line, with the implication that even so swift an animal will be caught by this monster of speed.

The **Raj** Term used from the mid-19C for British rule in *India, and by extension for India under the British. It derives from the Hindu word *raja* (a ruler).

Raj Quartet see Paul *Scott and *Jewel in the Crown.

The Rake's Progress (1733–5, Sir John *Soane's Museum) Series of eight paintings by *Hogarth, published as engravings in 1735. They tell the story of Tom Rakewell, who inherits a fortune, loses it through bad company and a fashionable life, gains another by marrying an old one-eyed heiress, loses that by gambling, and ends up as a debtor in the *Fleet prison and then as a lunatic in *Bedlam. Sarah Young, a girl whom he seduced as a young man and then abandoned, makes several attempts to save him. The story was made into a ballet in 1935, choreographed by Ninette *de Valois to music by Gavin Gordon; and into an opera in 1951, with music by Stravinksy and libretto by W.H. *Auden and Chester Kallman.

Walter **Raleigh** (also spelt Ralegh, *c.*1552–1618, kt 1584) The outstanding example of the Elizabethan adventurer, combining great talents with more than a dash of buccaneering bluster. His early career was as both sailor and soldier, in expeditions against Spanish galleons and Irish rebels. He came to the attention of the queen in about 1582 and rapidly became her chief favourite, acquiring much wealth and a knighthood; he remained in favour until her death, apart from a spell in the Tower in 1592 for having secretly married one of her maids of honour, Elizabeth Throckmorton. He had meanwhile been an energetic early promoter of English colonies in *America, sending out the expedition to Roanoke Island and naming the region Virginia in honour of the queen. In 1595 he himself sailed west and penetrated some 700km/435m up the Orinoco river in search of the fabled El Dorado, the supposed source of Spanish gold. Yet another major theme in his life was literature. He was a poet (mainly in private praise of Elizabeth) and he wrote several prose works of history and polemic. He was also a generous patron, introducing *Spenser at court and encouraging the publication of *The Faerie Queene*.

Raleigh's troubles began after the queen's death in 1603. The new king, James I, became convinced that he had plotted against his accession. A death sentence for treason was commuted to imprisonment, but this second spell in the Tower lasted for 13 years. During it Raleigh busied himself with chemical experiments and undertook a *History of the World* (his one completed volume reached no further than the 2nd century BC but long remained his most popular work). He was released in 1616 to lead another gold-seeking expedition to south America. It proved a disaster and on his return he was beheaded.

Such a life attracts romantic legends. There is no way of proving or disproving the two best-known (both from Thomas Fuller's *Worthies of England* 1662). In one Raleigh spreads his cloak over a puddle for the queen. In the other he writes with a diamond on a window pane 'Fain would I climb, yet fear I to fall', to which she replies by the same means 'If thy heart fails thee, climb not at all'. The often stated theory that his colonists brought the *potato back to Europe is untrue, but he may have introduced it to Ireland.

Marie **Rambert** (stage name of Myriam Ramberg, 1888–1982, DBE 1962) One of the founding figures of British ballet through Ballet Rambert (now the *Rambert Dance Company). Born in Warsaw, she danced with Diaghilev's Ballets Russes (1912–13) before opening a ballet school in London in 1920.

Rambert Dance Company (previously Ballet Rambert) Influential company which emerged from the ballet school founded in London in 1920 by Marie *Rambert.

Monthly rainfall, in millimetres (average 1951—90)

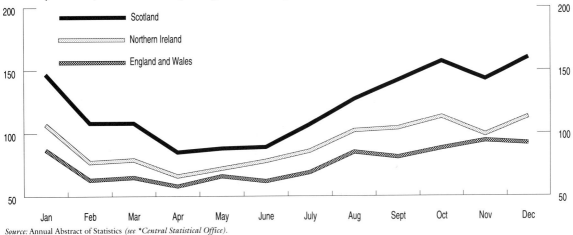

Source: Annual Abstract of Statistics *(see *Central Statistical Office).*

In 1926 she persuaded one of her students, Frederick *Ashton, to choreograph a new work, *A Tragedy of Fashion*, which virtually launched British ballet. By 1931 regular Sunday matinées were being given under the name of the Ballet Club, which in 1934 became Ballet Rambert; the location was the tiny Mercury Theatre in Notting Hill, an adapted school building of 1851 which remained the company's home until the 1960s. Antony *Tudor was another of the early choreographers. Rambert remained director until 1966. She was succeeded by Norman *Morrice, who gave the company a new image by concentrating exclusively on modern dance. The name was changed to the Rambert Dance Company in 1987, after Richard Alston became director – introducing an emphasis on the technique of the American dancer Merce Cunningham.

Ramblers' Association Pressure group established in 1935 with the twin purposes of encouraging people to enjoy the countryside and of ensuring that public access is protected. It formed part of a long and continuing campaign to prevent the closure of footpaths and rights of way; England's first footpath protection society was set up in York as early as 1824.

Allan **Ramsay** (1713–84) Scottish portrait painter who from 1739 had successful studios in both London and Edinburgh. In the 1750s he began to be overshadowed by Reynolds, ten years his junior. His talent lay in the delicacy of his style, seen at its best in portraits of women (for example his second wife, *c.*1757, in the National Gallery of Scotland).

William **Ramsay** (1852–1916, KCB 1902) Scottish experimental chemist with the unique distinction of having discovered an entire family of elements – the inert or noble gases – beginning with argon in 1894, through helium (1895, as an element on earth rather than in the sun) and neon, krypton and xenon (all 1898) to radon in 1910. He was awarded the Nobel prize for chemistry in 1904.

Alf **Ramsey** (b. 1920, kt 1967) Manager responsible for two of the greatest successes of English football. In eight years under his management (1955–63) *Ipswich Town rose from Division 3 to championship of the League, including the rare feat of winning Division 2 and Division 1 in successive years (1961, 62); astonishingly it was a feat which he had also achieved as a player with Tottenham Hotspur (1950, 51). As manager of the England team

(1963–74), he took them to their World Cup victory in 1966. His own playing career included 32 England caps.

Michael **Ramsey** (1904–88, baron 1974) Archbishop of Canterbury 1961–74, after being bishop of Durham (1952–6) and archbishop of York (1956–61). He was by training a theologian – he was professor of divinity at the university of Durham (1940–50) and at Cambridge (1950–52) – and he was the author of many books. His meeting with Pope Paul VI in 1966 developed a personal link between the leaders of the two churches which had been pioneered by his predecessor, Geoffrey *Fisher.

Mary **Rand** (Mary Bignall, b. 1940, m. Sidney Rand 1960) Athlete who by the age of 18 had set new British records for the long jump and the pentathlon. After a disappointing 1960 Olympic Games in Rome, she triumphed in Tokyo in 1964. She won the gold medal with a world-record long jump of 6.76m (22ft 2.25in) and added silver in the pentathlon as well as bronze in the 4x400 metres relay. She also won gold at the Commonwealth Games in 1966.

Ranelagh Gardens (London SW3) The site of the annual Chelsea Flower Show, running down to the Thames beside *Chelsea Hospital. The name survives from the pleasure gardens which opened here in 1742. They were the height of fashion for the rest of the 18c, competing successfully with the earlier *Vauxhall Gardens. A boating canal with a Chinese pavilion in it led to the great centrepiece, the domed Rotunda in which people promenaded and listened to music (the 9-year-old Mozart performed there in 1765). Canaletto painted both the gardens and the interior of the Rotunda, which was demolished in 1805.

Range Rover see *Rover.

Rangers, known as the Gers (Ibrox Park, Glasgow). Football club, founded in 1873, whose recent successes have given them the edge over their long-standing Glasgow rivals, *Celtic (though they are far from rivalling Celtic's record of nine sucessive league championships in 1966–74). The traditional religious divide between the two teams led to scenes of violence in 1989 when a leading Catholic player, Mo Johnston, was signed to play for Protestant Rangers. By the end of the 1992–3 season the club had won the Scottish FA Cup 26 times (Celtic 29), the Scottish League 43 times (Celtic 35) and the Scottish League Cup 18 times (Celtic 9).

Christ's call to St Peter, in one of the Raphael cartoons bought by Charles I for the Mortlake tapestry factory.

Ibrox Park has been the scene of two of soccer's tragedies. In 1902 a stand collapsed, killing 25; and in 1971 a crush of spectators on a stairway at the end of a game against Celtic left 66 dead in the worst national football disaster until *Hillsborough.

J. Arthur **Rank** (1882–1972, baron 1957) Entrepreneur responsible for two very different enterprises, each of which has developed into one of Britain's largest companies. He was son of a Yorkshire flour miller, Joseph Rank, who began the family business in a rented windmill in Hull in 1875. The firm was already large by the time Arthur Rank succeeded his elder brother as chairman in 1952; but Rank built it up enormously (in his own seventies and eighties), and acquired in 1962 two other long-established flour companies. The result is the present *Ranks Hovis McDougall.

The more famous side of Rank's life came about almost accidentally. He was a devout Methodist, and in 1933 he founded the Religious Film Society to spread the gospel on celluloid. The society's first film won a prize (*The Turn of the Tide* 1935) but Rank found it impossible to get distribution; his response was to buy a West End cinema to show it in. Irritated that American films dominated British screens, he joined the board of a new film production company, British National, and became one of the founders in 1935 of Pinewood Studios, about 27km/17m northwest of London (intended as Britain's answer to Hollywood, it is still in use today). In 1941 Rank acquired control of the Odeon Theatre group and of the Gaumont-British Picture Corporation. In the decades since then the majority of Britain's cinemas have been called either Odeon or Gaumont (though the Gaumonts have been phased out in recent years). These various activities were the basis of today's *Rank Organization.

Rank Organization For many years the dominant force in the British film industry – in all three fields of making films, distributing them and showing them in cinemas. Deriving from the activities of J. Arthur *Rank, it has diversified to become one of the country's largest leisure and entertainment groups. Subsidiary companies today, in addition to the original Pinewood Studios and Odeon cinemas, include Butlin's, Mecca, the Hard Rock Cafés and a large share in Rank Xerox. The company's logo, based on the famous opening image of all Rank films, is an athlete striking a gong.

Ranks Hovis McDougall (RHM) One of Europe's largest-food processing companies, deriving from the mill in Hull where the father of J. Arthur *Rank began trading in 1875. *Hovis and McDougall merged in 1957 and were acquired by Ranks in 1962. In 1992 RHM resisted a takeover bid by Hanson and agreed instead a merger with Tomkins.

Arthur **Ransome** (1884–1967) Children's author who was a successful foreign correspondent before he began the career which made him famous (his presence in Russia in 1917, covering the revolution for the *Daily News*, resulted in his marrying Trotsky's secretary). His 12 books of adventure stories for children began with *Swallows and Amazons* (1930), in which he introduced his main characters – the four Walker children, John, Susan, Titty and Roger. The story centres on sailing in the Lake District, where Ransome had spent his childhood holidays. The best of their later exploits, *We Didn't Mean to Go to Sea* (1937), takes the children accidentally to Holland when they are sailing off the coast of East Anglia.

Esther **Rantzen** see *That's Life!*

Rape of Lucrece see William *Shakespeare.

*The **Rape of the Lock*** (1712) Mock-heroic poem by *Pope, based on a real incident which had caused friction between two families of his acquaintance. At a party the 20-year-old Lord Petre had cut off a lock of Miss Arabella Fermor's hair. In treating the event as something out of Homer, Pope used laughter to defuse the issue. The result is a poem of delightful wit and delicacy following a nymph, named Belinda, through the rituals of her fashionable day up to the moment of the rape. The lock of hair ends as a new comet in the heavens. An extended version of the poem was published in 1714.

Raphael Cartoons (c.1514, Victoria and Albert Museum) Seven of the ten designs for tapestries on New Testament themes which were commissioned from Raphael by Leo X. In 1623 they were bought in Rome on behalf of the future Charles I, to serve as patterns for the factory recently established at *Mortlake. They miraculously survived the ravages of the Commonwealth, and the cartoon gallery at Hampton Court was designed for them by Wren in the late 17C. They have been on loan to the V&A since 1865.

Rastafarians (commonly known as Rastas) West Indian cult which began in the 1930s and has a number of followers in Britain, noticeable by their long matted hair (dreadlocks) and bright wollen hats or headbands in the Ethiopian colours of red, yellow and green. The sect is named after Ras Tafari (1892– 1975), better known as the Ethiopian emperor Haile Selassie; Rastafarians believe that he is divine and that he will bring to Zion in Africa the chosen people (all black but including the great figures of scripture, from Adam to Jesus). The smoking of marijuana is part of the cult, and reggae is its music (above all as performed by the best-known Rasta of all, Bob Marley, 1945–81).

rates see *local taxes.

rationing Introduced in Britain during the last year of World War I, rationing began with sugar in December 1917; in July 1918 it was extended to meat, bacon, ham, lard, butter and margarine. Rationing schemes were in place from the start of World War II, and the ration book became a familiar feature of the war and postwar years. Bacon, butter and sugar were the first commodities to be rationed (from Jan. 1940), soon followed by a wide range of commodities including meat, eggs, margarine and lard, tea, cheese and milk, jam and marmalade. In July 1942 chocolate and sweets were added. Rationed non-edible goods included petrol, domestic coal and clothing. It was not until the years of austerity after the war that bread was rationed (July 1946) or potatoes (Dec. 1947). Restrictions were gradually relaxed from April 1948, but butter and meat could not be freely bought until 1954 nor coal until 1958.

Ratners Chain of jewellery shops, operating at the lower end of the market, which grew rapidly during the 1980s and suffered a correspondingly sharp collapse in the early 1990s. Something of a turning point had been a widely publicized remark in April 1991 by the chairman and chief executive, Gerald Ratner; in a speech he jokingly described one of the items on sale in his shops, a sherry decanter set, as 'total crap'. Under pressure from shareholders Ratner resigned early in 1992 as chairman and in November of that year as chief executive.

Terence **Rattigan** (1911–77, kt 1971) Playwright known for a craftsmanlike skill combined with a considerable understanding of character, often of a rather bleak sort – as in *Separate Tables* (1954), a pair of one-act plays set in the dining room of a run-down residential hotel. He made his name with a light confection, *French without*

Tears (1936), but his work has lasted best in traditional plays of conflict and suspense such as The *Winslow Boy (1946). He invented Aunt *Edna three years before *Look Back in Anger changed the English theatrical scene; but his unfashionable concern for her caused his plays to be underrated during the last two decades of his life.

Simon **Rattle** (b. 1955) Conductor of great charisma who has put the *City of Birmingham Symphony Orchestra in the forefront of British musical life. He became its principal conductor in 1980, after three years as associate conductor of the Royal Liverpool Philharmonic. Liverpool is his home city, and he was playing percussion in the Merseyside Youth Orchestra at the age of eight. Since 1981 he has also been principal guest conductor of the Los Angeles Philharmonic.

Ratty see The *Wind in the Willows.

Ravenscraig Steel works at Motherwell, southeast of Glasgow, which were closed by *British Steel in 1992, bringing to an end Scotland's steel industry and causing much local indignation.

John **Ray** (1627–1705) Naturalist, born the son of a village blacksmith in Essex, who managed to get an education at Cambridge and then travelled Europe with a rich friend (Francis Willughby, 1635–72) looking for plant and animal specimens. They were hoping to provide a systematic description of all living species, and after Willughby's death Ray made an impressive start with his account of birds, fishes and above all plants (some 18,600). The concept of the species as a mutually fertile group is Ray's, earning him the title 'father of natural history'. Much of his system has remained at the heart of modern taxonomy.

Claire **Rayner** (b. 1931, m. Desmond Rayner 1957) A nurse by profession who began in journalism as a medical correspondent and then became one of Britain's leading agony aunts, both in print (*Sun* 1973–80, *Sunday Mirror* 1980–8, *Today* 1988–91) and in broadcasting (*TV-am Advice Spot* 1985–92). The trauma of her own childhood (she broke down when asked about it on radio by Anthony *Clare, and makes no mention of her parents or her maiden name in *Who's Who*) gave her the idea for *Myself When Young*, a series of interviews which she has conducted on radio since 1989.

Phil **Read** (b. 1939) Racing motorcyclist with a string of world championship victories from 1964 – mainly riding for Yamaha (1968 at 125cc, 1964–5, 1968 and 1971 at 250cc) but also in the more powerful 500cc class for MV Agusta (1973–4). He won the 1977 Isle of Man Senior TT on a Suzuki.

'Reader, I married him' see *Jane Eyre.

Reading (135,000 in 1991) Administrative centre of Berkshire, on the river Kennet. There are only fragmentary ruins of the great Benedictine abbey, founded in 1121, which made Reading a place of importance in the Middle Ages. In more recent centuries it has been famous above all for the manufacture of biscuits. The museum, in a redbrick building of the late 19C, has the finds from the nearby Roman site of *Silchester. Oscar *Wilde served most of his sentence (1895–7) in the prison at Reading.

real tennis (also called royal or court tennis) Game played with rackets, a ball and a net in an area imitating a courtyard, surrounded by sloping roofs. Perhaps originating in medieval monasteries, it became the sport of kings (tennis balls are the insultingly frivolous gift sent by the French to the young English king in *Henry V). The 16C was the heyday of the game, when a great house such as Hampton Court was likely to have its own tennis court. Lawn *tennis was an adaptation to a garden setting. The newcomer took on almost unaltered the older game's weirdly eccentric system of scoring, in which zero is 'love' and one is 'fifteen'.

Ray **Reardon** (b. 1932) Welsh snooker player who dominated the game in the 1970s. He won the World Professional Championship six times (1970, 73, 74, 75, 76, 78). In 1969 he was the first winner of the television tournament *Pot Black.

Rebecca (1938) Novel by Daphne *du Maurier about an unnamed young woman (the narrator) who marries a Cornish landowner and widower, Maxim de Winter, but finds his home, Manderley, unwelcoming for two reasons: the hostility of the sinister housekeeper, Mrs Danvers, and the all-pervasive memory of his apparently perfect first wife, Rebecca. The drama only lightens at the end when Rebecca's image is discovered to be a fraud. The book was filmed in 1940 by Hitchcock, with Laurence Olivier as de Winter, Joan Fontaine as the young wife and Judith Anderson as Mrs Danvers.

Rebecca Riots A series of attacks on tollgates in southwest Wales between 1839 and 1844, carried out by men disguised in women's clothes. There were many reasons for unrest at this time of considerable economic distress (it was the period also of the *Chartists), but the tollgates provided not only a good target but also the biblical justification for the female attire. In *Genesis* 24 it says: 'And they blessed Rebecca and said unto her . . . let thy seed possess the gate of those which hate them. And Rebecca arose, and her damsels, and they rode upon the camels.' The leader of each gang of rioters was known as Rebecca; but he and his damsels made do with horses for lack of Welsh camels.

Received Pronunciation (RP) A standardized form of educated southern English, without regional variations in vocabulary or pronunciation. A neutral accent of this kind, which came to be considered an indicator of class, was made possible by the *public schools in the 19C, bringing together upper-class boys who would otherwise have spoken in their own regional voices. For some decades such an accent was considered essential for advancement, being used by all announcers on the BBC and by many who had grown up speaking with other vowels. Fortunately this snobbery has ended, and accents of almost impenetrable authenticity can now be heard on radio and television. RP is sometimes called standard English – an ambiguous term used also of grammatically correct English.

recession An imprecise term for a downturn in the economy. It is sometimes defined as a period in which the *GDP declines over two successive quarters (allowing for seasonal adjustments) – a concept also stated as two quarters of negative growth. As the chart accompanying the GDP entry shows, the postwar recessions in Britain have been in the mid-1970s, the early 1980s and the early 1990s. The most recent has been the most severe, lasting from the middle of 1990 until at least the end of 1992.

Reckitt & Colman Company with a wide range of domestic products, resulting from the merger in 1954 of two 19C British family firms which were household names. Isaac Reckitt (1792–1862) was a Quaker miller, based in Hull, who diversified in the 1850s from his main product, starch; black grate polish and 'Reckitt's Blue' (to make

the laundry white) were early products, to which his descendants added others of a similarly homely kind such as Brasso and Dettol. From 1814 Jeremiah Colman (1777–1855) was milling mustard near Norwich, an activity which his family developed with such success that in England mustard and Colman became synonymous. A third company, merged with the other two in 1955, was Chiswick Products, which since 1886 had been making soap and then Cherry Blossom Shoe polish at Chiswick, in west London.

*The **Recruiting Officer*** (1706) Comedy by *Farquhar with a warm realism of character and detail, probably deriving from his own recent experience as a recruiting officer in Shrewsbury, where the play is set. Captain Plume's way of getting in contact with potential recruits is by making love to their sweethearts, while Sergeant Kite disguises himself as an astrologer to add the influence of the stars. Romance is provided by Sylvia, daughter of a local justice. Her father opposes her love for Plume. Her solution is ingenious and allows for one of the favourite pleasures of theatre-goers of that time, the sight of a pretty woman in breeches. Sylvia disguises herself as a man, gets herself arrested for bad behaviour, and is brought before her father; he hands her over to Plume as one of his recruits.

recusants see *Roman Catholics.

Red Arrows The aerobatic display team of the RAF, using nine red aircraft to perform complex formations at very high speed; they add to the already breathtaking spectacle by releasing trails of coloured vapour. Formed in 1965, they used Hawker Siddely Gnats until 1979; since then they have flown the British Aerospace Hawk T.1.

*The **Red Barn*** (1828) The first of many *melodramas on the most popular of real-life crimes. Maria Marten, daughter of a mole-catcher in Suffolk, was pregnant by William Corder when she arranged to meet him at the Red Barn on his father's farm so as to elope and get married in Ipswich. Her body was later found in the barn and Corder was hanged in August 1828 (little time was wasted in those days in getting a good story on to the stage).

'red books' see Humphry *Repton.

redbrick Term coined in the mid-20C for the universities founded in industrial cities in the late 19C and early 20C, many of them built in brick. A contrast with the stone of *Oxbridge was intended, though several colleges in the older universities are also of brick.

redcoats Term for British soldiers, whose uniform was a red tunic from the time of the *New Model Army in the 17C to the introduction of *khaki in the mid-19C. More recently a redcoat has been a 'holiday uncle' at a *Butlin's camp.

Red Devils The freefall display team of the *Parachute Regiment. They were formed in 1963 and the following year adopted their uniform of red jumpsuits and the name of Red Devils. Trailing plumes of coloured smoke, they 'swim' into a succession of formations as they fall, passing through hoops held for each other and landing in front of the public – often within target areas only a few yards across.

Red Ensign see *ensign.

*The **Red Flag*** An anthem of the Labour movement, written in 1889 by James Connell (1853–1929), an Irish poacher turned sheep farmer turned politician. It has featured prominently in British political life, at the end of each Labour party conference, with the party leaders and delegates seen on television singing this deeply improbable statement of past and future:

> The people's flag is deepest red;
> It shrouded oft our martyred dead,
> And ere their limbs grew stiff and cold,
> Their hearts' blood dyed its every fold.
> Then raise the scarlet standard high!
> Within its shade we'll live or die.
> Though cowards flinch and traitors sneer,
> We'll keep the red flag flying here.

Red Flag Act Popular name for the Locomotive Act of 1865, which put severe restrictions on the steam carriages then being developed. They were limited to 4 mph (6.4kph) in the country and 2 mph in towns, and they had to be preceded by someone on foot, at least 60 yards (55m) ahead, carrying a red flag. Early developments of the car in Britain were effectively stifled by these rules until the repeal of the act in 1896 – a liberation commemorated annually in the *Brighton Run.

Michael **Redgrave** (1908–85, kt 1959) Actor known in particular for his performances in Shakespeare and Chekhov, such as his Richard II at Stratford in 1951 and his Uncle Vanya in 1962–3 for Olivier's first National Theatre company. His film career had a notable early success in The *Lady Vanishes.

Steve **Redgrave** (b. 1962) Outstanding oarsman, with three gold medals in successive Olympic Games – for the coxed fours in 1984, for the coxless pairs in 1988 (with Andrew Holmes), and successfully defending that title in 1992 (with Matthew Pinsent). He also won a bronze in the coxed pairs in 1988. If he competes in the 1996 Olympics, he has a chance of equalling the five rowing medals of Jack *Beresford.

Vanessa **Redgrave** (b. 1937) Actress who, like her father Michael *Redgrave, has excelled in the roles of Chekhov and Shakespeare. Her film career began with several successes in the 1960s (*Morgan* 1966, *Blow-Up* 1967, *Isadora* 1968), and she won an Oscar for *Julia* (1977). She has been a vigorous campaigner for extreme left-wing causes, particularly on behalf of the Workers' Revolutionary party.

Red Hand of Ulster The badge of the province of Ulster and of the O'Neill family, in the form of a right hand cut off at the wrist (other organizations in Ulster use the left hand). There is an early legend – of no historical validity, and appearing also as a story in other places – that the origin is an occasion when territory on the other side of a stretch of water was promised to whoever could first place a hand upon it; the O'Neill chieftain's boat was trailing in the race, so he cut off his hand and flung it ahead to win the contest.

Red House see William *Morris.

Little **Red Riding Hood** Tale introduced to English readers in 1729 by *Mother Goose. The foolish girl, who accepts the wolf in bed in a bonnet as her grandmother, is eaten at the end of the original story without more ado. Modern versions insist on a less bleak conclusion.

Red Rum (foaled 1965) Bay gelding, by far the most famous racehorse of modern times for his unparalleled record in the *Grand National. In the period 1973–7 he won the race three times and was second in each of the

intervening years (1975, 76). He then retired to a profitable career making celebrity appearances (even opening supermarkets), being affectionately known to his adoring public as 'Rummy'. By the 1990s it had become the tradition for him to lead the procession before the big race at Aintree, where there has been a bronze statue of him since 1988.

The **Red Shoes** (1948) Film written and directed jointly by Michael Powell and Emeric Pressburger, which enjoyed great international success with its backstage view of the world of ballet. A young student, acted and danced by Moira *Shearer, has a meteoric rise to fame but commits suicide after a conflict between love and her new career.

red tape Term for excessive bureaucracy, deriving from the red tape around bundles of legal and official documents. It became widely used in its present pejorative sense in the mid-19C, by Thomas Carlyle and others.

Carol **Reed** (1906–76, kt 1952) Film director with theatre in his blood – he was an illegitimate son of the actor-manager Beerbohm Tree. His most creative period was just after the war. *Odd Man Out* (1947) was followed by The *Third Man* (1949), with a script by Graham Greene; their collaboration extended to two other films (*The Fallen Idol* 1948, *Our Man in Havana* 1960). An exuberant finale to Reed's career was his only musical, *Oliver!* (1968), which won him an Oscar.

Reed International Company with interests as wide-ranging as publishing and construction, fabrics and chemicals, but with paper at the heart of the business. It derives from the activities of Albert Reed (1846–1920), who managed paper mills in the west country before buying (from 1894) several of his own – mainly in the southeast. Part of his subsequent success came from supplying newsprint to the developing empire of Lord *Northcliffe. He floated his company on the Stock Exchange in 1903.

reels Folk dances, originating in the Highlands of Scotland, which in the 19C made the transition to the ballroom. Under the general name of Highland dancing, demonstrations of reels are now also a standard part of *Highland games.

Merlyn **Rees** (b. 1920, baron Merlyn-Rees 1992) Labour politician, MP for South Leeds (1963–83) and for Morley and Leeds South (1983–92), who entered the cabinet in

Red Riding Hood's first tremor of doubt about her grandmother: illustration by Gustave Doré for an edition of 1867.

Supporters of the Reform Act attack the rotten boroughs and nest eggs of the old guard in a caricature of 1832.

1974 as secretary of state for Northern Ireland and was subsequently home secretary (1976–9).

referendum By early 1993 there had only been one national referendum in British history, held in June 1975 on the issue of *EC membership. The question was 'Do you think that the Kingdom should stay in the European Community (the Common Market)?'. On a turnout of about 66% of the electorate, the answer was yes by a 2:1 majority (64.5% in favour). Four years later a referendum was held in Scotland and Wales on *devolution. In 1992–3 it was debated whether to hold a referendum on *Maastricht.

Reform Act (1832) The beginning of democracy in its modern form in Britain, following a tide of public indignation during the 1820s at the previous system (characterized at its worst by pocket and rotten *boroughs). The act was passed by the Whig administration of Earl *Grey, against prolonged and bitter opposition from many Tories but with the reluctant assistance of *William IV. It was the first of the extensions to the *franchise which led eventually to universal suffrage.

Reformation England and Scotland were affected very differently by the profound changes in Christian belief and worship launched in the early 16C by Luther in Germany, and carried further by Zwingli and Calvin in Switzerland.

There had been an English precursor of Protestant ideas in John *Wycliffe, but the actual break with Rome came more as a result of political and sexual intrigue than on any theological basis. It derived from *Henry VIII's determination to end one marriage and legitimize another. This was achieved by an extreme solution, the establishing of a separate *Church of England. Its eventual identity,

middle-of-the-road and relatively undogmatic, was itself largely the result of political wisdom, in a tradition going back to its founding father, Thomas *Cranmer.

The *Church of Scotland by contrast was intensely theological from the start. John *Knox, trained in Geneva, was a Protestant reformer of the sternest kind. Bringing the strict Calvinist creed to a country ruled by the Roman Catholic *Mary Queen of Scots, Knox and his followers were inevitably much involved in politics. But they were uncompromising in their doctrine. And so, whereas England in the Reformation created its own version of Protestantism, Scotland eventually established a church within the broader Presbyterian community.

In both countries the Reformation caused much destruction of art and architecture. The *dissolution of the monasteries was state policy; the destruction of frescoes and statues in cathedrals and village churches was the result of Puritan fervour, over-obedient to the Bible's prohibition of graven images.

Reform Club (London SW1) A *club founded in 1832 by Whig supporters of the *Reform Act; it continued with the same political allegiance to become later the leading *Liberal club. Charles *Barry won the 1837 competition to design the building, as he had earlier with its neighbour in Pall Mall, the *Travellers'; he again produced an Italian Renaissance palace, in this case even larger and grander. In 1981 the Reform became the first of the old London clubs to admit women as members.

Regency The period 1811–20, during which the prince of Wales was given the powers of regent because of the insanity of *George III. The term is most often used to describe a style in the decorative arts and in architecture (where balconies with fanciful metal roofs and the widespread use of stucco are characteristic). In this sense it is usually extended to cover the entire period from the beginning of the century to the start of the *Victorian era.

Regent's Park (London NW1) The main feature of John *Nash's development of central London for the Prince Regent. The area belonged to a convent until the 16C, when it was reserved as a royal hunting park after the *dissolution of the monasteries. Nash landscaped 197ha/487ac of open ground (a romantically meandering lake being the main feature) and enclosed the space with the elegant terraces which still survive. The park was completed in 1828, by which time it already had the new *London Zoo at its northern end. The Inner Circle now contains Queen Mary's Rose Garden, laid out in the 1930s, and the open-air theatre in which plays are performed each summer.

Regent Street (London W1) A thoroughfare driven through the West End by John *Nash in 1813–23, to join *Carlton House with the new *Regent's Park. Where it crossed *Piccadilly, it brought into being Piccadilly Circus. It then continued north in a stylish curving sweep known as the Quadrant. With covered pavements behind a colonnade, the Quadrant soon became London's most fashionable shopping area. The curve is all that remains of Nash's scheme, for this central part of Regent Street was redeveloped in a uniformly heavy style in the 1920s.

region The largest administrative unit in Scotland since the reorganization of *local government in 1975, when 33 former *counties were grouped into nine regions and three *islands areas. The regions are Borders, Central, Dumfries and Galloway, Fife, Grampian, Highland, Lothian, Strathclyde, Tayside.

Register House see *Scottish Record Office.

regnal year see *Act of Parliament.

Lord **Reith** (John Reith, 1889–1971, kt 1927, baron 1940) Creator of the *BBC from its beginnings in 1922 and pioneer of the concept of public service broadcasting. The Reith Lectures were established in his honour in 1948, the first series of six being given in that year by Bertrand Russell – who chose as his subject 'Authority and the Individual'. A new lecturer is appointed each year (it is radio's most prestigious invitation) and the lectures are first broadcast on Radio 4 in November and December.

Relate The name since 1988 of the Marriage Guidance Council. The organization was set up in 1938 by a group of clergy, magistrates, doctors and social workers – alarmed that the *divorce rate had risen to 7000 a year. A voluntary organization, Relate operates from some 160 centres around the country where advice and if necessary therapy is available to anyone whose marriage or relationship is in difficulties.

Remembrance Sunday see *Armistice.

remittance man Derogatory term in the colonies from the mid-19C for the type of emigrant supported by funds from Britain, the implication being that he had been bribed to leave. Such a man was defined in 1849 as a 'ne'er-do-well living in the colonies on quarterly remittances received from friends at home'.

Renaissance A notoriously elusive concept relating to western Europe in the 14–16C. In 14C Italy there was renewed interest in ancient Latin literature and this was followed, from around 1400, by a similar interest in Roman art and architecture. From these beginnings there developed humanism, an attitude giving man a central place in the attention of scholars, who had previously been more concerned with God. In the optimistic 18C this emergence from the Middle Ages was seen as the greatest single step in mankind's progress towards higher civilization. But in the 20C a certain loss of confidence in

John Nash's curving and arcaded Regent Street, viewed from Piccadilly Circus soon after its completion: aquatint c.1825.

man's perfectibility, combined with greater understanding of the Middle Ages, has dealt this simple view of the Renaissance a mortal blow. Nevertheless the emergence of humanism remains a demonstrable fact, and with it came certain changes in literature, art and architecture.

These changes came late in Britain. There were some early patrons of the new learning, such as Duke Humfrey of Gloucester (1390–1447) whose library went to the Bodleian at *Oxford, but it was not till the 16C, with the emergence of men such as Thomas *More, that humanism was clearly established. By then strong Tudor rule provided a setting in which the arts of the Renaissance could flourish. The people who look out of portraits by *Holbein are men and women of the Renaissance. So were *Spenser and *Sidney. So too were the patrons who commissioned the great houses such as *Longleat, *Wollaton, *Montacute or *Hardwick, in which elaborate symmetrical architecture emphasizes the owner's status.

Ruth **Rendell** (b. 1930) Popular crime novelist in the tradition of Agatha Christie and P.D. James. Her murder mysteries, taxing the ingenuity and often the sensibilities of the civilized Chief Inspector Wexford, tend to take place in very ordinary communities within the Home Counties. Several of her books have been televised in the past few years, including *Wolf to the Slaughter* (published 1967) and *The Veiled One* (1988); and her short stories have proved immensely popular as a television series under the title *Ruth Rendell Mysteries*. She also writes under the pseudonym Barbara Vine.

Renfrewshire Until 1975 a *county in the west of Scotland, to the south of the Clyde estuary, now part of the Strathclyde region.

John **Rennie** (1761–1821) Scottish engineer who contributed much to the appearance of 19C London, building Waterloo, Southwark and London bridges. All have been replaced in the 20C; his *London Bridge is the one now in Arizona. He also constructed the London and East India docks, together with many harbours and canals around the country.

Humphry **Repton** (1752–1818) The leading landscape gardener after the death of Capability *Brown. He modified his predecessor's example in various ways – particularly in contriving a more natural progression between house and park through arrangements of terraces and steps. He is remembered above all for his famous 'red books', bound in red leather for prospective patrons and containing watercolour views with hinged flaps to show house and landscape before and after his proposed improvements. More than 100 red books survive, of the 400 or so which Repton claimed to have made. He also published several books on the theory and practice of *landscape gardening.

Restoration (1660) The return of the monarch, *Charles II, to Britain and to his throne. The term is used of the event itself and of the period spanning the reigns of Charles II and James II, ending with the *Revolution of 1688. It was a time of frivolity and glamour (in reaction against the preceding years of the *Commonwealth), with the example of Charles II himself and of courtiers such as Lord *Rochester giving a veneer of licentiousness to London life.

The witty, cynical, aristocratic plays of the late 17C are often classed together as Restoration comedy. The style began in the reign of Charles II, and *Wycherley is the best-known exponent from that period. But the leading writers grouped under this heading were not born at the time of the Restoration and began writing after the departure of James II. They were *Vanbrugh (b. 1664, first play 1696), *Congreve (b. 1670, first play 1693) and *Farquhar (b. 1678, first play 1698).

Retail Price Index see *RPI.

retirement ages see *pensions.

Repton with a theodolite, supervising an improvement to the landscape: his professional trade card, engraved in 1788.

retrievers Sporting dogs used for retrieving game which has been shot. The most common breed is the Labrador retriever (usually shortened to Labrador). It originated in the region of Labrador, in northeast Canada, where it swam in the freezing waters to help fishermen place their nets. The breed has a short dense coat, usually black but sometimes brown or yellow. The golden retriever, with a wavy coat and feathering on legs and tail, was bred near Inverness in the mid-19C by selecting yellow puppies with these characteristics.

Reuters News and information services agency, founded in London in 1851 by a German-born immigrant, Paul Julius Reuter (1816–99). He set up an office near the Stock Exchange and telegraphed prices to Paris via the undersea cable between Dover and Calais (he had previously used carrier pigeons for the same purpose between Brussels and Aachen). By the end of the decade he was conveying general news as well, and as telegraphic links extended round the world his firm became the first international news agency.

Reuters was restructured in 1941 as a private company, jointly owned by the national newspapers and by the *Press Association (representing the regional press). In 1984, by which time the global electronic extension of its financial services had become very profitable, Reuters was floated as a public company.

HMS *Revenge* see entries on *Drake and *Grenville.

Don **Revie** (1927–89) Football manager who transformed *Leeds United after his appointment in 1961. By 1964 he had got them into Division 1, and before his retirement in 1974 they had twice won the League championship (1969, 74) and the European Fairs Cup (1968, 71), in addition to the League Cup (1968) and the FA Cup (1972). He managed England 1974–7, giving up the post to become the national team coach for the United Arab Emirates (1977–80).

Revised Version see *Bible in English.

Revolution of 1688 (also known as the Glorious Revolution) The coup which transferred the crown from *James II to *William III and Mary, considered glorious because it introduced *constitutional monarchy. It is also known as the Bloodless Revolution. In England and Wales the new monarchs were unopposed, but resistance in Scotland led to the massacre of *Glencoe; and in 1689 James II landed in Ireland for a campaign which ended with his defeat at the Battle of the *Boyne.

revue Theatrical entertainment composed of short sketches and songs of a relatively sophisticated and often satirical nature (as distinct from the more robust tradition of *music hall). Revues were a staple part of the London theatrical scene from the 1890s to 1960s (*Under the Clock* in 1893 is usually quoted as the first). Charles *Cochran was the foremost producer of revues; Noel *Coward was a frequent writer of revue sketches; and it was in revue that Joyce *Grenfell made her name. In the last years before the demise of the form John *Cranko produced a notable surrealist example in *Cranks* (1956); *Flanders and Swann had a very long run in *At the Drop of a Hat* (1957); and the convention went out with a blaze in *Beyond the Fringe* (1960). Since then the same skills have been alive and well on TV, in a wide range of series such as *That was the Week that Was*, *Monty Python's Flying Circus* or *Spitting Image*.

Joshua **Reynolds** (1723–92, kt 1769) Britain's leading portrait painter, remarkable for his range of response to his sitters ('Damn him, how various he is!' said his leading rival, Gainsborough). His years in Italy (1749–52) gave him a knowledge of classical ideals and a taste for the richness of Venetian colour, together with a conviction that painting was among the most dignified of callings and its practitioners worthy of equivalently high status. His own career greatly furthered this notion. He was rapidly successful and wealthy, coping with 150 sitters a year by 1758; and he was a natural choice in 1768 to be first president of the *Royal Academy. In his *Discourses*, delivered almost annually to the students of the academy, he offered a powerful testimony to what he called the Grand Manner in art. In doing so he made himself the bugbear of emerging romantics such as William *Blake. He was himself unsuccessful in history painting, which he considered the highest form of art, but he often added solemnity to his portraits through learned allusions or classical accessories. He is unsentimentally direct in his best portraits of children.

In spite of suffering from deafness he was a sociable man, at ease both in the aristocratic world of his sitters and in literary London. He was a close friend of *Johnson; the Club they founded together was his idea, and Boswell dedicated his life of the great man to Reynolds. He was buried in St Paul's Cathedral, the first artist to be granted this honour since another great portraitist of the English aristocracy, Van *Dyck.

Osborne **Reynolds** (1842–1912) Physicist and engineer whose researches in hydrodynamics led to practical improvements in the design of pumps and turbines. He is remembered in the Reynolds number, used in calculating aspects of fluid flow.

RFC see *Royal Air Force.

Cecil **Rhodes** (1853–1902) English-born entrepreneur and politician who made a vast fortune in the newly discovered diamond fields at Kimberley, in *South Africa, where he formed in 1880 the De Beers Mining Company; by 1891 he controlled 90% of the world production of diamonds. Meanwhile he had conceived the ambitious imperial dream of a British colony from the Cape to Cairo. He became a member of the Cape Colony parliament in 1881, and was prime minister by 1890. But there was a barrier to expansion in the Boer republic of the Transvaal to the northeast. Rhodes's admitted involvement in the early planning of the *Jameson Raid against the Transvaal led to his resignation as prime minister in 1896. His policy of commercial expansion to the north continued, under the aegis of the British South Africa Company which he had set up in 1889. The large area settled by the company's pioneers was in 1895 formally named Rhodesia (now *Zimbabwe); meanwhile the company was also pressing into the territory further north, which became Northern Rhodesia (now *Zambia).

Rhodes had been an undergraduate at Oriel College in Oxford. In his will he established the Rhodes Scholarships which enable young men (and more recently women) from the Commonwealth and the United States to study at Oxford.

Zandra **Rhodes** (b. 1940) Fashion and textile designer known for a painterly use of colour (extending at times to her own hair), as well as for bold printed fabrics, often cut in exotic shapes, and for unusual treatments of jersey as a fashion material. She has been involved in products as diverse as rugs, kitchen and bathroom accessories and china figurines.

Rhodesia and Nyasaland Federation of two British protectorates (Northern Rhodesia, later *Zambia, and

Nyasaland, later *Malawi) together with a self-governing colony (Southern Rhodesia, later *Zimbabwe). It lasted from 1953 to 1963 and had a colourful prime minister in Roy Welensky (1907–91). By 1963 all three wanted separate independence.

Rhondda Valley The area of south Wales, in Mid Glamorgan, which has become almost the symbol of Welsh mining, and of the chapel-going and choral-singing traditions of the mining community. It consists of two parallel valleys, Rhondda Fawr and Rhondda Fach, which in the 19–20C became heavily industrialized but which will now gradually revert to their original sparsely inhabited and scenic state. Coal was first mined here in the early 19C, when the population was under 1000; a century later, thanks to the voracious demands of steam engines, the valleys supported more than 150,000 people. The decline began in the *Depression, and the last Rhondda pit closed in 1990. An idealized community of this kind became the public image of Wales through the success of *How Green was my Valley*.

To the east of Rhondda several other valleys – Cynon, Taff, Rhymney, Ebbw, Sirhowy – run down in similar fashion from the south Wales mountains towards the coast. All have suffered the same rise and fall over the past two centuries.

rhyming slang Something between a secret language and an ongoing game of invention, first developed among London's *cockneys in the mid-19C. The principle is to find a phrase which rhymes with a real word, then to drop the rhyming part and use the rest as a synonym. A good example is the rhyming slang *titfer* (tit-for-tat) for hat; or more recently the *Sweeney* (from *Sweeney Todd) for the Flying Squad. Some phrases enter the language with the rhyme still attached; *trouble and strife* for wife is a well-known example. *Arthur* for cash (also used in full as *Arthur Ashe*) is proof that the game goes on.

Griff **Rhys Jones** see *Smith and Jones*.

rib vaulting Innovation at *Durham Cathedral in the late 11C, prefiguring the delicacy of *Gothic design. Rib vaults rise from points above adjacent pillars on each side of a nave, meeting in the centre like a four-branched starfish. Together they support the fabric of the roof, which can be of lighter material because it is not in itself structural.

David **Ricardo** (1772–1823) Economist who developed the theories of Adam *Smith, treating the subject more as a science than as a branch of philosophy. His main work was *On the Principles of Political Economy and Taxation* (1817). He was influential in the early stages of the campaign for free trade and for the abolition of the *Corn Laws. He made his career in the Stock Exchange and in 1819 was elected a member of parliament. Though Jewish by birth, of Dutch origin, he abandoned the Jewish faith as a young man and so was able to take his seat in the House of Commons.

David **Riccio** see *Mary Queen of Scots.

rice pudding Many countries have rice puddings, but a sweet pudding of this kind has been so much eaten in Britain since the 18C that it seemed for a while almost a national dish. The British version is at its best when the cream is allowed to bake into a yellowish brown skin on the surface.

Cliff **Richard** (stage name of Harry Webb, b. 1940) Singer who is the great survivor of the British pop scene, with no. 1 hit singles spanning a record 31 years from

Living Doll (1959) to *Saviour's Day* (1990); he has had in all more than 100 singles in the charts. He has occupied an unusual place in the world of pop as an icon of piety, having made much of his commitment to Christianity; press interest has frequently focused on his astonishingly youthful appearance and professed celibacy. In the 1960s he starred in a series of wholesome musical films, of which *The Young Ones* (1961) was the most successful. On the majority of his early records he was backed by the *Shadows.

Richard I (1157–99) King of England from 1189; third son of Henry II and Eleanor of Aquitaine; married Berengaria of Navarre in 1191. Growing up largely in his mother's province of Aquitaine in southwest France, and spending not more than six months in England during his entire 10-year reign, his link with the country was minimal – apart from exhausting its finances, first to raise an army for the third crusade and then to pay a massive ransom after he had been captured on his journey home. Nevertheless his skill and courage in warfare made him a hero in his own time, as reflected in his nickname *Coeur de Lion* (Lionheart) and in the later legend of *Blondel. Having no children, he was succeeded on the throne by his brother John (see the *royal house).

Richard II (1367–1400) King of England from 1377 (to 1399), succeeding Edward III; son of Edward the Black Prince and Joan of Kent; married Anne of Bohemia in 1382.

At the age of ten he succeeded his grandfather on the throne because his father, the Black Prince, had died the previous year. While still a minor he reacted with courage to the *Peasants' Revolt of 1381, but his unwisely chosen favourites provoked increasing hostility as he acquired more power. The civilized life of his court (the context in which *Chaucer flourished) was at odds with the more robust and military interests of his most powerful subjects. A plot against him in 1387 involved his cousin Bolingbroke. Richard banished Bolingbroke in 1398 and confiscated his lands in 1399, provoking the invasion which led to his own surrender at Conwy in August of that year (his capture was the outcome of a trick rather than a battle). Deposed and eventually imprisoned in Pontefract Castle, he died in February 1400. There is no evidence that he was murdered (as he is in Shakespeare's *Richard II*), but his death was certainly convenient to Bolingbroke who had taken the throne in 1399 as *Henry IV (see the *royal house).

Richard II (1595) Historical tragedy by *Shakespeare, in which the king brings his fate upon himself by his imperious behaviour, his weakness and his tendency to self-dramatization. At the start of the play he banishes two powerful nobles, one of them Bolingbroke, the son of *John of Gaunt. The confiscation of Bolingbroke's property leads, as in history, to his seizing the throne as *Henry IV. But a major element in the play is Richard's theatrical self-pity, inviting his followers to join him in telling 'sad stories of the death of kings' and making much of handing over the crown in a famous deposition scene. One of the charges against the earl of *Essex was that he and his followers had arranged a performance of a play about Richard II (almost certainly Shakespeare's) on the evening before his abortive uprising. At the end of the drama Richard is murdered on a hint from Henry IV, who then vows to make a pilgrimage to the Holy Land to expiate his guilt.

Richard III (1452–85) King of England from 1483. The youngest son of Richard, duke of York (see the *royal house), he succeeded his brother Edward IV and his

Richardson's Pamela suffers the first advance of the lascivious Mr B: detail of a painting of 1744 by Joseph Highmore.

nephew *Edward V. His traditional reputation, that of the deepest of villains (reinforced by Shakespeare's *Richard III*), derives partly from the need of the Tudor monarchs to blacken the name of the last representative of the royal house they had displaced. Richard's moral scruples were certainly few, even by the standards of the time, and it seems probable that he was responsible for the murder of *Henry VI and of the *princes in the Tower. On the other hand as duke of Gloucester he had been unusually loyal when his brother was on the throne, and had governed northern England with skill and good judgement. In 1471 he married Anne Neville, a daughter of *Warwick the Kingmaker, but their only son died in 1484. Richard himself was killed the following year in battle with his successor, *Henry VII, at Bosworth Field.

Richard III (*c*.1592) Historical melodrama by *Shakespeare, the first indication of the young author's ability to create a fascinating larger-than-life character. The villainous hunchback hero, Richard III, revels in his evil powers and takes us into his confidence from his famous opening couplet:

> Now is the winter of our discontent
> Made glorious summer by this sun of York.

His aside to the audience is in similar vein after he has virtually proposed marriage, in front of one of the coffins, to a woman whose husband and father-in-law he has murdered: ~ Was ever woman in this humour woo'd? ~ Was ever woman in this humour won?

After murdering his way to the throne, Richard is eventually challenged by the earl of Richmond. The final scenes depict their confrontation at *Bosworth Field. In the battle Richard is reduced to the indignity of fighting on foot, thus providing his most famous line: 'A horse! a horse! my kingdom for a horse!'. But he loses his kingdom to Richmond, who kills him on the battlefield and is crowned as Henry VII.

The play was superbly filmed in 1955, with Laurence Olivier both directing and giving one of his greatest performances in the title role.

Frank **Richards** see *Billy Bunter.

Gordon **Richards** (1904–86, kt 1953) Jockey who dominated more than 30 years of British racing. His career spanned 1920–54, and in the 28 seasons from 1925 to 1953 he was *champion jockey 26 times. He holds the record of 4870 wins in Britain and of 269 wins in one season (1947), but he only managed to win the Derby on the last of his 28 attempts (1953 on Pinza).

Ralph **Richardson** (1902–83, kt 1947) Actor with an ability to turn an apparently quite ordinary character into someone of intriguing mystery. In his middle years this was seen in several plays by J.B. Priestley, and in his old age it found a new outlet in deliberately strange and low-key modern works such as David Storey's *Home* (1970) and Harold Pinter's *No Man's Land* (1975) – in each case playing opposite John Gielgud in what became a famous geriatric partnership. It was Richardson who suggested to the National Theatre that a rocket should be fired on each first night, and 'Ralph's Rocket' was a regular feature until the early 1990s.

Samuel **Richardson** (1689–1761) Author whose use of letters as the medium for story-telling greatly extended the psychological range of the early novel. He had an immediate success with *Pamela, or Virtue Rewarded* (1740), in which the majority of the letters are written by Pamela herself, a 15-year-old maid who wards off the sexual designs of the young man of the house (including attempted rape and a mock marriage) until her virtue is at last rewarded with a genuine wedding ring. The book's somewhat scheming notion of virtue and its rewards had an excellent side-effect in provoking Henry *Fielding to attempt fiction. The much darker *Clarissa* (7 vols, 1747–8, and at more than a million words the longest novel in the English language) investigates similar pressures through the letters to their respective confidants of two upper-class characters, Clarissa Harlowe and Richard Lovelace. After hundreds of pages of failed attempts to have his way with Clarissa, Lovelace eventually drugs and rapes her. Clarissa goes mad for a while but recovers before declining to a slow death; Lovelace is killed by her cousin in a duel.

Richmond (7000 in 1981) Market town in North Yorkshire which grew up round the Norman castle, established *c*.1071 on a cliff above the river Swale. The somewhat ruined castle walls date from this time and the tall keep was added a century later. The town's Georgian theatre, which opened in 1788, is the second oldest surviving playhouse in the country (only Bristol is older). After long disuse it was restored and reopened in 1962.

Richmond (16km/10m SW of central London) Town on the south bank of the river Thames. Its importance, and its name, derived from 1499, when Henry VII, who had been earl of Richmond in Yorkshire, decided to build a palace here; the place had previously been known as Sheen. Of his fanciful many-turreted riverside creation only a gatehouse now remains. The town retains an elegant 18c atmosphere, from the time when the royal family spent much of their time at nearby *Kew.

Richmond-upon-Thames (163,000 in 1991) is one of the Greater London boroughs, formed in 1965 and stretching along the Thames from Hampton Court to Barnes.

Richmond Park Area of parkland, about 13km/8m southwest of central London, which was enclosed by Charles I for the hunting of deer. His wall around it was completed in 1637 and still stands. The park contains herds of fallow and red deer descended from those he hunted.

'a riddle wrapped in a mystery inside an enigma' Winston Churchill's description of Russia in a talk on the BBC on 1 October 1939. He was first lord of the Admiralty at the time, and was explaining that it was impossible to predict the actions of the USSR after Stalin's non-aggression pact with Hitler in August.

Ride a cockhorse to Banbury Cross Nursery rhyme, dating back at least to the 18c and much used when dandling a child upon the knee. There was a cross in the marketplace at *Banbury, but there is no historical evidence to support any of the popular candidates (ranging from Elizabeth I to Lady Godiva) for the fine lady who features in the best-known version of the rhyme:

> Ride a cockhorse to Banbury Cross,
> To see a fine lady upon a white horse;
> Rings on her fingers and bells on her toes,
> And she shall have music wherever she goes.

Ridgeway Pre-Roman grass track running northeast from *Avebury to the area of the *Uffington White Horse and then east along the Berkshire downs to Streatley, passsing many Iron Age forts and earthworks.

riding Word meaning a third part of something (from the Anglo-Saxon *thriding*), which has been applied to various regions divided into three parts and in particular to *Yorkshire.

Nicholas **Ridley** see *Oxford.

Nicholas **Ridley** (1929–93, baron 1992) Conservative politician, MP for the Cirencester and Tewkesbury division of Gloucestershire 1959–92. He entered the *cabinet in 1983 as secretary of state for transport, and was subsequently secretary of state for the environment (1986–9) and for trade and industry (1989–90).

Lucie **Rie** (b. 1902, DBE 1991) Austrian-born potter, living in England since 1939. She is known for her distinctively simple style (influenced by *Leach but more spare), as seen particularly in her elegant bowls and thin vertical vases.

Rievaulx Abbey (37km/23m N of York) Ruined Cistercian abbey, founded in 1132. The Early English walls of the choir and transepts survive to their full height in the beautiful Rye valley (the origin of the abbey's name). A long grassy terrace overlooking the ruins was laid out in the 18c with a classical temple at each end.

Malcolm **Rifkind** (b. 1946) Conservative politician, MP for Edinburgh Pentlands since 1974, who entered the *cabinet in 1986 as secretary of state for Scotland and was subsequently secretary of state for transport (1990–2) and for defence (from 1992).

Diana **Rigg** (b. 1938) Actress who was well known in leading Shakespearean roles with the Royal Shakespeare Company before becoming a favourite with a much wider television audience as Emma Peel in *The *Avengers.*

Right Honourable (abbreviated when written to Rt Hon.) Title of respect used for anyone who has been appointed a *privy councillor, and also more formally for appeal court judges, for peers and for certain lord mayors and lord provosts.

*The **Rights of Man*** see Thomas *Paine.

Bridget **Riley** (b. 1931) The leading British painter of op art, using optical illusion to create vibrant or seemingly three-dimensional images from a flat canvas. A painting of hers was on the cover of the catalogue of the first international exhibition of the style, 'The Responsive Eye', at the Museum of Modern Art in New York in 1965. At that

One of Bridget Riley's influential black-and-white canvases from the early 1960s: Hesitate (1964).

time she was working in black and white, but from the late 1960s she has used colour. She was awarded the international painting prize at the Venice Biennale in 1968.

Rillington Place A cul-de-sac in London's Notting Hill district, now demolished, which became notorious because of a succession of murders in no. 10. There was relatively little national attention in 1949 when Timothy Evans, the mentally retarded occupant of an upstairs flat, was hanged after confessing to the murder of his wife and baby girl, whose bodies had been found in the garden shed. The sensation came in 1953 with the discovery of the decaying remains of three young women, hidden in the ground-floor flat of John Christie; his wife's body was then found under the kitchen floorboards and there were skeletons of other female victims in the garden. Christie, a necrophiliac, confessed to these murders and to that of Mrs Evans. Timothy Evans was granted a posthumous pardon in 1966, after his case (taken up by Ludovic *Kennedy) had played a persuasive part in the campaign leading to the abolition of *capital punishment in the previous year.

Ring a ring o' roses Rhyme and tumbling game, in which the children dance in a ring and fall on the last line:

> Ring-a-ring o' roses,
> A pocket full of posies,
> A-tishoo! A-tishoo!
> We all fall down.

This has been a happy hunting ground for those who seek historical allusions in *nursery rhymes. It has been said to relate to the *Great Plague – a rosy rash being supposedly a symptom of the disease, posies being carried against it, sneezes a sign the end was near, and then the tumble into death. But the rhyme was first printed in 1881 and was for a while sung in many versions other than the best-known one quoted here, to which the interpretation is tailored.

Riot Act Legislation of 1715, passed after public disorder had greeted the accession of the house of *Hanover. It remained on the statute book until repealed in 1973. The act included a text be read verbatim by a magistrate to any unruly assembly of 12 or more people; if they had not dispersed within an hour they were guilty of a felony and liable to life imprisonment. The phrase 'reading the riot act' entered the language for any attempt to restore order.

Ripon (12,000 in 1981) Cathedral town in North Yorkshire, deriving from a monastery founded in about 660. The cathedral incorporates the crypt of the original monastery church. The carved wooden choir stalls and misericords of the late 15C are an outstanding feature. Ripon became a diocese in 1836.

Angela **Rippon** (b. 1944) TV presenter and the first woman to read the national news (on the BBC's *Nine O'Clock News* in 1976). She has since presented a wide range of programmes, including quiz games and *Come Dancing*. She was one of the five presenters who won the franchise for *TV-am in 1980.

ritual abuse see *child abuse.

Ritz Hotel (London W1) Hotel on the south side of Piccadilly, overlooking Green Park. In public perception it is the classiest in London – partly because this and the other hotels of the Swiss hotelier César Ritz (1850–1918) added the word 'ritzy' to the language. Before going into business on his own, he had been the manager at the *Savoy. The Ritz was the first important steel-framed building in London, though clad in a comforting Portland stone; it opened in 1906.

*The **Rivals*** (1775) Comedy by *Sheridan, in which a rich young man, Captain Jack Absolute, disguises himself as the impoverished Ensign Beverley because his loved one, Lydia Languish, finds the idea of a penniless suitor more romantic. Bob Acres, a friend of Jack's, also loves Lydia and challenges Beverley to a duel. When Beverley's identity is discovered, Bob Acres yields to his friend in the pursuit of Lydia; and Lydia finally forgives her loved one for being rich. The most memorable character is Lydia's aunt, Mrs Malaprop, whose wayward substitution of words ('as headstrong as an allegory on the banks of the Nile') has caused 'malapropism' to enter the language.

'rivers of blood' see Enoch *Powell.

Brian **Rix** (b. 1924, kt 1986, baron 1992) Actor and producer of farce, most notably at the *Whitehall Theatre in the 1950s, who retired in 1977 from full-time theatrical activity to devote himself to the mentally handicapped. In 1978–83 he presented *Let's Go...* (BBC), a television series for those with a mental handicap; and in 1980 he became the secretary general of *Mencap.

David **Rizzio** see *Mary Queen of Scots.

RLPO see *Royal Liverpool Philharmonic Orchestra.

RMT (National Union of Rail, Maritime and Transport Workers) Trade union formed in 1990 by the merger of two of the country's oldest unions – the NUR (National Union of Railwaymen) and the NUS (National Union of Seamen), with origins going back respectively to 1872 and 1887.

RNLI (Royal National Lifeboat Institution, Poole, Dorset) One of Britain's oldest and most popular charities, founded in 1824 for the purpose of maintaining boats round the coast to save people from shipwreck. Some government money was used in the early years, but since 1869 the costs have been entirely met by donations; and from the start the tradition has been that those manning a lifeboat are volunteers (nowadays with one full-time mechanic). On average three people have been rescued every day in recent years, with an estimated total of more than 120,000 lives saved since 1824.

road numbers Roads are numbered by the Department of Transport according to a system, introduced in 1919, which divides the country as if into slices of a cake. The six major routes leaving London are numbered A1 to A6, and the same number (1–6) is given to the section of country adjacent to each route, moving clockwise. All main roads originating in slice 1 have 1 as the first digit of their number, with A or B as a prefix depending on their greater or lesser importance for through traffic. The subsequent digits of a road's number are random, a new road being given the next unallocated number in its own section. A road originating in one section but then passing through others keeps its original number for its entire length.

The same applies in Scotland, where the slices are defined by the routes A7 to A9 radiating from Edinburgh. The motorway system has been organized on a similar basis, with the prefix M. The highest road number is B9175 in northeast Scotland.

road safety Although the number of cars on the roads has greatly increased, the level of fatal accidents has steadily declined since the mid-1960s – partly due to the introduction of breathalyzing in 1967. Since that year police have been allowed to stop drivers suspected of being under the influence of alcohol and to require them

Road safety

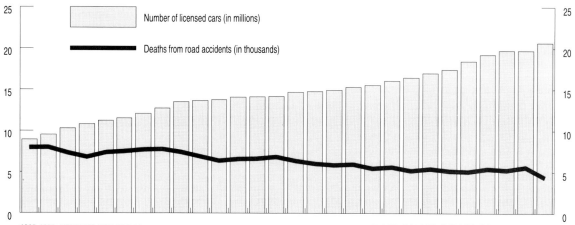

Source: Annual Abstract of Statistics (see *Central Statistical Office).

to breathe into a device, the Breathalyzer, in which the colour of crystals is changed by alcohol. A driver's legally permitted level of alcohol is 35 micrograms in 100 millilitres of breath (the equivalent of 80 milligrams in 100 millilitres of blood).

The **Road to Wigan Pier** (1937) First-hand account by George *Orwell of conditions in northern England during the *Depression. He sets out, imitating *Cobbett and his *Rural Rides*, to test his socialist ideals and his south-of-England preconceptions against the realities of industrial life. He reports from several other areas (particularly Sheffield) as well as Wigan.

Roamin' in the Gloamin' see Harry *Lauder.

Roaring Meg see *Londonderry.

O The **Roast Beef of Old England** (1748, Tate Gallery) The title by which *Hogarth's painting The Gate of Calais is commonly known. Painted after he had been arrested in Calais, suspected of being an English spy, it is a profoundly jingoistic statement by the outraged artist, who is seen sketching in the background. The central incident is the arrival of a succulent side of English beef, the sight of which is causing a fat Catholic friar and starving French soldiers to slaver with desire and admiration.

Roath Park see *Cardiff.

robbing Peter to pay Paul Phrase used for the diversion of funds from one good cause to another. It derives from medieval Christianity. St Peter and St Paul shared a feast day (June 29) and were two of the most popular patron saints – as is evidenced by London's two ancient churches, Westminster Abbey (dedicated to St Peter) and St Paul's Cathedral. This coincidence has led to a common belief, based on no evidence, that the phrase itself derives from London.

Robbins Report see *universities.

Robert I see *Robert the Bruce.

Robert II (1316–1390) King of Scotland from 1371, founding the royal house of *Stuart. He was the son of Walter, the hereditary steward of Scotland, and his claim to the throne came through his mother, Marjorie, daughter of *Robert the Bruce. His life was distinguished largely by the extraordinary number of his offspring – four sons and five daughters by his first marriage (to Elizabeth Mure, solemnized only after the nine births, and so of doubtful legitimacy), two sons and two daughters by his second marriage, and at least eight other illegitimate sons. He was succeeded by the eldest son of his first marriage, *Robert III (see the *royal house of Scotland).

Robert III (c.1337–1406) King of Scotland from 1390, son of Robert II and Elizabeth Mure. Two years before his accession he was severely crippled by a kick from a horse, so he was of necessity an ineffectual king in a very physical age. He married Annabella Drummond and was succeeded by his third son, James I (see the *royal house of Scotland).

Robert the Bruce (Robert I, 1274–1329) King of Scotland from 1306. He was a member of the Norman family of Bruce, in which the eldest son of every generation was called Robert de Bruce. Through marriage to the royal family the Bruces had a claim to the throne after the death in 1290 of *Margaret, the Maid of Norway. The crown went instead to John de *Balliol, whose subsequent removal by the English king Edward I left a hiatus in the royal house of Scotland. This ended in 1306, when Robert de Bruce murdered a rival claimant, John Comyn, in a church in Dumfries and had himself crowned at *Scone.

A succession of defeats by English armies led to three of Robert's brothers being executed and to his own flight, late in 1306, to the island of Rathlin off the northern Irish coast; his supposed place of refuge is *Bruce's Cave. The story of the lesson taught him by the persistent spider (failing six times to attach its web, just as he had failed six times against the English, and then succeeding on the seventh attempt) was first published in 1828 by Walter Scott, who claimed it to be a tradition within the Bruce family.

Like the spider, Robert did succeed when he persevered. From 1307 his supporters steadily recovered the Scottish castles which had fallen into English hands, and at *Bannockburn in 1314 he inflicted a decisive defeat on the English king – by now Edward II, a less formidable adversary than his father. In the following years Robert made continuous raids into the north of England. Finally, in 1328, the English recognized him as king of Scotland and renounced any claims to overlordship. He had only daughters (by his first wife, Isabella of Mar, and by his second, Elizabeth de Burgh) until the birth in his final years of a son, David II (see the *royal house of Scotland).

Gilbert **Roberts** (1899–1978, kt 1965) Designer of two of the most striking suspension bridges in Britain, over the *Forth and the *Severn.

George **Robey** (1869–1954, kt 1954) Actor, singer and *music-hall comedian, known as the 'prime minister of mirth'. His standard outfit was an incongruous combination of clergyman's black coat worn without a dog-collar, a raffish cane, a very shallow bowler hat, a pale face and enormous blacked eyebrows – which would rise in disapproval when the audience laughed at a double entendre. His best-known number was the duet *If you were the only girl in the world* in a London revue of 1916. In 1935 he performed Falstaff in a West End production of *Henry IV, Part 1*.

Robin Goodfellow see *Puck.

Robin Hood Legendary outlaw and the hero of *ballads dating back at least to the 14C. He was popular not only for his exciting exploits but for his tendency to redistribute wealth from rich to poor. The image of a band of merry men is a much later gloss on material which is as violent as its medieval times. In the ballads Robin is bled to death by the wicked prioress of Kirklees, whose lover is later fed to the dogs. The sturdy yeoman Little John is an early companion, whereas Friar Tuck and Maid Marian are later additions. No historical origin has been found for Robin himself, but details in the ballads seem to suggest that the stories have their roots in Yorkshire in spite of Robin's chief adversary being the sheriff of Nottingham.

Robert **Robinson** (b. 1927) Broadcaster with a remarkable talent for keeping a wide range of long-running shows on the air. On television he has presided since 1967 over the quiz *Ask The Family* and the celebrity panel game *Call My Bluff*. On radio he has been the questionmaster of *Brain of Britain* since 1973; and from 1974 until its demise in 1992 he was the exhaustingly articulate chairman of the exhibitionist chat show *Stop the Week*.

Robinson Crusoe (*The Life and Strange Surprising Adventures of Robinson Crusoe, of York, Mariner* 1719) Narrative by Daniel *Defoe, inspired by the real-life story of Alexander Selkirk – a Scottish sailor who spent five years, 1704–9, as a lone castaway on a Pacific island. Robinson Crusoe, also alone on an island after a shipwreck, uses great ingenuity to build a house and a boat, and to domesticate animals. He is later helped by a native whom he rescues from cannibals on a Friday (calling him therefore Man Friday). After overcoming a mutiny on a passing English ship, Crusoe and Friday sail on it for Europe. The thrill of adventure and survival has made *Robinson Crusoe* immensely popular at every period, while the realism with which Crusoe's predicament is imagined by Defoe has caused the book to be claimed as the first English novel.

Rob Roy The nickname (said to mean Rob the Red, relating to his red hair) which was given to the Scottish outlaw Robert MacGregor (1671–1734). He is often described as the Scottish *Robin Hood and has one clear advantage over his English counterpart, that of having undeniably existed.

Bobby **Robson** (b. 1933) Footballer and manager. His playing career was with Fulham (1950–6, 1962–7) and West Bromwich Albion (1956–62), and he had some 20 caps for England. He was manager for Ipswich Town (1969–82) before becoming manager of the England team and national coach in 1982 – a post he held until after the 1990 World Cup, in which he took England through to the semi-final. He then became manager of PSV Eindhoven in the Netherlands, followed by a move to the Portuguese club Sporting Lisbon.

Rochester (53,000 in 1981) City on the river Medway, of importance from Roman times as a river crossing on the route from the southeast coast to London. St *Augustine installed Justus, one of his monks from Canterbury, as the first bishop here in 604. A Norman bishop, Gundulf, began the present cathedral and the castle in the late 11C. The massive keep of the castle, still surviving, was added in the next century by an archbishop of Canterbury, and work continued on the cathedral, in a succession of styles, until the great Perpendicular window was added in the west front in the late 15C. Near the cathedral, but in 19C buildings, is the *King's School, the second oldest in the country, deriving from a cathedral school which began in that foundation year of 604 and was later attached to a Benedictine priory established by Gundulf.

Lord **Rochester** (John Wilmot, 1647–80, 2nd earl of Rochester 1658) Poet and leading wit in the circle of Charles II, whose personal debauchery and brilliant but risqué verses have made him a symbol of *Restoration society. He was frequently dismissed from court, for offences ranging from drunken indiscretions to the abduction of a young heiress, but he was as regularly reinstated.

Robert the Bruce with his first wife, Isabella of Mar, as imagined in a manuscript of the 16C.

His best-known verse is his suggested epitaph for his royal patron:

> Here lies a great and mighty king
> Whose promise none relies on;
> He never said a foolish thing,
> Nor ever did a wise one.

Charles replied with appropriate wit. 'This is very true: for my words are my own, and my actions are my ministers.'

Mr **Rochester** see *Jane Eyre.

rock An old word for any hard sweet, being short for 'rock sugar' and 'rock candy'. In recent times it has been specifically used of long brittle rods of hard sugar, brightly coloured on the outside, which are sold at holiday resorts. Rock often has the resort's name running miraculously through its length (Brighton rock being the best known in this respect) – a feat achieved by starting with large letters in a broad circle of soft sugar and rolling it into a long rod before it hardens. Edinburgh rock, by contrast, is a thinner stick of more crumbly texture – ridged on its surface and in pastel colours.

rock cake Bun-sized individual cake with a rough or 'rocky' surface, now invariably containing currants. The earliest known recipe, from the 1860s, was for a plain cake flavoured with lemon and brandy.

rockers see *mods and rockers.

rockery A favourite feature in many British gardens, providing a home for rock plants and the chance of a waterfall. Rock gardens derived from two impulses in the 18c – the fashion for *follies (which included grottoes made of carefully selected geological specimens) and the desire to nurture plants from mountainous habitats in *botanic gardens. In one of the earliest rock gardens mosses were grown on pieces of lava brought from Iceland by Joseph *Banks.

Rocket see *Rainhill trials.

Rock of Ages Hymn by Augustus Toplady (1740–78), which is believed in local tradition to have been inspired when he sheltered from a storm in the region of the *Cheddar Gorge. The theory relies on the opening couplet ('Rock of Ages, cleft for me, Let me hide myself in Thee') and on the fact that he was curate of nearby Blagdon (1762–4). It is possible; but the hymn was first published 11 years after the author had left Blagdon, and his rock of ages is Christ.

The **Rocky Horror Show** Gothic and camp musical by Richard O'Brien (b. 1941), which opened in 1973 in the small upstairs studio in London's Royal Court Theatre and went on to become an international cult – particularly after the film version of 1975, *The Rocky Horror Picture Show*. The story brings Brad and Janet, a wholesome couple of newly-weds, to the spooky castle of Dr Frank'n'Furter, a 'sweet transvestite' from Transylvania who has a ghoulish henchman by the name of Riff-Raff.

rococo Delicate style in decoration and furniture, using a flutter of unpredictable curves to dissolve solid form and to give an impression of gaiety and lightness, which developed in France during the first half of the 18c as both a reaction against and an offshoot from the heavier and more florid *baroque. It arrived late in England, where it appealed particularly in the form of *chinoiserie. The earlier furniture of Thomas *Chippendale is the essence of English rococo, but even he changed in mid-career to the sterner demands of *neoclassicism.

Roedean School One of the country's leading *public schools for girls. It began in a very small way in 1885 when three sisters, Dorothy, Penelope and Millicent Lawrence, opened a school in Brighton with ten pupils, 'six paying and four for show'; the prospectus promised 'a thorough education, physical, intellectual and moral', with the reassurance that 'special pains will be taken to guard against overwork'. Twelve years later (by which time there were no fewer than eight Lawrence sisters teaching at the school) the foundation stone was laid for the present building on a commanding site overlooking the sea, between Brighton and Rottingdean.

Sir **Roger de Coverley** The name of a country dance, surviving chiefly now as a *reel in Scotland, which was borrowed by Steele and Addison for a character in the early numbers of the *Spectator. Their Sir Roger de Coverley, supposedly descended from the inventor of the country dance, is an early example of the eccentric but fundamentally humane country gentleman who was to become part of the image of 18c England.

Richard **Rogers** (b. 1933, kt 1991) Architect with a proven ability to surprise and stimulate, being designer of the most talked about modern building in both Paris and London. In 1971 he and his partner, the Italian architect Renzo Piano, won the international competition for the Centre Pompidou in Paris. Their design was an early and striking example of the style known as Hi-Tech; the escalators are in transparent tubes on the outside of the building, as are the conduits for electricity, water and air (each with its own distinguishing colour). In 1978 Rogers won the competition for the new headquarters for *Lloyd's of London, for which he used a less brightly coloured but similar style; it was even more striking in a taller building. The puppet which occasionally appears as Richard Rogers in *Spitting Image has, appropriately enough, all his vital organs on the outside.

Roget's Thesaurus Dictionary of synonyms, first published in 1852 and compiled by Peter Mark Roget (1779–1869), a London-born physician whose father was a Protestant pastor from Geneva. His *Thesaurus of English Words and Phrases* went through 28 editions in his own lifetime, was edited by his son and grandson until 1953, and continues to be revised.

Rokeby Venus (c.1650, National Gallery) The name by which Velázquez's *Toilet of Venus* is known in Britain – because from 1813 to 1905 it was at Rokeby Park, a Palladian mansion in the county of Durham. The first masterpiece to be saved for the nation by the *National Art Collections Fund, it was the object of a notorious attack a few years later, in 1914, when it was slashed by a suffragette.

The **Rolling English Road** see G.K. *Chesterton.

Rolling Stones The band which shared with the Beatles the leading position in the British pop scene of the 1960s, but which has far outlasted them as a performing group. Formed in 1962 by Mick Jagger (b. 1943, vocals and harmonica), Keith Richard (later Richards, b. 1943, rhythm guitar) and Brian Jones (1942–69, lead guitar), the Stones were complete by early 1963 when Bill Wyman (William Perks, b. 1936, bass) and Charlie Watts (b. 1941, drums) had replaced earlier players. During that year they began to acquire a following through regular appearances at a club in Richmond, in southwest London, receiving their first write-up in the local *Richmond and Twickenham Times*. In 1963 they also acquired a manager, Andrew Loog Oldham, who saw their potential as a wild, rebellious and scruffy alternative to the clean-cut image of the Beatles. With violently noisy sounds (for the time) and Jagger's overtly sexual appeal as a singer, the Stones could be guaranteed to appal the middle-aged and thereby doubly delight the young.

They brought to British rock music the sound of black rhythm 'n' blues, which carried their first two LPs (both called *The Rolling Stones*) to the top of the UK charts. At this stage they were performing existing songs, but they hit a new peak when they began using their own material; never very precisely credited, the music has been mainly Keith Richards' and the lyrics usually by Jagger. Their first single to reach the top of the charts in both the UK and USA contained all the raw energy of the Stones at their best – *(I Can't Get No) Satisfaction* (1965). It was equalled if not outdone three years later by *Jumping Jack Flash*.

In 1969 Brian Jones left the group and a month later was found dead in his swimming pool; the coroner's verdict was accidental drowning under the influence of alcohol and drugs (the group's progress has been interspersed with drugs-related arrests and disasters). Jones's place was taken by Mick Taylor (b. 1948), who was himself replaced in 1975 by Ron Wood (b. 1942). In 1993 Bill Wyman announced that he was leaving the band after 30 years.

Nearly ten years on from their formation the Stones were producing some of their best music, notably the two albums *Sticky Fingers* (1971) and *Exile on Main Street* (1972), both of which reached the top of the UK charts – as did *Goat's Head Soup* (1973) and *Emotional Rescue* (1980). Touring and live performances have been a central thread in their career and 30 years on they are still in business, occasionally going on the road as well as producing albums. Jagger's much publicized private life has included marriages to the Nicaraguan Bianca Perez-Mora and the American model Jerry Hall.

Rolls-Royce Company with a long history in the manufacture of luxury cars and of aero-engines. Charles Stewart Rolls (1877–1910) was an early pioneer in both fields, as a driver and a pilot. In 1902 he began selling cars in Mayfair and in 1904 he met Henry Royce (1863– 1933), a one-time railway apprentice who had established his own electrical engineering company in Manchester in 1884. Royce had recently begun manufacturing cars to a high technical standard. Together they formed Rolls-Royce, setting up a factory in Derby in 1907 and in that first year producing their famous Silver Ghost. The firm moved into aircraft engines in World War I, but by then Rolls had died in a flying accident (a short while after becoming the first man to fly across the Channel and back non-stop).

In World War II Rolls-Royce engines powered the Spitfire, the Hurricane and Britain's first jet fighter, the Meteor. This head-start in turbine and jet technology meant that after the war Rolls-Royce engines were used in many aircraft, such as the Viscount, the Comet, the Caravelle and several Lockheed and Boeing wide-bodied jets. Nevertheless by 1971 the company was in severe financial difficulties, and in that year the aero-engine division was nationalized (it was privatized in 1987). Rolls-Royce Motors remained in the private sector and merged in 1980 with *Vickers.

'Roll up that map of Europe' see *Napoleonic Wars.

roly-poly pudding Pudding popular from the mid-19C; jam is spread on a flat layer of suet pastry, which is then rolled up before being steamed or baked.

Roman Baths see *Bath.

Roman Catholics The success of the *Reformation in England, Wales and Scotland meant that those who remained loyal to the Roman Catholic faith could worship only discreetly, becoming known as 'recusants' (from the Latin for 'refuse', meaning that they refused to attend the services of the *Church of England). In practice recusants were limited to the richer classes, who could afford chapels at home. Many old English houses boast a 'priest's hole', a secret chamber where a visiting priest could be hidden; but such precautions were necessary only at a few periods of extreme tension, particularly in the 16C. In normal times Catholic families were not directly persecuted (the case of the *Earl Marshal is the most striking example), but they were excluded from public life and from university education under restrictions suffered also by the *Nonconformists.

Pressure for change came from *Ireland, the only part of the king's realm with a large Roman Catholic population, indeed a majority. Unrest there put *emancipation firmly on the political agenda from the late 18C. This was followed in the early 19C by a large influx of Irish labourers to Britain's west-coast ports and developing industrial cities. By the 1840s there were also many influential converts from the Church of England in the wake of the *Oxford Movement. By 1850 these developments persuaded Pope Pius IX to restore a Roman Catholic diocesan hierarchy to Britain with the appointment of Cardinal *Wiseman as archbishop of Westminster. Today there are also archbishoprics in Birmingham, Cardiff, Liverpool, Southwark, St Andrews (with Edinburgh), Glasgow and Armagh. The centuries of hostility between Protestants and Catholics are now no more than a distant fact of history except in *Northern Ireland, where Protestant settlements in the 17C and subsequent restrictions on Roman Catholics lie behind the unrest of recent decades.

The archbishop of *Westminster is the head of the church in England and Wales, as the archbishop of *Glasgow is in Scotland and the archbishop of *Armagh in Ireland – where no distinction is made in ecclesiastical terms between north and south. In the early 1990s there are estimated to be nearly 6 million Roman Catholics in the United Kingdom (for the numbers attending church in England see *Christians).

Romanesque A word coined in the early 18C to describe the architecture of early medieval Europe, which adapted and developed the rounded arch of ancient Roman architecture and which was replaced in the 12C by the pointed arch of the *Gothic style.

English Romanesque, also known as Norman architecture, began relatively late, in the mid-11C, as a result of influence from Normandy during the reign of Edward the Confessor. It then spread rapidly through the country in the century after the Norman Conquest. (Anglo-Saxon churches had been mainly of wood; but when in stone they also used the rounded arch and are sometimes described as early Romanesque.)

The characteristics of English Romanesque are massively thick walls and huge round pillars, often decorated (as are arched doorways) with geometrical or zigzag patterns. The country is rich in examples, but none is more impressive than *Durham Cathedral.

Roman law see *law.

Romans The first direct contact between Britain and the Roman empire came with the invasions of Julius *Caesar in the 1st century BC, but the Roman conquest of southern Britain began only with the invasion of AD 43. In spite of the resistance led by *Caratacus, the Roman success was rapid. By the year 47 the *Fosse Way was in existence

Remains of Roman London: Bacchus with a tiger in a mosaic pavement discovered beneath Leadenhall Street in the 19C.

as a road to move troops along the northern border of a territory which stretched from Devon to Lincolnshire. The uprising of *Boudicca in 60 was a temporary setback for the Romans, but the conquest of Wales was completed in 78 by Agricola (the Roman governor of Britain 77–84). Agricola advanced far into Scotland, defeating the tribe of Caledones in 83 at *Mons Graupius. But the Caledonians proved difficult to subdue; the protective *Hadrian's Wall was built some 40 years later to seal off this troublesome area. Thus the Roman province of Britannia became established as what is now England and Wales.

With three protective legions permanently based in York, Chester and *Caerleon, Roman Britain settled down in the 2C to a period of prosperity. Trade with the Continent increased. An urban culture developed, of which traces are best seen now in *Bath. Many Celtic chieftains and landowners became Roman citizens and adopted Roman ways. Great villas were built and were decorated with mosaics, as at *Fishbourne, *Hinton St Mary, *Chedworth or *Lullingstone. With all this came the religions that were then competing in Italy, in particular Christianity and *Mithraism.

The decline of Roman Britain followed the decline of Rome itself in the 4–5C. As Goths, Vandals and Huns threatened the centre of empire (even reaching and plundering Rome herself), legions were withdrawn from the distant provinces – leaving them in turn exposed to invasion. By the 7C, after much upheaval, England was the territory of the *Anglo-Saxons.

Romantic Movement European cultural development, starting in the mid-18C, in which Britain played an important part. The movement involved so many diverging strands, in both literature and art, that a precise definition is impossible. The central theme was perhaps a rejection of the 18C faith in reason, preferring the power of the imagination and the intensity of individual experience. Untamed nature and the mysteries of the supernatural began to seem, from about 1760, more attractive than the orderly middle ground of polite society; and the rich chaos of the Middle Ages set the mind dreaming more fervently than the well-ordered discipline of classical architecture and literature.

Early manifestations of this mood in Britain were the

*Gothic Revival and the fashion for the *picturesque. In literature the poems of *Ossian and *Chatterton were fakes, but that hardly seemed to matter when they evoked so pleasantly a distant Celtic twilight. The fustian became more convincing, with greater evidence of solid research, in the influential recreations by Walter *Scott of a historical past. *Frankenstein raised the tingle level above anything available from earlier Gothic novels, but it was in *Wuthering Heights that the dark excitement of Romantic fiction proved its real power in an intensity of genuine feeling.

The all-importance of imagination in the Romantic movement is exemplified in the poetry and painting of William *Blake, a lone spirit in a strange mythological world of his own devising – one which would be ridiculous if not created with such conviction. With another type of artist the style of life becomes in itself a Romantic performance, in a tradition which peaks with *Byron but leads as far as *Wilde.

Four other writers share with Byron the heyday of the Romantic movement in English poetry – *Wordsworth and *Coleridge, *Shelley and *Keats. A good example of how nature and the supernatural can coexist under the umbrella term of Romanticism is *Lyrical Ballads; Wordsworth's poems, concentrating intently on everyday experience, share the volume with the fantastic nightmare of Coleridge's *Ancient Mariner. There is a similar contrast between Britain's two greatest Romantic painters. *Constable finds magic in the minutely observed fall of light on leaf and water, meadow and cloud; *Turner eventually allows light to overwhelm his images in such an intoxicating blaze of colour that detail vanishes. Between these two extremes of nature and the supernatural lies the area of least interest to the Romantic artist – the drawing-room, so sharply observed at the same period by Jane Austen.

Treaty of **Rome** see *EC.

Romeo and Juliet (c.1595) Romantic tragedy by *Shakespeare, set in Verona where the Capulets and the Montagues are bitter enemies. Romeo, son of the head of the Montague family, glimpses and falls in love with Juliet, the daughter of Capulet. Courted by him beneath her balcony, she overcomes her fear of who he is: 'O Romeo, Romeo! wherefore art thou Romeo?' is soon followed by 'What's in a name? that which we call a rose/By any other name would smell as sweet'. With the help of her old nurse and Friar Laurence, the couple secretly marry. But in a street brawl between the two families, Romeo's kinsman Mercutio is fatally wounded by Tybalt, a cousin of Juliet; Romeo in revenge kills Tybalt. The romance, with its exquisite love poetry, descends to a Gothic and improbable conclusion in which Juliet is given a potion to make her seem dead (so as to avoid another marriage, forced upon her by her father); the message telling Romeo about the potion fails to reach him; finding her apparently dead he kills himself; and waking to find him dead beside her, she does the same.

Prokofiev wrote the music for a full-length ballet of *Romeo and Juliet*, premiered in 1938 and interpreted since by many different choreographers – including Frederick Ashton in Copenhagen in 1955, John Cranko in Stuttgart in 1962 and Kenneth MacMillan for the Royal Ballet in 1965. MacMillan created his for Christopher Gable and Lynn Seymour; in the event the premiere was danced by Nureyev and Fonteyn, and MacMillan's ballet became probably the best-known example of their outstanding partnership. Antony Tudor choreographed a *Romeo and Juliet* to music by Delius in New York in 1943, and the American musical *West Side Story* (1957) is also based on the play.

George **Romney** (1734–1802) Portrait painter who in the 1760s was exceeded only by Reynolds and Gainsborough in the number of his fashionable sitters. In the 1780s he became infatuated with Emma Hart, later known as Lady *Hamilton, and used her as the model for more than 50 paintings in which she appears in such varied guises as Cassandra, Mary Magdalene and Joan of Arc.

Ronnie Scott's see Ronnie *Scott.

Roodee see *Chester.

Jean **Rook** (1931–91) For the two last decades of her life the best-known woman journalist in Britain, thanks to the punchy, down-to-earth and often controversial column in the *Daily Express* which won her the honorary title First Lady of Fleet Street. It was an essential part of her image that she came from Yorkshire – where, as she liked to say, they call a spade a shovel.

Room at the Top (1957) The first novel of John Braine (1922–86), in which Joe Lampton abandons the woman he loves in order to seduce and marry a young heiress in a small Yorkshire town. It was an immediate success, and the character of its cynical young hero caused Braine to be linked with the *angry young men who had been the publicity rage of the previous year. The story was filmed in 1958 with Laurence Harvey and Simone Signoret.

A Room with a View see E.M. *Forster.

Roots (1959) The central play of a trilogy by Arnold *Wesker. It takes place in a farm cottage in Norfolk, where Beatie Bryant awaits the arrival of her boyfriend, Ronnie Kahn, a young London intellectual. She patronizes her long-suffering family with his pretentious theories; but at the end, when a letter arrives from Ronnie breaking off their relationship, the shock makes her discover for the first time a voice of her own.

Rorke's Drift see *Zulu War.

Rosalind see *As You Like It.

Lord **Rosebery** (Archibald Philip Primrose, 1847–1929, 5th earl of Rosebery 1868) Liberal politician who held high office as foreign secretary (1886, 1892–4) and briefly as prime minister (1894–5). It was his initiative at the Home Office, when responsible for Scottish affairs in the early 1880s, which resulted in the establishment of the *Scottish Office. The 16 months of his premiership were made ineffectual by a Conservative majority in the House of Lords and by divisions in his own party, but they were distinguished by one unusual achievement: horses owned by him won both the *Derbies within that period, giving him, it was said, more satisfaction than any of his political successes.

Rosencrantz and Guildenstern see *Hamlet* and Tom *Stoppard.

Wars of the **Roses** see *Wars of the Roses.

Rose Theatre The first theatre on London's *Bankside, built in 1586–7 and demolished in 1606. Here *Alleyn made his name and it may have been here that Shakespeare's first play (one part of *Henry VI*) was performed. The theatre's foundations were discovered in the summer of 1989, during excavation for an office block, and an appeal was launched to preserve them. By the early 1990s they were intact but relatively inaccessible beneath the completed building.

Rosetta stone (British Museum) Black basalt slab found in 1799 by Napoleon's army in Egypt, at the village of Rashid (called Rosetta by Europeans). Captured by the British from the French, it was presented to the British Museum in 1802. Its significance is that it carries the same inscription (a text from the reign of Ptolemy V in the 2nd century BC) in three languages – hieroglyphic Egyptian, demotic Egyptian and Greek. It thus enabled hieroglyphs to be deciphered. After groundwork by several scholars, the solution was provided in the 1820s by the French linguist, Jean-François Champollion (1790–1832).

Roslin Chapel (10km/6m S of Edinburgh) This small 15c chapel (originally the choir of an uncompleted church) is known for its intricate stone carving and in particular for the Prentice Pillar, a richly decorated single column with spiral banding. It is named from the tradition that it was carved by an apprentice when his master was absent; the mason on his return, in a fit of professional jealousy, struck and killed the boy genius.

James Clark **Ross** (1800–62, kt 1843) Polar explorer who had been a member of five Arctic voyages before accompanying his uncle Sir John Ross (1777–1856) on the expedition which reached the north magnetic pole on 1 June 1831. The younger Ross then commanded the *Erebus* and *Terror* on a very successful expedition to the Antarctic (1839–43). In 1845 *Franklin sailed northwest in those same two ships and disappeared. Ross returned to the Arctic in 1848–9, leading one of the many attempts to discover what had happened to Franklin and his men.

Jonathan **Ross** (b. 1960) The youngest of Britain's chat-show hosts in the early 1990s, with a quick line in cockney humour. He established himself in 1989 with *The Last Resort*.

Ronald **Ross** (1857–1932, KCB 1911) Bacteriologist known for his discovery in 1897–8 of the life history of the malarial parasite and its transmission by the mosquito, thus proving the theory first put forward in 1894 by 'Mosquito Manson' (Patrick Manson, 1844–1922). He was awarded the Nobel prize for medicine in 1902, the second year of the awards.

Ross and Cromarty Until 1975 a *county spanning northern Scotland from coast to coast and including

Ross's Gull, named after James Clark Ross who shot the first recorded example on an Arctic voyage in 1823.

Lewis in the Outer Hebrides. The mainland territory is now part of the Highland region.

Rossetti family In 1824 Gabriele Rossetti (1783–1854) settled in London. He was a Neapolitan poet and radical, seeking asylum after a failed revolution. In 1826 he married Maria Polidori, the daughter of a teacher of Italian. They had three distinguished children.

Dante Gabriel Rossetti (1828–82) and William Michael (1829–1919) were founder members of the *Pre-Raphaelite Brotherhood. Dante Gabriel provided two of the most striking paintings of the early years of the movement – *The Girlhood of Mary Virgin* and *Ecce Ancilla Domini* (1849 and 1850, both Tate Gallery). William Michael's contribution was as the archivist of the brotherhood (his paid employment was with the Inland Revenue), and it is thanks to his publications that its activities are known in detail.

In those two paintings Dante Gabriel's model for the Virgin was his sister Christina, but he soon found another muse in Elizabeth Siddal, known to everyone in the group of friends as Guggums (she is Millais' *Ophelia). From 1850 she was Rossetti's regular model, seen in countless drawings, and in 1860 he married her; but in 1862 she died of an overdose of laudanum. In a macabre romantic gesture he placed in her coffin the only complete manuscript of his poems – he had written poetry from boyhood and his best-known work, *The Blessed Damozel*, dates from his early twenties. In 1869 some friends of Rossetti's arranged for the grave to be opened and retrieved the manuscript. The resulting volume (*Poems* 1870) provoked the famous phrase 'the fleshly school of poetry' in an attack by Robert Buchanan.

The younger second wave of Pre-Raphaelites, *Morris and *Burne-Jones, met Rossetti in 1856 and were much influenced by his romantic medievalism. Rossetti later had a brief involvement with Morris's design company and a long relationship with his wife, Jane. Hers is the face in most of the sultry and rather repetitive paintings from the mid-1860s onwards, and the photographs that Rossetti took of her in his garden reveal that the pout of her painted lips and the dark cloud of her hair is hardly exaggerated. From 1862 Rossetti lived at 16 Cheyne Walk, contributing greatly to *Chelsea's new bohemian image.

Christina Rossetti (1830–94) was as serious about Christianity as her appearance in her brother's early paintings might suggest; she broke off her engagement to the Pre-Raphaelite painter James Collinson (1825–81) when he became a Roman Catholic in 1850, for she herself could go no further than Anglo-Catholicism. The majority of her poems are devotional but she also had a rich streak of fantasy – seen in her best-known work, *Goblin Market* (1862). She often achieved a Pre-Raphaelite clarity of image, as for example in the opening lines of *Mid-Winter*, which in *Holst's setting has become a popular carol:

> In the bleak mid-winter
> Frosty wind made moan,
> Earth stood hard as iron,
> Water like a stone;
> Snow had fallen, snow on snow,
> Snow on snow,
> In the bleak mid-winter,
> Long ago.

Duke of **Rothesay** The oldest dukedom in Scotland, conferred by Robert III in 1398 on his eldest son. With the *union of the crowns in 1603 it became the highest Scottish title of the British monarch's eldest son, the Prince of *Wales, who is officially known as the Duke of Rothesay when north of the border.

Rothmans Tobacco company which derives from a shop opened in 1890 in London's Fleet Street by Louis Rothman (1869–1926), who was born in the Ukraine and came to London at the age of 18. After World War II Rothmans merged with other long-established British tobacco companies, notably Carreras in 1958 and Dunhill in 1972. Carreras was founded in London in 1852 by a Spanish nobleman, José Carreras; the company named its best-known blend of tobacco after an aristocratic customer, the 3rd earl of Craven. Alfred Dunhill (1872–1959) opened a tobacconist shop in London in 1907, and in 1910 began specializing in the manufacture of pipes.

Rothschild Jewish family from Frankfurt in Germany which has made an extraordinary contribution to British life over the past two centuries. In 1804 Nathan Mayer Rothschild (1777–1836) became a British citizen and established in London a branch of the family bank; under the name N.M. Rothschild and Sons it is still a major institution in the *City. In 1858 his son Lionel Nathan (1808–79) became the first Jew to sit in the House of Commons, after a prolonged and heroic struggle against the requirement to swear a Christian oath. He had first been elected (for the City of London) in 1847, and was re-elected five times during the next 11 years while a succession of bills to allow the oath to be made on the Old Testament were thrown out by the House of Lords. His son, Nathaniel Meyer (1840–1915), became in his turn the first Jew to sit in the House of Lords, when he was made a baron in 1885.

rotten borough see *borough.

Rotten Row The unpaved road along the south side of *Hyde Park, reserved now for riders of horses. The name is traditionally (but not very convincingly) said to derive from the French *route du roi* (road of the king), being the route taken by William III from *Kensington Palace to London.

Louis François **Roubiliac** (also spelt Roubillac, d. 1762) French sculptor, in England from the 1730s. No fewer than seven monuments in Westminster Abbey are by him; one of the least elaborate is that of *Handel, whose statue he had also done for *Vauxhall Gardens. His informal full-length bust of Shakespeare, commissioned by *Garrick, is in the British Museum.

rough cast see *pebble dash.

Rough Castle see the *Antonine Wall.

rounders Children's game in England since at least the early 18C, played to much the same rules as baseball and accepted now as its origin. The earliest known description of rounders, in an English alphabet book (*A Little Pretty Pocket-Book* 1744), lists it under B for Baseball. The crucial difference is that a player is out in rounders if struck by a thrown ball when running between bases. This requires a soft ball. The development in the American game, introduced in the first half of the 19C, was that a player became out when touched with a ball in the hand. This allowed a hard ball, turning baseball into a game for adults with fast deliveries from the pitcher and powerful hits by the batter.

Roundheads Supporters of the parliamentary cause in the *English Civil War. Like *Cavalier, the word was in use from the early 1640s; it referred derisively to the shorter hair preferred by the Puritans.

Round Table The table at which the knights of King *Arthur sat, its circular shape avoiding disputes over

Natural enmity between the short-haired Roundhead cur and the long-haired Cavalier dog: woodcut of 1642.

precedence. It was introduced to Arthurian legend by the Norman cleric Wace in the 12C, and later tradition added that it had been given to Arthur as part of Guinevere's dowry. One seat was kept vacant (the Siege Perilous, or dangerous seat), reserved for the knight who would complete the quest for the *Holy Grail; its rightful occupant turned out to be Galahad. Since about 1400 there has been in the Great Hall at *Winchester a round table described as King Arthur's (5.5m/18ft in diameter, attached now to a wall). The wood has been dated scientifically to the 14C. It was given its coat of paint by order of Henry VIII in 1522 for a visit of the emperor Charles V.

Round Tower see *Windsor.

round towers The most characteristic architectural feature of Celtic monasteries. Built from the 10C to 14C, they are tall structures of stone with a conical top and with the entrance too high for easy access from the ground. They served a double purpose, as a belfry calling the monks to prayer in normal times and as a place of refuge, with the wooden or rope ladder pulled up, during a *Viking raid. Many such towers survive in Ireland and three in Scotland.

Rover Company which began manufacturing cars in Coventry in 1900 and produced very successful models in two different areas of the market after World War II. The Rover 2000 (introduced in 1963) was a solidly luxurious car, as was the 3500 (1968, restyled in 1976). Meanwhile the 4-wheel-drive Land Rover, rugged and making no concessions to comfort, appeared in 1949 and rapidly established a secure place in British country life; the Range Rover (1970) was a more expensive version, as sturdy in rough conditions but with interior comforts and top speeds of a car rather than a jeep. Rover was taken over by Leyland in 1967, and a year later became part of *British Leyland. The major part of British Leyland was in turn given the name Rover Group when it was sold to *British Aerospace in 1988.

Rovers Return see *Coronation Street.

Rowallane (18km/11m S of Belfast) Garden created by two generations of the Moore family, uncle and nephew, starting in the 1860s. The thin soil and temperate climate led them to specialize in rhododendrons, and the garden is famous for the way the profuse shrubs hug the contours of the hillside, interspersed with patches of rock garden on the bare outcrops.

Thomas **Rowlandson** (1756–1827) English caricaturist, whose easy line and rich gallery of stock characters make his vast output instantly recognizable; the curves of the wenches' bosoms and buttocks, and of their elderly admirers' paunches, are a recurrent theme. His watercolours – in effect pen-and-ink drawings with a wash – range from often charming countryside scenes to the grosser delights of the town. His series of etchings include the adventures of Dr *Syntax (3 vols, 1813–21) and the many plates in Ackermann's *Microcosm of London* (3 vols, 1808–10), where he added the figures which enliven the architectural drawings of Augustus Charles Pugin. He also did some remarkably robust pornographic prints, which became more widely known after being published in book form in the 1980s.

Rowley Mile see *Newmarket.

Rows see *Chester.

Roxburghshire Until 1975 an inland *county in southeast Scotland, bordering England, which is now part of the Borders region.

Roxy Music Rock group formed in 1971 by Bryan Ferry (b. 1945, vocals), Brian Eno (b. 1948, keyboards) and Andy Mackay (b. 1946, saxophone and woodwinds), subsequently joined by Phil Manzanera (b. 1951, guitar) and Paul Thompson (b.1951, drums). The combination of Ferry's eclectic compositions and good looks and Eno's lavish costumes and innovative synthesizers brought the group immediate success with their first album, *Roxy Music* (1972). They later had three albums which topped the UK

The Royal Academy, with the maximum number of works on display at Somerset House: watercolour by George Scharf, 1828.

charts – *Stranded* (1973), *Flesh and Blood* (1980), *Avalon* (1982) – though Eno had left in 1973. Ferry disbanded the group in 1983 to concentrate on his solo career.

Royal Academy (London W1) Institution founded in 1768, with the active support of George III, for varied purposes – to dignify the profession of the artist, to provide space for the display and sale of members' work, and to give free training to talented newcomers. The academy's first established home was in *Somerset House; from 1837 it shared the National Gallery's building in Trafalgar Square; and since 1868 it has been at *Burlington House.

The first president was *Reynolds and until the late 19C the academy was acknowledged as representing the best in British art. During the mid-20C it adopted a reactionary stance, with the result that leading artists in the modern tradition ceased to be academicians – a split which has been largely healed in recent years. The summer exhibition, offering for sale paintings and prints selected from thousands submitted by the public, has long been a popular annual event in London. And in recent decades the academy's spacious rooms, extended in the 1990s by Norman *Foster's Sackler Galleries, have presented an outstanding series of loan exhibitions.

The academy's own collection has included two Renaissance masterpieces, the *Leonardo cartoon (now in the National Gallery) and Michelangelo's marble tondo of the Madonna and Child, on permanent show in the Sackler Galleries.

Royal Academy of Music see *music schools.

Royal Air Force The first British air force was the RFC (Royal Flying Corps), founded on 13 May 1912 as a joint army and navy enterprise. During World War I the naval side split off to become the RNAS (Royal Naval Air Service, later the *Fleet Air Arm), and in the last months of the war the two were absorbed in the new Royal Air Force, established on 1 April 1918. In the first year of World War II the RAF demonstrated, in the *Battle of

Britain, that it had now taken over a role which the navy had held for a millennium, that of being the country's main defence against invasion. The officer in command of the RAF is the chief of the air staff, and the government department controlling it is the air force department of the Ministry of *Defence. In 1992 the approximate numbers serving were 76,000 men and 7000 women.

Royal Air Force College see *Cranwell.

Royal Air Force Museum (London NW8) Museum illustrating the history of flight and of the RAF, opened in 1972 and situated on a historic airfield at Hendon. The main collection of aircraft is housed in two original hangars dating from 1917. Additional structures have been added for World War II planes – the Battle of Britain Hall (1978) and the Bomber Command Hall (1983).

Royal and Ancient The club at St Andrews, on the east coast of Scotland, which is the accepted international authority on the rules of *golf. It was established originally in 1754, as the Society of St Andrews Golfers; the only club of greater antiquity is the one now at *Muirfield. The Royal and Ancient also organizes and regularly plays host to the *Open. The course, known as the Old course, can lay claim to be the most famous in the world. It was reduced in 1764 from 22 holes to the 18 which subsequently became the standard number.

Royal Armoured Corps Formed in 1939 to combine under one central control the mechanized units of the army. These included all the ancient cavalry regiments except the *Household Cavalry; the units within the Royal Armoured Corps still bear their regimental cavalry names as Dragoon Guards, Hussars or Lancers. The other part of the new corps was the only section of the army to have begun its existence in mechanized form, the Royal Tank Regiment. The first *tanks went into action in 1916; by 1917 the Tank Corps was established, becoming the Royal Tank Corps in 1923 and then the Royal

Tank Regiment (still the name today) when absorbed in 1939 within the Royal Armoured Corps.

Royal Armouries Britain's oldest museum, deriving from the collection of armour and weapons gathered in the Tower of London by Henry VIII. After his death in 1547 this became virtually a private museum, until Charles II opened it in the 1660s to the paying public. Many rarities and a wide range of conventional weapons have been added in succeeding centuries; the activities of the East India Company brought in a superb selection of oriental armour. The long connection of the Armouries with the Tower is about to end, for the collection is scheduled to move in 1996 to a new building on the Clarence Dock site in Leeds. The artillery is mainly on show in Fort Nelson, at Fareham, overlooking Portsmouth harbour.

Royal Arms The personal arms of the sovereign, used in many contexts as a symbol of authority. The lion and the unicorn took their position as supporters (presenting the shield to the viewer) with the *union of the crowns in 1603, the lion representing England and the unicorn Scotland. The nursery rhyme about the *lion and the unicorn probably relates to their appearance here. The shield has had its present form only since the accession of Victoria, when the quartering of *Hanover was removed. The three lions passant (walking with one raised paw) in the first and fourth quarters represent England; the lion rampant (upright) in the second quarter stands for Scotland; and the harp in the third quarter for Ireland. Wales is not featured for it had its own heraldic device as a separate principality, in the arms of the Prince of *Wales, before the quarterings of Scotland and Ireland became part of the royal arms in the early 17C. The fleur-de-lis, which appeared in one or more quarters of the royal arms until late in the reign of George III, related to England's ancient claim to the throne of France (see the *Hundred Years' War).

The buckled belt surrounding the shield represents the *Garter and carries its motto *Honi soit qui mal y pense*, though only the first and last words are wholly visible. The words written below, *Dieu et mon droit* (French for 'God and my right') have been the royal motto since the reign of Henry V. The royal arms may be used on the premises and products of any firm holding a *royal warrant from the Queen.

The English lion in the royal arms was referred to from the 17C as the British lion and came gradually to be seen as a symbol of the nation. It provided political cartoonists, particularly in 19C issues of *Punch*, with rich opportunities; a hostile foreign power, for example, could be shown taking the risky course of 'twisting the tail of the British lion'.

Royal Artillery (Royal Regiment of Artillery) Originally formed in 1716, it was known in the 18C as the Foot Artillery; at that time civilian carters were used to haul the cannon around in support of the infantry. In 1793 the Royal Horse Artillery was established as a wing of the cavalry, manned entirely by mounted soldiers and able to move light artillery at speed across the battlefield (its style of operation can still be seen today in the performances of the *King's Troop). The next addition to the artillery's arsenal was anti-aircraft batteries, introduced during World War I but of much greater significance in World War II; their familiar name of 'ack ack' was a World War I signallers' version of AA (anti aircraft). After World War II the anti-aircraft regiments gradually exchanged their guns for today's surface-to-air guided missiles.

Royal Assent The final stage in the passage of a bill before it becomes an *act of parliament and passes into law. The bill is signed by the sovereign, and the fact of the royal assent having been granted is then announced in an ancient ceremony in the House of *Lords. The phrase still in use derives from Norman French: *La Reyne le veult* (the Queen wishes it), or with a king on the throne *Le Roy le veult*. The royal assent has not been withheld from a bill since 1707, in the reign of Queen Anne, but the phrase for such a case was *La Reyne s'avisera* (the Queen will consider).

Royal Automobile Club (RAC, London SW1) A *club founded in 1897 with a more practical purpose than most – 'for the protection, encouragement and development of automobilism'. The *Red Flag Act had been repealed in the previous year and there was an exhilarating new speed limit of 12mph (19kph). The club was so successful that by 1911 its present massive premises had been built on Pall Mall, complete with a large and elegant swimming pool in the basement. An offshoot of the club's activities is the motoring organization, also called the RAC but now a separate enterprise, which is second in size only to the Automobile Association in its recovery arrangements for stranded motorists; it has developed from services first offered in 1908 to associate members of the club.

Royal Ballet The company which dances at *Covent Garden. It descends from the Vic-Wells Ballet, founded by Ninette *de Valois in 1931 (so named because it performed both at the *Old Vic and at *Sadler's Wells). From the start *Ashton was the main choreographer alongside de Valois, *Lambert the chief conductor, and *Markova, *Dolin and *Helpmann were among the earliest leading dancers. After the war the company was renamed the Sadler's Wells Ballet but in 1946 it moved to Covent Garden, leaving Sadler's Wells theatre vacant (a new company formed there to fill the vacuum eventually became the *Birmingham Royal Ballet). A royal charter in 1956 transformed the Sadler's Wells Ballet into the Royal Ballet.

In the years after the war the undisputed star of the company was Margot *Fonteyn, who had been dancing leading roles since 1935. Her career had a glorious final chapter in her famous partnership with Rudolf Nureyev (1938–93). He defected from the Kirov Ballet when it was performing in Paris in 1961, and from 1962 he made the Royal Ballet his base – creating with Fonteyn in the following years one of the most famous partnerships of the 20C.

Among choreographers the 1950s saw the emergence of *Cranko and *MacMillan, and leading dancers of a slightly younger generation have included Lynn *Seymour,

One of the more eccentric items in the Royal Armouries: a grotesque helmet given to Henry VIII by Maximilian I.

Royal Family

The direct line of descent from George V, with brothers and sisters and first cousins

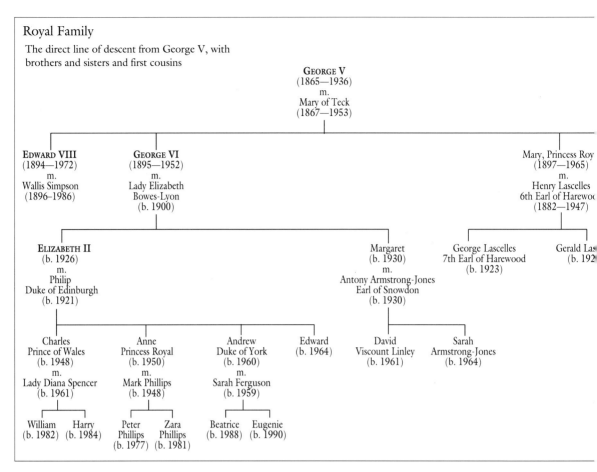

GEORGE V
(1865—1936)
m.
Mary of Teck
(1867—1953)

EDWARD VIII
(1894—1972)
m.
Wallis Simpson
(1896–1986)

GEORGE VI
(1895—1952)
m.
Lady Elizabeth
Bowes-Lyon
(b. 1900)

Mary, Princess Roy
(1897—1965)
m.
Henry Lascelles
6th Earl of Harewoo
(1882—1947)

ELIZABETH II
(b. 1926)
m.
Philip
Duke of Edinburgh
(b. 1921)

Margaret
(b. 1930)
m.
Antony Armstrong-Jones
Earl of Snowdon
(b. 1930)

George Lascelles
7th Earl of Harewood
(b. 1923)

Gerald Las
(b. 192

Charles
Prince of Wales
(b. 1948)
m.
Lady Diana Spencer
(b. 1961)

Anne
Princess Royal
(b. 1950)
m.
Mark Phillips
(b. 1948)

Andrew
Duke of York
(b. 1960)
m.
Sarah Ferguson
(b. 1959)

Edward
(b. 1964)

David
Viscount Linley
(b. 1961)

Sarah
Armstrong-Jones
(b. 1964)

William
(b. 1982)

Harry
(b. 1984)

Peter
Phillips
(b. 1977)

Zara
Phillips
(b. 1981)

Beatrice
(b. 1988)

Eugenie
(b. 1990)

Antoinette *Sibley and Anthony *Dowell. In the early 1990s the Royal Ballet is exceptionally strong. Jonathan *Cope and two young female principals, Viviana *Durante and Darcey *Bussell, emerged – like most of the company – from the Royal Ballet School, at White Lodge in Richmond Park. They have been joined by three brilliant partners from abroad – Sylvie Guillem (French, b. 1965), Irek Mukhamedov (Russian, b. 1960) and Zoltan Solymosi (Hungarian, b. 1967).

Royal Birkdale Golf course on the west coast of England, in Merseyside, which was laid out in about 1897 (the club itself is slightly older, having opened nearby in 1889). In recent decades the course has become one of the main English locations for international tournaments, including the *Open on seven occasions since 1954.

Royal College of Art see *art schools.

Royal College of Music see *music schools.

Royal Commission A body set up by the monarch, on the recommendation of the prime minister, to investigate a specific subject. Some are long-term ongoing activities: the Royal Commission on Historical Manuscripts, for example, was established in 1869 to report on surviving papers of historical importance and it continues to do so; and the Royal Commission for the Exhibition of 1851 still dispenses, for educational purposes, the income from the profits of the *Great Exhibition.

But most royal commissions are like any other major report instigated by government, except that they are given added resonance by the royal link. Such enquiries were virtually discontinued during the 1980s, until revived in 1991 with the Royal Commission on *Criminal Justice, chaired by Lord Runciman and scheduled to report in the summer of 1993.

Royal Court Theatre (London SW1) Theatre which has at two separate periods played a leading role in new British drama. In 1904–7 it was run by Harley Granville-Barker and others, presenting several new plays by G.B. Shaw. Since 1956 it has been the home of the *English Stage Company.

Royal Crescent see *Bath.

Royal Engineers (Corps of Royal Engineers) The engineers, a new technical wing for the army, were formed in 1717 – just one year after the *Royal Artillery. Many famous groups within the British armed forces have developed within the Royal Engineers and then become independent; among these were the Sappers and Miners, the Royal Corps of Signals and even the land-based section of the Royal Flying Corps, the World War I enterprise which in 1918 became the *Royal Air Force.

Royal Exchange (London EC3) Traditionally the central trading place for London's merchants and bankers. The first exchange, on the same site, was built 1566–8 by Thomas *Gresham and lasted until the Great Fire of 1666. Its successor was burnt in 1838, and the present Greek Revival building (by William Tite, 1798–1873) opened in 1844. Its original function as an exchange ended in 1939, since when it has been home to various financial institutions.

Royal Exchange Theatre company in Manchester which from its first season in 1976 established a high reputation. The boldly designed theatre-in-the-round occupies a cap-

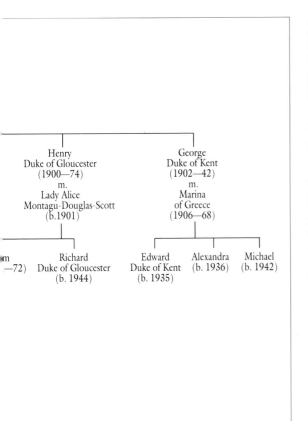

Henry
Duke of Gloucester
(1900—74)
m.
Lady Alice
Montagu-Douglas-Scott
(b.1901)

George
Duke of Kent
(1902—42)
m.
Marina
of Greece
(1906—68)

m —72)

Richard
Duke of Gloucester
(b. 1944)

Edward
Duke of Kent
(b. 1935)

Alexandra
(b. 1936)

Michael
(b. 1942)

Altrincham and Malcolm Muggeridge to be seen by many as enemies of the state. By the early 1990s this situation had drastically changed, though the hysterical adverse publicity caused by the failed marriages of younger members of the royal family was the reverse of the same coin. It implied that they were still expected to be better than the rest of us.

In the centuries before Victoria few expected the royal family to be morally superior; power was their business. The murderous excesses of Henry VIII in the 16c were followed by the adulterous excesses of Charles II in the 17c; but it was the undistinguished Hanoverians of the 18c who attracted a level of public criticism which puts such matters in perspective. A comment on the children of George III by Lord Grenville has often been quoted: 'Good God what a set they are. We talked over the Royal family and we agreed that the three Kingdoms cannot furnish such a brood, so many and so bad, rogues, blackguards, fools and whores.'

For the finances of the royal family, see the *civil list.

Royal Film Performance A major social event each year in the British film industry, consisting of the premiere of a selected new film before an audience including members of the royal family. The occasion raises money for the Cinema and Television Benevolent Fund. The tradition of what used to be called the Royal Command Film Performance goes back as far as 1896, when the prince of Wales (the future Edward VII) was shown at Marlborough House a programme of 20 short films – among them lively footage of a boxing kangaroo.

Royal Flying Corps see *Royal Air Force.

Royal Free Hospital (London NW3) Established in 1828 by a young surgeon, William Marsden (founder also of the *Marsden), it was the first hospital to take patients without either payment or a letter of recommendation. The previous year Marsden had found a young woman almost dead on the steps of a church and had been unable to get her admitted to any hospital. It was known as the Royal Free from 1837, when Queen Victoria became the patron. From 1843 it was in Gray's Inn Road, until it moved in 1975 to new buildings in Hampstead.

Royal Geographical Society (London SW7) Institution founded as the Geographical Society of London in 1830, when it absorbed the African Association (formed in 1788). From the start it has sponsored expeditions, including in its early days the great African adventures of Livingstone, Burton and Speke, and the society was always the natural first place for a returning explorer to recount his discoveries. Its central activity is the furthering of geographical knowledge through lectures and publications, including its own *Geographical Journal*. The society moved in 1913 to its premises on Kensington Gore, designed in the 1870s as a private house by Norman Shaw.

Royal Horticultural Society (London SW1) Britain's foremost society of gardeners, established in 1804 at a meeting at *Hatchard's convened by John Wedgwood and Joseph *Banks. The fortnightly flower shows for members at Vincent Square continue a tradition going back to the 1830s, and the Society's annual public show, now known as the *Chelsea Flower Show, has been held in *Ranelagh Gardens since 1913. In its centenary year, 1904, the RHS took possession of its famous garden at *Wisley. It also keeps smaller gardens elsewhere – since 1988 Rosemoor, near Great Torrington in Devon, and more recently Hyde Hall in Essex.

Royal Hospital see *Chelsea Hospital.

sule, seating up to 740 people, which is suspended from the pillars of the central hall of Manchester's 19c cotton exchange. The enterprise developed from the earlier 59 and 69 Theatre Companies, and the joint founding directors were Caspar Wrede, Michael Elliott, Braham Murray and James Maxwell. A drama school, the Arden School of Theatre, was launched with the company in 1990.

Royal Family In a dynastic sense the royal family encompasses all the descendants of George I, any of whom is eligible to inherit the British crown but who suffer certain restrictions under the terms of the Act of *Settlement (1701) and the Royal Marriages Act (1772). The former prevented a Roman Catholic or anyone married to a Roman Catholic from remaining in the line of succession; the latter, now largely a formality, required royal consent for the marriage of any British descendant of George II.

In everyday usage the phrase covers only the immediate family of the sovereign, a group which is roughly perceived by the public as stretching as far as first cousins – the effective limit of most modern families. By this yardstick the royal family is composed of the children and grandchildren of sovereigns, and living memory takes it as far back as George V. The tree shows those of his descendants who are first cousins or nearer to the direct line of descent.

The idea that the royal family should represent a national ideal of family life is relatively recent, deriving from the domestic bliss and numerous offspring of Victoria and Albert, but it soon became firmly established. The *abdication crisis was rooted in the assumption that the royal family would be irretrievably tainted by any connection with divorce. The adulation of everything royal reached a peak in the years after World War II, when even faint criticism of the family and its entourage caused Lord

Royal House

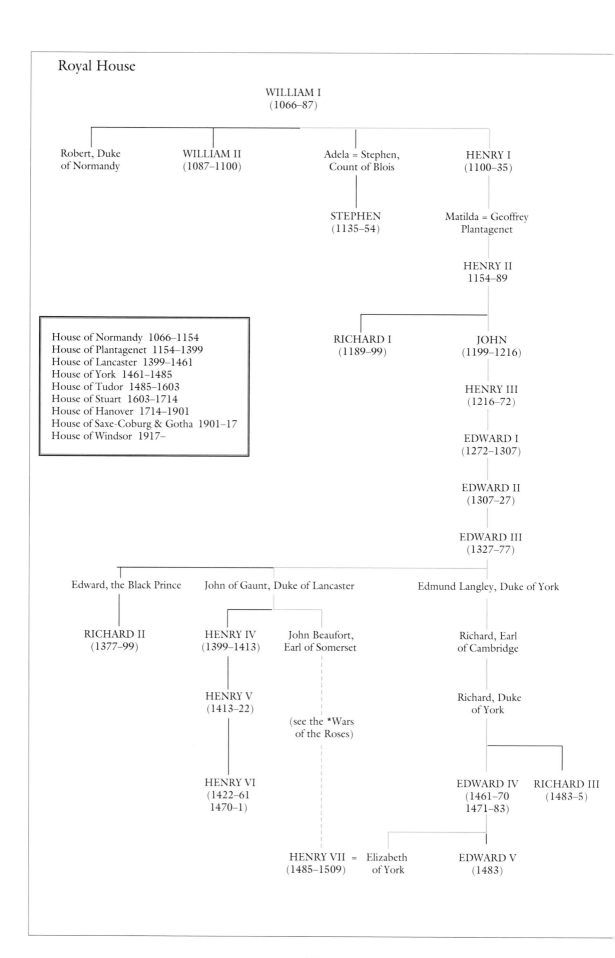

House of Normandy 1066–1154
House of Plantagenet 1154–1399
House of Lancaster 1399–1461
House of York 1461–1485
House of Tudor 1485–1603
House of Stuart 1603–1714
House of Hanover 1714–1901
House of Saxe-Coburg & Gotha 1901–17
House of Windsor 1917–

WILLIAM I
(1066–87)

Robert, Duke
of Normandy

WILLIAM II
(1087–1100)

Adela = Stephen,
Count of Blois

HENRY I
(1100–35)

STEPHEN
(1135–54)

Matilda = Geoffrey
Plantagenet

HENRY II
1154–89

RICHARD I
(1189–99)

JOHN
(1199–1216)

HENRY III
(1216–72)

EDWARD I
(1272–1307)

EDWARD II
(1307–27)

EDWARD III
(1327–77)

Edward, the Black Prince

John of Gaunt, Duke of Lancaster

Edmund Langley, Duke of York

RICHARD II
(1377–99)

HENRY IV
(1399–1413)

John Beaufort,
Earl of Somerset

Richard, Earl
of Cambridge

HENRY V
(1413–22)

(see the *Wars
of the Roses)

Richard, Duke
of York

HENRY VI
(1422–61
1470–1)

EDWARD IV
(1461–70
1471–83)

RICHARD III
(1483–5)

HENRY VII =
(1485–1509)

Elizabeth
of York

EDWARD V
(1483)

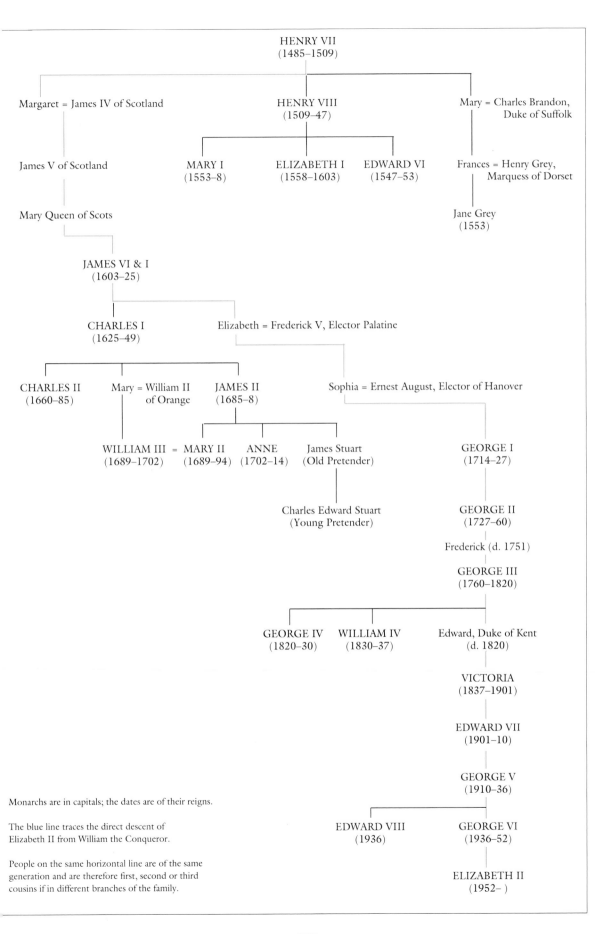

HENRY VII
(1485–1509)

Margaret = James IV of Scotland

HENRY VIII
(1509–47)

Mary = Charles Brandon,
Duke of Suffolk

James V of Scotland

MARY I
(1553–8)

ELIZABETH I
(1558–1603)

EDWARD VI
(1547–53)

Frances = Henry Grey,
Marquess of Dorset

Mary Queen of Scots

Jane Grey
(1553)

JAMES VI & I
(1603–25)

CHARLES I
(1625–49)

Elizabeth = Frederick V, Elector Palatine

CHARLES II
(1660–85)

Mary = William II
of Orange

JAMES II
(1685–8)

Sophia = Ernest August, Elector of Hanover

WILLIAM III = MARY II
(1689–1702)   (1689–94)

ANNE
(1702–14)

James Stuart
(Old Pretender)

GEORGE I
(1714–27)

Charles Edward Stuart
(Young Pretender)

GEORGE II
(1727–60)

Frederick (d. 1751)

GEORGE III
(1760–1820)

GEORGE IV
(1820–30)

WILLIAM IV
(1830–37)

Edward, Duke of Kent
(d. 1820)

VICTORIA
(1837–1901)

EDWARD VII
(1901–10)

GEORGE V
(1910–36)

Monarchs are in capitals; the dates are of their reigns.

The blue line traces the direct descent of
Elizabeth II from William the Conqueror.

People on the same horizontal line are of the same
generation and are therefore first, second or third
cousins if in different branches of the family.

EDWARD VIII
(1936)

GEORGE VI
(1936–52)

ELIZABETH II
(1952–)

551

royal house The beginnings of a royal house in Great Britain can be traced back to the *Anglo-Saxon kingdoms of the 8C, followed by the emergence in the 9C of *Alfred the Great as the first man who could lay claim to be king of the English. The entire English kingdom fell for a while to the *Danes (1016–42) and was conquered from 1066 by the *Normans.

The present royal house descends in an unbroken line from the house of *Normandy (see previous page). The marriage of the Norman princess *Matilda led to the rule of the house of *Plantagenet. *Wales was incorporated within this royal house once Edward I had conquered the principality in the late 13C and established his son as the *Prince of Wales. By the 15C rival Plantagenet branches, the houses of *Lancaster and *York, were fighting the internecine *Wars of the Roses. But at the end of that century the house of *Tudor healed the breach and introduced a period of strong centralized control.

By now *Ireland too was a possession of the English crown. Irish chieftains had first done homage to Henry II in the 12C; but it was not until the 16C that England was strong enough to dominate her smaller neighbour. And in 1603 Scotland became linked through the *union of the crowns, when the house of *Stuart (see the *royal house of Scotland) inherited the English throne. For the first time all parts of the British Isles were ruled by a single monarch, though in the form of three separate kingdoms – England (including the principality of Wales), Scotland and Ireland. They were eventually merged into a single country through the Acts of *Union.

Fears of a return to Roman Catholicism caused the *Revolution of 1688 and subsequently the change to the house of *Hanover; Queen Victoria's marriage introduced the brief house of *Saxe-Coburg & Gotha; and that in turn was transformed in the face of anti-German sentiment into the present house of *Windsor. Since the independence of the republic of Ireland in 1921, the realm has been the United Kingdom of Great Britain and Northern Ireland.

royal house of Scotland The gradual process of unifying *Scotland can be traced back to *Kenneth I in the 9C, but the kingdom was not stable until the 11C when *Malcolm III established a dynasty which lasted for more than 200 years. After the death of *Margaret, the Maid of Norway, there was a hiatus. *Robert the Bruce, distantly related to the royal family, seized the throne and re-established firm government in the early 14C. It was his daughter, Marjorie, who married Walter Stewart. The succession of their son to the throne in 1371, as Robert II, marked the beginning of the *Stuart dynasty from which the British *royal house descends. It has been traditional in the past to describe Scottish monarchs as the kings or queens 'of Scots' (as in Mary Queen of Scots) rather than of Scotland.

Royal Institution (London W1) Organization established in 1799 by Count Rumford; born Benjamin Thompson (1753–1814), he was an amateur English scientist who had been created a count in Bavaria. His stated purpose was to teach by lectures and experiments 'the application of science to the common purposes of life'. Still in its original headquarters in Albermarle Street, the institution continues to promote public knowledge of science. In 1801 Rumford employed *Davy to lecture in chemistry; in 1812 Davy took on *Faraday as his assistant. Faraday's laboratory and equipment are preserved at the institution, and the Friday Evening Discourses – begun by him in 1826 – are still a regular feature. The Christmas lectures for young people, also launched in 1826 and regularly given by Faraday, have remained another popular attraction.

Royal International Horse Show Annual show-jumping competition held over several days in June or July, first staged at Olympia in 1907. It was subsequently held at White City (1945–67) and at Wembley (1968–82), since when it has moved between several locations round the country. The two main contests are the King George V Gold Cup for men (competed for since 1911) and the Queen Elizabeth II Cup for women (since 1949). The record number of wins belong to a brother and sister. David *Broome has won most often among the men (six times), though *Foxhunter and Harry Llewellyn hold the record for a partnership (three wins). Liz *Edgar, with five victories, has been the outstanding performer among the women.

Royal Liverpool Philharmonic The name of a society, a choir and an orchestra. The Liverpool Philharmonic Society was established in 1840 to present musical performances, with its members as the choir. As early as 1846 they were sufficiently confident to commission an architect, John Cunningham, to build them a hall; the Liverpool Philharmonic Hall opened in 1849 and was used by the society until it was burnt in 1933; its replacement, the present Philharmonic Hall (by Herbert Rowse), opened in 1939. Meanwhile the society's orchestra – the Philharmonic Band, as it was called in the mid-19C – was becoming increasingly professional; by 1851 amateurs were excluded from the principal positions. In the first half of the 20C the chief conductors were Henry Wood and Thomas Beecham; Malcolm Sargent was in charge just after World War II, soon followed by John Pritchard (1957–63) and Charles Groves (1963–77); the present music director (since 1987) is Libor Pesek. Royal patronage changed the name in 1957 to the Royal Liverpool Philharmonic Orchestra (RLPO).

Royal Lytham (Royal Lytham and St Anne's) Golf course in Lancashire, Lytham and St Anne's being neighbouring towns on the north coast of the Ribble estuary. The club was founded in 1886, but moved to its present location in 1897. Since the 1950s Royal Lytham has been one of the regular locations for the *Open.

Royal Marines One of the oldest units in the British armed forces, formed in 1664 as the Duke of York's Maritime Regiment of Foot. They were described then as 'land soldiers prepared for sea service', and this has remained their task as the infantry of the Royal Navy, spearheading amphibious operations. During World War II they provided the majority of the new *commandos. The Commando Brigade has been since then the toughest operational branch of the marines, with expertise in fighting in very difficult circumstances – arctic conditions are one speciality. In 1992 there were about 7000 men serving in the Royal Marines.

Royal Mile see *Edinburgh.

Royal Military Academy see *Sandhurst.

Royal Mint see Royal *Mint.

Royal Museum of Scotland (Edinburgh) The name now shared by two institutions which merged in 1985. The Royal Museum in Chambers Street was until then the Royal Scottish Museum. Founded in 1854, it has wide-ranging holdings in natural history, archaeology, technology and the decorative arts. It occupies a superb building of 1861–5 by Francis Fowke (later architect of the *Albert Hall); behind a Venetian Renaissance façade there is a great entrance hall more in the style of the Crystal Palace. An ambitious extension is being built during the mid-1990s,

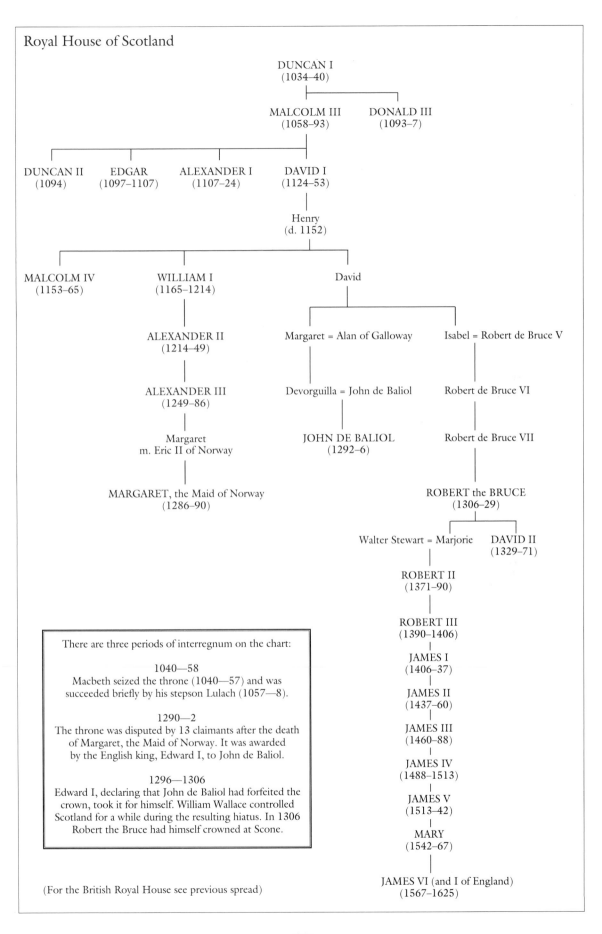

Royal House of Scotland

DUNCAN I
(1034–40)

MALCOLM III
(1058–93)

DONALD III
(1093–7)

DUNCAN II
(1094)

EDGAR
(1097–1107)

ALEXANDER I
(1107–24)

DAVID I
(1124–53)

Henry
(d. 1152)

MALCOLM IV
(1153–65)

WILLIAM I
(1165–1214)

David

ALEXANDER II
(1214–49)

Margaret = Alan of Galloway

Isabel = Robert de Bruce V

ALEXANDER III
(1249–86)

Devorguilla = John de Baliol

Robert de Bruce VI

Margaret
m. Eric II of Norway

JOHN DE BALIOL
(1292–6)

Robert de Bruce VII

MARGARET, the Maid of Norway
(1286–90)

ROBERT the BRUCE
(1306–29)

Walter Stewart = Marjorie

DAVID II
(1329–71)

ROBERT II
(1371–90)

ROBERT III
(1390–1406)

JAMES I
(1406–37)

JAMES II
(1437–60)

JAMES III
(1460–88)

JAMES IV
(1488–1513)

JAMES V
(1513–42)

MARY
(1542–67)

JAMES VI (and I of England)
(1567–1625)

There are three periods of interregnum on the chart:

1040—58
Macbeth seized the throne (1040—57) and was
succeeded briefly by his stepson Lulach (1057—8).

1290—2
The throne was disputed by 13 claimants after the death
of Margaret, the Maid of Norway. It was awarded
by the English king, Edward I, to John de Baliol.

1296—1306
Edward I, declaring that John de Baliol had forfeited the
crown, took it for himself. William Wallace controlled
Scotland for a while during the resulting hiatus. In 1306
Robert the Bruce had himself crowned at Scone.

(For the British Royal House see previous spread)

William and Mary in triumph: the central detail of Thornhill's ceiling (1707–27) in the Painted Hall at the Royal Naval College.

designed by Gordon Benson and Alan Forsyth; their design won in a competition with nearly 400 entrants, but the private nature of the selection process (left, in his words, to 'so-called experts') caused the prince of Wales to resign as patron of the museum in 1991.

The Royal Museum in Queen Street was previously the National Museum of Antiquities of Scotland. Founded in 1817, it covers Scottish history from Stone Age times to recent centuries. Among the greatest treasures are the Monymusk reliquary (8C) and a hoard of Celtic silver of the same period, found on St Ninian's Isle in the Shetlands and probably buried by monks to save it from marauding Vikings. The museum shares a building with the *Scottish National Portrait Gallery.

Royal National Institute for the Blind (London W1) Britain's main pressure group for the blind, which also provides training, runs schools for blind children and is a major publisher of books in braille. It descends from the British and Foreign Blind Association, a committee of blind people brought together in 1863 by Thomas Armitage (a surgeon who had recently gone blind) with the purpose of achieving education for the blind.

Royal National Institute for Deaf People (London WC1) The main pressure group for the deaf in Britain, involving itself also in research and education. It originated in the National Bureau for Promoting the General Welfare of the Deaf, founded in London in 1911 by Leo Bonn, a deaf merchant banker.

Royal National Lifeboat Institution see *RNLI.

Royal Naval College Imposing range of buildings facing the Thames at *Greenwich, designed mainly by *Wren with *Hawksmoor as his assistant. The gap between the two wings was designed to allow the *Queen's House to remain visible from the river. The famous Painted Hall has a ceiling by James Thornhill (1675–1734), showing William and Mary bringing peace to Europe. The buildings were designed as a Royal Naval Hospital, giving

sailors what the *Chelsea Hospital had recently provided for soldiers further up the Thames. The hospital continued until the mid-19C. In 1873 the buildings were adapted to their present use, as the country's main training college for naval officers.

Royal Naval Reserve (RNR) The main naval section of the *Volunteer Reserve Forces, consisting in the early 1990s of about 6000 men and women who train in their spare time. It replaced in 1957 the Royal Naval Volunteer Reserve (RNVR), famous in World War II as the Wavy Navy – from the wavy gold braid on the officers' sleeves as opposed to the straight braid of the regular navy.

Royal Navy Known as the senior service among the *armed forces, because there was a permanent fleet at the king's disposal for many centuries before there was a standing army. Alfred the Great established a navy in the 9C, and by the 13C there was an official called 'keeper of the king's ships'. Henry VIII had a fleet of some 80 vessels, with the *Great Harry as his flagship. In the 17C the Admiralty was established as the government department in charge of the navy, headed by the first lord of the Admiralty – a political appointment. By contrast the serving officer in command of the navy has been the first sea lord (now known as chief of naval staff and first sea lord). The Admiralty was abolished in 1964 and was replaced by the naval department of the Ministry of *Defence. In 1992 there were some 50,000 men and 4000 women (see *WRNS) serving in the navy. The main vessels in the fleet were 3 aircraft carriers (*Ark Royal, Illustrious* and *Invincible*), with 12 destroyers, 32 frigates and 16 submarines (of which 3 were Polaris *nuclear submarines). The first Trident nuclear submarine began tests in 1992.

Royal Northern College of Music see *music schools.

Royal Observatory Established at Greenwich in 1675 by Charles II. The astronomer John *Flamsteed was instructed to set about 'rectifying the tables of the motions of the heavens, and the places of the fixed stars, so as to find out the so much desired longitude of places for the perfecting the art of navigation'. This royal request for the much desired longitude led ultimately to the *Greenwich meridian and *Greenwich Mean Time.

The building, by Wren, was ready for occupation in 1676. It had a specially high ceiling in one room to accommodate pendulum clocks by Thomas *Tompion. The time ball on the roof was added in 1833; it drops down its mast at 1300 GMT each day, originally so that ships on the Thames could set their chronometers. In 1859 this control of the nation's time was extended when a telegraph line was run between Greenwich and *Big Ben for a twice-daily check on parliament's new clock. And in 1924 the Royal Observatory became responsible for the *pips on BBC radio.

Meanwhile the polluted atmosphere and bright lights of London were making observation difficult. In 1948 the Royal Observatory began the process of moving to new premises in Herstmonceux, a 15c castle in East Sussex; in 1990 it moved again, to Cambridge. Its work is also carried out from an observatory on La Palma in the Canary Islands. The original buildings at Greenwich are open to the public as part of the National Maritime Museum.

An independent Royal Observatory in Edinburgh was founded in 1818 by the Astronomical Institution and was given a royal charter in 1822. Its main telescopes are sited now in Hawaii.

Royal Opera House (London WC2) Home of the Royal Opera and the *Royal Ballet. The theatre is the third on the site, in an unbroken succession going back to 1732; it opened in 1858 to the design of E.M. Barry (1830–80, son of Charles *Barry). Situated in *Covent Garden, it is also widely known by that name. Its superb auditorium is virtually unaltered.

The Covent Garden theatre specialized in opera from 1847, except during the two world wars (in the second it was famous as a Mecca dance hall). It is only since World War II that it has combined opera and ballet. The Sadler's Wells Ballet reopened the theatre in 1946 with a perfor-

mance of *The Sleeping Beauty*; and in 1947 a newly formed Covent Garden Opera Company gave its first performance, with *Carmen*. The opera company, renamed the Royal Opera in 1968, presents as guest artists the greatest singers in the world with the operas performed in the original languages – complementing the British casts and English texts of London's other permanent opera house, *English National Opera.

Royal Pavilion, Brighton (also known as the Brighton Pavilion) Britain's most extravagantly fanciful piece of architecture, built in 1815–20 for the Prince Regent, the future *George IV, to the design of John *Nash. The prince had spent part of each year in *Brighton from 1784 and had built there in 1787 a Marine Pavilion, designed by Henry *Holland; it was this which he employed Nash to rebuild and enlarge. Nash's exterior is in a style derived from Mughal India, made fashionable by the aquatints of Thomas *Daniell and first used for an English country house at *Sezincote. But the predominant style inside is Chinese, seen at its most spectacular in the Banqueting Hall and the Music Room. The great kitchen, with the ceiling supported by palm-tree pillars and with the contemporary cooking equipment still in place, is also a major attraction.

Royal Philharmonic Orchestra (RPO) The second of the orchestras created by Thomas *Beecham, with whom it gave its first performance in 1946; the name reflected an informal arrangement with the *Royal Philharmonic Society that the new orchestra would be the one normally called upon for their concerts. Beecham remained in charge until his death in 1961; he was followed as artistic director by Rudolf Kempe, for an equally long spell (1961–75). In 1986 the orchestra became the first in the world to launch a recording company, RPO Records, and in 1987 it broke new ground with a sister orchestra for popular music, the Royal Philharmonic Pops. Since 1987 the Russian pianist and conductor Vladimir Ashkenazy has been the RPO's music director.

Oriental fantasies in Sussex: the main façade, or east front, of John Nash's Royal Pavilion at Brighton.

Royal Philharmonic Society Founded in London in 1813 for the promotion of concerts, a function which it still fulfils. Its greatest pride has been its patronage of Beethoven; amazingly the society commissioned his ninth symphony (first performed in Vienna in 1824), and when he was in his final illness its members sent him the large sum of £100. Since 1871 a bust of the great man has been on the platform at all the society's concerts.

Royal Prerogative The residue (small and possibly non-existent under *constitutional monarchy) of the monarch's ancient power to do whatever he or she likes in public affairs. In practice it is used now to cover all those acts of government requiring no specific authority from parliament; these include the appointment of high officials, some aspects of foreign affairs, and the summoning and dissolving of parliament. In the rare circumstance where it is not clear which political leader should be invited first to form a government, the sovereign might still be able to exercise a choice amounting to a genuine use of the royal prerogative; and theoretically, in a national crisis, it could be used in refusing the *royal assent.

The phrase most commonly comes to public attention in the form of the royal prerogative of mercy, for the sovereign has the exclusive right to grant pardons (a dispensation of great urgency before the abolition of *capital punishment). But even this form of royal prerogative is only exercised on government advice – that of the home secretary or of the secretary of state for Scotland.

Royal St George's see *Sandwich.

royal salute The firing of cannon on ceremonial occasions, such as the arrival of visiting heads of state, the state opening of parliament or certain royal anniversaries. The number of rounds fired varies according to the place and occasion; 21 is the minimum but a further 20 are added if the guns are in a royal park. In central London salutes are fired either in Hyde Park or Green Park (both of them royal), and the operation is carried out by the *King's Troop of the Royal Horse Artillery. They provide a colourful spectacle as they gallop into action in braided uniforms in the style of the Crimean War and with teams of six horses dragging 13-pounder field guns from World War I.

Royal Scottish Academy (Edinburgh) Institution founded in 1826 to fulfil much the same functions as the *Royal Academy in London. It occupies a Greek Revival building (1823–36, by William Playfair) which stands in front of the National Gallery of Scotland on the south side of Princes Street.

Royal Scottish Academy of Music and Drama see *music schools.

Royal Scottish Orchestra Formally established in Glasgow in 1891, though based on an earlier enterprise dating from 1844. It was then the Scottish Orchestra, but its role throughout Scotland was recognized with a change of name in 1950 to the Scottish National Orchestra (this in turn became the Royal Scottish Orchestra in 1991, the centenary year). The SNO greatly enhanced its reputation in the long period when Alexander Gibson was music director (1959–84), with British premieres of work by composers such as Schoenberg and Stockhausen. Walter Weller became music director in 1992.

Royal Shakespeare Company (RSC) Enterprise based in both Stratford-upon-Avon and London, which has developed from summer seasons in the original Shakespeare Memorial Theatre. This opened in Stratford in 1879. There had been earlier festivals to commemorate Shakespeare in the town of his birth (the first organized by *Garrick), but this first permanent theatre began a tradition which has made Stratford the undisputed centre of Shakespearean production in Britain. The original Shakespeare Memorial Theatre burnt down in 1926 and the present one opened in 1932.

The name Royal Shakespeare Company was adopted in 1961, during a period when the level of activity was greatly increased under Peter *Hall as artistic director (1960–8). The Aldwych Theatre became from 1960 the company's London home, enabling Shakespeare productions, transferred from Stratford, to play in repertoire with modern plays presented only in London. There was further expansion with Trevor *Nunn as artistic director (1968–87). The opening in 1974 of the Other Place, a small studio theatre in Stratford for experimental work, was followed in 1977 by the similarly intimate Warehouse in London, making transfers possible between these two. In 1982, the RSC moved to the newly completed *Barbican, a single location where the main auditorium and the smaller Pit replaced the Aldwych and the Warehouse. Finally, in 1986, the Swan opened in Stratford, modelled on a Jacobean indoor playhouse.

The result of all this is an extraordinarily wide and ambitious programme of work. From 1982 Terry Hands was joint artistic director with Trevor Nunn; in 1987 he became sole artistic director, and was followed in the post in 1991 by Adrian Noble.

Royal Society (London SW1) Britain's oldest scientific society, founded in 1660. Informal meetings had been held since 1645 to discuss 'natural philosophy' – meaning experimental science as opposed to theories inherited from classical authors. The publication of scientific papers in the society's *Philosophical Transactions* has been continuous from 1665. Until 1847 fellowship was open to anyone interested in science, but since then it has been awarded in recognition of original work. Up to 40 new fellows and six foreign members are elected each year. The society gives various awards of which the *Copley medal carries the greatest prestige.

Royal Society for the Protection of Birds see *RSPB.

Royal Society of Arts (Royal Society for the Encouragement of Arts, Manufactures & Commerce, London WC2) Founded in 1754 to fulfil the aims described in its unabbreviated title, the society has continued ever since to agitate and educate for improved standards in areas such as industrial design. This became an increasingly fashionable cause in the mid-19C, when Prince *Albert was president (1843–61), and the society was much involved in planning the *Great Exhibition. Since 1856 it has conducted examinations in the fields of craft and design (most recently in the *NVQ programme). The society still occupies the house built for it as part of the *Adelphi; the main room is decorated with murals by James Barry (1741–1806), offering a pleasantly eccentric view of *The Progress of Human Culture*.

Royal Society of Edinburgh Founded in 1783 with aims similar to those of the *Royal Society in London, but with an additional interest in the arts. It was formed largely from the members of the Philosophical Society, established in 1737 with the fuller title of the 'Edinburgh Society for improving Arts and Sciences and particularly Natural Knowledge'.

Royal Standard Flag bearing the four quarterings of the *royal arms. It is flown when the Queen is in residence in any of the royal palaces, and may be flown on secular buildings which she is visiting.

Royal Tank Regiment see *Royal Armoured Corps.

Royal Tournament Military display presented on successive evenings each July at Earl's Court in London. First held in 1880 in the Royal Agricultural Hall, Islington, the event moved to Olympia in 1905 and to Earl's Court in 1950. The army, navy and air force all take part, with one of the three in a leading role each year. The performances combine elements of spectacle and skill, often involving competition between rival units.

Royal Troon Golf course on the west coast of Scotland, in Strathclyde. Troon was established in 1878 (becoming Royal Troon in its centenary year) and was first used for the *Open in 1923. It has both the longest and the shortest holes of any course regularly used for the tournament: the 6th (the Turnberry) is 528m/577yds; the 8th (the Postage Stamp) is only 115m/126yds, but a player in the 1950 Open needed 15 shots to complete it, including five from a bunker on the left, five from a bunker on the right, and another three when he found himself back in the bunker on the left (he finished triumphantly with a single putt).

Royal Ulster Constabulary see *RUC.

Royal Variety Performance Annual show, attended by royalty and televised, to raise money for the Entertainment Artistes's Benevolent Fund. The acts cover the full traditional range of variety, with jugglers and acrobats, singers, comedians and dancers.

Royal Warrant An appointment as supplier of goods to any of four members of the royal family (the Queen, the Duke of Edinburgh, the Queen Mother and the Prince of Wales). The holder of a royal warrant may display the appropriate royal insignia (different for each of the four) and the words 'By Appointment'; these are usually shown on shop fronts, delivery vans and printed material.

royal we A former custom, by which monarchs talked of themselves in the first person plural. It is remembered now chiefly because of Queen Victoria's famous remark, 'We are not amused'. She was reported to have said this after seeing an imitation of herself by a member of the court. More recently the memory of the royal we was revived by Mrs Thatcher's tendency to use it. The element of ambiguity surrounding this mannerism (for she could always have been talking about herself and her government) was resolved in 1989 when she announced to the assembled press: 'We are a grandmother.'

Royal Yacht Squadron see *Cowes.

Henry **Royce** see *Rolls-Royce.

RP see *Received Pronunciation.

RPI (Retail Prices Index) The index, published monthly by the *Central Statistical Office, which is accepted as the main indicator of the level of inflation. It monitors changes in the price levels of the commodities and services believed to be bought by the average household; this average excludes the two extremes (approximately the richest 4% of households, and those where more than 75% of the income derives from state pensions or benefits), since their expenditure pattern is considered untypical. The reliability of the index depends not only on the price changes being accurately recorded, but on the correct weighting of each commodity within the overall pattern of expenditure. This is monitored in a continuous Family Expenditure Survey; any necessary change to the weighting in the basket of commodities and other domestic expenses is made each February. (For the cumulative effect of inflation on the spending power of money since 1965, see the *pound in your pocket.)

Statistical analysis of this sort began in the late 19c in the labour department of the Board of Trade. This developed into an official Cost of Living Index (1914–47), which was followed by an 'interim index' and finally, from 1 January 1956, by the RPI. The index was compiled by the Department of Employment until 1989, when the statistics division there was absorbed into the Central Statistical Office.

RPO see *Royal Philharmonic Orchestra.

RSC see *Royal Shakespeare Company.

RPI (Retail Prices Index): January 1987 = 100

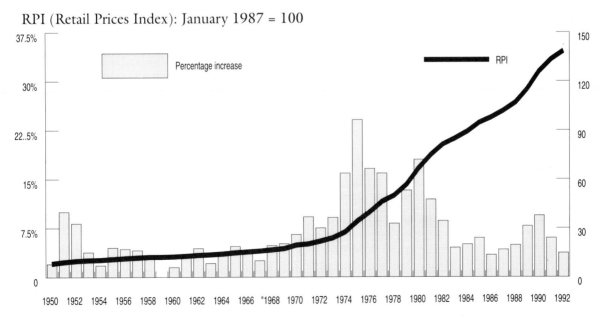

For the comparative value of money every five years from 1950 to 1990 see the *pound in your pocket.

Source: Economic Trends *(see *Central Statistical Office).*

RSPB (Royal Society for the Protection of Birds, Sandy, Bedfordshire) Pressure group founded in Manchester in 1889 by Mrs Robert Williamson, as a circle of ladies pledging themselves not to wear feathers in their hats. Thousands of egrets, birds of paradise and kingfishers were at that time being killed for this purpose, and London was the world centre of the plumage trade. The society now has some 750,000 members and its activities have extended to managing nature reserves (more than 100), assisting in the reintroduction of species to Britain (in particular the avocet and the osprey) and lobbying for protection of the environment and for anti-pollution measures.

RSPCA (Royal Society for the Prevention of Cruelty to Animals, Horsham, West Sussex) Founded in 1824 to enforce recent laws protecting animals and to campaign for further legislation, the society was granted the addition of 'Royal' in 1840 by an enthusiastic young Victoria. (It is an often mentioned fact of British life that the NSPCC, preventing cruelty to children, has remained only 'National'). The society's early campaigns achieved the banning of bull-baiting in the 1830s and of cockfighting in the 1840s, but the widespread maltreatment of horses remained at that time the central issue. The Protection of Animals Act (1911) is seen now as the society's greatest achievement. Today domestic pets are a prime concern (there are more than seven million dogs in Britain and almost as many cats), and the RSPCA has campaigned strongly for *dog registration. Its work is carried out by uniformed inspectors and is supported by a large number of local branches.

Rt Hon. see *Right Honourable.

Peter Paul **Rubens** (1577–1640, kt 1630) Flemish painter and diplomat. It was as a diplomat that Rubens spent nearly a year in London (1629–30), negotiating a peace between Spain and England. For this he was knighted by Charles I on his departure, while he in turn presented the king with a large allegorical painting of *Peace and War* (now in the National Gallery). Meanwhile it had also been agreed that he would provide his most important contribution to art in Britain – the ceiling for the *Banqueting House in Whitehall. The huge canvases were painted in Antwerp and sent to England.

RUC (Royal Ulster Constabulary) The police force in *Northern Ireland, which in the past two decades has had a high profile in the front line against *terrorism. It is the oldest police force in the United Kingdom, descending from the original 'peelers' set up by Robert Peel in Ireland in 1814 and organized on a more thorough basis by his Constabulary Act of 1822 (it was not until 1829 that he established the metropolitan police in London). The 'peelers' became in 1867 the Royal Irish Constabulary and subsequently in Northern Ireland, after 1921, the Royal Ulster Constabulary.

Since 1969 the British army has been in Northern Ireland to support the RUC in its difficult task of policing the province, but the effectiveness of their collaboration has recently been in doubt. In 1989 John Stevens, deputy chief constable of Cambridgeshire, was asked to enquire into allegations that members of the security forces were in collusion with the Ulster Defence Association, a Protestant terrorist organization. He uncovered a tangle of distrust between police and army, notably in the case of one of the army's undercover agents, Brian *Nelson. A few years earlier the RUC itself was the subject of an enquiry after three members of the IRA were shot in their car in 1982 by officers of the RUC Special Branch. John Stalker, deputy chief constable of Greater Manchester, was asked in 1984 to investigate charges that the RUC was operating a shoot-to-kill policy; the issue became even more controversial after Mr Stalker was for various reasons prevented in 1986 from completing his report.

Rugby (60,000 in 1981) Town in Warwickshire which has been an engineering centre since the arrival of the railway in the 19C. Its wider fame is due to Rugby School, founded in 1567 and influential in the 19C through the ideas of Dr *Arnold and from *Tom Brown's Schooldays. The school has given its name to rugby football.

rugby football (also known colloquially as rugger) Game in which an oval ball may be handled as well as kicked. Various rival forms of *football were competing with each other for predominance in the mid-19C; Rugby School was strongly associated with the handling game, which therefore became known by its name. The Rugby Football Union was formed in 1871 after the Football Association had officially banned the handling of the ball. Many local and traditional forms of football had allowed the use of hands, and it was not till the 1890s that Rugby School claimed to have actually invented such a game. An intrinsically improbable story surfaced at that time, for which there was no contemporary evidence; but it was cast in stone in 1923 in the famous inscription at the school commemorating 'William Webb Ellis, who, with a fine disregard for the rules of football as played in his time, first took the ball in his arms and ran with it, thus originating the distinctive feature of the Rugby game. AD 1823.'

Rugby football itself soon suffered a schism, as a result of the obsession of the Rugby Union with amateur status. The game had rapidly become popular in the north of England, where many of the players were from the working class. They could not afford to travel or take time off work without compensation, but the southern clubs, whose members were more likely to come from the public schools, refused to yield on this point. As a result 22 clubs formed their own breakaway Northern Union in 1895 (the name was changed to the Northern Rugby League in 1922 and in 1980 was reduced simply to the Rugby League). By 1898 there were full-time professionals in the northern game. A century later the distinction survives. Rugby Union remains an amateur game, though in the 1990s complex formulas have been devised by which players can earn money from sidelines (such as endorsement of products) without losing their supposed amateur status. The professional teams introduced several changes to the rules of their game, but the most noticeable difference is that a rugby league team consists (since 1906) of only 13 players instead of the 15 in rugby union (there are six rather than eight in the scrum).

There have been international contests in rugby union since early days, with England, Ireland, Scotland and Wales later joined by France to make a *Five Nations tournament. Since 1888 teams representing the four home countries (known in recent times as the *Lions) have played regular series abroad or at home against Australia, New Zealand and South Africa. The spread of rugby union round the world during the 20C is evident in the World Cup series, launched in 1987. The 16 teams competing in the second contest, in 1991, included countries as far-flung as Argentina, Italy, Zimbabwe, Japan and Western Samoa. Since 1954 there have also been rugby league international competitions (called at different periods the World Cup and the International Championship), with Great Britain, France, New Zealand, Australia and recently Papua New Guinea as the competing teams.

In the domestic game, the oldest rugby union contest is the English County Championship, introduced in 1889. Knockout competitions have been held since the 1971–2 season in both England and Wales – known in England as the John Player Special until 1988 (then as the Pilkington

Rugby Union

John Player Special/ Pilkington Cup		Schweppes Welsh Cup	
1972	Gloucester	1972	Neath
1973	Coventry	1973	Llanelli
1974	Coventry	1974	Llanelli
1975	Bedford	1975	Llanelli
1976	Gosforth	1976	Llanelli
1977	Gosforth	1977	Newport
1978	Gloucester	1978	Swansea
1979	Leicester	1979	Bridgend
1980	Leicester	1980	Bridgend
1981	Leicester	1981	Cardiff
1982	Gloucester/Moseley (tie)	1982	Cardiff
1983	Bristol	1983	Pontypool
1984	Bath	1984	Cardiff
1985	Bath	1985	Llanelli
1986	Bath	1986	Cardiff
1987	Bath	1987	Cardiff
1988	Harlequins	1988	Llanelli
1989	Bath	1989	Neath
1990	Bath	1990	Neath
1991	Harlequins	1991	Llanelli
1992	Bath	1992	Llanelli
1993	Leicester	1993	Llanelli

Rugby League

Challenge Cup

1965	Wigan	1980	Hull Kingston Rovers
1966	St Helens	1981	Widnes
1967	Featherstone Rovers	1982	Hull
1968	Leeds	1983	Featherstone Rovers
1969	Castleford	1984	Widnes
1970	Castleford	1985	Wigan
1971	Leigh	1986	Castleford
1972	St Helens	1987	Halifax
1973	Featherstone Rovers	1988	Wigan
1974	Warrington	1989	Wigan
1975	Widnes	1990	Wigan
1976	St Helens	1991	Wigan
1977	Leeds	1992	Wigan
1978	Leeds	1993	Wigan
1979	Widnes		

Cup) and in Wales as the Schweppes Welsh Cup. One of the most popular rugby union events in England, played in a fast and loose version of the game with only seven on each side instead of 15, is the Middlesex Sevens tournament. The two English knockout competitions have their finals at Twickenham, and that of the Schweppes Cup is held at Cardiff Arms Park.

The Rugby League Championship was first competed for in the 1895–6 season; its structure has been through many changes (there were two divisions from 1973 and there have been three since 1991, but with much discussion of changing back to two). The Challenge Cup, Rugby League's chief knockout tournament, had its first final at Leeds in 1897 (since 1933 the event has been held at Wembley).

rugger see *rugby football.

Rule, Britannia! Song by Thomas *Arne from the masque *Alfred* (1740), which has become almost a secular national anthem (with an honoured place, for example, at the last night of the *Proms).The words are by James Thomson (1700–48).

Rule 43 see *Strangeways.

Rumpole Fictional barrister, created by John *Mortimer, who combines two irresistible characteristics – he is both grumpy and warm-hearted. He defends the hopeless cases which no-one else will touch, while coping with rivalries in his chambers and the whims of his wife, 'she who must be obeyed' (see *She). Rumpole made his first appearance in a television play of 1976, was fleshed out in short stories (*Rumpole of the Bailey* 1978) and has featured since in a great many books and television series. He is played on television, in a perfect piece of casting, by Leo McKern.

Rump Parliament see the *Long Parliament.

Robert **Runcie** (b. 1921, baron 1991) Archbishop of Canterbury 1980–91, after being bishop of St Albans (1970–80). He guided the Church of England through a difficult period, with dissension rife on topics such as the *ordination of women. He was an outspoken critic of the uncaring social attitudes which he saw as prevailing during the 1980s; and he annoyed the prime minister, Mrs Thatcher, (but pleased many others) when he insisted on remembering and praying for the Argentinian dead as well as the British in the Falkland Islands Service in St Paul's Cathedral in 1982.

Steven **Runciman** (b. 1903, kt 1958) Historian of Byzantine civilization and related subjects, known in particular for his three-volume *History of the Crusades* (1951–4).

runes The letters of a Germanic alphabet, dating from the 3rd century AD or earlier and possibly derived from the Etruscan script. Common to northwest Europe and Scandinavia, runes were used for inscriptions in Britain by the *Anglo-Saxons, who adapted and enlarged the alphabet to accommodate the sounds of Old *English. One of the runic letters, the thorn, is still widely familiar on signs beginning with the words *'ye olde'.

Runnymede Meadow on the south bank of the Thames, just downstream from Windsor, where King John signed *Magna Carta in 1215. After the assassination in 1963 of John F. Kennedy, an acre of land here was given by the people of Britain to the people of the United States as a memorial to the president. At the top of the nearby Cooper's Hill is the Air Forces Memorial, commemorating the 20,456 airmen of the Allied forces who died in World War II and have no known grave.

Prince **Rupert** (1619–82) Son of the *Winter Queen and grandson of James I. He is also known as Rupert of the Rhine, because his title through his father was Count Palatine of the Rhine. He is remembered in two very different contexts. He was a dashing though not consistently successful cavalry commander on behalf of his uncle Charles I in the *English Civil War. And he was the first practitioner in England of a new form of print-making, the mezzotint, which later became almost exclusively British (providing richly toned monochrome reproductions of paintings, in particular portraits). A mezzotint by Prince Rupert was included as an illustration in John *Evelyn's book on engraving. Rupert is also credited with having invented prince's metal, a form of brass (an alloy of copper and zinc) used as a cheap substitute for gold.

Rupert Bear A bear in check trousers, jumper and scarf, who has had a lively career both in comic strips and on television since being launched in the *Daily Express* in 1920, together with his friends Algy Pug, Bill Badger and Edward Trunk (an elephant). They were created by Mary Tourtel (1874–1948).

rural protection Three separate bodies were set up in the 1920s to campaign for the protection of the countryside. All depend for their funds on membership fees and donations. Two were founded in 1926 (Council for the Protection of Rural England, London SW1; Association for the Protection of Rural Scotland, Edinburgh) and the third in 1928 (Campaign for the Protection of Rural Wales, Welshpool, Powys).

Rural Rides see William *Cobbett.

Ruritania see Anthony *Hope.

Salman **Rushdie** (b. 1947) Author born in Bombay who has lived in Britain since 1965. He made his reputation with *Midnight's Children* (1981), a novel about the family of an Indian boy, Saleem, who has magic powers because he was born (about two months after Rushdie) at midnight on 15 August 1947, the very moment of India's independence. The rich detail of the story-telling, combined with the hallucinatory nature of the material, made this a brilliant example of the style known as magic realism, and it won for Rushdie the Booker prize. *Shame* (1983) dealt with Pakistan's modern history in much the same oblique and satirical vein.

It was when the same literary technique was applied to Islam that Rushdie's own life turned to nightmare. The crisis over *The Satanic Verses* (1988) was a clash between cultures. The complex story, intermingling our century with the 7C (in which Islam has its origins), is not shocking within a context of modern western literature; but the content of a few scenes (in particular one in which a character dreams of a brothel where the women boost their takings by pretending to be the wives of the Prophet Muhammad) was sufficient to give profound offence when recounted among fundamentalist Muslims. In 1989 the Ayatollah Khomeini declared a *fatwa* (or edict) sentencing Rushdie to death for blasphemy. This incitement to murder was compounded when a foundation headed by another Iranian ayatollah, Hassan Sanei, offered a reward of $2 million to anyone carrying out the *fatwa*. As a result Rushdie has lived since then in hiding, under police protection.

John **Ruskin** (1819–1900) The most influential art critic of the 19C. He engaged in three main crusades. The first was a passionate advocacy of *Turner, whose impressionistic late style had met with criticism; in the first volume of *Modern Painters* (5 vols, 1843–60) Ruskin argued that he was a great artist because of his underlying truth to nature. The second was his crusade for Gothic architecture, as against classical or baroque, on the grounds that it was more spiritual and more structurally honest – the theme of *The Seven Lamps of Architecture* (1849) and *The Stones of Venice* (3 vols, 1851–3). And the third was his defence of the *Pre-Raphaelites, partly in response to intemperate attacks on them but also because he saw their minutely observed detail as a form of truth to nature, and one which he himself practised in his watercolours of mountains and rocks.

It was his friendship with the Pre-Raphaelites which brought to an end his disastrous and unconsummated marriage of 1848 to Effie Gray; in 1854 she had it annulled so that she could marry *Millais. In his later years Ruskin concentrated increasingly on the political side of his campaign against the crass modern world, spending much time and money trying to achieve for the working classes better living conditions, education in a craft and contact with objects of beauty (the collection which he gathered together for this purpose is displayed in the Ruskin Gallery in Sheffield). From 1872 he lived in Brantwood, a house beside *Coniston Water which is kept now as a museum.

Bertrand **Russell** (1872–1970, 3rd earl Russell 1931) Philosopher and mathematician, grandson of the prime minister Lord John Russell, whose special skill was the application of mathematical logic to philosophical problems. A similar clarity was characteristic of his prose, with the result that his *History of Western Philosophy* (1945) became a bestselling popular work on the subject. He had made his professional reputation with *A Critical Exposition of the Philosophy of Leibniz* (1900) and *The Principles of Mathematics* (1903). He then collaborated with his former teacher at Cambridge, A.N. Whitehead (1861–1947), in developing the principles of mathematical logic; they gave their joint work a title already used by Newton, *Principia Mathematica* (3 vols, 1910–13). At that same period Russell himself became the teacher of *Wittgenstein, and found his own philosophical tenets challenged and somewhat undermined by his brilliant pupil. Russell was irritated, on one occasion, at not being able to get Wittgenstein to agree that there was certainly no rhinoceros in the room.

The First World War introduced another important theme in Russell's life, that of pacifism and political protest. He was fined £100 in 1916 for a pamphlet in defence of a conscientious objector, and was removed from his lectureship at Trinity, Cambridge; in 1918 he was imprisoned for six months for an article which was judged, in the atmosphere of the time, to be seditious. But more than anything it was the threat of nuclear war in the 1950s which spurred him to action. After the first American H-bomb tests on the Bikini atoll, in 1954, he organized an anti-nuclear manifesto signed by Einstein and other scientists. In 1958 he became the first president of *CND, and he later headed the more militant Committee of 100. With them, at the age of 88, he took part in a mass sitdown in Whitehall in 1961; sentenced to two months in prison, he was released after a week for medical reasons. For much of the rest of his life, through his nineties, he became a slightly pathetic figure, taking exaggerated political stances in which he was orchestrated by an American follower, Ralph Schoenman.

Lord John **Russell** (1792–1878, Earl Russell 1861) Prime minister 1846–52 and 1865–6. Born into a great Whig family, he became an MP as soon as he was of age, in 1813; for most of his career he was known as Lord John Russell (his title as a son of the duke of Bedford), until he was himself created Earl Russell. He argued passionately in favour of the Emancipation Act of 1829 and was the most active member of Lord Grey's team in securing the Reform Act of 1832. During Melbourne's Whig administrations of the later 1830s he led the party in the House of Commons, and it was he who began to refer to it as the *Liberal party.

Russell formed an administration in 1846, after Peel's repeal of the *Corn Laws had split the Conservatives. One of the most significant measures of his government was the Ten Hours Act of 1847, an important step in the series of *Factory Acts; but Russell's violent opposition to the restoring of *Roman Catholic bishoprics in Britain in 1850 was in marked contrast to his earlier record on emancipation. From the mid-1850s he was eclipsed on the Liberal side of politics by *Palmerston, but he served as foreign secretary throughout Palmerston's second administration (1859–65) and was prime minister again for a few months after Palmerston's death in 1865.

Ken **Russell** (b. 1927) Director who established his reputation with a series of original and often provocative television biographies of composers (among them Elgar, Delius and Vaughan Williams) and whose films have included *Women in Love* (1969), *The Boy Friend* (1971) and the rock opera *Tommy* (1974).

Russell of the _Times_ (William Howard Russell, 1820–1907, kt 1895) The first war correspondent in the modern sense. He went out with the troops to the *Crimea in 1854 and sent back regular articles to the _Times_, written with a passionate intensity and describing the appalling conditions in which the men were living. Strongly disapproved of by the military authorities, these were the earliest first-hand immediate reports of a military action and they had an effect similar to the television news from Vietnam. They were largely what inspired Florence *Nightingale to undertake her mission. Russell continued to report from the front line until the Zulu War of 1879, by which time he was writing for the _Daily Telegraph_.

Ernest **Rutherford** (1871–1937, kt 1914, baron 1931) Physicist, born in New Zealand, whose researches on the atomic structure are the basis of modern nuclear physics. At the *Cavendish Laboratory in Cambridge (1895–8) and then at McGill University in Montreal (1898–1907) his early work was on radioactivity. He recognized with *Soddy in 1902 that radioactive substances are emitting rays while spontaneously transmuting into different elements, and thus formulated the concept of radioactive half-life; it was for his discoveries in this region that he received the Nobel prize for chemistry in 1908. Even greater work was to come, at the university of Manchester (1907–1919) and then back at the Cavendish, where he succeeded J.J. *Thomson as director.

The turning point into the age of nuclear physics was Rutherford's proof in 1911 that there was a very dense positively charged nucleus at the heart of the atom, tiny compared with the size of the atom as a whole; its existence had been suggested to him by the mysterious rebounding from metal foil of just a few out of many alpha particles (helium nuclei), implying that the obstacle they had struck was small but heavy. In 1919 he achieved the first artificially induced nuclear reaction, bombarding nitrogen with alpha particles and releasing particles which he named protons. He next showed (1920) that the proton formed the entire nucleus of the hydrogen atom and in differing numbers was present in all other nuclei. The brilliant team headed by Rutherford at the Cavendish went on to make further advances in subatomic physics – notably *Chadwick's discovery of the neutron.

Margaret **Rutherford** (1892–1972, DBE 1967) Actress whose solemn appearance and trembling chins made her a natural performer of a certain type of comedy. Two of her best-known stage roles featured also among her many film performances – Madame Arcati in _Blithe Spirit_ (1945) and Miss Prism in _The Importance of Being Earnest_ (1952).

Ruthwell (16km/10m SE of Dumfries) Village known for the outstanding Celtic cross in its parish church. The central shaft (5.5m/18ft high, carved in the 8C) is decorated with scenes from the life of Christ and has an inscription in *runes recounting (from the cross's point of view) the events of the crucifixion. The text is part of an Old English poem known as _The Dream of the Rood_.

Rutland Former *county in east central England. Long famous as the smallest English county (394sq.km/152sq.m), it became in 1974 part of Leicestershire.

Rydal Mount see *Grasmere.

Sue **Ryder** (b. 1923, baroness 1979) Founder of the Sue Ryder Homes, caring for the sick and disabled; in the early 1990s there were some 80 of them, in 15 countries. In World War II she worked with the Special Operations Executive, an organization coordinating resistance activities in countries occupied by the Germans; her own links were with Poland. In 1959 she married another great founder of charities for the disabled, Leonard *Cheshire.

Ryder Cup The major international professional golf tournament for teams of male players. An informal match between an American and a British team took place at Wentworth in Surrey in 1926, and the following year an English seed merchant, Samuel Ryder, presented a gold cup for a biennial contest between teams from the USA and from Great Britain and Ireland (listed as separate countries only from 1973). By the end of the 1977 match the team from the British Isles had won only three times, so since 1979 the contest has been between the USA and Europe. At present the three-day event consists of 4 foursomes and 4 four-ball games on each of the first two days, and 12 singles on the final day.

Martin **Ryle** (1918–84, kt 1966) Radio astronomer whose special contribution was the development of aperture synthesis – the use of widely separated aerials to pinpoint radio sources in space (by 1971 his Mullard Radio Astronomy Laboratory at Cambridge had the equivalent of a 5km/3m aperture). In 1955 his researches led him to the conclusion that the universe had evolved from a densely concentrated mass some ten billion years ago. This resulted in a lively dispute between himself and Fred *Hoyle, who argued that the universe is in a steady state of continuous creation; subsequent research has supported Ryle and the big bang. He won the Nobel prize in 1974 and was appointed *astronomer royal in 1972 (a post from which he retired in 1982 because of ill health).

S

S4C (Sianel Pedwar Cymru, Welsh for Channel 4 Wales) The only TV channel in Britain to have been the result of an intense political campaign. *Plaid Cymru and others had argued the case for a Welsh-language channel to preserve *Welsh against the encroachments of English and American, and the argument seemed to have been won when the first Queen's Speech of the new Conservative administration in 1979 included a commitment to 'seek an early start with the fourth television channel in Wales'. But in September of that year the home secretary, William Whitelaw, said there would be no Welsh TV channel. In May 1980 the leader of Plaid Cymru, Gwynfor Evans, declared that he would start a hunger strike in October. A summer of demonstrations was followed by the capitulation of the government in September. S4C began broadcasting in 1982 and was soon transmitting 23 hours a week in Welsh in peak evening time.

Saatchi & Saatchi Advertising agency founded in 1970 by two Saatchi brothers, Charles (b. 1943) and Maurice (b. 1946). By the late 1980s it had become one of the world's largest advertising groups, though there has been some retrenchment since. The agency became known to the wider public through its publicity for the Conservative party in the election of 1979; it played the same role in each of the party's three subsequent victories. Charles, something of a recluse (his younger brother has been chairman of the company since 1985), has built up Britain's leading private collection of contemporary art, which he opened to the public in a purpose-built gallery in north London.

Jonathan **Sacks** (b. 1948) The *Chief Rabbi since 1991, after being rabbi of the Golders Green Synagogue (1978–82) and minister of the Marble Arch Synagogue (1983–90).

Vita **Sackville-West** (1892–1962) Gardener and writer who grew up at *Knole – an experience which provided material for many of her books and inspired her greatest achievement, the creation of *Sissinghurst. Her partner in this was the diplomat and biographer Harold Nicolson (1886–1968), whom she married in 1913. It was a happy marriage, though both were more passionately involved in homosexual friendships. Two of Vita's have received much attention (with Violet Trefusis and Virginia *Woolf). Vita was short for Victoria.

Sadler's Wells (London E1) In 1683 Thomas Sadler opened a music house at some medicinal wells here, a short distance to the north of the old city of London. He thus began a link with entertainment which has lasted intermittently to this day. A theatre built in 1765 had

*Grimaldi as its star attraction from 1802. The present theatre was built by Lilian Baylis in 1927–31 and became the cradle of the *Royal Ballet, the *Birmingham Royal Ballet and the *English National Opera.

Sadler's Wells Ballet see *Royal Ballet.

Sadler's Wells Royal Ballet see *Birmingham Royal Ballet.

safari parks An idea introduced at *Longleat in 1966 and soon imitated elsewhere. It was the brainchild of a circus owner, Jimmy Chipperfield (1912–90). In pleasant English parkland he combined the close proximity of creatures in a zoo with the motorized viewing of an African game park, allowing tourists the pleasure of driving among concentrated groups of large wild animals.

Safeway see *Argyll Group.

Sainsbury Centre see *Norwich.

Sainsbury Family Charitable Trusts (London EC4) The largest privately funded charitable foundation in Britain, consisting of separate trusts financed by individual members of the grocery family. Support is given to the full spectrum of charitable purposes, while sometimes reflecting the individual interests of the various donors (which range from ballet to evangelical Christianity).

Sainsbury Wing see *National Gallery.

Sainsbury's Britain's oldest and largest food retailers, and in 1992 the largest retailer of any kind (a role in which it in that year replaced *Marks & Spencer). The first Sainsbury's was a small dairy in London's Drury Lane, opened in 1869 by John James and Mary Ann Sainsbury (1844–1928, 1849–1927); the company remained a private concern until 1973 and is still, in the 1990s, run by descendants of the founders. The early shops, which specialized in meat and bacon as well as dairy products, were famous for their tiled interiors; the last counter service shop of this kind, at Rye Lane in Peckham, closed in 1982. Self-service had been introduced in Croydon in 1950, and the first Sainsbury's supermarket (an American concept and word) opened in Southampton in 1954. Large supermarkets with parking facilities became the basis of the firm's subsequent expansion through the Midlands and the north of England; in the early 1990s there are more than 300 Sainsbury's supermarkets in England but, as yet, only about ten in Wales and Scotland. The firm's 19c slogan 'Quality Perfect, Prices Lower' has been recycled since 1960 in its present better-known form – 'Good food costs less at Sainsbury's'. Homebase, launched in 1979, is Sainsbury's chain of home improvement stores and garden centres.

The Saint The hero of romantic thrillers by Leslie Charteris (1907–93), being the name by which the gentleman burglar Simon Templar is known. There was a popular TV series of his exploits in the 1960s (ATV 1963–8), starring Roger Moore.

St Abb's Head (24km/15m N of Berwick-upon-Tweed) High promontory, with dramatic cliff scenery, which is an important bird sanctuary. Guillemots and kittiwakes nest in the spring, together with razorbills and fulmars, and many species gather here for the autumn migration.

St Albans (51,000 in 1981) City in Hertfordshire, on the other side of the river Ver from the Roman site of *Verulamium. The cathedral (11–14c) is the church of a Benedictine abbey, founded in the 8c on the hill where St *Alban was believed to have been martyred. The church was in a dilapidated state by 1877, when it was heavily restored to become the cathedral of a new diocese covering Hertfordshire and Bedfordshire.

St **Andrews** (11,000 in 1981) City on the east coast of Scotland, in Fife, which was a medieval centre of Christianity and learning. Legend states that a certain St Rule (or Regulus) was shipwrecked here in the 4c when he happened to have with him the mortal remains of St *Andrew. It is more likely that the relics were brought here in the 8c, when a Pictish king dedicated a church to St Andrew (who became the patron saint of the Picts, and then of the *Scots). The town was the seat of a bishop from the 9c and came to be considered the most important Scottish diocese, a status acknowledged with the appointment of an archbishop here in 1472 as the primate of Scotland. It was therefore the natural setting for the most violent clashes of the *Reformation. It was here that John *Knox demonstrated his qualities, preaching his first public sermon in 1547 in the 15c Holy Trinity Church. The two main medieval buildings are both now

ruins: the 12–14c cathedral, in its day the largest in Scotland; and the 13c castle on a rock by the sea, used by the bishops as a fortified palace. Close to the cathedral the choir survives of the 12c church of St Rule.

Scotland's first university was founded at St Andrews in 1412. The 15c St Salvator's College is the university centre (though only the chapel survives from that date), and several of the 16c buildings of St Mary's College are still in use. The bright red gowns of the students are a famous feature of St Andrews.

In spite of its strong medieval claims to fame, it is for a more recent distinction that the city is best known – as the home of *golf and of the *Royal and Ancient.

St Asaph (32km/20m east of Conwy) Cathedral town in Clwyd, in effect not much more than a village on a hill surmounted by the smallest of Britain's ancient cathedrals. A church is believed to have been established here in about 560 by St *Mungo, but the present building dates from the 13–14c and was much restored in the 19c. The cathedral has on display an excellent collection of early printed Bibles and prayer books in Welsh, including the Bible used at the investiture of the Prince of Wales at *Caernarfon in 1969.

St Bartholomew's Hospital see *Bart's.

St Bartholomew the Great (London EC1) The oldest surviving church in London, and all that remains of the priory founded in about 1123 by *Rahere alongside St Bartholomew's Hospital. The present church is the original choir, built in Rahere's time; it contains a 16c monument to him. The nave was demolished in the *dissolution of the monasteries.

St Bride's (London EC4) A church site of great antiquity, dedicated to St Brigid, an Irish saint of the 5–6c, and with the earliest foundations going back to her period. The present spire, the tallest of *Wren's many spires in London, is all that remained of his church after a night of bombing in 1940; the body of the church has been rebuilt to his design. The church has been associated with

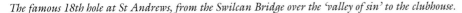

The famous 18th hole at St Andrews, from the Swilcan Bridge over the 'valley of sin' to the clubhouse.

printing ever since Wynkyn de Worde installed *Caxton's press nearby in 1500, and the later specialization of *Fleet Street gave St Bride's a special link also with journalism.

St Christopher and Nevis see *St Kitts-Nevis.

Lindi **St Clair** see *Corrective Party.

St Clement Danes (London WC2) Church by *Wren at the east end of the Strand where it joins Fleet Street, standing nowadays in the middle of the road with traffic streaming round it. Bombed in the war and reconstructed, it is now associated in particular with the RAF and contains many memorials and rolls of honour. Statues of the leaders of Fighter Command and Bomber Command, *Dowding and *Harris, stand in front of the church. It claims to be the St Clement's featured in *Oranges and Lemons* and these fruits are given to local children in an annual ceremony.

St David's (43km/27m NW of Pembroke) The tiniest of cathedral towns, in effect a village, occupying almost the most westerly point in mainland Wales, on a promontory in Dyfed. It was here that St *David established his monastery in the 6C. The present cathedral, set among fields in a small valley, was begun in 1180. It is known in particular for its ornate flat timber ceiling of the late 15C, and for the oddity of a gradual rise of some 4.25m/14ft in the floor level from the west door to the altar. Nearby are the ruins of a spectacularly large bishop's palace (12–14C).

St David's Hall see *Cardiff.

St Dunstan's (London W1) Charity for blind ex-service men and women founded in 1915 by Arthur Pearson (1866–1921), who was himself blind. The name was that of the first hostel, St Dunstan's House in Regent's Park, so called because it had in the grounds a great clock, with two giants striking the hours, which had come from the church of St Dunstan-in-the-West in Fleet Street (it was returned there in 1935).

St George's Channel see *Irish Sea.

St George's Chapel Chapel of the Order of the *Garter in *Windsor Castle. Built 1477–1528, it is an exquisite example of the Perpendicular style of *Gothic. Each knight of the Garter has his seat in the upper tier of stalls in the choir; above it hangs his banner. The chapel has been used as the burial place of monarchs during its own first century (Henry VI, Edward IV, Henry VIII with Jane Seymour) and in the 20C (Edward VII and Alexandra, George V and Mary). The vault beneath the choir also contains the bones of the beheaded Charles I. The most interesting of the monuments is that of an heir to the throne who died young, Princess Charlotte, the daughter of *George IV; in the Urswick Chapel her shrouded body is surrounded by veiled mourners in an extraordinary composition of marble drapery (by Matthew Cotes Wyatt, 1777–1862).

St George's Hospital Charity hospital established at London's Hyde Park Corner in 1733 by a splinter group from the *Westminster Hospital. It was rebuilt in the late 1820s by William Wilkins. In 1980 the hospital and its medical school moved to Tooting, in south London. The building at Hyde Park Corner was reopened in 1991 as the Lanesborough Hotel.

St Giles' Cathedral (Edinburgh) Gothic church of the 15C, in *Parliament Square, with a famous openwork structure (the Crown of St Giles) on top of its square tower. The building was dedicated to St Giles when a bone said to be from his arm was given in 1454; he was one of the most popular saints of the Middle Ages, the patron of cripples and believed to have been a French hermit, but nothing historical is known of him. John *Knox was the minister from 1559 until his death. The church is now incorrectly called a cathedral (the seat of a bishop), for it is the High Kirk of the *Church of the Scotland. Since the *Reformation it has only been a cathedral during two brief periods (1633–9 and 1660–90), when the Stuart kings imposed Anglican bishops on Scotland. It was in 1637 that Jenny Geddes, outraged at hearing a passage from the Anglican prayer book, flung her stool at the preacher; the spot from which she supposedly launched it is marked in the floor of the church. St Giles' contains many memorials to famous Scots, and in the southeast corner is the entrance to the Chapel of the *Thistle.

St Helena Island of volcanic origin in the south Atlantic, occupied from 1659 by the *East India Company as a port of call for their ships on the journey to and from the east. Ceded to the crown in 1834, it is now a British dependent territory. Its fame derives from the six years (1815–21) which Napoleon spent there, living and dying in Longwood (a house which survives) as a prisoner of the British after his defeat at Waterloo.

St Ives (10,000 in 1981) Resort on the north coast of Cornwall which has had strong artistic links since Bernard *Leach established his pottery here in 1920. Ben *Nicholson and Barbara *Hepworth arrived in 1939. Alfred Wallis (1855–1942), a retired rag-and-bone merchant of the town, was discovered to be painting naive images of ships, almost abstract in their simplicity; if this somewhat accidental group had any common artistic concern it was probably in this borderland between nature and abstraction. Barbara Hepworth's studio and garden are kept as a museum, and in 1993 a new gallery was opened in St Ives as an extension of the *Tate.

The choice of St Ives for the famous trick rhyme, known from at least the 18C, reflects nothing more than the need for a place to rhyme with 'wives':

> As I was going to St Ives,
> I met a man with seven wives,
> Each wife had seven sacks,
> Each sack had seven cats,
> Each cat had seven kits:
> Kits, cats, sacks and wives,
> How many were going to St Ives?

The answer is one, since 'met' is taken to mean that the man and his multitude of sevens were going in the opposite direction. 'None' has also been a traditional answer, limiting the question to the group being met.

St James's Hospital see *Jimmy's.

St James's Palace (London SW1) Redbrick Tudor palace lying between St James's Street and St James's Park. It was built by Henry VIII on the site of a convent which he had closed in 1532 (it had earlier been a leper hospital dedicated to St James the Less). The main unaltered part of his palace is the gatehouse at the bottom of St James's Street. After the destruction of *Whitehall Palace by fire in 1698, St James's became the official residence of the sovereign. It remains so today, with foreign diplomats accredited to the *Court of St James's, even though the actual royal residence in London has been *Buckingham Palace since Victoria's accession in 1837.

St James's Park (London SW1) Extensive landscaped gardens in front of Buckingham Palace, running almost the entire length of the Mall. This has always been the nearest open space to the royal palaces of central London, whether Whitehall, St James's or Buckingham. Since the reign of Charles II there has been a lake, as now, with a great variety of waterfowl.

Saint Joan (1923) Play by George Bernard *Shaw, first produced in New York in 1923 and in London the following year with Sybil Thorndike in the title role. It follows the inspirational career of Joan of Arc (who had been canonized only recently, in 1920) from her peasant beginnings, through her victories in battle against the English (in the *Hundred Years' War), to her capture, trial and execution. The 67-year-old playwright, who could argue any case by the agility of his intellect, was so inspired by his young illiterate teenage heroine, who could argue only one case by strength of conviction and by earthy commonsense, that he wrote his most powerful play, containing much forceful argument within a rich weave of comedy and tragedy.

St John Ambulance Brigade (London EC1) Charitable organization which provides volunteers, trained in first aid, to attend public events in Britain; the tradition began with Victoria's Golden Jubilee in 1887. The Brigade derives from the Order of the Hospital of St John of Jerusalem, which nursed pilgrims and crusaders to the Holy Land. The Knights Hospitaller, as they were known, retreated later to Rhodes (1309–1522) and then to Malta (1530–1798). They had an English branch from the 12C until it was suppressed by Henry VIII in 1540. An Order of St John was revived in Britain in the early 19C. It was this body which in 1877 set up the St John Ambulance Association (which still provides first-aid training for the public) and followed this in 1887 with the Brigade.

St John's, Smith Square see *Smith Square.

St Katharine's Dock (London E1) The furthest upstream of London's docks, designed by Thomas *Telford and constructed in 1826–8 on the north bank of the river near the Tower of London. In 1968 it was closed down as a working dock. It is now home to a collection of historic ships.

St Kilda Group of four islands, the most westerly point of the United Kingdom (72km/45m W of Lewis with Harris) and the first place in Scotland to be designated (in 1987) a UNESCO world heritage site. It has spectacular cliff scenery, a thriving colony of sea birds and some distinctive local mammals (including the sheep of the island of Soay). The St Kilda wren is a distinct sub-species, larger and greyer than the more familiar wren. The main island, Hirta, was occupied from prehistoric times until 1930, when the last 35 inhabitants left.

St **Kitts-Nevis** (more formally St Christopher and Nevis) Member of the *Commonwealth since independence in 1983, consisting of two islands in the eastern Caribbean. Christopher Columbus discovered St Christopher in 1493 and named it after his patron saint. Settlers arriving there in 1623 made it the earliest British colony in the Caribbean (it was they who shortened the name to St Kitts), but the French were not far behind, in 1627. Eventually the island was ceded by France to the British under the treaty of Utrecht in 1713. Nevis, just 3km/2m southeast of St Kitts, was settled by the British in 1682.

In 1882 St Kitts was grouped with Nevis and *Anguilla, and in 1967 the three islands were jointly granted semi-independent statehood in association with Britain. Three months later Anguilla dissociated itself from the others, reverting to the status of a British dependent territory.

St Leger The oldest of the five *Classics and the last in the season (run on a Saturday in September at Doncaster). It is for 3-year-old colts and fillies, nowadays over 2.8km/1.75m. Founded in 1776 by Colonel Barry St Leger (1737–89), it was an innovation in two respects; it was unusual at the time to race 3-year-olds, and most races were not in a single sprint like this (which later became standard) but in a succession of heats over a longer aggregate distance.

St Lucia One of the Windward Islands in the Caribbean and a member of the *Commonwealth since 1979. Visited by Columbus in 1502, it was constantly fought over by the British and French during the 17–18C until being ceded to the British in 1814 by the treaty of Paris. It became independent in 1979.

St Margaret's Westminster (London SW1) Church, mainly of the early 16C, which nestles beneath the walls of Westminster Abbey. It has been been regarded since 1614 as the parish church of the House of Commons.

St Martin-in-the-Fields (London WC2) Church built 1722–6 to the design of James *Gibbs. Its interior, with balconies along each side, and its pillared classical portico set in front of a tall steeple were details much copied elsewhere, particularly in America. The first church service to be broadcast on radio came from here in 1924, and this was the original home of the *Academy of St Martin-in-the-Fields. The church was also responsible for St Martin's *art school.

St Mary-le-Bow see *Bow Bells.

St Mary Redcliffe see *Bristol.

St Mary's see *Scilly Isles.

St Michael's Mount Island off the south coast of Cornwall, joined at low tide by a causeway to the village of Marazion. In 1070 it was granted to the Benedictine monks of Mont St Michel, an even more precipitous island off the coast of Normandy. Since 1647 the St Aubyn family have lived on the island, turning the priory buildings (which date back to the 14C) into the present castle-like house on top of the rock.

St Pancras One of London's main railway termini for trains to the north. The station, with an exceptionally broad span and high roof, was built in 1863–7 for the Great Northern Railway, to the design of William Henry Barlow (1812–1902). The Midland Grand Hotel, one of the most striking of London's Victorian buildings, was built in 1868–72 by George Gilbert *Scott. It closed as a hotel in 1935 and was used as railway offices, but in the 1990s British Rail undertook a major programme to restore it as a five-star hotel. The station, like the surrounding district, takes its name from that of a nearby church of St Pancras, an early 4C Roman martyr. He became part of British tradition after St *Augustine dedicated a church to him in Canterbury.

St Paul's Cathedral (London EC4) The present St Paul's is the fifth on the site. The first was founded in 604. The fourth, begun in the late 11C, was the one known now as Old St Paul's. Destroyed in the *Great Fire, it was considerably larger and taller than the present cathedral. This, the outstanding example of English *baroque, was built 1675–1710 to the design of Sir Christopher *Wren. Both Nelson and Wellington are buried in the cathedral, as well as Wren himself – whose famous epitaph *Si monumentum requiris, circumspice* (Latin for 'If you seek his monument,

The dome of St Paul's Cathedral, with scenes of St Paul by James Thornhill above the Whispering Gallery.

look about you') is attributed to his son. The walkway round the base of the dome, known as the Whispering Gallery, has long been famous for its acoustics; even a whispered word uttered close to the wall sounds clear to someone on the far side. One of the treasures of the cathedral is the Great Wooden Model (5.5m/18ft long), a version of Wren's proposed design made for him in 1673 and complete in even the tiniest details.

St Paul's, Covent Garden see *Covent Garden.

St Paul's School A *public school for boys was founded in 1509 by the dean of St Paul's Cathedral, John Colet. It stood in St Paul's Churchyard and was burnt, with the old cathedral, in the Great Fire of 1666. Two subsequent buildings housed the school on the same site, until it moved in 1884 to Hammersmith and then again, in 1968, to new premises in Barnes.

By the late 19c the funds of the Dean Colet Foundation had grown sufficiently for the trustees to build a girl's school. This opened in 1904 in Hammersmith as the St Paul's Girls' School, and rapidly acquired a high academic reputation.

St Peter's School see *York.

St Thomas's Hospital (London SE1) One of the two oldest hospitals in London (the other is *Bart's). It may have been founded as early as 1106, as part of a priory in Southwark. After the canonization of *Becket in 1173 it became the hospital of St Thomas the Martyr, but with the Reformation the patron saint was changed to St Thomas the Apostle. From the early 13c the hospital occupied a site on which *Guy's later became its neighbour; but in 1859 this was sold (to become London Bridge railway station) and St Thomas's moved to a riverside position on the opposite bank from the Houses of Parliament. Florence *Nightingale advised on the new building (1868–71) and set up in the hospital a school for nurses; those trained at

St Thomas's are still known as Nightingales. A report published in 1992 recommended that St Thomas's and Guy's should be merged, freeing the premises of one or the other.

St Trinian's see Ronald *Searle.

St Vincent and the Grenadines A group of the Windward Islands in the Caribbean which together have been a member of the *Commonwealth since 1979. St Vincent was visited by Columbus in 1498, and was claimed by both Britain and France in the 17–18c until being ceded to the British in 1763 at the end of the Seven Years' War. St Vincent and the Grenadines became independent in 1979.

Saki (pen name of Hector Hugh Munro, 1870–1916) Author of witty and cold-hearted short stories. The first of several volumes (*Reginald* 1904) contains the line most often quoted as an example of Saki's verbal dexterity: 'The cook was a good cook, as cooks go; and as cooks go she went.' He enlisted as a trooper in World War I (though much older than most) and was killed in the trenches. The choice of Saki as his pseudonym has not been explained, but the name appears in the final verse of *Omar Khayyám.

Salamanca see *Peninsular War.

Salford (98,000 in 1981) City in Greater Manchester, separated from Manchester only by the narrow river Irwell and indistinguishable on the ground from its larger neighbour. Its long-standing importance as a cotton town was greatly increased by the opening in 1894 of the *Manchester Ship Canal, on which it has extensive docks. It was given the status of a city in 1926. In recent times it has been best known for its link with L.S. *Lowry.

Salic Law Legal system of the 6c Salian Franks, which included a clause that daughters cannot inherit land. In 14c France this was quoted as the authority for a new restriction on women, preventing their succession to the throne. This late version of the Salic Law became accepted in many European kingdoms, though never in Britain. Victoria was therefore able to inherit the British crown in 1837 but not that of *Hanover.

Salisbury (35,000 in 1981) Cathedral town in Wiltshire, on the river Avon, with views over the meadows which have attracted many artists, most notably *Constable. The original settlement was at Old *Sarum, now an abandoned site just to the north of the town. Here an Iron Age hill fort was successively adapted by Romans, Anglo-Saxons and finally Normans, who in the 11c built a castle and a cathedral side by side. Friction between the two caused the bishop to move a little way south and to start the present cathedral in 1220. The body of the church, in the Early English style, was complete by 1258; the tower and spire (at 123m/404ft by far the tallest in the country) were added some 50 years later. The interior has been much tidied up in successive restorations, starting with that of *Wyatt, but it retains one very popular medieval detail – Britain's earliest clock mechanism, dating back to the 1380s and still working (it never had a clock face, its purpose being only to ring a bell in the tower). The Salisbury and South Wiltshire Museum contains all the finds from nearby *Stonehenge. Over the centuries Old Sarum faded to nothing, being remembered now as the most rotten of all rotten *boroughs.

Lord **Salisbury** (Robert Gascoyne-Cecil, 1830–1903, 3rd marquess of Salisbury 1868) Conservative politician, prime minister 1885–6, 1886–92 and 1895–1902, and the last to hold that office in the House of Lords. His first important political initiative was as foreign secretary (1878–80), when he played a major part (with Disraeli) in securing international agreement at the congress of Berlin (1878), defusing, albeit temporarily, the *Eastern Question. Foreign affairs remained Salisbury's main interest, and for the greater part of each of his three administrations he acted as his own foreign secretary. The great issue of the time was the expansion of empire, with European nations jockeying for territory in distant regions, particularly in Africa (see *British Empire). Salisbury gave strong support to colonial entrepreneurs, such as Cecil *Rhodes. His policy was that territories should be divided up into established spheres of national influence, agreed after tough negotiations between the European powers. His most far-reaching domestic legislation was the Local Government Act of 1888, which established county councils throughout England and Wales and the London County Council for the capital.

Salisbury Plain Large area of chalk downland (about 500sq.km/200sq.m), lying to the north and west of Salisbury and containing *Stonehenge. In recent decades it has been used for military ranges and encampments, a restriction paradoxically of great benefit to the local fauna and flora.

Sally Bowles see Christopher *Isherwood.

Sally in our Alley Song with words and music by Henry Carey (c.1690–1743), about an apprentice who is in love with a girl living in the same alley. He dreams of the day when the seven long years of his apprenticeship are done:
> And then we'll wed and then we'll bed,
> But not in our alley.

Sally Lunn Sponge tea-cake, usually served warm and buttered. Sally Lunns were a speciality of fashionable *Bath in the 18C; the earliest known reference (1780) describes them as 'spungy hot rolls'. The traditional explanation of the name was first printed in 1827, stating that Sally Lunn, a young woman of Bath, sold these cakes as a street-vendor until her recipe was taken up by one of the town's bakers.

salmonella see Edwina *Currie.

Johann Peter **Salomon** see *London Symphonies.

Titus **Salt** see *Saltaire.

Saltaire (8km/5m NW of Bradford) Model industrial village on the river Aire built between 1851 and 1872 by Titus Salt (1803–76, bt 1869) to house the workers for his spinning and weaving mills. It was a consciously paternalistic venture, with decent housing in a country setting, provision for education, health and worship, and no public house. The buildings survive virtually unchanged.

Mr **Salteena** see The *Young Visiters.

Saltram House (5km/3m E of Plymouth) House remodelled in the 1740s by an unknown architect for John Parker, who commissioned Robert *Adam to create the magnificent saloon (1768–71) and a library which Adam later converted to the present dining room (1781). Parker also gathered an excellent collection of paintings, including about a dozen by Reynolds, which are still in the house.

Salvation Army Evangelical Christian organization, now worldwide in scope, which evolved from the missionary work in the East End of London of William Booth (1829–1912), who had previously been a Methodist preacher. The name Salvation Army, adopted in 1878, reflected the fact that the mission was organized on military lines, with uniforms, brass bands to attract attention on the streets, and a hierarchy of ranks. Booth himself was the general

The dominant feature on Salisbury plain for at least the past 4000 years: the brooding mystery of Stonehenge.

and after his death was followed in that position by his son, William Bramwell Booth (1856–1929). Popular evangelism has remained the central purpose, with deliberately simple and cheerful services (much clapping and singing, no sacraments), but the 'Sally' also plays an important role in alleviating poverty and distress in the cities. The army's crusading publication, *The War Cry*, has been published weekly since 1879.

Samaritans (Slough, Berkshire) Organization set up to prevent suicide, by befriending and listening to the suicidal. It was established in 1953 by Chad Varah (b. 1911) with financial help from the Grocers' Company (one of the *City Livery Companies), which in that year had appointed him rector of St Stephen Walbrook. The work is largely done on the telephone, and by the early 1990s there were some 22,000 volunteers spending part of their time in more than 180 branches round the country, taking calls from those in need of reassurance.

Sam Browne Shiny leather belt worn by officers in the army and the police, with a strap passing from the left side (from which a sword hangs on ceremonial occasions) up and over the right shoulder. It is named after Samuel Browne (1824–1901), a general in the Indian army who designed it.

Samhain see *Hallowe'en.

Samson Agonistes (1671) Poetic drama by *Milton, similar to a Greek tragedy in the intensity with which it fills a narrow canvas. The action is limited to the final days of Samson, captive of the Philistines, who describes himself as 'eyeless in Gaza at the mill with slaves' (many have seen a parallel with the blind author himself, out of step in a society that had reverted to royalist rule with the *Restoration). During the drama Samson moves from self-pity to a new sense of strength and mission, which enables him to bring the hall of the Philistines crashing down.

Samuel French Publishers of acting editions of plays, whose products have long been an indispensable part of the amateur theatre in English-speaking countries. The British firm derives from a publishing house set up in London in 1830 by an actor, Thomas Lacy. In 1872 his business was bought by Samuel French, who moved to London in that year after establishing (from 1854) a similar enterprise in New York. The firm of Samuel French still has separate British and American branches.

Paul Sandby (1730–1809) Artist who was the first major figure in the British tradition of landscape *watercolours and the first to publish aquatints (beginning with views of Wales in 1775). With its ability to achieve the effect of a tonal wash, aquatint chimed perfectly with the fashion for watercolours and provided over the next half century the most attractive form of British topographical print.

Tessa Sanderson (b. 1956) Javelin-thrower who competed in five successive Olympic Games from 1976 to 1992. She won the gold medal in 1984 (the year in which Fatima *Whitbread took the bronze), and she won gold also in three Commonwealth Games (1978, 86, 90). She was much in the news in 1990 when she won libel damages of £30,000 against the *Sunday Mirror* and the *People* for printing allegations by Jewel Evans that Sanderson had stolen her husband.

Sandham Memorial Chapel see *Burghclere.

Sandhurst Village in Berkshire, location of the Royal Military Academy where officers are trained for the army.

Founded in 1799 as the Royal Military College, it merged in 1946 with the original Royal Military Academy (established at *Woolwich in 1741).

Sandown Park (24km/15m SW of central London) Racecourse opened in 1875 and unusual in that both flat and jumping races of top quality are run there. The highlight of the season is the April meeting, popularly known as the Whitbread meeting. The Whitbread Gold Cup, a steeplechase of 3 miles 5 furlongs (5.8km), was established in 1957 and was one of the first examples in Britain of the commercial sponsorship of sport. The important race of the July meeting is the Eclipse Stakes, a flat race for 3-year-olds and upwards over 1 mile 2 furlongs (2km); it was first run in 1886.

Sandringham (13km/8m NE of King's Lynn) The most informal of the queen's residences in England, being essentially a large country estate. It was bought for the prince of Wales, the future Edward VII, in 1861. In 1870 he replaced an existing building with the present Sandringham House, designed in a neo-Jacobean style by A.J. Humbert (1822–77).

sandwich In use since *c.*1760 for a slice of meat (or later any other filling) eaten between two pieces of bread. It is named after the 4th earl of Sandwich (1718–92), who is said to have devised it as a convenient way of eating without having to leave the gaming table.

Sandwich The name commonly used for the Royal St George's golf course, near Sandwich in Kent, which became in 1894 the location for the first *Open played outside Scotland. It was then only a few years old; the site had been chosen in 1887 by an Edinburgh player for its similarity to the links with which he was familiar at home. Sandwich has remained one of the regular courses for the Open.

Frederick Sanger (b. 1918) Biochemist and the only British scientist to have won two Nobel prizes. The first, in 1958, was for his work in establishing the sequence of 51 amino acids in insulin. The second, shared in 1980, was for the infinitely more complex analysis of the chains forming nucleic acids. Carried out with his team in Cambridge (where the secret of *DNA had earlier been discovered), this work laid the basis for the techniques of genetic engineering. He is a member of the Order of *Merit.

Santa Claus see *Father Christmas.

Sapper see *Bull-dog Drummond.

Saratoga see War of *American Independence.

Sarawak One of the states of *Malaysia, on the northwest coast of Borneo. For a century, from 1841, it was ruled by the family of Raja *Brooke. Occupied by the Japanese in 1942–5, it became a British crown colony in 1946 and joined the new federation of Malaysia in 1963.

John Singer Sargent (1856–1925) American artist based from 1884 in London, where he rapidly became the most fashionable portrait painter, with an easy elegance of style which perfectly matched the requirements of his sitters. After 1907 he declined almost every commission, spending each summer painting watercolours in Italy and the Alps and working in the winter on two large series of murals in the USA (in Boston). During a brief period as a war artist in World War I he produced the large and powerful *Gassed* (1918–19, Imperial War Museum).

Malcolm **Sargent** (1895–1967, kt 1947) Conductor who was perhaps the best known of his generation in Britain, partly because he conducted a large number of choral societies up and down the country, but also as the principal conductor of the *Proms from Wood's death in 1944 until his own. He was also famously svelte and had a reputation as a conversationalist, appearing as a guest on the wartime *Brains Trust*.

Sark see *Channel Islands.

Sarum Medieval Latin name for *Salisbury, probably an abbreviation of the older *Sarisburia*. It is still used in ecclesiastical contexts and in the place name of Old Sarum (see *borough); the present city is in these terms New Sarum.

SAS (Special Air Service) Commando unit formed in North Africa in 1941 by a Scots Guards officer, David Stirling (1915–90), with a special brief to operate behind enemy lines. In peace time their skills were turned to undercover and counter-terrorist activities. Their efficiency greatly impressed the British public in 1980, when an SAS team was seen on television storming the Iranian embassy in London. Six gunmen, demanding the release of Arab prisoners in Iran, had held the staff hostage for six days and killed two of them; neither the SAS nor the hostages suffered casualties during the rescue, but five of the terrorists were killed. More controversial was the SAS shooting of three IRA terrorists in 1988 in Gibraltar (see *Death on the Rock*). Since 1942 the SAS badge has carried the motto 'Who Dares Wins'.

sash windows An essential element in the rectilinear façades of *Georgian houses, which themselves are the most characteristic and lasting strand in English domestic architecture. Developed first in 17c Holland, this type of window became increasingly popular in Britain after the arrival of *William III. The sash is a frame (from the French *chassis*), and each window consists of two sashes, set one behind the other, which ride up and down within grooves at the side, counterbalanced by weights concealed within the wall.

Sassenach The Scottish word for an Englishman, or occasionally a Lowland Scot. Commonly used in a derogatory sense, it derives from the *Gaelic word for the unwelcome *Saxons.

Siegfried **Sassoon** (1886–1967) Author who acquired notoriety in World War I by winning an MC in the trenches and then throwing it away after his experiences had made him a pacifist. Sent to a hospital near Edinburgh as mentally ill, he met and influenced Wilfred *Owen. His own ferociously bleak war poems were published in two volumes (1917, 1918). *The Memoirs of a Fox-Hunting Man* (1928) was the first of a series of autobiographical novels with 'George Sherston' as the central character.

satanic abuse see *child abuse.

The **Satanic Verses** see Salman *Rushdie.

Saturday Night and Sunday Morning (1958) The first novel of Alan *Sillitoe, about an anarchic beer-swilling young Nottingham factory worker, Arthur Seaton, who is in a state of half-humorous rage against everyone around him – except, from time to time, the married woman with whom he has an affair. It was brilliantly filmed by Karel Reisz in 1960 with Albert Finney as Arthur and Rachel Roberts as Brenda, the married woman.

Sauchiehall Street see *Glasgow.

'savaged by a dead sheep' A phrase which caught the public's fancy after the chancellor of the exchequer, Denis Healey, had been attacked in 1978 in a speech by Geoffrey Howe; he described the experience as 'rather like being savaged by a dead sheep'.

Thomas **Savery** see *steam.

Save the Children (London SE5) The charity had its beginnings in the distress of an English woman, Eglantyne Jebb, when she saw children starving in Austria in 1919 in the aftermath of World War I. The public response to her appeal for them was such that relief work was almost immediately extended to other countries. Children in Britain were included from 1926, originally to cope with the suffering caused by the General Strike. A declaration of *The Rights of the Child*, drafted by Miss Jebb in 1923, was later incorporated as part of the United Nations charter. Since 1970 the charity has had a very committed president in the *Princess Royal, and it now has health, education and welfare programmes in more than 50 countries.

Jimmy **Savile** (b. 1926, kt 1990) Disc jockey who made his name in the 1960s on Radio Luxembourg before moving to Radio 1 in 1968. His television show *Jim'll Fix It* (BBC from 1975) reaches a large audience by arranging often elaborate wish fulfilments for children. He is a tireless fund-raiser and publicist for three hospitals (Stoke Mandeville, Broadmoor and Leeds Infirmary). In the interests of his good causes he runs a great many marathons and half-marathons (more than 200 by 1992), often hampered by eye-catching but far from aerodynamic costumes.

Savill Garden (8km/5m S of Windsor) Part of Windsor Great Park, turned in the 1930s into a 14ha/35ac garden by the deputy ranger of the park, Eric Savill (1895–1980). The emphasis is on woody plants, notably magnolias and rhododendrons.

savings The British have traditionally kept their savings with a *building society or in a Post Office savings account (now called *National Savings); the latter is money on loan to the government, at fixed rates of interest in a variety of schemes, which can be deposited or withdrawn at any post office or high-street bank. A savings scheme in the form of a lottery was introduced in 1956 as *premium bonds. A recent government attempt to encourage saving is the tax-exempt special savings account (Tessa), introduced in January 1991. Under its terms money may be saved with a bank or building society up to a maximum of £9000 over a five-year period; the interest, most of which can be taken out as it is earned, remains tax free as long as none of the capital is withdrawn from the Tessa before the end of the five years.

Savoy Hotel (London WC2) Built in 1884–9 by Richard *D'Oyly Carte as an adjunct to his *Savoy Theatre, and designed by T.E. Colcutt (1840–1924). Beginning in great style (César Ritz was the original manager, Auguste Escoffier the first chef), the hotel has retained its position as one of the grandest in London, situated with superb views (painted by *Monet) up and down the Thames.

Savoy operas Name given to the operettas of *Gilbert and *Sullivan, performed (from 1881) at the *Savoy Theatre. The librettist and composer had collaborated ineffectively in 1871 on *Thespis*, and their run of extraordinary successes began only when *D'Oyly Carte

Savoy opera poster using Oscar Wilde, whose trademark was a lily, to identify the satirical targets of Patience.

brought them together for *Trial by Jury* (1875); it continued with *The Sorcerer* (1877), *HMS Pinafore* (1878), *The Pirates of Penzance* (1880), *Patience* (1881), *Iolanthe* (1882), *Princess Ida* (1884), *The Mikado* (1885), *Ruddigore* (1887), *The Yeomen of the Guard* (1888) and *The Gondoliers* (1889).

At this point Gilbert and Sullivan fell out over a business dispute. When they resumed their collaboration, the results were less impressive (*Utopia Limited* 1893, *The Grand Duke* 1896). But in their heyday they had created something distinctively their own – witty and tuneful works, laced with contemporary references, which acquired the status almost of national treasures. Until the 1960s the D'Oyly Carte company maintained a monopoly on professional productions, presenting the operettas in a somewhat fossilized style. More imaginative interpretations, made possible by the lapse of copyright, have in recent years provided a new lease of life.

Savoy Theatre (London WC2) Built by Richard *D'Oyly Carte in 1881 with profits from Gilbert and Sullivan operettas, known later as the *Savoy operas. The name derived from the medieval Savoy Palace which stood here (the land was owned in the 13C by the count of Savoy). The theatre was the first public building in the world to be lit by electricity. A major reconstruction in 1929 gave it a magnificent Art Deco interior, destroyed when the theatre was gutted by fire in 1990 but restored by 1993.

House of Saxe-Coburg & Gotha (1901–1917) The name until World War I of the present ruling family in Britain. It was the royal house of *Albert, prince consort of Queen Victoria, and therefore also of his eldest son,

Edward VII, and of his grandson, George V. But anti-German feelings caused George V in 1917 to change the name of the royal house to *Windsor.

Saxons One of the three main Germanic tribes which together became known as the *Anglo-Saxons. Coming from the area that is now northwest Germany, they invaded England during the 5–6C and settled from the Midlands down to the south coast.

Dorothy **Sayers** (1893–1957) Writer of detective fiction and creator of the elegant amateur detective Lord Peter Wimsey, who first appeared, with his manservant Bunter, in *Whose Body?* (1923). In *Strong Poison* (1930) Wimsey cleared Harriet Vane, a female writer of detective stories, of a charge of murder; he also fell in love with her, and in *Busman's Honeymoon* (1937) they married. With this their creator brought to an end their careers, and her own as an author of detective fiction. Her later work included a radio play about the life of Christ (*The Man Born to be King*, broadcast at monthly intervals in 1941–2) and translations of Dante's *Inferno* (1949) and *Purgatorio* (1955).

Scafell Pike Peak in the *Lake District which is the highest point in England (978m/3210ft). In the same range, just to the southwest, is another peak called simply Scafell (964m/3162ft).

Prunella **Scales** Actress who has created a wide range of successful roles in comedy. Best known is Sybil Fawlty, Basil's strict wife in *Fawlty Towers* (1975–9), but almost equally celebrated is her subtle portrayal of the queen in Alan *Bennett's *A Question of Attribution* (1991). In *After Henry* (1985–91), on both radio and TV, she played a young widow caught in a generation war between a scheming old mother and a wilful teenage daughter. She is married to Timothy *West.

Scapa Flow Anchorage of about 24km/15m by 13km/8m, formed by a ring of the larger islands of the *Orkneys. It was the main base of the British fleet in both world wars. In 1919 the German High Sea Fleet, interned here and awaiting a decision on its fate, was scuttled by its skeleton crews. Early in World War II a U-boat penetrated Scapa Flow and sank the battleship *Royal Oak* with a loss of 833 lives on 14 October 1939 – a disaster which led to the construction of a much more elaborate defensive system. Scapa Flow was closed as a base in 1956.

The Scapegoat (1854–5, Lady Lever Art Gallery) Painting by Holman *Hunt, widely remembered for its surreal strangeness. It shows in immaculate detail a long-haired white goat staggering across a parched and salt-caked landscape, empty except for the bones of the animal's predecessors. The scene illustrates *Leviticus* 16, in which a goat is sent to die in the wilderness bearing the sins of mankind. To achieve an authentic effect, Hunt spent several months painting near the Dead Sea. A smaller version, in more lurid colours, is in.the Manchester City Art Gallery.

Scarborough (43,000 in 1981) Resort in North Yorkshire, popular as a spa town from the 17C and one of the first places to cater for the new fad for sea bathing in the 18C. There are two sandy bays either side of a rocky hill crowned by the ruins of a 12C castle. The extensive facilities have also made the town a popular conference location out of season. The very grand Grand Hotel (1860s) is by Cuthbert Brodrick, architect of the town hall in *Leeds.

Gerald **Scarfe** (b. 1936) Political cartoonist (mainly for the *Sunday Times*, from 1967), whose savagery is expressed in grotesquely distorted and angular images. He has created several animated films and has designed for the stage – notably *Orpheus in the Underworld* for English National Opera in 1985.

Arthur **Scargill** (b. 1938) President of the *NUM since 1981 and the trade union leader best known to the public during the past decade, because of his high profile during the *miners' strike of 1984–5 (he had first attracted attention as an organizer of flying pickets during the dispute of 1972). His persistent warnings of accelerating pit closures, often dismissed as scaremongering in the mid-1980s, have been amply justified by events; but his hectoring style, air of self-importance and love of left-wing jargon did disservice to his cause. He was much in the news again in 1990 when his own union took legal action against him over the whereabouts of a large sum of money donated to the NUM by Soviet miners during the strike; the action was dropped when the money was handed over by the International Miners' Organization, a group in Paris with which he was involved. Late in 1992 he found himself enjoying an unprecedented level of public support in the general outcry against the government's plans for pit closures (see *coal).

The **Scarlet Pimpernel** (1905) Historical romance by Baroness *Orczy, about the League of the Scarlet Pimpernel – a band of Englishmen, headed by Sir Percy Blakeney, who rescue aristocrats from the guillotine during the French Revolution. The story had succeeded as a play, adapted by Orczy herself from her much rejected manuscript, before a publisher was found for the original novel. Blakeney, a genius at disguise, baffles French and English alike:

> We seek him here, we seek him there,
> Those Frenchies seek him everywhere.
> Is he in heaven? – Is he in hell?
> That demmed, elusive Pimpernel?

The book was very successfully filmed by Alexander *Korda in 1934, with Leslie Howard in the role of the Pimpernel.

Lord **Scarman** (Leslie George Scarman, b. 1911, kt 1961, baron 1977) Judge who has been a prominent campaigner for both legal and constitutional reform. His report of 1981 was the first official response to the problems of the *inner cities.

SCE see *exams.

'sceptred isle' see *'precious stone set in the silver sea'.

School Certificate An *exam replaced in 1951 by the O level.

The **School for Scandal** (1777) Comedy by *Sheridan in which the title relates to the malicious gossiping salon presided over by the young Lady Teazle, with Lady Sneerwell as a star performer. The plot centres on two brothers, Charles and Joseph Surface. Charles is good-hearted but recklessly extravagant, whereas Joseph is a model of good behaviour and a hypocrite; both are courting Maria, Charles for love and Joseph for her money. Their real characters are revealed when their rich uncle, Sir Oliver Surface, arrives from India and disguises himself to test them. The comic climax of the play is the 'screen scene', in which Joseph's attempt to seduce Lady Teazle involves him in a farcical sequence of concealment, false explanations and ultimate embarrassment.

schools see *state school, *public school and *education.

Schweppes see *Cadbury Schweppes.

Schweppes Welsh Cup see *rugby football.

Science Museum (London SW7) The national museum of science and technology, which began as part of the wide-ranging collections of the *Victoria and Albert Museum. It became independent as the Science Museum in 1909, and in 1928 moved into its present building (architect Richard Allison, 1869–1958) on the opposite side of Exhibition Road from the V&A.

The view towards Scafell Pike across the Esk valley, from close to Hardknott Fort.

The exhibition halls contain many of the milestones of British technology – *Puffing Billy, for example, and a factory steam engine of 1788 by *Boulton and Watt – but there is also increasing emphasis on interactive displays, through which visitors can become involved in a scientific or technological process. Launch Pad, a pioneering children's gallery of this kind, was introduced in 1986, followed by Flight Lab in 1991; by the early 1990s there were more than 800 'hands-on' exhibits. The museum is the centre of the newly formed National Museum of Science and Industry, a grouping which includes the *National Museum of Photography, Film and Television in Bradford and the *National Railway Museum in York.

Scilly Isles (also known as the Scillies, 2000 in 1991) Group of about 140 rocky islands and islets, lying approximately 45km/28m southwest of *Land's End. Legend says that they are the only part of *Lyonesse remaining above the sea. Five islands are inhabited – St Agnes, Bryher, *Tresco, St Martin's and the largest, St Mary's, on which the majority live and which contains the capital, Hugh Town. An exceptionally mild climate (because of the *Gulf Stream) has enabled the Scillies to supply winter and spring flowers to the British market. The local fauna and flora, in several cases unique in Britain, have given the islands the status of a nature reserve. The granite reef of which they are a part makes this a treacherous region for shipping; the first lighthouse was constructed with great difficulty in 1858 on Bishop Rock, about 7km/4m to the southwest of St Agnes.

Paul **Scofield** (b. 1922) Actor who made his name in the postwar years in leading roles at Stratford-upon-Avon, including a famous Hamlet of 1948 (a role he repeated in Moscow in 1955, with the first English theatre company to visit Russia since the revolution). A long West End run in Anouilh's *Ring Round the Moon* (1950) was followed a decade later by his best-known role, both on stage and film – that of Thomas More in A *Man For All Seasons* (1960). The film brought him an Oscar.

scone Small round bun, with a brown top and white sides, made from a flaky dough with relatively little fat. Broken in half, and spread with butter, jam and cream, it is an essential ingredient of a *cream tea. By contrast a drop scone, also eaten at tea with butter and jam, is made from batter and is in effect a small thick pancake (an alternative name for it is a Scotch pancake).

Scone (pron. *Scoon*, 3km/2m N of Perth) The most important site in Scottish royal history. The Stone of Scone, a rectangular slab of reddish-grey sandstone also known as the Stone of Destiny, is traditionally believed to have been the stone which Jacob took for a pillow (*Genesis* 28); the story continues that it was used as a coronation throne in Ireland in the 6c and so came with the *Scots to Scotland. It enters the realms of history with the probability that it was brought to Scone, a Pictish centre, by *Kenneth I in the 9c in a gesture uniting the Picts and Scots under his rule. It was used for Scottish coronations until seized in 1296 by *Edward I, who made it the centrepiece of the *Coronation Chair in Westminster Abbey. On Christmas Eve 1950 it was taken from there as a Scottish nationalist gesture by four students from Glasgow university. It was returned in 1952.

There was an Augustinian abbey at Scone from the 11c, but it was destroyed in the Reformation. In its place is Scone Palace, a large castellated house of the *Gothic Revival, mainly dating from 1802–13 and designed by William Atkinson (*c*.1773–1839). It has fine interiors and contents.

Scoop (1938) Novel by Evelyn *Waugh about Fleet Street which has become the classic of its kind and has introduced to the language Lord Copper, proprietor of the *Beast*. He stands, somewhat like *Beaverbrook, for 'self-sufficiency at home, self-assertion abroad'. Mr Salter, the foreign editor, has developed a safe response to any totally inaccurate assertion by his employer; 'Up to a point, Lord Copper' he murmurs in reply. The comedy, of journalists competing to scoop each other in Africa, begins with mistaken identity. Julia Stitch has persuaded Lord Copper to send her young protégé, John Boot, to cover a local war. Copper tells Salter to fix it, but he mistakenly employs William Boot, nature correspondent on the *Beast*. William's style is typified in the sentence, 'Feather-footed through the plashy fens passes the questing vole'.

Scotch Historically the more usual form of the word 'Scottish', both in England and Scotland. A more recent tradition in Scotland is that the word should only be used of Scotch whisky. Scottish is now considered the only proper adjective for anything else from Scotland, and 'the Scots' the correct term for the people themselves.

Scotch broth A soup of beef or lamb stock thickened with vegetables and pearl barley.

Scotch egg A hard-boiled egg, encased in a layer of sausage meat, covered with breadcrumbs and deep fried. It is eaten cold.

Scotch pancake see *scone.

Scotland (land area 77,097sq.km/29,767sq.m, population 5 million in 1991) The mainland of *Great Britain north of a line from the Solway Firth in the west to the mouth of the Tweed on the east, together with three major island groups, the Hebrides, Orkneys and Shetlands. The mainland was to a large extent unified by the *Scots in the 9c; the islands remained for several more centuries under Scandinavian control. Edinburgh emerged as the capital city in the mid-15c. Scotland became linked with England in two stages, by the *union of the crowns in 1603 and the Act of *Union in 1707. Since 1885 the country has been administered by the *Scottish Office. In recent decades there has been fluctuating pressure for *devolution.

Scotland on Sunday see the *Scotsman*.

Scotland the brave A traditional tune to which new words were written in the 1950s by a Glasgow journalist, Cliff Hanley (b. 1922). For some years it was almost the unofficial Scottish anthem, sung by the crowd on sporting occasions, but it has been edged out by *Flower of Scotland*.

New **Scotland Yard** (London SW1) Headquarters of the Metropolitan *Police since 1967, just off Victoria Street. The name Scotland Yard is that of their previous building, designed by Norman *Shaw, on the north bank of the Thames just downstream from Westminster Bridge (it is now called the Norman Shaw Building and provides offices for members of parliament). The area was known as Scotland Yard from the Middle Ages because lodgings in this part of *Whitehall Palace were used by representatives of the Scottish crown.

Scotney Castle (14km/9m SE of Tunbridge Wells) Romantic garden making the most of water, a rocky quarry and the remains of a small medieval castle. It was designed from 1835 by William Sawrey Gilpin, nephew of the pioneer of the *picturesque.

Scots It is a famous oddity of British history that the Scots were Irish. They were a Celtic tribe of northern Ireland who began colonizing the west coast of Scotland, probably as early as the 5C, and formed the kingdom of *Dalriada. The same process brought Irish Christians, such as St Columba, to Scotland. The *Picts were the rival ethnic group in the area now known as the Highlands, but in the reign of *Kenneth I (9C) the Scots finally established themselves as the dominant group in the region.

Scots (the language) see *Lallans.

The Scotsman The first Scottish newspaper to achieve distribution throughout Scotland (by sending the papers carriage-paid on the railways from 1865) and to establish a national identity within Britain (as the first non-London newspaper to open an office in Fleet Street, in 1868). It was founded in Edinburgh in 1817 as a radical publication, and continues to interpret its masthead of three thistles as a symbol of prickliness. In 1988 it launched a sister paper, *Scotland on Sunday*.

Scots, wha hae (Lowland Scottish for 'Scots, who have') The opening words of a song by *Burns which is often sung at Scottish gatherings. It is supposedly the speech of Robert the Bruce to his troops on the eve of *Bannockburn. In the opening line he addresses them as 'Scots, wha hae wi' *Wallace bled'.

Captain **Scott** (Robert Falcon Scott, 1868–1912) Explorer whose expedition was the second to reach the South Pole. A serving officer in the navy, he was chosen to lead an Antarctic expedition (1901–4) in the *Discovery* (preserved now in *Dundee). He set off south again in 1910, this time in the *Terra Nova*. With four companions (H.R. Bowers, Edgar Evans, Lawrence Oates and Edward Wilson) he reached the pole on 17 January 1912, to find a tent pitched by the Norwegian Roald Amundsen. In it was a note for Scott, dated the previous month. The tragic drama of the British party's return journey became known after their final camp was found in November 1912. They were just 18km/11m short of safety. Scott's diary, ending with the words 'I do not think I can write any more', gave a graphic account of their sufferings, including the heroic suicide of Captain *Oates. His comment on the pole itself was unromantic: 'Great God! this is an awful place.'

George Gilbert **Scott** (1811–78, kt 1872) Prolific architect of the later *Gothic Revival and a controversial figure for his sometimes heavy-handed restoration of medieval buildings. His best-known works are the *Albert Memorial, *St Pancras Station Hotel, and the Government Offices (now occupied entirely by the Foreign Office) which form a large block between Whitehall and St James's Park. Unusually for him these offices are in a Renaissance style, the result of his losing what became known as the 'battle of the styles' with Palmerston, the prime minister, who rejected Scott's Gothic designs and forced him to buy 'some costly books on Italian architecture'.

Giles Gilbert **Scott** (1880–1960, kt 1924) Architect, grandson of George Gilbert *Scott, who in 1903 won the competition for the new Anglican cathedral in *Liverpool (alarming the selection committee when they discovered that he was only 22). Among his other works are the University Library at Cambridge, the new Bodleian at Oxford, *Battersea Power Station and the rebuilt lobby and chamber of the Commons in the *Houses of Parliament. He also designed Britain's traditional red telephone boxes, much lamented by many when replaced in recent years.

Paul **Scott** (1920–78) Novelist who tragically died of cancer just as he was about to acquire a wide and devoted following. The formative experience of his life was his service as a soldier in India during World War II. Nearly all his novels (from *Johnny Sahib* in 1952) were set in the subcontinent, to which he returned for several visits after 1964. The result was his great work, the four novels about the final years of the *Raj in the 1940s (*The Jewel in the Crown* 1966, *The Day of the Scorpion* 1968, *The Towers of Silence* 1971, *A Division of the Spoils* 1975); in 1976 they were published together under the combined title *The Raj Quartet*. Scott followed this with a short novel, *Staying On* (1977), about an old married couple remaining in India after independence. This won the *Booker prize in 1977 and was filmed for television by Granada in 1980, with Celia Johnson and Trevor Howard. It was followed in 1983 by Granada's triumphantly successful 13-part version of the quartet under the title *Jewel in the Crown*.

Peter **Scott** (1909–89, kt 1973) Naturalist and painter (particularly of geese and ducks in flight), who founded the Wildfowl Trust at *Slimbridge in 1946. He was the only son of Captain *Scott.

Ronnie **Scott** (b. 1927) Jazz musician who is a noted tenor saxophonist (joint leader with Tubby *Hayes of the Jazz Couriers in 1957–9, and playing with the Clarke-Boland big band from 1962), but who is best known as the founder of a jazz club. Ronnie Scott's has been the centre of British jazz, and the leading venue for visiting foreign players, since he opened it in London's Gerrard Street in 1959; it moved in 1965 to Frith Street. Since 1991 there has also been a Ronnie Scott's in Birmingham.

Sheila **Scott** (1927–88) British aviator who won many long-distance races. She flew three times solo round the world, and was the first to do so via the north pole in a light aircraft.

Walter **Scott** (1771–1832, bt 1820) Scotland's most prolific and, in his day, most successful author. He first won fame for his romantic poems set in earlier centuries, particularly *The *Lay of the Last Minstrel* (1805) and *The *Lady of the Lake* (1810). He started another even more successful career with his first novel, *Waverley*, published anonymously in 1814. This and its immediate successors, such as *The *Heart of Midlothian* (1818), were set in Scotland in the 17–18C. With *Ivanhoe* (1819) he moved not only to an English subject but to the Middle Ages, a period with which readers increasingly associated him.

Scott built himself a baronial hall, *Abbotsford, but two years later, in 1826, he went spectacularly bankrupt when the crash of a publishing venture left him with huge debts. In a premature example of Victorian high-mindedness he worked himself literally to his death, six years later, to pay off his creditors. It is a measure of his influence in the age of *Romanticism that so many contemporary operas, such as Rossini's *La Donna del Lago* or Donizetti's *Lucia di Lammermoor*, were based on his works.

Scottie see *terriers.

Scottish Ballet Company established in 1969 by Peter Darrell (1929–87), who was originally a dancer with the Sadler's Wells Theatre Ballet. He began his career as a choreographer with Festival Ballet in the 1950s, and in 1957 he founded the Western Theatre Ballet in Bristol. An invitation from the Scottish Arts Council prompted him to move his company in 1969 to Glasgow, where it has thrived as Scotland's ballet company; Elaine McDonald (b. 1934), one of those who moved north with him from

The romance of 19C Scottish baronial: the west front of Balmoral Castle, designed by William Smith of Aberdeen.

Bristol, became the company's leading ballerina. The Dance School of Scotland (the only full-time ballet school north of the border) was established in 1983, and Scottish Ballet now has several schemes taking dance out to the community; the Small Scale Touring Company performs ballet even in remote parts of the Highlands and Islands. Since 1991 the artistic director has been Galina Samsova (b. 1937), who was from 1980 a principal dancer with the Sadler's Wells Royal Ballet.

Scottish baronial Modern term for the style of architecture of Scottish fortified houses up to the 17C (such as Glamis or Craigievar), characterized by round turrets with steep conical roofs. The term is particularly applied to the 19C revival of this style, in which David *Bryce was the leading architect and of which *Balmoral is a prime example.

Scottish Blackface see *sheep.

Scottish Colourists Name given retrospectively to four artists who responded more rapidly and vigorously than their English contemporaries to the bright colours which had burst upon Paris in 1905 in the work of Matisse, Derain and others (classed together as the Fauves, French for wild beasts). The Scots who brightened their own palettes in response were S.J. Peploe (Samuel John Peploe, 1871–1935), J.D. Fergusson (John Duncan Fergusson, 1874–1961), G. Leslie Hunter (1877–1931) and F.C.B. Cadell (Francis Campbell Boileau Cadell, 1883–1937). Their work, long neglected, grew rapidly both in esteem and value during the 1980s.

Scottish FA Cup The cup and the Scottish Football Association were launched together at a meeting in Glasgow in 1873, inspired by the first *FA Cup in the previous year. Of the eight clubs at that meeting only *Queen's Park and Kilmarnock survive. Since 1924 the final has been played at *Hampden Park. By 1993 Celtic had won 29 times and Rangers 26.

Scottish law see *law.

Scottish League Established by ten clubs in 1890, following the example two years earlier of the *Football League. A 2nd division was added in 1893, and in 1975 ten leading clubs emerged to form a Premier division, with the other clubs still in a 1st and 2nd division. By 1993 Rangers had won 43 times and Celtic 35.

Scottish League Cup Established in 1946, well ahead of the *Football League Cup. Since the 1984–5 season it has been known as the Skol Cup. By the end of the 1992–3 season Rangers had won 18 times and Celtic 9.

Scottish National Gallery of Modern Art (Edinburgh) Collection established in 1960 and housed since 1984 behind the classical façade of John Watson's Hospital – built in 1825 for destitute children and designed by William Burn (1789–1870). The holdings cover the broad range of European 20C art, while allowing a certain emphasis on the national contribution (for example the *Scottish Colourists).

Scottish National Orchestra see entry on *Royal Scottish Orchestra.

Scottish National Party see *SNP.

Scottish National Portrait Gallery (Edinburgh) Founded in 1882 with similar aims to the slightly earlier *National Portrait Gallery in London. Its red sandstone Italian Gothic building of 1885–90 (by Robert Rowand Anderson, 1834–1921) is shared by part of the *Royal Museum of Scotland. The gallery has a particularly strong holding of one of the greatest of British portrait painters, Henry Raeburn. In 1984 it extended its range to include photography and it now has the largest collection of Edinburgh's pioneer photographers, *Adamson and *Hill.

Scottish National War Memorial see *Edinburgh Castle.

Scottish Office (Edinburgh) Government department created in 1885, responsible in Scotland for a wide range of matters which in the rest of the country are looked after by specialist departments, each with its own secretary of state; these devolved areas of responsibility include agriculture and fisheries, education, environment, home affairs, health and industry. The office of the secretary of state for Scotland is in Whitehall, but the Scottish civil service is based in Edinburgh. For secretaries of state since 1983 see the *cabinet.

Scottish Opera Company founded in Glasgow in 1962, largely on the initiative of Alexander *Gibson. It had from the start an adventurous policy; one of the only two operas in its first season was Debussy's *Pelléas et Mélisande*. Until 1975 it performed mainly in the King's Theatre in Glasgow, but in that year it moved to a permanent home in the refurbished Theatre Royal. The company tours in Scotland and increasingly also to English cities. An unusual initiative is Opera-Go-Round, which since 1978 has taken out to small towns and villages throughout Scotland specially adapted opera productions, performed by a small cast to a piano accompaniment.

Scottish play see *Macbeth.

Scottish Record Office (Edinburgh) Scotland's national archives were established in the 13C, with the appointment of a Clerk of the Rolls. The present building, the domed Register House on Princes Street, is Britain's oldest purpose-built record office. Designed by Robert Adam in 1774, it was not completed until 1827. An extension, the West Register House in Charlotte Square, was opened in 1971 in an adapted early 19C church, St George's. The equivalent archive for England and Wales is the *Public Record Office.

Scottish United Services Museum see *Edinburgh Castle.

Scott Monument see *Princes Street.

Scouse Slang term for anyone from Liverpool, derived from a meat stew of that name eaten locally (originally a sailor's dish, known as lobscouse).

Scouts Youth movement founded in 1908 by *Baden-Powell with the aim of training boys physically, mentally and spiritually to become responsible members of society. The summer camp was the focus of the year's activities, with much of the training being in skills needed for that outdoor adventure (the motto is 'Be Prepared'). The idea was immediately popular and in 1910 two new groups were established – the Girl *Guides and the Sea Scouts

---

Finalists in the Scottish FA Cup and winners of the Scottish League since 1950

Scottish FA Cup

Year	Winner		Runner-up			Year	Winner		Runner-up		
1950	Rangers	3	East Fife	0		1972	Celtic	6	Hibernian	1	
1951	Celtic	1	Motherwell	0		1973	Rangers	3	Celtic	2	
1952	Motherwell	4	Dundee	0		1974	Celtic	3	Dundee United	0	
1953	Rangers	1	Aberdeen	0	(on replay)	1975	Celtic	3	Airdrieonians	1	
1954	Celtic	2	Aberdeen	1		1976	Rangers	3	Hearts	1	
1955	Clyde	1	Celtic	0	(on replay)	1977	Celtic	1	Rangers	0	
1956	Hearts	3	Celtic	1		1978	Rangers	2	Aberdeen	1	
1957	Falkirk	2	Kilmarnock	1	(on replay)	1979	Rangers	3	Hibernian	2	(on 2nd replay)
1958	Clyde	1	Hibernian	0		1980	Celtic	1	Rangers	0	
1959	St Mirren	3	Aberdeen	1		1981	Rangers	4	Dundee United	1	(on replay)
1960	Rangers	2	Kilmarnock	0		1982	Aberdeen	4	Rangers	1	
1961	Dunfermline A	2	Celtic	0	(on replay)	1983	Aberdeen	1	Rangers	0	
1962	Rangers	2	St Mirren	0		1984	Aberdeen	2	Celtic	1	
1963	Rangers	3	Celtic	0	(on replay)	1985	Celtic	2	Dundee United	1	
1964	Rangers	3	Dundee	1		1986	Aberdeen	3	Hearts	0	
1965	Celtic	3	Dunfermline A	2		1987	St Mirren	1	Dundee United	0	
1966	Rangers	1	Celtic	0	(on replay)	1988	Celtic	2	Dundee United	1	
1967	Celtic	2	Aberdeen	0		1989	Celtic	1	Rangers	0	
1968	Dunfermline A	3	Hearts	1		1990	Aberdeen	0 *	Celtic	0	
1969	Celtic	4	Rangers	0		1991	Motherwell	4	Dundee United	3	
1970	Aberdeen	3	Celtic	1		1992	Rangers	2	Airdrieonians	1	
1971	Celtic	2	Rangers	1	(on replay)	1993	Rangers	2	Aberdeen	1	

* Aberdeen won 9-8 on penalties

Scottish League

Year	Winner	Year	Winner	Year	Winner	Year	Winner
1950	Rangers	1962	Dundee	1974	Celtic	1986	Celtic
1951	Hibernian	1963	Rangers	1975	Rangers	1987	Rangers
1952	Hibernian	1964	Rangers	1976	Rangers	1988	Celtic
1953	Rangers	1965	Kilmarnock	1977	Celtic	1989	Rangers
1954	Celtic	1966	Celtic	1978	Rangers	1990	Rangers
1955	Aberdeen	1967	Celtic	1979	Celtic	1991	Rangers
1956	Rangers	1968	Celtic	1980	Aberdeen	1992	Rangers
1957	Rangers	1969	Celtic	1981	Celtic	1993	Rangers
1958	Hearts	1970	Celtic	1982	Celtic		
1959	Rangers	1971	Celtic	1983	Dundee United		
1960	Hearts	1972	Celtic	1984	Aberdeen		
1961	Rangers	1973	Celtic	1985	Aberdeen		

(the Air Scouts followed in 1941). Younger boys were involved from 1914 as Wolf *Cubs; and the Beavers (8–10) were added in 1982. The first Jamboree was held in London's Olympia in 1920 and now there is a World Jamboree in a different country every four years; the word is 19C American slang of unknown origin. For many years the Scouts put on an annual public entertainment, *The Gang Show*, produced by Ralph Reader (1903–1982). There are now about 16 million Scouts and Cubs in more than 150 countries. The name was shortened from Boy Scouts to Scouts in 1967.

Screaming Lord Sutch see *Monster Raving Loony Party.

The Screwtape Letters (1942) Book by C.S. *Lewis which uses a satirical device to present a witty and challenging Christian view of life's temptations. The letters are written by a senior devil, Screwtape, to his subordinate, Wormwood, giving practical hints on how best to keep his patient out of God's clutches.

'scribble, scribble, scribble' see Edward *Gibbon.

Scrooge see A *Christmas Carol.

scrumpy Dialect word for a rough cider made from 'scrumps' (withered or stunted apples). It is particularly associated with the West Country.

Peter **Scudamore** (b. 1958) The most successful of all National Hunt jockeys. From 1986 he was *champion jockey each year in a run which was still unbroken in 1992. In 1989 he passed John Francome's previous record of 1138 winners in a career (by 1992 the Scudamore score had risen to 1534) and in that same year he rode the record number of winners in a season (221). There remain two tantalizing omissions in this catalogue of success; he had won (by 1992) neither of steeplechasing's two greatest trophies, the Grand National and the Cheltenham Gold Cup.

Scutari see Florence *Nightingale.

SDLP (Social Democratic and Labour Party) Political party formed in *Northern Ireland in 1970 by a group of independent nationalist MPs in the Stormont parliament. The immediate purpose was to give organized political expression to the civil rights movement, which was then gathering much public support in its demands for an end to discrimination against the Catholic community. From the start the SDLP has taken a committed stand against the violence in the nationalist cause perpetrated by the *IRA; it shares the ideal of a united Ireland, but believes that it can only be achieved by consensus between the communities (both within Northern Ireland and between north and south). The party's first leader was Gerry Fitt (b. 1926, MP for Belfast constituencies at Stormont 1962–72 and at Westminster 1966–79); he was succeeded in 1979 by John *Hume. Since 1989 the party has been the second largest in local government in Northern Ireland, after the Unionists; and the 1992 general election gave the SDLP four MPs at Westminster, its highest number to date. On most issues the SDLP votes with the Labour party.

SDP The abbreviation commonly used for the Social Democratic Party, which emerged during 1981. In January of that year four leading members of the Labour party (Roy Jenkins, Shirley Williams, David Owen and Bill Rodgers) held a press conference criticizing trends in the Labour party (such as its tolerance of the *Militant Tendency) and setting up a Council for Social Democracy. They became collectively known as the 'gang of four', after the widow of Mao Tse-tung and her three colleagues who tyrannized China in the mid-1970s and were imprisoned in 1981. During 1981 nearly 20 Labour members and one Conservative gave their support, so the new party was formed around a group of sitting MPs. The SDP and the *Liberal party, campaigning together as the *Alliance, pushed the centre vote in the next few years to unprecedented heights. After the 1987 election the party voted to merge with the Liberals, forming what became the *Liberal Democrats. But David Owen, who had succeeded Roy Jenkins as leader in 1983, rejected this decision and carried on with a small group (himself and two other MPs) which still called itself the SDP. This rump of the party was finally disbanded in 1990 for lack of support.

Sea Fever Poem from *Masefield's first book (*Salt-Water Ballads* 1902) which rapidly became popular, with its romantic evocation of a life of freedom and the yearning refrain which begins each verse, 'I must down to the seas again'. In 1913 it was set to music by John *Ireland, who changed the line to 'I must go down to the sea again'.

Sealyham see *terriers.

SEAQ (Stock Exchange Automated Quotations) Computer-based dealing system introduced by the *Stock Exchange in 1986 as part of the improvements connected with *Big Bang. Whereas dealing was previously only on the floor of the Stock Exchange itself, SEAQ brings to the computer screens of brokers and their clients, anywhere in the world, the best available up-to-the-minute bid and offer prices on some 2000 securities. Instant instructions to buy or sell can be made by telephone or computer link. The same technology also makes possible increasingly sophisticated *Financial Times Indices.

Ronald **Searle** (b. 1920) Artist and cartoonist, best known for his creation of the appalling schoolgirls of St Trinian's. Their cheerful anarchy was the subject of many of his cartoons from 1941 to 1953, and subsequently five feature films were created around them. His serious drawings include a powerful series from the war years, when he was a prisoner of the Japanese in Thailand and Malaya.

Sears see Charles *Clore.

seaside piers The popularity of the 18C seaside resorts, such as Scarborough, Lyme Regis and Brighton, led to the development in the early 19C of the seaside pier. Wooden piles driven into the sea bed carried a cast-iron superstructure and a wooden deck, to form in effect an open-ended bridge leading out to sea. A pier was ideal for promenading in the healthy sea breezes but was also a good place to separate the tourists from their money; a wide range of stalls and even full-scale theatres became a standard feature, particularly at the far end, known as the pier head. For most of the 19C the best-known piers were those at *Brighton, but in 1889 the pier at *Southend opened; extended in 1929, it is the world's longest. Blackpool is unique in Britain in having three piers.

seaside postcards From the Edwardian period it became a British tradition to send brightly coloured postcards from holidays at the seaside. The comic ones made much use of mild sexual double entendre, closely related to the humour of the *music halls (the outstanding exponent was Donald *McGill). Picture postcards had been developed on the Continent, and became a craze in Britain only after two concessions by the Post Office – first (from 1894) delivering them for a halfpenny, half the letter rate, and then (from 1897) allowing messages on the same side as the address, thus giving the artists space to indulge themselves on the other side.

SEATO (Southeast Asia Treaty Organization) An alliance against Communist aggression formed in 1954 after the French defeat in southeast Asia (the area known then as Indochina). The members were Australia, France, New Zealand, Pakistan, the Philippines, Thailand, the UK and the USA. It was never very effective (the SEATO nations did not support the USA in the Vietnam War) and it was dissolved in 1977.

Seaton Delaval Hall (19km/12m NE of Newcastle-upon-Tyne) An extraordinary late house by *Vanbrugh, built 1718–28, which is both bold and awkward in its clashing elements. The central block was gutted by fire in 1822 and was long left derelict, but in recent years the house has been under restoration. The remains of the great hall and gallery, and the undamaged stables in the east wing, are like settings for some heroic Roman opera, in keeping with the classicizing self-confidence of the early 18C.

Sebastopol see the *Crimean War.

Harry **Secombe** (b. 1921, kt 1981) Welsh comedian and tenor, who made his debut in 1947 at the *Windmill Theatre and became a celebrity on *The *Goon Show* (1952–60). His main career has been in variety (with frequent appearances in the *Royal Variety Performance), but he had a notable success in musical comedy with a long run in *Pickwick* (1963). Since 1983 he has presented *Highway* for Tyne Tees TV.

secondary school see *state school.

second best bed see Anne *Hathaway.

*The **Second Mrs Tanqueray*** (1893) Play by *Pinero which was the first Victorian drama with 'shocking' subject matter to be a commercial success (launching the career of Mrs Patrick *Campbell). Tanqueray, a respectable widower, marries Paula in spite of a sexual liaison in her past. But their love is undermined by the constant danger of shame and dishonour if her secret becomes known. Circumstances eventually conspire to force Paula to make public the truth, and she commits suicide.

Second Reading see *Act of Parliament.

Secretary of State The title given to the heads of the most important government departments. The monarch's chief administrator of state affairs was known from the 13C as the king's secretary. By the late 18C there were still only two secretaries of state, but the number has grown to more than a dozen in the modern *cabinet.

*The **Secret Garden*** (1911) Children's classic by Frances Hodgson *Burnett. A spoilt girl is transformed by her discovery of a long-closed-up garden in Yorkshire, which she begins secretly cultivating. Her own new strength and the magic of the growing garden inspire a bedridden boy, Colin, who experiences a similar voyage of self-discovery and growth.

Security Council see *United Nations.

Adam **Sedgwick** see *geological periods.

'See, the conquering hero comes!' see entry on duke of *Cumberland.

Segontium (SE outskirts of Caernarfon) *Roman fort established in the late 1st century AD. The foundations are excavated, and there is a museum of items found on the site.

Henry **Segrave** (1896–1930, kt 1929) Racing driver who set speed records on land and water. In 1927 at Daytona, in Florida, he became the first man to drive at more than 200 mph, reaching 328kph/203mph in a 1000 h.p. Sunbeam; in 1929 he achieved 372kph/231mph in *Golden Arrow* (both cars are now at *Beaulieu). He established a new water speed record of 98.76 mph on Lake Windermere in 1930, before being killed in a later run.

Selborne see Gilbert *White.

Select Committee see parliamentary *committees.

selective employment tax (SET) Tax introduced in 1966, payable by employers at varying rates on all employees and then refunded to selected areas of industry. The intention was to divert labour from the service industries into manufacturing, and to offset the effect of *purchase tax which fell more heavily on manufactured goods. SET was abolished in 1973 with the introduction of *VAT.

Self-Help see Samuel *Smiles.

Selfridges (London W1) Major department store on Oxford Street, unlike nearly all others in that it was established from the very beginning on the grandest scale. It was built in 1908–9 by an American, Gordon Selfridge (1857–1947), whose architects provided an open-plan steel structure behind a façade of massive Ionic columns. Selfridge had 1300 retail staff on the premises for two months before opening and he spent a fortune (£36,000) on newspaper advertisements to launch the venture. His bold marketing techniques included several innovations in Britain – such as bargain basements and annual sales.

Alexander **Selkirk** see *Robinson Crusoe.

Selkirkshire Until 1975 an inland *county in southern Scotland, now part of the Borders region.

Sellafield Site on the west coast of England, in Cumbria, run by British Nuclear Fuels and prominent in the story of Britain's *nuclear power. The first nuclear power station opened here, at Calder Hall, in 1956. At that time the area was known as Windscale, but on 10 October 1957 an atomic pile overheated in what could have developed into a major accident. To limit the harm done to the image of nuclear power, the name of the site was changed to Sellafield.

From as early as 1952 spent nuclear fuel was reprocessed here, and that has remained Sellafield's specialization. High-level waste is brought from all Britain's magnox nuclear power stations and from many plants abroad. About 97% of it is recyled into new fuel, but the other 3% remains extremely dangerous; until recently it has been stored in liquid form in stainless steel tanks within thick concrete walls, but a new process of vitrification converts it into glass which is then sealed within stainless steel. In 1992 a massive new thermal oxide reprocessing plant (Thorp) was opened. At the same time there were plans (criticized by many as dangerous) to excavate great storage caverns for intermediate and low-level nuclear waste deep in the rock below the site.

From the Windscale accident onwards, Sellafield has had the reputation of being an environmental and health hazard – a public image strenuously contested by British

Nuclear Fuels. The plant regularly pipes into the Irish Sea liquid waste which is said to be safe, but in 1986 half a ton of uranium was accidentally discharged. In 1983 a Yorkshire TV documentary, *Windscale, the Nuclear Laundry*, identified an incidence of leukaemia in the district considerably above the national average; this was confirmed in 1984 in a report by Sir Douglas Black.

Peter **Sellers** (1925–80) Comedian and actor who began his career in 1948 at the *Windmill Theatre. He was known on radio in *Ray's a Laugh* before his first major success, The *Goon Show* (1952–60). With brilliant timing and a genius for mimicry, his comedy also had a characteristic element of bottled-up severity – particularly on film. Some of his greatest cinema performances were as the shop steward in *I'm All Right Jack* (1959) and his three roles in *Dr Strangelove* (1963), but he is best known as Inspector Clouseau in the *Pink Panther* series (from 1963). Of his four marriages, the one which attracted most attention was to Britt Ekland (1964–9).

selling the family silver see *privatization.

send to Coventry see *Coventry.

senior service see the *Royal Navy.

Sense and Sensibility (1811) The first novel by Jane *Austen to be published, based on a story called *Elinor and Marianne* which she wrote in 1795. Elinor and Marianne Dashwood are two sisters of contrasting character, personifying sense and sensibility (Elinor reserved, Marianne extremely emotional). They are living in straitened circumstances with their widowed mother in a cottage in Devon, where they fall in love, respectively, with Edward Ferrars and John Willoughby. But when the sisters visit London, the young men treat them coolly – for different reasons, as it turns out. Ferrars has been secretly engaged for four years to Lucy Steele, a relationship which he now regrets. His mother, discovering the secret, is so angry that she settles her fortune upon his younger brother, whereupon Lucy becomes engaged to him instead. This double reversal liberates Ferrars; he is now free to pursue his real aim in life, that of becoming a clergyman, and to propose to Elinor. Willoughby, by contrast, is revealed as an adventurer; his mood to Marianne has changed because he has found an heiress. This shock has a sobering effect on her (inclining her from sensibility to sense), and she marries a family friend of sterling qualities, Colonel Brandon.

*A **Sentimental Journey*** see Laurence *Sterne.

Serious Fraud Office Body established in 1987 for the investigation and prosecution of serious or complex frauds; it is answerable directly to the attorney general. Major cases in the SFO's first years included the *Guinness Affair and *Barlow Clowes. The Fraud Squad, a *police operation, has been in existence since 1946.

Serpentine see *Hyde Park.

SERPS see *pensions.

SET see *selective employment tax.

setters Large dogs with long coats and long hanging ears, used when shooting game birds. A setter's function is to crouch ('set' derives from the same root as 'sit') when it scents a bird. There are three breeds, all developed in the British Isles. The English setter, used for hunting from the 16C but bred in its present form in the 19C, has a white coat flecked with a darker colour. The Gordon setter or black-and-tan (a black body with light brown at the extremities) was developed by the 4th duke of Gordon in Scotland in the late 18C. The Irish or red setter, deriving from Ireland in the 18C, was originally white and red but has been bred to have a pure red coat.

Act of **Settlement** (1701) Act of parliament settling the succession to the throne. The *Bill of Rights (1689) had limited the succession to the children of Mary and Anne (the daughters of James II) and of their cousin William III. But by 1701 Queen Mary had already died, childless, and her husband William III showed no likelihood of re-marrying. Anne, next in line to the throne, had no living heir in spite of 15 pregnancies. Parliament's main concern was to ensure that no Catholic descendant of the *Stuarts should inherit. So they settled the inheritance on the heirs of Sophia, a Protestant granddaughter of James I (see the *royal house), who had married the elector of Hanover. Her son became king, on the death of Queen Anne in 1714, as the first ruler of the house of *Hanover, George I. The act also imposed certain lasting restrictions on the *royal family.

seven ages of man The divisions of life, best known in English in the version recounted by Jaques in **As You Like It*. In the speech beginning 'All the world's a stage', he says that each of us plays many parts and that the acts of our play are seven ages: the puking infant; the whining schoolboy; the lover, sighing like a furnace; the soldier, full of strange oaths; the round-bellied justice; the lean and slippered pantaloon; and finally second childishness, 'sans teeth, sans eyes, sans taste, sans everything'.

*The **Seven Pillars of Wisdom*** see T.E. *Lawrence.

Seven Sisters see *Beachy Head.

Seven Years' War (1756–63) Conflict involving two separate rivalries. One was the struggle in central Europe between neighbouring Prussia and Austria, a continuation of the War of the *Austrian Succession; Britain was involved in this largely because of the need to protect *Hanover. The other was a persistent confrontation between Britain and France as colonial powers. From the start of the 18C there had been sporadic warfare between British America and French Canada, which flared up again in 1754; and from the late 1740s there were military engagements in India between the *East India Company and its French equivalent. These separate clashes, predating the outbreak of war between Britain and France in 1756, became part of the wider conflict in which Britain sided with Prussia against France, Austria, Russia and Sweden.

Britain took relatively little part in the European land war. Her main interest lay in winning control of the sea to avoid invasion by France, and in making territorial gains in north America. Both were achieved in 1759, which became known as the 'wonderful year'. The French fleet was severely damaged at Quiberon Bay (Nov. 20–1) on the southern side of the Brest peninsula; and in September Quebec fell to *Wolfe. In India the French province of Pondicherry surrendered in 1761. In the treaty of Paris, ending the war in 1763, France ceded to Britain the mainland of north America east of the Mississippi (except New Orleans), several Caribbean islands (others were restored by Britain to France), and recent French acquisitions in India and the East Indies. This settlement left Britain well placed to become the leading colonial power.

Severn The longest river in Great Britain if calculated at about 354km/220m (estimates as low as 290km/180m end the Severn at a different point in its long estuary and

The Severn, meandering through Wales near Welshpool shortly before crossing the English border on the way to Shrewsbury.

allow the *Thames to take the crown). It rises in Wales, in Powys, and flows northeast to Shrewsbury before entering a narrow gorge at Ironbridge. It continues south to Worcester and to Gloucester, where it becomes tidal. The estuary, narrowing from the great expanse of the *Bristol Channel, causes the phenomenon of the Severn Bore – a wave rushing upstream on a spring tide which can be more than 2.5m/8ft high and has been known to travel at 20kph/13mph.

The railway was brought under the Severn to join England and Wales in 1873–86; at 7km/4.35m this Victorian tunnel is still the longest in Britain (the engineer was John Hawkshaw, 1811–91). A suspension toll bridge a few miles north of Bristol (by Gilbert *Roberts) was opened in 1966 to carry the M4 motorway over the river; it was privatized in 1992 and its owners plan another bridge, 5km/3m downstream, which is scheduled for completion in 1996.

Anna **Sewell** see *Black Beauty.*

Sex Pistols The group which launched punk rock. With the support of Malcolm McLaren, owner of a King's Road boutique, the band was formed in 1975 with Johnny Rotten (John Lydon, b. 1956, vocals), Steve Jones (b. 1955, guitar) and Paul Cook (b. 1956, drums). Joined in 1977 by Sid Vicious (John Ritchie, 1957–79, bass), they claimed little in the way of talent other than a genius for causing offence. This rapidly brought them success, particularly after their contracts had been cancelled by both A&M and EMI (they were picked up by Virgin) and their single *God Save the Queen* (1977) had been banned by the BBC. Their first album, *Never Mind the Bollocks Here's*

the Sex Pistols (1977), went to the top of the charts. The broader public's lasting memory of them is of the two deaths which brought the group to an end. On a tour of America in 1978 Sid Vicious's girlfriend Nancy Spungen was stabbed; he was arrested and charged with her murder; four months later he died from an overdose of heroin.

sex discrimination see entry on *Equal Opportunities Commission.

Seychelles Archipelago in the Indian Ocean (more than 100 islands, but with nearly all the population living on Mahé), which has been a member of the *Commonwealth and a republic since 1976. Mahé was captured by the British from the French in 1794 and was ceded by the treaty of Paris in 1814. Seychelles became a crown colony in 1903 and achieved independence in 1976.

Lynn **Seymour** (b. 1939) Canadian-born dancer who made her career with the Royal Ballet, which she joined as a soloist in 1958. Famous for the dramatic quality of her dancing, she had many roles created for her by Kenneth MacMillan (*The Invitation* securely established her reputation in 1960) and by Frederick Ashton (including *A *Month in the Country*).

Sezincote (32km/20m NE of Cheltenham) House built 1798–1805 with an exterior using Indian motifs (some years before the *Royal Pavilion at Brighton). The architect, Samuel Pepys Cockerell (1754–1827), was surveyor to the East India Company and was advised on the design of the house by Thomas *Daniell. The interior is in the conventional neoclassical style of the time.

sgian-dhu see *Highland dress.

Ernest **Shackleton** (1874–1922, kt 1909) Explorer who made four expeditions to the Antarctic. The first was with Captain *Scott in 1901–4. He led the attempt of 1907–9 in the *Nimrod*, during which members of his party reached the summit of Mt Erebus and located the south magnetic pole. The third (1914–16 in the *Endurance*) was an extraordinary and heroic saga; the ship was crushed in pack ice; the party drifted on ice floes for five months before reaching the South Shetland islands; Shackleton and five others then made a further journey of 1300km/ 800m in a 7m/22ft open boat to South Georgia, where they crossed the mountainous interior to reach a Norwegian whaling station; after three failed attempts Shackleton rescued his men from the South Shetlands. He was again in South Georgia when he died, in 1922, at the start of a fourth expedition.

Shadow Cabinet see *Opposition.

Shadows Instrumental pop group which emerged from the Drifters, the early backing group for Cliff *Richard. The guitarists Hank Marvin and Bruce Welch (both b. 1941) joined the Drifters in 1958 and were the leading pair in a quartet which changed its name in 1959 to the Shadows; in the same year the group began an independent career, though continuing to back Cliff Richard. Their no. 1 hits (more than any other instrumental act) have been *Apache* (1960), *Kon-Tiki* (1961), *Wonderful Land* (1962), *Dance On* (1962) and *Foot Tapper* (1963). They are still issuing successful records; their album *Reflection* reached no. 6 in 1990.

Peter **Shaffer** (b. 1926) Playwright who has continued over a long period to produce serious plays, extraordinarily different one from another in character, which have had long runs in the West End and on Broadway. His first was *Five Finger Exercise* (1958); subsequent successes have included *The Royal Hunt of the Sun* (1964), *Equus* (1973) and above all *Amadeus* (1979).

Lord **Shaftesbury** (Anthony Ashley Cooper, 1801–85, 7th earl 1851) Philanthropist, reformer, evangelical Christian and an MP in the House of Commons from 1826 until he moved to the Lords in 1851. He is best known for his work in relation to the *Factory Acts (the Ten-Hour Act of 1847 was largely his achievement), but he was instrumental also in the Mines Act of 1842, which made it illegal for women and girls of any age and for boys under 13 to be employed underground. The condition of the slums of central London also caused him to be much involved with housing reform and public sanitation. During the first half of his career (from 1811, when his father inherited the earldom) he was known by the *courtesy title of Lord Ashley.

Shaftesbury Avenue (London W1) Street running northeast from *Piccadilly Circus, completed in 1886 and designed to improve traffic circulation. It broke through an area of squalid narrow streets, slums of the kind which had prompted Lord Shaftesbury's zeal in housing reform; its completion the year after his death caused him to be commemorated in its name and in *Eros at its southern end. Six theatres were built along the west side of the street, causing Shaftesbury Avenue to be used as a synonym for West End theatre.

William **Shakespeare** (1564–1616) The world's most performed playwright. The first record of him is his baptism in Stratford-upon-Avon on 26 April 1564, but the tradition is that he was born on April 23 (a date which has the added national attraction of being St *George's day). This was also the date on which he died 52 years later.

His father was a leading citizen of the town and his mother was born Mary *Arden. It is a safe assumption that Shakespeare was given a good education at Stratford's *grammar school. When he was 18 he married Anne *Hathaway, who was about seven years older than him. For the next ten years nothing is known of his life, but by the early 1590s he was in London and making a name for himself as poet, playwright and actor. The only works which he wrote for publication date from this period, being two rhetorical exercises in epic verse, *Venus and Adonis* (1593) and *The Rape of Lucrece* (1594). The *Sonnets, private poems for a circle of friends, were probably also written during the 1590s.

The social mix of the theatrical audience of the time helped develop Shakespeare's art, for no other playwright has so successfully combined the highest flights of poetry with such broad comedy. After three uneven chronicle plays on Henry VI, his first unqualified success was *Richard III*, which is thought to date from 1592–3. In the next few years he continued his coverage of English history of the previous two centuries, with *Richard II* and the two parts of *Henry IV* (where his ability to create a rounded comic character finds perfect expression in *Falstaff) and finally with *Henry V*.

By this time other sides of his multifaceted genius had revealed themselves – in the tragic romance of *Romeo and Juliet*, the comic romance of A *Midsummer Night's Dream*, *As You Like It* and *Twelfth Night*, the knockabout comedy of The *Taming of the Shrew* and The *Merry Wives of Windsor*, and the historical tragedy of *Julius Caesar*. All these are believed to have been written by about 1600, when Shakespeare was 36.

He had been for some years a leading member of London's best theatrical company, the *Chamberlain's Men, and as such he owned a share in the new theatre, the *Globe, which they built in 1599 on Bankside. So it was the patrons of the Globe who were the first audiences for the great series of tragedies which now followed, starting with *Hamlet* in about 1601, and continuing with *Othello*, *Macbeth* and *King Lear*.

The Droeshout portrait of Shakespeare in the First Folio.

The plays of Shakespeare with their approximate dates

1590–2	Henry VI, Parts 1, 2 and 3	1599–	As You Like It	1606	Macbeth	
	Titus Andronicus	1600	Henry V			
			Julius Caesar	1607	Antony and Cleopatra	
1592–3	The Comedy of Errors		The Merry Wives of Windsor		Timon of Athens	
	Richard III		Much Ado About Nothing			
	The Taming of the Shrew			1608	Coriolanus	
	The Two Gentlemen of Verona	1601	Hamlet		Pericles, Prince of Tyre	
			Twelfth Night			
1594–5	King John			1609	Cymbeline	
	Love's Labour's Lost	1602	Troilus and Cressida			
	Richard II			1611	The Tempest	
	Romeo and Juliet	1603	All's Well that Ends Well		The Winter's Tale	
			Othello			
1596	The Merchant of Venice			*and two plays possibly written in*		
	A Midsummer Night's Dream	1604	Measure for Measure	*collaboration with John Fletcher:*		
				1613	Henry VIII	
1597–8	Henry IV, Parts 1 and 2	1605	King Lear		The Two Noble Kinsmen	

NB There is no significance in the sequence within each date group; the plays are listed alphabetically.

Although Shakespeare is believed to have written parts of *Henry VIII* (during a performance of which in 1613 the Globe caught fire and was destroyed), *The *Tempest* is generally considered his last play. At the end of it the magician, Prospero, destroys his magic staff and book – an appropriate touch, since at about this time Shakespeare seems to have given up the theatre and retired to New Place, the house which he had bought in Stratford.

Since the age of 44 he had been a grandfather, his elder daughter Susanna having herself had a daughter in 1604 (who became his last surviving descendant, and died in 1670). His only son Hamnet had died at the age of 11, some four years before the writing of *Hamlet*. When Shakespeare himself died, he was buried in Holy Trinity Church at Stratford. Tradition maintains that he chose the doggerel verse above the grave:

Good friend, for Jesu's sake forbear
To dig the dust enclosed here.
Blest be the man that spares these stones,
And curst be he that moves my bones.

Within a few years of his death a bust of Shakespeare was put up on the wall of the church, where it may still be seen. It is one of the only two portraits which have any authenticity.

The other is the so-called Droeshout Portrait, the print commissioned from Martin Droeshout for the title-page of the *First Folio of Shakespeare's plays, published as a tribute to him in 1623 by his fellow actors. There was a strong disincentive to publish the plays when they were new (with no law of copyright, the authentic text was a closely guarded property of the theatre company), but during his life about half the plays had appeared as separate *quartos. Their titles differ not only from quarto to quarto but even in separate parts of the First Folio, with the result that some are still used in slightly varying forms today.

In spite of all the changes of fashion, Shakespeare's plays have held their own at every period as the most frequently performed works on the English-speaking stage. The theory that a boy from provincial Stratford could not have written them (the *Baconian theory) derives more from snobbery than scholarship.

Justice **Shallow** see *Henry IV*.

shamrock see national *emblems.

shandy Beer mixed half and half with lemonade or ginger beer. The origin of the name, in use since the 19c, is unknown.

Shandy Hall see Laurence *Sterne.

Shangri-La Term for any place of retreat from the cares of the world. It is the name of a utopian society in a remote valley of Tibet, where no-one grows old, featuring in *Lost Horizon*, a novel of 1933 by James Hilton (1900–54).

Bill **Shankly** (1913–81) Scottish footballer and manager. His playing career was with Preston North End (1933–49), but it is as a manager that he is remembered – for his transformation of *Liverpool. When he took over in 1959 the club was in Division 2. He took them into Division 1 in 1962, and by the time of his retirement in 1974 the club had won two FA Cups, three League championships and the UEFA Cup.

*The **Shape of Things to Come*** see * *Things to Come*.

George Bernard **Shaw** (1856–1950) Anglo-Irish playwright, born in Dublin, who lived in England from 1876. After writing five unsuccessful novels, he began to make his name as a critic, most notably of music and drama. His three years of weekly theatre reviews for the *Saturday Review* (1895–8) amounted to an impassioned plea for serious plays on moral or political themes instead of the frivolities then in vogue. He was in particular an early champion of the plays of Ibsen.

His own extensive contribution to English drama (some 30 full-length plays) began with what he classed as his three 'unpleasant plays'. These dealt with depressing social problems, such as his first, *Widowers' Houses* (1892), about a slum landlord, or *Mrs Warren's Profession* about organized prostitution (written 1893 but banned by the *lord chamberlain). The four 'pleasant plays' which followed, including * *Arms and the Man* (1894), revealed a more skittish side to the way in which Shaw enjoyed undermining the audience's expectations. At different levels

The white-faced hornless Cotswold sheep: a prize flock painted by Richard Whitford in 1861.

that remained his motive in such plays as *Major Barbara* and *Man and Superman*, both first performed in 1905. An oddity in his work was *Heartbreak House* (1920), somewhat in the style of Chekhov but with a message. Among his most lasting successes *Pygmalion* (1913) is more a comedy of character than ideas, and *Saint Joan* (1923) carried him further than usual in the direction of tragedy.

A life-long socialist, he became in 1884 an early and very active member of the *Fabian Society. Other less mainstream causes dear to his heart were vegetarianism and the reform of the perplexing inconsistencies of English spelling. His combination of passion, wit and eccentricity, combined with his command of the provocative paradox, gave him a role in society which he much relished – that of the serious jester. He had prolonged romantic attachments, mainly by letter, with Ellen *Terry and with Mrs Patrick *Campbell. In 1898 he married Charlotte Payne-Townshend (she died in 1943), and in 1906 they moved to *Ayot St Lawrence, where he lived until his death. He was awarded the Nobel prize for literature in 1925.

Norman **Shaw** (1831–1912) The leading architect in the late-19C revival of redbrick domestic architecture, in a style which became known as *Queen Anne. He designed country houses and many large town houses in London, but his single best-known work is New *Scotland Yard.

Sandie **Shaw** (b. 1947) Pop singer who had several no. 1 hits in the 1960s – *(There's) Always Something There to Remind Me* (1964), *Long Live Love* (1965) and *Puppet on a String* (1967, the song with which she won the *Eurovision Song Contest). She was famous at the time for singing in bare feet – a gimmick which she dropped when she returned to the profession, after some years of motherhood, in the 1980s.

She (1887) Exotic and mystical adventure story by Rider *Haggard about the quest of Leo Vincey to avenge the murder of his earliest ancestor by an unknown woman.

The trail leads to a kingdom in Africa, ruled over by a queen with the secret of eternal life – Ayesha, or She-Who-Must-Be-Obeyed. She recognizes Leo as the reincarnation of a man she murdered because he rejected her love. Attempting to give Leo immortal life in an underground ritual, she herself suddenly bears the marks of her immense age. Horrified by what they have seen, Leo and his companion struggle back to everyday life in England.

Alan **Shearer** (b. 1970) Footballer who became in 1992 the most expensive player transferred between British clubs, when *Blackburn Rovers bought him from Southampton for £3.6 million. His skill as a striker rapidly put Rovers ahead in the new Premier League.

Moira **Shearer** (Moira Shearer King, b. 1926) Ballerina and actress. She joined Sadler's Wells Ballet in 1942 and from 1944 danced most of the great classical roles as well as creating some important new ones, such as Ashton's *Cinderella* in 1948. In that same year she achieved international renown with her starring role in the film *The *Red Shoes*. In 1955 she joined the Bristol Old Vic and began a successful second career as an actress. She is married to Ludovic *Kennedy.

George **Shearing** (b. 1919) Jazz pianist, blind from birth, who won a wide following in Britain during World War II and moved in 1947 to the USA. He composes much of his own material, *Lullaby in Birdland* (1952) being his best-known number.

sheep The British climate and the profusion of grass make the country well suited to the rearing of sheep, which were introduced by the *Romans. By the late Middle Ages *wool was a source of great prosperity in many areas. Out of almost 300 breeds of sheep in existence today, many of the most widely known were developed in Britain; indeed almost every county of southern England has a variety named after it. The oldest English breed is the Southdown (dark-faced, hornless), raised on the Sussex *Downs and known for excellent meat production and for a very fine but light fleece. The broad term 'Down sheep' is also applied to the medium-wool and dark-faced Hampshire, Oxford, Shropshire and Suffolk sheep, all bred in similar conditions.

The Cheviot, from the border district of the *Cheviots between England and Scotland, is a hardy white-faced breed; like the Border Leicester (originally a cross between Cheviot and Leicester), it has no wool on its head or legs, giving it the neat picture-book image of the essential sheep. Also white-faced and hornless, but with longer and coarser wool, are the Leicester, Cotswold, Lincoln and Wensleydale. The best-known horned English sheep is the white-faced Dorset or Dorset Horn. Two hardy mountain breeds have become well established: the horned Scottish Blackface (or Blackface Highland), and the Welsh Mountain sheep, white-faced and with only the rams growing horns. The island of Soay, part of *St Kilda, has its own distinctive breed.

sheepdogs Dogs bred, like the *collies, for herding sheep or driving them to market. The Old English sheepdog is large and shaggy, with a coat usually of grey and white and with long hair obscuring its eyes. It was bred in the west of England and an important element in the strain is believed to have been the Scottish bearded collie. Certainly the working breed now known as the bearded collie is closely related, being similar in appearance but smaller, with a shorter coat and sometimes with a reddish tan colour instead of grey. The other well-known variety of sheepdog, the Shetland or 'sheltie' (originating in the Shetlands), looks like a small version of a long-haired collie and has a wide range of colours from black to a golden brown, with white or tan markings.

Sheffield (477,000 in 1981) City in South Yorkshire on the river Don, historically the centre of the British steel industry. Local iron ore, stone suitable for grinding, and power from the abundant streams tumbling from the Pennines enabled Sheffield to specialize in cutlery from at least the 15C. In the 1740s Benjamin *Huntsman made a breakthrough with the development of the crucible and Thomas Boulsover pioneered *Sheffield plate. When *Bessemer perfected his new technique for steel production in the 1850s, it was at Sheffield that he set up his works; and stainless steel was pioneered here from 1903 (it was developed separately at the same time in the USA and Germany). The vast tower of the Renaissance-style town hall (1897, by C.W. Mountford) is appropriately crowned by a statue of Vulcan, the Roman god of fire and metal. A more direct memento of Sheffield's achievement is the Abbeydale Industrial Hamlet, southwest of the city, where a restored scythe-making factory of 1742 is now the setting for a museum of steel, with a Huntsman crucible furnace and water-powered tilt-hammers. The City Museum has an outstanding collection of cutlery and Sheffield plate.

In 1914 Sheffield was made a diocese and the old parish church (15C) became the cathedral; the Roman Catholic cathedral, completed 1850, is by Matthew Hadfield, a pupil of Pugin. The Graves Art Gallery (given to the city in the 1930s by a local businessman who had established Britain's first mail-order firm) is particularly strong in British painting of the 19–20C and in oriental art. The Crucible Theatre (1971) is for most of the year one of the country's leading repertory theatres, but it has also played a major part in the modern promotion of *snooker. Sheffield has acquired in recent years outstanding sports facilities in the Don Valley Stadium and Pond's Forge water sports centre – both built at very great cost to accommodate the World Student Games of 1991. Meadowhall, a vast shopping centre opened in 1990 on an out-of-town area of abandoned steelworks, became a controversial issue because of its damaging effect on retail business in the heart of the city.

Sheffield Park Garden (16km/10m N of Lewes) Garden with superb shrubs and trees round five man-made lakes. The lakes were laid out by Capability *Brown in the 1770s, but two of them were later much enlarged. The planting as seen today is largely of 1909–34.

Sheffield plate Copper coated with silver in a technique discovered by Thomas Boulsover (1704–88) in *Sheffield in about 1742. A thin sheet of silver was placed above and below the copper, and the whole sandwich was then heated and rolled. Though at first used for small items such as buttons, it was soon realized that cheap versions of silver pots and dishes for the table could be produced. The standard achieved was extremely high, and

Sheffield Park, where the shrubs and trees make for a rich display of autumn colours.

Sheffield did a great trade until the discovery of *electroplating in the 1840s.

Sheffield United, known as the Blades (Bramall Lane, Sheffield). Football club formed in 1889 on the initiative of the Yorkshire County Cricket Club, which owned Bramall Lane (the ground continued to be used for cricket, including Test matches, until 1973). The club was professional from the start and was elected to the new Division 2 of the *Football League in 1892. It has been much of the time since then in the top division, though it sank to Division 4 in 1981–2. It was a founder member of the Premier League in 1992. Club victories: FA Cup 1899, 1902, 15, 25; League Champions 1898.

Sheffield Wednesday, known as the Owls (Hillsborough, Sheffield). Football club formed in 1867 by the Sheffield Wednesday Cricket Club, which itself dated from 1825. It was elected to Division 1 of the *Football League in 1892 and has spent the greater part of the time since then in the top division, becoming a founder member in 1992 of the Premier League. Club victories: FA Cup 1896, 1907, 35; League Champions 1903, 04, 29, 30.

Sheldonian Theatre see *Oxford.

Shell Oil company which since 1907 has traded in partnership with Royal Dutch. Shell derives ultimately from a small shop opened in 1833 by Marcus Samuel (1798–1870) in the East End of London. He dealt in curios and oriental sea shells. The latter became so popular in Victorian households that he began organizing transport from the Far East, and it was this trading link which provided the basis for future growth. In 1890 his son, also Marcus Samuel (1858–1927), decided that there was a large market for paraffin in the Far East which he could supply by bulk transport from Russian oil terminals on the Black Sea. The Suez authorities had until then refused all applications to transport oil through the canal, but Samuel had a tanker designed which met their safety regulations. The *Murex* passed through the canal in 1892 with 4000 tons of Russian paraffin en route for Singapore and Bangkok. By 1897 the transport of oil was so much the largest part of Samuel's business that he set up a new specialist company; and for its name he used the original basis of the family fortune, the shell. The following year he began successfully drilling for oil in the east, in Borneo.

Meanwhile Royal Dutch had been formed in 1890 to exploit an oil well in Sumatra. During the 1890s the two companies were in competition, but they were also threatened by the much larger US firm, Standard Oil. They decided to merge their interests while retaining separate identities.

By World War I Shell had acquired oil wells in two areas – the Middle East and Venezuela – which were to become of great importance. From 1959 it was involved in developing the vast natural gas field at Groningen in the Netherlands. And from the 1970s the company was active in the North Sea oil fields, where the discovery in 1971 of the largest UK source, the Brent field, was a major new enterprise.

Mary **Shelley** (1797–1851) Author of *Frankenstein* and daughter of William Godwin and Mary *Wollstonecraft. She married Percy Bysshe Shelley in 1816.

Percy Bysshe **Shelley** (1792–1822) Poet of the Romantic movement whose life has often received more attention than his poetry. At the age of 19 he was sent down from Oxford for circulating to the heads of colleges a pamphlet entitled *The Necessity of Atheism*. That same year, 1811, he eloped with the 16-year-old Harriet Westbrook and married her in Edinburgh. Three years later, in 1814, he eloped with another 16-year-old, Mary Godwin, and wrote from Switzerland to invite his wife to join them. She declined and in 1816 committed suicide in the Serpentine in Hyde Park, whereupon he immediately married Mary (see Mary *Shelley). In 1817, after a lengthy law case, he was denied custody of his and Harriet's two children. The following year he and Mary left England for Italy, where they spent the rest of his short life (much of it in the company of Byron), and where two of their own very young children died. Shelley's death was the final macabre tragedy. He was drowned with two others when sailing his boat, the *Don Juan*, in a heavy storm in the gulf of Spezia, off the west coast of Italy. His body was washed up ten days later, recognizable only by his clothes; his face had been eaten away. He was cremated on the beach, in a specially built iron furnace, in the presence of Byron.

A radical and utopian passion inspired Shelley's major poetry, dreaming of mankind free from the restrictions of authority and convention. His first long poem, *Queen Mab* (1813), foresees a future in which the shackles of monarchy, commerce and religion have been cast away by a republican atheist society devoted to free love and vegetarianism. Similar themes of liberation are central to his very complex *Prometheus Unbound* (1820). Often he wrote in furious response to distressing news: the *Peterloo massacre prompted *The Mask of Anarchy* (1819), which includes his famous couplet on *Castlereagh; *Adonais* (1821) was written in Pisa on hearing that Keats had died in Rome. The long poems bear powerful witness to Shelley's belief in the high importance of poetry and the poet, but it is his brilliantly easy short lyrics which have been more widely known and loved – in particular *Ozymandias, *Ode to the West Wind and *To a Skylark.

Shelter (London EC1) Pressure group and fund-raising charity, set up in 1966 as a national campaign on behalf of the *homeless and much helped in its early days by the impact of the TV play *Cathy Come Home. Shelter calculated in 1991 that the number of homeless in Britain had more than doubled in the previous decade.

E.H. **Shepard** (Ernest Howard Shepard, 1879–1976) Artist best known for his illustrations to the books of A.A. *Milne. He was one of the team of cartoonists on *Punch* for more than 50 years, and it was there that he first illustrated Milne's poems for children.

Gillian **Shephard** (Gillian Watts, b. 1940, m. Thomas Shephard 1975) Conservative politician, MP for South West Norfolk since 1987, who entered the *cabinet in 1992 as secretary of state for employment.

shepherd's pie (also called cottage pie) Dish of stewed minced meat covered with a layer of mashed potato, browned on top in the oven. First mentioned in the late 19C (when mincing machines were introduced), it is more a Victorian idea of what a shepherd or a cottager might eat than any traditional reality. When called shepherd's pie, the main ingredient should traditionally be mutton or lamb; but it is now as likely to be beef.

Jack **Sheppard** (1702–24) London criminal who became a major celebrity, and later a popular hero of *penny dreadfuls, by the frequency and daring of his escapes from prison during 1724. After freeing himself twice in the early months of that year, he spent the summer committing robbery or highway theft almost every day (in popular myth to satisfy the demands of his mistress, Edgeworth Bess). When he was sentenced to death in August, Bess helped him to escape from the condemned cell. Captured in September, he was chained to the floor in the deepest

Jack Sheppard, the Houdini of his time, plans his next escape from Newgate prison: anonymous 18C engraving.

dungeon of *Newgate, yet somehow was soon back in Bess's arms. He was finally hanged in November before an estimated crowd of 200,000.

Thomas **Sheraton** (1751–1806) Furniture designer whose wide influence derived from *The Cabinet-Maker and Upholsterer's Drawing Book* (issued in 4 parts, 1791–4). Its intention was to provide practical information about the best designs of the time, making it easily available to cabinet-makers. The style was still *neoclassical. In preparing his book Sheraton interviewed craftsmen in different sections of the trade about their special skills (there is no evidence that he himself had a workshop or ever made any furniture). The success of this book has given his name to the English furniture of the period immediately after *Hepplewhite.

Shergar (foaled 1978) Bay colt which won the Derby by a record ten lengths in 1981, ridden by Walter Swinburn (b. 1961). After winning several other races with equal ease, including the Irish Derby, he retired to stud in County Kildare in Ireland. There, in February 1983, he was abducted by armed and masked men. The horse was never seen again. A committee of enquiry concluded that he had been taken by members of the IRA and was probably killed soon afterwards.

Richard Brinsley **Sheridan** (1751–1816) Anglo-Irish playwright, born in Dublin but living in England from childhood. He achieved success in his twenties with *The *Rivals* and *The *School for Scandal*, and in 1776 succeeded David Garrick as owner and manager of the Drury Lane theatre. His wit and fame soon made him a figure in fashionable London, an intimate friend of the prince of Wales and of leading politicians. From 1780 he sat as a Whig in the House of Commons and soon became known as an orator; his five-hour speech about the begums of Oudh in 1787 was considered so brilliant that he was appointed manager of the impeachment of Warren *Hastings. Wildly extravagant and frequently drunk, he had ever-mounting debts which were not helped by the fire which destroyed Drury Lane in 1809 – though this did allow him one of his best witticisms. Rebuked for standing in the street with a glass in his hand, watching the disaster, he replied 'A man may surely be allowed to take a glass of wine by his own fireside'.

sheriff court A judge is known as a sheriff in Scotland, where sheriff courts try the majority of civil cases and of those criminal cases too serious to be dealt with in district courts by lay magistrates (see *courts of law). Above the sheriff court for civil cases is the *Court of Session, and on the criminal side the *High Court of Justiciary. The maximum sentence which can be imposed in a sheriff court is three years' imprisonment, so serious crimes such as murder or rape are tried automatically in the High Court. In England the *high sheriff plays a different role.

Sherlock Holmes see Sherlock *Holmes.

Charles Scott **Sherrington** (1857–1952, GBE 1922) Physiologist who did pioneering research into the nervous system. He demonstrated the interconnection of all reflexes (*The Integrative Action of the Nervous System* 1906), eventually even relating the mysterious human knee-jerk to the excited state of nerve cells in the spine. In 1932 he shared a Nobel prize with *Adrian.

sherry Spanish white wine, fortified nowadays with brandy or other spirits, which for centuries has been a favourite drink in Britain. The name is a version of Xeres (now Jerez de la Frontera) and it referred originally to any wine from that district of Spain; Falstaff's favourite drink is 'sherris sack', 'sack' being a general word for wine from Spain and the Canaries.

Sherwood Forest Ancient woodland which once covered most of the western part of Nottinghamshire, known above all for its legendary association with *Robin Hood. A tiny section of it survives unaltered in the Sherwood Forest Country Park, 32km/20m north of Nottingham – about 180ha/450ac, containing some huge old oaks. The best known is the Major Oak, supported on numerous crutches, which is at least 500 years old and is traditionally said to be where Robin Hood liked to set up his camp.

She Stoops to Conquer: or, the Mistakes of a Night (1773) Comedy by *Goldsmith about the courtship of Kate Hardcastle by young Marlow. When travelling to meet the young woman his father hopes he will marry, Marlow loses his way and asks at the Three Jolly Pigeons for lodgings in the district. He is directed to Kate's home by her oafish and mischievous half-brother, Tony Lumpkin. Marlow therefore treats Mr Hardcastle as the landlord of an inn and makes immediate advances to Kate, whom he takes for one of the servants. In the event this is fortunate. He is crippled by shyness with girls of his own class, but this disability is overcome by his being unaware that Kate is his intended and this the house where he was expected.

Shetland (23,000 in 1991, administrative centre Lerwick) Since 1975 the *islands area covering the Shetlands.

Shetland see *ponies and *sheepdogs.

Shetlands Group of islands at the extreme north of Scotland, stretching from Fair Isle in the south to Unst in the north. Lerwick (the capital and site of the midwinter festival of *Up-Helly-Aa) is on Mainland, which also has the important prehistoric site of *Jarlshof. On *Mousa, an uninhabited island off the east coast of Mainland, is the most complete of Scotland's many brochs. The islands have bred the Shetlands *sheepdog (like a miniature collie) and the famous Shetlands pony (the smallest of *ponies, but stronger for its size than any other horse); both sheepdogs and ponies are known informally as shelties. The Shetlands share with the *Orkneys a history of Scandinavian domination from the 8C until being transferred to the crown of Scotland as part of a Danish dowry in the 15C.

In recent years Sullom Voe, an inlet on the north coast of Mainland, has become Europe's largest oil terminal, receiving both the Brent and Ninian pipelines from the *North Sea oil fields. But it was not in any way linked with the pollution threat to the Shetlands in January 1993. The tanker *Braer* drifted on to the rocks of Fitful Head, at the southwest tip of Mainland, after an engine failure; it was on its way from Norway to Canada carrying 85,000 tons of oil. A gale-force storm frustrated attempts to stop the ship drifting on to the rocks, and subsequently prevented the pumping of oil from its ruptured tanks. But the same violent winds had the effect of dispersing the relatively light crude oil of the cargo, and the disaster proved less severe than expected.

She-Who-Must-Be-Obeyed see *She and *Rumpole.

shilling see *currency.

Peter **Shilton** (b. 1949) One of England's two greatest goalkeepers, following the other (Gordon *Banks) at Leicester City in 1967. He later moved to Stoke City (1974), Nottingham Forest (1977), Southampton (1982), Derby County (1987) and as player manager to Plymouth Argyle (1992). At the end of 1992 he held a probably unbeatable trio of British records: the most League appearances (968 by the end of the 1991–2 season), the greatest number of caps (125 for England), and the most games played in the final rounds of the World Cup (17).

shinty (officially known by its Gaelic name of *camanachd*) Early form of *hockey and the sport of the Scottish Highlands. It is closely related to the Irish game of *hurling and is believed to have been brought from Ireland by the *Scots in about the 6C. There were many local variants of the rules, which were eventually coordinated at Kingussie in 1893. The main trophy, the Camanachd Cup, has been competed for by the local clubs since 1895.

Manny **Shinwell** (Emmanuel Shinwell, 1884–1986, baron 1970) Politician whose great age made him the last surviving link with the early days of the Labour movement, and whose chirpy character caused him to be a popular favourite. A Londoner by birth, it was in Scotland that he became involved in politics; he was on the Glasgow trades council from 1911 and was one of those who served a prison sentence in 1921 for incitement to riot. He was Labour MP for Linlithgow (1922–4, 1928–31) and then for Durham (1935–70); in the postwar Labour government he was briefly in the cabinet as minister of defence (1950–1). On his 100th birthday he made a speech in the House of Lords replying to tributes from all the political parties.

One of the great prehistoric sites of the Shetlands: the so-called wheel-houses at Jarlshof, dating from the 3–8C.

ship money Tax by means of which *Charles I sought to avoid having to summon parliament during the 1630s. It was traditionally the right of the monarch to levy ship money on property in coastal counties and cities for defence in time of war, and to do so without the involvement of parliament. In 1634 the king levied it on the argument that there was a possibility of war; in 1635 he extended it to inland areas; and he made a further claim in 1636. It was beginning to seem like a permanent tax, bypassing *parliament's right to control revenue. A policy of non-payment was led by John *Hampden, and one of the first acts of the *Long Parliament in 1640 was to declare ship money illegal.

ship of the line Sailing ship of sufficient size to take its place in the formal line of battle in a naval engagement of the 18–19C. This was usually taken to mean a ship of 74 guns or more, ranged along two or three decks.

shipping forecast Information provided four times a day by the *Meteorological Office on wind conditions (see *Beaufort scale) and visibility at sea, described separately for each of 31 forecasting areas round the British Isles from Iceland to Norway in the north and down to Gibraltar in the south.

Mother **Shipton** A supposed prophetess of the early 16C who has provided pamphleteers and the gullible with much excellent material over the centuries. She first appears in a pamphlet of 1641, in which she is said to have foretold various events then known to have happened in the 16C. The pattern has continued up to the present time, particularly in the north of England (she is believed to have lived in York), with successive modern marvels and events retrospectively discovered among her prophecies.

shire horse see *carthorses.

Shires A term for the counties of the Midlands, used originally by their neighbours to the east and south (Norfolk, Suffolk, Essex, Middlesex, Kent, Sussex, Surrey) whose own names did not end in 'shire'. It later became applied in particular to Northamptonshire and Leicestershire, counties famous for *hunting. It was here in the late 17C that packs of hounds were first kept purely for the purpose of hunting foxes, and many of England's oldest and best-known hunts are in this region – in particular the Cottesmore (which lays claim to be the oldest hunt of all, dating back to 1666), the Quorn (1698), the Pytchley (1750) and the Belvoir (1762).

shooting The three main game birds in Britain are the *grouse, the pheasant (traditionally said to have been introduced to England by the Romans) and the partridge. Of these the pheasant is shot in the greatest numbers, being the chief game bird reared for the purpose. The best shooting is considered to be when the birds are driven by beaters to fly fast or high across a waiting line of guns, but birds are also flushed out and shot by people walking with dogs across the moors or through fields and woods. Other types of bird considered 'fair game' are snipe, woodcock and wildfowl (ducks and geese). Rabbits and hares are also shot. The chief game birds are protected during statutory *close seasons.

Shooting in its present form developed in the 18C, when more accurate shotguns made it possible to hit a flying bird. Until then the sport was closer to stalking, using a dog to sniff out game and then creeping as close as possible to shoot the birds on the ground.

Clay-pigeon shooting has its origins in England in the late 18C. It derives from trapshooting, in which live birds were released from box traps. The unpredictable direc-

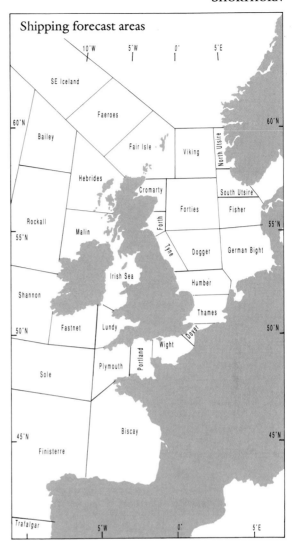

Shipping forecast areas

tion of their flight was imitated in the 19C by glass balls catapulted from spring-loaded devices (sometimes the balls were filled with feathers, to simulate a kill when the moving target was hit). By the late 19C versions of the modern clay saucers were already in use.

Nigel **Short** (b. 1965) Chess player whose early achievements did much to inspire a revival of the game in Britain. At the age of 15 he was runner-up to the 17-year-old Garry Kasparov in the World Junior Championship, and by the time he was 19 he was an international grandmaster. In January 1993 he defeated the Dutch grandmaster Jan Timman in the final of the candidates' contest to challenge Kasparov for his world title, becoming the first British-born player to reach such a level in the international chess scene. The only previous British challenger was Isidor Gunsberg (born in Hungary), who lost over seven weeks in 1890–1 to Wilhelm Steinitz.

shortbread Thick biscuit, sweet and rich, which is now particularly associated with Scotland. It is 'short' in the sense that the dough contains an unusually high proportion of butter, giving a crumbly quality.

Shorthorn (also called Durham) One of the earliest strains of cattle to have been improved by selection within a breed. Charles and Robert Colling, two brothers farming in county Durham, developed their herd of local cattle by selective breeding in the late 18C. Shorthorns were the first breed to have their own herdbook, begun in 1822. They are familiar now in many countries of the world and are found with any combination of white and red markings. The strain was bred originally to combine good beef and milking characteristics.

Henry **Shrapnel** (1761–1842) Artillery officer, remembered for the devastatingly effective exploding shell which he invented. Designed to scatter lead shot among enemy troops, it was adopted by the British army in 1803, was effective during the Battle of Waterloo, and has been in use in various forms throughout the world ever since.

Shrewsbury (60,000 in 1981) Town in a loop of the river Severn; administrative centre of Shropshire. It has been a place of strategic importance between Wales and England from at least the 5C. Leading out of the town across the river, in rival directions, are two beautiful bridges of the 18C, the Welsh Bridge and the English Bridge. The Norman castle was adapted for modern living by Telford and now provides the council chamber. Of the Benedictine abbey (founded 1083) only the church survives, much restored apart from its magnificent west end. The 12–15C St Mary's is famous for its stained glass, in particular a great Jesse window of the mid-14C. The Roman Catholic cathedral, never completed, is by one of Pugin's sons.

Among the steep streets there are many timber-frame Tudor houses, one of them (Rowley's House) containing Roman finds from nearby *Viroconium. The town's museum and library is in a 17C building near the castle. This previously belonged to Shrewsbury School, a leading *public school (founded 1552) which moved in 1882 to a new site outside the loop of the river.

Jean **Shrimpton** (b. 1942) The leading British model in the first half of the 1960s. David *Bailey photographed her from 1960 and their careers developed together, with his images of her characteristically sixties look (large eyes, provocative mouth and long, straight hair) soon appearing in the international fashion magazines.

Shropshire (413,000 in 1991, administrative centre Shrewsbury) *County in west central England, bordering on Wales.

A Shropshire Lad (1896) Volume of 63 poems, some of them named and others only numbered, which A.E. *Housman published at his own expense in 1896. Hardly noticed at first, they became extremely popular during World War I when a deep chord was struck by their mood of poignancy for the transience of youth and of nature's beauties. They share a mood of lyric melancholy with *Gray's *Elegy*, a similarly accessible work which has had an equally powerful effect.

Shrove Tuesday (also known as Pancake Day) The Tuesday 41 days before Easter. It is followed by Ash Wednesday, the first of the 40 days of Lent. The name relates back to pre-Reformation times, when the priest 'shrove' his parishioners on this day – meaning that he heard their confessions, enabling them to enter Lent with a clear conscience. The approach of lean times provoked in other countries the merry excesses of carnival (a farewell to meat), but in Britain the humble pancake has been the national indulgence. Traditionally it is turned in the pan by tossing it in the air. In many places (most famously at Olney in Buckinghamshire) this is done by women while running in a pancake race. An ancient ceremony at Westminster School, called the Pancake Greeze, involves the cook tossing a large pancake over a high bar before the boys scramble for it.

Shugborough (10km/6m E of Stafford) House begun in 1695 and much enlarged and altered throughout the 18C. It is known in particular for the series of early *Greek Revival monuments in the park, designed by 'Athenian' Stuart. The main ones, constructed in the 1760s, are the Tower of the Winds, the Triumphal Arch and the Lanthorn of Demosthenes. Shugborough is the home of Patrick *Lichfield.

Nevil **Shute** (pen name of Nevil Shute Norway, 1899–1960) Author whose professional background enabled him to write gripping novels about people confronting technological or scientific disaster. He worked as a designer in the aeronautic industry, notably on the successful airship R-100 (see *R-101). His specialist knowledge lay behind the drama of *No Highway* (1948), in which a desperate engineer struggles to persuade his superiors that he has identified metal fatigue in an airliner (this was some years before the *Comet was taken out of service for that very reason). From 1950 Shute lived in Australia; *On the Beach* (1957) is set in a Melbourne suburb, with people struggling to go about their everyday lives among nuclear fall-out from World War III.

Shylock see *The *Merchant of Venice*.

Antoinette **Sibley** (b. 1939) Dancer who joined the Royal Ballet in 1956 and went on to appear in all the ballerina roles of the standard repertory. In 1964 she created Titania in Ashton's *The Dream*; her Oberon was Anthony *Dowell. Together they went on to become the Royal Ballet's most romantic leading pair in the era after Fonteyn and Nureyev. MacMillan's *Manon* was another work in which they together created the leading roles.

Walter **Sickert** (1860-1942) Painter who was the leading spirit of the *Camden Town Group. His own art went through many phases, but always with a preference for a broad brush stroke and a sombre palette. His favourite early subject matter was the interiors of music halls (his first career, in his late teens, had been as an actor). Around the turn of the century he was living abroad and painting exterior scenes (Dieppe and Venice), but by the Camden Town period his speciality was drab interiors, often with a nude model on a bed. His best-known image, from about 1914, is of domestic dreariness – the marital scene, influenced in its composition by Degas, which is known simply as *Ennui* (there are several versions, of which one is in the Tate).

Mrs **Siddons** (Sarah Kemble, 1755–1831, m. William Siddons 1773) The greatest tragic actress of her age and perhaps in the history of the English theatre. She was one of 12 children in a family of strolling players; her brother John Philip Kemble (1757–1823) became a much admired tragic actor, and their niece Fanny *Kemble also had a successful career. Mrs Siddons' first season in London was a failure (the winter of 1775–6, in Garrick's company), but she then built up a faithful following round the country before returning to captivate Drury Lane in 1782. She avoided comedy, concentrating on the tragic roles in which she could transfix an audience with the intensity of her passion and grief. Lady Macbeth was considered her greatest part; when she chose it for her farewell performance, in 1812, the play was brought to an abrupt end after the character's final appearance in the sleepwalking scene.

Philip **Sidney** (1554–86, kt 1583) England's closest approach to the ideal of a Renaissance gentleman. Well travelled and well educated, he was at home in the great houses of the land. He was born at *Penshurst and his sister Mary, countess of Pembroke, lived at *Wilton. He wrote purely for the enjoyment of his own circle; nothing was published in his lifetime. *Arcadia* was mainly written at Wilton (*The Countesse of Pembrokes Arcadia* 1590) and is a long prose narrative in a pastoral setting. *Astrophel and Stella* was the first sequence of sonnets in English; its publication in 1591 made the writing of sonnets briefly but intensely fashionable. Sidney died after being wounded at Zutphen, in the Netherlands, from a bullet in the thigh. The famous story – that he refused a drink of water, telling a wounded soldier 'Thy necessity is yet greater than mine' – was current soon after his death.

Sidney Street siege (1911) Incident in a street in London's East End, when two armed anarchists died in a house where they had been trapped by police and a detachment of Scots Guards. The memory of it survives largely because the home secretary, Winston *Churchill, appeared in the street to direct operations himself – an involvement for which he was much criticized.

Siege Perilous see the *Round Table.

Siegfried line Name used by the Germans for two of their lines of fortification. The Siegfried line of World War I, known to the Allies as the Hindenburg line, was built behind the German trenches in Belgium as a fall-back position. The later Siegfried line was constructed between the wars along the border between Germany and France, facing France's equivalent Maginot line. It is this which features in the song popular with British soldiers in World War II: 'We're going to hang out the washing on the Siegfried line . . . if the Siegfried line's still there'.

William **Siemens** (1823–83, kt 1883) German-born inventor, naturalized in 1859, who made important contributions in many fields but is remembered above all for the open-hearth process of steel-making (see *iron and steel). This was an application of the regenerative principle, pioneered with his German brother Friedrich (1826–1904), by which waste heat from a process is reused – in this case both to increase the temperature of the furnace and to heat the inflow of oxygen.

Sierra Leone Member of the *Commonwealth since 1961. The country, on the west coast of Africa, has an indigenous population in the interior while the descendants of many generations of immigrants live on the coast around the capital, Freetown. This was founded in 1787 by British opponents of the *slave trade, as a refuge for freed slaves – a purpose reflected also in the name of the neighbouring state to the south, Liberia, established by American abolitionists in the 1820s. Freetown was a crown colony from 1808. From 1951 it was administered with the interior as Sierra Leone, which became independent in 1961.

Sikhs There are believed to be in Britain about 400,000 Sikhs – followers of a religion which developed during the 15C in India, in the Punjab. Following the teaching of a succession of *gurus*, beginning with Guru Nanak, Sikhism was an attempt to reconcile the two dominant religions of India, Hinduism and Islam. The majority of Sikh families arrived from the Punjab by *immigration in the years after World War II. The main Sikh communities in Britain are in London, Bradford, Birmingham, Coventry, Huddersfield, Leeds, Nottingham and Wolverhampton.

Silbury Hill (10km/6m W of Marlborough) The largest prehistoric mound in Europe, a flat-topped cone 40m/130ft high, erected some time before 2000 BC for an unknown purpose (there is no evidence of burial within

it). It was constructed with great care, of chalk blocks and infill. Though small compared to the pyramids, the traditional calculation is that it would have taken 700 men 10 years to build.

Silchester (16km/10m SW of Reading) The site of a Roman town, *Calleva Atrebatum*, with buildings from the 2–4C. The walls, about 2.5km/1.5m in length, are still in places 4m/13ft high. The town, laid out on a rectangular grid, was the capital of a local tribe. Excavations have revealed the foundations of a central forum, public baths, several temples and a 4C Christian church, the earliest to have been discovered in Britain. The main finds from the site are in the museum at Reading.

'silk' see *QC.

Alan **Sillitoe** (b. 1928) Novelist, much of whose work is directly based on his own working-class background in the city of Nottingham. With his first two books – *Saturday Night and Sunday Morning* and The *Loneliness of the Long Distance Runner* – he provided two of the most memorable anti-heroes of the anti-heroic 1950s.

Silurian see *geological periods.

Silverstone (23km/14m SW of Northampton) Britain's foremost motor racing circuit and the location of the *British Grand Prix (until 1987 the event alternated with *Brands Hatch). Silverstone was a World War II airfield; it was adapted for motor racing in 1948 and was opened with an RAC Grand Prix. The first official British Grand Prix (which happened to be also the first race in the newly established world championship for drivers) took place at Silverstone in 1950.

Lambert **Simnel** (*c.*1475–1535) A nonentity used by Yorkist opponents of *Henry VII to legitimize an uprising in 1487. They claimed him to be Edward of Warwick (son of the duke of Clarence, brother to Edward IV and Richard III) and he was crowned Edward VI in the cathedral in Dublin. They then invaded England with an army of German mercenaries, whom Henry defeated with some difficulty at Stoke in Nottinghamshire. Deciding that Simnel himself was harmless, Henry employed him in the royal kitchens.

simnel cake Traditional cake for *Mothering Sunday, recently associated also with Easter. It acquired in the mid-19C its present identity as a rich fruit cake with a layer of marzipan through the centre or on top. Earlier references make it sound more like a currant loaf, the name 'simnel' being that of the fine flour used.

'Si monumentum requiris, circumspice' see *St Paul's Cathedral.

Simply Red Pop group formed in Manchester in 1985 by singer and writer Mick Hucknall (b. 1961), who had previously fronted a punk band, the Frantic Elevators. Their 1985 single *Holding Back the Years* reached no. 2 in the UK when reissued in 1986, and was briefly no. 1 in the USA. In 1989 the LP *A New Flame* topped the UK charts. Its success was soon far exceeded by another no. 1 hit, *Stars* – one of the top bestselling albums of 1991, as subsequently also of 1992.

James **Simpson** (1811–70, bt 1866) Scottish obstetrician whose fame derives from his pioneering use of chloroform. In 1846 an American dentist, William Morton, demonstrated the pain-killing effects of ether. Simpson, a professor of midwifery in Edinburgh, recognized the need for a more reliable anaesthetic and in 1847 found the answer in chloroform (his first patient was so enthusiastic that she named her baby girl Anaesthesia). Initial public resistance crumbled after chloroform was given to Queen Victoria for the birth of Prince Leopold in 1853.

Wallis **Simpson** see the *abdication crisis.

Clive **Sinclair** (b. 1940, kt 1983) Inventor and entrepreneur who led the market in 1972 with Britain's first electronic pocket calculator, and held his lead later in the decade with a computer which sold for under £100. He had many production difficulties with both of these, but his first invention to fail commercially was the C5, an electric three-wheel vehicle which he launched in 1985. In 1992 he introduced the Zike, a lightweight electric bicycle.

Sindbad the Sailor One of the stories of The *Arabian Nights* which became popular in the late 19c as a subject for *pantomime (the marvels of Sindbad's seven journeys offer spectacular opportunities for stage effects). His best-known exploit concerns the terrifying Old Man of the Sea, who refuses to get off Sindbad's back after being given a lift over a stream.

Donald **Sinden** (b. 1923) Actor who has been closely linked with the Royal Shakespeare Company, but who is most widely known for his roles in three television series – as a young vicar in *Our Man at St Mark's* in the 1960s, as the very British butler to an American in London (Elaine Stritch) in *Two's Company* in the 1970s, and as one of a pair of antique dealers in *Never the Twain* in the 1980s.

Sinfonia Antartica see *Vaughan Williams.

Singapore Island off the southern tip of the Malay peninsula, which has been a member of the *Commonwealth and a republic since 1965. Measuring only 42km/26m by 23km/14m, it occupied an important position on the sea route from India to China after a settlement was established here for the East India Company by Stamford *Raffles in 1819. The island was grouped from 1826 with two other ports on the west coast of the peninsula, Malacca and Penang, to form the Straits Settlements. In 1946 Singapore became a separate colony and it was granted internal self-government in 1959. With full independence, in 1963, it joined the federation of *Malaysia, from which it seceded in 1965. The prime minister in 1959, Lee Kuan Yew (b. 1923), retained an unbroken spell of power until his resignation in 1990.

Sing a song of sixpence *Nursery rhyme first printed in about 1744 and very much interpreted ever since. According to the most fanciful theory, the blackbirds singing in the pie set before the king are the choirs of monasteries dissolved by Henry VIII, while the queen in the parlour is Catherine of Aragon and the maid in the garden her successor, Anne Boleyn.

'singeing the king of Spain's beard' see *Armada.

The *Singing Detective* (BBC 1986) Six-part television drama series by Dennis *Potter, building on the technique of his earlier *Pennies from Heaven* in interspersing the drama with song-and-dance routines based on popular songs. The central character, played by Michael *Gambon, suffers from a painful skin disease, psoriasis – as does Potter himself.

single cube room see *Wilton House.

sinking fund see William *Pitt.

Sinn Fein (*sinn féin* Irish Gaelic for 'we ourselves') Nationalist political party founded in *Ireland in 1902 by Arthur Griffith (1872–1922), with a policy of passive resistance by such means as non-payment of taxes. By the time of the *Easter Rising of 1916 the supporters of the cause were more militant. Eamon de Valera (1882–1975) was elected leader in 1917; unlike Griffith he had taken an active part in the rising. In the election of 1918 Sinn Fein won the majority of the Irish seats at Westminster, but the party did not accept the Anglo-Irish treaty of 1921 because of the exclusion of the *six counties. In conjunction with that part of the *IRA which also rejected the treaty, Sinn Fein fought and lost a civil war (1921–3) with the government of the newly independent Irish Free State.

De Valera himself accepted the status quo in 1926 and the following year his supporters within Sinn Fein entered parliament as a new party, Fianna Fail. A minority still refused to accept the validity of the parliament in Dublin and continued as a much reduced Sinn Fein – linked with those in the IRA who took the same line. Both organizations remained relatively obscure, though two Sinn Fein candidates were elected to Westminster in 1955 (they were subsequently disqualified, as felons). In 1969 breakaway groups, calling themselves Provisional Sinn Fein and the Provisional IRA, adopted a more violent policy in *Northern Ireland; and in 1983 Provisional Sinn Fein achieved its first success in a general election when its leader (Gerry Adams, b. 1948) became MP for West Belfast. Since the party does not recognize the authority of Westminster, he declined to take his seat; he held it in the general election of 1987 but lost it in 1992. In local government in Northern Ireland Sinn Fein has a considerable number of elected councillors.

Sir Title used by a *baronet or a knight (see *orders of chivalry).

siren suit One-piece garment, similar to overalls, which was in the shops in the autumn of 1939 as suitable apparel for women in air raid shelters; it was to be worn, therefore, after a siren rather than by one (the ambiguity was immediately pointed out). The garment was later made for both sexes, and its fame derives from its use by Winston Churchill. He had a blue siren suit which he referred to as his 'rompers'.

Sir Patrick Spens Ancient Scottish *ballad in which Sir Patrick, the best sailor in Scotland, is sent over the sea to fetch the daughter of the king of Norway. The greater part of the ballad is a vivid description of the storm which sends Sir Patrick and all his crew 50 fathoms deep.

Sissinghurst Castle (22km/14m S of Maidstone) Only a single low range of buildings and a tall central tower survive from the great Tudor house which once stood here, but from the sunken moat and the surrounding jumble of old walls Vita *Sackville-West and Harold Nicolson were able to create, from 1930, England's most influential garden of the 20c. He was the architect of the overall layout, she the gardener who planted it. Informality within a formal structure was their secret, developing a theme pioneered by Gertrude *Jekyll and adopted also in the succession of garden 'rooms' at *Hidcote. Among the best known of the strongly differentiated areas at Sissinghurst are the Cottage Garden, the Moat Walk, and the most celebrated of all, the White Garden.

Peter **Sissons** (b. 1942) Newsreader, at differing times for BBC TV and on Channel 4. In 1989 he followed Robin Day in the challenging role of chairman of *Question Time*, with the task of holding the ring between loquacious and obstinate politicians.

Ganesh **Sittampalam** see *infant prodigies.

Sitwell family Three children who grew up at Renishaw Hall, an ancestral seat in Derbyshire. Each became a writer. The eldest, Edith (1887–1964, DBE 1954), was the most original – in her work and also in her famously eccentric appearance and dress. The public became aware of her talent with the first public performance in 1923 of *Façade*, a piece which has grown steadily in popularity. Its jazzy rhythms and jagged speech patterns were untypical of most of her later work, which was often romantic and elegiac, with an increasingly Christian element; she became a Roman Catholic in 1955.

Her brother Osbert (1892–1969, 5th bt 1943) was a poet and novelist but is remembered in particular for his 5-volume autobiography (*Left Hand, Right Hand* 1944, *The Scarlet Tree* 1946, *Great Morning!* 1947, *Laughter in the Next Room* 1948, *Noble Essences* 1950).

The youngest of the three, Sacheverell (1897–1988, 6th bt 1969), was like the others a poet but was also an art historian; *Southern Baroque Art* (1924) and *German Baroque Art* (1927) appeared when the subject was far from fashionable.

Six Counties The counties of *Ulster which in 1921 remained part of the *United Kingdom as a result of the campaign against *Home Rule. They are Antrim, Armagh, Down, Fermanagh, Londonderry and Tyrone.

sixes and sevens Phrase for anything in a disordered state. To set all 'on six and seven' was an idiom in use from at least the 14C, deriving from dice and meaning to take a big gamble. The theme of disorder entered with a gradual change to 'at sixes and sevens'. The most likely influence is the ancient dispute between the Merchant Taylors and Skinners for the sixth and seventh places in the great twelve *City Livery Companies.

sixth form college see *state school.

Sizewell Village on the east coast of England, in Suffolk, which has become the nation's main site for *nuclear power. Twin magnox reactors (Sizewell A) began operating here in 1966. Sizewell B – Britain's first pressurized water reactor (PWR) – was under construction in the early 1990s. Visible for miles around, with a steel dome three times the size of the one on St Paul's Cathedral, it was scheduled to be functional in 1994. In 1992 Nuclear Electric announced plans to add a further two PWRs, to be known jointly as Sizewell C.

Skara Brae (Mainland, Orkney) The best preserved *Stone Age village in Europe, kept almost intact by two violent storms. The first of these, in about 2000 BC, is believed to have buried the houses in sand; the second, in 1850, revealed them again. On an island without trees everything was of stone and has survived, including items of furniture such as beds and tables and recessed cupboards. The one-room houses (some seven or eight forming the original village) had earth and rubbish banked up to the top of their stone walls and no doubt over the stone roofs, making them in effect underground shelters in a harsh climate. A drain from each dwelling led to a common sewer.

Skegness is so bracing The slogan on the most famous of all railway posters, first used by the Great Northern Railway in 1908 and reissued for many years in modified versions. In the drawing (by John Hassall, 1868–1948) the jolly pipe-smoking fisherman is bounding along the beach of Skegness, a resort on the east coast of England, in Lincolnshire.

The famous Skegness poster, adapted for use between the wars by the London and North Eastern Railway.

skinhead The term was coined in the USA to describe an army recruit with the shortest of crew cuts. In Britain it became associated from the 1960s with a minority youth fashion (later linked with *neo-Nazis), characterized by closely shaven heads, white T-shirts and Crombie jackets, braces and narrow jeans rolled up to reveal heavy boots (preferably 22-hole Doc Martens).

Dennis **Skinner** see *Bolsover.

Sky see *television.

*The **Sky at Night*** see Patrick *Moore.

Skye The largest island of the Inner Hebrides, lying just off the northwest coast of Scotland. It is also one of the most scenic, with several peaks of the Cuillin Hills rising above 950m/3120ft. The capital, Portree, is on the east coast and *Dunvegan Castle on an inlet to the northwest. There are several locations on the island associated with its most romantic moment, when Flora *MacDonald smuggled Bonnie Prince Charlie here in disguise. In 1992, among much litigation and controversy, work began to construct a bridge over the narrow channel (about 900m/1000yd) between Skye and the mainland at Kyle of Lochalsh.

Skye Boat Song A relatively recent song, based on the adapted tune of a sea shanty and with words written in 1884 by Harold Boulton (1859–1935). It has added greatly to the popular fame of Charles Edward *Stuart's escape from Benbecula to Skye in 1746 under the protection of Flora *Macdonald:

> Speed, bonnie boat, like a bird on the wing;
> Onward, the sailors cry:
> Carry the lad that's born to be king
> Over the sea to Skye.

Skye terrier see *terriers.

Slade Jokey rock group composed of Noddy Holder (b. 1952, guitar and vocals), Dave Hill (b. 1952, guitar), Jimmy Lea (b. 1952, bass, piano and violin) and Don Powell (b. 1950, drums). They were together in 1966 as the 'N Betweens, changing their name to Ambrose Slade and then to Slade in 1969. Their first no. 1 single was *Coz I Love You* (1971), followed by *Take Me Bak 'Ome* and *Mama Weer All Crazee Now* (both 1972), then *Cum On Feel The Noize*, *Skweeze Me Pleeze Me* and *Merry Xmas Everybody* (all 1973). Most of their songs are written by Holder and Lea. An album of 1987, *You Boyz Make Big Noize*, took its title from a comment made by the tea lady at the recording studio.

Felix **Slade** (1790–1868) Collector of ancient and modern glass (now in the British Museum) who also had a lasting effect on British education in the fine arts. A bequest in his will endowed Slade professorships at Oxford and Cambridge and at University College in London. An endowment of six art scholarships at University College led to the establishment of the *art school named after him.

Slade School of Fine Art see *art schools.

slave trade The transport of slaves from Africa to plantations in the New World followed soon after the voyage of Columbus in 1492. By 1517 Spain was granting licences for slaves to be taken to its colonies in the Caribbean. By the late 17C, when sugar plantations in the West Indies had become extremely profitable, the bulk of the slave trade was being carried out by the British; and in the 18C the *triangular trade became fully developed. The coastal area of Nigeria, to which captives were brought from the interior of Africa, became known as the Slave Coast.

From the late 17C there was a steady groundswell of opinion against slavery, in which the Quakers were active from the start and of which Aphra Behn's novel *Oroonoko* (1688) was an early expression. One important milestone was the judgement by Lord Mansfield in 1772 that a slave, James Somersett, held in irons on board a ship in the Thames after escaping and being recaptured, had automatically become free when he set foot in Britain. Another was the formation in 1787 of the Society for the Abolition of the Slave Trade, of which *Wilberforce was the most active member. But it took 20 years of pressure before parliament passed an act (1807) making it illegal for British ships to carry slaves or for British colonies to import them.

Meanwhile the world's first decree outlawing slavery itself had been passed, in 1794, by the revolutionary assembly in France; and various South American countries, winning independence from Spain in the early 19C, legislated to free their existing slaves. In 1823 Wilberforce formed the British and Foreign Anti-Slavery Society, and success followed this time in only ten years. The Abolition Act of 1833 provided for slaves in British colonies to be set free and for their owners to be compensated. The moral crusade then shifted to Africa itself, with *Livingstone and others trying to penetrate the interior in the hope of eventually stifling the trade at its source.

Wayne **Sleep** (b. 1948) Dancer who in 1966 joined the Royal Ballet, where his agility and humour won him the best character parts though his short stature denied him

the classic roles. He formed his own company, Dash, in 1980; played Mr Mistoffelees in the original cast of *Cats* (1981); and in 1983–4 starred in *The Hot Shoe Show* on television and stage.

General **Slim** (William Slim, 1891–1970, KCB 1944, viscount 1960) Commander who led the 14th army in the victories of 1944–5, driving the Japanese out of Burma. He was governor general of Australia 1953–60.

Slimbridge (24km/15m SW of Gloucester) Wetlands bird sanctuary on the Severn estuary, headquarters of the Wildfowl & Wetlands Trust established in 1946 by Peter *Scott (the name was changed from Wildfowl Trust in 1989). Many varieties of swans, geese and ducks winter here, in addition to Slimbridge's extensive resident collection of water birds and other species.

slipware Earthenware pottery decorated with diluted clay of various colours, usually standing in relief. Such wares were made to a high standard in Staffordshire in the late 17C, particularly in the form of circular dishes bearing figurative designs and a prominently displayed name. The names are most often those of the Toft family – in particular Thomas Toft, but also James and Ralph. It is assumed that these were the potters, but there is no firm evidence of this (see *Five Towns for illustration).

Hans **Sloane** (1660–1753, bt 1716) Physician and obsessive collector, whose coins and medals, books, prints and drawings, botanical specimens, ethnographic objects and other curiosities (amounting in all to some 80,000 items) became the basis of the *British Museum. He kept his treasures in a house in Chelsea, where he is commemorated in Sloane Street and Sloane Square.

Sloane Ranger Term coined by Peter York in *Harpers and Queen* in 1975 to describe the conventional upperclass young woman in fashionable areas of London, characteristically wearing informal country clothes. The phrase, combining London's Sloane Square with the Lone Ranger, had considerable currency during the 1980s.

slogan Used now for any repeated phrase in advertising or politics, the word is *Gaelic for a battle cry of the Highland clans of Scotland.

Mr **Slope** see *Barchester Towers*.

Slough of Despond see *Pilgrim's Progress*.

Slump see the *Depression.

small claims Procedure in England and Wales by which civil litigation for sums less than £1000 can be delegated by *county courts to a district judge sitting as an arbitrator, thus greatly reducing the cost for the litigant. There is a simple scale of fees (in 1992 10% of any sum claimed below £300, and then a reducing scale up to a maximum of £43). Most such cases are brought by customers against firms and a majority are judged on written evidence, without either side needing to attend the court. If the claim is successful, the fee is recovered from the defendant.

John **Smeaton** (1724–92) Engineer who made his reputation with his *Eddystone lighthouse and was responsible for the *Forth-Clyde canal.

Smike see *Nicholas Nickleby*.

Samuel **Smiles** (1812–1904) Scottish author who expressed the values and aspirations of the Victorian era, with an emphasis on hard work and making the most of one's opportunities. He wrote biographies of great men who had succeeded from humble beginnings (*Lives of the Engineers* 1861–2), but by far his most influential book was *Self-Help; with illustrations of character and conduct* (1859). Based on his lectures to young men in Leeds, telling them how to improve their chances in life, this book sold in vast numbers. *Character* (1871), *Thrift* (1875) and *Duty* (1880) went through fewer editions.

Smiley see John *Le Carré.

Robert **Smirke** (1781–1867, kt 1832) The leading *Greek Revival architect. The *British Museum is his most important building.

Adam **Smith** (1723–90) Scottish political philosopher and economist, whose *Inquiry into the nature and causes of the Wealth of Nations* (1776) has been an extremely influential work. He lectured from 1748 in Edinburgh, where he became a close friend of *Hume, and he was then a professor (1751–63) at the university of Glasgow. *The Wealth of Nations* analyzes the division of labour, the concept of value, the nature of capital and investment, and systems of government and taxation. Smith concludes that economic well-being derives from the combined self-interest of people operating in a free market, and that government intervention should therefore be limited to breaking up monopolies (which frustrate the working of the market); he allows government a role outside the market, in the provision of defence, major capital projects such as roads, and education where not otherwise available. His ideas have been vigorously championed in recent years – witness the *think-tank named after him – and they were central to government theory in the *Thatcher period.

Delia **Smith** Cookery writer, with a column for many years in London's *Evening Standard* (1972–85), and presenter of several cookery series on BBC TV. Her first book, with the endearing title *How to Cheat at Cooking* (1973), was followed by several with a special emphasis on 'country recipes'.

Doug **Smith** (b. 1917) The jockey who followed Gordon Richards' unbroken spell as *champion jockey; his own run of championship years, 1954–9, was interrupted only once (by Scobie Breasley in 1957). He excelled at the longer races, winning the Cesarewitch (over 2 miles and 2 furlongs) no less than six times.

F.E. **Smith** (Frederick Edwin Smith, 1872–1930, earl of Birkenhead 1922) Lawyer and Conservative politician, known for most of his life as F.E. Smith and famous for his wit. As attorney general (1915–18) he prosecuted *Casement for treason. His period as lord chancellor (1919–22) was notable for his reform of the laws of land and property.

Harvey **Smith** (b. 1938) Yorkshire rider who is the crowd-pulling showman of the jumping circuit, both for his determination and for his sometimes aggressive unpredictability. He was the first professional in the sport (from 1972) and one of the first to be sponsored (appearing on horses with names such as Sanyo Music Centre). His extremely successful career has not included a gold in the Olympics or World or European Championships, but one of his most impressive records is four wins, equalled only by the Irish rider Eddie Macken, in the Hickstead Derby (1970, 71, 74, 81).

His son Robert (b. 1961) made a spectacular entry into the profession; at the age of 18, in 1979, he won the King George V Gold Cup and was leading showjumper at the Horse of the Year Show.

John **Smith** (*c.*1579–1631) The leading colonist at Jamestown, in Virginia, which was the first successful English settlement in *America. He later went on to explore the coastal region which he named New England (he wrote books on both Virginia and New England). The best-known incident connected with him, possibly fabricated, is the saving of his life by *Pocahontas.

John **Smith** (b. 1938) Labour politician, MP for Monklands East since 1983 (previously Lanarkshire North 1970–83). Trained as a lawyer and called to the Bar in Scotland, he was briefly in the cabinet at the end of the Callaghan administration as secretary of state for trade (1978–9). He was shadow cabinet spokesman on trade and consumer protection (1979–82), on energy (1982–3) and on trade and industry (1984–7), before becoming shadow chancellor in 1987 for a five-year period (during which he suffered a heart attack, in 1989). In 1992 he succeeded Neil Kinnock as leader of the Labour party and of the Opposition, after an easy victory over the rival candidate, Bryan Gould. He immediately instituted a major review of the party's policy and programme, in the light of four successive electoral defeats. He is a keen climber of the *Munros.

Maggie **Smith** (b. 1934, DBE 1990) Actress who first appeared on the West End stage in a revue, *Share My Lettuce* (1957), and from 1963 was a founding member of Laurence Olivier's National Theatre company – playing Desdemona to his Othello in 1964. She soon established a major international career in films, winning an Oscar for *The *Prime of Miss Jean Brodie* (1969). Her most characteristic performances have been of tight-lipped and rather edgy women, as in *A Room with a View* (1986) or *The Lonely Passion of Judith Hearne* (1989).

Matthew **Smith** (1879–1959, kt 1954) Painter who studied in 1911 in Paris under Matisse and became the leading English exponent of the Fauve style, with bright contrasting colours. His later work consists mainly of nudes, made luscious by his strongly applied line and the richness of his tones.

Mel **Smith** see *Smith and Jones.

Paul **Smith** (b. 1946) Menswear designer who opened his first shop in Nottingham in 1970. He has since extended to London and New York, and there are 60 Paul Smith shops in Japan – all making much of the clothes' British origin and several of them with authentic interiors shipped out from England (the Tokyo branch was once a chocolate shop in Newcastle). His designs combine traditional styles with unusual fabrics and colours. In 1993 he marketed his first collection of clothes for women.

Stevie **Smith** (Florence Margaret Smith, 1902–71) Poet and novelist, known for a barbed wit masking an often bleak view of life. She had the same job for her entire professional career – as a private secretary in the publishing firm of Newnes – and she lived in the house of an adored aunt (the 'lion aunt') who died in 1966. In her last decade Stevie Smith had considerable success on the poetry-reading circuit of the 1960s. Glenda Jackson played her in *Stevie* (1977), a play and then a film based on her life and work. She has added to everyday English idiom a phrase, 'not waving but drowning', which was the title of one of her books (1957). The title poem includes the couplet:

I was much further out than you thought
And not waving but drowning.

Smithfield in its last decades as a market for live animals, brought to the slaughter: aquatint after Rowlandson, 1811.

Sydney Smith (1771–1845) Clergyman remembered for his wit. He said of Macaulay that 'the occasional flashes of silence make his conversation perfectly delightful', and declared his own idea of heaven to be 'eating *pâtés de foie gras* to the sound of trumpets'. He was a leading member of the *Holland House set.

W.H. Smith Newsagent, stationer and bookselling chain named after William Henry Smith (1792–1865), who developed a newspaper shop opened by his parents in London in 1792. By efficient use of the stage-coach network, William Henry beat his rivals in the distribution of newspapers from London. Subsequently his son, also William Henry, used the railways to change the business from a London shop into a national retail chain. In 1848 he secured an exclusive contract to place stalls selling newspapers and cheap books on the platforms of the London and North-Western Railway; the stalls flourished in a period when novels were sold in instalments and paperbacks were being introduced. In the early 20C the firm gave up its station bookstalls in favour of premises on station approaches and subsequently on high streets, but branches of W.H. Smith later reappeared on railway stations as well as featuring prominently in airports.

William Smith (1769–1839) Amateur geologist, variously known as the father of English geology or Strata Smith. His work as an engineer, carrying out surveys for canals, brought him in contact with rock strata of many kinds. His originality lay in realizing that they could be dated by the fossils which they contained. He kept records and drawings of his observations, which he published in his *Geological Map of England and Wales, with Part of Scotland* (1815) and in *Strata Identified by Organized Fossils* (1816–19).

Smith and Jones (BBC from 1982) Television revue series featuring Mel Smith (b. 1952) and Griff Rhys Jones (b. 1953). Its most characteristic sketch, a staple of all the shows, has the pair nose to nose in profile with their faces filling the screen, as they muse quietly on some lunatic or bone-headed theme. In its early series, until it transferred from BBC 2 to BBC 1, the show was known as *Alas Smith and Jones.*

Smithfield Market (London EC1) The capital's main meat market since the 12C, named because originally a 'smooth field' just to the northwest of the old walled city. Cattle, sheep and pigs arrived on the hoof and were slaughtered here in conditions of appalling squalor. In 1855 the live trade was moved to Islington. The present covered market, built in imitation of the Crystal Palace, opened in 1868. Lorries deliver carcasses which are cut up during the night and sold to the retail trade when the market opens at 3 a.m. After some doubts about its future in the early 1990s, Smithfield is now being expensively refurbished to meet EC regulations.

SmithKline Beecham One of the largest companies quoted on the Stock Exchange, formed in 1989 by the merger of two great pharmaceutical enterprises. Smith-Kline derived originally from a drugstore in Philadelphia, where from 1830 John Smith sold his own preparations as pills; Marlon Kline was a chemist who joined the company in 1875. The Beecham Group was the name from 1945 of the British company whose fortune was based on a similar product, *Beecham's Pills. Beecham achieved a major breakthrough in 1957 when their scientists isolated the penicillin nucleus 6-APA, making possible a wide new range of semi-synthetic penicillin products.

Smith Square (London SW1) Square much connected with politics, a few hundred yards south of the Houses of Parliament. The headquarters of the Conservative party are at no. 32 and 'Smith Square' is sometimes used to mean the party organization. Until recently the Labour party also had headquarters here, at *Transport House. In the middle of the square stands St John's, originally a baroque church of the early 18C; its interior, destroyed by a bomb in the war, has been rebuilt as a concert hall.

smog Word coined from 'smoke' and 'fog' in the first decade of the 20c to describe atmospheric conditions in Britain's cities. It was widely used after more than 1000 'smoke-fog' deaths were caused in Edinburgh and Glasgow alone during the autumn of 1909. The choking density of smog was caused by sulphur from coal-burning chimneys combining with the water particles of a normal fog. The elimination of the problem began with the *Clean Air Act of 1956. The smog that now threatens large cities in hot weather is different in kind, being the result of car exhausts and complex photochemical reactions.

Tobias **Smollett** (1721–71) Scottish author, by profession a surgeon, whose picaresque novels are characterized by a brutally harsh view of contemporary life, whether seen in the wartime experiences of a young man on sea and land (*The Adventures of Roderick Random* 1748) or among fashionable society at home and abroad (*The Adventures of Peregrine Pickle* 1751). Smollett took a slightly gentler line in his last book, *The Expedition of Humphry Clinker* (1771), in which a varied and comic picture of Britain emerges from the letters written by a Welsh squire, Matthew Bramble, and his family as they travel through England and Scotland with a faithful servant, Humphry Clinker.

Pat **Smythe** (b. 1928) Showjumper who won gold at the first European Championship in 1957 (at that stage there was a separate competition for men and women), and followed it with victories again in 1961, 1962 and 1963 (all on Flanagan). She won the Queen Elizabeth II Cup in 1958 and the Hickstead Derby in 1962.

Robert **Smythson** (*c*.1535–1614) England's first professional architect to be known by name; he is described on his tomb as 'architector and survayor'. He worked as the master mason on *Longleat, designed one of the most flamboyant of Elizabethan houses, *Wollaton, and almost certainly was responsible for the splendid *Hardwick Hall. His son John and grandson Huntingdon were also architects.

snakes and ladders Board game introduced in the early 20c. A player's counter slithers down a snake if it falls on the square at its head, or climbs up a ladder if it falls on the square at its foot.

Snape see *Aldeburgh.

'snapper-up of unconsidered trifles' see *The *Winter's Tale*.

Snettisham Village in Norfolk, near the coast north of King's Lynn, where the largest hoard of Iron Age gold and silver in Britain has been found. A magnificent gold torque or neck ring of the 1st century BC was unearthed by ploughing in 1950, and in 1990 extensive further discoveries were made. Several different hoards in the area

Nothing new about smog: A Thoroughbred November and London Particular *(aquatint of 1827).*

yielded 63 torques and bracelets, variously of gold, silver and bronze; these were the characteristic ornaments of the rulers of the Celtic tribes inhabiting Britain in the centuries before the Roman invasion. Coins deposited with the hoards have enabled the burial of the objects to be dated to about 70 BC. The Snettisham treasure is now in the British Museum.

snooker By the late 20c easily the most popular form of *billiards in Britain. It developed in about 1880 as a variant of two other billiard games, pool and pyramid (it was known at the time as 'snooker's pool', snooker being slang for a newly-joined cadet). The game remained relatively obscure until the great billiards player Joe *Davis took it up in the 1920s, recognizing it as more dramatic than billiards for exhibition games. Davis was the first to achieve, in 1955, the 'perfect' score of 147 (requiring the black to be potted after each of the 15 reds, followed by the coloured balls in the correct sequence, clearing the table in a single break). But the wide popularity of snooker began with the television programme *Pot Black*. The climax of each year's snooker season is the World Professional Championship, sponsored since 1976 by Embassy and televised in May from the Crucible Theatre in Sheffield.

Winners of the World Professional Snooker Championship since it became a knockout contest

1969	John Spencer	1976	Ray Reardon	1983	Steve Davis	1990	Stephen Hendry
1970	Ray Reardon	1977	John Spencer	1984	Steve Davis	1991	John Parrott
1971	John Spencer	1978	Ray Reardon	1985	Dennis Taylor	1992	Stephen Hendry
1972	Alex Higgins	1979	Terry Griffiths	1986	Joe Johnson		
1973	Ray Reardon	1980	Cliff Thorburn	1987	Steve Davis		
1974	Ray Reardon	1981	Steve Davis	1988	Steve Davis		
1975	Ray Reardon	1982	Alex Higgins	1989	Steve Davis		

Lord **Snooty** see the *Beano.

C.P. Snow (Charles Percy Snow, 1905–80, kt 1957, baron 1964) Novelist whose wide-ranging experience of university life, the civil service and politics provided the material for his sequence of novels entitled *Strangers and Brothers* (1940–70). The best known of them is *The Masters* (1951), about political intrigue among the fellows of a Cambridge college electing a new master (Snow was a fellow of Christ's). He entered the real *corridors of power (a phrase popularized by him) when he joined the House of Lords in 1964 and became a parliamentary secretary in the new Ministry of Technology. His own academic subject was physics; in his Rede lectures of 1959 he coined the phrase 'the two cultures' to express the deep 20c gulf between those trained in the sciences and the arts. He married in 1950 the novelist Pamela Hansford Johnson (1912–81).

Snowball see *Animal Farm.

Snowdon (Y Widdfa in Welsh) The highest mountain peak in England and Wales (1085m/3560ft), in the northwest corner of Wales, in Gwynedd. Its top can be reached in one hour from Llanberis on the country's only narrow-gauge rack-and-pinion railway, opened in 1896 and still using steam engines. The mountain's Welsh name, meaning 'great tomb', derives from the legend that a giant killed by King Arthur is buried at its summit.

Lord **Snowdon** (Antony Armstrong-Jones, b. 1930, earl 1961) Photographer whose work in fashion and the theatre had already extended to royal portraiture before he became engaged in 1960 to Princess *Margaret. They married in 1961 and divorced in 1978. In 1965 he designed a new aviary at London Zoo and in 1969, in his role as constable of *Caernarfon Castle, masterminded the ceremony of investiture of the *prince of Wales.

Snowdonia (2171sq.km/838sq.m) Mountainous area of Gwynedd, designated a *national park in 1951. It stretches from Cader Idris in the south, up past Snowdon, to reach the north coast at Conwy.

The Snowman see Raymond *Briggs.

The Snow Queen Fairy story by the Danish author Hans Christian Andersen which has become a popular subject for *pantomime, with scope for marvels of all sorts in the adventures of Gerda – a small girl who goes in search of her friend Kai, bewitched and carried off by the icily cruel Snow Queen.

Snow White One of the most popular subjects for *pantomime in Britain today, largely because of the Disney cartoon film of 1937. The tale of the cruel stepmother's attempts to kill Snow White, and of Snow White's friendship with the seven dwarfs, was one of the fairy stories collected in Germany by the brothers Grimm and translated into English in the 1820s.

SNP (Scottish National Party) Left-of-centre political party committed to the establishment of an independent Scottish parliament. It derives from the National Party of Scotland, formed in 1928 by Hugh *MacDiarmid and others; the name was changed to Scottish National Party in 1934, when it merged with a rival nationalist party founded in 1932, the Scottish Party. The SNP won its first parliamentary seat at Westminster in 1945, since when it has had fluctuating fortunes. Its best period was the 1970s with an upsurge of interest in *devolution and the development of a new source of Scottish wealth in

*North Sea oil; two famous by-election victories (Winifred Ewing's at Hamilton in 1967, Margo MacDonald's at Govan in 1973) were soon followed by the party's highest representation at Westminster (11 seats) after the second general election of 1974. In the 1992 election the SNP polled 21.5% of the Scottish vote but only won three of the 72 seats (see *two-party system). Since 1986 the SNP has formed an alliance at Westminster with *Plaid Cymru, the other leading nationalist party in the UK. In 1990 Alex Salmond (b. 1954, MP for Banff and Buchan since 1987) became the SNP leader.

John **Soane** (1753–1837, kt 1831) Architect and collector. He worked in a highly original neoclassical style, with much use of shallow domes for overhead lighting. His greatest building, the Bank of England, was almost entirely demolished and rebuilt in the 1930s. Surviving designs include *Dulwich Picture Gallery and his own London house at 13 Lincoln's Inn Fields. It was here that he built up his outstanding collection, ranging in the fashion of the time from the curious to the beautiful (the latter including Hogarth's *Rake's Progress and *Election* series). The objects are still *in situ*, for he left house and collection to the nation. It is known now as Sir John Soane's Museum.

soccer see *Football Association.

soccer hooliganism A disorder which had been growing since the 1960s but which came to a head in the *Heysel Stadium disaster of 1985. This tragedy focused much attention on the problem. Teenage gang warfare in deprived city streets had long existed, and there had often been violent scenes at football matches. What was new since the 1960s was a specifically territorial aggression on the football stands, an ugly new element of racism and possibly an added stimulus from the attention of television cameras. Steps have since been taken to ban alcohol, to improve safety barriers and to move towards all-seat stadiums. Identity card schemes for the fans were considered but rejected. By the early 1990s the situation had greatly improved, though there were some violent scenes at European Championship matches in Sweden in 1992.

Social Democratic and Labour Party see *SDLP.

Social Democratic Party see *SDP.

Department of **Social Security** (DSS, London SW1) Formed in 1988 when the Department of Health and Social Security was split in two (they had been merged in 1968). The department is responsible for national insurance, pensions, child benefit and benefits for the elderly or infirm. For secretaries of state since 1983 see the *cabinet.

Society of Antiquaries (London W1) Institution with an unbroken history from the first meeting in 1707, in a Fleet Street tavern, of a group of gentlemen with antiquarian interests. The society was more formally constituted in 1717, had premises in Somerset House from 1781, and since 1875 has been in Burlington House. Its main activity is the publication of antiquarian research and its first great achievement was *Vetusta Monumenta*, a series of large volumes containing descriptions and engravings of antiquities, issued from 1747.

Society of Antiquaries of Scotland (Edinburgh) Body founded in 1780 with purposes similar to the Society of Antiquaries in London. From the start it collected antiquities and manuscripts, and these later formed the nucleus of the National Museum of Antiquities of Scotland – now part of the *Royal Museum of Scotland, with which the society is closely connected.

soda bread It was discovered in the mid-19c that bread could be made to rise with bubbles of carbon dioxide instead of yeast. Baking powders became available made of two ingredients (bicarbonate of soda, cream of tartar) which would release the bubbles when in contact with water. Soda bread became a general term, but it is used most often of the wholemeal variety associated with Ireland.

Frederick **Soddy** (1877–1956) Experimental chemist who worked with *Rutherford at McGill in 1900–03 on the disintegration theory of radioactivity. He then became a lecturer at the university of Aberdeen, where he argued that certain elements could exist in two forms chemically identical but with differing atomic weights. Others were thinking along the same lines, but it was his name for such substances which stuck; he called them isotopes, from the Greek for 'same place' (they occupy the same place in the periodic table). He was awarded the Nobel prize for chemistry in 1921.

Softly Softly see *Z Cars.*

Some of the rare curiosities which can still be seen in Soane's house in Lincoln's Inn Fields: wood engraving of 1864.

SOGAT see *GPMU.

Soho (London W1) The area lying west of Charing Cross Road, bounded by Oxford Street to the north and Leicester Square to the south. It has traditionally been cosmopolitan, with many French and Italian restaurants (today the southern part of Soho is London's Chinatown), but in recent decades it has been increasingly taken over by strip clubs and sex shops.

Soho tapestries see *Mortlake tapestries.

solar topee Pith helmet with brim and rounded top which has become a caricature attribute of the British as empire builders, protecting pale skin from the blazing sun of the Asian and African colonies. It originated in India, where *topi* was a Hindi word for a hat; 'solar' merely relates it to the sun.

Solent The channel between the north coast of the Isle of Wight and Hampshire, forming the entrance to Southampton Water. Its eastern end, opposite Portsmouth, is separately known as Spithead. As the stretch of sea off *Cowes, the Solent is known in particular for yachting.

Solheim Cup Biennial contest between European and US teams of women golfers, the equivalent of the *Ryder Cup for men. Launched in 1990 (the gift of Mr and Mrs Karsten Solheim, manufacturers of golf clubs in Arizona), it was won first by the USA and in 1992 by Europe.

solicitor The term for the majority of lawyers in Britain, as distinct from *barristers. Solicitors undertake all the regular legal work of their clients, bringing in barristers only for specialized opinions on the likely outcome of litigation or to plead on their clients' behalf in the higher courts. With a few exceptions, solicitors have the right to plead only in *magistrates' courts and in the *county courts. However, a committee set up by the lord chancellor recommended in 1992 that such restrictions should in most cases be removed.

Solicitor General see *Attorney General.

Solomon Islands Scattered archipelago stretching some 1450km/900m southeast from New Guinea, which has been a member of the *Commonwealth since 1978. The islands were named in the 16c by a Spaniard who believed they were the source of the gold used by Solomon for his Temple in Jerusalem. Grouped together as a British protectorate during the 1890s, the islands became independent in 1978.

Georg **Solti** (b. 1912, KBE 1971) Hungarian-born British conductor who has made a major contribution to the nation's musical life, particularly during his years at Covent Garden (1961–71). His greatest achievement has been the high stature of the Chicago Symphony Orchestra, of which he was music director 1969–91. He was the first to conduct a complete studio recording of Wagner's *Ring* (with the Vienna Philharmonic in 1958–64).

Solway Firth Inlet of the Irish Sea separating northwest England (Cumbria) from southwest Scotland (Dumfries and Galloway). *Hadrian's Wall begins at Bowness on the southern shore of the firth.

Some Mothers Do 'Ave 'Em see Michael *Crawford.

Somerset (469,000 in 1991, administrative centre Taunton) *County in southwest England, on the Bristol Channel.

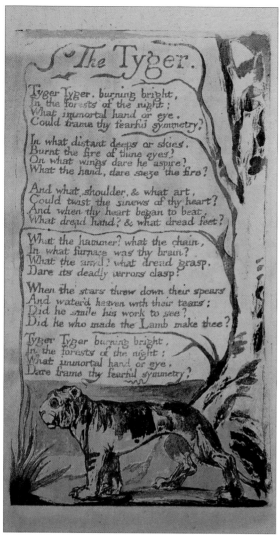

The page of the Tyger *in* Songs of Innocence and Experience, *with both text and illustration etched by Blake and hand-coloured by him or his wife.*

Protector **Somerset** see *Edward VI.

Somerset County Cricket Club Founded in 1875 and in the *county championship from 1891. The club has as yet never won the championship, but its record in *one-day cricket has been more impressive – winning the Gillette Cup or NatWest Bank Trophy twice (1979, 83), the Benson and Hedges Cup twice (1981, 82) and the Sunday League once (1979). The county ground is in Taunton, and the county also plays at Bath and Weston-super-Mare.

Somerset House (London WC2) On the site of a palace built in 1547–50 for the 1st duke of Somerset there now stands one of the most imposing 18c buildings in London, occupying a long stretch of river front and reaching back to the Strand. It was designed as government offices, by William *Chambers, and work started in 1776. The building is mostly associated in living memory with family records, for the General Register of Births, Deaths and Marriages had its offices here from 1836 to 1973. The fine rooms in the Strand block, originally occupied by the *Royal Academy and other learned societies, have recently been returned to art as the new home of the *Courtauld Institute.

Michael **Somes** (b. 1917) Dancer who joined the Vic-Wells Ballet at Sadler's Wells in 1934 and created his first major role, dancing opposite Margot Fonteyn, in Ashton's *Horoscope* (1938). When Helpmann left the Royal Ballet in 1950, Somes became Fonteyn's chief partner in the classics and in ballets created for them (such as *Ondine) until his retirement from dancing roles in 1961; he continued for some years to play acting parts with the company, such as Capulet in MacMillan's *Romeo and Juliet* (1965).

'Something is rotten in the state of Denmark' An entirely justifiable observation by a very minor character, Marcellus, in *Hamlet. Hamlet's father's ghost has just appeared on the ramparts at Elsinore and has beckoned to his son to follow him.

'something nasty in the woodshed' see entry on *Cold Comfort Farm.

Battles of the **Somme** (1916, 1918) Prolonged engagements in *World War I, resulting in massive loss of life and little military advantage. Part of the line of trenches ran along the valley of the river Somme in northern France. In July 1916 *Haig laid down a heavy bombardment of the German position, which he believed could be followed by a rapid infantry advance. Instead the first day claimed the highest number of casualties in British military history; 60,000 men fell as they struggled towards the enemy machine guns. By November, when prolonged rain brought the Somme offensive to an end, little had been achieved – except perhaps in relieving the pressure of the German assault on the French lines at Verdun (Feb.–Dec. 1916). By the end of the Somme offensive the British had lost 420,000 men, the French 195,000 and the Germans more than 600,000. There was one newcomer to the battlefield which played an insignificant part on this occasion but which had a very important future – the *tank.

The second Battle of the Somme began with a German attempt on 21 March 1918 to break through the Allied lines before the anticipated arrival of large numbers of US troops on the battlefields. The British retreated some 64km/40m before French reinforcements turned the tide. By April 5 the Germans had been forced back, but the casualties in a little over two weeks had been 163,000 British and 77,000 French, with a total of more than 200,000 on the German side.

Songs of Innocence (1789) Book of poems by William *Blake giving a gentle and childlike view of creation, as when the question 'Little Lamb, who made thee?' is answered:

> He is called by thy name,
> For he calls himself a Lamb.
> He is meek, and he is mild;
> He became a little child.

This was but one half of Blake's dual vision; it was balanced by the darker side, five years later, in his *Songs of Innocence and Experience.

Songs of Innocence and Experience (1794) Volume in which William *Blake added to his earlier *Songs of Innocence some deliberately contrasting poems which were variously more cynical, more indignant or more intense. Thus the innocent question in the previous book about the Creator of the lamb becomes savage when applied to the tiger:

> Tyger! Tyger! burning bright
> In the forests of the night,
> What immortal hand or eye
> Could frame thy fearful symmetry?

The **Sonnets** The general name for the best-known sequence of sonnets in the English language, those of *Shakespeare (154 in all). They are believed to have been written in about 1593–8 (a period when there was a craze for sonnet-writing in England, following the publication of *Sidney's *Astrophel and Stella*), but they were not printed until 1609. The volume was published by Thomas Thorpe with a dedication 'to the onlie begetter of these insuing sonnets Mr W.H.'. The search for the identity of W.H. has been ceaseless but inconclusive. On the assumption that he was the young aristocrat who inspired many of the sonnets, the leading contenders have been William Herbert (1580–1630, 3rd earl of Pembroke) and Henry Wriothesley (1573–1624, 3rd earl of Southampton). There is no firm evidence to support either. It has also been argued that W.H. may have been the man who procured the poems for Thorpe, for there is also no evidence that Shakespeare intended their publication.

In the early poems (1–17) the poet urges the young man to achieve immortality by marrying and having children, but in 18–25 he develops the thought that the recipient will be immortal anyway through the sonnets addressed to him. No. 18 ('Shall I compare thee to a summer's day?') introduces the theme and concludes:

So long as men can breathe, or eyes can see,
So long lives this, and this gives life to thee.

The poems up to 126 (addressed to 'my lovely boy') continue on the relationship with the young man, including passages of disillusion, betrayal and rival affection. In some (40–42) he appears to have been unfaithful with a woman, and it may be the same woman to whom the last sequence of sonnets (127–52) is addressed. This is the mysterious dark lady of the sonnets, described as dark both in her physical colouring and in the bitter turmoil she creates for her lover. With even less to go on, there has been almost as much speculation about her identity as that of Mr W.H.

Sons and Lovers (1913) Largely autobiographical novel by D.H. *Lawrence about Paul Morel, whose mother is an ex-schoolteacher and his father a drunken miner. The plot centres on the relationship between Paul, his mother and the other women in his life – the reserved and spiritual Miriam Leivers and Clara Dawes, a married feminist. In his despair after his mother's death he is unable to respond to Miriam's love for him, and turns away, alone, to find a new life.

Sooty Teddy bear with black ears, animated as a glove puppet by his creator Harry Corbett (b. 1918). Sooty was a children's favourite on television for many years from the 1950s, and has featured also in books.

Donald **Soper** (b. 1903, baron 1965) Methodist minister who became famous for his oratorical skills in holding forth not only in the service of his Christian mission but on any topic of moral or political importance. For many years he has appeared regularly among the public orators (most of them, unlike him, wildly eccentric) at London's Tower Hill and Speakers' Corner, fielding questions from the crowd.

Tommy **Sopwith** (1888-1989, kt 1953) Pilot and aircraft designer who formed the Sopwith Aviation company in 1912 at Kingston-upon-Thames. During World War I the factory produced eight varieties of biplane and a triplane. The Sopwith Pup (in service from summer 1916) and the Sopwith Camel (from summer 1917) were the main fighter planes of the RFC. Pilots flying the Camel, armed with two Vickers machine guns, claimed to have shot down some 3000 enemy planes, including the Red Baron himself (Manfred von Richthofen) in April 1918.

The Sopwith Aviation Company later developed into *Hawker Siddeley.

Sotheby's (Sotheby Parke Bernet, London W1) Auctioneers established in London by Samuel Baker in 1744; the name derives from John Sotheby, Baker's nephew, who joined the firm in 1776. For many years the leading auctioneers in books, in which at certain periods they specialized exclusively, Sotheby's moved in the 20c into the fine and decorative arts, gradually becoming the equal and great rival of *Christie's. They have been at their present address since 1917. In 1964 they bought the New York auctioneers, Parke Bernet.

The **South** Term for the entire south of England, often defined as the area below a line from the Bristol Channel on the west to the Wash on the east. It includes *East Anglia, the *Home Counties and the *West Country.

South Africa The Portuguese were the first Europeans to round the Cape of Good Hope (a feat achieved by Bartholomeu Dias in 1488), but the Dutch were the first to settle there, under Jan van Riebeeck in 1652. The Cape became of strategic importance during the Napoleonic Wars; the colony was seized by Britain in 1795, and British title to it was confirmed in the peace negotiations at the congress of Vienna in 1814.

To escape direct rule by the British (who were opposed to slavery), many Dutch settlers, known now as the *Voortrekkers*, made the Great Trek north between 1835 and 1843 to settle new lands. The result was that from the 1850s there were two virtually independent Boer republics (the Orange Free State and the Transvaal) to the east and northeast of Cape Colony. Meanwhile Natal, on the east coast, had been settled by the British in 1824 and was annexed to Cape Colony in 1843; it became a separate

The Sopwith triplane in a World War I dogfight with a German Albatross: painting by R.W. Bradford.

province in 1893. In 1897 Natal incorporated Zululand, to the north, as the long-term outcome of the *Zulu War.

In the 1870s and 1880s the economy of South Africa was transformed by the discovery of vast deposits of diamonds (particularly at Kimberley) and of gold (Witwatersrand). The Transvaal held the bulk of these precious minerals. The arrival of numerous *uitlanders* (foreign prospectors and businessmen, of whom a majority were British) proved a new threat to the Boer style of life so forcefully preserved by the *Voortrekkers* just a generation or two earlier. The response of the Transvaal government was to welcome the new wealth but to deny all political rights to the outsiders who were creating it. This in turn provoked the parliaments in Cape Town and in London to reconsider the question of the lapsed British sovereignty.

These clashes of interest lay behind the *Boer War. At its end the Transvaal and the Orange Free State were crown colonies, like Cape Colony and Natal. In 1909 the four provinces together formed the Union of South Africa, with *dominion status as an independent country. With the introduction of apartheid in 1948 South Africa became increasingly isolated within the *Commonwealth, from which it withdrew in 1961 after the white electorate had voted narrowly to become a republic.

Southampton (205,000 in 1991) City and seaport in Hampshire, standing on a peninsula between the mouths of the rivers Test and Itchen at the top of Southampton Water, an inlet of the *English Channel. There was a Roman settlement here and it became an important Norman town – the walls, considerably rebuilt, survive in an almost unbroken circuit of about 2km/1.25m. Ever since the departure of Richard I on crusade in 1190 this has been the main port of embarkation for English armies going abroad. And it was from here, through most of the 20c, that the great liners sailed for New York. The city itself is much rebuilt, having been heavily bombed in World War II. The Art Gallery, founded only in 1939, has rapidly built up an outstanding collection of 20c British sculpture and painting.

South Bank (London SE1) Area on the curving bank of the Thames, north of Waterloo Station, which has been a centre for the arts since the Festival of Britain in 1951. In addition to the *Festival Hall, there are two other concert halls (Queen Elizabeth Hall, Purcell Room) sharing a building opened in 1967. The exhibition and museum areas are the *Hayward Gallery and the *Museum of the Moving Image, while the performing arts are served by the *National Theatre and the *National Film Theatre. The predominant building material is the concrete of New Brutalism, which gives the whole complex a gloomy quality ill-suited to its purpose. In the early 1990s there was much talk of a more cheerful face-lift.

The **South Bank Show** (LWT from 1978) The most influential arts programme on television in recent years, edited and presented by Melvyn *Bragg. The name reflects the fact that the *South Bank is both a centre of London's cultural life and the location of the London Weekend Television studios.

Southdown see *sheep.

Southeast Alternative term for the *Home Counties.

Southend (Southend-on-Sea, 163,000 in 1991) London's seaside resort, 55km/34m east of the capital on the north coast of the Thames estuary, boasting 11km/7m of uninterrupted seafront and the world's longest *seaside pier (2.15km/1.34m, with a railway running along it).

Robert **Southey** (1774–1843) Poet and historian, remembered chiefly now as one of the *Lake Poets. In 1803 he moved into Greta Hall at Keswick, sharing it first with *Coleridge (the wives of the two poets were sisters). It remained Southey's home for the rest of his life. He later abandoned the radical views of his youth, which had been an important theme in his early friendship with Coleridge. In 1813 he was appointed *poet laureate.

South Georgia Island in the south Atlantic. Until 1985 it was a dependency of the *Falkland Islands, which lie some 1300km/800m to the northwest. It now forms a separate colony with the South Sandwich Islands, about 750km/470m to the southeast. The only inhabitants are a garrison and scientists of the British Antarctic Survey. A landing by Argentinians on South Georgia was the prelude to the *Falklands War.

South Glamorgan (406,000 in 1991, administrative centre Cardiff) Since 1974 a *county in Wales, formed from part of Glamorgan, a small section of Monmouthshire and the former county borough of Cardiff.

South Sea Bubble (1720) Term for the rapid rise in value of the shares of the South Sea Company, multiplying about eight times during a few months, followed by their collapse and the ruin of many speculators. The company was founded in 1711 to trade with South America, in the expectation of special advantages at the end of the War of the *Spanish Succession (no such advantages transpired). The shares became fashionable in 1718 when George I became a governor, but the wave of hysteria began only when the company agreed to take over the *national debt in 1720, offering its own shares (at an ever increasing premium) in exchange for government stocks. Large numbers of fraudulent ventures were launched on the market to take advantage of the new mania for speculation; the corrupt involvement of several leading politicians added to the subsequent scandal. The South Sea Company, in itself an honest venture, continued in business in a modest way until 1853.

South Stack Lighthouse which was built in 1808 by Daniel Alexander (1768–1846) on a rock off the west coast of Holy Island, off the west coast of *Anglesey, off the northwest coast of Wales.

Southwark (London SE1) One of the oldest districts of London and a focal point from Roman times, being on the bank of the Thames at the southern end of *London Bridge. The riverside area known still as *Bankside was London's entertainment district in the early 17c. With travellers arriving from the southern counties and the coast, Southwark was a place of inns. The Tabard was here, the starting point for the *Canterbury Tales; and the 17c George Inn has London's only surviving galleried courtyard, of the kind used for performances of plays before the permanent theatres were built. When Southwark was made a diocese, in 1905, the parish church of St Saviour became the cathedral; the building dates from the 13c, with an enlarged nave added in the 1890s.

Southwell (6000 in 1981) Town in Nottinghamshire with a medieval cathedral, known like its original parent house in York as the minster. There was a church on the site from the 8c. The earliest part of the present building is the Norman west front of *c.*1140, unique in having its twin towers surmounted by square and sharply pointed roofs, known as the 'Rhenish caps' because reminiscent of the style of the Rhineland. The Norman nave leads into an Early English chancel of the mid-13c, but the great glory of the minster is the sculpture in the late 13c chapter house; the columns are entwined with wonderfully naturalistic stone foliage, the 'leaves of Southwell'. This had always been the chief church of Nottinghamshire, but it only became a cathedral with the creation of a new diocese in 1884. Southwell's other claim to fame is as the home of the *Bramley seedling.

Southwest Alternative term for the *West Country.

South Yorkshire (1,263,000 in 1991) *Metropolitan county in northern England, consisting of four *districts – Barnsley, Doncaster, Rotherham and Sheffield.

sovereign Gold coin worth £1 (see *currency) when in circulation, in Tudor times and again from 1817 to 1914.

sovereignty A concept, previously little discussed, which became topical during the 1980s because of the supposed threat to Britain's sovereignty from the *EC. Parliament in Britain has until recently had absolute sovereignty in the sense that it may legislate as it pleases, and clearly British sovereignty is eroded when EC regulations take precedence over national laws. To counteract these dangers much emphasis was placed in the early 1990s on the principle of subsidiarity, a concept implying that decisions should always be taken at a lower level (in the EC at the national level) unless demonstrably better taken at the centre. The high passions raised by the rather abstract concept of sovereignty suggest that the dividing line is often blurred between it and national identity. But the two are very different. In a British context the Welsh have had no sovereignty since about 1300, but they retain a remarkably strong identity.

The spacious firmament on high see Joseph *Addison.

spaghetti junction Term coined in the 1960s to describe the particularly complex interlacing of flyovers where the M6 motorway links with the A38 and the A5127 north of Birmingham.

spaniels Small gun dogs with curly coats and drooping ears. The name derives from the French for 'Spanish'; the breed is believed to have originated in Spain, to have become popular in France and to have arrived in England in the 16c. The King Charles was one of several small or 'toy' breeds kept by Charles II in the late 17c. In the 18c several of today's varieties were bred to assist in the new sport of *shooting flying birds. The cocker spaniel derived from the toy spaniels, its size helping it through tight thickets in search of the small game bird, the woodcock, from which it takes its name. The springer spaniel, larger and quicker (known now in two varieties, the English and the Welsh) was bred to 'spring' partridges from their hiding places in open fields. The Clumber spaniel, one of the largest of its kind, slow-moving, with a white coat and a heavy head, was bred in the 19c at Clumber Park in Nottinghamshire, the seat of the dukes of Newcastle.

Spanish Armada see *Armada.

War of the **Spanish Succession** (1701–14) The first of the great 18c struggles to achieve a workable balance of power in Europe by preventing the dominance of either the Bourbon dynasty of France or the Hapsburg dynasty of Austria (or the Holy Roman Empire). It was prompted by the Spanish king Charles II dying without an heir in 1700; he left his extensive possessions and the Spanish crown to Philip, a 16-year-old grandson of the French king Louis XIV. This increase in French power was opposed by an alliance of Britain and Austria. The disputed Spanish territories within Europe were Spain herself, the Spanish

Netherlands (approximately modern Belgium) and large parts of Italy.

Full-scale hostilities developed slowly. In 1704 the Battle of *Blenheim prevented a French invasion of Austria; and in 1706 Marlborough's victory at Ramillies drove the French out of the Spanish Netherlands, while in the same year Prince Eugene of Savoy captured from them much of Italy. Peace negotiations alternated with continuing warfare, the main stumbling block being the allied insistence that Louis XIV should if necessary attack Spain to remove his grandson from the throne. Eventually France and Spain signed individual treaties at Utrecht (1713–14) with each of their opponents. That between Britain and France (11 Apr. 1713) gave Britain major French possessions in Canada (Newfoundland, Nova Scotia and the Hudson Bay territory); moreover France agreed to recognize *Anne rather than James *Stuart as the rightful British monarch. In the treaty between Britain and Spain (13 July 1713) Britain received *Gibraltar and *Minorca and was granted the right to be the only foreign nation supplying Spanish America with slaves for the next 30 years. Britain therefore emerged as a much stronger commercial power, but the original purpose of the war was not achieved; Philip V remained in Madrid as the founder of the Bourbon dynasty in Spain.

Muriel **Spark** (Muriel Camberg, b. 1918, m. S.O. Spark 1937) Author of elegant, witty, often macabre novels – a blend seen at its best in one of her earliest, *Memento Mori* (1959), about a group of old people receiving messages of impending death on the telephone. She converted to Roman Catholicism in 1954, and a thread of religious guilt underlies many of her black fables. Her education in Edinburgh, at James Gillespie's School for Girls, provided the theme of her best-known book, The *Prime of Miss Jean Brodie*.

Speakers of the House of Commons since 1943	
1943	Douglas Clifton Brown
1951	William Shepherd Morrison
1959	Harry Hylton-Foster
1965	Horace King
1971	Selwyn Lloyd
1976	George Thomas
1983	Bernard Weatherill
1992	Betty Boothroyd

Speaker The presiding officer of the House of *Commons, elected by *MPs from among themselves at the start of each parliament. It is conventional to re-elect the Speaker of the previous parliament if still in the House, so in practice the office ends only with retirement or death. The first to be given the title of Speaker was Sir Thomas Hungerford, appointed in 1377. The Speaker was often considered in the early centuries to be the king's man, but an eventual unswerving loyalty to the House was firmly established with Speaker Lenthall's conduct in the case of the *Five Members. The later tradition that the Speaker must also be above party was established in the long career of the man considered the greatest of all in the office, Arthur Onslow (1691–1768, Speaker 1728–61).

The Speaker entering the chamber of the House is preceded by the sergeant-at-arms bearing the *mace on his right shoulder; when the Speaker is in the Chair the mace lies on the table of the House, with the orb and cross pointing towards the government side. In the House of Lords the authority of the Speaker (the lord chancellor) is similarly indicated by a mace.

When the debates in the Commons were first heard on radio in 1975, the public reacted with some dismay to the often rowdy nature of the proceedings – a dismay later modified by the reassuring sight on television of a subsequent Speaker, Bernard *Weatherill, resolutely calling for 'Order! Order!'. History was made in 1992 when Betty *Boothroyd became the first woman to be elected Speaker. She was deputy Speaker from 1987, and on her first occasion in the chair she ushered in a new era (after so many centuries of 'Mr Speaker') with her ringing declaration 'Call me Madam'.

Speakers' Corner The northeast corner of *Hyde Park, which in the mid-19C became a favourite place for open-air public meetings and gatherings of protest. These were illegal until 1872, when this spot became recognized as a lawful place of free assembly where speakers would not be moved on unless their message transgressed the law (by being obscene, blasphemous or seditious). It is a right still energetically exercised every Sunday. Many of the soap-box orators and their hecklers are cranks, but the resulting confrontations provide very popular entertainment.

Special Branch see *police.

special relationship see *iron curtain.

The **Spectator** (1711–14) Periodical founded jointly by *Steele and *Addison. It appeared daily (with a long gap in 1712) and each issue consisted of a single essay, the vast majority written by Addison or Steele. Non-political, unlike its predecessor the *Tatler*, it was supposedly produced by a club of gentlemen representing different interests (the member that the public took most to heart was the country gentleman, Sir *Roger de Coverley). It ranged broadly over the cultural and moral aspects of civilized life, in a manner which proved immensely attractive to a developing middle class of both sexes. The title was revived in 1828 for a political weekly, still published today, which in recent decades has been a lively and often radical voice on the right of the political spectrum, balancing the *New Statesman* on the left.

Speech from the Throne see entry on *State Opening of Parliament.

John **Speed** (c.1552–1629) Cartographer whose engraved maps of separate counties, many with views of important buildings inset in the corners, became the first printed atlas of the country when published together as *The Theatre of the Empire of Great Britain* (1611–12). The maps were designed to accompany his *History of Great Britaine under the conquests of the Romans, Saxons, Danes and Normans . . . from Julius Caesar to our most gracious soveraigne King James* (1611).

Jonathan **Speelman** (b. 1956) Chess player who has been an international grandmaster since 1980. In 1989 he became the first Briton to reach the semi-finals among the candidates competing to challenge for the world title; he had defeated Nigel *Short on the way, but he lost in the semi-finals to the Dutch grandmaster Jan Timman. In the next world championship contest he was himself defeated by Short, who went on to beat Timman in the 1993 candidates' final.

John Hanning **Speke** (1827–64) Explorer and discoverer in 1858 of Lake Victoria as the main source of the *Nile. He had begun the expedition in 1856 with Richard *Burton, but they had gone separate ways before Speke reached the lake. To establish further proof he returned in 1860, with James Grant, and they found the river's exit

from the lake in what they called the Ripon Falls (after Lord Ripon, who had promoted their expedition). Burton published a book casting doubt on Speke's discovery. The British Association arranged a meeting in Bath on 18 September 1864 at which the two men were to debate their disagreement. The audience was already assembled when the news came that Speke, staying nearby, had accidentally shot himself that morning while shooting partridges.

Speke Hall (11km/7m SE of Liverpool) Timber-frame building, mainly of the 16C, built round a courtyard and very little altered. The great parlour has a spectacular stucco ceiling of the early 17C with motifs of fruits and flowers. The two yews in the courtyard, known as Adam and Eve, are believed to be even older than the house.

Basil **Spence** (1907–76, kt 1960) Architect whose first job was working for *Lutyens on the designs for New Delhi and who sprang to prominence on his own account in 1951 when he won the competition for the new *Coventry cathedral. A large number of commissions in the 1960s included the Edinburgh University library, the layout and first buildings of Sussex University, and Knightsbridge Barracks – highly controversial in that it placed a tower block on the very edge of Hyde Park.

Stanley **Spencer** (1891–1959, kt 1958) Painter of Christian visionary scenes in a highly individual style of primitive realism. His most notable works include the World War I murals at *Burghclere; the scenes of Christ at *Cookham which have brought fame to his native village; and the series deriving from his time as a war artist on the Clyde in the 1940s, ranging from detailed views of the process of shipbuilding to glimpses of the Resurrection at Port Glasgow. He also painted some exceptionally stark images of the nude female body which prefigure the work of Lucian Freud.

Stephen **Spender** (b. 1909, kt 1983) Poet and critic who was in the left-wing circle around W.H. Auden. Like Christopher Isherwood he spent some years in Berlin during the 1930s. 'The Pylons' (in his first major collection, *Poems* 1933) was taken as the key example of the industrial imagery used by this group of anti-Fascist writers, and they were even known for a while as the Pylon poets; but elsewhere Spender's poetry tended to be more personal and less directly political than that of the others. In later life he has mainly concerned himself with literary criticism.

Edmund **Spenser** (c.1552-99) A great English poet now more studied than read. His approach was essentially learned, in the manner of a Renaissance scholar. His first major work, *The Shepheardes Calender* (1579), is modelled on the pastoral poetry of Virgil, and *The *Faerie Queene* sets out to rival the Italian epics of Ariosto and Tasso. He lived most of his adult life in Ireland, where he acquired a large estate near Cork as part of the Elizabethan scheme to encourage English settlers.

Spey River in the Highlands of Scotland, flowing northeast for some 172km/107 miles to enter the North Sea near the Moray Firth. It is famous for its salmon fishing and is the chief river in the region which produces Scotland's best whisky.

spider see *Robert the Bruce.

spinning jenny see James *Hargreaves.

spinning mule see Samuel *Crompton.

Spitalfields (London E1) Area to the east of the *City, close to Liverpool Street Station. It was famous in the late 17c and 18c for the manufacture of silk; an important element in the success of the factories was the skill of *Huguenot weavers. Spitalfields Market, established in 1682 and long the centre of the East End's trade in fruit and vegetables, was moved in 1991 to new premises further east, in Leyton. Plans for developing the area, by Norman *Foster and others, were accepted in 1992.

Spitfire The fastest and most agile of the British aircraft in the *Battle of Britain, and the only one to match the German Messerschmitt 109. It was designed by Reginald Mitchell (1895–1937), who lived only long enough to see the prototype fly in 1936 – a blend of tragedy and triumph dramatized in the film *The First of the Few* (1942).

Spithead The channel between Portsmouth and the Isle of Wight, often used in modern times for reviewing the fleet and in the 17–18c as an anchorage. The sailors at Spithead mutinied over conditions on board ship in April 1797, during the French Revolutionary Wars, their example being shortly followed at the *Nore.

Spitting Image (Central TV from 1983) Television series in which grotesque sketches feature equally grotesque life-size rubbery versions of the famous and the infamous in local and world affairs; the faces make no attempt at realism, but the voices of the unseen actors provide uncannily convincing versions of the people being satirized. The show's appeal is its irreverence, and the producers achieved much publicity when they first introduced the royal family as regular characters. The animated figures are created by Peter Fluck and Roger Law (both b. 1941). The wrist of the puppeteer (concealed by the costume) becomes the character's neck, while the hand operates the mouth.

Spode pottery and porcelain Josiah Spode (1733–97) established a pottery at *Stoke-on-Trent during the 1760s and it was his son, also Josiah (1755–1827), who introduced *bone china. Early Spode pottery was noted for its excellent underglaze decorations in blue, the designs including the *willow pattern, but the porcelain was more often in the lavish French Empire style. In 1842 the firm, then owned by the Copeland family, became the first to introduce the so-called Parian ware – an unglazed porcelain, supposedly resembling marble from the Greek island of Paros, which was used for figures imitating statues. The company merged with *Wedgwood in 1964, but continues to manufacture under the name of Spode. A museum of its wares is attached to the factory.

William **Spooner** (1844–1930) Oxford cleric and don (Warden of New College) whose occasional habit of transposing his consonants has given the language the word 'spoonerism' for any such phrase – particularly one that is comic in its results, such as 'beating your Maker' instead of 'meeting your baker'. He has been traditionally credited with some magnificent accidental effects (such as his supposed rebuke to an undergraduate, 'You have deliberately tasted two worms and can leave Oxford by the town drain'), but these are apocryphal.

sporran see *Highland dress.

sport see *games.

The Sporting Life National daily newspaper, founded in 1859, which is primarily concerned with horse racing but gives brief coverage to any other sports or events on which a bet can be placed. The *Greyhound Life*, a guide to

The Spitting Image *puppet of the architect Richard Rogers, with inside-out anatomy in the style of his buildings.*

dog racing, has been since 1989 a separate pull-out section of the paper.

Sports Council Body set up in 1972 to promote sport and physical recreation, with an annual grant from central government; there are separate councils for England, Wales, Scotland and Northern Ireland. It runs various national sports centres, including Crystal Palace in London, Bisham Abbey in Buckinghamshire, Lilleshall in Shropshire, the Holme Pierrepont National Water Sports Centre in Nottingham and the Plas y Brenin National Centre for Mountain Activities in Gwynedd.

spotted dick One of the few old suet puddings to have retained its popularity, consisting of a plain mixture with currants or raisins. In the mid-19c it was as often called spotted dog.

Nicholas **Sprimont** see *Chelsea porcelain.

springer spaniel see *spaniels.

Dusty **Springfield** (stage name of Mary O'Brien, b. 1939) Singer who first became known as a member of a folk and country music trio, the Springfields. She went solo in 1963 and had several top-ten singles and one no. 1 (*You Don't Have to Say You Love Me* 1966). She later moved into soul music with albums such as *Dusty in Memphis* (1969).

Constance **Spry** (1886–1960) Influential author on floral decoration. From the late 1920s she had a flower shop in London, and she arranged the flowers for both the wedding and coronation of Elizabeth II. In 1945 she opened a Cordon Bleu cookery school with Rosemary Hume, her co-author in several cookery books.

Spy Pseudonym of Leslie Ward (1851–1922, kt 1918), who from 1873 to 1909 published portrait caricatures of the famous figures of the age in *Vanity Fair*. Immediately recognizable as by Spy, these elongated figures in muted colours can be found hanging in the corridors of innumerable clubs and country houses in Britain.

Spycatcher (1987) Confessional autobiography by a former member of *MI5, Peter Wright. Its account of secret service life and of his own seedy part in it had the ingredients of a bestseller, together with its argument that Roger Hollis was the fifth man of the *Cambridge spies and its account of a dirty tricks campaign by MI5 to destabilize the Labour government of Harold Wilson. But its success was assured by the British government's efforts to prevent people in Britain reading it. The resulting court case did popularize one very useful phrase, *'economical with the truth'. Wright was living in Australia when he published the book; in Britain his revelations would have led to prosecution under the *Official Secrets Act.

The Spy Who Came in from the Cold (1963) Bleak thriller by John *Le Carré about a failed British spy, Alec Leamas. He and his Communist girlfriend, Liz Gold, get fatally entangled in the undercover world of East Berlin in the first year of the Berlin Wall.

'square mile' see *City of London.

squash (short for squash rackets) A version of *rackets, played with a softer ball and in a smaller court. It began at Harrow School in the first half of the 19C, where the first players were boys awaiting their turn on the rackets court, who passed the time by knocking up in a smaller area nearby. For this they needed a soft ball and the solution was a rubber one which could be 'squashed' in the hand. Many private courts were built in the 19C, but it was not until the 1920s that the game began to acquire its widespread modern popularity. Individual players seem able to dominate the international scene in a manner unlike any other sport. In the British Open Championships, Jahangir Khan (Pakistan) had ten consecutive wins (1982–91) while Heather McKay (Australia) achieved no less than 16 victories in a row (1962–77).

squashed flies Colloquial term since the late 19C for a biscuit, consisting of two thin layers with currants between them, of which the proper name is a 'Garibaldi'.

Squeers see *Nicholas Nickleby.

Squirrel see Humphrey *Gilbert.

SR see *railways.

Sri Lanka (previously Ceylon) Member of the *Commonwealth since 1948. European control of the island began in the 16C with the Portuguese, from whom it was taken by the Dutch in the 17C. The British captured it in 1796, during the *French Revolutionary Wars, and it was ceded to Britain in 1802 by the treaty of Amiens. Ceylon became in that year a crown colony (unlike India, which was administered by the *East India Company until 1858), and it made rather easier progress than its neighbour towards independence, which was achieved in 1948. Ceylon was an exclusively European word; it was replaced in 1972 by Sri Lanka (the island's name in Pali, the language of the Buddhist scriptures).

Staffa Uninhabited island in the Hebrides, west of Mull, famous for its caves (in particular *Fingal's) and for its extraordinary rock formations, which have the same origin as the *Giant's Causeway.

Stafford (55,000 in 1981) Town on the river Sow; administrative centre of Staffordshire. Nothing remains of

the castle established by William the Conqueror, but there are many buildings from the 16C onwards. The town's main traditional industry has been the manufacture of boots and shoes.

Staffordshire (1,047,000 in 1991, administrative centre Stafford) *County in central England.

Staffordshire bull terrier see *bull terrier.

Staffordshire pottery Most British pottery has been produced in and around the *Five Towns of Staffordshire. Ceramics were an important part of the local economy from the 17C, deriving from the abundance of coal and clay in the area. The most notable firms, all still in business today, have been *Wedgwood, *Spode and *Minton.

Staffordshire is known first for its magnificent 17C *slipware. By the 18C the region was producing the immensely successful *Toby jug and a wide range of the famous Staffordshire figures. Usually primitive in style (such as the early 'pew groups' of two or three people on a high-backed seat), these figures were modelled in the round. But from the 1840s Staffordshire produced a range specifically designed as ornaments for cottage chimneys, a position which meant that the back could be disregarded. This saved cost by enabling the clay to be pressed into a flat mould. The resulting 'flatbacks', known collectively as Victorian Staffordshire or sometimes Cottage Staffordshire, were usually portraits of contemporary notables, whether royal, political, military or theatrical.

stag-hunting see *hunting.

Stalker enquiry see *RUC.

Stalky & Co (1899) Collection of stories by *Kipling, following the exploits of a trio of cheerfully unruly schoolboys. Beetle, editor of the school magazine, is Kipling himself; M'Turk and Stalky were based on the two boys he shared a study with at his Devon boarding school, the United Services College; and many of the incidents actually happened.

Stalybridge Old Band see *brass bands.

Stamford Bridge see *Harold II and *Chelsea Football Club.

stamp duty One of the oldest forms of taxation, in which an official charge is made for the seal or stamp giving a document legal status. Administered by the Inland Revenue, stamp duty is in some contexts a fixed amount but more often is *ad valorem*, meaning that the tax is a percentage of the sum involved. The purchase of a house or of shares are the two contexts in which it is most widely familiar. In the early 1990s the levels stood at 1% on houses or land and 0.5% on shares. In an attempt to revive the depressed housing market, the government abolished stamp duty on purchases below £250,000 from 20 December 1991 to 19 August 1992.

Evening Standard London's evening newspaper, descended from the *Standard* which was founded, also as an evening paper, in 1827. Its greatest period began in 1923 when it was acquired by Lord *Beaverbrook, who employed leading writers and political cartoonists (*Low followed by *Vicky). At that time it was in competition with two evening rivals, the *Star* (which later closed) and the *Evening News*. The *Standard* and the *News*) eventually merged in the present *Evening Standard*, which is now part of the *Mail* group of newspapers, Beaverbrook's main rivals.

standard English see *Received Pronunciation.

standard gauge (4ft 8.5in, now standardized as 1.432m) The width between the lines in more than half the *railways of the world. It was the gauge which happened to be in use for the early horse-drawn railways of northeast England. Adopted by George *Stephenson for his first steam locomotives, it later spread abroad with the export of British engines. The famous exception in the early days was *Brunel's Great Western railway, which opened in 1841 with a gauge of 7ft/2.134m. This was more expensive in construction but allowed greater stability and higher speeds. The company eventually lost what became known as the 'battle of the gauges'; its lines were converted to standard gauge in 1892.

standing stones Upright stones, most often arranged in circles, which are characteristic monuments of the late Stone Age and the Bronze Age in western Europe. They are also known as menhirs, from the Breton for 'long stone'. *Stonehenge and *Avebury are the two best-known examples of stone circles in Britain.

Myles **Standish** (c.1584–1656) The military leader in the first settlement of the *Pilgrim Fathers, best remembered now for the popular tradition that he asked John *Alden to woo Priscilla Mullens on his behalf.

Charles Villiers **Stanford** (1852–1924, kt 1902) Anglo-Irish composer, born in Dublin, known in particular for his numerous works for the voice – operas, choral music and songs. He was also a very influential teacher at a time when British music was experiencing something of a renaissance. In his many years teaching composition at the Royal College of Music (1883–1924), his pupils included *Vaughan Williams, *Holst, *Ireland and *Bliss.

Henry Morton **Stanley** (b. John Rowlands, 1841–1904, GCB 1899) Welsh journalist and explorer. As an illegitimate child he spent many of his early years in the St Asaph workhouse; at the age of 18 he emigrated to the USA and took the name of an adoptive parent, Henry Morton Stanley. He was working for the *New York Herald* in 1869 when his editor gave him the task of finding David *Livingstone. He did so, in November 1871 at Ujiji, greeting him with the famous line 'Dr Livingstone, I presume'. Inspired by this encounter to become an explorer, he succeeded in tracing the course of the Congo in a great journey described in his *Through the Dark Continent* (1878). He became a British subject again in 1892.

Stanley Gibbons Britain's leading firm of dealers in stamps, whose annual catalogues are a bible to philatelists and whose headquarters in London's Strand include the world's largest stamp shop. Stanley Gibbons (1840–1913), was born in the same year as the postage stamp (see *Post Office). He established his company largely on the strength of one brilliant purchase – a sackful of stamps, many of them rarities, which had been won by two sailors in a raffle in Cape Town. He secured this treasure in 1863 for £5, and sold from it for many years. In 1865 he began the Stanley Gibbons catalogue, which was then a 20-page list issued on a monthly basis.

Stannaries (from *stannum*, Latin for tin) Area of Devon and Cornwall in which tin was mined. From the Middle Ages until 1896 justice was dispensed there in local independent stannary courts.

Stansted (55km/34m NE of London) The site chosen for London's third major airport after many years of protest and indecision. Used for US bombers during World War II, and for occasional commercial flights from 1957, Stansted was designated London's third airport in a government white paper of 1967. Subsequent enquiries selected quite different sites – notably Maplin Sands, north of the Thames estuary – and Stansted seemed to have been spared. But it was under consideration again in the late 1970s, and in 1986 the decision was finally confirmed. A spectacular new terminal by Norman *Foster was opened in 1991. The airport is designed to handle 8 million passengers a year, with the option of expanding up to 15 million.

Daily Star Newspaper launched in Manchester in 1978 for the North and Midlands, and extended in the following year to cover the whole country. It competes with the *Sun* and *Mirror* at the bottom end of the *tabloid market (though in the early 1990s trailing far behind them in terms of circulation) and is part of the group which owns the *Daily* and *Sunday *Express.*

Star and Garter (Royal Star and Garter Home, Richmond, Surrey) Residential home for disabled servicemen. The massive building on top of Richmond Hill was completed in 1924. It takes its name from a famous hotel which had occupied the site since 1738.

Star Chamber Court of law which developed in the 14c. It consisted of the *privy council sitting as a court and was therefore not subject to the delays and constraints of the common-law courts (it also lacked their safeguards, dispensing justice without a jury). The Star Chamber was a familiar part of the Tudor legal scene, particularly in the time of Wolsey, but it acquired its lasting image of tyranny in the reign of Charles I, who used it to threaten and punish those who resisted his demands. With its almost arbitrary ability to impose heavy penalties, it came to symbolize royal restraints on the liberty of the subject. One of the first acts of the *Long Parliament was to abolish it (in 1641). There is no proven explanation for the name, but the first references are all to a 'starred' chamber. The traditional theory is therefore likely to be correct – that it relates to a room in the palace of Westminster with a ceiling decorated with gilt stars.

Freya **Stark** (1893–1993, DBE 1972) Traveller in the Middle East and author of several classics of travel writing, such as *The Valley of the Assassins* (1934) and *The Southern Gates of Arabia* (1936). She was also a prolific and vivid letter writer, with eight published volumes covering the years 1914–80.

'I've **started so I'll finish**' see *Mastermind.*

'your **starter for ten**' see *University Challenge.*

Start the Week (BBC from 1970) Programme on Radio 4 after the 9 a.m. news each Monday morning. It usually has four guests, each with some topical reason for being on the show and each interviewed separately before joining in a general discussion. Until 1987 the host and interviewer was Richard Baker; since 1988 Melvyn Bragg has been in the chair.

stately homes The large country houses of the aristocracy, particularly those open to the public. The phrase was perhaps coined and certainly popularized by Mrs Hemans in her lines:

> The stately homes of England
> How beautiful they stand!
> Amidst their tall ancestral trees,
> O'er all the pleasant land.

Noel Coward's song *The Stately Homes of England* borrows the first couplet and follows it with:

> To prove the upper classes
> Have still the upper hand.

State Opening of Parliament The ceremony which begins each session of *parliament, taking place immediately after a *general election and then each subsequent autumn, usually in late October or early November. After processing in a coach from Buckingham Palace to Westminster, the monarch is accompanied by heralds and other dignitaries into a crowded House of Lords. *Black Rod then summons the Commons to join the Lords in hearing the Queen's (or King's) Speech, also known as the Speech from the Throne. The Commons traditionally make a point of arriving in the upper house ambling and chatting, to emphasize that they are not overawed. Although read out by the sovereign, the speech is provided by the *cabinet; it outlines the government's proposed legislation for the coming session.

In a tradition going back to 1605 and the *Gunpowder Plot, the House of Lords and its cellars are ceremonially searched by the Yeomen of the Guard before the state opening takes place.

state school The term in general use for what is officially called a maintained school – maintained from public funds and offering free *education. The majority of the cost falls on central government, but until the introduction of *opting out the direct responsibility for all maintained schools has been with *LEAs (local education authorities). The schools fall into two categories: primary schools, which children enter at the age of five (four in Northern Ireland); and secondary schools to which most transfer at 11 (usually 12 in Scotland). Primary school education is sometimes divided betweeen an infant school (5–7) and a junior school (7–11).

In the early 1990s the majority of children in secondary state education were in *comprehensive schools. Where a comprehensive has no sixth form, pupils studying for A-levels transfer at 16 to a sixth-form college or a tertiary college (similar but offering vocational courses in addition to academic subjects). By the late 1980s about 80% of state schools were co-educational in England, Wales and Scotland (60% in Northern Ireland).

A few local authorities have kept their *grammar schools, and throughout the country at both primary and secondary level there are many so-called voluntary schools. These are independent establishments, usually religious foundations, which are funded by the state in return for supplying free education. The majority are Anglican or Roman Catholic, but they include other Christian denominations as well as Jewish schools. A topical issue in the early 1990s was the omission of Muslim schools from this category; legislation before parliament late in 1992 made it likely that they would soon achieve the same status. See also *opting out.

Brian **Statham** (b. 1930) Fast bowler who played *cricket for Lancashire (1950–68) and England (1950–65). For a while, from 1963, he held the world record for the number of wickets taken in *Test matches.

statistics see *Central Statistical Office and *'lies, damned lies'.

Status Quo Rock group consisting of Francis Rossi (b. 1949, guitar and vocals), Rick Parfitt (b. 1948, guitar and vocals), Alan Lancaster (b. 1949, bass) and John Coghlan (b. 1946, drums). Known as Status Quo from 1967, they had their first top-ten single with *Pictures of Matchstick Men* in 1968. *Down Down* (1974) has been

their only no. 1 single, but the albums *Hello* (1973), *On The Level* (1975), *Blue For You* (1976) and *1982* (1982) all reached the top of the charts. Coghlan and Lancaster left the band in the 1980s, but Rossi and Parfitt were still performing with others as Status Quo in the early 1990s.

Statute of Westminster see *Commonwealth of Nations and *dominion status.

Ralph **Steadman** (b. 1936) Cartoonist and illustrator who combines an exuberantly macabre imagination with a great precision of line. His skills are seen at their best in books written by himself – a biography of Freud illustrated in monochrome (*Sigmund Freud* 1979), the autobiography of Leonardo da Vinci in colour (*I, Leonardo* 1983) and the observations on humanity of a lonely and tormented GOD (*The Big I Am* 1988).

steak and kidney pudding Pieces of beef steak and kidney in a brown sauce, steamed in a bowl lined and covered with suet pastry. It is considered now the quintessentially English dish, but the kidney seems to have been added only in the mid-19C; it first appears in one of Mrs *Beeton's recipes. Before that a plain steak pudding filled the same national role, being known as *John Bull's pudding in a beef-oriented tradition which includes *O The *Roast Beef of Old England*.

steam The first practical steam engine was developed by a Devon man, Thomas Savery (*c.*1650–1715), who took out a patent for it in 1698. It was described in *The Miner's Friend* (1702) as suitable for pumping water from mines, but it seems to have been used mainly for supplying water to country houses and their gardens. It was the next generation of engine which became standard equipment in the mines for most of the 18C. This was developed by another native of Devon, Thomas Newcomen (1663–1729); first documented in a mine in Worcestershire in 1712, his engine was almost certainly in earlier use in the Cornish tin mines. It was in its turn made redundant by the great improvements introduced by James *Watt.

Engines of the kind developed by Watt were used to propel boats from as early as the 1780s in both France and America. Britain's first practical steamboat was a tug, the *Charlotte Dundas*, designed by William Symington (1763–1831) and in use in 1802 on the *Forth-Clyde canal. The first passenger-carrying steam boat in Britain was also on the Clyde – the *Comet*, designed by Henry Bell (1767–1830) and launched in 1812. The successful application of steam to travel on land came a little later, complicated by the great weight of the engines, but it was in these same years that the first steps were being taken by Richard *Trevithick. The era of the practical steam locomotive began with *Puffing Billy, followed by the machines of George and Robert *Stephenson. By the early 19C steam was also replacing water power in the cotton mills. The *Times* was printed on a steam press as early as 1814.

The final major advance in the development of steam power was the perfecting by Charles Parsons (1854–1931) of the steam turbine, in which jets of steam drive a bladed rotor (patented 1884). Parsons' interest was in providing power to generate electricity, for which the steam turbine is still the main method. The principle soon found another use in marine engines, first demonstrated when *Turbinia* broke the speed record at a naval review for Queen Victoria's jubilee in 1897.

steel see *iron and steel.

David **Steel** (b. 1938, KBE 1990) Scottish politician, MP for Roxburgh, Selkirk and Peebles 1965–83 and for Tweeddale, Ettrick and Lauderdale since 1983. He was

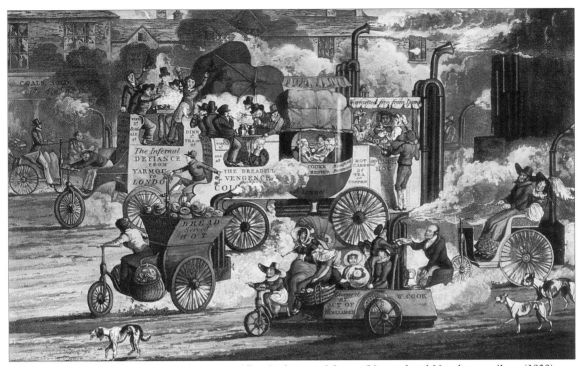

Nightmare vision of steam: aquatint after Henry Alken in the year of the new Liverpool and Manchester railway (1830).

the youngest MP when he entered the House of Commons as a Liberal in 1965, and he immediately distinguished himself by successfully sponsoring the controversial private member's bill which made *abortion legal (1967). He became leader of the Liberal party in 1976, after Jeremy *Thorpe resigned the post. In the 1980s Steel formed an electoral and parliamentary *Alliance with the SDP, and immediately after the 1987 election he set in motion the discussions which led to the merger of the parties in 1988 as the *Liberal Democrats. He did not stand for the leadership of the new party.

Richard **Steele** (1672–1729, kt 1715) Irish dramatist and essayist who made his career in London. His comedies were in a new sentimental style, a reaction against the cynically amoral (but much more enjoyable) *Restoration comedy. Steele's fame rests now on his founding of the *Tatler* in 1709, to be followed by the *Spectator* in 1711.

Tommy **Steele** (stage name of Thomas Hicks, b. 1936) Britain's first rock-and-roll star and teenage idol. He was in the merchant navy when he was spotted playing in a Soho coffee bar in 1956 and given a Decca contract. His first record, *Rock with the Caveman*, got into the charts in November of that year and his second, *Singing the Blues*, reached no. 1 after being launched in December. A film, *The Tommy Steele Story*, was ready for release by May 1957. There followed a succession of singles until 1961 but by then his humour, his good looks and his acting talents were leading him further afield. In a wide-ranging career, involving musicals, variety, pantomime and straight theatre, the highlight has probably been his leading role in *Half a Sixpence* (from 1963 in the West End, on Broadway and on film).

steeplechase A professional horse race run on a course of 2 miles (3.2km) or more, which includes birch fences, ditches and water jumps. Races over slightly lower fences, and without the other obstacles, are known as hurdle races; and jumping races for amateurs are *point-to-points. Originally the term 'steeplechase' meant precisely what it

says. In the 18C, first in Ireland and then in England, it became the custom to challenge other riders to a cross-country race with a distant steeple as the winning post. Competitors could take any course they chose, clearing whatever obstacles might intervene. The first recorded instance of a steeplechase is in County Cork in 1752, when Cornelius O'Callaghan and Edmund Blake raced the 6km/4m from Buttevant church to the St Leger steeple.

Sten gun Light sub-machine-gun used by the British army in World War II. It was named in imitation of the *Bren, the first two letters in this case standing for its inventors, R.V. Shepherd and H.J. Turpin.

Stones of **Stenness** see *Maes Howe.

Stephen (c.1097–1154) King of England from 1135, grandson of William the Conqueror (his mother, Adela, was William's daughter). He was brought up in the household of his uncle, Henry I, and was one of those who took an oath of loyalty to *Matilda as Henry's heir. But after Henry's death the barons, reluctant to be ruled by a queen, secured the throne for Stephen. His reign was a time of anarchy, fuelled by Matilda's efforts to claim her rights. A compromise was eventually reached by which Stephen retained the throne until his death in return for acknowledging her son, *Henry II, as his heir.

Leslie **Stephen** see The *Dictionary of National Biography.

George **Stephenson** (1781–1848) Engineer and pioneer of railways who was entirely self-taught in technology (he only learnt to read at 18). Born at Wylam in Northumberland, he was in charge of the engines in a colliery only 19km/12m away, at Killingworth, when *Puffing Billy was put to work at Wylam in 1813. Stephenson set about designing his own first locomotive; called *Blücher* (a year in advance of *Waterloo), it went into service in 1814. He also produced a safety lamp for miners similar to the model which, unknown to him, was being invented at the same time by *Davy.

Stephenson's career moved outside the world of the local collieries when he provided the locomotives for the *Stockton and Darlington railway in 1825; it progressed greatly when he was commissioned in 1826 to construct the line for the *Liverpool and Manchester railway; and it was crowned when *Rocket* (designed and built by his son Robert) won the *Rainhill trials in 1829. In 1823 he had established a business in Newcastle-upon-Tyne to manufacture locomotives, and until his retirement in 1845 he was chief engineer to many of the developing railway companies.

Robert **Stephenson** (1803–59) Engineer who built *Rocket* for his father, George Stephenson, and in doing so solved the crucial problem of attaching the copper tubes to the boiler. After assisting his father on the *Liverpool and Manchester railway, he became in 1833 the engineer on the London and Birmingham railway, the first main line into the capital city. Later his speciality was the design of bridges, starting with his famous high-level bridge at Newcastle-upon-Tyne. He pioneered the box-girder design, first used to carry the Chester and Holyhead railway over the river at Conwy and over the *Menai Strait. He used the same principle for the Victoria Bridge (1854–9) over the St Lawrence river at Montreal, which for many years was the longest span in the world. From 1847 till his death he was Conservative MP for Whitby.

Patrick **Steptoe** see *test-tube babies.

Steptoe and Son (BBC 1964–73) One of Britain's classic television series, finding both comedy and pathos in the relationship between a father and son in the rag-and-bone trade. The wilful and eccentric old father (Wilfrid Brambell) and the exasperated son (Harry H. Corbett) almost invariably frustrate each other's most cherished plans, either accidentally or deliberately. The scripts were by Ray Galton (b. 1930) and Alan Simpson (b. 1929).

sterling This name (of uncertain origin, but possibly deriving from a star on certain Norman coins) was used from the 12c for the English silver penny. Coins were traded by weight and the standard became 240 pennies to the pound (hence a pound sterling, as in *£.s.d.). The word is now used for the level of purity of British silver and gold, guaranteed by the *hallmark, and also as a general term for the currency of the UK. The *exchange rate of sterling has been expressed in the past mainly in terms of the US dollar, but recently its relationship to the German mark, the strongest currency in the *EMS, has been of greater importance.

Laurence **Sterne** (1713–68) One of the most original of British authors. His father was an impoverished army officer and he spent much of his early life in barracks in England and Ireland. Ordained in 1738, he was attached to the cathedral in York until the publication in 1760 of the first part of the wonderfully eccentric *Tristram Shandy*. This brought him instant fame and a lifetime curacy at Coxwold, in North Yorkshire, where he moved into a medieval house and named it Shandy Hall – it survives much as he left it, open now to the public.

His new reputation even enabled Sterne to publish the sermons he had preached in York Minster; they appeared with great success as *The Sermons of William Yorick* (7 vols, 1760–9). Yorick, the parson in *Tristram Shandy*, thus became Sterne's alter ego and pseudonym. He is the narrator of *A Sentimental Journey through France and Italy* (1768), a book based on Sterne's experiences on the Continent, where he spent 1762–4 with his wife and daughter for the sake of his health (he had tuberculosis). As a travel book, *A Sentimental Journey* is again unconventional. It begins in the middle of a conversation, ends in the middle of a sentence, and is not so much about the places visited as the effect of the journey on Yorick's sensibilities – particularly the effect of various young ladies. Sterne's greatest sentimental attachment came at the end of his life. In 1767 he fell in love with Elizabeth Draper, the wife of an official in the East India Company. *Letters from Yorick to Eliza*, based on a journal which he kept for her after her return to India, were published in 1775.

Shakin' **Stevens** (stage name of Michael Barratt, b. 1948) Rock singer whose talent for the styles of the past enabled him to play Presley on the West End stage in *Elvis* (1977–8) and subsequently brought him a succession of hit singles in a traditional rock-and-roll vein. Three which reached the no. 1 spot were *This Ole House* and *Green Door* (both 1981) and *Oh Julie* (1982).

Juliet **Stevenson** Actress whose career reached new heights in 1991 with superb performances in two leading roles – in the film *Truly, Madly, Deeply*, and in *Death and the Maiden* at the Royal Court and in the West End.

Robert Louis **Stevenson** (1850–94) Scottish author with a wide range of talents. He was a great traveller and his early wanderings in France with Modestine were described in *Travels with a Donkey in the Cevennes* (1879). In 1883 he achieved immediate and lasting success as a writer of adventure stories with *Treasure Island, followed in 1886 by *Kidnapped*; in the same year there appeared *The Strange Case of Dr *Jekyll and Mr Hyde*. A collection of his poems about childhood, *A Child's Garden of Verses*, came out in 1885. In 1889 he and his family went to the South Pacific for his health (he had severe lung problems) and settled on the island of Samoa. Stevenson's adult novels, including anti-colonial fiction written on Samoa, have recently been gaining in critical esteem.

Stewart see house of *Stuart.

Jackie **Stewart** (b. 1939) Scottish racing driver who is the only Briton to have won the world championship three times – in 1969, 1971 and 1973, driving for Tyrrell on each occasion (in 1969 in a Matra-Ford). He also held the British record for the greatest number of Grand Prix wins (27), until overtaken in 1992 by Nigel *Mansell.

Rod **Stewart** (b. 1945) London-born singer and guitarist, of Scottish descent, who was with the Faces for several years in the early 1970s while separately developing a solo career. He had his first no.1 hit single in 1971 with *Maggie May*, which came from the album *Every Picture Tells a Story* (also top of the charts in that year, and the first of a run of six no. 1 albums). Of many later hit singles, *Sailing* became almost his signature tune; it was issued in 1975, the year when he began a much publicized affair with Britt Ekland. His throaty voice and ear for a tune have kept at the top into the 1990s.

Stilton Britain's most distinguished cheese, and the only one with a name protected by law; Stilton is officially defined as a blue or white cheese made with full-cream milk in the district of Melton Mowbray (in Leicestershire) and surrounding areas. It first became famous in the early 18c, when it was sold in the Bell Inn – a coaching house on the Great North Road at Stilton (then in Huntingdonshire, now Cambridgeshire). The cheese has never been made at Stilton or in its vicinity, but it became known by the place where travellers had enjoyed it.

A Stilton starts cream-coloured and firm and then matures, within its protective crust, to a blue crumbling richness. There was an early tradition (not followed now, but mentioned by Defoe when he discovered the cheese at Stilton in 1722 during his tour of Great Britain) that it should be kept until crawling with mites and maggots; another theory is that port poured into the cheese improves its texture and flavour. A white Stilton is a different and less widely known product.

Sting see *Police.

Stirling (39,000 in 1991) University town and administrative centre of the Central *region of Scotland. Nature gave this site strategic importance, with its vast rock, sheer on two sides, guarding a crossing place over the Forth and thus the route north to the Highlands. The castle on the rock changed hands several times in the struggles between the English and the Scots which followed the invasion of Edward I in 1296, and two major battles – *Stirling Bridge (1297) and *Bannockburn (1314) – were fought (and won by the Scots) for control of it. A colossal modern statue of Robert the Bruce, the victor of Bannockburn, now dominates the esplanade up to the castle. The present buildings within the castle date from the 15–16C, when this was a royal residence of the *Stuart dynasty.

This aspect of Stirling's importance dwindled after the *union of the crowns in 1603, but the settlement below the castle is itself a historic town. The old bridge (a stone structure over the Forth, now used only by pedestrians) dates from about 1400; the bridge which gave its name to the battle of 1297 was of wood. The Church of the Holy Rude (rood, or crucifix) is a Gothic building of the 16C, in which the 9-month-old Mary was crowned Queen of Scots in 1543.

James **Stirling** (1926–92, kt 1992) Architect who made an early name with controversial, angular, brightly coloured designs – in particular the engineering building at the university of Leicester (1959), the history faculty building at Cambridge (1964) and the Florey building at Queen's College, Oxford (1966). In his later career he was more appreciated abroad than in Britain. By far his most famous building was the art gallery in Stuttgart; this became obliquely familiar to British viewers from a TV commercial for Rover, in which a German driving the British car looks approvingly at the façade of the gallery and murmurs '*Britischer Architekt*'. His only building of importance in Britain in recent decades was the Clore Gallery for the *Tate. In the years before his death his proposed design for an important site opposite the Mansion House in London was the subject of much debate, being dismissed by the prince of Wales as looking like a '1930s wireless set' but being eventually granted planning permission after long legal battles.

Robert **Stirling** (1790–1878) Scottish inventor and Presbyterian minister, who patented in 1816 an external combustion engine converting heat into mechanical energy through expansion of a gas. In the late 20C his concept is much discussed as a cleaner and quieter alternative to the internal combustion engine.

Stirling Bridge (11 Sept. 1297) Decisive victory by the Scottish leader, William *Wallace, over the English, led by the earl of Surrey. Wallace attacked after half the English army had crossed a narrow bridge over the river Forth at Stirling. Those on the northern bank were destroyed and Surrey made a hasty retreat to England with the remainder of his army.

Stirlingshire Until 1975 an inland *county in central Scotland, now mostly in the Central region but with part in Strathclyde.

Stock Exchange (London EC2) The institution through which all stocks and shares are traded in Britain. The first joint stock enterprise to be launched in London, with shares on offer to the public, was the Muscovy Company which in the 1550s established trade with Ivan the Terrible, the Russian tsar. By the late 17C brokers were dealing in stocks on a regular basis from *coffee houses; Jonathan's coffee house was their chief haunt and it was there that they first called themselves, in 1773, the Stock Exchange. In 1801 special premises were built on the site still occupied by the exchange (the present building dates from 1972).

There has been a traditional distinction in the Stock Exchange between brokers (buying and selling for their clients, and taking a percentage as commission) and jobbers (trading in much larger quantities on their own account). This distinction, together with the system of minimum commissions, was among the restrictive practices swept away in 1986 in *Big Bang. The other great change in recent years has been the introduction of computerized trading with *SEAQ.

stocks see *pillory.

Stockton and Darlington railway The world's first public *railway to use steam locomotion. In 1823 the engineer George *Stephenson began constructing a line between these two towns on Teesside, approximately 16km/10m apart; it opened on 27 September 1825, when Stephenson in his engine *Active* (later renamed *Locomotion*) drew a train of 450 passengers at about 24kph/15 mph. But his locomotives were not yet reliable and were usually kept on this line for freight, while passengers continued to travel in horse-drawn carriages. The railway provided goods from Darlington with easy access to transport by sea, for Stockton was the major port on the *Tees.

The original Darlington station has been restored and is now the Darlington Railway Centre and Museum; the prize exhibit is *Locomotion* itself.

Stoke Mandeville Hospital in Buckinghamshire with a worldwide reputation for its treatment of spinal injuries. It developed this role, together with its almost equally well-known plastic surgery programme, as a result of specializing in service casualties during World War II. In recent times Jimmy *Savile has played a leading role in fund-raising for the National Spinal Injuries Centre. The extensive site was in use for medical purposes from about 1920, when it was an isolation hospital for TB patients.

Ludwig Guttman (1899–1980) pioneered at Stoke Mandeville the use of athletics as therapy for those with paraplegia (paralysis from the waist down). In 1948, to coincide with the Wembley Olympic Games, he organized Stoke Mandeville Games in wheelchairs. The event was repeated four years later, when some Dutch ex-servicemen came to England to compete, and in 1960 in Rome the Paralympic Games became for the first time directly associated with the Olympics.

Stoke-on-Trent (250,000 in 1991) City on the river Trent, centre of the Staffordshire *Potteries. It derives from the amalgamation in 1910 of the *Five Towns plus Fenton, which together were given city status in 1925. Within the boundaries of the modern city are the factories of *Doulton, *Minton, *Spode and *Wedgwood. Each has a museum of its own wares, while the city's Museum and Art Gallery displays an outstanding general collection of pottery and porcelain. The Chatterley Whitfield Mining Museum at Tunstall uses both surface and underground areas of a redundant pit to reveal the everyday life of a coal mine.

Stoke Poges see *Gray's *Elegy*.

Stokesay Castle (34km/21m S of Shrewsbury) A rarity for its time, the 13C, in being more of a fortified manor house than a castle. Its most striking feature is the sturdy north tower of about 1240 (stone, with arrow slits) on top of which Lawrence of Ludlow added in the 1290s a projecting timbered storey of comfortable rooms. The Great Hall dates from his time, but the timber-frame gatehouse is an addition of the early 17C.

stone see *weight.

Stone Age General term for the entire span of human culture from the earliest beginnings (now estimated to be about 2.5 million years in the past) to a few thousand years ago. The Stone Age is divided into old, middle and new periods – palaeolithic, mesolithic, neolithic (*lithos* being the Greek for stone). The palaeolithic period came to an end in Britain about 10,000 years ago, when the ice cap receded at the end of the *ice age. The transition to mesolithic and then neolithic was inevitably gradual; archaeological remains are classified as one or the other according to the flint tools being used (progressing from chipped to polished), and by the sophistication of weapons and of hunting methods.

Agriculture, animal husbandry and pottery begin in the neolithic period, roughly from about 4000 BC in Britain. The use of metal provides the first clear-cut distinction, with the transition to the *Bronze Age in about 2000 BC. In *Skara Brae Scotland has an outstanding relic of Stone Age life, and it was in the Stone Age that *Avebury and *Stonehenge first acquired their ritual significance.

Stonehenge (13km/8m N of Salisbury) Britain's best-known prehistoric site, consisting of circles of huge *standing stones on Salisbury plain. Several pairs still have massive horizontal lintel stones on top of them. The name is recorded in literature from the 12C and is thought to relate to the idea of stones 'hanging' in the air.

Stonehenge seems to have been in continuous human use from about 3100 BC to 1100 BC. The earliest features are the ditch and bank surrounding the area, and the 56 pits inside the ditch which were first described by *Aubrey in the 17C and so are called the Aubrey holes; their original purpose is uncertain but they were later used for burial. The next stage, probably connected with the *Beaker folk, saw the creation of the earthwork approach known as the avenue and the erection of a double circle of standing stones; it was at this period that the sun became of significance, because the avenue and the circles are aligned with the position of sunrise at the summer solstice. Further circles and horseshoes of even larger stones were added later, with the curving lintels fitting on the standing stones with a precision more characteristic of carpentry.

The precise purpose of Stonehenge is unknown, and is anyway likely to have changed during almost two millennia of use; but clearly there was some element of either sun worship or astronomical calculation. The popular link with the *Druids is unhistoric, since the Celts arrived in Britain centuries after Stonehenge was abandoned. An even greater mystery than how these vast stones were raised into position has been how they reached this site. The larger stones, known as sarsens (the term for that particular variety of sandstone), are found naturally as huge boulders in an area about 32km/20m to the north – a distance over which it is just possible to imagine them being brought on rollers. But the smaller blue stones have been shown to come from the Preseli Hills in Wales. Since 1921 the accepted theory has been that they were somehow transported by man. The easy solution, that they

were brought to the Salisbury plain in a glacier, was until recently rejected by geologists as impossible. But in 1991 new evidence was found suggesting that this may, after all, be the answer.

A recent tradition is for large numbers of itinerant young people – usually described as hippies, *New Age travellers and ravers – to converge on Stonehenge for the summer solstice. The police, charged with protecting the monument and the local environment, mount expensive campaigns to prevent their even reaching its vicinity. The confrontation degenerated in 1985 into violence between the travellers and more than 800 police, in what became known as the Battle of the Beanfield.

In the early 1990s English Heritage and the National Trust put forward a joint plan to restore some sense of mystery and remoteness to the monument, by closing a road which passes nearby and placing the visitors' centre out of sight about a kilometre to the north.

John **Stonehouse** (b. 1925) Labour politician, with a succession of ministerial posts in the period 1964–70, who staged a fraudulent disappearance in 1974. His clothes were found in a beachside changing room in Miami and he was assumed to have drowned. He was subsequently discovered in Australia with his secretary, Sheila Buckley. He was sentenced in 1976 to seven years in prison on charges of forgery and theft, including false claims against insurance companies for his death.

Stone of Destiny see *Scone.

'Stone walls do not a prison make' see entry on Richard *Lovelace.

Marie **Stopes** (1880–1958) Passionate advocate of birth control, who did more than anyone else to make it a subject of open discussion. She was an academic botanist and geologist by profession, but in 1918 she published *Married Love* – a discussion of sexual relations, unusually frank for the time, which was greeted with uproar and was an immediate success. It led to so many practical enquiries about contraception that she rushed out a sequel, *Wise Parenthood* (also 1918, and an even greater success). She and her husband together founded in London in 1921 the Mothers' Clinic for Birth Control, the first of its kind. Her *Contraception; its theory, history and practice* (1923) remained for some time a standard work on the subject.

Tom **Stoppard** (b. 1937) Playwright born in Czechoslovakia, who lived as a young child in Singapore and India and came to Britain in 1946. He achieved international fame with *Rosencrantz and Guildenstern are Dead* (1967), a *tour de force* of farce and philosophy in which the tragic events of *Hamlet* are seen from the peripheral viewpoint of the two attendants Rosencrantz and Guildenstern. Similar mental agilities underly *Jumpers* (1972, a farcical parody of the contortions of philosophers) and *Travesties* (1974, with Lenin and James Joyce involved in an amateur production of *The Importance of Being Earnest*). *The Real Thing* (1982) derives more conventional drama from the collapse of a marriage.

David **Storey** (b. 1933) Novelist and playwright, whose early career as a rugby league footballer provided material for his first novel (*This Sporting Life* 1960) and for a play (*The Changing Room* 1972). A Yorkshire mining community, his own background, was the setting for a novel which won the Booker prize (*Saville* 1976). *Home* (1970), taking place in an asylum, was a success on both sides of the Atlantic with John Gielgud and Ralph Richardson.

Stormont see *Belfast.

Stornoway (9000 in 1981) Port on the east coast of *Lewis with Harris, in the outer Hebrides, and administrative headquarters of the Western Isles *region of Scotland. It is a centre for the marketing of the island's best-known product, *Harris tweed.

Paul **Storr** (1771–1844) Silversmith who established himself at the head of his profession from a young age, setting up on his own in 1796. He is famous for his elaborate presentation pieces, of which one of the earliest is also one of the best known – the 'Battle of the Nile Cup' (National Maritime Museum), presented to Nelson after his victory in 1798 near the mouth of the Nile.

Stourhead (45km/28m W of Salisbury) One of England's first *Palladian mansions, commissioned from Colen *Campbell by a successful banker, Henry Hoare, and completed in 1725. (The two projecting wings were added in the 1790s.) It was Henry Hoare's son, also Henry, who began in 1743 to create the *landscape garden which is now the primary cause of Stourhead's fame. He dammed the river Stour and placed a curving stone bridge across his new lake at the focal point of the view. He and his architect, Henry Flitcroft (1697–1769), then dotted the landscape with classical follies – a pantheon, temples of Apollo and of Flora, a grotto – to turn it into a living version of a painting by Claude.

John **Stow** (1525–1605) Antiquary whose *Survey of London* (1598) was the first account to combine the evidence of records and documents with personal observation. Like a modern guidebook, it deals with the city ward by ward and street by street, providing much fascinating detail about Elizabethan London. An enlarged edition was published in 1603.

Stowe (27km/17m E of Banbury) House of the late 17C, made more grandiose in the early 18C by *Vanbrugh (outside) and William *Kent (inside). Since 1923 it has been occupied by Stowe School, a boys' *public school.

The gardens are the glory of Stowe, being the most extensive of their kind in Britain (some 30 temples and other follies in about 162ha/400ac). Virtually a pattern book in the development of *landscape gardening, they are unique in having been created during three stylistic periods and in retaining traces of each. They were begun from 1713 in a formal style, with straight avenues, to the design of the royal gardener Charles Bridgeman (d. 1738). William Kent then took a hand, introducing heroic classical elements in an idealized landscape, with features such as the Temple of Ancient Virtue and the Temple of British Worthies (displaying 16 half-length busts of heroes from King Alfred to Alexander Pope). Finally the softer landscape of the Grecian Valley, more broadly sketched with belts and clumps of trees, was the contribution of Capability *Brown, who was head gardener here for ten years from 1841.

Lytton **Strachey** (1880–1932) Biographer and flamboyant member of the *Bloomsbury group. His witty and irreverent approach to the past made an instant success of *Eminent Victorians* (1918), which he followed in 1921 with a biography of Victoria herself.

Earl of **Strafford** (Thomas Wentworth, 1593–1641, baron 1628, earl 1640) Statesman who had been a leading parliamentary critic of Charles I in the 1620s but who by the time of the *Long Parliament in 1640 was seen as a symbol of royal misrule. He became close to the king after the death of *Buckingham, and was sent to govern northern England and then Ireland. He carried out these tasks with great efficiency but also with a high degree of self-enrichment. In the mood of 1640 an attack on Strafford seemed the most effective way to undermine royal authority. His impeachment for treason was launched within the first two weeks of the new parliament and his trial began in March 1641. He defended himself so convincingly that the charge was replaced by a bill of attainder, being a summary sentence of death by act of parliament. He was beheaded on Tower Hill.

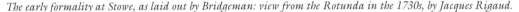

The early formality at Stowe, as laid out by Bridgeman: view from the Rotunda in the 1730s, by Jacques Rigaud.

Strait of Dover Strait at the eastern end of the *English Channel, joining it with the North Sea. At its narrowest it is only 32km/20m wide, between Dover and Calais. This is the stretch of water commonly referred to as the Channel, as in *swimming the Channel or *Channel tunnel.

Straits Settlements see *Singapore.

Strand Magazine (1891–1950) Illustrated magazine, specializing in short stories, which got off to an excellent start by featuring Conan Doyle and Sherlock *Holmes from its very first year. Many other distinguished authors were published in its pages, from Kipling and H.G. Wells to P.G. Wodehouse.

Strange Meeting Poem by Wilfred *Owen, in which he imagines coming face to face in Hell with an adversary from World War I ('I am the enemy you killed, my friend'). The dead man describes vividly how his death deprives the world of the truth he could tell about 'the pity of war'.

Strangeways The scene of Britain's most violent prison riot in recent years. The Manchester jail, designed in the 19C for 970 inmates, held 1647 in 1990. On April 1 of that year, during the Sunday morning service, prisoners in the chapel seized control. They held the prison for the next three weeks, doing £60m of damage and violently assaulting sexual offenders (known as Rule 43s, because kept in isolation for their own safety under Rule 43 of prison regulations); one such prisoner died after being thrown from a fourth-floor landing. Copy-cat riots soon followed in several other jails. Lord Justice Woolf's subsequent report on the event made widely accepted recommendations for reform in Britain's *prisons, and a rebuilt Strangeways was in 1992 declared to be an early candidate for *privatization.

Strata Florida Abbey (24km/15m SE of Aberystwyth) Ruins of a Cistercian abbey built in the 12–14c. At this period it was one of the most important centres in Wales, rich from local wool. It was the site of important assemblies and the burial place for several princely families. The name is Latin for 'carpets of flowers'.

Stratfield Saye (14km/9m S of Reading) House of about 1630, with its interiors largely remodelled during the 18C, which was bought by the duke of *Wellington in 1817. After his victory at Waterloo, parliament voted him £600,000 for a suitable home (following the precedent of Marlborough and *Blenheim Palace a century earlier). He chose Stratfield Saye, intending to build a palace in its grounds. Instead he settled into the existing house, modest only by palatial standards. It has remained the family home of his descendants, but is also a richly stocked museum of trophies and mementoes of the 'Iron Duke'.

Stratford-upon-Avon (21,000 in 1981) Town in Warwickshire, famous as the birthplace of William *Shakespeare. The economy of the town now depends largely on its famous son, but little attention was paid to the place until David Garrick organized a festival there in 1769 to commemorate the poet's birthday. Since 1879, by which time a permanent theatre had been built, there have been regular summer seasons of the plays. The original Memorial Theatre was burnt in 1926 and was replaced in 1932 by the present theatre (home of the *Royal Shakespeare Company). Several buildings connected with Shakespeare are now museums; these include his birthplace, a timber-frame building in Henley Street;

Hall's Croft, the house of John Hall, who married Shakespeare's daughter Susanna; and houses associated with the early years of his mother, Mary *Arden, and his wife, Anne *Hathaway. New Place, which he bought in 1597 and in which he died, was pulled down in 1759; the site is now a garden. The 13–14C Holy Trinity Church contains his grave, together with his wife's and Susanna's, and an almost contemporary half-length effigy of him by Gheerart Janssen. Harvard House is so named because it was the childhood home of the mother of John Harvard (1607–38), benefactor of the American university named after him.

Strathclyde (2,249,000 in 1991, administrative centre Glasgow) Since 1975 a *region of west central Scotland, comprising the former counties of Lanark, Ayr, Renfrew, Dunbarton, Bute, most of Argyll and part of Stirling.

Strathclyde Country Park (16km/10m SE of Glasgow) Recreational park created from 1973 on 668ha/1650ac of land left derelict after the closing of local mines. It opened in 1978 and rapidly became one of Britain's leading attractions, with an annual figure of about 4 million visitors in recent years. In addition to walking, riding and fishing, there are facilities for most kinds of games and water sports.

Strawberry Hill (21km/13m SW of central London) House which was an early and influential example of the *Gothic Revival. In 1749 Horace *Walpole bought a small house close to the Thames at Twickenham and set about transforming it into 'a little Gothic castle'. Over the next 20 years he added new wings and towers in a medieval-rococo style. The building was the ideal setting for his own life-long performance, which would be described nowadays as high camp. Strawberry Hill outraged the Victorians (more serious about their Gothic) but is today much appreciated. Since 1923 the house and grounds have been the home of St Mary's, a teacher training college.

Noel **Streatfield** (1895–1986) Author whose first book for children, the very successful *Ballet Shoes* (1936), set a vogue for stories about exciting careers. She developed the same theme in *Tennis Shoes* (1937) and *The Circus is Coming* (1938).

G.E. **Street** (George Edmund Street, 1824–1881) Prolific architect of the later Gothic Revival, responsible for the design of more than 250 buildings, the majority of them churches. Before setting up his practice he worked with George Gilbert Scott, and younger men among his own assistants included William Morris, Norman Shaw and Philip Webb. In 1866 he won a competition for the building by which he is best known, the *Law Courts in the Strand, but construction did not begin until 1874 and the great Gothic edifice was not completed until a year after Street's death. He had considerable influence on his contemporaries through two books illustrated with his own drawings: *Brick and Marble in the Middle Ages* (1855) and *Some Account of Gothic Architecture in Spain* (1865).

strikes In the 1960s and 1970s strikes seemed an endemic part of the British industrial scene, being often quoted as the main symptom of what was known on the Continent as the *'English disease'. The last winter of the Callaghan administration (1978–9) was marked by so many strikes that it became known as the *'winter of discontent', but the situation was even worse four months after the new Thatcher government had taken over; September 1979 registered the highest number of days lost through strikes in any month since the *General Strike in 1926. The total

Strikes: working days lost, in millions

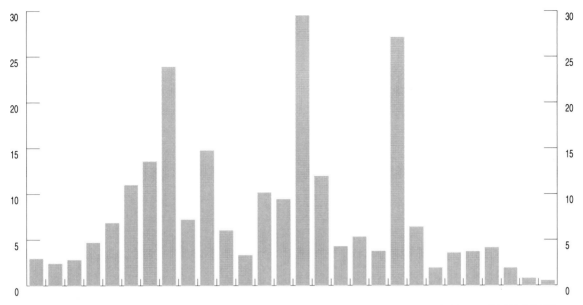

1965 1966 1967 1968 1969 1970 1971 1972 1973 1974 1975 1976 1977 1978 1979 1980 1981 1982 1983 1984 1985 1986 1987 1988 1989 1990 1991 1992

Source: Annual Abstract of Statistics *(see *Central Statistical Office)*.

of days lost fell steadily during the 1980s, as successive employment acts tightened the law on *picketing, abolished *closed shops and introduced pre-strike ballots. Government funds had been on offer since early in the 1980s to pay for a secret ballot in any union contemplating strike action, but until 1986 the *TUC made it a disciplinary offence for an affiliated union to accept such money. Under the Employment Act of 1988 it finally became illegal for a union to call its members out on strike unless a majority had previously voted for such action in a secret ballot.

strip-farming see *open-field system.

Stroller see Marion *Mould.

Patience **Strong** (pen name of Winifred Cushing, 1907–90) The nation's best-loved sentimental poet, whose verses – about everyday emotions and the sense of religious wonder – appeared for 40 years from 1935, in the *Daily Mirror* and subsequently the *Sunday Mirror*, under the heading 'The Quiet Corner'. She was particularly popular during World War II, when families were separated. The narrow width of a newspaper column caused her poems to be printed as if they were prose. The one most often quoted begins: 'If you stand very still in the heart of a wood you will hear many wonderful things, the snap of a twig, the wind in the trees and the whirr of invisible wings.'

'Athenian' **Stuart** see *Greek Revival.

House of **Stuart** (Scotland 1371–1603, Britain 1603–1714) The descendants on the thrones of Scotland and Britain of a family of hereditary stewards to the kings of Scotland, whose name for that reason became Stewart. In 1315 Marjorie, daughter of *Robert the Bruce, married Walter Stewart; in 1371 their son became king as Robert II (see the *royal house of Scotland). His reign was followed by those of Robert III, James I, James II, James III, James IV, James V, Mary Queen of Scots and James VI. In the 16c, when there were close links with France (Mary being married in her teens to the French king Francis II),

the spelling was gradually adjusted to Stuart, because there was no 'w' in the French alphabet.

When Elizabeth I died in 1603, James VI of Scotland was the senior descendant of Henry VII (see the *royal house). He therefore also became James I of England, bringing the two crowns together for the first time. The house of Stuart continued with Charles I, Charles II, James II, William III and Mary II, and finally Anne. The Act of *Settlement transferred the crown to the house of *Hanover, but the *Jacobites continued to press the Stuart claim until the mid-18c.

Charles Edward **Stuart** (1720–88) Claimant to the throne as grandson of James II and son of James *Stuart and Maria Sobieska, a Polish princess; he is known also as the Young Pretender and Bonnie Prince Charlie. On behalf of his father he landed in Scotland in 1745 to begin the *'45 Rebellion. After considerable early successes, the adventure ended nine months later in overwhelming defeat at *Culloden. The prince was in Scotland for a further five months, on the run from government troops (an ignominious period to which a touch of glamour was added by the heroism of Flora *Macdonald), until he escaped back to France in September 1746. From 1748 he was no longer welcome even there, with Britain and France at peace after the War of the Austrian Succession. Charles spent the last 40 years of his life wandering round Europe, virtually a fugitive, often in disguise. With the death of his younger brother Henry (the cardinal duke of York, 1725–1807), the male Stuart line came to an end.

James **Stuart** (1688–1766) Son of *James II and Mary of Modena, known as the Old Pretender (but by *Jacobites as James VIII and III). His birth raised the possibility of a Roman Catholic succession and provoked the *Revolution of 1688. Growing up in France, and living the later part of his life in Rome, he was known to his Jacobite supporters as the 'king over the water'. On several occasions he made preparations to recover his father's throne by force, but he only set foot in Britain during the brief *'15 Rebellion. From the 1740s he left the furtherance of the Jacobite cause to his son, Charles Edward *Stuart.

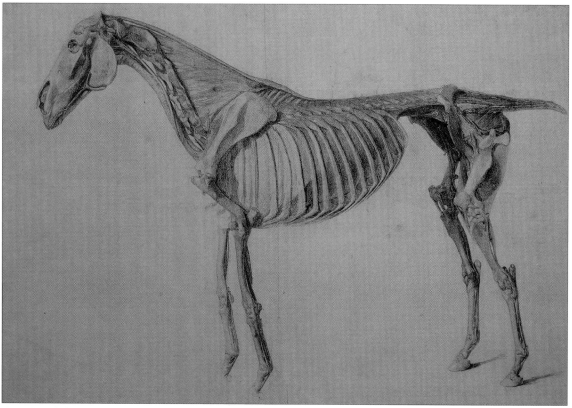

An original drawing by Stubbs for one of the etched plates in his Anatomy of the Horse *(1766).*

George **Stubbs** (1724–1806) Britain's outstanding painter of animals, particularly the horse. He first made his reputation with *The Anatomy of the Horse* (1766), a series of etched plates based on many months of painstaking dissection in a Lincolnshire farmhouse. He soon established a thriving career depicting his patrons' favourite horses, often with their grooms and carriages, in compositions which have a classical calm. The same mood pervades his scenes of country life, such as *Haymakers* and *Reapers* in the Tate Gallery. But his favourite single subject, painted many times, inclines more to the developing mood of romanticism; it is a horse attacked or frightened by a lion, inspired by a Roman marble sculpture of such an incident. In the 1770s he experimented with painting in enamel on ceramic panels provided by *Wedgwood, and achieved a high degree of finish. Largely forgotten in the 19C (his style could not be more at odds with that of the other great British animal painter, *Landseer), his reputation has soared in recent decades.

Studley Royal (6km/4m SW of Ripon) Landscape garden of the 18C with *Fountains Abbey as a climax to its vista of curving lakes and classical follies. The garden, with its architectural features such as the Octagon Tower and the Temples of Fame and Piety, was created between 1720 and 1781 by a father and son, John and William Aislabie. The house itself was severely damaged by fire in 1946 and was subsequently demolished.

*A **Study in Scarlet** see Sherlock *Holmes.*

Styal (16km/10m S of central Manchester) Largely unchanged early factory community, restored as a working museum. Samuel Greg (1758–1834) built a cotton-spinning mill on the river Bollin in 1784, and over the years followed it with houses for his manager, his adult workers and his own family, together with a counting house, a

bakery, a shop, a chapel, a school and an apprentice house for the pauper children who were a major part of his workforce. Here they were brought up under strict supervision and with long working hours, but with provision for health and some education. The buildings survive in beautiful surroundings, and a great water wheel now turns once again to demonstrate the spinning and weaving of cotton on 19C machinery.

*A **Subaltern's Love Song** see John *Betjeman.*

Sudan Independent republic since 1956, lying south of Egypt. The area came increasingly under the control of Egypt from 1820 and it was on behalf of the Egyptian khedive that General *Gordon governed the province. The expedition by *Kitchener to avenge Gordon's death at Khartoum led to the Sudan being jointly ruled by Britain and Egypt (1899–1955).

Sudbury Hall (21km/13m W of Derby) House built from about 1661 for George Vernon, remarkable for its eccentric combination of styles – thought to be due to Vernon acting as his own architect and discovering more modern fashions during the 30 years of construction. The exterior has a Jacobean appearance, by then about half a century out of date, but the interiors contain the richest display of baroque plasterwork and woodcarving to be seen in any English house of the late 17C. The main woodcarver was Edward Pierce, responsible for the superb staircase. The drawing room has an overmantel by Grinling *Gibbons, and the magnificent ceilings are by James Pettifer and Robert Bradbury.

Suez Canal The United Kingdom, protecting its own well-established systems of communication with India, opposed the construction (on French initiative) of a canal linking the Mediterranean with the Red Sea. The country therefore had no stake in the Suez Canal when it opened to ships in 1869. But in 1875 the bankrupt khedive of Egypt sold his shares to the British government, in a deal clinched by a bold gamble on the part of *Disraeli as prime minister. As a result of his action Britain became the largest single shareholder in the canal, a position which it still held at the time of the *Suez crisis of 1956.

Suez Crisis (more usually referred to in Britain just as Suez) In 1956 the United States and the United Kingdom withdrew financial support for the building of the Aswan dam in Egypt, and in retaliation President Nasser nationalized the *Suez Canal, without warning or compensation (the 99-year lease still had 12 years to run). Britain and France were the main shareholders in the canal, but they and Israel also had political reasons for wishing to reduce the power of Nasser. Israel attacked Egypt on 29 October 1956, and the next day Britain and France demanded that both sides withdraw 16km/10m from the canal. When Egypt refused, the British and French launched air attacks and landed troops. This swift action caused a bitterly divided response. Some applauded it as a reassertion of Britain's dwindling imperial might; others were appalled by an anachronistic reversion to *gunboat diplomacy. The most important reaction was that of the United Nations, which strongly condemned the invasion. By December 22 all British and French troops had been withdrawn, after an adventure widely agreed to have been a military and diplomatic disaster (in Britain it ended the career of Anthony *Eden). In 1958 Egypt paid compensation to the shareholders for the remainder of the lease on the canal.

Suffolk (662,000 in 1991, administrative centre Ipswich) *County on the east coast of southern England.

Suffolk Punch see *carthorses.

suffragettes Term in use from the early 20C for women campaigning for the suffrage (the right to vote). The cause went back as far as Mary *Wollstonecraft in the 18C, but it became of increasing urgency in the late 19C after the *franchise had been gradually extended to include virtually all men. Meanwhile in 1881 the *Tynwald on the Isle of Man had discreetly become the first parliament in the world to give women the vote (unmarried women and widows only, and with property qualifications), to be followed in 1893 by New Zealand.

In the early 20C Mrs *Pankhurst emerged as the leader of the movement in Britain, at a time when a succession of bills promising women the vote were being defeated in parliament. Under her guidance the suffragettes became more aggressive, chaining themselves to railings or damaging property. The most drastic protest of all was that of Emily Davison, who died after throwing herself among the galloping horses during the Derby of 1913 (it happened to be the king's horse that trampled her). By then the suffragettes in prison had evolved a new method of protest, the hunger strike, which the government countered with the *Cat and Mouse Act. The tension continued to mount until the greater urgency of World War I intervened. In the changed climate after the war, the cause was finally and easily won in 1918 – at first only for women over 30, but in 1928 this was reduced to 21 bringing full parity with men.

The last of the suffragettes, Victoria Lidiard, died in 1992 at the age of 102. She was one of 200 women jailed in 1912 after a window-smashing raid on Whitehall and the War Office.

Sulgrave Manor (29km/18m SW of Northampton) Manor house of the 16C, of interest as the family home from 1539 to 1626 of the ancestors of George Washington (his great-grandfather, John Washington, emigrated to Virginia in 1656). Since 1921 the house has been kept as a museum. In the porch are the Washington ancestral arms, composed of heraldic mullets and bars. These are similar to stars and stripes and are often inaccurately described as the origin of the US flag, which evolved gradually during the War of American Independence from earlier striped flags.

Arthur **Sullivan** (1842–1900, kt 1883) Composer of the *Savoy operas. With his brilliance at providing wit and parody in the music of the operettas, to match the verbal skills of W.S. *Gilbert, there went also an ability to tap a more solid and sentimental vein; his are the tunes for *Onward, Christian Soldiers and The *Lost Chord. But his ambition lay in serious music, where his large output included oratorios, cantatas (The Golden Legend 1886) and a grand romantic opera (Ivanhoe 1891). These were much admired in his time.

Sullom Voe see *Shetlands.

'**Sumer is icumen in**, lhude sing cuccu!' (Summer has come, loudly sing cuckoo) One of the earliest known English lyrics, exceptional also in having its music attached (to be sung as a canon). It features in a manuscript of about 1240, compiled at Reading Abbey.

summer pudding Pudding of berries (usually raspberries or blackberries with red or black currants), pressed until the juice has soaked through and darkened the

The suffragette leader, Mrs Pankhurst, arrested outside Buckingham Palace when trying to present a petition in 1914.

casing of white bread. Mrs *Beeton calls it a 'hydropathic pudding', saying that it derived from 18C spa towns, probably originally Bath, as a healthy dish for those taking the waters.

Summer Time (British Summer Time, or BST) The local time in the UK from the last Sunday in March to the Sunday following the fourth Saturday in October. It is one hour ahead of *Greenwich Mean Time and therefore gives an hour more daylight each evening. It was first introduced during World War I (in 1916) and since then there have been occasional variations in its duration, together with two major periods of change: there was Double Summer Time (two hours ahead) in 1941–5; and the extra hour of Summer Time was continued throughout the winters of 1968–70.

The **Sun** One of the main *tabloids at the bottom end of the market, competing directly with the *Mirror at a level not far short of 4 million copies. The paper has origins very different from its present character. In 1911 a news sheet was produced by striking trade unionists under the title *Daily Herald*; it became the official paper of the Trades Union Congress and by the early 1930s had a circulation of about 2 million. It was ailing by the 1960s, when an attempt was made to replace it with a livelier paper under the title *The Sun*. This failed to establish itself and was bought in 1969 by Rupert *Murdoch. A famous innovation of 1970 was the *page-three girl, and in 1976 the *Sun* overtook the *Mirror* to become for the first time Britain's largest-selling daily. In 1992 the two rivals were level-pegging a little below 3.7 million.

Sun Alliance Insurance group formed by the amalgamation of several of Britain's oldest companies in the field. The first was the Sun Fire Office, founded in London in 1710; its symbol of a smiling sun, with multiple rays like a starfish, can be seen on the outer walls of many 18C houses (meaning that the house was insured with the Sun). The company merged in 1959 with Alliance Assurance, launched in 1824 with the huge capital sum of £5 million provided by Nathan Rothschild. London Assurance, founded in 1720, joined the group in 1965; and Phoenix Assurance, dating from 1782, was included in 1984.

Sunday The Protestant tradition of a sober-suited Sunday, rather than the holiday mood preferred in many Roman Catholic countries, has historically been the strong preference of Anglicans and Nonconformists alike. The *Lord's Day Observance Society was founded by Anglicans in 1831. In spite of their vigilance there now remain relatively few restrictions on Sunday entertainment, yet as recently as 1982 district councils in Wales held a referendum on whether by-laws should be changed to allow local pubs to open on Sunday; two areas out of 15 decided against.

Gambling on Sunday is for many people a stumbling block, and it remains illegal under the Betting, Gaming and Lotteries Act of 1963; when Britain's first Sunday race meeting took place at Doncaster in July 1992, it was without the presence of bookies (in motor-racing the British Grand Prix, less associated with betting, was held on a Sunday as early as 1976).

The most topical issue in the early 1990s has been Sunday trading, which like gambling was still illegal in 1992 (under the Shops Act of 1950). The Lord's Day lobby, with the Keep Sunday Special Campaign playing a leading role, has stood on unusually firm ground on this issue, enjoying the support of trade unions concerned that shop assistants should not be exploited on their day of rest. An unprecedented situation developed in the 1991 Christmas season when major chains (headed by

A missionary brings the Word to ungodly bonnet makers: illustration in 'a Family Magazine for Sabbath Reading', 1861.

Sainsbury and Tesco, but with Marks & Spencer among those abstaining) deliberately flouted the law by opening on Sundays; they argued that the law in England and Wales was invalidated by EC regulations. The government, committed in principle to abolishing restrictions on Sunday trading, declared that it would wait for EC clarification; the European Court of Justice was expected to give its ruling during 1993. Meanwhile in January 1993 a majority of MPs voted in favour of a private member's bill to reinforce the Sunday restrictions.

Sunday Express see *Express.*

Sunday Mirror Launched in 1915 by Harold Harmsworth (younger brother of Lord *Northcliffe) as the *Sunday Pictorial*. It was a sister paper of the *Daily Mirror* and in 1963 was renamed the *Sunday Mirror*. With the other Mirror Group newspapers, it had the misfortune to be purchased in 1984 by Robert *Maxwell.

Sunday Night at the London Palladium see *London Palladium.

The **Sunday Post** Scotland's leading Sunday paper, launched in Glasgow in 1914 as the *Post Sunday Special* and given its present title in 1919. It is part of the D.C. Thomson stable, along with the *Courier. Its readership is calculated to be about 47% of the adult population of Scotland, earning it a place in *The Guinness Book of Records* as the most read national newspaper.

Sunday schools A movement pioneered in Gloucester in 1780 by Robert Raikes (1736–1811), prompted by the unruly behaviour of local children on the Lord's Day. Though linked with a parish church, and with compulsory attendance at the service, the educational purpose was to teach the children to read. The scheme was an immediate success, meeting a real need since the children worked every other day of the week. A Sunday School Society was formed in 1785 and the system spread rapidly through the country and even abroad. When the education acts offered all children a general *education, the Sunday schools adapted by concentrating on religious themes.

Sunday Telegraph see *Telegraph.*

*The **Sunday Times*** Paper launched in 1821 as *The New Observer* in direct competition with the *Observer (a rivalry which has persisted ever since); a few months later it was renamed *The Independent Observer*. In 1822, in another rapid change of name, it became *The Sunday Times* in the hope of imitating the success of the *Times – of which it finally became a sister paper in 1966 (they were both bought by Rupert Murdoch in 1981). In 1962 the *Sunday Times* was the first British newspaper to introduce a colour magazine, an idea since imitated in various forms by all its rivals.

Sunderland (196,000 in 1981) City and seaport on the northeast coast of England, at the mouth of the river Wear. It expanded greatly in the 17–18C, first as the port from which coal mined in the Wear valley was distributed and then as a shipbuilding centre. Glass and pottery became important products at the same period, both making much use of a famous local image, the iron bridge over the Wear which was opened in 1796. The Sunderland Museum and Art Gallery, established in 1846, has a fine collection of these wares. Sunderland was given the status of a city in 1992.

Sunderland, known as the Rokermen (Roker Park, Sunderland). Football club formed among Sunderland schoolmasters in 1879 as the District Teachers' Association Football Club. Membership was soon extended outside the teaching profession and the club was elected to Division 1 of the *Football League in 1890. It had many early successes – not matched in recent times, though Sunderland has usually been in the top division. Club victories: FA Cup 1937, 73; League Champions 1892, 93, 95, 1902, 13, 36.

Sunningdale Golf course near Ascot, in Berkshire, which was one of the first to be built inland (the origins of *golf being on seaside links). It was realized that the local heathland was in many ways equivalent to seaside conditions (hardy scrub, firm well-drained turf) and the Old course at Sunningdale was opened in 1901. The more demanding New course followed in 1922.

super-unions New term for giant *trade unions formed by mergers in a process which began in the late 1980s, though the *TGWU can be seen as a much earlier prototype. Examples in recent years are *Unison and the *AEEU, *GMB and *MSF.

supper see *dinner.

supplementary benefit see *income support.

Act of **Supremacy** (1534) Act which formally declared *Henry VIII to be head of the *Church of England and whch therefore denied the authority of the Pope. It was for refusing to affirm on oath their acceptance of this act that *Fisher and *More were executed (and both later canonized).

Supreme Court (in full Supreme Court of Judicature) The highest court in England and Wales other than the House of *Lords. It is composed of three separate entities: the *High Court of Justice, the *Crown Court and the *Court of Appeal. The High Court deals with civil cases; the Crown Court with criminal cases; and the Court of Appeal hears appeals from both sides. The nearest equivalent in Scotland is the *Court of Session.

Surrey (1,036,000 in 1991, administrative centre Kingston upon Thames) *County in southern England, southwest of London.

Surrey County Cricket Club Founded in 1845 and one of the original teams in the *county championship. The club's record in the championship (bettered only by Yorkshire's) included three wins before the points system was introduced in 1890 and 15 outright victories subsequently (1890, 91, 92, 94, 95, 99, 1914, 52, 53, 54, 55, 56, 57, 58, 71). In *one-day cricket the only wins have been the Benson and Hedges Cup in 1974 and the NatWest Trophy in 1982. Among the club's great players have been Jack *Hobbs, Jim *Laker and Peter *May. The county ground is the *Oval in London, and the county plays also at Guildford.

John **Surtees** Racing motorist with the unique distinction of having been world champion on two wheels and on four. Riding for MV Agusta in his motorcycling career he won seven world championships (1956 and 1958–60 on 500cc, 1958–60 on 350cc) and had four victories in the Isle of Man Senior TT (1956, 1958–60). He then changed to motor racing and was champion in 1964, driving for Ferrari, and runner-up in 1966.

R.S. **Surtees** see *Jorrocks.

Survey of London see John *Stow.

Survival (Anglia TV from 1960) Series of half-hour wildlife films, numbering 13 or more each year, which amount to an exceptionally distinguished achievement by the regional TV company based in Norwich.

survival of the fittest see Charles *Darwin.

Sussex Until 1974 a *county on the south coast of England, now divided officially into West Sussex and East Sussex (it had been administered as these two separate areas since the 16C). Sussex was in the 8C one of the seven *Anglo-Saxon kingdoms.

Sussex County Cricket Club Founded in 1839 and one of the original teams in the *county championship (which it has never won). The club's record in *one-day cricket has been better, with four victories in the Gillette Cup and NatWest Trophy (1963, 64, 78, 86, a total improved on only by Lancashire), and one in the Sunday League (1982). Ted *Dexter has been the most distinguished player in recent years. The county ground is at Hove, and the county plays also at Horsham, Eastbourne and Arundel.

Rosemary **Sutcliff** (1920–92) Author of numerous historical novels, the majority of them for teenage readers. She is best known for her series about the Roman occupation of Britain, beginning with *The Eagle of the Ninth* (1954), but her range extended to either side of that period; the hero of *Warrior Scarlet* (1958) is a boy with a withered arm in southern England in the Bronze Age, attempting the very difficult task of killing a wolf so as to achieve manhood; and *The Shield Ring* (1956) tells of Viking settlements in the Lake District resisting the encroachment of the Normans. A childhood illness confined Rosemary Sutcliff to a wheelchair, and her books (like many adolescents) have a strong sense of identity with the lonely and the excluded.

Herbert **Sutcliffe** (1894–1978) Batsman who played *cricket for Yorkshire (1919–39) and for England (1924–35). His aggregate of 1839 runs in 1919 is still (in 1992) the record for any player's first season, and he became part of two famous opening pairs – with *Hobbs for England and with Percy Holmes for Yorkshire (their stand of 555 against Essex in 1932 remains an English

The fragments of a warrior's ceremonial helmet from Sutton Hoo, with gilt-bronze moustache and eyebrows of inlaid garnet.

record). He effectively retired in 1939 but played one more match for Yorkshire in 1945.

Sutherland Until 1975 a *county in the extreme northwest of mainland Scotland, now part of the Highland region.

Graham **Sutherland** (1903–80) Artist who began his career as a printmaker (etching landscapes in a style influenced by the rediscovery of Samuel *Palmer) and did not take up painting until he was almost 30. His inspiration was the scenery of Wales, which he interpreted in a semi-abstract manner, finding in it metaphors for other forms of life and growth. Two new departures brought his art into the public eye. An interest from 1944 in Christian art and symbolism resulted in the great tapestry of *Christ in Glory* above the altar of *Coventry Cathedral. And his emergence as a vivid portraitist, beginning with Somerset Maugham (1949, Tate Gallery), led to the commission for an 80th-birthday portrait of Winston Churchill in 1954. This too was strikingly powerful, but it so distressed the sitter that Lady Churchill destroyed it a year or two later.

Sutton Hoo Ship Burial Anglo-Saxon treasure unearthed in 1939 at Sutton Hoo in Suffolk. It had been placed in a great wooden ship within a barrow or burial mound. The date of the burial was about 625, and it is believed to have been the tomb of an Anglo-Saxon king; a leading candidate is Raedwald, who ruled much of England south of the Humber. The king was buried with numerous gold and silver items, several of them decorated with delicate cloisonné work. The collection was judged not to be *treasure trove and so belonged to Mrs Pretty, who owned the land and had organized the excavation. She very generously presented the entire hoard to the British Museum.

Svengali see *Trilby.*

SVQ see *NVQ.

Swallows and Amazons see Arthur *Ransome.

Joseph **Swan** (1828–1914, kt 1904) Inventor of several improvements in photographic processes (he patented bromide paper in 1879), but known above all as a pioneer of electric lighting. There had been several unsuccessful experiments by others in which filaments were heated in a vacuum, but Swan was the first to demonstrate a practical source of electric light (to the Newcastle-upon-Tyne Chemical Society in 1878), using an incandescent carbon filament. Shortly afterwards Thomas Edison developed a similar lamp in the USA. This led to litigation over priority, but in 1883 the two merged their efforts in a single company.

Swan of Avon Ben Jonson's phrase for Shakespeare, the poet of *Stratford-upon-Avon, in his commemorative poem published in the *First Folio:

> Sweet Swan of Avon! what a sight it were
> To see thee in our waters yet appear,
> And make those flights upon the banks of Thames,
> That so did take Eliza, and our James!

Swansea (Abertawe in Welsh, 188,000 in 1991) City and port on the south coast of Wales, at the mouth of the river Tawe; administrative centre of West Glamorgan. Possibly deriving from a Viking settlement (the name is sometimes explained as coming from Sweyn, the father of Canute), it was certainly a place of importance for the Normans who built a castle here in the 12c. By the 17c Swansea was the largest port in Wales; shipbuilding, coal and metal became the basis of its prosperity. The docks expanded massively in the 19c and early 20c. With the recent reduction in shipping large sections of them have been developed for housing and as the Maritime and Industrial Museum, opened in 1977.

The city was severely bombed in World War II and much of the centre is now modern. One fortunate survival was the impressive Guildhall of the 1930s, by Percy Thomas (1883–1969); it contains the large bright 'British Empire' murals by Frank Brangwyn (1867–1956), commissioned but rejected for the House of Lords. The Glynn Vivian Art Gallery and Museum, opened in 1911, has an excellent collection of the local *Swansea porcelain and pottery. The University College of Swansea, founded in 1920, is one of the constituent colleges of the University of *Wales. Since 1974 all British driving licences and vehicle registrations have been issued from the Department of Transport's Driver and Vehicle Licensing Centre (DVLC Swansea, SA99).

Swansea porcelain Earthenware pottery was made at Swansea from the 1760s, but the factory is known in particular for the porcelain with delicately painted decoration which was produced from 1814, when William Billingsley brought the technology from *Nantgarw. The factory reverted to earthenware after only eight years, in 1822.

swan-upping Ancient ceremony, dating from the 15c, which is performed on the river Thames between Sunbury and Pangbourne on the Monday to Thursday of the third full week in July. As the largest British bird and the most impressive dish to set before a king, any swan living on open water has been held since the Middle Ages to belong to the monarch. The exceptions, from about 1470, were certain swans on the Thames which had been granted to two of the *City Livery Companies; they were identified by nicks on their bills, a single nick belonging to the Dyers and two nicks to the Vintners, while the royal swans remained unmarked. The purpose of the annual ceremony is to allocate the new cygnets in due proportion. The liveried swan-uppers process slowly upstream from Sunbury in six boats, cornering swan families, inspecting the bills of the adults (at some risk) and nicking the appropriate number of their offspring.

Swaythling Cup see *table tennis.

Swaziland Independent kingdom in southeast Africa, between South Africa and Mozambique, which has been a member of the *Commonwealth since 1968. The Swazi people, who had moved into the area in the early 19C, were by the 1880s under the control of the Boer republic of the Transvaal. After the *Boer War the territory was administered by a British High Commissioner, until independence in 1968.

The **Sweeney** (Thames TV 1974–8) Police drama series on television, set in London, with the Flying Squad as the central characters; the Sweeney is *rhyming slang for the squad (from Sweeney Todd). It distinguished itself by being considerably rougher and tougher than other similar series. Two of the regular detectives were played by John Thaw and Dennis Waterman, who went on to equally successful careers in, respectively, *Inspector Morse* and *Minder*.

Sweeney Todd The fictional 'demon barber of Fleet Street', who slit the throats of his customers to provide the fillings for Mrs Lovett's meat pies. He made his first appearance in *penny dreadfuls of the 1840s and went on to become a favourite character in *melodrama.

Sweetheart Abbey (10km/6m S of Dumfries) The ruins of a Cistercian abbey, destroyed in the Reformation.

Within the great protective wall (enclosing some 12ha/ 30ac) only the church remains, well preserved up to the beginning of the roof line. The abbey's name recalls its romantic origins. It was founded in 1273 by Devorguilla de Baliol in memory of her husband John (they were the parents of the Scottish king John de *Baliol). Until her death in 1290 she carried John's heart with her (this was a period of portable hearts, as with *Robert the Bruce), and then she and the heart were buried in the abbey church. Known originally as New Abbey, it gradually acquired its present name.

sweets Sweet titbits of various kinds had been made for centuries with honey before sugar from American plantations became widely available in Europe. The invention of the vacuum pan in England in the early 19C turned sugar refining from a cottage industry to one of mass production. In the same period the modern names of sweets first appeared, though they probably bore little relation to their present-day equivalents.

Toffee (under an earlier name of 'taffy') is first described in 1817 as 'treacle thickened by boiling and made into hard cakes'; modern toffee, by contrast, includes butter. Butterscotch, now a brittle version of toffee for sucking rather than chewing, is first mentioned in 1855 as a 'treacle ball, with an amalgamation of butter in it'.

Meanwhile the glutinous substances exuded by the acacia (known as gum arabic) or extracted from the root of the marsh mallow were making possible new pleasures such as gum drops, jujubes (named from the shape of the berry of the jujube tree) and marshmallows. The humbug was already a name for toffee flavoured with mint, though not as yet with its characteristic modern stripes. Fudge, a soft toffee whose name oddly shares with humbug the element of deception, was an import from America in the late 19C. The splendidly named gobstopper – originally a ball changing colour as successive layers are sucked away,

Swan-upping on the Thames: checking the ownership of the adult bird before the cygnets are marked.

Swift's best-known story in an 18C illustration: Gulliver wakes to find himself tied down by the tiny Lilliputians.

but now used of any huge sweet – was not introduced until the 20C.

Sweets consisting of hard sugar in stick form have been known generally as *rock.

Jonathan **Swift** (1667–1745) Anglo-Irish author, the greatest prose satirist in the English language. Born in Dublin and educated at Trinity College, he was ordained an Anglican priest in 1695. His literary talents became evident in 1704, with the publication of two works written during the 1690s when he was secretary to Sir William Temple at Moor Park in Surrey: *The Battle of the Books* is a mock-heroic account of a struggle between classical and modern authors; and *A Tale of a Tub* satirizes Roman Catholics and Presbyterians while finding relatively little fault with Anglicans. The tone of his irony is evident in the title of another attack, in 1708, on what he regarded as fashionable trends in religion – *An Argument to prove that the Abolishing of Christianity in England, may as Things now stand, be attended with some Inconveniences.*

In 1710 he became the leading polemicist for a new Tory administration in London. He described his daily life at this period in the letters which he sent to 'Stella' in Dublin. She was Esther Johnson, whom he had first known as an eight-year-old child when he gave her lessons at Moor Park. There has been much speculation about their relationship, which was probably just a close friendship. The letters, first published in 1766, became known as his *Journal to Stella.* The other important female friend in his life was 'Vanessa' – Esther Vanhomrigh, whom he met in London in 1708 and who followed him back to Ireland. His services to the Tories gave him hope of a bishopric, but he was appointed in 1713 dean of St Patrick's

Cathedral in Dublin, where he spent the rest of his life – apart from visiting London in 1726–7 to arrange for the publication of **Gulliver's Travels.*

His disappointment and relative seclusion served to sharpen his satirical talents. In addition to Gulliver the 1720s produced *The Drapier's Letters* (1724), a series of pamphlets which caused the government to back down on a corrupt scheme for supplying the copper coinage of Ireland (this victory made Swift something of a national hero). *A Modest Proposal for preventing the Children of poor People in Ireland, from being a Burden to their Parents or Country* (1729) is, though brief, the most savagely effective of all his works. The argument enables him to describe the dreadful conditions of poverty in Ireland, for his proposal is that everyone would be far better off if poor children were fattened up and eaten. He fully earned the Latin epitaph, written by himself, which is above his grave in St Patrick's. It says that he has gone where *saeva indignatio* (fierce indignation) can no longer tear his heart.

Swift was also an accomplished poet, usually in rhyming couplets of 8-syllable lines. Best known are his *Verses on the Death of Dr Swift* (1731), in which he surveys his life's achievement and the likely impact of the news in various quarters:

> My female Friends, whose tender Hearts,
> Have better learned to Act their Parts.
> Receive the News in doleful dumps,
> 'The Dean is Dead (and what is Trumps?).'

swimming the Channel The first man to swim across the Strait of Dover was a captain in the British merchant navy, Matthew Webb, who on 24–5 August 1875 swam the 34km/21m from Dover to Calais in 21hr 45min. It was another 51 years before the first woman achieved the feat (Gertrude Ederle from the USA, taking 14hr 39min on 6 August 1926).

Since then extraordinary records have proliferated, such as a fastest time by either sex of 7hr 40min (Penny Dean, USA, 29 July 1978); a girl of 12 making the crossing in 1983 (Samantha Druce, UK, 15hr 27min) and a boy of 11 in 1988 (Thomas Gregory, UK, 11hr 54min); a British swimmer, Michael Read, achieving a total of 31 crossings between 1969 and 1984, six of them in one year; and the fastest ever triple crossing (England to France, back to England and again to France in one continuous swim of 28hr 21min) by the New Zealander Philip Rush in 1987.

Algernon **Swinburne** (1837–1909) Poet of great virtuosity in his use of rhythm, who shot to fame in the 1860s as a figure of scandal, defying the conventions of Victorian respectability. The book which had this effect was *Poems and Ballads* (1866), with its themes of sexual perversion, masochism (he had acquired at Eton a taste for flagellation) and irreligion. One of its best-known lines (in 'Hymn to Proserpine') takes the traditional final capitulation of the Roman emperor Julian the Apostate ('thou hast conquered, Galilean') and gives it a twist very much less pleasing to the believing Christian: 'Thou hast conquered, O pale Galilean; the world has grown gray from thy breath'. In the 1870s Swinburne was at the centre of avant-garde London, defending *Rossetti in the battle over the 'fleshly school of poetry' and campaigning for all forms of liberty.

Alcohol and the physical excesses of his private life increasingly threatened his health, until he was taken in hand by a friend, Theodore Watts (1832–1914), a solicitor turned writer. Watts, who changed his name in 1896 to Watts-Dunton, took Swinburne in 1879 to live with him at the Pines in Putney. Here, for the rest of his life, the poet was restricted to a quiet regime, but one in which

Hot Coffee by Moonlight during Captain Webb's historic swimming of the Channel (contemporary wood engraving).

he remained immensely productive. By the early 20c the *enfant terrible* had become a grand old man of letters.

swingometer Primitive device, consisting of a vertical arrow which can be moved left or right to predict the effect of a swing to either party in an election. During BBC election coverage of the 1960s it became a familiar feature in the hands of the Canadian Robert McKenzie; by the time of the 1992 general election, after making remarkably few concessions to hi-tech, the swingometer was being manipulated in a famously excitable manner by Peter Snow.

St **Swithin's Day** A legend, known from at least the 13c, says that the feast day of St Swithin (July 15), be it dry or wet, will set the pattern for the next 40 days. Swithin was a counsellor to the kings of Wessex and became bishop of Winchester in 852. Various attempts have been made to explain the legend but it is not unique to Britain; other countries have similar traditions attached to different saints.

sword dance Two distinct versions of sword dancing have been traditional in Britain. In the linked-sword dances of northeast England the dancers hold the tips of each others' swords and perform feats of agility over and under the resulting barriers. In the solo sword dance of Scotland two swords are crossed on the ground and the dancer must perform rapid steps between them without touching the blades.

syllabub Something between a drink and a pudding, popular from Elizabethan to Victorian times and still served occasionally in more traditional dining rooms. The essen-

tial ingredients are alcohol and milk or cream. In its simplest form it was a rustic treat; a dairymaid milked the cow into a bowl of spiced cider or ale, providing her sophisticated visitors with some warm alcoholic curds and whey. The version made today also goes back to at least the 17c, blending cream, sugar and wine (and sometimes brandy) with spices and whisking the mixture to a light froth.

Symond's Yat Rock (32km/20m W of Gloucester) Rock rising high above the Wye valley, on the border of England and Wales, with a superb view over a great loop in the river.

Symphonic Variations (1946) One-act ballet in three movements by Frederick *Ashton, which has come to be considered one of his greatest masterpieces. It is without plot, following the emotional development of the score by César Franck (*Variations Symphoniques* 1885). The six dancers for whom it was created included Margot Fonteyn, Moira Shearer and Michael Somes.

Symphony Hall (Birmingham) Concert hall opened in 1991, as the home of the *City of Birmingham Symphony Orchestra. Its state-of-the-art acoustics are the work of an American specialist, Russell Johnson.

Synod of Whitby (664) The council held at *Whitby to decide whether the kingdom of Northumbria would follow the Celtic form of Christianity, brought by missionaries from Ireland, or the Roman rite introduced by St *Augustine. The choice of Rome, symbolized in particular by adopting the Roman date for Easter, led to the rest of England turning also in that direction.

Astonishing the locals, Dr Syntax pauses to sketch the picturesque: aquatint after Rowlandson from the 1813 Tour.

Dr Syntax A ludicrous wizened clergyman, illustrated by *Rowlandson and based on the Rev. William Gilpin. He became a popular character in a series of books beginning with his *Tour . . . in search of the *picturesque* (1813).

Syon House (18km/11m W of central London) House on the north bank of the Thames, built from 1547 by the 1st duke of *Somerset. His square brick building was later castellated, faced in stone and given sash windows, which explains its present unprepossessing exterior. But the interiors are a marvel of *neoclassicism, with rooms of breath-taking self-confidence by the young Robert *Adam; he was 34 when he started remodelling the house in 1762. The name, deriving from Mount Zion outside Jerusalem, is that of a convent of Bridgettine nuns established here in 1415 by Henry V; their buildings were given to the duke of Somerset after the *dissolution of the monasteries. In 1594 Syon came into the hands of the Percy family, whose main seat is *Alnwick Castle.

The modern tourist attractions in the grounds include the Heritage Motor Museum, a large collection of vehicles selected to show the development of the British motor industry.

T

Pat **Taaffe** see *Arkle.

*The **Tablet*** Weekly newspaper launched in 1840 as a voice for Britain's *Roman Catholic community; the first issue contained a letter from Daniel *O'Connell welcoming this new 'channel of communication'. It was founded by a convert, Frederick Lucas, whose intention was to be radical in politics but traditional in religion – an approach still followed, in principle, by the *Tablet* of the 1990s.

table tennis (also known as ping pong) Game which began as a pastime in Britain in the mid-19c, using cork or rubber balls and an improvised barrier (such as a row of books) across a table. By the 1880s balls and bats were being manufactured for sale. James Gibb pioneered the use of a celluloid ball in the early 1890s, and he and his partners patented the name Ping-Pong – from the sound of the ball on a table and on a bat of stretched parchment. There was a craze for the game at the turn of the century but it faded away until revived in the 1920s, by then with a pimpled rubber surface to the bat making spin an essential part of the player's skill. The name table tennis was officially adopted with the formation in 1926 of the International Table Tennis Federation. In that same year the Swaythling Cup, for national teams of men, was donated by Lady Swaythling, mother of the first president of the ITTF; and in 1933 the equivalent Corbillon Cup for women was given by Marcel Corbillon, president of the French association. Both competitions are now biennial.

tabloid press Tabloid newspapers are those small enough to be sold with the entire front page visible, by contrast with the more weighty 'broadsheet' papers which have a horizontal fold. The term is usually applied to the bottom end of the market (particularly the *Sun* and the *Star*) and so 'tabloid journalism' has come to mean trivial stories of a titillating, sensational and often xenophobic nature. But the tabloid format is also used by the *Mail*, the *Express*, the *Mirror* and *Today*.

   The word itself (a combination of tablet and alkaloid) was invented and registered in 1884 by Henry *Wellcome as a trade name for a patent medicine in the form of a small compressed tablet. It was used figuratively 12 years later of the first popular newspaper, the *Daily *Mail*, referring not to its shape (it was then a broadsheet) but to its short and pithy paragraphs ('all the news in the smallest space').

Taffy Nickname for a Welshman, deriving from the pronunciation in Wales of *Dafydd* (the Welsh version of David and one of the most common Welsh Christian names). From at least the 18c English children sang a nursery rhyme on St David's day to bait the Welsh, beginning:

   Taffy was a Welshman, Taffy was a thief,
   Taffy came to my house and stole a piece of beef.

tagging A government response in the early 1990s to the problem of Britain's overcrowded *prisons was a proposed policy of curfew and electronic tagging. Convicted men and women would have to stay wherever the court ordered – usually at home, for all or part of the day – and the tag would activate an alarm if they broke the curfew. The introduction of the scheme was delayed by the cost of the equipment and by the discovery, in trials, that it is very difficult to devise a tag which cannot be removed.

Take It From Here (BBC 1947–58) Radio comedy series on the Light Programme, starring Jimmy Edwards, Dick Bentley and Joy Nichols. June Whitfield replaced Nichols in 1953, the first year of the series' most popular item – a comic soap opera, 'The Glums', featuring the engaged couple Ron and Eth. The programme was the first collaboration of two young writers, Frank Muir (b. 1920) and Denis Norden (b. 1922), later known as performers of witty entertainment.

Fox **Talbot** (William Henry Fox Talbot, 1800–77) Pioneer photographer who in 1835 was the first to expose a successful negative; one of that summer's tiny paper negatives survives, showing an oriel window at *Lacock Abbey (it is now in the Science Museum in London). By 1840 he had speeded up the negative–positive process, reducing

A print from the oldest negative: Fox Talbot's view from inside a room at Lacock Abbey, 1835.

exposure times and increasing the paper size. In 1841 he patented this kind of image (the basis of all subsequent photography) under the name of calotype – derived from the Greek for 'beautiful impression'. His book *The Pencil of Nature* (1844–6) was the first to be illustrated with photographs.

A *Tale of Two Cities* (1859, after monthly publication that year in *All the Year Round*) Novel by *Dickens, with illustrations by *Phiz, which begins with one of the best-known opening passages in the language: 'It was the best of times, it was the worst of times, it was the age of wisdom, it was the age of foolishness . . .'. The time is that of the French Revolution, the cities are London and Paris. The story centres on Dr Manette, freed after 18 years of wrongful imprisonment in the Bastille; and on his daughter Lucie, married in London to a French aristocrat, Charles Darnay, but loved from afar by Sydney Carton. Her husband goes to France to rescue a family servant but is arrested and condemned to death. He is saved at the last moment when Carton, who luckily resembles him, takes his place on the scaffold. Carton's final thoughts end the book with a sentence almost as famous as its opening: 'It is a far, far better thing that I do, than I have ever done; it is a far, far better rest that I go to than I have ever known.'

Tales from Shakespeare see Charles *Lamb.

Thomas **Tallis** (*c*.1505–85) Composer and organist who was a leading member of the court musical establishment under four monarchs, from Henry VIII to Elizabeth I. He was the teacher of *Byrd; from 1572 they shared the post of organist at the Chapel Royal, and in 1575 Elizabeth gave them a joint monopoly to publish music. Their *Cantiones Sacrae* of that year is a shared collection of their motets. Tallis's main output was sacred music, often of extraordinary contrapuntal complexity – most notably in *Spem in alium* for 8 choirs of 5 voices, all 40 singers having individual parts. His name is best known now to a wide public through Vaughan Williams' *Fantasia on a Theme by Thomas Tallis*.

Tamar River which rises close to the Bristol Channel and flows south to the English Channel, forming for most of its length (97km/60m) the border between Cornwall and Devon. Two notable bridges cross its estuary, a suspension bridge carrying the A38 (opened 1961) and a railway bridge – the Royal Albert Bridge, by Isambard Kingdom Brunel, completed in 1859. The area of the estuary downstream of the bridges and west of *Plymouth has long been an anchorage and dockyard for the navy.

Tamburlaine the Great (*c*.1587) Drama by *Marlowe, published in 1590 but probably first performed in 1587. The play chronicles the rise of the 14c conqueror Tamburlaine, or Timur, from shepherd and bandit to emperor of vast dominions. In its rich use of *blank verse and in providing a towering role for an actor (in this case Edward *Alleyn), *Tamburlaine* set the pattern for the glories of Elizabethan and Jacobean tragedy.

The *Taming of the Shrew* (*c*.1593) Comedy by *Shakespeare in which Petruchio, visiting Padua in search of a wife, marries the notoriously difficult Katharina for the sake of her dowry. The comedy derives from his attempts to humiliate her into obedience and from her spirited resistance. By the end – in a final scene often embarrassing to modern sensibilities – she has been tamed into willing submission and is presented as a perfect wife. Petruchio's peremptory demand 'Kiss me, Kate' provided the title of the American musical of 1948 about a company performing Shakespeare's play.

Tam o' Shanter, on Meg, escapes over the river Doon from Cutty Sark and the witches: steel engraving, c.1840.

Tam o' Shanter (1791) Poem by Robert *Burns, telling the story of Tam o' Shanter, a farmer who spends a drunken evening in a tavern on market day at *Ayr. Riding home on his grey mare, Meg, he passes the church at *Alloway and sees witches dancing in it. He calls out to the only pretty one, wearing a 'cutty sark' (a short shirt or shift), and to his terror she pursues him with all her cronies behind her. If he can reach the bridge over the Doon he will be safe, for witches will not cross a running stream. He is over just in time, but poor Meg is not entirely so. Her tail is still on the wrong side of the keystone, and Cutty Sark pulls it off. Tam's circular woollen bonnet, with a bobble in the centre, was a common headdress in Scotland and has since become known as a tam o' shanter (from later illustrations to the poem, for Burns gives Tam only a 'gude blue bonnet').

Tamworth see *pigs.

Tanganyika A *mandated territory which was administered by Britain after World War I, having previously been German East Africa. Agreed spheres of influence in the late 19c had given this area to Germany and neighbouring *Kenya to Britain. Julius Nyerere (b. 1922) became in 1961 the first prime minister of the newly independent Tanganyika and in 1964 the president of *Tanzania, a post which he held until his resignation in 1985.

tanks Armoured chariots have long been familiar in war but an all-metal vehicle, moving on tracks and with the crew concealed inside, was not introduced until World War I. Such a design was proposed in Britain in the first months of the war, but the only politician to show an interest was Winston Churchill, who was then first lord of the Admiralty. As a result of this accidental origin under naval auspices, tanks still have parts referred to as hull, turret and deck. The name itself was a result of the need for secrecy. Those working in the factory where the hull was developed were told that it was to be a mobile water carrier for Mesopotamia; so they called it the water tank and the name stuck. Eleven tanks went into action at the *Somme on 15 September 1916. They had little effect on this first occasion, and it was not until Cambrai in November 1917 that they were used in large numbers. They then proved how effective they were against the most devastating weapon of that war, the machine gun. The Tank Corps of World War I was absorbed into the *Royal Armoured Corps at the start of World War II.

British tanks have traditionally (but not exclusively) been given names beginning with C: Churchills, Cromwells and Comets were prominent in World War II; they were followed in the postwar era by Centurions and then Chieftains; and the army's most recent tank is the Challenger (made by Vickers), which demonstrated its merits in the Gulf War. At Bovington Camp in Dorset the Royal Armoured Corps has a museum of more than 200 tanks and armoured vehicles, including several from World War I.

Tantallon Castle (45km/28m E of Edinburgh) One of Scotland's most dramatically situated castles, perched on a promontory jutting into the sea opposite *Bass Rock. A stronghold of the powerful and unruly Douglas family from the 14C, it was abandoned as a ruin after a siege in the 17C. Even so its crumbling red walls and towers still give a powerful and dramatic impression.

La **Tante Claire** (London SW3) One of only two restaurants in Britain to have three stars in the 1993 *Michelin Guide* (the other is the *Waterside Inn). Its proprietor is Pierre Koffman (b. 1948), a French chef who worked with Michel Roux at the Waterside Inn (1971–7) before opening La Tante Claire in 1978.

Tanzania Republic and member of the *Commonwealth since 1964, when it was formed by the merging of two existing member states, *Tanganyika and *Zanzibar.

tap dance see *clog dance.

Tarka the Otter (1927) Unsentimental story by Henry Williamson (1895–1977) about the life and death of an otter in Devon, which rapidly became a classic because of its closely observed realism. Tarka dies after being pursued for many hours by a hunt, but in a final underwater struggle he succeeds in killing one of the hounds.

Tarmac In the late 1980s one of Britain's largest companies, involved in roads, housing, and the manufacture of construction materials; by the early 1990s its market value had been much reduced by the recession in the building industry. The trade name dates back to a patent of 1902, taken out by Purnell Hooley (1860–1942), the county surveyor of Nottingham, for a road surface formed of tar mixed with iron slag – waste material from the blast furnaces of iron works. The general name tarmacadam had been in use since the 1880s for various improvements to *McAdam's famous road surface by the addition of tar, but Hooley's method proved the most effective. He formed his company in 1903.

tartan Cloth in brightly coloured rectangular patterns, worn as a kilt or other garment in Scotland. Scottish plaids were traditionally woven with designs of this kind and were recognized by the 18C as characteristic *Highland dress, but there were not at that time any firm links between individual tartans and particular *clans or regiments. After the collapse of the '45 Rebellion at *Culloden, Highland dress was forbidden (until 1782). From the late 18C Scottish regiments wore tartan again, each now using an individual pattern as an identifying feature. The creation of

clan tartans seems to have followed a surge of interest in all things Scottish, prompted by the works of Walter *Scott, and it gathered impetus after George IV, in Edinburgh in 1822, acknowledged the Scottish part of his ancestry by wearing the tartan now known as the Royal Stuart. The Scottish Tartans Society runs a museum at Comrie in Tayside, with a collection of some 1300 tartans, where traditional methods of dyeing and weaving are demonstrated.

TASS see *MSF.

Jeffrey **Tate** (b. 1943) Conductor who had qualified as a doctor before joining Covent Garden's music staff in 1970; he subsequently became principal conductor there from 1986 to 1991. He has held that role with the English Chamber Orchestra since 1985, and in 1991 he became the artistic director of the Rotterdam Philharmonic.

Tate & Lyle Sugar company formed by the merger of two firms established in the mid-19C. Henry Tate (1819–99, bt 1898) was a sugar refiner in Liverpool when an invention was brought to his notice in 1872 – a device for producing easily packaged cubes of sugar, instead of the jagged pieces previously chipped by grocers from large blocks. Tate patented the idea and it led to a massive increase in his business, which he transferred in 1880 to London. In the remaining two decades of his life he became an exceptionally generous philanthropist and an important collector of contemporary British art. He made major benefactions to Liverpool; in London he offered to give his collection to the nation and to build a home for it. The result was the *Tate Gallery.

Tate's main commercial rival had been his Scottish contemporary Abram Lyle (1820–91), who from 1865 had a sugar refinery at Greenock on the Clyde. He also moved his business to London, in 1883, and in 1885 introduced an extremely successful product, Golden Syrup. The Tate and Lyle families merged their interests in 1921 to form an enterprise of a size to match any foreign competition. The joint venture was floated on the Stock Exchange in 1928.

Tate Gallery (London SW1) Collection which fulfils a double purpose, as the nation's gallery of British art and as the national museum of modern art. It was founded by Sir Henry Tate (of *Tate and Lyle), who not only paid for the building on the north bank of the Thames at Millbank but also gave his own collection of contemporary British paintings. Designed by Sidney Smith (1858–1913), the gallery opened in 1897. Until 1954 it was administered as a department of the National Gallery. In 1988 the Tate opened a major outpost of its own, the Tate Gallery in *Liverpool; and this was followed in 1993 by the Tate Gallery in *St Ives.

The British collection is unsurpassed in its field and is broadly representative of all schools, from Tudor painting onwards. It has some famous Hogarths (among them *The Beggar's Opera* and *O the *Roast Beef of Old England*), superb paintings by Stubbs and an unrivalled collection of Blake. It contains some of the best-known images of 19C British art (Millais' *Ophelia*, for example, or Frith's *Derby Day*). But the most extraordinary holding is of Turner, for the Tate houses the collection which he left to the nation (some 300 paintings and 19,000 watercolours and drawings). His wish that a special gallery should be built for them was finally achieved when the Clore Gallery opened in 1987 – designed by James *Stirling and a gift from the *Clore Foundation.

In the modern collection international and British art is intermingled. The masters of European and American painting are here from Impressionism onwards, together with the Camden Town and Euston Road schools, the suburban mythologies of Stanley Spencer, the abstractions of Ben Nicholson and some of the most familiar images by Graham Sutherland (portrait of Somerset Maugham), Francis Bacon (*Three Studies for Figures at the Base of a Crucifixion*) and David Hockney (**Mr and Mrs Clark and Percy*). The modern collection also displays sculpture – Rodin and Giacometti alongside Epstein and Moore, Caro or Richard Long. It was the Tate's purchase in the early 1970s of a minimalist sculpture, the so-called 'bricks' by Carl Andre (actual title *Equivalent VIII*), which provoked the nation's most intense debate on the nature and value of modern art.

There are plans for the collection to be split by the year 2000, establishing a museum of modern art in a new building and making the present Tate a gallery of British art.

The *Tatler* (1709–11) Periodical founded by *Steele, which appeared three times a week in the form of a letter or essay supposedly penned in one of several fashionable *coffee houses, whose patrons were the enthusiastic readers. Steele, assisted soon by *Addison (a school friend from Charterhouse), wrote on a wide variety of topics in a lively and informal manner, with a consistent emphasis on the reasoned and moderate response considered suitable in a gentleman. The paper was Whig in its politics and Steele brought it to an end when a Tory administration came to power in 1711, replacing it almost immediately with the non-political **Spectator*. The name was revived in 1901 for an illustrated monthly magazine, specializing in social events, which is still published today.

Tattenham Corner see *Epsom.

Tattersalls The world's oldest auction house for *thoroughbred racehorses, founded by Richard Tattersall (1724–95). In 1745 he bought a share in Beevor's Horse Repository in London's St Martin's Lane; in 1766 he set up on his own as Tattersalls Sales at Hyde Park Corner. From 1838 sales were held also at Doncaster and from 1886 at *Newmarket, which has been since 1977 the centre of Tattersalls' activities. Of the ten sales a year at Park Paddocks in Newmarket, the most important are the Houghton sales for yearlings in the autumn.

Taunton (35,000 in 1981) Town on the river Tone; administrative centre of Somerset. There was an Anglo-Saxon castle here from the 8c. The present castle (12c, but much demolished and restored) houses the Somerset County Museum, which includes a Roman mosaic floor found in Low Ham, a village a few miles to the northeast. The church of St Mary Magdalene, mainly of the 15–16c, has a tall elaborately carved tower and a magnificent oak

Tudor roof in the nave. The town was one of the main locations of the Bloody Assizes held in 1685 by Judge *Jeffreys.

John **Tavener** (b. 1944) Composer who first became widely known with *The Whale* (1968), a large and raucous piece combining singers, chorus, orchestra, taped sounds and a speaker intoning factual information. He subsequently joined the Orthodox Church and his more recent work, such as *The Protecting Veil* (1989), has had a ritual simplicity.

R.H. **Tawney** (Richard Henry Tawney, 1880–1962) Economic historian and committed socialist, whose ideas were influential in the early decades of the Labour party. His works include *The Agrarian Problem in the Sixteenth Century* (1912), *The Acquisitive Society* (1921) and – probably the best known – *Religion and the Rise of Capitalism* (1926).

tax burden The money taken by government, central and local, in all forms of taxation. The main elements are taxes on income (*income tax for individuals, *corporation tax for companies), on capital (*capital gains tax, *inheritance tax) and on expenditure (*VAT), together with *national insurance contributions (from both employees and employers), excise (duties in addition to VAT on certain commodities, in particular petrol, alcohol and tobacco) and *local taxes. The overall level of taxation is usually expressed as a percentage of the *GDP or GNP.

People are much more aware of direct than indirect taxation. The reduction in the basic rate of income tax from 30% to 25% during the 1980s left the public with the impression that taxes had become lower. As the graph below shows, the opposite was the case: the level of taxation was unusually high in that period.

Tay The longest river in Scotland, flowing 193km/120m from the source of its main headwaters (the Dochart and Lochay) in the Grampians, through Loch Tay and eventually out to its firth in the North Sea. For centuries the last crossing place of the river was at Perth, but three great bridges have been constructed in modern times across the firth near Dundee, where it is about 2km/1.2m wide. The first was a railway bridge (1871–8), which collapsed during a gale on 28 December 1879 when a train was crossing it – from the start one of Britain's most famous disasters, made more so by William *MacGonagall's verses on the subject. The present railway bridge was built close to the original site in 1883–8. Two miles to the east, a road bridge was built in 1963–6.

A.J.P. **Taylor** (Alan John Percivale Taylor, 1906–90) Historian specializing in European events of the 19–20c,

Tax burden: percentage of the GNP taken by the government in taxes

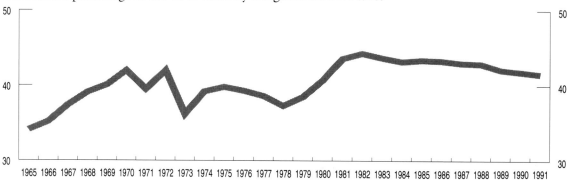

Source: United Kingdom National Accounts (see **Central Statistical Office*).

with a particular emphasis on the world wars. His compelling quality as a lecturer was first discovered by television audiences in 1958 through his account of the Russian revolution, spoken in a conversational style straight to the camera. He was also a lively columnist for the *Sunday Express* and wrote the official biography of his friend and employer (*Beaverbrook* 1972).

Dennis **Taylor** (b. 1949) Northern Irish snooker player known for his custom-built spectacles, rising high and square above the eyebrows to enable him to squint along the cue. His most dramatic success was beating Steve Davis in the 1985 final of the Embassy World Professional Championship, a tournament which he won on the final black of the final frame.

Elizabeth **Taylor** (b. 1932) Actress who moved with her parents to the USA at the start of World War II and was in films in Hollywood from the age of ten. She was in the first Lassie film (*Lassie Come Home* 1943) and then starred in *National Velvet* (1944). Her power as an adult actress was seen in *Cat on a Hot Tin Roof* (1958) and in her Oscar-winning performance in *Who's Afraid of Virginia Woolf?* (1966). In the latter her relationship with her husband, played by Richard *Burton, was as stormy on-screen as in real life. She and Burton married first in 1964, in one of the most publicized of Hollywood liaisons. The ongoing saga of her marriages, eight in all by the mid-1990s, is a feature of her biography to rank with her beauty and her talent. Her husbands have been: Conrad Hilton Jnr (1950), Michael Wilding (1952), Mike Todd (1957), Eddie Fisher (1959), Richard Burton (1964, divorced 1974, remarried 1975, divorced 1976), John Hills (1976), Larry Fortensky (1991).

Lord **Taylor** (Peter Taylor, kt 1980, baron 1992) Lord chief justice who entered office in 1992 with the determination, in his own words, to 'make the judiciary seem more accessible and user-friendly' – after a period during which the administration of *criminal justice had attracted much criticism. He had previously been best known for the *Taylor Report into the Hillsborough disaster.

Taylor Report The findings and recommendations of Lord Justice *Taylor after the *Hillsborough football disaster of 1989. His main proposal was that the terraces for standing fans, on one of which the tragedy had occurred, should be replaced in the grounds of 1st and 2nd division clubs by all-seated arrangements. In the early 1990s this is being gradually put into effect at very great cost (£650m was the Football League's estimate). The fans, attached to the more informal atmosphere of open terraces as well as to cheaper prices, staged in 1992 a succession of peaceful protests against the resulting changes.

Tayside (384,000 in 1991, administrative centre Dundee) Since 1975 a *region of east central Scotland, comprising the former county of Angus and most of Perth and Kinross.

tea Indigenous in western China and northeast India, tea was first imported to Europe by the Portuguese and the Dutch. It was brought to England from China in the 1650s by the *East India Company, which for the next two centuries was the world's largest dealer in the commodity. It was at first extremely expensive; a London advertisement of the 1660s offers the best quality tea at £2.50 per lb (£5 per kilo). Originally drunk only in the *coffee houses, it became a normal part of life in fashionable households during the 18C and by the 19C was the nation's main drink.

Tea in an English family, c.1720, when tea cups had not yet acquired handles: painting by Richard Collins.

In the first half of the 19C two new meals, both called 'tea', were introduced by the richer classes. One was 'afternoon tea', a lady-like affair of tea and cakes at five o'clock. The other, known from the start as 'high tea', was a robust meal including meat or fish, eaten later in the evening on occasions when it was not convenient to sit down to *dinner. The two different meals became separated on a class basis in the 20C. The tea of the middle classes is afternoon tea, while the meal traditionally called tea by the working classes was the old high tea – a cooked meal, eaten on the return home from work.

Edward **Teach** (d. 1718) Pirate, known as Blackbeard, who in 1717 captured a large French merchant ship and converted her into a man-of-war with 40 guns and a new name, *Queen Anne's Revenge*. He then terrorized the Caribbean and the eastern coast of north America, making his base in North Carolina, where he had a mutually advantageous arrangement with the governor. He died in a battle with two naval sloops from Virginia.

Norman **Tebbit** (b. 1931, baron 1992) Conservative politician, MP for Epping 1970–4 and Chingford (1974–92), who entered the *cabinet in 1981 as secretary of state for employment. He was subsequently secretary of state for trade and industry (1983–5) and chancellor of the duchy of Lancaster and chairman of the Conservative party (1985–7). He reduced his involvement in politics in the second half of the 1980s, after his wife Margaret was severely injured in the *Brighton bomb outrage of 1984 (in which he also was injured). In the 1990s he has been a pugnacious defender of the ideas of Margaret Thatcher, particularly in opposition to *Maastricht.

TECs (Training and Enterprise Councils) Bodies set up by the government in the early 1990s to channel state funds for employment-related training. There are 82 TECs in England and Wales and 22 similar LECs (Local Enterprise Companies) in Scotland. Industrialists and business people form the boards of both TECs and LECs, the intention being to put to more practical use the funds previously spent by the Department of Employment. The two main training schemes are *YT for the young and ET (Employment Training) for the long-term unemployed. In 1992 the councils found a common voice in G10, an elected group of ten of their chairmen who expressed strong dissatisfaction with the limitations imposed on them by government bureaucracy.

teds or **teddy boys** Followers of a teenage fashion in the 1950s, characterized by sideburns, long velvet-collared jackets and drain-pipe trousers; the name reflected the belief that this was the style of Edwardian dandies in the reign of Edward VII. Teddy boys and their accompanying teddy girls alarmed their elders by going about in gangs. By the 1960s they had been largely replaced by *mods and rockers.

Tees River rising in the northern Pennines and flowing about 113km/70m southeast and east to enter the North Sea at Middlesbrough. Historically it has been the border between Yorkshire and Durham, but in 1974 the heavily industrialized area round the estuary became the separate county of Cleveland. The river is navigable as far upstream as Stockton, a major port in the early 19c and the terminus of the *Stockton and Darlington railway.

Telegraph The name of two of Britain's leading national newspapers. The *Daily Telegraph* was launched in 1855 and built a rapid circulation by halving its price after three months to become the first penny paper. It amalgamated in 1937 with the *Morning Post*, and in 1939 broke with tradition among serious papers by putting news on the front page instead of advertisements (the *Guardian* followed in 1952 and the *Times* in 1966). The *Telegraph*, conservative in its image and policies, has a high reputation for the extent of its news coverage. A sister paper, the *Sunday Telegraph*, was launched in 1961. In 1987 the two left their grandiose Fleet Street building (completed in 1928) and moved to the Isle of Dogs in *Docklands. Editions of each are now printed simultaneously in London and at a new plant in Manchester, opened in 1986.

Telethon Charity deriving its funds from marathon broadcasts on independent television. The first two Telethons (1980, 85) were promoted by Thames TV and were limited to the London region, but since the third (1988) it has been a national event on the ITV network. Large sums of money are raised by telephone pledges from the audience, in addition to sponsorship. In 1990 a continuous 27-hour live broadcast resulted in donations of £24 million, but in 1992 the total fell to a little over £15 million.

television The *BBC launched the world's first public high-definition service in 1936, after a period of experiment with John Logie *Baird. Transmission resumed after the war, in 1946, but the coronation of Elizabeth II in 1953 was the first occasion on which a large audience in Britain saw TV. Two years later the BBC lost its monopoly. A commercial channel (Independent Television or ITV) was authorized by the Television Act of 1954, and franchises were then issued to successful applicants for the different regions of the country. Two London companies were the first on the air, in September 1955 – Associated-Rediffusion on weekdays and Associated Television (ATV) at weekends. Of the original companies granted franchises for the major regions at that time only one, *Granada, was still transmitting in the 1990s.

Commercial television proved extremely profitable, as Roy *Thomson of Scottish TV candidly admitted, and so the government charged the companies a levy – until 1974 on revenue and subsequently on profits. The franchises had to be competed for afresh every few years. In 1991 the basis of the competition was radically changed; any company passing a 'quality threshold' with its programme

plans for a region was then invited to submit a sealed bid for the amount it would pay the government each year. As a result of this widely criticized lottery, the commercial television companies transmitting from 1993 on Channel 3 carry annual fiscal burdens ranging from a few thousand pounds to many millions.

Until 1964 Britain had two television channels, known simply as BBC and ITV. In that year the BBC introduced a minority cultural channel, calling it BBC2; and in 1982 a second commercial channel was added, Channel 4, with a brief to cater for minority interests of any kind (the existence of Channel 4 has caused ITV to become known as Channel 3). Channel 4 was an innovation in that it is not a programme-making company. It buys its programmes from independent producers – a pattern increasingly followed by other channels, with the result that a proliferation of small production companies has become a feature of British television. In 1992 the franchise for a fifth terrestrial network, Channel 5, was offered; only Thames TV applied for the licence and its submission was rejected by the ITC. The reason for the lack of applicants was that reaching a sizable audience on the given wavelength would involve high technical costs.

In the early 1990s relatively few homes in Britain could receive television by cable, but the ownership of satellite dishes was growing. Two rival companies entered the field, BSB (British Satellite Broadcasting) and Sky; after spending a great deal of money they merged as BSkyB, though continuing to use Sky as the name of their various channels. BSkyB increased its audience share by lavish expenditure, notably the payment in 1992 of £304 million for an exclusive five-year contract to televise football matches in the *Premier League. In 1993 about 20% of the population was able to receive satellite programmes.

Telford see *new towns.

Thomas **Telford** (1757–1834) Scottish engineer, self-educated son of a shepherd, with a prodigious list of achievements in several fields. He amazed the world with his *Pont Cysyllte aqueduct, under construction from 1795 (it is astonishing even today to see a barge moving through the sky). In 1803 he was appointed by the government to undertake extensive works in his native Scotland; the result was 1480km/920m of roads (Southey called him the Colossus of Roads), 120 bridges and the *Caledonian Canal. He was commissioned next to improve the road along the north coast of Wales, from Chester to Holyhead in Anglesey (part of the main route between London and Dublin); this task involved constructing his two most famous bridges, at *Conwy and over the *Menai Strait. One of his last undertakings was *St Katharine's Dock in London.

temperature Britain has traditionally used the temperature scale introduced by Gabriel Fahrenheit (1686–1736), a German physicist who lived most of his life in the Netherlands. He invented the mercury thermometer, more accurate than its predecessors, but devised an extremely elaborate system for its scale. For zero he chose the freezing point of salt water. He then divided the gap between this and blood temperature into 96 equal degrees (12 sections of 8). Having selected his two fixed points of frozen brine as 0° and human blood as 96°, he calculated that fresh water froze at 32° and that it boiled at 212° (strangely his findings were more accurate for water than for blood, which is closer to 98° than 96°).

Britain adopted this first effective thermometric scale, and as a result it is still used in many countries which were once British colonies, including the USA. Anders Celsius (1701–44), a Swedish astronomer only a few years younger than Fahrenheit, proposed the more convenient centigrade scale, with 100° separating the freezing and boiling points of water. Celsius is gradually replacing Fahrenheit in late-20c Britain.

Britain's climate has a moderate temperature range. More than a few degrees below freezing seems exceptional in most parts of the country, as does a summer temperature above 30°C/86°F. The lowest officially recorded figure is –27.2°C/–17°F (oddly enough the same on two occasions a century apart in the same place, at Braemar in Scotland in 1895 and 1982), while the highest is 36.8°C/98.2°F in Kent and Surrey in 1911. But as the charts show, Britain's average temperature at sea level over an entire month is very rarely as low as freezing point or as high as 18°C/65°F. In the late 1980s the annual average temperature was consistently high, causing much debate on the ozone layer and the greenhouse effect, but in the mid-1980s it had been consistently low.

The Tempest (*c*.1611) Drama by *Shakespeare, usually considered his last, forming a magic interplay of discovery and enchantment, recrimination and reconciliation. Prospero, the rightful duke of Milan and a learned magician, has had his throne usurped by his brother Antonio. For 12 years he has been living on an island with his books and his daughter, Miranda. The only previous inhabitant of the island, Caliban, the misshapen offspring of the witch Sycorax, labours reluctantly for Prospero; so, with slightly better grace, does Ariel, a spirit imprisoned in a cloven pine by Sycorax and released by Prospero. Prospero uses his magic to summon a tempest, which wrecks on the island a shipload of enemies and friends from the courts of Milan and Naples.

As a result, the enchanted island becomes full of people wandering around in a daze. Ferdinand, son of the king of Naples, falls in love with Miranda, who is bowled over by her first glimpse of a young man. Caliban allies himself

Fahrenheit and Celsius equivalents

Air temperature		Body temperature	
F	C	F	C
120	48.88	106	41.11
113	45	105.8	41
110	43.33	105	40.55
104	40	104	40
100	37.77	103	39.44
95	35	102.2	39
90	32.22	102	38.88
86	30	101	38.33
80	26.66	100.4	38
77	25	100	37.77
70	21.11	99	37.22
68	20	98.6	37
60	15.55	98	36.66
59	15	97	36.11
50	10	96.8	36
41	5	96	35.55
40	4.4		
32	0		
25	-3.88		
23	-5		
20	-6.66		
14	-10		
10	-12.22		
5	-15		
0	-17.77		
-4	-20		
-10	-23.33		
-13	-25		
-20	-28.88		

Average daily temperature at sea level

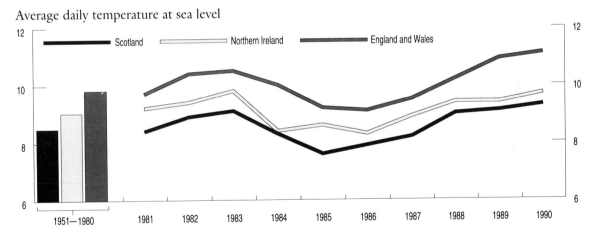

Average monthly temperature, 1951—90

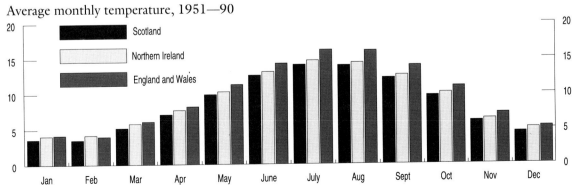

Source: Annual Abstract of Statistics (*see* *Central Statistical Office*).

The new delights of mixed doubles in the early years of lawn tennis: painting by Horace Cauty, 1885.

with two comic characters from the shipwreck (the jester Trinculo and the drunken butler Stephano), and tries to get them to murder his master Prospero. In the final scene the court characters settle their scores with each other; Prospero breaks his magic staff and releases Ariel from his service, before returning to his rightful place in Milan and to the promised wedding of Miranda and Ferdinand; and the island is left once again to Caliban.

Temple Bar Originally a simple barrier across Fleet Street marking the western limit of the *City of London. By the 14c it had become a gateway with a prison above it. Rebuilt in the 1670s to a design by Wren, it remained in position until 1878 when it was removed as an obstacle to traffic. A few years later it was rebuilt at Theobalds in Hertfordshire (near Waltham Cross), where it remains today. In 1880 the Temple Bar Memorial was erected near the Law Courts, to mark where the Temple Bar had been, and this now represents the transition, on the old east–west thoroughfare, between the cities of London and Westminster.

Temple Church see *Inns of Court.

Temple Newsam see *Leeds.

Tenby (5000 in 1981) Picturesque resort on the Bristol Channel, in Dyfed, perched on a rocky promontory between two sandy bays. It was a prosperous walled town in the late Middle Ages; part of the wall survives, and by the harbour is the 15c Tudor Merchant's House.

10cc Pop group comprising Eric Stewart and Graham Gouldman (both b. 1945, both vocals and guitar), Lol

Creme (b.1947, vocals and guitar) and Kevin Godley (b.1945, vocals and drums). The four came together in Manchester in 1969 as Hotlegs, and reached no. 2 with *Neanderthal Man* (1970). Renamed 10cc in 1972, they went again to no. 2 with *Donna* (1972). Subsequent no. 1 hits were *Rubber Bullets* (1973), *I'm not in Love* (1975) and *Dreadlock Holiday* (1978, by which time Godley and Creme had left the group).

Ten Hours Bill see *Factory Acts.

John **Tenniel** (1820–1914, kt 1893) Cartoonist and illustrator who spent most of his career with *Punch*. He joined in 1850 and provided the main political cartoon each week from 1862 to 1901. Out of more than 2000, his best known has long been *'Dropping the Pilot'. In spite of this huge output, his name would be relatively unfamiliar now if he had not also illustrated Lewis *Carroll's two books about Alice. It is thanks to Tenniel that we have such memorable images of Humpty Dumpty, Tweedledum and Tweedledee, the Mad Hatter, the Jabberwock and many more, including Alice herself.

tennis (also known as lawn tennis to distinguish it from *real tennis) Game which achieved a very rapid success after being introduced in Britain in the 1870s. There had been various attempts to adapt the indoor game of real tennis to one that could be played on a lawn, and the first lawn tennis club was probably established at Leamington Spa in 1872. But it was a version patented by Major Walter Wingfield in 1874 which triggered the explosion of interest. He called his game Sphairistiké (from a Greek root meaning 'playing at ball'); it had a court in the shape of an hour-glass, narrower at the net, and it was first tried out at a country-house party in Wales in 1873. Two factors were of importance in its surge of popularity: many middle-class homes now had smooth lawns, thanks to the recent success of *croquet; and lawn tennis was the first energetic game which could be played respectably by both sexes. Mixed doubles were of the essence from the start.

The crucial moment for the game was the involvement of the All-England Croquet Club at *Wimbledon, where the first championship was held in 1877 (an event which also established today's shape and size of court). Tennis then spread rapidly to the USA, where the men's championship dates from 1881 and the women's from 1887. The two most prominent international team cups were both donated by American players. Dwight F. Davis gave the Davis Cup in 1900, to be competed for by national teams of men; each contest involves four singles matches and one doubles. Hazel Wightman gave the Wightman Cup in 1923 for teams of women. Unlike the Davis Cup, it was restricted to the USA and Britain. It was discontinued in 1990 because the contests had become too uneven; the USA had won 7-0 in four of the previous five years.

Lord **Tennyson** (Alfred Tennyson, 1809–92, baron 1884) Poet who more than any other struck a chord with the Victorian public. At Trinity College, Cambridge, he became a close friend of Arthur Hallam. Hallam fell in love with Tennyson's sister, Emily, and was engaged to marry her when he suddenly died. The shock of this death inspired the poem which years later made Tennyson's reputation, *In Memoriam*. The queen was among its keenest admirers, and its publication in 1850 coincided with the death of the poet laureate, William Wordsworth. Tennyson was immediately appointed in his place.

His early work had not been so well received. *Poems* (1833) provoked savage reviews, causing him to publish nothing more until the 2-volume *Poems* of 1842 (the first volume contained revised versions of the 1833 poems, including 'The *Lady of Shalott'). But after 1850 he steadily consolidated his position, catching the national mood successfully with poems such as his ode on the death of Wellington in 1852 or with The *Charge of the Light Brigade* in 1854. The response to *Maud* (1854) was less warm, many finding it confusing and morbid, but the series grouped as *Idylls of the King* (1859–85) satisfied the Victorian appetite for medieval and Arthurian themes. The short poem *Crossing the Bar* (1889) revealed that he had not lost his touch in old age. It was written on the sea between the south coast and the Isle of Wight, where he and his wife had made their home since 1853 in a house called Farringford (now a hotel). A neighbour, Julia Margaret *Cameron, was responsible for several powerful images of his leonine features and shock of hair – a bohemian appearance which greatly pleased his public when combined with so respectable a life.

1066 and all that, A Memorable History of England (1930) Humorous classic by two schoolmasters, Walter Sellar (1898–1951) and Robert Yeatman (1898–1968), making splendid nonsense of the teaching and examining of English history. Typical is the explanation of why Julius Caesar so easily defeated the ancient Britons; hearing him declare *Veni, vidi, vici* they lost heart, for they were still using the old Latin pronunciation and thought that he had judged them to be 'weeny, weedy and weaky'.

Terrence Higgins Trust (London WC1) Britain's leading Aids charity, set up in 1982 by friends of Terrence Higgins, one of the first people in Britain to die of the condition. The aim is to provide support for those with Aids or HIV infection (achieved by a wide range of counselling services and a telephone helpline) and to serve as a pressure group for improved education on the subject.

terriers (from the French *terre* meaning 'earth') Dogs originally bred to go underground and flush out wild animals. The fox terrier was bred in England in the 18c, at a time when fox *hunting had become a popular sport. There are two distinct varieties, smooth and wire-haired; both are predominantly white, with markings ranging from fawn to black. The Jack Russell also emerged from a fox-hunting context. Smaller and with very short legs, but with colour and markings similar to the fox terrier, it is named after John Russell (1795–1883), the 'sporting parson' of Devon who spent considerably more time with his pack of hounds than with his parishioners. The Lakeland terrier, an older breed of varied colour, was developed in the Lake District to hunt otters as well as foxes.

The Airedale, the largest of the English terriers (with a black body and tan legs, chest and head), takes its name from the Yorkshire valley where it was bred in the 19c from the otter hound and a now extinct breed of terrier. The *bull terrier, bred for fighting, also descends from an extinct breed. The tiny Yorkshire terrier (blue-grey body and tan head and chest, with long silky hair) is a toy variety of the late 19c which rapidly became a fashionable pet; it was bred from a mix of Scottish terriers.

Scotland is the home of several very popular varieties. The Scottie (the abbreviation commonly used for the Scottish or Aberdeen terrier) is a very old breed used originally against many types of vermin, including foxes; it is small with a thick wiry coat, and although usually black is known in several colours. It is closely related to the cairn terrier, grey or tan in colour and named because it chased vermin out of 'cairns' (rocky piles of stone). The cairn terrier was bred originally on Skye – the home also of the Skye terrier, which has long hair falling over its eyes and which ranges in colour from black through grey and fawn to cream. The West Highland white terrier, known also as the Westie, was bred in Scotland in the 19c and has become very popular in the USA. The Dandie Dinmont,

The very image of a poet: Tennyson in an 1869 photograph by his neighbour, Julia Margaret Cameron.

with silky hair and short legs, derives from the border district and is named after a Lowland farmer who keeps terriers in Walter Scott's *Guy Mannering* (1815).

The Welsh terrier, with a black and tan coat, was bred in Wales in the 19C to hunt otters, badgers and foxes. The Sealyham, with its medium-length white coat, is named from Sealy Ham, a house near Haverfordwest in Dyfed where it was bred in the 19C.

Territorial Army (TA) The *militia of a district, ready to turn out when required, have long been valued in Britain. The modern Territorial Army, similarly drafted into the regular army in an emergency, was established in 1908 as part of the military reforms of Lord *Haldane. In the early 1990s it numbered about 90,000, as part of the wider *Volunteer Reserve Forces.

terrorism In Britain in recent decades this has mainly meant acts of sectarian violence resulting from the situation in *Northern Ireland. The earliest of the terrorist groups is the *IRA, dating back originally to 1919 but represented in Northern Ireland by a splinter group of 1969 – the Provisional IRA, known also as the Provisionals or Provos. A smaller terrorist organization on the republican side of the argument is the INLA (Irish National Liberation Army), which separated from the IRA in the mid-1970s. The INLA was itself split in the mid-1980s when internal feuds led to the assassination of several of its own members and the emergence of another breakaway faction, the IPLO (Irish People's Liberation Organization). By the end of 1992 the IPLO was in disarray, after one member had been killed by the IRA and several others kneecapped in retribution for drug pushing.

The chief terrorist group on the *loyalist side has been the UDA (Ulster Defence Association), formed in 1972 from various smaller paramilitary units. Unlike other terrorist enterprises the UDA remained until 1992 a legal organization, thanks to the fiction that its assassinations were carried out by a separate group, the UFF (Ulster Freedom Fighters). A murky insight into UDA activities was provided in 1992 by the trial of Brian *Nelson. A smaller and older Protestant terrorist group is the UVF (Ulster Volunteer Force). The name of Ulster Volunteers was first used by the violently partisan bands of men organized by *Carson in 1913. In modern times the UVF was declared an illegal organization as early as 1966, but it has remained very active.

Terrorist violence from both sides in Northern Ireland has been almost continuous since 1969, and the republican groups have engaged in periodic bombing campaigns and assassinations in mainland Britain – including the killing of Airey *Neave in 1979 by the INLA, and the bombing of the Grand Hotel in *Brighton in 1984 and the murder of Ian *Gow in 1990 by the IRA. By the early 1990s Ulster terrorists had caused more than 2000 civilian deaths, and the overall death toll due to terrorism in the province passed the 3000 level in 1992; in addition some 30,000 people had been injured.

Government measures to contain terrorism have included: a heavy deployment of British troops, from the first 1000 sent in August 1969 to a level of ten regular battalions on duty in the early 1990s; the formation of the *Ulster Defence Regiment; the experiment with *internment; the *Prevention of Terrorism Act; and a ban from 1988 on the broadcasting of interviews with members of any terrorist group (a category which in this context included *Sinn Fein).

A persistent campaign of arson has been carried out in recent decades by a militant Welsh nationalist group, Meibion Glyndwr (Welsh for the sons of Glendower); their target has been the property of English people living in Wales.

Ellen **Terry** (1847–1928, DBE 1925) The outstanding English actress of the late 19C. She was *Irving's leading lady during his entire period at the Lyceum theatre (1878–1901), forming an exceptionally successful partnership, both in Shakespeare and in contemporary plays. She had a varied career before joining him. Born into a theatrical family, she was a well-known child actress from the age of nine. At 17, in 1864, she left the stage to marry the 47-year-old painter G.F. *Watts, a disastrous ten-month relationship of which the only good outcome was some fine portraits of her. In 1868 she again gave up acting for six years to live with the scene designer Edward Godwin (1833–86); one of their two children was the designer Edward Gordon Craig (1872–1966). During the 1890s she carried on a brilliant and flirtatious correspondence with George Bernard *Shaw (published 1931). Smallhythe Place, a 16C timber-frame house in Kent which was her home from 1899 to 1928, is kept as a museum.

tertiary college see *state school.

Tesco Britain's second largest chain of food retailers, after Sainsbury's. It was founded by Jack Cohen (1898–1979), son of an immigrant Jewish tailor from Poland, who used the £30 given him on demobilization after World War I to start up a street market food stall in the London district of Hackney. He sold a great deal of tea and created his own brand by using the initials of his supplier (T.E. Stockwell) and the first two letters of Cohen to form the word Tesco. Under this name he opened in 1931 his first two grocery shops in London's suburbs; by World War II there were about 100 Tesco stores in and around the capital. After the war Cohen pioneered in Britain the American retailing method of self-service and check-out tills. The title of his authorized biography stated his marketing philosophy – *Pile it High, Sell it Cheap* (1971). By the early 1990s the firm had nearly 200 superstores in England, Wales and Scotland, and about the same number of smaller premises.

Tessa see *savings.

***Tess of the d'Urbervilles**: a pure woman, faithfully presented* (1891) Novel by Thomas *Hardy, the subject of immediate controversy because of the contrast between subtitle and plot. Tess Durbeyfield, a country girl descended from the Norman d'Urbervilles, is seduced by Alec d'Urberville, member of a *nouveau riche* family which has adopted the name; her child by him dies. Happiness seems possible when she marries a parson's son, Angel Clare, but he abandons her on hearing of her past. In desperation she succumbs again to Alec, now an itinerant preacher. Angel repents and returns to her; to escape from Alec she stabs and kills him. After a brief whirlwind of happiness with Angel, hiding together in the New Forest, she is arrested at Stonehenge and is hanged.

Test Acts Series of laws which made it impossible for anyone to hold public office, undertake military service, or receive university education unless professing the established religion of the Church of England. The best-known Test Act was passed in 1673. It was parliament's response to a measure of tolerance by Charles II, who by a declaration of indulgence (1672) removed the restrictions embodied in the *Clarendon Code. This Test Act required that anyone entering public service in England must take the sacrament in the Anglican manner. In other contexts the wording of oaths was sufficient to serve the purpose (a Christian oath excluded Jews, while the requirement to deny the Pope's authority did the same for Roman Catholics). The various tests and barriers were gradually dismantled during the 19C.

Test matches International *cricket matches, beginning with one between England and Australia in Melbourne in 1877. The phrase had been coined in 1862 when an England eleven visited Australia and played local teams (often numbering more than 11 players), who were in a real sense being 'tested'. From the Test series of 1882 derives the concept of the *Ashes. The other teams now competing in Tests are India, Pakistan, the West Indies, New Zealand, Sri Lanka and Zimbabwe (since 1992). South Africa took part until 1965, but was then excluded until 1992 because of the policy of apartheid. A national team visiting a rival country will usually play from three to five Test matches interspersed with games against other teams. See next page for a complete list of England test matches played since 1946.

The term is also now used in the same sense for international series in *rugby football.

test-tube babies The term in everyday use for babies resulting from IVF, standing for in-vitro fertilization – *in vitro* is Latin for 'in glass'. The process involves removing eggs from the mother's ovaries, fertilizing them with the father's sperm and allowing them to grow in an artificial environment (the test tube) until one or more can be implanted in the mother's womb; thereafter the pregnancy follows the normal course. The technique was developed in the 1970s by Patrick Steptoe (1913–88) and Robert Edwards (b. 1925). The world's first test-tube baby, Louise Brown, was born under their care in 1978 in Oldham, Greater Manchester. In 1980 they established a centre for this treatment at Bourn Hall, 16km/10m west of Cambridge, and here they achieved the next development – the freezing of unused embryos, so that the mother can return if the first pregnancy fails or if she wants a second child. The first such 'deep freeze' baby was born in 1984; her sister from the same batch of eggs followed in 1986, making Elizabeth and Amy Wright the first examples of what the press called 'time warp twins'. By 1990 Bourn Hall, combined by then with the Hallam Medical Centre in London's Harley Street, had achieved 2500 IVF births.

TGWU (Transport and General Workers' Union) The first of the *super-unions, formed in 1922 by the amalgamation of 14 separate trade unions covering a wide range of employment from dockers, stevedores, drivers and factory workers to clerks. The impetus for the merger had come from the National Transport Workers' Federation (in particular its dynamic secretary Ernest *Bevin) and from the Dockers' Union. Many factors have made the TGWU the most significant union in the history of the Labour party: its overwhelming size (350,000 members when founded); the political career of Bevin himself; and the fact that until 1980 Labour party headquarters were in the TGWU's building, *Transport House. With about 1.25 million members in the early 1990s the TGWU looked in danger of being outgrown by some of the new super-unions, but it was at the time engaged in its own merger discussions with other unions including the NUM.

William Makepeace **Thackeray** (1811-63) Journalist and novelist. He inherited a fortune of £20,000 on coming of age, but lost it through gambling and unlucky investments. From the mid-1830s he contributed to a large number of magazines under a wide range of pseudonyms (in particular Michael Angelo Titmarsh). A series of satirical character sketches, done for *Punch* in 1846-7, was published as *The Book of Snobs*. The first title to appear under his own name was his great historical novel *Vanity Fair* (1848). *The History of Pendennis* (1848–50) moved the focus to contemporary life and introduced the semi-autobiographical central character of Arthur Pendennis.

With *The History of Henry Esmond* (1852) he returned to the historical novel (set this time in the early 18c); and in its sequel, *The Virginians* (1858–9), he followed the fortunes of Esmond's twin grandsons at the time of the War of American Independence. Thackeray was an excellent artist, illustrating several of his own books. A personal tragedy was the mental breakdown of his wife, Isabella, in 1840 when they had two young daughters. From then on she was looked after in a home in the country, leaving him with the life, but not the freedom, of a widower.

Thames The longest river wholly in England (and some would say in Britain, see the *Severn). Its length is usually given as about 338km/210m from the Cotswolds to the Nore, the point where its estuary is joined by the Medway. There are two candidates for its source: the traditional one is Thames Head (5km/3m SW of Cirencester); the other, adding about 8km/5m to the overall length, is the source of a tributary, the Churn, at Seven Springs (6km/4m S of Cheltenham). The Thames links some of the most historic of English towns, castles and palaces: Oxford (where it is called the *Isis), Windsor, Hampton Court, London (with the Houses of Parliament and the Tower on its bank) and Greenwich.

London Bridge has been historically the lowest point at which the river could be crossed. In the late 19c Tower Bridge was built a few hundred yards downstream; and many miles further down the river the Queen Elizabeth Bridge at Dartford, connecting with the M25, was opened in 1991. The first tunnel under the Thames was begun by *Brunel's father in the 1820s and was completed in 1843. There are road tunnels at Rotherhithe (1908), at Blackwall (two of them, 1897 and 1967) and at Dartford (again two, 1963 and 1980). For about 16km/10m downstream from Tower Bridge the estuary was developed in the 19c as a series of extremely busy docks; it is now being redeveloped as *Docklands.

Thackeray's own 1848 illustration for the first scene in Vanity Fair: *Becky's departure from Miss Pinkerton's academy.*

England Test matches since World War II

				(*Captain*)
1946	India	home	WDD	Wally Hammond
1946–7	Australia	away	LLDDL	Wally Hammond (1–4)
				Norman Yardley (5)
1947	New Zealand	away	D	Wally Hammond
1947	South Africa	home	DWWWD	Norman Yardley
1947–8	West Indies	away	DDLL	Kenneth Cranston (1)
				Gubby Allen (2–4)
1948	Australia	home	LLDLL	Norman Yardley
1948–9	South Africa	away	WDDDW	George Mann
1949	New Zealand	home	DDDD	George Mann (1–2)
				Freddie Brown (3–4)
1950	West Indies	home	WLLL	Norman Yardley (1–3)
				Freddie Brown (4)
1950–1	Australia	away	LLLLW	Freddie Brown
1950–1	New Zealand	away	DW	Freddie Brown
1951	South Africa	home	LWWDW	Freddie Brown
1951–2	India	away	DDDWL	Nigel Howard (1–4)
				Donald Carr (5)
1952	India	home	WWWD	Len Hutton
1953	Australia	home	DDDDW	Len Hutton
1953–4	West Indies	away	LLWDW	Len Hutton
1954	Pakistan	home	DWDL	Len Hutton (1,4)
				David Sheppard (2,3)
1954–5	Australia	away	LWWWD	Len Hutton
1954–5	New Zealand	away	WW	Len Hutton
1955	South Africa	home	WWLLW	Peter May
1956	Australia	home	DLWWD	Peter May
1956–7	South Africa	away	WWDLL	Peter May
1957	West Indies	home	DWDWW	Peter May
1958	New Zealand	home	WWWWD	Peter May
1958–9	Australia	away	LLDLL	Peter May
1958–9	New Zealand	away	WD	Peter May
1959	India	home	WWWWW	Peter May (1–3)
				Colin Cowdrey (4–5)
1959–60	West Indies	away	DWDDD	Peter May (1–3)
				Colin Cowdrey (4–5)
1960	South Africa	home	WWWDD	Colin Cowdrey
1961	Australia	home	DLWLD	Colin Cowdrey (1–2)
				Peter May (3–5)
1961–2	Pakistan	away	WDD	Ted Dexter
1961–2	India	away	DDDLL	Ted Dexter
1962	Pakistan	home	WWWDW	Ted Dexter
1962–3	Australia	away	DWLDD	Ted Dexter
1962–3	New Zealand	away	WWW	Ted Dexter
1963	West Indies	home	LDWLL	Ted Dexter
1963–4	India	away	DDDDD	Mike Smith
1964	Australia	home	DDLDD	Ted Dexter
1964–5	South Africa	away	WDDDD	Mike Smith
1965	New Zealand	home	WWW	Mike Smith
1965	South Africa	home	DLD	Mike Smith
1965–6	Australia	away	DDWLD	Mike Smith
1965–6	New Zealand	away	DDD	Mike Smith
1966	West Indies	home	LDLLW	Mike Smith (1)
				Colin Cowdrey (2–4)
				Brian Close (5)
1967	India	home	WWW	Brian Close
1967	Pakistan	home	DWW	Brian Close
1967–8	West Indies	away	DDDWD	Colin Cowdrey
1968	Australia	home	LDDDW	Colin Cowdrey (1–3,5)
				Tom Graveney (4)
1968–9	Pakistan	away	DDD	Colin Cowdrey
1969	West Indies	home	WDW	Ray Illingworth
1969	New Zealand	home	WDW	Ray Illingworth
1970–1	Australia	away	DDWDDW	Ray Illingworth
1970–1	New Zealand	away	WD	Ray Illingworth
1971	Pakistan	home	DDW	Ray Illingworth
1971	India	home	DDL	Ray Illingworth
1972	Australia	home	WLDWL	Ray Illingworth
1972–3	India	away	WLLDD	Tony Lewis
1972–3	Pakistan	away	DDD	Tony Lewis
1973	New Zealand	home	WDW	Ray Illingworth
1973	West Indies	home	LDL	Ray Illingworth
1973–4	West Indies	away	LDDDW	Mike Denness
1974	India	home	WWW	Mike Denness
1974	Pakistan	home	DDD	Mike Denness

1974–5	Australia	away	LLDLLW	Mike Denness (1–3, 5–6)
				John Edrich (4)
1974–5	New Zealand	away	WD	Mike Denness
1975	Australia	home	LDDD	Mike Denness (1)
				Tony Greig (2–4)
1976	West Indies	home	DDLLL	Tony Greig
1976–7	India	away	WWWLD	Tony Greig
1976–7	Australia	away	L	Tony Greig
1977	Australia	home	DWWWD	Mike Brearley
1977–8	Pakistan	away	DDD	Mike Brearley (1–2)
				Geoff Boycott (3)
1977–8	New Zealand	away	LWD	Geoff Boycott
1978	Pakistan	home	WWD	Mike Brearley
1978	New Zealand	home	WWW	Mike Brearley
1978–9	Australia	away	WWLWWW	Mike Brearley
1979	India	home	WDDD	Mike Brearley
1979–80	Australia	away	LLL	Mike Brearley
1979–80	India	away	W	Mike Brearley
1980	West Indies	home	LDDDD	Ian Botham
1980	Australia	home	D	Ian Botham
1980–1	West Indies	away	LLDD	Ian Botham
1981	Australia	home	LDWWWD	Ian Botham (1–2)
				Mike Brearley (3–6)
1981–2	India	away	LDDDDD	Keith Fletcher
1981–2	Sri Lanka	away	W	Keith Fletcher
1982	India	home	WDD	Bob Willis
1982	Pakistan	home	WLW	Bob Willis (1,3)
				David Gower (2)
1982–3	Australia	away	DLLWD	Bob Willis
1983	New Zealand	home	WLWW	Bob Willis
1983–4	New Zealand	away	DLD	Bob Willis
1983–4	Pakistan	away	LDD	Bob Willis (1)
				David Gower (2,3)
1984	West Indies	home	LLLLL	David Gower
1984	Sri Lanka	home	D	David Gower
1984–5	India	away	LWDWD	David Gower
1985	Australia	home	WLDDWW	David Gower
1985–6	West Indies	away	LLLLL	David Gower
1986	India	home	LLD	David Gower (1)
				Mike Gatting (2,3)
1986	New Zealand	home	DLD	Mike Gatting
1986–7	Australia	away	WDDWL	Mike Gatting
1987	Pakistan	home	DDLDD	Mike Gatting
1987–8	Pakistan	away	LDD	Mike Gatting
1987–8	Australia	away	D	Mike Gatting
1987–8	New Zealand	away	DDD	Mike Gatting
1988	West Indies	home	DLLLL	Mike Gatting (1)
				John Emburey (2–3)
				Christopher Cowdrey (4)
				Graham Gooch (5)
1988	Sri Lanka	home	W	Graham Gooch
1989	Australia	home	LLDLL	David Gower
1989–90	West Indies	away	WADLL*	Graham Gooch (1–3)
				Allan Lamb (4–5)
1990	India	home	WDD	Graham Gooch
	New Zealand	home	DDW	Graham Gooch
1990–1	Australia	away	LLDDL	Allan Lamb (1)
				Graham Gooch (2–5)
1991	West Indies	home	WDLLW	Graham Gooch
1991	Sri Lanka	home	W	Graham Gooch
1991–2	New Zealand	away	WWD	Graham Gooch
1992	Pakistan	home	DLDWL	Graham Gooch
1992–3	India	away	LLL	Graham Gooch (1,3)
				Alec Stewart (2)
1992–3	Sri Lanka	away	L	Alec Stewart

The result of each successive game is given from England's point of view: W means won, L lost and D drawn. Thus WDW signifies a three-match series won 2–0 by England; LDLWDD is a six-match series lost 1–2 by England; and WDLD is a four-match draw.

* The A for the second Test in the 1989–90 series in the West Indies means '"abandoned"; there was so much rain that play was impossible.

Thames Tunnel Paper,

PRINTED BY AUTHORITY, 76 FEET BELOW HIGH-WATER MARK,

*To commemorate the day of opening the Tunnel as a Thoroughfare for Foot Passengers,
March 25, 1843.*

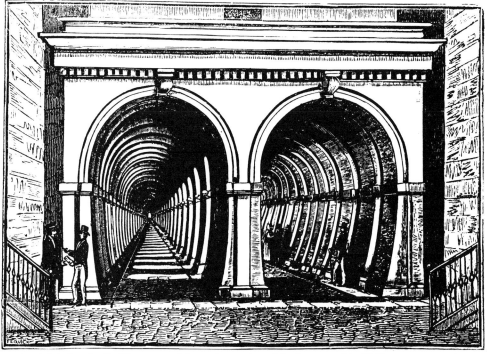

Wood engraving printed under the Thames, to celebrate the opening of the first tunnel in 1843.

The river is tidal throughout London (as far upstream as Teddington) and the capital city was in regular danger of flooding until the completion in 1982 of the Thames Barrier at Woolwich. The barrier, crossing the river where it is about 520m/569yds wide, consists above water level of a series of narrow islands supporting hydraulic machinery (in casings with a profile reminiscent of the Sydney Opera House). The machines control vast steel gates, which normally rest in concrete cavities on the river bed so that ships can pass above them; if the gates need to be raised against an unusually high tide (a precaution which happens on average about once a year), they rotate upwards to form a solid vertical wall. A routine exercise of closing the barrier for a full day is also carried out once a year – an event announced well in advance and something of a tourist attraction.

Thames Rowing Club (Putney, London) Founded in 1860, the club had an exceptional period between the wars when Jack *Beresford was its most distinguished member. The Thames eight achieved a silver medal at the 1928 Olympics and its coxless four won gold in 1932.

Isle of **Thanet** The northeast tip of Kent, jutting out into the sea and containing the resorts of Margate, Broadstairs and Ramsgate. In Roman times a boat could be rowed from a fort at Richborough, at the mouth of the river Stour on the east coast, to another fort at Reculver where a small tributary of the Stour almost reaches the north coast. This waterway, giving Thanet its status as an island, remained navigable by small boats until the 16C.

thatch The standard roof covering in England until tiles and slates began to be widely used in the 18C. It is still seen on many old cottages, particularly in the south. The most common material has been wheat straw (lasting 10–20 years) but by far the best is reeds, particularly those from Norfolk (50–60 years).

Margaret **Thatcher** (Margaret Roberts, b. 1925, m. Denis Thatcher 1951, baroness 1992) The longest-serving prime minister of the 20C (1979–90), but also the only one to be removed from office in peacetime by pressure from within her own party. Born in the Lincolnshire town of Grantham, daughter of a grocer who became mayor of the town, she studied chemistry at Oxford University (1947–51). She married Denis Thatcher in 1951 and their twins, Mark and Carol, were born in 1953. Meanwhile she was studying law, and she became a barrister in 1954. She was elected in 1959 for the safe Conservative seat of Finchley, in north London, and first entered the cabinet as secretary of state for education and science (1970–4) in the administration of Edward Heath. In 1975 she challenged Heath for the party leadership. Although apparently having only an outside chance, she won.

Her victory in the general election of 1979 began an era which became stamped with her name. 'Thatcherism' and 'Thatcherite' became part of the language, referring to her own brand of aggressive 'conviction' politics which rejected the broad consensus (characteristic of British attitudes since World War II), promoting instead the free play of market forces, often regardless of any socially harsh results, and dismantling the restrictive practices of both the trade unions and the professions. She was rescued from early unpopularity by her determined handling of the *Falklands War in 1982. Two years later her response to an internal problem, the *miners' strike of 1984–5, gave another boost to her reputation for toughness, which had been won originally through her intransigence on Britain's behalf in economic negotiations with the *EC.

It was the Russians who had first called her the Iron Lady, in 1976, because of her pronouncements on the Cold War as leader of the Opposition; and she herself proclaimed in 1980 that she was 'not for turning' (see *The *Lady's Not For Burning*).

Her qualities of strength and dominance later contributed to her downfall, as it came to seem that cabinet colleagues could not work with her and that certain deeply unpopular policies (in particular the *poll tax) were specifically her own. Two senior ministers resigned over the *Westland affair in 1986; her chancellor, Nigel *Lawson, resigned in 1989 over the ERM (see *EMS); and her longest surviving colleague, Sir Geoffrey *Howe, resigned in 1990 over his attitude to Europe, precipitating the leadership challenge in which John *Major emerged as her successor.

The Thatcher years polarized British politics in a way unknown since the 1930s. Her supporters saw *privatization as the creation of a new share-owning democracy; her opponents likened the same measures to selling the family silver (in Harold Macmillan's analogy), and argued that the unrepeatable benefits of *North Sea oil had been squandered. Her admirers talked much of the 'economic miracle' of the 1980s, a period which others saw as characterized by the two extremes of *yuppies and *homeless. 'There is no such thing as society', she said in 1987; 'there are individual men and women, and there are families.' She is a member of the Order of *Merit.

That's Life! (BBC from 1973) Television programme, presented by Esther Rantzen (b. 1940), which provides a popular blend of consumer indignation, contrived larks and comic street interviews. Of the others on the team, the longest serving regular has been the comedian Cyril Fletcher (b. 1913).

That Was The Week That Was (BBC 1962–3) Television's first satire show, popularly known as TW3 and produced late on Saturday nights by Ned Sherrin. It introduced a tone of irreverent informality, new then on television, with revue sketches and songs performed live by a regular team including Millicent Martin and William Rushton; there were impromptu cartoons drawn on camera by the brilliant Timothy Birdsall, who tragically died just after the run of the show; there were provocative monologues delivered from a high stool by Bernard *Levin, who was on one occasion assaulted by a member of the audience; and the central figure and linkman was David *Frost. Many of the same team returned for similar

Cartoon by Cummings in 1985, after Harold Macmillan had accused Mrs Thatcher of selling the family silver.

"Mʳ Kinnock! Would you care to buy some Georgian silver, antique family furniture and an old painting?"

follow-on series, *Not so Much a Programme, More a Way of Life* and *BBC3*.

Theatre Museum (London WC2) The nation's collection of theatricalia, housed appropriately in the vicinity of Covent Garden and Drury Lane. Opened in 1987, it is run as an outpost of the Victoria and Albert Museum.

Theatre Workshop see Joan *Littlewood.

'Their's not to reason why' see *Charge of the Light Brigade.

There is a green hill far away see Mrs *Alexander.

'The **rest is silence**' see *Hamlet*.

'They also serve who only stand and wait' see *Milton.

Things to Come (1936) Massive visionary and cautionary film, produced by Alexander *Korda and based on a text by H.G. *Wells (something between a film script and a novel), which had been published in 1933 as *The Shape of Things to Come*. The film is set in Everytown and foresees a war in 1940, followed by plague and rebellion and the emergence of a new type of society which sends rockets to the moon but is rigidly divided by class. The music was by *Bliss.

'Think of England' see *'close your eyes and think of England'.

think-tank The name, deriving from the USA, was first applied in Britain to the CPRS (Central Policy Review Staff). This was a small department established in 1971 by the prime minister, Edward Heath, to give in-depth advice to the cabinet on all aspects of government policy. Beginning under the leadership of Lord Rothschild (1910–90), it survived successive changes of government, first to Labour then back to Conservative, until it was disbanded by Mrs Thatcher at the start of her second term in 1983.

In the early 1990s there are four leading think-tanks in Britain, three on the right of the political spectrum and one on the left. By far the longest established is the IEA (Institute of Economic Affairs), launched in 1957; in its pamphlets it argued for financial deregulation and privatization long before such policies became associated with Margaret Thatcher; its bi-monthly journal *Economic Affairs* has been published since 1980. The CPS (Centre for Policy Studies) was founded by Mrs Thatcher and Keith Joseph in 1974, when the Conservative party was in opposition after two election defeats that year. Its political stance is in broad terms against state intervention and in favour of maximum freedom for the individual; it produces pamphlets on a wide range of issues and circulates them to cabinet ministers and government departments. The Adam Smith Institute, established in 1977, shares similar aims and methods (with a special emphasis on the free market, in keeping with the ideals of Adam *Smith himself), but it is less closely connected with government than the CPS has been during four successive Conservative administrations.

In a sense the left has the oldest think-tank of all, the *Fabian Society, though it is not usually described in those terms. But the IPPR (Institute for Public Policy Research) is entirely in the modern mould; it was launched in 1988 by a joint group of trade unionists, academics and business people with the specific aim of providing an alternative view of public policy to that offered by the free-market think-tanks. Its emphasis has been on how government can contribute to improvements in such areas as economic performance, education, transport or the environment, in ways that may be impossible to achieve by market forces alone.

thin red line Phrase for the *redcoats of the British army in line of battle. It first appeared in 1845 in a report from the Crimea by *Russell of the *Times* ('that thin red line tipped with steel').

*The **Third Man*** (1949) The most successful film of Carol *Reed, written by Graham *Greene. Set in a shattered and occupied Vienna, just after World War II, it follows the efforts of an American author, played by Joseph Cotten, to trace an old friend, the elusive Harry Lime – who turns out to be causing numerous deaths by the drugs he is adulterating. Orson Welles, playing Lime, has only a few scenes (notably a conversation while on Vienna's giant Ferris wheel and a chase in the sewers) but he successfully steals the film. The zither score (by Anton Karas) and the stark photography (Robert Krasker) are also famous features.

Third Programme see *radio.

Thirlestane Castle (45km/28m SE of Edinburgh) House in which three distinct periods of buildings coexist in an exotic jumble of peaked and turreted roofs. A four-square building of the 1590s (far more gracious than most Scottish castles of the period) acquired an extension by William *Bruce in the 1670s (in which the state rooms

The 'thin red line tipped with steel' at the Battle of Alma in the Crimea, by Richard Caton Woodville (1896).

are notable for their extravagantly baroque plaster ceilings) and the whole was enlarged in the *Scottish baronial style in the 19C.

Thirty days hath September The best-known mnemonic in the language and of great antiquity. Known in Latin and French in the Middle Ages, it was first printed in English in the 16C:

> Thirty days hath September,
> April, June and November;
> All the rest have thirty-one,
> Excepting February alone.

Thirty-nine Articles Historically the central statement of belief of the *Church of England. Based on the Forty-two Articles drawn up by Cranmer in 1553, they were given their final form in 1563 (with minor revisions in 1571), becoming the doctrine to which Anglican clergy had to assent. They took account of the broad spectrum of religious views in Elizabethan England, attempting to accommodate Catholics who might give up Rome (and five of the seven sacraments) as well as Puritans who could tolerate bishops. The Thirty-nine Articles have traditionally been printed at the end of *The *Book of Common Prayer*.

*The **Thirty-Nine Steps*** (1915) The thriller by John *Buchan which introduced his patriotic and resourceful hero, Richard Hannay. News of an elaborate international plot to invade Britain is given him by an American, who is then found murdered. Suspicion falls on Hannay, who has to outwit both the enemy and the police in his efforts to clarify his information and bring it to Scotland Yard, thus saving the country (the thirty-nine steps, one of his clues, lead up to the house occupied by the villains on the southeast coast). The film of 1935, with Robert Donat as Hannay and with considerable alterations to the plot, was one of Hitchcock's early successes.

thirty-year rule A restriction on government papers, which under the terms of the Public Records Act (1967) are made public only after 30 years. A new batch of material therefore becomes available at the *Public Record Office on the first working day in each January. Some papers are considered too sensitive even for this delay and have a longer restriction placed on them. Those arguing for a *freedom of information act in Britain point to the greater accessibility of comparable material in other countries, such as the USA.

This Is Your Life (from 1955) Long-running series of television programmes (based on an American format), in each of which an unsuspecting victim is ambushed by the presenter bearing a red book (the life encapsulated). The subject later meets, in a studio, a succession of unexpected people from his or her often distant past – guaranteeing an unfailing blend of sentiment and mild embarrassment. The programme has been broadcast at different periods by both BBC and ITV, and the only presenters have been Eamonn *Andrews, until his death in 1987, and then Michael *Aspel.

This little pig went to market Known from the early 18C and the most popular nursery rhyme for counting toes – the fifth pig being the little one, which cries 'wee-wee-wee-wee-wee' and can't find its way home.

thistle see national *emblems.

Order of the **Thistle** (The Most Ancient and Most Noble Order of the Thistle) The senior *order of chivalry in Scotland, second only to the *Garter in the United Kingdom.

It was probably founded by James III in the 15c and in its present form was revived by Queen Anne in 1703. The motto, which appears round the thistle in the star of the order, is *Nemo me impune lacessit* (Latin for 'No-one provokes me with impunity'); the same motto is used by Scottish regiments. Apart from royal members the maximum number of Knights, who place KT after their names, is 16; in 1987 it was made possible for ladies (LT) to be of this number, though none had been appointed by the early 1990s. Since 1911 the order has had its own chapel, designed by Robert Lorimer (1864– 1929), in St Giles' Cathedral in Edinburgh.

This Week (1956–78 and 1986–92) Weekly half-hour current affairs programme on independent television, made first by Associated-Rediffusion and then by Thames, transmitting often controversial material in peak evening time. It was in *This Week* that Jonathan Dimbleby drew Britain's attention to the famine in Ethiopia in 1973, and **Death on the Rock* was one of its documentaries. It came to an end at the start of 1993, when Carlton took over from Thames the weekday franchise for *television in the London region.

Dylan **Thomas** (1914–53) Welsh poet, born in Swansea, who developed a double reputation, for his romantic poems (much influenced by *Hopkins) and for his bucolic lifestyle – as seen in London's drinking clubs and on his four tours of the USA. Many of his best-known poems, including *'Fern Hill' and 'In my Craft or Sullen Art', were published in *Deaths and Entrances* (1946). *'Do not go gentle into that good night' was included in his much reprinted *Collected Poems* (1952).

His book *Portrait of the Artist as a Young Dog* (1940, echoing James Joyce's *Portrait of the Artist as a Young Man* 1915) is a collection of autobiographical short stories; they demonstrate Thomas's ability to find comedy and delight in a cast of everyday characters, which he later put to such good effect in his last work, *Under Milk Wood. He appeared in the first performance of this in New York in October 1953, and two weeks later died there of alcoholic poisoning.

Thomas, the Tank Engine The best known of the characters in the 'Railway Series' by the Rev. W. Awdry (Wilbert Awdry, b. 1911). The steam engines converse through their funnels (an idea which had occurred to Awdry in bed as a child, listening to the engines whistling and puffing on the railway), and Thomas is much bossed around by superior locomotives. The series ran to 26 volumes, from *The Three Railway Engines* (1945) to *Tramway Engines* (1972).

Daley **Thompson** (b. 1958) The greatest athlete there has ever been in the classic all-round contest – the decathlon, which involves running over three distances (100m, 400m, 1500m) in addition to seven other events (hurdling, long and high jump and pole vault, discus, javelin and putting the shot). Son of a Nigerian father and a Scottish mother, Thompson won the first of his three gold medals in the Commonwealth Games in 1978, when he was only 20; he successfully defended his title in 1982 and again in 1986. Meanwhile he had collected two golds in the Olympic Games (1980, 84), and had won his event in the European Championships of 1982 and the World Championships of 1983 – making him the first decathlete to hold the European, World and Olympic titles at the same time. In the course of these achievements he improved four times on the world record.

Emma **Thompson** (b. 1959) Actress who achieved an early success in two television drama serials, *Tutti Frutti*

Daley Thompson putting the shot during his gold-medal decathlon at the 1984 Los Angeles Olympics.

(1987) and *Fortunes of War* (1988). She gave an award-winning performance as the central character, Margaret Schlegel, in the 1992 film of **Howard's End. She is married to Kenneth *Branagh.

Charles Wyville **Thomson** see HMS **Challenger.

'Greek' **Thomson** see *Greek Revival.

J.J. **Thomson** (Joseph John Thomson, 1856–1940, kt 1908) Physicist who discovered the electron at the *Cavendish Laboratory, of which he was director from 1884 to 1918. His work on cathode rays in the 1890s led him to conclude that atoms of all kinds contain identical smaller particles, which he at first called corpuscles but later changed to electrons (a term coined a few years earlier by G.J. Stoney). In 1906 he received the Nobel prize for physics, for his work into the electrical conductivity of gases. In addition to his own scientific genius, Thomson was a superb director of a team; seven of his assistants later won Nobel prizes, as also did his son George Thomson (1892–1975).

Roy **Thomson** (1894–1976, baron 1964) Canadian newspaper proprietor who at the age of 60 began to build a new empire in Britain. In 1954 he bought the *Scotsman*, in 1959 the *Sunday Times* and in 1966 the *Times*. He was considered by many the ideal owner of newspapers, refusing to interfere in editorial policy. In 1956 he won the franchise for commercial television in central Scotland. It was this which he described, with disarming frankness, as 'a licence to print money'.

William **Thomson** (1824–1907, kt 1866, baron Kelvin 1892) Physicist who produced a stream of influential papers and inventions during his 53 years as professor of natural philosophy at the university of Glasgow, a chair to which he was appointed when only 22. Much of his work was in thermodynamics: he proposed in 1848 the absolute scale of temperature, later called the Kelvin scale; in 1852 he described with *Joule the effect now known by their joint names; and he formulated in the same year the second law of thermodynamics (an idea developed at the same time by Carnot in France and Clausius in Germany). He was also much involved in magnetism and electricity, the two fields in which he introduced many of his most useful inventions. He was responsible for major improvements in basic nautical equipment (including the compass, tide gauge and sounding apparatus), and he made important contributions to the development of telegraphy, particularly in the advances which made possible the laying of the great submarine cables.

Sybil **Thorndike** (1882–1976, DBE 1931) Actress who made her name in Shakespeare – notably at the Old Vic during World War I, where with so many actors away at the front her parts included Puck and even Prince Hal. She also excelled in modern plays, in particular *Saint Joan*. She often appeared with her husband, Lewis Casson (1875–1969). The Thorndike Theatre in Leatherhead, Surrey, is named after her.

thoroughbred Though used of any pure-bred animal, the term has had special significance in relation to racehorses, where it is applied to any appearing in the *General Stud Book*. This equine genealogy was first published in 1791 by James Weatherby and has since then been kept up to date by his descendants. Until 1948, when the rules were relaxed a little, every horse in it could trace its descent back to one of three 18C sires.

Of these, the Darley Arabian was bought by James Darley in 1704 (the majority of modern thoroughbreds descend in his line, through *Eclipse); the Byerley Turk was owned by Robert Byerley, who rode him in a cavalry charge in 1690 at the Battle of the Boyne (descent is through Herod, foaled 1758); and the Godolphin Arabian belonged to the 2nd earl of Godolphin in about 1730 (descent is through Matchem, foaled 1748). Only horses included in the *General Stud Book* can race on licensed racecourses in Britain.

Jeremy **Thorpe** (b. 1929) Liberal politician, MP for Devon North 1959–79 and leader of the Liberal party 1967–76. He resigned as leader of the party in May 1976, saying that 'a sustained press witch-hunt' had made it impossible for him to carry out his duties. The press campaign was the result of allegations by a former male model, Norman Scott, that they had once had a homosexual relationship. In June 1979 Thorpe and three others were acquitted, after a sensational trial, of charges that they had conspired to murder Scott.

1,000 Guineas Flat race for 3-year-old fillies run over 1.6km/1m at *Newmarket on a Thursday in late April or early May. The most recent of the five *Classics, established in 1814, it is the first to be run each year.

Threadneedle Street (London EC2) Thoroughfare at the heart of the *City. The *Bank of England moved here in 1734 and occupies a site facing the Mansion House and the Royal Exchange. It was Sheridan who first called the Bank the 'old lady of Threadneedle Street'.

Three blind mice Probably the most widely known of all nursery rhymes, with a tune which can be sung as a round. The three blind mice feature in a group of 'pleasant roundelaies' printed in 1609, but the incident of the farmer's wife cutting off their tails is a later addition.

Three Choirs Festival Europe's oldest surviving annual music festival. The cathedral choirs of Gloucester, Hereford and Worcester first came together to perform in about 1717; the purpose was to raise funds for 'widows and orphans of the Clergy of the three Dioceses'. The cities have taken it in turn since then (except during war years) to stage the event. By the early 1990s there have been some 265 festivals. The three choirs, augmented by other local singers, remain at the heart of the enterprise and most of the music is heard in the cathedrals (including orchestral works), but there are many related performances in other nearby locations.

three-day event Equestrian competition in which the competitor must ride the same horse on each of three days. The first is concerned with dressage; on the second there are four endurance tests, two of them over roads and tracks, one steeplechase and one cross-country; the third day's contest is showjumping.

The event has been included in the Olympic Games since 1912; there has been a European Championship since 1953 (biennial from 1965) and a World Championship every four years since 1966. In Britain the two most important annual competitions are at *Badminton and *Burghley.

three-day week see *miners' strikes and *oil crisis.

three-line whip see *Whips.

Three Men in a Boat – To say nothing of the Dog! (1889) Comic account of a disaster-prone journey in a rowing boat up the Thames from Kingston, and the only work which keeps alive the name of its author, the humorist and playwright Jerome K. Jerome (1859–1927). The three are the narrator, George and Harris; the dog (a speaking part) is Montmorency; and the author's unused middle name is Klapka.

three Rs Term in use since the early 19C for the three elements of a basic education (reading, writing and arithmetic), which can be spoken to sound as if they all begin with the letter R. Although the phrase is essentially a joke at the expense of education, it is now used even in the most solemn of contexts.

Through the Looking-Glass and What Alice Found There (1872) Children's book by Lewis *Carroll, with illustrations by *Tenniel. Alice, after playing with a set of red and white chess pieces, explores through the looking-glass into the Looking-Glass House, where the Red and White Queen and the vague theme of chess provide the link for a series of fantasy scenes. Alice first finds a poem written the wrong way round; when she holds it up to the mirror she reads the superbly sinister nonsense poem *Jabberwocky*, beginning ''Twas brillig, and the slithy toves/ Did gyre and gimble in the wabe'. Later encounters include Tweedledum and Tweedledee, two plump middle-aged schoolboys who dress up in pots and pans for a battle and who recite the poem about how the Walrus and the Carpenter deceived and ate the young oysters; Humpty Dumpty, enjoying riddles in the last moments before he falls off the wall; the Lion and the Unicorn, spoiling for another fight whether it be over a plum cake or a crown; and the White Knight, who has not yet mastered the art of staying on a horse. Alice eventually becomes a Queen herself before waking up.

Thunderbirds (ATV 1965–6) Series of 32 puppet films for children which have become an adult cult. The adventures in space are those of the Thunderbirds International Rescue Service, with the central characters Lady Penelope

Alice and the White Knight (based by Tenniel on his own appearance) in Through the Looking Glass.

(with blonde beehive hairdo) and her reliable chauffeur Parker; they are supported by the stammering scientist Brains and many others. The series and the puppets were the creation of Gerry Anderson (b. 1929) and his wife Sylvia.

Thunderer see the **Times*.

'Thy necessity is yet greater than mine' see Philip *Sidney.

Tichborne Dole Annual distribution of bread, or nowadays flour, to the parishioners of Tichborne in Hampshire, carried out since the 12C on Lady Day (March 25). The original bequest to the poor came with an accompanying curse, foretelling doom for the local family of landowners, also called Tichborne, if the dole were ever discontinued. The only attempt to end the charity, in the early 19C, was duly followed by a series of disasters including the famous case of the Tichborne Claimant. This resulted from the heir to the estate being lost at sea in 1854. In 1862 his younger brother inherited the property and the baronetcy; but their mother, refusing to believe in her elder son's death, began advertising round the world to find him. Eventually a butcher from Wagga Wagga in Australia convinced her that he was her missing son. A law suit of 1871–2, in which he claimed his inheritance, caused immense interest and brought him many supporters. The jury eventually decided that he was Arthur Orton, born the son of a butcher in Wapping, and he spent ten years in jail for perjury. But the cost of the case had almost ruined the Tichbornes.

Tiger Moth Two-seater biplane manufactured by de Havilland, on which nearly all the pilots of World War II were trained; in service with the RAF 1932–47.

Jean **Tijou** (active 1688–1712) The greatest craftsman in decorative wrought iron to have worked in England. He was of French origin but is not heard of before he began work at Chatsworth in 1688 (the date makes it likely that he was a *Huguenot). He provided gates (1695–1707) for St Paul's Cathedral but the very best of his work is at *Hampton Court (1689–99).

Till Death Us Do Part (BBC 1966–75) TV comedy series, written by Johnny Speight (b. 1920) and relying on dialogue rather than plot. The central character was a working-class reactionary, Alf Garnett, who spent most of each episode haranguing his long-suffering family with his outrageous views on a wide variety of topics (race and colour featured prominently). The bravura of the writing and of Warren *Mitchell's performance meant that his diatribes gave as much pleasure to those who ridiculed his views as to others who may have secretly agreed with them. Alf returned for another brief series in 1985–6 when his wife was ill and in a wheelchair (the real-life circumstance by then of the actress, Dandy Nichols). The title of the new series (*In Sickness and in Health*) was taken, like the earlier one, from the Anglican marriage service. The central situation, transferred to an American context, had a great success in the USA as *All in the Family*.

Tiller Girls Troupe of British dancers, famous for their precision when high-kicking in a line. From the 1920s several troupes of Tiller girls were regularly touring the world. Their origin was in the Manchester district of Moss Side, where a rich cotton merchant, John Tiller (1854–1925), organized amateur theatricals for local children. They had their first professional engagement in 1890, when he presented four 10-year-old girls in a Liverpool pantomime. Later Blackpool became the company's base.

Vesta **Tilley** (Matilda Powles, 1864–1952) The greatest of the male impersonators in the *music hall. Her petite feminine charm in gentleman's attire proved irresistible in

The corpulent Tichborne Claimant (foreground): anonymous artist's impression of the scene in court, 1872.

A collector's souvenir of a great performer: Vesta Tilley, dressed to kill in her number For the Weekend *(c.1897).*

songs such as *Burlington Bertie*, and she became an unofficial part of the nation's recruiting drive in World War I when she performed in uniform such numbers as *Jolly good luck to the girl who loves a sailor* and *The army of today's all right.*

timber-frame (also known as half-timber) The most common form of construction from about 1450 to 1650 in those parts of England (particularly the south and Midlands) where stone was scarce. In such buildings the dark timber frame was left visible and the spaces were filled either with red bricks or with lath and plaster, painted white in the style often described as black-and-white.

*The **Time Machine*** (1895) The title story of the first book of short stories by H.G. *Wells, developed from a series of articles which he wrote in a science journal for schools. The Time Traveller has invented a vehicle which can transport him to any period. His first stop is the year 802701, where he finds the leisurely and effete Eloi threatened by the Morlocks, descended from generations of underground labourers (a disastrous class division which is the theme of much of Wells's work). He later inspects the forms of life which have survived the extinction of man, and visits earth in its final era – a time of lurking monsters and terrifying eclipses of the sun.

*The **Times*** England's oldest daily newspaper (Ireland has the oldest in the country, with the *Belfast News Letter*, and Scotland follows with the *Press and Journal*). It was founded by John Walter and was first published in 1785 as *The Daily Universal Register*; the name was changed to *The Times* in 1788. It pioneered a new technology in 1814 when it became the first newspaper to be printed on a steam press, capable of producing 1100 sheets an hour; the machines were installed secretly in a nearby building for fear of a *Luddite response by the printers. At that time the paper was strongly committed to the Tories, but its hostile coverage of the *Peterloo massacre in 1819 signalled a change of direction. In 1830 a vigorous leader in support of political reform earned it the nickname of 'The Thunderer'; the editor had urged that 'the people, the people everywhere, come forward and petition, nay thunder for reform'. Gradually during the 19C the paper established itself as the main national forum of information, not only for its news coverage but for a court page where society announced family births, marriages and deaths, and a letters page where people of importance aired their views.

In 1966 Roy *Thomson, already owner of the *Sunday Times*, purchased the *Times* and thus brought together two titles which had long seemed, incorrectly, to be sister publications. During the Thomson ownership both titles suffered from disastrous industrial relations, and a strike by print unions in November 1978 kept them out of circulation for nearly a year. In 1981 his son, Kenneth Thomson, sold them to Rupert *Murdoch, whose move of the printing and editorial operations to a computerized plant at *Wapping in 1986 was prepared with as much secrecy as the introduction of the steam presses a century and a half earlier. The change, this time, was not achieved so peacefully. But the violent confrontations were followed by the introduction of new technology throughout the newspaper industry.

There has been a convention in British typography that newspapers should be printed with the definite article in roman type – the *Observer* or the *Sun* – but that *The Times* is an exception. The reason is given in *Hart's Rules*, dating from the 1890s, where it is explained that *The Times* 'prefers to have it so'. This seems insufficient reason to perpetuate the inconsistency, which is not followed in these pages.

The *Times* has some long-established offshoots in its famous supplements, in particular the *TLS and the *Times Educational Supplement* (first published in 1910).

Timon of Athens (*c.* 1607) Unrelievedly bleak tragedy by *Shakespeare about a rich Athenian who generously gives all his wealth away and is then spurned by his friends. Retiring to a cave to nurse his hatred of mankind, he finds a hoard of gold. The effect of this news on the Athenians does nothing to restore his spirits, and he commits suicide.

Timothy Whites see *Boots.

Tinker Bell see *Peter Pan.

Tinker, Tailor The main survivor of the many nursery rhymes used as fortune-telling games when counting. The eight possible destinies in store for the children are: 'Tinker, Tailor, Soldier, Sailor, Rich man, Poor man, Beggar man, Thief'.

Tintagel (80km/50m NW of Plymouth) Ruined castle, mainly of the 13C, on a rocky promontory on the north coast of Cornwall. Its great appeal derives from its being the supposed birthplace of King *Arthur, a legend first written down by *Geoffrey of Monmouth in the 11C.

Tintern Abbey (8km/5m N of Chepstow) Romantically situated ruin among wooded hills on a curve of the river Wye. It was founded as a Cistercian house in 1131, but the ruins are of 13–14C buildings. Although the roof of the abbey church was removed at the *dissolution of the monasteries, the walls with their great Gothic windows survive to their full height. The beauty of Tintern became appreciated in the late 18C, when the Wye valley was singled out as one of the first examples of the *picturesque. The abbey was much visited by watercolourists, J.M.W. Turner among them. But its status as Britain's foremost romantic ruin derives from the young Wordsworth having included in *Lyrical Ballads* his 'Lines composed a few miles above Tintern Abbey', verses suffused with tender melancholy:

> I have learned
> To look on nature, not as in the hour
> Of thoughtless youth; but hearing often-times
> The still, sad music of humanity. . .

Michael **Tippett** (b. 1905, kt 1966) Composer who started late but whose career has extended into a very productive old age. He began to establish a reputation with his Concerto for Double String Orchestra (1939), and secured it two years later with what remains his best-known work – the oratorio *A Child of our Time* (1941), an impassioned protest against tyranny and persecution (inspired by an outburst of anti-Semitic violence in 1938). This oratorio had a text by Tippett himself, as have his operas. The first was *The Midsummer Marriage* (1955), followed by *King Priam* (1962), *The Knot Garden* (1970) and *The Ice Break* (1977); a constant theme, consciously developed from Mozart, has been reconciliation. His most recent opera was *New Year* (1989), a space-age fable. One of his most popular instrumental works is the *Fantasia Concertante on a Theme of Corelli* (1953), commissioned for the Edinburgh Festival to celebrate the tercentenary of Corelli's birth. Tippett is also well known for his commitment to pacifism, which brought him a jail sentence of three months in World War II when he refused to comply with the conditions for exemption from active service. He is a member of the Order of *Merit.

Tippoo's Tiger (Victoria and Albert Museum) Life-size mechanical toy of a tiger devouring a prostrate European in the costume of the 1790s. It was made for Tippoo, the Sultan of Mysore, who fought two wars against the East India Company, and it was brought to London after the Company defeated him in 1799. Only the man's arm moves (up and down in agony) but a concealed organ reproduces the roars of the lion and the cries of the victim.

Sarah **Tisdall** see *moles.

James **Tissot** (1836–1902) French realist painter who lived in London from 1871 to 1882 and produced a large number of detailed pictures of English social life, much of it taking place on and around the Thames. The woman who appears in so many of them was his Irish mistress, Kathleen Newton. It was after her death from tuberculosis in 1882 that he returned to Paris.

Titania see *A *Midsummer Night's Dream.*

Titanic British luxury liner of the White Star line, at the time the largest in the world, which sank off Newfoundland on its maiden voyage from Southampton to New York in 1912. Just before midnight on April 14, travelling at the high speed of 22 knots, she struck an iceberg and sank within three hours. There were 2224 passengers on board but lifeboats for only about half that number; 1513 people drowned, and the number would have been greater if the Cunard liner *Carpathia* had not arrived just after the *Titanic* went down. Scandal and controversy long surrounded the details of who got into the few lifeboats and why another nearby liner, the *Californian*, failed to pick up the radio signals for help. The disaster prompted major improvements in safety at sea, in particular a new requirement that ships provide a lifeboat place for everyone aboard and keep a 24-hour radio watch. The hull of the *Titanic* was discovered in 1985 and has since been explored and filmed.

Titus Andronicus (*c.*1591) Tragedy by *Shakespeare, possibly with a collaborator, consisting of an unending succession of gory murders and mutilations in ancient Rome. Perhaps dating from as early as 1590, its main interest (shared with *Henry VI*) is as a work of apprenticeship.

TLS (*The Times Literary Supplement*) Specialist weekly paper, consisting mainly of book reviews, which was first issued in 1902 as a free supplement with Friday editions of the *Times*. It remained in that role, literally a supplement, until it was launched in 1914 as a separate paper under *Times* ownership. With its parent paper it became in 1981 part of Rupert *Murdoch's stable.

The Titanic *towed from Southampton by tugs, at the start of her first and only voyage (April 1912).*

Toad see *The *Wind in the Willows*.

toad-in-the-hole Now invariably sausages baked in batter, but in the 18C the meat lurking in the hole was good beef. A writer in 1797 argues that for Mrs Siddons to be performing at Sadler's Wells is as incongruous as 'a toad in a hole, putting a noble sirloin of beef into a poor paltry batter-pudding'.

To a Skylark (1820) Poem written by *Shelley in Italy after walking one summer evening with his wife Mary and together hearing a skylark. Beginning 'Hail to thee, blithe spirit!', the poet salutes what he sees as the freedom and intensity of the bird's rapture.

Tobago see *Trinidad and Tobago.

'To be, or not to be: that is the question' see entry on **Hamlet*.

Toby see *Punch and Judy.

Uncle **Toby** see **Tristram Shandy*.

Toby jug Pottery jug in the form of a seated figure, himself holding a jug to tipple from and usually wearing a three-cornered hat which doubles as lid and drinking cup. First made in the mid-18C at the Staffordshire factory of Ralph Wood (1715–72), many versions were later produced both in Britain and abroad – all of them male except the one featuring Martha Gunn, a famous 'dipper' at *Brighton. The original jug is said to have been based on Toby Philpot, a real-life toper featured in a song of 1761 called *The Brown Jug*.

Toc H (Wendover, Buckinghamshire) Christian fellowship, dedicated to service in the community, which derives from a club for British soldiers set up in 1915 at Poperinge in Belgium, behind the allied lines. The building was called Talbot House (after Gilbert Talbot, killed in that year) and the soldiers referred to it in the signallers' version of its initials, Toc H. It was run by an army chaplain, Philip Clayton (1885–1972), known to all because of his shape as 'Tubby'; it was he who extended the fellowship to a network of branches throughout Britain after the war.

Today (BBC from 1957) Breakfast-time programme on Radio 4 which the BBC likes to describe as 'setting the nation's agenda'. In its early days it was closer to light entertainment, but it now has a high reputation for its discussion of current affairs. The programme was presented from 1958 to 1970 by Jack De Manio (1914–88), and from 1975 to 1986 it had a particularly successful double-act of front men in John Timpson (b. 1928) and Brian Redhead (b. 1929). In the early 1990s Redhead, now with other co-presenters, remains a key figure. A regular five-minute feature on the programme, at about 7.45, is *Thought for the Day* in which someone of religious profession or persuasion delivers a homily, often connected with topical events. Most of the speakers are Christian, but one of the most popular has been Rabbi Lionel Blue (b. 1930).

Today Britain's first national newspaper to be printed in colour. Its production methods were technically in advance of its rivals when it was launched in 1986 by Eddy Shah, who had previously won a long-running battle with the print unions in Greater Manchester over the production of his *Stockport Messenger*. *Today* at first failed to live up to Shah's hopes; it was bought after a few months by Lonrho, and then in 1987 by Rupert *Murdoch. By the early 1990s it was established as a middle-of-the-market *tabloid.

toffee see *sweets.

Toft family see *slipware.

To his Coy Mistress see Andrew *Marvell.

J.R.R. **Tolkien** (John Ronald Reuel Tolkien, 1892–1973) Professor of Anglo-Saxon and bestselling author, whose love of medieval literature and legend lay behind the world which he created in miniature in *The *Hobbit* and then enlarged to epic scale in *The *Lord of the Rings*.

Tolpuddle Martyrs Six farm labourers from the Dorset village of Tolpuddle who were given this name after being sentenced in 1834 to transportation for seven years to Australia. Their leaders were two brothers, George and James Loveless, and their offence (with James Brine, James Hammett, Thomas Stanfield and his son John) had been to establish a lodge of the Friendly Society of Agricultural Labourers. This was not in itself illegal, but the government – alarmed at the growth of *trade union activity – charged them with administering unlawful oaths. Nationwide protests contributed to the development of the *Chartist movement. In 1836 the sentences of the six were remitted and they were brought back to England. Five of them later emigrated to Canada.

tomato ketchup The only one of the original ketchups (spicy sauces used as condiments for meat or fish) to have survived as an everyday feature of British life, used particularly now with fried fish and chips. The word 'ketchup' is a variant of a Chinese term for a brine of pickled fish; it entered the language in about 1700. In past centuries mushrooms and walnuts were the most popular ingredients for ketchup.

Tom Bowling Popular sentimental song about the death of 'poor Tom Bowling, the darling of our crew'. It was written by Charles Dibdin (1745–1814), apparently in memory of his elder brother, the captain of a ship plying the route to India, who had died at sea.

Tom Brown's Schooldays (1857) Novel by Thomas Hughes (1822–96), which from its first publication rapidly became Britain's best-known schoolboy story. It takes place at Rugby (Hughes's own school) and it idolizes the famous headmaster, Dr *Arnold. Under his influence Tom progresses from a mildly naughty small boy to a courageous and committed Christian, but the book's appeal derives from its realistic and often brutal portrayal of life in a boys' boarding school – most notably in Tom's persecution by the school bully, *Flashman.

Tom Jones (in full *The History of Tom Jones, a Foundling* 1749) Novel by Henry *Fielding with an immensely complex plot which includes: the boyhood of Tom in the household of Squire Allworthy (who has adopted him after returning home to find a baby abandoned on his bed); Tom's education at the hands of two malevolent tutors, Messrs Square and Thwackum; his developing love for Sophia, the daughter of the neighbouring Squire Western; the misfortunes which cause him to be driven unjustly from home; and his many sexual adventures before a final happy reunion with Sophia, leading to marriage and the blessing of both paternal squires.

A film (*Tom Jones* 1963) was directed in suitably rumbustious style by Tony Richardson, with a script by John Osborne and with Albert Finney as Tom and Susannah York as Sophia.

Tommy Atkins Popular term from the early 19C for a soldier. From 1815 the name Thomas Atkins was printed on all specimen forms in the army, showing how they should be filled up by a private in the infantry.

tommy shop see *Truck Act.

Tomorrow's World (BBC from 1957) Series of television programmes investigating the latest inventions and technological developments, of a kind likely to become of use to the consumer. For many years (1965–78) the main presenter was Raymond Baxter.

Thomas **Tompion** (1639–1713) English maker of clocks and watches whose mechanical brilliance, combined with the inventive genius of Robert Hooke (the balance spring) and of Edward Barlow (the cylinder escapement), enabled English watches to become smaller, flatter and yet more reliable than others. Repeating watches (striking the recent hour or quarter-hour when a spring is pressed) and clocks that ran for a year without winding were other Tompion specialities. In 1676 he was appointed clockmaker to the new *Royal Observatory, where accuracy in timekeeping was essential.

Tom Thumb A tiny man no taller than a thumb appears in the folk tales of many countries. He is mentioned under this name in England from the 16C, and by the 18C Tom Thumb was one of the most popular of characters for children. He was also the hero of a famous burlesque by Henry *Fielding.

ton see *weight.

Tonga Independent kingdom, comprising an archipelago of islands in the Pacific southeast of Fiji, which has been a member of the *Commonwealth since 1970. Ruled by a line of sacred kings from at least the 10C, the islands had been noted by various European explorers before the visits in the mid-18C of Captain *Cook, who called them the Friendly Islands. A constitutional monarchy was established in 1845 by King George Tupou I. His descendant Queen Salote became a firm favourite with the crowds watching the coronation of Elizabeth II in 1953; an impressively large figure, she was one of the few dignitaries to remain in an open carriage throughout the entire procession in a steady downpour of rain. Tonga was a British protectorate from 1900 and became independent in 1970.

tonic (Indian tonic water) Mineral water containing quinine. During the 18–19C quinine was the only known remedy against malaria, and was regularly taken as a protection in infested parts of the British empire. Tonic water, launched by Schweppes in the 1870s, was found to be extremely pleasant with gin and so survives regardless of malaria.

Tonight Title used for several BBC series of early evening magazine programmes, but particularly remembered among older viewers for the first series (from 1957), which had Cliff Michelmore as the front man and Alan Whicker, Derek Hart and Fyfe Robertson among its roving reporters.

Augustus **Toplady** see *Rock of Ages.

Top of the Pops (BBC from 1963) Weekly television showcase for the pop recordings currently heading the charts. Launched at a time when British rock music was making the headlines (1963 saw the first no. 1 hits by the Beatles and the first appearance in the charts of the Rolling Stones), the programme rapidly became something of a national institution.

Tories and Whigs The two names were first applied to opposing factions in the late 1670s, during the turmoil following the *Popish Plot. The issue was whether the duke of York (the future *James II) should be excluded from the throne as a Roman Catholic. The opponents of the duke tried various abusive names for his supporters and 'Tory' was the one which stuck. It was an Irish Gaelic word, meaning 'pursuer', and was the common name for Irish outlaws who plundered English settlers; the implication was of someone wild, foreign, Roman Catholic. The Tories soon found an equivalently offensive term for the other side. 'Whiggamore' was a Scottish Gaelic word, of unknown meaning, used of a group of Presbyterian rebels who had marched on royalist Edinburgh in 1648; the implied characteristics this time were wild, foreign, Nonconformist and probably regicidal as well. The rivalry was a clear extension of the alignments of the *English Civil War, and was recognized as such at the time: 'instead of Cavalier and Roundhead, now they are called Torys and Wiggs', noted a diarist, Oliver Heywood, in 1681.

The distinction between the two groups was somewhat blurred in the years after the *Revolution of 1688 (the change of monarch within the Stuart family had the support of many Tories), but under the next dynasty, the Hanoverians, the traditional Tory link with the Stuarts told against the party. The Whigs therefore had an unbroken period of ascendancy after 1714, which the Tories followed with an equally long tenure of office at the end of the century during the reign of George III. In the politics of the time allegiance to one side or the other was more often a matter of family or regional loyalty than an issue of principle. In so far as the two parties had an identity, the Whigs were associated with the nobility and the urban middle class, while the Tories had the support of the more traditional country squires. The political scene was transformed by the *Reform Act of 1832, after which the Tories and Whigs evolved into the *Conservative and *Liberal parties.

Torquay Resort in Devon, popular since the early 19C because of its beautiful sea views and the mild climate caused by the *Gulf Stream. There are ruins of Torre Abbey, founded in the 12C, and a house in the abbey grounds is now used as the art gallery. The town's museum has the finds from nearby *Kent's Cavern, one of the oldest inhabited sites in Britain. In 1968 Torquay was merged with two neighbouring towns to form the borough of Torbay (123,000 in 1991).

torques see *Snettisham.

Torres Vedras see *Peninsular War.

Torrey Canyon Kuwaiti tanker responsible in 1967 for Britain's worst oil pollution disaster. She was carrying 30,000 tons of oil when she ran aground on the Seven Stones reef west of Land's End. The ship was bombed by the RAF in an unsuccessful attempt to set the cargo on fire. Some 110km/70m of Cornish coast was polluted. A greater quantity of oil was spilled in the *Shetlands disaster of 1993, but it dispersed with less apparent or immediate damage.

Torvill and Dean Phenomenal ice-dancing duo from Nottingham, by trade an insurance clerk (Jane Torvill, b. 1957) and a policeman (Christopher Dean, b. 1958). They proved their pre-eminence in the sport in 1981, when they won both the European title and the world championship. Retaining their world championship title in each of the next three years, they made history at Helsinki in 1983 when all nine judges gave them the maximum six points for artistic impression. They repeated this feat in

London celebrates the opening of Tower Bridge and the first raising of the roadway for ships: painting by William Wyllie, 1894.

their most famous performance of all, when they won the gold medal at the 1984 Olympics (dancing to Ravel's *Bolero*); in the same event they collected another three sixes for technical merit. The total of 12 was unprecedented, but they improved on it themselves four weeks later in Ottawa, winning their fourth world title with 13 sixes.

tossing the caber The most specifically Scottish of the athletic events at *Highland games. The caber (Gaelic for a pole) is the size of a telegraph pole; the one used at the Braemar gathering is 5.8m/19ft long and weighs 54kg/119lb. The contestant must support it upright on his joined hands, and then toss it so that it lands on its other end and falls away from him. The winning throw is the caber which falls most nearly in a straight line (i.e. nearest to 12 o'clock from the contestant).

Tote (Horserace Totalisator Board) Government organization established in 1929 to take the public's bets at racecourses. The intention was to channel the profits back to racing rather than into the pockets of the private bookmakers. For serious punters it has traditionally had little appeal because it is run on the pool system (like the football *pools), meaning that individual winnings depend on how many other people have placed the same bet. The bookmakers' starting price system (by which the punter knows what he will collect and there is always the chance of the bookie losing a fortune) is considered a more challenging gamble. Since 1989 the Tote has accepted off-course telephone bets at starting prices.

To the Lighthouse (1927) Novel by Virginia *Woolf, in which she uses the interior monologue of her characters to weave a rich fabric of rivalries and disappointments within the Ramsay family. On holiday on the west coast of Scotland, they are unable to agree on whether to make an expedition to a nearby lighthouse. The father and son,

whose views were most directly opposed, reach the lighthouse together years later, after the death of Mrs Ramsay, the novel's central character.

Tottenham Hotspur, known as Spurs (White Hart Lane, London N17). Football club formed in 1882 by members of a cricket club, most of them old boys from two local schools. It was not until 1895 that it turned professional. In 1901 it became the only non-League club (since the formation of the *Football League in 1888) to win the FA Cup, and in 1908 it finally entered the League – in Division 2, winning promotion at the end of the first season. Achievements were relatively modest until the 1960s, but in 1961 Spurs became the first team in the 20c to win the FA Cup and the League in the same year. They went on to a phenomenal run of further successes in the FA Cup – bringing them, by 1991, a record eight victories. The club's fortunes were dramatic in two senses in the early 1990s: it nearly went bankrupt, until rescued by Alan Sugar (of Amstrad); meanwhile the team included England's two most charismatic players, Gary Lineker and Paul Gascoigne. Club victories: FA Cup 1901, 21, 61, 62, 67, 81, 82, 91; League Champions 1951, 61; League Cup, 1971, 73; European Cup-Winners' Cup 1963; UEFA Cup 1972, 84.

Tottenham Three Three young men – Winston Silcott, Engin Raghip and Mark Braithwaite – who were sentenced to life imprisonment in 1987 for 'having common cause' with the mob which murdered PC Blakelock in the brutal sequence of events on *Broadwater Farm. Their convictions were quashed in 1991, and the police superintendent in charge of the case suspended, after *ESDA tests revealed that Silcott's confession had been tampered with. The other two were released, but Silcott remained in jail as he was also serving a life sentence for the murder of Anthony Smith in 1984.

totting up System introduced in 1988 by which driving offences add up until they lead to disqualification. In place of the earlier total of three endorsements on the driving licence, disqualification is now likely if 12 points are incurred within three years. The most common offence, exceeding a speed limit, brings three points while reckless driving carries 10 and 'unlawful pillion riding' only one.

Tourist Trophy see *TT.

Tour of Britain see *Milk Race.

Tower Bridge (London EC3) One of London's best-known landmarks and the city's furthest bridge downstream over the Thames; it was built in 1886–94 a few hundred yards below *London Bridge. The engineer was John Wolfe-Barry (1836–1918), a son of the architect Charles Barry; and the Gothic exterior was designed by Horace Jones (1819–87). The tall towers conceal the machinery which raises the roadway, as two drawbridges, to let ships pass through. The towers also contain lifts to take pedestrians up to the high-level footbridge.

Tower Hill (London EC3) Rising ground to the north of the *Tower of London, where distinguished 'traitors' were brought from the Tower to be beheaded. Fewer than 100 such executions took place (among them Thomas More), but each had the importance of a state occasion, watched by large crowds on specially constructed stands. Ordinary criminals were hanged on the other side of town, at *Tyburn.

Tower of London (EC3) Fortress built just outside the city walls of London, to dominate rather than protect the citizens. Begun just after the Norman *Conquest and completed by the 13C, it symbolized the royal power. Political prisoners were held here or were executed on the nearby Tower Hill (women, such as Anne Boleyn or Catherine Howard, were more likely to be executed within the Tower). The so-called Traitors' Gate, a broad low arch under St Thomas's Tower, was the main entrance from the river and therefore the place of arrival for any prisoner brought down by water from Westminster.

Since 1303 the *crown jewels have been kept in the Tower and for 600 years, up to the 19C, lions were on show in the Royal Menagerie. The central keep (the original fortress, known as the White Tower) for centuries housed the *Royal Armouries. The yeoman warders, established by Edward VI and still wearing Tudor costume, are commonly known as 'beefeaters'. James I was the last monarch to occupy the Tower as a palace.

town crier Official appointed in a medieval town to shout proclamations in the street; the custom survives today in various ceremonial contexts. A town crier traditionally begins his announcement with the words *Oyez! Oyez!*, Norman French for 'Hear ye! Hear ye!'.

Towneley plays see *mystery plays.

Sue **Townsend** see *Adrian Mole.

Turnip **Townshend** (Charles Townshend, 1674–1738, 2nd viscount 1687) Whig statesman, responsible for British foreign policy during the 1720s, whose fame now is largely as an agriculturalist. Alexander Pope wrote that this great man liked nothing better than to talk about turnips, and tradition credits him with introducing the four-course rotation of this root crop on his Norfolk estate. It seems, however, that it was common practice there and that it was merely his enthusiasm which gave it prominence,

causing the turnip to become an important feed for cattle in other parts of the country.

Townswomen's Guilds Organization consisting of some 2000 guilds around Britain, meeting for social activities and functioning as a pressure group on women's issues. The guilds trace their origin to the Kensington Society, a ladies' discussion group established in London in 1865. Votes for women was the main theme of the following decades, and many of the members were *suffragettes. The equal franchise was finally achieved in 1928, and in 1929 the first four guilds on the present pattern were formed. The name Townswomen's Guilds was adopted in 1933.

Toxteth see *Liverpool.

Arnold **Toynbee** The name of two men of significance in the 19–20C. The elder (1852–83) was a social reformer who worked in the poor London district of *Whitechapel, where he was commemorated after his death in Toynbee Hall. His nephew (1889–1975) was a historian whose subject was Greece and Rome, but whose most challenging contribution was his massive 12-volume *Study of History* (1934–61); it reached a wide audience in the two-volume reduction by David Somervell (1946–57). Toynbee presents human history as a recurring cycle of growth and decay, and implies – more controversially – that some added spiritual dimension could break the mould and open the way to a higher civilization.

Toynbee Hall see *Whitechapel.

toy theatre (also known as juvenile drama) Nursery entertainment popular in Britain for a few decades from about 1810. The characters from plays on the adult stage were depicted in small etchings – usually six or eight to each sheet, sold for a penny plain or twopence hand-coloured. Also available was an abbreviated script of the play, together with scenery and a miniature theatre. The children cut out the characters, mounted each on the end of a rod and manipulated them on the stage while declaiming the text. The craze declined after about 1850, but reproductions of the old sheets are still published. Pollock's Toy Museum (London W1) is based on the stock in trade of Benjamin Pollock (1876–1937), whose predecessors in his business reach back to the early 19C and the beginning of juvenile drama.

Toytown see * *Children's Hour*.

Tractarians see *Oxford Movement.

Department of **Trade and Industry** (DTI, London SW1) Government department formed in 1970 by the merging of the Board of Trade and the Ministry of Technology. It is responsible for UK trade policy and for industry and technology, research and development, company legislation and consumer protection – together with the concerns taken on in 1992 when it absorbed the Department of *Energy. Michael *Heseltine, taking charge of the DTI in 1992, revived the earlier title of president of the Board of Trade. For secretaries of state since 1983 see the *cabinet.

trade gap see *balance of payments.

John **Tradescant** (*c*.1570–1638) Collector of curiosities and gardener to Charles I. He brought back large numbers of plants from his travels in Europe, and was responsible for stocking the gardens at *Hatfield. His son, also John (1608–62), followed him as gardener to the king and continued to build up the family collection, which became the basis of the *Ashmolean Museum. The Tradescants lived in Lambeth, south of the river in London, and were buried in St Mary's – which now houses a museum of garden history.

Trades Union Congress see the *TUC.

trade unions From the late Middle Ages there were occasional attempts by workers to stand together when arguing with those who paid them, but the common law made it illegal to combine 'in restraint of trade'. The issue did not become important until the *Industrial Revolution and the development of the factory system during the 18C, when groups of skilled artisans began to form associations. The example of the French Revolution alarmed the government into passing the Combination Acts of 1799 and 1800, which declared such associations to be criminal conspiracies against the public interest. These acts were repealed in 1824, and several of today's unions have their earliest roots in the years immediately after that event. The surge of enthusiasm for what was now legal provoked the government into finding other ways of making it illegal, but the conviction of the *Tolpuddle Martyrs in 1834 (for unlawfully administering oaths) proved only a brief check on the proliferation of unions. The umbrella organization of the *TUC (Trades Union Congress) was established in 1868, and by the end of the century the movement was powerful enough to play a major part in the founding of the *Labour party.

The *General Strike of 1926 was an important assertion of nationwide solidarity, but it was after World War II that the unions came into their own. In subsequent decades union leaders (in particular the general secretary of the TUC) were treated almost as partners in government; as representatives of the nation's workforce they negotiated with politicians and civil servants at the highest level, often over beer and sandwiches at 10 Downing Street. This cosy arrangement did nothing to improve Britain's appalling industrial relations (known elsewhere as the *English disease), and restrictive practices were rife on the shop floor.

There was an abrupt change with the election of the Conservative administration in 1979 after the *'winter of discontent', and many would point to the subsequent reduction of the unions' misuse of power as Mrs Thatcher's one undeniable achievement. Successive employment acts during the 1980s ended compulsory closed

shops, removed legal immunities if strikes were called without a secret ballot, and reformed the law on *picketing. The *miners' strike of 1984 was the central trial of strength, which the government won.

The resulting decline in union power has been reflected in a marked decrease in the number of days lost through *strikes. It has also been accompanied by a steep drop in union membership, a tendency for unions to merge into much larger *super-unions, and a growing campaign to reduce the influence of the block vote in the deliberations of the Labour party.

Trafalgar (21 Oct. 1805) Victory by *Nelson over a combined French and Spanish fleet (commanded by Pierre de Villeneuve) in the Atlantic outside the Straits of Gibraltar; the name derives from Cape Trafalgar in southwest Spain. The French fleet of 33 ships was attempting to sail from Cadiz into the Mediterranean to support Napoleon's planned invasion of Austria. Nelson, with 27 ships, began by flying from the masthead of the *Victory his famous signal (see *'England expects'). Both he and *Collingwood broke through the French line, and the battle would have been a largely painless victory (20 French and Spanish ships surrendered with no British losses) if a sniper firing with a musket from the topmast of the *Redoutable* had not put a bullet through Nelson's spine. He was alive for the last few hours of the battle. 'Kiss me, Hardy', one of his final requests to his captain on the *Victory*, has often struck people as odd; but in the context of a long death scene, recorded by a doctor who was tending him (William Beatty), it reads as a simple request for a comforting embrace. The victory gave Britain a reputation at sea which was unchallenged until World War I.

Trafalgar House Company founded in 1956, and floated on the Stock Exchange in 1963, which has become large by acquisitions and internal growth. Its main business is construction and engineering, but it includes also Cunard and the *QE2.

Trafalgar Square (London WC2) The capital city's largest square with unrestricted access, and therefore the traditional place for meetings of political protest and for New Year revels. It was laid out in 1830–41, on the site of earlier royal stables, as a memorial to the victory at *Trafalgar and with *Nelson's Column as its main feature.

training see *TECs.

Membership of trade unions, in millions

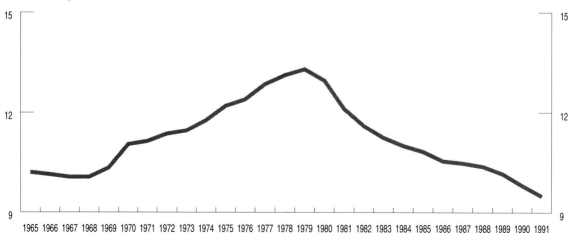

Source: Annual Abstract of Statistics (*see* *Central Statistical Office*).

UNDER WHICH FLAG?

JOHN BULL. "ONE OF THESE TWO FLAGS HAS GOT TO COME DOWN—AND IT WON'T BE MINE."

A far from impartial view of the trade unions by John Bull in 1926: caricature in Punch.

Traitors' Gate see *Tower of London.

Transjordan That part of the *mandated territory of *Palestine which lay east of the river Jordan. It was administered by Britain as a separate area, because the mandate specifically excluded it from the terms of the *Balfour Declaration. Abdullah (1882–1951), the brother of Faisal I of *Iraq, was appointed emir of Transjordan in 1921, becoming king on independence in 1946. The country's name was changed to Jordan in 1949 – reflecting the extension of the kingdom to the west bank of the Jordan, where territory was captured and annexed in the war of 1948–9 against Israel.

Department of **Transport** (London SW1) Government department responsible for all aspects of land, sea and air transport, including railways, motorways and trunk roads as well as airports and ports. It is invariably subject to political controversy over the relative amount of support it gives to road and rail. For secretaries of state since 1983 see the *cabinet.

Transport House The London headquarters, in Smith Square, of the *TGWU. The building was also the headquarters of the Labour party until 1980, when the party transferred to *Walworth Road.

Traquair House (48km/30m S of Edinburgh) Claimed to be the oldest inhabited house in Scotland. There is mention of a building here in the early 12C; the present house is mainly of the 17C, but it incorporates a fortified tower of an earlier period. Nowadays Traquair has another claim to fame. Since 1965 (six years before the founding of *CAMRA) beer has been brewed here by traditional methods in an ancient brewhouse. It is available only in relatively small quantities – in the early 1990s the output was eight barrels a week – but Traquair House ale is exported as far afield as Japan and the USA.

Travellers' Club (London SW1) A *club founded in 1819 for gentlemen who had travelled abroad – an adventure only recently possible again, with the ending of the Napoleonic Wars. In 1828 the club acquired its premises in Pall Mall, part of the site of *Carlton House; a competition to find the architect was won by Charles *Barry, who completed the Italian-Renaissance building in 1832.

Travels with a Donkey see Robert Louis *Stevenson.

Ben **Travers** (1886–1980) Author of a string of nine successful farces between the wars, which became known as the Aldwych farces because they were first produced at the Aldwych Theatre in London. The best known now are the first two, *A Cuckoo in the Nest* (1925) and *Rookery Nook* (1926). Two famous regulars in the casts were Robertson Hare and Ralph Lynn.

Traverse (Edinburgh) Theatre with a distinguished record in new drama; more than 400 new plays have been presented since it was founded in 1963 by Jim Haynes, with the intention of achieving throughout the year the vitality of the Fringe at the *Edinburgh Festival. The theatre was in those days a club (and remained so until 1988), functioning in tiny premises in the Lawnmarket. In 1969 it moved to a converted warehouse in the Grassmarket, and then in 1992 to a custom-built home with two auditoria (250 and 100 seats) next door to the Usher Hall.

Treasure Island (1883) Adventure story of 18C piracy, by Robert Louis *Stevenson. The boy hero, Jim Hawkins, finds a map of an island with buried treasure. He shows it to Squire Trelawney, who sails with Jim on the schooner *Hispaniola* to recover the booty. Among the crew are several pirates, led by the one-legged ship's cook, Long John Silver, whose plot to seize the ship is discovered by Jim. The pirates are overcome in a battle, and the treasure is found with the help of a castaway, Ben Gunn, whose years on the island have been enlivened by dreams of cheese, 'toasted, mostly'.

treasure-trove Objects of gold and silver which have been hidden, either in the ground or in a building, by an owner who intended to return and collect them and who cannot now be traced. Treasure of this kind belongs to the crown, with the British Museum given first refusal on accepting it. If the Museum or any other public collection wants the treasure, the finder is given the full market value. The definition excludes items which were accidentally lost (a single gold jewel found by a roadside, for example) but almost inevitably includes any large hoard unless part of a burial. The inquest on whether a find is treasure-trove is held by a *coroner.

Treasury (London SW1) The government department responsible for all financial matters. Three members of the Treasury are in the *cabinet – the first lord of the Treasury (an office held by the *prime minister), the *chancellor of the exchequer, and the *chief secretary to the Treasury.

Treasury Bench see *front bench.

Trelawny of the 'Wells' (1898) Romantic comedy by *Pinero about the appeal of theatre itself. Rose Trelawny, star of the Bagnigg Wells company in the heyday of *melodrama, leaves to marry into a respectable family; but even before the wedding she has returned to the stage. Romantic disappointments are avoided when her fiancé abandons his family to appear in the new production as her leading man.

Trevithick's steam locomotive as an attraction for paying customers in London's Euston Square: watercolour by Rowlandson, 1809.

Trelissick (8km/5m S of Truro) Garden on a hillside stretching down to the river Fal, with trees planted in the 1820s and a profusion of more recent flowering shrubs, particularly rhododendrons and hydrangeas, which thrive in the mild climate brought by the *Gulf Stream.

Trent The main river of the Midlands, flowing 274km/170m from north Staffordshire in a great loop (southeast through the Potteries and Stoke-on-Trent, then northeast again through Burton-upon-Trent and Nottingham) to enter the North Sea by the *Humber estuary. The river acquired great importance in the late 18C after the Grand Trunk Canal had joined the Mersey to the Trent, downstream of Burton, to provide in 1772 the first coast-to-coast route across England for barges.

Trent Bridge (Nottingham) County ground of *Nottinghamshire County Cricket Club. A pitch was laid out in 1838 behind the Trent Bridge Inn (still a famous feature just to the west of the ground), and the county club played there from its formation in 1841. Trent Bridge is one of the regular locations for *Test matches (first played at the ground in 1899).

Tresco One of the *Scilly Isles, notable for Tresco Abbey Gardens – developed round the ruins of a Benedictine abbey from 1834 by Augustus Smith and his descendants. The climate produced by the *Gulf Stream allows a great many exotic plants to thrive here which could not survive elsewhere in Britain, though an unprecedented spell of frost in January 1987 caused some damage. Ships have been wrecked on the Scillies for centuries, and a collection of their figureheads is displayed in the Valhalla Museum.

G.M. Trevelyan (George Macaulay Trevelyan, 1876–1962) Historian whose narrative and descriptive skills equalled those of his great uncle, Macaulay, and likewise brought his work to a wide popular audience. He established himself with a three-volume life of Garibaldi (1907–11), but thereafter he specialized in British history. His two most successful books with the public were *History of England* (1926) and *English Social History* (1942).

Richard **Trevithick** (1771–1833) The first man to carry passengers on a *steam vehicle. Born in Cornwall, he was familiar with steam engines in the mines. After the expiry of *Watt's patent in 1800 he began building engines, adapting one to drive a carriage. On this he took passengers over a short distance on Christmas Eve 1801 at Camborne, in Cornwall; in London in 1803 another version was driven from Holborn to Paddington and back; and in Wales in 1804 he ran the first locomotive on rails, pulling five wagons at Merthyr Tydfil at a speed of about 8kph/5mph with a load of ten tons of iron and 70 men. He went bankrupt in 1811 and later spent many years in Peru – where in 1827 he accidentally met Robert Stephenson (who gave him his passage money home).

Trewithen (8km/5m E of Truro) Woodland gardens created over two centuries by the descendants of Thomas Hawkins, who in the mid-18C planted many of the trees which now provide the essential framework. Among them, in the early 20C, George Johnstone added a profusion of shrubs and smaller trees from all over the world – in particular camellias, rhododendrons, magnolias, maples and birches – many of them of considerable rarity. The resulting 12ha/28ac garden is a delight to layman and specialist alike.

trews Gaelic word (older than 'trousers', which comes from the same root) for the breeches worn in Ireland and Scotland. It is now associated in particular with the tight-fitting tartan trousers worn by certain Scottish regiments.

T.Rex see Marc *Bolan.

Trial of the Pyx Annual ceremony, dating back in its present form to the 13C, in which the coin of the realm is tested to ensure that it is up to standard in weight and quality. During the course of the year one coin is taken from every batch produced at the Royal *Mint; these sample coins are brought to Goldsmiths' Hall in London for the Trial (the Pyx is an old name for the chest in which the coins are kept). Sample coins are again selected to be matched and weighed against a standard 'plate', before being assayed for the quality of the metal.

triangular trade The pattern of the *slave trade as carried on from Bristol and Liverpool in the 18C. Ships took metal goods, trinkets and liquor to the west of Africa, where they were exchanged for slaves; these were carried to the West Indies or the southern states of America; their sale financed the purchase of a cargo of rum, sugar or cotton for the third leg of the journey home.

Tribune Political newspaper of the left, supporting the Labour party but independent of it. It was founded in 1937 as the 'tribune of the people', announcing that its purpose was to smash capitalism. It has mellowed. In the 1992 parliament the so-called Tribune group of MPs formed the centre left of the party. The paper's editorial line was by then pro-Europe and also (slightly ahead of the Labour party) in favour of proportional representation.

Trident The name by which the three-engined de Havilland 121 jet became known. Manufactured by Hawker Siddeley, it was introduced by BEA in 1964 and was the main aircraft on Britain's domestic and European air routes for some 20 years.

Trident see *nuclear submarines.

trifle Dessert of pieces of sponge cake, mixed with jam and fruit and sometimes jelly, soaked in wine or sherry and topped with custard and whipped cream. The present meaning goes back to the 18C. Before that a trifle was a clotted-cream dish, in origin connected with the *fool.

trig point see *Ordnance Survey.

Trilby (1894) Romantic novel by George *du Maurier, set in the bohemian Paris which he had known as an art student. Trilby O'Ferrall (unusually tall but 'wistful and sweet') is an artist's model who becomes a successful singer when coached by her hypnotic guru, Svengali. But she grows so dependent on him that when he dies, poor Trilby has not long to live.

The word 'trilby' for a soft felt hat, with a brim and an indented crown, derives from one of du Maurier's illustrations in the book, showing Little Billee wearing just such a hat as he tells a dog, Tray, how much he loves Tray's mistress, Alice.

Corporal **Trim** see *Tristram Shandy*.

Tommy **Trinder** (1909–89) Cockney stand-up comic, in the music-hall tradition, who also became popular in films – one of which used his catch phrase as its title (*You Lucky People* 1954). He was compere of *Sunday Night at the London Palladium*, from its start on television in 1955 until 1958; and he had a famous link with Fulham Football Club, of which he was chairman (1955–76) and then president until his death.

Trinidad and Tobago Member of the *Commonwealth since 1962, consisting of the two most southerly of the Caribbean islands, just off the coast of Venezuela. Both were visited by Columbus in 1498. Trinidad was a Spanish colony from 1532 until ceded to Britain in 1802. Tobago was first settled by the Dutch in 1632 and was successively occupied by different European nations; it was eventually ceded to Britain by France in 1814, and was amalgamated administratively with Trinidad in 1888. Trinidad, like *Jamaica, seceded from the *West Indies Federation in 1962, opting for immediate independence.

Trinity House (London EC3) Corporation responsible for lighthouses, light vessels, buoys and beacons around the coasts of England and Wales. Its origins are obscure (it may have been a guild of mariners similar to the *City Livery Companies), but successive royal charters of the 16C gave the Guild of Trinity (known by the middle of that century as Trinity House) the right to place 'sea-marks'. The present Trinity House, on Tower Hill, was built for the corporation in 1792–4; almost entirely demolished in the blitz, it has been rebuilt behind the original façade.

The equivalent responsibility for the coastal waters of Scotland rests with the Commissioners of Northern Lighthouses, based in Edinburgh.

triple crown Term current from the 19C for victory in all three *classic English races open to colts – the 2,000 Guineas, the Derby and the St Leger. It is now used also for contests between the four countries of the British Isles (England, Ireland, Scotland, Wales), being achieved when any one of them beats the other three. Best known in relation to rugby union, a triple crown of this kind is competed for also in hockey and various other team sports.

Tristan and Iseult Though now widely thought of as a German legend, because of the fame of Wagner's *Tristan und Isolde*, the story is Celtic in origin. The Irish princess Iseult is to be married to King Mark of Cornwall. Her mother prepares a love potion for her and her husband to drink on their wedding night, but on the journey from Ireland it is accidentally drunk by Iseult and Tristan, Mark's nephew who has been sent to collect her – with predictable results, though this is only the beginning of a complex story. Developed from the 12C by poets in

The first trilby, worn by Little Billee as he bares his soul to the attentive Tray in du Maurier's own illustration.

France and Germany (most notably by Gottfried von Strassburg, Wagner's source), the story was later included by Malory in his *Morte d'Arthur. In his version the young Cornish hero is called Sir Tristram but is described as a prince of *Lyonesse, a birthplace acquired on his continental travels – which is how that name became attached to a supposed lost land stretching beyond Cornwall.

Tristan da Cunha Volcanic island in the south Atlantic, named after the Portuguese sailor who discovered it in 1506. Britain established a small garrison in 1816 which was withdrawn in 1817, but Corporal William Glass was given permission to remain with his wife and two children. Others later joined them and their descendants formed a settled community. An eruption in 1961 of the island's volcano, thought to be extinct, caused the islanders to be evacuated to Britain. Most of them returned in 1963. Since 1938 Tristan da Cunha has been administered as a dependency of *St Helena.

Tristram Shandy (*The Life and Opinions of Tristram Shandy, Gentleman* 1760–7) Novel by Laurence *Sterne – the most deliberately chaotic and, for those who find their way into it, one of the most endearing books in the English language. It is Tristram's autobiography and it begins, unusually but logically, with the scene at his conception. Thereafter, in a series of looping digressions,

Peter Green, head man of Tristan da Cunha, recorded in the 1870s by the photographer on the Challenger *expedition.*

Sterne brings vividly to life the hero's learned father; his good-hearted Uncle Toby (who shares with his servant, Corporal Trim, an obsession with military fortifications); the neighbouring Widow Wadman, who has sexual designs on Toby; the grossly incompetent family physician, Dr Slop; and Yorick, the opinionated parson in whom Sterne partly satirized himself. The book ends only because Sterne wrote no more of it. It is in many ways two centuries ahead of its time, resembling a modern demolition of the very idea of the novel (itself then a relatively new form).

Triumph Coventry-based firm which manufactured *motorcycles from 1902 and was one of the best-known names in the industry from the 1920s to the 1960s. It went bankrupt in 1983 but the name was bought by John Bloor, who set up a new design and manufacturing complex at Hinckley in Leicestershire. The first six new Triumph models went on sale in 1991.

The original Coventry firm began making cars in 1923 and this part of the business collapsed in 1939. After the war the name was revived by the Standard Motor Company, which soon had a great success with two series – the TR sports cars, beginning with the TR2 in 1953, and the Triumph Herald, introduced in 1959. Standard-Triumph was taken over by Leyland Motors in 1961 and became in 1968 a part of *British Leyland.

Trog Pseudonym of Wally Fawkes (b. 1924), best known as the creator of *Flook but also a widely published political cartoonist, with a very effective clarity both of idea and execution. As a sideline Fawkes is an accomplished jazz player, on the clarinet and soprano saxophone; he was a founder member in 1948 of Humphrey *Lyttelton's band.

Troilus and Cressida (*c.*1602) Tragedy by *Shakespeare, for which Chaucer's *Troilus and Criseyde* was merely one of the sources. Where Chaucer concentrated on the lovers, Shakespeare broadens the story to bring in the main scenes and the leading figures of the Trojan War itself. The heroes are for the most part presented as cynical and unscrupulous (Hector being the noble exception), and a running commentary on the nature of war is provided by the twisted and bitter Thersites. Pandarus is here more of the bustling unctuous bawd, giving the word 'pander' (in use from soon after Chaucer's time) its lasting flavour.

Troilus and Criseyde (*c.*1387) *Chaucer's longest single poem, and his most perfect, in which Boccaccio's story of a doomed pair of young Trojan lovers is retold with far greater subtlety and tenderness. Troilus falls in love with Criseyde and she with him after she has been gently coaxed by her uncle, Pandarus, into accepting his advances. All is well until Criseyde is sent to the Greek camp to join her father, an astronomer. There she is seduced by a Greek, Diomede. Troilus, discovering this, flings himself in despair into the battle and dies.

Anthony **Trollope** (1815–82) The outstanding English novelist of clerical and political intrigue. Until 1867 he had a successful full-time career in the Post Office (he is credited with inventing the pillar box), and he wrote his numerous books by a prodigious feat of self-discipline, rising at 5.30 each day and writing 2500 words before breakfast. He conceived the idea for his Barsetshire series when visiting Salisbury Cathedral (he was on a tour to inspect rural postal deliveries), and it got off to a magnificent start with The *Warden (1855) and *Barchester Towers (1857). After four more in the series, ending with The Last Chronicle of Barset (1866–7), he moved from the cathedral precinct to Westminster for the six Palliser novels (1864–80). These centre on the ambitions of Plantagenet Palliser and his wife Glencora; he eventually becomes duke of Omnium and prime minister. In 1868 Trollope himself stood unsuccessfully for parliament as a Liberal candidate. *The Way We Live Now* (1874–5), his longest and most ambitious novel, is a satirical panorama of a society which worships wealth.

The intrigues of the typical Trollope plot are ideal for a television serial, as was suggested in *The Pallisers* (BBC 1975) and then triumphantly proved in *The Barchester Chronicles* (BBC 1982, consisting of *The Warden* and *Barchester Towers*).

Troon see *Royal Troon.

Trooping the Colour Annual ceremony on *Horse Guards Parade, held on the *Queen's Birthday. Parading the colour (the regimental standard or flag) before the troops was a necessary military exercise in earlier centuries, so that soldiers could recognize their rallying point on the field of battle. The ceremony was first used in 1748 to mark the monarch's official birthday, and it has been an annual event since the early 19C. All seven regiments of the *Household Division take part, but the colour being trooped invariably belongs to a battalion of one of the five regiments of Foot Guards. The Queen comes from Buckingham Palace along the Mall to Horse Guards (each year from 1969 to 1986 she rode the same black mare, Burmese). She takes the salute at a colourful and famously precise military parade, before returning to the palace where she and her family watch from the balcony a fly-past by the RAF.

Trossachs see Loch *Katrine.

The **Troubles** A term used of various periods of unrest in *Ireland (including even the uprising of 1641) but applied in particular to the *Anglo-Irish War of 1919–21; this had been preceded by the *Easter Rising of 1916 and the formation of the *IRA in January 1919. The name has been revived for the new period of *terrorism in *Northern Ireland which began in the late 1960s.

Troubleshooter (BBC from 1990) Series of television business documentaries which have won large audiences thanks to the personality of the presenter, Sir John Harvey-Jones (b. 1924) – an amiably eccentric figure with hair dangling about his ears and a famous line in flashy ties. The format involves him storming into some troubled business (his own career included the chairmanship of ICI), then ferreting cheerfully around the works and telling the bosses in no uncertain terms what they are doing wrong.

Trowbridge (23,000 in 1981) Administrative centre of Wiltshire, prosperous originally from the weaving of woollen cloth and now a market town with a variety of light industries.

troy weight Medieval system of weights, deriving from Troyes in France. It was replaced by the *imperial system in 1878 except in the field of jewels and precious metals, where it is still used. The smallest unit is a grain; there are 24 grains in a pennyweight, 20 pennyweights in a troy ounce, and 12 ounces in a troy pound.

Trucial States Seven emirates in the Persian Gulf which by a series of treaties (or truces, hence the name) became from 1920 steadily more involved with Britain. Broadly speaking the early truces committed them to giving up piracy in return for British protection. Eventually, by a treaty of 1892, Britain undertook to deal with all the foreign affairs of the seven (Abu Dhabi, Dubai, Sharjah, Ajman, Umm al Qaiwain, Ras al Khaimah and Fujairah). The group became fully independent as the United Arab Emirates in 1971, though authority within each emirate remains with the hereditary sheikh.

Truck Act (1831) The first of several acts of parliament preventing the abuse by which factory owners paid their workers with 'truck' (goods instead of cash) or with tokens to be used in a specified shop (the 'tommy shop'). The acts made it illegal to pay wages for manual labour in anything other than currency of the realm. An amendment of 1960 allowed for payment by cheque or into a bank account.

Fred **Trueman** (b. 1931) Fast bowler who played for Yorkshire (1949–68) and England (1952–65). A flamboyant and controversial figure both on and off the pitch, he was the first bowler to take 300 wickets in Test *cricket (in 1964); his eventual total of 307 lasted as the England record until 1983, when it was improved on by Bob *Willis. Trueman's most famous achievement was probably his 5 wickets in a row for no runs against Australia at Headingley in 1961.

Trumpet Voluntary Title given by Henry *Wood to his transcription for organ, brass and kettledrums of a harpsichord piece by Jeremiah Clarke (*c.*1674–1707). The original work, published in 1700 with the name *The Prince of Denmark's March*, either imitated a trumpet or was itself transcribed from a piece for trumpet and wind ensemble.

Truro (16,000 in 1981) Cathedral town and administrative centre of Cornwall, on the river Truro. Situated a long way inland, it has access to the sea down its own river into the Fal and its estuary; the town's medieval prosperity came from exporting the products of the Cornish tin mines. The diocese of Truro was established in 1877. The Victorian Gothic cathedral was built 1880–1910 to the design of John Loughborough Pearson (1817–97). The Royal Institution of Cornwall was founded as early as 1818; its collections, mainly of local history but including also European paintings and drawings, are on public display.

trust status The status of *National Health Service hospitals which have been allowed to become 'self-governing trusts' under the terms of the National Health Service and Community Care Act of 1990. In December of that year 57 hospitals were selected for trust status, followed by another 99 in April 1992. A further 128 were granted trust status from April 1993, with a declared government policy of about 90% of all hospitals becoming self-governing before the end of 1994.

The best-known hospital in the original group of 57 was *Guy's, acting jointly with Lewisham. It was presented at the time as something of a flagship for the scheme, with a projected surplus of £1.5m for its first year of independence. But Guy's became the target of much adverse criticism four months later; on achieving independence in April 1991, it produced a revised estimate of a £6m deficit and announced 600 job cuts.

'truth universally acknowledged' see *Pride and Prejudice*.

'Try sparrowhawks, ma'am' see *Crystal Palace.

TSB (Trustee Savings Bank) One of the *clearing banks, formed as a public limited company in 1986. It derived from the many trustee savings banks which in the mid-19C looked after the savings of the working class, particularly in the industrial cities. The first was set up in 1810 by the Rev. Henry Duncan as the Parish Savings Bank at Ruthwell, in Dumfriesshire; by 1820 there were nearly 500 such banks around the country. Legislation was passed in 1817 requiring the trustees to invest the money in government bonds, and it subsequently became established that the interest should be tax free – two features adopted later in the century for the government's own *National Savings. Over the years the trustee savings banks tended to merge; in 1976 they were reduced from 70 to four (one each for England, Wales, Scotland and Northern Ireland). It was the Central Board of these four which moved the emphasis from savings to full-scale banking and so created the present TSB.

TT (Tourist Trophy Races) Britain's leading *motorcycle race meeting, held in the Isle of Man since 1907, now always in early June. The race track is 60km/37m of ordinary roads from Douglas to Ramsey and back, and it includes a mountain climb on Snaefell (an exceptionally dangerous course, it had by 1992 claimed 160 lives). The link between the Isle of Man and racing dates back to 1904. In that year the British parliament refused to enable cars to compete on the roads by putting a temporary ban on other traffic; but the *Tynwald agreed to do so, and motor racing remained a regular sporting fixture on the island until 1953. It was the success with cars in 1904 that prompted the first TT races three years later. The most prestigious event, the Senior TT, was long dominated by a British motorbike, Norton, with 15 wins out of the 17 races between 1931 and 1954; and in 1992 Norton finally ended an unbroken run of Japanese victories which had lasted since 1973.

tube The name in London for that part of the *underground railway system running in deep tunnels.

TUC (Trades Union Congress) National association representing the interests of its affiliated *trade unions. It was founded in 1868, and holds an annual congress (normally for four days starting on the first Monday in September). In 1957 it moved into new headquarters, Congress House (London WC1), built as a memorial to trade unionists who died in the two world wars. Recent general secretaries have been George Woodcock (1960–9), Vic Feather (1969–73), Len Murray (1973–84) and Norman Willis since 1984. The Scottish TUC, in Glasgow, was founded in 1897 and holds its annual congress in April.

Tudor A term which can be applied to any period of the Tudor dynasty (1485–1603) but is most often used by architectural historians for the years before 1558, the later part being known as *Elizabethan. The distinction, seen in secular buildings, is that Tudor detail is still essentially *Gothic – for example the stone windows set in the redbrick walls of Wolsey's *Hampton Court – whereas in the showy buildings of Elizabeth's reign (dubbed in recent years 'prodigy houses') the themes of the Renaissance begin to arrive from continental Europe.

Antony **Tudor** (1908–87) Dancer and choreographer who pioneered a form of ballet interpreting psychological states. His first works were for Ballet Rambert (*The Planets* 1934, *Jardin aux Lilas* 1936, *Dark Elegies* 1937), but during the war he went as choreographer to the newly formed American Ballet Theatre in New York. It was for them that he created *Pillar of Fire* (1942) and *Romeo and Juliet* (1943, to music by Delius). He danced in most of his own ballets.

Winners of the Senior TT since World War II		
1947	Harold Daniell	Norton
1948	Artie Bell	Norton
1949	Harold Daniell	Norton
1950	Geoff Duke	Norton
1951	Geoff Duke	Norton
1952	Reg Armstrong	Norton
1953	Ray Amm	Norton
1954	Ray Amm	Norton
1955	Geoff Duke	Gilera
1956	John Surtees	MV Agusta
1957	Bob McIntyre	Gilera
1958	John Surtees	MV Agusta
1959	John Surtees	MV Agusta
1960	John Surtees	MV Agusta
1961	Mike Hailwood	Norton
1962	Gary Hocking	MV Agusta
1963	Mike Hailwood	MV Agusta
1964	Mike Hailwood	MV Agusta
1965	Mike Hailwood	MV Agusta
1966	Mike Hailwood	Honda
1967	Mike Hailwood	Honda
1968	Giacomo Agostini	MV Agusta
1969	Giacomo Agostini	MV Agusta
1970	Giacomo Agostini	MV Agusta
1971	Giacomo Agostini	MV Agusta
1972	Giacomo Agostini	MV Agusta
1973	Jack Findlay	Suzuki
1974	Phil Carpenter	Yamaha
1975	Mick Grant	Kawasaki
1976	Tom Herron	Yamaha
1977	Phil Read	Suzuki
1978	Tom Herron	Suzuki
1979	Mike Hailwood	Suzuki
1980	Graeme Crosby	Suzuki
1981	Mick Grant	Suzuki
1982	Norman Brown	Suzuki
1983	Rob McElnea	Suzuki
1984	Rob McElnea	Suzuki
1985	Joey Dunlop	Honda
1986	Roger Burnett	Honda
1987	Joey Dunlop	Honda
1988	Joey Dunlop	Honda
1989	Steve Hislop	Honda
1990	Carl Fogarty	Honda
1991	Steve Hislop	Honda
1992	Steve Hislop	Norton

House of Tudor (1485–1603) The descendants on the throne of England of Owen Tudor (*c*.1400–1461), a Welsh adventurer in the service of Henry V who after the king's death married his widow, Catherine, the daughter of the king of France. Their eldest son, Edmund (*c*.1430–56) married Margaret Beaufort, who was descended from *John of Gaunt, duke of Lancaster, and so had a distant claim to the throne (see the *royal house). Her son, Henry VII, used this claim to overthrow the house of York at the end of the *Wars of the Roses. He then married a Yorkist princess (Elizabeth, daughter of Edward IV), and so was able to claim that their descendants reunited the two rival lines. The Tudor monarchs, after Henry VII himself, were Henry VIII, Edward VI, Mary I and Elizabeth I. They were followed by the house of *Stuart.

Tudor rose see *Wars of the Roses.

Tudor Trust (London W11) One of Britain's largest charitable foundations, set up by Godfrey Mitchell (1891–1982) – the creator of the firm of George

Wimpey, which he bought in 1919 as a small insolvent business and transformed into a major construction company. The Tudor Trust specializes in charitable projects connected with social welfare.

Jethro **Tull** (1674–1741) Inventor of the seed drill, which he used from 1701 on his father's farm near Wallingford in Oxfordshire. The machine, pulled by a horse, sowed three rows of seed at a time. The great advantage over scattering the seed corn was that it became possible to weed between the rows, for which Tull also invented a mechanical hoe. His results were so good that he published his method in *The New Horse-Hoeing Husbandry* (1731), an important early step in the mechanization of agriculture.

Royal **Tunbridge ware** Wooden objects, usually small, decorated with patterns of coloured mosaic. The method was developed in the late 17C in *Tunbridge Wells and in nearby Tonbridge, and was still in use in the early 20C. Sticks of wood of different colours, several inches long, were glued together so that their ends formed a pattern or image in mosaic. The completed bundle was then sliced into thin layers of veneer for application to boxes, trays, picture frames, or even occasionally cabinets and tables.

Royal **Tunbridge Wells** (45,000 in 1981) Resort town in Kent, in hilly countryside, which became fashionable after a chalybeate spring was discovered in 1606. Its heyday was after the Restoration; the church of King Charles the Martyr with its magnificent plaster ceiling dates from that period (1676–8). From 1735 Beau *Nash was in charge here as well as in Bath. The colonnaded street leading to the spring (where the water can still be drunk) is called the Pantiles because it was paved with tiles in 1700. The museum has a good collection of the local *Tunbridge ware. In 1909 Edward VII allowed the town to become Royal Tunbridge Wells, but the prefix is rarely used.

'turbulent priest' see Thomas *Becket.

Turf Club (London SW1) A *club, founded in 1868, which traditionally has an uncommonly large number of dukes among the members. The name reflects the fact that it is a favourite club for owners of race horses.

Alan **Turing** (1912–54) Mathematician who was an important pioneer in the theory of the computer. He made an early contribution with his 1937 paper *On Computable Numbers*, and during the war played a leading role in deciphering German codes at Bletchley Park in Buckinghamshire – particularly in the highly successful Ultra programme, unscrambling German radio messages transmitted in Enigma. Subsequently Turing supervised the construction of two computers known by acronyms – ACE (Automatic Computing Agency) at the National Physical Laboratory in Teddington, and MADAM (Manchester Automatic Digital Machine) at the university of Manchester. His early death was a tragic result of British law at that time; he committed suicide after being prosecuted for *homosexual activities.

Turks and Caicos Islands Group in the West Indies, lying south of the Bahamas. Used by Bermudans for salt-panning from the 17C, the islands have been administered at different periods from Bermuda, the Bahamas and Jamaica. Since 1962 they have been a British crown colony.

Turnberry Golf course on the west coast of Scotland, in Strathclyde, which was first laid out in about 1905 but was dug up in both world wars to provide a military air-field. Of the two courses reconstructed after World War II, the Ailsa is the one which has been selected twice (1977 and 1986) as the location for the *Open.

Eva **Turner** (1892–1990, DBE 1962) Dramatic soprano of great power who spent much of her career with the Chicago opera company but was also a star of the Covent Garden seasons from 1928 to 1948. She was known in particular for her performances in Verdi and Wagner, but the single part most strongly associated with her was Puccini's Turandot; she first sang it in Italy in 1926, only months after the premiere at La Scala, and Franco Alfano (the composer who had completed the work after Puccini's death) was said to consider her the ideal performer for the part.

J.M.W. Turner (Joseph Mallord William Turner, 1775–1851) Landscape painter of great originality in his use of light and colour. Son of a London barber, he entered the *Royal Academy schools when he was 14 and became a full academician at the exceptionally young age of 27. He first made his name supplying publishers with watercolours of *picturesque scenes from around the country, which were then turned by others into romantic topographical prints. This work established his life-long pattern of constant travelling and sketching. He later published his own choice of his best work in printed form – the famous *Liber Studiorum* (Latin for 'book of studies'), consisting of 70 landscapes issued from 1807 to 1819 in groups of five (each of them an etching with mezzotint). He frequently journeyed abroad, as well as round Britain, his favourite sources of inspiration being Venice and the mountain scenery of Switzerland.

Turner's watercolours, which in his early days were in a detailed topographical style, steadily became more impressionistic during his long career; and the same pattern prevailed in his oils. His early works show him inspired by Dutch seascapes of the 17C; he then set himself to rival the classical manner of Claude, with shimmering effects of sunlight on water (Turner gave two paintings in this vein to the National Gallery on condition that they hang beside his two favourite Claudes, which they have done ever since); and he finally progressed to his dazzling use of almost abstract colour, with the details of the landscape only hinted at in a blaze of light. This was the style which

Turner applying his customary last-minute touches of magic on varnishing day: painting by Samuel Parrott, c.1846.

Constable described as painting 'with tinted steam'. It was said that Turner often added tiny but crucial touches on varnishing day, the very last moment before the opening of the Royal Academy's annual exhibition, even choosing his colours to upstage neighbouring pictures. His paintings prefigured two later movements in art. The Impressionists were struck by his treatment of light (*Monet and *Pissarro saw his work in London in 1870), and the Abstract Expressionists of the mid-20c were excited by his free use of colour.

Two of his best-known paintings are in the National Gallery (*The *Fighting Téméraire*, *Rain, Steam and Speed*), and there is an interesting collection of his work at *Petworth, which became almost a second home in the 1830s. But the place to see Turner is in the *Tate, which houses the Turner Bequest – about 300 oil paintings and some 19,000 watercolours and drawings which came to the nation after his death. He left the finished oil paintings with the proviso that a gallery should be provided to house them. This was finally achieved with the opening of the Tate's Clore Gallery in 1987.

Turner Prize Established by the Tate Gallery in 1984 in the hope of achieving the level of public attention for modern art which the Booker prize had won for new fiction. The task has proved difficult, as the contest is inevitably less focused – rewarding an 'outstanding recent contribution' to art instead of a book widely available in any bookshop. From 1991 an age limit was introduced, with the prize (by then £20,000) restricted to artists under 50. The work of a short list of four is exhibited in the Tate each November before the winner is announced.

Dick **Turpin** (1706–39) The best known of the 18c highwaymen, working mainly round London but eventually hanged in York. The details of his legend – his horse Black Bess, his gallantry, his ride non-stop from London to York – were inventions of the 19c, when he was a popular hero of the *penny dreadfuls.

Madame **Tussaud's** see *Madame Tussaud's.

Tutankhamen see Howard *Carter.

Dorothy **Tutin** (b. 1931) Actress whose career has been in the mainstream of serious drama, performing frequently with the Royal Shakespeare Company and the National Theatre. On television she has been best known for the 13-part series *South Riding* (1974), set in Yorkshire in the 1930s.

Tuvalu Republic and member of the *Commonwealth since independence in 1978, known previously as the Ellice Islands and consisting of nine coral atolls in the Pacific (with a population of only about 9000). In 1892 they were made of the protectorate of the Gilbert and Ellice Islands (the Gilbert Islands became independent as *Kiribati).

TV-am The company providing breakfast programmes nationwide until 1992 on ITV. The franchise was granted in 1980 to a consortium headed by five well-known presenters (Anna Ford, David Frost, Robert Kee, Michael Parkinson and Angela Rippon), but with the exception of David Frost they were all eased out soon after transmission began in 1983, when the expected viewing figures did not materialize. A move down market from the level that the original group had promised, together with the appeal to children of a puppet rodent, Roland Rat, saved the company from early collapse. It later became extremely profitable, but lost its franchise in 1991 (see *television). The hi-tech studios, with exposed girders and tubes in bright colours, were among the first buildings by Terry *Farrell to win attention.

Twickenham's main contribution to architectural history: early Gothic Revival at Strawberry Hill (engraving, 1774).

TV Times Originally the programme-listing magazine of the commercial *television companies (ITV), appearing in a national format for its promotional stories but with individual listings for each region. Its BBC rival was the *Radio Times. Both magazines have since 1991 carried listings of all available programmes.

tweed Woollen twill cloth much used for jackets and suits, usually of a rough texture and particularly associated with Scotland. The word first appears in the mid-19C and the traditional explanation (not entirely convincing) is that a clerk in the London firm of James Lock accidentally transcribed the Scottish 'tweel' (for twill) as tweed, and that the name stuck because much of the cloth was made in the region of the river Tweed.

Tweed River in southern Scotland, 156km/97m long, which for much of its course forms the border between Scotland and England before entering the North Sea at Berwick. Not far from its mouth it is crossed by Britain's oldest suspension bridge, the *Union Chain Bridge.

Tweedledum and Tweedledee Two nursery-rhyme characters who are about to fight over a rattle when they are frightened out of it by a crow. They are now best known from their appearance, illustrated by Tenniel, in *Through the Looking-Glass, but they were familiar figures long before that. In 1725 a poet and diarist, John Byrom, compared two composers, Handel and Bononcini, to this indistinguishable pair of puny rivals.

'Twelfth' see *grouse and Battle of the *Boyne.

Twelfth Night, or What You Will (c.1601) Comedy by *Shakespeare, possibly written for court festivities on 6 January 1601, the twelfth night of *Christmas. The main plot is one of romantic misunderstandings between Orsino, duke of Illyria, who is in love with Olivia, who is in love with the page Cesario, who is in fact Viola in male disguise, whose love for Orsino completes the unhappy triangle. The arrival of Viola's identical twin, Sebastian, complicates matters further. The play contains superb lyric poetry, starting with Orsino's opening line: 'If music be the food of love, play on.'

The sub-plot, busy with the schemes of Olivia's courtiers, introduces three of Shakespeare's best-known comic characters: her uncle Sir Toby Belch, a hard-drinking knight in the Falstaff mould; her self-important steward, Malvolio, who is persuaded that she loves him; and the effete Sir Andrew Aguecheek.

Twelve Days of Christmas Secular *carol, with traditional words and tune, in which the full period of a medieval *Christmas is enlivened by the singer's true love sending him or her a crescendo of gifts – from a partridge in a pear tree on the first day to twelve lords a-leaping on the last.

Twickenham (18km/11m W of central London) District on the north bank of the river Thames, part of the Greater London borough of Richmond-upon-Thames. It became a fashionable area in the 18C after Alexander *Pope moved there; later in the century Horace Walpole built *Strawberry Hill nearby. Today it is more widely known for Twickenham stadium, England's national ground and the international centre for *rugby union football (headquarters of the Rugby Football Union).

Twiggy (stage name of Lesley Hornby, b. 1949) The leading British model of the second half of the 1960s. When she was 15 she met Justin de Villeneuve (real name Johnny Davies), who became her boyfriend and manager; it was a friend of his who began calling her, because she was extremely thin, first Sticks, then Twigs and finally Twiggy. A full-page photograph in the *Daily Express* in 1966 was the start of her fame, and soon the waif-like boyish look (very short hair, with the stick-like legs often accentuated by a miniskirt) was in all the magazines. She also became a well-known character, with her Cockney accent and humour. Her leading role in the 1971 film of The *Boy Friend was the beginning of a second career in cinema and television. In 1988 she married Leigh Lawson and she has performed since then as Twiggy Lawson.

Twinkle, twinkle, little star Nursery rhyme published in 1806 and unusual in having been written specifically as a poem for children (by Jane Taylor, 1783–1824) rather than emerging from obscure popular antecedents. The cliché of the star compared to a diamond in the sky provoked the Mad Hatter's famous parody in *Alice in Wonderland* ('Twinkle, twinkle, little bat'), where the bat is likened to a tea-tray in the sky.

The Two Gentlemen of Verona (c.1593) Comedy by *Shakespeare about the tortuous path of love between two gentlemen from Verona, Valentine and Proteus, and their respective maidens, Silvia and Julia. All ends happily after much confusion, brought about by disguises and temporary betrayals. Meanwhile Proteus's servant Launce, troubled by his ill-natured dog Crab, provides a level of more clownish humour.

Two Lovely Black Eyes see Charles *Coborn.

two-minute silence see *Armistice.

'two nations' see *Disraeli.

The Two Noble Kinsmen (c.1613) A tragi-comedy which may be partly by Shakespeare. It was not included in the *First Folio, but the title page of its first edition (1634) attributes it jointly to Shakespeare and John Fletcher (see *Beaumont and Fletcher). It contains passages which stylistically could be Shakespeare's. The plot is based loosely on Chaucer's 'Knight's Tale', one of *The Canterbury Tales*.

two-party system The arrangement that has prevailed from the start of British democracy. Deriving from the original emergence of two parties, the *Tories and Whigs, it has been perpetuated by the electoral system known as 'first past the post', in which a candidate is elected for a parliamentary constituency if he or she gets even a single vote more than the nearest rival. All the votes cast for other candidates are in effect wasted, and a party coming second in many seats can be almost unrepresented in the House of Commons (see the *Alliance and the *SNP for examples, and *general election for the balance of votes and seats since 1945). This has led in recent years to increasing pressure for *proportional representation. The two-party system is reflected in the rectangular shape of the chamber in the House of Commons, with one side for each party.

The Two Ronnies (BBC TV 1971–86) Comedy series of sketches featuring Ronnie *Barker and Ronnie *Corbett, making much of the eternal comic contrast between the large and laid-back (Barker) and the small and energetic (Corbett), and with scripts much inclined to naughty innuendo.

2,000 Guineas Flat race for 3-year-old colts and fillies (but usually entered only by colts), run over 1.6km/1m at *Newmarket on a Saturday in late April or early May, two days after the *1,000 Guineas. It was first run in 1809.

Tyburn The area now known as Marble Arch. From the late 14c it was London's main place of public execution, attracting large crowds in a holiday mood. The gallows (often referred to as Tyburn Tree) stood where Edgware Road joins Oxford Street. They were moved in 1783 to a position outside *Newgate prison.

'Tyger! Tyger! burning bright' see entry on *Songs of Experience*.

Wat **Tyler** (d. 1381) Leader of the Kentish rebels in the *Peasants' Revolt. His men took Canterbury on 10 June 1381 and the Tower of London four days later. At a meeting with Richard II at Smithfield, Tyler went so far as to demand the confiscation of all church property. During the argument he was wounded by the Lord Mayor of London, who later had him beheaded.

Kenneth **Tynan** (1927–80) The most influential British theatre critic of the mid-20c, reviewing in the *Observer* at a time when there was a wave of exciting new drama. His whole-hearted response to John Osborne's first play was typically arrresting: 'I doubt if I could love anyone who did not wish to see *Look Back in Anger*.' In 1963 he became literary manager of the new National Theatre and was largely responsible for its exciting repertoire in those early years. Always a professional *enfant terrible*, he deliberately provoked outrage in 1965 by becoming the first person to say 'fuck' on British television; similar in its

effect, but more rewarding commercially, was the sexually liberated revue *Oh! Calcutta!* which he devised and produced in 1969.

William **Tyndale** see *Bible in English.

Tyne River in northeast England, only 48km/30m in length from where the North Tyne (rising in Northumberland near the Scottish border) and the South Tyne (rising in Cumberland, in the Pennines) join at Hexham to flow together, as the Tyne, past Newcastle and into the North Sea between Tynemouth and Southshields. For more than half its length it is the artery of the industrial area of Tyneside.

Tyne and Wear (1,095,000 in 1991) *Metropolitan county in northeast England, encompassing the estuaries of the rivers Tyne and Wear and consisting of five *districts – Gateshead, Newcastle-upon-Tyne, North Tyneside, South Tyneside and Sunderland.

Tyneside Britain's earliest industrial district, in northeast England, along both banks of the river Tyne from west of Newcastle to the coast. Its advantages were plentiful coal and easy transport by water to the sea, so that by the early 17c it was supplying most of London's fuel. The region has suffered greatly since the mid-20c from the decline of both mining and heavy industry. It has been since 1974 part of the metropolitan county of Tyne and

Industry on the Tyne: scene near Newcastle's bridges in a mural by William Bell Scott at Wallington Hall, c.1855.

Wear. Those born on Tyneside are known colloquially as *Geordies.

Tynwald (in full the Tynwald Court) Parliament of the *Isle of Man, probably the oldest surviving legislative body in the world. It has been in existence since the Viking domination of the island in the 10–13C. The upper house, the Legislative Council, is appointed; the lower one, the House of Keys, has been elected since 1866 (by male suffrage only until 1881, when the Tynwald became the first body in the world to extend the franchise to women). As in the parliament at Westminster, bills must receive the *royal assent before they become law; but in the Isle of Man they must also be read out on July 5 on the Tynwald Hill, a circular mound at St John's near the centre of the island. Bills are declaimed there both in English and in Manx *Gaelic (by now virtually the only use on the island of the old Celtic language). The Tynwald normally meets in the Legislative Buildings (1894) in Douglas, having moved in 1869 from Castletown.

Tyrone One of the six *counties of Northern Ireland, but since 1973 no longer an administrative unit in *local government.

Ken **Tyrrell** (b. 1924) Motor racing manager and constructor closely linked with the career of Jackie *Stewart. Tyrrell formed a partnership in 1968 with the French aerospace company Matra, putting a Ford-Cosworth engine in a Matra chassis. It was for this team that Stewart won the 1969 world championship. By the end of the 1970 season Tyrrell was using the Ford engine in a car of

Engraving of Tyburn in the Newgate Calendar *of 1773, with the condemned man already in his shroud.*

his own design – a combination which brought him the constructors' championship in 1971 and gave Stewart his 1971 and 1973 world titles.

U

U and non-U A pernicious distinction, typical of the English obsession with class, between idioms and customs which are supposedly upper-class (U) or not (non-U), with the implication that the latter are incorrect. The terms were first used in 1954 by A.S.C. Ross as convenient abbreviations in a serious context; he was writing in a philological journal about class differences in language and pronunciation. Popularized by Nancy *Mitford (in *Noblesse Oblige* 1956), they had wide currency in the 1960s and 1970s.

UB40 The document number of the card issued by the Department of Employment to anyone registered as unemployed. Price concessions offered in Britain often include 'UB40s' along with the young or the old.

UB40 Reggae group formed in Birmingham in 1978 by Ali Campbell (b. 1959, lead vocals and guitar) and his brother Robin (b. 1954, lead guitar and vocals) with half a dozen others. Their name, the *UB40 of the unemployed, implies a political stance which has been reflected in much of their music; *One in Ten* (1981), for example, stated the level of unemployment. Two singles (*Red Red Wine* 1983, *I Got You Babe* 1985 with Chrissie Hynde) and one album (*Labour of Love* 1983) have reached the top of the charts.

UCAS (Universities and Colleges Admissions Service, Cheltenham) The body which in 1993 replaced UCCA (Universities' Central Council on Admissions) and PCAS (Polytechnics Central Admissions System), after the polytechnics had been transformed in 1992 into *universities. UCAS coordinates the applications of students for places in universities and colleges; it is usual to apply before taking A levels, and offers of places are dependent on specified grades being achieved. Results in the *exams are turned into an aggregate score of points in the competition for places: A level grades bring 10 points for an A, 8 for B, 6 for C, 4 for D and 2 for E; the same grades score half, from 5 down to 1, for AS levels. All British universities participate, except the *Open University which has its own admissions system.

UCATT (Union of Construction, Allied Trades and Technicians) The trade union for workers in the building trades, formed in 1970 by merging the Amalgamated Society of Woodworkers, the Amalgamated Society of Painters and Decorators and the Amalgamated Union of Building Trade Workers. The titles of the three constituent parts reveal that the amalgamation of 1970 was the last stage in a long process of smaller unions gradually coming together.

UCCA see *UCAS.

UCW (Union of Communications Workers) The trade union representing workers in the Post Office and in British Telecom. Known until 1980 as the UPW (Union of Post Office Workers), it was founded in 1920 after long struggles to establish a union within the country's first *nationalized concern. Until then successive attempts at staff combination (beginning with a Telegraphists Association in Manchester in 1871) had all been defeated by the Post Office.

UDA see *terrorism.

UDI see *Zimbabwe.

UDM (Union of Democratic Mineworkers) Independent trade union formed in 1985 by miners in Nottinghamshire and South Derbyshire as a result of the recent *miners' strike. The majority in these areas had continued working because of the refusal of the *NUM leadership to hold a ballot. The only British union to have 'democratic' in its name, the UDM's stance repudiates the past autocracy of union barons. It includes among its aims the replacement of the NUM as the union representing all miners; not surprisingly it is not (in 1992) affiliated to the *TUC.

UDR see *Ulster Defence Regiment.

UEFA Cup Contest organized by the Union of European Football Associations between leading teams which have not qualified for the *European Cup or the *European Cup-Winners' Cup. It was first held in 1958 and has been annual since 1960, but it has only been known as the UEFA Cup since 1971. It was originally the Intercities Fairs Cup and from 1966 the European Fairs Cup.

UFF see *terrorism.

Uffington White Horse (32km/20m SW of Oxford) One of the most authentic of England's hillside chalk figures. The stylized image of a horse, 114m/374ft long, is believed to have been cut in the turf by Britons in the 1st century BC (it is close to the ancient track known as the *Ridgeway), though local tradition has long maintained that Alfred the Great created it in celebration of his victory over the Danes somewhere nearby in the Battle of Ashdown (871).

Uganda Land-locked republic in east central Africa, a member of the *Commonwealth since 1962. The first European to reach the area was *Speke in 1862. In the following decades rival missionaries, imperialists and traders competed for influence in the territory, which became a

British protectorate through a piecemeal succession of treaties with local rulers (the first was with the kabaka of Buganda in 1894). The country became independent in 1962 with Milton Obote (b. 1924) as the first prime minister.

Ujiji see Henry Morton *Stanley.

UK see *United Kingdom.

Ullswater The most northeasterly of the lakes in the *Lake District, and the second largest lake in England (12km/7.5m long, exceeded only by *Windermere). The enclosing fells and crags become steadily grander with each twist on the way south towards the lake's head at Patterdale.

Ulster The most northerly of the ancient kingdoms and provinces of *Ireland, and often used now as an alternative name for *Northern Ireland. Conquered by the English in the 13C and turned into a feudal earldom, it had passed by 1461 to the crown (by descent and marriage). It was divided in the 16C into nine counties, of which six (the *six counties) remained in the United Kingdom in 1921, while the other three (Cavan, Donegal and Monaghan) became the province of Ulster in the republic of Ireland.

Ulster Defence Association see *terrorism.

Ulster Defence Regiment (UDR) Reserve force of soldiers, many of them part-time, established in 1970 in response to the upsurge of *terrorism in *Northern Ireland. Its predominantly Protestant membership (usually more than 95%) has made it controversial in a crisis caused by sectarian hostilities. In 1992 the UDR's nine battalions were merged – under the government's *Options for Change – with the two battalions of the Royal Irish Rangers, together forming a new Royal Irish Regiment. The UDR thus became for the first time a part of the regular British army, though battalions serving in Northern Ireland will still include part-time soldiers. The Royal Irish Rangers was about 25% Roman Catholic, with some 6% of its soldiers from south of the border. The Royal Irish Regiment (a name first used in 1684) will continue the policy of recruiting from the whole of Ireland.

Ulster Democratic Unionist Party see *Unionist.

Ulster Folk and Transport Museum (13km/8m NE of Belfast) The park of Cultra Manor, at Holywood, is the site of some 25 buildings of different kinds from Northern Ireland, re-erected here and appropriately furnished. Custom-built galleries also develop the theme of local crafts and domestic life. The Folk Museum, established in 1958, was combined in 1967 with the Belfast Transport Museum – adding to the collection a wide range of items used or made locally, from sledges and horse-drawn vehicles to aircraft.

Ulster Museum see *Belfast.

Ulster Orchestra The province's only professional orchestra, formed in 1966 and originally administered by the Arts Council of Northern Ireland. It made its first record in 1979 to celebrate the centenary of the birth of Ulster-born Hamilton Harty. In recent years it has established a reputation for its performances of the French repertoire under Yan Pascal Tortelier (principal conductor 1989–92).

Ulster Unionist see *Unionist.

Ulster Volunteer Force see *terrorism.

Ultra see Alan *Turing.

''umblest person going' see **David Copperfield*.

'the unacceptable face of capitalism' Phrase used by the prime minister, Edward Heath, in the House of Commons in 1973, in answer to a question about a former Tory cabinet minister. Duncan Sandys had received £130,000 in compensation for giving up a consultancy with Lonrho and had avoided British tax, quite legally, by paying it into a Cayman Islands account.

Uncle Mac see **Children's Hour*.

Uncle Tom Cobbleigh see **Widdicombe Fair*.

'unconscionable time dying' see *Charles II.

underground The abbreviation commonly used in London for the underground railway. The Metropolitan Railway, engineered by John *Fowler and opened in 1863, was the first of its kind in the world. It ran 6.5km/4m from Paddington to Farringdon Street and was later extended to become the District and Circle lines. These were built close to the surface and were covered over only where necessary. They could therefore use steam engines. The next development was deep tunnelling for a railway using only electric trains, in what became known as the 'tube'. The world's first stretch of underground electric railway opened in 1890 between the City and Stockwell (it is incorporated in today's Northern line). By 1907 the basis of the present system was in place, but it was owned by several private companies. They came together as part of London Transport in 1933. In recent decades there have been two major accidents on London's underground: 42 people were killed when a train crashed into the end of a cul de sac at Moorgate in 1975, and 31 died as a result of a fire at King's Cross in 1987. The only other cities in Britain to have underground systems are Glasgow, Liverpool and Newcastle.

Under Milk Wood (1953) A 'play for voices' by Dylan *Thomas which has become a perennial favourite in the theatre. The complete play was performed in October 1953, with Dylan Thomas himself as the First Voice, at the Poetry Center in New York; the first British production was on the BBC Third Programme early in 1954, with Richard Burton in Thomas's part. The play follows a single day, from one night to the next, in the small imaginary Welsh town of Llaregyb (in the early drafts Llareggub, or 'bugger all' in reverse), which had been inspired by Laugharne, where Thomas lived, along the coast from Swansea. The characters include Captain Cat, an old sea dog with rich memories; Mrs Ogmore-Pritchard, strict widow of two husbands, Ogmore (linoleum) and Pritchard (bookmaker); Mr Pugh, dreaming of how best to poison Mrs Pugh; Polly Garter, no better than she should be; beautiful beautiful Gossamer Beynon, butcher's daughter and schoolmistress; Organ Morgan, who thinks only of Bach and Palestrina; the Rev. Eli Jenkins, local historian; and many others.

Rory **Underwood** (b. 1963) Outstanding rugby union player, a wing three-quarter, with a record number of caps for England (56 by the end of 1992) and of tries scored (35). By profession he is a flight lieutenant in the RAF. In 1989, against Fiji at Twickenham, he became only the third man in the history of the game to score five tries in an international (the other two occasions were in 1887 and 1907). Against South Africa in 1992, again at

The unemployed in a 1910 Labour party poster, by Gerald Pryse, which was reissued in the 1920s.

Twickenham, he and his younger brother Tony were the first two brothers to play together for England since Harold and Arthur Wheatley in 1938.

unemployment The peaks of unemployment in 20C Britain have been in the *Depression of the 1930s and during the 1980s and early 1990s. In the recent period, high unemployment has resulted partly from government attempts to make Britain's economy more competitive, by withdrawing support from ailing industries and by pursuing a single-minded policy to reduce *inflation. During the same period the size of the total workforce has also grown (the increase has been almost entirely in

female employment), though many of the new jobs are part time. In October 1992 male unemployment, at 13.4%, reached its highest level since World War II; and early in 1993 two sensitive figures were passed, a total of 3 million unemployed and of 1 million long-term unemployed (those out of work for a year or more).

The figures should in fact be higher by comparison with those of previous decades. Since 1980 as many as 30 changes have been made in the method of counting the unemployed – a subject of controversy since most of the innovations had the effect of lowering the total. Among the more substantial have been: a new method of recording unemployed men aged over 60, reducing the unemployment level by some 162,000 in 1983; an adjustment for previous over-recording, bringing the number down by 50,000 in 1986; and the removal of unemployed school-leavers from the figures when all under 18 were offered places on training schemes.

unemployment benefit The official term for what is more often called the dole, paid to the unemployed by the *Employment Service and collected weekly from a local Unemployment Benefit office. To qualify for unemployment benefit, a worker must have made a certain level of *national insurance payments during the previous two years; benefit is paid for a maximum of one year in any period of unemployment (beyond that time the unemployed person has to rely on other social security benefits, in particular *income support). The high levels of *unemployment in recent years and the consequent drain on public funds have led to some political pressure for benefits to be paid for only six months, and for stricter insistence that anyone drawing unemployment benefit must show evidence of attempting to find work.

Britain was the first country to introduce unemployment benefit, with *Lloyd George's National Insurance Act of 1911. At that time it was limited to specific industries, but a succession of acts between the wars gradually extended its application until it became general with the National Insurance Act of 1946.

HMS *Unicorn* see *Dundee.

Act of **Uniformity** see *Clarendon Code.

unilateral disarmament The policy that Britain should give up its nuclear weapons without any corresponding concessions from other nuclear powers. It has been a

Numbers unemployed, in millions

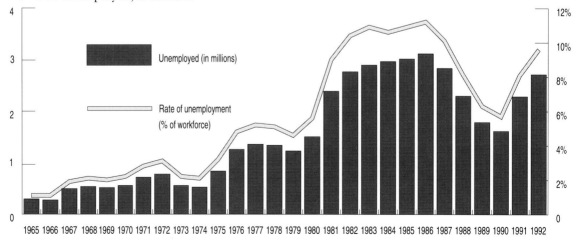

The figures are no more than approximate as a historical comparison, since the basis of calculation has been changed several times: see *unemployment.
Source: Annual Abstract of Statistics *(see *Central Statistical Office).*

much debated theme in the Labour party since the 1950s, with many members deeply committed to the concept; a resolution to adopt unilateral disarmament in 1957 prompted Aneurin Bevan's famous phrase that it would send a British foreign secretary 'naked into the conference chamber'. Hugh Gaitskell continued the struggle against it, and it was never the policy of the Labour governments of the 1960s and 1970s. But in 1980 the party conference passed a resolution that the next Labour government should renounce nuclear weapons unilaterally and close all US nuclear bases on British soil. The leader at the time, Michael Foot, was a member of *CND, as was his successor, Neil Kinnock. It became increasingly clear in the following years that this policy was an electoral liability, and in 1991 Kinnock let his membership of CND lapse. The party's election manifesto of 1992 proposed to retain Britain's Trident missiles as a bargaining pawn in nuclear disarmament negotiations (and thus not go naked into the conference chamber).

Unilever One of the largest companies in Britain, formed in 1930 by a merger between Lever Brothers (founded by Lord *Leverhulme) and the Dutch firm Margarine Unie (the latter providing the first half of the new joint name). Their interests were complementary, because they had been competitors for the same raw materials; the British firm needed oils and fats for soap, the Dutch firm used them for margarine. The resulting company, with headquarters in London and Rotterdam, expanded its two original concerns into a very wide range of cosmetic products and packaged foods and drink. Many of the best-known brand names in any British shopping basket are from the Unilever stable: Sunlight, Lux and Pears among soaps; Persil, Surf and Sun detergents; the Elizabeth Arden and Pond's cosmetics; Flora, Stork and Blue Band margarines; the Brooke Bond, Bird's Eye and Walls ranges of foods.

Acts of **Union** The acts of parliament which merged England with first Scotland (1707) and then Ireland (1800, effective from 1 Jan. 1801) to form a single *United Kingdom. The acts put an end to the parliaments in Edinburgh and Dublin, bringing MPs from Scotland and Ireland to the House of Commons in Westminster. In spite of minority opposition represented by the *SNP, the union with Scotland still holds. But the union with Ireland provoked the long 19C political crisis over *Home Rule and came to an end in 1921, except in *Northern Ireland.

Union Chain Bridge The first suspension bridge large enough to carry wheeled traffic, built over the river *Tweed about 8km/5m from its mouth in 1820 and still surviving. The engineer was Samuel Brown (1776–1852), who had patented improved methods for linking chain cables and for constructing bridges. His advances made possible the better-known examples by *Telford over the Menai Strait and at Conwy.

Unionist Term first used in British politics in 1886, when the Liberal party split over *Home Rule. Those opposing it, and in favour therefore of maintaining the Act of *Union of 1800, formed a coalition with the Conservatives and later merged with them. The Conservatives today are still officially called the Conservative and Unionist party.

In Northern Ireland, where the issue remains topical, the Ulster Unionists are an independent political party. On most topics their stance is what elsewhere would be called Conservative, and in the House of Commons they usually vote with the Conservatives. Their leader in the early 1990s is James *Molyneaux. The Ulster Democratic Unionist party is a splinter group headed by Ian *Paisley.

Union Jack (or Union Flag) The flag of the *United Kingdom since the *Union with Ireland in 1801. It is made up of the red cross of St George on a white ground (for England), the white diagonal cross or saltire of St Andrew on a blue ground (Scotland) and the red saltire of St Patrick on a white ground (Ireland). A simpler Union flag had been in use previously, combining just the English and Scottish elements. 'Jack' is the nautical term for a flag.

Union of the Crowns Phrase used to describe the constitutional change of 1603, when James VI of Scotland became *James I of England (uniting the two crowns on one head), as distinct from the Union of the Parliaments in 1707, effected by the Act of *Union.

unions see *trade unions.

Unison The largest of the *super-unions, formed in 1993 by a merger of three public service unions, NALGO, NUPE and COHSE. Its membership amounted at that time to about 1.4 million.

The largest of its constituent parts was NALGO (National and Local Government Officers Association), formed in 1905 as a *friendly society for local government officials. By 1920 it had developed into a *trade union, though it did not affiliate to the *TUC until 1965. With the process of *nationalization after World War II, NALGO members found themselves working in the gas and electricity industries, in the National Health Service, and in many other concerns newly run by the *civil service; the union grew accordingly, and in the early 1990s had about 750,000 members.

Unionist poster, part of a successful campaign of opposition to Asquith's Home Rule proposals of 1912.

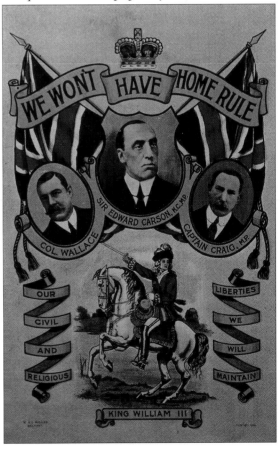

NUPE (National Union of Public Employees) had its origins in the late 19C among office workers of the London County Council. And COHSE (Confederation of Health Service Employees) evolved within the National Health Service.

United Arab Emirates see *Trucial States.

United Free Church see *Free Church of Scotland.

United Kingdom (land area 240,939sq.km/93,027sq.m, population 56.5 million in 1991) Abbreviation for the United Kingdom of Great Britain and Northern Ireland, and the name given to the country in all official contexts. The term seems to have developed informally during the 18C after the union of England and Scotland in 1707. It became official when the Act of *Union of 1800 brought in Ireland, the enlarged country being called the United Kingdom of Great Britain and Ireland. This full name was adjusted to its present form when the southern part of Ireland became independent in 1921. The British themselves refer to their country more informally as Britain.

United Nations (UN) International organization which after World War II replaced the *League of Nations. It had its origins in the *Atlantic Charter and in a Declaration of the United Nations; this was signed in 1942 by 26 states, setting out their aims in opposing the Axis powers, Germany, Italy and Japan. In 1945 the Charter of the United Nations was signed by 51 states, considered the founder members of the UN.

New York was selected as the location for the new organization, and in 1951 the UN moved into handsome new buildings on a riverside location in east Manhattan. Of its various constituent parts the two most important are the General Assembly, in which every member nation (178 in 1993) has an equal vote; and the Security Council, a group of 15 nations responsible for the UN's peace-keeping role around the world. Ten of the nations on the Security Council are temporary members, elected by the General Assembly for a two-year term, and five are permanent. The five permanent members, unchanged from the start, are those nations which took the leading role in the defeat of Fascism in World War II – China, France, the Russian Federation (previously USSR), the UK and USA.

The UN has played a more active peace-keeping role than the League of Nations, with major military engagements from the Korean War to the Gulf War and with peace-keeping forces establishing a long-term presence in disputed areas such as Cyprus.

United Reformed Church Formed in 1972 by the merger of the *Presbyterian Church of England and the *Congregational Church in England and Wales. In the early 1990s the United Reformed Church had something over 125,000 members (for numbers attending services see *Christians).

*The **Universe*** The Roman Catholic newspaper with the largest circulation in Britain. It was founded in 1860, is based in Manchester and is published weekly.

universities The oldest universities in England, *Oxford and *Cambridge, date from the 12–13C; by the end of the 15C Scotland had three, at *St Andrews, *Glasgow and *Aberdeen; *Edinburgh followed in 1582. Thereafter no new universities were founded, and very few new colleges within the existing establishments, until *University College in London in 1826, followed immediately by *King's. Later in the 19C many of the great industrial towns established their own local university colleges. At first the students sat the exams of an existing university,

usually London, but the colleges gradually established themselves as independent degree-giving bodies, becoming known collectively as the *redbrick universities.

A great many new universities were founded in the period after World War II, and they were joined in 1967 by 30 polytechnics with a more practical orientation towards industry, commerce and the professions. The polytechnics represented both a rationalization and an expansion of the existing non-university range of colleges of higher education, and they resulted largely from the Robbins Report of 1963 on higher education (chaired by Lionel Robbins). The original intention was that the polytechnics should remain different in kind from universities. But in 1992 they ceased, on paper, to exist; they were given university status and re-emerged under new names.

There are two exceptional cases among Britain's universities. One is the nationwide *Open University, in which the students study part-time and at home. The other is the country's only private or independent university, receiving no public grant; this is the university of Buckingham, which admitted its first undergraduates in 1976.

University Challenge (Granada TV 1962–87) TV quiz for teams of university students, based on a similar American game (*College Bowl*) and presented throughout its long British run by Bamber Gascoigne (b. 1935). Its catch phrase became 'your starter for ten', introducing a starter question to be raced for by all eight contestants individually.

University College, London The first university college established in England outside Oxford and Cambridge. It was set up in 1826 for *Nonconformists because only Anglicans were admitted to the two old universities (*King's College in London was the immediate Anglican response). The main building in Gower Street (1827–9) is by *Wilkins, and has Jeremy *Bentham as its oldest resident. The college was in existence before *London University, of which it is now a part. University College Hospital, a teaching hospital attached to the college from the 1830s, was in the early 1990s threatened with closure in a government revision of London's hospital needs.

Tomb of the **Unknown Warrior** A marble slab in the nave of *Westminster Abbey, which is the first detail to confront a visitor entering by the west door. It marks the grave in which the Unknown Warrior was buried on 11 November 1920, the second anniversary of the *Armistice. In an inspired symbolic act, a body was selected at random from the unmarked graves in British war cemeteries. The coffin was draped in the so-called Padre's Flag (a Union Jack which had been used at the front and which now hangs nearby in the Abbey), and was brought to London with great ceremony. The earth surrounding it, beneath its slab of Belgian marble, had also been brought from the battlefields. The inscription, in capital letters, begins: 'Beneath this stone rests the body of a British warrior unknown by name or rank brought from France to lie among the most illustrious of the land and buried here on Armistice Day.'

Unst Island in the *Shetlands, the most northerly inhabited part of the British Isles. The actual northernmost point is Muckle Flugga, a rock with a lighthouse about a mile off the coast.

Up-Helly-Aa A festivity held on the last Tuesday of January at *Lerwick, in the Shetlands. Originally a fire festival signalling the end of Yule, the north European pagan festivity which became absorbed in *Christmas, it was adapted in 1889 to emphasize the islands' Viking past; in that year, for the first time, the object to be burnt was a Viking longship. Surrounded by 'guizers' clad in Viking costume and carrying blazing torches, the wheeled ship moves in procession to the centre of the town, where the torches are tossed into it to start an almighty blaze and a long night of revelry.

Uppark (18km/11m NW of Chichester) Four-square redbrick house, built in the early 1690s and famous for its delicate rococo interiors of the mid-18C, many of them decorated until recently with the original fabrics and papers. In 1989 the upper floors were gutted by fire and the entire house damaged by water; but nearly all the contents were saved and the state rooms are being restored down to the smallest detail. Uppark was the first step in the lively extramarital career of Emma *Hamilton; and the mother of H.G. *Wells was housekeeper here during his boyhood.

Upstairs Downstairs (London Weekend 1970–5) Television series making excellent period drama out of the rigid class divisions upstairs and downstairs in a rich London household, that of the Bellamy family, in the first decades of the 20C. The downstairs characters became the most firmly established – in particular Hudson the butler (played by Gordon Jackson), Mrs Bridges the housekeeper (Angela Baddeley) and Rose, one of the housemaids (Jean Marsh, who was also partly responsible for the concept of the series).

'up with which' The idiocy of the rule once taught to children, that an English sentence should not end with a preposition, is said to have been exposed by Winston Churchill with the splendid example, 'This is the sort of English up with which I will not put'.

Uranus see *Herschel.

Urban Development Corporations The bodies carrying out ten major *enterprise zone schemes in areas of urban decay. Plans for the first two, London Docklands and Merseyside, were announced in September 1979, anticipating the launch of enterprise zones in 1981; the others (Black Country, Bristol, Central Manchester, Leeds, Sheffield, Teesside, Trafford Park, Tyne and Wear) were added from the mid-1980s. The corporations were closely involved in the building of offices and factories, and they therefore suffered from getting into their stride just before the major collapse of the property market in the early 1990s. The outstanding crisis was that of *Canary Wharf. Critics also argued that the corporations had soaked up far too much scarce public money (the equivalent of £2bn in grants and tax concessions by 1992) for a few prestige projects.

Urban Regeneration Agency see *inner cities.

Uriah Heep see *David Copperfield*.

USDAW (Union of Shop, Distributive and Allied Workers) The trade union for workers in the retail trade, with its origins in the Manchester and District Co-Operative Employees Association, founded in 1891; Manchester is still the union's headquarters. Shop workers were then among the most exploited of employees (in that same year, 1891, a bill was defeated in parliament which had proposed to limit the work of women and children in shops to 74 hours a week) and they remain today among the lowest paid. USDAW was formed in 1947 by the amalgamation of the Manchester-based union and a smaller rival.

Usher Hall Edinburgh's main concert hall, built with £100,000 donated for the purpose in 1896 by Andrew Usher (1826–98). The opening concert, on 4 August 1914, was attended by George V even though this was the day on which Britain had declared war on Germany. Seating nearly 3000 people, the hall has been used until recently only for classical music; but it now opens its doors to a wider range of entertainment, including pop concerts, causing local indignation in some circles.

Peter **Ustinov** (b. 1921, kt 1990) The most multi-talented of entertainers, as author, dramatist, actor, mimic and raconteur. Born in London of French-speaking Russian parents, his ability with languages and accents has always been an important theme in his comedy – as in his first major success as a dramatist, *The Love of Four Colonels* (1951), in which the four colonels were of different nationalities. He is best known as a witty character actor in films, in a career including Nero in *Quo Vadis* (1951) and Hercule Poirot in *Death on the Nile* (1978).

Uther Pendragon see King *Arthur.

Utilitarianism see Jeremy *Bentham.

utility Term during and after World War II (in use 1941–51) for clothes and household goods made to a government-approved standard, designed to make the most of scarce resources. They were identified by a utility mark – two circles with a wedge removed from each, and the figures 41 representing the year of its introduction.

Utopia (1516) Work of political and social speculation, written in Latin by Thomas *More. It describes a happy island, discovered by a traveller, in which the people live communally without private property, a national system of education is offered to boys and girls alike, and there is complete religious toleration. The name Utopia was coined by More and is based on two similar-sounding Greek phrases, one implying 'good place' and the other 'no place'.

Treaty of **Utrecht** see War of the *Spanish Succession.

UVF see *terrorism.

V

V1 and **V2** Pilotless bombs developed by Germany at the end of World War II. The initial V stood for *Vergeltungswaffe* (reprisal weapon). The V1, more commonly known in Britain as the doodle-bug or buzz-bomb, was literally a flying bomb – a cylinder with small wings carrying about 900kg/2000lb of explosives and powered by a ramjet engine at the tail. From June 1944 to March 1945 more than 2000 were launched against Britain. The V2 (about 1300 launched from September 1944 to March 1945) was the first modern rocket, a ballistic missile with a payload about the same as the V1, which left the earth's atmosphere in its trajectory and re-entered faster than the speed of sound. It was the basis of postwar rocket development in both the USA and the USSR.

V&A see *Victoria and Albert Museum.

vaccination see Edward *Jenner.

St Valentine's Day (Feb. 14) The lovers' day, deriving ultimately from a Roman fertility festival, the Lupercalia, which was held on February 15. St Valentine's was the nearest available Christian feast day; it is said to commemorate two early Christian martyrs, both called Valentine, but history records no trace of either. In medieval France and England St Valentine's day already had its modern connotation – explained at the time as deriving from the example of the birds, which begin at this season to look for a mate. The two main features were a partner for the day chosen by lot (a flirtatious game surviving until quite recent times) and a love message or 'valentine' sent anonymously. The latter led to a profusion of elaborately printed cards in the mid-19C. Valentine cards were eclipsed later in the century by the success of the *Christmas card, but they have become widely popular again in the second half of the 20C. A modern Valentine custom is the sending of exotic messages of love through the personal columns of newspapers.

Ninette de **Valois** see *de Valois.

Value Added Tax see *VAT.

John **Vanbrugh** (1664–1726, kt 1714) English dramatist and architect. He was the grandson of a Flemish merchant who had settled in London. After an early career as a soldier, he made his name in 1696 with his first comedy, *The Relapse*. This was followed by *The Provok'd Wife* (1697). Vanbrugh's lusty depiction of a dissolute aristocratic world contributed to the middle-class backlash which dominated the London theatre of the early 18C.

He began yet another career when he was invited, in about 1699, to design *Castle Howard. His lack of any architectural training was made up for by Nicholas

*Hawksmoor, officially his assistant but in effect probably more of a partner. Together they went on to win the biggest commission of the age, *Blenheim Palace, in which they achieved the outstanding example of English *baroque. *Seaton Delaval, a later project, was entirely Vanbrugh's own; so also was the house which he built for himself in the last years of his life in Greenwich, known as Vanbrugh Castle and still surviving. The scale of Blenheim prompted the satirical epitaph proposed for him by Abel Evans (1679–1737):

> Lie heavy on him, Earth! for he
> Laid many heavy loads on thee!

George **Vancouver** (1757–98) Explorer who joined the navy at 13 and whose first journeys were with Captain *Cook (1772–5, 1776–80). In 1791 he was put in command of an expedition to explore the northwest coast of America and to discover whether there was a channel leading through from the Pacific to Hudson Bay. In a three-year voyage he made detailed surveys of the entire Pacific coast of the United States and Canada, proving that any northwest passage between the Atlantic and Pacific must pass north of Alaska. He was the first to circumnavigate the large Canadian island now named after him.

Vanity Fair see *Pilgrim's Progress*.

Vanity Fair Weekly magazine 'of political, social and literary wares', published in London 1868–1912. It made a feature of its 'cartoons printed in chromolithography' and from 1873 these were mainly by *Spy. The title has subsequently been used for other magazines both in Britain and the USA.

Vanity Fair, a novel without a hero (1848) Novel by *Thackeray, with his own illustrations, published in monthly parts from January 1847. It is a social panorama of the early 19C, following the ups and downs of two school friends from Miss Pinkerton's academy for young ladies in Chiswick. Amelia Sedley is virtuous and rich (daughter of a merchant) while Rebecca Sharp, known as Becky, is scheming and poor (orphaned child of an artist and a dancer). Both see fortunes come and go – whether through marriage, disinheritance, financial disaster or secret admirers – and both accompany their soldier husbands to Belgium just before Waterloo. Only the death in the battle of Amelia's husband (George Osborne) prevents his elopement with Becky; and the discovery of this betrayal, years later, enables Amelia to shed her sentimental memories and to marry a more suitable long-standing admirer, William Dobbin. Meanwhile Becky has been living a suprisingly prosperous existence in London. The explanation emerges when her husband (Rawdon Crawley) discovers that she has a seedy old admirer, the rich Lord

Steyne. Rejected by both, Becky acquires her final fortune after persuading a dying admirer to take out a life-insurance policy in her favour. She settles down to charitable good works in fashionable Bath and Cheltenham.

Vanuatu Island group in the Pacific, west of Fiji, which has been a republic and a member of the *Commonwealth since 1980. The islands were named the New Hebrides by Captain Cook in 1774. By the late 19C both Britain and France had established strong interests in the area, resulting in a condominium (from 1906) in which the islands were jointly administered by the two countries. Independence was achieved under the new name of Vanuatu in 1980.

Harry **Vardon** (1870–1937) One of the greatest of all British golfers, whose six victories in the Open (1896, 98, 99, 1903, 11, 14) remain still an unbeaten record. He also won the US Open in 1900 before defending his 1899 British title, thus holding the two major trophies at the same time – a feat not repeated by a British player until *Jacklin 70 years later. His name is also widely known to golfers because of the popular Vardon grip (the little finger of the right hand overlapping the index finger of the left), but in fact it is wrongly attributed to him and was in use before his time.

Variety Club of Great Britain Show-business charity raising money for children through star-studded events organized by the members, known as Barkers. The British club, formed in 1949, is 'Tent no. 36' of a worldwide Variety Club launched in 1927 in the USA.

VAT (Value Added Tax) A tax operating in all *EC countries, in use in Britain since 1973 (when it replaced *purchase tax and *selective employment tax). It is levied on invoices at every stage in manufacturing, retailing or the providing of services (ostensibly as a tax on the value added at each stage). However the tax paid out to suppliers or consultants is claimed back as an expense, so the entire burden is carried by the end consumer. It is therefore in effect a sales tax, which skilfully avoids the need for difficult guidelines as to what constitutes a sale but generates instead a great deal of accountancy and paperwork. The levels of the tax vary within the EC. In Britain it was introduced at 10%; it was then for a while 8% on some commodities and 12.5% on others; in 1979 it became a flat 15%; and since 1991 it has been 17.5%. Many categories of goods pay no VAT, some of the more important being food, children's clothes, books and newspapers, education, health, insurance, travel and all exports. In the spring budget of 1993 VAT was imposed for the first time on domestic fuel and power, at 8% in 1994–5 and thereafter at the full rate.

Ralph **Vaughan Williams** (1872–1958) Composer with a distinctively English quality, resulting from a double enthusiasm – for music of the Tudor period and for English folk songs, of which he was an avid collector. The former inspired one of his best-known pieces, the *Fantasia on a Theme by Thomas Tallis*. He wrote nine very varied symphonies: the first (*A Sea Symphony* 1910) is a setting for soloists and chorus of poems by Walt Whitman; the second (*A London Symphony* 1914) echoes sounds from the life of the city; and the seventh (*Sinfonia Antartica* 1953) is based on the score which he wrote for the 1948 film *Scott of the Antarctic*. Among his many songs, the cycle *On Wenlock Edge* (1909) is outstanding, setting six poems from Housman's *A Shropshire Lad*. His romance for violin and orchestra, The *Lark Ascending*, is a firmly established concert favourite.

Vauxhall Car company which began production in 1903 in London's Vauxhall district and moved in 1905 to Luton, in Bedfordshire. The Vauxhall company was known before World War I for its expensive models, and in particular for one of the world's first sports cars – the Prince Henry, which later evolved into the Vauxhall 30/98. In 1925 the company was bought by the American firm of General Motors; Vauxhall then moved gradually into the position which it still holds, as one of the chief manufacturers in Britain of a wide range of everyday cars.

Vauxhall Gardens By far the most successful and long-lasting of London's pleasure gardens. They opened in 1660 on the south bank of the Thames (roughly opposite

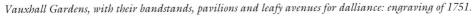

Vauxhall Gardens, with their bandstands, pavilions and leafy avenues for dalliance: engraving of 1751.

where the Tate Gallery now stands on the north bank) and did not finally close until 1859, when the area was developed. Avenues of trees, some well lit for promenading, others darker for assignations, were dotted with pavilions and supper rooms. There was a high level of musical entertainment – *Handel, for example, was a popular favourite and a life-size statue of him was placed in the gardens in 1738 (the first major work by *Roubiliac, it is now in the V&A). There were added excitements such as firework displays and, from the late 18c, ascents by balloon.

VC see *Victoria Cross.

VC10 The main jet in the *BOAC fleet during the 1960s and 1970s, manufactured by *Vickers.

V-E Day (Victory in Europe, 8 May 1945) The official end of *World War II in Europe. Germany's unconditional surrender was signed on May 7 and all hostilities were to cease by midnight on May 8 – the signal, in Churchill's words, 'for the greatest outburst of joy in the history of mankind'. At the centre of Britain's celebrations was a vast crowd in the Mall, jubilantly awaiting the appearance of Churchill with the king and queen on the balcony of Buckingham Palace. In his broadcast on that day Churchill warned of the continued sacrifices needed in the war against Japan. V-J Day (Victory in Japan, 15 Aug. 1945) was a more arbitrary date. The Japanese surrender was offered on August 10 with a proviso about the emperor's status, and it was not formally ratified until September 2.

vehicle registration see *Swansea.

'**Veni, vidi, vici**' (Latin for 'I came, I saw, I conquered') The famously brief account by Julius Caesar of his own military success. Usually believed in Britain to have been said about his conquests here in 55–4 BC, he in fact used the slogan on his triumphal return to Rome after a brief campaign in Turkey in 47 BC. According to *1066 and all that this remark was the cause of the Roman defeat of the Britons.

Michael **Ventris** see *Linear B.

Venus and Adonis see William *Shakespeare.

Verdun see Battles of the *Somme.

Treaty of **Versailles** see *World War I.

Verulamium (St Albans) One of the most prosperous towns of Roman Britain, and the only one to be given the status of *municipium* (a self-governing community, with specific obligations and privileges under Roman law). It was sacked by *Boudicca in AD 60 but rapidly recovered. Excavations have revealed remains of the forum, built some 20 years after Boudicca's encroachment, a theatre and temple, two triumphal arches, and several luxurious houses with mosaics and wall paintings (on show in a museum on the site).

In the early 1990s an exceptionally important discovery was being excavated – a Roman temple complex, built around a Celtic tomb in which a ruler was cremated, surrounded by his most precious possessions and accompanied by human sacrifice. Pottery in the tomb dates it to shortly before AD 50, in the very first years of the *Roman occupation. Archaeologists speculate that the tomb may be that of Adminius, who unlike his brother *Caratacus collaborated with Rome. Four centuries later, after the departure of the Romans, the local religious

centre shifted to a nearby Christian shrine – which developed into *St Albans.

'**Very flat, Norfolk**' see *Norfolk.

vestry see *parish.

veteran cars see *Brighton Run.

The **Vicar of Bray** see *Bray.

The **Vicar of Wakefield** (1766) Novel by Oliver *Goldsmith. The vicar is Dr Charles Primrose, whose good nature is more than matched by his ill fortune. This includes the loss of all his money and the burning down of his house; the seduction and abandonment of his daughter Olivia by the wicked Squire Thornhill, who then plans the same for another daughter, Sophia; and the assault and casting into jail of his son George. After many complications, all ends happily.

le vice anglais (French for 'the English vice') Early 20c term for a masochistic interest in flagellation, said with some justification to be a peculiarly English perversion. The most prominent example was *Swinburne. Victorian pornography abounds in scenes of flagellation; and titillating stories in today's tabloid press, of the naughty vicar variety, frequently include spanking. The origin is often said to be the rituals of birching and caning which until recently were characteristic of English *public schools. Certainly it has been a taste associated mainly with the upper classes.

Vickers Company which has played a major role in Britain's armament and aviation industries. In 1828 Naylor, Hutchinson, Vickers and Co. was established as a steel firm in Sheffield; from it there emerged in 1867 Vickers Sons and Co., which combined its business with *Maxim in 1897 (becoming well known for the Vickers Maxim machine gun). The company's contribution to aviation history has included the Vickers Vimy, in which *Alcock and Brown flew the Atlantic, followed by the *Wellington, *Spitfire, *Viscount and *VC10. The aircraft division was merged in 1960 with two other companies to form the British Aircraft Corporation, which was nationalized in 1977 and became part of *British Aerospace. In 1980 Vickers merged with *Rolls-Royce Motors. The Challenger tank is the best-known Vickers product of recent years in the armaments field.

Vicky Pseudonym of the cartoonist Victor Weisz (1913–66). By birth a Hungarian Jew, he was publishing anti-Nazi cartoons in Berlin in the 1930s and so had a double reason to flee to Britain. He was on the staff of the *News Chronicle* during the war, then moved to the *Daily Mirror*. In the last years of his life, when he and *Low were Britain's leading pair of cartoonists, his work appeared weekly in the *New Statesman* (from 1954) and six days a week in the *Evening Standard* (from 1958).

Victoria (1819–1901) Queen of the United Kingdom from 1837 and empress of India from 1876; only child of Edward, duke of Kent (d. 1820), and Victoria of Saxe-Coburg; married Albert of Saxe-Coburg & Gotha (1840).

Victoria's father, the fourth son of George III, was one of three royal dukes who married hurriedly in 1818, in an attempt to produce an heir to the throne; the death in 1817 of Princess Charlotte, only child of *George IV, had left not a single living legitimate grandchild of George III. Of those three marriages other children were born, senior to Victoria in order of succession, but they died as infants. Victoria was not told that she was heir to

Young Annie Paxton demonstrates the buoyancy of Victoria Amazonica: *wood engraving in the* Illustrated London News *(1849).*

her uncle, *William IV, until she was 12 – the occasion on which she solemnly declared 'I will be good'. She inherited the throne when she was 18, and in the early years of her reign was much influenced by her prime minister, Lord *Melbourne. He was the first of four men in whom she put a deeply emotional trust.

The next, and by far the most important of the four, was her husband, Prince *Albert. The virtues of moral rectitude and hard work, known now as Victorian values, were his rather than hers; and her admiration for his talents and ideas meant that she allowed him a prominent role in British affairs. Their family life (they had nine children) was intensely happy, much of it spent in the two country houses which they built, *Osborne and *Balmoral. Albert's early and sudden death devastated the queen and for her remaining 40 years she dressed as a widow. She next found comfort in the friendship of John Brown, a gillie from Balmoral. From 1864 until his death in 1883 she took him everywhere as her personal servant, in his distinctive Highland dress; she liked his forthright manner (he addressed her as 'woman'), though such informality inevitably led to gossip and jokes about Mrs John Brown.

The last of these intense friendships was with *Disraeli, who first became her prime minister in 1868. The queen shared his commitment to British imperial interests and was delighted in 1876 when he steered through parliament, against considerable opposition, a bill making her empress of India.

Through the marriages of her children Victoria was increasingly the matriarch of Europe, and the great celebrations of the last two decades of her reign (Golden Jubilee 1887, Diamond Jubilee 1897) brought together an astonishing array of interconnecting royal families. At the time of her death there were 37 great-grandchildren alive; in World War I one of her grandsons was the British king, another the German kaiser. Her reign, the longest of any British sovereign, saw the gradual effect of the *Reform Act, introducing what we now mean by *constitutional monarchy. But if the crown had lost much of its political power, it had gained greatly in symbolic stature

as the empire grew and with it Britain's power. Victoria ranks now with Elizabeth I, in public perception, as one of the country's two greatest monarchs.

Victoria amazonica (also called *Victoria Regia*) Giant water lily, named after the queen, which caused a sensation when it first flowered in England. Seeds had been sent from South America to *Kew Gardens, where three germinated in 1849; one was kept at Kew, one sent to nearby Syon and one to Chatsworth, where *Paxton was gardener. That year only Paxton's flowered. In celebration his 7-year-old daughter Annie was placed on one of of the great leaves, dressed as a fairy (though the *Illustrated London News* depicted her in her own clothes). Paxton said later that the light structure but great strength of the leaf had partly inspired the *Crystal Palace. In 1850 the lily flowered also at Kew, where it remains one of the great attractions.

Victoria and Albert Museum (London SW7) Familiarly known now as the V&A, the museum was conceived in the aftermath of the *Great Exhibition and was partly built from the profits. The intention was to improve standards of industrial design by displaying the art and technology of past centuries. Founded in 1852, it moved to its present site in 1857, being known then as the South Kensington Museum. As the collection grew, rapidly and randomly, galleries and wings were added in similar manner. The main building, on Cromwell Road, was designed by Aston *Webb; the foundation stone was laid in 1899 by Queen Victoria, who then gave the museum its present name. The scientific collection was increasingly administered as a separate department, and it 1909 it became independent as the *Science Museum.

The original educational purpose of the V&A is clearly seen in the Cast Court, with plaster casts of famous works of sculpture or relief (including even the massive Trajan's column). But at the same time original masterpieces were being gathered in. The Renaissance sculptures are particularly fine, as is a permanent loan from the royal collection

– the *Raphael cartoons. Splendid oddities such as the *Great Bed of Ware or *Tippoo's Tiger are perennially popular. But the real value and endless fascination of the collection is as the world's largest display of the decorative arts, with extensive coverage of all fields from metalwork to costumes.

The museum's library is the National Art Library. In 1983 the important collection of prints and drawings was rehoused in restored buildings on Exhibition Road – known now as the Henry Cole Wing, in honour of the man who was in charge of the museum in the early years (and who was also earned himself a place in history as the inventor of the *Christmas card). The V&A administers several outposts, including *Apsley House, the *Bethnal Green Museum and the *Theatre Museum.

Victoria Cross (VC) Britain's highest decoration, awarded for heroism in war. Instituted by Queen Victoria in 1856, the crosses are cast from guns captured in the *Crimea. It is awarded only to the armed forces and nursing services (or to civilians under orders from those services). Suspended from a crimson ribbon, the medal consists of a bronze cross with at its centre the royal crown, surmounted by a lion, and the words 'For Valour'.

Victoria Memorial (London SW1) A large sculptural group at the southwest end of the *Mall, in front of Buckingham Palace. It was designed by Thomas Brock (1847–1922) and was unveiled in 1911. Unfashionable in the past, this baroque profusion of white figures (using some 2300 tons of marble) is nevertheless a striking piece of public sculpture. Beneath a gilded figure of Victory, Victoria herself sits massively, staring down the Mall, accompanied by allegorical handmaidens.

Victorian Adjective relating to the reign of Victoria (1837–1901) which is used in many contexts: of morality (stuffy with more than a dash of hypocrisy); of values (self-help with an emphasis on the family); and most commonly of furniture (heavy and plush) and architecture (massive and ornate). Victorian taste was essentially eclectic, scouring the past for ideas and details. The favourite hunting ground was the Middle Ages, in a romantic reaction to the rational 18c which had preferred classical sources. The period therefore saw the climax of the *Gothic Revival, but Victorian architects also made much use of *Romanesque and even borrowed *Renaissance themes. After being reviled for much of the 20c, the detail and excellent craftsmanship of the Victorian style is now greatly appreciated.

Victoria plum Sweet plum first identified in 1840 and named after the young queen.

Victoria Station (London SW1) Terminus which now combines two adjacent stations built in the 1860s, one running trains to Brighton and the other serving Chatham and Dover. It was the Brighton company which built the Grosvenor Hotel in 1860–1. Victoria is now, like *Waterloo, a main commuter terminal for the region south of London.

Victoria Tower see *Houses of Parliament.

HMS **Victory** (2162 tons) Nelson's flagship at *Trafalgar, preserved in the Royal Dockyard at *Portsmouth. The oldest surviving *ship of the line, she was about 150 years afloat before being placed in a dry dock in the 1920s.

Vic-Wells Ballet see *Royal Ballet.

Congress of **Vienna** see *Napoleonic Wars.

Vikings A word meaning sailors or pirates, applied to any of the numerous groups who sailed from Scandinavia in the 9–11c either to plunder or settle. They are also known as Norsemen. Those who came west were mainly from Denmark and Norway, whereas the Swedes marauded east into the Baltic territories and Russia.

The first Viking raid on the British Isles is generally held to be their sacking of the monastery on Lindisfarne in 793. Two years later they attacked an unidentified Irish island (called Rechru in the chronicles). Within the next half century they established kingdoms of their own in much of Ireland, and an invasion by the *Danes in 865 led to their rapid conquest of northeast England.

The other Vikings of great significance in English history were those who invaded northwest France, establishing themselves there as the *Normans.

George **Villiers** see duke of *Buckingham.

Vindolanda see *Hadrian's Wall.

Virago Publishing firm, founded in 1973 by Carmen Callil (b. 1938), which has achieved rapid growth and high esteem by specializing in books by or about women. In addition to new works, a particularly successful venture has been the rediscovery of half forgotten books by leading female authors, reissued under the heading of Virago Modern Classics. The name of the firm was a brilliant piece of feminist public relations. Used in recent times as an abusive term for a shrewish woman, 'virago' was originally applied to a heroic woman or Amazon (the only slight snag is that it means a man-like woman, *vir* being Latin for man). The quintessential virago is Mrs Thatcher, who became leader of the Conservative party in 1975 – the year in which the firm's first book was published.

Virgin Company founded by Richard *Branson in 1970 as a mail-order record retailer. Within two years he had expanded to a shop in Oxford Street and a recording studio in Oxfordshire – where Virgin's first artist, Mike *Oldfield, recorded *Tubular Bells* (1973). Virgin developed into a major record company, with worldwide retailing and publishing interests. In 1992 Branson sold this side of his business to Thorn EMI for £560 million. But in 1993 he returned to rock music with Virgin Radio, Britain's first national commercial pop station.

In 1984 Branson had launched an airline, Virgin Atlantic Airways, and the money from the music business was applied to expanding Virgin Atlantic – already, by 1988, Britain's second long-haul carrier after British Airways. An acrimonious relationship between the giant national airline and its small competitor led to extended litigation which ended, early in 1993, with BA paying Branson substantial damages and admitting to a dirty tricks campaign to deter and sidetrack Virgin's customers. BA's methods had included hacking into the Virgin computer, impersonating Virgin staff on the telephone and contacting Virgin's passengers with false information.

Virgin Islands Group in the northeast Caribbean, visited by Columbus in 1493 and named in honour of St Ursula, supposedly martyred with 11,000 other virgins. The eastern islands form the colony of the British Virgin Islands. The largest of these, Tortola, was captured from the Dutch in 1666. The western islands were a Danish colony until 1917, when they were bought by the USA.

Virgin Queen see *Elizabeth I.

Viroconium (8km/5m SE of Shrewsbury) *Roman town, near the village of Wroxeter, established as a camp in about AD 50. It was unusual in becoming a civilian centre, occupied by the local tribe, when the garrison moved in 88 to Chester. The remains include the Roman baths, and a museum tells the story of the site.

viscount see *peerage.

Viscount The first turboprop civil aircraft, manufactured by *Vickers and put into service by BEA in 1950.

vital statistics see entries on *abortion, *birth rate, *divorce, *infant mortality, *life expectancy, *marriages, *population.

Vitoria see *Peninsular War.

Viyella Trade name for a yarn and a cloth, registered in 1893 by the Hollins family, owners of a mill near Matlock in Derbyshire where the new fabric was made; the mill's strange name, Via Gelia, was adapted to form the word Viyella. The material, a blend of 55% Merino wool and 45% long staple cotton, was the result of lengthy experiments to find a yarn which could be used for both weaving and knitting, while retaining the best qualities of both cotton and wool.

V-J Day see *V-E Day.

Volpone or *the Fox* (1606) Comedy by Ben *Jonson, using a series of character types based on animals to satirize grasping materialism. Volpone (the fox) pretends to be dying so as to extract gifts from people who believe they are his heir, for each is told so by his accomplice Mosca (the fly). A lawyer, Voltore (the vulture), proves all too willing to break the law; a feeble old man, Corbaccio (the crow), is happy to disinherit his son; and the self-righteous Corvino (the raven) even offers his wife to satisfy Volpone's needs. A sub-plot introduces a ludicrous English traveller and his pretentious bluestocking of a wife, Sir Politic and Lady Would-Be. Morality requires that the tricksters are unmasked, bringing punishment on themselves and public humiliation to their victims.

fluid volume The *imperial system has yielded to the metric in some areas (litres of petrol at filling stations),

Wyndham Lewis (centre, with hat) and fellow Vorticists in 1915: painting by William Roberts (on Lewis's right).

Measurements of volume		
Imperial		*Metric*
1 fluid ounce	=	0.0284 litre
(5 fluid ounces) **quarter pint**	=	0.142 litre
half pint	=	0.284 litre
0.88 pint	=	**half litre**
1 pint	=	0.568 litre
1.76 pints	=	**1 litre**
(2 pints) **1 quart**	=	1.136 litres
(4 pints) **half gallon**	=	2.272 litres
(8 pints) **1 gallon**	=	4.544 litres

Note: the US gallon is 17% smaller than the imperial gallon
0.83 imperial gallons = 1 US gallon 1 imperial gallon= 1.20 US gallon

while prevailing strongly in others (pints of beer in a pub). The smallest unit in the imperial system is the fluid ounce: there are 20 fluid ounces in a pint, 2 pints in a quart, and 4 quarts (or 8 pints) in a gallon.

Volunteer Reserve Forces Grouping which brings under central control the volunteer reserves of the army, navy and air force. It comprises the *Territorial Army, the *Royal Naval Reserve, the Royal Naval Auxiliary Service, the Royal Marines Reserve, the Royal Auxiliary Air Force and the Royal Air Force Volunteer Reserve.

Vorticism Art movement launched in 1914 by Wyndham Lewis (1882–1957) and others, including *Epstein. The Vorticists used the techniques of Cubism and Futurism to achieve a deliberately violent clash of angular forms; their magazine was appropriately entitled *Blast*.

Charles **Voysey** (1857–1941) Architect and designer, an exponent of the *Arts and Crafts movement. His houses were often in the simple style which he considered traditionally English, with strongly delineated roofs and chimneys above low white walls. His fabrics and wallpapers were in the tradition of William *Morris, but often with a more delicate touch.

V-sign (victory sign) One of the trademarks during World War II of Winston Churchill, who held out the first two fingers of his right hand in a V for Victory with the palm towards the crowd (the same gesture with the palm inwards and a flick of the fingers is a traditional symbol of contempt and provocation). The opening bar of Beethoven's 5th symphony also became a V-sign; having the same rhythm as the letter V in the morse code (. . . _), it was used by the BBC from 1941 as the identifying signal for its radio transmissions to occupied Europe.

VSO (Voluntary Service Overseas, London SW15) Aid organization set up in 1958 to give school-leavers a challenging year in a developing country before going to university. During the 1960s the emphasis shifted to sending graduates whose particular skills were needed, and today the operation is limited to trained people, usually in their thirties, who spend two years abroad. Their wages are paid at the appropriate local level by the host country – usually a member of the *Commonwealth, for reasons of the shared language. Medicine, building and business are the three areas in which volunteers are most in demand, and there are about 1000 of them abroad at any one time.

WAAF see *WRAF

Waddesdon Manor (42km/26m NE of Oxford) Renaissance-style château, built 1874–89 for Baron Ferdinand de Rothschild by a French architect (Gabriel-Hippolyte Destailleur) to house a rich profusion of paintings and objects, which still cram to bursting this museum of a house. French art of the 18c is the central theme, but there is much else. The baron left his exceptional medieval and Renaissance collection to the British Museum, where it is exhibited as the Waddesdon Bequest.

David **Waddington** (b. 1929, baron 1990) Conservative politician, MP for Nelson and Colne 1968–74, Clitheroe 1979–83, Ribble Valley 1983–90. He was government chief whip (1987–9) and served briefly in the *cabinet as home secretary (1989–90).

General **Wade** (George Wade, 1673–1748) Soldier who built a network of roads and bridges in the Highlands of Scotland. Although their purpose was military, to control the clans after the *'15 Rebellion, the excellence of the roads combined with Wade's own diplomacy meant that his name has been remembered warmly even in Scotland.

Virginia **Wade** (b. 1945) Britain's most successful tennis player since Fred *Perry in the 1930s. She won the US Open in 1968, the Italian championship in 1971 and the Australian in 1972; but she particularly delighted the British crowd by winning Wimbledon in the centenary year of 1977. She subsequently became a commentator for BBC television.

Louis **Wain** (1860–1939) Artist who painted a profusion of cats in an invariably cheerful manner; they are presented as feline humans, standing on their hind legs, usually in comic situations. Immensely successful from the 1890s, and illustrator of numerous books, he was certified insane in 1923 and spent his last years in an asylum.

Alfred **Wainwright** (1907–91) Author of walking guides to the fells of northern England which have acquired a high status with hikers (a million and a half copies sold since he published his first in 1952). The most popular is his *Coast to Coast Walk; St Bees Head to Robin Hood's Bay*, but this became the subject of controversy in the early 1990s when conservationists argued that the large number of ramblers following the route were damaging environmentally sensitive areas.

Terry **Waite** see *hostages.

Waitrose see *John Lewis Partnership.

Wakefield (61,000 in 1981) City in West Yorkshire on the river Calder, an important centre for the manufacture of woollen goods in the Middle Ages – the period of the chapel on its old bridge and of its cycle of *mystery plays. It was made a diocese in 1888; the 14c parish church of All Saints (with the tallest spire in Yorkshire) then became the cathedral.

John **Wakeham** (b. 1932, baron 1992) Conservative politician, MP for Maldon 1974–83 and for Colchester South and Maldon 1983–92. He was government chief whip 1983–7 and entered the *cabinet in 1987 as leader of the House of Commons. He was subsequently secretary of state for energy (1989–92) and leader of the House of Lords, from 1992. His wife Roberta was killed in the *Brighton bomb outrage of 1984, in which he was also injured.

Wakehurst Place (32km/20m N of Brighton) Garden created mainly between 1902 and 1936 by Gerald Loder and administered since 1965 as a companion to *Kew Gardens. Wakehurst now specializes in those plants and trees which prefer its rich moist earth to the dry soil of Kew (among them, superb rhododendrons). The many different areas of the extensive gardens (some 200ha/ 500ac) are planted according to species, with the result that the natural beauties of the place have an added appeal for the specialist.

wakes week Traditional term for holiday periods in northern industrial towns, deriving from the times when Victorian factories were closed during the annual local festivity or 'wake'. This meant originally just the eve of a saint's day, but it came to include the entire sequence of events celebrating the patron saint of the local church. The dates differed from parish to parish, so holidays were staggered within the region.

'**Wakey, Wakey!**' see Billy *Cotton and *Butlin's.

William **Waldegrave** (b. 1946) Conservative politician, MP for Bristol West since 1979. He entered the *cabinet in 1990 as secretary of state for health; in 1992 he was put in charge of the new Office of *Public Service and Science, while holding the cabinet position of chancellor of the duchy of Lancaster.

Wales (land area 20,636sq.km/7968sq.m, population 2.8 million in 1991) The western projection of *Great Britain, bounded by the Bristol Channel to the south and the Irish Sea to the north. Its eastern boundary was effectively defined by *Offa's Dyke, the line to which the Anglo-Saxons, moving west, had pushed the ancient

Britons by the 8C. Wales remains, therefore, the part of the United Kingdom with the strongest Celtic character and the only one in which a Celtic language, *Welsh, is still spoken as a first language by many people.

Wales became a political entity under *Llewelyn ap Iorwerth in the early 13C, but Welsh independence came to an end later in that century with the campaigns of *Edward I. The title of Prince of *Wales was thereafter reserved for the heir to the English throne, though it was not till 1536 that Wales was made formally a part of the kingdom. By then, under the *Tudors, the dynasty was itself in origin Welsh. Cardiff became in 1955 the official capital of Wales and since 1964 has housed the departments of the *Welsh Office.

Prince of Wales Title first assumed in 1244 by David ap Llewelyn, son of *Llewelyn ap Iorwerth. It was first recognized by the English crown in 1267, when it was held by *Llewelyn ap Gruffydd. In 1301, by which time the conquest of Wales was secure, Edward I conferred it on his heir, the future Edward II. It has been since then the highest of the titles conferred on the eldest son and heir apparent of the monarch; granted with it from the start have been the duchy of Cornwall and the earldom of Chester. The three ostrich plumes forming the crest of the principality, together with the motto *Ich dien* (German for 'I serve'), were won by the *Black Prince at the Battle of Crécy in 1346. The two best-known princes of Wales in history (because each bore the title for most of his life) have been the future George IV and Edward VII. The title was conferred on the present holder, Prince Charles, in 1958.

The Prince of Wales (Prince Charles, b. 1948) Eldest child of *Elizabeth II (see the *royal family) and heir apparent to the throne. He was created Prince of Wales in 1958, though his investiture at *Caernarfon Castle did not take place until 1969. His education was at *Gordonstoun and Trinity College, Cambridge. In 1971 he joined both the RAF and the Royal Navy, studying first at *Cranwell and then at *Dartmouth. For the next decade he served as an officer in the navy.

On 29 July 1981, in St Paul's Cathedral, he married Lady Diana Spencer (see the Princess of *Wales); they have two sons, Prince William (b.1982) and Prince Harry (b. 1984). He and the princess agreed to separate in 1992; subsequently his friendship with Camilla Parker Bowles received wide publicity because of the Camillagate tape (see *privacy).

The prince is known in particular for his interest in the environment and in architecture, on which his forcefully expressed views are often controversial; his intervention in the *National Gallery affair prompted a nationwide debate on the merits of modern architecture. He is also an enthusiastic advocate and practitioner of organic gardening and farming. In 1980 he published *The Old Man of Lochnagar*, a story for children written by himself and illustrated by Hugh Casson, which was translated into a dozen or more languages. His London home has been in Kensington Palace, and his country house is Highgrove – near Tetbury in Gloucestershire.

The Princess of Wales (Lady Diana Spencer, b. 1961, m. Prince Charles 1981) She was born at Park House, *Sandringham, which remained her childhood home until the age of 14; her father then inherited the family title, as the 8th earl of Spencer, and moved to his ancestral home at *Althorp. At 19 she was working as a kindergarten teacher in Pimlico when it was announced, in 1981, that she was engaged to Prince Charles (see the Prince of *Wales). Their marriage in St Paul's Cathedral was widely seen as an event of fairy-tale romance. The story remained

romantic with the rapid arrival of two boys, 2nd and 3rd in line to the throne – William in 1982 and Henry (invariably known as Harry) in 1984.

But within a few years there was persistent press speculation about her marriage. In 1992, apparently with the princess's tacit consent, a book was published (*Diana: Her True Story* by Andrew Morton) which depicted her as intensely unhappy; later that year the so-called Dianagate tape was revealed, said to be of a private telephone conversation between the princess and a male friend (see *privacy); and in December it was announced that the prince and princess had made an amicable agreement to separate.

Whatever the private realities, the public fact was that in the 11 years of the marriage a shy girl had transformed herself into one of the most accomplished and popular members of the royal family in the performance of her duties. She had also taken a courageous lead on important social issues, going out of her way – for example – to be seen comforting victims of Aids.

University of Wales Founded in 1893 to combine existing university colleges at Aberystwyth (1872) and at Bangor and Cardiff (both 1883). In 1920 Swansea was added and in 1971 St David's College, Lampeter – making a total of five in addition to a college of medicine in Cardiff. The four general colleges, apart from St David's, have subtly differing names. They are: University College of Wales, Aberystwyth; University College of North Wales, Bangor; University of Wales College of Cardiff; and University College, Swansea.

George Walker (b. 1929) Ex-boxer who built up from scratch a vast company, Brent Walker. The name came from his first major success, the Brent Cross shopping centre in north London, which he developed in the 1970s. By the late 1980s Brent Walker owned the William Hill chain of betting shops, the Brighton marina and much else. In 1991 Walker was ousted from his position as chairman and chief executive in a boardroom coup; and early in 1993 he was charged with the theft of £12.5 million from his former company.

Peter Walker (b. 1932, baron 1992) Conservative politician, MP for Worcester 1961–92. He entered the *cabinet in 1970 as secretary of state for the environment, and subsequently was in charge of trade and industry (1972–4), agriculture (1979–83) and energy (1983–7). A notably successful spell as secretary of state for Wales (1987–90) rounded off a run of 11 years in Mrs Thatcher's cabinet – a long period in view of his status as a leading *'wet'. In 1992 he was appointed to head a new Urban Regeneration Agency, with a brief to revive the *inner cities.

Walker Art Gallery see *Liverpool.

Walker Cup see *golf.

Max Wall (stage name of Maxwell Lorimer, 1908–90) Comedian whose lugubrious features, understated manner and impeccable timing brought him early success in variety and pantomime and eventually a high reputation as a straight actor – particularly in the plays of Samuel Beckett, where similar time-honoured techniques are put to good effect.

Alfred Russell Wallace (1823–1913) Naturalist who conceived the idea of evolution by natural selection independently of Charles *Darwin. Inspired by Darwin's account of his voyage on the *Beagle*, Wallace spent many years collecting specimens in the Malay archipelago. In 1858 the theories of *Malthus gave him the idea of natural selection, just as they had earlier with Darwin. On the following

One of Barnes Wallis's Wellington Bombers, with a fabric skin, in flight during World War II.

three evenings he wrote a paper *On the tendency of Varieties to depart indefinitely from the original Type*, which he sent to Darwin. The sharp division of species either side of a line east of Borneo and Bali (now known as Wallace's Line) had provided him with the same clue that Darwin found in the Galapagos islands.

Edgar **Wallace** (1875–1932) Exceptionally prolific author of thrillers and plays, producing four or five books a year (he was ahead of his time in dictating them on to the wax cylinders of a dictaphone) and sometimes having three plays running in the West End. His first success was *The Four Just Men* (1905); in *Sanders of the River* (1911) he introduced the famous district commissioner who 'kept the king's peace amongst the cannibals of West Africa'. Wallace died in Hollywood where he was writing stories for films. The first to reach the screen, after his death, was an enduring classic – *King Kong* (1933).

William **Wallace** (*c*.1270–1305) Scottish hero who frustrated the first attempt of *Edward I to overrun Scotland. His great victory was at *Stirling Bridge in 1297. He then briefly administered Scotland on behalf of John de *Baliol (a prisoner in the Tower of London), becoming known at this point as Sir William Wallace – though it is not clear by whom he had been knighted. Edward himself moved north to Scotland in 1298 and defeated Wallace near *Falkirk in July, after which Wallace's power gradually waned. He was eventually captured, in 1305; he owed no allegiance to the English king, but he was declared a traitor and was hanged, drawn and quartered in London. His four fragments were displayed in northern strongholds held by the English – Newcastle, Berwick, Stirling and Perth. But the resistance which he had inaugurated was continued by *Robert the Bruce.

Wallace Collection (London W1) Collection built up by Richard Wallace (1818–90, bt 1871, illegitimate son

of the 4th marquess of Hertford) and by four generations of his ancestors. All the treasures, together with the family home containing them (Hertford House, 1776–88), were bequeathed to the nation in 1897 by Wallace's widow. The best-known single item is *The *Laughing Cavalier*, but the most exceptional holdings are the French paintings, furniture and decorative arts of the 17–19C. There is also sculpture, metalwork, arms and armour, enamels and jewellery from Europe and the east, giving the collection the breadth of a museum of art.

Alfred **Wallis** see *St Ives.

Barnes **Wallis** (1887–1979, kt 1968) Aviation designer and inventor. He designed the successful airship R-100, taken out of service after the disaster of the *R-101, and it was the geodesic principles (he called them 'geodetics') of his rigid airship frame which led to his fabric-covered *Wellington bomber in World War II. His greatest stroke of genius was in devising the bombs of the *Dam Busters, which bounced on the water and were given a reverse spin, forcing them down the surface of the dam to be exploded at the most effective depth by a pressure device.

Wall's The company which pioneered the distribution of ice cream in Britain. Between the wars several thousand men on tricycles pedalled Wall's ice cream from numerous depots to the surrounding districts, with their famous slogan 'Stop me and buy one'. The origin of the company was the London meat pie and sausage shop of Richard Wall, which his descendants developed into a large national concern. Ice cream was introduced in 1922 as a side-line for the summer period, when the sausage business invariably slackened.

Wally Cheerful character, with owlish glasses and red and white sweater and bobble hat, who has become an international star in children's books. Known as Wally in

Britain, he is Waldo in the USA, Walter in Germany, Charlie (surprisingly) in France, Aref in Egypt, Efi in Israel and so on. He is the creation of Martin Handford (b. 1956) and he first featured in *Where's Wally?* (1987). The book, like its annual successors, consists of a series of pages crowded with tiny figures. On each spread Wally makes several appearances in the crowd; the game for the child is to find him.

Horace **Walpole** (1717–97, 4th earl of Orford 1791) Author and inspired dilettante, sixth and youngest child of Robert *Walpole. His prolific letters are an invaluable source for historians of the period and he was a major figure in the early *Gothic Revival, the example of *Strawberry Hill being followed by *The Castle of Otranto* (1764). This prototype of the Gothic novel is a spine-tingling tale of medieval villainies and wronged innocence. At the end the ghost of the murdered prince of Otranto grows larger and larger until his castle cannot take the strain and crumbles around him.

Robert **Walpole** (1676–1745, KB 1725, earl of Orford 1742) The first British *prime minister in the modern sense, the longest in the office and the first to inhabit 10 *Downing Street. Born the son of a country gentleman in Norfolk, he entered parliament in 1701 and rapidly established himself as a leading young Whig and a member of the *Kit-Kat Club. He held important positions in the War of the *Spanish Succession (secretary-at-war 1708, treasurer of the navy 1710). The Tories were in power from 1711 and Walpole became the effective leader of the opposition. In 1715, after the change to the Hanoverian dynasty, he was made first lord of the Treasury and chancellor of the exchequer; but he resigned these posts in 1717, in a disagreement over foreign policy. Three years later the *South Sea Bubble brought him a double advantage. He argued forcefully against the scheme in parliament and in print, thus keeping clear of the scandal, but he also managed to sell his own stock at the peak of the market, making 1000% profit and laying the foundation of his fortune. He was thus well placed to lead the country when reappointed first lord of the Treasury and chancellor of the exchequer in 1721. He held both offices until 1742.

He used his long tenure of office to secure the Hanoverian dynasty and the Whig supremacy, achieving both by shamelessly self-interested political appointments. The result was a period of relative stability in Britain, but one in which corruption became the norm in political life. The War of the *Austrian Succession was a national commitment for which he could find little enthusiasm and he resigned in 1742. He had made good use of his fortune in building *Houghton Hall and filling it with an outstanding collection of paintings. Sold by his grandson to Catherine the Great of Russia, they are now in the Hermitage.

The **Walrus and the Carpenter** see *Through the Looking-Glass.*

Walsingham (45km/28m NW of Norwich) Village which was one of the most popular places of pilgrimage in medieval England. In the late 11c a shrine was built here to the Virgin Mary, after she had appeared in a vision to a pious local lady. An Augustinian priory was founded in the 12c to cope with the pilgrims to Our Lady of Walsingham. The Reformation reduced it to ruins (still partly standing), but in modern times a restored shrine has again become a place of pilgrimage, in particular for *Anglo-Catholics.

Francis **Walsingham** (*c.*1532–90, kt 1577) Secretary of state to Elizabeth I from 1573 till his death. He is remembered in particular for his organization of an

extremely efficient secret service. His network of spies kept him one step ahead of numerous conspirators, including those hatching the *Babington plot.

Julie **Walters** (b. 1950) Actress who made her reputation with her performance on stage (1980) and film (1983) of the title role in *Educating Rita*. She has featured regularly on television in comedy series with Victoria *Wood.

Izaak **Walton** (1593–1683) Successful man of business who turned in middle age to writing literary biographies. At the age of 60 he published one of the best-loved books about English country life, *The *Compleat Angler*. Over the years it has been issued in more than 300 editions.

William **Walton** (1902–83, kt 1951) Composer who was virtually a member of the *Sitwell family from 1919 (he lived with them until 1934), and who first came to public attention with *Façade* in 1923. *Portsmouth Point* followed in 1925, an orchestral overture inspired by a Rowlandson etching. One of his most ambitious works was *Belshazzar's Feast* (1931). He was the most successful of British composers in turning his hand to film scores, above all for Laurence Olivier's *Henry V* (1944), with its famous music for the Agincourt sequence. He provided the scores for two other Olivier films of Shakespeare (*Hamlet* 1948, *Richard III* 1955) and for *The First of the Few* (1942), about the development of the Spitfire.

Walworth Road (London SE1) Street running southeast from the Elephant and Castle, to which the *Labour party moved its offices in 1980. The name is now often used for the central administration of the party.

Wapping (London E1) The western part of *Docklands, closest to the *City of London and the first part of the development to be occupied. The *Times* and other Murdoch newspapers moved there in 1986 and were printed on new machinery manned by members of the electricians' union, the EETPU. Security measures installed against the traditional print unions, who had been excluded from the plant, caused the area to be known as Fortress Wapping. Violent clashes between pickets and police in January 1987 led to many arrests and, two years later, to more than 20 police being charged with offences committed during the disturbance. But the failure of the print unions to disrupt the operation put an effective end to their previously great power.

Perkin **Warbeck** (*c.*1474–99) Pretender who was trained up by Yorkist opponents of *Henry VII, and in particular by Margaret, sister of Edward IV, to impersonate the younger of the *princes in the Tower. If alive, and if his elder brother was dead, this prince was the rightful king of England as Richard IV. From 1492 Warbeck was entertained in that role by the king of France, by the Holy Roman Emperor, and by James IV of Scotland – who in 1495 even gave him his cousin, Catherine Gordon, in marriage. Warbeck made various feeble attempts to invade England and was finally captured in Hampshire in 1497. His life was spared until further plots made his execution a necessary precaution.

The **War Cry** see *Salvation Army.

Judith **Ward** (b. 1949) English woman who invented a fantasy life as a terrorist and was sentenced in 1974 to 30 years in jail for placing three IRA bombs – on the *M62 coach in February of that year, at the National Defence Centre in Latimer a week later, and at Euston station in 1973. When the Court of Appeal freed her and quashed her conviction in 1992, it was revealed that the police had relied heavily on her uncorroborated confessions (though she was clearly in a disturbed state of mind), that there had been extensive non-disclosure of evidence to the defence, and that *forensic evidence used against Miss Ward had been both inaccurate and slanted. It was the fourth in a series of cases to raise major questions about the administration of *criminal justice.

The **Warden** (1855) The first novel in *Trollope's Barsetshire series, and the book which brought him his first success. The unworldly Rev. Septimus Harding has been appointed warden of Hiram's Hospital, an almshouse for 12 poor old men. The interplay of character and political intrigue (the rich vein which Trollope discovered in this book) arises here from a press campaign against Harding on the grounds that too much of the charity's income goes towards his salary and too little is spent on the old men in his care. In spite of being urged on by his pugnacious and ambitious son-in-law, Archdeacon Grantly, the warden resigns his post – for he rather agrees with the thrust of the objection. He moves into lodgings in the town. His small new parish contains part of the Cathedral Close, the setting for the next stage of the drama in *Barchester Towers.*

wardian case Glass case with a tightly fitting top, capable of containing a moist atmosphere in which plants such as ferns can live. It was an important element in the 19C transportation of plants over long distances, and it became a favourite item in Victorian drawing rooms. It is named after its inventor, Nathaniel Bagshaw Ward (1791–1868), who wrote *On the Growth of Plants in closely glazed cases* (1842).

Wardour Street (London W1) Street in Soho which since the 1930s has contained the offices of many film companies. The name is sometimes used as a general term for the film industry in Britain.

War Graves Commission (Commonwealth War Graves Commission) Established in 1917 as the Imperial War Graves Commission, the organization commemorates the 1,700,000 members of the forces of the UK, Australia, Canada, India, New Zealand, South Africa and other countries then in the Commonwealth, who died in the two World Wars. It maintains nearly a million graves throughout the world, together with monuments for those who were lost but never identified. The movingly simple epitaph on World War I graves of unidentified bodies (A Soldier of the Great War Known unto God) was chosen by *Kipling as literary adviser to the Commission.

warming-pan baby Phrase applied in the 17C to James *Stuart, resulting from popular incredulity at his birth and survival. His mother had not had a child for five years; the previous ones had all died in infancy; and a male heir was precisely what *James II needed if he was to re-establish Roman Catholicism in Britain. The rumour quickly spread that a changeling had been smuggled into the queen's bed in a warming pan. It is discounted by modern historians.

'Plum' Warner (Pelham Warner, 1873–1963, kt 1937) Batsman for Middlesex (1894–1920) and England (1898–1912, captain 1903–6), and in his retirement a prolific writer on *cricket. He was the first to score a century in his maiden Test match, but his lasting fame in cricketing circles derives as much from a lifetime of service to the game as from his own prowess.

War of 1812 (1812–15) War between Britain and the USA which was an offshoot of the *Napoleonic Wars.

American naval commerce suffered greatly from Napoleon's blockade of Britain and from the British response. The British regarded as hostile any vessel carrying cargo which had not paid dues at a port in Britain; moreover they began boarding American ships and press-ganging any sailors whom they suspected of being British. After the failure of lengthy negotiations, the USA declared war in June 1812. Hostilities took place mainly along the border with the British colony of Canada and on the eastern seaboard, where the British navy imposed an almost complete commercial blockade. The most dramatic event of the war was the burning by British troops in 1814 of the Capitol and the president's house in Washington, D.C., in reprisal for similar American acts in Toronto. Peace terms agreed at Ghent, in Belgium, were accepted by the American senate in February 1815.

War of American Independence see War of *American Independence.

War Office see the *Army.

War of the Spanish Succession see War of the *Spanish Succession.

War of the Worlds (1898) Immensely influential story by H.G. *Wells, first published as a serial in *Pearson's Magazine* in 1897. Others at the time had speculated about Martians sending messages to earth, but Wells produced the classic science-fiction scenario of them invading in a rocket. Their weapons prove irresistible, London is destroyed, and the survivors of the catastrophe subsist with difficulty until the Martians are overcome by an unexpected foe – earth's bacteria. A radio adaptation by Orson Welles in the USA in 1938, using the convention of a news bulletin, was so convincing that it caused widespread panic.

War on Want Overseas aid charity, founded in 1951, which got into serious financial difficulties in 1990 and was criticized by the *Charity Commissioners for its record of management and for inaccuracies in its accounts. It was attempting in the early 1990s to continue with a slimmed down programme.

War Requiem (1962) Choral work by Benjamin *Britten, setting World War I poems by Wilfred *Owen in the context of a Requiem mass. A powerful work in itself, it was also profoundly apt for its occasion; its first performance was in the new *Coventry Cathedral, which had risen phoenix-like among World War II ruins.

HMS **Warrior** (Royal Dockyard, Portsmouth) The Royal Navy's first ironclad steam frigate (9210 tons), launched at Blackwall on the Thames in 1860. From 1904 to 1924 she was used in a torpedo school at Portsmouth. She was then effectively forgotten until being rediscovered in the 1960s, in use as a floating jetty for unloading oil at Milford Haven. Fully restored in all her interior details, she is now on display in *Portsmouth.

Warsaw Concerto (1941) Popular pastiche of a romantic piano concerto, written by Richard Addinsell (1904–77) as a score for the film *Dangerous Moonlight* – about a Polish pianist, a refugee from the Nazis, who loses his memory after flying in the Battle of Britain.

Wars of the Roses (1455–87) The name which was later given to the dynastic wars in England between two rival lines of the royal family. They were known as the Lancastrians and the Yorkists because their rival claims went back to John of Gaunt, duke of Lancaster, and to Edward of Langley, duke of York, both of them sons of

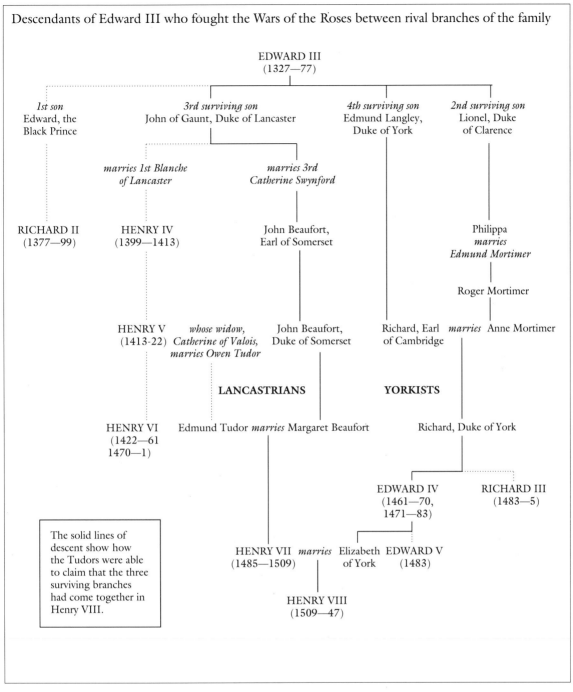

Descendants of Edward III who fought the Wars of the Roses between rival branches of the family

EDWARD III
(1327—77)

1st son
Edward, the
Black Prince

3rd surviving son
John of Gaunt, Duke of Lancaster

4th surviving son
Edmund Langley,
Duke of York

2nd surviving son
Lionel, Duke
of Clarence

*marries 1st Blanche
of Lancaster*

*marries 3rd
Catherine Swynford*

RICHARD II
(1377—99)

HENRY IV
(1399—1413)

John Beaufort,
Earl of Somerset

Philippa
*marries
Edmund Mortimer*

Roger Mortimer

HENRY V
(1413-22)

*whose widow,
Catherine of Valois,
marries Owen Tudor*

John Beaufort,
Duke of Somerset

Richard, Earl
of Cambridge

marries Anne Mortimer

LANCASTRIANS

YORKISTS

HENRY VI
(1422—61
1470—1)

Edmund Tudor *marries* Margaret Beaufort

Richard, Duke of York

EDWARD IV
(1461—70,
1471—83)

RICHARD III
(1483—5)

The solid lines of
descent show how
the Tudors were able
to claim that the three
surviving branches
had come together in
Henry VIII.

HENRY VII *marries* Elizabeth EDWARD V
(1485—1509)   of York   (1483)

HENRY VIII
(1509—47)

Edward III. Distinctive badges were worn by followers of feudal lords, and that of the Yorkists had long been a white rose. The corresponding red rose of the Lancastrians was not adopted as their main badge until the very end of the wars, in 1485.

The Lancastrians, descending in direct male line from John of Gaunt, seized the throne from Richard II in 1399. There followed three kings of their line – Henry IV, Henry V and Henry VI – but the chaos resulting from the weak reign of Henry VI caused his Yorkist cousins to press their claim. (Their ancestor, the duke of York, was a younger brother of John of Gaunt, but they were also descended through the female line from an elder brother, the duke of Clarence.) The first battle was fought at St Albans in 1455, and the first Yorkist king, Edward IV, was proclaimed in 1461. He was followed briefly by his

son, Edward V, and then by his brother, Richard III.

The final change of dynasty came after the Battle of Bosworth Field (1485), in which an army led by Henry VII defeated and killed Richard III. But the wars were not finally over until 1487, when Henry defeated a Yorkist army attempting to put a pretender, Lambert *Simnel, on the throne.

In three decades those suffering violent death in the direct royal line had included Henry VI, his son Prince Edward, Richard III and almost certainly the two *princes in the Tower (Edward V and his brother Richard). These events left England with a distaste for anarchy which enabled the new *Tudor dynasty to exercise a strong rule. Henry VII, claiming to unite the two lines (through his marriage to Elizabeth of York), combined the white and red roses in a new badge, the Tudor rose.

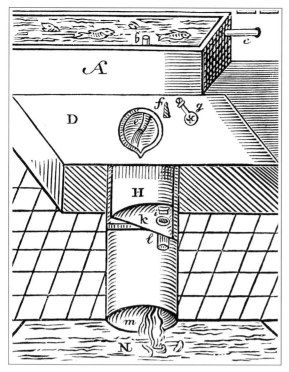

The 1596 diagram of a water closet, with fishes to make plain that the cistern holds water.

warts and all A phrase used for the unadorned truth. According to Horace Walpole's *Anecdotes of Painting* (1762–71), Oliver Cromwell instructed *Lely to paint him 'with all these roughnesses, pimples, warts and everything as you see me, otherwise I will never pay a farthing for it'.

Warwick (22,000 in 1981) Ancient town on the river Avon; administrative centre of Warwickshire. It is believed that Ethelfleda, a daughter of Alfred the Great, built a wooden fortress here against the Danes in about 915. Certainly the early Normans were able to enlarge an existing castle. The exterior of the present building, rising sheer from the river and with two impressive towers (Caesar's Tower and Guy's Tower) dates from the 14C, not long before this was the stronghold of *Warwick the Kingmaker. But the comfortable rooms inside the castle, giving on to a grassy courtyard, are of the 17–19C and are filled with treasures brought back from the *Grand Tour.

Though the town of Warwick was much damaged by a fire in 1694, a few medieval buildings survive. The Leycester Hospital occupies premises built in the 14–15C for religious guilds; since 1571 it has been an almshouse for 12 old soldiers, founded by Elizabeth's favourite, the earl of Leicester. His tomb and the elaborate Beauchamp Chapel (1443–64) are at the east end of St Mary's, the only part of Warwick's oldest church to have escaped the fire.

Warwickshire (490,000 in 1991, administrative centre Warwick) *County in central England, much reduced in 1974 by the creation of the *metropolitan county of West Midlands.

Warwickshire County Cricket Club Founded in 1884 and in the *county championship from 1894; it has won three times (1911, 51, 72). In *one-day cricket the club has had three victories in the Gillette Cup and NatWest Trophy (1966, 68, 89) and one in the Sunday League

(1980). The county ground is *Edgbaston in Birmingham, and the county plays also at Coventry.

Warwick the Kingmaker The name commonly given to Richard Neville, Earl of Warwick (1428–71), the most powerful baron of his time, because of his influence on whether *Edward IV or *Henry VI wore the crown during the *Wars of the Roses. He was killed fighting against Edward IV in the Battle of Barnet.

Warwick Vase Marble 18C reconstruction incorporating the fragments of a large Roman vase of the 2nd century AD, found among the ruins of the emperor Hadrian's villa at Tivoli. It was at Warwick Castle until 1979, and is now the central feature of the courtyard of the *Burrell Collection.

The **Wash** Shallow bay in the North Sea between Lincolnshire and Norfolk. It is being gradually filled by silt from the rivers Witham, Welland, Nene and Great Ouse, a process which in the past has created the *Fens. King John, campaigning here in 1216, lost all his baggage and some of his men when crossing the tidal estuary of the Welland – making possible a favourite joke in English school history, that King John lost all his things in the wash.

Washington Old Hall (8km/5m W of Sunderland) House on the site of the medieval home of the family of George Washington (the present building is of the 17C, though some walls survive from the earlier house). The direct ancestor of the first president of the USA left the village of Washington in the late 13C, and that branch of the family lived from the 16C at *Sulgrave Manor.

*The **Waste Land*** (1922) Poem by T.S. *Eliot which has come to symbolize a mood of lively unease in the period after World War I. In its deliberate fragmentation ('These fragments I have shored against my ruins') it juxtaposes literary allusion and commonplace everyday remarks, resulting in a sort of cubist collage of the jazz age. The poem consists of five sections – 'The Burial of the Dead', 'A Game of Chess', 'The Fire Sermon', the very brief 'Death by Water', and 'What the Thunder said'. When Eliot published it as a book (it had appeared in magazines earlier in 1922), he padded it out with learned notes about his sources. He later dismissed these as 'bogus scholarship', but they have added to the pleasure of researchers in exploring the poem. They revealed that his main inspiration, and the origin of the title, was a book about the legend of the *Holy Grail (Jessie Weston *From Ritual to Romance* 1920). The poem is dedicated to a fellow poet, Ezra Pound, whose advice had led to the original draft being greatly shortened.

John **Wastell** (d. *c*.1515) The leading English architect of the early Tudor period, responsible among other works for Bell Harry (the central tower of Canterbury Cathedral) and for the glorious fan vaulting in King's College Chapel, Cambridge.

watch committee see *police.

water The provision of conduits, wells and pumps to make water available in towns and villages was traditionally a civic or parish responsibility. But when technology made it possible to send water through pipes to individual houses, commercial interests took up the challenge of providing this service – from as early as the 17C. As with the later piping of *gas, the proliferation of private companies eventually became uneconomic. From the late 19C municipal authorities gradually took responsibility for the water supply. In London, for example, the newly formed

Metropolitan Water Board took over in 1904 the capital city's eight private water companies. Subsequently the Water Act of 1973 reorganized all the municipal water services of England and Wales into ten regional authorities.

It was these water authorities which were sold in 1989 as ten independent companies, in the most controversial of the Conservative government's acts of *privatization. Many in Britain felt that the supply of water, more than any other commodity, should remain a public service. It is still the responsibility of local authorities in Scotland and of a government department in Northern Ireland.

The **Water-Babies** (1863) An improving fantasy for young children by Charles *Kingsley. Tom, a small boy whose job is climbing up the inside of chimneys, escapes from his master, a cruel chimney-sweep, and is drowned in a stream. He gradually adapts to the more Christian behaviour of the little creatures who live there, the water-babies. They are kept in order by two memorable governess figures – the ferocious Mrs Bedonebyasyoudid, who dishes out punishments and rewards, and the loving Mrs Doasyouwouldbedoneby.

water closet It is a cherished English belief that the water closet or flush toilet was invented by Sir John Harington, the godson of Elizabeth I, and that he installed one to her great satisfaction in Richmond or Greenwich Palace. There is no direct evidence of this, but it is possible. His pamphlet of 1596, with its punning title *The Metamorphosis of Ajax* ('a jakes' was a contemporary name for a lavatory), includes a woodcut showing how a water closet should be installed. All the modern ingredients are there: the overhead cistern (complete with overflow pipe), from which tubes lead down to the lavatory pan; a shaped seat to sit on; and a water trap sealing off odours from the sewage tank below. The necessary parts for the carpenter and plumber are individually costed,

coming to a total of 30 shillings and 8 pence. If it was not built, it deserved to be; but it was certainly far ahead of its time. The term 'water closet' first appears in the 18C, as do patents for flushing systems – notably that of Joseph Bramah in 1778.

watercolours The form of painting in which the British have made the most distinctive contribution. Used only occasionally by artists in previous centuries (most notably by Dürer), watercolour proved ideally suited to the 18C British passion for topographical views – at first solemnly accurate, and then with an ever-increasing dash of the *picturesque. Paul *Sandby was the earliest master in this field. His relatively straightforward approach was followed by more impressionistic and romantic styles from the brushes of John Robert Cozens (1752–97), Thomas Girtin (1775–1802), Richard Parkes Bonington (1802–28), David Cox (1783–1859), Peter de Wint (1784–1849) and above all *Turner. Meanwhile Francis Towne (1740–1816) and John Sell Cotman (1782–1842) had evolved a method of suggesting landscape by almost abstract blocks of colour wash; and *Rowlandson, *Blake and *Palmer were each using watercolour in a distinctive manner suited to their differing subjects. Since the late 18C watercolour pigments had been available in small ready-made blocks, and equipment so easily portable proved ideal for the growing fashion of sketching out of doors. By the Victorian period every well-brought-up young lady, including the queen herself, was a keen and often accomplished watercolourist.

Alfred **Waterhouse** (1830–1905) Architect who began his career with an early success in a competion – for the assize courts in Manchester in 1859. He followed this by winning another competition (1868), this time for the *Manchester town hall, his most imposing work in the Gothic style. Unusually for him, he turned to a version of

Watercolour by Paul Sandby, c.1780, of the south front of Warwick Castle and the tall Caesar's Tower.

the Romanesque for an equally impressive building in London, the *Natural History Museum.

Keith **Waterhouse** (b. 1929) Novelist, playwright and journalist. He made his name with *Billy Liar* in 1959. He turned the novel into a successful play and film in collaboration with Willis Hall (b. 1929), with whom he has written much both for television (*Worzel Gummidge*) and in the theatre – though the recent *Jeffrey Bernard is Unwell* (1991, performed by Peter O'Toole) was his alone. Waterhouse is also a regular newspaper columnist, for the *Daily Mirror* (1970–86) and since 1986 for the *Daily Mail*.

Waterloo (18 June 1815) Defeat of the French army by *Wellington and the Prussian marshal Blücher, bringing to an end the *Napoleonic Wars. After Napoleon escaped from Elba, the allied nations (Britain, Prussia, Austria and Russia) agreed that each would put 150,000 men into the field to suppress him. The British and Prussians were the first to mobilize their troops in Belgium, and Napoleon decided to attack them before the arrival of the Russians and Austrians.

He marched north from Paris with about 124,000 men, the majority of them veterans of many battles. The allied forces were larger but relatively inexperienced. Blücher's army of Prussians, encamped southeast of Brussels, numbered about 120,000. Wellington's forces, occupying Brussels itself and the areas to the south and southwest, amounted to some 94,000 men; these were made up about equally of British, Dutch-Belgian and German troops. Napoleon's strategy was to advance directly upon Brussels, separating the two allied armies and hoping to contain one while destroying the other.

Quatre Bras, a crossroads 35km/22m south of Brussels, was a pivotal point of communication between the British and Prussian armies and therefore of great strategic importance to Napoleon. On June 16 he instructed Marshal Ney to capture it from the forward troops of Wellington's army; the battle continued all day, with heavy losses on both sides, but by nightfall the British still held Quatre Bras. Further east, on that same day, Napoleon attacked and defeated Blücher's army at Ligny. During June 17 Blücher's Prussians withdrew northwards in disarray, but Napoleon failed to pursue them effectively. Wellington, hearing of their defeat, ordered his own forces to withdraw from Quatre Bras and to occupy a strong defensive position on a ridge at Waterloo, 20km/12m south of Brussels.

The decisive battle on June 18 centred on the French attempts to drive Wellington's forces off that ridge. When the day started Wellington had in position about 68,000 men and 156 guns; Napoleon had some 72,000 men and 246 guns. The French army was likely to suffer heavy losses attacking a defensive position with successive waves of infantry and cavalry, but they had a well-deserved reputation as the best troops in Europe. Napoleon would certainly have won the day but for the arrival in the afternoon of Blücher's army, regrouped after its defeat and now attacking the French right wing from the northeast. By early evening the French were in flight. Wellington and Blücher met at 9.15 p.m. and each congratulated the other as the victor. The day's dead numbered 25,000 rench, 7000 Prussians and some 15,000 from the combined British forces.

Two remarks of Wellington's, much quoted later, testify to the narrowness of the victory. 'Hard pounding this, gentlemen; let's see who will pound longest', he had said during the battle; and he later described it as 'the nearest run thing you ever saw in your life', adding with characteristic self-confidence 'By God! I don't think it would have done if I had not been there'.

Waterloo Chamber see *Windsor.

Waterloo Cup see *greyhound racing.

Waterloo Gallery see *Apsley House.

Waterloo Station (London SE1) Terminus in two parts, serving the regions southwest of London from the main station (rebuilt 1902–22) and the southeastern regions from Waterloo East, from which trains cross the river to their final destination at *Charing Cross. In 1899 a direct underground link was constructed from the main station to the Bank in the City of London – a service still much used by commuters and known as 'the Drain'. Waterloo is to be the first international terminus for the *Channel Tunnel trains (another is planned at *King's Cross), and a new terminal building by Nicholas Grimshaw is scheduled for completion during 1993.

Water Music see George Frideric *Handel.

water polo Game which was developed informally in Britain in the second half of the 19C, being known at first as 'football in the water'. Some early versions used the round ball of association football and others the oval ball of rugby football. The round ball prevailed when official rules were drawn up by the Swimming Association of Great Britain in 1885. Scotland defeated England in the first international in 1890, and water polo was included in the Olympic Games from 1900.

Watership Down (1972) The bestselling first book of Richard Adams (b. 1920), who wrote it when he was a civil servant in the Department of the Environment. Told originally to his own daughters, the story follows a colony of rabbits (including Hazel, Fiver and Bigwig) as they are forced by a building development to move from their warren; they find a new home on Watership Down (in north Hampshire, just west of Kingsclere). The book's appeal reached far beyond the intended audience of children, partly because the social activities of the rabbits were treated so seriously. In this the author acknowledged his indebtedness to *The Private Life of the Rabbit* (1964), by Ronald Lockley.

Waterside Inn (Bray, Berkshire) One of only two restaurants in Britain to have three stars in the 1993 *Michelin Guide* (the other is La *Tante Claire). Its proprietor is Michel Roux (b. 1941), a French chef who came to England in 1967 and opened the Waterside Inn in 1972. His first restaurant in Britain was Le Gavroche, launched in London in 1967 with his brother Albert (b. 1935). Le Gavroche, run by Albert, also had three stars until losing one after his retirement in 1992.

'water, water, everywhere' see The *Ancient Mariner.

Watling Street The Roman road running northwest from London to the west Midlands, ending near Shrewsbury (at Wroxeter). The name derives from an Anglo-Saxon word for St Albans, which was the first place of importance on the journey out from London. The fame of the original Watling Steet caused its name to be applied later, unhistorically, to Roman roads in other parts of the country – in particular the one from Dover to London, more properly called Casinge Street.

Dr Watson see Sherlock *Holmes.

Michael Watson (b. 1965) Boxer whose severe injury in 1991 raised many questions about the sport. Twice in that year he challenged Chris Eubank for his WBO world middleweight title. On the first occasion, at Earl's Court in June, Watson lost on points – many thought unjustly. On the second, in September and also in London, he collapsed just after the referee had stopped the fight in the final round. He was in a coma for a month and had four brain operations; eventually, during 1992, he began to recover both movement and speech.

Robert **Watson-Watt** (1892–1973, kt 1942) Scottish physicist who from 1935 developed the system of radar used in wartime Britain; with a network of radar stations in place along the south coast by 1939, his work was a vital part of the defence against German air attack. Similar systems were being developed at the same time in the USA, France and Germany.

James **Watt** (1736–1819) Scottish inventor who made important advances in the development of the *steam engine. He was instrument-maker to the university of Glasgow in 1764 when he was given a model of Newcomen's engine to repair. He was struck by its wasteful consumption of steam, which he solved by separating the condenser from the cylinder, allowing the temperature in the condenser to be low while that in the cylinder remained high. In partnership with Matthew *Boulton, Watt developed this principle in an engine which used a quarter of the fuel previously required. The firm of Boulton and Watt was able to prosper by charging a royalty of 33% of the money saved. Watt's many later improvements included the double-action engine and a brilliantly simple self-regulating device, the centrifugal governor.

His engines had made the transition from simple pumping machines to adaptable sources of rotary power, suitable for the mechanical requirements of mills and factories. They thus made possible a major advance in the *Industrial Revolution.

G.F. **Watts** (George Frederick Watts, 1817–1904) Painter who used a wide variety of styles, often for heavily allegorical subjects. He is appreciated now mainly for his portraits (for example Ellen *Terry, who was briefly his child bride). *Hope* (1886, a version in the Tate) is so full of symbolist mystery that it has caught the public's fancy; on a globe, partly wreathed in mist, sits a hunched and blindfold maiden plucking an instrument with broken strings. Watts was also a sculptor, and *Physical Energy* in *Kensington Gardens shows yet another very different side of his talent. His high reputation in his lifetime is shown by his selection, at the age of 85, as the only artist among the founding members of the Order of *Merit. His house at Compton, near Guildford, is kept as a museum.

Isaac **Watts** (1674–1748) The first great writer of English hymns, author of some 700, many of them still much sung – for example *O God, our help in ages past*. Watts brought to hymn-writing a new note of subjective piety. *When I survey the wondrous Cross* (sung now to the late 18C tune called Rockingham) is believed to be the earliest hymn by any author to include the personal pronoun.

Evelyn **Waugh** (1902–66) Novelist who viewed life with a balefully intolerant eye, and derived from it some of the best fictional comedy of the 20C. His books were closely derived from his own experiences. After Oxford he became briefly a schoolmaster, enabling him to write his first success, * *Decline and Fall* (1928). Visits to Africa as a journalist in the 1930s provided *Black Mischief* (1932) and *Scoop* (1938). In all of these, as also in A *Handful of Dust* (1934), he made good use of the brittle social life of London, of which he was himself a part (his satirical wit did not prevent his being also a snob). In 1930 he

took a step of great importance in his personal life, converting to Roman Catholicism; his faith, his Oxford experiences and a fascination with the aristocracy all came together in a novel more solemn than his previous work, * *Brideshead Revisited* (1945).

His wartime experiences as a soldier, including spells in Crete and Yugoslavia, led to three novels with a rich new cast of characters including Apthorpe, an officer obsessed with his portable lavatory or 'thunder box'; the individual books (*Men at Arms* 1952, *Officers and Gentlemen* 1955, *Unconditional Surrender* 1961) were issued together in 1962 under the title *Sword of Honour*. A visit to Hollywood in 1947 resulted in a macabre comedy on Californian burial customs (*The Loved One* 1948), and *The Ordeal of Gilbert Pinfold* (1957) recounted, in barely fictional manner, some alarmingly self-revealing hallucinations which Waugh had suffered. By the end of his life his own personality – bigoted, reactionary and often spectacularly rude – had become almost as intriguing to the public as his perennially popular books.

Lord **Wavell** (1883–1950, KCB 1939, earl 1947) Commander of the British forces in the Middle East at the start of World War II , from 1939 to 1941. After proving no match for Rommel, he was moved to the post of commander-in-chief in India (where he was subsequently viceroy, 1943–7).

Waverley Edinburgh's main railway station, at the east end of Princes Street, which opened in 1846 as the General Station and was renamed in 1854 in honour of the *Waverley novels.

Waverley see *Glasgow.

Waverley novels Name by which the novels of Walter *Scott were known, because their titlepages just said 'by the author of Waverley' (the title of the first, in 1814). The anonymous and hugely popular author was referred to as the Great Unknown, until Scott finally announced at a public dinner in 1827 that he was the man.

*The **Waves*** (1931) The most fluid of Virginia *Woolf's 'stream of consciousness' novels, using the interior monologues of six characters (taught together as children in a seaside house, and meeting again on two later occasions) to reveal obliquely the individual development of each, seen in relation to the recurring patterns of nature and the seasons.

Wavy Navy see *Royal Naval Reserve.

Wayland Smith Anglo-Saxon version of the blacksmith with magical powers who appears in many Nordic legends. He became particularly associated with a Stone Age burial chamber, known as Wayland's Smithy, not far from the *Uffington White Horse. The legend, used by Walter Scott in *Kenilworth*, was that if a traveller left his horse outside the cave with a coin, and refrained from watching, his horse would be magically shod.

*The **Way of the World*** (1700) Comedy by *Congreve about the elaborate ruses required if Mirabell is to win the heart and hand of his beloved Millamant without losing her inheritance. Her own independent spirit is one of his obstacles, and a high point of the play is her listing of the 'provisos' (mainly the avoidance of fashionable behaviour) on which she might accept him: 'These articles subscrib'd, if I continue to endure you a little longer, I may by degrees dwindle into a wife.'

*The **Wealth of Nations*** see Adam *Smith.

'**We are a grandmother**' see the *royal we.

'**We are not amused**' see the *royal we.

Bernard **Weatherill** (b. 1920, baron 1992) Conservative politician, MP for Croydon North East 1964–92. Elected *Speaker of the House of Commons in 1983, he became more familiar to the public in that office than any of his predecessors – since he was the first to be seen controlling debates when the proceedings of the House were televised (from 1989).

Aston **Webb** (1849–1930, kt 1904) The most prolific architect of public buildings around the turn of the century. Among his best known are the Victoria and Albert Museum, the law courts and the university in Birmingham, and the entire processional route in central London from the façade of Buckingham Palace along the Mall to Admiralty Arch. He often worked in partnership with Edward Ingress Bell (1826–1914).

Beatrice and Sidney **Webb** Tireless couple in left-wing politics in the early 20c. In 1892 Sidney Webb (1859–1947, baron Passfield 1929) married Beatrice Potter (1858–1943). Together they wrote a succession of influential books on such subjects as trade unionism, industrial democracy, local government and the treatment of poverty; Beatrice's minority report of 1909 as a member of the Royal Commission on the poor law was an important step in the development of the welfare state. They were closely involved in the establishment of both the *London School of Economics and the *New Statesman*.

Matthew **Webb** see *swimming the Channel.

Philip **Webb** see William *Morris.

John **Webster** (active 1602–25) The leading English writer of poetic tragedy after Shakespeare. Almost nothing is known of his life except that he was born a Londoner and was dead by 1634. His two great plays, The *White Devil* and The *Duchess of Malfi*, are characterized by extremes of melodramatic evil shot through with flashes of sudden tenderness. Webster uses a powerful economy of language, as in the famous line in The *Duchess of Malfi* when Ferdinand sees the corpse of his twin sister, the duchess, who has been murdered on his behalf: 'Cover her face; mine eyes dazzle; she died young.'

'**We buried him darkly at dead of night**' see The *Burial of Sir John Moore*.

Wedgwood The leading make of British pottery from the mid-18c. Josiah Wedgwood (1730–95), a member of a long-established family of potters, set up in business on his own in 1759 in Burslem, one of Staffordshire's *Five Towns. He achieved rapid success with a cream-coloured earthenware; it was known as Queen's Ware from 1765, thanks to the patronage of Queen Charlotte. He next developed a black ware, which he called black basaltes. This was well suited to reproducing classical objects, such as urns, and with the addition of details in red encaustic it could imitate Greek red-figure vases (thought at the time to be Etruscan, which is why Wedgwood gave the name Etruria to the factory he built near Hanley in 1769). Finally there was his most important discovery, a dense stoneware fine enough to rival porcelain. He called it jasper. Introduced in 1775, jasper became the most characteristic of Wedgwood's wares. It was made in various colours, usually with white decorative patterns or figures standing up in relief. This cameo effect was in keeping with the contemporary taste for *neoclassical decoration,

A plate from Wedgwood's great Frog Service, hand-painted with a sepia scene of Castle Acre in Norfolk.

and the range of colours in jasper ware was similar to those appearing on walls and ceilings in the new *Adam style. Wedgwood was now the height of fashion.

The most famous product of the Wedgwood factory was the Frog Service supplied to Catherine the Great in 1774, now in the Hermitage in St Petersburg. It consists of 952 pieces, hand-painted with 1244 different British views. Each piece bears the crest of a green frog, because the service was intended for a palace near Petrodvorets at La Grenouillière (French for the Froggery). An equally distinguished production in jasper ware was Wedgwood's reproduction of the *Portland Vase. Capable of achievements such as these, he did not need to compete with lesser manufacturers in the difficult quest for porcelain. The Wedgwood factory produced no porcelain until 1812, and then only for a few years; it did not become a regular product (in the English form of *bone china) until 1878.

The link with the Wedgwood family lasted until 1986, and production continued at Etruria until the 1940s; the factory then moved to its present site at Barlaston (part of *Stoke-on-Trent), where there is a comprehensive museum of the company's history and products.

C.V. **Wedgwood** (Cicely Veronica Wedgwood, b. 1910, DBE 1968) Historian of the 17c, known in particular for her three-volume history of the English Civil War (*The King's Peace* 1955, *The King's War* 1958, *The Trial of Charles I* 1964). She was appointed in 1969 to the Order of *Merit.

We Didn't Mean to Go to Sea see Arthur *Ransome.

Wee Frees see *Free Church of Scotland.

'**A week is a long time in politics**' see Harold *Wilson.

'**We few, we happy few**' see St *Crispin.

weight In the early 1990s most ordinary commodities, such as groceries or fruit, are still bought by the public on the *imperial system; but packaged goods are more likely to be *metric. The smallest everyday unit in the imperial system is the ounce: there are 16 ounces in a pound, 14 pounds in a stone, 8 stone (or 112 pounds) in a hundredweight, and 20 hundredweight in a ton. The stone is now little used as a measure except in one very common context, the weight of a human being. Jewellers use an older measure, *troy weight.

weights and measures see *area, *length, fluid *volume and *weight.

welfare state The concept is most closely associated in Britain with the legislation introduced by the Labour government of 1945–50, including the *National Health Service and an extension of the existing *national insurance. But its origins are much earlier. In 1888 the American author Edward Bellamy published a widely read Utopian novel (*Looking Backward: 2000–1887*) in which he foresaw the community in the year 2000 guaranteeing 'the nurture, education, and comfortable maintenance of every citizen from the cradle to the grave'. In Germany, also in the 1880s, Bismarck introduced sickness and old-age insurance for wage earners. In Britain the Liberals brought in unemployment insurance in 1911, and laid the foundations for sickness benefit and old-age pensions. But the most comprehensive programme was laid out in the *Beveridge Report of 1942, which picked up the cradle-to-grave theme. The concept that all should have a right to free welfare on a broad front remained a consensus in Britain until the 1980s, when the *Thatcher government tended to ridicule the welfare state as the 'nanny' state. In 1993 a wide-ranging government review was launched, placing all aspects of the welfare state under close scrutiny in response to ever-mounting costs.

Wellcome A name of great significance in British medicine. The pharmaceutical group Wellcome, one of the largest companies in Britain, derives from the firm established in London in 1880 by two American chemists, Silas Burroughs (1846–95) and Henry Wellcome (1853–1936). Wellcome built the firm into a major enterprise, and in his will left the entire company to the Wellcome Trust – a charity to aid medical research. By the early 1990s the Trustees were funding research to the tune of about £100 million per year. Related projects are the Wellcome Institute and the Wellcome Museum for the History of Medicine. These have grown from the collections made by Wellcome himself during the last 40 years of his life. The institute, with a magnificent medical library of some 500,000 volumes, is now closely linked with London's University College; and since 1976 the museum has been on indefinite loan to the Science Museum, where part of it is on permanent exhibition.

In 1986 the Trustees sold a proportion of the company to diversify their investment. In 1992 another £2bn of shares was placed on the market, further reducing their holding in Wellcome (to a little over 40%).

Sam **Weller** see *Pickwick Papers*.

Wellington World War II bomber made by Vickers. It was the workhorse of Bomber Command until 1943, car-

Caricature portrait of the great duke as a Wellington boot: anonymous hand-coloured etching of 1827.

rying a crew of six on night raids (the smaller *Blenheim was used in daylight after the Wellington proved too vulnerable to fighters). Universally known at the time by its nickname, the Wimpy, it was produced in greater numbers than any other bomber (nearly 12,000 were made) and had a fabric skin on a geodesic frame designed by Barnes *Wallis; the great advantage of this was that it could fly even with the skin much damaged by flak. But it was unable to carry the heavier bombs of the later war years and was largely replaced by the *Lancaster, though remaining in service until 1953.

Duke of **Wellington** (Arthur Wellesley, 1769–1852, kt 1804, duke 1814) Britain's leading soldier in the Napoleonic Wars and later prime minister (1828–30). Born in Dublin, in the Protestant Irish gentry, he began his career in the pampered manner of the times, with commissions bought for him in various regiments and seats procured in the Irish and English houses of parliament. The first hint of his talents was seen in India (1796–1804), where he won a series of impressive victories in local wars. His military skill was confirmed in the *Peninsular War. When he finally broke through the Pyrenees in 1813, his was the first hostile army on French soil since the rise of Napoleon. The campaign not only propelled him rapidly through the ranks of the peerage, but brought financial awards from parliament amounting to £500,000.

In March 1815 he was at the congress of Vienna, deliberating on the future shape of Europe after the *Napoleonic Wars, when news came that Napoleon had escaped from Elba. Wellington returned to achieve his greatest victory, at *Waterloo. This not only brought him further wealth (another £200,000 from the government) but gave him the prestige to resume a political career at the highest level. In 1818 he joined Lord Liverpool's

Measurements of weight		
Imperial		*Metric*
1 ounce	=	28.35 grams
(16 ounces) **1 pound**	=	453.59 grams
2.2 pounds	=	**1 kilogram** (1000 grams)
(14 pounds) **1 stone**	=	6.35 kilograms
(112 pounds) **1 hundredweight**	=	50.8 kilograms
2204.6 pounds	=	**1000 kilograms** (1 tonne)
(2240 pounds, 20 hundredweight) **1 ton**	=	1016 kilograms

Tory cabinet. Ten years later, when the Tory party had split into factions over Catholic emancipation and *Canning's liberal foreign policy, Wellington seemed the only man who might hold the government together.

His two years as prime minister were marked by one great success (the *Emancipation Act of 1829, achieved in alliance with his home secretary, *Peel) and by one great disaster – Wellington's own blank assertion that no political reform of any kind was necessary, which lost him all credibility in the period of intense agitation leading up to the *Reform Act. He never fully adjusted to reform (he was long remembered for his comment on the members of the first reformed parliament, that he had never seen 'so many shocking bad hats'), but the memory of his earlier achievements gave him great stature at the end of his long life. With the bounty from his victories he bought *Apsley House and *Stratfield Saye. Tennyson, in his ode on Wellington's death, called him the 'ever-loyal iron leader' and the 'Great Duke'; and he has been frequently known as the 'Iron Duke'.

Wellington College Boys' *public school in Berkshire, founded in 1853 by public subscription in memory of the duke of *Wellington, who had died the previous year. In keeping with its origins the school long maintained a military tradition. Since 1978 girls have been admitted for the last two years, in the sixth form.

Wellington Museum see *Apsley House.

wellingtons Leather knee-length boots worn in the early 19C, usually higher over the knee than at the back, were named Wellington boots after the duke. Slightly shorter boots with level tops were made of rubber in the late 19C, and by the mid-20C wellingtons meant exclusively calf-length rubber boots of this type. They have traditionally been black, but in the past two decades 'green wellies' became a fashion (associated, but not exclusively so, with *Sloane Rangers). Gumboot was originally an American word for the same product.

The **Well of Loneliness** (1928) Novel by Radclyffe Hall (1883–1943), in which she presented a serious and sympathetic account of a lesbian relationship. On its first publication it was prosecuted for *obscenity and was banned. It was reissued in 1949.

Wells (8000 in 1981) Cathedral town in Somerset, renowned for the unspoilt perfection of an entire range of ecclesiastical buildings. A church is believed to have been established here in the early 8C and Wells became a diocese in 909. Over the centuries there were tussles as to whether the bishop's seat should be here or at Bath, but in 1245 the compromise was established whereby the bishop is of Bath and Wells but his seat is at Wells.

The glories of the cathedral begin with its extraordinary west front (mid-13C), decorated with some 300 separate statues, originally all coloured. The severe Early English nave is dominated by two curving scissor arches, boldly crossing it and interrupting the view; they were added in the early 14C to strengthen the base of the central tower shortly after its completion. In the north transept is a famous 24-hour astronomical clock, also of the 14C, with mounted knights emerging on the hour from a castle at the top; nearby a large seated figure known as Jack Blandiver strikes the quarters on a bell. Leading off the north transept is a magnificent flight of stone steps, part of which branches off into the beautiful early 14C octagonal chapter house, with its central column exploding like a firework into the multiple ribs of the roof.

Outside the cathedral there survives an entire street of 14C houses built for the clergy, Vicars' Close. There are two medieval gatehouses, the Penniless Porch and the Bishop's Eye; the latter leads to the 13C Bishop's Palace, which is still the episcopal residence. The palace is surrounded by a moat (fed by the springs from which Wells takes its name), and the swans on the moat are trained to ring a bell when they consider it time for a meal.

Allan **Wells** (b. 1952) Scottish athlete who won two gold medals (200m and 4x100m relay) and a silver (100m) in the 1978 Commonwealth Games. At the 1980 Olympic Games he won gold in the 100 metres and silver in the 200 metres (these were, admittedly, the Moscow Olympics, boycotted by the Americans). In the 1982 Commonwealth Games he won the 100 metres and shared his 200 metres title in a dead heat with another runner, Mike McFarlane.

H.G. **Wells** (Herbert George Wells, 1866–1946) Novelist and pioneer of science fiction. The son of an unsuccessful small shopkeeper and of a domestic servant (his mother was eventually housekeeper at *Uppark), and himself apprenticed to a draper after leaving school at 14, he used his own experiences as the basis for a series of novels about lower-middle-class life – *Love and Mr Lewisham* (1900), **Kipps* (1905), *Tono-Bungay* (1909) and *The *History of Mr Polly* (1910). But he had made his name earlier with some very original works of science fiction. Like their modern successors (but unlike the earlier Jules Verne), these use the dislocation of time and space to comment on our own society. *The *Time Machine* (1895) was the first; others include *The Invisible Man* (1897), *The *War of the Worlds* (1898) and *The First Men in the Moon* (1901). His famous film script for **Things to Come* (1936) was in the same tradition. *The Country of the Blind*, published in a collection in 1911, has remained a classic among short stories.

Many of Wells' early books are about society changing and improving, and from 1903 he became an active member of the *Fabian Society (briefly as it turned out, because he soon quarrelled with the star turn, G.B. *Shaw). He was also a firm advocate of sexual freedom, and had a long relationship with Rebecca *West.

Welsh By far the most successful survivor among the ancient *Celtic languages. There has been no period at which it was not a living language, and today it remains the first language of more than half a million people in *Wales (nearly 20% of the total), for whom programmes are broadcast on radio and television. There is a full and rich Welsh literature, ranging from the medieval tales of the *Mabinogion to the fiction of Daniel *Owen. The Welsh bardic tradition is enthusiastically kept alive by means of the *eisteddfod.

The **Welsh** Those *British citizens who were born in or now live in *Wales. Collectively they have a stronger Celtic strain than any other group in the country, because their region was the largest and most defensible territory of the ancient *Britons.

Welsh black cattle see *cattle.

Welsh corgi see *corgi.

Welsh dragon A red dragon, long associated with Wales, was officially recognized in 1801 as the royal badge of Wales. It also forms the central figure of the Welsh flag, on a green and white ground.

Welsh Folk Museum (7km/4m W of Cardiff) Branch of the *National Museum of Wales, occupying St Fagan's Castle (an Elizabethan mansion within the wall of an earlier stronghold) and the surrounding 32ha/80ac of parkland. In the house and in newly built galleries there are displays of Welsh social and agricultural history, and characteristic buildings of different kinds have been rescued from all over Wales and reconstructed in the grounds.

Welsh Industrial and Maritime Museum (Cardiff) Branch of the *National Museum of Wales, opened in 1977 to exhibit large engines and machines.

Welsh Mountain see *ponies and *sheep.

Welsh National War Memorial see *Cardiff.

Welsh National Opera The first of Britain's three regional opera companies (the others being Scottish Opera and Opera North), and the only one to have grown from amateur beginnings. It first performed in Cardiff in 1946. As a result of the great Welsh tradition of singing, the new company soon had enthusiastic choruses in both Cardiff and Swansea, each preparing separately for the next production. It was not until the 1970s that the enterprise became fully professional. In recent years it has had critical success with ambitious productions involving leading European artists – notably Verdi's *Otello* (1986) and *Falstaff* (1988) staged by the German director Peter Stein, who was also responsible for Debussy's *Pelléas et Mélisande* (1992) conducted by Pierre Boulez. When at home in Cardiff the company performs in the New Theatre, but it also tours throughout Wales and central England – sometimes, in small places, with the accompaniment reduced to a few instruments or even to a single piano.

Welsh Office (Cardiff) Government department responsible for the administration of Wales, created in 1964 along the lines of the *Scottish Office but with less fully devolved powers. Unlike for Scotland, the final responsibility in many areas of home policy remains with the appropriate departments in Whitehall. For secretaries of state since 1983 see the *cabinet.

Welsh rabbit Toast with cheese on it, which is heated under a grill until it flows over the edges. The dish was known under this name from the early 18C, when a very similar dish was called a Scotch rabbit. It is not known in what sense they were rabbits; perhaps it was a joke at the expense of regional cuisine, too poor to afford even real rabbit. The version 'Welsh rarebit' is a later attempt to explain the improbable name.

Welsh terrier see *terriers.

Welsh valleys see *Rhondda Valley.

Welwyn see *garden city.

Wembley Area of northwest London known in particular for the stadium and halls built for the British Empire Exhibition of 1924. The stadium was ready by 1923 to mount the sporting event with which it has become most associated, the *Cup Final; it was later the scene of the 1948 Olympic Games. Some of the original exhibition halls survive as warehouses.

The *Empire Pool, now known as the Wembley Arena, was added in 1934; and the Wembley Conference Centre was opened in 1977.

Great **Wen** see William *Cobbett.

Wendy see *Peter Pan.

Wensleydale A Yorkshire dale, the valley of the river Ure, known for its cheese as well as its beauty (Wensley is one of the villages). By the early 19C Wensleydale was a general name for cheese from any of the neighbouring dales. In the 1890s production began in a central creamery at Hawes, the first of several factories to produce the white and flaky variety now known as Wensleydale. By the late 1950s none was being made by the traditional method in farmhouses.

Wentworth Golf course at Virginia Water in Surrey, famous as the location for the annual World Matchplay Championship. Inaugurated in 1964, this is a knockout competition between 12 (originally 8) leading international players. It takes place on Wentworth's West course – designed in the 1920s and widely known in more recent years as the Burma Road.

'We shall fight on the beaches' The best remembered phrase from the speech made by Churchill to the House of Commons on 4 June 1940, immediately after the retreat from *Dunkirk: 'We shall defend our island whatever the cost may be, we shall fight on the beaches, we shall fight on the landing grounds, we shall fight in the fields and in the streets, we shall fight in the hills; we shall never surrender.'

Arnold **Wesker** (b. 1932) Playwright whose early work successfully turned his own experiences (growing up in a left-wing Jewish family in the East End of London) into a succession of plays rooted in everyday life but dealing with utopian hopes and failures. The character of Ronnie Kahn is the central figure of a trilogy: *Chicken Soup with Barley* (1958) and *I'm Talking about Jerusalem* (1960) feature his family, but in the best known of the three, *Roots* (1959), he is only an unseen influence. Wesker's first play, *The Kitchen* (not given a full production until 1961), makes virtuoso use of the streamlined chaos in a large commercial kitchen and was based on the author's experiences as a pastry cook.

Charles **Wesley** (1707–88) One of the founders of the *Methodist movement, with his elder brother John. Charles's greatest contribution was in the writing of hymns, which played an important part in the spiritual fervour of Methodist worship. Of some 7500 published under the joint names of the two brothers, nearly all were by Charles. They include such perennial favourites as *Jesu, lover of my soul* and *Love divine, all loves excelling*; and one that became a popular carol, *Hark! the herald angels sing*.

John **Wesley** (1703–91) Founder of the *Methodist movement. Ordained an Anglican clergyman in 1725, he became in 1729 the leading member of the Holy Club, a devotional group started in Oxford by his younger brother, Charles *Wesley. Their methodical programme of prayer and study caused the young men to be ridiculed as Methodists. Together with another member of their club, George *Whitefield, the Wesleys began preaching an intensely personal message of individual salvation, in which each listener was to be persuaded of God's eagerness to save him or her while being threatened with the alternative of a very vivid Hell – a technique familiar ever since in Christian evangelism. When conventional Anglican clergy closed their pulpits to sermons of such fervour (weeping and fainting were commonplace in Methodist congregations), Whitefield and Wesley began preaching in the open air.

From 1739 Wesley spent much of the rest of his life riding round the country (5000 miles each year, it was calculated), establishing and encouraging local congregations. In his view this was a revival within the *Church of England, but in 1784 he took the step of ordaining two of his preachers when a bishop refused to do so. This action signalled a rift which became absolute after his death; the Methodists then went their way as a separate church. The house where Wesley lived and died, in London's City Road, is kept as a museum. (For the number of practising Methodists in England in 1989, see under *Christians.)

Wessex The *Anglo-Saxon kingdom which eventually asserted control over the rest of the country and established a unified England. The heartland of Wessex was the southern counties of Hampshire, Wiltshire, Somerset and Dorset. During the 7–8c there was much pressure from *Mercia to the north, but in the early 9c the kings of Wessex gained control of the region of Devon and Cornwall to the west and of the Anglo-Saxon kingdoms of Sussex and Kent to the east. It was from this base, across the entire south of the island, that *Alfred in the late 9c successfully resisted the advance of the *Danes who had overrun eastern England and much of Mercia. That achievement caused him to be considered the king of all the English; and when the reconquest of the Danish territories was completed by his grandson Athelstan (by about 930), the rulers of other regions formally accepted Athelstan's overlordship as king of England.

Rebecca **West** (name adopted by Cicily Fairfield, 1892–1983, DBE 1959) Writer and committed feminist; her chosen name belongs to the independent-minded heroine of Ibsen's play *Rosmersholm*. Though author of many novels, she excelled in books where she took the role of reporter – *Black Lamb and Grey Falcon* (1941) on Yugoslavia or *The Meaning of Treason* (1949), based on the Nuremberg trials.

Her robust review of a book by H.G. *Wells advocating free love (*Marriage* 1912) led to his suggestion that they should meet and to the resulting ten-year love affair which was the dominant relationship of her life.

Timothy **West** (b. 1934) Actor whose performance as Edward VII in a 1973 television serial brought him a wide audience, and whose chunky bulldog quality makes him ideal for historical figures of similar character – as in *Churchill and the Generals* (1979) or *Beecham* (1980 on stage, 1989 TV). He has also portrayed similarly hard men in fiction (*Hard Times* 1977, *Brass* 1982–90). He is married to Prunella *Scales.

West Bromwich Albion, known as Throstles, Baggies and Albion (The Hawthorns, West Bromwich). Football club founded in 1879 as West Bromwich Strollers by employees of Salter's Spring Works. Strollers became Albion in 1881 and the club was a founder member of the *Football League in 1888. Club victories: FA Cup 1888, 92, 1931, 54, 68; League Champions 1920; League Cup 1966.

Westbury Court (14km/9m SW of Gloucester) Britain's only surviving example of a late-17c Dutch garden, laid out in 1696–1703 in the fashion brought from Holland by William III and Mary. Westbury escaped alteration in the romantic phase of *landscape gardening, but by the 20c the yews and hollies had grown too large for their original more regimented purpose. They have recently been replanted and clipped into the shapes which can be seen, together with the surviving canal and Tall Pavilion, in the bird's eye view engraved by Johannes Kip in about 1707.

Westbury White Horse (26km/16m SE of Bath) As at *Uffington, the local tradition is that the chalk figure

on the hillside commemorates a victory by Alfred the Great over the Danes, in this case at nearby Edington in 878. However, there is no evidence that the white horse at Westbury existed earlier than the 18c.

West Country Term used for the southwestern area of England, from Somerset and Dorset through to Devon and Cornwall.

West End Area of London, originally comprising Mayfair and Soho but now more extensive, which contains the theatres and the most expensive shops. It was the western end of 18c London.

Western Daily Press The morning newspaper of the West Country, based in Bristol and distributed in as many as eight counties. It was established in 1858 as Bristol's first daily paper.

Western European Union (WEU) Defence alliance within the *EC, of which the members in 1993 were Belgium, France, Germany, Italy, Luxembourg, the Netherlands, Portugal, Spain and the UK. It derives originally from a treaty signed in Brussels in 1948 by five of the member states (West Germany and Italy joined in 1954, Portugal and Spain in 1988). One of the decisions at *Maastricht in 1991 was that the WEU should be developed as an EC defence force, and WEU ships and aircraft were sent in 1992 to the Adriatic to enforce sanctions against Yugoslavia.

Western Isles (30,000 in 1991, administrative centre Stornoway) The *islands area covering the Outer *Hebrides (before 1975 divided between the *counties of Inverness and of Ross and Cromarty). The name Western Isles has in the past been used for the whole of the Hebrides.

Western Samoa Independent country from 1962 and a full member of the *Commonwealth since 1970. It comprises the greater part of Samoa, a group of islands in the south Pacific (the rest being American Samoa). During the 19c Britain, Germany and the USA competed for influence until a treaty of 1899 made Western Samoa a German colony. After World War I control passed to New Zealand under a League of Nations *mandate. Since independence Malietoa Tanumafili II has been head of state, in the role of a constitutional monarch.

West Glamorgan (369,000 in 1991, administrative centre Swansea) Since 1974 a *county in Wales, formed from part of Glamorgan and the former county borough of Swansea.

West Ham United, known as the Hammers (Upton Park, London E13). Football club formed in 1895 by employees of a shipbuilding yard, as the Thames Ironworks Football Club. It became professional in 1898 and was relaunched in 1900 as West Ham United. Elected to Division 2 of the *Football League in 1919, it had no major successes until the 1960s when Bobby Moore, Geoff Hurst and Martin Peters were in the team. Club victories: FA Cup 1964, 75, 80; European Cup-Winners' Cup 1965.

West Highland white terrier see *terriers.

West Indians see *ethnic and religious minorities.

West Indies Federation Political grouping of the ten main British colonies in the Caribbean, which lasted from 1958 to 1962. Widely separated geographically, and with different traditions, the group was formed in the belief that only together could its members achieve independence within the *Commonwealth. It was intended by Britain that the Federation should become independent in 1962. But *Jamaica and *Trinidad seceded and became separately independent in that year. The other eight were *Antigua, *Barbados, *Dominica, *Grenada, *Montserrat, *St Kitts (with Nevis and *Anguilla), *St Lucia and *St Vincent, most of whom later found their own separate paths to independence.

Westland (1986) The most public cabinet row during the Thatcher administration. The subject was the financially insecure Westland helicopter company, based in Yeovil in Somerset. Michael *Heseltine, the secretary of state for defence, favoured a rescue bid by a European consortium; Leon *Brittan, secretary of state for trade and industry, agreed with the Westland directors in preferring a deal with a US firm, Sikorski.

In January 1986 Heseltine caused a sensation by resigning in the middle of a cabinet meeting, when Mrs Thatcher insisted that ministerial statements on the issue should be approved by the Cabinet Office. Subsequently a letter from the solicitor general, critical of Heseltine, was leaked. By the end of January Brittan had also resigned, admitting that he had approved the leak. The Opposition argued that it must have been authorized at a higher level, by the prime minister; but she stated that she had not been informed, though her press secretary had known the details. The deal with Sikorski went through; and nearly five years later Heseltine challenged for the leadership of the Conservative party, starting a process which brought Mrs Thatcher's premiership to an end.

West Lothian Until 1975 a *county in east central Scotland, on the south shore of the Firth of Forth, now part of the Lothian region.

Richard **Westmacott** (1775–1856, kt 1837) Sculptor responsible for two of the best-known public statues in England, *Achilles* in *Hyde Park and the Copper Horse at *Windsor.

West Midlands (2,552,000 in 1991) *Metropolitan county in central England, consisting of seven *districts – Birmingham, Coventry, Dudley, Sandwell, Solihull, Walsall and Wolverhampton.

West Midlands Serious Crime Squad The group which has done most in recent years to damage the reputation of the *police. The squad was disbanded in 1989 after complaints about its methods, including the intimidation of suspects. Subsequently the convictions of more than ten people were quashed after *ESDA proof that evidence had been fabricated in their cases by members of the squad. Three former detectives from the squad were acquitted of perjury charges in June 1991, and in 1992 the Director of Public Prosecutions announced that there was insufficient evidence to bring charges against any other officers. Members of the squad helped to interrogate the *Birmingham Six in 1974, but the four officers charged in 1992 in relation to that case were part of the normal West Midlands police force.

Westminster (London SW1) One of the two historic centres of what is now *London, though not absorbed within the metropolis until the 18C. The other centre was the original walled *City of London. Westminster derived its name from being the monastery church to the west of the city. Legend takes the founding of the monastery back to a Saxon king of the 7C; but its importance began with the patronage in the 11C of Edward the Confessor, who began building a new abbey church (*Westminster Abbey) and established here the *Palace of Westminster. In 1900 Westminster was itself granted a charter as a city with its

The interior of Westminster Hall (see next page), with its superb 14C hammer-beam roof.

own Lord Mayor. Since 1965 it has also been a borough of *Greater London, extending west to Chelsea, east to the City and north as far as Regent's Park – an area including the three *Westminster cemeteries sold in 1987.

Archbishop of **Westminster** Senior Roman Catholic prelate in England and Wales and president of the church's governing body, the Bishop's Conference. The see was created in 1850, with Cardinal *Wiseman as the first archbishop, when Pius IX decided to restore a diocesan hierarchy in Britain in response to an increasing population of *Roman Catholics and a gradual easing of restrictions, as seen on the political front in the *Emancipation Act of 1829. The archiepiscopal seat is *Westminster Cathedral, and since 1976 the archbishop has been Cardinal *Hume.

Statute of **Westminster** see *Commonwealth of Nations and *dominion status.

Westminster Abbey (London SW1) There has been at *Westminster an abbey dedicated to St Peter since before the Norman Conquest. William I was crowned here on Christmas Day in 1066, and the abbey has been the site of every subsequent coronation. (The *Coronation Chair stands behind the high altar.) The present building dates largely from the 13–14C, apart from the two towers at the main entrance which were added in the 18C by Hawksmoor (adapting a design by Wren). The abbey contains memorials to many of the nation's most honoured dead – see *Poets' Corner and the *Unknown Warrior.

Westminster Bridge Bridge crossing the Thames beside the Houses of Parliament, the view from which prompted Wordsworth in 1802 to write his famous sonnet beginning 'Earth has not anything to show more fair'. The bridge that he stood on was the first to be built across the Thames in London since the medieval *London Bridge. It had opened in 1750 and was replaced by the present cast-iron bridge in 1862.

Westminster Cathedral (London SW1) Seat of the archbishop of *Westminster, whose Roman Catholic diocese was established in 1850 as the first in Britain since the *Reformation. The architect was John Francis Bentley (1839–1902). The fabric of the cathedral was completed in 1903, but the work of decoration still continues.

Westminster cemeteries Three cemeteries which were the subject of controversy after the Westminster City Council sold them to an estate agent for 5 pence each in 1987 – giving rise to the observation that in Britain at that time it was possible to buy half a pint of beer and three cemeteries and still have change from a pound. The council bought them back five years later for rather more.

Westminster Hall (London SW1) The nation's most historic secular interior (see previous page). Built by William II in the late 11C as a new great hall for the *Palace of Westminster, it was refashioned in its upper levels by Richard II in 1394–9, acquiring at that time its magnificent oak *hammer-beam roof. The hall has been used for parliaments (including the *Model Parliament),

for state trials (most notably that of *Charles I), and in the past hundred years for the lying-in-state of great political leaders; Gladstone in 1898 was the first, Churchill in 1965 the most recent.

Westminster Hospital (London SW1) London's first hospital to be funded by private donations, established in 1715. A minority group of trustees, dissatisfied with the available accommodation, founded *St George's Hospital in 1733 as a separate venture. The Westminster occupied several premises close to the abbey before moving in 1939 to a site near Lambeth Bridge; in 1993 it moved again, to Chelsea, becoming known as the Chelsea and Westminster Hospital.

Westminster School Boys' *public school, with ancient buildings behind *Westminster Abbey. There was a school here from at least the 12C, run by the abbey's Benedictine monks (their successors are still a teaching community, at *Ampleforth). At the Reformation Westminster was re-established as a Protestant school and its new foundation is taken as dating from 1560, when Elizabeth I gave it her royal patronage. Girls are now admitted for the last two years, in the sixth form.

Westmorland Former *county in northwest England with its administrative centre at Kendal, merged in 1974 with Cumberland and part of Lancashire to form Cumbria.

Westonbirt Arboretum (29km/18m N of Bath) Britain's finest collection of trees and shrubs, with some 17,000 specimens from all round the world, started in 1829 by Robert Holford and continued after his death by his son, Sir George. Since 1965 it has been maintained by the *Forestry Commission. Robert Holford also built Westonbirt House, one of the most magnificent of Victorian mansions, which has been a girls' school since 1928.

West Sussex (714,000 in 1991, administrative centre Chichester) Since 1974 a *county on the south coast of England, previously part of *Sussex.

Westward Ho! (1855) Novel by Charles *Kingsley, inspired by his sense of patriotic fervour over the *Crimean War. Intended for adults, it proved immensely popular with children. The exploits of heroic English seamen are set against the threat of the Armada, with scheming Jesuits in the background and the blood-curdling horrors of the Inquisition.

Vivienne **Westwood** (b. 1941) Designer who introduced to fashion the jagged brightness of *punk. In the 1970s she and her partner of that time, Malcolm McLaren, had a shop in the King's Road (with a bewildering succession of names) which was a centre of punk; indeed McLaren was instrumental in launching the first punk rock group, the *Sex Pistols. Westwood began in 1981 a series of fashion shows, each with a strongly differentiated theme – pirates 1981, savages 1982, muddy colours and bras over sweaters 1983, fluorescent with white 1984, company logos 1985. From the mid-1980s she has moved more towards traditional couture, with fine cutting and expensive fabrics, and has extended her range to include menswear. She is the only person to have won the British Designer of the Year Award in successive years (1990, 91).

West Wycombe Park (32km/20m SE of Oxford) House of the early 18C, remodelled from 1739 to 1781 in a variety of contemporary styles. It has baroque,

Palladian, rococo and neoclassical elements, and the temples in the park include early examples of the Greek Revival. The owner, following his own whims in these matters, was Sir Francis Dashwood (1708–81). He is known also as a leading member of the *Hellfire Club, which is believed to have met for its rituals in the caves to the north of the park.

West Yorkshire (2,014,000 in 1991) *Metropolitan county in northern England, consisting of five *districts – Bradford, Calderdale, Kirklees, Leeds and Wakefield.

wets Members of the Conservative party in parliament during the 1980s who did not agree with Mrs *Thatcher's right-wing policies, particularly *monetarism. The term, later adopted by the wets themselves as a name to be proud of, was the prime minister's favourite adjective for anyone who held less absolute views than herself. Such a person would also be described as 'not one of us'.

WEU see *Western European Union.

Mr **W.H.** see The *Sonnets.

'What do you think of it so far?' see The *Morecambe and Wise Show.

'What's in a name?' see *Romeo and Juliet.

What's My Line? American television game show which in the 1950s established a group of Britain's earliest television personalities. Isobel Barnett, David Nixon, Gilbert Harding and Barbara Kelly were the most regular of the panellists invited by Eamonn Andrews, in the chair, to discover by oblique questions the occupation of the contestant.

What the Papers Say (from 1956) Britain's longest-running weekly television programme, made by Granada TV and transmitted on ITV until transferred in the 1980s to Channel 4 and then to BBC2. Each week a leading journalist makes a selection from the week's newspapers and gives a guided tour (witty or forceful according to the context) through the assembled cuttings.

'Whaur's your Wullie Shakspear noo?' Triumphant question supposedly shouted by a member of the audience after the sensationally successful first night, in Edinburgh in 1756, of Douglas – a verse tragedy by the Scottish playwright John Home (1722–1808).

Charles **Wheatstone** (1802–75, kt 1868) Physicist who from 1834 was professor of experimental physics at King's College, London. He made many discoveries in the fields of acoustics and telegraphy, but is remembered chiefly for the simple device, known now as the Wheatstone bridge, which he designed for measuring electrical resistance.

Mortimer **Wheeler** (1890–1976, kt 1952) Archaeologist who with his wife, Tessa, excavated between the wars several Roman sites in Britain and the great Iron Age fort of *Maiden Castle. Their working partnership ended with her death in 1936. He became Britain's best-known archaeologist, to the broader public, through his regular appearances in the 1950s on the television panel game Animal, Vegetable and Mineral.

Huw **Wheldon** (1916–86, kt 1976) Welsh television producer, presenter and executive who had a major influence on the development in Britain of arts programmes and documentaries. His single greatest contribution was

Monitor, much enlivened by his own expansive and often partisan enthusiasms. He also had executive control over increasingly large sections of BBC TV between 1962 and 1975. His subsequent freelance career included a series on the royal palaces and collections (Royal Heritage 1977).

whelk stall For at least the past century the whelk stall has been proverbial as the smallest possible commercial enterprise ('he couldn't even run a whelk stall'), reflecting the popularity of these small open-air ventures in large cities and at seaside resorts. Sweet Molly Malone is in a similar business, in the traditional song, wheeling her barrow through Dublin's streets and crying 'Cockles and mussels! alive, alive, oh!'. The fare on a typical stall, eaten cold after being boiled and seasoned with vinegar, includes cockles, the whelk itself (a large snail-like gastropod), its cousin the winkle (so much smaller that it needs a pin to extract it, thus providing the name for the *winkle-pickers of the 1950s) and jellied eels (boiled freshwater eels, jellied in an aspic of their own juice).

'When I consider how my light is spent' see John *Milton.

When I survey the wondrous Cross see Isaac *Watts.

Which? The first and still the best-known publication by the Consumers' Association, formed in 1957 by Michael Young. As its name implies, Which? tests and reports on products available to the consumer. Its first issue appeared in October 1957 with a cover photograph of two housewives looking at four kettles. The issue brought in 10,000 subscribers (a subscription includes membership of the association), and the next year two of the manufacturers modified their kettles to answer the magazine's criticisms. Membership reached 100,000 in 1958, and in 1959 Which? changed from quarterly to monthly publication. The association's activities have extended greatly over the years both as publisher (of the *Good Food Guide among other titles) and as a pressure group. By the early 1990s there were nearly a million members.

Alan **Whicker** (b. 1925) Television reporter who began his career in 1947 on *Tonight and since 1959 has been busy with human-interest travel documentaries, mostly in series entitled Whicker's World or something similar. His quarry, as he roams the planet, is any exotic character – whom he will briskly describe and gently interview before moving on to pin down the next in line.

Whigs see *Tories and Whigs.

While shepherds watched their flocks by night Hymn by Nahum Tate (1652–1715), which is now also popular as a *carol. It was originally sung to a traditional tune (the one used today for God rest you merry, gentlemen), but this has long been replaced by the present one, known as 'Winchester Old', which was published in a metrical psalter of 1592.

Whips Members of parliament responsible for managing party business in both Houses and for ensuring the maximum vote from their own party at the end of an important debate. Their role began in the 18C with the increasing importance of the *two-party system. They were known then as whippers-in (the hunt servants responsible for ensuring that hounds do not stray). The government chief whip, whose office is at 12 *Downing Street, liaises closely with the chief whip of the Opposition to organize the day-to-day business of parliamentary debate; traditionally they do not themselves join in the debate, so

Stipple-engraved glass by Laurence Whistler (Farewell Festival, 1976), with the light glinting on the windscreens of the funeral cars.

as not to jeopardize their working relationship. Every week the whips send out to their party members a document (which itself is also known as 'the whip') detailing the forthcoming debates and underlining them in three categories of importance. A 'three-line whip' means that, except in case of illness, a member must be present to vote in the division.

Whipsnade (Whipsnade Wild Animal Park, 19km/12m to the NW of St Albans) Open zoo where the uncaged conservation of wild animals and the breeding in captivity of endangered species was pioneered from 1931 by the Zoological Society, as an extension of their activities at *London Zoo. The original purpose was scientific, but with the development of *safari parks elsewhere the freedom of the public to move among the animals has steadily increased; the African animals can even be viewed from a narrow-gauge steam train which itself derives from Africa.

whisky Strong alcoholic drink, originally local to Scotland and Ireland, distilled from a mash of fermented grain, traditionally malted barley. Whisky derives from the first word of *uisge beatha*, Gaelic for 'water of life'. Other spirits are known by the same phrase in different languages (*eau de vie, akvavit*); the reason is that *aqua vitae* (Latin for 'water of life') was the Roman term for any distilled alcohol. The Scots spell the word 'whisky' and the Irish 'whiskey', the latter being the version that has travelled to the USA.

It was not until the early 19C that whisky began to be distilled commercially in Scotland, instead of just for local use. The best-known Scottish distilleries are in the northeast, in the Grampian region. They provide the unblended Highland malts which are considered the finest of all whiskies, the normal commercial varieties being blended from several sources.

Whisky Galore (1949) One of the *Ealing comedies, based on a novel by Compton *Mackenzie which was inspired by a real event of World War II. A ship with a cargo of whisky goes aground off *Barra, provoking a war of nerves and ingenuity between excise officers and the thirsty islanders.

Whispering Gallery see *St Paul's Cathedral.

whist The most widely played of card games until replaced by its own progeny, the more complex game of bridge. Whist is believed to have developed in England, where it was known by the early 16C. The definitive rules were established in Edmond Hoyle's *Short Treatise on the Game of Whist* (1742). The essential feature of the game is two pairs of players competing to win seven or more of the 13 available tricks (from the pack of 52 cards), with one of the four suits declared as trumps. Bridge added much greater sophistication in two areas – the method of playing the hand and the system of scoring. It began to be developed in Greece and Turkey in the 1860s, and achieved its present form in the USA in the 1920s.

whistle-blowers People who speak out, at a risk to their own employment, about unacceptable practices of any kind. To encourage employees to reveal dangers to health and safety in places of work, the government put forward proposals in 1992 to protect whistle-blowers against dismissal or victimization. Whistle-blowers alerting the public to government practices are less popular and are more often described as *moles.

James McNeill **Whistler** (1834–1903) American artist, based in London from 1859 (he had over the years no less than eight different addresses in *Chelsea). As a student in Paris he had been influenced by the new fashion for everything Japanese, and there is an oriental elegance in the muted paintings to which he gave titles such as 'symphonies', 'arrangements' or 'nocturnes'; the best known is the portrait of his mother, now in the Louvre, which he called *Arrangement in Grey and Black*. He was an important influence on the *Aesthetic movement; it was Ruskin's hostile response to one of his paintings at the *Grosvenor Gallery which led to a famous lawsuit and Whistler's damages of one farthing. He was known both for a quarrelsome nature and a brilliant wit (answering Oscar Wilde's 'I wish I had said that' with 'You will, Oscar, you will'). The apt title which he chose for a collection of his own writing was *The Gentle Art of Making Enemies* (1890).

Whistler brothers The elder, Rex (1905–44), was a precociously talented decorative artist, book illustrator and set designer, best known now for two large murals – *The Pursuit of Rare Meats* in 1927 for the Tate Gallery (an appropriate theme in that the room was and remains a restaurant), and the more ambitious scheme of 1937 at *Plas Newydd. He was killed on active service in the war. His younger brother Laurence (b. 1912) led the revival of glass-engraving in Britain. He is known for the complex architectural scenes and landscapes which he is able to achieve on goblets, bowls and more recently windows, showing up in subtle shades of white against a black background.

Whitaker family Two brothers and a sister with a distinguished record in British showjumping. Michael (b. 1960) has won the King George V Gold Cup in 1982, 1989 and 1992 and the Hickstead Derby in 1992. Veronique (b. 1959) won the Queen Elizabeth II Cup in 1984. And John (b. 1955) won the King George V Gold Cup in 1986. But the most dramatic string of Whitaker successes came when John began riding the famous Milton – owned by the parents of Caroline *Bradley, who until her early death was the horse's first rider. John Whitaker and Milton took the individual gold medal at the 1989 European Championships, and followed this with two Volvo World Cups (1990, 91) and the 1990 King George V Gold Cup.

Whitaker's Almanack Invaluable annual publication, appearing every December with details of British institutions and office holders. It also provides information on Commonwealth and foreign countries, a survey of the previous year's events (September to August) and much else besides – together with the astronomical tables which justify the name 'almanack'. It has been published annually since the 1869 volume was issued in December 1868 by Joseph Whitaker (1820–95). He was then correspondence editor of the *Gentleman's Magazine*, and the published information was what he had gathered together for his own reference purposes.

Whitbread One of Britain's largest brewers and owners of *pubs, which has expanded into off-licences, restaurants and hotels. Samuel Whitbread (1720–96) established his first brewery in London in 1742, and rapidly made a success by undercutting his rivals with a beer known as porter – short for 'porter's ale', because market porters were the chief customers for a product which was strong, black, cloudy and cheap. The company was a pioneer of commercial sponsorship with the Whitbread Gold Cup at *Sandown Park, and in 1971 it launched the prize now known as the *Whitbread Book of the Year. Since 1973 it has sponsored the *Whitbread Round The World Race.

Fatima **Whitbread** (b. 1961) Javelin thrower who broke the world record in 1986 with a throw of 77.44 metres; it still stood, in 1992, as the UK and Commonwealth record. She went on to win gold in the European Championships of 1986 and the World Championships of 1987. In the Olympic Games she won bronze in 1984 (the year when Tessa *Sanderson took the gold) and followed this with silver in 1988.

Whitbread Gold Cup see *Sandown Park.

Whitbread Book of the Year Annual literary award which achieves a high profile not only by its generous prize money but by the tantalizing method of selection. The contest was organized differently when *Whitbread launched the prize in 1971, but in the 1990s it begins with the choice of a winner in each of five categories: novel, first novel, children's novel, book of poems and biography (they must have been published in the previous 12 months by an author living in the UK or Ireland). The five category winners are announced in November, and one of them is chosen in January as the Book of the Year.

Whitbread Round The World Race The world's longest regular race, held every four years since 1973 for ocean-going yachts with the start and the finish at Portsmouth or Southampton. It is organized by the Royal Naval Sailing Association and sponsored by Whitbread. Until 1985 the race was over four legs and a distance of about 27,000 nautical miles, but since 1989 there have been two extra legs – bringing the flotilla of contestants to the USA and extending the distance to nearly 32,000 miles.

Whitby (14,000 in 1981) Fishing port in North Yorkshire with an abbey, founded in 656, in which the poet *Caedmon was a monk in his old age. The present ruins are those of an abbey church built in the 13c. The town was the location in 664 of the *Synod of Whitby. Images of the place and its inhabitants around the turn of the century have become widely known through the camera of a local photographer, Frank Meadow Sutcliffe (1853–1941).

Gilbert **White** (1720–93) Naturalist who brought lasting fame to the Hampshire village of Selborne, about 26km/16m east of Winchester, where his home is kept as a museum. He was born in the village and spent almost his entire life there. Ordained an Anglican clergyman, he helped out locally as curate; but it was the fauna and flora of the surrounding countryside which claimed his attention. His letters on the subject to two friends form the basis of *The Natural History and Antiquities of Selborne* (1789), the charm of which comes from his keen but amateurish observations.

Jimmy **White** (b. 1962) Snooker player with a tantalizing record in the Embassy World Professional Championships, where he has been runner-up four times – in 1984 to Steve Davis, in 1991 to John Parrott, in 1990 and 1992 to Stephen Hendry. But he has had a high number of wins in other tournaments, and in the early 1990s was usually among the top three or four in the world rankings.

Whitechapel (London E1) The heart of the *East End, originally lying just to the northeast of the old walled *City. As one of the poorest areas close to the centre, it was here that successive waves of immigrants settled – most notably Jews from central Europe in the decades before World War I. Attempts to improve the life of the people of Whitechapel in the late 19c included two notable initiatives – the founding in 1884 of Toynbee Hall (a free educational venture at university level) and the building in 1897–9 of the Whitechapel Art Gallery. The gallery has been in recent years one of London's foremost exhibition areas for modern art. Whitechapel also received some less welcome publicity in the late 19c, for this was the area in which *Jack the Ripper operated.

One of the characters around Whitby harbour a century ago, with life-saving equipment; photograph by Sutcliffe.

White City Stadium in northwest London which was demolished during the 1980s. It was completed in 1908 as part of a 57ha/140ac complex laid out for a Franco-British exhibition. That same summer it staged the fourth Olympic Games, famous now on two counts in relation to the *marathon. It was here that the modern length of the race was fixed at 26 miles 385 yards (42.195km); it was intended to be 26 miles, until it was realized that a further 385 yards were required to bring the finishing line in front of the royal box. And it was over that finishing line that the leading runner, Dorando Pietri of Italy, was helped by a race official after he had collapsed just short of it, causing him to be disqualified. *Greyhound racing in the stadium began in 1927 and it remained till its final years the site of the Greyhound Derby.

*The **White Devil** (c.1612)* Remorseless tragedy of lust and revenge by *Webster, based on notorious events which had happened in Italy some 30 years before. Brachiano, with the help of the scheming Flamineo, seduces Vittoria Corombona; together they then arrange for the murder of Brachiano's wife and Vittoria's husband. The central scene of the play is Vittoria's lively self-defence when on trial for murder and adultery, after which she is confined in a 'house of penitent whores'. Her rescue by Brachiano is followed by their violent deaths, together with that of Flamineo, at the hands of those with a justified grudge.

White Ensign see *ensign.

George **Whitefield** (1714–70) Anglican clergyman, a member of the Holy Club with Charles and John *Wesley in the 1730s, who pioneered open-air preaching in the early years of the *Methodist movement. He eventually split from Wesley, for his own position was more Calvinist, but his powerful sermons were an important feature of the 18C evangelical revival – particularly in America, where he made several long visits.

Whitehall (London SW1) Street running north from the Houses of Parliament to Trafalgar Square. The *Cenotaph stands in it, and *Downing Street leads off to the left. Most of the buildings are government offices, so Whitehall is often used as a general term for the central administration.

The name was that of the palace built here by Henry VIII as his chief residence, in place of the earlier *Palace of Westminster just to the south. James I planned to rebuild it entirely, but of the ambitious scheme drawn up for him by Inigo Jones only the *Banqueting House was built; it was also the only structure to survive the fire which destroyed the palace in 1698.

Whitehall Theatre (London SW1) Famous in the decades after World War II as the home of farce. The tradition began in 1945 with R.F. Delderfield's long-running *Worm's Eye View*. In 1950 Brian *Rix took over the theatre and began with two resounding successes, Colin Morris's *Reluctant Heroes* (1950) and John Chapman's *Dry Rot* (1954).

Alfred North **Whitehead** see Bertrand *Russell.

'white heat of the technological revolution' see Harold *Wilson.

White Horse see *Uffington and *Westbury.

white house see *Whithorn.

Mary **Whitehouse** (b. 1910) Unofficial watchdog of the airwaves, leading a forceful pressure group in monitoring television and radio programmes for words or scenes offensive to the members' notions of respectability. She first became prominent in 1964 as one of the founders of a 'Clean up TV campaign', and in 1965 she launched the National Viewers' and Listeners' Association. She brought a private prosecution against *Gay News* in 1977.

White Knight see *Through the Looking-Glass.*

William **Whitelaw** (b. 1918, viscount 1983) Conservative politician, MP for Penrith and the Border division of Cumberland 1955–83. He entered the cabinet as leader of the House of Commons in 1970, and was subsequently secretary of state for Northern Ireland (1972–3) and for employment (1973–4). In Mrs Thatcher's administration he was home secretary (1979–83) and leader of the House of Lords (1983–8).

white paper Any document presented by government to parliament as a firm statement of policy, usually outlining future legislation. Its whiteness is that of the paper itself, for such documents have usually been slim enough to have no cover, the first printed page forming the outer surface. By contrast a 'blue book' meant originally a document of similar kind which was fat enough to require a cover, of a thick blue paper; nowadays this usually means official reports, from government enquiries or royal commissions. A green paper (for a while they had green covers) is a recent innovation, dating only from the 1960s; it differs from a white paper in putting forward, as a basis for discussion, policies which are as yet only at a formative stage.

White's (London SW1) The oldest of London's *clubs, having developed from a chocolate house opened by Francis White in 1693 lower down St James's Street (on the site of the present Boodle's). White's soon became notorious for its high stakes and the club's betting book, continuous from the mid-18C, reveals that anything was good for a gamble; £3000 was placed one rainy day on which of two drops would win the race to the bottom of the window pane. London's clubs were largely non-political until the end of the 18C, when White's became Tory because Pitt and his supporters congregated there – as opposed to Brooks's on the other side of St James's Street, where Charles James Fox held court.

The transition from a chocolate house seems to have occurred through inner rooms being reserved for a select group, who eventually became the club. White's moved to its present site in 1755 and the building was refashioned in 1787–8, probably by James Wyatt. The famous bow window on to the street (a vantage point virtually reserved when it was new for Beau *Brummell) was added in 1811.

White Ship The ship which in 1120 sailed from France for England, carrying many of the courtiers of Henry I. All on board died (except a butcher from Rouen) when it struck a rock off the Cherbourg peninsula. Among them was William the Aetheling, Henry's only legitimate son. The disaster caused the king to attempt, unsuccessfully, to establish his daughter *Matilda as his successor.

white tie see *evening dress.

White Tower see *Tower of London.

Whithorn (1000 in 1981) Town in Dumfries and Galloway which was an important pilgrimage site in the Middle Ages. It was believed to be the 'white house' (*huit aern* in Old English) of St *Ninian. There are remains of a 12–13C priory. On the coast, at Isle of Whithorn, is a 14C ruin called St Ninian's Chapel – probably built to welcome pilgrims arriving by sea.

Dick **Whittington** Favourite *pantomime character who was a historical figure, being three times lord mayor of London (in the years 1397, 1406 and 1419). His legend first surfaced in the 17c. It contains two main elements: that as an apprentice he was running away from London when he seemed to hear the bells chiming 'Turn again Whittington, Lord Mayor of London'; and that his fortune was made when his cat, sent abroad on a merchant ship, killed so many rats that the king of Barbary bought the animal for a large sum.

Frank **Whittle** (b. 1907, KBE 1948) Pioneer of the jet engine. He took out a patent in 1930 but the first jet to fly was the German Heinkel He 178, with an engine designed by Hans von Ohain (first patent 1935). In 1941 a Gloster E28/39 airframe flew with a Whittle jet engine, the development of which led to the *Meteor. He is a member of the Order of *Merit.

Joseph **Whitworth** (1803–87, bt 1869) Engineer who in his Manchester workshops revolutionized the making of machine tools by inventing a measuring device, eventually accurate to a millionth of an inch. In the Crimean War he began to study the design of gun barrels, a field in which he also made many innovations. The Whitworth Art Gallery in Manchester commemorates him.

The **Who** Rock group formed in 1962 by Pete Townshend (b. 1945, guitar), Roger Daltrey (b. 1945 vocals) and John Entwistle (b. 1944, bass); they were joined in 1964 by Keith Moon (1947–78, drums) and later in that year they called themselves the Who. They were essentially an elegant mod band (see *mods and rockers), and Pete Townshend's songs – particularly *My Generation*, the title of both a single and an album in 1965 – seemed indeed to speak for a generation. The Who became firmly established alongside the Beatles and the Rolling Stones as a third group in the vanguard of Britain's rock music of the 1960s. Their originality was further demonstrated in the rock musical *Tommy*, a double-LP of 1969 telling the story of a deaf, dumb and blind boy, a wizard at pinball, who becomes a cult figure and then is rejected by his followers; it was filmed in 1974 by Ken Russell with Elton *John as the Pinball Wizard.

Their only no. 1 album followed in 1971 – *Who's Next*, including 'Won't Get Fooled Again'. *Quadrophenia* (1973) was another rock opera, this time about a young mod; it was filmed in 1979. By then Keith Moon had died, from an overdose of a drug prescribed against alcoholism, but the group continued until 1983 with a replacement drummer, Kenny Jones (b. 1948).

Who Dares Wins see *SAS.

Who killed Cock Robin? *Nursery rhyme for which both a mythological and a historical source have been proposed. The former relates it to a Norse legend, the death of Balder, and the latter to the fall from power of Robert Walpole in 1742 (the rhyme was first printed in about 1744). But the sequence of everyday creatures offering to take part in the funeral of poor Cock Robin seems to need no explanation beyond that of being a simple childish entertainment.

Who's Who A reference book published annually since 1849, listing those considered by the editorial board to have achieved prominence (whether inherited, by office or through ability). Until 1897 it consisted of lists of people occupying specific positions. The present alphabetical format, with a brief biography of each person, was adopted in that year. The book then described 5500 people; in the 1993 edition there are some 29,000. *Who's Who* differs in two respects from other similar works of reference: the biographies are written by the biographees, and updated each year, with maximum opportunity for self-revelation under the heading 'recreations'; and only death removes an entry, however little may have been achieved after the first year of inclusion. The final entries of those who have died are published every ten years as *Who Was Who*.

The ultimate puff on one's own trumpet was perhaps achieved by the Rev. Sidney Swann (1862–1942). Among other sporting achievements the vicar mentions: 'first to cycle round Syria; rode Land's End to John o'Groats, Carlisle to London in a day; rowed home-made boat from Crosby Vicarage down the rapids of the Eden to the sea, and cut the record from England to France, 1911, rowing the Channel in 3 hours 50 minutes; built several flying machines; in 1917, when 55 years old, cycled, walked, ran, paddled, rode and swam six consecutive half-miles in 26 minutes 20 seconds in competition with Lieut. Muller of the Danish Army.'

'Who's your fat friend?' see Beau *Brummell.

Who would true valour see see The *Pilgrim's Progress.

Edward **Whymper** (1840–1911) The best known of the many British climbers who pioneered the sport of mountaineering, mainly in Switzerland, in the mid-19c. His most famous achievement was reaching the peak of the Matterhorn (4477m/14,688ft) on his seventh attempt, in 1865. On the way down one of the party slipped and fell. Three others were pulled off the slope before the rope broke – a failure of equipment which saved the life of Whymper and two guides.

Details such as this made bestsellers of Whymper's books about his adventures, embellished with his own illustrations (he was a trained wood engraver). In 1880 he climbed in the Andes and was able to describe for his readers a night on the volcanic summit of Cotopaxi (5897m/19,347ft).

WI see *Women's Institutes.

Widdicombe Fair A *ballad about the horse fair at Widecombe-in-the-Moor in Devon (still held on the second Tuesday in September), which has become a popular song because of the pleasure of repeating the names of Bill Brewer, Jan Stewer, Peter Gurney, Peter Davy, Dan'l Whiddon, Harry Hawk, old Uncle Tom Cobbleigh and all, who together go to the fair with the grey mare borrowed from Tom Pearse.

Widmerpool see Anthony *Powell.

Widnes One of the original clubs in rugby league football in 1895. Widnes has had seven victories in the Challenge Cup (1930, 37, 64, 75, 79, 81, 84) and three in the present version of the League Championship (1978, 88, 89).

Wife of Bath see The *Canterbury Tales.

Wigan (80,000 in 1981) Town in greater Manchester, with a history dating back to Roman and Anglo-Saxon times but in recent centuries associated with coal mining and the cotton industry. In the 19c it was the original home of *Beecham's pill, and its name has a particular modern resonance through featuring in Orwell's title, The *Road to Wigan Pier.

Wilberforce attempting to save the nation's blushes at the nude Achilles (see Hyde Park): caricature by Cruikshank (1822).

Wigan One of the original clubs in rugby league football in 1895, and in recent years by far the most successful – with an unprecedented run of six successive victories in the Challenge Cup up to 1993. This gave them a record total of 14 wins (1924, 29, 48, 51, 58, 59, 65, 85, 88, 89, 90, 91, 92, 93); Leeds, their nearest rival, trailed at that time with ten. In the present form of the League Championship they have won five times (1987, 90, 91, 92, 93), which is also a record. Their dominance of the game is likely to be increased by their 1992 purchase of Martin *Offiah.

Isle of **Wight** see *Isle of Wight.

Wightman Cup see *tennis.

Dafydd **Wigley** see *Plaid Cymru.

Wigmore Hall (London W1) Concert hall in Wigmore Street which has been particularly associated with artists making their debuts in London. It opened in 1901 as the Bechstein Hall, built by the German piano manufacturer Friedrich Bechstein as an extension of his London showrooms. Appropriated in 1914, on the outbreak of war, it reopened under its present name in 1917.

Wigtownshire Until 1975 a *county on the extreme southwest coast of mainland Scotland, now part of the Dumfries and Galloway region.

William **Wilberforce** (1759–1833) Evangelical Christian and member of the *Clapham Sect, who devoted most of his energies as a member of parliament (1780–1825) to the campaign against the *slave trade. He was the leading figure in Britain in the abolitionist cause. His birthplace in *Hull is kept as a museum.

Oscar **Wilde** (1854–1900) Anglo-Irish playwright, poet and wit, the most famous exponent of the lifestyle of the *Aesthetic movement and victim of the resulting clash with the morality of his day. Born in Dublin, son of a leading surgeon, he was christened with a string of names seeming to predestine him for a life of flamboyant affectation – Oscar Fingal O'Flahertie Wills Wilde. By 1882 he was sufficiently famous to make a very successful lecture tour of the United States as a living example of an aesthete. Legend relates that he told the customs officer 'I have nothing to declare except my genius'; the story may well be true, but was not reported at the time.

In the 1880s he produced a steady stream of essays, reviews, unsuccessful historical plays and successful fairy stories (*The Happy Prince* 1888), but his great literary success was compressed into a brief 4-year period preceding his downfall. His comedies delighted audiences with their wit (*Lady Windermere's Fan* 1892, *A Woman of No Importance* 1893, *An Ideal Husband* and *The *Importance of Being Earnest*, both 1895); a verse drama, *Salome*, showed that he could also shock (banned by the *lord chamberlain in Britain in 1893, it was performed in Paris in 1896 and is best known now in the operatic version of 1905 by Richard Strauss); and his only novel, *The *Picture of Dorian Gray* (1891), proved that he could delight and shock at the same time. But he was now causing much deeper offence by his personal behaviour, being seen openly in public with his young lover, Lord Alfred *Douglas.

Disaster struck in 1895, the direct result of a campaign against Wilde by Douglas's outraged father, the marquess of Queensberry. He left at Wilde's club an ill-spelt card saying 'To Oscar Wilde posing Somdomite'. Wilde sued him for libel and lost the case. The inevitable result was Wilde's arrest and prosecution for homosexuality, an illegal act at the time. He was sentenced to two years' imprisonment with hard labour. From the prison at Reading he wrote **De Profundis* to Douglas, and his experiences there were the basis of his **Ballad of Reading Gaol*. After his release in 1897 Wilde lived the few remaining years of his life in France and Italy, often using an assumed name, Sebastian Melmoth. St Sebastian was his favourite martyr (and his uniform as a convict had been decorated with arrows), while Melmoth was the satanic hero of a Gothic novel, *Melmoth the Wanderer* (1820), written by one of Wilde's ancestors. But even in ill health and in destitution Wilde was able to coin an aphorism which has long survived him, describing himself as 'dying beyond my means'.

Wildfowl & Wetlands Trust see *Slimbridge.

John **Wilkes** (1725–97) Political agitator and journalist who was as dissolute in his private life (joining in the revels of the *Hellfire Club, for example) as he was courageous in public matters. In 1762 he founded a weekly magazine, *The North Briton*, for the express purpose of attacking George III and his minister, Lord Bute. In no. 45 he went so far that a general warrant was issued against anyone, as yet unnamed, connected with this act of seditious libel. Nearly 50 people were arrested in the search for evidence, but Wilkes won the day when the court declared this type of warrant illegal.

The rest of his career (interrupted by lawsuits, forced exile and prison sentences) was spent using the power of the electorate and of independent bodies such as the *City of London against the king and his ministers, making him the figurehead of a wider campaign for personal liberty and political reform. In 1768–9 he was three times re-elected for Middlesex after the House of Commons refused to accept him as a member; the MPs even adopted the defeated candidate, Henry Luttrell, in direct disregard of the voters' wishes. In 1774 Wilkes became Lord Mayor of London. He was known for the quickness of his wit, most famously when Lord Sandwich told him he would die either on the gallows or of the pox: 'That must depend on whether I embrace your lordship's principles or your mistress.'

David **Wilkie** (b. 1954) Scottish swimmer who collected a glittering succession of breaststroke medals in the 1970s. In the world championships of 1973 he won the 200 metres in a world record time of 2:19.28; in 1975 he retained his title (with 2:18.23) and also won gold for the 100 metres. In the Commonwealth Games of 1974 he won both the breaststroke and the individual medley over 200 metres. At the Olympics he had won silver in 1972 over 200 metres, and he followed this with silver in 1976 for 100 metres; but it was the 200 metres in the 1976 Olympics which was his triumph. He not only took the gold medal, but shattered his own world record by a margin of more than three seconds (with a time of 2:15.11).

Maurice **Wilkins** see *DNA.

William **Wilkins** (1778–1839) Architect working in the style of the *Greek Revival, whose most important buildings were for universities – Downing College in Cambridge, and University College in London. He also designed the earliest part of the National Gallery.

William (known as the Lion, 1143–1214) King of Scotland from 1165, when he succeeded his brother

Oscar Wilde in Vanity Fair *by Ape (Carlo Pellegrini) in 1884, when Wilde had not yet succeeded as a playwright.*

Malcolm IV. After the murder of *Becket, he joined the sons of Henry II in their rebellion against the English king. His own interest was in recovering Northumberland, but he was captured at Alnwick in 1174 and was released later that year only after agreeing to a humiliating treaty. By its terms William handed over castles as far north as Edinburgh and accepted that he held the crown of Scotland as a vassal of the English king; he eventually bought back these concessions in 1189 for a large payment to Henry's son, Richard I, who was raising funds to go on crusade. Meanwhile he had pointedly founded an abbey at *Arbroath in honour of the martyred Becket. Within Scotland the royal authority was strengthened during his long reign. He was succeeded by his son Alexander II (see the *royal house of Scotland).

William (William Brown) Irrepressible schoolboy hero of short stories by Richmal *Crompton. At constant odds with adult intentions, the 11-year-old William slips away from his middle-class parents on every possible occasion to join the Outlaws, of whom he is the leader. The others are Henry, Douglas and Ginger, but they find it impossible to rid themselves of an intruder, Violet Elizabeth Bott (a new arrival in the village and much despised because her very rich father has made his money too recently and by means of Bott's Digestive Sauce). The characters first appeared in book form in *Just – William* (1922) and continued unchanged for some 350 stories up to the end of the author's life. Their illustrator was Thomas Henry (Thomas Henry Fisher, 1879–1962).

Prince **William** see the Prince of *Wales.

William I see *William the Conqueror.

William II (William Rufus, *c.*1056–1100) King of England from 1087, the third son of William the Conqueror and Matilda of Flanders. His eldest brother, Robert Curthose, inherited the duchy of Normandy; the next, Richard, had died hunting. William was an aggressive ruler, putting down with great severity revolts by his barons and pillaging the revenues of the church (one of the reasons for his continuing conflict with *Anselm). Like his elder brother he died in the hunting field, in his case hit by an arrow in the New Forest. It has been generally held to have come from the bow of Walter Tirel, and it is likely that the king was murdered on behalf of his brother and successor, *Henry I, who was in the hunting party (see the *royal house). William was unmarried and probably homosexual. His contemporaries called him *rufus*, the Latin for red, because of his ruddy complexion.

William III (1650–1702) Prince of *Orange from birth and king of England, Scotland and Ireland from 1689 (ruling jointly with Mary II till 1694); posthumous son of William II of Orange and of Mary, daughter of Charles I (see the *royal house); married Mary, elder daughter of James II, in 1677.
William's early adult years were spent leading the Dutch resistance to joint English and French aggression in the *Anglo-Dutch war of 1672. But from then on France alone was the enemy, for he made peace with England in 1674 and cemented that alliance three years later by marrying his cousin Mary. In 1685 his father-in-law, *James II, succeeded to the throne in Britain as a Roman Catholic; and in 1688 a Roman Catholic heir was born (James *Stuart). In the resulting crisis William and Mary, a Protestant couple, were invited to Britain to seize the crown in what became known as the *Revolution of 1688. William landed at Torbay in Devon in November and reached London unopposed. In January parliament offered the throne to William and Mary as joint

sovereigns, accompanied by a Declaration of Right which later became the basis for the *Bill of Rights.

William took all political decisions when ruling jointly with his wife; so her sudden death in 1694, though a great personal shock, made little difference in the affairs of state. He spent much of the 1690s campaigning in the Netherlands against the French in the War of the Grand Alliance (1689–97). In the treaties concluding the war, signed at Ryswick, Louis XIV acknowledged William as king of England and Scotland; but on the death of James II in 1701 Louis reversed this commitment and proclaimed the young James Stuart to be king, thus prolonging by half a century the *Jacobite cause. William was succeeded by his sister-in-law, *Anne.

William IV (known as the Sailor King, 1765–1837) King of Great Britain, Ireland and *Hanover from 1830; third son of George III and Charlotte of Mecklenburg-Strelitz; married Adelaide of Saxe-Meiningen (1818).

He saw active service as a midshipman from the age of 13 and continued in the navy until he was 25. In the following year, 1791, he began his long liaison with the actress Dorothea Jordan (1761–1816), by whom he eventually had ten illegitimate children – all given the surname FitzClarence, for he had been created Duke of Clarence in 1789. The death in 1817 of Princess Charlotte, the only child of *George IV, made Clarence the heir to the throne and caused all the king's bachelor brothers to look round for brides. After being rejected by several (he was somewhat uncouth), Clarence was accepted by Adelaide of Saxe-Meiningen; they had two daughters but both died in infancy. The early years of his short reign were dominated by the agitation surrounding the *Reform Act. A constitutional crisis loomed when the Tories in the Lords persistently rejected the reform bills passed in the Commons. It was only resolved when the king, wisely but against his own inclinations, agreed to create sufficient Whig peers to carry the legislation; the threat was enough. He was succeeded by his niece, Victoria (see the *royal house).

William Rufus see *William II.

Williams Motor-racing team, founded in 1967 by Frank Williams (b. 1942), which completely dominated the Grand Prix scene in 1992 with Nigel *Mansell as the leading driver. Previous victories in the constructors' championship had come in 1980 and 1981 (with Alan Jones and Carlos Reutemann driving) and in 1986 and 1987 (Nelson Piquet and Nigel Mansell). In 1989 Williams changed to Renault engines, and it was the Williams-Renault (with its sophisticated 'active-ride' suspension) which triumphed in 1992. Frank Williams broke his spine in a road accident in France in 1986, since when he has been paralysed from the shoulders down.

Emlyn **Williams** (1905–87) Welsh actor and dramatist. Of his plays, the semi-autobiographical *The Corn is Green* (1938) has lasted best; it concerns the education of a young Welsh miner, Morgan Evans, and his relationship with his teacher, Miss Moffat. As an actor he was particularly known for his solo performances, based on the life and work of Charles Dickens (from 1950) and of Dylan Thomas (from 1955).

John **Williams** (b. 1941) Australian guitarist, living in Britain from the 1960s; like Julian *Bream, with whom he often plays, he was a pupil of Segovia. In addition to playing the classic repertoire, he has used the classical techniques of the guitar in a more popular range of music – notably with his group Sky (their album *Sky 2* was in the charts for 53 weeks in 1980 and reached the top position).

J.P.R. **Williams** (John Peter Rhys Williams, b. 1949) Rugby union player, at fullback, with a record 55 caps for Wales (1969–81) and with another eight for the *Lions (1971–4). He is also a tennis player (winner of the junior singles at Wimbledon in 1966), and by profession is an orthopaedic surgeon.

Kenneth **Williams** (1926–88) Actor and comedian whose high camp manner and drawling nasal voice, brimming with innuendo, made him a perennial favourite in the *Carry On films and in radio programmes such as *Beyond Our Ken* and *Round the Horne* (both with Kenneth *Horne). With his quick wit he also excelled on *Just a Minute*, a radio programme where the panellists must improvise on a given theme without repeating themselves.

Shirley **Williams** (Shirley Brittain, b. 1930, m. Bernard Williams 1955, baroness 1993) Labour politician who was subsequently one of the founders of the *SDP. She was in the cabinet as secretary of state for prices and consumer protection (1974–6) and for education and science (1976–9). In 1981 she was the first MP to be elected for the SDP (for Crosby), but she lost her seat in 1983.

Malcolm **Williamson** (b. 1931) Australian composer, living in Britain from the 1950s and appointed *Master of the Queen's Music in 1975. His output has been prolific (in many forms and incorporating many influences, from serial music to jazz and pop) and he has provided the occasional music which is the main purpose of his royal office – such as *Mass of Christ the King* (1967, for the queen's silver jubilee) or *Songs for a Royal Baby* (1985).

William the Conqueror (William I, c.1028–87) King of England from 1066; illegitimate son of Robert I, duke of Normandy, and of Arlette (daughter of a tanner in Falaise); married Matilda of Flanders (c.1051).

Succeeding his father as duke in 1035, William only established his authority over Normandy after a long struggle. But strong links with England through *Edward the Confessor gave him hopes of the English crown, and his invasion in 1066 was supported by a pope dissatisfied with the English church. After the initial victory at *Hastings the Norman *Conquest was rapidly consolidated; a mere ten weeks later William was crowned in Westminster Abbey on Christmas Day (an auspicious day for a coronation ever since Charlemagne had been crowned in Rome on Christmas Day 800). Good relations with the church under *Lanfranc and good administration (culminating in the great *Domesday Book) meant that William's reign was one of consolidation. His eldest son, Robert Curthose, inherited the duchy of Normandy, while two others (William II and Henry I) followed him on the throne of England (see the *royal house).

Bob **Willis** (b. 1949) Fast bowler who played *cricket for Surrey (1969–71), Warwickshire (1972–84) and England (1970–84, captain 1982–4). In 1983 he exceeded Fred Trueman's 307 Test wickets for England, and his own eventual total of 325 remained the record until bettered in 1985 by Ian *Botham.

Ted **Willis** see *Dixon of Dock Green.

willow pattern A much repeated English ceramic design in the Chinese style, the ingredients of which are a bridge with figures on it, a willow tree, a pagoda, a boat and a distant island. There were many similar patterns in Europe at the time, but this particular group is believed to have been designed by Thomas *Minton for *Spode in about 1780. It was eventually copied even in China.

willow song see *Othello*.

Willy Lot's cottage see John *Constable.

Wilmington Long Man (24km/15m E of Brighton)
Chalk figure of a man with a staff in each hand, about
70m/230ft high, cut into the side of Windhover Hill.
First described in the 18C, and tidied up in the 19C, the
figure is nevertheless believed to date back to the Middle
Ages and possibly to Anglo-Saxon times.

Angus **Wilson** (1913–91, kt 1980) Novelist and writer
of short stories, with a keen eye for quirks of character
and oddities of social class. He was a librarian in the
British Museum (now the British Library) when his first
two books of short stories came out (*The Wrong Set*
1949, *Those Darling Dodos* 1950); the novels which followed included *Hemlock and After* (1952), *Anglo-Saxon
Attitudes* (1956) and *The Middle Age of Mrs Eliot* (1958).
All were notable for the wide range of characters (academics, society hostesses, chorus boys, rough trade)
among whom the author felt at ease. He himself said that
his passport was being, as a homosexual, a member of a
'half-secret society' transcending the class structure.

Charles **Wilson** (1869–1959) Scottish physicist who invented the cloud chamber, in which water vapour in a
sealed dust-free container is cooled by sudden expansion.
It thereby becomes possible to trace the path of particles
through the chamber; they ionize the molecules they
encounter, leaving a visible line of water droplets (which
can be photographed) as evidence of their presence and
passage. Wilson had perfected his cloud chamber by
1911, and it rapidly advanced the search for subatomic
particles (see *Blackett). He shared the 1927 Nobel prize
with the American physicist Arthur Compton.

Harold **Wilson** (b. 1916, KG 1976, baron 1983) Labour
politician, MP for Ormskirk 1945–50 and Huyton
1950–83, and twice prime minister (1964–70, 1974–6).
An economist and statistician by profession, he became
the youngest cabinet minister of the 20C when appointed
president of the Board of Trade in 1947. In 1963 the
sudden death of Hugh *Gaitskell left the leadership of
the party unexpectedly open, and Wilson was elected in a
contest with George Brown and James Callaghan.
  1963 was the year of the *Profumo affair. The Conservative administration seemed stale and tarnished, and
there was a marked contrast when Wilson held out the
promise of technology and of 'the Britain that is going to
be forged in the white heat of this revolution' (a phrase
used at that autumn's party conference, usually now
quoted as 'the white heat of the technological revolution'). The Labour party won by just five seats in the general election of October 1964, but Wilson returned to the
country in March 1966 and increased his majority to 99.
A balance of payments crisis, leading to devaluation in
1967 (see *exchange rate), frustrated the fulfilment of his
promises; and Britain's economic difficulties were under-
lined by nearly four years of the most stringent *exchange
controls. Meanwhile foreign affairs were dominated by
the issue of Rhodesia, on which Wilson took a personal
initiative in diplomacy with Ian Smith (see *Zimbabwe)
but failed to make any progress.
  Wilson lost the 1970 election, but returned to power
in February 1974 without an overall majority; a second
election in that year, in October, gave him a slender
majority of five. He then surprised the nation, early in
1976, by the sudden announcement of his resignation.
He had declared that he would retire before the next general election; but there was inevitable speculation that he
had some dark reason for going (if so, it has never been

discovered), and controversy followed his departure in
the form of the *lavender list. It was later revealed, in
Spycatcher, that there had been a dirty tricks campaign
– as Wilson himself suspected – to undermine his administration. He was succeeded as party leader and prime
minister by James Callaghan.
  Several of Wilson's phrases have found a secure place in
Britain's collective memory. One is the *'gnomes of
Zurich'; another the *'pound in your pocket'; and a third
the perennially useful 'a week is a long time in politics'. It
is uncertain precisely when he first said this, but it was
probably to lobby correspondents on the subject of a sterling crisis shortly after he took office in 1964.

Harriette **Wilson** (1786–1846) Courtesan whose *Memoirs*
(1825) are the source of two popular quotations. The first
is her own opening sentence: 'I shall not say why and how
I became, at the age of fifteen, the mistress of the earl of
Craven.' The second is the riposte of the duke of Wellington on receiving a blackmailing letter from the publisher
of the memoirs, in which he features as one of Harriette's
conquests. 'Publish and be damned', he was said to have
scrawled across the letter before sending it back.

Jocky **Wilson** see *darts.

Richard **Wilson** (1714–82) The first British landscape
painter of distinction, born in Wales, son of an Anglican
clergyman. His mature style derived from the years which
he spent in Rome (1752–7, after two years in Venice),
where he fell under the spell of the French 17C painter
Claude, who had lived and worked there. Back in Britain,
Wilson interpreted the local landscape with Claude's classical balance, sense of serenity and clarity of light.

Wilson the Wonder Athlete see *Hotspur*.

Wilton (5km/3m W of Salisbury) Small town in Wiltshire
long associated with the manufacture of carpets. A factory
for hand-made carpets was established here in 1655 and
was granted a royal charter in 1699. During the 18C the
Brussels style of carpet, woven with a pile made from
looped wool, was in fashion; Wilton modified this by cutting each loop to give a tufted pile. The mechanical looms
developed in the 19C for this type of carpet in either form
became known as Wilton looms, and the term Wilton
now describes any carpet, cut or uncut, which is woven
on such a loom. The vast bulk of modern mass-produced
carpet is either Wilton or *Axminster, with the development of which Wilton was also closely involved. The
Wilton Royal Carpet Museum, opened at Wilton in 1983,
shows the history of carpet making together with modern
methods, seen in a tour of the factory.

Wilton Diptych (*c*.1395, National Gallery) The name
commonly given to a pair of linked paintings which show
the English king Richard II (kneeling in the left panel)
being presented to the Virgin and Child (with attendant
angels in the right panel). It is not known whether it was
painted in England or on the Continent, for it is in the
style known as International Gothic, practised throughout western Europe. Its name derives from its having been
at *Wilton House for more than two centuries before it
came to the National Gallery.

Wilton House (6km/4m W of Salisbury) Originally a
Tudor house, built by the Herbert family on the site of
Wilton Abbey, but famous for its 17C south front. This is
traditionally attributed to Inigo Jones but is now believed
to have been built in Jones's Palladian style by a French
architect, Isaac de Caus, in 1636–7. There was a fire in
the new wing in 1647, after which the present rooms were

Singles champions at Wimbledon since World War II

	Men	Women
1946	Yvon Petra (Fra)	Pauline Betz (USA)
1947	Jack Kramer (USA)	Margaret Osborne (USA)
1948	Bob Falkenburg (USA)	Louise Brough (USA)
1949	Ted Schroeder (USA)	Louise Brough (USA)
1950	Budge Patty (USA)	Louise Brough (USA)
1951	Dick Savitt (USA)	Doris Hart (USA)
1952	Frank Sedgman (Aus)	Maureen Connolly (USA)
1953	Vic Seixas (USA)	Maureen Connolly (USA)
1954	Jaroslav Drobny (Egy)	Maureen Connolly (USA)
1955	Tony Trabert (USA)	Louise Brough (USA)
1956	Lew Hoad (Aus)	Shirley Fry (USA)
1957	Lew Hoad (Aus)	Althea Gibson (USA)
1958	Ashley Cooper (Aus)	Althea Gibson (USA)
1959	Alex Olmedo (USA)	Maria Bueno (Bra)
1960	Neale Fraser (Aus)	Maria Bueno (Bra)
1961	Rod Laver (Aus)	Angela Mortimer (UK)
1962	Rod Laver (Aus)	Karen Susman (USA)
1963	Chuck McKinley (USA)	Margaret Smith (Aus)
1964	Roy Emerson (Aus)	Maria Bueno (Bra)
1965	Roy Emerson (Aus)	Margaret Smith (Aus)
1966	Manuel Santana (Spa)	Billie Jean King (USA)
1967	John Newcombe (Aus)	Billie Jean King (USA)
1968	Rod Laver (Aus)	Billie Jean King (USA)
1969	Rod Laver (Aus)	Ann Jones (UK)
1970	John Newcombe (Aus)	Margaret Court (Aus)*
1971	John Newcombe (Aus)	Evonne Goolagong (Aus)
1972	Stan Smith (USA)	Billie Jean King (USA)
1973	Jan Kodes (Cze)	Billie Jean King (USA)
1974	Jimmy Connors (USA)	Chris Evert (USA)
1975	Arthur Ashe (USA)	Billie Jean King (USA)
1976	Björn Borg (Swe)	Chris Evert (USA)
1977	Björn Borg (Swe)	Virginia Wade (USA)
1978	Björn Borg (Swe)	Martina Navratilova (Cze)
1979	Björn Borg (Swe)	Martina Navratilova (Cze)
1980	Björn Borg (Swe)	Evonne Cawley (Aus)**
1981	John McEnroe (USA)	Chris Evert Lloyd (USA)
1982	Jimmy Connors (USA)	Martina Navratilova (USA)
1983	John McEnroe (USA)	Martina Navratilova (USA)
1984	John McEnroe (USA)	Martina Navratilova (USA)
1985	Boris Becker (FRG)	Martina Navratilova (USA)
1986	Boris Becker (FRG)	Martina Navratilova (USA)
1987	Pat Cash (Aus)	Martina Navratilova (USA)
1988	Stefan Edberg (Swe)	Steffi Graf (FRG)
1989	Boris Becker (FRG)	Steffi Graf (FRG)
1990	Stefan Edberg (Swe)	Martina Navratilova (USA)
1991	Michael Stich (Ger)	Steffi Graf (FRG)
1992	Andre Agassi (USA)	Steffi Graf (FRG)

*won previously as Margaret Smith and **as Evonne Goolagong

created by Inigo *Jones's assistant, John Webb (1611–72). The famous 'double cube' room (18m/60ft by 9m/30ft, and 9m/30ft high) was designed partly to hold a superb collection of paintings by Van Dyck, in particular the large Herbert family group which occupies an end wall. Next door is the 'single cube' room, 9m/30ft in each dimension. The interior of the courtyard was much altered in the early 19C when James Wyatt added a Gothic sculpture gallery.

Wiltshire (575,000 in 1991, administrative centre Trowbridge) *County in southwest England.

Wimbledon (London SW19) Area known above all as the first home of international *tennis. It was *croquet which provided Wimbledon's first link with sport, when the All England Croquet Club was founded here in 1868. Seven years later the club decided to adopt an even newer game, lawn tennis. A sub-committee was set up to look into the

rules. It opted for a rectangular court in place of the hourglass shape proposed elsewhere at the time; it established the dimensions of the playing area still in use today; and it laid down a basis of play and of scoring (borrowed from *real tennis) which has required little alteration. With these crucial details settled, the club was ready in 1877 to launch its first singles championship for men (women's singles followed in 1884). The prize was £25 – donated by the *Field*, a magazine energetically promoting the game in the early days – and the winner was Spencer Gore (1850–1906), who devastated the opposition by the cunning device of playing the ball on the volley. In that same year the name of the club was changed to the All England Croquet and Lawn Tennis Club; in 1882, acknowledging the dominance of the younger game, croquet was dropped from the title. It was restored for sentimental reasons in 1889, when the club became (as it still is) the All England Lawn Tennis and Croquet Club.

For most of its history Wimbledon has been an amateur championship; winners who turned professional could not reappear to defend their titles. But the British, in other contexts so fond of amateurism, were this time in the forefront of a long campaign for change. Against strong opposition from the International Lawn Tennis Federation, Wimbledon became in 1968 the first major tournament to admit professionals (the first open tournament anywhere, won by Ken Rosewall, was at Bournemouth earlier that year). As the world's original tennis event, Wimbledon has retained a certain pre-eminence among the four major competitions constituting the *Grand Slam; it is also the only one to be played on the game's original surface, grass.

Peter **Wimsey** see Dorothy *Sayers.

Winchester (31,000 in 1981) City on the river Itchen; administrative centre of Hampshire. A place of some significance in pre-Roman and Roman times, its real importance began when the Anglo-Saxon kings of *Wessex made it their capital. As they (and in particular *Alfred the Great) became pre-eminent among other Anglo-Saxon rulers, Winchester developed almost imperceptibly into the capital of England. It retained this position under the Norman kings, being in their time (and until about the 14C) a joint capital with London; it was at Winchester that the royal treasure was kept and the city had the advantage of being close to Southampton, the usual port of embarkation for Normandy.

Winchester was a diocese from the 7C and St *Swithin was bishop in the 9C. The cathedral, begun shortly after the Conquest, was ready to be consecrated by 1093 and the Norman church remains the basis of today's building. But its greatest glory derives from the Gothic columns and vaulted roof added in the Perpendicular style in the late 14C. The result is the astonishing vista of the interior – seemingly endless, for this is Europe's longest cathedral, at 160m/526ft.

The transformation of the nave was largely carried out for William of Wykeham (1324–1404), who was bishop from 1367 till his death. He was also the founder in 1382 of Winchester College (boys educated there are known as Wykehamists). The college, still in its original premises to the south of the cathedral close, provided the first pattern for what became the *public school. Of the medieval city's four gates only the Westgate survives, with its upper room used as a museum. And of the Norman castle (begun by William the Conqueror) all that remains is the Great Hall, known since the 15C for containing the supposed *Round Table of King Arthur.

A famous local hero is William Walker, a diver who worked for 6 years (1906–12) in liquid mud beneath the cathedral, underpinning it with concrete.

Bishop of **Winchester** One of the five *Lords Spiritual who invariably have a seat in the House of Lords. The bishopric was founded in the late 7C, and the office has been held since 1985 by Colin James (b. 1926). The bishop of Winchester signs with his Christian name followed by *Winton*.

The ***Wind Blew*** see Raymond *Briggs.

Windermere The chief lake in the *Lake District and the largest in England (17km/10.5m long). From its northern reach, near Ambleside, the distant peaks of Helvellyn and Scafell are visible. At the town of Windermere, on the east bank, there is a museum of working steam boats. It was on Windermere that Henry *Segrave died in 1930.

The ***Wind in the Willows*** (1908) Children's classic by Kenneth *Grahame, evolved from bedtime stories told to his only son, Alastair. The tentative Mole makes friends with Ratty (a water rat, whose chief passion is 'messing about in boats') and together they get involved with the owner of the local grand house, the larger-than-life Toad; his dangerous driving lands him in prison from which he escapes disguised as a washerwoman, only to find that Toad Hall has been taken over by stoats and weasels from the Wild Wood, who are evicted with difficulty. (It has often been pointed out that the story reflects an Edwardian leisured existence, complete with Toad the cad, with the perceived threat of social unrest in the background.) The book appeared first without pictures, but later illustrators have included E.H. Shepard, Arthur *Rackham and John Burningham. It was dramatized with great success by A.A. Milne in 1929 as *Toad of Toad Hall*, which was for many years a traditional Christmas entertainment in London. A recent adaptation by Alan *Bennett, directed by Nicholas Hytner at the National Theatre, seems likely to fill the same role in the future.

Windmill Theatre (London W1) Intimate theatre, built originally as a small cinema, which acquired a proud reputation in World War II as the only London theatre to have stayed open throughout the bombing; 'We never closed' became its slogan. In a continuous variety performance from approximately midday to midnight, fan dancers and tableaux of almost nude girls shared the bill with stand-up comics. Many successful comedians (notably Tony Hancock, Jimmy Edwards, Harry Secombe and Peter Sellers) first made their names at the Windmill. It finally closed as a theatre in 1964.

'wind of change' see Harold *Macmillan.

window tax First levied in 1695 on the number of windows in a house, and finally abolished in 1851 as a result of Lord Shaftesbury's campaign for improved standards of sanitation in lodging houses. Many old houses in Britain can still be seen with windows bricked up to save the tax.

Windscale see *Sellafield.

Windsor (28,000 in 1981) Town on the south bank of the Thames in Berkshire. It has grown up below Windsor Castle, a royal stronghold on a chalk bluff above the river. There was an Anglo-Saxon fort here, and William the Conqueror built his keep on the site of the central feature of today's castle, the Round Tower; replaced and altered by successive monarchs, the tower acquired its present appearance in the early 19C at the hands of *Wyatville. Windsor has remained since Norman times an important

The towers at the northeast corner of Windsor Castle, ablaze on the night of 20 November 1992.

royal residence. Its most distinguished architectural feature is *St George's Chapel; nearby is the contemporary but much restored *Albert Memorial Chapel. Most of the State Apartments were either created or remodelled by Wyatville in the early 19C. His most spectacular room is the Waterloo Chamber, a banqueting hall created by roofing over a courtyard; commissioned by George IV to celebrate the defeat of Napoleon, it contains portraits by Lawrence of the statesmen who between them carved up post-Napoleonic Europe. Among many great works of art in these apartments, a minor but irresistible treasure is *Queen Mary's Dolls' House.

In 1992 parts of the castle were severely damaged by a fire which started in a chapel in the private apartments around noon on November 20. Several rooms were gutted, including St George's Hall – the castle's principal banqueting room until replaced by the Waterloo Chamber. Amazingly, nearly all the works of art were saved. The only major loss was an equestrian portrait of George III by William Beechey, too massive to move.

Adjoining the castle is Windsor Home Park (265ha/655ac), which includes *Frogmore. Further to the south lie the 2150ha/5313ac of Windsor Great Park, originally a royal hunting ground and now much used for equestrian events. Deer are confined to the area around the Long Walk, a 4km/2.5m avenue running south from the castle; this was laid out in 1680 and has at its southern end a great equestrian statue of George III, known familiarly as the Copper Horse, by *Westmacott (1831).

Duke and Duchess of **Windsor** see *Edward VIII.

House of **Windsor** The name since 1917 (see *Saxe-Coburg & Gotha) of the ruling family in Britain, applying therefore to George V, Edward VIII, George VI and Elizabeth II (see the *royal house). All male descendants of George V have Windsor as their surname and daughters of male descendants have it as their maiden name.

Windsor chair General name for a type of chair made in England since the 17C and exported in the early 18C to America, where it also became a standard pattern. The distinctive feature is a solid wooden seat into which are fitted the round tops of the legs and the round bottoms of the spindles for the back. There are many variations – high or low-backed, armless or with a rail of wood curving round at elbow level. The separate ingredients could be made by different craftsmen and even on other premises, making possible an early form of mass production. A main centre for making the chairs has been High Wycombe, about 20km/12m northwest of Windsor (the reason for the name is unknown).

Orde **Wingate** (1903–44) The most successful British commander of guerrilla forces in World War II, first in Ethiopia and then in Burma, where he led his famous *'Chindits' in lengthy missions behind the Japanese lines – a form of campaign made possible by long-range radio communication and the dropping of supplies by air. In 1944 he was put in command of the reconquest of Burma. He died in an unexplained air crash in the jungle.

winkle-pickers Shoes with extremely long pointed toes, a fashion of the *teddy boys in the 1950s and named from the winkles available on *whelk stalls.

winkles see *whelk stall.

Winnie-the-Pooh see A.A. *Milne.

The **Winslow Boy** (1946) Play by Terence *Rattigan based on a real case in 1911. A 13-year-old cadet, Ronnie Winslow, has been expelled from the Royal Naval College at Osborne for stealing a five-shilling postal order. He protests his innocence and his stern father begins a long fight to clear his son's name. In the pursuit of justice the family suffers all sorts of privations and embarrassments, not least of which is the supercilious arrogance of the famous barrister who finally agrees to take the case and then wins it.

winter of discontent Phrase from the opening line of *Richard III ('Now is the winter of our discontent'), which has become the standard description of the winter of 1978–9 in Britain – marked by exceptional levels of industrial unrest and of days lost through strikes. That winter is remembered also for the remark 'Crisis? What crisis?', attributed to the prime minister, James Callaghan. The phrase was in fact a *Sun* headline, reporting an interview in which he had denied that there was 'mounting chaos'.

Winter Queen Name given to Elizabeth (1596–1662), eldest daughter of James I of England, because her husband, the elector palatine Frederick V, was chosen to be king of Bohemia in 1619 but was evicted the following year. One of her 13 children was Prince *Rupert.

The **Winter's Tale** (c.1611) Drama by *Shakespeare falling into two distinct parts, the first a tragedy of jealousy and the second a comedy of rebirth and reconciliation. The jealous tyranny of Leontes, king of Sicilia, leads to the apparent death both of his wife Hermione and of their infant daughter. But the child has been saved by Antigonus, who takes her to Bohemia and leaves her on the shore with some gold and a name, Perdita (the lost girl). This first half ends with the most famous stage direction in English drama: 'Exit, pursued by a bear'. The bear which thus hurries Antigonus off (and eats him, as we later hear) leaves the stage clear for a shepherd to find and bring up the baby. Sixteen years pass and the beautiful young shepherdess takes the fancy of a prince, thus bringing us back into the courtly world. Leontes has hardly heard the joyful news that his daughter lives before he is shown a statue of his wife, Hermione, which also comes to life (the story of her death had been invented, to save her from his vengeance). Comedy is provided in the second half by the pickpocket Autolycus, famous for his disarming definition of himself as a 'snapper-up of unconsidered trifles'.

Wisden (Wisden Cricketers' Almanack) The bible of cricketing statistics, published each year (since 1864) and including the detailed results of the previous 12 months of Test, first class, minor counties and school *cricket – together with cumulative records (of huge importance to enthusiasts) in all combinations of batting, bowling and fielding. John Wisden (1826–84) was a fast bowler and one of the leading cricketers of his day. The first issue of his Almanack provided much information of only marginal relevance to cricket (such as the battles of the Wars of the Roses), but he soon settled down to the intense specialization which has ensured the long-term success of his venture.

Ernie **Wise** see The *Morecambe and Wise Show.

Cardinal **Wiseman** (Nicholas Wiseman, 1802–65) Prelate of Irish ancestry who in 1850 became the first Roman Catholic archbishop in Britain since the *Reformation, as archbishop of *Westminster.

'The **wisest fool in Christendom**' In British tradition the French court's view of James I of England. The remark, known only in this English translation, is variously attributed to the French king Henri IV and to his chief minister, the duc de Sully.

Wisley (13km/8m NE of Guildford) The garden since 1904 of the *Royal Horticultural Society. In addition to being a large and beautiful garden (97ha/240ac), it has many small areas laid out in response to the needs and interests of the public. Some are planted according to species, others in relation to differing conditions and types of soil. Particularly popular are the 'model gardens' – including one each for fruit and herbs, one demonstrating hedge and ground cover, three showing what can be done with small areas, and one with suggestions for the disabled or elderly.

Ludwig **Wittgenstein** (1889–1951) Austrian-born philosopher who lived in England from 1929 and was naturalized in 1938. He studied engineering at the university of Manchester in 1908–11 and then philosophy under Bertrand *Russell at Cambridge in 1912–13, before serving in the Austrian army in World War I. In 1921 he published *Tractatus Logico-Philosophicus*, an influential work on the philosophy of logic. In 1929 he returned to Cambridge. His later concerns were with linguistic philosophy and 'language games'. His lecture notes and manuscripts provided the material for *Philosophical Investigations* (1953) and for several other volumes published after his death.

Woburn Abbey (24km/15m SW of Bedford) Site of a Cistercian abbey granted to the Russell family (now dukes of Bedford) in 1547. The house dates mainly from the 18C, with successive parts designed by Henry Flitcroft (1697–1769) and Henry *Holland, though a celebrated shell grotto survives from an earlier building of the 1620s. The most historic of the paintings in the house is the Armada Portrait of Elizabeth I, with the wrecked ships of the *Armada depicted behind her. The park, landscaped by *Repton from 1816, is notable for its herd of Père David's deer; the species was preserved here after dying out in China in the late 19C (22 animals were returned to China from Woburn in 1985). Also in the park is a temple of 1818 by *Wyatville, now empty because it was built to house *The Graces*, a group of three marble nudes by the Italian neoclassical sculptor Antonio Canova. In the late 1980s they were removed from the temple and offered for sale.

P.G. **Wodehouse** (Pelham Grenville Wodehouse, 1881–1975, KBE 1975) Comic writer with a notably idiosyncratic style, and creator in Jeeves and Wooster of a pair of characters rivalled in English literature only by Holmes and Watson. The humour of his fiction derives partly from the farcical muddles which afflict the idle young men of the Drones Club and their vacuous girlfriends, threatened always by a desperate shortage of funds and by hordes of terrifying elderly aunts. Equally important are the constant surprises in Wodehouse's use of English, whether in its vocabulary ('if not actually disgruntled, he was far from being gruntled') or in its imagery ('small, shrivelled chap – looks like a haddock with lung-trouble'). Bertie Wooster, innocent and gullible, and his manservant Jeeves – nobody's fool behind the formal deference – first appeared in a collection of short stories in 1917, *The Man with Two Left Feet*. Another favourite corner of the Wodehouse world is Blandings Castle, home of Lord Emsworth – the proud owner of a prize sow, the Empress of Blandings.

Early in his career Wodehouse wrote the lyrics for several successful American musical comedies, and from 1909 he lived mainly in the USA until settling in 1934 in France. He and his wife were captured there by the Germans in 1940 and were interned until 1941. On his release from prison he made five broadcasts to the USA, in his usual comic vein – an ill-judged action, even though the content was entirely non-political, and one that caused him to be seen in official circles in Britain as a traitor. Partly for this reason he returned to the USA after the war, becoming an American citizen in 1955, but peace was formally declared in the last year of his life with the offer and acceptance of a knighthood.

Terry **Wogan** (b. 1938) Irish broadcaster who first won a large following in Britain on radio. He was one of the original team of disc jockeys on the new Radio 1 in 1967, following this with the *Terry Wogan Show* – at breakfast time on Radio 2 from 1972 to 1984. He then transferred to television in a three-nights-a-week BBC chat show (*Wogan* 1984–92), which eventually proved an overdose of even his considerable charm. His line in gentle mockery is well exercised each year in presenting the *Eurovision Song Contest*.

Wolds The name of two ranges of hills in northeast England, separated by the Humber estuary. To the north are the old Yorkshire Wolds (now in Humberside and so appearing on maps just as the Wolds) and to the south are the Lincolnshire Wolds.

General **Wolfe** (James Wolfe, 1726–59) Soldier whose capture of Quebec in 1759 led to the ceding of Canada to Britain at the end of the *Seven Years' War, and whose death at the moment of victory was the most poignant scene in Britain's annals of war until eclipsed by that of Nelson at Trafalgar. He was already weak from tuberculosis when he led his men up a wooded cliff during the night of September 12 to reach the Heights of Abraham, just outside the city of Quebec, where a successful engagement was fought the following day. Wolfe was wounded three times before dying on the battlefield. The house in which he grew up, at Westerham in Kent, is known now as Quebec House and is kept as a museum.

Wolfenden Report (1957) The findings and recommendations of the Departmental Committee on Homosexual Offences and Prostitution, chaired by John Wolfenden. The report was an important step towards the legalization of *homosexuality, for it recommended that homosexual acts between consenting adults should cease to be a criminal offence.

Wolfson Foundation (London W1) One of Britain's largest charitable trusts, established by Isaac Wolfson (see *Great Universal Stores). It specializes in medicine, education and the arts. He and his wife Edith, followed by other members of the family, also funded the separate Wolfson Family Charitable Trust, originally for Jewish charities but now mainly giving grants to medical and educational institutions in the UK.

William Hyde **Wollaston** (1766–1828) Chemist who in 1803 isolated the elements palladium and rhodium. He also discovered a way of making platinum malleable and therefore of practical use. In doing so he pioneered the technique of powder metallurgy which later became standard in the treatment of many metals.

Wollaton Hall (4km/2.5m W of Nottingham) The most spectacularly ornate and self-important of Elizabethan houses, built in 1580–88 by Robert *Smythson for Sir Francis Willoughby. It inspired an equally grandiose Victorian building, *Mentmore Towers. Wollaton Hall now houses Nottingham's museum of natural history.

Mary **Wollstonecraft** (1759–97) Writer and early feminist. Her *Vindication of the Rights of Men* (1790) was an answer to Edmund Burke's reflections on the French Revolution. It was followed by her most famous work, *A Vindication of the Rights of Woman* (1792), which was a passionate protest against society's low expectations of women and their limited opportunities. In 1797 she married the philosopher William Godwin and died only 11 days after giving birth to a daughter, the writer Mary *Shelley.

Wolseley A three-wheeler under this name was produced in 1895 and a car in 1899, both designed by *Austin for the Wolseley Sheep Shearing Machine Company in Birmingham. The company was bought in 1927 by *Morris, but the name continued to be used on new models.

Cardinal **Wolsey** (Thomas Wolsey, *c.*1475–1530) The leading political figure in the first half of the reign of Henry VIII. He was born into a relatively humble family in Ipswich; early rumours made his father a butcher, but he owned houses and land in the town. Wolsey's talents caused him to shine both at Oxford and in the church. Ordained in 1498, he was chaplain to the archbishop of Canterbury by 1501 and was soon an adviser in royal circles. When the 18-year-old Henry VIII became king, in 1509, he left the details of administration very largely to Wolsey. Rapid preferment followed. Wolsey became bishop of Lincoln in 1514 and archbishop of York later that same year (it was typical of the age that he did not visit York till 1530); by the end of the following year, 1515, he was a cardinal and lord chancellor of England.

Wolsey's main interest, like the king's, was in foreign affairs – the *Field of Cloth of Gold was an event much to their liking. But it was a domestic issue, admittedly with foreign ramifications, which prompted his downfall – the king's divorce from Catherine of Aragon. Wolsey suggested in 1527 that the necessary annulment could be procured from the pope, but he failed to deliver it. In 1529 Wolsey was dismissed as lord chancellor. Losing his greater powers, he travelled to York to be enthroned as archbishop, but he was arrested and brought south to face charges of treason. They would certainly have led to his execution but illness saved him this indignity; he died on the journey, at Leicester.

A reputation for tyranny, sometimes imputed to him, is not justified. Wolsey made great use of the *Star Chamber, but under his control it was subject to fewer delays and probably less injustice than other courts (its evil reputation was earned in the next century). He was nevertheless an extreme example of the greedy and worldly pre-Reformation prelate. His opulence can be seen still in his own house (*Hampton Court) and in his most munificent foundation (Christ Church at *Oxford).

Wolverhampton (249,000 in 1991) Industrial town in West Midlands, often considered the capital of the *Black Country. It was an ancient market town (the large church of St Peter is 15C and the grammar school was founded in the 16C) before becoming an important centre for the iron industry in the 18C. Decorative *japanning was a speciality of nearby Bilston, and there is a good collection of these wares in Bantock House, Wolverhampton's museum of applied art. The neoclassical Art Gallery, designed by Julius Chatwin (1829–1907) and opened in 1884, is strongest in British painting of the 18–19C.

Wolverhampton Wanderers, known as Wolves (Molineux Grounds, Wolverhampton). Football club believed to have been formed in 1879 by members from two other clubs (themselves dating from 1876 and 1877). A founder member of the *Football League in 1888, the club had early successes before a long bleak period in Division 2 in the early decades of the 20C. It returned to glory in the 1950s, when Billy Wright was the team's star performer and captain. Club victories: FA Cup 1893, 1908, 49, 60; League Champions 1954, 58, 59; League Cup 1974, 80.

Woman, Woman's Own, Woman's Weekly Three magazines, all owned by IPC and each selling more than half a million copies a week, which between them cover the market described as Britain's 'housewives'. The biggest seller, *Woman's Weekly*, was launched in 1911 and aims at the 45–64 age group; *Woman's Own* (1932) and *Woman* (1937) cater for those aged 25–44.

The **Woman in White** (1860) Tale of suspense and melodrama by Wilkie *Collins, published as a serial in *All the Year Round* from 1859. There are two women in white, each in turn the wife of an evil baronet (in fact an impostor) who confines them in a lunatic asylum. The young second wife, Laura Fairlie, is rescued by her half-sister, Marian Halcombe, the narrator, Walter Hartright, marries Laura after her husband has burnt to death while trying to destroy the evidence of his own illegitimacy.

Woman's Hour (BBC from 1946) Weekday radio programme which in nearly half a century of broadcasting has changed gradually but radically to reflect the shift in women's lives – from mainly domestic and often frivolous items in the early years to a much wider range of issues. One regular feature, the serialized book, has remained constant and popular. There has been a remarkable constancy too in the presenters – Marjorie Anderson from 1958 to 1972, then Sue MacGregor until 1987, followed by Jenni Murray. There was something of a furore in 1990 when the programme was moved from its hallowed time of 2 p.m. to 10.30 a.m., but there it remains.

Wombles Creatures with long snouts and eccentric clothes who live underground, originally under Wimbledon Common in London. Created by Elizabeth Beresford, they made their first appearance in a book for children (*The Wombles* 1968) and went on to become extremely popular in animated form on television. They were environment-friendly ahead of their time, for their night-time hobby is collecting and making imaginative use of the rubbish left by humans.

Women in Love see D.H. *Lawrence.

Women's Institutes (WI) Social and educational organization, catering particularly for women in rural districts. The movement began in Canada in 1897, with classes on domestic science at Stoney Creek, Ontario. The first WI in Britain was established at *Llanfair PG in 1915; several other branches were formed elsewhere in Wales and in England before the end of that year. In the early 1990s there are approximately 8900 WIs in England, Wales, the Channel Islands and the Isle of Man. In Scotland the Scottish Women's Rural Institutes are an equivalent organization.

Henry **Wood** (1869–1944, kt 1911) Conductor whose lasting memorial is the *Proms, where a traditional feature of the last night is his *Fantasia on British Sea Songs*. The piece known as the *Trumpet Voluntary* is also one of his arrangements. He greatly raised the standard of British orchestral playing, insisting upon a permanent team (he rejected the convention by which musicians could send deputies in their place) and bringing female players into the orchestra. He premiered in Britain the works of many leading continental composers, including Tchaikovsky, Sibelius, Richard Strauss, Debussy, Mahler and Schoenberg.

John **Wood** (the Elder, 1704–54; the Younger, 1728–81) Architects, father and son, who between them were responsible for much of *Bath. The father, also known as 'Wood of Bath', had worked as a young man on terraces being built in London in the developing *Georgian style of neo-classicism. Deciding to improve his own native city in the same manner, he returned in 1727 and began the process which transformed it into the greatest of England's 18C urban landscapes.

Victoria **Wood** (b. 1953) Writer and performer of comedy, with several series on television from the early 1980s. Her regular partner has been Julie *Walters, starting with *Wood and Walters* (1981–2).

Woodchester (20km/12m W of Cirencester) Site of one of the largest Roman buildings in Britain, little known because its 15 mosaic pavements are kept under a metre of protective earth. The villa, of the early 4C, was discovered in the late 18C and was last uncovered for a few weeks in 1973.

'**wooden O**' see the *Globe.

Sydney **Wooderson** (b. 1914) Shining hero to any schoolboy in mid-20C Britain, as the man who defeated the mighty Czech athlete Emil Zatopek to win the 5000 metres in the 1946 European Championships. In the years before World War II Wooderson held several world records, including the 800 metres, half mile and mile. His 1945 mile record of 4:4.2 lasted until defeated by *Bannister.

Parson **Woodforde** see *Diary of a Country Parson*.

Elizabeth **Woodville** (1437–92) Queen of *Edward IV. The marriage caused great offence at the Yorkist court, particularly to *Warwick the Kingmaker, because her family, now heaped with wealth and favours, had previously been Lancastrian supporters. Her two sons by Edward, the *princes in the Tower, are assumed to have been murdered soon after their father's death. But her descendants continued on the throne through the marriage of her daughter, Elizabeth, to *Henry VII.

Wookey Hole (3km/2m N of Wells) Series of caves worn by the river Axe on its course through the Mendips. They have been continuously either lived in or visited since prehistoric times. The most spectacular of the stalagmites, known as the Witch of Wookey, is traditionally said to be a petrified old woman.

wool The major source of English prosperity from the late Middle Ages (as reflected in the *Woolsack). The climate is well suited to the rearing of sheep, and at first the product was mainly exported as raw wool. But from the 14C England increasingly became a manufacturer and exporter of cloth. Areas with strong and reliable streams, such as the Cotswolds, were soon dotted with water-driven mills where primitive machinery replaced muscle power in the exhausting process of fulling – the pounding of the loosely woven fabric to make it more compact. Spinning and weaving were mainly done as piecework in people's homes. Other areas particularly known for the production of woollen cloth were Yorkshire and East Anglia (worsted derives its name from the Norfolk village of Worstead).

In the 17C woollen goods made up half of Britain's exports. This figure had fallen to about a quarter by the mid-18C. Wool was then still the country's largest single export, but by the early 19C it had been overtaken by *cotton – the commodity which had benefited from many of the most significant advances of the early *Industrial Revolution.

Virginia **Woolf** (Virginia Stephen, 1882–1941, m. Leonard Woolf 1912) Novelist, critic and central figure of the

The spinning of woollen yarn, still a cottage industry in the early 19C: hand-coloured aquatint, 1814.

*Bloomsbury Group. The early deaths of her mother, her father (editor of the *Dictionary of National Biography*) and her brother Thoby, all between 1895 and 1906, threatened her with successive nervous breakdowns and all her life she remained a manic depressive. Her growing reputation as a leading novelist in a modernist style, using the 'stream of consciousness' technique, was consolidated in 1925 with *Mrs Dalloway*, which follows the heroine's thoughts through one London day as she prepares for her party in the evening. Later books included *To the Lighthouse*, *Orlando* (1928, a fantasy inspired by her friendship with Vita *Sackville-West) and The *Waves. In recent years her essays about the obstacles placed in the way of women's creativity (in particular *A Room of One's Own* 1929) have made her a heroine of the feminist movement. In a final fit of depression she drowned herself in the river Ouse near her home, Monk's House at Rodmell in Sussex, which is kept now partly as a museum.

Leonard **Woolley** (1880–1960, kt 1935) Archaeologist who from 1922 to 1934 excavated the royal cemetery at Ur of the Chaldees, in Iraq. The spectacular Sumerian treasures, dating from the 3rd millennium BC, were divided between the museum in Baghdad, the British Museum and the university of Pennsylvania.

Woolsack Large square cushion-like seat in the House of Lords, without back, arms or legs, traditionally said to have been placed there in the 14C and to have been stuffed at that time with *wool clippings, in token of the importance of the trade to England. After several centuries of a more normal hair stuffing, the Woolsack was in 1938 filled once again with wool from Britain and the Commonwealth. It is the seat of the *lord chancellor as Speaker of the House.

Woolwich (London SE18) Ancient town downstream of London on the south bank of the Thames. Its economic importance derived from 1512 when Henry VIII established a royal dockyard here to build the *Great Harry. The dockyard closed in 1869, but Woolwich by then had another identity as a military town. The Woolwich Arsenal was Britain's chief arms factory in the 18C; it developed into the Royal Ordnance, now privatized as a division of British Aerospace. The Royal Military Academy, part of the Arsenal from 1741, moved to *Sandhurst in 1946. The fame of the *Arsenal lives on in the football club founded in Woolwich in 1886.

The **Woolwich** Britain's third largest *building society, founded in 1847 in the upstairs room of a pub in *Woolwich. It became particularly well known in the 1970s as the first building society to advertise on television, with the simple but effective slogan 'We're with the Woolwich'.

Woolworths International chain which developed from the first 'five cent' store opened by F.W. Woolworth in Utica (in the state of New York) in 1879. From the launch of its first shop in Liverpool in 1909, with a top price of sixpence, the British subsidiary of Woolworths rapidly acquired a dominant position on the high street; it was the leading UK retailer until overtaken in 1968 by Marks & Spencer. Woolworths was bought in 1982 by *Kingfisher, under whose management its range of goods has been more clearly focused and its fortunes have revived.

Ian **Woosnam** (b. 1958) Welsh golfer, known for a while for a brilliant career which nevertheless lacked a victory in any of the four major tournaments. In 1987 he topped the money list, breaking the record with £439,075 in a single season; in 1991 he reached the top

position in the world rankings; and later in that year there followed at last the elusive major, with a win in the US Masters.

Bertie **Wooster** see P.G. *Wodehouse.

Worcester (84,000 in 1991) City on the river Severn; administrative centre of Hereford and Worcester. Situated at the lowest convenient fording place of the Severn, it became a walled Anglo-Saxon town after being made a diocese in about 680. The present cathedral was begun in the late 11C, and the Norman crypt survives from that time; the rest of the building is mainly of the 14C. The oldest secular buildings in the city are three timber-frame houses of the 15C; the Greyfriars is kept as an example of domestic architecture of the period, while both the Tudor House and the Commandery (originally founded as a hospice for travellers in the 11C) are now museums of local history. The Guildhall, completed in 1721, is by Thomas White, a local pupil of Wren. Wool was the source of Worcester's medieval wealth and glove-making became a later specialization (a tall spire, all that remains of St Andrew's church, is known locally as the Glover's Needle). But the production of *Worcester porcelain has been the city's best-known activity since 1751; the Royal Porcelain Works have occupied their present site in Severn Street since 1840. Worcester is one of the cities of the *Three Choirs Festival; and Edward *Elgar was born in the village of Broadheath, 5km/3m to the west.

Battle of **Worcester** see *Charles II.

Worcester Pearmain Apple first grown in about 1875 by Richard Smith, a nurseryman in Worcestershire. Pearmain is an old word for apple.

Worcester porcelain The British porcelain with the longest history of production, continuous from 1751 until the present day. The early wares were mainly white, decorated in underglaze blue with the fashionable Chinese motifs of the time. In the late 1750s the factory pioneered transfer-printing from engravings – the image of Britain's ally Frederick the Great was particularly popular (partly because of the crippling effect of his military campaigns on the output of porcelain from Meissen). The company has been known as Royal Worcester since 1862. Close to the factory is the Dyson Perrins Museum, formed in 1946, with a very full collection including the 'Wigornia' creamboat – believed to be the very first Worcester design, produced in 1751.

Worcester sauce The common term now for Worcestershire sauce (which is still the name on the Lea and Perrins bottle). Tradition relates that in 1835 Messrs Lea and Perrins, chemists in Worcester, were asked by a retired governor of Bengal to recreate a sauce which he had enjoyed in India. The method of making and maturing it has remained a secret, but the sauce includes anchovies, shallots, tamarind, spices, garlic, vinegar and molasses. In 1837 Lea and Perrins began to produce it commercially, and it is still made in Worcester. In addition to its original purpose as a condiment for meat dishes, it is now widely used to give an edge to tomato juice.

Worcestershire Former *county in west central England, merged in 1974 with Herefordshire to form Hereford and Worcester.

Worcestershire County Cricket Club Founded in 1865 and in the *county championship from 1899; it has won five times (1964, 65, 74, 88, 89). In *one-day cricket the club has won the Benson and Hedges Cup once (1991) and the Sunday League three times (1971, 87, 88). The successes of the period since 1987 coincided with the five years (1986–91) which Ian *Botham spent in the team. The county ground is at Worcester – famous for its beautiful location, with the cathedral as a backdrop – and the county plays also at Kidderminster.

William **Wordsworth** (1770–1850) A leading poet of the *Romantic movement, inspired by an intense experience of nature. He was born in the *Lake District (the house at Cockermouth is kept as a museum) and spent nearly all his life there. His most formative period elsewhere was the year 1791–2 which he spent in France, recalled later in his *French Revolution, as it Appeared to Enthusiasts at its Commencement* (1809):
> Bliss was it in that dawn to be alive,
> But to be young was very heaven!

Back in England, the year 1795 brought two important developments. A small inheritance enabled him to set up house with his remarkable sister Dorothy (1771–1855), who had a profound influence on him; her ability to observe and describe nature equalled his own, and he was not above pinching good phrases from her journal for his poems. They lived together for the rest of his life, even after his marriage in 1802 to their mutual friend Mary Hutchinson and the birth of five children. The other great event of 1795 was meeting *Coleridge. Dorothy and William moved to Somerset in 1797 to be near him, and the friendship between the two poets led in 1798 to *Lyrical Ballads*, a turning point in English romantic poetry. Dorothy and William lived from 1799 in *Dove Cottage, and in 1800 Coleridge followed them to the Lake District.

Dorothy kept her *Grasmere Journal* during the early years at Dove Cottage, recording a simple life of walks, conversation, reading. It was here that her brother wrote many of the short lyric poems for which he is best known, published in *Poems* (2 vols, 1807). The collection included 'I wandered lonely as a cloud' (with its host of golden daffodils), 'My heart leaps up' (beholding a rainbow in the sky), and the sonnet on *Westminster Bridge. Published with these was 'Intimations of Immortality from Recollections of early Childhood', making the painful observation that such intense and mystical experiences of nature seem linked to youth; in it he describes how the beauties of the earth still move him but somehow lack the 'celestial light' and 'visionary gleam' that once they had. His autobiographical account of those inspirational years was published after his death as *The Prelude* (1850). It had been conceived as the prelude to a major poem on man and nature which Coleridge had urged him to write. *The Excursion* (1814), a political and philosophical treatise, was the only other completed part of this large project.

In 1813 the Wordsworth household moved to Rydal Mount, a larger house nearby, where he lived for the rest of his life. His reputation suffered from the effects of a young romantic living to the age of 80. He became *poet laureate in 1843. As early as 1818 the young Keats, attempting to visit the famous radical at Rydal Mount, had been surprised at the reason why he was unavailable; he was out campaigning for the Tory candidate in a forthcoming election.

Work see Ford Madox *Brown.

'**work expands**' see *Parkinson's Law.

workhouse see *Poor Laws.

working men's club A social institution of great importance over the past century in industrial communities, particularly in the Midlands and north of England. In recent decades, when an evening's convivial drinking and entertainment has become the central purpose, the clubs have been famous as a circuit on which stand-up comics often first make a name for themselves. But in their origins the clubs were more solemn, with local clergy active in setting up the first examples in the 1850s. They were seen as somewhere for working men to relax, talk and read – a role similar to that of the gentlemen's *clubs, such as the Travellers' or Athenaeum, founded in London earlier in the century. The movement spread rapidly after the Rev. Henry Solly established in 1862 a central organization, the Working Men's Club and Institute Union.

*The **World at One*** (BBC from 1965) Lunchtime programme on Radio 4, known for reacting fast and in a popular style to the news stories of the day. For the first ten years the presenter was William Hardcastle; among his successors have been Robin Day (1979–88) and, since 1988, the Scottish journalist James Naughtie.

World Cup The Jules Rimet Trophy was the prize offered by FIFA (Fédération Internationale de Football Association) for the first World Cup of association *football in 1930. Won on that occasion by Uruguay, and subsequently competed for every fourth year, the cup became the property of Brazil with their third win, in 1970. The new trophy is the FIFA World Cup. England won in July 1966, captained by Bobby *Moore. In March of that year the World Cup had been stolen, when on exhibition in Westminster Hall; it was discovered a week later, in a south London garden, by a mongrel called Pickles.

A World Cup in cricket, competed for in one-day matches, has been held every four years since 1975. And there are World Cups, also on a 4-year cycle, in rugby union and rugby league.

World in Action (Granada TV from 1963) The oldest surviving weekly programme of investigative journalism on independent television, with an established position at 8.30 p.m. on Mondays.

BBC **World Service** Originally the name for the English-language programmes broadcast around the world from 1932 by the *BBC, but extended in 1988 to include also the 35 foreign-language channels (previously called the External Services); together they amount to the entire output from *Bush House, with an estimated global audience of 120 million. The importance of these transmissions and of the BBC's reputation for impartiality became evident in World War II and has hardly lessened since; there was therefore considerable opposition in the early 1980s when the government proposed pruning the World Service (it is funded by the Foreign Office).

World War I (also known as the Great War, 1914–18) The war which more than any other in European history has come to symbolize senseless slaughter. Its origins were so complex that no short answer is ever given as to why it was fought. But a central theme was the underlying tension between great imperial powers – some old and disintegrating, others new and growing in strength.

The empires in decline were Turkey (whose plight had long been known as the *Eastern Question) and Austria-Hungary. A widely recognized danger point was in the Balkan territories lying between these ailing giants – Croatia, Bosnia-Herzegovina, Serbia, Albania, Bulgaria, Greece, all of which had at some time been subject to one empire or the other. Nationalist movements had won freedom for some, but relationships remained uneasy. Meanwhile a third great empire to the north, Russia, was eager to exploit any trouble in this region so as to acquire access to the Mediterranean.

Death at the front: the ironically entitled Paths of Glory *by an official war artist, Christopher Nevinson (1917).*

The newest empire, Germany, had recently established itself as the dominant power in continental Europe. But the event which had emphasized this status – Germany's invasion and defeat of France in the Franco-Prussian War of 1870–1 – had also left France, the second greatest continental power, with deep-seated grounds for hostility; after her defeat she had been forced to cede to Germany two border regions, Alsace and Lorraine, in which the population was of mixed French and German origin.

Outside Europe, particularly in Africa, German expansionism was now rivalling the other leading imperial power, Britain. The British relied on their own traditional form of national security, that of controlling the seas. But this too seemed threatened in the early 20C by a rapid build-up of the German navy.

Increasing nervousness between the powers led to several crises in the early years of the century, including a succession of local wars in the Balkans. The final explosion was triggered by a single dramatic event. On 28 June 1914, in the Bosnian city of Sarajevo, a Serbian nationalist assassinated the Archduke Franz Ferdinand, heir to the Austrian throne. Austria used this as a pretext for strong demands on Serbia and, when they were not fully met, declared war. On 29 July Austrian artillery shelled Belgrade and within a week almost the whole of Europe was in arms. In quick succession Russia ordered her army to mobilize against Austria; Germany declared war on Russia; France prepared for action, whereupon Germany declared war on her and sent an army of invasion through Belgium; Britain, committed by a treaty of 1839 to preserving Belgian neutrality, declared war on Germany. And it was still only August 4, a mere six days after the assassination at Sarajevo.

The German plan was for a quick thrust to Paris and to the Channel ports facing Britain, after which the victori-

ous armies could be transferred to an eastern front against Russia. This scheme was frustrated by the resolution of the French, supported by a relatively small *British Expeditionary Force. Engagements in the autumn of 1914 at *Mons, the Marne and *Ypres resulted in the Germans being held at a line roughly along the French-Belgian border and along the French-German border down to Switzerland.

The only flat part of this territory was in Belgium, and it was there (in 'Flanders fields') that the rival armies settled in for nearly four years of devastating trench warfare. It is a measure of the static situation underlying successive campaigns that battles were fought again and again at the same places: the Marne (1914, 1918), the *Somme (1916, 1918) or *Ypres (every year except 1916). There were innovations – the Germans used gas on occasion (chlorine in 1915 and mustard gas in 1917, both at Ypres) and the British introduced *tanks (the Somme, 1916). Otherwise little changed except the spiralling casualty figures, until at last the Allies began to push the Germans back after the second Battle of the Marne in 1918.

There were two other major fronts in Europe. The Italians entered the fray in May 1915, declaring war on Austria in return for an Allied promise that Austrian territory south of the Alps would become Italian. The result was a prolonged localized war between Italy and Austria in this region. More important were Russia's assaults on Germany and Austria from the north and east. The only route by which the Allies could get supplies to Russia was through the Bosphorus and the Black Sea, and this was blocked from November 1914 when Turkey joined the war on the German side. The disastrous *Gallipoli campaign of 1915 was a British attempt to force Turkey out of the war, reopening the gateway to Russia.

The most important front outside Europe was in the Middle East, an area which had long been part of the Turkish empire and where the Suez canal was of great strategic importance to the Allies. There were reverses here in the early years of the war, but by 1917–18 a two-pronged campaign was yielding results. *Allenby moved up the coast with conventional military forces, capturing Jerusalem, while further inland T.E. *Lawrence fostered an Arab revolt to pin down Turkish resistance. Early in October 1918 Allenby took Damascus and Beirut; soon he was close to the Turkish border and before the end of the month Turkey signed an armistice.

Meanwhile a deadly conflict had been carried on at sea throughout the entire four years. Both Britain and Germany entered the war with large fleets of heavily armed battle cruisers and battleships (of the *'dreadnought' type), but there was only one major engagement between these leviathans – at *Jutland. More significant was the threat to Britain from Germany's extremely successful submarines. The U-boats sank so many merchant ships that Britain was in serious danger of being starved of supplies, until the adoption in May 1917 of the convoy system with armed escort vessels. But in another way the U-boats harmed Germany's chances; several ships were sunk with American passengers on board, the *Lusitania being the best known. Such provocation eroded the isolationist stance of the USA, as did an intercepted message from Zimmermann, the German foreign minister, promising Mexico the prize of Texas, Arizona and New Mexico in the event of war. In April 1917 the US Congress approved a declaration of war on Germany.

The arrival of US troops in large numbers on the western front in the summer of 1918 coincided with the Allies breaking through the *Siegfried line. For the first time the

Life at home: powerful blackmail in a notorious World War I recruiting poster by Savile Lumley.

balance tipped decisively, for Allied troop levels would now steadily increase while those of Germany could only decline. As the front line crumbled, so did the political structure within Germany. Sparked by a mutiny in the fleet, revolt spread through the country in October 1918. On November 9 a socialist government took power and proclaimed a republic. The German emperor William II (Kaiser Bill to the British) fled to the neutral Netherlands, where he lived until his death in 1941. Two days later, on November 11, the new government negotiated the *armistice. Alsace and Lorraine were to be returned to France; German troops were to withdraw from all occupied territories; military hardware and submarines were to be handed over and surface warships interned. The German fleet was moved to the security of *Scapa Flow, where the sailors on 21 June 1919 pulled off a remarkable feat of defiance. In spite of British precautions they managed to scuttle every one of their 50 warships, in protest against the terms imposed at Versailles.

The Versailles conference, convened in January 1919 to settle the details of the peace, had gone far beyond the reasonable demands of the armistice. The Germans had assumed that peace would be based on the conciliatory Fourteen Points of Woodrow Wilson, the US president. These were concerned with avoiding war, and their main purpose – the founding of the *League of Nations – was achieved. But to the distress of Woodrow Wilson, the Allies were more concerned with punishing Germany. The final treaty imposed crippling financial penalties, to be paid by Germany to the Allies as reparation for war damages. The resulting instability in Germany proved a fertile ground for the rise of the Nazis and did much to ensure a continuation of the conflict in *World War II.

The real damage, for which reparation from either side was impossible, had been in the lives of a generation. Deaths in the armed services alone amounted to some 8 million. The countries suffering the highest losses of military personnel were Germany (1.8m), Russia (1.7m), France (1.35m), Austria-Hungary (1m), Britain and the empire (0.9m). Civilian deaths worldwide are believed to have been in the region of 7 million.

World War II (1939–45) A rarity among wars in having a clear moral purpose, to defeat Nazi tyranny. Fascism had thrived in Germany's devastated economy between the wars (partly a result of the terms of the treaty of Versailles after *World War I), and in 1933 the Nazis were voted into power. By 1938 Hitler's expansionist plans were unmistakable, but supporters of *appeasement felt that they could best be contained by diplomacy. In March of that year Hitler invaded Austria (the *Anschluss* or 'joining' of the two countries), and in September he demanded that Czechoslovakia cede the Sudetenland to Germany; this was an area with a large proportion of German speakers, which had been included in 1919 in the newly established Czech state (previously part of the Austrian empire). Chamberlain and Daladier agreed at *Munich to Hitler's demand for the Sudetenland, but in March 1939 he went beyond the agreement by invading and occupying the rest of Czechoslovakia. By now it was clear that he had similar designs on Poland. On March 31 Britain and France guaranteed to defend Poland against aggression. Hitler's tanks crossed the Polish frontier on September 1 and two days later Britain and France declared war.

In 1936 Hitler had entered a vague alliance with the other Fascist country in Europe at that time, Mussolini's Italy; the pact was described as an 'axis' between Rome and Berlin. In the same year Hitler had made an anti-Soviet alliance with Japan. Italy entered the war on Germany's side in 1940, to be followed by Japan in 1941; together the three nations became known as the Axis powers. But during the first year of the war Hitler had a different and more improbable ally. In August 1939 he and Stalin, ideologically the most committed of enemies, had made a cynical non-aggression pact containing an agreement about the future of Poland. The following month, shortly after Hitler's invasion of Poland from the west, Stalin's troops marched in from the east and the country was partitioned.

In western Europe the first six months of the war were quiet. This was the period of the so-called phony war, a time of feverish preparation. The action began in April 1940, when German forces invaded Denmark and Norway. British and French troops were sent to Norway, but they maintained only a small foothold before retreating in June. The feebleness of this campaign provoked intense criticism of *Chamberlain in the House of Commons on May 7–8. There followed, on May 10, the news that Germany had marched into the Netherlands and Belgium. Chamberlain resigned and was replaced by Winston *Churchill.

The new prime minister's powers of leadership were severely tested and triumphantly proved by the events of that summer. The German army moved fast in its successful technique of *blitzkrieg* (lightning war). Holland fell in five days, Belgium in three weeks, and by June 14 the Germans were in Paris. The *British Expeditionary Force avoided capture at the coast only by the rescue operation at *Dunkirk in late May; the same undertaking brought to Britain the French soldiers who continued to take an active part in the war, as the Free French, under the leadership of Charles de Gaulle.

In June 1940 Hitler launched an aerial assault on southern England, leading to a life-and-death struggle which became known – without any exaggeration of its importance – as the *Battle of Britain. Meanwhile the fall of France had given Germany submarine bases on the Atlantic coast for the almost equally crucial Battle of the *Atlantic. Supplies from Canada and the USA were the main external lifeline for Britain. The USA was not yet in the war, but in March 1941 American aid was established on the regular basis of *Lend-Lease; and in August the *Atlantic Charter expressed a shared vision of the future.

Two major developments in that same year shaped the future course of events. In June Hitler abandoned his own non-aggression pact and launched a *blitzkrieg* on Russia; ideology (a hatred of both Slavs and Communists), together with an appetite for Russia's grain and oil, had made him abandon his more prudent earlier policy. And on December 7 the Japanese air force launched a surprise attack on the American fleet at Pearl Harbor, killing more than 2000 men, destroying 18 ships and some 200 aircraft, and bringing the USA unequivocally into the war. By the end of the month the Japanese had taken Hong Kong and the Philippines, as well as sinking two powerful British warships based in Singapore, the *Prince of Wales* and the *Repulse*; early in 1942 they occupied Malaya, Singapore and Burma.

Japan had been at war with China since 1937; this older conflict now became a strand in the world war, with China (under Chiang Kai-shek) a new member of the Allied nations. The events of 1941 had finally set in place the main combatants: the USA, USSR, China, Britain and the Commonwealth countries on the Allied side, with support from the Free French; Germany, Italy and Japan as the Axis powers.

In 1941–2 the main theatre of the land war in the west was north Africa. In 1940 Italy held most of the north African coast (Mussolini dreamt of making the Mediterranean a Roman sea again). But the Suez canal was essential to Britain's links with India. In the winter of 1940–1 *Wavell drove the Italians west through Libya. The arrival of Rommel and the Afrika Corps turned the

tables until the two battles of El *Alamein. After the second of these, in November 1942, a joint US and British force under Eisenhower landed in western north Africa. By May 1943 Eisenhower's forces from the west and *Montgomery's 8th army from the east had converged to trap the enemy. Some 250,000 German and Italian soldiers surrendered.

The conclusion of the north Africa campaign in May 1943 was the first significant Allied achievement of the war. It was followed in July by the successful invasion of Sicily. This development, combined with the bombing of Rome, prompted Mussolini's colleagues to overthrow him; a new Italian government made peace with the Allies on September 3. On that same day British and American forces crossed from Sicily to southern Italy, beginning the long Italian campaign as the Allies slowly fought their way up the country against strong German resistance (Italy declared war on Germany in October 1943). The *Anzio landing was in January 1944, the struggle for *Monte Cassino in February–May, and Rome fell in June. In April Italian partisans captured Mussolini and his mistress near Lake Como and executed them both.

Throughout this central period of the war, Germany's eastern front against Russia had been a severe drain on Hitler's resources. The initial invasion in the summer of 1941 went with the usual *blitzkrieg* bravura; German troops were surrounding Leningrad before the end of August. But the Russians demonstrated their fabled powers of resistance, which in the previous century had humbled even Napoleon. Leningrad withstood a siege of 900 days, until January 1944. When the Germans succeeded in entering Stalingrad in September 1942, the resulting battle left 300,000 of their troops dead and another 100,000 in Russian hands. By the autumn of 1943 the Russians were driving the Germans back on all fronts. By the summer of 1944 the Red Army was in Poland and pressing towards the eastern frontiers of Germany.

This was the moment at which the Allies launched the most dramatic campaign of the war, with the invasion of Normandy. *D-day was 6 June 1944. Paris was liberated on August 25 and Brussels on September 3. On October 21 the US 1st army took Aachen, the first German city to be captured. By then the Allied advance was faltering after the disaster at *Arnhem, but a strong German counter-attack in the Ardennes region in December was contained (the Battle of the Bulge). In the early months of 1945 the Allies in the west were moving fast into Germany, while the Russians were pressing through east Prussia to Berlin. It was now that the two armies came upon the first harrowing evidence of what has since become known as the Holocaust, the Nazi 'final solution' for the Jews. The Russians reached Auschwitz in Poland as the British and Americans came upon Buchenwald, Belsen and Dachau.

The Russians surrounded Berlin on April 25 and on that same day their advance guard joined up with the US 9th army at the river Elbe, about 100km/62m west of the city. Hitler committed suicide in his Berlin bunker on April 30. The German unconditional surrender came into effect on May 8 (*V-E day). One threat of tyranny in Europe had been brought to an end, but the germ of another already existed. The Russians, having advanced from the east, were now in Romania, Bulgaria, Hungary, Czechoslovakia and Poland as well as eastern Germany. At *Yalta the Allied leaders – Roosevelt, Churchill and Stalin – had all pledged themselves to fostering democracy in the liberated and conquered countries. But there was nothing the western powers could do to hold Soviet Russia to such an improbable commitment, short of fighting another war. The conditions were in place for what Churchill later called the *'iron curtain', the blight of eastern Europe until the late 1980s.

The war against Japan was also being slowly won. By the summer of 1945 Burma had been liberated by *Slim and the Philippines by the US general Douglas MacArthur, while heavy bombing of Tokyo and other Japanese cities was the clear prelude to an invasion. On July 26, from *Potsdam, Truman and Churchill (together with Chiang Kai-shek) sent an ultimatum to Japan demanding unconditional surrender. The text did not mention the new weapon which had been successfully tested in the USA. The Japanese refused to surrender, and an atom bomb was dropped on August 6 on Hiroshima, followed by another on Nagasaki on August 9 (between the two bombs, on August 8, Russia declared war on Japan, exercising an option agreed at Yalta). On August 10 the Japanese offered to surrender and the formalities were completed on September 2.

The horrors of Hiroshima and Nagasaki were the culmination of something new in World War II, the bombing of civilians. Serious air raids were first suffered by London and other British cities (such as *Coventry) in the *blitz that began in 1940, but later in the war the same techniques were used to even more devastating effect against German cities. The extreme example was the controversial carpet bombing by the RAF of Dresden during the night of 13–14 February 1945, engulfing the city in a fire storm which is estimated by some to have killed as many as 135,000 people (the immediate death toll at Hiroshima was about 75,000). Meanwhile the Germans had inaugurated in 1944 new techniques of aerial warfare against civilians with unmanned missiles and rockets, the *V1 and V2 – at that time more psychologically alarming than massively destructive. The *Geneva Convention was amended after the war to take into account the bombing of cities.

The cost of the war in lives far exceeded any previous conflict. The total of military deaths in World War I had been about 8 million, to which a very rough figure of some 7 million civilian deaths is usually added. The figures for World War II are even more inexact, largely because they are unreliable for the two nations with the highest number of casualties, Russia and China. International totals often quoted are in the region of 15–20 million military deaths and 25 million civilian deaths. For the eight main combatant nations the usual estimates of military/civilian deaths are approximately as follows: USSR 7.5 million military/10 million civilian; China 2.2m/6m; Germany 3.5m/500,000; Japan 1.5m/ 600,000; France 200,000/ 400,000; Britain 300,000/ 65,000; Italy 200,000/ 150,000; USA 300,000/6000. About 6 million Jews were murdered by the Nazis, the majority of them from Poland.

The precedent of charging prominent figures with war crimes was set in the Nuremberg trials (1945–6), which resulted in the execution of 11 Nazi leaders and the imprisonment of seven others. (The treaty of Versailles had provided for the trial of the German emperor after World War I, but it was not carried out.) Germany and Austria were occupied after the war by the four western Allies (USA, USSR, Britain, France); Berlin, which fell within the Russian sector of Germany, was similarly divided into four sections. Austria became free and neutral in 1955, when the four powers withdrew their occupying forces. At the same period (1954–5) the three western zones of Germany became the Federal Republic of Germany and the Russian zone became a separate state as the German Democratic Republic. Berlin was similarly divided, and the rigid isolation of east Germany from the west was symbolized from 1961 by the Berlin Wall. Its dismantling in 1989 was the prelude to the reunification of Germany in 1990.

The economic recovery of Europe was greatly advanced by the *Marshall Plan of 1947, while the evident

The classic image of the Blitz, which St Paul's Cathedral miraculously survived at the heart of London.

"*Strictly between you & me....*"

CARELESS TALK COSTS LIVES

World War II poster by Fougasse (Kenneth Bird) on the need for security in the fight against Hitler.

need for co-ordinated western defence led to the establishment in 1949 of *NATO. In 1950 the first steps were taken towards what became the *EC, prompted by a desire to end the long history of conflict between the nations of Europe. On the broader international scene the war led directly to the creation of the *United Nations, with the five main Allies (USA, USSR, Britain, France, China) occupying the only permanent seats on the Security Council.

Wormwood Scrubs Victorian prison in west London, with a name of Dickensian appropriateness whether used in full or in its common abbreviation – the Scrubs. It was built (1874–90) by the convicts themselves, described in an account of the time as 'felon bees'. Contractors built the first nine lock-up cells, after which the first nine prisoners built more cells and were joined by more prisoners to build more cells, and so on until at last the prison was both complete and full.

worsted General term for woollen fabric made from long-staple wool with the fibres combed to lie in one direction. It derives from the village of Worstead, north of Norwich. Flemish weavers brought the craft there in the 12c, and cloth of this kind was soon widely known as worsted.

Worzel Gummidge Scarecrow who first appeared in *Worzel Gummidge, or the Scarecrow of Scatterbrook Farm* (1936), by Barbara Euphan Todd (*c.*1900–76); the book was selected by *Penguin in 1941 as the first Puffin. Worzel's many scarecrow friends and relations included at that time Earthy Mangold as his fiancée. He became

widely known through a television series which began in 1979, written by Keith *Waterhouse and Willis Hall; in this context Worzel, played by Jon Pertwee, had Aunt Sally in place of Earthy as his sweetheart.

WRAC (Women's Royal Army Corps) Until 1992 the women's branch of the regular army, formed in 1949 but descending directly from the ATS (Auxiliary Territorial Service) of World War II and before that from the WAC (Women's Auxiliary Corps) of World War I. The WAC was formed in 1917, was renamed Queen Mary's Army Auxiliary Corps in 1918, and was disbanded in 1919; the ATS was established in 1939. The WRAC numbered about 6000 women in 1992, when it came to an end as a separate entity. In the interests of sexual equality it was incorporated within a new Adjutant General's Corps, bringing under single control all the administrative services of the army.

WRAF (Women's Royal Air Force) A female section under this name was established in 1918 on the same day as the *Royal Air Force, and was disbanded in 1920. It was re-established in 1939 for World War II under a different name, the WAAF (Women's Auxiliary Air Force), which was changed to WRAF in 1949. Women are involved in nearly all air force activities, serving now even in aircrews.

Christopher **Wren** (1632–1723, kt 1673) English architect, designer of *St Paul's Cathedral and of some 50 other London churches after the *Great Fire of 1666. His early career was as an astronomer, and he was a founder member of the *Royal Society. His first major architectural commission was in 1663 for the Sheldonian Theatre at *Oxford, where he had been Savilian professor of astronomy since 1661. He carried on the classicism introduced to English architecture by Inigo *Jones and added to it elements of the *baroque style which was well established in Europe. His secular buildings include *Chelsea Hospital, the *Royal Naval College and *Hampton Court. He is buried in St Paul's.

Wrens see *WRNS.

wrestling Two traditional forms of wrestling in Britain have become better known than others: that of Cumberland and Westmorland, in which the contestants start in a clinch or 'hold', chest to chest, and try to wrestle each other to the ground from that position; and that of Devon and Cornwall, where the wrestlers wear jackets and attempt to throw each other from a standing position by holding the opponent's collar and one sleeve.

Billy **Wright** (b. 1924) Footballer, at centre back, who led Wolverhampton Wanderers to many victories (FA Cup 1949, League Champions 1954, 58, 59). In 1959 he became the first player to win 100 caps for England. Of his final total of 105 international appearances, 70 were in consecutive games; and he captained the country on 90 occasions.

Peter **Wright** (b. 1926) Dancer, choreographer and ballet director. Much of his early career was with the Sadler's Wells Theatre Ballet (1949–55), the company of which he became director in 1977 and which he transformed in 1990 into the *Birmingham Royal Ballet. As a choreographer he has specialized in reworking the classic 19c ballets. From 1961 he was associate director to John *Cranko in developing the Stuttgart ballet company.

Wright of Derby (Joseph Wright, 1734–97) Painter whose career was made in the industrial Midlands around his home town of *Derby. His strong and direct style of portraiture suited his patrons, men of business who were more robust than the fashionable clientele in London; and his personal fascination with the effects of artificial light, whether candles, furnaces or fireworks, made science and industry a natural subject matter. His two most celebrated works are candle-lit and scientific, both dating from about 1768 – *A Philosopher giving that Lecture on the Orrery, in which a lamp is put in place of the Sun* (Derby Art Gallery) and *An Experiment on a Bird in the Air Pump* (National Gallery). A trip to Italy in 1773–5 provided him with two other favourite themes – a firework display at the Castel Sant'Angelo in Rome, and an eruption of Vesuvius.

WRNS (Women's Royal Naval Service) A female branch of the *Royal Navy was formed under this name in 1917, was disbanded after the war and was reformed again just before World War II; from the start members of the service were affectionately known as Wrens. They were limited to shore duties until 1990. In that year 16 Wrens ended a taboo of seven decades when they joined the crew of HMS *Brilliant* for five weeks' operational training at sea (provoking a protest march by some of the wives left on shore). In the early 1990s the WRNS was about 3500 strong.

Wroxeter see *Viroconium.

WRVS (Women's Royal Voluntary Service) The name since 1966 of the WVS, which played a major part on the home front during World War II. The Women's Voluntary Service was formed in 1938 to recruit women for air raid service. During the war it had more than a million members, most of them housewives involved on a part-time basis in a wide range of emergency and welfare activities. A smaller membership (about 150,000 in the early 1990s) has continued in peacetime with similar activities, such as caring for disaster victims, doing voluntary work in hospitals and delivering 'meals on wheels' to the elderly.

Wuthering Heights (1847) The only novel by Emily *Brontë, a turbulent story set among the Yorkshire moors and one of the most powerful late works of the *Romantic movement. Dark deeds are discovered in flashbacks narrated by two characters more prosaic than the events they describe – Mr Lockwood, a visitor to the district, and the housekeeper Nelly Dean. The tragic story involves two generations of two families, the passionate Earnshaws in Wuthering Heights, a wind-buffeted house on the hill, and the gentler Lintons in Thrushcross Grange.

The relationship which provoked the tragedy was between Catherine Earnshaw and Heathcliff, a foundling from Liverpool brought into their home by Catherine's father. The childhood friendship between these two develops into adult passion, of a wildness reflected in the rocky moorland setting. Catherine will not marry him, for reasons of class, and Heathcliff leaves. He returns, three years later, rich – only to find Catherine married to Edgar Linton. In his revenge Heathcliff dominates and largely destroys both families. His activities hasten the death of Catherine, with whom he is still obsessed; and soon he owns the two houses. He is the brooding, sullen inhabitant of Wuthering Heights from whom Mr Lockwood rents a cottage.

The dark complexities of the book are impossible to attempt in the cinema, but a famous film version of the first half of the story was directed in 1939 by William Wyler, with Laurence Olivier as Heathcliff and Merle Oberon as Catherine.

James **Wyatt** (1746–1813) Architect who worked both in the neo-classical style (the interior of *Heveningham) and in neo-Gothic (most notably the extravaganza of Fonthill Abbey for *Beckford). His ignorant 'improvements' of several cathedrals later earned him the title of 'the Destroyer'.

Wyatt's father and two of his brothers were architects; his son Benjamin (1775–c.1850) followed him in the profession; and *Wyatville was related.

Jeffry **Wyatville** (b. Wyatt, 1766–1840, kt 1828) Architect and nephew of James *Wyatt, whose pseudo-historical change of name (in keeping with the flavour of his architecture) was prompted by his winning a competition in 1824 to remodel much of *Windsor Castle. George IV granted him the improved name when laying the foundation stone of the proposed work, and gave him a knighthood on its completion four years later. Wyatville was working at the same period on *Chatsworth.

William **Wycherley** (c.1640–1716) The earliest writer of *Restoration comedy to survive in today's repertoire. With Lord *Rochester he was part of the dissolute court circle of *Charles II, and his plays satirize a cynical world which he knew intimately. His best, *The Country Wife* (1675), brings together two themes brimming with potential for bawdy comedy: the arrival in town of Pinchwife and the young country girl he has married, Margery, who has heard much of the wickedness of London and would like to hear more; and the subterfuge of the libertine, Horner, who puts it about that he is impotent and therefore the perfect man to chaperone the wives of jealous husbands.

A distinctly glamorous view of the ATS (subsequently the WRAC) in a World War II recruiting poster designed by Abram Games.

John **Wycliffe** (*c*.1330–84) Important precursor of the *Reformation. After a brilliant career as a theologian at Oxford, he became in his last years a powerful opponent of the claims of the papacy – the worldliness of which was emphasized in 1378, when the Great Schism produced two rival popes. At about this time Wycliffe wrote a series of works not only attacking the wealth of the Church but emphasizing various points which were later central to the Reformation. He argued that the scriptures provide the only firm basis for religious authority; that the Bible must therefore be available to Christians in their own languages; and that the bread and wine of the sacrament do not literally become, through transubstantiation, the body and blood of Christ.

In Oxford in 1381 his opinions were pronounced heretical, but he had not been brought to trial by the time he died in 1384 in his Leicestershire parish of Lutterworth. His ideas lived on among the *Lollards and inspired the great Czech reformer, John Huss (or Jan Hus). The Council of Constance (1414–18) finally ended the Schism but also burned Huss and condemned Wycliffe; his remains were dug up, burnt and thrown into the river Swift at Lutterworth.

Wye River which rises in central Wales, in Powys, and follows a tortuous course of 210km/130m southeast into England, passing through Hereford and Ross-on-Wye before forming for its last few miles, below Monmouth, the border between Wales and England; at Chepstow it flows into the Severn estuary. Deservedly the birthplace of the *picturesque, it is rich in both natural and man-made beauties (*Symonds Yat, *Tintern Abbey). Some of its tributaries have been dammed to form the *Elan Valley reservoirs.

William of **Wykeham** see *Winchester.

Wylan Dilly see *Puffing Billy*.

Wynkyn de Worde see William *Caxton.

X·Y·Z

Xanadu see **Kubla Khan.*

Yahoos see **Gulliver's Travels.*

Yalta Resort city in the Ukraine, on the Black Sea, where Roosevelt, Churchill and Stalin met during 4–11 February 1945 to plan the final strategies of *World War II and their postwar policy. Stalin and Churchill, meeting three months earlier in Moscow, had already agreed a relative share of influence for Britain and the USSR in the countries of eastern Europe (a deal which Churchill himself considered 'rather cynical'). The brutal fact, of which Roosevelt and Churchill were all too aware at Yalta, was that Russian armies would be in place throughout eastern Europe when the war ended. The two leaders had little option but to accept Stalin's assurance that the people of those countries would be free to decide their own futures. A secret deal which also tainted the image of Yalta was the promise that Russia could have certain Japanese territory (including the Kuril islands, still a major bone of contention today) if she declared war on Japan within two or three months of the end of the war in Europe. Stalin exercised this option two days after the atom bomb was dropped on Hiroshima. Discussion of similar topics was continued at *Potsdam.

One of the agreements made at Yalta was that Soviet citizens captured fighting on the German side should be returned to the Soviet Union. The term 'victims of Yalta', used broadly for all who were forcibly repatriated to almost certain death, applies more particularly to Russians wrongly returned under this agreement – those who had left Russia after the revolution of 1917 and had never been Soviet citizens.

yard see *length.

The Yard Abbreviation often used for *Scotland Yard.

Dornford **Yates** (pen name of Cecil Mercer, 1885–1960) Popular author between the wars of light society novels about 'Berry' Pleydell and his friends, and the somewhat Ruritanian adventures in which they become involved.

*The **Yellow Book*** (1894–7) Illustrated quarterly, with *Beardsley as art editor, which represented both the elegance and the self-conscious air of decadence of the last years of the *Aesthetic movement.

ye olde This archaic phrase, often seen on mock-Tudor tea shops or inns, is correctly written; but 'ye' merely spells 'the'. In medieval manuscripts and early printed books there was a letter known as the thorn (deriving from *runes) which stood for 'th'. In its written form it became almost indistinguishable from 'y' and so printers often used the same letter.

yeoman Originally a free man living on enough freehold land to support his family and his independence, but the term was later taken to include tenant farmers who had progressed from being villeins to copyholders. Emerging from the disintegration of *feudalism, the yeomen were seen by many from the 15c onwards as the backbone of England. It was they who had been the foot soldiers at Crécy and Agincourt. With *gentlemen above and wage-labouring peasants below, they were the beginnings of a middle class.

Yeomen of the Guard The personal bodyguard of the monarch, established for the coronation of Henry VII in 1485 and surviving today for ceremonial functions. Although wearing a similar Tudor costume, they are distinct from the yeoman warders of the *Tower of London.

*The **Yeomen of the Guard*** or, *The Merryman and His Maid* (1888) Unusual among the *Savoy operas of Gilbert and Sullivan in having a sad ending. Colonel Fairfax, about

The Beardsley design that was featured, in black on yellow paper, on the cover of the first Yellow Book *(1894).*

713

to be executed in the Tower of London in the 16c, has legal reasons for getting married just before his death. He persuades Elsie Maynard, the partner of a strolling jester (Jack Point) to go through the charade with him, but just after the wedding a pardon arrives for Fairfax. The bridal pair are delighted. But Jack Point, singing 'the song of a merryman moping mum', spoils the festivities by falling 'insensible at their feet'.

Yes, Minister (BBC 1980–5) The wittiest of TV comedy series, combining the ingredients of farce with wickedly observed satire on the British establishment's methods, manners and morals. The sparring partners are an unscrupulous senior civil servant, Sir Humphrey (played by Nigel *Hawthorne) and his bumbling but sometimes wily minister, Jim Hacker (Paul *Eddington). The scriptwriters, Antony Jay (b. 1930) and Jonathan Lynn (b 1943), somehow contrived the impossible and got the ineffective Hacker into 10 Downing Street, thus providing for an equally brilliant sequel, *Yes, Prime Minister* (1986–7).

Henry **Yevele** (c.1325–1400) England's most distinguished medieval architect, who became mason to the Black Prince in about 1357. Among many works attributed to him, the most important is the nave of Canterbury Cathedral. He was in charge of the alterations made in 1394–9 to Westminster Hall.

YMCA (Young Men's Christian Association) Worldwide organization formed originally in London in 1844 by George Williams (1821–1905) with several other young men in the drapery firm of Hitchock and Rogers, where he worked as an assistant. Beginning with prayer meetings – in an *evangelical tradition going back to John Wesley in the previous century – the YMCA soon adopted the wider aim of improving 'the spiritual condition of young men engaged in the drapery and other trades' and within months had broadened this again to 'the improvement of the spiritual and mental condition of young men'. Educational and recreational programmes, combined with the provision of low-cost accommodation in cities, have remained at the heart of the fellowship's activities. The movement is strongest in the USA, where the first YMCA was opened in 1851.

Yonghy-Bonghy-Bò Central character in Edward *Lear's nonsense song *The Courtship of the Yonghy-Bonghy-Bò*. He lives on the coast of Coromandel and courts the Lady Jingly Jones, offering her all his worldly goods (two old chairs, and half a candle, one old jug without a handle). But he is too late. To her great regret she already has a husband in England, Handel Jones, who sends her an unceasing supply of Dorking chickens.

Yorick see *Hamlet* and Laurence *Sterne.

York (103,000 in 1991) City in North Yorkshire, on the river Ouse. In the 1st century AD the *Romans established here a garrison town, Eboracum, which became the military headquarters of the province of Britain. By the 7c York was the capital of the Anglo-Saxon kingdom of *Northumbria; from this period comes its religious pre-eminence and the status of the archbishop of *York as the primate of England. The Danes captured York in 867 and, as Jorvik, it remained an important centre.

The city's present appearance reflects its prosperity in the Middle Ages, as a port and market town. The Merchant Adventurers' Hall (1357–68) is famous for its timber work. Clifford's Tower is a 14c keep on a mound created for William the Conqueror's original wooden fortress. The city walls are complete for almost the entire

circuit (parts of them on Roman foundations). The name of one of the oldest streets in the city, the Shambles, reflects its origin as a place of butchers' stalls. And medieval York provided one of the four surviving cycles of English *mystery plays, now performed every three years.

The greatest glory of the city is the cathedral, known as York Minster (13–15c). It is the largest medieval cathedral in Britain and contains the most extensive array of medieval stained glass, including the famous windows in the north transept known as the Five Sisters. The glass luckily survived the fire, caused by lightning, which on 9 July 1984 destroyed the roof of the south transept. A survival from the earliest days of Christian York is St Peter's School, founded in 627 by the first archbishop of York, St Paulinus; it has the high distinction of including *Alcuin among its early teachers, and the more dubious one of Guy Fawkes being its most famous old boy. It is now a co-educational independent school.

York is well provided with museums. The City Art Gallery has a broadly based collection with a strong holding of York's own painter, William Etty (1787–1849). The Castle Museum is known in particular for its recreation of a cobbled street lined with old York shop fronts and with contemporary wares on show inside. The Yorkshire Museum was founded in 1825, specializing in archaeology and natural history; it has strong medieval holdings, and in 1991 succeeded in securing the *Middleham Jewel. The Jorvik Viking Centre, opened in 1984, reflects the period of invasion from Scandinavia. Since 1975 the city has been the home of the *National Railway Museum.

Window (14c) in York Minster, showing a kneeling donor in stained glass presenting a stained glass window.

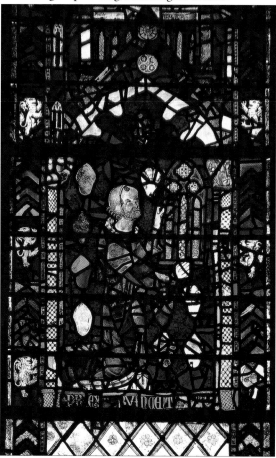

York has long played an important part in the horse-racing calendar, with the Knavesmire course in use since 1731. The three-day August meeting is the annual highlight.

Archbishop of York (Primate of England) Second to the archbishop of *Canterbury in the hierarchy of the *Church of England. St Paulinus (d. 644) is accepted as the first archbishop of York. He was consecrated at Canterbury in 625 before accompanying a Kentish princess on her journey north to marry Edwin of Northumbria, who was as yet unconverted. Paulinus baptized Edwin and his nobles in 627, whereupon Edwin appointed him bishop of York; the pope later recognized him as archbishop. The title Primate of England reflects York's long claim to be equal with Canterbury; Pope Gregory's original plan, when he first sent *Augustine to England, had been for two equal archbishoprics in the north and south of the country. John *Habgood was consecrated in 1983, as the 95th in line of succession. His immediate predecessors were Michael Ramsey (1956), Donald Coggan (1961) and Stuart Blanch (1975). The archbishop signs with his Christian name followed by *Ebor*.

Duke of York (Prince Andrew, b. 1960) Third child and second son of Elizabeth II (see the *royal family). Educated at Gordonstoun, he joined the Royal Navy in 1979 and trained as a helicopter pilot – seeing active service in that capacity in 1982 in the Falklands War. In 1986, in Westminster Abbey, he married Sarah Ferguson, popularly known as Fergie (b. 1959). They moved in 1990 to a new house, Sunninghill Park, built for them in Berkshire, but they separated in 1992. They have two daughters, Princess Beatrice (b.1988) and Princess Eugenie (b. 1990).

Duke of York (Prince Frederick, 1763–1827) Second son of George III and commander-in-chief of the army from 1798. He introduced useful reforms but was not himself a success in the field. The nursery rhyme which has perpetuated his name, though no precise origin has been found for it, has perhaps an oblique ring of truth:

> Oh, the grand old duke of York,
> He had ten thousand men;
> He marched them up to the top of the hill,
> And he marched them down again.

He stands in London at the top of the duke of York's steps, surveying St James's Park from a high column (high enough to be out of reach of his creditors, the joke went), which was put up in 1831–4 on the site of *Carlton House.

House of York (1461–1485) The descendants on the throne of England of Edmund of Langley, duke of York, who was the fourth surviving son of Edward III (see the *royal house and the *Wars of the Roses). They were Edward IV, Edward V and Richard III; they were followed by the house of *Tudor.

Yorkshire Historically the largest *county of England, split for administrative purposes into east, west and north *ridings. In 1974 it was divided into two new counties (North Yorkshire and Humberside) and two *metropolitan counties (West Yorkshire and South Yorkshire).

Yorkshire County Cricket Club Founded in 1863 and one of the original teams in the *county championship; it has won far more often than any other county, with two outright victories before the points system was introduced in 1890 and 29 subsequent wins (1893, 96, 98, 1900, 01, 02, 05, 08, 12, 19, 22, 23, 24, 25, 31, 32, 33, 35, 37, 38, 39, 46, 59, 60, 62, 63, 66, 67, 68). The club also shared the championship twice (1869 with

Nottinghamshire, 1949 with Middlesex). The great players contributing to this string of successes have included Herbert *Sutcliffe, Len *Hutton, Freddie *Trueman and Geoff *Boycott.

Yorkshire had long been famous as the only club to insist on its players being born in the county, but this came to seem an unwise restriction with no win in the championship since 1968. The policy was ended in dramatic fashion when the club signed up for the 1992 season the Indian boy wonder of Test cricket, Sachin Tendulkar, who had made his first Test century at the age of 17 (against England in 1990). Tendulkar became popular with the Yorkshire crowds, but even so the club ended the season in 16th place (as opposed to 14th in 1991).

In *one-day cricket Yorkshire has won the Gillette Cup twice (1965, 69), the Benson and Hedges Cup once (1987) and the Sunday League once (1983). The county ground is *Headingley in Leeds, and the county plays also in Sheffield, Harrogate, Scarborough and Middlesbrough.

Yorkshire Dales Section of the *Pennines, mainly in North Yorkshire but partly in Cumbria. It was designated in 1954 a *national park (1762sq.km/680sq.m).

Yorkshire Post Yorkshire's daily newspaper, based in Leeds and descending from a weekly founded in 1754 – the *Leeds Intelligencer*. After more than a century it was given the name *Yorkshire Post*, in 1866, and was at the same time transformed by the Yorkshire Conservative Newspaper Company into a daily paper supporting the Conservative cause (a commitment no longer automatically applying). For much of the 20c the *Yorkshire Post* and the *Manchester Guardian*, either side of the Pennines, were seen as a pair – England's two leading regional newspapers. But the *Yorkshire Post* has not followed the *Guardian* in moving to a fully national status and circulation.

Yorkshire pudding A baked batter of flour, eggs and milk which is the traditional accompaniment in Britain for roast beef. Originally baked in the same pan as the joint (or beneath the joint in a spit oven) so that it mingled with the juices of the meat, it is now almost invariably cooked on its own.

Yorkshire Ripper The name given, by analogy with *Jack the Ripper, to a man who in the late 1970s killed a succession of women, most of them in Yorkshire. He had murdered 13 and attempted to kill another seven before he was caught, early in 1981, and was discovered to be a 34-year-old long-distance lorry driver, Peter Sutcliffe. He was jailed for life, with a recommendation of a minimum 30 years. The gruesome case was followed by an unusual sequence of legal actions. Some of the women who had survived his attacks and parents of some of his victims successfully sued Sutcliffe for damages. Meanwhile his wife, Sonia, won a succession of libel actions against the press. The extraordinary £600,000 awarded to her in 1989 against *Private Eye* was later reduced to £60,000. But she had also received more than £200,000 from other cases before losing in 1990 against the *News of the World* and having to meet their very heavy costs.

Yorkshire Sculpture Park (8km/5m SW of Wakefield) Britain's first open-air sculpture gallery, mounting a series of exhibitions in the rolling parkland (landscaped in the late 18c) of Bretton Hall. The sculpture park, established in 1977, includes studios open to the public showing work in progress. In 1992 some pieces by Henry Moore were added to the works on permanent exhibition in the park.

Yorkshire terrier see *terriers.

Yorktown see War of *American Independence.

You are old, Father William see *Alice in Wonderland.*

Arthur **Young** (1741–1820) Author who did much to advance the improvements taking place in agriculture. He publicized them in a series of books based on his own travels through the country (starting with *A Six Weeks Tour through the Southern Counties of England and Wales*, 1768) and discussed them in a periodical which he edited (*Annals of Agriculture* 1784–1815).

Jimmy **Young** (b. 1923) Broadcaster, with a Gloucestershire origin and accent, who began as a singer and had two no. 1 hits in 1955 (*Unchained Melody; The Man from Laramie*). He was by then already an occasional disc jockey; he became a regular on Radio Luxembourg and was one of the original team in 1967 on Radio 1. The *Jimmy Young Programme* has been on BBC radio consistently from that time (Radio 2 from 1973), and has developed an orginal and very successful format – combining records with consumer news, current affairs and serious interviews. The wide range of people interviewed have included, quite regularly, Britain's prime ministers.

Lord **Young** (David Young, b. 1932, baron 1984) Businessman who became an industrial adviser to the government at the start of the Thatcher administration in 1979, and in 1984 was given a peerage and a seat in the *cabinet as minister without portfolio. He was subsequently secretary of state for employment (1985–7) and for trade and industry (1987–9).

Young England see *Disraeli.

George **Younger** (b. 1931, baron 1992) Conservative politician, MP for Ayr 1964–92, who entered the *cabinet in 1979 as secretary of state for Scotland (1979–86) and was subsequently secretary of state for defence (1986–9).

young offender institution (previously called detention centre) Place of detention for children aged 15–17 sentenced in a *youth court and for young people aged 18–20 (18–21 in Scotland and Northern Ireland) who are sentenced in an adult court. The equivalent *borstals were replaced by detention centres in 1983.

The Young Ones (BBC 1982–4) The first undiluted dose of 'alternative' comedy on British television, featuring the frenetically offensive antics of a group of student dropouts sharing a squat. The four regulars were Rik Mayall, Nigel Planer, Adrian Edmondson and Christopher Ryan.

The Young Person's Guide to the Orchestra (1946) Work by Benjamin *Britten in which a narrator describes the various sections of the orchestra; his words are illustrated in Britten's variations on an incidental tune from a play of 1695, *Abdelazer* (the subtitle is *Variations and Fugue on a Theme of Purcell*). The piece was originally the score for a documentary film.

Young Pretender see Charles Edward *Stuart.

Young Roscius see *infant prodigies.

The Young Visiters (1890) Classic child's-eye-view of romance and high society. Written at the age of nine by Daisy Ashford (1881–1972), the manuscript was rediscovered in 1917 and published in 1919 with a preface by J.M. *Barrie. In racy narrative and wildly eccentric spelling, the book tells of the love of Ethel Monticue for Bernard Clark and of the efforts to rise in society of the irrepressible Mr Salteena, who says of himself 'I am parshial to ladies if they are nice I suppose it is my nature' and 'I am not quite a gentleman but you would hardly notice it'.

'Your country needs you' see *Kitchener.

Youth Clubs Premises offering social and recreational facilities, with historical origins in deprived areas of Victorian cities similar to those of the *boys' clubs – though most youth clubs are for both sexes and have a higher age limit (usually 21). Many are affiliated to Youth Clubs UK, formed in 1911 as the National Council of Girls' Clubs.

youth court (previously juvenile court) *Magistrates' court before which a child or young person appears if between the ages of 10 and 17. The court is presided over by three *JPs, at least one of whom must be a woman. The hearings are in private and offenders' names may not be published except by specific order. Children under the age of 10 are deemed incapable of committing a crime, and a child aged 10–14 will only be considered guilty if the prosecution can show that he or she knew the act to be morally or legally wrong. Apart from fines, which the parents may be ordered to pay, the youth court can impose a *community service order or a specified number of days at an *attendance centre. Any custodial sentence will be to a *young offender institution.

'You will, Oscar, you will' see *Whistler.

Battles of **Ypres** (1914–18) The town of Ypres is in Belgium, about 40km/25m southeast of Dunkirk. In October 1914, in *World War I, the German army was racing to reach the coast before turning south to the Channel ports. At the same time the Allies were moving to prevent their doing so. When the two armies met, the *British Expeditionary Force held a projecting salient in the first battle of Ypres (19 Oct.–22 Nov.), though they were nearly wiped out in the encounter. This salient remained for the next four years a key British section of the line. In the second battle (22 Apr.–25 May 1915) it was the area chosen by the Germans to launch an experimental assault with chlorine, the first use of poison gas on the western front; it gained them part of the projecting territory. The third battle (June–Nov. 1917) painfully extended the salient again for the Allies, ending with the capture by Canadian forces of Passchendaele as a new forward position; this campaign, winning a devastated terrain deep in mud at a cost of nearly 300,000 Allied lives (and as many German) has become one of the bleakest symbols of the war. In April 1918 the Germans made one final successful thrust against the Ypres salient; the Allies won it back in August.

The road out of Ypres in the direction of Menin, about 19km/12m to the southeast, was the way to the front. So it was there that a new triple-arched Menin Gate was built in 1927, to a design by Reginald Blomfield, as a memorial to the armies of the British empire and in particular to the fallen who have no known grave. Inscribed on the walls are the names of some 55,000 men who fell in the salient and were listed as missing. Every evening, at 8 p.m., the traffic comes to a halt and the Last Post is sounded.

YT (Youth Training) Scheme administered in the early 1990s by the *TECs. The government guaranteed a YT place (with a weekly payment) for any school-leaver unable to find unemployment – a promise which became the subject of controversy in 1992 when not enough places were available. As a result many of the young unemployed fell into a Catch-22 poverty trap, for the Social Securities Act of 1986 (modified in 1988) denied *income support to anyone under 18 not enrolled on a YT scheme.

yuppies Both the concept and the word are American, but yuppies became a familiar part of the British scene when young people began earning huge salaries in the City in the excitement surrounding *Big Bang. The letters stand for 'young urban professional people' but in Britain are often taken to mean 'young upwardly mobile people' – a group separately identified in the USA as yumpies.

YWCA (Young Women's Christian Association) Organization which is entirely separate from the *YMCA, though influenced by it in its origin and largely sharing its aims. It was established in 1855 by two groups of women in London, whose twin aims combined the spiritual and practical sides of the movement; one was to pray for women (princesses and factory girls were among those for whom prayers were specified), and the other was to found a home for nurses returning from the Crimean War. A similar group, the Ladies' Christian Association, was formed in New York in 1858, and the present worldwide organization was established in 1894.

Zambia Republic and member of the *Commonwealth since 1964. This part of east central Africa was explored by *Livingstone, but the first Europeans to settle in any number were employees of Cecil *Rhodes and the British South Africa Company in the 1890s. The region, known as Northern Rhodesia and of increasing importance for its copper mines, was made a British protectorate in 1924. Northern Rhodesia was a member of the Federation of *Rhodesia and Nyasaland, before becoming independent as Zambia in 1964 with Kenneth Kaunda (b. 1924) as its first president.

Zanzibar Island off the east coast of Africa which from the late 17C was an Arab sultanate, originally controlled from Oman but under a local sultan from 1856. It was Africa's largest slave market and had long been a target of British anti-slavery efforts. A treaty for the suppression of the slave trade was signed in 1873, and the island was declared a British protectorate in 1890. It became independent in 1963. The following year the sultan was deposed and Zanzibar joined with Tanganyika to form the republic of *Tanzania.

Z Cars (BBC 1960–78) Popular and influential television series, with police in their crime cars tackling the problems of two contrasted Liverpool suburbs. Prominent among the policemen were Stratford Johns as Inspector Barlow and Frank Windsor as Inspector Watt. *Softly Softly* (BBC 1966–76) was originally a spin-off, aiming to follow more closely the adventures of Inspector Barlow.

zebra crossing Pedestrian crossing marked by black and white stripes on the road surface. The stripes were added in 1950 to give greater visibility to the crossings, previously marked only by a *Belisha beacon at each end.

Zeebrugge see *Herald of Free Enterprise*.

Zimbabwe Republic and member of the *Commonwealth since 1980. This region of Africa, immediately to the north of South Africa, was developed from the early 1890s by Cecil *Rhodes and the British South Africa Company. It was known as Rhodesia from 1895. In 1922, when there were some 34,000 European settlers, a majority voted to become a self-governing British colony rather than the fifth province of independent South Africa. It was known by then as Southern Rhodesia, by contrast with the northern area (now *Zambia) which had been pioneered a little later by the same company. After the ten years in which Southern Rhodesia led the Federation of *Rhodesia and Nyasaland (1953–63), it alone of the three was unable to gain independence because it rejected the principle of majority rule (there were then about 220,000 Europeans and 3.8 million Africans).

In 1965 the prime minister, Ian Smith (b. 1919), made a unilateral declaration of independence (UDI). In spite of two series of talks between him and the British prime minister, Harold Wilson, on warships off Gibraltar (the *Tiger* in 1966 and the *Fearless* in 1968), no solution was found; sanctions imposed by Britain and the UN remained in force. These, together with a prolonged guerrilla campaign inside Rhodesia, led to the concession of universal suffrage and the election in 1979 of the country's first black prime minister, Abel Muzorewa (b. 1925). Talks in London later that year, involving for the first time the rebel leaders Joshua Nkomo (b. 1917) and Robert Mugabe (b. 1924), resulted at last in an agreed constitution. Mugabe became the prime minister of the newly independent Zimbabwe in 1980 and president in 1987.

Zinoviev letter A document, probably a forgery, which was supposedly sent to the British Communist party by Grigori Zinoviev, head of the Communist International, urging armed revolution. It was published in the press a few days before the general election of 1924, and as an anti-leftist scare contributed to the defeat of Ramsay *MacDonald's coalition government.

Johann **Zoffany** (1733–1810) German-born painter, based in England from about 1760, who brought a new life to the formal conversation piece. His single most striking work is *The Tribuna of the Uffizi* (1772–7, Royal Collection). It was commissioned by Queen Charlotte, who sent Zoffany to Florence because she wanted to see the treasures of the Medici but protocol prevented her going on the *Grand Tour. He brought back this detailed view of the gallery and its assembled masterpieces, which he enlivened with excellent portraits of some 20 British noblemen and connoisseurs enjoying the art. These living figures make his painting, but the queen considered them an unseemly intrusion.

Zuleika Dobson see Max *Beerbohm.

Zulu War (1879) In the mid-19C two areas of *South Africa were settled by whites on the borders of a powerful Zulu kingdom, recently formed out of many separate tribes by Shaka (c.1787–1828); they were Natal to the south and the Transvaal to the west. Border disputes and other minor transgressions were used by the British early in 1878 as a pretext to attack Cetshwayo (c.1834–84), a nephew of Shaka who was by then king. Disaster followed almost immediately. On January 22 an ill-prepared British camp at Isandhlwana was surprised by a Zulu army and some 1200 troops were massacred. The Zulus moved on to attack a much smaller garrison nearby at Rorke's Drift, where a force of only about 100 men put up a heroic defence and by dawn the next morning had repelled the enemy, inflicting casualties of some 350 for only 17 British dead. In the way of selective national memories, Rorke's Drift is the name famous in Britain from that day of two battles. A decisive victory over the Zulus in July at Ulundi effectively brought the war to an end. After a period as a crown colony, Zululand became in 1897 a part of Natal.

BIBLIOGRAPHY

Much of this book has been written from material supplied at my request by organizations or individuals. Nevertheless my main sources have been the works described below. For the sake of brevity the list has been limited to books designed specifically for reference. Most of them consist of separate entries arranged alphabetically.

Where no year is given, the work is issued annually. In other cases I have given the date of the volume used by me; but many of the titles are kept regularly in print in updated editions.

General and Biographical

Annual Abstract of Statistics (Central Statistical Office).

Britain, an Official Handbook (HMSO).

Chambers Biographical Dictionary, ed. Magnus Magnusson (5th edn, 1990).

Chronicle of the 20th Century, ed. Derrik Mercer (1988).

The Dictionary of National Biography (1885–1900, with successive supplements covering the years up to 1985).

Encyclopaedia Britannica (1972).

The Macmillan Family Encyclopedia (1989).

The Reader's Digest Complete Atlas of the British Isles (1965).

Social Trends (Central Statistical Office).

Webster's Biographical Dictionary (1971).

Whitaker's Almanack.

Who's Who.

Who Was Who.

Architecture

Briggs, Martin *Everyman's Concise Encyclopaedia of Architecture* (1959).

The Country Life Book of Castles and Houses in Britain (1988).

Gascoigne, Christina *Castles of Britain* (1975).

The Penguin Dictionary of Architecture, ed. John Fleming, Hugh Honour and Nikolaus Pevsner (3rd edn, 1980).

Pevsner, Nikolaus (and others) *The Buildings of England* (46 vols, 1941–74).

Thorold, Henry *Cathedrals, Abbeys and Priories of England and Wales* (1986).

Vayne, Stella *Nicholson's Guide to English Churches* (1984).

Art, Fine and Decorative

The Fine and Decorative Art Collections of Britain and Ireland, ed. Jeannie Chapel and Charlotte Gere (1985).

Fleming, John and Hugh Honour *The Penguin Dictionary of Decorative Arts* (1977).

Godden, Geoffrey *British Porcelain* (1974).

Godden, Geoffrey *British Pottery* (1974).

Houfe, Simon *The Dictionary of British Book Illustrators and Caricaturists, 1800–1914* (1978).

Jervis, Simon *The Penguin Dictionary of Design and Designers* (1984).

Murray, Peter and Linda *The Penguin Dictionary of Art and Artists* (4th edn, 1976).

Museums and Art Galleries in Great Britain and Ireland.

Museums Yearbook.

Newman, Harold *An Illustrated Dictionary of Glass* (1977).

The Oxford Companion to Art, ed. Harold Osborne (1970).

The Oxford Dictionary of Art, ed. Ian Chilvers and Harold Osborne (1988).

Pugh, P.D.G. *Staffordshire Portrait Figures of the Victorian Era* (1970).

Reilly, Robin and George Savage *The Dictionary of Wedgwood* (1980).

Savage, George and Harold Newman *An Illustrated Dictionary of Ceramics* (2nd edn, 1976).

The Thames and Hudson Encyclopaedia of British Art, ed. David Bindman (1985).

Waterhouse, Ellis *The Dictionary of British 18th Century Painters* (1981).

Wood, Christopher *The Dictionary of Victorian Painters* (2nd edn, 1978).

Broadcasting

Donovan, Paul *The Radio Companion* (1991).

Halliwell, Leslie with Philip Purser *Halliwell's Television Companion* (3rd edn, 1986).

Screen International Film and TV Year Book.

Who's Who on Television, ed. Alan Curthoys, Jane Struthers and John Doyle (1982).

Commerce, Economics and Industry

Bannock, Graham, R.E. Baxter and Evan Davis *The Penguin Dictionary of Economics* (4th edn, 1987).

Economic Trends (Central Statistical Office).

Greener, Michael *The Penguin Business Dictionary* (1987).

Hanson, J.L. *A Dictionary of Economics and Commerce* (3rd edn, 1969).

Sinclair, W.I. *Allied Dunbar Tax Guide.*

Gardens

Hollis, Sarah and Derry Moore *The Shell Guide to the Gardens of England and Wales* (1989).

The Oxford Companion to Gardens, ed. Geoffrey and Susan Jellicoe, Patrick Goode and Michael Lancaster (1986).

Thacker, Christopher and John Bethell *England's Historic Gardens* (1989).

Government and Politics

Butler, David and Gareth *British Political Facts* (6th edn, 1986).

Wilding, Norman and Philip Laundy *An Encyclopaedia of Parliament* (4th edn, 1972).

Language

Brewer's Dictionary of Phrase and Fable (centenary edn by Ivor Evans, 1970).

Brewer's Dictionary of 20th-Century Phrase and Fable, ed. David Pickering, Alan Isaacs and Elizabeth Martin (1991).

The Collins English Dictionary, ed. Patrick Hanks (2nd edn, 1986).

Grose, Francis *Dictionary of the Vulgar Tongue* (1811 edn, paperback facsimile 1981).

The Oxford Dictionary of Modern Quotations, ed. Tony Augarde (1991).

The Oxford Dictionary of Quotations (3rd edn, 1979).

The Oxford English Dictionary (1884–1933, supplement 1972–86, integrated as 2nd edn 1989).

Partridge, Eric *A Dictionary of Catch Phrases* (1977).

Partridge, Eric *A Dictionary of Historical Slang* (1972).

The Penguin Dictionary of Modern Quotations, ed. J.M. and M.J. Cohen (2nd edn, 1980).

The Penguin Dictionary of Quotations, ed. J.M. and M.J. Cohen (1960).

Rees, Nigel *Dictionary of Popular Phrases* (1990).

Law

A Concise Dictionary of Law, ed. Elizabeth Martin (2nd edn, 1990).

Literature

Bartlett's Familiar Quotations (15th edn, 1980).

The Cambridge Guide to Literature in English, ed. Ian Ousby (1988).

Carpenter, Humphrey and Mari Prichard *The Oxford Companion to Children's Literature* (1984).

The International Authors and Writers Who's Who, ed. Ernest Kay (12th edn, 1991).

McLeish, Kenneth *Good Reading Guide* (2nd edn, 1990).

The Oxford Book of Ballads, ed. Arthur Quiller-Couch (1946).

The Oxford Book of English Verse, ed. Arthur Quiller-Couch (2nd edn, 1939).

The Oxford Companion to English Literature, ed. Margaret Drabble (5th edn, 1985).

The Oxford Dictionary of Nursery Rhymes, ed. Iona and Peter Opie (2nd edn, 1980).

The Reader's Encyclopedia, ed. William Rose Benét (2nd edn, 1965).

London

Banks, F.R. *The Penguin Guide to London* (7th edn, 1977).

London, ed. Nikolaus Pevsner and Bridget Cherry (3 vols, 1973–91).

The London Encyclopedia, ed. Ben Weinreb and Christopher Hibbert (1983).

Mander, Raymond and Joe Mitchenson *The Theatres of London* (1961).

Piper, David *The Companion Guide to London* (2nd edn, 1972).

Performing Arts

BALLET AND DANCE

The Dance Encyclopedia, ed. Anatole Chujoy and P.W. Manchester (1967).

Koegler, Horst *The Concise Oxford Dictionary of Ballet* (1977).

FILM

Halliwell, Leslie *Halliwell's Filmgoer's Companion* (8th edn, 1984).

Halliwell, Leslie *Halliwell's Film Guide* (4th edn, 1983).

Screen International Film and TV Year Book.

Shipman, David *The Great Movie Stars* (3 vols, 1989–91).

The Time Out Film Guide, ed. Tom Milne (1989).

MUSIC, CLASSICAL

The Concise Oxford Dictionary of Music, ed. Michael Kennedy (3rd edn, 1980).

The Concise Oxford Dictionary of Opera, ed. Harold Rosenthal and John Warrack (2nd edn, 1979).

Jacobs, Arthur *The New Penguin Dictionary of Music* (4th edn, 1977).

Kobbé's Complete Opera Book, ed. the earl of Harewood (9th edn, 1976).

The New Grove Dictionary of Music and Musicians, ed. Stanley Sadie (6th edn, 20 vols, 1980).

Osborne, Charles *The Dictionary of Opera* (1983).

MUSIC, POP

Book of Rock Stars, ed. Dafydd Rees and Luke Crampton with Barry Lazell (1989).

British Hit Albums, ed. Paul Gambaccini, Tim Rice and Jonathan Rice (5th edn, 1992).

British Hit Singles, ed. Paul Gambaccini, Tim Rice and Jonathan Rice (8th edn, 1991).

Gammond, Peter *The Oxford Companion to Popular Music* (1991).

The Penguin Encyclopedia of Popular Music, ed. Donald Clarke (1989).

THEATRE

The Concise Oxford Companion to the Theatre, ed. Phyllis Hartnoll (1972).

Gammond, Peter *Your Own, Your Very Own! a Music-Hall Scrapbook* (1971).

Mander, Raymond and Joe Mitchenson *British Music Hall* (1965).

Who's Who in the Theatre (17th edn, 1981).

Religion

Attwater, Donald *A Dictionary of Saints* (1965).

Brierley, Peter *'Christian' England: What the 1989 English Church Census reveals* (1991).

The Oxford Book of Carols, ed. Percy Dearmer, Ralph Vaughan Williams and Martin Shaw (1928).

The Penguin Book of Hymns, ed. Ian Bradley (1989).

Science and Technology

A Biographical Dictionary of Scientists, ed. Trevor Williams (1969).

Chambers Concise Dictionary of Scientists, ed. David, Ian, John and Margaret Millar (1989).

Chambers Dictionary of Science and Technology, ed. T.C. Collocott (1971).

Sports and Games

Buchanan, Ian *British Olympians: a Hundred Years of Gold Medallists* (1991).

The Guinness Encyclopedia of International Sports Records and Results, ed. Peter Matthews and Ian Morrison (2nd edn, 1990).

The Oxford Companion to Sports and Games, ed. John Arlott (1975).

The Sportspages Almanac, ed. Matthew Engel and Ian Morrison (issued annually 1989–91 but then discontinued).

Wallechinsky, David *The Complete Book of the Olympics* (1992).

BOXING

Hugman, Barry J. *British Boxing Yearbook*.

CRICKET

Frindall, Bill *England Test Cricketers* (1989).

Powell, William *The Wisden Guide to Cricket Grounds* (1989).

Wisden: Cricketers' Almanack

FOOTBALL

Brooking, Trevor *100 Great British Footballers* (1988).

The Guinness Football Encyclopedia, ed. Graham Hart (1991).

Rothman's Football Yearbook.

GOLF

Alliss, Peter *100 Greatest Golfers* (1989).

Campbell, Malcolm *The Encyclopedia of Golf* (1991).

RACING

The Illustrated Encyclopedia of World Racing, ed. Richard Dawes (1989).

Magee, Sean *The Racing Year* (1990).

BIBLIOGRAPHY

RUGBY FOOTBALL

Quinn, Keith *The Encyclopedia of World Rugby* (1991).
Rothman's Rugby League Yearbook.
Rothman's Rugby Union Yearbook.

SNOOKER

Morrison, Ian *Who's Who in Snooker* (1988).
Rothman's Snooker Yearbook.

Town and Country

Bennett, Linda *The Macmillan Guide to Britain's Nature Reserves* (2nd edn, 1989).
Blue Guide: England, ed. Stuart Rossiter (9th edn, 1980).
Blue Guide: Ireland, ed. Ian Robertson (5th edn, 1987).
Blue Guide: Scotland, ed. John Tomes (9th edn, 1986).
Blue Guide: Wales, ed. John Tomes (6th edn, 1979).
Book of the British Countryside (AA, 2nd edn, 1988).
Book of British Villages (AA, 2nd edn, 1985).
English Heritage *Guide to English Heritage Properties open to the public.*

Greeves, Lydia and Michael Trinick *The National Trust Guide* (4th edn, 1989).
Historic Houses, Castles and Gardens open to the public.
The Historic House and Garden Directory.
National Trust for Scotland: Guide to over 100 Properties.
The National Trust Handbook.
Places to Visit in Britain (AA, 1988).
Tinniswood, Adrian *Historic Houses of the National Trust* (1991).
Treasures of Britain (AA, 3rd edn, 1976).
The Visitor's Guide to Britain, ed. Esmond Wright (1987).

Miscellaneous

The Encyclopedia of the British Press 1422–1992, ed. Dennis Griffiths (1992).
The Guinness Book of Records.
Kightly, Charles *The Customs and Ceremonies of Britain* (1986).
The Oxford Companion to Ships and the Sea, ed. Peter Kemp (1988).
The Royal Encyclopedia, ed. Ronald Allison and Sarah Riddell (1991).

PICTURE ACKNOWLEDGEMENTS